Essential
English
Thesaurus

Plus Word Power supplement

Essential
English
Thesaurus

Plus Word Power supplement

Collins
An imprint of HarperCollinsPublishers

first published 2003

© HarperCollins Publishers 2003

latest reprint 2003

HarperCollins Publishers
Westerhill Road, Bishopbriggs, Glasgow G64 2QT
Great Britain

www.collinsdictionaries.com

Collins® and Bank of English® are registered trademarks of
HarperCollins Publishers Limited

ISBN 0-00-716261-8

Acknowledgements

We would like to thank those authors and publishers who kindly
gave permission for copyright material to be used in the Bank of
English. We would also like to thank Times Newspapers Ltd for
providing valuable data.

Note

Entered words that we have reason to believe constitute trademarks
have been designated as such. However, neither the presence nor
absence of such designation should be regarded as affecting the legal
status of any trademark.

A catalogue record for this book is available from the British Library

Computing support and typesetting by John Podbielski

Supplement typeset by Wordcraft

Printed and bound by William Clowes Ltd.,
Beccles and London.

EDITORIAL STAFF

Editor
Lorna Gilmour

Supplement typesetting
Wordcraft

Series Editor
Lorna Sinclair Knight

Editorial Direction
Elaine Higgleton

BANK *of* ENGLISH

This book has been compiled by referring to the Bank of English, a unique database of the English language with examples of over 520 million words enabling Collins lexicographers to analyse how English is actually used and how it is changing. This is the evidence on which the material in this book is based.

The Bank of English was set up as a joint initiative by HarperCollins Publishers and Birmingham University to be a resource for language research and lexicography. It contains a very wide range of material from books, newspapers, radio, TV, magazines, letters, and talks reflecting the whole spectrum of English today. Its size and range make it an unequalled resource and the purpose-built software for its analysis is unique to Collins Dictionaries.

This ensures that Collins Dictionaries accurately reflect English as it is used today in a way that is most helpful to the dictionary or thesaurus user as well as including the full range of rarer and historical words and meanings.

FOREWORD

Collins Essential English Thesaurus is an immensely practical and helpful language resource. It allows you to look up a word and find a wide selection of alternatives that can replace it. It is, therefore, tremendously helpful when you are trying to find different ways of expressing yourself, as well as being an invaluable aid for crosswords and puzzles.

The thesaurus has been designed to give the user as much help as possible in finding the right word for any occasion. Its A-Z arrangement of main entry words lets you go straight to any word without having to resort to an index, just as easily as if you were looking up a dictionary. The wide number of main entry words gives you a greater chance of finding the word you want. At the same time, the generous number of alternative words (synonyms) for each main entry word means the widest possible choice of the most helpful alternatives is included in each case. The book also takes account of recent changes in the language, with terms like *gridlock, nerd* and *Internet* included as main entry words, and words and idioms like *gut-wrenching, in the loop, big hitter* and *go pear-shaped* being found among the synonyms.

The **Collins Essential English Thesaurus** also includes lists of opposites (antonyms) at many of the main entry words. These lists give a range of opposites which provide you with another way of expressing yourself. For instance, if you want to say that something is *difficult*, it can sometimes be effective to use a negative construction and, taking a word from the antonym list, you may think of a phrase such as *"by no means straightforward"*.

This thesaurus further demonstrates Collins' commitment to helping the user. As part of an innovative design, key synonyms have been highlighted in bold type and placed first in each list. This layout enables you to see immediately which sense of the word is referred to. This is particularly helpful when a main entry word has a number of different senses. It also gives you an idea of which synonym is the closest alternative to the word you have looked up. Where helpful, the key synonym is also given in bold type at the start of the appropriate list of antonyms in the entry, allowing you to identify at once the particular sense for which these can be used as opposites.

The Word Power supplement gives you another, uniquely practical, kind of language help. It lists famous people such as actors, artists, composers, politicians, and writers, all arranged by their occupations. It also lists geographical information such as countries, capitals, currencies, and political parties, arranged by subject. It therefore provides invaluable information for solving general-knowledge clues in crosswords and puzzles, and for boosting home study.

All these features mean that the **Collins Essential English Thesaurus** is a treasury of useful and practical words and information, arranged in the most helpful way possible.

GUIDE TO THE TEXT

Main entry word ——— **above** *preposition* **1** = **over**, atop, beyond, exceeding, higher than, on top of, upon **2** = **superior to**, before, beyond, exceeding, surpassing ♦ *adverb* **3** = **overhead**, aloft, atop, in heaven, on high ♦ *adjective* **4** = **preceding**, aforementioned, aforesaid, earlier, foregoing, previous, prior

Synonyms, listed in alphabetical order, that can be used in place of the main entry word

➤ **Antonyms**
preposition ≠**over**: below, beneath, under, underneath ≠**superior to**: inferior, lesser, less than, lower than, subordinate

Key synonym given first and highlighted ——— **above board** *adjective* **1** = **honest**, candid, fair and square, forthright, frank, guileless, honourable, kosher (*informal*), legitimate, on the up and up, open, overt, square, straight, straightforward, true, trustworthy, truthful, upfront (*informal*), upright, veracious ♦ *adverb* **2** = **honestly**, candidly, forthrightly, frankly, honourably, openly, overtly, straightforwardly, truly, truthfully, uprightly, veraciously, without guile

Labels show context of use

➤ **Antonyms**
adjective ≠**honest**: clandestine, crooked, deceitful, deceptive, devious, dishonest, fraudulent, furtive, secret, secretive, shady, sly, sneaky, underhand

Parts of speech ——— **abracadabra** *noun* = **spell**, chant, charm, conjuration, hocus-pocus, incantation, invocation, magic, mumbo jumbo, sorcery, voodoo, witchcraft

abrade *verb* = **scrape**, erase, erode, file, grind, rub off, scour, scrape away, scrape out, wear away, wear down, wear off

abrasion *noun* **1** *Medical* = **graze**, chafe, scrape, scratch, scuff, surface injury, trauma (*Pathology*) **2** = **scraping**, abrading, chafing, erosion, friction, grating, rubbing, scouring, scratching, scuffing, wearing away, wearing down

a label which is not in brackets relates to the whole of that particular sense

a label in brackets applies only to the word preceding it

abrasive *adjective* **1** = **unpleasant**, annoying, biting, caustic, cutting, galling, grating, hurtful, irritating, nasty, rough, sharp, vitriolic **2** = **rough**, chafing, erosive, frictional, grating, scraping, scratching,

GUIDE TO THE TEXT

abreast *adjective* **1** = **alongside**, beside, level, neck and neck, shoulder to shoulder, side by side **2 abreast of** = **informed about**, acquainted with, *au courant* with, *au fait* with, conversant with, familiar with, in the picture about, in touch with, keeping one's finger on the pulse of, knowledgeable about, up to date with, up to speed with

abridge *verb* = **shorten**, abbreviate, abstract, clip, compress, concentrate, condense, contract, curtail, cut, cut down, decrease, digest, diminish, downsize, epitomize, lessen, précis, reduce, summarize, synopsize (*U.S.*), trim
➤ **Antonyms**
amplify, augment, enlarge, expand, extend, go into detail, lengthen, prolong, protract, spin out, stretch out

abridgment *noun* = **shortening**, abbreviation, abstract, compendium, condensation, conspectus, contraction, curtailment, cutting, decrease, digest, diminishing, diminution, epitome, lessening, limitation, outline, précis, reduction, restraint, restriction, résumé, summary, synopsis

abroad *adverb* **1** = **overseas**, beyond the sea, in foreign lands, out of the country **2** = **about**, at large, away, circulating, current, elsewhere, extensively, far, far and wide, forth, in circulation, out, out-of-doors, outside, publicly, widely, without

abrupt *adjective* **1** = **sudden**, hasty, headlong, hurried, precipitate, quick, surprising, swift, unanticipated, unexpected, unforeseen **2** = **steep**, precipitous, sharp, sheer, sudden **3** = **uneven**, broken, disconnected, discontinuous, irregular, jerky **4** = **curt**, blunt, brisk, brusque, clipped, direct, discourteous, gruff, impatient, impolite, monosyllabic, rough, rude, short, snappish, snappy, terse, unceremonious, uncivil, ungracious
➤ **Antonyms**
≠**sudden**: easy, leisurely, slow, thoughtful, unhurried ≠**steep**: gradual ≠**curt**: civil, courteous, gracious, polite

A a

abaft *adverb, adjective Nautical* = **behind**, aft, astern

abandon *verb* **1** = **leave**, desert, forsake, jilt, leave behind, leave in the lurch, let (someone) stew in their own juice, strand **2** = **evacuate**, quit, vacate, withdraw from **3** = **give up**, abdicate, cede, relinquish, renounce, resign, surrender, waive, yield **4** = **stop**, desist, discontinue, drop, forgo, kick (*informal*) ◆ *noun* **5** = **wildness**, careless freedom, dash, recklessness, unrestraint, wantonness, wild impulse
➤ **Antonyms**
verb ≠**evacuate**: defend, maintain, uphold ≠**give up**: claim, hold, keep, take ≠**stop**: continue ◆ *noun* ≠**wildness**: control, moderation, restraint

abandoned *adjective* **1** = **left**, cast aside, cast away, cast out, derelict, deserted, discarded, ditched, dropped, forlorn, forsaken, jilted, neglected, outcast, out of the window, rejected, relinquished, stranded **2** = **unoccupied**, vacant **3** = **depraved**, corrupt, debauched, dissipated, dissolute, profligate, reprobate, sinful, wanton, wicked **4** = **uninhibited**, uncontrolled, unrestrained, wild
➤ **Antonyms**
≠**unoccupied**: claimed, kept, maintained, occupied ≠**depraved**: good, high-principled, honest, moral, pure, reputable, righteous, upright, virtuous, worthy ≠**uninhibited**: conscious, inhibited, restrained

abandonment *noun* **1** = **leaving**, dereliction, desertion, forsaking, jilting **2** = **evacuation**, quitting, withdrawal from **3** = **giving up**, abdication, cession, relinquishment, renunciation, resignation, surrender, waiver **4** = **stopping**, desistance, discontinuation, dropping

abase *verb* = **humble**, belittle, bring low, cast down, debase, degrade, demean, demote, denigrate, depress, disgrace, dishonour, downgrade, humiliate, lower, mortify, put in one's place, reduce
➤ **Antonyms**
advance, aggrandize, dignify, elevate, exalt, glorify, honour, prefer, promote, raise, upgrade

abasement *noun* = **humbling**, belittlement, debasement, degradation, demotion, depression, disgrace, dishonour, downgrading, humiliation, lowering, mortification, reduction, shame

abashed *adjective* = **embarrassed**, affronted, ashamed, astounded, bewildered, chagrined, confounded, confused, discomfited, discomposed, disconcerted, discountenanced, dismayed, humbled, humiliated, mortified, perturbed, shamefaced, taken aback
➤ **Antonyms**
at ease, blatant, bold, brazen, composed, confident, unabashed, unashamed, undaunted, undismayed, unperturbed

abate *verb* = **decrease**, alleviate, appease, attenuate, decline, diminish, dull, dwindle, ease, ebb, fade, lessen, let up, mitigate, moderate, quell, reduce, relax, relieve, sink, slacken, slake, slow, subside, taper off, wane, weaken
➤ **Antonyms**
add to, amplify, augment, boost, enhance, escalate, increase, intensify, magnify, multiply, strengthen

abatement *noun* = **decrease**, alleviation, allowance, attenuation, cessation, decline, diminution, dulling, dwindling, easing, extenuation, fading, lessening, let-up (*informal*), mitigation, moderation, quelling, reduction, relief, remission, slackening, slaking, slowing, tapering off, waning, weakening

abbey *noun* = **monastery**, cloister, convent, friary, nunnery, priory

abbreviate *verb* = **shorten**, abridge, abstract, clip, compress, condense, contract, curtail, cut, epitomize, précis, reduce, summarize, trim, truncate
➤ **Antonyms**
amplify, draw out, elongate, expand, extend, increase, lengthen, prolong, protract, spin out, stretch out

abbreviation *noun* = **shortening**, abridgment, abstract, clipping, compendium, compression, condensation, conspectus, contraction, curtailment, digest, epitome, précis, reduction, résumé, summary, synopsis, trimming, truncation

abdicate *verb* = **give up**, abandon, abjure, abnegate, cede, forgo, quit, relinquish, renounce, resign, retire, step down (*informal*), surrender, vacate, waive, yield

abdication *noun* = **giving up**, abandonment, abjuration, abnegation, cession, quitting, relinquishment, renunciation, resignation, retiral (*especially Scot.*), retirement, surrender, waiver, yielding

abdominal *adjective* = **gastric**, intestinal, stomachic, stomachical, visceral

abduct *verb* = **kidnap**, carry off, make off with, run away with, run off with, seize, snatch (*slang*)

abduction *noun* = **kidnapping**, carrying off, seizure

aberration *noun* = **oddity**, aberrancy, abnormality, anomaly, defect, deviation, divergence, eccentricity, irregularity, lapse, peculiarity, quirk, rambling, straying, wandering

abet *verb* **1** = **help**, aid, assist, back, condone, connive at, promote, sanction, second, succour, support, sustain, uphold **2** = **encourage**, egg on, incite, prompt, spur, urge

abeyance *noun* **in abeyance** = **shelved**, hanging fire, in cold storage (*informal*), on ice (*informal*), pending, suspended

abhor *verb* = **hate**, abominate, detest, execrate, loathe, recoil from, regard with repugnance *or* horror, shrink from, shudder at
➤ **Antonyms**
admire, adore, cherish, delight in, desire, enjoy, like, love, relish

abhorrent *adjective* = **hateful**, abominable, detestable, disgusting, distasteful, execrable, hated, heinous, horrible, horrid, loathsome, obnoxious, obscene, odious, offensive, repellent, repugnant, repulsive, revolting, yucky *or* yukky (*slang*)

abide *verb* **1** = **tolerate**, accept, bear, brook, endure, hack (*slang*), put up with, stand, stomach, submit to, suffer **2** = **last**, continue, endure, persist, remain, survive **3** = **stay**, dwell, linger, live, lodge, reside, rest, sojourn, stop, tarry, wait

abide by *verb* **1** = **obey**, acknowledge, agree to, comply with, conform to, follow, observe, submit to, toe the line **2** = **carry out**, adhere to, discharge, fulfil, hold to, keep to, persist in, stand by

abiding *adjective* = **everlasting**, constant, continuing, durable, enduring, eternal, fast, firm, immortal, immutable, indissoluble, lasting, permanent, persistent, persisting, steadfast, surviving, tenacious, unchanging, unending
➤ **Antonyms**
brief, ephemeral, evanescent, fleeting, momentary, passing, short, short-lived,

temporary, transient, transitory

ability *noun* = **skill**, adeptness, aptitude, capability, capacity, competence, competency, craft, dexterity, endowment, energy, expertise, expertness, facility, faculty, flair, force, gift, knack, know-how (*informal*), potentiality, power, proficiency, qualification, talent
➤ **Antonyms**
inability, incapability, incapacity, incompetence, powerlessness, weakness

abject *adjective* **1** = **miserable**, deplorable, forlorn, hopeless, outcast, pitiable, wretched **2** = **servile**, base, contemptible, cringing, debased, degraded, despicable, dishonourable, fawning, grovelling, humiliating, ignoble, ignominious, low, mean, slavish, sordid, submissive, vile, worthless
➤ **Antonyms**
≠servile: august, dignified, distinguished, elevated, eminent, exalted, grand, great, high, lofty, noble, patrician, worthy

abjectness *noun* **1** = **misery**, destitution, forlornness, hopelessness, pitiableness, pitifulness, squalor, wretchedness **2** = **degradation**, abjection, baseness, contemptibleness, debasement, dishonour, humbleness, humiliation, ignominy, lowness, meanness, servility, slavishness, sordidness, submissiveness, vileness, worthlessness

ablaze *adjective* **1** = **on fire**, afire, aflame, alight, blazing, burning, fiery, flaming, ignited, lighted **2** = **glowing**, aglow, brilliant, flashing, gleaming, illuminated, incandescent, luminous, radiant, sparkling **3** = **furious**, angry, fit to be tied (*slang*), foaming at the mouth, fuming, incandescent, incensed, on the warpath, raging **4** = **aroused**, enthusiastic, excited, fervent, frenzied, impassioned, passionate, stimulated

able *adjective* = **capable**, accomplished, adept, adequate, adroit, clever, competent, effective, efficient, experienced, expert, fit, fitted, gifted, highly endowed, masterful, masterly, powerful, practised, proficient, qualified, skilful, skilled, strong, talented
➤ **Antonyms**
amateurish, inadequate, incapable, incompetent, ineffective, inefficient, inept, mediocre, no great shakes (*informal*), unfit, unskilful, weak

able-bodied *adjective* = **strong**, firm, fit, hale, hardy, healthy, hearty, lusty, powerful, right as rain (*Brit. informal*), robust, sound, staunch, stout, strapping, sturdy, vigorous

ablutions

about

➤ **Antonyms**
ailing, debilitated, feeble, frail, sickly, weak

ablutions *plural noun* = **washing**, bath, bathing, cleansing, lavation, purification, shower, wash

abnegation *noun* = **giving up**, abandonment, abjuration, abstinence, continence, disallowance, eschewal, forbearance, refusal, rejection, relinquishment, renunciation, sacrifice, self-denial, surrender, temperance

abnormal *adjective* = **unusual**, aberrant, anomalous, atypical, curious, deviant, eccentric, erratic, exceptional, extraordinary, irregular, monstrous, odd, oddball (*informal*), off-the-wall (*slang*), outré, peculiar, queer, singular, strange, uncommon, unexpected, unnatural, untypical, wacko (*slang*), weird
➤ **Antonyms**
common, conventional, customary, familiar, natural, normal, ordinary, regular, unexceptional, usual

abnormality *noun* = **oddity**, aberration, anomaly, atypicalness, bizarreness, deformity, deviation, eccentricity, exception, extraordinariness, flaw, irregularity, monstrosity, peculiarity, queerness, singularity, strangeness, uncommonness, unexpectedness, unnaturalness, untypicalness, unusualness, weirdness

abode *noun* = **home**, domicile, dwelling, dwelling-place, habitat, habitation, house, lodging, pad (*slang*), quarters, residence

abolish *verb* = **do away with**, abrogate, annihilate, annul, axe (*informal*), blot out, cancel, destroy, eliminate, end, eradicate, expunge, exterminate, extinguish, extirpate, invalidate, nullify, obliterate, overthrow, overturn, put an end to, quash, repeal, repudiate, rescind, revoke, stamp out, subvert, suppress, terminate, vitiate, void, wipe out
➤ **Antonyms**
authorize, continue, create, establish, found, institute, introduce, legalize, promote, reinstate, reintroduce, restore, revive, sustain

abolition *noun* = **ending**, abrogation, annihilation, annulment, blotting out, cancellation, destruction, elimination, end, eradication, expunction, extermination, extinction, extirpation, invalidation, nullification, obliteration, overthrow, overturning, quashing, repeal, repudiation, rescission, revocation, stamping out, subversion, suppression, termination, vitiation, voiding, wiping out, withdrawal

abominable *adjective* = **terrible**, abhorrent, accursed, atrocious, base, contemptible, despicable, detestable, disgusting, execrable, foul, godawful (*slang*), hateful, heinous, hellish, horrible, horrid, loathsome, nauseous, obnoxious, obscene, odious, repellent, reprehensible, repugnant, repulsive, revolting, vile, villainous, wretched, yucky *or* yukky (*slang*)
➤ **Antonyms**
admirable, agreeable, charming, commendable, delightful, desirable, good, laudable, likable *or* likeable, lovable, pleasant, pleasing, wonderful

abominate *verb* = **hate**, abhor, detest, execrate, loathe, recoil from, regard with repugnance, shudder at
➤ **Antonyms**
admire, adore, cherish, dote on, esteem, idolize, love, revere, treasure, worship

abomination *noun* 1 = **hatred**, abhorrence, antipathy, aversion, detestation, disgust, distaste, execration, hate, horror, loathing, odium, repugnance, revulsion 2 = **evil**, anathema, bête noire, bugbear, curse, disgrace, horror, plague, shame, torment

aboriginal *adjective* = **native**, ancient, autochthonous, earliest, first, indigenous, original, primary, primeval, primitive, primordial, pristine

abort *verb* 1 = **terminate** (*a pregnancy*), miscarry 2 = **stop**, arrest, axe (*informal*), call off, check, end, fail, halt, terminate

abortion *noun* 1 = **termination**, aborticide, deliberate miscarriage, feticide, miscarriage 2 = **failure**, disappointment, fiasco, misadventure, monstrosity, vain effort

abortive *adjective* 1 = **failed**, bootless, failing, fruitless, futile, idle, ineffectual, miscarried, unavailing, unsuccessful, useless, vain 2 *Biology* = **imperfectly developed**, incomplete, rudimentary, stunted

abound *verb* = **be plentiful**, be jammed with, be packed with, crowd, flourish, increase, infest, luxuriate, overflow, proliferate, superabound, swarm, swell, teem, thrive

abounding *adjective* = **plentiful**, abundant, bountiful, copious, filled, flourishing, flowing, flush, full, lavish, luxuriant, overflowing, plenteous, profuse, prolific, rank, replete, rich, superabundant, teeming, thick on the ground, two a penny

about *preposition* 1 = **regarding**, anent (*Scot.*), as regards, concerned with, concerning, connected with, dealing with, on, re, referring to, relating to, relative to, respecting, touching, with respect to **2** = **near**, adjacent to, beside, circa (*used with dates*), close to, nearby **3** = **around**, encircling, on all sides, round, surrounding **4** = **throughout**, all over, over, through ♦ *adverb* **5** = **nearly**, almost, approaching, approximately, around, close to, more or less, nearing, roughly **6** = **here and there**, from place to place, hither and thither, to and fro ♦ *adjective* **7** = **around**, active, astir, in motion, present, stirring

about to *adverb* = **on the point of**, intending to, on the verge *or* brink of, ready to

above *preposition* **1** = **over**, atop, beyond, exceeding, higher than, on top of, upon **2** = **superior to**, before, beyond, exceeding, surpassing ♦ *adverb* **3** = **overhead**, aloft, atop, in heaven, on high ♦ *adjective* **4** = **preceding**, aforementioned, aforesaid, earlier, foregoing, previous, prior
➤ **Antonyms**
preposition ≠**over**: below, beneath, under, underneath ≠**superior to**: inferior, lesser, less than, lower than, subordinate

above board *adjective* **1** = **honest**, candid, fair and square, forthright, frank, guileless, honourable, kosher (*informal*), legitimate, on the up and up, open, overt, square, straight, straightforward, true, trustworthy, truthful, upfront (*informal*), upright, veracious ♦ *adverb* **2** = **honestly**, candidly, forthrightly, frankly, honourably, openly, overtly, straightforwardly, truly, truthfully, uprightly, veraciously, without guile
➤ **Antonyms**
adjective ≠**honest**: clandestine, crooked, deceitful, deceptive, devious, dishonest, fraudulent, furtive, secret, secretive, shady, sly, sneaky, underhand

abracadabra *noun* = **spell**, chant, charm, conjuration, hocus-pocus, incantation, invocation, magic, mumbo jumbo, sorcery, voodoo, witchcraft

abrade *verb* = **scrape**, erase, erode, file, grind, rub off, scour, scrape away, scrape out, wear away, wear down, wear off

abrasion *noun* **1** *Medical* = **graze**, chafe, scrape, scratch, scuff, surface injury, trauma (*Pathology*) **2** = **scraping**, abrading, chafing, erosion, friction, grating, rubbing, scouring, scratching, scuffing, wearing away, wearing down

abrasive *adjective* **1** = **unpleasant**, annoying, biting, caustic, cutting, galling, grating, hurtful, irritating, nasty, rough, sharp, vitriolic **2** = **rough**, chafing, erosive, frictional, grating, scraping, scratching,

scratchy, scuffing ♦ *adjective, noun* **3** = **scourer**, abradant, burnisher, grinder, scarifier

abreast *adjective* **1** = **alongside**, beside, level, neck and neck, shoulder to shoulder, side by side **2 abreast of** = **informed about**, acquainted with, *au courant* with, *au fait* with, conversant with, familiar with, in the picture about, in touch with, keeping one's finger on the pulse of, knowledgeable about, up to date with, up to speed with

abridge *verb* = **shorten**, abbreviate, abstract, clip, compress, concentrate, condense, contract, curtail, cut, cut down, decrease, digest, diminish, downsize, epitomize, lessen, précis, reduce, summarize, synopsize (*U.S.*), trim
➤ **Antonyms**
amplify, augment, enlarge, expand, extend, go into detail, lengthen, prolong, protract, spin out, stretch out

abridgment *noun* = **shortening**, abbreviation, abstract, compendium, condensation, conspectus, contraction, curtailment, cutting, decrease, digest, diminishing, diminution, epitome, lessening, limitation, outline, précis, reduction, restraint, restriction, résumé, summary, synopsis

abroad *adverb* **1** = **overseas**, beyond the sea, in foreign lands, out of the country **2** = **about**, at large, away, circulating, current, elsewhere, extensively, far, far and wide, forth, in circulation, out, out-of-doors, outside, publicly, widely, without

abrupt *adjective* **1** = **sudden**, hasty, headlong, hurried, precipitate, quick, surprising, swift, unanticipated, unexpected, unforeseen **2** = **steep**, precipitous, sharp, sheer, sudden **3** = **uneven**, broken, disconnected, discontinuous, irregular, jerky **4** = **curt**, blunt, brisk, brusque, clipped, direct, discourteous, gruff, impatient, impolite, monosyllabic, rough, rude, short, snappish, snappy, terse, unceremonious, uncivil, ungracious
➤ **Antonyms**
≠**sudden**: easy, leisurely, slow, thoughtful, unhurried ≠**steep**: gradual ≠**curt**: civil, courteous, gracious, polite

abscond *verb* = **flee**, bolt, clear out, decamp, disappear, do a bunk (*Brit. slang*), do a runner (*slang*), escape, flit (*informal*), fly, fly the coop (*U.S. & Canad. informal*), make off, run off, skedaddle (*informal*), slip away, sneak away, steal away, take a powder (*U.S. & Canad. slang*), take it on the lam (*U.S. & Canad. slang*)

absence *noun* **1** = **nonattendance**, absenteeism, nonappearance, truancy **2** = **lack**, default, defect, deficiency, need, nonexistence, omission, privation, unavailability, want

absent *adjective* **1** = **missing**, away, elsewhere, gone, lacking, nonattendant, nonexistent, not present, out, truant, unavailable, wanting **2** = **absent-minded**, absorbed, abstracted, bemused, blank, daydreaming, distracted, dreamy, empty, faraway, heedless, inattentive, musing, oblivious, preoccupied, unaware, unconscious, unheeding, unthinking, vacant, vague ◆ *verb* **3 absent oneself** = **stay away**, abscond, bunk off (*slang*), depart, keep away, play truant, remove, slope off (*informal*), truant, withdraw
➤ Antonyms
adjective ≠**missing**: attendant, in attendance, present ≠**absent-minded**: alert, attentive, aware, conscious, thoughtful ◆ *verb* ≠**stay away**: attend, show up (*informal*)

absently *adverb* = **absent-mindedly**, abstractedly, bemusedly, blankly, distractedly, dreamily, emptily, heedlessly, inattentively, obliviously, on automatic pilot, unconsciously, unheedingly, vacantly, vaguely

absent-minded *adjective* = **vague**, absent, absorbed, abstracted, bemused, distracted, ditzy *or* ditsy (*slang*), dreaming, dreamy, engrossed, faraway, forgetful, heedless, in a brown study, inattentive, musing, oblivious, preoccupied, unaware, unconscious, unheeding, unthinking
➤ Antonyms
alert, awake, observant, on one's toes, on the ball, perceptive, quick, vigilant, wary, wide-awake

absolute *adjective* **1** = **total**, arrant, complete, consummate, deep-dyed (*usually derogatory*), downright, entire, full-on (*informal*), out-and-out, outright, perfect, pure, sheer, thorough, unadulterated, unalloyed, unmitigated, unmixed, unqualified, utter **2** = **supreme**, absolutist, arbitrary, autarchical, autocratic, autonomous, despotic, dictatorial, full, peremptory, sovereign, tyrannical, unbounded, unconditional, unlimited, unqualified, unquestionable, unrestrained, unrestricted **3** = **definite**, actual, categorical, certain, conclusive, decided, decisive, exact, genuine, infallible, positive, precise, sure, unambiguous, unequivocal, unquestionable

absolutely *adverb* **1** = **totally**, completely, consummately, entirely, every inch, fully, lock, stock and barrel, one hundred per cent, perfectly, purely, thoroughly, to the hilt, unmitigatedly, utterly, wholly **2** = **supremely**, arbitrarily, autocratically, autonomously, despotically, dictatorially, fully, peremptorily, sovereignly, tyrannically, unconditionally, unquestionably, unrestrainedly, without qualification **3** = **definitely**, actually, categorically, certainly, conclusively, decidedly, decisively, exactly, genuinely, infallibly, positively, precisely, surely, truly, unambiguously, unequivocally, unquestionably
➤ Antonyms
≠**totally**: fairly, probably, reasonably, somewhat

absoluteness *noun* **1** = **totality**, consummateness, entirety, perfection, purity, thoroughness, unmitigatedness, wholeness **2** = **supremacy**, arbitrariness, autonomy, despotism, dictatorialness, fullness, peremptoriness, tyranny, unboundedness, unquestionability, unrestrainedness, unrestrictedness **3** = **certainty**, assuredness, certitude, conclusiveness, correctness, decidedness, decisiveness, definiteness, exactitude, genuineness, infallibility, positiveness, precision, sureness, surety, truth, unambiguousness, unequivocalness

absolution *noun* = **forgiveness**, acquittal, amnesty, deliverance, discharge, dispensation, exculpation, exemption, exoneration, freeing, indulgence, liberation, mercy, pardon, release, remission, setting free, shriving, vindication

absolutism *noun* = **dictatorship**, absoluteness, arbitrariness, autarchy, authoritarianism, autocracy, despotism, totalitarianism, tyranny

absolutist *noun* = **dictator**, arbiter, authoritarian, autocrat, despot, totalitarian, tyrant

absolve *verb* = **forgive**, acquit, clear, deliver, discharge, exculpate, excuse, exempt, exonerate, free, let off, liberate, loose, pardon, release, remit, set free, shrive, vindicate
➤ Antonyms
blame, censure, charge, condemn, convict, damn, denounce, excoriate, pass sentence on, reprehend, reproach, reprove, sentence, upbraid

absorb *verb* **1** = **soak up**, assimilate, consume, devour, digest, drink in, exhaust, imbibe, incorporate, ingest, osmose, receive, suck up, take in **2**

= **preoccupy**, captivate, engage, engross, enwrap, fascinate, fill, fill up, fix, hold, immerse, monopolize, occupy, rivet

absorbed adjective 1 = **preoccupied**, captivated, concentrating, engaged, engrossed, fascinated, fixed, held, immersed, involved, lost, occupied, rapt, riveted, up to one's ears, wrapped up 2 = **digested**, assimilated, consumed, devoured, exhausted, imbibed, incorporated, received, soaked up

absorbent adjective = **permeable**, porous, receptive, spongy

absorbing adjective = **fascinating**, arresting, captivating, engrossing, gripping, interesting, intriguing, preoccupying, riveting, spellbinding
➤ **Antonyms**
boring, dreary, dull, humdrum, mind-numbing, monotonous, tedious, tiresome, unexciting

absorption noun 1 = **soaking up**, assimilation, consumption, digestion, exhaustion, incorporation, osmosis, sucking up 2 = **concentration**, captivation, engagement, fascination, holding, immersion, intentness, involvement, occupation, preoccupation, raptness

abstain verb = **refrain**, avoid, cease, decline, deny (oneself), desist, fast, forbear, forgo, give up, keep from, kick (informal), refuse, renounce, shun, stop, withhold
➤ **Antonyms**
abandon oneself, give in, indulge, partake, yield

abstemious adjective = **self-denying**, abstinent, ascetic, austere, continent, frugal, moderate, sober, sparing, temperate
➤ **Antonyms**
gluttonous, greedy, immoderate, incontinent, intemperate, self-indulgent

abstention noun = **refusal**, abstaining, abstinence, avoidance, desistance, eschewal, forbearance, nonindulgence, refraining, self-control, self-denial, self-restraint

abstinence noun = **self-denial**, abstemiousness, asceticism, avoidance, continence, forbearance, moderation, refraining, self-restraint, soberness, sobriety, teetotalism, temperance
➤ **Antonyms**
abandon, acquisitiveness, covetousness, excess, gluttony, greediness, indulgence, self-indulgence, wantonness

abstinent adjective = **self-denying**, abstaining, abstemious, continent, forbearing, moderate, self-controlled,

self-restraining, sober, temperate

abstract adjective 1 = **theoretical**, abstruse, arcane, complex, conceptual, deep, general, generalized, hypothetical, indefinite, intellectual, nonconcrete, notional, occult, philosophical, profound, recondite, separate, subtle, theoretic, unpractical, unrealistic ◆ noun 2 = **summary**, abridgment, compendium, condensation, digest, epitome, essence, outline, précis, recapitulation, résumé, synopsis ◆ verb 3 = **summarize**, abbreviate, abridge, condense, digest, epitomize, outline, précis, shorten, synopsize (U.S.) 4 = **remove**, detach, dissociate, extract, isolate, separate, steal, take away, take out, withdraw
➤ **Antonyms**
adjective actual ≠**theoretical**: concrete, definite, factual, material, real, specific ◆ noun ≠**summary**: enlargement, expansion ◆ verb ≠**remove**: add, combine, inject

abstracted adjective = **preoccupied**, absent, absent-minded, bemused, daydreaming, dreamy, faraway, inattentive, remote, withdrawn, woolgathering

abstraction noun 1 = **idea**, concept, formula, generality, generalization, hypothesis, notion, theorem, theory, thought 2 = **absent-mindedness**, absence, bemusedness, dreaminess, inattention, pensiveness, preoccupation, remoteness, woolgathering

abstruse adjective = **obscure**, abstract, arcane, complex, dark, deep, Delphic, enigmatic, esoteric, hidden, incomprehensible, mysterious, mystical, occult, perplexing, profound, puzzling, recondite, subtle, unfathomable, vague
➤ **Antonyms**
apparent, bold, clear, conspicuous, evident, manifest, open, overt, patent, perceptible, plain, self-evident, transparent, unsubtle

absurd adjective = **ridiculous**, crazy (informal), daft (informal), dumb-ass (slang), farcical, foolish, idiotic, illogical, inane, incongruous, irrational, laughable, ludicrous, meaningless, nonsensical, preposterous, senseless, silly, stupid, unreasonable
➤ **Antonyms**
intelligent, logical, prudent, rational, reasonable, sagacious, sensible, smart, wise

absurdity noun = **ridiculousness**, bêtise (rare), craziness (informal), daftness (informal), farce, farcicality, farcicalness, folly, foolishness, idiocy, illogicality, illogicalness, incongruity, irrationality, joke, ludicrousness, meaninglessness, nonsense, preposterousness, senselessness, silliness, stupidity, unreasonableness

abundance *noun* 1 = **plenty**, affluence, ampleness, bounty, copiousness, exuberance, fullness, heap (*informal*), plenitude, plenteousness, profusion 2 = **wealth**, affluence, big bucks (*informal, chiefly U.S.*), big money, fortune, megabucks (*U.S. & Canad. slang*), opulence, pretty penny (*informal*), riches, tidy sum (*informal*), wad (*U.S. & Canad. slang*)
➤ **Antonyms**
≠**plenty**: dearth, deficiency, lack, need, paucity, scantiness, scarcity, sparseness

abundant *adjective* = **plentiful**, ample, bounteous, bountiful, copious, exuberant, filled, full, lavish, luxuriant, overflowing, plenteous, profuse, rank, rich, teeming, thick on the ground, two a penny, well-provided, well-supplied
➤ **Antonyms**
deficient, few, few and far between, inadequate, in short supply, insufficient, lacking, rare, scant, scanty, scarce, short, sparse, thin on the ground

abuse *noun* 1 = **ill-treatment**, damage, exploitation, harm, hurt, imposition, injury, maltreatment, manhandling, oppression, spoiling, wrong 2 = **insults**, blame, calumniation, castigation, censure, character assassination, contumely, curses, cursing, defamation, derision, disparagement, invective, libel, opprobrium, reproach, revilement, scolding, slander, swearing, tirade, traducement, upbraiding, vilification, vituperation 3 = **misuse**, misapplication
♦ *verb* 4 = **ill-treat**, damage, dump on (*slang, chiefly U.S.*), exploit, harm, hurt, impose upon, injure, maltreat, manhandle, mar, misapply, misuse, oppress, shit on (*taboo slang*), spoil, take advantage of, wrong 5 = **insult**, calumniate, castigate, curse, defame, disparage, inveigh against, libel, malign, revile, scold, slander, slate (*informal, chiefly Brit.*), smear, swear at, traduce, upbraid, vilify, vituperate
➤ **Antonyms**
verb ≠**ill-treat**: care for, protect ≠**insult**: acclaim, commend, compliment, extol, flatter, praise, respect

abusive *adjective* 1 = **insulting**, calumniating, castigating, censorious, contumelious, defamatory, derisive, disparaging, invective, libellous, maligning, offensive, opprobrious, reproachful, reviling, rude, scathing, scolding, slanderous, traducing,

upbraiding, vilifying, vituperative 2 = **harmful**, brutal, cruel, destructive, hurtful, injurious, rough
➤ **Antonyms**
≠**insulting**: approving, complimentary, eulogistic, flattering, laudatory, panegyrical, praising

abysmal *adjective* = **terrible**, appalling, awful, bad, dire, dreadful, godawful (*informal*)

abyss *noun* = **pit**, abysm, bottomless depth, chasm, crevasse, fissure, gorge, gulf, void

academic *adjective* 1 = **scholarly**, bookish, campus, college, collegiate, erudite, highbrow, learned, lettered, literary, scholastic, school, studious, university 2 = **hypothetical**, abstract, conjectural, impractical, notional, speculative, theoretical ♦ *noun* 3 = **scholar**, academician, don, fellow, lecturer, master, professor, pupil, scholastic, schoolman, student, tutor

accede *verb* 1 = **agree**, accept, acquiesce, admit, assent, comply, concede, concur, consent, endorse, grant, own, yield 2 = **inherit**, assume, attain, come to, enter upon, succeed, succeed to (*as heir*)

accelerate *verb* = **speed up**, advance, expedite, forward, further, hasten, hurry, pick up speed, precipitate, quicken, speed, spur, step up (*informal*), stimulate
➤ **Antonyms**
decelerate, delay, hinder, impede, obstruct, slow down

acceleration *noun* = **speeding up**, expedition, hastening, hurrying, quickening, spurring, stepping up (*informal*), stimulation

accent *noun* 1 = **pronunciation**, articulation, brogue, enunciation, inflection, intonation, modulation, tone 2 = **emphasis**, beat, cadence, force, ictus, pitch, rhythm, stress, timbre, tonality
♦ *verb* 3 = **emphasize**, accentuate, stress, underline, underscore

accentuate *verb* = **emphasize**, accent, draw attention to, foreground, highlight, stress, underline, underscore
➤ **Antonyms**
gloss over, make light *or* little of, minimize, play down, soft-pedal (*informal*), underplay

accept *verb* 1 = **receive**, acquire, gain, get, have, obtain, secure, take 2 = **agree to**, accede, acknowledge, acquiesce, admit, adopt, affirm, approve, believe, buy (*slang*), buy into (*slang*), concur with, consent to, cooperate with, recognize, swallow (*informal*), take on board 3 = **stand**, bear, bow to, brook, defer to, like

it or lump it (*informal*), put up with, submit to, suffer, take, tolerate, yield to **4** = **take on**, acknowledge, admit, assume, avow, bear, undertake
➤ **Antonyms**
≠**agree to**: decline, deny, disown, rebut, refuse, reject, repudiate, spurn

acceptable *adjective* **1** = **satisfactory**, adequate, admissible, all right, fair, moderate, passable, so-so (*informal*), standard, suitable, tolerable, up to scratch (*informal*) **2** = **pleasant**, agreeable, delightful, grateful, gratifying, pleasing, welcome
➤ **Antonyms**
≠**satisfactory**: unacceptable, unsatisfactory, unsuitable

acceptance *noun* **1** = **accepting**, acquiring, gaining, getting, having, obtaining, receipt, securing, taking **2** = **agreement**, accedence, accession, acknowledgment, acquiescence, admission, adoption, affirmation, approbation, approval, assent, belief, compliance, concession, concurrence, consensus, consent, cooperation, credence, O.K. *or* okay (*informal*), permission, recognition, stamp *or* seal of approval **3** = **submission**, deference, standing, taking, yielding **4** = **taking on**, acknowledgment, admission, assumption, avowal, undertaking

accepted *adjective* = **agreed**, acceptable, acknowledged, admitted, agreed upon, approved, authorized, common, confirmed, conventional, customary, established, normal, received, recognized, regular, sanctioned, standard, time-honoured, traditional, universal, usual
➤ **Antonyms**
abnormal, irregular, strange, unconventional, uncustomary, unorthodox, unusual, unwonted

access *noun* **1** = **entrance**, admission, admittance, approach, avenue, course, door, entering, entrée, entry, gateway, key, passage, passageway, path, road, way in **2** *Medical* = **attack**, fit, onset, outburst, paroxysm

accessibility *noun* **1** = **handiness**, approachability, attainability, availability, nearness, obtainability, possibility, readiness **2** = **approachability**, affability, conversableness, cordiality, friendliness, informality **3** = **openness**, exposedness, susceptibility

accessible *adjective* **1** = **handy**, achievable, a hop, skip and a jump away, at hand, at one's fingertips, attainable, available, get-at-able (*informal*), near, nearby,

obtainable, on hand, possible, reachable, ready **2** = **approachable**, affable, available, cordial, friendly, informal **3** = **open**, exposed, liable, subject, susceptible, vulnerable, wide-open
➤ **Antonyms**
≠**handy**: far-off, inaccessible, unavailable, unobtainable, unreachable

accession *noun* **1** = **taking up**, assumption, attaining to, attainment of, entering upon, succession (*to a throne, dignity, or office*), taking on, taking over **2** = **agreement**, accedence, acceptance, acquiescence, assent, concurrence, consent **3** = **increase**, addition, augmentation, enlargement, extension

accessory *noun* **1** = **addition**, accent, accompaniment, add-on, adjunct, adornment, aid, appendage, attachment, component, convenience, decoration, extension, extra, frill, help, supplement, trim, trimming **2** = **accomplice**, abettor, assistant, associate (*in crime*), colleague, confederate, helper, partner ◆ *adjective* **3** = **additional**, abetting, aiding, ancillary, assisting in, auxiliary, contributory, extra, secondary, subordinate, supplemental, supplementary

accident *noun* **1** = **misfortune**, blow, calamity, casualty, chance, collision, crash, disaster, misadventure, mischance, mishap, pile-up (*informal*) **2** = **chance**, fate, fluke, fortuity, fortune, hazard, luck

accidental *adjective* = **unintentional**, adventitious, casual, chance, contingent, fortuitous, haphazard, inadvertent, incidental, inessential, nonessential, random, uncalculated, uncertain, unessential, unexpected, unforeseen, unintended, unlooked-for, unplanned, unpremeditated, unwitting
➤ **Antonyms**
calculated, designed, expected, foreseen, intended, intentional, planned, prepared

accidentally *adverb* = **unintentionally**, adventitiously, by accident, by chance, by mistake, casually, fortuitously, haphazardly, inadvertently, incidentally, randomly, unconsciously, undesignedly, unexpectedly, unwittingly
➤ **Antonyms**
by design, consciously, deliberately, designedly, on purpose, wilfully

acclaim *verb* **1** = **praise**, applaud, approve, celebrate, cheer, clap, commend, crack up (*informal*), eulogize, exalt, extol, hail, honour, laud, salute, welcome ◆ *noun* **2** = **praise**, acclamation, applause, approbation, approval, celebration, cheering, clapping, commendation,

eulogizing, exaltation, honour, kudos, laudation, plaudits, welcome
➤ **Antonyms**
noun ≠**praise**: bad press, brickbats, censure, criticism, denigration, disparagement, fault-finding, flak (*informal*), panning (*informal*), stick (*slang*), vituperation
acclamation *noun* = **praise**, acclaim, adulation, approbation, approval, cheer, cheering, cheers, enthusiasm, kudos, laudation, loud homage, ovation, plaudit, salutation, shouting, tribute
acclimatization *noun* = **adaptation**, acclimation, accommodation, acculturation, adjustment, habituation, inurement, naturalization
acclimatize *verb* = **adapt**, accommodate, acculturate, acculture, accustom, adjust, become seasoned to, get used to, habituate, inure, naturalize
accolade *noun* = **praise**, acclaim, applause, approval, commendation, compliment, ovation, recognition, tribute
accommodate *verb* 1 = **house**, billet, board, cater for, entertain, harbour, lodge, put up, quarter, shelter 2 = **help**, afford, aid, assist, furnish, oblige, provide, purvey, serve, supply 3 = **adapt**, accustom, adjust, comply, compose, conform, fit, harmonize, modify, reconcile, settle
accommodating *adjective* = **helpful**, complaisant, considerate, cooperative, friendly, hospitable, kind, obliging, polite, unselfish, willing
➤ **Antonyms**
disobliging, inconsiderate, rude, uncooperative, unhelpful
accommodation *noun* 1 = **housing**, board, digs (*Brit. informal*), harbouring, house, lodging(s), quartering, quarters, shelter, sheltering 2 = **help**, aid, assistance, provision, service, supply 3 = **adaptation**, adjustment, compliance, composition, compromise, conformity, fitting, harmony, modification, reconciliation, settlement
accompaniment *noun* 1 = **supplement**, accessory, companion, complement 2 = **backing music**, backing
accompany *verb* 1 = **go with**, attend, chaperon, conduct, convoy, escort, hold (someone's) hand, squire, usher 2 = **occur with**, belong to, coexist with, coincide with, come with, follow, go cheek by jowl, go together with, join with, supplement
accompanying *adjective* = **additional**, accessory, added, appended, associate, associated, attached, attendant, complementary, concomitant, concurrent, connected, fellow, joint, related,

supplemental, supplementary
accomplice *noun* = **helper**, abettor, accessory, ally, assistant, associate, coadjutor, collaborator, colleague, confederate, henchman, partner
accomplish *verb* = **do**, achieve, attain, bring about, bring off (*informal*), carry out, complete, conclude, consummate, effect, effectuate, execute, finish, fulfil, manage, perform, produce, put the tin lid on, realize
➤ **Antonyms**
fail, fall short, forsake, give up
accomplished *adjective* 1 = **skilled**, adept, consummate, cultivated, expert, gifted, masterly, polished, practised, proficient, skilful, talented 2 = **done**, achieved, attained, brought about, carried out, completed, concluded, consummated, effected, executed, finished, fulfilled, in the can (*informal*), managed, performed, produced, realized
➤ **Antonyms**
≠**skilled**: amateurish, incapable, incompetent, inexpert, unestablished, unproven, unrealized, unskilled, untalented
accomplishment *noun* 1 = **completion**, achievement, attainment, bringing about, carrying out, conclusion, consummation, doing, effecting, execution, finishing, fulfilment, management, performance, production, realization 2 = **achievement**, act, attainment, coup, deed, exploit, feat, stroke, triumph 3 *often plural* = **skill**, ability, achievement, art, attainment, capability, craft, gift, proficiency, talent
accord *noun* 1 = **agreement**, accordance, assent, concert, concurrence, conformity, congruence, correspondence, harmony, rapport, sympathy, unanimity, unison ♦ *verb* 2 = **grant**, allow, bestow, concede, confer, endow, give, present, render, tender, vouchsafe 3 = **agree**, assent, be in tune (*informal*), concur, conform, correspond, fit, harmonize, match, suit, tally
➤ **Antonyms**
noun ≠**agreement**: conflict, contention, disagreement, discord ♦ *verb* ≠**grant**: hold back, refuse, withhold ≠**agree**: conflict, contrast, differ, disagree, discord
accordance *noun* As in **in accordance with** = **agreement**, accord, assent, concert, concurrence, conformity, congruence, correspondence, harmony, rapport, sympathy, unanimity
accordingly *adverb* 1 = **appropriately**, correspondingly, fitly, properly, suitably 2 = **consequently**, as a result, ergo, hence, in consequence, so, therefore, thus

according to *adverb* **1** = **as stated by**, as believed by, as maintained by, in the light of, on the authority of, on the report of **2** = **in keeping with**, after, after the manner of, consistent with, in accordance with, in compliance with, in conformity with, in harmony with, in line with, in obedience to, in step with, in the manner of, obedient to **3** = **in relation**, commensurate with, in proportion

accost *verb* = **approach**, buttonhole, confront, greet, hail

account *noun* **1** = **description**, chronicle, detail, explanation, history, narration, narrative, recital, record, relation, report, statement, story, tale, version **2** *Commerce* = **statement**, balance, bill, book, books, charge, computation, inventory, invoice, ledger, reckoning, register, score, tally **3** = **importance**, advantage, benefit, consequence, distinction, esteem, honour, import, merit, note, profit, rank, repute, significance, standing, use, value, worth **4** = **reason**, basis, cause, consideration, ground, grounds, interest, motive, regard, sake, score ♦ *verb* **5** = **consider**, appraise, assess, believe, calculate, compute, count, deem, esteem, estimate, explain, gauge, hold, judge, rate, reckon, regard, think, value, weigh

accountability *noun* = **responsibility**, answerability, chargeability, culpability, liability

accountable *adjective* = **responsible**, amenable, answerable, charged with, liable, obligated, obliged

accountant *noun* = **auditor**, bean counter (*informal*), book-keeper

account for *verb* **1** = **explain**, answer for, clarify, clear up, elucidate, illuminate, justify, rationalize **2** = **put out of action**, destroy, incapacitate, kill, put paid to

accredit *verb* **1** = **authorize**, appoint, certify, commission, depute, empower, endorse, entrust, guarantee, license, recognize, sanction, vouch for **2** = **attribute**, ascribe, assign, credit

accredited *adjective* = **authorized**, appointed, certified, commissioned, deputed, deputized, empowered, endorsed, guaranteed, licensed, official, recognized, sanctioned, vouched for

accrue *verb* = **increase**, accumulate, amass, arise, be added, build up, collect, enlarge, ensue, flow, follow, grow, issue, spring up

accumulate *verb* = **collect**, accrue, amass, build up, cumulate, gather, grow, hoard, increase, pile up, stockpile, store
➤ **Antonyms**
diffuse, disperse, disseminate, dissipate,

distribute, propagate, scatter

accumulation *noun* = **collection**, aggregation, augmentation, build-up, conglomeration, gathering, growth, heap, hoard, increase, mass, pile, rick, stack, stock, stockpile, store

accuracy *noun* = **exactness**, accurateness, authenticity, carefulness, closeness, correctness, exactitude, faithfulness, faultlessness, fidelity, meticulousness, niceness, nicety, precision, strictness, truth, truthfulness, veracity, verity
➤ **Antonyms**
carelessness, erroneousness, imprecision, inaccuracy, incorrectness, inexactitude, laxity, laxness

accurate *adjective* = **exact**, authentic, careful, close, correct, faithful, faultless, just, meticulous, nice, on the money (*U.S.*), precise, proper, regular, right, scrupulous, spot-on (*Brit. informal*), strict, true, truthful, unerring, veracious
➤ **Antonyms**
careless, defective, faulty, imperfect, imprecise, inaccurate, incorrect, inexact, wrong

accurately *adverb* = **exactly**, authentically, carefully, closely, correctly, faithfully, faultlessly, justly, meticulously, nicely, precisely, properly, regularly, rightly, scrupulously, strictly, to the letter, truly, truthfully, unerringly, veraciously

accursed *adjective* **1** = **cursed**, bedevilled, bewitched, condemned, damned, doomed, hopeless, ill-fated, ill-omened, jinxed, luckless, ruined, undone, unfortunate, unlucky, wretched **2** = **hateful**, abominable, despicable, detestable, execrable, hellish, horrible
➤ **Antonyms**
≠cursed: blessed, charmed, favoured, fortunate, lucky

accusation *noun* = **charge**, allegation, arraignment, attribution, citation, complaint, denunciation, impeachment, imputation, incrimination, indictment, recrimination

accuse *verb* = **charge**, allege, arraign, attribute, blame, censure, cite, denounce, impeach, impute, incriminate, indict, point a *or* the finger at, recriminate, tax
➤ **Antonyms**
absolve, defend, exonerate, vindicate

accustom *verb* = **adapt**, acclimatize, acquaint, discipline, exercise, familiarize, habituate, inure, season, train

accustomed *adjective* **1** = **usual**, common, conventional, customary, established, everyday, expected, fixed, general, habitual, normal, ordinary, regular,

routine, set, traditional, wonted **2 = used**, acclimatized, acquainted, adapted, disciplined, exercised, familiar, familiarized, given to, habituated, in the habit of, inured, seasoned, trained
➤ **Antonyms**
≠**usual**: abnormal, infrequent, occasional, odd, peculiar, rare, strange, unaccustomed, uncommon, unfamiliar, unusual ≠**used**: unaccustomed, unfamiliar, unused

ace noun **1** *Cards, dice, etc.* **= one**, single point **2** *Informal* **= expert**, adept, buff (*informal*), champion, dab hand (*Brit. informal*), genius, hotshot (*informal*), master, maven (*U.S.*), star, virtuoso, whizz (*informal*), winner, wizard (*informal*)
♦ *adjective* **3** *Informal* **= excellent**, awesome (*slang*), brilliant, champion, expert, fine, great, masterly, outstanding, superb, virtuoso

ache verb **1** **= hurt**, pain, pound, smart, suffer, throb, twinge **2** **= suffer**, agonize, eat one's heart out, grieve, mourn, sorrow **3** **= long**, covet, crave, desire, eat one's heart out over, hanker, hope, hunger, need, pine, set one's heart on, thirst, yearn
♦ *noun* **4** **= pain**, hurt, pang, pounding, smart, smarting, soreness, suffering, throb, throbbing **5** **= suffering**, anguish, grief, mourning, sorrow **6** **= longing**, craving, desire, hankering, hope, hunger, need, pining, thirst, yearning

achievable *adjective* **= attainable**, accessible, accomplishable, acquirable, feasible, obtainable, possible, practicable, reachable, realizable, winnable, within one's grasp

achieve verb **= attain**, accomplish, acquire, bring about, carry out, complete, consummate, do, earn, effect, execute, finish, fulfil, gain, get, obtain, perform, procure, put the tin lid on, reach, realize, win

achievement noun **1 = accomplishment**, act, deed, effort, exploit, feat, feather in one's cap, stroke **2** accomplishment, **= fulfilment**, acquirement, attainment, completion, execution, performance, production, realization

acid *adjective* **1** **= sour**, acerb, acerbic, acetic, acidulous, acrid, biting, pungent, sharp, tart, vinegarish, vinegary **2** **= sharp**, acerbic, biting, bitter, caustic, cutting, harsh, hurtful, mordacious, mordant, pungent, stinging, trenchant, vitriolic
➤ **Antonyms**
≠**sour**: alkaline, bland, mild, pleasant, sweet ≠**sharp**: benign, bland, gentle, kindly, mild, pleasant, sweet

acidity noun **1** **= sourness**, acerbity, acidulousness, acridity, acridness, bitterness, pungency, sharpness, tartness, vinegariness, vinegarishness **2** **= sharpness**, acerbity, acridity, acridness, bitterness, causticity, causticness, harshness, hurtfulness, mordancy, pungency, trenchancy

acknowledge verb **1** **= accept**, accede, acquiesce, admit, allow, concede, confess, declare, grant, own, profess, recognize, yield **2** **= greet**, address, hail, notice, recognize, salute **3** **= reply to**, answer, notice, react to, recognize, respond to, return
➤ **Antonyms**
≠**accept**: contradict, deny, disclaim, discount, reject, renounce, repudiate ≠**greet**: disdain, disregard, ignore, reject, snub, spurn ≠**reply to**: deny, disavow, disregard, ignore, rebut

acknowledged *adjective* **= accepted**, accredited, admitted, answered, approved, conceded, confessed, declared, professed, recognized, returned

acknowledgment noun **1** **= acceptance**, accession, acquiescence, admission, allowing, confession, declaration, profession, realization, yielding **2** **= greeting**, addressing, hail, hailing, notice, recognition, salutation, salute **3** **= appreciation**, answer, credit, gratitude, reaction, recognition, reply, response, return, thanks

acme noun **= high point**, apex, climax, crest, crown, culmination, height, optimum, peak, pinnacle, summit, top, vertex, zenith
➤ **Antonyms**
bottom, depths, low point, minimum, nadir, rock bottom, zero

acquaint verb **= tell**, advise, announce, apprise, disclose, divulge, enlighten, familiarize, inform, let (someone) know, notify, reveal

acquaintance noun **1** **= associate**, colleague, contact **2** **= knowledge**, association, awareness, cognizance, companionship, conversance, conversancy, experience, familiarity, fellowship, intimacy, relationship, social contact, understanding
➤ **Antonyms**
≠**associate**: buddy, good friend, intimate ≠**knowledge**: ignorance, unfamiliarity

acquainted with *adjective* **= familiar with**, alive to, apprised of, *au fait* with, aware of, cognizant of, conscious of, conversant with, experienced in, informed of, in on, knowledgeable about, privy to, up to speed with, versed in

acquiesce verb = **agree**, accede, accept, allow, approve, assent, bow to, comply, concur, conform, consent, give in, go along with, play ball (informal), submit, yield
➤ Antonyms
balk at, contest, demur, disagree, dissent, fight, object, protest, refuse, resist, veto

acquiescence noun = **agreement**, acceptance, accession, approval, assent, compliance, concurrence, conformity, consent, giving in, obedience, submission, yielding

acquiescent adjective = **agreeing**, acceding, accepting, agreeable, approving, assenting, compliant, concurrent, conforming, consenting, obedient, submissive, yielding

acquire verb = **get**, achieve, amass, attain, buy, collect, earn, gain, gather, land, obtain, pick up, procure, realize, receive, score (slang), secure, win
➤ Antonyms
be deprived of, forfeit, forgo, give up, lose, relinquish, renounce, surrender, waive

acquirement noun 1 = **acquisition**, accomplishment, achievement, attainment, gathering, grip 2 = **skill**, knowledge, learning, mastery, qualification

acquisition noun 1 = **possession**, buy, gain, prize, property, purchase 2 = **acquiring**, achievement, acquirement, attainment, gaining, obtainment, procurement, pursuit

acquisitive adjective = **greedy**, avaricious, avid, covetous, grabbing, grasping, predatory, rapacious
➤ Antonyms
bounteous, bountiful, generous, lavish, liberal, munificent, open-handed, unselfish, unstinting

acquisitiveness noun = **greed**, avarice, avidity, avidness, covetousness, graspingness, predatoriness, rapaciousness, rapacity

acquit verb 1 = **clear**, absolve, deliver, discharge, exculpate, exonerate, free, fulfil, liberate, release, relieve, vindicate 2 = **pay off**, discharge, pay, repay, satisfy, settle 3 = **behave**, bear, comport, conduct, perform
➤ Antonyms
≠clear: blame, charge, condemn, convict, damn, find guilty, sentence

acquittal noun = **clearance**, absolution, deliverance, discharge, exculpation, exoneration, freeing, liberation, release, relief, vindication

acrid adjective 1 = **pungent**, acerb, acid, astringent, biting, bitter, burning, caustic, harsh, irritating, sharp, stinging, vitriolic 2 = **sharp**, acrimonious, biting, bitter, caustic, cutting, harsh, mordacious, mordant, nasty, sarcastic, trenchant, vitriolic

acrimonious adjective = **bitter**, acerbic, astringent, biting, caustic, censorious, churlish, crabbed, cutting, irascible, mordacious, mordant, peevish, petulant, pungent, rancorous, sarcastic, severe, sharp, spiteful, splenetic, tart, testy, trenchant, vitriolic
➤ Antonyms
affable, benign, forgiving, good-tempered

acrimony noun = **bitterness**, acerbity, asperity, astringency, churlishness, harshness, ill will, irascibility, mordancy, peevishness, pungency, rancour, sarcasm, spleen, tartness, trenchancy, virulence
➤ Antonyms
amity, friendliness, friendship, good feelings, goodwill, liking, warmth

act noun 1 = **deed**, accomplishment, achievement, action, blow, doing, execution, exertion, exploit, feat, move, operation, performance, step, stroke, undertaking 2 = **law**, bill, decree, edict, enactment, measure, ordinance, resolution, statute 3 = **performance**, routine, show, sketch, turn 4 = **pretence**, affectation, attitude, counterfeit, dissimulation, fake, feigning, front, performance, pose, posture, sham, show, stance ◆ verb 5 = **do**, acquit, bear, behave, carry, carry out, comport, conduct, enact, execute, exert, function, go about, make, move, operate, perform, react, serve, strike, take effect, undertake, work 6 = **perform**, act out, characterize, enact, impersonate, mime, mimic, personate, personify, play, play or take the part of, portray, represent 7 = **pretend**, affect, assume, counterfeit, dissimulate, feign, imitate, perform, pose, posture, put on, seem, sham

act for verb = **stand in for**, cover for, deputize for, fill in for, function in place of, replace, represent, serve, substitute for, take the place of

acting noun 1 = **performance**, characterization, dramatics, enacting, impersonation, performing, playing, portrayal, portraying, stagecraft, theatre ◆ adjective 2 = **temporary**, interim, pro tem, provisional, substitute, surrogate

action noun 1 = **deed**, accomplishment, achievement, act, blow, exercise, exertion, exploit, feat, move, operation, performance, step, stroke, undertaking **2** = **lawsuit**, case, cause, litigation, proceeding, prosecution, suit **3** = **energy**, activity, force, liveliness, spirit, vigour, vim, vitality **4** = **movement**, activity, effect, effort, exertion, force, functioning, influence, motion, operation, power, process, work, working **5** = **battle**, affray, clash, combat, conflict, contest, encounter, engagement, fight, fighting, fray, skirmish, sortie, warfare

actions *plural noun* = **behaviour**, bearing, comportment, conduct, demeanour, deportment, manners, ways

activate *verb* = **start**, actuate, animate, arouse, energize, galvanize, get going, impel, initiate, kick-start (*informal*), mobilize, motivate, move, prod, prompt, propel, rouse, set going, set in motion, set off, stimulate, stir, switch on, trigger (off), turn on
➤ **Antonyms**
arrest, check, deactivate, halt, impede, stall, stop, terminate, turn off

active *adjective* **1** = **busy**, bustling, engaged, full, hard-working, involved, occupied, on the go (*informal*), on the move, strenuous **2** = **energetic**, alert, alive and kicking, animated, diligent, industrious, lively, nimble, on the go (*informal*), quick, spirited, sprightly, spry, vibrant, vigorous, vital, vivacious **3** = **enthusiastic**, activist, aggressive, ambitious, assertive, committed, devoted, energetic, engaged, enterprising, forceful, forward, hard-working, industrious, militant, zealous **4** = **in operation**, acting, astir, at work, doing, effectual, functioning, in action, in business, in force, live, moving, operative, running, stirring, working
➤ **Antonyms**
dormant, dull, idle, inactive, inoperative, lazy, sedentary, slow, sluggish, torpid, unimaginative, unoccupied

activist *noun* = **militant**, organizer, partisan

activity *noun* **1** = **action**, activeness, animation, bustle, enterprise, exercise, exertion, hurly-burly, hustle, labour, life, liveliness, motion, movement, stir, work **2** = **pursuit**, act, avocation, deed, endeavour, enterprise, hobby, interest, job, labour, occupation, pastime, project, scheme, task, undertaking, venture, work
➤ **Antonyms**
≠**action:** dullness, idleness, immobility, inaction, inactivity, indolence, inertia, lethargy, passivity, sluggishness, torpor

act on, act upon *verb* **1** = **obey**, act in accordance with, carry out, comply with,

conform to, follow, heed, yield to **2** = **affect**, alter, change, impact, influence, modify, sway, transform

actor *noun* = **performer**, actress, dramatic artist, leading man, luvvie (*informal*), play-actor, player, thesp (*informal*), Thespian, tragedian, trouper

actress *noun* = **performer**, actor, dramatic artist, leading lady, play-actor, player, starlet, Thespian, tragedienne, trouper

actual *adjective* **1** = **definite**, absolute, categorical, certain, concrete, corporeal, factual, indisputable, indubitable, physical, positive, real, substantial, tangible, undeniable, unquestionable **2** = **real**, authentic, confirmed, genuine, realistic, true, truthful, verified
➤ **Antonyms**
fictitious, hypothetical, made-up, probable, supposed, theoretical, unreal, untrue

actually *adverb* = **really**, absolutely, as a matter of fact, de facto, essentially, indeed, in fact, in point of fact, in reality, in truth, literally, truly, veritably

actuate *verb* = **motivate**, animate, arouse, cause, dispose, drive, excite, get going, impel, incite, induce, influence, inspire, instigate, move, prompt, quicken, rouse, spur, stimulate, stir, urge

act up *verb* = **misbehave**, be naughty, carry on, cause trouble, give bother, give trouble, horse around (*informal*), malfunction, mess about, piss about (*taboo slang*), piss around (*taboo slang*), play up (*Brit. informal*), raise Cain

act upon *see* ACT ON

acumen *noun* = **judgment**, acuteness, astuteness, cleverness, discernment, ingenuity, insight, intelligence, keenness, penetration, perception, perspicacity, perspicuity, sagacity, sharpness, shrewdness, smartness, smarts (*slang, chiefly U.S.*), wisdom, wit

acute *adjective* **1** = **serious**, critical, crucial, dangerous, decisive, essential, grave, important, severe, sudden, urgent, vital **2** = **sharp**, cutting, distressing, excruciating, exquisite, fierce, harrowing, intense, overpowering, overwhelming, piercing, poignant, powerful, racking, severe, shooting, shrill, stabbing, sudden, violent **3** = **perceptive**, astute, canny, clever, discerning, discriminating, incisive, ingenious, insightful, intuitive, keen, observant, on the ball (*informal*), penetrating, perspicacious, piercing, sensitive, sharp, smart, subtle
➤ **Antonyms**
≠**perceptive:** dense, dim, dim-witted, dull,

obtuse, slow, stupid, unintelligent

acuteness noun 1 = **seriousness**, criticality, criticalness, cruciality, danger, dangerousness, decisiveness, essentiality, gravity, importance, severity, suddenness, urgency, vitalness 2 = **sharpness**, distressingness, exquisiteness, fierceness, intenseness, intensity, poignancy, powerfulness, severity, shrillness, suddenness, violence 3 = **perceptiveness**, acuity, astuteness, canniness, cleverness, discernment, discrimination, ingenuity, insight, intuition, intuitiveness, keenness, perception, perspicacity, sensitivity, sharpness, smartness, subtleness, subtlety, wit

adage noun = **saying**, aphorism, apophthegm, axiom, by-word, dictum, maxim, motto, precept, proverb, saw

adamant adjective = **determined**, firm, fixed, immovable, inexorable, inflexible, insistent, intransigent, obdurate, relentless, resolute, rigid, set, stiff, stubborn, unbending, uncompromising, unrelenting, unshakable, unyielding
➤ **Antonyms**
compliant, compromising, easy-going, flexible, lax, pliant, receptive, responsive, susceptible, tractable, yielding

adapt verb = **adjust**, acclimatize, accommodate, alter, apply, change, comply, conform, convert, customize, familiarize, fashion, fit, habituate, harmonize, make, match, modify, prepare, qualify, remodel, shape, suit, tailor, tweak (informal)

adaptability noun = **flexibility**, adaptableness, adjustability, alterability, changeability, compliancy, convertibility, malleability, modifiability, plasticity, pliability, pliancy, resilience, variability, versatility

adaptable adjective = **flexible**, adjustable, alterable, changeable, compliant, conformable, convertible, easy-going, easy-oasy (slang), malleable, modifiable, plastic, pliant, resilient, variable, versatile

adaptation noun 1 = **acclimatization**, accustomedness, familiarization, habituation, naturalization 2 = **conversion**, adjustment, alteration, change, modification, refitting, remodelling, reworking, shift, transformation, variation, version

add verb 1 = **count up**, add up, compute, reckon, sum up, total, tot up 2 = **include**, adjoin, affix, amplify, annex, append, attach, augment, enlarge by, increase by, supplement
➤ **Antonyms**

deduct, diminish, lessen, reduce, remove, subtract, take away, take from

addendum noun = **addition**, adjunct, affix, appendage, appendix, attachment, augmentation, codicil, extension, extra, postscript, supplement

addict noun 1 = **junkie** (informal), dope-fiend (slang), fiend (informal), freak (informal), head (slang), pill-popper (informal), user (informal) 2 = **fan**, adherent, buff (informal), devotee, enthusiast, follower, freak (informal), nut (slang)

addicted adjective = **hooked** (slang), absorbed, accustomed, dedicated, dependent, devoted, disposed, fond, habituated, inclined, obsessed, prone

addiction noun = **dependence**, craving, enslavement, habit, obsession

addition noun 1 = **inclusion**, accession, adding, adjoining, affixing, amplification, annexation, attachment, augmentation, enlargement, extension, increasing 2 = **extra**, addendum, additive, adjunct, affix, appendage, appendix, extension, gain, increase, increment, supplement 3 = **counting up**, adding up, computation, reckoning, summation, summing up, totalling, totting up 4 **in addition (to)** = **as well (as)**, additionally, also, besides, into the bargain, moreover, over and above, to boot, too, withal
➤ **Antonyms**
≠inclusion, counting up: deduction, detachment, diminution, lessening, reduction, removal, subtraction

additional adjective = **extra**, added, add-on, affixed, appended, fresh, further, increased, more, new, other, over-and-above, spare, supplementary

address noun 1 = **location**, abode, domicile, dwelling, home, house, lodging, pad (slang), place, residence, situation, whereabouts 2 = **direction**, inscription, superscription 3 = **speech**, discourse, disquisition, dissertation, harangue, lecture, oration, sermon, talk ✦ verb 4 = **speak to**, accost, apostrophize, approach, greet, hail, invoke, salute, talk to 5 = **give a speech**, discourse, give a talk, harangue, lecture, orate, sermonize, speak, spout, talk 6 **address (oneself) to** = **concentrate on**, apply (oneself) to, attend to, devote (oneself) to, engage in, focus on, knuckle down to, look to, take care of, take up, turn to, undertake

adduce verb = **mention**, advance, allege, cite, designate, name, offer, present, quote

add up verb 1 = **count up**, add, compute, count, reckon, sum up, total, tot up 2

= **mean**, amount, come to, imply, indicate, reveal, signify **3** = **make sense**, be plausible, be reasonable, hold water, ring true, stand to reason

adept *adjective* **1** = **skilful**, able, accomplished, adroit, dexterous, expert, masterful, masterly, practised, proficient, skilled, versed ♦ *noun* **2** = **expert**, buff (*informal*), dab hand (*Brit. informal*), genius, hotshot (*informal*), master, maven (*U.S.*), whizz (*informal*)
➤ **Antonyms**
adjective ≠ **skilful**: amateurish, awkward, clumsy, inept, unskilled

adequacy *noun* = **sufficiency**, capability, commensurateness, competence, fairness, requisiteness, satisfactoriness, suitability, tolerability

adequate *adjective* = **enough**, capable, commensurate, competent, fair, passable, requisite, satisfactory, sufficient, suitable, tolerable, up to scratch (*informal*)
➤ **Antonyms**
deficient, inadequate, insufficient, lacking, meagre, scant, short, unsatisfactory, unsuitable

adhere *verb* **1** = **stick**, attach, cement, cleave, cling, cohere, fasten, fix, glue, glue on, hold fast, paste, stick fast, unite **2** = **support**, abide by, be attached, be constant, be devoted, be faithful, be loyal, be true, cleave to, cling, follow, fulfil, heed, keep, keep to, maintain, mind, obey, observe, respect, stand by

adherent *noun* **1** = **supporter**, admirer, advocate, devotee, disciple, fan, follower, hanger-on, henchman, partisan, protagonist, sectary, upholder, votary ♦ *adjective* **2** = **sticky**, adhering, adhesive, clinging, gluey, glutinous, gummy, holding, mucilaginous, sticking, tacky, tenacious
➤ **Antonyms**
noun ≠ **supporter**: adversary, antagonist, disputant, enemy, foe, opponent, opposer, opposition, rival

adhesive *adjective* **1** = **sticky**, adhering, attaching, clinging, cohesive, gluey, glutinous, gummy, holding, mucilaginous, sticking, tacky, tenacious ♦ *noun* **2** = **glue**, cement, gum, mucilage, paste

adieu *noun* = **goodbye**, congé, farewell, leave-taking, parting, valediction

adipose *adjective* = **fatty**, fat, greasy, obese, oily, oleaginous, sebaceous

adjacent *adjective* = **next**, abutting, adjoining, alongside, beside, bordering, cheek by jowl, close, contiguous, near, neighbouring, next door, proximate, touching, within sniffing distance

(*informal*)
➤ **Antonyms**
distant, far away, remote, separated

adjoin *verb* = **connect**, abut, add, affix, annex, append, approximate, attach, border, combine, communicate with, couple, impinge, interconnect, join, link, neighbour, touch, unite, verge

adjoining *adjective* = **connecting**, abutting, adjacent, bordering, contiguous, interconnecting, joined, joining, near, neighbouring, next door, touching, verging

adjourn *verb* = **postpone**, defer, delay, discontinue, interrupt, prorogue, put off, put on the back burner (*informal*), recess, stay, suspend, take a rain check on (*U.S. & Canad. informal*)
➤ **Antonyms**
assemble, continue, convene, gather, open, remain, reopen, stay

adjournment *noun* = **postponement**, deferment, deferral, delay, discontinuation, interruption, prorogation, putting off, recess, stay, suspension

adjudge *verb* = **judge**, adjudicate, allot, apportion, assign, award, decide, declare, decree, determine, distribute, order, pronounce

adjudicate *verb* = **judge**, adjudge, arbitrate, decide, determine, mediate, referee, settle, umpire

adjudication *noun* = **judgment**, adjudgment, arbitration, conclusion, decision, determination, finding, pronouncement, ruling, settlement, verdict

adjunct *noun* = **addition**, accessory, addendum, add-on, appendage, appurtenance, auxiliary, complement, supplement

adjure *verb* **1** = **beg**, appeal to, beseech, entreat, implore, invoke, pray, supplicate **2** = **order**, charge, command, direct, enjoin

adjust *verb* = **alter**, acclimatize, accommodate, accustom, adapt, arrange, compose, convert, customize, dispose, fit, fix, harmonize, make conform, measure, modify, order, reconcile, rectify, redress, regulate, remodel, set, settle, suit, tune (up), tweak (*informal*)

adjustable *adjective* = **alterable**, adaptable, flexible, malleable, modifiable, mouldable, movable, tractable

adjustment *noun* **1** = **alteration**, adaptation, arrangement, arranging, fitting, fixing, modification, ordering, rectification, redress, regulation, remodelling, setting, tuning **2** = **acclimatization**, harmonization, orientation, reconciliation, settlement, settling in

ad-lib *verb* **1 = improvise**, busk, extemporize, make up, speak extemporaneously, speak impromptu, speak off the cuff, vamp, wing it (*informal*) ♦ *adjective* **2 = improvised**, extemporaneous, extempore, extemporized, impromptu, made up, off-the-cuff (*informal*), off the top of one's head, unprepared, unrehearsed ♦ *adverb* **3 ad lib = off the cuff**, extemporaneously, extempore, impromptu, off the top of one's head (*informal*), spontaneously, without preparation, without rehearsal

administer *verb* **1 = manage**, conduct, control, direct, govern, handle, oversee, run, superintend, supervise **2 = give**, apply, contribute, dispense, distribute, execute, impose, mete out, perform, provide

administration *noun* **1 = management**, administering, application, conduct, control, direction, dispensation, distribution, execution, governing, government, overseeing, performance, provision, running, superintendence, supervision **2 = government**, executive, governing body, management, ministry, term of office

administrative *adjective* **= managerial**, directorial, executive, governmental, gubernatorial (*chiefly U.S.*), management, organizational, regulatory, supervisory

administrator *noun* **= manager**, bureaucrat, executive, official, organizer, supervisor

admirable *adjective* **= excellent**, choice, commendable, estimable, exquisite, fine, laudable, meritorious, praiseworthy, rare, sterling, superior, valuable, wonderful, worthy
➤ **Antonyms**
bad, commonplace, deplorable, disappointing, displeasing, mediocre, no great shakes (*informal*), worthless

admiration *noun* **= regard**, adoration, affection, amazement, appreciation, approbation, approval, astonishment, delight, esteem, pleasure, praise, respect, surprise, veneration, wonder, wonderment

admire *verb* **1 = respect**, adore, appreciate, approve, esteem, idolize, look up to, praise, prize, take one's hat off to, think highly of, value, venerate, worship **2 = marvel at**, appreciate, delight in, take pleasure in, wonder at
➤ **Antonyms**
contemn, deride, despise, look down on, look down one's nose at (*informal*), misprize, scorn, sneer at, spurn, undervalue

admirer *noun* **1 = suitor**, beau, boyfriend, lover, sweetheart, wooer **2 = fan**, adherent, buff (*informal*), devotee, disciple, enthusiast, follower, partisan, protagonist, supporter, votary, worshipper

admissible *adjective* **= permissible**, acceptable, allowable, allowed, passable, permitted, tolerable, tolerated
➤ **Antonyms**
disallowed, inadmissible, intolerable, unacceptable

admission *noun* **1 = entrance**, acceptance, access, admittance, entrée, entry, ingress, initiation, introduction **2 = confession**, acknowledgment, admitting, affirmation, allowance, avowal, concession, declaration, disclosure, divulgence, profession, revelation

admit *verb* **1 = confess**, acknowledge, affirm, avow, concede, cough (*slang*), declare, disclose, divulge, 'fess up (*U.S. slang*), own, profess, reveal **2 = allow**, agree, grant, let, permit, recognize **3 = let in**, accept, allow, allow to enter, give access, initiate, introduce, receive, take in
➤ **Antonyms**
≠**allow**: deny, dismiss, forbid, negate, prohibit, reject ≠**let in**: exclude, keep out

admittance *noun* **= letting in**, acceptance, access, admitting, allowing, entrance, entry, passage, reception

admonish *verb* **= reprimand**, advise, bawl out (*informal*), berate, carpet (*informal*), caution, censure, check, chew out (*U.S. & Canad. informal*), chide, counsel, enjoin, exhort, forewarn, give a rocket (*Brit. & N.Z. informal*), rap over the knuckles, read the riot act, rebuke, reprove, scold, slap on the wrist, tear into (*informal*), tear (someone) off a strip (*Brit. informal*), tell off (*informal*), upbraid, warn
➤ **Antonyms**
applaud, commend, compliment, congratulate, praise

admonition *noun* **= reprimand**, advice, berating, caution, chiding, counsel, rebuke, remonstrance, reproach, reproof, scolding, telling off (*informal*), upbraiding, warning

admonitory *adjective* **= reprimanding**, admonishing, advisory, cautionary, rebuking, reproachful, reproving, scolding, warning

ado *noun* **= fuss**, agitation, bother, bustle, commotion, confusion, delay, disturbance, excitement, flurry, pother, stir, to-do, trouble

adolescence *noun* **1 = youth**, boyhood, girlhood, juvenescence, minority, teens **2 = youthfulness**, boyishness, childishness, girlishness, immaturity, juvenility, puerility

adolescent *adjective* **1** = **young**, boyish, girlish, growing, immature, juvenile, puerile, teenage, youthful ◆ *noun* **2** = **youth**, juvenile, minor, teenager, youngster

adopt *verb* **1** = **foster**, take in **2** = **choose**, accept, appropriate, approve, assume, embrace, endorse, espouse, follow, maintain, ratify, select, support, take on, take over, take up
➤ **Antonyms**
≠**choose**: abandon, abnegate, cast aside, cast off, disavow, disclaim, disown, forswear, give up, reject, renounce, repudiate, spurn, wash one's hands of

adoption *noun* **1** = **fostering**, adopting, fosterage, taking in **2** = **choice**, acceptance, approbation, appropriation, approval, assumption, embracing, endorsement, espousal, following, maintenance, ratification, selection, support, taking on, taking over, taking up

adorable *adjective* = **lovable**, appealing, attractive, captivating, charming, cute, darling, dear, delightful, fetching, pleasing, precious, sweet
➤ **Antonyms**
despicable, displeasing, hateful, unlikable or unlikeable, unlovable

adoration *noun* = **love**, admiration, esteem, estimation, exaltation, glorification, honour, idolatry, idolization, reverence, veneration, worship, worshipping

adore *verb* = **love**, admire, bow to, cherish, dote on, esteem, exalt, glorify, honour, idolize, revere, reverence, venerate, worship
➤ **Antonyms**
abhor, abominate, despise, detest, execrate, hate, loathe

adoring *adjective* = **loving**, admiring, affectionate, devoted, doting, fond
➤ **Antonyms**
despising, detesting, hating, loathing

adorn *verb* = **decorate**, array, beautify, bedeck, deck, embellish, emblazon, engarland, enhance, enrich, festoon, garnish, gild the lily, grace, ornament, trim

adornment *noun* **1** = **decoration**, accessory, embellishment, festoon, frill, frippery, ornament, supplement, trimming **2** = **ornamentation**, beautification, decorating, decoration, embellishment, trimming

adrift *adjective* **1** = **drifting**, afloat, unanchored, unmoored **2** = **aimless**, directionless, goalless, purposeless
◆ *adverb* **3** = **wrong**, amiss, astray, off course

adroit *adjective* = **skilful**, able, adept, apt, artful, bright (*informal*), clever, cunning, deft, dexterous, expert, ingenious, masterful, neat, nimble, proficient, quick-witted, skilled
➤ **Antonyms**
awkward, blundering, bungling, cack-handed (*informal*), clumsy, ham-fisted or ham-handed (*informal*), inept, inexpert, maladroit, uncoordinated, unhandy, unskilful

adroitness *noun* = **skill**, ability, ableness, address, adeptness, aptness, artfulness, cleverness, craft, cunning, deftness, dexterity, expertise, ingeniousness, ingenuity, knack, masterfulness, mastery, nimbleness, proficiency, quick-wittedness, skilfulness

adulation *noun* = **worship**, blandishment, bootlicking (*informal*), extravagant flattery, fawning, fulsome praise, servile flattery, sycophancy
➤ **Antonyms**
abuse, calumniation, censure, condemnation, disparagement, revilement, ridicule, vilification, vituperation

adulatory *adjective* = **worshipping**, blandishing, bootlicking (*informal*), fawning, flattering, obsequious, praising, servile, slavish, sycophantic

adult *noun* **1** = **grown-up**, grown or grown-up person (man or woman), person of mature age ◆ *adjective* **2** = **fully grown**, full grown, fully developed, grown-up, mature, of age, ripe

adulterate *verb* **1** = **debase**, attenuate, bastardize, contaminate, corrupt, depreciate, deteriorate, devalue, make impure, mix with, thin, vitiate, water down, weaken ◆ *adjective* **2** = **debased**, adulterated, attenuated, bastardized, contaminated, corrupt, depreciated, deteriorated, devalued, mixed, thinned, vitiated, watered down, weakened

adumbrate *verb* = **foreshadow**, augur, forecast, foretell, portend, predict, prefigure, presage, prognosticate, prophesy

adumbration *noun* = **foretelling**, augury, forecast, foreshadowing, omen, portent, prediction, prefiguration, prefigurement, presage, prognostication, prophecy, sign

advance *verb* **1** = **progress**, accelerate, come forward, go ahead, go forward, go on, make inroads, move onward, move up, press on, proceed **2** = **promote**, accelerate, bring forward, bring up, elevate, hasten, send forward, send up,

speed, upgrade **3 = benefit**, further, grow, improve, multiply, prosper, thrive **4 = suggest**, adduce, allege, cite, offer, present, proffer, put forward, submit **5 = lend**, pay beforehand, supply on credit
♦ *noun* **6 = progress**, advancement, development, forward movement, headway, inroads, onward movement **7 = improvement**, advancement, amelioration, betterment, breakthrough, furtherance, gain, growth, progress, promotion, step **8 = loan**, credit, deposit, down payment, increase (*in price*), prepayment, retainer, rise (*in price*) **9 advances = overtures**, approach, approaches, moves, proposals, proposition
♦ *adjective* **10 = prior**, beforehand, early, foremost, forward, in front, leading **11 in advance = beforehand**, ahead, earlier, in the forefront, in the lead, in the van, on the barrelhead, previously
➤ Antonyms
verb ≠**progress**: decrease, diminish, lessen, move back, regress, retreat, weaken ≠**promote**: demote, hold back, impede, retard, set back ≠**suggest**: hide, hold back, suppress, withhold ≠**lend**: defer payment, withhold payment

advanced *adjective* **= foremost**, ahead, avant-garde, extreme, forward, higher, leading, precocious, progressive
➤ Antonyms
backward, behind, late, retarded, underdeveloped, undeveloped

advancement *noun* **1 = promotion**, advance, amelioration, betterment, gain, growth, improvement, preferment, progress, rise **2 = progress**, advance, forward movement, headway, onward movement

advantage *noun* **= benefit**, ace in the hole, ace up one's sleeve, aid, ascendancy, asset, assistance, avail, blessing, boon, boot (*obsolete*), convenience, dominance, edge, gain, good, help, inside track, interest, lead, mileage (*informal*), precedence, pre-eminence, profit, service, start, superiority, sway, upper hand, use, utility, welfare
➤ Antonyms
curse, difficulty, disadvantage, downside, drawback, handicap, hindrance, inconvenience, snag

advantageous *adjective* **1 = beneficial**, convenient, expedient, helpful, of service, profitable, useful, valuable, worthwhile **2 = superior**, dominant, dominating, favourable
➤ Antonyms
≠**beneficial**: detrimental, unfavourable, unfortunate, unhelpful, useless

advent *noun* **= coming**, appearance, approach, arrival, entrance, occurrence, onset, visitation

adventitious *adjective* **= accidental**, casual, chance, extraneous, foreign, fortuitous, incidental, nonessential, unexpected

adventure *noun* **= escapade**, chance, contingency, enterprise, experience, exploit, hazard, incident, occurrence, risk, speculation, undertaking, venture

adventurer *noun* **1 = mercenary**, charlatan, fortune-hunter, gambler, opportunist, rogue, speculator **2 = hero**, daredevil, heroine, knight-errant, soldier of fortune, swashbuckler, traveller, venturer, voyager, wanderer

adventurous *adjective* **= daring**, adventuresome, audacious, bold, dangerous, daredevil, enterprising, foolhardy, have-a-go (*informal*), hazardous, headstrong, intrepid, rash, reckless, risky, temerarious (*rare*), venturesome
➤ Antonyms
careful, cautious, chary, circumspect, hesitant, prudent, safe, tentative, timid, timorous, unadventurous, wary

adversary *noun* **= opponent**, antagonist, competitor, contestant, enemy, foe, opposer, rival
➤ Antonyms
accomplice, ally, associate, collaborator, colleague, confederate, co-worker, friend, helper, partner, supporter

adverse *adjective* **= unfavourable**, antagonistic, conflicting, contrary, detrimental, disadvantageous, hostile, inexpedient, inimical, injurious, inopportune, negative, opposing, opposite, reluctant, repugnant, unfortunate, unfriendly, unlucky, unpropitious, unwilling
➤ Antonyms
advantageous, auspicious, beneficial, favourable, fortunate, helpful, lucky, opportune, promising, propitious, suitable

adversity *noun* **= hardship**, affliction, bad luck, calamity, catastrophe, deep water, disaster, distress, hard times, ill-fortune, ill-luck, misery, misfortune, mishap, reverse, sorrow, suffering, trial, trouble, woe, wretchedness

advert *noun* *Brit. informal* **= advertisement**, ad (*informal*), announcement, bill, blurb, circular, commercial, display, notice, placard, plug (*informal*), poster, promotion, publicity, puff

advertise *verb* **= publicize**, advise, announce, apprise, blazon, crack up (*informal*), declare, display, flaunt, inform, make known, notify, plug (*informal*), praise, proclaim, promote, promulgate, publish, puff, push (*informal*), tout

advertisement *noun* = **advert** (*Brit. informal*), ad (*informal*), announcement, bill, blurb, circular, commercial, display, notice, placard, plug (*informal*), poster, promotion, publicity, puff

advice *noun* 1 = **guidance**, admonition, caution, counsel, help, injunction, opinion, recommendation, suggestion, view 2 = **notification**, information, instruction, intelligence, notice, warning, word

advisability *noun* = **wisdom**, appropriateness, aptness, desirability, expediency, fitness, judiciousness, profitability, propriety, prudence, seemliness, soundness, suitability

advisable *adjective* = **wise**, appropriate, apt, desirable, expedient, fit, fitting, judicious, politic, profitable, proper, prudent, recommended, seemly, sensible, sound, suggested, suitable
➤ **Antonyms**
ill-advised, impolitic, improper, imprudent, inappropriate, inexpedient, injudicious, silly, stupid, undesirable, unfitting, unprofitable, unseemly, unsound, unsuitable, unwise

advise *verb* 1 = **recommend**, admonish, caution, commend, counsel, enjoin, prescribe, suggest, urge 2 = **notify**, acquaint, apprise, inform, let (someone) know, make known, report, tell, warn

adviser *noun* = **guide**, aide, authority, coach, confidant, consultant, counsel, counsellor, guru, helper, lawyer, mentor, right-hand man, solicitor, teacher, tutor

advisory *adjective* = **advising**, consultative, counselling, helping, recommending

advocacy *noun* = **recommendation**, advancement, argument for, backing, campaigning for, championing, defence, encouragement, espousal, justification, pleading for, promotion, promulgation, propagation, proposal, spokesmanship, support, upholding, urging

advocate *verb* 1 = **recommend**, advise, argue for, campaign for, champion, commend, countenance, defend, encourage, espouse, favour, hold a brief for (*informal*), justify, plead for, prescribe, press for, promote, propose, speak for, support, uphold, urge ♦ *noun* 2 = **supporter**, apologist, apostle, backer, campaigner, champion, counsellor, defender, pleader, promoter, proponent, proposer, speaker, spokesman, upholder 3 *Law* = **lawyer**, attorney, barrister, counsel,

solicitor
➤ **Antonyms**
verb ≠ **recommend**: contradict, oppose, resist, speak against, take a stand against, take issue with

aegis *noun* As in **under the aegis of** = **protection**, advocacy, auspices, backing, favour, guardianship, patronage, shelter, sponsorship, support, wing

affability *noun* = **friendliness**, amiability, amicability, approachability, benevolence, benignity, civility, congeniality, cordiality, courtesy, geniality, good humour, good nature, graciousness, kindliness, mildness, obligingness, pleasantness, sociability, urbanity, warmth

affable *adjective* = **friendly**, amiable, amicable, approachable, benevolent, benign, civil, congenial, cordial, courteous, genial, good-humoured, good-natured, gracious, kindly, mild, obliging, pleasant, sociable, urbane, warm
➤ **Antonyms**
brusque, cold, discourteous, distant, haughty, rude, stand-offish, surly, unapproachable, uncivil, unfriendly, ungracious, unpleasant, unsociable

affair *noun* 1 = **event**, activity, business, circumstance, concern, episode, happening, incident, interest, matter, occurrence, proceeding, project, question, subject, transaction, undertaking 2 = **relationship**, amour, intrigue, liaison, romance

affect[1] *verb* 1 = **influence**, act on, alter, bear upon, change, concern, impact, impinge upon, interest, involve, modify, prevail over, regard, relate to, sway, transform 2 = **move**, disturb, impress, overcome, perturb, stir, touch, tug at (someone's) heartstrings (*often facetious*), upset

affect[2] *verb* = **put on**, adopt, aspire to, assume, contrive, counterfeit, feign, imitate, pretend, sham, simulate

affectation *noun* = **pretence**, act, affectedness, appearance, artificiality, assumed manners, façade, fakery, false display, insincerity, mannerism, pose, pretension, pretentiousness, sham, show, simulation, unnatural imitation

affected *adjective* 1 = **influenced**, afflicted, altered, changed, concerned, damaged, deeply moved, distressed, hurt, impaired, impressed, injured, melted, stimulated, stirred, touched, troubled, upset 2 = **pretended**, artificial, arty-farty (*informal*), assumed, camp (*informal*), conceited, contrived, counterfeit, feigned, insincere, la-di-da (*informal*), mannered,

mincing, phoney or phony (informal),
pompous, precious, pretentious, put-on,
sham, simulated, spurious, stiff, studied,
unnatural
➤ Antonyms
≠**influenced**: cured, unaffected,
unconcerned, unharmed, uninjured,
unmoved, untouched ≠**pretended**:
genuine, natural, real, unaffected
affecting adjective = **moving**, pathetic,
piteous, pitiable, pitiful, poignant, sad,
saddening, touching
affection noun = **fondness**, amity,
attachment, care, desire, feeling,
friendliness, goodwill, inclination,
kindness, liking, love, passion, propensity,
tenderness, warmth
affectionate adjective = **fond**, attached,
caring, devoted, doting, friendly, kind,
loving, tender, warm, warm-hearted
➤ Antonyms
cold, cool, glacial, indifferent, stony,
uncaring, undemonstrative, unfeeling,
unresponsive
affiliate verb = **join**, ally, amalgamate,
annex, associate, band together, combine,
confederate, connect, incorporate, link,
unite
affiliation noun = **connection**, alliance,
amalgamation, association, banding
together, coalition, combination,
confederation, incorporation, joining,
league, merging, relationship, union
affinity noun 1 = **attraction**, fondness,
inclination, leaning, liking, partiality,
rapport, sympathy 2 = **similarity**, alliance,
analogy, closeness, compatibility,
connection, correspondence, kinship,
likeness, relation, relationship,
resemblance
➤ Antonyms
≠**attraction**: abhorrence, animosity,
antipathy, aversion, dislike, hatred,
hostility, loathing, repugnance, revulsion
≠**similarity**: difference, disparity,
dissimilarity
affirm verb = **declare**, assert, asseverate,
attest, aver, avouch, avow, certify,
confirm, maintain, pronounce, ratify, state,
swear, testify
➤ Antonyms
deny, disallow, rebut, refute, reject,
renounce, repudiate, rescind, retract
affirmation noun = **declaration**, assertion,
asseveration, attestation, averment,
avouchment, avowal, certification,
confirmation, oath, pronouncement,
ratification, statement, testimony
affirmative adjective = **agreeing**,
approving, assenting, concurring,

confirming, consenting, corroborative,
favourable, positive
➤ Antonyms
denying, disagreeing, disapproving,
dissenting, negating, negative
affix verb = **attach**, add, annex, append,
bind, fasten, glue, join, paste, put on,
stick, subjoin, tack, tag
➤ Antonyms
detach, disconnect, remove, take off,
unfasten, unglue
afflict verb = **torment**, ail, beset, burden,
distress, grieve, harass, hurt, oppress, pain,
plague, rack, smite, trouble, try, wound
affliction noun = **suffering**, adversity,
calamity, cross, curse, depression, disease,
distress, grief, hardship, misery,
misfortune, ordeal, pain, plague, scourge,
sickness, sorrow, torment, trial, tribulation,
trouble, woe, wretchedness
affluence noun = **wealth**, abundance, big
bucks (informal, chiefly U.S.), big money,
exuberance, fortune, megabucks (U.S. &
Canad. slang), opulence, plenty, pretty
penny (informal), profusion, prosperity,
riches, tidy sum (informal), wad (U.S. &
Canad. slang)
affluent adjective 1 = **wealthy**, loaded
(slang), moneyed, opulent, prosperous,
rich, rolling in money (slang), well-heeled
(informal), well-off, well-to-do 2
= **plentiful**, abundant, copious, exuberant,
plenteous
➤ Antonyms
≠**wealthy**: broke (informal), destitute,
down at heel, hard-up (informal),
impecunious, impoverished, indigent, on
the breadline, penniless, penurious, poor,
poverty-stricken, skint (Brit. slang),
stony-broke (Brit. slang)
afford verb 1 As in can afford = **spare**, bear,
manage, stand, sustain 2 = **give**, bestow,
furnish, grant, impart, offer, produce,
provide, render, supply, yield
affordable adjective = **inexpensive**, cheap,
economical, low-cost, moderate, modest,
reasonable
➤ Antonyms
beyond one's means, costly, dear,
exorbitant, expensive, unaffordable,
uneconomical
affray noun = **fight**, bagarre, brawl, contest,
disturbance, dogfight, encounter, feud,
fracas, free-for-all (informal), mêlée,
outbreak, quarrel, scrap, scrimmage,
scuffle, set-to (informal), shindig
(informal), shindy (informal), skirmish,
tumult
affront noun 1 = **insult**, abuse, indignity,
injury, offence, outrage, provocation, slap

in the face (*informal*), slight, slur, vexation, wrong ♦ *verb* **2 = offend**, abuse, anger, annoy, displease, insult, outrage, pique, provoke, put or get one's back up, slight, vex

afire *adjective* **1 = burning**, ablaze, aflame, alight, blazing, fiery, flaming, ignited, lighted, lit, on fire **2 = passionate**, aglow, aroused, excited, fervent, impassioned, stimulated

aflame *adjective* **1 = burning**, ablaze, afire, alight, blazing, fiery, flaming, ignited, lighted, lit, on fire **2 = passionate**, afire, aroused, excited, fervent, impassioned, stimulated **3 = red**, aglow, flushed, inflamed, ruddy

afoot *adjective* **= going on**, about, abroad, afloat, astir, brewing, circulating, current, happening, hatching, in preparation, in progress, in the wind, on the go (*informal*), operating, up (*informal*)

afraid *adjective* **1 = scared**, alarmed, anxious, apprehensive, cowardly, faint-hearted, fearful, frightened, intimidated, nervous, reluctant, suspicious, timid, timorous **2 = sorry**, regretful, unhappy
➤ **Antonyms**
≠**scared**: audacious, bold, fearless, inapprehensive, indifferent, unafraid ≠**sorry**: happy, pleased

afresh *adverb* **= again**, anew, newly, once again, once more, over again

after *adverb* **= following**, afterwards, behind, below, later, subsequently, succeeding, thereafter
➤ **Antonyms**
before, earlier, in advance, in front, previously, prior to, sooner

aftermath *noun* **= effects**, aftereffects, consequences, end, end result, outcome, results, sequel, upshot, wake

again *adverb* **1 = once more**, afresh, anew, another time **2 = also**, besides, furthermore, in addition, moreover **3 = on the other hand**, on the contrary

against *preposition* **1 = beside**, abutting, close up to, facing, fronting, in contact with, on, opposite to, touching, upon **2 = opposed to**, anti (*informal*), averse to, contra (*informal*), counter, hostile to, in defiance of, in opposition to, in the face of, opposing, resisting, versus **3 = in preparation for**, in anticipation of, in expectation of, in provision for

age *noun* **1 = time**, date, day(s), duration, epoch, era, generation, lifetime, period, span **2 = old age**, advancing years, decline (*of life*), majority, maturity, senescence, senility, seniority ♦ *verb* **3 = grow old**,

decline, deteriorate, mature, mellow, ripen
➤ **Antonyms**
noun ≠**old age**: adolescence, boyhood or girlhood, childhood, immaturity, salad days, young days, youth

aged *adjective* **= old**, age-old, ancient, antiquated, antique, cobwebby, elderly, getting on, grey, hoary, past it (*informal*), senescent, superannuated
➤ **Antonyms**
adolescent, boyish or girlish, childish, immature, juvenile, young, youthful

agency *noun* **1 = business**, bureau, department, office, organization **2** *Old-fashioned* **= medium**, action, activity, auspices, efficiency, force, influence, instrumentality, intercession, intervention, means, mechanism, mediation, operation, power, work

agenda *noun* **= list**, calendar, diary, plan, programme, schedule, timetable

agent *noun* **1 = representative**, advocate, deputy, emissary, envoy, factor, go-between, negotiator, rep (*informal*), substitute, surrogate **2 = worker**, actor, author, doer, executor, mover, officer, operative, operator, performer **3 = force**, agency, cause, instrument, means, power, vehicle

aggravate *verb* **1 = make worse**, add insult to injury, exacerbate, exaggerate, fan the flames of, heighten, increase, inflame, intensify, magnify, worsen **2** *Informal* **= annoy**, be on one's back (*slang*), bother, exasperate, gall, get in one's hair (*informal*), get on one's nerves (*informal*), get on one's wick (*Brit. slang*), get under one's skin (*informal*), get up one's nose (*informal*), hassle (*informal*), irk, irritate, nark (*Brit., Austral., & N.Z. slang*), needle (*informal*), nettle, pester, piss one off (*taboo slang*), provoke, rub (someone) up the wrong way (*informal*), tease, vex
➤ **Antonyms**
≠**make worse**: alleviate, assuage, calm, diminish, ease, improve, lessen, mitigate, smooth ≠**annoy**: assuage, calm, pacify, please

aggravation *noun* **1 = worsening**, exacerbation, exaggeration, heightening, increase, inflaming, intensification, magnification **2** *Informal* **= annoyance**, exasperation, gall, grief (*informal*), hassle (*informal*), irksomeness, irritation, provocation, teasing, vexation

aggregate *noun* **1 = total**, accumulation, agglomeration, amount, assemblage, body, bulk, collection, combination, heap, lump, mass, mixture, pile, sum, whole ♦ *adjective* **2 = total**, accumulated, added, assembled, collected, collective, combined, composite, corporate, cumulative, mixed ♦ *verb* **3 = combine**, accumulate, amass, assemble, collect, heap, mix, pile

aggression *noun* **1 = hostility**, aggressiveness, antagonism, belligerence, destructiveness, pugnacity **2 = attack**, assault, encroachment, injury, invasion, offence, offensive, onslaught, raid

aggressive *adjective* **1 = hostile**, belligerent, destructive, offensive, pugnacious, quarrelsome **2 = forceful**, assertive, bold, dynamic, energetic, enterprising, in-your-face (*slang*), militant, pushing, pushy (*informal*), vigorous, zealous
➤ **Antonyms**
≠**hostile**: friendly, peaceful ≠**forceful**: mild, quiet, retiring, submissive

aggressor *noun* **= attacker**, assailant, assaulter, invader

aggrieved *adjective* **= hurt**, afflicted, distressed, disturbed, harmed, ill-used, injured, peeved (*informal*), saddened, unhappy, woeful, wronged

aghast *adjective* **= horrified**, afraid, amazed, appalled, astonished, astounded, awestruck, confounded, frightened, horror-struck, shocked, startled, stunned, thunder-struck

agile *adjective* **1 = nimble**, active, brisk, limber, lissom(e), lithe, lively, quick, sprightly, spry, supple, swift **2 = acute**, alert, bright (*informal*), clever, lively, nimble, prompt, quick, quick-witted, sharp
➤ **Antonyms**
≠**nimble**: awkward, clumsy, heavy, lumbering, ponderous, slow, slow-moving, stiff, ungainly, unsupple

agility *noun* **1 = nimbleness**, activity, briskness, litheness, liveliness, quickness, sprightliness, spryness, suppleness, swiftness **2 = acuteness**, alertness, cleverness, liveliness, promptitude, promptness, quickness, quick-wittedness, sharpness

agitate *verb* **1 = upset**, alarm, arouse, confuse, disconcert, disquiet, distract, disturb, excite, faze, ferment, fluster, incite, inflame, perturb, rouse, ruffle, stimulate, trouble, unnerve, work up, worry **2 = stir**, beat, churn, convulse, disturb, rock, rouse, shake, toss
➤ **Antonyms**
≠**upset**: appease, assuage, calm, calm down, mollify, pacify, placate, quiet, quieten, soothe, still, tranquillize

agitation *noun* **1 = turmoil**, alarm, arousal, clamour, commotion, confusion,

discomposure, disquiet, distraction, disturbance, excitement, ferment, flurry, fluster, incitement, lather (*informal*), outcry, stimulation, tizzy, tizz *or* tiz-woz (*informal*), trouble, tumult, upheaval, upset, worry **2 = turbulence**, churning, convulsion, disturbance, rocking, shake, shaking, stir, stirring, tossing, upheaval

agitator *noun* **= troublemaker**, agent provocateur, demagogue, firebrand, inciter, instigator, rabble-rouser, revolutionary, stirrer (*informal*)

agog *adjective* **= eager**, avid, curious, enthralled, enthusiastic, excited, expectant, impatient, in suspense, keen
➤ **Antonyms**
apathetic, incurious, indifferent, unconcerned, uninterested

agonize *verb* **= suffer**, be distressed, be in agony, be in anguish, go through the mill, labour, strain, strive, struggle, worry, writhe

agony *noun* **= suffering**, affliction, anguish, distress, misery, pain, pangs, throes, torment, torture, woe

agree *verb* **1 = concur**, accede, acquiesce, admit, allow, assent, be of the same mind, be of the same opinion, comply, concede, consent, engage, grant, permit, see eye to eye, settle, shake hands **2 = get on (together)**, accord, answer, chime, coincide, conform, correspond, fit, harmonize, match, square, suit, tally
➤ **Antonyms**
≠**concur**: contradict, deny, differ, disagree, dispute, dissent, rebut, refute, retract

agreeable *adjective* **1 = pleasant**, acceptable, congenial, delightful, enjoyable, gratifying, likable *or* likeable, pleasing, pleasurable, satisfying, to one's liking, to one's taste **2 = consenting**, acquiescent, agreeing, amenable, approving, complying, concurring, in accord, onside (*informal*), responsive, sympathetic, well-disposed, willing
➤ **Antonyms**
≠**pleasant**: disagreeable, displeasing, horrid, offensive, unlikable *or* unlikeable, unpleasant

agreement *noun* **1 = concurrence**, agreeing, assent, compliance, concord, consent, harmony, union, unison **2 = correspondence**, accord, accordance, affinity, agreeing, analogy, compatibility, conformity, congruity, consistency, similarity, suitableness **3 = contract**, arrangement, bargain, compact, covenant, deal (*informal*), pact, settlement, treaty, understanding
➤ **Antonyms**

≠**concurrence:** altercation, argument, clash, conflict, discord, dispute, dissent, division, falling-out, quarrel, row, squabble, strife, tiff, wrangle
≠**correspondence:** difference, discrepancy, disparity, dissimilarity, diversity, incompatibility, incongruity

agricultural adjective = **farming**, agrarian, country, rural, rustic

agriculture noun = **farming**, agronomics, agronomy, cultivation, culture, husbandry, tillage

aground adverb = **beached**, ashore, foundered, grounded, high and dry, on the rocks, stranded, stuck

ahead adverb = **in front**, along, at an advantage, at the head, before, forwards, in advance, in the foreground, in the lead, in the vanguard, leading, on, onwards, to the fore, winning

aid noun 1 = **help**, assistance, benefit, encouragement, favour, promotion, relief, service, succour, support 2 = **helper**, abettor, adjutant, aide, aide-de-camp, assistant, second, supporter ◆ verb 3 = **help**, abet, assist, befriend, encourage, favour, give a leg up (informal), promote, relieve, second, serve, subsidize, succour, support, sustain
➤ **Antonyms**
noun ≠**help:** hindrance ◆ verb ≠**help:** detract from, harm, hinder, hurt, impede, obstruct, oppose, thwart

aide noun = **assistant**, attendant, helper, right-hand man, second, supporter

ailing adjective = **ill**, indisposed, infirm, poorly, sick, under the weather (informal), unwell, weak

ailment noun = **illness**, affliction, complaint, disease, disorder, infirmity, malady, sickness

aim verb 1 = **intend**, aspire, attempt, design, direct, draw a bead (on), endeavour, level, mean, plan, point, propose, purpose, resolve, seek, set one's sights on, sight, strive, take aim (at), train, try, want, wish ◆ noun 2 = **intention**, ambition, aspiration, course, design, desire, direction, end, goal, Holy Grail (informal), intent, mark, object, objective, plan, purpose, scheme, target, wish

aimless adjective = **purposeless**, chance, directionless, erratic, frivolous, goalless, haphazard, pointless, random, stray, undirected, unguided, unpredictable, vagrant, wayward
➤ **Antonyms**
decided, deliberate, determined, firm, fixed, positive, purposeful, resolute, resolved, settled, single-minded

air noun 1 = **atmosphere**, heavens, sky 2 = **wind**, blast, breath, breeze, draught, puff, waft, whiff, zephyr 3 = **manner**, ambience, appearance, atmosphere, aura, bearing, character, demeanour, effect, feeling, flavour, impression, look, mood, quality, style, tone, vibes (slang) 4 = **tune**, aria, lay, melody, song 5 = **circulation**, display, dissemination, exposure, expression, publicity, utterance, vent, ventilation ◆ verb 6 = **publicize**, circulate, communicate, declare, disclose, display, disseminate, divulge, exhibit, expose, express, give vent to, make known, make public, proclaim, reveal, take the wraps off, tell, utter, ventilate, voice 7 = **ventilate**, aerate, expose, freshen

airborne adjective = **flying**, floating, gliding, hovering, in flight, in the air, on the wing

airily adverb = **light-heartedly**, animatedly, blithely, breezily, buoyantly, gaily, happily, high-spiritedly, jauntily

airiness noun 1 = **freshness**, breeziness, draughtiness, gustiness, lightness, openness, windiness 2 = **light-heartedness**, animation, blitheness, breeziness, buoyancy, gaiety, happiness, high spirits, jauntiness, lightness of heart

airing noun 1 = **ventilation**, aeration, drying, freshening 2 = **exposure**, circulation, display, dissemination, expression, publicity, utterance, vent, ventilation

airless adjective = **stuffy**, breathless, close, heavy, muggy, oppressive, stale, stifling, suffocating, sultry, unventilated
➤ **Antonyms**
airy, blowy, breezy, draughty, fresh, gusty, light, open, spacious, well-ventilated

airs plural noun = **affectation**, affectedness, arrogance, haughtiness, hauteur, pomposity, pretensions, superciliousness, swank (informal)

airy adjective 1 = **well-ventilated**, blowy, breezy, draughty, fresh, gusty, light, lofty, open, spacious, uncluttered, windy 2 = **light-hearted**, animated, blithe, buoyant, cheerful, cheery, chirpy (informal), debonair, frolicsome, gay, genial, graceful, happy, high-spirited, jaunty, light, lively, merry, nonchalant, sprightly, upbeat (informal) 3 = **insubstantial**, aerial, delicate, ethereal, fanciful, flimsy, illusory, imaginary, immaterial, incorporeal, light, vaporous, visionary, weightless, wispy
➤ **Antonyms**
≠**well-ventilated:** airless, close, heavy,

muggy, oppressive, stale, stifling, stuffy, suffocating, unventilated ≠**light-hearted:** cheerless, dismal, gloomy, glum, melancholy, miserable, morose, sad ≠**insubstantial:** concrete, corporeal, material, real, realistic, substantial, tangible

aisle *noun* = **passageway,** alley, corridor, gangway, lane, passage, path

alacrity *noun* = **eagerness,** alertness, avidity, briskness, cheerfulness, dispatch, enthusiasm, gaiety, hilarity, joyousness, liveliness, promptness, quickness, readiness, speed, sprightliness, willingness, zeal
➤ **Antonyms**
apathy, dullness, inertia, lethargy, reluctance, slowness, sluggishness, unconcern, unwillingness

alarm *noun* **1** = **fear,** anxiety, apprehension, consternation, dismay, distress, fright, nervousness, panic, scare, terror, trepidation, unease, uneasiness **2** = **danger signal,** alarm bell, alert, bell, distress signal, hooter, siren, tocsin, warning ◆ *verb* **3** = **frighten,** daunt, dismay, distress, give (someone) a turn (*informal*), make (someone's) hair stand on end, panic, put the wind up (someone) (*informal*), scare, startle, terrify, unnerve
➤ **Antonyms**
noun ≠**fear:** calm, calmness, composure, sang-froid, serenity ◆ *verb* ≠**frighten:** assure, calm, comfort, reassure, relieve, soothe

alarming *adjective* = **frightening,** daunting, dismaying, distressing, disturbing, dreadful, scaring, shocking, startling, terrifying, unnerving

alcoholic *noun* **1** = **drunkard,** bibber, boozer (*informal*), dipsomaniac, drinker, drunk, hard drinker, inebriate, soak (*slang*), sot, sponge (*informal*), tippler, toper, tosspot (*informal*), wino (*informal*) ◆ *adjective* **2** = **intoxicating,** brewed, distilled, fermented, hard, inebriant, inebriating, spirituous, strong, vinous

alcove *noun* = **recess,** bay, bower, compartment, corner, cubbyhole, cubicle, niche, nook

alert *adjective* **1** = **watchful,** active, agile, attentive, awake, bright-eyed and bushy-tailed (*informal*), brisk, careful, circumspect, heedful, keeping a weather eye on, lively, nimble, observant, on guard, on one's toes, on the ball (*informal*), on the lookout, on the watch, perceptive, quick, ready, spirited, sprightly, vigilant, wary, wide-awake ◆ *noun* **2** = **warning,** alarm, signal, siren ◆ *verb* **3** = **warn,** alarm, forewarn, inform,

notify, signal
➤ **Antonyms**
adjective ≠**watchful:** careless, heedless, inactive, languid, lethargic, listless, oblivious, slow, unaware, unconcerned, unwary ◆ *noun* ≠**warning:** all clear ◆ *verb* ≠**warn:** lull

alertness *noun* = **watchfulness,** activeness, agility, attentiveness, briskness, carefulness, circumspection, heedfulness, liveliness, nimbleness, perceptiveness, promptitude, quickness, readiness, spiritedness, sprightliness, vigilance, wariness

alias *adverb* **1** = **also known as,** also called, otherwise, otherwise known as ◆ *noun* **2** = **pseudonym,** assumed name, nom de guerre, nom de plume, pen name, stage name

alibi *noun* = **excuse,** defence, explanation, justification, plea, pretext, reason

alien *adjective* **1** = **strange,** adverse, beyond one's ken, conflicting, contrary, estranged, exotic, foreign, inappropriate, incompatible, incongruous, not native, not naturalized, opposed, outlandish, remote, repugnant, separated, unfamiliar ◆ *noun* **2** = **foreigner,** newcomer, outsider, stranger
➤ **Antonyms**
adjective ≠**strange:** affiliated, akin, alike, allied, analogous, cognate, connected, corresponding, kindred, like, parallel, related, similar ◆ *noun* ≠**foreigner:** citizen, countryman, dweller, inhabitant, national, resident

alienate *verb* **1** = **set against,** break off, disaffect, divert, divorce, estrange, make unfriendly, separate, turn away, withdraw **2** *Law* = **transfer,** abalienate, convey

alienation *noun* **1** = **setting against,** breaking off, disaffection, diversion, divorce, estrangement, indifference, remoteness, rupture, separation, turning away, withdrawal **2** *Law* = **transfer,** abalienation, conveyance

alight[1] *verb* **1** = **get off,** descend, disembark, dismount, get down **2** = **land,** come down, come to rest, descend, light, perch, settle, touch down
➤ **Antonyms**
≠**land:** ascend, climb, float up, fly up, go up, lift off, mount, move up, rise, scale, soar, take off

alight[2] *adjective* **1** = **on fire,** ablaze, aflame, blazing, burning, fiery, flaming, flaring, ignited, lighted, lit **2** = **lit up,** bright, brilliant, illuminated, shining

align *verb* **1** = **ally,** affiliate, agree, associate, cooperate, join, side, sympathize **2** = **line up,** arrange in line, coordinate, even, even up, make parallel, order, range, regulate, sequence, straighten

alignment noun 1 = alliance, affiliation, agreement, association, cooperation, sympathy, union 2 = lining up, adjustment, arrangement, coordination, evening, evening up, line, order, ranging, regulating, sequence, straightening up

alike adjective 1 = similar, akin, analogous, corresponding, cut from the same cloth, duplicate, equal, equivalent, even, identical, like two peas in a pod, of a piece, parallel, resembling, the same, uniform ♦ adverb 2 = similarly, analogously, correspondingly, equally, evenly, identically, uniformly
➤ Antonyms
adjective ≠ similar: different, dissimilar, diverse, separate, unlike ♦ adverb ≠ similarly: differently, distinctly, unequally

alive adjective 1 = living, animate, breathing, having life, in the land of the living (informal), subsisting 2 = in existence, active, existent, existing, extant, functioning, in force, operative, unquenched 3 = lively, active, alert, animated, awake, brisk, cheerful, chirpy (informal), eager, energetic, full of beans (informal), full of life, quick, spirited, sprightly, spry, vigorous, vital, vivacious, zestful
➤ Antonyms
≠ living: dead, deceased, departed, expired, extinct, gone, inanimate, lifeless ≠ in existence: extinct, inactive, inoperative, lost ≠ lively: apathetic, dull, inactive, lifeless, spiritless

alive to adjective = aware of, alert to, awake to, cognizant of, eager for, sensible of, sensitive to, susceptible to

alive with adjective = swarming with, abounding in, bristling with, bustling with, buzzing with, crawling with, hopping with, infested with, jumping with, lousy with (slang), overrun by, packed with, teeming with, thronged with

all adjective 1 = the whole of, every bit of, the complete, the entire, the sum of, the totality of, the total of 2 = every, each, each and every, every one of, every single 3 = complete, entire, full, greatest, perfect, total, utter ♦ adverb 4 = completely, altogether, entirely, fully, totally, utterly, wholly ♦ noun 5 = whole amount, aggregate, entirety, everything, sum, sum total, total, total amount, totality, utmost, whole

allegation noun = claim, accusation, affirmation, assertion, asseveration, averment, avowal, charge, declaration,

deposition, plea, profession, statement

allege verb = claim, advance, affirm, assert, asseverate, aver, avow, charge, declare, depose, maintain, plead, profess, put forward, state
➤ Antonyms
abjure, contradict, deny, disagree with, disavow, disclaim, gainsay (archaic or literary), oppose, refute, renounce, repudiate

alleged adjective 1 = stated, affirmed, asserted, averred, declared, described, designated 2 = supposed, doubtful, dubious, ostensible, professed, purported, so-called, suspect, suspicious, unproved

allegiance noun = loyalty, adherence, constancy, devotion, duty, faithfulness, fealty, fidelity, homage, obedience, obligation, troth (archaic)
➤ Antonyms
disloyalty, faithlessness, falseness, inconstancy, infidelity, perfidy, treachery, treason, unfaithfulness

allegorical adjective = symbolic, emblematic, figurative, parabolic, symbolizing

allegory noun = symbol, apologue, emblem, fable, myth, parable, story, symbolism, tale

allergic adjective 1 = sensitive, affected by, hypersensitive, sensitized, susceptible 2 Informal = averse, antipathetic, disinclined, hostile, loath, opposed

allergy noun 1 = sensitivity, antipathy, hypersensitivity, susceptibility 2 Informal = dislike, antipathy, aversion, disinclination, hostility, loathing, opposition

alleviate verb = ease, allay, lessen, lighten, moderate, reduce, relieve, soothe

alley noun = passage, alleyway, backstreet, lane, passageway, pathway, walk

alliance noun = union, affiliation, affinity, agreement, association, coalition, combination, compact, concordat, confederacy, confederation, connection, federation, league, marriage, pact, partnership, treaty
➤ Antonyms
alienation, breach, break, disaffection, dissociation, disunion, disunity, division, rupture, separation, severance, split, split-up

allied adjective = united, affiliated, amalgamated, associated, bound, combined, confederate, connected, hand in glove (informal), in cahoots (U.S. informal), in league, joined, joint, kindred, leagued, linked, married, related, unified, wed

allocate verb = **assign**, allot, allow, apportion, appropriate, budget, designate, earmark, mete, set aside, share out

allocation noun = **assignment**, allotment, allowance, apportionment, appropriation, grant, lot, measure, portion, quota, ration, share, stint, stipend

allot verb = **assign**, allocate, apportion, appropriate, budget, designate, earmark, mete, set aside, share out

allotment noun 1 = **plot**, kitchen garden, patch, tract 2 = **assignment**, allocation, allowance, apportionment, appropriation, grant, lot, measure, portion, quota, ration, share, stint, stipend

all-out adjective = **total**, complete, determined, exhaustive, full, full-on (informal), full-scale, maximum, optimum, outright, resolute, supreme, thorough, thoroughgoing, undivided, unlimited, unremitting, unrestrained, unstinted, utmost
➤ **Antonyms**
careless, cursory, half-hearted, negligent, off-hand, perfunctory, unenthusiastic

allow verb 1 = **permit**, approve, authorize, bear, brook, enable, endure, give leave, let, put up with (informal), sanction, stand, suffer, tolerate 2 = **give**, allocate, allot, assign, deduct, grant, provide, remit, set aside, spare 3 = **acknowledge**, acquiesce, admit, concede, confess, grant, own
➤ **Antonyms**
≠**permit**: ban, disallow, forbid, prohibit, proscribe, refuse ≠**give**: deny, forbid, refuse ≠**acknowledge**: contradict, deny, disagree with, gainsay (archaic or literary), oppose

allowable adjective = **permissible**, acceptable, admissible, all right, appropriate, approved, sanctionable, sufferable, suitable, tolerable

allowance noun 1 = **portion**, allocation, allotment, amount, annuity, apportionment, grant, lot, measure, pension, quota, ration, remittance, share, stint, stipend, subsidy 2 = **concession**, deduction, discount, rebate, reduction

allow for verb = **take into account**, arrange for, consider, foresee, keep in mind, make allowances for, make concessions for, make provision for, plan for, provide for, set (something) aside for, take into consideration

alloy noun 1 = **mixture**, admixture, amalgam, blend, combination, composite, compound, hybrid, meld ♦ verb 2 = **mix**, admix, amalgamate, blend, combine, compound, fuse, meld

all right adjective 1 = **satisfactory**, acceptable, adequate, average, fair, O.K. or okay (informal), passable, so-so (informal), standard, unobjectionable, up to scratch (informal) 2 = **well**, hale, healthy, O.K. or okay (informal), out of the woods, safe, sound, unharmed, unimpaired, uninjured, whole ♦ adverb 3 = **satisfactorily**, acceptably, adequately, O.K. or okay (informal), passably, unobjectionably, well enough
➤ **Antonyms**
adjective ≠**satisfactory**: bad, inadequate, not good enough, not up to scratch (informal), objectionable, poor, unacceptable, unsatisfactory ≠**well**: ailing, bad, ill, injured, off colour, out of sorts, poorly, sick, sickly, unhealthy, unwell

allude verb = **refer**, hint, imply, intimate, mention, suggest, touch upon

allure noun 1 = **attractiveness**, appeal, attraction, charm, enchantment, enticement, glamour, lure, persuasion, seductiveness, temptation ♦ verb 2 = **attract**, beguile, cajole, captivate, charm, coax, decoy, enchant, entice, inveigle, lead on, lure, persuade, seduce, tempt, win over

alluring adjective = **attractive**, beguiling, bewitching, captivating, come-hither, enchanting, fascinating, fetching, glamorous, intriguing, seductive, sexy, tempting
➤ **Antonyms**
abhorrent, off-putting (Brit. informal), repellent, repugnant, repulsive, unattractive

allusion noun = **reference**, casual remark, glance, hint, implication, indirect reference, innuendo, insinuation, intimation, mention, suggestion

ally noun 1 = **partner**, abettor, accessory, accomplice, associate, coadjutor, collaborator, colleague, confederate, co-worker, friend, helper ♦ verb 2 = **unite**, affiliate, associate, band together, collaborate, combine, confederate, connect, join, join battle with, join forces, league, marry, unify
➤ **Antonyms**
noun ≠**partner**: adversary, antagonist, competitor, enemy, foe, opponent, rival ♦ verb ≠**unite**: alienate, disaffect, disunite, divide, drive apart, separate, set at odds

almighty adjective 1 = **all-powerful**, absolute, invincible, omnipotent, supreme, unlimited 2 Informal = **great**, awful, desperate, enormous, excessive, intense, loud, severe, terrible
➤ **Antonyms**

≠**all-powerful**: helpless, impotent, powerless, weak ≠**great**: feeble, insignificant, paltry, poor, slight, tame, weak

almost *adverb* = **nearly**, about, all but, approximately, as good as, close to, just about, not far from, not quite, on the brink of, practically, so near (and) yet so far, virtually, well-nigh

alone *adjective* = **by oneself**, abandoned, apart, by itself, deserted, desolate, detached, forlorn, forsaken, isolated, lonely, lonesome, only, on one's tod (*slang*), out on a limb, separate, single, single-handed, sole, solitary, unaccompanied, unaided, unassisted, unattended, uncombined, unconnected, under one's own steam, unescorted
➤ **Antonyms**
accompanied, aided, among others, assisted, escorted, helped, joint, together

aloof *adjective* = **distant**, chilly, cold, cool, detached, forbidding, formal, haughty, indifferent, remote, reserved, standoffish, supercilious, unapproachable, unfriendly, uninterested, unresponsive, unsociable, unsympathetic
➤ **Antonyms**
friendly, gregarious, neighbourly, open, sociable, sympathetic, warm

aloud *adverb* = **out loud**, audibly, clearly, distinctly, intelligibly, plainly

already *adverb* = **before now**, as of now, at present, before, by now, by that time, by then, by this time, even now, heretofore, just now, previously

also *adverb* = **too**, additionally, along with, and, as well, as well as, besides, further, furthermore, in addition, including, into the bargain, moreover, on top of that, plus, to boot

alter *verb* = **change**, adapt, adjust, amend, convert, diversify, metamorphose, modify, recast, reform, remodel, reshape, revise, shift, transform, transmute, turn, tweak (*informal*), vary

alteration *noun* = **change**, adaptation, adjustment, amendment, conversion, difference, diversification, metamorphosis, modification, reformation, remodelling, reshaping, revision, shift, transformation, transmutation, variance, variation

alternate *verb* **1** = **change**, act reciprocally, alter, fluctuate, follow in turn, follow one another, interchange, intersperse, oscillate, rotate, substitute, take turns ♦ *adjective* **2** = **every other**, alternating, every second, interchanging, rotating **3** = **second**, alternative, another, different, substitute

alternative *noun* **1** = **choice**, option, other (*of two*), preference, recourse, selection, substitute ♦ *adjective* **2** = **different**, alternate, another, other, second, substitute

alternatively *adverb* = **or**, as an alternative, by way of alternative, if not, instead, on the other hand, otherwise

although *conjunction* = **though**, albeit, despite the fact that, even if, even supposing, even though, notwithstanding, tho' (*U.S. or poetic*), while

altitude *noun* = **height**, elevation, loftiness, peak, summit

altogether *adverb* **1** = **completely**, absolutely, every inch, fully, lock, stock and barrel, perfectly, quite, thoroughly, totally, utterly, wholly **2** = **on the whole**, all in all, all things considered, as a whole, collectively, generally, in general, *in toto* **3** = **in total**, all told, everything included, in all, in sum, *in toto*, taken together
➤ **Antonyms**
≠**completely**: halfway, incompletely, in part, in some measure, not fully, partially, relatively, slightly, somewhat, to a certain degree *or* extent, up to a certain point

altruistic *adjective* = **selfless**, benevolent, charitable, considerate, generous, humanitarian, philanthropic, public-spirited, self-sacrificing, unselfish
➤ **Antonyms**
egoistic(al), egotistic(al), greedy, looking out for number one (*informal*), mean, self-centred, self-interested, selfish, self-seeking, ungenerous

always *adverb* = **continually**, aye (*Scot.*), consistently, constantly, eternally, ever, everlastingly, evermore, every time, forever, *in perpetuum*, invariably, perpetually, repeatedly, unceasingly, without exception
➤ **Antonyms**
hardly, hardly ever, infrequently, once in a blue moon, once in a while, only now and then, on rare occasions, rarely, scarcely ever, seldom

amalgamate *verb* = **combine**, alloy, ally, blend, coalesce, commingle, compound, fuse, incorporate, integrate, intermix, meld, merge, mingle, unite
➤ **Antonyms**
disunite, divide, part, separate, split, split up

amalgamation *noun* = **combination**, admixture, alliance, alloy, amalgam, amalgamating, blend, coalition, commingling, composite, compound, fusion, incorporation, integration, joining, meld, merger, mingling, mixing, mixture, union

amass *verb* = **collect**, accumulate, aggregate, assemble, compile, garner, gather, heap up, hoard, pile up, rake up, scrape together

amateur *noun* = **nonprofessional**, dabbler, dilettante, layman

amateurish *adjective* = **unprofessional**, amateur, bungling, clumsy, crude, inexpert, unaccomplished, unskilful
➤ **Antonyms**
experienced, expert, practised, professional, skilled

amaze *verb* = **astonish**, alarm, astound, bewilder, boggle the mind, bowl over (*informal*), confound, daze, dumbfound, electrify, flabbergast, shock, stagger, startle, stun, stupefy, surprise

amazement *noun* = **astonishment**, admiration, bewilderment, confusion, marvel, perplexity, shock, stupefaction, surprise, wonder

amazing *adjective* = **astonishing**, astounding, breathtaking, eye-opening, jaw-dropping, overwhelming, staggering, startling, stunning, surprising

ambassador *noun* = **representative**, agent, consul, deputy, diplomat, emissary, envoy, legate, minister, plenipotentiary

ambiguity *noun* = **vagueness**, doubt, doubtfulness, dubiety, dubiousness, enigma, equivocacy, equivocality, equivocation, inconclusiveness, indefiniteness, indeterminateness, obscurity, puzzle, tergiversation, uncertainty

ambiguous *adjective* = **unclear**, clear as mud (*informal*), cryptic, Delphic, doubtful, dubious, enigmatic, enigmatical, equivocal, inconclusive, indefinite, indeterminate, obscure, oracular, puzzling, uncertain, vague
➤ **Antonyms**
clear, definite, explicit, obvious, plain, simple, specific, unequivocal, unmistakable, unquestionable

ambition *noun* 1 = **enterprise**, aspiration, avidity, desire, drive, eagerness, get-up-and-go (*informal*), hankering, longing, striving, yearning, zeal 2 = **goal**, aim, aspiration, desire, dream, end, Holy Grail (*informal*), hope, intent, objective, purpose, wish

ambitious *adjective* 1 = **enterprising**, aspiring, avid, desirous, driving, eager, hopeful, intent, purposeful, striving, zealous 2 = **demanding**, arduous, bold, challenging, difficult, elaborate, energetic, exacting, formidable, grandiose, hard, impressive, industrious, pretentious, severe, strenuous

➤ **Antonyms**
≠**enterprising**: apathetic, good-for-nothing, lazy, unambitious, unaspiring ≠**demanding**: easy, modest, simple, unambitious

ambivalence *noun* = **indecision**, clash, conflict, contradiction, doubt, equivocation, fluctuation, hesitancy, irresolution, opposition, uncertainty, vacillation, wavering

ambivalent *adjective* = **undecided**, clashing, conflicting, contradictory, debatable, doubtful, equivocal, fluctuating, hesitant, inconclusive, in two minds, irresolute, mixed, opposed, uncertain, unresolved, unsure, vacillating, warring, wavering
➤ **Antonyms**
certain, clear, conclusive, convinced, decided, definite, free from doubt, positive, sure, unwavering

amble *verb* = **stroll**, dawdle, meander, mosey (*informal*), ramble, saunter, walk, wander

ambush *noun* 1 = **trap**, ambuscade, attack, concealment, cover, hiding, hiding place, lying in wait, retreat, shelter, waylaying
◆ *verb* 2 = **trap**, ambuscade, attack, bushwhack (*U.S.*), ensnare, surprise, waylay

amenable *adjective* = **receptive**, able to be influenced, acquiescent, agreeable, compliant, open, persuadable, responsive, susceptible, tractable
➤ **Antonyms**
inflexible, intractable, mulish, obdurate, obstinate, pig-headed, recalcitrant, stiff-necked, stubborn, unbending, unyielding

amend *verb* = **change**, alter, ameliorate, better, correct, enhance, fix, improve, mend, modify, rectify, reform, remedy, repair, revise, tweak (*informal*)

amendment *noun* 1 = **change**, alteration, amelioration, betterment, correction, emendation, enhancement, improvement, mending, modification, rectification, reform, remedy, repair, revision 2 = **alteration**, addendum, addition, adjunct, attachment, clarification

amends *plural noun As in* **make amends for** = **compensation**, apology, atonement, expiation, indemnity, recompense, redress, reparation, requital, restitution, restoration, satisfaction

amenity *noun* 1 = **facility**, advantage, comfort, convenience, service 2 = **courtesy**, affability, agreeableness, amiability, complaisance, mildness, pleasantness, politeness, refinement,

suavity
➤ Antonyms
≠**courtesy:** bad manners, discourtesy, impoliteness, incivility, rudeness, ungraciousness

amiability noun = **pleasantness**, affability, agreeableness, amiableness, attractiveness, benignity, charm, cheerfulness, delightfulness, engagingness, friendliness, friendship, geniality, good humour, good nature, kindliness, kindness, lovableness, pleasingness, sociability, sweetness, sweetness and light (informal), sweet temper, winsomeness

amiable adjective = **pleasant**, affable, agreeable, attractive, benign, charming, cheerful, congenial, delightful, engaging, friendly, genial, good-humoured, good-natured, kind, kindly, likable or likeable, lovable, obliging, pleasing, sociable, sweet-tempered, winning, winsome
➤ Antonyms
disagreeable, displeasing, hostile, ill-natured, loathsome, repellent, sour, unfriendly, unpleasant

amicable adjective = **friendly**, amiable, brotherly, civil, cordial, courteous, fraternal, good-humoured, harmonious, kind, kindly, neighbourly, peaceable, peaceful, polite, sociable
➤ Antonyms
antagonistic, bellicose, belligerent, disagreeable, hostile, ill-disposed, impolite, inimical, pugnacious, quarrelsome, uncivil, unfriendly, unkind, unsociable

amid, amidst preposition = **in the middle of**, among, amongst, in the midst of, in the thick of, surrounded by

amiss adverb 1 = **wrongly**, erroneously, faultily, improperly, inappropriately, incorrectly, mistakenly, unsuitably 2 As in take (something) amiss = **as an insult**, as offensive, out of turn, wrongly ♦ adjective 3 = **wrong**, awry, confused, defective, erroneous, fallacious, false, faulty, improper, inaccurate, inappropriate, incorrect, mistaken, out of order, unsuitable, untoward
➤ Antonyms
adverb ≠**wrongly:** appropriately, correctly, properly, rightly, suitably, well ♦ adjective ≠**wrong:** accurate, appropriate, correct, in order, O.K. or okay (informal), perfect, proper, right, suitable, true

ammunition noun = **munitions**, armaments, cartridges, explosives, materiel, powder, rounds, shells, shot, shot and shell

amnesty noun = **general pardon**, absolution, condonation, dispensation, forgiveness, immunity, oblivion, remission (of penalty), reprieve

amok, amuck adverb As in run amok = **madly**, berserk, destructively, ferociously, frenziedly, in a frenzy, insanely, maniacally, murderously, savagely, uncontrollably, violently, wildly

among, amongst preposition 1 = **in the midst of**, amid, amidst, in association with, in the middle of, in the thick of, midst, surrounded by, together with, with 2 = **in the group of**, in the class of, in the company of, in the number of, out of 3 = **to each of**, between ♦ adverb 4 = **with one another**, by all of, by the joint action of, by the whole of, mutually

amorous adjective = **loving**, affectionate, amatory, ardent, attached, doting, enamoured, erotic, fond, impassioned, in love, lovesick, lustful, passionate, tender
➤ Antonyms
aloof, cold, distant, frigid, frosty, indifferent, passionless, stand-offish, undemonstrative, unfeeling, unloving

amorphous adjective = **shapeless**, characterless, formless, inchoate, indeterminate, irregular, nebulous, nondescript, unformed, unshaped, unshapen, unstructured, vague
➤ Antonyms
definite, distinct, regular, shaped, structured

amount noun 1 = **quantity**, bulk, expanse, extent, lot, magnitude, mass, measure, number, supply, volume 2 = **total**, addition, aggregate, entirety, extent, lot, sum, sum total, whole

amount to verb = **add up to**, aggregate, become, come to, develop into, equal, grow, mean, purport, total

ample adjective = **plenty**, abounding, abundant, big, bountiful, broad, capacious, commodious, copious, enough and to spare, expansive, extensive, full, generous, great, large, lavish, liberal, plenteous, plentiful, profuse, rich, roomy, spacious, substantial, two a penny, unrestricted, voluminous, wide
➤ Antonyms
inadequate, insufficient, little, meagre, restricted, scant, skimpy, small, sparse, unsatisfactory

amplification noun 1 = **explanation**, augmentation, development, elaboration, expansion, expatiation, fleshing out, rounding out, supplementing 2 = **increase**, augmentation, boosting, deepening, dilation, enlargement, expansion, extension, heightening, intensification, lengthening, magnification, raising, strengthening, stretching, widening

amplify verb 1 = **go into detail**, augment, develop, elaborate, enlarge, expand, expatiate, explain, flesh out, round out, supplement 2 = **expand**, augment, boost, deepen, dilate, enlarge, extend, heighten, increase, intensify, lengthen, magnify, raise, strengthen, stretch, widen
➤ **Antonyms**
≠**go into detail**: abbreviate, abridge, simplify ≠**expand**: boil down, condense, curtail, cut down, decrease, reduce

amply adverb = **fully**, abundantly, bountifully, capaciously, completely, copiously, extensively, generously, greatly, lavishly, liberally, plenteously, plentifully, profusely, richly, substantially, thoroughly, unstintingly, well, with a blank cheque, with a free hand, without stinting
➤ **Antonyms**
inadequately, insufficiently, meagrely, poorly, scantily, skimpily, sparsely, thinly

amputate verb = **cut off**, curtail, lop, remove, separate, sever, truncate

amuck see AMOK

amuse verb = **entertain**, beguile, charm, cheer, delight, divert, enliven, gladden, gratify, interest, occupy, please, recreate, regale, tickle
➤ **Antonyms**
be tedious, bore, jade, pall on, send to sleep, tire, weary

amusement noun 1 = **entertainment**, beguilement, cheer, delight, diversion, enjoyment, fun, gladdening, gratification, hilarity, interest, jollies (slang), laughter, merriment, mirth, pleasing, pleasure, recreation, regalement, sport 2 = **pastime**, distraction, diversion, entertainment, game, hobby, joke, lark, prank, recreation, sport
➤ **Antonyms**
≠**entertainment**: boredom, displeasure, monotony, sadness, tedium

amusing adjective = **funny**, charming, cheerful, cheering, comical, delightful, diverting, droll, enjoyable, entertaining, facetious, gladdening, gratifying, humorous, interesting, jocular, laughable, lively, merry, pleasant, pleasing, rib-tickling, waggish, witty
➤ **Antonyms**
boring, dead, dull, flat, humdrum, monotonous, stale, tedious, tiresome, unamusing, unexciting, unfunny, uninteresting, wearisome

anaemic adjective = **pale**, ashen, bloodless, characterless, colourless, dull, enervated, feeble, frail, infirm, like death warmed up

(informal), pallid, sickly, wan, weak
➤ **Antonyms**
blooming, florid, full-blooded, glowing, hearty, radiant, rosy, rosy-cheeked, rubicund, ruddy, sanguine

anaesthetic noun 1 = **painkiller**, analgesic, anodyne, narcotic, opiate, sedative, soporific, stupefacient, stupefactive
◆ adjective 2 = **pain-killing**, analgesic, anodyne, deadening, dulling, narcotic, numbing, opiate, sedative, sleep-inducing, soporific, stupefacient, stupefactive

analogous adjective = **similar**, agreeing, akin, alike, comparable, corresponding, equivalent, homologous, like, of a piece, parallel, related, resembling
➤ **Antonyms**
contrasting, different, discrepant, disparate, dissimilar, diverse, unlike

analogy noun = **similarity**, agreement, comparison, correlation, correspondence, equivalence, homology, likeness, parallel, relation, resemblance, similitude

analyse verb 1 = **examine**, assay, estimate, evaluate, interpret, investigate, judge, research, test, work over 2 = **break down**, anatomize, consider, dissect, dissolve, divide, resolve, separate, study, think through

analysis noun 1 = **examination**, anatomization, anatomy, assay, breakdown, dissection, dissolution, division, inquiry, investigation, perusal, resolution, scrutiny, separation, sifting, test 2 = **finding**, estimation, evaluation, interpretation, judgment, opinion, reasoning, study

analytic, analytical adjective = **rational**, detailed, diagnostic, discrete, dissecting, explanatory, expository, inquiring, inquisitive, interpretative, interpretive, investigative, logical, organized, problem-solving, questioning, searching, studious, systematic, testing

anarchic adjective = **lawless**, chaotic, confused, disordered, disorganized, misgoverned, misruled, off the rails, rebellious, revolutionary, rioting, riotous, ungoverned
➤ **Antonyms**
controlled, decorous, disciplined, law-abiding, ordered, peaceable, peaceful, quiet, restrained, well-behaved

anarchist noun = **revolutionary**, insurgent, nihilist, rebel, terrorist

anarchy noun = **lawlessness**, chaos, confusion, disorder, disorganization, misgovernment, misrule, rebellion, revolution, riot
➤ **Antonyms**

control, discipline, government, law, law and order, order, peace, rule

anathema *noun* = **abomination**, bane, bête noire, bugbear, enemy, pariah

anathematize *verb* = **curse**, abominate, ban, condemn, damn, denounce, excommunicate, execrate, imprecate, proscribe

anatomize *verb* = **examine**, analyse, break down, dissect, dissolve, divide, resolve, scrutinize, separate, study

anatomy *noun* 1 = **examination**, analysis, dismemberment, dissection, division, inquiry, investigation, study 2 = **structure**, build, composition, frame, framework, make-up

ancestor *noun* = **forefather**, forebear, forerunner, precursor, predecessor, progenitor
➤ **Antonyms**
descendant, inheritor, issue, offspring, progeny, successor

ancestry *noun* = **origin**, ancestors, antecedents, blood, derivation, descent, extraction, family, forebears, forefathers, genealogy, house, line, lineage, parentage, pedigree, progenitors, race, stock

ancient *adjective* = **old**, aged, age-old, antediluvian, antiquated, antique, archaic, bygone, cobwebby, early, hoary, obsolete, old as the hills, olden, old-fashioned, outmoded, out-of-date, primeval, primordial, superannuated, timeworn
➤ **Antonyms**
current, fresh, in vogue, late, modern, modish, new, newfangled, new-fashioned, novel, recent, state-of-the-art, up-to-date, with it (*informal*), young

ancillary *adjective* = **supplementary**, accessory, additional, auxiliary, contributory, extra, secondary, subordinate, subsidiary, supporting
➤ **Antonyms**
cardinal, chief, main, major, premier, primary, prime, principal

and *conjunction* = **also**, along with, as well as, furthermore, in addition to, including, moreover, plus, together with

anecdote *noun* = **story**, reminiscence, short story, sketch, tale, urban legend, urban myth, yarn

anew *adverb* = **again**, afresh, another time, from scratch, from the beginning, once again, once more, over again

angel *noun* 1 = **divine messenger**, archangel, cherub, guardian spirit, seraph, spiritual being 2 *Informal* = **dear**, beauty, darling, dream, gem, ideal, jewel, paragon, saint, treasure

angelic *adjective* 1 = **pure**, adorable, beatific, beautiful, entrancing, innocent, lovely, saintly, virtuous 2 = **heavenly**, celestial, cherubic, ethereal, seraphic
➤ **Antonyms**
≠heavenly: demonic, devilish, diabolic, diabolical, fiendish, hellish, infernal, satanic

anger *noun* 1 = **rage**, annoyance, antagonism, choler, displeasure, exasperation, fury, ill humour, ill temper, indignation, ire, irritability, irritation, outrage, passion, pique, resentment, seeing red, spleen, temper, vexation, wrath ♦ *verb* 2 = **enrage**, affront, aggravate (*informal*), annoy, antagonize, be on one's back (*slang*), displease, exasperate, excite, fret, gall, get in one's hair (*informal*), get one's back up, get one's dander up (*informal*), get on one's nerves (*informal*), hassle (*informal*), incense, infuriate, irritate, madden, make one's blood boil, nark (*Brit., Austral., & N.Z. slang*), nettle, offend, outrage, pique, piss one off (*taboo slang*), provoke, put one's back up, rile, vex
➤ **Antonyms**
noun ≠rage: acceptance, amiability, approval, calmness, forgiveness, goodwill, gratification, liking, patience, peace, pleasure ♦ *verb* ≠enrage: appease, calm, pacify, placate, please, soothe

angle¹ *noun* 1 = **intersection**, bend, corner, crook, crotch, cusp, edge, elbow, knee, nook, point 2 = **point of view**, approach, aspect, outlook, perspective, position, side, slant, standpoint, take (*informal*), viewpoint

angle² *verb* = **fish**, cast

angle for *verb* = **be after** (*informal*), aim for, cast about or around for, contrive, fish for, hunt, invite, look for, scheme, seek, set one's sights on, solicit, try for

angry *adjective* = **furious**, annoyed, antagonized, as black as thunder, at daggers drawn, choked, choleric, cross, displeased, enraged, exasperated, fit to be tied (*slang*), foaming at the mouth, hacked (off) (*U.S. slang*), heated, hot, hot under the collar (*informal*), ill-tempered, incandescent, incensed, indignant, infuriated, in high dudgeon, irascible, irate, ireful, irritable, irritated, mad (*informal*), nettled, on the warpath, outraged, passionate, piqued, pissed (*taboo slang*), pissed off (*taboo slang*), provoked, raging, resentful, riled, splenetic, tumultuous, up in arms, uptight (*informal*), wrathful
➤ **Antonyms**
agreeable, amiable, calm, congenial,

friendly, gratified, happy, loving, mild, peaceful, pleasant, pleased

angst *noun* = **anxiety**, apprehension, unease, worry
➤ **Antonyms**
calmness, composure, contentment, ease, nonchalance, peace of mind, satisfaction

anguish *noun* = **suffering**, agony, distress, grief, heartache, heartbreak, misery, pain, pang, sorrow, throe, torment, torture, woe

anguished *adjective* = **suffering**, afflicted, agonized, brokenhearted, distressed, grief-stricken, tormented, tortured, wounded, wretched

angular *adjective* = **skinny**, bony, gaunt, lank, lanky, lean, macilent (*rare*), rangy, rawboned, scrawny, spare

animal *noun* **1** = **creature**, beast, brute **2** *Applied to a person* = **brute**, barbarian, beast, monster, savage, wild man
♦ *adjective* **3** = **physical**, bestial, bodily, brutish, carnal, fleshly, gross, sensual

animate *verb* **1** = **enliven**, activate, breathe life into, embolden, encourage, energize, excite, fire, gee up, gladden, impel, incite, inspire, inspirit, instigate, invigorate, kick-start (*informal*), kindle, liven up, move, prod, quicken, revive, rouse, spark, spur, stimulate, stir, urge, vitalize, vivify
♦ *adjective* **2** = **living**, alive, alive and kicking, breathing, live, moving
➤ **Antonyms**
verb ≠**enliven**: check, curb, deaden, deter, devitalize, discourage, dull, inhibit, kill, make lifeless, put a damper on, restrain

animated *adjective* = **lively**, active, airy, alive and kicking, ardent, brisk, buoyant, dynamic, ebullient, elated, energetic, enthusiastic, excited, fervent, full of beans (*informal*), gay, passionate, quick, sparky, spirited, sprightly, vibrant, vigorous, vital, vivacious, vivid, zealous, zestful
➤ **Antonyms**
apathetic, boring, dejected, depressed, dull, inactive, lethargic, lifeless, listless, monotonous, passive

animation *noun* = **liveliness**, action, activity, airiness, ardour, brio, briskness, buoyancy, dynamism, ebullience, elation, energy, enthusiasm, excitement, exhilaration, fervour, gaiety, high spirits, life, passion, pep, pizzazz *or* pizazz (*informal*), sparkle, spirit, sprightliness, verve, vibrancy, vigour, vitality, vivacity, zeal, zest, zing (*informal*)

animosity *noun* = **hostility**, acrimony, animus, antagonism, antipathy, bad blood, bitterness, enmity, hate, hatred, ill will, malevolence, malice, malignity, rancour, resentment, virulence

➤ **Antonyms**
amity, benevolence, congeniality, friendliness, friendship, goodwill, harmony, kindness, love, rapport, sympathy

annals *plural noun* = **records**, accounts, archives, chronicles, history, journals, memorials, registers

annex *verb* **1** = **seize**, acquire, appropriate, arrogate, conquer, expropriate, occupy, take over **2** = **join**, add, adjoin, affix, append, attach, connect, fasten, subjoin, tack, unite
➤ **Antonyms**
≠**join**: detach, disconnect, disengage, disjoin, disunite, remove, separate, unfasten

annexation *noun* = **seizure**, annexing, appropriation, arrogation, conquest, expropriation, occupation, takeover

annexe *noun* **1** = **extension**, ell, supplementary building, wing **2** = **addition**, addendum, adjunct, affix, appendix, attachment, supplement

annihilate *verb* = **destroy**, abolish, eradicate, erase, exterminate, extinguish, extirpate, liquidate, nullify, obliterate, root out, wipe from the face of the earth, wipe out

annihilation *noun* = **destruction**, abolition, eradication, erasure, extermination, extinction, extinguishing, extirpation, liquidation, nullification, obliteration, rooting out, wiping out

annotate *verb* = **make notes**, commentate, comment on, elucidate, explain, footnote, gloss, illustrate, interpret, make observations, note

annotation *noun* = **note**, comment, commentary, elucidation, exegesis, explanation, explication, footnote, gloss, illustration, interpretation, observation

announce *verb* **1** = **make known**, advertise, blow wide open (*slang*), broadcast, declare, disclose, divulge, give out, intimate, proclaim, promulgate, propound, publish, report, reveal, shout from the rooftops (*informal*), tell **2** = **be a sign of**, augur, betoken, foretell, harbinger, herald, portend, presage, signal, signify
➤ **Antonyms**
≠**make known**: bury, conceal, cover up, hide, hold back, hush (up), keep back, keep quiet, keep secret, suppress, withhold

announcement *noun* = **statement**, advertisement, broadcast, bulletin, communiqué, declaration, disclosure, divulgence, intimation, proclamation, promulgation, publication, report, revelation

announcer noun = **presenter**, anchor man, broadcaster, commentator, master of ceremonies, newscaster, newsreader, reporter

annoy verb = **irritate**, aggravate (informal), anger, badger, bedevil, be on one's back (slang), bore, bother, bug (informal), displease, disturb, exasperate, gall, get (informal), get in one's hair (informal), get one's back up, get one's dander up (informal), get one's goat (slang), get on one's nerves (informal), get on one's wick (Brit. slang), get under one's skin (informal), get up one's nose (informal), harass, harry, hassle (informal), incommode, irk, madden, make one's blood boil, molest, nark (Brit., Austral., & N.Z. slang), needle (informal), nettle, peeve, pester, piss one off (taboo slang), plague, provoke, put one's back up, rile, rub (someone) up the wrong way (informal), ruffle, tease, trouble, vex
➤ **Antonyms**
appease, calm, comfort, console, mollify, solace, soothe

annoyance noun **1** = **irritation**, aggravation, anger, bedevilment, bother, displeasure, disturbance, exasperation, grief (informal), harassment, hassle (informal), nuisance, provocation, trouble, vexation **2** = **nuisance**, bind (informal), bore, bother, drag (informal), gall, pain (informal), pain in the arse (taboo informal), pain in the neck (informal), pest, plague, tease

annoying adjective = **irritating**, aggravating, bedevilling, boring, bothersome, displeasing, disturbing, exasperating, galling, harassing, irksome, maddening, peeving (informal), provoking, teasing, troublesome, vexatious
➤ **Antonyms**
agreeable, amusing, charming, delightful, diverting, enjoyable, entertaining, gratifying, pleasant

annual adjective = **yearly**, once a year, yearlong

annually adverb = **yearly**, by the year, each year, every year, once a year, per annum, per year, year after year

annul verb = **invalidate**, abolish, abrogate, cancel, countermand, declare or render null and void, negate, nullify, obviate, recall, repeal, rescind, retract, reverse, revoke, void
➤ **Antonyms**
bring back, re-enforce, re-establish, reimpose, reinstate, reintroduce, restore

annulment noun = **invalidation**, abolition, abrogation, cancellation, countermanding, negation, nullification, recall, repeal, rescindment, rescission, retraction, reversal, revocation, voiding

anodyne noun **1** = **painkiller**, analgesic, narcotic, pain reliever, palliative ♦ adjective **2** = **pain-killing**, analgesic, deadening, dulling, narcotic, numbing, pain-relieving, palliative

anoint verb **1** = **smear**, daub, embrocate, grease, oil, rub, spread over **2** = **consecrate**, anele (archaic), bless, hallow, sanctify

anomalous adjective = **unusual**, aberrant, abnormal, atypical, bizarre, deviating, eccentric, exceptional, incongruous, inconsistent, irregular, odd, oddball (informal), off-the-wall (slang), outré, peculiar, rare
➤ **Antonyms**
common, customary, familiar, natural, normal, ordinary, regular, typical, usual

anomaly noun = **irregularity**, aberration, abnormality, departure, deviation, eccentricity, exception, incongruity, inconsistency, oddity, peculiarity, rarity

anon adverb Old-fashioned or informal = **soon**, before long, betimes (archaic), erelong (archaic or poetic), forthwith, in a couple of shakes (informal), presently, promptly, shortly

anonymous adjective **1** = **unnamed**, incognito, innominate, nameless, unacknowledged, unattested, unauthenticated, uncredited, unidentified, unknown, unsigned **2** = **nondescript**, characterless, undistinguished, unexceptional
➤ **Antonyms**
≠unnamed: accredited, acknowledged, attested, authenticated, credited, identified, known, named, signed

answer verb **1** = **reply**, acknowledge, explain, react, refute, rejoin, resolve, respond, retort, return, solve **2** = **do**, conform, correlate, correspond, fill, fit, fulfil, measure up, meet, pass, qualify, satisfy, serve, suffice, suit, work ♦ noun **3** = **reply**, acknowledgment, comeback, counterattack, defence, explanation, plea, reaction, refutation, rejoinder, report, resolution, response, retort, return, riposte, solution, vindication
➤ **Antonyms**
verb ≠reply: ask, inquire, interrogate, query, question ♦ noun ≠reply: inquiry, interrogation, query, question

answerable adjective, usually with **for** or **to** = **responsible**, accountable, amenable, chargeable, liable, subject, to blame

answer back *verb* = **be impertinent**, argue, be cheeky, cheek (*informal*), contradict, disagree, dispute, rebut, retort, talk back

answer for *verb* **1** = **be responsible for**, be accountable for, be answerable for, be chargeable for, be liable for, be to blame for, take the rap for (*slang*) **2** = **pay for**, atone for, make amends for, suffer for

answer to *verb* **1** = **be responsible to**, be accountable to, be answerable to, be ruled by, obey **2** = **fit**, agree, confirm, correspond, match, meet

antagonism *noun* = **hostility**, antipathy, competition, conflict, contention, discord, dissension, friction, opposition, rivalry
➤ **Antonyms**
accord, agreement, amity, friendship, harmony, love, peacefulness, sympathy

antagonist *noun* = **opponent**, adversary, competitor, contender, enemy, foe, opposer, rival

antagonistic *adjective* = **hostile**, adverse, antipathetic, at odds, at variance, averse, conflicting, contentious, ill-disposed, incompatible, in dispute, inimical, opposed, unfriendly

antagonize *verb* = **annoy**, aggravate (*informal*), alienate, anger, be on one's back (*slang*), disaffect, estrange, gall, get in one's hair (*informal*), get on one's nerves (*informal*), get on one's wick (*Brit. slang*), get under one's skin (*informal*), get up one's nose (*informal*), hassle (*informal*), insult, irritate, nark (*Brit., Austral., & N.Z. slang*), offend, piss one off (*taboo slang*), repel, rub (someone) up the wrong way (*informal*)
➤ **Antonyms**
appease, calm, conciliate, disarm, mollify, pacify, placate, propitiate, soothe, win over

antecedent *adjective* = **preceding**, anterior, earlier, foregoing, former, precursory, preliminary, previous, prior
➤ **Antonyms**
after, coming, consequent, ensuing, following, later, posterior, subsequent, succeeding, successive

antecedents *plural noun* **1** = **ancestors**, ancestry, blood, descent, extraction, family, forebears, forefathers, genealogy, line, progenitors, stock **2** = **past**, background, history

antediluvian *adjective* **1** = **prehistoric**, primeval, primitive, primordial **2** = **old-fashioned**, ancient, antiquated, antique, archaic, obsolete, old as the hills, out-of-date, out of the ark (*informal*), passé

anteroom *noun* = **outer room**, antechamber, foyer, lobby, reception room, vestibule, waiting room

anthem *noun* **1** = **hymn**, canticle, carol, chant, chorale, psalm **2** = **song of praise**, paean

anthology *noun* = **collection**, analects, choice, compendium, compilation, digest, garland, miscellany, selection, treasury

anticipate *verb* **1** = **expect**, apprehend, await, count upon, forecast, foresee, foretell, hope for, look for, look forward to, predict, prepare for **2** = **forestall**, antedate, beat (someone) to it (*informal*), intercept, prevent

anticipation *noun* = **expectation**, apprehension, awaiting, expectancy, foresight, foretaste, forethought, hope, preconception, premonition, prescience, presentiment

anticlimax *noun* = **disappointment**, bathos, comedown (*informal*), letdown
➤ **Antonyms**
climax, culmination, height, highlight, high point, peak, summit, top, zenith

antics *plural noun* = **clowning**, buffoonery, capers, escapades, foolishness, frolics, horseplay, larks, mischief, monkey tricks, playfulness, pranks, silliness, skylarking, stunts, tomfoolery, tricks

antidote *noun* = **cure**, antitoxin, antivenin, corrective, counteragent, countermeasure, neutralizer, nostrum, preventive, remedy, specific

antipathetic *adjective* = **hostile**, abhorrent, antagonistic, averse, disgusting, distasteful, hateful, incompatible, invidious, loathsome, obnoxious, odious, offensive, repellent, repugnant, repulsive, revolting, yucky *or* yukky (*slang*)

antipathy *noun* = **hostility**, abhorrence, animosity, animus, antagonism, aversion, bad blood, contrariety, disgust, dislike, distaste, enmity, hatred, ill will, incompatibility, loathing, odium, opposition, rancour, repugnance, repulsion
➤ **Antonyms**
affection, affinity, attraction, bond, empathy, fellow-feeling, goodwill, harmony, partiality, rapport, sympathy, tie

antiquated *adjective* **1** = **obsolete**, antediluvian, antique, archaic, dated, old-fashioned, old hat, outmoded, out-of-date, outworn, passé, past it (*informal*), superannuated **2** = **old**, aged, ancient, cobwebby, elderly, hoary, old as the hills
➤ **Antonyms**

≠**obsolete**: all-singing, all-dancing, current, fashionable, fresh, modern, modish, new, state-of-the-art, stylish, up-to-date, young

antique *noun* **1** = **period piece**, bygone, heirloom, object of virtu, relic ♦ *adjective* **2** = **vintage**, antiquarian, classic, olden **3** = **old**, aged, ancient, elderly, superannuated **4** = **old-fashioned**, archaic, obsolete, outdated

antiquity *noun* **1** = **old age**, age, ancientness, elderliness, oldness **2** = **distant past**, ancient times, olden days, time immemorial **3** = **antique**, relic, ruin

antiseptic *adjective* **1** = **hygienic**, aseptic, clean, germ-free, pure, sanitary, sterile, uncontaminated, unpolluted ♦ *noun* **2** = **disinfectant**, bactericide, germicide, purifier
➤ Antonyms
adjective ≠**hygienic**: contaminated, dirty, impure, infected, insanitary, polluted, septic, unhygienic

antisocial *adjective* **1** = **unsociable**, alienated, asocial, misanthropic, reserved, retiring, uncommunicative, unfriendly, withdrawn **2** = **disruptive**, antagonistic, belligerent, disorderly, hostile, menacing, rebellious, uncooperative
➤ Antonyms
≠**unsociable**: companionable, friendly, gregarious, philanthropic, sociable, social

antithesis *noun* **1** = **opposite**, antipode, contrary, contrast, converse, inverse, reverse **2** = **contrast**, contradiction, contraposition, contrariety, inversion, opposition, reversal

anxiety *noun* = **uneasiness**, angst, apprehension, care, concern, disquiet, disquietude, distress, foreboding, fretfulness, misgiving, nervousness, restlessness, solicitude, suspense, tension, trepidation, unease, watchfulness, worry
➤ Antonyms
assurance, calmness, confidence, contentment, relief, security, serenity

anxious *adjective* **1** = **uneasy**, angsty, antsy (*informal*), apprehensive, careful, concerned, disquieted, distressed, disturbed, fearful, fretful, hot and bothered, in suspense, nervous, neurotic, on pins and needles, on tenterhooks, overwrought, restless, solicitous, taut, tense, troubled, twitchy (*informal*), unquiet (*chiefly literary*), watchful, wired (*slang*), worried **2** = **eager**, ardent, avid, desirous, expectant, impatient, intent, itching, keen, yearning
➤ Antonyms
≠**uneasy**: assured, calm, certain, collected,

composed, confident, cool, nonchalant, unfazed (*informal*), unperturbed ≠**eager**: disinclined, hesitant, loath, nonchalant, reluctant

apart *adverb* **1** = **to pieces**, asunder, in bits, in pieces, into parts, to bits **2** = **separate**, afar, alone, aloof, aside, away, by itself, by oneself, cut off, distant, distinct, divorced, excluded, independent, independently, isolated, out on a limb, piecemeal, separated, separately, singly, to itself, to oneself, to one side **3 apart from** = **except for**, aside from, besides, but, excluding, not counting, other than, save

apartment *noun* = **room**, accommodation, chambers, compartment, flat, living quarters, penthouse, quarters, rooms, suite

apathetic *adjective* = **uninterested**, cold, cool, emotionless, impassive, indifferent, insensible, listless, passive, phlegmatic, sluggish, stoic, stoical, torpid, unconcerned, unemotional, unfeeling, unmoved, unresponsive
➤ Antonyms
active, anxious, aroused, bothered, caring, committed, concerned, emotional, enthusiastic, excited, interested, moved, passionate, responsive, troubled, worried, zealous

apathy *noun* = **lack of interest**, coldness, coolness, emotionlessness, impassibility, impassivity, indifference, inertia, insensibility, listlessness, nonchalance, passiveness, passivity, phlegm, sluggishness, stoicism, torpor, unconcern, unfeelingness, uninterestedness, unresponsiveness
➤ Antonyms
anxiety, attention, concern, emotion, enthusiasm, feeling, interest, zeal

ape *verb* = **imitate**, affect, caricature, copy, counterfeit, echo, mimic, mirror, mock, parody, parrot

aperture *noun* = **opening**, breach, chink, cleft, crack, eye, eyelet, fissure, gap, hole, interstice, orifice, passage, perforation, rent, rift, slit, slot, space, vent

apex *noun* = **highest point**, acme, apogee, climax, crest, crown, culmination, height, peak, pinnacle, point, summit, tip, top, vertex, zenith
➤ Antonyms
base, bottom, depths, lowest point, nadir, perigee, rock bottom

aphorism *noun* = **saying**, adage, apothegm, axiom, dictum, gnome, maxim, precept, proverb, saw

apiece *adverb* = **each**, for each, from each, individually, respectively, separately, severally, to each

> ➤ **Antonyms**
all together, as a group, collectively, en masse, overall, together

aplomb *noun* = **self-possession**, balance, calmness, composure, confidence, coolness, equanimity, level-headedness, poise, sang-froid, self-assurance, self-confidence, stability
➤ **Antonyms**
awkwardness, chagrin, confusion, discomfiture, discomposure, embarrassment, self-consciousness

apocryphal *adjective* = **dubious**, doubtful, equivocal, fictitious, legendary, mythical, questionable, spurious, unauthenticated, uncanonical, unsubstantiated, unverified
➤ **Antonyms**
attested, authentic, authenticated, authorized, canonical, credible, factual, substantiated, true, undisputed, unquestionable, verified

apologetic *adjective* = **regretful**, contrite, penitent, remorseful, rueful, sorry

apologist *noun* = **defender**, advocate, arguer, champion, justifier, maintainer, pleader, spokesman, supporter, vindicator

apologize *verb* = **say sorry**, ask forgiveness, beg pardon, express regret, say one is sorry

apology *noun* 1 = **defence**, acknowledgment, confession, excuse, explanation, extenuation, justification, plea, vindication 2 *As in* **an apology for** = **mockery**, caricature, excuse, imitation, travesty

apostate *noun* 1 = **deserter**, backslider, defector, heretic, recreant (*archaic*), renegade, traitor, turncoat ♦ *adjective* 2 = **disloyal**, backsliding, faithless, false, heretical, perfidious, recreant, traitorous, treacherous, unfaithful, untrue

apostle *noun* 1 = **evangelist**, herald, messenger, missionary, preacher, proselytizer 2 = **supporter**, advocate, champion, pioneer, propagandist, propagator, proponent

apotheosis *noun* = **deification**, elevation, exaltation, glorification, idealization, idolization

appal *verb* = **horrify**, alarm, astound, daunt, dishearten, dismay, frighten, harrow, intimidate, make one's hair stand on end (*informal*), outrage, petrify, scare, shock, terrify, unnerve

appalling *adjective* = **horrifying**, alarming, astounding, awful, daunting, dire, disheartening, dismaying, dreadful, fearful, frightening, frightful, from hell (*informal*), ghastly, godawful (*slang*), grim, harrowing, hellacious (*U.S. slang*),

hideous, horrible, horrid, horrific, intimidating, petrifying, scaring, shocking, terrible, terrifying, unnerving
➤ **Antonyms**
comforting, consolatory, consoling, encouraging, heartening, reassuring

apparatus *noun* 1 = **equipment**, appliance, contraption (*informal*), device, gear, implements, machine, machinery, materials, means, mechanism, outfit, tackle, tools, utensils 2 = **organization**, bureaucracy, chain of command, hierarchy, network, setup (*informal*), structure, system

apparel *noun* Old-fashioned = **clothing**, accoutrements, array (*poetic*), attire, clothes, costume, dress, equipment, garb, garments, gear (*informal*), habiliments, habit, outfit, raiment (*archaic or poetic*), robes, threads (*slang*), trappings, vestments

apparent *adjective* 1 = **obvious**, blatant, bold, clear, conspicuous, discernible, distinct, evident, indubitable, manifest, marked, open, overt, patent, plain, plain as the nose on your face, salient, understandable, unmistakable, visible 2 = **seeming**, ostensible, outward, specious, superficial
➤ **Antonyms**
≠**obvious**: ambiguous, doubtful, dubious, hazy, indefinite, indistinct, obscure, uncertain, unclear, vague ≠**seeming**: actual, authentic, bona fide, genuine, honest, intrinsic, real, sincere, true

apparently *adverb* = **it appears that**, it seems that, on the face of it, ostensibly, outwardly, seemingly, speciously, superficially

apparition *noun* = **ghost**, chimera, eidolon, phantom, revenant, shade (*literary*), spectre, spirit, spook (*informal*), visitant, wraith

appeal *verb* 1 = **plead**, adjure, apply, ask, beg, beseech, call, call upon, entreat, implore, petition, pray, refer, request, resort to, solicit, sue, supplicate 2 = **attract**, allure, charm, engage, entice, fascinate, interest, invite, please, tempt ♦ *noun* 3 = **plea**, adjuration, application, entreaty, invocation, petition, prayer, request, solicitation, suit, supplication 4 = **attraction**, allure, attractiveness, beauty, charm, engagingness, fascination, interestingness, pleasingness
➤ **Antonyms**
verb ≠**plead**: deny, refuse, reject, repudiate, repulse ≠**attract**: alienate, bore, repulse, revolt ♦ *noun* ≠**plea**: denial, refusal, rejection, repudiation ≠**attraction**:

repulsiveness

appealing *adjective* = **attractive**, alluring, charming, desirable, engaging, winsome
➤ **Antonyms**
disgusting, forbidding, loathsome, objectionable, obnoxious, odious, offensive, repellent, repugnant, repulsive, revolting, sickening, unalluring, unappealing, unattractive, undesirable

appear *verb* **1** = **come into view**, arise, arrive, attend, be present, come forth, come into sight, come out, come to light, crop up (*informal*), develop, emerge, issue, loom, materialize, occur, show (*informal*), show one's face, show up (*informal*), surface, turn out, turn up **2** = **look (like** *or* **as if)**, occur, seem, strike one as **3** = **be obvious**, be apparent, be clear, be evident, be manifest, be patent, be plain **4** = **perform**, act, be exhibited, come on, come onstage, enter, play, play a part, take part **5** = **come into being**, become available, be created, be developed, be invented, be published, come into existence, come out
➤ **Antonyms**
≠**come into view**: disappear, vanish ≠**be obvious**: be doubtful, be unclear

appearance *noun* **1** = **arrival**, advent, appearing, coming, debut, emergence, introduction, presence, showing up (*informal*), turning up **2** = **look**, air, aspect, bearing, demeanour, expression, face, figure, form, image, looks, manner, mien (*literary*) **3** = **impression**, front, guise, illusion, image, outward show, pretence, semblance

appease *verb* **1** = **pacify**, calm, conciliate, mollify, placate, pour oil on troubled waters, quiet, satisfy, soothe **2** = **ease**, allay, alleviate, assuage, blunt, calm, compose, diminish, lessen, lull, mitigate, quell, quench, quiet, relieve, satisfy, soothe, subdue, tranquillize
➤ **Antonyms**
≠**pacify**: aggravate (*informal*), anger, annoy, antagonize, arouse, be on one's back (*slang*), disturb, enrage, get in one's hair (*informal*), get on one's nerves (*informal*), hassle (*informal*), incense, inflame, infuriate, irritate, madden, nark (*Brit., Austral., & N.Z. slang*), piss one off (*taboo slang*), provoke, rile, upset

appeasement *noun* **1** = **pacification**, acceding, accommodation, compromise, concession, conciliation, mollification, placation, propitiation **2** = **easing**, abatement, alleviation, assuagement, blunting, lessening, lulling, mitigation, quelling, quenching, quieting, relieving,

satisfaction, softening, solace, soothing, tranquillization

appellation *noun Formal* = **name**, address, description, designation, epithet, sobriquet, style, term, title

append *verb Formal* = **add**, adjoin, affix, annex, attach, fasten, hang, join, subjoin, tack on, tag on
➤ **Antonyms**
detach, disconnect, disengage, remove, separate, take off

appendage *noun* **1** = **attachment**, accessory, addendum, addition, adjunct, affix, ancillary, annexe, appendix, appurtenance, auxiliary, supplement **2** *Zoology* = **limb**, extremity, member, projection, protuberance

appendix *noun* = **supplement**, addendum, addition, add-on, adjunct, appendage, codicil, postscript

appertain *verb* **appertain to** = **relate to**, apply to, bear upon, be characteristic of, be connected to, belong to, be part of, be pertinent to, be proper to, be relevant to, have to do with, inhere in, pertain to, refer to, touch upon

appetence, appetency *noun* **1** = **desire**, ache, appetite, craving, hankering, hunger, longing, need, yearning **2** = **inclination**, bent, drive, instinct, leaning, penchant, propensity **3** = **liking**, affection, affinity, allurement, attraction, fondness, partiality

appetite *noun* = **desire**, appetence, appetency, craving, demand, hankering, hunger, inclination, liking, longing, passion, proclivity, propensity, relish, stomach, taste, willingness, yearning, zeal, zest
➤ **Antonyms**
abhorrence, aversion, disgust, disinclination, dislike, distaste, loathing, repugnance, repulsion, revulsion

appetizer *noun* **1** = **hors d'oeuvre**, antipasto, canapé, titbit **2** = **apéritif**, cocktail

appetizing *adjective* = **delicious**, appealing, inviting, mouthwatering, palatable, savoury, scrumptious (*informal*), succulent, tasty, tempting
➤ **Antonyms**
distasteful, nauseating, unappetizing, unpalatable, unsavoury

applaud *verb* = **praise**, acclaim, approve, cheer, clap, commend, compliment, crack up (*informal*), encourage, eulogize, extol, give (someone) a big hand, laud, magnify (*archaic*)
➤ **Antonyms**
blast, boo, censure, condemn, criticize,

decry, deprecate, deride, disparage, excoriate, hiss, lambast(e), pan (*informal*), put down, ridicule, run down, slag (off) (*slang*), tear into (*informal*), vilify

applause *noun* = **ovation**, acclaim, acclamation, accolade, approbation, approval, big hand, cheering, cheers, clapping, commendation, eulogizing, hand, hand-clapping, laudation, plaudit, praise

appliance *noun* = **device**, apparatus, gadget, implement, instrument, machine, mechanism, tool, waldo

applicable *adjective* = **appropriate**, apposite, apropos, apt, befitting, fit, fitting, germane, pertinent, relevant, suitable, suited, to the point, to the purpose, useful
➤ **Antonyms**
inapplicable, inappropriate, irrelevant, unsuitable, wrong

applicant *noun* = **candidate**, aspirant, claimant, inquirer, petitioner, postulant, suitor, suppliant

application *noun* **1** = **request**, appeal, claim, inquiry, petition, requisition, solicitation, suit **2** = **relevance**, appositeness, appropriateness, exercise, function, germaneness, pertinence, practice, purpose, use, value **3** = **effort**, assiduity, attention, attentiveness, commitment, dedication, diligence, hard work, industry, perseverance, study **4** = **lotion**, balm, cream, dressing, emollient, ointment, poultice, salve, unguent

apply *verb* **1** = **request**, appeal, claim, inquire, make application, petition, put in, requisition, solicit, sue **2** = **use**, administer, assign, bring into play, bring to bear, carry out, employ, engage, execute, exercise, exert, implement, practise, put to use, utilize **3** = **put on**, anoint, bring into contact with, cover with, lay on, paint, place, smear, spread on, touch to **4** = **be relevant**, appertain, be applicable, be appropriate, bear upon, be fitting, fit, pertain, refer, relate, suit **5 apply oneself** = **try**, address oneself, be assiduous, be diligent, be industrious, buckle down (*informal*), commit oneself, concentrate, dedicate oneself, devote oneself, make an effort, pay attention, persevere, study, work hard

appoint *verb* **1** = **assign**, choose, commission, delegate, elect, install, name, nominate, select **2** = **decide**, allot, arrange, assign, choose, designate, determine, establish, fix, set, settle **3** = **equip**, fit out, furnish, provide, supply
➤ **Antonyms**

≠**assign**: discharge, dismiss, fire, give the sack (*informal*), sack (*informal*) ≠**decide**: cancel ≠**equip**: dismantle, divest, strip

appointed *adjective* **1** = **assigned**, chosen, commissioned, delegated, elected, installed, named, nominated, selected **2** = **decided**, allotted, arranged, assigned, chosen, designated, determined, established, fixed, set, settled **3** = **equipped**, fitted out, furnished, provided, supplied

appointment *noun* **1** = **meeting**, arrangement, assignation, consultation, date, engagement, interview, rendezvous, session, tryst (*archaic*) **2** = **selection**, allotment, assignment, choice, choosing, commissioning, delegation, designation, election, installation, naming, nomination **3** = **appointee**, candidate, delegate, nominee, office-holder, representative **4** = **job**, assignment, berth (*informal*), office, place, position, post, situation, station **5 appointments** = **fittings**, accoutrements, appurtenances, equipage, fixtures, furnishings, gear, outfit, paraphernalia, trappings

apportion *verb* = **divide**, allocate, allot, assign, deal, dispense, distribute, dole out, give out, measure out, mete out, parcel out, ration out, share

apportionment *noun* = **division**, allocation, allotment, assignment, dealing out, dispensing, distribution, doling out, measuring out, meting out, parcelling out, rationing out, sharing

apposite *adjective* = **appropriate**, appertaining, applicable, apropos, apt, befitting, fitting, germane, pertinent, proper, relevant, suitable, suited, to the point, to the purpose
➤ **Antonyms**
inapplicable, inappropriate, inapt, irrelevant, unsuitable, unsuited

appraisal *noun* **1** = **assessment**, estimate, estimation, evaluation, judgment, opinion, recce (*slang*), sizing up (*informal*) **2** = **valuation**, assay, pricing, rating, reckoning, survey

appraise *verb* = **assess**, assay, estimate, evaluate, eye up, gauge, inspect, judge, price, rate, recce (*slang*), review, size up (*informal*), survey, value

appreciable *adjective* = **significant**, ascertainable, clear-cut, considerable, definite, detectable, discernible, distinguishable, evident, marked, material, measurable, noticeable, obvious, perceivable, perceptible, pronounced, recognizable, substantial, visible
➤ **Antonyms**

immaterial, imperceptible, inappreciable, indiscernible, indistinguishable, insignificant, invisible, minor, minute, negligible, small, trivial, undetectable, unnoticeable, unsubstantial

appreciate verb 1 = **value**, admire, cherish, enjoy, esteem, like, prize, rate highly, regard, relish, respect, savour, treasure 2 = **be aware of**, acknowledge, be alive to, be cognizant of, be conscious of, comprehend, estimate, know, perceive, realize, recognize, sympathize with, take account of, understand 3 = **be grateful for**, be appreciative, be indebted, be obliged, be thankful for, give thanks for 4 = **increase**, enhance, gain, grow, improve, inflate, raise the value of, rise
➤ Antonyms
≠**value**: belittle, denigrate, disdain, disparage, scorn ≠**be aware of**: be unaware of, misunderstand, underrate ≠**be grateful for**: be ungrateful for ≠**increase**: deflate, depreciate, devaluate, fall

appreciation noun 1 = **gratitude**, acknowledgment, gratefulness, indebtedness, obligation, thankfulness, thanks 2 = **awareness**, admiration, appraisal, assessment, cognizance, comprehension, enjoyment, esteem, estimation, knowledge, liking, perception, realization, recognition, regard, relish, respect, responsiveness, sensitivity, sympathy, understanding, valuation 3 = **praise**, acclamation, criticism, critique, notice, recognition, review, tribute 4 = **increase**, enhancement, gain, growth, improvement, inflation, rise
➤ Antonyms
≠**gratitude**: ingratitude ≠**awareness**: ignorance, incomprehension ≠**increase**: decline, depreciation, devaluation, fall

appreciative adjective 1 = **grateful**, beholden, indebted, obliged, thankful 2 = **aware**, admiring, cognizant, conscious, enthusiastic, in the know (informal), knowledgeable, mindful, perceptive, pleased, regardful, respectful, responsive, sensitive, supportive, sympathetic, understanding

apprehend verb 1 = **arrest**, bust (informal), capture, catch, collar (informal), feel one's collar (slang), lift (slang), nab (informal), nail (informal), nick (slang, chiefly Brit.), pinch (informal), run in (slang), seize, take, take prisoner 2 = **understand**, appreciate, believe, comprehend, conceive, get the message, get the picture, grasp, imagine, know, perceive, realize, recognize, think
➤ Antonyms
≠**arrest**: discharge, free, let go, liberate,

release ≠**understand**: be at cross-purposes, be unaware of, be unconscious of, get one's lines crossed, misapprehend, misconceive, miss, misunderstand

apprehension noun 1 = **anxiety**, alarm, apprehensiveness, concern, disquiet, doubt, dread, fear, foreboding, misgiving, mistrust, pins and needles, premonition, suspicion, trepidation, unease, uneasiness, worry 2 = **arrest**, capture, catching, seizure, taking 3 = **awareness**, comprehension, grasp, intellect, intelligence, ken, knowledge, perception, understanding 4 = **idea**, belief, concept, conception, conjecture, impression, notion, opinion, sentiment, thought, view
➤ Antonyms
≠**anxiety**: assurance, composure, confidence, nonchalance, serenity, unconcern ≠**arrest**: discharge, liberation, release ≠**awareness**: incomprehension

apprehensive adjective = **anxious**, afraid, alarmed, antsy (informal), concerned, disquieted, doubtful, fearful, foreboding, mistrustful, nervous, neurotic, suspicious, twitchy (informal), uneasy, worried
➤ Antonyms
assured, at ease, composed, confident, nonchalant, unafraid

apprentice noun = **trainee**, beginner, learner, neophyte, novice, probationer, pupil, student, tyro
➤ Antonyms
ace (informal), adept, dab hand (Brit. informal), expert, master, past master, pro

approach verb 1 = **move towards**, advance, catch up, come close, come near, come to, draw near, gain on, meet, near, push forward, reach 2 = **be like**, approximate, be comparable to, come close to, come near to, compare with, resemble 3 = **make a proposal to**, appeal to, apply to, broach the matter with, make advances to, make overtures to, sound out 4 = **set about**, begin work on, commence, embark on, enter upon, make a start, undertake ◆ noun 5 = **coming**, advance, advent, arrival, drawing near, nearing 6 often plural = **proposal**, advance, appeal, application, invitation, offer, overture, proposition 7 = **access**, avenue, entrance, passage, road, way 8 = **way**, attitude, course, manner, means, method, mode, modus operandi, procedure, style, technique 9 = **likeness**, approximation, semblance

approachable adjective 1 = **friendly**, affable, congenial, cordial, open, sociable 2 = **accessible**, attainable, come-at-able

(*informal*), get-at-able (*informal*),
reachable
➤ Antonyms
≠**friendly:** aloof, chilly, cold as ice, cool,
distant, frigid, remote, reserved,
standoffish, unfriendly, unsociable,
withdrawn ≠**accessible:** inaccessible, out
of reach, out-of-the-way, remote,
un-get-at-able (*informal*), unreachable

approbation *noun* = **approval,**
acceptance, acclaim, applause, assent,
commendation, congratulation,
encouragement, endorsement, favour,
laudation, praise, ratification, recognition,
sanction, support
➤ Antonyms
blame, censure, condemnation,
disapprobation, disapproval, disfavour,
dislike, displeasure, dissatisfaction, reproof,
stricture

appropriate *adjective* 1 = **suitable,**
adapted, applicable, apposite,
appurtenant, apropos, apt, becoming,
befitting, belonging, congruous, correct,
felicitous, fit, fitting, germane, meet
(*archaic*), opportune, pertinent, proper,
relevant, right, seemly, to the point, to the
purpose, well-suited, well-timed ♦ *verb* 2
= **seize,** annex, arrogate, assume,
commandeer, confiscate, expropriate,
impound, pre-empt, take, take over, take
possession of, usurp 3 = **steal,** embezzle,
filch, misappropriate, pilfer, pocket 4
= **allocate,** allot, apportion, assign, devote,
earmark, set aside
➤ Antonyms
adjective ≠**suitable:** improper,
inappropriate, incompatible, incorrect,
inopportune, irrelevant, unfitting,
unsuitable, untimely ♦ *verb* ≠**seize:** cede,
donate, give, relinquish ≠**allocate:**
withhold

appropriateness *noun* = **suitability,**
applicability, appositeness, aptness,
becomingness, congruousness,
correctness, felicitousness, felicity, fitness,
fittingness, germaneness, opportuneness,
pertinence, properness, relevance,
rightness, seemliness, timeliness,
well-suitedness

appropriation *noun* 1 = **setting aside,**
allocation, allotment, apportionment,
assignment, earmarking 2 = **seizure,**
annexation, arrogation, assumption,
commandeering, confiscation,
expropriation, impoundment,
pre-emption, takeover, taking, usurpation

approval *noun* 1 = **consent,** acquiescence,
agreement, assent, authorization, blessing,
compliance, concurrence, confirmation,

countenance, endorsement, imprimatur,
leave, licence, mandate, O.K. or okay
(*informal*), permission, ratification,
recommendation, sanction, the go-ahead
(*informal*), the green light, validation 2
= **favour,** acclaim, admiration, applause,
appreciation, approbation, Brownie
points, commendation, esteem, good
opinion, liking, praise, regard, respect
➤ Antonyms
≠**favour:** denigration, disapproval, dislike,
disparagement, displeasure, dissatisfaction

approve *verb* 1 = **favour,** acclaim, admire,
applaud, appreciate, be pleased with,
commend, esteem, have a good opinion
of, like, praise, regard highly, respect,
think highly of 2 = **agree to,** accede to,
accept, advocate, allow, assent to,
authorize, bless, buy into (*informal*),
concur in, confirm, consent to,
countenance, endorse, give the go-ahead
(*informal*), give the green light, go along
with, mandate, O.K. or okay (*informal*),
pass, permit, ratify, recommend, sanction,
second, subscribe to, uphold, validate
➤ Antonyms
≠**favour:** blame, censure, condemn,
deplore, deprecate, disapprove, dislike,
find unacceptable, frown on, look down
one's nose at (*informal*), object to, take
exception to ≠**agree to:** disallow,
discountenance, veto

approximate *adjective* 1 = **close,** almost
accurate, almost exact, near 2 = **rough,**
estimated, inexact, loose 3 = **like,**
analogous, close, comparable, near,
relative, similar, verging on ♦ *verb* 4
= **come close,** approach, border on, come
near, reach, resemble, touch, verge on
➤ Antonyms
adjective ≠**close, rough:** accurate, correct,
definite, exact, precise, specific

approximately *adverb* = **almost,** about,
around, circa (*used with dates*), close to,
generally, in the neighbourhood of, in the
region of, in the vicinity of, just about,
loosely, more or less, nearly, not far off,
relatively, roughly

approximation *noun* 1 = **guess,** ballpark
estimate (*informal*), ballpark figure
(*informal*), conjecture, estimate,
estimation, guesswork, rough calculation,
rough idea 2 = **likeness,** approach,
correspondence, resemblance, semblance

appurtenances *plural noun*
= **accompaniments,** accessories,
accoutrements, appendages, equipment,
impedimenta, paraphernalia, trappings

a priori *adjective* = **deduced,** deductive,
from cause to effect, inferential

apron noun = **pinny** (informal), pinafore

apropos adjective **1** = **appropriate**, applicable, apposite, apt, befitting, belonging, correct, fit, fitting, germane, meet (archaic), opportune, pertinent, proper, related, relevant, right, seemly, suitable, to the point, to the purpose ♦ adverb **2** = **appropriately**, aptly, opportunely, pertinently, relevantly, suitably, timely, to the point, to the purpose **3** = **incidentally**, by the bye, by the way, in passing, parenthetically, while on the subject

apropos of preposition = **regarding**, in respect of, on the subject of, re, respecting, with reference to, with regard to, with respect to

apt adjective **1** = **inclined**, disposed, given, liable, likely, of a mind, prone, ready **2** = **appropriate**, applicable, apposite, apropos, befitting, correct, fit, fitting, germane, meet (archaic), pertinent, proper, relevant, seemly, suitable, timely, to the point, to the purpose **3** = **gifted**, astute, bright, clever, expert, ingenious, intelligent, prompt, quick, sharp, skilful, smart, talented, teachable
➤ **Antonyms**
≠**appropriate**: ill-fitted, ill-suited, ill-timed, improper, inapplicable, inapposite, inappropriate, infelicitous, inopportune, irrelevant, unsuitable, untimely ≠**gifted**: awkward, clumsy, dull, gauche, incompetent, inept, inexpert, maladroit, slow, stupid

aptitude noun **1** = **tendency**, bent, disposition, inclination, leaning, predilection, proclivity, proneness, propensity **2** = **gift**, ability, aptness, capability, capacity, cleverness, faculty, flair, giftedness, intelligence, knack, proficiency, quickness, talent

aptness noun **1** = **tendency**, aptitude, bent, disposition, inclination, leaning, liability, likelihood, likeliness, predilection, proclivity, proneness, propensity, readiness **2** = **appropriateness**, applicability, appositeness, becomingness, congruousness, correctness, felicitousness, felicity, fitness, fittingness, germaneness, opportuneness, pertinence, properness, relevance, rightness, seemliness, suitability, timeliness, well-suitedness **3** = **gift**, ability, capability, capacity, cleverness, faculty, fitness, flair, giftedness, intelligence, knack, proficiency, quickness, suitability, talent

arable adjective = **productive**, cultivable, farmable, fecund, fertile, fruitful, ploughable, tillable

arbiter noun **1** = **judge**, adjudicator, arbitrator, referee, umpire **2** = **authority**, controller, dictator, expert, governor, lord, master, pundit, ruler

arbitrariness noun **1** = **randomness**, capriciousness, fancifulness, inconsistency, subjectivity, unreasonableness, whimsicality, wilfulness **2** = **dictatorialness**, absoluteness, despotism, dogmatism, domineeringness, high-handedness, imperiousness, magisterialness, overbearingness, peremptoriness, summariness, tyrannicalness, tyrannousness, tyranny, uncontrolledness, unlimitedness, unrestrainedness

arbitrary adjective **1** = **random**, capricious, chance, discretionary, erratic, fanciful, inconsistent, optional, personal, subjective, unreasonable, whimsical, wilful **2** = **dictatorial**, absolute, autocratic, despotic, dogmatic, domineering, high-handed, imperious, magisterial, overbearing, peremptory, summary, tyrannical, tyrannous, uncontrolled, unlimited, unrestrained
➤ **Antonyms**
≠**random**: consistent, judicious, logical, objective, rational, reasonable, reasoned, sensible, sound

arbitrate verb = **settle**, adjudge, adjudicate, decide, determine, judge, mediate, pass judgment, referee, sit in judgment, umpire

arbitration noun = **settlement**, adjudication, arbitrament, decision, determination, judgment

arbitrator noun = **judge**, adjudicator, arbiter, referee, umpire

arc noun = **curve**, arch, bend, bow, crescent, half-moon

arcade noun = **gallery**, cloister, colonnade, covered walk, mall, portico

arcane adjective = **mysterious**, cabbalistic, esoteric, hidden, occult, recondite, secret

arch[1] noun **1** = **archway**, curve, dome, span, vault **2** = **curve**, arc, bend, bow, curvature, hump, semicircle ♦ verb **3** = **curve**, arc, bend, bow, bridge, span

arch[2] adjective = **playful**, frolicsome, mischievous, pert, roguish, saucy, sly, waggish

arch- adjective = **chief**, accomplished, consummate, expert, finished, first, foremost, greatest, head, highest, lead, leading, main, major, master, pre-eminent, primary, principal, top

archaic adjective **1** = **old**, ancient, antique, bygone, olden (archaic), primitive **2** = **old-fashioned**, antiquated, behind the

times, obsolete, old hat, outmoded, out of
date, passé, superannuated
➤ **Antonyms**
≠**old**: contemporary, current, modern,
new, present, recent ≠**old-fashioned**:
fresh, latest, modern, modish, new,
newfangled, novel, state-of-the-art,
up-to-date, up-to-the-minute, with it
(*informal*)

arched *adjective* = **curved**, domed,
embowed, vaulted

archer *noun* = **bowman** (*archaic*),
toxophilite (*formal*)

archetypal *adjective* **1** = **typical**, classic,
ideal, model, standard **2** = **original**,
prototypic *or* prototypical

archetype *noun* **1** = **standard**, classic,
exemplar, form, ideal, model, norm,
paradigm, pattern, prime example **2**
= **original**, prototype

architect *noun* **1** = **designer**, master
builder, planner **2** = **creator**, author,
contriver, deviser, engineer, founder,
instigator, inventor, maker, originator,
planner, prime mover, shaper

architecture *noun* **1** = **design**,
architectonics, building, construction,
planning **2** = **structure**, construction,
design, framework, make-up, style

archive *noun* **1** = **record office**, museum,
registry, repository **2 archives** = **records**,
annals, chronicles, documents, papers,
registers, rolls

arctic *adjective Informal* = **freezing**, chilly,
cold, cold as ice, frigid, frost-bound, frosty,
frozen, gelid, glacial, icy

Arctic *adjective* = **polar**, far-northern,
hyperborean

ardent *adjective* **1** = **passionate**, ablaze,
amorous, fervent, fervid, fierce, fiery,
flaming, hot, hot-blooded, impassioned,
intense, lusty, spirited, vehement, warm,
warm-blooded **2** = **enthusiastic**, avid,
eager, keen, keen as mustard, zealous
➤ **Antonyms**
≠**passionate**: cold, cool, frigid, impassive
≠**enthusiastic**: apathetic, indifferent,
lukewarm, unenthusiastic

ardour *noun* **1** = **passion**, devotion, feeling,
fervour, fierceness, fire, heat, intensity,
spirit, vehemence, warmth **2**
= **enthusiasm**, avidity, eagerness,
earnestness, keenness, zeal

arduous *adjective* = **difficult**, backbreaking,
burdensome, exhausting, fatiguing,
formidable, gruelling, hard, harsh, heavy,
laborious, onerous, painful, punishing,
rigorous, severe, steep, strenuous, taxing,
tiring, toilsome, tough, troublesome,

trying
➤ **Antonyms**
child's play (*informal*), easy, easy-peasy
(*slang*), effortless, facile, light, no bother,
no trouble, painless, simple, undemanding

area *noun* **1** = **region**, district, domain,
locality, neck of the woods (*informal*),
neighbourhood, patch, plot, realm, sector,
sphere, stretch, territory, tract, turf (*U.S.
slang*), zone **2** = **part**, portion, section,
sector **3** = **field**, arena, department,
domain, province, realm, sphere, territory
4 = **sunken space**, yard **5** = **range**, ambit,
breadth, compass, expanse, extent, scope,
size, width

arena *noun* **1** = **ring**, amphitheatre, bowl,
coliseum, enclosure, field, ground, park
(*U.S. & Canad.*), stadium, stage **2**
= **sphere**, area, domain, field, province,
realm, scene, scope, sector, territory,
theatre

argot *noun* = **jargon**, cant, dialect, idiom,
lingo (*informal*), parlance, patois, patter,
slang, vernacular

argue *verb* **1** = **discuss**, assert, claim,
contend, controvert, debate, dispute,
expostulate, hold, maintain, plead,
question, reason, remonstrate **2** = **quarrel**,
altercate, bandy words, be at sixes and
sevens, bicker, cross swords, disagree,
dispute, fall out (*informal*), feud, fight,
fight like cat and dog, go at it hammer and
tongs, have an argument, squabble,
wrangle **3** = **persuade**, convince, prevail
upon, talk into, talk round **4** = **suggest**,
demonstrate, denote, display, evince,
exhibit, imply, indicate, manifest, point to,
show

argument *noun* **1** = **quarrel**, altercation,
barney (*informal*), bickering, clash,
controversy, difference of opinion,
disagreement, dispute, falling out
(*informal*), feud, fight, row, squabble,
wrangle **2** = **discussion**, assertion, claim,
contention, debate, dispute,
expostulation, plea, pleading, questioning,
remonstrance, remonstration **3** = **reason**,
argumentation, case, defence, dialectic,
ground(s), line of reasoning, logic,
polemic, reasoning
➤ **Antonyms**
≠**quarrel**: accord, agreement, concurrence

argumentative *adjective* = **quarrelsome**,
belligerent, combative, contentious,
contrary, disputatious, litigious,
opinionated
➤ **Antonyms**
accommodating, amenable, complaisant,
compliant, conciliatory, easy-going,
obliging

arid *adjective* **1** = **dry**, barren, desert, dried up, moistureless, parched, sterile, torrid, waterless **2** = **boring**, as dry as dust, colourless, dreary, dry, dull, flat, jejune, lifeless, spiritless, tedious, tiresome, uninspired, uninteresting, vapid
➤ **Antonyms**
≠**dry**: fertile, fruitful, lush, rich, verdant ≠**boring**: exciting, interesting, lively, sexy (*informal*), spirited, stimulating, vivacious

aridity, aridness *noun* **1** = **dryness**, barrenness, moisturelessness, parchedness, sterility, waterlessness **2** = **boredom**, colourlessness, dreariness, dryness, dullness, flatness, jejuneness, jejunity, lifelessness, spiritlessness, tediousness, tedium, uninspiredness, uninterestingness, vapidity, vapidness

aright *adverb* = **correctly**, accurately, appropriately, aptly, duly, exactly, fitly, in due order, justly, properly, rightly, suitably, truly, without error

arise *verb* **1** = **happen**, appear, begin, come into being, come to light, commence, crop up (*informal*), emanate, emerge, ensue, follow, issue, occur, originate, proceed, result, set in, spring, start, stem **2** *Old-fashioned* = **get up**, get to one's feet, go up, rise, stand up, wake up **3** = **ascend**, climb, lift, mount, move upward, rise, soar, tower

aristocracy *noun* = **upper class**, body of nobles, elite, gentry, *haut monde,* nobility, noblesse (*literary*), patricians, patriciate, peerage, ruling class, upper crust (*informal*)
➤ **Antonyms**
commoners, common people, hoi polloi, lower classes, masses, plebeians, plebs, proles (*derogatory slang, chiefly Brit.*), proletariat, working classes

aristocrat *noun* = **noble**, aristo (*informal*), childe (*archaic*), grandee, lady, lord, nobleman, noblewoman, patrician, peer, peeress

aristocratic *adjective* **1** = **upper-class**, blue-blooded, elite, gentle (*archaic*), gentlemanly, highborn, lordly, noble, patrician, titled, well-born **2** = **refined**, courtly, dignified, elegant, fine, haughty, polished, snobbish, stylish, well-bred
➤ **Antonyms**
≠**upper-class**: common, lower-class, plebeian, proletarian, working-class ≠**refined**: boorish, coarse, common, crass, crude, ill-bred, uncouth, unrefined, vulgar

arm[1] *noun* **1** = **upper limb**, appendage, limb **2** = **section**, bough, branch, department, detachment, division, extension, offshoot, projection, sector **3**

= **power**, authority, command, force, might, potency, strength, sway

arm[2] *verb* **1** *Especially with weapons* = **equip**, accoutre, array, deck out, furnish, issue with, outfit, provide, rig, supply **2** = **mobilize**, muster forces, prepare for war, take up arms **3** = **provide**, brace, equip, forearm, fortify, gird one's loins, guard, make ready, outfit, prepare, prime, protect, strengthen

armada *noun* = **fleet**, flotilla, navy, squadron

armaments *plural noun* = **weapons**, ammunition, arms, guns, materiel, munitions, ordnance, weaponry

armed *adjective* = **carrying weapons**, accoutred, arrayed, equipped, fitted out, forearmed, fortified, furnished, girded, guarded, in arms, prepared, primed, protected, provided, ready, rigged out, strengthened, supplied, tooled up (*slang*), under arms

armistice *noun* = **truce**, ceasefire, peace, suspension of hostilities

armour *noun* = **protection**, armour plate, covering, sheathing, shield

armoured *adjective* = **protected**, armour-plated, bombproof, bulletproof, ironclad, mailed, steel-plated

armoury *noun* = **arsenal**, ammunition dump, arms depot, magazine, ordnance depot

arms *plural noun* **1** = **weapons**, armaments, firearms, guns, instruments of war, ordnance, weaponry **2** = **heraldry**, blazonry, crest, escutcheon, insignia

army *noun* **1** = **soldiers**, armed force, host (*archaic*), land forces, legions, military, military force, soldiery, troops **2** = **vast number**, array, horde, host, multitude, pack, swarm, throng

aroma *noun* = **scent**, bouquet, fragrance, odour, perfume, redolence, savour, smell

aromatic *adjective* = **fragrant**, balmy, odoriferous, perfumed, pungent, redolent, savoury, spicy, sweet-scented, sweet-smelling
➤ **Antonyms**
acrid, bad-smelling, fetid, foul, foul-smelling, malodorous, niffy (*Brit. slang*), noisome, olid, rank, reeking, smelly, stinking, whiffy (*Brit. slang*)

around *preposition* **1** = **surrounding**, about, encircling, enclosing, encompassing, environing, on all sides of, on every side of **2** = **approximately**, about, circa (*used with dates*), roughly ♦ *adverb* **3** = **everywhere**, about, all over, here and there, in all directions, on all sides, throughout, to and fro **4** = **near**, at hand, close, close at hand, close by, nearby, nigh (*archaic or dialect*)

arouse *verb* **1** = **stimulate**, agitate, animate, call forth, enliven, excite, foment, foster, goad, incite, inflame, instigate, kindle, move, prod, provoke, quicken, sharpen, spark, spur, stir up, summon up, warm, whet, whip up **2** = **awaken**, rouse, waken, wake up
➤ **Antonyms**
≠**stimulate**: allay, alleviate, assuage, calm, dampen, dull, end, lull, pacify, quell, quench, still

arrange *verb* **1** = **plan**, construct, contrive, devise, fix up, organize, prepare, project, schedule **2** = **agree**, adjust, come to terms, compromise, determine, settle **3** = **put in order**, align, array, class, classify, dispose, file, form, group, line up, marshal, order, organize, position, range, rank, sequence, set out, sort, sort out (*informal*), systematize, tidy **4** = **adapt**, instrument, orchestrate, score
➤ **Antonyms**
≠**put in order**: disarrange, disorganize, disturb, mess up, scatter

arrangement *noun* **1** *often plural* = **plan**, construction, devising, organization, planning, preparation, provision, schedule **2** = **agreement**, adjustment, compact, compromise, deal, settlement, terms **3** = **order**, alignment, array, classification, design, display, disposition, form, grouping, line-up, marshalling, ordering, organization, ranging, rank, setup (*informal*), structure, system **4** = **adaptation**, instrumentation, interpretation, orchestration, score, version

arrant *adjective* = **total**, absolute, atrocious, blatant, complete, deep-dyed (*usually derogatory*), downright, egregious, extreme, flagrant, gross, infamous, monstrous, notorious, out-and-out, outright, rank, thorough, thoroughgoing, undisguised, unmitigated, utter, vile

array *noun* **1** = **arrangement**, collection, display, disposition, exhibition, formation, line-up, marshalling, muster, order, parade, show, supply **2** *Poetic* = **clothing**, apparel, attire, clothes, dress, finery, garb, garments, raiment (*archaic or poetic*), regalia, schmutter (*slang*), threads (*slang*)
♦ *verb* **3** = **arrange**, align, display, dispose, draw up, exhibit, form up, group, line up, marshal, muster, order, parade, place in order, range, sequence, set in line (*Military*), show **4** = **dress**, accoutre, adorn, apparel (*archaic*), attire, bedeck, caparison, clothe, deck, decorate, equip, festoon, fit out, garb, get ready, outfit,

robe, supply, wrap

arrest *verb* **1** = **capture**, apprehend, bust (*informal*), catch, collar (*informal*), detain, feel one's collar (*slang*), lay hold of, lift (*slang*), nab (*informal*), nail (*informal*), nick (*slang, chiefly Brit.*), pinch (*informal*), run in (*slang*), seize, take, take into custody, take prisoner **2** = **stop**, block, check, delay, end, halt, hinder, hold, inhibit, interrupt, obstruct, restrain, retard, slow, stall, stay, suppress **3** = **grip**, absorb, catch, engage, engross, fascinate, hold, intrigue, occupy
♦ *noun* **4** = **capture**, apprehension, bust (*informal*), cop (*slang*), detention, seizure **5** = **stopping**, blockage, check, delay, end, halt, hindrance, inhibition, interruption, obstruction, restraint, stalling, stay, suppression
➤ **Antonyms**
verb ≠**capture**: free, let go, release, set free ≠**stop**: accelerate, encourage, precipitate, promote, quicken, speed up ♦ *noun* ≠**capture**: freeing, release ≠**stopping**: acceleration, encouragement, precipitation, promotion, quickening

arresting *adjective* = **striking**, conspicuous, dramatic, engaging, extraordinary, impressive, jaw-dropping, noticeable, outstanding, remarkable, salient, stunning, surprising
➤ **Antonyms**
inconspicuous, unimpressive, unnoticeable, unremarkable

arrival *noun* **1** = **coming**, advent, appearance, arriving, entrance, happening, occurrence, taking place **2** = **newcomer**, arriver, caller, comer, entrant, incomer, visitant, visitor

arrive *verb* **1** = **come**, appear, attain, befall, enter, get to, happen, occur, reach, show up (*informal*), take place, turn up **2** *Informal* = **succeed**, achieve recognition, become famous, make good, make it (*informal*), make one's mark (*informal*), make the grade (*informal*), reach the top
➤ **Antonyms**
≠**come**: depart, disappear, exit, go, go away, leave, pack one's bags (*informal*), retire, take (one's) leave, vanish, withdraw

arrogance *noun* = **conceit**, bluster, conceitedness, contemptuousness, disdainfulness, haughtiness, hauteur, high-handedness, hubris, imperiousness, insolence, loftiness, lordliness, overweeningness, pomposity, pompousness, presumption, pretension, pretentiousness, pride, scornfulness, superciliousness, swagger, uppishness (*Brit. informal*)
➤ **Antonyms**

bashfulness, diffidence, humility, meekness, modesty, politeness, shyness

arrogant *adjective* = **conceited**, assuming, blustering, contemptuous, disdainful, haughty, high and mighty (*informal*), high-handed, imperious, insolent, looking down one's nose at, lordly, overbearing, overweening, pompous, presumptuous, pretentious, proud, scornful, supercilious, swaggering, too big for one's boots *or* breeches, turning up one's nose at, uppish (*Brit. informal*)
➤ **Antonyms**
bashful, deferential, diffident, humble, modest, polite, servile, shy, unassuming

arrogate *verb* = **seize**, appropriate, assume, claim unduly, commandeer, demand, expropriate, presume, usurp

arrogation *noun* = **seizure**, appropriation, assumption, commandeering, demand, expropriation, presumption, usurpation

arrow *noun* **1** = **dart**, bolt, flight, quarrel, reed (*archaic*), shaft (*archaic*) **2** = **pointer**, indicator

arsenal *noun* = **armoury**, ammunition dump, arms depot, magazine, ordnance depot, stock, stockpile, store, storehouse, supply

art *noun* **1** = **skill**, adroitness, aptitude, artifice (*archaic*), artistry, craft, craftsmanship, dexterity, expertise, facility, ingenuity, knack, knowledge, mastery, method, profession, trade, virtuosity **2** = **cunning**, artfulness, artifice, astuteness, craftiness, deceit, duplicity, guile, trickery, wiliness

artful *adjective* **1** = **cunning**, clever, crafty, deceitful, designing, foxy, intriguing, politic, scheming, sharp, shrewd, sly, smart, subtle, tricky, wily **2** = **skilful**, adept, adroit, clever, dexterous, ingenious, masterly, proficient, resourceful, smart, subtle
➤ **Antonyms**
≠**cunning**: artless, frank, ingenuous, open, simple, straightforward ≠**skilful**: artless, clumsy, unadept, unskilled, untalented

article *noun* **1** = **piece**, composition, discourse, essay, feature, item, paper, story, treatise **2** = **thing**, commodity, item, object, piece, substance, unit **3** = **clause**, branch, count, detail, division, head, heading, item, matter, paragraph, part, particular, passage, piece, point, portion, section

articulate *adjective* **1** = **expressive**, clear, coherent, comprehensible, eloquent, fluent, intelligible, lucid, meaningful, understandable, vocal, well-spoken ◆ *verb* **2** = **express**, enounce, enunciate, pronounce, say, speak, state, talk, utter, verbalize, vocalize, voice
➤ **Antonyms**
adjective ≠**expressive**: dumb, faltering, halting, hesitant, incoherent, incomprehensible, indistinct, mumbled, mute, poorly-spoken, silent, speechless, stammering, stuttering, tongue-tied, unclear, unintelligible, voiceless

articulation *noun* **1** = **expression**, delivery, diction, enunciation, pronunciation, saying, speaking, statement, talking, utterance, verbalization, vocalization, voicing **2** = **joint**, connection, coupling, hinge, jointing, juncture

artifice *noun* **1** = **trick**, contrivance, device, dodge, expedient, hoax, machination, manoeuvre, ruse, stratagem, subterfuge, tactic, wile **2** = **cunning**, artfulness, chicanery, craft, craftiness, deception, duplicity, guile, scheming, slyness, trickery **3** = **cleverness**, adroitness, deftness, facility, finesse, ingenuity, invention, inventiveness, skill

artificer *noun* = **craftsman**, artisan, mechanic

artificial *adjective* **1** = **synthetic**, man-made, manufactured, non-natural, plastic **2** = **fake**, bogus, counterfeit, ersatz, imitation, mock, phoney *or* phony (*informal*), pseudo (*informal*), sham, simulated, specious, spurious **3** = **insincere**, affected, assumed, contrived, false, feigned, forced, hollow, meretricious, phoney *or* phony (*informal*), pretended, spurious, unnatural
➤ **Antonyms**
≠**fake**: authentic ≠**insincere**: frank, genuine, honest, natural, sincere, true, unaffected

artillery *noun* = **big guns**, battery, cannon, cannonry, gunnery, ordnance

artisan *noun* = **craftsman**, artificer, handicraftsman, journeyman, mechanic, skilled workman, technician

artistic *adjective* = **creative**, aesthetic, beautiful, cultivated, cultured, decorative, elegant, exquisite, graceful, imaginative, ornamental, refined, sensitive, sophisticated, stylish, tasteful
➤ **Antonyms**
inartistic, inelegant, tasteless, unattractive, untalented

artistry *noun* = **skill**, accomplishment, art, artistic ability, brilliance, craft, craftsmanship, creativity, finesse, flair, genius, mastery, proficiency, sensibility, style, talent, taste, touch, virtuosity, workmanship

artless *adjective* **1** = **straightforward**,

candid, direct, fair, frank, genuine,
guileless, honest, open, plain, round,
sincere, true, undesigning, upfront
(*informal*) **2** = **natural**, humble, plain, pure,
simple, unadorned, unaffected,
uncontrived, unpretentious **3** = **unskilled**,
awkward, bungling, clumsy, crude,
incompetent, inept, maladroit, primitive,
rude, untalented
➤ Antonyms
≠**straightforward**: artful, crafty, cunning,
designing, dishonest, false, insincere
≠**natural**: affected, artificial, unnatural
≠**unskilled**: aesthetic, artful, artistic, crafty,
cunning, sophisticated

as *conjunction* **1** = **when**, at the time that,
during the time that, just as, while **2** = **in
the way that**, in the manner that, like **3**
= **what**, that which **4** = **since**, because,
considering that, seeing that **5** = **for
instance**, like, such as ♦ *preposition* **6**
= **being**, in the character of, in the role of,
under the name of **7 as for** = **with regard
to**, as regards, in reference to, on the
subject of, with reference to, with respect
to **8 as it were** = **in a way**, in a manner of
speaking, so to say, so to speak

ascend *verb* = **move up**, climb, float up, fly
up, go up, lift off, mount, rise, scale, slope
upwards, soar, take off, tower
➤ Antonyms
alight, descend, dip, drop, fall, go down,
incline, move down, plummet, plunge,
sink, slant, slope, subside, tumble

ascendancy, ascendence *noun*
= **influence**, authority, command, control,
dominance, domination, dominion,
hegemony, mastery, power,
predominance, pre-eminence, prevalence,
reign, rule, sovereignty, superiority,
supremacy, sway, upper hand
➤ Antonyms
inferiority, servility, subjection,
subordination, weakness

ascendant, ascendent *adjective* **1**
= **influential**, authoritative, commanding,
controlling, dominant, powerful,
predominant, pre-eminent, prevailing,
ruling, superior, supreme, uppermost
♦ *noun* **2 in the ascendant** = **rising**,
ascending, climbing, commanding,
dominant, dominating, flourishing,
growing, increasing, influential, mounting,
on the rise, on the way up, powerful,
prevailing, supreme, up-and-coming,
uppermost, winning

ascent *noun* **1** = **rise**, ascending, ascension,
clambering, climb, climbing, mounting,
rising, scaling, upward movement **2**
= **upward slope**, acclivity, gradient,
incline, ramp, rise, rising ground

ascertain *verb* = **find out**, confirm,
determine, discover, establish, ferret out,
fix, identify, learn, make certain, settle,
suss (out) (*slang*), verify

ascetic *noun* **1** = **monk**, abstainer,
anchorite, hermit, nun, recluse, self-denier
♦ *adjective* **2** = **self-denying**, abstemious,
abstinent, austere, celibate, frugal, harsh,
plain, puritanical, rigorous, self-disciplined,
severe, Spartan, stern
➤ Antonyms
noun ≠**monk**: hedonist, sensualist,
voluptuary ♦ *adjective* ≠**self-denying**:
abandoned, comfortable, luxurious,
self-indulgent, sensuous, voluptuous

asceticism *noun* = **self-denial**,
abstemiousness, abstinence, austerity,
celibacy, frugality, harshness, mortification
of the flesh, plainness, puritanism,
rigorousness, rigour, self-abnegation,
self-discipline, self-mortification

ascribe *verb* = **attribute**, assign, charge,
credit, impute, put down, refer, set down

ashamed *adjective* = **embarrassed**,
abashed, bashful, blushing, chagrined,
conscience-stricken, crestfallen,
discomfited, distressed, guilty, humbled,
humiliated, mortified, prudish, reluctant,
remorseful, shamefaced, sheepish, shy,
sorry
➤ Antonyms
gratified, honoured, pleased, proud,
satisfied, unashamed, vain

ashen *adjective* = **pale**, anaemic, ashy,
colourless, grey, leaden, like death
warmed up (*informal*), livid, pallid, pasty,
wan, white
➤ Antonyms
blooming, blushing, florid, flushed,
glowing, radiant, red, reddish, rosy,
rosy-cheeked, rubicund, ruddy

ashore *adverb* = **on land**, aground,
landwards, on dry land, on the beach, on
the shore, shorewards, to the shore

aside *adverb* **1** = **to one side**, alone,
alongside, apart, away, beside, in isolation,
in reserve, on one side, out of mind, out of
the way, privately, separately, to the side
♦ *noun* **2** = **interpolation**, interposition,
parenthesis **3** = **digression**, departure,
excursion, excursus, tangent

asinine *adjective* = **stupid**, braindead
(*informal*), brainless, daft (*informal*), dead
from the neck up (*informal*), dumb-ass
(*slang*), dunderheaded, fatuous, foolish,
goofy (*informal*), gormless (*Brit. informal*),
halfwitted, idiotic, imbecile, imbecilic,
inane, moronic, senseless, silly,
thickheaded, thick-witted

➤ **Antonyms**
brainy (*informal*), bright, clever,
intelligent, quick-witted, sage, sane,
sensible, sharp, smart, wise

ask *verb* **1** = **inquire**, interrogate, query,
question, quiz **2** = **request**, appeal, apply,
beg, beseech, claim, crave, demand,
entreat, implore, petition, plead, pray,
seek, solicit, sue, supplicate **3** = **invite**, bid,
summon
➤ **Antonyms**
≠**inquire:** answer, reply, respond

askance *adverb As in* **look askance at 1**
= **out of the corner of one's eye**, awry,
indirectly, obliquely, sideways, with a side
glance **2** = **suspiciously**, disapprovingly,
distrustfully, doubtfully, dubiously,
mistrustfully, sceptically

askew *adverb* **1** = **crookedly**, aslant, awry,
obliquely, off-centre, to one side
♦ *adjective* **2** = **crooked**, awry, cockeyed
(*informal*), lopsided, oblique, off-centre,
skewwhiff (*Brit. informal*)
➤ **Antonyms**
adverb ≠**crookedly:** aligned, evenly, in
line, level, right, squarely, straight, true
♦ *adjective* ≠**crooked:** aligned, even, in
line, level, right, square, straight, true

asleep *adjective* = **sleeping**, crashed out
(*slang*), dead to the world (*informal*),
dormant, dozing, fast asleep, napping, out
for the count, slumbering, snoozing
(*informal*), sound asleep

aspect *noun* **1** = **feature**, angle, facet, side
2 = **position**, bearing, direction, exposure,
outlook, point of view, prospect, scene,
situation, view **3** = **appearance**, air,
attitude, bearing, condition, countenance,
demeanour, expression, look, manner,
mien (*literary*)

asperity *noun* = **sharpness**, acerbity,
acrimony, bitterness, churlishness,
crabbedness, crossness, harshness,
irascibility, irritability, moroseness,
peevishness, roughness, ruggedness,
severity, sourness, sullenness

asphyxiate *verb* = **suffocate**, choke,
smother, stifle, strangle, strangulate,
throttle

aspirant *noun* **1** = **candidate**, applicant,
aspirer, hopeful, postulant, seeker, suitor
♦ *adjective* **2** = **hopeful**, ambitious,
aspiring, eager, endeavouring, longing,
striving, wishful

aspiration *noun* = **aim**, ambition, craving,
desire, dream, eagerness, endeavour, goal,
hankering, Holy Grail (*informal*), hope,
longing, object, objective, wish, yearning

aspire *verb* = **aim**, be ambitious, be eager,
crave, desire, dream, hanker, hope, long,

pursue, seek, set one's heart on, wish,
yearn

aspiring *adjective* = **hopeful**, ambitious,
aspirant, eager, endeavouring, longing,
striving, wannabe (*informal*), wishful,
would-be

ass *noun* **1** = **donkey**, jennet, moke (*slang*)
2 = **fool**, airhead (*slang*), berk (*Brit. slang*),
blockhead, bonehead (*slang*), charlie (*Brit.
informal*), coot, daftie (*informal*), dickhead
(*slang*), dickwit (*slang*), dipstick (*Brit.
slang*), divvy (*Brit. slang*), dolt, dope
(*informal*), dork (*slang*), dumb-ass (*slang*),
dunce, dweeb (*U.S. slang*), fathead
(*informal*), fuckwit (*taboo slang*), geek
(*slang*), gobshite (*Irish taboo slang*), gonzo
(*slang*), halfwit, idiot, jackass, jerk (*slang,
chiefly U.S. & Canad.*), nerd *or* nurd
(*slang*), nincompoop, ninny, nitwit
(*informal*), numbskull *or* numskull, numpty
(*Scot. informal*), oaf, pillock (*Brit. slang*),
plank (*Brit. slang*), plonker (*slang*), prat
(*slang*), prick (*slang*), schmuck (*U.S.
slang*), simpleton, twerp *or* twirp
(*informal*), twit (*informal, chiefly Brit.*),
wally (*slang*), weenie (*U.S. informal*)

assail *verb* **1** = **attack**, assault, belabour,
beset, charge, encounter, fall upon,
invade, lay into (*informal*), maltreat, set
about, set upon **2** = **criticize**, abuse,
berate, blast, go for the jugular, impugn,
lambast(e), malign, put down, revile, tear
into (*informal*), vilify

assailant *noun* = **attacker**, aggressor,
assailer, assaulter, invader

assassin *noun* = **murderer**, eliminator
(*slang*), executioner, hatchet man (*slang*),
hit man (*slang*), killer, liquidator, slayer

assassinate *verb* = **murder**, blow away
(*slang, chiefly U.S.*), eliminate (*slang*), hit
(*slang*), kill, liquidate, slay, take out (*slang*)

assault *noun* **1** = **attack**, aggression,
campaign, charge, incursion, inroad,
invasion, offensive, onset, onslaught,
storm, storming, strike ♦ *verb* **2** = **attack**,
assail, belabour, beset, charge, fall upon,
invade, lay into (*informal*), set about, set
upon, storm, strike at
➤ **Antonyms**
noun ≠**attack:** defence, protection,
resistance ♦ *verb* ≠**attack:** defend, protect,
resist

assay *verb* **1** = **analyse**, appraise, assess,
evaluate, examine, inspect, investigate,
prove, test, try, weigh ♦ *noun* **2** = **analysis**,
examination, inspection, investigation,
test, trial

assemble *verb* **1** = **gather**, accumulate,
amass, bring together, call together,
collect, come together, congregate,

convene, convoke, flock, foregather, marshal, meet, muster, rally, round up, summon **2 = put together**, build up, connect, construct, erect, fabricate, fit together, join, make, manufacture, piece together, set up
➤ **Antonyms**
≠**gather**: adjourn, break up (*informal*), disband, dismiss, disperse, distribute, scatter ≠**put together**: disassemble, divide, take apart

assembly *noun* **1 = gathering**, accumulation, aggregation, assemblage, body, collection, company, conclave, conference, congregation, congress, convention, convocation, council, crowd, diet, flock, group, house, mass, meeting, multitude, rally, synod, throng **2 = putting together**, building up, connecting, construction, erection, fabrication, fitting together, joining, manufacture, piecing together, setting up

assent *noun* **1 = agreement**, acceptance, accession, accord, acquiescence, approval, compliance, concurrence, consent, permission, sanction ◆ *verb* **2 = agree**, accede, accept, acquiesce, allow, approve, comply, concur, consent, fall in with, go along with, grant, permit, sanction, subscribe
➤ **Antonyms**
noun ≠**agreement**: denial, disagreement, disapproval, dissension, dissent, objection, refusal ◆ *verb* ≠**agree**: deny, differ, disagree, dissent, object, protest, rebut, reject, retract

assert *verb* **1 = state**, affirm, allege, asseverate, attest, aver, avouch (*archaic*), avow, contend, declare, maintain, predicate, profess, pronounce, swear **2 = insist upon**, claim, defend, press, put forward, stand up for, stress, uphold, vindicate **3 assert oneself = be forceful**, exert one's influence, make one's presence felt, put oneself forward, put one's foot down (*informal*)
➤ **Antonyms**
≠**state, insist upon**: deny, disavow, disclaim, rebut, refute, retract

assertion *noun* **1 = statement**, affirmation, allegation, asseveration, attestation, avowal, claim, contention, declaration, predication, profession, pronouncement **2 = insistence**, defence, maintenance, stressing, vindication

assertive *adjective* **= confident**, aggressive, can-do (*informal*), decided, decisive, demanding, dogmatic, domineering, emphatic, feisty (*informal, chiefly U.S. & Canad.*), firm, forceful, forward, insistent,

in-your-face (*Brit. slang*), overbearing, positive, pushy (*informal*), self-assured, strong-willed
➤ **Antonyms**
backward, bashful, diffident, hesitant, insecure, meek, modest, reserved, retiring, self-conscious, self-effacing, sheepish, shrinking, shy, timid, timorous, unassertive, unobtrusive

assess *verb* **1 = judge**, appraise, compute, determine, estimate, evaluate, eye up, fix, gauge, rate, size up (*informal*), value, weigh **2 = evaluate**, demand, fix, impose, levy, rate, tax, value

assessment *noun* **1 = judgment**, appraisal, computation, determination, estimate, estimation, evaluation, rating, valuation **2 = evaluation**, charge, demand, duty, fee, impost, levy, rate, rating, tariff, tax, taxation, toll, valuation

asset *noun* **1 = benefit**, ace in the hole, ace up one's sleeve, advantage, aid, blessing, boon, feather in one's cap, help, resource, service **2 assets = property**, capital, estate, funds, goods, holdings, means, money, possessions, reserves, resources, valuables, wealth
➤ **Antonyms**
≠**benefit**: albatross, burden, disadvantage, drag, drawback, encumbrance, handicap, hindrance, impediment, liability, millstone, minus (*informal*), nuisance

assiduous *adjective* **= diligent**, attentive, constant, hard-working, indefatigable, industrious, laborious, persevering, persistent, sedulous, steady, studious, unflagging, untiring, unwearied
➤ **Antonyms**
careless, idle, inattentive, indolent, lax, lazy, negligent, slack

assign *verb* **1 = select**, appoint, choose, delegate, designate, name, nominate **2 = give**, allocate, allot, apportion, consign, distribute, give out, grant, make over **3 = attribute**, accredit, ascribe, put down **4 = fix**, appoint, appropriate, determine, set apart, stipulate

assignation *noun* **1 = secret meeting**, clandestine meeting, illicit meeting, rendezvous, tryst (*archaic*) **2 = selection**, appointment, assignment, choice, delegation, designation, nomination **3 = giving**, allocation, allotment, apportionment, consignment, distribution, grant **4 = attribution**, accrediting, ascription **5 = fixing**, appointment, appropriation, determination, specification, stipulation

assignment *noun* **1 = task**, appointment, charge, commission, duty, job, mission, position, post, responsibility **2 = selection**, appointment, choice, delegation, designation, nomination **3 = giving**, allocation, allotment, apportionment, assignation (*Law, chiefly Scot.*), consignment, distribution, grant **4 = attribution**, accrediting, ascription **5 = fixing**, appointment, appropriation, determination, specification, stipulation

assimilate *verb* **1 = learn**, absorb, digest, imbibe (*literary*), incorporate, ingest, take in **2 = adjust**, acclimatize, accommodate, acculturate, accustom, adapt, become like, become similar, blend in, conform, fit, homogenize, intermix, mingle

assist *verb* **= help**, abet, aid, back, benefit, boost, collaborate, cooperate, encourage, expedite, facilitate, further, give a leg up (*informal*), lend a helping hand, promote, reinforce, relieve, second, serve, succour, support, sustain, work for, work with
➤ Antonyms
frustrate, hamper, handicap, hinder, hold back, hold up, impede, obstruct, resist, thwart, work against

assistance *noun* **= help**, abetment, aid, backing, benefit, boost, collaboration, cooperation, encouragement, furtherance, helping hand, promotion, reinforcement, relief, service, succour, support, sustenance
➤ Antonyms
hindrance, obstruction, opposition, resistance

assistant *noun* **= helper**, abettor, accessory, accomplice, aide, aider, ally, associate, auxiliary, backer, coadjutor (*rare*), collaborator, colleague, confederate, cooperator, helpmate, henchman, partner, protagonist, right-hand man, second, supporter

associate *verb* **1 = connect**, affiliate, ally, combine, confederate, conjoin, correlate, couple, identify, join, league, link, lump together, mention in the same breath, mix, pair, relate, think of together, unite, yoke **2 = mix**, accompany, befriend, be friends, consort, fraternize, hang (*informal, chiefly U.S.*), hang about, hang out (*informal*), hobnob, mingle, run around (*informal*), socialize ♦ *noun* **3 = partner**, collaborator, colleague, confederate, co-worker **4 = friend**, ally, companion, compeer, comrade, confrère, mate (*informal*)
➤ Antonyms
verb ≠**connect**: detach, disconnect, dissociate, distance, distinguish, divorce, isolate, segregate, separate, set apart
≠**mix**: avoid, be alienated, be estranged,

break off, part company

association *noun* **1 = group**, affiliation, alliance, band, clique, club, coalition, combine, company, confederacy, confederation, cooperative, corporation, federation, fraternity, league, order, organization, partnership, society, syndicate, union **2 = connection**, blend, bond, combination, concomitance, correlation, identification, joining, juxtaposition, linkage, linking, lumping together, mixing, mixture, pairing, relation, tie, union, yoking **3 = friendship**, affinity, companionship, comradeship, familiarity, fellowship, fraternization, intimacy, liaison, partnership, relations, relationship

assort *verb* **= group**, arrange, array, categorize, classify, dispose, distribute, file, grade, range, rank, sort, type

assorted *adjective* **1 = various**, different, diverse, diversified, heterogeneous, manifold, miscellaneous, mixed, motley, sundry, varied, variegated **2 = grouped**, arranged, arrayed, categorized, classified, disposed, filed, graded, matched, ranged, ranked, sorted, typed
➤ Antonyms
≠**various**: alike, homogeneous, identical, like, same, similar, uniform, unvaried

assortment *noun* **1 = variety**, array, choice, collection, diversity, farrago, hotchpotch, jumble, medley, *mélange*, miscellany, mishmash, mixed bag (*informal*), mixture, pick 'n' mix, potpourri, salmagundi, selection **2 = sorting**, arrangement, categorizing, classification, disposition, distribution, filing, grading, grouping, ranging, ranking, typing

assuage *verb* **1 = relieve**, allay, alleviate, calm, ease, lessen, lighten, mitigate, moderate, palliate, quench, soothe, temper **2 = calm**, appease, lull, mollify, pacify, pour oil on troubled waters, quiet, relax, satisfy, soften, soothe, still, tranquillize
➤ Antonyms
≠**relieve**: aggravate, exacerbate, heighten, increase, intensify, worsen ≠**calm**: aggravate, embitter, enrage, infuriate, madden, provoke

assume *verb* **1 = take for granted**, accept, believe, expect, fancy, guess (*informal, chiefly U.S. & Canad.*), imagine, infer, presume, presuppose, suppose, surmise, suspect, think **2 = take on**, accept, acquire, attend to, begin, don, embark upon, embrace, enter upon, put on, set about, shoulder, take over, take responsibility for,

take up, undertake **3 = put on**, adopt, affect, counterfeit, feign, imitate, impersonate, mimic, pretend to, sham, simulate **4 = take over**, acquire, appropriate, arrogate, commandeer, expropriate, pre-empt, seize, take, usurp
➤ Antonyms
≠**take for granted**: know, prove ≠**take on, take over**: give up, hand over, leave, put aside, relinquish

assumed *adjective* **1 = false**, affected, bogus, counterfeit, fake, feigned, fictitious, imitation, made-up, make-believe, phoney *or* phony (*informal*), pretended, pseudonymous, sham, simulated, spurious **2 = taken for granted**, accepted, expected, hypothetical, presumed, presupposed, supposed, surmised
➤ Antonyms
≠**false**: actual, authentic, natural, real ≠**taken for granted**: known, positive, stated, true

assumption *noun* **1 = presumption**, acceptance, belief, conjecture, expectation, fancy, guess, hypothesis, inference, postulate, postulation, premise, premiss, presupposition, supposition, surmise, suspicion, theory **2 = taking on**, acceptance, acquisition, adoption, embracing, entering upon, putting on, shouldering, takeover, taking up, undertaking **3 = taking**, acquisition, appropriation, arrogation, expropriation, pre-empting, seizure, takeover, usurpation **4 = presumptuousness**, arrogance, conceit, imperiousness, pride, self-importance

assurance *noun* **1 = assertion**, affirmation, declaration, guarantee, oath, pledge, profession, promise, protestation, statement, vow, word, word of honour **2 = confidence**, assertiveness, assuredness, boldness, certainty, certitude, conviction, coolness, courage, faith, firmness, nerve, poise, positiveness, security, self-confidence, self-reliance, sureness
➤ Antonyms
≠**assertion**: falsehood, lie ≠**confidence**: apprehension, diffidence, distrust, doubt, self-doubt, self-effacement, shyness, timidity, uncertainty

assure *verb* **1 = promise**, affirm, attest, certify, confirm, declare confidently, give one's word to, guarantee, pledge, swear, vow **2 = convince**, comfort, embolden, encourage, hearten, persuade, reassure, soothe **3 = make certain**, clinch, complete, confirm, ensure, guarantee, make sure, seal, secure

assured *adjective* **1 = confident**, assertive,

audacious, bold, brazen, certain, complacent, overconfident, poised, positive, pushy (*informal*), resting on one's laurels, self-assured, self-confident, self-possessed, sure of oneself **2 = certain**, beyond doubt, clinched, confirmed, dependable, ensured, fixed, guaranteed, indubitable, in the bag (*slang*), irrefutable, made certain, sealed, secure, settled, sure, unquestionable
➤ Antonyms
≠**confident**: bashful, diffident, hesitant, retiring, self-conscious, self-effacing, timid ≠**certain**: ambiguous, doubtful, indefinite, questionable, uncertain, unconfirmed, unsettled, unsure

astonish *verb* **= amaze**, astound, bewilder, boggle the mind, confound, daze, dumbfound, flabbergast (*informal*), stagger, stun, stupefy, surprise

astonishing *adjective* **= amazing**, astounding, bewildering, breathtaking, brilliant, impressive, jaw-dropping, sensational (*informal*), staggering, striking, stunning, stupefying, surprising, wondrous (*archaic or literary*)

astonishment *noun* **= amazement**, awe, bewilderment, confusion, consternation, stupefaction, surprise, wonder, wonderment

astound *verb* **= amaze**, astonish, bewilder, boggle the mind, confound, daze, dumbfound, flabbergast (*informal*), overwhelm, stagger, stun, stupefy, surprise, take one's breath away

astounding *adjective* **= amazing**, astonishing, bewildering, breathtaking, brilliant, impressive, jaw-dropping, sensational (*informal*), staggering, striking, stunning, stupefying, surprising, wondrous (*archaic or literary*)

astray *adjective, adverb* **1 = off the right track**, adrift, afield, amiss, lost, off, off course, off the mark, off the subject ♦ *adverb* **2 = into sin**, into error, to the bad, wrong

astronaut *noun* **= space traveller**, cosmonaut, spaceman, space pilot, spacewoman

astute *adjective* **= intelligent**, adroit, artful, bright, calculating, canny, clever, crafty, cunning, discerning, foxy, insightful, keen, knowing, on the ball (*informal*), penetrating, perceptive, politic, sagacious, sharp, shrewd, sly, subtle, wily
➤ Antonyms
dull, ingenuous, naive, slow, straightforward, stupid, unintelligent, unknowing

astuteness *noun* **= intelligence**, acumen,

adroitness, artfulness, brightness,
canniness, cleverness, craftiness, cunning,
discernment, foxiness, insight, keenness,
knowledge, penetration, perceptiveness,
sagacity, sharpness, shrewdness, slyness,
smarts (*slang, chiefly U.S.*), subtlety, suss
(*slang*), wiliness

asylum *noun* **1** = **refuge**, harbour, haven,
preserve, retreat, safety, sanctuary, shelter
2 *Old-fashioned* = **mental hospital**, funny
farm (*facetious*), hospital, institution,
laughing academy (*U.S. slang*), loony bin
(*slang*), madhouse (*informal*), nuthouse
(*slang*), psychiatric hospital, rubber room
(*U.S. slang*)

atheism *noun* = **nonbelief**, disbelief,
freethinking, godlessness, heathenism,
infidelity, irreligion, paganism, scepticism,
unbelief

atheist *noun* = **nonbeliever**, disbeliever,
freethinker, heathen, infidel, irreligionist,
pagan, sceptic, unbeliever

athlete *noun* = **sportsperson**, competitor,
contender, contestant, games player,
gymnast, player, runner, sportsman,
sportswoman

athletic *adjective* = **fit**, able-bodied, active,
brawny, energetic, herculean, husky
(*informal*), lusty, muscular, powerful,
robust, sinewy, strapping, strong, sturdy,
vigorous, well-proportioned
➤ **Antonyms**
delicate, feeble, frail, puny, sickly, weedy
(*informal*)

athletics *plural noun* = **sports**, contests,
exercises, games of strength, gymnastics,
races, track and field events

atmosphere *noun* **1** = **air**, aerosphere,
heavens, sky **2** = **feeling**, air, ambience,
aura, character, climate, environment, feel,
flavour, mood, quality, spirit,
surroundings, tone, vibes (*slang*)

atom *noun* = **particle**, bit, crumb, dot,
fragment, grain, iota, jot, mite, molecule,
morsel, mote, scintilla (*rare*), scrap, shred,
speck, spot, tittle, trace, whit

atone *verb, usually with* **for** = **make
amends**, answer for, compensate, do
penance, make redress, make reparation,
make up for, pay for, recompense, redress

atonement *noun* = **amends**,
compensation, expiation, payment,
penance, propitiation, recompense,
redress, reparation, restitution, satisfaction

atrocious *adjective* **1** = **cruel**, barbaric,
brutal, diabolical, fiendish, flagrant,
godawful (*slang*), heinous, hellacious (*U.S.
slang*), infamous, infernal, inhuman,
monstrous, nefarious, ruthless, savage,

vicious, villainous, wicked **2** *Informal*
= **shocking**, appalling, detestable,
execrable, grievous, horrible, horrifying,
terrible
➤ **Antonyms**
≠**cruel**: civilized, generous, gentle, good,
honourable, humane, kind, merciful
≠**shocking**: admirable, fine, tasteful

atrocity *noun* **1** = **cruelty**, atrociousness,
barbarity, barbarousness, brutality,
enormity, fiendishness, grievousness,
heinousness, horror, infamy, inhumanity,
monstrousness, nefariousness,
ruthlessness, savagery, shockingness,
viciousness, villainousness, wickedness **2**
= **act of cruelty**, abomination, barbarity,
brutality, crime, cruelty, enormity, evil,
horror, monstrosity, outrage, villainy

attach *verb* **1** = **connect**, add, adhere, affix,
annex, append, bind, couple, fasten, fix,
join, link, make fast, secure, stick, subjoin,
tie, unite **2** = **put**, ascribe, assign, associate,
attribute, connect, impute, invest with,
lay, place **3 attach oneself** *or* **be attached
to** = **join**, accompany, affiliate oneself with,
associate with, become associated with,
combine with, join forces with, latch on to,
sign on with, sign up with, unite with
➤ **Antonyms**
≠**connect**: detach, disconnect, dissociate,
loosen, remove, retire, separate, untie,
withdraw

attached *adjective* **1** = **spoken for**,
accompanied, engaged, married,
partnered **2 attached to** = **fond of**,
affectionate towards, devoted to, full of
regard for

attachment *noun* **1** = **fondness**, affection,
affinity, attraction, bond, devotion,
fidelity, friendship, liking, love, loyalty,
partiality, possessiveness, predilection,
regard, tenderness **2** = **accessory**,
accoutrement, adaptor *or* adapter,
addition, add-on, adjunct, appendage,
appurtenance, auxiliary, extension, extra,
fitting, fixture, supplement, supplementary
part **3** = **connector**, adaptor *or* adapter,
bond, clamp, connection, coupling,
fastener, fastening, joint, junction, link, tie
➤ **Antonyms**
≠**fondness**: animosity, antipathy, aversion,
disinclination, distaste, hatred, hostility,
loathing

attack *verb* **1** = **assault**, assail, charge, fall
upon, invade, lay into (*informal*), raid,
rush, set about, set upon, storm, strike (at)
2 = **criticize**, abuse, berate, bite someone's
head off, blame, blast, censure, excoriate,
go for the jugular, have a go (at)
(*informal*), impugn, lambast(e), malign,

put down, revile, snap someone's head off, tear into (*informal*), vilify ♦ *noun* **3** = **assault**, aggression, campaign, charge, foray, incursion, inroad, invasion, offensive, onset, onslaught, raid, rush, strike **4** = **criticism**, abuse, blame, calumny, censure, character assassination, denigration, impugnment, stick (*slang*), vilification **5** = **bout**, access, convulsion, fit, paroxysm, seizure, spasm, spell, stroke
➤ Antonyms
verb ≠**assault**: defend, guard, protect, retreat, support, sustain, withdraw ♦ *noun* ≠**assault**: defence, retreat, support, withdrawal

attacker *noun* = **assailant**, aggressor, assaulter, intruder, invader, raider

attain *verb* = **achieve**, accomplish, acquire, arrive at, bring off, complete, earn, effect, fulfil, gain, get, grasp, land, obtain, procure, reach, realize, reap, score (*slang*), secure, win

attainable *adjective* = **achievable**, accessible, accomplishable, at hand, feasible, gettable, graspable, likely, obtainable, possible, potential, practicable, probable, procurable, reachable, realizable, within reach
➤ Antonyms
impossible, impracticable, improbable, inaccessible, out of reach, unattainable, unfeasible, unlikely, unobtainable, unprocurable, unreachable

attainment *noun* **1** = **achievement**, accomplishment, acquirement, acquisition, arrival at, completion, feat, fulfilment, gaining, getting, obtaining, procurement, reaching, realization, reaping, winning **2** = **skill**, ability, accomplishment, achievement, art, capability, competence, gift, mastery, proficiency, talent

attempt *verb* **1** = **try**, endeavour, essay, experiment, have a crack, have a go (*informal*), have a shot (*informal*), have a stab (*informal*), jump through hoops (*informal*), seek, strive, tackle, take on, take the bit between one's teeth, try one's hand at, undertake, venture ♦ *noun* **2** = **try**, assault, attack, bid, crack (*informal*), effort, endeavour, essay, experiment, go (*informal*), shot (*informal*), stab (*informal*), trial, undertaking, venture

attend *verb* **1** = **be present**, appear, be at, be here, be there, frequent, go to, haunt, make one (*archaic*), put in an appearance, show oneself, show up (*informal*), turn up, visit **2** = **look after**, care for, mind, minister to, nurse, take care of, tend **3** = **pay attention**, follow, hear, hearken (*archaic*),

heed, listen, look on, mark, mind, note, notice, observe, pay heed, regard, take to heart, watch **4** = **escort**, accompany, chaperon, companion, convoy, guard, squire, usher **5** = **accompany**, arise from, be associated with, be connected with, be consequent on, follow, go hand in hand with, issue from, occur with, result from **6** = **serve**, be in the service of, wait upon, work for **7 attend to** = **apply oneself to**, concentrate on, devote oneself to, get to work on, look after, occupy oneself with, see to, take care of
➤ Antonyms
≠**be present**: be absent, miss, play truant ≠**look after**, apply oneself to: neglect ≠**pay attention**: discount, disregard, ignore, neglect ≠**accompany**: dissociate

attendance *noun* **1** = **presence**, appearance, attending, being there **2** = **turnout**, audience, crowd, gate, house, number present

attendant *noun* **1** = **assistant**, aide, auxiliary, chaperon, companion, custodian, escort, flunky, follower, guard, guide, helper, lackey, menial, page, servant, steward, underling, usher, waiter ♦ *adjective* **2** = **accompanying**, accessory, associated, concomitant, consequent, related

attention *noun* **1** = **concentration**, consideration, contemplation, deliberation, heed, heedfulness, intentness, mind, scrutiny, thinking, thought, thoughtfulness **2** = **notice**, awareness, consciousness, consideration, observation, recognition, regard **3** = **care**, concern, looking after, ministration, treatment **4 attentions** = **courtesy**, assiduities, care, civility, compliment, consideration, deference, gallantry, mindfulness, politeness, regard, respect, service
➤ Antonyms
≠**concentration**, **notice**: carelessness, disregard, disrespect, distraction, inattention, laxity, laxness, thoughtlessness, unconcern ≠**care**: negligence ≠**courtesy**: discourtesy, impoliteness

attentive *adjective* **1** = **intent**, alert, awake, careful, concentrating, heedful, listening, mindful, observant, on one's toes, regardful, studious, watchful **2** = **considerate**, accommodating, civil, conscientious, courteous, devoted, gallant, gracious, helpful, kind, obliging, polite, respectful, thoughtful
➤ Antonyms
≠**intent**: absent-minded, careless, distracted, dreamy, heedless, inattentive,

preoccupied, unheeding, unmindful
≠**considerate**: neglectful, negligent,
remiss, thoughtless

attest verb = **testify**, adjure, affirm, assert,
authenticate, aver, bear out, bear witness,
certify, confirm, corroborate, declare,
demonstrate, display, evince, exhibit, give
evidence, invoke, manifest, prove, ratify,
seal, show, substantiate, swear, verify,
vouch for, warrant, witness
➤ Antonyms
contradict, controvert, deny, disprove,
gainsay (archaic or literary), give the lie to,
make a nonsense of, prove false, rebut,
refute

attic noun = **loft**, garret

attire noun 1 = **clothes**, accoutrements,
apparel, array (poetic), clothing, costume,
dress, garb, garments, gear (informal),
habiliments, habit, outfit, raiment (archaic
or poetic), robes, threads (slang), uniform,
vestment, wear ♦ verb 2 = **dress**, accoutre,
apparel (archaic), array, clothe, costume,
deck out, equip, fit out, garb, get ready,
rig out, robe, turn out

attitude noun 1 = **disposition**, approach,
frame of mind, mood, opinion, outlook,
perspective, point of view, position,
stance, view 2 = **manner**, air, aspect,
bearing, carriage, condition, demeanour,
mien (literary) 3 = **position**, pose, posture,
stance

attract verb = **appeal to**, allure, bewitch,
captivate, catch (someone's) eye, charm,
decoy, draw, enchant, endear, engage,
entice, fascinate, incline, induce, interest,
invite, lure, pull (informal), tempt
➤ Antonyms
disgust, give one the creeps (informal), put
one off, repel, repulse, revolt, turn one off
(informal)

attraction noun = **appeal**, allure,
attractiveness, bait, captivation, charm,
come-on (informal), draw, enchantment,
endearment, enticement, fascination,
incentive, inducement, interest, invitation,
lure, magnetism, pull (informal),
temptation, temptingness

attractive adjective = **appealing**,
agreeable, alluring, beautiful, bonny,
captivating, charming, comely, cute,
engaging, enticing, fair, fascinating,
fetching, glamorous, good-looking,
gorgeous, handsome, interesting, inviting,
likable or likeable, lovely, magnetic,
pleasant, pleasing, prepossessing, pretty,
seductive, tempting, winning, winsome
➤ Antonyms
disagreeable, displeasing, distasteful,
offensive, repulsive, ugly, unappealing,

unbecoming, uninviting, unlikable or
unlikeable, unpleasant, unsightly

attribute verb 1 = **ascribe**, apply, assign,
blame, charge, credit, impute, lay at the
door of, put down to, refer, set down to,
trace to ♦ noun 2 = **quality**, aspect,
character, characteristic, facet, feature,
idiosyncrasy, indication, mark, note,
peculiarity, point, property, quirk, sign,
symbol, trait, virtue

attrition noun = **wearing down**,
attenuation, debilitation, harassment,
harrying, thinning out, weakening

attune verb = **accustom**, acclimatize,
accord, adapt, adjust, coordinate,
familiarize, harmonize, modulate, regulate,
set, tune

auburn adjective = **reddish-brown**,
chestnut-coloured, copper-coloured,
henna, nutbrown, russet, rust-coloured,
tawny, Titian red

audacious adjective 1 = **daring**,
adventurous, bold, brave, courageous,
daredevil, dauntless, death-defying,
enterprising, fearless, intrepid, rash,
reckless, risky, valiant, venturesome 2
= **cheeky**, assuming, brazen, defiant,
disrespectful, forward, fresh (informal),
impertinent, impudent, insolent,
in-your-face (Brit. slang), pert,
presumptuous, rude, sassy (U.S. informal),
shameless
➤ Antonyms
≠**daring**: careful, cautious, cowardly,
frightened, guarded, prudent, timid,
unadventurous, unenterprising ≠**cheeky**:
deferential, gracious, tactful, unassuming

audacity noun 1 = **daring**,
adventurousness, audaciousness, boldness,
bravery, courage, dauntlessness,
enterprise, face (informal), fearlessness,
front, guts (informal), intrepidity, nerve,
rashness, recklessness, valour,
venturesomeness 2 = **cheek**,
audaciousness, brass neck (Brit. informal),
chutzpah (U.S. & Canad. informal),
defiance, disrespectfulness, effrontery,
forwardness, gall (informal), impertinence,
impudence, insolence, neck (informal),
nerve, pertness, presumption, rudeness,
sassiness (U.S. informal), shamelessness

audible adjective = **clear**, detectable,
discernible, distinct, hearable, perceptible
➤ Antonyms
faint, imperceptible, inaudible, indistinct,
low, out of earshot

audience noun 1 = **spectators**,
assemblage, assembly, congregation,
crowd, gallery, gathering, house, listeners,
onlookers, turnout, viewers 2 = **public**,

devotees, fans, following, market **3** = **interview**, consultation, hearing, meeting, reception

audit *Accounting* ♦ *noun* **1** = **inspection**, balancing, check, checking, examination, investigation, review, scrutiny, verification ♦ *verb* **2** = **inspect**, balance, check, examine, go over, go through, investigate, review, scrutinize, verify

au fait *adjective* = **fully informed**, abreast of, *au courant*, clued-up (*informal*), conversant, expert, familiar, in the know, in the loop, in touch, knowledgeable, on the ball (*informal*), up to speed, well-acquainted, well up

augment *verb* = **increase**, add to, amplify, boost, build up, dilate, enhance, enlarge, expand, extend, grow, heighten, inflate, intensify, magnify, multiply, raise, reinforce, strengthen, swell
➤ **Antonyms**
contract, curtail, cut down, decrease, diminish, lessen, lower, reduce, shrink

augmentation *noun* = **increase**, accession, addition, amplification, boost, build-up, dilation, enhancement, enlargement, expansion, extension, growth, heightening, inflation, intensification, magnification, multiplication, reinforcement, rise, strengthening, swelling

augur *verb* = **bode**, be an omen of, bespeak (*archaic*), betoken, foreshadow, harbinger, herald, portend, predict, prefigure, presage, promise, prophesy, signify

augury *noun* **1** = **prediction**, divination, prophecy, soothsaying, sortilege **2** = **omen**, auspice, forerunner, forewarning, harbinger, herald, portent, precursor, presage, prognostication, promise, prophecy, sign, token, warning

august *adjective* = **noble**, dignified, exalted, glorious, grand, high-ranking, imposing, impressive, kingly, lofty, magnificent, majestic, monumental, regal, solemn, stately, superb

aura *noun* = **air**, ambience, aroma, atmosphere, emanation, feel, feeling, mood, odour, quality, scent, suggestion, tone, vibes (*slang*), vibrations (*slang*)

auspice *noun* As in **under the auspices of** = **support**, advocacy, aegis, authority, backing, care, championship, charge, control, countenance, guidance, influence, patronage, protection, sponsorship, supervision

auspicious *adjective* = **favourable**, bright, encouraging, felicitous, fortunate, happy, hopeful, lucky, opportune, promising, propitious, prosperous, rosy, timely

➤ **Antonyms**
bad, black, discouraging, ill-omened, inauspicious, infelicitous, ominous, unfavourable, unfortunate, unlucky, unpromising, unpropitious

austere *adjective* **1** = **stern**, cold, exacting, forbidding, formal, grave, grim, hard, harsh, inflexible, rigorous, serious, severe, solemn, stiff, strict, stringent, unfeeling, unrelenting **2** = **ascetic**, abstemious, abstinent, chaste, continent, economical, exacting, puritanical, rigid, self-denying, self-disciplined, sober, solemn, Spartan, strait-laced, strict, unrelenting **3** = **plain**, bleak, economical, harsh, severe, simple, spare, Spartan, stark, subdued, unadorned, unornamented
➤ **Antonyms**
≠**stern**: affable, cheerful, convivial, flexible, free-and-easy, genial, indulgent, jovial, kindly, permissive, sweet ≠**ascetic**: abandoned, free-and-easy, immoral, indulgent, loose, permissive ≠**plain**: comfortable, indulgent, luxurious

austerity *noun* **1** = **sternness**, coldness, exactingness, forbiddingness, formality, gravity, grimness, hardness, harshness, inflexibility, rigour, seriousness, severity, solemnity, stiffness, strictness **2** = **asceticism**, abstemiousness, abstinence, chasteness, chastity, continence, economy, exactingness, puritanism, rigidity, self-denial, self-discipline, sobriety, solemnity, Spartanism, strictness **3** = **plainness**, economy, severity, simplicity, spareness, Spartanism, starkness

authentic *adjective* = **genuine**, accurate, actual, authoritative, bona fide, certain, dependable, factual, faithful, legitimate, on the level (*informal*), original, pure, real, reliable, simon-pure (*rare*), the real McCoy, true, true-to-life, trustworthy, valid, veritable
➤ **Antonyms**
counterfeit, fake, false, fictitious, fraudulent, hypothetical, imitation, misleading, mock, pseudo (*informal*), spurious, supposed, synthetic, unfaithful, unreal, untrue

authenticate *verb* = **verify**, attest, authorize, avouch, certify, confirm, endorse, guarantee, validate, vouch for, warrant
➤ **Antonyms**
annul, invalidate, render null and void

authenticity *noun* = **genuineness**, accuracy, actuality, authoritativeness, certainty, dependability, factualness, faithfulness, legitimacy, purity, realness, reliability, trustworthiness, truth, truthfulness, validity, veritableness, verity

author noun 1 = **writer**, composer, creator
2 = **creator**, architect, designer, doer,
fabricator, father, founder, framer,
initiator, inventor, maker, mover,
originator, parent, planner, prime mover,
producer

authoritarian adjective 1 = **strict**, absolute,
autocratic, despotic, dictatorial,
disciplinarian, doctrinaire, dogmatic,
domineering, harsh, imperious, rigid,
severe, tyrannical, unyielding ♦ noun 2
= **disciplinarian**, absolutist, autocrat,
despot, dictator, tyrant
➤ Antonyms
adjective ≠**strict**: broad-minded,
democratic, flexible, indulgent, lenient,
liberal, permissive, tolerant

authoritative adjective 1 = **reliable**,
accurate, authentic, definitive,
dependable, factual, faithful, learned,
scholarly, sound, true, trustworthy,
truthful, valid, veritable 2 = **official**,
approved, authorized, commanding,
legitimate, sanctioned, sovereign 3
= **commanding**, assertive, autocratic,
confident, decisive, dictatorial, dogmatic,
dominating, imperative, imperious,
imposing, lordly, masterly, peremptory,
self-assured
➤ Antonyms
≠**reliable**: deceptive, undependable,
unreliable ≠**official**: unauthorized,
unofficial, unsanctioned ≠**commanding**:
humble, subservient, timid, weak

authority noun 1 = **power**, ascendancy,
charge, command, control, direction,
domination, dominion, force,
government, influence, jurisdiction, might,
prerogative, right, rule, say-so, strength,
supremacy, sway, weight 2 usually plural
= **powers that be**, administration,
government, management, officialdom,
police, the Establishment 3 = **expert**,
arbiter, bible, connoisseur, guru, judge,
master, professional, scholar, specialist,
textbook 4 = **permission**, a blank cheque,
authorization, justification, licence, permit,
sanction, say-so, warrant

authorization noun 1 = **power**, ability,
authority, right, say-so, strength 2
= **permission**, a blank cheque, approval,
credentials, leave, licence, permit,
sanction, say-so, warrant

authorize verb 1 = **empower**, accredit,
commission, enable, entitle, give authority
2 = **permit**, accredit, allow, approve,
confirm, countenance, give a blank
cheque to, give authority for, give leave,
give the green light for, license, ratify,

sanction, vouch for, warrant
➤ Antonyms
ban, debar, disallow, exclude, forbid,
outlaw, preclude, prohibit, proscribe, rule
out, veto

autocracy noun = **dictatorship**,
absolutism, despotism, tyranny

autocrat noun = **dictator**, absolutist,
despot, tyrant

autocratic adjective = **dictatorial**, absolute,
all-powerful, despotic, domineering,
imperious, tyrannical, tyrannous, unlimited

automatic adjective 1 = **mechanical**,
automated, mechanized, push-button,
robot, self-acting, self-activating,
self-moving, self-propelling, self-regulating
2 = **involuntary**, instinctive, instinctual,
mechanical, natural, reflex, spontaneous,
unconscious, unwilled 3 = **inevitable**,
assured, certain, inescapable, necessary,
routine, unavoidable
➤ Antonyms
≠**mechanical**: done by hand,
hand-operated, human, manual, physical
≠**involuntary**: conscious, deliberate,
intentional, voluntary

autonomous adjective = **self-ruling**, free,
independent, self-determining,
self-governing, sovereign

autonomy noun = **independence**,
freedom, home rule, self-determination,
self-government, self-rule, sovereignty
➤ Antonyms
dependency, foreign rule, subjection

autopsy noun = **postmortem**, dissection,
necropsy, postmortem examination

auxiliary adjective 1 = **supplementary**,
back-up, emergency, fall-back, reserve,
secondary, subsidiary, substitute 2
= **supporting**, accessory, aiding, ancillary,
assisting, helping ♦ noun 3 = **backup**,
reserve 4 = **helper**, accessory, accomplice,
ally, assistant, associate, companion,
confederate, henchman, partner,
protagonist, subordinate, supporter
➤ Antonyms
adjective ≠**supplementary, supporting**:
cardinal, chief, essential, first, leading,
main, primary, prime, principal

avail verb 1 = **benefit**, aid, assist, be of
advantage, be useful, help, profit ♦ noun 2
= **benefit**, advantage, aid, good, help,
profit, use

availability noun = **accessibility**,
attainability, handiness, readiness

available adjective = **accessible**, applicable,
at hand, at one's disposal, at one's
fingertips, attainable, convenient, free,
handy, obtainable, on hand, on tap, ready,

ready for use, to hand, vacant
➤ **Antonyms**
busy, engaged, inaccessible, in use,
occupied, spoken for, taken, unattainable,
unavailable, unobtainable

avalanche *noun* **1** = **snow-slide**, landslide,
landslip, snow-slip **2** = **flood**, barrage,
deluge, inundation, torrent

avant-garde *adjective* = **progressive**,
experimental, far-out (*slang*),
ground-breaking, innovative, innovatory,
pioneering, unconventional, way-out
(*informal*)
➤ **Antonyms**
conservative, conventional, hidebound,
reactionary, traditional

avarice *noun* = **greed**, acquisitiveness,
close-fistedness, covetousness, cupidity,
graspingness, greediness, meanness,
miserliness, niggardliness, parsimony,
penny-pinching, penuriousness, rapacity,
stinginess
➤ **Antonyms**
benevolence, bountifulness, extravagance,
generosity, largesse *or* largess, liberality,
unselfishness

avaricious *adjective* = **grasping**,
acquisitive, close-fisted, covetous, greedy,
mean, miserable, miserly, niggardly,
parsimonious, penny-pinching, penurious,
rapacious, snoep (*S. Afr. informal*), stingy,
tight-arsed (*taboo slang*), tight as a duck's
arse (*taboo slang*), tight-assed (*U.S. taboo
slang*)

avenge *verb* = **get revenge for**, even the
score for, get even for (*informal*), get one's
own back, hit back, pay (someone) back
for, pay (someone) back in his *or* her own
coin, punish, repay, requite, retaliate,
revenge, take revenge for, take satisfaction
for, take vengeance

avenue *noun* = **street**, access, alley,
approach, boulevard, channel, course,
drive, driveway, entrance, entry, pass,
passage, path, pathway, road, route,
thoroughfare, way

aver *verb* = **state**, affirm, allege, assert,
asseverate, avouch, avow, declare,
maintain, proclaim, profess, pronounce,
protest, say, swear

average *noun* **1** = **usual**, common run,
mean, medium, midpoint, norm, normal,
par, rule, run, run of the mill, standard **2**
on average = **usually**, as a rule, for the
most part, generally, normally, typically
♦ *adjective* **3** = **usual**, common,
commonplace, fair, general, normal,
ordinary, regular, standard, typical **4**
= **mean**, intermediate, median, medium,
middle **5** = **mediocre**, banal, bog-standard

(*Brit. & Irish slang*), indifferent,
middle-of-the-road, middling, moderate,
no great shakes (*informal*), not bad,
passable, run-of-the-mill, so-so (*informal*),
tolerable, undistinguished, unexceptional,
vanilla (*slang*) ♦ *verb* **6** = **make on
average**, balance out to, be on average,
do on average, even out to
➤ **Antonyms**
adjective ≠**usual**: abnormal, awful, bad,
different, exceptional, great, memorable,
notable, outstanding, remarkable, special,
terrible, unusual ≠**mean**: maximum,
minimum

averse *adjective* = **opposed**, antipathetic,
backward, disinclined, hostile, ill-disposed,
indisposed, inimical, loath, reluctant,
unfavourable, unwilling
➤ **Antonyms**
agreeable, amenable, disposed, eager,
favourable, inclined, keen, sympathetic,
willing

aversion *noun* = **hatred**, abhorrence,
animosity, antipathy, detestation, disgust,
disinclination, dislike, distaste, hate,
horror, hostility, indisposition, loathing,
odium, opposition, reluctance,
repugnance, repulsion, revulsion,
unwillingness
➤ **Antonyms**
desire, inclination, liking, love, willingness

avert *verb* **1** = **turn away**, turn, turn aside **2**
= **ward off**, avoid, fend off, forestall,
frustrate, preclude, prevent, stave off

aviation *noun* = **flying**, aeronautics, flight,
powered flight

aviator *noun* = **pilot**, aeronaut, airman, flyer

avid *adjective* **1** = **enthusiastic**, ardent,
devoted, eager, fanatical, fervent, intense,
keen, keen as mustard, passionate, zealous
2 = **insatiable**, acquisitive, athirst,
avaricious, covetous, grasping, greedy,
hungry, rapacious, ravenous, thirsty,
voracious
➤ **Antonyms**
≠**enthusiastic**: apathetic, impassive,
indifferent, lukewarm, unenthusiastic

avidity *noun* **1** = **enthusiasm**, ardour,
devotion, eagerness, fervour, keenness,
zeal **2** = **insatiability**, acquisitiveness,
avarice, covetousness, cupidity, desire,
graspingness, greediness, hankering,
hunger, longing, rapacity, ravenousness,
thirst, voracity

avocation *noun* *Old-fashioned* **1** = **job**,
business, calling, employment,
occupation, profession, pursuit, trade,
vocation, work **2** = **hobby**, diversion,
occupation, pastime, recreation

avoid *verb* **1** = **refrain from**, dodge, duck

(out of) (*informal*), eschew, fight shy of, shirk **2 = prevent**, avert **3 = keep away from**, body-swerve (*Scot.*), bypass, circumvent, dodge, elude, escape, evade, give a wide berth to, keep aloof from, shun, sidestep, slip through the net, steer clear of
➤ Antonyms
≠**keep away from:** approach, confront, contact, face, face up to, find, invite, pursue, seek out, solicit

avoidance *noun* **1 = refraining**, dodging, eschewal, shirking **2 = prevention 3 = evasion**, body swerve (*Scot.*), circumvention, dodging, eluding, escape, keeping away, shunning, steering clear

avowed *adjective* **1 = declared**, open, professed, self-proclaimed, sworn **2 = confessed**, acknowledged, admitted

await *verb* **1 = wait for**, abide, anticipate, expect, look for, look forward to, stay for **2 = be in store for**, attend, be in readiness for, be prepared for, be ready for, wait for

awake *adjective* **1 = not sleeping**, aroused, awakened, aware, bright-eyed and bushy-tailed, conscious, wakeful, waking, wide-awake **2 = alert**, alive, attentive, aware, heedful, observant, on guard, on one's toes, on the alert, on the lookout, vigilant, watchful ♦ *verb* **3 = wake up**, awaken, rouse, wake **4 = alert**, activate, animate, arouse, awaken, breathe life into, call forth, enliven, excite, fan, incite, kick-start (*informal*), kindle, provoke, revive, stimulate, stir up, vivify
➤ Antonyms
adjective ≠**not sleeping:** asleep, crashed out (*slang*), dead to the world (*informal*), dormant, dozing, napping, sleeping, unconscious ≠**alert:** inattentive, unaware

awaken *verb* **1 = awake**, arouse, revive, rouse, wake **2 = alert**, activate, animate, breathe life into, call forth, enliven, excite, fan, incite, kick-start (*informal*), kindle, provoke, stimulate, stir up, vivify

awakening *noun* **= waking up**, activation, animating, arousal, awaking, birth, enlivening, incitement, kindling, provocation, revival, rousing, stimulation, stirring up, vivification, waking

award *verb* **1 = give**, accord, adjudge, allot, apportion, assign, bestow, confer, decree, distribute, endow, gift, grant, hand out, present, render ♦ *noun* **2 = prize**, bonsela (*S. Afr.*), decoration, gift, grant, trophy, verdict **3 = giving**, allotment, bestowal, conferment, conferral, endowment, hand-out, order, presentation, stipend **4** *Law* **= decision**, adjudication, decree

aware *adjective* **1 aware of = knowing**

about, acquainted with, alive to, appreciative of, apprised of, attentive to, cognizant of, conscious of, conversant with, familiar with, hip to (*slang*), mindful of, sensible of, wise to (*slang*) **2 = informed**, *au courant*, clued-up (*informal*), enlightened, in the loop, in the picture, keeping one's finger on the pulse, knowledgeable
➤ Antonyms
ignorant, insensible, oblivious, unaware, unfamiliar with, unknowledgeable

awareness *noun* **= knowledge**, acquaintance, appreciation, attention, cognizance, consciousness, enlightenment, familiarity, mindfulness, perception, realization, recognition, sensibility, sentience, understanding

away *adverb* **1 = off**, abroad, elsewhere, from here, from home, hence **2 = at a distance**, apart, far, remote **3 = aside**, out of the way, to one side **4 = continuously**, incessantly, interminably, relentlessly, repeatedly, uninterruptedly, unremittingly ♦ *adjective* **5 = not present**, abroad, absent, elsewhere, gone, not at home, not here, not there, out ♦ *interjection* **6 = go away**, beat it (*slang*), begone, be off, bugger off (*taboo slang*), fuck off (*offensive taboo slang*), get lost (*informal*), get out, go, on your bike (*slang*), on your way

awe *noun* **1 = wonder**, admiration, amazement, astonishment, dread, fear, horror, respect, reverence, terror, veneration ♦ *verb* **2 = impress**, amaze, astonish, cow, daunt, frighten, horrify, intimidate, put the wind up (*informal*), stun, terrify
➤ Antonyms
noun ≠**wonder:** arrogance, boldness, contempt, disrespect, fearlessness, irreverence, scorn

awe-inspiring *adjective* **= impressive**, amazing, astonishing, awesome, breathtaking, daunting, fearsome, intimidating, jaw-dropping, magnificent, striking, stunning (*informal*), wonderful, wondrous (*archaic or literary*)
➤ Antonyms
bland, boring, dull, flat, humdrum, insipid, prosaic, tame, tedious, unimpressive, uninspiring, vapid

awesome *adjective* **= awe-inspiring**, alarming, amazing, astonishing, awful, breathtaking, daunting, dreadful, fearful, fearsome, formidable, frightening, horrible, horrifying, imposing, impressive, intimidating, jaw-dropping, magnificent, majestic, overwhelming, redoubtable, shocking, solemn, striking, stunning, stupefying, terrible, terrifying, wonderful, wondrous (*archaic or literary*)

awestruck *or* **awe-stricken** *adjective* = **impressed**, afraid, amazed, astonished, awed, awe-inspired, cowed, daunted, dumbfounded, fearful, frightened, horrified, intimidated, shocked, struck dumb, stunned, terrified, wonder-stricken, wonder-struck

awful *adjective* **1** = **terrible**, abysmal, alarming, appalling, deplorable, dire, distressing, dreadful, fearful, frightful, from hell (*informal*), ghastly, godawful (*slang*), gruesome, harrowing, hellacious (*U.S. slang*), hideous, horrendous, horrible, horrid, horrific, horrifying, nasty, shocking, tremendous, ugly, unpleasant, unsightly **2** *Obsolete* = **awe-inspiring**, amazing, awesome, dread, fearsome, majestic, portentous, solemn
➤ **Antonyms**
≠**terrible**: amazing, brilliant, excellent, fabulous (*informal*), fantastic, great (*informal*), magnificent, marvellous, miraculous, sensational (*informal*), smashing (*informal*), super (*informal*), superb, terrific, tremendous, wonderful

awfully *adverb* **1** = **badly**, disgracefully, disreputably, dreadfully, inadequately, reprehensibly, shoddily, unforgivably, unpleasantly, wickedly, woefully, wretchedly **2** *Informal* = **very**, badly, dreadfully, exceedingly, exceptionally, excessively, extremely, greatly, immensely, quite, seriously (*informal*), terribly, very much

awhile *adverb* = **for a while**, briefly, for a little while, for a moment, for a short time

awkward *adjective* **1** = **clumsy**, all thumbs, artless, blundering, bungling, clownish, coarse, gauche, gawky, graceless, ham-fisted *or* ham-handed (*informal*), ill-bred, inelegant, inept, inexpert, lumbering, maladroit, oafish, rude, skill-less, stiff, uncoordinated, uncouth, ungainly, ungraceful, unpolished, unrefined, unskilful, unskilled **2** = **uncooperative**, annoying, bloody-minded (*Brit. informal*), difficult, disobliging, exasperating, hard to handle, intractable, irritable, perverse, prickly, stubborn, touchy, troublesome, trying, unhelpful, unpredictable, vexatious, vexing **3** = **risky**, chancy (*informal*), dangerous, difficult, hazardous, perilous **4** = **inconvenient**, clunky (*informal*), cumbersome, difficult, troublesome, unhandy, unmanageable, unwieldy **5** = **embarrassing**, compromising, cringe-making (*Brit. informal*),

cringeworthy (*Brit. informal*), delicate, difficult, embarrassed, ill at ease, inconvenient, inopportune, painful, perplexing, sticky (*informal*), thorny, ticklish, toe-curling (*slang*), troublesome, trying, uncomfortable, unpleasant, untimely
➤ **Antonyms**
≠**clumsy**: adept, adroit, dexterous, graceful, skilful ≠**inconvenient**: convenient, easy, handy ≠**embarrassing**: comfortable, pleasant

awkwardness *noun* **1** = **clumsiness**, artlessness, clownishness, coarseness, gaucheness, gaucherie, gawkiness, gracelessness, ill-breeding, inelegance, ineptness, inexpertness, maladroitness, oafishness, rudeness, stiffness, uncoordination, uncouthness, ungainliness, unskilfulness, unskilledness **2** = **uncooperativeness**, bloody-mindedness (*Brit. informal*), difficulty, disobligingness, intractability, irritability, perversity, prickliness, stubbornness, touchiness, unhelpfulness, unpredictability ♦ *adjective* **3** = **difficulty**, chanciness (*informal*), danger, hazardousness, peril, perilousness, risk, riskiness **4** = **unwieldiness**, cumbersomeness, difficulty, inconvenience, troublesomeness, unhandiness, unmanageability **5** = **embarrassment**, delicacy, difficulty, discomfort, inconvenience, inopportuneness, painfulness, perplexingness, stickiness (*informal*), thorniness, ticklishness, unpleasantness, untimeliness

axe *noun* **1** = **hatchet**, adze, chopper **2 an axe to grind** = **pet subject**, grievance, personal consideration, private ends, private purpose, ulterior motive **3 the axe** *Informal* = **the sack** (*informal*), cancellation, cutback, discharge, dismissal, termination, the boot (*slang*), the chop (*slang*), the (old) heave-ho (*informal*), the order of the boot (*slang*), wind-up ♦ *verb* **4** = **cut down**, chop, fell, hew **5** *Informal* = **cut back**, cancel, discharge, dismiss, dispense with, eliminate, fire (*informal*), get rid of, give (someone) their marching orders, give the boot to (*slang*), give the bullet to (*Brit. slang*), give the push, oust, pull, pull the plug on, relegate, remove, sack (*informal*), terminate, throw out, turn off (*informal*), wind up

axiom *noun* = **principle**, adage, aphorism, apophthegm, dictum, fundamental, gnome, maxim, postulate, precept, truism

axiomatic *adjective* **1** = **epigrammatic**, aphoristic, apophthegmatic, gnomic, pithy, terse **2** = **self-evident**, absolute, accepted, apodictic *or* apodeictic, assumed, certain, fundamental, given, granted, indubitable, manifest, presupposed, understood, unquestioned

axis *noun* = **pivot**, axle, centre line, shaft, spindle

axle *noun* = **shaft**, arbor, axis, mandrel, pin, pivot, rod, spindle

azure *adjective* = **sky-blue**, blue, cerulean, clear blue, sky-coloured, ultramarine

B b

babble *verb* 1 = **gabble**, burble, chatter, jabber, prate, prattle, rabbit (on) (*Brit. informal*), waffle (*informal, chiefly Brit.*) 2 = **gibber**, gurgle 3 = **blab**, run off at the mouth (*slang*) ♦ *noun* 4 = **gabble**, burble, drivel, gibberish, waffle (*informal, chiefly Brit.*)

babe *noun* 1 = **baby**, ankle-biter (*Austral. slang*), bairn (*Scot.*), child, infant, nursling, rug rat (*slang*), sprog (*slang*), suckling 2 = **innocent**, babe in arms, ingénue or (*masc.*) ingénu

baby *noun* 1 = **infant**, ankle-biter (*Austral. slang*), babe, babe in arms, bairn (*Scot.*), child, newborn child, rug rat (*slang*), sprog (*slang*) ♦ *adjective* 2 = **small**, diminutive, dwarf, little, midget, mini, miniature, minute, pygmy or pigmy, teensy-weensy, teeny-weeny, tiny, wee ♦ *verb* 3 = **mollycoddle**, coddle, cosset, humour, indulge, overindulge, pamper, pet, spoil, spoon-feed

babyish *adjective* = **childish**, baby, foolish, immature, infantile, juvenile, namby-pamby, puerile, silly, sissy, soft (*informal*), spoiled
➤ **Antonyms**
adult, grown-up, mature, of age

back *noun* 1 = **rear**, backside, end, far end, hind part, hindquarters, posterior, reverse, stern, tail end 2 **behind one's back** = **secretly**, covertly, deceitfully, sneakily, surreptitiously ♦ *verb* 3 = **move back**, back off, backtrack, go back, regress, retire, retreat, reverse, turn tail, withdraw 4 = **support**, abet, advocate, assist, champion, countenance, encourage, endorse, espouse, favour, finance, promote, sanction, second, side with, sponsor, subsidize, sustain, underwrite ♦ *adjective* 5 = **rear**, end, hind, hindmost, posterior, tail 6 = **previous**, delayed, earlier, elapsed, former, overdue, past
➤ **Antonyms**
noun ≠**rear**: face, fore, front, head ♦ *verb* ≠**move back**: advance, approach, move forward, progress ≠**support**: attack, combat, hinder, thwart, undermine, weaken ♦ *adjective* ≠**rear**: advance, fore, front ≠**previous**: future, late

backbiting *noun* = **slander**, abuse, aspersion, bitchiness (*slang*), calumniation, calumny, cattiness (*informal*), defamation, denigration, detraction, disparagement, gossip, malice, maligning, scandalmongering, spite, spitefulness, vilification, vituperation

backbone *noun* 1 *Medical* = **spinal column**, spine, vertebrae, vertebral column 2 = **strength of character**, bottle (*Brit. slang*), character, courage, determination, firmness, fortitude, grit, hardihood, mettle, moral fibre, nerve, pluck, resolution, resolve, stamina, steadfastness, tenacity, toughness, will, willpower 3 = **foundation**, basis, mainstay, support

backbreaking *adjective* = **exhausting**, arduous, crushing, gruelling, hard, killing, laborious, punishing, strenuous, toilsome, wearing, wearying

back down *verb* = **give in**, accede, admit defeat, back-pedal, cave in (*informal*), concede, surrender, withdraw, yield

backer *noun* = **supporter**, advocate, angel (*informal*), benefactor, patron, promoter, second, sponsor, subscriber, underwriter, well-wisher

backfire *verb* = **fail**, boomerang, disappoint, flop (*informal*), miscarry, rebound, recoil

background *noun* = **history**, breeding, circumstances, credentials, culture, education, environment, experience, grounding, milieu, preparation, qualifications, tradition, upbringing

backhanded *adjective* = **ambiguous**, double-edged, equivocal, indirect, ironic, oblique, sarcastic, sardonic, two-edged, with tongue in cheek

backing *noun* = **support**, abetment, accompaniment, advocacy, aid, assistance, championing, encouragement, endorsement, espousal, funds, grant, moral support, patronage, promotion, sanction, seconding, sponsorship, subsidy

backlash *noun* = **reaction**, backfire, boomerang, counteraction, counterblast, kickback, recoil, repercussion, resentment, resistance, response, retaliation, retroaction

backlog *noun* = **build-up**, accumulation, excess, hoard, reserve, reserves, resources, stock, supply

back out *verb, often with* **of** = **withdraw**,

abandon, cancel, chicken out (*informal*), cop out (*slang*), give up, go back on, recant, renege, resign, retreat

backslide *verb* = **relapse**, fall from grace, go astray, go wrong, lapse, regress, renege, retrogress, revert, sin, slip, stray, weaken

backslider *noun* = **relapser**, apostate, deserter, recidivist, recreant, renegade, reneger, turncoat

back up *verb* = **support**, aid, assist, bolster, confirm, corroborate, reinforce, second, stand by, substantiate

backward *adjective* 1 = **slow**, behind, behindhand, braindead (*informal*), dead from the neck up (*informal*), dense, dozy (*Brit. informal*), dull, obtuse, retarded, stupid, subnormal, underdeveloped, undeveloped 2 = **shy**, bashful, diffident, hesitating, late, reluctant, sluggish, tardy, unwilling, wavering ♦ *adverb* 3 = **towards the rear**, behind, in reverse, rearward
➤ Antonyms
adjective ≠**shy**: bold, brash, eager, forward, pushy (*informal*), willing ♦ *adverb* ≠**towards the rear**: forward, frontward

backwards, backward *adverb* = **towards the rear**, behind, in reverse, rearward

backwoods *plural noun* = **sticks** (*informal*), back country (*U.S.*), backlands (*U.S.*), back of beyond, middle of nowhere, outback

bacteria *plural noun* = **microorganisms**, bacilli, bugs (*slang*), germs, microbes, pathogens, viruses

bad *adjective* 1 = **inferior**, chickenshit (*U.S. slang*), defective, deficient, duff (*Brit. informal*), erroneous, fallacious, faulty, imperfect, inadequate, incorrect, low-rent (*informal, chiefly U.S.*), of a sort or of sorts, pants (*informal*), pathetic, poor, poxy (*slang*), substandard, unsatisfactory 2 = **harmful**, damaging, dangerous, deleterious, detrimental, hurtful, injurious, ruinous, unhealthy 3 = **wicked**, base, corrupt, criminal, delinquent, evil, immoral, mean, sinful, vile, villainous, wrong 4 = **naughty**, disobedient, mischievous, unruly 5 = **rotten**, decayed, mouldy, off, putrid, rancid, sour, spoiled 6 = **severe**, disastrous, distressing, grave, harsh, painful, serious, terrible 7 = **sorry**, apologetic, conscience-stricken, contrite, guilty, regretful, remorseful, sad, upset 8 = **unfavourable**, adverse, discouraged, discouraging, distressed, distressing, gloomy, grim, low, melancholy, troubled, troubling, unfortunate, unpleasant 9 = **ill**, ailing, diseased, sick, unwell 10 **not bad** *Informal* = **O.K.** or **okay** (*informal*), all right, average, fair, fair to middling (*informal*),

moderate, passable, respectable, so-so (*informal*), tolerable
➤ Antonyms
≠**inferior**: adequate, fair, satisfactory ≠**harmful**: agreeable, beneficial, good, healthful, safe, sound, wholesome ≠**wicked**: ethical, fine, first-rate, good, moral, righteous, virtuous ≠**naughty**: biddable, docile, good, obedient, well-behaved

bad blood *noun* = **ill feeling**, acrimony, anger, animosity, antagonism, dislike, enmity, feud, hatred, ill will, malevolence, malice, rancour, resentment, seeing red

badge *noun* = **mark**, brand, device, emblem, identification, insignia, sign, stamp, token

badger *verb* = **pester**, bend someone's ear (*informal*), bully, chivvy, goad, harass, harry, hound, importune, nag, plague, torment

badinage *noun* = **wordplay**, banter, chaff, drollery, mockery, persiflage, pleasantry, raillery, repartee, teasing, waggery

badly *adverb* 1 = **poorly**, carelessly, defectively, erroneously, faultily, imperfectly, inadequately, incorrectly, ineptly, shoddily, wrong, wrongly 2 = **unfavourably**, unfortunately, unsuccessfully 3 = **severely**, acutely, deeply, desperately, exceedingly, extremely, gravely, greatly, intensely, painfully, seriously
➤ Antonyms
≠**poorly**: ably, competently, correctly, properly, rightly, satisfactorily, splendidly, well

bad manners *plural noun* = **rudeness**, boorishness, churlishness, coarseness, discourtesy, disrespect, impoliteness, incivility, inconsideration, indelicacy, unmannerliness
➤ Antonyms
civility, cordiality, courteousness, courtesy, good manners, graciousness, politeness, urbanity

baffle *verb* 1 = **puzzle**, amaze, astound, bewilder, boggle the mind, confound, confuse, daze, disconcert, dumbfound, elude, flummox, mystify, nonplus, perplex, stump, stun 2 = **frustrate**, balk, check, defeat, foil, hinder, thwart, upset
➤ Antonyms
≠**puzzle**: clarify, clear up, elucidate, explain, explicate, interpret, make plain, shed or throw light upon, spell out

bag *noun* 1 = **container**, poke (*Scot.*), receptacle, sac, sack ♦ *verb* 2 = **bulge**, balloon, droop, sag, swell 3 = **catch**, acquire, capture, gain, get, kill, land, shoot, take, trap

baggage *noun* = **luggage**, accoutrements, bags, belongings, equipment, gear, impedimenta, paraphernalia, suitcases, things

baggy *adjective* = **loose**, billowing, bulging, droopy, floppy, ill-fitting, oversize, roomy, sagging, seated, slack
➤ **Antonyms**
close, close-fitting, constricted, cramped, narrow, snug, stretched, taut, tight, tight-fitting

bail¹, bale *verb* = **scoop**, dip, drain off, ladle

bail² *noun Law* = **security**, bond, guarantee, guaranty, pledge, surety, warranty

bail out *see* BALE OUT

bait *noun* 1 = **lure**, allurement, attraction, bribe, carrot and stick, decoy, enticement, incentive, inducement, snare, temptation
♦ *verb* 2 = **tease**, aggravate (*informal*), annoy, be on one's back (*slang*), bother, gall, get in one's hair (*informal*), get one's back up, get on one's nerves (*informal*), get or take a rise out of, harass, hassle (*informal*), hound, irk, irritate, nark (*Brit., Austral., & N.Z. slang*), needle (*informal*), persecute, piss one off (*taboo slang*), provoke, put one's back up, torment, wind up (*Brit. slang*) 3 = **lure**, allure, beguile, entice, seduce, tempt

baked *adjective* = **dry**, arid, desiccated, parched, scorched, seared, sun-baked, torrid

balance *noun* 1 = **stability**, composure, equanimity, poise, self-control, self-possession, steadiness 2 = **equilibrium**, correspondence, equipoise, equity, equivalence, evenness, parity, symmetry 3 = **remainder**, difference, residue, rest, surplus ♦ *verb* 4 = **stabilize**, level, match, parallel, poise, steady 5 = **compare**, assess, consider, deliberate, estimate, evaluate, weigh 6 = **equalize**, adjust, compensate for, counteract, counterbalance, counterpoise, equate, make up for, neutralize, offset 7 *Accounting* = **calculate**, compute, settle, square, tally, total
➤ **Antonyms**
noun ≠**equilibrium**: disproportion, instability, unbalance ♦ *verb* ≠**stabilize**: outweigh, overbalance, upset

balanced *adjective* = **unbiased**, disinterested, equitable, even-handed, fair, impartial, just, unprejudiced
➤ **Antonyms**
biased, distorted, jaundiced, lopsided, one-sided, partial, predisposed, prejudiced, slanted, unfair, warped, weighted

balance sheet *noun* = **statement**, account, budget, credits and debits, ledger, report

balcony *noun* 1 = **terrace**, veranda 2 = **upper circle**, gallery, gods

bald *adjective* 1 = **hairless**, baldheaded, baldpated, depilated, glabrous (*Biology*) 2 = **barren**, bleak, exposed, naked, stark, treeless, uncovered 3 = **plain**, bare, blunt, direct, downright, forthright, outright, severe, simple, straight, straightforward, unadorned, unvarnished, upfront (*informal*)

balderdash *noun* = **nonsense**, balls (*taboo slang*), bilge (*informal*), bosh (*informal*), bull (*slang*), bullshit (*taboo slang*), bunk (*informal*), bunkum or buncombe (*chiefly U.S.*), claptrap (*informal*), cobblers (*Brit. taboo slang*), crap (*slang*), drivel, eyewash (*informal*), garbage (*informal*), gibberish, guff (*slang*), hogwash, hokum (*slang, chiefly U.S. & Canad.*), horsefeathers (*U.S. slang*), hot air (*informal*), kak (*S. Afr. slang*), moonshine, pap, piffle (*informal*), poppycock (*informal*), rot, rubbish, shit (*taboo slang*), tommyrot, tosh (*slang, chiefly Brit.*), trash, tripe (*informal*), twaddle, waffle

baldness *noun* 1 = **hairlessness**, alopecia (*Pathology*), baldheadedness, baldpatedness, glabrousness (*Biology*) 2 = **barrenness**, bleakness, nakedness, sparseness, starkness, treelessness 3 = **plainness**, austerity, bluntness, severity, simplicity

bale *see* BAIL¹

baleful *adjective* = **menacing**, calamitous, deadly, evil, harmful, hurtful, injurious, maleficent, malevolent, malignant, mournful, noxious, ominous, pernicious, ruinous, sinister, venomous, vindictive, woeful
➤ **Antonyms**
beneficial, benevolent, benign, friendly, good, healthy, salubrious

bale out, bail out *verb* 1 *Informal* = **help**, aid, relieve, rescue, save (someone's) bacon (*informal, chiefly Brit.*) 2 = **escape**, quit, retreat, withdraw

balk, baulk *verb* 1 = **recoil**, demur, dodge, evade, flinch, hesitate, jib, refuse, resist, shirk, shrink from 2 = **foil**, baffle, bar, check, counteract, defeat, disconcert, forestall, frustrate, hinder, obstruct, prevent, thwart
➤ **Antonyms**
≠**recoil**: accede, accept, acquiesce, comply, relent, submit, yield ≠**foil**: abet, advance, aid, assist, further, help, promote, support, sustain

ball *noun* 1 = **sphere**, drop, globe, globule,

orb, pellet, spheroid **2 = shot,**
ammunition, bullet, grapeshot, pellet, slug

ballast *noun* **= counterbalance,** balance,
counterweight, equilibrium, sandbag,
stability, stabilizer, weight

balloon *verb* **= swell,** belly, billow, bloat,
blow up, dilate, distend, enlarge, expand,
grow rapidly, inflate, puff out

ballot *noun* **= vote,** election, poll, polling,
voting

ballyhoo *noun Informal* **1 = fuss,** babble,
commotion, hubbub, hue and cry,
hullabaloo, noise, racket, to-do **2
= publicity,** advertising, build-up, hype,
PR, promotion, propaganda

balm *noun* **1 = ointment,** balsam, cream,
embrocation, emollient, lotion, salve,
unguent **2 = comfort,** anodyne,
consolation, curative, palliative,
restorative, solace

balmy *adjective* **1 = mild,** clement,
pleasant, summery, temperate **2** *see* BARMY
➤ **Antonyms**
annoying, discomforting, harsh,
inclement, intense, irksome, rough, stormy

bamboozle *verb Informal* **1 = cheat,** con
(*informal*), deceive, defraud, delude, dupe,
fool, hoax, hoodwink, pull a fast one on
(*informal*), skin (*slang*), swindle, trick **2
= puzzle,** baffle, befuddle, confound,
confuse, mystify, perplex, stump

ban *verb* **1 = prohibit,** banish, bar, black,
blackball, block, boycott, debar, disallow,
disqualify, exclude, forbid, interdict,
outlaw, proscribe, restrict, suppress ♦ *noun*
2 = prohibition, block, boycott,
censorship, disqualification, embargo,
interdict, interdiction, proscription,
restriction, stoppage, suppression, taboo
➤ **Antonyms**
verb ≠**prohibit:** allow, approve, authorize,
enable, let, permit, sanction ♦ *noun*
≠**prohibition:** allowance, approval,
permission, sanction

banal *adjective* **= unoriginal,** clichéd,
cliché-ridden, commonplace, everyday,
hackneyed, humdrum, mundane, old hat,
ordinary, pedestrian, platitudinous, stale,
stereotyped, stock, threadbare, tired, trite,
unimaginative, vanilla (*slang*), vapid
➤ **Antonyms**
challenging, distinctive, fresh,
ground-breaking, imaginative, interesting,
new, novel, original, stimulating, unique,
unusual

banality *noun* **= unoriginality,** bromide
(*informal*), cliché, commonplace,
platitude, triteness, trite phrase, triviality,
truism, vapidity

band¹ *noun* **1 = ensemble,** combo, group,
orchestra **2 = gang,** assembly, association,
bevy, body, camp, clique, club, company,
coterie, crew (*informal*), group, horde,
party, posse (*informal*), society, troop
♦ *verb* **3 = unite,** affiliate, ally, consolidate,
federate, gather, group, join, merge
➤ **Antonyms**
verb ≠**unite:** cleave, disperse, disunite,
divide, part, segregate, separate, split,
sunder

band² *noun* **= strip,** bandage, belt, binding,
bond, chain, cord, fetter, fillet, ligature,
manacle, ribbon, shackle, strap, tie

bandage *noun* **1 = dressing,** compress,
gauze, plaster ♦ *verb* **2 = dress,** bind,
cover, swathe

bandit *noun* **= robber,** brigand, crook,
desperado, footpad, freebooter, gangster,
gunman, highwayman, hijacker,
marauder, outlaw, pirate, racketeer, thief

bandy *adjective* **1 = bow-legged,**
bandy-legged, bent, bowed, crooked,
curved ♦ *verb* **2 = exchange,** barter,
interchange, pass, shuffle, swap, throw,
toss, trade

bane *noun* **= plague,** affliction, bête noire,
blight, burden, calamity, curse, despair,
destruction, disaster, downfall, misery,
nuisance, pest, ruin, scourge, torment,
trial, trouble, woe
➤ **Antonyms**
blessing, comfort, consolation, joy,
pleasure, relief, solace, support

baneful *adjective* **= harmful,** baleful,
calamitous, deadly, deleterious,
destructive, disastrous, fatal, hurtful,
injurious, maleficent, noxious, pernicious,
pestilential, ruinous, venomous

bang *noun* **1 = explosion,** boom, burst,
clang, clap, clash, detonation, peal, pop,
report, shot, slam, thud, thump **2 = blow,**
belt (*informal*), box, bump, cuff, hit,
knock, punch, smack, stroke, wallop
(*informal*), whack ♦ *verb* **3 = hit,** bash
(*informal*), beat, belt (*informal*), bump,
clatter, crash, hammer, knock, pound,
pummel, rap, slam, strike, thump, tonk
(*informal*) **4 = explode,** boom, burst,
clang, detonate, drum, echo, peal,
resound, thump, thunder ♦ *adverb* **5
= hard,** abruptly, headlong, noisily,
suddenly **6 = straight,** precisely, slap,
smack

banish *verb* **1 = expel,** deport, drive away,
eject, evict, exclude, excommunicate,
exile, expatriate, ostracize, outlaw, shut
out, transport **2 = get rid of,** ban, cast out,
discard, dislodge, dismiss, dispel,
eliminate, eradicate, oust, remove, shake

> **Antonyms**
≠**expel:** accept, admit, embrace, hail, invite, offer hospitality to, receive, welcome

banishment noun = **expulsion**, deportation, exile, expatriation, proscription, transportation

banisters plural noun = **railing**, balusters, balustrade, handrail, rail

bank¹ noun 1 = **storehouse**, depository, repository 2 = **store**, accumulation, fund, hoard, reserve, reservoir, savings, stock, stockpile ◆ verb 3 = **save**, deposit, keep 4 = **deal with**, transact business with

bank² noun 1 = **mound**, banking, embankment, heap, mass, pile, ridge 2 = **side**, brink, edge, margin, shore ◆ verb 3 = **pile**, amass, heap, mass, mound, stack 4 = **tilt**, camber, cant, heel, incline, pitch, slant, slope, tip

bank³ noun = **row**, arrangement, array, file, group, line, rank, sequence, series, succession, tier, train

bank on verb = **rely on**, assume, believe in, count on, depend on, lean on, look to, trust

bankrupt adjective = **insolvent**, beggared, broke (informal), depleted, destitute, exhausted, failed, impoverished, in queer street, in the red, lacking, on one's uppers, on the rocks, ruined, spent, wiped out (informal)
> **Antonyms**
in the money (informal), on the up and up, prosperous, solvent, sound, wealthy

bankruptcy noun = **insolvency**, crash, disaster, exhaustion, failure, indebtedness, lack, liquidation, ruin

banner noun = **flag**, banderole, burgee, colours, ensign, fanion, gonfalon, pennant, pennon, placard, standard, streamer

banquet noun = **feast**, dinner, meal, repast, revel, treat

banter verb 1 = **joke**, chaff, deride, jeer, jest, josh (slang, chiefly U.S. & Canad.), kid (informal), make fun of, rib (informal), ridicule, take the mickey (informal), taunt, tease, twit ◆ noun 2 = **joking**, badinage, chaff, chaffing, derision, jeering, jesting, kidding (informal), mockery, persiflage, pleasantry, raillery, repartee, ribbing (informal), ridicule, teasing, wordplay

baptism noun 1 Christianity = **christening**, immersion, purification, sprinkling 2 = **initiation**, beginning, debut, dedication, introduction, launching, rite of passage

baptize verb 1 Christianity = **purify**, besprinkle, cleanse, immerse 2 = **initiate**,

admit, enrol, recruit 3 = **name**, call, christen, dub, title

bar noun 1 = **rod**, batten, crosspiece, paling, palisade, pole, rail, shaft, stake, stick 2 = **obstacle**, barricade, barrier, block, deterrent, hindrance, impediment, interdict, obstruction, rail, railing, stop 3 = **public house**, boozer (Brit., Austral. & N.Z. informal), canteen, counter, hostelry (archaic or facetious), inn, lounge, pub (informal, chiefly Brit.), saloon, taproom, tavern, watering hole (facetious slang) 4 = **dock**, bench, court, courtroom, law court ◆ verb 5 = **fasten**, barricade, bolt, latch, lock, secure 6 = **obstruct**, hinder, prevent, restrain 7 = **exclude**, ban, black, blackball, forbid, keep out, prohibit
> **Antonyms**
noun ≠**obstacle:** aid, benefit, help ◆ verb ≠**exclude:** accept, admit, allow, let, permit, receive

Bar noun **the Bar** Law = **barristers**, body of lawyers, counsel, court, judgment, tribunal

barb noun 1 = **dig**, affront, cut, gibe, insult, rebuff, sarcasm, scoff, sneer 2 = **point**, bristle, prickle, prong, quill, spike, spur, thorn

barbarian noun 1 = **savage**, brute, yahoo 2 = **lout**, bigot, boor, hooligan, ignoramus, illiterate, lowbrow, ned (slang), philistine, ruffian, vandal ◆ adjective 3 = **uncivilized**, boorish, crude, lowbrow, philistine, primitive, rough, uncouth, uncultivated, uncultured, unsophisticated, vulgar, wild
> **Antonyms**
adjective ≠**uncivilized:** civil, civilized, cultured, genteel, highbrow, refined, sophisticated, urbane, well-mannered

barbaric adjective 1 = **uncivilized**, primitive, rude, wild 2 = **brutal**, barbarous, boorish, coarse, crude, cruel, fierce, inhuman, savage, uncouth, vulgar
> **Antonyms**
civilized, cultivated, cultured, gentlemanly, gracious, humane, refined, sophisticated, urbane

barbarism noun 1 = **atrocity**, barbarity, enormity, outrage 2 = **savagery**, coarseness, crudity, uncivilizedness 3 = **misuse**, corruption, misusage, solecism, vulgarism

barbarity noun = **viciousness**, brutality, cruelty, inhumanity, ruthlessness, savagery

barbarous adjective 1 = **uncivilized**, barbarian, brutish, primitive, rough, rude, savage, uncouth, wild 2 = **brutal**, barbaric, cruel, ferocious, heartless, inhuman, monstrous, ruthless, vicious 3 = **ignorant**, coarse, crude, uncultured, unlettered, unrefined, vulgar

barbed *adjective* **1** = **cutting**, critical, hostile, hurtful, nasty, pointed, scathing, unkind **2** = **spiked**, hooked, jagged, prickly, spiny, thorny

bare *adjective* **1** = **naked**, buck naked (*slang*), denuded, exposed, in the bare scud (*slang*), in the raw (*informal*), naked as the day one was born (*informal*), nude, peeled, scuddy (*slang*), shorn, stripped, unclad, unclothed, uncovered, undressed, without a stitch on (*informal*) **2** = **empty**, barren, lacking, mean, open, poor, scanty, scarce, unfurnished, vacant, void, wanting **3** = **plain**, bald, basic, cold, essential, hard, literal, sheer, simple, stark, unembellished **4** = **simple**, austere, basic, severe, spare, spartan, unadorned, unembellished, unfussy, unvarnished
➤ **Antonyms**
≠**naked**: attired, clad, clothed, concealed, covered, dressed, hidden ≠**empty**: abundant, full, plentiful, profuse, well-stocked ≠**simple**: adorned

barefaced *adjective* **1** = **obvious**, bald, blatant, flagrant, glaring, manifest, naked, open, palpable, patent, transparent, unconcealed **2** = **shameless**, audacious, bold, brash, brazen, impudent, insolent
➤ **Antonyms**
≠**obvious**: concealed, covered, hidden, inconspicuous, masked, obscured, secret, tucked away, unseen

barely *adverb* = **only just**, almost, at a push, by the skin of one's teeth, hardly, just, scarcely
➤ **Antonyms**
amply, completely, fully, profusely

bargain *noun* **1** = **agreement**, arrangement, business, compact, contract, convention, engagement, negotiation, pact, pledge, promise, stipulation, transaction, treaty, understanding **2** = **good buy**, (cheap) purchase, discount, giveaway, good value, good value, reduction, snip (*informal*), steal (*informal*)
♦ *verb* **3** = **negotiate**, agree, contract, covenant, cut a deal, promise, stipulate, transact **4** = **haggle**, barter, buy, deal, sell, trade, traffic

bargain for *verb* = **anticipate**, contemplate, expect, foresee, imagine, look for, plan for

bargain on *verb* = **depend on**, assume, bank on, count on, plan on, rely on

barge *noun* = **canal boat**, flatboat, lighter, narrow boat, scow

barge in *verb Informal* = **interrupt**, break in, burst in, butt in, infringe, intrude, muscle in (*informal*)

barge into *verb Informal* = **bump into**, cannon into, collide with, hit, push, shove

bark¹ *noun, verb* **1** = **yap**, bay, growl, howl, snarl, woof, yelp ♦ *verb* **2** = **shout**, bawl, bawl at, berate, bluster, growl, snap, snarl, yell

bark² *noun* **1** = **covering**, casing, cortex (*Anatomy, botany*), crust, husk, rind, skin ♦ *verb* **2** = **scrape**, abrade, flay, rub, shave, skin, strip

barmy *adjective Also* **balmy** *Slang* = **insane**, crackpot (*informal*), crazy, daft (*informal*), dippy, doolally, dumb-ass (*slang*) (*slang*), foolish, gonzo (*slang*), goofy (*informal*), idiotic, loony (*slang*), loopy (*informal*), nuts (*slang*), nutty (*slang*), odd, off one's rocker (*slang*), off one's trolley (*slang*), out of one's mind, out to lunch (*informal*), round the twist (*Brit. slang*), silly, stupid, up the pole (*informal*), wacko *or* whacko (*informal*)
➤ **Antonyms**
all there (*informal*), in one's right mind, of sound mind, rational, reasonable, sane, sensible

baroque *adjective* = **ornate**, bizarre, convoluted, elaborate, extravagant, flamboyant, florid, grotesque, overdecorated, rococo

barracks *plural noun* = **camp**, billet, cantonment, casern, encampment, garrison, quarters

barrage *noun* **1** = **torrent**, assault, attack, burst, deluge, hail, mass, onslaught, plethora, profusion, rain, storm, stream **2** *Military* = **bombardment**, battery, cannonade, curtain of fire, fusillade, gunfire, salvo, shelling, volley

barred *adjective* **1** = **striped**, banded, crosshatched, lined, marked, ribbed, ridged, streaked, veined **2** = **excluded**, banned, forbidden, off limits, outlawed, prohibited, proscribed, taboo

barren *adjective* **1** = **infertile**, childless, infecund, sterile, unprolific **2** = **unproductive**, arid, desert, desolate, dry, empty, unfruitful, waste **3** = **unprofitable**, fruitless, unsuccessful, useless **4** = **dull**, boring, flat, lacklustre, stale, uninformative, uninspiring, uninstructive, uninteresting, unrewarding, vapid
➤ **Antonyms**
≠**unproductive**: fecund, fertile, fruitful, lush, productive, profitable, rich, useful ≠**unprofitable**: productive, profitable, useful ≠**dull**: instructive, interesting

barricade *noun* **1** = **barrier**, blockade, bulwark, fence, obstruction, palisade, rampart, stockade ♦ *verb* **2** = **bar**, block, blockade, defend, fortify, obstruct, protect, shut in

barrier noun 1 = **barricade**, bar, block, blockade, boundary, ditch, fence, fortification, obstacle, obstruction, pale, railing, rampart, stop, wall 2 = **hindrance**, check, difficulty, drawback, handicap, hazard, hurdle, impediment, limitation, obstacle, restriction, stumbling block

barter verb = **trade**, bargain, drive a hard bargain, exchange, haggle, sell, swap, traffic

base¹ noun 1 = **bottom**, bed, foot, foundation, groundwork, pedestal, rest, stand, support 2 = **basis**, core, essence, essential, fundamental, heart, key, origin, principle, root, source 3 = **centre**, camp, headquarters, home, post, settlement, starting point, station ♦ verb 4 = **found**, build, construct, depend, derive, establish, ground, hinge 5 = **place**, locate, post, station
➤ **Antonyms**
noun ≠**bottom**: apex, crest, crown, peak, summit, top, vertex

base² adjective 1 = **dishonourable**, abject, contemptible, corrupt, depraved, despicable, disreputable, evil, ignoble, immoral, infamous, scandalous, shameful, sordid, vile, villainous, vulgar, wicked 2 = **inferior**, downtrodden, grovelling, low, lowly, mean, menial, miserable, paltry, pitiful, poor, servile, slavish, sorry, subservient, worthless, wretched 3 = **counterfeit**, adulterated, alloyed, debased, fake, forged, fraudulent, impure, pinchbeck, spurious
➤ **Antonyms**
≠**dishonourable**: admirable, good, honest, honourable, just, moral, noble, pure, rare, righteous, upright, valuable, virtuous ≠**inferior**: lofty, noble ≠**counterfeit**: pure, unalloyed

baseless adjective = **unfounded**, groundless, unconfirmed, uncorroborated, ungrounded, unjustifiable, unjustified, unsubstantiated, unsupported
➤ **Antonyms**
authenticated, confirmed, corroborated, proven, substantiated, supported, validated, verified, well-founded

baseness noun 1 = **depravity**, contemptibility, degradation, depravation, despicability, disgrace, ignominy, infamy, notoriety, obloquy, turpitude 2 = **inferiority**, lowliness, meanness, misery, poverty, servility, slavishness, subservience, worthlessness, wretchedness

bash verb 1 Informal = **hit**, belt (informal), biff (slang), break, chin (slang), crash, crush, deck, lay one on (slang), punch, slosh (Brit. slang), smash, sock

(slang), strike, tonk (informal), wallop (informal) ♦ noun 2 Informal = **attempt**, crack (informal), go (informal), shot (informal), stab (informal), try

bashful adjective = **shy**, abashed, blushing, confused, constrained, coy, diffident, easily embarrassed, nervous, overmodest, reserved, reticent, retiring, self-conscious, self-effacing, shamefaced, sheepish, shrinking, timid, timorous
➤ **Antonyms**
aggressive, arrogant, bold, brash, conceited, confident, egoistic, fearless, forward, immodest, impudent, intrepid, pushy (informal), self-assured

bashfulness noun = **shyness**, constraint, coyness, diffidence, embarrassment, hesitation, modesty, reserve, self-consciousness, sheepishness, timidity, timorousness

basic adjective = **essential**, bog-standard (informal), central, elementary, fundamental, immanent, indispensable, inherent, intrinsic, key, necessary, primary, radical, underlying, vital
➤ **Antonyms**
complementary, minor, peripheral, secondary, supplementary, supporting, trivial, unessential

basically adverb = **essentially**, at bottom, at heart, au fond, firstly, fundamentally, inherently, in substance, intrinsically, mostly, primarily, radically

basics plural noun = **essentials**, brass tacks (informal), core, facts, fundamentals, hard facts, necessaries, nitty-gritty (informal), nuts and bolts (informal), practicalities, principles, rudiments

basis noun 1 = **foundation**, base, bottom, footing, ground, groundwork, support 2 = **principle**, chief ingredient, core, essential, fundamental, heart, premise, principal element, theory

bask verb 1 = **lie in**, laze, loll, lounge, relax, sunbathe, swim in, toast oneself, warm oneself 2 = **enjoy**, delight in, indulge oneself, luxuriate, relish, revel, savour, take pleasure, wallow

bass adjective = **deep**, deep-toned, grave, low, low-pitched, resonant, sonorous

bastard noun 1 Informal, offensive = **rogue**, blackguard, caitiff (archaic), criminal, evildoer, knave (archaic), libertine, malefactor, miscreant, profligate, rapscallion, reprobate, scoundrel, villain, wretch 2 = **illegitimate child**, by-blow (archaic), love child, natural child, whoreson (archaic) ♦ adjective 3 = **illegitimate**, baseborn, misbegotten 4 = **false**, adulterated, counterfeit, illegitimate, imperfect, impure, inferior, irregular, sham, spurious

bastion noun = **stronghold**, bulwark, citadel, defence, fastness, fortress, mainstay, prop, rock, support, tower of strength

bat noun, verb = **hit**, bang, punch, rap, smack, strike, swat, thump, wallop (informal), whack

batch noun = **group**, accumulation, aggregation, amount, assemblage, bunch, collection, crowd, lot, pack, quantity, set

bath noun 1 = **wash**, ablution, cleansing, douche, douse, scrubbing, shower, soak, soaping, sponging, tub, washing ◆ verb 2 = **wash**, bathe, clean, douse, lave (archaic), scrub down, shower, soak, soap, sponge, tub

bathe verb 1 = **swim** 2 = **wash**, cleanse, rinse 3 = **cover**, flood, immerse, steep, suffuse ◆ noun 4 Brit. = **swim**, dip, dook (Scot.)

bathing costume noun = **swimming costume**, bathing suit, bikini, swimsuit, trunks

bathos noun = **anticlimax**, false pathos, letdown, mawkishness, sentimentality

baton noun = **stick**, club, crook, mace, rod, sceptre, staff, truncheon, wand

battalion noun = **army**, brigade, company, contingent, division, force, horde, host, legion, multitude, regiment, squadron, team, throng, troop

batten[1] verb, usually with **down** = **fasten**, board up, clamp down, cover up, fasten down, fix, nail down, secure, tighten

batten[2] verb, usually with **on** = **thrive**, fatten, flourish, gain, grow, increase, prosper

batter verb 1 = **beat**, assault, bash (informal), beat the living daylights out of, belabour, break, buffet, clobber (slang), dash against, lambast(e), lash, pelt, pound, pummel, smash, smite, thrash, wallop (informal) 2 = **damage**, bruise, crush, deface, demolish, destroy, disfigure, hurt, injure, mangle, mar, maul, ruin, shatter, shiver, total (slang), trash (slang)

battered adjective 1 = **beaten**, beat-up (informal), black-and-blue, bruised, crushed, injured, squashed 2 = **damaged**, beat-up (informal), broken-down, dilapidated, ramshackle

battery noun 1 = **series**, chain, ring, sequence, set, suite 2 Criminal law = **beating**, assault, attack, mayhem, onslaught, physical violence, thumping 3 = **artillery**, cannon, cannonry, gun emplacements, guns

battle noun 1 = **fight**, action, attack, combat, encounter, engagement, fray, hostilities, skirmish, war, warfare 2 = **conflict**, agitation, campaign, clash, contest, controversy, crusade, debate, disagreement, dispute, head-to-head, strife, struggle ◆ verb 3 = **struggle**, agitate, argue, clamour, combat, contend, contest, dispute, feud, fight, lock horns, strive, war
➤ **Antonyms**
noun ≠**fight, conflict**: accord, agreement, armistice, ceasefire, concord, entente, peace, suspension of hostilities, truce

battle-axe noun = **harridan**, ballbreaker (slang), disciplinarian, fury, scold, shrew, tartar, termagant, virago, vixen

battle cry noun 1 = **slogan**, catchword, motto, watchword 2 = **war cry**, war whoop

battlefield noun = **battleground**, combat zone, field, field of battle, front

battlement noun = **rampart**, barbican, bartizan, bastion, breastwork, bulwark, crenellation, fortification, parapet

battleship noun = **warship**, capital ship, gunboat, man-of-war, ship of the line

batty adjective = **crazy**, as daft as a brush (informal, chiefly Brit.), barking (slang), barking mad (slang), barmy (slang), bats (slang), bonkers (slang, chiefly Brit.), cracked (slang), crackers (Brit. slang), crackpot (informal), cranky (informal), daft (informal), doolally (slang), dotty (slang, chiefly Brit.), eccentric, gonzo (slang), insane, loony (slang), loopy (informal), lunatic, mad, not the full shilling (informal), nuts (slang), nutty (slang), odd, oddball (informal), off one's rocker (slang), off one's trolley (slang), off the rails, off-the-wall (slang), out of one's mind, outré, out to lunch (informal), peculiar, potty (Brit. informal), queer (informal), round the twist (Brit. slang), screwy (informal), touched, up the pole (informal), wacko or whacko (slang)

bauble noun = **trinket**, bagatelle, gewgaw, gimcrack, kickshaw, knick-knack, plaything, toy, trifle

baulk see BALK

bawd noun = **madam**, brothel-keeper, pimp, procuress, prostitute, whore, working girl (facetious slang)

bawdy adjective = **rude**, blue, coarse, dirty, erotic, gross, indecent, indecorous, indelicate, lascivious, lecherous, lewd, libidinous, licentious, lustful, near the knuckle (informal), obscene, prurient, ribald, risqué, salacious, smutty, steamy (informal), suggestive, vulgar, X-rated (informal)
➤ **Antonyms**

chaste, clean, decent, good, modest, moral, respectable, seemly, undefiled, upright, virtuous

bawl verb 1 = **cry**, blubber, sob, squall, wail, weep 2 = **shout**, bellow, call, clamour, halloo, howl, roar, vociferate, yell

bay[1] noun = **inlet**, bight, cove, gulf, natural harbour, sound

bay[2] noun = **recess**, alcove, compartment, embrasure, niche, nook, opening

bay[3] verb, noun 1 = **howl**, bark, bell, clamour, cry, growl, yelp ♦ noun 2 **at bay** = **cornered**, caught, trapped

bayonet verb = **stab**, impale, knife, run through, spear, stick, transfix

bays plural noun = **garland**, chaplet, glory, laurel crown, praise, prize, renown, trophy, wreath

bazaar noun 1 = **fair**, bring-and-buy, fête, sale of work 2 = **market**, exchange, marketplace, mart

be verb 1 = **exist**, be alive, breathe, inhabit, live 2 = **take place**, befall, come about, come to pass, happen, occur, transpire (informal) 3 = **remain**, abide, continue, endure, last, obtain, persist, prevail, stand, stay, survive

beach noun = **shore**, coast, lido, littoral, margin, plage, sands, seaboard (chiefly U.S.), seashore, seaside, shingle, strand, water's edge

beachcomber noun = **scavenger**, forager, loafer, scrounger, tramp, vagabond, vagrant, wanderer

beached adjective = **stranded**, abandoned, aground, ashore, deserted, grounded, high and dry, marooned, wrecked

beacon noun = **signal**, beam, bonfire, flare, lighthouse, pharos, rocket, sign, signal fire, smoke signal, watchtower

bead noun = **drop**, blob, bubble, dot, droplet, globule, pellet, pill, spherule

beads plural noun = **necklace**, chaplet, choker, necklet, pearls, pendant

beady adjective = **bright**, gleaming, glinting, glittering, sharp, shining

beak noun 1 = **bill**, mandible, neb (archaic or dialect), nib 2 Slang = **nose**, proboscis, snout

beam noun 1 = **smile**, grin 2 = **ray**, bar, emission, gleam, glimmer, glint, glow, radiation, shaft, streak, stream 3 = **rafter**, girder, joist, plank, spar, support, timber ♦ verb 4 = **smile**, grin 5 = **radiate**, emit, glare, gleam, glitter, glow, shine 6 = **send out**, broadcast, emit, transmit

beaming adjective 1 = **smiling**, cheerful, grinning, happy, joyful, sunny 2

= **radiating**, beautiful, bright, brilliant, flashing, gleaming, glistening, glittering, radiant, scintillating, shining, sparkling

bear verb 1 = **support**, cherish, entertain, exhibit, harbour, have, hold, maintain, possess, shoulder, sustain, uphold, weigh upon 2 = **carry**, bring, convey, hump (Brit. slang), move, take, tote (informal), transport 3 = **produce**, beget, breed, bring forth, develop, engender, generate, give birth to, yield 4 = **tolerate**, abide, admit, allow, brook, endure, hack (slang), permit, put up with (informal), stomach, suffer, undergo
➤ Antonyms
≠**support**: abandon, cease, desert, discontinue, drop, give up, leave, quit, relinquish ≠**carry**: drop, put down, shed

bearable adjective = **tolerable**, admissible, endurable, manageable, passable, sufferable, supportable, sustainable
➤ Antonyms
insufferable, insupportable, intolerable, oppressive, too much (informal), unacceptable, unbearable, unendurable

beard noun 1 = **whiskers**, bristles, five-o'clock shadow, stubble ♦ verb 2 = **confront**, brave, dare, defy, face, oppose, tackle

bearded adjective = **unshaven**, bewhiskered, bristly, bushy, hairy, hirsute, shaggy, stubbly, whiskered

beardless adjective = **clean-shaven**, barefaced, hairless, smooth, smooth-faced

bear down verb 1 = **press down**, burden, compress, encumber, push, strain, weigh down 2 = **approach**, advance on, attack, close in, converge on, move in

bearer noun 1 = **carrier**, agent, conveyor, messenger, porter, runner, servant 2 = **payee**, beneficiary, consignee

bearing noun 1 usually with **on** or **upon** = **relevance**, application, connection, import, pertinence, reference, relation, significance 2 = **manner**, air, aspect, attitude, behaviour, carriage, demeanour, deportment, mien, posture 3 Nautical = **position**, course, direction, point of compass
➤ Antonyms
≠**relevance**: inappositeness, inappropriateness, inaptness, inconsequence, irrelevance, irrelevancy, non sequitur

bearings plural noun = **position**, aim, course, direction, location, orientation, situation, track, way, whereabouts

bear on verb = **be relevant to**, affect, appertain to, belong to, concern, involve, pertain to, refer to, relate to, touch upon

bear out *verb* = **support**, confirm, corroborate, endorse, justify, prove, substantiate, uphold, vindicate

bear up *verb* = **cope**, bear the brunt, carry on, endure, go through the mill, grin and bear it (*informal*), keep one's chin up, persevere, suffer, take it on the chin (*informal*), withstand

bear with *verb* = **be patient with**, make allowances for, put up with (*informal*), suffer, tolerate, wait for

beast *noun* 1 = **animal**, brute, creature 2 = **brute**, barbarian, fiend, ghoul, monster, ogre, sadist, savage, swine

beastly *adjective* 1 *Informal* = **brutal**, animal, barbarous, bestial, brutish, coarse, cruel, depraved, inhuman, monstrous, repulsive, sadistic, savage 2 = **unpleasant**, awful, disagreeable, foul, horrid, mean, nasty, rotten, shitty (*taboo slang*), terrible
➤ **Antonyms**
≠**brutal**: humane, sensitive ≠**unpleasant**: agreeable, fine, good, pleasant

beat *verb* 1 = **hit**, bang, batter, belt (*informal*), break, bruise, buffet, cane, chin (*slang*), clobber (*slang*), cudgel, deck (*slang*), drub, flog, knock, lambast(e), lash, lay one on (*slang*), lick (*informal*), maul, pelt, pound, punch, strike, thrash, thwack, tonk (*informal*), whip 2 = **flap**, flutter 3 = **throb**, palpitate, pound, pulsate, pulse, quake, quiver, shake, thump, tremble, vibrate 4 = **shape**, fashion, forge, form, hammer, model, work 5 = **defeat**, best, blow out of the water (*slang*), bring to their knees, clobber (*slang*), conquer, excel, knock spots off (*informal*), lick (*informal*), make mincemeat of (*informal*), master, outdo, outrun, outstrip, overcome, overwhelm, pip at the post, put in the shade (*informal*), run rings around (*informal*), stuff (*slang*), subdue, surpass, tank (*slang*), undo, vanquish, wipe the floor with (*informal*) 6 **beat it** *Slang* = **go away**, bugger off (*taboo slang*), depart, exit, fuck off (*offensive taboo slang*), get lost (*informal*), get on one's bike (*Brit. slang*), go to hell (*informal*), hook it (*slang*), hop it (*slang*), leave, make tracks, pack one's bags (*informal*), piss off (*taboo slang*), scarper (*Brit. slang*), scram (*informal*), shoo, skedaddle (*informal*), sling one's hook (*Brit. slang*), vamoose (*slang, chiefly U.S.*) ♦ *noun* 7 = **blow**, belt (*informal*), hit, lash, punch, shake, slap, strike, swing, thump 8 = **throb**, palpitation, pulsation, pulse 9 = **route**, circuit, course, path, rounds, way 10 = **rhythm**, accent, cadence, ictus, measure (*Prosody*), metre, stress, time ♦ *adjective* 11

Slang = **exhausted**, clapped out (*Austral. & N.Z. informal*), fatigued, on one's last legs, shagged out (*Brit. slang*), tired, wearied, wiped out (*informal*), worn out, zonked (*slang*)

beaten *adjective* 1 = **stirred**, blended, foamy, frothy, mixed, whipped, whisked 2 = **shaped**, forged, formed, hammered, stamped, worked 3 = **defeated**, baffled, cowed, disappointed, disheartened, frustrated, overcome, overwhelmed, thwarted, vanquished 4 = **well-trodden**, much travelled, trampled, trodden, well-used, worn

beating *noun* 1 = **thrashing**, belting (*informal*), caning, chastisement, corporal punishment, flogging, pasting (*slang*), slapping, smacking, whipping 2 = **defeat**, conquest, downfall, overthrow, pasting (*slang*), rout, ruin

beatitude *noun* = **blessedness**, beatification, bliss, ecstasy, exaltation, felicity, happiness, holy joy, saintliness

beat up *verb* *Informal* = **assault**, attack, batter, beat the living daylights out of (*informal*), clobber (*slang*), do over (*Brit., Austral. & N.Z. slang*), duff up (*Brit. slang*), fill in (*Brit. slang*), knock about *or* around, lambast(e), put the boot in (*slang*), thrash, work over (*slang*)

beau *noun* 1 *Chiefly U.S.* = **boyfriend**, admirer, escort, fancy man (*slang*), fiancé, guy (*informal*), leman (*archaic*), lover, suitor, swain, sweetheart 2 = **dandy**, cavalier, coxcomb, fop, gallant, ladies' man, popinjay, swell (*informal*)

beautiful *adjective* = **attractive**, alluring, appealing, charming, comely, delightful, drop-dead (*slang*), exquisite, fair, fine, glamorous, good-looking, gorgeous, graceful, handsome, lovely, pleasing, radiant, ravishing, stunning (*informal*)
➤ **Antonyms**
awful, bad, hideous, repulsive, terrible, ugly, unattractive, unpleasant, unsightly

beautify *verb* = **make beautiful**, adorn, array, bedeck, deck, decorate, embellish, enhance, festoon, garnish, gild, glamorize, grace, ornament

beauty *noun* 1 = **attractiveness**, allure, bloom, charm, comeliness, elegance, exquisiteness, fairness, glamour, grace, handsomeness, loveliness, pulchritude, seemliness, symmetry 2 = **belle**, charmer, cracker (*slang*), goddess, good-looker, humdinger (*slang*), lovely (*slang*), stunner (*informal*), Venus 3 *Informal* = **advantage**, asset, attraction, benefit, blessing, boon, excellence, feature, good thing
➤ **Antonyms**

≠**attractiveness:** repulsiveness, ugliness, unpleasantness, unseemliness
≠**advantage:** detraction, disadvantage, flaw

beaver away *verb* = **work**, exert oneself, graft (*informal*), hammer away, keep one's nose to the grindstone, peg away, persevere, persist, plug away (*informal*), slog

becalmed *adjective* = **still**, motionless, settled, stranded, stuck

because *conjunction* = **since**, as, by reason of, in that, on account of, owing to, thanks to

beckon *verb* 1 = **gesture**, bid, gesticulate, motion, nod, signal, summon, wave at 2 = **lure**, allure, attract, call, coax, draw, entice, invite, pull, tempt

become *verb* 1 = **come to be**, alter to, be transformed into, change into, develop into, evolve into, grow into, mature into, metamorphose into, ripen into 2 = **suit**, embellish, enhance, fit, flatter, grace, harmonize, ornament, set off

becoming *adjective* 1 = **appropriate**, befitting, *comme il faut*, compatible, congruous, decent, decorous, fit, fitting, in keeping, meet (*archaic*), proper, seemly, suitable, worthy 2 = **flattering**, attractive, comely, enhancing, graceful, neat, pretty, tasteful
➤ **Antonyms**
≠**appropriate:** improper, inappropriate, unfit, unsuitable, unworthy ≠**flattering:** ugly, unattractive, unbecoming, unflattering

bed *noun* 1 = **bedstead**, berth, bunk, cot, couch, divan, pallet 2 = **plot**, area, border, garden, patch, row, strip 3 = **bottom**, base, foundation, groundwork, substratum
♦ *verb* 4 = **fix**, base, embed, establish, found, implant, insert, plant, settle, set up

bedaub *verb* = **smear**, besmear, smirch, soil, spatter, splash, stain

bedazzle *verb* = **dazzle**, amaze, astound, bewilder, blind, captivate, confuse, daze, dumbfound, enchant, overwhelm, stagger, stun, sweep off one's feet

bedclothes *plural noun* = **bedding**, bed linen, blankets, coverlets, covers, duvets, eiderdowns, pillowcases, pillows, quilts, sheets

bed down *verb* = **sleep**, hit the hay (*slang*), lie, retire, settle down, turn in (*informal*)

bedeck *verb* = **decorate**, adorn, array, bedight (*archaic*), bedizen (*archaic*), embellish, engarland, festoon, garnish, ornament, trim

bedevil *verb* 1 = **torment**, afflict, aggravate

(*informal*), annoy, be on one's back (*slang*), breathe down someone's neck, distress, frustrate, get in one's hair (*informal*), get on one's nerves (*informal*), get on one's wick (*Brit. slang*), get under one's skin (*informal*), get up one's nose (*informal*), harass, hassle (*informal*), irk, irritate, pester, plague, torture, trouble, vex, worry 2 = **confuse**, confound

bedlam *noun* = **pandemonium**, chaos, clamour, commotion, confusion, furore, hubbub, hullabaloo, madhouse (*informal*), noise, tumult, turmoil, uproar

bedraggled *adjective* = **messy**, dirty, dishevelled, disordered, drenched, dripping, muddied, muddy, sodden, soiled, stained, sullied, unkempt, untidy

bedridden *adjective* = **confined to bed**, confined, flat on one's back, incapacitated, laid up (*informal*)

bedrock *noun* 1 = **bottom**, bed, foundation, rock bottom, substratum, substructure 2 = **basics**, basis, core, essentials, fundamentals, nuts and bolts (*informal*), roots

beef *noun* 1 *Informal* = **flesh**, brawn, heftiness, muscle, physique, robustness, sinew, strength 2 *Slang* = **complaint**, criticism, dispute, grievance, gripe (*informal*), grouch (*informal*), grouse, grumble, objection, protest, protestation

beefy *adjective Informal* = **brawny**, bulky, burly, hulking, muscular, stalwart, stocky, strapping, sturdy, thickset
➤ **Antonyms**
feeble, frail, puny, scrawny, skinny, weak

beetling *adjective* = **overhanging**, hanging over, jutting, leaning over, pendent, projecting, prominent, protruding, sticking out, swelling over

befall *verb Archaic or literary* = **happen**, bechance, betide, chance, come to pass, ensue, fall, follow, materialize, occur, supervene, take place, transpire (*informal*)

befitting *adjective* = **appropriate**, apposite, becoming, fit, fitting, meet (*archaic*), proper, right, seemly, suitable
➤ **Antonyms**
improper, inappropriate, irrelevant, unbecoming, unfit, unsuitable, wrong

before *preposition* 1 = **ahead of**, in advance of, in front of 2 = **earlier than**, in advance of, prior to 3 = **in the presence of**, in front of ♦ *adverb* 4 = **previously**, ahead, earlier, formerly, in advance, sooner 5 = **in front**, ahead
➤ **Antonyms**
preposition ≠**ahead of, earlier than:** after, behind, following, succeeding ♦ *adverb* ≠**previously, in front:** after, afterwards,

behind, later, subsequently, thereafter

beforehand *adverb* = **in advance**, ahead of time, already, before, before now, earlier, early, in anticipation, previously, sooner

befriend *verb* = **help**, advise, aid, assist, back, benefit, encourage, favour, patronize, side with, stand by, succour, support, sustain, uphold, welcome

befuddle *verb* = **confuse**, baffle, bewilder, daze, disorient, intoxicate, muddle, puzzle, stupefy
➤ **Antonyms**
clarify, clear up, elucidate, explicate, illuminate, interpret, make clear, make plain, resolve, simplify, throw *or* shed light on

befuddled *adjective* = **confused**, at sea, dazed, fuddled, groggy (*informal*), inebriated, intoxicated, muddled, woozy (*informal*)

beg *verb* **1** = **scrounge**, blag (*slang*), cadge, call for alms, mooch (*slang*), seek charity, solicit charity, sponge on, touch (someone) for (*slang*) **2** = **implore**, beseech, crave, desire, entreat, importune, petition, plead, pray, request, solicit, supplicate **3** *As in* **beg the question** = **dodge**, avoid, duck (*informal*), equivocate, eschew, evade, fend off, flannel (*Brit. informal*), hedge, parry, shirk, shun, sidestep
➤ **Antonyms**
≠**scrounge**: claim, demand, exact, extort, insist on ≠**implore**: apportion, award, bestow, commit, confer, contribute, donate, give, grant, impart, present

beget *verb Old-fashioned* **1** = **cause**, bring, bring about, create, effect, engender, give rise to, occasion, produce, result in **2** = **father**, breed, generate, get, procreate, propagate, sire

beggar *noun* **1** = **scrounger** (*informal*), cadger, mendicant, sponger (*informal*), supplicant **2** = **tramp**, bag lady (*chiefly U.S.*), bankrupt, bum (*informal*), down-and-out, pauper, starveling, vagrant
♦ *verb* **3** *As in* **beggar description** = **defy**, baffle, challenge, surpass

beggarly *adjective* **1** = **poor**, abject, base, contemptible, despicable, destitute, impoverished, indigent, needy, pathetic, pitiful, poverty-stricken, vile, wretched **2** = **mean**, inadequate, low, meagre, miserly, niggardly, stingy

beggary *noun* = **poverty**, bankruptcy, destitution, indigence, need, pauperism, vagrancy, want, wretchedness

begin *verb* **1** = **start**, commence, embark on, get the show on the road (*informal*), inaugurate, initiate, instigate, institute,

prepare, set about, set on foot **2** = **happen**, appear, arise, be born, come into being, come into existence, commence, crop up (*informal*), dawn, emerge, originate, spring, start
➤ **Antonyms**
cease, complete, end, finish, stop, terminate

beginner *noun* = **novice**, amateur, apprentice, cub, fledgling, freshman, greenhorn (*informal*), initiate, learner, neophyte, recruit, starter, student, tenderfoot, trainee, tyro
➤ **Antonyms**
authority, expert, master, old hand, old stager, old-timer, past master *or* past mistress, pro (*informal*), professional, trouper, veteran

beginning *noun* **1** = **start**, birth, commencement, inauguration, inception, initiation, onset, opening, opening move, origin, outset, overture, preface, prelude, rise, rudiments, source, starting point **2** = **seed**, embryo, fount, fountainhead, germ, root
➤ **Antonyms**
≠**start**: closing, completion, conclusion, end, ending, finish, termination

begrudge *verb* = **resent**, be jealous, be reluctant, be stingy, envy, grudge

beguile *verb* **1** = **fool**, befool, cheat, deceive, delude, dupe, hoodwink, impose on, mislead, take for a ride (*informal*), trick **2** = **charm**, amuse, cheer, delight, distract, divert, engross, entertain, occupy, solace, tickle the fancy of
➤ **Antonyms**
≠**fool**: alarm, alert, enlighten, put right

beguiling *adjective* = **charming**, alluring, attractive, bewitching, captivating, diverting, enchanting, entertaining, enthralling, interesting, intriguing

behalf *noun* = **benefit**, account, advantage, defence, good, interest, part, profit, sake, side, support

behave *verb* **1** = **act**, function, operate, perform, run, work **2** = **conduct oneself properly**, act correctly, keep one's nose clean, mind one's manners
➤ **Antonyms**
≠**conduct oneself properly**: act up (*informal*), be bad, be insubordinate, be naughty, carry on (*informal*), get up to mischief (*informal*), misbehave, muck about (*Brit. slang*)

behaviour *noun* **1** = **conduct**, actions, bearing, carriage, comportment, demeanour, deportment, manner, manners, ways **2** = **action**, functioning, operation, performance

behest noun = **command**, bidding, canon, charge, commandment, decree, dictate, direction, expressed desire, injunction, instruction, mandate, order, precept, wish

behind preposition 1 = **after**, at the back of, at the heels of, at the rear of, following, later than 2 = **causing**, at the bottom of, initiating, instigating, responsible for 3 = **supporting**, backing, for, in agreement, on the side of ♦ adverb 4 = **after**, afterwards, following, in the wake (of), next, subsequently 5 = **overdue**, behindhand, in arrears ♦ noun 6 Informal = **bottom**, arse (taboo slang), ass (U.S. & Canad. taboo slang), bum (Brit. slang), buns (U.S. slang), butt (U.S. & Canad. informal), buttocks, derrière (euphemistic), jacksy (Brit. slang), posterior, rump, seat, tail (informal), tush (U.S. slang)
➤ Antonyms
adverb ≠ **after**: earlier than, in advance of, in front of, in the presence of, prior to ≠ **overdue**: ahead, earlier, formerly, in advance, previously, sooner

behindhand adjective = **late**, behind time, dilatory, remiss, slow, tardy

behind the times adjective = **out of the ark** (informal), antiquated, dated, démodé, obsolete, old-fashioned, old hat, outmoded, out of date, passé
➤ Antonyms
advanced, avant-garde, experimental, far-out (slang), ground-breaking, innovative, pioneering, progressive, trendy (Brit. informal), unconventional, way-out (informal)

behold verb Archaic or literary = **look at**, check, check out (informal), clock (Brit. slang), consider, contemplate, discern, eye, eyeball (slang), get a load of (informal), observe, perceive, recce (slang), regard, scan, survey, take a dekko at (Brit. slang), view, watch, witness

beholden adjective = **indebted**, bound, grateful, obligated, obliged, owing, under obligation

beige adjective, noun = **fawn**, biscuit, buff, café au lait, camel, cinnamon, coffee, cream, ecru, khaki, mushroom, neutral, oatmeal, sand, tan

being noun 1 = **existence**, actuality, animation, life, living, reality 2 = **nature**, entity, essence, soul, spirit, substance 3 = **creature**, animal, beast, body, human being, individual, living thing, mortal, thing
➤ Antonyms
≠ **existence**: nonbeing, nonexistence, nothingness, nullity, oblivion

belabour verb 1 = **beat**, batter, clobber (slang), flog, lambast(e), thrash, whip 2 = **attack**, berate, blast, castigate, censure, criticize, excoriate, flay, go for the jugular, lambast(e), lay into (informal), put down, tear into (informal)

belated adjective = **late**, behindhand, behind time, delayed, late in the day, overdue, tardy

belch verb 1 = **burp** (informal), eruct, eructate, hiccup 2 = **emit**, discharge, disgorge, erupt, give off, gush, spew forth, vent, vomit

beleaguered adjective 1 = **harassed**, aggravated (informal), annoyed, badgered, hassled (informal), persecuted, pestered, plagued, put upon, vexed 2 = **besieged**, assailed, beset, blockaded, encompassed, environed, hemmed in, surrounded

belie verb 1 = **disprove**, confute, contradict, deny, gainsay (archaic or literary), give the lie to, make a nonsense of, negate, rebut, repudiate 2 = **misrepresent**, conceal, deceive, disguise, falsify, gloss over, mislead

belief noun 1 = **trust**, admission, assent, assurance, confidence, conviction, credit, feeling, impression, judgment, notion, opinion, persuasion, presumption, reliance, theory, view 2 = **faith**, credence, credo, creed, doctrine, dogma, ideology, principles, tenet
➤ Antonyms
≠ **trust**: disbelief, distrust, doubt, dubiety, incredulity, mistrust, scepticism

believable adjective = **credible**, acceptable, authentic, creditable, imaginable, likely, plausible, possible, probable, reliable, trustworthy, verisimilar
➤ Antonyms
cock-and-bull (informal), doubtful, dubious, fabulous, implausible, incredible, questionable, unacceptable, unbelievable

believe verb 1 = **accept**, be certain of, be convinced of, buy (slang), count on, credit, depend on, have faith in, hold, place confidence in, presume true, rely on, swallow (informal), swear by, take as gospel, take on board, trust 2 = **think**, assume, conjecture, consider, gather, guess (informal, chiefly U.S. & Canad.), imagine, judge, maintain, postulate, presume, reckon, speculate, suppose
➤ Antonyms
disbelieve, distrust, doubt, know, question

believer noun = **follower**, adherent, convert, devotee, disciple, proselyte, protagonist, supporter, upholder, zealot
➤ Antonyms
agnostic, atheist, disbeliever, doubting

Thomas, infidel, sceptic, unbeliever

belittle *verb* = **disparage**, decry, denigrate, deprecate, depreciate, deride, derogate, detract, diminish, downgrade, minimize, scoff at, scorn, sneer at, underestimate, underrate, undervalue
➤ **Antonyms**
boast about, elevate, exalt, magnify, praise, vaunt

belligerent *adjective* **1** = **aggressive**, antagonistic, argumentative, bellicose, combative, contentious, hostile, litigious, pugnacious, quarrelsome, unfriendly, warlike, warring ♦ *noun* **2** = **fighter**, combatant, warring nation
➤ **Antonyms**
adjective ≠**aggressive**: amicable, benign, conciliatory, friendly, harmonious, nonviolent, without hostility

bellow *noun, verb* = **shout**, bawl, bell, call, clamour, cry, howl, roar, scream, shriek, yell

belly *noun* **1** = **stomach**, abdomen, breadbasket (*slang*), corporation (*informal*), gut, insides (*informal*), paunch, potbelly, tummy, vitals ♦ *verb* **2** = **swell out**, billow, bulge, fill, spread, swell

bellyful *noun* = **surfeit**, enough, excess, glut, plateful, plenty, satiety, superabundance, too much

belonging *noun* = **relationship**, acceptance, affiliation, affinity, association, attachment, fellowship, inclusion, kinship, loyalty, rapport

belongings *plural noun* = **possessions**, accoutrements, chattels, effects, gear, goods, paraphernalia, personal property, stuff, things

belong to *verb* **1** = **be the property of**, be at the disposal of, be held by, be owned by **2** = **be a member of**, be affiliated to, be allied to, be associated with, be included in **3** = **go with**, attach to, be connected with, be fitting, be part of, fit, have as a proper place, pertain to, relate to

beloved *adjective* = **dear**, admired, adored, cherished, darling, dearest, loved, pet, precious, prized, revered, sweet, treasured, valued, worshipped

below *preposition* **1** = **lesser**, inferior, subject, subordinate **2** = **less than**, lower than **3** = **unworthy of**, beneath **4 below par** = **poor**, below average, imperfect, inferior, off colour, off form, second-rate, unfit ♦ *adverb* **5** = **lower**, beneath, down, under, underneath

belt *noun* **1** = **waistband**, band, cincture, cummerbund, girdle, girth, sash **2** *Geography* = **zone**, area, district, layer,

region, stretch, strip, tract **3 below the belt** *Informal* = **unfair**, cowardly, foul, not playing the game (*informal*), unjust, unscrupulous, unsporting, unsportsmanlike

bemoan *verb* = **lament**, bewail, cry over spilt milk, deplore, express sorrow, grieve for, moan over, mourn, regret, rue, weep for

bemuse *verb* = **puzzle**, amaze, bewilder, confuse, daze, flummox, muddle, nonplus, overwhelm, perplex, stun

bemused *adjective* = **puzzled**, absent-minded, at sea, bewildered, confused, dazed, engrossed, flummoxed, fuddled, half-drunk, muddled, nonplussed, perplexed, preoccupied, stunned, stupefied, tipsy

bench *noun* **1** = **seat**, form, pew, settle, stall **2** = **worktable**, board, counter, table, trestle table, workbench **3 the bench** = **court**, courtroom, judge, judges, judiciary, magistrate, magistrates, tribunal

benchmark *noun* = **reference point**, criterion, example, gauge, level, measure, model, norm, par, reference, standard, touchstone, yardstick

bend *verb* **1** = **curve**, arc, arch, bow, buckle, contort, crouch, deflect, diverge, flex, incline, incurvate, lean, stoop, swerve, turn, twist, veer, warp **2** = **submit**, yield **3** = **force**, compel, direct, influence, mould, persuade, shape, subdue, sway ♦ *noun* **4** = **curve**, angle, arc, arch, bow, corner, crook, hook, loop, turn, twist, zigzag

beneath *preposition* **1** = **under**, below, lower than, underneath **2** = **inferior to**, below, less than **3** = **unworthy of**, unbefitting ♦ *adverb* **4** = **underneath**, below, in a lower place
➤ **Antonyms**
preposition ≠**under**: above, atop, higher than, on top of, over, upon ≠**inferior to**: higher than, over

benediction *noun* = **benison**, beatitude, *benedictus*, blessing, consecration, favour, grace, gratitude, invocation, orison, prayer, thankfulness, thanksgiving

benefactor *noun* = **supporter**, angel (*informal*), backer, contributor, donor, helper, patron, philanthropist, promoter, sponsor, subscriber, subsidizer, well-wisher

beneficial *adjective* = **helpful**, advantageous, benign, expedient, favourable, gainful, healthful, profitable, salubrious, salutary, serviceable, useful, valuable, wholesome
➤ **Antonyms**
detrimental, disadvantageous, harmful, pernicious, useless

beneficiary noun = **recipient**, assignee, heir, inheritor, legatee, payee, receiver, successor

benefit noun 1 = **help**, advantage, aid, asset, assistance, avail, betterment, blessing, boon, boot (*obsolete*), favour, gain, good, inside track (*informal*), interest, mileage (*informal*), profit, use, utility ♦ verb 2 = **help**, advance, advantage, aid, ameliorate, assist, avail, better, enhance, further, improve, profit, promote, serve
➤ **Antonyms**
noun ≠**help**: damage, detriment, disadvantage, downside, harm, impairment, injury, loss ♦ verb ≠**help**: damage, deprive, detract from, harm, impair, injure, worsen

benevolence noun = **kindness**, altruism, charity, compassion, fellow feeling, generosity, goodness, goodwill, humanity, kind-heartedness, sympathy
➤ **Antonyms**
ill will, malevolence, selfishness, stinginess, unkindness

benevolent adjective = **kind**, affable, altruistic, beneficent, benign, bounteous, bountiful, caring, charitable, compassionate, considerate, generous, humane, humanitarian, kind-hearted, liberal, philanthropic, tender-hearted, warm-hearted, well-disposed

benighted adjective = **uncivilized**, backward, crude, ignorant, illiterate, primitive, uncultivated, unenlightened

benign adjective 1 = **kindly**, affable, amiable, complaisant, friendly, generous, genial, gracious, kind, liberal, obliging, sympathetic 2 = **favourable**, advantageous, auspicious, beneficial, encouraging, good, lucky, propitious, salutary 3 *Medical* = **harmless**, curable, limited, remediable, slight, superficial
➤ **Antonyms**
≠**kindly**: bad, disobliging, harsh, hateful, inhumane, malicious, malign, severe, stern, unfavourable, unkind, unpleasant, unsympathetic ≠**favourable**: bad, unfavourable, unlucky ≠**harmless**: malignant

bent adjective 1 = **curved**, angled, arched, bowed, crooked, hunched, stooped, twisted 2 **bent on** = **determined to**, disposed to, fixed on, inclined to, insistent on, predisposed to, resolved on, set on ♦ noun 3 = **inclination**, ability, aptitude, bag (*slang*), cup of tea (*informal*), facility, faculty, flair, forte, knack, leaning, penchant, preference, proclivity, propensity, talent, tendency

➤ **Antonyms**
adjective ≠**curved**: aligned, erect, even, horizontal, in line, level, perpendicular, plumb, smooth, square, straight, true, upright, vertical

bequeath verb = **leave**, bestow, commit, endow, entrust, give, grant, hand down, impart, leave to by will, pass on, transmit, will

bequest noun = **legacy**, bequeathal, bestowal, dower, endowment, estate, gift, heritage, inheritance, settlement, trust

berate verb = **scold**, bawl out (*informal*), blast, carpet (*informal*), castigate, censure, chew out (*U.S. & Canad. informal*), chide, criticize, excoriate, give a rocket (*Brit. & N.Z. informal*), harangue, lambast(e), put down, rail at, rap over the knuckles, read the riot act, rebuke, reprimand, reproach, reprove, revile, slap on the wrist, slate (*informal, chiefly Brit.*), tear into (*informal*), tear (someone) off a strip (*Brit. informal*), tell off (*informal*), upbraid, vituperate
➤ **Antonyms**
acclaim, admire, applaud, approve, cheer, commend, compliment, congratulate, extol, laud, praise, take one's hat off to

bereavement noun = **loss**, affliction, death, deprivation, misfortune, tribulation

bereft adjective = **deprived**, cut off, destitute, devoid, lacking, minus, parted from, robbed of, shorn, wanting

berserk adverb = **crazy**, amok, ape (*slang*), apeshit (*slang*), enraged, frantic, frenzied, insane, mad, maniacal, manic, rabid, raging, uncontrollable, violent, wild

berth noun 1 = **bunk**, bed, billet, cot (*Nautical*), hammock 2 *Nautical* = **anchorage**, dock, harbour, haven, pier, port, quay, slip, wharf 3 = **job**, appointment, employment, living, position, post, situation ♦ verb 4 *Nautical* = **anchor**, dock, drop anchor, land, moor, tie up

beseech verb = **beg**, adjure, ask, call upon, crave, entreat, implore, importune, petition, plead, pray, solicit, sue, supplicate

beset verb 1 = **plague**, badger, bedevil, embarrass, entangle, harass, perplex, pester, trouble 2 = **attack**, assail, besiege, encircle, enclose, encompass, environ, hem in, surround

besetting adjective = **troublesome**, habitual, harassing, inveterate, persistent, prevalent

beside preposition 1 = **next to**, abreast of, adjacent to, alongside, at the side of, cheek by jowl, close to, near, nearby, neighbouring, next door to, overlooking 2

beside oneself = distraught, apoplectic, at the end of one's tether, berserk, crazed, delirious, demented, deranged, desperate, frantic, frenzied, insane, mad, out of one's mind, unbalanced, uncontrolled, unhinged

besides *adverb* **1 = too**, also, as well, further, furthermore, in addition, into the bargain, moreover, otherwise, what's more ♦ *preposition* **2 = apart from**, barring, excepting, excluding, in addition to, other than, over and above, without

beside the point *adjective* **= irrelevant**, extraneous, immaterial, inapplicable, inapposite, inappropriate, inconsequent, neither here nor there, unconnected
➤ **Antonyms**
admissible, applicable, apposite, appropriate, appurtenant, apt, fitting, germane, pertinent, relevant, significant, to the point

besiege *verb* **1 = surround**, beleaguer, beset, blockade, confine, encircle, encompass, environ, hedge in, hem in, invest (*rare*), lay siege to, shut in **2 = harass**, badger, bend someone's ear (*informal*), bother, harry, hassle (*informal*), hound, importune, nag, pester, plague, trouble

besotted *adjective* **1 = infatuated**, doting, hypnotized, smitten, spellbound **2 = drunk**, befuddled, bevvied (*dialect*), bladdered (*slang*), blitzed (*slang*), blotto (*slang*), bombed (*slang*), Brahms and Liszt (*slang*), intoxicated, legless (*informal*), lit up (*slang*), out of it (*slang*), out to it (*Austral. & N.Z. slang*), paralytic (*informal*), pissed (*taboo slang*), rat-arsed (*taboo slang*), smashed (*slang*), steamboats (*Scot. slang*), steaming (*slang*), stupefied, wasted (*slang*), wrecked (*slang*), zonked (*slang*) **3 = foolish**, confused, muddled, witless

bespatter *verb* **1 = splatter**, bedaub, befoul, begrime, besprinkle, muddy, smear, spatter **2 = slander**, besmirch, dishonour, sully

best *adjective* **1 = finest**, chief, first, first-class, first-rate, foremost, highest, leading, most excellent, outstanding, perfect, pre-eminent, principal, superlative, supreme, unsurpassed **2 = most fitting**, advantageous, apt, correct, golden, most desirable, right **3 = greatest**, largest, most ♦ *adverb* **4 = most highly**, extremely, greatly, most deeply, most fully **5 = excellently**, advantageously, attractively, most fortunately ♦ *noun* **6 = finest**, choice, cream, *crème de la crème*, elite, favourite, first, flower, pick, prime, top **7 = utmost**, hardest, highest endeavour ♦ *verb* **8 = defeat**, beat, blow

out of the water (*slang*), conquer, get the better of, lick (*informal*), master, outclass, outdo, put in the shade (*informal*), run rings around (*informal*), stuff (*slang*), surpass, tank (*slang*), thrash, triumph over, trounce, undo, wipe the floor with (*informal*)

bestial *adjective* **= brutal**, animal, barbaric, barbarous, beastlike, beastly, brutish, carnal, degraded, depraved, gross, inhuman, low, savage, sensual, sordid, vile

bestow *verb* **= present**, accord, allot, apportion, award, commit, confer, donate, endow, entrust, give, grant, hand out, honour with, impart, lavish, render to
➤ **Antonyms**
acquire, attain, come by, earn, gain, get, land, make, net, obtain, procure, secure

bestride *verb* **= straddle**, bestraddle, bridge, dominate, extend, mount, span, step over, tower over

bet *noun* **1 = gamble**, ante, hazard, long shot, pledge, risk, speculation, stake, venture, wager ♦ *verb* **2 = gamble**, chance, hazard, pledge, punt (*chiefly Brit.*), put money on, put one's shirt on, risk, speculate, stake, venture, wager

betide *verb* **= happen**, bechance, befall, chance, come to pass, crop up (*informal*), ensue, occur, overtake, supervene, take place, transpire (*informal*)

betimes *adverb* **= early**, anon, beforehand, before long, erelong (*archaic or poetic*), first thing, in good time, punctually, seasonably, soon

betoken *verb* **= indicate**, augur, bespeak, bode, declare, denote, evidence, manifest, mark, portend, presage, prognosticate, promise, represent, signify, suggest, typify

betray *verb* **1 = be disloyal**, be treacherous, be unfaithful, break one's promise, break with, double-cross (*informal*), grass (*Brit. slang*), grass up (*slang*), inform on or against, put the finger on (*informal*), sell down the river (*informal*), sell out (*informal*), sell the pass (*informal*), shop (*slang, chiefly Brit.*), stab in the back **2 = give away**, blurt out, disclose, divulge, evince, expose, lay bare, let slip, manifest, reveal, show, tell, tell on, uncover, unmask **3 = abandon**, desert, forsake, jilt, walk out on

betrayal *noun* **1 = disloyalty**, deception, double-cross (*informal*), double-dealing, duplicity, falseness, perfidy, sell-out (*informal*), treachery, treason, trickery, unfaithfulness **2 = giving away**, blurting out, disclosure, divulgence, revelation, telling
➤ **Antonyms**

≠**disloyalty**: allegiance, constancy, devotion, faithfulness, fealty, fidelity, loyalty, steadfastness, trustiness, trustworthiness ≠**giving away**: guarding, keeping, keeping secret, preserving, safeguarding

betrayer *noun* = **traitor**, apostate, conspirator, deceiver, renegade, snake in the grass

betrothal *noun Old-fashioned* = **engagement**, affiancing, betrothing, espousal (*archaic*), marriage compact, plight, promise, troth, vow

better *adjective* **1** = **superior**, bigger, excelling, finer, fitter, greater, higher-quality, larger, more appropriate, more desirable, more expert, more fitting, more suitable, more useful, more valuable, preferable, streets ahead, surpassing, worthier **2** = **well**, cured, fitter, fully recovered, healthier, improving, less ill, mending, more healthy, on the mend (*informal*), progressing, recovering, stronger **3** = **greater**, bigger, larger, longer ◆ *adverb* **4** = **in a more excellent manner**, in a superior way, more advantageously, more attractively, more competently, more effectively **5** = **to a greater degree**, more completely, more thoroughly ◆ *noun* **6 get the better of** = **defeat**, beat, best, get the upper hand, outdo, outsmart (*informal*), outwit, prevail over, score off, surpass, triumph over, worst ◆ *verb* **7** = **improve**, advance, ameliorate, amend, correct, enhance, forward, further, meliorate, mend, promote, raise, rectify, reform **8** = **beat**, cap (*informal*), clobber (*slang*), exceed, excel, improve on *or* upon, knock spots off (*informal*), lick (*informal*), outdo, outstrip, put in the shade (*informal*), run rings around (*informal*), surpass, top
➤ **Antonyms**
adjective ≠**superior**: inferior, lesser, smaller, substandard, worse ≠**well**: worse ◆ *adverb* ≠**in a more excellent manner**: worse ◆ *verb* ≠**improve**: depress, devaluate, go downhill, impoverish, lessen, lower, weaken, worsen

between *preposition* = **amidst**, among, betwixt, in the middle of, mid

beverage *noun* = **drink**, bevvy (*dialect*), draught, libation (*facetious*), liquid, liquor, potable, potation, refreshment

bevy *noun* **1** = **group**, band, bunch (*informal*), collection, company, crowd, gathering, pack, troupe **2** = **flock**, covey, flight

bewail *verb* = **lament**, bemoan, cry over, deplore, express sorrow, grieve for, keen, moan, mourn, regret, repent, rue, wail, weep over

beware *verb* = **be careful**, avoid, be cautious, be wary, guard against, heed, look out, mind, refrain from, shun, steer clear of, take heed, watch out

bewilder *verb* = **confound**, baffle, befuddle, bemuse, confuse, daze, flummox, mix up, mystify, nonplus, perplex, puzzle, stun, stupefy

bewildered *adjective* = **confused**, at a loss, at sea, awed, baffled, bamboozled (*informal*), disconcerted, dizzy, flummoxed, giddy, mystified, nonplussed, perplexed, puzzled, speechless, startled, stunned, surprised, taken aback, uncertain

bewitch *verb* = **enchant**, absorb, allure, attract, beguile, captivate, charm, enrapture, entrance, fascinate, hypnotize, ravish, spellbind
➤ **Antonyms**
disgust, give one the creeps (*informal*), make one sick, offend, repel, repulse, sicken, turn off (*informal*)

bewitched *adjective* = **enchanted**, charmed, entranced, fascinated, mesmerized, possessed, spellbound, transformed, under a spell, unrecognizable

beyond *preposition* **1** = **past**, above, apart from, at a distance, away from, outwith (*Scot.*), over **2** = **exceeding**, out of reach of, superior to, surpassing

bias *noun* **1** = **prejudice**, bent, bigotry, favouritism, inclination, intolerance, jobs for the boys (*informal*), leaning, narrow-mindedness, nepotism, one-sidedness, partiality, penchant, predilection, predisposition, proclivity, proneness, propensity, tendency, turn, unfairness **2** = **slant**, angle, cross, diagonal line ◆ *verb* **3** = **prejudice**, distort, influence, predispose, slant, sway, twist, warp, weight
➤ **Antonyms**
noun ≠**prejudice**: equality, equity, fairness, impartiality, neutrality, objectivity, open-mindedness

biased *adjective* = **prejudiced**, distorted, embittered, jaundiced, one-sided, partial, predisposed, slanted, swayed, twisted, warped, weighted

bicker *verb* = **quarrel**, argue, cross swords, disagree, dispute, fight, fight like cat and dog, go at it hammer and tongs, row (*informal*), scrap (*informal*), spar, squabble, wrangle
➤ **Antonyms**
accord, acquiesce, agree, assent, concur, cooperate, get on, harmonize

bid *verb* **1** = **offer**, proffer, propose, submit,

tender 2 = **say**, call, greet, tell, wish 3 = **tell**, ask, call, charge, command, desire, direct, enjoin, instruct, invite, order, require, solicit, summon ♦ *noun* 4 = **offer**, advance, amount, price, proposal, proposition, submission, sum, tender 5 = **attempt**, crack (*informal*), effort, endeavour, go (*informal*), stab (*informal*), try, venture

biddable *adjective* = **obedient**, amenable, complaisant, cooperative, docile, teachable, tractable
➤ **Antonyms**
awkward, difficult, disobedient, intractable, petulant, querulous, refractory, unruly

bidding *noun* 1 = **order**, beck, beck and call, behest, call, canon, charge, command, demand, direction, injunction, instruction, invitation, request, summons 2 = **offers**, auction, offer, proposal, tender

big *adjective* 1 = **large**, bulky, burly, colossal, considerable, elephantine, enormous, extensive, gigantic, great, huge, hulking, humongous *or* humungous (*U.S. slang*), immense, mammoth, massive, ponderous, prodigious, sizable *or* sizeable, spacious, stellar (*informal*), substantial, vast, voluminous 2 = **important**, big-time (*informal*), eminent, influential, leading, main, major league (*informal*), momentous, paramount, powerful, prime, principal, prominent, serious, significant, valuable, weighty 3 = **grown-up**, adult, elder, grown, mature 4 = **generous**, altruistic, benevolent, gracious, heroic, magnanimous, noble, princely, unselfish 5 = **boastful**, arrogant, bragging, conceited, haughty, inflated, pompous, pretentious, proud
➤ **Antonyms**
≠**large**: diminutive, insignificant, little, mini, miniature, petite, pint-sized (*informal*), pocket-sized, pygmy *or* pigmy, small, tiny, wee ≠**important**: humble, ignoble, insignificant, minor, modest, ordinary, unimportant, unknown ≠**grown-up**: immature, young

bighead *noun Informal* = **boaster**, braggart, know-all (*informal*)

bigheaded *adjective* = **boastful**, arrogant, bumptious, cocky, conceited, egotistic, full of oneself, immodest, overconfident, swollen-headed, too big for one's boots *or* breeches

bigot *noun* = **fanatic**, dogmatist, persecutor, racist, sectarian, zealot

bigoted *adjective* = **intolerant**, biased, dogmatic, illiberal, narrow-minded, obstinate, opinionated, prejudiced, sectarian, twisted, warped
➤ **Antonyms**
broad-minded, equitable, open-minded, tolerant, unbiased, unbigoted, unprejudiced

bigotry *noun* = **intolerance**, bias, discrimination, dogmatism, fanaticism, ignorance, injustice, mindlessness, narrow-mindedness, pig-ignorance (*slang*), prejudice, provincialism, racialism, racism, sectarianism, sexism, unfairness
➤ **Antonyms**
broad-mindedness, forbearance, open-mindedness, permissiveness, tolerance

bigwig *noun Informal* = **important person**, big cheese (*slang, old-fashioned*), big gun (*informal*), big hitter (*informal*), big name, big noise (*informal*), big shot (*informal*), celeb (*informal*), celebrity, dignitary, heavy hitter (*informal*), heavyweight (*informal*), mogul, nob (*slang*), notability, notable, panjandrum, personage, somebody, V.I.P.
➤ **Antonyms**
cipher, lightweight (*informal*), nobody, nonentity, nothing, zero

bile *noun* = **bitterness**, anger, churlishness, ill humour, irascibility, irritability, nastiness, peevishness, rancour, spleen

bilious *adjective* 1 = **sick**, liverish, nauseated, nauseous, out of sorts, queasy 2 *Informal* = **bad-tempered**, cantankerous, crabby, cross, crotchety, edgy, grouchy (*informal*), grumpy, ill-humoured, ill-tempered, irritable, like a bear with a sore head, nasty, peevish, ratty (*Brit. & N.Z. informal*), short-tempered, testy, tetchy, touchy

bilk *verb* = **cheat**, bamboozle (*informal*), con (*informal*), cozen, deceive, defraud, do (*slang*), fleece, pull a fast one on (*informal*), rook (*slang*), sell a pup, skin (*slang*), stiff (*slang*), swindle, trick

bill¹ *noun* 1 = **charges**, account, invoice, note of charge, reckoning, score, statement, tally 2 = **proposal**, measure, piece of legislation, projected law 3 = **advertisement**, broadsheet, bulletin, circular, handbill, handout, leaflet, notice, placard, playbill, poster 4 = **list**, agenda, card, catalogue, inventory, listing, programme, roster, schedule, syllabus ♦ *verb* 5 = **charge**, debit, figure, invoice, reckon, record 6 = **advertise**, announce, give advance notice of, post

bill² *noun* = **beak**, mandible, neb (*archaic or dialect*), nib

billet *verb* 1 = **quarter**, accommodate, berth, station ♦ *noun* 2 = **quarters**, accommodation, barracks, lodging

billow noun 1 = **wave**, breaker, crest, roller, surge, swell, tide 2 = **surge**, cloud, deluge, flood, outpouring, rush, wave ♦ verb 3 = **surge**, balloon, belly, puff up, rise up, roll, swell

billowy adjective 1 = **wavy**, rippling, undulating, waving 2 = **surging**, heaving, rolling, swelling, swirling

bind verb 1 = **tie**, attach, fasten, glue, hitch, lash, paste, rope, secure, stick, strap, tie up, truss, wrap 2 = **oblige**, compel, constrain, engage, force, necessitate, obligate, prescribe, require 3 = **restrict**, confine, detain, hamper, hinder, restrain 4 = **edge**, border, finish, hem, trim 5 = **bandage**, cover, dress, encase, swathe, wrap ♦ noun 6 Informal = **nuisance**, bore, difficulty, dilemma, drag (informal), hot water (informal), pain in the arse (taboo informal), pain in the neck (informal), predicament, quandary, spot (informal), tight spot
➤ Antonyms
verb ≠**tie**: free, loosen, release, unbind, undo, unfasten, untie

binding adjective = **compulsory**, conclusive, imperative, indissoluble, irrevocable, mandatory, necessary, obligatory, unalterable
➤ Antonyms
discretionary, free, noncompulsory, optional, uncompelled, unconstrained, unforced, voluntary

binge noun Informal = **bout**, beano (Brit. slang), bender (informal), blind (slang), feast, fling, jag (slang), orgy, spree

biography noun = **life story**, account, curriculum vitae, CV, life, life history, memoir, memoirs, profile, record

birth noun 1 = **childbirth**, delivery, nativity, parturition 2 = **beginning**, emergence, fountainhead, genesis, origin, rise, source 3 = **ancestry**, background, blood, breeding, derivation, descent, extraction, forebears, genealogy, line, lineage, nobility, noble extraction, parentage, pedigree, race, stock, strain
➤ Antonyms
≠**childbirth**: death, demise, end, extinction, passing, passing away or on

bisect verb = **cut in two**, bifurcate, cross, cut across, cut in half, divide in two, halve, intersect, separate, split, split down the middle

bisexual adjective 1 = **bi** (slang), AC/DC (slang), ambidextrous (slang), swinging both ways (slang) 2 = **hermaphrodite**, androgyne, androgynous, epicene, gynandromorphic or gynandromorphous (Entomology), gynandrous,

hermaphroditic, monoclinous (Botany)

bishopric noun = **diocese**, episcopacy, episcopate, primacy, see

bit[1] noun 1 = **piece**, atom, chip, crumb, fragment, grain, iota, jot, mite, morsel, mouthful, part, remnant, scrap, segment, slice, small piece, speck, tittle, whit 2 = **little while**, instant, jiffy (informal), minute, moment, period, second, spell, tick (Brit. informal), time

bit[2] noun 1 = **curb**, brake, check, restraint, snaffle 2 **take the bit in** or **between one's teeth** = **get to grips with**, get stuck into (informal), set about

bitchy adjective Informal = **spiteful**, backbiting, catty (informal), cruel, malicious, mean, nasty, rancorous, shrewish, snide, venomous, vicious, vindictive, vixenish
➤ Antonyms
charitable, generous, gracious, kindly, magnanimous, nice

bite verb 1 = **cut**, champ, chew, clamp, crunch, crush, gnaw, grip, hold, masticate, nibble, nip, pierce, pinch, rend, seize, snap, tear, wound 2 = **eat into**, burn, corrode, eat away, erode, smart, sting, tingle, wear away ♦ noun 3 = **wound**, itch, nip, pinch, prick, smarting, sting, tooth marks 4 = **snack**, food, light meal, morsel, mouthful, piece, refreshment, taste 5 = **kick** (informal), edge, piquancy, punch (informal), pungency, spice

biting adjective 1 = **piercing**, bitter, blighting, cold, cold as ice, cutting, freezing, harsh, nipping, penetrating, sharp 2 = **sarcastic**, caustic, cutting, incisive, mordacious, mordant, scathing, severe, sharp, stinging, trenchant, vitriolic, withering

bitter adjective 1 = **sour**, acerb, acid, acrid, astringent, harsh, sharp, tart, unsweetened, vinegary 2 = **resentful**, acrimonious, begrudging, crabbed, embittered, hostile, morose, rancorous, sore, sour, sullen, with a chip on one's shoulder 3 = **grievous**, calamitous, cruel, dire, distressing, galling, gut-wrenching, harsh, heartbreaking, merciless, painful, poignant, ruthless, savage, vexatious 4 = **freezing**, biting, fierce, intense, severe, stinging
➤ Antonyms
≠**sour**: bland, mellow, mild, pleasant, sugary, sweet ≠**resentful**: appreciative, friendly, gentle, grateful, happy, mellow, mild, pleasant, sweet, thankful ≠**grievous**: fortunate, happy, pleasant ≠**freezing**: balmy, gentle, mild, pleasant

bitterness noun 1 = **sourness**, acerbity,

acidity, sharpness, tartness, vinegariness **2** = **resentment**, acrimony, animosity, asperity, chip on one's shoulder (*informal*), grudge, hostility, pique, rancour, sarcasm, venom, virulence

bizarre *adjective* = **strange**, abnormal, comical, curious, eccentric, extraordinary, fantastic, freakish, grotesque, left-field (*informal*), ludicrous, odd, oddball (*informal*), off-beat, off the rails, off-the-wall (*slang*), outlandish, outré, peculiar, queer, ridiculous, rum (*Brit. slang*), unusual, wacko (*slang*), way-out (*informal*), weird, zany
➤ **Antonyms**
common, customary, normal, ordinary, regular, routine, standard, typical

blab *verb* = **tell**, blow the gaff (*Brit. slang*), blow wide open (*slang*), blurt out, disclose, divulge, give away, gossip, let slip, let the cat out of the bag, open one's mouth, reveal, shop (*slang, chiefly Brit.*), sing (*slang, chiefly U.S.*), spill one's guts (*slang*), spill the beans (*informal*), tattle, tell all, tell on

blabber *noun* **1** = **gossip**, busybody, informer, rumour-monger, scandalmonger, talebearer, tattler, telltale
♦ *verb* **2** = **prattle**, blather, blether (*Scot.*), chatter, gab (*informal*), jabber, run off at the mouth

black *adjective* **1** = **dark**, coal-black, dusky, ebony, inky, jet, murky, pitch-black, pitchy, raven, sable, starless, stygian, swarthy **2** = **gloomy**, atrocious, depressing, dismal, distressing, doleful, foreboding, funereal, hopeless, horrible, lugubrious, mournful, ominous, sad, sombre **3** = **dirty**, dingy, filthy, grimy, grubby, soiled, sooty, stained **4** = **angry**, furious, hostile, menacing, resentful, sullen, threatening **5** = **wicked**, bad, evil, iniquitous, nefarious, villainous ♦ *noun* **6 in the black** = **in credit**, in funds, solvent, without debt ♦ *verb* **7** = **boycott**, ban, bar, blacklist
➤ **Antonyms**
adjective ≠**dark**: bright, illuminated, light, lighted, lit, moonlit, sunny ≠**gloomy**: cheerful, happy, warm ≠**dirty**: clean, pure, white ≠**angry**: amicable, cheerful, friendly, happy, pleased, warm ≠**wicked**: good, honourable, moral, pure

blackball *verb* = **exclude**, ban, bar, blacklist, debar, drum out, expel, ostracize, oust, repudiate, snub, vote against

blacken *verb* **1** = **darken**, befoul, begrime, cloud, dirty, grow black, make black, smudge, soil **2** = **discredit**, bad-mouth (*slang, chiefly U.S. & Canad.*), calumniate, decry, defame, defile, denigrate,

dishonour, knock (*informal*), malign, rubbish (*informal*), slag (off) (*slang*), slander, smear, smirch, stain, sully, taint, tarnish, traduce, vilify

blackguard *noun* = **scoundrel**, bad egg (*old-fashioned informal*), bastard (*offensive*), blighter (*Brit. informal*), bounder (*old-fashioned Brit. slang*), bugger (*taboo slang*), miscreant, rascal, rogue, scumbag (*slang*), shit (*taboo slang*), skelm (*S. Afr.*), son-of-a-bitch (*slang, chiefly U.S. & Canad.*), swine, villain, wretch

blacklist *verb* = **exclude**, ban, bar, blackball, boycott, debar, expel, ostracize, preclude, proscribe, reject, repudiate, snub, vote against

black magic *noun* = **witchcraft**, black art, diabolism, necromancy, sorcery, voodoo, wizardry

blackmail *noun* **1** = **threat**, exaction, extortion, hush money (*slang*), intimidation, milking, pay-off (*informal*), protection (*informal*), ransom, shakedown ♦ *verb* **2** = **threaten**, bleed (*informal*), coerce, compel, demand, exact, extort, force, hold to ransom, intimidate, milk, squeeze

blackness *noun* = **darkness**, duskiness, gloom, inkiness, melanism, murkiness, nigrescence, nigritude (*rare*), swarthiness
➤ **Antonyms**
brightness, brilliance, effulgence, incandescence, lambency, light, lightness, luminescence, luminosity, phosphorescence, radiance

blackout *noun* **1** = **unconsciousness**, coma, faint, loss of consciousness, oblivion, swoon, syncope (*Pathology*) **2** = **power cut**, power failure **3** = **noncommunication**, censorship, radio silence, secrecy, suppression, withholding news

black out *verb* **1** = **darken**, conceal, cover, eclipse, obfuscate, shade **2** = **pass out**, collapse, faint, flake out (*informal*), lose consciousness, swoon

black sheep *noun* = **disgrace**, bad egg (*old-fashioned informal*), dropout, ne'er-do-well, outcast, prodigal, renegade, reprobate, wastrel

blame *verb* **1** = **hold responsible**, accuse, point a *or* the finger at **2** = **criticize**, admonish, blast, censure, charge, chide, condemn, disapprove, express disapprobation, find fault with, lambast(e), put down, reprehend, reproach, reprove, tax, tear into (*informal*), upbraid ♦ *noun* **3** = **responsibility**, accountability, accusation, culpability, fault, guilt, incrimination, liability, onus, rap (*slang*) **4**

= condemnation, castigation, censure, charge, complaint, criticism, recrimination, reproach, reproof, stick (*slang*)
➤ Antonyms
verb ≠**hold responsible**: absolve, acquit, clear, excuse, exonerate, forgive, vindicate ≠**criticize**: acclaim, approve of, commend, compliment, praise ♦ *noun* ≠**responsibility**: absolution, alibi, excuse, exoneration, vindication ≠**condemnation**: acclaim, Brownie points, commendation, credit, honour, praise, tribute

blameless *adjective* = **innocent**, above suspicion, clean, faultless, guiltless, immaculate, impeccable, in the clear, irreproachable, perfect, squeaky-clean, stainless, unblemished, unimpeachable, unoffending, unspotted, unsullied, untarnished, upright, virtuous
➤ Antonyms
at fault, censurable, culpable, guilty, reprovable, responsible, to blame

blameworthy *adjective* = **reprehensible**, discreditable, disreputable, indefensible, inexcusable, iniquitous, reproachable, shameful

bland *adjective* **1** = **dull**, boring, flat, humdrum, insipid, monotonous, tasteless, tedious, tiresome, undistinctive, unexciting, uninspiring, uninteresting, unstimulating, vanilla (*informal*), vapid, weak **2** = **smooth**, affable, amiable, congenial, courteous, debonair, friendly, gentle, gracious, suave, unemotional, urbane
➤ Antonyms
≠**dull**: distinctive, exciting, inspiring, interesting, rousing, stimulating, turbulent, volatile

blandishments *plural noun* = **flattery**, blarney, cajolery, coaxing, compliments, fawning, ingratiation, inveiglement, soft soap (*informal*), soft words, sweet talk (*informal*), wheedling, winning caresses

blank *adjective* **1** = **unmarked**, bare, clean, clear, empty, plain, spotless, uncompleted, unfilled, void, white **2** = **expressionless**, deadpan, dull, empty, hollow, impassive, inane, lifeless, poker-faced (*informal*), vacant, vacuous, vague **3** = **puzzled**, at a loss, at sea, bewildered, confounded, confused, disconcerted, dumbfounded, flummoxed, muddled, nonplussed, uncomprehending **4** = **absolute**, complete, out and out, outright, thorough, total, unqualified, utter ♦ *noun* **5** = **empty space**, emptiness, gap, nothingness, space, tabula rasa, vacancy, vacuity, vacuum, void

➤ Antonyms
adjective ≠**unmarked**: busy, completed, filled in, full, marked ≠**expressionless**: alert, expressive, intelligent, interested, lively, thoughtful

blanket *noun* **1** = **cover**, afghan, coverlet, rug **2** = **covering**, carpet, cloak, coat, coating, envelope, film, layer, mantle, sheet, wrapper, wrapping ♦ *adjective* **3** = **comprehensive**, across-the-board, all-inclusive, overall, sweeping, wide-ranging ♦ *verb* **4** = **cover**, cloak, cloud, coat, conceal, eclipse, hide, mask, obscure, suppress, surround

blankness *noun* = **vacancy**, abstraction, fatuity, inanity, indifference, obliviousness, vacuity

blare *verb* = **sound out**, blast, boom, clamour, clang, honk, hoot, peal, resound, roar, scream, toot, trumpet

blarney *noun* = **flattery**, blandishment, cajolery, coaxing, exaggeration, honeyed words, overpraise, soft soap (*informal*), spiel, sweet talk (*informal*), wheedling

blasé *adjective* = **indifferent**, apathetic, bored, cloyed, glutted, jaded, lukewarm, nonchalant, offhand, satiated, surfeited, unconcerned, unexcited, uninterested, unmoved, weary, world-weary
➤ Antonyms
affected, caring, enthusiastic, excited, interested, responsive, stimulated

blaspheme *verb* = **curse**, abuse, anathematize, damn, desecrate, execrate, profane, revile, swear

blasphemous *adjective* = **irreverent**, godless, impious, irreligious, profane, sacrilegious, ungodly
➤ Antonyms
devout, God-fearing, godly, pious, religious, respectful, reverent, reverential

blasphemy *noun* = **irreverence**, cursing, desecration, execration, impiety, impiousness, indignity (*to God*), profanation, profaneness, profanity, sacrilege, swearing

blast *noun* **1** = **explosion**, bang, blow-up, burst, crash, detonation, discharge, eruption, outburst, salvo, volley **2** = **gust**, gale, squall, storm, strong breeze, tempest **3** = **blare**, blow, clang, honk, peal, scream, toot, wail ♦ *verb* **4** = **blow up**, blow sky-high, break up, burst, demolish, destroy, explode, put paid to, ruin, shatter **5** = **blight**, kill, shrivel, wither **6** = **criticize**, attack, castigate, flay, lambast(e), put down, rail at, tear into (*informal*)

blasted *adjective* = **ruined**, blighted, desolated, destroyed, devastated, ravaged, shattered, spoiled, wasted, withered

blastoff *noun* = **launch**, discharge, expulsion, firing, launching, liftoff, projection, shot

blatant *adjective* = **obvious**, bald, brazen, conspicuous, flagrant, flaunting, glaring, naked, obtrusive, ostentatious, outright, overt, prominent, pronounced, sheer, unmitigated
➤ **Antonyms**
hidden, inconspicuous, quiet, soft, subtle, tasteful, unnoticeable, unobtrusive

blather *noun* = **jabbering**, blether (*Scot.*), claptrap (*informal*), drivel, gibberish, gobbledegook, jabber, moonshine, pap, twaddle

blaze *noun* **1** = **fire**, bonfire, conflagration, flame, flames **2** = **glare**, beam, brilliance, flare, flash, gleam, glitter, glow, light, radiance **3** = **outburst**, blast, burst, eruption, flare-up, fury, outbreak, rush, storm, torrent ◆ *verb* **4** = **burn**, fire, flame **5** = **shine**, beam, flare, flash, glare, gleam, glow **6** = **flare up**, boil, explode, fume, seethe

blazon *verb* = **proclaim**, broadcast, celebrate, flourish, make known, renown, trumpet

bleach *verb* = **whiten**, blanch, etiolate, fade, grow pale, lighten, peroxide, wash out

bleached *adjective* = **whiten**, achromatic, etiolated, faded, lightened, peroxided, stone-washed, washed-out

bleak *adjective* **1** = **exposed**, bare, barren, chilly, cold, desolate, gaunt, open, raw, stark, unsheltered, weather-beaten, windswept, windy **2** = **dismal**, cheerless, comfortless, depressing, discouraging, disheartening, dreary, gloomy, grim, hopeless, joyless, sombre, unpromising
➤ **Antonyms**
≠**exposed**: protected, sheltered, shielded ≠**dismal**: cheerful, cosy, encouraging, promising

bleary *adjective* = **dim**, blurred, blurry, fogged, foggy, fuzzy, hazy, indistinct, misty, murky, rheumy, watery

bleed *verb* **1** = **lose blood**, exude, flow, gush, ooze, run, seep, shed blood, spurt, trickle, weep **2** = **draw** *or* **take blood**, extract, leech, phlebotomize (*Medical*) **3** *Informal* = **extort**, drain, exhaust, fleece, milk, squeeze **4** = **drain**, extract

blemish *noun* **1** = **mark**, blot, blotch, blot on one's escutcheon, blur, defect, demerit, disfigurement, disgrace, dishonour, fault, flaw, imperfection, scar, smirch, smudge, speck, spot, stain, taint ◆ *verb* **2** = **mark**, blot, blotch, blur, damage, deface, disfigure, flaw, impair, injure, mar, smirch,

smudge, spoil, spot, stain, sully, taint, tarnish
➤ **Antonyms**
noun ≠**mark**: enhancement, improvement, ornament, perfection, purity, refinement ◆ *verb* ≠**mark**: correct, enhance, improve, perfect, purify, refine, restore

blend *verb* **1** = **mix**, amalgamate, coalesce, combine, compound, fuse, intermix, meld, merge, mingle, synthesize, unite **2** = **go well**, complement, fit, go with, harmonize, suit ◆ *noun* **3** = **mixture**, alloy, amalgam, amalgamation, combination, composite, compound, concoction, fusion, meld, mix, synthesis, union

bless *verb* **1** = **sanctify**, anoint, consecrate, dedicate, exalt, hallow, invoke happiness on, ordain **2** = **praise**, extol, give thanks to, glorify, magnify, thank **3** = **endow**, bestow, favour, give, grace, grant, provide
➤ **Antonyms**
≠**sanctify**: anathematize, curse, damn, excommunicate, execrate, fulminate, imprecate ≠**endow**: afflict, blight, burden, curse, destroy, doom, plague, scourge, torment, trouble, vex

blessed *adjective* **1** = **holy**, adored, beatified, divine, hallowed, revered, sacred, sanctified **2** = **endowed**, favoured, fortunate, granted, jammy (*Brit. slang*), lucky **3** = **happy**, blissful, contented, glad, joyful, joyous

blessedness *noun* **1** = **sanctity**, beatitude, heavenly joy, state of grace, *summum bonum* **2** = **happiness**, bliss, blissfulness, content, felicity, pleasure

blessing *noun* **1** = **benediction**, benison, commendation, consecration, dedication, grace, invocation, thanksgiving **2** = **approval**, approbation, backing, concurrence, consent, favour, good wishes, leave, permission, regard, sanction, support **3** = **benefit**, advantage, boon, boot (*obsolete*), bounty, favour, gain, gift, godsend, good fortune, help, kindness, manna from heaven, profit, service, windfall
➤ **Antonyms**
≠**benediction**: condemnation, curse, malediction ≠**approval**: disapproval, disfavour, objection, reproof ≠**benefit**: damage, deprivation, disadvantage, drawback, harm, misfortune

blether *noun Scot.* = **jabbering**, blather, claptrap (*informal*), drivel, gibberish, gobbledegook, jabber, moonshine, pap, twaddle

blight *noun* **1** = **curse**, affliction, bane, contamination, corruption, evil, plague, pollution, scourge, woe **2** = **disease**,

canker, decay, fungus, infestation, mildew, pest, pestilence, rot ◆ *verb* **3 = destroy,** blast, injure, nip in the bud, ruin, shrivel, taint with mildew, wither **4 = frustrate,** annihilate, crush, dash, disappoint, mar, nullify, put a damper on, ruin, spoil, undo, wreck
➤ **Antonyms**
noun ≠**curse:** benefaction, blessing, boon, bounty, favour, godsend, help, service

blind *adjective* **1 = sightless,** destitute of vision, eyeless, stone-blind, unseeing, unsighted, visionless **2 = unaware of,** careless, heedless, ignorant, inattentive, inconsiderate, indifferent, injudicious, insensitive, neglectful, oblivious, thoughtless, unconscious of, uncritical, undiscerning, unmindful of, unobservant **3 = unreasoning,** indiscriminate, prejudiced **4 = unthinking,** hasty, impetuous, irrational, mindless, rash, reckless, senseless, uncontrollable, uncontrolled, violent, wild **5 = hidden,** concealed, dim, obscured **6 = dead-end,** closed, dark, leading nowhere, obstructed, without exit ◆ *noun* **7 = cover,** camouflage, cloak, façade, feint, front, mask, masquerade, screen, smoke screen
➤ **Antonyms**
adjective ≠**sightless:** seeing, sighted ≠**unaware of:** alive to, attentive, aware, concerned, conscious, discerning, heedful, knowledgeable, noticeable, observant ≠**hidden:** obvious, open

blindly *adverb* **1 = thoughtlessly,** carelessly, heedlessly, impulsively, inconsiderately, passionately, recklessly, regardlessly, senselessly, unreasonably, wilfully **2 = aimlessly,** at random, confusedly, frantically, indiscriminately, instinctively, madly, purposelessly, wildly

blink *verb* **1 = wink,** bat, flutter, glimpse, nictate, nictitate, peer, squint **2 = flicker,** flash, gleam, glimmer, scintillate, shine, sparkle, twinkle, wink **3 = turn a blind eye to,** condone, connive at, disregard, ignore, overlook, pass by ◆ *noun* **4 on the blink** *Slang* = **not working (properly),** faulty, malfunctioning, on the fritz (*U.S. slang*), out of action, out of order, playing up

bliss *noun* **= joy,** beatitude, blessedness, blissfulness, ecstasy, euphoria, felicity, gladness, happiness, heaven, nirvana, paradise, rapture
➤ **Antonyms**
affliction, anguish, distress, grief, heartbreak, misery, mourning, regret, sadness, sorrow, unhappiness, woe, wretchedness

blissful *adjective* **= joyful,** cock-a-hoop,

delighted, ecstatic, elated, enchanted, enraptured, euphoric, happy, heavenly (*informal*), in ecstasies, joyous, over the moon (*informal*), rapt, rapturous

blister *noun* **= sore,** abscess, blain, bleb, boil, bubble, canker, carbuncle, cyst, furuncle (*Pathology*), pimple, pustule, swelling, ulcer, welt, wen

blithe *adjective* **1 = heedless,** careless, casual, indifferent, nonchalant, thoughtless, unconcerned, untroubled **2 = happy,** animated, buoyant, carefree, cheerful, cheery, chirpy (*informal*), debonair, gay, genial, gladsome (*archaic*), jaunty, light-hearted, merry, mirthful, sprightly, sunny, upbeat (*informal*), vivacious
➤ **Antonyms**
≠**heedless:** concerned, preoccupied, thoughtful ≠**happy:** dejected, depressed, gloomy, melancholy, morose, sad, unhappy

blitz *noun* **= attack,** assault, blitzkrieg, bombardment, campaign, offensive, onslaught, raid, strike

blizzard *noun* **= snowstorm,** blast, gale, squall, storm, tempest

bloat *verb* **= puff up,** balloon, blow up, dilate, distend, enlarge, expand, inflate, swell
➤ **Antonyms**
contract, deflate, shrink, shrivel, wither, wrinkle

blob *noun* **= drop,** ball, bead, bubble, dab, dewdrop, droplet, glob, globule, lump, mass, pearl, pellet, pill

bloc *noun* **= group,** alliance, axis, cabal, clique, coalition, combine, entente, faction, league, ring, schism, union, wing

block *noun* **1 = piece,** bar, brick, cake, chunk, cube, hunk, ingot, lump, mass, nugget, square **2 = obstruction,** bar, barrier, blockage, hindrance, impediment, jam, obstacle, occlusion, stoppage ◆ *verb* **3 = obstruct,** bung up (*informal*), choke, clog, close, plug, stem the flow, stop up **4 = stop,** arrest, bar, check, deter, halt, hinder, hobble, impede, obstruct, put a spoke in someone's wheel, throw a spanner in the works, thwart
➤ **Antonyms**
verb ≠**obstruct:** clear, open, unblock, unclog ≠**stop:** advance, aid, expedite, facilitate, foster, further, lend support to, promote, push, support

blockade *noun* **= stoppage,** barricade, barrier, block, closure, encirclement, hindrance, impediment, obstacle, obstruction, restriction, siege

blockage *noun* **= obstruction,** block,

blocking, impediment, occlusion, stoppage, stopping up

blockhead *noun* = **idiot**, berk (*Brit. slang*), bimbo (*slang*), bonehead (*slang*), charlie (*Brit. informal*), chump (*informal*), coot, dickhead (*slang*), dimwit (*informal*), dipstick (*Brit. slang*), divvy (*Brit. slang*), dolt, dork (*slang*), dullard, dumb-ass (*slang*), dunce, dweeb (*U.S. slang*), fathead (*informal*), fool, fuckwit (*taboo slang*), geek (*slang*), gobshite (*Irish taboo slang*), gonzo (*slang*), ignoramus, jerk (*slang, chiefly U.S. & Canad.*), nerd *or* nurd (*slang*), nitwit, noodle, numbskull *or* numskull, numpty (*Scot. informal*), pillock (*Brit. slang*), plank (*Brit. slang*), plonker (*slang*), prat (*slang*), prick (*slang*), schmuck (*U.S. slang*), thickhead, twit (*informal, chiefly Brit.*), wally (*slang*)

block out *verb* = **outline**, chart, map out, plan, sketch

bloke *noun Informal* = **man**, bastard (*informal*), bod (*informal*), body, boy, bugger (*slang*), chap, character (*informal*), customer (*informal*), fellow, guy (*informal*), individual, person, punter (*informal*)

blond, blonde *adjective* = **fair**, fair-haired, fair-skinned, flaxen, golden-haired, light, light-coloured, light-complexioned, tow-headed

blood *noun* 1 = **lifeblood**, gore, vital fluid 2 = **family**, ancestry, birth, consanguinity, descendants, descent, extraction, kindred, kinship, lineage, noble extraction, relations 3 = **feeling**, anger, disposition, passion, spirit, temper

bloodcurdling *adjective* = **terrifying**, appalling, chilling, dreadful, fearful, frightening, hair-raising, horrendous, horrifying, scaring, spine-chilling

bloodless *adjective* 1 = **pale**, anaemic, ashen, chalky, colourless, like death warmed up (*informal*), pallid, pasty, sallow, sickly, wan 2 = **listless**, cold, languid, lifeless, passionless, spiritless, torpid, unemotional, unfeeling

bloodshed *noun* = **killing**, blood bath, blood-letting, butchery, carnage, gore, massacre, murder, slaughter, slaying

bloodthirsty *adjective* = **cruel**, barbarous, brutal, cut-throat, ferocious, gory, inhuman, murderous, ruthless, savage, vicious, warlike

bloody *adjective* 1 = **bloodstained**, bleeding, blood-soaked, blood-spattered, gaping, raw, unstaunched 2 = **cruel**, ferocious, fierce, sanguinary, savage

bloom *noun* 1 = **flower**, blossom, blossoming, bud, efflorescence, opening

(*of flowers*) 2 = **prime**, beauty, flourishing, health, heyday, perfection, vigour 3 = **glow**, blush, flush, freshness, lustre, radiance, rosiness ♦ *verb* 4 = **blossom**, blow, bud, burgeon, open, sprout 5 = **flourish**, develop, fare well, grow, prosper, succeed, thrive, wax
➤ **Antonyms**
noun ≠**glow**: bloodlessness, paleness, pallor, wanness, whiteness ♦ *verb* ≠**blossom, flourish**: decay, decline, die, droop, fade, fail, languish, perish, shrink, shrivel, wane, waste, wilt, wither

blossom *noun* 1 = **flower**, bloom, bud, floret, flowers ♦ *verb* 2 = **flower**, bloom, burgeon 3 = **grow**, bloom, develop, flourish, mature, progress, prosper, thrive

blot *noun* 1 = **spot**, blotch, mark, patch, smear, smudge, speck, splodge 2 = **stain**, blemish, blot on one's escutcheon, blur, defect, demerit, disgrace, fault, flaw, scar, smirch, spot, taint ♦ *verb* 3 = **stain**, bespatter, disfigure, disgrace, mark, smirch, smudge, spoil, spot, sully, tarnish 4 = **soak up**, absorb, dry, take up 5 **blot out**: **a** = **obliterate**, darken, destroy, eclipse, efface, obscure, shadow **b** = **erase**, cancel, expunge

blotch *noun*, *verb* = **mark**, blemish, blot, patch, scar, smirch, smudge, smutch, splash, splodge, spot, stain

blotchy *adjective* = **spotty**, blemished, macular, patchy, reddened, scurvy, uneven

blow¹ *verb* 1 = **carry**, bear, buffet, drive, fling, flutter, move, sweep, waft, whirl, whisk 2 = **exhale**, breathe, pant, puff 3 = **play**, blare, mouth, pipe, sound, toot, trumpet, vibrate 4 **blow one's top** *Informal* = **lose one's temper**, blow up (*informal*), do one's nut (*Brit. slang*), explode, flip one's lid (*slang*), fly into a temper, fly off the handle (*informal*), go spare (*Brit. slang*), have a fit (*informal*), lose it (*informal*), lose the plot (*informal*), see red (*informal*), throw a tantrum ♦ *noun* 5 = **gust**, blast, draught, flurry, gale, puff, strong breeze, tempest, wind

blow² *noun* 1 = **knock**, bang, bash (*informal*), belt (*informal*), buffet, clomp (*slang*), clout (*informal*), clump (*slang*), punch, rap, slosh (*Brit. slang*), smack, sock (*slang*), stroke, thump, tonk (*informal*), wallop (*informal*), whack 2 = **setback**, affliction, bolt from the blue, bombshell, bummer (*slang*), calamity, catastrophe, choker (*informal*), comedown (*informal*), disappointment, disaster, jolt, misfortune, reverse, shock, sucker punch, upset, whammy (*informal, chiefly U.S.*)

blowout *noun* 1 = **burst**, break, flat, flat

tyre, leak, puncture, rupture, tear **2**
= **explosion**, blast, detonation, eruption **3**
Slang = **binge** (*informal*), beano (*Brit.
slang*), carousal, carouse, feast, hooley *or*
hoolie (*chiefly Irish & N.Z.*), party, rave
(*Brit. slang*), rave-up (*Brit. slang*), spree

blow out *verb* **1** = **put out**, extinguish,
snuff **2** = **burst**, erupt, explode, rupture,
shatter

blow over *verb* = **die down**, be forgotten,
cease, disappear, end, finish, pass, pass
away, subside, vanish

blowsy, blowzy *adjective* **1** = **slovenly**,
bedraggled, dishevelled, frowzy, slatternly,
slipshod, sloppy, sluttish, tousled,
unkempt, untidy **2** = **red-faced**, florid,
ruddy

blow up *verb* **1** = **explode**, blast, blow
sky-high, bomb, burst, detonate,
dynamite, go off, rupture, shatter **2**
= **inflate**, bloat, distend, enlarge, expand,
fill, puff up, pump up, swell **3**
= **exaggerate**, blow out of (all) proportion,
enlarge, enlarge on, heighten, magnify,
make a mountain out of a molehill, make a
production out of, overstate **4** *Informal*
= **lose one's temper**, become angry,
become enraged, blow a fuse (*slang,
chiefly U.S.*), crack up (*informal*), erupt, flip
one's lid (*slang*), fly off the handle
(*informal*), go ballistic (*slang, chiefly U.S.*),
go off the deep end (*informal*), go up the
wall (*slang*), hit the roof (*informal*), lose it
(*informal*), lose the plot (*informal*), rage,
see red (*informal*), wig out (*slang*)

bludgeon *noun* **1** = **club**, cosh (*Brit.*),
cudgel, shillelagh, truncheon ♦ *verb* **2**
= **club**, beat, beat up, cosh (*Brit.*), cudgel,
knock down, strike **3** = **bully**, browbeat,
bulldoze (*informal*), coerce, dragoon,
force, hector, put the screws on, railroad
(*informal*), steamroller

blue *adjective* **1** = **azure**, cerulean, cobalt,
cyan, navy, sapphire, sky-coloured,
ultramarine **2** = **depressed**, dejected,
despondent, dismal, downcast,
down-hearted, down in the dumps
(*informal*), down in the mouth, fed up,
gloomy, glum, low, melancholy, sad,
unhappy **3** = **smutty**, bawdy, dirty,
indecent, lewd, naughty, near the knuckle
(*informal*), obscene, risqué, vulgar, X-rated
(*informal*)
➤ Antonyms
≠**depressed**: blithe, cheerful, cheery,
chirpy (*informal*), elated, genial, happy,
jolly, merry, optimistic, sunny ≠**smutty**:
decent, respectable

blueprint *noun* = **plan**, design, draft,
layout, norm, outline, pattern, pilot

scheme, project, prototype, scheme, sketch

blues *plural noun* = **depression**, dejection,
despondency, doldrums, dumps
(*informal*), gloom, gloominess, glumness,
low spirits, melancholy, moodiness, the
hump (*Brit. informal*), unhappiness

bluff[1] *verb* **1** = **deceive**, con, defraud,
delude, fake, feign, humbug, lie, mislead,
pretend, pull the wool over someone's
eyes, sham ♦ *noun* **2** = **deception**, bluster,
boast, braggadocio, bragging, bravado,
deceit, fake, feint, fraud, humbug, idle
boast, lie, mere show, pretence, sham,
show, subterfuge

bluff[2] *noun* **1** = **precipice**, bank, cliff, crag,
escarpment, headland, peak, promontory,
ridge, scarp ♦ *adjective* **2** = **hearty**, abrupt,
blunt, blustering, downright, frank, genial,
good-natured, open, outspoken,
plain-spoken **3** = **steep**, abrupt,
perpendicular, precipitous, sheer,
towering
➤ Antonyms
adjective ≠**hearty**: delicate, diplomatic,
discreet, judicious, sensitive, tactful,
thoughtful

blunder *noun* **1** = **mistake**, bloomer (*Brit.
informal*), boob (*Brit. slang*), boo-boo
(*informal*), clanger (*informal*), faux pas,
gaffe, gaucherie, howler (*informal*),
impropriety, indiscretion **2** = **error**, fault,
inaccuracy, mistake, oversight, slip, slip-up
(*informal*) ♦ *verb* **3** = **make a mistake**,
bodge (*informal*), botch, bungle, drop a
brick (*Brit. informal*), drop a clanger
(*informal*), err, flub (*U.S. slang*), put one's
foot in it (*informal*), slip up (*informal*) **4**
= **stumble**, bumble, confuse, flounder,
misjudge
➤ Antonyms
noun ≠**error**: accuracy, correctness ♦ *verb*
≠**make a mistake**: be correct, be exact,
get it right

blunt *adjective* **1** = **dull**, dulled, edgeless,
pointless, rounded, unsharpened **2**
= **forthright**, bluff, brusque, discourteous,
downright, explicit, frank, impolite,
outspoken, plain-spoken, rude,
straightforward, straight from the
shoulder, tactless, trenchant, uncivil,
unpolished, upfront (*informal*) ♦ *verb* **3**
= **dull**, dampen, deaden, numb, soften,
take the edge off, water down, weaken
➤ Antonyms
adjective ≠**dull**: keen, pointed, sharp
≠**forthright**: acute, courteous, diplomatic,
keen, pointed, sensitive, sharp, subtle,
tactful ♦ *verb* ≠**dull**: animate, put an edge
on, sharpen, stimulate, vitalize

blur *verb* **1** = **make indistinct**, becloud,

bedim, befog, blear, cloud, darken, dim, fog, make hazy, make vague, mask, obscure, soften **2** = **smudge**, blot, smear, spot, stain ♦ *noun* **3** = **indistinctness**, blear, blurredness, cloudiness, confusion, dimness, fog, haze, obscurity **4** = **smudge**, blot, smear, spot, stain

blurred *adjective* = **indistinct**, bleary, blurry, dim, faint, foggy, fuzzy, hazy, ill-defined, lacking definition, misty, nebulous, out of focus, unclear, vague

blurt out *verb* = **exclaim**, babble, blab, blow the gaff (*Brit. slang*), cry, disclose, gush, let the cat out of the bag, reveal, run off at the mouth (*slang*), spill, spill one's guts (*slang*), spill the beans (*informal*), spout (*informal*), sputter, tattle, tell all, utter suddenly

blush *verb* **1** = **turn red**, colour, crimson, flush, go red (as a beetroot), redden, turn scarlet ♦ *noun* **2** = **reddening**, colour, flush, glow, pink tinge, rosiness, rosy tint, ruddiness
➤ **Antonyms**
verb ≠**turn red**: blanch, blench, drain, fade, pale, turn pale, whiten

bluster *verb* **1** = **roar**, bulldoze, bully, domineer, hector, rant, roister, storm **2** = **boast**, blow one's own horn (*U.S. & Canad.*), blow one's own trumpet, brag, swagger, swell, vaunt ♦ *noun* **3** = **hot air** (*informal*), bluff, boasting, boisterousness, bombast, bragging, bravado, crowing, swagger, swaggering

blustery *adjective* = **gusty**, blusterous, boisterous, inclement, squally, stormy, tempestuous, violent, wild, windy

board *noun* **1** = **plank**, panel, piece of timber, slat, timber **2** = **directors**, advisers, advisory group, committee, conclave, council, directorate, panel, quango, trustees **3** = **meals**, daily meals, provisions, victuals ♦ *verb* **4** = **get on**, embark, embus, enplane, enter, entrain, mount **5** = **lodge**, accommodate, feed, house, put up, quarter, room
➤ **Antonyms**
verb ≠**get on**: alight, arrive, disembark, dismount, get off, go ashore, land

boast *verb* **1** = **brag**, blow one's own trumpet, bluster, crow, exaggerate, puff, strut, swagger, talk big (*slang*), vaunt **2** = **possess**, be proud of, congratulate oneself on, exhibit, flatter oneself, pride oneself on, show off ♦ *noun* **3** = **brag**, avowal, gasconade (*rare*), rodomontade (*literary*), swank (*informal*), vaunt **4** = **source of pride**, gem, joy, pride, pride and joy, treasure
➤ **Antonyms**

verb ≠**brag**: cover up, depreciate, disavow, disclaim ♦ *noun* ≠**brag**: disavowal, disclaimer

boastful *adjective* = **bragging**, cocky, conceited, crowing, egotistical, full of oneself, puffed-up, swaggering, swanky (*informal*), swollen-headed, vainglorious, vaunting
➤ **Antonyms**
deprecating, humble, modest, self-belittling, self-effacing, unassuming

bob *verb* = **duck**, bounce, hop, jerk, leap, nod, oscillate, quiver, skip, waggle, weave, wobble

bode *verb* = **portend**, augur, be an omen of, betoken, forebode, foreshadow, foretell, forewarn, omen, predict, presage, prophesy, signify, threaten

bodily *adjective* = **physical**, actual, carnal, corporal, corporeal, fleshly, material, substantial, tangible

body *noun* **1** = **physique**, build, figure, form, frame, shape **2** = **torso**, trunk **3** = **corpse**, cadaver, carcass, dead body, relics, remains, stiff (*slang*) **4** = **organization**, association, band, bloc, collection, company, confederation, congress, corporation, society **5** = **mass**, crowd, horde, majority, mob, multitude, throng **6** = **main part**, bulk, essence, mass, material, matter, substance **7** = **consistency**, density, firmness, richness, solidity, substance **8** *Informal* = **person**, being, creature, human, human being, individual, mortal

boffin *noun Brit. informal* = **expert**, authority, bluestocking (*usually disparaging*), brain(s) (*informal*), brainbox, egghead, genius, guru, intellect, intellectual, inventor, mastermind, maven (*U.S.*), planner, thinker, virtuoso, wizard

bog *noun* = **marsh**, fen, marshland, mire, morass, moss (*Scot. & Northern English dialect*), peat bog, quagmire, slough, swamp, wetlands

bog down *verb* = **hold up**, delay, halt, impede, sink, slow down, slow up, stall, stick

bogey *noun* **1** = **spirit**, apparition, bogeyman, goblin, hobgoblin, imp, spectre, spook (*informal*), sprite **2** = **bugbear**, bête noire, bugaboo, nightmare

boggle *verb* **1** = **be confused**, be alarmed, be surprised, be taken aback, shy, stagger, startle, take fright **2** = **hesitate**, demur, dither (*chiefly Brit.*), doubt, equivocate, falter, hang back, hover, jib, shillyshally (*informal*), shrink from, vacillate, waver

boggy *adjective* = **marshy**, fenny, miry, muddy, oozy, quaggy, soft, spongy, swampy, waterlogged, yielding

bogus *adjective* = **fake**, artificial, counterfeit, dummy, ersatz, false, forged, fraudulent, imitation, phoney *or* phony (*informal*), pseudo (*informal*), sham, spurious
➤ Antonyms
actual, authentic, genuine, real, true

bohemian *adjective* **1** = **unconventional**, alternative, artistic, arty (*informal*), avant-garde, eccentric, exotic, left bank, nonconformist, oddball (*informal*), offbeat, off-the-wall (*slang*), outré, unorthodox, way-out (*informal*) ◆ *noun* **2** = **nonconformist**, beatnik, dropout, hippy, iconoclast
➤ Antonyms
adjective ≠**unconventional**: bourgeois, conservative, conventional, Pooterish, square (*informal*), straight (*slang*), straight-laced, stuffy

boil¹ *verb* **1** = **bubble**, agitate, churn, effervesce, fizz, foam, froth, seethe **2** = **be furious**, be angry, be indignant, blow a fuse (*slang, chiefly U.S.*), crack up (*informal*), fly off the handle (*informal*), foam at the mouth (*informal*), fulminate, fume, go ballistic (*slang, chiefly U.S.*), go off the deep end (*informal*), go up the wall (*slang*), rage, rave, see red (*informal*), storm, wig out (*slang*)

boil² *noun* = **pustule**, blain, blister, carbuncle, furuncle (*Pathology*), gathering, swelling, tumour, ulcer

boil down *verb* = **reduce**, come down, condense, decrease

boiling *adjective* **1** = **very hot**, baking, blistering, hot, roasting, scorching, tropical **2** = **furious**, angry, choked, cross, enraged, foaming at the mouth, fuming, incandescent, incensed, indignant, infuriated, on the warpath

boisterous *adjective* **1** = **unruly**, bouncy, clamorous, disorderly, impetuous, loud, noisy, obstreperous, riotous, rollicking, rowdy, rumbustious, unrestrained, uproarious, vociferous, wild **2** = **stormy**, blustery, gusty, raging, rough, squally, tempestuous, tumultuous, turbulent
➤ Antonyms
≠**unruly**: calm, controlled, peaceful, quiet, restrained, self-controlled, subdued ≠**stormy**: calm, peaceful, quiet

bold *adjective* **1** = **fearless**, adventurous, audacious, brave, courageous, daring, dauntless, enterprising, gallant, gritty, heroic, intrepid, lion-hearted, valiant, valorous **2** = **impudent**, barefaced, brash,

brazen, cheeky, confident, feisty (*informal*, chiefly U.S. & Canad.*), forward, fresh (*informal*), insolent, in-your-face (*Brit. slang*), pert, pushy (*informal*), rude, sassy (*U.S. informal*), saucy, shameless **3** = **conspicuous**, bright, colourful, eye-catching, flashy, forceful, lively, loud, prominent, pronounced, salient, showy, spirited, striking, strong, vivid
➤ Antonyms
≠**fearless**: cowardly, faint-hearted, fearful, timid, timorous ≠**impudent**: conservative, cool, courteous, meek, modest, polite, retiring, shy, tactful ≠**conspicuous**: dull, ordinary, pale, soft

bolster *verb* = **support**, aid, assist, augment, boost, brace, buoy up, buttress, cushion, give a leg up (*informal*), help, hold up, maintain, pillow, prop, reinforce, shore up, stay, strengthen

bolt *noun* **1** = **bar**, catch, fastener, latch, lock, sliding bar **2** = **pin**, peg, rivet, rod **3** = **dash**, bound, dart, escape, flight, rush, spring, sprint **4** = **arrow**, dart, missile, projectile, shaft, thunderbolt ◆ *verb* **5** = **run away**, abscond, bound, dash, decamp, do a runner (*slang*), escape, flee, fly, fly the coop (*U.S. & Canad. informal*), hurtle, jump, leap, make a break (for it), run, run for it, rush, skedaddle (*informal*), spring, sprint, take a powder (*U.S. & Canad. slang*), take it on the lam (*U.S. & Canad. slang*) **6** = **lock**, bar, fasten, latch, secure **7** = **gobble**, cram, devour, gorge, gulp, guzzle, stuff, swallow whole, wolf

bomb *noun* **1** = **explosive**, bombshell, charge, device, grenade, mine, missile, projectile, rocket, shell, torpedo ◆ *verb* **2** = **blow up**, attack, blow sky-high, bombard, destroy, shell, strafe, torpedo

bombard *verb* **1** = **bomb**, assault, blast, blitz, cannonade, fire upon, open fire, pound, shell, strafe **2** = **attack**, assail, barrage, batter, beset, besiege, harass, hound, pester

bombardment *noun* = **bombing**, assault, attack, barrage, blitz, cannonade, fire, flak, fusillade, shelling, strafe

bombast *noun* = **grandiloquence**, bluster, brag, braggadocio, extravagant boasting, fustian, gasconade (*rare*), grandiosity, hot air (*informal*), magniloquence, pomposity, rant, rodomontade (*literary*)

bombastic *adjective* = **grandiloquent**, declamatory, fustian, grandiose, high-flown, histrionic, inflated, magniloquent, pompous, ranting, turgid, verbose, windy, wordy

bona fide *adjective* = **genuine**, actual, authentic, honest, kosher (*informal*),

lawful, legal, legitimate, on the level (*informal*), real, the real McCoy, true
➤ **Antonyms**
bogus, counterfeit, ersatz, fake, false, imitation, phoney *or* phony (*informal*), sham

bond *noun* 1 = **fastening**, band, binding, chain, cord, fetter, ligature, link, manacle, shackle, tie 2 = **tie**, affiliation, affinity, attachment, connection, link, relation, union 3 = **agreement**, compact, contract, covenant, guarantee, obligation, pledge, promise, word ♦ *verb* 4 = **hold together**, bind, connect, fasten, fix together, fuse, glue, gum, paste

bondage *noun* = **slavery**, captivity, confinement, enslavement, imprisonment, subjugation

bonny *adjective Scot. & N English dialect* = **beautiful**, comely, fair, handsome, lovely, pretty, sweet

bonus *noun* = **extra**, benefit, bounty, commission, dividend, gift, gratuity, hand-out, honorarium, icing on the cake, perk (*Brit. informal*), plus, premium, prize, reward

bon vivant *noun* = **gourmet**, bon viveur, epicure, epicurean, foodie, gastronome, hedonist, luxurist, pleasure-seeker, voluptuary
➤ **Antonyms**
abstainer, ascetic, celibate, self-denier

bony *adjective* = **thin**, angular, emaciated, gangling, gaunt, lanky, lean, macilent (*rare*), rawboned, scrawny, skin and bone, skinny

book *noun* 1 = **work**, hardback, manual, paperback, publication, roll, scroll, textbook, title, tome, tract, volume 2 = **notebook**, album, diary, exercise book, jotter, pad ♦ *verb* 3 = **reserve**, arrange for, bill, charter, engage, line up, make reservations, organize, procure, programme, schedule 4 = **note**, enrol, enter, insert, list, log, mark down, post, put down, record, register, write down

bookish *adjective* = **studious**, academic, donnish, erudite, intellectual, learned, literary, pedantic, scholarly, well-read

booklet *noun* = **brochure**, leaflet, pamphlet

boom *verb* 1 = **bang**, blast, crash, explode, resound, reverberate, roar, roll, rumble, thunder 2 = **flourish**, develop, expand, gain, grow, increase, intensify, prosper, spurt, strengthen, succeed, swell, thrive ♦ *noun* 3 = **bang**, blast, burst, clap, crash, explosion, roar, rumble, thunder 4 = **expansion**, advance, boost, development, gain, growth, improvement, increase, jump, push, spurt, upsurge,

upswing, upturn
➤ **Antonyms**
verb ≠**flourish**: crash, fail, fall, slump ♦ *noun* ≠**expansion**: bust (*informal*), collapse, crash, decline, depression, downturn, failure, hard times, recession, slump

boomerang *verb* = **rebound**, backfire, come back, come home to roost, recoil, return, reverse, ricochet

boon[1] *noun* = **benefit**, advantage, benefaction, blessing, donation, favour, gift, godsend, grant, gratuity, hand-out, manna from heaven, present, windfall

boon[2] *adjective* = **intimate**, close, special

boor *noun* = **lout**, barbarian, brute, bumpkin, churl, clodhopper (*informal*), clodpole, hayseed (*U.S. & Canad. informal*), hick (*informal, chiefly U.S. & Canad.*), oaf, peasant, philistine, redneck (*U.S. slang*), vulgarian

boorish *adjective* = **loutish**, awkward, barbaric, bearish, churlish, clownish, coarse, crude, gross, gruff, hick (*informal, chiefly U.S. & Canad.*), ill-bred, lubberly, oafish, rude, rustic, uncivilized, uncouth, uneducated, unrefined, vulgar
➤ **Antonyms**
cultured, gallant, genteel, polite, refined, sophisticated, urbane

boost *noun* 1 = **help**, encouragement, gee-up, hype, improvement, praise, promotion 2 = **push**, heave, hoist, lift, raise, shove, thrust 3 = **rise**, addition, expansion, improvement, increase, increment, jump ♦ *verb* 4 = **increase**, add to, amplify, develop, enlarge, expand, heighten, hoick, jack up, magnify, raise 5 = **promote**, advance, advertise, assist, crack up (*informal*), encourage, foster, further, gee up, hype, improve, inspire, plug (*informal*), praise, support, sustain 6 = **raise**, elevate, heave, hoist, lift, push, shove, thrust
➤ **Antonyms**
noun ≠**help**: condemnation, criticism, knock (*informal*) ≠**rise**: cut-back, decline, decrease, deterioration, fall, reduction ♦ *verb* ≠**increase**: cut, decrease, diminish, drop, lessen, lower, moderate, pare, reduce, scale down ≠**promote**: condemn, criticize, hinder, hold back, knock (*informal*) ≠**raise**: drop, let down, lower

boot *verb* = **kick**, drive, drop-kick, knock, punt, put the boot in(to) (*slang*), shove

bootless *adjective* = **useless**, fruitless, futile, ineffective, profitless, to no avail, unavailing, unsuccessful, vain

boot out *verb Informal* 1 = **throw out**, eject, give the bum's rush (*slang*), kick out, show one the door, throw out on one's ear (*informal*) **2 = sack** (*informal*), dismiss, expel, give (someone) their marching orders, give the boot (*slang*), give the bullet (*Brit. slang*), give the heave *or* push (*informal*), kick out, kiss off (*slang, chiefly U.S. & Canad.*), oust, relegate

booty *noun* **= plunder**, boodle (*slang, chiefly U.S.*), gains, haul, loot, pillage, prey, spoil, spoils, swag (*slang*), takings, winnings

border *noun* **1 = frontier**, borderline, boundary, line, march **2 = edge**, bound, boundary, bounds, brim, brink, confine, confines, flange, hem, limit, limits, lip, margin, pale, rim, skirt, verge ♦ *verb* **3 = edge**, bind, decorate, fringe, hem, rim, trim

borderline *adjective* **= marginal**, ambivalent, doubtful, equivocal, indecisive, indefinite, indeterminate, inexact, unclassifiable

border on *verb* **1 = adjoin**, abut, connect, contact, impinge, join, march, neighbour, touch, verge on **2 = come close to**, approach, approximate, be like, be similar to, come near, echo, match, parallel, resemble

bore¹ *verb* **1 = drill**, burrow, gouge out, mine, penetrate, perforate, pierce, sink, tunnel ♦ *noun* **2 = hole**, borehole, calibre, drill hole, shaft, tunnel

bore² *verb* **1 = tire**, annoy, be tedious, bother, exhaust, fatigue, jade, pall on, pester, send to sleep, trouble, vex, wear out, weary, worry ♦ *noun* **2 = nuisance**, anorak (*informal*), bother, drag (*informal*), dullard, dull person, headache (*informal*), pain (*informal*), pain in the arse (*taboo informal*), pain in the neck (*informal*), pest, tiresome person, wearisome talker, yawn (*informal*)
➤ **Antonyms**
verb ≠ **tire:** amuse, divert, engross, excite, fascinate, hold the attention of, interest, stimulate

bored *adjective* **= fed up**, listless, tired, uninterested, wearied

boredom *noun* **= tedium**, apathy, doldrums, dullness, ennui, flatness, irksomeness, monotony, sameness, tediousness, weariness, world-weariness
➤ **Antonyms**
amusement, entertainment, excitement, interest, stimulation

boring *adjective* **= uninteresting**, dead, dull, flat, ho-hum (*informal*), humdrum, insipid, mind-numbing, monotonous, old, repetitious, routine, stale, tedious, tiresome, tiring, unexciting, unvaried,

wearisome

borrow *verb* **1 = take on loan**, blag (*slang*), cadge, mooch (*slang*), scrounge (*informal*), take and return, touch (someone) for (*slang*), use temporarily **2 = steal**, acquire, adopt, appropriate, copy, filch, imitate, obtain, pilfer, pirate, plagiarize, simulate, take, use, usurp
➤ **Antonyms**
≠ **take on loan:** advance, give, lend, loan, provide, return, supply

bosom *noun* **1 = breast**, bust, chest **2 = feelings**, affections, emotions, heart, sentiments, soul, spirit, sympathies **3 = midst**, centre, circle, core, protection, shelter ♦ *adjective* **4 = intimate**, boon, cherished, close, confidential, dear, very dear

boss¹ *noun* **1 = head**, administrator, big cheese (*slang, old-fashioned*), chief, director, employer, executive, foreman, gaffer (*informal, chiefly Brit.*), governor (*informal*), kingpin, leader, manager, master, Mister Big (*slang, chiefly U.S.*), numero uno (*informal*), overseer, owner, superintendent, supervisor, torchbearer ♦ *verb* **2 = be in charge**, administrate, call the shots, call the tune, command, control, direct, employ, manage, oversee, run, superintend, supervise, take charge

boss² *noun* **= stud**, knob, nub, nubble, point, protuberance, tip

boss around *verb Informal* **= domineer**, bully, dominate, oppress, order, overbear, push around (*slang*), put upon, ride roughshod over, tyrannize

bossy *adjective Informal* **= domineering**, arrogant, authoritarian, autocratic, despotic, dictatorial, hectoring, high-handed, imperious, lordly, overbearing, tyrannical

botch *verb* **1 = spoil**, balls up (*taboo slang*), blunder, bodge (*informal*), bungle, butcher, cobble, cock up (*Brit. slang*), flub (*U.S. slang*), fuck up (*offensive taboo slang*), fumble, make a nonsense of (*informal*), make a pig's ear of (*informal*), mar, mend, mess up, mismanage, muff, patch, screw up (*informal*) ♦ *noun* **2 = mess**, balls-up (*taboo slang*), blunder, bungle, bungling, cock-up (*Brit. slang*), failure, fuck-up (*offensive taboo slang*), fumble, hash, miscarriage, pig's breakfast (*informal*), pig's ear (*informal*)

bother *verb* **1 = trouble**, alarm, annoy, bend someone's ear (*informal*), breathe down someone's neck, concern, dismay, distress, disturb, gall, get on one's nerves (*informal*), get on one's wick (*Brit. slang*), harass, hassle (*informal*), inconvenience,

irritate, molest, nag, nark (*Brit., Austral. & N.Z. slang*), pester, plague, put out, upset, vex, worry ♦ *noun* **2 = trouble**, aggravation, annoyance, bustle, difficulty, flurry, fuss, gall, grief (*informal*), hassle (*informal*), inconvenience, irritation, molestation, nuisance, perplexity, pest, problem, strain, vexation, worry
➤ **Antonyms**
verb ≠**trouble**: aid, assist, facilitate, further, help, relieve, succour, support ♦ *noun* ≠**trouble**: advantage, aid, benefit, comfort, convenience, help, service, use

bothersome *adjective* = **troublesome**, aggravating, annoying, distressing, exasperating, inconvenient, irritating, tiresome, vexatious, vexing
➤ **Antonyms**
appropriate, beneficial, commodious, convenient, handy, helpful, serviceable, useful

bottleneck *noun* = **hold-up**, block, blockage, congestion, impediment, jam, obstacle, obstruction, snarl-up (*informal, chiefly Brit.*)

bottle up *verb* = **suppress**, check, contain, curb, keep back, restrict, shut in, trap

bottom *noun* **1 = lowest part**, base, basis, bed, deepest part, depths, floor, foot, foundation, groundwork, pedestal, support **2 = underside**, lower side, sole, underneath **3 = buttocks**, arse (*taboo slang*), ass (*U.S. & Canad. taboo slang*), backside, behind (*informal*), bum (*Brit. slang*), buns (*U.S. slang*), butt (*U.S. & Canad. informal*), derrière (*euphemistic*), fundament, jacksy (*Brit. slang*), posterior, rear, rear end, rump, seat, tail (*informal*), tush (*U.S. slang*) **4 = basis**, base, cause, core, essence, ground, heart, mainspring, origin, principle, root, source, substance ♦ *adjective* **5 = lowest**, base, basement, basic, ground, last, undermost
➤ **Antonyms**
noun ≠**lowest part**: cover, crown, height, lid, peak, summit, surface, top ♦ *adjective* ≠**lowest**: higher, highest, top, upper

bottomless *adjective* = **unlimited**, boundless, deep, fathomless, immeasurable, inexhaustible, infinite, unfathomable

bounce *verb* **1 = rebound**, bob, bound, bump, jounce, jump, leap, recoil, resile, ricochet, spring, thump **2** *Slang* = **throw out**, boot out (*informal*), eject, fire (*informal*), kick out (*informal*), oust, relegate ♦ *noun* **3** *Informal* = **life**, animation, brio, dynamism, energy, go (*informal*), liveliness, pep, vigour, vitality, vivacity, zip (*informal*) **4 = springiness**,

bound, elasticity, give, rebound, recoil, resilience, spring

bouncing *adjective* = **lively**, alive and kicking, blooming, bonny, fighting fit, fit as a fiddle (*informal*), healthy, robust, thriving, vigorous

bound[1] *adjective* **1 = tied**, cased, fastened, fixed, pinioned, secured, tied up **2 = certain**, destined, doomed, fated, sure **3 = obliged**, beholden, committed, compelled, constrained, duty-bound, forced, obligated, pledged, required

bound[2] *verb* = **limit**, circumscribe, confine, define, delimit, demarcate, encircle, enclose, hem in, restrain, restrict, surround, terminate

bound[3] *verb, noun* = **leap**, bob, bounce, caper, frisk, gambol, hurdle, jump, lope, pounce, prance, skip, spring, vault

boundary *noun* = **limits**, barrier, border, borderline, bounds, brink, confines, edge, extremity, fringe, frontier, march, margin, pale, precinct, termination, verge

boundless *adjective* = **unlimited**, endless, illimitable, immeasurable, immense, incalculable, inexhaustible, infinite, limitless, measureless, the sky's the limit, unbounded, unconfined, unending, untold, vast
➤ **Antonyms**
bounded, confined, limited, little, restricted, small

bounds *plural noun* **1 = boundary**, border, confine, edge, extremity, fringe, limit, line, march, margin, pale, periphery, rim, termination, verge **2 out of bounds = forbidden**, banned, barred, off-limits (*chiefly U.S. military*), prohibited, taboo

bountiful *adjective* *Literary* **1 = plentiful**, abundant, ample, bounteous, copious, exuberant, lavish, luxuriant, plenteous, prolific **2 = generous**, beneficent, bounteous, liberal, magnanimous, munificent, open-handed, princely, prodigal, unstinting

bounty *noun* *Literary* **1 = generosity**, benevolence, charity, kindness, largesse *or* largess, liberality, philanthropy **2 = reward**, bonus, gift, present

bouquet *noun* **1 = bunch of flowers**, boutonniere, buttonhole, corsage, garland, nosegay, posy, spray, wreath **2 = aroma**, fragrance, perfume, redolence, savour, scent

bourgeois *adjective* = **middle-class**, conventional, hidebound, materialistic, Pooterish, traditional

bout *noun* **1 = period**, course, fit, round, run, session, spell, spree, stint, stretch, term, time, turn **2** = **fight**, battle, boxing match, competition, contest, encounter, engagement, head-to-head, match, set-to, struggle

bovine *adjective* = **dull**, dense, dozy (*Brit. informal*), slow, sluggish, stolid, stupid, thick

bow[1] *verb* **1** = **bend**, bob, droop, genuflect, incline, make obeisance, nod, stoop **2** = **give in**, accept, acquiesce, comply, concede, defer, kowtow, relent, submit, succumb, surrender, yield ◆ *noun* **3** = **bending**, bob, genuflexion, inclination, kowtow, nod, obeisance, salaam

bow[2] *noun Nautical* = **prow**, beak, fore, head, stem

bowdlerize *verb* = **censor**, blue-pencil, clean up, expurgate, mutilate, sanitize

bowels *plural noun* **1** = **guts**, entrails, innards (*informal*), insides (*informal*), intestines, viscera, vitals **2** = **depths**, belly, core, deep, hold, inside, interior

bower *noun* = **arbour**, alcove, grotto, leafy shelter, shady recess, summerhouse

bowl[1] *noun* = **basin**, dish, vessel

bowl[2] *verb* **1** = **roll**, revolve, rotate, spin, trundle, whirl **2** = **throw**, fling, hurl, pitch

bowl over *verb* **1** *Informal* = **surprise**, amaze, astonish, astound, dumbfound, stagger, startle, stun, sweep off one's feet **2** = **knock down**, bring down, deck (*slang*), fell, floor, overthrow, overturn

bow out *verb* = **give up**, abandon, back out, call it a day *or* night, cop out (*slang*), get out, pull out, quit, resign, retire, step down (*informal*), throw in the sponge, throw in the towel, withdraw

box[1] *noun* **1** = **container**, ark (*dialect*), carton, case, casket, chest, coffret, kist (*Scot. & Northern English dialect*), pack, package, portmanteau, receptacle, trunk ◆ *verb* **2** = **pack**, package, wrap

box[2] *verb* **1** = **fight**, exchange blows, spar **2** = **punch**, belt (*informal*), buffet, butt, chin (*slang*), clout (*informal*), cuff, deck (*slang*), hit, lay one on (*slang*), slap, sock (*slang*), strike, thwack, tonk (*informal*), wallop (*informal*), whack ◆ *noun* **3** = **punch**, belt (*informal*), blow, buffet, clout (*informal*), cuff, slap, stroke, thumping, wallop (*informal*)

boxer *noun* = **fighter**, prizefighter, pugilist, sparrer, sparring partner

box in *verb* = **confine**, cage, contain, coop up, enclose, hem in, isolate, shut in, surround, trap

boxing *noun* = **prizefighting**, fisticuffs, pugilism, sparring, the fight game (*informal*), the ring

boy *noun* = **lad**, fellow, junior, schoolboy, stripling, youngster, youth

boycott *verb* = **embargo**, ban, bar, black, blackball, blacklist, exclude, ostracize, outlaw, prohibit, proscribe, refrain from, refuse, reject, spurn
➤ **Antonyms**
accept, advocate, back, champion, defend, espouse, help, patronize, promote, support, welcome

boyfriend *noun* = **sweetheart**, admirer, beau, date, follower, leman (*archaic*), lover, man, steady, suitor, swain, toy boy, young man

boyish *adjective* = **youthful**, adolescent, childish, immature, innocent, juvenile, puerile, young

brace *noun* **1** = **support**, bolster, bracer, bracket, buttress, prop, reinforcement, stanchion, stay, strut, truss ◆ *verb* **2** = **support**, bandage, bind, bolster, buttress, fasten, fortify, hold up, prop, reinforce, shove, shove up, steady, strap, strengthen, tie, tighten

bracing *adjective* = **refreshing**, brisk, chilly, cool, crisp, energizing, exhilarating, fortifying, fresh, invigorating, lively, restorative, reviving, rousing, stimulating, tonic, vigorous
➤ **Antonyms**
debilitating, draining, enervating, exhausting, fatiguing, sapping, soporific, taxing, tiring, weakening

brackish *adjective* = **salty**, bitter, brak (*S. Afr.*), briny, saline, salt, undrinkable
➤ **Antonyms**
clean, clear, fresh, pure, sweet, unpolluted

brag *verb* = **boast**, blow one's own horn (*U.S. & Canad.*), blow one's own trumpet, bluster, crow, swagger, talk big (*slang*), vaunt

braggart *noun* = **boaster**, bigmouth (*slang*), bluffer, blusterer, brag, braggadocio, bragger, hot dog (*chiefly U.S.*), show-off (*informal*), swaggerer, swashbuckler

braid *verb* = **interweave**, entwine, interlace, intertwine, lace, plait, ravel, twine, weave

brain *noun Informal* = **intellectual**, bluestocking (*usually disparaging*), brainbox, egghead (*informal*), genius, highbrow, intellect, mastermind, prodigy, pundit, sage, scholar

brainless *adjective* = **stupid**, braindead (*informal*), dead from the neck up (*informal*), dumb-ass (*slang*), foolish, idiotic, inane, inept, mindless, senseless, thoughtless, unintelligent, witless

brains *plural noun* = **intelligence**, capacity,

intellect, mind, nous (*Brit. slang*), reason, sagacity, savvy (*slang*), sense, shrewdness, smarts (*slang, chiefly U.S.*), suss (*slang*), understanding, wit

brainwashing *noun* = **indoctrination**, alteration, conditioning, persuasion, re-education

brainwave *noun* = **idea**, bright idea, stroke of genius, thought

brainy *adjective Informal* = **intelligent**, bright, brilliant, clever, smart

brake *noun* 1 = **control**, check, constraint, curb, rein, restraint ◆ *verb* 2 = **slow**, check, decelerate, halt, moderate, reduce speed, slacken, stop

branch *noun* 1 = **bough**, arm, limb, offshoot, prong, ramification, shoot, spray, sprig 2 = **division**, chapter, department, local office, office, part, section, subdivision, subsection, wing

branch out *verb* = **expand**, add to, develop, diversify, enlarge, extend, have a finger in every pie, increase, multiply, proliferate, ramify, spread out

brand *noun* 1 = **label**, emblem, hallmark, logo, mark, marker, sign, stamp, symbol, trademark 2 = **kind**, cast, class, grade, make, quality, sort, species, type, variety 3 = **stigma**, blot, disgrace, infamy, mark, reproach, slur, smirch, stain, taint ◆ *verb* 4 = **mark**, burn, burn in, label, scar, stamp 5 = **stigmatize**, censure, denounce, discredit, disgrace, expose, mark

brandish *verb* = **wave**, display, exhibit, flaunt, flourish, parade, raise, shake, swing, wield

brash *adjective* = **bold**, brazen, cocky, forward, heedless, impertinent, impudent, insolent, pushy (*informal*), rude
➤ **Antonyms**
careful, cautious, polite, prudent, reserved, respectful, thoughtful, timid, uncertain

brass *noun Informal* = **nerve** (*informal*), audacity, brass neck (*Brit. informal*), cheek, chutzpah (*U.S. & Canad. informal*), effrontery, face (*informal*), front, gall, impertinence, impudence, insolence, neck (*informal*), presumption, rudeness, sassiness (*U.S. informal*)

brassy *adjective* 1 = **brazen**, barefaced, bold, brash, forward, impudent, insolent, loud-mouthed, pert, pushy (*informal*), saucy 2 = **flashy**, blatant, garish, gaudy, hard, jazzy (*informal*), loud, obtrusive, showy, vulgar 3 = **strident**, blaring, cacophonous, dissonant, grating, harsh, jangling, jarring, loud, noisy, piercing, raucous, shrill
➤ **Antonyms**

≠**flashy**: discreet, low-key, modest, played down, quiet, restrained, subdued, toned down, understated

bravado *noun* = **swagger**, bluster, boast, boastfulness, boasting, bombast, brag, braggadocio, fanfaronade (*rare*), swaggering, swashbuckling, vaunting

brave *adjective* 1 = **courageous**, ballsy (*taboo slang*), bold, daring, dauntless, fearless, gallant, gritty, heroic, intrepid, plucky, resolute, undaunted, valiant, valorous ◆ *verb* 2 = **confront**, bear, beard, challenge, dare, defy, endure, face, face the music, go through the mill, stand up to, suffer, tackle, walk into the lion's den, withstand
➤ **Antonyms**
adjective ≠**courageous**: afraid, cowardly, craven, faint-hearted, fearful, frightened, scared, shrinking, timid ◆ *verb* ≠**confront**: give in to, retreat from, surrender to

bravery *noun* = **courage**, balls (*taboo slang*), ballsiness (*taboo slang*), boldness, bravura, daring, dauntlessness, doughtiness, fearlessness, fortitude, gallantry, grit, guts (*informal*), hardihood, hardiness, heroism, indomitability, intrepidity, mettle, pluck, pluckiness, spirit, spunk (*informal*), valour
➤ **Antonyms**
cowardice, faint-heartedness, fearfulness, fright, timidity

bravo *noun* = **hired killer**, assassin, bandit, brigand, cut-throat, desperado, murderer, villain

bravura *noun* = **brilliance**, animation, audacity, boldness, brio, daring, dash, display, élan, energy, exhibitionism, ostentation, panache, punch (*informal*), spirit, verve, vigour, virtuosity

brawl *noun* 1 = **fight**, affray (*Law*), altercation, argument, *bagarre*, battle, broil, clash, disorder, dispute, donnybrook, fracas, fray, free-for-all (*informal*), melee *or* mêlée, punch-up (*Brit. informal*), quarrel, row (*informal*), ruckus (*informal*), rumpus, scrap (*informal*), scrimmage, scuffle, shindig (*informal*), shindy (*informal*), skirmish, squabble, tumult, uproar, wrangle ◆ *verb* 2 = **fight**, altercate, argue, battle, dispute, fight like Kilkenny cats, go at it hammer and tongs, quarrel, row (*informal*), scrap (*informal*), scuffle, tussle, wrangle, wrestle

brawn *noun* = **muscle**, beef (*informal*), beefiness (*informal*), brawniness, flesh, might, muscles, muscularity, power, robustness, strength, vigour

brawny *adjective* = **muscular**, athletic, beefy (*informal*), bulky, burly, fleshy,

hardy, hefty (*informal*), herculean, husky
(*informal*), lusty, powerful, robust, sinewy,
stalwart, strapping, strong, sturdy, thewy,
thickset, vigorous, well-built, well-knit
➤ **Antonyms**
frail, scrawny, skinny, thin, undeveloped,
weak, weakly, weedy (*informal*), wimpish
or wimpy (*informal*), wussy (*slang*)

bray *verb* 1 = **heehaw**, bell, bellow, blare,
hoot, roar, screech, trumpet ◆ *noun* 2
= **heehaw**, bawl, bell, bellow, blare, cry,
harsh sound, hoot, roar, screech, shout

brazen *adjective* 1 = **bold**, audacious,
barefaced, brash, brassy (*informal*),
defiant, forward, immodest, impudent,
insolent, pert, pushy (*informal*), saucy,
shameless, unabashed, unashamed 2
= **brassy**, brass, bronze, metallic ◆ *verb* 3
brazen it out = **be unashamed**, be
impenitent, confront, defy, outface,
outstare, persevere
➤ **Antonyms**
adjective ≠**bold**: cautious, decorous,
diffident, mannerly, modest, reserved,
respectful, reticent, secret, shy, stealthy,
timid

breach *noun* 1 = **nonobservance**,
contravention, disobedience, infraction,
infringement, noncompliance, offence,
transgression, trespass, violation 2
= **disagreement**, alienation, difference,
disaffection, dissension, division,
estrangement, falling-out (*informal*),
parting of the ways, quarrel, schism,
separation, severance, variance 3 = **crack**,
aperture, break, chasm, cleft, fissure, gap,
hole, opening, rent, rift, rupture, split
➤ **Antonyms**
≠**nonobservance**: adherence to, attention,
compliance, discharge, fulfilment,
heeding, honouring, observation,
performance

bread *noun* 1 = **food**, aliment, diet, fare,
necessities, nourishment, nutriment,
provisions, subsistence, sustenance,
viands, victuals 2 *Slang* = **money**, ackers
(*slang*), brass (*Northern English dialect*),
cash, dibs (*slang*), dosh (*Brit. & Austral.
slang*), dough (*slang*), finance, funds,
necessary (*informal*), needful (*informal*),
rhino (*Brit. slang*), shekels (*informal*), silver,
spondulicks (*slang*), tin (*slang*)

breadth *noun* 1 = **width**, beam (*of a ship*),
broadness, latitude, span, spread,
wideness 2 = **extent**, amplitude, area,
compass, comprehensiveness, dimension,
expanse, extensiveness, magnitude,
measure, range, reach, scale, scope, size,
space, spread, sweep, vastness 3
= **broad-mindedness**, freedom, latitude,

liberality, open-mindedness, openness,
permissiveness

break *verb* 1 = **separate**, batter, burst,
crack, crash, demolish, destroy,
disintegrate, divide, fracture, fragment,
part, rend, sever, shatter, shiver, smash,
snap, splinter, split, tear, total (*slang*),
trash (*slang*) 2 = **disobey**, breach,
contravene, disregard, infract (*Law*),
infringe, renege on, transgress, violate 3
= **reveal**, announce, come out, come out
in the wash, disclose, divulge, impart,
inform, let out, make public, proclaim, tell
4 = **stop**, abandon, cut, discontinue, give
up, interrupt, pause, rest, suspend 5
= **weaken**, cow, cripple, demoralize,
dispirit, enervate, enfeeble, impair,
incapacitate, subdue, tame, undermine 6
Of a record, etc. = **beat**, better, cap
(*informal*), exceed, excel, go beyond,
outdo, outstrip, surpass, top 7 = **reduce**,
cushion, diminish, lessen, lighten,
moderate, soften, weaken 8 = **ruin**,
bankrupt, bust (*informal*), degrade,
demote, discharge, dismiss, humiliate,
impoverish, make bankrupt, reduce 9
= **happen**, appear, burst out, come forth
suddenly, emerge, erupt, occur ◆ *noun* 10
= **division**, breach, cleft, crack, fissure,
fracture, gap, gash, hole, opening, rent,
rift, rupture, split, tear 11 = **breach**,
alienation, disaffection, dispute,
divergence, estrangement, rift, rupture,
schism, separation, split 12 = **rest**, breather
(*informal*), breathing space, entr'acte, halt,
hiatus, interlude, intermission,
interruption, interval, let-up (*informal*), lull,
pause, recess, respite, suspension 13
Informal = **stroke of luck**, advantage,
chance, fortune, opening, opportunity
➤ **Antonyms**
verb ≠**separate**: attach, bind, connect,
fasten, join, repair, unite ≠**disobey**: abide
by, adhere to, conform, discharge, follow,
obey, observe

breakable *adjective* = **fragile**, brittle,
crumbly, delicate, flimsy, frail, frangible,
friable
➤ **Antonyms**
durable, indestructible, lasting,
nonbreakable, resistant, rugged,
shatterproof, solid, strong, toughened,
unbreakable

break away *verb* 1 = **flee**, decamp, escape,
fly, hook it (*slang*), make a break for it,
make a run for it (*informal*), make off, run
away 2 = **break with**, detach, part
company, secede, separate

breakdown *noun* 1 = **collapse**, crackup
(*informal*), disintegration, disruption,
failure, mishap, stoppage 2 = **analysis**,

categorization, classification, detailed list, diagnosis, dissection, itemization

break down *verb* **1** = **collapse**, come unstuck, conk out (*informal*), fail, go kaput (*informal*), go phut, seize up, stop, stop working **2** = **be overcome**, crack up (*informal*), go to pieces

breaker *noun* = **wave**, billow, comber, roller, whitecap, white horse

break-in *noun* = **burglary**, breaking and entering, invasion, robbery

break in *verb* **1** = **burgle**, break and enter, invade, rob **2** = **interrupt**, barge in, burst in, butt in, interfere, interject, interpose, intervene, intrude, put one's oar in, put one's two cents in (*U.S. slang*) **3** = **get used to**, accustom, condition, habituate, initiate, prepare, tame, train

break into *verb* = **begin**, burst into, burst out, commence, dissolve into, give way to, launch into

break off *verb* **1** = **detach**, divide, part, pull off, separate, sever, snap off, splinter **2** = **stop**, belay (*Nautical*), cease, desist, discontinue, end, finish, halt, pause, pull the plug on, suspend, terminate

break out *verb* **1** = **begin**, appear, arise, commence, emerge, happen, occur, set in, spring up, start **2** = **escape**, abscond, bolt, break loose, burst out, flee, get free **3** = **erupt**, burst out

breakthrough *noun* = **development**, advance, discovery, find, finding, gain, improvement, invention, leap, progress, quantum leap, step forward

break-up *noun* = **separation**, breakdown, breaking, crackup (*informal*), disintegration, dispersal, dissolution, divorce, ending, parting, rift, split, splitting, termination, wind-up

break up *verb* **1** = **separate**, dissolve, divide, divorce, end, part, scatter, sever, split **2** = **stop**, adjourn, disband, dismantle, disperse, disrupt, end, suspend, terminate

breakwater *noun* = **sea wall**, groyne, jetty, mole, spur

breast *noun* **1** = **bosom**, boob (*slang*), bust, chest, front, teat, thorax, tit (*slang*), udder **2** = **heart**, being, conscience, core, emotions, feelings, seat of the affections, sentiments, soul, thoughts

breath *noun* **1** = **respiration**, air, animation, breathing, exhalation, gasp, gulp, inhalation, pant, wheeze **2** = **odour**, aroma, niff (*Brit. slang*), smell, vapour, whiff **3** = **gust**, faint breeze, flutter, puff, sigh, slight movement, waft, zephyr **4** = **rest**, break, breather, breathing-space, instant, moment, pause, respite, second **5**
= **suggestion**, hint, murmur, suspicion, undertone, whisper **6** = **life**, animation, energy, existence, lifeblood, life force, vitality

breathe *verb* **1** = **inhale and exhale**, draw in, gasp, gulp, pant, puff, respire, wheeze **2** = **instil**, imbue, impart, infuse, inject, inspire, transfuse **3** = **whisper**, articulate, express, murmur, say, sigh, utter, voice

breather *noun Informal* = **rest**, break, breathing space, breath of air, halt, pause, recess, respite

breathless *adjective* **1** = **out of breath**, choking, exhausted, gasping, gulping, out of wind (*informal*), panting, short-winded, spent, wheezing, winded **2** = **excited**, agog, anxious, astounded, avid, eager, flabbergasted (*informal*), gobsmacked (*Brit. slang*), on tenterhooks, open-mouthed, thunderstruck, with bated breath

breathtaking *adjective* = **amazing**, astonishing, awe-inspiring, awesome, brilliant, dramatic, exciting, heart-stirring, impressive, jaw-dropping, magnificent, moving, overwhelming, sensational, striking, stunning (*informal*), thrilling, wondrous (*archaic or literary*)

breed *verb* **1** = **reproduce**, bear, beget, bring forth, engender, generate, hatch, multiply, originate, procreate, produce, propagate **2** = **bring up**, cultivate, develop, discipline, educate, foster, instruct, nourish, nurture, raise, rear **3** = **produce**, arouse, bring about, cause, create, generate, give rise to, induce, make, occasion, originate, stir up ♦ *noun* **4** = **variety**, pedigree, race, species, stock, strain, type **5** = **kind**, brand, sort, stamp, type, variety **6** = **lineage**, class, extraction, family, ilk, line, pedigree, race, stock

breeding *noun* **1** = **upbringing**, ancestry, cultivation, development, lineage, nurture, raising, rearing, reproduction, training **2** = **refinement**, civility, conduct, courtesy, cultivation, culture, gentility, manners, polish, sophistication, urbanity

breeze *noun* **1** = **light wind**, air, breath of wind, capful of wind, current of air, draught, flurry, gust, puff of air, waft, whiff, zephyr ♦ *verb* **2** = **move briskly**, flit, glide, hurry, pass, sail, sally, sweep, trip

breezy *adjective* **1** = **windy**, airy, blowing, blowy, blusterous, blustery, fresh, gusty, squally **2** = **carefree**, airy, animated, blithe, buoyant, casual, cheerful, chirpy (*informal*), debonair, easy-going, free and easy, full of beans (*informal*), genial, informal, jaunty, light, light-hearted, lively, sparkling, sparky, spirited, sprightly,

sunny, upbeat (*informal*), vivacious
➤ **Antonyms**
≠**windy**: calm, heavy, oppressive, windless
≠**carefree**: calm, depressed, dull, heavy,
lifeless, mournful, sad, serious

brevity *noun* **1** = **shortness**, briefness,
ephemerality, impermanence, transience,
transitoriness **2** = **conciseness**, concision,
condensation, crispness, curtness,
economy, pithiness, succinctness,
terseness
➤ **Antonyms**
≠**conciseness**: diffuseness, discursiveness,
long-windedness, prolixity, rambling,
redundancy, tautology, tediousness,
verbiage, verboseness, verbosity, wordiness

brew *verb* **1** = **make** (*beer*), boil, ferment,
infuse (*tea*), prepare by fermentation,
seethe, soak, steep, stew **2** = **develop**,
breed, concoct, contrive, devise, excite,
foment, form, gather, hatch, plan, plot,
project, scheme, start, stir up ♦ *noun* **3**
= **drink**, beverage, blend, concoction,
distillation, fermentation, infusion, liquor,
mixture, preparation

bribe *verb* **1** = **buy off**, corrupt, get at,
grease the palm *or* hand of (*slang*),
influence by gifts, lure, oil the palm of
(*informal*), pay off (*informal*), reward,
square, suborn ♦ *noun* **2** = **inducement**,
allurement, backhander (*slang*), boodle
(*slang, chiefly U.S.*), corrupting gift,
enticement, graft (*informal*), hush money
(*slang*), incentive, kickback (*U.S.*), pay-off
(*informal*), payola (*informal*), reward for
treachery, sop, sweetener (*slang*)

bribery *noun* = **buying off**, corruption,
graft (*informal*), inducement,
palm-greasing (*slang*), payola (*informal*),
protection, subornation

bric-a-brac *noun* = **knick-knacks**, baubles,
bibelots, curios, gewgaws, kickshaws,
objects of virtu, *objets d'art*, ornaments,
trinkets

bridal *adjective* = **matrimonial**, bride's,
conjugal, connubial, hymeneal, marital,
marriage, nuptial, spousal, wedding

bridge *noun* **1** = **arch**, flyover, overpass,
span, viaduct **2** = **link**, band, bond,
connection, tie ♦ *verb* **3** = **connect**, arch
over, attach, bind, couple, cross, cross
over, extend across, go over, join, link,
reach across, span, traverse, unite
➤ **Antonyms**
verb ≠**connect**: cleave, come apart, disjoin,
divide, keep apart, separate, sever, split,
sunder, widen

bridle *noun* **1** = **curb**, check, control, rein,
restraint, trammels ♦ *verb* **2** = **curb**, check,
constrain, control, govern, have in one's

pocket, keep a tight rein on, keep in check,
keep on a string, master, moderate, rein,
repress, restrain, subdue **3** = **get angry**, be
indignant, bristle, draw (oneself) up, get
one's back up, raise one's hackles, rear up

brief *adjective* **1** = **short**, ephemeral, fast,
fleeting, hasty, little, momentary, quick,
quickie (*informal*), short-lived, swift,
temporary, transitory **2** = **curt**, abrupt,
blunt, brusque, sharp, short, surly **3**
= **concise**, clipped, compendious,
compressed, crisp, curt, laconic, limited,
monosyllabic, pithy, short, succinct, terse,
thumbnail, to the point ♦ *noun* **4**
= **summary**, abridgment, abstract, digest,
epitome, outline, précis, sketch, synopsis **5**
= **case**, argument, contention, data,
defence, demonstration ♦ *verb* **6** = **inform**,
advise, clue in (*informal*), explain, fill in
(*informal*), gen up (*Brit. informal*), give
(someone) a rundown, give (someone) the
gen (*Brit. informal*), instruct, keep posted,
prepare, prime, put (someone) in the
picture (*informal*)
➤ **Antonyms**
adjective ≠**short**: extensive, lengthy, long,
protracted ≠**concise**: circuitous, detailed,
diffuse, lengthy, long, long-drawn-out,
long-winded

briefing *noun* = **instructions**, conference,
directions, guidance, information,
instruction, meeting, preamble,
preparation, priming, rundown

briefly *adverb* = **shortly**, abruptly, briskly,
casually, concisely, cursorily, curtly,
fleetingly, hastily, hurriedly, in a few
words, in a nutshell, in brief, in outline, in
passing, momentarily, precisely, quickly,
temporarily

brigade *noun* = **group**, band, body, camp,
company, contingent, corps, crew, force,
organization, outfit, party, squad, team,
troop, unit

brigand *noun* = **bandit**, desperado,
footpad (*archaic*), freebooter, gangster,
highwayman, marauder, outlaw,
plunderer, robber, ruffian

bright *adjective* **1** = **shining**, beaming,
blazing, brilliant, dazzling, effulgent,
flashing, gleaming, glistening, glittering,
glowing, illuminated, intense, lambent,
luminous, lustrous, radiant, resplendent,
scintillating, shimmering, sparkling,
twinkling, vivid **2** = **promising**, auspicious,
encouraging, excellent, favourable,
golden, good, hopeful, optimistic, palmy,
propitious, prosperous, rosy **3** = **cheerful**,
chirpy (*informal*), full of beans (*informal*),
gay, genial, glad, happy, jolly, joyful,
joyous, light-hearted, lively, merry, sparky,

upbeat (*informal*), vivacious **4**
= intelligent, acute, astute, aware, brainy,
brilliant, clear-headed, clever, ingenious,
inventive, keen, quick, quick-witted, sharp,
smart, wide-awake **5 = sunny**, clear,
clement, cloudless, fair, limpid, lucid,
pellucid, pleasant, translucent,
transparent, unclouded
➤ **Antonyms**
≠**intelligent**: dense, dim, dim-witted
(*informal*), dull, dumb (*informal*),
dumb-ass (*slang*), foolish, idiotic, ignorant,
retarded, simple, slow, stupid, thick,
unintelligent, witless ≠**sunny**: cloudy,
dark, dim, dusky, gloomy, grey, overcast,
poorly lit

brighten *verb* **1 = light up**, clear up,
enliven, gleam, glow, illuminate, lighten,
make brighter, shine **2 = cheer up**,
become cheerful, buck up (*informal*), buoy
up, encourage, enliven, gladden, hearten,
make happy, perk up
➤ **Antonyms**
≠**light up**: becloud, blacken, cloud over *or*
up, dim, dull, obscure, overshadow,
shade, shadow ≠**cheer up**: become angry,
become gloomy, blacken, cloud, deject,
depress, dispirit, look black, sadden

brightness *noun* **1 = shine**, brilliance,
glare, incandescence, intensity, light,
luminosity, radiance, vividness **2**
= intelligence, acuity, cleverness,
quickness, sharpness, smartness
➤ **Antonyms**
≠**shine**: dimness, dullness

brilliance, brilliancy *noun* **1 = brightness**,
blaze, dazzle, effulgence, gleam, glitter,
intensity, luminosity, lustre, radiance,
refulgence, resplendence, sheen, sparkle,
vividness **2 = cleverness**, acuity, aptitude,
braininess, distinction, excellence, genius,
giftedness, greatness, inventiveness, talent,
wisdom **3 = splendour**, éclat, gilt,
glamour, gorgeousness, grandeur,
illustriousness, magnificence, pizzazz *or*
pizazz (*informal*)
➤ **Antonyms**
≠**brightness**: darkness, dimness, dullness,
paleness ≠**cleverness**: folly, idiocy,
inanity, incompetence, ineptitude,
silliness, simple-mindedness, stupidity

brilliant *adjective* **1 = shining**, ablaze,
bright, coruscating, dazzling, glittering,
glossy, intense, luminous, lustrous, radiant,
refulgent, resplendent, scintillating,
sparkling, vivid **2 = splendid**, celebrated,
eminent, exceptional, famous, glorious,
illustrious, magnificent, notable,
outstanding, superb **3 = intelligent**,
accomplished, acute, astute, brainy,
clever, discerning, expert, gifted,

intellectual, inventive, masterly,
penetrating, profound, quick, talented
➤ **Antonyms**
≠**shining**: dark, dim, dull, gloomy
≠**splendid**: dull, ordinary, run-of-the-mill,
unaccomplished, unexceptional,
untalented ≠**intelligent**: dim, simple,
slow, stupid

brim *noun* **1 = rim**, border, brink,
circumference, edge, flange, lip, margin,
skirt, verge ♦ *verb* **2 = be full**, fill, fill up,
hold no more, overflow, run over, spill,
well over

brimful *adjective* **= full**, brimming, filled,
flush, level with, overflowing, overfull,
packed, running over

bring *verb* **1 = take**, accompany, bear,
carry, conduct, convey, deliver, escort,
fetch, gather, guide, import, lead, transfer,
transport, usher **2 = cause**, contribute to,
create, effect, engender, inflict, occasion,
produce, result in, wreak **3 = make**,
compel, convince, dispose, force, induce,
influence, move, persuade, prevail on *or*
upon, prompt, sway **4 = sell for**,
command, earn, fetch, gross, net,
produce, return, yield

bring about *verb* **= cause**, accomplish,
achieve, bring to pass, compass, create,
effect, effectuate, generate, give rise to,
make happen, manage, occasion,
produce, realize

bring down *verb* **1 = lower**, cut down,
drop, fell, floor, lay low, level, pull down,
shoot down, upset **2 = overthrow**, abase,
overturn, reduce, undermine

bring in *verb* **= produce**, accrue, bear, be
worth, fetch, generate, gross, net, profit,
realize, return, yield

bring off *verb* **= accomplish**, achieve, bring
home the bacon (*informal*), bring to pass,
carry off, carry out, crack it (*informal*), cut
it (*informal*), discharge, execute, perform,
pull off, succeed

bring up *verb* **1 = rear**, breed, develop,
educate, form, nurture, raise, support,
teach, train **2 = mention**, advance, allude
to, broach, introduce, move, propose, put
forward, raise, submit

brink *noun* **= edge**, border, boundary,
brim, fringe, frontier, limit, lip, margin,
point, rim, skirt, threshold, verge

brisk *adjective* **1 = lively**, active, agile, alert,
animated, bustling, busy, energetic,
nimble, no-nonsense, quick, sparky,
speedy, sprightly, spry, vigorous, vivacious
2 = invigorating, biting, bracing, crisp,
exhilarating, fresh, keen, nippy, refreshing,
sharp, snappy, stimulating
➤ **Antonyms**

≠**lively**: heavy, lazy, lethargic, slow, sluggish, unenergetic ≠**invigorating**: boring, dull, enervating, tiring, wearisome

briskly adverb = **quickly**, actively, apace, brusquely, coolly, decisively, efficiently, energetically, firmly, incisively, nimbly, pdq (slang), posthaste, promptly, pronto (informal), rapidly, readily, smartly, vigorously

bristle noun **1** = **hair**, barb, prickle, spine, stubble, thorn, whisker ♦ verb **2** = **stand up**, horripilate, prickle, rise, stand on end **3** = **be angry**, be infuriated, be maddened, bridle, flare up, get one's dander up (slang), go ballistic (slang, chiefly U.S.), rage, see red, seethe, spit (informal), wig out (slang) **4** = **be thick**, abound, be alive, crawl, hum, swarm, teem

bristly adjective = **hairy**, bearded, bewhiskered, prickly, rough, stubbly, unshaven, whiskered

brittle adjective **1** = **fragile**, breakable, crisp, crumbling, crumbly, delicate, frail, frangible, friable, shatterable, shivery **2** = **tense**, curt, edgy, irritable, nervous, prim, stiff, stilted, wired (slang)
➤ **Antonyms**
≠**fragile**: durable, elastic, flexible, infrangible, nonbreakable, resistant, rugged, shatterproof, strong, sturdy, toughened

broach verb **1** = **bring up**, approach, hint at, introduce, mention, open up, propose, raise the subject, speak of, suggest, talk of, touch on **2** = **open**, crack, draw off, pierce, puncture, start, tap, uncork

broad adjective **1** = **wide**, ample, beamy (of a ship), capacious, expansive, extensive, generous, large, roomy, spacious, vast, voluminous, widespread **2** = **general**, all-embracing, catholic, comprehensive, encyclopedic, far-reaching, global, inclusive, nonspecific, overarching, sweeping, undetailed, universal, unlimited, wide, wide-ranging **3** As in **broad daylight** = **clear**, full, obvious, open, plain, straightforward, undisguised **4** = **tolerant**, broad-minded, liberal, open, open-minded, permissive, progressive, unbiased **5** = **vulgar**, blue, coarse, gross, improper, indecent, indelicate, near the knuckle (informal), unrefined
➤ **Antonyms**
≠**wide**: close, confined, constricted, cramped, limited, meagre, narrow, restricted, tight

broadcast noun **1** = **transmission**, programme, show, telecast ♦ verb **2** = **transmit**, air, beam, cable, put on the air, radio, relay, show, televise **3** = **make**

public, advertise, announce, circulate, disseminate, proclaim, promulgate, publish, report, shout from the rooftops (informal), spread

broaden verb = **expand**, augment, develop, enlarge, extend, fatten, increase, open up, spread, stretch, supplement, swell, widen
➤ **Antonyms**
circumscribe, constrain, diminish, narrow, reduce, restrict, tighten

broad-minded adjective = **tolerant**, catholic, cosmopolitan, dispassionate, flexible, free-thinking, indulgent, liberal, open-minded, permissive, responsive, unbiased, unbigoted, undogmatic, unprejudiced
➤ **Antonyms**
biased, bigoted, closed-minded, dogmatic, inflexible, intolerant, narrow-minded, prejudiced, uncharitable

broadside noun = **attack**, abuse, assault, battering, bombardment, censure, criticism, denunciation, diatribe, philippic, stick (slang), swipe

brochure noun = **booklet**, advertisement, circular, folder, handbill, hand-out, leaflet, mailshot, pamphlet

broke adjective Informal = **penniless**, bankrupt, bust (informal), cleaned out (slang), dirt-poor (informal), down and out, flat broke (informal), impoverished, in queer street, insolvent, in the red, on one's uppers, penurious, ruined, short, skint (Brit. slang), stony-broke (Brit. slang), strapped for cash (informal), without a penny to one's name, without two pennies to rub together (informal)
➤ **Antonyms**
affluent, comfortable, flush (informal), in the money (informal), prosperous, rich, solvent, wealthy, well-to-do

broken adjective **1** = **smashed**, burst, demolished, destroyed, fractured, fragmented, rent, ruptured, separated, severed, shattered, shivered **2** = **interrupted**, disconnected, discontinuous, disturbed, erratic, fragmentary, incomplete, intermittent, spasmodic **3** = **not working**, defective, imperfect, kaput (informal), not functioning, on its last legs, on the blink (slang), out of order, ruined **4** = **violated**, dishonoured, disobeyed, disregarded, forgotten, ignored, infringed, isolated, not kept, retracted, traduced, transgressed **5** = **imperfect**, disjointed, halting, hesitating, stammering **6** = **defeated**, beaten, browbeaten, crippled, crushed, demoralized, humbled, oppressed, overpowered, subdued, tamed, vanquished

broken-down adjective = **not in working order**, collapsed, dilapidated, in disrepair, inoperative, kaput (informal), not functioning, old, on the blink (slang), on the fritz (U.S. slang), out of commission, out of order, worn out

brokenhearted adjective = **heartbroken**, choked, crestfallen, desolate, despairing, devastated, disappointed, disconsolate, down in the dumps (informal), grief-stricken, heart-sick, inconsolable, miserable, mournful, prostrated, sorrowful, wretched

broker noun = **dealer**, agent, factor, go-between, intermediary, middleman, negotiator

bronze adjective = **reddish-brown**, brownish, chestnut, copper, copper-coloured, metallic brown, reddish-tan, rust, tan, yellowish-brown

brood noun 1 = **offspring**, breed, chicks, children, clutch, family, hatch, infants, issue, litter, progeny, young ♦ verb 2 = **incubate**, cover, hatch, set, sit upon 3 = **think upon**, agonize, dwell upon, eat one's heart out, fret, have a long face, meditate, mope, mull over, muse, obsess, ponder, repine, ruminate

brook noun = **stream**, beck, burn, gill (dialect), rill, rivulet, runnel (literary), streamlet, watercourse

brothel noun = **whorehouse**, bagnio, bawdy house (archaic), bordello, cathouse (U.S. slang), house of ill fame, house of ill repute, house of prostitution, knocking shop (slang), red-light district, stews (archaic)

brother noun 1 = **sibling**, blood brother, kin, kinsman, relation, relative 2 = **comrade**, associate, chum (informal), cock (Brit. informal), colleague, companion, compeer, confrère, fellow member, mate, pal (informal), partner 3 = **monk**, cleric, friar, regular, religious

brotherhood noun 1 = **fellowship**, brotherliness, camaraderie, companionship, comradeship, friendliness, kinship 2 = **association**, alliance, clan, clique, community, coterie, fraternity, guild, league, order, society, union

brotherly adjective = **kind**, affectionate, altruistic, amicable, benevolent, cordial, fraternal, friendly, neighbourly, philanthropic, sympathetic

brow noun 1 = **forehead**, air, appearance, aspect, bearing, countenance, eyebrow, face, front, mien, temple 2 = **top**, brim,

brink, crest, crown, edge, peak, rim, summit, tip, verge

browbeat verb = **bully**, badger, bulldoze (informal), coerce, cow, domineer, dragoon, hector, intimidate, lord it over, oppress, overawe, overbear, ride roughshod over, threaten, tyrannize
➤ **Antonyms**
beguile, cajole, coax, entice, flatter, inveigle, lure, manoeuvre, seduce, sweet-talk (informal), tempt, wheedle

brown adjective 1 = **brunette**, auburn, bay, brick, bronze, bronzed, browned, chestnut, chocolate, coffee, dark, donkey brown, dun, dusky, fuscous, ginger, hazel, rust, sunburnt, tan, tanned, tawny, toasted, umber ♦ verb 2 = **fry**, cook, grill, sauté, seal, sear

browned off adjective = **fed up**, cheesed off (Brit. slang), discontented, discouraged, disgruntled, disheartened, pissed off (taboo slang), sick as a parrot (informal), weary

brown study noun = **preoccupation**, absorption, abstractedness, abstraction, contemplation, meditation, musing, reflection, reverie, rumination

browse verb 1 = **skim**, dip into, examine cursorily, flip through, glance at, leaf through, look round, look through, peruse, scan, survey 2 = **graze**, crop, eat, feed, nibble, pasture

bruise verb 1 = **discolour**, blacken, blemish, contuse, crush, damage, deface, injure, mar, mark, pound, pulverize 2 = **hurt**, displease, grieve, injure, insult, offend, pain, sting, wound ♦ noun 3 = **discoloration**, black-and-blue mark, black mark, blemish, contusion, injury, mark, swelling, trauma (Pathology)

brunt noun = **full force**, burden, force, impact, pressure, shock, strain, stress, thrust, violence

brush[1] noun 1 = **broom**, besom, sweeper 2 = **encounter**, clash, conflict, confrontation, fight, fracas, scrap (informal), set-to (informal), skirmish, slight engagement, spot of bother (informal), tussle ♦ verb 3 = **clean**, buff, paint, polish, sweep, wash 4 = **touch**, caress, contact, flick, glance, graze, kiss, scrape, stroke, sweep

brush[2] noun = **shrubs**, brushwood, bushes, copse, scrub, thicket, undergrowth, underwood

brush aside verb = **dismiss**, discount, disregard, have no time for, ignore, kiss off (slang, chiefly U.S. & Canad.), override, sweep aside

brush-off noun Slang = **snub**, bum's rush

(*slang*), cold shoulder, cut, dismissal, go-by (*slang*), kick in the teeth (*slang*), kiss-off (*slang, chiefly U.S. & Canad.*), knock-back (*slang*), rebuff, refusal, rejection, repudiation, repulse, slight, the (old) heave-ho (*informal*)

brush off *verb Slang* = **ignore**, blank (*slang*), cold-shoulder, cut, deny, disdain, dismiss, disown, disregard, kiss off (*slang, chiefly U.S. & Canad.*), put down, rebuff, refuse, reject, repudiate, scorn, send to Coventry, slight, snub, spurn

brush up *verb* = **revise**, bone up (*informal*), cram, go over, polish up, read up, refresh one's memory, relearn, study

brusque *adjective* = **curt**, abrupt, blunt, discourteous, gruff, hasty, impolite, monosyllabic, sharp, short, surly, tart, terse, unmannerly
➤ **Antonyms**
accommodating, civil, courteous, gentle, patient, polite, well-mannered

brutal *adjective* **1** = **cruel**, barbarous, bloodthirsty, ferocious, heartless, inhuman, merciless, pitiless, remorseless, ruthless, savage, uncivilized, vicious **2** = **harsh**, bearish, callous, gruff, impolite, insensitive, rough, rude, severe, uncivil, unfeeling, unmannerly **3** = **bestial**, animal, beastly, brute, brutish, carnal, coarse, crude, sensual
➤ **Antonyms**
≠**cruel**: civilized, gentle, humane, kind, merciful, soft-hearted ≠**harsh**: polite, refined, sensitive

brutality *noun* = **cruelty**, atrocity, barbarism, bloodthirstiness, ferocity, inhumanity, ruthlessness, savagery, viciousness

brutally *adverb* = **cruelly**, barbarically, barbarously, brutishly, callously, ferociously, fiercely, hardheartedly, heartlessly, in cold blood, inhumanly, meanly, mercilessly, murderously, pitilessly, remorselessly, ruthlessly, savagely, unkindly, viciously

brute *noun* **1** = **savage**, barbarian, beast, devil, fiend, ghoul, monster, ogre, sadist, swine **2** = **animal**, beast, creature, wild animal ◆ *adjective* **3** = **mindless**, bodily, carnal, fleshly, instinctive, physical, senseless, unthinking **4** = **coarse**, animal, bestial, depraved, gross, sensual

bubble *noun* **1** = **air ball**, bead, blister, blob, drop, droplet, globule, vesicle ◆ *verb* **2** = **foam**, boil, effervesce, fizz, froth, percolate, seethe, sparkle **3** = **gurgle**, babble, burble, murmur, purl, ripple, trickle, trill

bubbly *adjective* **1** = **lively**, alive and

kicking, animated, bouncy, elated, excited, full of beans (*informal*), happy, merry, sparky **2** = **frothy**, carbonated, curly, effervescent, fizzy, foamy, lathery, sparkling, sudsy

buccaneer *noun* = **pirate**, corsair, freebooter, privateer, sea-rover

buckle *noun* **1** = **fastener**, catch, clasp, clip, hasp **2** = **distortion**, bulge, contortion, kink, warp ◆ *verb* **3** = **fasten**, catch, clasp, close, hook, secure **4** = **distort**, bend, bulge, cave in, collapse, contort, crumple, fold, twist, warp

buckle down *verb Informal* = **apply oneself**, exert oneself, launch into, pitch in, put one's shoulder to the wheel, set to

buck up *verb* **1** = **cheer up**, brighten, encourage, hearten, inspirit, perk up, rally, take heart **2** *Informal* = **hurry up**, get a move on, hasten, shake a leg, speed up

bucolic *adjective* = **rustic**, agrarian, agrestic, agricultural, country, pastoral, rural

bud *noun* **1** = **shoot**, embryo, germ, sprout ◆ *verb* **2** = **develop**, burgeon, burst forth, grow, pullulate, shoot, sprout

budding *adjective* = **developing**, beginning, burgeoning, embryonic, fledgling, flowering, germinal, growing, incipient, nascent, potential, promising

budge *verb* **1** = **move**, dislodge, give way, inch, propel, push, remove, roll, shift, slide, stir **2** = **change**, bend, convince, give way, influence, persuade, sway, yield

budget *noun* **1** = **allowance**, allocation, cost, finances, financial statement, fiscal estimate, funds, means, resources ◆ *verb* **2** = **plan**, allocate, apportion, cost, cost out, estimate, ration

buff¹ *adjective* **1** = **yellowish-brown**, sandy, straw, tan, yellowish ◆ *noun* **2 in the buff** = **naked**, bare, buck naked (*slang*), in one's birthday suit (*informal*), in the altogether (*informal*), in the bare scud (*slang*), in the raw (*informal*), nude, scuddy (*slang*), unclad, unclothed, with bare skin, without a stitch on (*informal*) ◆ *verb* **3** = **polish**, brush, burnish, rub, shine, smooth

buff² *noun Informal* = **expert**, addict, admirer, aficionado, connoisseur, devotee, enthusiast, fan, fiend (*informal*), freak (*informal*), grandmaster, hotshot (*informal*), maven (*U.S.*), whizz (*informal*)

buffer *noun* = **safeguard**, bulwark, bumper, cushion, fender, intermediary, screen, shield, shock absorber

buffet¹ *noun* = **snack bar**, brasserie, café, cafeteria, cold table, counter, cupboard, refreshment counter, salad bar, sideboard, smorgasbord

buffet² verb 1 = **batter**, bang, beat, box, bump, clobber (slang), cuff, flail, knock, lambast(e), pound, pummel, punch, push, rap, shove, slap, strike, thump, wallop (informal) ♦ noun 2 = **blow**, bang, box, bump, cuff, jolt, knock, push, rap, shove, slap, smack, thump, wallop (informal)

buffoon noun = **clown**, comedian, comic, droll, fool, harlequin, jester, joculator or (fem.) joculatrix, joker, merry-andrew, silly billy (informal), wag

bug noun 1 Informal = **illness**, disease, infection, lurgy (informal), virus 2 Informal = **mania**, craze, fad, obsession, rage 3 = **fault**, blemish, catch, defect, error, failing, flaw, glitch, gremlin, imperfection, snarl-up (informal, chiefly Brit.), virus ♦ verb 4 Informal = **annoy**, aggravate (informal), badger, be on one's back (slang), bother, disturb, gall, get in one's hair (informal), get on one's nerves (informal), get on one's wick (Brit. slang), get under one's skin (informal), get up one's nose (informal), harass, hassle (informal), irk, irritate, nark (Brit., Austral. & N.Z. slang), needle (informal), nettle, pester, piss one off (taboo slang), plague, vex 5 = **tap**, eavesdrop, listen in, spy, wiretap

bugbear noun = **pet hate**, anathema, bane, bête noire, bogey, bogeyman, bugaboo, devil, dread, fiend, horror, nightmare

build verb 1 = **construct**, assemble, erect, fabricate, form, make, put up, raise 2 = **establish**, base, begin, constitute, formulate, found, inaugurate, initiate, institute, originate, set up, start 3 = **increase**, accelerate, amplify, augment, develop, enlarge, escalate, extend, improve, intensify, strengthen ♦ noun 4 = **physique**, body, figure, form, frame, shape, structure
➤ **Antonyms**
verb ≠**construct**: demolish, dismantle, tear down ≠**establish**: end, finish, relinquish, suspend ≠**increase**: decline, decrease, impair, lower, reduce, weaken

building noun 1 = **structure**, domicile, dwelling, edifice, fabric, house, pile 2 = **construction**, architecture, erection, fabricating, raising

build-up noun 1 = **increase**, accumulation, development, enlargement, escalation, expansion, gain, growth 2 = **accumulation**, accretion, heap, load, mass, rick, stack, stockpile, store 3 = **hype**, ballyhoo (informal), plug (informal), promotion, publicity, puff

built-in adjective = **integral**, essential, immanent, implicit, in-built, included, incorporated, inherent, inseparable, part and parcel of

bulbous adjective = **bulging**, bloated, convex, rounded, swelling, swollen

bulge noun 1 = **swelling**, bump, hump, lump, projection, protrusion, protuberance 2 = **increase**, boost, intensification, rise, surge ♦ verb 3 = **swell out**, bag, dilate, distend, enlarge, expand, project, protrude, puff out, sag, stand out, stick out, swell
➤ **Antonyms**
noun ≠**swelling**: bowl, cave, cavity, concavity, crater, dent, depression, hole, hollow, indentation, pit, trough

bulk noun 1 = **size**, amplitude, bigness, dimensions, immensity, largeness, magnitude, massiveness, substance, volume, weight 2 = **main part**, better part, body, generality, lion's share, majority, major part, mass, most, nearly all, plurality, preponderance ♦ verb 3 **bulk large** = **be important**, carry weight, dominate, loom, loom large, preponderate, stand out, threaten

bulky adjective = **large**, big, colossal, cumbersome, elephantine, enormous, ginormous (informal), heavy, huge, hulking, humongous or humungous (U.S. slang), immense, mammoth, massive, massy, mega (slang), ponderous, substantial, unmanageable, unwieldy, very large, voluminous, weighty
➤ **Antonyms**
convenient, handy, manageable, neat, slim, small

bulldoze verb 1 = **demolish**, flatten, level, raze 2 Informal = **force**, browbeat, bully, coerce, cow, dragoon, hector, intimidate, put the screws on, railroad (informal) 3 = **push**, drive, force, propel, shove, thrust

bullet noun = **projectile**, ball, missile, pellet, shot, slug

bulletin noun = **announcement**, account, communication, communiqué, dispatch, message, news flash, notification, report, statement

bull-headed adjective = **stubborn**, headstrong, inflexible, mulish, obstinate, pig-headed, stiff-necked, stupid, tenacious, uncompromising, unyielding, wilful

bully noun 1 = **persecutor**, big bully, browbeater, bully boy, coercer, intimidator, oppressor, ruffian, tormentor, tough ♦ verb 2 = **persecute**, bluster, browbeat, bulldoze (informal), bullyrag, coerce, cow, domineer, hector, intimidate, oppress, overbear, push around (slang), ride roughshod over, swagger, terrorize, tyrannize ♦ *interjection* **3** *As in* **bully for you, him,** *etc.* = **well done**, bravo, capital, good, grand, great

bulwark *noun* **1** = **fortification**, bastion, buttress, defence, embankment, outwork, partition, rampart, redoubt **2** = **defence**, buffer, guard, mainstay, safeguard, security, support

bumbling *adjective* = **clumsy**, awkward, blundering, botching, bungling, incompetent, inefficient, inept, lumbering, maladroit, muddled
➤ **Antonyms**
able, capable, competent, efficient, fit

bump *verb* **1** = **knock**, bang, collide (with), crash, hit, slam, smash into, strike **2** = **jerk**, bounce, jar, jolt, jostle, jounce, rattle, shake **3** = **move**, budge, dislodge, displace, remove, shift ♦ *noun* **4** = **knock**, bang, blow, collision, crash, hit, impact, jar, jolt, rap, shock, smash, thud, thump **5** = **lump**, bulge, contusion, hump, knob, knot, node, nodule, protuberance, swelling

bumper *adjective* = **exceptional**, abundant, bountiful, excellent, jumbo (*informal*), massive, mega (*slang*), prodigal, spanking (*informal*), teeming, unusual, whacking (*informal, chiefly Brit.*), whopping (*informal*)

bump into *verb Informal* = **meet**, chance upon, come across, encounter, happen upon, light upon, meet up with, run across, run into

bumpkin *noun* = **yokel**, boor, clodhopper, clown, country bumpkin, hayseed (*U.S. & Canad. informal*), hick (*informal, chiefly U.S. & Canad.*), hillbilly, lout, lubber, oaf, peasant, rustic

bump off *verb Slang* = **murder**, assassinate, blow away (*slang, chiefly U.S.*), dispatch, do away with, do in (*slang*), eliminate, finish off, kill, knock off (*slang*), liquidate, remove, rub out (*U.S. slang*), take out (*slang*), wipe out (*informal*)

bumptious *adjective* = **cocky**, arrogant, boastful, brash, conceited, egotistic, forward, full of oneself, impudent, overbearing, overconfident, presumptuous, pushy (*informal*), self-assertive, showy, swaggering, vainglorious, vaunting

bumpy *adjective* = **rough**, bone-breaking, bouncy, choppy, irregular, jarring, jerky, jolting, jolty, knobby, lumpy, pitted, potholed, rutted, uneven

bunch *noun* **1** = **number**, assortment, batch, bouquet, bundle, clump, cluster, collection, heap, lot, mass, parcel, pile, quantity, rick, sheaf, spray, stack, tuft **2** = **group**, band, bevy, crew (*informal*), crowd, flock, gang, gathering, knot, mob, multitude, party, posse (*informal*), swarm, team, troop ♦ *verb* **3** = **group**, assemble, bundle, cluster, collect, congregate, cram together, crowd, flock, herd, huddle, mass, pack

bundle *noun* **1** = **bunch**, accumulation, assortment, batch, collection, group, heap, mass, pile, quantity, rick, stack **2** = **package**, bag, bale, box, carton, crate, pack, packet, pallet, parcel, roll ♦ *verb* **3** = **package**, bale, bind, fasten, pack, palletize, tie, tie together, tie up, truss, wrap **4** *with* **out, off, into,** *etc.* = **push**, hurry, hustle, rush, shove, throw, thrust

bundle up *verb* = **wrap up**, clothe warmly, muffle up, swathe

bungle *verb* = **mess up**, blow (*slang*), blunder, bodge (*informal*), botch, butcher, cock up (*Brit. slang*), drop a brick *or* clanger (*informal*), flub (*U.S. slang*), foul up, fuck up (*offensive taboo slang*), fudge, louse up (*slang*), make a mess of, make a nonsense of (*informal*), make a pig's ear of (*informal*), mar, miscalculate, mismanage, muff, ruin, screw up (*informal*), spoil
➤ **Antonyms**
accomplish, achieve, carry off, effect, fulfil, succeed, triumph

bungling *adjective* = **incompetent**, awkward, blundering, botching, cack-handed (*informal*), clumsy, ham-fisted (*informal*), ham-handed (*informal*), inept, maladroit, unskilful

bunk, bunkum *noun Informal* = **nonsense**, balderdash, balls (*taboo slang*), baloney (*informal*), bilge (*informal*), bosh (*informal*), bullshit (*taboo slang*), cobblers (*Brit. taboo slang*), crap (*slang*), eyewash (*informal*), garbage (*informal*), guff (*slang*), havers (*Scot.*), hogwash, hokum (*slang, chiefly U.S. & Canad.*), hooey (*slang*), horsefeathers (*U.S. slang*), hot air (*informal*), kak (*S. Afr. slang*), moonshine, piffle (*informal*), poppycock (*informal*), rot, rubbish, shit (*taboo slang*), stuff and nonsense, tarradiddle, tomfoolery, tommyrot, tosh (*slang, chiefly Brit.*), trash, tripe (*informal*), truck (*informal*), twaddle

buoy *noun* **1** = **marker**, beacon, float, guide, signal ♦ *verb* **2 buoy up** = **encourage**, boost, cheer, cheer up, gee up, hearten, keep afloat, lift, raise, support, sustain

buoyancy *noun* **1** = **lightness**, floatability, weightlessness **2** = **cheerfulness**, animation, bounce (*informal*), cheeriness, good humour, high spirits, liveliness, pep, spiritedness, sunniness, zing (*informal*)

buoyant *adjective* **1** = **floating**, afloat,

floatable, light, weightless **2 = cheerful,**
animated, blithe, bouncy, breezy, bright,
carefree, chirpy (*informal*), debonair, full of
beans (*informal*), genial, happy, jaunty,
joyful, light-hearted, lively, peppy
(*informal*), sparky, sunny, upbeat
(*informal*), vivacious
➤ Antonyms
≠**cheerful:** cheerless, depressed,
despairing, dull, forlorn, gloomy, glum,
hopeless, melancholy, moody, morose,
pessimistic, sad, sullen, unhappy

burden *noun* **1 = load,** encumbrance,
weight **2 = trouble,** affliction, albatross,
anxiety, care, clog, encumbrance,
grievance, millstone, obstruction, onus,
pigeon (*informal*), responsibility, sorrow,
strain, stress, trial, weight, worry **3** *Nautical*
= tonnage, cargo, freight, lading ♦ *verb* **4**
= weigh down, bother, encumber,
handicap, load, oppress, overload,
overwhelm, saddle with, strain, tax, worry

bureau *noun* **1 = office,** agency, branch,
department, division, service **2 = desk,**
writing desk

bureaucracy *noun* **1 = government,**
administration, authorities, civil service,
corridors of power, directorate, ministry,
officialdom, officials, the system **2 = red
tape,** bumbledom, officialdom, officialese,
regulations

bureaucrat *noun* **= official,** administrator,
apparatchik, civil servant, functionary,
mandarin, minister, office-holder, officer,
public servant

burglar *noun* **= housebreaker,** cat burglar,
filcher, picklock, pilferer, robber, sneak
thief, thief

burglary *noun* **= breaking and entering,**
break-in, filching, housebreaking, larceny,
pilferage, robbery, stealing, theft, thieving

burial *noun* **= interment,** burying,
entombment, exequies, funeral,
inhumation, obsequies, sepulture

buried *adjective* **1 = interred,** coffined,
consigned to the grave, entombed, laid to
rest **2 = hidden,** cloistered, concealed,
private, sequestered, tucked away **3**
= engrossed, caught up, committed,
concentrating, devoted, immersed, intent,
lost, occupied, preoccupied, rapt **4**
= forgotten, covered, hidden, repressed,
sunk in oblivion, suppressed

burlesque *noun* **1 = parody,** caricature,
mock, mockery, satire, send-up (*Brit.
informal*), spoof (*informal*), takeoff
(*informal*), travesty ♦ *adjective* **2 = satirical,**
caricatural, comic, farcical, hudibrastic,
ironical, ludicrous, mock, mock-heroic,
mocking, parodic, travestying ♦ *verb* **3**

= satirize, ape, caricature, exaggerate,
imitate, lampoon, make a monkey out of,
make fun of, mock, parody, ridicule, send
up (*Brit. informal*), spoof (*informal*), take
off (*informal*), take the piss out of (*taboo
slang*), travesty

burly *adjective* **= brawny,** beefy (*informal*),
big, bulky, hefty, hulking, muscular,
powerful, stocky, stout, strapping, strong,
sturdy, thickset, well-built
➤ Antonyms
lean, puny, scraggy, scrawny, slight, spare,
thin, weak, weedy (*informal*), wimpish *or*
wimpy (*informal*), wussy (*slang*)

burn *verb* **1 = be on fire,** be ablaze, blaze,
flame, flare, flash, flicker, glow, go up in
flames, smoke **2 = set on fire,** brand,
calcine, char, ignite, incinerate, kindle,
light, parch, reduce to ashes, scorch, sear,
shrivel, singe, toast, wither **3 = sting,** bite,
hurt, pain, smart, tingle **4 = be passionate,**
be angry, be aroused, be excited, be
inflamed, blaze, desire, fume, seethe,
simmer, smoulder, yearn

burning *adjective* **1 = intense,** ablaze, afire,
all-consuming, ardent, eager, earnest,
fervent, fervid, flaming, frantic, frenzied,
impassioned, passionate, vehement,
zealous **2 = crucial,** acute, compelling,
critical, essential, important, now or never,
pressing, significant, urgent, vital **3**
= blazing, fiery, flaming, flashing,
gleaming, glowing, hot, illuminated,
scorching, smouldering **4 = stinging,** acrid,
biting, caustic, irritating, painful, piercing,
prickling, pungent, reeking, smarting,
tingling
➤ Antonyms
≠**intense:** apathetic, calm, cool, faint,
indifferent, mild, passive ≠**stinging:**
cooling, mild, numbing, soothing

burnish *verb* **1 = polish,** brighten, buff,
furbish, glaze, rub up, shine, smooth
♦ *noun* **2 = shine,** gloss, lustre, patina,
polish, sheen
➤ Antonyms
verb ≠**polish:** abrade, graze, scratch, scuff

burrow *noun* **1 = hole,** den, lair, retreat,
shelter, tunnel ♦ *verb* **2 = dig,** delve,
excavate, hollow out, scoop out, tunnel

burst *verb* **1 = explode,** blow up, break,
crack, disintegrate, fly open, fragment,
puncture, rend asunder, rupture, shatter,
shiver, split, tear apart **2 = rush,** barge,
break, break out, erupt, gush forth, run,
spout ♦ *noun* **3 = explosion,** bang, blast,
blasting, blowout, blow-up, breach, break,
crack, discharge, rupture, split **4 = rush,**
eruption, fit, gush, gust, outbreak,
outburst, outpouring, spate, spurt, surge,

torrent ♦ *adjective* 5 = **ruptured**, flat, punctured, rent, split

bury *verb* 1 = **inter**, consign to the grave, entomb, inearth, inhume, lay to rest, sepulchre 2 = **embed**, drive in, engulf, implant, sink, submerge 3 = **hide**, conceal, cover, cover up, draw a veil over, enshroud, secrete, shroud, stash (*informal*), stow away 4 = **engross**, absorb, engage, immerse, interest, occupy
➤ **Antonyms**
≠**inter, hide**: bring to light, dig up, discover, disinter, dredge up, exhume, expose, find, reveal, turn up, uncover, unearth

bush *noun* 1 = **shrub**, hedge, plant, shrubbery, thicket 2 **the bush = the wild**, back country (*U.S.*), backlands (*U.S.*), backwoods, brush, scrub, scrubland, woodland

bushy *adjective* = **thick**, bristling, bristly, fluffy, fuzzy, luxuriant, rough, shaggy, spreading, stiff, unruly, wiry

busily *adverb* = **actively**, assiduously, briskly, carefully, diligently, earnestly, energetically, industriously, intently, purposefully, speedily, strenuously

business *noun* 1 = **trade**, bargaining, commerce, dealings, industry, manufacturing, merchandising, selling, trading, transaction 2 = **establishment**, company, concern, corporation, enterprise, firm, organization, venture 3 = **profession**, calling, career, craft, employment, function, job, line, métier, occupation, pursuit, trade, vocation, work 4 = **concern**, affair, assignment, duty, function, issue, matter, pigeon (*informal*), point, problem, question, responsibility, subject, task, topic

businesslike *adjective* = **efficient**, correct, matter-of-fact, methodical, orderly, organized, practical, professional, regular, routine, systematic, thorough, well-ordered, workaday
➤ **Antonyms**
careless, disorderly, disorganized, frivolous, impractical, inefficient, irregular, sloppy, unprofessional, unsystematic, untidy

businessman, businesswoman *noun* = **executive**, capitalist, employer, entrepreneur, financier, *homme d'affaires*, industrialist, merchant, tradesman, tycoon

bust[1] *noun* = **bosom**, breast, chest, front, torso

bust[2] *Informal* ♦ *verb* 1 = **break**, burst, fracture, rupture 2 = **arrest**, catch, collar (*informal*), cop (*slang*), feel one's collar (*slang*), lift (*slang*), nab (*informal*), nail

(*informal*), raid, search ♦ *adjective* 3 **go bust = go bankrupt**, become insolvent, be ruined, break, fail ♦ *noun* 4 = **arrest**, capture, cop (*slang*), raid, search, seizure

bustle *verb* 1 = **hurry**, beetle, bestir, dash, flutter, fuss, hasten, rush, scamper, scramble, scurry, scuttle, stir, tear ♦ *noun* 2 = **activity**, ado, agitation, commotion, excitement, flurry, fuss, haste, hurly-burly, hurry, pother, stir, to-do, tumult
➤ **Antonyms**
verb ≠**hurry**: be indolent, idle, laze, lie around, loaf, loiter, loll, relax, rest, take it easy ♦ *noun* ≠**activity**: inaction, inactivity, quiet, quietness, stillness, tranquillity

bustling *adjective* = **busy**, active, buzzing, crowded, full, humming, lively, swarming, teeming

busy *adjective* 1 = **occupied**, active, assiduous, brisk, diligent, employed, engaged, engrossed, hard at work, industrious, in harness, on active service, on duty, persevering, rushed off one's feet, slaving, working 2 = **lively**, active, energetic, exacting, full, hectic, hustling, on the go (*informal*), restless, strenuous, tireless, tiring ♦ *verb* 3 = **occupy**, absorb, employ, engage, engross, immerse, interest
➤ **Antonyms**
adjective ≠**occupied, lively**: idle, inactive, indolent, lackadaisical, lazy, off duty, relaxed, slothful, unoccupied

busybody *noun* = **nosy parker** (*informal*), eavesdropper, gossip, intriguer, intruder, meddler, pry, scandalmonger, snoop, snooper, stirrer (*informal*), troublemaker

but *conjunction* 1 = **however**, further, moreover, nevertheless, on the contrary, on the other hand, still, yet ♦ *preposition* 2 = **except**, bar, barring, excepting, excluding, notwithstanding, save, with the exception of ♦ *adverb* 3 = **only**, just, merely, simply, singly, solely

butcher *noun* 1 = **murderer**, destroyer, killer, slaughterer, slayer ♦ *verb* 2 = **slaughter**, carve, clean, cut, cut up, dress, joint, prepare 3 = **kill**, assassinate, cut down, destroy, exterminate, liquidate, massacre, put to the sword, slaughter, slay 4 = **mess up**, bodge (*informal*), botch, destroy, mutilate, ruin, spoil, wreck

butchery *noun* = **slaughter**, blood bath, blood-letting, bloodshed, carnage, killing, massacre, mass murder, murder

butt[1] *noun* 1 = **end**, haft, handle, hilt, shaft, shank, stock 2 = **stub**, base, end, fag end (*informal*), foot, leftover, tail, tip

butt[2] *noun* = **target**, Aunt Sally, dupe, laughing stock, mark, object, point, subject, victim

butt³ verb, noun **1** With or of the head or horns = **knock**, buck, buffet, bump, bunt, jab, poke, prod, punch, push, ram, shove, thrust ♦ verb **2 butt in = interfere**, chip in (informal), cut in, interrupt, intrude, meddle, put one's oar in, put one's two cents in (U.S. slang), stick one's nose in

butt⁴ noun = **cask**, barrel, pipe

buttonhole verb = **detain**, accost, bore, catch, grab, importune, persuade importunately, take aside, waylay

buttress noun **1** = **support**, abutment, brace, mainstay, pier, prop, reinforcement, shore, stanchion, stay, strut ♦ verb **2** = **support**, augment, back up, bolster, brace, prop, prop up, reinforce, shore, shore up, strengthen, sustain, uphold

buxom adjective = **plump**, ample, bosomy, busty, comely, curvaceous, debonair, fresh-looking, full-bosomed, healthy, hearty, jocund, jolly, lively, lusty, merry, robust, sprightly, voluptuous, well-rounded, winsome
➤ Antonyms
delicate, frail, slender, slight, slim, svelte, sylphlike, thin, trim

buy verb **1** = **purchase**, acquire, get, invest in, obtain, pay for, procure, score (slang), shop for **2 buy off = bribe**, corrupt, fix (informal), grease someone's palm (slang), square, suborn ♦ noun **3** = **purchase**, acquisition, bargain, deal
➤ Antonyms
verb ≠purchase: auction, barter, retail, sell, vend

buzz noun **1** = **hum**, bombilation or bombination (literary), buzzing, drone, hiss, murmur, purr, ring, ringing, sibilation, susurration or susurrus (literary), whir, whisper **2** Informal = **gossip**, dirt (U.S.

slang), gen (Brit. informal), hearsay, latest (informal), news, report, rumour, scandal, scuttlebutt (U.S. slang), whisper, word ♦ verb **3** = **hum**, bombilate or bombinate (literary), drone, fizzle, murmur, reverberate, ring, sibilate, susurrate (literary), whir, whisper, whizz **4** = **gossip**, chatter, natter, rumour, tattle

by preposition **1** = **via**, by way of, over **2** = **through**, through the agency of, under the aegis of **3** = **near**, along, beside, close to, next to, past ♦ adverb **4** = **near**, at hand, close, handy, in reach **5** = **past**, aside, away, to one side

by and by adverb = **presently**, anon, before long, erelong (archaic or poetic), eventually, in a while, in the course of time, one day, shortly, soon

bygone adjective = **past**, ancient, antiquated, departed, erstwhile, extinct, forgotten, former, gone by, lost, of old, of yore, olden, one-time, past recall, previous, sunk in oblivion
➤ Antonyms
coming, forthcoming, future, prospective, to be, to come

bypass verb = **go round**, avoid, body-swerve (Scot.), circumvent, depart from, detour round, deviate from, get round, give a wide berth to, pass round
➤ Antonyms
abut, adjoin, come together, connect, converge, cross, intersect, join, link, meet, touch, unite

bystander noun = **onlooker**, eyewitness, looker-on, observer, passer-by, spectator, viewer, watcher, witness
➤ Antonyms
contributor, partaker, participant, party

byword noun = **saying**, adage, maxim, motto, precept, proverb, slogan

C c

cab noun = **taxi**, hackney, hackney carriage, minicab, taxicab

cabal noun 1 = **clique**, caucus, conclave, faction, league, party, set 2 = **plot**, conspiracy, intrigue, machination, scheme

cabin noun 1 = **room**, berth, compartment, deckhouse, quarters 2 = **hut**, berth, bothy, chalet, cot, cottage, crib, hovel, lodge, shack, shanty, shed

cabinet noun = **cupboard**, case, chiffonier, closet, commode, dresser, escritoire, locker

Cabinet noun = **council**, administration, assembly, counsellors, ministry

cackle verb 1 = **laugh**, chuckle, giggle, snicker, snigger, titter 2 = **squawk**, babble, chatter, cluck, crow, gabble, gibber, jabber, prattle

cad noun Old-fashioned, informal = **scoundrel**, bounder (old-fashioned Brit. slang), churl, cur, dastard (archaic), heel (slang), knave, rat (informal), rotter (slang, chiefly Brit.), scumbag (slang)

cadaverous adjective = **deathly**, ashen, blanched, bloodless, corpse-like, deathlike, emaciated, exsanguinous, gaunt, ghastly, haggard, hollow-eyed, like death warmed up (informal), pale, pallid, wan

caddish adjective = **ungentlemanly**, despicable, ill-bred, low, unmannerly
➤ Antonyms
gentlemanly, honourable, mannerly

cadence noun 1 = **rhythm**, beat, lilt, measure (Prosody), metre, pulse, swing, tempo, throb 2 = **intonation**, accent, inflection, modulation

café noun = **snack bar**, brasserie, cafeteria, coffee bar, coffee shop, eatery or eaterie, lunchroom, restaurant, tearoom

cage noun 1 = **enclosure**, corral (U.S.), pen, pound ◆ verb 2 = **shut up**, confine, coop up, fence in, immure, impound, imprison, incarcerate, lock up, mew, pound, restrain

cagey, cagy adjective Informal = **wary**, careful, cautious, chary, discreet, guarded, noncommittal, shrewd, wily
➤ Antonyms
careless, imprudent, indiscreet, reckless, unthinking, unwary

cajole verb = **persuade**, beguile, coax, decoy, dupe, entice, entrap, flatter, inveigle, lure, manoeuvre, mislead, seduce,

sweet-talk (informal), tempt, wheedle

cake noun 1 = **block**, bar, cube, loaf, lump, mass, slab ◆ verb 2 = **encrust**, bake, cement, coagulate, congeal, consolidate, dry, harden, inspissate (archaic), ossify, solidify, thicken

calamitous adjective = **disastrous**, blighting, cataclysmic, catastrophic, deadly, devastating, dire, fatal, pernicious, ruinous, tragic, woeful
➤ Antonyms
advantageous, beneficial, favourable, fortunate, good, helpful

calamity noun = **disaster**, adversity, affliction, cataclysm, catastrophe, distress, downfall, hardship, misadventure, mischance, misfortune, mishap, reverse, ruin, scourge, tragedy, trial, tribulation, woe, wretchedness
➤ Antonyms
advantage, benefit, blessing, boon, good fortune, good luck, help

calculate verb 1 = **work out**, adjust, compute, consider, count, determine, enumerate, estimate, figure, gauge, judge, rate, reckon, value, weigh 2 = **plan**, aim, design, intend

calculated adjective = **deliberate**, considered, intended, intentional, planned, premeditated, purposeful
➤ Antonyms
haphazard, hasty, heedless, hurried, impetuous, impulsive, rash, spontaneous, unintentional, unplanned, unpremeditated

calculating adjective = **scheming**, canny, cautious, contriving, crafty, cunning, designing, devious, Machiavellian, manipulative, politic, sharp, shrewd, sly
➤ Antonyms
blunt, direct, downright, frank, guileless, honest, open, outspoken, sincere, undesigning

calculation noun 1 = **working out**, answer, computation, estimate, estimation, figuring, forecast, judgment, reckoning, result 2 = **planning**, caution, circumspection, contrivance, deliberation, discretion, foresight, forethought, precaution

calibre noun 1 = **worth**, ability, capacity, distinction, endowment, faculty, force, gifts, merit, parts, quality, scope, stature, strength, talent **2 = diameter**, bore, gauge, measure

call verb **1 = name**, christen, denominate, describe as, designate, dub, entitle, label, style, term **2 = consider**, estimate, judge, regard, think **3 = cry**, announce, arouse, awaken, cry out, hail, halloo, proclaim, rouse, shout, waken, yell **4 = phone**, give (someone) a bell (*Brit. slang*), ring up (*informal, chiefly Brit.*), telephone **5 = summon**, assemble, bid, collect, contact, convene, convoke, gather, invite, muster, rally ◆ noun **6 = cry**, hail, scream, shout, signal, whoop, yell **7 = summons**, announcement, appeal, command, demand, invitation, notice, order, plea, request, supplication, visit **8 = need**, cause, claim, excuse, grounds, justification, occasion, reason, right, urge
➤ **Antonyms**
verb ≠**cry**: be quiet, be silent, murmur, mutter, speak softly, whisper ≠**summon**: call off, cancel, dismiss, disperse, excuse, release ◆ noun ≠**cry**: murmur, mutter, whisper ≠**summons**: dismissal, release

call for verb **1 = require**, demand, entail, involve, necessitate, need, occasion, suggest **2 = fetch**, collect, pick up, uplift (*Scot.*)

calling noun **= profession**, business, career, employment, life's work, line, métier, mission, occupation, province, pursuit, trade, vocation, walk of life, work

call on verb **1 = visit**, drop in on, look in on, look up, see **2 = request**, appeal to, ask, bid, call upon, entreat, invite, invoke, summon, supplicate

callous adjective **= heartless**, affectless, apathetic, case-hardened, cold, hard-bitten, hard-boiled (*informal*), hardened, hardhearted, harsh, indifferent, indurated (*rare*), insensate, insensible, insensitive, inured, obdurate, soulless, thick-skinned, torpid, uncaring, unfeeling, unresponsive, unsusceptible, unsympathetic
➤ **Antonyms**
caring, compassionate, considerate, gentle, sensitive, soft, sympathetic, tender, understanding

callow adjective **= inexperienced**, green, guileless, immature, naive, raw, unsophisticated

calm adjective **1 = cool**, as cool as a cucumber, collected, composed, dispassionate, equable, impassive, imperturbable, keeping one's cool, relaxed, sedate, self-possessed, undisturbed, unemotional, unexcitable, unexcited, unfazed (*informal*), unflappable

(*informal*), unmoved, unruffled **2 = still**, balmy, halcyon, mild, pacific, peaceful, placid, quiet, restful, serene, smooth, tranquil, windless ◆ noun **3 = peacefulness**, calmness, hush, peace, quiet, repose, serenity, stillness ◆ verb **4 = quieten**, hush, mollify, placate, relax, soothe
➤ **Antonyms**
adjective ≠**cool**: agitated, aroused, discomposed, disturbed, emotional, excited, fierce, frantic, heated, perturbed, shaken, troubled, worried ≠**still**: rough, stormy, wild ◆ noun ≠**peacefulness**: agitation, disturbance, wildness ◆ verb ≠**quieten**: aggravate, agitate, arouse, disturb, excite, irritate, stir

calmness noun **1 = coolness**, composure, cool (*slang*), dispassion, equanimity, impassivity, imperturbability, poise, sang-froid, self-possession **2 = peacefulness**, calm, hush, motionlessness, peace, placidity, quiet, repose, restfulness, serenity, smoothness, stillness, tranquillity

calumny noun **= slander**, abuse, aspersion, backbiting, calumniation, defamation, denigration, derogation, detraction, evil-speaking, insult, libel, lying, misrepresentation, obloquy, revilement, smear, stigma, vilification, vituperation

camouflage noun **1 = disguise**, blind, cloak, concealment, cover, deceptive markings, false appearance, front, guise, mask, masquerade, mimicry, protective colouring, screen, subterfuge ◆ verb **2 = disguise**, cloak, conceal, cover, hide, mask, obfuscate, obscure, screen, veil
➤ **Antonyms**
verb ≠**disguise**: bare, display, exhibit, expose, reveal, show, uncover, unmask, unveil

camp[1] noun **= camp site**, bivouac, camping ground, cantonment (*Military*), encampment, tents

camp[2] adjective Informal **= effeminate**, affected, artificial, camped up (*informal*), campy (*informal*), mannered, ostentatious, poncy (*slang*), posturing

campaign noun **= operation**, attack, crusade, drive, expedition, jihad (*rare*), movement, offensive, push

canal noun **= waterway**, channel, conduit, duct, passage, watercourse

cancel verb **1 = call off**, abolish, abort, abrogate, annul, blot out, countermand, cross out, delete, do away with, efface, eliminate, erase, expunge, obliterate, obviate, quash, repeal, repudiate, rescind, revoke **2 cancel out = make up for**, balance out, compensate for, counterbalance, neutralize, nullify, obviate, offset, redeem

cancellation *noun* = **abandonment**, abandoning, abolition, annulment, deletion, elimination, quashing, repeal, revocation

cancer *noun* = **growth**, blight, canker, carcinoma (*Pathology*), corruption, evil, malignancy, pestilence, rot, sickness, tumour

candid *adjective* 1 = **honest**, blunt, downright, fair, forthright, frank, free, guileless, impartial, ingenuous, just, open, outspoken, plain, round, sincere, straightforward, truthful, unbiased, unequivocal, unprejudiced, upfront (*informal*) 2 = **informal**, impromptu, uncontrived, unposed
➤ Antonyms
≠honest: biased, complimentary, diplomatic, flattering, kind, subtle

candidate *noun* = **contender**, applicant, aspirant, claimant, competitor, contestant, entrant, nominee, possibility, runner, solicitant, suitor

candour *noun* = **honesty**, artlessness, directness, fairness, forthrightness, frankness, guilelessness, impartiality, ingenuousness, naïveté, openness, outspokenness, simplicity, sincerity, straightforwardness, truthfulness, unequivocalness
➤ Antonyms
bias, cunning, deceit, diplomacy, dishonesty, flattery, insincerity, prejudice, subtlety

canker *noun* 1 = **disease**, bane, blight, blister, cancer, corrosion, corruption, infection, lesion, rot, scourge, sore, ulcer ♦ *verb* 2 = **rot**, blight, consume, corrode, corrupt, embitter, envenom, inflict, poison, pollute, rust, waste away

cannon *noun* = **gun**, artillery piece, big gun, field gun, mortar

cannonade *noun* = **bombardment**, barrage, battery, broadside, gunfire, pounding, salvo, shelling, volley

canny *adjective* = **shrewd**, acute, artful, astute, careful, cautious, circumspect, clever, judicious, knowing, on the ball (*informal*), perspicacious, prudent, sagacious, sharp, subtle, wise, worldly-wise
➤ Antonyms
bumbling, inept, obtuse, unskilled

canon *noun* 1 = **rule**, criterion, dictate, formula, precept, principle, regulation, standard, statute, yardstick 2 = **list**, catalogue, roll

canopy *noun* = **awning**, baldachin, covering, shade, sunshade, tester

cant¹ *noun* 1 = **hypocrisy**, affected piety, humbug, insincerity, lip service, pious platitudes, pretence, pretentiousness, sanctimoniousness, sham holiness 2 = **jargon**, argot, lingo, patter, slang, vernacular

cant² *verb* = **tilt**, angle, bevel, incline, rise, slant, slope

cantankerous *adjective* = **bad-tempered**, captious, choleric, contrary, crabby, cranky (*U.S., Canad., & Irish informal*), crotchety (*informal*), crusty, difficult, disagreeable, grouchy (*informal*), grumpy, ill-humoured, irascible, irritable, liverish, peevish, perverse, quarrelsome, ratty (*Brit. & N.Z. informal*), testy, tetchy, waspish
➤ Antonyms
agreeable, amiable, breezy, cheerful, complaisant, congenial, genial, good-natured, happy, kindly, merry, placid, pleasant, vivacious

canter *noun* 1 = **jog**, amble, dogtrot, easy gait, lope ♦ *verb* 2 = **jog**, amble, lope

canting *adjective* = **hypocritical**, insincere, Janus-faced, sanctimonious, two-faced

canvass *verb* 1 = **campaign**, electioneer, solicit, solicit votes 2 = **poll**, analyse, examine, fly a kite, inspect, investigate, scan, scrutinize, sift, study, ventilate ♦ *noun* 3 = **poll**, examination, investigation, scrutiny, survey, tally

canyon *noun* = **gorge**, coulee (*U.S.*), gulch (*U.S.*), gulf, gully, ravine, valley

cap *verb Informal* = **beat**, better, clobber (*slang*), complete, cover, crown, eclipse, exceed, excel, finish, lick (*informal*), outdo, outstrip, overtop, put in the shade, run rings around (*informal*), surpass, top, transcend

capability *noun* = **ability**, capacity, competence, facility, faculty, means, potential, potentiality, power, proficiency, qualification(s), wherewithal
➤ Antonyms
inability, incompetence, inefficiency, ineptitude, powerlessness

capable *adjective* = **able**, accomplished, adapted, adept, adequate, apt, clever, competent, efficient, experienced, fitted, gifted, intelligent, masterly, proficient, qualified, skilful, suited, susceptible, talented
➤ Antonyms
incapable, incompetent, ineffective, inept, inexpert, unqualified, unskilled

capacious *adjective* = **spacious**, ample, broad, comfortable, commodious,

comprehensive, expansive, extended, extensive, generous, liberal, roomy, sizable or sizeable, substantial, vast, voluminous, wide
➤ **Antonyms**
confined, constricted, cramped, enclosed, incommodious, insubstantial, limited, narrow, poky, restricted, small, tight, tiny, uncomfortable, ungenerous

capacity *noun* **1** = **size**, amplitude, compass, dimensions, extent, magnitude, range, room, scope, space, volume **2** = **ability**, aptitude, aptness, brains, capability, cleverness, competence, competency, efficiency, facility, faculty, forte, genius, gift, intelligence, power, readiness, strength **3** = **function**, appointment, office, position, post, province, role, service, sphere

cape *noun* = **headland**, chersonese (*poetic*), head, ness (*archaic*), peninsula, point, promontory

caper *noun* **1** = **escapade**, antic, dido (*informal*), gambol, high jinks, hop, jape, jest, jump, lark (*informal*), leap, mischief, practical joke, prank, revel, shenanigan (*informal*), sport, stunt ◆ *verb* **2** = **dance**, bounce, bound, cavort, cut a rug (*informal*), frisk, frolic, gambol, hop, jump, leap, romp, skip, spring, trip

capital *noun* **1** = **money**, assets, cash, finance, finances, financing, funds, investment(s), means, principal, property, resources, stock, wealth, wherewithal ◆ *adjective* **2** = **principal**, cardinal, central, chief, controlling, essential, foremost, important, leading, main, major, overruling, paramount, pre-eminent, primary, prime, prominent, vital **3** *Old-fashioned* = **first-rate**, excellent, fine, first, prime, splendid, sterling, superb, world-class

capitalism *noun* = **private enterprise**, free enterprise, laissez faire or laisser faire, private ownership

capitalize on *verb* = **take advantage of**, benefit from, cash in on (*informal*), exploit, gain from, make the most of, profit from

capitulate *verb* = **give in**, cave in (*informal*), come to terms, give up, relent, submit, succumb, surrender, yield
➤ **Antonyms**
beat, conquer, crush, defeat, get the better of, lick (*informal*), overcome, overpower, subdue, subjugate, vanquish

capitulation *noun* = **surrender**, accedence, cave-in (*informal*), submission, yielding

caprice *noun* = **whim**, changeableness, fad, fancy, fickleness, fitfulness, freak, humour,

impulse, inconstancy, notion, quirk, vagary, whimsy

capricious *adjective* = **unpredictable**, changeful, crotchety (*informal*), erratic, fanciful, fickle, fitful, freakish, impulsive, inconsistent, inconstant, mercurial, odd, queer, quirky, variable, wayward, whimsical
➤ **Antonyms**
certain, consistent, constant, decisive, determined, firm, immovable, resolute, responsible, stable, unchangeable, unwavering

capsize *verb* = **overturn**, invert, keel over, tip over, turn over, turn turtle, upset

capsule *noun* **1** = **pill**, bolus, lozenge, tablet, troche (*Medical*) **2** *Botany* = **pod**, case, pericarp (*Botany*), receptacle, seed case, sheath, shell, vessel

captain *noun* = **leader**, boss, chief, chieftain, commander, head, master, number one (*informal*), officer, (senior) pilot, skipper, torchbearer

captivate *verb* = **charm**, absorb, allure, attract, beguile, bewitch, dazzle, enamour, enchant, enrapture, enslave, ensnare, enthral, entrance, fascinate, hypnotize, infatuate, lure, mesmerize, ravish, seduce, sweep off one's feet, win
➤ **Antonyms**
alienate, disenchant, disgust, repel, repulse

captive *noun* **1** = **prisoner**, bondservant, convict, detainee, hostage, internee, prisoner of war, slave ◆ *adjective* **2** = **confined**, caged, enslaved, ensnared, imprisoned, incarcerated, locked up, penned, restricted, subjugated

captivity *noun* = **confinement**, bondage, custody, detention, durance (*archaic*), duress, enthralment, imprisonment, incarceration, internment, restraint, servitude, slavery, thraldom, vassalage

capture *verb* **1** = **catch**, apprehend, arrest, bag, collar (*informal*), feel one's collar (*slang*), lift (*slang*), nab (*informal*), nail (*informal*), secure, seize, take, take into custody, take prisoner ◆ *noun* **2** = **catching**, apprehension, arrest, imprisonment, seizure, taking, taking captive, trapping
➤ **Antonyms**
verb ≠**catch**: free, let go, let out, liberate, release, set free, turn loose

car *noun* **1** = **vehicle**, auto (*U.S.*), automobile, jalopy (*informal*), machine, motor, motorcar, wheels (*informal*) **2** *U.S. & Canad.* = **(railway) carriage**, buffet car, cable car, coach, dining car, sleeping car, van

carafe *noun* = **jug**, decanter, flagon, flask,

pitcher

carcass *noun* = **body**, cadaver (*Medical*), corpse, corse (*archaic*), dead body, framework, hulk, remains, shell, skeleton

cardinal *adjective* = **principal**, capital, central, chief, essential, first, foremost, fundamental, greatest, highest, important, key, leading, main, paramount, pre-eminent, primary, prime
➤ **Antonyms**
dispensable, inessential, least important, lowest, secondary, subordinate

care *verb* **1** = **be concerned**, be bothered, be interested, mind ♦ *noun* **2** = **caution**, attention, carefulness, circumspection, consideration, direction, forethought, heed, management, meticulousness, pains, prudence, regard, vigilance, watchfulness **3** = **protection**, charge, control, custody, guardianship, keeping, management, ministration, supervision, ward **4** = **worry**, affliction, anxiety, burden, concern, disquiet, hardship, interest, perplexity, pressure, responsibility, solicitude, stress, tribulation, trouble, vexation, woe
➤ **Antonyms**
noun ≠**caution**: abandon, carelessness, heedlessness, inattention, indifference, laxity, laxness, neglect, negligence, unconcern ≠**worry**: pleasure, relaxation

career *noun* **1** = **occupation**, calling, employment, life's work, livelihood, pursuit, vocation **2** = **progress**, course, passage, path, procedure, race, walk ♦ *verb* **3** = **rush**, barrel (along) (*informal, chiefly U.S. & Canad.*), bolt, burn rubber (*informal*), dash, hurtle, race, speed, tear

care for *verb* **1** = **look after**, attend, foster, mind, minister to, nurse, protect, provide for, tend, watch over **2** = **like**, be fond of, desire, enjoy, find congenial, love, prize, take to, want

carefree *adjective* = **untroubled**, airy, blithe, breezy, buoyant, careless, cheerful, cheery, chirpy (*informal*), easy-going, halcyon, happy, happy-go-lucky, insouciant, jaunty, light-hearted, lightsome (*archaic*), radiant, sunny
➤ **Antonyms**
blue, careworn, cheerless, dejected, depressed, desolate, despondent, down, down in the dumps (*informal*), gloomy, low, melancholy, miserable, sad, unhappy, worried

careful *adjective* **1** = **cautious**, accurate, attentive, chary, circumspect, conscientious, discreet, fastidious, heedful, painstaking, precise, prudent, punctilious, scrupulous, thoughtful, thrifty **2**

= **thorough**, conscientious, meticulous, painstaking, particular, precise
➤ **Antonyms**
abandoned, careless, casual, inaccurate, inattentive, inexact, neglectful, negligent, reckless, remiss, slovenly, thoughtless, unconcerned, untroubled

careless *adjective* **1** = **slapdash**, cavalier, inaccurate, irresponsible, lackadaisical, neglectful, offhand, slipshod, sloppy (*informal*) **2** = **negligent**, absent-minded, cursory, forgetful, hasty, heedless, incautious, inconsiderate, indiscreet, perfunctory, regardless, remiss, thoughtless, unconcerned, unguarded, unmindful, unthinking **3** = **nonchalant**, artless, casual, unstudied
➤ **Antonyms**
≠**slapdash**: accurate, careful, neat, orderly, painstaking, tidy ≠**negligent**: alert, anxious, attentive, careful, cautious, concerned, correct, on the ball (*informal*), wary, watchful

carelessness *noun* = **negligence**, inaccuracy, inattention, inconsiderateness, indiscretion, irresponsibility, laxity, laxness, neglect, omission, remissness, slackness, sloppiness (*informal*), thoughtlessness

caress *verb* **1** = **stroke**, cuddle, embrace, fondle, hug, kiss, neck (*informal*), nuzzle, pet ♦ *noun* **2** = **stroke**, cuddle, embrace, fondling, hug, kiss, pat

caretaker *noun* **1** = **warden**, concierge, curator, custodian, janitor, keeper, porter, superintendent, watchman ♦ *adjective* **2** = **temporary**, holding, interim, short-term

cargo *noun* = **load**, baggage, consignment, contents, freight, goods, lading, merchandise, shipment, tonnage, ware

caricature *noun* **1** = **parody**, burlesque, cartoon, distortion, farce, lampoon, mimicry, pasquinade, satire, send-up (*Brit. informal*), takeoff (*informal*), travesty ♦ *verb* **2** = **parody**, burlesque, distort, lampoon, mimic, mock, ridicule, satirize, send up (*Brit. informal*), take off (*informal*)

carnage *noun* = **slaughter**, blood bath, bloodshed, butchery, havoc, holocaust, massacre, mass murder, murder, shambles

carnal *adjective* = **sexual**, amorous, animal, erotic, fleshly, impure, lascivious, lecherous, lewd, libidinous, licentious, lustful, prurient, randy (*informal, chiefly Brit.*), raunchy (*slang*), salacious, sensual, sensuous, sexy (*informal*), steamy (*informal*), unchaste, voluptuous, wanton

carnival *noun* = **festival**, celebration, fair, fête, fiesta, gala, holiday, jamboree, jubilee, Mardi Gras, merrymaking, revelry

carol *noun* = **song**, canticle, canzonet,

chorus, ditty, hymn, lay, noel, strain

carouse *verb* = **drink**, bend the elbow (*informal*), bevvy (*dialect*), booze (*informal*), imbibe, make merry, quaff, roister, wassail

carp *verb* = **find fault**, beef (*slang*), cavil, censure, complain, criticize, hypercriticize, knock (*informal*), kvetch (*U.S. slang*), nag, pick holes, quibble, reproach
➤ **Antonyms**
admire, applaud, approve, commend, compliment, extol, laud (*literary*), pay tribute to, praise, sing the praises of, speak highly of

carpenter *noun* = **joiner**, cabinet-maker, woodworker

carping *adjective* = **fault-finding**, captious, cavilling, critical, grouchy (*informal*), hard to please, hypercritical, nagging, nit-picking (*informal*), on someone's back (*informal*), picky (*informal*), reproachful

carriage *noun* **1** = **vehicle**, cab, coach, conveyance **2** = **bearing**, air, behaviour, comportment, conduct, demeanour, deportment, gait, manner, mien, posture, presence **3** = **transportation**, carrying, conveyance, conveying, delivery, freight, transport

carry *verb* **1** = **transport**, bear, bring, conduct, convey, fetch, haul, hump (*Brit. slang*), lift, lug, move, relay, take, tote (*informal*), transfer, transmit **2** = **support**, bear, bolster, hold up, maintain, shoulder, stand, suffer, sustain, underpin, uphold **3** = **include**, broadcast, communicate, display, disseminate, give, offer, publish, release, stock **4** = **win**, accomplish, capture, effect, gain, secure

carry on *verb* **1** = **continue**, endure, keep going, last, maintain, perpetuate, persevere, persist **2** = **run**, administer, manage, operate **3** *Informal* = **make a fuss**, create (*slang*), misbehave, raise Cain

carry out *verb* = **perform**, accomplish, achieve, carry through, consummate, discharge, effect, execute, fulfil, implement, realize

carton *noun* = **box**, case, container, pack, package, packet

cartoon *noun* **1** = **drawing**, caricature, comic strip, lampoon, parody, satire, sketch, takeoff (*informal*) **2** = **animation**, animated cartoon, animated film

cartridge *noun* **1** = **shell**, charge, round **2** = **container**, capsule, case, cassette, cylinder, magazine

carve *verb* = **cut**, chip, chisel, divide, engrave, etch, fashion, form, grave (*archaic*), hack, hew, incise, indent,

inscribe, mould, sculpt, sculpture, slash, slice, whittle

cascade *noun* **1** = **waterfall**, avalanche, cataract, deluge, downpour, falls, flood, fountain, outpouring, shower, torrent
◆ *verb* **2** = **flow**, descend, fall, flood, gush, overflow, pitch, plunge, pour, spill, surge, teem, tumble

case[1] *noun* **1** = **instance**, example, illustration, occasion, occurrence, specimen **2** = **situation**, circumstance(s), condition, context, contingency, dilemma, event, plight, position, predicament, state **3** *Law* = **lawsuit**, action, cause, dispute, proceedings, process, suit, trial

case[2] *noun* **1** = **container**, box, cabinet, canister, capsule, carton, cartridge, casket, chest, coffret, compact, crate, holder, receptacle, suitcase, tray, trunk **2** = **covering**, capsule, casing, cover, envelope, folder, integument, jacket, sheath, shell, wrapper, wrapping

cash *noun* = **money**, ackers (*slang*), banknotes, brass (*Northern English dialect*), bread (*slang*), bullion, change, coin, coinage, currency, dibs (*slang*), dosh (*Brit. & Austral. slang*), dough (*slang*), funds, necessary (*informal*), needful (*informal*), notes, payment, ready (*informal*), ready money, resources, rhino (*Brit. slang*), shekels (*informal*), silver, specie, spondulicks (*slang*), tin (*slang*), wherewithal

cashier[1] *noun* = **teller**, accountant, bank clerk, banker, bursar, clerk, purser, treasurer

cashier[2] *verb* = **dismiss**, break, cast off, discard, discharge, drum out, expel, give the boot to (*slang*)

casket *noun* = **box**, ark (*dialect*), case, chest, coffer, coffret, jewel box, kist (*Scot. & Northern English dialect*)

cast *noun* **1** = **actors**, characters, company, dramatis personae, players, troupe **2** = **type**, air, appearance, complexion, demeanour, look, manner, mien, semblance, shade, stamp, style, tinge, tone, turn **3** = **throw**, fling, lob, thrust, toss
◆ *verb* **4** = **choose**, allot, appoint, assign, name, pick, select **5** = **give out**, bestow, deposit, diffuse, distribute, emit, radiate, scatter, shed, spread **6** = **form**, found, model, mould, set, shape **7** = **throw**, chuck (*informal*), drive, drop, fling, hurl, impel, launch, lob, pitch, project, shed, shy, sling, thrust, toss

cast down *verb* = **discourage**, deject, depress, desolate, dishearten, dispirit

caste *noun* = **class**, estate, grade, lineage, order, race, rank, social order, species, station, status, stratum

castigate verb = **reprimand**, bawl out (*informal*), beat, berate, blast, cane, carpet (*informal*), censure, chasten, chastise, chew out (*U.S. & Canad. informal*), correct, criticize, discipline, dress down (*informal*), excoriate, flail, flay, flog, give a rocket (*Brit. & N.Z. informal*), haul over the coals (*informal*), lambast(e), lash, put down, rap over the knuckles, read the riot act, rebuke, scold, scourge, slap on the wrist, slate (*informal, chiefly Brit.*), tear into (*informal*), tear (someone) off a strip (*Brit. informal*), whip

cast-iron adjective = **certain**, copper-bottomed, definite, established, fixed, guaranteed, settled

castle noun = **fortress**, chateau, citadel, donjon, fastness, keep, mansion, palace, peel, stronghold, tower

cast-off adjective 1 = **unwanted**, discarded, rejected, scrapped, surplus to requirements, unneeded, useless ♦ noun 2 = **reject**, discard, failure, outcast, second

castrate verb = **neuter**, emasculate, geld

casual adjective 1 = **careless**, apathetic, blasé, cursory, indifferent, informal, insouciant, lackadaisical, nonchalant, offhand, perfunctory, relaxed, unconcerned 2 = **chance**, accidental, contingent, fortuitous, hit-and-miss *or* hit-or-miss (*informal*), incidental, irregular, occasional, random, serendipitous, uncertain, unexpected, unforeseen, unintentional, unpremeditated 3 = **informal**, non-dressy, sporty
➤ Antonyms
≠**careless**: committed, concerned, direct, enthusiastic, passionate, serious ≠**chance**: arranged, deliberate, expected, fixed, foreseen, intentional, planned, premeditated ≠**informal**: ceremonial, dressy, formal

casualty noun 1 = **victim**, death, fatality, loss, sufferer, wounded 2 = **accident**, calamity, catastrophe, disaster, misadventure, misfortune, mishap

cat noun = **feline**, gib, grimalkin, kitty (*informal*), malkin (*archaic*), moggy (*slang*), mouser, puss (*informal*), pussy (*informal*), tabby

catacombs plural noun = **vault**, crypt, tomb

catalogue noun 1 = **list**, directory, gazetteer, index, inventory, record, register, roll, roster, schedule ♦ verb 2 = **list**, accession, alphabetize, classify, file, index, inventory, register, tabulate

catapult noun 1 = **sling**, ballista, slingshot

(*U.S.*), trebuchet ♦ verb 2 = **shoot**, heave, hurl, hurtle, pitch, plunge, propel, toss

cataract noun 1 *Medical* = **opacity** (*of the eye*) 2 = **waterfall**, cascade, deluge, downpour, falls, Niagara, rapids, torrent

catastrophe noun = **disaster**, adversity, affliction, blow, bummer (*slang*), calamity, cataclysm, deep water, devastation, failure, fiasco, ill, meltdown (*informal*), mischance, misfortune, mishap, reverse, tragedy, trial, trouble, whammy (*informal, chiefly U.S.*)

catcall noun 1 = **jeer**, boo, gibe, hiss, raspberry, whistle ♦ verb 2 = **jeer**, boo, deride, gibe, give the bird to (*informal*), hiss, whistle

catch verb 1 = **seize**, clutch, get, grab, grasp, grip, lay hold of, snatch, take 2 = **capture**, apprehend, arrest, ensnare, entangle, entrap, feel one's collar (*slang*), lift (*slang*), nab (*informal*), nail (*informal*), snare, trap 3 = **discover**, catch in the act, detect, expose, find out, surprise, take unawares, unmask 4 = **contract**, develop, get, go down with, incur, succumb to, suffer from 5 = **attract**, bewitch, captivate, capture, charm, delight, enchant, enrapture, fascinate 6 = **make out**, apprehend, comprehend, discern, feel, follow, get, grasp, hear, perceive, recognize, sense, take in, twig (*Brit. informal*) ♦ noun 7 = **fastener**, bolt, clasp, clip, hasp, hook, hook and eye, latch, sneck (*dialect, chiefly Scot. & N. English*), snib (*Scot.*) 8 *Informal* = **drawback**, disadvantage, fly in the ointment, hitch, snag, stumbling block, trap, trick
➤ Antonyms
verb ≠**seize**: drop, free, give up, liberate, loose, release ≠**contract**: avert, avoid, escape, ward off ≠**attract**: alienate, bore, disenchant, disgust, fail to interest, repel ♦ noun ≠**drawback**: advantage, benefit, bonus, boon, reward

catching adjective = **infectious**, communicable, contagious, infective, transferable, transmittable
➤ Antonyms
incommunicable, non-catching, non-contagious, non-infectious, non-transmittable

catch on verb *Informal* = **understand**, comprehend, find out, get the picture, grasp, see, see the light of day, see through, twig (*Brit. informal*)

catchword noun = **slogan**, byword, motto, password, refrain, watchword

catchy adjective = **memorable**, captivating, haunting, popular

catechize verb = **question**, cross-examine,

drill, examine, grill (*informal*), interrogate

categorical *adjective* = **absolute**, direct, downright, emphatic, explicit, express, positive, unambiguous, unconditional, unequivocal, unqualified, unreserved
➤ **Antonyms**
conditional, hesitant, indefinite, qualified, questionable, uncertain, vague

category *noun* = **class**, classification, department, division, grade, grouping, head, heading, list, order, rank, section, sort, type

cater *verb* = **provide**, furnish, outfit, provision, purvey, supply, victual

catharsis *noun* = **release**, abreaction, cleansing, lustration, purgation, purging, purification

catholic *adjective* = **wide**, all-embracing, all-inclusive, broad-minded, charitable, comprehensive, eclectic, ecumenical, general, global, liberal, tolerant, unbigoted, universal, unsectarian, whole, world-wide
➤ **Antonyms**
bigoted, exclusive, illiberal, limited, narrow-minded, parochial, sectarian

cattle *plural noun* = **cows**, beasts, bovines, kine (*archaic*), livestock, neat (*archaic*), stock

catty *adjective* = **spiteful**, backbiting, bitchy (*informal*), ill-natured, malevolent, malicious, mean, rancorous, shrewish, snide, venomous
➤ **Antonyms**
benevolent, charitable, compassionate, considerate, generous, kind, pleasant

caucus *noun* = **meeting**, assembly, conclave, congress, convention, get-together (*informal*), parley, session

cause *noun* 1 = **origin**, agent, beginning, creator, genesis, mainspring, maker, originator, prime mover, producer, root, source, spring 2 = **reason**, account, agency, aim, basis, consideration, end, grounds, incentive, inducement, justification, motivation, motive, object, purpose, the why and wherefore 3 = **aim**, attempt, belief, conviction, enterprise, ideal, movement, principle, purpose, undertaking ♦ *verb* 4 = **produce**, begin, bring about, compel, create, effect, engender, generate, give rise to, incite, induce, lead to, motivate, occasion, precipitate, provoke, result in
➤ **Antonyms**
noun ≠**origin**: consequence, effect, end, outcome, result ♦ *verb* ≠**produce**: deter, foil, inhibit, prevent, stop

caustic *adjective* 1 = **burning**, acrid, astringent, biting, corroding, corrosive,

keen, mordant, vitriolic 2 = **sarcastic**, acrimonious, cutting, mordacious, pungent, scathing, severe, stinging, trenchant, virulent, vitriolic
➤ **Antonyms**
≠**sarcastic**: agreeable, bland, gentle, kind, loving, mild, pleasant, soft, soothing, sweet

caution *noun* 1 = **care**, alertness, belt and braces, carefulness, circumspection, deliberation, discretion, forethought, heed, heedfulness, prudence, vigilance, watchfulness 2 = **warning**, admonition, advice, counsel, injunction ♦ *verb* 3 = **warn**, admonish, advise, tip off, urge
➤ **Antonyms**
noun ≠**care**: carelessness, daring, imprudence, rashness, recklessness ♦ *verb* ≠**warn**: dare

cautious *adjective* = **careful**, alert, belt-and-braces, cagey (*informal*), chary, circumspect, discreet, guarded, heedful, judicious, keeping a weather eye on, on one's toes, prudent, tentative, vigilant, wary, watchful
➤ **Antonyms**
adventurous, bold, careless, daring, foolhardy, heedless, impetuous, inattentive, incautious, indiscreet, madcap, rash, reckless, unguarded, unheedful, venturesome, venturous

cavalcade *noun* = **parade**, array, march-past, procession, spectacle, train

cavalier *adjective* 1 = **haughty**, arrogant, condescending, curt, disdainful, insolent, lofty, lordly, offhand, scornful, supercilious ♦ *noun* 2 = **gentleman**, beau, blade (*archaic*), escort, gallant 3 = **knight**, chevalier, equestrian, horseman

cavalry *noun* = **horsemen**, horse, mounted troops
➤ **Antonyms**
foot soldiers, infantrymen

cave *noun* = **hollow**, cavern, cavity, den, grotto

caveat *noun* = **warning**, admonition, caution

cavern *noun* = **cave**, hollow, pothole

cavernous *adjective* 1 = **deep**, concave, hollow, sunken, yawning 2 = **resonant**, echoing, reverberant, sepulchral

cavil *verb* = **find fault**, beef (*slang*), carp, censure, complain, hypercriticize, kvetch (*U.S. slang*), object, quibble

cavity *noun* = **hollow**, crater, dent, gap, hole, pit

cease *verb* = **stop**, belay (*Nautical*), break off, bring or come to an end, conclude, culminate, desist, die away, discontinue, end, fail, finish, halt, leave off, refrain, stay,

terminate
➤ **Antonyms**
begin, commence, continue, initiate, start
ceaseless *adjective* = **continual**, constant, continuous, endless, eternal, everlasting, incessant, indefatigable, interminable, never-ending, nonstop, perennial, perpetual, unending, unremitting, untiring
➤ **Antonyms**
broken, erratic, intermittent, irregular, occasional, periodic, spasmodic, sporadic
cede *verb* = **surrender**, abandon, abdicate, allow, concede, convey, grant, hand over, make over, relinquish, renounce, resign, step down (*informal*), transfer, yield
celebrate *verb* **1** = **rejoice**, commemorate, drink to, keep, kill the fatted calf, observe, put the flags out, toast **2** = **perform**, bless, honour, reverence, solemnize **3** = **praise**, commend, crack up (*informal*), eulogize, exalt, extol, glorify, honour, laud, proclaim, publicize
celebrated *adjective* = **well-known**, acclaimed, distinguished, eminent, famed, famous, glorious, illustrious, lionized, notable, outstanding, popular, pre-eminent, prominent, renowned, revered
➤ **Antonyms**
dishonoured, forgotten, insignificant, obscure, trivial, unacclaimed, undistinguished, unknown, unnotable, unpopular
celebration *noun* **1** = **party**, beano (*Brit. slang*), carousal, -fest (*in combination*), festival, festivity, gala, hooley or hoolie (*chiefly Irish & N.Z.*), jollification, jubilee, junketing, merrymaking, rave (*Brit. slang*), rave-up (*Brit. slang*), red-letter day, revelry **2** = **performance**, anniversary, commemoration, honouring, observance, remembrance, solemnization
celebrity *noun* **1** = **personality**, big name, big shot (*informal*), bigwig (*informal*), celeb (*informal*), dignitary, face (*informal*), lion, luminary, megastar (*informal*), name, personage, star, superstar, V.I.P. **2** = **fame**, distinction, éclat, glory, honour, notability, popularity, pre-eminence, prestige, prominence, renown, reputation, repute, stardom
➤ **Antonyms**
≠**personality**: has-been, nobody, unknown ≠**fame**: obscurity
celerity *noun Formal* = **speed**, dispatch, expedition, fleetness, haste, promptness, quickness, rapidity, swiftness, velocity
celestial *adjective* = **heavenly**, angelic, astral, divine, elysian, empyrean (*poetic*), eternal, ethereal, godlike, immortal,

seraphic, spiritual, sublime, supernatural
celibacy *noun* = **chastity**, continence, purity, singleness, virginity
cell *noun* **1** = **room**, cavity, chamber, compartment, cubicle, dungeon, stall **2** = **unit**, caucus, core, coterie, group, nucleus
cement *noun* **1** = **mortar**, adhesive, binder, glue, gum, paste, plaster, sealant ◆ *verb* **2** = **stick together**, attach, bind, bond, cohere, combine, glue, gum, join, plaster, seal, solder, unite, weld
cemetery *noun* = **graveyard**, burial ground, churchyard, God's acre, necropolis
censor *verb* = **cut**, blue-pencil, bowdlerize, expurgate
censorious *adjective* = **critical**, captious, carping, cavilling, condemnatory, disapproving, disparaging, fault-finding, hypercritical, scathing, severe
censure *noun* **1** = **disapproval**, blame, castigation, condemnation, criticism, dressing down (*informal*), obloquy, rebuke, remonstrance, reprehension, reprimand, reproach, reproof, stick (*slang*), stricture ◆ *verb* **2** = **criticize**, abuse, bawl out (*informal*), berate, blame, blast, carpet (*informal*), castigate, chew out (*U.S. & Canad. informal*), chide, condemn, denounce, excoriate, give (someone) a rocket (*Brit. & N.Z. informal*), lambast(e), put down, rap over the knuckles, read the riot act, rebuke, reprehend, reprimand, reproach, reprove, scold, slap on the wrist, slate (*informal, chiefly U.S.*), tear into (*informal*), tear (someone) off a strip (*Brit. informal*), upbraid
➤ **Antonyms**
noun ≠**disapproval**: approval, commendation, compliment, encouragement ◆ *verb* ≠**criticize**: applaud, commend, compliment
central *adjective* **1** = **middle**, inner, interior, mean, median, mid **2** = **main**, chief, essential, focal, fundamental, key, primary, principal
➤ **Antonyms**
≠**middle**: exterior, outer, outermost ≠**main**: minor, secondary, subordinate, subsidiary
centralize *verb* = **unify**, amalgamate, compact, concentrate, concentre, condense, converge, incorporate, rationalize, streamline
centre *noun* **1** = **middle**, bull's-eye, core, crux, focus, heart, hub, kernel, mid (*archaic*), midpoint, nucleus, pivot ◆ *verb* **2** = **focus**, cluster, concentrate, converge, revolve

➤ **Antonyms**
noun ≠**middle**: border, boundary, brim, circumference, edge, fringe, limit, lip, margin, perimeter, periphery, rim

centrepiece *noun* = **focus**, cynosure, epergne, highlight, hub, star

ceremonial *adjective* **1** = **ritual**, formal, liturgical, ritualistic, solemn, stately ♦ *noun* **2** = **ritual**, ceremony, formality, rite, solemnity
➤ **Antonyms**
adjective ≠**ritual**: casual, informal, relaxed, simple

ceremonious *adjective* = **formal**, civil, courteous, courtly, deferential, dignified, exact, precise, punctilious, ritual, solemn, starchy (*informal*), stately, stiff

ceremony *noun* **1** = **ritual**, commemoration, function, observance, parade, rite, service, show, solemnities **2** = **formality**, ceremonial, decorum, etiquette, form, formal courtesy, niceties, pomp, propriety, protocol

certain *adjective* **1** = **sure**, assured, confident, convinced, positive, satisfied **2** = **known**, ascertained, conclusive, incontrovertible, indubitable, irrefutable, plain, true, undeniable, undoubted, unequivocal, unmistakable, valid **3** = **inevitable**, bound, definite, destined, fated, ineluctable, inescapable, inexorable, sure **4** = **fixed**, decided, definite, established, settled **5** = **particular**, express, individual, precise, special, specific
➤ **Antonyms**
disputable, doubtful, dubious, equivocal, fallible, indefinite, questionable, uncertain, unconvinced, undecided, unlikely, unreliable, unsettled, unsure

certainly *adverb* = **definitely**, assuredly, indisputably, indubitably, surely, truly, undeniably, undoubtedly, without doubt

certainty *noun* **1** = **sureness**, assurance, authoritativeness, certitude, confidence, conviction, faith, indubitableness, inevitability, positiveness, trust, validity **2** = **fact**, banker, reality, sure thing (*informal*), surety, truth
➤ **Antonyms**
≠**sureness**: disbelief, doubt, indecision, qualm, scepticism, uncertainty, unsureness

certificate *noun* = **document**, authorization, credential(s), diploma, licence, testimonial, voucher, warrant

certify *verb* = **confirm**, ascertain, assure, attest, authenticate, aver, avow, corroborate, declare, endorse, guarantee, notify, show, testify, validate, verify, vouch, witness

chafe *verb* **1** = **rub**, abrade, rasp, scrape,

scratch **2** = **be annoyed**, be angry, be exasperated, be impatient, be incensed, be inflamed, be irritated, be narked (*Brit., Austral., & N.Z. slang*), be offended, be ruffled, be vexed, fret, fume, rage, worry

chaff[1] *noun* = **waste**, dregs, glumes, hulls, husks, refuse, remains, rubbish, trash

chaff[2] *verb* **1** = **tease**, banter, deride, jeer, josh (*slang, chiefly U.S. & Canad.*), mock, rib (*informal*), ridicule, scoff, take the piss out of (*taboo slang*), taunt ♦ *noun* **2** = **teasing**, badinage, banter, joking, josh (*slang, chiefly U.S. & Canad.*), persiflage, raillery

chagrin *noun* **1** = **annoyance**, discomfiture, discomposure, displeasure, disquiet, dissatisfaction, embarrassment, fretfulness, humiliation, ill-humour, irritation, mortification, peevishness, spleen, vexation ♦ *verb* **2** = **annoy**, discomfit, discompose, displease, disquiet, dissatisfy, embarrass, humiliate, irk, irritate, mortify, peeve, vex

chain *noun* **1** = **link**, bond, coupling, fetter, manacle, shackle, union **2** = **series**, concatenation, progression, sequence, set, string, succession, train ♦ *verb* **3** = **bind**, confine, enslave, fetter, gyve (*archaic*), handcuff, manacle, restrain, shackle, tether, trammel, unite

chairman *noun* = **director**, chairperson, chairwoman, master of ceremonies, president, presider, speaker, spokesman, toastmaster

chalk up *verb Informal* = **score**, accumulate, achieve, attain, credit, enter, gain, log, mark, record, register, tally, win

challenge *noun* **1** = **test**, confrontation, dare, defiance, face-off (*slang*), interrogation, provocation, question, summons to contest, trial, ultimatum ♦ *verb* **2** = **test**, accost, arouse, beard, brave, call out, call (someone's) bluff, claim, confront, dare, defy, demand, dispute, face off (*slang*), impugn, investigate, object to, provoke, question, require, stimulate, summon, tackle, tax, throw down the gauntlet, try

chamber *noun* **1** = **room**, apartment, bedroom, cavity, compartment, cubicle, enclosure, hall, hollow **2** = **council**, assembly, legislative body, legislature

champion *noun* **1** = **winner**, challenger, conqueror, hero, nonpareil, title holder, victor, warrior **2** = **defender**, backer, guardian, patron, protector, upholder, vindicator ♦ *verb* **3** = **support**, advocate, back, commend, defend, encourage, espouse, fight for, promote, stick up for (*informal*), uphold

chance noun 1 = **probability**, liability, likelihood, odds, possibility, prospect 2 = **opportunity**, occasion, opening, scope, time, window 3 = **luck**, accident, casualty, coincidence, contingency, destiny, fate, fortuity, fortune, misfortune, peril, providence 4 = **risk**, gamble, hazard, jeopardy, speculation, uncertainty ♦ verb 5 = **risk**, endanger, gamble, go out on a limb, hazard, jeopardize, skate on thin ice, stake, try, venture, wager 6 = **happen**, befall, betide, come about, come to pass, fall out, occur ♦ adjective 7 = **accidental**, casual, contingent, fortuitous, inadvertent, incidental, random, serendipitous, unforeseeable, unforeseen, unintentional, unlooked-for
➤ **Antonyms**
noun ≠**probability**: certainty, design, impossibility, improbability, intention, surety, unlikelihood ♦ adjective ≠**accidental**: arranged, deliberate, designed, expected, foreseen, intentional, planned

chancy adjective Informal = **risky**, dangerous, dicey (informal, chiefly Brit.), dodgy (Brit., Austral., & N.Z. slang), hazardous, perilous, problematical, speculative, uncertain
➤ **Antonyms**
certain, reliable, safe, secure, sound, stable, sure

change noun 1 = **alteration**, difference, innovation, metamorphosis, modification, mutation, permutation, revolution, transformation, transition, transmutation, vicissitude 2 = **variety**, break (informal), departure, diversion, novelty, variation, whole new ball game (informal) 3 = **exchange**, conversion, interchange, substitution, swap, trade ♦ verb 4 = **alter**, convert, diversify, fluctuate, metamorphose, moderate, modify, mutate, reform, remodel, reorganize, restyle, shift, transform, transmute, vacillate, vary, veer 5 = **exchange**, alternate, barter, convert, displace, interchange, remove, replace, substitute, swap, trade, transmit
➤ **Antonyms**
noun ≠**alteration, variety**: constancy, invariability, monotony, permanence, stability, uniformity ♦ verb ≠**alter**: hold, keep, remain, stay

changeable adjective = **variable**, capricious, changeful, chequered, erratic, fickle, fitful, fluid, inconstant, irregular, kaleidoscopic, labile (Chemistry), mercurial, mobile, mutable, protean, shifting, temperamental, uncertain, uneven, unpredictable, unreliable, unsettled, unstable, unsteady, vacillating, versatile, volatile, wavering, whimsical
➤ **Antonyms**
constant, invariable, irreversible, regular, reliable, stable, steady, unchangeable

changeless adjective = **unchanging**, abiding, consistent, constant, eternal, everlasting, fixed, immovable, immutable, permanent, perpetual, regular, reliable, resolute, settled, stationary, steadfast, steady, unalterable, uniform, unvarying

channel noun 1 = **route**, approach, artery, avenue, course, means, medium, path, way 2 = **passage**, canal, chamber, conduit, duct, fluting, furrow, groove, gutter, main, route, strait ♦ verb 3 = **direct**, conduct, convey, guide, transmit

chant verb 1 = **sing**, carol, chorus, croon, descant, intone, recite, warble ♦ noun 2 = **song**, carol, chorus, melody, psalm

chaos noun = **disorder**, anarchy, bedlam, confusion, disorganization, entropy, lawlessness, mayhem, pandemonium, tumult
➤ **Antonyms**
neatness, orderliness, organization, tidiness

chaotic adjective = **disordered**, anarchic, confused, deranged, disorganized, lawless, purposeless, rampageous, riotous, topsy-turvy, tumultuous, uncontrolled

chap noun Informal = **fellow**, bloke (Brit. informal), character, cove (slang), customer (informal), dude (U.S. & Canad. informal), guy (informal), individual, man, person, sort, type

chaperone noun 1 = **escort**, companion, duenna, governess ♦ verb 2 = **escort**, accompany, attend, protect, safeguard, shepherd, watch over

chapter noun = **section**, clause, division, episode, part, period, phase, stage, topic

char verb = **scorch**, carbonize, cauterize, sear, singe

character noun 1 = **nature**, attributes, bent, calibre, cast, complexion, constitution, disposition, individuality, kidney, make-up, marked traits, personality, quality, temper, temperament, type 2 = **reputation**, honour, integrity, rectitude, strength, uprightness 3 = **role**, part, persona, portrayal 4 = **eccentric**, card (informal), nut (slang), oddball (informal), odd bod (informal), oddity, original, queer fish (Brit. informal), wacko or whacko (informal) 5 Informal = **person**, fellow, guy (informal), individual, sort, type 6 = **symbol**, cipher, device, emblem, figure, hieroglyph, letter, logo, mark, rune, sign, type

characteristic *noun* **1** = **feature**, attribute, faculty, idiosyncrasy, mark, peculiarity, property, quality, quirk, trait ♦ *adjective* **2** = **typical**, distinctive, distinguishing, idiosyncratic, individual, peculiar, representative, singular, special, specific, symbolic, symptomatic
➤ **Antonyms**
adjective ≠**typical**: rare, uncharacteristic, unrepresentative, unusual

characterize *verb* = **identify**, brand, distinguish, indicate, inform, mark, represent, stamp, typify

charade *noun* = **pretence**, fake, farce, pantomime, parody, travesty

charge *verb* **1** = **accuse**, arraign, blame, impeach, incriminate, indict, involve **2** = **attack**, assail, assault, rush, stampede, storm **3** = **fill**, instil, lade, load, suffuse **4** *Formal* = **command**, bid, commit, demand, enjoin, entrust, exhort, instruct, order, require ♦ *noun* **5** = **price**, amount, cost, damage (*informal*), expenditure, expense, outlay, payment, rate, toll **6** = **accusation**, allegation, imputation, indictment **7** = **attack**, assault, onset, onslaught, rush, sortie, stampede **8** = **care**, custody, duty, office, responsibility, safekeeping, trust **9** = **ward**, burden, concern **10** = **instruction**, canon, command, demand, dictate, direction, exhortation, injunction, mandate, order, precept
➤ **Antonyms**
verb ≠**accuse**: absolve, acquit, clear, exonerate, pardon ≠**attack**: back off, retreat, withdraw ♦ *noun* ≠**accusation**: absolution, acquittal, clearance, exoneration, pardon, reprieve ≠**attack**: retreat, withdrawal

charisma *noun* = **charm**, allure, attraction, lure, magnetism, personality

charismatic *adjective* = **charming**, alluring, attractive, enticing, influential, magnetic

charitable *adjective* **1** = **kind**, broad-minded, considerate, favourable, forgiving, gracious, humane, indulgent, lenient, magnanimous, sympathetic, tolerant, understanding **2** = **generous**, beneficent, benevolent, bountiful, eleemosynary, kind, lavish, liberal, philanthropic
➤ **Antonyms**
≠**kind**: inconsiderate, mean, strict, uncharitable, unforgiving, unkind, unsympathetic ≠**generous**: mean, stingy, ungenerous

charity *noun* **1** = **donations**, alms-giving, assistance, benefaction, contributions, endowment, fund, gift, hand-out, help, largesse *or* largess, philanthropy, relief **2** = **kindness**, affection, Agape, altruism, benevolence, benignity, bountifulness, bounty, compassion, fellow feeling, generosity, goodness, goodwill, humanity, indulgence, love, pity, tenderheartedness
➤ **Antonyms**
≠**donations**: meanness, miserliness, selfishness, stinginess ≠**kindness**: hatred, ill will, intolerance, malice

charlatan *noun* = **fraud**, cheat, con man (*informal*), fake, fraudster, grifter (*slang, chiefly U.S. & Canad.*), impostor, mountebank, phoney *or* phony (*informal*), pretender, quack, sham, swindler

charm *noun* **1** = **attraction**, allure, allurement, appeal, desirability, fascination, magnetism **2** = **spell**, enchantment, magic, sorcery **3** = **talisman**, amulet, fetish, good-luck piece, lucky piece, periapt (*rare*), trinket ♦ *verb* **4** = **attract**, absorb, allure, beguile, bewitch, cajole, captivate, delight, enamour, enchant, enrapture, entrance, fascinate, mesmerize, please, ravish, win, win over
➤ **Antonyms**
noun ≠**attraction**: repulsiveness, unattractiveness ♦ *verb* ≠**attract**: alienate, repel, repulse

charming *adjective* = **attractive**, appealing, bewitching, captivating, cute, delectable, delightful, engaging, eye-catching, fetching, irresistible, likable *or* likeable, lovely, pleasant, pleasing, seductive, winning, winsome
➤ **Antonyms**
disgusting, horrid, repulsive, unappealing, unattractive, unlikable *or* unlikeable, unpleasant, unpleasing

chart *noun* **1** = **table**, blueprint, diagram, graph, map, plan, tabulation ♦ *verb* **2** = **plot**, delineate, draft, graph, map out, outline, shape, sketch

charter *noun* **1** = **document**, bond, concession, contract, deed, franchise, indenture, licence, permit, prerogative, privilege, right ♦ *verb* **2** = **hire**, commission, employ, lease, rent **3** = **authorize**, sanction

chase *verb* **1** = **pursue**, course, follow, hunt, run after, track **2** = **drive away**, drive, expel, hound, put to flight ♦ *noun* **3** = **pursuit**, hunt, hunting, race, venery (*archaic*)

chasm *noun* = **gulf**, abyss, alienation, breach, cavity, cleft, crack, crater, crevasse, fissure, gap, gorge, hiatus, hollow, opening, ravine, rent, rift, split, void

chassis *noun* = **frame**, anatomy, bodywork, framework, fuselage, skeleton, substructure

chaste adjective = **pure,** austere, decent, decorous, elegant, immaculate, incorrupt, innocent, modest, moral, neat, quiet, refined, restrained, simple, unaffected, uncontaminated, undefiled, unsullied, vestal, virginal, virtuous, wholesome
➤ **Antonyms**
corrupt, dirty, dishonourable, immoral, impure, promiscuous, self-indulgent, tainted, unchaste, unclean, unrestrained, wanton

chasten verb = **subdue,** afflict, castigate, chastise, correct, cow, curb, discipline, humble, humiliate, put in one's place, repress, soften, tame

chastise verb 1 = **scold,** berate, castigate, censure, correct, discipline, upbraid 2 Old-fashioned = **beat,** flog, lash, lick (informal), punish, scourge, whip
➤ **Antonyms**
≠scold: commend, compliment, congratulate, praise, reward ≠beat: caress, cuddle, embrace, fondle, hug

chastity noun = **purity,** celibacy, continence, innocence, maidenhood, modesty, virginity, virtue
➤ **Antonyms**
debauchery, immorality, lewdness, licentiousness, profligacy, promiscuity, wantonness

chat noun 1 = **talk,** chatter, chinwag (Brit. informal), confab (informal), conversation, gossip, heart-to-heart, natter, schmooze (slang), tête-à-tête ◆ verb 2 = **talk,** chatter, chew the rag or fat (slang), gossip, jaw (slang), natter, rabbit (on) (Brit. informal), run off at the mouth (U.S. slang), schmooze (slang), shoot the breeze (U.S. slang)

chatter noun 1 = **prattle,** babble, blather, chat, gab (informal), gossip, jabber, natter, rabbit (Brit. informal), tattle, twaddle ◆ verb 2 = **prattle,** babble, blather, chat, gab (informal), gossip, jabber, natter, prate, rabbit (on) (Brit. informal), run off at the mouth (U.S. slang), schmooze (slang), tattle

chatty adjective = **talkative,** colloquial, familiar, friendly, gossipy, informal, newsy (informal)
➤ **Antonyms**
aloof, cold, distant, formal, hostile, quiet, reserved, shy, silent, standoffish, taciturn, timid, unfriendly, unsociable

cheap adjective 1 = **inexpensive,** bargain, cheapo (informal), cut-price, economical, economy, keen, low-cost, low-priced, reasonable, reduced, sale 2 = **inferior,** bush-league (Austral. & N.Z. informal), chickenshit (U.S. slang), common, crappy (slang), dime-a-dozen (informal), low-rent (informal, chiefly U.S.), paltry, piss-poor (U.S. taboo slang), poor, poxy (slang), second-rate, shoddy, tatty, tawdry, tinhorn (U.S. slang), two a penny, two-bit (U.S. & Canad. slang), worthless 3 Informal = **despicable,** base, contemptible, low, mean, scurvy, sordid, vulgar
➤ **Antonyms**
≠inexpensive: costly, dear, expensive, pricey (informal), steep ≠inferior: admirable, decent, elegant, good, high-class, superior, tasteful, valuable ≠despicable: admirable, decent, generous, good, honourable

cheapen verb = **degrade,** belittle, debase, demean, denigrate, depreciate, derogate, devalue, discredit, disparage, lower

cheat verb 1 = **deceive,** bamboozle (informal), beguile, bilk, con (informal), cozen, defraud, diddle (informal), do (informal), do the dirty on (Brit. informal), double-cross (informal), dupe, finagle (informal), fleece, fool, gull (archaic), hoax, hoodwink, kid (informal), mislead, pull a fast one on (informal), rip off (slang), skin (slang), stiff (slang), sting (informal), stitch up (slang), swindle, take for a ride (informal), take in (informal), thwart, trick, victimize 2 = **foil,** baffle, check, defeat, deprive, frustrate, prevent, thwart ◆ noun 3 = **deceiver,** charlatan, cheater, chiseller (informal), con man (informal), dodger, double-crosser (informal), fraudster, grifter (slang, chiefly U.S. & Canad.), impostor, knave (archaic), rogue, shark, sharper, swindler, trickster 4 = **deception,** artifice, deceit, fraud, imposture, rip-off (slang), scam (slang), sting (informal), swindle, trickery

check verb 1 = **examine,** check out (informal), compare, confirm, inquire into, inspect, investigate, look at, look over, make sure, monitor, note, probe, research, scrutinize, study, take a dekko at (Brit. slang), test, tick, verify, vet, work over 2 = **stop,** arrest, bar, bridle, control, curb, delay, halt, hinder, hobble, impede, inhibit, limit, nip in the bud, obstruct, pause, put a spoke in someone's wheel, rein, repress, restrain, retard, stem the flow, thwart ◆ noun 3 = **examination,** inspection, investigation, once-over (informal), research, scrutiny, test 4 = **stoppage,** constraint, control, curb, damper, hindrance, impediment, inhibition, limitation, obstacle, obstruction, rein, restraint 5 = **setback,** blow, disappointment, frustration, rejection, reverse, whammy (informal,

chiefly U.S.)
➤ **Antonyms**
verb ≠**examine**: disregard, ignore, neglect, overlook, pass over, pay no attention to ≠**stop**: accelerate, advance, begin, encourage, further, give free rein, help, release, start

cheek noun Informal = **impudence**, audacity, brass neck (Brit. informal), brazenness, chutzpah (U.S. & Canad. informal), disrespect, effrontery, face (informal), front, gall (informal), impertinence, insolence, lip (slang), neck (informal), nerve, sassiness (U.S. informal), sauce (informal), temerity

cheeky adjective = **impudent**, audacious, disrespectful, forward, fresh (informal), impertinent, insolent, insulting, lippy (U.S. & Canad. slang), pert, sassy (U.S. informal), saucy
➤ **Antonyms**
civil, complaisant, courteous, decorous, deferential, mannerly, polite, respectful, well-behaved, well-mannered

cheer verb 1 = **applaud**, acclaim, clap, hail, hurrah 2 = **cheer up**, animate, brighten, buoy up, comfort, console, elate, elevate, encourage, enliven, exhilarate, gladden, hearten, incite, inspire, inspirit, solace, uplift, warm ♦ noun 3 = **applause**, acclamation, ovation, plaudits 4 = **cheerfulness**, animation, buoyancy, comfort, gaiety, gladness, glee, hopefulness, joy, liveliness, merriment, merry-making, mirth, optimism, solace
➤ **Antonyms**
verb ≠**applaud**: blow a raspberry, boo, hiss, jeer, ridicule ≠**cheer up**: darken, depress, discourage, dishearten, sadden

cheerful adjective = **happy**, animated, blithe, bright, bucked (informal), buoyant, cheery, chirpy (informal), contented, enlivening, enthusiastic, gay, genial, glad, gladsome (archaic), hearty, jaunty, jolly, joyful, light-hearted, lightsome (archaic), merry, optimistic, pleasant, sparkling, sprightly, sunny, upbeat (informal)
➤ **Antonyms**
cheerless, dejected, depressed, depressing, despondent, dismal, down, downcast, down in the dumps (informal), dull, gloomy, low, melancholy, miserable, morose, pensive, sad, unhappy, unpleasant

cheerfulness noun = **happiness**, buoyancy, exuberance, gaiety, geniality, gladness, good cheer, good humour, high spirits, jauntiness, joyousness, light-heartedness

cheering adjective = **encouraging**, auspicious, bright, comforting, heartening, promising, propitious

cheerless adjective = **gloomy**, austere, bleak, comfortless, dark, dejected, depressed, desolate, despondent, disconsolate, dismal, dolorous, drab, dreary, dull, forlorn, funereal, grim, joyless, melancholy, miserable, mournful, sad, sombre, sorrowful, sullen, unhappy, woebegone, woeful
➤ **Antonyms**
cheerful, cheery, elated, happy, jolly, joyful, light-hearted, merry

cheer up verb 1 = **comfort**, brighten, encourage, enliven, gee up, gladden, hearten, jolly along (informal) 2 = **take heart**, buck up (informal), perk up, rally

cheery adjective = **cheerful**, breezy, carefree, chirpy (informal), full of beans (informal), genial, good-humoured, happy, jovial, lively, pleasant, sunny, upbeat (informal)

chemical noun = **compound**, drug, potion, substance, synthetic

chemist noun = **pharmacist**, apothecary (obsolete), dispenser, pharmacologist

cherish verb 1 = **cling to**, cleave to, encourage, entertain, foster, harbour, hold dear, nurture, prize, sustain, treasure 2 = **care for**, comfort, cosset, hold dear, love, nourish, nurse, shelter, support, treasure
➤ **Antonyms**
abandon, desert, despise, disdain, dislike, forsake, hate, neglect

cherubic adjective = **angelic**, adorable, heavenly, innocent, lovable, seraphic, sweet

chest noun = **box**, ark (dialect), case, casket, coffer, crate, kist (Scot. & Northern English dialect), strongbox, trunk

chew verb 1 = **bite**, champ, chomp, crunch, gnaw, grind, masticate, munch 2 **chew over** = **consider**, deliberate upon, meditate, mull (over), muse on, ponder, reflect upon, ruminate, weigh

chewy adjective = **tough**, as tough as old boots, fibrous, leathery

chic adjective = **stylish**, elegant, fashionable, modish, sexy (informal), smart, trendy (Brit. informal), up-to-date, urbane
➤ **Antonyms**
dinosaur, inelegant, naff (Brit. slang), old-fashioned, outmoded, out-of-date, passé, shabby, unfashionable

chide verb Old-fashioned = **scold**, admonish, bawl out (informal), berate, blame, blast, carpet (informal), censure, check, chew out (U.S. & Canad. informal), criticize, find fault, give (someone) a rocket

(*Brit. & N.Z. informal*), give (someone) a
row (*Scot. informal*), lambast(e), lecture,
put down, rap over the knuckles, read the
riot act, rebuke, reprehend, reprimand,
reproach, reprove, slap on the wrist, slate
(*informal, chiefly Brit.*), tear into (*informal*),
tear (someone) off a strip (*Brit. informal*),
tell off (*informal*), tick off (*informal*),
upbraid

chief *noun* 1 = **head**, boss (*informal*),
captain, chieftain, commander, director,
governor, leader, lord, manager, master,
principal, ringleader, ruler,
superintendent, superior, suzerain,
torchbearer ♦ *adjective* 2 = **primary**,
big-time (*informal*), capital, cardinal,
central, especial, essential, foremost,
grand, highest, key, leading, main, major
league (*informal*), most important,
outstanding, paramount, predominant,
pre-eminent, premier, prevailing, prime,
principal, superior, supreme, uppermost,
vital
➤ Antonyms
noun ≠**head**: follower, subject,
subordinate ♦ *adjective* ≠**primary**: least,
minor, subordinate, subsidiary

chiefly *adverb* 1 = **especially**, above all,
essentially, primarily, principally 2
= **mainly**, in general, in the main, largely,
mostly, on the whole, predominantly,
usually

child *noun* = **youngster**, ankle-biter
(*Austral. slang*), babe, babe in arms
(*informal*), baby, bairn (*Scot.*), brat, chit,
descendant, infant, issue, juvenile, kid
(*informal*), little one, minor, nipper
(*informal*), nursling, offspring, progeny,
rug rat (*slang*), sprog (*slang*), suckling,
toddler, tot, wean (*Scot.*)

childbirth *noun* = **child-bearing**,
accouchement, confinement, delivery,
labour, lying-in, parturition, travail

childhood *noun* = **youth**, boyhood *or*
girlhood, immaturity, infancy, minority,
schooldays

childish *adjective* = **immature**, boyish *or*
girlish, foolish, frivolous, infantile, juvenile,
puerile, silly, simple, trifling, weak, young
➤ Antonyms
adult, grown-up, manly *or* womanly,
mature, sensible, sophisticated

childlike *adjective* = **innocent**, artless,
credulous, guileless, ingenuous, naive,
simple, trustful, trusting, unfeigned

chill *noun* 1 = **cold**, bite, coldness, coolness,
crispness, frigidity, nip, rawness, sharpness
♦ *verb* 2 = **cool**, congeal, freeze, refrigerate
3 = **dishearten**, dampen, deject, depress,
discourage, dismay ♦ *adjective* 4 = **cold**,

biting, bleak, chilly, freezing, frigid, parky
(*Brit. informal*), raw, sharp, wintry 5
= **unfriendly**, aloof, cool, depressing,
distant, frigid, hostile, stony, ungenial,
unresponsive, unwelcoming

chilly *adjective* 1 = **cool**, blowy, breezy,
brisk, crisp, draughty, fresh, nippy, parky
(*Brit. informal*), penetrating, sharp 2
= **unfriendly**, cold as ice, frigid, hostile,
unresponsive, unsympathetic,
unwelcoming
➤ Antonyms
≠**cool**: balmy, hot, mild, scorching, sunny,
sweltering, warm ≠**unfriendly**: affable,
chummy (*informal*), congenial, cordial,
friendly, responsive, sociable, sympathetic,
warm, welcoming

chime *verb, noun* = **ring**, boom, clang,
dong, jingle, peal, sound, tinkle, toll

china *noun* = **pottery**, ceramics, crockery,
porcelain, service, tableware, ware

chink *noun* = **opening**, aperture, cleft,
crack, cranny, crevice, cut, fissure, flaw,
gap, rift

chip *noun* 1 = **scratch**, dent, flake, flaw,
fragment, nick, notch, paring, scrap,
shard, shaving, sliver, wafer ♦ *verb* 2
= **nick**, chisel, damage, gash, whittle

chip in *verb Informal* = **contribute**, donate,
go Dutch (*informal*), interpose, interrupt,
pay, subscribe

chirp *verb* = **chirrup**, cheep, peep, pipe,
tweet, twitter, warble

chivalrous *adjective* = **courteous**, bold,
brave, courageous, courtly, gallant,
gentlemanly, heroic, high-minded,
honourable, intrepid, knightly,
magnanimous, true, valiant
➤ Antonyms
boorish, cowardly, dishonourable, disloyal,
rude, uncourtly, ungallant, unmannerly

chivalry *noun* = **courtesy**, courage,
courtliness, gallantry, gentlemanliness,
knight-errantry, knighthood, politeness

chivvy *verb Brit.* = **nag**, annoy, badger,
bend someone's ear (*informal*), breathe
down someone's neck (*informal*), bug
(*informal*), harass, hassle (*informal*),
hound, pester, plague, pressure (*informal*),
prod, torment

choice *noun* 1 = **option**, alternative,
discrimination, election, pick, preference,
say 2 = **selection**, range, variety ♦ *adjective*
3 = **best**, bad (*slang*), crucial (*slang*),
dainty, def (*slang*), elect, elite, excellent,
exclusive, exquisite, hand-picked, nice,
precious, prime, prize, rare, select, special,
superior, uncommon, unusual, valuable

choke *verb* 1 = **strangle**, asphyxiate, gag,

overpower, smother, stifle, suffocate, suppress, throttle 2 = **block**, bar, bung, clog, close, congest, constrict, dam, obstruct, occlude, stop

choleric *adjective* = **bad-tempered**, angry, cross, fiery, hasty, hot, hot-tempered, ill-tempered, irascible, irritable, passionate, petulant, quick-tempered, ratty (*Brit. & N.Z. informal*), testy, tetchy, touchy

choose *verb* = **pick**, adopt, cherry-pick, cull, designate, desire, elect, espouse, fix on, opt for, predestine, prefer, see fit, select, settle upon, single out, take, wish
➤ **Antonyms**
decline, dismiss, exclude, forgo, leave, refuse, reject, throw aside

choosy *adjective Informal* = **fussy**, discriminating, exacting, faddy, fastidious, finicky, particular, picky (*informal*), selective
➤ **Antonyms**
easy (*informal*), easy to please, indiscriminate, undemanding, unselective

chop *verb* 1 = **cut**, axe, cleave, fell, hack, hew, lop, sever, shear, slash, truncate
♦ *noun* 2 **the chop** *Slang, chiefly Brit.* = **the sack** (*informal*), dismissal, one's cards, sacking (*informal*), termination, the axe (*informal*), the boot (*slang*), the (old) heave-ho (*informal*), the order of the boot (*slang*)

choppy *adjective* = **rough**, blustery, broken, ruffled, squally, tempestuous
➤ **Antonyms**
calm, smooth, windless

chop up *verb* = **cut up**, cube, dice, divide, fragment, mince

chore *noun* = **task**, burden, duty, errand, fag (*informal*), job, no picnic

chortle *verb, noun* = **chuckle**, cackle, crow, guffaw

chorus *noun* 1 = **choir**, choristers, ensemble, singers, vocalists 2 = **refrain**, burden, response, strain 3 = **unison**, accord, concert, harmony

christen *verb* 1 = **baptize** 2 = **name**, call, designate, dub, style, term, title

Christmas *noun* = **festive season**, Noel, Xmas (*informal*), Yule (*archaic*), Yuletide (*archaic*)

chronic *adjective* 1 = **habitual**, confirmed, deep-rooted, deep-seated, incessant, incurable, ineradicable, ingrained, inveterate, persistent 2 *Informal* = **dreadful**, abysmal, appalling, atrocious, awful
➤ **Antonyms**
≠**habitual**: infrequent, occasional, temporary

chronicle *noun* 1 = **record**, account, annals, diary, history, journal, narrative, register, story ♦ *verb* 2 = **record**, enter, narrate, put on record, recount, register, relate, report, set down, tell

chronicler *noun* = **recorder**, annalist, diarist, historian, historiographer, narrator, reporter, scribe

chronological *adjective* = **in order**, consecutive, historical, in sequence, ordered, progressive, sequential
➤ **Antonyms**
haphazard, intermittent, irregular, out-of-order, random

chubby *adjective* = **plump**, buxom, flabby, fleshy, podgy, portly, roly-poly, rotund, round, stout, tubby
➤ **Antonyms**
lean, skinny, slender, slight, slim, sylphlike, thin

chuck *verb Informal* = **throw**, cast, discard, fling, heave, hurl, pitch, shy, sling, toss

chuckle *verb* = **laugh**, chortle, crow, exult, giggle, snigger, titter

chum *noun Informal* = **friend**, cock (*Brit. informal*), companion, comrade, crony, mate (*informal*), pal (*informal*)

chunk *noun* = **piece**, block, dollop (*informal*), hunk, lump, mass, nugget, portion, slab, wad, wodge (*Brit. informal*)

chunky *adjective* = **thickset**, beefy (*informal*), dumpy, stocky, stubby

churl *noun* 1 = **boor**, lout, oaf 2 *Archaic* = **peasant**, bumpkin, clodhopper (*informal*), clown, hayseed (*U.S. & Canad. informal*), hick (*informal, chiefly U.S. & Canad.*), hillbilly, rustic, yokel

churlish *adjective* 1 = **boorish**, loutish, oafish, uncouth, unmannerly, vulgar 2 = **rude**, brusque, crabbed, harsh, ill-tempered, impolite, morose, sullen, surly, uncivil
➤ **Antonyms**
≠**boorish**: cultivated, mannerly, noble, well-bred ≠**rude**: agreeable, amiable, civil, courteous, good-tempered, pleasant, polite

churlishness *noun* 1 = **boorishness**, crassness, crudeness, loutishness, oafishness, uncouthness 2 = **rudeness**, surliness

churn *verb* = **stir up**, agitate, beat, boil, convulse, foam, froth, seethe, swirl, toss

cigarette *noun* = **fag** (*Brit. slang*), cancer stick (*slang*), ciggy (*informal*), coffin nail (*slang*), gasper (*slang*), smoke

cinema *noun* = **films**, big screen (*informal*), flicks (*slang*), motion pictures, movies, pictures

cipher *noun* 1 = **code**, cryptograph 2

= **symbol**, character, digit, figure, number,
numeral **3** = **monogram**, device, logo,
mark **4** = **nobody**, nonentity **5** *Obsolete*
= **zero**, nil, nothing, nought

circle *noun* **1** = **ring**, band, circumference,
coil, cordon, cycle, disc, globe, lap, loop,
orb, perimeter, periphery, revolution,
round, sphere, turn **2** = **area**, bounds,
circuit, compass, domain, enclosure, field,
orbit, province, range, realm, region,
scene, sphere **3** = **group**, assembly, class,
clique, club, company, coterie, crowd,
fellowship, fraternity, order, school, set,
society ♦ *verb* **4** = **go round**, belt,
circumnavigate, circumscribe, coil,
compass, curve, encircle, enclose,
encompass, envelop, enwreath, gird, hem
in, pivot, revolve, ring, rotate, surround,
tour, wheel, whirl

circuit *noun* **1** = **course**, area, compass,
journey, lap, orbit, perambulation,
revolution, round, route, tour, track **2**
= **range**, boundary, bounding line,
bounds, circumference, compass, district,
limit, pale, region, tract

circuitous *adjective* = **indirect**, ambagious
(*archaic*), devious, labyrinthine,
meandering, oblique, rambling,
roundabout, tortuous, winding
➤ **Antonyms**
as the crow flies, direct, straight,
undeviating, unswerving

circular *adjective* **1** = **round**, ring-shaped,
rotund, spherical **2** = **orbital**, circuitous,
cyclical ♦ *noun* **3** = **advertisement**, notice

circulate *verb* **1** = **spread**, broadcast,
diffuse, disseminate, distribute, issue, make
known, promulgate, propagate, publicize,
publish **2** = **flow**, gyrate, radiate, revolve,
rotate

circulation *noun* **1** = **bloodstream 2**
= **flow**, circling, motion, rotation **3**
= **distribution**, currency, dissemination,
spread, transmission, vogue

circumference *noun* = **boundary**, ambit,
border, bounds, circuit, edge, extremity,
fringe, limits, outline, pale, perimeter,
periphery, rim, verge

circumscribe *verb Formal* = **restrict**,
bound, confine, define, delimit, delineate,
demarcate, encircle, enclose, encompass,
environ, hem in, limit, mark off, restrain,
straiten, surround

circumspect *adjective* = **cautious**,
attentive, canny, careful, deliberate,
discreet, discriminating, guarded, heedful,
judicious, observant, politic, prudent,
sagacious, sage, vigilant, wary, watchful
➤ **Antonyms**
bold, careless, daring, foolhardy, heedless,

imprudent, rash, venturous

circumstance *noun* = **event**, accident,
condition, contingency, detail, element,
fact, factor, happening, incident, item,
occurrence, particular, position, respect,
situation

circumstances *plural noun* = **situation**, lie
of the land, lifestyle, means, position,
resources, state, state of affairs, station,
status, times

circumstantial *adjective* **1** = **conjectural**,
contingent, founded on circumstances,
hearsay, incidental, indirect, inferential,
presumptive, provisional **2** = **detailed**,
particular, specific

cistern *noun* = **tank**, basin, reservoir, sink,
vat

citadel *noun* = **fortress**, bastion, fastness,
fortification, keep, stronghold, tower

citation *noun* **1** = **commendation**, award,
mention **2** = **quotation**, commendation,
excerpt, illustration, passage, quote,
reference, source

cite *verb* **1** = **quote**, adduce, advance,
allude to, enumerate, evidence, extract,
mention, name, specify **2** *Law* = **summon**,
call, subpoena

citizen *noun* = **inhabitant**, burgess,
burgher, denizen, dweller, freeman,
ratepayer, resident, subject, townsman

city *noun* **1** = **town**, conurbation,
megalopolis, metropolis, municipality
♦ *adjective* **2** = **urban**, civic, metropolitan,
municipal

civic *adjective* = **public**, borough,
communal, community, local, municipal

civil *adjective* **1** = **civic**, domestic, home,
interior, municipal, political **2** = **polite**,
accommodating, affable, civilized,
complaisant, courteous, courtly, obliging,
polished, refined, urbane, well-bred,
well-mannered
➤ **Antonyms**
≠**civic**: military, religious, state ≠**polite**:
discourteous, ill-mannered, impolite, rude,
uncivil, unfriendly, ungracious, unpleasant

civility *noun* = **politeness**, affability,
amiability, breeding, complaisance,
cordiality, courteousness, courtesy, good
manners, graciousness, politesse, tact,
urbanity

civilization *noun* **1** = **culture**,
advancement, cultivation, development,
education, enlightenment, progress,
refinement, sophistication **2** = **society**,
community, nation, people, polity **3**
= **customs**, mores, way of life

civilize *verb* = **cultivate**, educate,
enlighten, humanize, improve, polish,

refine, sophisticate, tame

civilized *adjective* = **cultured**, educated, enlightened, humane, polite, sophisticated, tolerant, urbane
➤ **Antonyms**
ignorant, naive, primitive, simple, uncivilized, uncultivated, uncultured, undeveloped, unenlightened, unsophisticated, wild

claim *verb* **1** = **assert**, allege, challenge, exact, hold, insist, maintain, profess, uphold **2** = **demand**, ask, call for, insist, need, require **3** = **take**, collect, pick up ♦ *noun* **4** = **assertion**, affirmation, allegation, pretension, privilege, protestation **5** = **demand**, application, call, petition, request, requirement **6** = **right**, title

clairvoyant *noun* **1** = **psychic**, diviner, fortune-teller, visionary ♦ *adjective* **2** = **psychic**, extrasensory, second-sighted, telepathic, visionary

clamber *verb* = **climb**, claw, scale, scrabble, scramble, shin

clammy *adjective* = **moist**, close, damp, dank, sticky, sweaty

clamorous *adjective* = **noisy**, blaring, deafening, insistent, loud, lusty, riotous, strident, tumultuous, uproarious, vehement, vociferous

clamour *noun* = **noise**, agitation, babel, blare, brouhaha, commotion, din, exclamation, hubbub, hullabaloo, outcry, racket, shout, shouting, uproar, vociferation

clamp *noun* **1** = **vice**, bracket, fastener, grip, press ♦ *verb* **2** = **fasten**, brace, clinch, fix, impose, make fast, secure

clan *noun* = **family**, band, brotherhood, clique, coterie, faction, fraternity, gens, group, house, order, race, schism, sect, sept, set, society, sodality, tribe

clandestine *adjective* = **secret**, cloak-and-dagger, concealed, covert, furtive, private, stealthy, surreptitious, underground

clang *verb* **1** = **ring**, bong, chime, clank, clash, jangle, resound, reverberate, toll ♦ *noun* **2** = **ringing**, clangour, ding-dong, knell, reverberation

clap *verb* **1** = **applaud**, acclaim, cheer, give (someone) a big hand **2** = **strike**, bang, pat, punch, slap, thrust, thwack, wallop (*informal*), whack
➤ **Antonyms**
≠**applaud**: blow a raspberry, boo, catcall, hiss, jeer

claptrap *noun Informal* = **nonsense**, affectation, balls (*taboo slang*), bilge

(*informal*), blarney, bombast, bosh (*informal*), bull (*slang*), bullshit (*taboo slang*), bunk (*informal*), bunkum or buncombe (*chiefly U.S.*), cobblers (*Brit. taboo slang*), crap (*slang*), drivel, eyewash (*informal*), flannel (*Brit. informal*), garbage (*informal*), guff (*slang*), hogwash, hokum (*slang, chiefly U.S. & Canad.*), horsefeathers (*U.S. slang*), hot air (*informal*), humbug, insincerity, moonshine, pap, piffle (*informal*), poppycock (*informal*), rodomontade (*literary*), rot, rubbish, shit (*taboo slang*), tommyrot, tosh (*slang, chiefly Brit.*), trash, tripe (*informal*), twaddle

clarification *noun* = **explanation**, elucidation, exposition, illumination, interpretation, simplification

clarify *verb* **1** = **explain**, clear the air, clear up, elucidate, explicate, illuminate, interpret, make plain, resolve, simplify, throw *or* shed light on **2** = **refine**, cleanse, purify

clarity *noun* = **clearness**, comprehensibility, definition, explicitness, intelligibility, limpidity, lucidity, obviousness, precision, simplicity, transparency
➤ **Antonyms**
cloudiness, complexity, complication, dullness, haziness, imprecision, intricacy, murkiness, obscurity

clash *verb* **1** = **conflict**, cross swords, feud, grapple, lock horns, quarrel, war, wrangle **2** = **crash**, bang, clang, clank, clatter, jangle, jar, rattle ♦ *noun* **3** = **conflict**, brush, collision, confrontation, difference of opinion, disagreement, fight, showdown (*informal*)

clasp *noun* **1** = **fastening**, brooch, buckle, catch, clip, fastener, grip, hasp, hook, pin, press stud, snap **2** = **grasp**, embrace, grip, hold, hug ♦ *verb* **3** = **grasp**, attack, clutch, embrace, enfold, grapple, grip, hold, hug, press, seize, squeeze **4** = **fasten**, concatenate, connect

class *noun* **1** = **group**, caste, category, classification, collection, denomination, department, division, genre, genus, grade, grouping, kind, league, order, rank, set, sort, species, sphere, stamp, status, type, value ♦ *verb* **2** = **classify**, brand, categorize, codify, designate, grade, group, label, rank, rate

classic *adjective* **1** = **definitive**, archetypal, exemplary, ideal, master, model, paradigmatic, quintessential, standard **2** = **typical**, characteristic, regular, standard, time-honoured, usual **3** = **best**, consummate, finest, first-rate, masterly, world-class **4** = **lasting**, abiding, ageless,

deathless, enduring, immortal, undying
♦ noun 5 = **standard**, exemplar,
masterpiece, masterwork, model,
paradigm, prototype
➤ **Antonyms**
adjective ≠**best**: inferior, modern, poor,
second-rate, terrible

classical adjective 1 = **pure**, chaste,
elegant, harmonious, refined, restrained,
symmetrical, understated,
well-proportioned 2 = **Greek**, Attic,
Augustan, Grecian, Hellenic, Latin, Roman

classification noun = **categorization**,
analysis, arrangement, cataloguing,
codification, grading, sorting, taxonomy

classify verb = **categorize**, arrange,
catalogue, codify, dispose, distribute, file,
grade, pigeonhole, rank, sort, systematize,
tabulate

classy adjective Informal = **high-class**,
elegant, exclusive, posh (informal, chiefly
Brit.), stylish, superior, top-drawer,
up-market

clause noun 1 = **section**, article, chapter,
condition, paragraph, part, passage 2
= **point**, heading, item, provision, proviso,
rider, specification, stipulation

claw noun 1 = **nail**, nipper, pincer, talon,
tentacle, unguis ♦ verb 2 = **scratch**, dig,
graze, lacerate, mangle, maul, rip,
scrabble, scrape, tear

clean adjective 1 = **pure**, faultless, flawless,
fresh, hygienic, immaculate, impeccable,
laundered, sanitary, spotless,
squeaky-clean, unblemished, unsoiled,
unspotted, unstained, unsullied, washed 2
= **hygienic**, antiseptic, clarified,
decontaminated, natural, purified, sterile,
sterilized, unadulterated, uncontaminated,
unpolluted 3 = **moral**, chaste, decent,
exemplary, good, honourable,
impeccable, innocent, pure, respectable,
undefiled, upright, virtuous 4 = **complete**,
conclusive, decisive, entire, final, perfect,
thorough, total, unimpaired, whole 5
= **neat**, delicate, elegant, graceful, simple,
tidy, trim, uncluttered ♦ verb 6 = **cleanse**,
bath, deodorize, disinfect, do up, dust,
launder, lave, mop, purge, purify, rinse,
sanitize, scour, scrub, sponge, swab,
sweep, vacuum, wash, wipe
➤ **Antonyms**
adjective ≠**pure**: dirty, filthy, mucky, scuzzy
(slang, chiefly U.S.), soiled, sullied,
unwashed ≠**hygienic**: adulterated,
contaminated, infected, polluted ≠**moral**:
dishonourable, immoral, impure, indecent,
unchaste ≠**neat**: chaotic, disorderly,
disorganized, higgledy-piggledy
(informal), shambolic (informal), untidy

♦ verb ≠**cleanse**: adulterate, defile, dirty,
infect, mess up, pollute, soil, stain

clean-cut adjective = **clear**, chiselled,
definite, etched, neat, outlined, sharp,
trim, well-defined

cleanse verb = **clean**, absolve, clear,
lustrate, purge, purify, rinse, scour, scrub,
wash

cleanser noun = **detergent**, disinfectant,
purifier, scourer, soap, soap powder,
solvent

clear adjective 1 = **certain**, convinced,
decided, definite, positive, resolved,
satisfied, sure 2 = **obvious**, apparent,
articulate, audible, blatant, bold, coherent,
comprehensible, conspicuous,
cut-and-dried (informal), definite, distinct,
evident, explicit, express, incontrovertible,
intelligible, lucid, manifest, palpable,
patent, perceptible, plain, pronounced,
recognizable, unambiguous, unequivocal,
unmistakable, unquestionable 3
= **transparent**, crystalline, glassy, limpid,
pellucid, see-through, translucent 4
= **bright**, cloudless, fair, fine, halcyon,
light, luminous, shining, sunny,
unclouded, undimmed 5 = **unobstructed**,
empty, free, open, smooth, unhampered,
unhindered, unimpeded, unlimited 6
= **unblemished**, clean, guiltless,
immaculate, innocent, pure, sinless,
stainless, undefiled, untarnished,
untroubled ♦ verb 7 = **unblock**, disengage,
disentangle, extricate, free, loosen, open,
rid, unclog, unload, unpack 8 = **pass over**,
jump, leap, miss, vault 9 = **brighten**, break
up, clarify, lighten 10 = **clean**, cleanse,
erase, purify, refine, sweep away, tidy (up),
wipe 11 = **absolve**, acquit, excuse,
exonerate, justify, vindicate 12 = **gain**,
acquire, earn, make, reap, secure
➤ **Antonyms**
adjective ≠**obvious**: ambiguous, confused,
doubtful, equivocal, hidden, inarticulate,
inaudible, incoherent, indistinct, inexplicit,
obscured, unrecognizable ≠**transparent**:
cloudy, muddy, non-translucent,
non-transparent, opaque, turbid ≠**bright**:
cloudy, dark, dull, foggy, hazy, misty,
murky, overcast, stormy ≠**unobstructed**:
barricaded, blocked, closed, hampered,
impeded, obstructed ♦ verb ≠**absolve**:
accuse, blame, charge, condemn, convict,
find guilty

clearance noun 1 = **evacuation**,
depopulation, emptying, eviction,
removal, unpeopling, withdrawal 2
= **permission**, authorization, blank cheque,
consent, endorsement, go-ahead
(informal), green light, leave, O.K. or okay

(*informal*), sanction **3** = **space**, allowance, gap, headroom, margin

clear-cut *adjective* = **straightforward**, black-and-white, cut-and-dried (*informal*), definite, explicit, plain, precise, specific, unambiguous, unequivocal

clearly *adverb* = **obviously**, beyond doubt, distinctly, evidently, incontestably, incontrovertibly, markedly, openly, overtly, undeniably, undoubtedly

clear out *verb* **1** = **get rid of**, empty, exhaust, sort, tidy up **2** *Informal* = **go away**, beat it (*slang*), decamp, depart, hook it (*slang*), leave, make oneself scarce, make tracks, pack one's bags (*informal*), retire, slope off, take oneself off, withdraw

clear up *verb* **1** = **tidy (up)**, order, rearrange **2** = **solve**, answer, clarify, elucidate, explain, resolve, straighten out, unravel

cleave[1] *verb* = **split**, crack, dissever, disunite, divide, hew, open, part, rend, rive, sever, slice, sunder, tear asunder

cleave[2] *verb* = **stick**, abide by, adhere, agree, attach, be devoted to, be true, cling, cohere, hold, remain, stand by

clergy *noun* = **priesthood**, churchmen, clergymen, clerics, ecclesiastics, first estate, holy orders, ministry, the cloth

clergyman *noun* = **minister**, chaplain, churchman, cleric, curate, divine, father, man of God, man of the cloth, padre, parson, pastor, priest, rabbi, rector, reverend (*informal*), vicar

clerical *adjective* **1** = **office**, book-keeping, clerkish, clerkly, secretarial, stenographic **2** = **ecclesiastical**, pastoral, priestly, sacerdotal

clever *adjective* = **intelligent**, able, adroit, apt, astute, brainy (*informal*), bright, canny, capable, cunning, deep, dexterous, discerning, expert, gifted, ingenious, inventive, keen, knowing, knowledgeable, quick, quick-witted, rational, resourceful, sagacious, sensible, shrewd, skilful, smart, talented, witty
➤ **Antonyms**
awkward, clumsy, dense, dull, dumb (*informal*), ham-fisted (*informal*), inept, inexpert, maladroit, slow, stupid, thick, unaccomplished, unimaginative, witless

cleverness *noun* = **intelligence**, ability, adroitness, astuteness, brains, brightness, canniness, dexterity, flair, gift, gumption (*Brit. informal*), ingenuity, nous (*Brit. slang*), quickness, quick wits, resourcefulness, sagacity, sense, sharpness, shrewdness, smartness, smarts (*slang, chiefly U.S.*), suss (*slang*), talent, wit

cliché *noun* = **platitude**, banality, bromide, chestnut (*informal*), commonplace, hackneyed phrase, old saw, stereotype, truism

click *noun, verb* **1** = **snap**, beat, clack, tick ♦ *verb* **2** *Informal* = **become clear**, come home (to), fall into place, make sense **3** *Slang* = **get on**, be compatible, be on the same wavelength, feel a rapport, get on like a house on fire (*informal*), go over, hit it off (*informal*), make a hit, succeed, take to each other

client *noun* = **customer**, applicant, buyer, consumer, dependant, habitué, patient, patron, protégé, shopper

clientele *noun* = **customers**, business, clients, following, market, patronage, regulars, trade

cliff *noun* = **rock face**, bluff, crag, escarpment, face, overhang, precipice, scar, scarp

climactic *adjective* = **crucial**, climactical, critical, decisive, paramount, peak

climate *noun* **1** = **weather**, clime, country, region, temperature **2** = **trend**, ambience, disposition, feeling, mood, temper, tendency

climax *noun* **1** = **culmination**, acme, apogee, crest, head, height, highlight, high point, high spot (*informal*), ne plus ultra, pay-off (*informal*), peak, summit, top, zenith ♦ *verb* **2** = **culminate**, come to a head, peak

climb *verb* = **ascend**, clamber, mount, rise, scale, shin up, soar, top

climb down *verb* **1** = **descend**, dismount **2** = **back down**, eat crow (*U.S. informal*), eat one's words, retract, retreat

clinch *verb* **1** = **settle**, assure, cap, conclude, confirm, decide, determine, seal, secure, set the seal on, sew up (*informal*), tip the balance, verify **2** = **secure**, bolt, clamp, fasten, fix, make fast, nail, rivet **3** = **grasp**, clutch, cuddle, embrace, hug, squeeze

cling *verb* = **stick**, adhere, attach to, be true to, clasp, cleave to, clutch, embrace, fasten, grasp, grip, hug, twine round

clinical *adjective* = **unemotional**, analytic, cold, detached, dispassionate, impersonal, objective, scientific

clip[1] *verb* **1** = **trim**, crop, curtail, cut, cut short, dock, pare, prune, shear, shorten, snip ♦ *noun, verb* **2** *Informal* = **smack**, belt (*informal*), box, clout (*informal*), cuff, knock, punch, skelp (*dialect*), strike, thump, wallop (*informal*), whack ♦ *noun* **3** *Informal* = **speed**, gallop, lick (*informal*), rate, velocity

clip² *verb* = **attach**, fasten, fix, hold, pin, staple

clique *noun* = **group**, cabal, circle, clan, coterie, crew (*informal*), crowd, faction, gang, mob, pack, posse (*informal*), schism, set

cloak *noun* **1** = **cape**, coat, mantle, wrap **2** = **cover**, blind, front, mask, pretext, shield ♦ *verb* **3** = **cover**, camouflage, conceal, disguise, hide, mask, obscure, screen, veil

clodhopper *noun Informal* = **oaf**, booby, boor, bumpkin, clown, galoot (*slang, chiefly U.S.*), loon (*informal*), lout, yokel

clog *verb* = **obstruct**, block, bung, burden, congest, dam up, hamper, hinder, impede, jam, occlude, shackle, stop up

cloistered *adjective* = **sheltered**, cloistral, confined, hermitic, insulated, protected, reclusive, restricted, secluded, sequestered, shielded, shut off, withdrawn ➤ Antonyms
extrovert, genial, gregarious, outgoing, public, sociable, social

close¹ *verb* **1** = **shut**, bar, block, bung, choke, clog, confine, cork, fill, lock, obstruct, plug, seal, secure, shut up, stop up **2** = **end**, axe (*informal*), cease, complete, conclude, culminate, discontinue, finish, mothball, shut down, terminate, wind up **3** = **connect**, come together, couple, fuse, grapple, join, unite ♦ *noun* **4** = **end**, cessation, completion, conclusion, culmination, denouement, ending, finale, finish, run-in, termination ➤ Antonyms
verb ≠**shut**: clear, free, open, release, unblock, unclog, uncork, unstop, widen ≠**end**: begin, commence, initiate, open, start ≠**connect**: disconnect, disjoin, disunite, divide, part, separate, split, uncouple

close² *adjective* **1** = **near**, adjacent, adjoining, a hop, skip and a jump away, approaching, at hand, cheek by jowl, handy, hard by, imminent, impending, just round the corner, nearby, neighbouring, nigh, proximate, upcoming, within sniffing distance, within spitting distance (*informal*), within striking distance (*informal*) **2** = **intimate**, attached, confidential, dear, devoted, familiar, inseparable, loving **3** = **careful**, alert, assiduous, attentive, concentrated, detailed, dogged, earnest, fixed, intense, intent, keen, minute, painstaking, rigorous, searching, thorough **4** = **compact**, congested, cramped, cropped, crowded, dense, impenetrable, jam-packed, packed, short, solid, thick, tight **5** = **accurate**, conscientious, exact,

faithful, literal, precise, strict **6** = **stifling**, airless, confined, frowsty, fuggy, heavy, humid, muggy, oppressive, stale, stuffy, suffocating, sweltering, thick, unventilated **7** = **secretive**, hidden, private, reticent, retired, secluded, secret, taciturn, uncommunicative, unforthcoming **8** = **mean**, illiberal, mingy (*Brit. informal*), miserly, near, niggardly, parsimonious, penurious, stingy, tight as a duck's arse (*taboo slang*), tight-fisted, ungenerous ➤ Antonyms
≠**near**: distant, far, far away, far off, future, outlying, remote ≠**intimate**: alienated, aloof, chilly, cold, cool, distant, indifferent, standoffish, unfriendly ≠**compact**: dispersed, empty, free, loose, penetrable, porous, uncongested, uncrowded ≠**stifling**: airy, fresh, refreshing, roomy, spacious ≠**mean**: charitable, extravagant, generous, lavish, liberal, magnanimous, unstinting

closed *adjective* **1** = **shut**, fastened, locked, out of business, out of service, sealed **2** = **exclusive**, restricted **3** = **finished**, concluded, decided, ended, over, resolved, settled, terminated ➤ Antonyms
≠**shut**: ajar, open, unclosed, unfastened, unlocked, unsealed

cloth *noun* = **fabric**, dry goods, material, stuff, textiles

clothe *verb* = **dress**, accoutre, apparel, array, attire, bedizen (*archaic*), caparison, cover, deck, doll up (*slang*), drape, endow, enwrap, equip, fit out, garb, get ready, habit, invest, outfit, rig, robe, swathe ➤ Antonyms
disrobe, divest, expose, strip, strip off, unclothe, uncover, undress

clothes *plural noun* = **clothing**, apparel, attire, clobber (*Brit. slang*), costume, dress, duds (*informal*), ensemble, garb, garments, gear (*informal*), get-up (*informal*), glad rags (*informal*), habits, outfit, raiment (*archaic or poetic*), rigout (*informal*), schmutter (*slang*), threads (*slang*), togs (*informal*), vestments, vesture, wardrobe, wear

clothing *noun* = **clothes**, apparel, attire, clobber (*Brit. slang*), costume, dress, duds (*informal*), ensemble, garb, garments, gear (*informal*), get-up (*informal*), glad rags (*informal*), habits, outfit, raiment (*archaic or poetic*), rigout (*informal*), schmutter (*slang*), threads (*slang*), togs (*informal*), vestments, vesture, wardrobe, wear

cloud *noun* **1** = **mist**, billow, darkness, fog, gloom, haze, murk, nebula, nebulosity, obscurity, vapour **2** = **dense mass**, crowd, flock, horde, host, multitude, shower, swarm, throng ♦ *verb* **3** = **obscure**, becloud, darken, dim, eclipse, obfuscate, overcast, overshadow, shade, shadow, veil **4** = **confuse**, disorient, distort, impair, muddle, muddy the waters

cloudy *adjective* **1** = **dull**, dark, dim, dismal, dusky, gloomy, leaden, louring *or* lowering, nebulous, obscure, overcast, sombre, sullen, sunless **2** = **opaque**, emulsified, muddy, murky **3** = **confused**, blurred, hazy, indistinct, unclear
➤ **Antonyms**
≠**dull**: bright, clear, fair, sunny, uncloudy ≠**confused**: clear, distinct, obvious, plain

clout *Informal* ♦ *noun* **1** = **influence**, authority, bottom, power, prestige, pull, standing, weight ♦ *verb* **2** = **hit**, box, chin (*slang*), clobber (*slang*), cuff, deck (*slang*), lay one on (*slang*), punch, skelp (*dialect*), sock (*slang*), strike, thump, tonk (*informal*), wallop (*informal*), wham

clown *noun* **1** = **comedian**, buffoon, comic, dolt, fool, harlequin, jester, joculator *or* (*fem.*) joculatrix, joker, merry-andrew, mountebank, pierrot, prankster, punchinello **2** = **boor**, clodhopper (*informal*), hind (*obsolete*), peasant, swain (*archaic*), yahoo, yokel ♦ *verb* **3** = **play the fool**, act the fool, act the goat, jest, mess about, piss about *or* around (*taboo slang*), play the goat

club *noun* **1** = **association**, circle, clique, company, fraternity, group, guild, lodge, order, set, society, sodality, union **2** = **stick**, bat, bludgeon, cosh (*Brit.*), cudgel, truncheon ♦ *verb* **3** = **beat**, bash, baste, batter, bludgeon, clobber (*slang*), clout (*informal*), cosh (*Brit.*), hammer, pommel (*rare*), pummel, strike

clue *noun* = **indication**, evidence, hint, inkling, intimation, lead, pointer, sign, suggestion, suspicion, tip, tip-off, trace

clueless *adjective* = **stupid**, dense, dim, dopey (*informal*), dozy (*Brit. informal*), dull, dumb (*informal*), half-witted, moronic, naive, simple, simple-minded, slow, slow on the uptake (*informal*), thick, unintelligent, witless

clump *noun* **1** = **cluster**, bunch, bundle, group, mass, shock ♦ *verb* **2** = **stomp**, bumble, clomp, lumber, plod, stamp, stump, thud, thump, tramp

clumsy *adjective* = **awkward**, accident-prone, blundering, bumbling, bungling, butterfingered (*informal*), cack-handed (*informal*), clunky (*informal*), gauche, gawky, ham-fisted (*informal*), ham-handed (*informal*), heavy, ill-shaped, inept, inexpert, klutzy (*U.S. & Canad.*

slang), like a bull in a china shop, lumbering, maladroit, ponderous, uncoordinated, uncouth, ungainly, unhandy, unskilful, unwieldy
➤ **Antonyms**
adept, adroit, competent, deft, dexterous, expert, graceful, handy, proficient, skilful

cluster *noun* **1** = **gathering**, assemblage, batch, bunch, clump, collection, group, knot ♦ *verb* **2** = **gather**, assemble, bunch, collect, flock, group

clutch *verb* = **seize**, catch, clasp, cling to, embrace, fasten, grab, grapple, grasp, grip, snatch

clutches *plural noun* = **power**, claws, control, custody, grasp, grip, hands, keeping, possession, sway

clutter *verb* **1** = **litter**, scatter, strew ♦ *noun* **2** = **untidiness**, confusion, disarray, disorder, hotchpotch, jumble, litter, mess, muddle
➤ **Antonyms**
verb ≠**litter**: arrange, order, organize, straighten, tidy ♦ *noun* ≠**untidiness**: neatness, order, organization, tidiness

coach *noun* **1** = **bus**, car, carriage, charabanc, vehicle **2** = **instructor**, handler, teacher, trainer, tutor ♦ *verb* **3** = **instruct**, cram, drill, exercise, prepare, train, tutor

coalesce *verb* = **blend**, amalgamate, cohere, combine, come together, commingle, commix, consolidate, fraternize, fuse, incorporate, integrate, meld, merge, mix, unite

coalition *noun* = **alliance**, affiliation, amalgam, amalgamation, association, bloc, combination, compact, confederacy, confederation, conjunction, fusion, integration, league, merger, union

coarse *adjective* **1** = **rough**, coarse-grained, crude, homespun, impure, rough-hewn, unfinished, unpolished, unprocessed, unpurified, unrefined **2** = **loutish**, boorish, brutish, coarse-grained, foul-mouthed, gruff, rough, rude, uncivil **3** = **vulgar**, bawdy, earthy, immodest, impolite, improper, impure, indecent, indelicate, mean, offensive, raunchy (*slang*), ribald, rude, smutty
➤ **Antonyms**
≠**rough**: fine-grained, polished, purified, refined, smooth, soft ≠**loutish**: civilized, cultured, fine, genteel, refined, sophisticated, urbane, well-bred, well-mannered ≠**vulgar**: inoffensive, polite, proper

coarsen *verb* = **roughen**, anaesthetize, blunt, callous, deaden, desensitize, dull, harden, indurate

coarseness *noun* **1** = **roughness**, crudity,

unevenness 2 = **vulgarity**, bawdiness, boorishness, crudity, earthiness, indelicacy, offensiveness, poor taste, ribaldry, roughness, smut, smuttiness, uncouthness

coast noun 1 = **shore**, beach, border, coastline, littoral, seaboard, seaside, strand ◆ verb 2 = **cruise**, drift, freewheel, get by, glide, sail, taxi

coat noun 1 = **fur**, fleece, hair, hide, pelt, skin, wool 2 = **layer**, coating, covering, overlay ◆ verb 3 = **cover**, apply, Artex (*Trademark*), plaster, smear, spread

coating noun = **layer**, blanket, coat, covering, dusting, film, finish, glaze, lamination, membrane, patina, sheet, skin, varnish, veneer

coax verb = **persuade**, allure, beguile, cajole, decoy, entice, flatter, inveigle, prevail upon, soft-soap (*informal*), soothe, sweet-talk (*informal*), talk into, twist (someone's) arm, wheedle
➤ Antonyms
browbeat, bully, coerce, force, harass, intimidate, pressurize, threaten

cock noun 1 = **cockerel**, chanticleer, rooster ◆ verb 2 = **raise**, perk up, prick, stand up

cockeyed adjective Informal 1 = **crooked**, askew, asymmetrical, awry, lopsided, skewwhiff (*Brit. informal*), squint (*informal*) 2 = **absurd**, crazy, ludicrous, nonsensical, preposterous

cocktail noun = **mixture**, amalgamation, blend, combination, mix

cocky adjective = **overconfident**, arrogant, brash, cocksure, conceited, egotistical, full of oneself, lordly, swaggering, swollen-headed, vain
➤ Antonyms
hesitant, lacking confidence, modest, self-effacing, uncertain, unsure

coddle verb = **pamper**, baby, cosset, humour, indulge, mollycoddle, nurse, pet, spoil, wet-nurse (*informal*)

code noun 1 = **cipher**, cryptograph 2 = **principles**, canon, convention, custom, ethics, etiquette, manners, maxim, regulations, rules, system

cogency noun = **conviction**, force, potency, power, strength

cogent adjective = **convincing**, compelling, compulsive, conclusive, effective, forceful, forcible, influential, irresistible, potent, powerful, strong, urgent, weighty

cogitate verb = **think**, consider, contemplate, deliberate, meditate, mull over, muse, ponder, reflect, ruminate

cogitation noun = **thought**, consideration, contemplation, deliberation, meditation, reflection, rumination

cognate adjective = **related**, affiliated, akin, alike, allied, analogous, associated, connected, kindred, similar

cognition noun Formal = **perception**, apprehension, awareness, comprehension, discernment, insight, intelligence, reasoning, understanding

coherent adjective 1 = **consistent**, logical, lucid, meaningful, orderly, organized, rational, reasoned, systematic 2 = **intelligible**, articulate, comprehensible
➤ Antonyms
≠consistent: confusing, disjointed, illogical, inconsistent, meaningless, rambling, vague ≠intelligible: incomprehensible, unintelligible

coil verb = **wind**, convolute, curl, entwine, loop, snake, spiral, twine, twist, wreathe, writhe

coin noun 1 = **money**, cash, change, copper, dosh (*Brit. & Austral. slang*), silver, specie ◆ verb 2 = **invent**, conceive, create, fabricate, forge, formulate, frame, make up, mint, mould, originate, think up

coincide verb 1 = **occur simultaneously**, be concurrent, coexist, synchronize 2 = **agree**, accord, concur, correspond, harmonize, match, square, tally
➤ Antonyms
≠agree: be inconsistent, be unlike, contradict, differ, disagree, diverge, divide, part, separate

coincidence noun 1 = **chance**, accident, eventuality, fluke, fortuity, happy accident, luck, stroke of luck 2 = **coinciding**, concomitance, concurrence, conjunction, correlation, correspondence, synchronism

coincident adjective = **coinciding**, concomitant, concurring, consonant, contemporaneous, coordinate, correspondent, synchronous

coincidental adjective 1 = **chance**, accidental, casual, fluky (*informal*), fortuitous, unintentional, unplanned 2 = **coinciding**, coincident, concomitant, concurrent, simultaneous, synchronous
➤ Antonyms
≠chance: calculated, deliberate, done on purpose, intentional, planned, prearranged

cold adjective 1 = **chilly**, arctic, biting, bitter, bleak, brumal, chill, cool, freezing, frigid, frosty, frozen, gelid, harsh, icy, inclement, parky (*Brit. informal*), raw, wintry 2 = **numb**, benumbed, chilled, chilly, freezing, frozen to the marrow, shivery 3 = **unfriendly**, affectless, aloof, apathetic, cold-blooded, dead, distant, frigid, glacial, indifferent, inhospitable, lukewarm, passionless, phlegmatic, reserved, spiritless, standoffish, stony,

undemonstrative, unfeeling, unmoved, unresponsive, unsympathetic **4 give (someone) the cold shoulder = snub**, cut (*informal*), ignore, ostracize, put down, rebuff, send (someone) to Coventry, shun ♦ *noun* **5 = coldness**, chill, chilliness, frigidity, frostiness, iciness, inclemency
➤ **Antonyms**
adjective ≠**chilly:** balmy, heated, hot, mild, sunny, warm ≠**unfriendly:** alive, animated, caring, compassionate, demonstrative, emotional, friendly, loving, open, passionate, responsive, spirited, sympathetic, warm

cold-blooded *adjective* **= callous**, barbarous, brutal, cruel, dispassionate, heartless, inhuman, merciless, pitiless, ruthless, savage, steely, stony-hearted, unemotional, unfeeling, unmoved
➤ **Antonyms**
caring, charitable, civilized, concerned, emotional, feeling, friendly, humane, involved, kind, kind-hearted, merciful, open, passionate, sensitive, warm

cold-hearted *adjective* **= heartless**, callous, detached, frigid, hardhearted, harsh, indifferent, inhuman, insensitive, stony-hearted, uncaring, unfeeling, unkind, unsympathetic

collaborate *verb* **1 = work together**, cooperate, coproduce, join forces, participate, play ball (*informal*), team up **2 = conspire**, collude, cooperate, fraternize

collaboration *noun* **= teamwork**, alliance, association, concert, cooperation, partnership

collaborator *noun* **1 = co-worker**, associate, colleague, confederate, partner, team-mate **2 = traitor**, collaborationist, fraternizer, quisling, turncoat

collapse *verb* **1 = fall down**, cave in, crumple, fall, fall apart at the seams, give way, subside **2 = fail**, come to nothing, fold, founder, go belly-up (*informal*) **3 = faint**, break down, crack up (*informal*) ♦ *noun* **4 = falling down**, cave-in, disintegration, falling apart, ruin, subsidence **5 = failure**, downfall, flop, slump **6 = faint**, breakdown, exhaustion, prostration

collar *verb Informal* **= seize**, apprehend, appropriate, arrest, capture, catch, catch in the act, grab, lay hands on, nab (*informal*), nail (*informal*)

colleague *noun* **= fellow worker**, aider, ally, assistant, associate, auxiliary, coadjutor (*rare*), collaborator, companion, comrade, confederate, confrère, helper, partner, team-mate, workmate

collect *verb* **1 = assemble**, cluster,

congregate, convene, converge, flock together, rally **2 = gather**, accumulate, aggregate, amass, assemble, heap, hoard, save, stockpile **3 = obtain**, acquire, muster, raise, secure, solicit
➤ **Antonyms**
≠**gather:** disperse, distribute, scatter, spread, strew

collected *adjective* **= calm**, as cool as a cucumber, composed, confident, cool, keeping one's cool, placid, poised, sedate, self-controlled, self-possessed, serene, together (*slang*), unfazed (*informal*), unperturbable, unperturbed, unruffled
➤ **Antonyms**
agitated, antsy (*informal*), distressed, emotional, excitable, irritable, nervous, perturbed, ruffled, shaky, troubled, twitchy (*informal*)

collection *noun* **1 = accumulation**, anthology, compilation, congeries, heap, hoard, mass, pile, set, stockpile, store **2 = group**, assemblage, assembly, assortment, cluster, company, congregation, convocation, crowd, gathering **3 = contribution**, alms, offering, offertory

collective *adjective* **= combined**, aggregate, common, composite, concerted, cooperative, corporate, cumulative, joint, shared, unified, united
➤ **Antonyms**
divided, individual, piecemeal, split, uncombined, uncooperative

collide *verb* **1 = crash**, clash, come into collision, meet head-on **2 = conflict**, clash

collision *noun* **1 = crash**, accident, bump, impact, pile-up (*informal*), prang (*informal*), smash **2 = conflict**, clash, clashing, confrontation, encounter, opposition, skirmish

colloquial *adjective* **= informal**, conversational, demotic, everyday, familiar, idiomatic, vernacular

collusion *noun* **= conspiracy**, cahoots (*informal*), complicity, connivance, craft, deceit, fraudulent artifice, intrigue, secret understanding

colonist *noun* **= settler**, colonial, colonizer, frontiersman, homesteader (*U.S.*), immigrant, pioneer, planter

colonize *verb* **= settle**, open up, people, pioneer, populate, put down roots

colonnade *noun* **= cloisters**, arcade, covered walk, peristyle, portico

colony *noun* **= settlement**, community, dependency, dominion, outpost, possession, province, satellite state, territory

colossal *adjective* = **huge**, Brobdingnagian, elephantine, enormous, gargantuan, gigantic, ginormous (*informal*), herculean, humongous *or* humungous (*U.S. slang*), immense, mammoth, massive, monstrous, monumental, mountainous, prodigious, stellar (*informal*), titanic, vast
➤ Antonyms
average, diminutive, little, miniature, minute, ordinary, pygmy *or* pigmy, slight, small, tiny, weak, wee

colour *noun* 1 = **hue**, colorant, coloration, complexion, dye, paint, pigment, pigmentation, shade, tincture, tinge, tint 2 = **rosiness**, animation, bloom, blush, brilliance, flush, glow, liveliness, ruddiness, vividness 3 = **pretext**, appearance, disguise, excuse, façade, false show, guise, plea, pretence, semblance ♦ *verb* 4 = **paint**, colourwash, dye, stain, tinge, tint 5 = **blush**, burn, crimson, flush, go as red as a beetroot, go crimson, redden 6 = **misrepresent**, disguise, distort, embroider, exaggerate, falsify, garble, gloss over, pervert, prejudice, slant, taint

colourful *adjective* 1 = **bright**, brilliant, Day-glo (*Trademark*), intense, jazzy (*informal*), kaleidoscopic, motley, multicoloured, psychedelic, rich, variegated, vibrant, vivid 2 = **interesting**, characterful, distinctive, graphic, lively, picturesque, rich, stimulating, unusual, vivid
➤ Antonyms
≠**bright**: colourless, dark, drab, dreary, dull, faded, pale, washed out
≠**interesting**: boring, characterless, dull, flat, lifeless, monotonous, unexciting, uninteresting, unvaried

colourless *adjective* 1 = **drab**, achromatic, achromic, anaemic, ashen, bleached, faded, neutral, sickly, wan, washed out 2 = **uninteresting**, characterless, dreary, dull, insipid, lacklustre, tame, unmemorable, vacuous, vapid
➤ Antonyms
≠**drab**: blooming, flushed, glowing, healthy, radiant, robust, ruddy
≠**uninteresting**: animated, bright, colourful, compelling, distinctive, exciting, interesting, unusual

colours *plural noun* 1 = **flag**, banner, emblem, ensign, standard 2 As in **show one's true colours** = **nature**, aspect, breed, character, identity, stamp, strain

column *noun* 1 = **pillar**, caryatid, obelisk, pilaster, post, shaft, support, upright 2 = **line**, cavalcade, file, list, procession, queue, rank, row, string, train

columnist *noun* = **journalist**, correspondent, critic, editor, gossip columnist, journo (*slang*), reporter, reviewer

coma *noun* = **unconsciousness**, insensibility, lethargy, oblivion, somnolence, stupor, torpor, trance

comatose *adjective* = **unconscious**, drugged, insensible, lethargic, somnolent, stupefied, torpid

comb *verb* 1 = **untangle**, arrange, curry, dress, groom 2 *Of flax, wool, etc.* = **card**, tease, teasel, teazle 3 = **search**, forage, go through with a fine-tooth comb, hunt, rake, ransack, rummage, scour, screen, sift, sweep

combat *noun* 1 = **fight**, action, battle, conflict, contest, encounter, engagement, skirmish, struggle, war, warfare ♦ *verb* 2 = **fight**, battle, contend, contest, cope, defy, do battle with, engage, oppose, resist, strive, struggle, withstand
➤ Antonyms
noun ≠**fight**: agreement, armistice, peace, surrender, truce ♦ *verb* ≠**fight**: accept, acquiesce, declare a truce, give up, make peace, support, surrender

combatant *noun* 1 = **fighter**, adversary, antagonist, belligerent, contender, enemy, fighting man, gladiator, opponent, serviceman, soldier, warrior ♦ *adjective* 2 = **fighting**, battling, belligerent, combative, conflicting, contending, opposing, warring

combative *adjective* = **aggressive**, antagonistic, bellicose, belligerent, contentious, militant, pugnacious, quarrelsome, truculent, warlike
➤ Antonyms
nonaggressive, nonbelligerent, nonviolent, pacific, pacifist, peaceable, peaceful, peace-loving

combination *noun* 1 = **mixture**, amalgam, amalgamation, blend, coalescence, composite, connection, meld, mix 2 = **association**, alliance, cabal, cartel, coalition, combine, compound, confederacy, confederation, consortium, conspiracy, federation, merger, syndicate, unification, union

combine *verb* = **join together**, amalgamate, associate, bind, blend, bond, compound, connect, cooperate, fuse, incorporate, integrate, link, marry, meld, merge, mix, pool, put together, synthesize, unify, unite
➤ Antonyms
detach, dissociate, dissolve, disunite, divide, part, separate, sever

combustible *adjective* = **flammable**, explosive, incendiary, inflammable

come verb 1 = **move towards**, advance, appear, approach, arrive, become, draw near, enter, happen, materialize, move, near, occur, originate, show up (informal), turn out, turn up (informal) 2 = **arrive**, appear, attain, enter, materialize, reach, show up (informal), turn up (informal) 3 = **happen**, fall, occur, take place 4 = **result**, arise, emanate, emerge, end up, flow, issue, originate, turn out 5 = **reach**, extend 6 = **be available**, be made, be offered, be on offer, be produced

come about verb = **happen**, arise, befall, come to pass, occur, result, take place, transpire (informal)

come across verb = **find**, bump into (informal), chance upon, discover, encounter, happen upon, hit upon, light upon, meet, notice, stumble upon, unearth

come along verb = **improve**, develop, mend, perk up, pick up, progress, rally, recover, recuperate

come apart verb = **fall to pieces**, break, come unstuck, crumble, disintegrate, give way, separate, split, tear

come at verb = **attack**, assail, assault, charge, fall upon, fly at, go for, light into, rush, rush at

comeback noun 1 Informal = **return**, rally, rebound, recovery, resurgence, revival, triumph 2 = **response**, rejoinder, reply, retaliation, retort, riposte

come back verb = **return**, reappear, recur, re-enter

come between verb = **separate**, alienate, divide, estrange, interfere, meddle, part, set at odds

come by verb = **get**, acquire, land, lay hold of, obtain, procure, score (slang), secure, take possession of, win

come clean verb Informal = **confess**, acknowledge, admit, come out of the closet, cough up (slang), get (something) off one's chest (informal), make a clean breast of, own up, reveal, sing (slang, chiefly U.S.), spill one's guts (slang)

comedian noun = **comic**, card (informal), clown, funny man, humorist, jester, joculator or (fem.) joculatrix, joker, laugh (informal), wag, wit

comedown noun 1 = **decline**, deflation, demotion, reverse 2 Informal = **disappointment**, anticlimax, blow, humiliation, letdown, whammy (informal, chiefly U.S.)

come down verb 1 = **descend**, go downhill 2 = **decline**, degenerate, deteriorate, fall, go to pot (informal), reduce, worsen 3 = **decide**, choose, favour, recommend

come down on verb = **reprimand**, bawl out (informal), blast, carpet (informal), chew out (U.S. & Canad. informal), criticize, dress down (informal), give (someone) a rocket (Brit. & N.Z. informal), jump on (informal), lambast(e), put down, rap over the knuckles, read the riot act, rebuke, tear into (informal), tear (someone) off a strip (Brit. informal)

come down to verb = **amount to**, boil down to, end up as, result in

come down with verb = **catch**, ail, be stricken with, contract, fall ill, fall victim to, get, sicken, take, take sick

comedy noun = **humour**, chaffing, drollery, facetiousness, farce, fun, hilarity, jesting, joking, light entertainment, sitcom (informal), slapstick, wisecracking, witticisms
➤ Antonyms
high drama, melancholy, melodrama, sadness, seriousness, serious play, soap opera, solemnity, tragedy

come forward verb = **volunteer**, offer one's services, present or proffer oneself

come in verb 1 = **enter**, appear, arrive, cross the threshold, show up (informal) 2 = **finish**, reach

come in for verb = **receive**, acquire, bear the brunt of, endure, get, suffer

comely adjective 1 Old-fashioned = **good-looking**, attractive, beautiful, becoming, blooming, bonny, buxom, cute, fair, graceful, handsome, lovely, pleasing, pretty, wholesome, winsome 2 Archaic = **proper**, decent, decorous, fit, fitting, seemly, suitable
➤ Antonyms
≠good-looking: disagreeable, distasteful, faded, homely, mumsy, plain, repulsive, ugly, unattractive, unpleasant ≠proper: improper, indecorous, unbecoming, unfitting, unnatural, unseemly

come off verb Informal = **happen**, go off, occur, succeed, take place, transpire (informal)

come on verb 1 = **progress**, advance, develop, improve, make headway, proceed 2 = **begin**, appear, take place

come out verb 1 = **be revealed**, appear, be announced, be divulged, be issued, be published, be released, be reported 2 = **end up**, result, turn out

come out with verb = **say**, acknowledge, come clean, declare, disclose, divulge, lay open, own, own up

come round verb 1 = **regain consciousness**, come to, rally, recover, revive **2 = change one's opinion**, accede, acquiesce, allow, concede, grant, mellow, relent, yield **3 = call**, drop in, pop in, stop by, visit

come through *verb* **1 = survive**, endure, weather the storm, withstand **2 = accomplish**, achieve, make the grade (*informal*), prevail, succeed, triumph

come up *verb* **= happen**, arise, crop up, occur, rise, spring up, turn up

comeuppance *noun Informal* **= punishment**, chastening, deserts, due reward, dues, merit, recompense, requital, retribution

come up to *verb* **= compare with**, admit of comparison with, approach, equal, match, measure up to, meet, resemble, rival, stand *or* bear comparison with

come up with *verb* **= produce**, advance, create, discover, furnish, offer, present, propose, provide, submit, suggest

comfort *noun* **1 = luxury**, cosiness, creature comforts, ease, opulence, snugness, wellbeing **2 = relief**, aid, alleviation, cheer, compensation, consolation, ease, encouragement, enjoyment, help, satisfaction, succour, support ◆ *verb* **3 = console**, alleviate, assuage, cheer, commiserate with, ease, encourage, enliven, gladden, hearten, inspirit, invigorate, reassure, refresh, relieve, solace, soothe, strengthen

➤ **Antonyms**
noun ≠**relief**: aggravation, annoyance, discouragement, displeasure, hassle (*informal*), inconvenience, irritation ◆ *verb* ≠**console**: aggravate (*informal*), agitate, annoy, bother, depress, discomfort, distress, excite, hassle (*informal*), irk, irritate, rile, ruffle, sadden, trouble

comfortable *adjective* **1 = pleasant**, agreeable, convenient, cosy, delightful, easy, enjoyable, homely, relaxing, restful **2 = happy**, at ease, at home, contented, gratified, relaxed, serene **3** *Informal* **= well-off**, affluent, in clover (*informal*), prosperous, well-to-do

➤ **Antonyms**
≠**pleasant**: inadequate, uncomfortable, unpleasant ≠**happy**: distressed, disturbed, ill at ease, like a fish out of water, miserable, nervous, on tenterhooks, tense, troubled, uncomfortable, uneasy

comforting *adjective* **= consoling**, cheering, consolatory, encouraging, heart-warming, inspiriting, reassuring, soothing

➤ **Antonyms**
alarming, dismaying, disturbing, perplexing, upsetting, worrying

comic *adjective* **1 = funny**, amusing, comical, droll, facetious, farcical, humorous, jocular, joking, light, rich, waggish, witty ◆ *noun* **2 = comedian**, buffoon, clown, funny man, humorist, jester, joculator *or* (*fem.*) joculatrix, wag, wit

➤ **Antonyms**
adjective ≠**funny**: depressing, melancholy, pathetic, sad, serious, solemn, touching, tragic

comical *adjective* **= funny**, absurd, amusing, comic, diverting, droll, entertaining, farcical, hilarious, humorous, laughable, ludicrous, priceless, ridiculous, risible, side-splitting, silly, whimsical, zany

coming *adjective* **1 = approaching**, at hand, due, en route, forthcoming, future, imminent, impending, in store, in the wind, just round the corner, near, next, nigh, on the cards, upcoming **2 = up-and-coming**, aspiring, future, promising ◆ *noun* **3 = arrival**, accession, advent, approach

command *verb* **1 = order**, bid, charge, compel, demand, direct, enjoin, require **2 = have authority over**, administer, call the shots, call the tune, control, dominate, govern, handle, head, lead, manage, reign over, rule, supervise, sway ◆ *noun* **3 = order**, behest, bidding, canon, commandment, decree, demand, direction, directive, edict, fiat, injunction, instruction, mandate, precept, requirement, ultimatum **4 = authority**, charge, control, direction, domination, dominion, government, grasp, management, mastery, power, rule, supervision, sway, upper hand

➤ **Antonyms**
verb ≠**order**: appeal (to), ask, beg, beseech, plead, request, supplicate ≠**have authority over**: be inferior, be subordinate, follow

commandeer *verb* **= seize**, appropriate, confiscate, expropriate, hijack, requisition, sequester, sequestrate, usurp

commander *noun* **= officer**, boss, captain, chief, C in C, C.O., commander-in-chief, commanding officer, director, head, leader, ruler

commanding *adjective* **1 = controlling**, advantageous, decisive, dominant, dominating, superior **2 = authoritative**, assertive, autocratic, compelling, forceful, imposing, impressive, peremptory

➤ **Antonyms**
≠**authoritative**: retiring, shrinking, shy, submissive, timid, unassertive, unimposing, weak

commemorate *verb* = remember, celebrate, honour, immortalize, keep, memorialize, observe, pay tribute to, recognize, salute, solemnize
➤ **Antonyms**
disregard, forget, ignore, omit, overlook, pass over, take no notice of

commemoration *noun* = remembrance, ceremony, honouring, memorial service, observance, tribute

commemorative *adjective* = memorial, celebratory, dedicatory, in honour, in memory, in remembrance

commence *verb* = begin, embark on, enter upon, get the show on the road (*informal*), inaugurate, initiate, open, originate, start
➤ **Antonyms**
bring *or* come to an end, cease, complete, conclude, desist, end, finish, halt, stop, terminate, wind up

commend *verb* **1** = praise, acclaim, applaud, approve, compliment, crack up (*informal*), eulogize, extol, recommend, speak highly of **2** = entrust, commit, confide, consign, deliver, hand over, yield
➤ **Antonyms**
≠praise: attack, blast, censure, condemn, criticize, denounce, disapprove, knock (*informal*), lambast(e), put down, slam, tear into (*informal*) ≠entrust: hold back, keep, keep back, retain, withdraw, withhold

commendable *adjective* = praiseworthy, admirable, creditable, deserving, estimable, exemplary, laudable, meritorious, worthy

commendation *noun* = praise, acclaim, acclamation, approbation, approval, Brownie points, credit, encomium, encouragement, good opinion, panegyric, recommendation

commensurate *adjective* = proportionate, adequate, appropriate, coextensive, comparable, compatible, consistent, corresponding, due, equivalent, fit, fitting, in accord, sufficient

comment *noun* **1** = remark, animadversion, observation, statement **2** = note, annotation, commentary, criticism, elucidation, explanation, exposition, illustration ♦ *verb* **3** = remark, animadvert, interpose, mention, note, observe, opine, point out, say, utter **4** = annotate, criticize, elucidate, explain, interpret

commentary *noun* **1** = narration, description, voice-over **2** = notes, analysis, critique, exegesis, explanation, review, treatise

commentator *noun* **1** = reporter, commenter, special correspondent, sportscaster **2** = critic, annotator, expositor, interpreter, scholiast

commerce *noun* **1** = trade, business, dealing, exchange, merchandising, traffic **2** *Literary* = relations, communication, dealings, intercourse, socializing

commercial *adjective* **1** = mercantile, business, profit-making, sales, trade, trading **2** = profitable, in demand, marketable, popular, saleable **3** = materialistic, exploited, mercenary, monetary, pecuniary, profit-making, venal

commingle *verb* = mix, amalgamate, blend, combine, commix, intermingle, intermix, join, meld, mingle, unite

commiserate *verb* = sympathize, console, feel for, pity

commission *noun* **1** = duty, appointment, authority, charge, employment, errand, function, mandate, mission, task, trust, warrant **2** = fee, allowance, brokerage, compensation, cut, percentage, rake-off (*slang*), royalties **3** = committee, board, body of commissioners, commissioners, delegation, deputation, representatives ♦ *verb* **4** = appoint, authorize, contract, delegate, depute, empower, engage, nominate, order, select, send

commit *verb* **1** = do, carry out, enact, execute, perform, perpetrate **2** = give, commend, confide, consign, deliver, deposit, engage, entrust, hand over **3** = pledge, align, bind, compromise, endanger, make liable, obligate, rank **4** = put in custody, confine, imprison
➤ **Antonyms**
≠do: omit ≠give: receive, withhold ≠pledge: disavow, vacillate, waver ≠put in custody: free, let out, release, set free

commitment *noun* **1** = dedication, adherence, devotion, involvement, loyalty **2** = responsibility, duty, engagement, liability, obligation, tie **3** = pledge, assurance, guarantee, promise, undertaking, vow, word
➤ **Antonyms**
≠dedication: indecisiveness, vacillation, wavering ≠pledge: disavowal, negation

common *adjective* **1** = average, a dime a dozen, bog-standard (*Brit. & Irish slang*), commonplace, conventional, customary, daily, everyday, familiar, frequent, general, habitual, humdrum, obscure, ordinary, plain, regular, routine, run-of-the-mill, simple, standard, stock, usual, vanilla (*slang*), workaday **2** = popular, accepted, general, prevailing, prevalent, universal, widespread **3** = collective, communal,

community, popular, public, social **4** = **vulgar**, coarse, hackneyed, inferior, low, pedestrian, plebeian, stale, trite, undistinguished
➤ **Antonyms**
≠**average**: abnormal, famous, formal, important, infrequent, noble, outstanding, rare, scarce, sophisticated, strange, superior, uncommon, unknown, unusual ≠**collective**: personal, private ≠**vulgar**: cultured, distinguished, gentle, refined, sensitive

commonplace *adjective* **1** = **everyday**, banal, common, customary, dime-a-dozen (*informal*), humdrum, mundane, obvious, ordinary, pedestrian, run-of-the-mill, stale, threadbare, trite, uninteresting, vanilla (*slang*), widespread, worn out ♦ *noun* **2** = **cliché**, banality, platitude, truism
➤ **Antonyms**
adjective ≠**everyday**: exciting, extraordinary, ground-breaking, infrequent, interesting, left-field (*informal*), new, novel, original, rare, strange, uncommon, unfamiliar, unique, unusual

common-sense, common-sensical *adjective* = **sensible**, astute, down-to-earth, hard-headed, judicious, level-headed, matter-of-fact, practical, realistic, reasonable, sane, shrewd, sound
➤ **Antonyms**
airy-fairy (*informal*), daft (*informal*), foolish, impractical, irrational, unrealistic, unreasonable, unthinking, unwise

common sense *noun* = **good sense**, gumption (*Brit. informal*), horse sense, level-headedness, mother wit, native intelligence, nous (*Brit. slang*), practicality, prudence, reasonableness, smarts (*slang, chiefly U.S.*), sound judgment, soundness, wit

commotion *noun* = **disturbance**, ado, agitation, brouhaha, bustle, disorder, excitement, ferment, furore, fuss, hubbub, hue and cry, hullabaloo, hurly-burly, perturbation, racket, riot, rumpus, to-do, tumult, turmoil, upheaval, uproar

communal *adjective* = **public**, collective, communistic, community, general, joint, neighbourhood, shared
➤ **Antonyms**
exclusive, individual, personal, private, single, unshared

commune *noun* = **community**, collective, cooperative, kibbutz

commune with *verb* **1** = **contemplate**, meditate on, muse on, ponder, reflect on **2** = **talk to**, communicate with, confer with, confide in, converse with, discourse with, discuss with, parley with

communicable *adjective* = **infectious**, catching, contagious, taking, transferable, transmittable

communicate *verb* = **make known**, acquaint, announce, be in contact, be in touch, connect, convey, correspond, declare, disclose, disseminate, divulge, impart, inform, pass on, phone, proclaim, publish, report, reveal, ring up (*informal, chiefly Brit.*), signify, spread, transmit, unfold
➤ **Antonyms**
conceal, cover up, hold back, hush up, keep back, keep secret, keep under wraps, repress, sit on (*informal*), suppress, whitewash (*informal*), withhold

communication *noun* **1** = **passing on**, connection, contact, conversation, correspondence, dissemination, intercourse, link, transmission **2** = **message**, announcement, disclosure, dispatch, information, intelligence, news, report, statement, word

communications *plural noun* **1** = **transport**, routes, travel **2** = **information technology**, media, publicity, public relations, telecommunications

communicative *adjective* = **talkative**, candid, chatty, conversable, expansive, forthcoming, frank, informative, loquacious, open, outgoing, unreserved, voluble
➤ **Antonyms**
quiet, reserved, reticent, secretive, taciturn, uncommunicative, uninformative, untalkative

communion *noun* = **closeness**, accord, affinity, agreement, communing, concord, consensus, converse, fellowship, harmony, intercourse, participation, rapport, sympathy, togetherness, unity

Communion *noun Church* = **Eucharist**, Lord's Supper, Mass, Sacrament

communiqué *noun* = **announcement**, bulletin, dispatch, news flash, official communication, report

Communism *noun* = **socialism**, Bolshevism, collectivism, Eurocommunism, Maoism, Marxism, Marxism-Leninism, Stalinism, state socialism, Titoism, Trotskyism

Communist *noun* = **socialist**, Bolshevik, collectivist, Marxist, Red (*informal*)

community *noun* = **society**, association, body politic, brotherhood, commonwealth, company, district, general public, locality, people, populace, population, public, residents, state

commute *verb* **1** *Law: of penalties, etc.*

= **reduce**, alleviate, curtail, mitigate, modify, remit, shorten, soften **2** = **substitute**, barter, exchange, interchange, switch, trade

commuter noun = **daily traveller**, straphanger (informal), suburbanite

compact¹ adjective **1** = **closely packed**, compressed, condensed, dense, firm, impenetrable, impermeable, pressed together, solid, thick **2** = **brief**, compendious, concise, epigrammatic, laconic, pithy, pointed, succinct, terse, to the point ♦ verb = **pack closely**, compress, condense, cram, stuff, tamp
➤ Antonyms
adjective ≠closely packed: dispersed, large, loose, roomy, scattered, spacious, sprawling ≠brief: circumlocutory, garrulous, lengthy, long-winded, prolix, rambling, verbose, wordy ♦ verb ≠pack closely: disperse, loosen, separate

compact² noun = **agreement**, alliance, arrangement, bargain, bond, concordat, contract, covenant, deal, entente, pact, stipulation, treaty, understanding

companion noun **1** = **friend**, accomplice, ally, associate, buddy (informal), colleague, comrade, confederate, consort, crony, gossip (archaic), homeboy (slang, chiefly U.S.), mate (informal), partner **2** = **escort**, aide, assistant, attendant, chaperon, duenna, squire **3** = **mate**, complement, counterpart, fellow, match, twin

companionable adjective = **friendly**, affable, congenial, conversable, convivial, cordial, familiar, genial, gregarious, neighbourly, outgoing, sociable

companionship noun = **fellowship**, amity, camaraderie, company, comradeship, conviviality, esprit de corps, fraternity, friendship, rapport, togetherness

company noun **1** = **business**, association, concern, corporation, establishment, firm, house, partnership, syndicate **2** = **group**, assemblage, assembly, band, bevy, body, camp, circle, collection, community, concourse, convention, coterie, crew, crowd, ensemble, gathering, league, party, set, throng, troop, troupe, turnout **3** = **companionship**, fellowship, presence, society **4** = **guests**, callers, party, visitors

comparable adjective **1** = **on a par**, a match for, as good as, commensurate, equal, equivalent, in a class with, proportionate, tantamount **2** = **similar**, akin, alike, analogous, cognate, corresponding, cut from the same cloth, of a piece, related
➤ Antonyms

different, dissimilar, incommensurable, incomparable, unequal

comparative adjective = **relative**, approximate, by comparison, qualified

compare verb **1** = **weigh**, balance, collate, contrast, juxtapose, set against **2** usually with **with** = **be on a par with**, approach, approximate to, bear comparison, be in the same class as, be the equal of, come up to, compete with, equal, hold a candle to, match, vie **3 compare to** = **liken to**, correlate to, equate to, identify with, mention in the same breath as, parallel, resemble

comparison noun **1** = **contrast**, collation, distinction, juxtaposition **2** = **similarity**, analogy, comparability, correlation, likeness, resemblance

compartment noun **1** = **section**, alcove, bay, berth, booth, carrel, carriage, cell, chamber, cubbyhole, cubicle, locker, niche, pigeonhole **2** = **category**, area, department, division, section, subdivision

compass noun **1** = **range**, area, bound, boundary, circle, circuit, circumference, enclosure, extent, field, limit, reach, realm, round, scope, sphere, stretch, zone ♦ verb **2** = **surround**, beset, besiege, blockade, circumscribe, encircle, enclose, encompass, environ, hem in, invest (rare)

compassion noun = **sympathy**, charity, clemency, commiseration, compunction, condolence, fellow feeling, heart, humanity, kindness, mercy, pity, quarter, ruth (archaic), soft-heartedness, sorrow, tender-heartedness, tenderness, understanding
➤ Antonyms
apathy, cold-heartedness, indifference, mercilessness, unconcern

compassionate adjective = **sympathetic**, benevolent, charitable, humane, humanitarian, indulgent, kind-hearted, kindly, lenient, merciful, pitying, tender, tender-hearted, understanding
➤ Antonyms
callous, harsh, heartless, inhumane, pitiless, uncaring, unfeeling, unmerciful, unsympathetic

compatibility noun = **harmony**, affinity, agreement, amity, concord, congeniality, empathy, like-mindedness, rapport, single-mindedness, sympathy

compatible adjective = **harmonious**, accordant, adaptable, agreeable, congenial, congruent, congruous, consistent, consonant, in harmony, in keeping, like-minded, reconcilable, suitable
➤ Antonyms

contradictory, inappropriate, inapt, incompatible, unfitting, unharmonious, unsuitable

compatriot *noun* = **fellow countryman**, countryman, fellow citizen

compel *verb* = **force**, bulldoze (*informal*), coerce, constrain, dragoon, drive, enforce, exact, hustle (*slang*), impel, make, necessitate, oblige, railroad (*informal*), restrain, squeeze, urge

compelling *adjective* **1** = **fascinating**, enchanting, enthralling, gripping, hypnotic, irresistible, mesmeric, spellbinding **2** = **pressing**, binding, coercive, imperative, overriding, peremptory, unavoidable, urgent **3** = **convincing**, cogent, conclusive, forceful, irrefutable, powerful, telling, weighty
➤ **Antonyms**
≠**fascinating**: boring, dull, humdrum, monotonous, ordinary, repetitious, tiresome, uneventful, uninteresting, wearisome

compensate *verb* **1** = **recompense**, atone, indemnify, make amends, make good, make restitution, refund, reimburse, remunerate, repay, requite, reward, satisfy **2** = **cancel (out)**, balance, counteract, counterbalance, countervail, make up for, offset, redress

compensation *noun* = **recompense**, amends, atonement, damages, indemnification, indemnity, meed (*archaic*), offset, payment, reimbursement, remuneration, reparation, requital, restitution, reward, satisfaction

compete *verb* = **contend**, be in the running, challenge, contest, emulate, fight, pit oneself against, rival, strive, struggle, vie

competence *noun* = **ability**, adequacy, appropriateness, capability, capacity, competency, craft, expertise, fitness, proficiency, skill, suitability
➤ **Antonyms**
inability, inadequacy, incompetence

competent *adjective* = **able**, adapted, adequate, appropriate, capable, clever, endowed, equal, fit, pertinent, proficient, qualified, sufficient, suitable
➤ **Antonyms**
inadequate, incapable, incompetent, inexperienced, inexpert, unqualified, unskilled

competition *noun* **1** = **rivalry**, contention, contest, emulation, one-upmanship (*informal*), opposition, strife, struggle **2** = **contest**, championship, event, head-to-head, puzzle, quiz, tournament **3** = **opposition**, challengers, field, rivals

competitive *adjective* **1** = **cut-throat**, aggressive, antagonistic, at odds, dog-eat-dog, opposing, rival, vying **2** = **ambitious**, combative

competitor *noun* = **contestant**, adversary, antagonist, challenger, competition, emulator, opponent, opposition, rival

compilation *noun* = **collection**, accumulation, anthology, assemblage, assortment, treasury

compile *verb* = **put together**, accumulate, amass, anthologize, collect, cull, garner, gather, marshal, organize

complacency *noun* = **self-satisfaction**, contentment, gratification, pleasure, satisfaction, smugness

complacent *adjective* = **self-satisfied**, contented, gratified, pleased, pleased with oneself, resting on one's laurels, satisfied, self-assured, self-contented, self-righteous, serene, smug, unconcerned
➤ **Antonyms**
discontent, dissatisfied, insecure, troubled, uneasy, unsatisfied

complain *verb* = **find fault**, beef (*slang*), bellyache (*slang*), bemoan, bewail, bitch (*slang*), bleat, carp, deplore, fuss, grieve, gripe (*informal*), groan, grouch (*informal*), grouse, growl, grumble, kick up a fuss (*informal*), kvetch (*U.S. slang*), lament, moan, put the boot in (*slang*), whine, whinge (*informal*)

complaint *noun* **1** = **criticism**, accusation, annoyance, beef (*slang*), bitch (*slang*), charge, dissatisfaction, fault-finding, grievance, gripe (*informal*), grouch (*informal*), grouse, grumble, lament, moan, plaint, protest, remonstrance, trouble, wail **2** = **illness**, affliction, ailment, disease, disorder, indisposition, malady, sickness, upset

complement *noun* **1** = **completion**, companion, consummation, correlative, counterpart, finishing touch, rounding-off, supplement **2** = **total**, aggregate, capacity, entirety, quota, totality, wholeness ♦ *verb* **3** = **complete**, cap (*informal*), crown, round off, set off

complementary *adjective* = **completing**, companion, correlative, corresponding, fellow, interdependent, interrelating, matched, reciprocal
➤ **Antonyms**
contradictory, different, incompatible, incongruous, uncomplementary

complete *adjective* **1** = **total**, absolute, consummate, deep-dyed (*usually derogatory*), dyed-in-the-wool, outright, perfect, thorough, thoroughgoing, utter **2** = **finished**, accomplished, achieved,

concluded, ended **3** = **entire**, all, faultless, full, intact, integral, plenary, unabridged, unbroken, undivided, unimpaired, whole ♦ *verb* **4** = **finish**, accomplish, achieve, cap, close, conclude, crown, discharge, do, end, execute, fill in, finalize, fulfil, perfect, perform, put the tin lid on, realize, round off, settle, terminate, wrap up (*informal*)
➤ **Antonyms**
adjective ≠**total**: partial ≠**finished**: inconclusive, unaccomplished, unfinished, unsettled ≠**entire**: deficient, imperfect, incomplete, spoilt ♦ *verb* ≠**finish**: begin, commence, initiate, mar, spoil, start

completely *adverb* = **totally**, absolutely, a hundred per cent, altogether, down to the ground, en masse, entirely, every inch, from A to Z, from beginning to end, fully, heart and soul, hook, line and sinker, in full, *in toto,* lock, stock and barrel, one hundred per cent, perfectly, quite, root and branch, solidly, thoroughly, utterly, wholly

completion *noun* = **finishing**, accomplishment, attainment, bitter end, close, conclusion, consummation, culmination, end, expiration, finalization, fruition, fulfilment, realization

complex *adjective* **1** = **compound**, composite, compounded, heterogeneous, manifold, multifarious, multiple **2** = **complicated**, circuitous, convoluted, Daedalian (*literary*), elaborate, intricate, involved, knotty, labyrinthine, mingled, mixed, tangled, tortuous ♦ *noun* **3** = **structure**, aggregate, composite, network, organization, scheme, synthesis, system **4** *Informal* = **obsession**, fixation, fixed idea, *idée fixe,* phobia, preoccupation
➤ **Antonyms**
adjective ≠**complicated**: clear, easy, easy-peasy (*slang*), elementary, obvious, simple, straightforward, uncomplicated

complexion *noun* **1** = **skin**, colour, colouring, hue, pigmentation, skin tone **2** = **nature**, appearance, aspect, cast, character, countenance, disposition, guise, light, look, make-up, stamp

complexity *noun* = **complication**, convolution, elaboration, entanglement, intricacy, involvement, multiplicity, ramification

compliance *noun* = **obedience**, acquiescence, agreement, assent, complaisance, concession, concurrence, conformity, consent, deference, observance, passivity, submission, submissiveness, yielding
➤ **Antonyms**
defiance, disobedience, non-compliance,

nonconformity, opposition, refusal, resistance, revolt

complicate *verb* = **make difficult**, confuse, embroil, entangle, interweave, involve, make intricate, muddle, ravel, snarl up
➤ **Antonyms**
clarify, clear up, disentangle, elucidate, explain, facilitate, simplify, spell out, unsnarl

complicated *adjective* **1** = **difficult**, involved, perplexing, problematic, puzzling, troublesome **2** = **involved**, Byzantine (*of attitudes, etc.*), complex, convoluted, elaborate, interlaced, intricate, labyrinthine
➤ **Antonyms**
≠**difficult**: clear, easy, easy-peasy (*slang*), undemanding, understandable, user-friendly ≠**involved**: simple, straightforward, uncomplicated, uninvolved

complication *noun* **1** = **complexity**, combination, confusion, entanglement, intricacy, mixture, web **2** = **problem**, aggravation, difficulty, drawback, embarrassment, factor, obstacle, snag

complicity *noun* = **collusion**, abetment, collaboration, concurrence, connivance

compliment *noun* **1** = **praise**, admiration, bouquet, commendation, congratulations, courtesy, eulogy, favour, flattery, honour, tribute ♦ *verb* **2** = **praise**, commend, congratulate, crack up (*informal*), extol, felicitate, flatter, laud, pat on the back, pay tribute to, salute, sing the praises of, speak highly of, wish joy to
➤ **Antonyms**
noun ≠**praise**: complaint, condemnation, criticism, disparagement, insult, reproach ♦ *verb* ≠**praise**: blast, condemn, criticize, decry, disparage, insult, lambast(e), put down, reprehend, reproach, tear into (*informal*)

complimentary *adjective* **1** = **flattering**, appreciative, approving, commendatory, congratulatory, eulogistic, laudatory, panegyrical **2** = **free**, courtesy, donated, free of charge, gratis, gratuitous, honorary, on the house
➤ **Antonyms**
≠**flattering**: abusive, critical, disparaging, fault-finding, insulting, scathing, uncomplimentary, unflattering

compliments *plural noun* = **greetings**, good wishes, regards, remembrances, respects, salutation

comply *verb* = **obey**, abide by, accede, accord, acquiesce, adhere to, agree to, conform to, consent to, defer, discharge, follow, fulfil, observe, perform, play ball (*informal*), respect, satisfy, submit, toe the line, yield

➤ **Antonyms**
break, defy, disobey, disregard, fight, ignore, oppose, refuse to obey, reject, repudiate, resist, spurn, violate

component *noun* 1 = **part**, constituent, element, ingredient, item, piece, unit ♦ *adjective* 2 = **constituent**, composing, inherent, intrinsic

compose *verb* 1 = **put together**, build, compound, comprise, constitute, construct, fashion, form, make, make up 2 = **create**, contrive, devise, frame, imagine, indite, invent, produce, write 3 = **calm**, appease, assuage, collect, control, pacify, placate, quell, quiet, soothe, still, tranquillize 4 = **arrange**, adjust, reconcile, regulate, resolve, settle

➤ **Antonyms**
≠**put together**: bulldoze, demolish, destroy, dismantle, obliterate, raze ≠**calm**: agitate, disturb, excite, perturb, trouble, unsettle, upset

composed *adjective* = **calm**, as cool as a cucumber, at ease, collected, confident, cool, imperturbable, keeping one's cool, laid-back (*informal*), level-headed, poised, relaxed, sedate, self-controlled, self-possessed, serene, together (*slang*), tranquil, unfazed (*informal*), unflappable, unruffled, unworried

➤ **Antonyms**
agitated, antsy (*informal*), anxious, disturbed, excited, hot and bothered (*informal*), nervous, ruffled, twitchy (*informal*), uncontrolled, uneasy, unpoised, upset

composite *adjective* 1 = **compound**, blended, combined, complex, conglomerate, mixed, synthesized ♦ *noun* 2 = **compound**, amalgam, blend, conglomerate, fusion, meld, synthesis

composition *noun* 1 = **creation**, compilation, fashioning, formation, formulation, invention, making, mixture, production, putting together 2 = **design**, arrangement, configuration, constitution, form, formation, layout, make-up, organization, structure 3 = **arrangement**, balance, concord, consonance, harmony, placing, proportion, symmetry 4 = **essay**, creation, exercise, literary work, opus, piece, study, treatise, work, writing

compost *noun* = **organic fertilizer**, humus, mulch

composure *noun* = **calmness**, aplomb, calm, collectedness, cool (*slang*), coolness, dignity, ease, equanimity, imperturbability, placidity, poise,

sang-froid, sedateness, self-assurance, self-possession, serenity, tranquillity

➤ **Antonyms**
agitation, discomposure, excitability, impatience, nervousness, perturbation, uneasiness

compound *noun* 1 = **combination**, alloy, amalgam, blend, composite, composition, conglomerate, fusion, medley, meld, mixture, synthesis ♦ *verb* 2 = **combine**, amalgamate, blend, coalesce, concoct, fuse, intermingle, meld, mingle, mix, synthesize, unite 3 = **intensify**, add insult to injury, add to, aggravate, augment, complicate, exacerbate, heighten, magnify, worsen 4 *Used of a dispute, difference, etc.* = **settle**, adjust, arrange, compose ♦ *adjective* 5 = **complex**, composite, conglomerate, intricate, multiple, not simple

➤ **Antonyms**
noun ≠**combination**: element ♦ *verb* ≠**combine**: divide, part, segregate ≠**intensify**: decrease, lessen, minimize, moderate, modify ♦ *adjective* ≠**complex**: pure, simple, single, unmixed

comprehend *verb* 1 = **understand**, apprehend, assimilate, conceive, discern, fathom, get the hang of (*informal*), get the picture, grasp, know, make out, perceive, see, see the light of day, take in 2 = **include**, comprise, contain, embody, embrace, enclose, encompass, involve, take in

➤ **Antonyms**
≠**understand**: be at cross-purposes, get (it) wrong, get one's lines crossed, get the wrong end of the stick, misapprehend, misconceive, misconstrue, misinterpret, miss the point of, mistake, misunderstand, pervert

comprehensible *adjective* = **understandable**, clear, coherent, conceivable, explicit, graspable, intelligible, plain, user-friendly

comprehension *noun* 1 = **understanding**, conception, discernment, grasp, intelligence, judgment, knowledge, perception, realization, sense 2 = **inclusion**, compass, domain, field, limits, province, range, reach, scope

➤ **Antonyms**
≠**understanding**: incomprehension, misapprehension, misunderstanding, unawareness

comprehensive *adjective* = **broad**, all-embracing, all-inclusive, blanket, catholic, complete, encyclopedic, exhaustive, extensive, full, inclusive, overarching, sweeping, thorough,

umbrella, wide
> **Antonyms**
incomplete, limited, narrow, restricted,
specialized, specific
compress verb = **squeeze**, abbreviate,
compact, concentrate, condense,
constrict, contract, cram, crowd, crush,
knit, press, pucker, shorten, squash,
summarize, wedge
compressed adjective = **squeezed**,
abridged, compact, compacted,
concentrated, concise, consolidated,
constricted, flattened, reduced, shortened,
squashed
compression noun = **squeezing**,
condensation, consolidation, constriction,
crushing, pressure, wedging
comprise verb **1** = **be composed of**,
comprehend, consist of, contain, embrace,
encompass, include, take in **2** = **make up**,
compose, constitute, form
compromise noun **1** = **give-and-take**,
accommodation, accord, adjustment,
agreement, concession, half measures,
middle ground, settlement, trade-off
♦ verb **2** = **meet halfway**, adjust, agree,
arbitrate, compose, compound, concede,
give and take, go fifty-fifty (*informal*),
settle, strike a balance **3** = **weaken**,
discredit, dishonour, embarrass, endanger,
expose, hazard, imperil, implicate,
jeopardize, prejudice
> **Antonyms**
noun ≠**give-and-take**: contention,
controversy, difference, disagreement,
dispute, quarrel ♦ verb ≠**meet halfway**:
argue, contest, differ, disagree ≠**weaken**:
assure, boost, enhance, support
compulsion noun **1** = **urge**, drive,
necessity, need, obsession, preoccupation
2 = **force**, coercion, constraint, demand,
duress, obligation, pressure, urgency
compulsive adjective = **irresistible**,
besetting, compelling, driving, neurotic,
obsessive, overwhelming, uncontrollable,
urgent
compulsory adjective = **obligatory**,
binding, de rigueur, forced, imperative,
mandatory, required, requisite
> **Antonyms**
discretionary, elective, non-obligatory,
non-requisite, optional, unimperative,
unnecessary, voluntary
compute verb = **calculate**, add up, cast up,
cipher, count, enumerate, estimate, figure,
figure out, measure, rate, reckon, sum,
tally, total
comrade noun = **companion**, ally,
associate, buddy (*informal*), cock (*Brit.
informal*), colleague, compatriot, compeer,

confederate, co-worker, crony, fellow,
friend, homeboy (*slang, chiefly U.S.*), mate
(*informal*), pal (*informal*), partner
con Informal ♦ noun **1** = **swindle**,
deception, fraud, scam (*slang*), sting
(*informal*), trick ♦ verb **2** = **swindle**, cheat,
deceive, defraud, double-cross (*informal*),
dupe, hoodwink, rip off (*slang*), trick
concave adjective = **hollow**, cupped,
depressed, excavated, hollowed, incurved,
indented, scooped, sunken
> **Antonyms**
bulging, convex, curving, protuberant,
rounded
conceal verb = **hide**, bury, camouflage,
cover, disguise, dissemble, draw a veil
over, keep dark, keep secret, keep under
one's hat, mask, obscure, screen, secrete,
shelter, stash (*informal*)
> **Antonyms**
disclose, display, divulge, expose, lay bare,
reveal, show, uncover, unmask, unveil
concealed adjective = **hidden**, covered,
covert, inconspicuous, masked, obscured,
screened, secret, secreted, tucked away,
under wraps, unseen
concealment noun = **hiding**, camouflage,
cover, disguise, hideaway, hide-out,
secrecy
> **Antonyms**
disclosure, display, exposure, give-away,
leak, revelation, showing, uncovering
concede verb **1** = **admit**, accept,
acknowledge, allow, confess, grant, own **2**
= **give up**, cede, hand over, relinquish,
surrender, yield
> **Antonyms**
≠**admit**: contest, deny, disclaim, dispute,
protest, refute, reject ≠**give up**: beat,
conquer, defeat, fight to the bitter end,
make a stand
conceit noun **1** = **self-importance**,
amour-propre, arrogance, complacency,
egotism, narcissism, pride, self-love,
swagger, vainglory, vanity **2** Archaic
= **fancy**, belief, fantasy, idea, image,
imagination, judgment, notion, opinion,
quip, thought, vagary, whim, whimsy
conceited adjective = **self-important**,
arrogant, bigheaded (*informal*), cocky,
egotistical, full of oneself, immodest,
narcissistic, overweening, puffed up, stuck
up (*informal*), swollen-headed, too big for
one's boots or breeches, vain, vainglorious
> **Antonyms**
humble, modest, self-effacing, unassuming
conceivable adjective = **imaginable**,
believable, credible, possible, thinkable
> **Antonyms**
inconceivable, incredible, unbelievable,

unimaginable, unthinkable

conceive *verb* 1 = **imagine**, appreciate, apprehend, believe, comprehend, envisage, fancy, get the picture, grasp, realize, suppose, think, understand 2 = **think up**, contrive, create, design, develop, devise, form, formulate, produce, project, purpose 3 = **become pregnant**, become impregnated

concentrate *verb* 1 = **focus one's attention on**, be engrossed in, consider closely, give all one's attention to, put one's mind to, rack one's brains 2 = **focus**, bring to bear, centre, cluster, converge 3 = **gather**, accumulate, cluster, collect, congregate, huddle
➤ **Antonyms**
≠**focus one's attention on**: disregard, let one's mind wander, lose concentration, pay no attention to, pay no heed to ≠**focus, gather**: diffuse, disperse, dissipate, scatter, spread out

concentrated *adjective* 1 = **intense**, all-out (*informal*), deep, hard, intensive 2 = **condensed**, boiled down, evaporated, reduced, rich, thickened, undiluted

concentration *noun* 1 = **single-mindedness**, absorption, application, heed 2 = **focusing**, bringing to bear, centralization, centring, combination, compression, consolidation, convergence, intensification 3 = **convergence**, accumulation, aggregation, cluster, collection, horde, mass
➤ **Antonyms**
≠**single-mindedness**: absent-mindedness, disregard, distraction, inattention ≠**focusing, convergence**: diffusion, dispersal, scattering, spreading-out

concept *noun* = **idea**, abstraction, conception, conceptualization, hypothesis, image, impression, notion, theory, view

conception *noun* 1 = **idea**, concept, design, image, notion, plan 2 = **understanding**, appreciation, clue, comprehension, impression, inkling, perception, picture 3 = **impregnation**, fertilization, germination, insemination 4 = **origin**, beginning, birth, formation, inception, initiation, invention, launching, outset

concern *noun* 1 = **worry**, anxiety, apprehension, attention, burden, care, consideration, disquiet, disquietude, distress, heed, responsibility, solicitude 2 = **importance**, bearing, interest, reference, relation, relevance 3 = **business**, affair, charge, department, field, interest, involvement, job, matter, mission,

occupation, pigeon (*informal*), responsibility, task, transaction 4 = **business**, company, corporation, enterprise, establishment, firm, house, organization ♦ *verb* 5 = **worry**, bother, disquiet, distress, disturb, make anxious, make uneasy, perturb, trouble 6 = **be relevant to**, affect, apply to, bear on, interest, involve, pertain to, regard, touch

concerned *adjective* 1 = **involved**, active, implicated, interested, mixed up, privy to 2 = **worried**, anxious, bothered, distressed, disturbed, exercised, troubled, uneasy, upset 3 = **caring**, attentive, interested, solicitous
➤ **Antonyms**
aloof, carefree, detached, indifferent, neglectful, unconcerned, uninterested, untroubled, without a care

concerning *preposition* = **regarding**, about, anent (*Scot.*), apropos of, as regards, as to, in the matter of, on the subject of, re, relating to, respecting, touching, with reference to

concert *noun* 1 = **agreement**, accord, concord, concordance, harmony, unanimity, union, unison 2 **in concert** = **together**, concertedly, in collaboration, in league, in unison, jointly, shoulder to shoulder, unanimously

concerted *adjective* = **coordinated**, agreed upon, collaborative, combined, joint, planned, prearranged, united
➤ **Antonyms**
disunited, separate, uncontrived, uncooperative, unplanned

concession *noun* 1 = **grant**, adjustment, allowance, boon, compromise, indulgence, permit, privilege, sop 2 = **conceding**, acknowledgment, admission, assent, confession, surrender, yielding

conciliate *verb* = **pacify**, appease, clear the air, disarm, mediate, mollify, placate, pour oil on troubled waters, propitiate, reconcile, restore harmony, soothe, win over

conciliation *noun* = **pacification**, appeasement, disarming, mollification, placation, propitiation, reconciliation, soothing

conciliatory *adjective* = **pacifying**, appeasing, disarming, irenic, mollifying, pacific, peaceable, placatory, propitiative

concise *adjective* = **brief**, compact, compendious, compressed, condensed, epigrammatic, in a nutshell, laconic, pithy, short, succinct, summary, synoptic, terse, to the point
➤ **Antonyms**

diffuse, discursive, garrulous, lengthy, long-winded, prolix, rambling, verbose, wordy

conclave noun = **secret** or **private meeting**, assembly, cabinet, conference, congress, council, parley, session

conclude verb **1** = **decide**, assume, clinch, deduce, determine, establish, fix, gather, infer, judge, reckon (informal), resolve, settle, sum up, suppose, surmise, work out **2** = **end**, bring down the curtain, cease, close, come to an end, complete, draw to a close, finish, round off, terminate, wind up **3** = **accomplish**, bring about, carry out, effect, pull off
➤ Antonyms
≠**end**: begin, commence, initiate, open, start

conclusion noun **1** = **decision**, agreement, conviction, deduction, inference, judgment, opinion, resolution, settlement, verdict **2** = **end**, bitter end, close, completion, ending, finale, finish, result, termination **3** = **outcome**, consequence, culmination, end result, issue, result, sequel, upshot **4 in conclusion** = **finally**, in closing, lastly, to sum up

conclusive adjective = **decisive**, clinching, convincing, definite, definitive, final, irrefutable, ultimate, unanswerable, unarguable
➤ Antonyms
contestable, disputable, doubtful, dubious, inconclusive, indecisive, indefinite, questionable, refutable, unconvincing, vague

concoct verb = **make up**, brew, contrive, cook up (informal), design, devise, fabricate, formulate, hatch, invent, manufacture, mature, plot, prepare, project, think up, trump up

concoction noun = **mixture**, blend, brew, combination, compound, contrivance, creation, preparation

concrete noun **1** = **cement** (not in technical usage), concretion ♦ adjective **2** = **specific**, definite, explicit **3** = **real**, actual, factual, material, sensible, substantial, tangible
➤ Antonyms
adjective ≠**specific**: indefinite, unspecified, vague ≠**real**: abstract, immaterial, insubstantial, intangible, notional, theoretical

concubine noun Old-fashioned = **mistress**, courtesan, kept woman, leman (archaic), odalisque, paramour

concupiscence noun Formal = **lust**, appetite, desire, horniness (slang), lasciviousness, lechery, libidinousness, libido, lickerishness (archaic), lustfulness,

randiness (informal, chiefly Brit.)

concur verb = **agree**, accede, accord, acquiesce, approve, assent, buy into (informal), coincide, combine, consent, cooperate, harmonize, join

concurrent adjective **1** = **simultaneous**, coexisting, coincident, concerted, concomitant, contemporaneous, synchronous **2** = **converging**, confluent, convergent, uniting **3** = **in agreement**, agreeing, at one, compatible, consentient, consistent, cooperating, harmonious, in rapport, like-minded, of the same mind

concussion noun = **shaking**, clash, collision, crash, impact, jarring, jolt, jolting, shock

condemn verb **1** = **disapprove**, blame, censure, criticize, damn, denounce, excoriate, reprehend, reproach, reprobate, reprove, upbraid **2** = **sentence**, convict, damn, doom, pass sentence on, proscribe
➤ Antonyms
≠**disapprove**: acclaim, applaud, approve, commend, compliment, condone, praise ≠**sentence**: acquit, free, liberate

condemnation noun **1** = **disapproval**, blame, censure, denouncement, denunciation, reproach, reprobation, reproof, stricture **2** = **sentence**, conviction, damnation, doom, judgment, proscription

condensation noun **1** = **distillation**, condensate, deliquescence, liquefaction, precipitate, precipitation **2** = **abridgment**, contraction, digest, précis, synopsis **3** = **concentration**, compression, consolidation, crystallization, curtailment, reduction

condense verb **1** = **abridge**, abbreviate, compact, compress, concentrate, contract, curtail, encapsulate, epitomize, précis, shorten, summarize **2** = **concentrate**, boil down, coagulate, decoct, precipitate (Chemistry), reduce, solidify, thicken
➤ Antonyms
≠**abridge**: elaborate, enlarge, expand, expatiate, increase, lengthen, pad out, spin out ≠**concentrate**: dilute, make thinner, thin (out), water down, weaken

condensed adjective **1** = **abridged**, compressed, concentrated, curtailed, shortened, shrunken, slimmed-down, summarized **2** = **concentrated**, boiled down, clotted, coagulated, precipitated (Chemistry), reduced, thickened

condescend verb **1** = **patronize**, talk down to **2** = **lower oneself**, be courteous, bend, come down off one's high horse (informal), humble or demean oneself, see fit, stoop, submit, unbend (informal), vouchsafe

condescending *adjective* = **patronizing**, disdainful, lofty, lordly, on one's high horse (*informal*), snobbish, snooty (*informal*), supercilious, superior, toffee-nosed (*slang, chiefly Brit.*)

condition *noun* 1 = **state**, case, circumstances, lie of the land, plight, position, predicament, shape, situation, state of affairs, status quo 2 = **requirement**, arrangement, article, demand, limitation, modification, prerequisite, provision, proviso, qualification, requisite, restriction, rider, rule, stipulation, terms 3 = **health**, fettle, fitness, kilter, order, shape, state of health, trim 4 = **ailment**, complaint, infirmity, malady, problem, weakness ♦ *verb* 5 = **accustom**, adapt, educate, equip, habituate, inure, make ready, prepare, ready, tone up, train, work out

conditional *adjective* = **dependent**, contingent, limited, provisional, qualified, subject to, with reservations
➤ **Antonyms**
absolute, categorical, unconditional, unrestricted

conditioned *adjective* = **accustomed**, acclimatized, adapted, adjusted, familiarized, habituated, inured, made ready, prepared, seasoned, trained, used

conditioning *noun* 1 = **accustoming**, familiarization, grooming, hardening, inurement, preparation, readying, reorientation, seasoning, training ♦ *adjective* 2 = **toning**, astringent

conditions *plural noun* = **circumstances**, environment, milieu, situation, surroundings, way of life

condom *noun* = **sheath**, French letter (*slang*), French tickler (*slang*), rubber (*U.S. slang*), rubber johnny (*Brit. slang*), safe (*U.S. & Canad. slang*)

condone *verb* = **overlook**, disregard, excuse, forgive, let pass, look the other way, make allowance for, pardon, turn a blind eye to, wink at
➤ **Antonyms**
censure, condemn, denounce, disapprove, punish

conduct *noun* 1 = **behaviour**, attitude, bearing, carriage, comportment, demeanour, deportment, manners, mien (*literary*), ways 2 = **management**, administration, control, direction, guidance, handling, leadership, organization, running, supervision ♦ *verb* 3 = **carry out**, administer, control, direct, govern, handle, manage, organize, preside over, regulate, run, supervise 4 = **behave**, acquit, act, carry, comport, deport 5 = **accompany**, attend, chair, convey,

escort, guide, lead, pilot, steer, usher

confederacy *noun* = **union**, alliance, bund, coalition, compact, confederation, conspiracy, covenant, federation, league

confederate *noun* 1 = **associate**, abettor, accessory, accomplice, ally, colleague, partner ♦ *adjective* 2 = **allied**, associated, combined, federal, federated, in alliance ♦ *verb* 3 = **unite**, ally, amalgamate, associate, band together, combine, federate, merge

confer *verb* 1 = **discuss**, consult, converse, deliberate, discourse, parley, talk 2 = **grant**, accord, award, bestow, give, hand out, present, vouchsafe

conference *noun* = **meeting**, colloquium, congress, consultation, convention, convocation, discussion, forum, seminar, symposium, teach-in

confess *verb* 1 = **admit**, acknowledge, allow, blurt out, come clean (*informal*), come out of the closet, concede, confide, disclose, divulge, 'fess up (*U.S.*), get (something) off one's chest (*informal*), grant, make a clean breast of, own, own up, recognize, sing (*slang, chiefly U.S.*), spill one's guts (*slang*) 2 = **declare**, affirm, assert, attest, aver, confirm, evince, manifest, profess, prove, reveal
➤ **Antonyms**
≠**admit:** button one's lips, conceal, cover, deny, hide, hush up, keep mum, keep secret, keep under wraps, repudiate, suppress, withhold

confession *noun* = **admission**, acknowledgment, avowal, disclosure, divulgence, exposure, revelation, unbosoming

confidant, confidante *noun* = **close friend**, alter ego, bosom friend, crony, familiar, intimate

confide *verb* 1 = **tell**, admit, breathe, confess, disclose, divulge, impart, reveal, whisper 2 *Formal* = **entrust**, commend, commit, consign

confidence *noun* 1 = **trust**, belief, credence, dependence, faith, reliance 2 = **self-assurance**, aplomb, assurance, boldness, courage, firmness, nerve, self-possession, self-reliance 3 **in confidence** = **in secrecy**, between you and me (and the gatepost), confidentially, privately
➤ **Antonyms**
≠**trust:** disbelief, distrust, doubt, misgiving, mistrust ≠**self-assurance:** apprehension, fear, self-doubt, shyness, uncertainty

confident *adjective* 1 = **certain**, convinced, counting on, positive, satisfied, secure,

sure 2 = **self-assured**, assured, bold, can-do (*informal*), dauntless, fearless, self-reliant
> Antonyms
≠**certain**: doubtful, dubious, not sure, tentative, uncertain, unconvinced, unsure ≠**self-assured**: afraid, hesitant, insecure, jittery, lacking confidence, mousy, nervous, scared, self-doubting, unsure

confidential *adjective* 1 = **secret**, classified, hush-hush (*informal*), intimate, off the record, private, privy 2 = **trusted**, faithful, familiar, trustworthy, trusty

confidentially *adverb* = **in secret**, behind closed doors, between ourselves, in camera, in confidence, personally, privately, sub rosa

confine *verb* = **restrict**, bind, bound, cage, circumscribe, clip someone's wings, enclose, hem in, hold back, immure, imprison, incarcerate, intern, keep, limit, repress, restrain, shut up, straiten

confined *adjective* 1 = **restricted**, enclosed, limited 2 = **in childbirth**, in childbed, lying-in

confinement *noun* 1 = **imprisonment**, custody, detention, incarceration, internment, porridge (*slang*) 2 = **childbirth**, *accouchement*, childbed, labour, lying-in, parturition, time, travail

confines *plural noun* = **limits**, boundaries, bounds, circumference, edge, pale, precincts

confirm *verb* 1 = **prove**, approve, authenticate, bear out, corroborate, endorse, ratify, sanction, substantiate, validate, verify 2 = **strengthen**, assure, buttress, clinch, establish, fix, fortify, reinforce, settle

confirmation *noun* 1 = **proof**, authentication, corroboration, evidence, substantiation, testimony, validation, verification 2 = **sanction**, acceptance, agreement, approval, assent, endorsement, ratification
> Antonyms
≠**proof**: contradiction, denial, disavowal, repudiation ≠**sanction**: annulment, cancellation, disapproval, refusal, rejection

confirmed *adjective* = **long-established**, chronic, dyed-in-the-wool, habitual, hardened, ingrained, inured, inveterate, rooted, seasoned

confiscate *verb* = **seize**, appropriate, commandeer, expropriate, impound, sequester, sequestrate
> Antonyms
free, give, give back, hand back, release, restore, return

confiscation *noun* = **seizure**, appropriation, expropriation, forfeiture, impounding, sequestration, takeover

conflict *noun* 1 = **opposition**, antagonism, bad blood, difference, disagreement, discord, dissension, divided loyalties, friction, hostility, interference, strife, variance 2 = **battle**, clash, collision, combat, contention, contest, encounter, engagement, fight, fracas, head-to-head, set-to (*informal*), strife, war, warfare ♦ *verb* 3 = **be incompatible**, be at variance, clash, collide, combat, contend, contest, differ, disagree, fight, interfere, strive, struggle
> Antonyms
noun ≠**opposition**, **battle**: accord, agreement, harmony, peace, treaty, truce ♦ *verb* ≠**be incompatible**: agree, coincide, harmonize, reconcile

conflicting *adjective* = **incompatible**, antagonistic, clashing, contradictory, contrary, discordant, inconsistent, opposed, opposing, paradoxical
> Antonyms
accordant, agreeing, compatible, congruous, consistent, harmonious, similar, unopposing

conform *verb* 1 = **comply**, adapt, adjust, fall in with, follow, follow the crowd, obey, run with the pack, toe the line, yield 2 = **agree**, accord, assimilate, correspond, harmonize, match, square, suit, tally

conformation *noun* = **shape**, anatomy, arrangement, build, configuration, form, framework, outline, structure

conformist *noun* = **traditionalist**, Babbitt (*U.S.*), conventionalist, stick-in-the-mud (*informal*), yes man

conformity *noun* 1 = **compliance**, allegiance, Babbittry (*U.S.*), conventionality, observance, orthodoxy, traditionalism 2 = **likeness**, affinity, agreement, conformance, congruity, consonance, correspondence, harmony, resemblance, similarity

confound *verb* 1 = **bewilder**, amaze, astonish, astound, baffle, be all Greek to (*informal*), boggle the mind, confuse, dumbfound, flabbergast (*informal*), flummox, mix up, mystify, nonplus, perplex, startle, surprise 2 = **destroy**, annihilate, contradict, demolish, explode, make a nonsense of, overthrow, overwhelm, refute, ruin

confront *verb* = **face**, accost, beard, brave, bring face to face with, call out, challenge, defy, encounter, face off (*slang*), face the music, face up to, oppose, stand up to, tackle, walk into the lion's den
> Antonyms

avoid, body-swerve (*Scot.*), circumvent, dodge, evade, flee, give a wide berth to, keep *or* steer clear of, sidestep

confrontation *noun* = **conflict**, contest, crisis, encounter, face-off (*slang*), fight, head-to-head, set-to (*informal*), showdown (*informal*)

confuse *verb* **1** = **mix up**, blend, confound, disarrange, disorder, intermingle, involve, jumble, mingle, mistake, muddle, ravel, snarl up (*informal*), tangle **2** = **bewilder**, baffle, be all Greek to (*informal*), bemuse, darken, faze, flummox, muddy the waters, mystify, nonplus, obscure, perplex, puzzle **3** = **disconcert**, abash, addle, demoralize, discomfit, discompose, discountenance, disorient, embarrass, fluster, mortify, nonplus, rattle (*informal*), shame, throw into disorder, throw off balance, unnerve, upset

confused *adjective* **1** = **bewildered**, at a loss, at sea, at sixes and sevens, baffled, dazed, discombobulated (*informal, chiefly U.S. & Canad.*), disorganized, disorientated, flummoxed, muddled, muzzy (*U.S. informal*), nonplussed, not knowing if one is coming or going, not with it (*informal*), perplexed, puzzled, taken aback, thrown off balance, upset **2** = **disordered**, at sixes and sevens, chaotic, disarranged, disarrayed, disorderly, disorganized, higgledy-piggledy (*informal*), hugger-mugger (*archaic*), in disarray, jumbled, mistaken, misunderstood, mixed up, out of order, topsy-turvy, untidy
➤ **Antonyms**
≠**bewildered**: aware, enlightened, informed, on the ball (*informal*), with it (*informal*) ≠**disordered**: arranged, in order, ordered, orderly, organized, tidy

confusing *adjective* = **bewildering**, ambiguous, baffling, clear as mud (*informal*), complicated, contradictory, disconcerting, inconsistent, misleading, muddling, perplexing, puzzling, unclear
➤ **Antonyms**
clear, definite, explicit, plain, simple, straightforward, uncomplicated, understandable

confusion *noun* **1** = **bewilderment**, befuddlement, bemusement, disorientation, mystification, perplexity, puzzlement **2** = **disconcertion**, abashment, chagrin, demoralization, discomfiture, distraction, embarrassment, fluster, mind-fuck (*taboo slang*), perturbation **3** = **disorder**, bustle, chaos, clutter, commotion, disarrangement, disarray, disorganization, hodgepodge (*U.S.*),

hotchpotch, jumble, mess, muddle, pig's breakfast (*informal*), shambles, state, tangle, turmoil, untidiness, upheaval
➤ **Antonyms**
≠**bewilderment**: clarification, enlightenment, explanation, solution ≠**disorder**: arrangement, neatness, order, organization, tidiness

congenial *adjective* **1** = **pleasant**, affable, agreeable, companionable, complaisant, favourable, friendly, genial, kindly, pleasing **2** = **compatible**, adapted, fit, kindred, like-minded, suitable, sympathetic, well-suited

congenital *adjective* **1** = **inborn**, constitutional, immanent, inbred, inherent, innate, natural **2** *Informal* = **complete**, deep-dyed (*usually derogatory*), inveterate, thorough, utter

congested *adjective* **1** = **overcrowded**, crowded, teeming **2** = **clogged**, blocked-up, crammed, jammed, overfilled, overflowing, packed, stuffed, stuffed-up
➤ **Antonyms**
≠**overcrowded**: empty, half-full, uncrowded ≠**clogged**: clear, free, uncongested, unhampered, unhindered, unimpeded, unobstructed

congestion *noun* **1** = **overcrowding**, crowding **2** = **clogging**, bottleneck, jam, mass, snarl-up (*informal, chiefly Brit.*), surfeit

conglomerate *noun* **1** = **corporation**, agglomerate, aggregate, multinational ◆ *verb* **2** = **amass**, accumulate, agglomerate, aggregate, cluster, coalesce, snowball ◆ *adjective* **3** = **amassed**, clustered, composite, heterogeneous, massed

conglomeration *noun* = **mass**, accumulation, aggregation, assortment, combination, composite, hotchpotch, medley, miscellany, mishmash, potpourri

congratulate *verb* = **compliment**, felicitate, pat on the back, wish joy to

congratulations *plural noun, interjection* = **good wishes**, best wishes, compliments, felicitations, greetings, pat on the back

congregate *verb* = **come together**, assemble, collect, concentrate, convene, converge, convoke, flock, forgather, gather, mass, meet, muster, rally, rendezvous, throng
➤ **Antonyms**
break up, dispel, disperse, dissipate, part, scatter, separate, split up

congregation *noun* = **assembly**, brethren, crowd, fellowship, flock, host, laity, multitude, parish, parishioners, throng

congress noun = **meeting**, assembly, chamber of deputies, conclave, conference, convention, convocation, council, delegates, diet, house, legislative assembly, legislature, parliament, quango, representatives

conic, conical adjective = **cone-shaped**, conoid, funnel-shaped, pointed, pyramidal, tapered, tapering

conjecture noun **1** = **guess**, assumption, conclusion, fancy, guesstimate (informal), guesswork, hypothesis, inference, notion, presumption, shot in the dark, speculation, supposition, surmise, theorizing, theory ♦ verb **2** = **guess**, assume, fancy, hypothesize, imagine, infer, speculate, suppose, surmise, suspect, theorize

conjugal adjective = **marital**, bridal, connubial, hymeneal, married, matrimonial, nuptial, spousal, wedded

conjunction noun = **joining**, association, coincidence, combination, concurrence, juxtaposition, union

conjure verb **1** = **perform tricks**, juggle **2** = **summon up**, bewitch, call upon, cast a spell, charm, enchant, invoke, raise, rouse **3** Formal = **appeal to**, adjure, beg, beseech, crave, entreat, implore, importune, pray, supplicate

conjure up verb = **bring to mind**, contrive, create, evoke, produce as if by magic, recall, recollect

conjuror, conjurer noun = **magician**, illusionist, miracle-worker, sorcerer, thaumaturge (rare), wizard

connect verb = **link**, affix, ally, associate, attach, cohere, combine, couple, fasten, join, relate, unite
➤ Antonyms
detach, disconnect, dissociate, divide, part, separate, sever, unfasten

connected adjective **1** = **linked**, affiliated, akin, allied, associated, banded together, bracketed, combined, coupled, joined, related, united **2** Of speech = **coherent**, comprehensible, consecutive, intelligible

connection noun **1** = **association**, affiliation, affinity, bond, commerce, communication, correlation, correspondence, intercourse, interrelation, liaison, link, marriage, nexus, relation, relationship, relevance, tie-in **2** = **link**, alliance, association, attachment, coupling, fastening, junction, tie, union **3** = **contact**, acquaintance, ally, associate, friend, sponsor **4** = **relative**, kin, kindred, kinsman, kith, relation **5** = **context**, frame of reference, reference

connivance noun = **collusion**, abetment,

abetting, complicity, conspiring, tacit consent

connive verb **1** = **conspire**, cabal, collude, cook up (informal), intrigue, plot, scheme **2 connive at** = **turn a blind eye to**, abet, aid, be an accessory to, be a party to, be in collusion with, blink at, disregard, lend oneself to, let pass, look the other way, overlook, pass by, shut one's eyes to, wink at

connoisseur noun = **expert**, aficionado, appreciator, arbiter, authority, buff (informal), cognoscente, devotee, judge, maven (U.S.), savant, specialist, whiz (informal)

conquer verb **1** = **defeat**, beat, blow out of the water (slang), bring to their knees, checkmate, clobber (slang), crush, discomfit, get the better of, humble, lick (informal), make mincemeat of (informal), master, overcome, overpower, overthrow, prevail, put in their place, quell, rout, run rings around (informal), stuff (slang), subdue, subjugate, succeed, surmount, tank (slang), triumph, undo, vanquish, wipe the floor with (informal) **2** = **seize**, acquire, annex, obtain, occupy, overrun, win
➤ Antonyms
≠defeat: be defeated, capitulate, give in, give up, lose, quit, submit, surrender, throw in the towel, yield

conqueror noun = **winner**, champion, conquistador, defeater, hero, lord, master, subjugator, vanquisher, victor

conquest noun **1** = **defeat**, discomfiture, mastery, overthrow, pasting (slang), rout, triumph, vanquishment, victory **2** = **takeover**, acquisition, annexation, appropriation, coup, invasion, occupation, subjection, subjugation **3** = **captivation**, enchantment, enthralment, enticement, seduction **4** = **catch**, acquisition, adherent, admirer, fan, feather in one's cap, follower, prize, supporter, worshipper

conscience noun **1** = **principles**, moral sense, scruples, sense of right and wrong, still small voice **2 in all conscience** = **in fairness**, assuredly, certainly, fairly, honestly, in truth, rightly, truly

conscience-stricken adjective = **guilty**, ashamed, compunctious, contrite, disturbed, penitent, remorseful, repentant, sorry, troubled

conscientious adjective **1** = **thorough**, careful, diligent, exact, faithful, having one's nose to the grindstone, meticulous, painstaking, particular, punctilious **2** = **honourable**, high-minded, high-principled, honest, incorruptible, just,

moral, responsible, scrupulous, straightforward, strict, upright
> **Antonyms**
≠**thorough**: careless, irresponsible, negligent, remiss, slack, thoughtless, unconscientious, unreliable, untrustworthy
≠**honourable**: unprincipled, unscrupulous
conscious *adjective* **1** = **aware**, alert, alive to, awake, clued-up (*informal*), cognizant, percipient, responsive, sensible, sentient, wise to (*slang*) **2** = **deliberate**, calculated, intentional, knowing, premeditated, rational, reasoning, reflective, responsible, self-conscious, studied, wilful
> **Antonyms**
≠**aware**: ignorant, insensible, oblivious, unaware, unconscious ≠**deliberate**: accidental, uncalculated, unintended, unintentional, unplanned, unpremeditated, unwitting
consciousness *noun* = **awareness**, apprehension, knowledge, realization, recognition, sensibility
consecrate *verb* = **sanctify**, dedicate, devote, exalt, hallow, ordain, set apart, venerate
consecutive *adjective* = **successive**, chronological, following, in sequence, in turn, running, sequential, seriatim, succeeding, uninterrupted
consensus *noun* = **agreement**, assent, common consent, concord, concurrence, general agreement, harmony, unanimity, unity
consent *noun* **1** = **agreement**, acquiescence, approval, assent, compliance, concession, concurrence, go-ahead (*informal*), green light, O.K. or okay (*informal*), permission, sanction
♦ *verb* **2** = **agree**, accede, acquiesce, allow, approve, assent, comply, concede, concur, permit, play ball (*informal*), yield
> **Antonyms**
noun ≠**agreement**: disagreement, disapproval, dissent, refusal, unwillingness
♦ *verb* ≠**agree**: decline, demur, disagree, disapprove, dissent, refuse, resist
consequence *noun* **1** = **result**, effect, end, end result, event, issue, outcome, repercussion, sequel, upshot **2** = **importance**, account, concern, import, interest, moment, note, portent, significance, value, weight **3** = **status**, bottom, distinction, eminence, notability, rank, repute, standing **4 in consequence** = **as a result**, because, following
consequent *adjective* = **following**, ensuing, resultant, resulting, sequential, subsequent, successive
consequently *adverb* = **as a result**,

accordingly, ergo, hence, necessarily, subsequently, therefore, thus
conservation *noun* = **protection**, custody, economy, guardianship, husbandry, maintenance, preservation, safeguarding, safekeeping, saving, upkeep
conservative *adjective* **1** = **traditional**, cautious, conventional, die-hard, guarded, hidebound, middle-of-the-road, moderate, quiet, reactionary, sober ♦ *noun* **2** = **traditionalist**, die-hard, middle-of-the-roader, moderate, reactionary, stick-in-the-mud (*informal*)
> **Antonyms**
adjective ≠**traditional**: imaginative, innovative, liberal, progressive, radical
♦ *noun* ≠**traditionalist**: changer, innovator, progressive, radical
Conservative *adjective* **1** = **Tory**, right-wing ♦ *noun* **2** = **Tory**, right-winger
conservatory *noun* = **greenhouse**, glasshouse, hothouse
conserve *verb* = **protect**, go easy on, hoard, husband, keep, nurse, preserve, save, store up, take care of, use sparingly
> **Antonyms**
be extravagant, blow (*slang*), dissipate, fritter away, misspend, misuse, spend, spend like water, squander, use up, waste
consider *verb* **1** = **think**, believe, deem, hold to be, judge, rate, regard as **2** = **think about**, chew over, cogitate, consult, contemplate, deliberate, discuss, examine, eye up, meditate, mull over, muse, ponder, reflect, revolve, ruminate, study, turn over in one's mind, weigh, work over **3** = **bear in mind**, care for, keep in view, make allowance for, reckon with, regard, remember, respect, take into account
considerable *adjective* **1** = **large**, abundant, ample, appreciable, comfortable, goodly, great, lavish, marked, much, noticeable, plentiful, reasonable, sizable or sizeable, substantial, tidy, tolerable **2** = **important**, distinguished, influential, notable, noteworthy, renowned, significant, venerable
> **Antonyms**
≠**large**: insignificant, insubstantial, meagre, paltry, small ≠**important**: insignificant, ordinary, unimportant, unremarkable
considerably *adverb* = **greatly**, appreciably, markedly, noticeably, remarkably, seriously (*informal*), significantly, substantially, very much
considerate *adjective* = **thoughtful**, attentive, charitable, circumspect, concerned, discreet, forbearing, kind,

kindly, mindful, obliging, patient, tactful, unselfish
➤ **Antonyms**
heedless, inconsiderate, selfish, thoughtless
consideration *noun* 1 = **thought**, analysis, attention, cogitation, contemplation, deliberation, discussion, examination, perusal, reflection, regard, review, scrutiny, study 2 = **factor**, concern, issue, point 3 = **thoughtfulness**, concern, considerateness, friendliness, kindliness, kindness, respect, solicitude, tact 4 = **payment**, fee, perquisite, recompense, remuneration, reward, tip 5 **take into consideration = bear in mind**, make allowance for, take into account, weigh
considering *preposition* 1 = **taking into account**, in the light of, in view of ♦ *adverb* 2 *Informal* = **all things considered**, all in all
consignment *noun* 1 = **shipment**, batch, delivery, goods 2 = **handing over**, assignment, committal, entrusting, relegation 3 = **sending**, dispatch, distribution, shipment, transmittal
consist *verb* 1 **consist of = be made up of**, amount to, be composed of, comprise, contain, embody, include, incorporate, involve 2 **consist in = lie in**, be expressed by, be found *or* contained in, inhere in, reside in
consistency *noun* 1 = **texture**, compactness, density, firmness, thickness, viscosity 2 = **constancy**, evenness, regularity, steadfastness, steadiness, uniformity
consistent *adjective* 1 = **unchanging**, constant, dependable, persistent, regular, steady, true to type, undeviating 2 = **agreeing**, accordant, all of a piece, coherent, compatible, congruous, consonant, harmonious, logical
➤ **Antonyms**
≠**unchanging**: changing, deviating, erratic, inconsistent, irregular ≠**agreeing**: contradictory, contrary, discordant, incompatible, incongruous, inconsistent, inharmonious
consolation *noun* = **comfort**, alleviation, assuagement, cheer, ease, easement, encouragement, help, relief, solace, succour, support
console *verb* = **comfort**, assuage, calm, cheer, encourage, express sympathy for, relieve, solace, soothe
➤ **Antonyms**
aggravate (*informal*), agitate, annoy, discomfort, distress, hassle (*informal*), hurt, sadden, torment, trouble, upset
consolidate *verb* 1 = **strengthen**, fortify,

reinforce, secure, stabilize 2 = **combine**, amalgamate, cement, compact, condense, conjoin, federate, fuse, harden, join, solidify, thicken, unite
consolidation *noun* 1 = **strengthening**, fortification, reinforcement 2 = **combination**, alliance, amalgamation, association, compression, condensation, federation, fusion
consort *verb* 1 = **associate**, fraternize, go around with, hang about, around *or* out with, hang with (*informal, chiefly U.S.*), keep company, mingle, mix 2 = **agree**, accord, be consistent, correspond, harmonize, square, tally ♦ *noun* 3 = **spouse**, associate, companion, fellow, husband, partner, significant other (*U.S. informal*), wife
conspicuous *adjective* 1 = **obvious**, apparent, blatant, clear, discernible, easily seen, evident, manifest, noticeable, patent, perceptible, salient, visible 2 = **noteworthy**, celebrated, distinguished, eminent, famous, illustrious, notable, outstanding, prominent, remarkable, salient, signal, striking
➤ **Antonyms**
≠**obvious**: concealed, hidden, imperceptible, inconspicuous, indiscernible, invisible, obscure, unnoticeable ≠**noteworthy**: humble, inconspicuous, insignificant, ordinary, unacclaimed, undistinguished, unmemorable, unnotable
conspiracy *noun* = **plot**, cabal, collusion, confederacy, frame-up (*slang*), intrigue, league, machination, scheme, treason
conspirator *noun* = **plotter**, cabalist, conspirer, intriguer, schemer, traitor
conspire *verb* 1 = **plot**, cabal, confederate, contrive, devise, hatch treason, intrigue, machinate, manoeuvre, plan, scheme 2 = **work together**, combine, concur, conduce, contribute, cooperate, tend
constancy *noun* 1 = **steadiness**, firmness, fixedness, permanence, perseverance, regularity, stability, steadfastness, tenacity, uniformity 2 = **faithfulness**, devotion, fidelity
constant *adjective* 1 = **continuous**, ceaseless, continual, endless, eternal, everlasting, incessant, interminable, never-ending, nonstop, perpetual, persistent, relentless, sustained, uninterrupted, unrelenting, unremitting 2 = **unchanging**, continual, even, firm, fixed, habitual, immovable, immutable, invariable, permanent, perpetual, regular, stable, steadfast, steady, unalterable, unbroken, uniform, unvarying 3 = **faithful**,

attached, dependable, devoted, loyal, stalwart, staunch, tried-and-true, true, trustworthy, trusty, unfailing
➤ Antonyms
≠**continuous:** erratic, inconstant, intermittent, irregular, occasional, random, unsustained ≠**unchanging:** changeable, changing, deviating, uneven, unstable, variable ≠**faithful:** disloyal, fickle, irresolute, undependable

constantly *adverb* = **continuously**, all the time, always, aye (*Scot.*), continually, endlessly, everlastingly, incessantly, interminably, invariably, morning, noon and night, night and day, nonstop, perpetually, persistently, relentlessly
➤ Antonyms
(every) now and then, every so often, from time to time, intermittently, irregularly, now and again, occasionally, off and on, periodically, sometimes

consternation *noun* = **dismay**, alarm, amazement, anxiety, awe, bewilderment, confusion, distress, dread, fear, fright, horror, panic, shock, terror, trepidation

constituent *noun* 1 = **voter**, elector 2 = **component**, element, essential, factor, ingredient, part, principle, unit ◆ *adjective* 3 = **component**, basic, elemental, essential, integral

constitute *verb* 1 = **make up**, compose, comprise, create, enact, establish, fix, form, found, make, set up 2 = **set up**, appoint, authorize, commission, delegate, depute, empower, name, nominate, ordain

constitution *noun* 1 = **health**, build, character, disposition, physique, temper, temperament 2 = **structure**, composition, form, make-up, nature 3 = **establishment**, composition, formation, organization

constitutional *adjective* 1 = **statutory**, chartered, vested 2 = **inherent**, congenital, immanent, inborn, intrinsic, organic ◆ *noun* 3 = **walk**, airing, stroll, turn

constrain *verb* 1 = **force**, bind, coerce, compel, drive, impel, necessitate, oblige, pressure, pressurize, urge 2 = **restrict**, chain, check, confine, constrict, curb, hem in, rein, restrain, straiten

constrained *adjective* = **forced**, embarrassed, guarded, inhibited, reserved, reticent, subdued, unnatural

constraint *noun* 1 = **restriction**, check, curb, damper, deterrent, hindrance, limitation, rein 2 = **force**, coercion, compulsion, necessity, pressure, restraint 3 = **repression**, bashfulness, diffidence, embarrassment, inhibition, reservation, restraint, timidity

construct *verb* = **build**, assemble,

compose, create, design, elevate, engineer, erect, establish, fabricate, fashion, form, formulate, found, frame, make, manufacture, organize, put together, put up, raise, set up, shape
➤ Antonyms
bulldoze, demolish, destroy, devastate, dismantle, flatten, knock down, level, pull down, raze, tear down

construction *noun* 1 = **building**, assembly, composition, creation, edifice, erection, fabrication, formation 2 = **structure**, composition, fabric, figure, form, shape 3 *Formal* = **interpretation**, explanation, inference, reading, rendering, take (*informal, chiefly U.S.*)

constructive *adjective* = **helpful**, positive, practical, productive, useful, valuable
➤ Antonyms
destructive, futile, ineffective, limp-wristed, negative, unhelpful, unproductive, useless, vain, worthless

consult *verb* 1 = **ask**, ask advice of, commune, compare notes, confer, consider, debate, deliberate, interrogate, pick (someone's) brains, question, refer to, take counsel, turn to 2 = **consider**, have regard for, regard, respect, take account of, take into consideration

consultant *noun* = **specialist**, adviser, authority

consultation *noun* = **seminar**, appointment, conference, council, deliberation, dialogue, discussion, examination, hearing, interview, meeting, session

consume *verb* 1 = **eat**, devour, eat up, gobble (up), guzzle, polish off (*informal*), put away, swallow 2 = **use up**, absorb, deplete, dissipate, drain, eat up, employ, exhaust, expend, finish up, fritter away, lavish, lessen, spend, squander, use, utilize, vanish, waste, wear out 3 = **destroy**, annihilate, decay, demolish, devastate, lay waste, ravage 4 *often passive* = **obsess**, absorb, devour, dominate, eat up, engross, monopolize, preoccupy

consumer *noun* = **buyer**, customer, purchaser, shopper, user

consuming *adjective* = **overwhelming**, absorbing, compelling, devouring, engrossing, excruciating, gripping, immoderate, tormenting

consummate *verb* 1 = **complete**, accomplish, achieve, carry out, compass, conclude, crown, effectuate, end, finish, fulfil, perfect, perform, put the tin lid on ◆ *adjective* 2 = **skilled**, accomplished, matchless, perfect, polished, practised, superb, supreme 3 = **complete**, absolute,

conspicuous, deep-dyed (*usually derogatory*), extreme, supreme, total, transcendent, ultimate, unqualified, utter
➤ **Antonyms**
verb ≠**complete**: begin, commence, conceive, get under way, inaugurate, initiate, originate, start

consumption *noun* **1** = **using up**, consuming, decay, decrease, depletion, destruction, diminution, dissipation, drain, exhaustion, expenditure, loss, use, utilization, waste **2** *Old-fashioned* = **tuberculosis**, atrophy, emaciation, phthisis, T.B.

contact *noun* **1** = **communication**, association, connection **2** = **touch**, approximation, contiguity, junction, juxtaposition, union **3** = **acquaintance**, connection ♦ *verb* **4** = **get** *or* **be in touch with**, approach, call, communicate with, get hold of, phone, reach, ring (up) (*informal, chiefly Brit.*), speak to, touch base with (*U.S. & Canad. informal*), write to

contagious *adjective* = **infectious**, catching, communicable, epidemic, epizootic (*Veterinary medicine*), pestiferous, pestilential, spreading, taking (*informal*), transmissible

contain *verb* **1** = **hold**, accommodate, enclose, have capacity for, incorporate, seat **2** = **include**, comprehend, comprise, consist of, embody, embrace, involve **3** = **restrain**, control, curb, hold back, hold in, keep a tight rein on, repress, stifle

container *noun* = **holder**, receptacle, repository, vessel

contaminate *verb* = **pollute**, adulterate, befoul, corrupt, defile, deprave, infect, radioactivate, smirch, soil, stain, sully, taint, tarnish, vitiate
➤ **Antonyms**
clean, cleanse, decontaminate, deodorize, disinfect, fumigate, purify, sanitize, sterilize

contamination *noun* = **pollution**, adulteration, contagion, corruption, decay, defilement, dirtying, filth, foulness, impurity, infection, poisoning, radioactivation, rottenness, taint

contemplate *verb* **1** = **think about**, brood over, consider, deliberate, meditate, meditate on, mull over, muse over, observe, ponder, reflect upon, revolve *or* turn over in one's mind, ruminate (upon) **2** = **consider**, aspire to, design, envisage, expect, foresee, have in view *or* in mind, intend, mean, plan, propose, think of **3** = **look at**, behold, check out (*informal*), examine, eye, eye up, gaze at, inspect, recce (*slang*), regard, scrutinize, stare at, study, survey, view, weigh

contemplation *noun* **1** = **thought**, cogitation, consideration, deliberation, meditation, musing, pondering, reflection, reverie, rumination **2** = **looking at**, examination, gazing at, inspection, observation, recce (*slang*), scrutiny, survey, viewing

contemplative *adjective* = **thoughtful**, deep *or* lost in thought, in a brown study, intent, introspective, meditative, musing, pensive, rapt, reflective, ruminative

contemporary *adjective* **1** = **coexisting**, coetaneous (*rare*), coeval, coexistent, concurrent, contemporaneous, synchronous **2** = **modern**, à la mode, current, happening (*informal*), in fashion, latest, newfangled, present, present-day, recent, trendy (*Brit. informal*), ultramodern, up-to-date, up-to-the-minute, with it (*informal*) ♦ *noun* **3** = **peer**, compeer, fellow
➤ **Antonyms**
adjective ≠**modern**: antecedent, antique, early, obsolete, old, old-fashioned, out-of-date, passé

contempt *noun* = **scorn**, condescension, contumely, derision, despite (*archaic*), disdain, disregard, disrespect, mockery, neglect, slight
➤ **Antonyms**
admiration, esteem, honour, liking, regard, respect

contemptible *adjective* = **despicable**, abject, base, cheap, degenerate, detestable, ignominious, low, low-down (*informal*), mean, measly, paltry, pitiful, scurvy, shabby, shameful, vile, worthless
➤ **Antonyms**
admirable, attractive, honourable, laudable, pleasant, praiseworthy

contemptuous *adjective* = **scornful**, arrogant, cavalier, condescending, derisive, disdainful, haughty, high and mighty, insolent, insulting, on one's high horse (*informal*), sneering, supercilious, withering
➤ **Antonyms**
civil, courteous, deferential, gracious, humble, mannerly, obsequious, polite, respectful

contend *verb* **1** = **compete**, clash, contest, cope, emulate, fight, grapple, jostle, litigate, skirmish, strive, struggle, vie **2** = **argue**, affirm, allege, assert, aver, avow, debate, dispute, hold, maintain

content[1] *noun* **1** = **meaning**, burden, essence, gist, ideas, matter, significance, substance, text, thoughts **2** = **amount**, capacity, load, measure, size, volume

content[2] *adjective* **1** = **satisfied**, agreeable, at ease, comfortable, contented, fulfilled, willing to accept ♦ *verb* **2 = satisfy**, appease, delight, gladden, gratify, humour, indulge, mollify, placate, please, reconcile, sate, suffice ♦ *noun* **3 = satisfaction**, comfort, contentment, ease, gratification, peace, peace of mind, pleasure

contented *adjective* **= satisfied**, at ease, at peace, cheerful, comfortable, complacent, content, glad, gratified, happy, pleased, serene, thankful
➤ **Antonyms**
annoyed, discontented, displeased, dissatisfied, pissed off (*taboo slang*), troubled, uncomfortable, uneasy

contention *noun* **1 = dispute**, bone of contention, competition, contest, disagreement, discord, dissension, enmity, feuding, hostility, rivalry, row, strife, struggle, wrangling **2 = assertion**, affirmation, allegation, argument, asseveration, belief, claim, declaration, ground, idea, maintaining, opinion, position, profession, stand, thesis, view

contentious *adjective* **= argumentative**, bickering, cantankerous, captious, cavilling, combative, cross, disputatious, factious, litigious, peevish, perverse, pugnacious, quarrelsome, querulous, wrangling

contentment *noun* **= satisfaction**, comfort, complacency, content, contentedness, ease, equanimity, fulfilment, gladness, gratification, happiness, peace, pleasure, repletion, serenity
➤ **Antonyms**
discomfort, discontent, discontentment, displeasure, dissatisfaction, uneasiness, unhappiness

contents *plural noun* **1 = constituents**, elements, ingredients, load **2 = chapters**, divisions, subject matter, subjects, themes, topics

contest *noun* **1 = competition**, game, head-to-head, match, tournament, trial **2 = struggle**, affray, altercation, battle, combat, conflict, controversy, debate, discord, dispute, encounter, fight, shock ♦ *verb* **3 = dispute**, argue, call in or into question, challenge, debate, doubt, litigate, object to, oppose, question **4 = compete**, contend, fight, fight over, strive, vie

contestant *noun* **= competitor**, aspirant, candidate, contender, entrant, participant, player

context *noun* **1 = circumstances**, ambience, conditions, situation **2 = frame**

of reference, background, connection, framework, relation

continent *adjective* **= self-restrained**, abstemious, abstinent, ascetic, austere, celibate, chaste, sober

contingency *noun* **= possibility**, accident, chance, emergency, event, eventuality, fortuity, happening, incident, juncture, uncertainty

contingent *noun* **1 = group**, batch, body, bunch (*informal*), deputation, detachment, mission, quota, section, set ♦ *adjective* **2 = chance**, accidental, casual, fortuitous, haphazard, random, uncertain **3 contingent on** or **upon = dependent on**, conditional on, controlled by, subject to

continual *adjective* **= constant**, continuous, endless, eternal, everlasting, frequent, incessant, interminable, oft-repeated, perpetual, recurrent, regular, repeated, repetitive, unceasing, uninterrupted, unremitting
➤ **Antonyms**
broken, ceasing, erratic, fluctuating, fragmentary, infrequent, intermittent, interrupted, irregular, occasional, periodic, spasmodic, sporadic

continually *adverb* **= constantly**, all the time, always, aye (*Scot.*), endlessly, eternally, everlastingly, forever, incessantly, interminably, nonstop, persistently, repeatedly

continuance *noun* **= duration**, continuation, period, protraction, term

continuation *noun* **1 = continuing**, maintenance, perpetuation, prolongation, resumption **2 = addition**, extension, furtherance, postscript, sequel, supplement

continue *verb* **1 = remain**, abide, carry on, endure, last, live on, persist, rest, stay, stay on, survive **2 = keep on**, carry on, go on, keep at, keep one's hand in, keep the ball rolling, keep up, maintain, persevere, persist in, prolong, pursue, stick at, stick to, sustain **3 = resume**, carry on, pick up where one left off, proceed, recommence, return to, take up **4 = go on**, draw out, extend, lengthen, project, prolong, reach
➤ **Antonyms**
≠**remain**: abdicate, leave, quit, resign, retire, step down ≠**keep on**, **resume**: break off, call it a day, cease, discontinue, give up, leave off, pack in (*Brit. informal*), quit, stop

continuing *adjective* **= lasting**, enduring, in progress, ongoing, sustained

continuity *noun* **= sequence**, cohesion, connection, flow, interrelationship, progression, succession, whole

continuous adjective = **constant**, connected, continued, extended, prolonged, unbroken, unceasing, undivided, uninterrupted
➤ Antonyms
broken, disconnected, ending, inconstant, intermittent, interrupted, occasional, passing, spasmodic

contour noun = **outline**, curve, figure, form, lines, profile, relief, shape, silhouette

contraband noun 1 = **smuggling**, black-marketing, bootlegging, moonshine (U.S.), rum-running, trafficking ◆ adjective 2 = **smuggled**, banned, black-market, bootleg, bootlegged, forbidden, hot (informal), illegal, illicit, interdicted, prohibited, unlawful

contract noun 1 = **agreement**, arrangement, bargain, bond, commission, commitment, compact, concordat, convention, covenant, deal (informal), engagement, pact, settlement, stipulation, treaty, understanding ◆ verb 2 = **agree**, arrange, bargain, clinch, close, come to terms, commit oneself, covenant, engage, enter into, negotiate, pledge, shake hands, stipulate 3 = **shorten**, abbreviate, abridge, compress, condense, confine, constrict, curtail, diminish, dwindle, epitomize, knit, lessen, narrow, pucker, purse, reduce, shrink, shrivel, tighten, wither, wrinkle 4 = **catch**, acquire, be afflicted with, develop, get, go down with, incur
➤ Antonyms
verb ≠**agree**: decline, disagree, refuse, turn down ≠**shorten**: broaden, develop, distend, enlarge, expand, grow, increase, inflate, multiply, spread, stretch, swell, widen ≠**catch**: avert, avoid, escape, ward off

contraction noun = **shortening**, abbreviation, compression, constriction, diminution, drawing in, elision, narrowing, reduction, shrinkage, shrivelling, tensing, tightening

contradict verb = **deny**, be at variance with, belie, challenge, contravene, controvert, counter, counteract, dispute, fly in the face of, gainsay (archaic or literary), impugn, make a nonsense of, negate, oppose, rebut
➤ Antonyms
affirm, agree, authenticate, confirm, defend, endorse, support, verify

contradiction noun = **denial**, conflict, confutation, contravention, incongruity, inconsistency, negation, opposite

contradictory adjective = **inconsistent**, antagonistic, antithetical, conflicting, contrary, discrepant, incompatible, irreconcilable, opposed, opposite, paradoxical, repugnant

contraption noun Informal = **device**, apparatus, contrivance, gadget, instrument, mechanism, rig, waldo

contrary noun 1 = **opposite**, antithesis, converse, reverse 2 **on the contrary** = **quite the opposite** or **reverse**, conversely, in contrast, not at all, on the other hand ◆ adjective 3 = **opposed**, adverse, antagonistic, clashing, contradictory, counter, discordant, hostile, inconsistent, inimical, opposite, paradoxical 4 = **perverse**, awkward, balky, cantankerous, cussed (informal), difficult, disobliging, froward (archaic), intractable, obstinate, stroppy (Brit. slang), thrawn (Northern English dialect), unaccommodating, wayward, wilful
➤ Antonyms
adjective ≠**opposed**: accordant, congruous, consistent, harmonious, in agreement, parallel, unopposed ≠**perverse**: accommodating, agreeable, amiable, cooperative, eager to please, helpful, obliging, tractable, willing

contrast noun 1 = **difference**, comparison, contrariety, differentiation, disparity, dissimilarity, distinction, divergence, foil, opposition ◆ verb 2 = **differentiate**, compare, differ, distinguish, oppose, set in opposition, set off

contribute verb 1 = **give**, add, afford, bestow, chip in (informal), donate, furnish, provide, subscribe, supply 2 **contribute to** = **be partly responsible for**, be conducive to, be instrumental in, conduce to, help, lead to, tend to

contribution noun = **gift**, addition, bestowal, donation, grant, input, offering, stipend, subscription

contributor noun 1 = **giver**, backer, bestower, conferrer, donor, patron, subscriber, supporter 2 = **writer**, correspondent, freelance, freelancer, journalist, journo (slang), reporter

contrite adjective = **sorry**, chastened, conscience-stricken, humble, in sackcloth and ashes, penitent, regretful, remorseful, repentant, sorrowful

contrivance noun 1 = **device**, apparatus, appliance, contraption, equipment, gadget, gear, implement, instrument, invention, machine, mechanism 2 = **plan**, artifice, design, dodge, expedient, fabrication, formation, intrigue, inventiveness, machination, measure, plot, project, ruse, scheme, stratagem, trick

contrive verb 1 = **bring about**, arrange, effect, hit upon, manage, manoeuvre, plan, plot, scheme, succeed **2 = devise,** concoct, construct, create, design, engineer, fabricate, frame, improvise, invent, manufacture, wangle (*informal*)

contrived *adjective* = **forced,** artificial, elaborate, laboured, overdone, planned, recherché, strained, unnatural
➤ **Antonyms**
genuine, natural, relaxed, spontaneous, unaffected, unconstrained, unfeigned, unforced, unpretentious

control *noun* **1 = power,** authority, charge, command, direction, discipline, government, guidance, jurisdiction, management, mastery, oversight, rule, superintendence, supervision, supremacy **2 = restraint,** brake, check, curb, limitation, regulation ◆ *verb* **3 = have power over,** administer, boss (*informal*), call the shots, call the tune, command, conduct, direct, dominate, govern, handle, have charge of, have (someone) in one's pocket, hold the purse strings, keep a tight rein on, keep on a string, lead, manage, manipulate, oversee, pilot, reign over, rule, steer, superintend, supervise **4 = restrain,** bridle, check, constrain, contain, curb, hold back, limit, master, rein in, repress, subdue

controls *plural noun* = **instruments,** console, control panel, dash, dashboard, dials

controversial *adjective* = **disputed,** at issue, contended, contentious, controvertible, debatable, disputable, open to question, polemic, under discussion

controversy *noun* = **argument,** altercation, contention, debate, discussion, dispute, dissension, polemic, quarrel, row, squabble, strife, wrangle, wrangling

convalescence *noun* = **recovery,** improvement, recuperation, rehabilitation, return to health

convalescent *adjective* = **recovering,** getting better, improving, mending, on the mend, recuperating

convene *verb* = **gather,** assemble, bring together, call, come together, congregate, convoke, meet, muster, rally, summon

convenience *noun* **1 = usefulness,** accessibility, advantage, appropriateness, availability, benefit, fitness, handiness, opportuneness, serviceability, suitability, utility **2 = suitable time,** chance, leisure, opportunity, spare moment, spare time **3 = appliance,** amenity, comfort, facility, help, labour-saving device
➤ **Antonyms**
≠**usefulness:** inconvenience, uselessness

convenient *adjective* **1 = useful,** adapted, appropriate, beneficial, commodious, fit, fitted, handy, helpful, labour-saving, opportune, seasonable, serviceable, suitable, suited, timely, well-timed **2 = nearby,** accessible, at hand, available, close at hand, handy, just round the corner, within reach
➤ **Antonyms**
≠**useful:** awkward, inconvenient, unsuitable, useless ≠**nearby:** distant, inaccessible, inconvenient, out-of-the-way

convent *noun* = **nunnery,** convent school, religious community

convention *noun* **1 = custom,** code, etiquette, formality, practice, propriety, protocol, tradition, usage **2 = agreement,** bargain, compact, concordat, contract, pact, protocol, stipulation, treaty **3 = assembly,** conference, congress, convocation, council, delegates, meeting, representatives

conventional *adjective* **1 = ordinary,** accepted, bog-standard (*Brit. & Irish slang*), common, correct, customary, decorous, expected, formal, habitual, normal, orthodox, prevailing, prevalent, proper, regular, ritual, standard, traditional, usual, wonted **2 = unoriginal,** banal, bourgeois, commonplace, hackneyed, hidebound, pedestrian, Pooterish, prosaic, routine, run-of-the-mill, stereotyped, vanilla (*slang*)
➤ **Antonyms**
abnormal, left-field (*informal*), off-the-wall (*slang*), uncommon, unconventional, unorthodox

converge *verb* = **come together,** coincide, combine, concentrate, focus, gather, join, meet, merge, mingle

conversant *adjective* **conversant with = experienced in,** acquainted with, *au fait* with, familiar with, knowledgeable about, practised in, proficient in, skilled in, versed in, well-informed about, well up in (*informal*)

conversation *noun* = **talk,** chat, chinwag (*Brit. informal*), colloquy, communication, communion, confab (*informal*), confabulation, conference, converse, dialogue, discourse, discussion, exchange, gossip, intercourse, powwow, tête-à-tête

conversational *adjective* = **chatty,** colloquial, communicative, informal

converse[1] *verb* = **talk,** chat, commune, confer, discourse, exchange views

converse[2] *noun* **1 = opposite,** antithesis, contrary, obverse, other side of the coin, reverse ◆ *adjective* **2 = opposite,** contrary, counter, reverse, reversed, transposed

conversion noun 1 = **change,** metamorphosis, transfiguration, transformation, transmogrification (jocular), transmutation 2 = **adaptation,** alteration, modification, reconstruction, remodelling, reorganization 3 = **reformation,** change of heart, proselytization, rebirth, regeneration

convert verb 1 = **change,** alter, interchange, metamorphose, transform, transmogrify (jocular), transmute, transpose, turn 2 = **adapt,** apply, appropriate, customize, modify, remodel, reorganize, restyle, revise 3 = **reform,** baptize, bring to God, convince, proselytize, regenerate, save ♦ noun 4 = **neophyte,** catechumen, disciple, proselyte

convex adjective = **rounded,** bulging, gibbous, outcurved, protuberant
➤ **Antonyms**
concave, cupped, depressed, excavated, hollowed, indented, sunken

convey verb 1 = **communicate,** disclose, impart, make known, relate, reveal, tell 2 = **carry,** bear, bring, conduct, fetch, forward, grant, guide, move, send, support, transmit, transport 3 Law = **transfer,** bequeath, cede, deliver, demise, devolve, grant, lease, will

conveyance noun 1 Old-fashioned = **vehicle,** transport 2 = **transportation,** carriage, movement, transfer, transference, transmission, transport

convict verb 1 = **find guilty,** condemn, imprison, pronounce guilty, sentence ♦ noun 2 = **prisoner,** con (slang), criminal, culprit, felon, jailbird, lag (slang), malefactor, villain

conviction noun 1 = **belief,** creed, faith, opinion, persuasion, principle, tenet, view 2 = **confidence,** assurance, certainty, certitude, earnestness, fervour, firmness, reliance

convince verb = **persuade,** assure, bring round, gain the confidence of, prevail upon, prove to, satisfy, sway, win over

convincing adjective = **persuasive,** cogent, conclusive, credible, impressive, incontrovertible, likely, plausible, powerful, probable, telling, verisimilar
➤ **Antonyms**
beyond belief, cock-and-bull (informal), dubious, far-fetched, implausible, improbable, inconclusive, incredible, unconvincing, unlikely

convoy noun 1 = **escort,** armed guard, attendance, attendant, guard, protection ♦ verb 2 = **escort,** accompany, attend, guard, pilot, protect, shepherd, usher

convulse verb = **shake,** agitate, churn up, derange, disorder, disturb, shatter, twist, work

convulsion noun 1 = **spasm,** contortion, contraction, cramp, fit, paroxysm, seizure, throe (rare), tremor 2 = **upheaval,** agitation, commotion, disturbance, furore, shaking, tumult, turbulence

cook up verb Informal = **invent,** concoct, contrive, devise, dream up, fabricate, improvise, manufacture, plot, prepare, scheme, trump up

cool adjective 1 = **cold,** chilled, chilling, chilly, coldish, nippy, refreshing 2 = **calm,** collected, composed, deliberate, dispassionate, imperturbable, laid-back (informal), level-headed, placid, quiet, relaxed, sedate, self-controlled, self-possessed, serene, together (slang), unemotional, unexcited, unfazed (informal), unruffled 3 = **unfriendly,** aloof, apathetic, distant, frigid, incurious, indifferent, lukewarm, offhand, reserved, standoffish, uncommunicative, unconcerned, unenthusiastic, uninterested, unresponsive, unwelcoming 4 = **impudent,** audacious, bold, brazen, cheeky, impertinent, presumptuous, shameless 5 Informal = **sophisticated,** cosmopolitan, elegant, urbane ♦ verb 6 = **chill,** cool off, freeze, lose heat, refrigerate 7 = **calm (down),** abate, allay, assuage, dampen, lessen, moderate, quiet, temper ♦ noun 8 Slang = **calmness,** composure, control, poise, self-control, self-discipline, self-possession, temper
➤ **Antonyms**
adjective ≠**cold:** lukewarm, moderately hot, sunny, tepid, warm ≠**calm:** agitated, antsy (informal), delirious, excited, impassioned, nervous, overwrought, perturbed, tense, troubled, twitchy (informal) ≠**unfriendly:** amiable, chummy (informal), cordial, friendly, outgoing, receptive, responsive, sociable, warm ♦ verb ≠**chill:** heat, reheat, take the chill off, thaw, warm (up)

coop noun 1 = **pen,** box, cage, corral (chiefly U.S. & Canad.), enclosure, hutch, pound ♦ verb 2 coop up = **confine,** cage, immure, impound, imprison, pen, pound, shut up

cooperate verb 1 = **work together,** collaborate, combine, concur, conduce, conspire, coordinate, join forces, pool resources, pull together 2 = **help,** abet, aid, assist, contribute, go along with, lend a helping hand, pitch in, play ball (informal)
➤ **Antonyms**
conflict, contend with, fight, hamper,

hamstring, hinder, impede, obstruct, oppose, prevent, put the mockers on (*informal*), resist, struggle against, stymie, thwart

cooperation *noun* 1 = **teamwork**, collaboration, combined effort, concert, concurrence, esprit de corps, give-and-take, unity 2 = **help**, assistance, helpfulness, participation, responsiveness
➤ **Antonyms**
discord, dissension, hindrance, opposition, rivalry

cooperative *adjective* 1 = **helpful**, accommodating, obliging, onside (*informal*), responsive, supportive 2 = **shared**, coactive, collective, combined, concerted, coordinated, joint, unified, united

coordinate *verb* 1 = **bring together**, correlate, harmonize, integrate, match, mesh, organize, relate, synchronize, systematize ◆ *adjective* 2 = **equivalent**, coequal, correlative, correspondent, equal, parallel, tantamount

cope *verb* 1 = **manage**, carry on, get by (*informal*), hold one's own, make out (*informal*), make the grade, rise to the occasion, struggle through, survive 2 **cope with** = **deal with**, contend with, dispatch, encounter, grapple with, handle, struggle with, tangle with, tussle with, weather, wrestle with

copious *adjective* = **abundant**, ample, bounteous, bountiful, extensive, exuberant, full, generous, lavish, liberal, luxuriant, overflowing, plenteous, plentiful, profuse, rich, superabundant

copulate *verb* = **have intercourse**, ball (*taboo slang, chiefly U.S.*), bonk (*informal*), fuck (*taboo slang*), have sex, hump (*taboo slang*), screw (*taboo slang*), shag (*taboo slang, chiefly Brit.*)

copy *noun* 1 = **reproduction**, archetype, carbon copy, counterfeit, duplicate, facsimile, fake, fax, forgery, image, imitation, likeness, model, pattern, photocopy, Photostat (*Trademark*), print, replica, replication, representation, transcription, Xerox (*Trademark*) ◆ *verb* 2 = **reproduce**, counterfeit, duplicate, photocopy, Photostat (*Trademark*), replicate, transcribe, Xerox (*Trademark*) 3 = **imitate**, act like, ape, behave like, echo, emulate, follow, follow suit, follow the example of, mimic, mirror, parrot, repeat, simulate
➤ **Antonyms**
noun ≠**reproduction**: model, original, pattern, prototype, the real thing ◆ *verb* ≠**reproduce**: create, originate

cord *noun* = **rope**, line, string, twine

cordial *adjective* = **warm**, affable, affectionate, agreeable, cheerful, congenial, earnest, friendly, genial, heartfelt, hearty, invigorating, sociable, warm-hearted, welcoming, wholehearted
➤ **Antonyms**
aloof, cold, distant, formal, frigid, reserved, unfriendly, ungracious

cordiality *noun* = **warmth**, affability, amiability, friendliness, geniality, heartiness, sincerity, wholeheartedness

cordon *noun* 1 = **chain**, barrier, line, ring ◆ *verb* 2 **cordon off** = **surround**, close off, encircle, enclose, fence off, isolate, picket, separate

core *noun* = **centre**, crux, essence, gist, heart, kernel, nub, nucleus, pith

corner *noun* 1 = **angle**, bend, crook, joint 2 = **space**, cavity, cranny, hideaway, hide-out, hidey-hole (*informal*), hole, niche, nook, recess, retreat 3 = **tight spot**, hole (*informal*), hot water (*informal*), pickle (*informal*), predicament, spot (*informal*) ◆ *verb* 4 = **trap**, bring to bay, run to earth 5 *As in* **corner the market** = **monopolize**, dominate, engross, hog (*slang*)

cornerstone *noun* 1 = **basis**, bedrock, key, premise, starting point 2 = **quoin**

corny *adjective Slang* = **unoriginal**, banal, commonplace, dull, feeble, hackneyed, maudlin, mawkish, old-fashioned, old hat, sentimental, stale, stereotyped, trite

corporal *adjective* = **bodily**, anatomical, carnal, corporeal (*archaic*), fleshly, material, physical, somatic

corporate *adjective* = **collective**, allied, collaborative, combined, communal, joint, merged, pooled, shared, united

corporation *noun* 1 = **business**, association, corporate body, society 2 = **town council**, civic authorities, council, municipal authorities 3 *Informal* = **paunch**, beer belly (*informal*), middle-age spread (*informal*), pod, pot, potbelly, spare tyre (*Brit. slang*), spread (*informal*)

corps *noun* = **team**, band, body, company, contingent, crew, detachment, division, regiment, squad, squadron, troop, unit

corpse *noun* = **body**, cadaver, carcass, remains, stiff (*slang*)

corpulent *adjective* = **fat**, beefy (*informal*), bulky, burly, fattish, fleshy, large, lusty, obese, overweight, plump, portly, roly-poly, rotund, stout, tubby, well-padded
➤ **Antonyms**
anorexic, bony, emaciated, gaunt, scrawny, skin and bones (*informal*), skinny,

slim, thin, thin as a rake, underweight

correct *adjective* **1 = true**, accurate, equitable, exact, faultless, flawless, just, O.K. *or* okay (*informal*), on the right lines, precise, regular, right, strict **2 = proper**, acceptable, appropriate, diplomatic, fitting, kosher (*informal*), O.K. *or* okay (*informal*), seemly, standard ♦ *verb* **3 = rectify**, adjust, amend, cure, emend, improve, redress, reform, regulate, remedy, right, set the record straight **4 = punish**, admonish, chasten, chastise, chide, discipline, rebuke, reprimand, reprove
➤ **Antonyms**
adjective ≠**true**: false, inaccurate, incorrect, untrue, wrong ≠**proper**: improper, inappropriate, unacceptable, unfitting, unsuitable ♦ *verb* ≠**rectify**: damage, harm, impair, ruin, spoil ≠**punish**: compliment, excuse, praise

correction *noun* **1 = rectification**, adjustment, alteration, amendment, emendation, improvement, modification, righting **2 = punishment**, admonition, castigation, chastisement, discipline, reformation, reproof

corrective *adjective* **1 = remedial**, palliative, rehabilitative, restorative, therapeutic **2 = disciplinary**, penal, punitive, reformatory

correctly *adverb* **= rightly**, accurately, aright, perfectly, precisely, properly, right

correctness *noun* **1 = truth**, accuracy, exactitude, exactness, faultlessness, fidelity, preciseness, precision, regularity **2 = decorum**, *bon ton,* civility, good breeding, propriety, seemliness

correlate *verb* **= correspond**, associate, compare, connect, coordinate, equate, interact, parallel, tie in

correlation *noun* **= correspondence**, alternation, equivalence, interaction, interchange, interdependence, interrelationship, reciprocity

correspond *verb* **1 = be consistent**, accord, agree, be related, coincide, complement, conform, correlate, dovetail, fit, harmonize, match, square, tally **2 = communicate**, exchange letters, keep in touch, write
➤ **Antonyms**
≠**be consistent**: be at variance, be dissimilar, be inconsistent, belie, be unlike, differ, disagree, diverge, vary

correspondence *noun* **1 = letters**, communication, mail, post, writing **2 = relation**, agreement, analogy, coincidence, comparability, comparison, concurrence, conformity, congruity,

correlation, fitness, harmony, match, similarity

correspondent *noun* **1 = letter writer**, pen friend *or* pal **2 = reporter**, contributor, gazetteer (*archaic*), journalist, journo (*slang*), special correspondent ♦ *adjective* **3 = corresponding**, analogous, comparable, like, of a piece, parallel, reciprocal, similar

corresponding *adjective* **= related**, analogous, answering, complementary, correlative, correspondent, equivalent, identical, interrelated, matching, reciprocal, similar, synonymous

corridor *noun* **= passage**, aisle, alley, hallway, passageway

corroborate *verb* **= support**, authenticate, back up, bear out, confirm, document, endorse, establish, ratify, substantiate, sustain, validate
➤ **Antonyms**
contradict, disprove, invalidate, negate, rebut, refute

corrode *verb* **= eat away**, canker, consume, corrupt, deteriorate, erode, gnaw, impair, oxidize, rust, waste, wear away

corrosive *adjective* **1 = corroding**, acrid, biting, caustic, consuming, erosive, virulent, vitriolic, wasting, wearing **2 = cutting**, caustic, incisive, mordant, sarcastic, trenchant, venomous, vitriolic

corrugated *adjective* **= furrowed**, channelled, creased, crinkled, fluted, grooved, puckered, ridged, rumpled, wrinkled

corrupt *adjective* **1 = dishonest**, bent (*slang*), bribable, crooked (*informal*), fraudulent, rotten, shady (*informal*), unethical, unprincipled, unscrupulous, venal **2 = depraved**, abandoned, debased, defiled, degenerate, demoralized, dishonoured, dissolute, profligate, vicious **3 = contaminated**, adulterated, decayed, defiled, infected, polluted, putrescent, putrid, rotten, tainted **4 = distorted**, altered, doctored, falsified ♦ *verb* **5 = bribe**, buy off, entice, fix (*informal*), grease (someone's) palm (*slang*), lure, square, suborn **6 = deprave**, debauch, demoralize, pervert, subvert **7 = contaminate**, adulterate, debase, defile, infect, putrefy, spoil, taint, vitiate **8 = distort**, doctor, tamper with
➤ **Antonyms**
adjective ≠**dishonest, depraved**: ethical, honest, honourable, moral, noble, principled, righteous, scrupulous, straight, upright, virtuous ♦ *verb* ≠**deprave**: correct, reform ≠**contaminate**: purify

corruption *noun* **1 = dishonesty**, breach of

trust, bribery, bribing, crookedness (*informal*), demoralization, extortion, fiddling (*informal*), fraud, fraudulency, graft (*informal*), jobbery, profiteering, shadiness, shady dealings (*informal*), unscrupulousness, venality **2 = depravity**, baseness, decadence, degeneration, degradation, evil, immorality, impurity, iniquity, perversion, profligacy, sinfulness, turpitude, vice, viciousness, wickedness **3 = rotting**, adulteration, debasement, decay, defilement, foulness, infection, pollution, putrefaction, putrescence, rot, rottenness **4 = distortion**, doctoring, falsification

corset *noun* **= girdle**, belt, bodice, corselet, foundation garment, panty girdle, stays (*rare*)

cosmetic *adjective* **= beautifying**, nonessential, superficial, surface, touching-up

cosmic *adjective* **1 = universal**, stellar **2 = vast**, grandiose, huge, immense, infinite, limitless, measureless

cosmonaut *noun* **= astronaut**, spaceman, space pilot

cosmopolitan *adjective* **1 = sophisticated**, broad-minded, catholic, open-minded, universal, urbane, well-travelled, worldly, worldly-wise ◆ *noun* **2 = man** *or* **woman of the world**, cosmopolite, jet-setter, sophisticate
➤ **Antonyms**
adjective ≠**sophisticated:** hidebound, illiberal, insular, limited, narrow-minded, parochial, provincial, restricted, rustic, unsophisticated

cost *noun* **1 = price**, amount, charge, damage (*informal*), expenditure, expense, figure, outlay, payment, rate, worth **2 = loss**, damage, deprivation, detriment, expense, harm, hurt, injury, penalty, sacrifice, suffering ◆ *verb* **3 = sell at**, come to, command a price of, set (someone) back (*informal*) **4 = lose**, do disservice to, harm, hurt, injure, necessitate

costly *adjective* **1 = splendid**, gorgeous, lavish, luxurious, opulent, precious, priceless, rich, sumptuous **2 = expensive**, dear, excessive, exorbitant, extortionate, highly-priced, steep (*informal*), stiff, valuable **3 = damaging**, catastrophic, deleterious, disastrous, harmful, loss-making, ruinous, sacrificial
➤ **Antonyms**
≠**expensive:** cheap, cheapo (*informal*), dirt-cheap, economical, fair, inexpensive, low-priced, reasonable, reduced

costs *plural noun* **1 = expenses**, budget, outgoings, overheads **2 at all costs = no**

matter what, at any price, regardless, without fail

costume *noun* **= outfit**, apparel, attire, clothing, dress, ensemble, garb, get-up (*informal*), livery, national dress, robes, uniform

cosy *adjective* **= snug**, comfortable, comfy (*informal*), cuddled up, homely, intimate, secure, sheltered, snuggled down, tucked up, warm

cottage *noun* **= cabin**, but-and-ben (*Scot.*), chalet, cot, hut, lodge, shack

couch *noun* **1 = sofa**, bed, chaise longue, chesterfield, day bed, divan, ottoman, settee ◆ *verb* **2 = express**, frame, phrase, set forth, utter, word

cough *noun* **1 = frog** *or* **tickle in one's throat**, bark, hack ◆ *verb* **2 = clear one's throat**, bark, hack, hawk, hem

cough up *verb Informal* **= give up**, ante up (*informal, chiefly U.S.*), come across, deliver, fork out (*slang*), hand over, shell out (*informal*), surrender

council *noun* **= governing body**, assembly, board, cabinet, chamber, committee, conclave, conference, congress, convention, convocation, diet, house, ministry, panel, parliament, quango, synod

counsel *noun* **1 = advice**, admonition, caution, consideration, consultation, deliberation, direction, forethought, guidance, information, recommendation, suggestion, warning **2 = legal adviser**, advocate, attorney, barrister, lawyer, solicitor ◆ *verb* **3 = advise**, admonish, advocate, caution, exhort, instruct, prescribe, recommend, urge, warn

count *verb* **1 = add (up)**, calculate, cast up, check, compute, enumerate, estimate, number, reckon, score, tally, tot up **2 = matter**, be important, carry weight, cut any ice (*informal*), enter into consideration, rate, signify, tell, weigh **3 = consider**, deem, esteem, impute, judge, look upon, rate, regard, think **4 = take into account** *or* **consideration**, include, number among ◆ *noun* **5 = calculation**, computation, enumeration, numbering, poll, reckoning, sum, tally

countenance *noun* **1** *Literary* **= face**, appearance, aspect, expression, features, look, mien, physiognomy, visage **2 = support**, aid, approval, assistance, backing, endorsement, favour, sanction ◆ *verb* **3 = support**, abet, aid, approve, back, champion, commend, condone, encourage, endorse, help, sanction **4 = tolerate**, brook, endure, hack (*slang*), put up with (*informal*), stand for (*informal*)

counter *verb* **1** = **retaliate**, answer, hit back, meet, obviate, offset, oppose, parry, resist, respond, return, ward off ♦ *adverb* **2** = **opposite to**, against, at variance with, contrarily, contrariwise, conversely, in defiance of, versus ♦ *adjective* **3** = **opposing**, adverse, against, conflicting, contradictory, contrary, contrasting, obverse, opposed, opposite
➤ **Antonyms**
verb ≠**retaliate**: accept, cave in (*informal*), give in, surrender, take, yield ♦ *adverb* ≠**opposite to**: in agreement, parallel ♦ *adjective* ≠**opposing**: accordant, parallel, similar

counteract *verb* = **act against**, annul, check, contravene, counterbalance, countervail, cross, defeat, foil, frustrate, hinder, invalidate, negate, neutralize, obviate, offset, oppose, resist, thwart

counterbalance *verb* = **offset**, balance, compensate, counterpoise, countervail, make up for, set off

counterfeit *adjective* **1** = **fake**, bogus, copied, ersatz, false, feigned, forged, fraudulent, imitation, phoney *or* phony (*informal*), pseud *or* pseudo (*informal*), sham, simulated, spurious, supposititious ♦ *noun* **2** = **fake**, copy, forgery, fraud, imitation, phoney *or* phony (*informal*), reproduction, sham ♦ *verb* **3** = **fake**, copy, fabricate, feign, forge, imitate, impersonate, pretend, sham, simulate
➤ **Antonyms**
adjective ≠**fake**: authentic, genuine, good, original, real, the real thing

countermand *verb* = **cancel**, annul, override, repeal, rescind, retract, reverse, revoke

counterpart *noun* **1** = **opposite number**, complement, correlative, equal, fellow, match, mate, supplement, tally, twin **2** = **copy**, duplicate

countless *adjective* = **innumerable**, endless, immeasurable, incalculable, infinite, legion, limitless, measureless, multitudinous, myriad, numberless, uncounted, untold
➤ **Antonyms**
finite, limited, restricted

count on *or* **upon** *verb* = **depend on**, bank on, believe (in), lean on, pin one's faith on, reckon on, rely on, take for granted, take on trust, trust

count out *verb Informal* = **leave out**, disregard, except, exclude, leave out of account, pass over

country *noun* **1** = **nation**, commonwealth, kingdom, people, realm, sovereign state, state **2** = **territory**, land, part, region,

terrain **3** = **people**, citizenry, citizens, community, electors, grass roots, inhabitants, nation, populace, public, society, voters **4** = **countryside**, back country (*U.S.*), backlands (*U.S.*), backwoods, boondocks (*U.S. slang*), farmland, green belt, outback (*Austral. & N.Z.*), outdoors, provinces, rural areas, sticks (*informal*), the back of beyond, the middle of nowhere, wide open spaces (*informal*) **5** = **native land**, fatherland, homeland, motherland, nationality, *patria* ♦ *adjective* **6** = **rural**, agrarian, agrestic, Arcadian, bucolic, georgic (*literary*), landed, pastoral, provincial, rustic
➤ **Antonyms**
noun ≠**countryside**: city, metropolis, town ♦ *adjective* ≠**rural**: city, cosmopolitan, sophisticated, urban, urbane

countryman *noun* **1** = **compatriot**, fellow citizen **2** = **yokel**, bumpkin, cockie (*N.Z.*), country dweller, farmer, hayseed (*U.S. & Canad. informal*), hick (*informal, chiefly U.S. & Canad.*), hind (*obsolete*), husbandman, peasant, provincial, rustic, swain

countryside *noun* = **country**, farmland, green belt, outback (*Austral. & N.Z.*), outdoors, panorama, sticks (*informal*), view, wide open spaces (*informal*)

count up *verb* = **add**, reckon up, sum, tally, total

county *noun* **1** = **province**, shire ♦ *adjective* **2** *Informal* = **upper-class**, green-wellie, huntin', shootin', and fishin' (*informal*), plummy (*informal*), tweedy, upper-crust (*informal*)

coup *noun* = **masterstroke**, accomplishment, action, deed, exploit, feat, manoeuvre, stratagem, stroke, stroke of genius, stunt, *tour de force*

couple *noun* **1** = **pair**, brace, duo, item, span (*of horses or oxen*), twain (*archaic*), two, twosome ♦ *verb* **2** = **link**, buckle, clasp, conjoin, connect, hitch, join, marry, pair, unite, wed, yoke

coupon *noun* = **slip**, card, certificate, detachable portion, ticket, token, voucher

courage *noun* = **bravery**, balls (*taboo slang*), ballsiness (*taboo slang*), boldness, bottle (*Brit. slang*), daring, dauntlessness, fearlessness, firmness, fortitude, gallantry, grit, guts (*informal*), hardihood, heroism, intrepidity, lion-heartedness, mettle, nerve, pluck, resolution, spunk (*informal*), valour
➤ **Antonyms**
cowardice, cravenness, faint-heartedness, fear, timidity

courageous *adjective* = **brave**, audacious, ballsy (*taboo slang*), bold, daring,

dauntless, fearless, gallant, gritty, hardy, heroic, indomitable, intrepid, lion-hearted, plucky, resolute, stalwart, stouthearted, valiant, valorous
➤ **Antonyms**
chicken (*slang*), chicken-hearted, chickenshit (*U.S. slang*), cowardly, craven, dastardly, faint-hearted, gutless (*informal*), lily-livered, pusillanimous, scared, spineless, timid, timorous, yellow (*informal*)

courier noun 1 = **guide**, representative 2 = **messenger**, bearer, carrier, emissary, envoy, herald, runner

course noun 1 = **classes**, course of study, curriculum, lectures, programme, schedule, studies 2 = **progression**, advance, advancement, continuity, development, flow, furtherance, march, movement, order, progress, sequence, succession, tenor, unfolding 3 = **route**, channel, direction, line, orbit, passage, path, road, tack, track, trail, trajectory, way 4 = **racecourse**, cinder track, circuit, lap, race, round 5 = **procedure**, behaviour, conduct, manner, method, mode, plan, policy, programme, regimen 6 = **period**, duration, lapse, passage, passing, sweep, term, time 7 **in due course** = **in time**, eventually, finally, in the course of time, in the end, sooner or later 8 **of course** = **naturally**, certainly, definitely, indubitably, needless to say, obviously, undoubtedly, without a doubt ♦ verb 9 = **run**, dash, flow, gush, move apace, race, scud, scurry, speed, stream, surge, tumble 10 = **hunt**, chase, follow, pursue

court noun 1 = **law court**, bar, bench, court of justice, seat of judgment, tribunal 2 = **courtyard**, cloister, piazza, plaza, quad (*informal*), quadrangle, square, yard 3 = **palace**, hall, manor 4 = **royal household**, attendants, cortege, entourage, retinue, suite, train ♦ verb 5 = **woo**, chase, date, go (out) with, go steady with (*informal*), keep company with, make love to, pay court to, pay one's addresses to, pursue, run after, serenade, set one's cap at, sue (*archaic*), take out, walk out with 6 = **cultivate**, curry favour with, fawn upon, flatter, pander to, seek, solicit 7 = **invite**, attract, bring about, incite, prompt, provoke, seek

courteous adjective = **polite**, affable, attentive, ceremonious, civil, courtly, elegant, gallant, gracious, mannerly, polished, refined, respectful, urbane, well-bred, well-mannered
➤ **Antonyms**
discourteous, disrespectful, ill-mannered, impolite, insolent, rude, uncivil, ungracious, unkind

courtesy noun 1 = **politeness**, affability, civility, courteousness, courtliness, elegance, gallantness, gallantry, good breeding, good manners, grace, graciousness, polish, urbanity 2 = **favour**, benevolence, consent, consideration, generosity, indulgence, kindness

courtier noun = **attendant**, follower, henchman, liegeman, pursuivant (*Historical*), squire, train-bearer

courtly adjective = **ceremonious**, affable, aristocratic, chivalrous, civil, decorous, dignified, elegant, flattering, formal, gallant, highbred, lordly, obliging, polished, refined, stately, urbane

courtship noun = **wooing**, courting, engagement, keeping company, pursuit, romance, suit

courtyard noun = **yard**, area, enclosure, peristyle, playground, quad, quadrangle

cove noun = **bay**, anchorage, bayou, creek, firth or frith (*Scot.*), inlet, sound

covenant noun 1 = **promise**, agreement, arrangement, bargain, commitment, compact, concordat, contract, convention, pact, pledge, stipulation, treaty, trust 2 *Law* = **deed**, bond ♦ verb 3 = **promise**, agree, bargain, contract, engage, pledge, shake hands, stipulate, undertake

cover verb 1 = **clothe**, dress, envelop, invest, put on, wrap 2 = **overlay**, canopy, coat, daub, encase, envelop, layer, mantle, overspread 3 = **submerge**, engulf, flood, overrun, wash over 4 = **conceal**, camouflage, cloak, cover up, curtain, disguise, eclipse, enshroud, hide, hood, house, mask, obscure, screen, secrete, shade, shroud, veil 5 = **travel over**, cross, pass through or over, range, traverse 6 = **protect**, defend, guard, reinforce, shelter, shield, watch over 7 = **report**, describe, detail, investigate, narrate, recount, relate, tell of, write up 8 = **make up for**, balance, compensate, counterbalance, insure, make good, offset 9 = **deal with**, comprehend, comprise, consider, contain, embody, embrace, encompass, examine, include, incorporate, involve, provide for, refer to, survey, take account of 10 **cover for** = **stand in for**, double for, fill in for, hold the fort (*informal*), relieve, substitute, take over, take the rap for (*slang*) ♦ noun 11 = **covering**, awning, binding, canopy, cap, case, clothing, coating, dress, envelope, jacket, lid, sheath, top, wrapper 12 = **disguise**, cloak, cover-up, façade, front, mask, pretence, pretext, screen, smoke screen, veil, window-dressing 13 = **protection**, camouflage, concealment,

defence, guard, hiding place, refuge, sanctuary, shelter, shield, undergrowth, woods **14 = insurance**, compensation, indemnity, payment, protection, reimbursement
➤ **Antonyms**
verb ≠**conceal:** exhibit, expose, reveal, show, unclothe, uncover, unmask, unwrap ≠**deal with:** exclude, omit ◆ *noun* ≠**covering:** base, bottom

covering *adjective* **1 = explanatory,** accompanying, descriptive, introductory ◆ *noun* **2 = cover,** blanket, casing, clothing, coating, housing, layer, overlay, protection, shelter, top, wrap, wrapper, wrapping

cover-up *noun* **= concealment,** complicity, conspiracy, front, smoke screen, whitewash (*informal*)

cover up *verb* **= conceal,** cover one's tracks, draw a veil over, feign ignorance, hide, hush up, keep dark, keep secret, keep silent about, keep under one's hat (*informal*), repress, stonewall, suppress, sweep under the carpet, whitewash (*informal*)

covet *verb* **= long for,** aspire to, begrudge, crave, desire, envy, fancy (*informal*), hanker after, have one's eye on, lust after, set one's heart on, thirst for, would give one's eyeteeth for, yearn for

covetous *adjective* **= envious,** acquisitive, avaricious, close-fisted, grasping, greedy, jealous, mercenary, rapacious, yearning

cow *verb* **= intimidate,** awe, browbeat, bully, daunt, dishearten, dismay, frighten, overawe, psych out (*informal*), scare, subdue, terrorize, unnerve

coward *noun* **= wimp** (*informal*), caitiff (*archaic*), chicken (*slang*), craven, dastard (*archaic*), faint-heart, funk (*informal*), poltroon, recreant (*archaic*), renegade, scaredy-cat (*informal*), skulker, sneak, yellow-belly (*slang*)

cowardice *noun* **= faint-heartedness,** fearfulness, spinelessness, weakness

cowardly *adjective* **= faint-hearted,** abject, base, boneless, caitiff (*archaic*), chicken (*slang*), chicken-hearted, chickenshit (*U.S. slang*), craven, dastardly, fearful, gutless (*informal*), lily-livered, pusillanimous, recreant (*archaic*), scared, shrinking, soft, spineless, timorous, weak, weak-kneed (*informal*), white-livered, yellow (*informal*)
➤ **Antonyms**
audacious, bold, brave, courageous, daring, dauntless, doughty, intrepid, plucky, valiant

cowboy *noun* **= cowhand,** broncobuster (*U.S.*), buckaroo (*U.S.*), cattleman,

cowpuncher (*U.S. informal*), drover, gaucho (*S. American*), herder, herdsman, rancher, ranchero (*U.S.*), stockman, wrangler (*U.S.*)

cower *verb* **= cringe,** crouch, draw back, fawn, flinch, grovel, quail, shrink, skulk, sneak, tremble, truckle

coy *adjective* **= shy,** arch, backward, bashful, coquettish, demure, evasive, flirtatious, kittenish, modest, overmodest, prudish, reserved, retiring, self-effacing, shrinking, skittish, timid
➤ **Antonyms**
bold, brash, brass-necked (*Brit. informal*), brassy (*informal*), brazen, flip (*informal*), forward, impertinent, impudent, pert, pushy (*informal*), saucy, shameless

crabbed *adjective* **1 = unreadable,** awkward, cramped, hieroglyphical, illegible, indecipherable, laboured, squeezed **2 = bad-tempered,** acrid, acrimonious, captious, churlish, cross, cynical, difficult, fretful, harsh, ill-tempered, irritable, morose, perverse, petulant, prickly, ratty (*Brit. & N.Z. informal*), sour, splenetic, surly, tart, testy, tetchy, tough, trying

crack *verb* **1 = break,** burst, chip, chop, cleave, crackle, craze, fracture, rive, snap, splinter, split **2 = snap,** burst, crash, detonate, explode, pop, ring **3 = give in,** break down, collapse, give way, go to pieces, lose control, succumb, yield **4** *Informal* **= hit,** buffet, clip (*informal*), clout (*informal*), cuff, slap, smack, thump, wallop (*informal*), whack **5 = solve,** decipher, fathom, get the answer to, work out ◆ *noun* **6 = snap,** burst, clap, crash, explosion, pop, report **7 = break,** breach, chink, chip, cleft, cranny, crevice, fissure, fracture, gap, interstice, rift **8** *Informal* **= blow,** buffet, clip (*informal*), clout (*informal*), cuff, slap, smack, thump, wallop (*informal*), whack **9** *Informal* **= attempt,** go (*informal*), opportunity, shot, stab (*informal*), try **10** *Informal* **= joke,** dig, funny remark, gag (*informal*), insult, jibe, quip, smart-alecky remark, wisecrack, witticism ◆ *adjective* **11** *Slang* **= first-class,** ace, choice, elite, excellent, first-rate, hand-picked, superior, world-class

crackdown *noun* **= suppression,** clampdown, crushing, repression

cracked *adjective* **1 = broken,** chipped, crazed, damaged, defective, faulty, fissured, flawed, imperfect, split **2** *Informal* **= crazy** (*informal*), bats (*slang*), batty (*slang*), crackbrained, crackpot (*informal*), daft (*informal*), doolally (*slang*), eccentric, gonzo (*slang*), insane, loony (*slang*), loopy (*informal*), nuts (*slang*), nutty (*slang*), oddball (*informal*), off one's head or nut (*slang*), off one's rocker (*slang*), off one's trolley (*slang*), off-the-wall (*slang*), out of one's mind, outré, out to lunch (*informal*), round the bend (*slang*), round the twist (*Brit. slang*), touched, up the pole (*informal*), wacko or whacko (*informal*)

cracked up adjective As in **not all it is cracked up to be = overrated**, blown up, exaggerated, hyped (up), overpraised, puffed up

crack up verb Informal = **have a breakdown**, break down, collapse, come apart at the seams (*informal*), flip one's lid (*slang*), fly off the handle (*informal*), freak out (*informal*), go ape (*slang*), go apeshit (*slang*), go berserk, go crazy (*informal*), go off one's head (*slang*), go off one's rocker (*slang*), go off the deep end (*informal*), go out of one's mind, go to pieces, throw a wobbly (*slang*)

cradle noun 1 = **crib**, bassinet, cot, Moses basket 2 = **birthplace**, beginning, fount, fountainhead, origin, source, spring, wellspring ◆ verb 3 = **hold**, lull, nestle, nurse, rock, support

craft noun 1 = **occupation**, business, calling, employment, handicraft, handiwork, line, pursuit, trade, vocation, work 2 = **skill**, ability, aptitude, art, artistry, cleverness, dexterity, expertise, expertness, ingenuity, knack, know-how (*informal*), technique, workmanship 3 = **cunning**, artfulness, artifice, contrivance, craftiness, deceit, duplicity, guile, ruse, scheme, shrewdness, stratagem, subterfuge, subtlety, trickery, wiles 4 = **vessel**, aircraft, barque, boat, plane, ship, spacecraft

craftiness noun = **cunning**, artfulness, astuteness, canniness, deviousness, duplicity, foxiness, guile, shrewdness, slyness, subtlety, trickiness, wiliness

craftsman noun = **skilled worker**, artificer, artisan, maker, master, smith, technician, wright

craftsmanship noun = **workmanship**, artistry, expertise, mastery, technique

crafty adjective = **cunning**, artful, astute, calculating, canny, deceitful, designing, devious, duplicitous, foxy, fraudulent, guileful, insidious, knowing, scheming, sharp, shrewd, sly, subtle, tricksy, tricky, wily
➤ **Antonyms**
as green as grass, candid, ethical, frank, honest, ingenuous, innocent, naive, open, simple, wet behind the ears

crag noun = **rock**, aiguille, bluff, peak, pinnacle, tor

cram verb 1 = **stuff**, compact, compress, crowd, crush, fill to overflowing, force, jam, overcrowd, overfill, pack, pack in, press, ram, shove, squeeze 2 = **overeat**, glut, gorge, gormandize, guzzle, overfeed, pig out (*slang*), put or pack away, satiate, stuff 3 = **study**, bone up (*informal*), con, grind, mug up (*slang*), revise, swot, swot up

cramp[1] noun = **spasm**, ache, contraction, convulsion, crick, pain, pang, shooting pain, stiffness, stitch, twinge

cramp[2] verb = **restrict**, check, circumscribe, clip someone's wings, clog, confine, constrain, encumber, hamper, hamstring, handicap, hinder, impede, inhibit, obstruct, shackle, stymie, thwart

cramped adjective 1 = **closed in**, awkward, circumscribed, confined, congested, crowded, hemmed in, jammed in, narrow, overcrowded, packed, restricted, squeezed, uncomfortable 2 = **small**, crabbed, indecipherable, irregular
➤ **Antonyms**
≠**closed in**: capacious, commodious, large, open, roomy, sizable or sizeable, spacious, uncongested, uncrowded

crank noun Informal = **eccentric**, case (*informal*), character (*informal*), freak (*informal*), kook (*U.S. & Canad. informal*), nut (*slang*), oddball (*informal*), odd fish (*informal*), queer fish (*Brit. informal*), rum customer (*Brit. slang*), screwball (*slang, chiefly U.S. & Canad.*), wacko or whacko (*informal*), weirdo or weirdie (*informal*)

cranky adjective Informal = **eccentric**, bizarre, capricious, erratic, freakish, freaky (*slang*), funny (*informal*), idiosyncratic, odd, oddball (*informal*), off-the-wall (*slang*), outré, peculiar, queer, quirky, rum (*Brit. slang*), strange, wacko or whacko (*informal*), wacky (*slang*)

cranny noun = **crevice**, breach, chink, cleft, crack, fissure, gap, hole, interstice, nook, opening, rift

crash noun 1 = **collision**, accident, bump, jar, jolt, pile-up (*informal*), prang (*informal*), smash, smash-up, thud, thump, wreck 2 = **smash**, bang, boom, clang, clash, clatter, clattering, din, racket, smashing, thunder 3 = **collapse**, bankruptcy, debacle, depression, downfall, failure, ruin, smash ◆ verb 4 = **collide**, bang, bump (into), crash-land (*an aircraft*), drive into, have an accident, hit, hurtle into, plough into, run together, wreck 5 = **smash**, break, break up, dash to pieces, disintegrate, fracture, fragment, shatter, shiver, splinter 6 = **collapse**, be ruined, fail, fold, fold up, go belly up (*informal*), go broke (*informal*), go bust (*informal*), go to the wall, go under, smash **7 = hurtle**, come a cropper (*informal*), dash, fall, fall headlong, give way, lurch, overbalance, pitch, plunge, precipitate oneself, sprawl, topple ♦ *adjective* **8 = intensive**, emergency, immediate, round-the-clock, speeded-up, telescoped, urgent

crass *adjective* = **insensitive**, asinine, blundering, boorish, bovine, coarse, dense, doltish, gross, indelicate, lumpish, oafish, obtuse, stupid, unrefined, witless
➤ **Antonyms**
brainy (*informal*), bright, clever, elegant, intelligent, polished, refined, sensitive, sharp, smart

crate *noun* **1 = container**, box, case, packing case, tea chest ♦ *verb* **2 = box**, case, encase, enclose, pack, pack up

crater *noun* = **hollow**, depression, dip, shell hole

crave *verb* **1 = long for**, be dying for, cry out for (*informal*), desire, eat one's heart out over, fancy (*informal*), hanker after, hope for, hunger after, lust after, need, pant for, pine for, require, set one's heart on, sigh for, thirst for, want, would give one's eyeteeth for, yearn for **2** *Informal* = **beg**, ask, beseech, entreat, implore, petition, plead for, pray for, seek, solicit, supplicate

craven *adjective* **1 = cowardly**, abject, caitiff (*archaic*), chicken-hearted, chickenshit (*U.S. slang*), dastardly, fearful, lily-livered, mean-spirited, niddering (*archaic*), pusillanimous, scared, timorous, weak, yellow (*informal*) ♦ *noun* **2 = coward**, base fellow (*archaic*), caitiff (*archaic*), dastard (*archaic*), niddering (*archaic*), poltroon, recreant (*archaic*), renegade, wheyface, yellow-belly (*slang*)

craving *noun* = **longing**, ache, appetite, cacoethes, desire, hankering, hope, hunger, lust, thirst, urge, yearning, yen (*informal*)

crawl *verb* **1 = creep**, advance slowly, drag, go on all fours, inch, move at a snail's pace, move on hands and knees, pull *or* drag oneself along, slither, worm one's way, wriggle, writhe **2 = grovel**, abase oneself, brown-nose (*taboo slang*), creep, cringe, fawn, humble oneself, kiss ass (*U.S. & Canad. taboo slang*), lick someone's arse (*taboo slang*), lick someone's boots (*slang*), pander to, suck up to someone (*slang*), toady, truckle **3 = be full of**, be alive, be lousy, be overrun (*slang*), swarm, teem
➤ **Antonyms**

≠**creep**: dart, dash, fly, hasten, hurry, race, run, rush, sprint, step on it (*informal*), walk

craze *noun* **1 = fad**, enthusiasm, fashion, infatuation, mania, mode, novelty, passion, preoccupation, rage, the latest (*informal*), thing, trend, vogue ♦ *verb* **2 = drive mad**, bewilder, confuse, dement, derange, distemper, enrage, infatuate, inflame, madden, make insane, send crazy *or* berserk, unbalance, unhinge, unsettle

crazy *adjective* **1** *Informal* = **ridiculous**, absurd, bird-brained (*informal*), cockeyed (*informal*), derisory, fatuous, foolhardy, foolish, half-baked (*informal*), idiotic, ill-conceived, impracticable, imprudent, inane, inappropriate, irresponsible, ludicrous, nonsensical, potty (*Brit. informal*), preposterous, puerile, quixotic, senseless, short-sighted, unrealistic, unwise, unworkable, wild **2 = strange**, bizarre, eccentric, fantastic, odd, oddball (*informal*), outrageous, peculiar, ridiculous, rum (*Brit. slang*), silly, wacko *or* whacko (*informal*), weird **3 = fanatical**, ablaze, ardent, devoted, eager, enamoured, enthusiastic, hysterical, infatuated, into (*informal*), mad, passionate, smitten, very keen, wild (*informal*), zealous **4 = insane**, a bit lacking upstairs (*informal*), as daft as a brush (*informal, chiefly Brit.*), barking (*slang*), barking mad (*slang*), barmy (*slang*), batty (*slang*), berserk, bonkers (*slang, chiefly Brit.*), cracked (*slang*), crackpot (*informal*), crazed, cuckoo (*informal*), daft (*informal*), delirious, demented, deranged, doolally (*slang*), idiotic, loopy (*informal*), lunatic, mad, mad as a hatter, mad as a March hare, maniacal, mental (*slang*), not all there (*informal*), not right in the head, not the full shilling (*informal*), nuts (*slang*), nutty (*slang*), nutty as a fruitcake (*slang*), off one's head (*slang*), off one's rocker (*slang*), off one's trolley (*slang*), off-the-wall (*slang*), of unsound mind, out of one's mind, out to lunch (*informal*), potty (*Brit. informal*), round the bend (*slang*), round the twist (*Brit. slang*), touched, unbalanced, unhinged, up the pole (*informal*)
➤ **Antonyms**
≠**ridiculous**: appropriate, brilliant, feasible, possible, practicable, prudent, realistic, responsible, sensible, wise, workable ≠**strange**: common, conventional, normal, ordinary, orthodox, regular, usual ≠**fanatical**: cool, indifferent, uncaring, unenthusiastic, uninterested ≠**insane**: all there (*informal*), compos mentis, down-to-earth, in one's right mind, intelligent, mentally sound, practical,

prudent, rational, reasonable, sane, sensible, smart, wise

creak *verb* = **squeak**, grate, grind, groan, rasp, scrape, scratch, screech, squeal

cream *noun* **1** = **lotion**, cosmetic, emulsion, essence, liniment, oil, ointment, paste, salve, unguent **2** = **best**, *crème de la crème*, elite, flower, pick, prime ♦ *adjective* **3** = **off-white**, yellowish-white

creamy *adjective* = **smooth**, buttery, creamed, lush, milky, oily, rich, soft, velvety

crease *noun* **1** = **line**, bulge, corrugation, fold, groove, overlap, pucker, ridge, ruck, tuck, wrinkle ♦ *verb* **2** = **wrinkle**, corrugate, crimp, crinkle, crumple, double up, fold, pucker, ridge, ruck up, rumple, screw up

create *verb* **1** = **make**, beget, bring into being *or* existence, coin, compose, concoct, design, develop, devise, dream up (*informal*), form, formulate, generate, give birth to, give life to, hatch, initiate, invent, originate, produce, spawn **2** = **cause**, bring about, lead to, occasion **3** = **appoint**, constitute, establish, found, install, invest, make, set up
➤ **Antonyms**
≠**make**: annihilate, demolish, destroy

creation *noun* **1** = **making**, conception, formation, generation, genesis, procreation, siring **2** = **setting up**, constitution, development, establishment, formation, foundation, inception, institution, laying down, origination, production **3** = **invention**, achievement, brainchild (*informal*), chef-d'oeuvre, concept, concoction, handiwork, magnum opus, *pièce de résistance*, production **4** = **universe**, all living things, cosmos, life, living world, natural world, nature, world

creative *adjective* = **imaginative**, artistic, clever, fertile, gifted, ingenious, inspired, inventive, original, productive, stimulating, visionary

creativity *noun* = **imagination**, cleverness, fecundity, fertility, imaginativeness, ingenuity, inspiration, inventiveness, originality, productivity, talent

creator *noun* = **maker**, architect, author, begetter, designer, father, framer, initiator, inventor, originator, prime mover

creature *noun* **1** = **living thing**, animal, beast, being, brute, critter (*U.S. dialect*), dumb animal, lower animal, quadruped **2** = **person**, body, character, fellow, human being, individual, man, mortal, soul, wight (*archaic*), woman **3** = **minion**, cohort (*chiefly U.S.*), dependant, hanger-on, hireling, instrument (*informal*), lackey, puppet, retainer, tool, wretch

credentials *plural noun* = **certification**, attestation, authorization, card, deed, diploma, docket, document, letter of recommendation *or* introduction, letters of credence, licence, missive, papers, passport, recommendation, reference(s), testament, testimonial, title, voucher, warrant

credibility *noun* = **believability**, believableness, integrity, plausibility, reliability, tenability, trustworthiness

credible *adjective* **1** = **believable**, conceivable, imaginable, likely, plausible, possible, probable, reasonable, supposable, tenable, thinkable, verisimilar **2** = **reliable**, dependable, honest, sincere, trustworthy, trusty
➤ **Antonyms**
≠**believable**: doubtful, implausible, inconceivable, incredible, questionable, unbelievable, unlikely ≠**reliable**: dishonest, insincere, not dependable, unreliable, untrustworthy

credit *noun* **1** = **praise**, acclaim, acknowledgment, approval, Brownie points, commendation, fame, glory, honour, kudos, merit, recognition, thanks, tribute **2** *As in* **be a credit to** = **source of satisfaction** *or* **pride**, feather in one's cap, honour **3** = **prestige**, character, clout (*informal*), esteem, estimation, good name, influence, position, regard, reputation, repute, standing, status **4** = **belief**, confidence, credence, faith, reliance, trust **5 on credit** = **on account**, by deferred payment, by instalments, on hire-purchase, on (the) H.P., on the slate (*informal*), on tick (*informal*) ♦ *verb* **6** = **believe**, accept, bank on, buy (*slang*), depend on, fall for, have faith in, rely on, swallow (*informal*), trust **7 credit with** = **attribute to**, accredit to, ascribe to, assign to, chalk up to (*informal*), impute to, refer to

creditable *adjective* = **praiseworthy**, admirable, commendable, deserving, estimable, exemplary, honourable, laudable, meritorious, reputable, respectable, worthy

credulity *noun* = **gullibility**, blind faith, credulousness, naïveté, silliness, simplicity, stupidity

credulous *adjective* = **gullible**, as green as grass, born yesterday (*informal*), dupable, green, naive, overtrusting, trustful, uncritical, unsuspecting, unsuspicious, wet behind the ears (*informal*)
➤ **Antonyms**
cynical, incredulous, sceptical, suspecting, unbelieving, wary

creed noun = **belief**, articles of faith, canon, catechism, confession, credo, doctrine, dogma, persuasion, principles, profession (*of faith*), tenet

creek noun **1** = **inlet**, bay, bight, cove, firth or frith (*Scot.*) **2** *U.S., Canad., Austral., & N.Z.* = **stream**, bayou, brook, rivulet, runnel, streamlet, tributary, watercourse

creep verb **1** = **sneak**, approach unnoticed, skulk, slink, steal, tiptoe **2** = **crawl**, crawl on all fours, glide, insinuate, slither, squirm, worm, wriggle, writhe **3** = **drag**, crawl, dawdle, edge, inch, proceed at a snail's pace **4** = **grovel**, bootlick (*informal*), brown-nose (*taboo slang*), cower, cringe, fawn, kiss (someone's) ass (*U.S. & Canad. taboo slang*), kowtow, pander to, scrape, suck up to (*informal*), toady, truckle ♦ noun **5** *Slang* = **bootlicker** (*informal*), ass-kisser (*U.S. & Canad. taboo slang*), brown-noser (*taboo slang*), crawler (*slang*), sneak, sycophant, toady

creeper noun = **climbing plant**, climber, rambler, runner, trailing plant, vine (*chiefly U.S.*)

creeps plural noun **give one the creeps** *Informal* = **disgust**, frighten, horrify, make one flinch, make one quail, make one's hair stand on end, make one shrink, make one squirm, make one wince, repel, repulse, scare, terrify, terrorize

creepy adjective *Informal* = **disturbing**, awful, direful, disgusting, eerie, forbidding, frightening, ghoulish, goose-pimply (*informal*), gruesome, hair-raising, horrible, macabre, menacing, nightmarish, ominous, scary (*informal*), sinister, terrifying, threatening, unpleasant, weird

crescent noun **1** = **meniscus**, half-moon, new moon, old moon, sickle, sickle-shape ♦ adjective **2** = **sickle-shaped**, arched, bow-shaped, curved, falcate, semicircular **3** *Archaic* = **waxing**, growing, increasing

crest noun **1** = **top**, apex, crown, head, height, highest point, peak, pinnacle, ridge, summit **2** = **tuft**, aigrette, caruncle (*Zoology*), cockscomb, comb, crown, mane, panache, plume, tassel, topknot **3** = **emblem**, badge, bearings, charge, device, insignia, symbol

crestfallen adjective = **disappointed**, chapfallen, choked, dejected, depressed, despondent, disconsolate, discouraged, disheartened, downcast, downhearted, sick as a parrot (*informal*)
➤ **Antonyms**
cock-a-hoop, elated, encouraged, exuberant, happy, in seventh heaven, joyful, on cloud nine (*informal*), over the

moon (*informal*)

crevice noun = **gap**, chink, cleft, crack, cranny, fissure, fracture, hole, interstice, opening, rent, rift, slit, split

crew noun **1** = **(ship's) company**, hands, (ship's) complement **2** = **team**, company, corps, gang, party, posse, squad, working party **3** *Informal* = **crowd**, assemblage, band, bunch (*informal*), camp, company, gang, herd, horde, lot, mob, pack, posse (*informal*), set, swarm, troop

crib noun **1** *Informal* = **translation**, key, trot (*U.S. slang*) **2** = **cradle**, bassinet, bed, cot **3** = **manger**, bin, box, bunker, rack, stall ♦ verb **4** *Informal* = **copy**, cheat, pass off as one's own work, pilfer, pirate, plagiarize, purloin, steal **5** = **confine**, box up, cage, coop, coop up, enclose, fence, imprison, limit, pen, rail, restrict, shut in

crime noun **1** = **offence**, atrocity, fault, felony, job (*informal*), malfeasance, misdeed, misdemeanour, outrage, transgression, trespass, unlawful act, violation, wrong **2** = **lawbreaking**, corruption, delinquency, guilt, illegality, iniquity, malefaction, misconduct, sin, unrighteousness, vice, villainy, wickedness, wrong, wrongdoing

criminal noun **1** = **lawbreaker**, con (*slang*), con man (*informal*), convict, crook (*informal*), culprit, delinquent, evildoer, felon, jailbird, lag (*slang*), malefactor, offender, sinner, skelm (*S. Afr.*), transgressor, villain ♦ adjective **2** = **unlawful**, bent (*slang*), corrupt, crooked (*informal*), culpable, felonious, illegal, illicit, immoral, indictable, iniquitous, lawless, nefarious, under-the-table, unrighteous, vicious, villainous, wicked, wrong **3** *Informal* = **disgraceful**, deplorable, foolish, preposterous, ridiculous, scandalous, senseless
➤ **Antonyms**
adjective ≠**unlawful**: commendable, honest, honourable, innocent, law-abiding, lawful, legal, right

criminality noun = **illegality**, corruption, culpability, delinquency, depravity, guiltiness, sinfulness, turpitude, villainy, wickedness

cringe verb **1** = **shrink**, blench, cower, dodge, draw back, duck, flinch, quail, quiver, recoil, shy, start, tremble, wince **2** = **grovel**, bend, bootlick (*informal*), bow, brown-nose (*taboo slang*), crawl, creep, crouch, fawn, kiss ass (*U.S. & Canad. taboo slang*), kneel, kowtow, pander to, sneak, stoop, toady, truckle

cripple verb **1** = **disable**, debilitate, enfeeble, hamstring, incapacitate, lame,

maim, mutilate, paralyse, weaken **2** = **damage**, bring to a standstill, cramp, destroy, halt, impair, put out of action, put paid to, ruin, spoil, vitiate
➤ **Antonyms**
≠**damage**: advance, aid, assist, assist the progress of, ease, expedite, facilitate, further, help, promote

crippled *adjective* = **disabled**, bedridden, deformed, enfeebled, handicapped, housebound, incapacitated, laid up (*informal*), lame, paralysed

crisis *noun* **1** = **critical point**, climacteric, climax, confrontation, crunch (*informal*), crux, culmination, height, moment of truth, point of no return, turning point **2** = **emergency**, catastrophe, critical situation, deep water, dilemma, dire straits, disaster, exigency, extremity, meltdown (*informal*), mess, panic stations (*informal*), pass, plight, predicament, quandary, strait, trouble

crisp *adjective* **1** = **firm**, brittle, crispy, crumbly, crunchy, fresh, unwilted **2** = **clean**, clean-cut, neat, orderly, smart, snappy, spruce, tidy, trig (*archaic or dialect*), trim, well-groomed, well-pressed **3** = **bracing**, brisk, fresh, invigorating, refreshing **4** = **brief**, brusque, clear, incisive, pithy, short, succinct, tart, terse
➤ **Antonyms**
≠**firm**: drooping, droopy, flaccid, floppy, limp, soft, wilted, withered ≠**bracing**: balmy, clement, mild, pleasant, warm

criterion *noun* = **standard**, bench mark, canon, gauge, measure, norm, par, principle, proof, rule, test, touchstone, yardstick

critic *noun* **1** = **judge**, analyst, arbiter, authority, commentator, connoisseur, expert, expositor, pundit, reviewer **2** = **fault-finder**, attacker, carper, caviller, censor, censurer, detractor, knocker (*informal*), Momus, reviler, vilifier

critical *adjective* **1** = **crucial**, all-important, dangerous, deciding, decisive, grave, hairy (*slang*), high-priority, momentous, now or never, perilous, pivotal, precarious, pressing, psychological, risky, serious, urgent, vital **2** = **disparaging**, captious, carping, cavilling, censorious, derogatory, disapproving, fault-finding, nagging, niggling, nit-picking (*informal*), on someone's back (*informal*), scathing **3** = **analytical**, accurate, diagnostic, discerning, discriminating, fastidious, judicious, penetrating, perceptive, precise
➤ **Antonyms**
≠**crucial**: safe, secure, settled, unimportant ≠**disparaging**: appreciative, approving,

complimentary, uncritical ≠**analytical**: undiscriminating

criticism *noun* **1** = **fault-finding**, animadversion, bad press, brickbats (*informal*), censure, character assassination, critical remarks, denigration, disapproval, disparagement, flak (*informal*), knocking (*informal*), panning (*informal*), slagging (*slang*), slam (*slang*), slating (*informal*), stick (*slang*), stricture **2** = **analysis**, appraisal, appreciation, assessment, comment, commentary, critique, elucidation, evaluation, judgment, notice, review

criticize *verb* **1** = **find fault with**, animadvert on *or* upon, blast, carp, censure, condemn, disapprove of, disparage, excoriate, give (someone *or* something) a bad press, have a go (at) (*informal*), knock (*informal*), lambast(e), nag at, pan (*informal*), pass strictures upon, pick holes in, pick to pieces, put down, slam (*slang*), slate (*informal*), tear into (*informal*) **2** = **analyse**, appraise, assess, comment upon, evaluate, give an opinion, judge, pass judgment on, review
➤ **Antonyms**
≠**find fault with**: commend, compliment, extol, laud (*literary*), praise

critique *noun* = **essay**, analysis, appraisal, assessment, commentary, examination, review, treatise

croak *verb* **1** = **squawk**, caw, gasp, grunt, utter *or* speak harshly, utter *or* speak huskily, utter *or* speak throatily, wheeze **2** *Slang* = **die**, buy it (*U.S. slang*), buy the farm (*U.S. slang*), check out (*U.S. slang*), expire, go belly-up (*slang*), hop the twig (*informal*), kick it (*slang*), kick the bucket (*informal*), pass away, peg it (*informal*), peg out (*informal*), perish, pop one's clogs (*informal*)

crook *noun* **1** *Informal* = **criminal**, cheat, chiseller (*informal*), fraudster, grifter (*slang, chiefly U.S. & Canad.*), knave (*archaic*), lag (*slang*), racketeer, robber, rogue, shark, skelm (*S. Afr.*), swindler, thief, villain ♦ *verb* **2** = **bend**, angle, bow, curve, flex, hook

crooked *adjective* **1** = **bent**, anfractuous, bowed, crippled, curved, deformed, deviating, disfigured, distorted, hooked, irregular, meandering, misshapen, out of shape, tortuous, twisted, twisting, warped, winding, zigzag **2** = **at an angle**, angled, askew, asymmetric, awry, lopsided, off-centre, skewwhiff (*Brit. informal*), slanted, slanting, squint, tilted, to one side, uneven, unsymmetrical **3** *Informal* = **dishonest**, bent (*slang*), corrupt, crafty, criminal, deceitful, dishonourable,

dubious, fraudulent, illegal, knavish, nefarious, questionable, shady (*informal*), shifty, treacherous, underhand, under-the-table, unlawful, unprincipled, unscrupulous
> **Antonyms**
≠**bent:** flat, straight ≠**dishonest:** ethical, fair, honest, honourable, lawful, legal, straight, upright

croon *verb* = **sing**, breathe, hum, purr, warble

crop *noun* **1** = **produce**, fruits, gathering, harvest, reaping, season's growth, vintage, yield ♦ *verb* **2** = **cut**, clip, curtail, dock, lop, mow, pare, prune, reduce, shear, shorten, snip, top, trim **3** = **harvest**, bring home, bring in, collect, garner, gather, mow, pick, reap **4** = **graze**, browse, nibble

crop up *verb Informal* = **happen**, appear, arise, emerge, occur, spring up, turn up

cross *verb* **1** = **go across**, bridge, cut across, extend over, ford, meet, move across, pass over, ply, span, traverse, zigzag **2** = **intersect**, crisscross, intertwine, lace, lie athwart of **3** = **oppose**, block, deny, foil, frustrate, hinder, impede, interfere, obstruct, resist, thwart **4** = **interbreed**, blend, crossbreed, cross-fertilize, cross-pollinate, hybridize, intercross, mix, mongrelize ♦ *noun* **5** = **crucifix**, rood **6** = **crossroads**, crossing, intersection, junction **7** = **crossbreed**, cur, hybrid, mongrel, mutt (*slang*) **8** = **mixture**, amalgam, blend, combination **9** = **trouble**, affliction, burden, grief, load, misery, misfortune, trial, tribulation, woe, worry ♦ *adjective* **10** = **angry**, annoyed, cantankerous, captious, choked, churlish, crotchety (*informal*), crusty, disagreeable, fractious, fretful, grouchy (*informal*), grumpy, hacked (off) (*U.S. slang*), ill-humoured, ill-tempered, impatient, in a bad mood, irascible, irritable, liverish, out of humour, peeved (*informal*), peevish, pettish, petulant, pissed (*taboo slang*), pissed off (*taboo slang*), put out, querulous, ratty (*Brit. & N.Z. informal*), shirty (*slang, chiefly Brit.*), short, snappish, snappy, splenetic, sullen, surly, testy, tetchy, vexed, waspish **11** = **transverse**, crosswise, diagonal, intersecting, oblique **12** = **opposing**, adverse, contrary, opposed, unfavourable **13** = **reciprocal**, opposite
> **Antonyms**
adjective ≠**angry:** affable, agreeable, calm, cheerful, civil, congenial, even-tempered, genial, good-humoured, good-natured, nice, placid, pleasant, sweet

cross-examine *verb* = **question**, catechize, grill (*informal*), interrogate, pump, quiz

cross out *or* **off** *verb* = **strike off** *or* **out**, blue-pencil, cancel, delete, eliminate, score off *or* out

crotch *noun* = **groin**, crutch

crotchety *adjective Informal* = **bad-tempered**, awkward, cantankerous, contrary, crabby, cross, crusty, curmudgeonly, difficult, disagreeable, fractious, grumpy, irritable, liverish, obstreperous, peevish, ratty (*Brit. & N.Z. informal*), surly, testy, tetchy

crouch *verb* = **bend down**, bow, duck, hunch, kneel, squat, stoop

crow *verb* = **gloat**, blow one's own trumpet, bluster, boast, brag, drool, exult, flourish, glory in, strut, swagger, triumph, vaunt

crowd *noun* **1** = **multitude**, army, assembly, bevy, company, concourse, flock, herd, horde, host, mass, mob, pack, press, rabble, swarm, throng, troupe **2** = **group**, bunch (*informal*), circle, clique, lot, set **3** = **audience**, attendance, gate, house, spectators **4 the crowd** = **masses**, hoi polloi, mob, people, populace, proletariat, public, rabble, rank and file, riffraff, vulgar herd ♦ *verb* **5** = **flock**, cluster, congregate, cram, foregather, gather, huddle, mass, muster, press, push, stream, surge, swarm, throng **6** = **squeeze**, bundle, congest, cram, pack, pile **7** *Informal* = **jostle**, batter, butt, elbow, shove

crowded *adjective* = **packed**, busy, congested, cramped, crushed, full, huddled, jam-packed, mobbed, overflowing, populous, swarming, teeming, thronged

crown *noun* **1** = **coronet**, chaplet, circlet, coronal (*poetic*), diadem, tiara **2** = **laurel wreath**, bays, distinction, garland, honour, kudos, laurels, prize, trophy, wreath **3** = **high point**, acme, apex, crest, head, perfection, pinnacle, summit, tip, top, ultimate, zenith ♦ *verb* **4** = **honour**, adorn, dignify, festoon, invest, reward **5** = **cap**, be the climax *or* culmination of, complete, consummate, finish, fulfil, perfect, put the finishing touch to, put the tin lid on, round off, surmount, terminate, top **6** *Slang* = **strike**, belt (*informal*), biff (*slang*), box, cuff, hit over the head, punch

Crown *noun* **1** = **monarchy**, royalty, sovereignty **2** = **monarch**, emperor *or* empress, king *or* queen, rex, ruler, sovereign

crowning *adjective* = **supreme**, climactic, consummate, culminating, final, mother of all (*informal*), paramount, sovereign, ultimate

crucial *adjective* **1** *Informal* = **vital**, essential, high-priority, important, momentous, now or never, pressing, urgent **2** = **critical**, central, decisive, pivotal, psychological, searching, testing, trying

crucify *verb* **1** = **execute**, harrow, persecute, rack, torment, torture **2** *Slang* = **pan** (*informal*), lampoon, ridicule, tear to pieces, wipe the floor with (*informal*)

crude *adjective* **1** = **primitive**, clumsy, makeshift, outline, rough, rough-and-ready, rough-hewn, rude, rudimentary, simple, sketchy, undeveloped, unfinished, unformed, unpolished **2** = **vulgar**, boorish, coarse, crass, dirty, gross, indecent, lewd, obscene, smutty, tactless, tasteless, uncouth, X-rated (*informal*) **3** = **unrefined**, natural, raw, unmilled, unpolished, unprepared, unprocessed
➤ **Antonyms**
≠**vulgar**: genteel, polished, refined, subtle, tasteful ≠**unrefined**: fine, fine-grained, polished, prepared, processed, refined

crudely *adverb* = **vulgarly**, bluntly, clumsily, coarsely, impolitely, indecently, pulling no punches (*informal*), roughly, rudely, sketchily, tastelessly

crudity *noun* **1** = **roughness**, clumsiness, crudeness, primitiveness, rudeness **2** = **vulgarity**, coarseness, crudeness, impropriety, indecency, indelicacy, lewdness, loudness, lowness, obscenity, obtrusiveness, smuttiness

cruel *adjective* **1** = **brutal**, atrocious, barbarous, bitter, bloodthirsty, brutish, callous, cold-blooded, depraved, excruciating, fell (*archaic*), ferocious, fierce, flinty, grim, hard, hard-hearted, harsh, heartless, hellish, implacable, inclement, inexorable, inhuman, inhumane, malevolent, murderous, painful, poignant, ravening, raw, relentless, remorseless, sadistic, sanguinary, savage, severe, spiteful, stony-hearted, unfeeling, unkind, unnatural, vengeful, vicious **2** = **merciless**, pitiless, ruthless, unrelenting
➤ **Antonyms**
benevolent, caring, compassionate, gentle, humane, kind, merciful, sympathetic, warm-hearted

cruelly *adverb* **1** = **brutally**, barbarously, brutishly, callously, ferociously, fiercely, heartlessly, in cold blood, mercilessly, pitilessly, sadistically, savagely, spitefully, unmercifully, viciously **2** = **bitterly**, deeply, fearfully, grievously, monstrously, mortally, severely

cruelty *noun* = **brutality**, barbarity, bestiality, bloodthirstiness, brutishness, callousness, depravity, ferocity, fiendishness, hardheartedness, harshness, heartlessness, inhumanity, mercilessness, murderousness, ruthlessness, sadism, savagery, severity, spite, spitefulness, venom, viciousness

cruise *noun* **1** = **sail**, boat trip, sea trip, voyage ♦ *verb* **2** = **sail**, coast, voyage **3** = **travel along**, coast, drift, keep a steady pace

crumb *noun* = **bit**, atom, fragment, grain, mite, morsel, particle, scrap, shred, sliver, snippet, soupçon, speck

crumble *verb* **1** = **disintegrate**, break down, break up, collapse, come to dust, decay, decompose, degenerate, deteriorate, fall apart, go to pieces, go to wrack and ruin, moulder, perish, tumble down **2** = **crush**, bruise, crumb, fragment, granulate, grind, pound, powder, pulverize, triturate

crumple *verb* **1** = **crush**, crease, pucker, rumple, screw up, scrumple, wrinkle **2** = **collapse**, break down, cave in, fall, give way, go to pieces

crunch *verb* **1** = **chomp**, champ, chew noisily, grind, masticate, munch ♦ *noun* **2** *Informal* = **critical point**, crisis, crux, emergency, hour of decision, moment of truth, test

crusade *noun* = **campaign**, cause, drive, holy war, jihad, movement, push

crusader *noun* = **campaigner**, advocate, champion, reformer

crush *verb* **1** = **squash**, break, bruise, comminute, compress, contuse, crease, crumble, crumple, crunch, mash, pound, press, pulverize, rumple, scrumple, smash, squeeze, wrinkle **2** = **squeeze**, embrace, enfold, hug, press **3** = **overcome**, conquer, extinguish, overpower, overwhelm, put down, quell, stamp out, subdue, vanquish **4** = **humiliate**, abash, browbeat, chagrin, dispose of, mortify, put down (*slang*), quash, shame ♦ *noun* **5** = **crowd**, huddle, jam, party

crust *noun* = **layer**, caking, coat, coating, concretion, covering, film, incrustation, outside, scab, shell, skin, surface

crusty *adjective* **1** = **crispy**, brittle, crisp, friable, hard, short, well-baked, well-done **2** = **irritable**, brusque, cantankerous, captious, choleric, crabby, cross, curt, gruff, ill-humoured, peevish, prickly, ratty (*Brit. & N.Z. informal*), short, short-tempered, snappish, snarling, splenetic, surly, testy, tetchy, touchy

cry verb 1 = **weep**, bawl, bewail, blubber, boohoo, greet (*Scot. or archaic*), howl one's eyes out, keen, lament, mewl, pule, shed tears, snivel, sob, wail, whimper, whine, whinge (*informal*), yowl 2 = **shout**, bawl, bell, bellow, call, call out, ejaculate, exclaim, hail, halloo, holler (*informal*), howl, roar, scream, screech, shriek, sing out, vociferate, whoop, yell ♦ noun 3 = **weeping**, bawling, blubbering, crying, greet (*Scot. or archaic*), howl, keening, lament, lamentation, plaint (*archaic*), snivel, snivelling, sob, sobbing, sorrowing, wailing, weep 4 = **shout**, bawl, bell, bellow, call, ejaculation, exclamation, holler (*informal*), hoot, howl, outcry, roar, scream, screech, shriek, squawk, whoop, yell, yelp, yoo-hoo 5 = **appeal**, plea
➤ Antonyms
verb ≠**weep**: chortle, chuckle, giggle, laugh, snicker, snigger ≠**shout**: drone, mumble, murmur, mutter, speak in hushed tones, speak softly, utter indistinctly, whisper

cry down verb = **run down**, asperse, bad-mouth (*slang, chiefly U.S. & Canad.*), belittle, decry, denigrate, disparage, knock (*informal*), rubbish (*informal*), slag (off) (*slang*)

cry off verb *Informal* = **back out**, beg off, cop out (*slang*), excuse oneself, quit, withdraw, withdraw from

crypt noun = **vault**, catacomb, ossuary, tomb, undercroft

cub noun 1 = **young**, offspring, whelp 2 = **youngster**, babe (*informal*), beginner, fledgling, greenhorn (*informal*), lad, learner, puppy, recruit, tenderfoot, trainee, whippersnapper

cubbyhole noun 1 = **compartment**, niche, pigeonhole, recess, slot 2 = **hideaway**, den, hole, snug

cuddle verb = **hug**, bill and coo, canoodle (*slang*), clasp, cosset, embrace, fondle, nestle, pet, snuggle

cuddly adjective = **soft**, buxom, cuddlesome, curvaceous, huggable, lovable, plump, warm

cudgel noun 1 = **club**, bastinado, baton, bludgeon, cosh (*Brit.*), shillelagh, stick, truncheon ♦ verb 2 = **beat**, bang, baste, batter, bludgeon, cane, cosh (*Brit.*), drub, maul, pound, pummel, thrash, thump, thwack

cue noun = **signal**, catchword, hint, key, nod, prompting, reminder, sign, suggestion

cuff noun off the cuff *Informal* = **impromptu**, ad lib, extempore, improvised, offhand, off the top of one's head, on the spur of the moment, spontaneous, spontaneously, unrehearsed

cul-de-sac noun = **dead end**, blind alley

culminate verb = **end up**, climax, close, come to a climax, come to a head, conclude, end, finish, rise to a crescendo, terminate, wind up

culmination noun = **climax**, acme, apex, apogee, completion, conclusion, consummation, crown, crowning touch, finale, height, *ne plus ultra*, peak, perfection, pinnacle, punch line, summit, top, zenith

culpable adjective = **blameworthy**, answerable, at fault, blamable, censurable, found wanting, guilty, in the wrong, liable, reprehensible, sinful, to blame, wrong
➤ Antonyms
blameless, clean (*slang*), guiltless, innocent, in the clear, not guilty, squeaky-clean

culprit noun = **offender**, criminal, delinquent, evildoer, felon, guilty party, malefactor, miscreant, person responsible, rascal, sinner, transgressor, villain, wrongdoer

cult noun 1 = **sect**, body, church, clique, denomination, faction, faith, following, party, religion, school 2 = **devotion**, admiration, craze, idolization, reverence, veneration, worship

cultivate verb 1 = **farm**, bring under cultivation, fertilize, harvest, plant, plough, prepare, tend, till, work 2 = **develop**, ameliorate, better, bring on, cherish, civilize, discipline, elevate, enrich, foster, improve, polish, promote, refine, train 3 = **encourage**, aid, devote oneself to, forward, foster, further, help, patronize, promote, pursue, support 4 = **court**, associate with, butter up, consort with, dance attendance upon, run after, seek out, seek someone's company or friendship, take trouble or pains with

cultivation noun 1 = **farming**, agronomy, gardening, husbandry, planting, ploughing, tillage, tilling, working 2 = **development**, advancement, advocacy, encouragement, enhancement, fostering, furtherance, help, nurture, patronage, promotion, support 3 = **devotion to**, pursuit, study 4 = **refinement**, breeding, civility, civilization, culture, discernment, discrimination, education, enlightenment, gentility, good taste, learning, letters, manners, polish, sophistication, taste

cultural adjective = **artistic**, broadening, civilizing, developmental, edifying, educational, educative, elevating, enlightening, enriching, humane, humanizing, liberal, liberalizing

culture noun 1 = **civilization**, customs, lifestyle, mores, society, stage of development, the arts, way of life 2 = **refinement**, accomplishment, breeding, education, elevation, enlightenment, erudition, gentility, good taste, improvement, polish, politeness, sophistication, urbanity 3 = **farming**, agriculture, agronomy, cultivation, husbandry

cultured adjective = **refined**, accomplished, advanced, educated, enlightened, erudite, genteel, highbrow, knowledgeable, polished, scholarly, sophisticated, urbane, versed, well-bred, well-informed, well-read
➤ **Antonyms**
coarse, common, inelegant, uncultivated, uneducated, unpolished, unrefined, vulgar

culvert noun = **drain**, channel, conduit, gutter, watercourse

cumbersome adjective = **awkward**, bulky, burdensome, clumsy, clunky (informal), cumbrous, embarrassing, heavy, hefty (informal), incommodious, inconvenient, oppressive, unmanageable, unwieldy, weighty
➤ **Antonyms**
compact, convenient, easy to use, handy, manageable, practical, serviceable, wieldy

cumulative adjective = **collective**, accruing, accumulative, aggregate, amassed, heaped, increasing, snowballing

cunning adjective 1 = **crafty**, artful, astute, canny, devious, foxy, guileful, knowing, Machiavellian, sharp, shifty, shrewd, sly, subtle, tricky, wily 2 = **skilful**, adroit, deft, dexterous, imaginative, ingenious ♦ noun 3 = **craftiness**, artfulness, astuteness, deceitfulness, deviousness, foxiness, guile, shrewdness, slyness, trickery, wiliness 4 = **skill**, ability, adroitness, art, artifice, cleverness, craft, deftness, dexterity, finesse, ingenuity, subtlety
➤ **Antonyms**
adjective ≠**crafty**: artless, dull, ethical, frank, honest, ingenuous ≠**skilful**: maladroit ♦ noun ≠**craftiness**: candour, ingenuousness, sincerity ≠**skill**: clumsiness

cup noun 1 = **mug**, beaker, bowl, cannikin, chalice, demitasse, goblet, teacup 2 = **trophy**

cupboard noun = **cabinet**, ambry (obsolete), closet, locker, press

Cupid noun = **god of love**, amoretto, Eros, love

curb noun 1 = **restraint**, brake, bridle, check, control, deterrent, limitation, rein ♦ verb 2 = **restrain**, bite back, bridle, check, constrain, contain, control, hinder, impede, inhibit, keep a tight rein on, moderate, muzzle, repress, restrict, retard, stem the flow, subdue, suppress

curdle verb = **congeal**, clot, coagulate, condense, curd, solidify, thicken, turn sour
➤ **Antonyms**
deliquesce, dissolve, liquefy, melt, soften, thaw

cure verb 1 = **make better**, alleviate, correct, ease, heal, help, mend, rehabilitate, relieve, remedy, restore, restore to health 2 = **preserve**, dry, kipper, pickle, salt, smoke ♦ noun 3 = **remedy**, alleviation, antidote, corrective, healing, medicine, nostrum, panacea, recovery, restorative, specific, treatment

cure-all noun = **panacea**, catholicon, elixir, elixir vitae, nostrum

curiosity noun 1 = **inquisitiveness**, interest, nosiness (informal), prying, snooping (informal) 2 = **oddity**, celebrity, freak, marvel, novelty, phenomenon, rarity, sight, spectacle, wonder 3 = **collector's item**, bibelot, bygone, curio, knick-knack, objet d'art, trinket

curious adjective 1 = **inquiring**, inquisitive, interested, puzzled, questioning, searching 2 = **inquisitive**, meddling, nosy (informal), peeping, peering, prying, snoopy (informal) 3 = **unusual**, bizarre, exotic, extraordinary, marvellous, mysterious, novel, odd, peculiar, puzzling, quaint, queer, rare, rum (Brit. slang), singular, strange, unconventional, unexpected, unique, unorthodox, wonderful
➤ **Antonyms**
≠**inquiring**: incurious, indifferent, uninquisitive, uninterested ≠**unusual**: common, everyday, familiar, ordinary

curl verb 1 = **twirl**, bend, coil, convolute, corkscrew, crimp, crinkle, crisp, curve, entwine, frizz, loop, meander, ripple, spiral, turn, twine, twist, wind, wreathe, writhe ♦ noun 2 = **twist**, coil, curlicue, kink, ringlet, spiral, whorl

curly adjective = **curling**, corkscrew, crimped, crimpy, crinkly, crisp, curled, frizzy, fuzzy, kinky, permed, spiralled, waved, wavy, winding

currency noun 1 = **money**, bills, coinage, coins, dosh (Brit. & Austral. slang), medium of exchange, notes 2 = **acceptance**, circulation, exposure, popularity, prevalence, publicity, transmission, vogue

current adjective 1 = **present**, contemporary, fashionable, happening (informal), in, in fashion, in vogue, now (informal), present-day, sexy (informal), trendy (Brit. informal), up-to-date, up-to-the-minute 2 = **prevalent**, accepted,

circulating, common, customary, general, going around, in circulation, in progress, in the air, in the news, ongoing, popular, prevailing, rife, topical, widespread ♦ *noun* **3** = **flow**, course, draught, jet, progression, river, stream, tide, tideway, undertow **4** = **mood**, atmosphere, drift, feeling, inclination, tendency, trend, undercurrent, vibes (*slang*)
➤ Antonyms
adjective ≠**present**: archaic, obsolete, old-fashioned, outmoded, out-of-date, passé, past

curse *verb* **1** = **swear**, be foul-mouthed, blaspheme, cuss (*informal*), take the Lord's name in vain, turn the air blue (*informal*), use bad language **2** = **damn**, accurse, anathematize, excommunicate, execrate, fulminate, imprecate **3** = **afflict**, blight, burden, destroy, doom, plague, scourge, torment, trouble, vex ♦ *noun* **4** = **oath**, blasphemy, expletive, obscenity, swearing, swearword **5** = **denunciation**, anathema, ban, evil eye, excommunication, execration, hoodoo (*informal*), imprecation, jinx, malediction, malison (*archaic*) **6** = **affliction**, bane, burden, calamity, cross, disaster, evil, hardship, misfortune, ordeal, plague, scourge, torment, tribulation, trouble, vexation

cursed *adjective* **1** = **damned**, accursed, bedevilled, blighted, cast out, confounded, doomed, excommunicate, execrable, fey (*Scot.*), foredoomed, ill-fated, star-crossed, unholy, unsanctified, villainous **2** = **hateful**, abominable, damnable, detestable, devilish, fell (*archaic*), fiendish, infamous, infernal, loathsome, odious, pernicious, pestilential, vile

curt *adjective* = **short**, abrupt, blunt, brief, brusque, concise, gruff, monosyllabic, offhand, pithy, rude, sharp, snappish, succinct, summary, tart, terse, unceremonious, uncivil, ungracious

curtail *verb* = **cut short**, abbreviate, abridge, contract, cut, cut back, decrease, diminish, dock, lessen, lop, pare down, reduce, retrench, shorten, trim, truncate

curtailment *noun* = **cutting short**, abbreviation, abridgment, contraction, cutback, cutting, docking, retrenchment, truncation

curtain *noun* **1** = **hanging**, drape (*chiefly U.S.*) ♦ *verb* **2** = **conceal**, drape, hide, screen, shroud, shut off, shutter, veil

curve *noun* **1** = **bend**, arc, camber, curvature, half-moon, loop, trajectory, turn ♦ *verb* **2** = **bend**, arc, arch, bow, coil, hook, inflect, spiral, swerve, turn, twist, wind

curved *adjective* = **bent**, arced, arched, bowed, crooked, humped, rounded, serpentine, sinuous, sweeping, turned, twisted, twisty

cushion *noun* **1** = **pillow**, beanbag, bolster, hassock, headrest, pad, scatter cushion, squab ♦ *verb* **2** = **soften**, bolster, buttress, cradle, dampen, deaden, muffle, pillow, protect, stifle, support, suppress

cushy *adjective* *Informal* = **easy**, comfortable, jammy (*Brit. slang*), soft, undemanding

custody *noun* **1** = **safekeeping**, aegis, auspices, care, charge, custodianship, guardianship, keeping, observation, preservation, protection, supervision, trusteeship, tutelage, ward, watch **2** = **imprisonment**, arrest, confinement, detention, durance (*archaic*), duress, incarceration

custom *noun* **1** = **tradition**, convention, etiquette, fashion, form, formality, matter of course, observance, observation, policy, practice, praxis, ritual, rule, style, unwritten law, usage, use **2** = **habit**, habitude (*rare*), manner, mode, practice, procedure, routine, way, wont **3** = **customers**, patronage, trade

customarily *adverb* = **usually**, as a rule, commonly, generally, habitually, in the ordinary way, normally, ordinarily, regularly, traditionally

customary *adjective* = **usual**, accepted, accustomed, acknowledged, bog-standard (*Brit. & Irish slang*), common, confirmed, conventional, established, everyday, familiar, fashionable, general, habitual, normal, ordinary, popular, regular, routine, traditional, wonted
➤ Antonyms
exceptional, infrequent, irregular, occasional, rare, uncommon, unusual

customer *noun* = **client**, buyer, consumer, habitué, patron, prospect, purchaser, regular (*informal*), shopper

customs *plural noun* = **duty**, import charges, tariff, tax, toll

cut *verb* **1** = **penetrate**, chop, cleave, divide, gash, incise, lacerate, lance, nick, notch, pierce, score, sever, slash, slice, slit, wound **2** = **divide**, bisect, carve, cleave, cross, dissect, interrupt, intersect, part, segment, sever, slice, split, sunder **3** = **trim**, clip, dock, fell, gather, hack, harvest, hew, lop, mow, pare, prune, reap, saw down, shave, snip **4** = **abridge**, abbreviate, condense, curtail, delete, edit out, excise, precis, shorten **5** = **reduce**, contract, cut back, decrease, diminish, downsize, ease up on,

lower, rationalize, slash, slim (down) **6 = shape**, carve, chip, chisel, chop, engrave, fashion, form, inscribe, saw, sculpt, sculpture, whittle **7 = hurt**, grieve, insult, pain, put down, snub, sting, wound **8** *Informal* **= ignore**, avoid, cold-shoulder, freeze (someone) out (*informal*), look straight through (someone), send to Coventry, slight, spurn, turn one's back on ♦ *noun* **9 = incision**, gash, graze, groove, laceration, nick, rent, rip, slash, slit, snip, stroke, wound **10 = reduction**, cutback, decrease, decrement, diminution, economy, fall, lowering, saving **11** *Informal* **= share**, chop (*slang*), division, kickback (*chiefly U.S.*), percentage, piece, portion, rake-off (*slang*), section, slice **12 = style**, configuration, fashion, form, look, mode, shape **13 a cut above** *Informal* **= superior to**, better than, higher than, more capable than, more competent than, more efficient than, more reliable than, more trustworthy than, more useful than ♦ *adjective* **14 cut and dried** *Informal* **= prearranged**, automatic, fixed, organized, predetermined, settled, sorted out (*informal*)
➤ **Antonyms**
verb ≠**abridge, reduce**: add to, augment, enlarge, expand, extend, fill out, increase ≠**ignore**: accept gladly, embrace, greet, hail, receive, welcome with open arms
cutback *noun* **= reduction**, cut, decrease, economy, lessening, retrenchment
cut back *verb* **1 = trim**, prune, shorten **2 = reduce**, check, curb, decrease, downsize, draw *or* pull in one's horns (*informal*), economize, lessen, lower, retrench, slash
cut down *verb* **1 = fell**, hew, level, lop, raze **2 = reduce**, decrease, lessen, lower **3 = kill**, blow away (*slang, chiefly U.S.*), dispatch, massacre, mow down, slaughter, slay (*archaic*), take out (*slang*) **4 cut (someone) down to size = make (someone) look small**, abash, humiliate, take the wind out of (someone's) sails
cute *adjective* **= appealing**, attractive, charming, delightful, engaging, lovable, sweet, winning, winsome
cut in *verb* **= interrupt**, break in, butt in, interpose, intervene, intrude, move in (*informal*)
cut off *verb* **1 = separate**, isolate, sever **2 = interrupt**, disconnect, intercept, intersect **3 = halt**, bring to an end, discontinue, obstruct, suspend **4 = disinherit**, disown, renounce
cut out *verb* **1 = stop**, cease, delete,

extract, give up, kick (*informal*), refrain from, remove, sever **2** *Informal* **= exclude**, displace, eliminate, oust, supersede, supplant
cut out for *adjective* **= suited**, adapted, adequate, competent, designed, eligible, equipped, fitted, qualified, suitable
cut-price *adjective* **= cheap**, bargain, cheapo (*informal*), cut-rate (*chiefly U.S.*), reduced, sale
cut short *verb* **= interrupt**, abort, break off, bring to an end, check, dock, halt, leave unfinished, postpone, pull the plug on, stop, terminate, truncate
cutthroat *adjective* **1 = competitive**, dog-eat-dog, fierce, relentless, ruthless, unprincipled **2 = murderous**, barbarous, bloodthirsty, bloody, cruel, death-dealing, ferocious, homicidal, savage, thuggish, violent ♦ *noun* **3 = murderer**, assassin, bravo, butcher, executioner, heavy (*slang*), hit man (*slang*), homicide, killer, liquidator, slayer (*archaic*), thug
cutting *adjective* **1 = hurtful**, acid, acrimonious, barbed, bitter, caustic, malicious, mordacious, pointed, sarcastic, sardonic, scathing, severe, trenchant, vitriolic, wounding **2 = piercing**, biting, bitter, chilling, keen, numbing, penetrating, raw, sharp, stinging
➤ **Antonyms**
≠**hurtful**: consoling, flattering, kind, mild ≠**piercing**: balmy, pleasant, soothing
cut up *verb* **1 = chop**, carve, dice, divide, mince, slice **2 = slash**, injure, knife, lacerate, wound ♦ *adjective* **3** *Informal* **= upset**, agitated, dejected, desolated, distressed, disturbed, heartbroken, stricken, wretched
cycle *noun* **= era**, aeon, age, circle, period, phase, revolution, rotation, round (*of years*)
cynic *noun* **= sceptic**, doubter, misanthrope, misanthropist, pessimist, scoffer
cynical *adjective* **= sceptical**, contemptuous, derisive, distrustful, ironic, misanthropic, misanthropical, mocking, mordacious, pessimistic, sarcastic, sardonic, scoffing, scornful, sneering, unbelieving
➤ **Antonyms**
credulous, green, gullible, hopeful, optimistic, trustful, trusting, unsceptical, unsuspecting
cynicism *noun* **= scepticism**, disbelief, doubt, misanthropy, pessimism, sarcasm, sardonicism

D d

dab *verb* **1** = **pat**, daub, stipple, tap, touch ♦ *noun* **2** = **spot**, bit, drop, pat, smudge, speck **3** = **pat**, flick, stroke, tap, touch

dabble *verb* **1** = **play at**, dally, dip into, potter, tinker, trifle (with) **2** = **splash**, dip, guddle (*Scot.*), moisten, paddle, spatter, sprinkle, wet

dabbler *noun* = **amateur**, dilettante, potterer, tinkerer, trifler

dab hand *noun Brit. informal* = **expert**, ace (*informal*), adept, buff (*informal*), dabster (*dialect*), hotshot (*informal*), maven (*U.S.*), past master, whizz (*informal*), wizard

daft *adjective Informal, chiefly Brit.* **1** = **foolish**, absurd, asinine, crackpot (*informal*), crazy, doolally (*slang*), dopey (*informal*), dumb-ass (*slang*), giddy, gonzo (*slang*), goofy (*informal*), idiotic, inane, loopy (*informal*), off one's head (*informal*), off one's trolley (*slang*), out to lunch (*informal*), scatty (*Brit. informal*), silly, simple, stupid, up the pole (*informal*), wacko *or* whacko (*slang*), witless **2** = **crazy**, barking (*slang*), barking mad (*slang*), crackers (*Brit. slang*), demented, deranged, insane, lunatic, mental (*slang*), not right in the head, not the full shilling (*informal*), nuts (*slang*), nutty (*slang*), round the bend (*Brit. slang*), touched, unhinged **3 daft about** = **enthusiastic**, besotted, crazy (*informal*), doting, dotty (*slang, chiefly Brit.*), infatuated by, mad, nuts (*slang*), nutty (*informal*), potty (*Brit. informal*), sweet on

dagger *noun* **1** = **knife**, bayonet, dirk, poniard, skean, stiletto **2 at daggers drawn** = **on bad terms**, at enmity, at loggerheads, at odds, at war, up in arms **3 look daggers** = **glare**, frown, glower, look black, lour *or* lower, scowl

daily *adjective* **1** = **everyday**, circadian, diurnal, quotidian **2** = **day-to-day**, common, commonplace, everyday, ordinary, quotidian, regular, routine ♦ *adverb* **3** = **every day**, constantly, day after day, day by day, often, once a day, per diem, regularly

dainty *adjective* **1** = **delicate**, charming, elegant, exquisite, fine, graceful, neat, petite, pretty **2** = **delectable**, choice, delicious, palatable, savoury, tasty, tender, toothsome **3** = **particular**, choosy, fastidious, finical, finicky, fussy, mincing, nice, picky (*informal*), refined, scrupulous ♦ *noun* **4** = **delicacy**, *bonne bouche*, fancy, sweetmeat, titbit

➤ **Antonyms**
adjective ≠ **delicate**: awkward, clumsy, coarse, gauche, inelegant, maladroit, uncouth, ungainly

dale *noun* = **valley**, bottom, coomb, dell, dingle, glen, strath (*Scot.*), vale

dally *verb* **1** *Old-fashioned* = **waste time**, dawdle, delay, dilly-dally (*informal*), drag one's feet *or* heels, fool (about *or* around), fritter away, hang about, linger, loiter, procrastinate, tarry, while away **2 dally with** = **flirt**, caress, fondle, fool (about *or* around), frivol (*informal*), lead on, play, play fast and loose (*informal*), tamper, tease, toy, trifle

➤ **Antonyms**
≠ **waste time**: hasten, hurry (up), make haste, push forward *or* on, run, step on it (*informal*)

dam *noun* **1** = **barrier**, barrage, embankment, hindrance, obstruction, wall ♦ *verb* **2** = **block up**, barricade, block, check, choke, confine, hold back, hold in, obstruct, restrict

damage *verb* **1** = **harm**, deface, hurt, impair, incapacitate, injure, mar, mutilate, play (merry) hell with (*informal*), ruin, spoil, tamper with, undo, weaken, wreck ♦ *noun* **2** = **harm**, destruction, detriment, devastation, hurt, impairment, injury, loss, mischief, mutilation, suffering **3** *Informal* = **cost**, bill, charge, expense, total

➤ **Antonyms**
verb ≠ **harm**: better, fix, improve, mend, repair ♦ *noun* ≠ **harm**: gain, improvement, reparation

damages *plural noun Law* = **compensation**, fine, indemnity, reimbursement, reparation, satisfaction

damaging *adjective* = **harmful**, deleterious, detrimental, disadvantageous, hurtful, injurious, prejudicial, ruinous

➤ **Antonyms**
advantageous, favourable, healthful, helpful, profitable, salutary, useful, valuable, wholesome

dame *noun* = **noblewoman**, baroness, dowager, *grande dame*, lady, matron (*archaic*), peeress

damn *verb* 1 = **criticize**, blast, castigate, censure, condemn, denounce, denunciate, excoriate, inveigh against, lambast(e), pan (*informal*), put down, slam (*slang*), slate (*informal*), tear into (*informal*) 2 = **curse**, abuse, anathematize, blaspheme, execrate, imprecate, revile, swear 3 = **sentence**, condemn, doom ♦ *noun* 4 **not give a damn** *Informal* = **not care**, be indifferent, not care a brass farthing, not care a jot, not care a whit, not give a hoot, not give a tinker's curse *or* damn (*slang*), not give two hoots, not mind
➤ **Antonyms**
verb ≠**criticize**: acclaim, admire, applaud, approve, cheer, compliment, congratulate, extol, honour, laud, praise, take one's hat off to ≠**curse**: adore, bless, exalt, glorify, pay homage to

damnable *adjective* = **detestable**, abominable, accursed, atrocious, culpable, cursed, despicable, execrable, hateful, horrible, offensive, wicked
➤ **Antonyms**
admirable, commendable, creditable, excellent, exemplary, fine, honourable, laudable, meritorious, praiseworthy, worthy

damnation *noun Theology* = **condemnation**, anathema, ban, consigning to perdition, damning, denunciation, doom, excommunication, objurgation, proscription, sending to hell

damned *adjective* 1 = **doomed**, accursed, anathematized, condemned, infernal, lost, reprobate, unhappy 2 *Slang* = **detestable**, confounded, despicable, hateful, infamous, infernal, loathsome, revolting

damning *adjective* = **incriminating**, accusatorial, condemnatory, damnatory, dooming, implicating, implicative

damp *adjective* 1 = **moist**, clammy, dank, dewy, dripping, drizzly, humid, misty, muggy, sodden, soggy, sopping, vaporous, wet ♦ *noun* 2 = **moisture**, clamminess, dampness, dankness, dew, drizzle, fog, humidity, mist, mugginess, vapour ♦ *verb* 3 = **moisten**, dampen, wet 4 **damp down** = **curb**, allay, check, chill, cool, dash, deaden, deject, depress, diminish, discourage, dispirit, dull, inhibit, moderate, pour cold water on, reduce, restrain, stifle
➤ **Antonyms**
adjective ≠**moist**: arid, dry, watertight ♦ *noun* ≠**moisture**: aridity, dryness ♦ *verb* ≠**curb**: encourage, gee up, hearten, inspire

dampen *verb* 1 = **reduce**, check, dull, lessen, moderate, restrain, stifle 2

= **moisten**, make damp, spray, wet

damper *noun As in* **put a damper on** = **discouragement**, chill, cloud, cold water (*informal*), curb, gloom, hindrance, killjoy, pall, restraint, wet blanket (*informal*)

dance *verb* 1 = **prance**, bob up and down, caper, cut a rug (*informal*), frolic, gambol, hop, jig, rock, skip, spin, sway, swing, trip, whirl ♦ *noun* 2 = **ball**, dancing party, disco, discotheque, hop (*informal*), knees-up (*Brit. informal*), social

dancer *noun* = **ballerina**, Terpsichorean

dandy *noun* 1 = **fop**, beau, blade (*archaic*), blood (*rare*), buck (*archaic*), coxcomb, dude (*U.S. & Canad. informal*), exquisite (*obsolete*), macaroni (*obsolete*), man about town, peacock, popinjay, swell (*informal*), toff (*Brit. slang*) ♦ *adjective* 2 *Informal* = **excellent**, capital, fine, first-rate, great, splendid

danger *noun* = **peril**, endangerment, hazard, insecurity, jeopardy, menace, pitfall, precariousness, risk, threat, venture, vulnerability

dangerous *adjective* = **perilous**, alarming, breakneck, chancy (*informal*), exposed, hairy (*slang*), hazardous, insecure, menacing, nasty, parlous (*archaic*), precarious, risky, threatening, treacherous, ugly, unchancy (*Scot.*), unsafe, vulnerable
➤ **Antonyms**
harmless, innocuous, O.K. *or* okay (*informal*), out of danger, out of harm's way, protected, safe, safe and sound, secure

dangerously *adverb* 1 = **perilously**, alarmingly, carelessly, daringly, desperately, harmfully, hazardously, precariously, recklessly, riskily, unsafely, unsecurely 2 = **seriously**, critically, gravely, severely

dangle *verb* 1 = **hang**, depend, flap, hang down, sway, swing, trail 2 = **wave**, brandish, entice, flaunt, flourish, lure, tantalize, tempt

dangling *adjective* = **hanging**, disconnected, drooping, loose, swaying, swinging, trailing, unconnected

dapper *adjective* = **neat**, active, brisk, chic, dainty, natty (*informal*), nice, nimble, smart, soigné *or* soignée, spruce, spry, stylish, trig (*archaic or dialect*), trim, well-groomed, well turned out
➤ **Antonyms**
blowsy, disarrayed, dishevelled, dowdy, frowzy, ill-groomed, rumpled, slobby (*informal*), sloppy (*informal*), slovenly, unkempt, untidy

dapple *verb* = **mottle**, bespeckle, dot, fleck,

freckle, speckle, spot, stipple

dappled *adjective* = **mottled**, brindled, checkered, flecked, freckled, piebald, pied, speckled, spotted, stippled, variegated

dare *verb* 1 = **risk**, brave, endanger, gamble, hazard, make bold, presume, skate on thin ice, stake, venture 2 = **challenge**, defy, goad, provoke, taunt, throw down the gauntlet ♦ *noun* 3 = **challenge**, defiance, provocation, taunt

daredevil *noun* 1 = **adventurer**, adrenalin junky (*slang*), desperado, exhibitionist, hot dog (*chiefly U.S.*), madcap, show-off (*informal*), stunt man ♦ *adjective* 2 = **daring**, adventurous, audacious, bold, death-defying, madcap, reckless

daring *adjective* 1 = **brave**, adventurous, audacious, ballsy (*taboo slang*), bold, daredevil, fearless, game (*informal*), have-a-go (*informal*), impulsive, intrepid, plucky, rash, reckless, valiant, venturesome ♦ *noun* 2 = **bravery**, audacity, balls (*taboo slang*), ballsiness (*taboo slang*), boldness, bottle (*Brit. slang*), courage, derring-do (*archaic*), face (*informal*), fearlessness, grit, guts (*informal*), intrepidity, nerve (*informal*), pluck, rashness, spirit, spunk (*informal*), temerity
➤ **Antonyms**
adjective ≠**brave**: anxious, careful, cautious, cowardly, faint-hearted, fearful, timid, uncourageous, wary ♦ *noun* ≠**bravery**: anxiety, caution, cowardice, fear, timidity

dark *adjective* 1 = **dim**, cloudy, darksome (*literary*), dingy, indistinct, murky, overcast, pitch-black, pitchy, shadowy, shady, sunless, unlit 2 = **brunette**, black, dark-skinned, dusky, ebony, sable, swarthy 3 = **gloomy**, bleak, cheerless, dismal, doleful, drab, grim, joyless, morbid, morose, mournful, sad, sombre 4 = **evil**, atrocious, damnable, foul, hellish, horrible, infamous, infernal, nefarious, satanic, sinful, sinister, vile, wicked 5 = **secret**, abstruse, arcane, concealed, cryptic, deep, Delphic, enigmatic, hidden, mysterious, mystic, obscure, occult, puzzling, recondite 6 = **angry**, dour, forbidding, frowning, glowering, glum, ominous, scowling, sulky, sullen, threatening ♦ *noun* 7 = **darkness**, dimness, dusk, gloom, murk, murkiness, obscurity, semi-darkness 8 = **night**, evening, nightfall, night-time, twilight
➤ **Antonyms**
adjective ≠**brunette**: blond, blonde, fair, fair-haired, flaxen-haired, light, light-complexioned, towheaded
≠**gloomy**: bright, cheerful, clear, genial,

glad, hopeful, pleasant, sunny

darken *verb* 1 = **make dark**, becloud, blacken, cloud up *or* over, deepen, dim, eclipse, make darker, make dim, obscure, overshadow, shade, shadow 2 = **become gloomy**, become angry, blacken, cast a pall over, cloud, deject, depress, dispirit, grow troubled, look black, sadden
➤ **Antonyms**
≠**make dark**: brighten, clear up, enliven, gleam, glow, illuminate, lighten, light up, make bright, shine ≠**become gloomy**: become cheerful, cheer, encourage, gladden, hearten, make happy, perk up

darkness *noun* 1 = **dark**, blackness, dimness, dusk, duskiness, gloom, murk, murkiness, nightfall, obscurity, shade, shadiness, shadows 2 = **secrecy**, blindness, concealment, ignorance, mystery, privacy, unawareness

darling *noun* 1 = **beloved**, dear, dearest, love, sweetheart, truelove 2 = **favourite**, apple of one's eye, blue-eyed boy, fair-haired boy (*U.S.*), pet, spoilt child ♦ *adjective* 3 = **beloved**, adored, cherished, dear, precious, treasured 4 = **adorable**, attractive, captivating, charming, cute, enchanting, lovely, sweet

darn *verb* 1 = **mend**, cobble up, patch, repair, sew up, stitch ♦ *noun* 2 = **mend**, invisible repair, patch, reinforcement

dart *verb* 1 = **dash**, bound, flash, flit, fly, race, run, rush, scoot, shoot, spring, sprint, start, tear, whistle, whizz 2 = **throw**, cast, fling, hurl, launch, propel, send, shoot, sling

dash *verb* 1 = **rush**, barrel (along) (*informal, chiefly U.S. & Canad.*), bolt, bound, burn rubber (*informal*), dart, fly, haste, hasten, hurry, race, run, speed, spring, sprint, tear 2 = **throw**, cast, fling, hurl, slam, sling 3 = **crash**, break, destroy, shatter, shiver, smash, splinter 4 = **frustrate**, blight, foil, ruin, spoil, thwart, undo 5 = **disappoint**, abash, chagrin, confound, dampen, discomfort, discourage ♦ *noun* 6 = **rush**, bolt, dart, haste, onset, race, run, sortie, sprint, spurt 7 = **little**, bit, drop, flavour, hint, pinch, smack, soupçon, sprinkling, suggestion, tinge, touch 8 = **style**, brio, élan, flair, flourish, panache, spirit, verve, vigour, vivacity
➤ **Antonyms**
verb ≠**rush**: crawl, dawdle, walk
≠**frustrate**: enhance, improve ♦ *noun*
≠**little**: lot, much

dashing *adjective* 1 = **bold**, daring, debonair, exuberant, gallant, lively, plucky, spirited, swashbuckling 2 = **stylish**, dapper, dazzling, elegant, flamboyant, jaunty, showy, smart, sporty, swish (*informal, chiefly Brit.*), urbane

> ➤ Antonyms

≠**bold**: boring, dreary, dull, lacklustre, stolid, unexciting, uninteresting

data *noun* = **information**, details, documents, dope (*informal*), facts, figures, info (*informal*), input, materials, statistics

date *noun* **1** = **time**, age, epoch, era, period, stage **2** = **appointment**, assignation, engagement, meeting, rendezvous, tryst **3** = **partner**, escort, friend, steady (*informal*) **4 out of date** = **old-fashioned**, antiquated, archaic, dated, obsolete, old, passé **5 to date** = **up to now**, now, so far, up to the present, up to this point, yet **6 up-to-date** = **modern**, à la mode, contemporary, current, fashionable, trendy (*Brit. informal*), up-to-the-minute ♦ *verb* **7** = **put a date on**, assign a date to, determine the date of, fix the period of **8** = **become old-fashioned**, be dated, obsolesce, show one's age **9 date from** *or* **date back to** = **come from**, bear a date of, belong to, exist from, originate in

dated *adjective* = **old-fashioned**, antiquated, archaic, *démodé,* obsolete, old hat, out, outdated, outmoded, out of date, out of the ark (*informal*), passé, unfashionable, untrendy (*Brit. informal*)

> ➤ Antonyms

à la mode, all the rage, chic, cool (*informal*), current, hip (*slang*), in vogue, latest, modern, modish, popular, stylish, trendy (*Brit. informal*), up-to-date

daub *verb* **1** = **smear**, coat, cover, paint, plaster, slap on (*informal*) **2** = **stain**, bedaub, begrime, besmear, blur, deface, dirty, grime, smirch, smudge, spatter, splatter, sully ♦ *noun* **3** = **smear**, blot, blotch, smirch, splodge, splotch, spot, stain

daunt *verb* **1** = **intimidate**, alarm, appal, cow, dismay, frighten, frighten off, overawe, scare, subdue, terrify **2** = **discourage**, deter, dishearten, dispirit, put off, shake

> ➤ Antonyms

cheer, comfort, encourage, hearten, inspire, reassure, spur, support

daunted *adjective* = **intimidated**, alarmed, cowed, demoralized, deterred, discouraged, disillusioned, dismayed, dispirited, downcast, frightened, hesitant, overcome, put off, unnerved

daunting *adjective* = **intimidating**, alarming, demoralizing, disconcerting, discouraging, disheartening, frightening, off-putting (*Brit. informal*), unnerving

> ➤ Antonyms

cheering, comforting, encouraging, heartening, reassuring

dauntless *adjective* = **fearless**, bold, brave, courageous, daring, doughty, gallant, gritty, heroic, indomitable, intrepid, lion-hearted, resolute, stouthearted, undaunted, unflinching, valiant, valorous

dawdle *verb* = **waste time**, dally, delay, dilly-dally (*informal*), drag one's feet *or* heels, fritter away, hang about, idle, lag, loaf, loiter, potter, trail

> ➤ Antonyms

fly, get a move on (*informal*), hasten, hurry, lose no time, make haste, rush, scoot, step on it (*informal*)

dawn *noun* **1** = **daybreak**, aurora (*poetic*), cockcrow, crack of dawn, dawning, daylight, dayspring (*poetic*), morning, sunrise, sunup **2** = **beginning**, advent, birth, dawning, emergence, genesis, inception, onset, origin, outset, rise, start, unfolding ♦ *verb* **3** = **grow light**, break, brighten, gleam, glimmer, lighten **4** = **begin**, appear, develop, emerge, initiate, open, originate, rise, unfold **5 dawn on** *or* **upon** = **hit**, become apparent, come into one's head, come to mind, cross one's mind, flash across one's mind, occur, register (*informal*), strike

day *noun* **1** = **twenty-four hours**, daylight, daylight hours, daytime, working day **2** = **point in time**, date, particular day, set time, time **3** = **time**, age, ascendancy, cycle, epoch, era, generation, height, heyday, period, prime, zenith **4 call it a day** *Informal* = **stop**, end, finish, knock off (*informal*), leave off, pack it in (*slang*), pack up (*informal*), shut up shop **5 day after day** = **continually**, monotonously, persistently, regularly, relentlessly **6 day by day** = **gradually**, daily, progressively, steadily

daybreak *noun* = **dawn**, break of day, cockcrow, crack of dawn, dayspring (*poetic*), first light, morning, sunrise, sunup

daydream *noun* **1** = **fantasy**, castle in the air *or* in Spain, dream, fancy, figment of the imagination, fond hope, imagining, pipe dream, reverie, wish ♦ *verb* **2** = **fantasize**, dream, envision, fancy, hallucinate, imagine, muse, stargaze

daydreamer *noun* = **fantasizer**, castle-builder, dreamer, pipe dreamer, visionary, Walter Mitty, wishful thinker, woolgatherer

daylight *noun* **1** = **sunlight**, light of day, sunshine **2** = **daytime**, broad day, daylight hours **3** = **full view**, light of day, openness, public attention

daze *verb* **1** = **stun**, benumb, numb,

paralyse, shock, stupefy **2 = confuse,** amaze, astonish, astound, befog, bewilder, blind, dazzle, dumbfound, flabbergast (*informal*), flummox, nonplus, perplex, stagger, startle, surprise ♦ *noun* **3 = shock,** bewilderment, confusion, distraction, mind-fuck (*taboo slang*), stupor, trance, trancelike state

dazed *adjective* **= shocked,** at sea, baffled, bemused, bewildered, confused, disorientated, dizzy, dopey (*slang*), flabbergasted (*informal*), flummoxed, fuddled, groggy (*informal*), light-headed, muddled, nonplussed, numbed, perplexed, punch-drunk, staggered, stunned, stupefied, woozy (*informal*)

dazzle *verb* **1 = impress,** amaze, astonish, awe, bowl over (*informal*), fascinate, hypnotize, overawe, overpower, overwhelm, strike dumb, stupefy, take one's breath away **2 = blind,** bedazzle, blur, confuse, daze ♦ *noun* **3 = splendour,** brilliance, éclat, flash, glitter, magnificence, razzle-dazzle (*slang*), razzmatazz (*slang*), sparkle

dazzling *adjective* **= splendid,** brilliant, divine, drop-dead (*slang*), glittering, glorious, radiant, ravishing, scintillating, sensational (*informal*), shining, sparkling, stunning, sublime, superb, virtuoso

➤ **Antonyms**
dull, ordinary, tedious, unexceptional, unexciting, uninspiring, uninteresting, unmemorable, unremarkable, vanilla (*slang*)

dead *adjective* **1 = deceased,** defunct, departed, extinct, gone, late, passed away, perished, pushing up (the) daisies **2 = inanimate,** lifeless **3 = not working,** barren, inactive, inoperative, obsolete, stagnant, sterile, still, unemployed, unprofitable, useless **4 = spiritless,** apathetic, callous, cold, dull, frigid, glassy, glazed, indifferent, lukewarm, torpid, unresponsive, wooden **5 = numb,** inert, paralysed **6 = total,** absolute, complete, downright, entire, outright, thorough, unqualified, utter **7** *Informal* **= exhausted,** dead beat (*informal*), spent, tired, worn out **8 = boring,** dead-and-alive, dull, flat, ho-hum (*informal*), insipid, stale, tasteless, uninteresting, vapid ♦ *noun* **9 = middle,** depth, midst ♦ *adverb* **10** *Informal* **= exactly,** absolutely, completely, directly, entirely, totally

➤ **Antonyms**
adjective ≠**deceased:** alive, alive and kicking, animate, existing, living
≠**inanimate:** animated, lively, responsive
≠**not working:** active, alive, effective, in use, operative, productive, working

≠**spiritless:** active, alive, alive and kicking, animated, full of beans (*informal*), lively, vivacious

deaden *verb* **= reduce,** abate, alleviate, anaesthetize, benumb, blunt, check, cushion, damp, dampen, diminish, dull, hush, impair, lessen, muffle, mute, numb, paralyse, quieten, smother, stifle, suppress, weaken

deadline *noun* **= time limit,** cutoff point, limit, target date

deadlock *noun* **= impasse,** cessation, dead heat, draw, full stop, gridlock, halt, stalemate, standoff, standstill, tie

deadlocked *adjective* **= even,** equal, level, neck and neck

deadly *adjective* **1 = lethal,** baleful, baneful, dangerous, death-dealing, deathly, destructive, fatal, malignant, mortal, noxious, pernicious, poisonous, venomous **2** *Informal* **= boring,** as dry as dust, dull, ho-hum (*informal*), mind-numbing, monotonous, tedious, tiresome, uninteresting, wearisome **3 = deathly,** ashen, deathlike, ghastly, ghostly, pallid, wan, white **4 = ruthless,** cruel, grim, implacable, mortal, savage, unrelenting **5 = accurate,** effective, exact, on target, precise, sure, true, unerring, unfailing

deadpan *adjective* **= expressionless,** blank, empty, impassive, inexpressive, inscrutable, poker-faced, straight-faced

deaf *adjective* **1 = hard of hearing,** stone deaf, without hearing **2 = oblivious,** indifferent, unconcerned, unhearing, unmoved

deafen *verb* **= make deaf,** din, drown out, split *or* burst the eardrums

deafening *adjective* **= ear-piercing,** booming, dinning, ear-splitting, intense, overpowering, piercing, resounding, ringing, thunderous

deal *noun* **1** *Informal* **= agreement,** arrangement, bargain, contract, pact, transaction, understanding **2 = amount,** degree, distribution, extent, portion, quantity, share, transaction **3 = hand,** cut and shuffle, distribution, round, single game ♦ *verb* **4 = sell,** bargain, buy and sell, do business, negotiate, stock, trade, traffic

dealer *noun* **= trader,** chandler, marketer, merchandiser, merchant, purveyor, supplier, tradesman, wholesaler

dealings *plural noun* **= business,** business relations, commerce, trade, traffic, transactions, truck

deal out *verb* **= distribute,** allot, apportion, assign, bestow, dispense, divide, dole out, give, mete out, reward, share

deal with *verb* 1 = **handle**, attend to, come to grips with, cope with, get to grips with, manage, oversee, see to, take care of, treat 2 = **be concerned with**, consider, treat of 3 = **behave towards**, act towards, conduct oneself towards

dear *noun* 1 = **beloved**, angel, darling, loved one, precious, treasure ♦ *adjective* 2 = **beloved**, cherished, close, darling, esteemed, familiar, favourite, intimate, precious, prized, respected, treasured 3 = **expensive**, at a premium, costly, high-priced, overpriced, pricey (*informal*) ♦ *adverb* 4 = **dearly**, at a heavy cost, at a high price, at great cost
➤ Antonyms
adjective ≠**beloved**: disliked, hated ≠**expensive**: cheap, common, inexpensive, worthless

dearly *adverb* 1 = **very much**, extremely, greatly, profoundly 2 = **at great cost**, at a heavy cost, at a high price, dear

dearth *noun* = **scarcity**, deficiency, inadequacy, insufficiency, lack, paucity, poverty, shortage, want

death *noun* 1 = **dying**, bereavement, cessation, curtains (*informal*), decease, demise, departure, dissolution, end, exit, expiration, loss, passing, quietus, release 2 = **destruction**, annihilation, downfall, ending, eradication, extermination, extinction, finish, grave, obliteration, ruin, ruination, undoing 3 *sometimes capital* = **grim reaper**, Dark Angel
➤ Antonyms
≠**dying**: birth ≠**destruction**: beginning, emergence, genesis, growth, origin, rise, source

deathless *adjective* = **eternal**, everlasting, immortal, imperishable, incorruptible, timeless, undying
➤ Antonyms
corporeal, earthly, ephemeral, human, mortal, passing, temporal, transient, transitory

deathly *adjective* 1 = **deathlike**, cadaverous, gaunt, ghastly, grim, haggard, like death warmed up (*informal*), pale, pallid, wan 2 = **fatal**, deadly, extreme, intense, mortal, terrible

debacle *noun* = **disaster**, catastrophe, collapse, defeat, devastation, downfall, fiasco, havoc, overthrow, reversal, rout, ruin, ruination

debase *verb* 1 = **degrade**, abase, cheapen, demean, devalue, disgrace, dishonour, drag down, humble, humiliate, lower, reduce, shame 2 = **contaminate**, adulterate, bastardize, corrupt, defile, depreciate, impair, pollute, taint, vitiate

➤ Antonyms
≠**degrade**: elevate, enhance, exalt, improve, uplift ≠**contaminate**: purify

debased *adjective* 1 = **degraded**, abandoned, base, corrupt, debauched, depraved, devalued, fallen, low, perverted, sordid, vile 2 = **contaminated**, adulterated, depreciated, impure, lowered, mixed, polluted, reduced
➤ Antonyms
≠**degraded**: chaste, decent, ethical, good, honourable, incorruptible, innocent, moral, pure, upright, virtuous ≠**contaminated**: pure

debasement *noun* 1 = **degradation**, abasement, baseness, corruption, depravation, devaluation, perversion 2 = **contamination**, adulteration, depreciation, pollution, reduction

debatable *adjective* = **doubtful**, arguable, borderline, controversial, disputable, dubious, iffy (*informal*), in dispute, moot, open to question, problematical, questionable, uncertain, undecided, unsettled

debate *noun* 1 = **discussion**, altercation, argument, contention, controversy, disputation, dispute, polemic, row 2 = **consideration**, cogitation, deliberation, meditation, reflection ♦ *verb* 3 = **discuss**, argue, contend, contest, controvert, dispute, question, wrangle 4 = **consider**, cogitate, deliberate, meditate upon, mull over, ponder, reflect, revolve, ruminate, weigh

debauched *adjective* = **corrupt**, abandoned, debased, degenerate, degraded, depraved, dissipated, dissolute, immoral, licentious, perverted, pervy (*slang*), profligate, sleazy, wanton

debauchery *noun* = **depravity**, dissipation, dissoluteness, excess, indulgence, intemperance, lewdness, overindulgence

debilitate *verb* = **weaken**, devitalize, enervate, enfeeble, exhaust, incapacitate, prostrate, relax, sap, undermine, wear out
➤ Antonyms
animate, brighten, energize, enliven, excite, fire, invigorate, pep up, perk up, rouse, stimulate, vitalize

debility *noun* = **weakness**, decrepitude, enervation, enfeeblement, exhaustion, faintness, feebleness, frailty, incapacity, infirmity, languor, malaise, sickliness

debonair *adjective* = **elegant**, affable, buoyant, charming, cheerful, courteous, dashing, jaunty, light-hearted, refined, smooth, sprightly, suave, urbane, well-bred

debrief *verb* = **interrogate**, cross-examine, examine, probe, question, quiz

debris noun = **remains**, bits, brash, detritus, dross, fragments, litter, pieces, rubbish, rubble, ruins, waste, wreck, wreckage

debt noun 1 = **debit**, arrears, bill, claim, commitment, due, duty, liability, obligation, score 2 **in debt** = **owing**, accountable, beholden, in arrears, in hock (*informal, chiefly U.S.*), in the red (*informal*), liable, responsible

debtor noun = **borrower**, defaulter, insolvent, mortgagor

debunk verb *Informal* = **expose**, cut down to size, deflate, disparage, lampoon, mock, puncture, ridicule, show up

debut noun = **introduction**, beginning, bow, coming out, entrance, first appearance, inauguration, initiation, launching, presentation

decadence noun = **degeneration**, corruption, debasement, decay, decline, deterioration, dissipation, dissolution, fall, perversion, retrogression

decadent adjective = **degenerate**, abandoned, corrupt, debased, debauched, decaying, declining, degraded, depraved, dissolute, immoral, self-indulgent
➤ Antonyms
decent, ethical, good, high-minded, honourable, incorruptible, moral, principled, proper, upright, upstanding, virtuous

decant verb = **pour out**, drain, draw off, tap

decapitate verb = **behead**, execute, guillotine

decay verb 1 = **decline**, atrophy, break down, crumble, degenerate, deteriorate, disintegrate, dissolve, dwindle, moulder, shrivel, sink, spoil, wane, waste away, wear away 2 = **rot**, corrode, decompose, mortify, perish, putrefy ♦ noun 3 = **decline**, atrophy, collapse, decadence, degeneracy, degeneration, deterioration, dying, fading, failing, wasting, withering 4 = **rot**, caries, cariosity, decomposition, gangrene, mortification, perishing, putrefaction, putrescence, putridity, rotting
➤ Antonyms
verb ≠**decline**: expand, flourish, flower, grow, increase ♦ noun ≠**decline**: growth

decayed adjective = **rotten**, bad, carious, carrion, corroded, decomposed, perished, putrefied, putrid, rank, spoiled, wasted, withered

decaying adjective = **rotting**, crumbling, deteriorating, disintegrating, gangrenous, perishing, putrefacient, wasting away, wearing away

decease noun *Formal* = **death**, demise, departure, dissolution, dying, release

deceased adjective = **dead**, defunct, departed, expired, finished, former, gone, late, lifeless, lost, pushing up daisies

deceit noun 1 = **dishonesty**, artifice, cheating, chicanery, craftiness, cunning, deceitfulness, deception, dissimulation, double-dealing, duplicity, fraud, fraudulence, guile, hypocrisy, imposition, lying, pretence, slyness, treachery, trickery, underhandedness 2 = **lie**, artifice, blind, cheat, chicanery, deception, duplicity, fake, feint, fraud, imposture, misrepresentation, pretence, ruse, scam (*slang*), sham, shift, sting (*informal*), stratagem, subterfuge, swindle, trick, wile
➤ Antonyms
≠**dishonesty**: candour, frankness, honesty, openness, sincerity, truthfulness

deceitful adjective = **dishonest**, counterfeit, crafty, deceiving, deceptive, designing, disingenuous, double-dealing, duplicitous, fallacious, false, fraudulent, guileful, hypocritical, illusory, insincere, knavish (*archaic*), sneaky, treacherous, tricky, two-faced, underhand, untrustworthy

deceive verb 1 = **take in** (*informal*), bamboozle (*informal*), beguile, betray, cheat, con (*informal*), cozen, delude, disappoint, double-cross (*informal*), dupe, ensnare, entrap, fool, hoax, hoodwink, impose upon, kid (*informal*), lead (someone) on (*informal*), mislead, outwit, pull a fast one (*slang*), pull the wool over (someone's) eyes, stiff (*slang*), sting (*informal*), swindle, take for a ride (*informal*), trick 2 **be deceived by** = **be taken in (by)**, be made a fool of, be the dupe of, bite, fall for, fall into a trap, swallow (*informal*), swallow hook, line, and sinker (*informal*), take the bait

deceiver noun = **liar**, cheat, con man (*informal*), double-dealer, fraud, impostor, swindler, trickster

decency noun = **respectability**, appropriateness, civility, correctness, courtesy, decorum, etiquette, fitness, good form, good manners, modesty, propriety, seemliness

decent adjective 1 = **satisfactory**, acceptable, adequate, ample, average, competent, fair, passable, reasonable, sufficient, tolerable 2 = **respectable**, chaste, decorous, delicate, modest, nice, polite, presentable, proper, pure 3 = **proper**, appropriate, becoming, befitting, comely, *comme il faut*, fit, fitting, seemly, suitable 4 *Informal* = **kind**, accommodating, courteous, friendly, generous, gracious, helpful, obliging, thoughtful

➤ **Antonyms**
≠**satisfactory**: clumsy, inept,
unsatisfactory ≠**proper**: awkward,
immodest, improper, incorrect, indecent,
unseemly, unsuitable ≠**kind**: awkward,
discourteous

deception noun 1 = **trickery**, craftiness,
cunning, deceit, deceitfulness,
deceptiveness, dissimulation, duplicity,
fraud, fraudulence, guile, hypocrisy,
imposition, insincerity, legerdemain,
treachery 2 = **trick**, artifice, bluff, canard,
cheat, decoy, feint, fraud, hoax, hokum
(slang, chiefly U.S. & Canad.), illusion,
imposture, leg-pull (Brit. informal), lie, pork
pie (Brit. slang), porky (Brit. slang), ruse,
sham, snare, snow job (slang, chiefly U.S. &
Canad.), stratagem, subterfuge, wile
➤ **Antonyms**
≠**trickery**: artlessness, candour, fidelity,
frankness, honesty, openness,
scrupulousness, straightforwardness,
trustworthiness, truthfulness

deceptive adjective = **misleading**,
ambiguous, deceitful, delusive, dishonest,
fake, fallacious, false, fraudulent, illusory,
mock, specious, spurious, unreliable

decide verb = **reach** or **come to a decision**,
adjudge, adjudicate, choose, come to a
conclusion, commit oneself, conclude,
decree, determine, elect, end, make a
decision, make up one's mind, purpose,
resolve, settle, tip the balance
➤ **Antonyms**
be indecisive, be unable to decide, blow
hot and cold (informal), dither (chiefly
Brit.), falter, fluctuate, hesitate, hum and
haw, seesaw, shillyshally (informal),
swither (Scot.), vacillate

decided adjective 1 = **definite**, absolute,
categorical, certain, clear-cut, distinct,
express, indisputable, positive,
pronounced, unambiguous, undeniable,
undisputed, unequivocal, unquestionable
2 = **determined**, assertive, decisive,
deliberate, emphatic, firm, resolute,
strong-willed, unfaltering, unhesitating
➤ **Antonyms**
≠**definite**: doubtful, dubious,
questionable, undetermined
≠**determined**: hesitant, indecisive,
irresolute, undetermined, weak

decidedly adverb = **definitely**, absolutely,
certainly, clearly, decisively, distinctly,
downright, positively, unequivocally,
unmistakably

deciding adjective = **determining**, chief,
conclusive, critical, crucial, decisive,
influential, prime, principal, significant

decimate verb = **devastate**, destroy, lay
waste, ravage, wreak havoc on

decipher verb = **figure out** (informal),
construe, crack, decode, deduce, explain,
interpret, make out, read, reveal, solve,
suss (out) (slang), understand, unfold,
unravel

decision noun 1 = **judgment**, arbitration,
conclusion, finding, outcome, resolution,
result, ruling, sentence, settlement, verdict
2 = **decisiveness**, determination, firmness,
purpose, purposefulness, resoluteness,
resolution, resolve, strength of mind or will

decisive adjective 1 = **crucial**, absolute,
conclusive, critical, definite, definitive,
fateful, final, influential, momentous,
positive, significant 2 = **resolute**, decided,
determined, firm, forceful, incisive,
strong-minded, trenchant
➤ **Antonyms**
≠**crucial**: doubtful, indecisive, uncertain,
undecided ≠**resolute**: hesitant, hesitating,
indecisive, in two minds (informal),
irresolute, pussy-footing (informal),
uncertain, undecided, vacillating

deck verb 1 = **decorate**, adorn, apparel
(archaic), array, attire, beautify, bedeck,
bedight (archaic), bedizen (archaic),
clothe, dress, embellish, engarland,
festoon, garland, grace, ornament, trim 2
deck up or **out** = **dress up**, doll up (slang),
get ready, prettify, pretty up, prink, rig
out, tog up or out, trick out

declaim verb 1 = **orate**, harangue, hold
forth, lecture, perorate, proclaim, rant,
recite, speak, spiel (informal) 2 **declaim**
against = **protest against**, attack, decry,
denounce, inveigh, rail

declamation noun = **oration**, address,
harangue, lecture, rant, recitation, speech,
tirade

declaration noun 1 = **statement**,
acknowledgment, affirmation, assertion,
attestation, averment, avowal, deposition,
disclosure, protestation, revelation,
testimony 2 = **announcement**, edict,
manifesto, notification, proclamation,
profession, promulgation,
pronouncement, pronunciamento

declaratory, declarative adjective
= **affirmative**, definite, demonstrative,
enunciatory, explanatory, expository,
expressive, positive

declare verb 1 = **state**, affirm, announce,
assert, asseverate, attest, aver, avow,
certify, claim, confirm, maintain, notify,
proclaim, profess, pronounce, swear,
testify, utter, validate 2 = **make known**,
confess, convey, disclose, manifest, reveal,
show

decline verb 1 = **lessen**, decrease, diminish,

drop, dwindle, ebb, fade, fail, fall, fall off, flag, shrink, sink, wane **2** = **deteriorate**, decay, degenerate, droop, languish, pine, weaken, worsen **3** = **refuse**, abstain, avoid, deny, forgo, reject, say 'no', send one's regrets, turn down **4** = **slope**, descend, dip, sink, slant ◆ *noun* **5** = **lessening**, abatement, diminution, downturn, drop, dwindling, falling off, recession, slump **6** = **deterioration**, decay, decrepitude, degeneration, enfeeblement, failing, senility, weakening, worsening **7** = **consumption**, phthisis, tuberculosis **8** = **slope**, declivity, hill, incline
➤ **Antonyms**
verb ≠**lessen**: increase, rise ≠**deteriorate**: improve ≠**refuse**: accept, agree, consent ◆ *noun* ≠**lessening**: rise, upswing ≠**deterioration**: improvement

decode *verb* = **decipher**, crack, decrypt, interpret, solve, unscramble, work out
➤ **Antonyms**
encipher, encode, encrypt, scramble

decompose *verb* **1** = **rot**, break up, crumble, decay, fall apart, fester, putrefy, spoil **2** = **break down**, analyse, atomize, break up, decompound, disintegrate, dissect, dissolve, distil, separate

decomposition *noun* **1** = **rot**, corruption, decay, putrefaction, putrescence, putridity **2** = **breakdown**, atomization, disintegration, dissolution, division

decor *noun* = **decoration**, colour scheme, furnishing style, ornamentation

decorate *verb* **1** = **adorn**, beautify, bedeck, deck, embellish, engarland, enrich, festoon, grace, ornament, trim **2** = **do up** (*informal*), colour, furbish, paint, paper, renovate, wallpaper **3** = **pin a medal on**, cite, confer an honour on *or* upon

decoration *noun* **1** = **adornment**, beautification, elaboration, embellishment, enrichment, garnishing, ornamentation, trimming **2** = **ornament**, arabesque, bauble, cartouch(e), curlicue, falderal, festoon, flounce, flourish, frill, furbelow, garnish, scroll, spangle, trimmings, trinket **3** = **medal**, award, badge, colours, emblem, garter, order, ribbon, star

decorative *adjective* = **ornamental**, adorning, arty-crafty, beautifying, enhancing, fancy, nonfunctional, pretty

decorous *adjective* = **proper**, appropriate, becoming, befitting, comely, *comme il faut*, correct, decent, dignified, fit, fitting, mannerly, polite, refined, sedate, seemly, staid, suitable, well-behaved
➤ **Antonyms**
inapposite, inappropriate, malapropos, out of keeping, unbefitting, undignified,

unseemly

decorum *noun* = **propriety**, behaviour, breeding, courtliness, decency, deportment, dignity, etiquette, gentility, good grace, good manners, gravity, politeness, politesse, protocol, punctilio, respectability, seemliness
➤ **Antonyms**
bad manners, churlishness, impoliteness, impropriety, indecorum, rudeness, unseemliness

decoy *noun* **1** = **lure**, attraction, bait, ensnarement, enticement, inducement, pretence, trap ◆ *verb* **2** = **lure**, allure, bait, deceive, ensnare, entice, entrap, inveigle, seduce, tempt

decrease *verb* **1** = **lessen**, abate, contract, curtail, cut down, decline, diminish, drop, dwindle, ease, fall off, lower, peter out, reduce, shrink, slacken, subside, wane ◆ *noun* **2** = **lessening**, abatement, contraction, cutback, decline, diminution, downturn, dwindling, ebb, falling off, loss, reduction, shrinkage, subsidence
➤ **Antonyms**
verb ≠**lessen**: enlarge, expand, extend, increase ◆ *noun* ≠**lessening**: expansion, extension, growth

decree *noun* **1** = **law**, act, canon, command, demand, dictum, edict, enactment, mandate, order, ordinance, precept, proclamation, regulation, ruling, statute ◆ *verb* **2** = **order**, command, decide, demand, determine, dictate, enact, establish, lay down, ordain, prescribe, proclaim, pronounce, rule

decrepit *adjective* **1** = **weak**, aged, crippled, debilitated, doddering, effete, feeble, frail, incapacitated, infirm, past it, superannuated, wasted **2** = **worn-out**, antiquated, battered, beat-up (*informal*), broken-down, deteriorated, dilapidated, ramshackle, rickety, run-down, tumbledown, weather-beaten

decry *verb* = **condemn**, abuse, asperse, belittle, blame, blast, censure, criticize, cry down, denigrate, denounce, depreciate, derogate, detract, devalue, discredit, disparage, excoriate, lambast(e), put down, rail against, run down, tear into (*informal*), traduce, underestimate, underrate, undervalue

dedicate *verb* **1** = **devote**, commit, give over to, pledge, surrender **2** = **inscribe**, address, assign, offer **3** = **consecrate**, bless, hallow, sanctify, set apart

dedicated *adjective* = **devoted**, committed, enthusiastic, given over to, purposeful, single-minded, sworn, wholehearted, zealous

➤ **Antonyms**
indifferent, uncaring, uncommitted, unconcerned, uninterested

dedication *noun* 1 = **devotion**, adherence, allegiance, commitment, devotedness, faithfulness, loyalty, single-mindedness, wholeheartedness 2 = **inscription**, address, message 3 = **consecration**, hallowing, sanctification
➤ **Antonyms**
≠**devotion**: apathy, coolness, indifference, insensibility, torpor, unconcern, uninterestedness

deduce *verb* = **conclude**, derive, draw, gather, glean, infer, put two and two together, read between the lines, reason, take to mean, understand

deduct *verb* = **subtract**, decrease by, knock off (*informal*), reduce by, remove, take away, take from, take off, take out, withdraw
➤ **Antonyms**
add, add to, enlarge

deduction *noun* 1 = **subtraction**, abatement, allowance, decrease, diminution, discount, reduction, withdrawal 2 = **conclusion**, assumption, consequence, corollary, finding, inference, reasoning, result

deed *noun* 1 = **action**, achievement, act, exploit, fact, feat, performance, reality, truth 2 *Law* = **document**, contract, indenture, instrument, title, title deed, transaction

deem *verb* = **consider**, account, believe, conceive, esteem, estimate, hold, imagine, judge, reckon, regard, suppose, think

deep *adjective* 1 = **wide**, abyssal, bottomless, broad, far, profound, unfathomable, yawning 2 = **mysterious**, abstract, abstruse, arcane, esoteric, hidden, obscure, recondite, secret 3 = **intense**, extreme, grave, great, profound, serious (*informal*), unqualified 4 = **wise**, acute, discerning, learned, penetrating, sagacious 5 = **cunning**, artful, astute, canny, designing, devious, insidious, knowing, scheming, shrewd 6 = **absorbed**, engrossed, immersed, lost, preoccupied, rapt 7 = **dark**, intense, rich, strong, vivid 8 = **low**, bass, booming, full-toned, low-pitched, resonant, sonorous ♦ *noun* 9 = **middle**, culmination, dead, mid point 10 **the deep** *Poetic* = **ocean**, briny (*informal*), high seas, main, sea ♦ *adverb* 11 = **far into**, deeply, far down, late
➤ **Antonyms**
adjective ≠**wide**: shallow ≠**mysterious**: shallow ≠**intense**: shallow, superficial

≠**wise**: simple ≠**cunning**: shallow, simple ≠**dark**: light, pale ≠**low**: high, sharp

deepen *verb* 1 = **dig out**, dredge, excavate, hollow, scoop out, scrape out 2 = **intensify**, grow, increase, magnify, reinforce, strengthen

deeply *adverb* 1 = **thoroughly**, completely, gravely, profoundly, seriously, severely, to the core, to the heart, to the quick 2 = **intensely**, acutely, affectingly, distressingly, feelingly, mournfully, movingly, passionately, sadly

deep-rooted *or* **deep-seated** *adjective* = **fixed**, confirmed, dyed-in-the-wool, entrenched, ineradicable, ingrained, inveterate, rooted, settled, subconscious, unconscious
➤ **Antonyms**
eradicable, exterior, external, on the surface, shallow, skin-deep, slight, superficial, surface

deface *verb* = **vandalize**, blemish, damage, deform, destroy, disfigure, impair, injure, mar, mutilate, obliterate, spoil, sully, tarnish, total (*slang*), trash (*slang*)

defacement *noun* = **vandalism**, blemish, damage, destruction, disfigurement, distortion, impairment, injury, mutilation

de facto *adverb* 1 = **in fact**, actually, in effect, in reality, really ♦ *adjective* 2 = **actual**, existing, real

defamation *noun* = **slander**, aspersion, calumny, character assassination, denigration, disparagement, libel, obloquy, opprobrium, scandal, slur, smear, traducement, vilification

defamatory *adjective* = **slanderous**, abusive, calumnious, contumelious, denigrating, derogatory, disparaging, injurious, insulting, libellous, vilifying, vituperative

defame *verb* = **slander**, asperse, bad-mouth (*slang, chiefly U.S. & Canad.*), belie, besmirch, blacken, calumniate, cast a slur on, cast aspersions on, denigrate, detract, discredit, disgrace, dishonour, disparage, knock (*informal*), libel, malign, rubbish (*informal*), slag (off) (*slang*), smear, speak evil of, stigmatize, traduce, vilify, vituperate

default *noun* 1 = **failure**, absence, defect, deficiency, dereliction, evasion, fault, lack, lapse, neglect, nonpayment, omission, want ♦ *verb* 2 = **fail**, bilk, defraud, dodge, evade, levant (*Brit.*), neglect, rat (*informal*), swindle, welsh (*slang*)

defaulter *noun* = **nonpayer**, delinquent, embezzler, levanter (*Brit.*), offender, peculator, welsher (*slang*)

defeat *verb* **1** = **beat**, blow out of the water (*slang*), clobber (*slang*), conquer, crush, lick (*informal*), make mincemeat of (*informal*), master, outplay, overpower, overthrow, overwhelm, pip at the post, quell, repulse, rout, run rings around (*informal*), stuff (*slang*), subdue, subjugate, tank (*slang*), trounce, undo, vanquish, wipe the floor with (*informal*), worst **2** = **frustrate**, baffle, balk, confound, disappoint, discomfit, foil, get the better of, ruin, thwart ♦ *noun* **3** = **conquest**, beating, debacle, overthrow, pasting (*slang*), repulse, rout, trouncing, vanquishment **4** = **frustration**, disappointment, discomfiture, failure, rebuff, repulse, reverse, setback, thwarting
➤ **Antonyms**
verb ≠**beat**: bow, cave in (*informal*), lose, submit, succumb, surrender, yield ♦ *noun* ≠**conquest**: success, triumph, victory

defeated *adjective* = **beaten**, balked, bested, checkmated, conquered, crushed, licked (*informal*), overcome, overpowered, overwhelmed, routed, thrashed, thwarted, trounced, vanquished, worsted
➤ **Antonyms**
conquering, dominant, glorious, successful, triumphal, triumphant, undefeated, victorious, winning

defeatist *noun* **1** = **pessimist**, prophet of doom, quitter, submitter, yielder ♦ *adjective* **2** = **pessimistic**

defect *noun* **1** = **imperfection**, blemish, blotch, error, failing, fault, flaw, foible, mistake, spot, taint, want **2** = **deficiency**, absence, default, frailty, inadequacy, lack, shortcoming, weakness ♦ *verb* **3** = **desert**, abandon, apostatize, break faith, change sides, go over, rebel, revolt, tergiversate, walk out on (*informal*)

defection *noun* = **desertion**, abandonment, apostasy, backsliding, dereliction, rebellion, revolt

defective *adjective* **1** = **faulty**, broken, deficient, flawed, imperfect, inadequate, incomplete, insufficient, not working, on the blink (*slang*), out of order, scant, short **2** = **abnormal**, mentally deficient, retarded, subnormal
➤ **Antonyms**
≠**faulty**: adequate, intact, perfect, whole, working ≠**abnormal**: normal

defector *noun* = **deserter**, apostate, rat (*informal*), recreant (*archaic*), renegade, runagate (*archaic*), tergiversator, turncoat

defence *noun* **1** = **protection**, armament, cover, deterrence, guard, immunity, resistance, safeguard, security, shelter **2** = **shield**, barricade, bastion, buckler, bulwark, buttress, fastness, fortification, rampart **3** = **argument**, apologia, apology, excuse, exoneration, explanation, extenuation, justification, plea, vindication **4** *Law* = **plea**, alibi, case, declaration, denial, pleading, rebuttal, testimony

defenceless *adjective* = **helpless**, endangered, exposed, naked, powerless, unarmed, unguarded, unprotected, vulnerable, wide open
➤ **Antonyms**
free from harm, guarded, out of harm's way, protected, safe, safe and sound, secure

defend *verb* **1** = **protect**, cover, fortify, guard, keep safe, preserve, safeguard, screen, secure, shelter, shield, ward off, watch over **2** = **support**, assert, champion, endorse, espouse, justify, maintain, plead, speak up for, stand by, stand up for, stick up for (*informal*), sustain, uphold, vindicate

defendant *noun* = **the accused**, appellant, defence, litigant, offender, prisoner at the bar, respondent

defender *noun* **1** = **protector**, bodyguard, escort, guard **2** = **supporter**, advocate, champion, patron, sponsor, vindicator

defensible *adjective* **1** = **justifiable**, pardonable, permissible, plausible, tenable, valid, vindicable **2** = **secure**, holdable, impregnable, safe, unassailable
➤ **Antonyms**
≠**justifiable**: inexcusable, insupportable, unforgivable, unjustifiable, unpardonable, untenable, wrong

defensive *adjective* = **on guard**, averting, defending, on the defensive, opposing, protective, safeguarding, uptight (*informal*), watchful, withstanding

defensively *adverb* = **in self-defence**, at bay, in defence, on guard, on the defensive, suspiciously

defer[1] *verb* = **postpone**, adjourn, delay, hold over, procrastinate, prorogue, protract, put off, put on ice (*informal*), put on the back burner (*informal*), set aside, shelve, suspend, table, take a rain check on (*U.S. & Canad. informal*)

defer[2] *verb* = **comply**, accede, bow, capitulate, give in, give way to, respect, submit, yield

deference *noun* **1** = **respect**, attention, civility, consideration, courtesy, esteem, homage, honour, obeisance, politeness, regard, reverence, thoughtfulness, veneration **2** = **obedience**, acquiescence, capitulation, complaisance, compliance, obeisance, submission, yielding
➤ **Antonyms**
≠**respect**: contempt, discourtesy,

dishonour, disregard, disrespect,
impertinence, impoliteness, impudence,
incivility, insolence, irreverence, lack of
respect, rudeness ≠**obedience:**
disobedience, insubordination,
noncompliance, nonobservance, revolt

deferential *adjective* = **respectful**, civil,
complaisant, considerate, courteous,
dutiful, ingratiating, obedient, obeisant,
obsequious, polite, regardful, reverential,
submissive

deferment, deferral *noun*
= **postponement**, adjournment, delay,
moratorium, putting off, stay, suspension

defiance *noun* = **resistance**, challenge,
confrontation, contempt, contumacy,
disobedience, disregard, insolence,
insubordination, opposition, provocation,
rebelliousness, recalcitrance, spite
➤ **Antonyms**
accordance, acquiescence, compliance,
deference, obedience, observance, regard,
respect, subservience

defiant *adjective* = **resisting**, aggressive,
audacious, bold, challenging,
contumacious, daring, disobedient,
insolent, insubordinate, mutinous,
provocative, rebellious, recalcitrant,
refractory, truculent
➤ **Antonyms**
cowardly, meek, obedient, respectful,
submissive

deficiency *noun* 1 = **lack**, absence, dearth,
deficit, inadequacy, insufficiency,
scantiness, scarcity, shortage 2 = **failing**,
defect, demerit, fault, flaw, frailty,
imperfection, shortcoming, weakness
➤ **Antonyms**
≠**lack:** abundance, adequacy, sufficiency,
superfluity, surfeit

deficient *adjective* 1 = **lacking**, exiguous,
inadequate, insufficient, meagre, pathetic,
scant, scanty, scarce, short, skimpy,
wanting 2 = **unsatisfactory**, defective,
faulty, flawed, impaired, imperfect,
incomplete, inferior, weak

deficit *noun* = **shortfall**, arrears, default,
deficiency, loss, shortage

defiled *adjective* 1 = **unclean**, besmirched,
dirtied, impure, polluted, spoilt, tainted 2
= **desecrated**, profaned 3 = **dishonoured**,
ravished, violated
➤ **Antonyms**
≠**unclean:** clean, immaculate, spotless,
uncontaminated, uncorrupted, undefiled,
unstained, unsullied, untainted
≠**dishonoured:** chaste, innocent

define *verb* 1 = **describe**, characterize,
designate, detail, determine, explain,
expound, interpret, specify, spell out 2

= **mark out**, bound, circumscribe, delimit,
delineate, demarcate, limit, outline

definite *adjective* 1 = **clear**,
black-and-white, clear-cut, clearly defined,
cut-and-dried (*informal*), determined,
exact, explicit, express, fixed, marked,
obvious, particular, precise, specific 2
= **certain**, assured, decided, guaranteed,
positive, settled, sure
➤ **Antonyms**
≠**clear:** confused, fuzzy, general, hazy,
ill-defined, imprecise, indefinite,
indeterminate, indistinct, inexact, loose,
obscure, unclear, undetermined, vague
≠**certain:** uncertain, undecided

definitely *adverb* = **certainly**, absolutely,
beyond any doubt, categorically, clearly,
come hell or high water (*informal*),
decidedly, easily, far and away, finally,
indubitably, needless to say, obviously,
plainly, positively, surely, undeniably,
unequivocally, unmistakably,
unquestionably, without doubt, without
fail, without question

definition *noun* 1 = **explanation**,
clarification, elucidation, exposition,
statement of meaning 2 = **description**,
delimitation, delineation, demarcation,
determination, fixing, outlining, settling 3
= **sharpness**, clarity, contrast, distinctness,
focus, precision

definitive *adjective* 1 = **final**, absolute,
complete, conclusive, decisive 2
= **authoritative**, exhaustive, mother of all
(*informal*), perfect, reliable, ultimate

deflate *verb* 1 = **collapse**, contract, empty,
exhaust, flatten, puncture, shrink, void 2
= **humiliate**, chasten, dash, debunk
(*informal*), disconcert, dispirit, humble,
mortify, put down (*slang*), squash, take
the wind out of (someone's) sails 3
Economics = **reduce**, decrease, depreciate,
depress, devalue, diminish
➤ **Antonyms**
≠**collapse:** balloon, bloat, blow up, dilate,
distend, enlarge, expand, increase, inflate,
puff up *or* out, pump up, swell
≠**humiliate:** boost, expand, increase,
inflate

deflect *verb* = **turn aside**, bend, deviate,
diverge, glance off, ricochet, shy,
sidetrack, slew, swerve, turn, twist, veer,
wind

deflection *noun* = **deviation**, aberration,
bend, declination, divergence, drift,
refraction, swerve, turning aside, veer

deform *verb* 1 = **distort**, buckle, contort,
gnarl, malform, mangle, misshape, twist,
warp 2 = **disfigure**, cripple, deface, injure,
maim, mar, mutilate, ruin, spoil

deformed *adjective* **1** = **distorted**, bent, blemished, crooked, malformed, mangled, misshapen, twisted, warped **2** = **disfigured**, crippled, maimed, marred, misbegotten

deformity *noun* **1** = **abnormality**, defect, disfigurement, malformation **2** = **distortion**, irregularity, misproportion, misshapenness

defraud *verb* = **cheat**, beguile, bilk, con (*informal*), cozen, delude, diddle (*informal*), do (*slang*), dupe, embezzle, fleece, gull (*archaic*), gyp (*slang*), outwit, pilfer, pull a fast one on (*informal*), rip off (*slang*), rob, rook (*slang*), skin (*slang*), stiff (*slang*), stitch up (*slang*), swindle, trick

deft *adjective* = **skilful**, able, adept, adroit, agile, clever, dexterous, expert, handy, neat, nimble, proficient
➤ **Antonyms**
awkward, bumbling, cack-handed (*informal*), clumsy, gauche, inept, maladroit, unskilful

defunct *adjective* **1** = **dead**, deceased, departed, extinct, gone **2** = **obsolete**, a dead letter, bygone, expired, inoperative, invalid, nonexistent, not functioning, out of commission

defy *verb* **1** = **resist**, beard, brave, confront, contemn, despise, disobey, disregard, face, flout, hurl defiance at, scorn, slight, spurn **2** = **foil**, baffle, call (someone's) bluff, defeat, elude, frustrate, repel, repulse, thwart, withstand **3** *Formal* = **challenge**, dare, provoke

degenerate *adjective* **1** = **depraved**, base, corrupt, debased, debauched, decadent, degenerated, degraded, deteriorated, dissolute, fallen, immoral, low, mean, perverted, pervy (*slang*) ♦ *verb* **2** = **worsen**, decay, decline, decrease, deteriorate, fall off, go to pot, lapse, regress, retrogress, rot, sink, slip

degeneration *noun* = **deterioration**, debasement, decline, degeneracy, descent, dissipation, dissolution, regression

degradation *noun* **1** = **disgrace**, discredit, dishonour, humiliation, ignominy, mortification, shame **2** = **deterioration**, abasement, debasement, decadence, decline, degeneracy, degeneration, demotion, derogation, downgrading, perversion

degrade *verb* **1** = **demean**, cheapen, corrupt, debase, discredit, disgrace, dishonour, humble, humiliate, impair, injure, pervert, shame, vitiate **2** = **adulterate**, dilute, doctor, mix, thin, water, water down, weaken **3** = **demote**, break, cashier, depose, downgrade, lower, reduce to inferior rank
➤ **Antonyms**
≠**demean**: dignify, enhance, ennoble, honour, improve ≠**demote**: elevate, promote, raise

degraded *adjective* = **disgraced**, abandoned, base, corrupt, debased, debauched, decadent, depraved, despicable, disreputable, dissolute, low, mean, profligate, sordid, vicious, vile

degrading *adjective* = **demeaning**, cheapening, contemptible, debasing, disgraceful, dishonourable, humiliating, infra dig (*informal*), lowering, shameful, undignified, unworthy

degree *noun* **1** = **stage**, division, extent, gradation, grade, interval, limit, mark, measure, notch, point, rung, scale, step, unit **2** = **rank**, class, grade, level, order, position, standing, station, status **3** = **extent**, ambit, calibre, intensity, level, measure, proportion, quality, quantity, range, rate, ratio, scale, scope, severity, standard **4 by degrees** = **little by little**, bit by bit, gently, gradually, imperceptibly, inch by inch, slowly, step by step

deign *verb* = **condescend**, consent, deem worthy, lower oneself, see fit, stoop, think fit

deity *noun* = **god**, celestial being, divine being, divinity, goddess, godhead, idol, immortal, supreme being

dejected *adjective* = **downhearted**, blue, cast down, crestfallen, depressed, despondent, disconsolate, disheartened, dismal, doleful, down, downcast, down in the dumps (*informal*), gloomy, glum, low, low-spirited, melancholy, miserable, morose, sad, sick as a parrot (*informal*), woebegone, wretched
➤ **Antonyms**
blithe, cheerful, chirpy (*informal*), encouraged, genial, happy, joyous, light-hearted, upbeat (*informal*)

dejection *noun* = **low spirits**, blues, depression, despair, despondency, doldrums, downheartedness, dumps (*informal*), gloom, gloominess, heavy-heartedness, melancholy, sadness, sorrow, the hump (*Brit. informal*), unhappiness

de jure *adverb* = **legally**, according to the law, by right, rightfully

delay *verb* **1** = **put off**, beat about the bush, defer, hold over, play for time, postpone, procrastinate, prolong, protract, put on the back burner (*informal*), shelve, stall, suspend, table, take a rain check on (*U.S. & Canad. informal*), temporize **2** = **hold up**, arrest, bog down, check, detain, halt,

hinder, hold back, impede, obstruct, retard, set back, slow up, stop, throw a spanner in the works **3 = drag one's feet** or **heels** (*informal*), dawdle, dilly-dally (*informal*), drag, lag, linger, loiter, tarry ♦ *noun* **4 = putting off**, deferment, postponement, procrastination, stay, suspension **5 = hold-up**, check, detention, hindrance, impediment, interruption, interval, obstruction, setback, stoppage, wait **6 = dawdling**, dilly-dallying (*informal*), lingering, loitering, tarrying
➤ **Antonyms**
verb ≠**hold up**: accelerate, advance, dispatch, expedite, facilitate, forward, hasten, hurry, precipitate, press, promote, quicken, rush, speed (up), urge

delectable *adjective* = **delicious**, adorable, agreeable, appetizing, charming, dainty, delightful, enjoyable, enticing, gratifying, inviting, luscious, lush, pleasant, pleasurable, satisfying, scrumptious (*informal*), tasty, toothsome, yummy (*slang*)
➤ **Antonyms**
awful, disagreeable, disgusting, distasteful, dreadful, horrible, horrid, nasty, offensive, terrible, unappetizing, unpleasant, yucky or yukky (*slang*)

delectation *noun Formal* = **enjoyment**, amusement, delight, diversion, entertainment, gratification, happiness, jollies (*slang*), pleasure, refreshment, relish, satisfaction

delegate *noun* **1 = representative**, agent, ambassador, commissioner, deputy, envoy, legate, vicar ♦ *verb* **2 = entrust**, assign, consign, devolve, give, hand over, pass on, relegate, transfer **3 = appoint**, accredit, authorize, commission, depute, designate, empower, mandate

delegation *noun* **1 = deputation**, commission, contingent, embassy, envoys, legation, mission **2 = devolution**, assignment, commissioning, committal, deputizing, entrustment, relegation

delete *verb* = **remove**, blot out, blue-pencil, cancel, cross out, cut out, dele, edit, edit out, efface, erase, excise, expunge, obliterate, rub out, strike out

deliberate *adjective* **1 = intentional**, calculated, conscious, considered, designed, planned, prearranged, premeditated, purposeful, studied, thoughtful, wilful **2 = unhurried**, careful, cautious, circumspect, heedful, measured, methodical, ponderous, prudent, slow, thoughtful, wary ♦ *verb* **3 = consider**, cogitate, consult, debate, discuss, meditate, mull over, ponder, reflect, think,

weigh
➤ **Antonyms**
adjective ≠**intentional**: accidental, inadvertent, unconscious, unintended, unpremeditated, unthinking ≠**unhurried**: fast, haphazard, hasty, heedless, hurried, impetuous, impulsive, rash

deliberately *adverb* = **intentionally**, by design, calculatingly, consciously, determinedly, emphatically, in cold blood, knowingly, on purpose, pointedly, resolutely, studiously, wilfully, wittingly

deliberation *noun* **1 = consideration**, calculation, care, carefulness, caution, circumspection, cogitation, coolness, forethought, meditation, prudence, purpose, reflection, speculation, study, thought, wariness **2 = discussion**, conference, consultation, debate

delicacy *noun* **1 = fineness**, accuracy, daintiness, elegance, exquisiteness, lightness, nicety, precision, subtlety **2 = fragility**, debility, flimsiness, frailness, frailty, infirmity, slenderness, tenderness, weakness **3 = treat**, *bonne bouche*, dainty, luxury, relish, savoury, titbit **4 = fastidiousness**, discrimination, finesse, purity, refinement, sensibility, taste **5 = sensitivity**, sensitiveness, tact

delicate *adjective* **1 = fine**, accurate, deft, detailed, elegant, exquisite, graceful, minute, precise, skilled, subtle **2 = subtle**, choice, dainty, delicious, fine, savoury, tender **3 = soft**, faint, muted, pastel, subdued, subtle **4 = fragile**, flimsy, frail, slender, slight, tender, weak **5 = sickly**, ailing, debilitated, frail **6 = difficult**, built on sand, critical, precarious, sensitive, sticky (*informal*), ticklish, touchy **7 = considerate**, diplomatic, discreet, sensitive, tactful **8 = fastidious**, careful, critical, discriminating, nice, prudish, pure, refined, scrupulous, squeamish
➤ **Antonyms**
≠**fine**: coarse, crude, indelicate, unrefined ≠**subtle**: harsh, strong ≠**soft**: bright, harsh, rough ≠**sickly**: healthy, strong ≠**considerate**: harsh, inconsiderate, indelicate, insensitive, rough ≠**fastidious**: careless, crude, rough

delicately *adverb* **1 = finely**, carefully, daintily, deftly, elegantly, exquisitely, gracefully, lightly, precisely, skilfully, softly, subtly **2 = tactfully**, diplomatically, sensitively

delicious *adjective* **1 = delectable**, ambrosial, appetizing, choice, dainty, luscious, mouthwatering, nectareous, palatable, savoury, scrumptious (*informal*), tasty, toothsome, yummy (*slang*) **2**

= **delightful**, agreeable, charming, enjoyable, entertaining, exquisite, pleasant, pleasing
➤ Antonyms
≠**delectable**: disagreeable, distasteful, unpleasant

delight noun 1 = **pleasure**, ecstasy, enjoyment, felicity, gladness, glee, gratification, happiness, jollies (slang), joy, rapture, transport ♦ verb 2 = **please**, amuse, charm, cheer, divert, enchant, gratify, ravish, rejoice, satisfy, thrill 3 **delight in** = **take pleasure in**, appreciate, enjoy, feast on, glory in, indulge in, like, love, luxuriate in, relish, revel in, savour
➤ Antonyms
noun ≠**pleasure**: disapprobation, disfavour, dislike, displeasure, dissatisfaction, distaste ♦ verb ≠**please**: disgust, displease, dissatisfy, gall, irk, offend, upset, vex

delighted adjective = **pleased**, blissed out, captivated, charmed, cock-a-hoop, ecstatic, elated, enchanted, gladdened, happy, in seventh heaven, joyous, jubilant, overjoyed, over the moon (informal), rapt, sent, thrilled

delightful adjective = **pleasant**, agreeable, amusing, captivating, charming, congenial, delectable, enchanting, engaging, enjoyable, entertaining, fascinating, gratifying, heavenly, pleasing, pleasurable, rapturous, ravishing, thrilling
➤ Antonyms
disagreeable, displeasing, distasteful, horrid, nasty, unpleasant

delinquency noun = **crime**, fault, misbehaviour, misconduct, misdeed, misdemeanour, offence, wrongdoing

delinquent noun = **criminal**, culprit, defaulter, juvenile delinquent, lawbreaker, malefactor, miscreant, offender, villain, wrongdoer, young offender

delirious adjective 1 = **mad**, crazy, demented, deranged, gonzo (slang), incoherent, insane, light-headed, raving, unhinged 2 = **ecstatic**, beside oneself, blissed out, carried away, Corybantic, excited, frantic, frenzied, hysterical, sent, wild
➤ Antonyms
calm, clear-headed, coherent, compos mentis, in one's right mind, lucid, rational, sane, sensible

delirium noun 1 = **madness**, aberration, derangement, hallucination, insanity, lunacy, raving 2 = **frenzy**, ecstasy, fever, fury, hysteria, passion, rage

deliver verb 1 = **carry**, bear, bring, cart, convey, distribute, transport 2 = **hand**

over, cede, commit, give up, grant, make over, relinquish, resign, surrender, transfer, turn over, yield 3 = **give**, announce, declare, give forth, present, proclaim, pronounce, publish, read, utter 4 = **release**, acquit, discharge, emancipate, free, liberate, loose, ransom, redeem, rescue, save 5 = **strike**, administer, aim, deal, direct, give, inflict, launch, throw 6 = **provide**, discharge, dispense, feed, give forth, purvey, release, supply

deliverance noun = **release**, emancipation, escape, liberation, ransom, redemption, rescue, salvation

delivery noun 1 = **handing over**, consignment, conveyance, dispatch, distribution, surrender, transfer, transmission, transmittal 2 = **speech**, articulation, elocution, enunciation, intonation, utterance 3 = **childbirth**, confinement, labour, parturition 4 = **release**, deliverance, escape, liberation, rescue

delude verb = **deceive**, bamboozle (informal), beguile, cheat, con (informal), cozen, dupe, fool, gull (archaic), hoax, hoodwink, impose on, kid (informal), lead up the garden path (informal), misguide, mislead, pull the wool over someone's eyes, take for a ride (informal), take in (informal), trick

deluge noun 1 = **flood**, cataclysm, downpour, inundation, overflowing, spate, torrent 2 = **rush**, avalanche, barrage, flood, spate, torrent ♦ verb 3 = **flood**, douse, drench, drown, inundate, soak, submerge, swamp 4 = **overwhelm**, engulf, inundate, overload, overrun, swamp

delusion noun = **misconception**, deception, error, fallacy, false impression, fancy, hallucination, illusion, misapprehension, misbelief, mistake, phantasm, self-deception

de luxe adjective = **luxurious**, choice, costly, elegant, exclusive, expensive, gorgeous, grand, opulent, palatial, plush (informal), rich, select, special, splendid, splendiferous (facetious), sumptuous, superior

delve verb = **research**, burrow, dig into, examine, explore, ferret out, forage, investigate, look into, probe, ransack, rummage, search, unearth

demagogue noun = **agitator**, firebrand, haranguer, rabble-rouser, soapbox orator

demand verb 1 = **request**, ask, challenge, inquire, interrogate, question 2 = **require**, call for, cry out for, entail, involve, necessitate, need, take, want 3 = **claim**, exact, expect, insist on, order ♦ noun 4

= **request**, bidding, charge, inquiry, interrogation, order, question, requisition **5** = **need**, call, claim, market, necessity, requirement, want **6 in demand** = **sought after**, fashionable, in vogue, like gold dust, needed, popular, requested
➤ **Antonyms**
verb ≠**require**, **claim**: come up with, contribute, furnish, give, grant, produce, provide, supply, yield

demanding *adjective* **1** = **difficult**, challenging, exacting, exhausting, exigent, hard, taxing, tough, trying, wearing **2** = **insistent**, clamorous, imperious, importunate, nagging, pressing, urgent
➤ **Antonyms**
≠**difficult**: a piece of cake (*informal*), child's play (*informal*), easy, easy-peasy (*slang*), effortless, facile, no bother, painless, simple, straightforward, uncomplicated, undemanding

demarcate *verb* = **delimit**, define, determine, differentiate, distinguish between, fix, mark, separate

demarcation *noun* **1** = **delimitation**, differentiation, distinction, division, separation **2** = **limit**, bound, boundary, confine, enclosure, margin, pale

demean *verb* = **lower**, abase, debase, degrade, descend, humble, stoop

demeanour *noun* = **behaviour**, air, bearing, carriage, comportment, conduct, deportment, manner, mien

demented *adjective* = **mad**, barking (*slang*), barking mad (*slang*), crackbrained, crackpot (*informal*), crazed, crazy, daft (*informal*), deranged, distraught, doolally (*slang*), dotty (*slang, chiefly Brit.*), foolish, frenzied, gonzo (*slang*), idiotic, insane, loopy (*informal*), lunatic, maniacal, manic, *non compos mentis*, not the full shilling (*informal*), off one's trolley (*slang*), out to lunch (*informal*), unbalanced, unhinged, up the pole (*informal*), wacko or whacko (*slang*)
➤ **Antonyms**
all there (*informal*), compos mentis, in one's right mind, lucid, mentally sound, normal, of sound mind, rational, reasonable, sensible, sound

demise *noun* **1** = **failure**, collapse, downfall, end, fall, ruin **2** *Euphemistic* = **death**, decease, departure

democracy *noun* = **self-government**, commonwealth, government by the people, representative government, republic

democratic *adjective* = **self-governing**, autonomous, egalitarian, popular, populist, representative, republican

demolish *verb* **1** = **knock down**, bulldoze, destroy, dismantle, flatten, level, overthrow, pulverize, raze, ruin, tear down, total (*slang*), trash (*slang*) **2** = **defeat**, annihilate, blow out of the water (*slang*), destroy, lick (*informal*), master, overthrow, overturn, stuff (*slang*), tank (*slang*), undo, wipe the floor with (*informal*), wreck **3** *Facetious* = **devour**, consume, eat, gobble up, put away
➤ **Antonyms**
≠**knock down**: build, construct, create, repair, restore, strengthen

demolition *noun* = **knocking down**, bulldozing, destruction, explosion, levelling, razing, tearing down, wrecking

demon *noun* **1** = **evil spirit**, devil, fiend, ghoul, goblin, malignant spirit **2** = **monster**, devil, fiend, ghoul, rogue, villain **3** = **wizard**, ace (*informal*), addict, fanatic, fiend, master

demonic, demoniac, demoniacal *adjective* **1** = **devilish**, diabolic, diabolical, fiendish, hellish, infernal, satanic **2** = **frenzied**, crazed, frantic, frenetic, furious, hectic, like one possessed, mad, maniacal, manic

demonstrable *adjective* = **provable**, attestable, axiomatic, certain, evident, evincible, incontrovertible, indubitable, irrefutable, obvious, palpable, positive, self-evident, undeniable, unmistakable, verifiable

demonstrate *verb* **1** = **prove**, display, establish, evidence, evince, exhibit, indicate, manifest, show, testify to **2** = **show how**, describe, explain, illustrate, make clear, teach **3** = **march**, parade, picket, protest, rally

demonstration *noun* **1** = **march**, mass lobby, parade, picket, protest, rally, sit-in **2** = **explanation**, description, exposition, presentation, test, trial **3** = **proof**, affirmation, confirmation, display, evidence, exhibition, expression, illustration, manifestation, substantiation, testimony, validation

demonstrative *adjective* **1** = **open**, affectionate, effusive, emotional, expansive, expressive, gushing, loving, unreserved, unrestrained **2** = **indicative**, evincive, explanatory, expository, illustrative, symptomatic
➤ **Antonyms**
≠**open**: aloof, cold, contained, distant, formal, impassive, reserved, restrained, stiff, unaffectionate, undemonstrative, unemotional, unresponsive

demoralize *verb* = **dishearten**, cripple,

daunt, deject, depress, disconcert, discourage, dispirit, enfeeble, psych out (*informal*), rattle (*informal*), sap, shake, undermine, unnerve, weaken
➤ **Antonyms**
boost, cheer, egg on, encourage, gee up, hearten, spur

demoralized *adjective* = **disheartened**, broken, crushed, depressed, discouraged, dispirited, downcast, sick as a parrot (*informal*), subdued, unmanned, unnerved, weakened

demote *verb* = **downgrade**, declass, degrade, disrate (*Naval*), kick downstairs (*slang*), lower in rank, relegate
➤ **Antonyms**
advance, elevate, kick upstairs (*informal*), prefer, promote, raise, upgrade

demur *verb* 1 = **object**, balk, cavil, disagree, dispute, doubt, hesitate, pause, protest, refuse, take exception, waver ♦ *noun* 2 *As in* **without demur** = **objection**, compunction, demurral, demurrer, dissent, hesitation, misgiving, protest, qualm, scruple

demure *adjective* 1 = **shy**, decorous, diffident, grave, modest, reserved, reticent, retiring, sedate, sober, staid, unassuming 2 = **coy**, affected, bashful, niminy-piminy, priggish, prim, prissy (*informal*), prudish, strait-laced
➤ **Antonyms**
brash, brazen, forward, immodest, impudent, shameless

den *noun* 1 = **lair**, cave, cavern, haunt, hide-out, hole, shelter 2 *Chiefly U.S.* = **study**, cloister, cubbyhole, hideaway, retreat, sanctuary, sanctum, snuggery

denial *noun* 1 = **negation**, adjuration, contradiction, disavowal, disclaimer, dismissal, dissent, renunciation, repudiation, retraction 2 = **refusal**, prohibition, rebuff, rejection, repulse, veto
➤ **Antonyms**
≠**negation**: acknowledgment, admission, affirmation, avowal, confession, declaration, disclosure, divulgence, profession, revelation

denigrate *verb* = **disparage**, asperse, bad-mouth (*slang, chiefly U.S. & Canad.*), belittle, besmirch, blacken, calumniate, decry, defame, impugn, knock (*informal*), malign, revile, rubbish (*informal*), run down, slag (off) (*slang*), slander, vilify
➤ **Antonyms**
acclaim, admire, approve, cheer, compliment, eulogize, extol, honour, laud, praise, take one's hat off to

denigration *noun* = **disparagement**, aspersion, backbiting, defamation,

detraction, obloquy, scandal, scurrility, slander, vilification

denominate *verb* = **name**, call, christen, designate, dub, entitle, phrase, style, term

denomination *noun* 1 = **religious group**, belief, communion, creed, persuasion, school, sect 2 = **unit**, grade, size, value 3 = **name**, appellation, designation, label, style, term, title 4 = **classification**, body, category, class, group

denote *verb* = **indicate**, betoken, designate, express, imply, import, mark, mean, show, signify, typify

denounce *verb* = **condemn**, accuse, arraign, attack, brand, castigate, censure, declaim against, decry, denunciate, excoriate, impugn, point a *or* the finger at, proscribe, revile, stigmatize, vilify

dense *adjective* 1 = **thick**, close, close-knit, compact, compressed, condensed, heavy, impenetrable, opaque, solid, substantial, thickset 2 *Informal* = **stupid**, blockish, braindead (*informal*), crass, dead from the neck up (*informal*), dozy (*Brit. informal*), dull, dumb (*informal*), obtuse, slow, slow-witted, stolid, thick, thick-witted
➤ **Antonyms**
≠**thick**: light, scattered, sparse, thin, transparent ≠**stupid**: alert, bright, clever, intelligent, quick

density *noun* 1 = **tightness**, body, bulk, closeness, compactness, consistency, crowdedness, denseness, impenetrability, mass, solidity, thickness 2 *Informal* = **stupidity**, crassness, dullness, obtuseness, slowness, stolidity, thickness

dent *noun* 1 = **hollow**, chip, concavity, crater, depression, dimple, dip, impression, indentation, pit ♦ *verb* 2 = **make a dent in**, depress, dint, gouge, hollow, imprint, make concave, press in, push in

denude *verb* = **strip**, bare, divest, expose, lay bare, uncover

deny *verb* 1 = **contradict**, disagree with, disprove, gainsay (*archaic or literary*), oppose, rebuff, rebut, refute 2 = **refuse**, begrudge, decline, disallow, forbid, negate, reject, turn down, veto, withhold 3 = **renounce**, abjure, disavow, discard, disclaim, disown, recant, renege, repudiate, retract, revoke
➤ **Antonyms**
≠**contradict**: accept, acknowledge, admit, affirm, agree, allow, concede, confirm, recognize, take on board ≠**refuse**: accept, grant, let, permit, receive

deodorant *noun* = **antiperspirant**, air freshener, deodorizer, disinfectant, fumigant

depart *verb* **1** = **leave**, absent (oneself), decamp, disappear, escape, exit, go, go away, hook it (*slang*), make tracks, migrate, pack one's bags (*informal*), quit, remove, retire, retreat, set forth, slope off, start out, take (one's) leave, vanish, withdraw **2** = **deviate**, differ, digress, diverge, stray, swerve, turn aside, vary, veer
➤ **Antonyms**
≠**leave**: arrive, remain, show up (*informal*), stay, turn up

departed *adjective Euphemistic* = **dead**, deceased, expired, late

department *noun* **1** = **section**, branch, bureau, division, office, station, subdivision, unit **2** = **region**, district, division, province, sector **3** *Informal* = **speciality**, area, domain, function, line, province, realm, responsibility, sphere

departure *noun* **1** = **leaving**, exit, exodus, going, going away, leave-taking, removal, retirement, withdrawal **2** = **divergence**, abandonment, branching off, deviation, digression, variation, veering **3** = **shift**, branching out, change, difference, innovation, novelty, whole new ball game (*informal*)
➤ **Antonyms**
≠**leaving**: advent, appearance, arrival, coming, entrance, return

depend *verb* **1** = **trust in**, bank on, build upon, calculate on, confide in, count on, lean on, reckon on, rely upon, turn to **2** = **be determined by**, be based on, be contingent on, be subject to, be subordinate to, hang on, hinge on, rest on, revolve around

dependable *adjective* = **reliable**, faithful, reputable, responsible, staunch, steady, sure, trustworthy, trusty, unfailing
➤ **Antonyms**
irresponsible, undependable, unreliable, unstable, untrustworthy

dependant *noun* = **relative**, child, client, cohort (*chiefly U.S.*), hanger-on, henchman, minion, minor, protégé, retainer, subordinate, vassal

dependent *adjective* **1** = **reliant**, counting on, defenceless, helpless, immature, relying on, vulnerable, weak **2 dependent on** *or* **upon** = **determined by**, conditional on, contingent on, depending on, influenced by, liable to, relative to, subject to
➤ **Antonyms**
≠**reliant**: autarkic, autonomous, independent, self-determining, self-governing, self-reliant

depict *verb* **1** = **draw**, delineate, illustrate, limn, outline, paint, picture, portray, render, reproduce, sculpt, sketch **2** = **describe**, characterize, detail, narrate, outline, represent, sketch

depiction *noun* = **representation**, delineation, description, picture, portrayal, sketch

deplete *verb* = **use up**, bankrupt, consume, decrease, drain, empty, evacuate, exhaust, expend, impoverish, lessen, milk, reduce
➤ **Antonyms**
add to, augment, enhance, expand, increase, raise, step up (*informal*), swell

depleted *adjective* = **used (up)**, consumed, decreased, depreciated, devoid of, drained, effete, emptied, exhausted, lessened, out of, reduced, short of, spent, wasted, weakened, worn out

depletion *noun* = **using up**, attenuation, consumption, decrease, deficiency, diminution, drain, dwindling, exhaustion, expenditure, lessening, lowering, reduction

deplorable *adjective* **1** = **terrible**, calamitous, dire, disastrous, distressing, grievous, heartbreaking, lamentable, melancholy, miserable, pitiable, regrettable, sad, unfortunate, wretched **2** = **disgraceful**, blameworthy, dishonourable, disreputable, execrable, opprobrious, reprehensible, scandalous, shameful
➤ **Antonyms**
≠**terrible**: A1 *or* A-one (*informal*), bad (*slang*), bodacious (*slang, chiefly U.S.*), brilliant, excellent, fantastic, great (*informal*), marvellous, outstanding, super (*informal*), superb ≠**disgraceful**: admirable, laudable, notable, praiseworthy

deplore *verb* **1** = **disapprove of**, abhor, censure, condemn, denounce, deprecate, excoriate, object to, take a dim view of **2** = **lament**, bemoan, bewail, grieve for, mourn, regret, rue, sorrow over

deploy *verb* = **position**, arrange, dispose, extend, redistribute, set out, set up, spread out, station, use, utilize

deployment *noun* = **position**, arrangement, disposition, organization, setup, spread, stationing, use, utilization

deport *verb* **1** = **expel**, banish, exile, expatriate, extradite, oust **2 deport oneself** = **behave**, acquit oneself, act, bear oneself, carry oneself, comport oneself, conduct oneself, hold oneself

deportation *noun* = **expulsion**, banishment, eviction, exile, expatriation, extradition, transportation

deportment *noun* = **bearing**, air, appearance, aspect, behaviour, carriage, cast, comportment, conduct, demeanour, manner, mien, posture, stance

depose *verb* **1** = **remove from office**, break, cashier, degrade, demote, dethrone, dismiss, displace, downgrade, oust **2** *Law* = **testify**, avouch, declare, make a deposition

deposit *verb* **1** = **put**, drop, lay, locate, place, precipitate, settle, sit down **2** = **store**, amass, bank, consign, entrust, hoard, lodge, save ♦ *noun* **3** = **down payment**, instalment, money (*in bank*), part payment, pledge, retainer, security, stake, warranty **4** = **sediment**, accumulation, alluvium, deposition, dregs, lees, precipitate, silt

deposition *noun* **1** *Law* = **sworn statement**, affidavit, declaration, evidence, testimony **2** = **removal**, dethronement, dismissal, displacement, ousting

depository *noun* = **storehouse**, depot, repository, safe-deposit box, store, warehouse

depot *noun* **1** = **storehouse**, depository, repository, warehouse **2** *Chiefly U.S. & Canad.* = **bus station**, garage, terminus **3** *Military* = **arsenal**, dump

deprave *verb* = **corrupt**, brutalize, debase, debauch, degrade, demoralize, lead astray, pervert, seduce, subvert, vitiate

depraved *adjective* = **corrupt**, abandoned, debased, debauched, degenerate, degraded, dissolute, evil, immoral, lascivious, lewd, licentious, perverted, pervy (*slang*), profligate, shameless, sinful, vicious, vile, wicked
➤ **Antonyms**
chaste, decent, ethical, good, honourable, innocent, moral, principled, proper, pure, upright, virtuous, wholesome

depravity *noun* = **corruption**, baseness, contamination, criminality, debasement, debauchery, degeneracy, depravation, evil, immorality, iniquity, profligacy, sinfulness, turpitude, vice, viciousness, vitiation, wickedness

depreciate *verb* **1** = **decrease**, deflate, devaluate, devalue, lessen, lose value, lower, reduce **2** = **disparage**, belittle, decry, denigrate, deride, detract, look down on, ridicule, run down, scorn, sneer at, traduce, underestimate, underrate, undervalue
➤ **Antonyms**
≠**decrease**: add to, appreciate, augment, enhance, enlarge, expand, grow, increase, rise ≠**disparage**: admire, appreciate, cherish, esteem, like, prize, rate highly, regard, respect, value

depreciation *noun* **1** = **devaluation**,

deflation, depression, drop, fall, slump **2** = **disparagement**, belittlement, denigration, deprecation, derogation, detraction, pejoration

depress *verb* **1** = **sadden**, cast down, chill, damp, daunt, deject, desolate, discourage, dishearten, dispirit, make despondent, oppress, weigh down **2** = **lower**, cheapen, depreciate, devaluate, devalue, diminish, downgrade, impair, lessen, reduce **3** = **press down**, flatten, level, lower, push down
➤ **Antonyms**
≠**sadden**: cheer, elate, hearten, heighten, increase, lift, raise, strengthen, uplift ≠**lower**: heighten, increase, raise, strengthen

depressed *adjective* **1** = **low-spirited**, blue, crestfallen, dejected, despondent, discouraged, dispirited, down, downcast, downhearted, down in the dumps (*informal*), fed up, glum, low, melancholy, moody, morose, pessimistic, sad, unhappy **2** = **poverty-stricken**, deprived, destitute, disadvantaged, distressed, grey, needy, poor, run-down **3** = **lowered**, cheapened, depreciated, devalued, impaired, weakened **4** = **sunken**, concave, hollow, indented, recessed, set back

depressing *adjective* = **bleak**, black, daunting, dejecting, depressive, discouraging, disheartening, dismal, dispiriting, distressing, dreary, funereal, gloomy, harrowing, heartbreaking, hopeless, melancholy, sad, saddening, sombre

depression *noun* **1** = **low spirits**, dejection, despair, despondency, dolefulness, downheartedness, dumps (*informal*), gloominess, hopelessness, melancholia, melancholy, sadness, the blues, the hump (*Brit. informal*) **2** = **recession**, dullness, economic decline, hard or bad times, inactivity, lowness, slump, stagnation **3** = **hollow**, bowl, cavity, concavity, dent, dimple, dip, excavation, impression, indentation, pit, sag, sink, valley

deprivation *noun* **1** = **withholding**, denial, deprival, dispossession, divestment, expropriation, removal, withdrawal **2** = **want**, destitution, detriment, disadvantage, distress, hardship, need, privation

deprive *verb* = **withhold**, bereave, despoil, dispossess, divest, expropriate, rob, strip, wrest

deprived *adjective* = **poor**, bereft, denuded, destitute, disadvantaged, down at heel, forlorn, in need, in want, lacking, necessitous, needy

> ➤ **Antonyms**

born with a silver spoon in one's mouth, favoured, fortunate, golden, happy, having a charmed life, lucky, prosperous, sitting pretty (*informal*), successful, well-off

depth *noun* 1 = **deepness**, drop, extent, measure, profoundness, profundity 2 = **profoundness**, astuteness, discernment, insight, penetration, profundity, sagacity, wisdom 3 = **complexity**, abstruseness, obscurity, reconditeness 4 = **intensity**, richness, strength 5 **in depth** = **thoroughly**, comprehensively, extensively, intensively

> ➤ **Antonyms**

≠**deepness**: apex, apogee, crest, crown, height, peak, pinnacle, summit, top, vertex, zenith ≠**profoundness**: emptiness, lack of depth *or* substance, superficiality, triviality

depths *plural noun* = **deepest part**, abyss, bowels of the earth, furthest part, innermost part, middle, midst, most intense part, remotest part

deputation *noun* 1 = **delegation**, commission, delegates, deputies, embassy, envoys, legation 2 = **appointment**, assignment, commission, designation, nomination

deputize *verb* 1 = **stand in for**, act for, take the place of, understudy 2 = **appoint**, commission, delegate, depute

deputy *noun* 1 = **substitute**, agent, ambassador, commissioner, delegate, legate, lieutenant, number two, nuncio, proxy, representative, second-in-command, surrogate, vicegerent ◆ *adjective* 2 = **assistant**, depute (*Scot.*), subordinate

derange *verb* 1 = **disorder**, confound, confuse, disarrange, disarray, discompose, disconcert, displace, disturb, ruffle, unsettle, upset 2 = **drive mad**, craze, dement (*rare*), madden, make insane, unbalance, unhinge

deranged *adjective* = **mad**, barking (*slang*), barking mad (*slang*), berserk, crackpot (*informal*), crazed, crazy, delirious, demented, distracted, doolally (*slang*), frantic, frenzied, gonzo (*slang*), insane, irrational, loopy (*informal*), lunatic, maddened, not the full shilling (*informal*), off one's trolley (*slang*), out to lunch (*informal*), unbalanced, unhinged, up the pole (*informal*), wacko *or* whacko (*slang*)

> ➤ **Antonyms**

all there (*informal*), calm, *compos mentis*, in one's right mind, lucid, mentally sound, normal, of sound mind

derelict *adjective* 1 = **abandoned**, deserted,

dilapidated, discarded, forsaken, neglected, ruined 2 = **negligent**, careless, irresponsible, lax, remiss, slack ◆ *noun* 3 = **tramp**, bag lady, bum (*informal*), down-and-out, good-for-nothing, ne'er-do-well, outcast, vagrant, wastrel

dereliction *noun* 1 = **abandonment**, abdication, desertion, forsaking, relinquishment, renunciation 2 = **negligence**, delinquency, evasion, failure, faithlessness, fault, neglect, nonperformance, remissness

deride *verb* = **mock**, chaff, contemn, detract, disdain, disparage, flout, gibe, insult, jeer, knock (*informal*), pooh-pooh, ridicule, scoff, scorn, sneer, take the piss out of (*taboo slang*), taunt

derision *noun* = **mockery**, contempt, contumely, denigration, disdain, disparagement, disrespect, insult, laughter, raillery, ridicule, satire, scoffing, scorn, sneering

derisory *adjective* = **ridiculous**, contemptible, insulting, laughable, ludicrous, outrageous, preposterous

derivation *noun* 1 = **origin**, ancestry, basis, beginning, descent, etymology, foundation, genealogy, root, source 2 = **obtaining**, acquiring, deriving, extraction, getting

derivative *adjective* 1 = **unoriginal**, copied, imitative, plagiaristic, plagiarized, rehashed, secondary, second-hand, uninventive ◆ *noun* 2 = **by-product**, derivation, descendant, offshoot, outgrowth, spin-off

> ➤ **Antonyms**

adjective ≠**unoriginal**: archetypal, authentic, first-hand, genuine, master, original, prototypical, seminal

derive *verb* = **obtain**, collect, deduce, draw, elicit, extract, follow, gain, gather, get, glean, infer, procure, receive, trace

derive from *verb* = **come from**, arise from, descend from, emanate from, flow from, issue from, originate from, proceed from, spring from, stem from

derogatory *adjective* = **disparaging**, belittling, damaging, defamatory, depreciative, detracting, discreditable, dishonouring, injurious, offensive, slighting, uncomplimentary, unfavourable, unflattering

> ➤ **Antonyms**

appreciative, complimentary, flattering, fulsome

descend *verb* 1 = **move down**, alight, dismount, drop, fall, go down, plummet, plunge, sink, subside, tumble 2 = **slope**, dip, gravitate, incline, slant 3 = **lower**

oneself, abase oneself, condescend, degenerate, deteriorate, stoop **4 be descended = originate**, be handed down, be passed down, derive, issue, proceed, spring **5 descend on = attack**, arrive, assail, assault, come in force, invade, pounce, raid, swoop
➤ Antonyms
≠**move down**: ascend, climb, go up, mount, rise, scale, soar

descent noun **1 = coming down**, drop, fall, plunge, swoop **2 = slope**, declination, declivity, dip, drop, incline, slant **3 = ancestry**, extraction, family tree, genealogy, heredity, lineage, origin, parentage **4 = decline**, debasement, decadence, degeneration, degradation, deterioration

describe verb **1 = relate**, characterize, define, depict, detail, explain, express, illustrate, narrate, portray, recount, report, specify, tell **2 = trace**, delineate, draw, mark out, outline

description noun **1 = account**, characterization, delineation, depiction, detail, explanation, narration, narrative, portrayal, report, representation, sketch **2 = kind**, brand, breed, category, class, genre, genus, ilk, kidney, order, sort, species, type, variety

descriptive adjective **= graphic**, circumstantial, depictive, detailed, explanatory, expressive, illustrative, pictorial, picturesque, vivid

desecrate verb **= commit sacrilege**, abuse, blaspheme, contaminate, defile, despoil, dishonour, pervert, pollute, profane, violate
➤ Antonyms
esteem, exalt, glorify, hallow, prize, respect, revere, value, venerate, worship

desert[1] noun **1 = wilderness**, solitude, waste, wasteland, wilds ♦ adjective **2 = barren**, arid, bare, desolate, infertile, lonely, solitary, uncultivated, uninhabited, unproductive, untilled, waste, wild

desert[2] verb **= abandon**, abscond, betray, decamp, defect, forsake, give up, go over the hill (Military slang), jilt, leave, leave high and dry, leave (someone) in the lurch, leave stranded, maroon, quit, rat (on) (informal), relinquish, renounce, resign, run out on (informal), strand, throw over, vacate, walk out on (informal)
➤ Antonyms
be a source of strength to, look after, maintain, provide for, succour, sustain, take care of

deserted adjective **= abandoned**, bereft, cast off, derelict, desolate, empty, forlorn, forsaken, godforsaken, isolated, left in the lurch, left stranded, lonely, neglected, solitary, unfriended, unoccupied, vacant

deserter noun **= defector**, absconder, apostate, escapee, fugitive, rat (informal), renegade, runaway, traitor, truant

desertion noun **= abandonment**, absconding, apostasy, betrayal, defection, departure, dereliction, escape, evasion, flight, forsaking, relinquishment, truancy

deserve verb **= merit**, be entitled to, be worthy of, earn, gain, justify, procure, rate, warrant, win

deserved adjective **= well-earned**, appropriate, condign, due, earned, fair, fitting, just, justifiable, justified, meet (archaic), merited, proper, right, rightful, suitable, warranted

deserving adjective **= worthy**, commendable, estimable, laudable, meritorious, praiseworthy, righteous
➤ Antonyms
not deserving of, not good enough, not worth, undeserving, unworthy

design verb **1 = plan**, delineate, describe, draft, draw, outline, sketch, trace **2 = create**, conceive, fabricate, fashion, invent, originate, think up **3 = intend**, aim, contrive, destine, devise, make, mean, plan, project, propose, purpose, scheme, tailor ♦ noun **4 = plan**, blueprint, delineation, draft, drawing, model, outline, scheme, sketch **5 = arrangement**, configuration, construction, figure, form, motif, organization, pattern, shape, style **6 = intention**, aim, end, goal, intent, meaning, object, objective, point, purport, purpose, target, view

designate verb **1 = name**, call, christen, dub, entitle, label, nominate, style, term **2 = appoint**, allot, assign, choose, delegate, depute, nominate, select **3 = specify**, characterize, define, denote, describe, earmark, indicate, pinpoint, show, stipulate

designation noun **1 = name**, denomination, description, epithet, label, mark, title **2 = appointment**, classification, delegation, indication, selection, specification

designer noun **= creator**, architect, artificer, couturier, deviser, inventor, originator, planner, stylist

designing adjective **= scheming**, artful, astute, conniving, conspiring, crafty, crooked (informal), cunning, deceitful, devious, intriguing, Machiavellian, plotting, sharp, shrewd, sly, treacherous, tricky, unscrupulous, wily

desirability noun **= worth**, advantage,

benefit, merit, profit, usefulness, value

desirable *adjective* **1** = **agreeable**, advantageous, advisable, beneficial, covetable, eligible, enviable, good, pleasing, preferable, profitable, to die for (*informal*), worthwhile **2** = **attractive**, adorable, alluring, fascinating, fetching, glamorous, seductive, sexy (*informal*)
➤ **Antonyms**
≠**agreeable**: disagreeable, distasteful, unacceptable, unappealing, unattractive, undesirable, unpleasant, unpopular ≠**attractive**: unappealing, unattractive, undesirable, unsexy (*informal*)

desire *verb* **1** = **want**, aspire to, covet, crave, desiderate, fancy, hanker after, hope for, long for, set one's heart on, thirst for, wish for, yearn for **2** *Formal* = **request**, ask, entreat, importune, petition, solicit ♦ *noun* **3** = **wish**, ache, appetite, aspiration, craving, hankering, hope, longing, need, thirst, want, yearning, yen (*informal*) **4** = **request**, appeal, entreaty, importunity, petition, solicitation, supplication **5** = **lust**, appetite, concupiscence, lasciviousness, lechery, libido, lustfulness, passion

desired *adjective* = **required**, accurate, appropriate, correct, exact, expected, express, fitting, necessary, particular, proper, right

desirous *adjective* = **wishing**, ambitious, anxious, aspiring, avid, craving, desiring, eager, hopeful, hoping, keen, longing, ready, willing, yearning
➤ **Antonyms**
averse, disinclined, grudging, indisposed, loath, opposed, reluctant, unenthusiastic, unwilling

desist *verb* = **stop**, abstain, belay (*Nautical*), break off, cease, discontinue, end, forbear, give over (*informal*), give up, have done with, kick (*informal*), leave off, pause, refrain from, remit, suspend

desolate *adjective* **1** = **uninhabited**, bare, barren, bleak, desert, dreary, godforsaken, ruined, solitary, unfrequented, waste, wild **2** = **miserable**, abandoned, bereft, cheerless, comfortless, companionless, dejected, depressing, despondent, disconsolate, dismal, downcast, down in the dumps (*informal*), forlorn, forsaken, gloomy, lonely, melancholy, wretched ♦ *verb* **3** = **lay waste**, depopulate, despoil, destroy, devastate, lay low, pillage, plunder, ravage, ruin **4** = **deject**, daunt, depress, discourage, dishearten, dismay, distress, grieve
➤ **Antonyms**
adjective ≠**uninhabited**: inhabited, populous ≠**miserable**: cheerful, happy,

joyous, light-hearted ♦ *verb* ≠**lay waste**: develop ≠**deject**: cheer, encourage, hearten

desolation *noun* **1** = **ruin**, destruction, devastation, havoc, ravages, ruination **2** = **bleakness**, barrenness, desolateness, forlornness, isolation, loneliness, solitariness, solitude, wildness **3** = **misery**, anguish, dejection, despair, distress, gloom, gloominess, melancholy, sadness, unhappiness, woe, wretchedness

despair *noun* **1** = **despondency**, anguish, dejection, depression, desperation, disheartenment, gloom, hopelessness, melancholy, misery, wretchedness **2** = **hardship**, burden, cross, ordeal, pain, trial, tribulation ♦ *verb* **3** = **lose hope**, despond, give up, lose heart

despairing *adjective* = **hopeless**, anxious, at the end of one's tether, broken-hearted, dejected, depressed, desperate, despondent, disconsolate, dismal, downcast, down in the dumps (*informal*), frantic, grief-stricken, inconsolable, melancholy, miserable, suicidal, wretched

despatch *see* DISPATCH

desperado *noun* = **criminal**, bandit, cut-throat, gangster, gunman, heavy (*slang*), hoodlum (*chiefly U.S.*), lawbreaker, mugger (*informal*), outlaw, ruffian, skelm (*S. African*), thug, villain

desperate *adjective* **1** = **reckless**, audacious, dangerous, daring, death-defying, determined, foolhardy, frantic, furious, hasty, hazardous, headstrong, impetuous, madcap, precipitate, rash, risky, violent, wild **2** = **grave**, acute, critical, dire, drastic, extreme, great, urgent, very grave **3** = **hopeless**, at the end of one's tether, despairing, despondent, forlorn, inconsolable, irrecoverable, irremediable, irretrievable, wretched

desperately *adverb* **1** = **gravely**, badly, dangerously, perilously, seriously, severely **2** = **hopelessly**, appallingly, fearfully, frightfully, shockingly

desperation *noun* **1** = **recklessness**, defiance, foolhardiness, frenzy, heedlessness, impetuosity, madness, rashness **2** = **misery**, agony, anguish, anxiety, despair, despondency, distraction, heartache, hopelessness, pain, sorrow, torture, trouble, unhappiness, worry

despicable *adjective* = **contemptible**, abject, base, beyond contempt, cheap, degrading, detestable, disgraceful, disreputable, hateful, ignominious, infamous, low, mean, pitiful, reprehensible, scurvy, shameful, sordid,

vile, worthless, wretched
➤ **Antonyms**
admirable, estimable, ethical, exemplary, good, honest, honourable, moral, noble, praiseworthy, righteous, upright, virtuous, worthy

despise *verb* = **look down on**, abhor, contemn, deride, detest, disdain, disregard, flout, have a down on (*informal*), loathe, neglect, revile, scorn, slight, spurn, undervalue
➤ **Antonyms**
admire, adore, be fond of, be keen on, cherish, dig (*slang*), esteem, fancy (*informal*), love, relish, revel in, take to

despite *preposition* = **in spite of**, against, even with, in contempt of, in defiance of, in the face of, in the teeth of, notwithstanding, regardless of, undeterred by

despoil *verb Formal* = **plunder**, denude, deprive, destroy, devastate, dispossess, divest, loot, pillage, ravage, rifle, rob, strip, total (*slang*), trash (*slang*), vandalize, wreak havoc upon, wreck

despondency *noun* = **dejection**, depression, despair, desperation, disconsolateness, discouragement, dispiritedness, downheartedness, gloom, hopelessness, low spirits, melancholy, misery, sadness, the hump (*Brit. informal*), wretchedness

despondent *adjective* = **dejected**, blue, depressed, despairing, disconsolate, discouraged, disheartened, dismal, dispirited, doleful, down, downcast, downhearted, down in the dumps (*informal*), gloomy, glum, hopeless, in despair, low, low-spirited, melancholy, miserable, morose, sad, sick as a parrot (*informal*), sorrowful, woebegone, wretched
➤ **Antonyms**
buoyant, cheerful, cheery, chirpy (*informal*), genial, glad, happy, hopeful, joyful, light-hearted, optimistic, upbeat (*informal*)

despot *noun* = **tyrant**, autocrat, dictator, monocrat, oppressor

despotic *adjective* = **tyrannical**, absolute, arbitrary, arrogant, authoritarian, autocratic, dictatorial, domineering, imperious, monocratic, oppressive, unconstitutional

despotism *noun* = **tyranny**, absolutism, autarchy, autocracy, dictatorship, monocracy, oppression, totalitarianism

destination *noun* **1** = **journey's end**, harbour, haven, landing-place, resting-place, station, stop, terminus **2**

= **objective**, aim, ambition, design, end, goal, intention, object, purpose, target

destine *verb* = **fate**, allot, appoint, assign, consecrate, decree, design, devote, doom, earmark, intend, mark out, ordain, predetermine, preordain, purpose, reserve

destined *adjective* **1** = **fated**, bound, certain, designed, doomed, foreordained, ineluctable, inescapable, inevitable, intended, meant, ordained, predestined, unavoidable **2** = **bound for**, assigned, booked, directed, en route, heading for, on the road to, routed, scheduled

destiny *noun* = **fate**, cup, divine decree, doom, fortune, karma, kismet, lot, portion

destitute *adjective* **1** = **penniless**, dirt-poor (*informal*), distressed, down and out, flat broke (*informal*), impecunious, impoverished, indigent, in queer street (*informal*), insolvent, moneyless, necessitous, needy, on one's uppers, on the breadline (*informal*), on the rocks, penurious, poor, poverty-stricken, short, without two pennies to rub together (*informal*) **2** = **lacking**, bereft of, deficient in, depleted, deprived of, devoid of, drained, empty of, in need of, wanting, without

destitution *noun* = **pen! lessness**, beggary, dire straits, distress, impecuniousness, indigence, neediness, pauperism, penury, privation, utter poverty, want
➤ **Antonyms**
affluence, fortune, good fortune, life of luxury, luxury, plenty, prosperity, riches, wealth

destroy *verb* = **ruin**, annihilate, blow sky-high, blow to bits, break down, crush, demolish, desolate, devastate, dismantle, dispatch, eradicate, extinguish, extirpate, gut, kill, put paid to, ravage, raze, shatter, slay, smash, torpedo, total (*slang*), trash (*slang*), waste, wipe out, wreck

destruction *noun* = **ruin**, annihilation, crushing, demolition, devastation, downfall, end, eradication, extermination, extinction, havoc, liquidation, massacre, overthrow, overwhelming, ruination, shattering, slaughter, undoing, wreckage, wrecking

destructive *adjective* **1** = **damaging**, baleful, baneful, calamitous, cataclysmic, catastrophic, deadly, deleterious, detrimental, devastating, fatal, harmful, hurtful, injurious, lethal, maleficent, noxious, pernicious, ruinous **2** = **negative**, adverse, antagonistic, contrary, derogatory, discouraging, discrediting, disparaging, hostile, invalidating, opposed, undermining, vicious

detach verb = **separate**, cut off, disconnect, disengage, disentangle, disjoin, disunite, divide, free, isolate, loosen, remove, segregate, sever, tear off, unbridle, uncouple, unfasten, unhitch
➤ Antonyms
attach, bind, connect, fasten

detached adjective 1 = **separate**, disconnected, discrete, disjoined, divided, free, loosened, severed, unconnected 2 = **uninvolved**, aloof, disinterested, dispassionate, impartial, impersonal, neutral, objective, reserved, unbiased, uncommitted, unprejudiced
➤ Antonyms
≠uninvolved: biased, concerned, interested, involved, partisan, prejudiced

detachment noun 1 = **indifference**, aloofness, coolness, nonchalance, remoteness, unconcern 2 = **impartiality**, disinterestedness, fairness, neutrality, nonpartisanship, objectivity 3 Military = **unit**, body, detail, force, party, patrol, squad, task force 4 = **separation**, disconnection, disengagement, disjoining, severing

detail noun 1 = **point**, aspect, component, count, element, fact, factor, feature, item, particular, respect, specific, technicality 2 = **fine point**, minutiae, nicety, part, particular, triviality 3 Military = **party**, assignment, body, detachment, duty, fatigue, force, squad 4 **in detail** = **comprehensively**, exhaustively, inside out, item by item, point by point, thoroughly ◆ verb 5 = **list**, catalogue, delineate, depict, describe, enumerate, individualize, itemize, narrate, particularize, portray, recite, recount, rehearse, relate, specify, tabulate 6 = **appoint**, allocate, assign, charge, commission, delegate, detach, send

detailed adjective = **comprehensive**, blow-by-blow, circumstantial, elaborate, exact, exhaustive, full, intricate, itemized, meticulous, minute, particular, particularized, specific, thorough
➤ Antonyms
brief, compact, concise, condensed, limited, pithy, short, slight, succinct, summary, superficial, terse

detain verb 1 = **delay**, check, hinder, hold up, impede, keep, keep back, retard, slow up (or down), stay, stop 2 = **hold**, arrest, confine, intern, restrain

detect verb 1 = **notice**, ascertain, catch, descry, distinguish, identify, note, observe, perceive, recognize, scent, spot 2 = **discover**, catch, disclose, expose, find,

reveal, track down, uncover, unmask

detection noun = **discovery**, exposé, exposure, ferreting out, revelation, tracking down, uncovering, unearthing, unmasking

detective noun = **investigator**, bizzy (slang), C.I.D. man, constable, cop (slang), copper (slang), dick (slang, chiefly U.S.), gumshoe (U.S. slang), private eye, private investigator, sleuth (informal), tec (slang)

detention noun = **imprisonment**, confinement, custody, delay, hindrance, holding back, incarceration, keeping in, porridge (slang), quarantine, restraint, withholding
➤ Antonyms
acquittal, discharge, emancipation, freedom, liberation, liberty, release

deter verb = **discourage**, caution, check, damp, daunt, debar, dissuade, frighten, hinder, inhibit from, intimidate, prevent, prohibit, put off, restrain, stop, talk out of

detergent noun 1 = **cleaner**, cleanser ◆ adjective 2 = **cleansing**, abstergent, cleaning, detersive, purifying

deteriorate verb 1 = **decline**, corrupt, debase, degenerate, degrade, deprave, depreciate, go downhill (informal), go to pot, go to the dogs (informal), impair, injure, lower, slump, spoil, worsen 2 = **disintegrate**, be the worse for wear (informal), break down, crumble, decay, decline, decompose, ebb, fade, fall apart, lapse, retrogress, weaken, wear away
➤ Antonyms
≠decline: advance, ameliorate, get better, improve

deterioration noun 1 = **decline**, debasement, degeneration, degradation, dégringolade, depreciation, descent, downturn, drop, fall, retrogression, slump, vitiation, worsening 2 = **disintegration**, atrophy, corrosion, dilapidation, lapse, meltdown (informal)

determination noun 1 = **resolution**, backbone, constancy, conviction, dedication, doggedness, drive, firmness, fortitude, indomitability, perseverance, persistence, resoluteness, resolve, single-mindedness, steadfastness, tenacity, willpower 2 = **decision**, conclusion, judgment, purpose, resolve, result, settlement, solution, verdict
➤ Antonyms
≠resolution: doubt, hesitancy, hesitation, indecision, instability, irresolution, vacillation

determine verb 1 = **settle**, arbitrate, conclude, decide, end, finish, fix upon, ordain, regulate, terminate 2 = **find out**, ascertain, certify, check, detect, discover, establish, learn, verify, work out **3 = affect**, condition, control, decide, dictate, direct, govern, impel, impose, incline, induce, influence, lead, modify, regulate, rule, shape **4 = decide**, choose, elect, establish, fix, make up one's mind, purpose, resolve

determined _adjective_ = **resolute**, bent on, constant, dogged, firm, fixed, immovable, intent, persevering, persistent, purposeful, set on, single-minded, stalwart, steadfast, strong-minded, strong-willed, tenacious, unflinching, unwavering

determining _adjective_ = **deciding**, conclusive, critical, crucial, decisive, definitive, essential, final, important, settling

deterrent _noun_ = **discouragement**, check, curb, defensive measures, determent, disincentive, hindrance, impediment, obstacle, restraint
➤ **Antonyms**
bait, carrot (_informal_), enticement, incentive, inducement, lure, motivation, spur, stimulus

detest _verb_ = **hate**, abhor, abominate, despise, dislike intensely, execrate, feel aversion towards, feel disgust towards, feel hostility towards, loathe, recoil from
➤ **Antonyms**
adore, cherish, dig (_slang_), dote on, love, relish

detonate _verb_ = **explode**, blast, blow up, discharge, fulminate, set off, touch off, trigger

detonation _noun_ = **explosion**, bang, blast, blow-up, boom, discharge, fulmination, report

detour _noun_ = **diversion**, bypass, byway, circuitous route, deviation, indirect course, roundabout way

detract _verb_ **1 = lessen**, derogate, devaluate, diminish, lower, reduce, take away from **2 = divert**, deflect, distract, shift
➤ **Antonyms**
≠lessen: add to, augment, boost, complement, enhance, improve, reinforce, strengthen

detraction _noun_ = **disparagement**, abuse, aspersion, belittlement, calumny, defamation, denigration, deprecation, innuendo, insinuation, misrepresentation, muckraking, running down, scandalmongering, scurrility, slander, traducement, vituperation

detractor _noun_ = **slanderer**, backbiter, belittler, defamer, denigrator, derogator (_rare_), disparager, muckraker, scandalmonger, traducer

detriment _noun_ = **damage**, disadvantage, disservice, harm, hurt, impairment, injury, loss, mischief, prejudice

detrimental _adjective_ = **damaging**, adverse, baleful, deleterious, destructive, disadvantageous, harmful, inimical, injurious, mischievous, pernicious, prejudicial, unfavourable
➤ **Antonyms**
advantageous, beneficial, efficacious, favourable, good, helpful, salutary

devastate _verb_ **1 = destroy**, demolish, desolate, despoil, lay waste, level, pillage, plunder, ravage, raze, ruin, sack, spoil, total (_slang_), trash (_slang_), waste, wreck **2** _Informal_ = **overwhelm**, chagrin, confound, discomfit, discompose, disconcert, floor (_informal_), nonplus, overpower, take aback

devastating _adjective_ = **overwhelming**, caustic, cutting, effective, incisive, keen, mordant, overpowering, ravishing, sardonic, satirical, savage, stunning, trenchant, vitriolic, withering

devastation _noun_ = **destruction**, demolition, depredation, desolation, havoc, pillage, plunder, ravages, ruin, ruination, spoliation

develop _verb_ **1 = advance**, blossom, cultivate, evolve, flourish, foster, grow, mature, progress, promote, prosper, ripen **2 = form**, acquire, begin, breed, commence, contract, establish, generate, invent, originate, pick up, start **3 = expand**, amplify, augment, broaden, dilate upon, elaborate, enlarge, unfold, work out **4 = result**, be a direct result of, break out, come about, ensue, follow, happen

development _noun_ **1 = growth**, advance, advancement, evolution, expansion, improvement, increase, maturity, progress, progression, spread, unfolding, unravelling **2 = event**, change, circumstance, happening, incident, issue, occurrence, outcome, phenomenon, result, situation, turn of events, upshot

deviant _adjective_ **1 = perverted**, aberrant, abnormal, bent (_slang_), deviate, devious, freaky (_slang_), heretical, kinky (_slang_), perverse, pervy (_slang_), queer (_informal, derogatory_), sick (_informal_), sicko (_informal_), twisted, warped, wayward
♦ _noun_ **2 = pervert**, deviate, freak, misfit, odd type, queer (_informal, derogatory_), sicko (_informal_)
➤ **Antonyms**
adjective ≠perverted: conventional, normal, orthodox, straight, straightforward

deviate _verb_ = **differ**, avert, bend, deflect, depart, digress, diverge, drift, err, meander, part, stray, swerve, turn, turn aside, vary, veer, wander

deviation *noun* = **departure**, aberration, alteration, change, deflection, digression, discrepancy, disparity, divergence, fluctuation, inconsistency, irregularity, shift, variance, variation

device *noun* 1 = **gadget**, apparatus, appliance, contraption, contrivance, gimmick, gizmo *or* gismo (*slang, chiefly U.S. & Canad.*), implement, instrument, invention, machine, tool, utensil, waldo 2 = **ploy**, artifice, design, dodge, expedient, gambit, improvisation, manoeuvre, plan, project, purpose, ruse, scheme, shift, stratagem, strategy, stunt, trick, wile 3 = **emblem**, badge, colophon, crest, design, figure, insignia, logo, motif, motto, symbol, token

devil *noun* 1 **the Devil** = **Satan**, Abbadon, Apollyon, archfiend, Beelzebub, Belial, Clootie (*Scot.*), deil (*Scot.*), demon, Deuce, Evil One, fiend, Foul Fiend, Lord of the Flies, Lucifer, Mephisto, Mephistopheles, Old Gentleman (*informal*), Old Harry (*informal*), Old Hornie (*informal*), Old Nick (*informal*), Old One, Old Scratch (*informal*), Prince of Darkness, Tempter, Wicked One 2 = **brute**, beast, demon, fiend, ghoul, monster, ogre, rogue, savage, terror, villain 3 = **scamp**, imp, monkey (*informal*), pickle (*Brit. informal*), rascal, rogue, scoundrel 4 = **person**, beggar, creature, thing, unfortunate, wretch 5 = **enthusiast**, demon, fiend, go-getter (*informal*)

devilish *adjective* = **fiendish**, accursed, atrocious, damnable, detestable, diabolic, diabolical, execrable, hellish, infernal, satanic, wicked

devil-may-care *adjective* = **happy-go-lucky**, careless, casual, easy-going, flippant, heedless, insouciant, nonchalant, reckless, swaggering, swashbuckling, unconcerned

devilry *noun* 1 = **mischief**, devilment, jiggery-pokery (*informal, chiefly Brit.*), knavery, mischievousness, monkey-business (*informal*), rascality, roguery 2 = **wickedness**, cruelty, evil, malevolence, malice, vice, viciousness, villainy 3 = **sorcery**, black magic, diablerie, diabolism

devious *adjective* 1 = **sly**, calculating, crooked (*informal*), deceitful, dishonest, double-dealing, evasive, indirect, insidious, insincere, not straightforward, scheming, surreptitious, treacherous, tricky, underhand, wily 2 = **indirect**, circuitous, confusing, crooked, deviating, erratic,

excursive, misleading, rambling, roundabout, tortuous, wandering
➤ **Antonyms**
≠**sly**: blunt, candid, direct, downright, forthright, frank, honest, straight, straightforward ≠**indirect**: blunt, direct, downright, forthright, straight, straightforward, undeviating, unswerving

devise *verb* = **work out**, arrange, conceive, concoct, construct, contrive, design, dream up, form, formulate, frame, imagine, invent, plan, plot, prepare, project, scheme, think up

devoid *adjective* = **lacking**, barren, bereft, deficient, denuded, destitute, empty, free from, sans (*archaic*), vacant, void, wanting, without

devolution *noun* = **decentralization**, delegation

devolve *verb* 1 = **fall upon** *or* **to**, be transferred, commission, consign, delegate, depute, entrust, rest with, transfer 2 *Law* = **be handed down**, alienate, convey

devote *verb* = **dedicate**, allot, apply, appropriate, assign, commit, concern oneself, consecrate, enshrine, give, occupy oneself, pledge, reserve, set apart

devoted *adjective* = **dedicated**, ardent, caring, committed, concerned, constant, devout, faithful, fond, loving, loyal, staunch, steadfast, true
➤ **Antonyms**
disloyal, inconstant, indifferent, uncommitted, undedicated, unfaithful

devotee *noun* = **enthusiast**, addict, adherent, admirer, aficionado, buff (*informal*), disciple, fan, fanatic, follower, supporter, votary

devotion *noun* 1 = **dedication**, adherence, allegiance, commitment, consecration, constancy, faithfulness, fidelity, loyalty 2 = **love**, affection, ardour, attachment, earnestness, fervour, fondness, intensity, passion, zeal 3 = **devoutness**, adoration, godliness, holiness, piety, prayer, religiousness, reverence, sanctity, spirituality, worship 4 **devotions** = **prayers**, church service, divine office, religious observance
➤ **Antonyms**
≠**dedication**: carelessness, disregard, inattention, indifference, laxity, laxness, neglect, thoughtlessness ≠**devoutness**: derision, disrespect, impiety, irreverence

devour *verb* 1 = **eat**, bolt, consume, cram, dispatch, gobble, gorge, gulp, guzzle, pig out on (*slang*), polish off (*informal*), stuff, swallow, wolf 2 = **destroy**, annihilate, consume, ravage, spend, waste, wipe out

3 = enjoy, absorb, appreciate, be engrossed by, be preoccupied, delight in, drink in, feast on, go through, read compulsively *or* voraciously, relish, revel in, take in

devouring *adjective* = **overwhelming**, consuming, excessive, flaming, insatiable, intense, passionate, powerful

devout *adjective* **1 = religious**, godly, holy, orthodox, pious, prayerful, pure, reverent, saintly **2 = sincere**, ardent, deep, devoted, earnest, fervent, genuine, heartfelt, intense, passionate, profound, serious, zealous
➤ **Antonyms**
≠**religious**: impious, irreligious, irreverent, sacrilegious ≠**sincere**: indifferent, passive

devoutly *adverb* = **with all one's heart**, fervently, heart and soul, profoundly, sincerely

dexterity *noun* **1 = skill**, adroitness, artistry, craft, deftness, effortlessness, expertise, facility, finesse, handiness, knack, mastery, neatness, nimbleness, proficiency, smoothness, touch **2 = cleverness**, ability, address, adroitness, aptitude, aptness, art, expertness, ingenuity, readiness, skilfulness, tact
➤ **Antonyms**
clumsiness, gaucheness, inability, incapacity, incompetence, ineptitude, uselessness

diabolical *adjective Informal* = **dreadful**, abysmal, appalling, atrocious, damnable, difficult, disastrous, excruciating, fiendish, from hell (*informal*), hellacious (*U.S. slang*), hellish, nasty, outrageous, shocking, terrible, tricky, unpleasant, vile

diagnose *verb* = **identify**, analyse, determine, distinguish, interpret, investigate, pinpoint, pronounce, put one's finger on, recognize

diagnosis *noun* **1 = examination**, analysis, investigation, scrutiny **2 = opinion**, conclusion, interpretation, pronouncement

diagonal *adjective* = **slanting**, angled, cater-cornered (*U.S. informal*), cornerways, cross, crossways, crosswise, oblique

diagonally *adverb* = **aslant**, at an angle, cornerwise, crosswise, obliquely, on the bias, on the cross

diagram *noun* = **plan**, chart, drawing, figure, graph, layout, outline, representation, sketch

dialect *noun* = **language**, accent, brogue, idiom, jargon, lingo (*informal*), localism, patois, pronunciation, provincialism, speech, tongue, vernacular

dialectic *noun* **1 = debate**, argumentation, contention, discussion, disputation, logic, polemics, ratiocination, reasoning
♦ *adjective* **2 = logical**, analytic, argumentative, dialectical, polemical, rational, rationalistic

dialogue *noun* **1 = conversation**, colloquy, communication, confabulation, conference, converse, discourse, discussion, duologue, exchange, interlocution **2 = lines**, conversation, script, spoken part

diametric, diametrical *adjective* = **opposed**, antipodal, antithetical, conflicting, contrary, contrasting, counter, opposite, poles apart

diametrically *adverb* = **completely**, absolutely, entirely, totally, utterly

diarrhoea *noun* = **the runs**, dysentery, gippy tummy, holiday tummy, looseness, Montezuma's revenge (*informal*), Spanish tummy, the skits (*informal*), the skitters (*informal*), the trots (*informal*)

diary *noun* = **journal**, appointment book, chronicle, daily record, day-to-day account, engagement book, Filofax (*Trademark*)

diatribe *noun* = **tirade**, abuse, castigation, criticism, denunciation, disputation, harangue, invective, philippic, reviling, stream of abuse, stricture, verbal onslaught, vituperation

dicey *adjective Informal, chiefly Brit.* = **dangerous**, chancy (*informal*), difficult, hairy (*slang*), risky, ticklish, tricky

dicky *adjective Brit. informal* = **weak**, fluttery, queer, shaky, unreliable, unsound, unsteady

dictate *verb* **1 = speak**, read out, say, transmit, utter **2 = order**, command, decree, demand, direct, enjoin, establish, impose, lay down, lay down the law, ordain, prescribe, pronounce ♦ *noun* **3 = command**, behest, bidding, decree, demand, direction, edict, fiat, injunction, mandate, order, ordinance, requirement, statute, ultimatum, word **4 = principle**, canon, code, dictum, law, precept, rule

dictator *noun* = **absolute ruler**, autocrat, despot, oppressor, tyrant

dictatorial *adjective* **1 = absolute**, arbitrary, autocratic, despotic, totalitarian, tyrannical, unlimited, unrestricted **2 = domineering**, authoritarian, bossy (*informal*), dogmatical, imperious, iron-handed, magisterial, oppressive, overbearing
➤ **Antonyms**
≠**absolute**: constitutional, democratic, egalitarian, restricted ≠**domineering**:

humble, servile, suppliant, tolerant

dictatorship *noun* = **absolute rule**, absolutism, authoritarianism, autocracy, despotism, reign of terror, totalitarianism, tyranny

diction *noun* = **pronunciation**, articulation, delivery, elocution, enunciation, fluency, inflection, intonation, speech

dictionary *noun* = **wordbook**, concordance, encyclopedia, glossary, lexicon, vocabulary

didactic *adjective* = **instructive**, edifying, educational, enlightening, homiletic, moral, moralizing, pedagogic, pedantic, preceptive

die *verb* 1 = **pass away**, breathe one's last, buy it (*U.S. slang*), buy the farm (*U.S. slang*), check out (*U.S. slang*), croak (*slang*), decease, depart, expire, finish, give up the ghost, go belly-up (*slang*), hop the twig (*slang*), kick it (*slang*), kick the bucket (*slang*), peg it (*informal*), peg out (*informal*), perish, pop one's clogs (*informal*), snuff it (*slang*) 2 = **dwindle**, decay, decline, disappear, ebb, end, fade, lapse, pass, sink, subside, vanish, wane, wilt, wither 3 = **stop**, break down, fade out *or* away, fail, fizzle out, halt, lose power, peter out, run down 4 **be dying for** = **long for**, ache for, be eager for, desire, hunger for, languish for, pine for, set one's heart on, swoon over, yearn for 5 **be dying of** *Informal* = **be overcome with**, collapse with, succumb to
➤ **Antonyms**
≠**pass away**: be born, begin, come to life, exist, live, survive ≠**dwindle, stop**: flourish, grow, increase

die-hard *noun* 1 = **reactionary**, fanatic, intransigent, old fogey, stick-in-the-mud (*informal*), ultraconservative, zealot
♦ *adjective* 2 = **reactionary**, dyed-in-the-wool, immovable, inflexible, intransigent, ultraconservative, uncompromising, unreconstructed (*chiefly U.S.*)

diet[1] *noun* 1 = **food**, aliment, comestibles, commons, edibles, fare, nourishment, nutriment, provisions, rations, subsistence, sustenance, viands, victuals 2 = **regime**, abstinence, dietary, fast, regimen ♦ *verb* 3 = **slim**, abstain, eat sparingly, fast, lose weight
➤ **Antonyms**
verb ≠**slim**: get fat, glut, gobble, gormandize, guzzle, indulge, overindulge, pig out (*slang*), stuff oneself

diet[2] *noun* = **council**, chamber, congress, convention, legislative assembly, legislature, meeting, parliament, sitting

differ *verb* 1 = **be dissimilar**, be distinct, contradict, contrast, depart from, diverge, run counter to, stand apart, vary 2 = **disagree**, clash, contend, debate, demur, dispute, dissent, oppose, take exception, take issue
➤ **Antonyms**
≠**be dissimilar**: accord, coincide, harmonize ≠**disagree**: accord, acquiesce, agree, assent, concur, cooperate

difference *noun* 1 = **dissimilarity**, alteration, change, contrast, deviation, differentiation, discrepancy, disparity, distinction, distinctness, divergence, diversity, unlikeness, variation, variety 2 = **distinction**, exception, idiosyncrasy, particularity, peculiarity, singularity 3 = **disagreement**, argument, clash, conflict, contention, contrariety, contretemps, controversy, debate, discordance, dispute, quarrel, row, set-to (*informal*), strife, tiff, wrangle 4 = **remainder**, balance, rest, result
➤ **Antonyms**
≠**dissimilarity**: affinity, comparability, conformity, congruence, likeness, relation, resemblance, sameness, similarity, similitude ≠**disagreement**: agreement, concordance

different *adjective* 1 = **unlike**, altered, at odds, at variance, changed, clashing, contrasting, deviating, discrepant, disparate, dissimilar, divergent, diverse, inconsistent, opposed, streets apart 2 = **various**, assorted, divers (*archaic*), diverse, manifold, many, miscellaneous, multifarious, numerous, several, some, sundry, varied 3 = **unusual**, another story, atypical, bizarre, distinctive, extraordinary, left-field (*informal*), out of the ordinary, peculiar, rare, singular, something else, special, strange, uncommon, unconventional, unique 4 = **other**, another, discrete, distinct, individual, separate

differential *adjective* 1 = **distinctive**, diacritical, discriminative, distinguishing
♦ *noun* 2 = **difference**, amount of difference, discrepancy, disparity

differentiate *verb* 1 = **distinguish**, contrast, discern, discriminate, make a distinction, mark off, separate, set off *or* apart, tell apart 2 = **make different**, adapt, alter, change, convert, modify, transform

difficult *adjective* 1 = **hard**, arduous, burdensome, demanding, formidable, laborious, like getting blood out of a stone, no picnic (*informal*), onerous, painful, strenuous, toilsome, uphill, wearisome 2 = **problematical**, abstract, abstruse,

baffling, complex, complicated, delicate, enigmatical, intricate, involved, knotty, obscure, perplexing, thorny, ticklish **3 = troublesome**, demanding, fastidious, fractious, fussy, hard to please, intractable, obstreperous, perverse, refractory, rigid, tiresome, trying, unaccommodating, unamenable, unmanageable **4 = tough**, dark, full of hardship, grim, hard, straitened, trying
➤ **Antonyms**
≠**hard:** easy, easy-peasy (*slang*), light, manageable, obvious, plain, simple, straightforward, uncomplicated ≠**troublesome:** accommodating, amenable, cooperative, pleasant ≠**tough:** easy, pleasant

difficulty *noun* **1 = laboriousness**, arduousness, awkwardness, hardship, labour, pain, painfulness, strain, strenuousness, tribulation **2 = predicament**, deep water, dilemma, distress, embarrassment, fix (*informal*), hot water (*informal*), jam (*informal*), mess, perplexity, pickle (*informal*), plight, quandary, spot (*informal*), straits, tight spot, trial, trouble **3 = problem**, complication, hassle (*informal*), hazard, hindrance, hurdle, impediment, objection, obstacle, opposition, pitfall, protest, snag, stumbling block

diffidence *noun* **= shyness**, backwardness, bashfulness, constraint, doubt, fear, hesitancy, hesitation, humility, insecurity, lack of self-confidence, meekness, modesty, reluctance, reserve, self-consciousness, sheepishness, timidity, timidness, timorousness, unassertiveness
➤ **Antonyms**
assurance, boldness, confidence, courage, firmness, self-confidence, self-possession

diffident *adjective* **= shy**, backward, bashful, constrained, distrustful, doubtful, hesitant, insecure, meek, modest, reluctant, reserved, self-conscious, self-effacing, sheepish, shrinking, suspicious, timid, timorous, unassertive, unassuming, unobtrusive, unsure, withdrawn

diffuse *verb* **1 = spread**, circulate, dispel, dispense, disperse, disseminate, dissipate, distribute, propagate, scatter ◆ *adjective* **2 = spread out**, dispersed, scattered, unconcentrated **3 = rambling**, circumlocutory, copious, diffusive, digressive, discursive, long-winded, loose, maundering, meandering, prolix, vague, verbose, waffling (*informal*), wordy
➤ **Antonyms**
adjective ≠**spread out:** concentrated ≠**rambling:** apposite, brief, compendious,

concise, succinct, terse, to the point

diffusion *noun* **1 = spread**, circulation, dispersal, dispersion, dissemination, dissipation, distribution, expansion, propaganda, propagation, scattering **2 = rambling**, circuitousness, diffuseness, digressiveness, discursiveness, long-windedness, prolixity, verbiage, verbosity, wandering, wordiness

dig *verb* **1 = excavate**, break up, burrow, delve, gouge, grub, hoe, hollow out, mine, penetrate, pierce, quarry, scoop, till, tunnel, turn over **2 = investigate**, delve, dig down, go into, probe, research, search **3** *with* **out** *or* **up = find**, bring to light, come across, come up with, discover, expose, extricate, retrieve, root (*informal*), rootle, uncover, unearth, uproot **4** *Informal* **= like**, appreciate, enjoy, follow, groove (*dated slang*), understand **5 = poke**, drive, jab, prod, punch, thrust ◆ *noun* **6 = poke**, jab, prod, punch, thrust **7 = cutting remark**, barb, crack (*slang*), gibe, insult, jeer, quip, sneer, taunt, wisecrack (*informal*)

digest *verb* **1 = ingest**, absorb, assimilate, concoct, dissolve, incorporate, macerate **2 = take in**, absorb, assimilate, con, consider, contemplate, grasp, master, meditate, ponder, study, understand ◆ *noun* **3 = summary**, abridgment, abstract, compendium, condensation, epitome, précis, résumé, synopsis

digestion *noun* **= ingestion**, absorption, assimilation, conversion, incorporation, transformation

dig in *verb Informal* **1 = start eating**, begin, fall to, set about, tuck in (*informal*) **2 = entrench**, defend, establish, fortify, maintain

dignified *adjective* **= distinguished**, august, decorous, exalted, formal, grave, honourable, imposing, lofty, lordly, noble, reserved, solemn, stately, upright
➤ **Antonyms**
crass, inelegant, unbecoming, undignified, unseemly, vulgar

dignify *verb* **= distinguish**, adorn, advance, aggrandize, elevate, ennoble, exalt, glorify, grace, honour, promote, raise

dignitary *noun* **= public figure**, bigwig (*informal*), celeb (*informal*), high-up (*informal*), notability, notable, personage, pillar of society, pillar of the church, pillar of the state, V.I.P., worthy

dignity *noun* **1 = decorum**, courtliness, grandeur, gravity, hauteur, loftiness, majesty, nobility, propriety, solemnity, stateliness **2 = honour**, elevation, eminence, excellence, glory, greatness,

importance, nobleness, rank,
respectability, standing, station, status **3**
= **self-importance**, *amour-propre,* pride,
self-esteem, self-possession, self-regard,
self-respect

digress *verb* = **wander**, be diffuse, depart,
deviate, diverge, drift, expatiate, get off
the point *or* subject, go off at a tangent,
meander, ramble, stray, turn aside

digression *noun* = **departure**, apostrophe,
aside, detour, deviation, divergence,
diversion, footnote, obiter dictum,
parenthesis, straying, wandering

dilapidated *adjective* = **ruined**, battered,
beat-up (*informal*), broken-down,
crumbling, decayed, decaying, decrepit,
fallen in, falling apart, gone to rack and
ruin, in ruins, neglected, ramshackle,
rickety, ruinous, run-down, shabby, shaky,
tumbledown, uncared for, worn-out

dilate *verb* **1** = **enlarge**, broaden, distend,
expand, extend, puff out, stretch, swell,
widen **2** = **expand**, amplify, be profuse, be
prolix, descant, detail, develop, dwell on,
enlarge, expatiate, expound, spin out
➤ **Antonyms**
≠**enlarge**: compress, constrict, contract,
narrow, shrink

dilation *noun* = **enlargement**, broadening,
dilatation, distension, expansion,
extension, increase, spread

dilatory *adjective* = **time-wasting**,
backward, behindhand, dallying, delaying,
laggard, lingering, loitering,
procrastinating, putting off, slack, slow,
sluggish, snail-like, tardy, tarrying
➤ **Antonyms**
on-the-ball (*informal*), prompt, punctual,
sharp (*informal*)

dilemma *noun* **1** = **predicament**, difficulty,
embarrassment, fix (*informal*),
how-do-you-do (*informal*), jam (*informal*),
mess, perplexity, pickle (*informal*), plight,
problem, puzzle, quandary, spot
(*informal*), strait, tight corner *or* spot **2 on
the horns of a dilemma** = **between the
devil and the deep blue sea**, between a
rock and a hard place (*informal*), between
Scylla and Charybdis

dilettante *noun* = **amateur**, aesthete,
dabbler, nonprofessional, trifler

diligence *noun* = **application**, activity,
assiduity, assiduousness, attention,
attentiveness, care, constancy,
earnestness, heedfulness, industry,
intentness, laboriousness, perseverance,
sedulousness

diligent *adjective* = **hard-working**, active,
assiduous, attentive, busy, careful,
conscientious, constant, earnest,

indefatigable, industrious, laborious,
painstaking, persevering, persistent,
sedulous, studious, tireless
➤ **Antonyms**
careless, dilatory, good-for-nothing,
inconstant, indifferent, lazy

dilly-dally *verb Informal* = **dawdle**, dally,
delay, dither (*chiefly Brit.*), falter, fluctuate,
hesitate, hover, hum and haw, linger,
loiter, potter, procrastinate, shillyshally
(*informal*), trifle, vacillate, waver

dilute *verb* **1** = **water down**, adulterate, cut,
make thinner, thin (out), weaken **2**
= **reduce**, attenuate, decrease, diffuse,
diminish, lessen, mitigate, temper, weaken
➤ **Antonyms**
≠**water down**: concentrate, condense,
strengthen, thicken ≠**reduce**: intensify,
strengthen

dim *adjective* **1** = **poorly lit**, caliginous
(*archaic*), cloudy, dark, darkish, dusky,
grey, overcast, shadowy, tenebrous,
unilluminated **2** = **unclear**, bleary, blurred,
faint, fuzzy, ill-defined, indistinct,
obscured, shadowy **3** *Informal* = **stupid**,
braindead (*informal*), dense, doltish, dozy
(*Brit. informal*), dull, dumb (*informal*),
obtuse, slow, slow on the uptake
(*informal*), thick **4** = **obscure**, confused,
hazy, imperfect, indistinct, intangible,
remote, shadowy, vague **5** = **dull**, dingy,
feeble, lacklustre, muted, opaque, pale,
sullied, tarnished, weak **6** = **unfavourable**,
depressing, discouraging, gloomy,
sombre, unpromising **7 take a dim view**
= **disapprove**, be displeased, be sceptical,
look askance, reject, suspect, take
exception, view with disfavour ♦ *verb* **8**
= **dull**, bedim, blur, cloud, darken, fade,
lower, obscure, tarnish, turn down
➤ **Antonyms**
adjective ≠**poorly lit**: bright, clear,
cloudless, fair, limpid, pleasant, sunny,
unclouded ≠**unclear**: bright, brilliant,
clear, distinct, limpid ≠**stupid**: acute,
astute, aware, brainy, bright, clever,
intelligent, keen, quick-witted, sharp, smart

dimension *noun, often plural*
= **measurement**, amplitude, bulk,
capacity, extent, proportions, size, volume

dimensions *plural noun* = **extent**, bigness,
greatness, importance, largeness,
magnitude, measure, range, scale, scope

diminish *verb* **1** = **decrease**, abate,
contract, curtail, cut, downsize, lessen,
lower, reduce, retrench, shrink, taper,
weaken **2** = **dwindle**, decline, die out, ebb,
fade away, peter out, recede, shrivel,
slacken, subside, wane **3** = **belittle**,
cheapen, demean, depreciate, devalue

➤ **Antonyms**
≠**decrease:** amplify, augment, enhance, enlarge, expand, grow, heighten, increase

diminution *noun* = **decrease**, abatement, contraction, curtailment, cut, cutback, decay, decline, deduction, lessening, reduction, retrenchment, weakening

diminutive *adjective* = **small**, bantam, Lilliputian, little, midget, mini, miniature, minute, petite, pocket(-sized), pygmy *or* pigmy, teensy-weensy, teeny-weeny, tiny, undersized, wee
➤ **Antonyms**
big, colossal, enormous, giant, gigantic, great, immense, jumbo (*informal*), king-size, massive (*informal*)

din *noun* 1 = **noise**, babel, clamour, clangour, clash, clatter, commotion, crash, hubbub, hullabaloo, outcry, pandemonium, racket, row, shout, uproar
♦ *verb* 2 **din (something) into (someone)** = **instil**, drum into, go on at, hammer into, inculcate, instruct, teach
➤ **Antonyms**
noun ≠**noise:** calm, calmness, hush, peace, quiet, quietness, silence, tranquillity

dine *verb* 1 = **eat**, banquet, chow down (*slang*), feast, lunch, sup 2 **dine on** *or* **off** = **eat**, consume, feed on

dingy *adjective* 1 = **dull**, bedimmed, colourless, dark, dim, drab, dreary, dusky, faded, gloomy, murky, obscure, sombre 2 = **discoloured**, dirty, grimy, seedy, shabby, soiled, tacky (*informal*)

dinky *adjective Brit. informal* = **cute**, dainty, mini, miniature, natty (*informal*), neat, petite, small, trim

dinner *noun* = **meal**, banquet, beanfeast (*Brit. informal*), blowout (*slang*), collation, feast, main meal, refection, repast, spread (*informal*)

dip *verb* 1 = **plunge**, bathe, douse, duck, dunk, immerse, rinse, souse 2 = **slope**, decline, descend, disappear, droop, drop (down), fade, fall, lower, sag, set, sink, slump, subside, tilt ♦ *noun* 3 = **plunge**, douche, drenching, ducking, immersion, soaking 4 = **bathe**, dive, plunge, swim 5 = **hollow**, basin, concavity, depression, hole, incline, slope 6 = **drop**, decline, fall, lowering, sag, slip, slump 7 = **mixture**, concoction, dilution, infusion, preparation, solution, suspension

dip into *verb* 1 = **draw upon**, reach into 2 = **sample**, browse, dabble, glance at, peruse, play at, run over, skim, try

diplomacy *noun* 1 = **statesmanship**, international negotiation, statecraft 2 = **tact**, artfulness, craft, delicacy, discretion, finesse, savoir-faire, skill, subtlety
➤ **Antonyms**
≠**tact:** awkwardness, clumsiness, ineptness, tactlessness, thoughtlessness

diplomat *noun* = **negotiator**, conciliator, go-between, mediator, moderator, politician, public relations expert, tactician

diplomatic *adjective* = **tactful**, adept, discreet, polite, politic, prudent, sensitive, subtle
➤ **Antonyms**
impolitic, insensitive, rude, tactless, thoughtless, undiplomatic, unsubtle

dire *adjective* 1 = **disastrous**, alarming, appalling, awful, calamitous, cataclysmic, catastrophic, cruel, godawful (*slang*), horrible, horrid, ruinous, terrible, woeful 2 = **desperate**, critical, crucial, crying, drastic, exigent, extreme, now or never, pressing, urgent 3 = **grim**, bodeful, dismal, dreadful, fearful, gloomy, ominous, portentous

direct *adjective* 1 = **straight**, nonstop, not crooked, shortest, through, unbroken, undeviating, uninterrupted 2 = **first-hand**, face-to-face, head-on, immediate, personal 3 = **straightforward**, candid, downright, frank, honest, man-to-man, matter-of-fact, open, outspoken, plain-spoken, round, sincere, straight, upfront (*informal*) 4 = **explicit**, absolute, blunt, categorical, downright, express, plain, point-blank, unambiguous, unequivocal ♦ *verb* 5 = **control**, administer, advise, call the shots, call the tune, conduct, dispose, govern, guide, handle, lead, manage, mastermind, oversee, preside over, regulate, rule, run, superintend, supervise 6 = **order**, bid, charge, command, demand, dictate, enjoin, instruct 7 = **guide**, indicate, lead, point in the direction of, point the way, show 8 = **address**, label, mail, route, send, superscribe 9 = **aim**, address, cast, fix, focus, intend, level, mean, point, train, turn
➤ **Antonyms**
adjective ≠**straight:** circuitous, crooked, indirect ≠**first-hand:** indirect, mediated ≠**straightforward:** circuitous, crooked, devious, indirect, sly, subtle ≠**explicit:** ambiguous, circuitous, indirect

direction *noun* 1 = **way**, aim, bearing, course, line, path, road, route, track 2 = **tendency**, bent, bias, current, drift, end, leaning, orientation, proclivity, tack, tenor, trend 3 = **management**, administration, charge, command, control, government, guidance, leadership, order, oversight, superintendence, supervision

directions plural noun = **instructions**, briefing, guidance, guidelines, indication, plan, recommendation, regulations

directive noun = **order**, canon, charge, command, decree, dictate, edict, fiat, imperative, injunction, instruction, mandate, notice, ordinance, regulation, ruling

directly adverb 1 = **straight**, by the shortest route, exactly, in a beeline, precisely, unswervingly, without deviation 2 = **honestly**, candidly, face-to-face, in person, openly, overtly, personally, plainly, point-blank, straightforwardly, truthfully, unequivocally, without prevarication 3 = **at once**, as soon as possible, dead, due, forthwith, immediately, in a second, instantaneously, instantly, pdq (slang), posthaste, presently, promptly, pronto (informal), quickly, right away, soon, speedily, straightaway

director noun = **controller**, administrator, boss (informal), chairman, chief, executive, governor, head, leader, manager, organizer, principal, producer, supervisor

dirge noun = **lament**, coronach (Scot. & Irish), dead march, elegy, funeral song, requiem, threnody

dirt noun 1 = **filth**, crap (slang), crud (slang), dust, excrement, grime, grot (slang), impurity, kak (S. African slang), mire, muck, mud, shit (taboo slang), slime, slob (Irish), smudge, stain, tarnish 2 = **soil**, clay, earth, loam 3 = **obscenity**, indecency, pornography, sleaze, smut

dirty adjective 1 = **filthy**, begrimed, foul, grimy, grotty (slang), grubby, grungy (slang, chiefly U.S.), messy, mucky, muddy, nasty, polluted, scuzzy (slang, chiefly U.S.), soiled, sullied, unclean 2 = **dark**, clouded, dull, miry, muddy, not clear 3 = **dishonest**, corrupt, crooked, fraudulent, illegal, treacherous, unfair, unscrupulous, unsporting 4 = **despicable**, base, beggarly, contemptible, cowardly, ignominious, low, low-down (informal), mean, nasty, scurvy, shabby, sordid, squalid, vile 5 = **obscene**, blue, indecent, off-colour, pornographic, risqué, salacious, sleazy, smutty, vulgar, X-rated (informal) 6 As in **a dirty look** = **angry**, annoyed, bitter, choked, indignant, offended, resentful, scorching 7 = **stormy**, gusty, louring or lowering, rainy, squally ♦ verb 8 = **soil**, begrime, blacken, defile, foul, mess up, muddy, pollute, smear, smirch, smudge, spoil, stain, sully
➤ **Antonyms**
adjective ≠**filthy**: clean, pure ≠**dishonest**: decent, honest, moral, reputable, respectable, upright ≠**obscene**: clean,

decent ≠**stormy**: pleasant ♦ verb ≠**soil**: clean, tidy up

disability noun 1 = **handicap**, affliction, ailment, complaint, defect, disablement, disorder, impairment, infirmity, malady 2 = **incapacity**, disqualification, impotency, inability, incompetency, unfitness, weakness

disable verb 1 = **handicap**, cripple, damage, debilitate, enfeeble, hamstring, immobilize, impair, incapacitate, paralyse, prostrate, put out of action, render hors de combat, render inoperative, unfit, unman, weaken 2 = **disqualify**, disenable, invalidate, render or declare incapable

disabled adjective = **handicapped**, bedridden, crippled, incapacitated, infirm, lame, maimed, mangled, mutilated, paralysed, weak, weakened, wrecked
➤ **Antonyms**
able-bodied, fit, hale, healthy, hearty, robust, sound, strong, sturdy

disadvantage noun 1 = **harm**, damage, detriment, disservice, hurt, injury, loss, prejudice 2 = **drawback**, burden, downside, flaw, fly in the ointment (informal), handicap, hardship, hindrance, impediment, inconvenience, liability, minus (informal), nuisance, privation, snag, trouble, weakness, weak point 3 at a disadvantage = **vulnerable**, boxed in, cornered, handicapped, in a corner, with one's hands tied behind one's back
➤ **Antonyms**
≠**harm**, **drawback**: advantage, aid, benefit, convenience, gain, help, merit, profit

disadvantageous adjective = **unfavourable**, adverse, damaging, deleterious, detrimental, harmful, hurtful, ill-timed, inconvenient, inexpedient, injurious, inopportune, prejudicial

disaffected adjective = **alienated**, antagonistic, discontented, disloyal, dissatisfied, estranged, hostile, mutinous, rebellious, seditious, uncompliant, unsubmissive

disaffection noun = **alienation**, animosity, antagonism, antipathy, aversion, breach, disagreement, discontent, dislike, disloyalty, dissatisfaction, estrangement, hostility, ill will, repugnance, resentment, unfriendliness

disagree verb 1 = **differ (in opinion)**, argue, be at sixes and sevens, bicker, clash, contend, contest, cross swords, debate, dispute, dissent, fall out (informal), have words (informal), object, oppose, quarrel, take issue with, wrangle 2 = **conflict**, be discordant, be dissimilar, contradict,

counter, depart, deviate, differ, diverge, run counter to, vary **3 = make ill**, be injurious, bother, discomfort, distress, hurt, nauseate, sicken, trouble, upset
➤ **Antonyms**
≠**differ (in opinion)**: agree, concur, get on (together) ≠**conflict**: accord, coincide, harmonize

disagreeable *adjective* **1 = nasty**, disgusting, displeasing, distasteful, horrid, objectionable, obnoxious, offensive, repellent, repugnant, repulsive, uninviting, unpalatable, unpleasant, unsavoury, yucky *or* yukky (*slang*) **2 = ill-natured**, bad-tempered, brusque, churlish, contrary, cross, difficult, disobliging, irritable, nasty, peevish, ratty (*Brit. & N.Z. informal*), rude, surly, tetchy, unfriendly, ungracious, unlikable *or* unlikeable, unpleasant
➤ **Antonyms**
≠**nasty**: agreeable, delightful, enjoyable, lovely, nice, pleasant ≠**ill-natured**: agreeable, congenial, delightful, friendly, good-natured, lovely, nice, pleasant

disagreement *noun* **1 = incompatibility**, difference, discrepancy, disparity, dissimilarity, dissimilitude, divergence, diversity, incongruity, unlikeness, variance **2 = argument**, altercation, clash, conflict, debate, difference, discord, dispute, dissent, division, falling out, misunderstanding, quarrel, row, squabble, strife, tiff, wrangle **3 in disagreement = at odds**, at daggers drawn, at loggerheads, at variance, disunited, in conflict, in disharmony
➤ **Antonyms**
≠**incompatibility**: correspondence, harmony, similarity ≠**argument**: accord, agreement, assent, consensus, unison, unity

disallow *verb* **1 = reject**, abjure, disavow, disclaim, dismiss, disown, rebuff, refuse, repudiate **2 = cancel**, ban, boycott, embargo, forbid, prohibit, proscribe, veto

disappear *verb* **1 = vanish**, be lost to view, drop out of sight, ebb, evanesce, fade away, pass, recede, vanish off the face of the earth, wane **2 = flee**, abscond, depart, escape, fly, go, retire, withdraw **3 = cease**, cease to be known, cease to exist, die out, dissolve, end, evaporate, expire, fade, leave no trace, melt away, pass away, perish, vanish
➤ **Antonyms**
appear, arrive, materialize, reappear

disappearance *noun* **= vanishing**, departure, desertion, disappearing, disappearing trick, eclipse, evanescence,

evaporation, fading, flight, going, loss, melting, passing, vanishing point

disappoint *verb* **1 = let down**, chagrin, dash, deceive, delude, disenchant, disgruntle, dishearten, disillusion, dismay, dissatisfy, fail, sadden, vex **2 = frustrate**, baffle, balk, defeat, disconcert, foil, hamper, hinder, thwart

disappointed *adjective* **= let down**, balked, cast down, choked, depressed, despondent, discontented, discouraged, disenchanted, disgruntled, disillusioned, dissatisfied, distressed, downhearted, foiled, frustrated, saddened, thwarted, upset
➤ **Antonyms**
content, contented, fulfilled, happy, pleased, satisfied

disappointing *adjective* **= unsatisfactory**, depressing, disagreeable, disconcerting, discouraging, failing, inadequate, inferior, insufficient, lame, not much cop (*Brit. slang*), pathetic, sad, second-rate, sorry, unexpected, unhappy, unworthy, upsetting

disappointment *noun* **1 = frustration**, chagrin, discontent, discouragement, disenchantment, disillusionment, displeasure, dissatisfaction, distress, failure, ill-success, mortification, regret, unfulfilment **2 = letdown**, blow, calamity, choker (*informal*), disaster, failure, fiasco, miscarriage, misfortune, setback, washout (*informal*), whammy (*informal, chiefly U.S.*)

disapproval *noun* **= displeasure**, censure, condemnation, criticism, denunciation, deprecation, disapprobation, dissatisfaction, objection, reproach, stick (*slang*)

disapprove *verb* **1 = condemn**, blame, censure, deplore, deprecate, discountenance, dislike, find unacceptable, frown on, have a down on (*informal*), look down one's nose at (*informal*), object to, raise an *or* one's eyebrow, reject, take a dim view of, take exception to **2 = turn down**, disallow, reject, set aside, spurn, veto
➤ **Antonyms**
≠**condemn**: applaud, approve, commend, compliment (*informal*), like ≠**turn down**: endorse, give the go-ahead (to), O.K. *or* okay (*informal*)

disarm *verb* **1 = render defenceless**, disable **2 = win over**, persuade, set at ease **3 = demilitarize**, deactivate, demobilize, disband

disarmament *noun* **= arms reduction**, arms limitation, de-escalation, demilitarization, demobilization

disarming *adjective* = **charming**, irresistible, likable *or* likeable, persuasive, winning

disarrange *verb* = **disorder**, confuse, derange, discompose, disorganize, disturb, jumble (up), mess (up), scatter, shake (up), shuffle, unsettle, untidy

disarray *noun* **1** = **confusion**, discomposure, disharmony, dismay, disorder, disorderliness, disorganization, disunity, indiscipline, unruliness, upset **2** = **untidiness**, chaos, clutter, dishevelment, hodgepodge (*U.S.*), hotchpotch, jumble, mess, mix-up, muddle, pig's breakfast (*informal*), shambles, state, tangle
➤ **Antonyms**
arrangement, harmony, method, neatness, order, orderliness, organization, pattern, plan, regularity, symmetry, system, tidiness

disaster *noun* = **catastrophe**, accident, act of God, adversity, blow, bummer (*slang*), calamity, cataclysm, misadventure, mischance, misfortune, mishap, reverse, ruin, ruination, stroke, tragedy, trouble, whammy (*informal, chiefly U.S.*)

disastrous *adjective* = **terrible**, adverse, calamitous, cataclysmal, cataclysmic, catastrophic, destructive, detrimental, devastating, dire, dreadful, fatal, hapless, harmful, ill-fated, ill-starred, ruinous, tragic, unfortunate, unlucky, unpropitious, untoward

disbelief *noun* = **scepticism**, distrust, doubt, dubiety, incredulity, mistrust, unbelief
➤ **Antonyms**
belief, credence, credulity, faith, trust

disbelieve *verb* = **doubt**, discount, discredit, give no credence to, mistrust, not accept, not buy (*slang*), not credit, not swallow (*informal*), reject, repudiate, scoff at, suspect

disbeliever *noun* = **sceptic**, agnostic, atheist, doubter, doubting Thomas, questioner, scoffer
➤ **Antonyms**
adherent, believer, devotee, disciple, follower, supporter, upholder, zealot

disbelievingly *adverb* = **sceptically**, askance, cynically, doubtingly, incredulously, mistrustfully, quizzically, suspiciously, with a pinch of salt

discard *verb* = **get rid of**, abandon, axe (*informal*), cast aside, chuck (*informal*), dispense with, dispose of, ditch (*slang*), drop, dump (*informal*), jettison, junk (*informal*), reject, relinquish, remove, repudiate, scrap, shed, throw away *or* out
➤ **Antonyms**

hang *or* hold on to, hold back, keep, reserve, retain, save

discerning *adjective* = **discriminating**, acute, astute, clear-sighted, critical, ingenious, intelligent, judicious, knowing, penetrating, perceptive, percipient, perspicacious, piercing, sagacious, sensitive, sharp, shrewd, subtle, wise

discharge *verb* **1** = **release**, absolve, acquit, allow to go, clear, exonerate, free, liberate, pardon, set free **2** = **dismiss**, cashier, discard, eject, expel, fire (*informal*), give (someone) the boot (*slang*), give (someone) the sack (*informal*), oust, remove, sack (*informal*) **3** = **fire**, detonate, explode, let loose (*informal*), let off, set off, shoot **4** = **pour forth**, disembogue, dispense, emit, empty, excrete, exude, give off, gush, leak, ooze, release, void **5** = **off-load**, disburden, lighten, remove, unburden, unload **6** = **carry out**, accomplish, do, execute, fulfil, observe, perform **7** = **pay**, clear, honour, meet, relieve, satisfy, settle, square up ♦ *noun* **8** = **release**, acquittal, clearance, exoneration, liberation, pardon, remittance **9** = **dismissal**, congé, demobilization, ejection, the boot (*slang*), the (old) heave-ho (*informal*), the order of the boot (*slang*), the sack (*informal*) **10** = **firing**, blast, burst, detonation, discharging, explosion, fusillade, report, salvo, shot, volley **11** = **emission**, emptying, excretion, flow, ooze, pus, secretion, seepage, suppuration, vent, voiding **12** = **unloading**, disburdening, emptying, unburdening **13** = **carrying out**, accomplishment, achievement, execution, fulfilment, observance, performance **14** = **payment**, satisfaction, settlement

disciple *noun* = **follower**, adherent, apostle, believer, catechumen, convert, devotee, learner, partisan, proselyte, pupil, student, supporter, votary
➤ **Antonyms**
guru, leader, master, swami, teacher

disciplinarian *noun* = **authoritarian**, despot, drill sergeant, hard master, martinet, stickler, strict teacher, taskmaster, tyrant

discipline *noun* **1** = **training**, drill, exercise, method, practice, regimen, regulation **2** = **punishment**, castigation, chastisement, correction **3** = **self-control**, conduct, control, orderliness, regulation, restraint, strictness **4** = **field of study**, area, branch of knowledge, course, curriculum, speciality, subject ♦ *verb* **5** = **train**, break in, bring up, check, control, drill, educate, exercise, form, govern, instruct, inure, prepare, regulate, restrain **6 = punish**, bring to book, castigate, chasten, chastise, correct, penalize, reprimand, reprove

disclaim *verb* = **deny**, abandon, abjure, abnegate, decline, disaffirm, disallow, disavow, disown, forswear, rebut, reject, renege, renounce, repudiate, retract

disclose *verb* **1 = make known**, blow wide open (*slang*), broadcast, communicate, confess, divulge, get off one's chest (*informal*), impart, leak, let slip, make public, out (*informal*), publish, relate, reveal, spill one's guts about (*slang*), spill the beans about (*informal*), tell, unveil, utter **2 = show**, bring to light, discover, exhibit, expose, lay bare, reveal, take the wraps off, uncover, unveil
➤ **Antonyms**
conceal, cover, dissemble, hide, keep dark, keep secret, mask, obscure, veil

disclosure *noun* = **revelation**, acknowledgment, admission, announcement, broadcast, confession, declaration, discovery, divulgence, exposé, exposure, leak, publication, uncovering

discolour *verb* = **stain**, fade, mar, mark, rust, soil, streak, tarnish, tinge

discomfort *noun* **1 = pain**, ache, hurt, irritation, malaise, soreness **2 = uneasiness**, annoyance, disquiet, distress, gall, hardship, inquietude, irritation, nuisance, trouble, unpleasantness, vexation ♦ *verb* **3 = make uncomfortable**, discomfit, discompose, disquiet, distress, disturb, embarrass
➤ **Antonyms**
noun ≠**pain**: comfort, ease ≠**uneasiness**: ease, reassurance, solace ♦ *verb* ≠**make uncomfortable**: alleviate, assuage, comfort, ease, reassure, solace, soothe

discomposure *noun* = **disturbance**, agitation, anxiety, confusion, discomfiture, disquiet, disquietude, distraction, embarrassment, fluster, inquietude, malaise, nervousness, perturbation, trepidation, uneasiness

disconcert *verb* **1 = disturb**, abash, agitate, bewilder, discompose, faze, flummox, flurry, fluster, nonplus, perplex, perturb, put out of countenance, rattle (*informal*), ruffle, shake up (*informal*), take aback, throw off balance, trouble, unbalance, unnerve, unsettle, upset, worry **2 = frustrate**, baffle, balk, confuse, defeat, disarrange, hinder, put off, thwart, undo

disconcerted *adjective* = **disturbed**, annoyed, at sea, bewildered, caught off balance, confused, distracted, embarrassed, fazed, flummoxed, flurried, flustered, mixed-up, nonplussed, out of

countenance, perturbed, rattled (*informal*), ruffled, shook up (*informal*), taken aback, thrown (*informal*), troubled, unsettled, upset, worried

disconcerting *adjective* = **disturbing**, alarming, awkward, baffling, bewildering, bothersome, confusing, dismaying, distracting, embarrassing, off-putting (*Brit. informal*), perplexing, upsetting

disconnect *verb* = **cut off**, detach, disengage, divide, part, separate, sever, take apart, uncouple

disconnected *adjective* = **illogical**, confused, disjointed, garbled, incoherent, irrational, jumbled, mixed-up, rambling, uncoordinated, unintelligible, wandering

disconnection *noun* = **cutting off**, cessation, cut-off, discontinuation, discontinuity, interruption, separation, severance, stoppage, suspension

disconsolate *adjective* = **inconsolable**, crushed, dejected, desolate, despairing, dismal, down in the dumps (*informal*), forlorn, gloomy, grief-stricken, heartbroken, hopeless, low, melancholy, miserable, sad, unhappy, woeful, wretched

discontent *noun* = **dissatisfaction**, discontentment, displeasure, envy, fretfulness, regret, restlessness, uneasiness, unhappiness, vexation

discontented *adjective* = **dissatisfied**, brassed off (*Brit. slang*), cheesed off (*Brit. slang*), complaining, disaffected, disgruntled, displeased, exasperated, fed up, fretful, miserable, pissed off (*taboo slang*), unhappy, vexed, with a chip on one's shoulder (*informal*)
➤ **Antonyms**
cheerful, content, contented, happy, pleased, satisfied

discontinue *verb* = **stop**, abandon, axe (*informal*), belay (*Nautical*), break off, cease, drop, end, finish, give up, halt, interrupt, kick (*informal*), leave off, pause, pull the plug on, put an end to, quit, refrain from, suspend, terminate, throw in the sponge, throw in the towel

discontinued *adjective* = **stopped**, abandoned, ended, finished, given up *or* over, halted, no longer made, terminated

discord *noun* **1 = disagreement**, clashing, conflict, contention, difference, discordance, dispute, dissension, disunity, division, friction, incompatibility, lack of concord, opposition, row, rupture, strife, variance, wrangling **2 = disharmony**, cacophony, din, dissonance, harshness, jangle, jarring, racket, tumult
➤ **Antonyms**
≠**disagreement**: accord, agreement,

concord, friendship, harmony, peace, understanding, unison, unity ≠**disharmony**: concord, euphony, harmony, melody, tunefulness, unison

discordant *adjective* **1** = **disagreeing**, at odds, clashing, conflicting, contradictory, contrary, different, divergent, incompatible, incongruous, inconsistent, opposite **2** = **inharmonious**, cacophonous, dissonant, grating, harsh, jangling, jarring, shrill, strident, unmelodious

discount *verb* **1** = **leave out**, brush off (*slang*), disbelieve, disregard, ignore, overlook, pass over **2** = **deduct**, lower, mark down, rebate, reduce, take off ♦ *noun* **3** = **deduction**, abatement, allowance, concession, cut, cut price, drawback, percentage (*informal*), rebate, reduction

discountenance *verb* **1** = **embarrass**, abash, chagrin, confuse, discompose, disconcert, humiliate, put down (*slang*), shame **2** = **disapprove**, condemn, discourage, disfavour, frown on, object to, oppose, resist, take exception to, veto

discourage *verb* **1** = **dishearten**, abash, awe, cast down, cow, damp, dampen, dash, daunt, deject, demoralize, depress, dismay, dispirit, frighten, intimidate, overawe, psych out (*informal*), put a damper on, scare, unman, unnerve **2** = **put off**, check, curb, deprecate, deter, discountenance, disfavour, dissuade, divert from, hinder, inhibit, prevent, restrain, talk out of, throw cold water on (*informal*) **3** = **prevent**, check, curb, deter, hinder, inhibit
➤ **Antonyms**
≠**dishearten**: embolden, encourage, gee up, hearten, inspire ≠**put off**: bid, countenance, encourage, urge

discouraged *adjective* = **put off**, crestfallen, dashed, daunted, deterred, disheartened, dismayed, dispirited, downcast, down in the mouth, glum, pessimistic, sick as a parrot (*informal*)

discouragement *noun* **1** = **loss of confidence**, cold feet (*informal*), dejection, depression, despair, despondency, disappointment, discomfiture, dismay, downheartedness, hopelessness, low spirits, pessimism **2** = **deterrent**, constraint, curb, damper, disincentive, hindrance, impediment, obstacle, opposition, rebuff, restraint, setback

discouraging *adjective* = **disheartening**, dampening, daunting, depressing, disappointing, dispiriting, off-putting (*Brit. informal*), unfavourable, unpropitious

discourse *noun* **1** = **conversation**, chat,

communication, converse, dialogue, discussion, seminar, speech, talk **2** = **speech**, address, disquisition, dissertation, essay, homily, lecture, oration, sermon, talk, treatise ♦ *verb* **3** = **hold forth**, confer, converse, debate, declaim, discuss, expatiate, speak, talk

discourteous *adjective* = **rude**, abrupt, bad-mannered, boorish, brusque, curt, disrespectful, ill-bred, ill-mannered, impolite, insolent, offhand, uncivil, uncourteous, ungentlemanly, ungracious, unmannerly
➤ **Antonyms**
civil, courteous, courtly, gracious, mannerly, polite, respectful, well-mannered

discourtesy *noun* **1** = **rudeness**, bad manners, disrespectfulness, ill-breeding, impertinence, impoliteness, incivility, insolence, ungraciousness, unmannerliness **2** = **insult**, affront, cold shoulder, kick in the teeth (*slang*), rebuff, slight, snub

discover *verb* **1** = **find**, bring to light, come across, come upon, dig up, light upon, locate, turn up, uncover, unearth **2** = **find out**, ascertain, descry, detect, determine, discern, disclose, espy, get wise to (*informal*), learn, notice, perceive, realize, recognize, reveal, see, spot, suss (out) (*slang*), turn up, uncover **3** = **invent**, conceive, contrive, design, devise, originate, pioneer

discoverer *noun* = **inventor**, author, explorer, founder, initiator, originator, pioneer

discovery *noun* **1** = **finding**, ascertainment, detection, disclosure, espial, exploration, introduction, locating, location, origination, revelation, uncovering **2** = **breakthrough**, bonanza, coup, find, findings, godsend, innovation, invention, secret

discredit *verb* **1** = **disgrace**, blame, bring into disrepute, censure, defame, degrade, detract from, dishonour, disparage, reproach, slander, slur, smear, vilify **2** = **doubt**, challenge, deny, disbelieve, discount, dispute, distrust, mistrust, question ♦ *noun* **3** = **disgrace**, aspersion, censure, dishonour, disrepute, ignominy, ill-repute, imputation, odium, reproach, scandal, shame, slur, smear, stigma **4** = **doubt**, distrust, mistrust, question, scepticism, suspicion
➤ **Antonyms**
verb ≠**disgrace**: acclaim, applaud, commend, honour, laud, pay tribute to, praise ♦ *noun* ≠**disgrace**: acclaim, acknowledgment, approval,

commendation, credit, honour, merit, praise

discreditable *adjective* = **disgraceful**, blameworthy, degrading, dishonourable, humiliating, ignominious, improper, infamous, reprehensible, scandalous, shameful, unprincipled, unworthy

discredited *adjective* = **debunked**, discarded, exploded, exposed, obsolete, outworn, refuted, rejected

discreet *adjective* = **tactful**, careful, cautious, circumspect, considerate, diplomatic, discerning, guarded, judicious, politic, prudent, reserved, sagacious, sensible, wary
➤ **Antonyms**
incautious, indiscreet, injudicious, rash, tactless, undiplomatic, unthinking, unwise

discrepancy *noun* = **disagreement**, conflict, contradiction, contrariety, difference, discordance, disparity, dissimilarity, dissonance, divergence, incongruity, inconsistency, variance, variation

discretion *noun* 1 = **tact**, acumen, care, carefulness, caution, circumspection, consideration, diplomacy, discernment, good sense, heedfulness, judgment, judiciousness, maturity, prudence, sagacity, wariness 2 = **choice**, disposition, inclination, liking, mind, option, pleasure, predilection, preference, responsibility, volition, will, wish
➤ **Antonyms**
≠tact: carelessness, indiscretion, insensitivity, rashness, tactlessness, thoughtlessness

discretionary *adjective* = **optional**, arbitrary (*Law*), elective, nonmandatory, open, open to choice, unrestricted

discriminate *verb* 1 = **show prejudice**, disfavour, favour, show bias, single out, treat as inferior, treat differently, victimize 2 = **differentiate**, assess, discern, distinguish, draw a distinction, evaluate, segregate, separate, separate the wheat from the chaff, sift, tell the difference

discriminating *adjective* = **discerning**, acute, astute, critical, cultivated, fastidious, keen, particular, refined, selective, sensitive, tasteful
➤ **Antonyms**
careless, desultory, general, hit or miss (*informal*), indiscriminate, random, undiscriminating, unselective, unsystematic

discrimination *noun* 1 = **prejudice**, bias, bigotry, favouritism, inequity, intolerance, unfairness 2 = **discernment**, acumen, acuteness, clearness, insight, judgment, keenness, penetration, perception,

refinement, sagacity, subtlety, taste

discriminatory *adjective* 1 = **prejudiced**, biased, favouring, inequitable, one-sided, partial, partisan, preferential, prejudicial, unjust, weighted 2 = **discerning**, analytical, astute, differentiating, discriminating, perceptive, perspicacious

discuss *verb* = **talk about**, argue, confer, consider, consult with, converse, debate, deliberate, examine, exchange views on, get together, go into, reason about, review, sift, thrash out, ventilate, weigh up the pros and cons

discussion *noun* = **talk**, analysis, argument, colloquy, confabulation, conference, consideration, consultation, conversation, debate, deliberation, dialogue, discourse, examination, exchange, review, scrutiny, seminar, symposium

disdain *noun* 1 = **contempt**, arrogance, contumely, derision, dislike, haughtiness, hauteur, indifference, scorn, sneering, snobbishness, superciliousness ♦ *verb* 2 = **scorn**, belittle, contemn, deride, despise, disregard, look down on, look down one's nose at (*informal*), misprize, pooh-pooh, reject, slight, sneer at, spurn, undervalue

disdainful *adjective* = **contemptuous**, aloof, arrogant, derisive, haughty, high and mighty (*informal*), hoity-toity (*informal*), insolent, looking down one's nose (at), on one's high horse (*informal*), proud, scornful, sneering, supercilious, superior, turning up one's nose (at)

disease *noun* 1 = **illness**, affliction, ailment, complaint, condition, disorder, ill health, indisposition, infection, infirmity, lurgy (*informal*), malady, sickness, upset 2 = **malady**, blight, cancer, canker, contagion, contamination, disorder, plague

diseased *adjective* = **sick**, ailing, infected, rotten, sickly, tainted, unhealthy, unsound, unwell, unwholesome

disembark *verb* = **land**, alight, arrive, get off, go ashore, step out of

disembodied *adjective* = **bodiless**, ghostly, immaterial, incorporeal, intangible, phantom, spectral, spiritual, unbodied

disembowel *verb* = **eviscerate**, draw, gut, paunch

disenchanted *adjective* = **disillusioned**, blasé, cynical, disappointed, indifferent, jaundiced, let down, out of love, sick of, soured, undeceived

disenchantment *noun* = **disillusionment**, disappointment, disillusion, revulsion, rude awakening

disengage *verb* 1 = **release**, disentangle,

ease, extricate, free, liberate, loosen, set free, unbridle, unloose, untie **2 = detach**, disconnect, disjoin, disunite, divide, separate, undo, withdraw

disengaged *adjective* **1 = unconnected**, apart, detached, free, loose, out of gear, released, separate, unattached, uncoupled **2 = free**, at ease, at leisure, not busy, uncommitted, unoccupied, vacant

disengagement *noun* **= disconnection**, detachment, disentanglement, division, separation, withdrawal

disentangle *verb* **1 = untangle**, detach, disconnect, disengage, extricate, free, loose, separate, sever, unfold, unravel, unsnarl, untwist **2 = sort out**, clarify, clear (up), resolve, simplify, work out

disfavour *noun* **1 = disapproval**, disapprobation, dislike, displeasure **2** *As in* **fall into disfavour = unpopularity**, bad books (*informal*), discredit, disesteem, disgrace, doghouse (*informal*), shame

disfigure *verb* **= damage**, blemish, deface, deform, disfeature, distort, injure, maim, make ugly, mar, mutilate, scar

disfigurement *noun* **= damage**, blemish, defacement, defect, deformity, distortion, impairment, injury, mutilation, scar, spot, stain, trauma (*Pathology*)

disgorge *verb* **1 = vomit**, barf (*U.S. slang*), belch, blow lunch (*U.S. slang*), chuck (up) (*slang, chiefly U.S.*), chunder (*slang, chiefly Austral.*), discharge, do a technicolour yawn (*slang*), eject, empty, expel, lose one's lunch (*U.S. slang*), regurgitate, spew, spit up, spout, throw up, toss one's cookies (*U.S. slang*), upchuck (*U.S. slang*) **2 = give up**, cede, relinquish, renounce, resign, surrender, yield

disgrace *noun* **1 = shame**, baseness, degradation, dishonour, disrepute, ignominy, infamy, odium, opprobrium **2 = stain**, aspersion, blemish, blot, blot on one's escutcheon, defamation, reproach, scandal, slur, stigma **3 = discredit**, contempt, disesteem, disfavour, obloquy ♦ *verb* **4 = bring shame upon**, abase, defame, degrade, discredit, disfavour, dishonour, disparage, humiliate, reproach, shame, slur, stain, stigmatize, sully, taint
➤ **Antonyms**
noun ≠**shame**: credit, esteem, favour, grace, honour, repute ♦ *verb* ≠**bring shame upon**: credit, grace, honour

disgraced *adjective* **= shamed**, branded, degraded, discredited, dishonoured, humiliated, in disgrace, in the doghouse (*informal*), mortified, stigmatized, under a cloud

disgraceful *adjective* **= shameful**,

blameworthy, contemptible, degrading, detestable, discreditable, dishonourable, disreputable, ignominious, infamous, low, mean, opprobrious, scandalous, shocking, unworthy

disgruntled *adjective* **= discontented**, annoyed, cheesed off (*Brit. slang*), displeased, dissatisfied, grumpy, hacked (off) (*U.S. slang*), huffy, irritated, malcontent, peeved, peevish, petulant, pissed off (*taboo slang*), put out, sulky, sullen, testy, vexed

disguise *verb* **1 = hide**, camouflage, cloak, conceal, cover, mask, screen, secrete, shroud, veil **2 = misrepresent**, deceive, dissemble, dissimulate, fake, falsify, fudge, gloss over ♦ *noun* **3 = costume**, camouflage, cloak, cover, get-up (*informal*), mask, screen, veil **4 = façade**, deception, dissimulation, front, pretence, semblance, trickery, veneer

disguised *adjective* **= in disguise**, camouflaged, cloaked, covert, fake, false, feigned, incognito, masked, pretend, undercover, unrecognizable

disgust *noun* **1 = loathing**, abhorrence, abomination, antipathy, aversion, detestation, dislike, distaste, hatefulness, hatred, nausea, odium, repugnance, repulsion, revulsion ♦ *verb* **2 = sicken**, cause aversion, displease, fill with loathing, gross out (*U.S. slang*), nauseate, offend, outrage, put off, repel, revolt, turn one's stomach
➤ **Antonyms**
noun ≠**loathing**: liking, love, pleasure, satisfaction, taste ♦ *verb* ≠**sicken**: delight, impress, please

disgusted *adjective* **= sickened**, appalled, nauseated, offended, outraged, repelled, repulsed, scandalized, sick and tired of (*informal*), sick of (*informal*)

disgusting *adjective* **= sickening**, abominable, cringe-making (*Brit. informal*), detestable, distasteful, foul, gross, grotty (*slang*), hateful, loathsome, nasty, nauseating, nauseous, noisome, objectionable, obnoxious, odious, offensive, repellent, repugnant, revolting, shameless, stinking, vile, vulgar, yucky *or* yukky (*slang*)

dish *noun* **1 = bowl**, plate, platter, salver **2 = food**, fare, recipe ♦ *verb* **3** *Slang* **= ruin**, finish, muck up (*slang*), spoil, torpedo, wreck

dishearten *verb* **= discourage**, cast down, crush, damp, dampen, dash, daunt, deject, depress, deter, dismay, dispirit, put a damper on
➤ **Antonyms**

buck up (*informal*), cheer up, encourage, gee up, hearten, lift, perk up, rally

disheartened *adjective* = **discouraged**, choked, crestfallen, crushed, daunted, dejected, depressed, disappointed, dismayed, dispirited, downcast, downhearted, sick as a parrot (*informal*)

dishevelled *adjective* = **untidy**, bedraggled, blowsy, disarranged, disarrayed, disordered, frowzy, hanging loose, messy, ruffled, rumpled, tousled, uncombed, unkempt
➤ **Antonyms**
chic, dapper, neat, smart, soigné *or* soignée, spick-and-span, spruce, tidy, trim, well-groomed

dishonest *adjective* = **deceitful**, bent (*slang*), cheating, corrupt, crafty, crooked (*informal*), deceiving, deceptive, designing, disreputable, double-dealing, false, fraudulent, guileful, knavish (*archaic*), lying, mendacious, perfidious, shady (*informal*), swindling, treacherous, unfair, unprincipled, unscrupulous, untrustworthy, untruthful
➤ **Antonyms**
honest, honourable, law-abiding, lawful, principled, true, trustworthy, upright

dishonesty *noun* = **deceit**, cheating, chicanery, corruption, craft, criminality, crookedness, duplicity, falsehood, falsity, fraud, fraudulence, graft (*informal*), improbity, mendacity, perfidy, sharp practice, stealing, treachery, trickery, unscrupulousness, wiliness

dishonour *verb* **1** = **disgrace**, abase, blacken, corrupt, debase, debauch, defame, degrade, discredit, shame, sully **2** = **seduce**, defile, deflower, pollute, rape, ravish ◆ *noun* **3** = **disgrace**, abasement, degradation, discredit, disfavour, disrepute, ignominy, infamy, obloquy, odium, opprobrium, reproach, scandal, shame **4** = **insult**, abuse, affront, discourtesy, indignity, offence, outrage, sacrilege, slight
➤ **Antonyms**
verb ≠**disgrace**: esteem, exalt, respect, revere, worship ◆ *noun* ≠**disgrace**: decency, goodness, honour, integrity, morality, principles, rectitude

dishonourable *adjective* **1** = **shameful**, base, contemptible, despicable, discreditable, disgraceful, ignoble, ignominious, infamous, not cricket (*informal*), scandalous **2** = **untrustworthy**, blackguardly, corrupt, disreputable, shameless, treacherous, unprincipled, unscrupulous

dish out *verb Informal* = **distribute**, allocate, dole out, hand out, inflict, mete out

dish up *verb* = **serve**, hand out, ladle, prepare, present, produce, scoop, spoon

disillusion *verb* = **shatter one's illusions**, break the spell, bring down to earth, disabuse, disenchant, open the eyes of, undeceive

disillusioned *adjective* = **disenchanted**, disabused, disappointed, enlightened, indifferent, out of love, sadder and wiser, undeceived

disincentive *noun* = **discouragement**, damper, determent, deterrent, dissuasion, impediment

disinclination *noun* = **reluctance**, alienation, antipathy, aversion, demur, dislike, hesitance, lack of desire, lack of enthusiasm, loathness, objection, opposition, repugnance, resistance, unwillingness

disinclined *adjective* = **reluctant**, antipathetic, averse, balking, hesitating, indisposed, loath, not in the mood, opposed, resistant, unwilling

disinfect *verb* = **sterilize**, clean, cleanse, decontaminate, deodorize, fumigate, purify, sanitize
➤ **Antonyms**
contaminate, defile, infect, poison, pollute, taint

disinfectant *noun* = **antiseptic**, germicide, sanitizer, sterilizer

disingenuous *adjective* = **insincere**, artful, cunning, deceitful, designing, dishonest, duplicitous, feigned, guileful, insidious, shifty, sly, two-faced, uncandid, underhanded, unfair, wily

disinherit *verb Law* = **cut off**, cut off without a penny, disown, dispossess, oust, repudiate

disintegrate *verb* = **break up**, break apart, crumble, disunite, fall apart, fall to pieces, go to pieces, go to seed, reduce to fragments, separate, shatter, splinter

disinterest *noun* = **impartiality**, candidness, detachment, disinterestedness, dispassionateness, equity, fairness, justice, neutrality, unbiasedness

disinterested *adjective* = **impartial**, candid, detached, dispassionate, equitable, even-handed, free from self-interest, impersonal, neutral, objective, outside, unbiased, uninvolved, unprejudiced, unselfish
➤ **Antonyms**
biased, involved, partial, prejudiced, selfish

disjointed *adjective* **1** = **incoherent**,

aimless, confused, disconnected, disordered, fitful, loose, rambling, spasmodic, unconnected 2 = **disconnected**, dislocated, displaced, disunited, divided, separated, split

dislike verb 1 = **be averse to**, abhor, abominate, despise, detest, disapprove, disfavour, disrelish, hate, have a down on (informal), have no taste or stomach for, loathe, not be able to bear or abide or stand, object to, scorn, shun, take a dim view of ◆ noun 2 = **aversion**, animosity, animus, antagonism, antipathy, detestation, disapprobation, disapproval, disgust, disinclination, displeasure, distaste, enmity, hatred, hostility, loathing, odium, repugnance
➤ Antonyms
verb ≠ **be averse to**: esteem, favour, like ◆ noun ≠ **aversion**: admiration, attraction, delight, esteem, inclination, liking

dislocate verb 1 = **put out of joint**, disarticulate, disconnect, disengage, disjoint, disunite, luxate (Medical), unhinge 2 = **shift**, disorder, displace, disrupt, disturb, misplace

dislocation noun 1 = **putting out of joint**, disarticulation, disconnection, disengagement, luxation (Medical), unhinging 2 = **shift**, disarray, disorder, disorganization, disruption, disturbance, misplacement

dislodge verb = **displace**, disturb, extricate, force out, knock loose, oust, remove, uproot

disloyal adjective = **treacherous**, apostate, disaffected, faithless, false, perfidious, seditious, subversive, traitorous, treasonable, two-faced, unfaithful, unpatriotic, untrustworthy
➤ Antonyms
constant, dependable, dutiful, faithful, loyal, steadfast, true, trustworthy, trusty

disloyalty noun = **treachery**, betrayal of trust, breach of trust, breaking of faith, deceitfulness, double-dealing, falseness, falsity, inconstancy, infidelity, perfidy, Punic faith, treason, unfaithfulness

dismal adjective = **gloomy**, black, bleak, cheerless, dark, depressing, despondent, discouraging, dolorous, dreary, forlorn, funereal, gruesome, lonesome, louring or lowering, lugubrious, melancholy, sad, sombre, sorrowful, wretched
➤ Antonyms
bright, cheerful, cheery, glad, happy, joyful, light-hearted, sunny

dismantle verb = **take apart**, demolish, disassemble, strip, take to pieces

dismay verb 1 = **alarm**, affright, appal,

distress, fill with consternation, frighten, horrify, paralyse, scare, terrify, unnerve 2 = **disappoint**, daunt, discourage, dishearten, disillusion, dispirit, put off ◆ noun 3 = **alarm**, agitation, anxiety, apprehension, consternation, distress, dread, fear, fright, horror, panic, terror, trepidation 4 = **disappointment**, chagrin, discouragement, disillusionment, upset

dismember verb = **cut into pieces**, amputate, anatomize, disjoint, dislocate, dissect, divide, mutilate, rend, sever

dismiss verb 1 = **sack** (informal), axe (informal), cashier, discharge, fire (informal), give notice to, give (someone) their marching orders, give the boot to (slang), give the bullet to (Brit. slang), kiss off (slang, chiefly U.S. & Canad.), lay off, oust, remove, send packing (informal) 2 = **let go**, disband, disperse, dissolve, free, release, send away 3 = **put out of one's mind**, banish, discard, dispel, disregard, drop, lay aside, pooh-pooh, reject, relegate, repudiate, set aside, shelve, spurn

dismissal noun 1 = **the sack** (informal), discharge, expulsion, kiss-off (slang, chiefly U.S. & Canad.), marching orders (informal), notice, one's books or cards (informal), removal, the boot (slang), the bum's rush (slang), the (old) heave-ho (informal), the order of the boot (slang), the push (slang) 2 = **permission to go**, adjournment, congé, end, freedom to depart, release

disobedience noun = **defiance**, indiscipline, infraction, insubordination, mutiny, noncompliance, nonobservance, recalcitrance, revolt, unruliness, waywardness

disobedient adjective = **defiant**, contrary, contumacious, disorderly, froward (archaic), insubordinate, intractable, mischievous, naughty, noncompliant, nonobservant, obstreperous, refractory, undisciplined, unruly, wayward, wilful
➤ Antonyms
biddable, compliant, dutiful, manageable, obedient, submissive, well-behaved

disobey verb = **refuse to obey**, contravene, defy, dig one's heels in (informal), disregard, flout, go counter to, ignore, infringe, overstep, rebel, resist, transgress, violate

disorder noun 1 = **untidiness**, chaos, clutter, confusion, disarray, jumble, mess, muddle, shambles 2 = **disturbance**, commotion, riot, turmoil, unrest, unruliness, uproar 3 = **illness**, affliction, ailment, complaint, disease, malady, sickness

disorderly *adjective* **1** = **untidy**, chaotic, confused, disorganized, higgledy-piggledy (*informal*), indiscriminate, irregular, jumbled, messy, shambolic (*informal*), unsystematic **2** = **unruly**, boisterous, disruptive, indisciplined, lawless, obstreperous, rebellious, refractory, riotous, rowdy, stormy, tumultuous, turbulent, ungovernable, unlawful, unmanageable
➤ **Antonyms**
≠**untidy**: arranged, neat, orderly, organized, tidy

disorganize *verb* = **disrupt**, break up, confuse, convulse, derange, destroy, disarrange, discompose, disorder, disturb, jumble, make a shambles of, muddle, turn topsy-turvy, unsettle, upset

disorganized *adjective* = **muddled**, chaotic, confused, disordered, haphazard, jumbled, off the rails, shuffled, unmethodical, unorganized, unsystematic

disown *verb* = **deny**, abandon, abnegate, cast off, disallow, disavow, disclaim, rebut, refuse to acknowledge *or* recognize, reject, renounce, repudiate, retract

disparage *verb* = **run down**, asperse, bad-mouth (*slang, chiefly U.S. & Canad.*), belittle, blast, criticize, decry, defame, degrade, denigrate, deprecate, depreciate, deride, derogate, detract from, discredit, disdain, dismiss, knock (*informal*), lambast(e), malign, minimize, put down, ridicule, rubbish (*informal*), scorn, slag (off) (*slang*), slander, tear into (*informal*), traduce, underestimate, underrate, undervalue, vilify

disparagement *noun* = **contempt**, aspersion, belittlement, condemnation, contumely, criticism, debasement, degradation, denigration, denunciation, depreciation, derision, derogation, detraction, discredit, disdain, impairment, lessening, prejudice, reproach, ridicule, scorn, slander, underestimation

dispassionate *adjective* **1** = **unemotional**, calm, collected, composed, cool, imperturbable, moderate, quiet, serene, sober, temperate, unexcitable, unexcited, unfazed (*informal*), unmoved, unruffled **2** = **objective**, candid, detached, disinterested, fair, impartial, impersonal, indifferent, neutral, unbiased, uninvolved, unprejudiced
➤ **Antonyms**
≠**unemotional**: ablaze, ardent, emotional, excited, fervent, impassioned, intense, passionate ≠**objective**: biased, concerned, interested, involved, partial, prejudiced

dispatch, despatch *verb* **1** = **send**, accelerate, consign, dismiss, express, forward, hasten, hurry, quicken, remit, transmit **2** = **carry out**, conclude, discharge, dispose of, expedite, finish, make short work of (*informal*), perform, settle **3** = **murder**, assassinate, blow away (*slang, chiefly U.S.*), bump off (*slang*), butcher, eliminate (*slang*), execute, finish off, kill, put an end to, slaughter, slay, take out (*slang*) ♦ *noun* **4** = **message**, account, bulletin, communication, communiqué, document, instruction, item, letter, missive, news, piece, report, story **5** *As in* with dispatch = **promptness**, alacrity, celerity, expedition, haste, precipitateness, promptitude, quickness, rapidity, speed, swiftness

dispel *verb* = **drive away**, allay, banish, chase away, dismiss, disperse, dissipate, eliminate, expel, resolve, rout, scatter

dispensable *adjective* = **expendable**, disposable, inessential, needless, nonessential, superfluous, unnecessary, unrequired, useless
➤ **Antonyms**
crucial, essential, important, indispensable, necessary, requisite, vital

dispensation *noun* **1** = **distribution**, allotment, appointment, apportionment, bestowal, conferment, consignment, dealing out, disbursement, endowment, supplying **2** = **exemption**, exception, immunity, indulgence, licence, permission, privilege, relaxation, relief, remission, reprieve

dispense *verb* **1** = **distribute**, allocate, allot, apportion, assign, deal out, disburse, dole out, mete out, share **2** = **prepare**, measure, mix, supply **3** = **administer**, apply, carry out, direct, discharge, enforce, execute, implement, operate, undertake **4** = **exempt**, except, excuse, exonerate, let off (*informal*), release, relieve, reprieve **5** dispense with: **a** = **do away with**, abolish, brush aside, cancel, dispose of, disregard, get rid of, ignore, pass over, render needless, shake off **b** = **do without**, abstain from, forgo, give up, omit, relinquish, waive

disperse *verb* **1** = **scatter**, broadcast, circulate, diffuse, disseminate, distribute, spread, strew **2** = **break up**, disappear, disband, dismiss, dispel, dissolve, rout, scatter, send off, separate, vanish
➤ **Antonyms**
amass, assemble, collect, concentrate, congregate, convene, gather, muster, pool

dispirited *adjective* = **disheartened**, crestfallen, dejected, depressed, despondent, discouraged, down, downcast, gloomy, glum, in the doldrums, low, morose, sad, sick as a parrot (*informal*)

displace *verb* 1 = **move**, derange, disarrange, disturb, misplace, shift, transpose 2 = **dismiss**, cashier, depose, discard, discharge, fire (*informal*), remove, sack (*informal*) 3 = **replace**, crowd out, oust, succeed, supersede, supplant, take the place of 4 = **force out**, dislocate, dislodge, dispossess, eject, evict, unsettle

display *verb* 1 = **show**, betray, demonstrate, disclose, evidence, evince, exhibit, expose, manifest, open, open to view, present, reveal, take the wraps off, unveil 2 = **spread out**, expand, extend, model, open out, stretch out, unfold, unfurl 3 = **show off**, boast, flash (*informal*), flaunt, flourish, parade, vaunt ♦ *noun* 4 = **exhibition**, array, demonstration, exposition, exposure, manifestation, presentation, revelation, show 5 = **show**, flourish, ostentation, pageant, parade, pomp, spectacle
➤ **Antonyms**
verb ≠**show**: conceal, cover, hide, keep dark, keep secret, mask, secrete, veil

displease *verb* = **annoy**, aggravate (*informal*), anger, disgust, dissatisfy, exasperate, gall, hassle (*informal*), incense, irk, irritate, nark (*Brit., Austral., & N.Z. slang*), nettle, offend, pique, piss one off (*taboo slang*), provoke, put one's back up, put out, rile, upset, vex

displeasure *noun* = **annoyance**, anger, disapprobation, disapproval, disfavour, disgruntlement, dislike, dissatisfaction, distaste, indignation, irritation, offence, pique, resentment, vexation, wrath
➤ **Antonyms**
approval, pleasure, satisfaction

disposable *adjective* 1 = **throwaway**, biodegradable, compostable, decomposable, nonreturnable, paper 2 = **available**, at one's service, consumable, expendable, free for use, spendable

disposal *noun* 1 = **throwing away**, clearance, discarding, dumping (*informal*), ejection, jettisoning, parting with, relinquishment, removal, riddance, scrapping 2 = **arrangement**, array, dispensation, disposition, distribution, grouping, placing, position 3 = **transfer**, assignment, bequest, bestowal, consignment, conveyance, dispensation, gift, settlement 4 **at one's disposal** = **available**, at one's service, consumable, expendable, free for use, spendable

dispose *verb* 1 = **arrange**, adjust, array, determine, distribute, fix, group, marshal,

order, place, put, range, rank, regulate, set, settle, stand 2 = **lead**, actuate, adapt, bias, condition, incline, induce, influence, motivate, move, predispose, prompt, tempt

disposed *adjective* = **inclined**, apt, given, liable, likely, of a mind to, predisposed, prone, ready, subject, tending towards

dispose of *verb* 1 = **get rid of**, bin (*informal*), chuck (*informal*), destroy, discard, dump (*informal*), get shot of, jettison, junk (*informal*), scrap, throw out or away, unload 2 = **give**, bestow, make over, part with, sell, transfer 3 = **deal with**, decide, determine, end, finish with, settle

disposition *noun* 1 = **character**, constitution, make-up, nature, spirit, temper, temperament 2 = **tendency**, bent, bias, habit, inclination, leaning, predisposition, proclivity, proneness, propensity, readiness 3 = **arrangement**, adjustment, classification, disposal, distribution, grouping, ordering, organization, placement 4 = **control**, direction, disposal, management, regulation

disproportion *noun* = **inequality**, asymmetry, discrepancy, disparity, imbalance, inadequacy, insufficiency, lopsidedness, unevenness, unsuitableness
➤ **Antonyms**
balance, congruity, harmony, proportion, symmetry

disproportionate *adjective* = **unequal**, excessive, incommensurate, inordinate, out of proportion, too much, unbalanced, uneven, unreasonable

disprove *verb* = **prove false**, blow out of the water (*slang*), confute, contradict, controvert, discredit, expose, give the lie to, invalidate, make a nonsense of, negate, rebut, refute
➤ **Antonyms**
ascertain, bear out, confirm, evince, prove, show, substantiate, verify

disputation *noun* = **dispute**, argumentation, controversy, debate, dissension, polemics

dispute *noun* 1 = **disagreement**, altercation, argument, *bagarre*, brawl, conflict, discord, disturbance, feud, friction, quarrel, shindig (*informal*), shindy (*informal*), strife, wrangle 2 = **argument**, contention, controversy, debate, discussion, dissension ♦ *verb* 3 = **doubt**, challenge, contest, contradict, controvert, deny, impugn, question, rebut 4 = **argue**, altercate, brawl, clash, contend, cross swords, debate, discuss, quarrel, row, spar, squabble, wrangle

disqualification *noun* **1** = **ban**, debarment, disenablement, disentitlement, elimination, exclusion, incompetence, ineligibility, rejection **2** = **unfitness**, disability, disablement, incapacitation, incapacity

disqualified *adjective* = **ineligible**, debarred, eliminated, knocked out, out of the running

disqualify *verb* **1** = **ban**, debar, declare ineligible, disentitle, preclude, prohibit, rule out **2** = **invalidate**, disable, incapacitate, unfit (*rare*)

disquiet *noun* **1** = **uneasiness**, alarm, angst, anxiety, concern, disquietude, distress, disturbance, fear, foreboding, fretfulness, nervousness, restlessness, trepidation, trouble, unrest, worry ♦ *verb* **2** = **make uneasy**, agitate, annoy, bother, concern, discompose, distress, disturb, fret, harass, hassle (*informal*), incommode, perturb, pester, plague, trouble, unsettle, upset, vex, worry

disquieting *adjective* = **worrying**, annoying, bothersome, disconcerting, distressing, disturbing, harrowing, irritating, perturbing, troubling, unnerving, unsettling, upsetting, vexing

disregard *verb* **1** = **ignore**, brush aside *or* away, discount, disobey, laugh off, leave out of account, make light of, neglect, overlook, pass over, pay no attention to, pay no heed to, take no notice of, turn a blind eye to **2** = **snub**, brush off (*slang*), cold-shoulder, contemn, despise, disdain, disparage, send to Coventry, slight ♦ *noun* **3** = **inattention**, brushoff (*slang*), contempt, disdain, disrespect, heedlessness, ignoring, indifference, neglect, negligence, oversight, slight, the cold shoulder
➤ Antonyms
verb ≠**ignore**: attend, heed, listen to, mind, note, pay attention to, regard, respect, take into consideration, take notice of

disrepair *noun* **1** = **dilapidation**, collapse, decay, deterioration, ruination **2 in disrepair** = **out of order**, broken, bust (*informal*), decayed, decrepit, kaput (*informal*), not functioning, on the blink (*slang*), out of commission, worn-out

disreputable *adjective* **1** = **discreditable**, base, contemptible, derogatory, disgraceful, dishonourable, disorderly, ignominious, infamous, louche, low, mean, notorious, opprobrious, scandalous, shady (*informal*), shameful, shocking, unprincipled, vicious, vile **2** = **scruffy**, bedraggled, dilapidated, dingy, dishevelled, down at heel, seedy, shabby, threadbare, worn
➤ Antonyms
≠**discreditable**: decent, reputable, respectable, respected, upright, worthy

disrepute *noun* = **discredit**, disesteem, disfavour, disgrace, dishonour, ignominy, ill favour, ill repute, infamy, obloquy, shame, unpopularity

disrespect *noun* = **contempt**, cheek, discourtesy, dishonour, disregard, impertinence, impoliteness, impudence, incivility, insolence, irreverence, lack of respect, lese-majesty, rudeness, sauce, unmannerliness
➤ Antonyms
esteem, regard, respect

disrespectful *adjective* = **contemptuous**, bad-mannered, cheeky, discourteous, ill-bred, impertinent, impolite, impudent, insolent, insulting, irreverent, misbehaved, rude, uncivil

disrupt *verb* **1** = **disturb**, agitate, confuse, convulse, disorder, disorganize, spoil, throw into disorder, upset **2** = **interrupt**, break up *or* into, interfere with, intrude, obstruct, unsettle, upset

disruption *noun* = **disturbance**, confusion, disarray, disorder, disorderliness, interference, interruption, stoppage

disruptive *adjective* = **disturbing**, confusing, disorderly, distracting, obstreperous, troublemaking, troublesome, unruly, unsettling, upsetting
➤ Antonyms
biddable, compliant, cooperative, docile, obedient, well-behaved

dissatisfaction *noun* = **discontent**, annoyance, chagrin, disappointment, discomfort, dislike, dismay, displeasure, distress, exasperation, frustration, irritation, regret, resentment, unhappiness

dissatisfied *adjective* = **discontented**, disappointed, disgruntled, displeased, fed up, frustrated, not satisfied, unfulfilled, ungratified, unhappy, unsatisfied
➤ Antonyms
content, contented, pleased, satisfied

dissect *verb* **1** = **cut up** *or* **apart**, anatomize, dismember, lay open **2** = **analyse**, break down, explore, inspect, investigate, research, scrutinize, study

dissection *noun* **1** = **cutting up**, anatomization, anatomy, autopsy, dismemberment, necropsy, postmortem (examination) **2** = **analysis**, breakdown, examination, inspection, investigation, research, scrutiny

disseminate *verb* = **spread**, broadcast,

circulate, diffuse, disperse, dissipate, distribute, proclaim, promulgate, propagate, publicize, publish, scatter, sow

dissemination *noun* = **spread**, broadcasting, circulation, diffusion, distribution, promulgation, propagation, publication, publishing

dissension *noun* = **disagreement**, conflict, conflict of opinion, contention, difference, discord, discordance, dispute, dissent, friction, quarrel, row, strife, variance

dissent *verb* 1 = **disagree**, decline, differ, object, protest, refuse, withhold assent *or* approval ♦ *noun* 2 = **disagreement**, difference, discord, dissension, dissidence, nonconformity, objection, opposition, refusal, resistance
➤ Antonyms
verb ≠**disagree**: agree, assent, concur ♦ *noun* ≠**disagreement**: accord, agreement, assent, concurrence, consensus

dissenter *noun* = **objector**, disputant, dissident, nonconformist, protestant

dissenting *adjective* = **disagreeing**, conflicting, differing, dissident, opposing, protesting

dissertation *noun* = **thesis**, critique, discourse, disquisition, essay, exposition, treatise

disservice *noun* = **bad turn**, disfavour, harm, ill turn, injury, injustice, unkindness, wrong
➤ Antonyms
courtesy, good turn, indulgence, kindness, obligement (*Scot. or archaic*), service

dissident *adjective* 1 = **dissenting**, differing, disagreeing, discordant, dissentient, heterodox, nonconformist, schismatic ♦ *noun* 2 = **protester**, agitator, dissenter, rebel, recusant

dissimilar *adjective* = **different**, disparate, divergent, diverse, heterogeneous, manifold, mismatched, not alike, not capable of comparison, not similar, unlike, unrelated, various
➤ Antonyms
alike, comparable, congruous, corresponding, in agreement, much the same, resembling, uniform

dissimilarity *noun* = **difference**, discrepancy, disparity, dissimilitude, distinction, divergence, heterogeneity, incomparability, nonuniformity, unlikeness, unrelatedness

dissipate *verb* 1 = **squander**, burn up, consume, deplete, expend, fritter away, indulge oneself, lavish, misspend, run through, spend, waste 2 = **disperse**, disappear, dispel, dissolve, drive away,

evaporate, scatter, vanish

dissipated *adjective* 1 = **debauched**, abandoned, dissolute, intemperate, profligate, rakish, self-indulgent 2 = **squandered**, consumed, destroyed, exhausted, scattered, wasted

dissipation *noun* 1 = **dispersal**, disappearance, disintegration, dissemination, dissolution, scattering, vanishing 2 = **debauchery**, abandonment, dissoluteness, drunkenness, excess, extravagance, indulgence, intemperance, lavishness, prodigality, profligacy, squandering, wantonness, waste

dissociate *verb* 1 = **break away**, break off, disband, disrupt, part company, quit 2 = **separate**, detach, disconnect, distance, divorce, isolate, segregate, set apart

dissolute *adjective* = **immoral**, abandoned, corrupt, debauched, degenerate, depraved, dissipated, lax, lewd, libertine, licentious, loose, profligate, rakish, unrestrained, vicious, wanton, wild
➤ Antonyms
chaste, clean-living, good, moral, squeaky-clean, upright, virtuous, worthy

dissolution *noun* 1 = **breaking up**, disintegration, division, divorce, parting, resolution, separation 2 = **adjournment**, conclusion, disbandment, discontinuation, dismissal, end, ending, finish, suspension, termination 3 = **debauchery**, corruption, dissipation, intemperance, wantonness
➤ Antonyms
≠**breaking up**: alliance, amalgamation, coalition, combination, unification, union

dissolve *verb* 1 = **melt**, deliquesce, flux, fuse, liquefy, soften, thaw 2 = **disappear**, break down, crumble, decompose, diffuse, disintegrate, disperse, dissipate, dwindle, evanesce, evaporate, fade, melt away, perish, vanish, waste away 3 = **break up**, collapse, disorganize, disunite, divorce, loose, resolve into, separate, sever 4 = **end**, axe (*Informal*), break up, destroy, discontinue, dismiss, overthrow, ruin, suspend, terminate, wind up

dissuade *verb* = **deter**, advise against, discourage, disincline, divert, expostulate, persuade not to, put off, remonstrate, talk out of, urge not to, warn
➤ Antonyms
bring round (*informal*), coax, convince, persuade, sway, talk into

distance *noun* 1 = **space**, absence, extent, gap, interval, lapse, length, range, reach, remoteness, remove, separation, span, stretch, width 2 = **reserve**, aloofness, coldness, coolness, frigidity, remoteness, restraint, stiffness 3 **go the distance**

= **finish**, bring to an end, complete, see through, stay the course **4 in the distance** = **far off**, afar, far away, on the horizon, yonder **5 keep one's distance** = **be reserved**, avoid, be aloof, be indifferent, keep (someone) at arm's length, shun ◆ verb **6 distance oneself** = **separate oneself**, be distanced from, dissociate oneself, put in proportion

distant adjective **1** = **far-off**, abroad, afar, far, faraway, far-flung, outlying, out-of-the-way, remote, removed **2** = **apart**, disparate, dispersed, distinct, scattered, separate **3** = **reserved**, aloof, at arm's length, ceremonious, cold, cool, formal, haughty, restrained, reticent, standoffish, stiff, unapproachable, unfriendly, withdrawn **4** = **faint**, indistinct, obscure, slight, uncertain
➤ **Antonyms**
≠**far-off**: adjacent, adjoining, at hand, close, handy, imminent, just round the corner, near, nearby, neighbouring, nigh, proximate, within sniffing distance (informal) ≠**reserved**: close, friendly, intimate, warm

distaste noun = **dislike**, abhorrence, antipathy, aversion, detestation, disfavour, disgust, disinclination, displeasure, disrelish, dissatisfaction, horror, loathing, odium, repugnance, revulsion

distasteful adjective = **unpleasant**, abhorrent, disagreeable, displeasing, loathsome, nauseous, objectionable, obnoxious, obscene, offensive, repugnant, repulsive, undesirable, uninviting, unpalatable, unsavoury
➤ **Antonyms**
agreeable, charming, enjoyable, pleasing, pleasurable

distend verb = **swell**, balloon, bloat, bulge, dilate, enlarge, expand, increase, inflate, puff, stretch, widen

distended adjective = **swollen**, bloated, dilated, enlarged, expanded, inflated, puffy, stretched, tumescent

distil verb = **extract**, condense, draw out, evaporate, express, press out, purify, rectify, refine, sublimate, vaporize

distillation noun = **essence**, elixir, extract, quintessence, spirit

distinct adjective **1** = **different**, detached, discrete, dissimilar, individual, separate, unconnected **2** = **definite**, apparent, black-and-white, blatant, bold, clear, clear-cut, decided, evident, lucid, manifest, marked, noticeable, obvious, palpable, patent, plain, recognizable, sharp, unambiguous, unmistakable, well-defined

➤ **Antonyms**
≠**different**: common, connected, identical, indistinct, similar ≠**definite**: fuzzy, indefinite, indistinct, obscure, unclear, vague

distinction noun **1** = **differentiation**, discernment, discrimination, penetration, perception, separation **2** = **feature**, characteristic, distinctiveness, individuality, mark, particularity, peculiarity, quality **3** = **difference**, contrast, differential, division, fine line, separation **4** = **excellence**, account, celebrity, consequence, credit, eminence, fame, greatness, honour, importance, merit, name, note, prominence, quality, rank, renown, reputation, repute, superiority, worth

distinctive adjective = **characteristic**, different, distinguishing, extraordinary, idiosyncratic, individual, original, peculiar, singular, special, typical, uncommon, unique
➤ **Antonyms**
common, ordinary, run-of-the-mill, typical

distinctly adverb = **definitely**, clearly, decidedly, evidently, manifestly, markedly, noticeably, obviously, palpably, patently, plainly, precisely, sharply, unmistakably

distinctness noun **1** = **clearness**, clarity, lucidity, obviousness, plainness, sharpness, vividness **2** = **difference**, detachment, discreteness, disparateness, dissimilarity, dissociation, distinctiveness, individuality, separation

distinguish verb **1** = **differentiate**, ascertain, decide, determine, discriminate, judge, tell apart, tell between, tell the difference **2** = **characterize**, categorize, classify, individualize, make distinctive, mark, separate, set apart, single out **3** = **make out**, discern, know, perceive, pick out, recognize, see, tell **4** = **make famous**, celebrate, dignify, honour, immortalize, signalize

distinguishable adjective = **recognizable**, bold, clear, conspicuous, discernible, evident, manifest, noticeable, obvious, perceptible, plain, well-marked

distinguished adjective **1** = **eminent**, acclaimed, celebrated, conspicuous, famed, famous, illustrious, notable, noted, renowned, well-known **2** = **marked**, conspicuous, extraordinary, outstanding, signal, striking
➤ **Antonyms**
common, inferior, undistinguished, unknown

distinguishing adjective = **characteristic**, different, differentiating, distinctive, individualistic, marked, peculiar, typical

distort verb 1 = **misrepresent**, bias, colour, falsify, garble, pervert, slant, twist 2 = **deform**, bend, buckle, contort, disfigure, misshape, twist, warp, wrench, wrest

distortion noun 1 = **misrepresentation**, bias, colouring, falsification, perversion, slant 2 = **deformity**, bend, buckle, contortion, crookedness, malformation, twist, twistedness, warp

distract verb 1 = **divert**, draw away, sidetrack, turn aside 2 = **amuse**, beguile, engross, entertain, occupy 3 = **agitate**, bewilder, confound, confuse, derange, discompose, disconcert, disturb, harass, madden, perplex, puzzle, torment, trouble

distracted adjective 1 = **agitated**, at sea, bemused, bewildered, confounded, confused, flustered, harassed, in a flap (informal), perplexed, puzzled, troubled 2 = **frantic**, at the end of one's tether, crazy, deranged, desperate, distraught, frenzied, gonzo (slang), grief-stricken, insane, mad, overwrought, raving, wild

distracting adjective = **disturbing**, bewildering, bothering, confusing, disconcerting, dismaying, off-putting (Brit. informal), perturbing

distraction noun 1 = **diversion**, disturbance, interference, interruption 2 = **entertainment**, amusement, beguilement, diversion, divertissement, pastime, recreation 3 = **agitation**, abstraction, bewilderment, commotion, confusion, discord, disorder, disturbance 4 = **frenzy**, aberration, alienation, delirium, derangement, desperation, hallucination, incoherence, insanity, mania

distraught adjective = **frantic**, agitated, anxious, at the end of one's tether, beside oneself, crazed, desperate, distracted, distressed, hysterical, mad, out of one's mind, overwrought, raving, wild, worked-up, wrought-up

distress noun 1 = **worry**, affliction, agony, anguish, anxiety, desolation, discomfort, grief, heartache, misery, pain, sadness, sorrow, suffering, torment, torture, woe, wretchedness 2 = **need**, adversity, calamity, destitution, difficulties, hardship, indigence, misfortune, poverty, privation, straits, trial, trouble ◆ verb 3 = **upset**, afflict, agonize, bother, disturb, grieve, harass, harrow, pain, perplex, sadden, torment, trouble, worry, wound

distressed adjective 1 = **upset**, afflicted, agitated, anxious, distracted, distraught, saddened, tormented, troubled, worried, wretched 2 = **poverty-stricken**, destitute, down at heel, indigent, needy, poor, straitened

distressing adjective = **upsetting**, affecting, afflicting, distressful, disturbing, grievous, gut-wrenching, harrowing, heart-breaking, hurtful, lamentable, nerve-racking, painful, sad, worrying

distribute verb 1 = **hand out**, circulate, convey, deliver, pass round 2 = **spread**, diffuse, disperse, disseminate, scatter, strew 3 = **share**, administer, allocate, allot, apportion, assign, deal, dispense, dispose, divide, dole out, give, measure out, mete 4 = **classify**, arrange, assort, categorize, class, file, group

distribution noun 1 = **delivery**, dealing, handling, mailing, marketing, trading, transport, transportation 2 = **spreading**, circulation, diffusion, dispersal, dispersion, dissemination, propagation, scattering 3 = **sharing**, allocation, allotment, apportionment, dispensation, division, dole, partition 4 = **classification**, arrangement, assortment, disposition, grouping, location, organization, placement

district noun = **area**, community, locale, locality, neck of the woods (informal), neighbourhood, parish, quarter, region, sector, vicinity, ward

distrust verb 1 = **suspect**, be sceptical of, be suspicious of, be wary of, disbelieve, discredit, doubt, misbelieve, mistrust, question, smell a rat (informal), wonder about ◆ noun 2 = **suspicion**, disbelief, doubt, dubiety, lack of faith, misgiving, mistrust, qualm, question, scepticism, wariness

➤ **Antonyms**

verb ≠**suspect**: believe, depend, have confidence, have faith, trust ◆ noun ≠**suspicion**: confidence, faith, reliance, trust

disturb verb 1 = **interrupt**, bother, butt in on, disrupt, interfere with, intrude on, pester, rouse, startle 2 = **upset**, agitate, alarm, annoy, confound, discompose, distract, distress, excite, fluster, harass, hassle (informal), perturb, ruffle, shake, trouble, unnerve, unsettle, worry 3 = **muddle**, confuse, derange, disarrange, disorder, disorganize, unsettle

➤ **Antonyms**

≠**upset**: calm, compose, lull, pacify, quiet, quieten, reassure, relax, relieve, settle, soothe

disturbance noun 1 = **interruption**, agitation, annoyance, bother, confusion, derangement, disorder, distraction, hindrance, intrusion, molestation, perturbation, upset 2 = **disorder**, bother (*informal*), brawl, commotion, fracas, fray, hubbub, riot, ruckus (*informal*), ruction (*informal*), rumpus, shindig (*informal*), shindy (*informal*), tumult, turmoil, upheaval, uproar

disturbed *adjective* 1 *Psychiatry* = **unbalanced**, disordered, maladjusted, neurotic, troubled, upset 2 = **worried**, agitated, angsty (*informal*), antsy (*informal*), anxious, apprehensive, bothered, concerned, disquieted, nervous, troubled, uneasy, upset
➤ Antonyms
≠**unbalanced**: balanced, untroubled
≠**worried**: calm, collected, self-possessed, unfazed (*informal*), untroubled

disturbing *adjective* = **worrying**, agitating, alarming, disconcerting, discouraging, dismaying, disquieting, distressing, frightening, harrowing, perturbing, startling, threatening, troubling, unsettling, upsetting

disuse *noun* = **neglect**, abandonment, decay, desuetude, discontinuance, idleness, non-employment, nonuse
➤ Antonyms
application, employment, practice, service, usage, use

ditch *noun* 1 = **channel**, drain, dyke, furrow, gully, moat, trench, watercourse
♦ *verb* 2 *Slang* = **get rid of**, abandon, axe (*informal*), bin (*informal*), chuck (*informal*), discard, dispose of, drop, dump (*informal*), jettison, junk (*informal*), scrap, throw out *or* overboard

dither *verb* 1 *Chiefly Brit.* = **vacillate**, faff about (*Brit. informal*), falter, haver, hesitate, hum and haw, oscillate, shillyshally (*informal*), swither (*Scot.*), teeter, waver ♦ *noun* 2 *Chiefly Brit.* = **flutter**, bother, flap (*informal*), fluster, pother, stew (*informal*), tiz-woz (*informal*), tizzy (*informal*), twitter (*informal*)
➤ Antonyms
verb ≠**vacillate**: come to a conclusion, conclude, decide, make a decision, make up one's mind, reach *or* come to a decision, resolve, settle

dive *verb* 1 = **plunge**, descend, dip, disappear, drop, duck, fall, go underwater, jump, leap, nose-dive, pitch, plummet, submerge, swoop ♦ *noun* 2 = **plunge**, dash, header (*informal*), jump, leap, lunge, nose dive, spring 3 *Slang* = **sleazy bar**, honky-tonk (*U.S. slang*), joint (*slang*)

diverge *verb* 1 = **separate**, bifurcate, branch, divaricate, divide, fork, part, radiate, split, spread 2 = **be at variance**, be at odds, conflict, differ, disagree, dissent 3 = **deviate**, depart, digress, meander, stray,

turn aside, wander

divergence *noun* = **separation**, branching out, deflection, departure, deviation, difference, digression, disparity, divagation, ramification, varying

divergent *adjective* = **separate**, conflicting, deviating, different, differing, disagreeing, dissimilar, diverging, diverse, variant

divers *adjective Archaic or literary* = **various**, different, manifold, many, multifarious, numerous, several, some, sundry, varied

diverse *adjective* 1 = **various**, assorted, diversified, manifold, miscellaneous, of every description, several, sundry, varied 2 = **different**, differing, discrete, disparate, dissimilar, distinct, divergent, separate, unlike, varying

diversify *verb* = **vary**, alter, assort, branch out, change, expand, have a finger in every pie, mix, modify, spread out, transform, variegate

diversion *noun* 1 *Chiefly Brit.* = **detour**, alteration, change, deflection, departure, deviation, digression, variation 2 = **pastime**, amusement, beguilement, delight, distraction, divertissement, enjoyment, entertainment, game, gratification, jollies (*slang*), play, pleasure, recreation, relaxation, sport

diversity *noun* = **difference**, assortment, dissimilarity, distinctiveness, divergence, diverseness, diversification, heterogeneity, medley, multiplicity, range, unlikeness, variance, variegation, variety

divert *verb* 1 = **redirect**, avert, deflect, switch, turn aside 2 = **distract**, detract, draw *or* lead away from, lead astray, sidetrack 3 = **entertain**, amuse, beguile, delight, gratify, recreate, regale

diverting *adjective* = **entertaining**, amusing, beguiling, enjoyable, fun, humorous, pleasant

divest *verb* 1 = **strip**, denude, disrobe, doff, remove, take off, unclothe, undress 2 = **deprive**, despoil, dispossess, strip

divide *verb* 1 = **separate**, bisect, cleave, cut (up), detach, disconnect, part, partition, segregate, sever, shear, split, subdivide, sunder 2 = **share**, allocate, allot, apportion, deal out, dispense, distribute, divvy (up) (*informal*), dole out, measure out, portion 3 = **cause to disagree**, alienate, break up, come between, disunite, estrange, set at variance *or* odds, set *or* pit against one another, sow dissension, split 4 = **classify**, arrange, categorize, grade, group, put in order, separate, sort
➤ Antonyms
≠**separate**: combine, come together,

connect, join, knit, marry, splice, unite

dividend *noun* = **bonus**, cut (*informal*), divvy (*informal*), extra, gain, plus, portion, share, surplus

divine *adjective* **1** = **heavenly**, angelic, celestial, godlike, holy, spiritual, superhuman, supernatural **2** = **sacred**, consecrated, holy, religious, sanctified, spiritual **3** = **mystical**, beatific, blissful, exalted, rapturous, supreme, transcendent, transcendental, transmundane **4** *Informal* = **wonderful**, beautiful, excellent, glorious, marvellous, perfect, splendid, superlative ♦ *noun* **5** = **priest**, churchman, clergyman, cleric, ecclesiastic, minister, pastor, reverend ♦ *verb* **6** = **infer**, apprehend, conjecture, deduce, discern, foretell, guess, intuit, perceive, prognosticate, suppose, surmise, suspect, understand **7** *Of water or minerals* = **dowse**

diviner *noun* **1** = **seer**, astrologer, augur, oracle, prophet, sibyl, soothsayer **2** *Of water or minerals* = **dowser**

divinity *noun* **1** = **theology**, religion, religious studies **2** = **god** *or* **goddess**, daemon, deity, genius, guardian spirit, spirit **3** = **godliness**, deity, divine nature, godhead, godhood, holiness, sanctity

divisible *adjective* = **dividable**, fractional, separable, splittable

division *noun* **1** = **separation**, bisection, cutting up, detaching, dividing, partition, splitting up **2** = **sharing**, allotment, apportionment, distribution **3** = **dividing line**, border, boundary, demarcation, divide, divider, partition **4** = **part**, branch, category, class, compartment, department, group, head, portion, section, sector, segment **5** = **disagreement**, breach, difference of opinion, discord, disunion, estrangement, feud, rupture, split, variance
➤ **Antonyms**
≠**disagreement**: accord, agreement, concord, harmony, peace, union, unity

divisive *adjective* = **disruptive**, alienating, damaging, detrimental, discordant, estranging, inharmonious, pernicious, troublesome, unsettling

divorce *noun* **1** = **separation**, annulment, breach, break, decree nisi, dissolution, disunion, rupture, severance, split-up ♦ *verb* **2** = **separate**, annul, disconnect, dissociate, dissolve (*marriage*), disunite, divide, part, sever, split up, sunder

divulge *verb* = **make known**, betray, blow wide open (*slang*), communicate, confess, cough (*slang*), declare, disclose, exhibit, expose, get off one's chest (*informal*),

impart, leak, let slip, out (*informal*), proclaim, promulgate, publish, reveal, spill (*informal*), spill one's guts about (*slang*), tell, uncover
➤ **Antonyms**
conceal, hide, keep secret

dizzy *adjective* **1** = **giddy**, faint, light-headed, off balance, reeling, shaky, staggering, swimming, vertiginous, weak at the knees, wobbly, woozy (*informal*) **2** = **confused**, at sea, befuddled, bemused, bewildered, dazed, dazzled, muddled **3** = **steep**, lofty, vertiginous **4** *Informal* = **scatterbrained**, capricious, ditzy *or* ditsy (*slang*), fickle, flighty, foolish, frivolous, giddy, light-headed, silly

do *verb* **1** = **perform**, accomplish, achieve, act, carry out, complete, conclude, discharge, end, execute, produce, transact, undertake, work **2** = **be adequate**, answer, be enough, be of use, be sufficient, cut the mustard, pass muster, satisfy, serve, suffice, suit **3** = **get ready**, arrange, be responsible for, fix, look after, make, make ready, organize, prepare, see to, take on **4** = **solve**, decipher, decode, figure out, puzzle out, resolve, work out **5** = **behave**, bear oneself, carry oneself, comport oneself, conduct oneself **6** = **cause**, bring about, create, effect, produce **7** = **get on**, fare, get along, make out, manage, proceed **8** *Informal* = **visit**, cover, explore, journey through *or* around, look at, stop in, tour, travel **9** *Informal* = **cheat**, con (*informal*), cozen, deceive, defraud, diddle (*informal*), dupe, fleece, hoax, pull a fast one on (*informal*), skin (*slang*), stiff (*slang*), swindle, take (someone) for a ride (*informal*), trick **10** = **perform**, act, give, present, produce, put on ♦ *noun* **11** *Informal, chiefly Brit. & N.Z.* = **event**, affair, function, gathering, occasion, party **12** **do's and don'ts** *Informal* = **rules**, code, customs, etiquette, instructions, regulations, standards

do away with *verb* **1** = **kill**, blow away (*slang, chiefly U.S.*), bump off (*slang*), destroy, do in (*slang*), exterminate, liquidate, murder, slay, take out (*slang*) **2** = **get rid of**, abolish, axe (*informal*), chuck (*informal*), discard, discontinue, eliminate, junk (*informal*), pull, put an end to, put paid to, remove

docile *adjective* = **submissive**, amenable, biddable, compliant, ductile, manageable, obedient, pliant, teachable (*rare*), tractable
➤ **Antonyms**
difficult, intractable, obstreperous, troublesome, trying, uncooperative, unmanageable

docility *noun* = **submissiveness**, amenability, biddableness, compliance, ductility, manageability, meekness, obedience, pliancy, tractability

dock[1] *noun* 1 = **wharf**, harbour, pier, quay, waterfront ◆ *verb* 2 = **moor**, anchor, berth, drop anchor, land, put in, tie up 3 *Of spacecraft* = **link up**, couple, hook up, join, rendezvous, unite

dock[2] *verb* 1 = **deduct**, decrease, diminish, lessen, reduce, subtract, withhold 2 = **cut off**, clip, crop, curtail, cut short, diminish, lessen, shorten
➤ **Antonyms**
≠deduct: augment, boost, increase, raise

docket *noun* 1 = **label**, bill, certificate, chit, chitty, counterfoil, receipt, tab, tag, tally, ticket, voucher ◆ *verb* 2 = **label**, catalogue, file, index, mark, register, tab, tag, ticket

doctor *noun* 1 = **G.P.**, general practitioner, medic (*informal*), medical practitioner, physician ◆ *verb* 2 = **change**, alter, disguise, falsify, fudge, misrepresent, pervert, tamper with 3 = **add to**, adulterate, cut, dilute, mix with, spike, water down

doctrinaire *adjective* 1 = **dogmatic**, biased, fanatical, inflexible, insistent, opinionated, rigid 2 = **impractical**, hypothetical, ideological, speculative, theoretical, unpragmatic, unrealistic

doctrine *noun* = **teaching**, article, article of faith, belief, canon, concept, conviction, creed, dogma, opinion, precept, principle, tenet

document *noun* 1 = **paper**, certificate, instrument, legal form, record, report ◆ *verb* 2 = **support**, authenticate, back up, certify, cite, corroborate, detail, give weight to, instance, particularize, substantiate, validate, verify

doddering *adjective* = **tottering**, aged, decrepit, doddery, faltering, feeble, floundering, infirm, senile, shaky, shambling, trembly, unsteady, weak

doddle *noun Brit. informal* = **piece of cake** (*informal*), cakewalk (*informal*), child's play (*informal*), cinch (*slang*), easy-peasy (*slang*), money for old rope, no sweat (*slang*), picnic (*informal*), pushover (*slang*)

dodge *verb* 1 = **duck**, body-swerve (*Scot.*), dart, shift, sidestep, swerve, turn aside 2 = **evade**, avoid, body-swerve (*Scot.*), deceive, elude, equivocate, fend off, flannel (*Brit. informal*), fudge, get out of, hedge, parry, shirk, shuffle, trick ◆ *noun* 3 = **trick**, contrivance, device, feint, flannel (*Brit. informal*), machination, ploy, ruse, scheme, stratagem, subterfuge, wheeze (*Brit. slang*), wile

doer *noun* = **achiever**, active person, activist, bustler, dynamo, go-getter (*informal*), live wire (*slang*), organizer, powerhouse (*slang*), wheeler-dealer (*informal*)

doff *verb* 1 *Of a hat* = **tip**, lift, raise, remove, take off, touch 2 *Of clothing* = **take off**, cast off, discard, remove, shed, slip off, slip out of, throw off, undress

dog *noun* 1 = **hound**, bitch, canine, cur, kuri or goorie (*N.Z.*), man's best friend, mongrel, mutt (*slang*), pooch (*slang*), pup, puppy, tyke 2 *Informal* = **scoundrel**, beast, blackguard, cur, heel (*slang*), knave (*archaic*), villain 3 **dog-eat-dog** = **ruthless**, cut-throat, ferocious, fierce, vicious, with no holds barred 4 **go to the dogs** *Informal* = **go to ruin**, degenerate, deteriorate, go down the drain, go to pot ◆ *verb* 5 = **trouble**, follow, haunt, hound, plague, pursue, shadow, tail (*informal*), track, trail

dogged *adjective* = **determined**, firm, immovable, indefatigable, obstinate, persevering, persistent, pertinacious, resolute, single-minded, staunch, steadfast, steady, stiff-necked, stubborn, tenacious, unflagging, unshakable, unyielding
➤ **Antonyms**
doubtful, half-hearted, hesitant, irresolute, undetermined, unsteady

doggedness *noun* = **determination**, bulldog tenacity, endurance, obstinacy, perseverance, persistence, pertinacity, relentlessness, resolution, single-mindedness, steadfastness, steadiness, stubbornness, tenaciousness, tenacity

dogma *noun* = **doctrine**, article, article of faith, belief, credo, creed, opinion, precept, principle, teachings, tenet

dogmatic *adjective* 1 = **opinionated**, arbitrary, arrogant, assertive, categorical, dictatorial, doctrinaire, downright, emphatic, imperious, magisterial, obdurate, overbearing, peremptory 2 = **doctrinal**, authoritative, canonical, categorical, ex cathedra, oracular, positive

dogmatism *noun* = **opinionatedness**, arbitrariness, arrogance, dictatorialness, imperiousness, peremptoriness, positiveness, presumption

dogsbody *noun Informal* = **drudge**, general factotum, maid or man of all work, menial, skivvy (*chiefly Brit.*), slave

do in *verb Slang* 1 = **kill**, blow away (*slang, chiefly U.S.*), butcher, dispatch, eliminate (*slang*), execute, liquidate, murder, slaughter, slay, take out (*slang*) 2 = **exhaust**, fag (*informal*), fatigue, knacker (*slang*), shatter (*informal*), tire, wear out, weary

doing *noun* = **carrying out** *or* **through**, achievement, act, action, deed, execution, exploit, handiwork, implementation, performance

doings *plural noun* = **deeds**, actions, affairs, concerns, dealings, events, exploits, goings-on (*informal*), handiwork, happenings, proceedings, transactions

doldrums *noun* **the doldrums** = **inactivity**, apathy, blues, boredom, depression, dullness, dumps (*informal*), ennui, gloom, inertia, lassitude, listlessness, malaise, stagnation, tedium, the hump (*Brit. informal*), torpor

dole *noun* **1** *Brit. & Austral. informal* = **benefit**, allowance, alms, donation, gift, grant, gratuity, handout, modicum, parcel, pittance, portion, quota, share ♦ *verb* **2 dole out** = **give out**, administer, allocate, allot, apportion, assign, deal, dispense, distribute, divide, hand out, mete, share

dollop *noun* = **lump**, helping, portion, scoop, serving

doll up *verb Slang* = **dress up**, deck out, get ready, gussy up (*slang*), preen, primp, prink, tart up (*slang*), titivate, trick out

dolt *noun* = **idiot**, ass, berk (*Brit. slang*), blockhead, booby, charlie (*Brit. informal*), chump (*informal*), clot (*Brit. informal*), coot, dickwit (*slang*), dimwit (*informal*), dipstick (*Brit. slang*), dope (*informal*), dork (*slang*), dullard, dumb-ass (*slang*), dunce, dweeb (*U.S. slang*), fathead (*informal*), fool, fuckwit (*taboo slang*), geek (*slang*), gobshite (*Irish taboo slang*), gonzo (*slang*), ignoramus, jerk (*slang, chiefly U.S. & Canad.*), lamebrain (*informal*), nerd *or* nurd (*slang*), nitwit (*informal*), numbskull *or* numskull, numpty (*Scot. informal*), oaf, plank (*Brit. slang*), plonker (*slang*), prat (*slang*), prick (*slang*), schmuck (*U.S. slang*), simpleton, thickhead, twit (*informal, chiefly Brit.*), wally (*slang*)

domestic *adjective* **1** = **home**, domiciliary, family, household, private **2** = **home-loving**, domesticated, homely, housewifely, stay-at-home **3** = **domesticated**, house, house-trained, pet, tame, trained **4** = **native**, indigenous, internal, not foreign ♦ *noun* **5** = **servant**, char (*informal*), charwoman, daily, daily help, help, maid, woman (*informal*)

domesticate *verb* **1** = **tame**, break, gentle, house-train, train **2** = **accustom**, acclimatize, familiarize, habituate, naturalize

domesticated *adjective* **1** *Of plants or*

animals = **tame**, broken (in), naturalized, tamed **2** = **home-loving**, domestic, homely, house-trained (*jocular*), housewifely
➤ **Antonyms**
≠**tame**: feral, ferocious, savage, unbroken, undomesticated, untamed, wild

dominant *adjective* **1** = **controlling**, ascendant, assertive, authoritative, commanding, governing, leading, presiding, ruling, superior, supreme **2** = **main**, chief, influential, outstanding, paramount, predominant, pre-eminent, prevailing, prevalent, primary, principal, prominent
➤ **Antonyms**
ancillary, auxiliary, inferior, junior, lesser, lower, minor, secondary, subservient, subsidiary

dominate *verb* **1** = **control**, direct, domineer, govern, have the upper hand over, have the whip hand over, keep under one's thumb, lead, lead by the nose (*informal*), master, monopolize, overbear, rule, rule the roost, tyrannize **2** = **tower above**, bestride, loom over, overlook, stand head and shoulders above, stand over, survey **3** = **predominate**, detract from, eclipse, outshine, overrule, overshadow, prevail over

domination *noun* **1** = **control**, ascendancy, authority, command, influence, mastery, power, rule, superiority, supremacy, sway **2** = **dictatorship**, despotism, oppression, repression, subjection, subordination, suppression, tyranny

domineer *verb* = **boss around** *or* **about** (*informal*), bluster, browbeat, bully, hector, intimidate, lord it over, menace, overbear, ride roughshod over, swagger, threaten, tyrannize

domineering *adjective* = **overbearing**, arrogant, authoritarian, autocratic, bossy (*informal*), coercive, despotic, dictatorial, high-handed, imperious, iron-handed, magisterial, masterful, oppressive, tyrannical
➤ **Antonyms**
meek, obsequious, servile, shy, submissive, subservient

dominion *noun* **1** = **control**, ascendancy, authority, command, domination, government, jurisdiction, mastery, power, rule, sovereignty, supremacy, sway **2** = **kingdom**, country, domain, empire, patch, province, realm, region, territory, turf (*U.S. slang*)

don *verb* = **put on**, clothe oneself in, dress in, get into, pull on, slip on *or* into

donate *verb* = **give**, bequeath, bestow,

chip in (*informal*), contribute, gift, hand out, make a gift of, present, subscribe

donation *noun* = **contribution**, alms, benefaction, boon, gift, grant, gratuity, hand-out, largesse *or* largess, offering, present, stipend, subscription

done *interjection* 1 = **agreed**, it's a bargain, O.K. *or* okay (*informal*), settled, you're on (*informal*) ♦ *adjective* 2 = **finished**, accomplished, completed, concluded, consummated, ended, executed, in the can (*informal*), over, perfected, realized, terminated, through 3 = **cooked enough**, cooked, cooked sufficiently, cooked to a turn, ready 4 = **used up**, depleted, exhausted, finished, spent 5 = **acceptable**, conventional, de rigueur, proper 6 *Informal* = **cheated**, conned (*informal*), duped, taken for a ride (*informal*), tricked 7 **done for** *Informal* = **finished**, beaten, broken, dashed, defeated, destroyed, doomed, foiled, lost, ruined, undone, wrecked 8 **done in** *or* **up** *Informal* = **exhausted**, all in (*slang*), bushed (*informal*), clapped out (*Austral. & N.Z. informal*), creamcrackered (*Brit. slang*), dead (*informal*), dead beat (*informal*), dog-tired (*informal*), fagged out (*informal*), knackered (*slang*), on one's last legs, ready to drop, tired out, worn out, worn to a frazzle (*informal*), zonked (*slang*) ♦ *verb* 9 **have done with** = **be through with**, be finished with, desist, end relations with, give up, throw over, wash one's hands of

donnish *adjective* = **scholarly**, bookish, erudite, formalistic, pedagogic, pedantic, precise, scholastic

donor *noun* = **giver**, almsgiver, benefactor, contributor, donator, grantor (*Law*), philanthropist
➤ **Antonyms**
assignee, beneficiary, inheritor, legatee, payee, receiver, recipient

doom *noun* 1 = **destruction**, catastrophe, death, destiny, downfall, fate, fortune, lot, portion, ruin 2 = **sentence**, condemnation, decision, decree, judgment, verdict ♦ *verb* 3 = **condemn**, consign, damn, decree, destine, foreordain, judge, predestine, preordain, sentence, sound the death knell, threaten

doomed *adjective* = **condemned**, bedevilled, bewitched, cursed, fated, hopeless, ill-fated, ill-omened, luckless, star-crossed

door *noun* 1 = **opening**, doorway, egress, entrance, entry, exit, ingress 2 **lay at the door of** = **blame**, censure, charge, hold responsible, impute to 3 **out of doors** = **in the open air**, alfresco, out, outdoors, outside 4 **show someone the door** = **throw out**, ask to leave, boot out (*informal*), bounce (*slang*), eject, oust, show out

do out of *verb* = **cheat**, balk, bilk, con (*informal*), cozen, deprive, diddle (*informal*), swindle, trick

dope *noun* 1 *Slang* = **drug**, narcotic, opiate 2 *Informal* = **idiot**, berk (*Brit. slang*), blockhead, charlie (*Brit. informal*), coot, dickhead (*slang*), dickwit (*slang*), dimwit (*informal*), dipstick (*Brit. slang*), divvy (*Brit. slang*), dolt, dork (*slang*), dumb-ass (*slang*), dunce, dweeb (*U.S. slang*), fathead (*informal*), fool, fuckwit (*taboo slang*), geek (*slang*), gobshite (*Irish taboo slang*), gonzo (*slang*), jerk (*slang, chiefly U.S. & Canad.*), lamebrain (*informal*), nerd *or* nurd (*slang*), nitwit (*informal*), numbskull *or* numskull, numpty (*Scot. informal*), oaf, pillock (*Brit. slang*), plank (*Brit. slang*), plonker (*slang*), prat (*slang*), prick (*slang*), schmuck (*U.S. slang*), simpleton, twit (*informal, chiefly Brit.*), wally (*slang*) 3 = **information**, details, facts, gen (*Brit. informal*), info (*informal*), inside information, lowdown (*informal*), news, tip ♦ *verb* 4 = **drug**, anaesthetize, doctor, inject, knock out, narcotize, sedate, stupefy

dormant *adjective* = **inactive**, asleep, comatose, fallow, hibernating, inert, inoperative, latent, quiescent, sleeping, sluggish, slumbering, suspended, torpid
➤ **Antonyms**
active, alert, alive and kicking, aroused, awake, awakened, conscious, wakeful, wide-awake

dose *noun* = **quantity**, dosage, draught, drench, measure, portion, potion, prescription

dot *noun* 1 = **spot**, atom, circle, dab, fleck, full stop, iota, jot, mark, mite, mote, point, speck, speckle 2 **on the dot** = **on time**, exactly, on the button (*informal*), precisely, promptly, punctually, to the minute ♦ *verb* 3 = **spot**, dab, dabble, fleck, speckle, sprinkle, stipple, stud

dotage *noun* = **senility**, decrepitude, eld (*archaic*), feebleness, imbecility, old age, second childhood, weakness

dote on *or* **upon** *verb* = **adore**, admire, hold dear, idolize, lavish affection on, prize, treasure

doting *adjective* = **adoring**, devoted, fond, foolish, indulgent, lovesick

double *adjective* 1 = **twice**, binate (*Botany*), coupled, doubled, dual, duplicate, in pairs, paired, twin, twofold 2 = **deceitful**, dishonest, false, hypocritical, insincere,

Janus-faced, knavish (*archaic*), perfidious, treacherous, two-faced, vacillating ♦ *verb* **3** = **multiply**, duplicate, enlarge, fold, grow, increase, magnify, plait, repeat ♦ *noun* **4** = **twin**, clone, copy, counterpart, dead ringer (*slang*), Doppelgänger, duplicate, fellow, impersonator, lookalike, mate, replica, ringer (*slang*), spitting image (*informal*) **5 at** *or* **on the double** = **quickly**, at full speed, briskly, immediately, in double-quick time, pdq (*slang*), posthaste, without delay

double-cross *verb* = **betray**, cheat, cozen, defraud, hoodwink, mislead, sell down the river (*informal*), swindle, trick, two-time (*informal*)

double-dealer *noun* = **cheat**, betrayer, con man (*informal*), cozener, deceiver, dissembler, double-crosser (*informal*), fraud, fraudster, grifter (*slang, chiefly U.S. & Canad.*), hypocrite, rogue, snake in the grass (*informal*), swindler, traitor, two-timer (*informal*)

double-dealing *noun* **1** = **treachery**, bad faith, betrayal, cheating, deceit, deception, dishonesty, duplicity, foul play, hypocrisy, mendacity, perfidy, trickery, two-timing (*informal*) ♦ *adjective* **2** = **treacherous**, cheating, crooked (*informal*), deceitful, dishonest, duplicitous, fraudulent, hypocritical, lying, perfidious, sneaky, swindling, tricky, two-faced, two-timing (*informal*), underhanded, untrustworthy, wily

double entendre *noun* = **double meaning**, ambiguity, innuendo, play on words, pun

doubt *noun* **1** = **uncertainty**, dubiety, hesitancy, hesitation, indecision, irresolution, lack of conviction, suspense, vacillation **2** = **suspicion**, apprehension, disquiet, distrust, fear, incredulity, lack of faith, misgiving, mistrust, qualm, scepticism **3** = **difficulty**, ambiguity, can of worms (*informal*), confusion, dilemma, perplexity, problem, quandary **4 no doubt** = **certainly**, admittedly, assuredly, doubtless, doubtlessly, probably, surely ♦ *verb* **5** = **be uncertain**, be dubious, demur, fluctuate, hesitate, scruple, vacillate, waver **6** = **suspect**, discredit, distrust, fear, lack confidence in, misgive, mistrust, query, question
➤ Antonyms
noun ≠**uncertainty:** belief, certainty, confidence, conviction ≠**suspicion:** confidence, trust ♦ *verb* ≠**suspect:** accept, believe, buy (*slang*), have faith in, swallow (*informal*), take on board, trust

doubter *noun* = **sceptic**, agnostic,

disbeliever, doubting Thomas, questioner, unbeliever

doubtful *adjective* **1** = **unlikely**, ambiguous, debatable, dodgy (*Brit., Austral., & N.Z. informal*), dubious, equivocal, hazardous, iffy (*informal*), improbable, inconclusive, indefinite, indeterminate, inexact, obscure, precarious, problematic(al), questionable, unclear, unconfirmed, unsettled, vague **2** = **unsure**, distrustful, hesitating, in two minds (*informal*), irresolute, leery (*slang*), perplexed, sceptical, suspicious, tentative, uncertain, unconvinced, undecided, unresolved, unsettled, vacillating, wavering **3** = **questionable**, disreputable, dodgy (*Brit., Austral., & N.Z. informal*), dubious, shady (*informal*), suspect, suspicious
➤ Antonyms
≠**unlikely:** certain, definite, indubitable ≠**unsure:** certain, decided, positive, resolute

doubtless *adverb* **1** = **certainly**, assuredly, clearly, indisputably, of course, precisely, surely, truly, undoubtedly, unquestionably, without doubt **2** = **probably**, apparently, most likely, ostensibly, presumably, seemingly, supposedly

dour *adjective* = **gloomy**, dismal, dreary, forbidding, grim, morose, sour, sullen, unfriendly
➤ Antonyms
carefree, cheerful, cheery, chirpy (*informal*), genial, good-humoured, happy, jovial, pleasant, sunny

dovetail *verb* **1** = **fit together**, fit, interlock, join, link, mortise, tenon, unite **2** = **correspond**, accord, agree, coincide, conform, harmonize, match, tally

dowdy *adjective* = **frumpy**, dingy, drab, frowzy, frumpish, ill-dressed, old-fashioned, scrubby (*Brit. informal*), shabby, slovenly, tacky (*U.S. informal*), unfashionable
➤ Antonyms
chic, dressy, fashionable, neat, smart, spruce, trim, well-dressed

dower *noun* = **dowry**, inheritance, legacy, portion, provision, share

do without *verb* = **manage without**, abstain from, dispense with, forgo, get along without, give up, kick (*informal*)

down *adjective* **1** = **depressed**, blue, dejected, disheartened, dismal, downcast, down in the dumps (*informal*), low, miserable, sad, sick as a parrot (*informal*), unhappy ♦ *verb* **2** *Informal* = **swallow**, drain, drink (down), gulp, put away, toss off **3** = **bring down**, deck (*slang*), fell, floor, knock down, overthrow, prostrate, subdue, tackle, throw, trip ♦ *noun* **4** = **drop**, decline, descent, dropping, fall, falling, reverse **5 have a down on** *Informal* = **be antagonistic** *or* **hostile to,** be anti (*informal*), bear a grudge towards, be contra (*informal*), be prejudiced against, be set against, feel ill will towards, have it in for (*slang*)

down-and-out *noun* **1** = **tramp,** bag lady, beggar, bum (*informal*), derelict, dosser (*Brit. slang*), loser, outcast, pauper, vagabond, vagrant ♦ *adjective* **2** = **destitute,** derelict, dirt-poor (*informal*), flat broke (*informal*), impoverished, on one's uppers (*informal*), penniless, ruined, short, without two pennies to rub together (*informal*)

downcast *adjective* = **dejected,** cheerless, choked, crestfallen, daunted, depressed, despondent, disappointed, disconsolate, discouraged, disheartened, dismal, dismayed, dispirited, down in the dumps (*informal*), miserable, sad, sick as a parrot (*informal*), unhappy
➤ **Antonyms**
cheerful, cheery, chirpy (*informal*), contented, elated, genial, happy, joyful, light-hearted, optimistic

downfall *noun* **1** = **ruin,** breakdown, collapse, comedown, comeuppance (*slang*), debacle, descent, destruction, disgrace, fall, overthrow, undoing **2** = **rainstorm,** cloudburst, deluge, downpour

downgrade *verb* **1** = **demote,** degrade, humble, lower *or* reduce in rank, take down a peg (*informal*) **2** = **run down,** decry, denigrate, detract from, disparage
➤ **Antonyms**
≠**demote:** advance, better, elevate, enhance, improve, promote, raise, upgrade

downhearted *adjective* = **dejected,** blue, chapfallen, crestfallen, depressed, despondent, discouraged, disheartened, dismayed, dispirited, downcast, low-spirited, sad, sick as a parrot (*informal*), sorrowful, unhappy

downpour *noun* = **rainstorm,** cloudburst, deluge, flood, inundation, torrential rain

downright *adjective* **1** = **complete,** absolute, arrant, blatant, categorical, clear, deep-dyed (*usually derogatory*), explicit, out-and-out, outright, plain, positive, simple, thoroughgoing, total, undisguised, unequivocal, unqualified, utter **2** = **blunt,** candid, forthright, frank, honest, open, outspoken, plain, sincere, straightforward, straight-from-the-shoulder, upfront (*informal*)

down-to-earth *adjective* = **sensible,** common-sense, hard-headed, matter-of-fact, mundane, no-nonsense, plain-spoken, practical, realistic, sane, unsentimental

downtrodden *adjective* = **oppressed,** abused, afflicted, distressed, exploited, helpless, subjugated, subservient, tyrannized

downward *adjective* = **descending,** declining, earthward, heading down, sliding, slipping

doze *verb* **1** = **nap,** catnap, drop off (*informal*), drowse, kip (*Brit. slang*), nod, nod off (*informal*), sleep, sleep lightly, slumber, snooze (*informal*), zizz (*Brit. informal*) ♦ *noun* **2** = **nap,** catnap, forty winks (*informal*), kip (*Brit. slang*), little sleep, shuteye (*slang*), siesta, snooze (*informal*), zizz (*Brit. informal*)

drab *adjective* = **dull,** cheerless, colourless, dingy, dismal, dreary, flat, gloomy, grey, lacklustre, shabby, sombre, uninspired, vapid
➤ **Antonyms**
bright, cheerful, colourful, jazzy (*informal*), vibrant, vivid

draft *noun* **1** = **outline,** abstract, delineation, plan, preliminary form, rough, sketch, version **2** = **order,** bill (*of exchange*), cheque, postal order ♦ *verb* **3** = **outline,** compose, delineate, design, draw, draw up, formulate, plan, sketch

drag *verb* **1** = **pull,** draw, hale, haul, lug, tow, trail, tug, yank **2** = **go slowly,** crawl, creep, inch, limp along, shamble, shuffle **3** = **lag behind,** dawdle, draggle, linger, loiter, straggle, trail behind **4 drag on** *or* **out** = **last,** draw out, extend, keep going, lengthen, persist, prolong, protract, spin out, stretch out **5 drag one's feet** *Informal* = **stall,** block, hold back, obstruct, procrastinate ♦ *noun* **6** *Slang* = **nuisance,** annoyance, bore, bother, pain (*informal*), pain in the arse (*taboo informal*), pest

dragging *adjective* = **tedious,** boring, dull, going slowly, humdrum, mind-numbing, monotonous, tiresome, wearisome

dragoon *verb* = **force,** browbeat, bully, coerce, compel, constrain, drive, impel, intimidate, railroad (*informal*), strong-arm (*informal*)

drain *noun* **1** = **pipe,** channel, conduit, culvert, ditch, duct, outlet, sewer, sink, trench, watercourse **2** = **reduction,** depletion, drag, exhaustion, expenditure, sap, strain, withdrawal **3 down the drain** = **wasted,** gone, gone for good, lost, ruined ♦ *verb* **4** = **remove,** bleed, draw off, dry, empty, evacuate, milk, pump off *or* out, tap, withdraw **5 = flow out**, discharge, effuse, exude, leak, ooze, seep, trickle, well out **6 = drink up**, finish, gulp down, quaff, swallow **7 = exhaust**, consume, deplete, dissipate, empty, sap, strain, tax, use up, weary

drainage *noun* **= sewerage**, bilge (water), seepage, sewage, waste

dram *noun* **= shot** (*informal*), drop, glass, measure, slug, snifter (*informal*), snort (*slang*), tot

drama *noun* **1 = play**, dramatization, show, stage play, stage show, theatrical piece **2 = theatre**, acting, dramatic art, dramaturgy, stagecraft, Thespian art **3 = excitement**, crisis, dramatics, histrionics, scene, spectacle, theatrics, turmoil

dramatic *adjective* **1 = theatrical**, dramaturgic, dramaturgical, Thespian **2 = powerful**, affecting, effective, expressive, impressive, moving, striking, vivid **3 = exciting**, breathtaking, climactic, electrifying, emotional, high-octane (*informal*), melodramatic, sensational, shock-horror (*facetious*), startling, sudden, suspenseful, tense, thrilling
➤ **Antonyms**
≠**powerful**: ordinary, run-of-the-mill, undramatic, unexceptional, unmemorable

dramatist *noun* **= playwright**, dramaturge, screenwriter, scriptwriter

dramatize *verb* **= exaggerate**, act, lay it on (thick) (*slang*), make a performance of, overdo, overstate, play-act, play to the gallery

drape *verb* **1 = cover**, adorn, array, cloak, fold, swathe, wrap **2 = hang**, dangle, droop, drop, lean over, let fall, suspend

drastic *adjective* **= extreme**, desperate, dire, forceful, harsh, radical, severe, strong

draught *noun* **1 = breeze**, current, flow, influx, movement, puff **2 = drink**, cup, dose, drench, potion, quantity **3 = pulling**, dragging, drawing, haulage, traction

draw *verb* **1 = sketch**, delineate, depict, design, map out, mark out, outline, paint, portray, trace **2 = pull**, drag, haul, tow, tug **3 = take out**, extort, extract, pull out **4 = attract**, allure, bring forth, call forth, elicit, engage, entice, evoke, induce, influence, invite, persuade **5 = deduce**, derive, get, infer, make, take **6 = choose**, pick, select, single out, take **7 = stretch**, attenuate, elongate, extend, lengthen **8 = inhale**, breathe in, drain, inspire, puff, pull, respire, suck **9 = draft**, compose, formulate, frame, prepare, write ◆ *noun* **10** *Informal* **= attraction**, enticement, lure, pull (*informal*) **11 = tie**, dead heat, deadlock, impasse, stalemate

drawback *noun* **= disadvantage**, defect, deficiency, detriment, difficulty, downside, fault, flaw, fly in the ointment (*informal*), handicap, hazard, hindrance, hitch, impediment, imperfection, nuisance, obstacle, snag, stumbling block, trouble
➤ **Antonyms**
advantage, asset, benefit, gain, help, service, use

draw back *verb* **= recoil**, back off, retract, retreat, shrink, start back, withdraw

drawing *noun* **= picture**, cartoon, delineation, depiction, illustration, outline, portrayal, representation, sketch, study

drawl *verb* **= draw out**, drag out, extend, lengthen, prolong, protract

drawling *adjective* **= droning**, dragging, drawly, dull, twanging, twangy

drawn *adjective* **= tense**, fatigued, fraught, haggard, harassed, harrowed, pinched, sapped, strained, stressed, taut, tired, worn

draw on *verb* **= make use of**, employ, exploit, extract, fall back on, have recourse to, rely on, take from, use

draw out *verb* **= extend**, drag out, lengthen, make longer, prolong, prolongate, protract, spin out, stretch, string out
➤ **Antonyms**
curtail, cut, cut short, dock, pare down, reduce, shorten, trim, truncate

draw up *verb* **1 = draft**, compose, formulate, frame, prepare, write out **2 = halt**, bring to a stop, pull up, run in, stop, stop short

dread *verb* **1 = fear**, anticipate with horror, cringe at, have cold feet (*informal*), quail, shrink from, shudder, tremble ◆ *noun* **2 = fear**, affright, alarm, apprehension, aversion, awe, dismay, fright, funk (*informal*), heebie-jeebies (*slang*), horror, terror, trepidation ◆ *adjective* **3** *Literary* **= frightening**, alarming, awe-inspiring, awful, dire, dreaded, dreadful, frightful, horrible, terrible, terrifying

dreadful *adjective* **= terrible**, abysmal, alarming, appalling, atrocious, awful, dire, distressing, fearful, formidable, frightful, from hell (*informal*), ghastly, godawful (*slang*), grievous, hellacious (*U.S. slang*), hideous, horrendous, horrible, monstrous, shocking, tragic, tremendous

dream *noun* **1 = vision**, delusion, hallucination, illusion, imagination, reverie, speculation, trance, vagary **2 = daydream**, fantasy, pipe dream **3 = ambition**, aim, aspiration, design, desire, goal, Holy Grail (*informal*), hope, notion, thirst, wish **4 = delight**, beauty, gem, joy, marvel, pleasure, treasure ♦ verb 5 = **have dreams**, conjure up, envisage, fancy, hallucinate, imagine, think, visualize 6 = **daydream**, build castles in the air or in Spain, fantasize, stargaze

dreamer noun = **idealist**, daydreamer, Don Quixote, escapist, fantasist, fantasizer, fantast, romancer, theorizer, utopian, visionary, Walter Mitty

dreamland noun = **land of make-believe**, cloud-cuckoo-land, cloudland, dream world, fairyland, fantasy, illusion, land of dreams, land of Nod, never-never land (informal)

dream up verb = **invent**, concoct, contrive, cook up (informal), create, devise, hatch, imagine, spin, think up

dreamy adjective 1 = **vague**, absent, abstracted, daydreaming, faraway, in a reverie, musing, pensive, preoccupied, with one's head in the clouds 2 = **impractical**, airy-fairy, dreamlike, fanciful, imaginary, quixotic, speculative, surreal, vague, visionary 3 = **unreal**, chimerical, dreamlike, fantastic, intangible, misty, phantasmagoric, phantasmagorical, shadowy 4 = **relaxing**, calming, gentle, lulling, romantic, soothing

➤ **Antonyms**

≠**vague, impractical**: common-sense, down-to-earth, feet-on-the-ground, practical, pragmatic, realistic, unromantic

dreary adjective 1 = **dull**, as dry as dust, boring, colourless, drab, ho-hum (informal), humdrum, lifeless, mind-numbing, monotonous, routine, tedious, tiresome, uneventful, uninteresting, wearisome 2 = **dismal**, bleak, cheerless, comfortless, depressing, doleful, downcast, drear, forlorn, funereal, gloomy, glum, joyless, lonely, lonesome, melancholy, mournful, sad, solitary, sombre, sorrowful, wretched

➤ **Antonyms**

≠**dull**: bright, interesting ≠**dismal**: cheerful, happy, joyful

dregs plural noun 1 = **sediment**, deposit, draff, dross, grounds, lees, residue, residuum, scourings, scum, trash, waste 2 = **scum**, canaille, down-and-outs, good-for-nothings, outcasts, rabble, ragtag and bobtail, riffraff

drench verb 1 = **soak**, drown, duck, flood, imbrue, inundate, saturate, souse, steep, swamp, wet ♦ noun 2 Veterinary = **dose**, physic, purge

dress noun 1 = **frock**, costume, ensemble, garment, get-up (informal), gown, outfit, rigout (informal), robe, suit 2 = **clothing**, apparel, attire, clothes, costume, garb, garments, gear (informal), guise, habiliment, raiment (archaic or poetic), schmutter (slang), threads (slang), togs, vestment ♦ verb 3 = **put on**, attire, change, clothe, don, garb, robe, slip on or into 4 = **decorate**, adorn, apparel (archaic), array, bedeck, deck, drape, embellish, festoon, furbish, ornament, rig, trim 5 = **bandage**, bind up, plaster, treat 6 = **arrange**, adjust, align, comb (out), dispose, do (up), fit, get ready, groom, prepare, set, straighten

➤ **Antonyms**

verb ≠**put on**: disrobe, divest oneself of, peel off (slang), shed, strip, take off one's clothes

dress down verb Informal = **reprimand**, bawl out (informal), berate, carpet (informal), castigate, chew out (U.S. & Canad. informal), give a rocket (Brit. & N.Z. informal), haul over the coals, rap over the knuckles, read the riot act, rebuke, reprove, scold, slap on the wrist, tear (informal), tear (someone) off a strip (Brit. informal), tell off (informal), upbraid

dressmaker noun = **seamstress**, couturier, modiste, sewing woman, tailor

dress up verb 1 = **dress formally**, doll up (slang), dress for dinner, put on one's best bib and tucker (informal), put on one's glad rags (informal) 2 = **put on fancy dress**, disguise, play-act, wear a costume

dribble verb 1 = **run**, drip, drop, fall in drops, leak, ooze, seep, trickle 2 = **drool**, drip saliva, drivel, slaver, slobber

drift verb 1 = **float**, be carried along, coast, go (aimlessly), meander, stray, waft, wander 2 = **pile up**, accumulate, amass, bank up, drive, gather ♦ noun 3 = **pile**, accumulation, bank, heap, mass, mound 4 = **meaning**, aim, design, direction, gist, implication, import, intention, object, purport, scope, significance, tendency, tenor, thrust 5 = **current**, course, direction, flow, impulse, movement, rush, sweep, trend

drifter noun = **wanderer**, beachcomber, bum (informal), hobo (U.S.), itinerant, rolling stone, vagrant

drill noun 1 = **boring tool**, bit, borer, gimlet, rotary tool 2 = **training**, discipline, exercise, instruction, practice, preparation, repetition ♦ verb 3 = **bore**, penetrate, perforate, pierce, puncture, sink in 4 = **train**, coach, discipline, exercise, instruct, practise, rehearse, teach

drink verb 1 = **swallow**, absorb, drain, gulp, guzzle, imbibe, partake of, quaff, sip, suck, sup, swig (informal), swill, toss off, wash down, wet one's whistle (informal) 2 = **booze** (informal), bend the elbow (*informal*), bevvy (*dialect*), carouse, go on a binge *or* bender (*informal*), hit the bottle (*informal*), indulge, pub-crawl (*informal, chiefly Brit.*), revel, tipple, tope, wassail ♦ *noun* **3** = **beverage**, liquid, potion, refreshment, thirst quencher **4** = **alcohol**, booze (*informal*), Dutch courage, hooch *or* hootch (*informal, chiefly U.S. & Canad.*), liquor, spirits, the bottle (*informal*) **5** = **glass**, cup, draught, gulp, noggin, sip, snifter (*informal*), swallow, swig (*informal*), taste, tipple **6 the drink** *Informal* = **the sea**, the briny (*informal*), the deep, the main, the ocean

drinker *noun* = **alcoholic**, bibber, boozer (*informal*), dipsomaniac, drunk, drunkard, guzzler, inebriate, lush (*slang*), soak (*slang*), sot, sponge (*informal*), tippler, toper, wino (*informal*)

drink in *verb* = **pay attention**, absorb, assimilate, be all ears (*informal*), be fascinated by, be rapt, hang on (someone's) words, hang on the lips of

drink to *verb* = **toast**, pledge, pledge the health of, salute

drip *verb* **1** = **drop**, dribble, drizzle, exude, filter, plop, splash, sprinkle, trickle ♦ *noun* **2** = **drop**, dribble, dripping, leak, trickle **3** *Informal* = **weakling**, milksop, mummy's boy (*informal*), namby-pamby, ninny, softie (*informal*), weed (*informal*), wet (*Brit. informal*)

drive *verb* **1** = **operate**, direct, go, guide, handle, manage, motor, ride, steer, travel **2** = **goad**, actuate, coerce, compel, constrain, dragoon, force, harass, impel, motivate, oblige, overburden, overwork, press, prick, prod, prompt, railroad (*informal*), rush, spur **3** = **push**, herd, hurl, impel, propel, send, urge **4** = **thrust**, dig, hammer, plunge, push, ram, sink, stab ♦ *noun* **5** = **run**, excursion, hurl (*Scot.*), jaunt, journey, outing, ride, spin (*informal*), trip, turn **6** = **campaign**, action, advance, appeal, crusade, effort, push (*informal*), surge **7** = **initiative**, ambition, effort, energy, enterprise, get-up-and-go (*informal*), motivation, pep, pressure, push (*informal*), vigour, zip (*informal*)

drive at *verb Informal* = **mean**, aim, allude to, get at, have in mind, hint at, imply, indicate, insinuate, intend, intimate, refer to, signify, suggest

drivel *noun* **1** = **nonsense**, balderdash, balls (*taboo slang*), bilge (*informal*), blah (*slang*), bosh (*informal*), bull (*slang*), bullshit (*taboo slang*), bunk (*informal*), bunkum *or* buncombe (*chiefly U.S.*), cobblers (*Brit. taboo slang*), crap (*slang*), dross, eyewash (*informal*), fatuity, garbage

(*informal*), gibberish, guff (*slang*), hogwash, hokum (*slang, chiefly U.S. & Canad.*), horsefeathers (*U.S. slang*), hot air (*informal*), moonshine, pap, piffle (*informal*), poppycock (*informal*), prating, rot, rubbish, shit (*taboo slang*), stuff, tommyrot, tosh (*slang, chiefly Brit.*), trash, tripe (*informal*), twaddle, waffle (*informal, chiefly Brit.*) **2** = **saliva**, slaver, slobber ♦ *verb* **3** = **babble**, blether, gab (*informal*), gas (*informal*), maunder, prate, ramble, waffle (*informal, chiefly Brit.*) **4** = **dribble**, drool, slaver, slobber

driving *adjective* = **forceful**, compelling, dynamic, energetic, galvanic, storming (*informal*), sweeping, vigorous, violent

drizzle *noun* **1** = **fine rain**, Scotch mist, smir (*Scot.*) ♦ *verb* **2** = **rain**, mizzle (*dialect*), shower, spot *or* spit with rain, spray, sprinkle

droll *adjective* = **amusing**, clownish, comic, comical, diverting, eccentric, entertaining, farcical, funny, humorous, jocular, laughable, ludicrous, odd, oddball (*informal*), off-the-wall (*slang*), quaint, ridiculous, risible, waggish, whimsical

drone¹ *noun* = **parasite**, couch potato (*slang*), idler, leech, loafer, lounger, scrounger (*informal*), skiver (*Brit. slang*), sluggard, sponger (*informal*)

drone² *verb* **1** = **hum**, buzz, purr, thrum, vibrate, whirr **2 drone on** = **speak monotonously**, be boring, chant, drawl, intone, prose about, spout, talk interminably ♦ *noun* **3** = **hum**, buzz, murmuring, purr, thrum, vibration, whirr, whirring

drool *verb* **1** = **dribble**, drivel, salivate, slaver, slobber, water at the mouth **2 drool over** = **gloat over**, dote on, fondle, gush, make much of, pet, rave about (*informal*), slobber over, spoil

droop *verb* **1** = **sag**, bend, dangle, drop, fall down, hang (down), sink **2** = **flag**, decline, diminish, fade, faint, languish, slump, wilt, wither

drop *verb* **1** = **fall**, decline, depress, descend, diminish, dive, droop, lower, plummet, plunge, sink, tumble **2** = **drip**, dribble, fall in drops, trickle **3** = **set down**, deposit, leave, let off, unload **4** = **discontinue**, abandon, axe (*informal*), cease, desert, forsake, give up, kick (*informal*), leave, quit, relinquish, remit, terminate **5** *Informal* = **reject**, disown, ignore, jilt, renounce, repudiate, throw over ♦ *noun* **6** = **droplet**, bead, bubble, driblet, drip, globule, pearl, tear **7** = **dash**, dab, mouthful, nip, pinch, shot (*informal*), sip, spot, taste, tot, trace, trickle **8**

= **decrease**, cut, decline, deterioration, downturn, fall-off, lowering, reduction, slump **9** = **fall**, abyss, chasm, declivity, descent, plunge, precipice, slope

drop in (on) *verb Informal* = **visit**, blow in (*informal*), call, call in, go and see, look in (on), look up, pop in (*informal*), roll up (*informal*), stop, turn up

drop off *verb* **1** = **set down**, allow to alight, deliver, leave, let off **2** *Informal* = **fall asleep**, catnap, doze (off), drowse, have forty winks (*informal*), nod (off), snooze (*informal*) **3** = **decrease**, decline, diminish, dwindle, fall off, lessen, slacken

drop out *verb* = **leave**, abandon, back out, cop out (*slang*), fall by the wayside, forsake, give up, quit, renege, stop, withdraw

drought *noun* **1** = **dry spell**, aridity, dehydration, drouth (*Scot.*), dryness, dry weather, parchedness **2** = **shortage**, dearth, deficiency, insufficiency, lack, need, scarcity, want
➤ **Antonyms**
≠**dry spell**: deluge, downpour, flood, flow, inundation, outpouring, rush, stream, torrent ≠**shortage**: abundance, profusion

drove *noun* = **herd**, collection, company, crowd, flock, gathering, horde, mob, multitude, press, swarm, throng

drown *verb* **1** = **drench**, deluge, engulf, flood, go down, go under, immerse, inundate, sink, submerge, swamp **2** = **overpower**, deaden, engulf, muffle, obliterate, overcome, overwhelm, stifle, swallow up, wipe out

drowse *verb* **1** = **be sleepy**, be drowsy, be lethargic, doze, drop off (*informal*), kip (*Brit. slang*), nap, nod, sleep, slumber, snooze (*informal*), zizz (*Brit. informal*)
◆ *noun* **2** = **sleep**, doze, forty winks (*informal*), kip (*Brit. slang*), nap, slumber, zizz (*Brit. informal*)

drowsy *adjective* **1** = **sleepy**, comatose, dazed, dopey (*slang*), dozy, drugged, half asleep, heavy, lethargic, nodding, somnolent, tired, torpid **2** = **peaceful**, dreamy, lulling, quiet, restful, sleepy, soothing, soporific
➤ **Antonyms**
≠**sleepy**: alert, awake, bright-eyed and bushy-tailed, full of beans (*informal*), lively, perky

drubbing *noun* **1** = **beating**, clobbering (*slang*), flogging, hammering (*informal*), licking (*informal*), pasting (*slang*), pounding, pummelling, thrashing, walloping (*informal*), whipping **2** = **defeat**, clobbering (*slang*), hammering (*informal*), licking (*informal*), pasting (*slang*),

thrashing, trouncing

drudge *noun* **1** = **menial**, dogsbody (*informal*), factotum, hack, maid or man of all work, plodder, scullion (*archaic*), servant, skivvy (*chiefly Brit.*), slave, toiler, worker ◆ *verb* **2** = **toil**, grind (*informal*), keep one's nose to the grindstone, labour, moil (*archaic or dialect*), plod, plug away (*informal*), slave, work

drudgery *noun* = **menial labour**, chore, donkey-work, fag (*informal*), grind (*informal*), hack work, hard work, labour, skivvying (*Brit.*), slavery, slog, sweat (*informal*), sweated labour, toil

drug *noun* **1** = **medication**, medicament, medicine, physic, poison, remedy **2** = **dope** (*slang*), narcotic, opiate, stimulant ◆ *verb* **3** = **dose**, administer a drug, dope (*slang*), medicate, treat **4** = **knock out**, anaesthetize, deaden, numb, poison, stupefy

drug addict *noun* = **junkie** (*informal*), acid head (*informal*), crack-head (*informal*), dope-fiend (*slang*), head (*informal*), hop-head (*informal*), tripper (*informal*)

drugged *adjective* = **stoned** (*slang*), bombed (*slang*), comatose, doped (*slang*), dopey (*slang*), flying (*slang*), high (*informal*), on a trip (*informal*), out of it (*slang*), out of one's mind (*slang*), out to it (*Austral. & N.Z. slang*), smashed (*slang*), spaced out (*slang*), stupefied, tripping (*informal*), turned on (*slang*), under the influence (*informal*), wasted (*slang*), wrecked (*slang*), zonked (*slang*)

drum *verb* **1** = **beat**, pulsate, rap, reverberate, tap, tattoo, throb **2 drum into** = **drive home**, din into, hammer away, harp on, instil into, reiterate

drum up *verb* = **canvass**, attract, bid for, obtain, petition, round up, solicit

drunk *adjective* **1** = **intoxicated**, babalas (*S. African*), bacchic, bevvied (*dialect*), bladdered (*slang*), blitzed (*slang*), blotto (*slang*), bombed (*slang*), Brahms and Liszt (*slang*), canned (*slang*), drunken, flying (*slang*), fu' (*Scot.*), fuddled, half seas over (*informal*), inebriated, legless (*informal*), lit up (*slang*), loaded (*slang, chiefly U.S. & Canad.*), maudlin, merry (*Brit. informal*), muddled, out of it (*slang*), out to it (*Austral. & N.Z. slang*), paralytic (*informal*), pickled (*informal*), pie-eyed (*slang*), pissed (*taboo slang*), plastered (*slang*), rat-arsed (*taboo slang*), sloshed (*slang*), smashed (*slang*), soaked (*informal*), steamboats (*Scot. slang*), steaming (*slang*), stewed (*slang*), stoned (*slang*), tanked up (*slang*), tiddly (*slang, chiefly Brit.*), tight (*informal*), tipsy, tired and emotional (*euphemistic*), under the influence (*informal*), wasted (*slang*), well-oiled (*slang*), wrecked (*slang*), zonked (*slang*) ♦ *noun* **2** = **drunkard**, alcoholic, boozer (*informal*), inebriate, lush (*slang*), soak (*slang*), sot, toper, wino (*informal*)

drunkard *noun* = **drinker**, alcoholic, carouser, dipsomaniac, drunk, lush (*slang*), soak (*slang*), sot, tippler, toper, wino (*informal*)

drunken *adjective* **1** = **intoxicated**, bevvied (*dialect*), bibulous, bladdered (*slang*), blitzed (*slang*), blotto (*slang*), bombed (*slang*), boozing (*informal*), Brahms and Liszt (*slang*), drunk, flying (*slang*), (gin-)sodden, inebriate, legless (*informal*), lit up (*slang*), out of it (*slang*), out to it (*Austral. & N.Z. slang*), paralytic (*informal*), pissed (*taboo slang*), rat-arsed (*taboo slang*), red-nosed, smashed (*slang*), sottish, steamboats (*Scot. slang*), steaming (*slang*), tippling, toping, under the influence (*informal*), wasted (*slang*), wrecked (*slang*), zonked (*slang*) **2** = **debauched**, bacchanalian, bacchic, boozy (*informal*), dionysian, dissipated, orgiastic, riotous, saturnalian

drunkenness *noun* = **intoxication**, alcoholism, bibulousness, dipsomania, inebriation, insobriety, intemperance, sottishness, tipsiness

dry *adjective* **1** = **dehydrated**, arid, barren, desiccated, dried up, juiceless, moistureless, parched, sapless, thirsty, torrid, waterless **2** = **dull**, boring, dreary, ho-hum (*informal*), monotonous, plain, tedious, tiresome, uninteresting **3** = **sarcastic**, cutting, deadpan, droll, keen, low-key, quietly humorous, sharp, sly ♦ *verb* **4** = **dehydrate**, dehumidify, desiccate, drain, make dry, parch, sear
➤ **Antonyms**
adjective ≠ **dehydrated**: damp, humid, moist, wet ≠ **dull**: entertaining, interesting, lively ♦ *verb* ≠ **dehydrate**: moisten, wet

dryness *noun* = **aridity**, aridness, dehumidification, dehydration, drought, thirst, thirstiness

dry out *or* **up** *verb* = **become dry**, become unproductive, harden, mummify, shrivel up, wilt, wither, wizen

dual *adjective* = **twofold**, binary, coupled, double, duplex, duplicate, matched, paired, twin

dubious *adjective* **1** = **suspect**, dodgy (*Brit., Austral., & N.Z. informal*), fishy (*informal*), questionable, shady (*informal*), suspicious, undependable, unreliable, untrustworthy **2** = **doubtful**, ambiguous, debatable, dodgy

(*Brit., Austral., & N.Z. informal*), equivocal **3** = **unsure**, doubtful, hesitant, iffy (*informal*), leery (*slang*), sceptical, uncertain, unconvinced, undecided, wavering
➤ **Antonyms**
≠ **suspect**: dependable, reliable, trustworthy ≠ **unsure**: certain, definite, positive, sure

duck *verb* **1** = **bob**, bend, bow, crouch, dodge, drop, lower, stoop **2** = **plunge**, dip, dive, douse, dunk, immerse, souse, submerge, wet **3** *Informal* = **dodge**, avoid, body-swerve (*Scot.*), escape, evade, shirk, shun, sidestep

duct *noun* = **pipe**, canal, channel, conduit, funnel, passage, tube

dud *Informal* ♦ *noun* **1** = **failure**, clinker (*slang, chiefly U.S.*), clunker (*informal*), flop (*informal*), washout (*informal*) ♦ *adjective* **2** = **useless**, broken, bust (*informal*), duff (*Brit. informal*), failed, inoperative, kaput (*informal*), not functioning, valueless, worthless

dudgeon *noun* in high dudgeon = **indignant**, angry, choked, fuming, offended, resentful, vexed

due *adjective* **1** = **expected**, expected to arrive, scheduled **2** = **payable**, in arrears, outstanding, owed, owing, unpaid **3** = **fitting**, appropriate, becoming, bounden, deserved, fit, just, justified, merited, obligatory, proper, requisite, right, rightful, suitable, well-earned ♦ *noun* **4** = **right(s)**, comeuppance (*slang*), deserts, merits, prerogative, privilege ♦ *adverb* **5** = **directly**, dead, direct, exactly, straight, undeviatingly

duel *noun* **1** = **single combat**, affair of honour **2** = **contest**, clash, competition, encounter, engagement, fight, head-to-head, rivalry ♦ *verb* **3** = **fight**, clash, compete, contend, contest, lock horns, rival, struggle, vie with

dues *plural noun* = **membership fee**, charge, charges, contribution, fee, levy

duffer *noun Informal* = **clot** (*Brit. informal*), blunderer, booby, bungler, clod, galoot (*slang, chiefly U.S.*), lubber, lummox (*informal*), oaf

dulcet *adjective* = **sweet**, agreeable, charming, delightful, euphonious, harmonious, honeyed, mellifluent, mellifluous, melodious, musical, pleasant, pleasing, soothing

dull *adjective* **1** = **boring**, as dry as dust, commonplace, dozy, dreary, dry, flat, ho-hum (*informal*), humdrum, mind-numbing, monotonous, plain, prosaic, run-of-the-mill, tedious, tiresome,

unimaginative, uninteresting, vapid **2
= stupid**, braindead (*informal*), daft, dense,
dim, dim-witted (*informal*), doltish, dozy
(*Brit. informal*), obtuse, slow, stolid, thick,
unintelligent **3 = cloudy**, dim, dismal,
gloomy, leaden, opaque, overcast, turbid **4
= lifeless**, apathetic, blank, callous, dead,
empty, heavy, indifferent, insensible,
insensitive, listless, passionless, slow,
sluggish, unresponsive, unsympathetic,
vacuous **5 = drab**, faded, feeble, murky,
muted, sombre, subdued, subfusc,
toned-down **6 = blunt**, blunted, dulled,
edgeless, not keen, not sharp,
unsharpened ♦ *verb* **7 = dampen**, deject,
depress, discourage, dishearten, dispirit,
sadden **8 = relieve**, allay, alleviate,
assuage, blunt, lessen, mitigate, moderate,
palliate, paralyse, soften, stupefy, take the
edge off **9 = cloud**, darken, dim, fade,
obscure, stain, sully, tarnish
➤ **Antonyms**
adjective ≠**boring**: exciting, interesting
≠**stupid**: bright, clever, intelligent, sharp
≠**cloudy**: bright ≠**lifeless**: active, full of
beans (*informal*), lively ≠**blunt**: sharp

duly *adverb* **1 = properly**, accordingly,
appropriately, befittingly, correctly,
decorously, deservedly, fittingly, rightfully,
suitably **2 = on time**, at the proper time,
punctually

dumb *adjective* **1 = mute**, at a loss for
words, inarticulate, mum, silent,
soundless, speechless, tongue-tied,
voiceless, wordless **2** *Informal* **= stupid**,
asinine, braindead (*informal*), dense,
dim-witted (*informal*), dozy (*Brit. informal*),
dull, foolish, obtuse, thick, unintelligent
➤ **Antonyms**
≠**mute**: articulate ≠**stupid**: bright, clever,
intelligent, quick-witted, smart

dumbfounded, dumfounded *adjective*
= amazed, astonished, astounded, at sea,
bewildered, bowled over (*informal*),
breathless, confounded, confused, dumb,
flabbergasted (*informal*), flummoxed,
gobsmacked (*Brit. slang*), knocked for six
(*informal*), knocked sideways (*informal*),
lost for words, nonplussed, overcome,
overwhelmed, speechless, staggered,
startled, stunned, taken aback, thrown,
thunderstruck

dummy *noun* **1 = model**, figure, form, lay
figure, manikin, mannequin **2 = copy**,
counterfeit, duplicate, imitation, sham,
substitute **3** *Slang* **= fool**, berk (*Brit. slang*),
blockhead, charlie (*Brit. informal*), coot,
dickhead (*slang*), dickwit (*slang*), dimwit
(*informal*), dipstick (*Brit. slang*), divvy (*Brit.
slang*), dolt, dork (*slang*), dullard,
dumb-ass (*slang*), dunce, dweeb (*U.S.*

slang), fathead (*informal*), fuckwit (*taboo
slang*), geek (*slang*), gobshite (*Irish taboo
slang*), gonzo (*slang*), idiot, jerk (*slang,
chiefly U.S. & Canad.*), lamebrain
(*informal*), nerd *or* nurd (*slang*), nitwit
(*informal*), numbskull *or* numskull, numpty
(*Scot. informal*), oaf, pillock (*Brit. slang*),
plank (*Brit. slang*), plonker (*slang*), prat
(*slang*), prick (*slang*), schmuck (*U.S.
slang*), simpleton, wally (*slang*), weenie
(*U.S. informal*) ♦ *adjective* **4 = imitation**,
artificial, bogus, fake, false, mock, phoney
or phony (*informal*), sham, simulated **5
= practice**, mock, simulated, trial

dump *verb* **1 = drop**, deposit, fling down,
let fall, throw down **2 = get rid of**, coup
(*Scot.*), discharge, dispose of, ditch
(*slang*), empty out, jettison, scrap, throw
away *or* out, tip, unload ♦ *noun* **3
= rubbish tip**, junkyard, refuse heap,
rubbish heap, tip **4** *Informal* **= pigsty**, hole
(*informal*), hovel, joint (*slang*), mess,
shack, shanty, slum

dumps *plural noun* As in **down in the
dumps** **= low spirits**, blues, dejection,
depression, despondency, dolour, gloom,
gloominess, melancholy, mopes, sadness,
the hump (*Brit. informal*), unhappiness,
woe

dunce *noun* **= simpleton**, ass, blockhead,
bonehead (*slang*), dimwit (*informal*), dolt,
donkey, duffer (*informal*), dullard,
dunderhead, fathead (*informal*), goose
(*informal*), halfwit, ignoramus, lamebrain
(*informal*), loon (*informal*), moron,
nincompoop, nitwit (*informal*), numbskull
or numskull, oaf, thickhead

dungeon *noun* **= prison**, cage, calaboose
(*U.S. informal*), cell, donjon, lockup,
oubliette, vault

duplicate *adjective* **1 = identical**,
corresponding, matched, matching, twin,
twofold ♦ *noun* **2 = copy**, carbon copy,
clone, dead ringer (*slang*), double,
facsimile, fax, likeness, lookalike, match,
mate, photocopy, Photostat (*Trademark*),
replica, reproduction, ringer (*slang*), twin,
Xerox (*Trademark*) ♦ *verb* **3 = copy**, clone,
double, echo, fax, photocopy, Photostat
(*Trademark*), reinvent the wheel, repeat,
replicate, reproduce, Xerox (*Trademark*)

duplicity *noun* **= deceit**, artifice, chicanery,
deception, dishonesty, dissimulation,
double-dealing, falsehood, fraud, guile,
hypocrisy, perfidy
➤ **Antonyms**
candour, honesty, straightforwardness

durability *noun* **= durableness**, constancy,
endurance, imperishability, lastingness,
permanence, persistence

durable *adjective* = **long-lasting**, abiding, constant, dependable, enduring, fast, firm, fixed, hard-wearing, lasting, permanent, persistent, reliable, resistant, sound, stable, strong, sturdy, substantial, tough
➤ **Antonyms**
breakable, brittle, delicate, fragile, impermanent, perishable, weak

duration *noun* = **length**, extent, period, span, spell, stretch, term, time

duress *noun* **1** = **pressure**, coercion, compulsion, constraint, threat **2** = **imprisonment**, captivity, confinement, constraint, hardship, incarceration, restraint

dusk *noun* **1** = **twilight**, dark, evening, eventide, gloaming (*Scot. or poetic*), nightfall, sundown, sunset **2** *Poetic* = **shade**, darkness, gloom, murk, obscurity, shadowiness
➤ **Antonyms**
≠**twilight**: aurora (*poetic*), cockcrow, dawn, dawning, daybreak, daylight, morning, sunlight, sunup

dusky *adjective* **1** = **dark**, dark-complexioned, dark-hued, sable, swarthy **2** = **dim**, caliginous (*archaic*), cloudy, crepuscular, darkish, gloomy, murky, obscure, overcast, shadowy, shady, tenebrous, twilight, twilit, veiled

dust *noun* **1** = **grime**, fine fragments, grit, particles, powder, powdery dirt **2** = **earth**, dirt, ground, soil **3 bite the dust** *Informal* = **die**, drop dead, expire, fall in battle, pass away, perish **4 throw dust in the eyes of** = **mislead**, con (*slang*), confuse, deceive, fool, have (someone) on, hoodwink, take in (*informal*) ♦ *verb* **5** = **sprinkle**, cover, dredge, powder, scatter, sift, spray, spread

dusty *adjective* **1** = **dirty**, grubby, sooty, unclean, undusted, unswept **2** = **powdery**, chalky, crumbly, friable, granular, sandy

dutiful *adjective* = **conscientious**, compliant, deferential, devoted, docile, filial, obedient, punctilious, respectful, reverential, submissive
➤ **Antonyms**
disobedient, disrespectful, insubordinate, remiss, uncaring

duty *noun* **1** = **responsibility**, assignment, business, calling, charge, engagement, function, job, mission, obligation, office, onus, pigeon (*informal*), province, role, service, task, work **2** = **loyalty**, allegiance, deference, obedience, respect, reverence **3** = **tax**, customs, due, excise, impost, levy, tariff, toll **4 be the duty of** = **be up to** (*informal*), behove (*archaic*), be incumbent upon, belong to, be (someone's) pigeon (*Brit. informal*), devolve upon, pertain to,

rest with **5 off duty** = **off work**, at leisure, free, off, on holiday **6 on duty** = **at work**, busy, engaged, on active service

dwarf *verb* **1** = **tower above** *or* **over**, dim, diminish, dominate, minimize, overshadow **2** = **stunt**, check, cultivate by bonsai, lower, retard ♦ *adjective* **3** = **miniature**, baby, bonsai, diminutive, dwarfed, Lilliputian, petite, pint-sized, pocket, small, teensy-weensy, teeny-weeny, tiny, undersized ♦ *noun* **4** = **midget**, bantam, homunculus, hop-o'-my-thumb, Lilliputian, manikin, munchkin (*informal, chiefly U.S.*), pygmy *or* pigmy, Tom Thumb **5** = **gnome**, goblin

dwell *verb* *Formal, literary* = **live**, abide, establish oneself, hang out (*informal*), inhabit, lodge, quarter, remain, reside, rest, settle, sojourn, stay, stop

dwelling *noun* *Formal, literary* = **home**, abode, domicile, dwelling house, establishment, habitation, house, lodging, pad (*slang*), quarters, residence

dwell on *or* **upon** *verb* = **go on about** (*informal*), be engrossed in, continue, elaborate, emphasize, expatiate, harp on, linger over, tarry over

dwindle *verb* = **lessen**, abate, contract, decay, decline, decrease, die away, die down, die out, diminish, ebb, fade, fall, grow less, peter out, pine, shrink, shrivel, sink, subside, taper off, wane, waste away, weaken, wither
➤ **Antonyms**
advance, amplify, develop, dilate, enlarge, escalate, expand, grow, heighten, increase, magnify, multiply, swell, wax

dye *noun* **1** = **colouring**, colorant, colour, pigment, stain, tinge, tint ♦ *verb* **2** = **colour**, pigment, stain, tincture, tinge, tint

dyed-in-the-wool *adjective* = **confirmed**, complete, deep-dyed (*usually derogatory*), deep-rooted, die-hard, entrenched, established, inveterate, through-and-through

dying *adjective* = **expiring**, at death's door, ebbing, fading, failing, final, going, *in extremis*, moribund, mortal, not long for this world, passing, perishing, sinking

dynamic *adjective* = **energetic**, active, alive and kicking, driving, electric, forceful, full of beans (*informal*), go-ahead, go-getting (*informal*), high-octane (*informal*), high-powered, lively, magnetic, powerful, storming (*informal*), vigorous, vital, zippy (*informal*)
➤ **Antonyms**
apathetic, couldn't-care-less (*informal*), impassive, inactive, listless, sluggish,

torpid, undynamic, unenergetic

dynasty *noun* = **empire**, ascendancy, dominion, government, house, regime, rule, sovereignty, sway

E e

each *adjective* **1** = **every** ♦ *pronoun* **2** = **every one**, each and every one, each one, one and all ♦ *adverb* **3** = **apiece**, for each, from each, individually, per capita, per head, per person, respectively, singly, to each

eager *adjective* = **keen**, agog, anxious, ardent, athirst, avid, bright-eyed and bushy-tailed (*informal*), earnest, enthusiastic, fervent, fervid, greedy, hot, hungry, impatient, intent, keen as mustard, longing, raring, up for it (*informal*), vehement, yearning, zealous
  ➤ **Antonyms**
  apathetic, blasé, impassive, indifferent, lazy, nonchalant, opposed, unambitious, unconcerned, unenthusiastic, unimpressed, uninterested

eagerness *noun* = **keenness**, ardour, avidity, earnestness, enthusiasm, fervour, greediness, heartiness, hunger, impatience, impetuosity, intentness, longing, thirst, vehemence, yearning, zeal

ear *noun* **1** = **sensitivity**, appreciation, discrimination, musical perception, taste **2** = **attention**, consideration, hearing, heed, notice, regard

early *adjective* **1** = **premature**, advanced, forward, untimely **2** = **primitive**, primeval, primordial, undeveloped, young ♦ *adverb* **3** = **too soon**, ahead of time, beforehand, betimes (*archaic*), in advance, in good time, prematurely
  ➤ **Antonyms**
  adjective ≠**primitive**: developed, mature, ripe, seasoned ♦ *adverb* ≠**too soon**: behind, belated, late, overdue, tardy

earmark *verb* = **set aside**, allocate, designate, flag, label, mark out, reserve

earn *verb* **1** = **make**, bring in, collect, draw, gain, get, gross, net, obtain, procure, realize, reap, receive **2** = **deserve**, acquire, attain, be entitled to, be worthy of, merit, rate, warrant, win

earnest[1] *adjective* **1** = **serious**, close, constant, determined, firm, fixed, grave, intent, resolute, resolved, sincere, solemn, stable, staid, steady, thoughtful **2** = **heartfelt**, ablaze, ardent, devoted, eager, enthusiastic, fervent, fervid, impassioned, keen, keen as mustard, passionate, purposeful, urgent, vehement, warm, zealous ♦ *noun* **3** *As in* **in earnest** = **seriousness**, determination, reality, resolution, sincerity, truth
  ➤ **Antonyms**
  adjective ≠**serious**: flippant, frivolous, insincere, trifling ≠**heartfelt**: apathetic, couldn't-care-less, half-hearted, indifferent, unconcerned, unenthusiastic, uninterested ♦ *noun* ≠**seriousness**: apathy, indifference, unconcern

earnest[2] *noun* *Old-fashioned* = **down payment**, assurance, deposit, earnest money (*Law*), foretaste, guarantee, pledge, promise, security, token

earnings *plural noun* = **income**, emolument, gain, pay, proceeds, profits, receipts, remuneration, return, reward, salary, stipend, takings, wages

earth *noun* **1** = **world**, globe, orb, planet, sphere, terrestrial sphere **2** = **soil**, clay, clod, dirt, ground, land, loam, mould, sod, topsoil, turf

earthenware *noun* = **crockery**, ceramics, crocks, pots, pottery, terracotta

earthly *adjective* **1** = **worldly**, human, material, mortal, non-spiritual, profane, secular, temporal **2** *Informal* = **possible**, conceivable, feasible, imaginable, likely, practical **3** = **terrestrial**, mundane, sublunary, tellurian, telluric, terrene, worldly **4** = **carnal**, base, fleshly, gross, low, materialistic, physical, sensual, sordid, vile
  ➤ **Antonyms**
  ≠**worldly**: ethereal, heavenly, immaterial, immortal, otherworldly, spiritual, supernatural, unearthly

earthy *adjective* = **crude**, bawdy, coarse, raunchy (*slang*), ribald, robust, uninhibited, unsophisticated

ease *noun* **1** = **effortlessness**, easiness, facility, readiness, simplicity **2** = **peace of mind**, calmness, comfort, content, contentment, enjoyment, happiness, peace, quiet, quietude, serenity, tranquillity **3** = **leisure**, relaxation, repose, rest, restfulness **4** = **freedom**, flexibility, informality, liberty, naturalness, unaffectedness, unconstraint, unreservedness ♦ *verb* **5** = **relieve**, abate, allay, alleviate, appease, assuage, calm, comfort, disburden, lessen, lighten,

mitigate, moderate, mollify, pacify, palliate, quiet, relax, relent, slacken, soothe, still, tranquillize **6 = make easier**, aid, assist, expedite, facilitate, forward, further, give a leg up (*informal*), lessen the labour of, simplify, smooth, speed up **7 = move carefully**, edge, guide, inch, manoeuvre, slide, slip, squeeze, steer
➤ **Antonyms**
≠**effortlessness**: arduousness, awkwardness, clumsiness, difficulty, effort, exertion, toil ≠**peace of mind**: agitation, awkwardness, clumsiness, discomfort, disturbance, tension *noun* ≠**leisure**: difficulty, discomfort, hardship, irritation, pain, poverty, tribulation ≠**freedom**: awkwardness, clumsiness, constraint, formality ♦ *verb* ≠**relieve**: aggravate, discomfort, exacerbate, irritate, worsen ≠**make easier**: hinder, retard

easily *adverb* **1 = without difficulty**, comfortably, effortlessly, facilely, like a knife through butter, readily, simply, smoothly, standing on one's head, with ease, with one hand tied behind one's back, with one's eyes closed *or* shut, without trouble **2 = without a doubt**, absolutely, beyond question, by far, certainly, clearly, definitely, doubtlessly, far and away, indisputably, indubitably, plainly, surely, undeniably, undoubtedly, unequivocally, unquestionably

easy *adjective* **1 = not difficult**, a bed of roses, a piece of cake (*informal*), a piece of piss (*taboo slang*), a pushover (*slang*), child's play (*informal*), clear, easy-peasy (*slang*), effortless, facile, light, no bother, no trouble, painless, plain sailing, simple, smooth, straightforward, uncomplicated, undemanding **2 = carefree**, calm, comfortable, contented, cushy (*informal*), easeful, leisurely, peaceful, pleasant, quiet, relaxed, satisfied, serene, tranquil, undisturbed, untroubled, unworried, well-to-do **3 = tolerant**, easy-going, flexible, indulgent, lenient, liberal, light, mild, permissive, unburdensome, unoppressive **4 = relaxed**, affable, casual, easy-going, friendly, gentle, graceful, gracious, informal, laid-back (*informal*), mild, natural, open, pleasant, smooth, tolerant, unaffected, unceremonious, unconstrained, undemanding, unforced, unpretentious **5** *Informal* = **accommodating**, amenable, biddable, compliant, docile, gullible, manageable, pliant, soft, submissive, suggestible, susceptible, tractable, trusting, yielding
➤ **Antonyms**
≠**not difficult**: arduous, complex, demanding, difficult, exacting, exhausting,

formidable, hard, impossible, onerous, stiff ≠**carefree**: difficult, insecure, stressful, uncomfortable, worried ≠**tolerant**: demanding, dictatorial, difficult, exacting, hard, harsh, inflexible, intolerant, rigid, stern, strict, unyielding ≠**relaxed**: affected, anxious, forced, formal, self-conscious, stiff, uncomfortable, unnatural, worried ≠**accommodating**: difficult, impossible, unyielding

easy-going *adjective* = **relaxed**, amenable, calm, carefree, casual, complacent, easy, easy-oasy (*slang*), even-tempered, flexible, happy-go-lucky, indulgent, insouciant, laid-back (*informal*), lenient, liberal, mild, moderate, nonchalant, permissive, placid, serene, tolerant, unconcerned, uncritical, undemanding, unhurried
➤ **Antonyms**
anxious, edgy, fussy, hung-up (*slang*), intolerant, irritated, nervy (*Brit. informal*), neurotic, on edge, strict, tense, uptight (*informal*)

eat *verb* **1 = consume**, chew, devour, gobble, ingest, munch, scoff (*slang*), swallow **2 = have a meal**, break bread, chow down (*slang*), dine, feed, take food, take nourishment **3 = destroy**, corrode, crumble, decay, dissolve, erode, rot, waste away, wear away **4 eat one's words = retract**, abjure, recant, rescind, take (a statement) back

eavesdrop *verb* = **listen in**, bug (*informal*), earwig (*informal*), monitor, overhear, snoop (*informal*), spy, tap

ebb *verb* **1 = flow back**, abate, fall away, fall back, go out, recede, retire, retreat, retrocede, sink, subside, wane, withdraw **2 = decline**, decay, decrease, degenerate, deteriorate, diminish, drop, dwindle, fade away, fall away, flag, lessen, peter out, shrink, sink, slacken, weaken ♦ *noun* **3 = flowing back**, ebb tide, going out, low tide, low water, reflux, regression, retreat, retrocession, subsidence, wane, waning, withdrawal **4 = decline**, decay, decrease, degeneration, deterioration, diminution, drop, dwindling, fading away, flagging, lessening, petering out, shrinkage, sinking, slackening, weakening

eccentric *adjective* **1 = odd**, aberrant, abnormal, anomalous, bizarre, capricious, erratic, freakish, idiosyncratic, irregular, oddball (*informal*), off the rails, off-the-wall (*slang*), outlandish, outré, peculiar, queer (*informal*), quirky, rum (*Brit. slang*), singular, strange, uncommon, unconventional, wacko (*slang*), weird, whimsical ♦ *noun* **2 = crank** (*informal*), card (*informal*), case (*informal*), character

(*informal*), freak (*informal*), kook (*U.S. & Canad. informal*), loose cannon, nonconformist, nut (*slang*), oddball (*informal*), odd fish (*informal*), oddity, queer fish (*Brit. informal*), rum customer (*Brit. slang*), screwball (*slang, chiefly U.S. & Canad.*), wacko (*slang*), weirdo or weirdie (*informal*)
➤ **Antonyms**
adjective ≠**odd**: average, conventional, normal, ordinary, regular, run-of-the-mill, straightforward, typical

eccentricity *noun* = **oddity**, aberration, abnormality, anomaly, bizarreness, caprice, capriciousness, foible, freakishness, idiosyncrasy, irregularity, nonconformity, oddness, outlandishness, peculiarity, queerness (*informal*), quirk, singularity, strangeness, unconventionality, waywardness, weirdness, whimsicality, whimsicalness

ecclesiastic *noun* **1** = **clergyman**, churchman, cleric, divine, holy man, man of the cloth, minister, parson, pastor, priest ◆ *adjective* **2** *Also* **ecclesiastical** = **clerical**, church, churchly, divine, holy, pastoral, priestly, religious, spiritual

echo *noun* **1** = **repetition**, answer, reverberation **2** = **copy**, imitation, mirror image, parallel, reflection, reiteration, reproduction **3** = **reminder**, allusion, evocation, hint, intimation, memory, suggestion, trace **4** *often plural* = **repercussion**, aftereffect, aftermath, consequence ◆ *verb* **5** = **repeat**, resound, reverberate **6** = **copy**, ape, imitate, mirror, parallel, parrot, recall, reflect, reiterate, reproduce, resemble, ring, second

eclipse *noun* **1** = **obscuring**, darkening, dimming, extinction, occultation, shading **2** = **decline**, diminution, failure, fall, loss ◆ *verb* **3** = **surpass**, exceed, excel, outdo, outshine, put in the shade (*informal*), transcend **4** = **obscure**, blot out, cloud, darken, dim, extinguish, overshadow, shroud, veil

economic *adjective* **1** = **financial**, business, commercial, industrial, mercantile, trade **2** = **profitable**, money-making, productive, profit-making, remunerative, solvent, viable **3** = **monetary**, bread-and-butter (*informal*), budgetary, financial, fiscal, material, pecuniary **4** *Informal Also* **economical** = **inexpensive**, cheap, fair, low, low-priced, modest, reasonable

economical *adjective* **1** *Also* **economic** = **inexpensive**, cheap, fair, low, low-priced, modest, reasonable **2** = **thrifty**, careful, economizing, frugal, prudent, saving, scrimping, sparing **3**

= **cost-effective**, efficient, money-saving, neat, sparing, time-saving, unwasteful, work-saving
➤ **Antonyms**
≠**inexpensive**: exorbitant, expensive, unprofitable ≠**thrifty**: extravagant, generous, imprudent, lavish, profligate, spendthrift, uneconomical, unthrifty, wasteful ≠**cost-effective**: loss-making, uneconomical, unprofitable, wasteful

economize *verb* = **cut back**, be economical, be frugal, be on a shoestring, be sparing, draw in one's horns, husband, pull in one's horns, retrench, save, scrimp, tighten one's belt
➤ **Antonyms**
be extravagant, push the boat out (*informal*), spend, splurge, squander

economy *noun* = **thrift**, frugality, husbandry, parsimony, providence, prudence, restraint, retrenchment, saving, sparingness, thriftiness

ecstasy *noun* = **rapture**, bliss, delight, elation, enthusiasm, euphoria, exaltation, fervour, frenzy, joy, ravishment, rhapsody, seventh heaven, trance, transport
➤ **Antonyms**
affliction, agony, anguish, distress, hell, misery, pain, suffering, torment, torture

ecstatic *adjective* = **rapturous**, blissed out, blissful, cock-a-hoop, delirious, elated, enraptured, enthusiastic, entranced, euphoric, fervent, floating on air, frenzied, in exaltation, in seventh heaven, in transports of delight, joyful, joyous, on cloud nine (*informal*), overjoyed, over the moon (*informal*), rhapsodic, sent, transported, walking on air

eddy *noun* **1** = **swirl**, counter-current, counterflow, tideway, undertow, vortex, whirlpool ◆ *verb* **2** = **swirl**, whirl

edge *noun* **1** = **border**, bound, boundary, brim, brink, contour, flange, fringe, limit, line, lip, margin, outline, perimeter, periphery, rim, side, threshold, verge **2** = **sharpness**, acuteness, animation, bite, effectiveness, force, incisiveness, interest, keenness, point, pungency, sting, urgency, zest **3** *As in* **have the edge on** = **advantage**, ascendancy, dominance, lead, superiority, upper hand **4** *on* **edge** = **nervous**, antsy (*informal*), apprehensive, eager, edgy, excited, ill at ease, impatient, irritable, keyed up, on tenterhooks, tense, tetchy, twitchy (*informal*), uptight (*informal*), wired (*slang*) ◆ *verb* **5** = **border**, bind, fringe, hem, rim, shape, trim **6** = **inch**, creep, ease, sidle, steal, work, worm **7** = **sharpen**, hone, strop, whet

edgy *adjective* = **nervous**, antsy (*informal*),

anxious, ill at ease, irascible, irritable, keyed up, nervy (*Brit. informal*), neurotic, on edge, on pins and needles, on tenterhooks, restive, tense, tetchy, touchy, twitchy (*informal*), uptight (*informal*), wired (*slang*)

edible *adjective* = **eatable**, comestible (*rare*), digestible, esculent, fit to eat, good, harmless, palatable, wholesome
➤ **Antonyms**
baneful, harmful, indigestible, inedible, noxious, pernicious, poisonous, uneatable

edict *noun* = **decree**, act, canon, command, demand, dictate, dictum, enactment, fiat, injunction, law, mandate, manifesto, order, ordinance, proclamation, pronouncement, pronunciamento, regulation, ruling, statute, ukase (*rare*)

edifice *noun* = **building**, construction, erection, fabric (*rare*), habitation, house, pile, structure

edify *verb* = **instruct**, educate, elevate, enlighten, guide, improve, inform, nurture, school, teach, uplift

edit *verb* **1** = **revise**, adapt, annotate, censor, check, condense, correct, emend, polish, redact, rephrase, rewrite **2** = **put together**, assemble, compose, rearrange, reorder, select

edition *noun* = **version**, copy, impression, issue, number, printing, programme (*TV, Radio*), volume

educate *verb* = **teach**, civilize, coach, cultivate, develop, discipline, drill, edify, enlighten, exercise, foster, improve, indoctrinate, inform, instruct, mature, rear, school, train, tutor

educated *adjective* **1** = **taught**, coached, informed, instructed, nurtured, schooled, tutored **2** = **cultured**, civilized, cultivated, enlightened, experienced, informed, knowledgeable, learned, lettered, literary, polished, refined, sophisticated, tasteful
➤ **Antonyms**
≠**taught**: ignorant, illiterate, uneducated, unlettered, unread, unschooled, untaught ≠**cultured**: benighted, lowbrow, philistine, uncultivated, uncultured, uneducated

education *noun* = **teaching**, breeding, civilization, coaching, cultivation, culture, development, discipline, drilling, edification, enlightenment, erudition, improvement, indoctrination, instruction, knowledge, nurture, scholarship, schooling, training, tuition, tutoring

educational *adjective* = **instructive**, cultural, didactic, edifying, educative, enlightening, heuristic, improving, informative

educative *adjective* = **instructive**, didactic, edifying, educational, enlightening, heuristic, improving, informative

eerie *adjective* = **frightening**, awesome, creepy (*informal*), eldritch (*poetic*), fearful, ghostly, mysterious, scary (*informal*), spectral, spooky (*informal*), strange, uncanny, unearthly, uneasy, weird

efface *verb* **1** = **obliterate**, annihilate, blot out, cancel, cross out, delete, destroy, dim, eradicate, erase, excise, expunge, extirpate, raze, rub out, wipe out **2 efface oneself** = **make oneself inconspicuous**, be bashful, be diffident, be modest, be retiring, be timid, be unassertive, humble oneself, lower oneself, withdraw

effect *noun* **1** = **result**, aftermath, conclusion, consequence, end result, event, fruit, issue, outcome, upshot **2** = **power**, clout (*informal*), effectiveness, efficacy, efficiency, fact, force, influence, reality, strength, use, validity, vigour, weight **3** = **operation**, action, enforcement, execution, force, implementation **4** = **impression**, drift, essence, impact, import, meaning, purport, purpose, sense, significance, tenor **5 in effect** = **in fact**, actually, effectively, essentially, for practical purposes, in actuality, in reality, in truth, really, to all intents and purposes, virtually **6 take effect** = **produce results**, become operative, begin, come into force, work ♦ *verb* **7** = **bring about**, accomplish, achieve, actuate, carry out, cause, complete, consummate, create, effectuate, execute, fulfil, give rise to, initiate, make, perform, produce

effective *adjective* **1** = **efficient**, able, active, adequate, capable, competent, effectual, efficacious, energetic, operative, productive, serviceable, useful **2** = **in operation**, active, actual, current, in effect, in execution, in force, operative, real **3** = **powerful**, cogent, compelling, convincing, emphatic, forceful, forcible, impressive, moving, persuasive, potent, striking, telling
➤ **Antonyms**
≠**efficient**: futile, inadequate, incompetent, ineffective, inefficient, insufficient, otiose, unimpressive, unproductive, useless, vain, worthless ≠**in operation**: inactive, inoperative ≠**powerful**: feeble, ineffectual, pathetic, powerless, tame, weak

effectiveness *noun* = **power**, bottom, capability, clout (*informal*), cogency, effect, efficacy, efficiency, force, influence, potency, strength, success, use, validity, vigour, weight

effects *plural noun* = **belongings**, chattels, furniture, gear, goods, movables, paraphernalia, possessions, property, things, trappings

effeminacy *noun* = **womanliness**, delicacy, femininity, softness, tenderness, unmanliness, weakness, womanishness

effeminate *adjective* = **womanly**, camp (*informal*), delicate, feminine, poofy (*slang*), sissy, soft, tender, unmanly, weak, wimpish *or* wimpy (*informal*), womanish, womanlike, wussy (*slang*)
➤ **Antonyms**
butch (*slang*), he-man (*informal*), macho, manly, virile

effervesce *verb* = **bubble**, ferment, fizz, foam, froth, sparkle

effervescence *noun* **1** = **bubbling**, ferment, fermentation, fizz, foam, foaming, froth, frothing, sparkle **2** = **liveliness**, animation, brio, buoyancy, ebullience, enthusiasm, excitedness, excitement, exhilaration, exuberance, gaiety, high spirits, pizzazz *or* pizazz (*informal*), vim (*slang*), vitality, vivacity, zing (*informal*)

effervescent *adjective* **1** = **bubbling**, bubbly, carbonated, fermenting, fizzing, fizzy, foaming, foamy, frothing, frothy, sparkling **2** = **lively**, animated, bubbly, buoyant, ebullient, enthusiastic, excited, exhilarated, exuberant, gay, in high spirits, irrepressible, merry, vital, vivacious, zingy (*informal*)
➤ **Antonyms**
≠**bubbling**: flat, flavourless, insipid, stale, watery, weak ≠**lively**: boring, dull, flat, insipid, jejune, lacklustre, lifeless, spiritless, stale, unexciting, vapid

effete *adjective* **1** = **decadent**, corrupt, debased, decayed, decrepit, degenerate, dissipated, enervated, enfeebled, feeble, ineffectual, overrefined, spoiled, weak **2** = **worn out**, burnt out, drained, enervated, exhausted, played out, spent, used up, wasted **3** = **sterile**, barren, fruitless, infecund, infertile, unfruitful, unproductive, unprolific

efficacious *adjective* = **effective**, active, adequate, capable, competent, effectual, efficient, energetic, operative, potent, powerful, productive, serviceable, successful, useful
➤ **Antonyms**
abortive, futile, ineffective, ineffectual, inefficacious, unavailing, unproductive, unsuccessful, useless

efficacy *noun* = **effectiveness**, ability, capability, competence, effect, efficaciousness, efficiency, energy, force, influence, potency, power, strength, success, use, vigour, virtue, weight

efficiency *noun* = **competence**, ability, adeptness, capability, economy, effectiveness, efficacy, power, productivity, proficiency, readiness, skilfulness, skill

efficient *adjective* = **competent**, able, adept, businesslike, capable, economic, effective, effectual, organized, powerful, productive, proficient, ready, skilful, well-organized, workmanlike
➤ **Antonyms**
cowboy (*informal*), disorganized, incompetent, ineffectual, inefficient, inept, slipshod, sloppy, unbusinesslike, unproductive, wasteful

effigy *noun* = **likeness**, dummy, figure, guy, icon, idol, image, picture, portrait, representation, statue

effluent *noun* **1** = **waste**, effluvium, pollutant, sewage **2** = **outflow**, discharge, effluence, efflux, emanation, emission, exhalation, flow, issue, outpouring
♦ *adjective* **3** = **outflowing**, discharged, emanating, emitted

effort *noun* **1** = **exertion**, application, blood, sweat, and tears (*informal*), elbow grease (*facetious*), endeavour, energy, force, labour, pains, power, strain, stress, stretch, striving, struggle, toil, travail (*literary*), trouble, work **2** = **attempt**, endeavour, essay, go (*informal*), shot (*informal*), stab (*informal*), try **3** = **creation**, accomplishment, achievement, act, deed, feat, job, product, production

effortless *adjective* = **easy**, easy-peasy (*slang*), facile, painless, plain sailing, simple, smooth, uncomplicated, undemanding, untroublesome
➤ **Antonyms**
demanding, difficult, formidable, hard, onerous, uphill

effrontery *noun* = **insolence**, arrogance, audacity, brazenness, cheek (*informal*), impertinence, impudence, nerve, presumption, temerity

effulgent *adjective* = **radiant**, beaming, blazing, bright, brilliant, Day-Glo, dazzling, flaming, fluorescent, fulgent (*poetic*), glowing, incandescent, lucent, luminous, lustrous, refulgent (*literary*), resplendent, shining, splendid, vivid

effusion *noun* **1** = **talk**, address, outpouring, speech, utterance, writing **2** = **outpouring**, discharge, effluence, efflux, emission, gush, issue, outflow, shedding, stream

effusive *adjective* = **demonstrative**, ebullient, enthusiastic, expansive, extravagant, exuberant, free-flowing, fulsome, gushing, lavish, overflowing, profuse, talkative, unreserved, unrestrained, wordy

egg on *verb* = **encourage**, exhort, goad, incite, prod, prompt, push, spur, urge
➤ **Antonyms**
deter, discourage, dissuade, hold back, put off, talk out of

egocentric *adjective* = **self-centred**, egoistic, egoistical, egotistic, egotistical, selfish

egotism, egoism *noun* = **self-centredness**, conceitedness, egocentricity, egomania, narcissism, self-absorption, self-admiration, self-conceit, self-esteem, self-importance, self-interest, selfishness, self-love, self-praise, self-regard, self-seeking, superiority, vainglory, vanity

egotist, egoist *noun* = **egomaniac**, bighead (*informal*), blowhard (*informal*), boaster, braggadocio, braggart, narcissist, self-admirer, self-seeker, swaggerer

egotistic, egotistical, egoistic *or* **egoistical** *adjective* = **self-centred**, boasting, bragging, conceited, egocentric, egomaniacal, full of oneself, narcissistic, opinionated, self-absorbed, self-admiring, self-important, self-seeking, superior, vain, vainglorious

egress *noun Formal* = **exit**, departure, emergence, escape, exodus, issue, outlet, passage out, vent, way out, withdrawal

eject *verb* **1** = **emit**, cast out, discharge, disgorge, expel, spew, spout, throw out, vomit **2** = **throw out**, banish, boot out (*informal*), bounce (*slang*), deport, dispossess, drive out, evacuate, evict, exile, expel, give the bum's rush (*slang*), oust, relegate, remove, show one the door, throw out on one's ear (*informal*), turn out **3** = **dismiss**, discharge, dislodge, fire (*informal*), get rid of, kick out (*informal*), oust, sack (*informal*), throw out

ejection *noun* **1** = **emission**, casting out, disgorgement, expulsion, spouting, throwing out **2** = **expulsion**, banishment, deportation, dispossession, evacuation, eviction, exile, ouster (*Law*), removal, the bum's rush (*slang*) **3** = **dismissal**, discharge, dislodgement, firing (*informal*), sacking (*informal*), the boot (*slang*), the sack (*informal*)

eke out *verb* = **be sparing with**, be economical with, be frugal with, economize on, husband, stretch out

elaborate *adjective* **1** = **detailed**, careful, exact, intricate, laboured, minute, painstaking, perfected, precise, skilful,

studied, thorough **2** = **complicated**, complex, decorated, detailed, extravagant, fancy, fussy, involved, ornamented, ornate, ostentatious, showy ◆ *verb* **3** = **expand (upon)**, add detail, amplify, complicate, decorate, develop, devise, embellish, enhance, enlarge, flesh out, garnish, improve, ornament, polish, produce, refine, work out
➤ **Antonyms**
adjective ≠**complicated**: basic, minimal, modest, plain, severe, simple, unadorned, unembellished, unfussy ◆ *verb* ≠**expand (upon)**: abbreviate, condense, put in a nutshell, reduce to essentials, simplify, streamline, summarize, truncate

elapse *verb* = **pass**, glide by, go, go by, lapse, pass by, roll by, roll on, slip away, slip by

elastic *adjective* **1** = **flexible**, ductile, plastic, pliable, pliant, resilient, rubbery, springy, stretchable, stretchy, supple, tensile, yielding **2** = **adaptable**, accommodating, adjustable, complaisant, compliant, flexible, supple, tolerant, variable, yielding
➤ **Antonyms**
≠**flexible**: firm, immovable, inflexible, rigid, set, stiff, unyielding ≠**adaptable**: firm, immovable, inflexible, intractable, obdurate, resolute, rigid, set, stiff, strict, stringent, unyielding

elated *adjective* = **joyful**, animated, blissed out, blissful, cheered, cock-a-hoop, delighted, ecstatic, elevated, euphoric, excited, exhilarated, exultant, floating *or* walking on air, gleeful, in high spirits, in seventh heaven, joyous, jubilant, overjoyed, over the moon (*informal*), proud, puffed up, rapt, roused, sent
➤ **Antonyms**
dejected, depressed, discouraged, dispirited, downcast, down in the dumps (*informal*), miserable, sad, unhappy, woebegone

elation *noun* = **joy**, bliss, delight, ecstasy, euphoria, exaltation, exhilaration, exultation, glee, high spirits, joyfulness, joyousness, jubilation, rapture

elbow *noun* **1** = **joint**, angle, bend, corner, turn **2 at one's elbow** = **within reach**, at hand, close by, handy, near, to hand **3 out at elbow(s)** = **impoverished**, beggarly, down at heel, in rags, ragged, seedy, shabby, tattered **4 rub elbows with** = **associate**, fraternize, hang out (*informal*), hobnob, mingle, mix, socialize **5 up to the elbows** = **occupied**, absorbed, busy, engaged, engrossed, immersed, tied up, up to the ears, wrapped up ◆ *verb* **6**

= **push**, bump, crowd, hustle, jostle, knock, nudge, shoulder, shove

elbow room noun = **scope**, freedom, latitude, leeway, play, room, space

elder adjective 1 = **older**, ancient, earlier born, first-born, senior ♦ noun 2 = **older person**, senior 3 Presbyterianism = **church official**, office bearer, presbyter

elect verb 1 = **choose**, appoint, decide upon, designate, determine, opt for, pick, pick out, prefer, select, settle on, vote ♦ adjective 2 = **selected**, choice, chosen, elite, hand-picked, picked, preferred, select

election noun = **voting**, appointment, choice, choosing, decision, determination, judgment, preference, selection, vote

elector noun = **voter**, chooser, constituent, selector

electric adjective = **charged**, dynamic, exciting, high-octane (informal), rousing, stimulating, stirring, tense, thrilling

electrify verb = **startle**, amaze, animate, astonish, astound, excite, fire, galvanize, invigorate, jolt, rouse, shock, stimulate, stir, take one's breath away, thrill
➤ **Antonyms**
be tedious, bore, exhaust, fatigue, jade, send to sleep, tire, weary

elegance noun = **style**, beauty, courtliness, dignity, exquisiteness, gentility, grace, gracefulness, grandeur, luxury, polish, politeness, refinement, sumptuousness, taste

elegant adjective 1 = **stylish**, à la mode, artistic, beautiful, chic, choice, comely, courtly, cultivated, delicate, exquisite, fashionable, fine, genteel, graceful, handsome, luxurious, modish, nice, polished, refined, sumptuous, tasteful, urbane 2 = **ingenious**, appropriate, apt, clever, effective, neat, simple
➤ **Antonyms**
≠**stylish**: awkward, clumsy, clunky (informal), coarse, gauche, graceless, inelegant, misshapen, plain, tasteless, tawdry, ugly, uncouth, undignified, ungraceful, unrefined

elegy noun = **lament**, coronach (Scot. & Irish), dirge, keen, plaint (archaic), requiem, threnody

element noun 1 = **component**, basis, constituent, essential factor, factor, feature, ingredient, member, part, section, subdivision, unit 2 As in **in one's element** = **environment**, domain, field, habitat, medium, milieu, sphere

elementary adjective 1 = **simple**, clear, easy, facile, plain, rudimentary, straightforward, uncomplicated 2 = **basic**, bog-standard (informal), elemental, fundamental, initial, introductory, original, primary, rudimentary
➤ **Antonyms**
≠**simple**: complex, complicated, sophisticated ≠**basic**: advanced, higher, highly-developed, progressive, secondary

elements plural noun 1 = **basics**, essentials, foundations, fundamentals, nuts and bolts (informal), principles, rudiments 2 = **weather conditions**, atmospheric conditions, atmospheric forces, powers of nature

elevate verb 1 = **raise**, heighten, hoist, lift, lift up, uplift, upraise 2 = **promote**, advance, aggrandize, exalt, prefer, upgrade 3 = **cheer**, animate, boost, brighten, buoy up, elate, excite, exhilarate, hearten, lift up, perk up, raise, rouse, uplift

elevated adjective 1 = **high-minded**, dignified, exalted, grand, high, high-flown, inflated, lofty, noble, sublime 2 = **in high spirits**, animated, bright, cheerful, cheery, elated, excited, exhilarated, gleeful, overjoyed
➤ **Antonyms**
≠**high-minded**: humble, lowly, modest, simple

elevation noun 1 = **promotion**, advancement, aggrandizement, exaltation, preferment, upgrading 2 = **altitude**, height 3 = **rise**, acclivity, eminence, height, hill, hillock, mountain, rising ground

elicit verb 1 = **bring about**, bring forth, bring out, bring to light, call forth, cause, derive, evolve, give rise to 2 = **obtain**, draw out, educe, evoke, exact, extort, extract, wrest

eligible adjective = **qualified**, acceptable, appropriate, desirable, fit, preferable, proper, suitable, suited, worthy
➤ **Antonyms**
inappropriate, ineligible, unacceptable, unqualified, unsuitable, unsuited

eliminate verb 1 = **get rid of**, cut out, dispose of, do away with, eradicate, exterminate, get shot of, remove, stamp out, take out, wipe from the face of the earth 2 = **drop**, axe (informal), dispense with, disregard, eject, exclude, expel, ignore, knock out, leave out, omit, put out, reject, throw out 3 Slang = **murder**, annihilate, blow away (slang, chiefly U.S.), bump off (slang), kill, liquidate, rub out (U.S. slang), slay, take out (slang), terminate, waste (informal)

elite noun 1 = **best**, aristocracy, cream, crème de la crème, elect, flower, gentry, high society, nobility, pick, upper class

♦ *adjective* **2** = **best**, aristocratic, choice, crack (*slang*), elect, exclusive, first-class, noble, pick, selected, upper-class
➤ **Antonyms**
noun ≠**best**: dregs, hoi polloi, rabble, riffraff

elitist *adjective* **1** = **snobbish**, exclusive, selective ♦ *noun* **2** = **snob**

elixir *noun* = **panacea**, nostrum

elocution *noun* = **diction**, articulation, declamation, delivery, enunciation, oratory, pronunciation, public speaking, rhetoric, speech, speechmaking, utterance, voice production

elongate *verb* = **make longer**, draw out, extend, lengthen, prolong, protract, stretch

elope *verb* = **run away**, abscond, bolt, decamp, disappear, escape, leave, run off, slip away, steal away

eloquence *noun* = **expressiveness**, expression, fluency, forcefulness, oratory, persuasiveness, rhetoric, way with words

eloquent *adjective* **1** = **silver-tongued**, articulate, fluent, forceful, graceful, moving, persuasive, stirring, well-expressed **2** = **expressive**, meaningful, pregnant, revealing, suggestive, telling, vivid
➤ **Antonyms**
≠**silver-tongued**: faltering, halting, hesitant, inarticulate, speechless, stumbling, tongue-tied, wordless

elsewhere *adverb* = **in** *or* **to another place**, abroad, away, hence (*archaic*), not here, somewhere else

elucidate *verb* = **clarify**, annotate, clear the air, clear up, explain, explicate, expound, gloss, illuminate, illustrate, interpret, make plain, shed *or* throw light upon, spell out, unfold

elucidation *noun* = **clarification**, annotation, comment, commentary, explanation, explication, exposition, gloss, illumination, illustration, interpretation

elude *verb* **1** = **escape**, avoid, body-swerve (*Scot.*), circumvent, dodge, duck (*informal*), evade, flee, get away from, outrun, shirk, shun, slip through one's fingers, slip through the net **2** = **baffle**, be beyond (someone), confound, escape, foil, frustrate, puzzle, stump, thwart

elusive *adjective* **1** = **difficult to catch**, shifty, slippery, tricky **2** = **indefinable**, baffling, fleeting, intangible, puzzling, subtle, transient, transitory **3** = **evasive**, ambiguous, deceitful, deceptive, elusory, equivocal, fallacious, fraudulent, illusory, misleading, oracular, unspecific

emaciated *adjective* = **skeletal**, atrophied, attenuate, attenuated, cadaverous, gaunt, haggard, lank, lean, macilent (*rare*), meagre, pinched, scrawny, thin, undernourished, wasted

emaciation *noun* = **thinness**, atrophy, attenuation, gauntness, haggardness, leanness, meagreness, scrawniness, wasting away

emanate *verb* **1** = **flow**, arise, come forth, derive, emerge, issue, originate, proceed, spring, stem **2** = **give out**, discharge, emit, exhale, give off, issue, radiate, send forth

emanation *noun* **1** = **flow**, arising, derivation, emergence, origination, proceeding **2** = **emission**, discharge, effluent, efflux, effusion, exhalation, radiation

emancipate *verb* = **free**, deliver, discharge, disencumber, disenthral, enfranchise, liberate, manumit, release, set free, unbridle, unchain, unfetter, unshackle
➤ **Antonyms**
bind, capture, enchain, enslave, enthral, fetter, shackle, subjugate, yoke

emancipation *noun* = **freedom**, deliverance, discharge, enfranchisement, liberation, liberty, manumission, release
➤ **Antonyms**
bondage, captivity, confinement, detention, enthralment, imprisonment, servitude, slavery, thraldom, vassalage

embalm *verb* **1** = **preserve**, mummify **2** = **enshrine**, cherish, consecrate, conserve, immortalize, store, treasure

embargo *noun* **1** = **ban**, bar, barrier, block, blockage, boycott, check, hindrance, impediment, interdict, interdiction, prohibition, proscription, restraint, restriction, stoppage ♦ *verb* **2** = **ban**, bar, block, boycott, check, impede, interdict, prohibit, proscribe, restrict, stop

embark *verb* **1** = **go aboard**, board ship, put on board, take on board, take ship **2** **embark on** *or* **upon** = **begin**, broach, commence, engage, enter, get the show on the road (*informal*), initiate, launch, plunge into, set about, set out, start, take up, undertake
➤ **Antonyms**
≠**go aboard**: alight, arrive, get off, go ashore, land, step out of

embarrass *verb* = **shame**, abash, chagrin, confuse, discomfit, discompose, disconcert, discountenance, distress, faze, fluster, humiliate, mortify, put out of countenance, show up (*informal*)

embarrassed *adjective* = **ashamed**, awkward, blushing, discomfited, disconcerted, humiliated, mortified, red-faced, self-conscious, sheepish

embarrassing *adjective* = **humiliating**, awkward, blush-making, compromising, cringe-making (*Brit. informal*), cringeworthy (*Brit. informal*), discomfiting, disconcerting, distressing, mortifying, sensitive, shameful, shaming, toe-curling (*slang*), touchy, tricky, uncomfortable

embarrassment *noun* 1 = **shame**, awkwardness, bashfulness, chagrin, confusion, discomfiture, discomposure, distress, humiliation, mortification, self-consciousness, showing up (*informal*) 2 = **predicament**, bind (*informal*), difficulty, mess, pickle (*informal*), scrape (*informal*)

embellish *verb* = **decorate**, adorn, beautify, bedeck, deck, dress up, elaborate, embroider, enhance, enrich, exaggerate, festoon, garnish, gild, gild the lily, grace, ornament, tart up (*slang*), varnish

embellishment *noun* = **decoration**, adornment, elaboration, embroidery, enhancement, enrichment, exaggeration, gilding, ornament, ornamentation, trimming

embezzle *verb* = **misappropriate**, abstract, appropriate, defalcate (*Law*), filch, have one's hand in the till (*informal*), misapply, misuse, peculate, pilfer, purloin, rip off (*slang*), steal

embezzlement *noun* = **misappropriation**, abstraction, appropriation, defalcation (*Law*), filching, fraud, larceny, misapplication, misuse, peculation, pilferage, pilfering, purloining, stealing, theft, thieving

embitter *verb* 1 = **make bitter** or **resentful**, alienate, anger, disaffect, disillusion, envenom, poison, sour 2 = **aggravate**, exacerbate, exasperate, worsen

embittered *adjective* = **resentful**, angry, bitter, disaffected, disillusioned, rancorous, soured, with a chip on one's shoulder (*informal*)

emblazon *verb* 1 = **decorate**, adorn, blazon, colour, embellish, illuminate, ornament, paint 2 = **publicize**, crack up (*informal*), extol, glorify, laud (*literary*), praise, proclaim, publish, trumpet

emblem *noun* = **symbol**, badge, crest, device, figure, image, insignia, mark, representation, sigil (*rare*), sign, token, type

embodiment *noun* 1 = **personification**, bodying forth, epitome, example, exemplar, exemplification, expression, incarnation, incorporation, manifestation,

realization, reification, representation, symbol, type 2 = **incorporation**, bringing together, codification, collection, combination, comprehension, concentration, consolidation, inclusion, integration, organization, systematization

embody *verb* 1 = **personify**, exemplify, manifest, represent, stand for, symbolize, typify 2 = **incorporate**, collect, combine, comprise, contain, include

embolden *verb* = **encourage**, animate, cheer, fire, gee up, hearten, inflame, inspirit, invigorate, nerve, reassure, rouse, stimulate, stir, strengthen, vitalize

embrace *verb* 1 = **hug**, clasp, cuddle, encircle, enfold, envelop, grasp, hold, neck (*informal*), seize, squeeze, take or hold in one's arms 2 = **accept**, adopt, avail oneself of, espouse, grab, make use of, receive, seize, take on board, take up, welcome 3 = **include**, comprehend, comprise, contain, cover, deal with, embody, enclose, encompass, involve, provide for, subsume, take in, take into account ◆ *noun* 4 = **hug**, canoodle (*slang*), clasp, clinch (*slang*), cuddle, squeeze

embroil *verb* = **involve**, complicate, compromise, confound, confuse, disorder, disturb, encumber, enmesh, ensnare, entangle, implicate, incriminate, mire, mix up, muddle, perplex, stitch up (*slang*), trouble

embryo *noun* = **germ**, beginning, nucleus, root, rudiment

embryonic *adjective* = **early**, beginning, germinal, immature, inchoate, incipient, primary, rudimentary, seminal, undeveloped
➤ **Antonyms**
advanced, developed, progressive

emend *verb* = **revise**, amend, correct, edit, improve, rectify, redact

emendation *noun* = **revision**, amendment, correction, editing, improvement, rectification, redaction

emerge *verb* 1 = **come into view**, appear, arise, become visible, come forth, come out, come up, emanate, issue, proceed, rise, spring up, surface 2 = **become apparent**, become known, come out, come out in the wash, come to light, crop up, develop, materialize, transpire, turn up
➤ **Antonyms**
≠**come into view**: depart, disappear, fade, fall, recede, retreat, sink, submerge, vanish from sight, wane, withdraw

emergence *noun* = **coming**, advent, apparition, appearance, arrival, dawn, development, disclosure, emanation, issue, materialization, rise

emergency *noun* = **crisis**, danger,
difficulty, exigency, extremity, necessity,
panic stations (*informal*), pass, pinch,
plight, predicament, quandary, scrape
(*informal*), strait

emigrate *verb* = **move abroad**, migrate,
move, remove

emigration *noun* = **departure**, exodus,
migration, removal

eminence *noun* 1 = **prominence**, celebrity,
dignity, distinction, esteem, fame,
greatness, illustriousness, importance,
notability, note, pre-eminence, prestige,
rank, renown, reputation, repute,
superiority 2 = **high ground**, elevation,
height, hill, hillock, knoll, rise, summit

eminent *adjective* = **prominent**, big-time
(*informal*), celebrated, conspicuous,
distinguished, elevated, esteemed,
exalted, famous, grand, great, high,
high-ranking, illustrious, important, major
league (*informal*), notable, noted,
noteworthy, outstanding, paramount,
pre-eminent, prestigious, renowned,
signal, superior, well-known
➤ **Antonyms**
anonymous, commonplace, infamous,
lowly, ordinary, undistinguished,
unheard-of, unimportant, unknown,
unremarkable, unsung

eminently *adverb* = **extremely**,
conspicuously, exceedingly, exceptionally,
greatly, highly, notably, outstandingly,
prominently, remarkably, seriously
(*informal*), signally, strikingly, surpassingly,
well

emission *noun* = **giving off** *or* **out**,
diffusion, discharge, ejaculation, ejection,
emanation, exhalation, exudation,
issuance, issue, radiation, shedding,
transmission, utterance, venting

emit *verb* = **give off**, breathe forth, cast out,
diffuse, discharge, eject, emanate, exhale,
exude, give out, give vent to, issue,
radiate, send forth, send out, shed, throw
out, transmit, utter, vent
➤ **Antonyms**
absorb, assimilate, consume, devour,
digest, drink in, incorporate, ingest,
receive, soak up, suck up, take in

emolument *noun* = **fee**, benefit,
compensation, earnings, gain, hire, pay,
payment, profits, recompense,
remuneration, return, reward, salary,
stipend, wages

emotion *noun* = **feeling**, agitation, ardour,
excitement, fervour, passion, perturbation,
sensation, sentiment, vehemence, warmth

emotional *adjective* 1 = **sensitive**,
demonstrative, excitable, feeling,
hot-blooded, passionate, responsive,
sentimental, susceptible, temperamental,
tender, touchy-feely (*informal*), warm 2
= **moving**, affecting, emotive, exciting,
heart-warming, pathetic, poignant,
sentimental, stirring, tear-jerking
(*informal*), three-hankie (*informal*),
thrilling, touching 3 = **passionate**, ablaze,
ardent, enthusiastic, fervent, fervid, fiery,
flaming, heated, impassioned, roused,
stirred, zealous
➤ **Antonyms**
≠**sensitive**: apathetic, cold, detached,
insensitive, phlegmatic, undemonstrative,
unemotional, unfeeling, unmoved,
unsentimental ≠**passionate**:
dispassionate, unenthusiastic, unexcitable,
unruffled

emotive *adjective* 1 = **sensitive**,
argumentative, controversial, delicate,
touchy 2 = **moving**, affecting, emotional,
exciting, heart-warming, pathetic,
poignant, sentimental, stirring, tear-jerking
(*informal*), three-hankie (*informal*),
thrilling, touching

emphasis *noun* = **stress**, accent,
accentuation, attention, decidedness,
force, importance, impressiveness,
insistence, intensity, moment,
positiveness, power, pre-eminence,
priority, prominence, significance,
strength, underscoring, weight

emphasize *verb* = **stress**, accent,
accentuate, dwell on, foreground, give
priority to, highlight, insist on, lay stress
on, play up, press home, put the accent
on, underline, underscore, weight
➤ **Antonyms**
gloss over, make light of, make little of,
minimize, play down, soft-pedal
(*informal*), underplay

emphatic *adjective* = **forceful**, absolute,
categorical, certain, decided, definite,
direct, distinct, earnest, energetic, forcible,
important, impressive, insistent, in spades,
marked, momentous, positive, powerful,
pronounced, resounding, significant,
storming (*informal*), striking, strong,
telling, unequivocal, unmistakable,
vigorous
➤ **Antonyms**
commonplace, equivocal, hesitant,
insignificant, tame, tentative, uncertain,
undecided, unremarkable, unsure, weak

empire *noun* 1 = **kingdom**,
commonwealth, domain, imperium (*rare*),
realm 2 = **power**, authority, command,
control, dominion, government, rule,
sovereignty, supremacy, sway

empirical, empiric *adjective* = **first-hand**,

experiential, experimental, observed, practical, pragmatic
➤ **Antonyms**
academic, assumed, conjectural, hypothetical, putative, speculative, theoretic(al)

emplacement *noun* **1** = **position**, location, lodgment, platform, site, situation, station **2** = **positioning**, placement, placing, putting in place, setting up, stationing

employ *verb* **1** = **hire**, commission, engage, enlist, retain, take on **2** = **keep busy**, engage, fill, make use of, occupy, spend, take up, use up **3** = **use**, apply, bring to bear, exercise, exert, make use of, ply, put to use, utilize ◆ *noun* **4** *As in* **in the employ of** = **service**, employment, engagement, hire

employed *adjective* = **working**, active, busy, engaged, in a job, in employment, in work, occupied
➤ **Antonyms**
idle, jobless, laid off, on the dole (*Brit. informal*), out of a job, out of work, redundant, unoccupied

employee *noun* = **worker**, hand, job-holder, staff member, wage-earner, workman

employer *noun* = **boss** (*informal*), business, company, establishment, firm, gaffer (*informal, chiefly Brit.*), organization, outfit (*informal*), owner, patron, proprietor

employment *noun* **1** = **taking on**, engagement, enlistment, hire, retaining **2** = **use**, application, exercise, exertion, utilization **3** = **job**, avocation (*archaic*), business, calling, craft, employ, line, métier, occupation, profession, pursuit, service, trade, vocation, work

emporium *noun* *Old-fashioned* = **shop**, bazaar, market, mart, store, warehouse

empower *verb* = **enable**, allow, authorize, commission, delegate, entitle, license, permit, qualify, sanction, warrant

emptiness *noun* **1** = **bareness**, blankness, desertedness, desolation, destitution, vacancy, vacantness, vacuum, void, waste **2** = **purposelessness**, aimlessness, banality, barrenness, frivolity, futility, hollowness, inanity, ineffectiveness, meaninglessness, senselessness, silliness, unreality, unsatisfactoriness, unsubstantiality, vainness, valuelessness, vanity, worthlessness **3** = **insincerity**, cheapness, hollowness, idleness, triviality, trivialness **4** = **blankness**, absentness, expressionlessness, unintelligence, vacancy, vacantness, vacuity, vacuousness

empty *adjective* **1** = **bare**, blank, clear, deserted, desolate, destitute, hollow,

unfurnished, uninhabited, unoccupied, untenanted, vacant, void, waste **2** = **purposeless**, aimless, banal, bootless, frivolous, fruitless, futile, hollow, inane, ineffective, meaningless, otiose, senseless, silly, unreal, unsatisfactory, unsubstantial, vain, valueless, worthless **3** = **insincere**, cheap, hollow, idle, trivial **4** = **blank**, absent, expressionless, unintelligent, vacant, vacuous **5** *Informal* = **hungry**, esurient, famished, ravenous, starving (*informal*), unfed, unfilled ◆ *verb* **6** = **evacuate**, clear, consume, deplete, discharge, drain, dump, exhaust, gut, pour out, unburden, unload, use up, vacate, void
➤ **Antonyms**
adjective ≠**bare**: full, inhabited, occupied, packed, stuffed ≠**purposeless**: busy, fulfilled, full, interesting, meaningful, occupied, purposeful, satisfying, serious, significant, useful, valuable, worthwhile ◆ *verb* ≠**evacuate**: cram, fill, pack, replenish, stock, stuff

empty-headed *adjective* = **scatterbrained**, brainless, ditzy *or* ditsy (*slang*), dizzy (*informal*), featherbrained, flighty, frivolous, giddy, goofy (*informal*), harebrained, inane, silly, skittish, vacuous

emulate *verb* = **imitate**, challenge, compete with, contend with, copy, echo, follow, follow in the footsteps of, follow suit, follow the example of, mimic, rival, take after, take a leaf out of someone's book, vie with

enable *verb* = **allow**, authorize, capacitate, commission, empower, entitle, facilitate, fit, license, permit, prepare, qualify, sanction, warrant
➤ **Antonyms**
bar, block, hinder, impede, obstruct, prevent, stop, thwart

enact *verb* **1** = **establish**, authorize, command, decree, legislate, ordain, order, pass, proclaim, ratify, sanction **2** = **perform**, act, act out, appear as, depict, personate, play, play the part of, portray, represent

enactment *noun* **1** = **decree**, authorization, canon, command, commandment, dictate, edict, law, legislation, order, ordinance, proclamation, ratification, regulation, statute **2** = **portrayal**, acting, depiction, performance, personation, play-acting, playing, representation

enamoured *adjective* = **in love**, bewitched, captivated, charmed, crazy about (*informal*), enchanted, enraptured, entranced, fascinated, fond, infatuated, nuts on or about (*slang*), smitten, swept off one's feet, taken, wild about (*informal*)

encampment *noun* = **camp**, base, bivouac, camping ground, campsite, cantonment, quarters, tents

encapsulate, incapsulate *verb* = **sum up**, abridge, compress, condense, digest, epitomize, précis, summarize

enchant *verb* = **fascinate**, beguile, bewitch, captivate, cast a spell on, charm, delight, enamour, enrapture, enthral, hypnotize, mesmerize, ravish, spellbind

enchanter *noun* = **sorcerer**, conjuror, magician, magus, necromancer, spellbinder, warlock, witch, wizard

enchanting *adjective* = **fascinating**, alluring, appealing, attractive, bewitching, captivating, charming, delightful, endearing, entrancing, lovely, Orphean, pleasant, ravishing, winsome

enchantment *noun* **1** = **fascination**, allure, allurement, beguilement, bliss, charm, delight, hypnotism, mesmerism, rapture, ravishment, transport **2** = **spell**, charm, conjuration, incantation, magic, necromancy, sorcery, witchcraft, wizardry

enchantress *noun* **1** = **sorceress**, conjuror, lamia, magician, necromancer, spellbinder, witch **2** = **seductress**, charmer, *femme fatale*, siren, vamp (*informal*)

enclose, inclose *verb* **1** = **surround**, bound, circumscribe, cover, encase, encircle, encompass, environ, fence, hedge, hem in, impound, pen, pound, shut in, wall in, wrap **2** = **send with**, include, insert, put in **3** = **include**, comprehend, contain, embrace, hold, incorporate

encompass *verb* **1** = **surround**, circle, circumscribe, encircle, enclose, envelop, environ, enwreath, girdle, hem in, ring **2** = **include**, admit, comprehend, comprise, contain, cover, embody, embrace, hold, incorporate, involve, subsume, take in

encounter *verb* **1** = **meet**, bump into (*informal*), chance upon, come upon, confront, experience, face, happen on or upon, run across, run into (*informal*) **2** = **battle with**, attack, clash with, combat, come into conflict with, contend, cross swords with, do battle with, engage, face off (*slang*), fight, grapple with, join battle with, strive, struggle ♦ *noun* **3** = **meeting**, brush, confrontation, rendezvous **4** = **battle**, action, clash, collision, combat, conflict, contest, dispute, engagement, face-off (*slang*), fight, head-to-head, run-in (*informal*), set to (*informal*), skirmish

encourage *verb* **1** = **inspire**, animate, buoy up, cheer, comfort, console, embolden, gee up, hearten, incite, inspirit, rally, reassure, rouse, stimulate **2** = **spur**, abet, advance, advocate, aid, boost, commend, egg on, favour, forward, foster, further, help, promote, prompt, strengthen, succour, support, urge
➤ **Antonyms**
daunt, depress, deter, discourage, dishearten, dispirit, dissuade, hinder, inhibit, intimidate, prevent, retard, scare, throw cold water on (*informal*)

encouragement *noun* = **inspiration**, advocacy, aid, boost, cheer, clarion call, consolation, favour, gee-up, help, incitement, inspiritment, promotion, reassurance, security blanket (*informal*), stimulation, stimulus, succour, support, urging

encouraging *adjective* = **promising**, bright, cheerful, cheering, comforting, good, heartening, hopeful, reassuring, rosy, satisfactory, stimulating
➤ **Antonyms**
daunting, depressing, disappointing, discouraging, disheartening, dispiriting, off-putting (*informal*), unfavourable, unpropitious

encroach *verb* = **intrude**, appropriate, arrogate, impinge, infringe, invade, make inroads, overstep, trench, trespass, usurp

encroachment *noun* = **intrusion**, appropriation, arrogation, impingement, incursion, infringement, inroad, invasion, trespass, usurpation, violation

encumber *verb* = **burden**, clog, cramp, embarrass, hamper, handicap, hinder, impede, incommode, inconvenience, make difficult, obstruct, oppress, overload, retard, saddle, slow down, trammel, weigh down

encumbrance *noun* = **burden**, albatross, clog, difficulty, drag, embarrassment, handicap, hindrance, impediment, inconvenience, liability, load, millstone, obstacle, obstruction

end *noun* **1** = **extremity**, bound, boundary, edge, extent, extreme, limit, point, terminus, tip **2** = **finish**, cessation, close, closure, ending, expiration, expiry, stop, termination, wind-up **3** = **conclusion**, attainment, completion, consequence, consummation, culmination, denouement, ending, end result, finale, issue, outcome, resolution, result, sequel, upshot **4** = **remnant**, bit, butt, fragment, leftover, oddment, remainder, scrap, stub, tag end, tail end **5** = **destruction**, annihilation, death, demise, dissolution, doom, extermination, extinction, ruin,

ruination **6** = **purpose**, aim, aspiration, design, drift, goal, intent, intention, object, objective, point, reason **7 the end** *Slang* = **the worst**, beyond endurance, insufferable, intolerable, the final blow, the last straw, the limit (*informal*), too much (*informal*), unbearable, unendurable
♦ *verb* **8** = **finish**, axe (*informal*), belay (*Nautical*), bring to an end, cease, close, complete, conclude, culminate, dissolve, expire, nip in the bud, pull the plug on, put paid to, resolve, stop, terminate, wind up **9** = **destroy**, abolish, annihilate, exterminate, extinguish, kill, put to death, ruin
➤ **Antonyms**
noun ≠**finish**: beginning, birth, commencement, inception, launch, opening, origin, outset, prelude, source, start ♦ *verb* ≠**finish**: begin, come into being, commence, initiate, launch, originate, start

endanger *verb* = **put at risk**, compromise, hazard, imperil, jeopardize, put in danger, risk, threaten
➤ **Antonyms**
defend, guard, preserve, protect, safeguard, save, secure

endear *verb* = **attract**, attach, bind, captivate, charm, engage, win

endearing *adjective* = **attractive**, adorable, captivating, charming, cute, engaging, lovable, sweet, winning, winsome

endearment *noun* **1** = **loving word**, affectionate utterance, sweet nothing **2** = **affection**, attachment, fondness, love

endeavour *Formal* ♦ *verb* **1** = **try**, aim, aspire, attempt, bend over backwards (*informal*), break one's neck (*informal*), bust a gut (*informal*), do one's best, do one's damnedest (*informal*), essay, give it one's all (*informal*), give it one's best shot (*informal*), go for broke (*slang*), go for it (*informal*), have a crack (*informal*), have a go, have a shot (*informal*), have a stab (*informal*), jump through hoops (*informal*), knock oneself out (*informal*), labour, make an all-out effort (*informal*), make an effort, rupture oneself (*informal*), strive, struggle, take pains, undertake ♦ *noun* **2** = **effort**, aim, attempt, crack (*informal*), enterprise, essay, go (*informal*), shot (*informal*), stab (*informal*), trial, try, undertaking, venture

ending *noun* = **finish**, cessation, close, completion, conclusion, consummation, culmination, denouement, end, finale, resolution, termination, wind-up
➤ **Antonyms**
birth, commencement, inauguration, inception, onset, opening, origin, preface,

source, start, starting point

endless *adjective* **1** = **eternal**, boundless, ceaseless, constant, continual, everlasting, immortal, incessant, infinite, interminable, limitless, measureless, perpetual, unbounded, unbroken, undying, unending, uninterrupted, unlimited **2** = **interminable**, monotonous, overlong **3** = **continuous**, unbroken, undivided, whole
➤ **Antonyms**
≠**eternal**: bounded, brief, circumscribed, finite, limited, passing, restricted, temporary, terminable, transient, transitory

endorse, indorse *verb* **1** = **approve**, advocate, affirm, authorize, back, champion, confirm, espouse, favour, prescribe, promote, ratify, recommend, sanction, subscribe to, support, sustain, vouch for, warrant **2** = **sign**, countersign, superscribe, undersign

endorsement, indorsement *noun* **1** = **approval**, advocacy, affirmation, approbation, authorization, backing, championship, confirmation, espousal, favour, fiat, O.K. *or* okay (*informal*), promotion, ratification, recommendation, sanction, seal of approval, subscription to, support, warrant **2** = **signature**, comment, countersignature, qualification, superscription

endow *verb* = **provide**, award, bequeath, bestow, confer, donate, endue, enrich, favour, finance, fund, furnish, give, grant, invest, leave, make over, purvey, settle on, supply, will

endowment *noun* **1** = **provision**, award, benefaction, bequest, bestowal, boon, donation, fund, gift, grant, hand-out, income, largesse *or* largess, legacy, presentation, property, revenue, stipend **2** *often plural* = **talent**, ability, aptitude, attribute, capability, capacity, faculty, flair, genius, gift, power, qualification, quality

end up *verb* **1** = **arrive**, come to a halt, fetch up (*informal*), finish up, stop, wind up **2** = **turn out to be**, become eventually, finish as, finish up, pan out (*informal*)

endurable *adjective* = **bearable**, acceptable, sufferable, supportable, sustainable, tolerable
➤ **Antonyms**
insufferable, insupportable, intolerable, too much (*informal*), unbearable, unendurable

endurance *noun* **1** = **staying power**, bearing, fortitude, patience, perseverance, persistence, pertinacity, resignation, resolution, stamina, strength, submission, sufferance, tenacity, toleration **2** = **permanence**, continuation, continuity, durability, duration, immutability, lastingness, longevity, stability

endure *verb* **1** = **bear**, brave, cope with, experience, go through, stand, stick it out (*informal*), suffer, support, sustain, take it (*informal*), thole (*Scot.*), undergo, weather, withstand **2** = **put up with**, abide, allow, bear, brook, countenance, hack (*slang*), permit, stand, stick (*slang*), stomach, submit to, suffer, swallow, take patiently, tolerate **3** = **last**, abide, be durable, continue, have a good innings, hold, live, live on, persist, prevail, remain, stand, stay, survive, wear well

enduring *adjective* = **long-lasting**, abiding, continuing, durable, eternal, firm, immortal, immovable, imperishable, lasting, living, perennial, permanent, persistent, persisting, prevailing, remaining, steadfast, steady, surviving, unfaltering, unwavering
➤ **Antonyms**
brief, ephemeral, fleeting, momentary, passing, short, short-lived, temporary, transient, transitory

enemy *noun* = **foe**, adversary, antagonist, competitor, opponent, rival, the opposition, the other side
➤ **Antonyms**
ally, confederate, friend, supporter

energetic *adjective* = **vigorous**, active, alive and kicking, animated, bright-eyed and bushy-tailed (*informal*), brisk, dynamic, forceful, forcible, full of beans (*informal*), high-octane (*informal*), high-powered, indefatigable, lively, potent, powerful, spirited, storming (*informal*), strenuous, strong, tireless, zippy (*informal*)
➤ **Antonyms**
debilitated, dull, enervated, inactive, lazy, lethargic, lifeless, listless, slow, sluggish, torpid, weak

energy *noun* = **vigour**, activity, animation, ardour, brio, drive, efficiency, élan, elbow grease (*facetious*), exertion, fire, force, forcefulness, get-up-and-go (*informal*), go (*informal*), intensity, life, liveliness, pep, pluck, power, spirit, stamina, strength, strenuousness, verve, vim (*slang*), vitality, vivacity, zeal, zest, zip (*informal*)

enfold, infold *verb* = **wrap**, clasp, embrace, enclose, encompass, envelop, enwrap, fold, hold, hug, shroud, swathe, wrap up

enforce *verb* = **impose**, administer, apply, carry out, coerce, compel, constrain, exact, execute, implement, insist on, oblige, prosecute, put in force, put into effect, reinforce, require, urge

enforced *adjective* = **imposed**, compelled,

compulsory, constrained, dictated, involuntary, necessary, ordained, prescribed, required, unavoidable, unwilling

enforcement *noun* = **imposition**, administration, application, carrying out, exaction, execution, implementation, prosecution, reinforcement

enfranchise *verb* **1** = **give the vote to**, grant suffrage to, grant the franchise to, grant voting rights to **2** = **free**, emancipate, liberate, manumit, release, set free

enfranchisement *noun* **1** = **giving the vote**, granting suffrage *or* the franchise, granting voting rights **2** = **freeing**, emancipation, freedom, liberating, liberation, manumission, release, setting free

engage *verb* **1** = **participate**, embark on, enter into, join, partake, practise, set about, take part, undertake **2** = **occupy**, absorb, busy, engross, grip, involve, preoccupy, tie up **3** = **captivate**, allure, arrest, attach, attract, catch, charm, draw, enamour, enchant, fascinate, fix, gain, win **4** = **employ**, appoint, commission, enlist, enrol, hire, retain, take on **5** = **book**, bespeak, charter, hire, lease, prearrange, rent, reserve, secure **6** = **promise**, affiance, agree, betroth (*archaic*), bind, commit, contract, covenant, guarantee, obligate, oblige, pledge, undertake, vouch, vow **7** *Military* = **begin battle with**, assail, attack, combat, come to close quarters with, encounter, face off (*slang*), fall on, fight with, give battle to, join battle with, meet, take on **8** = **set going**, activate, apply, bring into operation, energize, switch on **9** = **interlock**, dovetail, interact, interconnect, join, mesh
➤ **Antonyms**
≠**employ**: axe (*informal*), discharge, dismiss, fire (*informal*), give notice to, lay off, oust, remove, sack (*informal*)

engaged *adjective* **1** = **betrothed** (*archaic*), affianced, pledged, promised, spoken for **2** = **occupied**, absorbed, busy, committed, employed, engrossed, in use, involved, preoccupied, tied up, unavailable
➤ **Antonyms**
≠**betrothed**: available, fancy-free, free, unattached, uncommitted, unengaged
≠**occupied**: available, free, uncommitted, unengaged

engagement *noun* **1** = **appointment**, arrangement, commitment, date, meeting **2** = **betrothal**, troth (*archaic*) **3** = **promise**, assurance, bond, compact, contract, oath, obligation, pact, pledge, undertaking, vow, word **4** = **job**, commission, employment, gig (*informal*), post, situation, stint, work **5** = **battle**, action, combat, conflict, confrontation, contest, encounter, face-off (*slang*), fight

engaging *adjective* = **charming**, agreeable, appealing, attractive, captivating, cute, enchanting, fascinating, fetching (*informal*), likable *or* likeable, lovable, pleasant, pleasing, winning, winsome
➤ **Antonyms**
disagreeable, objectionable, obnoxious, offensive, repulsive, unattractive, unlikable *or* unlikeable, unlovely, unpleasant

engender *verb* = **produce**, beget, breed, bring about, cause, create, excite, foment, generate, give rise to, hatch, incite, induce, instigate, lead to, make, occasion, precipitate, provoke

engine *noun* = **machine**, mechanism, motor

engineer *verb* = **bring about**, cause, concoct, contrive, control, create, devise, effect, encompass, finagle (*informal*), manage, manoeuvre, mastermind, originate, plan, plot, scheme, wangle (*informal*)

engrave *verb* **1** = **carve**, chase, chisel, cut, enchase (*rare*), etch, grave (*archaic*), inscribe **2** = **imprint**, impress, print **3** = **fix**, embed, impress, imprint, infix, ingrain, lodge

engraving *noun* **1** = **cutting**, carving, chasing, chiselling, dry point, enchasing (*rare*), etching, inscribing, inscription **2** = **carving**, block, etching, inscription, plate, woodcut **3** = **print**, etching, impression

engross *verb* = **absorb**, arrest, engage, engulf, hold, immerse, involve, occupy, preoccupy

engrossed *adjective* = **absorbed**, captivated, caught up, deep, enthralled, fascinated, gripped, immersed, intent, intrigued, lost, preoccupied, rapt, riveted

engrossing *adjective* = **absorbing**, captivating, compelling, enthralling, fascinating, gripping, interesting, intriguing, riveting

engulf *verb* = **immerse**, envelop, inundate, overrun, overwhelm, submerge, swallow up, swamp

enhance *verb* = **improve**, add to, augment, boost, complement, elevate, embellish, exalt, heighten, increase, intensify, lift, magnify, raise, reinforce, strengthen, swell
➤ **Antonyms**
debase, decrease, depreciate, devalue, diminish, lower, minimize, reduce, spoil

enigma *noun* = **mystery**, conundrum,

problem, puzzle, riddle, teaser

enigmatic, enigmatical *adjective* = **mysterious**, ambiguous, cryptic, Delphic, doubtful, equivocal, incomprehensible, indecipherable, inexplicable, inscrutable, obscure, oracular, perplexing, puzzling, recondite, sphinxlike, uncertain, unfathomable, unintelligible
➤ **Antonyms**
clear, comprehensible, simple, straightforward, uncomplicated

enjoin *verb* **1** = **order**, advise, bid, call upon, charge, command, counsel, demand, direct, instruct, prescribe, require, urge, warn **2** *Law* = **prohibit**, ban, bar, disallow, forbid, interdict, place an injunction on, preclude, proscribe, restrain

enjoy *verb* **1** = **take pleasure in** *or* **from**, appreciate, be entertained by, be pleased with, delight in, like, rejoice in, relish, revel in, take joy in **2** = **have**, be blessed *or* favoured with, experience, have the benefit of, have the use of, own, possess, reap the benefits of, use **3 enjoy oneself** = **have a good time**, have a ball (*informal*), have a field day (*informal*), have fun, let one's hair down, make merry
➤ **Antonyms**
≠**take pleasure in** *or* **from**: abhor, despise, detest, dislike, hate, have no taste *or* stomach for, loathe

enjoyable *adjective* = **pleasurable**, agreeable, amusing, delectable, delicious, delightful, entertaining, gratifying, pleasant, pleasing, satisfying, to one's liking
➤ **Antonyms**
despicable, disagreeable, displeasing, hateful, loathsome, obnoxious, offensive, repugnant, unenjoyable, unpleasant, unsatisfying, unsavoury

enjoyment *noun* = **pleasure**, amusement, beer and skittles (*informal*), delectation, delight, diversion, entertainment, fun, gladness, gratification, gusto, happiness, indulgence, joy, recreation, relish, satisfaction, zest

enlarge *verb* **1** = **increase**, add to, amplify, augment, blow up (*informal*), broaden, diffuse, dilate, distend, elongate, expand, extend, grow, heighten, inflate, lengthen, magnify, make *or* grow larger, multiply, stretch, swell, wax, widen **2 enlarge on** = **expand on**, descant on, develop, elaborate on, expatiate on, give further details about
➤ **Antonyms**
≠**increase**: compress, condense, curtail, decrease, diminish, lessen, narrow, reduce,

shorten, shrink, trim, truncate ≠**expand**
on: abbreviate, abridge, condense, shorten

enlighten *verb* = **inform**, advise, apprise, cause to understand, civilize, counsel, edify, educate, instruct, make aware, teach

enlightened *adjective* = **informed**, aware, broad-minded, civilized, cultivated, educated, knowledgeable, liberal, literate, open-minded, reasonable, refined, sophisticated
➤ **Antonyms**
ignorant, narrow-minded, short-sighted, small-minded, unaware, uneducated, unenlightened

enlightenment *noun* = **understanding**, awareness, broad-mindedness, civilization, comprehension, cultivation, edification, education, information, insight, instruction, knowledge, learning, literacy, open-mindedness, refinement, sophistication, teaching, wisdom

enlist *verb* **1** = **join up**, enrol, enter (into), gather, join, muster, register, secure, sign up, volunteer **2** = **obtain**, engage, procure, recruit

enliven *verb* = **cheer up**, animate, brighten, buoy up, cheer, excite, exhilarate, fire, gladden, hearten, inspire, inspirit, invigorate, pep up, perk up, quicken, rouse, spark, stimulate, vitalize, vivify, wake up
➤ **Antonyms**
chill, dampen, deaden, depress, put a damper on, repress, subdue

enmity *noun* = **hostility**, acrimony, animosity, animus, antagonism, antipathy, aversion, bad blood, bitterness, hate, hatred, ill will, malevolence, malice, malignity, rancour, spite, venom
➤ **Antonyms**
affection, amity, cordiality, friendliness, friendship, geniality, goodwill, harmony, love, warmth

ennoble *verb* = **dignify**, aggrandize, elevate, enhance, exalt, glorify, honour, magnify, raise

ennui *noun Literary* = **boredom**, dissatisfaction, lassitude, listlessness, tedium, the doldrums

enormity *noun* **1** = **wickedness**, atrociousness, atrocity, depravity, disgrace, evilness, heinousness, monstrousness, nefariousness, outrageousness, turpitude, viciousness, vileness, villainy **2** = **atrocity**, abomination, crime, disgrace, evil, horror, monstrosity, outrage, villainy **3** *Informal* = **hugeness**, enormousness, greatness, immensity, magnitude, massiveness, vastness

enormous *adjective* = **huge**, astronomic,

Brobdingnagian, colossal, elephantine, excessive, gargantuan, gigantic, ginormous (*informal*), gross, humongous *or* humungous (*U.S. slang*), immense, jumbo (*informal*), mammoth, massive, monstrous, mountainous, prodigious, stellar (*informal*), titanic, tremendous, vast
➤ **Antonyms**
diminutive, dwarf, infinitesimal, insignificant, Lilliputian, little, meagre, microscopic, midget, minute, petite, pint-sized (*informal*), small, tiny, trivial, wee

enough *adjective* **1** = **sufficient**, abundant, adequate, ample, plenty ♦ *noun* **2** = **sufficiency**, abundance, adequacy, ample supply, plenty, right amount
♦ *adverb* **3** = **sufficiently**, abundantly, adequately, amply, fairly, moderately, passably, reasonably, satisfactorily, tolerably

enquire *see* INQUIRE

enquiry *see* INQUIRY

enrage *verb* = **anger**, aggravate (*informal*), exasperate, gall, get one's back up, incense, incite, inflame, infuriate, irritate, madden, make one's blood boil, make one see red (*informal*), nark (*Brit., Austral., & N.Z. slang*), provoke, put one's back up
➤ **Antonyms**
appease, assuage, calm, conciliate, mollify, pacify, placate, soothe

enraged *adjective* = **furious**, aggravated (*informal*), angered, angry, boiling mad, choked, cross, exasperated, fuming, incandescent, incensed, inflamed, infuriated, irate, irritated, livid (*informal*), mad (*informal*), on the warpath, pissed (*taboo slang*), pissed off (*taboo slang*), raging, raging mad, wild

enrich *verb* **1** = **enhance**, aggrandize, ameliorate, augment, cultivate, develop, endow, improve, refine, supplement **2** = **make rich**, make wealthy

enrol *verb* **1** = **enlist**, accept, admit, engage, join up, matriculate, recruit, register, sign up *or* on, take on **2** = **record**, chronicle, inscribe, list, note

enrolment *noun* = **enlistment**, acceptance, admission, engagement, matriculation, recruitment, registration

en route *adverb* = **on** *or* **along the way**, in transit, on the road

ensemble *noun* **1** = **whole**, aggregate, assemblage, collection, entirety, set, sum, total, totality, whole thing **2** = **outfit**, costume, get-up (*informal*), suit **3** = **group**, band, cast, chorus, company, supporting cast, troupe

enshrine *verb* = **preserve**, apotheosize,

cherish, consecrate, dedicate, embalm, exalt, hallow, revere, sanctify, treasure

enshroud verb = **cover**, cloak, cloud, conceal, enclose, enfold, envelop, enwrap, hide, obscure, pall, shroud, veil, wrap

ensign noun = **flag**, badge, banner, colours, jack, pennant, pennon, standard, streamer

enslave verb = **subjugate**, bind, dominate, enchain, enthral, reduce to slavery, yoke

ensue verb = **follow**, arise, attend, be consequent on, befall, come after, come next, come to pass (archaic), derive, flow, issue, proceed, result, stem, succeed, supervene, turn out or up

➤ **Antonyms**
antecede, come first, forerun, go ahead of, go before, introduce, lead, pave the way, precede, usher

ensure, insure verb 1 = **make certain**, certify, confirm, effect, guarantee, make sure, secure, warrant 2 = **protect**, guard, make safe, safeguard, secure

entail verb = **involve**, bring about, call for, cause, demand, encompass, give rise to, impose, lead to, necessitate, occasion, require, result in

entangle verb 1 = **tangle**, catch, compromise, embroil, enmesh, ensnare, entrap, foul, implicate, involve, knot, mat, mix up, ravel, snag, snare, trammel, trap 2 = **mix up**, bewilder, complicate, confuse, jumble, muddle, perplex, puzzle, snarl, twist

➤ **Antonyms**
≠**tangle**: detach, disconnect, disengage, disentangle, extricate, free, loose, separate, sever, unfold, unravel, unsnarl, untangle, untwist ≠**mix up**: clarify, clear (up), resolve, simplify, work out

entanglement noun 1 = **tangle**, complication, confusion, ensnarement, entrapment, imbroglio, involvement, jumble, knot, mesh, mess, mix-up, muddle, snare, snarl-up (informal, chiefly Brit.), toils, trap 2 = **difficulty**, embarrassment, imbroglio, involvement, liaison, predicament, tie

enter verb 1 = **come or go in or into**, arrive, insert, introduce, make an entrance, pass into, penetrate, pierce 2 = **join**, become a member of, begin, commence, commit oneself to, embark upon, enlist, enrol, participate in, set about, set out on, sign up, start, take part in, take up 3 = **record**, inscribe, list, log, note, register, set down, take down

➤ **Antonyms**
≠**come or go in or into**: depart, exit, go, issue from, leave, take one's leave,

withdraw ≠**join**: drop out, go, leave, pull out, resign, retire, withdraw

enterprise noun 1 = **firm**, business, company, concern, establishment, operation 2 = **undertaking**, adventure, effort, endeavour, essay, operation, plan, programme, project, venture 3 = **initiative**, activity, adventurousness, alertness, audacity, boldness, daring, dash, drive, eagerness, energy, enthusiasm, get-up-and-go (informal), gumption (informal), pep, push (informal), readiness, resource, resourcefulness, spirit, vigour, zeal

enterprising adjective = **resourceful**, active, adventurous, alert, audacious, bold, daring, dashing, eager, energetic, enthusiastic, go-ahead, intrepid, keen, ready, spirited, stirring, up-and-coming, venturesome, vigorous, zealous

entertain verb 1 = **amuse**, charm, cheer, delight, divert, occupy, please, recreate (rare), regale 2 = **show hospitality to**, accommodate, be host to, harbour, have company, have guests or visitors, lodge, put up, treat 3 = **consider**, cherish, cogitate on, conceive, contemplate, foster, harbour, hold, imagine, keep in mind, maintain, muse over, ponder, support, think about, think over

entertaining adjective = **enjoyable**, amusing, charming, cheering, delightful, diverting, funny, humorous, interesting, pleasant, pleasing, pleasurable, recreative (rare), witty

entertainment noun = **enjoyment**, amusement, beer and skittles (informal), cheer, distraction, diversion, fun, good time, leisure activity, pastime, play, pleasure, recreation, satisfaction, sport, treat

enthral verb = **fascinate**, absorb, beguile, captivate, charm, enchant, enrapture, entrance, grip, hold spellbound, hypnotize, intrigue, mesmerize, ravish, rivet, spellbind

enthralling adjective = **fascinating**, beguiling, captivating, charming, compelling, compulsive, enchanting, entrancing, gripping, hypnotizing, intriguing, mesmerizing, riveting, spellbinding

enthusiasm noun 1 = **keenness**, ardour, avidity, devotion, eagerness, earnestness, excitement, fervour, frenzy, interest, passion, relish, vehemence, warmth, zeal, zest, zing (informal) 2 = **passion**, craze, fad (informal), hobby, hobbyhorse, interest, mania, rage

enthusiast noun = **lover**, admirer,

aficionado, buff (*informal*), devotee, fan, fanatic, fiend (*informal*), follower, freak (*informal*), supporter, zealot

enthusiastic *adjective* = **keen**, ablaze, ardent, avid, bright-eyed and bushy-tailed (*informal*), devoted, eager, earnest, ebullient, excited, exuberant, fervent, fervid, forceful, full of beans (*informal*), hearty, keen as mustard, lively, passionate, spirited, unqualified, unstinting, vehement, vigorous, warm, wholehearted, zealous
➤ **Antonyms**
apathetic, blasé, bored, cool, dispassionate, half-hearted, indifferent, nonchalant, unconcerned, unenthusiastic, uninterested

entice *verb* = **attract**, allure, beguile, cajole, coax, dangle a carrot in front of (someone's) nose, decoy, draw, inveigle, lead on, lure, persuade, prevail on, seduce, tempt, wheedle

entire *adjective* **1** = **whole**, complete, full, gross, total **2** = **total**, absolute, full, outright, thorough, undiminished, unmitigated, unreserved, unrestricted **3** = **intact**, perfect, sound, unbroken, undamaged, unmarked, unmarred, whole, without a scratch **4** = **continuous**, integrated, unbroken, undivided, unified

entirely *adverb* **1** = **completely**, absolutely, altogether, every inch, fully, in every respect, lock, stock and barrel, perfectly, thoroughly, totally, unreservedly, utterly, wholly, without exception, without reservation **2** = **only**, exclusively, solely
➤ **Antonyms**
≠**completely**: incompletely, moderately, partially, partly, piecemeal, slightly, somewhat, to a certain extent *or* degree

entirety *noun* **1** = **whole**, aggregate, sum, total, unity **2** = **wholeness**, absoluteness, completeness, fullness, totality, undividedness, unity

entitle *verb* **1** = **give the right to**, accredit, allow, authorize, empower, enable, enfranchise, fit for, license, make eligible, permit, qualify for, warrant **2** = **call**, characterize, christen, denominate, designate, dub, label, name, style, term, title

entity *noun* = **thing**, being, body, creature, existence, individual, object, organism, presence, quantity, substance

entourage *noun* = **retinue**, associates, attendants, companions, company, cortege, court, escort, followers, following, retainers, staff, suite, train

entrails *plural noun* = **intestines**, bowels, guts, innards (*informal*), insides (*informal*),

offal, viscera

entrance [1] *noun* **1** = **way in**, access, avenue, door, doorway, entry, gate, ingress, inlet, opening, passage, portal **2** = **appearance**, arrival, coming in, entry, ingress, introduction **3** = **admission**, access, admittance, entrée, entry, ingress, permission to enter
➤ **Antonyms**
≠**way in**: exit, outlet, way out
≠**appearance**: departure, egress, exit, exodus, leave-taking

entrance [2] *verb* **1** = **enchant**, absorb, bewitch, captivate, charm, delight, enrapture, enthral, fascinate, gladden, ravish, spellbind, transport **2** = **mesmerize**, hypnotize, put in a trance
➤ **Antonyms**
≠**enchant**: bore, disenchant, irritate, offend, put off, turn off (*informal*)

entrant *noun* **1** = **competitor**, candidate, contestant, entry, participant, player **2** = **new member**, beginner, convert, initiate, neophyte, newcomer, novice, probationer, tyro

entreaty *noun* = **plea**, appeal, earnest request, exhortation, importunity, petition, prayer, request, solicitation, suit, supplication

entrench *verb* **1** = **fix**, anchor, dig in, embed, ensconce, establish, implant, ingrain, install, lodge, plant, root, seat, set, settle **2** *Military* = **fortify**, construct defences, dig in, dig trenches

entrenched *adjective* = **fixed**, deep-rooted, deep-seated, firm, indelible, ineradicable, ingrained, rooted, set, unshakable, well-established

entrepreneur *noun* = **businessman** *or* **businesswoman**, contractor, director, financier, impresario, industrialist, magnate, tycoon

entrust *verb* = **give custody of**, assign, authorize, charge, commend, commit, confide, consign, delegate, deliver, hand over, invest, trust, turn over

entry *noun* **1** = **way in**, access, avenue, door, doorway, entrance, gate, ingress, inlet, opening, passage, passageway, portal **2** = **coming in**, appearance, entering, entrance, initiation, introduction **3** = **admission**, access, entrance, entrée, free passage, permission to enter **4** = **record**, account, item, jotting, listing, memo, memorandum, minute, note, registration **5** = **competitor**, attempt, candidate, contestant, effort, entrant, participant, player, submission
➤ **Antonyms**
≠**way in**: exit, way out ≠**coming in**:

departure, egress, exit, leave, leave-taking, withdrawal

entwine *verb* = **twist**, braid, embrace, encircle, entwist (*archaic*), interlace, intertwine, interweave, knit, plait, ravel, surround, twine, weave, wind
➤ **Antonyms**
disentangle, extricate, free, separate, straighten out, undo, unravel, untangle, unwind

enumerate *verb* 1 = **list**, cite, detail, itemize, mention, name, quote, recapitulate, recite, recount, rehearse, relate, specify, spell out, tell 2 = **count**, add up, calculate, compute, number, reckon, sum up, tally, total

enunciate *verb* 1 = **pronounce**, articulate, enounce, say, sound, speak, utter, vocalize, voice 2 = **state**, declare, proclaim, promulgate, pronounce, propound, publish

envelop *verb* = **enclose**, blanket, cloak, conceal, cover, embrace, encase, encircle, encompass, enfold, engulf, enwrap, hide, obscure, sheathe, shroud, surround, swaddle, swathe, veil, wrap

envelope *noun* = **wrapping**, case, casing, coating, cover, covering, jacket, sheath, shell, skin, wrapper

enviable *adjective* = **desirable**, advantageous, blessed, covetable, favoured, fortunate, lucky, much to be desired, privileged, to die for (*informal*)
➤ **Antonyms**
disagreeable, painful, thankless, uncomfortable, undesirable, unenviable, unpleasant

envious *adjective* = **covetous**, begrudging, green-eyed, green with envy, grudging, jaundiced, jealous, malicious, resentful, spiteful

environment *noun* = **surroundings**, atmosphere, background, conditions, context, domain, element, habitat, locale, medium, milieu, scene, setting, situation, territory

environmental *adjective* = **ecological**, green

environmentalist *noun* = **conservationist**, ecologist, friend of the earth, green

environs *plural noun* = **surrounding area**, district, locality, neighbourhood, outskirts, precincts, purlieus, suburbs, vicinity

envisage *verb* 1 = **imagine**, conceive (of), conceptualize, contemplate, fancy, picture, think up, visualize 2 = **foresee**, anticipate, envision, predict, see

envision *verb* = **conceive of**, anticipate,

contemplate, envisage, foresee, predict, see, visualize

envoy *noun* = **messenger**, agent, ambassador, courier, delegate, deputy, diplomat, emissary, intermediary, legate, minister, plenipotentiary, representative

envy *noun* 1 = **covetousness**, enviousness, grudge, hatred, ill will, jealousy, malice, malignity, resentfulness, resentment, spite, the green-eyed monster (*informal*) ◆ *verb* 2 = **covet**, be envious (of), begrudge, be jealous (of), grudge, resent

ephemeral *adjective* = **brief**, evanescent, fleeting, flitting, fugacious, fugitive, impermanent, momentary, passing, short, short-lived, temporary, transient, transitory
➤ **Antonyms**
abiding, durable, enduring, eternal, immortal, lasting, long-lasting, persisting, steadfast

epicure *noun* 1 = **gourmet**, bon vivant, epicurean, foodie, gastronome 2 = **hedonist**, glutton, gourmand, sensualist, sybarite, voluptuary

epicurean *adjective* 1 = **hedonistic**, bacchanalian, gluttonous, gourmandizing, libertine, luscious, lush, luxurious, pleasure-seeking, self-indulgent, sensual, sybaritic, voluptuous ◆ *noun* 2 = **gourmet**, bon vivant, epicure, foodie, gastronome

epidemic *noun* 1 = **spread**, contagion, growth, outbreak, plague, rash, upsurge, wave ◆ *adjective* 2 = **widespread**, general, pandemic, prevailing, prevalent, rampant, rife, sweeping, wide-ranging

epigram *noun* = **witticism**, aphorism, bon mot, quip

epilogue *noun* = **conclusion**, afterword, coda, concluding speech, postscript
➤ **Antonyms**
exordium, foreword, introduction, preamble, preface, prelude, prologue

episode *noun* 1 = **event**, adventure, affair, business, circumstance, escapade, experience, happening, incident, matter, occurrence 2 = **part**, chapter, instalment, passage, scene, section

epistle *noun* = **letter**, communication, message, missive, note

epitaph *noun* = **monument**, inscription

epithet *noun* = **name**, appellation, description, designation, moniker *or* monicker (*slang*), nickname, sobriquet, tag, title

epitome *noun* 1 = **personification**, archetype, embodiment, essence, exemplar, norm, quintessence, representation, type, typical example 2 = **summary**, abbreviation, abridgment, abstract, compendium, condensation, conspectus, contraction, digest, précis, résumé, syllabus, synopsis

epitomize *verb* **1 = typify**, embody, exemplify, illustrate, incarnate, personify, represent, symbolize **2 = summarize**, abbreviate, abridge, abstract, condense, contract, curtail, cut, encapsulate, précis, reduce, shorten, synopsize

epoch *noun* **= era**, age, date, period, time

equable *adjective* **1 = even-tempered**, agreeable, calm, composed, easy-going, imperturbable, level-headed, placid, serene, temperate, unexcitable, unfazed (*informal*), unflappable (*informal*), unruffled **2 = constant**, consistent, even, on an even keel, regular, smooth, stable, steady, temperate, tranquil, unchanging, uniform, unvarying
➤ **Antonyms**
≠**even-tempered**: excitable, nervous, temperamental ≠**constant**: changeable, fitful, inconsistent, irregular, temperamental, uneven, unstable, volatile

equal *adjective* **1 = identical**, alike, commensurate, corresponding, equivalent, like, matched, one and the same, proportionate, tantamount, the same, uniform **2 = regular**, symmetrical, uniform, unvarying **3 = even**, balanced, evenly balanced, evenly matched, evenly proportioned, fifty-fifty (*informal*), level pegging (*Brit. informal*) **4 = fair**, egalitarian, equable, even-handed, impartial, just, unbiased **5 equal to = capable of**, able to, adequate for, competent to, fit for, good enough for, ready for, strong enough, suitable for, up to ♦ *noun* **6 = match**, brother, compeer, counterpart, equivalent, fellow, mate, parallel, peer, rival, twin ♦ *verb* **7 = match**, agree with, amount to, balance, be equal to, be even with, be level with, be tantamount to, come up to, correspond to, equalize, equate, even, level, parallel, rival, square with, tally with, tie with
➤ **Antonyms**
adjective ≠**identical**: different, disproportionate, dissimilar, diverse, unequal, unlike ≠**regular**: irregular ≠**even**: unbalanced, unequal, uneven, unmatched ≠**fair**: biased, inequitable, partial, unequal, unfair, unjust ≠**capable of**: inadequate, incapable, incompetent, not good enough, not up to, unequal, unfit ♦ *verb* ≠**match**: be different, be unequal, disagree

equality *noun* **1 = sameness**, balance, coequality, correspondence, equatability, equivalence, evenness, identity, likeness, similarity, uniformity **2 = fairness**, egalitarianism, equal opportunity, parity
➤ **Antonyms**
≠**sameness**: disparity, lack of balance, unevenness ≠**fairness**: bias, discrimination, imparity, inequality, prejudice, unfairness

equalize *verb* **= make equal**, balance, equal, equate, even up, level, match, regularize, smooth, square, standardize

equate *verb* **= make** *or* **be equal**, agree, balance, be commensurate, compare, correspond with *or* to, equalize, liken, match, mention in the same breath, offset, pair, parallel, square, tally, think of together

equation *noun* **= equating**, agreement, balancing, comparison, correspondence, equality, equalization, equivalence, likeness, match, pairing, parallel

equestrian *adjective* **1 = on horseback**, in the saddle, mounted ♦ *noun* **2 = rider**, cavalier (*archaic*), horseman, knight

equilibrium *noun* **1 = stability**, balance, counterpoise, equipoise, evenness, rest, steadiness, symmetry **2 = composure**, calm, calmness, collectedness, coolness, equanimity, poise, self-possession, serenity, stability, steadiness

equip *verb* **= supply**, accoutre, arm, array, attire, deck out, dress, endow, fit out, fit up, furnish, kit out, outfit, prepare, provide, rig, stock

equipment *noun* **= apparatus**, accoutrements, appurtenances, baggage, equipage, furnishings, furniture, gear, materiel, outfit, paraphernalia, rig, stuff, supplies, tackle, tools

equitable *adjective* **= fair**, candid, disinterested, dispassionate, due, even-handed, honest, impartial, just, nondiscriminatory, proper, proportionate, reasonable, right, rightful, unbiased, unprejudiced

equity *noun* **= fairness**, disinterestedness, equitableness, even-handedness, fair-mindedness, fair play, honesty, impartiality, integrity, justice, reasonableness, rectitude, righteousness, uprightness
➤ **Antonyms**
bias, discrimination, injustice, partiality, preference, prejudice, unfairness

equivalence *noun* **= equality**, agreement, alikeness, conformity, correspondence, evenness, identity, interchangeableness, likeness, match, parallel, parity, sameness, similarity, synonymy

equivalent *noun* **1 = equal**, correspondent, counterpart, match, opposite number, parallel, peer, twin ♦ *adjective* **2** = **equal**, alike, commensurate, comparable, correspondent, corresponding, even, homologous, interchangeable, of a kind, of a piece, same, similar, synonymous, tantamount

➤ **Antonyms**

adjective ≠**equal**: different, dissimilar, incomparable, unequal, unlike

equivocal *adjective* = **ambiguous**, ambivalent, doubtful, dubious, evasive, indefinite, indeterminate, misleading, oblique, obscure, oracular, prevaricating, questionable, suspicious, uncertain, vague

➤ **Antonyms**

absolute, certain, clear, clear-cut, cut-and-dried (*informal*), decisive, definite, evident, explicit, incontrovertible, indubitable, manifest, plain, positive, straight, unambiguous, unequivocal

equivocate *verb* = **be evasive**, avoid the issue, beat about the bush (*informal*), dodge, evade, fence, flannel (*Brit. informal*), fudge, hedge, parry, prevaricate, pussyfoot (*informal*), quibble, shuffle, sidestep, tergiversate, waffle (*informal, chiefly Brit.*)

equivocation *noun* = **ambiguity**, double talk, doubtfulness, evasion, hedging, prevarication, quibbling, shuffling, tergiversation, waffle (*informal, chiefly Brit.*), weasel words (*informal, chiefly U.S.*)

era *noun* = **age**, aeon, cycle, date, day *or* days, epoch, generation, period, stage, time

eradicate *verb* = **wipe out**, abolish, annihilate, deracinate, destroy, efface, eliminate, erase, excise, expunge, exterminate, extinguish, extirpate, get rid of, obliterate, put paid to, remove, root out, stamp out, uproot, weed out, wipe from the face of the earth

eradication *noun* = **wiping out**, abolition, annihilation, deracination, destruction, effacement, elimination, erasure, expunction, extermination, extinction, extirpation, obliteration, removal

erase *verb* = **wipe out**, blot, cancel, delete, efface, excise, expunge, obliterate, remove, rub out, scratch out

erect *verb* **1** = **build**, construct, elevate, lift, mount, pitch, put up, raise, rear, set up, stand up **2** = **found**, create, establish, form, initiate, institute, organize, set up ♦ *adjective* **3** = **upright**, elevated, firm, perpendicular, pricked-up, raised, rigid, standing, stiff, straight, vertical

➤ **Antonyms**

verb ≠**build**: demolish, destroy, dismantle, raze, tear down ♦ *adjective* ≠**upright**:

bent, flaccid, horizontal, leaning, limp, prone, recumbent, relaxed, supine

erection *noun* **1** = **building**, assembly, construction, creation, elevation, establishment, fabrication, manufacture **2** = **structure**, building, construction, edifice, pile

erode *verb* = **wear down** *or* **away**, abrade, consume, corrode, destroy, deteriorate, disintegrate, eat away, grind down, spoil

erosion *noun* = **deterioration**, abrasion, attrition, consumption, corrasion, corrosion, destruction, disintegration, eating away, grinding down, spoiling, wear, wearing down *or* away

erotic *adjective* = **sexual**, amatory, aphrodisiac, carnal, erogenous, lustful, rousing, seductive, sensual, sexy (*informal*), steamy (*informal*), stimulating, suggestive, titillating, voluptuous

err *verb* **1** = **make a mistake**, be inaccurate, be incorrect, be in error, blot one's copybook (*informal*), blunder, drop a brick *or* clanger (*informal*), go astray, go wrong, misapprehend, miscalculate, misjudge, mistake, put one's foot in it (*informal*), slip up (*informal*) **2** = **sin**, be out of order, blot one's copybook (*informal*), deviate, do wrong, fall, go astray, lapse, misbehave, offend, transgress, trespass

errand *noun* = **job**, charge, commission, message, mission, task

errant *adjective* **1** = **sinning**, aberrant, deviant, erring, offending, straying, wayward, wrong **2** *Old-fashioned or literary* = **wandering**, itinerant, journeying, nomadic, peripatetic, rambling, roaming, roving

erratic *adjective* = **unpredictable**, aberrant, abnormal, capricious, changeable, desultory, eccentric, fitful, inconsistent, inconstant, irregular, shifting, uneven, unreliable, unstable, variable, wayward

➤ **Antonyms**

certain, consistent, constant, dependable, invariable, natural, normal, predictable, regular, reliable, stable, steady, straight, unchanging, undeviating

erroneous *adjective* = **incorrect**, amiss, fallacious, false, faulty, flawed, inaccurate, inexact, invalid, mistaken, spurious, unfounded, unsound, untrue, wide of the mark, wrong

➤ **Antonyms**

accurate, correct, factual, faultless, flawless, precise, right, true, veracious

error *noun* **1** = **mistake**, bloomer (*Brit. informal*), blunder, boner (*slang*), boob (*Brit. slang*), delusion, erratum, fallacy, fault, flaw, howler (*informal*), inaccuracy, misapprehension, miscalculation, misconception, oversight, slip, solecism **2** = **wrongdoing**, delinquency, deviation, fault, lapse, misdeed, offence, sin, transgression, trespass, wrong

erstwhile *adjective* = **former**, bygone, ex (*informal*), late, old, once, one-time, past, previous, quondam, sometime

erudite *adjective* = **learned**, cultivated, cultured, educated, knowledgeable, lettered, literate, scholarly, well-educated, well-read
➤ **Antonyms**
ignorant, illiterate, shallow, uneducated, uninformed, unlettered, unschooled, untaught, unthinking

erupt *verb* **1** = **explode**, be ejected, belch forth, blow up, break out, burst forth, burst into, burst out, discharge, flare up, gush, pour forth, spew forth *or* out, spit out, spout, throw off, vent, vomit **2** *Medical* = **break out**, appear

eruption *noun* **1** = **explosion**, discharge, ejection, flare-up, outbreak, outburst, sally, venting **2** *Medical* = **inflammation**, outbreak, rash

escalate *verb* = **increase**, amplify, ascend, be increased, enlarge, expand, extend, grow, heighten, intensify, magnify, mount, raise, rise, step up
➤ **Antonyms**
abate, contract, decrease, descend, diminish, fall, lessen, limit, lower, shrink, wane, wind down

escapade *noun* = **adventure**, antic, caper, fling, lark (*informal*), mischief, prank, romp, scrape (*informal*), spree, stunt, trick

escape *verb* **1** = **get away**, abscond, bolt, break free *or* out, decamp, do a bunk (*Brit. slang*), do a runner (*slang*), flee, fly, fly the coop (*U.S. & Canad. informal*), hook it (*slang*), make one's getaway, make *or* effect one's escape, run away *or* off, skedaddle (*informal*), skip, slip away, slip through one's fingers, take a powder (*U.S. & Canad. slang*), take it on the lam (*U.S. & Canad. slang*) **2** = **avoid**, body-swerve (*Scot.*), circumvent, dodge, duck, elude, evade, pass, shun, slip **3** = **leak**, discharge, drain, emanate, exude, flow, gush, issue, pour forth, seep, spurt **4** = **be forgotten by**, baffle, be beyond (someone), elude, puzzle, stump ◆ *noun* **5** = **getaway**, bolt, break, break-out, decampment, flight **6** = **avoidance**, circumvention, elusion, evasion **7** = **relaxation**, distraction, diversion, pastime, recreation, relief **8** = **leak**, discharge, drain, effluence, efflux, emanation, emission, gush, leakage, outflow, outpour, seepage, spurt

eschew *verb* = **avoid**, abandon, abjure, abstain from, elude, fight shy of, forgo, forswear, give a wide berth to, give up, have nothing to do with, keep *or* steer clear of, kick (*informal*), refrain from, renounce, shun, swear off

escort *noun* **1** = **guard**, bodyguard, company, convoy, cortege, entourage, protection, retinue, safeguard, train **2** = **companion**, attendant, beau, chaperon, guide, partner, protector, squire (*rare*)
◆ *verb* **3** = **accompany**, chaperon, conduct, convoy, guard, guide, hold (someone's) hand, lead, partner, protect, shepherd, squire, usher

especial *adjective* **1** *Formal* = **exceptional**, chief, distinguished, extraordinary, marked, notable, noteworthy, outstanding, principal, signal, special, uncommon, unusual **2** = **particular**, exclusive, express, individual, peculiar, personal, private, singular, special, specific, unique

especially *adverb* **1** = **exceptionally**, chiefly, conspicuously, extraordinarily, largely, mainly, markedly, notably, outstandingly, principally, remarkably, seriously (*informal*), signally, specially, strikingly, supremely, uncommonly, unusually **2** = **particularly**, exclusively, expressly, peculiarly, singularly, specifically, uniquely

espionage *noun* = **spying**, counter-intelligence, intelligence, surveillance, undercover work

espousal *noun* **1** = **support**, adoption, advocacy, backing, championing, championship, defence, embracing, maintenance, promotion, taking up **2** *Old-fashioned* = **engagement**, affiancing, betrothal, betrothing (*archaic*), espousing (*archaic*), marriage, nuptials, plighting, wedding

espouse *verb* **1** = **support**, adopt, advocate, back, champion, defend, embrace, maintain, promote, stand up for, take up, uphold **2** *Old-fashioned* = **marry**, betroth (*archaic*), plight one's troth (*old-fashioned*), take as spouse, take to wife, wed

essay *noun* **1** = **composition**, article, discourse, disquisition, dissertation, paper, piece, tract, treatise ◆ *verb* **2** *Formal* = **attempt**, aim, endeavour, try, undertake

essence *noun* **1** = **fundamental nature**, being, bottom line, core, crux, entity, heart, kernel, life, lifeblood, meaning, nature, pith, principle, quiddity, quintessence, significance, soul, spirit, substance **2** = **concentrate**, distillate, elixir,

extract, spirits, tincture **3 in essence**
= **essentially**, basically, fundamentally, in
effect, in substance, in the main,
materially, substantially, to all intents and
purposes, virtually **4 of the essence**
= **vitally important**, crucial, essential,
indispensable, of the utmost importance,
vital

essential *adjective* **1** = **vital**, crucial,
important, indispensable, necessary,
needed, requisite **2** = **fundamental**, basic,
cardinal, constitutional, elemental,
elementary, immanent, inherent, innate,
intrinsic, key, main, principal, radical **3**
= **perfect**, absolute, complete, ideal,
quintessential **4** = **concentrated**, distilled,
extracted, rectified, refined, volatile
♦ *noun* **5** = **prerequisite**, basic,
fundamental, must, necessity, principle,
requisite, rudiment, *sine qua non*, vital part
➤ **Antonyms**
adjective ≠**vital**, **fundamental**: accessory,
dispensable, expendable, extra,
extraneous, incidental, inessential, lesser,
minor, nonessential, optional, secondary,
superfluous, surplus, trivial, unimportant,
unnecessary

establish *verb* **1** = **create**, base, constitute,
decree, enact, ensconce, entrench, fix,
form, found, ground, implant, inaugurate,
install, institute, organize, plant, put down
roots, root, secure, settle, set up, sow the
seeds, start **2** = **prove**, authenticate, certify,
confirm, corroborate, demonstrate, ratify,
show, substantiate, validate, verify

establishment *noun* **1** = **creation**,
enactment, formation, foundation,
founding, inauguration, installation,
institution, organization, setting up **2**
= **organization**, business, company,
concern, corporation, enterprise, firm,
house, institute, institution, outfit
(*informal*), setup (*informal*), structure,
system **3** = **office**, building, factory, house,
plant, quarters **4** = **house**, abode, domicile,
dwelling, home, household, pad (*slang*),
residence **5 the Establishment** = **the
authorities**, established order,
institutionalized authority, ruling class, the
powers that be, the system

estate *noun* **1** = **lands**, area, demesne,
domain, holdings, manor, property **2** *Law*
= **property**, assets, belongings, effects,
fortune, goods, possessions, wealth **3**
History = **class**, caste, order, rank **4**
= **status**, condition, lot, period, place,
position, quality, rank, situation, standing,
state, station

esteem *noun* **1** = **respect**, admiration,
Brownie points, consideration, credit,

estimation, good opinion, honour, regard,
reverence, veneration ♦ *verb* **2** = **respect**,
admire, be fond of, cherish, honour, like,
love, prize, regard highly, revere,
reverence, take off one's hat to, think
highly of, treasure, value, venerate **3**
Formal = **consider**, account, believe,
calculate, deem, estimate, hold, judge,
rate, reckon, regard, think, view

estimate *verb* **1** = **calculate roughly**,
appraise, assess, evaluate, gauge, guess,
judge, number, reckon, value **2** = **form an
opinion**, assess, believe, conjecture,
consider, guess, judge, rank, rate, reckon,
surmise, think ♦ *noun* **3** = **approximate
calculation**, appraisal, appraisement,
assessment, ballpark estimate (*informal*),
ballpark figure (*informal*), evaluation,
guess, guesstimate (*informal*), judgment,
reckoning, valuation **4** = **opinion**,
appraisal, appraisement, assessment,
belief, conjecture, educated guess,
estimation, judgment, surmise, thought(s)

estimation *noun* **1** = **opinion**, appraisal,
appreciation, assessment, belief,
consideration, considered opinion,
estimate, evaluation, judgment, view **2**
= **respect**, admiration, Brownie points,
credit, esteem, good opinion, honour,
regard, reverence, veneration

estrange *verb* = **alienate**, antagonize,
disaffect, disunite, divide, drive apart, lose
or destroy the affection of, make hostile,
part, separate, set at odds, withdraw,
withhold
➤ **Antonyms**
ally, associate, couple, fuse, join, link,
marry, unite

estrangement *noun* = **alienation**,
antagonization, breach, break-up,
disaffection, dissociation, disunity, division,
hostility, parting, separation, split,
withdrawal, withholding

estuary *noun* = **inlet**, creek, firth, fjord,
mouth

et cetera *adverb* **1** = **and so on**, and so
forth ♦ *noun* **2** = **and the rest**, and others,
and the like, et al.

etch *verb* = **cut**, carve, corrode, eat into,
engrave, furrow, impress, imprint, incise,
ingrain, inscribe, stamp

etching *noun* = **print**, carving, engraving,
impression, imprint, inscription

eternal *adjective* **1** = **everlasting**, abiding,
ceaseless, constant, deathless, endless,
immortal, infinite, interminable,
never-ending, perennial, perpetual,
sempiternal (*literary*), timeless, unceasing,
undying, unending, unremitting, without
end **2** = **permanent**, deathless, enduring,

everlasting, immortal, immutable, imperishable, indestructible, lasting, unchanging

➤ **Antonyms**

≠**everlasting**: finite, fleeting, infrequent, irregular, mortal, occasional, random, rare, temporal ≠**permanent**: changing, ephemeral, evanescent, perishable, transient, transitory

eternity *noun* **1** = **infinity**, age, ages, endlessness, immortality, infinitude, perpetuity, timelessness, time without end **2** *Theology* = **the afterlife**, heaven, paradise, the hereafter, the next world

ethical *adjective* = **moral**, conscientious, correct, decent, fair, fitting, good, honest, honourable, just, principled, proper, right, righteous, upright, virtuous

➤ **Antonyms**

dishonourable, disreputable, immoral, improper, indecent, low-down (*informal*), not cricket (*informal*), underhand, unethical, unfair, unscrupulous, unseemly

ethics *plural noun* = **moral code**, conscience, morality, moral philosophy, moral values, principles, rules of conduct, standards

ethnic, ethnical *adjective* = **cultural**, folk, indigenous, national, native, racial, traditional

etiquette *noun* = **good** *or* **proper behaviour**, civility, code, convention, courtesy, customs, decorum, formalities, manners, politeness, politesse, propriety, protocol, p's and q's, rules, usage

eulogize *verb* = **praise**, acclaim, applaud, commend, compliment, crack up (*informal*), cry up, exalt, extol, glorify, laud, magnify (*archaic*), panegyrize, pay tribute to, sing *or* sound the praises of

eulogy *noun* = **praise**, acclaim, acclamation, accolade, applause, commendation, compliment, encomium, exaltation, glorification, laudation, paean, panegyric, plaudit, tribute

euphoria *noun* = **elation**, bliss, ecstasy, exaltation, exhilaration, exultation, glee, high spirits, intoxication, joy, joyousness, jubilation, rapture, transport

➤ **Antonyms**

depression, despair, despondency, dolefulness, downheartedness, dumps (*informal*), gloominess, hopelessness, low spirits, melancholia, melancholy, sadness, the blues

evacuate *verb* **1** = **clear**, abandon, decamp, depart, desert, forsake, leave, move out, pull out, quit, relinquish, remove, vacate, withdraw **2** *Physiology* = **excrete**, crap (*taboo slang*), defecate, discharge, eject, eliminate, empty, expel, shit (*taboo slang*), void

evade *verb* **1** = **avoid**, body-swerve (*Scot.*), circumvent, decline, dodge, duck, elude, escape, escape the clutches of, eschew, get away from, shirk, shun, sidestep, slip through one's fingers, slip through the net, steer clear of **2** = **avoid answering**, balk, beat about the bush, circumvent, cop out (*slang*), equivocate, fence, fend off, flannel (*Brit. informal*), fudge, hedge, parry, prevaricate, quibble, waffle (*informal, chiefly Brit.*)

➤ **Antonyms**

≠**avoid**: brave, confront, encounter, face, meet, meet face to face

evaluate *verb* = **assess**, appraise, assay, calculate, estimate, gauge, judge, rank, rate, reckon, size up (*informal*), value, weigh

evaluation *noun* = **assessment**, appraisal, calculation, estimate, estimation, judgment, opinion, rating, valuation

evanescent *adjective Formal* = **ephemeral**, brief, fading, fleeting, fugacious, fugitive, impermanent, momentary, passing, short-lived, transient, transitory, vanishing

evangelical, evangelistic *adjective* = **crusading**, missionary, propagandizing, proselytizing, zealous

evaporate *verb* **1** = **dry up**, dehydrate, desiccate, dry, vaporize **2** = **disappear**, dematerialize, dispel, disperse, dissipate, dissolve, evanesce, fade, fade away, melt, melt away, vanish

evaporation *noun* **1** = **drying up**, dehydration, desiccation, drying, vaporization **2** = **disappearance**, dematerialization, dispelling, dispersal, dissipation, dissolution, evanescence, fading, fading away, melting, melting away, vanishing

evasion *noun* **1** = **avoidance**, circumvention, dodging, elusion, escape **2** = **deception**, artifice, cop-out (*slang*), cunning, equivocation, evasiveness, excuse, fudging, obliqueness, pretext, prevarication, ruse, shift, shirking, shuffling, sophism, sophistry, subterfuge, trickery, waffle (*informal, chiefly Brit.*)

evasive *adjective* = **deceptive**, cagey (*informal*), casuistic, casuistical, cunning, deceitful, devious, dissembling, equivocating, indirect, misleading, oblique, prevaricating, shifty, shuffling, slippery, sophistical, tricky

➤ **Antonyms**

candid, direct, frank, guileless, honest, open, straight, straightforward, truthful, unequivocating

eve *noun* **1 = night before**, day before, vigil **2 = brink**, edge, point, threshold, verge

even *adjective* **1 = level**, flat, flush, horizontal, parallel, plane, plumb, smooth, steady, straight, true, uniform **2 = regular**, constant, metrical, smooth, steady, unbroken, uniform, uninterrupted, unvarying, unwavering **3 = equal**, coequal, commensurate, comparable, drawn, equalized, equally balanced, fifty-fifty (*informal*), identical, level, level pegging (*Brit. informal*), like, matching, neck and neck, on a par, parallel, similar, square, the same, tied, uniform **4 = fair**, balanced, disinterested, dispassionate, equitable, fair and square, impartial, just, unbiased, unprejudiced **5 = calm**, composed, cool, equable, equanimous, even-tempered, imperturbable, peaceful, placid, serene, stable, steady, tranquil, undisturbed, unexcitable, unruffled, well-balanced **6 get even (with)** *Informal* **= pay back**, be revenged *or* revenge oneself, even the score, get one's own back, give tit for tat, pay (someone) back in his *or* her own coin, reciprocate, repay, requite, return like for like, settle the score, take an eye for an eye, take vengeance ♦ *adverb* **7 = despite**, disregarding, in spite of, notwithstanding **8 = all the more**, much, still, yet **9 even as = while**, at the same time as, at the time that, during the time that, exactly as, just as, whilst **10 even so = nevertheless**, all the same, be that as it may, despite (that), however, in spite of (that), nonetheless, notwithstanding (that), still, yet ♦ *verb* **11 even out = make** *or* **become level**, align, flatten, level, regularize, smooth, square, stabilize, steady **12 even the score = pay (someone) back**, be revenged *or* revenge oneself, equalize, get even (*informal*), get one's own back, give tit for tat, reciprocate, repay, requite, return like for like, settle the score, take an eye for an eye, take vengeance **13 even up = equalize**, balance, equal, match
➤ **Antonyms**
adjective ≠**level:** asymmetrical, awry, bumpy, curving, rough, twisting, undulating, uneven, wavy ≠**regular:** broken, changeable, changing, different, fluctuating, irregular, odd, uneven, variable ≠**equal:** disproportionate, ill-matched, imbalanced, irregular, unequal, uneven ≠**fair:** biased, partial, prejudiced, unbalanced, unequal, unfair ≠**calm:** agitated, changeable, emotional, excitable, quick-tempered, unpredictable

even-handed *adjective* **= fair**, balanced, disinterested, equitable, fair and square, impartial, just, unbiased, unprejudiced

evening *noun* **= dusk**, crepuscule, e'en (*archaic or poetic*), eve, even (*archaic*), eventide (*archaic or poetic*), gloaming (*Scot. or poetic*), twilight, vesper (*archaic*)

event *noun* **1 = incident**, adventure, affair, business, circumstance, episode, escapade, experience, fact, happening, matter, milestone, occasion, occurrence **2 = competition**, bout, contest, game, tournament **3 As in in the event = outcome**, conclusion, consequence, effect, end, issue, result, termination, upshot **4 at all events = whatever happens**, at any rate, come what may, in any case, in any event, regardless

even-tempered *adjective* **= calm**, composed, cool, cool-headed, equable, imperturbable, level-headed, peaceful, placid, serene, steady, tranquil, unexcitable, unruffled
➤ **Antonyms**
emotional, excitable, hasty, highly-strung, hot-headed, hot-tempered, irascible, quick-tempered, temperamental, touchy, volatile

eventful *adjective* **= exciting**, active, busy, consequential, critical, crucial, decisive, dramatic, fateful, full, historic, important, lively, memorable, momentous, notable, noteworthy, remarkable, significant
➤ **Antonyms**
commonplace, dull, humdrum, insignificant, ordinary, trivial, uneventful, unexceptional, unexciting, unimportant, uninteresting, unremarkable

eventual *adjective* **= final**, concluding, consequent, ensuing, future, later, overall, prospective, resulting, ultimate

eventuality *noun* **= possibility**, case, chance, contingency, event, likelihood, probability

eventually *adverb* **= in the end**, after all, at the end of the day, finally, in the course of time, in the fullness of time, in the long run, one day, some day, some time, sooner or later, ultimately, when all is said and done

ever *adverb* **1 = at any time**, at all, at any period, at any point, by any chance, in any case, on any occasion **2 = always**, at all times, aye (*Scot.*), constantly, continually, endlessly, eternally, everlastingly, evermore, for ever, incessantly, perpetually, relentlessly, to the end of time, unceasingly, unendingly

everlasting *adjective* **1 = eternal**, abiding, deathless, endless, immortal, imperishable, indestructible, infinite, interminable, never-ending, perpetual, timeless, undying **2 = continual**, ceaseless, constant, continuous, endless, incessant, interminable, never-ending, unceasing, uninterrupted, unremitting

➤ **Antonyms**

≠**eternal**: brief, ephemeral, fleeting, impermanent, passing, short-lived, temporary, transient, transitory

evermore adverb = **for ever**, always, eternally, ever, in perpetuum, to the end of time

every adjective = **each**, all, each one, the whole number

everybody pronoun = **everyone**, all and sundry, each one, each person, every person, one and all, the whole world

everyday adjective 1 = **ordinary**, accustomed, banal, bog-standard (Brit. & Irish slang), common, common or garden (informal), commonplace, conventional, customary, dime-a-dozen (informal), dull, familiar, frequent, habitual, informal, mundane, routine, run-of-the-mill, stock, unexceptional, unimaginative, usual, vanilla (slang), wonted, workaday 2 = **daily**, quotidian

➤ **Antonyms**

≠**ordinary**: best, exceptional, exciting, extraordinary, incidental, individual, infrequent, interesting, irregular, now and then, occasional, original, outlandish, periodic, special, uncommon, unusual ≠**daily**: infrequent, irregular, now and then, occasional, periodic

everyone pronoun = **everybody**, all and sundry, each one, each person, every person, one and all, the whole world

everything pronoun = **all**, each thing, the aggregate, the entirety, the lot, the sum, the total, the whole, the whole caboodle (informal), the whole kit and caboodle (informal), the whole lot

everywhere adverb = **to or in every place**, all around, all over, far and wide or near, high and low, in each place, in every nook and cranny, omnipresent, the world over, ubiquitous, ubiquitously

evict verb = **expel**, boot out (informal), chuck out (informal), dislodge, dispossess, eject, kick out (informal), oust, put out, remove, show the door (to), throw on to the streets, throw out, turf out (informal), turn out

eviction noun = **expulsion**, clearance, dislodgement, dispossession, ejection, ouster (Law), removal

evidence noun 1 = **proof**, affirmation, attestation, averment, confirmation, corroboration, data, declaration, demonstration, deposition, grounds, indication, manifestation, mark, sign,

substantiation, testimony, token, witness ♦ verb 2 = **show**, demonstrate, denote, display, evince, exhibit, indicate, manifest, prove, reveal, signify, testify to, witness

evident adjective = **obvious**, apparent, blatant, bold, clear, conspicuous, incontestable, incontrovertible, indisputable, manifest, noticeable, palpable, patent, perceptible, plain, plain as the nose on your face, salient, tangible, unmistakable, visible

➤ **Antonyms**

ambiguous, concealed, doubtful, dubious, hidden, imperceptible, obscure, questionable, secret, uncertain, unclear, unknown, vague

evidently adverb 1 = **obviously**, clearly, doubtless, doubtlessly, incontestably, incontrovertibly, indisputably, manifestly, patently, plainly, undoubtedly, unmistakably, without question 2 = **apparently**, it seems, it would seem, ostensibly, outwardly, seemingly, to all appearances

evil noun 1 = **wickedness**, badness, baseness, corruption, curse, depravity, heinousness, immorality, iniquity, maleficence, malignity, sin, sinfulness, turpitude, vice, viciousness, villainy, wrong, wrongdoing 2 = **harm**, affliction, calamity, catastrophe, disaster, hurt, ill, injury, mischief, misery, misfortune, pain, ruin, sorrow, suffering, woe ♦ adjective 3 = **wicked**, bad, base, corrupt, depraved, heinous, immoral, iniquitous, maleficent, malevolent, malicious, malignant, nefarious, reprobate, sinful, unholy, vicious, vile, villainous, wrong 4 = **harmful**, baneful (archaic), calamitous, catastrophic, deleterious, destructive, detrimental, dire, disastrous, hurtful, inauspicious, injurious, mischievous, painful, pernicious, ruinous, sorrowful, unfortunate, unlucky, woeful 5 = **offensive**, foul, mephitic, noxious, pestilential, putrid, unpleasant, vile

evoke verb 1 = **arouse**, awaken, call, excite, give rise to, induce, recall, rekindle, stimulate, stir up, summon up 2 = **provoke**, call forth, educe (rare), elicit, produce

➤ **Antonyms**

≠**arouse**: contain, hold in check, inhibit, muffle, repress, restrain, smother, stifle, suppress

evolution noun = **development**, enlargement, evolvement, expansion, growth, increase, maturation, progress, progression, unfolding, unrolling, working out

evolve verb = **develop**, disclose, educe,

elaborate, enlarge, expand, grow, increase, mature, open, progress, unfold, unroll, work out

exact *adjective* **1** = **accurate**, careful, correct, definite, explicit, express, faithful, faultless, identical, literal, methodical, on the money (*U.S.*), orderly, particular, precise, right, specific, true, unequivocal, unerring, veracious, very **2** = **meticulous**, careful, exacting, painstaking, punctilious, rigorous, scrupulous, severe, strict ♦ *verb* **3** = **demand**, call for, claim, command, compel, extort, extract, force, impose, insist upon, require, squeeze, wrest, wring
➤ **Antonyms**
adjective ≠**accurate**: approximate, careless, imprecise, inaccurate, incorrect, indefinite, inexact, loose, rough, slovenly

exacting *adjective* = **demanding**, difficult, hard, harsh, imperious, oppressive, painstaking, rigid, rigorous, severe, stern, strict, stringent, taxing, tough, unsparing
➤ **Antonyms**
easy, easy-peasy (*slang*), effortless, no bother, simple, undemanding

exactly *adverb* **1** = **precisely**, accurately, carefully, correctly, definitely, explicitly, faithfully, faultlessly, literally, methodically, rigorously, scrupulously, severely, strictly, truly, truthfully, unequivocally, unerringly, veraciously **2** = **in every respect**, absolutely, bang, explicitly, expressly, indeed, just, on the button (*informal*), particularly, precisely, prompt (*informal*), quite, specifically, to the letter **3** *not exactly Ironical* = **not at all**, by no means, certainly not, hardly, in no manner, in no way, not by any means, not quite, not really ♦ *interjection* **4** = **precisely**, absolutely, assuredly, as you say, certainly, indeed, just so, of course, quite, quite so, spot-on (*Brit. informal*), truly

exactness *noun* = **precision**, accuracy, carefulness, correctness, exactitude, faithfulness, faultlessness, nicety, orderliness, painstakingness, preciseness, promptitude, regularity, rigorousness, rigour, scrupulousness, strictness, truth, unequivocalness, veracity
➤ **Antonyms**
imprecision, inaccuracy, incorrectness, inexactness, unfaithfulness

exaggerate *verb* = **overstate**, amplify, blow out of all proportion, embellish, embroider, emphasize, enlarge, exalt, hyperbolize, inflate, lay it on thick (*informal*), magnify, make a federal case of (*U.S. informal*), make a mountain out of a molehill (*informal*), make a production (out) of (*informal*), overdo,

overemphasize, overestimate

exaggerated *adjective* = **overstated**, amplified, exalted, excessive, extravagant, fulsome, highly coloured, hyped, hyperbolic, inflated, overblown, overdone, overestimated, over the top (*informal*), pretentious, tall (*informal*)

exaggeration *noun* = **overstatement**, amplification, embellishment, emphasis, enlargement, exaltation, excess, extravagance, hyperbole, inflation, magnification, overemphasis, overestimation, pretension, pretentiousness
➤ **Antonyms**
litotes, restraint, underplaying, understatement

exalt *verb* **1** = **praise**, acclaim, apotheosize, applaud, bless, crack up (*informal*), extol, glorify, idolize, laud, magnify (*archaic*), pay homage to, pay tribute to, reverence, set on a pedestal, worship **2** = **raise**, advance, aggrandize, dignify, elevate, ennoble, honour, promote, upgrade **3** = **stimulate**, animate, arouse, electrify, elevate, excite, fire the imagination (of), heighten, inspire, inspirit, uplift **4** = **elate**, delight, exhilarate, fill with joy, thrill

exaltation *noun* **1** = **praise**, acclaim, acclamation, apotheosis, applause, blessing, extolment, glorification, glory, homage, idolization, laudation, lionization, magnification, panegyric, plaudits, reverence, tribute, worship **2** = **rise**, advancement, aggrandizement, dignity, elevation, eminence, ennoblement, grandeur, high rank, honour, loftiness, prestige, promotion, upgrading **3** = **stimulation**, animation, elevation, excitement, inspiration, uplift **4** = **elation**, bliss, delight, ecstasy, exhilaration, exultation, joy, joyousness, jubilation, rapture, transport

exalted *adjective* **1** = **high-ranking**, august, dignified, elevated, eminent, grand, high, honoured, lofty, prestigious **2** = **noble**, elevated, high-minded, ideal, intellectual, lofty, sublime, superior, uplifting **3** *Informal* = **inflated**, elevated, exaggerated, excessive, overblown, pretentious **4** = **elated**, animated, blissful, cock-a-hoop, ecstatic, elevated, excited, exhilarated, exultant, in high spirits, in seventh heaven, inspired, inspirited, joyous, jubilant, on cloud nine (*informal*), over the moon (*informal*), rapturous, stimulated, transported, uplifted

examination *noun* **1** = **inspection**, analysis, assay, checkup, exploration, interrogation, investigation, observation, once-over (*informal*), perusal, recce (*slang*), research, review, scrutiny, search, study, survey, test, trial **2 = questioning**, catechism, inquiry, inquisition, probe, quiz, test

examine *verb* **1 = inspect**, analyse, appraise, assay, check, check out, consider, explore, go over *or* through, investigate, look over, peruse, ponder, pore over, probe, recce (*slang*), research, review, scan, scrutinize, sift, study, survey, take stock of, test, vet, weigh, work over **2 = question**, catechize, cross-examine, grill (*informal*), inquire, interrogate, quiz, test

example *noun* **1 = specimen**, case, case in point, exemplification, illustration, instance, sample **2 = model**, archetype, exemplar, ideal, illustration, norm, paradigm, paragon, pattern, precedent, prototype, standard **3 = warning**, admonition, caution, lesson **4 for example = as an illustration**, by way of illustration, e.g., *exempli gratia*, for instance, to cite an instance, to illustrate

exasperate *verb* **= irritate**, aggravate (*informal*), anger, annoy, bug (*informal*), embitter, enrage, exacerbate, excite, gall, get (*informal*), get in one's hair (*informal*), get on one's nerves (*informal*), get on one's wick (*Brit. slang*), hassle (*informal*), incense, inflame, infuriate, irk, madden, nark (*Brit., Austral., & N.Z. slang*), needle (*informal*), nettle, peeve (*informal*), pique, piss one off (*taboo slang*), provoke, rankle, rile (*informal*), rouse, try the patience of, vex

➤ **Antonyms**
appease, assuage, calm, conciliate, mollify, pacify, placate, soothe

exasperation *noun* **= irritation**, aggravation (*informal*), anger, annoyance, exacerbation, fury, ire (*literary*), passion, pique, provocation, rage, vexation, wrath

excavate *verb* **= dig out**, burrow, cut, delve, dig, dig up, gouge, hollow, mine, quarry, scoop, trench, tunnel, uncover, unearth

excavation *noun* **= hole**, burrow, cavity, cut, cutting, dig, diggings, ditch, dugout, hollow, mine, pit, quarry, shaft, trench, trough

exceed *verb* **1 = surpass**, beat, be superior to, better, cap (*informal*), eclipse, excel, go beyond, knock spots off (*informal*), outdistance, outdo, outreach, outrun, outshine, outstrip, overtake, pass, put in the shade (*informal*), surmount, top, transcend **2 = go over the limit of**, go beyond the bounds of, go over the top, overstep

exceeding *adjective* **= extraordinary**, enormous, exceptional, excessive, great, huge, pre-eminent, streets ahead, superior, superlative, surpassing, vast

exceedingly *adverb* **= extremely**, enormously, especially, exceptionally, excessively, extraordinarily, greatly, highly, hugely, inordinately, seriously (*informal*), superlatively, surpassingly, to a fault, to the nth degree, unusually, vastly, very

excel *verb* **1 = be superior**, beat, better, cap (*informal*), eclipse, exceed, go beyond, outdo, outrival, outshine, pass, put in the shade (*informal*), run rings around (*informal*), steal the show (*informal*), surmount, surpass, top, transcend **2 excel in** *or* **at = be good at**, be master of, be proficient in, be skilful at, be talented at, have (something) down to a fine art, predominate in, shine at, show talent in

excellence *noun* **= high quality**, distinction, eminence, fineness, goodness, greatness, merit, perfection, pre-eminence, purity, superiority, supremacy, transcendence, virtue, worth

excellent *adjective* **= outstanding**, A1 *or* A-one (*informal*), admirable, bitchin' (*U.S. slang*), bodacious (*slang, chiefly U.S.*), boffo (*slang*), brill (*informal*), brilliant, capital, champion, chillin' (*U.S. slang*), choice, cracking (*Brit. informal*), crucial (*slang*), def (*slang*), distinguished, dope (*slang*), estimable, exemplary, exquisite, fine, first-class, first-rate, good, great, jim-dandy (*slang*), mean (*slang*), mega (*slang*), meritorious, notable, noted, prime, select, sovereign, sterling, superb, superior, superlative, the dog's bollocks (*taboo slang*), tiptop, top-notch (*informal*), topping (*Brit. slang*), world-class, worthy

➤ **Antonyms**
abysmal, bad, dreadful, faulty, imperfect, incompetent, inexpert, inferior, lousy (*slang*), mediocre, no great shakes (*informal*), piss-poor (*taboo slang*), poor, rotten (*informal*), second-class, second-rate, substandard, terrible, unskilled

except *preposition* **1** Also **except for = apart from**, bar, barring, besides, but, excepting, excluding, exclusive of, omitting, other than, save (*archaic*), saving, with the exception of ♦ *verb* **2 = exclude**, ban, bar, disallow, leave out, omit, pass over, reject, rule out

exception *noun* **1 = special case**, anomaly, departure, deviation, freak, inconsistency, irregularity, oddity, peculiarity, quirk **2 = exclusion**, debarment, disallowment, excepting, leaving out, omission, passing over, rejection **3 take exception to**

= **object to**, be offended at, be resentful of, demur at, disagree with, quibble at, take offence at, take umbrage at

exceptional *adjective* **1** = **unusual**, aberrant, abnormal, anomalous, atypical, deviant, extraordinary, inconsistent, irregular, odd, peculiar, rare, singular, special, strange, uncommon **2** = **remarkable**, bodacious (*slang, chiefly U.S.*), excellent, extraordinary, marvellous, notable, one in a million, outstanding, phenomenal, prodigious, special, superior
➤ **Antonyms**
≠**unusual**: average, common, customary, familiar, normal, ordinary, regular, straightforward, typical, unexceptional, unremarkable, usual ≠**remarkable**: average, awful, bad, lousy (*slang*), mediocre, no great shakes (*informal*), second-rate

excerpt *noun* = **extract**, fragment, part, passage, piece, quotation, section, selection

excess *noun* **1** = **surfeit**, glut, leftover, overabundance, overdose, overflow, overload, plethora, remainder, superabundance, superfluity, surplus, too much **2** = **overindulgence**, debauchery, dissipation, dissoluteness, exorbitance, extravagance, immoderation, intemperance, prodigality, unrestraint
♦ *adjective* **3** = **spare**, extra, leftover, redundant, remaining, residual, superfluous, surplus
➤ **Antonyms**
noun ≠**surfeit**: dearth, deficiency, insufficiency, lack, shortage, want ≠**overindulgence**: moderation, restraint, self-control, self-discipline, self-restraint, temperance

excessive *adjective* = **immoderate**, disproportionate, enormous, exaggerated, exorbitant, extravagant, extreme, fulsome, inordinate, intemperate, needless, O.T.T. (*slang*), overdone, overmuch, over the odds, over the top (*slang*), prodigal, profligate, superfluous, too much, unconscionable, undue, unfair, unreasonable

exchange *verb* **1** = **interchange**, bandy, barter, change, commute, convert into, reciprocate, swap, switch, trade, truck
♦ *noun* **2** = **interchange**, barter, dealing, quid pro quo, reciprocity, substitution, swap, switch, tit for tat, trade, traffic, truck **3** = **market**, Bourse

excitable *adjective* = **nervous**, edgy, emotional, hasty, highly strung, hot-headed, hot-tempered, irascible, mercurial, passionate, quick-tempered,

sensitive, susceptible, temperamental, testy, touchy, uptight (*informal*), violent, volatile
➤ **Antonyms**
calm, cool, cool-headed, even-tempered, imperturbable, laid-back (*informal*), placid, unexcitable, unruffled

excite *verb* **1** = **arouse**, agitate, animate, awaken, elicit, evoke, fire, foment, galvanize, incite, inflame, inspire, instigate, kindle, move, provoke, quicken, rouse, stimulate, stir up, waken, whet, work up **2** = **thrill**, electrify, titillate

excited *adjective* = **worked up**, aflame, agitated, animated, aroused, awakened, discomposed, disturbed, enthusiastic, feverish, flurried, high (*informal*), hot and bothered (*informal*), moved, nervous, overwrought, roused, stimulated, stirred, thrilled, tumultuous, wild

excitement *noun* **1** = **agitation**, action, activity, ado, adventure, animation, commotion, discomposure, elation, enthusiasm, ferment, fever, flurry, furore, heat, kicks (*informal*), passion, perturbation, thrill, tumult, warmth **2** = **stimulus**, impulse, incitement, instigation, motivation, motive, provocation, stimulation, thrill, urge

exciting *adjective* = **stimulating**, dramatic, electrifying, exhilarating, inspiring, intoxicating, moving, provocative, rip-roaring (*informal*), rousing, sensational, sexy (*informal*), stirring, thrilling, titillating
➤ **Antonyms**
boring, dreary, dull, flat, humdrum, mind-numbing, monotonous, unexciting, uninspiring, uninteresting

exclaim *verb* = **cry out**, call, call out, cry, declare, ejaculate, proclaim, shout, utter, vociferate, yell

exclamation *noun* = **cry**, call, ejaculation, expletive, interjection, outcry, shout, utterance, vociferation, yell

exclude *verb* **1** = **keep out**, ban, bar, black, blackball, boycott, debar, disallow, embargo, forbid, interdict, ostracize, prohibit, proscribe, refuse, shut out, veto **2** = **remove**, bounce (*slang*), drive out, eject, evict, expel, force out, get rid of, oust, throw out **3** = **leave out**, count out, eliminate, except, ignore, not count, omit, pass over, preclude, reject, repudiate, rule out, set aside
➤ **Antonyms**
≠**keep out, remove**: accept, admit, allow, let in, permit, receive, welcome ≠**leave out**: accept, count, include

exclusion *noun* **1** = **ban**, bar, boycott, debarment, disqualification, embargo,

forbiddance, interdict, nonadmission,
preclusion, prohibition, proscription,
refusal, veto **2 = removal**, eviction,
expulsion **3 = elimination**, exception,
omission, rejection, repudiation

exclusive *adjective* **1 = sole**, absolute,
complete, entire, full, only, private, single,
total, undivided, unique, unshared, whole
2 = limited, confined, peculiar, restricted,
unique **3 = select**, aristocratic, chic, choice,
clannish, classy (*slang*), cliquish, closed,
discriminative, elegant, fashionable,
high-toned, limited, narrow, posh
(*informal, chiefly Brit.*), private, restricted,
restrictive, ritzy (*slang*), selfish, snobbish,
swish (*informal, chiefly Brit.*), top-drawer,
up-market **4 exclusive of = except for**,
debarring, excepting, excluding, leaving
aside, not counting, omitting, restricting,
ruling out
➤ **Antonyms**
≠**sole, limited:** inclusive, nonexclusive,
partial, shared ≠**select:** common,
communal, open, popular, public,
unrestricted

excommunicate *verb* **= expel**,
anathematize, ban, banish, cast out,
denounce, eject, exclude, proscribe,
remove, repudiate, unchurch

excruciating *adjective* **= agonizing**, acute,
burning, exquisite, extreme, harrowing,
insufferable, intense, piercing, racking,
searing, severe, tormenting, torturous,
unbearable, unendurable, violent

exculpate *verb* **= absolve**, acquit, clear,
discharge, dismiss, excuse, exonerate, free,
justify, pardon, release, vindicate

excursion *noun* **1 = trip**, airing, day trip,
expedition, jaunt, journey, outing,
pleasure trip, ramble, tour **2 = digression**,
detour, deviation, episode, excursus,
wandering

excusable *adjective* **= forgivable**,
allowable, defensible, justifiable, minor,
pardonable, permissible, slight,
understandable, venial, warrantable

excuse *noun* **1 = justification**, apology,
defence, explanation, grounds, mitigation,
plea, pretext, reason, vindication **2
= pretext**, cop-out (*slang*), disguise,
evasion, expedient, makeshift, pretence,
semblance, shift, subterfuge **3** *Informal*
= poor substitute, apology, makeshift,
mockery, travesty ♦ *verb* **4 = justify**,
apologize for, condone, defend, explain,
mitigate, vindicate **5 = forgive**, absolve,
acquit, bear with, exculpate, exonerate,
extenuate, indulge, make allowances for,
overlook, pardon, pass over, tolerate, turn
a blind eye to, wink at **6 = free**, absolve,

discharge, exempt, let off, liberate, release,
relieve, spare
➤ **Antonyms**
noun ≠**justification:** accusation, charge,
imputation, indictment ♦ *verb* ≠**justify:**
accuse, blame, censure, chasten, chastise,
compel, condemn, correct, criticize, hold
responsible, oblige, point a *or* the finger at,
punish ≠**free:** arraign, charge, convict,
indict, sentence

execrate *verb* **1 = loathe**, abhor,
abominate, condemn, denounce, deplore,
despise, detest, excoriate, hate, revile,
slam (*slang*), vilify **2 = curse**, anathematize,
damn, imprecate

execration *noun* **1 = loathing**, abhorrence,
abomination, condemnation, contempt,
detestation, excoriation, hate, hatred,
odium, vilification **2 = curse**, anathema,
damnation, imprecation, malediction

execute *verb* **1 = put to death**, behead,
electrocute, guillotine, hang, kill, shoot **2
= carry out**, accomplish, achieve,
administer, bring off, complete,
consummate, discharge, do, effect, enact,
enforce, finish, fulfil, implement, perform,
prosecute, put into effect, realize, render **3**
Law **= validate**, deliver, seal, serve, sign

execution *noun* **1 = carrying out**,
accomplishment, achievement,
administration, completion,
consummation, discharge, effect,
enactment, enforcement, implementation,
operation, performance, prosecution,
realization, rendering **2 = killing**, capital
punishment, hanging, necktie party
(*informal*) **3 = technique**, delivery,
manner, mode, performance, rendition,
style

executioner *noun* **1 = hangman**,
headsman **2 = killer**, assassin,
exterminator, hit man (*slang*), liquidator,
murderer, slayer

executive *noun* **1 = administrator**,
director, manager, official **2
= administration**, directorate, directors,
government, hierarchy, leadership,
management ♦ *adjective* **3
= administrative**, controlling,
decision-making, directing, governing,
managerial

exemplary *adjective* **1 = ideal**, admirable,
commendable, correct, estimable,
excellent, fine, good, honourable,
laudable, meritorious, model,
praiseworthy, punctilious, sterling **2
= warning**, admonitory, cautionary,
monitory **3 = typical**, characteristic,
illustrative, representative

exemplify *verb* **= show**, demonstrate,

depict, display, embody, evidence, exhibit, illustrate, instance, manifest, represent, serve as an example of

exempt *adjective* 1 = **immune**, absolved, clear, discharged, excepted, excused, favoured, free, liberated, not liable, not subject, privileged, released, spared ♦ *verb* 2 = **grant immunity**, absolve, discharge, except, excuse, exonerate, free, let off, liberate, release, relieve, spare
➤ **Antonyms**
adjective ≠**immune**: accountable, answerable, chargeable, liable, obligated, responsible, subject

exemption *noun* = **immunity**, absolution, discharge, dispensation, exception, exoneration, freedom, privilege, release

exercise *noun* 1 = **exertion**, action, activity, discipline, drill, drilling, effort, labour, toil, training, work, work-out 2 = **task**, drill, lesson, practice, problem, schooling, schoolwork, work 3 = **use**, accomplishment, application, discharge, employment, enjoyment, exertion, fulfilment, implementation, practice, utilization ♦ *verb* 4 = **put to use**, apply, bring to bear, employ, enjoy, exert, practise, use, utilize, wield 5 = **train**, discipline, drill, habituate, inure, practise, work out 6 = **worry**, afflict, agitate, annoy, burden, distress, disturb, occupy, pain, perturb, preoccupy, trouble, try, vex

exert *verb* 1 = **use**, apply, bring into play, bring to bear, employ, exercise, expend, make use of, put forth, utilize, wield 2 **exert oneself** = **make an effort**, apply oneself, bend over backwards (*informal*), break one's neck (*informal*), bust a gut (*informal*), do one's best, do one's damnedest (*informal*), endeavour, get one's finger out (*Brit. informal*), give it one's all (*informal*), give it one's best shot (*informal*), go for broke (*slang*), go for it (*informal*), knock oneself out (*informal*), labour, make an all-out effort (*informal*), pull one's finger out (*Brit. informal*), rupture oneself (*informal*), spare no effort, strain, strive, struggle, toil, try hard, work

exertion *noun* 1 = **effort**, action, attempt, elbow grease (*facetious*), endeavour, exercise, industry, labour, pains, strain, stretch, struggle, toil, travail (*literary*), trial 2 = **use**, application, employment, utilization

exhaust *verb* 1 = **tire out**, bankrupt, cripple, debilitate, disable, drain, enervate, enfeeble, fatigue, impoverish, prostrate, sap, tire, weaken, wear out 2 = **use up**, consume, deplete, dissipate, expend, finish, run through, spend, squander,

waste 3 = **empty**, drain, dry, strain, void

exhausted *adjective* 1 = **worn out**, all in (*slang*), beat (*slang*), buggered (*slang*), clapped out (*Austral. & N.Z. informal*), creamcrackered (*Brit. slang*), crippled, dead (*informal*), dead beat (*informal*), dead tired, debilitated, disabled, dog-tired (*informal*), done in (*informal*), drained, effete, enervated, enfeebled, fatigued, jaded, knackered (*slang*), on one's last legs (*informal*), out on one's feet (*informal*), prostrated, ready to drop, sapped, shagged out (*Brit. slang*), spent, tired out, wasted, weak, wiped out (*informal*), worn to a frazzle (*informal*), zonked (*slang*) 2 = **used up**, at an end, consumed, depleted, dissipated, done, expended, finished, gone, spent, squandered, wasted 3 = **empty**, bare, drained, dry, void
➤ **Antonyms**
≠**worn out**: active, alive and kicking, animated, enlivened, invigorated, refreshed, rejuvenated, restored, revived, stimulated ≠**used up**: conserved, kept, preserved, replenished, restored

exhausting *adjective* = **tiring**, arduous, backbreaking, crippling, debilitating, difficult, draining, enervating, fatiguing, gruelling, hard, laborious, punishing, sapping, strenuous, taxing, testing

exhaustion *noun* 1 = **tiredness**, debilitation, enervation, fatigue, feebleness, lassitude, prostration, weariness 2 = **depletion**, consumption, emptying, using up

exhaustive *adjective* = **thorough**, all-embracing, all-inclusive, all-out (*informal*), complete, comprehensive, detailed, encyclopedic, extensive, far-reaching, full, full-scale, in-depth, intensive, sweeping, thoroughgoing, total
➤ **Antonyms**
casual, cursory, desultory, incomplete, perfunctory, sketchy, superficial

exhibit *verb* 1 = **display**, air, demonstrate, disclose, evidence, evince, expose, express, flaunt, indicate, make clear *or* plain, manifest, offer, parade, present, put on view, reveal, show ♦ *noun* 2 = **display**, exhibition, illustration, model, show

exhibition *noun* = **display**, airing, demonstration, exhibit, expo (*informal*), exposition, fair, manifestation, performance, presentation, representation, show, showing, spectacle

exhilarating *adjective* = **exciting**, breathtaking, cheering, enlivening, exalting, exhilarant, exhilarative, exhilaratory, gladdening, invigorating, stimulating, thrilling, vitalizing

exhilaration noun = excitement, animation, cheerfulness, delight, elation, exaltation, gaiety, gladness, gleefulness, high spirits, hilarity, joy, joyfulness, liveliness, mirth, sprightliness, vivacity
➤ Antonyms
dejection, depression, despondency, gloom, low spirits, melancholy, misery, sadness

exhort verb Formal = urge, admonish, advise, beseech, bid, call upon, caution, counsel, encourage, enjoin, entreat, goad, incite, persuade, press, prompt, spur, warn

exhortation noun Formal = urging, admonition, advice, beseeching, bidding, caution, clarion call, counsel, encouragement, enjoinder (rare), entreaty, goading, incitement, lecture, persuasion, sermon, warning

exhume verb Formal = dig up, disentomb, disinter, unbury, unearth
➤ Antonyms
bury, entomb, inter

exigency, exigence noun 1 = need, constraint, demand, necessity, requirement, wont 2 = urgency, acuteness, constraint, criticalness, demandingness, difficulty, distress, emergency, imperativeness, necessity, needfulness, pressingness, pressure, stress 3 = emergency, crisis, difficulty, extremity, fix (informal), hardship, jam (informal), juncture, panic stations (informal), pass, pickle (informal), pinch, plight, predicament, quandary, scrape (informal), strait

exigent adjective Formal 1 = urgent, acute, constraining, critical, crucial, imperative, importunate, insistent, necessary, needful, pressing 2 = demanding, arduous, difficult, exacting, hard, harsh, rigorous, severe, stiff, strict, stringent, taxing, tough

exile noun 1 = banishment, deportation, expatriation, expulsion, ostracism, proscription, separation 2 = expatriate, deportee, émigré, outcast, refugee ♦ verb 3 = banish, deport, drive out, eject, expatriate, expel, ostracize, oust, proscribe

exist verb 1 = be, abide, be extant, be living, be present, breathe, continue, endure, happen, last, live, obtain, occur, prevail, remain, stand, survive 2 = survive, eke out a living, get along or by, keep one's head above water, stay alive, subsist

existence noun 1 = being, actuality, animation, breath, continuance, continuation, duration, endurance, life, subsistence, survival 2 = creature, being, entity, thing 3 = creation, life, reality, the world

existent adjective = in existence, abiding, alive, around, current, enduring, existing, extant, living, obtaining, present, prevailing, remaining, standing, surviving, to the fore (Scot.)

exit noun 1 = way out, door, egress, gate, outlet, passage out, vent 2 = departure, adieu, evacuation, exodus, farewell, going, goodbye, leave-taking, retirement, retreat, withdrawal ♦ verb 3 = depart, bid farewell, go away, go offstage (Theatre), go out, issue, leave, make tracks, retire, retreat, say goodbye, take one's leave, withdraw
➤ Antonyms
noun ≠way out: entrance, entry, ingress, inlet, opening, way in ♦ verb ≠depart: arrive, come or go in or into, enter, make an entrance

exodus noun = departure, evacuation, exit, flight, going out, leaving, migration, retirement, retreat, withdrawal

exonerate verb 1 = clear, absolve, acquit, discharge, dismiss, exculpate, excuse, justify, pardon, vindicate 2 = exempt, discharge, dismiss, except, excuse, free, let off, liberate, release, relieve

exorbitant adjective = excessive, enormous, extortionate, extravagant, extreme, immoderate, inordinate, outrageous, preposterous, ridiculous, unconscionable, undue, unreasonable, unwarranted
➤ Antonyms
cheap, fair, moderate, reasonable

exorcise verb = drive out, adjure, cast out, deliver (from), expel, purify

exorcism noun = driving out, adjuration, casting out, deliverance, expulsion, purification

exotic adjective 1 = unusual, beyond one's ken, bizarre, colourful, curious, different, extraordinary, fascinating, glamorous, mysterious, outlandish, peculiar, strange, striking, unfamiliar 2 = foreign, alien, external, extraneous, extrinsic, imported, introduced, naturalized, not native
➤ Antonyms
≠unusual: conventional, familiar, ordinary, pedestrian, plain, run-of-the-mill, unmemorable, unremarkable

expand verb 1 = increase, amplify, augment, bloat, blow up, broaden, develop, dilate, distend, enlarge, extend, fatten, fill out, grow, heighten, inflate, lengthen, magnify, multiply, prolong, protract, swell, thicken, wax, widen 2 = spread (out), diffuse, open (out), outspread, stretch (out), unfold, unfurl, unravel, unroll 3 expand on = go into detail about, amplify, develop, dilate,

elaborate on, embellish, enlarge on,
expatiate on, expound on, flesh out
➤ **Antonyms**
≠**increase:** condense, contract, decrease,
reduce, shorten, shrink ≠**go into detail
about:** abbreviate, condense, shorten

expanse noun = **area**, breadth, extent,
field, plain, range, space, stretch, sweep,
tract

expansion noun = **increase**, amplification,
augmentation, development, diffusion,
dilatation, distension, enlargement,
expanse, growth, inflation, magnification,
multiplication, opening out, spread,
swelling, unfolding, unfurling

expansive adjective **1** = **wide**,
all-embracing, broad, comprehensive,
extensive, far-reaching, inclusive,
thorough, voluminous, wide-ranging,
widespread **2** = **talkative**, affable,
communicative, easy, effusive, free,
friendly, garrulous, genial, loquacious,
open, outgoing, sociable, unreserved,
warm **3** = **expanding**, dilating, distending,
elastic, enlargeable, extendable, inflatable,
stretching, stretchy, swelling

expatiate verb Formal = **go into detail**,
amplify, descant, develop, dilate, dwell on,
elaborate, embellish, enlarge, expound

expatriate adjective **1** = **exiled**, banished,
emigrant, émigré ◆ noun **2** = **exile**,
emigrant, émigré, refugee ◆ verb **3** = **exile**,
banish, expel, ostracize, proscribe

expect verb **1** = **think**, assume, believe,
calculate, conjecture, forecast, foresee,
imagine, presume, reckon, suppose,
surmise, trust **2** = **look forward to**,
anticipate, await, bargain for,
contemplate, envisage, hope for, look
ahead to, look for, predict, watch for **3**
= **require**, call for, count on, demand,
insist on, look for, rely upon, want, wish

expectancy noun **1** = **likelihood**, outlook,
prospect **2** = **expectation**, anticipation,
assumption, belief, conjecture, hope,
looking forward, prediction, presumption,
probability, supposition, surmise,
suspense, waiting

expectant adjective **1** = **expecting**,
anticipating, anxious, apprehensive,
awaiting, eager, hopeful, in suspense,
ready, watchful **2** = **pregnant**, enceinte,
expecting (informal), gravid

expectation noun **1** = **probability**,
assumption, assurance, belief, calculation,
confidence, conjecture, forecast,
likelihood, presumption, supposition,
surmise, trust **2** = **anticipation**,
apprehension, chance, expectancy, fear,
hope, looking forward, outlook, possibility,

prediction, promise, prospect, suspense **3**
= **requirement**, demand, insistence,
reliance, trust, want, wish

expecting adjective = **pregnant**, enceinte,
expectant, gravid, in the club (Brit. slang),
in the family way (informal), with child

expediency, expedience noun **1**
= **means**, contrivance, device, expedient,
makeshift, manoeuvre, measure, method,
resort, resource, scheme, shift, stopgap,
stratagem, substitute **2** = **suitability**,
advantageousness, advisability,
appropriateness, aptness, benefit,
convenience, desirability, effectiveness,
fitness, helpfulness, judiciousness,
meetness, practicality, pragmatism,
profitability, properness, propriety,
prudence, usefulness, utilitarianism, utility

expedient noun **1** = **means**, contrivance,
device, expediency, makeshift,
manoeuvre, measure, method, resort,
resource, scheme, shift, stopgap,
stratagem, substitute ◆ adjective **2**
= **advantageous**, advisable, appropriate,
beneficial, convenient, desirable, effective,
fit, helpful, judicious, meet, opportune,
politic, practical, pragmatic, profitable,
proper, prudent, suitable, useful,
utilitarian, worthwhile
➤ **Antonyms**
adjective ≠**advantageous:** detrimental,
disadvantageous, futile, harmful,
ill-advised, impractical, imprudent,
inadvisable, inappropriate, ineffective,
inexpedient, unwise, wrong

expedite verb Formal = **speed (up)**,
accelerate, advance, assist, dispatch,
facilitate, forward, hasten, hurry,
precipitate, press, promote, quicken, rush,
urge
➤ **Antonyms**
block, curb, decelerate, delay, handicap,
hold up, obstruct, restrict, slow up or down

expedition noun **1** = **journey**, enterprise,
excursion, exploration, mission, quest,
safari, tour, trek, trip, undertaking, voyage
2 = **team**, company, crew, explorers,
travellers, voyagers, wayfarers **3** = **speed**,
alacrity, celerity, dispatch, expeditiousness,
haste, hurry, promptness, quickness,
rapidity, readiness, swiftness

expeditious adjective = **quick**, active, alert,
brisk, diligent, efficient, fast, hasty,
immediate, instant, nimble, prompt, rapid,
ready, speedy, swift

expel verb **1** = **drive out**, belch, cast out,
discharge, dislodge, eject, remove, spew,
throw out **2** = **dismiss**, ban, banish, bar,
black, blackball, discharge, drum out,
evict, exclude, exile, expatriate, give the

bum's rush (*slang*), oust, proscribe, relegate, send packing, show one the door, throw out, throw out on one's ear (*informal*), turf out (*informal*)
➤ **Antonyms**
≠**dismiss**: admit, allow to enter, give access, let in, receive, take in, welcome

expend *verb Formal* = **spend**, consume, disburse, dissipate, employ, exhaust, fork out (*slang*), go through, lay out (*informal*), pay out, shell out (*informal*), use (up)

expendable *adjective* = **dispensable**, inessential, nonessential, replaceable, unimportant, unnecessary
➤ **Antonyms**
crucial, essential, indispensable, key, necessary, vital

expenditure *noun* = **spending**, application, charge, consumption, cost, disbursement, expense, outgoings, outlay, output, payment, use

expense *noun* = **cost**, charge, consumption, disbursement, expenditure, loss, outlay, output, payment, sacrifice, spending, toll, use

expensive *adjective* = **dear**, costly, excessive, exorbitant, extravagant, high-priced, inordinate, lavish, overpriced, rich, steep (*informal*), stiff
➤ **Antonyms**
bargain, budget, cheap, cut-price, economical, inexpensive, low-cost, low-priced, reasonable

experience *noun* 1 = **knowledge**, contact, doing, evidence, exposure, familiarity, involvement, know-how (*informal*), observation, participation, practice, proof, training, trial, understanding 2 = **event**, adventure, affair, encounter, episode, happening, incident, occurrence, ordeal, test, trial ♦ *verb* 3 = **undergo**, apprehend, become familiar with, behold, encounter, endure, face, feel, go through, have, know, live through, meet, observe, participate in, perceive, sample, sense, suffer, sustain, taste, try

experienced *adjective* 1 = **knowledgeable**, accomplished, adept, capable, competent, expert, familiar, master, practised, professional, qualified, seasoned, skilful, tested, trained, tried, veteran, well-versed 2 = **worldly-wise**, knowing, mature, sophisticated, wise, worldly
➤ **Antonyms**
≠**knowledgeable**: apprentice, green, incompetent, inexperienced, new, unqualified, unskilled, untrained, untried

experiment *noun* 1 = **test**, assay, attempt, examination, experimentation, investigation, procedure, proof, research,

trial, trial and error, trial run, venture ♦ *verb* 2 = **test**, assay, examine, investigate, put to the test, research, sample, try, verify

experimental *adjective* = **test**, empirical, exploratory, pilot, preliminary, probationary, provisional, speculative, tentative, trial, trial-and-error

expert *noun* 1 = **master**, ace (*informal*), adept, authority, buff (*informal*), connoisseur, dab hand (*Brit. informal*), guru, hotshot (*informal*), maven (*U.S.*), past master, pro (*informal*), professional, specialist, virtuoso, whizz (*informal*), wizard ♦ *adjective* 2 = **skilful**, able, adept, adroit, apt, clever, deft, dexterous, experienced, facile, handy, knowledgeable, master, masterly, practised, professional, proficient, qualified, skilled, trained, virtuoso
➤ **Antonyms**
noun ≠**master**: amateur, dabbler, ham, layman, nonprofessional, novice
♦ *adjective* ≠**skilful**: amateurish, cack-handed (*informal*), clumsy, incompetent, inexperienced, unpractised, unqualified, unskilled, untrained

expertise *noun* = **skill**, ableness, adroitness, aptness, cleverness, command, craft, deftness, dexterity, expertness, facility, grasp, grip, judgment, knack, know-how (*informal*), knowing inside out, knowledge, masterliness, mastery, proficiency, skilfulness

expertness *noun* = **skill**, ableness, adroitness, aptness, command, craft, deftness, dexterity, expertise, facility, grasp, grip, judgment, know-how (*informal*), knowing inside out, knowledge, masterliness, mastery, proficiency, skilfulness

expire *verb* 1 = **finish**, cease, close, come to an end, conclude, end, lapse, run out, stop, terminate 2 = **breathe out**, emit, exhale, expel 3 = **die**, buy it (*U.S. slang*), check out (*U.S. slang*), croak (*slang*), decease, depart, go belly-up (*slang*), kick it (*slang*), kick the bucket (*informal*), pass away *or* on, peg it (*informal*), peg out (*informal*), perish, pop one's clogs (*informal*), snuff it (*informal*)

explain *verb* 1 = **make clear** *or* **plain**, clarify, clear up, define, demonstrate, describe, disclose, elucidate, explicate (*formal*), expound, illustrate, interpret, resolve, solve, teach, unfold 2 = **account for**, excuse, give an explanation for, give a reason for, justify

explanation *noun* 1 = **reason**, account, answer, cause, excuse, justification, meaning, mitigation, motive, sense, significance, the why and wherefore, vindication **2 = description**, clarification, definition, demonstration, elucidation, explication, exposition, illustration, interpretation, resolution

explanatory *adjective* **= descriptive**, demonstrative, elucidatory, explicative, expository, illuminative, illustrative, interpretive, justifying

explicit *adjective* **= clear**, absolute, categorical, certain, definite, direct, distinct, exact, express, frank, open, outspoken, patent, plain, positive, precise, specific, stated, straightforward, unambiguous, unequivocal, unqualified, unreserved, upfront (*informal*)
➤ **Antonyms**
ambiguous, cryptic, general, implicit, implied, indefinite, indirect, inexact, obscure, oracular, suggested, uncertain, vague

explode *verb* **1 = blow up**, burst, detonate, discharge, erupt, go off, set off, shatter, shiver **2 = disprove**, belie, blow out of the water (*slang*), debunk, discredit, give the lie to, invalidate, refute, repudiate

exploit *verb* **1 = take advantage of**, abuse, dump on (*slang, chiefly U.S.*), impose upon, manipulate, milk, misuse, play on *or* upon, shit on (*taboo slang*) **2 = make the best use of**, capitalize on, cash in on (*informal*), live off the backs of, make capital out of, profit by *or* from, put to use, turn to account, use, use to advantage, utilize ♦ *noun* **3 = feat**, accomplishment, achievement, adventure, attainment, deed, escapade, stunt

exploitation *noun* **= misuse**, abuse, manipulation, using

exploration *noun* **1 = investigation**, analysis, examination, inquiry, inspection, once-over (*informal*), probe, research, scrutiny, search, study **2 = expedition**, recce (*slang*), reconnaissance, survey, tour, travel, trip

exploratory *adjective* **= investigative**, analytic, experimental, fact-finding, probing, searching, trial

explore *verb* **1 = investigate**, analyse, examine, inquire into, inspect, look into, probe, prospect, research, scrutinize, search, work over **2 = travel**, case (*slang*), have *or* take a look around, range over, recce (*slang*), reconnoitre, scout, survey, tour, traverse

explosion *noun* **1 = bang**, blast, burst, clap, crack, detonation, discharge, outburst, report **2 = outburst**, eruption, fit, outbreak, paroxysm

explosive *adjective* **1 = unstable**, volatile **2 = violent**, fiery, stormy, touchy, vehement **3 = dangerous**, charged, hazardous, overwrought, perilous, tense, ugly

exponent *noun* **1 = advocate**, backer, champion, defender, promoter, propagandist, proponent, spokesman, spokeswoman, supporter, upholder **2 = performer**, executant, interpreter, player, presenter **3 = interpreter**, commentator, demonstrator, elucidator, expositor, expounder, illustrator

expose *verb* **1 = uncover**, display, exhibit, manifest, present, put on view, reveal, show, take the wraps off, unveil **2 = reveal**, air, betray, blow wide open (*slang*), bring to light, denounce, detect, disclose, divulge, lay bare, let out, make known, out (*informal*), show up, smoke out, uncover, unearth, unmask **3 = make vulnerable**, endanger, hazard, imperil, jeopardize, lay open, leave open, risk, subject **4 expose (someone) to = introduce to**, acquaint with, bring into contact with, familiarize with, make conversant with
➤ **Antonyms**
≠**uncover:** conceal, cover, hide, mask, protect, screen, shelter, shield ≠**reveal:** conceal, cover, hide, keep secret

exposed *adjective* **1 = unconcealed**, bare, exhibited, laid bare, made manifest, made public, on display, on show, on view, revealed, shown, uncovered, unveiled **2 = unsheltered**, open, open to the elements, unprotected **3 = vulnerable**, in danger, in peril, laid bare, laid open, left open, liable, open, susceptible, wide open

exposition *noun* **1 = explanation**, account, commentary, critique, description, elucidation, exegesis, explication, illustration, interpretation, presentation **2 = exhibition**, demonstration, display, expo (*informal*), fair, presentation, show

expostulate *verb* **= reason (with)**, argue (with), dissuade, protest, remonstrate (with)

exposure *noun* **1 = vulnerability**, danger, hazard, jeopardy, risk **2 = revelation**, airing, betrayal, denunciation, detection, disclosure, divulgence, divulging, exposé, unmasking **3 = publicity**, baring, display, exhibition, manifestation, presentation, revelation, showing, uncovering, unveiling **4 = contact**, acquaintance, conversancy, experience, familiarity, introduction, knowledge **5 = position**, aspect, frontage, location, outlook, setting, view

expound *verb* **= explain**, describe, elucidate, explicate (*formal*), illustrate, interpret, set forth, spell out, unfold

express *verb* 1 = **state**, articulate, assert, asseverate, communicate, couch, declare, enunciate, phrase, pronounce, put, put across, put into words, say, speak, tell, utter, verbalize, voice, word 2 = **show**, bespeak, convey, denote, depict, designate, disclose, divulge, embody, evince, exhibit, indicate, intimate, make known, manifest, represent, reveal, signify, stand for, symbolize, testify 3 = **squeeze out**, extract, force out, press out
♦ *adjective* 4 = **explicit**, accurate, categorical, certain, clear, definite, direct, distinct, exact, outright, plain, pointed, precise, unambiguous 5 = **specific**, clear-cut, deliberate, especial, particular, singular, special 6 = **fast**, direct, high-speed, nonstop, quick, quickie (*informal*), rapid, speedy, swift

expression *noun* 1 = **statement**, announcement, assertion, asseveration, communication, declaration, enunciation, mention, pronouncement, speaking, utterance, verbalization, voicing 2 = **indication**, demonstration, embodiment, exhibition, manifestation, representation, show, sign, symbol, token 3 = **look**, air, appearance, aspect, countenance, face, mien (*literary*) 4 = **phrase**, idiom, locution, remark, set phrase, term, turn of phrase, word 5 = **choice of words**, delivery, diction, emphasis, execution, intonation, language, phraseology, phrasing, speech, style, wording

expressive *adjective* 1 = **vivid**, eloquent, emphatic, energetic, forcible, lively, mobile, moving, poignant, striking, strong, sympathetic, telling 2 = **meaningful**, allusive, demonstrative, indicative, pointed, pregnant, revealing, significant, suggestive, thoughtful
➤ **Antonyms**
≠**vivid**: blank, dead-pan, dull, empty, impassive, inscrutable, poker-faced (*informal*), straight-faced, vacuous, wooden

expressly *adverb* 1 = **definitely**, absolutely, categorically, clearly, decidedly, distinctly, explicitly, in no uncertain terms, manifestly, outright, plainly, pointedly, positively, unambiguously, unequivocally, unmistakably 2 = **specifically**, deliberately, especially, exactly, intentionally, on purpose, particularly, precisely, purposely, specially

expropriate *verb Formal* = **seize**, appropriate, arrogate, assume, commandeer, confiscate, impound, requisition, take, take over

expulsion *noun* = **ejection**, banishment, debarment, discharge, dislodgment, dismissal, eviction, exclusion, exile, expatriation, extrusion, proscription, removal

expurgate *verb* = **censor**, blue-pencil, bowdlerize, clean up (*informal*), cut, purge, purify, sanitize

exquisite *adjective* 1 = **beautiful**, attractive, charming, comely, lovely, pleasing, striking 2 = **fine**, beautiful, dainty, delicate, elegant, lovely, precious 3 = **refined**, appreciative, consummate, cultivated, discerning, discriminating, fastidious, impeccable, meticulous, polished, selective, sensitive 4 = **intense**, acute, excruciating, keen, piercing, poignant, sharp 5 = **excellent**, admirable, choice, consummate, delicious, divine, fine, flawless, incomparable, matchless, outstanding, peerless, perfect, rare, select, splendid, superb, superlative
➤ **Antonyms**
≠**beautiful**: ill-favoured, ugly, unattractive, unlovely, unsightly ≠**excellent**: flawed, imperfect

extempore *adverb, adjective* = **impromptu**, ad lib, extemporaneous, extemporary, freely, improvised, offhand, off the cuff (*informal*), off the top of one's head, on the spot, spontaneously, unplanned, unpremeditated, unprepared

extemporize *verb* = **improvise**, ad-lib, busk, make up, play (it) by ear, vamp, wing it (*informal*)

extend *verb* 1 = **make longer**, carry on, continue, drag out, draw out, elongate, lengthen, prolong, protract, spin out, spread out, stretch, unfurl, unroll 2 = **reach**, amount to, attain, go as far as, spread 3 = **last**, carry on, continue, go on, take 4 = **widen**, add to, amplify, augment, broaden, develop, dilate, enhance, enlarge, expand, increase, spread, supplement 5 = **offer**, advance, bestow, confer, give, grant, hold out, impart, present, proffer, put forth, reach out, stretch out, yield
➤ **Antonyms**
≠**make longer**: condense, contract, curtail, cut, decrease, limit, reduce, restrict, shorten, take back ≠**widen**: abbreviate, abridge, condense, contract, cut, decrease, reduce, restrict, shorten ≠**offer**: take back, withdraw

extended *adjective* 1 = **lengthened**, continued, drawn-out, elongated, enlarged, long, prolonged, protracted, spread (out), stretched out, unfolded, unfurled, unrolled 2 = **broad**, comprehensive, enlarged, expanded, extensive, far-reaching, large-scale, sweeping, thorough, wide, widespread **3** = **outstretched**, conferred, proffered, stretched out

extension *noun* **1** = **annexe**, addendum, addition, add-on, adjunct, appendage, appendix, branch, ell, supplement, wing **2** = **lengthening**, amplification, augmentation, broadening, continuation, delay, development, dilatation, distension, elongation, enlargement, expansion, extent, increase, postponement, prolongation, protraction, spread, stretching, widening

extensive *adjective* = **wide**, all-inclusive, broad, capacious, commodious, comprehensive, expanded, extended, far-flung, far-reaching, general, great, huge, humongous *or* humungous (*U.S. slang*), large, large-scale, lengthy, long, pervasive, prevalent, protracted, spacious, sweeping, thorough, universal, vast, voluminous, wholesale, widespread
➤ **Antonyms**
circumscribed, confined, constricted, limited, narrow, restricted, tight

extent *noun* **1** = **size**, amount, amplitude, area, breadth, bulk, degree, duration, expanse, expansion, length, magnitude, measure, quantity, stretch, term, time, volume, width **2** = **range**, ambit, bounds, compass, play, reach, scope, sphere, sweep

extenuating *adjective* = **mitigating**, justifying, moderating, qualifying, serving as an excuse

exterior *noun* **1** = **outside**, appearance, aspect, coating, covering, façade, face, finish, shell, skin, surface ◆ *adjective* **2** = **outside**, external, outer, outermost, outward, superficial, surface **3** = **external**, alien, exotic, extraneous, extrinsic, foreign, outside
➤ **Antonyms**
noun ≠**outside**: inner, inside, interior ◆ *adjective* ≠**outside**: inherent, inside, interior, internal, intrinsic ≠**external**: domestic, internal, intrinsic

exterminate *verb* = **destroy**, abolish, annihilate, eliminate, eradicate, extirpate

external *adjective* **1** = **outer**, apparent, exterior, outermost, outside, outward, superficial, surface, visible **2** = **outside**, alien, exotic, exterior, extramural, extraneous, extrinsic, foreign, independent
➤ **Antonyms**
≠**outer**: inherent, inner, inside, interior, internal, intrinsic ≠**outside**: inside, interior, intrinsic

extinct *adjective* **1** = **dead**, defunct, gone,

lost, vanished **2** = **obsolete**, abolished, defunct, ended, terminated, void **3** = **inactive**, doused, extinguished, out, quenched, snuffed out
➤ **Antonyms**
≠**dead**: active, alive, existing, extant, flourishing, living, surviving, thriving

extinction *noun* = **dying out**, abolition, annihilation, death, destruction, eradication, excision, extermination, extirpation, obliteration, oblivion

extinguish *verb* **1** = **put out**, blow out, douse, quench, smother, snuff out, stifle **2** = **destroy**, abolish, annihilate, eliminate, end, eradicate, erase, expunge, exterminate, extirpate, kill, obscure, put paid to, remove, suppress, wipe out

extol *verb* = **praise**, acclaim, applaud, celebrate, commend, crack up (*informal*), cry up, eulogize, exalt, glorify, laud, magnify (*archaic*), panegyrize, pay tribute to, sing the praises of

extort *verb* = **force**, blackmail, bleed (*informal*), bully, coerce, exact, extract, squeeze, wrest, wring

extortion *noun* **1** = **force**, blackmail, coercion, compulsion, demand, exaction, oppression, rapacity, shakedown (*U.S. slang*) **2** = **overcharging**, enormity, exorbitance, expensiveness

extortionate *adjective* = **exorbitant**, excessive, extravagant, immoderate, inflated, inordinate, outrageous, preposterous, sky-high, unreasonable
➤ **Antonyms**
fair, inexpensive, moderate, modest, reasonable

extra *adjective* **1** = **additional**, accessory, added, add-on, ancillary, auxiliary, fresh, further, more, new, other, supplemental, supplementary **2** = **surplus**, excess, extraneous, inessential, leftover, needless, redundant, reserve, spare, supererogatory, superfluous, supernumerary, unnecessary, unneeded, unused ◆ *noun* **3** = **addition**, accessory, addendum, add-on, adjunct, affix, appendage, appurtenance, attachment, bonus, complement, extension, supernumerary, supplement ◆ *adverb* **4** = **exceptionally**, especially, extraordinarily, extremely, particularly, remarkably, uncommonly, unusually
➤ **Antonyms**
adjective ≠**additional**: compulsory, essential, mandatory, necessary, needed, obligatory, required, requisite, vital ◆ *noun* ≠**addition**: essential, must, necessity, precondition, prerequisite, requirement, requisite

extract *verb* **1** = **pull out**, draw, extirpate,

pluck out, pull, remove, take out, uproot, withdraw **2 = derive**, bring out, draw, elicit, evoke, exact, gather, get, glean, obtain, reap, wrest, wring **3 = obtain**, distil, draw out, express, press out, separate out, squeeze, take out **4 = copy out**, abstract, choose, cite, cull, cut out, quote, select **5 = develop**, deduce, derive, educe, elicit, evolve ♦ *noun* **6 = passage**, abstract, citation, clipping, cutting, excerpt, quotation, selection **7 = essence**, concentrate, decoction, distillate, distillation, juice

extraction *noun* **1 = taking out**, drawing, extirpation, pulling, removal, uprooting, withdrawal **2 = distillation**, derivation, separation **3 = origin**, ancestry, birth, blood, derivation, descent, family, lineage, parentage, pedigree, race, stock

extraneous *adjective* **1 = nonessential**, accidental, additional, adventitious, extra, incidental, inessential, needless, peripheral, redundant, superfluous, supplementary, unessential, unnecessary, unneeded **2 = irrelevant**, beside the point, immaterial, impertinent, inadmissible, inapplicable, inapposite, inappropriate, inapt, off the subject, unconnected, unrelated **3 = external**, adventitious, alien, exotic, extrinsic, foreign, out of place, strange

extraordinary *adjective* **= unusual**, amazing, beyond one's ken, bizarre, curious, exceptional, fantastic, marvellous, notable, odd, out of this world (*informal*), outstanding, particular, peculiar, phenomenal, rare, remarkable, serious (*informal*), singular, special, strange, surprising, uncommon, unfamiliar, unheard-of, unique, unprecedented, unwonted, weird, wonderful, wondrous (*archaic or literary*)
➤ **Antonyms**
banal, common, commonplace, customary, everyday, ordinary, unexceptional, unremarkable, usual

extravagance *noun* **1 = waste**, improvidence, lavishness, overspending, prodigality, profligacy, profusion, squandering, wastefulness **2 = excess**, absurdity, dissipation, exaggeration, exorbitance, folly, immoderation, outrageousness, preposterousness, recklessness, unreasonableness, unrestraint, wildness

extravagant *adjective* **1 = wasteful**, excessive, having money to burn, improvident, imprudent, lavish, prodigal, profligate, spendthrift **2 = overpriced**, costly, excessive, exorbitant, expensive,

extortionate, inordinate, steep (*informal*), unreasonable **3 = excessive**, absurd, exaggerated, exorbitant, fanciful, fantastic, foolish, immoderate, inordinate, O.T.T. (*slang*), outrageous, outré, over the top (*slang*), preposterous, reckless, unreasonable, unrestrained, wild **4 = showy**, fancy, flamboyant, flashy, garish, gaudy, grandiose, ornate, ostentatious, pretentious
➤ **Antonyms**
≠**wasteful**: careful, close, economical, frugal, miserly, moderate, prudent, sensible, sparing, thrifty, tight-fisted (*informal*) ≠**overpriced**: economical, moderate, reasonable ≠**excessive**: conservative, down-to-earth, moderate, prudent, realistic, reasonable, restrained, sensible, sober ≠**showy**: conservative, moderate, restrained, sober

extreme *adjective* **1 = maximum**, acute, great, greatest, high, highest, intense, mother of all (*informal*), severe, supreme, ultimate, utmost, uttermost, worst **2 = severe**, dire, drastic, harsh, radical, rigid, stern, strict, unbending, uncompromising **3 = excessive**, downright, egregious, exaggerated, exceptional, extraordinary, extravagant, fanatical, immoderate, inordinate, intemperate, O.T.T. (*slang*), out-and-out, outrageous, over the top (*slang*), radical, remarkable, sheer, uncommon, unconventional, unreasonable, unusual, utter, zealous **4 = farthest**, faraway, far-off, final, last, most distant, outermost, remotest, terminal, ultimate, utmost, uttermost ♦ *noun* **5 = limit**, acme, apex, apogee, boundary, climax, consummation, depth, edge, end, excess, extremity, height, maximum, minimum, nadir, pinnacle, pole, termination, top, ultimate, zenith
➤ **Antonyms**
adjective ≠**maximum**: average, common, mild, moderate, modest, ordinary, reasonable, traditional, unremarkable ≠**farthest**: nearest

extremely *adverb* **= very**, acutely, awfully (*informal*), exceedingly, exceptionally, excessively, extraordinarily, greatly, highly, inordinately, intensely, markedly, quite, severely, terribly, to a fault, to *or* in the extreme, to the nth degree, ultra, uncommonly, unusually, utterly

extremist *noun* **= fanatic**, die-hard, radical, ultra, zealot

extremity *noun* **1 = limit**, acme, apex, apogee, border, bound, boundary, brim, brink, edge, end, extreme, farthest point, frontier, margin, maximum, minimum, nadir, pinnacle, pole, rim, terminal, termination, terminus, tip, top, ultimate, verge, zenith **2** = **crisis**, adversity, dire straits, disaster, emergency, exigency, hardship, pass, pinch, plight, setback, trouble **3 extremities** = **hands and feet**, fingers and toes, limbs

extricate *verb* = **free**, clear, deliver, disembarrass, disengage, disentangle, get out, get (someone) off the hook (*slang*), liberate, release, relieve, remove, rescue, withdraw, wriggle out of

extrovert *adjective* = **outgoing**, amiable, exuberant, gregarious, hearty, sociable, social
➤ **Antonyms**
introspective, introverted, inward-looking, self-contained, withdrawn

exuberance *noun* **1** = **high spirits**, animation, brio, buoyancy, cheerfulness, eagerness, ebullience, effervescence, energy, enthusiasm, excitement, exhilaration, life, liveliness, pep, spirit, sprightliness, vigour, vitality, vivacity, zest **2** = **luxuriance**, abundance, copiousness, lavishness, lushness, plenitude, profusion, rankness, richness, superabundance, teemingness **3** = **fulsomeness**, effusiveness, exaggeration, excessiveness, lavishness, prodigality, superfluity

exuberant *adjective* **1** = **high-spirited**, animated, buoyant, cheerful, chirpy (*informal*), eager, ebullient, effervescent, elated, energetic, enthusiastic, excited, exhilarated, full of beans (*informal*), full of life, in high spirits, lively, sparkling, spirited, sprightly, upbeat (*informal*), vigorous, vivacious, zestful **2** = **luxuriant**, abundant, copious, lavish, lush, overflowing, plenteous, plentiful, profuse, rank, rich, superabundant, teeming **3** = **fulsome**, effusive, exaggerated, excessive, lavish, overdone, prodigal, superfluous
➤ **Antonyms**
≠**high-spirited**: apathetic, dull, lifeless, subdued, unenthusiastic

exult *verb* **1** = **be joyful**, be delighted, be elated, be in high spirits, be jubilant, be overjoyed, celebrate, jubilate, jump for joy, make merry, rejoice **2** = **triumph**, boast, brag, crow, drool, gloat, glory (in), revel, take delight in, taunt, vaunt

exultant *adjective* = **joyful**, cock-a-hoop, delighted, elated, exulting, flushed, gleeful, joyous, jubilant, overjoyed, over the moon (*informal*), rapt, rejoicing,

revelling, transported, triumphant

exultation *noun* **1** = **joy**, celebration, delight, elation, glee, high spirits, joyousness, jubilation, merriness, rejoicing, transport **2** = **triumph**, boasting, bragging, crowing, gloating, glory, glorying, revelling

eye *noun* **1** = **eyeball**, optic (*informal*), orb (*poetic*), peeper (*slang*) **2** = **appreciation**, discernment, discrimination, judgment, perception, recognition, taste **3** *often plural* = **opinion**, belief, judgment, mind, point of view, viewpoint **4 an eye for an eye** = **retaliation**, justice, reprisal, requital, retribution, revenge, vengeance **5 clap, lay** *or* **set eyes on** = **see**, behold, come across, encounter, meet, notice, observe, run into **6 keep an** *or* **one's eye on** = **watch**, guard, keep in view, keep tabs on (*informal*), keep under surveillance, look after, look out for, monitor, observe, pay attention to, regard, scrutinize, supervise, survey, watch like a hawk, watch over **7 see eye to eye** = **agree**, accord, back, be in unison, coincide, concur, fall in, get on, go along, harmonize, jibe (*informal*), speak the same language, subscribe to **8 up to one's eyes** = **busy**, caught up, engaged, flooded out, fully occupied, inundated, overwhelmed, up to here, up to one's elbows, wrapped up in ♦ *verb* **9** = **look at**, behold (*archaic or literary*), check, check out (*informal*), clock (*Brit. slang*), contemplate, eyeball (*slang*), gaze at, get a load of (*informal*), glance at, have *or* take a look at, inspect, peruse, recce (*slang*), regard, scan, scrutinize, stare at, study, survey, take a dekko at (*Brit. slang*), view, watch **10** = **ogle**, eye up (*informal*), give (someone) the (glad) eye, leer at, make eyes at

eyeful *noun Slang* **1** = **look**, butcher's (*Brit. slang*), gander (*informal*), gaze, glance, shufti (*Brit. slang*), sight, view **2** = **spectacle**, beauty, dazzler, humdinger (*slang*), knockout (*informal*), show, sight, sight for sore eyes (*informal*), stunner (*informal*), vision

eyesight *noun* = **vision**, observation, perception, range of vision, sight

eyesore *noun* = **mess**, atrocity, blemish, blight, blot, disfigurement, disgrace, horror, monstrosity, sight (*informal*), ugliness

eyewitness *noun* = **observer**, bystander, looker-on, onlooker, passer-by, spectator, viewer, watcher, witness

F f

fable *noun* **1** = **story**, allegory, apologue, legend, myth, parable, tale **2** = **fiction**, fabrication, fairy story (*informal*), falsehood, fantasy, fib, figment, invention, lie, romance, tall story (*informal*), untruth, urban legend, urban myth, white lie, yarn (*informal*)
➤ **Antonyms**
actuality, certainty, fact, reality, truth, verity

fabled *adjective* = **legendary**, fabulous, famed, famous, fictional, mythical

fabric *noun* **1** = **cloth**, material, stuff, textile, web **2** = **framework**, constitution, construction, foundations, infrastructure, make-up, organization, structure

fabricate *verb* **1** = **make up**, coin, concoct, devise, fake, falsify, feign, forge, form, invent, trump up **2** = **build**, assemble, construct, erect, fashion, form, frame, make, manufacture, shape

fabrication *noun* **1** = **forgery**, cock-and-bull story (*informal*), concoction, fable, fairy story (*informal*), fake, falsehood, fiction, figment, invention, lie, myth, pork pie (*Brit. slang*), porky (*Brit. slang*), untruth **2** = **construction**, assemblage, assembly, building, erection, manufacture, production

fabulous *adjective* **1** *Informal* = **wonderful**, brilliant, fantastic (*informal*), magic (*informal*), marvellous, out-of-this-world (*informal*), sensational (*informal*), spectacular, superb **2** = **astounding**, amazing, breathtaking, fictitious, immense, inconceivable, incredible, legendary, phenomenal, unbelievable **3** = **legendary**, apocryphal, fantastic, fictitious, imaginary, invented, made-up, mythical, unreal
➤ **Antonyms**
actual, common, commonplace, credible, genuine, natural, ordinary, real

façade *noun* = **appearance**, exterior, face, front, frontage, guise, mask, pretence, semblance, show, veneer

face *noun* **1** = **countenance**, clock (*Brit. slang*), dial (*Brit. slang*), features, kisser (*slang*), lineaments, mug (*slang*), phiz *or* phizog (*slang*), physiognomy, visage **2** = **expression**, appearance, aspect, look **3** = **scowl**, frown, grimace, *moue*, pout,

smirk **4** = **side**, aspect, cover, exterior, facet, front, outside, right side, surface **5** *As in* **save** *or* **lose face** = **self-respect**, authority, dignity, honour, image, prestige, reputation, standing, status **6** *As in* **put a good face on** = **façade**, air, appearance, disguise, display, exterior, front, mask, pretence, semblance, show **7 on the face of it** = **to all appearances**, apparently, at first sight, seemingly, to the eye **8 to one's face** = **directly**, in one's presence, openly, straight ♦ *verb* **9** = **look onto**, be opposite, front onto, give towards *or* onto, overlook **10** = **confront**, be confronted by, brave, come up against, cope with, deal with, defy, encounter, experience, face off (*slang*), meet, oppose, tackle **11** = **coat**, clad, cover, dress, finish, level, line, overlay, sheathe, surface, veneer

faceless *adjective* = **impersonal**, anonymous, remote, unidentified, unknown

face-lift *noun* **1** = **cosmetic surgery**, plastic surgery **2** = **renovation**, restoration

facer *noun Brit. old-fashioned* = **problem**, difficulty, dilemma, how-do-you-do (*informal*), poser, puzzle, teaser

facet *noun* = **aspect**, angle, face, part, phase, plane, side, slant, surface

facetious *adjective* = **funny**, amusing, comical, droll, flippant, frivolous, humorous, jesting, jocose, jocular, merry, playful, pleasant, tongue in cheek, unserious, waggish, witty
➤ **Antonyms**
earnest, genuine, grave, lugubrious, pensive, sedate, serious, sincere, sober, thoughtful

face up to *verb* = **accept**, acknowledge, come to terms with, confront, cope with, deal with, face the music, meet head-on, tackle

facile *adjective* **1** = **superficial**, cursory, glib, hasty, shallow, slick **2** = **easy**, adept, adroit, dexterous, effortless, fluent, light, proficient, quick, ready, simple, skilful, smooth, uncomplicated
➤ **Antonyms**
≠**easy**: awkward, careful, clumsy, difficult, maladroit, slow, unskilful

facilitate *verb* = **promote**, assist the progress of, ease, expedite, forward,

further, help, make easy, oil the wheels, pave the way for, smooth the path of, speed up
➤ **Antonyms**
delay, encumber, frustrate, hamper, handicap, hinder, hold up *or* back, impede, obstruct, prevent, restrain, thwart

facility *noun* 1 *often plural* = **equipment**, advantage, aid, amenity, appliance, convenience, means, opportunity, resource 2 = **ease**, ability, adroitness, craft, dexterity, efficiency, effortlessness, expertness, fluency, gift, knack, proficiency, quickness, readiness, skilfulness, skill, smoothness, talent
➤ **Antonyms**
≠**ease:** awkwardness, clumsiness, difficulty, hardship, ineptness, maladroitness, pains

facing *noun* 1 = **overlay**, cladding, coating, façade, false front, front, plaster, reinforcement, stucco, surface, trimming, veneer ♦ *adjective* 2 = **opposite**, fronting, partnering

facsimile *noun* = **copy**, carbon, carbon copy, duplicate, fax, photocopy, Photostat (*Trademark*), print, replica, reproduction, transcript, Xerox (*Trademark*)

fact *noun* 1 = **event**, act, deed, *fait accompli*, happening, incident, occurrence, performance 2 = **truth**, actuality, certainty, gospel (truth), naked truth, reality 3 = **detail**, circumstance, feature, item, particular, point, specific 4 **in fact** = **actually**, indeed, in point of fact, in reality, in truth, really, truly
➤ **Antonyms**
≠**truth:** delusion, fable, fabrication, falsehood, fiction, invention, lie, tall story, untruth, yarn (*informal*)

faction *noun* 1 = **group**, bloc, cabal, camp, caucus, clique, coalition, combination, confederacy, contingent, coterie, division, gang, ginger group, junta, lobby, minority, party, pressure group, schism, section, sector, set, splinter group 2 = **dissension**, conflict, disagreement, discord, disharmony, disunity, division, divisiveness, friction, infighting, rebellion, sedition, strife, tumult, turbulence
➤ **Antonyms**
≠**dissension:** accord, agreement, amity, assent, concord, consensus, friendship, goodwill, harmony, peace, rapport, unanimity, unity

factitious *adjective* = **artificial**, affected, assumed, counterfeited, engineered, fabricated, fake, false, imitation, insincere, made-up, manufactured, mock, phoney *or* phony (*informal*), pinchbeck, pseudo

(*informal*), put-on, sham, simulated, spurious, synthetic, unnatural, unreal

factor *noun* 1 = **element**, aspect, cause, circumstance, component, consideration, determinant, influence, item, part, point, thing 2 *Scot.* = **agent**, deputy, estate manager, middleman, reeve, steward

factory *noun* = **works**, manufactory (*obsolete*), mill, plant

factotum *noun* = **Man Friday** *or* **Girl Friday**, handyman, jack of all trades, man of all work, odd job man

facts *plural noun* = **information**, data, details, gen (*Brit. informal*), info (*informal*), ins and outs, the lowdown (*informal*), the score (*informal*), the whole story

factual *adjective* = **true**, accurate, authentic, circumstantial, close, correct, credible, exact, faithful, genuine, literal, matter-of-fact, objective, precise, real, sure, true-to-life, unadorned, unbiased, veritable
➤ **Antonyms**
embellished, fanciful, fictitious, fictive, figurative, imaginary, unreal

faculties *plural noun* = **powers**, capabilities, intelligence, reason, senses, wits

faculty *noun* 1 = **ability**, adroitness, aptitude, bent, capability, capacity, cleverness, dexterity, facility, gift, knack, power, propensity, readiness, skill, talent, turn 2 = **department**, branch of learning, discipline, profession, school, teaching staff (*chiefly U.S.*)
➤ **Antonyms**
≠**ability:** failing, inability, shortcoming, unskilfulness, weakness, weak point

fad *noun* = **craze**, affectation, fancy, fashion, mania, mode, rage, trend, vogue, whim

fade *verb* 1 = **pale**, blanch, bleach, blench, dim, discolour, dull, grow dim, lose colour, lose lustre, wash out 2 *As in* **fade away** *or* **out** = **dwindle**, decline, die away, die out, dim, disappear, disperse, dissolve, droop, ebb, etiolate, evanesce, fail, fall, flag, languish, melt away, perish, shrivel, vanish, vanish into thin air, wane, waste away, wilt, wither

faded *adjective* = **discoloured**, bleached, dim, dull, etiolated, indistinct, lustreless, pale, washed out

fading *adjective* = **declining**, decreasing, disappearing, dying, on the decline, vanishing

faeces *plural noun* = **excrement**, bodily waste, droppings, dung, excreta, ordure, stools

fag[1] *noun Informal* = **chore**, bind (*informal*),

bore, bother, drag (*informal*), inconvenience, irritation, nuisance, pain in the arse (*taboo informal*)

fag[2] *noun Offensive slang* = **homosexual**, bender (*slang*), catamite, fairy (*slang*), gay, homo (*informal*), nancy boy (*slang*), poof (*slang*), poofter (*slang*), queen (*slang*), queer (*informal, derogatory*), woofter (*slang*)

fagged out *adjective Informal* = **exhausted**, all in (*slang*), beat (*slang*), clapped out (*Austral. & N.Z. informal*), creamcrackered (*Brit. informal*), fatigued, jaded, jiggered (*informal*), knackered (*slang*), on one's last legs (*informal*), shagged out (*Brit. slang*), wasted, weary, wiped out (*informal*), worn out, zonked (*slang*)

fail *verb* **1** = **be unsuccessful**, be defeated, be found lacking *or* wanting, be in vain, bite the dust, break down, come a cropper (*informal*), come to grief, come to naught, come to nothing, come unstuck, fall, fall by the wayside, fall flat, fall flat on one's face, fall short, fall short of, fall through, fizzle out (*informal*), flop (*informal*), founder, go astray, go belly-up (*slang*), go by the board, go down, go down like a lead balloon (*informal*), go up in smoke, lay an egg (*slang, chiefly U.S. & Canad.*), meet with disaster, miscarry, misfire, miss, not make the grade (*informal*), run aground, turn out badly **2** = **give out**, be on one's last legs (*informal*), cease, conk out (*informal*), cut out, decline, die, disappear, droop, dwindle, fade, fall apart at the seams, give up, go phut, gutter, languish, peter out, sicken, sink, stop working, wane, weaken **3** = **disappoint**, abandon, break one's word, desert, forget, forsake, let down, neglect, omit, turn one's back on **4** = **go bankrupt**, become insolvent, close down, crash, fold (*informal*), go broke (*informal*), go bust (*informal*), go into receivership, go out of business, go to the wall, go under, smash ♦ *noun* **5 without fail** = **regularly**, conscientiously, constantly, dependably, like clockwork, punctually, religiously, without exception
➤ **Antonyms**
verb ≠**be unsuccessful**: bloom, flourish, grow, pass, prosper, strengthen, succeed, thrive, triumph

failing *noun* **1** = **weakness**, blemish, blind spot, defect, deficiency, drawback, error, failure, fault, flaw, foible, frailty, imperfection, lapse, miscarriage, misfortune, shortcoming ♦ *preposition* **2** = **in the absence of**, in default of, lacking
➤ **Antonyms**
noun ≠**weakness**: advantage, asset, forte,

metier, speciality, strength, strong suit

failure *noun* **1** = **lack of success**, abortion, breakdown, collapse, defeat, downfall, fiasco, frustration, miscarriage, overthrow, wreck **2** = **shortcoming**, default, deficiency, dereliction, neglect, negligence, nonobservance, nonperformance, nonsuccess, omission, remissness, stoppage **3** = **loser**, black sheep, clinker (*slang, chiefly U.S.*), clunker (*informal*), dead duck (*slang*), disappointment, dud (*informal*), flop (*informal*), incompetent, ne'er-do-well, no-good, no-hoper (*chiefly Austral.*), nonstarter, washout (*informal*) **4** = **breakdown**, decay, decline, deterioration, failing, loss **5** = **bankruptcy**, crash, downfall, folding (*informal*), insolvency, liquidation, ruin
➤ **Antonyms**
≠**lack of success**: effectiveness, success, triumph ≠**shortcoming**: care, observance ≠**bankruptcy**: fortune, prosperity

fain *adverb Old-fashioned* = **gladly**, as lief (*rare*), as soon, cheerfully, eagerly, willingly

faint *adjective* **1** = **dim**, bleached, delicate, distant, dull, faded, faltering, feeble, hazy, hushed, ill-defined, indistinct, light, low, muffled, muted, soft, subdued, thin, vague, whispered **2** = **dizzy**, drooping, enervated, exhausted, faltering, fatigued, giddy, languid, lethargic, light-headed, muzzy, vertiginous, weak, woozy (*informal*) **3** = **slight**, feeble, remote, unenthusiastic, weak ♦ *verb* **4** = **pass out**, black out, collapse, fade, fail, flake out (*informal*), keel over (*informal*), languish, lose consciousness, swoon (*literary*), weaken ♦ *noun* **5** = **blackout**, collapse, swoon (*literary*), syncope (*Pathology*), unconsciousness
➤ **Antonyms**
adjective ≠**dim**: bright, clear, conspicuous, distinct, loud, powerful, strong ≠**dizzy**: energetic, fresh, hearty, vigorous

faint-hearted *adjective* = **timid**, chickenshit (*U.S. slang*), cowardly, diffident, half-arsed (*Brit. slang*), half-assed (*U.S. & Canad. slang*), half-hearted, irresolute, spineless, timorous, weak, yellow
➤ **Antonyms**
audacious, bold, brave, courageous, daring, dauntless, fearless, game (*informal*), intrepid, plucky, stouthearted

faintly *adverb* **1** = **softly**, feebly, in a whisper, indistinctly, weakly **2** = **slightly**, a little, dimly, somewhat

fair[1] *adjective* **1** = **unbiased**, above board, according to the rules, clean, disinterested, dispassionate, equal, equitable, even-handed, honest, honourable, impartial, just, lawful, legitimate, objective, on the level (*informal*), proper, square, trustworthy, unprejudiced, upright **2 = light**, blond, blonde, fair-haired, flaxen-haired, light-complexioned, tow-haired, towheaded **3 = beautiful**, beauteous, bonny, comely, handsome, lovely, pretty, well-favoured **4 = respectable**, adequate, all right, average, decent, mediocre, middling, moderate, not bad, O.K. or okay (*informal*), passable, reasonable, satisfactory, so-so (*informal*), tolerable **5 = fine**, bright, clear, clement, cloudless, dry, favourable, sunny, sunshiny, unclouded

➤ **Antonyms**

≠**unbiased**: bad, biased, bigoted, discriminatory, dishonest, inequitable, one-sided, partial, partisan, prejudiced, unfair, unjust ≠**beautiful**: homely, plain, ugly

fair² *noun* = **carnival**, bazaar, expo (*informal*), exposition, festival, fête, gala, market, show

fair and square *adjective* = **just**, above board, correct, honest, kosher (*informal*), on the level (*informal*), straight

fairly *adverb* **1 = moderately**, adequately, pretty well, quite, rather, reasonably, somewhat, tolerably **2 = positively**, absolutely, in a manner of speaking, really, veritably **3 = deservedly**, equitably, honestly, impartially, justly, objectively, properly, without fear or favour

fairness *noun* = **impartiality**, decency, disinterestedness, equitableness, equity, justice, legitimacy, rightfulness, uprightness

fairy *noun* = **sprite**, brownie, elf, hob, leprechaun, peri, pixie, Robin Goodfellow

fairy tale *or* **fairy story** *noun* **1 = folk tale**, romance **2 = lie**, cock-and-bull story (*informal*), fabrication, fantasy, fiction, invention, pork pie (*Brit. slang*), porky (*Brit. slang*), tall story, untruth, urban legend, urban myth

faith *noun* **1 = confidence**, assurance, conviction, credence, credit, dependence, reliance, trust **2 = religion**, belief, church, communion, creed, denomination, dogma, persuasion **3 = allegiance**, constancy, faithfulness, fealty, fidelity, loyalty, troth (*archaic*), truth, truthfulness **4** *As in* **bad faith** *or* **good faith = honesty**, honour, pledge, promise, sincerity, vow, word, word of honour

➤ **Antonyms**

≠**confidence**: apprehension, denial, disbelief, distrust, doubt, incredulity,

misgiving, mistrust, rejection, scepticism, suspicion, uncertainty ≠**religion**: agnosticism ≠**allegiance**: infidelity

faithful *adjective* **1 = loyal**, attached, constant, dependable, devoted, immovable, reliable, staunch, steadfast, true, true-blue, trusty, truthful, unswerving, unwavering **2 = accurate**, close, exact, just, precise, strict, true **3 the faithful = believers**, adherents, brethren, communicants, congregation, followers, the elect

➤ **Antonyms**

≠**loyal**: disloyal, faithless, false, false-hearted, fickle, inconstant, perfidious, traitorous, treacherous, unfaithful, unreliable, untrue, untrustworthy

faithfulness *noun* **1 = loyalty**, adherence, constancy, dependability, devotion, fealty, fidelity, trustworthiness **2 = accuracy**, closeness, exactness, justice, strictness, truth

faithless *adjective* = **disloyal**, doubting, false, false-hearted, fickle, inconstant, perfidious, recreant (*archaic*), traitorous, treacherous, unbelieving, unfaithful, unreliable, untrue, untrustworthy, untruthful

faithlessness *noun* = **disloyalty**, betrayal, fickleness, inconstancy, infidelity, perfidy, treachery, unfaithfulness

fake *verb* **1 = sham**, affect, assume, copy, counterfeit, fabricate, feign, forge, pretend, put on, simulate ♦ *noun* **2 = impostor**, charlatan, copy, forgery, fraud, hoax, imitation, mountebank, phoney *or* phony (*informal*), reproduction, sham ♦ *adjective* **3 = artificial**, affected, assumed, counterfeit, false, forged, imitation, mock, phoney *or* phony (*informal*), pinchbeck, pseudo (*informal*), reproduction, sham

➤ **Antonyms**

adjective ≠**artificial**: actual, authentic, bona fide, faithful, genuine, honest, legitimate, real, true, veritable

fall *verb* **1 = descend**, be precipitated, cascade, collapse, come a cropper (*informal*), crash, dive, drop, drop down, go head over heels, keel over, nose-dive, pitch, plummet, plunge, settle, sink, stumble, subside, topple, trip, trip over, tumble **2 = decrease**, abate, become lower, decline, depreciate, diminish, drop, dwindle, ebb, fall off, flag, go down, lessen, slump, subside **3 = slope**, incline, incline downwards **4 = die**, be a casualty, be killed, be lost, be slain, meet one's end, perish **5 = be overthrown**, be taken, capitulate, give in *or* up, give way,

go out of office, pass into enemy hands, resign, succumb, surrender, yield **6 = occur**, become, befall, chance, come about, come to pass, fall out, happen, take place **7 = lapse**, backslide, err, go astray, offend, sin, transgress, trespass, yield to temptation **8 fall short = be inadequate**, disappoint, fail, fall down on (*informal*), not come up to expectations *or* scratch (*informal*) ♦ *noun* **9 = descent**, dive, drop, nose dive, plummet, plunge, slip, spill, tumble **10 = decrease**, cut, decline, diminution, dip, drop, dwindling, falling off, lessening, lowering, reduction, slump **11 = collapse**, capitulation, death, defeat, destruction, downfall, failure, overthrow, resignation, ruin, surrender **12 = lapse**, degradation, failure, sin, slip, transgression
➤ **Antonyms**
verb ≠**descend**: ascend, climb, go up, increase, mount, rise, scale, soar ≠**decrease**: advance, appreciate, climb, escalate, extend, heighten, increase, wax ≠**die**: endure, hold out, survive ≠**be overthrown**: prevail, triumph

fallacious *adjective* **= incorrect**, deceptive, delusive, delusory, erroneous, false, fictitious, illogical, illusory, misleading, mistaken, sophistic, sophistical, spurious, untrue, wrong

fallacy *noun* **= error**, casuistry, deceit, deception, delusion, falsehood, faultiness, flaw, illusion, inconsistency, misapprehension, misconception, mistake, sophism, sophistry, untruth

fall apart *verb* **= break up**, come apart at the seams, crumble, disband, disintegrate, disperse, dissolve, fall to bits, go *or* come to pieces, go to seed, lose cohesion, shatter

fall asleep *verb* **= drop off** (*informal*), doze off, go out like a light, go to sleep, nod off (*informal*)

fall back *verb* **= retreat**, back off, draw back, recede, recoil, retire, withdraw

fall back on *verb* **= resort to**, call upon, employ, have recourse to, make use of, press into service

fall behind *verb* **1 = lag**, drop back, get left behind, lose one's place, trail **2 = be in arrears**

fall down *verb* **= fail**, disappoint, fail to make the grade, fall short, go wrong, prove unsuccessful

fallen *adjective* **1 = collapsed**, decayed, flat, on the ground, ruinous, sunken **2** *Old-fashioned* **= dishonoured**, disgraced, immoral, loose, lost, ruined, shamed, sinful, unchaste **3 = killed**, dead, lost, perished, slain, slaughtered

fall for *verb* **1 = fall in love with**, become

infatuated with, desire, lose one's head over, succumb to the charms of **2 = be fooled by**, accept, be deceived by, be duped by, be taken in by, buy (*slang*), give credence to, swallow (*informal*), take on board

fallible *adjective* **= imperfect**, erring, frail, ignorant, mortal, prone to error, uncertain, weak
➤ **Antonyms**
divine, faultless, impeccable, infallible, omniscient, perfect, superhuman, unerring, unimpeachable

fall in *verb* **= collapse**, cave in, come down about one's ears, fall apart at the seams, sink

falling off *noun* **= decrease**, deceleration, decline, deterioration, downward trend, drop, slackening, slowing down, slump, waning, worsening

fall in with *verb* **= go along with**, accept, agree with, assent, buy into (*informal*), concur with, cooperate with, support, take on board

fall off *verb* **1 = tumble**, be unseated, come a cropper *or* purler (*informal*), plummet, take a fall *or* tumble, topple **2 = decrease**, decline, diminish, drop, dwindle, ebb away, fade, fall away, go down *or* downhill, lessen, peter out, reduce, shrink, slacken, slump, subside, tail off (*informal*), wane, weaken
➤ **Antonyms**
≠**decrease**: improve, increase, pick up, rally, recover, revive

fall on *or* **fall upon** *verb* **= attack**, assail, assault, belabour, descend upon, lay into, pitch into (*informal*), set upon *or* about, snatch, tear into (*informal*)

fall out *verb* *Informal* **= argue**, altercate, clash, come to blows, differ, disagree, fight, quarrel, squabble

fallow *adjective* **= uncultivated**, dormant, idle, inactive, inert, resting, undeveloped, unplanted, untilled, unused

falls *plural noun* **= waterfall**, cascade, cataract, force (*Northern English dialect*), linn (*Scot.*), rapids

fall short *verb* **= be lacking**, be deficient, be wanting, fail, miss, prove inadequate

fall through *verb* **= fail**, come to nothing, fizzle out (*informal*), go by the board, miscarry

fall to *verb* **1 = be the responsibility of**, be up to, come down to, devolve upon **2 = begin**, apply oneself to, commence, set about, start

false *adjective* **1 = incorrect**, concocted, erroneous, faulty, fictitious, improper,

inaccurate, inexact, invalid, mistaken, unfounded, unreal, wrong **2** = **artificial**, bogus, counterfeit, ersatz, fake, feigned, forged, imitation, mock, pretended, pseudo (*informal*), sham, simulated, spurious, synthetic **3** = **untrue**, lying, mendacious, truthless, unreliable, unsound, untrustworthy, untruthful **4** = **deceptive**, deceitful, deceiving, delusive, fallacious, fraudulent, hypocritical, misleading, trumped up **5** = **treacherous**, dishonest, dishonourable, disloyal, double-dealing, duplicitous, faithless, false-hearted, hypocritical, perfidious, treasonable, two-faced, unfaithful, untrustworthy
➤ **Antonyms**
≠**incorrect:** correct, exact, right, sound, valid ≠**artificial:** authentic, bona fide, genuine, honest, kosher (*informal*), real, sincere ≠**untrue:** reliable, true ≠**treacherous:** faithful, loyal, trustworthy

falsehood *noun* **1** = **untruthfulness**, deceit, deception, dishonesty, dissimulation, inveracity (*rare*), mendacity, perjury, prevarication **2** = **lie**, fabrication, fib, fiction, misstatement, pork pie (*Brit. slang*), porky (*Brit. slang*), story, untruth

falsification *noun* = **misrepresentation**, adulteration, deceit, dissimulation, distortion, forgery, perversion, tampering with

falsify *verb* = **alter**, belie, cook (*slang*), counterfeit, distort, doctor, fake, forge, garble, misrepresent, misstate, pervert, tamper with

falsity *noun* **1** = **untruth**, deceit, deceptiveness, dishonesty, double-dealing, duplicity, fraudulence, hypocrisy, inaccuracy, mendacity, perfidy, treachery, unreality **2** = **lie**, cheating, deception, fraud, pork pie (*Brit. slang*), porky (*Brit. slang*)

falter *verb* = **hesitate**, break, shake, speak haltingly, stammer, stumble, stutter, totter, tremble, vacillate, waver
➤ **Antonyms**
continue, endure, keep going, last, persevere, persist, proceed, stand firm, stick at

faltering *adjective* = **hesitant**, broken, irresolute, stammering, tentative, timid, uncertain, weak

fame *noun* = **prominence**, celebrity, credit, eminence, glory, honour, illustriousness, name, public esteem, renown, reputation, repute, stardom
➤ **Antonyms**
disgrace, dishonour, disrepute, ignominy, infamy, oblivion, obscurity, shame

famed *adjective* = **renowned**, acclaimed, celebrated, recognized, widely-known

familiar *adjective* **1** = **well-known**, accustomed, common, common or garden (*informal*), conventional, customary, domestic, everyday, frequent, household, mundane, ordinary, recognizable, repeated, routine, stock **2** = **friendly**, amicable, buddy-buddy (*slang, chiefly U.S. & Canad.*), chummy (*informal*), close, confidential, cordial, easy, free, free-and-easy, hail-fellow-well-met, informal, intimate, near, open, palsy-walsy (*informal*), relaxed, unceremonious, unconstrained, unreserved **3** = **disrespectful**, bold, forward, impudent, intrusive, overfree, presuming, presumptuous **4 familiar with** = **acquainted with**, abreast of, at home with, *au courant with, au fait with,* aware of, conscious of, conversant with, introduced to, knowledgeable about, no stranger to, on speaking terms with, versed in, well up in
➤ **Antonyms**
≠**well-known:** infrequent, unaccustomed, uncommon, unfamiliar, unknown, unusual ≠**friendly:** aloof, cold, detached, distant, formal, unfriendly ≠**acquainted with:** ignorant, unaccustomed, unacquainted, unfamiliar, uninformed, unskilled

familiarity *noun* **1** = **acquaintance**, acquaintanceship, awareness, experience, grasp, understanding **2** = **friendliness**, absence of reserve, closeness, ease, fellowship, freedom, friendship, informality, intimacy, naturalness, openness, sociability, unceremoniousness **3** = **disrespect**, boldness, forwardness, liberties, liberty, presumption
➤ **Antonyms**
≠**acquaintance:** ignorance, inexperience, unfamiliarity ≠**friendliness:** distance, formality, reserve ≠**disrespect:** constraint, decorum, propriety, respect

familiarize *verb* = **accustom**, bring into common use, coach, get to know (about), habituate, instruct, inure, make conversant, make used to, prime, school, season, train

family *noun* **1** = **relations**, brood, children, descendants, folk (*informal*), household, issue, kin, kindred, kinsfolk, kinsmen, kith and kin, ménage, offspring, one's nearest and dearest, one's own flesh and blood, people, progeny, relatives **2** = **clan**, ancestors, ancestry, birth, blood, descent, dynasty, extraction, forebears, forefathers, genealogy, house, line, lineage, parentage, pedigree, race, sept, stemma, stirps, strain, tribe **3** = **group**, class, classification, genre, kind, network, subdivision, system

family tree noun = **lineage**, ancestry, extraction, genealogy, line, line of descent, pedigree, stemma, stirps

famine noun = **hunger**, dearth, destitution, scarcity, starvation

famished adjective = **starving**, ravening, ravenous, ready to eat a horse (informal), starved, voracious

famous adjective = **well-known**, acclaimed, celebrated, conspicuous, distinguished, eminent, excellent, far-famed, glorious, honoured, illustrious, legendary, lionized, much-publicized, notable, noted, prominent, remarkable, renowned, signal
➤ **Antonyms**
forgotten, mediocre, obscure, uncelebrated, undistinguished, unexceptional, unknown, unremarkable

fan¹ noun **1** = **blower**, air conditioner, blade, propeller, punkah (in India), vane, ventilator ♦ verb **2** = **blow**, air-condition, air-cool, cool, refresh, ventilate, winnow (rare) **3** = **stimulate**, add fuel to the flames, agitate, arouse, enkindle, excite, impassion, increase, provoke, rouse, stir up, whip up, work up

fan² noun = **supporter**, addict, adherent, admirer, aficionado, buff (informal), devotee, enthusiast, fiend (informal), follower, freak (informal), groupie (slang), lover, rooter (U.S.), zealot

fanatic noun = **extremist**, activist, addict, bigot, buff (informal), devotee, energumen, enthusiast, militant, visionary, zealot

fanatical adjective = **obsessive**, bigoted, burning, enthusiastic, extreme, fervent, frenzied, immoderate, mad, overenthusiastic, passionate, rabid, visionary, wild, zealous

fanaticism noun = **immoderation**, bigotry, dedication, devotion, enthusiasm, extremism, infatuation, madness, monomania, obsessiveness, overenthusiasm, single-mindedness, zeal, zealotry

fancier noun = **expert**, aficionado, amateur, breeder, connoisseur

fanciful adjective = **unreal**, capricious, chimerical, curious, extravagant, fabulous, fairy-tale, fantastic, ideal, imaginary, imaginative, mythical, poetic, romantic, visionary, whimsical, wild
➤ **Antonyms**
conventional, down-to-earth, dry, dull, literal, matter of fact, ordinary, pedestrian, predictable, routine, sensible, sober, unimaginative, uninspired

fancy adjective **1** = **elaborate**, baroque, decorated, decorative, elegant, embellished, extravagant, fanciful, intricate, ornamental, ornamented, ornate ♦ noun **2** = **whim**, caprice, desire, humour, idea, impulse, inclination, notion, thought, urge **3** = **partiality**, fondness, hankering, inclination, liking, predilection, preference, relish, thirst **4** Old-fashioned or literary = **imagination**, conception, image, impression **5** = **delusion**, chimera, daydream, dream, fantasy, nightmare, phantasm, vision ♦ verb **6** Informal = **be attracted to**, be captivated by, desire, favour, go for, have an eye for, like, lust after, prefer, take a liking to, take to **7** = **wish for**, be attracted to, crave, desire, dream of, hanker after, have a yen for, hope for, long for, relish, thirst for, would like, yearn for **8** = **suppose**, be inclined to think, believe, conceive, conjecture, guess (informal, chiefly U.S. & Canad.), imagine, infer, reckon, surmise, think, think likely
➤ **Antonyms**
adjective ≠**elaborate**: basic, cheap, common, inferior, ordinary, plain, simple, unadorned, undecorated, unfussy ♦ noun ≠**partiality**: aversion, disinclination, dislike

fanfare noun = **trumpet call**, flourish, trump (archaic)

fang noun = **tooth**, tusk

fan out verb = **spread out**, disperse, lay out, open out, space out, spread, unfurl

fantasize verb = **daydream**, dream, envision, imagine

fantastic adjective **1** Informal = **wonderful**, awesome (slang), bitchin' (U.S. slang), boffo (slang), brill (informal), chillin' (U.S. slang), cracking (Brit. informal), crucial (slang), def (slang), dope (slang), excellent, first-rate, jim-dandy (slang), marvellous, mean (slang), mega (slang), out of this world (informal), sensational (informal), sovereign, superb, the dog's bollocks (taboo slang), topping (Brit. slang), world-class **2** Informal = **enormous**, extreme, great, overwhelming, severe, tremendous **3** = **strange**, comical, eccentric, exotic, fanciful, freakish, grotesque, imaginative, odd, oddball (informal), off-the-wall (slang), outlandish, outré, peculiar, phantasmagorical, quaint, queer, rococo, unreal, weird, whimsical, zany **4** = **unrealistic**, ambitious, chimerical, extravagant, far-fetched, grandiose, illusory, ludicrous, ridiculous, visionary, wild **5** = **implausible**, absurd, capricious, cock-and-bull (informal), incredible, irrational, mad, preposterous, unlikely
➤ **Antonyms**

≠**wonderful**: common, everyday, normal, ordinary, poor, typical ≠**unrealistic**, **implausible**: credible, moderate, rational, realistic, sensible

fantasy noun 1 = **imagination**, creativity, fancy, invention, originality 2 = **daydream**, apparition, delusion, dream, fancy, figment of the imagination, flight of fancy, hallucination, illusion, mirage, nightmare, pipe dream, reverie, vision

far adverb 1 = **a long way**, afar, a good way, a great distance, deep, miles 2 = **much**, considerably, decidedly, extremely, greatly, incomparably, very much 3 **by far** = **very much**, by a long chalk (informal), by a long shot, by a long way, easily, far and away, immeasurably, incomparably, to a great degree 4 **far and wide** = **extensively**, broadly, everywhere, far and near, here, there and everywhere, in every nook and cranny, widely, worldwide 5 **so far** = **up to now**, thus far, to date, until now, up to the present ♦ adjective 6 = **remote**, distant, faraway, far-flung, far-off, far-removed, long, outlying, out-of-the-way, removed
➤ **Antonyms**
adjective ≠**remote**: adjacent, adjoining, alongside, at close quarters, beside, bordering, close, contiguous, just round the corner, near, nearby, neighbouring, proximate, within sniffing distance (informal)

faraway adjective 1 = **distant**, beyond the horizon, far, far-flung, far-off, far-removed, outlying, remote 2 = **dreamy**, absent, abstracted, distant, lost, vague

farce noun 1 = **comedy**, broad comedy, buffoonery, burlesque, satire, slapstick 2 = **mockery**, absurdity, joke, nonsense, parody, ridiculousness, sham, travesty

farcical adjective = **ludicrous**, absurd, amusing, comic, custard-pie, derisory, diverting, droll, funny, laughable, nonsensical, preposterous, ridiculous, risible, slapstick

fare noun 1 = **charge**, passage money, price, ticket money, transport cost 2 = **passenger**, pick-up (informal), traveller 3 = **food**, commons, diet, eatables, feed, meals, menu, nosebag (slang), provisions, rations, sustenance, table, tack (informal), victuals, vittles (obsolete or dialect) ♦ verb 4 = **get on**, do, get along, make out, manage, prosper

farewell noun = **goodbye**, adieu, adieux or adieus, departure, leave-taking, parting, sendoff (informal), valediction

far-fetched adjective = **unconvincing**, cock-and-bull (informal), doubtful, dubious, fantastic, hard to swallow

(informal), implausible, improbable, incredible, preposterous, strained, unbelievable, unlikely, unnatural, unrealistic
➤ **Antonyms**
acceptable, authentic, believable, credible, feasible, imaginable, likely, plausible, possible, probable, realistic, reasonable

farm noun 1 = **smallholding**, acreage, acres, croft (Scot.), farmstead, grange, holding, homestead, land, plantation, ranch (chiefly North American), station (Austral. & N.Z.) ♦ verb 2 = **cultivate**, bring under cultivation, operate, plant, practise husbandry, till the soil, work

farmer noun = **agriculturist**, agronomist, cockie (N.Z.), husbandman, smallholder, yeoman

farming noun = **agriculture**, agronomy, husbandry

far-out adjective = **strange**, advanced, avant-garde, bizarre, off-the-wall (slang), outlandish, outré, unconventional, unusual, weird, wild

farrago noun = **hotchpotch**, gallimaufry, hash, hodgepodge, jumble, medley, mélange, miscellany, mishmash, mixed bag, mixture, potpourri, salmagundi

far-reaching adjective = **extensive**, broad, important, momentous, pervasive, significant, sweeping, widespread

far-sighted adjective = **prudent**, acute, canny, cautious, discerning, far-seeing, judicious, politic, prescient, provident, sage, shrewd, wise

fascinate verb = **entrance**, absorb, allure, beguile, bewitch, captivate, charm, delight, enamour, enchant, engross, enrapture, enthral, hold spellbound, hypnotize, infatuate, intrigue, mesmerize, ravish, rivet, spellbind, transfix
➤ **Antonyms**
alienate, bore, disenchant, disgust, irritate, jade, put one off, sicken, turn one off (informal)

fascinated adjective = **entranced**, absorbed, beguiled, bewitched, captivated, charmed, engrossed, enthralled, hooked on, hypnotized, infatuated, smitten, spellbound, under a spell

fascinating adjective = **captivating**, alluring, bewitching, compelling, enchanting, engaging, engrossing, enticing, gripping, intriguing, irresistible, ravishing, riveting, seductive
➤ **Antonyms**
boring, dull, mind-numbing, unexciting, uninteresting

fascination *noun* = **attraction**, allure, charm, enchantment, glamour, lure, magic, magnetism, pull, sorcery, spell

fascism *noun* = **authoritarianism**, absolutism, autocracy, dictatorship, Hitlerism, totalitarianism

fashion *noun* **1** = **style**, convention, craze, custom, fad, latest, latest style, look, mode, prevailing taste, rage, trend, usage, vogue **2** = **method**, attitude, demeanour, manner, mode, style, way **3 after a fashion** = **to some extent**, in a manner of speaking, in a way, moderately, somehow, somehow or other, to a degree ♦ *verb* **4** = **make**, construct, contrive, create, design, forge, form, manufacture, mould, shape, work

fashionable *adjective* = **popular**, à la mode, all the go (*informal*), all the rage, chic, cool (*slang*), current, customary, genteel, happening (*informal*), hip (*slang*), in (*informal*), in vogue, latest, modern, modish, prevailing, smart, stylish, trendsetting, trendy (*Brit. informal*), up-to-date, up-to-the-minute, usual, voguish (*informal*), with it (*informal*)
➤ **Antonyms**
behind the times, dated, frumpy, obsolete, old-fashioned, old-hat, outmoded, out of date, out of the ark (*informal*), uncool (*slang*), unfashionable, unpopular, unstylish, untrendy (*Brit. informal*)

fast¹ *adjective* **1** = **quick**, accelerated, brisk, fleet, flying, hasty, hurried, mercurial, nippy (*Brit. informal*), quickie (*informal*), rapid, speedy, swift, winged **2** = **dissipated**, dissolute, extravagant, gadabout (*informal*), giddy, immoral, intemperate, licentious, loose, profligate, promiscuous, rakish, reckless, self-indulgent, wanton, wild **3** = **fixed**, close, constant, fastened, firm, fortified, immovable, impregnable, lasting, loyal, permanent, secure, sound, stalwart, staunch, steadfast, tight, unwavering **4 pull a fast one** *Informal* = **trick**, bamboozle (*informal*), cheat, con (*informal*), deceive, defraud, hoodwink, put one over on (*informal*), swindle, take advantage of, take for a ride (*informal*) ♦ *adverb* **5** = **quickly**, apace, at a rate of knots, hastily, hell for leather (*informal*), hotfoot, hurriedly, in haste, like a bat out of hell (*slang*), like a flash, like a shot (*informal*), like greased lightning (*informal*), like lightning, like nobody's business (*informal*), like the clappers (*Brit. informal*), pdq (*slang*), posthaste, presto, rapidly, speedily, swiftly, with all haste **6** = **soundly**, deeply, firmly, fixedly, securely, tightly
➤ **Antonyms**

adjective ≠**quick**: leisurely, plodding, slow, slow moving, unhurried ≠**fixed**: inconstant, irresolute, unfaithful, unreliable, unstable, wavering, weak ♦ *adverb* ≠**quickly**: at a snail's pace, at one's leisure, gradually, leisurely, slowly, steadily, unhurriedly

fast² *verb* **1** = **go hungry**, abstain, deny oneself, go without food, practise abstention, refrain from food *or* eating ♦ *noun* **2** = **fasting**, abstinence

fasten *verb* **1** = **fix**, affix, anchor, attach, bind, bolt, chain, connect, grip, join, lace, link, lock, make fast, make firm, seal, secure, tie, unite **2** = **direct**, aim, bend, concentrate, fix, focus, rivet

fastening *noun* = **tie**, affixation, attachment, binding, bond, concatenation, connection, coupling, fusion, joint, junction, ligature, link, linking, union

fastidious *adjective* = **particular**, choosy, critical, dainty, difficult, discriminating, finicky, fussy, hard to please, hypercritical, meticulous, nice, overdelicate, overnice, pernickety, picky (*informal*), punctilious, squeamish
➤ **Antonyms**
careless, casual, disorderly, easy-going, lenient, slack, slipshod, sloppy, slovenly, unsystematic

fat *adjective* **1** = **overweight**, beefy (*informal*), broad in the beam (*informal*), corpulent, elephantine, fleshy, gross, heavy, obese, plump, podgy, portly, roly-poly, rotund, solid, stout, tubby **2** = **fatty**, adipose, greasy, lipid, oily, oleaginous, suety **3** = **profitable**, affluent, cushy (*slang*), fertile, flourishing, fruitful, jammy (*Brit. slang*), lucrative, lush, productive, prosperous, remunerative, rich, thriving ♦ *noun* **4** = **fatness**, adipose tissue, beef (*informal*), blubber, bulk, cellulite, corpulence, flab, flesh, obesity, overweight, paunch, weight problem
➤ **Antonyms**
adjective ≠**overweight**: angular, bony, gaunt, lank, lean, scrawny, skinny, slender, slight, slim, spare, thin ≠**fatty**: lean ≠**profitable**: barren, poor, scanty, scarce, unproductive, unprofitable, unrewarding

fatal *adjective* **1** = **lethal**, deadly, destructive, final, incurable, killing, malignant, mortal, pernicious, terminal **2** = **disastrous**, baleful, baneful, calamitous, catastrophic, lethal, ruinous
➤ **Antonyms**
≠**lethal**: beneficial, benign, harmless, innocuous, inoffensive, non-lethal, non-toxic, wholesome ≠**disastrous**:

inconsequential, minor

fatalism *noun* = **resignation**, acceptance, determinism, necessitarianism, passivity, predestinarianism, stoicism

fatality *noun* = **death**, casualty, deadliness, disaster, fatal accident, lethalness, loss, mortality

fate *noun* 1 = **destiny**, chance, divine will, fortune, kismet, nemesis, predestination, providence, weird (*archaic*) 2 = **fortune**, cup, horoscope, lot, portion, stars 3 = **downfall**, death, destruction, doom, end, ruin

fated *adjective* = **destined**, doomed, foreordained, ineluctable, inescapable, inevitable, marked down, predestined, pre-elected, preordained, sure, written

fateful *adjective* 1 = **crucial**, critical, decisive, important, portentous, significant 2 = **disastrous**, deadly, destructive, fatal, lethal, ominous, ruinous
➤ **Antonyms**
≠**crucial**: inconsequential, insignificant, nugatory, ordinary, unimportant

fathead *noun Informal* = **idiot**, ass, berk (*Brit. slang*), booby, charlie (*Brit. informal*), coot, dimwit (*informal*), divvy (*Brit. slang*), dope (*informal*), dumb-ass (*slang*), dunderhead, fool, goose, imbecile, jackass, jerk (*slang, chiefly U.S. & Canad.*), lamebrain (*informal*), nerd or nurd (*slang*), nincompoop, nitwit (*informal*), numbskull or numskull, pillock (*Brit. slang*), plonker (*slang*), prat (*slang*), prick (*derogatory slang*), schmuck (*U.S. slang*), twerp or twirp (*informal*), twit (*informal, chiefly Brit.*), wally (*slang*)

father *noun* 1 = **daddy** (*informal*), begetter, dad (*informal*), governor (*informal*), old boy (*informal*), old man (*informal*), pa (*informal*), papa (*old-fashioned informal*), pater, paterfamilias, patriarch, pop (*informal*), sire 2 = **forefather**, ancestor, forebear, predecessor, progenitor 3 = **founder**, architect, author, creator, inventor, maker, originator, prime mover 4 = **leader**, city father, elder, patriarch, patron, senator 5 = **priest**, abbé, confessor, curé, padre (*informal*), pastor ♦ *verb* 6 = **sire**, beget, get, procreate

fatherland *noun* = **homeland**, land of one's birth, land of one's fathers, motherland, native land, old country

fatherly *adjective* = **paternal**, affectionate, benevolent, benign, forbearing, indulgent, kind, kindly, patriarchal, protective, supportive, tender

fathom *verb* = **understand**, comprehend, get to the bottom of, grasp, interpret

fathomless *adjective* = **profound**, abysmal, bottomless, deep, immeasurable, impenetrable, incomprehensible, unfathomable, unplumbed

fatigue *noun* 1 = **tiredness**, debility, ennui, heaviness, languor, lethargy, listlessness, overtiredness ♦ *verb* 2 = **tire**, drain, drain of energy, exhaust, fag (out) (*informal*), jade, knacker (*slang*), overtire, poop (*informal*), take it out of (*informal*), weaken, wear out, weary, whack (*Brit. informal*)
➤ **Antonyms**
noun ≠**tiredness**: alertness, animation, energy, freshness, get-up-and-go (*informal*), go, indefatigability, life, vigour, zest ♦ *verb* ≠**tire**: refresh, rejuvenate, relieve, rest, revive, stimulate

fatness *noun* = **obesity**, beef (*informal*), bulkiness, corpulence, *embonpoint,* flab, flesh, fleshiness, girth, grossness, heaviness, overweight, podginess, rotundity, size, stoutness, weight, weight problem

fatten *verb* 1 = **grow fat**, broaden, coarsen, expand, gain weight, put on weight, spread, swell, thicken, thrive 2 *often with* **up** = **feed up**, bloat, build up, cram, distend, feed, nourish, overfeed, stuff

fatty *adjective* = **greasy**, adipose, fat, oily, oleaginous, rich

fatuity *noun* = **foolishness**, absurdity, brainlessness, daftness (*informal*), denseness, fatuousness, folly, idiocy, imbecility, insanity, ludicrousness, lunacy, mindlessness, stupidity

fatuous *adjective* = **foolish**, absurd, asinine, brainless, dense, dull, dumb-ass (*slang*), idiotic, inane, ludicrous, lunatic, mindless, moronic, puerile, silly, stupid, vacuous, weak-minded, witless

fault *noun* 1 = **responsibility**, accountability, culpability, liability 2 = **mistake**, blunder, boob (*Brit. slang*), error, error of judgment, inaccuracy, indiscretion, lapse, negligence, offence, omission, oversight, slip, slip-up 3 = **flaw**, blemish, defect, deficiency, demerit, drawback, failing, imperfection, infirmity, lack, shortcoming, snag, weakness, weak point 4 *at fault* = **guilty**, answerable, blamable, culpable, in the wrong, responsible, to blame 5 *find fault with* = **criticize**, carp at, complain, pick holes in, pull to pieces, quibble, take to task 6 *to a fault* = **excessively**, immoderately, in the extreme, needlessly, out of all proportion, overly (*U.S.*), overmuch, preposterously, ridiculously, unduly ♦ *verb* 7 = **criticize**, blame, call to account, censure, find fault

with, find lacking, hold (someone) accountable, hold (someone) responsible, hold (someone) to blame, impugn
➤ **Antonyms**
noun ≠**flaw**: asset, attribute, credit, goodness, merit, perfection, strength, virtue

fault-finding *noun* = **criticism**, carping, hairsplitting, nagging, niggling, nit-picking (*informal*)

faultless *adjective* **1** = **flawless**, accurate, classic, correct, exemplary, faithful, foolproof, impeccable, model, perfect, unblemished **2** = **blameless**, above reproach, guiltless, immaculate, impeccable, innocent, irreproachable, pure, sinless, spotless, squeaky-clean, stainless, unblemished, unspotted, unsullied

faulty *adjective* = **defective**, bad, blemished, broken, damaged, erroneous, fallacious, flawed, impaired, imperfect, imprecise, inaccurate, incorrect, invalid, malfunctioning, not working, on the blink, out of order, unsound, weak, wrong

faux pas *noun* = **gaffe**, bloomer (*Brit. informal*), blunder, boob (*Brit. slang*), breach of etiquette, clanger (*informal*), gaucherie, impropriety, indiscretion, solecism

favour *noun* **1** = **approval**, approbation, backing, bias, championship, espousal, esteem, favouritism, friendliness, good opinion, goodwill, grace, kindness, kind regard, partiality, patronage, promotion, support **2** = **good turn**, benefit, boon, courtesy, indulgence, kindness, obligement (*Scot. or archaic*), service **3 in favour of** = **for**, all for (*informal*), backing, on the side of, pro, supporting, to the benefit of ◆ *verb* **4** = **prefer**, incline towards, single out **5** = **indulge**, be partial to, esteem, have in one's good books, pamper, pull strings for (*informal*), reward, side with, smile upon, spoil, treat with partiality, value **6** = **support**, advocate, approve, back, be in favour of, champion, choose, commend, countenance, encourage, espouse, fancy, like, opt for, patronize
➤ **Antonyms**
noun ≠**approval**: animosity, antipathy, disapproval, disfavour, ill will, malevolence ≠**good turn**: disservice, harm, injury, wrong ◆ *verb* ≠**prefer**: disapprove, disdain, dislike, object to ≠**support**: oppose, thwart

favourable *adjective* **1** = **advantageous**, appropriate, auspicious, beneficial, convenient, encouraging, fair, fit, good, helpful, hopeful, opportune, promising, propitious, suitable, timely **2** = **positive**, affirmative, agreeable, amicable, approving, benign, encouraging, enthusiastic, friendly, kind, reassuring, sympathetic, understanding, welcoming, well-disposed
➤ **Antonyms**
≠**advantageous**: disadvantageous, inauspicious, unfavourable, unhelpful, unpromising, useless ≠**positive**: disapproving, ill-disposed, unfavourable, unfriendly, unsympathetic

favourably *adverb* **1** = **advantageously**, auspiciously, conveniently, fortunately, opportunely, profitably, to one's advantage, well **2** = **positively**, agreeably, approvingly, enthusiastically, genially, graciously, helpfully, in a kindly manner, with approbation, with approval, with cordiality, without prejudice

favourite *adjective* **1** = **preferred**, best-loved, choice, dearest, esteemed, fave (*informal*), favoured ◆ *noun* **2** = **darling**, beloved, blue-eyed boy (*informal*), choice, dear, fave (*informal*), idol, pet, pick, preference, teacher's pet, the apple of one's eye

favouritism *noun* = **preferential treatment**, bias, jobs for the boys (*informal*), nepotism, one-sidedness, partiality, partisanship, preference
➤ **Antonyms**
equality, equity, even-handedness, fairness, impartiality, neutrality, objectivity, open-mindedness

fawn[1] *verb, often with* **on** *or* **upon** = **ingratiate oneself**, be obsequious, be servile, bow and scrape, brown-nose (*taboo slang*), court, crawl, creep, cringe, curry favour, dance attendance, flatter, grovel, kiss ass (*U.S. & Canad. taboo slang*), kneel, kowtow, lick (someone's) arse (*taboo slang*), lick (someone's) boots, pander to, pay court, toady, truckle

fawn[2] *adjective* = **beige**, buff, greyish-brown, neutral

fawning *adjective* = **obsequious**, abject, bootlicking (*informal*), bowing and scraping, crawling, cringing, deferential, flattering, grovelling, prostrate, servile, slavish, sycophantic

fealty *noun* = **loyalty**, allegiance, devotion, faith, faithfulness, fidelity, homage, obeisance, submission, troth (*archaic*)

fear *noun* **1** = **dread**, alarm, apprehensiveness, awe, blue funk (*informal*), consternation, cravenness, dismay, fright, horror, panic, qualms, terror, timidity, tremors, trepidation **2**

= **bugbear**, bête noire, bogey, horror, nightmare, phobia, spectre ♦ *verb* **3** = **be afraid**, apprehend, be apprehensive, be frightened, be in a blue funk (*informal*), be scared, dare not, dread, have a horror of, have a phobia about, have butterflies in one's stomach (*informal*), have qualms, live in dread of, shake in one's shoes, shudder at, take fright, tremble at **4 fear for** = **worry about**, be anxious about, be concerned about, be disquieted over, be distressed about, feel concern for, tremble for

fearful *adjective* **1** = **scared**, afraid, alarmed, anxious, apprehensive, diffident, faint-hearted, frightened, hellacious (*U.S. slang*), hesitant, intimidated, jittery (*informal*), jumpy, nervous, nervy (*Brit. informal*), neurotic, panicky, pusillanimous, shrinking, tense, timid, timorous, uneasy, wired (*slang*) **2** = **frightful**, appalling, atrocious, awful, dire, distressing, dreadful, ghastly, grievous, grim, gruesome, hair-raising, harrowing, hideous, horrendous, horrible, horrific, monstrous, shocking, terrible, unspeakable
➤ **Antonyms**
≠**scared**: ballsy (*taboo slang*), bold, brave, confident, courageous, daring, dauntless, doughty, gallant, game (*informal*), gutsy (*slang*), heroic, indomitable, intrepid, lion-hearted, plucky, unabashed, unafraid, undaunted, unflinching, valiant, valorous

fearfully *adverb* **1** = **nervously**, apprehensively, diffidently, in fear and trembling, timidly, timorously, uneasily, with bated breath, with many misgivings or forebodings, with one's heart in one's mouth **2** = **very**, awfully, exceedingly, excessively, frightfully, terribly, tremendously

fearless *adjective* = **brave**, ballsy (*taboo slang*), bold, confident, courageous, daring, dauntless, doughty, gallant, game (*informal*), gutsy (*slang*), heroic, indomitable, intrepid, lion-hearted, plucky, unabashed, unafraid, undaunted, unflinching, valiant, valorous

fearlessness *noun* = **bravery**, balls (*taboo slang*), ballsiness (*taboo slang*), boldness, confidence, courage, dauntlessness, guts (*informal*), indomitability, intrepidity, lion-heartedness, nerve, pluckiness

fearsome *adjective* = **terrifying**, alarming, appalling, awe-inspiring, awesome, awful, baleful, daunting, dismaying, formidable, frightening, hair-raising, hellacious (*U.S. slang*), horrendous, horrifying, menacing, unnerving

feasibility *noun* = **possibility**, expediency,

practicability, usefulness, viability, workability

feasible *adjective* = **possible**, achievable, attainable, likely, practicable, realizable, reasonable, viable, workable
➤ **Antonyms**
impossible, impracticable, inconceivable, unreasonable, untenable, unviable, unworkable

feast *noun* **1** = **banquet**, barbecue, beanfeast (*Brit. informal*), beano (*Brit. slang*), blowout (*slang*), carousal, carouse, dinner, entertainment, festive board, jollification, junket, repast, revels, slap-up meal (*Brit. informal*), spread (*informal*), treat **2** = **treat**, delight, enjoyment, gratification, pleasure **3** = **festival**, celebration, -fest, fête, gala day, holiday, holy day, red-letter day, saint's day ♦ *verb* **4** = **eat one's fill**, eat to one's heart's content, fare sumptuously, gorge, gormandize, indulge, overindulge, pig out (*slang*), stuff, stuff one's face (*slang*), wine and dine **5** = **treat**, entertain, hold a reception for, kill the fatted calf for, regale, wine and dine

feat *noun* = **accomplishment**, achievement, act, attainment, deed, exploit, feather in one's cap, performance

feathers *plural noun* = **plumage**, down, plumes

feathery *adjective* = **downy**, feathered, fluffy, plumate *or* plumose (*Botany & Zoology*), plumed, plumy, wispy

feature *noun* **1** = **aspect**, attribute, characteristic, facet, factor, hallmark, mark, peculiarity, point, property, quality, trait **2** = **highlight**, attraction, crowd puller (*informal*), draw, innovation, main item, special, special attraction, speciality, specialty **3** = **article**, column, comment, item, piece, report, story ♦ *verb* **4** = **spotlight**, accentuate, call attention to, emphasize, foreground, give prominence to, give the full works (*slang*), headline, play up, present, promote, set off, star

features *plural noun* = **face**, countenance, lineaments, physiognomy

febrile *adjective* *Formal* = **feverish**, delirious, fevered, fiery, flushed, hot, inflamed, pyretic (*Medical*)

feckless *adjective* = **irresponsible**, aimless, feeble, futile, good-for-nothing, hopeless, incompetent, ineffectual, shiftless, useless, weak, worthless

fecund *adjective* *Literary* = **fertile**, fructiferous, fruitful, productive, prolific, teeming

fecundity *noun* = **fertility**, fruitfulness,

productiveness

federate *verb* = **unite**, amalgamate, associate, combine, confederate, integrate, syndicate, unify

federation *noun* = **union**, alliance, amalgamation, association, *Bund*, coalition, combination, confederacy, copartnership, entente, federacy, league, syndicate

fed up *adjective* = **dissatisfied**, annoyed, blue, bored, brassed off (*Brit. slang*), browned-off (*informal*), depressed, discontented, dismal, down, down in the mouth, gloomy, glum, hacked (off) (*U.S. slang*), pissed off (*taboo slang*), sick and tired (*informal*), tired, weary

fee *noun* = **charge**, account, bill, compensation, emolument, hire, honorarium, meed (*archaic*), pay, payment, recompense, remuneration, reward, toll

feeble *adjective* **1** = **weak**, debilitated, delicate, doddering, effete, enervated, enfeebled, etiolated, exhausted, failing, faint, frail, infirm, languid, powerless, puny, shilpit (*Scot.*), sickly, weakened, weedy (*informal*) **2** = **flimsy**, flat, inadequate, incompetent, indecisive, ineffective, ineffectual, inefficient, insignificant, insufficient, lame, paltry, pathetic, poor, slight, tame, thin, unconvincing, weak
➤ Antonyms
≠**weak:** energetic, hale, healthy, hearty, lusty, robust, stalwart, strong, sturdy, vigorous ≠**flimsy:** effective, forceful, successful

feeble-minded *adjective* = **half-witted**, addle-pated, bone-headed (*slang*), braindead (*informal*), deficient, dim-witted (*informal*), dozy (*Brit. informal*), dull, dumb (*informal*), dumb-ass (*slang*), idiotic, imbecilic, lacking, moronic, obtuse, retarded, simple, slow on the uptake, slow-witted, soft in the head (*informal*), stupid, vacant, weak-minded
➤ Antonyms
astute, aware, bright, clear-headed, clever, intelligent, keen, quick-witted, smart

feebleness *noun* **1** = **weakness**, debility, delicacy, effeteness, enervation, etiolation, exhaustion, frailness, frailty, incapacity, infirmity, lack of strength, languor, lassitude, sickliness **2** = **flimsiness**, inadequacy, incompetence, indecisiveness, ineffectualness, insignificance, insufficiency, lameness, weakness

feed *verb* **1** = **cater for**, nourish, provide for, provision, supply, sustain, victual, wine and dine **2** *sometimes with* **on** = **eat**,
devour, exist on, fare, graze, live on, nurture, partake of, pasture, subsist, take nourishment **3** = **encourage**, augment, bolster, foster, fuel, minister to, strengthen, supply ♦ *noun* **4** = **food**, fodder, forage, pasturage, provender, silage **5** *Informal* = **meal**, feast, nosh (*slang*), nosh-up (*Brit. slang*), repast, spread (*informal*), tuck-in (*informal*)

feel *verb* **1** = **touch**, caress, finger, fondle, handle, manipulate, maul, paw, run one's hands over, stroke **2** = **experience**, be aware of, be sensible of, endure, enjoy, go through, have, have a sensation of, know, notice, observe, perceive, suffer, take to heart, undergo **3** = **explore**, fumble, grope, sound, test, try **4** = **sense**, be convinced, feel in one's bones, have a hunch, have the impression, intuit **5** = **believe**, be of the opinion that, consider, deem, hold, judge, think **6** *with* **for** = **feel compassion for**, be moved by, be sorry for, bleed for, commiserate, condole with, empathize, pity, sympathize with **7** **feel like** = **fancy**, could do with, desire, feel inclined, feel the need for, feel up to, have the inclination, want ♦ *noun* **8** = **texture**, finish, surface, touch **9** = **impression**, air, ambience, atmosphere, feeling, quality, sense, vibes (*slang*)

feeler *noun* **1** = **antenna**, tentacle, whisker **2** *As in* **put out feelers** = **approach**, advance, probe

feeling *noun* **1** = **emotion**, affection, ardour, fervour, fondness, heat, intensity, passion, sentiment, sentimentality, warmth **2** = **impression**, apprehension, consciousness, hunch, idea, inkling, notion, presentiment, sense, suspicion **3** = **opinion**, inclination, instinct, point of view, view **4** = **sympathy**, appreciation, compassion, concern, empathy, pity, sensibility, sensitivity, understanding **5** = **sense of touch**, feel, perception, sensation, sense, touch **6** = **atmosphere**, air, ambience, aura, feel, mood, quality, vibes (*slang*) **7** **bad feeling** = **hostility**, anger, dislike, distrust, enmity, upset

feelings *plural noun* = **emotions**, ego, self-esteem, sensitivities, susceptibilities

feign *verb* = **pretend**, act, affect, assume, counterfeit, fake, forge, give the appearance of, imitate, make a show of, put on, sham, simulate

feigned *adjective* = **pretended**, affected, artificial, assumed, counterfeit, ersatz, fake, false, imitation, insincere, pseudo (*informal*), sham, simulated

feint *noun* = **bluff**, artifice, blind, distraction, dodge, expedient, gambit, manoeuvre, mock attack, play, pretence, ruse, stratagem, subterfuge, wile

felicitous *adjective* = **fitting**, apposite, appropriate, apropos, apt, happy, inspired, neat, opportune, pat, propitious, suitable, timely, well-chosen, well-timed

felicity *noun* 1 = **happiness**, blessedness, bliss, blissfulness, delectation, ecstasy, joy 2 = **aptness**, applicability, appropriateness, becomingness, effectiveness, grace, propriety, suitability, suitableness

feline *adjective* 1 = **catlike**, leonine 2 = **graceful**, flowing, sinuous, sleek, slinky, smooth, stealthy

fell *verb* = **cut down**, cut, deck (*slang*), demolish, flatten, floor, hew, knock down, level, prostrate, raze, strike down

fellow *noun* 1 *Old-fashioned* = **man**, bloke (*Brit. informal*), boy, chap (*informal*), character, customer (*informal*), guy (*informal*), individual, person, punter (*informal*) 2 = **associate**, colleague, companion, compeer, comrade, co-worker, equal, friend, member, partner, peer ♦ *adjective* 3 = **co-**, affiliated, akin, allied, associate, associated, like, related, similar

fellow feeling *noun* = **sympathy**, compassion, empathy, pity, understanding

fellowship *noun* 1 = **camaraderie**, amity, brotherhood, communion, companionability, companionship, familiarity, fraternization, intercourse, intimacy, kindliness, sociability 2 = **society**, association, brotherhood, club, fraternity, guild, league, order, sisterhood, sodality

feminine *adjective* = **womanly**, delicate, gentle, girlie, girlish, graceful, ladylike, modest, soft, tender
➤ Antonyms
Amazonian, butch, indelicate, manly, mannish, masculine, rough, unfeminine, unladylike, unwomanly, virile

femininity *noun* = **womanliness**, delicacy, feminineness, gentleness, girlishness, muliebrity, softness, womanhood

femme fatale *noun* = **seductress**, charmer, Circe, enchantress, siren, vamp (*informal*)

fen *noun* = **marsh**, bog, holm (*dialect*), morass, moss (*Scot.*), quagmire, slough, swamp

fence *noun* 1 = **barrier**, barbed wire, barricade, defence, guard, hedge, paling, palisade, railings, rampart, shield, stockade, wall 2 **on the fence** = **uncommitted**, between two stools, irresolute, uncertain, undecided, vacillating ♦ *verb* 3 *often with* **in** *or* **off**

= **enclose**, bound, circumscribe, confine, coop, defend, encircle, fortify, guard, hedge, impound, pen, pound, protect, restrict, secure, separate, surround 4 = **evade**, beat about the bush, cavil, dodge, equivocate, flannel (*Brit. informal*), hedge, parry, prevaricate, quibble, shift, stonewall, tergiversate

fend for *verb* = **look after**, make do, make provision for, provide for, shift for, support, sustain, take care of

fend off *verb* = **turn aside**, avert, beat off, deflect, drive back, hold *or* keep at bay, keep off, parry, repel, repulse, resist, stave off, ward off

feral *adjective* 1 = **wild**, unbroken, uncultivated, undomesticated, untamed 2 = **savage**, bestial, brutal, fell, ferocious, fierce, vicious

ferment *noun* 1 = **commotion**, agitation, brouhaha, disruption, excitement, fever, frenzy, furore, glow, heat, hubbub, imbroglio, state of unrest, stew, stir, tumult, turbulence, turmoil, unrest, uproar 2 = **yeast**, bacteria, barm, fermentation agent, leaven, leavening ♦ *verb* 3 = **brew**, boil, bubble, concoct, effervesce, foam, froth, heat, leaven, rise, seethe, work
➤ Antonyms
noun ≠**commotion**: calmness, hush, peacefulness, quiet, restfulness, stillness, tranquillity

ferocious *adjective* 1 = **fierce**, feral, predatory, rapacious, ravening, savage, violent, wild 2 = **cruel**, barbaric, barbarous, bloodthirsty, brutal, brutish, merciless, pitiless, relentless, ruthless, tigerish, vicious
➤ Antonyms
≠**fierce**: calm, docile, gentle, mild, subdued, submissive, tame

ferocity *noun* = **savagery**, barbarity, bloodthirstiness, brutality, cruelty, ferociousness, fierceness, inhumanity, rapacity, ruthlessness, savageness, viciousness, wildness

ferret out *verb* = **track down**, bring to light, dig up, disclose, discover, drive out, elicit, get at, nose out, root out, run to earth, search out, smell out, trace, unearth

ferry *noun* 1 = **ferry boat**, packet, packet boat ♦ *verb* 2 = **carry**, chauffeur, convey, run, ship, shuttle, transport

fertile *adjective* = **productive**, abundant, fat, fecund, flowering, flowing with milk and honey, fruit-bearing, fruitful, generative, luxuriant, plenteous, plentiful, prolific, rich, teeming, yielding
➤ Antonyms
barren, dry, impotent, infecund, infertile, poor, sterile, unfruitful, unproductive

fertility *noun* = **fruitfulness**, abundance, fecundity, luxuriance, productiveness, richness

fertilization *noun* **1** = **propagation**, implantation, impregnation, insemination, pollination, procreation **2** = **manuring**, dressing, mulching, top dressing

fertilize *verb* **1** = **make fruitful**, fecundate, fructify, impregnate, inseminate, make pregnant, pollinate **2** = **feed**, compost, dress, enrich, manure, mulch, top-dress

fertilizer *noun* = **compost**, dressing, dung, guano, manure, marl

fervent, fervid *adjective* = **intense**, animated, ardent, devout, eager, earnest, ecstatic, emotional, enthusiastic, excited, fiery, flaming, heartfelt, impassioned, passionate, perfervid (*literary*), vehement, warm, zealous
➤ **Antonyms**
apathetic, cold, cool, detached, dispassionate, frigid, impassive, unfeeling, unimpassioned

fervour *noun* = **intensity**, animation, ardour, eagerness, earnestness, enthusiasm, excitement, fervency, passion, vehemence, warmth, zeal

fester *verb* **1** = **intensify**, aggravate, chafe, gall, irk, rankle, smoulder **2** = **putrefy**, become inflamed, decay, gather, maturate, suppurate, ulcerate

festival *noun* **1** = **celebration**, carnival, entertainment, -fest, festivities, fête, field day, gala, jubilee, treat **2** = **holy day**, anniversary, commemoration, feast, fête, fiesta, holiday, red-letter day, saint's day

festive *adjective* = **celebratory**, back-slapping, carnival, cheery, Christmassy, convivial, festal, gala, gay, gleeful, happy, hearty, holiday, jolly, jovial, joyful, joyous, jubilant, light-hearted, merry, mirthful, sportive
➤ **Antonyms**
depressing, drab, dreary, funereal, gloomy, lugubrious, mournful, sad

festivity *noun* **1** = **merrymaking**, amusement, conviviality, fun, gaiety, jollification, joviality, joyfulness, merriment, mirth, pleasure, revelry, sport **2** *often plural* = **celebration**, beano (*Brit. slang*), carousal, entertainment, festival, festive event, festive proceedings, fun and games, hooley *or* hoolie (*chiefly Irish & N.Z.*), jollification, party, rave (*Brit. slang*), rave-up (*Brit. slang*)

festoon *verb* **1** = **decorate**, array, bedeck, beribbon, deck, drape, engarland, garland, hang, swathe, wreathe ♦ *noun* **2** = **decoration**, chaplet, garland, lei, swag, swathe, wreath

fetch *verb* **1** = **bring**, carry, conduct, convey, deliver, escort, get, go for, lead, obtain, retrieve, transport **2** = **sell for**, bring in, earn, go for, make, realize, yield

fetching *adjective* = **attractive**, alluring, captivating, charming, cute, enchanting, enticing, fascinating, intriguing, sweet, taking, winsome

fetch up *verb* = **end up**, arrive, come, finish up, halt, land, reach, stop, turn up

fête, fete *noun* **1** = **fair**, bazaar, festival, gala, garden party, sale of work ♦ *verb* **2** = **entertain**, bring out the red carpet for (someone), hold a reception for (someone), honour, kill the fatted calf for (someone), lionize, make much of, treat, wine and dine

fetid *adjective* = **stinking**, corrupt, foul, malodorous, mephitic, noisome, noxious, offensive, olid, rancid, rank, reeking

fetish *noun* **1** = **fixation**, idée fixe, mania, obsession, thing (*informal*) **2** = **talisman**, amulet, cult object

fetter *verb* **1** = **restrict**, bind, clip someone's wings, confine, curb, encumber, hamper, hamstring, restrain, straiten **2** = **chain**, hobble, hold captive, manacle, put a straitjacket on, shackle, tie, tie up

fetters *plural noun* **1** = **restraint**, bondage, captivity, check, curb, hindrance, obstruction **2** = **chains**, bonds, irons, leg irons, manacles, shackles

feud *noun* **1** = **hostility**, argument, bad blood, bickering, broil, conflict, contention, disagreement, discord, dissension, enmity, estrangement, faction, falling out, grudge, quarrel, rivalry, row, strife, vendetta ♦ *verb* **2** = **quarrel**, be at daggers drawn, be at odds, bicker, brawl, clash, contend, dispute, duel, fall out, row, squabble, war

fever *noun* **1** = **ague**, pyrexia (*Medical*) **2** = **excitement**, agitation, delirium, ecstasy, ferment, fervour, flush, frenzy, heat, intensity, passion, restlessness, turmoil, unrest

feverish *or* **fevered** *adjective* **1** = **hot**, burning, febrile, fevered, flaming, flushed, hectic, inflamed, pyretic (*Medical*) **2** = **excited**, agitated, desperate, distracted, frantic, frenetic, frenzied, impatient, obsessive, overwrought, restless
➤ **Antonyms**
≠**excited:** calm, collected, composed, cool, dispassionate, nonchalant, offhand, serene, tranquil, unemotional, unexcitable, unfazed (*informal*), unruffled

few *adjective* **1** = **not many**, hardly any, inconsiderable, infrequent, insufficient,

meagre, negligible, rare, scant, scanty, scarce, scarcely any, scattered, sparse, sporadic, thin **2 few and far between** = **scarce**, at great intervals, hard to come by, infrequent, in short supply, irregular, rare, scattered, seldom met with, thin on the ground, uncommon, unusual, widely spaced ♦ *pronoun* **3 = small number**, handful, scarcely any, scattering, some
> **Antonyms**
adjective ≠**not many, scarce:** abundant, bounteous, divers (*archaic*), inexhaustible, manifold, many, multifarious, plentiful, sundry

fiancé, fiancée *noun* = **husband-** *or* **wife-to-be**, betrothed, intended, prospective spouse

fiasco *noun* = **flop** (*informal*), balls-up (*taboo slang*), catastrophe, cock-up (*Brit. slang*), debacle, disaster, failure, fuck-up (*offensive taboo slang*), mess, rout, ruin, washout (*informal*)

fiat *noun* **1 = order**, command, decree, demand, dictate, dictum, edict, mandate, ordinance, proclamation **2 = permission**, authorization, sanction, warrant

fib *noun* = **lie**, fiction, pork pie (*Brit. slang*), porky (*Brit. slang*), prevarication, story, untruth, white lie, whopper (*informal*)

fibre *noun* **1 = thread**, fibril, filament, pile, staple, strand, texture, wisp **2** *As in* **moral fibre** = **strength of character**, resolution, stamina, strength, toughness **3 = essence**, nature, quality, spirit, substance

fickle *adjective* = **changeable**, blowing hot and cold, capricious, faithless, fitful, flighty, inconstant, irresolute, mercurial, mutable, quicksilver, temperamental, unfaithful, unpredictable, unstable, unsteady, vacillating, variable, volatile
> **Antonyms**
changeless, constant, faithful, firm, invariable, loyal, reliable, resolute, settled, stable, staunch, steadfast, true, trustworthy

fickleness *noun* = **inconstancy**, capriciousness, fitfulness, flightiness, mutability, unfaithfulness, unpredictability, unsteadiness, volatility

fiction *noun* **1 = tale**, fable, fantasy, legend, myth, novel, romance, story, storytelling, work of imagination, yarn (*informal*) **2** = **lie**, cock and bull story (*informal*), concoction, fabrication, falsehood, fancy, fantasy, figment of the imagination, imagination, improvisation, invention, pork pie (*Brit. slang*), porky (*Brit. slang*), tall story, untruth, urban legend, urban myth

fictional *adjective* = **imaginary**, invented, legendary, made-up, nonexistent, unreal

fictitious *adjective* = **false**, apocryphal, artificial, assumed, bogus, counterfeit, fabricated, fanciful, feigned, imaginary, imagined, improvised, invented, made-up, make-believe, mythical, spurious, unreal, untrue
> **Antonyms**
actual, authentic, genuine, legitimate, real, true, truthful, veracious, veritable

fiddle *noun* **1 = violin 2** *Brit. informal* = **fraud**, fix, graft (*informal*), piece of sharp practice, racket, scam (*slang*), sting (*informal*), swindle, wangle (*informal*) **3 fit as a fiddle** *Informal* = **healthy**, blooming, hale and hearty, in fine fettle, in good form, in good shape, in rude health, in the pink, sound, strong ♦ *verb* **4** *Informal* = **cheat**, cook the books (*informal*), diddle (*informal*), finagle (*informal*), fix, gerrymander, graft (*informal*), manoeuvre, racketeer, sting (*informal*), swindle, wangle (*informal*) **5** = **fidget**, finger, interfere with, mess about *or* around, play, tamper with, tinker, toy, trifle

fiddling *adjective* = **trivial**, futile, insignificant, nickel-and-dime (*U.S. slang*), pettifogging, petty, trifling

fidelity *noun* **1 = loyalty**, allegiance, constancy, dependability, devotedness, devotion, faith, faithfulness, fealty, integrity, lealty (*archaic or Scot.*), staunchness, troth (*archaic*), true-heartedness, trustworthiness **2** = **accuracy**, adherence, closeness, correspondence, exactitude, exactness, faithfulness, preciseness, precision, scrupulousness
> **Antonyms**
≠**loyalty:** disloyalty, faithlessness, falseness, infidelity, perfidiousness, treachery, unfaithfulness, untruthfulness ≠**accuracy:** inaccuracy, inexactness

fidget *verb* **1 = move restlessly**, be like a cat on hot bricks (*informal*), bustle, chafe, fiddle (*informal*), fret, jiggle, jitter (*informal*), squirm, twitch, worry ♦ *noun* **2 the fidgets = restlessness**, fidgetiness, jitters (*informal*), nervousness, unease, uneasiness

fidgety *adjective* = **restless**, antsy (*informal*), impatient, jerky, jittery (*informal*), jumpy, nervous, on edge, restive, twitchy (*informal*), uneasy

field *noun* **1 = meadow**, grassland, green, greensward (*archaic or literary*), lea (*poetic*), mead (*archaic*), pasture **2** = **competitors**, applicants, candidates, competition, contestants, entrants, possibilities, runners **3 = speciality**, area, bailiwick, bounds, confines, department, discipline, domain, environment, limits, line, metier, pale, province, purview, range, scope, specialty, sphere of activity, sphere of influence, sphere of interest, sphere of study, territory ♦ *verb* **4** *Sport* = **retrieve**, catch, pick up, return, stop **5** *Informal* = **deal with**, deflect, handle, turn aside

fiend *noun* **1** = **demon**, devil, evil spirit, hellhound **2** = **brute**, barbarian, beast, degenerate, ghoul, monster, ogre, savage **3** *Informal* = **enthusiast**, addict, energumen, fanatic, freak (*informal*), maniac

fiendish *adjective* = **wicked**, accursed, atrocious, black-hearted, cruel, demoniac, devilish, diabolical, hellish, implacable, infernal, inhuman, malevolent, malicious, malignant, monstrous, satanic, savage, ungodly, unspeakable

fierce *adjective* **1** = **wild**, baleful, barbarous, brutal, cruel, dangerous, fell (*archaic*), feral, ferocious, fiery, menacing, murderous, passionate, savage, threatening, tigerish, truculent, uncontrollable, untamed, vicious **2** = **stormy**, blustery, boisterous, furious, howling, inclement, powerful, raging, strong, tempestuous, tumultuous, uncontrollable, violent **3** = **intense**, cut-throat, keen, relentless, strong
➤ Antonyms
≠**wild**: affectionate, calm, civilized, cool, docile, domesticated, gentle, harmless, kind, mild, peaceful, submissive, tame
≠**stormy**: temperate, tranquil

fiercely *adverb* = **ferociously**, frenziedly, furiously, in a frenzy, like cat and dog, menacingly, passionately, savagely, tempestuously, tigerishly, tooth and nail, uncontrolledly, viciously, with bared teeth, with no holds barred

fiery *adjective* **1** = **burning**, ablaze, afire, aflame, blazing, flaming, on fire **2** = **excitable**, fierce, hot-headed, impetuous, irascible, irritable, passionate

fiesta *noun* = **carnival**, celebration, fair, feast, festival, festivity, fête, gala, holiday, merrymaking, party, revel, revelry

fight *verb* **1** = **battle**, assault, bear arms against, box, brawl, carry on war, clash, close, combat, come to blows, conflict, contend, cross swords, do battle, engage, engage in hostilities, exchange blows, feud, fight like Kilkenny cats, go to war, grapple, joust, lock horns, row, scrap (*informal*), spar, struggle, take the field, take up arms against, tilt, tussle, wage war, war, wrestle **2** = **oppose**, contest, defy, dispute, make a stand against, resist, stand

up to, strive, struggle, withstand **3** = **quarrel**, argue, bicker, dispute, fall out (*informal*), squabble, wrangle **4** = **engage in**, carry on, conduct, prosecute, wage **5 fight shy of** = **avoid**, duck out of (*informal*), keep aloof from, keep at arm's length, shun, steer clear of ♦ *noun* **6** = **battle**, action, affray (*Law*), altercation, *bagarre*, bout, brawl, brush, clash, combat, conflict, contest, dispute, dissension, dogfight, duel, encounter, engagement, exchange of blows, fracas, fray, free-for-all (*informal*), head-to-head, hostilities, joust, melee *or* mêlée, passage of arms, riot, row, rumble (*U.S. & N.Z. slang*), scrap (*informal*), scrimmage, scuffle, set-to (*informal*), shindig (*informal*), shindy (*informal*), skirmish, sparring match, struggle, tussle, war **7** = **resistance**, belligerence, gameness, mettle, militancy, pluck, spirit, will to resist

fighter *noun* **1** = **boxer**, bruiser (*informal*), prize fighter, pugilist **2** = **soldier**, fighting man, man-at-arms, warrior **3** = **combatant**, antagonist, battler, belligerent, contender, contestant, disputant, militant

fighting *noun* = **battle**, bloodshed, blows struck, combat, conflict, hostilities, warfare

fight off *verb* = **repel**, beat off, drive away, keep *or* hold at bay, repress, repulse, resist, stave off, ward off

figment *noun* As in **figment of one's imagination** = **invention**, creation, fable, fabrication, falsehood, fancy, fiction, improvisation, production

figurative *adjective* **1** = **symbolical**, allegorical, emblematical, metaphorical, representative, typical **2** = **poetical**, descriptive, fanciful, florid, flowery, ornate, pictorial
➤ Antonyms
≠**symbolical**: accurate, exact, factual, faithful, literal ≠**poetical**: prosaic, simple, true, unpoetical, unvarnished

figure *noun* **1** = **number**, character, cipher, digit, numeral, symbol **2** = **amount**, cost, price, sum, total, value **3** = **outline**, form, shadow, shape, silhouette **4** = **shape**, body, build, chassis (*slang*), frame, physique, proportions, torso **5** = **character**, big name, celebrity, dignitary, face (*informal*), force, leader, notability, notable, personage, personality, presence, somebody, worthy **6** = **diagram**, depiction, design, device, drawing, emblem, illustration, motif, pattern, representation, sketch ♦ *verb* **7** = **calculate**, add, compute, count, reckon, sum, tally, tot up, work out **8** *usually with* **in** = **feature**, act, appear, be conspicuous, be featured, be included, be mentioned, contribute to, have a place in, play a part **9 it figures = it is to be expected**, it follows, it goes without saying

figured *adjective* = **decorated**, adorned, embellished, marked, ornamented, patterned, variegated

figurehead *noun* = **front man**, cipher, dummy, leader in name only, man of straw, mouthpiece, name, nonentity, puppet, straw man (*chiefly U.S.*), titular *or* nominal head, token

figure of speech *noun* = **expression**, conceit, image, trope, turn of phrase

figure out *verb* **1** = **calculate**, compute, reckon, work out **2** = **understand**, comprehend, decipher, fathom, make head or tail of (*informal*), make out, resolve, see, suss (out) (*slang*)

filament *noun* = **strand**, cilium (*Biology & Zoology*), fibre, fibril, pile, staple, string, thread, wire, wisp

filch *verb* = **steal**, abstract, cabbage (*Brit. slang*), crib (*informal*), embezzle, half-inch (*old-fashioned slang*), lift (*informal*), misappropriate, nick (*slang, chiefly Brit.*), pilfer, pinch (*informal*), purloin, rip off (*slang*), snaffle (*Brit. informal*), swipe (*slang*), take, thieve, walk off with

file¹ *noun* **1** = **folder**, case, data, documents, dossier, information, portfolio **2** = **line**, column, list, queue, row, string ◆ *verb* **3** = **register**, document, enter, pigeonhole, put in place, record, slot in (*informal*) **4** = **march**, parade, troop

file² *verb* = **smooth**, abrade, burnish, furbish, polish, rasp, refine, rub, rub down, scrape, shape

filibuster *noun* **1** *Chiefly U.S., with reference to legislation* = **obstruction**, delay, hindrance, postponement, procrastination ◆ *verb* **2** *Chiefly U.S., with reference to legislation* = **obstruct**, delay, hinder, play for time, prevent, procrastinate, put off

filigree *noun* = **wirework**, lace, lacework, lattice, tracery

fill *verb* **1** = **stuff**, brim over, cram, crowd, furnish, glut, gorge, inflate, pack, pervade, replenish, sate, satiate, satisfy, stock, store, supply, swell **2** = **saturate**, charge, imbue, impregnate, overspread, pervade, suffuse **3** = **plug**, block, bung, close, cork, seal, stop **4** = **perform**, assign, carry out, discharge, engage, execute, fulfil, hold, occupy, officiate, take up ◆ *noun* **5 one's fill** = **sufficient**, all one wants, ample, a sufficiency, enough, plenty
➤ **Antonyms**
verb ≠**stuff:** diminish, drain, empty,

exhaust, shrink, subside, vacate, void

filler *noun* = **padding**, makeweight, stopgap

fill in *verb* **1** = **complete**, answer, fill out (*U.S.*), fill up **2** = **replace**, deputize, represent, stand in, sub, substitute, take the place of **3** *Informal* = **inform**, acquaint, apprise, bring up to date, give the facts *or* background, put wise (*slang*)

filling *noun* **1** = **stuffing**, contents, filler, innards (*informal*), inside, insides, padding, wadding ◆ *adjective* **2** = **satisfying**, ample, heavy, square, substantial

fillip *noun* = **stimulus**, goad, incentive, prod, push, spice, spur, zest

film *noun* **1** = **movie**, flick (*slang*), motion picture **2** = **layer**, coat, coating, covering, dusting, gauze, integument, membrane, pellicle, scum, skin, tissue ◆ *verb* **3** = **photograph**, shoot, take, video, videotape **4 film over** = **cloud**, blear, blur, dull, haze, mist, veil

filmy *adjective* = **transparent**, chiffon, cobwebby, delicate, diaphanous, fine, finespun, flimsy, floaty, fragile, gauzy, gossamer, insubstantial, see-through, sheer

filter *noun* **1** = **sieve**, gauze, membrane, mesh, riddle, strainer ◆ *verb* **2** = **purify**, clarify, filtrate, refine, screen, sieve, sift, strain, winnow **3** = **trickle**, dribble, escape, exude, leach, leak, ooze, penetrate, percolate, seep, well

filth *noun* **1** = **dirt**, carrion, contamination, crap (*slang*), crud (*slang*), defilement, dung, excrement, excreta, faeces, filthiness, foul matter, foulness, garbage, grime, grot (*slang*), kak (*S. African slang*), muck, nastiness, ordure, pollution, putrefaction, putrescence, refuse, sewage, shit (*taboo slang*), slime, sludge, squalor, uncleanness **2** = **obscenity**, corruption, dirty-mindedness, impurity, indecency, pornography, smut, vileness, vulgarity

filthy *adjective* **1** = **dirty**, faecal, feculent, foul, nasty, polluted, putrid, scummy, scuzzy (*slang, chiefly U.S.*), slimy, squalid, unclean, vile **2** = **muddy**, begrimed, black, blackened, grimy, grubby, miry, mucky, mud-encrusted, scuzzy (*slang, chiefly U.S.*), smoky, sooty, unwashed **3** = **obscene**, bawdy, coarse, corrupt, depraved, dirty-minded, foul, foul-mouthed, impure, indecent, lewd, licentious, pornographic, smutty, suggestive, X-rated (*informal*)

final *adjective* **1** = **last**, closing, concluding, end, eventual, last-minute, latest, terminal, terminating, ultimate **2** = **conclusive**, absolute, decided, decisive, definite, definitive, determinate, finished, incontrovertible, irrevocable, settled
➤ **Antonyms**

≠**last**: earliest, first, initial, introductory, maiden, opening, original, precursory, prefatory, premier, preparatory

finale *noun* = **ending**, climax, close, conclusion, crowning glory, culmination, denouement, epilogue, finis, last act
➤ **Antonyms**
commencement, exordium, foreword, intro (*informal*), lead-in, opening, overture, preamble, preface, preliminaries, prelude, proem, prolegomenon, prologue

finality *noun* = **conclusiveness**, certitude, decidedness, decisiveness, definiteness, inevitableness, irrevocability, resolution, unavoidability

finalize *verb* = **complete**, agree, clinch, conclude, decide, settle, sew up (*informal*), shake hands, tie up, work out, wrap up (*informal*)

finally *adverb* **1** = **eventually**, at last, at length, at long last, at the end of the day, at the last, at the last moment, in the end, in the fullness of time, in the long run, lastly, ultimately, when all is said and done **2** = **in conclusion**, in summary, lastly, to conclude **3** = **conclusively**, beyond the shadow of a doubt, completely, convincingly, decisively, for all time, for ever, for good, inescapably, inexorably, irrevocably, once and for all, permanently

finance *verb* **1** = **fund**, back, bankroll (*U.S.*), float, guarantee, pay for, provide security for, set up in business, subsidize, support, underwrite ♦ *noun* **2** = **economics**, accounts, banking, business, commerce, financial affairs, investment, money, money management

finances *plural noun* = **resources**, affairs, assets, capital, cash, financial condition, funds, money, wherewithal

financial *adjective* = **economic**, budgeting, fiscal, monetary, money, pecuniary

find *verb* **1** = **discover**, catch sight of, chance upon, come across, come up with, descry, encounter, espy, expose, ferret out, hit upon, lay one's hand on, light upon, locate, meet, recognize, run to earth, run to ground, spot, stumble upon, track down, turn up, uncover, unearth **2** = **realise**, arrive at, ascertain, become aware, detect, discover, experience, learn, note, notice, observe, perceive, remark **3** = **get**, achieve, acquire, attain, earn, gain, obtain, procure, win **4** = **provide**, be responsible for, bring, contribute, cough up (*informal*), furnish, purvey, supply ♦ *noun* **5** = **discovery**, acquisition, asset, bargain, catch, good buy
➤ **Antonyms**
verb ≠**discover**: lose, mislay, misplace,

miss, overlook

finding *noun* = **conclusion**, award, decision, decree, judgment, pronouncement, recommendation, verdict

find out *verb* **1** = **learn**, detect, discover, note, observe, perceive, realize **2** = **detect**, bring to light, catch, disclose, expose, reveal, rumble (*Brit. informal*), suss (out) (*slang*), uncover, unmask

fine[1] *adjective* **1** = **excellent**, accomplished, admirable, beautiful, choice, divine, exceptional, exquisite, first-class, first-rate, great, magnificent, masterly, ornate, outstanding, rare, select, showy, skilful, splendid, sterling, superior, supreme, world-class **2** = **sunny**, balmy, bright, clear, clement, cloudless, dry, fair, pleasant **3** = **satisfactory**, acceptable, agreeable, all right, convenient, good, hunky-dory (*informal*), O.K. or okay (*informal*), suitable **4** = **delicate**, dainty, elegant, expensive, exquisite, fragile, quality **5** = **subtle**, abstruse, acute, critical, discriminating, fastidious, hairsplitting, intelligent, keen, minute, nice, precise, quick, refined, sensitive, sharp, tasteful, tenuous **6** = **slender**, delicate, diaphanous, fine-grained, flimsy, gauzy, gossamer, light, lightweight, powdered, powdery, pulverized, sheer, small, thin **7** = **sharp**, brilliant, cutting, honed, keen, polished, razor-sharp **8** = **good-looking**, attractive, bonny, handsome, lovely, smart, striking, stylish, well-favoured
➤ **Antonyms**
≠**excellent**: indifferent, inferior, poor, second rate, substandard ≠**sunny**: cloudy, dull, overcast, unpleasant ≠**delicate**: blunt, coarse, crude, dull, heavy, rough

fine[2] *noun* **1** = **penalty**, amercement (*obsolete*), damages, forfeit, punishment ♦ *verb* **2** = **penalize**, amerce (*archaic*), mulct, punish

finery *noun* = **splendour**, best bib and tucker (*informal*), decorations, frippery, gear (*informal*), gewgaws, glad rags (*informal*), ornaments, showiness, Sunday best, trappings, trinkets

finesse *noun* **1** = **skill**, adeptness, adroitness, artfulness, cleverness, craft, delicacy, diplomacy, discretion, know-how (*informal*), polish, quickness, savoir-faire, sophistication, subtlety, tact ♦ *verb* **2** = **manoeuvre**, bluff, manipulate

finger *verb* **1** = **touch**, feel, fiddle with (*informal*), handle, manipulate, maul, meddle with, paw (*informal*), play about with, toy with ♦ *noun* **2 put one's finger on** = **identify**, bring to mind, discover, find out, hit the nail on the head, hit upon, indicate, locate, pin down, place, recall, remember

finicky *adjective* = **fussy**, choosy (*informal*), critical, dainty, difficult, fastidious, finicking, hard to please, nit-picking (*informal*), overnice, overparticular, particular, picky (*informal*), scrupulous, squeamish

finish *verb* **1** = **stop**, accomplish, achieve, bring to a close *or* conclusion, carry through, cease, close, complete, conclude, culminate, deal with, discharge, do, end, execute, finalize, fulfil, get done, get out of the way, make short work of, put the finishing touch(es) to, put the tin lid on, round off, settle, terminate, wind up, wrap up (*informal*) **2** = **consume**, deplete, devour, dispatch, dispose of, drain, drink, eat, empty, exhaust, expend, spend, use, use up **3** = **perfect**, elaborate, polish, refine **4** = **coat**, face, gild, lacquer, polish, smooth off, stain, texture, veneer, wax **5** = **destroy**, administer *or* give the coup de grâce, annihilate, best, bring down, defeat, dispose of, drive to the wall, exterminate, get rid of, kill, move in for the kill, overcome, overpower, put an end to, put paid to, rout, ruin, worst ♦ *noun* **6** = **end**, cessation, close, closing, completion, conclusion, culmination, denouement, ending, finale, last stage(s), run-in, termination, winding up (*informal*), wind-up **7** = **defeat**, annihilation, bankruptcy, curtains (*informal*), death, end, end of the road, liquidation, ruin **8** = **surface**, appearance, grain, lustre, patina, polish, shine, smoothness, texture **9** = **polish**, cultivation, culture, elaboration, perfection, refinement, sophistication

► Antonyms

verb ≠**stop**: begin, commence, create, embark on, instigate, start, undertake ♦ *noun* ≠**end**: beginning, birth, commencement, conception, genesis, inauguration, inception, instigation, preamble, preface, prologue

finished *adjective* **1** = **over**, accomplished, achieved, closed, complete, completed, concluded, done, ended, entire, final, finalized, full, in the past, over and done with, sewed up (*informal*), shut, terminated, through, tied up, wrapped up (*informal*) **2** = **spent**, done, drained, empty, exhausted, gone, played out (*informal*), used up **3** = **polished**, accomplished, classic, consummate, cultivated, elegant, expert, flawless, impeccable, masterly, perfected, professional, proficient, refined, skilled, smooth, urbane **4** = **ruined**, bankrupt, defeated, devastated, done for (*informal*),

doomed, gone, liquidated, lost, through, undone, washed up (*informal, chiefly U.S.*), wiped out, wound up, wrecked

► Antonyms

≠**over**: begun, incomplete ≠**polished**: basic, coarse, crude, imperfect, rough, unfinished, unrefined, unskilled, unsophisticated

finite *adjective* = **limited**, bounded, circumscribed, conditioned, delimited, demarcated, restricted, subject to limitations, terminable

► Antonyms

boundless, endless, eternal, everlasting, immeasurable, infinite, interminable, limitless, perpetual, unbounded

fire *noun* **1** = **flames**, blaze, combustion, conflagration, inferno **2** = **bombardment**, barrage, cannonade, flak, fusillade, hail, salvo, shelling, sniping, volley **3** = **passion**, animation, ardour, brio, burning passion, dash, eagerness, élan, enthusiasm, excitement, fervency, fervour, force, heat, impetuosity, intensity, life, light, lustre, pizzazz *or* pizazz (*informal*), radiance, scintillation, sparkle, spirit, splendour, verve, vigour, virtuosity, vivacity **4 on fire**: **a** = **burning**, ablaze, aflame, alight, blazing, fiery, flaming, in flames **b** = **ardent**, eager, enthusiastic, excited, inspired, passionate ♦ *verb* **5** = **shoot**, detonate, discharge, eject, explode, hurl, launch, let loose (*informal*), let off, loose, pull the trigger, set off, shell, touch off **6** *Informal* = **dismiss**, cashier, discharge, give marching orders, give the boot (*slang*), give the bullet (*Brit. slang*), give the push, kiss off (*slang, chiefly U.S. & Canad.*), make redundant, sack (*informal*), show the door **7** = **set fire to**, enkindle, ignite, kindle, light, put a match to, set ablaze, set aflame, set alight, set on fire, torch **8** = **inspire**, animate, arouse, electrify, enliven, excite, galvanize, impassion, incite, inflame, inspirit, irritate, quicken, rouse, stir

firearm *noun* = **weapon**, gun, handgun, piece (*slang*), pistol, revolver, shooter (*slang*)

firebrand *noun* = **rabble-rouser**, agitator, demagogue, fomenter, incendiary, instigator, soapbox orator, tub-thumper

fireworks *plural noun* **1** = **pyrotechnics**, illuminations **2** *Informal* = **trouble**, fit of rage, hysterics, paroxysms, rage, row, storm, temper, uproar

firm[1] *adjective* **1** = **hard**, close-grained, compact, compressed, concentrated, congealed, dense, inelastic, inflexible, jelled, jellified, rigid, set, solid, solidified, stiff, unyielding **2** = **secure**, anchored, braced, cemented, embedded, fast, fastened, fixed, immovable, motionless, riveted, robust, rooted, secured, stable, stationary, steady, strong, sturdy, taut, tight, unfluctuating, unmoving, unshakable **3** = **determined**, adamant, constant, definite, fixed, immovable, inflexible, obdurate, resolute, resolved, set on, settled, stalwart, staunch, steadfast, strict, true, unalterable, unbending, unfaltering, unflinching, unshakable, unshaken, unswerving, unwavering, unyielding

➤ **Antonyms**
≠**hard**: flabby, flaccid, limp, soft ≠**secure**: flimsy, insecure, loose, shaky, unreliable, unstable, unsteady ≠**determined**: inconstant, irresolute, wavering

firm² *noun* = **company**, association, business, concern, conglomerate, corporation, enterprise, house, organization, outfit (*informal*), partnership

firmament *noun Literary* = **sky**, heaven, heavens, the blue, the skies, vault, vault of heaven

firmly *adverb* **1** = **securely**, enduringly, immovably, like a rock, motionlessly, steadily, tightly, unflinchingly, unshakably **2** = **resolutely**, determinedly, staunchly, steadfastly, strictly, through thick and thin, unchangeably, unwaveringly, with a rod of iron, with decision

firmness *noun* **1** = **hardness**, compactness, density, fixedness, inelasticity, inflexibility, resistance, rigidity, solidity, stiffness **2** = **steadiness**, immovability, soundness, stability, strength, tautness, tensile strength, tension, tightness **3** = **resolve**, constancy, fixedness, fixity of purpose, inflexibility, obduracy, resolution, staunchness, steadfastness, strength of will, strictness

first *adjective* **1** = **earliest**, initial, introductory, maiden, opening, original, premier, primeval, primitive, primordial, pristine **2** = **elementary**, basic, cardinal, fundamental, key, primary, rudimentary **3** = **foremost**, chief, head, highest, leading, pre-eminent, prime, principal, ruling ◆ *noun* **4** *As in* **from the first** = **start**, beginning, commencement, inception, introduction, outset, starting point, word "go" (*informal*) ◆ *adverb* **5** = **to begin with**, at the beginning, at the outset, before all else, beforehand, firstly, initially, in the first place, to start with

first-class *adjective* = **excellent**, A1 or A-one (*informal*), ace (*informal*), bad (*slang*), bitchin' (*U.S. slang*), boffo (*slang*),

brill (*informal*), brilliant, capital, champion, choice, crack (*slang*), cracking (*Brit. informal*), crucial (*slang*), dope (*slang*), elite, exceptional, exemplary, first-rate, five-star, great, jim-dandy (*slang*), marvellous, matchless, mean (*slang*), outstanding, premium, prime, second to none, sovereign, superb, superlative, tiptop, top, top-class, top-drawer, top-flight, top-notch (*informal*), topping (*Brit. slang*), tops (*slang*), twenty-four carat, very good, world-class

➤ **Antonyms**
inferior, second-class, second-rate, shocking (*informal*), terrible, third-rate

first-hand *adjective, adverb* = **direct**, straight from the horse's mouth

first-rate *adjective* = **excellent**, A1 or A-one (*informal*), admirable, bitchin' (*U.S. slang*), bodacious (*slang, chiefly U.S.*), boffo (*slang*), brill (*informal*), chillin' (*U.S. slang*), crack (*slang*), cracking (*Brit. informal*), crucial (*slang*), def (*slang*), dope (*slang*), elite, exceptional, exclusive, first class, jim-dandy (*slang*), mean (*slang*), mega (*slang*), outstanding, prime, second to none, sovereign, superb, superlative, the dog's bollocks (*taboo slang*), tiptop, top, top-notch (*informal*), topping (*Brit. slang*), tops (*slang*), world-class

fiscal *adjective* = **financial**, budgetary, economic, monetary, money, pecuniary

fish for *verb* = **seek**, angle for, elicit, hint at, hope for, hunt for, invite, look for, search for, solicit

fish out *verb* = **pull out**, extract, extricate, find, haul out, produce

fishy *adjective* **1** *Informal* = **suspicious**, cock-and-bull (*informal*), dodgy (*Brit., Austral., & N.Z. informal*), doubtful, dubious, funny (*informal*), implausible, improbable, odd, queer, questionable, rum (*Brit. slang*), suspect, unlikely **2** = **fishlike**, piscatorial, piscatory, piscine

fission *noun* = **splitting**, breaking, cleavage, division, parting, rending, rupture, schism, scission

fissure *noun* = **crack**, breach, break, chink, cleavage, cleft, cranny, crevice, fault, fracture, gap, hole, interstice, opening, rent, rift, rupture, slit, split

fit¹ *verb* **1** = **suit**, accord, agree, be consonant, belong, concur, conform, correspond, dovetail, go, interlock, join, match, meet, tally **2** = **adapt**, adjust, alter, arrange, customize, dispose, fashion, modify, place, position, shape, tweak (*informal*) **3** = **equip**, accommodate, accoutre, arm, fit out, kit out, outfit, prepare, provide, rig out ◆ *adjective* **4**

= **appropriate**, able, adapted, adequate, apposite, apt, becoming, capable, competent, convenient, correct, deserving, equipped, expedient, fitted, fitting, good enough, meet (*archaic*), prepared, proper, qualified, ready, right, seemly, suitable, trained, well-suited, worthy **5** = **healthy**, able-bodied, as right as rain, hale, in good condition, in good shape, in good trim, robust, strapping, toned up, trim, well
➤ **Antonyms**
adjective ≠**appropriate**: amiss, ill-fitted, ill-suited, improper, inadequate, inappropriate, unfit, unprepared, unseemly, unsuitable, untimely ≠**healthy**: flabby, in poor condition, out of shape, out of trim, unfit, unhealthy

fit² *noun* **1** = **seizure**, attack, bout, convulsion, paroxysm, spasm **2** = **outbreak**, bout, burst, outburst, spell **3 by fits and starts** = **spasmodically**, erratically, fitfully, intermittently, irregularly, on and off, sporadically, unsystematically

fitful *adjective* = **irregular**, broken, desultory, disturbed, erratic, flickering, fluctuating, haphazard, impulsive, inconstant, intermittent, spasmodic, sporadic, uneven, unstable, variable
➤ **Antonyms**
constant, equable, even, orderly, predictable, regular, steady, systematic, unchanging, uniform

fitfully *adverb* = **irregularly**, by fits and starts, desultorily, erratically, in fits and starts, in snatches, intermittently, interruptedly, off and on, spasmodically, sporadically

fitness *noun* **1** = **appropriateness**, adaptation, applicability, aptness, competence, eligibility, pertinence, preparedness, propriety, qualifications, readiness, seemliness, suitability **2** = **health**, good condition, good health, robustness, strength, vigour, wellness

fitted *adjective* **1** *often with* **with** = **equipped**, accoutred, appointed, armed, furnished, outfitted, provided, rigged out, set up, supplied **2** = **built-in**, permanent

fitting *adjective* **1** = **appropriate**, apposite, becoming, *comme il faut*, correct, decent, decorous, desirable, meet (*archaic*), proper, right, seemly, suitable ♦ *noun* **2** = **accessory**, attachment, component, connection, part, piece, unit
➤ **Antonyms**
adjective ≠**appropriate**: ill-suited, improper, unfitting, unseemly, unsuitable

fittings *plural noun* = **furnishings**, accessories, accoutrements, appointments, appurtenances, bells and whistles, conveniences, equipment, extras, furniture, trimmings

fix *verb* **1** = **place**, anchor, embed, establish, implant, install, locate, plant, position, root, set, settle **2** = **repair**, adjust, correct, mend, patch up, put to rights, regulate, see to, sort **3** = **fasten**, attach, bind, cement, connect, couple, glue, link, make fast, pin, secure, stick, tie **4** = **decide**, agree on, appoint, arrange, arrive at, conclude, define, determine, establish, limit, name, resolve, set, settle, specify **5** = **focus**, direct, level at, rivet **6** *Informal* = **rig**, bribe, fiddle (*informal*), influence, manipulate, manoeuvre, pull strings (*informal*) **7** *Slang* = **sort (someone) out** (*informal*), cook (someone's) goose (*informal*), get even with (*informal*), get revenge on, pay back, settle (someone's) hash (*informal*), take retribution on, wreak vengeance on
♦ *noun* **8** *Informal* = **predicament**, difficult situation, difficulty, dilemma, embarrassment, hole (*slang*), hot water (*informal*), jam (*informal*), mess, pickle (*informal*), plight, quandary, spot (*informal*), ticklish situation, tight spot

fixated *adjective* = **obsessed**, absorbed, attached, besotted, captivated, caught up in, devoted, engrossed, fascinated, hung up on (*slang*), hypnotized, infatuated, mesmerized, preoccupied, single-minded, smitten, spellbound, taken up with, wrapped up in
➤ **Antonyms**
detached, disinterested, dispassionate, indifferent, open-minded, uncommitted, unconcerned, uninvolved

fixation *noun* = **obsession**, addiction, complex, hang-up (*informal*), *idée fixe*, infatuation, mania, preoccupation, thing (*informal*)

fixed *adjective* **1** = **immovable**, anchored, attached, established, made fast, permanent, rigid, rooted, secure, set **2** = **steady**, intent, level, resolute, unbending, unblinking, undeviating, unflinching, unwavering **3** = **agreed**, arranged, decided, definite, established, planned, resolved, settled **4** = **mended**, going, in working order, put right, repaired, sorted **5** *Informal* = **rigged**, framed, manipulated, packed, put-up
➤ **Antonyms**
≠**immovable**: bending, mobile, motile, moving, pliant, unfixed ≠**steady**: inconstant, varying, wavering

fixity *noun* = **steadiness**, doggedness, intentness, perseverance, persistence, stability

fix up verb 1 = **arrange**, agree on, fix, organize, plan, settle, sort out 2 often with **with = provide**, accommodate, arrange for, bring about, furnish, lay on

fizz verb = **bubble**, effervesce, fizzle, froth, hiss, sparkle, sputter

fizzle out verb Informal = **die away**, abort, collapse, come to nothing, end in disappointment, fail, fall through, fold (informal), miss the mark, peter out

fizzy adjective = **bubbly**, bubbling, carbonated, effervescent, gassy, sparkling

flab noun = **fat**, beef (informal), flabbiness, flesh, fleshiness, heaviness, overweight, plumpness, slackness, weight

flabbergasted adjective = **astonished**, abashed, amazed, astounded, bowled over (informal), confounded, dazed, disconcerted, dumbfounded, gobsmacked (Brit. slang), lost for words, nonplussed, overcome, overwhelmed, rendered speechless, speechless, staggered, struck dumb, stunned

flabby adjective 1 = **limp**, baggy, drooping, flaccid, floppy, hanging, lax, loose, pendulous, sagging, slack, sloppy, toneless, unfit, yielding 2 = **weak**, effete, enervated, feeble, impotent, ineffective, ineffectual, nerveless, spineless, wimpish or wimpy (informal), wussy (slang)
➤ Antonyms
≠limp: firm, hard, solid, strong, taut, tense, tight, tough

flaccid adjective = **limp**, drooping, flabby, lax, loose, nerveless, slack, soft, weak

flaccidity noun = **limpness**, flabbiness, looseness, nervelessness, slackness, softness

flag¹ noun 1 = **banner**, banderole, colours, ensign, gonfalon, jack, pennant, pennon, standard, streamer ♦ verb 2 = **mark**, docket, indicate, label, note, tab 3 sometimes with **down** = **hail**, salute, signal, warn, wave

flag² verb = **weaken**, abate, decline, die, droop, ebb, fade, fail, faint, fall, fall off, feel the pace, languish, peter out, pine, sag, sink, slump, succumb, taper off, wane, weary, wilt

flagellate verb = **whip**, beat, castigate, chastise, flay, flog, lambast(e), lash, scourge, thrash

flagellation noun = **whipping**, beating, flogging, lashing, thrashing

flagging adjective = **weakening**, declining, decreasing, deteriorating, ebbing, fading, failing, faltering, giving up, sinking, slowing down, tiring, waning, wilting

flagrant adjective = **outrageous**, arrant, atrocious, awful, barefaced, blatant, bold, brazen, crying, dreadful, egregious, enormous, flagitious, flaunting, glaring, heinous, immodest, infamous, notorious, open, ostentatious, out-and-out, scandalous, shameless, undisguised
➤ Antonyms
delicate, faint, implied, indirect, insinuated, slight, subtle, understated

flagstone noun = **paving stone**, block, flag, slab

flail verb = **thrash**, beat, thresh, windmill

flair noun 1 = **ability**, accomplishment, aptitude, faculty, feel, genius, gift, knack, mastery, talent 2 = **style**, chic, dash, discernment, elegance, panache, stylishness, taste

flak noun = **criticism**, abuse, bad press, censure, complaints, condemnation, denigration, disapprobation, disapproval, disparagement, fault-finding, hostility, opposition, stick (slang)

flake noun 1 = **chip**, disk, lamina, layer, peeling, scale, shaving, sliver, squama (Biology), wafer ♦ verb 2 = **chip**, blister, desquamate, peel (off), scale (off)

flake out verb = **collapse**, faint, keel over, lose consciousness, pass out, swoon (literary)

flamboyance noun = **showiness**, bravura, brio, chic, dash, élan, exhibitionism, extravagance, flair, flamboyancy, flashiness, ostentation, panache, pizzazz or pizazz (informal), pomp, show, sparkle, style, stylishness, swagger, swank (informal), theatricality
➤ Antonyms
drabness, dullness, flatness, restraint, simplicity, unobtrusiveness

flamboyant adjective 1 = **showy**, actorly, baroque, camp (informal), dashing, elaborate, extravagant, florid, ornate, ostentatious, over the top (informal), rich, rococo, swashbuckling, theatrical 2 = **colourful**, brilliant, dazzling, exciting, glamorous, glitzy (slang)

flame noun 1 = **fire**, blaze, brightness, light 2 = **passion**, affection, ardour, enthusiasm, fervency, fervour, fire, intensity, keenness, warmth 3 Informal = **sweetheart**, beau, beloved, boyfriend, girlfriend, heart-throb (Brit.), ladylove, lover ♦ verb 4 = **burn**, blaze, flare, flash, glare, glow, shine

flaming adjective 1 = **burning**, ablaze, afire, blazing, brilliant, fiery, glowing, ignited, in flames, raging, red, red-hot 2 = **intense**, angry, ardent, aroused, frenzied, hot, impassioned, raging, scintillating, vehement, vivid

flammable *adjective* = **combustible**, ignitable, incendiary, inflammable

flank *noun* **1** = **side**, ham, haunch, hip, loin, quarter, thigh **2** = **wing**, side ♦ *verb* **3** = **border**, book-end, bound, edge, fringe, line, screen, skirt, wall

flannel *noun* **1** *Informal* = **prevarication**, baloney (*informal*), blarney, equivocation, flattery, hedging, soft soap (*informal*), sweet talk (*U.S. informal*), waffle (*informal, chiefly Brit.*), weasel words (*informal, chiefly U.S.*) ♦ *verb* **2** *Informal* = **prevaricate**, blarney, butter up, equivocate, flatter, hedge, pull the wool over (someone's) eyes, soft-soap (*informal*), sweet-talk (*informal*), waffle (*informal, chiefly Brit.*)

flap *verb* **1** = **flutter**, agitate, beat, flail, shake, swing, swish, thrash, thresh, vibrate, wag, wave ♦ *noun* **2** = **flutter**, bang, banging, beating, shaking, swinging, swish, waving **3** = **cover**, apron, fly, fold, lapel, lappet, overlap, skirt, tab, tail **4** *Informal* = **panic**, agitation, commotion, fluster, state (*informal*), stew (*informal*), sweat (*informal*), tizzy (*informal*), twitter (*informal*)

flare *verb* **1** = **blaze**, burn up, dazzle, flicker, flutter, glare, waver **2** = **widen**, broaden, spread out ♦ *noun* **3** = **flame**, blaze, burst, dazzle, flash, flicker, glare

flare up *verb* **1** = **lose one's temper**, blaze, blow one's top (*informal*), boil over, break out, explode, fire up, fly off the handle (*informal*), lose control, lose it (*informal*), lose one's cool (*informal*), lose the plot (*informal*), throw a tantrum

flash *noun* **1** = **blaze**, burst, coruscation, dazzle, flare, flicker, gleam, ray, scintillation, shaft, shimmer, spark, sparkle, streak, twinkle **2** = **burst**, demonstration, display, manifestation, outburst, show, sign, touch **3** = **moment**, bat of an eye (*informal*), instant, jiffy (*informal*), second, shake, split second, trice, twinkling, twinkling of an eye, two shakes of a lamb's tail (*informal*) ♦ *adjective* **4** *Informal* = **ostentatious**, cheap, glamorous, naff (*Brit. slang*), tacky (*informal*), tasteless, vulgar ♦ *verb* **5** = **blaze**, coruscate, flare, flicker, glare, gleam, glint, glisten, glitter, light, scintillate, shimmer, sparkle, twinkle **6** = **speed**, barrel (along) (*informal, chiefly U.S. & Canad.*), bolt, burn rubber (*informal*), dart, dash, fly, race, shoot, sprint, streak, sweep, whistle, zoom **7** *Informal* = **show**, display, exhibit, expose, flaunt, flourish

flashy *adjective* = **showy**, brash, cheap, cheap and nasty, flamboyant, flaunting, garish, gaudy, glittery, glitzy (*slang*), in poor taste, jazzy (*informal*), loud, meretricious, naff (*Brit. slang*), ostentatious, over the top (*informal*), snazzy (*informal*), tacky (*informal*), tasteless, tawdry, tinselly

➤ **Antonyms**
downbeat, low-key, modest, natural, plain, unaffected, understated

flat[1] *adjective* **1** = **even**, horizontal, level, levelled, low, planar, plane, smooth, unbroken **2** = **horizontal**, laid low, lying full length, outstretched, prone, prostrate, reclining, recumbent, supine **3** = **punctured**, blown out, burst, collapsed, deflated, empty **4** = **absolute**, categorical, direct, downright, explicit, final, fixed, out-and-out, peremptory, plain, positive, straight, unconditional, unequivocal, unmistakable, unqualified **5** = **dull**, boring, dead, flavourless, ho-hum (*informal*), insipid, jejune, lacklustre, lifeless, monotonous, pointless, prosaic, spiritless, stale, tedious, tiresome, uninteresting, vapid, watery, weak ♦ *adverb* **6** = **completely**, absolutely, categorically, exactly, point blank, precisely, utterly **7 flat out** *Informal* = **at full speed**, all out, at full gallop, at full tilt, for all one is worth, hell for leather (*informal*), posthaste, under full steam ♦ *noun* **8** *often plural* = **plain**, lowland, marsh, mud flat, shallow, shoal, strand, swamp

➤ **Antonyms**
adjective ≠**even**: broken, hilly, irregular, rolling, rough, rugged, slanting, sloping, uneven, up and down ≠**horizontal**: on end, perpendicular, straight, upright, vertical ≠**dull**: bubbly, effervescent, exciting, fizzy, sparkling, zestful

flat[2] *noun* = **apartment**, rooms

flatly *adverb* = **absolutely**, categorically, completely, positively, unhesitatingly

flatness *noun* **1** = **evenness**, horizontality, levelness, smoothness, uniformity **2** = **dullness**, emptiness, insipidity, monotony, staleness, tedium, vapidity

flatten *verb* **1** = **level**, compress, even out, iron out, plaster, raze, roll, smooth off, squash, trample **2** *Informal* = **knock down**, bowl over, deck (*slang*), fell, floor, knock off one's feet, prostrate **3** *Informal* = **crush**, subdue

flatter *verb* **1** = **praise**, blandish, butter up, cajole, compliment, court, fawn, flannel (*Brit. informal*), humour, inveigle, lay it on (thick) (*slang*), pander to, puff, soft-soap (*informal*), sweet-talk (*informal*), wheedle **2** = **suit**, become, do something for, enhance, set off, show to advantage

flattering *adjective* **1** = **ingratiating**,

adulatory, complimentary, fawning, fulsome, gratifying, honeyed, honey-tongued, laudatory, sugary **2 = becoming**, effective, enhancing, kind, well-chosen

➤ **Antonyms**

≠**ingratiating**: blunt, candid, honest, straight, uncomplimentary ≠**becoming**: not shown in the best light, not shown to advantage, plain, unattractive, unbecoming, unflattering, warts and all

flattery noun **= obsequiousness**, adulation, blandishment, blarney, cajolery, false praise, fawning, flannel (*Brit. informal*), fulsomeness, honeyed words, servility, soft-soap (*informal*), sweet-talk (*informal*), sycophancy, toadyism

flatulence noun **= wind**, borborygmus (*Medical*), eructation

flaunt verb **= show off**, boast, brandish, display, disport, exhibit, flash about, flourish, make a (great) show of, make an exhibition of, parade, sport (*informal*), vaunt

flavour noun **1 = taste**, aroma, essence, extract, flavouring, odour, piquancy, relish, savour, seasoning, smack, tang, zest, zing (*informal*) **2 = quality**, aspect, character, essence, feel, feeling, property, *soupçon*, stamp, style, suggestion, tinge, tone, touch ♦ verb **3 = season**, ginger up, imbue, infuse, lace, leaven, spice

➤ **Antonyms**

noun ≠**taste**: blandness, flatness, insipidity, tastelessness

flavouring noun **= essence**, extract, spirit, tincture, zest

flaw noun **= weakness**, blemish, chink in one's armour, defect, disfigurement, failing, fault, imperfection, scar, speck, spot, weak spot

flawed adjective **= damaged**, blemished, broken, chipped, cracked, defective, erroneous, faulty, imperfect, unsound

flawless adjective **= perfect**, faultless, impeccable, spotless, unblemished, unsullied

flay verb **1 = skin**, excoriate **2 = upbraid**, castigate, excoriate, execrate, give a tongue-lashing, pull to pieces (*informal*), revile, slam (*slang*), tear a strip off, tear into (*informal*)

fleabite noun **= trifle**, drop in the ocean, nothing, piddling amount, pinprick

flea-bitten adjective *Informal* **= shabby**, crawling, decrepit, fetid, flea-ridden, frowsty, grotty (*slang*), grubby, infested, insalubrious, lousy, mean, mucky, pediculous (*Medical*), run-down, scabby,

scruffy, scurfy, sleazy, slummy, sordid, squalid, tatty, unhygienic

fleck noun **1 = mark**, dot, pinpoint, speck, speckle, spot, streak ♦ verb **2 = speckle**, bespeckle, besprinkle, dapple, dot, dust, mark, mottle, spot, stipple, streak, variegate

fledgling noun **= chick**, nestling

flee verb **= run away**, abscond, avoid, beat a hasty retreat, bolt, cut and run (*informal*), decamp, depart, do a runner (*slang*), escape, fly, fly the coop (*U.S. & Canad. informal*), get away, hook it (*slang*), leave, make a quick exit, make off, make oneself scarce (*informal*), make one's escape, make one's getaway, scarper (*Brit. slang*), shun, skedaddle (*informal*), slope off, split (*slang*), take a powder (*U.S. & Canad. slang*), take flight, take it on the lam (*U.S. & Canad. slang*), take off (*informal*), take to one's heels, turn tail, vanish

fleece noun **1 = wool** ♦ verb **2 = cheat**, bleed (*informal*), con (*informal*), cozen, defraud, despoil, diddle (*informal*), mulct, overcharge, plunder, rifle, rip off (*slang*), rob, rook (*slang*), sell a pup, skin (*slang*), soak (*U.S. & Canad. slang*), steal, stiff (*slang*), swindle, take for a ride (*informal*), take to the cleaners (*slang*) **3 = shear**, clip

fleecy adjective **= woolly**, downy, fluffy, shaggy, soft

fleet[1] noun **= navy**, argosy, armada, flotilla, naval force, sea power, squadron, task force, vessels, warships

fleet[2] adjective **= swift**, fast, flying, mercurial, meteoric, nimble, nimble-footed, quick, rapid, speedy, winged

fleeting adjective **= momentary**, brief, ephemeral, evanescent, flitting, flying, fugacious, fugitive, here today, gone tomorrow, passing, short, short-lived, temporary, transient, transitory

➤ **Antonyms**

abiding, continuing, durable, enduring, eternal, imperishable, lasting, long-lasting, long-lived, permanent

flesh noun **1 = meat**, beef (*informal*), body, brawn, fat, fatness, food, tissue, weight **2 = physical nature**, animality, body, carnality, flesh and blood, human nature, physicality, sensuality **3 one's own flesh and blood = family**, blood, kin, kindred, kinsfolk, kith and kin, relations, relatives

fleshly adjective **1 = carnal**, animal, bodily, erotic, lascivious, lecherous, lustful, sensual **2 = worldly**, corporal, corporeal, earthly, human, material, mundane, of this world, physical, secular, terrestrial

fleshy *adjective* = **plump**, ample, beefy (*informal*), brawny, chubby, chunky, corpulent, fat, hefty, meaty, obese, overweight, podgy, stout, tubby, well-padded

flex *verb* = **bend**, angle, contract, crook, curve, tighten

flexibility *noun* **1** = **pliancy**, elasticity, give (*informal*), pliability, resilience, springiness, tensility **2** = **adaptability**, adjustability, complaisance

flexible *adjective* **1** = **pliable**, bendable, ductile, elastic, limber, lissom(e), lithe, mouldable, plastic, pliant, springy, stretchy, supple, tensile, willowy, yielding **2** = **adaptable**, adjustable, discretionary, open, variable
➤ **Antonyms**
≠**pliable**: fixed, immovable, inflexible, rigid, stiff, tough, unyielding ≠**adaptable**: absolute, inflexible

flick *verb* **1** = **strike**, dab, fillip, flip, hit, jab, peck, rap, tap, touch **2 flick through** = **browse**, flip through, glance at, skim, skip, thumb ♦ *noun* **3** = **tap**, fillip, flip, jab, peck, rap, touch

flicker *verb* **1** = **twinkle**, flare, flash, glimmer, gutter, shimmer, sparkle **2** = **flutter**, quiver, vibrate, waver ♦ *noun* **3** = **glimmer**, flare, flash, gleam, spark **4** = **trace**, atom, breath, drop, glimmer, iota, spark, vestige

flier *see* FLYER

flight[1] *noun* **1** *Of air travel* = **journey**, trip, voyage **2** = **aviation**, aerial navigation, aeronautics, air transport, flying **3** = **flying**, mounting, soaring, winging **4** = **flock**, cloud, formation, squadron, swarm, unit, wing

flight[2] *noun* **1** = **escape**, departure, exit, exodus, fleeing, getaway, retreat, running away **2 take (to) flight** = **run away** *or* **off**, abscond, beat a retreat, bolt, decamp, do a bunk (*Brit. slang*), do a runner (*slang*), flee, fly the coop (*U.S. & Canad. informal*), light out (*informal*), make a hasty retreat, skedaddle (*informal*), take a powder (*U.S. & Canad. slang*), take it on the lam (*U.S. & Canad. slang*), turn tail, withdraw hastily **3 put to flight** = **drive off**, chase off, disperse, rout, scare off, scatter, send packing, stampede

flightiness *noun* = **frivolity**, capriciousness, fickleness, flippancy, giddiness, irresponsibility, levity, lightness, mercurialness, volatility

flighty *adjective* = **frivolous**, capricious, changeable, ditzy *or* ditsy (*slang*), dizzy, fickle, giddy, harebrained, impetuous, impulsive, irresponsible, light-headed,

mercurial, scatterbrained, skittish, thoughtless, unbalanced, unstable, unsteady, volatile, wild

flimsy *adjective* **1** = **fragile**, delicate, frail, gimcrack, insubstantial, makeshift, rickety, shaky, shallow, slight, superficial, unsubstantial **2** = **thin**, chiffon, gauzy, gossamer, light, sheer, transparent **3** = **unconvincing**, feeble, frivolous, implausible, inadequate, pathetic, poor, tenuous, thin, transparent, trivial, unsatisfactory, weak
➤ **Antonyms**
≠**fragile**: durable, heavy, robust, solid, sound, stout, strong, sturdy, substantial

flinch *verb* = **recoil**, back off, baulk, blench, cower, cringe, draw back, duck, flee, quail, retreat, shirk, shrink, shy away, start, swerve, wince, withdraw

fling *verb* **1** = **throw**, cast, catapult, chuck (*informal*), heave, hurl, jerk, let fly, lob (*informal*), pitch, precipitate, propel, send, shy, sling, toss ♦ *noun* **2** = **binge** (*informal*), bash, beano (*Brit. slang*), bit of fun, good time, hooley *or* hoolie (*chiefly Irish & N.Z.*), indulgence, party, rave (*Brit. slang*), rave-up (*Brit. slang*), spree **3** = **try**, attempt, bash (*informal*), crack (*informal*), gamble, go (*informal*), shot (*informal*), stab (*informal*), trial, venture, whirl (*informal*)

flip *verb, noun* = **toss**, cast, flick, jerk, pitch, snap, spin, throw, twist

flippancy *noun* = **frivolity**, cheek (*informal*), cheekiness, disrespectfulness, impertinence, irreverence, levity, pertness, sauciness

flippant *adjective* = **frivolous**, cheeky, disrespectful, flip (*informal*), glib, impertinent, impudent, irreverent, offhand, pert, rude, saucy, superficial
➤ **Antonyms**
gracious, mannerly, polite, respectful, serious, sincere, solicitous, well-mannered

flirt *verb* **1** = **chat up** (*informal*), coquet, dally, lead on, make advances, make eyes at, make sheep's eyes at, philander **2** *usually with* **with** = **toy with**, consider, dabble in, entertain, expose oneself to, give a thought to, play with, trifle with ♦ *noun* **3** = **tease**, coquette, heart-breaker, philanderer, trifler, wanton

flirtation *noun* = **teasing**, coquetry, dalliance, intrigue, philandering, toying, trifling

flirtatious *adjective* = **teasing**, amorous, arch, come-hither, come-on (*informal*), coquettish, coy, enticing, flirty, provocative, sportive

flit *verb* = **fly**, dart, flash, fleet, flutter, pass, skim, speed, whisk, wing

float *verb* 1 = **be buoyant**, be *or* lie on the surface, displace water, hang, hover, poise, rest on water, stay afloat 2 = **glide**, bob, drift, move gently, sail, slide, slip along 3 = **launch**, get going, promote, push off, set up
➤ **Antonyms**
≠**be buoyant**: dip, drown, founder, go down, settle, sink, submerge ≠**launch**: abolish, annul, cancel, dissolve, terminate

floating *adjective* = **free**, fluctuating, migratory, movable, unattached, uncommitted, unfixed, variable, wandering

flock *noun* 1 = **herd**, colony, drove, flight, gaggle, skein 2 = **crowd**, assembly, bevy, collection, company, congregation, convoy, gathering, group, herd, host, mass, multitude, throng ♦ *verb* 3 = **gather**, collect, congregate, converge, crowd, group, herd, huddle, mass, throng, troop

flog *verb* = **beat**, castigate, chastise, flagellate, flay, lambast(e), lash, scourge, thrash, trounce, whack, whip

flogging *noun* = **beating**, caning, flagellation, hiding (*informal*), horsewhipping, lashing, scourging, thrashing, trouncing, whipping

flood *noun* 1 = **deluge**, downpour, flash flood, freshet, inundation, overflow, spate, tide, torrent 2 = **torrent**, abundance, flow, glut, multitude, outpouring, profusion, rush, stream ♦ *verb* 3 = **immerse**, brim over, deluge, drown, inundate, overflow, pour over, submerge, swamp, teem 4 = **engulf**, flow, gush, overwhelm, rush, surge, swarm, sweep 5 = **oversupply**, choke, fill, glut, saturate

floor *noun* 1 = **tier**, level, stage, storey ♦ *verb* 2 = **knock down**, deck (*slang*), prostrate 3 *Informal* = **disconcert**, baffle, beat, bewilder, bowl over (*informal*), bring up short, confound, conquer, defeat, discomfit, dumbfound, faze, nonplus, overthrow, perplex, puzzle, stump, throw (*informal*)

flop *verb* 1 = **fall**, collapse, dangle, droop, drop, hang limply, sag, slump, topple, tumble 2 *Informal* = **fail**, bomb (*U.S. & Canad. slang*), close, come to nothing, come unstuck, fall flat, fall short, fold (*informal*), founder, go belly-up (*slang*), go down like a lead balloon (*informal*), misfire ♦ *noun* 3 *Informal* = **failure**, cockup (*Brit. slang*), debacle, disaster, fiasco, loser, nonstarter, washout (*informal*)
➤ **Antonyms**
verb ≠**fail**: flourish, make a hit, make it (*informal*), prosper, succeed, triumph, work ♦ *noun* ≠**failure**: hit, success, triumph

floppy *adjective* = **droopy**, baggy, flaccid, limp, loose, pendulous, sagging, soft

floral *adjective* = **flowery**, flower-patterned

florid *adjective* 1 = **flushed**, blowsy, high-coloured, high-complexioned, rubicund, ruddy 2 = **ornate**, baroque, busy, embellished, euphuistic, figurative, flamboyant, flowery, fussy, grandiloquent, high-flown, overelaborate
➤ **Antonyms**
≠**flushed**: anaemic, bloodless, pale, pallid, pasty, wan, washed out ≠**ornate**: bare, dull, plain, unadorned

flotsam *noun* = **debris**, detritus, jetsam, junk, odds and ends, sweepings, wreckage

flounce *verb* = **bounce**, fling, jerk, spring, stamp, storm, throw, toss

flounder *verb* = **struggle**, be in the dark, blunder, fumble, grope, muddle, plunge, stumble, thrash, toss, tumble, wallow

flourish *verb* 1 = **thrive**, bear fruit, be in one's prime, be successful, be vigorous, bloom, blossom, boom, burgeon, develop, do well, flower, get ahead, get on, go great guns (*slang*), go up in the world, grow, grow fat, increase, prosper, succeed 2 = **wave**, brandish, display, flaunt, flutter, shake, sweep, swing, swish, twirl, vaunt, wag, wield ♦ *noun* 3 = **wave**, brandishing, dash, display, fanfare, parade, shaking, show, showy gesture, twirling 4 = **ornamentation**, curlicue, decoration, embellishment, plume, sweep
➤ **Antonyms**
verb ≠**thrive**: decline, diminish, dwindle, fade, fail, grow less, pine, shrink, wane

flourishing *adjective* = **successful**, blooming, burgeoning, doing well, going places, going strong, in the pink, in top form, lush, luxuriant, mushrooming, on a roll, on the up and up (*informal*), prospering, rampant, thriving

flout *verb* = **defy**, deride, gibe at, insult, jeer at, laugh in the face of, mock, outrage, ridicule, scoff at, scorn, scout (*archaic*), show contempt for, sneer at, spurn, take the piss out of (*taboo slang*), taunt, treat with disdain
➤ **Antonyms**
esteem, heed, honour, mind, note, pay attention to, regard, respect, revere, value

flow *verb* 1 = **run**, circulate, course, glide, move, purl, ripple, roll, slide 2 = **pour**, cascade, deluge, flood, gush, inundate, issue, overflow, run, run out, rush, spew, spill, spurt, squirt, stream, surge, sweep, swirl, teem, well forth, whirl 3 = **issue**, arise, emanate, emerge, pour, proceed, result, spring ♦ *noun* 4 = **stream**, course, current, drift, flood, flux, gush, issue, outflow, outpouring, spate, tide, tideway, undertow **5 = outpouring**, abundance, deluge, effusion, emanation, outflow, plenty, plethora, succession, train

flower *noun* **1 = bloom**, blossom, efflorescence **2 = elite**, best, choicest part, cream, *crème de la crème*, freshness, greatest *or* finest point, height, pick, vigour ◆ *verb* **3 = bloom**, blossom, blow, burgeon, effloresce, flourish, mature, open, unfold

flowering *adjective* **= blooming**, abloom, blossoming, florescent, in bloom, in blossom, in flower, open, out, ready

flowery *adjective* **= ornate**, baroque, embellished, euphuistic, fancy, figurative, florid, high-flown, overwrought, rhetorical
➤ **Antonyms**
austere, bare, basic, modest, muted, plain, restrained, simple, spartan, unadorned, unembellished

flowing *adjective* **1 = streaming**, falling, gushing, rolling, rushing, smooth, sweeping **2 = fluent**, continuous, cursive, easy, smooth, unbroken, uninterrupted **3 = abundant**, abounding, brimming over, flooded, full, overrun, prolific, rich, teeming

fluctuate *verb* **= change**, alter, alternate, ebb and flow, go up and down, hesitate, oscillate, rise and fall, seesaw, shift, swing, undulate, vacillate, vary, veer, waver

fluctuation *noun* **= change**, alternation, fickleness, inconstancy, instability, oscillation, shift, swing, unsteadiness, vacillation, variation, wavering

fluency *noun* **= ease**, articulateness, assurance, command, control, facility, glibness, readiness, slickness, smoothness, volubility

fluent *adjective* **= effortless**, articulate, easy, facile, flowing, glib, natural, ready, smooth, smooth-spoken, voluble, well-versed
➤ **Antonyms**
faltering, halting, hesitant, hesitating, inarticulate, stammering, stumbling, tongue-tied

fluff *noun* **1 = fuzz**, down, dust, dustball, lint, nap, oose (*Scot.*), pile ◆ *verb* **2** *Informal* **= mess up** (*informal*), bungle, cock up (*Brit. slang*), foul up (*informal*), fuck up (*offensive taboo slang*), make a mess off, make a nonsense of, muddle, screw up (*informal*), spoil

fluffy *adjective* **= soft**, downy, feathery, fleecy, fuzzy

fluid *noun* **1 = liquid**, liquor, solution
◆ *adjective* **2 = liquid**, aqueous, flowing, in

solution, liquefied, melted, molten, running, runny, watery **3 = changeable**, adaptable, adjustable, flexible, floating, fluctuating, indefinite, mercurial, mobile, mutable, protean, shifting
➤ **Antonyms**
adjective ≠**liquid**: firm, hard, rigid, set, solid ≠**changeable**: definite, firm, fixed, immobile, immutable

fluke *noun* **= stroke of luck**, accident, blessing, break, chance, chance occurrence, coincidence, fortuity, freak, lucky break, quirk, quirk of fate, serendipity, stroke, windfall

flummox *verb* **= baffle**, bamboozle (*informal*), bewilder, bring up short, defeat, fox, mystify, nonplus, perplex, puzzle, stump, stymie

flummoxed *adjective* **= baffled**, at a loss, at sea, bewildered, foxed, mystified, nonplussed, puzzled, stumped, stymied

flunk *Informal verb* **= fail**, be found lacking, be unsuccessful, fall short, flop (*informal*), founder, miss, not come up to scratch, not come up to the mark (*informal*), not make the grade (*informal*), screw up (*informal*), underachieve, underperform
➤ **Antonyms**
be successful, get by *or* through, make it, pass

flunky *noun* **1 = manservant**, footman, lackey, valet **2 = minion**, assistant, cohort (*chiefly U.S.*), drudge, hanger-on, menial, slave, toady, tool, underling, yes man

flurry *noun* **1 = commotion**, ado, agitation, bustle, disturbance, excitement, ferment, flap, fluster, flutter, furore, fuss, hurry, stir, to-do, tumult, whirl **2 = burst**, outbreak, spell, spurt **3 = gust**, flaw, squall ◆ *verb* **4 = confuse**, agitate, bewilder, bother, disconcert, disturb, faze, fluster, flutter, fuss, hassle (*informal*), hurry, hustle, rattle (*informal*), ruffle, unnerve, unsettle, upset

flush¹ *verb* **1 = blush**, burn, colour, colour up, crimson, flame, glow, go as red as a beetroot, go red, redden, suffuse **2 = rinse out**, cleanse, douche, drench, eject, expel, flood, hose down, swab, syringe, wash out
◆ *noun* **3 = blush**, bloom, colour, freshness, glow, redness, rosiness

flush² *adjective* **1 = level**, even, flat, plane, square, true **2** *Informal* **= wealthy**, in funds, in the money (*informal*), moneyed, rich, rolling (*slang*), well-heeled (*informal*), well-off, well-supplied ◆ *adverb* **3 = level with**, even with, hard against, in contact with, squarely, touching

flush³ *verb* **= drive out**, discover, disturb, put to flight, rouse, start, uncover

flushed *adjective* **1 = blushing**, burning,

crimson, embarrassed, feverish, glowing, hot, red, rosy, rubicund, ruddy **2** *often with* **with** = **exhilarated**, animated, aroused, elated, enthused, excited, high (*informal*), inspired, intoxicated, thrilled

fluster *verb* **1** = **upset**, agitate, bother, bustle, confound, confuse, disturb, excite, flurry, hassle (*informal*), heat, hurry, make nervous, perturb, rattle (*informal*), ruffle, throw off balance, unnerve ♦ *noun* **2** = **turmoil**, agitation, bustle, commotion, disturbance, dither (*chiefly Brit.*), flap (*informal*), flurry, flutter, furore, perturbation, ruffle, state (*informal*)

fluted *adjective* = **grooved**, channelled, corrugated, furrowed

flutter *verb* **1** = **beat**, agitate, bat, flap, flicker, flit, flitter, fluctuate, hover, palpitate, quiver, ripple, ruffle, shiver, tremble, vibrate, waver ♦ *noun* **2** = **vibration**, palpitation, quiver, quivering, shiver, shudder, tremble, tremor, twitching **3** = **agitation**, commotion, confusion, dither (*chiefly Brit.*), excitement, flurry, fluster, perturbation, state (*informal*), state of nervous excitement, tremble, tumult

flux *noun* **1** = **change**, alteration, fluctuation, instability, modification, mutability, mutation, transition, unrest **2** = **flow**, fluidity, motion

fly[1] *verb* **1** = **take wing**, flit, flutter, hover, mount, sail, soar, take to the air, wing **2** = **pilot**, aviate, be at the controls, control, manoeuvre, operate **3** = **display**, flap, float, flutter, show, wave **4** = **rush**, barrel (along) (*informal, chiefly U.S. & Canad.*), be off like a shot (*informal*), bolt, burn rubber (*informal*), career, dart, dash, hare (*Brit. informal*), hasten, hurry, race, scamper, scoot, shoot, speed, sprint, tear, whizz (*informal*), zoom **5** = **pass**, elapse, flit, glide, pass swiftly, roll on, run its course, slip away **6** = **flee**, abscond, avoid, beat a retreat, clear out (*informal*), cut and run (*informal*), decamp, disappear, do a runner (*slang*), escape, fly the coop (*U.S. & Canad. informal*), get away, hightail (*informal, chiefly U.S.*), light out (*informal*), make a getaway, make a quick exit, make one's escape, run, run for it, run from, show a clean pair of heels, skedaddle (*informal*), take a powder (*U.S. & Canad. slang*), take flight, take it on the lam (*U.S. & Canad. slang*), take off, take to one's heels **7 let fly: a** *Informal* = **lose one's temper**, burst forth, give free reign, keep nothing back, lash out, let (someone) have it, tear into (*informal*), vent **b** = **throw**, cast, chuck (*informal*), fire, fling, heave, hurl, hurtle, launch, let off, lob (*informal*), shoot, sling

fly[2] *adjective Slang, chiefly Brit.* = **cunning**, astute, canny, careful, knowing, nobody's fool, not born yesterday, on the ball (*informal*), sharp, shrewd, smart, wide-awake

fly at *verb* = **attack**, assail, assault, belabour, fall upon, get stuck into (*informal*), go for, go for the jugular, have a go at (*informal*), lay about, pitch into (*informal*), rush at

fly-by-night *adjective Informal* = **unreliable**, cowboy (*informal*), dubious, questionable, shady, undependable, untrustworthy

flyer, flier *noun* **1** = **leaflet**, advert (*Brit. informal*), bill, booklet, circular, handbill, handout, leaf, literature (*informal*), notice, pamphlet, promotional material, publicity material, release **2** = **goer**, racer, runner, sprinter **3** *Old-fashioned* = **pilot**, aeronaut, airman *or* airwoman, aviator *or* aviatrix

flying *adjective* **1** = **hurried**, brief, fleeting, fugacious, hasty, rushed, short-lived, transitory **2** = **fast**, express, fleet, mercurial, mobile, rapid, speedy, winged **3** = **airborne**, flapping, floating, fluttering, gliding, hovering, in the air, soaring, streaming, waving, wind-borne

foam *noun* **1** = **froth**, bubbles, head, lather, spray, spume, suds ♦ *verb* **2** = **bubble**, boil, effervesce, fizz, froth, lather

foamy *adjective* = **bubbly**, foaming, frothy, lathery, spumescent, sudsy

fob off *verb* **1** = **put off**, appease, deceive, equivocate with, flannel (*Brit. informal*), give (someone) the run-around (*informal*), stall **2** = **pass off**, dump, foist, get rid of, inflict, palm off, unload

focus *verb* **1** = **concentrate**, aim, bring to bear, centre, converge, direct, fix, join, meet, pinpoint, rivet, spotlight, zero in (*informal*), zoom in ♦ *noun* **2** = **centre**, bull's eye, centre of activity, centre of attraction, core, cynosure, focal point, headquarters, heart, hub, meeting place, target **3 in focus** = **clear**, distinct, sharp-edged, sharply defined **4 out of focus** = **blurred**, fuzzy, ill-defined, indistinct, muzzy, unclear

fodder *noun* = **feed**, food, foodstuff, forage, provender, rations, tack (*informal*), victuals, vittles (*obsolete or dialect*)

foe *noun* = **enemy**, adversary, antagonist, foeman (*archaic*), opponent, rival
➤ **Antonyms**
ally, companion, comrade, confederate, friend, partner

fog *noun* **1** = **mist**, gloom, miasma, murk,

murkiness, peasouper (*informal*), smog
♦ *verb* **2** = **mist over** *or* **up**, cloud, steam
up **3** = **obscure**, becloud, bedim, befuddle,
bewilder, blear, blind, cloud, confuse,
darken, daze, dim, muddle, muddy the
waters, obfuscate, perplex, stupefy

fogey, fogy *noun* = **fuddy-duddy**
(*informal*), dinosaur, dodo (*informal*), fossil
(*informal*), square (*informal*),
stick-in-the-mud (*informal*)

foggy *adjective* **1** = **misty**, blurred, cloudy,
dim, grey, hazy, indistinct, murky,
nebulous, obscure, smoggy, soupy,
vaporous **2** = **unclear**, befuddled,
bewildered, clouded, cloudy, confused,
dark, dazed, dim, indistinct, muddled,
obscure, stupefied, stupid, vague
➤ **Antonyms**
≠**misty**: bright, clear ≠**unclear**: alert,
awake, clear, distinct, lucid, sharp,
undimmed

foible *noun* = **idiosyncrasy**, defect, failing,
fault, imperfection, infirmity, peculiarity,
quirk, weakness, weak point

foil¹ *verb* = **thwart**, baffle, balk, check,
checkmate, circumvent, cook (someone's)
goose (*informal*), counter, defeat,
disappoint, elude, frustrate, nip in the bud,
nullify, outwit, put a spoke in (someone's)
wheel (*Brit.*), stop

foil² *noun* = **contrast**, antithesis,
background, complement, setting

foist *verb* = **impose**, fob off, get rid of,
insert, insinuate, interpolate, introduce,
palm off, pass off, put over, sneak in,
unload

fold *verb* **1** = **bend**, crease, crumple,
dog-ear, double, double over, gather,
intertwine, overlap, pleat, tuck, turn under
2 = **wrap**, do up, enclose, enfold, entwine,
envelop, wrap up **3** *Informal* = **go
bankrupt**, be ruined, close, collapse, crash,
fail, go belly-up (*slang*), go bust (*informal*),
go by the board, go down like a lead
balloon (*informal*), go to the wall, go
under, shut down ♦ *noun* **4** = **crease**,
bend, double thickness, folded portion,
furrow, knife-edge, layer, overlap, pleat,
turn, wrinkle

folder *noun* = **file**, binder, envelope,
portfolio

folk *noun* = **people**, clan, ethnic group,
family, kin, kindred, race, tribe

follow *verb* **1** = **come after**, come next,
step into the shoes of, succeed, supersede,
supplant, take the place of **2** = **accompany**,
attend, bring up the rear, come after,
come *or* go with, escort, tag along, tread
on the heels of **3** = **pursue**, chase, dog,
hound, hunt, run after, shadow, stalk, tail

(*informal*), track, trail **4** = **result**, arise, be
consequent, develop, emanate, ensue,
flow, issue, proceed, spring, supervene **5**
= **obey**, act in accordance with, be guided
by, comply, conform, give allegiance to,
heed, mind, note, observe, regard, toe the
line, watch **6** = **copy**, adopt, emulate,
imitate, live up to, pattern oneself upon,
take a leaf out of someone's book, take as
example **7** = **understand**, appreciate,
catch, catch on (*informal*), comprehend,
fathom, get, get the hang of (*informal*),
get the picture, grasp, keep up with,
realize, see, take in **8** = **be interested in**, be
a devotee *or* supporter of, be devoted to,
cultivate, keep abreast of, support
➤ **Antonyms**
≠**come after**: guide, lead, precede
≠**pursue**: avoid, elude, escape ≠**obey**:
abandon, desert, disobey, flout, forsake,
give up, ignore, reject, renounce, shun

follower *noun* = **supporter**, adherent,
admirer, apostle, backer, believer, cohort
(*chiefly U.S.*), convert, devotee, disciple,
fan, fancier, habitué, henchman, partisan,
protagonist, pupil, representative, votary,
worshipper
➤ **Antonyms**
guru, leader, mentor, svengali, swami,
teacher, tutor

following *adjective* **1** = **next**, coming,
consequent, consequential, ensuing, later,
specified, subsequent, succeeding,
successive ♦ *noun* **2** = **supporters**,
audience, circle, clientele, coterie,
entourage, fans, patronage, public,
retinue, suite, support, train

follow through *verb* = **complete**, bring to
a conclusion, conclude, consummate,
pursue, see through

follow up *verb* **1** = **investigate**, check out,
find out about, look into, make inquiries,
pursue, research **2** = **continue**, consolidate,
make sure, reinforce

folly *noun* = **foolishness**, absurdity, bêtise
(*rare*), daftness (*informal*), desipience,
fatuity, idiocy, imbecility, imprudence,
indiscretion, irrationality, lunacy, madness,
nonsense, preposterousness, rashness,
recklessness, silliness, stupidity
➤ **Antonyms**
judgment, level-headedness, moderation,
prudence, rationality, reason, sanity, sense,
wisdom

foment *verb* = **stir up**, abet, agitate, arouse,
brew, encourage, excite, fan the flames,
foster, goad, incite, instigate, promote,
provoke, quicken, raise, rouse, sow the
seeds of, spur, stimulate, whip up

fond *adjective* **1** = **loving**, adoring,

affectionate, amorous, caring, devoted, doting, indulgent, tender, warm **2 = foolish,** absurd, credulous, deluded, delusive, delusory, empty, indiscreet, naive, overoptimistic, vain **3 fond of = keen on,** addicted to, attached to, enamoured of, having a fancy for, having a liking for, having a soft spot for, having a taste for, hooked on, into (*informal*), partial to, predisposed towards

➤ **Antonyms**

≠**loving:** aloof, austere, averse, disinterested, indifferent, unaffectionate, unconcerned, undemonstrative ≠**foolish:** rational, sensible

fondle *verb* **= caress,** cuddle, dandle, pat, pet, stroke

fondly *adverb* **1 = lovingly,** affectionately, dearly, indulgently, possessively, tenderly, with affection **2 = foolishly,** credulously, naively, stupidly, vainly

fondness *noun* **1 = liking,** attachment, fancy, love, partiality, penchant, predilection, preference, soft spot, susceptibility, taste, weakness **2 = devotion,** affection, attachment, kindness, love, tenderness

➤ **Antonyms**

abhorrence, animosity, animus, antagonism, antipathy, aversion, bad blood, coldness, contempt, detestation, dislike, enmity, harshness, hatred, hostility, ill will, loathing, malevolence, malice, repugnance, repulsion, resentment, unfriendliness

food *noun* **1 = nourishment,** board, bread, chow (*informal*), comestibles, commons, cooking, cuisine, diet, eatables (*slang*), eats (*slang*), fare, feed, foodstuffs, grub (*slang*), meat, nosh (*slang*), nutriment, nutrition, provender, provisions, rations, refreshment, scoff (*slang*), stores, subsistence, survival rations, sustenance, tack (*informal*), tuck (*informal*), tucker (*Austral. & N.Z. informal*), viands, victuals, vittles (*obsolete or dialect*) **2** *Cattle, etc.* **= fodder,** feed, forage, provender

foodie *noun Informal* **= gourmet,** *bon vivant, bon viveur,* connoisseur, epicure, gastronome, gourmand

fool *noun* **1 = simpleton,** ass, berk (*Brit. slang*), bird-brain (*informal*), blockhead, bonehead (*slang*), charlie (*Brit. informal*), chump (*informal*), clot (*Brit. informal*), coot, dickhead (*slang*), dickwit (*slang*), dimwit (*informal*), dipstick (*Brit. slang*), divvy (*Brit. slang*), dolt, dope (*informal*), dork (*slang*), dumb-ass (*slang*), dunce, dunderhead, fathead (*informal*), geek (*slang*), goose (*informal*), halfwit, idiot,

ignoramus, illiterate, imbecile (*informal*), jackass, jerk (*slang, chiefly U.S. & Canad.*), lamebrain (*informal*), moron, nerd or nurd (*slang*), nincompoop, ninny, nit (*informal*), nitwit (*informal*), numbskull or numskull, numpty (*Scot. informal*), oaf, pillock (*Brit. slang*), prat (*slang*), prick (*derogatory slang*), sap (*slang*), schmuck (*U.S. slang*), silly, twerp or twirp (*informal*), twit (*informal, chiefly Brit.*), wally (*slang*) **2 = dupe,** butt, chump (*informal*), easy mark (*informal*), fall guy (*informal*), greenhorn (*informal*), gull (*archaic*), laughing stock, mug (*Brit. slang*), stooge (*slang*), sucker (*slang*) **3 = clown,** buffoon, comic, harlequin, jester, joculator or (*fem.*) jocularrix, merry-andrew, motley, pierrot, punchinello **4 act** or **play the fool = clown,** act the goat, act up, be silly, frolic, lark about (*informal*), mess about, piss about (*taboo slang*), piss around (*taboo slang*), play (silly) games, play the goat, show off (*informal*) ♦ *verb* **5 = deceive,** bamboozle, beguile, bluff, cheat, con (*informal*), delude, dupe, have (someone) on, hoax, hoodwink, kid (*informal*), make a fool of, mislead, play a trick on, pull a fast one on (*informal*), put one over on (*informal*), take for a ride (*informal*), take in, trick **6 with with, around with,** or **about with** *Informal* **= play,** fiddle (*informal*), meddle, mess, monkey, piss about (*taboo slang*), piss around (*taboo slang*), tamper, toy, trifle

➤ **Antonyms**

noun ≠**simpleton:** expert, genius, master, sage, savant, scholar, wise man

fool around or **about** *verb Informal* **= mess about,** act the fool, dawdle, footle (*informal*), hang around, idle, kill time, lark, play about, play the fool, waste time

foolery *noun* **= nonsense,** antics, capers, carry-on (*informal, chiefly Brit.*), childishness, clowning, despience, folly, fooling, horseplay, larks, mischief, monkey tricks (*informal*), practical jokes, pranks, shenanigans (*informal*), silliness, tomfoolery

foolhardy *adjective* **= rash,** adventurous, bold, hot-headed, impetuous, imprudent, incautious, irresponsible, madcap, precipitate, reckless, temerarious, venturesome, venturous

➤ **Antonyms**

alert, careful, cautious, chary, circumspect, heedful, judicious, prudent, shrewd, solicitous, thoughtful, wary, watchful

foolish *adjective* **1 = unwise,** absurd, asinine, ill-advised, ill-considered, ill-judged, imprudent, inane, incautious, indiscreet, injudicious, nonsensical, senseless, short-sighted, silly, unintelligent, unreasonable **2 = silly,** as daft as a brush

(*informal, chiefly Brit.*), braindead (*informal*), brainless, crackpot (*informal*), crazy, daft (*informal*), doltish, dumb-ass (*slang*), fatuous, goofy (*informal*), half-baked (*informal*), half-witted, harebrained, idiotic, imbecilic, inane, loopy (*informal*), ludicrous, mad, moronic, off one's head (*informal*), potty (*Brit. informal*), ridiculous, senseless, simple, stupid, weak, witless
➤ **Antonyms**
bright, cautious, clever, commonsensical, intelligent, judicious, prudent, rational, sagacious, sane, sensible, sharp, smart, sound, thoughtful, wise

foolishly *adverb* = **unwisely**, absurdly, idiotically, ill-advisedly, imprudently, incautiously, indiscreetly, injudiciously, like a fool, mistakenly, short-sightedly, stupidly, without due consideration

foolishness *noun* 1 = **stupidity**, absurdity, bêtise (*rare*), folly, idiocy, imprudence, inanity, indiscretion, irresponsibility, silliness, weakness 2 = **nonsense**, bunk (*informal*), bunkum *or* buncombe (*chiefly U.S.*), carrying-on (*informal, chiefly Brit.*), claptrap (*informal*), foolery, rigmarole, rubbish, trash

foolproof *adjective* = **infallible**, certain, guaranteed, never-failing, safe, sure-fire (*informal*), unassailable, unbreakable

footing *noun* 1 = **basis**, establishment, foot-hold, foundation, ground, groundwork, installation, settlement 2 = **relationship**, condition, grade, position, rank, relations, standing, state, status, terms

footling *adjective* = **trivial**, fiddling, fussy, hairsplitting, immaterial, insignificant, irrelevant, minor, nickel-and-dime (*U.S. slang*), niggly, petty, pointless, silly, time-wasting, trifling, unimportant

footstep *noun* 1 = **step**, footfall, tread 2 = **footprint**, footmark, trace, track

footwear *noun* = **footgear**

fop *noun* = **dandy**, beau, Beau Brummel, clotheshorse, coxcomb (*archaic*), peacock, popinjay, swell

foppish *adjective* = **dandyish**, dapper, dressy (*informal*), natty (*informal*), spruce

forage *verb* 1 = **search**, cast about, explore, hunt, look round, plunder, raid, ransack, rummage, scavenge, scour, scrounge (*informal*), seek ♦ *noun* 2 *Cattle, etc.* = **fodder**, feed, food, foodstuffs, provender

foray *noun* = **raid**, incursion, inroad, invasion, sally, sortie, swoop

forbear *verb* = **refrain**, abstain, avoid, cease, decline, desist, eschew, hold back, keep from, omit, pause, resist the temptation to, restrain oneself, stop, withhold

forbearance *noun* 1 = **patience**, indulgence, leniency, long-suffering, resignation, restraint, self-control, temperance, tolerance 2 = **abstinence**, avoidance, refraining
➤ **Antonyms**
≠**patience**: anger, impatience, impetuosity, intolerance, irritability, shortness

forbearing *adjective* = **patient**, clement, easy, forgiving, indulgent, lenient, long-suffering, merciful, mild, moderate, tolerant

forbid *verb* = **prohibit**, ban, debar, disallow, exclude, hinder, inhibit, interdict, outlaw, preclude, proscribe, rule out, veto
➤ **Antonyms**
allow, approve, authorize, bid, enable, endorse, grant, let, license, O.K. *or* okay (*informal*), order, permit, sanction

forbidden *adjective* = **prohibited**, banned, outlawed, out of bounds, proscribed, taboo, *verboten*, vetoed

forbidding *adjective* = **threatening**, baleful, bodeful, daunting, foreboding, frightening, grim, hostile, menacing, ominous, sinister, unfriendly
➤ **Antonyms**
alluring, attractive, beguiling, enticing, inviting, magnetic, tempting, welcoming, winning

force *noun* 1 = **power**, dynamism, energy, impact, impulse, life, might, momentum, muscle, potency, pressure, stimulus, strength, stress, vigour 2 = **compulsion**, arm-twisting (*informal*), coercion, constraint, duress, enforcement, pressure, violence 3 = **influence**, bite, cogency, effect, effectiveness, efficacy, persuasiveness, power, punch (*informal*), strength, validity, weight 4 = **intensity**, drive, emphasis, fierceness, persistence, vehemence, vigour 5 = **army**, battalion, body, corps, detachment, division, host, legion, patrol, regiment, squad, squadron, troop, unit 6 **in force: a** = **valid**, binding, current, effective, in operation, on the statute book, operative, working **b** = **in great numbers**, all together, in full strength ♦ *verb* 7 = **compel**, bring pressure to bear upon, coerce, constrain, dragoon, drive, impel, impose, make, necessitate, obligate, oblige, overcome, press, press-gang, pressure, pressurize, put the screws on (*informal*), put the squeeze on (*informal*), railroad (*informal*), strong-arm (*informal*), twist (someone's) arm, urge 8

= **extort**, drag, exact, wring **9** = **push**,
propel, thrust **10** = **break open**, blast,
prise, use violence on, wrench, wrest
➤ **Antonyms**
noun ≠**power**: debility, enervation,
feebleness, fragility, frailty, impotence,
ineffectiveness, irresolution, powerlessness,
weakness ♦ *verb* ≠**extort**: coax, convince,
induce, persuade, prevail, talk into

forced *adjective* **1** = **compulsory**,
conscripted, enforced, involuntary,
mandatory, obligatory, slave, unwilling **2**
= **false**, affected, artificial, contrived,
insincere, laboured, stiff, strained,
unnatural, wooden
➤ **Antonyms**
≠**compulsory**: spontaneous, voluntary
≠**false**: easy, natural, simple, sincere,
spontaneous, unforced, unpretending

forceful *adjective* = **powerful**, cogent,
compelling, convincing, dynamic,
effective, persuasive, pithy, potent, telling,
vigorous, weighty
➤ **Antonyms**
enervated, exhausted, faint, feeble, frail,
powerless, spent, weak

forcible *adjective* **1** = **violent**, aggressive,
armed, coercive, compulsory, drastic **2**
= **compelling**, active, cogent, effective,
efficient, energetic, forceful, impressive,
mighty, potent, powerful, strong, telling,
valid, weighty

forcibly *adverb* = **by force**, against one's
will, by main force, compulsorily, under
compulsion, under protest, willy-nilly

forebear *noun* = **ancestor**, father,
forefather, forerunner, predecessor,
progenitor

foreboding *noun* = **dread**, anxiety,
apprehension, apprehensiveness, chill,
fear, misgiving, premonition, presentiment

forecast *verb* **1** = **predict**, anticipate,
augur, calculate, call, divine, estimate,
foresee, foretell, plan, prognosticate,
prophesy ♦ *noun* **2** = **prediction**,
anticipation, conjecture, foresight,
forethought, guess, outlook, planning,
prognosis, projection, prophecy

forefather *noun* = **ancestor**, father,
forebear, forerunner, predecessor,
primogenitor, procreator, progenitor

forefront *noun* = **lead**, centre, fore,
foreground, front, prominence, spearhead,
van, vanguard

forego *see* FORGO

foregoing *adjective* = **preceding**, above,
antecedent, anterior, former, previous,
prior

foreground *noun* = **front**, centre,

forefront, limelight, prominence

foreign *adjective* **1** = **alien**, beyond one's
ken, borrowed, distant, exotic, external,
imported, outlandish, outside, overseas,
remote, strange, unfamiliar, unknown **2**
= **extraneous**, extrinsic, incongruous,
irrelevant, unassimilable, uncharacteristic,
unrelated
➤ **Antonyms**
≠**alien**: customary, domestic, familiar,
native, well-known ≠**extraneous**:
characteristic, intrinsic, relevant

foreigner *noun* = **alien**, immigrant,
incomer, newcomer, outlander, stranger

foreknowledge *noun* = **prior knowledge**,
clairvoyance, foresight, forewarning,
precognition, prescience, prevision

foremost *adjective* = **leading**, chief, first,
front, headmost, highest, inaugural, initial,
paramount, pre-eminent, primary, prime,
principal, supreme

foreordain *verb* = **predestine**, doom, fate,
prearrange, predetermine, preordain

forerunner *noun* **1** = **precursor**, ancestor,
announcer, forebear, foregoer, harbinger,
herald, predecessor, progenitor, prototype
2 = **omen**, augury, foretoken, indication,
portent, premonition, sign, token

foresee *verb* = **predict**, anticipate, divine,
envisage, forebode, forecast, foretell,
prophesy

foreshadow *verb* = **predict**, augur,
betoken, bode, forebode, imply, indicate,
portend, prefigure, presage, promise,
prophesy, signal

foresight *noun* = **forethought**,
anticipation, care, caution,
circumspection, far-sightedness,
precaution, premeditation, preparedness,
prescience, provision, prudence
➤ **Antonyms**
carelessness, hindsight, imprudence,
inconsideration, lack of foresight, neglect,
thoughtlessness, unpreparedness

forestall *verb* = **prevent**, anticipate, balk,
circumvent, frustrate, head off, hinder,
intercept, nip in the bud, obviate, parry,
preclude, provide against, thwart

forestry *noun* = **woodcraft**, arboriculture,
woodmanship

foretaste *noun* = **sample**, example,
foretoken, indication, prelude, preview,
trailer, warning

foretell *verb* = **predict**, augur, bode, call,
forebode, forecast, foreshadow, foreshow,
forewarn, portend, presage,
prognosticate, prophesy, signify

forethought *noun* = **anticipation**,
far-sightedness, foresight, precaution,

providence, provision, prudence
➤ **Antonyms**
carelessness, imprudence, impulsiveness, inconsideration, neglect, unpreparedness

forever *adverb* **1 = evermore**, always, for all time, for good and all (*informal*), for keeps, in perpetuity, till Doomsday, till the cows come home (*informal*), till the end of time, world without end **2 = constantly**, all the time, continually, endlessly, eternally, everlastingly, incessantly, interminably, perpetually, unremittingly

forewarn *verb* **= caution**, admonish, advise, alert, apprise, dissuade, give fair warning, put on guard, tip off

foreword *noun* **= introduction**, preamble, preface, preliminary, prolegomenon, prologue

forfeit *noun* **1 = penalty**, amercement (*obsolete*), damages, fine, forfeiture, loss, mulct ♦ *verb* **2 = lose**, be deprived of, be stripped of, give up, relinquish, renounce, say goodbye to, surrender

forfeiture *noun* **= loss**, confiscation, giving up, relinquishment, sequestration (*Law*), surrender

forge *verb* **1 = create**, construct, contrive, devise, fabricate, fashion, form, frame, hammer out, invent, make, mould, shape, work **2 = fake**, coin, copy, counterfeit, falsify, feign, imitate

forger *noun* **= counterfeiter**, coiner, falsifier

forgery *noun* **1 = fake**, counterfeit, falsification, imitation, phoney *or* phony (*informal*), sham **2 = falsification**, coining, counterfeiting, fraudulence, fraudulent imitation

forget *verb* **1 = neglect**, leave behind, lose sight of, omit, overlook **2 = dismiss from one's mind**, consign to oblivion, let bygones be bygones, let slip from the memory
➤ **Antonyms**
bring to mind, mind, recall, recollect, remember, retain

forgetful *adjective* **= absent-minded**, apt to forget, careless, dreamy, having a memory like a sieve, heedless, inattentive, lax, neglectful, negligent, oblivious, slapdash, slipshod, unmindful, vague
➤ **Antonyms**
attentive, careful, mindful, unforgetful, unforgetting

forgive *verb* **= excuse**, absolve, accept (someone's) apology, acquit, bear no malice, condone, exonerate, let bygones be bygones, let off (*informal*), pardon, remit
➤ **Antonyms**

blame, censure, charge, condemn, find fault with, reproach, reprove

forgiveness *noun* **= pardon**, absolution, acquittal, amnesty, condonation, exoneration, mercy, overlooking, remission

forgiving *adjective* **= lenient**, clement, compassionate, forbearing, humane, magnanimous, merciful, mild, soft-hearted, tolerant

forgo, forego *verb* **= give up**, abandon, abjure, cede, do without, kick (*informal*), leave alone *or* out, relinquish, renounce, resign, sacrifice, say goodbye to, surrender, waive, yield

forgotten *adjective* **= unremembered**, blotted out, buried, bygone, consigned to oblivion, gone (clean) out of one's mind, left behind, lost, obliterated, omitted, past, past recall

fork *verb* **= branch**, bifurcate, branch off, diverge, divide, go separate ways, part, split

forked *adjective* **= branching**, angled, bifurcate(d), branched, divided, pronged, split, tined, zigzag

forlorn *adjective* **= miserable**, abandoned, bereft, desolate, disconsolate, down in the dumps (*informal*), forgotten, forsaken, helpless, homeless, hopeless, lonely, lost, pathetic, pitiable, pitiful, unhappy, woebegone, wretched
➤ **Antonyms**
busy, cheerful, happy, hopeful, optimistic, thriving

form *noun* **1 = shape**, appearance, cast, configuration, construction, cut, fashion, formation, model, mould, pattern, stamp, structure **2 = build**, anatomy, being, body, figure, frame, outline, person, physique, shape, silhouette **3 = mode**, arrangement, character, design, guise, manifestation, semblance **4 = type**, description, kind, manner, method, order, practice, sort, species, stamp, style, system, variety, way **5 = condition**, fettle, fitness, good condition, good spirits, health, shape, trim **6 = document**, application, paper, sheet **7 = class**, grade, rank **8 = procedure**, behaviour, ceremony, conduct, convention, custom, done thing, etiquette, formality, manners, protocol, ritual, rule **9 = structure**, format, framework, harmony, order, orderliness, organization, plan, proportion, symmetry ♦ *verb* **10 = make**, assemble, bring about, build, concoct, construct, contrive, create, devise, establish, fabricate, fashion, forge, found, invent, manufacture, model, mould, produce, put together, set up, shape, stamp **11 = arrange**, combine, design, dispose, draw up, frame, organize, pattern, plan, think up **12 = take shape**, accumulate, appear, become visible, come into being, crystallize, grow, materialize, rise, settle, show up (*informal*) **13 = train**, bring up, discipline, educate, instruct, rear, school, teach **14 = develop**, acquire, contract, cultivate, get into (*informal*), pick up **15 = constitute**, compose, comprise, make, make up, serve as

formal *adjective* **1 = official**, approved, ceremonial, fixed, lawful, legal, methodical, prescribed, *pro forma,* regular, rigid, ritualistic, set, solemn, strict **2 = conventional**, affected, aloof, ceremonious, correct, exact, precise, prim, punctilious, reserved, starched, stiff, unbending
➤ **Antonyms**
casual, easy-going, informal, laid-back (*informal*), relaxed, unceremonious, unofficial

formality *noun* **1 = convention**, ceremony, conventionality, custom, form, matter of form, procedure, red tape, rite, ritual **2 = correctness**, ceremoniousness, decorum, etiquette, politesse, protocol, p's and q's, punctilio

format *noun* **= arrangement**, appearance, construction, form, layout, look, make-up, plan, style, type

formation *noun* **1 = development**, accumulation, compilation, composition, constitution, crystallization, establishment, evolution, forming, generation, genesis, manufacture, organization, production **2 = arrangement**, configuration, design, disposition, figure, grouping, pattern, rank, structure

formative *adjective* **1 = impressionable**, malleable, mouldable, pliant, sensitive, susceptible **2 = developmental**, determinative, influential, moulding, shaping

former *adjective* **1 = previous**, antecedent, anterior, earlier, erstwhile, ex-, late, one-time, prior, quondam **2 = past**, ancient, bygone, departed, long ago, long gone, of yore, old, old-time **3 = aforementioned**, above, aforesaid, first mentioned, foregoing, preceding
➤ **Antonyms**
≠**previous**: coming, current, ensuing, following, future, latter, subsequent, succeeding ≠**past**: current, future, modern, present, present-day

formerly *adverb* **= previously**, already, at one time, before, heretofore, lately, once

formidable *adjective* **1 = intimidating**, appalling, baleful, dangerous, daunting, dismaying, dreadful, fearful, frightful, horrible, menacing, shocking, terrifying, threatening **2 = difficult**, arduous, challenging, colossal, mammoth, onerous, overwhelming, staggering **3 = impressive**, awesome, great, indomitable, mighty, powerful, puissant, redoubtable, terrific, tremendous
➤ **Antonyms**
≠**intimidating**: cheering, comforting, encouraging, genial, heartening, pleasant, reassuring ≠**difficult**: easy

formless *adjective* **= shapeless**, amorphous, disorganized, inchoate, incoherent, indefinite, nebulous, unformed, vague

formula *noun* **1 = method**, blueprint, modus operandi, precept, prescription, principle, procedure, recipe, rule, way **2 = form of words**, rite, ritual, rubric

formulate *verb* **1 = define**, codify, detail, express, frame, give form to, particularize, set down, specify, systematize **2 = devise**, coin, develop, evolve, forge, invent, map out, originate, plan, work out

fornication *noun* **= adultery**, extra-curricular sex (*informal*), extra-marital congress *or* relations *or* sex, infidelity, living in sin, pre-marital congress *or* relations *or* sex, unfaithfulness

forsake *verb* **1 = desert**, abandon, cast off, disown, jettison, jilt, leave, leave in the lurch, quit, repudiate, strand, throw over **2 = give up**, abdicate, forgo, forswear, have done with, kick (*informal*), relinquish, renounce, set aside, surrender, turn one's back on, yield

forsaken *adjective* **= deserted**, abandoned, cast off, destitute, disowned, ditched, forlorn, friendless, ignored, isolated, jilted, left behind, left in the lurch, lonely, marooned, outcast, solitary, stranded

forswear *verb* **1 = renounce**, abandon, abjure, drop (*informal*), forgo, forsake, give up, swear off **2 = reject**, deny, disavow, disclaim, disown, recant, repudiate, retract **3 = lie**, perjure oneself, renege, swear falsely

fort *noun* **1 = fortress**, blockhouse, camp, castle, citadel, fastness, fortification, garrison, station, stronghold **2 hold the fort** *Informal* **= carry on**, keep things moving, keep things on an even keel, maintain the status quo, stand in, take over the reins

forte *noun* **= speciality**, gift, long suit (*informal*), métier, strength, strong point, talent
➤ **Antonyms**
Achilles heel, chink in one's armour,

defect, failing, imperfection, shortcoming, weak point

forth *adverb Formal or old-fashioned*
= **forward**, ahead, away, into the open, onward, out, out of concealment, outward

forthcoming *adjective* 1 = **approaching**, coming, expected, future, imminent, impending, prospective, upcoming 2 = **available**, accessible, at hand, in evidence, obtainable, on tap (*informal*), ready 3 = **communicative**, chatty, expansive, free, informative, open, sociable, talkative, unreserved

forthright *adjective* = **outspoken**, above-board, blunt, candid, direct, downright, frank, open, plain-spoken, straightforward, straight from the shoulder (*informal*), upfront (*informal*)
➤ **Antonyms**
dishonest, furtive, secret, secretive, sneaky, underhand, untruthful

forthwith *adverb* = **at once**, directly, immediately, instantly, quickly, right away, straightaway, *tout de suite*, without delay

fortification *noun* 1 = **strengthening**, embattlement, reinforcement 2 = **defence**, bastion, bulwark, castle, citadel, fastness, fort, fortress, keep, protection, stronghold

fortify *verb* 1 = **protect**, augment, brace, buttress, embattle, garrison, reinforce, secure, shore up, strengthen, support 2 = **strengthen**, brace, cheer, confirm, embolden, encourage, hearten, invigorate, reassure, stiffen, sustain
➤ **Antonyms**
≠**strengthen**: debilitate, demoralize, dilute, dishearten, impair, reduce, sap the strength of, weaken

fortitude *noun* = **courage**, backbone, bravery, dauntlessness, determination, endurance, fearlessness, firmness, grit, guts (*informal*), hardihood, intrepidity, patience, perseverance, pluck, resolution, staying power, stoutheartedness, strength, strength of mind, valour

fortress *noun* = **castle**, citadel, fastness, fort, redoubt, stronghold

fortuitous *adjective* 1 = **chance**, accidental, arbitrary, casual, contingent, incidental, random, unforeseen, unplanned 2 = **lucky**, fluky (*informal*), fortunate, happy, providential, serendipitous

fortunate *adjective* 1 = **lucky**, born with a silver spoon in one's mouth, bright, favoured, golden, happy, having a charmed life, in luck, jammy (*Brit. slang*), on a roll, prosperous, rosy, sitting pretty (*informal*), successful, well-off 2 = **providential**, advantageous, auspicious, convenient, encouraging, expedient, favourable, felicitous, fortuitous, helpful, opportune, profitable, promising, propitious, timely
➤ **Antonyms**
hapless, ill-fated, ill-starred, miserable, poor, unfortunate, unhappy, unlucky, unsuccessful, wretched

fortunately *adverb* = **luckily**, by a happy chance, by good luck, happily, providentially

fortune *noun* 1 = **luck**, accident, chance, contingency, destiny, fate, hazard, kismet, providence 2 **fortunes** = **destiny**, adventures, circumstances, doom, experiences, history, life, lot, portion, star, success 3 = **wealth**, affluence, an arm and a leg (*informal*), big bucks (*informal, chiefly U.S.*), big money, bomb (*Brit. slang*), bundle (*slang*), gold mine, king's ransom, megabucks (*U.S. & Canad. slang*), mint, opulence, packet (*slang*), pile (*informal*), possessions, pretty penny (*informal*), property, prosperity, riches, tidy sum (*informal*), treasure, wad (*U.S. & Canad. slang*)
➤ **Antonyms**
≠**wealth**: destitution, hardship, indigence, penury, poverty, privation

forum *noun* = **meeting**, assemblage, assembly, body, caucus (*chiefly U.S. & Canad.*), colloquium, conclave, conference, congregation, congress, convention, convergence, convocation, council, court, gathering, get-together (*informal*), parliament, rally, seminar, senate, symposium, synod, tribunal (*archaic or literary*)

forward *adjective* 1 = **leading**, advance, first, fore, foremost, front, head 2 = **presumptuous**, bare-faced, bold, brash, brass-necked (*Brit. informal*), brazen, brazen-faced, cheeky, confident, familiar, fresh (*informal*), impertinent, impudent, overassertive, overweening, pert, presuming, pushy (*informal*), sassy (*U.S. informal*) 3 = **well-developed**, advanced, advancing, early, forward-looking, onward, precocious, premature, progressive ♦ *adverb* 4 *Also* **forwards** = **forth**, ahead, on, onward 5 = **to the front**, into consideration, into prominence, into the open, into view, out, to light, to the surface ♦ *verb* 6 = **send**, dispatch, post, route, send on, ship, transmit 7 = **promote**, advance, aid, assist, back, encourage, expedite, favour, foster, further, hasten, help, hurry, speed, support
➤ **Antonyms**
adjective ≠**presumptuous**: backward, diffident, modest, regressive, retiring, shy

♦ *adverb* ≠**forth**: backward(s) ♦ *verb*
≠**promote**: bar, block, hinder, hold up,
impede, obstruct, retard, thwart

foster *verb* 1 = **bring up**, mother, nurse,
raise, rear, take care of 2 = **promote**,
cultivate, encourage, feed, foment,
nurture, stimulate, support, uphold
➤ Antonyms
≠**promote**: combat, curb, curtail, hold out
against, inhibit, oppose, resist, restrain,
subdue, suppress, withstand

foul *adjective* 1 = **offensive**, abhorrent,
abominable, base, despicable, detestable,
disgraceful, dishonourable, egregious,
hateful, heinous, infamous, iniquitous,
nefarious, notorious, scandalous,
shameful, shitty (*taboo slang*), vicious, vile,
wicked 2 = **dirty**, contaminated,
disgusting, fetid, filthy, grotty (*slang*),
grungy (*slang, chiefly U.S.*), impure,
loathsome, malodorous, mephitic, nasty,
nauseating, noisome, offensive, polluted,
putrid, rank, repulsive, revolting, rotten,
scuzzy (*slang, chiefly U.S.*), squalid,
stinking, sullied, tainted, unclean, yucky *or*
yukky (*slang*) 3 = **obscene**, abusive,
blasphemous, blue, coarse, dirty, filthy,
foul-mouthed, gross, indecent, lewd, low,
profane, scatological, scurrilous, smutty,
vulgar 4 = **unfair**, crooked, dirty,
dishonest, fraudulent, inequitable, shady
(*informal*), underhand, unjust,
unscrupulous, unsportsmanlike 5
= **stormy**, bad, blustery, disagreeable,
foggy, murky, rainy, rough, wet, wild
♦ *verb* 6 = **dirty**, begrime, besmear,
besmirch, contaminate, defile, pollute,
smear, smirch, soil, stain, sully, taint 7
= **clog**, block, catch, choke, ensnare,
entangle, jam, snarl, twist
➤ Antonyms
adjective ≠**offensive**: admirable, attractive,
decent, pleasant, respectable ≠**dirty**:
clean, clear, fair, fragrant, fresh, pure,
spotless, undefiled ♦ *verb* ≠**dirty**: clean,
cleanse, clear, purge, purify, sanitize

foul-mouthed *adjective* = **profane**,
abusive, blasphemous, coarse, obscene,
offensive

foul play *noun* = **crime**, chicanery,
corruption, deception, dirty work,
double-dealing, duplicity, fraud, perfidy,
roguery, sharp practice, skulduggery,
treachery, villainy

foul up *verb* = **bungle**, bodge (*informal*),
botch, cock up (*Brit. slang*), make a mess
of, make a nonsense of, make a pig's ear of
(*informal*), mismanage, muck up (*slang*),
put a spanner in the works (*Brit. informal*),
spoil

found *verb* 1 = **establish**, bring into being,
constitute, construct, create, endow, erect,
fix, inaugurate, institute, organize,
originate, plant, raise, settle, set up, start 2
= **base**, bottom, build, ground, rest, root,
sustain

foundation *noun* 1 = **basis**, base, bedrock,
bottom, footing, groundwork,
substructure, underpinning 2 = **setting up**,
endowment, establishment, inauguration,
institution, organization, settlement

founder[1] *noun* = **initiator**, architect,
author, beginner, benefactor, builder,
constructor, designer, establisher, father,
framer, generator, institutor, inventor,
maker, organizer, originator, patriarch

founder[2] *verb* 1 = **fail**, abort, bite the dust,
break down, collapse, come to grief, come
to nothing, come unstuck, fall by the
wayside, fall through, go belly-up (*slang*),
go down like a lead balloon (*informal*),
miscarry, misfire 2 = **sink**, be lost, go
down, go to the bottom, submerge 3
= **stumble**, collapse, fall, go lame, lurch,
sprawl, stagger, trip

foundling *noun* = **orphan**, outcast, stray,
waif

fountain *noun* 1 = **jet**, font, fount,
reservoir, spout, spray, spring, well 2
= **source**, beginning, cause,
commencement, derivation, fount,
fountainhead, genesis, origin, rise,
wellhead, wellspring

fountainhead *noun* = **source**, fount,
inspiration, mainspring, origin, spring,
well, wellspring

foursquare *adverb* 1 = **squarely**, firmly,
resolutely ♦ *adjective* 2 = **strong**, firm,
firmly-based, immovable, resolute, solid,
steady, unyielding

foxy *adjective* = **crafty**, artful, astute, canny,
cunning, devious, guileful, knowing,
sharp, shrewd, sly, tricky, wily

foyer *noun* = **entrance hall**, antechamber,
anteroom, lobby, reception area, vestibule

fracas *noun* = **brawl**, affray (*Law*), aggro
(*slang*), disturbance, fight, free-for-all
(*informal*), melee *or* mêlée, quarrel, riot,
row, rumpus, scrimmage, scuffle, shindig
(*informal*), shindy (*informal*), skirmish,
trouble, uproar

fraction *noun* 1 = **piece**, cut, division,
moiety, part, percentage, portion,
proportion, quota, ratio, section, sector,
segment, share, slice, subdivision 2
= **fragment**, atom, bit, bite, chip, crumb,
drop, flake, grain, granule, iota, jot,
morsel, mote, particle, scrap, shard, shred,
sliver, smithereen (*informal*), splinter, whit

fractious *adjective* = **irritable**, awkward, captious, crabby, cross, fretful, froward (*archaic*), grouchy (*informal*), peevish, pettish, petulant, querulous, ratty (*Brit. & N.Z. informal*), recalcitrant, refractory, testy, tetchy, touchy, unruly
➤ **Antonyms**
affable, agreeable, amiable, biddable, complaisant, genial, good-natured, good-tempered, tractable

fracture *noun* 1 = **break**, breach, cleft, crack, fissure, gap, opening, rent, rift, rupture, schism, split ♦ *verb* 2 = **break**, crack, rupture, splinter, split

fragile *adjective* = **delicate**, breakable, brittle, dainty, feeble, fine, flimsy, frail, frangible, infirm, slight, weak
➤ **Antonyms**
durable, elastic, flexible, hardy, lasting, reliable, resilient, robust, strong, sturdy, tough

fragility *noun* = **delicacy**, brittleness, feebleness, frailty, frangibility, infirmity, weakness

fragment *noun* 1 = **piece**, bit, chip, fraction, morsel, oddment, part, particle, portion, remnant, scrap, shiver, shred, sliver ♦ *verb* 2 = **break**, break up, come apart, come to pieces, crumble, disintegrate, disunite, divide, shatter, shiver, splinter, split, split up
➤ **Antonyms**
verb ≠**break**: bond, combine, compound, fuse, join together, link, marry, merge, synthesize, unify

fragmentary *adjective* = **incomplete**, bitty, broken, disconnected, disjointed, incoherent, partial, piecemeal, scattered, scrappy, sketchy, unsystematic

fragrance *noun* = **scent**, aroma, bouquet, perfume, redolence, smell, sweet odour
➤ **Antonyms**
effluvium, miasma, niff (*Brit. slang*), offensive smell, pong (*Brit. informal*), reek, smell, stink, whiff (*Brit. slang*)

fragrant *adjective* = **aromatic**, ambrosial, balmy, odoriferous, odorous, perfumed, redolent, sweet-scented, sweet-smelling
➤ **Antonyms**
fetid, foul-smelling, malodorous, niffy (*Brit. slang*), noisome, olid, pongy (*Brit. informal*), reeking, smelling, smelly, stinking

frail *adjective* = **weak**, breakable, brittle, decrepit, delicate, feeble, flimsy, fragile, frangible, infirm, insubstantial, puny, slight, tender, unsound, vulnerable, wispy
➤ **Antonyms**
hale, healthy, robust, sound, stalwart, strong, sturdy, substantial, tough, vigorous

frailty *noun* 1 = **weakness**, fallibility, feebleness, frailness, infirmity, puniness, susceptibility 2 = **fault**, blemish, chink in one's armour, defect, deficiency, failing, flaw, foible, imperfection, shortcoming, vice, weak point
➤ **Antonyms**
≠**weakness**: fortitude, might, robustness, strength ≠**fault**: asset, strong point, virtue

frame *noun* 1 = **casing**, construction, fabric, form, framework, scheme, shell, structure, system 2 = **mounting**, mount, setting 3 = **physique**, anatomy, body, build, carcass, morphology, skeleton 4 **frame of mind** = **mood**, attitude, disposition, fettle, humour, outlook, spirit, state, temper ♦ *verb* 5 = **construct**, assemble, build, constitute, fabricate, fashion, forge, form, institute, invent, make, manufacture, model, mould, put together, set up 6 = **devise**, block out, compose, conceive, concoct, contrive, cook up, draft, draw up, form, formulate, hatch, map out, plan, shape, sketch 7 = **mount**, case, enclose, surround

frame-up *noun Slang* = **false charge**, fabrication, fit-up (*slang*), put-up job, trumped-up charge

framework *noun* = **structure**, core, fabric, foundation, frame, frame of reference, groundwork, plan, schema, shell, skeleton, the bare bones

franchise *noun* 1 = **vote**, suffrage 2 = **right**, authorization, charter, exemption, freedom, immunity, prerogative, privilege

frank *adjective* = **honest**, artless, blunt, candid, direct, downright, forthright, free, ingenuous, open, outright, outspoken, plain, plain-spoken, round, sincere, straightforward, straight from the shoulder (*informal*), transparent, truthful, unconcealed, undisguised, unreserved, unrestricted, upfront (*informal*)
➤ **Antonyms**
artful, crafty, cunning, evasive, indirect, inscrutable, reserved, reticent, secretive, shifty, shy, underhand

frankly *adverb* 1 = **honestly**, candidly, in truth, to be honest 2 = **openly**, bluntly, directly, freely, overtly, plainly, straight, straight from the shoulder, without reserve

frankness *noun* = **outspokenness**, absence of reserve, bluntness, candour, forthrightness, ingenuousness, laying it on the line, openness, plain speaking, truthfulness

frantic *adjective* 1 = **distraught**, at one's wits' end, at the end of one's tether, berserk, beside oneself, distracted, furious, mad, overwrought, raging, raving, uptight

(*informal*), wild **2** = **hectic**, desperate,
fraught (*informal*), frenetic, frenzied
➤ **Antonyms**
calm, collected, composed, cool,
laid-back, poised, self-possessed, together
(*slang*), unfazed (*informal*), unruffled

fraternity *noun* **1** = **association**,
brotherhood, circle, clan, club, company,
guild, league, order, set, sodality, union **2**
= **companionship**, brotherhood,
camaraderie, comradeship, fellowship,
kinship

fraternize *verb* = **associate**, concur,
consort, cooperate, go around with, hang
out (*informal*), hang with (*informal, chiefly
U.S.*), hobnob, keep company, mingle,
mix, socialize, sympathize, unite
➤ **Antonyms**
avoid, eschew, keep away from, shun,
steer clear of

fraud *noun* **1** = **deception**, cheat,
chicanery, deceit, double-dealing,
duplicity, guile, hoax, humbug, imposture,
scam (*slang*), sharp practice, spuriousness,
sting (*informal*), stratagems, swindling,
treachery, trickery **2** *Informal* = **impostor**,
bluffer, charlatan, cheat, counterfeit,
double-dealer, fake, forgery, fraudster,
grifter (*slang, chiefly U.S. & Canad.*), hoax,
hoaxer, phoney *or* phony (*informal*),
pretender, quack, sham, swindler
➤ **Antonyms**
≠**deception:** fairness, good faith, honesty,
integrity, probity, rectitude,
trustworthiness, virtue

fraudulent *adjective* = **deceitful**,
counterfeit, crafty, criminal, crooked
(*informal*), deceptive, dishonest,
double-dealing, duplicitous, false, phoney
or phony (*informal*), sham, spurious,
swindling, treacherous
➤ **Antonyms**
above board, genuine, honest,
honourable, lawful, principled, reputable,
true, trustworthy, upright

fraught *adjective* **1** *with* with = **filled**,
abounding, accompanied, attended,
bristling, charged, full, heavy, laden,
stuffed **2** *Informal* = **tense**, agitated,
anxious, difficult, distracted, distressed,
distressing, emotionally charged, emotive,
on tenterhooks, strung-up, tricky, trying,
uptight (*informal*), wired (*slang*)

fray¹ *noun* = **fight**, battle, brawl, broil,
clash, combat, conflict, disturbance, melee
or mêlée, quarrel, riot, row, ruckus
(*informal*), rumpus, scrimmage, scuffle,
set-to (*informal*), shindig (*informal*), shindy
(*informal*), skirmish

fray² *verb* = **wear thin**, become threadbare,

chafe, fret, rub, wear, wear away

frayed *adjective* = **worn**, frazzled, out at
elbows, ragged, tattered, threadbare

freak *noun* **1** = **oddity**, aberration,
abnormality, abortion, anomaly,
grotesque, malformation, monster,
monstrosity, mutant, queer fish (*Brit.
informal*), weirdo *or* weirdie (*informal*) **2**
Informal = **enthusiast**, addict, aficionado,
buff (*informal*), devotee, fan, fanatic, fiend
(*informal*), nut (*slang*) ◆ *adjective* **3**
= **abnormal**, aberrant, atypical, bizarre,
erratic, exceptional, fluky (*informal*),
fortuitous, odd, queer, unaccountable,
unexpected, unforeseen, unparalleled,
unpredictable, unusual

freakish *adjective* = **odd**, aberrant,
abnormal, fantastic, freaky (*slang*),
grotesque, malformed, monstrous,
outlandish, outré, preternatural, strange,
unconventional, weird

freaky *adjective* = **weird**, abnormal, bizarre,
crazy, far-out (*slang*), freakish, odd, queer,
rum (*Brit. slang*), strange, unconventional,
wild

free *adjective* **1** = **at liberty**, at large,
footloose, independent, liberated, loose,
off the hook (*slang*), on the loose,
uncommitted, unconstrained, unengaged,
unfettered, unrestrained **2** = **allowed**, able,
clear, disengaged, loose, open, permitted,
unattached, unengaged, unhampered,
unimpeded, unobstructed, unregulated,
unrestricted, untrammelled **3** *with*
= **unaffected by**, above, beyond, deficient
in, devoid of, exempt from, immune to,
lacking (in), not liable to, safe from,
unencumbered by, untouched by, without
4 = **independent**, autarchic, autonomous,
democratic, emancipated, self-governing,
self-ruling, sovereign **5** = **complimentary**,
for free (*informal*), for nothing, free of
charge, gratis, gratuitous, on the house,
unpaid, without charge **6** = **available**, at
leisure, empty, extra, idle, not tied down,
spare, unemployed, uninhabited,
unoccupied, unused, vacant **7** = **generous**,
big (*informal*), bounteous, bountiful,
charitable, eager, hospitable, lavish,
liberal, munificent, open-handed,
prodigal, unsparing, unstinting, willing **8**
free and easy = **relaxed**, casual,
easy-going, informal, laid-back (*informal*),
lax, lenient, liberal, tolerant,
unceremonious ◆ *adverb* **9** = **freely**,
abundantly, copiously, idly, loosely **10**
= **without charge**, at no cost, for love,
gratis ◆ *verb* **11** = **release**, deliver,
discharge, emancipate, let go, let out,
liberate, loose, set at liberty, set free, turn

loose, unbridle, uncage, unchain, unfetter, unleash, untie **12** = **clear**, cut loose, disengage, disentangle, extricate, relieve, rescue, rid, unburden, undo
➤ **Antonyms**
adjective ≠**at liberty**: bound, captive, confined, dependent, fettered, immured, incarcerated, restrained, restricted, secured ≠**generous**: close, mean, mingy (*informal*), stingy, tight, ungenerous ◆ *verb* ≠**release**: confine, imprison, incarcerate, inhibit, limit, restrain, restrict, straiten

freebooter *noun* = **pirate**, bandit, brigand, buccaneer, looter, marauder, pillager, plunderer, raider, reiver (*dialect*), robber

freedom *noun* **1** = **liberty**, autonomy, deliverance, emancipation, home rule, independence, manumission, release, self-government **2** = **exemption**, immunity, impunity, privilege **3** = **licence**, ability, a free hand, blank cheque, carte blanche, discretion, elbowroom, facility, flexibility, free rein, latitude, leeway, opportunity, play, power, range, scope **4** = **openness**, abandon, candour, directness, ease, familiarity, frankness, informality, ingenuousness, lack of restraint *or* reserve, unconstraint **5** = **overfamiliarity**, boldness, brazenness, disrespect, forwardness, impertinence, laxity, licence, presumption
➤ **Antonyms**
≠**liberty**: bondage, captivity, dependence, imprisonment, servitude, slavery, thraldom ≠**licence**: limitation, restriction ≠**openness**: caution, restraint ≠**overfamiliarity**: respectfulness

free-for-all *noun Informal* = **fight**, brawl, dust-up (*informal*), fracas, melee *or* mêlée, riot, row, scrimmage, shindig (*informal*), shindy (*informal*)

free hand *noun* = **freedom**, authority, blank cheque, carte blanche, discretion, latitude, liberty, scope

freely *adverb* **1** = **willingly**, of one's own accord, of one's own free will, spontaneously, voluntarily, without prompting **2** = **openly**, candidly, frankly, plainly, unreservedly, without reserve **3** = **without restraint**, as you please, unchallenged, without let or hindrance **4** = **abundantly**, amply, bountifully, copiously, extravagantly, lavishly, liberally, like water, open-handedly, unstintingly, with a free hand **5** = **easily**, cleanly, loosely, readily, smoothly

freethinker *noun* = **unbeliever**, agnostic, doubter, sceptic

freewheel *verb* = **coast**, drift, float, glide

freeze *verb* **1** = **chill**, benumb, congeal,

glaciate, harden, ice over *or* up, stiffen **2** = **suspend**, fix, hold up, inhibit, peg, stop

freezing *adjective* = **icy**, arctic, biting, bitter, chill, chilled, cold as ice, cutting, frost-bound, frosty, glacial, numbing, parky (*Brit. informal*), penetrating, polar, raw, Siberian, wintry

freight *noun* **1** = **transportation**, carriage, conveyance, shipment **2** = **cargo**, bales, bulk, burden, consignment, contents, goods, haul, lading, load, merchandise, payload, tonnage

French *adjective* = **Gallic**

frenetic *adjective* = **wild**, demented, distraught, excited, fanatical, frantic, frenzied, hyped up (*slang*), insane, mad, maniacal, obsessive, overwrought, unbalanced

frenzied *adjective* = **uncontrolled**, agitated, all het up (*informal*), berserk, convulsive, distracted, distraught, excited, feverish, frantic, frenetic, furious, hysterical, mad, maniacal, rabid, wild

frenzy *noun* **1** = **fury**, aberration, agitation, delirium, derangement, distraction, hysteria, insanity, lunacy, madness, mania, paroxysm, passion, rage, seizure, transport, turmoil **2** = **fit**, bout, burst, convulsion, outburst, paroxysm, spasm
➤ **Antonyms**
≠**fury**: calm, collectedness, composure, coolness, sanity

frequency *noun* = **recurrence**, constancy, frequentness, periodicity, prevalence, repetition

frequent *adjective* **1** = **common**, constant, continual, customary, everyday, familiar, habitual, incessant, numerous, persistent, recurrent, recurring, reiterated, repeated, usual ◆ *verb* **2** = **visit**, attend, be a regular customer of, be found at, hang out at (*informal*), haunt, patronize, resort
➤ **Antonyms**
adjective ≠**common**: few, few and far between, infrequent, occasional, rare, scanty, sporadic ◆ *verb* ≠**visit**: avoid, keep away, shun, spurn

frequently *adverb* = **often**, commonly, customarily, habitually, many a time, many times, much, not infrequently, over and over again, repeatedly, thick and fast, very often
➤ **Antonyms**
hardly ever, infrequently, occasionally, once in a blue moon (*informal*), rarely, seldom

fresh *adjective* **1** = **new**, different, ground-breaking, latest, left-field (*informal*), modern, modernistic, new-fangled, novel, original, recent,

unconventional, unusual, up-to-date **2** = **additional**, added, auxiliary, extra, further, more, other, renewed, supplementary **3** = **natural**, crude, green, raw, uncured, undried, unprocessed, unsalted **4** = **invigorating**, bracing, bright, brisk, clean, clear, cool, crisp, pure, refreshing, sparkling, stiff, sweet, unpolluted **5** = **lively**, alert, bouncing, bright, bright-eyed and bushy-tailed (*informal*), chipper (*informal*), energetic, full of beans (*informal*), full of vim and vigour (*informal*), invigorated, keen, like a new man, refreshed, rested, restored, revived, sprightly, spry, vigorous, vital **6** = **vivid**, dewy, undimmed, unfaded, unwearied, unwithered, verdant **7** = **rosy**, blooming, clear, fair, florid, glowing, good, hardy, healthy, ruddy, wholesome **8** = **inexperienced**, artless, callow, green, natural, new, raw, uncultivated, untrained, untried, youthful **9** *Informal* = **cheeky**, bold, brazen, disrespectful, familiar, flip (*informal*), forward, impudent, insolent, pert, presumptuous, sassy (*U.S. informal*), saucy, smart-alecky (*informal*)
➤ **Antonyms**
≠**new**: dull, old, ordinary, stereotyped, trite ≠**natural**: frozen, pickled, preserved, salted, tinned ≠**invigorating**: impure, musty, stale, warm ≠**lively**: exhausted, weary ≠**vivid**: old, weary ≠**rosy**: pallid, sickly ≠**inexperienced**: experienced, old ≠**cheeky**: well-mannered

freshen *verb* = **refresh**, enliven, freshen up, liven up, restore, revitalize, rouse, spruce up, titivate

freshness *noun* **1** = **novelty**, innovativeness, inventiveness, newness, originality **2** = **cleanness**, bloom, brightness, clearness, dewiness, glow, shine, sparkle, vigour, wholesomeness

fret *verb* **1** = **worry**, agonize, anguish, brood, lose sleep over, obsess about, upset *or* distress oneself **2** = **rub**, abrade, chafe, erode, fray, gall, wear, wear away **3** = **annoy**, agitate, bother, distress, disturb, gall, goad, grieve, harass, irk, irritate, nag, nettle, peeve (*informal*), pique, provoke, rankle with, rile, ruffle, torment, trouble, vex

fretful *adjective* = **irritable**, captious, complaining, cross, crotchety (*informal*), edgy, fractious, out of sorts, peevish, petulant, querulous, ratty (*Brit. & N.Z. informal*), short-tempered, splenetic, testy, tetchy, touchy, uneasy

friable *adjective* = **crumbly**, brittle, crisp, powdery, pulverizable

friction *noun* **1** = **rubbing**, abrasion,

attrition, chafing, erosion, fretting, grating, irritation, rasping, resistance, scraping, wearing away **2** = **hostility**, animosity, antagonism, bad blood, bad feeling, bickering, conflict, disagreement, discontent, discord, disharmony, dispute, dissension, incompatibility, opposition, resentment, rivalry, wrangling

friend *noun* **1** = **companion**, alter ego, boon companion, bosom friend, buddy (*informal*), china (*Brit. slang*), chum (*informal*), comrade, confidant, crony, intimate, mate (*informal*), pal, partner, playmate, soul mate **2** = **supporter**, adherent, advocate, ally, associate, backer, benefactor, partisan, patron, protagonist, well-wisher
➤ **Antonyms**
adversary, antagonist, competitor, enemy, foe, opponent, rival

friendless *adjective* = **alone**, abandoned, alienated, all alone, cut off, deserted, estranged, forlorn, forsaken, isolated, lonely, lonesome, ostracized, shunned, solitary, unattached, with no one to turn to, without a friend in the world, without ties

friendliness *noun* = **amiability**, affability, companionability, congeniality, conviviality, geniality, kindliness, mateyness *or* matiness (*Brit. informal*), neighbourliness, open arms, sociability, warmth

friendly *adjective* = **amiable**, affable, affectionate, amicable, attached, attentive, auspicious, beneficial, benevolent, benign, chummy (*informal*), close, companionable, comradely, conciliatory, confiding, convivial, cordial, familiar, favourable, fond, fraternal, genial, good, helpful, intimate, kind, kindly, matey *or* maty (*Brit. informal*), neighbourly, on good terms, on visiting terms, outgoing, pally (*informal*), peaceable, propitious, receptive, sociable, sympathetic, thick (*informal*), welcoming, well-disposed
➤ **Antonyms**
antagonistic, belligerent, cold, contentious, distant, inauspicious, sinister, uncongenial, unfriendly

friendship *noun* = **friendliness**, affection, affinity, alliance, amity, attachment, benevolence, closeness, concord, familiarity, fondness, good-fellowship, goodwill, harmony, intimacy, love, rapport, regard
➤ **Antonyms**
animosity, antagonism, antipathy, aversion, bad blood, conflict, enmity, hatred, hostility, resentment, strife,

unfriendliness

fright *noun* **1** = **fear**, alarm, apprehension, (blue) funk (*informal*), cold sweat, consternation, dismay, dread, fear and trembling, horror, panic, quaking, scare, shock, terror, the shivers, trepidation **2** *Informal* = **sight** (*informal*), eyesore, frump, mess (*informal*), scarecrow
➤ **Antonyms**
≠**fear**: boldness, bravery, courage, pluck, valor

frighten *verb* = **scare**, alarm, appal, cow, daunt, dismay, freeze one's blood, get the wind up, intimidate, make one's blood run cold, make one's hair stand on end (*informal*), make (someone) jump out of his skin (*informal*), petrify, put the wind up (someone) (*informal*), scare (someone) stiff, scare the living daylights out of (someone) (*informal*), shock, startle, terrify, terrorize, throw into a fright, throw into a panic, unnerve
➤ **Antonyms**
allay, assuage, calm, comfort, encourage, hearten, reassure, soothe

frightened *adjective* = **afraid**, abashed, alarmed, cowed, dismayed, frozen, in a cold sweat, in a panic, in fear and trepidation, numb with fear, panicky, petrified, scared, scared shitless (*taboo slang*), scared stiff, shit-scared (*taboo slang*), startled, terrified, terrorized, terror-stricken, unnerved

frightening *adjective* = **terrifying**, alarming, appalling, baleful, bloodcurdling, daunting, dismaying, dreadful, fearful, fearsome, hair-raising, horrifying, intimidating, menacing, scary (*informal*), shocking, spooky (*informal*), unnerving

frightful *adjective* **1** = **terrifying**, alarming, appalling, awful, dire, dread, dreadful, fearful, from hell (*informal*), ghastly, godawful (*slang*), grim, grisly, gruesome, harrowing, hellacious (*U.S. slang*), hideous, horrendous, horrible, horrid, lurid, macabre, petrifying, shocking, terrible, traumatic, unnerving, unspeakable **2** = **dreadful**, annoying, awful, disagreeable, extreme, great, insufferable, terrible, terrific, unpleasant
➤ **Antonyms**
≠**terrifying**: attractive, beautiful, calming, lovely, nice, pleasant, soothing ≠**dreadful**: moderate, pleasant, slight

frigid *adjective* **1** = **unresponsive**, aloof, austere, cold as ice, cold-hearted, forbidding, formal, icy, lifeless, passionless, passive, repellent, rigid, stiff, unapproachable, unbending, unfeeling,

unloving **2** = **cold**, arctic, chill, cool, frost-bound, frosty, frozen, gelid, glacial, hyperboreal, icy, Siberian, wintry
➤ **Antonyms**
≠**unresponsive**: ardent, cordial, friendly, hospitable, hot, impassioned, passionate, responsive, sensual, warm ≠**cold**: hot, stifling, sweltering, warm

frigidity *noun* = **unresponsiveness**, aloofness, austerity, chill, cold-heartedness, coldness, frostiness, iciness, impassivity, lack of response, lifelessness, passivity, touch-me-not attitude, unapproachability, wintriness

frill *noun* = **ruffle**, flounce, gathering, ruche, ruching, ruff, tuck

frills *plural noun* = **trimmings**, additions, bells and whistles, bits and pieces, decoration(s), dressing up, embellishments, extras, fanciness, finery, frilliness, frippery, fuss, gewgaws, icing on the cake, jazz (*slang*), mannerisms, nonsense, ornamentation, ostentation

frilly *adjective* = **ruffled**, fancy, flouncy, frothy, lacy, ruched

fringe *noun* **1** = **border**, binding, edging, hem, tassel, trimming **2** = **edge**, borderline, limits, march, marches, margin, outskirts, perimeter, periphery ♦ *adjective* **3** = **unofficial**, unconventional, unorthodox ♦ *verb* **4** = **border**, edge, enclose, skirt, surround, trim

fringed *adjective* = **edged**, befringed, bordered, margined, outlined, overhung

frippery *noun* **1** = **frills**, fanciness, finery, flashiness, frilliness, fussiness, gaudiness, glad rags (*informal*), nonsense, ostentation, showiness **2** = **decoration**, adornment, bauble, fandangle, gewgaw, icing on the cake, knick-knack, ornament, toy, trinket

frisk *verb* **1** = **frolic**, bounce, caper, cavort, curvet, dance, gambol, hop, jump, play, prance, rollick, romp, skip, sport, trip **2** *Informal* = **search**, check, inspect, run over, shake down (*U.S. slang*)

frisky *adjective* = **lively**, bouncy, coltish, frolicsome, full of beans (*informal*), full of joie de vivre, high-spirited, in high spirits, kittenish, playful, rollicking, romping, spirited, sportive
➤ **Antonyms**
demure, dull, lacklustre, pensive, sedate, stodgy, stolid, wooden

fritter away *verb* = **waste**, dally away, dissipate, idle away, misspend, run through, spend like water, squander

frivolity *noun* = **flippancy**, childishness, desipience, flightiness, flummery, folly,

frivolousness, fun, gaiety, giddiness, jest, levity, light-heartedness, lightness, nonsense, puerility, shallowness, silliness, superficiality, trifling, triviality
➤ **Antonyms**
earnestness, gravity, humourlessness, importance, sedateness, seriousness, significance, soberness, sobriety

frivolous *adjective* **1** = **flippant**, childish, ditzy *or* ditsy (*slang*), dizzy, empty-headed, flighty, flip (*informal*), foolish, giddy, idle, ill-considered, juvenile, light-minded, nonserious, puerile, silly, superficial **2** = **trivial**, footling (*informal*), impractical, light, minor, nickel-and-dime (*U.S. slang*), niggling, paltry, peripheral, petty, pointless, shallow, trifling, unimportant
➤ **Antonyms**
≠**flippant**: earnest, mature, practical, responsible, sensible, serious, solemn ≠**trivial**: important, serious, vital

frizzle *verb* = **crisp**, fry, hiss, roast, scorch, sizzle, sputter

frolic *verb* **1** = **play**, caper, cavort, cut capers, frisk, gambol, lark, make merry, romp, sport ♦ *noun* **2** = **merriment**, amusement, drollery, fun, fun and games, gaiety, high jinks, skylarking (*informal*), sport **3** = **revel**, antic, escapade, gambol, game, lark, prank, romp, spree

frolicsome *adjective* = **playful**, coltish, frisky, full of beans (*informal*), gay, kittenish, lively, merry, rollicking, sportive, sprightly

front *noun* **1** = **exterior**, anterior, façade, face, facing, foreground, forepart, frontage, obverse **2** = **forefront**, beginning, fore, front line, head, lead, top, van, vanguard **3** = **appearance**, air, aspect, bearing, countenance, demeanour, expression, exterior, face, manner, mien, show **4** *Informal* = **disguise**, blind, cover, cover-up, façade, mask, pretext, show **5 in front** = **in advance**, ahead, before, first, in the lead, in the van, leading, preceding, to the fore ♦ *adjective* **6** = **foremost**, first, head, headmost, lead, leading, topmost ♦ *verb* **7** = **face onto**, look over *or* onto, overlook
➤ **Antonyms**
adjective ≠**foremost**: aft, back, back end, behind, hindmost, nethermost, rear

frontier *noun* = **boundary**, borderland, borderline, bound, confines, edge, limit, marches, perimeter, verge

frost *noun* = **hoarfrost**, freeze, freeze-up, Jack Frost, rime

frosty *adjective* **1** = **cold**, chilly, frozen, ice-capped, icicled, icy, parky (*Brit. informal*), wintry **2** = **unfriendly**, cold as

ice, discouraging, frigid, off-putting (*Brit. informal*), standoffish, unenthusiastic, unwelcoming

froth *noun* **1** = **foam**, bubbles, effervescence, head, lather, scum, spume, suds ♦ *verb* **2** = **fizz**, bubble over, come to a head, effervesce, foam, lather

frothy *adjective* **1** = **foamy**, foaming, spumescent, spumous, spumy, sudsy **2** = **trivial**, empty, frilly, frivolous, light, petty, slight, trifling, unnecessary, unsubstantial, vain

frown *verb* **1** = **scowl**, give a dirty look, glare, glower, knit one's brows, look daggers, lour *or* lower **2 frown on** = **disapprove of**, discountenance, discourage, dislike, look askance at, not take kindly to, show disapproval *or* displeasure, take a dim view of, view with disfavour

frowsty *adjective* = **stale**, close, fuggy, fusty, ill-smelling, musty, stuffy

frowzy *adjective* = **slovenly**, blowsy, dirty, frumpy, messy, slatternly, sloppy, sluttish, ungroomed, unkempt, untidy, unwashed

frozen *adjective* **1** = **icy**, arctic, chilled, chilled to the marrow, frigid, frosted, icebound, ice-cold, ice-covered, numb **2** = **fixed**, pegged (*of prices*), stopped, suspended **3** = **motionless**, petrified, rooted, stock-still, turned to stone

frugal *adjective* = **thrifty**, abstemious, careful, cheeseparing, economical, meagre, niggardly, parsimonious, penny-wise, provident, prudent, saving, sparing
➤ **Antonyms**
excessive, extravagant, imprudent, lavish, luxurious, prodigal, profligate, spendthrift, wasteful

frugality *noun* = **thrift**, carefulness, conservation, economizing, economy, good management, husbandry, moderation, providence, thriftiness

fruit *noun* **1** = **produce**, crop, harvest, product, yield **2** *plural* = **result**, advantage, benefit, consequence, effect, end result, outcome, profit, return, reward

fruitful *adjective* **1** = **useful**, advantageous, beneficial, effective, gainful, productive, profitable, rewarding, successful, well-spent, worthwhile **2** = **fertile**, fecund **3** = **plentiful**, abundant, copious, flush, plenteous, productive, profuse, prolific, rich, spawning
➤ **Antonyms**
≠**useful**: fruitless, futile, ineffectual, pointless, unfruitful, unproductive, useless, vain ≠**fertile**: barren, fruitless, infertile, sterile, unfruitful, unproductive

≠**plentiful**: scarce

fruition noun = **fulfilment**, actualization, attainment, completion, consummation, enjoyment, materialization, maturation, maturity, perfection, realization, ripeness

fruitless adjective **1** = **useless**, abortive, bootless, futile, idle, ineffectual, in vain, pointless, profitless, to no avail, to no effect, unavailing, unfruitful, unproductive, unprofitable, unsuccessful, vain **2** = **barren**, unfruitful, unproductive, unprolific
➤ **Antonyms**
≠**useless**: effective, fruitful, productive, profitable, useful ≠**barren**: abundant, fecund, fertile, fruitful, productive, prolific

fruity adjective **1** = **rich**, full, mellow, resonant **2** Informal, chiefly Brit. = **risqué**, bawdy, blue, hot, indecent, indelicate, juicy, near the knuckle (informal), racy, ripe, salacious, sexy, smutty, spicy (informal), suggestive, titillating, vulgar

frumpy, frumpish adjective = **dowdy**, badly-dressed, dated, dingy, drab, dreary, mumsy, out of date

frustrate verb = **thwart**, baffle, balk, block, check, circumvent, confront, counter, defeat, disappoint, foil, forestall, inhibit, neutralize, nullify, render null and void, stymie
➤ **Antonyms**
advance, encourage, endorse, forward, further, promote, satisfy, stimulate

frustrated adjective = **disappointed**, carrying a chip on one's shoulder (informal), choked, discontented, discouraged, disheartened, embittered, foiled, irked, resentful, sick as a parrot (informal)

frustration noun **1** = **annoyance**, disappointment, dissatisfaction, grievance, irritation, resentment, vexation **2** = **obstruction**, blocking, circumvention, contravention, curbing, failure, foiling, nonfulfilment, nonsuccess, thwarting

fuddled adjective **1** = **confused**, muddled, muzzy **2** = **drunk**, bevvied (dialect), blitzed (slang), blotto (slang), bombed (slang), flying (slang), inebriated, intoxicated, legless (informal), lit up (slang), out of it (slang), paralytic (informal), pissed (taboo slang), rat-arsed (taboo slang), smashed (slang), sozzled (informal), steamboats (Scot. slang), steaming (slang), stupefied, tipsy, wasted (slang), woozy (informal), wrecked (slang), zonked (slang)

fuddy-duddy noun Informal = **conservative**, dinosaur, dodo (informal), fossil, museum piece, (old) fogey, square (informal), stick-in-the-mud (informal),

stuffed shirt (informal)

fudge verb = **misrepresent**, avoid, cook (slang), dodge, equivocate, evade, fake, falsify, flannel (Brit. informal), hedge, stall

fuel noun **1** = **incitement**, ammunition, encouragement, fodder, food, material, means, nourishment, provocation ♦ verb **2** = **inflame**, charge, fan, feed, fire, incite, nourish, stoke up, sustain

fug noun = **stale air**, fetidity, fetor, frowst, frowstiness, fustiness, reek, staleness, stink

fuggy adjective = **stuffy**, airless, fetid, foul, frowsty, noisome, noxious, stale, suffocating, unventilated

fugitive noun **1** = **runaway**, deserter, escapee, refugee ♦ adjective **2** = **momentary**, brief, ephemeral, evanescent, fleeing, fleeting, flitting, flying, passing, short, short-lived, temporary, transient, transitory

fulfil verb **1** = **achieve**, accomplish, bring to completion, carry out, complete, conclude, discharge, effect, execute, finish, keep, perfect, perform, realise, satisfy **2** = **comply with**, answer, conform to, fill, meet, obey, observe
➤ **Antonyms**
disappoint, dissatisfy, fail in, fail to meet, fall short of, neglect

fulfilment noun = **achievement**, accomplishment, attainment, carrying out or through, completion, consummation, discharge, discharging, effecting, end, implementation, observance, perfection, realization

full adjective **1** = **filled**, brimful, brimming, bursting at the seams, complete, entire, gorged, intact, loaded, replete, sated, satiated, satisfied, saturated, stocked, sufficient **2** = **crammed**, chock-a-block, chock-full, crowded, in use, jammed, occupied, packed, taken **3** = **extensive**, abundant, adequate, all-inclusive, ample, broad, comprehensive, copious, detailed, exhaustive, generous, maximum, plenary, plenteous, plentiful, thorough, unabridged **4** = **plump**, buxom, curvaceous, rounded, voluptuous **5** = **rich**, clear, deep, distinct, loud, resonant, rounded **6** = **voluminous**, baggy, balloon-like, capacious, large, loose, puffy ♦ noun **7 in full** = **completely**, in its entirety, in total, in toto, without exception **8 to the full** = **thoroughly**, completely, entirely, fully, to the utmost, without reservation
➤ **Antonyms**
adjective ≠**filled, crammed**: blank, devoid, empty, vacant, void ≠**extensive**: abridged, incomplete, limited, partial ≠**rich**: faint, thin ≠**voluminous**: restricted,

tight

full-blooded *adjective* = **vigorous**, ballsy (*taboo slang*), gutsy (*slang*), hearty, lusty, mettlesome, red-blooded, virile

full-blown *adjective* = **fully developed**, advanced, complete, developed, entire, full, full-scale, full-sized, fully fledged, fully formed, fully grown, progressed, total, whole
➤ **Antonyms**
dormant, latent, potential, undeveloped

full-bodied *adjective* = **rich**, fruity, full-flavoured, heady, heavy, mellow, redolent, strong, well-matured

fullness *noun* 1 = **plenty**, abundance, adequateness, ampleness, copiousness, fill, glut, profusion, repletion, satiety, saturation, sufficiency 2 = **completeness**, broadness, comprehensiveness, entirety, extensiveness, totality, vastness, wealth, wholeness 3 = **roundness**, curvaceousness, voluptuousness 4 = **richness**, clearness, loudness, resonance, strength

full-scale *adjective* = **major**, all-encompassing, all-out, comprehensive, exhaustive, extensive, full-dress, in-depth, proper, sweeping, thorough, thoroughgoing, wide-ranging

fully *adverb* 1 = **totally**, absolutely, altogether, completely, entirely, every inch, from first to last, heart and soul, in all respects, intimately, lock, stock and barrel, one hundred per cent, perfectly, positively, thoroughly, to the hilt, utterly, wholly 2 = **adequately**, abundantly, amply, comprehensively, enough, plentifully, satisfactorily, sufficiently 3 = **at least**, quite, without (any) exaggeration, without a word of a lie (*informal*)

fulminate *verb* = **criticize**, berate, blast, castigate, censure, denounce, denunciate, fume, inveigh against, lambast(e), protest against, rage, rail against, tear into (*informal*), upbraid, vilify, vituperate

fulmination *noun* = **condemnation**, denunciation, diatribe, invective, reprobation, tirade

fulsome *adjective* = **extravagant**, adulatory, cloying, excessive, fawning, gross, icky (*informal*), immoderate, ingratiating, inordinate, insincere, nauseating, overdone, over the top, saccharine, sickening, smarmy (*Brit. informal*), sycophantic, unctuous

fumble *verb* 1 = **grope**, feel around, flounder, paw (*informal*), scrabble 2 = **bungle**, bodge (*informal*), botch, cock up (*Brit. slang*), fuck up (*offensive taboo slang*), make a hash of (*informal*), make a nonsense of, mess up, misfield, mishandle, mismanage, muff, spoil

fume *verb* = **rage**, blow a fuse (*slang, chiefly U.S.*), boil, chafe, champ at the bit (*informal*), crack up (*informal*), fly off the handle (*informal*), get hot under the collar (*informal*), get steamed up about (*slang*), go ballistic (*slang, chiefly U.S.*), go off the deep end (*informal*), go up the wall (*slang*), rant, rave, see red (*informal*), seethe, smoulder, storm, wig out (*slang*)

fumes *noun* = **smoke**, effluvium, exhalation, exhaust, gas, haze, miasma, pollution, reek, smog, stench, vapour

fumigate *verb* = **disinfect**, clean out *or* up, cleanse, purify, sanitize, sterilize

fuming *adjective* = **furious**, all steamed up (*slang*), angry, at boiling point (*informal*), choked, enraged, fit to be tied (*slang*), foaming at the mouth, in a rage, incandescent, incensed, on the warpath (*informal*), pissed (*taboo slang*), pissed off (*taboo slang*), raging, roused, seething, up in arms

fun *noun* 1 = **enjoyment**, amusement, beer and skittles (*informal*), cheer, distraction, diversion, entertainment, frolic, gaiety, good time, high jinks, jollity, joy, living it up, merriment, merrymaking, mirth, pleasure, recreation, romp, sport, treat 2 = **joking**, clowning, foolery, game, horseplay, jesting, jocularity, nonsense, play, playfulness, skylarking (*informal*), sport, teasing 3 **in** *or* **for fun** = **for a joke**, facetiously, for a laugh, in jest, jokingly, light-heartedly, mischievously, playfully, roguishly, teasingly, tongue in cheek, with a gleam *or* twinkle in one's eye, with a straight face 4 **make fun of** = **mock**, deride, hold up to ridicule, lampoon, laugh at, make a fool of, make a monkey of, make game of, make sport of, parody, poke fun at, rag, rib (*informal*), ridicule, satirize, scoff at, send up (*Brit. informal*), sneer at, take off, take the piss out of (*taboo slang*), taunt ◆ *adjective* 5 = **enjoyable**, amusing, convivial, diverting, entertaining, lively, witty
➤ **Antonyms**
noun ≠**enjoyment**: depression, desolation, despair, distress, gloom, grief, melancholy, misery, sadness, sorrow, unhappiness, woe

function *noun* 1 = **purpose**, activity, business, capacity, charge, concern, duty, employment, exercise, job, mission, occupation, office, operation, part, post, province, *raison d'être*, responsibility, role, situation, task 2 = **reception**, affair, do (*informal*), gathering, social occasion ◆ *verb* 3 = **work**, act, act the part of, behave, be in business, be in commission, be in operation or action, be in running order, do duty, go, officiate, operate, perform, run, serve, serve one's turn

functional adjective 1 = **practical**, hard-wearing, serviceable, useful, utilitarian, utility 2 = **working**, operative

functionary noun = **officer**, dignitary, employee, office bearer, office holder, official

fund noun 1 = **reserve**, capital, endowment, fall-back, foundation, kitty, pool, stock, store, supply 2 = **store**, hoard, mine, repository, reserve, reservoir, source, treasury, vein ◆ verb 3 = **finance**, capitalize, endow, float, pay for, promote, stake, subsidize, support

fundamental adjective 1 = **essential**, basic, cardinal, central, constitutional, crucial, elementary, first, important, indispensable, integral, intrinsic, key, necessary, organic, primary, prime, principal, radical, rudimentary, underlying, vital ◆ noun 2 = **principle**, axiom, basic, cornerstone, essential, first principle, law, rudiment, rule, sine qua non
➤ Antonyms
adjective ≠**essential**: advanced, back-up, extra, incidental, lesser, secondary, subsidiary, superfluous

fundamentally adverb = **essentially**, at bottom, at heart, basically, intrinsically, primarily, radically

funds plural noun = **money**, brass (Northern English dialect), bread (slang), capital, cash, dosh (Brit. & Austral. slang), dough (slang), finance, hard cash, necessary (informal), needful (informal), ready money, resources, savings, the ready (informal), the wherewithal

funeral noun = **burial**, cremation, inhumation, interment, obsequies

funereal adjective = **gloomy**, dark, depressing, dismal, dreary, grave, lugubrious, mournful, sad, sepulchral, solemn, sombre, woeful

funk verb = **chicken out of** (informal), dodge, duck out of (informal), flinch from, recoil from, take fright, turn tail

funnel verb = **channel**, conduct, convey, direct, filter, move, pass, pour

funny adjective 1 = **humorous**, absurd, a card (informal), a caution (informal), amusing, a scream, comic, comical, diverting, droll, entertaining, facetious, farcical, hilarious, jocose, jocular, jolly, laughable, ludicrous, rich, ridiculous, riotous, risible, side-splitting, silly, witty 2 = **peculiar**, curious, dubious, mysterious, odd, perplexing, puzzling, queer,

remarkable, rum (Brit. slang), strange, suspicious, unusual, weird
➤ Antonyms
≠**humorous**: grave, humourless, melancholy, serious, sober, solemn, stern, unfunny

furbish verb Formal = **renovate**, brighten, burnish, polish, restore, rub, shine, smarten up, spruce up

furious adjective 1 = **angry**, beside oneself, boiling, choked, cross, enraged, fit to be tied (slang), foaming at the mouth, frantic, frenzied, fuming, incandescent, incensed, infuriated, in high dudgeon, livid (informal), mad, maddened, on the warpath (informal), pissed (taboo slang), pissed off (taboo slang), raging, up in arms, wrathful 2 = **violent**, agitated, boisterous, fierce, impetuous, intense, savage, stormy, tempestuous, tumultuous, turbulent, ungovernable, unrestrained, vehement, wild
➤ Antonyms
≠**angry**: calm, dispassionate, impassive, imperturbable, mild, placated, pleased, serene, tranquil

furnish verb 1 = **decorate**, appoint, equip, fit, fit out, fit up, outfit, provide, provision, purvey, rig, stock, store, supply 2 = **supply**, afford, bestow, endow, give, grant, hand out, offer, present, provide, reveal

furniture noun = **household goods**, appliances, appointments, chattels, effects, equipment, fittings, furnishings, goods, movable property, movables, possessions, things (informal)

furore noun = **commotion**, brouhaha, disturbance, excitement, flap (informal), frenzy, fury, hullabaloo, outburst, outcry, stir, to-do, uproar

furrow noun 1 = **groove**, channel, corrugation, crease, hollow, line, rut, seam, trench, wrinkle ◆ verb 2 = **wrinkle**, corrugate, crease, draw together, knit, seam

further adverb 1 = **in addition**, additionally, also, as well as, besides, furthermore, into the bargain, moreover, on top of, over and above, to boot, what's more, yet
◆ adjective 2 = **additional**, extra, fresh, more, new, other, supplementary ◆ verb 3 = **promote**, advance, aid, assist, champion, contribute to, encourage, expedite, facilitate, forward, foster, hasten, help, lend support to, pave the way for, plug (informal), push, speed, succour, work for
➤ Antonyms
verb ≠**promote**: foil, frustrate, hinder, hobble, impede, obstruct, oppose,

prevent, retard, stop, thwart

furtherance noun = **promotion**, advancement, advocacy, backing, boosting, carrying-out, championship, prosecution, pursuit

furthermore adverb = **besides**, additionally, as well, further, in addition, into the bargain, moreover, not to mention, to boot, too, what's more

furthest adjective = **most distant**, extreme, farthest, furthermost, outermost, outmost, remotest, ultimate, uttermost

furtive adjective = **sly**, behind someone's back, clandestine, cloaked, conspiratorial, covert, hidden, secret, secretive, skulking, slinking, sneaking, sneaky, stealthy, surreptitious, underhand, under-the-table
➤ **Antonyms**
above-board, candid, forthright, frank, open, public, straightforward, undisguised, unreserved

fury noun 1 = **anger**, frenzy, impetuosity, ire, madness, passion, rage, red mist (informal), wrath 2 = **violence**, ferocity, fierceness, force, intensity, power, savagery, severity, tempestuousness, turbulence, vehemence 3 = **spitfire**, hellcat, shrew, termagant, virago, vixen
➤ **Antonyms**
≠anger: calm, calmness, composure, equanimity ≠violence: hush, peace, peacefulness, serenity, stillness, tranquillity

fuse verb = **join**, amalgamate, blend, coalesce, combine, commingle, dissolve, integrate, intermingle, intermix, meld, melt, merge, run together, solder, unite, weld
➤ **Antonyms**
diffuse, dispense, disseminate, dissipate, disunite, scatter, separate, spread, strew

fusillade noun = **barrage**, broadside, burst, fire, hail, outburst, salvo, volley

fusion noun = **merging**, alloy, amalgam, amalgamation, blend, blending, coalescence, commingling, commixture, integration, meld, merger, mixture, smelting, union, uniting, welding

fuss noun 1 = **bother**, ado, agitation, bustle, commotion, confusion, excitement, fidget, flap (informal), flurry, fluster, flutter, hue and cry, hurry, palaver, stir, storm in a teacup (Brit.), to-do, upset, worry 2 = **argument**, altercation, bother, complaint, difficulty, display, furore, hassle (informal), objection, row, squabble, trouble, unrest, upset ♦ verb 3 = **worry**, bustle, chafe, fidget, flap (informal), fret, fume, get in a stew (informal), get worked

up, labour over, make a meal of (informal), make a thing of (informal), niggle, take pains

fusspot noun Brit. informal = **nit-picker** (informal), fidget, old woman, perfectionist, worrier

fussy adjective 1 = **particular**, choosy (informal), dainty, difficult, discriminating, exacting, faddish, faddy, fastidious, finicky, hard to please, nit-picking (informal), old-maidish, old womanish, overparticular, pernickety, picky (informal), squeamish 2 = **overelaborate**, busy, cluttered, overdecorated, overembellished, overworked, rococo

fusty adjective 1 = **stale**, airless, damp, frowsty, mildewed, mouldering, mouldy, musty, stuffy 2 = **old-fashioned**, antediluvian, antiquated, archaic, old-fogeyish, outdated, out-of-date, out of the ark (informal), passé

futile adjective 1 = **useless**, abortive, barren, bootless, empty, forlorn, fruitless, hollow, ineffectual, in vain, profitless, to no avail, unavailing, unproductive, unprofitable, unsuccessful, vain, valueless, worthless 2 = **trivial**, idle, pointless, trifling, unimportant
➤ **Antonyms**
≠useless: constructive, effective, fruitful, profitable, purposeful, successful, useful, valuable, worthwhile ≠trivial: important, significant

futility noun 1 = **uselessness**, bootlessness, emptiness, fruitlessness, hollowness, ineffectiveness 2 = **triviality**, pointlessness, unimportance, vanity

future noun 1 = **time to come**, hereafter 2 = **prospect**, expectation, outlook ♦ adjective 3 = **forthcoming**, approaching, coming, destined, eventual, expected, fated, impending, in the offing, later, prospective, subsequent, to be, to come, ultimate, unborn
➤ **Antonyms**
adjective ≠forthcoming: bygone, erstwhile, ex-, former, late, past, preceding, previous, quondam

fuzz noun = **fluff**, down, fibre, floss, hair, nap, pile

fuzzy adjective 1 = **fluffy**, down-covered, downy, flossy, frizzy, woolly 2 = **indistinct**, bleary, blurred, distorted, faint, ill-defined, muffled, out of focus, shadowy, unclear, unfocused, vague
➤ **Antonyms**
≠indistinct: clear, defined, detailed, distinct, in focus, precise

G g

gabble *verb* **1** = **prattle**, babble, blab, blabber, cackle, chatter, gaggle, gibber, gush, jabber, rabbit (*Brit. informal*), rattle, run off at the mouth (*slang*), splutter, spout, sputter, waffle (*informal, chiefly Brit.*) ◆ *noun* **2** = **gibberish**, babble, blabber, cackling, chatter, drivel, jargon, pap, prattle, twaddle, waffle (*informal, chiefly Brit.*)

gad *verb, with* **about** *or* **around** = **gallivant**, ramble, range, roam, rove, run around, stravaig (*Scot. & Northern English dialect*), stray, traipse (*informal*), wander

gadabout *noun* = **pleasure-seeker**, gallivanter, rambler, rover, wanderer

gadget *noun* = **device**, appliance, contraption (*informal*), contrivance, gimmick, gizmo (*slang, chiefly U.S.*), instrument, invention, novelty, thing, tool, waldo

gaffe *noun* = **blunder**, bloomer (*informal*), boob (*Brit. slang*), boo-boo (*informal*), clanger (*informal*), faux pas, gaucherie, howler, indiscretion, lapse, mistake, slip, solecism

gaffer *noun* **1** *Informal* = **manager**, boss (*informal*), foreman, ganger, overseer, superintendent, supervisor **2** = **old man**, granddad, greybeard, old boy (*informal*), old fellow, old-timer (*U.S.*)

gag¹ *verb* **1** = **choke**, gasp, pant, struggle for breath **2** = **retch**, barf (*slang*), disgorge, heave, puke (*slang*), spew, throw up (*informal*), vomit **3** = **suppress**, curb, muffle, muzzle, quiet, silence, stifle, still, stop up, throttle

gag² *noun* = **joke**, crack (*slang*), funny (*informal*), hoax, jest, wisecrack (*informal*), witticism

gaiety *noun* **1** = **cheerfulness**, animation, blitheness, blithesomeness (*literary*), effervescence, elation, exhilaration, glee, good humour, high spirits, hilarity, *joie de vivre*, jollity, joviality, joyousness, light-heartedness, liveliness, merriment, mirth, sprightliness, vivacity **2** = **merrymaking**, celebration, conviviality, festivity, fun, jollification, revelry, revels **3** = **colour**, brightness, brilliance, colourfulness, gaudiness, glitter, show, showiness, sparkle
➤ **Antonyms**

≠**cheerfulness**: despondency, gloom, melancholy, misery, sadness

gaily *adverb* **1** = **cheerfully**, blithely, gleefully, happily, joyfully, light-heartedly, merrily **2** = **colourfully**, brightly, brilliantly, flamboyantly, flashily, gaudily, showily

gain *verb* **1** = **acquire**, achieve, attain, bag, bring in, capture, clear, collect, earn, gather, get, glean, harvest, land, make, net, obtain, procure, realize, reap, score (*slang*), secure, win **2** = **improve**, advance, build up, increase, pick up, profit **3** = **reach**, arrive at, attain, come to, get to **4** **gain on** = **get nearer**, approach, catch up with, close, narrow the gap, overtake **5** **gain time** = **stall**, delay, procrastinate, temporize, use delaying tactics ◆ *noun* **6** = **profit**, accretion, achievement, acquisition, advantage, attainment, benefit, dividend, earnings, emolument, headway, income, lucre, proceeds, produce, return, winnings, yield **7** = **increase**, advance, advancement, growth, improvement, increment, progress, rise
➤ **Antonyms**
verb ≠**acquire**: forfeit, lose ≠**improve**: fail, worsen ◆ *noun* ≠**profit**: forfeiture, loss ≠**increase**: damage, injury

gainful *adjective* = **profitable**, advantageous, beneficial, expedient, fruitful, lucrative, moneymaking, paying, productive, remunerative, rewarding, useful, worthwhile

gains *plural noun* = **profits**, booty, earnings, gainings, pickings, prize, proceeds, revenue, takings, winnings

gainsay *verb* = **contradict**, contravene, controvert, deny, disaffirm, disagree with, dispute, rebut, retract
➤ **Antonyms**
agree with, back, confirm, support

gait *noun* = **walk**, bearing, carriage, pace, step, stride, tread

gala *noun* **1** = **festival**, beano (*Brit. slang*), carnival, celebration, festivity, fête, hooley *or* hoolie (*chiefly Irish & N.Z.*), jamboree, pageant, party, rave (*Brit. slang*), rave-up (*Brit. slang*) ◆ *adjective* **2** = **festive**, celebratory, convivial, festal, gay, jovial, joyful, merry

gale *noun* **1** = **storm**, blast, cyclone,

hurricane, squall, tempest, tornado, typhoon **2** *Informal* = **outburst**, burst, eruption, explosion, fit, howl, outbreak, paroxysm, peal, shout, shriek, storm

gall¹ *noun* **1** *Informal* = **impudence**, brass (*informal*), brass neck (*Brit. informal*), brazenness, cheek (*informal*), chutzpah (*U.S. & Canad. informal*), effrontery, face (*informal*), impertinence, insolence, neck (*informal*), nerve (*informal*), sassiness (*U.S. informal*), sauciness **2** = **bitterness**, acrimony, animosity, animus, antipathy, bad blood, bile, enmity, hostility, malevolence, malice, malignity, rancour, sourness, spite, spleen, venom

gall² *verb* **1** = **annoy**, aggravate (*informal*), be on one's back (*slang*), bother, exasperate, fret, get in one's hair (*informal*), get on one's nerves (*informal*), harass, hassle (*informal*), irk, irritate, nag, nark (*Brit., Austral., & N.Z. slang*), nettle, peeve (*informal*), pester, piss one off (*taboo slang*), plague, provoke, rankle, rile (*informal*), rub up the wrong way, ruffle, vex **2** = **scrape**, abrade, bark, chafe, excoriate, fret, graze, irritate, rub raw, skin ◆ *noun* **3** = **irritation**, aggravation (*informal*), annoyance, bother, botheration (*informal*), exasperation, harassment, irritant, nuisance, pest, provocation, vexation **4** = **sore**, abrasion, chafe, excoriation, raw spot, scrape, sore spot, wound

gallant *adjective* **1** = **brave**, bold, courageous, daring, dashing, dauntless, doughty, fearless, game (*informal*), heroic, high-spirited, honourable, intrepid, lion-hearted, manful, manly, mettlesome, noble, plucky, valiant, valorous **2** = **courteous**, attentive, chivalrous, courtly, gentlemanly, gracious, magnanimous, noble, polite **3** = **elegant**, august, dignified, glorious, grand, imposing, lofty, magnificent, noble, splendid, stately ◆ *noun* **4** = **ladies' man**, beau, blade (*archaic*), buck (*informal*), dandy, fop, lady-killer (*informal*), man about town, man of fashion

➤ **Antonyms**
adjective ≠**brave**: cowardly, fearful, ignoble ≠**courteous**: churlish, discourteous, ill-mannered, impolite, rude

gallantry *noun* **1** = **courtesy**, attentiveness, chivalry, courteousness, courtliness, elegance, gentlemanliness, graciousness, nobility, politeness **2** = **bravery**, audacity, boldness, courage, courageousness, daring, dauntlessness, derring-do (*archaic*), fearlessness, heroism, intrepidity, manliness, mettle, nerve, pluck, prowess, spirit, valiance, valour

➤ **Antonyms**
≠**courtesy**: churlishness, discourtesy, rudeness, ungraciousness ≠**bravery**: cowardice, irresolution

galling *adjective* = **annoying**, aggravating (*informal*), bitter, bothersome, exasperating, harassing, humiliating, irksome, irritating, nettlesome, plaguing, provoking, rankling, vexatious, vexing

gallivant *verb* = **wander**, gad about, ramble, roam, rove

gallop *verb* = **run**, barrel (along) (*informal, chiefly U.S. & Canad.*), bolt, career, dart, dash, fly, hasten, hie (*archaic*), hurry, race, rush, scud, shoot, speed, sprint, tear along, zoom

galore *adverb* = **in abundance**, à gogo (*informal*), all over the place, aplenty, everywhere, in great quantity, in numbers, in profusion, to spare

galvanize *verb* = **stimulate**, arouse, awaken, electrify, excite, fire, inspire, invigorate, jolt, kick-start, move, prod, provoke, put a bomb under (*informal*), quicken, shock, spur, startle, stir, thrill, vitalize, wake

gamble *verb* **1** = **bet**, back, game, have a flutter (*informal*), lay *or* make a bet, play, punt, put one's shirt on, stake, try one's luck, wager **2** = **risk**, back, chance, hazard, put one's faith *or* trust in, skate on thin ice (*informal*), speculate, stake, stick one's neck out (*informal*), take a chance, take the plunge, venture ◆ *noun* **3** = **bet**, flutter (*informal*), punt, wager **4** = **risk**, chance, leap in the dark, lottery, speculation, uncertainty, venture

➤ **Antonyms**
noun ≠**risk**: banker, certainty, foregone conclusion, safe bet, sure thing

gambol *verb* **1** = **frolic**, caper, cavort, curvet, cut a caper, frisk, hop, jump, prance, rollick, skip ◆ *noun* **2** = **frolic**, antic, caper, gambado, hop, jump, prance, skip, spring

game *noun* **1** = **pastime**, amusement, distraction, diversion, entertainment, frolic, fun, jest, joke, lark, merriment, play, recreation, romp, sport **2** = **match**, competition, contest, event, head-to-head, meeting, round, tournament **3** = **undertaking**, adventure, business, enterprise, line, occupation, plan, proceeding, scheme **4** = **wild animals**, chase, prey, quarry **5** = **scheme**, design, device, plan, plot, ploy, stratagem, strategy, tactic, trick ◆ *adjective* **6** = **brave**, ballsy (*taboo slang*), bold, courageous, dauntless, dogged, fearless, feisty (*informal, chiefly U.S. & Canad.*), gallant,

gritty, have-a-go (*informal*), heroic, intrepid, persevering, persistent, plucky, resolute, spirited, unflinching, valiant, valorous **7 = willing**, desirous, disposed, eager, inclined, interested, keen, prepared, ready, up for it (*informal*)
➤ **Antonyms**
noun ≠**pastime**: business, chore, duty, job, labour, toil, work ♦ *adjective* ≠**brave**: cowardly, fearful, irresolute

gamut *noun* **= range**, area, catalogue, compass, field, scale, scope, series, sweep

gang *noun* **= group**, band, bevy, camp, circle, clique, club, company, coterie, crew (*informal*), crowd, herd, horde, lot, mob, pack, party, posse (*slang*), ring, set, shift, squad, team, troupe

gangling, gangly *adjective* **= tall**, angular, awkward, lanky, loose-jointed, rangy, rawboned, skinny, spindly

gangster *noun* **= racketeer**, bandit, brigand, crook (*informal*), desperado, gang member, heavy (*slang*), hood (*U.S. slang*), hoodlum (*chiefly U.S.*), mobster (*U.S. slang*), robber, ruffian, thug, tough, tsotsi (*S. African*)

gap *noun* **1 = opening**, blank, breach, break, chink, cleft, crack, cranny, crevice, discontinuity, divide, hole, interstice, rent, rift, space, vacuity, void **2 = interval**, breathing space, entr'acte, hiatus, interlude, intermission, interruption, lacuna, lull, pause, recess, respite **3 = difference**, disagreement, disparity, divergence, inconsistency

gape *verb* **1 = stare**, gawk, gawp (*Brit. slang*), goggle, wonder **2 = open**, crack, split, yawn

gaping *adjective* **= wide**, broad, cavernous, great, open, vast, wide open, yawning

garb *noun* **1 = clothes**, apparel, array, attire, clothing, costume, dress, garment, gear (*slang*), habiliment, habit, outfit, raiment (*archaic*), robes, threads (*slang*), uniform, vestments, wear **2 = fashion**, cut, look, mode, style **3 = appearance**, aspect, attire, covering, guise, outward form ♦ *verb* **4 = clothe**, apparel, attire, cover, dress, rig out, robe

garbage *noun* **1 = junk**, bits and pieces, debris, detritus, litter, odds and ends, rubbish, scraps **2 = waste**, dreck (*slang, chiefly U.S.*), dross, filth, muck, offal, refuse, rubbish, scourings, slops, sweepings, swill, trash (*chiefly U.S.*), wack (*U.S. slang*) **3 = nonsense**, balderdash, balls (*taboo slang*), bilge (*informal*), bosh (*informal*), bull (*slang*), bullshit (*taboo slang*), bunkum *or* buncombe (*chiefly U.S.*), claptrap (*informal*), cobblers (*Brit.*

taboo slang), codswallop (*Brit. slang*), crap (*slang*), drivel, eyewash (*informal*), flapdoodle (*slang*), gibberish, guff (*slang*), havers (*Scot.*), hogwash, hokum (*slang, chiefly U.S. & Canad.*), horsefeathers (*U.S. slang*), hot air (*informal*), kak (*S. African slang*), moonshine, pap, piffle (*informal*), poppycock (*informal*), rot, shit (*taboo slang*), stuff and nonsense, tommyrot, tosh (*informal*), trash, tripe (*informal*), twaddle

garble *verb* **1 = jumble**, confuse, mix up **2 = distort**, corrupt, doctor, falsify, misinterpret, misquote, misreport, misrepresent, misstate, mistranslate, mutilate, pervert, slant, tamper with, twist
➤ **Antonyms**
clarify, decipher, make intelligible

garbled *adjective* **= jumbled**, confused, distorted, double-Dutch, incomprehensible, mixed up, unintelligible

gargantuan *adjective* **= huge**, big, Brobdingnagian, colossal, elephantine, enormous, giant, gigantic, ginormous (*informal*), humongous *or* humungous (*U.S. slang*), immense, mammoth, massive, monstrous, monumental, mountainous, prodigious, stellar (*informal*), titanic, towering, tremendous, vast
➤ **Antonyms**
little, meagre, miniature, minute, paltry, petite, puny, pygmy *or* pigmy, small, tiny

garish *adjective* **= gaudy**, brash, brassy, brummagem, cheap, flash (*informal*), flashy, flaunting, glaring, glittering, loud, meretricious, naff (*Brit. slang*), raffish, showy, tacky (*informal*), tasteless, tawdry, vulgar
➤ **Antonyms**
conservative, elegant, modest, plain, refined, sedate, sombre, unobtrusive

garland *noun* **1 = wreath**, bays, chaplet, coronal, crown, festoon, honours, laurels ♦ *verb* **2 = adorn**, crown, deck, festoon, wreathe

garments *plural noun* **= clothes**, apparel, array, articles of clothing, attire, clothing, costume, dress, duds (*informal*), garb, gear (*slang*), habiliment, habit, outfit, raiment (*archaic*), robes, schmutter (*slang*), threads (*slang*), togs, uniform, vestments, wear

garner *verb* **1 = collect**, accumulate, amass, assemble, deposit, gather, hoard, husband, lay in *or* up, put by, reserve, save, stockpile, store, stow away, treasure ♦ *noun* **2** *Literary* **= storehouse**, depository, granary, store, vault

garnish *verb* **1 = decorate**, adorn, beautify, bedeck, deck, embellish, enhance, festoon, grace, ornament, set off, trim ♦ *noun* **2**

= **decoration**, adornment, embellishment, enhancement, festoon, garniture, ornament, ornamentation, trim, trimming
➤ **Antonyms**
verb ≠**decorate**: denude, spoil, strip

garrison *noun* 1 = **troops**, armed force, command, detachment, unit 2 = **fort**, base, camp, encampment, fortification, fortress, post, station, stronghold ♦ *verb* 3 = **station**, assign, mount, position, post, put on duty 4 = **occupy**, defend, guard, man, protect, supply with troops

garrulity *noun* 1 = **talkativeness**, babble, babbling, chatter, chattering, chattiness, effusiveness, gabbiness (*informal*), garrulousness, gift of the gab (*informal*), glibness, loquacity, mouthiness, prating, prattle, verbosity, volubility 2 = **long-windedness**, diffuseness, prolixity, prosiness, verbosity, windiness, wordiness

garrulous *adjective* 1 = **talkative**, babbling, chattering, chatty, effusive, gabby (*informal*), glib, gossiping, gushing, loquacious, mouthy, prating, prattling, verbose, voluble 2 = **long-winded**, diffuse, gassy (*slang*), prolix, prosy, verbose, windy, wordy
➤ **Antonyms**
≠**talkative**: reserved, reticent, taciturn, tight-lipped, uncommunicative
≠**long-winded**: concise, succinct, terse

gash *verb* 1 = **cut**, cleave, gouge, incise, lacerate, rend, slash, slit, split, tear, wound ♦ *noun* 2 = **cut**, cleft, gouge, incision, laceration, rent, slash, slit, split, tear, wound

gasp *verb* 1 = **gulp**, blow, catch one's breath, choke, fight for breath, pant, puff ♦ *noun* 2 = **gulp**, blow, ejaculation, exclamation, intake of breath, pant, puff, sharp intake of breath

gate *noun* = **barrier**, access, door, doorway, egress, entrance, exit, gateway, opening, passage, port (*Scot.*), portal

gather *verb* 1 = **assemble**, accumulate, amass, bring *or* get together, collect, congregate, convene, flock, foregather, garner, group, heap, hoard, marshal, mass, muster, pile up, round up, stack up, stockpile 2 = **intensify**, build, deepen, enlarge, expand, grow, heighten, increase, rise, swell, thicken, wax 3 = **learn**, assume, be led to believe, conclude, deduce, draw, hear, infer, make, surmise, understand 4 = **fold**, pleat, pucker, ruffle, shirr, tuck 5 = **pick**, crop, cull, garner, glean, harvest, pluck, reap, select 6 = **enfold**, clasp, draw, embrace, hold, hug
➤ **Antonyms**
≠**assemble**: diffuse, disperse, dissipate,

scatter, separate

gathering *noun* 1 = **assembly**, assemblage, company, conclave, concourse, congregation, congress, convention, convocation, crowd, flock, get-together (*informal*), group, knot, meeting, muster, party, rally, throng, turnout 2 = **accumulation**, acquisition, aggregate, collecting, collection, concentration, gain, heap, hoard, mass, pile, procuring, roundup, stock, stockpile 3 *Informal* = **pimple**, abscess, boil, carbuncle, pustule, sore, spot, tumour, ulcer

gauche *adjective* = **awkward**, clumsy, graceless, ignorant, ill-bred, ill-mannered, inelegant, inept, insensitive, lacking in social graces, maladroit, tactless, uncultured, unpolished, unsophisticated
➤ **Antonyms**
elegant, gracious, polished, polite, refined, sophisticated, tasteful, urbane, well-mannered

gaudy *adjective* = **garish**, brash, bright, brilliant, brummagem, flash (*informal*), flashy, florid, gay, gimcrack, glaring, jazzy (*informal*), loud, meretricious, naff (*Brit. slang*), ostentatious, raffish, showy, tacky (*informal*), tasteless, tawdry, vulgar
➤ **Antonyms**
colourless, conservative, dull, elegant, modest, quiet, refined, sedate, subtle, tasteful

gauge *verb* 1 = **judge**, adjudge, appraise, assess, estimate, evaluate, guess, rate, reckon, value 2 = **measure**, ascertain, calculate, check, compute, count, determine, weigh ♦ *noun* 3 = **indicator**, basis, criterion, example, exemplar, guide, guideline, measure, meter, model, par, pattern, rule, sample, standard, test, touchstone, yardstick 4 = **size**, bore, capacity, degree, depth, extent, height, magnitude, measure, scope, span, thickness, width

gaunt *adjective* 1 = **thin**, angular, attenuated, bony, cadaverous, emaciated, haggard, lank, lean, macilent (*rare*), meagre, pinched, rawboned, scraggy, scrawny, skeletal, skin and bone, skinny, spare, wasted 2 = **bleak**, bare, desolate, dismal, dreary, forbidding, forlorn, grim, harsh, stark
➤ **Antonyms**
≠**thin**: chubby, corpulent, fat, lush, obese, plump, stout, well-fed ≠**bleak**: inviting, lush, luxurious

gawk *verb* 1 = **stare**, gape, gawp (*slang*), gaze open-mouthed, goggle ♦ *noun* 2 = **oaf**, boor, churl, clod, clodhopper (*informal*), dolt, dunderhead, galoot (*slang*), ignoramus, lout, lubber, lummox (*informal*)

gawky *adjective* = **awkward**, clownish, clumsy, gauche, loutish, lumbering, lumpish, maladroit, oafish, uncouth, ungainly
➤ Antonyms
elegant, graceful, self-assured, well-coordinated

gay *adjective* **1** = **homosexual**, bent (*offensive slang*), dykey (*slang*), lesbian, moffie (*S. African slang*), pink (*informal*), poofy (*offensive slang*), queer (*informal, derogatory*) **2** = **cheerful**, animated, blithe, carefree, debonair, full of beans (*informal*), glad, gleeful, happy, hilarious, insouciant, jolly, jovial, joyful, joyous, light-hearted, lively, merry, sparkling, sunny, vivacious **3** = **colourful**, bright, brilliant, flamboyant, flashy, fresh, garish, gaudy, rich, showy, vivid **4** = **merry**, convivial, festive, frivolous, frolicsome, fun-loving, gamesome, playful, pleasure-seeking, rakish, rollicking, sportive, waggish ♦ *noun* **5** = **homosexual**, bull dyke (*offensive slang*), dyke (*offensive slang*), faggot (*U.S. offens. slang*), fairy (*offensive slang*), invert, lesbian, poof (*offensive slang*), queer (*offensive slang*)
➤ Antonyms
adjective, noun ≠**homosexual**: heterosexual, straight ♦ *adjective* ≠**cheerful**: cheerless, down in the dumps (*informal*), grave, grim, melancholy, miserable, sad, sedate, serious, sober, solemn, sombre, unhappy ≠**colourful**: colourless, conservative, drab, dull, sombre

gaze *verb* **1** = **stare**, contemplate, eyeball (*slang*), gape, look, look fixedly, regard, view, watch, wonder ♦ *noun* **2** = **stare**, fixed look, look

gazette *noun* = **newspaper**, journal, news-sheet, organ, paper, periodical

gear *noun* **1** = **cog**, cogwheel, gearwheel, toothed wheel **2** = **mechanism**, cogs, gearing, machinery, works **3** = **clothing**, apparel, array, attire, clothes, costume, dress, garb, garments, habit, outfit, rigout (*informal*), schmutter (*slang*), threads (*slang*), togs, wear **4** = **belongings**, baggage, effects, kit, luggage, stuff, things **5** = **equipment**, accessories, accoutrements, apparatus, harness, instruments, outfit, paraphernalia, rigging, supplies, tackle, tools, trappings ♦ *verb* **6** = **equip**, adapt, adjust, fit, rig, suit, tailor

gelatinous *adjective* = **jelly-like**, gluey, glutinous, gummy, mucilaginous, sticky, viscid, viscous

gem *noun* **1** = **precious stone**, jewel, semiprecious stone, stone **2** = **prize**,

flower, jewel, masterpiece, pearl, pick, treasure

genealogy *noun* = **ancestry**, blood line, derivation, descent, extraction, family tree, line, lineage, pedigree, progeniture, stemma, stirps, stock, strain

general *adjective* **1** = **common**, accepted, broad, extensive, popular, prevailing, prevalent, public, universal, widespread **2** = **universal**, across-the-board, all-inclusive, blanket, broad, catholic, collective, comprehensive, encyclopedic, generic, indiscriminate, miscellaneous, overall, overarching, panoramic, sweeping, total **3** = **ordinary**, accustomed, conventional, customary, everyday, habitual, normal, regular, typical, usual **4** = **imprecise**, approximate, ill-defined, inaccurate, indefinite, inexact, loose, undetailed, unspecific, vague
➤ Antonyms
≠**common, universal**: distinctive, exceptional, extraordinary, individual, peculiar, special, unusual ≠**ordinary**: infrequent, rare ≠**imprecise**: definite, exact, particular, precise, specific

generality *noun* **1** = **generalization**, abstract principle, loose statement, sweeping statement, vague notion **2** = **commonness**, acceptedness, extensiveness, popularity, prevalence, ubiquity, universality **3** = **universality**, breadth, catholicity, completeness, comprehensiveness, miscellaneity, sweepingness **4** = **impreciseness**, approximateness, indefiniteness, inexactness, lack of detail, looseness, vagueness

generally *adverb* **1** = **usually**, almost always, as a rule, by and large, conventionally, customarily, for the most part, habitually, in most cases, largely, mainly, normally, on average, on the whole, ordinarily, regularly, typically **2** = **commonly**, extensively, popularly, publicly, universally, widely **3** = **broadly**, approximately, chiefly, for the most part, in the main, largely, mainly, mostly, on the whole, predominantly, principally
➤ Antonyms
≠**usually**: especially, occasionally, rarely, unusually ≠**commonly**: individually, particularly

generate *verb* = **produce**, beget, breed, bring about, cause, create, engender, form, give rise to, initiate, make, originate, procreate, propagate, spawn, whip up
➤ Antonyms
annihilate, crush, destroy, end, extinguish, kill, terminate

generation *noun* 1 = **age group**, breed, crop 2 = **age**, day, days, epoch, era, period, time, times 3 = **production**, begetting, breeding, creation, engenderment, formation, genesis, origination, procreation, propagation, reproduction

generic *adjective* = **collective**, all-encompassing, blanket, common, comprehensive, general, inclusive, sweeping, universal, wide
➤ **Antonyms**
individual, particular, precise, specific

generosity *noun* 1 = **liberality**, beneficence, benevolence, bounteousness, bounty, charity, kindness, largesse *or* largess, munificence, open-handedness 2 = **unselfishness**, disinterestedness, goodness, high-mindedness, magnanimity, nobleness

generous *adjective* 1 = **liberal**, beneficent, benevolent, bounteous, bountiful, charitable, free, hospitable, kind, lavish, munificent, open-handed, princely, prodigal, ungrudging, unstinting 2 = **unselfish**, big-hearted, disinterested, good, high-minded, lofty, magnanimous, noble 3 = **plentiful**, abundant, ample, copious, full, fulsome, lavish, liberal, overflowing, rich, unstinting
➤ **Antonyms**
≠**liberal**: avaricious, close-fisted, greedy, mean, miserly, parsimonious, selfish, stingy, tight ≠**plentiful**: cheap, minimal, scanty, small, tiny

genesis *noun* = **beginning**, birth, commencement, creation, dawn, engendering, formation, generation, inception, origin, outset, propagation, root, source, start
➤ **Antonyms**
completion, conclusion, end, finish, termination

genial *adjective* = **cheerful**, affable, agreeable, amiable, cheery, congenial, convivial, cordial, easy-going, enlivening, friendly, glad, good-natured, happy, hearty, jolly, jovial, joyous, kind, kindly, merry, pleasant, sunny, warm, warm-hearted
➤ **Antonyms**
cheerless, cool, discourteous, frigid, morose, rude, sardonic, sullen, unfriendly, ungracious, unpleasant

geniality *noun* = **cheerfulness**, affability, agreeableness, amiability, cheeriness, congenialness, conviviality, cordiality, friendliness, gladness, good cheer, good nature, happiness, heartiness, jollity, joviality, joy, joyousness, kindliness,

kindness, mirth, pleasantness, sunniness, warm-heartedness, warmth

genitals *plural noun* = **sex organs**, genitalia, loins, private parts, pudenda, reproductive organs

genius *noun* 1 = **master**, adept, brain (*informal*), brainbox, buff (*informal*), expert, hotshot (*informal*), intellect (*informal*), maestro, master-hand, mastermind, maven (*U.S.*), virtuoso, whiz (*informal*) 2 = **brilliance**, ability, aptitude, bent, capacity, creative power, endowment, faculty, flair, gift, inclination, knack, propensity, talent, turn
➤ **Antonyms**
≠**master**: dolt, dunce, fool, half-wit, idiot, imbecile, nincompoop, simpleton

genre *noun* = **type**, brand, category, character, class, fashion, genus, group, kind, school, sort, species, stamp, style

genteel *adjective* = **refined**, aristocratic, civil, courteous, courtly, cultivated, cultured, elegant, fashionable, formal, gentlemanly, ladylike, mannerly, polished, polite, respectable, sophisticated, stylish, urbane, well-bred, well-mannered
➤ **Antonyms**
discourteous, ill-bred, impolite, inelegant, low-bred, natural, plebeian, rude, unaffected, uncultured, unmannerly, unpolished, unrefined

gentility *noun* 1 = **nobility**, blue blood, gentle birth, good family, high birth, rank 2 = **refinement**, breeding, civility, courtesy, courtliness, cultivation, culture, decorum, elegance, etiquette, formality, good breeding, good manners, mannerliness, polish, politeness, propriety, respectability, sophistication, urbanity 3 = **aristocracy**, elite, gentlefolk, gentry, nobility, nobles, ruling class, upper class

gentle *adjective* 1 = **mild**, amiable, benign, bland, compassionate, dove-like, humane, kind, kindly, lenient, meek, merciful, pacific, peaceful, placid, quiet, soft, sweet-tempered, tender 2 = **moderate**, balmy, calm, clement, easy, light, low, mild, muted, placid, quiet, serene, slight, smooth, soft, soothing, temperate, tranquil, untroubled 3 = **gradual**, easy, imperceptible, light, mild, moderate, slight, slow 4 = **tame**, biddable, broken, docile, manageable, placid, tractable 5 *Archaic* = **well-bred**, aristocratic, civil, courteous, cultured, elegant, genteel, gentlemanlike, gentlemanly, high-born, ladylike, noble, polished, polite, refined, upper-class, well-born
➤ **Antonyms**
≠**mild**: aggressive, cruel, fierce, hard,

harsh, heartless, impolite, rough, savage, sharp, unkind ≠**tame:** fierce, savage, unmanageable, wild ≠**moderate:** powerful, strong, violent, wild ≠**gradual:** sudden

gentlemanly *adjective* = **polite,** civil, civilized, courteous, cultivated, debonair, gallant, genteel, gentlemanlike, honourable, mannerly, noble, obliging, polished, refined, reputable, suave, urbane, well-bred, well-mannered

gentleness *noun* = **tenderness,** compassion, kindness, mildness, softness, sweetness

gentry *noun* = **nobility,** aristocracy, elite, upper class, upper crust (*informal*)

genuine *adjective* 1 = **authentic,** actual, bona fide, honest, legitimate, natural, on the level, original, pure, real, sound, sterling, the real McCoy, true, unadulterated, unalloyed, veritable 2 = **sincere,** artless, candid, earnest, frank, heartfelt, honest, unaffected, unfeigned
➤ Antonyms
≠**authentic:** artificial, bogus, counterfeit, fake, false, fraudulent, imitation, phoney, pseudo (*informal*), sham, simulated, spurious ≠**sincere:** affected, false, feigned, hypocritical, insincere, phoney

germ *noun* 1 = **microbe,** bacterium, bug (*informal*), microorganism, virus 2 = **embryo,** bud, egg, nucleus, ovule, ovum, seed, spore, sprout 3 = **beginning,** bud, cause, embryo, origin, root, rudiment, seed, source, spark

germane *adjective* = **relevant,** akin, allied, apposite, appropriate, apropos, apt, cognate, connected, fitting, kindred, material, pertinent, proper, related, suitable, to the point or purpose
➤ Antonyms
extraneous, foreign, immaterial, inappropriate, irrelevant, unrelated

germinate *verb* = **sprout,** bud, develop, generate, grow, originate, pullulate, shoot, swell, vegetate

gestation *noun* = **development,** evolution, incubation, maturation, pregnancy, ripening

gesticulate *verb* = **signal,** gesture, indicate, make a sign, motion, sign, wave

gesture *noun* 1 = **signal,** action, gesticulation, indication, motion, sign
♦ *verb* 2 = **signal,** gesticulate, indicate, motion, sign, wave

get *verb* 1 = **obtain,** achieve, acquire, attain, bag, bring, come by, come into possession of, earn, fall heir to, fetch, gain, glean, inherit, land, make, net, pick up, procure,

realize, reap, receive, score (*slang*), secure, succeed to, win 2 = **contract,** be afflicted with, become infected with, be smitten by, catch, come down with, fall victim to, take 3 = **become,** come to be, grow, turn, wax 4 = **arrange,** contrive, fix, manage, succeed, wangle (*informal*) 5 = **understand,** catch, comprehend, fathom, follow, get the picture, hear, notice, perceive, see, suss (out) (*slang*), take in, work out 6 = **arrive,** come, make it (*informal*), reach 7 = **persuade,** coax, convince, induce, influence, prevail upon, sway, talk into, wheedle, win over 8 *Informal* = **annoy,** bother, bug (*informal*), gall, get (someone's) goat (*slang*), irk, irritate, nark (*Brit., Austral., & N.Z. slang*), pique, rub (someone) up the wrong way, upset, vex 9 = **puzzle,** baffle, confound, mystify, nonplus, perplex, stump 10 = **capture,** arrest, collar (*informal*), grab, lay hold of, nab (*informal*), nail (*informal*), seize, take, trap 11 *Informal* = **impress,** affect, arouse, excite, have an effect on, impact on, move, stimulate, stir, touch, tug at (someone's) heartstrings (*often facetious*) 12 = **contact,** communicate with, get in touch with, reach

get across *verb* 1 = **cross,** ford, negotiate, pass over, traverse 2 = **communicate,** bring home to, convey, get (something) through to, impart, make clear or understood, put over, transmit

get ahead *verb* 1 = **prosper,** advance, be successful, cut it (*informal*), do well, flourish, get on, make good, make one's mark, progress, succeed, thrive 2 = **overtake,** excel, leave behind, outdo, outmanoeuvre, surpass

get along *verb* 1 = **go away,** be off, depart, get on one's bike (*Brit. slang*), go, go to hell (*informal*), leave, make tracks, move off, sling one's hook (*Brit. slang*), slope off 2 = **cope,** develop, fare, get by (*informal*), make out (*informal*), manage, progress, shift 3 = **be friendly,** agree, be compatible, be on good terms, get on, harmonize, hit it off (*informal*)

get at *verb* 1 = **gain access to,** acquire, attain, come to grips with, get, get hold of, reach 2 = **imply,** hint, intend, lead up to, mean, suggest 3 = **criticize,** annoy, attack, be on one's back (*slang*), blame, carp, find fault with, hassle (*informal*), irritate, nag, nark (*Brit., Austral., & N.Z. slang*), pick on, put the boot into (*slang*), taunt 4 = **corrupt,** bribe, buy off, influence, suborn, tamper with

getaway *noun* = **escape,** break, break-out, decampment, flight

get away *verb* = **escape**, abscond, break free, break out, decamp, depart, disappear, flee, leave, make good one's escape, slope off

get back *verb* **1** = **regain**, recoup, recover, repossess, retrieve **2** = **return**, arrive home, come back *or* home, revert, revisit **3 get back at** = **retaliate**, be avenged, get even with, get one's own back, give tit for tat, hit back, settle the score with, take vengeance on

get by *verb* **1** = **pass**, circumvent, get ahead of, go around, go past, overtake, round **2** = **manage**, contrive, cope, exist, fare, get along, keep one's head above water, make both ends meet, subsist, survive

get down *verb* **1** = **descend**, alight, bring down, climb down, disembark, dismount, get off, lower, step down **2** = **dishearten**, bring down, depress, dispirit

get in *verb* = **enter**, alight, appear, arrive, collect, come, embark, include, infiltrate, insert, interpose, land, make inroads (into), mount, penetrate

get off *verb* **1** = **leave**, alight, depart, descend, disembark, dismount, escape, exit **2** = **remove**, detach, shed, take off

get on *verb* **1** = **board**, ascend, climb, embark, mount **2** = **be friendly**, agree, be compatible, concur, get along, harmonize, hit it off (*informal*) **3** = **progress**, advance, cope, cut it (*informal*), fare, get along, make out (*informal*), manage, prosper, succeed

get out *verb* = **leave**, alight, break out, clear out (*informal*), decamp, escape, evacuate, extricate oneself, free oneself, vacate, withdraw

get out of *verb* = **avoid**, body-swerve (*Scot.*), dodge, escape, evade, shirk

get over *verb* **1** = **cross**, ford, get across, pass, pass over, surmount, traverse **2** = **recover from**, come round, get better, mend, pull through, rally, revive, survive **3** = **overcome**, defeat, get the better of, master, shake off **4** = **communicate**, convey, get *or* put across, impart, make clear *or* understood

get round *verb* **1** = **bypass**, circumvent, edge, evade, outmanoeuvre, skirt **2** *Informal* = **win over**, cajole, coax, convert, persuade, prevail upon, talk round, wheedle

get together *verb* = **meet**, accumulate, assemble, collect, congregate, convene, converge, gather, join, muster, rally, unite

get up *verb* = **arise**, ascend, climb, increase, mount, rise, scale, stand

ghastly *adjective* = **horrible**, ashen, cadaverous, deathlike, deathly pale, dreadful, frightful, from hell (*informal*), godawful (*slang*), grim, grisly, gruesome, hideous, horrendous, horrid, like death warmed up (*informal*), livid, loathsome, pale, pallid, repellent, shocking, spectral, terrible, terrifying, wan
➤ **Antonyms**
appealing, attractive, beautiful, blooming, charming, healthy, lovely, pleasing

ghost *noun* **1** = **spirit**, apparition, eidolon, manes, phantasm, phantom, revenant, shade (*literary*), soul, spectre, spook (*informal*), wraith **2** = **trace**, glimmer, hint, possibility, semblance, shadow, suggestion

ghostly *adjective* = **supernatural**, eerie, ghostlike, illusory, insubstantial, phantasmal, phantom, spectral, spooky (*informal*), uncanny, unearthly, weird, wraithlike

ghoulish *adjective* = **macabre**, disgusting, grisly, gruesome, morbid, sick (*informal*), unwholesome

giant *noun* **1** = **ogre**, behemoth, colossus, Hercules, leviathan, monster, titan
♦ *adjective* **2** = **huge**, Brobdingnagian, colossal, elephantine, enormous, gargantuan, gigantic, ginormous (*informal*), humongous *or* humungous (*U.S. slang*), immense, jumbo (*informal*), large, mammoth, monstrous, prodigious, stellar (*informal*), titanic, vast
➤ **Antonyms**
adjective ≠**huge**: dwarf, Lilliputian, miniature, pygmy *or* pigmy, tiny

gibberish *noun* = **nonsense**, all Greek (*informal*), babble, balderdash, balls (*taboo slang*), bilge (*informal*), blather, bosh (*informal*), bull (*slang*), bullshit (*taboo slang*), bunkum *or* buncombe (*chiefly U.S.*), cobblers (*Brit. taboo slang*), crap (*slang*), double talk, drivel, eyewash (*informal*), gabble, garbage (*informal*), gobbledegook (*informal*), guff (*slang*), hogwash, hokum (*slang, chiefly U.S. & Canad.*), horsefeathers (*U.S. slang*), hot air (*informal*), jabber, jargon, moonshine, mumbo jumbo, pap, piffle (*informal*), poppycock (*informal*), prattle, shit (*taboo slang*), tommyrot, tosh (*slang, chiefly Brit.*), tripe (*informal*), twaddle, yammer (*informal*)

gibe, jibe *noun* **1** = **taunt**, barb, crack (*slang*), cutting remark, derision, dig, jeer, mockery, ridicule, sarcasm, scoffing, sneer
♦ *verb* **2** = **taunt**, deride, flout, jeer, make fun of, mock, poke fun at, ridicule, scoff, scorn, sneer, take the piss out of (*slang*), twit

giddiness *noun* = **dizziness**, faintness,

light-headedness, vertigo

giddy *adjective* **1** = **dizzy**, dizzying, faint, light-headed, reeling, unsteady, vertiginous **2** = **scatterbrained**, capricious, careless, changeable, changeful, ditzy *or* ditsy (*slang*), dizzy, erratic, fickle, flighty, frivolous, heedless, impulsive, inconstant, irresolute, irresponsible, reckless, silly, thoughtless, unbalanced, unstable, unsteady, vacillating, volatile, wild
➤ **Antonyms**
≠**scatterbrained**: calm, constant, determined, earnest, resolute, serious, steady

gift *noun* **1** = **donation**, benefaction, bequest, bonus, boon, bounty, contribution, grant, gratuity, hand-out, largesse *or* largess, legacy, offering, present **2** = **talent**, ability, aptitude, attribute, bent, capability, capacity, endowment, faculty, flair, genius, knack, power, turn

gifted *adjective* = **talented**, able, accomplished, adroit, brilliant, capable, clever, expert, ingenious, intelligent, masterly, skilled
➤ **Antonyms**
amateur, backward, dull, incapable, inept, retarded, slow, talentless, unskilled

gigantic *adjective* = **enormous**, Brobdingnagian, colossal, Cyclopean, elephantine, gargantuan, giant, herculean, huge, humongous *or* humungous (*U.S. slang*), immense, mammoth, monstrous, prodigious, stellar (*informal*), stupendous, titanic, tremendous, vast
➤ **Antonyms**
diminutive, insignificant, little, miniature, puny, small, tiny, weak

giggle *verb, noun* = **laugh**, cackle, chortle, chuckle, snigger, tee-hee, titter, twitter

gild *verb* = **embellish**, adorn, beautify, bedeck, brighten, coat, deck, dress up, embroider, enhance, enrich, garnish, grace, ornament

gimmick *noun* = **stunt**, contrivance, device, dodge, gadget, gambit, gizmo (*slang, chiefly U.S.*), ploy, scheme, stratagem, trick

gingerly *adverb* **1** = **cautiously**, carefully, charily, circumspectly, daintily, delicately, fastidiously, hesitantly, reluctantly, squeamishly, suspiciously, timidly, warily
♦ *adjective* **2** = **cautious**, careful, chary, circumspect, dainty, delicate, fastidious, hesitant, reluctant, squeamish, suspicious, timid, wary
➤ **Antonyms**
adverb ≠**cautiously**: boldly, carelessly, confidently, rashly

gird *verb* **1** = **girdle**, belt, bind **2** = **surround**, blockade, encircle, enclose, encompass, enfold, engird, environ, hem in, pen, ring **3** *As in* **gird up one's loins** = **prepare**, brace, fortify, make ready, ready, steel

girdle *noun* **1** = **belt**, band, cincture, cummerbund, fillet, sash, waistband
♦ *verb* **2** = **surround**, bind, bound, encircle, enclose, encompass, engird, environ, enwreath, gird, hem, ring

girl *noun* = **female child**, bird (*slang*), chick (*slang*), colleen (*Irish*), damsel (*archaic*), daughter, lass, lassie (*informal*), maid (*archaic*), maiden (*archaic*), miss, wench

girth *noun* = **circumference**, bulk, measure, size

gist *noun* = **point**, core, drift, essence, force, idea, import, marrow, meaning, nub, pith, quintessence, sense, significance, substance

give *verb* **1** = **present**, accord, administer, allow, award, bestow, commit, confer, consign, contribute, deliver, donate, entrust, furnish, grant, hand over *or* out, make over, permit, provide, purvey, supply, vouchsafe **2** = **announce**, be a source of, communicate, emit, impart, issue, notify, pronounce, publish, render, transmit, utter **3** = **produce**, cause, do, engender, lead, make, occasion, perform **4** = **surrender**, cede, devote, hand over, lend, relinquish, yield **5** = **concede**, allow, grant **6** = **break**, bend, collapse, fall, recede, retire, sink **7** = **demonstrate**, display, evidence, indicate, manifest, offer, proffer, provide, set forth, show
➤ **Antonyms**
≠**present**: accept, get, hold, keep, receive, take, withdraw

give away *verb* = **reveal**, betray, disclose, divulge, expose, grass (*Brit. slang*), grass up (*slang*), inform on, leak, let out, let slip, let the cat out of the bag (*informal*), put the finger on (*informal*), shop (*slang, chiefly Brit.*), uncover

give in *verb* = **admit defeat**, capitulate, cave in (*informal*), collapse, comply, concede, quit, submit, succumb, surrender, yield

given *adjective* = **inclined**, addicted, apt, disposed, liable, likely, prone

give off *verb* = **emit**, discharge, exhale, exude, produce, release, send out, throw out, vent

give out *verb* **1** = **emit**, discharge, exhale, exude, produce, release, send out, throw out, vent **2** = **make known**, announce, broadcast, communicate, disseminate, impart, notify, publish, shout from the rooftops (*informal*), transmit, utter

give up *verb* = **abandon**, call it a day *or* night, capitulate, cave in (*informal*), cease, cede, cut out, desist, despair, fall by the wayside, forswear, hand over, kick (*informal*), kiss (something) goodbye, leave off, quit, relinquish, renounce, resign, say goodbye to, step down (*informal*), stop, surrender, throw in the sponge, throw in the towel, waive

glacial *adjective* **1** = **icy**, arctic, biting, bitter, chill, chilly, cold, freezing, frigid, frosty, frozen, gelid, piercing, polar, raw, wintry **2** = **unfriendly**, antagonistic, cold, frigid, hostile, icy, inimical

glad *adjective* **1** = **happy**, blithesome (*literary*), cheerful, chuffed (*slang*), contented, delighted, gay, gleeful, gratified, jocund, jovial, joyful, overjoyed, pleased, willing **2** *Archaic* = **pleasing**, animated, cheerful, cheering, cheery, delightful, felicitous, gratifying, joyous, merry, pleasant
➤ **Antonyms**
≠**happy**: depressed, discontented, displeased, melancholy, miserable, sad, sorrowful, unhappy

gladden *verb* = **please**, cheer, delight, elate, enliven, exhilarate, gratify, hearten, rejoice

gladly *adverb* = **happily**, cheerfully, freely, gaily, gleefully, jovially, joyfully, joyously, lief (*rare*), merrily, readily, willingly, with (a) good grace, with pleasure
➤ **Antonyms**
dolefully, grudgingly, reluctantly, sadly, unenthusiastically, unwillingly

gladness *noun* = **happiness**, animation, blitheness, cheerfulness, delight, felicity, gaiety, glee, high spirits, hilarity, jollity, joy, joyousness, mirth, pleasure

glamorous *adjective* = **elegant**, alluring, attractive, beautiful, bewitching, captivating, charming, dazzling, enchanting, entrancing, exciting, fascinating, glittering, glitzy (*slang*), glossy, lovely, prestigious, smart
➤ **Antonyms**
colourless, dull, plain, unattractive, unexciting, unglamorous

glamour *noun* = **charm**, allure, appeal, attraction, beauty, bewitchment, enchantment, fascination, magnetism, prestige, ravishment, witchery

glance *noun* **1** = **peek**, brief look, butcher's (*Brit. slang*), dekko (*slang*), gander (*informal*), glimpse, look, peep, quick look, shufti (*Brit. slang*), squint, view **2** = **gleam**, flash, glimmer, glint, reflection, sparkle, twinkle **3** = **allusion**, passing mention,

reference ♦ *verb* **4** = **peek**, check, check out (*informal*), clock (*Brit. informal*), gaze, glimpse, look, peep, scan, take a dekko at (*Brit. slang*), view **5** = **gleam**, flash, glimmer, glint, glisten, glitter, reflect, shimmer, shine, twinkle **6** = **graze**, bounce, brush, rebound, ricochet, skim **7** with **over, through,** *etc.* = **scan**, browse, dip into, flip through, leaf through, riffle through, run over *or* through, skim through, thumb through
➤ **Antonyms**
noun ≠**peek**: examination, good look, inspection, perusal ♦ *verb* ≠**peek**: peruse, scrutinize, study

glare *verb* **1** = **scowl**, frown, give a dirty look, glower, look daggers, lour *or* lower, stare angrily **2** = **dazzle**, blaze, flame, flare ♦ *noun* **3** = **scowl**, angry stare, black look, dirty look, frown, glower, lour *or* lower **4** = **dazzle**, blaze, brilliance, flame, flare, glow

glaring *adjective* **1** = **conspicuous**, audacious, blatant, egregious, flagrant, gross, manifest, obvious, open, outrageous, outstanding, overt, patent, rank, unconcealed, visible **2** = **dazzling**, blazing, bright, flashy, florid, garish, glowing, loud
➤ **Antonyms**
≠**conspicuous**: concealed, hidden, inconspicuous, obscure ≠**dazzling**: soft, subdued, subtle

glassy *adjective* **1** = **transparent**, clear, glossy, icy, shiny, slick, slippery, smooth **2** = **expressionless**, blank, cold, dazed, dull, empty, fixed, glazed, lifeless, vacant

glaze *verb* **1** = **coat**, burnish, enamel, furbish, gloss, lacquer, polish, varnish ♦ *noun* **2** = **coat**, enamel, finish, gloss, lacquer, lustre, patina, polish, shine, varnish

gleam *noun* **1** = **glow**, beam, flash, glimmer, ray, sparkle **2** = **trace**, flicker, glimmer, hint, inkling, ray, suggestion **3** = **brightness**, brilliance, coruscation, flash, gloss, lustre, sheen, splendour ♦ *verb* **4** = **shine**, coruscate, flare, flash, glance, glimmer, glint, glisten, glitter, glow, scintillate, shimmer, sparkle

glee *noun* = **delight**, cheerfulness, elation, exhilaration, exuberance, exultation, fun, gaiety, gladness, hilarity, jocularity, jollity, joviality, joy, joyfulness, joyousness, liveliness, merriment, mirth, sprightliness, triumph, verve
➤ **Antonyms**
depression, gloom, melancholy, misery, sadness

gleeful *adjective* = **delighted**, cheerful,

chirpy (*informal*), cock-a-hoop, elated, exuberant, exultant, gay, gratified, happy, jocund, jovial, joyful, joyous, jubilant, merry, mirthful, overjoyed, over the moon (*informal*), pleased, rapt, triumphant

glib *adjective* = **smooth**, artful, easy, fast-talking, fluent, garrulous, insincere, plausible, quick, ready, slick, slippery, smooth-tongued, suave, talkative, voluble
➤ **Antonyms**
halting, hesitant, implausible, sincere, tongue-tied

glide *verb* = **slide**, coast, drift, float, flow, fly, roll, run, sail, skate, skim, slip, soar

glimmer *verb* 1 = **flicker**, blink, gleam, glisten, glitter, glow, shimmer, shine, sparkle, twinkle ♦ *noun* 2 = **trace**, flicker, gleam, grain, hint, inkling, ray, suggestion 3 = **gleam**, blink, flicker, glow, ray, shimmer, sparkle, twinkle

glimpse *noun* 1 = **look**, brief view, butcher's (*Brit. slang*), gander (*informal*), glance, peek, peep, quick look, shufti (*Brit. slang*), sight, sighting, squint ♦ *verb* 2 = **catch sight of**, clock (*Brit. informal*), descry, espy, sight, spot, spy, view

glint *verb* 1 = **gleam**, flash, glimmer, glitter, shine, sparkle, twinkle ♦ *noun* 2 = **gleam**, flash, glimmer, glitter, shine, sparkle, twinkle, twinkling

glisten *verb* = **gleam**, coruscate, flash, glance, glare, glimmer, glint, glitter, scintillate, shimmer, shine, sparkle, twinkle

glitch *noun* = **problem**, blip, bug (*informal*), difficulty, fault, flaw, fly in the ointment, gremlin, hitch, interruption, kink, malfunction, snag

glitter *verb* 1 = **shine**, coruscate, flare, flash, glare, gleam, glimmer, glint, glisten, scintillate, shimmer, sparkle, twinkle ♦ *noun* 2 = **shine**, beam, brightness, brilliance, flash, glare, gleam, lustre, radiance, scintillation, sheen, shimmer, sparkle 3 = **glamour**, display, gaudiness, gilt, pageantry, show, showiness, splendour, tinsel

gloat *verb* = **relish**, crow, drool, exult, glory, revel in, rub it in (*informal*), rub one's hands, rub someone's nose in it, triumph, vaunt

global *adjective* 1 = **worldwide**, international, pandemic, planetary, universal, world 2 = **comprehensive**, all-encompassing, all-inclusive, all-out, encyclopedic, exhaustive, general, thorough, total, unbounded, unlimited
➤ **Antonyms**
≠**comprehensive**: limited, narrow, parochial, restricted, sectional

globe *noun* = **sphere**, ball, earth, orb, planet, round, world

globule *noun* = **droplet**, bead, bubble, drop, particle, pearl, pellet

gloom *noun* 1 = **depression**, blues, dejection, desolation, despair, despondency, downheartedness, low spirits, melancholy, misery, sadness, sorrow, the hump (*Brit. informal*), unhappiness, woe 2 = **darkness**, blackness, cloud, cloudiness, dark, dimness, dullness, dusk, duskiness, gloominess, murk, murkiness, obscurity, shade, shadow, twilight
➤ **Antonyms**
≠**depression**: brightness, cheerfulness, delight, happiness, high spirits, jollity, joy, mirth ≠**darkness**: daylight, light, radiance

gloomy *adjective* 1 = **miserable**, blue, chapfallen, cheerless, crestfallen, dejected, despondent, dismal, dispirited, down, downcast, downhearted, down in the dumps (*informal*), down in the mouth, glum, in low spirits, low, melancholy, moody, morose, pessimistic, sad, saturnine, sullen 2 = **depressing**, bad, black, cheerless, comfortless, disheartening, dismal, dispiriting, dreary, funereal, joyless, sad, saddening, sombre 3 = **dark**, black, crepuscular, dim, dismal, dreary, dull, dusky, grey, murky, obscure, overcast, shadowy, sombre, Stygian, tenebrous
➤ **Antonyms**
≠**miserable**: blithe, bright, cheerful, chirpy (*informal*), happy, high-spirited, jolly, jovial, light, merry, upbeat (*informal*) ≠**dark**: brilliant, light, radiant, sunny

glorify *verb* 1 = **enhance**, add lustre to, adorn, aggrandize, augment, dignify, elevate, ennoble, illuminate, immortalize, lift up, magnify, raise 2 = **praise**, celebrate, crack up (*informal*), cry up (*informal*), eulogize, extol, hymn, laud, lionize, magnify, panegyrize, sing *or* sound the praises of 3 = **worship**, adore, apotheosize, beatify, bless, canonize, deify, enshrine, exalt, honour, idolize, pay homage to, revere, sanctify, venerate
➤ **Antonyms**
≠**enhance**: debase, defile, degrade ≠**praise**: condemn, humiliate, mock ≠**worship**: desecrate, dishonour

glorious *adjective* 1 = **splendid**, beautiful, bright, brilliant, dazzling, divine, effulgent, gorgeous, radiant, resplendent, shining, splendiferous (*facetious*), superb 2 = **delightful**, enjoyable, excellent, fine, gorgeous, great, heavenly (*informal*), marvellous, pleasurable, splendid,

splendiferous (*facetious*), wonderful **3**
= **famous**, celebrated, distinguished,
elevated, eminent, excellent, famed,
grand, honoured, illustrious, magnificent,
majestic, noble, noted, renowned,
sublime, triumphant
➤ **Antonyms**
≠**splendid**, **delightful**: awful, dreary, dull,
gloomy, horrible, unimpressive,
unpleasant ≠**famous**: minor, ordinary,
trivial, unimportant, unknown

glory *noun* **1** = **honour**, celebrity, dignity,
distinction, eminence, exaltation, fame,
illustriousness, immortality, kudos, praise,
prestige, renown **2** = **splendour**, éclat,
grandeur, greatness, magnificence,
majesty, nobility, pageantry, pomp,
sublimity, triumph **3** = **worship**, adoration,
benediction, blessing, gratitude, homage,
laudation, praise, thanksgiving, veneration
4 = **beauty**, brilliance, effulgence,
gorgeousness, lustre, radiance,
resplendence ♦ *verb* **5** = **triumph**, boast,
crow, drool, exult, gloat, pride oneself,
relish, revel, take delight
➤ **Antonyms**
noun ≠**honour**: condemnation, disgrace,
dishonour, disrepute, infamy, shame
≠**splendour**: triviality ≠**worship**:
blasphemy ≠**beauty**: ugliness

gloss[1] *noun* **1** = **shine**, brightness,
brilliance, burnish, gleam, lustre, patina,
polish, sheen, varnish, veneer **2** = **façade**,
appearance, front, mask, semblance,
show, surface ♦ *verb* **3** = **glaze**, burnish,
finish, furbish, lacquer, polish, shine,
varnish, veneer **4 gloss over** = **conceal**,
camouflage, cover up, disguise, hide,
mask, smooth over, sweep under the
carpet (*informal*), veil, whitewash (*informal*)

gloss[2] *noun* **1** = **comment**, annotation,
commentary, elucidation, explanation,
footnote, interpretation, note, scholium,
translation ♦ *verb* **2** = **interpret**, annotate,
comment, construe, elucidate, explain,
translate

glossy *adjective* = **shiny**, bright, brilliant,
burnished, glassy, glazed, lustrous,
polished, sheeny, shining, silken, silky,
sleek, smooth
➤ **Antonyms**
drab, dull, mat *or* matt, subfusc

glow *noun* **1** = **light**, burning, gleam,
glimmer, incandescence, lambency,
luminosity, phosphorescence **2** = **radiance**,
brightness, brilliance, effulgence,
splendour, vividness **3** = **blush**, bloom,
flush, reddening, rosiness **4** = **passion**,
ardour, earnestness, enthusiasm,
excitement, fervour, gusto, impetuosity,

intensity, vehemence, warmth ♦ *verb* **5**
= **shine**, brighten, burn, gleam, glimmer,
redden, smoulder **6** = **blush**, be suffused,
colour, fill, flush, radiate, thrill, tingle
➤ **Antonyms**
noun ≠**radiance**: dullness, greyness
≠**blush**: paleness, pallor, wanness
≠**passion**: chill, coolness, half-heartedness,
iciness, indifference

glower *verb* **1** = **scowl**, frown, give a dirty
look, glare, look daggers, lour *or* lower
♦ *noun* **2** = **scowl**, angry stare, black look,
dirty look, frown, glare, lour *or* lower

glowing *adjective* **1** = **bright**, aglow,
beaming, flaming, florid, flushed, lambent,
luminous, radiant, red, rich, ruddy,
suffused, vibrant, vivid, warm **2**
= **complimentary**, adulatory, ecstatic,
enthusiastic, eulogistic, laudatory,
panegyrical, rave (*informal*), rhapsodic
➤ **Antonyms**
≠**bright**: colourless, cool, dull, grey, pale,
pallid, wan ≠**complimentary**: cruel,
dispassionate, scathing, unenthusiastic

glue *noun* **1** = **adhesive**, cement, gum,
mucilage, paste ♦ *verb* **2** = **stick**, affix,
agglutinate, cement, fix, gum, paste, seal

glum *adjective* = **gloomy**, chapfallen,
churlish, crabbed, crestfallen, crusty,
dejected, doleful, down, gruff, grumpy,
huffy, ill-humoured, low, moody, morose,
pessimistic, saturnine, sour, sulky, sullen,
surly
➤ **Antonyms**
cheerful, cheery, chirpy (*informal*), jolly,
joyful, merry, upbeat (*informal*)

glut *noun* **1** = **surfeit**, excess,
overabundance, oversupply, plethora,
saturation, superabundance, superfluity,
surplus ♦ *verb* **2** = **saturate**, choke, clog,
deluge, flood, inundate, overload,
oversupply **3** = **overfeed**, cram, fill, gorge,
satiate, stuff
➤ **Antonyms**
noun ≠**surfeit**: dearth, lack, paucity,
scarcity, shortage, want

glutinous *adjective* = **sticky**, adhesive,
cohesive, gluey, gooey, gummy,
mucilaginous, viscid, viscous

glutton *noun* = **gourmand**, gannet (*slang*),
gobbler, gorger, gormandizer, pig
(*informal*)

gluttonous *adjective* = **greedy**,
gormandizing, insatiable, piggish,
ravenous, voracious

gluttony *noun* = **greed**, edacity,
gormandizing, gourmandism, greediness,
piggishness, rapacity, voraciousness,
voracity

gnarled *adjective* = **twisted**, contorted,

knotted, knotty, knurled, leathery, rough, rugged, weather-beaten, wrinkled

gnaw verb 1 = **bite**, chew, munch, nibble, worry 2 = **distress**, fret, harry, haunt, nag, plague, prey on one's mind, trouble, worry 3 = **erode**, consume, devour, eat away or into, fret, wear away or down

go verb 1 = **move**, advance, fare (archaic), journey, make for, pass, proceed, repair, set off, travel 2 = **leave**, decamp, depart, make tracks, move out, slope off, withdraw 3 = **lead**, connect, extend, fit, give access, reach, run, span, spread, stretch 4 = **function**, move, operate, perform, run, work 5 = **fare**, develop, eventuate, fall out, happen, pan out (informal), proceed, result, turn out, work out 6 = **die**, buy it (U.S. slang), check out (U.S. slang), croak (slang), expire, give up the ghost, go belly-up (slang), kick it (slang), kick the bucket (slang), pass away, peg it (informal), peg out (informal), perish, pop one's clogs (informal), snuff it (informal) 7 = **elapse**, expire, flow, lapse, pass, slip away 8 = **contribute**, avail, concur, conduce, incline, lead to, serve, tend, work towards 9 = **harmonize**, accord, agree, blend, chime, complement, correspond, fit, match, suit ♦ noun 10 = **attempt**, bid, crack (informal), effort, essay, shot (informal), stab (informal), try, turn, whack (informal), whirl (informal) 11 Informal = **energy**, activity, animation, brio, drive, force, get-up-and-go (informal), life, oomph (informal), pep, spirit, verve, vigour, vitality, vivacity
➤ **Antonyms**
verb ≠**move**: arrive, halt, reach, remain, stay, stop ≠**function**: break (down), fail, malfunction, stop

go about verb 1 = **move around**, circulate, pass around, wander 2 = **tackle**, approach, begin, get the show on the road, set about, take the bit between one's teeth, undertake 3 = **busy** or **occupy oneself with**, devote oneself to

goad verb 1 = **provoke**, annoy, arouse, be on one's back (slang), drive, egg on, exhort, harass, hassle (informal), hound, impel, incite, instigate, irritate, lash, nark (Brit., Austral., & N.Z. slang), prick, prod, prompt, propel, spur, stimulate, sting, urge, worry ♦ noun 2 = **provocation**, impetus, incentive, incitement, irritation, motivation, pressure, spur, stimulation, stimulus, urge

go-ahead noun 1 Informal = **permission**, assent, authorization, consent, green light, leave, O.K. or okay (informal) ♦ adjective 2 = **enterprising**, ambitious, go-getting

(informal), pioneering, progressive, up-and-coming

go ahead verb = **advance**, begin, continue, go forward, go on, proceed, progress

goal noun = **aim**, ambition, design, destination, end, Holy Grail (informal), intention, limit, mark, object, objective, purpose, target

go along verb 1 = **accompany**, carry on, escort, join, keep up, move, pass, travel 2 = **agree**, acquiesce, assent, concur, cooperate, follow

go away verb = **leave**, decamp, depart, exit, get on one's bike (Brit. slang), go to hell (informal), hook it (slang), make tracks, move out, pack one's bags (informal), recede, sling one's hook (Brit. slang), slope off, withdraw

go back verb = **return**, retrocede, revert

go back on verb = **repudiate**, change one's mind about, desert, forsake, renege on, retract

gobble verb = **devour**, bolt, cram, gorge, gulp, guzzle, pig out on (U.S. & Canad. slang), stuff, swallow, wolf

gobbledegook noun = **nonsense**, babble, cant, gabble, gibberish, hocus-pocus, jargon, mumbo jumbo, twaddle

go-between noun = **intermediary**, agent, broker, dealer, factor, liaison, mediator, medium, middleman

go by verb 1 = **pass**, elapse, exceed, flow on, move onward, proceed 2 = **follow**, adopt, be guided by, heed, judge from, observe, take as guide

godforsaken adjective = **desolate**, abandoned, backward, bleak, deserted, dismal, dreary, forlorn, gloomy, lonely, neglected, remote, wretched

godless adjective 1 = **wicked**, depraved, evil, impious, unprincipled, unrighteous 2 = **profane**, atheistic, irreligious, ungodly

godlike adjective = **divine**, celestial, deific, deiform, heavenly, superhuman, transcendent

godly adjective = **devout**, god-fearing, good, holy, pious, religious, righteous, saintly

go down verb 1 = **fall**, be beaten, collapse, decline, decrease, drop, founder, go under, lose, set, sink, submerge, submit, suffer defeat 2 = **be recorded**, be commemorated, be recalled, be remembered

godsend noun = **blessing**, boon, manna, stroke of luck, windfall

go far verb = **be successful**, advance, cut it (informal), do well, get ahead (informal), get on (*informal*), make a name for oneself, make one's mark, progress, succeed

go for *verb* **1** = **favour**, admire, be attracted to, be fond of, choose, hold with, like, prefer **2** = **attack**, assail, assault, launch oneself at, rush upon, set about *or* upon, spring upon **3** = **seek**, clutch at, fetch, obtain, reach, stretch for

go in for *verb* = **enter**, adopt, embrace, engage in, espouse, practise, pursue, take up, undertake

go into *verb* **1** = **enter**, begin, develop, participate in, undertake **2** = **investigate**, analyse, consider, delve into, discuss, examine, inquire into, look into, probe, pursue, research, review, scrutinize, study, work over

golden *adjective* **1** = **yellow**, blond *or* blonde, bright, brilliant, flaxen, resplendent, shining **2** = **successful**, best, blissful, delightful, flourishing, glorious, halcyon, happy, joyful, joyous, precious, prosperous, rich **3** = **promising**, advantageous, auspicious, excellent, favourable, opportune, propitious, rosy, valuable
➤ **Antonyms**
≠**yellow**: black, brunette, dark, dull ≠**successful**: poorest, sad, unfavourable, worst ≠**promising**: black, dark, sad, unfavourable, untimely, wretched

gone *adjective* **1** = **used up**, consumed, done, finished, spent **2** = **past**, elapsed, ended, finished, over **3** = **missing**, absent, astray, away, lacking, lost, vanished **4** = **dead**, deceased, defunct, departed, extinct, no more

good *adjective* **1** = **excellent**, acceptable, admirable, agreeable, awesome (*slang*), bad (*slang*), bitchin' (*U.S. slang*), capital, choice, commendable, crucial (*slang*), divine, dope (*slang*), fine, first-class, first-rate, great, hunky-dory (*informal*), pleasant, pleasing, positive, precious, satisfactory, splendid, super (*informal*), superior, tiptop, valuable, wicked (*slang*), world-class, worthy **2** = **honourable**, admirable, estimable, ethical, exemplary, honest, moral, praiseworthy, right, righteous, trustworthy, upright, virtuous, worthy **3** = **favourable**, adequate, advantageous, auspicious, beneficial, convenient, fit, fitting, healthy, helpful, opportune, profitable, propitious, salubrious, salutary, suitable, useful, wholesome **4** = **kind**, altruistic, approving, beneficent, benevolent, charitable, friendly, gracious, humane, kind-hearted, kindly, merciful, obliging, well-disposed **5**

= **expert**, able, accomplished, adept, adroit, capable, clever, competent, dexterous, efficient, first-rate, proficient, reliable, satisfactory, serviceable, skilled, sound, suitable, talented, thorough, useful **6** = **well-behaved**, decorous, dutiful, mannerly, obedient, orderly, polite, proper, seemly, well-mannered **7** = **valid**, authentic, bona fide, dependable, genuine, honest, legitimate, proper, real, reliable, sound, true, trustworthy **8** = **full**, adequate, ample, complete, considerable, entire, extensive, large, long, sizable *or* sizeable, solid, substantial, sufficient, whole **9** = **enjoyable**, agreeable, cheerful, congenial, convivial, gratifying, happy, pleasant, pleasing, pleasurable, satisfying **10** = **best**, fancy, finest, newest, nicest, precious, smartest, special, valuable **11** *Of weather* = **sunny**, balmy, bright, calm, clear, clement, cloudless, fair, halcyon, mild, sunshiny, tranquil **12** = **eatable**, fit to eat, sound, uncorrupted, untainted, whole ♦ *noun* **13** = **benefit**, advantage, avail, behalf, gain, interest, mileage (*informal*), profit, service, use, usefulness, welfare, wellbeing, worth **14** = **virtue**, excellence, goodness, merit, morality, probity, rectitude, right, righteousness, uprightness, worth **15 for good** = **permanently**, finally, for ever, irrevocably, never to return, once and for all, *sine die*
➤ **Antonyms**
adjective ≠**excellent**: awful, bad, boring, disagreeable, dull, inadequate, rotten, tedious, unpleasant ≠**honourable**: bad, base, corrupt, dishonest, dishonourable, evil, immoral, improper, sinful ≠**favourable**: inappropriate, pathetic, unbecoming, unbefitting, unfavourable, unfitting, unsuitable, useless ≠**kind**: cruel, evil, mean (*informal*), selfish, unkind, vicious, wicked ≠**expert**: bad, incompetent, inefficient, unsatisfactory, unskilled ≠**well-behaved**: ill-mannered, mischievous, naughty, rude ≠**valid**: counterfeit, false, fraudulent, invalid, phoney ≠**full**: scant, short ≠**eatable**: bad, decayed, mouldy, off, rotten, unsound ♦ *noun* ≠**benefit**: detriment, disadvantage, failure, ill-fortune, loss ≠**virtue**: badness, baseness, corruption, cruelty, dishonesty, evil, immorality, meanness, wickedness

goodbye *noun* = **farewell**, adieu, leave-taking, parting

good-for-nothing *noun* **1** = **layabout**, black sheep, idler, ne'er-do-well, numb-nut (*U.S. slang*), profligate, rapscallion, scapegrace, skiver (*Brit. slang*),

slacker (*informal*), waster, wastrel
♦ *adjective* **2** = **worthless**, feckless, idle, irresponsible, useless

good-humoured *adjective* = **cheerful**, affable, amiable, congenial, genial, good-tempered, happy, pleasant

good-looking *adjective* = **attractive**, comely, fair, handsome, personable, pretty, well-favoured

goodly *adjective* **1** = **considerable**, ample, large, significant, sizable *or* sizeable, substantial, tidy (*informal*) **2** = **attractive**, agreeable, comely, desirable, elegant, fine, good-looking, graceful, handsome, personable, pleasant, pleasing, well-favoured

good-natured *adjective* = **kindly**, agreeable, amiable, benevolent, friendly, good-hearted, helpful, kind, tolerant, warm-hearted, well-disposed, willing to please

goodness *noun* **1** = **excellence**, merit, quality, superiority, value, worth **2** = **virtue**, honesty, honour, integrity, merit, morality, probity, rectitude, righteousness, uprightness **3** = **benefit**, advantage, nourishment, nutrition, salubriousness, wholesomeness **4** = **kindness**, beneficence, benevolence, friendliness, generosity, goodwill, graciousness, humaneness, kind-heartedness, kindliness, mercy, obligingness
➤ **Antonyms**
≠**virtue**: badness, corruption, dishonesty, evil, immorality, wickedness, worthlessness ≠**benefit**: detriment, disadvantage

goods *plural noun* **1** = **merchandise**, commodities, stock, stuff, wares **2** = **property**, appurtenances, belongings, chattels, effects, furnishings, furniture, gear, movables, paraphernalia, possessions, things, trappings

goodwill *noun* = **friendliness**, amity, benevolence, favour, friendship, heartiness, kindliness, zeal

go off *verb* **1** = **leave**, decamp, depart, go away, hook it (*slang*), move out, pack one's bags (*informal*), part, quit, slope off **2** = **explode**, blow up, detonate, fire **3** = **happen**, occur, take place **4** *Informal* = **rot**, go bad, go stale

go on *verb* **1** = **continue**, endure, happen, last, occur, persist, proceed, stay **2** = **chatter**, blether, carry on, prattle, rabbit (*Brit. informal*), ramble on, waffle (*informal, chiefly Brit.*), witter (on) (*informal*)

go out *verb* **1** = **leave**, depart, exit **2** = **be extinguished**, die out, expire, fade out

go over *verb* **1** = **examine**, inspect,

rehearse, reiterate, review, revise, study, work over **2** = **scan**, peruse, read, skim

gore[1] *noun* = **blood**, bloodshed, butchery, carnage, slaughter

gore[2] *verb* = **pierce**, impale, spit, stab, transfix, wound

gorge *noun* **1** = **ravine**, canyon, chasm, cleft, clough (*dialect*), defile, fissure, pass ♦ *verb* **2** = **overeat**, bolt, cram, devour, feed, fill, glut, gobble, gormandize, gulp, guzzle, pig out (*U.S. & Canad. slang*), raven, sate, satiate, stuff, surfeit, swallow, wolf

gorgeous *adjective* **1** = **beautiful**, brilliant, dazzling, drop-dead (*slang*), elegant, glittering, grand, luxuriant, magnificent, opulent, ravishing, resplendent, showy, splendid, splendiferous (*facetious*), stunning (*informal*), sumptuous, superb **2** *Informal* = **pleasing**, attractive, bright, delightful, enjoyable, exquisite, fine, glorious, good, good-looking, lovely
➤ **Antonyms**
cheap, dismal, dreary, dull, gloomy, homely, plain, repulsive, shabby, shoddy, sombre, ugly, unattractive, unsightly

gory *adjective* = **bloodthirsty**, blood-soaked, bloodstained, bloody, ensanguined (*literary*), murderous, sanguinary

gospel *noun* **1** = **doctrine**, credo, creed, message, news, revelation, tidings **2** = **truth**, certainty, fact, the last word, verity

gossamer *adjective* = **delicate**, airy, diaphanous, fine, flimsy, gauzy, light, sheer, silky, thin, transparent

gossip *noun* **1** = **idle talk**, blether, bush telegraph, buzz, chinwag (*Brit. informal*), chitchat, clishmaclaver (*Scot.*), dirt (*U.S. slang*), gen (*Brit. informal*), hearsay, jaw (*slang*), latest (*informal*), newsmongering (*old-fashioned*), prattle, scandal, scuttlebutt (*U.S. slang*), small talk, tittle-tattle **2** = **busybody**, babbler, blatherskite, blether, chatterbox (*informal*), chatterer, flibbertigibbet, gossipmonger, newsmonger (*old-fashioned*), prattler, quidnunc, scandalmonger, tattler, telltale ♦ *verb* **3** = **chat**, blather, blether, chew the fat *or* rag (*slang*), dish the dirt (*informal*), gabble, jaw (*slang*), prate, prattle, schmooze (*slang*), shoot the breeze (*slang, chiefly U.S.*), tattle

go through *verb* **1** = **suffer**, bear, brave, endure, experience, tolerate, undergo, withstand **2** = **examine**, check, explore, forage, hunt, look, search, work over **3** = **use up**, consume, exhaust, squander

gouge *verb* **1** = **scoop**, chisel, claw, cut, dig

(out), hollow (out) ♦ *noun* **2 = gash**, cut, furrow, groove, hollow, scoop, scratch, trench

go under *verb* **= sink**, default, die, drown, fail, fold (*informal*), founder, go down, submerge, succumb

gourmet *noun* **= connoisseur**, *bon vivant*, epicure, foodie (*informal*), gastronome

govern *verb* **1 = rule**, administer, be in power, call the shots, call the tune, command, conduct, control, direct, guide, handle, hold sway, lead, manage, order, oversee, pilot, reign, steer, superintend, supervise **2 = determine**, decide, guide, influence, rule, sway, underlie **3 = restrain**, bridle, check, contain, control, curb, direct, discipline, get the better of, hold in check, inhibit, keep a tight rein on, master, regulate, subdue, tame

government *noun* **1 = executive**, administration, ministry, powers-that-be, regime **2 = rule**, administration, authority, dominion, execution, governance, law, polity, sovereignty, state, statecraft **3 = guidance**, authority, command, control, direction, domination, management, regulation, restraint, superintendence, supervision, sway

governor *noun* **= leader**, administrator, boss (*informal*), chief, commander, comptroller, controller, director, executive, head, manager, overseer, ruler, superintendent, supervisor

go with *verb* **= match**, agree, blend, complement, concur, correspond, fit, harmonize, suit

go without *verb* **= be deprived of**, abstain, be denied, deny oneself, do without, go short, lack, want

gown *noun* **= dress**, costume, frock, garb, garment, habit, robe

grab *verb* **= snatch**, bag, capture, catch, catch *or* take hold of, clutch, grasp, grip, latch on to, nab (*informal*), nail (*informal*), pluck, seize, snap up

grace *noun* **1 = elegance**, attractiveness, beauty, charm, comeliness, ease, finesse, gracefulness, loveliness, pleasantness, poise, polish, refinement, shapeliness, tastefulness **2 = manners**, breeding, consideration, cultivation, decency, decorum, etiquette, mannerliness, propriety, tact **3 = indulgence**, charity, clemency, compassion, forgiveness, leniency, lenity, mercy, pardon, quarter, reprieve **4 = goodwill**, benefaction, beneficence, benevolence, favour, generosity, goodness, kindliness, kindness **5 = prayer**, benediction, blessing, thanks, thanksgiving ♦ *verb* **6 = honour**, adorn,

beautify, bedeck, deck, decorate, dignify, distinguish, elevate, embellish, enhance, enrich, favour, garnish, glorify, ornament, set off

➤ **Antonyms**
noun ≠**elegance**: awkwardness, clumsiness, inelegance, stiffness, tastelessness, ugliness, ungainliness ≠**manners**: bad manners, tactlessness ≠**goodwill**: disfavour, ill will ♦ *verb* ≠**honour**: desecrate, dishonour, insult, ruin, spoil

graceful *adjective* **= elegant**, agile, beautiful, becoming, charming, comely, easy, fine, flowing, gracile (*rare*), natural, pleasing, smooth, symmetrical, tasteful

➤ **Antonyms**
awkward, clumsy, gawky, inelegant, plain, ponderous, stiff, ugly, ungainly, ungraceful

gracious *adjective* **= kind**, accommodating, affable, amiable, beneficent, benevolent, benign, benignant, charitable, chivalrous, civil, compassionate, considerate, cordial, courteous, courtly, friendly, hospitable, indulgent, kindly, lenient, loving, merciful, mild, obliging, pleasing, polite, well-mannered

➤ **Antonyms**
brusque, cold, discourteous, gruff, haughty, impolite, mean, remote, rude, surly, unfriendly, ungracious, unpleasant

grade *noun* **1 = level**, brand, category, class, condition, degree, echelon, group, mark, notch, order, place, position, quality, rank, rung, size, stage, station, step **2 make the grade** *Informal* **= succeed**, come through with flying colours, come up to scratch (*informal*), measure up, measure up to expectations, pass muster, prove acceptable, win through ♦ *verb* **3 = classify**, arrange, brand, class, evaluate, group, order, range, rank, rate, sequence, sort, value

gradient *noun* **= slope**, acclivity, bank, declivity, grade, hill, incline, rise

gradual *adjective* **= steady**, continuous, even, gentle, graduated, moderate, piecemeal, progressive, regular, slow, successive, unhurried

➤ **Antonyms**
abrupt, broken, instantaneous, overnight, sudden

gradually *adverb* **= steadily**, bit by bit, by degrees, drop by drop, evenly, gently, little by little, moderately, piece by piece, piecemeal, progressively, slowly, step by step, unhurriedly

graduate *verb* **1 = mark off**, calibrate, grade, measure out, proportion, regulate **2 = classify**, arrange, grade, group, order, range, rank, sequence, sort

graft *noun* 1 = **shoot**, bud, implant, scion, splice, sprout ♦ *verb* 2 = **transplant**, affix, implant, ingraft, insert, join, splice

grain *noun* 1 = **seed**, grist, kernel 2 = **cereals**, corn 3 = **bit**, atom, crumb, fragment, granule, iota, jot, mite, modicum, molecule, morsel, mote, ounce, particle, piece, scintilla (*rare*), scrap, scruple, spark, speck, suspicion, trace, whit 4 = **texture**, fibre, nap, pattern, surface, weave 5 *As in* **go against the grain** = **inclination**, character, disposition, humour, make-up, temper

grand *adjective* 1 = **impressive**, ambitious, august, dignified, elevated, eminent, exalted, fine, glorious, gorgeous, grandiose, great, haughty, illustrious, imposing, large, lofty, lordly, luxurious, magnificent, majestic, monumental, noble, opulent, ostentatious, palatial, pompous, pretentious, princely, regal, splendid, splendiferous (*facetious*), stately, striking, sublime, sumptuous, superb 2 = **excellent**, admirable, awesome (*slang*), divine, fine, first-class, first-rate, great (*informal*), hunky-dory (*informal*), marvellous (*informal*), outstanding, smashing (*informal*), splendid, splendiferous (*facetious*), super (*informal*), superb, terrific (*informal*), very good, wonderful, world-class 3 = **chief**, big-time (*informal*), head, highest, lead, leading, main, major league (*informal*), pre-eminent, principal, supreme
➤ **Antonyms**
≠**impressive**: undignified, unimposing ≠**excellent**: awful, bad, chickenshit (*U.S. slang*), common, contemptible, crappy (*slang*), mean, pants (*informal*), petty, poor, poxy (*slang*), terrible, worthless ≠**chief**: inferior, insignificant, little, secondary, small, trivial, unimportant

grandeur *noun* = **splendour**, augustness, dignity, greatness, importance, loftiness, magnificence, majesty, nobility, pomp, state, stateliness, sublimity
➤ **Antonyms**
commonness, inferiority, insignificance, lowliness, pettiness, smallness, triviality, unimportance

grandiose *adjective* 1 = **imposing**, ambitious, grand, impressive, lofty, magnificent, majestic, monumental, stately 2 = **pretentious**, affected, ambitious, bombastic, extravagant, flamboyant, high-flown, ostentatious, pompous, showy
➤ **Antonyms**
≠**imposing**: humble, modest, small-scale

≠**pretentious**: down-to-earth, unpretentious

grant *verb* 1 = **give**, allocate, allot, assign, award, bestow, confer, donate, hand out, impart, present, vouchsafe 2 = **consent to**, accede to, accord, agree to, allow, permit 3 = **admit**, acknowledge, cede, concede 4 *Law* = **transfer**, assign, convey, transmit ♦ *noun* 5 = **award**, admission, allocation, allotment, allowance, benefaction, bequest, boon, bounty, concession, donation, endowment, gift, hand-out, present, stipend, subsidy

granule *noun* = **grain**, atom, crumb, fragment, iota, jot, molecule, particle, scrap, speck

graphic *adjective* 1 = **vivid**, clear, descriptive, detailed, explicit, expressive, forcible, illustrative, lively, lucid, picturesque, striking, telling, well-drawn 2 = **pictorial**, delineated, diagrammatic, drawn, illustrative, representational, seen, visible, visual
➤ **Antonyms**
≠**vivid**: generalized, imprecise, unspecific, vague, woolly ≠**pictorial**: impressionistic

grapple *verb* 1 = **deal with**, address oneself to, attack, battle, clash, combat, confront, contend, cope, do battle, encounter, engage, face, fight, get to grips with, struggle, tackle, take on, tussle, wrestle 2 = **grip**, catch, clasp, clutch, come to grips, fasten, grab, grasp, hold, hug, lay *or* take hold, make fast, seize, wrestle

grasp *verb* 1 = **grip**, catch, clasp, clinch, clutch, grab, grapple, hold, lay *or* take hold of, seize, snatch 2 = **understand**, catch on, catch *or* get the drift of, comprehend, follow, get, get the hang of (*informal*), get the message, get the picture, realize, see, take in ♦ *noun* 3 = **grip**, clasp, clutches, embrace, hold, possession, tenure 4 = **understanding**, awareness, comprehension, grip, ken, knowledge, mastery, perception, realization 5 = **control**, capacity, compass, extent, mastery, power, range, reach, scope, sway, sweep

grasping *adjective* = **greedy**, acquisitive, avaricious, close-fisted, covetous, mean, miserly, niggardly, penny-pinching (*informal*), rapacious, selfish, snoep (*S. African informal*), stingy, tight-arsed (*taboo slang*), tight as a duck's arse (*taboo slang*), tight-assed (*U.S. taboo slang*), tightfisted, usurious, venal
➤ **Antonyms**
altruistic, generous, unselfish

grate *verb* 1 = **shred**, mince, pulverize, triturate 2 = **scrape**, creak, grind, rasp, rub, scratch **3 = annoy**, aggravate (*informal*), chafe, exasperate, fret, gall, get one down, get on one's nerves (*informal*), get on one's wick (*Brit. slang*), get under someone's skin (*informal*), get up someone's nose (*informal*), irk, irritate, jar, nark (*Brit., Austral., & N.Z. slang*), nettle, peeve, rankle, rub one up the wrong way, set one's teeth on edge, vex

grateful *adjective* = **thankful**, appreciative, beholden, indebted, obliged

gratification *noun* = **satisfaction**, delight, enjoyment, fruition, fulfilment, glee, indulgence, joy, kick or kicks (*informal*), pleasure, recompense, relish, reward, thrill
➤ **Antonyms**
control, denial, disappointment, discipline, dissatisfaction, frustration, pain, restraint, sorrow

gratify *verb* = **please**, cater to, delight, favour, fawn on, feed, fulfil, give pleasure, gladden, humour, indulge, pander to, recompense, requite, satisfy, thrill

grating¹ *noun* = **grille**, grate, grid, gridiron, lattice, trellis

grating² *adjective* = **irritating**, annoying, disagreeable, discordant, displeasing, grinding, harsh, irksome, jarring, offensive, rasping, raucous, scraping, squeaky, strident, unpleasant, vexatious
➤ **Antonyms**
agreeable, calming, mellifluous, musical, pleasing, soft, soothing

gratis *adjective* = **free**, buckshee (*Brit. slang*), for nothing, freely, free of charge, gratuitously, on the house, unpaid

gratitude *noun* = **thankfulness**, appreciation, gratefulness, indebtedness, obligation, recognition, sense of obligation, thanks
➤ **Antonyms**
ingratitude, ungratefulness, unthankfulness

gratuitous *adjective* **1 = unjustified**, assumed, baseless, causeless, groundless, irrelevant, needless, superfluous, uncalled-for, unfounded, unmerited, unnecessary, unprovoked, unwarranted, wanton **2 = voluntary**, buckshee (*Brit. slang*), complimentary, free, gratis, spontaneous, unasked-for, unpaid, unrewarded
➤ **Antonyms**
≠**unjustified**: justifiable, provoked, relevant, well-founded ≠**voluntary**: compulsory, involuntary, paid

gratuity *noun* = **tip**, baksheesh, benefaction, bonsela (*S. African*), bonus, boon, bounty, donation, gift, largesse *or* largess, perquisite, *pourboire,* present, recompense, reward

grave¹ *adjective* **1 = important**, acute, critical, crucial, dangerous, exigent, hazardous, life-and-death, momentous, of great consequence, perilous, pressing, serious, severe, significant, threatening, urgent, vital, weighty **2 = solemn**, dignified, dour, dull, earnest, gloomy, grim-faced, heavy, leaden, long-faced, muted, quiet, sage (*obsolete*), sedate, serious, sober, sombre, staid, subdued, thoughtful, unsmiling
➤ **Antonyms**
≠**important**: frivolous, insignificant, mild, trifling, unimportant ≠**solemn**: carefree, exciting, flippant, happy, joyous, merry, undignified

grave² *noun* = **tomb**, burying place, crypt, last resting place, mausoleum, pit, sepulchre, vault

graveyard *noun* = **cemetery**, boneyard (*informal*), burial ground, charnel house, churchyard, God's acre (*literary*), necropolis

gravitas *noun* = **seriousness**, gravity, solemnity

gravitate *verb* **1 with to** *or* **towards = be drawn**, be attracted, be influenced, be pulled, incline, lean, move, tend **2 = fall**, be precipitated, descend, drop, precipitate, settle, sink

gravity *noun* **1 = importance**, acuteness, consequence, exigency, hazardousness, moment, momentousness, perilousness, pressingness, seriousness, severity, significance, urgency, weightiness **2 = solemnity**, demureness, dignity, earnestness, gloom, gravitas, grimness, reserve, sedateness, seriousness, sobriety, thoughtfulness
➤ **Antonyms**
≠**importance**: inconsequentiality, insignificance, triviality, unimportance ≠**solemnity**: flippancy, frivolity, gaiety, happiness, joy, levity, merriment, thoughtlessness

graze¹ *verb* = **feed**, browse, crop, pasture

graze² *verb* **1 = scratch**, abrade, bark, chafe, scrape, skin **2 = touch**, brush, glance off, kiss, rub, scrape, shave, skim ♦ *noun* **3 = scratch**, abrasion, scrape

greasy *adjective* **1 = fatty**, oily, oleaginous, slick, slimy, slippery **2 = sycophantic**, fawning, glib, grovelling, ingratiating, oily, slick, smarmy (*Brit. informal*), smooth, toadying, unctuous

great *adjective* **1 = large**, big, bulky, colossal, elephantine, enormous, extensive, gigantic, ginormous (*informal*), huge, humongous *or* humungous (*U.S. slang*), immense, mammoth, prodigious,

stellar (*informal*), stupendous, tremendous, vast, voluminous **2 = long**, extended, lengthy, prolonged, protracted **3 = major**, big-time (*informal*), capital, chief, grand, head, lead, leading, main, major league (*informal*), paramount, primary, principal, prominent, superior **4 = extreme**, considerable, decided, excessive, extravagant, grievous, high, inordinate, prodigious, pronounced, serious (*informal*), strong **5 = important**, consequential, critical, crucial, grave, heavy, momentous, serious, significant, weighty **6 = famous**, celebrated, distinguished, eminent, exalted, excellent, famed, glorious, illustrious, notable, noteworthy, outstanding, prominent, remarkable, renowned, superb, superlative, talented, world-class **7 = skilful**, able, adept, adroit, crack (*slang*), expert, good, masterly, proficient, skilled **8** *Informal* **= excellent**, admirable, awesome (*slang*), bitchin', boffo (*slang*), brill (*informal*), chillin' (*U.S. slang*), cracking (*Brit. informal*), crucial (*slang*), def (*informal*), dope (*slang*) fantastic (*informal*), fine, first-rate, good, hunky-dory (*informal*), jim-dandy (*slang*), marvellous (*informal*), mean (*slang*), mega (*slang*), sovereign, superb, terrific (*informal*), the dog's bollocks (*taboo slang*), topping (*Brit. slang*), tremendous (*informal*), wonderful **9 = noble**, august, chivalrous, dignified, distinguished, exalted, fine, glorious, grand, heroic, high-minded, idealistic, impressive, lofty, magnanimous, princely, sublime **10 = enthusiastic**, active, devoted, keen, zealous **11 = utter**, absolute, arrant, complete, consummate, downright, egregious, flagrant, out-and-out, perfect, positive, thoroughgoing, thundering (*informal*), total, unmitigated, unqualified
➤ **Antonyms**
≠**large**: diminutive, little, small ≠**important**: inconsequential, inconsiderable, insignificant, petty, trivial, unimportant ≠**skilful**: inexperienced, unskilled, untrained ≠**excellent**: average, inferior, poor, secondary, second-rate, undistinguished, unnotable ≠**noble**: base, ignoble, inhumane, mean, unkind

greatly *adverb* **= very much**, abundantly, by leaps and bounds, by much, considerably, enormously, exceedingly, extremely, highly, hugely, immensely, markedly, mightily, much, notably, powerfully, remarkably, seriously (*informal*), to the nth degree, tremendously, vastly

greatness *noun* **1 = immensity**, bulk, enormity, hugeness, largeness, length, magnitude, mass, prodigiousness, size, vastness **2 = intensity**, amplitude, force, high degree, potency, power, strength **3 = importance**, gravity, heaviness, import, moment, momentousness, seriousness, significance, urgency, weight **4 = fame**, celebrity, distinction, eminence, glory, grandeur, illustriousness, lustre, note, renown **5 = grandeur**, chivalry, dignity, disinterestedness, generosity, heroism, high-mindedness, idealism, loftiness, majesty, nobility, nobleness, stateliness, sublimity

greed, greediness *noun* **1 = gluttony**, edacity, esurience, gormandizing, hunger, insatiableness, ravenousness, voracity **2 = avarice**, acquisitiveness, avidity, covetousness, craving, cupidity, desire, eagerness, graspingness, longing, rapacity, selfishness
➤ **Antonyms**
≠**avarice**: altruism, benevolence, generosity, largesse *or* largess, munificence, self-restraint, unselfishness

greedy *adjective* **1 = gluttonous**, edacious, esurient, gormandizing, hoggish, hungry, insatiable, piggish, ravenous, voracious **2 = grasping**, acquisitive, avaricious, avid, covetous, craving, desirous, eager, hungry, impatient, rapacious, selfish
➤ **Antonyms**
≠**grasping**: altruistic, benevolent, generous, munificent, self-restrained, unselfish

Greek *adjective* **1 = Hellenic** ♦ *noun* **2 = Hellene**

green *adjective* **1 = leafy**, blooming, budding, flourishing, fresh, grassy, new, undecayed, verdant, verdurous **2 = ecological**, conservationist, ecologically sound, environment-friendly, non-polluting, ozone-friendly **3 = new**, fresh, immature, raw, recent, unripe **4 = nauseous**, ill, pale, sick, under the weather, unhealthy, wan **5 = inexperienced**, callow, credulous, gullible, ignorant, immature, inexpert, ingenuous, innocent, naive, new, raw, unpolished, unpractised, unskilful, unsophisticated, untrained, unversed, wet behind the ears (*informal*) **6 = jealous**, covetous, envious, grudging, resentful ♦ *noun* **7 = lawn**, common, grassplot, sward, turf

green light *noun* **= permission**, approval, authorization, blessing, clearance, confirmation, go-ahead (*informal*), imprimatur, O.K. *or* okay (*informal*), sanction

greet *verb* = **welcome**, accost, address, compliment, hail, meet, nod to, receive, salute, tip one's hat to

greeting *noun* 1 = **welcome**, address, hail, reception, salutation, salute 2 **greetings** = **best wishes**, compliments, devoirs, good wishes, regards, respects, salutations

gregarious *adjective* = **outgoing**, affable, companionable, convivial, cordial, friendly, sociable, social
➤ **Antonyms**
antisocial, reserved, solitary, standoffish, unsociable, withdrawn

grey *adjective* 1 = **pale**, ashen, bloodless, colourless, like death warmed up (*informal*), livid, pallid, wan 2 = **dismal**, cheerless, cloudy, dark, depressing, dim, drab, dreary, dull, foggy, gloomy, misty, murky, overcast, sunless 3 = **characterless**, anonymous, colourless, dull, indistinct, neutral, unclear, unidentifiable 4 = **old**, aged, ancient, elderly, experienced, hoary, mature, venerable

gridlock *noun* = **standstill**, deadlock, full stop, halt, impasse, stalemate

grief *noun* 1 = **sadness**, affliction, agony, anguish, bereavement, dejection, distress, grievance, hardship, heartache, heartbreak, misery, mournfulness, mourning, pain, regret, remorse, sorrow, suffering, trial, tribulation, trouble, woe 2 **come to grief** *Informal* = **fail**, come unstuck, fall flat on one's face, meet with disaster, miscarry
➤ **Antonyms**
≠**sadness**: cheer, comfort, consolation, delight, gladness, happiness, joy, rejoicing, solace

grievance *noun* = **complaint**, affliction, axe to grind, beef (*slang*), chip on one's shoulder (*informal*), damage, distress, grief, gripe (*informal*), hardship, injury, injustice, protest, resentment, sorrow, trial, tribulation, trouble, unhappiness, wrong

grieve *verb* 1 = **mourn**, ache, bemoan, bewail, complain, deplore, lament, regret, rue, sorrow, suffer, wail, weep 2 = **sadden**, afflict, agonize, break the heart of, crush, distress, hurt, injure, make one's heart bleed, pain, wound
➤ **Antonyms**
≠**sadden**: cheer, comfort, console, ease, gladden, please, rejoice, solace

grievous *adjective* 1 = **severe**, afflicting, calamitous, damaging, distressing, dreadful, grave, harmful, heavy, hurtful, injurious, lamentable, oppressive, painful, wounding 2 = **deplorable**, appalling, atrocious, dreadful, egregious, flagrant, glaring, heinous, intolerable, lamentable,

monstrous, offensive, outrageous, shameful, shocking, unbearable
➤ **Antonyms**
≠**severe**: insignificant, mild, trivial, unimportant ≠**deplorable**: delightful, pleasant

grim *adjective* = **forbidding**, cruel, ferocious, fierce, formidable, frightful, ghastly, godawful (*slang*), grisly, gruesome, hard, harsh, hideous, horrible, horrid, implacable, merciless, morose, relentless, resolute, ruthless, severe, shocking, sinister, stern, sullen, surly, terrible, unrelenting, unyielding
➤ **Antonyms**
amiable, attractive, benign, cheerful, easy, genial, gentle, happy, kind, pleasant, soft, sympathetic

grimace *noun* 1 = **scowl**, face, frown, mouth, sneer, wry face ♦ *verb* 2 = **scowl**, frown, lour *or* lower, make a face *or* faces, mouth, sneer

grime *noun* = **dirt**, filth, grot (*slang*), smut, soot

grimy *adjective* = **dirty**, begrimed, besmeared, besmirched, filthy, foul, grubby, scuzzy (*slang*), smutty, soiled, sooty, unclean

grind *verb* 1 = **crush**, abrade, comminute, granulate, grate, kibble, mill, pound, powder, pulverize, triturate 2 = **smooth**, file, polish, sand, sharpen, whet 3 = **scrape**, gnash, grate, grit 4 **grind down** = **oppress**, afflict, harass, hold down, hound, persecute, plague, trouble, tyrannize (over) ♦ *noun* 5 *Informal* = **hard work**, chore, drudgery, labour, sweat (*informal*), task, toil

grip *noun* 1 = **clasp**, handclasp (*U.S.*), hold, purchase 2 = **control**, clutches, domination, influence, keeping, possession, power, tenure 3 = **understanding**, command, comprehension, grasp, mastery, perception 4 **come** *or* **get to grips (with)** = **tackle**, close with, confront, contend with, cope with, deal with, encounter, face up to, grapple with, grasp, handle, meet, take on, take the bit between one's teeth, undertake ♦ *verb* 5 = **grasp**, clasp, clutch, hold, latch on to, seize, take hold of 6 = **engross**, absorb, catch up, compel, enthral, entrance, fascinate, hold, involve, mesmerize, rivet, spellbind

gripping *adjective* = **fascinating**, compelling, compulsive, engrossing, enthralling, entrancing, exciting, riveting, spellbinding, thrilling, unputdownable (*informal*)

grisly *adjective* = **gruesome**, abominable,

appalling, awful, dreadful, frightful,
ghastly, grim, hellacious (*U.S. slang*),
hideous, horrible, horrid, macabre,
shocking, sickening, terrible, terrifying
➤ **Antonyms**
agreeable, attractive, charming,
innocuous, nice, pleasant

grit *noun* **1** = **gravel**, dust, pebbles, sand **2**
= **courage**, backbone, balls (*taboo slang*),
determination, doggedness, fortitude,
gameness, guts (*informal*), hardihood,
mettle, nerve, perseverance, pluck,
resolution, spirit, tenacity, toughness
♦ *verb* **3** = **grind**, clench, gnash, grate

gritty *adjective* **1** = **courageous**, ballsy
(*taboo slang*), brave, determined, dogged,
feisty (*informal, chiefly U.S. & Canad.*),
game, hardy, mettlesome, plucky,
resolute, spirited, steadfast, tenacious,
tough **2** = **rough**, abrasive, dusty, grainy,
granular, gravelly, rasping, sandy

groan *noun* **1** = **moan**, cry, sigh, whine **2**
Informal = **complaint**, beef (*slang*), gripe
(*informal*), grouse, grumble, objection,
protest ♦ *verb* **3** = **moan**, cry, sigh, whine **4**
Informal = **complain**, beef (*slang*),
bemoan, bitch (*slang*), gripe (*informal*),
grouse, grumble, lament, object

groggy *adjective* = **dizzy**, befuddled,
confused, dazed, faint, muzzy,
punch-drunk, reeling, shaky, staggering,
stunned, stupefied, unsteady, weak,
wobbly, woozy (*informal*)

groom *noun* **1** = **stableman**, currier (*rare*),
hostler *or* ostler (*archaic*), stableboy ♦ *verb*
2 = **rub down**, brush, clean, curry, tend **3**
= **smarten up**, clean, dress, get up
(*informal*), gussy up (*slang, chiefly U.S.*),
preen, primp, spruce up, tidy, turn out **4**
= **train**, coach, drill, educate, make ready,
nurture, prepare, prime, ready

groove *noun* = **indentation**, channel, cut,
cutting, flute, furrow, gutter, hollow,
rebate, rut, score, trench, trough

grope *verb* = **feel**, cast about, finger, fish,
flounder, forage, fumble, grabble,
scrabble, search

gross *adjective* **1** = **blatant**, apparent,
arrant, downright, egregious, flagrant,
glaring, grievous, heinous, manifest,
obvious, outrageous, plain, rank, serious,
shameful, sheer, shocking, unmitigated,
unqualified, utter **2** = **vulgar**, coarse,
crude, improper, impure, indecent,
indelicate, lewd, low, obscene, offensive,
ribald, rude, sensual, smutty, unseemly,
X-rated (*informal*) **3** = **fat**, big, bulky,
corpulent, dense, great, heavy, hulking,
large, lumpish, massive, obese,
overweight, thick **4** = **total**, aggregate,

before deductions, before tax, entire,
whole **5** = **coarse**, boorish, callous, crass,
dull, ignorant, imperceptive, insensitive,
tasteless, uncultured, undiscriminating,
unfeeling, unrefined, unsophisticated
♦ *verb* **6** = **earn**, bring in, make, rake in
(*informal*), take
➤ **Antonyms**
≠**blatant**: partial, qualified ≠**vulgar**:
decent, delicate, proper, pure *adjective*
≠**fat**: delicate, little, petite, slim, small,
svelte, thin ≠**total**: net ≠**coarse**:
cultivated, elegant

grotesque *adjective* = **unnatural**, absurd,
bizarre, deformed, distorted, extravagant,
fanciful, fantastic, freakish, incongruous,
ludicrous, malformed, misshapen, odd,
outlandish, preposterous, ridiculous,
strange, weird, whimsical
➤ **Antonyms**
average, classic, graceful, natural, normal,
realistic

ground *noun* **1** = **earth**, clod, dirt, dry land,
dust, field, land, loam, mould, sod, soil,
terra firma, terrain, turf **2** = **stadium**, arena,
field, park (*informal*), pitch **3** *often plural*
= **land**, area, country, district, domain,
estate, fields, gardens, habitat, holding,
property, realm, terrain, territory, tract **4**
usually plural = **dregs**, deposit, grouts, lees,
sediment, settlings **5 grounds** = **reason**,
account, argument, base, basis, call, cause,
excuse, factor, foundation, inducement,
justification, motive, occasion, premise,
pretext, rationale ♦ *verb* **6** = **instruct**,
acquaint with, coach, familiarize with,
inform, initiate, prepare, teach, train, tutor
7 = **base**, establish, fix, found, set, settle

groundless *adjective* = **unjustified**,
baseless, chimerical, empty, false, idle,
illusory, imaginary, unauthorized,
uncalled-for, unfounded, unprovoked,
unsupported, unwarranted
➤ **Antonyms**
justified, logical, proven, real, reasonable,
substantial, supported, true, well-founded

groundwork *noun* = **preliminaries**, base,
basis, cornerstone, footing, foundation,
fundamentals, preparation, spadework,
underpinnings

group *noun* **1** = **set**, aggregation,
assemblage, association, band, batch,
bevy, bunch, camp, category, circle, class,
clique, clump, cluster, collection,
company, congregation, coterie, crowd,
faction, formation, gang, gathering,
organization, pack, party, posse (*slang*),
troop ♦ *verb* **2** = **arrange**, assemble,
associate, assort, bracket, class, classify,
dispose, gather, marshal, order, organize,

put together, range, sort **3** = **get together**, associate, band together, cluster, congregate, consort, fraternize, gather

grouse *verb* **1** = **complain**, beef (*slang*), bellyache (*slang*), bitch (*slang*), bleat, carp, find fault, gripe (*informal*), grouch (*informal*), grumble, kvetch (*U.S. slang*), moan, whine, whinge (*informal*) ♦ *noun* **2** = **complaint**, beef (*slang*), grievance, gripe (*informal*), grouch (*informal*), grumble, moan, objection, protest

grove *noun* = **wood**, coppice, copse, covert, plantation, spinney, thicket

grovel *verb* = **humble oneself**, abase oneself, bootlick (*informal*), bow and scrape, brown-nose (*taboo slang*), cower, crawl, creep, cringe, crouch, demean oneself, fawn, flatter, kiss ass (*taboo slang*), kowtow, lick someone's arse (*taboo slang*), lick someone's boots, pander to, sneak, toady
➤ **Antonyms**
be proud, domineer, face, hold one's head high, intimidate

grow *verb* **1** = **increase**, develop, enlarge, expand, extend, fill out, get bigger, get taller, heighten, multiply, spread, stretch, swell, thicken, widen **2** = **spring up**, develop, flourish, germinate, shoot, sprout, vegetate **3** = **cultivate**, breed, farm, nurture, produce, propagate, raise **4** = **improve**, advance, expand, flourish, progress, prosper, succeed, thrive **5** = **originate**, arise, issue, spring, stem **6** = **become**, come to be, develop (into), get, turn, wax
➤ **Antonyms**
≠**increase**: decline, decrease, die, diminish, dwindle, fail, lessen, shrink, subside, wane

grown-up *adjective* **1** = **mature**, adult, fully-grown, of age ♦ *noun* **2** = **adult**, man, woman

growth *noun* **1** = **increase**, aggrandizement, augmentation, development, enlargement, evolution, expansion, extension, growing, heightening, multiplication, proliferation, stretching, thickening, widening **2** = **progress**, advance, advancement, expansion, improvement, prosperity, rise, success **3** = **cultivation**, crop, development, germination, produce, production, shooting, sprouting, vegetation **4** *Medical* = **tumour**, excrescence, lump
➤ **Antonyms**
≠**increase**: decline, decrease, drop, dwindling, failure, fall, lessening, shrinkage, slackening, subsiding

grub *noun* **1** *Slang* = **food**, eats (*slang*), feed, nosebag (*slang*), nosh (*slang*), rations, sustenance, tack (*informal*), victuals, vittles (*obsolete or dialect*) **2** = **larva**, caterpillar, maggot ♦ *verb* **3** = **search**, ferret, forage, hunt, rummage, scour, uncover, unearth **4** = **dig up**, burrow, probe, pull up, root (*informal*), rootle (*Brit.*), search for, uproot

grubby *adjective* = **dirty**, besmeared, filthy, frowzy, grimy, grungy (*slang chiefly U.S. & Canad.*), manky (*Scot. dialect*), mean, messy, mucky, scruffy, scuzzy (*slang*), seedy, shabby, slovenly, smutty, soiled, sordid, squalid, unkempt, untidy, unwashed

grudge *noun* **1** = **resentment**, animosity, animus, antipathy, aversion, bitterness, chip on one's shoulder (*informal*), dislike, enmity, grievance, hard feelings, hate, ill will, malevolence, malice, pique, rancour, spite, venom ♦ *verb* **2** = **resent**, begrudge, be reluctant, complain, covet, envy, hold back, mind, stint
➤ **Antonyms**
noun ≠**resentment**: appreciation, goodwill, liking, thankfulness ♦ *verb* ≠**resent**: be glad for, celebrate, welcome

gruelling *adjective* = **exhausting**, arduous, backbreaking, brutal, crushing, demanding, difficult, fatiguing, fierce, grinding, hard, harsh, laborious, punishing, severe, stiff, strenuous, taxing, tiring, trying
➤ **Antonyms**
cushy (*informal*), easy, enjoyable, light, pleasant, undemanding

gruesome *adjective* = **horrific**, abominable, awful, fearful, from hell (*informal*), ghastly, grim, grisly, hellacious (*U.S. slang*), hideous, horrendous, horrible, horrid, horrifying, loathsome, macabre, obscene, repugnant, repulsive, shocking, spine-chilling, terrible
➤ **Antonyms**
appealing, benign, cheerful, pleasant, sweet

gruff *adjective* **1** = **surly**, bad-tempered, bearish, blunt, brusque, churlish, crabbed, crusty, curt, discourteous, grouchy (*informal*), grumpy, ill-humoured, ill-natured, impolite, rough, rude, sour, sullen, uncivil, ungracious, unmannerly **2** = **hoarse**, croaking, guttural, harsh, husky, low, rasping, rough, throaty
➤ **Antonyms**
≠**surly**: courteous, good-tempered, gracious, kind, pleasant, polite ≠**hoarse**: mellifluous, smooth, sweet

grumble *verb* **1** = **complain**, beef (*slang*),

bellyache (*slang*), bitch (*slang*), bleat, carp, find fault, gripe (*informal*), grouch (*informal*), grouse, kvetch (*U.S. slang*), moan, repine, whine, whinge (*informal*) **2** = **rumble**, growl, gurgle, murmur, mutter, roar ♦ *noun* **3** = **complaint**, beef (*slang*), grievance, gripe (*informal*), grouch (*informal*), grouse, moan, objection, protest **4** = **rumble**, growl, gurgle, murmur, muttering, roar

grumpy *adjective* = **irritable**, bad-tempered, cantankerous, crotchety (*informal*), peevish, sulky, sullen, surly, testy

guarantee *noun* **1** = **assurance**, bond, certainty, collateral, covenant, earnest, guaranty, pledge, promise, security, surety, undertaking, warranty, word, word of honour ♦ *verb* **2** = **ensure**, answer for, assure, certify, insure, maintain, make certain, pledge, promise, protect, secure, stand behind, swear, vouch for, warrant

guarantor *noun* = **underwriter**, backer, bailsman (*rare*), bondsman (*Law*), guarantee, sponsor, supporter, surety, voucher, warrantor

guard *verb* **1** = **watch over**, cover, defend, escort, keep, mind, oversee, patrol, police, preserve, protect, safeguard, save, screen, secure, shelter, shield, supervise, tend, watch ♦ *noun* **2** = **protector**, custodian, defender, lookout, picket, sentinel, sentry, warder, watch, watchman **3** = **escort**, convoy, patrol **4** = **protection**, buffer, bulwark, bumper, defence, pad, rampart, safeguard, screen, security, shield **5** = **watchfulness**, attention, care, caution, heed, vigilance, wariness **6 off guard** = **unprepared**, napping, unready, unwary, with one's defences down **7 on guard** = **prepared**, alert, cautious, circumspect, on the alert, on the lookout, on the qui vive, ready, vigilant, wary, watchful

guarded *adjective* = **cautious**, cagey (*informal*), careful, circumspect, discreet, leery (*slang*), noncommittal, prudent, reserved, restrained, reticent, suspicious, wary

guardian *noun* = **keeper**, attendant, champion, curator, custodian, defender, escort, guard, preserver, protector, trustee, warden, warder

guerrilla *noun* = **freedom fighter**, irregular, member of the underground *or* resistance, partisan, underground fighter

guess *verb* **1** = **estimate**, conjecture, fathom, hypothesize, penetrate, predict, solve, speculate, work out **2** = **suppose**, believe, conjecture, dare say, deem, divine, fancy, hazard, imagine, judge, reckon, surmise, suspect, think ♦ *noun* **3**

= **supposition**, ballpark figure (*informal*), conjecture, feeling, hypothesis, judgment, notion, prediction, reckoning, shot in the dark, speculation, surmise, suspicion, theory
➤ **Antonyms**
verb ≠**estimate, suppose**: be certain, be sure, know, prove, show ♦ *noun* ≠**supposition**: certainty, fact

guesswork *noun* = **speculation**, conjecture, estimation, presumption, supposition, surmise, suspicion, theory

guest *noun* = **visitor**, boarder, caller, company, lodger, visitant

guidance *noun* = **advice**, auspices, conduct, control, counsel, counselling, direction, government, help, instruction, intelligence, leadership, management, teaching

guide *noun* **1** = **escort**, adviser, attendant, chaperon, cicerone, conductor, controller, counsellor, director, dragoman, guru, leader, mentor, monitor, pilot, steersman, teacher, torchbearer, usher **2** = **pointer**, beacon, clue, guiding light, key, landmark, lodestar, mark, marker, sign, signal, signpost **3** = **guidebook**, Baedeker, catalogue, directory, handbook, instructions, key, manual, vade mecum **4** = **model**, criterion, example, exemplar, ideal, imago (*Psychoanalysis*), inspiration, lodestar, master, par, paradigm, standard ♦ *verb* **5** = **lead**, accompany, attend, conduct, convoy, direct, escort, pilot, shepherd, show the way, steer, usher **6** = **steer**, command, control, direct, handle, manage, manoeuvre **7** = **supervise**, advise, counsel, educate, govern, influence, instruct, oversee, regulate, rule, superintend, sway, teach, train

guild *noun* = **society**, association, brotherhood, club, company, corporation, fellowship, fraternity, league, lodge, order, organization, union

guile *noun* = **cunning**, art, artfulness, artifice, cleverness, craft, craftiness, deceit, deception, duplicity, gamesmanship (*informal*), knavery, ruse, sharp practice, slyness, treachery, trickery, trickiness, wiliness
➤ **Antonyms**
candour, frankness, honesty, sincerity, truthfulness

guileful *adjective* = **cunning**, artful, clever, crafty, deceitful, duplicitous, foxy, sly, sneaky, treacherous, tricky, underhand, wily

guilt *noun* **1** = **culpability**, blame, blameworthiness, criminality, delinquency, guiltiness, iniquity, misconduct,

responsibility, sinfulness, wickedness, wrong, wrongdoing **2 = remorse**, bad conscience, contrition, disgrace, dishonour, guiltiness, guilty conscience, infamy, regret, self-condemnation, self-reproach, shame, stigma
➤ **Antonyms**
≠**culpability**: blamelessness, innocence, righteousness, sinlessness, virtue
≠**remorse**: honour, pride, self-respect

guiltless *adjective* **= innocent**, blameless, clean (*slang*), clear, immaculate, impeccable, irreproachable, pure, sinless, spotless, squeaky-clean, unimpeachable, unsullied, untainted, untarnished

guilty *adjective* **1 = culpable**, at fault, blameworthy, convicted, criminal, delinquent, erring, evil, felonious, iniquitous, offending, reprehensible, responsible, sinful, to blame, wicked, wrong **2 = remorseful**, ashamed, conscience-stricken, contrite, hangdog, regretful, rueful, shamefaced, sheepish, sorry
➤ **Antonyms**
≠**culpable**: blameless, innocent, moral, righteous, virtuous ≠**remorseful**: proud

guise *noun* **= form**, appearance, aspect, demeanour, disguise, mode, pretence, semblance, shape

gulf *noun* **1 = bay**, bight, sea inlet **2 = chasm**, abyss, breach, cleft, gap, opening, rent, rift, separation, split, void, whirlpool

gullibility *noun* **= credulity**, innocence, naïveté, simplicity, trustingness

gullible *adjective* **= naive**, as green as grass, born yesterday, credulous, easily taken in, foolish, green, innocent, silly, simple, trusting, unsceptical, unsophisticated, unsuspecting, wet behind the ears (*informal*)
➤ **Antonyms**
cynical, sophisticated, suspicious, untrusting, worldly

gully *noun* **= channel**, ditch, gutter, watercourse

gulp *verb* **1 = swallow**, bolt, devour, gobble, guzzle, knock back (*informal*), quaff, swig (*informal*), swill, toss off, wolf **2 = gasp**, choke, stifle, swallow ♦ *noun* **3 = swallow**, draught, mouthful, swig (*informal*)

gum *noun* **1 = glue**, adhesive, cement, exudate, mucilage, paste, resin ♦ *verb* **2 = stick**, affix, cement, clog, glue, paste, stiffen

gumption *noun* **= resourcefulness**, ability, acumen, astuteness, cleverness, common sense, discernment, enterprise,

get-up-and-go (*informal*), horse sense, initiative, mother wit, nous (*Brit. slang*), sagacity, savvy (*slang*), shrewdness, spirit, wit(s)

gun *noun* **= firearm**, handgun, piece (*slang*), shooter (*slang*)

gunman *noun* **= terrorist**, assassin, bandit, bravo, desperado, gangster, gunslinger (*U.S. slang*), heavy (*slang*), hit man (*slang*), killer, mobster (*U.S. slang*), murderer, thug

gurgle *verb* **1 = murmur**, babble, bubble, burble, crow, lap, plash, purl, ripple, splash ♦ *noun* **2 = murmur**, babble, purl, ripple

guru *noun* **= teacher**, authority, guiding light, leader, maharishi, mahatma, master, mentor, sage, Svengali, swami, torchbearer, tutor

gush *verb* **1 = flow**, burst, cascade, flood, issue, jet, pour, run, rush, spout, spurt, stream **2 = enthuse**, babble, blather, chatter, effervesce, effuse, jabber, overstate, spout ♦ *noun* **3 = stream**, burst, cascade, flood, flow, issue, jet, outburst, outflow, rush, spout, spurt, torrent **4 = babble**, blather, chatter, effusion, exuberance

gust *noun* **1 = blast**, blow, breeze, flurry, gale, puff, rush, squall **2 = surge**, burst, eruption, explosion, fit, gale, outburst, paroxysm, passion, storm ♦ *verb* **3 = blow**, blast, puff, squall

gusto *noun* **= relish**, appetite, appreciation, brio, delight, enjoyment, enthusiasm, exhilaration, fervour, liking, pleasure, savour, verve, zeal, zest, zing (*informal*)
➤ **Antonyms**
apathy, coolness, disinterest, distaste, inertia

gusty *adjective* **= windy**, blowy, blustering, blustery, breezy, inclement, squally, stormy, tempestuous

gut *noun* **1** *Informal* **= paunch**, belly, potbelly, spare tyre (*Brit. slang*) **2 guts: a = intestines**, belly, bowels, entrails, innards (*informal*), insides (*informal*), inwards, stomach, viscera **b** *Informal* **= courage**, audacity, backbone, boldness, bottle (*slang*), daring, forcefulness, grit, hardihood, mettle, nerve, pluck, spirit, spunk (*informal*), willpower ♦ *verb* **3 = disembowel**, clean, draw, dress, eviscerate **4 = ravage**, clean out, despoil, empty, pillage, plunder, ransack, rifle, sack, strip ♦ *adjective* **5** *As in* **gut reaction = instinctive**, basic, deep-seated, emotional, heartfelt, innate, intuitive, involuntary, natural, spontaneous, unthinking, visceral

gutless *adjective* = **faint-hearted**, abject, chicken (*slang*), chickenshit (*U.S. slang*), cowardly, craven, feeble, irresolute, lily-livered, spineless, submissive, timid, weak

➤ **Antonyms**

bold, brave, courageous, determined, resolute

gutsy *adjective* = **brave**, bold, courageous, determined, gritty, indomitable, plucky, resolute, spirited

gutter *noun* = **drain**, channel, conduit, ditch, duct, pipe, sluice, trench, trough, tube

guttersnipe *noun* = **street urchin**, gamin, mudlark (*slang*), ragamuffin, street Arab (*offensive*), waif

guttural *adjective* = **throaty**, deep, gravelly, gruff, hoarse, husky, low, rasping, rough, thick

guy *noun Informal* = **man**, bloke (*Brit. informal*), cat (*slang*), chap, fellow, lad, person, youth

guzzle *verb* = **devour**, bolt, carouse, cram, drink, gobble, gorge, gormandize, knock back (*informal*), pig out (*U.S. & Canad. slang*), quaff, stuff (oneself), swill, tope, wolf

Gypsy, Gipsy *noun* = **traveller**, Bohemian, nomad, rambler, roamer, Romany, rover, vagabond, vagrant, wanderer

gyrate *verb* = **rotate**, circle, pirouette, revolve, spin, spiral, twirl, whirl

gyration *noun* = **rotation**, convolution, pirouette, revolution, spin, spinning, spiral, whirl, whirling

H h

habiliments *plural noun* = **clothes**, apparel, array, attire, clothing, costume, dress, garb, garment, habit, raiment (*archaic or poetic*), robes, uniform, vestments

habit *noun* **1** = **mannerism**, bent, custom, disposition, manner, practice, proclivity, propensity, quirk, tendency, way **2** = **custom**, convention, mode, practice, routine, rule, second nature, tradition, usage, wont **3** = **addiction**, dependence, fixation, obsession, weakness **4** = **disposition**, constitution, frame of mind, make-up, nature **5** = **dress**, apparel, garb, garment, habiliment, riding dress

habitat *noun* = **home**, abode, element, environment, home ground, locality, natural home, surroundings, terrain, territory

habitation *noun* **1** = **occupation**, inhabitance, inhabitancy, occupancy, tenancy **2** *Formal* = **dwelling**, abode, domicile, dwelling house, home, house, living quarters, lodging, pad (*slang*), quarters, residence

habit-forming *adjective* = **addictive**, compulsive, moreish (*informal*)

habitual *adjective* **1** = **customary**, accustomed, common, familiar, fixed, natural, normal, ordinary, regular, routine, standard, traditional, usual, wonted **2** = **persistent**, chronic, confirmed, constant, established, frequent, hardened, ingrained, inveterate, recurrent
➤ **Antonyms**
≠**customary**: abnormal, exceptional, extraordinary, irregular, rare, strange, uncommon, unusual ≠**persistent**: infrequent, irregular, occasional

habituate *verb* = **accustom**, acclimatize, acquaint, break in, condition, discipline, familiarize, harden, inure, make used to, school, season, train

habituated *adjective* = **accustomed**, acclimatized, adapted, broken in, conditioned, disciplined, familiarized, hardened, inured, schooled, seasoned, trained, used (to)
➤ **Antonyms**
unaccustomed, unfamiliar, unused (to)

habitué *noun* = **frequent visitor**, constant customer, frequenter, regular (*informal*), regular patron

hack¹ *verb* **1** = **cut**, chop, gash, hew, kick, lacerate, mangle, mutilate, notch, slash
♦ *noun* **2** = **cut**, chop, gash, notch, slash

hack² *noun* **1** = **scribbler**, literary hack **2** = **horse**, crock, hired horse, jade, nag
♦ *adjective* **3** = **unoriginal**, banal, mediocre, pedestrian, poor, stereotyped, tired, undistinguished, uninspired

hackles *plural noun* **make one's hackles rise** = **infuriate**, anger, annoy, cause resentment, get one's dander up (*slang*), make one see red (*informal*), rub one up the wrong way

hackneyed *adjective* = **unoriginal**, banal, clichéd, common, commonplace, overworked, pedestrian, played out (*informal*), run-of-the-mill, stale, stereotyped, stock, threadbare, timeworn, tired, trite, worn-out
➤ **Antonyms**
fresh, imaginative, new, novel, original, striking, unusual

Hades *noun* = **underworld**, hell, infernal regions, lower world, nether regions, realm of Pluto, (the) inferno

haft *noun* = **handle**, shaft

hag *noun* = **witch**, crone, fury, harridan, shrew, termagant, virago, vixen

haggard *adjective* = **gaunt**, careworn, drawn, emaciated, ghastly, hollow-eyed, pinched, shrunken, thin, wan, wasted, wrinkled
➤ **Antonyms**
bright-eyed, brisk, energetic, fresh, hale, robust, sleek, vigorous

haggle *verb* **1** = **bargain**, barter, beat down, drive a hard bargain **2** = **wrangle**, bicker, dispute, quarrel, squabble

hag-ridden *adjective* = **careworn**, angst-ridden, anxiety-ridden, ground down, harassed, tormented, with all the troubles of the world on one's shoulders, worn down, worried

hail¹ *noun* **1** = **shower**, barrage, bombardment, downpour, pelting, rain, storm, volley ♦ *verb* **2** = **shower**, barrage, batter, beat down upon, bombard, pelt, rain, rain down on, storm, volley

hail² *verb* **1** = **salute**, greet, welcome **2** = **acclaim**, acknowledge, applaud, cheer,

exalt, glorify, honour **3** = **flag down**, accost, address, call, halloo, shout to, signal to, sing out, speak to, wave down **4 hail from** = **come from**, be a native of, be born in, originate in
➤ **Antonyms**
≠**salute:** avoid, cut (*informal*), ignore, snub ≠**acclaim:** boo, condemn, criticize, hiss, insult, jeer

hail-fellow-well-met *adjective*
= **overfriendly**, back-slapping, familiar, free-and-easy, genial, hearty, unceremonious

hair *noun* **1** = **locks**, head of hair, mane, mop, shock, tresses **2 by a hair** = **by a narrow margin**, by a fraction of an inch, by a hair's-breadth, by a split second, by a whisker, by the skin of one's teeth **3 get in one's hair** *Informal* = **annoy**, aggravate (*informal*), be on one's back (*slang*), exasperate, get on one's nerves (*informal*), get on one's wick (*Brit. slang*), get up one's nose (*informal*), harass, hassle (*informal*), irritate, nark (*Brit., Austral., & N.Z. slang*), pester, piss one off (*taboo slang*), plague **4 let one's hair down** = **let oneself go**, chill out (*slang, chiefly U.S.*), let it all hang out (*informal*), let off steam (*informal*), mellow out (*informal*), relax, veg out (*slang, chiefly U.S.*) **5 not turn a hair** = **remain calm**, keep one's cool (*slang*), keep one's hair on (*Brit. informal*), not bat an eyelid **6 split hairs** = **quibble**, cavil, find fault, pettifog

hairdresser *noun* = **stylist**, barber, coiffeur *or* coiffeuse

hairless *adjective* = **bare**, bald, baldheaded, beardless, clean-shaven, depilated, shorn

hairpiece *noun* = **wig**, toupee

hair-raising *adjective* = **frightening**, alarming, bloodcurdling, breathtaking, creepy, exciting, horrifying, petrifying, scary, shocking, spine-chilling, startling, terrifying, thrilling

hair's-breadth *noun* = **fraction**, hair, jot, narrow margin, whisker

hairsplitting *adjective* = **fault-finding**, captious, carping, cavilling, fine, finicky, nice, niggling, nit-picking (*informal*), overrefined, quibbling, subtle

hairstyle *noun* = **haircut**, coiffure, cut, hairdo, style

hairy *adjective* **1** = **shaggy**, bearded, bewhiskered, bushy, fleecy, furry, hirsute, stubbly, unshaven, woolly **2** *Slang* = **dangerous**, difficult, hazardous, perilous, risky, scaring

halcyon *adjective* **1** = **peaceful**, calm,

gentle, mild, placid, quiet, serene, still, tranquil, undisturbed, unruffled **2** *As in* **halcyon days** = **happy**, carefree, flourishing, golden, palmy, prosperous

hale *adjective* = **healthy**, able-bodied, blooming, fit, flourishing, hearty, in fine fettle, in the pink, right as rain (*Brit. informal*), robust, sound, strong, vigorous, well

half *noun* **1** = **equal part**, bisection, division, fifty per cent, fraction, hemisphere, portion, section **2 by half** = **excessively**, considerably, very much ♦ *adjective* **3** = **partial**, divided, fractional, halved, incomplete, limited, moderate ♦ *adverb* **4** = **partially**, after a fashion, all but, barely, inadequately, incompletely, in part, partly, pretty nearly, slightly

half-baked *adjective Informal* = **poorly planned**, ill-conceived, ill-judged, impractical, short-sighted, unformed, unthought out *or* through

half-hearted *adjective* = **unenthusiastic**, apathetic, cool, half-arsed (*Brit. slang*), half-assed (*U.S. & Canad. slang*), indifferent, lacklustre, listless, lukewarm, neutral, passive, perfunctory, spiritless, tame, uninterested
➤ **Antonyms**
ambitious, animated, avid, concerned, determined, eager, emotional, energetic, enthusiastic, excited, spirited, warm, wholehearted, zealous

halfway *adverb* **1** = **midway**, to *or* in the middle, to the midpoint **2** = **partially**, incompletely, moderately, nearly, partly, rather **3 meet halfway** = **compromise**, accommodate, come to terms, concede, give and take, strike a balance, trade off ♦ *adjective* **4** = **midway**, central, equidistant, intermediate, mid, middle **5** = **partial**, imperfect, incomplete, moderate, part-way

halfwit *noun* = **fool**, airhead (*slang*), berk (*Brit. slang*), charlie (*Brit. informal*), dickhead (*slang*), dimwit (*informal*), divvy (*Brit. slang*), dolt, dumb-ass (*slang*), dunce, dunderhead, fathead (*informal*), idiot, imbecile (*informal*), jerk (*slang, chiefly U.S. & Canad.*), lamebrain (*informal*), mental defective, moron, nerd *or* nurd (*slang*), nitwit (*informal*), numbskull *or* numskull, numpty (*Scot. informal*), oaf, pillock (*Brit. slang*), prat (*slang*), prick (*slang*), schmuck (*U.S. slang*), simpleton, twit (*informal, chiefly Brit.*), wally (*slang*)

half-witted *adjective* = **foolish**, addle-brained, barmy (*slang*), batty (*slang*), crazy, doltish, doolally (*slang*), dull, dull-witted, dumb (*informal*), dumb-ass (*slang*), feeble-minded, goofy (*informal*), idiotic, moronic, obtuse, silly, simple, simple-minded, stupid

hall *noun* **1** = **entrance hall**, corridor, entry, foyer, hallway, lobby, passage, passageway, vestibule **2** = **meeting place**, assembly room, auditorium, chamber, concert hall

hallmark *noun* **1** = **indication**, badge, emblem, sure sign, telltale sign **2** *Brit.* = **seal**, authentication, device, endorsement, mark, sign, signet, stamp, symbol

hallowed *adjective* = **sanctified**, blessed, consecrated, dedicated, holy, honoured, revered, sacred, sacrosanct

hallucinate *verb* = **imagine**, daydream, envision, fantasize, freak out (*informal*), have hallucinations, trip (*informal*)

hallucination *noun* = **illusion**, apparition, delusion, dream, fantasy, figment of the imagination, mirage, phantasmagoria, vision

hallucinogenic *adjective* = **psychedelic**, hallucinatory, mind-blowing (*informal*), mind-expanding, psychoactive

halo *noun* = **ring of light**, aura, aureole *or* aureola, corona, nimbus, radiance

halt *verb* **1** = **stop**, belay (*Nautical*), break off, call it a day, cease, close down, come to an end, desist, draw up, pull up, rest, stand still, wait **2** = **hold back**, arrest, block, bring to an end, check, curb, cut short, end, impede, nip in the bud, obstruct, staunch, stem, stem the flow, terminate ♦ *noun* **3** = **stop**, arrest, break, close, end, impasse, interruption, pause, stand, standstill, stoppage, termination
➤ **Antonyms**
verb ≠ **stop**: begin, commence, continue, go ahead, maintain, proceed, resume, start ≠ **hold back**: aid, boost, encourage, forward ♦ *noun* ≠ **stop**: beginning, commencement, continuation, resumption, start

halting *adjective* = **faltering**, awkward, hesitant, imperfect, laboured, stammering, stumbling, stuttering

halve *verb* **1** = **bisect**, cut in half, divide equally, reduce by fifty per cent, share equally, split in two ♦ *noun* **2** *plural* **by halves** = **incompletely**, imperfectly, scrappily, skimpily

ham-fisted *adjective Informal* = **clumsy**, all fingers and thumbs (*informal*), awkward, bungling, butterfingered (*informal*), cack-handed (*informal*), ham-handed (*informal*), inept, maladroit

hammer *verb* **1** = **hit**, bang, beat, drive, knock, strike, tap **2** *often with* **into** = **impress upon**, din into, drive home, drub into, drum into, grind into, instruct, repeat **3** *often with* **away** (**at**) = **work**, beaver away (*Brit. informal*), drudge, grind, keep on, peg away (*chiefly Brit.*), persevere, persist, plug away (*informal*), pound away, stick at **4** *Informal* = **defeat**, beat, blow out of the water (*slang*), clobber (*slang*), drub, lick (*informal*), master, run rings around (*informal*), tank (*slang*), thrash, trounce, wipe the floor with (*informal*), worst

hammer out *verb* = **work out**, accomplish, bring about, come to a conclusion, complete, finish, form a resolution, make a decision, negotiate, produce, settle, sort out, thrash out

hamper *verb* = **hinder**, bind, cramp, curb, encumber, entangle, fetter, frustrate, hamstring, handicap, hold up, impede, interfere with, obstruct, prevent, restrain, restrict, slow down, thwart
➤ **Antonyms**
aid, assist, boost, encourage, expedite, forward, further, help, promote, speed

hamstring *verb* = **thwart**, balk, foil, frustrate, prevent, ruin, stop

hand *noun* **1** = **palm**, fist, hook, mitt (*slang*), paw (*informal*) **2** = **penmanship**, calligraphy, handwriting, longhand, script **3** = **influence**, agency, direction, part, participation, share **4** = **assistance**, aid, help, support **5** = **worker**, artificer, artisan, craftsman, employee, hired man, labourer, operative, workman **6** = **round of applause**, clap, ovation **7** **at** *or* **on hand** = **nearby**, approaching, at one's fingertips, available, close, handy, imminent, just round the corner, near, on tap (*informal*), ready, within reach **8** **from hand to mouth** = **in poverty**, by necessity, improvidently, insecurely, on the breadline (*informal*), precariously, uncertainly **9** **hand in glove** = **in league**, allied, in cahoots (*informal*), in partnership **10** **hand over fist** = **steadily**, by leaps and bounds, easily, swiftly **11** **in hand: a** = **under control**, in order, receiving attention **b** = **in reserve**, available for use, put by, ready ♦ *verb* **12** = **give**, deliver, hand over, pass

handbook *noun* = **guidebook**, guide, instruction book, manual

handcuff *verb* = **shackle**, fetter, manacle

handcuffs *plural noun* = **shackles**, cuffs (*informal*), fetters, manacles

hand down *or* **on** *verb* = **pass on** *or* **down**, bequeath, give, grant, transfer, will

handful *noun* = **few**, small number, small

quantity, smattering, sprinkling
➤ **Antonyms**
a lot, crowd, heaps, horde, large number, large quantity, loads (*informal*), masses (*informal*), mob, plenty, scores, stacks

handicap *noun* 1 = **disability**, defect, impairment 2 = **disadvantage**, barrier, block, drawback, encumbrance, hazard, hindrance, impediment, limitation, millstone, obstacle, restriction, shortcoming, stumbling block 3 = **advantage**, edge, head start, odds, penalty ♦ *verb* 4 = **hinder**, burden, encumber, hamper, hamstring, hobble, hold back, impede, limit, place at a disadvantage, restrict, retard
➤ **Antonyms**
noun ≠**disadvantage**: advantage, asset, benefit, boost, edge ♦ *verb* ≠**hinder**: aid, assist, benefit, boost, forward, further, help, promote

handicraft *noun* = **craftsmanship**, art, artisanship, craft, handiwork, skill, workmanship

handiwork *noun* 1 = **handicraft**, craft, handwork 2 = **creation**, achievement, artefact, design, invention, product, production, result

handkerchief *noun* = **hanky** (*informal*), tissue

handle *noun* 1 = **grip**, haft, handgrip, hilt, stock 2 **fly off the handle** *Informal* = **lose one's temper**, blow one's top, explode, flip one's lid (*slang*), fly into a rage, go ballistic (*slang, chiefly U.S.*), have a tantrum, hit or go through the roof (*informal*), let fly (*informal*), lose it (*informal*), lose one's cool (*slang*), lose the plot (*informal*), wig out (*slang*) ♦ *verb* 3 = **hold**, feel, finger, fondle, grasp, maul, paw (*informal*), pick up, poke, touch 4 = **control**, direct, guide, manage, manipulate, manoeuvre, operate, steer, use, wield 5 = **discuss**, discourse, treat 6 = **deal with**, administer, conduct, cope with, manage, supervise, take care of, treat 7 = **deal in**, carry, market, sell, stock, trade, traffic in

handling *noun* = **management**, administration, approach, conduct, direction, manipulation, running, treatment

hand-out *noun* 1 = **charity**, alms, dole 2 = **leaflet**, bulletin, circular, free sample, literature (*informal*), mailshot, press release

hand out *verb* = **distribute**, deal out, disburse, dish out (*informal*), dispense, disseminate, give out

hand over *verb* = **give**, deliver, donate, fork out or up (*slang*), present, release,

surrender, transfer, turn over, yield

hand-picked *adjective* = **selected**, choice, chosen, elect, elite, select
➤ **Antonyms**
haphazard, indiscriminate, random, run-of-the-mill, wholesale

hands *plural noun* 1 = **control**, authority, care, charge, command, custody, disposal, guardianship, keeping, possession, power, supervision 2 **hands down** = **easily**, effortlessly, with no contest, with no trouble

handsome *adjective* 1 = **good-looking**, admirable, attractive, becoming, comely, dishy (*informal, chiefly Brit.*), elegant, fine, gorgeous, graceful, personable 2 = **generous**, abundant, ample, bountiful, considerable, gracious, large, liberal, magnanimous, plentiful, sizable or sizeable
➤ **Antonyms**
≠**good-looking**: inelegant, tasteless, ugly, unattractive, unprepossessing, unsightly ≠**generous**: base, cheap, meagre, mean, miserly, selfish, small, stingy, ungenerous

handsomely *adverb* = **generously**, abundantly, amply, bountifully, liberally, magnanimously, munificently, plentifully, richly

handwriting *noun* = **penmanship**, calligraphy, fist, hand, longhand, scrawl, script

handy *adjective* 1 = **convenient**, accessible, at hand, at one's fingertips, available, close, just round the corner, near, nearby, on hand, within reach 2 = **useful**, convenient, easy to use, helpful, manageable, neat, practical, serviceable, user-friendly 3 = **skilful**, adept, adroit, clever, deft, dexterous, expert, proficient, ready, skilled
➤ **Antonyms**
≠**convenient**: awkward, inaccessible, inconvenient, out of the way, unavailable ≠**useful**: awkward, inconvenient, unwieldy, useless ≠**skilful**: clumsy, ham-fisted, incompetent, inept, inexpert, maladroit, unaccomplished, unskilful, unskilled, useless

handyman *noun* = **odd-jobman**, DIY expert, jack-of-all-trades

hang *verb* 1 = **suspend**, be pendent, dangle, depend, droop, incline 2 = **execute**, lynch, send to the gallows, string up (*informal*) 3 = **hover**, be poised, drift, float, remain, swing 4 = **fasten**, attach, cover, deck, decorate, drape, fix, furnish 5 **hang fire** = **put off**, be slow, be suspended, delay, hang back, procrastinate, stall, vacillate ♦ *noun* 6 **get the hang of** = **grasp**, comprehend, get the knack *or* technique, understand

hang about *or* **around** *verb* **1** = **loiter**, dally, linger, roam, tarry, waste time **2** = **associate with**, frequent, hang out (*informal*), hang with (*informal, chiefly U.S.*), haunt, resort

hang back *verb* = **be reluctant**, be backward, demur, hesitate, hold back, recoil

hangdog *adjective* = **guilty**, abject, browbeaten, cowed, cringing, defeated, downcast, furtive, shamefaced, sneaking, wretched

hanger-on *noun* = **parasite**, dependant, follower, freeloader (*slang*), lackey, leech, minion, sponger (*informal*), sycophant

hang on *verb* **1** *Informal* = **wait**, hold on, hold the line, remain, stop **2** = **continue**, carry on, endure, go on, hold on, hold out, persevere, persist, remain, stay the course **3** = **grasp**, cling, clutch, grip, hold fast **4** = **depend on**, be conditional upon, be contingent on, be dependent on, be determined by, hinge, rest, turn on **5** *Also* **hang onto** *or* **hang upon** = **listen attentively**, be rapt, give ear

hang-out *noun* = **haunt**, den, home, joint (*slang*), resort

hangover *noun* = **aftereffects**, head (*informal*), morning after (*informal*)

hang over *verb* = **loom**, be imminent, impend, menace, threaten

hang-up *noun Informal* = **preoccupation**, block, difficulty, inhibition, obsession, problem, thing (*informal*)

hank *noun* = **coil**, length, loop, piece, roll, skein

hanker *verb, with* **for** *or* **after** = **desire**, ache, covet, crave, eat one's heart out over, hope, hunger, itch, long, lust, pine, set one's heart on, thirst, want, wish, yearn, yen (*informal*)

hankering *noun* = **desire**, ache, craving, hope, hunger, itch, longing, pining, thirst, urge, wish, yearning, yen (*informal*)

hanky-panky *noun Informal* = **mischief**, chicanery, deception, funny business (*informal*), jiggery-pokery (*informal, chiefly Brit.*), monkey business (*informal*), shenanigans (*informal*), subterfuge, trickery

haphazard *adjective* **1** = **random**, accidental, arbitrary, chance, fluky (*informal*) **2** = **unsystematic**, aimless, careless, casual, disorderly, disorganized, hit or miss (*informal*), indiscriminate, slapdash, slipshod, unmethodical
➤ **Antonyms**
≠**random**: arranged, deliberate, planned
≠**unsystematic**: careful, considered,

methodical, orderly, organized, systematic, thoughtful

hapless *adjective* = **unlucky**, cursed, ill-fated, ill-starred, jinxed, luckless, miserable, unfortunate, unhappy, wretched

happen *verb* **1** = **occur**, appear, arise, come about, come off (*informal*), come to pass, crop up (*informal*), develop, ensue, eventuate, follow, materialize, present itself, result, see the light of day, take place, transpire (*informal*) **2** = **chance**, fall out, have the fortune to be, pan out (*informal*), supervene, turn out **3** = **befall**, become of, betide

happening *noun* = **event**, accident, adventure, affair, case, chance, episode, escapade, experience, incident, occasion, occurrence, phenomenon, proceeding, scene

happily *adverb* **1** = **joyfully**, blithely, cheerfully, gaily, gleefully, joyously, merrily **2** = **luckily**, auspiciously, favourably, fortunately, opportunely, propitiously, providentially **3** = **willingly**, agreeably, contentedly, delightedly, enthusiastically, freely, gladly, heartily, with pleasure

happiness *noun* = **joy**, blessedness, bliss, cheer, cheerfulness, cheeriness, contentment, delight, ecstasy, elation, enjoyment, exuberance, felicity, gaiety, gladness, high spirits, jubilation, light-heartedness, merriment, pleasure, prosperity, satisfaction, wellbeing
➤ **Antonyms**
annoyance, bane, depression, despondency, distress, grief, low spirits, misery, misfortune, sadness, sorrow, unhappiness

happy *adjective* **1** = **joyful**, blessed, blissful, blithe, cheerful, cock-a-hoop, content, contented, delighted, ecstatic, elated, floating on air, glad, gratified, jolly, joyous, jubilant, merry, on cloud nine (*informal*), overjoyed, over the moon (*informal*), pleased, thrilled, walking on air (*informal*) **2** = **fortunate**, advantageous, appropriate, apt, auspicious, befitting, convenient, favourable, felicitous, lucky, opportune, promising, propitious, satisfactory, seasonable, successful, timely, well-timed
➤ **Antonyms**
≠**joyful**: depressed, despondent, discontented, displeased, down in the dumps (*informal*), forlorn, gloomy, joyless, low, melancholy, miserable, mournful, sad, sombre, sorrowful, sorry, unhappy
≠**fortunate**: inapt, unfortunate, unhappy, unlucky

happy-go-lucky *adjective* = **carefree**, blithe, casual, devil-may-care, easy-going,

heedless, improvident, insouciant, irresponsible, light-hearted, nonchalant, unconcerned, untroubled
➤ **Antonyms**
careworn, cheerless, gloomy, melancholy, morose, sad, serious, unhappy

harangue verb 1 = **rant**, address, declaim, exhort, hold forth, lecture, spout (informal) ◆ noun 2 = **speech**, address, declamation, diatribe, exhortation, lecture, oration, screed, spiel (informal), tirade

harass verb = **annoy**, badger, bait, be on one's back (slang), bother, breathe down someone's neck, chivvy (Brit.), disturb, fatigue, harry, hassle (informal), hound, persecute, pester, plague, tease, torment, trouble, vex, weary, worry

harassed adjective = **hassled** (informal), careworn, distraught, harried, plagued, strained, tormented, troubled, under pressure, under stress, vexed, worried

harassment noun = **hassle** (informal), aggravation (informal), annoyance, badgering, bedevilment, bother, grief (informal), irritation, molestation, nuisance, persecution, pestering, torment, trouble, vexation

harbinger noun Literary = **herald**, forerunner, foretoken, indication, messenger, omen, portent, precursor, sign

harbour noun 1 = **port**, anchorage, destination, haven 2 = **sanctuary**, asylum, covert, haven, refuge, retreat, sanctum, security, shelter ◆ verb 3 = **maintain**, believe, brood over, cherish, cling to, entertain, foster, hold, imagine, nurse, nurture, retain 4 = **shelter**, conceal, hide, lodge, protect, provide refuge, relieve, secrete, shield

hard adjective 1 = **tough**, compact, dense, firm, impenetrable, inflexible, rigid, rocklike, solid, stiff, stony, strong, unyielding 2 = **strenuous**, arduous, backbreaking, burdensome, exacting, exhausting, fatiguing, formidable, laborious, rigorous, toilsome, tough, uphill, wearying 3 = **difficult**, baffling, complex, complicated, intricate, involved, knotty, perplexing, puzzling, tangled, thorny, unfathomable 4 = **harsh**, callous, cold, cruel, exacting, grim, hardhearted, implacable, obdurate, pitiless, ruthless, severe, stern, strict, stubborn, unfeeling, unjust, unkind, unrelenting, unsparing, unsympathetic 5 = **grim**, calamitous, dark, disagreeable, disastrous, distressing, grievous, intolerable, painful, unpleasant 6 = **forceful**, driving, fierce, heavy, powerful, strong, violent 7 Of truth or facts = **indisputable**, actual, bare, cold, definite,

plain, undeniable, unvarnished, verified 8 Of feelings or words = **bitter**, acrimonious, angry, antagonistic, hostile, rancorous, resentful ◆ adverb 9 = **energetically**, fiercely, forcefully, forcibly, heavily, intensely, powerfully, severely, sharply, strongly, vigorously, violently, with all one's might, with might and main 10 = **intently**, assiduously, determinedly, diligently, doggedly, earnestly, industriously, persistently, steadily, strenuously, untiringly 11 = **with difficulty**, agonizingly, badly, distressingly, harshly, laboriously, painfully, roughly, severely
➤ **Antonyms**
adjective ≠**tough**: flexible, malleable, pliable, soft, weak ≠**strenuous**: easy, easy-peasy (slang), lazy, light, soft ≠**difficult**: clear, direct, easy, easy-peasy (slang), simple, straightforward, uncomplicated ≠**harsh**: agreeable, amiable, careless, flexible, friendly, gentle, good, humane, kind, lenient, merciful, mild, permissive, pleasant ◆ adverb ≠**energetically**: lazily, lightly, loosely, softly, weakly ≠**intently**: easily, gently, softly

hard-and-fast adjective = **fixed**, binding, immutable, incontrovertible, inflexible, invariable, rigid, set, strict, stringent, unalterable

hard-bitten or **hard-boiled** adjective Informal = **tough**, case-hardened, cynical, down-to-earth, hard-headed, hard-nosed (informal), matter-of-fact, practical, realistic, shrewd, unsentimental
➤ **Antonyms**
benign, compassionate, gentle, humane, idealistic, mild, romantic, sympathetic

hard-core adjective 1 = **explicit**, obscene, X-rated (informal) 2 = **dyed-in-the-wool**, dedicated, die-hard, extreme, intransigent, obstinate, rigid, staunch, steadfast

harden verb 1 = **solidify**, anneal, bake, cake, freeze, set, stiffen 2 = **accustom**, brutalize, case-harden, habituate, inure, season, train 3 = **reinforce**, brace, buttress, fortify, gird, indurate, nerve, steel, strengthen, toughen

hardened adjective 1 = **habitual**, chronic, fixed, incorrigible, inveterate, irredeemable, shameless 2 = **seasoned**, accustomed, habituated, inured, toughened
➤ **Antonyms**
infrequent, irregular, occasional, rare, unaccustomed

hard-headed adjective = **shrewd**, astute, cool, hard-boiled (informal), level-headed, practical, pragmatic, realistic, sensible,

tough, unsentimental
➤ **Antonyms**
idealistic, impractical, sentimental, unrealistic

hardhearted *adjective* = **unsympathetic**, affectless, callous, cold, cruel, hard, hard as nails, heartless, indifferent, inhuman, insensitive, intolerant, merciless, pitiless, stony, uncaring, unfeeling, unkind
➤ **Antonyms**
compassionate, forgiving, gentle, humane, kind, loving, merciful, sensitive, soft-hearted, sympathetic, understanding, warm, warm-hearted

hardihood *noun* = **courage**, backbone, boldness, bottle (*Brit. slang*), bravery, daring, determination, firmness, grit, guts (*informal*), intrepidity, mettle, nerve, pluck, resolution, spirit, spunk (*informal*), strength

hardiness *noun* = **resilience**, boldness, courage, fortitude, intrepidity, resolution, robustness, ruggedness, sturdiness, toughness, valour

hardline *adjective* = **tough**, inflexible, intransigent, uncompromising, unyielding

hardly *adverb* = **barely**, almost not, at a push, by no means, faintly, infrequently, just, not at all, not quite, no way, only, only just, scarcely, with difficulty
➤ **Antonyms**
abundantly, amply, by all means, certainly, completely, easily, fully, indubitably, more than, really, truly, undoubtedly, well over

hard-pressed *adjective* = **under pressure**, harried, hotly pursued, in difficulties, pushed (*informal*), under attack, up against it (*informal*), with one's back to the wall

hardship *noun* = **suffering**, adversity, affliction, burden, calamity, destitution, difficulty, grievance, labour, misery, misfortune, need, oppression, persecution, privation, toil, torment, trial, tribulation, trouble, want
➤ **Antonyms**
aid, blessing, boon, comfort, ease, good fortune, happiness, help, prosperity, relief

hard up *adjective* = **poor**, bankrupt, broke (*informal*), bust (*informal*), cleaned out (*slang*), dirt-poor (*informal*), down and out, flat broke (*informal*), impecunious, impoverished, in the red (*informal*), on one's uppers (*informal*), on the breadline, out of pocket, penniless, short, short of cash or funds, skint (*Brit. slang*), strapped for cash (*informal*), without two pennies to rub together (*informal*)
➤ **Antonyms**
affluent, comfortable (*informal*), fortunate,

loaded (*slang*), rich, wealthy, well-heeled (*informal*), well-off

hard-wearing *adjective* = **durable**, resilient, rugged, stout, strong, tough, well-made

hard-working *adjective* = **industrious**, assiduous, busy, conscientious, diligent, energetic
➤ **Antonyms**
careless, good-for-nothing, lazy

hardy *adjective* = **strong**, firm, fit, hale, healthy, hearty, lusty, robust, rugged, sound, stalwart, stout, sturdy, tough, vigorous
➤ **Antonyms**
delicate, feeble, fragile, frail, sickly, soft, weak, weedy

harebrained *adjective* = **foolish**, asinine, empty-headed, flighty, half-baked (*informal*), inane, mindless, rash, reckless, unstable, unsteady, wild

hark *verb* Old-fashioned = **listen**, attend, give ear, give heed, hear, mark, notice, pay attention

hark back *verb* = **return**, look back, recall, recollect, regress, remember, revert, think back

harlot *noun* Literary = **prostitute**, call girl, fallen woman, hussy, loose woman, pro (*slang*), scrubber (*Brit. & Austral. slang*), slag (*Brit. slang*), slapper (*Brit. slang*), streetwalker, strumpet, tart (*informal*), tramp (*slang*), whore, working girl (*facetious slang*)

harm *verb* 1 = **injure**, abuse, blemish, damage, hurt, ill-treat, ill-use, impair, lay a finger on, maltreat, mar, molest, ruin, spoil, wound ♦ *noun* 2 = **injury**, abuse, damage, detriment, hurt, ill, impairment, loss, mischief, misfortune
➤ **Antonyms**
verb ≠**injure**: aid, alleviate, ameliorate, assist, benefit, better, cure, heal, help, improve, repair ♦ *noun* ≠**injury**: aid, assistance, benefit, blessing, boon, gain, good, help, improvement, reparation

harmful *adjective* = **injurious**, baleful, baneful, damaging, deleterious, destructive, detrimental, disadvantageous, evil, hurtful, noxious, pernicious
➤ **Antonyms**
beneficial, good, harmless, healthy, helpful, innocuous, safe, wholesome

harmless *adjective* = **innocuous**, gentle, innocent, innoxious, inoffensive, nontoxic, not dangerous, safe, unobjectionable
➤ **Antonyms**
dangerous, destructive, harmful, unhealthy, unsafe, unwholesome

harmonious   348   haste

harmonious *adjective* **1** = **compatible**, agreeable, congruous, consonant, coordinated, correspondent, matching **2** = **friendly**, agreeable, amicable, compatible, concordant, congenial, cordial, *en rapport*, fraternal, in accord, in harmony, in unison, of one mind, sympathetic **3** = **melodious**, concordant, dulcet, euphonic, euphonious, harmonic, harmonizing, mellifluous, musical, sweet-sounding, tuneful
➤ **Antonyms**
≠**compatible**: contrasting, discordant, incompatible, inconsistent, unlike ≠**friendly**: discordant, unfriendly ≠**melodious**: cacophonous, discordant, grating, harsh, unmelodious

harmonize *verb* = **go together**, accord, adapt, agree, arrange, attune, be in unison, be of one mind, blend, coordinate, correspond, match, reconcile, suit, tally, tone in with

harmony *noun* **1** = **agreement**, accord, amicability, amity, assent, compatibility, concord, conformity, consensus, cooperation, friendship, goodwill, like-mindedness, order, peace, rapport, sympathy, unanimity, understanding, unity **2** = **tunefulness**, euphony, melodiousness, melody, tune, unison **3** = **compatibility**, balance, concord, congruity, consistency, consonance, coordination, correspondence, fitness, parallelism, suitability, symmetry
➤ **Antonyms**
≠**agreement**: antagonism, conflict, contention, disagreement, dissension, hostility, opposition ≠**tunefulness**: cacophony ≠**compatibility**: conflict, disagreement, incongruity, inconsistency, unsuitability

harness *noun* **1** = **equipment**, gear, tack, tackle, trappings **2 in harness** = **working**, active, at work, busy, in action ♦ *verb* **3** = **put in harness**, couple, hitch up, saddle, yoke **4** = **exploit**, apply, channel, control, employ, make productive, mobilize, render useful, turn to account, utilize

harp *verb*, *with* **on** *or* **upon** = **go on**, dwell on, labour, press, reiterate, renew, repeat, rub it in

harridan *noun* = **shrew**, ballbreaker (*slang*), battle-axe (*informal*), nag, scold, tartar, termagant, virago, witch

harrowing *adjective* = **distressing**, agonizing, alarming, chilling, disturbing, excruciating, frightening, gut-wrenching, heartbreaking, heart-rending, nerve-racking, painful, racking, scaring, terrifying, tormenting, traumatic

harry *verb* = **pester**, annoy, badger, bedevil, be on one's back (*slang*), bother, breathe down someone's neck, chivvy, get in one's hair (*informal*), harass, hassle (*informal*), persecute, plague, tease, torment, trouble, vex, worry

harsh *adjective* **1** = **severe**, abusive, austere, bitter, bleak, brutal, comfortless, cruel, dour, Draconian, drastic, grim, hard, pitiless, punitive, relentless, ruthless, sharp, Spartan, stern, stringent, tough, unfeeling, unkind, unpleasant, unrelenting **2** = **raucous**, coarse, croaking, crude, discordant, dissonant, grating, guttural, jarring, rasping, rough, strident, unmelodious
➤ **Antonyms**
≠**severe**: agreeable, gentle, kind, loving, merciful, mild, pleasant, sweet ≠**raucous**: harmonious, mellifluous, smooth, soft, soothing, sweet

harshly *adverb* = **severely**, brutally, cruelly, grimly, roughly, sharply, sternly, strictly

harshness *noun* = **severity**, acerbity, acrimony, asperity, bitterness, brutality, coarseness, hardness, ill-temper, rigour, roughness, sourness, sternness

harum-scarum *adjective* = **reckless**, careless, hasty, impetuous, imprudent, inconstant, irresponsible, precipitate, rash, scatterbrained, scatty (*Brit. informal*), wild

harvest *noun* **1** = **gathering**, harvesting, harvest-time, reaping **2** = **crop**, produce, yield **3** = **product**, consequence, effect, fruition, result, return ♦ *verb* **4** = **gather**, mow, pick, pluck, reap

hash *noun* **make a hash of** *Informal* = **mess up**, bodge (*informal*), botch, bungle, cock up (*Brit. slang*), flub (*U.S. slang*), fuck up (*offensive taboo slang*), jumble, make a nonsense of (*informal*), make a pig's ear of (*informal*), mishandle, mismanage, mix, muddle

hassle *Informal* ♦ *noun* **1** = **trouble**, bother, difficulty, grief (*informal*), inconvenience, problem, struggle, trial, upset **2** = **argument**, altercation, bickering, disagreement, dispute, fight, quarrel, row, squabble, tussle, wrangle ♦ *verb* **3** = **bother**, annoy, badger, be on one's back (*slang*), breath down someone's neck, bug (*informal*), get in one's hair (*informal*), get on one's nerves (*informal*), harass, harry, hound, pester

haste *noun* **1** = **speed**, alacrity, briskness, dispatch, expedition, fleetness, nimbleness, promptitude, quickness, rapidity, rapidness, swiftness, urgency, velocity **2** = **rush**, bustle, hastiness, hurry, hustle, impetuosity, precipitateness,

rashness, recklessness
➤ **Antonyms**
≠**speed**: slowness, sluggishness ≠**rush**: calmness, care, delay, deliberation, leisureliness, sureness

hasten verb **1** = **rush**, barrel (along) (*informal, chiefly U.S. & Canad.*), beetle, bolt, burn rubber (*informal*), dash, fly, get one's skates on (*informal*), haste, hurry (up), make haste, race, run, scurry, scuttle, speed, sprint, step on it (*informal*), tear (along) **2** = **hurry (up)**, accelerate, advance, dispatch, expedite, goad, precipitate, press, push forward, quicken, speed (up), step up (*informal*), urge
➤ **Antonyms**
≠**rush**: crawl, creep, dawdle, move slowly ≠**hurry (up)**: decelerate, delay, hinder, impede, retard, slow, slow down

hastily adverb **1** = **quickly**, apace, double-quick, fast, hotfoot, pdq (*slang*), posthaste, promptly, pronto (*informal*), rapidly, speedily, straightaway **2** = **hurriedly**, heedlessly, impetuously, impulsively, on the spur of the moment, precipitately, rashly, recklessly, too quickly

hasty adjective **1** = **speedy**, brisk, eager, expeditious, fast, fleet, hurried, prompt, rapid, swift, urgent **2** = **brief**, cursory, fleeting, passing, perfunctory, rushed, short, superficial **3** = **rash**, foolhardy, headlong, heedless, impetuous, impulsive, indiscreet, precipitate, reckless, thoughtless, unduly quick
➤ **Antonyms**
≠**speedy**: leisurely, slow ≠**brief**: long, protracted ≠**rash**: careful, cautious, detailed, thorough, thoughtful

hatch verb **1** = **incubate**, breed, bring forth, brood **2** = **devise**, conceive, concoct, contrive, cook up (*informal*), design, dream up (*informal*), manufacture, plan, plot, project, scheme, think up, trump up

hatchet noun = **axe**, cleaver, machete, tomahawk

hate verb **1** = **detest**, abhor, abominate, be hostile to, be repelled by, be sick of, despise, dislike, have an aversion to, loathe, recoil from **2** = **be unwilling**, be loath, be reluctant, be sorry, dislike, feel disinclined, have no stomach for, shrink from ◆ noun **3** = **dislike**, abhorrence, abomination, animosity, animus, antagonism, antipathy, aversion, detestation, enmity, hatred, hostility, loathing, odium
➤ **Antonyms**
verb ≠**detest**: be fond of, cherish, dote on, enjoy, esteem, fancy, like, love, relish, treasure, wish ◆ noun ≠**dislike**: affection,

amity, devotion, fondness, goodwill, liking, love

hateful adjective = **despicable**, abhorrent, abominable, detestable, disgusting, foul, heinous, horrible, loathsome, obnoxious, obscene, odious, offensive, repellent, repugnant, repulsive, revolting, vile
➤ **Antonyms**
attractive, beautiful, charming, desirable, good, likable or likeable, lovable, pleasant, wonderful

hatred noun = **dislike**, abomination, animosity, animus, antagonism, antipathy, aversion, detestation, enmity, hate, ill will, odium, repugnance, revulsion
➤ **Antonyms**
affection, amity, attachment, devotion, fondness, friendliness, goodwill, liking, love

haughtiness noun = **pride**, airs, aloofness, arrogance, conceit, contempt, contemptuousness, disdain, hauteur, insolence, loftiness, pomposity, snobbishness, superciliousness

haughty adjective = **proud**, arrogant, assuming, conceited, contemptuous, disdainful, high, high and mighty (*informal*), hoity-toity (*informal*), imperious, lofty, on one's high horse (*informal*), overweening, scornful, snobbish, snooty (*informal*), stuck-up (*informal*), supercilious, uppish (*Brit. informal*)
➤ **Antonyms**
humble, meek, mild, modest, self-effacing, subservient, wimpish or wimpy (*informal*)

haul verb **1** = **drag**, draw, hale, heave, lug, pull, tow, trail, tug **2** = **transport**, carry, cart, convey, hump (*Brit. slang*), move ◆ noun **3** = **drag**, heave, pull, tug **4** = **yield**, booty, catch, find, gain, harvest, loot, spoils, takings

haunt verb **1** = **visit**, walk **2** = **plague**, beset, come back, obsess, possess, prey on, recur, stay with, torment, trouble, weigh on **3** = **frequent**, hang around or about, resort, visit ◆ noun **4** = **meeting place**, den, gathering place, hangout (*informal*), rendezvous, resort, stamping ground

haunted adjective **1** = **possessed**, cursed, eerie, ghostly, jinxed, spooky (*informal*) **2** = **preoccupied**, obsessed, plagued, tormented, troubled, worried

haunting adjective = **evocative**, disturbing, eerie, indelible, nostalgic, persistent, poignant, recurrent, recurring, unforgettable

hauteur noun = **haughtiness**, affectedness, airs, arrogance, contempt, dignity, disdain, loftiness, pride, snobbishness, stateliness, superciliousness

have *verb* **1 = possess**, hold, keep, obtain, occupy, own, retain **2 = receive**, accept, acquire, gain, get, obtain, procure, secure, take **3 = experience**, endure, enjoy, feel, meet with, suffer, sustain, undergo **4** *Slang* **= cheat**, deceive, dupe, fool, outwit, swindle, take in (*informal*), trick **5 = put up with** (*informal*), allow, consider, entertain, permit, think about, tolerate **6 = give birth to**, bear, beget, bring forth, bring into the world, deliver **7 have to = be obliged**, be bound, be compelled, be forced, have got to, must, ought, should **8 have had it** *Informal* **= be exhausted**, be defeated, be finished, be out, be past it (*informal*)

haven *noun* **1 = sanctuary**, asylum, refuge, retreat, sanctum, shelter **2 = harbour**, anchorage, port

have on *verb* **1 = wear**, be clothed in, be dressed in **2 = have planned**, be committed to, be engaged to, have on the agenda **3** *Informal* **= tease**, deceive, kid (*informal*), play a joke on, pull someone's leg, take the mickey, trick, wind up (*Brit. slang*)

havoc *noun* **1** *Informal* **= disorder**, chaos, confusion, disruption, mayhem, shambles **2 play havoc (with) = wreck**, bring into chaos, confuse, convulse, demolish, destroy, devastate, disorganize, disrupt

haw *verb* **hem and haw** *or* **hum and haw = hesitate**, falter, fumble, pause, stammer, stutter

hawk *verb* **= peddle**, sell, tout (*informal*)

hawker *noun* **= pedlar**, barrow boy (*Brit.*), huckster, vendor

hawk-eyed *adjective* **= sharp-eyed**, Argus-eyed, gimlet-eyed, having eyes in the back of one's head (*informal*), keen-sighted, lynx-eyed, observant, perceptive, vigilant

haywire *adjective* **As in go haywire = chaotic**, confused, disordered, disorganized, mixed up, on the blink (*slang*), on the fritz (*slang*), out of order, shambolic (*informal*), topsy-turvy

hazard *noun* **1 = danger**, jeopardy, peril, pitfall, risk, threat ◆ *verb* **2 = jeopardize**, endanger, expose, imperil, risk, threaten **3** *As in* **hazard a guess = conjecture**, advance, offer, presume, throw out, venture, volunteer

hazardous *adjective* **= dangerous**, dicey (*informal, chiefly Brit.*), difficult, fraught with danger, insecure, perilous, precarious, risky, unsafe
➤ **Antonyms**
reliable, safe, secure, sound, stable, sure

haze *noun* **= mist**, cloud, dimness, film, fog, obscurity, smog, smokiness, steam, vapour

hazy *adjective* **1 = misty**, blurry, cloudy, dim, dull, faint, foggy, nebulous, obscure, overcast, smoky, veiled **2 = vague**, fuzzy, ill-defined, indefinite, indistinct, loose, muddled, muzzy, nebulous, uncertain, unclear
➤ **Antonyms**
≠**misty**: bright, clear, light, sunny
≠**vague**: certain, clear, detailed, well-defined

head *noun* **1 = skull**, bean (*U.S. & Canad. slang*), cranium, crown, loaf (*slang*), noddle (*informal, chiefly Brit.*), noggin, nut (*slang*), pate **2 = mind**, ability, aptitude, brain, brains (*informal*), capacity, faculty, flair, intellect, intelligence, mentality, talent, thought, understanding **3 = front**, cutting edge, first place, fore, forefront, van, vanguard **4 = top**, apex, crest, crown, height, peak, pinnacle, pitch, summit, tip, vertex **5 = leader**, boss (*informal*), captain, chief, chieftain, commander, director, headmaster *or* headmistress, head teacher, manager, master, principal, superintendent, supervisor **6 = culmination**, climax, conclusion, crisis, end, turning point **7 = source**, beginning, commencement, origin, rise, start **8** *Geography* **= headland**, cape, foreland, point, promontory **9 = heading**, branch, category, class, department, division, section, subject, topic **10 go to one's head = excite**, dizzy, intoxicate, make conceited, puff up **11 head over heels = completely**, intensely, thoroughly, uncontrollably, utterly, wholeheartedly **12 put (our, their, etc.) heads together** *Informal* **= consult**, confab (*informal*), confabulate, confer, deliberate, discuss, palaver, powwow, talk over ◆ *adjective* **13 = chief**, arch, first, foremost, front, highest, leading, main, pre-eminent, premier, prime, principal, supreme, topmost ◆ *verb* **14 = lead**, be *or* go first, cap, crown, lead the way, precede, top **15 = be in charge of**, command, control, direct, govern, guide, lead, manage, rule, run, supervise **16 = make for**, aim, go to, make a beeline for, point, set off for, set out, start towards, steer, turn

headache *noun* **1 = migraine**, head (*informal*), neuralgia **2** *Informal* **= problem**, bane, bother, inconvenience, nuisance, trouble, vexation, worry

headfirst *adverb* **1 = headlong**, diving, head-on **2 = recklessly**, carelessly, hastily, head over heels, precipitately, rashly

heading *noun* **1 = title**, caption, headline, name, rubric **2 = division**, category, class, section

headland *noun* = **promontory**, bill, bluff, cape, cliff, foreland, head, mull (*Scot.*), point

headlong *adverb, adjective* **1** = **headfirst**, headforemost, head-on ♦ *adverb* **2** = **hastily**, heedlessly, helter-skelter, hurriedly, pell-mell, precipitately, rashly, thoughtlessly, wildly ♦ *adjective* **3** = **hasty**, breakneck, dangerous, impetuous, impulsive, inconsiderate, precipitate, reckless, thoughtless

headmaster *or* **headmistress** *noun* = **principal**, head, head teacher, rector

head off *verb* **1** = **intercept**, block off, cut off, deflect, divert, interpose, intervene **2** = **prevent**, avert, fend off, forestall, parry, stop, ward off

headstrong *adjective* = **obstinate**, contrary, foolhardy, heedless, imprudent, impulsive, intractable, mulish, perverse, pig-headed, rash, reckless, self-willed, stiff-necked, stubborn, ungovernable, unruly, wilful
➤ **Antonyms**
cautious, impressionable, manageable, pliant, subservient, tractable

headway *noun* **1** = **advance**, improvement, progress, progression, way **2 make headway** = **progress**, advance, come *or* get on, cover ground, develop, gain, gain ground, make inroads (into), make strides

heady *adjective* **1** = **exciting**, exhilarating, intoxicating, overwhelming, stimulating, thrilling **2** = **intoxicating**, inebriating, potent, spirituous, strong **3** = **rash**, hasty, impetuous, impulsive, inconsiderate, precipitate, reckless, thoughtless

heal *verb* **1** = **cure**, make well, mend, regenerate, remedy, restore, treat **2** = **patch up**, alleviate, ameliorate, conciliate, harmonize, reconcile, settle, soothe
➤ **Antonyms**
aggravate, exacerbate, harm, hurt, inflame, injure, make worse, reopen, wound

healing *adjective* **1** = **medicinal**, curative, remedial, restorative, restoring, therapeutic **2** = **soothing**, assuaging, comforting, gentle, mild, mitigative, palliative

health *noun* **1** = **condition**, constitution, fettle, form, shape, state, tone **2** = **wellbeing**, fitness, good condition, haleness, healthiness, robustness, soundness, strength, vigour, wellness
➤ **Antonyms**
≠**wellbeing**: debility, disease, frailty, illness, sickness, weakness

healthful *adjective* = **healthy**, beneficial, bracing, good for one, health-giving, invigorating, nourishing, nutritious, salubrious, salutary, wholesome

healthy *adjective* **1** = **well**, active, alive and kicking, blooming, fighting fit, fit, fit as a fiddle (*informal*), flourishing, hale, hale and hearty, hardy, hearty, in fine feather, in fine fettle, in fine form, in good condition, in good shape (*informal*), in the pink, physically fit, right as rain (*Brit. informal*), robust, sound, strong, sturdy, vigorous **2** = **wholesome**, beneficial, bracing, good for one, healthful, health-giving, hygienic, invigorating, nourishing, nutritious, salubrious, salutary
➤ **Antonyms**
≠**well**: ailing, at death's door, debilitated, delicate, diseased, feeble, fragile, frail, ill, infirm, poorly (*informal*), sick, sickly, unfit, unhealthy, unsound, unwell, weak, weedy (*informal*) ≠**wholesome**: unhealthy, unwholesome

heap *noun* **1** = **pile**, accumulation, aggregation, collection, hoard, lot, mass, mound, mountain, rick, stack, stockpile, store **2** *often plural, Informal* = **a lot**, abundance, great deal, lashings (*Brit. informal*), load(s) (*informal*), lots (*informal*), mass, mint, ocean(s), oodles (*informal*), plenty, pot(s) (*informal*), quantities, stack(s), tons ♦ *verb* **3** = **pile**, accumulate, amass, augment, bank, collect, gather, hoard, increase, mound, stack, stockpile, store **4** = **confer**, assign, bestow, burden, load, shower upon

hear *verb* **1** = **listen to**, attend, be all ears (*informal*), catch, eavesdrop, give attention, hark, hearken (*archaic*), heed, listen in, overhear **2** = **learn**, ascertain, be informed, be told of, discover, find out, gather, get wind of (*informal*), hear tell (*dialect*), pick up, understand **3** *Law* = **try**, examine, investigate, judge

hearing *noun* **1** = **perception**, audition, ear **2** = **chance to speak**, audience, audition, interview **3** = **earshot**, auditory range, hearing distance, range, reach, sound **4** = **inquiry**, industrial tribunal, investigation, review, trial

hearsay *noun* = **rumour**, buzz, dirt (*U.S. slang*), gossip, grapevine (*informal*), idle talk, mere talk, report, talk, talk of the town, tittle-tattle, word of mouth

heart *noun* **1** = **nature**, character, disposition, emotion, feeling, inclination, sentiment, soul, sympathy, temperament **2** = **tenderness**, affection, benevolence, compassion, concern, humanity, love, pity, understanding **3 = courage**, balls (*taboo slang*), boldness, bravery, fortitude, guts (*informal*), mettle, mind, nerve, pluck, purpose, resolution, spirit, spunk (*informal*), will **4 = centre**, central part, core, crux, essence, hub, kernel, marrow, middle, nucleus, pith, quintessence, root **5 by heart = by memory**, by rote, off pat, parrot-fashion (*informal*), pat, word for word **6 take heart = be encouraged**, be comforted, be heartened, brighten up, buck up (*informal*), cheer up, perk up, revive

heartache *noun* **= sorrow**, affliction, agony, anguish, despair, distress, grief, heartbreak, pain, remorse, suffering, torment, torture

heartbreak *noun* **= grief**, anguish, desolation, despair, misery, pain, sorrow, suffering

heartbreaking *adjective* **= sad**, agonizing, bitter, desolating, disappointing, distressing, grievous, gut-wrenching, harrowing, heart-rending, pitiful, poignant, tragic
➤ **Antonyms**
cheerful, cheery, comic, glorious, happy, jolly, joyful, joyous, light-hearted

heartbroken *adjective* **= miserable**, brokenhearted, choked, crestfallen, crushed, dejected, desolate, despondent, disappointed, disconsolate, disheartened, dismal, dispirited, downcast, down in the dumps (*informal*), grieved, heartsick
➤ **Antonyms**
cheerful, cock-a-hoop, elated, exuberant, happy, in seventh heaven, joyful, joyous, on cloud nine, over the moon (*informal*)

hearten *verb* **= encourage**, buck up (*informal*), buoy up, cheer, comfort, console, gee up, raise someone's spirits, reassure, rouse, stimulate

heartfelt *adjective* **= sincere**, ardent, cordial, deep, devout, earnest, fervent, genuine, hearty, honest, profound, unfeigned, warm, wholehearted
➤ **Antonyms**
false, feigned, flippant, fraudulent, frivolous, half-hearted, hypocritical, insincere, phoney *or* phony (*informal*), pretended, put on

heartily *adverb* **1 = sincerely**, cordially, deeply, feelingly, genuinely, profoundly, unfeignedly, warmly **2 = enthusiastically**, eagerly, earnestly, resolutely, vigorously, zealously **3 = thoroughly**, absolutely, completely, totally, very

heartless *adjective* **= cruel**, brutal, callous, cold, cold-blooded, cold-hearted, hard, hardhearted, harsh, inhuman, merciless, pitiless, uncaring, unfeeling, unkind
➤ **Antonyms**
compassionate, generous, humane, kind, merciful, sensitive, sympathetic, warm-hearted

heart-rending *adjective* **= moving**, affecting, distressing, gut-wrenching, harrowing, heartbreaking, pathetic, piteous, pitiful, poignant, sad, tragic

heart-to-heart *adjective* **1 = intimate**, candid, open, personal, sincere, unreserved ♦ *noun* **2 = cosy chat**, tête-à-tête

heart-warming *adjective* **= moving**, affecting, cheering, encouraging, heartening, touching, warming

hearty *adjective* **1 = friendly**, affable, ardent, back-slapping, cordial, eager, ebullient, effusive, enthusiastic, generous, genial, jovial, unreserved, warm **2 = wholehearted**, earnest, genuine, heartfelt, honest, real, sincere, true, unfeigned **3 = substantial**, ample, filling, nourishing, sizable *or* sizeable, solid, square
➤ **Antonyms**
≠**friendly**: cold, cool, unfriendly
≠**wholehearted**: half-hearted, insincere, mild

heat *verb* **1 = warm up**, become warm, chafe, flush, glow, grow hot, make hot, reheat ♦ *noun* **2 = hotness**, fever, fieriness, high temperature, hot spell, sultriness, swelter, torridity, warmness, warmth **3 = passion**, agitation, ardour, earnestness, excitement, fervour, fever, fury, impetuosity, intensity, vehemence, violence, warmth, zeal
➤ **Antonyms**
verb ≠**warm up**: chill, cool, cool off, freeze ♦ *noun* ≠**hotness**: cold, coldness, coolness ≠**passion**: calmness, coldness, composure, coolness

heated *adjective* **= impassioned**, angry, bitter, excited, fierce, fiery, frenzied, furious, intense, passionate, raging, stormy, tempestuous, vehement, violent
➤ **Antonyms**
calm, civilized, dispassionate, friendly, half-hearted, mellow, mild, peaceful, quiet, rational, reasoned, serene, subdued, unemotional, unfazed (*informal*), unruffled

heathen *noun* Old-fashioned **1 = pagan**, idolater, idolatress, infidel, unbeliever ♦ *adjective* **2 = pagan**, godless, heathenish, idolatrous, infidel, irreligious

heave *verb* **1 = lift**, drag (up), elevate, haul (up), heft (*informal*), hoist, lever, pull (up), raise, tug **2 = throw**, cast, fling, hurl, pitch, send, sling, toss **3 = sigh**, breathe heavily, groan, puff, sob, utter wearily **4** = **surge**, billow, breathe, dilate, exhale, expand, palpitate, pant, rise, swell, throb **5** = **vomit**, barf (*U.S. slang*), be sick, chuck (up) (*slang, chiefly U.S.*), chunder (*slang, chiefly Austral.*), do a technicolour yawn (*slang*), gag, retch, spew, throw up (*informal*), upchuck (*U.S. slang*)

heaven *noun* **1** = **paradise**, abode of God, bliss, Elysium *or* Elysian fields (*Greek myth*), happy hunting ground (*Native American legend*), hereafter, life everlasting, life to come, next world, nirvana (*Buddhism, Hinduism*), Valhalla (*Norse myth*), Zion (*Christianity*) **2** = **happiness**, bliss, dreamland, ecstasy, enchantment, felicity, paradise, rapture, seventh heaven, sheer bliss, transport, utopia **3 the heavens** = **sky**, empyrean (*poetic*), ether, firmament, welkin (*archaic*)

heavenly *adjective* **1** *Informal* = **wonderful**, alluring, beautiful, blissful, delightful, divine (*informal*), entrancing, exquisite, glorious, lovely, rapturous, ravishing, sublime **2** = **celestial**, angelic, beatific, blessed, blest, cherubic, divine, extraterrestrial, godlike, holy, immortal, paradisaical, seraphic, superhuman, supernatural
➤ **Antonyms**
≠**wonderful**: abominable, abysmal, appalling, awful, bad, depressing, dire, disagreeable, dreadful, dreary, dull, frightful, gloomy, grim, hellacious (*U.S. slang*), horrible, horrid, lousy (*slang*), miserable, rotten (*informal*), terrible, unpleasant, vile ≠**celestial**: earthly, human, secular, worldly

heavily *adverb* **1** = **densely**, closely, compactly, fast, hard, thick, thickly **2** = **considerably**, a great deal, copiously, excessively, frequently, to excess, very much **3** = **laboriously**, painfully, with difficulty **4** = **ponderously**, awkwardly, clumsily, weightily

heaviness *noun* **1** = **weight**, gravity, heftiness, ponderousness **2** = **onerousness**, arduousness, burdensomeness, grievousness, oppressiveness, severity, weightiness **3** = **sluggishness**, deadness, dullness, languor, lassitude, numbness, torpor **4** = **sadness**, dejection, depression, despondency, gloom, gloominess, glumness, melancholy, seriousness

heavy *adjective* **1** = **weighty**, bulky, hefty, massive, ponderous, portly **2** = **considerable**, abundant, copious, excessive, large, profuse **3** = **onerous**, burdensome, difficult, grievous, hard, harsh, intolerable, laborious, oppressive,

severe, tedious, vexatious, wearisome **4** = **sluggish**, apathetic, drowsy, dull, inactive, indolent, inert, listless, slow, stupid, torpid, wooden **5** = **sad**, crestfallen, dejected, depressed, despondent, disconsolate, downcast, gloomy, grieving, melancholy, sorrowful **6** = **overcast**, cloudy, dull, gloomy, leaden, louring *or* lowering **7** = **serious**, complex, deep, difficult, grave, profound, solemn, weighty
➤ **Antonyms**
≠**weighty**: agile, compact, handy, light, slight, small ≠**considerable**: light, moderate, slight, sparse ≠**onerous**: bearable, easy, gentle, light, mild, moderate, soft ≠**sluggish**: agile, alert, brisk, quick ≠**sad**: calm, cheerful, happy, joyful ≠**serious**: inconsequential, trivial, unimportant

heavy-handed *adjective* **1** = **clumsy**, awkward, bungling, graceless, ham-fisted (*informal*), ham-handed (*informal*), inept, inexpert, like a bull in a china shop (*informal*), maladroit **2** = **tactless**, bungling, inconsiderate, insensitive, thoughtless
➤ **Antonyms**
≠**clumsy**: adept, adroit, competent, dexterous, effectual, efficient, gentle, graceful, skilful, smooth ≠**tactless**: considered, diplomatic, prudent, sensible, tactful, well-advised, well-thought-out, wise

heavy-hearted *adjective* = **sad**, crushed, depressed, despondent, discouraged, disheartened, dismal, downcast, downhearted, down in the dumps (*informal*), forlorn, heartsick, melancholy, miserable, morose, mournful, sick as a parrot (*informal*), sorrowful

heckle *verb* = **jeer**, bait, barrack (*informal*), boo, disrupt, interrupt, pester, shout down, taunt

hectic *adjective* = **frantic**, animated, boisterous, chaotic, excited, fevered, feverish, flurrying, flustering, frenetic, frenzied, furious, heated, riotous, rumbustious, tumultuous, turbulent, wild
➤ **Antonyms**
calm, peaceful, relaxing, tranquil

hector *verb* = **bully**, bluster, boast, browbeat, intimidate, menace, provoke, ride roughshod over, threaten, worry

hedge *noun* **1** = **hedgerow 2** = **barrier**, boundary, screen, windbreak **3** = **insurance cover**, compensation, counterbalance, guard, protection ♦ *verb* **4** = **dodge**, beg the question, be noncommittal, duck, equivocate, evade, flannel (*Brit. informal*), prevaricate, pussyfoot (*informal*), quibble, sidestep, temporize, waffle (*informal, chiefly Brit.*) **5 = insure**, cover, fortify, guard, protect, safeguard, shield

hedonism *noun* = **pursuit of pleasure**, dolce vita, gratification, luxuriousness, pleasure-seeking, self-indulgence, sensualism, sensuality

hedonist *noun* **1** = **pleasure seeker**, *bon vivant*, sensualist, voluptuary **2** = **sybarite**, epicure, epicurean

heed *Formal* ♦ *noun* **1** = **care**, attention, caution, consideration, ear, heedfulness, mind, note, notice, regard, respect, thought, watchfulness ♦ *verb* **2** = **pay attention to**, attend, bear in mind, be guided by, consider, follow, listen to, mark, mind, note, obey, observe, regard, take notice of, take to heart
➤ **Antonyms**
noun ≠**care**: carelessness, disregard, inattention, laxity, laxness, neglect, thoughtlessness ♦ *verb* ≠**pay attention to**: be inattentive to, discount, disobey, disregard, flout, ignore, neglect, overlook, reject, shun, turn a deaf ear to

heedless *adjective* = **careless**, foolhardy, imprudent, inattentive, incautious, neglectful, negligent, oblivious, precipitate, rash, reckless, thoughtless, unmindful, unobservant, unthinking
➤ **Antonyms**
attentive, aware, careful, cautious, concerned, heedful, mindful, observant, thoughtful, vigilant, wary, watchful

heel[1] *noun* **1** *Slang* = **swine**, blackguard, bounder (*old-fashioned Brit. slang*), cad (*Brit. informal*), rotter (*slang, chiefly Brit.*), scally (*Northwest English dialect*), scoundrel, scumbag (*slang*) **2 down at heel** = **shabby**, dowdy, impoverished, out at elbows, run-down, seedy, slipshod, slovenly, worn **3 take to one's heels** = **flee**, escape, hook it (*slang*), run away *or* off, show a clean pair of heels, skedaddle (*informal*), take flight, turn tail, vamoose (*slang, chiefly U.S.*)

heel[2] *verb* = **lean over**, cant, careen, incline, keel over, list, tilt

hefty *adjective Informal* **1** = **big**, beefy (*informal*), brawny, burly, hulking, husky (*informal*), massive, muscular, robust, strapping, strong **2** = **heavy**, ample, awkward, bulky, colossal, cumbersome, large, massive, ponderous, substantial, tremendous, unwieldy, weighty **3** = **forceful**, heavy, powerful, thumping (*slang*), vigorous
➤ **Antonyms**
≠**big**: diminutive, inconsequential,

ineffectual, infinitesimal, insignificant, little, minute, narrow, pocket-sized, scanty, short, slight, slim, small, thin, tiny ≠**heavy**: agile, light ≠**forceful**: feeble, frail, mild, soft, weak, weedy (*informal*), wimpish *or* wimpy (*informal*)

height *noun* **1** = **altitude**, elevation, highness, loftiness, stature, tallness **2** = **peak**, apex, apogee, crest, crown, elevation, hill, mountain, pinnacle, summit, top, vertex, zenith **3** = **culmination**, climax, extremity, limit, maximum, *ne plus ultra*, ultimate, utmost degree, uttermost
➤ **Antonyms**
≠**altitude**: depth, lowness, shortness, smallness ≠**peak**: abyss, base, bottom, canyon, chasm, depth, lowland, nadir, ravine, valley ≠**culmination**: low point, minimum, nadir

heighten *verb* = **intensify**, add to, aggravate, amplify, augment, enhance, improve, increase, magnify, sharpen, strengthen

heinous *adjective* = **shocking**, abhorrent, abominable, atrocious, awful, evil, execrable, flagrant, grave, hateful, hideous, infamous, iniquitous, monstrous, nefarious, odious, outrageous, revolting, unspeakable, vicious, villainous

heir *noun* = **successor**, beneficiary, heiress (*fem.*), inheritor, inheritress *or* inheritrix (*fem.*), next in line, scion

hell *noun* **1** = **underworld**, abode of the damned, abyss, bottomless pit, fire and brimstone, Gehenna (*New Testament, Judaism*), Hades (*Greek myth*), hellfire, infernal regions, inferno, lower world, nether world, Tartarus (*Greek myth*) **2** *Informal* = **torment**, affliction, agony, anguish, martyrdom, misery, nightmare, ordeal, suffering, trial, wretchedness **3 hell for leather** = **speedily**, at a rate of knots, at the double, full-tilt, headlong, hotfoot, hurriedly, like a bat out of hell (*slang*), pell-mell, posthaste, quickly, swiftly

hellbent *adjective Informal* = **intent**, bent, determined, fixed, resolved, set, settled

hellish *adjective* **1** = **devilish**, damnable, damned, demoniacal, diabolical, fiendish, infernal **2** *Informal* = **atrocious**, abominable, accursed, barbarous, cruel, detestable, execrable, inhuman, monstrous, nefarious, vicious, wicked
➤ **Antonyms**
≠**atrocious**: admirable, agreeable, delightful, fine, good, humane, innocuous, kind, merciful, pleasant, wonderful

hello *interjection* = **hi** (*Informal*), good afternoon, good evening, good morning, greetings, how do you do?, welcome

helm noun 1 Nautical = **tiller**, rudder, steering gear, wheel 2 at the helm = **in charge**, at the wheel, directing, in command, in control, in the driving seat, in the saddle

help verb 1 = **aid**, abet, assist, back, befriend, cooperate, encourage, give a leg up (informal), lend a hand, lend a helping hand, promote, relieve, save, second, serve, stand by, succour, support 2 = **improve**, alleviate, ameliorate, cure, ease, facilitate, heal, mitigate, relieve, remedy, restore 3 = **refrain from**, abstain, avoid, control, eschew, forbear, hinder, keep from, prevent, resist, shun, withstand ♦ noun 4 = **assistance**, advice, aid, avail, benefit, cooperation, guidance, helping hand, promotion, service, support, use, utility 5 = **assistant**, employee, hand, helper, worker 6 = **remedy**, cure, relief, restorative
➤ Antonyms
verb ≠**aid**: bar, block, discourage, fight, foil, frustrate, hinder, hobble, impede, obstruct, oppose ≠**improve**: aggravate, harm, hurt, injure, irritate, make worse ♦ noun ≠**assistance**: aggravation, bane, block, discouragement, hindrance, irritant, obstruction, opposition

helper noun = **assistant**, abettor, aide, aider, ally, attendant, auxiliary, collaborator, colleague, deputy, helpmate, henchman, mate, partner, protagonist, right-hand man, second, subsidiary, supporter

helpful adjective 1 = **useful**, advantageous, beneficial, constructive, favourable, fortunate, practical, productive, profitable, serviceable, timely 2 = **cooperative**, accommodating, beneficent, benevolent, caring, considerate, friendly, kind, neighbourly, supportive, sympathetic

helpfulness noun 1 = **usefulness**, advantage, assistance, benefit 2 = **kindness**, cooperation, friendliness, rallying round, support

helping noun = **portion**, dollop (informal), piece, plateful, ration, serving

helpless adjective 1 = **vulnerable**, abandoned, defenceless, dependent, destitute, exposed, forlorn, stranded, unprotected, wide open 2 = **powerless**, debilitated, disabled, feeble, impotent, incapable, incompetent, infirm, paralysed, unfit, weak
➤ Antonyms
≠**vulnerable**: invulnerable, safe, secure, well-protected ≠**powerless**: able, capable, competent, equipped, fit, hardy, healthy,

hearty, mighty, powerful, robust, solid, strong, sturdy, thriving, tough

helplessness noun 1 = **vulnerability**, defencelessness, exposed position, forlornness 2 = **weakness**, disability, feebleness, impotence, infirmity, powerlessness

helpmate noun = **partner**, assistant, associate, companion, consort, helper, helpmeet, husband, significant other (U.S. informal), spouse, support, wife

helter-skelter adjective 1 = **haphazard**, confused, disordered, higgledy-piggledy (informal), hit-or-miss, jumbled, muddled, random, topsy-turvy ♦ adverb 2 = **carelessly**, anyhow, hastily, headlong, hurriedly, pell-mell, rashly, recklessly, wildly

hem noun = **edge**, border, fringe, margin, trimming

he-man noun Informal = **muscle man**, Atlas, bit of beefcake, Hercules, hunk (slang), Tarzan (informal)

hem in verb = **surround**, beset, border, circumscribe, confine, edge, enclose, environ, hedge in, restrict, shut in, skirt

hence conjunction = **therefore**, ergo, for this reason, on that account, thus

henceforth adverb = **from now on**, from this day forward, hence, hereafter, in the future

henchman noun = **attendant**, aide, associate, bodyguard, follower, heavy (slang), minder (slang), right-hand man, sidekick (slang), subordinate, supporter

henpecked adjective = **dominated**, browbeaten, bullied, cringing, led by the nose, meek, subject, subjugated, tied to someone's apron strings, timid, treated like dirt
➤ Antonyms
aggressive, assertive, bossy (informal), dominating, domineering, forceful, macho, overbearing, self-assertive, spirited, wilful

herald noun 1 = **messenger**, bearer of tidings, crier 2 Often literary = **forerunner**, harbinger, indication, omen, precursor, sign, signal, token ♦ verb 3 = **announce**, advertise, broadcast, proclaim, publicize, publish, trumpet 4 = **indicate**, foretoken, harbinger, pave the way, portend, precede, presage, promise, show, usher in

herculean adjective 1 = **arduous**, demanding, difficult, exhausting, formidable, gruelling, hard, heavy, laborious, onerous, prodigious, strenuous, toilsome, tough 2 = **strong**, athletic, brawny, husky (informal), mighty, muscular, powerful, rugged, sinewy, stalwart, strapping, sturdy

herd noun 1 = **flock**, assemblage, collection, crowd, crush, drove, horde, mass, mob, multitude, press, swarm, throng 2 Often disparaging = **mob**, populace, rabble, riffraff, the hoi polloi, the masses, the plebs ◆ verb 3 = **congregate**, assemble, associate, collect, flock, gather, huddle, muster, rally 4 = **drive**, force, goad, guide, lead, shepherd, spur

herdsman noun Chiefly Brit. = **stockman**, cowherd, cowman, drover, grazier

hereafter adverb 1 = **in future**, after this, from now on, hence, henceforth, henceforward ◆ noun 2 **the hereafter** = **afterlife**, future life, life after death, next world, the beyond

hereditary adjective 1 = **genetic**, family, inborn, inbred, inheritable, transmissible 2 Law = **inherited**, ancestral, bequeathed, handed down, patrimonial, traditional, transmitted, willed

heredity noun = **genetics**, congenital traits, constitution, genetic make-up, inheritance

heresy noun = **unorthodoxy**, apostasy, dissidence, error, heterodoxy, iconoclasm, impiety, revisionism, schism

heretic noun = **nonconformist**, apostate, dissenter, dissident, renegade, revisionist, schismatic, sectarian, separatist

heretical adjective = **unorthodox**, freethinking, heterodox, iconoclastic, idolatrous, impious, revisionist, schismatic

heritage noun = **inheritance**, bequest, birthright, endowment, estate, legacy, lot, patrimony, portion, share, tradition

hermaphrodite noun = **androgyne**, bisexual

hermaphroditic adjective = **androgynous**, AC/DC (informal), bisexual, gynandrous

hermetic, hermetical adjective = **airtight**, sealed, shut

hermit noun = **recluse**, anchoret, anchorite, eremite, loner (informal), monk, solitary, stylite

hero noun 1 = **leading man**, lead actor, male lead, principal male character, protagonist 2 = **idol**, celeb (informal), celebrity, champion, conqueror, great man, heart-throb (Brit.), man of the hour, megastar (informal), popular figure, star, superstar, victor

heroic adjective = **courageous**, bold, brave, daring, dauntless, doughty, fearless, gallant, intrepid, lion-hearted, stouthearted, undaunted, valiant, valorous
➤ **Antonyms**
base, chicken (slang), cowardly, craven, faint-hearted, ignoble, mean, timid

heroine noun 1 = **leading lady**, diva, female lead, lead actress, prima donna, principal female character, protagonist 2 = **idol**, celeb (informal), celebrity, goddess, megastar (informal), woman of the hour

heroism noun = **bravery**, boldness, courage, courageousness, daring, fearlessness, fortitude, gallantry, intrepidity, prowess, spirit, valour

hero worship noun = **idolization**, admiration, adoration, adulation, idealization, putting on a pedestal, veneration

hesitant adjective = **uncertain**, diffident, doubtful, half-hearted, halting, hanging back, hesitating, irresolute, lacking confidence, reluctant, shy, timid, unsure, vacillating, wavering
➤ **Antonyms**
arrogant, avid, can-do (informal), clear, confident, definite, determined, dogmatic, eager, enthusiastic, firm, forceful, keen, positive, resolute, self-assured, spirited, sure, unhesitating, unwavering

hesitate verb 1 = **waver**, be uncertain, delay, dither (chiefly Brit.), doubt, haver (Brit.), hum and haw, pause, shillyshally (informal), swither (Scot.), vacillate, wait 2 = **be reluctant**, balk, be unwilling, boggle, demur, hang back, scruple, shrink from, think twice 3 = **falter**, fumble, hem and haw or hum and haw, stammer, stumble, stutter
➤ **Antonyms**
≠waver: be confident, be decisive, be firm, continue ≠be reluctant: be determined, resolve, welcome

hesitation noun 1 = **indecision**, delay, doubt, dubiety, hesitancy, irresolution, uncertainty, vacillation 2 = **reluctance**, demurral, misgiving(s), qualm(s), scruple(s), unwillingness 3 = **faltering**, fumbling, hemming and hawing, stammering, stumbling, stuttering

heterodox adjective = **unorthodox**, dissident, heretical, iconoclastic, revisionist, schismatic, unsound

heterogeneous adjective = **varied**, assorted, contrary, contrasted, different, disparate, dissimilar, divergent, diverse, diversified, incongruous, manifold, miscellaneous, mixed, motley, opposed, unlike, unrelated

hew verb 1 = **cut**, axe, chop, hack, lop, split 2 = **carve**, fashion, form, make, model, sculpt, sculpture, shape, smooth

heyday noun = **prime**, bloom, flowering, pink, prime of life, salad days

hiatus noun = **pause**, blank, breach, break, discontinuity, gap, interruption, interval, lacuna, lapse, opening, respite, space

hibernate verb = **lie dormant**, hole up, overwinter, remain torpid, sleep snug, vegetate, winter

hidden adjective = **concealed**, abstruse, clandestine, close, covered, covert, cryptic, dark, latent, masked, mysterious, mystic, mystical, obscure, occult, recondite, secret, shrouded, ulterior, under wraps, unrevealed, unseen, veiled

hide¹ verb 1 = **conceal**, cache, secrete, stash (informal) 2 = **go into hiding**, go to ground, go underground, hole up, lie low, take cover 3 = **suppress**, draw a veil over, hush up, keep dark, keep secret, keep under one's hat, withhold 4 = **disguise**, blot out, bury, camouflage, cloak, conceal, cover, eclipse, mask, obscure, screen, shelter, shroud, veil
➤ **Antonyms**
admit, bare, confess, disclose, display, divulge, exhibit, expose, find, flaunt, reveal, show, uncover, unveil

hide² noun = **skin**, fell, pelt

hideaway noun = **hiding place**, haven, hide-out, nest, refuge, retreat, sanctuary, sequestered nook

hidebound adjective = **conventional**, narrow, narrow-minded, puritan, rigid, set, set in one's ways, strait-laced, ultraconservative
➤ **Antonyms**
broad-minded, flexible, liberal, open, receptive, tolerant, unconventional, unorthodox

hideous adjective = **ugly**, ghastly, grim, grisly, grotesque, gruesome, monstrous, repulsive, revolting, unsightly
➤ **Antonyms**
appealing, beautiful, captivating, charming, entrancing, lovely, pleasant, pleasing

hide-out noun = **hiding place**, den, hideaway, lair, secret place, shelter

hiding noun = **beating**, caning, drubbing, flogging, licking (informal), spanking, tanning (slang), thrashing, walloping (informal), whipping

hierarchy noun = **grading**, pecking order, ranking

hieroglyphic adjective = **indecipherable**, enigmatical, figurative, obscure, runic, symbolical

higgledy-piggledy Informal ♦ adverb 1 = **haphazardly**, all over the place, all over the shop (informal), anyhow, any old how, confusedly, helter-skelter, pell-mell, topsy-turvy ♦ adjective 2 = **haphazard**, helter-skelter, indiscriminate, jumbled,

muddled, pell-mell, topsy-turvy

high adjective 1 = **tall**, elevated, lofty, soaring, steep, towering 2 = **extreme**, excessive, extraordinary, great, intensified, sharp, strong 3 = **expensive**, costly, dear, exorbitant, high-priced, steep (informal), stiff 4 = **high-pitched**, acute, penetrating, piercing, piping, sharp, shrill, soprano, strident, treble 5 = **gamey**, niffy (Brit. slang), pongy (Brit. informal), strong-flavoured, tainted, whiffy (Brit. slang) 6 = **important**, arch, big-time (informal), chief, consequential, distinguished, eminent, exalted, influential, leading, major league (informal), notable, powerful, prominent, ruling, significant, superior 7 = **cheerful**, boisterous, bouncy (informal), elated, excited, exhilarated, exuberant, joyful, light-hearted, merry 8 Informal = **intoxicated**, delirious, euphoric, freaked out (informal), hyped up (slang), inebriated, on a trip (informal), spaced out (slang), stoned (informal), tripping (informal), turned on (slang), zonked (slang) 9 = **luxurious**, extravagant, grand, lavish, rich 10 high and dry = **abandoned**, bereft, destitute, helpless, stranded 11 high and low = **everywhere**, all over, exhaustively, far and wide, in every nook and cranny 12 high and mighty Informal = **self-important**, arrogant, cavalier, conceited, disdainful, haughty, imperious, overbearing, snobbish, stuck-up (informal), superior ♦ adverb 13 = **aloft**, at great height, far up, way up ♦ noun 14 = **peak**, apex, crest, height, record level, summit, top 15 Informal = **intoxication**, delirium, ecstasy, euphoria, trip (informal)
➤ **Antonyms**
adjective ≠**tall**: dwarfed, low, short, stunted ≠**extreme**: average, low, mild, moderate, restrained, suppressed ≠**high-pitched**: alto, bass, deep, gruff, low, low-pitched ≠**important**: average, common, inconsequential, insignificant, low, lowly, low-ranking, menial, secondary, undistinguished, unimportant ≠**cheerful**: dejected, depressed, gloomy, low, melancholy, sad

highbrow Often disparaging ♦ adjective 1 = **intellectual**, bookish, brainy (informal), cultivated, cultured, deep, highbrowed, sophisticated ♦ noun 2 = **intellectual**, aesthete, Brahmin (U.S.), brain (informal), brainbox (slang), egghead (informal), mastermind, savant, scholar
➤ **Antonyms**
adjective ≠**intellectual**: ignorant, lowbrow, philistine, shallow, uncultivated, uninformed, unintellectual, unlearned,

unsophisticated ♦ *noun* ≠**intellectual:** idiot, ignoramus, illiterate, imbecile (*informal*), lowbrow, moron, philistine

highfalutin *adjective* = **pompous,** big, bombastic, florid, grandiose, high-flown, high-sounding, lofty, magniloquent, pretentious

high-flown *adjective* = **extravagant,** arty-farty (*informal*), elaborate, exaggerated, florid, grandiose, high-falutin (*informal*), inflated, lofty, magniloquent, overblown, pretentious
➤ Antonyms
down-to-earth, moderate, modest, practical, pragmatic, realistic, reasonable, restrained, sensible, simple, straightforward, unpretentious

high-handed *adjective* = **dictatorial,** arbitrary, autocratic, bossy (*informal*), despotic, domineering, imperious, oppressive, overbearing, peremptory, tyrannical, wilful

highlands *plural noun* = **uplands,** heights, hill country, hills, mesa, mountainous region, plateau, tableland

highlight *noun* 1 = **high point,** best part, climax, feature, focal point, focus, high spot, main feature, memorable part, peak ♦ *verb* 2 = **emphasize,** accent, accentuate, bring to the fore, feature, focus attention on, foreground, give prominence to, play up, set off, show up, spotlight, stress, underline
➤ Antonyms
noun ≠**high point:** disappointment, lowlight, low point ♦ *verb* ≠**emphasize:** de-emphasize, gloss over, neglect, overlook, play down

highly *adverb* 1 = **extremely,** decidedly, eminently, exceptionally, extraordinarily, greatly, immensely, seriously (*informal*), supremely, tremendously, vastly, very, very much 2 = **favourably,** appreciatively, approvingly, enthusiastically, warmly, well

highly strung *adjective* = **nervous,** easily upset, edgy, excitable, irascible, irritable, nervy (*Brit. informal*), neurotic, on pins and needles, on tenterhooks, restless, sensitive, stressed, taut, temperamental, tense, tetchy, twitchy (*informal*), wired (*slang*)
➤ Antonyms
calm, collected, easy-going, even-tempered, laid-back (*informal*), placid, relaxed, serene, unfazed (*informal*)

high-minded *adjective* = **principled,** elevated, ethical, fair, good, honourable, idealistic, magnanimous, moral, noble, pure, righteous, upright, virtuous, worthy
➤ Antonyms
dishonest, dishonourable, unethical, unfair

high-powered *adjective* = **dynamic,** aggressive, driving, effective, energetic, enterprising, fast-track, forceful, go-ahead, go-getting (*informal*), vigorous

high-pressure *Informal (of salesmanship) adjective* = **forceful,** aggressive, bludgeoning, coercive, compelling, high-powered, importunate, insistent, intensive, in-your-face (*slang*), persistent, persuasive, pushy (*informal*)

high-spirited *adjective* = **lively,** alive and kicking, animated, boisterous, bold, bouncy, daring, dashing, ebullient, effervescent, energetic, exuberant, frolicsome, full of beans (*informal*), full of life, fun-loving, gallant, mettlesome, sparky, spirited, spunky (*informal*), vibrant, vital, vivacious

hijack *verb* = **seize,** commandeer, expropriate, skyjack, take over

hike *noun* 1 = **walk,** journey on foot, march, ramble, tramp, trek ♦ *verb* 2 = **walk,** back-pack, hoof it (*slang*), leg it (*informal*), ramble, tramp 3 **hike up** = **raise,** hitch up, jack up, lift, pull up

hiker *noun* = **walker,** backpacker, rambler

hilarious *adjective* = **funny,** amusing, comical, entertaining, humorous, jolly, merry, mirthful, rollicking, side-splitting, uproarious
➤ Antonyms
dull, gloomy, quiet, sad, sedate, serious

hilarity *noun* = **merriment,** amusement, cheerfulness, exhilaration, exuberance, gaiety, glee, high spirits, jollity, joviality, laughter, levity, mirth

hill *noun* 1 = **mount,** brae (*Scot.*), elevation, eminence, fell, height, hillock, hilltop, knoll, mound, prominence, tor 2 = **heap,** drift, hummock, mound, pile, rick, stack 3 = **slope,** brae (*Scot.*), climb, gradient, incline, rise

hillock *noun* = **mound,** barrow, hummock, knoll

hilly *adjective* = **mountainous,** rolling, steep, undulating

hilt *noun* 1 = **handle,** grip, haft, handgrip 2 **to the hilt** = **fully,** completely, entirely, totally, wholly

hind *adjective* = **back,** after, hinder, posterior, rear

hinder *verb* = **obstruct,** arrest, block, check, debar, delay, deter, encumber, frustrate, hamper, hamstring, handicap, hobble, hold up *or* back, impede, interrupt, oppose, prevent, retard, slow down, stop, stymie, throw a spanner in the works, thwart, trammel
➤ Antonyms

accelerate, advance, aid, benefit, encourage, expedite, facilitate, further, help, hurry, promote, quicken, speed, support

hindmost *adjective* = **last**, concluding, final, furthest, furthest behind, most remote, rearmost, terminal, trailing, ultimate

hindrance *noun* = **obstacle**, bar, barrier, block, check, deterrent, difficulty, drag, drawback, encumbrance, handicap, hazard, hitch, impediment, interruption, limitation, obstruction, restraint, restriction, snag, stoppage, stumbling block, trammel
➤ **Antonyms**
advancement, advantage, aid, asset, assistance, benefit, boon, boost, encouragement, furtherance, help, support

hinge *verb* **hinge on** = **depend on**, be contingent on, be subject to, hang on, pivot on, rest on, revolve around, turn on

hint *noun* **1** = **indication**, allusion, clue, implication, inkling, innuendo, insinuation, intimation, mention, reminder, suggestion, tip-off, word to the wise **2** = **advice**, help, pointer, suggestion, tip, wrinkle (*informal*) **3** = **trace**, breath, dash, soupçon, speck, suggestion, suspicion, taste, tinge, touch, undertone, whiff, whisper ♦ *verb* **4** = **suggest**, allude, cue, imply, indicate, insinuate, intimate, let it be known, mention, prompt, tip off, tip the wink (*informal*)

hip *adjective Slang* = **with it** (*informal*), aware, clued-up (*informal*), fashionable, in, informed, in on, knowledgeable, onto, trendy (*Brit. informal*), wise (*slang*)

hippy *noun* = **bohemian**, beatnik, dropout, flower child

hire *verb* **1** = **employ**, appoint, commission, engage, sign up, take on **2** = **rent**, charter, engage, lease, let ♦ *noun* **3** = **rental**, charge, cost, fee, price, rent

hirsute *adjective* = **hairy**, bearded, bewhiskered, bristly, shaggy, unshaven

hiss *noun* **1** = **sibilation**, buzz, hissing, sibilance **2** = **catcall**, boo, contempt, derision, jeer, raspberry ♦ *verb* **3** = **whistle**, rasp, shrill, sibilate, wheeze, whirr, whiz **4** = **jeer**, blow a raspberry, boo, catcall, condemn, damn, decry, deride, hoot, mock, revile, ridicule

historian *noun* = **chronicler**, annalist, biographer, historiographer, recorder

historic *adjective* = **significant**, celebrated, consequential, epoch-making, extraordinary, famous, ground-breaking, momentous, notable, outstanding,

red-letter, remarkable
➤ **Antonyms**
ordinary, uncelebrated, unimportant, unknown

historical *adjective* = **factual**, actual, archival, attested, authentic, chronicled, documented, real, verifiable
➤ **Antonyms**
fabulous, fictional, legendary, mythical

history *noun* **1** = **chronicle**, account, annals, autobiography, biography, memoirs, narration, narrative, recapitulation, recital, record, relation, saga, story **2** = **the past**, ancient history, antiquity, bygone times, days of old, days of yore, olden days, the good old days, the old days, yesterday, yesteryear

histrionic *adjective* = **theatrical**, actorly, actressy, affected, artificial, bogus, camp (*informal*), dramatic, forced, insincere, melodramatic, sensational, unnatural

histrionics *plural noun* = **dramatics**, performance, scene, staginess, tantrums, temperament, theatricality

hit *verb* **1** = **strike**, bang, bash (*informal*), batter, beat, belt (*informal*), chin (*slang*), clip (*informal*), clobber (*slang*), clout (*informal*), cuff, deck (*slang*), flog, knock, lambast(e), lay one on (*slang*), lob, punch, slap, smack, smite (*archaic*), sock (*slang*), swat, thump, wallop (*informal*), whack **2** = **collide with**, bang into, bump, clash with, crash against, meet head-on, run into, smash into **3** = **affect**, damage, devastate, impact on, impinge on, influence, leave a mark on, make an impact *or* impression on, move, overwhelm, touch **4** = **reach**, accomplish, achieve, arrive at, attain, gain, secure, strike, touch **5 hit it off** *Informal* = **get on (well) with**, be on good terms, click (*slang*), get on like a house on fire (*informal*), take to, warm to ♦ *noun* **6** = **stroke**, belt (*informal*), blow, bump, clash, clout (*informal*), collision, cuff, impact, knock, rap, shot, slap, smack, swipe (*informal*), wallop (*informal*) **7** = **success**, sellout, sensation, smash (*informal*), smasheroo (*informal*), triumph, winner

hitch *noun* **1** = **problem**, catch, check, delay, difficulty, drawback, hassle (*informal*), hazard, hindrance, hold-up, impediment, mishap, obstacle, snag, trouble ♦ *verb* **2** *Informal* = **hitchhike**, thumb a lift **3** = **fasten**, attach, connect, couple, harness, join, make fast, tether, tie, unite, yoke **4 hitch up** = **pull up**, hoick, jerk, tug, yank

hither *adverb* = **here**, close, closer, near,

nearer, nigh (*archaic*), over here, to this place

hitherto *adverb Formal* = **previously**, heretofore, so far, thus far, till now, until now, up to now

hit on *or* **upon** *verb* = **think up**, arrive at, chance upon, come upon, discover, guess, invent, light upon, realize, strike upon, stumble on

hit-or-miss *or* **hit-and-miss** *adjective* = **haphazard**, aimless, casual, cursory, disorganized, indiscriminate, perfunctory, random, undirected, uneven
➤ **Antonyms**
arranged, deliberate, organized, planned, systematic

hit out (at) *verb* = **attack**, assail, castigate, condemn, denounce, inveigh against, lash out, rail against, strike out at

hive *noun* **1** = **colony**, cluster, swarm **2** *As in* **hive of activity** = **centre**, heart, hub

hoard *noun* **1** = **store**, accumulation, cache, fall-back, fund, heap, mass, pile, reserve, stash, stockpile, supply, treasure-trove
♦ *verb* **2** = **save**, accumulate, amass, buy up, cache, collect, deposit, garner, gather, hive, lay up, put away, put by, stash away (*informal*), stockpile, store, treasure

hoarder *noun* = **saver**, collector, miser, niggard, tight-arse (*taboo slang*), tight-ass (*U.S. taboo slang*)

hoarse *adjective* = **rough**, croaky, discordant, grating, gravelly, growling, gruff, guttural, harsh, husky, rasping, raucous, throaty
➤ **Antonyms**
harmonious, mellifluous, mellow, melodious, smooth

hoarseness *noun* = **croakiness**, a frog in one's throat, gruffness, huskiness, rasping, sore throat, throatiness, wheeziness

hoary *adjective* **1** = **white-haired**, frosty, grey, grey-haired, grizzled, hoar, silvery, white **2** = **old**, aged, ancient, antiquated, antique, venerable

hoax *noun* **1** = **trick**, cheat, con (*informal*), deception, fast one (*informal*), fraud, imposture, joke, practical joke, prank, ruse, spoof (*informal*), swindle ♦ *verb* **2** = **deceive**, bamboozle (*informal*), befool, bluff, con (*slang*), delude, dupe, fool, hoodwink, hornswoggle (*slang*), kid (*informal*), swindle, take in (*informal*), take (someone) for a ride (*informal*), trick, wind up (*Brit. slang*)

hobble *verb* **1** = **limp**, dodder, falter, shamble, shuffle, stagger, stumble, totter **2** = **tie**, fasten, fetter, hamstring, restrict, shackle

hobby *noun* = **pastime**, diversion, favourite occupation, (leisure) activity, leisure pursuit, relaxation, sideline

hobgoblin *noun* = **imp**, bogey, goblin, hob, spectre, spirit, sprite

hobnob *verb* = **socialize**, associate, consort, fraternize, hang about, hang out (*informal*), keep company, mingle, mix

hocus-pocus *noun Informal* = **trickery**, artifice, cheat, chicanery, deceit, deception, delusion, hoax, humbug, imposture, swindle

hog *verb Slang* = **monopolize**, be a dog in the manger, corner, corner the market in, dominate, tie up

hogwash *noun Informal* = **nonsense**, balderdash, balls (*taboo slang*), bilge (*informal*), bosh (*informal*), bull (*slang*), bullshit (*taboo slang*), bunk (*informal*), bunkum *or* buncombe (*chiefly U.S.*), cobblers (*Brit. taboo slang*), crap (*slang*), drivel, eyewash (*informal*), garbage (*informal*), guff (*slang*), hot air (*informal*), moonshine, piffle (*informal*), poppycock (*informal*), rot, rubbish, shit (*taboo slang*), tommyrot, tosh (*slang, chiefly Brit.*), trash, tripe (*informal*), twaddle

hoi polloi *noun* = **the common people**, admass, *canaille*, commonalty, riffraff, the (common) herd, the great unwashed (*informal & derogatory*), the lower orders, the masses, the plebs, the populace, the proles (*derogatory slang, chiefly Brit.*), the proletariat, the rabble, the third estate, the underclass

hoist *verb* **1** = **raise**, elevate, erect, heave, lift, rear, upraise ♦ *noun* **2** = **lift**, crane, elevator, tackle, winch

hoity-toity *adjective Informal* = **haughty**, arrogant, conceited, disdainful, high and mighty (*informal*), lofty, overweening, proud, scornful, snobbish, snooty (*informal*), stuck-up (*informal*), supercilious, toffee-nosed (*slang, chiefly Brit.*), uppish (*Brit. informal*)

hold *verb* **1** = **grasp**, clasp, cleave, clinch, cling, clutch, cradle, embrace, enfold, grip **2** = **support**, bear, brace, carry, prop, shoulder, sustain, take **3** = **continue**, endure, last, persevere, persist, remain, resist, stay, wear **4** = **accommodate**, comprise, contain, have a capacity for, seat, take **5** = **restrain**, arrest, bind, check, confine, curb, detain, impound, imprison, pound, stay, stop, suspend **6** = **own**, have, keep, maintain, occupy, possess, retain **7** = **consider**, assume, believe, deem, entertain, esteem, judge, maintain, presume, reckon, regard, think, view **8** = **convene**, assemble, call, carry on,

celebrate, conduct, have, officiate at, preside over, run **9 = apply**, be in force, be the case, exist, hold good, operate, remain true, remain valid, stand up ♦ *noun* **10 = grip**, clasp, clutch, grasp **11 = foothold**, anchorage, footing, leverage, prop, purchase, stay, support, vantage **12 = control**, ascendancy, authority, clout (*informal*), dominance, dominion, influence, mastery, pull (*informal*), sway
➤ **Antonyms**
verb ≠**support**: break, come undone, give way, loosen ≠**restrain**: free, let go, let loose, release ≠**own**: bestow, give, give away, give up, hand over, offer, turn over ≠**consider**: deny, disavow, disclaim, put down, refute, reject ≠**convene**: call off, cancel, postpone

hold back *verb* **1 = restrain**, check, control, curb, inhibit, rein, repress, stem the flow, suppress **2 = withhold**, desist, forbear, keep back, refuse

holder *noun* **1 = case**, container, cover, housing, receptacle, sheath **2 = owner**, bearer, custodian, incumbent, keeper, occupant, possessor, proprietor, purchaser

hold forth *verb* **= speak**, declaim, descant, discourse, go on, harangue, lecture, orate, preach, speechify, spiel (*informal*), spout (*informal*)

holding *noun* **= property**, assets, estate, investments, land interests, possessions, resources, securities, stocks and shares

hold off *verb* **1 = fend off**, keep off, rebuff, repel, repulse, stave off **2 = put off**, avoid, defer, delay, keep from, postpone, refrain

hold out *verb* **1 = offer**, extend, give, present, proffer **2 = last**, carry on, continue, endure, hang on, persevere, persist, stand fast, stay the course, withstand

hold over *verb* **= postpone**, adjourn, defer, delay, put off, suspend, take a rain check on (*U.S. & Canad. informal*), waive

hold-up *noun* **1 = robbery**, burglary, mugging (*informal*), stick-up (*slang, chiefly U.S.*), theft **2 = delay**, bottleneck, difficulty, hitch, obstruction, setback, snag, stoppage, traffic jam, trouble, wait

hold up *verb* **1 = delay**, detain, hinder, impede, retard, set back, slow down, stop **2 = support**, bolster, brace, buttress, jack up, prop, shore up, sustain **3 = rob**, mug (*informal*), stick up (*slang, chiefly U.S.*), waylay **4 = exhibit**, display, flaunt, present, show

hold with *verb* **= approve of**, agree to *or* with, be in favour of, countenance, subscribe to, support, take kindly to
➤ **Antonyms**

be against, disagree with, disapprove of, hold out against, oppose

hole *noun* **1 = cavity**, cave, cavern, chamber, depression, excavation, hollow, pit, pocket, scoop, shaft **2 = opening**, aperture, breach, break, crack, fissure, gap, orifice, outlet, perforation, puncture, rent, split, tear, vent **3 = burrow**, covert, den, earth, lair, nest, retreat, shelter **4 = fault**, defect, discrepancy, error, fallacy, flaw, inconsistency, loophole **5** *Informal* **= hovel**, dive (*slang*), dump (*informal*), joint (*slang*), slum **6** *Informal* **= predicament**, dilemma, fix (*informal*), hot water (*informal*), jam (*informal*), mess, quandary, scrape (*informal*), spot (*informal*), tangle, tight spot **7 pick holes in = criticize**, bad-mouth (*slang, chiefly U.S. & Canad.*), cavil, crab (*informal*), denigrate, disparage, disprove, find fault, knock (*informal*), pull to pieces, put down, rubbish (*informal*), run down, slag (off) (*slang*), slate (*informal*)

hole-and-corner *adjective* **= furtive**, backstairs, clandestine, secret, secretive, sneaky (*informal*), stealthy, surreptitious, underhand, under the counter (*informal*)
➤ **Antonyms**
above-board, candid, frank, open, public

hole up *verb* **= hide**, go into hiding, go to earth, hibernate, shelter, take cover, take refuge

holiday *noun* **1 = vacation**, away day, break, leave, recess, time off **2 = festival**, anniversary, bank holiday, celebration, feast, festivity, fête, gala, name day, public holiday, red-letter day, saint's day

holier-than-thou *adjective* **= self-righteous**, goody-goody (*informal*), pietistic, pietistical, priggish, religiose, sanctimonious, self-satisfied, smug, squeaky-clean, unctuous

holiness *noun* **= sanctity**, blessedness, devoutness, divinity, godliness, piety, purity, religiousness, righteousness, sacredness, saintliness, spirituality, virtuousness

holler *Informal* ♦ *verb, noun* **= yell**, bawl, bellow, call, cheer, clamour, cry, hail, halloo, roar, shout, whoop

hollow *adjective* **1 = empty**, not solid, unfilled, vacant, void **2 = sunken**, cavernous, concave, deep-set, depressed, indented **3 = toneless**, deep, dull, expressionless, flat, low, muffled, muted, reverberant, rumbling, sepulchral **4 = worthless**, empty, fruitless, futile, meaningless, pointless, unavailing, useless, vain **5 beat (someone) hollow** *Brit. informal* **= defeat**, hammer (*informal*), outdo,

overcome, rout, thrash, trounce, worst
♦ *noun* **6** = **cavity**, basin, bowl, cave,
cavern, concavity, crater, cup, den, dent,
depression, dimple, excavation, hole,
indentation, pit, trough **7** = **valley**,
bottom, dale, dell, dingle, glen ♦ *verb* **8**
= **scoop**, channel, dig, excavate, furrow,
gouge, groove, pit
➤ **Antonyms**
adjective ≠**empty:** full, occupied, solid
≠**sunken:** convex, rounded ≠**toneless:**
expressive, vibrant ≠**worthless:** gratifying,
meaningful, pleasing, satisfying, valuable,
worthwhile ♦ *noun* ≠**cavity:** bump,
mound, projection ≠**valley:** bluff, height,
hill, knoll, mountain, rise

holocaust *noun* = **genocide**, annihilation,
carnage, conflagration, destruction,
devastation, fire, inferno, massacre, mass
murder, pogrom

holy *adjective* **1** = **sacred**, blessed,
consecrated, dedicated, hallowed,
sacrosanct, sanctified, venerable,
venerated **2** = **devout**, divine, faithful,
god-fearing, godly, hallowed, pious, pure,
religious, righteous, saintly, sublime,
virtuous
➤ **Antonyms**
≠**sacred:** desecrated, unconsecrated,
unhallowed, unholy, unsanctified
≠**devout:** blasphemous, corrupt, earthly,
evil, human, immoral, impious, irreligious,
sacrilegious, secular, sinful, unholy,
wicked, worldly

homage *noun* = **respect**, admiration,
adoration, adulation, awe, deference,
devotion, duty, esteem, honour,
reverence, worship
➤ **Antonyms**
condemnation, contempt, disdain,
disregard, disrespect, irreverence, scorn

home *noun* **1** = **dwelling**, abode, domicile,
dwelling place, habitation, house, pad
(*slang*), residence **2** = **birthplace**, family,
fireside, hearth, homestead, home town,
household **3** = **territory**, abode, element,
environment, habitat, habitation, haunt,
home ground, range, stamping ground **4**
at home: a = **in**, available, present **b** = **at
ease**, comfortable, familiar, relaxed **c**
= **having guests**, entertaining, giving a
party, receiving **5 bring home to** = **make
clear**, drive home, emphasize, impress
upon, press home ♦ *adjective* **6**
= **domestic**, central, familiar, family,
household, inland, internal, local, national,
native

homeland *noun* = **native land**, country of
origin, fatherland, mother country,
motherland

homeless *adjective* **1** = **destitute**,
abandoned, displaced, dispossessed,
down-and-out, exiled, forlorn, forsaken,
outcast, unsettled ♦ *noun* **2 the homeless**
= **vagrants**, dossers (*Brit. slang*), squatters

homely *adjective* = **comfortable**, comfy
(*informal*), cosy, domestic, down-to-earth,
everyday, familiar, friendly, homelike,
homespun, homy, informal, modest,
natural, ordinary, plain, simple,
unaffected, unassuming, unfussy,
unpretentious, welcoming
➤ **Antonyms**
affected, elaborate, elegant, grand,
ostentatious, pretentious, refined, regal,
sophisticated, splendid

homespun *adjective* = **unsophisticated**,
artless, coarse, homely, home-made,
inelegant, plain, rough, rude, rustic,
unpolished

homicidal *adjective* = **murderous**, deadly,
death-dealing, lethal, maniacal, mortal

homicide *noun* **1** = **murder**, bloodshed,
killing, manslaughter, slaying **2**
= **murderer**, killer, slayer

homily *noun* = **sermon**, address, discourse,
lecture, preaching, preachment

homogeneity *noun* = **uniformity**,
analogousness, comparability, consistency,
correspondence, identicalness, oneness,
sameness, similarity

homogeneous *adjective* = **uniform**, akin,
alike, analogous, cognate, comparable,
consistent, identical, kindred, similar,
unvarying
➤ **Antonyms**
different, disparate, dissimilar, divergent,
diverse, heterogeneous, manifold, mixed,
unlike, unrelated, varied, various, varying

homologous *adjective* = **similar**,
analogous, comparable, correspondent,
corresponding, like, parallel, related

homosexual *adjective* = **gay**, bent (*slang*),
camp (*informal*), dykey (*slang*),
homoerotic, lesbian, moffie (*S. African
slang*), pink (*informal*), queer (*informal,
derogatory*), sapphic

hone *verb* = **sharpen**, edge, file, grind,
point, polish, whet

honest *adjective* **1** = **trustworthy**,
conscientious, decent, ethical,
high-minded, honourable, law-abiding,
reliable, reputable, scrupulous, trusty,
truthful, upright, veracious, virtuous **2**
= **open**, candid, direct, forthright, frank,
ingenuous, outright, plain, round, sincere,
straightforward, undisguised, unfeigned,
upfront (*informal*) **3** = **fair**, equitable, fair
and square, impartial, just

➤ **Antonyms**

≠**trustworthy**: bad, corrupt, crooked, deceitful, dishonest, guilty, immoral, treacherous, unethical, unfair, unfaithful, unlawful, unprincipled, unreliable, unrighteous, unscrupulous, untrustworthy, untruthful ≠**open**: disguised, false, insincere, secretive

honestly adverb **1** = **frankly**, candidly, in all sincerity, in plain English, plainly, straight (out), to one's face, truthfully **2** = **ethically**, by fair means, cleanly, honourably, in good faith, lawfully, legally, legitimately, on the level (informal), with clean hands

honesty noun **1** = **integrity**, faithfulness, fidelity, honour, incorruptibility, morality, probity, rectitude, reputability, scrupulousness, straightness, trustworthiness, truthfulness, uprightness, veracity, virtue **2** = **frankness**, bluntness, candour, equity, even-handedness, fairness, genuineness, openness, outspokenness, plainness, sincerity, straightforwardness

honorary adjective = **nominal**, complimentary, ex officio, in name or title only, titular, unofficial, unpaid

honour noun **1** = **integrity**, decency, fairness, goodness, honesty, morality, principles, probity, rectitude, righteousness, trustworthiness, uprightness **2** = **prestige**, credit, dignity, distinction, elevation, eminence, esteem, fame, glory, high standing, rank, renown, reputation, repute **3** = **tribute**, acclaim, accolade, adoration, Brownie points, commendation, deference, homage, kudos, praise, recognition, regard, respect, reverence, veneration **4** = **privilege**, compliment, credit, favour, pleasure, source of pride or satisfaction **5** Old-fashioned = **virginity**, chastity, innocence, modesty, purity, virtue ♦ verb **6** = **respect**, admire, adore, appreciate, esteem, exalt, glorify, hallow, prize, revere, reverence, value, venerate, worship **7** = **acclaim**, celebrate, commemorate, commend, compliment, crack up (informal), decorate, dignify, exalt, glorify, laud, lionize, praise **8** = **pay**, accept, acknowledge, cash, clear, credit, pass, take **9** = **fulfil**, be as good as (informal), be faithful to, be true to, carry out, discharge, keep, live up to, observe

➤ **Antonyms**

noun ≠**integrity**: degradation, dishonesty, dishonour, insincerity, lowness, meanness, unscrupulousness ≠**prestige**: disgrace, dishonour, disrepute, disrespect, infamy, shame ≠**tribute**: condemnation, contempt, disfavour, insult, scorn, slight

♦ verb ≠**respect**, **acclaim**: condemn, defame, degrade, dishonour, insult, offend, scorn, slight ≠**pay**: refuse

honourable adjective **1** = **principled**, ethical, fair, high-minded, honest, just, moral, true, trustworthy, trusty, upright, upstanding, virtuous **2** = **respected**, creditable, estimable, proper, reputable, respectable, right, righteous, virtuous

honours plural noun = **titles**, awards, decorations, distinctions, laurels

hoodoo noun Informal = **jinx**, bad luck, curse, evil eye, evil star, hex (U.S. & Canad. informal), nemesis, voodoo

hoodwink verb = **deceive**, bamboozle (informal), befool, cheat, con (informal), delude, dupe, fool, hoax, kid (informal), lead up the garden path (informal), mislead, pull a fast one on (informal), rook (slang), sell a pup, swindle, take (someone) for a ride (informal), trick

hook noun **1** = **fastener**, catch, clasp, hasp, holder, link, lock, peg **2 by hook or by crook** = **by any means**, by fair means or foul, somehow, somehow or other, someway **3 hook, line, and sinker** Informal = **completely**, entirely, lock, stock and barrel, thoroughly, through and through, totally, utterly, wholly **4 off the hook** Slang = **let off**, acquitted, cleared, exonerated, in the clear, under no obligation, vindicated ♦ verb **5** = **fasten**, catch, clasp, fix, hasp, secure **6** = **catch**, enmesh, ensnare, entrap, snare, trap

hooked adjective **1** = **bent**, aquiline, curved, hook-shaped **2** Slang = **addicted**, devoted, enamoured, obsessed, taken, turned on (slang)

hooligan noun = **delinquent**, casual, hoodlum (chiefly U.S.), lager lout, ned (Scot. slang), rowdy, ruffian, tough, vandal, yob or yobbo (Brit. slang)

hooliganism noun = **delinquency**, disorder, loutishness, rowdiness, vandalism, violence, yobbishness

hoop noun = **ring**, band, circlet, girdle, loop, round, wheel

hoot noun **1** = **toot 2** = **cry**, call **3** = **catcall**, boo, hiss, jeer, yell **4** Informal = **laugh**, card (informal), caution (informal), scream (informal) ♦ verb **5** = **toot 6** = **cry**, scream, shout, shriek, whoop, yell **7** = **jeer**, boo, catcall, condemn, decry, hiss, howl down, yell at

hop verb **1** = **jump**, bound, caper, dance, leap, skip, spring, trip, vault ♦ noun **2** = **jump**, bounce, bound, leap, skip, spring, step, vault

hope verb **1** = **desire**, anticipate, aspire,

await, believe, contemplate, count on, cross one's fingers, expect, foresee, keep one's fingers crossed, long, look forward to, rely, set one's heart on, trust ◆ *noun* **2** = **belief**, ambition, anticipation, assumption, confidence, desire, dream, expectancy, expectation, faith, light at the end of the tunnel, longing
➤ **Antonyms**
noun ≠**belief**: despair, distrust, doubt, dread, hopelessness

hopeful *adjective* **1** = **optimistic**, anticipating, assured, buoyant, confident, expectant, looking forward to, sanguine **2** = **promising**, auspicious, bright, cheerful, encouraging, heartening, propitious, reassuring, rosy
➤ **Antonyms**
≠**optimistic**: cheerless, dejected, despairing, hopeless, pessimistic
≠**promising**: depressing, discouraging, disheartening, unpromising

hopefully *adverb* **1** = **optimistically**, confidently, expectantly, sanguinely **2** *Informal* = **it is hoped**, all being well, conceivably, expectedly, feasibly, probably

hopeless *adjective* **1** = **pessimistic**, abject, defeatist, dejected, demoralized, despairing, desperate, despondent, disconsolate, downhearted, forlorn, in despair, woebegone **2** = **impossible**, forlorn, futile, impracticable, not having a prayer, no-win, pointless, unachievable, unattainable, useless, vain **3** = **incurable**, helpless, irremediable, irreparable, irreversible, lost, past remedy, remediless **4** *Informal* = **no good**, inadequate, incompetent, ineffectual, inferior, pants (*informal*), pathetic, poor, useless (*informal*)
➤ **Antonyms**
≠**pessimistic**: assured, cheerful, confident, expectant, happy, heartened, hopeful, optimistic, uplifted ≠**incurable**: curable, remediable

hopelessly *adverb* **1** = **without hope**, beyond all hope, despairingly, in despair, irredeemably, irremediably **2** = **completely**, impossibly, totally, utterly

horde *noun* = **crowd**, band, crew, drove, gang, host, mob, multitude, pack, press, swarm, throng, troop

horizon *noun* **1** = **skyline**, field of vision, vista **2** *plural* = **scope**, ambit, compass, ken, perspective, prospect, purview, range, realm, sphere, stretch

horizontal *adjective* = **level**, flat, parallel

horny *adjective* = **aroused**, amorous, excited, lustful, randy (*informal, chiefly Brit.*), raunchy (*slang*), turned on (*slang*)

horrible *adjective* **1** = **dreadful**, awful, beastly (*informal*), cruel, disagreeable, ghastly (*informal*), horrid, mean, nasty, terrible, unkind, unpleasant **2** = **terrifying**, abhorrent, abominable, appalling, awful, dreadful, fearful, frightful, from hell (*informal*), ghastly, grim, grisly, gruesome, heinous, hideous, horrid, loathsome, obscene, repulsive, revolting, shameful, shocking, terrible
➤ **Antonyms**
agreeable, appealing, attractive, charming, cute, delightful, enchanting, fetching, lovely, pleasant, wonderful

horrid *adjective* **1** = **unpleasant**, awful, disagreeable, disgusting, dreadful, horrible, nasty, obscene, offensive, terrible, yucky *or* yukky (*slang*) **2** *Informal* = **unkind**, beastly (*informal*), cruel, mean, nasty

horrific *adjective* = **horrifying**, appalling, awful, dreadful, frightful, ghastly, grisly, horrendous, shocking, terrifying

horrify *verb* **1** = **terrify**, affright, alarm, frighten, gross out (*U.S. slang*), intimidate, make one's hair stand on end, petrify, put the wind up (*informal*), scare, terrorize **2** = **shock**, appal, disgust, dismay, outrage, sicken
➤ **Antonyms**
comfort, delight, enchant, encourage, gladden, hearten, please, reassure, soothe

horror *noun* **1** = **terror**, alarm, apprehension, awe, consternation, dismay, dread, fear, fright, panic **2** = **hatred**, abhorrence, abomination, antipathy, aversion, detestation, disgust, loathing, odium, repugnance, revulsion
➤ **Antonyms**
≠**hatred**: affinity, approval, attraction, delight, liking, love

horse *noun* = **nag**, colt, filly, gee-gee (*slang*), gelding, mare, mount, stallion, steed (*archaic or literary*)

horse around *or* **about** *verb Informal* = **play around**, clown, fool about *or* around, misbehave, play the fool, play the goat, roughhouse (*slang*)

horseman *noun* = **rider**, cavalier, cavalryman, dragoon, equestrian, horse-soldier, knight

horseplay *noun* = **rough-and-tumble**, buffoonery, clowning, fooling around, high jinks, pranks, romping, roughhousing (*slang*), skylarking (*informal*)

horse sense *noun* = **common sense**, gumption (*Brit. informal*), judgment, mother wit, nous (*Brit. slang*), practicality

hospitable *adjective* = **welcoming**, amicable, bountiful, cordial, friendly, generous, genial, gracious, kind, liberal,

sociable
➤ **Antonyms**
inhospitable, parsimonious

hospitality *noun* = **welcome**, cheer, conviviality, cordiality, friendliness, heartiness, hospitableness, neighbourliness, sociability, warmth

host¹ *noun* **1** = **master of ceremonies**, entertainer, innkeeper, landlord *or* landlady, proprietor **2** = **presenter**, anchorman *or* anchorwoman, compere (*Brit.*) ♦ *verb* **3** = **present**, compere (*Brit.*), front (*informal*), introduce

host² *noun* = **multitude**, army, array, drove, horde, legion, myriad, swarm, throng

hostage *noun* = **prisoner**, captive, pawn, pledge, security, surety

hostile *adjective* **1** = **unfriendly**, antagonistic, anti (*informal*), bellicose, belligerent, contrary, ill-disposed, inimical, malevolent, opposed, opposite, rancorous, unkind, warlike **2** = **inhospitable**, adverse, alien, unpropitious, unsympathetic, unwelcoming
➤ **Antonyms**
≠**unfriendly**: affable, agreeable, amiable, approving, cordial, friendly, kind, peaceful, sympathetic, warm ≠**inhospitable**: congenial

hostilities *plural noun* = **warfare**, conflict, fighting, state of war, war
➤ **Antonyms**
alliance, ceasefire, peace, treaty, truce

hostility *noun* = **unfriendliness**, abhorrence, animosity, animus, antagonism, antipathy, aversion, bad blood, detestation, enmity, hatred, ill will, malevolence, malice, opposition, resentment
➤ **Antonyms**
agreement, amity, approval, congeniality, cordiality, friendliness, goodwill, sympathy

hot *adjective* **1** = **heated**, blistering, boiling, burning, fiery, flaming, piping hot, roasting, scalding, scorching, searing, steaming, sultry, sweltering, torrid, warm **2** = **spicy**, acrid, biting, peppery, piquant, pungent, sharp **3** = **passionate**, ablaze, animated, ardent, excited, fervent, fervid, fierce, fiery, flaming, impetuous, inflamed, intense, irascible, lustful, raging, stormy, touchy, vehement, violent **4** = **new**, fresh, just out, latest, recent, up to the minute **5** = **popular**, approved, favoured, in demand, in vogue, sought-after **6** = **following closely**, close, in hot pursuit, near
➤ **Antonyms**
≠**heated**: chilly, cold, cool, freezing, frigid, frosty, icy, parky (*Brit. informal*) ≠**spicy**:

mild ≠**passionate**: apathetic, calm, dispassionate, half-hearted, indifferent, mild, moderate ≠**new**: old, stale, trite ≠**popular**: out of favour, unpopular ≠**following closely**: cold

hot air *noun* = **empty talk**, blather, blether, bombast, bosh (*informal*), bunkum *or* buncombe (*chiefly U.S.*), claptrap (*informal*), gas (*informal*), guff (*slang*), rant, tall talk (*informal*), verbiage, wind

hotbed *noun* = **breeding ground**, den, forcing house, nest, nursery, seedbed

hot-blooded *adjective* = **passionate**, ardent, excitable, fervent, fiery, heated, impulsive, rash, spirited, temperamental, wild
➤ **Antonyms**
apathetic, calm, cold, cool, frigid, impassive, restrained, unenthusiastic

hotchpotch *noun* = **mixture**, conglomeration, farrago, hash, hodgepodge (*U.S.*), jumble, medley, *mélange*, mess, miscellany, mishmash, potpourri

hotfoot *adverb* = **speedily**, hastily, helter-skelter, hurriedly, pell-mell, posthaste, quickly

hot-headed *adjective* = **rash**, fiery, foolhardy, hasty, hot-tempered, impetuous, precipitate, quick-tempered, reckless, unruly, volatile

hothouse *noun* = **greenhouse**, conservatory, glasshouse

hotly *adverb* **1** = **passionately**, angrily, fiercely, heatedly, impetuously, indignantly, vehemently, with indignation **2** = **enthusiastically**, closely, eagerly, hotfoot, with enthusiasm

hound *verb* **1** = **pursue**, chase, drive, give chase, hunt, hunt down **2** = **harass**, badger, goad, harry, impel, persecute, pester, prod, provoke

house *noun* **1** = **home**, abode, building, domicile, dwelling, edifice, habitation, homestead, pad (*slang*), residence **2** = **household**, family, ménage **3** = **dynasty**, ancestry, clan, family tree, kindred, line, lineage, race, tribe **4** = **firm**, business, company, concern, establishment, organization, outfit (*informal*), partnership **5** = **assembly**, Commons, legislative body, parliament **6 on the house** = **free**, for nothing, gratis, without expense ♦ *verb* **7** = **accommodate**, billet, board, domicile, harbour, lodge, put up, quarter, take in **8** = **contain**, cover, keep, protect, sheathe, shelter, store

household *noun* **1** = **family**, home, house, ménage ♦ *adjective* **2** = **domestic**, family

householder noun = **occupant**, homeowner, resident, tenant

housekeeping noun = **household management**, home economy, homemaking (*U.S.*), housecraft, housewifery

housing noun 1 = **accommodation**, dwellings, homes, houses 2 = **case**, casing, container, cover, covering, enclosure, sheath

hovel noun = **hut**, cabin, den, hole, shack, shanty, shed

hover verb 1 = **float**, be suspended, drift, flutter, fly, hang, poise 2 = **linger**, hang about, wait nearby 3 = **waver**, alternate, dither (*chiefly Brit.*), falter, fluctuate, haver (*Brit.*), oscillate, pause, seesaw, swither (*Scot. dialect*), vacillate

however adverb = **nevertheless**, after all, anyhow, be that as it may, but, even though, nonetheless, notwithstanding, on the other hand, still, though, yet

howl noun 1 = **cry**, bawl, bay, bellow, clamour, groan, hoot, outcry, roar, scream, shriek, ululation, wail, yelp, yowl ♦ verb 2 = **cry**, bawl, bellow, cry out, lament, roar, scream, shout, shriek, ululate, wail, weep, yell, yelp

howler noun Informal = **mistake**, bloomer (*Brit. informal*), blunder, boob (*Brit. slang*), booboo (*informal*), bull (*slang*), clanger (*informal*), error, malapropism, schoolboy howler

hoyden noun Old-fashioned = **tomboy**

hoydenish adjective Old-fashioned = **unladylike**, boisterous, bold, ill-mannered, inelegant, uncouth, unfeminine, ungenteel, unruly

hub noun = **centre**, core, focal point, focus, heart, middle, nerve centre, pivot

hubbub noun = **noise**, babel, bedlam, brouhaha, clamour, confusion, din, disorder, disturbance, hue and cry, hullabaloo, hurly-burly, pandemonium, racket, riot, ruckus (*informal*), ruction (*informal*), rumpus, tumult, uproar

hubris noun = **pride**, arrogance, nemesis

huckster noun = **pedlar**, barker (*informal*), hawker, salesman, vendor

huddle noun 1 = **crowd**, confusion, disorder, heap, jumble, mass, mess, muddle 2 Informal = **conference**, confab (*informal*), discussion, meeting, powwow ♦ verb 3 = **crowd**, cluster, converge, flock, gather, press, throng 4 = **curl up**, crouch, cuddle, hunch up, make oneself small, nestle, snuggle

hue noun = **colour**, dye, shade, tincture, tinge, tint, tone

hue and cry noun = **outcry**, brouhaha, clamour, furore, hullabaloo, much ado, ruction (*informal*), rumpus, uproar

huff noun 1 = **sulk**, anger, bad mood, miff (*informal*), passion, pet, pique, rage, temper 2 in a huff = **offended**, angered, annoyed, hacked (off) (*U.S. slang*), hurt, in high dudgeon, irked, miffed (*informal*), nettled, peeved, piqued, pissed off (*taboo slang*), put out (*informal*), sulking (*informal*)

huffy adjective = **resentful**, angry, choked, cross, disgruntled, moody, moping, offended, peevish, pettish, petulant, querulous, snappy, sulky, sullen, surly
➤ Antonyms
amiable, cheerful, friendly, gay, good-humoured, happy, pleasant, sunny

hug verb 1 = **clasp**, cuddle, embrace, enfold, hold close, squeeze, take in one's arms 2 = **follow closely**, cling to, keep close, stay near ♦ noun 3 = **embrace**, bear hug, clasp, clinch (*slang*), squeeze

huge adjective = **enormous**, Brobdingnagian, bulky, colossal, elephantine, extensive, gargantuan, giant, gigantic, ginormous (*informal*), great, humongous *or* humungous (*U.S. slang*), immense, jumbo (*informal*), large, mammoth, massive, mega (*slang*), monumental, mountainous, prodigious, stellar (*informal*), stupendous, titanic, tremendous, vast
➤ Antonyms
insignificant, little, microscopic, minute, petty, puny, small, tiny

huggermugger noun Archaic = **confusion**, disarray, disorder, disorganization, guddle (*Scot.*), hodgepodge (*U.S.*), hotchpotch, huddle, jumble, mess, muddle, pig's breakfast (*informal*), shambles, state

hulk noun 1 = **wreck**, derelict, frame, hull, shell, shipwreck 2 Disparaging = **oaf**, lout, lubber, lump (*informal*)

hulking adjective = **ungainly**, awkward, bulky, clumsy, clunky (*informal*), cumbersome, gross, lubberly, lumbering, lumpish, massive, oafish, overgrown, ponderous, unwieldy

hull noun 1 = **frame**, body, casing, covering, framework, skeleton 2 = **husk**, peel, pod, rind, shell, shuck, skin ♦ verb 3 = **peel**, husk, shell, shuck, skin, trim

hullabaloo noun = **commotion**, babel, bedlam, brouhaha, clamour, confusion, din, disturbance, furore, hubbub, hue and cry, hurly-burly, noise, outcry, pandemonium, racket, ruckus (*informal*), ruction (*informal*), rumpus, to-do, tumult, turmoil, upheaval, uproar

hum *verb* **1** = **drone**, buzz, croon, mumble, murmur, purr, sing, throb, thrum, vibrate, whir **2** *Informal* = **be busy**, be active, bustle, buzz, move, pulsate, pulse, stir, vibrate

human *adjective* **1** = **mortal**, anthropoid, fleshly, manlike **2** = **kind**, approachable, compassionate, considerate, fallible, forgivable, humane, kindly, natural, understandable, understanding, vulnerable ♦ *noun* **3** = **human being**, body, child, creature, individual, man *or* woman, mortal, person, soul
➤ **Antonyms**
adjective ≠**mortal**: animal, nonhuman ≠**kind**: beastly, brutish, cruel, inhuman, unsympathetic ♦ *noun* ≠**human being**: animal, god, nonhuman

humane *adjective* = **kind**, benevolent, benign, charitable, clement, compassionate, forbearing, forgiving, gentle, good, good-natured, kind-hearted, kindly, lenient, merciful, mild, sympathetic, tender, understanding
➤ **Antonyms**
barbarous, brutal, cruel, inhuman, inhumane, ruthless, uncivilized, unkind, unmerciful, unsympathetic

humanitarian *adjective* **1** = **philanthropic**, altruistic, beneficent, benevolent, charitable, compassionate, humane, public-spirited ♦ *noun* **2** = **philanthropist**, altruist, benefactor, Good Samaritan

humanitarianism *noun* = **philanthropy**, beneficence, benevolence, charity, generosity, goodwill, humanism

humanities *plural noun* = **classical studies**, classics, liberal arts, literae humaniores

humanity *noun* **1** = **human race**, flesh, Homo sapiens, humankind, man, mankind, men, mortality, people **2** = **human nature**, humanness, mortality **3** = **kindness**, benevolence, benignity, brotherly love, charity, compassion, fellow feeling, kind-heartedness, mercy, philanthropy, sympathy, tenderness, tolerance, understanding

humanize *verb* = **civilize**, cultivate, educate, enlighten, improve, mellow, polish, reclaim, refine, soften, tame

humble *adjective* **1** = **modest**, meek, self-effacing, submissive, unassuming, unostentatious, unpretentious **2** = **lowly**, common, commonplace, insignificant, low, low-born, mean, modest, obscure, ordinary, plebeian, poor, simple, undistinguished, unimportant, unpretentious ♦ *verb* **3** = **humiliate**, abase, abash, break, bring down, chagrin, chasten, crush, debase, degrade, demean,

disgrace, lower, mortify, put down (*slang*), put (someone) in their place, reduce, shame, sink, subdue, take down a peg (*informal*)
➤ **Antonyms**
adjective ≠**modest**: arrogant, assuming, conceited, haughty, immodest, lordly, ostentatious, overbearing, pompous, presumptuous, pretentious, proud, snobbish, superior, vain ≠**lowly**: aristocratic, distinguished, elegant, famous, glorious, high, important, rich, significant, superior, wealthy ♦ *verb* ≠**humiliate**: elevate, exalt, magnify, raise

humbly *adverb* = **meekly**, cap in hand, deferentially, diffidently, modestly, obsequiously, on bended knee, respectfully, servilely, submissively, subserviently, unassumingly

humbug *noun* **1** = **nonsense**, baloney (*informal*), cant, claptrap (*informal*), eyewash (*informal*), hypocrisy, quackery, rubbish, trash **2** = **deception**, bluff, canard, cheat, deceit, dodge, feint, fraud, hoax, imposition, imposture, ruse, sham, swindle, trick, trickery, wile **3** = **fraud**, charlatan, cheat, con man (*informal*), faker, fraudster, impostor, phoney *or* phony (*informal*), quack, swindler, trickster

humdrum *adjective* = **dull**, banal, boring, commonplace, dreary, ho-hum (*informal*), mind-numbing, monotonous, mundane, ordinary, repetitious, routine, tedious, tiresome, uneventful, uninteresting, unvaried, wearisome
➤ **Antonyms**
dramatic, entertaining, exciting, extraordinary, interesting, lively, sexy (*informal*), stimulating

humid *adjective* = **damp**, clammy, dank, moist, muggy, steamy, sticky, sultry, watery, wet
➤ **Antonyms**
arid, dry, sunny, torrid

humidity *noun* = **damp**, clamminess, dampness, dankness, dew, humidness, moistness, moisture, mugginess, sogginess, wetness

humiliate *verb* = **embarrass**, abase, abash, bring low, chasten, crush, debase, degrade, discomfit, disgrace, humble, make (someone) eat humble pie, mortify, put down, put (someone) in their place, shame, subdue, take down a peg (*informal*), take the wind out of someone's sails
➤ **Antonyms**
elevate, honour, magnify, make proud

humiliating *adjective* = **embarrassing**, cringe-making (*Brit. informal*), cringeworthy (*Brit. informal*), crushing, degrading, disgracing, humbling, ignominious, mortifying, shaming, toe-curling (*slang*)

humiliation *noun* = **embarrassment**, abasement, affront, chagrin, condescension, degradation, disgrace, dishonour, humbling, ignominy, indignity, loss of face, mortification, put-down, resignation, self-abasement, shame, submission, submissiveness

humility *noun* = **modesty**, diffidence, humbleness, lack of pride, lowliness, meekness, self-abasement, servility, submissiveness, unpretentiousness
➤ **Antonyms**
arrogance, conceit, disdain, haughtiness, pomposity, presumption, pretentiousness, pride, snobbishness, superciliousness, superiority, vanity

hummock *noun* = **hillock**, hump, knoll, mound

humorist *noun* = **comedian**, card (*informal*), comic, eccentric, funny man, jester, joker, wag, wit

humorous *adjective* = **funny**, amusing, comic, comical, droll, entertaining, facetious, farcical, hilarious, jocose, jocular, laughable, ludicrous, merry, playful, side-splitting, waggish, whimsical, witty
➤ **Antonyms**
earnest, grave, sad, serious, sober, solemn

humour *noun* 1 = **funniness**, amusement, comedy, drollery, facetiousness, fun, jocularity, ludicrousness 2 = **joking**, comedy, farce, gags (*informal*), jesting, jests, jokes, pleasantry, wisecracks (*informal*), wit, witticisms, wittiness 3 = **mood**, disposition, frame of mind, spirits, temper ◆ *verb* 4 = **indulge**, accommodate, cosset, favour, fawn on, feed, flatter, go along with, gratify, mollify, pamper, pander to, spoil
➤ **Antonyms**
noun ≠**funniness**: gravity, grief, melancholy, sadness, seriousness, sobriety, solemnity, sorrow ◆ *verb* ≠**indulge**: aggravate, excite, oppose, rouse, stand up to

humourless *adjective* = **serious**, dour, dry, heavy-going, intense, po-faced, solemn, straight, unamused, unamusing, unfunny, unsmiling

hump *noun* 1 = **lump**, bulge, bump, hunch, knob, mound, projection, protrusion, protuberance, swelling 2 *As in* **get the hump** *Brit. informal* = **sulks**, blues, doldrums, dumps (*informal*), grumps (*informal*), megrims (*rare*), mopes ◆ *verb* 3 *Slang* = **carry**, heave, hoist, lug, shoulder

hunch *noun* 1 = **feeling**, idea, impression, inkling, intuition, premonition, presentiment, suspicion ◆ *verb* 2 = **draw in**, arch, bend, crouch, curve, huddle, hump, squat, stoop, tense

hunchback *noun* = **humpback**, Quasimodo

hunchbacked *adjective* = **humpbacked**, deformed, humped, malformed, misshapen, stooped

hunger *noun* 1 = **appetite**, emptiness, hungriness, ravenousness, voracity 2 = **starvation**, famine 3 = **desire**, ache, appetite, craving, greediness, itch, lust, thirst, yearning, yen (*informal*) ◆ *verb* 4 = **want**, ache, crave, desire, hanker, hope, itch, long, pine, starve, thirst, wish, yearn

hungry *adjective* 1 = **empty**, famished, famishing, hollow, peckish (*informal, chiefly Brit.*), ravenous, sharp-set, starved, starving, voracious 2 = **eager**, athirst, avid, covetous, craving, desirous, greedy, keen, yearning

hunk *noun* = **lump**, block, chunk, gobbet, mass, nugget, piece, slab, wedge, wodge (*Brit. informal*)

hunt *verb* 1 = **stalk**, chase, gun for, hound, pursue, track, trail 2 = **search**, ferret about, forage, go in quest of, look, look high and low, rummage through, scour, seek, try to find ◆ *noun* 3 = **search**, chase, hunting, investigation, pursuit, quest

hunter *noun* = **huntsman** *or* **huntress**, sportsman *or* sportswoman

hurdle *noun* 1 = **fence**, barricade, barrier, block, hedge, wall 2 = **obstacle**, barrier, block, complication, difficulty, handicap, hazard, hindrance, impediment, obstruction, snag, stumbling block

hurl *verb* = **throw**, cast, chuck (*informal*), fire, fling, heave, launch, let fly, pitch, project, propel, send, shy, sling, toss

hurly-burly *noun* = **commotion**, bedlam, brouhaha, chaos, confusion, disorder, furore, hubbub, pandemonium, tumult, turbulence, turmoil, upheaval, uproar
➤ **Antonyms**
composure, order, organization, tidiness

hurricane *noun* = **storm**, cyclone, gale, tempest, tornado, twister (*U.S. informal*), typhoon, windstorm

hurried *adjective* = **hasty**, breakneck, brief, cursory, hectic, perfunctory, precipitate, quick, quickie (*informal*), rushed, short, slapdash, speedy, superficial, swift

hurriedly *adverb* = **hastily**, hurry-scurry, in a rush, perfunctorily, quickly

hurry *verb* 1 = **rush**, barrel (along) (*informal, chiefly U.S. & Canad.*), burn rubber (*informal*), dash, fly, get a move on

(*informal*), get one's skates on (*informal*), lose no time, make haste, scoot, scurry, step on it (*informal*) **2 = speed (up)**, accelerate, expedite, goad, hasten, hustle, push on, quicken, urge ♦ *noun* **3 = haste**, bustle, celerity, commotion, dispatch, expedition, flurry, precipitation, promptitude, quickness, rush, speed, urgency
➤ **Antonyms**
verb ≠**rush**: crawl, creep, dawdle, drag one's feet, move slowly ≠**speed (up)**: delay, retard, slow, slow down ♦ *noun* ≠**haste**: calmness, slowness

hurt *verb* **1 = harm**, bruise, damage, disable, impair, injure, lay a finger on, mar, spoil, wound **2 = ache**, be sore, be tender, burn, smart, sting, throb **3 = upset**, afflict, aggrieve, annoy, cut to the quick, distress, grieve, pain, sadden, sting, wound ♦ *noun* **4 = distress**, discomfort, pain, pang, soreness, suffering ♦ *adjective* **5 = injured**, bruised, cut, damaged, grazed, harmed, scarred, scraped, scratched, wounded **6 = upset**, aggrieved, crushed, injured, miffed (*informal*), offended, pained, piqued, rueful, sad, wounded
➤ **Antonyms**
verb ≠**harm**: alleviate, cure, heal, relieve, repair, restore, soothe ♦ *noun* ≠**distress**: delight, happiness, joy, pleasure, pride, satisfaction ♦ *adjective* ≠**injured**: alleviated, assuaged, healed, relieved, repaired, restored, soothed ≠**upset**: calmed, consoled, placated

hurtful *adjective* **= unkind**, cruel, cutting, damaging, destructive, detrimental, disadvantageous, distressing, harmful, injurious, malicious, mean, mischievous, nasty, spiteful, upsetting, wounding

hurtle *verb* **= rush**, charge, crash, fly, plunge, race, shoot, speed, stampede, tear

husband *noun* **1 = partner**, better half (*humorous*), bridegroom, man (*informal*), mate, old man (*informal*), significant other (*U.S. informal*), spouse ♦ *verb* **2 = economize**, budget, conserve, hoard, manage thriftily, save, store, use sparingly
➤ **Antonyms**
verb ≠**economize**: be extravagant, fritter away, spend, splash out (*informal, chiefly Brit.*), squander

husbandry *noun* **1 = farming**, agriculture, agronomy, cultivation, land management, tillage **2 = thrift**, careful management, economy, frugality, good housekeeping

hush *verb* **1 = quieten**, mute, muzzle, shush, silence, still, suppress ♦ *noun* **2 = quiet**, calm, peace, peacefulness, silence, still (*poetic*), stillness, tranquillity

hush-hush *adjective* **= secret**, classified, confidential, restricted, top-secret, under wraps

hush up *verb* **= cover up**, conceal, draw a veil over, keep dark, keep secret, sit on (*informal*), smother, squash, suppress, sweep under the carpet (*informal*)

husk *noun* **= rind**, bark, chaff, covering, hull, shuck

huskiness *noun* **= hoarseness**, dryness, harshness, raspingness, roughness

husky *adjective* **1 = hoarse**, croaking, croaky, gruff, guttural, harsh, rasping, raucous, rough, throaty **2** *Informal* **= muscular**, beefy (*informal*), brawny, burly, hefty, powerful, rugged, stocky, strapping, thickset

hussy *noun* *Old-fashioned* **= slut**, baggage (*informal, old-fashioned*), floozy (*slang*), jade, scrubber (*Brit. & Austral. slang*), slapper (*Brit. slang*), strumpet, tart (*informal*), tramp (*slang*), trollop, wanton

hustle *verb* **= jostle**, bustle, crowd, elbow, force, haste, hasten, hurry, impel, jog, push, rush, shove, thrust

hut *noun* **= shed**, cabin, den, hovel, lean-to, refuge, shanty, shelter

hybrid *noun* **= crossbreed**, amalgam, composite, compound, cross, half-blood, half-breed, mixture, mongrel, mule

hygiene *noun* **= cleanliness**, hygienics, sanitary measures, sanitation

hygienic *adjective* **= clean**, aseptic, disinfected, germ-free, healthy, pure, salutary, sanitary, sterile
➤ **Antonyms**
dirty, filthy, germ-ridden, harmful, insanitary, polluted, unhealthy, unhygienic, unwholesome

hymn *noun* **= song of praise**, anthem, canticle, carol, chant, doxology, paean, psalm

hype *noun* *Slang* **= publicity**, ballyhoo (*informal*), brouhaha, build-up, plugging (*informal*), promotion, puffing, razzmatazz (*slang*)

hyperbole *noun* **= exaggeration**, amplification, enlargement, magnification, overstatement

hypercritical *adjective* **= fault-finding**, captious, carping, cavilling, censorious, finicky, fussy, hairsplitting, niggling, overcritical, overexacting, overscrupulous, pernickety (*informal*), strict

hypnotic *adjective* **= mesmerizing**, mesmeric, narcotic, sleep-inducing, somniferous, soothing, soporific, spellbinding

hypnotize *verb* **1 = mesmerize**, put in a

trance, put to sleep **2** = **fascinate**, absorb, entrance, magnetize, spellbind

hypochondria *noun* = **valetudinarianism**

hypochondriac *adjective, noun* = **valetudinarian**

hypocrisy *noun* = **insincerity**, cant, deceit, deceitfulness, deception, dissembling, duplicity, falsity, imposture, phoneyness *or* phoniness (*informal*), pretence, sanctimoniousness, speciousness, two-facedness
➤ **Antonyms**
honesty, sincerity, truthfulness

hypocrite *noun* = **fraud**, charlatan, deceiver, dissembler, impostor, pharisee, phoney *or* phony (*informal*), pretender, whited sepulchre

hypocritical *adjective* = **insincere**, canting, deceitful, deceptive, dissembling, duplicitous, false, fraudulent, hollow, pharisaical, phoney *or* phony (*informal*), sanctimonious, specious, spurious, two-faced

hypodermic *noun* = **syringe**, needle

hypothesis *noun* = **assumption**, postulate, premise, premiss, proposition, supposition, theory, thesis

hypothetical *adjective* = **theoretical**, academic, assumed, conjectural, imaginary, putative, speculative, supposed
➤ **Antonyms**
actual, confirmed, established, known, proven, real, true

hysteria *noun* = **frenzy**, agitation, delirium, hysterics, madness, panic, unreason

hysterical *adjective* **1** = **frenzied**, berserk, beside oneself, convulsive, crazed, distracted, distraught, frantic, mad, overwrought, raving, uncontrollable **2** *Informal* = **hilarious**, comical, farcical, screaming, side-splitting, uproarious, wildly funny
➤ **Antonyms**
≠**frenzied**: calm, composed, poised, self-possessed, unfazed (*informal*)
≠**hilarious**: grave, melancholy, sad, serious

I i

ice *noun* **1 break the ice = begin**, initiate the proceedings, kick off (*informal*), lead the way, make a start, start *or* set the ball rolling (*informal*), take the plunge (*informal*) **2 on thin ice = unsafe**, at risk, in jeopardy, open to attack, out on a limb, sticking one's neck out (*informal*), vulnerable

ice-cold *adjective* **= freezing**, arctic, biting, bitter, chilled to the bone *or* marrow, frozen, glacial, icy, raw, refrigerated, shivering

icy *adjective* **1 = cold**, arctic, biting, bitter, chill, chilling, chilly, freezing, frost-bound, frosty, frozen over, ice-cold, parky (*Brit. informal*), raw **2 = slippery**, glacial, glassy, like a sheet of glass, rimy, slippy (*informal or dialect*) **3 = unfriendly**, aloof, cold, distant, forbidding, frigid, frosty, glacial, hostile, indifferent, steely, stony, unwelcoming
➤ **Antonyms**
≠**cold**: blistering, boiling, hot, sizzling, warm ≠**unfriendly**: cordial, friendly, gracious, warm

idea *noun* **1 = thought**, abstraction, concept, conception, conclusion, fancy, impression, judgment, perception, understanding **2 = plan**, design, hypothesis, recommendation, scheme, solution, suggestion, theory **3 = belief**, conviction, doctrine, interpretation, notion, opinion, teaching, view, viewpoint **4 = impression**, approximation, ballpark figure, clue, estimate, guess, hint, inkling, intimation, notion, suspicion **5 = intention**, aim, end, import, meaning, object, objective, plan, purpose, *raison d'être*, reason, sense, significance

ideal *noun* **1 = model**, archetype, criterion, epitome, example, exemplar, last word, nonpareil, paradigm, paragon, pattern, perfection, prototype, standard, standard of perfection **2 often plural = principle**, moral value, standard ◆ *adjective* **3 = perfect**, archetypal, classic, complete, consummate, model, optimal, quintessential, supreme **4 = imaginary**, fanciful, impractical, ivory-tower, unattainable, unreal, Utopian, visionary
➤ **Antonyms**
adjective ≠**perfect**: deficient, flawed, impaired, imperfect, unsuitable

≠**imaginary**: actual, factual, literal, mundane, ordinary, real

idealist *noun* **= romantic**, dreamer, Utopian, visionary

idealistic *adjective* **= perfectionist**, impracticable, optimistic, quixotic, romantic, starry-eyed, Utopian, visionary
➤ **Antonyms**
down-to-earth, practical, pragmatic, realistic, sensible

idealize *verb* **= romanticize**, apotheosize, ennoble, exalt, glorify, magnify, put on a pedestal, worship

ideally *adverb* **= in a perfect world**, all things being equal, if one had one's way, under the best of circumstances

identical *adjective* **= alike**, a dead ringer (*slang*), corresponding, duplicate, equal, equivalent, indistinguishable, interchangeable, like, like two peas in a pod, matching, selfsame, the dead spit (*informal*), the same, twin
➤ **Antonyms**
different, disparate, distinct, diverse, separate, unlike

identification *noun* **1 = recognition**, cataloguing, classifying, establishment of identity, labelling, naming, pinpointing **2 = sympathy**, association, connection, empathy, fellow feeling, involvement, rapport, relationship **3 = identity card**, credentials, ID, letters of introduction, papers

identify *verb* **1 = recognize**, catalogue, classify, diagnose, flag, label, make out, name, pick out, pinpoint, place, put one's finger on (*informal*), single out, spot, tag **2 identify with = relate to**, ally with, associate with, empathize with, feel for, put in the same category as, put oneself in the place *or* shoes of, respond to, see through another's eyes, think of in connection with

identity *noun* **1 = existence**, distinctiveness, individuality, oneness, particularity, personality, self, selfhood, singularity, uniqueness **2 = sameness**, accord, correspondence, empathy, rapport, unanimity, unity

idiocy *noun* **= foolishness**, abject stupidity, asininity, cretinism, fatuity, fatuousness, imbecility, inanity, insanity, lunacy,

senselessness, tomfoolery
➤ **Antonyms**
acumen, sagacity, sanity, sense, soundness, wisdom

idiom *noun* 1 = **phrase**, expression, locution, set phrase, turn of phrase 2 = **language**, jargon, mode of expression, parlance, style, talk, usage, vernacular

idiomatic *adjective* = **vernacular**, dialectal, native

idiosyncrasy *noun* = **peculiarity**, affectation, characteristic, eccentricity, habit, mannerism, oddity, personal trait, quirk, singularity, trick

idiot *noun* = **fool**, airhead (*slang*), ass, berk (*Brit. slang*), blockhead, booby, charlie (*Brit. informal*), chump, coot, cretin, dickhead (*slang*), dickwit (*slang*), dimwit (*informal*), dipstick (*Brit. slang*), divvy (*Brit. slang*), dork (*slang*), dumb-ass (*slang*), dunderhead, dweeb (*U.S. slang*), fuckwit (*taboo slang*), geek (*slang*), gobshite (*Irish taboo slang*), gonzo (*slang*), halfwit, imbecile, jerk (*slang, chiefly U.S. & Canad.*), lamebrain (*informal*), mooncalf, moron, nerd *or* nurd (*slang*), nincompoop, nitwit (*informal*), numbskull *or* numskull, numpty (*Scot. informal*), oaf, pillock (*Brit. slang*), plank (*Brit. slang*), plonker (*slang*), prat (*slang*), prick (*derogatory slang*), schmuck (*U.S. slang*), simpleton, twit (*informal, chiefly Brit.*), wally (*slang*)

idiotic *adjective* = **foolish**, asinine, braindead (*informal*), crackpot (*informal*), crazy, daft (*informal*), dumb (*informal*), dumb-ass (*slang*), fatuous, foolhardy, halfwitted, harebrained, imbecile, imbecilic, inane, insane, loopy (*informal*), lunatic, moronic, senseless, stupid, unintelligent
➤ **Antonyms**
brilliant, commonsensical, intelligent, sensible, thoughtful, wise

idle *adjective* 1 = **inactive**, dead, empty, gathering dust, jobless, mothballed, out of action *or* operation, out of work, redundant, stationary, ticking over, unemployed, unoccupied, unused, vacant 2 = **lazy**, good-for-nothing, indolent, lackadaisical, shiftless, slothful, sluggish 3 = **useless**, abortive, bootless, fruitless, futile, groundless, ineffective, of no avail, otiose, pointless, unavailing, unproductive, unsuccessful, vain, worthless 4 = **trivial**, frivolous, insignificant, irrelevant, nugatory, superficial, unhelpful, unnecessary ◆ *verb* 5 *often with* **away** = **laze**, dally, dawdle, fool, fritter, hang out (*informal*), kill time, loaf, loiter, lounge, potter, waste, while 6 = **skive** (*Brit. slang*),

bob off (*Brit. slang*), coast, drift, mark time, shirk, sit back and do nothing, slack, slow down, take it easy, vegetate, veg out (*slang*)
➤ **Antonyms**
adjective ≠**inactive, lazy:** active, busy, employed, energetic, functional, industrious, occupied, operative, working ≠**useless:** advantageous, effective, fruitful, profitable, useful, worthwhile ≠**trivial:** important, meaningful

idleness *noun* 1 = **inactivity**, inaction, leisure, time on one's hands, unemployment 2 = **laziness**, hibernation, inertia, shiftlessness, sloth, sluggishness, torpor, vegetating 3 = **loafing**, dilly-dallying (*informal*), lazing, pottering, skiving (*Brit. slang*), time-wasting, trifling

idling *noun, adjective* = **loafing**, dawdling, drifting, pottering, resting, resting on one's oars, taking it easy, ticking over

idol *noun* 1 = **hero**, beloved, darling, fave (*informal*), favourite, pet, pin-up (*slang*), superstar 2 = **graven image**, deity, god, image, pagan symbol

idolater *noun* 1 = **heathen**, idol-worshipper, pagan 2 = **admirer**, adorer, devotee, idolizer, votary, worshipper

idolatrous *adjective* = **adoring**, adulatory, reverential, uncritical, worshipful

idolatry *noun* = **adoration**, adulation, apotheosis, deification, exaltation, glorification, hero worship, idolizing

idolize *verb* = **worship**, admire, adore, apotheosize, bow down before, deify, dote upon, exalt, glorify, hero-worship, look up to, love, revere, reverence, venerate, worship to excess

idyllic *adjective* = **idealized**, arcadian, charming, halcyon, heavenly, ideal, peaceful, picturesque, unspoiled

if *conjunction* 1 = **provided**, admitting, allowing, assuming, granting, in case, on condition that, on the assumption that, providing, supposing, though, whenever, wherever, whether ◆ *noun* 2 = **doubt**, condition, hesitation, stipulation, uncertainty

ignite *verb* 1 = **catch fire**, burn, burst into flames, fire, flare up, inflame, take fire 2 = **set fire to**, kindle, light, put a match to (*informal*), set alight, torch, touch off

ignominious *adjective* = **humiliating**, abject, despicable, discreditable, disgraceful, dishonourable, disreputable, indecorous, inglorious, mortifying, scandalous, shameful, sorry, undignified
➤ **Antonyms**

creditable, honourable, reputable, worthy

ignominy noun = **disgrace**, bad odour, contempt, discredit, dishonour, disrepute, humiliation, infamy, mortification, obloquy, odium, opprobrium, reproach, shame, stigma
➤ Antonyms
credit, honour, repute

ignorance noun 1 = **unawareness**, greenness, inexperience, innocence, nescience (literary), oblivion, unconsciousness, unfamiliarity 2 = **lack of education**, benightedness, blindness, illiteracy, mental darkness, unenlightenment, unintelligence
➤ Antonyms
≠lack of education: comprehension, enlightenment, insight, intelligence, knowledge, understanding, wisdom

ignorant adjective 1 = **uninformed**, benighted, blind to, inexperienced, innocent, in the dark about, oblivious, out of the loop, unaware, unconscious, unenlightened, uninitiated, unknowing, unschooled, unwitting 2 = **uneducated**, as green as grass, green, illiterate, naive, unaware, uncultivated, unknowledgeable, unlearned, unlettered, unread, untaught, untrained, untutored, wet behind the ears (informal) 3 = **insensitive**, crass, crude, gross, half-baked (informal), rude, shallow, superficial, uncomprehending, unscholarly
➤ Antonyms
≠uninformed: aware, conscious, informed, in the loop ≠uneducated: astute, brilliant, cultured, educated, knowledgeable, learned, literate, sagacious, sophisticated, wise

ignore verb = **overlook**, be oblivious to, blank (slang), bury one's head in the sand, cold-shoulder, cut (informal), discount, disregard, give the cold shoulder to, neglect, pass over, pay no attention to, reject, send (someone) to Coventry, shut one's eyes to, take no notice of, turn a blind eye to, turn a deaf ear to, turn one's back on
➤ Antonyms
acknowledge, heed, note, pay attention to, recognize, regard

ill adjective 1 = **unwell**, ailing, at death's door, dicky (Brit. informal), diseased, funny (informal), green about the gills, indisposed, infirm, laid up (informal), not up to snuff (informal), off-colour, on the sick list (informal), out of sorts (informal), poorly (informal), queasy, queer, seedy (informal), sick, under the weather (informal), unhealthy, valetudinarian 2 = **harmful**, bad, damaging, deleterious,

detrimental, evil, foul, iniquitous, injurious, ruinous, unfortunate, unlucky, vile, wicked, wrong 3 = **hostile**, acrimonious, adverse, antagonistic, cantankerous, cross, harsh, hateful, hurtful, inimical, malevolent, malicious, sullen, surly, unfriendly, unkind 4 = **ominous**, bodeful, disturbing, foreboding, inauspicious, sinister, threatening, unfavourable, unhealthy, unlucky, unpromising, unpropitious, unwholesome ♦ noun 5 = **harm**, affliction, hardship, hurt, injury, misery, misfortune, pain, trial, tribulation, trouble, unpleasantness, woe 6 = **evil**, abuse, badness, cruelty, damage, depravity, destruction, ill usage, malice, mischief, suffering, wickedness ♦ adverb 7 = **badly**, hard, inauspiciously, poorly, unfavourably, unfortunately, unluckily 8 = **hardly**, barely, by no means, insufficiently, scantily 9 As in ill-gotten = **illegally**, criminally, dishonestly, foully, fraudulently, illegitimately, illicitly, unlawfully, unscrupulously
➤ Antonyms
adjective ≠unwell: hale, healthy, strong, well ≠harmful: favourable, good ≠hostile: generous, kind ♦ noun ≠evil: good, kindness ♦ adverb ≠hardly: easily, well

ill-advised adjective = **misguided**, foolhardy, foolish, ill-considered, ill-judged, impolitic, imprudent, inappropriate, incautious, indiscreet, injudicious, overhasty, rash, reckless, short-sighted, thoughtless, unseemly, unwise, wrong-headed
➤ Antonyms
appropriate, cautious, discreet, judicious, politic, prudent, seemly, sensible, wise

ill-assorted adjective = **incompatible**, incongruous, inharmonious, mismatched, uncongenial, unsuited

ill at ease adjective = **uncomfortable**, antsy (informal), anxious, awkward, disquieted, disturbed, edgy, faltering, fidgety, hesitant, like a fish out of water, nervous, neurotic, on edge, on pins and needles (informal), on tenterhooks, out of place, restless, self-conscious, strange, tense, twitchy (informal), uneasy, unquiet, unrelaxed, unsettled, unsure, wired (slang)
➤ Antonyms
at ease, at home, comfortable, easy, quiet, relaxed, settled, sure

ill-bred adjective = **bad-mannered**, boorish, churlish, coarse, crass, discourteous, ill-mannered, impolite, indelicate, rude, uncivil, uncivilized, uncouth, ungallant, ungentlemanly, unladylike, unmannerly, unrefined, vulgar

➤ **Antonyms**
civil, courteous, delicate, mannerly,
refined, urbane, well-bred

ill-defined *adjective* = **unclear**, blurred,
dim, fuzzy, indistinct, nebulous, shadowy,
vague, woolly
➤ **Antonyms**
apparent, bold, clear, conspicuous,
cut-and-dried, distinct, evident, manifest,
obvious, plain

ill-disposed *adjective* = **unfriendly**,
against, antagonistic, anti (*informal*),
antipathetic, averse, disobliging, down on
(*informal*), hostile, inimical, opposed,
uncooperative, unwelcoming
➤ **Antonyms**
amicable, cooperative, friendly, obliging,
welcoming, well-disposed

illegal *adjective* = **unlawful**, actionable
(*Law*), banned, black-market, bootleg,
criminal, felonious, forbidden, illicit,
lawless, off limits, outlawed, prohibited,
proscribed, unauthorized,
unconstitutional, under-the-counter,
under-the-table, unlicensed, unofficial,
wrongful
➤ **Antonyms**
lawful, legal, licit, permissible

illegality *noun* = **crime**, criminality, felony,
illegitimacy, illicitness, lawlessness,
unlawfulness, wrong, wrongness

illegible *adjective* = **indecipherable**,
crabbed, faint, hard to make out,
hieroglyphic, obscure, scrawled,
undecipherable, unreadable
➤ **Antonyms**
clear, decipherable, legible, plain, readable

illegitimate *adjective* **1** = **born out of
wedlock**, baseborn (*archaic*), bastard,
born on the wrong side of the blanket,
fatherless, misbegotten (*literary*) **2**
= **unlawful**, illegal, illicit, improper,
unauthorized, unconstitutional,
under-the-table, unsanctioned **3** = **invalid**,
illogical, incorrect, spurious, unsound
➤ **Antonyms**
≠**unlawful**: authorized, constitutional,
lawful, legal, legitimate, proper, sanctioned

ill-fated *adjective* = **doomed**, blighted,
hapless, ill-omened, ill-starred, luckless,
star-crossed, unfortunate, unhappy,
unlucky

ill feeling *noun* = **hostility**, animosity,
animus, antagonism, bad blood,
bitterness, chip on one's shoulder,
disgruntlement, dissatisfaction, dudgeon
(*archaic*), enmity, frustration, hard
feelings, ill will, indignation, offence,
rancour, resentment
➤ **Antonyms**

amity, benevolence, favour, friendship,
goodwill, satisfaction

ill-founded *adjective* = **groundless**,
baseless, empty, idle, unjustified,
unproven, unreliable, unsubstantiated,
unsupported

ill-humoured *adjective* = **bad-tempered**,
acrimonious, crabbed, crabby, cross,
disagreeable, grumpy, huffy, impatient,
irascible, irritable, like a bear with a sore
head (*informal*), liverish, mardy (*dialect*),
moody, morose, out of sorts, out of
temper, petulant, ratty (*Brit. & N.Z.
informal*), sharp, snappish, snappy, sulky,
sullen, tart, testy, tetchy, thin-skinned,
touchy, unpleasant, waspish
➤ **Antonyms**
affable, agreeable, amiable, charming,
congenial, delightful, genial,
good-humoured, good-natured, pleasant

illiberal *adjective* **1** = **intolerant**, bigoted,
hidebound, narrow-minded, prejudiced,
reactionary, small-minded, uncharitable,
ungenerous **2** = **mean**, close-fisted,
miserly, niggardly, parsimonious, selfish,
sordid, stingy, tight, tight-arsed (*taboo
slang*), tight as a duck's arse (*taboo slang*),
tight-assed (*U.S. taboo slang*), tightfisted,
ungenerous
➤ **Antonyms**
≠**intolerant**: broad-minded, charitable,
generous, liberal, open-minded, politically
correct *or* PC, right-on (*informal*), tolerant

illicit *adjective* **1** = **illegal**, black-market,
bootleg, contraband, criminal, felonious,
illegitimate, off limits, prohibited,
unauthorized, unlawful, unlicensed **2**
= **forbidden**, clandestine, furtive, guilty,
immoral, improper, wrong
➤ **Antonyms**
≠**illegal**: above-board, lawful, legal,
legitimate, licit, permissible

illiteracy *noun* = **lack of education**,
benightedness, ignorance, illiterateness

illiterate *adjective* = **uneducated**,
benighted, ignorant, uncultured,
unlettered, untaught, untutored
➤ **Antonyms**
cultured, educated, lettered, literate,
taught, tutored

ill-judged *adjective* = **misguided**, foolish,
ill-advised, ill-considered, injudicious,
overhasty, rash, short-sighted, unwise,
wrong-headed

ill-mannered *adjective* = **rude**, badly
behaved, boorish, churlish, coarse,
discourteous, ill-behaved, ill-bred,
impolite, insolent, loutish, uncivil,
uncouth, unmannerly
➤ **Antonyms**

civil, courteous, cultivated, mannerly, polished, polite, refined, well-mannered

ill-natured *adjective* = **unkind**, bad-tempered, catty (*informal*), churlish, crabbed, cross, cross-grained, disagreeable, disobliging, malevolent, malicious, mean, nasty, perverse, petulant, shrewish, spiteful, sulky, sullen, surly, unfriendly, unpleasant
➤ **Antonyms**
agreeable, amiable, cheerful, congenial, friendly, good-natured, kind, obliging, pleasant

illness *noun* = **sickness**, affliction, ailment, attack, complaint, disability, disease, disorder, ill health, indisposition, infirmity, lurgy (*informal*), malady, malaise, poor health

illogical *adjective* = **irrational**, absurd, fallacious, faulty, inconclusive, inconsistent, incorrect, invalid, meaningless, senseless, sophistical, specious, spurious, unreasonable, unscientific, unsound
➤ **Antonyms**
coherent, consistent, correct, logical, rational, reasonable, scientific, sound, valid

ill-starred *adjective* = **doomed**, hapless, ill-fated, ill-omened, inauspicious, star-crossed, unfortunate, unhappy, unlucky

ill temper *noun* = **irascibility**, annoyance, bad temper, crossness, curtness, impatience, irritability, petulance, sharpness, spitefulness, tetchiness

ill-tempered *adjective* = **irascible**, annoyed, bad-tempered, choleric, cross, curt, grumpy, ill-humoured, impatient, irritable, liverish, ratty (*Brit. & N.Z. informal*), sharp, spiteful, testy, tetchy, touchy
➤ **Antonyms**
benign, cheerful, good-natured, mild-mannered, patient, pleasant, sweet-tempered

ill-timed *adjective* = **inopportune**, awkward, inappropriate, inconvenient, inept, unseasonable, untimely, unwelcome
➤ **Antonyms**
appropriate, convenient, opportune, seasonable, timely, well-timed

ill-treat *verb* = **abuse**, damage, dump on (*slang, chiefly U.S.*), handle roughly, harass, harm, harry, ill-use, injure, knock about *or* around, maltreat, mishandle, misuse, oppress, shit on (*taboo slang*), wrong

ill-treatment *noun* = **abuse**, damage, harm, ill-use, injury, mistreatment, misuse, rough handling

illuminate *verb* **1** = **light up**, brighten, illumine (*literary*), irradiate, light **2** = **clarify**, clear up, elucidate, enlighten, explain, explicate, give insight into, instruct, interpret, make clear, shed light on **3** = **decorate**, adorn, illustrate, ornament
➤ **Antonyms**
≠**light up**: black out, darken, dim, obscure, overshadow ≠**clarify**: befog, cloud, dull, obfuscate, overcast, shade, veil

illuminating *adjective* = **informative**, enlightening, explanatory, helpful, instructive, revealing
➤ **Antonyms**
confusing, obscuring, puzzling, unhelpful

illumination *noun* **1** = **light**, beam, brightening, brightness, lighting, lighting up, lights, radiance, ray **2** = **enlightenment**, awareness, clarification, edification, insight, inspiration, instruction, perception, revelation, understanding

illusion *noun* **1** = **fantasy**, chimera, daydream, figment of the imagination, hallucination, ignis fatuus, mirage, mockery, phantasm, semblance, will-o'-the-wisp **2** = **misconception**, deception, delusion, error, fallacy, false impression, fancy, misapprehension
➤ **Antonyms**
actuality, fact, reality, truth

illusory *or* **illusive** *adjective* = **unreal**, apparent, Barmecide, beguiling, chimerical, deceitful, deceptive, delusive, fallacious, false, hallucinatory, misleading, mistaken, seeming, sham, untrue
➤ **Antonyms**
authentic, down-to-earth, factual, genuine, real, reliable, solid, true

illustrate *verb* **1** = **demonstrate**, bring home, clarify, elucidate, emphasize, exemplify, exhibit, explain, explicate, instance, interpret, make clear, make plain, point up, show **2** = **draw**, adorn, decorate, depict, ornament, picture, sketch

illustrated *adjective* = **pictorial**, decorated, embellished, graphic, illuminated, picture, pictured, with illustrations

illustration *noun* **1** = **picture**, adornment, decoration, figure, plate, sketch **2** = **example**, analogy, case, case in point, clarification, demonstration, elucidation, exemplification, explanation, instance, interpretation, specimen

illustrious *adjective* = **famous**, brilliant, celebrated, distinguished, eminent, exalted, famed, glorious, great, noble, notable, noted, prominent, remarkable, renowned, resplendent, signal, splendid
➤ **Antonyms**

humble, ignoble, infamous, lowly, meek, notorious, obscure, unassuming

ill will noun = **hostility**, acrimony, animosity, animus, antagonism, antipathy, aversion, bad blood, dislike, enmity, envy, grudge, hard feelings, hatred, malevolence, malice, no love lost, rancour, resentment, spite, unfriendliness, venom
➤ **Antonyms**
amiability, amity, charity, congeniality, cordiality, friendship, goodwill

image noun 1 = **concept**, conception, idea, impression, mental picture, perception 2 = **figure**, conceit, trope 3 = **representation**, appearance, effigy, figure, icon, idol, likeness, picture, portrait, reflection, statue 4 = **replica**, chip off the old block (informal), counterpart, (dead) ringer (slang), Doppelgänger, double, facsimile, similitude, spit (informal, chiefly Brit.), spitting image (informal)

imaginable adjective = **possible**, believable, comprehensible, conceivable, credible, likely, plausible, supposable, thinkable, under the sun, within the bounds of possibility
➤ **Antonyms**
impossible, incomprehensible, inconceivable, incredible, unbelievable, unimaginable, unlikely, unthinkable

imaginary adjective = **fictional**, assumed, chimerical, dreamlike, fancied, fanciful, fictitious, hallucinatory, hypothetical, ideal, illusive, illusory, imagal (Psychoanal.), imagined, invented, legendary, made-up, mythological, nonexistent, phantasmal, shadowy, supposed, suppositious, supposititious, unreal, unsubstantial, visionary
➤ **Antonyms**
actual, factual, genuine, known, proven, real, substantial, tangible, true

imagination noun 1 = **unreality**, chimera, conception, idea, ideality, illusion, image, invention, notion, supposition 2 = **creativity**, enterprise, fancy, ingenuity, insight, inspiration, invention, inventiveness, originality, resourcefulness, vision, wit, wittiness

imaginative adjective = **creative**, clever, dreamy, enterprising, fanciful, fantastic, ingenious, inspired, inventive, original, poetical, visionary, vivid, whimsical
➤ **Antonyms**
literal, mundane, ordinary, uncreative, unimaginative, uninspired, unoriginal, unpoetical, unromantic

imagine verb 1 = **envisage**, conceive, conceptualize, conjure up, create, devise, dream up (informal), fantasize, form a

mental picture of, frame, invent, picture, plan, project, scheme, see in the mind's eye, think of, think up, visualize 2 = **believe**, apprehend, assume, conjecture, deduce, deem, fancy, gather, guess (informal, chiefly U.S. & Canad.), infer, realize, suppose, surmise, suspect, take for granted, take it, think

imbecile noun 1 = **idiot**, berk (Brit. slang), bungler, charlie (Brit. informal), chump, coot, cretin, dickhead (slang), dickwit (slang), dipstick (Brit. slang), divvy (Brit. slang), dolt, dork (slang), dotard, dumb-ass (slang), dweeb (U.S. slang), fool, fuckwit (taboo slang), geek (slang), gobshite (Irish taboo slang), gonzo (slang), halfwit, jerk (slang, chiefly U.S. & Canad.), moron, nerd or nurd (slang), numbskull or numskull, numpty (Scot. informal), pillock (Brit. slang), plank (Brit. slang), plonker (slang), prat (slang), prick (derogatory slang), schmuck (U.S. slang), thickhead, tosser (Brit. slang), twit (informal, chiefly Brit.), wally (slang) ◆ adjective 2 = **stupid**, asinine, braindead (informal), dead from the neck up, dumb-ass (slang), fatuous, feeble-minded, foolish, idiotic, imbecilic, inane, ludicrous, moronic, simple, simple-minded, thick, witless

imbecility noun = **stupidity**, asininity, childishness, cretinism, fatuity, foolishness, idiocy, inanity, incompetency
➤ **Antonyms**
comprehension, intelligence, perspicacity, reasonableness, sagacity, sense, soundness, wisdom

imbibe verb Formal 1 = **drink**, consume, knock back (informal), quaff, sink (informal), suck, swallow, swig (informal) 2 = **absorb**, acquire, assimilate, gain, gather, ingest, receive, take in

imbroglio noun = **complication**, complexity, embarrassment, entanglement, involvement, misunderstanding, quandary

imitate verb = **copy**, affect, ape, burlesque, caricature, counterfeit, do (informal), do an impression of, duplicate, echo, emulate, follow, follow in the footsteps of, follow suit, impersonate, mimic, mirror, mock, parody, personate, repeat, send up (Brit. informal), simulate, spoof (informal), take a leaf out of (someone's) book, take off (informal), travesty

imitation noun 1 = **replica**, carbon copy (informal), fake, forgery, impersonation, impression, mockery, parody, reflection, reproduction, sham, substitution, takeoff (informal), travesty 2 = **mimicry**, aping, copy, counterfeit, counterfeiting,

duplication, echoing, likeness, resemblance, simulation ♦ *adjective* **3** = **artificial**, dummy, ersatz, man-made, mock, phoney *or* phony (*informal*), pseudo (*informal*), repro, reproduction, sham, simulated, synthetic
➤ Antonyms
adjective ≠**artificial**: authentic, genuine, original, real, true, valid

imitative *adjective* = **derivative**, copied, copycat (*informal*), copying, echoic, mimetic, mimicking, mock, onomatopoeic, parrot-like, plagiarized, pseudo (*informal*), put-on, second-hand, simulated, unoriginal

imitator *noun* = **impersonator**, aper, carbon copy (*informal*), copier, copycat (*informal*), echo, epigone (*rare*), follower, impressionist, mimic, parrot, shadow

immaculate *adjective* **1** = **clean**, impeccable, neat, neat as a new pin, spick-and-span, spotless, spruce, squeaky-clean, trim **2** = **pure**, above reproach, faultless, flawless, guiltless, impeccable, incorrupt, innocent, perfect, sinless, squeaky-clean, stainless, unblemished, uncontaminated, undefiled, unexceptionable, unpolluted, unsullied, untarnished, virtuous
➤ Antonyms
≠**clean**: dirty, filthy, unclean ≠**pure**: contaminated, corrupt, impeachable, impure, polluted, stained, tainted

immaterial *adjective* **1** = **irrelevant**, a matter of indifference, extraneous, impertinent, inapposite, inconsequential, inconsiderable, inessential, insignificant, of little account, of no consequence, of no importance, trifling, trivial, unimportant, unnecessary **2** = **spiritual**, airy, disembodied, ethereal, ghostly, incorporeal, metaphysical, unembodied, unsubstantial
➤ Antonyms
≠**irrelevant**: crucial, essential, germane, important, material, relevant, significant, substantial ≠**spiritual**: earthly, physical, real, tangible

immature *adjective* **1** = **young**, adolescent, crude, green, imperfect, premature, raw, undeveloped, unfinished, unfledged, unformed, unripe, unseasonable, untimely **2** = **childish**, babyish, callow, inexperienced, infantile, jejune, juvenile, puerile, wet behind the ears (*informal*)
➤ Antonyms
adult, developed, fully-fledged, mature, mellow, ripe

immaturity *noun* **1** = **unripeness**, crudeness, crudity, greenness,

imperfection, rawness, unpreparedness **2** = **childishness**, babyishness, callowness, inexperience, juvenility, puerility

immeasurable *adjective* = **incalculable**, bottomless, boundless, endless, illimitable, immense, inestimable, inexhaustible, infinite, limitless, measureless, unbounded, unfathomable, unlimited, vast
➤ Antonyms
bounded, calculable, estimable, exhaustible, fathomable, finite, limited, measurable

immediate *adjective* **1** = **instant**, instantaneous **2** = **nearest**, adjacent, close, contiguous, direct, near, next, primary, proximate, recent **3** = **current**, actual, existing, extant, on hand, present, pressing, up to date, urgent
➤ Antonyms
≠**instant**: delayed, late, later, leisurely, postponed, slow, tardy ≠**nearest**: distant, far, remote

immediately *adverb* **1** = **at once**, before you could say Jack Robinson (*informal*), directly, forthwith, instantly, now, on the nail, posthaste, promptly, pronto (*informal*), right away, right now, straight away, this instant, this very minute, *tout de suite*, unhesitatingly, without delay, without hesitation **2** = **closely**, at first hand, directly, nearly

immemorial *adjective* = **age-old**, ancient, archaic, fixed, long-standing, of yore, olden (*archaic*), rooted, time-honoured, traditional

immense *adjective* = **huge**, Brobdingnagian, colossal, elephantine, enormous, extensive, giant, gigantic, ginormous (*informal*), great, humongous *or* humungous (*U.S. slang*), illimitable, immeasurable, infinite, interminable, jumbo (*informal*), large, mammoth, massive, mega (*slang*), monstrous, monumental, prodigious, stellar (*informal*), stupendous, titanic, tremendous, vast
➤ Antonyms
infinitesimal, little, microscopic, minuscule, minute, puny, small, tiny

immensity *noun* = **size**, bulk, enormity, expanse, extent, greatness, hugeness, infinity, magnitude, massiveness, scope, sweep, vastness

immerse *verb* **1** = **plunge**, bathe, dip, douse, duck, dunk, sink, submerge **2** = **engross**, absorb, busy, engage, involve, occupy, take up

immersion *noun* **1** = **dipping**, baptism, bathe, dip, dousing, ducking, dunking, plunging, submerging **2** = **involvement**, absorption, concentration, preoccupation

immigrant *noun* = **settler**, incomer, newcomer

imminent *adjective* = **near**, at hand, brewing, close, coming, fast-approaching, forthcoming, gathering, impending, in the air, in the offing, in the pipeline, just round the corner, looming, menacing, nigh (*archaic*), on the cards, on the horizon, on the way, threatening, upcoming
➤ **Antonyms**
delayed, distant, far-off, remote

immobile *adjective* = **stationary**, at a standstill, at rest, fixed, frozen, immobilized, immotile, immovable, like a statue, motionless, rigid, riveted, rooted, stable, static, stiff, still, stock-still, stolid, unmoving
➤ **Antonyms**
active, mobile, movable, on the move, pliant, portable, vigorous

immobility *noun* = **stillness**, absence of movement, firmness, fixity, immovability, inertness, motionlessness, stability, steadiness

immobilize *verb* = **paralyse**, bring to a standstill, cripple, disable, freeze, halt, lay up (*informal*), put out of action, render inoperative, stop, transfix

immoderate *adjective* = **excessive**, egregious, enormous, exaggerated, exorbitant, extravagant, extreme, inordinate, intemperate, O.T.T. (*slang*), over the odds (*informal*), over the top (*slang*), profligate, steep (*informal*), uncalled-for, unconscionable, uncontrolled, undue, unjustified, unreasonable, unrestrained, unwarranted, wanton
➤ **Antonyms**
controlled, judicious, mild, moderate, reasonable, restrained, temperate

immodesty *noun* 1 = **lewdness**, bawdiness, coarseness, impurity, indecorousness, indelicacy, obscenity 2 = **shamelessness**, audacity, balls (*taboo slang*), boldness, brass neck (*Brit. informal*), forwardness, gall (*informal*), impudence, temerity
➤ **Antonyms**
≠**lewdness**: decency, decorousness, delicacy, modesty, restraint, sobriety

immoral *adjective* = **wicked**, abandoned, bad, corrupt, debauched, degenerate, depraved, dishonest, dissolute, evil, impure, indecent, iniquitous, lewd, licentious, nefarious, obscene, of easy virtue, pornographic, profligate, reprobate, sinful, sink, unchaste, unethical, unprincipled, vicious, vile, wrong
➤ **Antonyms**

conscientious, good, honourable, inoffensive, law-abiding, moral, pure, upright, virtuous

immorality *noun* = **wickedness**, badness, corruption, debauchery, depravity, dissoluteness, evil, iniquity, licentiousness, profligacy, sin, turpitude, vice, wrong
➤ **Antonyms**
goodness, honesty, lawfulness, morality, purity

immortal *adjective* 1 = **eternal**, abiding, constant, death-defying, deathless, endless, enduring, everlasting, imperishable, incorruptible, indestructible, lasting, perennial, perpetual, sempiternal (*literary*), timeless, undying, unfading
♦ *noun* 2 = **great**, genius, hero, paragon 3 = **god**, goddess, Olympian
➤ **Antonyms**
adjective ≠**eternal**: ephemeral, fading, fleeting, mortal, passing, perishable, temporary, transitory

immortality *noun* 1 = **eternity**, deathlessness, endlessness, everlasting life, incorruptibility, indestructibility, perpetuity, timelessness 2 = **fame**, celebrity, glorification, gloriousness, glory, greatness, renown

immortalize *verb* = **commemorate**, apotheosize, celebrate, enshrine, eternalize, eternize, exalt, glorify, memorialize, perpetuate, solemnize

immovable *adjective* 1 = **fixed**, fast, firm, immutable, jammed, rooted, secure, set, stable, stationary, stuck, unbudgeable 2 = **inflexible**, adamant, constant, impassive, obdurate, resolute, steadfast, stony-hearted, unchangeable, unimpressionable, unshakable, unshaken, unwavering, unyielding
➤ **Antonyms**
≠**inflexible**: changeable, flexible, impressionable, movable, shakable, wavering, yielding

immune *adjective* = **exempt**, clear, free, insusceptible, invulnerable, let off (*informal*), not affected, not liable, not subject, proof (against), protected, resistant, safe, unaffected
➤ **Antonyms**
exposed, liable, prone, susceptible, unprotected, vulnerable

immunity *noun* 1 = **resistance**, immunization, protection 2 = **exemption**, amnesty, charter, exoneration, franchise, freedom, indemnity, invulnerability, liberty, licence, prerogative, privilege, release, right
➤ **Antonyms**
≠**resistance**: exposure, liability, openness,

proneness, susceptibility, vulnerability

immunize *verb* = **vaccinate**, inoculate, protect, safeguard

imp *noun* **1** = **demon**, devil, sprite **2** = **rascal**, brat, gamin, minx, pickle (*Brit. informal*), rogue, scamp, urchin

impact *noun* **1** = **effect**, brunt, burden, consequences, full force, impression, influence, meaning, power, repercussions, significance, thrust, weight **2** = **collision**, bang, blow, bump, concussion, contact, crash, force, jolt, knock, shock, smash, stroke, thump ◆ *verb* **3** = **hit**, clash, collide, crash, crush, strike

impair *verb* = **worsen**, blunt, damage, debilitate, decrease, deteriorate, diminish, enervate, enfeeble, harm, hinder, injure, lessen, mar, reduce, spoil, undermine, vitiate, weaken
➤ **Antonyms**
ameliorate, amend, better, enhance, facilitate, improve, strengthen

impaired *adjective* = **damaged**, defective, faulty, flawed, imperfect, unsound

impart *verb* **1** = **communicate**, convey, disclose, discover, divulge, make known, pass on, relate, reveal, tell **2** = **give**, accord, afford, bestow, confer, contribute, grant, lend, offer, yield

impartial *adjective* = **neutral**, detached, disinterested, equal, equitable, even-handed, fair, just, nondiscriminating, nonpartisan, objective, open-minded, unbiased, unprejudiced, without fear or favour
➤ **Antonyms**
biased, bigoted, influenced, partial, prejudiced, swayed, unfair, unjust

impartiality *noun* = **neutrality**, detachment, disinterest, disinterestedness, dispassion, equality, equity, even-handedness, fairness, lack of bias, nonpartisanship, objectivity, open-mindedness
➤ **Antonyms**
bias, favouritism, partiality, partisanship, subjectivity, unfairness

impassable *adjective* = **blocked**, closed, impenetrable, obstructed, pathless, trackless, unnavigable

impasse *noun* = **deadlock**, blind alley (*informal*), dead end, stalemate, standoff, standstill

impassioned *adjective* = **intense**, ablaze, animated, ardent, blazing, excited, fervent, fervid, fiery, flaming, furious, glowing, heated, inflamed, inspired, passionate, rousing, stirring, vehement, violent, vivid, warm, worked up

➤ **Antonyms**
apathetic, cool, impassive, indifferent, objective, reasoned

impatience *noun* **1** = **irritability**, intolerance, irritableness, quick temper, shortness, snappiness **2** = **haste**, hastiness, heat, impetuosity, rashness, vehemence, violence **3** = **restlessness**, agitation, anxiety, avidity, disquietude, eagerness, edginess, fretfulness, nervousness, restiveness, uneasiness
➤ **Antonyms**
≠**irritability**: control, forbearance, patience, restraint, tolerance
≠**restlessness**: calm, composure, serenity

impatient *adjective* **1** = **irritable**, demanding, hot-tempered, intolerant, quick-tempered, snappy, testy **2** = **hasty**, abrupt, brusque, curt, headlong, impetuous, indignant, sudden, vehement, violent **3** = **restless**, agog, athirst, chafing, eager, edgy, fretful, like a cat on hot bricks (*informal*), straining at the leash
➤ **Antonyms**
≠**irritable**: easy-going, tolerant ≠**restless**: calm, composed, cool, imperturbable, patient, quiet, serene

impeach *verb* **1** = **charge**, accuse, arraign, blame, censure, criminate (*rare*), denounce, indict, tax **2** = **challenge**, call into question, cast aspersions on, cast doubt on, disparage, impugn, question

impeachment *noun* = **accusation**, arraignment, indictment

impeccable *adjective* = **faultless**, above suspicion, blameless, exact, exquisite, flawless, immaculate, incorrupt, innocent, irreproachable, perfect, precise, pure, sinless, squeaky-clean, stainless, unblemished, unerring, unimpeachable
➤ **Antonyms**
blameworthy, corrupt, defective, deficient, faulty, flawed, shallow, sinful

impecunious *adjective* = **poor**, broke (*informal*), cleaned out (*slang*), destitute, dirt-poor (*informal*), down and out, flat broke (*informal*), indigent, in queer street, insolvent, penniless, poverty-stricken, short, skint (*Brit. slang*), stony (*Brit. slang*), strapped (*slang*), without two pennies to rub together (*informal*)
➤ **Antonyms**
affluent, prosperous, rich, wealthy, well-off, well-to-do

impede *verb* = **hinder**, bar, block, brake, check, clog, cumber, curb, delay, disrupt, encumber, hamper, hold up, obstruct, restrain, retard, slow (down), stop, throw a spanner in the works (*Brit. informal*), thwart

> ➤ **Antonyms**
advance, aid, assist, further, help, promote

impediment *noun* = **obstacle**, bar, barrier, block, check, clog, curb, defect, difficulty, encumbrance, fly in the ointment, hazard, hindrance, millstone around one's neck, obstruction, snag, stumbling block
> ➤ **Antonyms**
advantage, aid, assistance, benefit, encouragement, relief, support

impedimenta *plural noun* = **baggage**, accoutrements, belongings, effects, equipment, gear, junk (*informal*), luggage, odds and ends, paraphernalia, possessions, stuff, things, trappings

impel *verb* = **force**, actuate, chivy, compel, constrain, drive, goad, incite, induce, influence, inspire, instigate, motivate, move, oblige, power, prod, prompt, propel, push, require, spur, stimulate, urge
> ➤ **Antonyms**
check, discourage, dissuade, rebuff, repulse, restrain

impending *adjective* = **looming**, approaching, brewing, coming, forthcoming, gathering, hovering, imminent, in the offing, in the pipeline, menacing, near, nearing, on the horizon, threatening, upcoming

impenetrable *adjective* 1 = **impassable**, dense, hermetic, impermeable, impervious, inviolable, solid, thick, unpierceable 2 = **incomprehensible**, arcane, baffling, cabbalistic, dark, enigmatic, enigmatical, hidden, indiscernible, inexplicable, inscrutable, mysterious, obscure, unfathomable, unintelligible
> ➤ **Antonyms**
≠**impassable**: accessible, enterable, passable, penetrable, pierceable, vulnerable ≠**incomprehensible**: clear, explicable, obvious, soluble, understandable

imperative *adjective* 1 = **urgent**, compulsory, crucial, essential, exigent, indispensable, insistent, obligatory, pressing, vital 2 = **commanding**, authoritative, autocratic, dictatorial, domineering, high-handed, imperious, lordly, magisterial, peremptory
> ➤ **Antonyms**
≠**urgent**: avoidable, discretional, nonessential, optional, unimportant, unnecessary

imperceptible *adjective* = **undetectable**, faint, fine, gradual, impalpable, inappreciable, inaudible, indiscernible, indistinguishable, infinitesimal, insensible, invisible, microscopic, minute, shadowy,

slight, small, subtle, teensy-weensy, teeny-weeny, tiny, unnoticeable
> ➤ **Antonyms**
audible, detectable, discernible, distinguishable, noticeable, perceptible, visible

imperceptibly *adverb* = **invisibly**, by a hair's-breadth, inappreciably, indiscernibly, little by little, slowly, subtly, unnoticeably, unobtrusively, unseen

imperfect *adjective* = **flawed**, broken, damaged, defective, deficient, faulty, immature, impaired, incomplete, inexact, limited, partial, patchy, rudimentary, sketchy, undeveloped, unfinished
> ➤ **Antonyms**
complete, developed, exact, finished, flawless, perfect

imperfection *noun* = **fault**, blemish, defect, deficiency, failing, fallibility, flaw, foible, frailty, inadequacy, incompleteness, infirmity, insufficiency, peccadillo, scar, shortcoming, stain, taint, weakness, weak point
> ➤ **Antonyms**
adequacy, completeness, consummation, excellence, faultlessness, flawlessness, perfection, sufficiency

imperial *adjective* 1 = **royal**, kingly, majestic, princely, queenly, regal, sovereign 2 = **supreme**, august, exalted, grand, great, high, imperious, lofty, magnificent, noble, superior

imperil *verb* = **endanger**, expose, hazard, jeopardize, risk
> ➤ **Antonyms**
care for, guard, protect, safeguard, secure

imperishable *adjective* = **indestructible**, abiding, enduring, eternal, everlasting, immortal, perennial, permanent, perpetual, undying, unfading, unforgettable
> ➤ **Antonyms**
dying, fading, forgettable, mortal, perishable

impermeable *adjective* = **impenetrable**, hermetic, impassable, impervious, nonporous, proof, resistant

impersonal *adjective* = **detached**, aloof, bureaucratic, businesslike, cold, dispassionate, formal, inhuman, neutral, remote
> ➤ **Antonyms**
friendly, intimate, outgoing, personal, warm

impersonate *verb* = **imitate**, act, ape, caricature, do (*informal*), do an impression of, enact, masquerade as, mimic, parody, pass oneself off as, personate, pose as (*informal*), take off (*informal*)

impersonation *noun* = **imitation**, caricature, impression, mimicry, parody, takeoff (*informal*)

impertinence *noun* = **rudeness**, assurance, audacity, backchat (*informal*), boldness, brass neck (*Brit. informal*), brazenness, cheek (*informal*), chutzpah (*U.S. & Canad. informal*), disrespect, effrontery, face (*informal*), forwardness, front, impudence, incivility, insolence, neck (*informal*), nerve (*informal*), pertness, presumption, sauce (*informal*)

impertinent *adjective* = **rude**, bold, brazen, cheeky (*informal*), discourteous, disrespectful, flip (*informal*), forward, fresh (*informal*), impolite, impudent, insolent, interfering, lippy (*U.S. & Canad. slang*), pert, presumptuous, sassy (*U.S. informal*), saucy (*informal*), uncivil, unmannerly
➤ **Antonyms**
mannerly, polite, respectful

imperturbable *adjective* = **calm**, collected, complacent, composed, cool, equanimous, nerveless, sedate, self-possessed, serene, stoic, stoical, tranquil, undisturbed, unexcitable, unfazed (*informal*), unflappable (*informal*), unmoved, unruffled
➤ **Antonyms**
agitated, excitable, frantic, jittery (*informal*), nervous, panicky, ruffled, touchy, upset

impervious *adjective* **1** = **sealed**, hermetic, impassable, impenetrable, impermeable, imperviable, invulnerable, resistant **2** = **unaffected**, closed, immune, invulnerable, proof against, unmoved, unreceptive, unswayable, untouched

impetuosity *noun* = **haste**, hastiness, impulsiveness, precipitancy, precipitateness, rashness, vehemence, violence

impetuous *adjective* = **rash**, ardent, eager, fierce, furious, hasty, headlong, impassioned, impulsive, passionate, precipitate, spontaneous, spur-of-the-moment, unbridled, unplanned, unpremeditated, unreflecting, unrestrained, unthinking, vehement, violent
➤ **Antonyms**
cautious, leisurely, mild, slow, wary

impetuously *adverb* = **rashly**, helter-skelter, impulsively, in the heat of the moment, on the spur of the moment, passionately, recklessly, spontaneously, unthinkingly, vehemently, without thinking

impetus *noun* **1** = **incentive**, catalyst, goad, impulse, impulsion, motivation, push, spur, stimulus **2** = **force**, energy, momentum, power

impiety *noun* = **sacrilege**, godlessness, iniquity, irreligion, irreverence, profaneness, profanity, sinfulness, ungodliness, unholiness, unrighteousness, wickedness
➤ **Antonyms**
devoutness, godliness, holiness, piety, respect, reverence, righteousness

impinge *verb* **1** = **encroach**, infringe, invade, make inroads, obtrude, trespass, violate **2** = **affect**, bear upon, have a bearing on, impact, influence, relate to, touch, touch upon

impious *adjective* = **sacrilegious**, blasphemous, godless, iniquitous, irreligious, irreverent, profane, sinful, ungodly, unholy, unrighteous, wicked
➤ **Antonyms**
devout, godly, holy, pious, religious, reverent, righteous

impish *adjective* = **mischievous**, devilish, elfin, prankish, puckish, rascally, roguish, sportive, waggish

implacability *noun* = **pitilessness**, implacableness, inexorability, inflexibility, intractability, mercilessness, relentlessness, ruthlessness, unforgivingness, vengefulness

implacable *adjective* = **unyielding**, cruel, inexorable, inflexible, intractable, merciless, pitiless, rancorous, relentless, remorseless, ruthless, unappeasable, unbending, uncompromising, unforgiving, unrelenting
➤ **Antonyms**
appeasable, flexible, lenient, merciful, relenting, tolerant, yielding

implant *verb* **1** = **instil**, inculcate, infix, infuse, inseminate, sow **2** = **insert**, embed, fix, graft, ingraft, place, plant, root, sow

implement *verb* **1** = **carry out**, bring about, complete, effect, enforce, execute, fulfil, perform, put into action *or* effect, realize ♦ *noun* **2** = **tool**, agent, apparatus, appliance, device, gadget, instrument, utensil
➤ **Antonyms**
verb ≠**carry out**: delay, hamper, hinder, impede, weaken

implementation *noun* = **carrying out**, accomplishment, discharge, effecting, enforcement, execution, fulfilment, performance, performing, realization

implicate *verb* = **incriminate**, associate, compromise, concern, embroil, entangle, imply, include, inculpate, involve, mire, stitch up (*slang*), tie up with
➤ **Antonyms**
acquit, disentangle, dissociate, eliminate, exclude, exculpate, rule out

implicated *adjective* = **involved**, incriminated, suspected, under suspicion

implication *noun* 1 = **suggestion**, conclusion, inference, innuendo, meaning, overtone, presumption, ramification, significance, signification 2 = **involvement**, association, connection, entanglement, incrimination

implicit *adjective* 1 = **implied**, contained, inferred, inherent, latent, tacit, taken for granted, undeclared, understood, unspoken 2 = **absolute**, constant, entire, firm, fixed, full, steadfast, total, unhesitating, unqualified, unreserved, unshakable, unshaken, wholehearted
➤ **Antonyms**
≠**implied**: declared, explicit, expressed, obvious, patent, spoken, stated

implicitly *adverb* = **absolutely**, completely, firmly, unconditionally, unhesitatingly, unreservedly, utterly, without reservation

implied *adjective* = **unspoken**, hinted at, implicit, indirect, inherent, insinuated, suggested, tacit, undeclared, unexpressed, unstated

implore *verb* = **beg**, beseech, conjure, crave, entreat, go on bended knee to, importune, plead with, pray, solicit, supplicate

imply *verb* 1 = **hint**, connote, give (someone) to understand, insinuate, intimate, signify, suggest 2 = **entail**, betoken, denote, evidence, import, include, indicate, involve, mean, point to, presuppose

impolite *adjective* = **bad-mannered**, boorish, churlish, discourteous, disrespectful, ill-bred, ill-mannered, indecorous, indelicate, insolent, loutish, rough, rude, uncivil, uncouth, ungallant, ungentlemanly, ungracious, unladylike, unmannerly, unrefined
➤ **Antonyms**
courteous, decorous, gallant, gracious, mannerly, polite, refined, respectful, well-bred

impoliteness *noun* = **bad manners**, boorishness, churlishness, discourtesy, disrespect, incivility, indelicacy, insolence, rudeness, unmannerliness
➤ **Antonyms**
civility, courtesy, delicacy, mannerliness, politeness, respect

impolitic *adjective* = **unwise**, ill-advised, ill-judged, imprudent, indiscreet, inexpedient, injudicious, maladroit, misguided, undiplomatic, untimely
➤ **Antonyms**
diplomatic, discreet, expedient, judicious, politic, prudent, timely, wise

import *verb* 1 = **bring in**, introduce, land
♦ *noun* 2 *Formal* = **importance**, bottom, consequence, magnitude, moment, significance, substance, weight 3 = **meaning**, bearing, drift, gist, implication, intention, message, purport, sense, significance, thrust

importance *noun* 1 = **significance**, concern, consequence, import, interest, moment, momentousness, substance, usefulness, value, weight, worth 2 = **prestige**, bottom, distinction, eminence, esteem, influence, mark, pre-eminence, prominence, standing, status

important *adjective* 1 = **significant**, far-reaching, grave, large, material, meaningful, momentous, of substance, primary, salient, seminal, serious, signal, substantial, urgent, weighty 2 = **powerful**, big-time (*informal*), eminent, foremost, high-level, high-ranking, influential, leading, major league (*informal*), notable, noteworthy, of note, outstanding, pre-eminent, prominent 3 *usually with* **to** = **of concern**, basic, essential, of interest, relevant, valuable, valued
➤ **Antonyms**
inconsequential, insignificant, minor, needless, negligible, secondary, trivial, undistinctive, unimportant, unnecessary

importunate *adjective Formal* = **persistent**, burning, clamant, clamorous, demanding, dogged, earnest, exigent, insistent, pertinacious, pressing, solicitous, troublesome, urgent

impose *verb* 1 = **establish**, decree, exact, fix, institute, introduce, lay, levy, ordain, place, promulgate, put, set 2 = **inflict**, appoint, charge with, dictate, enforce, enjoin, prescribe, saddle (someone) with 3 **impose on**: **a** = **intrude on**, butt in on, encroach on, foist on, force oneself on, gate-crash (*informal*), horn in (*informal*), inflict on, obtrude on, presume upon, take liberties with, trespass on **b** = **take advantage of**, abuse, exploit, play on, use **c** = **deceive**, con (*informal*), dupe, hoodwink, pull the wool over (somebody's) eyes, trick

imposing *adjective* = **impressive**, august, commanding, dignified, effective, grand, majestic, stately, striking
➤ **Antonyms**
insignificant, mean, modest, ordinary, petty, poor, unimposing

imposition *noun* 1 = **application**, decree, introduction, laying on, levying, promulgation 2 = **intrusion**, cheek (*informal*), encroachment, liberty, presumption 3 = **constraint**, burden, charge, duty, levy, tax

impossibility *noun* = **hopelessness**, impracticability, inability, inconceivability

impossible *adjective* **1** = **inconceivable**, beyond one, beyond the bounds of possibility, hopeless, impracticable, not to be thought of, out of the question, unachievable, unattainable, unobtainable, unthinkable **2** = **absurd**, inadmissible, insoluble, intolerable, ludicrous, outrageous, preposterous, unacceptable, unanswerable, ungovernable, unreasonable, unsuitable, unworkable
➤ **Antonyms**
≠**inconceivable**: conceivable, imaginable, likely, plausible, possible, reasonable

impostor *noun* = **impersonator**, charlatan, cheat, deceiver, fake, fraud, hypocrite, knave (*archaic*), phoney *or* phony (*informal*), pretender, quack, rogue, sham, trickster

impotence *noun* = **powerlessness**, disability, enervation, feebleness, frailty, helplessness, inability, inadequacy, incapacity, incompetence, ineffectiveness, inefficacy, inefficiency, infirmity, paralysis, uselessness, weakness
➤ **Antonyms**
ability, adequacy, competence, effectiveness, efficacy, efficiency, powerfulness, strength, usefulness

impotent *adjective* = **powerless**, disabled, emasculate, enervated, feeble, frail, helpless, incapable, incapacitated, incompetent, ineffective, infirm, nerveless, paralysed, unable, unmanned, weak
➤ **Antonyms**
able, capable, competent, effective, potent, powerful, strong

impoverish *verb* **1** = **bankrupt**, beggar, break, pauperize, ruin **2** = **diminish**, deplete, drain, exhaust, reduce, sap, use up, wear out

impoverished *adjective* **1** = **poor**, bankrupt, destitute, distressed, impecunious, indigent, in reduced *or* straitened circumstances, necessitous, needy, on one's uppers, penurious, poverty-stricken, ruined, straitened **2** = **depleted**, barren, denuded, drained, empty, exhausted, played out, reduced, spent, sterile, worn out
➤ **Antonyms**
≠**poor**: affluent, rich, wealthy, well-off
≠**depleted**: fecund, fertile, productive

impracticability *noun* = **impracticality**, futility, hopelessness, impossibility, unsuitableness, unworkability, uselessness

impracticable *adjective* **1** = **unfeasible**, impossible, out of the question,

unachievable, unattainable, unworkable **2** = **unsuitable**, awkward, impractical, inapplicable, inconvenient, unserviceable, useless
➤ **Antonyms**
≠**unfeasible**: feasible, possible, practicable
≠**unsuitable**: practical, serviceable, suitable

impractical *adjective* **1** = **unworkable**, impossible, impracticable, inoperable, nonviable, unrealistic, unserviceable, visionary, wild **2** = **idealistic**, romantic, starry-eyed, unbusinesslike, unrealistic, visionary
➤ **Antonyms**
≠**unworkable**: possible, practical, serviceable, viable, workable ≠**idealistic**: down-to-earth, realistic, sensible

impracticality *noun* = **unworkability**, hopelessness, impossibility, inapplicability, romanticism

imprecise *adjective* = **indefinite**, ambiguous, blurred round the edges, careless, equivocal, estimated, fluctuating, hazy, ill-defined, inaccurate, indeterminate, inexact, inexplicit, loose, rough, sloppy (*informal*), vague, wide of the mark, woolly
➤ **Antonyms**
accurate, careful, definite, determinate, exact, explicit, precise

impregnable *adjective* = **invulnerable**, immovable, impenetrable, indestructible, invincible, secure, strong, unassailable, unbeatable, unconquerable, unshakable
➤ **Antonyms**
destructible, exposed, insecure, open, pregnable, shakable, vulnerable

impregnate *verb* **1** = **saturate**, fill, imbrue (*rare*), imbue, infuse, percolate, permeate, pervade, seep, soak, steep, suffuse **2** = **fertilize**, fecundate, fructify, get with child, inseminate, make pregnant

impress *verb* **1** = **excite**, affect, grab (*informal*), influence, inspire, make an impression, move, stir, strike, sway, touch **2** = **stress**, bring home to, emphasize, fix, inculcate, instil into **3** = **imprint**, emboss, engrave, indent, mark, print, stamp

impression *noun* **1** = **effect**, feeling, impact, influence, reaction, sway **2** = **idea**, belief, concept, conviction, fancy, feeling, funny feeling (*informal*), hunch, memory, notion, opinion, recollection, sense, suspicion **3** = **imitation**, impersonation, parody, send-up (*Brit. informal*), takeoff (*informal*) **4** = **mark**, brand, dent, hollow, impress, imprint, indentation, outline, stamp, stamping **5** = **edition**, imprinting, issue, printing **6 make an impression** = **cause a stir**, arouse comment, be conspicuous, excite notice, find favour, make a hit (*informal*), make an impact, stand out

impressionable *adjective* = **suggestible**, feeling, gullible, ingenuous, open, receptive, responsive, sensitive, susceptible, vulnerable
➤ **Antonyms**
blasé, hardened, insensitive, jaded, unresponsive

impressive *adjective* = **grand**, affecting, awesome, dramatic, exciting, forcible, moving, powerful, stirring, striking, touching
➤ **Antonyms**
ordinary, unimposing, unimpressive, uninspiring, unmemorable, weak

imprint *noun* 1 = **mark**, impression, indentation, print, sign, stamp ◆ *verb* 2 = **fix**, engrave, establish, etch, impress, print, stamp

imprison *verb* = **jail**, confine, constrain, detain, immure, incarcerate, intern, lock up, put away, put under lock and key, send down (*informal*), send to prison
➤ **Antonyms**
discharge, emancipate, free, liberate, release

imprisoned *adjective* = **jailed**, behind bars, captive, confined, immured, incarcerated, in irons, in jail, inside (*slang*), interned, locked up, put away, under lock and key

imprisonment *noun* = **custody**, confinement, detention, durance (*archaic*), duress, incarceration, internment, porridge (*slang*)

improbability *noun* = **doubt**, doubtfulness, dubiety, uncertainty, unlikelihood

improbable *adjective* = **doubtful**, cock-and-bull (*informal*), dubious, fanciful, far-fetched, implausible, questionable, unbelievable, uncertain, unconvincing, unlikely, weak
➤ **Antonyms**
certain, convincing, doubtless, likely, plausible, probable, reasonable

impromptu *adjective* 1 = **unprepared**, ad-lib, extemporaneous, extempore, extemporized, improvised, offhand, off the cuff (*informal*), spontaneous, unpremeditated, unrehearsed, unscripted, unstudied ◆ *adverb* 2 = **spontaneously**, ad lib, off the cuff (*informal*), off the top of one's head (*informal*), on the spur of the moment, without preparation
➤ **Antonyms**
adjective ≠**unprepared**: considered, planned, premeditated, prepared, rehearsed

improper *adjective* 1 = **indecent**, impolite, indecorous, indelicate, off-colour, risqué, smutty, suggestive, unbecoming, unfitting, unseemly, untoward, vulgar 2 = **inappropriate**, ill-timed, inapplicable, inapposite, inapt, incongruous, infelicitous, inopportune, malapropos, out of place, uncalled-for, unfit, unseasonable, unsuitable, unsuited, unwarranted 3 = **incorrect**, abnormal, erroneous, false, inaccurate, irregular, wrong
➤ **Antonyms**
≠**indecent**: becoming, decent, decorous, delicate, fitting, proper, seemly
≠**inappropriate**: apposite, appropriate, apt, felicitous, opportune, seasoned, suitable

impropriety *noun Formal* 1 = **indecency**, bad taste, immodesty, incongruity, indecorum, unsuitability, vulgarity 2 = **lapse**, bloomer (*Brit. informal*), blunder, faux pas, gaffe, gaucherie, mistake, slip, solecism
➤ **Antonyms**
≠**indecency**: decency, decorum, delicacy, modesty, propriety, suitability

improve *verb* 1 = **enhance**, ameliorate, amend, augment, better, correct, help, increase, mend, polish, rectify, touch up, upgrade 2 = **progress**, advance, develop, gain strength, look up (*informal*), make strides, perk up, pick up, rally, reform, rise, take a turn for the better (*informal*), take on a new lease of life (*informal*) 3 = **recuperate**, be on the mend, convalesce, gain ground, gain strength, grow better, make progress, mend, recover, turn the corner 4 = **reform**, clean up one's act (*informal*), get it together (*informal*), get one's act together (*informal*), pull one's socks up (*Brit. informal*), shape up (*informal*), turn over a new leaf
➤ **Antonyms**
≠**enhance**: damage, harm, impair, injure, mar, worsen

improvement *noun* 1 = **enhancement**, advancement, amelioration, amendment, augmentation, betterment, correction, face-lift, gain, increase, rectification 2 = **progress**, advance, development, furtherance, rally, recovery, reformation, rise, upswing

improvident *adjective* = **imprudent**, careless, heedless, inconsiderate, negligent, prodigal, profligate, reckless, shiftless, short-sighted, spendthrift, thoughtless, thriftless, uneconomical, unthrifty, wasteful
➤ **Antonyms**
careful, considerate, economical, heedful, provident, prudent, thrifty

improvisation *noun* 1 = spontaneity, ad-libbing, extemporizing, invention 2 = makeshift, ad-lib, expedient, impromptu

improvise *verb* 1 = concoct, contrive, devise, make do, throw together 2 = extemporize, ad-lib, busk, coin, invent, play it by ear (*informal*), speak off the cuff (*informal*), vamp, wing it (*informal*)

improvised *adjective* = unprepared, ad-lib, extemporaneous, extempore, extemporized, makeshift, off the cuff (*informal*), spontaneous, spur-of-the-moment, unrehearsed

imprudent *adjective* = unwise, careless, foolhardy, foolish, heedless, ill-advised, ill-considered, ill-judged, impolitic, improvident, incautious, inconsiderate, indiscreet, injudicious, irresponsible, overhasty, rash, reckless, temerarious, unthinking
➤ **Antonyms**
careful, cautious, considerate, discreet, judicious, politic, provident, prudent, responsible, wise

impudence *noun* = boldness, assurance, audacity, backchat (*informal*), brass neck (*Brit. informal*), brazenness, bumptiousness, cheek (*informal*), chutzpah (*U.S. & Canad. informal*), effrontery, face (*informal*), front, impertinence, insolence, lip (*slang*), neck (*informal*), nerve (*informal*), pertness, presumption, rudeness, sassiness (*U.S. informal*), sauciness, shamelessness

impudent *adjective* = bold, audacious, bold-faced, brazen, bumptious, cheeky (*informal*), cocky (*informal*), forward, fresh (*informal*), immodest, impertinent, insolent, lippy (*U.S. & Canad. slang*), pert, presumptuous, rude, sassy (*U.S. informal*), saucy (*informal*), shameless
➤ **Antonyms**
courteous, modest, polite, respectful, retiring, self-effacing, timid, well-behaved

impulse *noun* 1 = urge, caprice, drive, feeling, incitement, inclination, influence, instinct, motive, notion, passion, resolve, whim, wish 2 = force, catalyst, impetus, momentum, movement, pressure, push, stimulus, surge, thrust

impulsive *adjective* = instinctive, devil-may-care, emotional, hasty, headlong, impetuous, intuitive, passionate, precipitate, quick, rash, spontaneous, unconsidered, unpredictable, unpremeditated
➤ **Antonyms**
calculating, cautious, considered, cool, deliberate, halting, planned, premeditated, rehearsed, restrained

impunity *noun* = security, dispensation, exemption, freedom, immunity, liberty, licence, nonliability, permission

impure *adjective* 1 = unrefined, admixed, adulterated, alloyed, debased, mixed 2 = immoral, carnal, coarse, corrupt, gross, immodest, indecent, indelicate, lascivious, lewd, licentious, lustful, obscene, prurient, ribald, salacious, smutty, unchaste, unclean, X-rated (*informal*) 3 = unclean, contaminated, defiled, dirty, filthy, foul, infected, polluted, sullied, tainted, unwholesome, vitiated
➤ **Antonyms**
≠immoral: chaste, decent, delicate, modest, moral, pure, wholesome
≠unclean: clean, immaculate, spotless, squeaky-clean, undefiled, unsullied

impurity *noun* 1 *often plural* = dirt, bits, contaminant, dross, foreign body, foreign matter, grime, marks, pollutant, scum, spots, stains 2 = contamination, befoulment, defilement, dirtiness, filth, foulness, infection, pollution, taint, uncleanness 3 = immorality, carnality, coarseness, corruption, grossness, immodesty, indecency, lasciviousness, lewdness, licentiousness, obscenity, prurience, salaciousness, smuttiness, unchastity, vulgarity

imputation *noun* = blame, accusation, ascription, aspersion, attribution, censure, charge, insinuation, reproach, slander, slur

impute *verb* = attribute, accredit, ascribe, assign, credit, lay at the door of, refer, set down to

inability *noun* = incapability, disability, disqualification, impotence, inadequacy, incapacity, incompetence, ineptitude, powerlessness
➤ **Antonyms**
ability, adequacy, capability, capacity, competence, potential, power, talent

inaccessible *adjective* = out of reach, impassable, out of the way, remote, unapproachable, unattainable, un-get-at-able (*informal*), unreachable
➤ **Antonyms**
accessible, approachable, attainable, reachable

inaccuracy *noun* 1 = imprecision, erroneousness, incorrectness, inexactness, unfaithfulness, unreliability 2 = error, blunder, boob (*Brit. slang*), corrigendum, defect, erratum, fault, howler (*informal*), lapse, literal (*Printing*), miscalculation, mistake, slip, typo (*informal, Printing*)

inaccurate *adjective* = incorrect, careless, defective, discrepant, erroneous, faulty, imprecise, in error, inexact, mistaken, off

base (*U.S. & Canad. informal*), off beam (*informal*), out, unfaithful, unreliable, unsound, way off beam (*informal*), wide of the mark, wild, wrong
➤ Antonyms
accurate, correct, exact, precise, reliable, sound

inaccurately *adverb* = **imprecisely**, carelessly, clumsily, inexactly, unfaithfully, unreliably

inaction *noun* = **inactivity**, dormancy, idleness, immobility, inertia, rest, torpidity, torpor

inactive *adjective* 1 = **unused**, abeyant, dormant, idle, immobile, inert, inoperative, jobless, kicking one's heels, latent, mothballed, out of service, out of work, unemployed, unoccupied 2 = **slothful**, dull, indolent, lazy, lethargic, low-key (*informal*), passive, quiet, sedentary, slow, sluggish, somnolent, torpid
➤ Antonyms
≠unused: employed, mobile, occupied, operative, running, used, working
≠slothful: active, busy, diligent, energetic, industrious

inactivity *noun* 1 = **immobility**, dormancy, hibernation, inaction, passivity, unemployment 2 = **sloth**, dilatoriness, dolce far niente, dullness, heaviness, indolence, inertia, inertness, lassitude, laziness, lethargy, quiescence, sluggishness, stagnation, torpor, vegetation
➤ Antonyms
action, activeness, bustle, employment, exertion, mobility, movement

inadequacy *noun* 1 = **shortage**, dearth, inadequateness, incompleteness, insufficiency, meagreness, paucity, poverty, scantiness, skimpiness 2 = **incompetence**, defectiveness, deficiency, faultiness, inability, inaptness, incapacity, incompetency, ineffectiveness, inefficacy, unfitness, unsuitableness 3 = **shortcoming**, defect, failing, imperfection, lack, shortage, weakness

inadequate *adjective* 1 = **insufficient**, incommensurate, incomplete, insubstantial, meagre, niggardly, scant, scanty, short, sketchy, skimpy, sparse 2 = **incapable**, defective, deficient, faulty, found wanting, imperfect, inapt, incompetent, not up to scratch (*informal*), pathetic, unequal, unfitted, unqualified
➤ Antonyms
≠insufficient: adequate, ample, complete, perfect, satisfactory, substantial, sufficient
≠incapable: apt, capable, competent,

equal, fit, qualified

inadequately *adverb* = **insufficiently**, imperfectly, meagrely, poorly, scantily, sketchily, skimpily, sparsely, thinly

inadmissible *adjective* = **unacceptable**, immaterial, improper, inappropriate, incompetent, irrelevant, unallowable, unqualified, unreasonable

inadvertently *adverb* 1 = **unintentionally**, accidentally, by accident, by mistake, involuntarily, mistakenly, unwittingly 2 = **carelessly**, heedlessly, in an unguarded moment, negligently, thoughtlessly, unguardedly, unthinkingly
➤ Antonyms
carefully, consciously, deliberately, heedfully, intentionally

inadvisable *adjective* = **unwise**, ill-advised, impolitic, imprudent, inexpedient, injudicious

inane *adjective* = **senseless**, asinine, daft (*informal*), devoid of intelligence, empty, fatuous, frivolous, futile, goofy (*informal*), idiotic, imbecilic, mindless, puerile, silly, stupid, trifling, unintelligent, vacuous, vain, vapid, worthless
➤ Antonyms
meaningful, profound, sensible, serious, significant, weighty, worthwhile

inanimate *adjective* = **lifeless**, cold, dead, defunct, extinct, inactive, inert, insensate, insentient, quiescent, soulless, spiritless
➤ Antonyms
active, alive, alive and kicking, animate, full of beans (*informal*), lively, living, moving

inanity *noun* = **senselessness**, asininity, bêtise (*rare*), daftness (*informal*), emptiness, fatuity, folly, frivolity, imbecility, puerility, silliness, vacuity, vapidity, worthlessness

inapplicable *adjective* = **irrelevant**, inapposite, inappropriate, inapt, unsuitable, unsuited
➤ Antonyms
applicable, apposite, appropriate, apt, fitting, pertinent, relevant, suitable

inappropriate *adjective* = **unsuitable**, disproportionate, ill-fitted, ill-suited, ill-timed, improper, incongruous, malapropos, out of place, tasteless, unbecoming, unbefitting, unfit, unfitting, unseemly, untimely
➤ Antonyms
appropriate, becoming, congruous, fitting, proper, seemly, suitable, timely

inapt *adjective* 1 = **inappropriate**, ill-fitted, ill-suited, inapposite, infelicitous, unsuitable, unsuited 2 = **incompetent**, awkward, clumsy, dull, gauche, inept, inexpert, maladroit, slow, stupid

> ➤ Antonyms
≠**inappropriate**: apposite, appropriate, apt, felicitous, fitting, suitable, suited

inarticulate *adjective* 1 = **faltering**, halting, hesitant, tongue-tied 2 = **incoherent**, blurred, incomprehensible, indistinct, muffled, mumbled, poorly spoken, unclear, unintelligible
> ➤ Antonyms
≠**incoherent**: articulate, clear, coherent, comprehensible, intelligible, well-spoken

inattention *noun* = **neglect**, absent-mindedness, carelessness, daydreaming, disregard, forgetfulness, heedlessness, inadvertence, inattentiveness, indifference, preoccupation, thoughtlessness, woolgathering

inattentive *adjective* = **preoccupied**, absent-minded, careless, distracted, distrait, ditzy *or* ditsy (*slang*), dreamy, heedless, inadvertent, neglectful, negligent, regardless, remiss, slapdash, slipshod, thoughtless, unheeding, unmindful, unobservant, vague
> ➤ Antonyms
attentive, aware, careful, considerate, heeding, mindful, observant, thoughtful

inaudible *adjective* = **indistinct**, low, mumbling, out of earshot, stifled, unheard
> ➤ Antonyms
audible, clear, discernible, distinct, perceptible

inaugural *adjective* = **first**, dedicatory, initial, introductory, maiden, opening

inaugurate *verb* 1 = **open**, commission, dedicate, ordain 2 = **invest**, induct, install, instate 3 = **launch**, begin, commence, get under way, initiate, institute, introduce, kick off (*informal*), originate, set in motion, set up, usher in

inauguration *noun* 1 = **investiture**, induction, installation 2 = **launch**, initiation, institution, launching, opening, setting up

inauspicious *adjective* = **unpromising**, bad, black, bodeful, discouraging, ill-omened, ominous, unfavourable, unfortunate, unlucky, unpropitious, untoward
> ➤ Antonyms
auspicious, encouraging, favourable, fortunate, good, lucky, promising, propitious

inborn *adjective* = **natural**, congenital, connate, hereditary, immanent, inbred, ingrained, inherent, inherited, innate, in one's blood, instinctive, intuitive, native

inbred *adjective* = **innate**, constitutional, deep-seated, immanent, ingrained,

inherent, native, natural

incalculable *adjective* = **countless**, boundless, enormous, immense, incomputable, inestimable, infinite, innumerable, limitless, measureless, numberless, uncountable, untold, vast, without number

incantation *noun* = **chant**, abracadabra, charm, conjuration, formula, hex (*U.S. & Canad. informal*), invocation, spell

incapable *adjective* 1 = **incompetent**, feeble, inadequate, ineffective, inept, inexpert, insufficient, not equal to, not up to, unfit, unfitted, unqualified, weak 2 = **unable**, helpless, impotent, powerless, unfit 3 **incapable of** = **not susceptible to**, impervious to, not admitting of, resistant to
> ➤ Antonyms
≠**incompetent**: adequate, capable, competent, efficient, expert, fit, qualified, sufficient

incapacitate *verb* = **disable**, cripple, disqualify, immobilize, lay up (*informal*), paralyse, prostrate, put out of action (*informal*), scupper (*Brit. slang*), unfit (*rare*)

incapacitated *adjective* = **indisposed**, disqualified, *hors de combat,* immobilized, laid up (*informal*), out of action (*informal*), unfit

incapacity *noun* = **inability**, disqualification, feebleness, impotence, inadequacy, incapability, incompetency, ineffectiveness, powerlessness, unfitness, weakness

incarcerate *verb* = **imprison**, commit, confine, coop up, detain, immure, impound, intern, jail *or* gaol, lock up, put under lock and key, restrain, restrict, send down (*Brit.*), throw in jail

incarceration *noun* = **imprisonment**, bondage, captivity, confinement, detention, internment, porridge (*slang*), restraint

incarnate *adjective* 1 = **made flesh**, in bodily form, in human form, in the flesh 2 = **personified**, embodied, typified

incarnation *noun* = **embodiment**, avatar, bodily form, epitome, exemplification, impersonation, manifestation, personification, type

incautious *adjective* = **careless**, hasty, heedless, ill-advised, ill-judged, improvident, imprudent, impulsive, inconsiderate, indiscreet, injudicious, negligent, precipitate, rash, reckless, thoughtless, unguarded, unthinking, unwary
> ➤ Antonyms

careful, cautious, considerate, discreet, guarded, heedful, judicious, prudent, thoughtful, wary

incautiously *adverb* = **rashly**, imprudently, impulsively, indiscreetly, precipitately, recklessly, thoughtlessly, unthinkingly

incendiary *adjective* **1** = **inflammatory**, dissentious, provocative, rabble-rousing, seditious, subversive ♦ *noun* **2** = **arsonist**, firebug (*informal*), fire raiser, pyromaniac

incense[1] *noun* = **perfume**, aroma, balm, bouquet, fragrance, redolence, scent

incense[2] *verb* = **anger**, enrage, exasperate, excite, gall, get one's hackles up, inflame, infuriate, irritate, madden, make one's blood boil (*informal*), make one see red (*informal*), make one's hackles rise, nark (*Brit., Austral., & N.Z. slang*), provoke, raise one's hackles, rile (*informal*), rub one up the wrong way

incensed *adjective* = **angry**, choked, cross, enraged, exasperated, fit to be tied (*slang*), fuming, furious, hot under the collar (*informal*), incandescent, indignant, infuriated, irate, ireful (*literary*), mad (*informal*), maddened, on the warpath (*informal*), pissed (*taboo slang*), pissed off (*taboo slang*), steamed up (*slang*), up in arms, wrathful

incentive *noun* = **encouragement**, bait, carrot (*informal*), carrot and stick, enticement, goad, impetus, impulse, inducement, lure, motivation, motive, spur, stimulant, stimulus
➤ Antonyms
deterrent, discouragement, disincentive, dissuasion, warning

inception *noun* = **beginning**, birth, commencement, dawn, inauguration, initiation, kickoff (*informal*), origin, outset, rise, start
➤ Antonyms
completion, conclusion, end, ending, finish, termination

incessant *adjective* = **endless**, ceaseless, constant, continual, continuous, eternal, everlasting, interminable, never-ending, nonstop, perpetual, persistent, relentless, unbroken, unceasing, unending, unrelenting, unremitting
➤ Antonyms
infrequent, intermittent, occasional, periodic, rare, sporadic

incessantly *adverb* = **endlessly**, all the time, ceaselessly, constantly, continually, eternally, everlastingly, interminably, nonstop, perpetually, persistently, without a break

incidence *noun* = **prevalence**, amount, degree, extent, frequency, occurrence, rate

incident *noun* **1** = **happening**, adventure, circumstance, episode, event, fact, matter, occasion, occurrence **2** = **disturbance**, brush, clash, commotion, confrontation, contretemps, mishap, scene, skirmish

incidental *adjective* **1** = **accompanying**, attendant, by-the-way, concomitant, contingent, contributory, related **2** = **secondary**, ancillary, minor, nonessential, occasional, subordinate, subsidiary **3** = **accidental**, casual, chance, fortuitous, odd, random
➤ Antonyms
≠secondary: crucial, essential, important, necessary, vital

incidentally *adverb* **1** = **parenthetically**, by the bye, by the way, in passing **2** = **accidentally**, by chance, casually, fortuitously

incidentals *plural noun* = **odds and ends**, contingencies, extras, minutiae

incinerate *verb* = **burn up**, carbonize, char, consume by fire, cremate, reduce to ashes

incipient *adjective* = **beginning**, commencing, developing, embryonic, inceptive, inchoate, nascent, originating, starting

incise *verb* = **cut into**, carve, chisel, engrave, etch, inscribe

incision *noun* = **cut**, gash, notch, opening, slash, slit

incisive *adjective* = **penetrating**, acute, keen, perspicacious, piercing, sharp, trenchant
➤ Antonyms
dense, dull, superficial, vague, woolly

incisiveness *noun* = **perspicacity**, keenness, penetration, sharpness, trenchancy

incite *verb* = **provoke**, agitate for *or* against, animate, drive, egg on, encourage, excite, foment, goad, impel, inflame, instigate, prod, prompt, put up to, rouse, set on, spur, stimulate, stir up, urge, whip up
➤ Antonyms
dampen, deter, discourage, dishearten, dissuade, restrain

incitement *noun* = **provocation**, agitation, clarion call, encouragement, goad, impetus, impulse, inducement, instigation, motivation, motive, prompting, spur, stimulus

incivility *noun* = **rudeness**, bad manners, boorishness, discourteousness, discourtesy, disrespect, ill-breeding, impoliteness, unmannerliness
➤ Antonyms
civility, courteousness, courtesy, good manners, mannerliness, politeness, respect

inclemency *noun Formal* **1** = **storminess**, bitterness, boisterousness, rawness, rigour, roughness, severity **2** = **harshness**, callousness, cruelty, mercilessness, severity, tyranny, unfeelingness

inclement *adjective Formal* **1** = **stormy**, bitter, boisterous, foul, harsh, intemperate, rigorous, rough, severe, tempestuous **2** = **cruel**, callous, draconian, harsh, intemperate, merciless, pitiless, rigorous, severe, tyrannical, unfeeling, unmerciful
➤ **Antonyms**
≠**stormy:** balmy, calm, clement, fine, mild, pleasant, temperate ≠**cruel:** compassionate, gentle, humane, kind, merciful, tender

inclination *noun* **1** = **tendency**, affection, aptitude, bent, bias, desire, disposition, fancy, fondness, leaning, liking, partiality, penchant, predilection, predisposition, prejudice, proclivity, proneness, propensity, stomach, taste, thirst, turn, turn of mind, wish **2** = **slope**, angle, bend, bending, deviation, gradient, incline, leaning, pitch, slant, tilt **3** = **bow**, bending, bowing, nod
➤ **Antonyms**
≠**tendency:** antipathy, aversion, disinclination, dislike, revulsion

incline *verb* **1** = **slope**, bend, bevel, cant, deviate, diverge, heel, lean, slant, tend, tilt, tip, veer **2** = **predispose**, be disposed *or* predisposed, bias, influence, persuade, prejudice, sway, tend, turn **3** = **bend**, bow, lower, nod, nutate (*rare*), stoop ♦ *noun* **4** = **slope**, acclivity, ascent, declivity, descent, dip, grade, gradient, ramp, rise

inclined *adjective* = **disposed**, apt, given, liable, likely, minded, of a mind (*informal*), predisposed, prone, willing

inclose *see* ENCLOSE

include *verb* **1** = **contain**, comprehend, comprise, cover, embody, embrace, encompass, incorporate, involve, subsume, take in, take into account **2** = **introduce**, add, allow for, build in, count, enter, insert, number among
➤ **Antonyms**
eliminate, exclude, leave out, omit, rule out

including *preposition* = **together with**, as well as, containing, counting, inclusive of, plus, with

inclusion *noun* = **addition**, incorporation, insertion
➤ **Antonyms**
exception, exclusion, omission, rejection

inclusive *adjective* = **comprehensive**, across-the-board, all-embracing, all in, all together, blanket, catch-all (*chiefly U.S.*), full, general, global, *in toto*, overall, overarching, sweeping, umbrella, without exception
➤ **Antonyms**
confined, exclusive, limited, narrow, restricted, unique

incognito *adjective* = **in disguise**, disguised, under an assumed name, unknown, unrecognized

incoherence *noun* = **unintelligibility**, disconnectedness, disjointedness, inarticulateness

incoherent *adjective* = **unintelligible**, confused, disconnected, disjointed, disordered, inarticulate, inconsistent, jumbled, loose, muddled, rambling, stammering, stuttering, unconnected, uncoordinated, wandering, wild
➤ **Antonyms**
coherent, connected, intelligible, logical, rational

incombustible *adjective* = **fireproof**, flameproof, noncombustible, nonflammable, noninflammable

income *noun* = **revenue**, earnings, gains, interest, means, pay, proceeds, profits, receipts, salary, takings, wages

incoming *adjective* = **arriving**, approaching, entering, homeward, landing, new, returning, succeeding
➤ **Antonyms**
departing, exiting, leaving, outgoing

incomparable *adjective* = **unequalled**, beyond compare, inimitable, matchless, paramount, peerless, superlative, supreme, transcendent, unmatched, unparalleled, unrivalled

incomparably *adverb* = **immeasurably**, beyond compare, by far, easily, eminently, far and away

incompatibility *noun* = **inconsistency**, antagonism, conflict, discrepancy, disparateness, incongruity, irreconcilability, uncongeniality

incompatible *adjective* = **inconsistent**, antagonistic, antipathetic, conflicting, contradictory, discordant, discrepant, disparate, ill-assorted, incongruous, inconsonant, irreconcilable, mismatched, uncongenial, unsuitable, unsuited
➤ **Antonyms**
alike, appropriate, compatible, congenial, consistent, harmonious, reconcilable, suitable, suited

incompetence *noun* = **ineptitude**, inability, inadequacy, incapability, incapacity, incompetency, ineffectiveness, ineptness, insufficiency, skill-lessness, unfitness, uselessness

incompetent *adjective* = **inept**, bungling,

cowboy (*informal*), floundering, incapable, incapacitated, ineffectual, inexpert, insufficient, skill-less, unable, unfit, unfitted, unskilful, useless
➤ **Antonyms**
able, capable, competent, expert, fit, proficient, skilful

incomplete *adjective* = **unfinished**, broken, defective, deficient, fragmentary, imperfect, insufficient, lacking, partial, short, unaccomplished, undeveloped, undone, unexecuted, wanting
➤ **Antonyms**
accomplished, complete, developed, finished, perfect, unified, whole

incomprehensible *adjective*
= **unintelligible**, above one's head, all Greek to one (*informal*), baffling, beyond comprehension, beyond one's grasp, enigmatic, impenetrable, inconceivable, inscrutable, mysterious, obscure, opaque, perplexing, puzzling, unfathomable, unimaginable, unthinkable
➤ **Antonyms**
apparent, clear, comprehensible, conceivable, evident, intelligible, manifest, obvious, understandable

inconceivable *adjective* = **unimaginable**, beyond belief, impossible, incomprehensible, incredible, mind-boggling (*informal*), not to be thought of, out of the question, staggering (*informal*), unbelievable, unheard-of, unknowable, unthinkable
➤ **Antonyms**
believable, comprehensible, conceivable, credible, imaginable, likely, plausible, possible, reasonable

inconclusive *adjective* = **indecisive**, ambiguous, indeterminate, open, uncertain, unconvincing, undecided, unsettled, up in the air (*informal*), vague

incongruity *noun* = **inappropriateness**, conflict, discrepancy, disparity, inaptness, incompatibility, inconsistency, inharmoniousness, unsuitability

incongruous *adjective* = **inappropriate**, absurd, conflicting, contradictory, contrary, disconsonant, discordant, extraneous, improper, inapt, incoherent, incompatible, inconsistent, out of keeping, out of place, unbecoming, unsuitable, unsuited
➤ **Antonyms**
appropriate, becoming, compatible, consistent, harmonious, suitable, suited

inconsiderable *adjective* = **insignificant**, exiguous, inconsequential, light, minor, negligible, petty, slight, small, small-time (*informal*), trifling, trivial, unimportant

inconsiderate *adjective* = **selfish**, careless, indelicate, insensitive, intolerant, rude, self-centred, tactless, thoughtless, uncharitable, ungracious, unkind, unthinking
➤ **Antonyms**
attentive, careful, considerate, gracious, kind, sensitive, tactful, thoughtful, tolerant

inconsistency *noun* 1 = **unreliability**, fickleness, instability, unpredictability, unsteadiness 2 = **incompatibility**, contrariety, disagreement, discrepancy, disparity, divergence, incongruity, inconsonance, paradox, variance

inconsistent *adjective* 1 = **changeable**, capricious, erratic, fickle, inconstant, irregular, uneven, unpredictable, unstable, unsteady, vagarious (*rare*), variable 2 = **incompatible**, at odds, at variance, conflicting, contradictory, contrary, discordant, discrepant, incoherent, in conflict, incongruous, inconstant, irreconcilable, out of step
➤ **Antonyms**
≠**changeable**: consistent, constant, predictable, reliable, stable, steady, unchanging ≠**incompatible**: coherent, compatible, homogeneous, orderly, reconcilable, uniform

inconsistently *adverb* = **unpredictably**, contradictorily, differently, eccentrically, erratically, inequably, randomly, unequally, unfairly, variably

inconsolable *adjective* = **heartbroken**, brokenhearted, desolate, despairing, heartsick, prostrate with grief, sick at heart

inconspicuous *adjective* = **unobtrusive**, camouflaged, hidden, insignificant, modest, muted, ordinary, plain, quiet, retiring, unassuming, unnoticeable, unostentatious
➤ **Antonyms**
bold, conspicuous, noticeable, obtrusive, obvious, salient, significant, visible

incontestable *adjective* = **certain**, beyond doubt, beyond question, incontrovertible, indisputable, indubitable, irrefutable, self-evident, sure, undeniable, unquestionable

incontinent *adjective* = **unrestrained**, unbridled, unchecked, uncontrollable, uncontrolled, ungovernable, ungoverned

incontrovertible *adjective* = **indisputable**, beyond dispute, certain, established, incontestable, indubitable, irrefutable, positive, sure, undeniable, unquestionable, unshakable

inconvenience *noun* 1 = **trouble**, annoyance, awkwardness, bother, difficulty, disadvantage, disruption, disturbance, downside, drawback, fuss, hassle (*informal*), hindrance, nuisance, uneasiness, upset, vexation **2** = **awkwardness**, cumbersomeness, unfitness, unhandiness, unsuitableness, untimeliness, unwieldiness ♦ *verb* **3** = **trouble**, bother, discommode, disrupt, disturb, give (someone) bother *or* trouble, hassle (*informal*), irk, make (someone) go out of his way, put out, put to trouble, upset

inconvenient *adjective* **1** = **troublesome**, annoying, awkward, bothersome, disadvantageous, disturbing, embarrassing, inopportune, tiresome, unseasonable, unsuitable, untimely, vexatious **2** = **difficult**, awkward, cumbersome, unhandy, unmanageable, unwieldy
➤ **Antonyms**
≠**troublesome**: convenient, handy, opportune, seasonable, suitable, timely

incorporate *verb* = **include**, absorb, amalgamate, assimilate, blend, coalesce, combine, consolidate, embody, fuse, integrate, meld, merge, mix, subsume, unite

incorrect *adjective* = **false**, erroneous, faulty, flawed, improper, inaccurate, inappropriate, inexact, mistaken, off base (*U.S. & Canad. informal*), off beam (*informal*), out, specious, unfitting, unsuitable, untrue, way off beam (*informal*), wide of the mark (*informal*), wrong
➤ **Antonyms**
accurate, correct, exact, faultless, fitting, flawless, right, suitable, true

incorrectness *noun* = **inaccuracy**, erroneousness, error, fallacy, faultiness, impreciseness, imprecision, impropriety, inexactness, speciousness, unsoundness, unsuitability, wrongness

incorrigible *adjective* = **incurable**, hardened, hopeless, intractable, inveterate, irredeemable, unreformed

incorruptibility *noun* = **integrity**, honesty, honour, justness, uprightness

incorruptible *adjective* **1** = **honest**, above suspicion, honourable, just, straight, trustworthy, unbribable, upright **2** = **imperishable**, everlasting, undecaying

increase *verb* **1** = **grow**, add to, advance, aggrandize, amplify, augment, boost, build up, develop, dilate, enhance, enlarge, escalate, expand, extend, heighten, inflate, intensify, magnify, mount, multiply, proliferate, prolong, raise, snowball, spread, step up (*informal*), strengthen, swell, wax ♦ *noun* **2** = **growth**,

addition, augmentation, boost, development, enlargement, escalation, expansion, extension, gain, increment, intensification, rise, upsurge, upturn **3 on the increase** = **growing**, developing, escalating, expanding, increasing, multiplying, on the rise, proliferating, spreading
➤ **Antonyms**
verb ≠**grow**: abate, abbreviate, abridge, condense, curtail, decline, decrease, deflate, diminish, dwindle, lessen, reduce, shorten, shrink

increasingly *adverb* = **progressively**, more and more, to an increasing extent

incredible *adjective* **1** = **implausible**, absurd, beyond belief, cock-and-bull (*informal*), far-fetched, impossible, improbable, inconceivable, not able to hold water, preposterous, unbelievable, unimaginable, unthinkable **2** *Informal* = **amazing**, ace (*informal*), astonishing, astounding, awe-inspiring, brilliant, def (*slang*), extraordinary, far-out (*slang*), great, marvellous, mega (*slang*), prodigious, rad (*informal*), sensational (*informal*), superhuman, wonderful

incredulity *noun* = **disbelief**, distrust, doubt, scepticism, unbelief

incredulous *adjective* = **disbelieving**, distrustful, doubtful, doubting, dubious, mistrustful, sceptical, suspicious, unbelieving, unconvinced
➤ **Antonyms**
believing, credulous, gullible, naive, trusting, unsuspecting, wet behind the ears (*informal*)

increment *noun* = **increase**, accretion, accrual, accruement, addition, advancement, augmentation, enlargement, gain, step up, supplement

incriminate *verb* = **implicate**, accuse, arraign, blacken the name of, blame, charge, impeach, inculpate, indict, involve, point the finger at (*informal*), stigmatize

incumbent *adjective Formal* = **obligatory**, binding, compulsory, mandatory, necessary

incur *verb* = **earn**, arouse, bring (upon oneself), contract, draw, expose oneself to, gain, induce, lay oneself open to, meet with, provoke

incurable *adjective* **1** = **fatal**, inoperable, irrecoverable, irremediable, remediless, terminal **2** = **incorrigible**, dyed-in-the-wool, hopeless, inveterate

indebted *adjective* = **grateful**, beholden, in debt, obligated, obliged, under an obligation

indecency *noun* = **obscenity**, bawdiness, coarseness, crudity, foulness, grossness, immodesty, impropriety, impurity, indecorum, indelicacy, lewdness, licentiousness, outrageousness, pornography, smut, smuttiness, unseemliness, vileness, vulgarity
➤ **Antonyms**
decency, decorum, delicacy, modesty, propriety, purity, seemliness

indecent *adjective* **1** = **lewd**, blue, coarse, crude, dirty, filthy, foul, gross, immodest, improper, impure, indelicate, licentious, pornographic, salacious, scatological, smutty, vile **2** = **unbecoming**, ill-bred, improper, in bad taste, indecorous, offensive, outrageous, tasteless, unseemly, vulgar
➤ **Antonyms**
decent, decorous, delicate, modest, proper, pure, respectable, seemly, tasteful

indecipherable *adjective* = **illegible**, crabbed, indistinguishable, unintelligible, unreadable

indecision *noun* = **hesitation**, ambivalence, dithering (*chiefly Brit.*), doubt, hesitancy, indecisiveness, irresolution, shilly-shallying (*informal*), uncertainty, vacillation, wavering

indecisive *adjective* **1** = **hesitating**, dithering (*chiefly Brit.*), doubtful, faltering, in two minds (*informal*), irresolute, pussyfooting (*informal*), tentative, uncertain, undecided, undetermined, vacillating, wavering **2** = **inconclusive**, indefinite, indeterminate, unclear, undecided
➤ **Antonyms**
≠**hesitating**: certain, decided, determined, positive, resolute, unhesitating
≠**inconclusive**: clear, conclusive, decisive, definite, determinate, final

indeed *adverb* = **really**, actually, certainly, doubtlessly, in point of fact, in truth, positively, strictly, to be sure, truly, undeniably, undoubtedly, verily (*archaic*), veritably

indefensible *adjective* = **unforgivable**, faulty, inexcusable, insupportable, unjustifiable, unpardonable, untenable, unwarrantable, wrong
➤ **Antonyms**
defensible, excusable, forgivable, justifiable, legitimate, pardonable, supportable, tenable, warrantable

indefinable *adjective* = **inexpressible**, dim, hazy, impalpable, indescribable, indistinct, nameless, obscure, unrealized, vague

indefinite *adjective* = **unclear**, ambiguous, confused, doubtful, equivocal, evasive, general, ill-defined, imprecise, indeterminate, indistinct, inexact, loose, obscure, oracular, uncertain, undefined, undetermined, unfixed, unknown, unlimited, unsettled, vague
➤ **Antonyms**
certain, clear, definite, determinate, distinct, exact, fixed, settled, specific

indefinitely *adverb* = **endlessly**, ad infinitum, continually, for ever, *sine die,* till the cows come home (*informal*)

indelible *adjective* = **permanent**, enduring, indestructible, ineffaceable, ineradicable, inexpungible, inextirpable, ingrained, lasting
➤ **Antonyms**
eradicable, erasable, impermanent, removable, short-lived, temporary, washable

indelicacy *noun* = **vulgarity**, bad taste, coarseness, crudity, grossness, immodesty, impropriety, indecency, obscenity, offensiveness, rudeness, smuttiness, suggestiveness, tastelessness

indelicate *adjective* = **offensive**, blue, coarse, crude, embarrassing, gross, immodest, improper, indecent, indecorous, low, near the knuckle (*informal*), obscene, off-colour, risqué, rude, suggestive, tasteless, unbecoming, unseemly, untoward, vulgar, X-rated (*informal*)
➤ **Antonyms**
becoming, decent, decorous, delicate, modest, proper, refined, seemly

indemnify *verb* **1** = **insure**, endorse, guarantee, protect, secure, underwrite **2** = **compensate**, pay, reimburse, remunerate, repair, repay, requite, satisfy

indemnity *noun* **1** = **insurance**, guarantee, protection, security **2** = **compensation**, redress, reimbursement, remuneration, reparation, requital, restitution, satisfaction **3** *Law* = **exemption**, immunity, impunity, privilege

indent *verb* **1** = **order**, ask for, request, requisition **2** = **notch**, cut, dint, mark, nick, pink, scallop, score, serrate

independence *noun* = **freedom**, autarchy, autonomy, home rule, liberty, self-determination, self-government, self-reliance, self-rule, self-sufficiency, separation, sovereignty
➤ **Antonyms**
bondage, dependence, subjection, subjugation, subordination, subservience

independent *adjective* **1** = **free**, absolute, liberated, separate, unconnected, unconstrained, uncontrolled, unrelated **2** = **self-governing**, autarchic, autarchical,

autonomous, decontrolled, nonaligned, self-determining, separated, sovereign **3** = **self-sufficient**, bold, individualistic, liberated, self-contained, self-reliant, self-supporting, unaided, unconventional
➤ **Antonyms**
≠**free:** controlled, dependent, restrained, subject ≠**self-governing:** aligned, controlled, dependent, subject, submissive, subordinate, subservient, subsidiary

independently adverb = **separately**, alone, autonomously, by oneself, individually, on one's own, solo, unaided, under one's own steam

indescribable adjective = **unutterable**, beggaring description, beyond description, beyond words, incommunicable, indefinable, ineffable, inexpressible

indestructible adjective = **permanent**, abiding, durable, enduring, everlasting, immortal, imperishable, incorruptible, indelible, indissoluble, lasting, nonperishable, unbreakable, unfading
➤ **Antonyms**
breakable, corruptible, destructible, fading, impermanent, mortal, perishable

indeterminate adjective = **uncertain**, imprecise, inconclusive, indefinite, inexact, undefined, undetermined, unfixed, unspecified, unstipulated, vague
➤ **Antonyms**
certain, clear, conclusive, definite, determinate, exact, fixed, precise, specified, stipulated

index noun = **indication**, clue, guide, mark, sign, symptom, token

indicate verb **1** = **signify**, add up to (informal), bespeak, be symptomatic of, betoken, denote, evince, imply, manifest, point to, reveal, show, signal, suggest **2** = **point out**, designate, point to, specify **3** = **show**, display, express, mark, read, record, register

indication noun = **sign**, clue, evidence, explanation, forewarning, hint, index, inkling, intimation, manifestation, mark, note, omen, portent, signal, suggestion, symptom, warning

indicative adjective = **suggestive**, exhibitive, indicatory, indicial, pointing to, significant, symptomatic

indicator noun = **sign**, display, gauge, guide, index, mark, marker, meter, pointer, signal, signpost, symbol

indict verb = **charge**, accuse, arraign, impeach, prosecute, serve with a summons, summon, summons, tax

indictment noun = **charge**, accusation, allegation, impeachment, prosecution, summons

indifference noun **1** = **disregard**, absence of feeling, aloofness, apathy, callousness, carelessness, coldness, coolness, detachment, heedlessness, inattention, lack of interest, negligence, nonchalance, stoicalness, unconcern **2** = **irrelevance**, insignificance, triviality, unimportance **3** = **objectivity**, disinterestedness, dispassion, equity, impartiality, neutrality
➤ **Antonyms**
≠**disregard:** attention, care, commitment, concern, enthusiasm, heed, interest, regard

indifferent adjective **1** = **unconcerned**, aloof, apathetic, callous, careless, cold, cool, detached, distant, heedless, impervious, inattentive, not giving a monkey's (slang), regardless, uncaring, unimpressed, uninterested, unmoved, unresponsive, unsympathetic **2** = **mediocre**, average, fair, middling, moderate, no great shakes (informal), ordinary, passable, perfunctory, so-so (informal), undistinguished, uninspired **3** = **unimportant**, immaterial, insignificant, of no consequence **4** = **impartial**, disinterested, dispassionate, equitable, neutral, nonaligned, nonpartisan, objective, unbiased, uninvolved, unprejudiced
➤ **Antonyms**
≠**unconcerned:** avid, compassionate, concerned, eager, enthusiastic, interested, keen, responsive, sensitive, susceptible, sympathetic ≠**mediocre:** excellent, exceptional, fine, first-class, notable, remarkable

indigent adjective Formal = **destitute**, dirt-poor, down and out, down at heel (informal), flat broke (informal), impecunious, impoverished, in want, necessitous, needy, on one's uppers (informal), on the breadline, penniless, penurious, poor, poverty-stricken, short, straitened, without two pennies to rub together (informal)
➤ **Antonyms**
affluent, prosperous, rich, wealthy, well-off, well-to-do

indigestion noun = **heartburn**, dyspepsia, dyspepsy, upset stomach

indignant adjective = **resentful**, angry, annoyed, choked, disgruntled, exasperated, fuming (informal), furious, hacked (off) (U.S. slang), heated, hot under the collar (informal), huffy (informal), in a huff, incensed, in high dudgeon, irate, livid (informal), mad (*informal*), miffed (*informal*), narked (*Brit., Austral., & N.Z. slang*), peeved (*informal*), pissed off (*taboo slang*), provoked, riled, scornful, seeing red (*informal*), sore (*informal*), up in arms (*informal*), wrathful

indignation *noun* = **resentment**, anger, exasperation, fury, ire (*literary*), pique, rage, righteous anger, scorn, umbrage, wrath

indignity *noun* = **humiliation**, abuse, affront, contumely, dishonour, disrespect, injury, insult, obloquy, opprobrium, outrage, reproach, slap in the face (*informal*), slight, snub

indirect *adjective* 1 = **incidental**, ancillary, collateral, contingent, secondary, subsidiary, unintended 2 = **circuitous**, backhanded, circumlocutory, crooked, devious, long-drawn-out, meandering, oblique, periphrastic, rambling, roundabout, tortuous, wandering, winding, zigzag
➤ **Antonyms**
≠**circuitous**: direct, straight, straightforward, undeviating, uninterrupted

indirectly *adverb* = **second-hand**, by implication, circumlocutorily, in a roundabout way, obliquely, periphrastically

indiscernible *adjective* = **invisible**, hidden, impalpable, imperceptible, indistinct, indistinguishable, unapparent, undiscernible
➤ **Antonyms**
apparent, clear, discernible, distinct, distinguishable, perceptible, visible

indiscreet *adjective* = **tactless**, foolish, hasty, heedless, ill-advised, ill-considered, ill-judged, impolitic, imprudent, incautious, injudicious, naive, rash, reckless, undiplomatic, unthinking, unwise
➤ **Antonyms**
cautious, diplomatic, discreet, judicious, politic, prudent, tactful, wise

indiscretion *noun* = **mistake**, bloomer (*Brit. informal*), boob (*Brit. slang*), error, faux pas, folly, foolishness, gaffe, gaucherie, imprudence, lapse, rashness, recklessness, slip, slip of the tongue, tactlessness

indiscriminate *adjective* 1 = **random**, aimless, careless, desultory, general, hit or miss (*informal*), sweeping, uncritical, undiscriminating, unmethodical, unselective, unsystematic, wholesale 2 = **jumbled**, chaotic, confused, haphazard, higgledy-piggledy (*informal*), mingled, miscellaneous, mixed, mongrel, motley, promiscuous, undistinguishable
➤ **Antonyms**

≠**random**: deliberate, discriminating, exclusive, methodical, selective, systematic

indispensable *adjective* = **essential**, crucial, imperative, key, necessary, needed, needful, requisite, vital
➤ **Antonyms**
dispensable, disposable, nonessential, superfluous, unimportant, unnecessary

indisposed *adjective* 1 = **ill**, ailing, confined to bed, laid up (*informal*), on the sick list (*informal*), poorly (*informal*), sick, under the weather, unwell 2 = **unwilling**, averse, disinclined, loath, reluctant
➤ **Antonyms**
≠**ill**: fine, fit, hardy, healthy, sound, well

indisposition *noun* 1 = **illness**, ailment, ill health, sickness 2 = **reluctance**, aversion, disinclination, dislike, distaste, hesitancy, unwillingness

indisputable *adjective* = **undeniable**, absolute, beyond doubt, certain, evident, incontestable, incontrovertible, indubitable, irrefutable, positive, sure, unassailable, unquestionable
➤ **Antonyms**
assailable, disputable, doubtful, indefinite, questionable, refutable, uncertain, vague

indissoluble *adjective* = **permanent**, abiding, binding, enduring, eternal, fixed, imperishable, incorruptible, indestructible, inseparable, lasting, solid, unbreakable

indistinct *adjective* = **unclear**, ambiguous, bleary, blurred, confused, dim, doubtful, faint, fuzzy, hazy, ill-defined, indefinite, indeterminate, indiscernible, indistinguishable, misty, muffled, obscure, out of focus, shadowy, undefined, unintelligible, vague, weak
➤ **Antonyms**
clear, defined, determinate, discernible, distinct, distinguishable, evident, intelligible

indistinguishable *adjective* 1 = **identical**, alike, cut from the same cloth, like as two peas in a pod (*informal*), (the) same, twin 2 = **imperceptible**, indiscernible, invisible, obscure

individual *adjective* 1 = **personal**, characteristic, discrete, distinct, distinctive, exclusive, identical, idiosyncratic, own, particular, peculiar, personalized, proper, respective, separate, several, single, singular, special, specific, unique ◆ *noun* 2 = **person**, being, body (*informal*), character, creature, mortal, party, personage, soul, type, unit
➤ **Antonyms**
adjective ≠**personal**: collective, common, conventional, general, indistinct, ordinary, universal

individualism noun = **self-interest**, egocentricity, egoism, freethinking, independence, originality, self-direction, self-reliance

individualist noun = **maverick**, freethinker, independent, loner, lone wolf, nonconformist, original

individuality noun = **distinctiveness**, character, discreteness, distinction, originality, peculiarity, personality, separateness, singularity, uniqueness

individually adverb = **separately**, apart, independently, one at a time, one by one, personally, severally, singly

indoctrinate verb = **train**, brainwash, drill, ground, imbue, initiate, instruct, school, teach

indoctrination noun = **training**, brainwashing, drilling, grounding, inculcation, instruction, schooling

indolent adjective = **lazy**, fainéant, good-for-nothing, idle, inactive, inert, lackadaisical, languid, lethargic, listless, lumpish, slack, slothful, slow, sluggish, torpid, workshy
➤ Antonyms
active, assiduous, busy, conscientious, diligent, energetic, industrious, vigorous

indomitable adjective = **invincible**, bold, resolute, set, staunch, steadfast, unbeatable, unconquerable, unflinching, untameable, unyielding
➤ Antonyms
cowardly, faltering, feeble, shrinking, wavering, weak, yielding

indubitable adjective = **certain**, evident, incontestable, incontrovertible, indisputable, irrefutable, obvious, open-and-shut, sure, unarguable, undeniable, undoubted, unquestionable, veritable

induce verb 1 = **persuade**, actuate, convince, draw, encourage, get, impel, incite, influence, instigate, move, press, prevail upon, prompt, talk into 2 = **cause**, bring about, effect, engender, generate, give rise to, lead to, occasion, produce, set in motion, set off
➤ Antonyms
curb, deter, discourage, dissuade, hinder, prevent, restrain, stop, suppress

inducement noun = **incentive**, attraction, bait, carrot (informal), cause, clarion call, come-on (informal), consideration, encouragement, impulse, incitement, influence, lure, motive, reward, spur, stimulus, urge

indulge verb 1 = **gratify**, cater to, feed, give way to, pander to, regale, satiate, satisfy, treat oneself to, yield to 2 = **spoil**, baby, coddle, cosset, favour, fawn on, foster, give in to, go along with, humour, mollycoddle, pamper, pet

indulgence noun 1 = **luxury**, extravagance, favour, privilege, treat 2 = **gratification**, appeasement, fulfilment, satiation, satisfaction 3 = **intemperance**, excess, fondness, immoderation, intemperateness, kindness, leniency, pampering, partiality, permissiveness, profligacy, profligateness, spoiling 4 = **tolerance**, courtesy, forbearance, goodwill, patience, understanding
➤ Antonyms
≠intemperance: moderation, strictness, temperance, temperateness

indulgent adjective = **lenient**, compliant, easy-going, favourable, fond, forbearing, gentle, gratifying, kind, kindly, liberal, mild, permissive, tender, tolerant, understanding
➤ Antonyms
austere, demanding, harsh, intolerant, rigorous, stern, strict, stringent, unmerciful

industrialist noun = **capitalist**, baron, big businessman, boss, captain of industry, financier, magnate, manufacturer, producer, tycoon

industrious adjective = **hard-working**, active, assiduous, busy, conscientious, diligent, energetic, laborious, persevering, persistent, productive, purposeful, sedulous, steady, tireless, zealous
➤ Antonyms
good-for-nothing, idle, indolent, lackadaisical, lazy, shiftless, slothful

industriously adverb = **diligently**, assiduously, conscientiously, doggedly, hard, like a Trojan, nose to the grindstone (informal), perseveringly, sedulously, steadily, without slacking

industry noun 1 = **business**, commerce, commercial enterprise, manufacturing, production, trade 2 = **effort**, activity, application, assiduity, determination, diligence, labour, perseverance, persistence, tirelessness, toil, vigour, zeal

inebriated adjective = **drunk**, babalas (S. African), befuddled, bevvied (dialect), blind drunk, blitzed (slang), blotto (slang), bombed (slang), Brahms and Liszt (slang), drunk as a skunk, flying (slang), fou or fu' (Scot.), half-cut (informal), half seas over (informal), high (informal), high as a kite (informal), inebriate, in one's cups, intoxicated, legless (informal), lit up (slang), merry (Brit. informal), out of it (slang), out to it (Austral. & N.Z. slang), paralytic (informal), pie-eyed (slang), pissed (*taboo slang*), plastered (*slang*), rat-arsed (*taboo slang*), smashed (*slang*), sozzled (*informal*), steamboats (*Scot. slang*), steaming (*slang*), stoned (*slang*), the worse for drink, three sheets in the wind (*informal*), tight (*informal*), tipsy, under the influence (*informal*), under the weather (*informal*), wasted (*slang*), wrecked (*slang*), zonked (*slang*)

ineffective *adjective* = **useless**, barren, basket case, bootless, feeble, fruitless, futile, idle, impotent, inadequate, ineffectual, inefficacious, inefficient, pathetic, unavailing, unproductive, vain, weak, worthless
➤ **Antonyms**
effective, efficacious, efficient, fruitful, potent, productive, useful, worthwhile

ineffectual *adjective* = **weak**, abortive, basket case, bootless, emasculate, feeble, fruitless, futile, idle, impotent, inadequate, incompetent, ineffective, inefficacious, inefficient, inept, lame, pathetic, powerless, unavailing, useless, vain

inefficiency *noun* = **incompetence**, carelessness, disorganization, muddle, slackness, sloppiness

inefficient *adjective* = **incompetent**, cowboy (*informal*), disorganized, feeble, incapable, ineffectual, inefficacious, inept, inexpert, slipshod, sloppy, wasteful, weak
➤ **Antonyms**
able, capable, competent, effective, efficient, expert, organized, skilled

ineligible *adjective* = **unqualified**, disqualified, incompetent (*Law*), objectionable, ruled out, unacceptable, undesirable, unequipped, unfit, unfitted, unsuitable

inept *adjective* **1** = **incompetent**, awkward, bumbling, bungling, cack-handed (*informal*), clumsy, cowboy (*informal*), gauche, inexpert, maladroit, unhandy, unskilful, unworkmanlike **2** = **unsuitable**, absurd, improper, inappropriate, inapt, infelicitous, malapropos, meaningless, out of place, pointless, ridiculous, unfit
➤ **Antonyms**
≠**incompetent**: able, adroit, competent, dexterous, efficient, qualified, skilful, talented ≠**unsuitable**: appropriate, apt, effectual, germane, sensible, suitable

ineptitude *noun* **1** = **incompetence**, clumsiness, gaucheness, incapacity, inexpertness, unfitness, unhandiness **2** = **inappropriateness**, absurdity, pointlessness, uselessness

inequality *noun* = **disparity**, bias, difference, disproportion, diversity, imparity, irregularity, lack of balance,

preferentiality, prejudice, unevenness

inequitable *adjective* = **unfair**, biased, discriminatory, one-sided, partial, partisan, preferential, prejudiced, unjust
➤ **Antonyms**
even-handed, fair, impartial, just, unbiased, unprejudiced

inert *adjective* = **inactive**, dead, dormant, dull, idle, immobile, inanimate, indolent, lazy, leaden, lifeless, motionless, passive, quiescent, slack, slothful, sluggish, slumberous (*chiefly poetic*), static, still, torpid, unmoving, unreactive, unresponsive
➤ **Antonyms**
active, alive, alive and kicking, animated, energetic, full of beans (*informal*), living, mobile, moving, reactive, responsive, vital

inertia *noun* = **inactivity**, apathy, deadness, disinclination to move, drowsiness, dullness, idleness, immobility, indolence, languor, lassitude, laziness, lethargy, listlessness, passivity, sloth, sluggishness, stillness, stupor, torpor, unresponsiveness
➤ **Antonyms**
action, activity, animation, brio, energy, liveliness, vigour, vitality

inescapable *adjective* = **unavoidable**, certain, destined, fated, ineluctable, ineludible (*rare*), inevitable, inexorable, sure

inestimable *adjective* = **incalculable**, beyond price, immeasurable, invaluable, precious, priceless, prodigious

inevitable *adjective* = **unavoidable**, assured, certain, decreed, destined, fixed, ineluctable, inescapable, inexorable, necessary, ordained, settled, sure, unpreventable
➤ **Antonyms**
avoidable, escapable, evadable, preventable, uncertain

inevitably *adverb* = **unavoidably**, as a necessary consequence, as a result, automatically, certainly, necessarily, of necessity, perforce, surely, willy-nilly

inexcusable *adjective* = **unforgivable**, indefensible, inexpiable, outrageous, unjustifiable, unpardonable, unwarrantable
➤ **Antonyms**
defensible, excusable, forgivable, justifiable, pardonable

inexhaustible *adjective* **1** = **endless**, bottomless, boundless, illimitable, infinite, limitless, measureless, never-ending, unbounded **2** = **tireless**, indefatigable, undaunted, unfailing, unflagging, untiring, unwearied, unwearying
➤ **Antonyms**

≠**endless**: bounded, exhaustible, finite, limitable, limited, measurable ≠**tireless**: daunted, enervated, failing, flagging, tiring, wearied

inexorable *adjective* = **unrelenting**, adamant, cruel, hard, harsh, immovable, implacable, ineluctable, inescapable, inflexible, merciless, obdurate, pitiless, relentless, remorseless, severe, unappeasable, unbending, unyielding
➤ **Antonyms**
bending, flexible, lenient, movable, relenting, yielding

inexorably *adverb* = **relentlessly**, implacably, inevitably, irresistibly, remorselessly, unrelentingly

inexpensive *adjective* = **cheap**, bargain, budget, economical, low-cost, low-priced, modest, reasonable
➤ **Antonyms**
costly, dear, exorbitant, expensive, high-priced, pricey, uneconomical

inexperience *noun* = **unfamiliarity**, callowness, greenness, ignorance, newness, rawness, unexpertness

inexperienced *adjective* = **immature**, amateur, callow, fresh, green, new, raw, unaccustomed, unacquainted, unfamiliar, unfledged, unpractised, unschooled, unseasoned, unskilled, untrained, untried, unused, unversed, wet behind the ears (*informal*)
➤ **Antonyms**
experienced, familiar, knowledgeable, practised, seasoned, skilled, trained, versed

inexpert *adjective* = **amateurish**, awkward, bungling, cack-handed (*informal*), clumsy, inept, maladroit, skill-less, unhandy, unpractised, unprofessional, unskilful, unskilled, unworkmanlike

inexplicable *adjective* = **unaccountable**, baffling, beyond comprehension, enigmatic, incomprehensible, inscrutable, insoluble, mysterious, mystifying, strange, unfathomable, unintelligible
➤ **Antonyms**
comprehensible, explainable, explicable, fathomable, intelligible, soluble, understandable

inexpressible *adjective* = **indescribable**, incommunicable, indefinable, ineffable, unspeakable, unutterable

inexpressive *adjective* = **impassive**, bland, blank, cold, dead, deadpan, emotionless, empty, expressionless, inanimate, inscrutable, lifeless, stony, vacant

inextricably *adverb* = **inseparably**, indissolubly, indistinguishably, intricately, irretrievably, totally

infallibility *noun* **1** = **perfection**, faultlessness, impeccability, irrefutability, omniscience, supremacy, unerringness **2** = **reliability**, dependability, safety, sureness, trustworthiness

infallible *adjective* **1** = **perfect**, faultless, impeccable, omniscient, unerring, unimpeachable **2** = **sure**, certain, dependable, foolproof, reliable, sure-fire (*informal*), trustworthy, unbeatable, unfailing
➤ **Antonyms**
≠**perfect**: errant, fallible, human, imperfect, mortal ≠**sure**: doubtful, dubious, uncertain, undependable, unreliable, unsure

infamous *adjective* = **notorious**, abominable, atrocious, base, detestable, disgraceful, dishonourable, disreputable, egregious, flagitious, hateful, heinous, ignominious, ill-famed, iniquitous, loathsome, monstrous, nefarious, odious, opprobrious, outrageous, scandalous, scurvy, shameful, shocking, vile, villainous, wicked
➤ **Antonyms**
esteemed, glorious, honourable, noble, reputable, virtuous

infancy *noun* **1** = **early childhood**, babyhood **2** = **beginnings**, cradle, dawn, early stages, emergence, inception, origins, outset, start
➤ **Antonyms**
≠**beginnings**: close, conclusion, death, end, expiration, finish, termination

infant *noun* **1** = **baby**, ankle-biter (*Austral. slang*), babe, babe in arms, bairn (*Scot.*), child, little one, neonate, newborn child, rug rat (*slang*), sprog (*slang*), suckling, toddler, tot, wean (*Scot.*) ♦ *adjective* **2** = **early**, baby, dawning, developing, emergent, growing, immature, initial, nascent, newborn, unfledged, young

infantile *adjective* = **childish**, babyish, immature, puerile, tender, weak, young
➤ **Antonyms**
adult, developed, mature

infatuate *verb* = **obsess**, befool, beguile, besot, bewitch, captivate, delude, enchant, enrapture, fascinate, make a fool of, mislead, stupefy, sweep one off one's feet, turn (someone's) head

infatuated *adjective* = **obsessed**, beguiled, besotted, bewitched, captivated, carried away, crazy about (*informal*), enamoured, enraptured, fascinated, head over heels in love with, inflamed, intoxicated, possessed, smitten (*informal*), spellbound, swept off one's feet, under the spell of

infatuation *noun* = **obsession**, crush

(*informal*), fixation, folly, foolishness, madness, passion, thing (*informal*)

infect *verb* = **contaminate**, affect, blight, corrupt, defile, influence, poison, pollute, spread to *or* among, taint, touch, vitiate

infection *noun* = **contamination**, contagion, corruption, defilement, poison, pollution, septicity, virus

infectious *adjective* = **catching**, communicable, contagious, contaminating, corrupting, defiling, infective, pestilential, poisoning, polluting, spreading, transmittable, virulent, vitiating

infer *verb* = **deduce**, conclude, conjecture, derive, gather, presume, put two and two together, read between the lines, surmise, understand

inference *noun* = **deduction**, assumption, conclusion, conjecture, consequence, corollary, illation (*rare*), presumption, reading, surmise

inferior *adjective* **1** = **lower**, junior, lesser, menial, minor, secondary, subordinate, subsidiary, under, underneath **2** = **substandard**, bad, bush-league (*Austral. & N.Z. informal*), chickenshit (*U.S. slang*), crappy (*slang*), dime-a-dozen (*informal*), duff (*Brit. informal*), end-of-the-pier (*Brit. informal*), for the birds (*informal*), imperfect, indifferent, low-grade, low-rent (*informal, chiefly U.S.*), mean, mediocre, no great shakes (*informal*), not a patch on, not much cop (*Brit. slang*), of a sort *or* of sorts, pants (*informal*), piss-poor (*taboo slang*), poor, poorer, poxy (*slang*), second-class, second-rate, shoddy, strictly for the birds (*informal*), tinhorn (*U.S. slang*), two-bit (*U.S. & Canad. slang*), worse ♦ *noun* **3** = **underling**, junior, menial, subordinate
➤ **Antonyms**
adjective ≠**lower**: greater, higher, senior, superior, top ≠**substandard**: excellent, fine, first-class

inferiority *noun* **1** = **inadequacy**, badness, deficiency, imperfection, insignificance, meanness, mediocrity, shoddiness, unimportance, worthlessness **2** = **subservience**, abasement, inferior status *or* standing, lowliness, subordination
➤ **Antonyms**
≠**inadequacy**: eminence, excellence, superiority ≠**subservience**: advantage, ascendancy, dominance, superiority

infernal *adjective* **1** = **hellish**, chthonian, Hadean, lower, nether, Plutonian, Stygian, Tartarean (*literary*), underworld **2** = **devilish**, accursed, damnable, damned, demonic, diabolical, fiendish, hellish, malevolent, malicious, satanic

➤ **Antonyms**
≠**hellish**: celestial, heavenly ≠**devilish**: angelic, glorious, godlike, seraphic

infertile *adjective* = **barren**, infecund, nonproductive, sterile, unfruitful, unproductive
➤ **Antonyms**
fecund, fertile, fruitful, generative, productive

infertility *noun* = **sterility**, barrenness, infecundity, unfruitfulness, unproductiveness

infest *verb* = **overrun**, beset, flood, invade, penetrate, permeate, ravage, swarm, throng

infested *adjective* = **overrun**, alive, beset, crawling, lousy (*slang*), pervaded, plagued, ravaged, ridden, swarming, teeming

infiltrate *verb* = **penetrate**, creep in, filter through, insinuate oneself, make inroads (into), percolate, permeate, pervade, sneak in (*informal*), work *or* worm one's way into

infinite *adjective* = **never-ending**, absolute, all-embracing, bottomless, boundless, enormous, eternal, everlasting, illimitable, immeasurable, immense, inestimable, inexhaustible, interminable, limitless, measureless, numberless, perpetual, stupendous, total, unbounded, uncounted, untold, vast, wide, without end, without number
➤ **Antonyms**
bounded, circumscribed, finite, limited, measurable, restricted

infinitesimal *adjective* = **microscopic**, atomic, inappreciable, insignificant, minuscule, minute, negligible, teensy-weensy, teeny, teeny-weeny, tiny, unnoticeable, wee
➤ **Antonyms**
enormous, great, huge, infinite, large, vast

infinity *noun* = **eternity**, boundlessness, endlessness, immensity, infinitude, perpetuity, vastness

infirm *adjective* **1** = **frail**, ailing, debilitated, decrepit, doddering, doddery, enfeebled, failing, feeble, lame, weak **2** = **irresolute**, faltering, indecisive, insecure, shaky, unsound, unstable, vacillating, wavering, weak, wobbly
➤ **Antonyms**
≠**frail**: healthy, hearty, robust, sound, strong, sturdy, vigorous

infirmity *noun* **1** = **frailty**, debility, decrepitude, deficiency, feebleness, ill health, imperfection, sickliness, vulnerability **2** = **ailment**, defect, disorder, failing, fault, malady, sickness, weakness

➤ **Antonyms**

≠**frailty**: health, soundness, stability, strength, vigour, wellness

inflame verb **1** = **enrage**, agitate, anger, arouse, embitter, exasperate, excite, fire, foment, heat, ignite, impassion, incense, infuriate, intoxicate, kindle, madden, make one's blood boil, provoke, rile, rouse, stimulate **2** = **aggravate**, exacerbate, exasperate, fan, increase, intensify, worsen

➤ **Antonyms**

allay, calm, cool, discourage, extinguish, pacify, quench, quiet, soothe, suppress

inflamed adjective = **sore**, angry, chafing, festering, fevered, heated, hot, infected, red, septic, swollen

inflammable adjective = **flammable**, combustible, incendiary

inflammation noun = **soreness**, burning, heat, painfulness, rash, redness, sore, tenderness

inflammatory adjective = **provocative**, anarchic, demagogic, explosive, fiery, incendiary, inflaming, instigative, insurgent, intemperate, like a red rag to a bull, rabble-rousing, rabid, riotous, seditious

inflate verb = **expand**, aerate, aggrandize, amplify, balloon, bloat, blow up, boost, dilate, distend, enlarge, escalate, exaggerate, increase, puff up or out, pump up, swell

➤ **Antonyms**

collapse, compress, contract, deflate, diminish, lessen, shrink

inflated adjective = **exaggerated**, bombastic, grandiloquent, ostentatious, overblown, swollen

inflation noun = **expansion**, aggrandizement, blowing up, distension, enhancement, enlargement, escalation, extension, increase, intensification, puffiness, rise, spread, swelling, tumefaction

inflection noun **1** = **intonation**, accentuation, modulation **2** Grammar = **conjugation**, declension **3** = **bend**, angle, arc, arch, bow, crook, curvature

inflexibility noun **1** = **obstinacy**, fixity, intransigence, obduracy, steeliness **2** = **rigidity**, hardness, immovability, inelasticity, stiffness, stringency

inflexible adjective **1** = **obstinate**, adamant, brassbound, dyed-in-the-wool, firm, fixed, hard and fast, immovable, immutable, implacable, inexorable, intractable, iron, obdurate, relentless, resolute, rigorous, set, set in one's ways, steadfast, steely, stiff-necked, strict, stringent, stubborn, unadaptable, unbending, unchangeable, uncompromising, unyielding **2** = **inelastic**, hard, hardened, nonflexible, rigid, stiff, taut

➤ **Antonyms**

≠**obstinate**: flexible, irresolute, movable, variable, yielding ≠**inelastic**: elastic, flexible, lissom(e), pliable, pliant, supple, yielding

inflict verb = **impose**, administer, apply, deliver, exact, levy, mete or deal out, visit, wreak

infliction noun **1** = **imposition**, administration, exaction, perpetration, wreaking **2** = **affliction**, penalty, punishment, trouble, visitation, worry

influence noun **1** = **effect**, hold, magnetism, power, rule, spell, sway, weight **2** = **control**, ascendancy, authority, direction, domination, mastery **3** = **power**, bottom, clout (informal), connections, good offices, importance, leverage, prestige, pull (informal), weight ♦ verb **4** = **affect**, act or work upon, control, direct, guide, impact on, manipulate, modify, sway **5** = **persuade**, arouse, dispose, incite, incline, induce, instigate, move, predispose, prompt, rouse **6** = **carry weight with**, bring pressure to bear upon, cut any ice with (informal), make oneself felt, pull strings (informal)

influential adjective = **important**, authoritative, controlling, effective, efficacious, forcible, guiding, instrumental, leading, meaningful, momentous, moving, persuasive, potent, powerful, significant, telling, weighty

➤ **Antonyms**

impotent, ineffective, ineffectual, powerless, unimportant, uninfluential, unpersuasive, weak

influx noun = **arrival**, convergence, flow, incursion, inflow, inrush, inundation, invasion, rush

inform verb **1** = **tell**, acquaint, advise, apprise, clue in (informal), communicate, enlighten, give (someone) to understand, instruct, keep (someone) posted, leak to, let know, make conversant (with), notify, put (someone) in the picture (informal), send word to, teach, tip off **2** = **betray**, blab, blow the gaff (Brit. slang), blow the whistle on (informal), clype (Scot.), denounce, grass (Brit. slang), incriminate, inculpate, let the cat out of the bag, nark (Brit., Austral., & N.Z. slang), peach (slang), put the finger on (informal), rat (informal), shop (slang, chiefly Brit.), sing (slang, chiefly U.S.), snitch (slang), spill

one's guts (*slang*), spill the beans
(*informal*), squeal (*slang*), tell all, tell on
(*informal*) **3** = **inspire**, animate,
characterize, illuminate, imbue, permeate,
suffuse, typify

informal *adjective* = **relaxed**, casual,
colloquial, cosy, easy, familiar, natural,
simple, unceremonious, unconstrained,
unofficial
➤ **Antonyms**
ceremonious, constrained, conventional,
formal, official, stiff

informality *noun* = **familiarity**, casualness,
ease, lack of ceremony, naturalness,
relaxation, simplicity

information *noun* = **facts**, advice, blurb,
counsel, data, dope (*informal*), gen (*Brit.
informal*), info (*informal*), inside story,
instruction, intelligence, knowledge, latest
(*informal*), lowdown (*informal*), material,
message, news, notice, report, tidings,
word

informative *adjective* = **instructive**, chatty,
communicative, edifying, educational,
enlightening, forthcoming, gossipy,
illuminating, newsy, revealing

informed *adjective* = **knowledgeable**,
abreast, acquainted, *au courant, au fait*,
briefed, conversant, enlightened, erudite,
expert, familiar, genned up (*Brit. informal*),
in the know (*informal*), in the loop, in the
picture, keeping one's finger on the pulse,
learned, posted, primed, reliable, up, up to
date, versed, well-read

informer *noun* = **betrayer**, accuser, grass
(*Brit. slang*), Judas, nark (*Brit., Austral., &
N.Z. slang*), sneak, squealer (*slang*), stool
pigeon

infrequent *adjective* = **occasional**, few and
far between, once in a blue moon, rare,
sporadic, uncommon, unusual
➤ **Antonyms**
common, customary, frequent, habitual,
often, regular, usual

infringe *verb* **1** = **break**, contravene,
disobey, transgress, violate **2 infringe on** *or*
upon = **intrude on**, encroach on, trespass
on

infringement *noun* = **contravention**,
breach, infraction, noncompliance,
nonobservance, transgression, trespass,
violation

infuriate *verb* = **enrage**, anger, be like a
red rag to a bull, exasperate, gall, get
one's back up, get one's goat (*slang*),
incense, irritate, madden, make one's
blood boil, make one see red (*informal*),
make one's hackles rise, nark (*Brit., Austral.,
& N.Z. slang*), provoke, put one's back up,
raise one's hackles, rile

➤ **Antonyms**
appease, calm, mollify, pacify, placate,
propitiate, soothe

infuriating *adjective* = **annoying**,
aggravating (*informal*), exasperating,
galling, irritating, maddening, mortifying,
pestilential, provoking, vexatious

ingenious *adjective* = **creative**, adroit,
bright, brilliant, clever, crafty, dexterous,
fertile, inventive, masterly, original, ready,
resourceful, shrewd, skilful, subtle
➤ **Antonyms**
artless, clumsy, unimaginative,
uninventive, unoriginal, unresourceful,
unskilful

ingenuity *noun* = **originality**, adroitness,
cleverness, faculty, flair, genius, gift,
ingeniousness, inventiveness, knack,
resourcefulness, sharpness, shrewdness,
skill, turn
➤ **Antonyms**
clumsiness, dullness, incompetence,
ineptitude, ineptness

ingenuous *adjective* = **naive**, artless,
candid, childlike, frank, guileless, honest,
innocent, open, plain, simple, sincere,
trustful, trusting, unreserved,
unsophisticated, unstudied
➤ **Antonyms**
artful, crafty, devious, insincere, reserved,
sly, sophisticated, subtle, wily

ingenuousness *noun* = **naivety**,
artlessness, candour, frankness,
guilelessness, innocence, openness,
trustingness, unsuspiciousness
➤ **Antonyms**
artfulness, craftiness, insincerity, slyness,
sophistication, subterfuge, subtlety

inglorious *adjective* = **dishonourable**,
discreditable, disgraceful, disreputable,
failed, humiliating, ignoble, ignominious,
infamous, obscure, shameful, unheroic,
unknown, unsuccessful, unsung

ingratiate *verb* = **pander to**, be a yes man,
blandish, brown-nose (*taboo slang*), crawl,
curry favour, fawn, flatter, get in with, get
on the right side of, grovel, insinuate
oneself, keep (someone) sweet, kiss
(someone's) ass (*U.S. & Canad. taboo
slang*), lick someone's arse (*taboo slang*),
lick (someone's) boots, play up to, rub
(someone) up the right way (*informal*),
seek the favour (of someone), suck up to
(*informal*), toady, worm oneself into
(someone's) favour

ingratiating *adjective* = **sycophantic**,
bootlicking (*informal*), crawling, fawning,
flattering, humble, obsequious, servile,
timeserving, toadying, unctuous

ingratitude *noun* = **ungratefulness**,

thanklessness, unappreciativeness
➤ **Antonyms**
appreciation, gratefulness, gratitude,
thankfulness, thanks, thanksgiving

ingredient *noun* = **component**,
constituent, element, part

inhabit *verb* = **live**, abide, dwell, lodge,
make one's home, occupy, people,
populate, possess, reside, take up
residence in, tenant

inhabitant *noun* = **dweller**, aborigine,
citizen, denizen, indigene, indweller,
inmate, native, occupant, occupier,
resident, tenant

inhabited *adjective* = **populated**,
colonized, developed, held, occupied,
peopled, settled, tenanted

inhale *verb* = **breathe in**, draw in, gasp,
respire, suck in
➤ **Antonyms**
blow, breathe out, exhale, expire

inherent *adjective* = **innate**, basic,
congenital, connate, essential, hereditary,
immanent, inborn, inbred, inbuilt,
ingrained, inherited, in one's blood,
instinctive, intrinsic, native, natural
➤ **Antonyms**
alien, extraneous, extrinsic, imposed,
superficial, supplementary

inherit *verb* = **be left**, accede to, be
bequeathed, come into, fall heir to,
succeed to

inheritance *noun* = **legacy**, bequest,
birthright, heritage, patrimony

inhibit *verb* = **restrain**, arrest, bar, bridle,
check, constrain, cramp (someone's) style
(*informal*), curb, debar, discourage, forbid,
frustrate, hinder, hold back *or* in, impede,
obstruct, prevent, prohibit, stem the flow,
stop, throw a spanner in the works
➤ **Antonyms**
abet, allow, enable, encourage, further,
let, permit, support

inhibited *adjective* = **shy**, constrained,
frustrated, guarded, repressed, reserved,
reticent, self-conscious, subdued, uptight
(*informal*), withdrawn
➤ **Antonyms**
free, natural, outgoing, relaxed,
spontaneous, uninhibited, unreserved

inhibition *noun* = **shyness**, bar, block,
check, embargo, hang-up (*informal*),
hindrance, interdict, mental blockage,
obstacle, prohibition, reserve, restraint,
restriction, reticence, self-consciousness

inhospitable *adjective* **1** = **unfriendly**,
cool, uncongenial, ungenerous, unkind,
unreceptive, unsociable, unwelcoming,
xenophobic **2** = **bleak**, bare, barren,

desolate, empty, forbidding, godforsaken,
hostile, lonely, sterile, unfavourable,
uninhabitable
➤ **Antonyms**
≠**unfriendly**: amicable, friendly, generous,
genial, gracious, hospitable, sociable,
welcoming

inhuman *adjective* = **cruel**, animal,
barbaric, barbarous, bestial, brutal,
cold-blooded, diabolical, fiendish,
heartless, merciless, pitiless, remorseless,
ruthless, savage, unfeeling, vicious
➤ **Antonyms**
charitable, compassionate, feeling,
humane, merciful, sensitive, tender,
warmhearted

inhumane *adjective* = **cruel**, brutal,
heartless, pitiless, uncompassionate,
unfeeling, unkind, unsympathetic

inhumanity *noun* = **cruelty**, atrocity,
barbarism, brutality, brutishness,
cold-bloodedness, cold-heartedness,
hardheartedness, heartlessness,
pitilessness, ruthlessness, unkindness,
viciousness

inimical *adjective* = **hostile**, adverse,
antagonistic, antipathetic, contrary,
destructive, disaffected, harmful, hurtful,
ill-disposed, injurious, noxious, opposed,
oppugnant (*rare*), pernicious, repugnant,
unfavourable, unfriendly, unwelcoming
➤ **Antonyms**
affable, amicable, congenial, favourable,
friendly, good, helpful, kindly,
sympathetic, welcoming

inimitable *adjective* = **unique**,
consummate, incomparable, matchless,
nonpareil, peerless, supreme, unequalled,
unexampled, unmatched, unparalleled,
unrivalled, unsurpassable

iniquitous *adjective* = **wicked**, abominable,
accursed, atrocious, base, criminal, evil,
heinous, immoral, infamous, nefarious,
reprehensible, reprobate, sinful, unjust,
unrighteous, vicious

iniquity *noun* = **wickedness**, abomination,
baseness, crime, evil, evildoing,
heinousness, infamy, injustice, misdeed,
offence, sin, sinfulness, unrighteousness,
wrong, wrongdoing
➤ **Antonyms**
fairness, goodness, honesty, integrity,
justice, morality, righteousness,
uprightness, virtue

initial *adjective* = **first**, beginning,
commencing, early, inaugural, inceptive,
inchoate, incipient, introductory, opening,
primary
➤ **Antonyms**
closing, concluding, ending, final, last,

terminal, ultimate

initially *adverb* = **at first**, at *or* in the beginning, at the outset, at the start, first, firstly, in the early stages, originally, primarily, to begin with

initiate *verb* **1** = **begin**, break the ice, commence, get under way, inaugurate, institute, kick off (*informal*), kick-start, launch, lay the foundations of, open, originate, pioneer, set going, set in motion, set the ball rolling, start **2** = **induct**, indoctrinate, instate, introduce, invest **3** = **instruct**, acquaint with, coach, familiarize with, teach, train ♦ *noun* **4** = **novice**, beginner, convert, entrant, learner, member, probationer, proselyte, tyro

initiation *noun* = **introduction**, admission, baptism of fire, commencement, debut, enrolment, entrance, inauguration, inception, induction, installation, instatement, investiture

initiative *noun* **1** = **first step**, advantage, beginning, commencement, first move, lead **2** = **resourcefulness**, ambition, drive, dynamism, enterprise, get-up-and-go (*informal*), inventiveness, leadership, originality, push (*informal*), resource

inject *verb* **1** = **vaccinate**, inoculate, jab (*informal*), shoot (*informal*) **2** = **introduce**, bring in, infuse, insert, instil, interject

injection *noun* **1** = **vaccination**, inoculation, jab (*informal*), shot (*informal*), vaccine **2** = **introduction**, dose, infusion, insertion, interjection

injudicious *adjective* = **unwise**, foolish, hasty, ill-advised, ill-judged, ill-timed, impolitic, imprudent, incautious, inconsiderate, indiscreet, inexpedient, rash, unthinking
➤ **Antonyms**
cautious, considerate, discreet, expedient, judicious, prudent, well-timed, wise

injunction *noun* = **order**, admonition, command, dictate, exhortation, instruction, mandate, precept, ruling

injure *verb* = **hurt**, abuse, blemish, blight, break, damage, deface, disable, harm, impair, maltreat, mar, ruin, spoil, tarnish, undermine, vitiate, weaken, wound, wrong

injured *adjective* **1** = **hurt**, broken, damaged, disabled, lamed, undermined, weakened, wounded **2** = **wronged**, abused, blackened, blemished, defamed, ill-treated, maligned, maltreated, offended, tarnished, vilified **3** = **upset**, cut to the quick, disgruntled, displeased, hurt, long-suffering, put out, reproachful, stung, unhappy, wounded

injury *noun* = **harm**, abuse, damage, detriment, disservice, evil, grievance, hurt, ill, injustice, mischief, ruin, trauma (*Pathology*), wound, wrong

injustice *noun* = **unfairness**, bias, discrimination, favouritism, inequality, inequity, iniquity, one-sidedness, oppression, partiality, partisanship, prejudice, unjustness, unlawfulness, wrong
➤ **Antonyms**
equality, equity, fairness, impartiality, justice, lawfulness, rectitude, right

inkling *noun* = **suspicion**, clue, conception, faintest *or* foggiest idea, glimmering, hint, idea, indication, intimation, notion, suggestion, whisper

inland *adjective* = **interior**, domestic, internal, upcountry

inlet *noun* = **bay**, arm (of the sea), bight, cove, creek, entrance, firth *or* frith (*Scot.*), fjord, ingress, passage, sea loch (*Scot.*)

inmost *or* **innermost** *adjective* = **deepest**, basic, buried, central, deep, essential, intimate, personal, private, secret

innate *adjective* = **inborn**, congenital, connate, constitutional, essential, immanent, inbred, indigenous, ingrained, inherent, inherited, in one's blood, instinctive, intrinsic, intuitive, native, natural
➤ **Antonyms**
accidental, acquired, affected, assumed, cultivated, fostered, incidental, learned, nurtured, unnatural

inner *adjective* **1** = **inside**, central, essential, interior, internal, intestinal, inward, middle **2** = **mental**, emotional, psychological, spiritual **3** = **hidden**, esoteric, intimate, personal, private, repressed, secret, unrevealed
➤ **Antonyms**
≠**inside**: exterior, external, outer, outside, outward ≠**hidden**: exposed, obvious, overt, revealed, surface, unconcealed, unrepressed, visible

innkeeper *noun* = **publican**, host *or* hostess, hotelier, landlord *or* landlady, mine host

innocence *noun* **1** = **guiltlessness**, blamelessness, chastity, clean hands, incorruptibility, probity, purity, righteousness, sinlessness, stainlessness, uprightness, virginity, virtue **2** = **naïveté**, artlessness, credulousness, freshness, guilelessness, gullibility, inexperience, ingenuousness, simplicity, unsophistication, unworldliness **3** = **harmlessness**, innocuousness, innoxiousness, inoffensiveness **4** = **ignorance**, lack of knowledge, nescience

(*literary*), unawareness, unfamiliarity
➤ **Antonyms**
≠**guiltlessness:** corruption, guilt, impurity,
offensiveness, sinfulness, wrongness
≠**naïveté:** artfulness, cunning,
disingenuousness, guile, wiliness,
worldliness

innocent *adjective* **1** = **not guilty,**
blameless, clear, faultless, guiltless, honest,
in the clear, squeaky-clean, uninvolved,
unoffending **2** = **pure,** chaste, immaculate,
impeccable, incorrupt, pristine, righteous,
sinless, spotless, stainless, unblemished,
unsullied, upright, virgin, virginal **3**
= **harmless,** innocuous, inoffensive,
unmalicious, unobjectionable,
well-intentioned, well-meant **4** = **naive,**
artless, childlike, credulous, frank,
guileless, gullible, ingenuous, open,
simple, unsuspicious, unworldly, wet
behind the ears (*informal*) **5 innocent of**
= **lacking,** clear of, empty of, free from,
ignorant, nescient, unacquainted with,
unaware, unfamiliar with, untouched by
♦ *noun* **6** = **child,** babe (in arms)
(*informal*), greenhorn (*informal*), ingénue
or (*masc.*) ingénu
➤ **Antonyms**
adjective ≠**not guilty:** blameworthy,
culpable, guilty, responsible ≠**pure:**
corrupt, dishonest, immoral, impure,
sinful, wrong ≠**harmless:** evil, harmful,
iniquitous, malicious, offensive, wicked
≠**naive:** artful, disingenuous,
sophisticated, worldly

innovation *noun* = **modernization,**
alteration, change, departure,
introduction, modernism, newness,
novelty, variation

innovative *adjective* = **novel,** inventive,
new, transformational, variational

innuendo *noun* = **insinuation,** aspersion,
hint, implication, imputation, intimation,
overtone, suggestion, whisper

innumerable *adjective* = **countless,**
beyond number, incalculable, infinite,
many, multitudinous, myriad, numberless,
numerous, unnumbered, untold
➤ **Antonyms**
calculable, computable, finite, limited,
measurable, numbered

inoffensive *adjective* = **harmless,** humble,
innocent, innocuous, innoxious, mild,
neutral, nonprovocative, peaceable, quiet,
retiring, unobjectionable, unobtrusive,
unoffending
➤ **Antonyms**
abrasive, harmful, irksome, irritating,
malicious, objectionable, offensive,
provocative

inoperative *adjective* = **out of action,**
broken, broken-down, buggered (*slang,
chiefly Brit.*), defective, *hors de combat,*
ineffective, ineffectual, inefficacious,
invalid, nonactive, null and void, on the
fritz (*U.S. slang*), out of commission, out of
order, out of service, unserviceable,
unworkable, useless

inopportune *adjective* = **inconvenient,**
ill-chosen, ill-timed, inappropriate,
inauspicious, malapropos, mistimed,
unfavourable, unfortunate, unpropitious,
unseasonable, unsuitable, untimely
➤ **Antonyms**
appropriate, auspicious, convenient,
favourable, fortunate, opportune,
seasonable, suitable, timely, well-timed

inordinate *adjective* = **excessive,**
disproportionate, exorbitant, extravagant,
immoderate, intemperate, preposterous,
unconscionable, undue, unreasonable,
unrestrained, unwarranted
➤ **Antonyms**
inhibited, moderate, reasonable,
restrained, rightful, sensible, temperate

inorganic *adjective* = **artificial,** chemical,
man-made, mineral

inquest *noun* = **inquiry,** inquisition,
investigation, probe

inquire, enquire *verb* **1** = **ask,** query,
question, request information, seek
information **2** = **investigate,** examine,
explore, inspect, look into, make inquiries,
probe, research, scrutinize, search

inquiring *adjective* = **inquisitive,** analytical,
curious, doubtful, interested, investigative,
nosy (*informal*), outward-looking, probing,
questioning, searching, wondering

inquiry, enquiry *noun* **1** = **question,** query
2 = **investigation,** examination,
exploration, inquest, interrogation, probe,
research, scrutiny, search, study, survey

inquisition *noun* = **investigation,**
cross-examination, examination, grilling
(*informal*), inquest, inquiry, questioning,
quizzing, third degree (*informal*)

inquisitive *adjective* = **curious,** inquiring,
intrusive, nosy (*informal*), nosy-parkering
(*informal*), peering, probing, prying,
questioning, scrutinizing, snooping
(*informal*), snoopy (*informal*)
➤ **Antonyms**
apathetic, incurious, indifferent,
unconcerned, uninterested, unquestioning

inroad *noun* **make inroads upon**
= **encroach upon,** consume, eat away, eat
up or into, use up

insane *adjective* **1** = **mad,** barking (*slang*),
barking mad (*slang*), cracked (*slang*),

crackers (*Brit. slang*), crazed, crazy, cuckoo (*informal*), demented, deranged, doolally (*slang*), gaga (*informal*), having a screw loose (*informal*), loopy (*informal*), mental (*slang*), mentally disordered, mentally ill, *non compos mentis*, not right in the head, not the full shilling (*informal*), nuts (*slang*), off one's rocker (*slang*), off one's trolley (*slang*), of unsound mind, out of one's mind, round the bend (*informal*), round the twist (*informal*), screwy (*informal*) **2** = **stupid**, bizarre, daft (*informal*), dumb-ass (*slang*), fatuous, foolish, idiotic, impractical, inane, irrational, irresponsible, lunatic, preposterous, senseless
➤ **Antonyms**
logical, lucid, normal, practical, rational, reasonable, reasoned, sane, sensible, sound

insanitary *adjective* = **unhealthy**, contaminated, dirtied, dirty, disease-ridden, feculent, filthy, impure, infected, infested, insalubrious, noxious, polluted, unclean, unhygienic
➤ **Antonyms**
clean, healthy, hygienic, pure, salubrious, unpolluted

insanity *noun* **1** = **madness**, aberration, craziness, delirium, dementia, frenzy, mental derangement, mental disorder, mental illness **2** = **stupidity**, folly, irresponsibility, lunacy, preposterousness, senselessness
➤ **Antonyms**
logic, lucidity, normality, rationality, reason, sanity, sense, soundness, wisdom

insatiable *adjective* = **unquenchable**, edacious, gluttonous, greedy, insatiate, intemperate, quenchless, rapacious, ravenous, unappeasable, voracious
➤ **Antonyms**
appeasable, limited, quenchable, satiable, temperate

inscribe *verb* **1** = **carve**, cut, engrave, etch, impress, imprint **2** = **dedicate**, address **3** = **enrol**, engross, enlist, enter, record, register, write

inscription *noun* = **engraving**, dedication, label, legend, lettering, saying, words

inscrutable *adjective* **1** = **enigmatic**, blank, deadpan, impenetrable, poker-faced (*informal*), sphinxlike, unreadable **2** = **mysterious**, hidden, incomprehensible, inexplicable, undiscoverable, unexplainable, unfathomable, unintelligible
➤ **Antonyms**
≠**enigmatic**: open, penetrable, readable, revealing, transparent ≠**mysterious**: clear, comprehensible, evident, explainable, explicable, intelligible, lucid, manifest,

obvious, palpable, patent, plain, understandable

insecure *adjective* **1** = **anxious**, afraid, uncertain, unconfident, unsure **2** = **unsafe**, dangerous, defenceless, exposed, hazardous, ill-protected, open to attack, perilous, unguarded, unprotected, unshielded, vulnerable, wide-open **3** = **unstable**, built upon sand, flimsy, frail, insubstantial, loose, on thin ice, precarious, rickety, rocky, shaky, unreliable, unsound, unsteady, weak, wobbly
➤ **Antonyms**
≠**anxious**: assured, certain, confident, decisive, secure ≠**unsafe**: protected, safe, secure ≠**unstable**: firm, reliable, secure, sound, stable, steady, substantial, sure

insecurity *noun* **1** = **anxiety**, fear, uncertainty, unsureness, worry **2** = **vulnerability**, danger, defencelessness, hazard, peril, risk, uncertainty, weakness **3** = **unsteadiness**, dubiety, frailness, instability, precariousness, shakiness, uncertainty, unreliability, weakness
➤ **Antonyms**
≠**anxiety**: assurance, certainty, confidence, security ≠**vulnerability**: dependability, safety ≠**unsteadiness**: firmness, reliability, security, stability, steadiness

insensibility *noun* **1** = **unconsciousness**, inertness, numbness **2** = **insensitivity**, apathy, callousness, dullness, indifference, inertia, lethargy, torpor

insensible *adjective* **1** = **benumbed**, anaesthetized, dull, inert, insensate, numbed, torpid **2** = **unaware**, apathetic, callous, cold, deaf, hard-hearted, impassive, impervious, indifferent, oblivious, unaffected, unconscious, unfeeling, unmindful, unmoved, unresponsive, unsusceptible, untouched **3** = **imperceptible**, imperceivable, minuscule, negligible, unnoticeable
➤ **Antonyms**
≠**unaware**: affected, aware, conscious, feeling, mindful, responsive, sensible

insensitive *adjective* **1** = **unfeeling**, callous, crass, hardened, imperceptive, indifferent, obtuse, tactless, thick-skinned, tough, uncaring, unconcerned, unresponsive, unsusceptible **2 insensitive to** = **unaffected by**, dead to, immune to, impervious to, proof against, unmoved by
➤ **Antonyms**
≠**unfeeling**: caring, concerned, perceptive, responsive, sensitive, susceptible, sympathetic, tactful, tender

inseparable *adjective* **1** = **devoted**, bosom, close, intimate **2** = **indivisible**, conjoined, inalienable, indissoluble, inseverable

insert *verb* = **enter**, embed, implant, infix, interject, interpolate, interpose, introduce, place, pop in (*informal*), put, set, stick in, tuck in, work in
➤ **Antonyms**
delete, extract, pull out, remove, take out, withdraw

insertion *noun* = **inclusion**, addition, implant, insert, inset, interpolation, introduction, supplement

inside *adjective* **1** = **inner**, innermost, interior, internal, intramural, inward **2** = **confidential**, classified, esoteric, exclusive, internal, limited, private, restricted, secret ◆ *adverb* **3** = **indoors**, under cover, within ◆ *noun* **4** = **interior**, contents, inner part **5 insides** *Informal* = **stomach**, belly, bowels, entrails, gut, guts, innards (*informal*), internal organs, viscera, vitals
➤ **Antonyms**
adjective ≠**inner**: exterior, external, extramural, outer, outermost, outside, outward

insidious *adjective* = **stealthy**, artful, crafty, crooked, cunning, deceitful, deceptive, designing, disingenuous, duplicitous, guileful, intriguing, Machiavellian, slick, sly, smooth, sneaking, subtle, surreptitious, treacherous, tricky, wily
➤ **Antonyms**
artless, conspicuous, forthright, honest, ingenuous, obvious, open, sincere, straightforward, upright

insight *noun* = **understanding**, acumen, awareness, comprehension, discernment, intuition, intuitiveness, judgment, observation, penetration, perception, perspicacity, vision

insignia *noun* = **badge**, crest, decoration, distinguishing mark, earmark, emblem, ensign, symbol

insignificance *noun* = **unimportance**, immateriality, inconsequence, irrelevance, meaninglessness, negligibility, paltriness, pettiness, triviality, worthlessness
➤ **Antonyms**
consequence, importance, matter, meaningfulness, relevance, significance, weight, worth

insignificant *adjective* = **unimportant**, flimsy, immaterial, inconsequential, inconsiderable, irrelevant, meagre, meaningless, measly, minor, negligible, nickel-and-dime (*U.S. slang*), nondescript, nonessential, not worth mentioning, nugatory, of no account, of no consequence, of no moment, paltry, petty, scanty, small potatoes, trifling, trivial,

unsubstantial, wanky (*taboo slang*)
➤ **Antonyms**
consequential, considerable, essential, important, meaningful, momentous, relevant, significant, substantial, vital, weighty

insincere *adjective* = **deceitful**, deceptive, devious, dishonest, disingenuous, dissembling, dissimulating, double-dealing, duplicitous, evasive, faithless, false, hollow, hypocritical, Janus-faced, lying, mendacious, perfidious, pretended, two-faced, unfaithful, untrue, untruthful, with tongue in cheek
➤ **Antonyms**
direct, earnest, faithful, genuine, honest, sincere, straightforward, true, truthful

insincerity *noun* = **deceitfulness**, deviousness, dishonesty, disingenuousness, dissimulation, duplicity, faithlessness, hypocrisy, lip service, mendacity, perfidy, pretence, untruthfulness
➤ **Antonyms**
directness, faithfulness, honesty, sincerity, truthfulness

insinuate *verb* **1** = **imply**, allude, hint, indicate, intimate, suggest **2** = **ingratiate**, curry favour, get in with, worm *or* work one's way in

insinuation *noun* = **implication**, allusion, aspersion, hint, innuendo, slur, suggestion

insipid *adjective* **1** = **bland**, anaemic, banal, characterless, colourless, drab, dry, dull, flat, ho-hum (*informal*), jejune, lifeless, limp, pointless, prosaic, prosy, spiritless, stale, stupid, tame, tedious, tiresome, trite, unimaginative, uninteresting, vapid, weak, wearisome, wishy-washy (*informal*) **2** = **tasteless**, bland, flavourless, savourless, unappetizing, watered down, watery, wishy-washy (*informal*)
➤ **Antonyms**
≠**bland**: colourful, engaging, exciting, interesting, lively, provocative, spirited, stimulating ≠**tasteless**: appetizing, fiery, palatable, piquant, pungent, savoury, tasty

insipidity, insipidness *noun* **1** = **dullness**, banality, colourlessness, flatness, lack of imagination, pointlessness, staleness, tameness, tediousness, triteness, uninterestingness, vapidity **2** = **tastelessness**, blandness, flavourlessness, lack of flavour
➤ **Antonyms**
≠**dullness**: animation, character, dynamism, gaiety, liveliness, spirit, vitality, vivacity

insist *verb* **1** = **demand**, be firm, brook no refusal, lay down the law, not take no for an answer, persist, press (someone), put one's foot down (*informal*), require, stand firm, stand one's ground, take *or* make a stand, urge **2** = **assert**, asseverate, aver, claim, contend, hold, maintain, reiterate, repeat, swear, urge, vow

insistence *noun* = **persistence**, assertion, contention, demands, emphasis, importunity, insistency, pressing, reiteration, stress, urging

insistent *adjective* = **persistent**, demanding, dogged, emphatic, exigent, forceful, importunate, incessant, peremptory, persevering, pressing, unrelenting, urgent

insolence *noun* = **rudeness**, abuse, audacity, backchat (*informal*), boldness, cheek (*informal*), chutzpah (*U.S. & Canad. informal*), contemptuousness, contumely, disrespect, effrontery, front, gall (*informal*), impertinence, impudence, incivility, insubordination, offensiveness, pertness, sassiness (*U.S. informal*), sauce (*informal*), uncivility
➤ **Antonyms**
civility, courtesy, deference, esteem, mannerliness, politeness, respect, submission

insolent *adjective* = **rude**, abusive, bold, brazen-faced, contemptuous, fresh (*informal*), impertinent, impudent, insubordinate, insulting, pert, saucy, uncivil
➤ **Antonyms**
civil, courteous, deferential, mannerly, polite, respectful, submissive

insoluble *adjective* = **inexplicable**, baffling, impenetrable, indecipherable, mysterious, mystifying, obscure, unaccountable, unfathomable, unsolvable
➤ **Antonyms**
accountable, comprehensible, explicable, fathomable, penetrable, soluble, solvable

insolvency *noun* = **bankruptcy**, failure, liquidation, ruin

insolvent *adjective* = **bankrupt**, broke (*informal*), failed, gone bust (*informal*), gone to the wall, in queer street (*informal*), in receivership, in the hands of the receivers, on the rocks (*informal*), ruined

insomnia *noun* = **sleeplessness**, wakefulness

inspect *verb* = **examine**, audit, check, check out (*informal*), eye, eyeball (*slang*), give (something *or* someone) the once-over (*informal*), go over *or* through, investigate, look over, oversee, recce (*slang*), research, scan, scrutinize, search, superintend, supervise, survey, take a dekko at (*Brit. slang*), vet, work over

inspection *noun* = **examination**, check, checkup, investigation, look-over, once-over (*informal*), recce (*slang*), review, scan, scrutiny, search, superintendence, supervision, surveillance, survey

inspector *noun* = **examiner**, auditor, censor, checker, critic, investigator, overseer, scrutineer, scrutinizer, superintendent, supervisor

inspiration *noun* **1** = **revelation**, arousal, awakening, creativity, elevation, encouragement, enthusiasm, exaltation, genius, illumination, insight, stimulation **2** = **influence**, muse, spur, stimulus
➤ **Antonyms**
depressant, deterrent, discouragement, disenchantment

inspire *verb* **1** = **stimulate**, animate, be responsible for, encourage, enliven, fire *or* touch the imagination of, galvanize, gee up, hearten, imbue, influence, infuse, inspirit, instil, rouse, spark off, spur **2** = **arouse**, enkindle, excite, give rise to, produce, quicken, rouse, stir
➤ **Antonyms**
≠**stimulate**: daunt, deflate, depress, discourage, disenchant, dishearten, dispirit

inspired *adjective* **1** = **brilliant**, dazzling, enthralling, exciting, impressive, memorable, of genius, outstanding, superlative, thrilling, wonderful **2** *Of a guess* = **instinctive**, instinctual, intuitive **3** = **uplifted**, aroused, elated, enthused, exalted, exhilarated, galvanized, possessed, stimulated, stirred up

inspiring *adjective* = **uplifting**, affecting, encouraging, exciting, exhilarating, heartening, moving, rousing, stimulating, stirring
➤ **Antonyms**
boring, depressing, discouraging, disheartening, dispiriting, dull, uninspiring

instability *noun* = **unpredictability**, capriciousness, changeableness, disequilibrium, fickleness, fitfulness, fluctuation, fluidity, frailty, imbalance, impermanence, inconstancy, insecurity, irresolution, mutability, oscillation, precariousness, restlessness, shakiness, transience, unsteadiness, vacillation, variability, volatility, wavering, weakness
➤ **Antonyms**
balance, constancy, equilibrium, permanence, predictability, resolution, security, stability, steadiness, strength

install *verb* **1** = **set up**, fix, lay, lodge, place, position, put in, station **2** = **induct**, establish, inaugurate, instate, institute, introduce, invest, set up **3** = **settle**, ensconce, position

installation noun 1 = **setting up**, establishment, fitting, instalment, placing, positioning 2 = **induction**, inauguration, instatement, investiture 3 = **equipment**, machinery, plant, system 4 *Military* = **establishment**, base, post, station

instalment noun = **portion**, chapter, division, episode, part, repayment, section

instance noun 1 = **example**, case, case in point, illustration, occasion, occurrence, precedent, situation, time 2 = **insistence**, application, behest, demand, entreaty, importunity, impulse, incitement, instigation, pressure, prompting, request, solicitation, urging ♦ verb 3 = **quote**, adduce, cite, mention, name, specify

instant noun 1 = **second**, bat of an eye (*informal*), flash, jiffy (*informal*), moment, shake (*informal*), split second, tick (*Brit. informal*), trice, twinkling, twinkling of an eye (*informal*), two shakes of a lamb's tail (*informal*) 2 = **juncture**, moment, occasion, point, time ♦ adjective 3 = **immediate**, direct, instantaneous, on-the-spot, prompt, quick, quickie (*informal*), split-second, urgent 4 = **precooked**, convenience, fast, ready-mixed 5 = **urgent**, burning, exigent, imperative, importunate, pressing

instantaneous adjective = **immediate**, direct, instant, on-the-spot, prompt

instantaneously adverb = **immediately**, at once, forthwith, in a fraction of a second, instantly, in the bat of an eye (*informal*), in the same breath, in the twinkling of an eye (*informal*), like a bat out of hell (*slang*), like greased lightning (*informal*), on the instant, on the spot, posthaste, promptly, pronto (*informal*), quick as lightning, straight away, then and there

instantly adverb = **immediately**, at once, directly, forthwith, instantaneously, instanter (*Law*), now, on the spot, posthaste, pronto (*informal*), right away, right now, straight away, there and then, this minute, *tout de suite,* without delay

instead adverb 1 = **rather**, alternatively, in lieu, in preference, on second thoughts, preferably 2 **instead of** = **in place of**, as an alternative *or* equivalent to, in lieu of, rather than

instigate verb = **provoke**, actuate, bring about, encourage, foment, get going, impel, incite, influence, initiate, kick-start, kindle, move, persuade, prod, prompt, rouse, set off, set on, spur, start, stimulate, stir up, trigger, urge, whip up
➤ **Antonyms**
discourage, repress, restrain, stop, suppress

instigation noun = **prompting**, behest, bidding, encouragement, incentive, incitement, urging

instigator noun = **ringleader**, agitator, firebrand, fomenter, goad, incendiary, inciter, leader, mischief-maker, motivator, prime mover, spur, stirrer (*informal*), troublemaker

instil, instill verb = **introduce**, engender, engraft, imbue, implant, impress, inculcate, infix, infuse, insinuate, sow the seeds

instinct noun = **intuition**, aptitude, faculty, feeling, gift, gut feeling (*informal*), gut reaction (*informal*), impulse, knack, natural inclination, predisposition, proclivity, sixth sense, talent, tendency, urge

instinctive adjective = **inborn**, automatic, inherent, innate, instinctual, intuitional, intuitive, involuntary, mechanical, native, natural, reflex, spontaneous, unlearned, unpremeditated, unthinking, visceral
➤ **Antonyms**
acquired, calculated, considered, learned, premeditated, thinking, voluntary, willed

instinctively adverb = **intuitively**, automatically, by instinct, in one's bones, involuntarily, naturally, without thinking

institute noun 1 = **society**, academy, association, college, conservatory, foundation, guild, institution, school, seat of learning, seminary 2 = **custom**, decree, doctrine, dogma, edict, law, maxim, precedent, precept, principle, regulation, rule, tenet ♦ verb 3 = **establish**, appoint, begin, bring into being, commence, constitute, enact, fix, found, induct, initiate, install, introduce, invest, launch, ordain, organize, originate, pioneer, put into operation, set in motion, settle, set up, start
➤ **Antonyms**
verb ≠ **establish**: abandon, abolish, cancel, cease, discontinue, end, stop, suspend, terminate

institution noun 1 = **establishment**, academy, college, foundation, hospital, institute, school, seminary, society, university 2 = **custom**, convention, fixture, law, practice, ritual, rule, tradition 3 = **creation**, constitution, enactment, establishment, formation, foundation, initiation, introduction, investiture, investment, organization

institutional adjective 1 = **conventional**, accepted, bureaucratic, established, establishment (*informal*), formal, organized, orthodox, societal 2 = **routine**, cheerless, clinical, cold, drab, dreary, dull, forbidding, formal, impersonal, monotonous, regimented, uniform, unwelcoming

instruct *verb* **1** = **order**, bid, canon, charge, command, direct, enjoin, tell **2** = **teach**, coach, discipline, drill, educate, enlighten, ground, guide, inform, school, train, tutor **3** = **brief**, acquaint, advise, apprise, counsel, inform, notify, tell

instruction *noun* **1** = **order**, briefing, command, demand, direction, directive, injunction, mandate, ruling **2** = **teaching**, apprenticeship, coaching, discipline, drilling, education, enlightenment, grounding, guidance, information, lesson(s), preparation, schooling, training, tuition, tutelage

instructions *plural noun* = **orders**, advice, directions, guidance, information, key, recommendations, rules

instructive *adjective* = **informative**, cautionary, didactic, edifying, educational, enlightening, helpful, illuminating, instructional, revealing, useful

instructor *noun* = **teacher**, adviser, coach, demonstrator, exponent, guide, guru, handler, master *or* mistress, mentor, pedagogue, preceptor (*rare*), schoolmaster *or* schoolmistress, trainer, tutor

instrument *noun* **1** = **tool**, apparatus, appliance, contraption (*informal*), contrivance, device, gadget, implement, mechanism, utensil, waldo **2** *Informal* = **puppet**, cat's-paw, dupe, pawn, tool **3** = **means**, agency, agent, channel, factor, force, mechanism, medium, organ, vehicle

instrumental *adjective* = **active**, assisting, auxiliary, conducive, contributory, helpful, helping, influential, involved, of help *or* service, subsidiary, useful

insubordinate *adjective* = **disobedient**, contumacious, defiant, disorderly, fractious, insurgent, mutinous, rebellious, recalcitrant, refractory, riotous, seditious, turbulent, undisciplined, ungovernable, unruly
➤ **Antonyms**
compliant, deferential, disciplined, docile, obedient, orderly, submissive, subservient

insubordination *noun* = **disobedience**, defiance, indiscipline, insurrection, mutinousness, mutiny, rebellion, recalcitrance, revolt, riotousness, sedition, ungovernability
➤ **Antonyms**
acquiescence, compliance, deference, discipline, docility, obedience, submission, subordination

insubstantial *adjective* **1** = **flimsy**, feeble, frail, poor, slight, tenuous, thin, weak **2**

= **imaginary**, chimerical, ephemeral, false, fanciful, idle, illusory, immaterial, incorporeal, unreal
➤ **Antonyms**
≠**flimsy**: firm, solid, strong, substantial, weighty

insufferable *adjective* = **unbearable**, detestable, dreadful, enough to test the patience of a saint, enough to try the patience of Job, impossible, insupportable, intolerable, more than flesh and blood can stand, outrageous, past bearing, too much, unendurable, unspeakable
➤ **Antonyms**
appealing, attractive, bearable, charming, disarming, pleasant

insufficient *adjective* = **inadequate**, deficient, incapable, incommensurate, incompetent, lacking, scant, short, unfitted, unqualified
➤ **Antonyms**
adequate, ample, commensurate, competent, enough, plentiful, qualified, sufficient

insular *adjective* = **narrow-minded**, blinkered, circumscribed, closed, contracted, cut off, illiberal, inward-looking, isolated, limited, narrow, parish-pump, parochial, petty, prejudiced, provincial
➤ **Antonyms**
broad-minded, cosmopolitan, liberal, open-minded, tolerant, worldly

insulate *verb* = **isolate**, close off, cocoon, cushion, cut off, protect, sequester, shield, wrap up in cotton wool

insult *verb* **1** = **offend**, abuse, affront, call names, give offence to, injure, miscall (*dialect*), outrage, put down, revile, slag (off) (*slang*), slander, slight, snub ♦ *noun* **2** = **abuse**, affront, aspersion, contumely, indignity, insolence, offence, outrage, put-down, rudeness, slap in the face (*informal*), slight, snub
➤ **Antonyms**
verb ≠**offend**: flatter, please, praise ♦ *noun* ≠**abuse**: compliment, flattery, honour

insulting *adjective* = **offensive**, abusive, affronting, contemptuous, degrading, disparaging, insolent, rude, scurrilous, slighting
➤ **Antonyms**
complimentary, deferential, flattering, laudatory, respectful

insuperable *adjective* = **insurmountable**, impassable, invincible, unconquerable
➤ **Antonyms**
conquerable, possible, surmountable

insupportable *adjective* **1** = **intolerable**, insufferable, past bearing, unbearable, unendurable **2** = **unjustifiable**, indefensible, untenable

insurance *noun* = **protection**, assurance, cover, coverage, guarantee, indemnification, indemnity, provision, safeguard, security, something to fall back on (*informal*), warranty

insure *verb* = **protect**, assure, cover, guarantee, indemnify, underwrite, warrant

insurgent *adjective* **1** = **rebellious**, disobedient, insubordinate, insurrectionary, mutinous, revolting, revolutionary, riotous, seditious ♦ *noun* **2** = **rebel**, insurrectionist, mutineer, resister, revolter, revolutionary, revolutionist, rioter

insurmountable *adjective* = **insuperable**, hopeless, impassable, impossible, invincible, overwhelming, unconquerable

insurrection *noun* = **rebellion**, coup, insurgency, mutiny, putsch, revolt, revolution, riot, rising, sedition, uprising

intact *adjective* = **undamaged**, all in one piece, complete, entire, perfect, scatheless, sound, together, unbroken, undefiled, unharmed, unhurt, unimpaired, uninjured, unscathed, untouched, unviolated, virgin, whole
➤ **Antonyms**
broken, damaged, harmed, impaired, injured

integral *adjective* **1** = **essential**, basic, component, constituent, elemental, fundamental, indispensable, intrinsic, necessary, requisite **2** = **whole**, complete, entire, full, intact, undivided
➤ **Antonyms**
≠**essential**: inessential, unimportant, unnecessary ≠**whole**: fractional

integrate *verb* = **join**, accommodate, amalgamate, assimilate, blend, coalesce, combine, fuse, harmonize, incorporate, intermix, knit, meld, merge, mesh, unite
➤ **Antonyms**
disperse, divide, segregate, separate

integration *noun* = **assimilation**, amalgamation, blending, combining, commingling, fusing, harmony, incorporation, mixing, unification

integrity *noun* **1** = **honesty**, candour, goodness, honour, incorruptibility, principle, probity, purity, rectitude, righteousness, uprightness, virtue **2** = **soundness**, coherence, cohesion, completeness, unity, wholeness
➤ **Antonyms**
≠**honesty**: corruption, deceit, dishonesty, disrepute, immorality

intellect *noun* **1** = **intelligence**, brains (*informal*), judgment, mind, reason, sense,

understanding **2** *Informal* = **thinker**, brain (*informal*), egghead (*informal*), genius, intellectual, intelligence, mind

intellectual *adjective* **1** = **scholarly**, bookish, cerebral, highbrow, intelligent, mental, rational, studious, thoughtful ♦ *noun* **2** = **academic**, bluestocking (*usually disparaging*), egghead (*informal*), highbrow, thinker
➤ **Antonyms**
adjective ≠**scholarly**: ignorant, illiterate, material, physical, stupid, unintellectual, unlearned ♦ *noun* ≠**academic**: idiot, moron

intelligence *noun* **1** = **understanding**, acumen, alertness, aptitude, brain power, brains (*informal*), brightness, capacity, cleverness, comprehension, discernment, grey matter (*informal*), intellect, mind, nous (*Brit. slang*), penetration, perception, quickness, reason, sense, smarts (*slang, chiefly U.S.*) **2** = **information**, advice, data, disclosure, facts, findings, gen (*Brit. informal*), knowledge, low-down (*informal*), news, notice, notification, report, rumour, tidings, tip-off, word
➤ **Antonyms**
≠**understanding**: dullness, ignorance, stupidity ≠**information**: concealment, misinformation

intelligent *adjective* = **clever**, acute, alert, apt, brainy (*informal*), bright, discerning, enlightened, instructed, knowing, penetrating, perspicacious, quick, quick-witted, rational, sharp, smart, thinking, well-informed
➤ **Antonyms**
dim-witted, dull, foolish, ignorant, obtuse, stupid, unintelligent

intelligentsia *noun* = **intellectuals**, eggheads (*informal*), highbrows, illuminati, literati, masterminds, the learned

intelligibility *noun* = **clarity**, clearness, comprehensibility, distinctness, explicitness, lucidity, plainness, precision, simplicity

intelligible *adjective* = **understandable**, clear, comprehensible, distinct, lucid, open, plain
➤ **Antonyms**
confused, garbled, incomprehensible, puzzling, unclear, unintelligible

intemperate *adjective* = **excessive**, extravagant, extreme, immoderate, incontinent, inordinate, intoxicated, O.T.T. (*slang*), over the top (*slang*), passionate, prodigal, profligate, self-indulgent, severe, tempestuous, unbridled, uncontrollable, ungovernable, unrestrained, violent, wild
➤ **Antonyms**
continent, disciplined, moderate,

restrained, self-controlled, temperate

intend verb 1 = **plan**, aim, be resolved or determined, contemplate, determine, have in mind or view, mean, meditate, propose, purpose, scheme 2 often with for = **destine**, aim, consign, design, earmark, mark out, mean, set apart

intense adjective 1 = **extreme**, acute, agonizing, close, concentrated, deep, drastic, excessive, exquisite, fierce, forceful, great, harsh, intensive, powerful, profound, protracted, serious (informal), severe, strained, unqualified 2 = **passionate**, ardent, burning, consuming, eager, earnest, energetic, fanatical, fervent, fervid, fierce, flaming, forcible, heightened, impassioned, keen, speaking, vehement
➤ **Antonyms**
≠**extreme**: easy, gentle, mild, moderate, relaxed, slight ≠**passionate**: casual, cool, indifferent, subdued, weak

intensely adverb = **strongly**, deeply, extremely, fiercely, passionately, profoundly, seriously (informal)

intensify verb = **increase**, add fuel to the flames (informal), add to, aggravate, augment, boost, concentrate, deepen, emphasize, enhance, escalate, exacerbate, fan the flames of, heighten, magnify, quicken, redouble, reinforce, set off, sharpen, step up (informal), strengthen, whet
➤ **Antonyms**
damp down, decrease, dilute, diminish, dull, lessen, minimize, weaken

intensity noun = **force**, ardour, concentration, depth, earnestness, emotion, energy, excess, extremity, fanaticism, fervency, fervour, fierceness, fire, intenseness, keenness, passion, potency, power, severity, strain, strength, tension, vehemence, vigour

intensive adjective = **concentrated**, all-out, comprehensive, demanding, exhaustive, in-depth, thorough, thoroughgoing

intent noun 1 = **intention**, aim, design, end, goal, meaning, object, objective, plan, purpose 2 to all intents and purposes = **virtually**, as good as, practically ♦ adjective 3 = **intense**, absorbed, alert, attentive, committed, concentrated, earnest, engrossed, fixed, industrious, occupied, piercing, preoccupied, rapt, steadfast, steady, watchful, wrapped up 4 = **resolved**, bent, determined, eager, hellbent (informal), resolute, set
➤ **Antonyms**
noun ≠**intention**: chance, fortune

♦ adjective ≠**intense**: casual, indifferent
≠**resolved**: irresolute, unsteady, wavering

intention noun = **purpose**, aim, design, end, end in view, goal, idea, intent, meaning, object, objective, point, scope, target, view

intentional adjective = **deliberate**, calculated, designed, done on purpose, intended, meant, planned, prearranged, preconcerted, premeditated, purposed, studied, wilful
➤ **Antonyms**
accidental, inadvertent, unintentional, unplanned

intentionally adverb = **deliberately**, by design, designedly, on purpose, wilfully

intently adverb = **attentively**, closely, fixedly, hard, keenly, searchingly, steadily, watchfully

inter verb = **bury**, entomb, inhume, inurn, lay to rest, sepulchre

intercede verb = **mediate**, advocate, arbitrate, interpose, intervene, plead, speak

intercept verb = **seize**, arrest, block, catch, check, cut off, deflect, head off, interrupt, obstruct, stop, take

intercession noun = **pleading**, advocacy, entreaty, good offices, intervention, mediation, plea, prayer, solicitation, supplication

interchange verb 1 = **switch**, alternate, bandy, barter, exchange, reciprocate, swap, trade ♦ noun 2 = **junction**, alternation, crossfire, exchange, give and take, intersection, reciprocation

interchangeable adjective = **identical**, commutable, equivalent, exchangeable, reciprocal, synonymous, the same, transposable

intercourse noun 1 = **sexual intercourse**, carnal knowledge, coition, coitus, congress, copulation, intimacy, legover (slang), nookie (slang), rumpy-pumpy (slang), sex (informal), sexual act, sexual relations, the other (informal) 2 = **communication**, association, commerce, communion, connection, contact, converse, correspondence, dealings, intercommunication, trade, traffic, truck

interest noun 1 = **curiosity**, affection, attention, attentiveness, attraction, concern, notice, regard, suspicion, sympathy 2 = **importance**, concern, consequence, moment, note, relevance, significance, weight 3 = **hobby**, activity, diversion, leisure activity, pastime, preoccupation, pursuit, relaxation 4 often plural = **advantage**, benefit, boot (dialect), gain, good, profit 5 = **stake**, authority,

claim, commitment, influence, investment, involvement, participation, portion, right, share **6** *often plural* = **business**, affair, care, concern, matter
♦ *verb* **7** = **arouse one's curiosity**, amuse, attract, catch one's eye, divert, engross, fascinate, hold the attention of, intrigue, move, touch **8** = **engage**, affect, concern, involve
➤ **Antonyms**
noun ≠ **curiosity**: boredom, coolness, disinterest, dispassion, disregard, unconcern ≠ **importance**: inconsequence, insignificance, irrelevance, worthlessness
♦ *verb* ≠ **arouse one's curiosity**: bore, burden, irk, repel, tire, weary

interested *adjective* **1** = **curious**, affected, attentive, attracted, drawn, excited, fascinated, intent, into (*informal*), keen, moved, responsive, stimulated **2** = **involved**, biased, concerned, implicated, partial, partisan, predisposed, prejudiced
➤ **Antonyms**
≠ **curious**: apathetic, bored, detached, inattentive, indifferent, unconcerned, uninterested, wearied

interesting *adjective* = **intriguing**, absorbing, amusing, appealing, attractive, compelling, curious, engaging, engrossing, entertaining, gripping, pleasing, provocative, stimulating, stirring, suspicious, thought-provoking, unusual
➤ **Antonyms**
boring, dull, mind-numbing, tedious, tiresome, uninteresting

interface *noun* **1** = **connection**, border, boundary, frontier, link ♦ *verb* **2** = **connect**, combine, couple, join together, link

interfere *verb* **1** = **intrude**, butt in, get involved, intermeddle, intervene, meddle, poke one's nose in (*informal*), put one's two cents in (*U.S. slang*), stick one's oar in (*informal*), tamper **2** *often with* **with** = **conflict**, be a drag upon (*informal*), block, clash, collide, cramp, frustrate, get in the way of, hamper, handicap, hinder, impede, inhibit, obstruct, trammel

interference *noun* **1** = **intrusion**, intermeddling, intervention, meddlesomeness, meddling, prying **2** = **conflict**, clashing, collision, impedance, obstruction, opposition

interim *adjective* **1** = **temporary**, acting, caretaker, improvised, intervening, makeshift, pro tem, provisional, stopgap
♦ *noun* **2** = **interval**, entr'acte, interregnum, meantime, meanwhile, respite

interior *noun* **1** = **inside**, bosom, centre,

contents, core, heart, innards (*informal*) **2** *Geography* = **heartland**, centre, upcountry
♦ *adjective* **3** = **inside**, inner, internal, inward **4** = **mental**, hidden, inner, intimate, personal, private, secret, spiritual **5** *Politics* = **domestic**, home
➤ **Antonyms**
adjective ≠ **inside**: exterior, external, outer, outside, outward

interjection *noun* = **exclamation**, cry, ejaculation, interpolation, interposition

interloper *noun* = **trespasser**, gate-crasher (*informal*), intermeddler, intruder, meddler, uninvited guest, unwanted visitor

interlude *noun* = **interval**, break, breathing space, delay, entr'acte, episode, halt, hiatus, intermission, pause, respite, rest, spell, stop, stoppage, wait

intermediary *noun* = **mediator**, agent, broker, entrepreneur, go-between, middleman

intermediate *adjective* = **middle**, halfway, in-between (*informal*), intermediary, interposed, intervening, mean, mid, midway, transitional

interment *noun* = **burial**, burying, funeral, inhumation, sepulture

interminable *adjective* = **endless**, boundless, ceaseless, dragging, everlasting, immeasurable, infinite, limitless, long, long-drawn-out, long-winded, never-ending, perpetual, protracted, unbounded, unlimited, wearisome
➤ **Antonyms**
bounded, finite, limited, measurable, restricted, temporary

intermingle *verb* = **mix**, amalgamate, blend, combine, commingle, commix, fuse, interlace, intermix, interweave, meld, merge

intermission *noun* = **interval**, break, breathing space, cessation, entr'acte, interlude, interruption, let-up (*informal*), lull, pause, recess, respite, rest, stop, stoppage, suspense, suspension

intermittent *adjective* = **periodic**, broken, discontinuous, fitful, irregular, occasional, punctuated, recurrent, recurring, spasmodic, sporadic, stop-go (*informal*)
➤ **Antonyms**
continuous, steady, unceasing

intern *verb* = **imprison**, confine, detain, hold, hold in custody

internal *adjective* **1** = **inner**, inside, interior **2** = **domestic**, civic, home, in-house, intramural **3** = **private**, intimate, subjective
➤ **Antonyms**
≠ **inner**: exterior, external, outer,

outermost, outside ≠**private**: exposed, revealed, unconcealed

international *adjective* = **universal**, cosmopolitan, ecumenical (*rare*), global, intercontinental, worldwide

Internet *noun* = **information superhighway**, cyberspace, the net (*informal*), the web (*informal*), World Wide Web

interpolate *verb* = **insert**, add, intercalate, introduce

interpolation *noun* = **insertion**, addition, aside, insert, intercalation, interjection, introduction

interpose *verb* **1** = **intervene**, come *or* place between, intercede, interfere, intermediate, intrude, mediate, step in **2** = **interrupt**, insert, interject, introduce, put forth, put one's oar in

interpret *verb* = **explain**, adapt, clarify, construe, decipher, decode, define, elucidate, explicate, expound, make sense of, paraphrase, read, render, solve, spell out, take, throw light on, translate, understand

interpretation *noun* = **explanation**, analysis, clarification, construction, diagnosis, elucidation, exegesis, explication, exposition, meaning, performance, portrayal, reading, rendering, rendition, sense, signification, translation, understanding, version

interpreter *noun* = **translator**, annotator, commentator, exponent, scholiast

interrogate *verb* = **question**, ask, catechize, cross-examine, cross-question, enquire, examine, give (someone) the third degree (*informal*), grill (*informal*), inquire, investigate, pump, put the screws on (*informal*), quiz

interrogation *noun* = **questioning**, cross-examination, cross-questioning, examination, grilling (*informal*), inquiry, inquisition, probing, third degree (*informal*)

interrogative *adjective* = **questioning**, curious, inquiring, inquisitive, inquisitorial, quizzical

interrupt *verb* **1** = **intrude**, barge in (*informal*), break in, break (someone's) train of thought, butt in, disturb, heckle, hinder, interfere (with), obstruct, punctuate, separate, sever **2** = **suspend**, break, break off, check, cut, cut off, cut short, delay, disconnect, discontinue, disjoin, disunite, divide, hold up, lay aside, stay, stop

interrupted *adjective* = **disturbed**, broken, cut off, disconnected, discontinuous,

incomplete, intermittent, uneven

interruption *noun* = **stoppage**, break, cessation, disconnection, discontinuance, disruption, dissolution, disturbance, disuniting, division, halt, hiatus, hindrance, hitch, impediment, intrusion, obstacle, obstruction, pause, separation, severance, stop, suspension

intersect *verb* = **cross**, bisect, crisscross, cut, cut across, divide, meet

intersection *noun* = **junction**, crossing, crossroads, interchange

interval *noun* = **break**, delay, distance, entr'acte, gap, hiatus, interim, interlude, intermission, meantime, meanwhile, opening, pause, period, playtime, respite, rest, season, space, spell, term, time, wait

intervene *verb* **1** = **step in** (*informal*), arbitrate, intercede, interfere, interpose oneself, intrude, involve oneself, mediate, put one's oar in, put one's two cents in (*U.S. slang*), take a hand (*informal*) **2** = **happen**, befall, come to pass, ensue, occur, succeed, supervene, take place

intervention *noun* = **mediation**, agency, intercession, interference, interposition, intrusion

interview *noun* **1** = **meeting**, audience, conference, consultation, dialogue, evaluation, oral (examination), press conference, talk ♦ *verb* **2** = **question**, examine, interrogate, sound out, talk to

interviewer *noun* = **questioner**, examiner, interlocutor, interrogator, investigator, reporter

interwoven *adjective* = **interconnected**, blended, connected, entwined, inmixed, interlaced, interlocked, intermingled, knit

intestinal *adjective* = **abdominal**, coeliac, duodenal, gut (*informal*), inner, stomachic, visceral

intestines *plural noun* = **guts**, bowels, entrails, innards (*informal*), insides (*informal*), internal organs, viscera, vitals

intimacy *noun* = **familiarity**, closeness, confidence, confidentiality, fraternization, understanding
> **Antonyms**
alienation, aloofness, coldness, detachment, distance, estrangement, remoteness, separation

intimate[1] *adjective* **1** = **close**, bosom, cherished, confidential, dear, friendly, near, nearest and dearest, thick (*informal*), warm **2** = **private**, confidential, personal, privy, secret **3** = **detailed**, deep, exhaustive, experienced, first-hand, immediate, in-depth, penetrating, personal, profound, thorough **4** = **snug**,

comfy (*informal*), cosy, friendly, tête-à-tête, warm ♦ *noun* 5 = **friend**, bosom friend, buddy (*informal*), china (*Brit. slang*), chum (*informal*), close friend, cock (*Brit. informal*), comrade, confidant *or* confidante, (constant) companion, crony, familiar, gossip (*archaic*), homeboy (*slang, chiefly U.S.*), mate (*informal*), mucker (*Brit. slang*), pal
➤ **Antonyms**
adjective ≠**close**: distant, remote, superficial ≠**private**: known, open, public ♦ *noun* ≠**friend**: enemy, foe, stranger

intimate[2] *verb* 1 = **suggest**, allude, drop a hint, give (someone) to understand, hint, imply, indicate, insinuate, let it be known, tip (someone) the wink (*Brit. informal*), warn 2 = **announce**, communicate, declare, impart, make known, remind, state

intimately *adverb* 1 = **confidingly**, affectionately, closely, confidentially, familiarly, personally, tenderly, very well, warmly 2 = **in detail**, fully, inside out, thoroughly, through and through, to the core, very well

intimation *noun* 1 = **hint**, allusion, indication, inkling, insinuation, reminder, suggestion, warning 2 = **announcement**, communication, declaration, notice

intimidate *verb* = **frighten**, affright (*archaic*), alarm, appal, browbeat, bully, coerce, cow, daunt, dishearten, dismay, dispirit, lean on (*informal*), overawe, scare, scare off (*informal*), subdue, terrify, terrorize, threaten, twist someone's arm (*informal*)

intimidation *noun* = **bullying**, arm-twisting (*informal*), browbeating, coercion, fear, menaces, pressure, terror, terrorization, threat(s)

intolerable *adjective* = **unbearable**, beyond bearing, excruciating, impossible, insufferable, insupportable, more than flesh and blood can stand, not to be borne, painful, unendurable
➤ **Antonyms**
bearable, endurable, painless, possible, sufferable, supportable, tolerable

intolerance *noun* = **narrow-mindedness**, bigotry, chauvinism, discrimination, dogmatism, fanaticism, illiberality, impatience, jingoism, narrowness, prejudice, racialism, racism, xenophobia
➤ **Antonyms**
broad-mindedness, liberality, open-mindedness, patience, tolerance, understanding

intolerant *adjective* = **narrow-minded**, bigoted, chauvinistic, dictatorial, dogmatic, fanatical, illiberal, impatient,

narrow, one-sided, prejudiced, racialist, racist, small-minded, uncharitable, xenophobic
➤ **Antonyms**
broad-minded, charitable, lenient, liberal, open-minded, patient, tolerant, understanding

intonation *noun* 1 = **tone**, accentuation, cadence, inflection, modulation 2 = **incantation**, chant

intone *verb* = **recite**, chant, croon, intonate, sing

intoxicate *verb* 1 = **go to one's head**, addle, befuddle, fuddle, inebriate, put (someone) under the table (*informal*), stupefy 2 = **exhilarate**, elate, excite, go to one's head, inflame, make one's head spin, stimulate

intoxicated *adjective* 1 = **drunk**, babalas (*S. African*), bevvied (*dialect*), blitzed (*slang*), blotto (*slang*), bombed (*slang*), Brahms and Liszt (*slang*), canned (*slang*), cut (*Brit. slang*), drunk as a skunk, drunken, flying (*slang*), fuddled, half seas over (*Brit. informal*), high (*informal*), inebriated, in one's cups (*informal*), legless (*informal*), lit up (*slang*), out of it (*slang*), out to it (*Austral. & N.Z. slang*), paralytic (*informal*), pissed (*taboo slang*), plastered (*slang*), rat-arsed (*taboo slang*), smashed (*slang*), sozzled (*informal*), steamboats (*Scot. slang*), steaming (*slang*), stewed (*slang*), stiff (*slang*), stoned (*slang*), the worse for drink, three sheets in the wind (*informal*), tight (*informal*), tipsy, under the influence, wasted (*slang*), wrecked (*slang*), zonked (*slang*) 2 = **euphoric**, dizzy, ecstatic, elated, enraptured, excited, exhilarated, high (*informal*), infatuated, sent (*slang*), stimulated

intoxicating *adjective* 1 = **alcoholic**, inebriant, intoxicant, spirituous, strong 2 = **exciting**, exhilarating, heady, sexy (*informal*), stimulating, thrilling

intoxication *noun* 1 = **drunkenness**, inebriation, inebriety, insobriety, tipsiness 2 = **excitement**, delirium, elation, euphoria, exaltation, exhilaration, infatuation

intransigent *adjective* = **uncompromising**, hardline, immovable, intractable, obdurate, obstinate, stiff-necked, stubborn, tenacious, tough, unbending, unbudgeable, unyielding
➤ **Antonyms**
acquiescent, compliant, compromising, flexible, open-minded

intrepid *adjective* = **fearless**, audacious, bold, brave, courageous, daring, dauntless, doughty, gallant, game

(*informal*), have-a-go (*informal*), heroic, lion-hearted, nerveless, plucky, resolute, stalwart, stouthearted, unafraid, undaunted, unflinching, valiant, valorous
➤ **Antonyms**
afraid, cautious, cowardly, craven, daunted, faint-hearted, fearful, flinching, irresolute, timid

intricacy *noun* = **complexity**, complication, convolutions, elaborateness, entanglement, intricateness, involution, involvement, knottiness, obscurity

intricate *adjective* = **complicated**, baroque, Byzantine, complex, convoluted, daedal (*literary*), difficult, elaborate, fancy, involved, knotty, labyrinthine, obscure, perplexing, rococo, sophisticated, tangled, tortuous
➤ **Antonyms**
clear, easy, obvious, plain, simple, straightforward

intrigue *verb* 1 = **interest**, arouse the curiosity of, attract, charm, fascinate, pique, rivet, tickle one's fancy, titillate 2 = **plot**, connive, conspire, machinate, manoeuvre, scheme ♦ *noun* 3 = **plot**, cabal, chicanery, collusion, conspiracy, double-dealing, knavery, machination, manipulation, manoeuvre, ruse, scheme, sharp practice, stratagem, trickery, wile 4 = **affair**, amour, intimacy, liaison, romance

intriguing *adjective* = **interesting**, beguiling, compelling, diverting, exciting, fascinating, tantalizing, titillating

intrinsic *adjective* = **inborn**, basic, built-in, central, congenital, constitutional, elemental, essential, fundamental, genuine, inbred, inherent, native, natural, radical, real, true, underlying
➤ **Antonyms**
acquired, added, appended, artificial, extraneous, extrinsic, incidental

introduce *verb* 1 = **present**, acquaint, do the honours, familiarize, make known, make the introduction 2 = **bring up**, advance, air, broach, moot, offer, propose, put forward, recommend, set forth, submit, suggest, ventilate 3 = **bring in**, begin, commence, establish, found, inaugurate, initiate, institute, launch, organize, pioneer, set up, start, usher in 4 = **insert**, add, inject, interpolate, interpose, put in, throw in (*informal*) 5 = **lead into**, announce, lead off, open, preface

introduction *noun* 1 = **launch**, baptism, debut, establishment, first acquaintance, inauguration, induction, initiation, institution, pioneering, presentation 2 = **opening**, commencement, exordium, foreword, intro (*informal*), lead-in,

opening passage, opening remarks, overture, preamble, preface, preliminaries, prelude, proem, prolegomena, prolegomenon, prologue 3 = **insertion**, addition, interpolation
➤ **Antonyms**
≠**launch**: completion, elimination, termination ≠**opening**: conclusion, end, epilogue ≠**insertion**: extraction, removal, withdrawal

introductory *adjective* = **preliminary**, early, elementary, first, inaugural, initial, initiatory, opening, precursory, prefatory, preparatory, starting
➤ **Antonyms**
closing, concluding, final, last, terminating

introspective *adjective* = **inward-looking**, brooding, contemplative, inner-directed, introverted, meditative, pensive, subjective

introverted *adjective* = **introspective**, indrawn, inner-directed, inward-looking, self-centred, self-contained, withdrawn

intrude *verb* = **interfere**, butt in, encroach, infringe, interrupt, meddle, obtrude, push in, put one's two cents in (*U.S. slang*), thrust oneself in *or* forward, trespass, violate

intruder *noun* = **trespasser**, burglar, gate-crasher (*informal*), infiltrator, interloper, invader, prowler, raider, snooper (*informal*), squatter, thief

intrusion *noun* = **invasion**, encroachment, infringement, interference, interruption, trespass, violation

intrusive *adjective* = **interfering**, disturbing, forward, impertinent, importunate, invasive, meddlesome, nosy (*informal*), officious, presumptuous, pushy (*informal*), uncalled-for, unwanted

intuition *noun* = **instinct**, discernment, hunch, insight, perception, presentiment, sixth sense

intuitive *adjective* = **instinctive**, innate, instinctual, involuntary, spontaneous, unreflecting, untaught

inundate *verb* = **flood**, deluge, drown, engulf, glut, immerse, overflow, overrun, overwhelm, submerge, swamp

inundation *noun* = **flood**, deluge, overflow, tidal wave, torrent

invade *verb* 1 = **attack**, assail, assault, burst in, descend upon, encroach, infringe, make inroads, occupy, raid, violate 2 = **infest**, infect, overrun, overspread, penetrate, permeate, pervade, swarm over

invader *noun* = **attacker**, aggressor, alien, looter, plunderer, raider, trespasser

invalid[1] *noun* 1 = **patient**, convalescent, valetudinarian ♦ *adjective* 2 = **disabled**, ailing, bedridden, feeble, frail, ill, infirm, poorly (*informal*), sick, sickly, valetudinarian, weak

invalid² *adjective* = **null and void**, baseless, fallacious, false, ill-founded, illogical, inoperative, irrational, not binding, nugatory, null, unfounded, unscientific, unsound, untrue, void, worthless
➤ **Antonyms**
logical, operative, rational, solid, sound, true, valid, viable

invalidate *verb* = **nullify**, abrogate, annul, cancel, overrule, overthrow, quash, render null and void, rescind, undermine, undo, weaken
➤ **Antonyms**
authorize, empower, ratify, sanction, strengthen, validate

invaluable *adjective* = **precious**, beyond price, costly, inestimable, priceless, valuable, worth one's or its weight in gold
➤ **Antonyms**
cheap, rubbishy, valueless, worthless

invariable *adjective* = **regular**, changeless, consistent, constant, fixed, immutable, inflexible, rigid, set, unalterable, unchangeable, unchanging, unfailing, uniform, unvarying, unwavering
➤ **Antonyms**
alterable, changeable, changing, differing, flexible, inconsistent, irregular, uneven, variable, varying

invariably *adverb* = **consistently**, always, customarily, day in, day out, ever, every time, habitually, inevitably, on every occasion, perpetually, regularly, unfailingly, without exception

invasion *noun* **1** = **attack**, aggression, assault, campaign, foray, incursion, inroad, irruption, offensive, onslaught, raid **2** = **intrusion**, breach, encroachment, infiltration, infraction, infringement, overstepping, usurpation, violation

invective *noun* = **abuse**, berating, billingsgate, castigation, censure, contumely, denunciation, diatribe, obloquy, philippic(s), reproach, revilement, sarcasm, tirade, tongue-lashing, vilification, vituperation

invent *verb* **1** = **create**, coin, come up with (*informal*), conceive, contrive, design, devise, discover, dream up (*informal*), formulate, imagine, improvise, originate, think up **2** = **make up**, concoct, cook up (*informal*), fabricate, feign, forge, manufacture, trump up

invention *noun* **1** = **creation**, brainchild (*informal*), contraption, contrivance, design, development, device, discovery, gadget, instrument, waldo **2** = **creativity**,

coinage, creativeness, genius, imagination, ingenuity, inspiration, inventiveness, originality, resourcefulness **3** = **fiction**, deceit, fabrication, fake, falsehood, fantasy, fib (*informal*), figment or product of (someone's) imagination, forgery, lie, prevarication, sham, story, tall story (*informal*), untruth, urban legend, urban myth, yarn

inventive *adjective* = **creative**, fertile, gifted, ground-breaking, imaginative, ingenious, innovative, inspired, original, resourceful
➤ **Antonyms**
imitative, pedestrian, trite, unimaginative, uninspired, uninventive

inventor *noun* = **creator**, architect, author, coiner, designer, father, framer, maker, originator

inventory *noun* = **list**, account, catalogue, file, record, register, roll, roster, schedule, stock book

inverse *adjective* = **opposite**, contrary, converse, inverted, reverse, reversed, transposed

inversion *noun* **1** = **reversal**, contraposition, contrariety, transposal, transposition **2** = **opposite**, antipode, antithesis, contrary

invert *verb* = **overturn**, capsize, introvert, intussuscept (*Pathology*), invaginate (*Pathology*), overset, reverse, transpose, turn inside out, turn turtle, turn upside down, upset, upturn

invest *verb* **1** = **spend**, advance, devote, lay out, put in, sink **2** = **empower**, authorize, charge, license, sanction, vest **3** = **install**, adopt, consecrate, enthrone, establish, inaugurate, induct, ordain **4** = **provide**, endow, endue, supply

investigate *verb* = **examine**, consider, explore, go into, inquire into, inspect, look into, make inquiries, probe, put to the test, recce (*slang*), research, scrutinize, search, sift, study, work over

investigation *noun* = **examination**, analysis, exploration, fact finding, hearing, inquest, inquiry, inspection, probe, recce (*slang*), research, review, scrutiny, search, study, survey

investigator *noun* = **examiner**, dick (*slang, chiefly U.S.*), gumshoe (*U.S. slang*), inquirer, (private) detective, private eye (*informal*), researcher, reviewer, sleuth

investiture *noun* = **installation**, admission, enthronement, inauguration, induction, instatement, investing, investment, ordination

investment *noun* **1** = **transaction**, asset,

investing, speculation, venture **2** = **stake**, ante (*informal*), contribution

inveterate *adjective* = **long-standing**, chronic, confirmed, deep-dyed (*usually derogatory*), deep-rooted, deep-seated, dyed-in-the-wool, entrenched, established, habitual, hard-core, hardened, incorrigible, incurable, ineradicable, ingrained, obstinate

invidious *adjective* = **undesirable**, hateful, thankless, unpleasant
➤ **Antonyms**
desirable, pleasant, pleasing

invigilate *verb* = **watch over**, conduct, keep an eye on, oversee, preside over, run, superintend, supervise

invigorate *verb* = **refresh**, animate, brace, buck up (*informal*), energize, enliven, exhilarate, fortify, freshen (up), galvanize, harden, liven up, nerve, pep up, perk up, put new heart into, quicken, rejuvenate, revitalize, stimulate, strengthen

invincible *adjective* = **unbeatable**, impregnable, indestructible, indomitable, inseparable, insuperable, invulnerable, unassailable, unconquerable, unsurmountable, unyielding
➤ **Antonyms**
assailable, beatable, conquerable, defenceless, fallible, powerless, unprotected, vulnerable, weak, yielding

inviolable *adjective* = **sacrosanct**, hallowed, holy, inalienable, sacred, unalterable

inviolate *adjective* = **intact**, entire, pure, sacred, stainless, unbroken, undefiled, undisturbed, unhurt, unpolluted, unstained, unsullied, untouched, virgin, whole
➤ **Antonyms**
abused, broken, defiled, polluted, stained, sullied, touched, violated

invisible *adjective* **1** = **unseen**, imperceptible, indiscernible, out of sight, unperceivable **2** = **hidden**, concealed, disguised, inappreciable, inconspicuous, infinitesimal, microscopic
➤ **Antonyms**
≠unseen: discernible, distinct, obvious, perceptible, seen, visible

invitation *noun* **1** = **request**, asking, begging, bidding, call, invite (*informal*), solicitation, summons, supplication **2** = **inducement**, allurement, challenge, come-on (*informal*), coquetry, enticement, glad eye (*informal*), incitement, open door, overture, provocation, temptation

invite *verb* **1** = **request**, ask, beg, bid, call, request the pleasure of (someone's) company, solicit, summon **2** = **encourage**,

allure, ask for (*informal*), attract, bring on, court, draw, entice, lead, leave the door open to, provoke, solicit, tempt, welcome

inviting *adjective* = **tempting**, alluring, appealing, attractive, beguiling, captivating, delightful, engaging, enticing, fascinating, intriguing, magnetic, mouthwatering, pleasing, seductive, warm, welcoming, winning
➤ **Antonyms**
disagreeable, offensive, off-putting (*Brit. informal*), repellent, unappealing, unattractive, undesirable, uninviting, unpleasant

invocation *noun* = **appeal**, beseeching, entreaty, petition, prayer, supplication

invoke *verb* **1** = **apply**, call in, have recourse to, implement, initiate, put into effect, resort to, use **2** = **call upon**, adjure, appeal to, beg, beseech, conjure, entreat, implore, petition, pray, solicit, supplicate

involuntary *adjective* = **unintentional**, automatic, blind, conditioned, instinctive, instinctual, reflex, spontaneous, unconscious, uncontrolled, unthinking
➤ **Antonyms**
calculated, deliberate, intentional, planned, purposed, volitional, voluntary, wilful

involve *verb* **1** = **include**, comprehend, comprise, contain, cover, embrace, incorporate, number among, take in **2** = **entail**, imply, mean, necessitate, presuppose, require **3** = **concern**, affect, associate, compromise, connect, draw in, implicate, incriminate, inculpate, mix up (*informal*), stitch up (*slang*), touch **4** = **complicate**, embroil, enmesh, entangle, link, mire, mix up, snarl up, tangle **5** = **preoccupy**, absorb, bind, commit, engage, engross, grip, hold, rivet, wrap up

involved *adjective* **1** = **complicated**, Byzantine, complex, confusing, convoluted, difficult, elaborate, intricate, knotty, labyrinthine, sophisticated, tangled, tortuous **2** = **concerned**, caught (up), implicated, in on (*informal*), mixed up in or with, occupied, participating, taking part, up to one's ears in
➤ **Antonyms**
≠complicated: easy, easy-peasy (*slang*), elementary, simple, simplified, straightforward, uncomplicated, unsophisticated

involvement *noun* **1** = **connection**, association, commitment, concern, dedication, interest, participation, responsibility **2** = **complication**, complexity, difficulty, embarrassment, entanglement, imbroglio, intricacy, problem, ramification

invulnerable *adjective* = **safe**,
impenetrable, indestructible, insusceptible,
invincible, proof against, secure,
unassailable
➤ **Antonyms**
assailable, defenceless, insecure,
susceptible, unprotected, vulnerable, weak

inward *adjective* **1** = **incoming**, entering,
inbound, inflowing, ingoing, inpouring,
penetrating **2** = **internal**, inner, inside,
interior **3** = **private**, confidential, hidden,
inmost, innermost, personal, privy, secret
➤ **Antonyms**
≠**internal**: exterior, external, outer,
outermost, outside, outward ≠**private**:
open, public

inwardly *adverb* = **privately**, at heart, deep
down, in one's head, in one's inmost
heart, inside, secretly, to oneself, within

irate *adjective* = **angry**, annoyed, cross,
enraged, furious, incensed, indignant,
infuriated, livid

Irish *adjective* = **Hibernian**, green

irksome *adjective* = **irritating**, aggravating,
annoying, boring, bothersome,
burdensome, disagreeable, exasperating,
tedious, tiresome, troublesome, trying,
uninteresting, unwelcome, vexatious,
vexing, wearisome
➤ **Antonyms**
agreeable, enjoyable, gratifying,
interesting, pleasant, pleasing, welcome

iron *adjective* **1** = **ferrous**, chalybeate, ferric,
irony **2** = **inflexible**, adamant, cruel, hard,
heavy, immovable, implacable,
indomitable, obdurate, rigid, robust, steel,
steely, strong, tough, unbending,
unyielding
➤ **Antonyms**
≠**inflexible**: bending, easy, flexible, light,
malleable, pliable, soft, weak, yielding

ironic, ironical *adjective* **1** = **sarcastic**,
double-edged, mocking, mordacious,
sardonic, satirical, scoffing, sneering, with
tongue in cheek, wry **2** = **paradoxical**,
incongruous

iron out *verb* = **settle**, clear up, eliminate,
eradicate, erase, expedite, get rid of,
harmonize, put right, reconcile, resolve,
simplify, smooth over, sort out, straighten
out, unravel

irons *plural noun* = **chains**, bonds, fetters,
gyves (*archaic*), manacles, shackles

irony *noun* **1** = **sarcasm**, mockery, satire **2**
= **paradox**, contrariness, incongruity

irrational *adjective* **1** = **illogical**, absurd,
crackpot (*informal*), crazy, foolish,
injudicious, loopy (*informal*), nonsensical,

preposterous, silly, unreasonable,
unreasoning, unsound, unthinking, unwise
2 = **senseless**, aberrant, brainless, crazy,
demented, insane, mindless,
muddle-headed, raving, unstable, wild
➤ **Antonyms**
≠**illogical**: circumspect, judicious, logical,
rational, reasonable, sensible, sound, wise

irrationality *noun* = **senselessness**,
absurdity, brainlessness, illogicality,
insanity, lack of judgment, lunacy,
madness, preposterousness,
unreasonableness, unsoundness

irreconcilable *adjective* **1** = **incompatible**,
clashing, conflicting, diametrically
opposed, incongruous, inconsistent,
opposed **2** = **inflexible**, hardline,
implacable, inexorable, intransigent,
unappeasable, uncompromising

irrecoverable *adjective* = **lost**, gone for
ever, irreclaimable, irredeemable,
irremediable, irreparable, irretrievable,
unregainable, unsalvageable, unsavable

irrefutable *adjective* = **undeniable**,
apodeictic, apodictic, beyond question,
certain, incontestable, incontrovertible,
indisputable, indubitable, invincible,
irrefragable, irresistible, sure,
unanswerable, unassailable,
unquestionable

irregular *adjective* **1** = **uneven**,
asymmetrical, broken, bumpy, craggy,
crooked, elliptic, elliptical, holey, jagged,
lopsided, lumpy, pitted, ragged, rough,
serrated, unequal, unsymmetrical **2**
= **variable**, desultory, disconnected,
eccentric, erratic, fitful, fluctuating,
fragmentary, haphazard, inconstant,
intermittent, nonuniform, occasional, out
of order, patchy, random, shifting,
spasmodic, sporadic, uncertain, uneven,
unmethodical, unpunctual, unsteady,
unsystematic, wavering **3**
= **unconventional**, abnormal, anomalous,
capricious, disorderly, eccentric,
exceptional, extraordinary, immoderate,
improper, inappropriate, inordinate, odd,
peculiar, queer, quirky, rum (*Brit. slang*),
unofficial, unorthodox, unsuitable, unusual
♦ *noun* **4** = **guerrilla**, partisan, volunteer
➤ **Antonyms**
adjective ≠**uneven**: balanced, equal, even,
regular, smooth, symmetrical ≠**variable**:
certain, invariable, methodical, punctual,
reliable, steady, systematic
≠**unconventional**: appropriate,
conventional, normal, orthodox, proper,
regular, standard, usual

irregularity *noun* **1** = **unevenness**,
asymmetry, bumpiness, crookedness,

jaggedness, lack of symmetry, lopsidedness, lumpiness, patchiness, raggedness, roughness, spottiness **2 = uncertainty**, confusion, desultoriness, disorderliness, disorganization, haphazardness, lack of method, randomness, unpunctuality, unsteadiness **3 = abnormality**, aberration, anomaly, breach, deviation, eccentricity, freak, malfunction, malpractice, oddity, peculiarity, singularity, unconventionality, unorthodoxy

irregularly *adverb* = **erratically**, anyhow, by fits and starts, disconnectedly, eccentrically, fitfully, haphazardly, in snatches, intermittently, jerkily, now and again, occasionally, off and on, out of sequence, spasmodically, unevenly, unmethodically, unpunctually

irrelevance, irrelevancy *noun* = **inappropriateness**, inappositeness, inaptness, inconsequence, non sequitur
➤ **Antonyms**
appositeness, appropriateness, aptness, consequence, pertinence, point, relevance, suitability

irrelevant *adjective* = **unconnected**, beside the point, extraneous, immaterial, impertinent, inapplicable, inapposite, inappropriate, inapt, inconsequent, neither here nor there, unrelated
➤ **Antonyms**
applicable, apposite, appropriate, apt, connected, fitting, pertinent, related, relevant, suitable

irreparable *adjective* = **beyond repair**, incurable, irrecoverable, irremediable, irreplaceable, irretrievable, irreversible

irreplaceable *adjective* = **indispensable**, invaluable, priceless, unique, vital

irrepressible *adjective* = **ebullient**, boisterous, bubbling over, buoyant, effervescent, insuppressible, uncontainable, uncontrollable, unmanageable, unquenchable, unrestrainable, unstoppable

irreproachable *adjective* = **blameless**, beyond reproach, faultless, guiltless, impeccable, inculpable, innocent, irreprehensible, irreprovable, perfect, pure, squeaky-clean, unblemished, unimpeachable

irresistible *adjective* **1 = overwhelming**, compelling, compulsive, imperative, overmastering, overpowering, potent, urgent **2 = seductive**, alluring, beckoning, enchanting, fascinating, ravishing, tempting **3 = inescapable**, ineluctable, inevitable, inexorable, unavoidable

irresolute *adjective* = **indecisive**, doubtful,

fickle, half-arsed (*Brit. slang*), half-assed (*U.S. & Canad. slang*), half-hearted, hesitant, hesitating, infirm, in two minds, tentative, undecided, undetermined, unsettled, unstable, unsteady, vacillating, wavering, weak
➤ **Antonyms**
decisive, determined, firm, fixed, resolute, resolved, settled, stable, stalwart, steadfast, steady, strong

irrespective of *preposition* = **despite**, apart from, discounting, in spite of, notwithstanding, regardless of, without reference to, without regard to

irresponsible *adjective* = **thoughtless**, careless, featherbrained, flighty, giddy, good-for-nothing, harebrained, harum-scarum, ill-considered, immature, reckless, scatterbrained, shiftless, undependable, unreliable, untrustworthy, wild
➤ **Antonyms**
careful, dependable, level-headed, mature, reliable, responsible, sensible, trustworthy

irreverence *noun* = **disrespect**, cheek (*informal*), cheekiness (*informal*), chutzpah (*U.S. & Canad. informal*), derision, flippancy, impertinence, impudence, lack of respect, mockery, sauce (*informal*)

irreverent *adjective* = **disrespectful**, cheeky (*informal*), contemptuous, derisive, flip (*informal*), flippant, fresh (*informal*), iconoclastic, impertinent, impious, impudent, mocking, sassy (*U.S. informal*), saucy, tongue-in-cheek
➤ **Antonyms**
awed, deferential, meek, pious, respectful, reverent, submissive

irreversible *adjective* = **irrevocable**, final, incurable, irreparable, unalterable

irrevocable *adjective* = **fixed**, changeless, fated, immutable, invariable, irremediable, irretrievable, irreversible, predestined, predetermined, settled, unalterable, unchangeable, unreversible

irrigate *verb* = **water**, flood, inundate, moisten, wet

irritability *noun* = **bad temper**, ill humour, impatience, irascibility, peevishness, petulance, prickliness, testiness, tetchiness, touchiness
➤ **Antonyms**
bonhomie, cheerfulness, complacence, good humour, patience

irritable *adjective* = **bad-tempered**, cantankerous, choleric, crabbed, crabby, cross, crotchety (*informal*), dyspeptic, edgy, exasperated, fiery, fretful, hasty, hot, ill-humoured, ill-tempered, irascible, narky (*Brit. slang*), out of humour, oversensitive,

peevish, petulant, prickly, ratty (*Brit. & N.Z. informal*), snappish, snappy, snarling, tense, testy, tetchy, touchy
➤ **Antonyms**
agreeable, calm, cheerful, complacent, composed, even-tempered, good-natured, imperturbable, patient, unexcitable

irritate *verb* **1 = annoy**, aggravate (*informal*), anger, bother, drive one up the wall (*slang*), enrage, exasperate, fret, gall, get in one's hair (*informal*), get one's back up, get one's dander up (*informal*), get one's goat (*slang*), get one's hackles up, get on one's nerves (*informal*), get on one's wick (*informal*), get under one's skin (*informal*), harass, incense, inflame, infuriate, nark (*Brit., Austral., & N.Z. slang*), needle (*informal*), nettle, offend, pester, piss one off (*taboo slang*), provoke, put one's back up, raise one's hackles, rankle with, rub up the wrong way (*informal*), ruffle, try one's patience, vex **2 = rub**, aggravate, chafe, fret, inflame, intensify, pain
➤ **Antonyms**
≠**annoy**: calm, comfort, gratify, mollify, placate, please, soothe

irritated *adjective* **= annoyed**, angry, bothered, cross, displeased, exasperated, flustered, hacked (off) (*U.S. slang*), harassed, impatient, irritable, nettled, out of humour, peeved (*informal*), piqued, pissed (*taboo slang*), pissed off (*taboo slang*), put out, ruffled, vexed

irritating *adjective* **= annoying**, aggravating (*informal*), displeasing, disquieting, disturbing, galling, infuriating, irksome, maddening, nagging, pestilential, provoking, thorny, troublesome, trying, upsetting, vexatious, worrisome
➤ **Antonyms**
agreeable, assuaging, calming, comforting, mollifying, pleasant, pleasing, quieting, soothing

irritation *noun* **1 = annoyance**, anger, crossness, displeasure, exasperation, ill humour, ill temper, impatience, indignation, irritability, resentment, shortness, snappiness, testiness, vexation, wrath **2 = nuisance**, aggravation (*informal*), annoyance, drag (*informal*), gall, goad, irritant, pain (*informal*), pain in the arse (*taboo informal*), pain in the neck (*informal*), pest, provocation, tease, thorn in one's flesh
➤ **Antonyms**
≠**annoyance**: calm, composure, ease, pleasure, quietude, satisfaction, serenity, tranquillity

island *noun* **= isle**, ait *or* eyot (*dialect*), atoll,

cay *or* key, islet

isolate *verb* **= separate**, cut off, detach, disconnect, divorce, insulate, quarantine, segregate, sequester, set apart

isolated *adjective* **1 = remote**, backwoods, hidden, incommunicado, in the middle of nowhere, lonely, off the beaten track, outlying, out-of-the-way, retired, secluded, unfrequented **2 = random**, abnormal, anomalous, exceptional, freak, out on a limb, single, solitary, special, unique, unrelated, untypical, unusual

isolation *noun* **= separation**, aloofness, detachment, disconnection, exile, insularity, insulation, ivory tower, loneliness, quarantine, remoteness, retirement, seclusion, segregation, self-sufficiency, solitude, withdrawal

issue *noun* **1 = topic**, affair, argument, bone of contention, can of worms (*informal*), concern, controversy, matter, matter of contention, point, point in question, problem, question, subject **2 = edition**, copy, impression, instalment, number, printing **3 = outcome**, conclusion, consequence, culmination, effect, end, end result, finale, pay-off (*informal*), result, termination, upshot **4 = children**, descendants, heirs, offspring, progeny, scions, seed (*chiefly biblical*) **5 = distribution**, circulation, delivery, dispersal, dissemination, granting, issuance, issuing, publication, sending out, supply, supplying **6 at issue = under discussion**, at variance, controversial, in disagreement, in dispute, to be decided, unsettled **7 take issue = disagree**, challenge, dispute, object, oppose, raise an objection, take exception ♦ *verb* **8 = give out**, announce, broadcast, circulate, deliver, distribute, emit, promulgate, publish, put in circulation, put out, release **9 = emerge**, arise, be a consequence of, come forth, emanate, flow, originate, proceed, rise, spring, stem
➤ **Antonyms**
noun ≠**outcome**: beginning, cause, inception, start ≠**children**: parent, sire ≠**distribution**: cancellation, recall ♦ *verb* ≠**give out**: revoke, withdraw ≠**emerge**: cause

isthmus *noun* **= strip**, spit

itch *noun* **1 = irritation**, itchiness, prickling, tingling **2 = desire**, craving, hankering, hunger, longing, lust, passion, restlessness, yearning, yen (*informal*) ♦ *verb* **3 = prickle**, crawl, irritate, tickle, tingle **4 = long**, ache, burn, crave, hanker, hunger, lust, pant, pine, yearn

itching *adjective* **= longing**, agog, aquiver,

atremble, avid, burning, consumed with curiosity, eager, impatient, inquisitive, mad keen (*informal*), raring, spoiling for

itchy *adjective* = **impatient**, eager, edgy, fidgety, restive, restless, unsettled

item *noun* 1 = **detail**, article, aspect, component, consideration, entry, matter, particular, point, thing 2 = **report**, account, article, bulletin, dispatch, feature, note, notice, paragraph, piece

itemize *verb* = **list**, count, detail, document, enumerate, instance, inventory, number, particularize, record,

set out, specify

itinerant *adjective* = **wandering**, ambulatory, Gypsy, journeying, migratory, nomadic, peripatetic, roaming, roving, travelling, unsettled, vagabond, vagrant, wayfaring

➤ **Antonyms**
established, fixed, resident, rooted, settled, stable

itinerary *noun* 1 = **schedule**, circuit, journey, line, programme, route, timetable, tour 2 = **guidebook**, Baedeker, guide

J j

jab *verb, noun* = **poke**, dig, lunge, nudge, prod, punch, stab, tap, thrust

jabber *verb* = **chatter**, babble, blether, gabble, mumble, prate, rabbit (on) (*Brit. informal*), ramble, yap (*informal*)

jacket *noun* = **covering**, case, casing, coat, envelope, folder, sheath, skin, wrapper, wrapping

jackpot *noun* = **prize**, award, bonanza, kitty, pool, pot, pot of gold at the end of the rainbow, reward, winnings

jack up *verb* 1 = **lift**, elevate, heave, hoist, lift up, raise, rear 2 = **increase**, accelerate, augment, boost, escalate, inflate, put up, raise

jaded *adjective* 1 = **tired**, clapped out (*Austral. & N.Z. informal*), exhausted, fagged (out) (*informal*), fatigued, spent, tired-out, weary, zonked (*slang*) 2 = **bored**, cloyed, dulled, glutted, gorged, sated, satiated, surfeited, tired
➤ **Antonyms**
≠**tired**: bright-eyed and bushy-tailed (*informal*), fresh, refreshed ≠**bored**: eager, enthusiastic, keen

jagged *adjective* = **uneven**, barbed, broken, cleft, craggy, denticulate, indented, notched, pointed, ragged, ridged, rough, serrated, snaggy, spiked, toothed
➤ **Antonyms**
glassy, level, regular, rounded, smooth

jail, gaol *noun* 1 = **prison**, borstal, brig (*chiefly U.S.*), calaboose (*U.S. informal*), can (*slang*), clink (*slang*), cooler (*slang*), inside (*slang*), jailhouse (*Southern U.S.*), jug (*slang*), lockup, nick (*Brit. slang*), penitentiary (*U.S.*), poky or pokey (*U.S. & Canad. slang*), quod (*slang*), reformatory, slammer (*slang*), stir (*slang*) ♦ *verb* 2 = **imprison**, confine, detain, immure, impound, incarcerate, lock up, send down

jailer, gaoler *noun* = **guard**, captor, keeper, screw (*slang*), turnkey (*archaic*), warden, warder

jam *verb* 1 = **pack**, cram, force, press, ram, squeeze, stuff, wedge 2 = **crowd**, crush, throng 3 = **congest**, block, cease, clog, halt, obstruct, stall, stick ♦ *noun* 4 = **crush**, crowd, horde, mass, mob, multitude, pack, press, swarm, throng 5 = **predicament**, bind, deep water, dilemma, fix (*informal*), hole (*slang*), hot

water, pickle (*informal*), plight, quandary, scrape (*informal*), spot (*informal*), strait, tight spot, trouble

jamboree *noun* = **festival**, beano (*Brit. slang*), blast (*U.S. slang*), carnival, carousal, carouse, celebration, festivity, fête, frolic, hooley *or* hoolie (*chiefly Irish & N.Z.*), jubilee, merriment, party, rave (*Brit. slang*), rave-up (*Brit. slang*), revelry, spree

jangle *verb* 1 = **rattle**, chime, clank, clash, clatter, jingle, vibrate ♦ *noun* 2 = **clash**, cacophony, clang, clangour, din, dissonance, jar, racket, rattle, reverberation
➤ **Antonyms**
noun ≠**clash**: harmoniousness, mellifluousness, quiet, silence

janitor *noun* = **caretaker**, concierge, custodian, doorkeeper, porter

jar¹ *noun* = **pot**, amphora, carafe, container, crock, flagon, jug, pitcher, receptacle, urn, vase, vessel

jar² *verb* 1 = **irritate**, annoy, clash, discompose, gall, get on one's nerves (*informal*), grate, grind, irk, nark (*Brit., Austral., & N.Z. slang*), nettle, offend, piss one off (*taboo slang*) 2 = **clash**, bicker, contend, disagree, interfere, oppose, quarrel, wrangle 3 = **jolt**, agitate, bump, convulse, disturb, grate, rasp, rattle, rock, shake, vibrate ♦ *noun* 4 = **jolt**, bump, convulsion, shock, vibration

jargon *noun* 1 = **parlance**, argot, cant, dialect, idiom, lingo (*informal*), patois, patter, slang, tongue, usage 2 = **gobbledegook**, balderdash, bunkum *or* buncombe (*chiefly U.S.*), drivel, gabble, gibberish, Greek (*informal*), mumbo jumbo, nonsense, palaver, rigmarole, twaddle

jaundiced *adjective* 1 = **cynical**, preconceived, sceptical 2 = **bitter**, biased, bigoted, distorted, envious, hostile, jealous, partial, prejudiced, resentful, spiteful, suspicious
➤ **Antonyms**
≠**cynical**: credulous, ingenuous, naive, optimistic ≠**bitter**: open-minded, trusting, unbiased

jaunt *noun* = **outing**, airing, excursion, expedition, promenade, ramble, stroll, tour, trip

jaunty *adjective* = **sprightly**, airy, breezy, buoyant, carefree, dapper, gay, high-spirited, lively, perky, self-confident, showy, smart, sparky, spruce, trim
➤ **Antonyms**
dignified, dull, lifeless, sedate, serious, staid

jaw *Slang* ♦ *noun* **1** = **chat**, chinwag (*Brit. informal*), conversation, gabfest (*informal, chiefly U.S. & Canad.*), gossip, natter, talk ♦ *verb* **2** = **talk**, babble, chat, chatter, chew the fat *or* rag (*slang*), gossip, lecture, run off at the mouth (*slang*), spout

jaws *plural noun* = **opening**, abyss, aperture, entrance, gates, ingress, maw, mouth, orifice

jazz up *verb* = **enliven**, animate, enhance, heighten, improve

jazzy *adjective* = **flashy**, animated, fancy, gaudy, lively, smart, snazzy (*informal*), spirited, vivacious, wild, zestful

jealous *adjective* **1** = **suspicious**, anxious, apprehensive, attentive, guarded, mistrustful, possessive, protective, solicitous, vigilant, wary, watchful, zealous **2** = **envious**, covetous, desirous, emulous, green, green-eyed, grudging, intolerant, invidious, resentful, rival
➤ **Antonyms**
≠**suspicious**: carefree, indifferent, trusting ≠**envious**: satisfied

jealousy *noun* = **envy**, covetousness, distrust, heart-burning, ill-will, mistrust, possessiveness, resentment, spite, suspicion

jeans *plural noun* = **denims**, Levis (*Trademark*)

jeer *verb* **1** = **mock**, banter, barrack, cock a snook at (*Brit.*), contemn (*formal*), deride, flout, gibe, heckle, hector, knock (*informal*), ridicule, scoff, sneer, taunt ♦ *noun* **2** = **mockery**, abuse, aspersion, boo, catcall, derision, gibe, hiss, hoot, obloquy, ridicule, scoff, sneer, taunt
➤ **Antonyms**
verb ≠**mock**: acclaim, applaud, cheer, clap, praise ♦ *noun* ≠**mockery**: adulation, applause, cheers, encouragement, praise

jell *verb* **1** = **take shape**, come together, crystallize, finalize, form, materialize **2** = **solidify**, congeal, harden, set, thicken

jeopardize *verb* = **endanger**, chance, expose, gamble, hazard, imperil, risk, stake, venture

jeopardy *noun* = **danger**, endangerment, exposure, hazard, insecurity, liability, peril, pitfall, precariousness, risk, venture, vulnerability

jeremiad *noun* = **complaint**, groan, keen, lament, lamentation, moan, plaint, wail

jerk *verb, noun* = **tug**, jolt, lurch, pull, throw, thrust, tweak, twitch, wrench, yank

jerky *adjective* = **bumpy**, bouncy, convulsive, fitful, jolting, jumpy, rough, shaky, spasmodic, tremulous, twitchy, uncontrolled
➤ **Antonyms**
flowing, frictionless, gliding, smooth

jerry-built *adjective* = **ramshackle**, cheap, defective, faulty, flimsy, rickety, shabby, slipshod, thrown together, unsubstantial
➤ **Antonyms**
sturdy, substantial, well-built, well-constructed

jest *noun* **1** = **joke**, banter, bon mot, crack (*slang*), fun, gag (*informal*), hoax, jape, josh (*slang, chiefly U.S. & Canad.*), play, pleasantry, prank, quip, sally, sport, wisecrack (*informal*), witticism ♦ *verb* **2** = **joke**, banter, chaff, deride, gibe, jeer, josh (*slang, chiefly U.S. & Canad.*), kid (*informal*), mock, quip, scoff, sneer, tease

jester *noun* **1** = **clown**, buffoon, fool, harlequin, madcap, mummer, pantaloon, prankster, zany **2** = **humorist**, comedian, comic, joculator *or (fem.)* joculatrix, joker, quipster, wag, wit

jet¹ *noun* **1** = **stream**, flow, fountain, gush, spout, spray, spring **2** = **nozzle**, atomizer, nose, rose, spout, sprayer, sprinkler ♦ *verb* **3** = **fly**, soar, zoom **4** = **stream**, flow, gush, issue, rush, shoot, spew, spout, squirt, surge

jet² *adjective* = **black**, coal-black, ebony, inky, pitch-black, raven, sable

jettison *verb* = **abandon**, discard, dump, eject, expel, heave, scrap, throw overboard, unload

jetty *noun* = **pier**, breakwater, dock, groyne, mole, quay, wharf

jewel *noun* **1** = **gemstone**, brilliant, ornament, precious stone, rock (*slang*), sparkler (*informal*), trinket **2** = **rarity**, charm, collector's item, find, gem, humdinger (*slang*), masterpiece, paragon, pearl, prize, treasure, wonder

jewellery *noun* = **jewels**, finery, gems, ornaments, precious stones, regalia, treasure, trinkets

Jezebel *noun* = **harlot**, harridan, hussy, jade, virago, wanton, witch

jib *verb* = **refuse**, balk, recoil, retreat, shrink, stop short

jibe *see* GIBE

jig *verb* = **skip**, bob, bounce, caper, jiggle, jounce, prance, shake, twitch, wiggle, wobble

jingle *noun* **1** = **song**, chorus, ditty, doggerel, limerick, melody, tune **2** = **rattle**, clang, clangour, clink, reverberation, ringing, tinkle ◆ *verb* **3** = **ring**, chime, clatter, clink, jangle, rattle, tinkle, tintinnabulate

jinx *noun* **1** = **curse**, black magic, evil eye, hex (*U.S. & Canad. informal*), hoodoo (*informal*), nemesis, plague, voodoo ◆ *verb* **2** = **curse**, bewitch, hex (*U.S. & Canad. informal*)

jitters *plural noun* = **nerves**, anxiety, butterflies (in one's stomach) (*informal*), cold feet (*informal*), fidgets, heebie-jeebies (*slang*), nervousness, tenseness, the shakes (*informal*), the willies (*informal*)

jittery *adjective* = **nervous**, agitated, antsy (*informal*), anxious, fidgety, hyper (*informal*), jumpy, neurotic, quivering, shaky, trembling, twitchy (*informal*), wired (*slang*)
➤ **Antonyms**
calm, composed, laid-back (*informal*), relaxed, together (*slang*), unfazed (*informal*), unflustered

job *noun* **1** = **occupation**, activity, bread and butter (*informal*), business, calling, capacity, career, craft, employment, function, livelihood, métier, office, position, post, profession, situation, trade, vocation **2** = **task**, affair, assignment, charge, chore, concern, contribution, duty, enterprise, errand, function, pursuit, responsibility, role, stint, undertaking, venture, work **3** = **consignment**, allotment, assignment, batch, commission, contract, lot, output, piece, portion, product, share

jobless *adjective* = **unemployed**, idle, inactive, out of work, unoccupied

jockey *verb* = **manoeuvre**, cajole, engineer, finagle (*informal*), ingratiate, insinuate, manage, manipulate, negotiate, trim, wheedle

jocular *adjective* = **humorous**, amusing, comical, droll, facetious, frolicsome, funny, jesting, jocose, jocund, joking, jolly, jovial, ludic (*literary*), playful, roguish, sportive, teasing, waggish, whimsical, witty
➤ **Antonyms**
earnest, humourless, serious, solemn

jog *verb* **1** = **run**, canter, dogtrot, lope, trot **2** = **nudge**, activate, arouse, prod, prompt, push, remind, shake, stimulate, stir, suggest **3** = **plod**, lumber, traipse (*informal*), tramp, trudge

joie de vivre *noun* = **enthusiasm**, ebullience, enjoyment, gaiety, gusto, joy, joyfulness, pleasure, relish, zest
➤ **Antonyms**
apathy, depression, distaste

join *verb* **1** = **enrol**, affiliate with, associate with, enlist, enter, sign up **2** = **meet**, adjoin, border, border on, butt, conjoin,

extend, reach, touch, verge on **3** = **connect**, accompany, add, adhere, annex, append, attach, cement, combine, couple, fasten, knit, link, marry, splice, tie, unite, yoke
➤ **Antonyms**
≠**enrol**: leave, part, quit, resign ≠**connect**: detach, disconnect, disengage, disentangle, divide, separate, sever, unfasten

joint *adjective* **1** = **shared**, collective, combined, communal, concerted, consolidated, cooperative, joined, mutual, united ◆ *noun* **2** = **junction**, articulation, connection, hinge, intersection, juncture, knot, nexus, node, seam, union ◆ *verb* **3** = **join**, connect, couple, fasten, fit, unite **4** = **divide**, carve, cut up, dismember, dissect, segment, sever, sunder

jointly *adverb* = **collectively**, as one, in common, in conjunction, in league, in partnership, mutually, together, unitedly
➤ **Antonyms**
individually, separately, singly

joke *noun* **1** = **jest**, frolic, fun, gag (*informal*), jape, josh (*slang, chiefly U.S. & Canad.*), lark, play, prank, pun, quip, quirk, sally, sport, whimsy, wisecrack (*informal*), witticism, yarn **2** = **laughing stock**, buffoon, butt, clown, simpleton, target ◆ *verb* **3** = **jest**, banter, chaff, deride, frolic, gambol, josh (*slang, chiefly U.S. & Canad.*), kid (*informal*), mock, play the fool, quip, ridicule, taunt, tease, wind up (*Brit. slang*)

joker *noun* = **comedian**, buffoon, clown, comic, humorist, jester, kidder (*informal*), prankster, trickster, wag, wit

jolly *adjective* = **happy**, blithesome, carefree, cheerful, chirpy (*informal*), convivial, festive, frolicsome, funny, gay, genial, gladsome (*archaic*), hilarious, jocund, jovial, joyful, joyous, jubilant, ludic (*literary*), merry, mirthful, playful, sportive, sprightly, upbeat (*informal*)
➤ **Antonyms**
doleful, down in the dumps (*informal*), grave, lugubrious, miserable, morose, serious, solemn

jolt *noun* **1** = **surprise**, blow, bolt from the blue, bombshell, reversal, setback, shock, thunderbolt, whammy (*informal, chiefly U.S.*) **2** = **jerk**, bump, jar, jog, jump, lurch, quiver, shake, start ◆ *verb* **3** = **surprise**, astonish, discompose, disturb, perturb, stagger, startle, stun, upset **4** = **jerk**, jar, jog, jostle, knock, push, shake, shove

jostle *verb* = **push**, bump, butt, crowd, elbow, hustle, jog, joggle, jolt, press, scramble, shake, shove, squeeze, throng, thrust

jot *verb* 1 = **note down**, list, note, record, register, scribble, tally ♦ *noun* 2 = **bit**, ace, atom, detail, fraction, grain, iota, mite, morsel, particle, scintilla, scrap, smidgen *or* smidgin (*informal, chiefly U.S. & Canad.*), speck, tad (*informal, chiefly U.S.*), tittle, trifle, whit

journal *noun* 1 = **newspaper**, chronicle, daily, gazette, magazine, monthly, paper, periodical, record, register, review, tabloid, weekly, zine (*informal*) 2 = **diary**, chronicle, commonplace book, daybook, log, record

journalist *noun* = **reporter**, broadcaster, columnist, commentator, contributor, correspondent, hack, journo (*slang*), newsman *or* newswoman, newspaperman *or* newspaperwoman, pressman, scribe (*informal*), stringer

journey *noun* 1 = **trip**, excursion, expedition, jaunt, odyssey, outing, passage, peregrination, pilgrimage, progress, ramble, tour, travel, trek, voyage ♦ *verb* 2 = **travel**, fare, fly, go, peregrinate, proceed, ramble, range, roam, rove, tour, traverse, trek, voyage, wander, wend

jovial *adjective* = **cheerful**, airy, animated, blithe, buoyant, cheery, convivial, cordial, gay, glad, happy, hilarious, jocose, jocund, jolly, jubilant, merry, mirthful
➤ **Antonyms**
antisocial, doleful, grumpy, morose, solemn, unfriendly

joy *noun* 1 = **delight**, bliss, ecstasy, elation, exaltation, exultation, felicity, festivity, gaiety, gladness, glee, hilarity, pleasure, rapture, ravishment, satisfaction, transport 2 = **treasure**, charm, delight, gem, jewel, pride, prize, treat, wonder
➤ **Antonyms**
≠**delight:** despair, grief, misery, sorrow, tribulation, unhappiness ≠**treasure:** bane

joyful *adjective* = **delighted**, blithesome, cock-a-hoop, elated, enraptured, floating on air, glad, gladsome (*archaic*), gratified, happy, jocund, jolly, jovial, jubilant, light-hearted, merry, on cloud nine (*informal*), over the moon (*informal*), pleased, rapt, satisfied

joyless *adjective* = **unhappy**, cheerless, dejected, depressed, dismal, dispirited, downcast, down in the dumps (*informal*), dreary, gloomy, miserable, sad

joyous *adjective* = **joyful**, blithe, cheerful, festive, heartening, merry, rapturous

jubilant *adjective* = **overjoyed**, cock-a-hoop, elated, enraptured, euphoric, excited, exuberant, exultant, glad, joyous, over the moon (*informal*), rejoicing, rhapsodic, thrilled, triumphal,

triumphant
➤ **Antonyms**
despondent, doleful, downcast, melancholy, sad, sorrowful

jubilation *noun* = **joy**, celebration, ecstasy, elation, excitement, exultation, festivity, jamboree, jubilee, triumph

jubilee *noun* = **celebration**, carnival, festival, festivity, fête, gala, holiday

judge *noun* 1 = **magistrate**, beak (*Brit. slang*), justice 2 = **referee**, adjudicator, arbiter, arbitrator, moderator, umpire 3 = **critic**, appraiser, arbiter, assessor, authority, connoisseur, evaluator, expert ♦ *verb* 4 = **adjudicate**, adjudge, arbitrate, ascertain, conclude, decide, determine, discern, distinguish, mediate, referee, umpire 5 = **consider**, appraise, appreciate, assess, criticize, esteem, estimate, evaluate, examine, rate, review, value 6 = **try**, adjudge, condemn, decree, doom, find, pass sentence, pronounce sentence, rule, sentence, sit

judgment *noun* 1 = **opinion**, appraisal, assessment, belief, conviction, deduction, diagnosis, estimate, finding, valuation, view 2 = **verdict**, arbitration, award, conclusion, decision, decree, determination, finding, order, result, ruling, sentence 3 = **sense**, acumen, common sense, discernment, discrimination, intelligence, penetration, percipience, perspicacity, prudence, sagacity, shrewdness, smarts (*slang, chiefly U.S.*), taste, understanding, wisdom 4 = **punishment**, damnation, doom, fate, misfortune, retribution

judicial *adjective* 1 = **legal**, judiciary, juridical, official 2 = **discriminating**, distinguished, impartial, judgelike, magisterial, magistral

judicious *adjective* = **sensible**, acute, astute, careful, cautious, circumspect, considered, diplomatic, discerning, discreet, discriminating, enlightened, expedient, informed, politic, prudent, rational, reasonable, sagacious, sage, sane, sapient, shrewd, skilful, sober, sound, thoughtful, well-advised, well-judged, wise
➤ **Antonyms**
imprudent, indiscreet, injudicious, tactless, thoughtless

jug *noun* = **container**, carafe, crock, ewer, jar, pitcher, urn, vessel

juggle *verb* = **manipulate**, alter, change, disguise, doctor (*informal*), falsify, fix (*informal*), manoeuvre, misrepresent, modify, tamper with

juice *noun* = **liquid**, extract, fluid, liquor, nectar, sap, secretion, serum

juicy *adjective* **1** = **moist**, lush, sappy, succulent, watery **2** *Informal* = **interesting**, colourful, provocative, racy, risqué, sensational, spicy (*informal*), suggestive, vivid

jumble *noun* **1** = **muddle**, chaos, clutter, confusion, disarrangement, disarray, disorder, farrago, gallimaufry, hodgepodge, hotchpotch (*U.S.*), litter, medley, *mélange,* mess, miscellany, mishmash, mixture, pig's breakfast (*informal*) ♦ *verb* **2** = **mix**, confound, confuse, disarrange, dishevel, disorder, disorganize, entangle, mistake, muddle, ravel, shuffle, tangle

jumbo *adjective* = **giant**, elephantine, gigantic, ginormous (*informal*), huge, humongous *or* humungous (*U.S. slang*), immense, large, mega (*informal*), oversized
➤ **Antonyms**
baby, dwarf, micro, mini, pocket, tiny, wee

jump *verb* **1** = **leap**, bounce, bound, caper, clear, gambol, hop, hurdle, skip, spring, vault **2** = **recoil**, flinch, jerk, start, wince **3** = **increase**, advance, ascend, boost, escalate, gain, hike, mount, rise, surge **4** = **miss**, avoid, digress, evade, omit, overshoot, skip, switch ♦ *noun* **5** = **leap**, bound, buck, caper, hop, skip, spring, vault **6** = **rise**, advance, augmentation, boost, increase, increment, upsurge, upturn **7** = **interruption**, breach, break, gap, hiatus, lacuna, space **8** = **jolt**, jar, jerk, lurch, shock, start, swerve, twitch, wrench **9** = **hurdle**, barricade, barrier, fence, impediment, obstacle, rail

jumped-up *adjective* = **conceited**, arrogant, cocky, immodest, insolent, overbearing, pompous, presumptuous, puffed up, self-opinionated, stuck-up, toffee-nosed, too big for one's boots *or* breeches

jumper *noun* = **sweater**, jersey, pullover, woolly

jumpy *adjective* = **nervous**, agitated, antsy (*informal*), anxious, apprehensive, fidgety, hyper (*informal*), jittery (*informal*), neurotic, on edge, restless, shaky, tense, timorous, twitchy (*informal*), wired (*slang*)
➤ **Antonyms**
calm, composed, laid-back (*informal*), together (*slang*), unfazed (*informal*), unflustered

junction *noun* = **connection**, alliance, combination, coupling, joint, juncture, linking, seam, union

juncture *noun* **1** = **moment**, conjuncture, contingency, crisis, crux, emergency, exigency, occasion, point, predicament, strait, time **2** = **junction**, bond, connection, convergence, edge, intersection, link, seam, weld

junior *adjective* = **minor**, inferior, lesser, lower, secondary, subordinate, younger
➤ **Antonyms**
elder, higher-ranking, older, senior, superior

junk *noun* = **rubbish**, clutter, debris, dreck (*slang, chiefly U.S.*), leavings, litter, oddments, odds and ends, refuse, rummage, scrap, trash, waste

jurisdiction *noun* **1** = **authority**, command, control, dominion, influence, power, prerogative, rule, say, sway **2** = **range**, area, bounds, circuit, compass, district, dominion, field, orbit, province, scope, sphere, zone

just *adverb* **1** = **recently**, hardly, lately, only now, scarcely **2** = **merely**, at a push, at most, but, by the skin of one's teeth, no more than, nothing but, only, simply, solely **3** = **exactly**, absolutely, completely, entirely, perfectly, precisely ♦ *adjective* **4** = **fair**, blameless, conscientious, decent, equitable, fair-minded, good, honest, honourable, impartial, lawful, pure, right, righteous, unbiased, upright, virtuous **5** = **correct**, accurate, exact, faithful, normal, precise, proper, regular, sound, true **6** = **fitting**, appropriate, apt, condign, deserved, due, justified, legitimate, merited, proper, reasonable, rightful, sensible, suitable, well-deserved
➤ **Antonyms**
adjective ≠**fair**: corrupt, devious, dishonest, inequitable, prejudiced, unfair, unjust, unlawful ≠**correct**: untrue ≠**fitting**: inappropriate, undeserved, unfit, unreasonable

just about *adverb* = **practically**, all but, almost, around, close to, nearly, not quite, virtually, well-nigh

justice *noun* **1** = **fairness**, equity, honesty, impartiality, integrity, justness, law, legality, legitimacy, reasonableness, rectitude, right **2** = **amends**, compensation, correction, penalty, recompense, redress, reparation **3** = **judge**, magistrate
➤ **Antonyms**
≠**fairness**: dishonesty, favouritism, inequity, injustice, partiality, unfairness, unlawfulness, unreasonableness, wrong

justifiable *adjective* = **reasonable**, acceptable, defensible, excusable, fit, lawful, legitimate, proper, right, sensible, sound, tenable, understandable, valid, vindicable, warrantable, well-founded
➤ **Antonyms**

arbitrary, capricious, indefensible, inexcusable, unreasonable, unwarranted

justification *noun* **1** = **explanation**, absolution, apology, approval, defence, exculpation, excuse, exoneration, extenuation, plea, rationalization, vindication **2** = **reason**, basis, defence, grounds, plea, warrant

justify *verb* = **explain**, absolve, acquit, approve, confirm, defend, establish, exculpate, excuse, exonerate, legalize, legitimize, maintain, substantiate, support, sustain, uphold, validate, vindicate, warrant

justly *adverb* = **properly**, accurately, correctly, equally, equitably, fairly, honestly, impartially, lawfully

jut *verb* = **stick out**, bulge, extend, impend, overhang, poke, project, protrude

juvenile *adjective* **1** = **young**, babyish, boyish, callow, childish, girlish, immature, inexperienced, infantile, jejune, puerile, undeveloped, unsophisticated, youthful
♦ *noun* **2** = **child**, adolescent, boy, girl, infant, minor, youth
➤ **Antonyms**
adjective ≠**young**: adult, grown-up, mature ♦ *noun* ≠**child**: adult, grown-up

juxtaposition *noun* = **proximity**, adjacency, closeness, contact, contiguity, nearness, propinquity, vicinity

K k

kaleidoscopic *adjective* **1** = **changeable**, fluctuating, fluid, many-coloured, mobile, motley, mutable, unstable, variegated **2** = **complicated**, complex, confused, convoluted, disordered, intricate, jumbled, varied

kamikaze *adjective* = **self-destructive**, foolhardy, suicidal

keel over *verb* = **collapse**, black out (*informal*), capsize, faint, founder, overturn, pass out, swoon (*literary*), topple over, upset

keen *adjective* **1** = **eager**, ardent, avid, bright-eyed and bushy-tailed (*informal*), devoted to, earnest, ebullient, enthusiastic, fervid, fierce, fond of, impassioned, intense, into (*informal*), zealous **2** = **astute**, brilliant, canny, clever, discerning, discriminating, perceptive, perspicacious, quick, sagacious, sapient, sensitive, shrewd, wise **3** = **sharp**, acid, acute, biting, caustic, cutting, edged, finely honed, incisive, penetrating, piercing, pointed, razor-like, sardonic, satirical, tart, trenchant, vitriolic
➤ **Antonyms**
≠**eager**: apathetic, half-hearted, indifferent, lukewarm, unenthusiastic, uninterested ≠**astute**: dull, obtuse, unperceptive ≠**sharp**: blunt, dull

keenness *noun* **1** = **eagerness**, ardour, avidity, avidness, diligence, earnestness, ebullience, enthusiasm, fervour, impatience, intensity, passion, zeal, zest **2** = **astuteness**, canniness, cleverness, discernment, insight, sagacity, sapience, sensitivity, shrewdness, wisdom **3** = **sharpness**, acerbity, harshness, incisiveness, mordancy, penetration, pungency, rigour, severity, sternness, trenchancy, unkindness, virulence

keep *verb* **1** = **retain**, conserve, control, hold, maintain, possess, preserve **2** = **look after**, care for, defend, guard, maintain, manage, mind, operate, protect, safeguard, shelter, shield, tend, watch over **3** = **store**, accumulate, amass, carry, deal in, deposit, furnish, garner, heap, hold, pile, place, stack, stock, trade in **4** = **support**, board, feed, foster, maintain, nourish, nurture, provide for, provision, subsidize, sustain, victual **5** = **detain**,

arrest, block, check, constrain, control, curb, delay, deter, hamper, hamstring, hinder, hold, hold back, impede, inhibit, keep back, limit, obstruct, prevent, restrain, retard, shackle, stall, withhold **6** = **comply with**, adhere to, celebrate, commemorate, fulfil, hold, honour, obey, observe, perform, respect, ritualize, solemnize **7** = **associate with**, accompany, consort with, fraternize with ♦ *noun* **8** = **board**, food, livelihood, living, maintenance, means, nourishment, subsistence, support **9** = **tower**, castle, citadel, donjon, dungeon, fastness, stronghold
➤ **Antonyms**
verb ≠**retain**: abandon, discard, give up, lose ≠**detain**: free, liberate, release ≠**comply with**: disregard, ignore

keep at *verb* = **persist**, be steadfast, carry on, complete, continue, drudge, endure, finish, grind, labour, last, maintain, persevere, remain, slave, stay, stick, toil

keep back *verb* **1** = **restrain**, check, constrain, control, curb, delay, hold back, keep a tight rein on, limit, prohibit, restrict, retard, withhold **2** = **suppress**, censor, conceal, hide, keep dark, keep under one's hat, reserve, withhold

keeper *noun* = **guardian**, attendant, caretaker, curator, custodian, defender, governor, guard, jailer *or* gaoler, overseer, preserver, steward, superintendent, warden, warder

keeping *noun* **1** = **care**, aegis, auspices, charge, custody, guardianship, keep, maintenance, patronage, possession, protection, safekeeping, trust **2** *As in* **in keeping with** = **agreement**, accord, balance, compliance, conformity, congruity, consistency, correspondence, harmony, observance, proportion

keep on *verb* = **continue**, carry on, endure, last, persevere, persist, prolong, remain

keepsake *noun* = **souvenir**, emblem, favour, memento, relic, remembrance, reminder, symbol, token

keep up *verb* = **maintain**, balance, compete, contend, continue, emulate, keep pace, match, persevere, preserve, rival, sustain, vie

keg *noun* = **barrel**, cask, drum, firkin,

hogshead, tun, vat

kernel *noun* = **essence**, core, germ, gist, grain, marrow, nub, pith, seed, substance

key *noun* 1 = **opener**, latchkey 2 = **answer**, clue, cue, explanation, guide, indicator, interpretation, lead, means, pointer, sign, solution, translation ♦ *adjective* 3 = **essential**, basic, chief, crucial, decisive, fundamental, important, leading, main, major, pivotal, principal
➤ **Antonyms**
adjective ≠ **essential**: minor, secondary, subsidiary, superficial

key in *verb* = **type**, enter, input, keyboard

keynote *noun* = **heart**, centre, core, essence, gist, kernel, marrow, pith, substance, theme

kick *verb* 1 = **boot**, punt, put the boot in(to) (*slang*) 2 *Informal* = **resist**, complain, gripe (*informal*), grumble, object, oppose, protest, rebel, spurn 3 *Informal* = **give up**, abandon, desist from, leave off, quit, stop ♦ *noun* 4 *Informal* = **thrill**, buzz (*slang*), enjoyment, excitement, fun, gratification, jollies (*slang*), pleasure, stimulation 5 *Informal* = **pungency**, force, intensity, pep, power, punch, snap (*informal*), sparkle, strength, tang, verve, vitality, zest

kickoff *noun Informal* = **start**, beginning, commencement, opening, outset

kick off *verb Informal* = **begin**, commence, get the show on the road, get under way, initiate, kick-start, open, start

kick out *verb Informal* = **dismiss**, discharge, eject, evict, expel, get rid of, give (someone) their marching orders, give the boot (*slang*), give the bum's rush (*slang*), give the push, kiss off (*slang, chiefly U.S. & Canad.*), oust, reject, remove, sack (*informal*), show one the door, throw out on one's ear (*informal*), toss out

kid¹ *noun Informal* = **child**, ankle-biter (*Austral. slang*), baby, bairn, boy, girl, infant, lad, lass, little one, rug rat (*U.S. & Canad. informal*), sprog (*slang*), stripling, teenager, tot, youngster, youth

kid² *verb* = **tease**, bamboozle, beguile, cozen, delude, fool, gull (*archaic*), hoax, hoodwink, jest, joke, mock, plague, pretend, rag (*Brit.*), ridicule, trick, wind up (*Brit. slang*)

kidnap *verb* = **abduct**, capture, hijack, hold to ransom, remove, seize, steal

kill *verb* 1 = **slay**, annihilate, assassinate, blow away (*slang, chiefly U.S.*), bump off (*slang*), butcher, destroy, dispatch, do away with, do in (*slang*), eradicate, execute, exterminate, extirpate, knock off (*slang*), liquidate, massacre, murder,

neutralize, obliterate, slaughter, take out (*slang*), take (someone's) life, waste (*informal*), wipe from the face of the earth (*informal*) 2 *Informal* = **suppress**, cancel, cease, deaden, defeat, extinguish, halt, quash, quell, ruin, scotch, smother, stifle, still, stop, veto

killer *noun* = **assassin**, butcher, cut-throat, destroyer, executioner, exterminator, gunman, hit man (*slang*), liquidator, murderer, slaughterer, slayer

killing *adjective* 1 *Informal* = **tiring**, debilitating, enervating, exhausting, fatiguing, punishing 2 *Informal* = **hilarious**, absurd, amusing, comical, ludicrous, uproarious 3 = **deadly**, death-dealing, deathly, fatal, lethal, mortal, murderous ♦ *noun* 4 = **slaughter**, bloodshed, carnage, execution, extermination, fatality, homicide, manslaughter, massacre, murder, necktie party (*informal*), slaying 5 *Informal* = **bonanza**, bomb (*slang*), cleanup (*informal*), coup, gain, profit, success, windfall

killjoy *noun* = **spoilsport**, dampener, damper, wet blanket (*informal*)

kin *noun* = **family**, connections, kindred, kinsfolk, kinsmen, kith, people, relations, relatives

kind¹ *adjective* = **considerate**, affectionate, amiable, amicable, beneficent, benevolent, benign, bounteous, charitable, clement, compassionate, congenial, cordial, courteous, friendly, generous, gentle, good, gracious, humane, indulgent, kind-hearted, kindly, lenient, loving, mild, neighbourly, obliging, philanthropic, propitious, sympathetic, tender-hearted, thoughtful, understanding
➤ **Antonyms**
cruel, hard-hearted, harsh, heartless, merciless, severe, unkind, unsympathetic, vicious

kind² *noun* 1 = **class**, brand, breed, family, genus, ilk, race, set, sort, species, stamp, variety 2 = **nature**, character, description, essence, habit, manner, mould, persuasion, sort, style, temperament, type

kind-hearted *adjective* = **sympathetic**, altruistic, amicable, compassionate, considerate, generous, good-natured, gracious, helpful, humane, kind, tender, tender-hearted
➤ **Antonyms**
cold, cold-hearted, cruel, hard-hearted, harsh, heartless, selfish, severe, unkind, unsympathetic

kindle *verb* 1 = **set fire to**, fire, ignite, inflame, light 2 = **arouse**, agitate, animate,

awaken, bestir, enkindle, exasperate, excite, foment, incite, induce, inflame, inspire, provoke, rouse, sharpen, stimulate, stir, thrill
➤ **Antonyms**
douse, extinguish, quell, quench

kindliness *noun* = **kindness**, amiability, beneficence, benevolence, benignity, charity, compassion, friendliness, gentleness, humanity, kind-heartedness, sympathy

kindly *adjective* **1** = **benevolent**, affable, beneficial, benign, compassionate, cordial, favourable, genial, gentle, good-natured, hearty, helpful, kind, mild, pleasant, polite, sympathetic, warm ♦ *adverb* **2**
= **benevolently**, agreeably, cordially, graciously, politely, tenderly, thoughtfully
➤ **Antonyms**
adjective ≠**benevolent**: cruel, harsh, malevolent, malicious, mean, severe, spiteful, unkindly, unsympathetic ♦ *adverb*
≠**benevolently**: cruelly, harshly, malevolently, maliciously, meanly, spitefully, unkindly, unsympathetically

kindness *noun* **1** = **goodwill**, affection, amiability, beneficence, benevolence, charity, clemency, compassion, decency, fellow-feeling, generosity, gentleness, goodness, grace, hospitality, humanity, indulgence, kindliness, magnanimity, patience, philanthropy, tenderness, tolerance, understanding **2** = **good deed**, aid, assistance, benefaction, bounty, favour, generosity, help, service
➤ **Antonyms**
≠**goodwill**: animosity, callousness, cold-heartedness, cruelty, hard-heartedness, heartlessness, ill will, inhumanity, malevolence, malice, misanthropy, viciousness

kindred *adjective* **1** = **similar**, affiliated, akin, allied, cognate, congenial, corresponding, kin, like, matching, related ♦ *noun* **2** = **relationship**, affinity, consanguinity **3** = **family**, connections, flesh, kin, kinsfolk, kinsmen, lineage, relations, relatives

king *noun* = **ruler**, crowned head, emperor, majesty, monarch, overlord, prince, sovereign

kingdom *noun* **1** = **country**, commonwealth, division, nation, province, realm, state, territory, tract **2** = **domain**, area, field, province, sphere, territory

kink *noun* **1** = **twist**, bend, coil, corkscrew, crimp, entanglement, frizz, knot, tangle, wrinkle **2** = **flaw**, complication, defect, difficulty, hitch, imperfection, knot, tangle **3** = **quirk**, crotchet, eccentricity, fetish,

foible, idiosyncrasy, singularity, vagary, whim

kinky *adjective* **1** *Slang* = **perverted**, degenerated, depraved, deviant, licentious, pervy (*slang*), unnatural, warped **2** = **twisted**, coiled, crimped, curled, curly, frizzled, frizzy, tangled **3** *Slang* = **weird**, bizarre, eccentric, odd, oddball (*informal*), off-the-wall (*slang*), outlandish, outré, peculiar, queer, quirky, strange, unconventional, wacko (*slang*)

kinsfolk *plural noun* = **family**, connections, kin, kindred, kinsmen, relations, relatives

kinship *noun* **1** = **relation**, blood relationship, consanguinity, kin, ties of blood **2** = **similarity**, affinity, alliance, association, bearing, connection, correspondence, relationship

kinsman *noun* = **relative**, blood relative, fellow clansman, fellow tribesman, relation

kiosk *noun* = **booth**, bookstall, counter, newsstand, stall, stand

kiss *verb* **1** = **osculate**, buss (*archaic*), canoodle (*slang*), greet, neck (*informal*), peck (*informal*), salute, smooch (*informal*) **2** = **brush**, caress, glance, graze, scrape, touch ♦ *noun* **3** = **osculation**, buss (*archaic*), peck (*informal*), smacker (*slang*)

kit *noun* = **equipment**, accoutrements, apparatus, effects, gear, impedimenta, implements, instruments, outfit, paraphernalia, provisions, rig, supplies, tackle, tools, trappings, utensils

kitchen *noun* = **cookhouse**, galley, kitchenette

kit out *or* **up** *verb* = **equip**, accoutre, arm, deck out, fit out, fix up, furnish, outfit, provide with, supply

knack *noun* = **skill**, ability, adroitness, aptitude, bent, capacity, dexterity, expertise, expertness, facility, flair, forte, genius, gift, handiness, ingenuity, propensity, quickness, skilfulness, talent, trick
➤ **Antonyms**
awkwardness, clumsiness, disability, ineptitude

knave *noun* *Archaic* = **rogue**, blackguard, bounder (*old-fashioned Brit. slang*), cheat, cocksucker (*taboo slang*), rapscallion, rascal, reprobate, rotter (*slang, chiefly Brit.*), scally (*Northwest English dialect*), scallywag (*informal*), scamp, scapegrace, scoundrel, scumbag (*slang*), swindler, varlet (*archaic*), villain

knavery *noun* *Old-fashioned* = **dishonesty**, chicanery, corruption, deceit, deception, double-dealing, duplicity, fraud, imposture, rascality, roguery, trickery, villainy

knavish *adjective Old-fashioned*
= **dishonest**, deceitful, deceptive,
dishonourable, fraudulent, lying, rascally,
roguish, scoundrelly, tricky, unprincipled,
unscrupulous, villainous
➤ Antonyms
honest, honourable, noble, principled,
trustworthy

knead *verb* = **squeeze**, blend, form,
manipulate, massage, mould, press, rub,
shape, stroke, work

kneel *verb* = **genuflect**, bow, bow down,
curtsey, curtsy, get down on one's knees,
kowtow, make obeisance, stoop

knell *noun* **1** = **ringing**, chime, peal, sound,
toll ◆ *verb* **2** = **ring**, announce, chime,
herald, peal, resound, sound, toll

knickers *plural noun* = **underwear**,
bloomers, briefs, drawers, panties, smalls

knick-knack *noun* = **trinket**, bagatelle,
bauble, bibelot, bric-a-brac, gewgaw,
gimcrack, kickshaw, plaything, trifle

knife *noun* **1** = **blade**, cutter, cutting tool
◆ *verb* **2** = **cut**, impale, lacerate, pierce,
slash, stab, wound

knit *verb* **1** = **join**, affix, ally, bind, connect,
contract, fasten, heal, interlace, intertwine,
link, loop, mend, secure, tie, unite, weave
2 = **wrinkle**, crease, furrow, knot, pucker

knob *noun* = **lump**, boss, bulk, bump,
bunch, hump, knot, knurl, nub, projection,
protrusion, protuberance, snag, stud,
swell, swelling, tumour

knock *verb* **1** = **hit**, belt (*informal*), buffet,
chin (*slang*), clap, cuff, deck (*slang*), lay
one on (*slang*), punch, rap, slap, smack,
smite (*archaic*), strike, thump, thwack **2**
Informal = **criticize**, abuse, asperse, belittle,
carp, cavil, censure, condemn, denigrate,
deprecate, disparage, find fault, have a go
(at) (*informal*), lambast(e), run down, slag
(off) (*slang*), slam (*slang*) ◆ *noun* **3** = **blow**,
belt (*informal*), box, clip, clout (*informal*),
cuff, hammering, rap, slap, smack, thump
4 *Informal* = **setback**, defeat, failure, rebuff,
rejection, reversal **5** *Informal* = **criticism**,
blame, censure, condemnation, heat
(*slang, chiefly U.S. & Canad.*), slagging (off)
(*slang*), stick (*slang*), stricture

knockabout *adjective* = **boisterous**,
farcical, harum-scarum, rambunctious
(*informal*), riotous, rollicking,
rough-and-tumble, rumbustious, slapstick

knock about *or* **around** *verb* **1** = **wander**,
ramble, range, roam, rove, traipse, travel **2**
= **hit**, abuse, batter, beat up (*informal*),
bruise, buffet, clobber (*slang*), damage,
hurt, lambast(e), maltreat, manhandle,

maul, mistreat, strike, work over (*slang*),
wound

knock down *verb* = **demolish**, batter,
clout (*informal*), deck (*slang*), destroy, fell,
floor, level, pound, raze, smash, wallop
(*informal*), wreck

knock off *verb* **1** *Informal* = **stop work**,
clock off, clock out, complete, conclude,
finish, terminate **2** *Slang* = **kill**, assassinate,
blow away (*slang, chiefly U.S.*), bump off
(*slang*), do away with, do in (*slang*),
liquidate, murder, slay, take out (*slang*),
waste (*informal*) **3** *Slang* = **steal**, blag
(*slang*), cabbage (*Brit. slang*), filch, nick
(*slang, chiefly Brit.*), pilfer, pinch, purloin,
rob, thieve

knockout *noun* **1** = **killer blow**, coup de
grâce, kayo (*slang*), KO *or* K.O. (*slang*) **2**
Informal = **success**, hit, sensation, smash,
smasheroo (*informal*), smash hit, stunner
(*informal*), triumph, winner
➤ Antonyms
≠**success**: clunker (*informal*), failure, flop
(*informal*), turkey (*informal*)

knot *noun* **1** = **connection**, bond, bow,
braid, joint, ligature, loop, rosette, tie **2**
= **cluster**, aggregation, bunch, clump,
collection, heap, mass, pile, tuft **3** = **group**,
assemblage, band, circle, clique, company,
crew (*informal*), crowd, gang, mob, pack,
set, squad ◆ *verb* **4** = **tie**, bind, complicate,
entangle, knit, loop, secure, tether, weave

know *verb* **1** = **understand**, apprehend,
comprehend, experience, fathom, feel
certain, ken (*Scot.*), learn, notice, perceive,
realize, recognize, see, undergo **2** = **be
acquainted with**, associate with, be
familiar with, fraternize with, have dealings
with, have knowledge of, recognize **3**
= **distinguish**, differentiate, discern,
identify, make out, perceive, recognize,
see, tell
➤ Antonyms
≠**understand**: misunderstand ≠**be
acquainted with**: be ignorant, be
unfamiliar with

know-how *noun Informal* = **capability**,
ability, adroitness, aptitude, craft,
dexterity, experience, expertise, faculty,
flair, ingenuity, knack, knowledge,
proficiency, savoir-faire, skill, talent

knowing *adjective* **1** = **meaningful**,
eloquent, expressive, significant **2**
= **cunning**, acute, astute, perceptive,
sagacious, shrewd **3** = **deliberate**, aware,
conscious, intended, intentional **4**
= **well-informed**, clever, clued-up
(*informal*), competent, discerning,
experienced, expert, intelligent, qualified,
skilful

➤ **Antonyms**

≠**cunning**: ingenuous, naive, wet behind the ears (*informal*) ≠**deliberate**: accidental, unintentional ≠**well-informed**: ignorant, obtuse

knowingly *adverb* = **deliberately**, consciously, intentionally, on purpose, purposely, wilfully, wittingly

knowledge *noun* 1 = **learning**, education, enlightenment, erudition, instruction, intelligence, scholarship, schooling, science, tuition, wisdom 2 = **understanding**, ability, apprehension, cognition, comprehension, consciousness, discernment, grasp, judgment, recognition 3 = **acquaintance**, cognizance, familiarity, information, intimacy, notice

➤ **Antonyms**

≠**learning**: ignorance, illiteracy ≠**understanding**: misunderstanding, unawareness ≠**acquaintance**: unfamiliarity

knowledgeable *adjective* 1 = **well-informed**, acquainted, *au courant*, *au fait*, aware, clued-up (*informal*), cognizant, conscious, conversant, experienced, familiar, in the know (*informal*), in the loop, understanding 2 = **intelligent**, educated, erudite, learned, lettered, scholarly

known *adjective* = **famous**, acknowledged, admitted, avowed, celebrated, common, confessed, familiar, manifest, noted, obvious, patent, plain, popular, published, recognized, well-known

➤ **Antonyms**

closet (*informal*), concealed, hidden, secret, unfamiliar, unknown, unrecognized, unrevealed

knuckle under *verb* = **give way**, accede, acquiesce, capitulate, cave in (*informal*), give in, submit, succumb, surrender, yield

➤ **Antonyms**

be defiant, dig one's heels in (*informal*), hold out (against), kick up (a fuss *or* stink), rebel, resist

L l

label *noun* 1 = **tag**, docket (*chiefly Brit.*), flag, marker, sticker, tally, ticket 2 = **epithet**, characterization, classification, description ♦ *verb* 3 = **tag**, docket (*chiefly Brit.*), flag, mark, stamp, sticker, tally 4 = **describe**, brand, call, characterize, class, classify, define, designate, identify, name

laborious *adjective* = **hard**, arduous, backbreaking, burdensome, difficult, exhausting, fatiguing, herculean, onerous, strenuous, tiresome, tiring, toilsome, tough, uphill, wearing, wearisome
➤ **Antonyms**
easy, easy-peasy (*slang*), effortless, light

labour *noun* 1 = **work**, industry, toil 2 = **workers**, employees, hands, labourers, workforce, workmen 3 = **childbirth**, contractions, delivery, labour pains, pains, parturition, throes, travail 4 = **toil**, donkey-work, drudgery, effort, exertion, grind (*informal*), industry, pains, painstaking, sweat (*informal*), travail 5 = **chore**, job, task, undertaking ♦ *verb* 6 = **work**, drudge, endeavour, grind (*informal*), peg along *or* away (*chiefly Brit.*), plod, plug along *or* away (*informal*), slave, strive, struggle, sweat (*informal*), toil, travail 7 = **overemphasize**, dwell on, elaborate, go on about, make a federal case of (*U.S. informal*), make a production (out) of (*informal*), overdo, strain 8 *usually with* **under** = **be disadvantaged**, be a victim of, be burdened by, suffer
➤ **Antonyms**
noun ≠ **toil**: ease, idleness, leisure, relaxation, repose, respite, rest ♦ *verb* ≠ **work**: relax, rest

laboured *adjective* = **difficult**, awkward, forced, heavy, stiff, strained

labourer *noun* = **worker**, blue-collar worker, drudge, hand, labouring man, manual worker, navvy (*Brit. informal*), unskilled worker, working man, workman

labyrinth *noun* = **maze**, complexity, complication, convolution, entanglement, intricacy, jungle, perplexity, puzzle, riddle, tangle

labyrinthine *adjective* = **complex**, Byzantine, confused, convoluted, intricate, involved, knotty, mazelike, perplexing, puzzling, tangled, tortuous, winding

lace *noun* 1 = **netting**, filigree, openwork,

tatting 2 = **cord**, bootlace, shoelace, string, thong, tie ♦ *verb* 3 = **fasten**, attach, bind, close, do up, thread, tie 4 = **mix in**, add to, fortify, spike 5 = **intertwine**, interweave, twine

lacerate *verb* 1 = **tear**, claw, cut, gash, jag, maim, mangle, rend, rip, slash, wound 2 = **hurt**, afflict, distress, harrow, rend, torment, torture, wound

laceration *noun* = **cut**, gash, injury, mutilation, rent, rip, slash, tear, wound

lachrymose *adjective* = **tearful**, crying, mournful, sad, weeping, weepy (*informal*), woeful

lack *noun* 1 = **shortage**, absence, dearth, deficiency, deprivation, destitution, insufficiency, need, privation, scantiness, scarcity, shortcoming, shortness, want ♦ *verb* 2 = **need**, be deficient in, be short of, be without, miss, require, want
➤ **Antonyms**
noun ≠ **shortage**: abundance, adequacy, excess, plentifulness, sufficiency, surplus ♦ *verb* ≠ **need**: enjoy, have, own, possess

lackadaisical *adjective* 1 = **lethargic**, apathetic, dull, enervated, half-hearted, indifferent, languid, languorous, limp, listless, spiritless 2 = **lazy**, abstracted, dreamy, idle, indolent, inert
➤ **Antonyms**
ambitious, diligent, excited, inspired, spirited

lackey *noun* 1 = **hanger-on**, fawner, flatterer, instrument, menial, minion, parasite, pawn, sycophant, toady, tool, yes man 2 = **manservant**, attendant, cohort (*chiefly U.S.*), flunky, footman, valet, varlet (*archaic*)

lacking *adjective* = **without**, defective, deficient, flawed, impaired, inadequate, minus (*informal*), missing, needing, sans (*archaic*), wanting

lacklustre *adjective* = **flat**, boring, dim, drab, dry, dull, leaden, lifeless, lustreless, muted, prosaic, sombre, unimaginative, uninspired, vapid

laconic *adjective* = **terse**, brief, clipped, compact, concise, crisp, curt, monosyllabic, pithy, sententious, short, succinct, to the point
➤ **Antonyms**
long-winded, loquacious, rambling,

verbose, voluble, wordy

lacuna *noun* = **gap**, blank, break, hiatus, omission, space, void

lacy *adjective* = **filigree**, delicate, fine, lace-like, meshy, net-like, open

lad *noun* = **boy**, chap (*informal*), fellow, guy (*informal*), juvenile, kid (*informal*), laddie (*Scot.*), schoolboy, stripling, youngster, youth

laden *adjective* = **loaded**, burdened, charged, encumbered, fraught, full, hampered, oppressed, taxed, weighed down, weighted

la-di-da *adjective Informal* = **affected**, arty-farty (*informal*), conceited, highfalutin (*informal*), mannered, mincing, overrefined, posh (*informal, chiefly Brit.*), precious, pretentious, snobbish, snooty (*informal*), stuck-up (*informal*), toffee-nosed (*slang, chiefly Brit.*)

lady *noun* **1** = **gentlewoman**, dame **2** = **woman**, female

lady-killer *noun* = **womanizer**, Casanova, Don Juan, heartbreaker, ladies' man, libertine, Lothario, philanderer, rake, roué, wolf (*informal*)

ladylike *adjective* = **refined**, courtly, cultured, decorous, elegant, genteel, modest, polite, proper, respectable, sophisticated, well-bred
➤ **Antonyms**
discourteous, ill-bred, ill-mannered, impolite, rude, uncultured, unladylike, unmannerly, unrefined

lag *verb* **1** = **hang back**, be behind, dawdle, delay, drag (behind), drag one's feet (*informal*), idle, linger, loiter, saunter, straggle, tarry, trail **2** = **flag**, decrease, diminish, ebb, fail, fall off, lose strength, slacken, wane

laggard *noun* = **straggler**, dawdler, idler, lingerer, loafer, loiterer, lounger, saunterer, skiver (*Brit. slang*), slowcoach (*Brit. informal*), slowpoke (*U.S. & Canad. informal*), sluggard, snail

laid-back *adjective* = **relaxed**, at ease, casual, easy-going, easy-oasy (*slang*), free and easy, together (*slang*), unflappable (*informal*), unhurried
➤ **Antonyms**
antsy (*informal*), edgy, jittery (*informal*), jumpy, keyed-up, nervous, on edge, tense, twitchy (*informal*), uptight (*informal*), wound-up (*informal*)

lair *noun* **1** = **nest**, burrow, den, earth, form, hole, resting place **2** *Informal* = **hide-out**, den, refuge, retreat, sanctuary

laissez faire *or* **laisser faire** *noun* = **nonintervention**, free enterprise, free trade, individualism, live and let live

lake *noun* = **pond**, lagoon, loch (*Scot.*), lough (*Irish*), mere, reservoir, tarn

lam *verb Slang* = **attack**, batter, beat, hit, knock, lambast(e), pelt, pound, strike, thrash

lambast(e) *verb* **1** = **beat**, bludgeon, cosh (*Brit.*), cudgel, drub, flog, strike, thrash, whip **2** = **reprimand**, bawl out (*informal*), berate, carpet (*informal*), castigate, censure, chew out (*U.S. & Canad. informal*), give a rocket (*Brit. & N.Z. informal*), rap over the knuckles, read the riot act, rebuke, scold, slap on the wrist, tear into (*informal*), tear (someone) off a strip (*Brit. informal*), upbraid

lambent *adjective* **1** = **flickering**, dancing, fluttering, twinkling **2** *Of wit or humour* = **brilliant**, light, sparkling

lame *adjective* **1** = **disabled**, crippled, defective, game, halt (*archaic*), handicapped, hobbling, limping **2** = **unconvincing**, feeble, flimsy, inadequate, insufficient, pathetic, poor, thin, unsatisfactory, weak

lament *verb* **1** = **bemoan**, bewail, complain, deplore, grieve, mourn, regret, sorrow, wail, weep ♦ *noun* **2** = **complaint**, keening, lamentation, moan, moaning, plaint, ululation, wail, wailing **3** = **dirge**, coronach (*Scot. & Irish*), elegy, requiem, threnody

lamentable *adjective* **1** = **regrettable**, deplorable, distressing, grievous, gut-wrenching, harrowing, mournful, sorrowful, tragic, unfortunate, woeful **2** = **disappointing**, low, meagre, mean, miserable, not much cop (*Brit. slang*), pitiful, poor, unsatisfactory, wretched

lamentation *noun* = **sorrow**, dirge, grief, grieving, keening, lament, moan, mourning, plaint, sobbing, ululation, wailing, weeping

laminate *verb* **1** = **cover**, coat, face, foliate, layer, stratify, veneer **2** = **split**, exfoliate, flake, separate

lampoon *noun* **1** = **satire**, burlesque, caricature, parody, send-up (*Brit. informal*), skit, takeoff (*informal*) ♦ *verb* **2** = **ridicule**, burlesque, caricature, make fun of, mock, parody, satirize, send up (*Brit. informal*), take off (*informal*)

land *noun* **1** = **ground**, dry land, earth, terra firma **2** = **soil**, dirt, ground, loam **3** = **countryside**, farming, farmland, rural districts **4** *Law* = **property**, acres, estate, grounds, real property, realty **5** = **country**, district, fatherland, motherland, nation, province, region, territory, tract ♦ *verb* **6**

= **alight**, arrive, berth, come to rest, debark, disembark, dock, touch down **7** *Informal* = **obtain**, acquire, gain, get, score (*slang*), secure, win

landing *noun* **1** = **coming in**, arrival, disembarkation, disembarkment, touchdown **2** = **platform**, jetty, landing stage, quayside

landlord *noun* **1** = **owner**, freeholder, lessor, proprietor **2** = **innkeeper**, host, hotelier, hotel-keeper

landmark *noun* **1** = **feature**, monument **2** = **milestone**, crisis, turning point, watershed

landscape *noun* = **scenery**, countryside, outlook, panorama, prospect, scene, view, vista

landslide *noun* = **landslip**, avalanche, rockfall

land up *verb* = **end up**, arrive, lead, turn up, wind up

lane *noun* = **road**, alley, footpath, passageway, path, pathway, street, way

language *noun* **1** = **speech**, communication, conversation, discourse, expression, interchange, parlance, talk, utterance, verbalization, vocalization **2** = **tongue**, argot, cant, dialect, idiom, jargon, lingo (*informal*), lingua franca, patois, patter, speech, terminology, vernacular, vocabulary **3** = **style**, diction, expression, phraseology, phrasing, wording

languid *adjective* **1** = **feeble**, drooping, faint, languorous, limp, pining, sickly, weak, weary **2** = **lazy**, indifferent, lackadaisical, languorous, listless, spiritless, unenthusiastic, uninterested **3** = **lethargic**, dull, heavy, inactive, inert, sluggish, torpid
➤ **Antonyms**
active, alive and kicking, energetic, strong, tireless, vigorous

languish *verb* **1** *Literary* = **waste away**, be abandoned, be disregarded, be neglected, rot, suffer **2** = **decline**, droop, fade, fail, faint, flag, sicken, waste, weaken, wilt, wither **3** *often with* **for** = **pine**, desire, eat one's heart out over, hanker, hunger, long, sigh, want, yearn
➤ **Antonyms**
≠**waste away**, **decline**: bloom, flourish, prosper, thrive

languishing *adjective* **1** = **fading**, declining, deteriorating, drooping, droopy, failing, flagging, sickening, sinking, wasting away, weak, weakening, wilting, withering **2** = **lovesick**, dreamy, longing, lovelorn, melancholic, nostalgic, pensive, pining, soulful, tender, wistful, woebegone, yearning

languor *noun* *Literary* = **relaxation**, dreaminess, drowsiness, indolence, laziness, lotus-eating, sleepiness, sloth

lank *adjective* **1** = **limp**, dull, lifeless, long, lustreless, straggling **2** = **thin**, emaciated, gaunt, lanky, lean, rawboned, scraggy, scrawny, skinny, slender, slim, spare

lanky *adjective* = **gangling**, angular, bony, gaunt, loose-jointed, rangy, rawboned, scraggy, scrawny, spare, tall, thin, weedy (*informal*)
➤ **Antonyms**
brawny, burly, chubby, fat, muscular, plump, portly, rotund, rounded, short, sinewy, stocky, stout

lap¹ *noun* **1** = **circuit**, circle, course, distance, loop, orbit, round, tour ◆ *verb* **2** = **wrap**, cover, enfold, envelop, fold, swaddle, swathe, turn, twist

lap² *verb* **1** = **ripple**, gurgle, plash, purl, slap, splash, swish, wash **2** = **drink**, lick, sip, sup

lapse *noun* **1** = **mistake**, error, failing, fault, indiscretion, negligence, omission, oversight, slip **2** = **interval**, break, breathing space, gap, intermission, interruption, lull, passage, pause **3** = **drop**, backsliding, decline, descent, deterioration, fall, relapse ◆ *verb* **4** = **drop**, decline, degenerate, deteriorate, fail, fall, sink, slide, slip **5** = **end**, become obsolete, become void, expire, run out, stop, terminate

lapsed *adjective* **1** = **expired**, discontinued, ended, finished, invalid, out of date, run out, unrenewed **2** = **backsliding**, lacking faith, nonpractising

larceny *noun* *Law* = **theft**, burglary, misappropriation, pilfering, purloining, robbery, stealing

large *adjective* **1** = **big**, bulky, colossal, considerable, elephantine, enormous, giant, gigantic, ginormous (*informal*), goodly, great, huge, humongous *or* humungous (*U.S. slang*), immense, jumbo (*informal*), king-size, man-size, massive, mega (*slang*), monumental, sizable *or* sizeable, substantial, tidy (*informal*), vast **2** = **comprehensive**, abundant, ample, broad, capacious, copious, extensive, full, generous, grand, grandiose, liberal, plentiful, roomy, spacious, sweeping, wide **3 at large: a** = **in general**, as a whole, chiefly, generally, in the main, mainly **b** = **free**, at liberty, on the loose, on the run, roaming, unconfined **c** = **at length**, considerably, exhaustively, greatly, in full detail
➤ **Antonyms**

≠**big**: inconsiderable, infinitesimal, little, minute, petty, short, slender, slight, slim, small, tiny, trivial ≠**comprehensive**: brief, narrow, scanty, scarce, sparse, thin

largely *adverb* = **mainly**, as a rule, by and large, chiefly, considerably, extensively, generally, mostly, predominantly, primarily, principally, to a great extent, widely

large-scale *adjective* = **wide-ranging**, broad, extensive, far-reaching, global, sweeping, vast, wholesale, wide

largesse, largess *noun* = **generosity**, alms-giving, benefaction, bounty, charity, liberality, munificence, open-handedness, philanthropy

lark *Informal* ♦ *noun* 1 = **prank**, antic, caper, escapade, fling, frolic, fun, gambol, game, jape, mischief, revel, rollick, romp, skylark, spree ♦ *verb* 2 **lark about** = **play**, caper, cavort, cut capers, frolic, gambol, have fun, make mischief, rollick, romp, sport

lascivious *adjective* 1 = **lustful**, horny (*slang*), lecherous, lewd, libidinous, licentious, prurient, randy (*informal, chiefly Brit.*), salacious, sensual, unchaste, voluptuous, wanton 2 = **bawdy**, blue, coarse, crude, dirty, indecent, obscene, offensive, pornographic, ribald, scurrilous, smutty, suggestive, vulgar, X-rated (*informal*)

lash[1] *noun* 1 = **blow**, hit, stripe, stroke, swipe (*informal*) ♦ *verb* 2 = **whip**, beat, birch, chastise, flagellate, flog, horsewhip, lam (*slang*), lambast(e), scourge, thrash 3 = **pound**, beat, buffet, dash, drum, hammer, hit, knock, lambast(e), larrup (*dialect*), punch, smack, strike 4 = **censure**, attack, belabour, berate, blast, castigate, criticize, flay, lambast(e), lampoon, put down, ridicule, satirize, scold, slate (*informal, chiefly Brit.*), tear into (*informal*), upbraid

lash[2] *verb* = **fasten**, bind, join, make fast, rope, secure, strap, tie

lass *noun* = **girl**, bird (*slang*), chick (*slang*), colleen (*Irish*), damsel, lassie (*informal*), maid, maiden, miss, schoolgirl, wench (*facetious*), young woman

lassitude *noun* = **weariness**, apathy, drowsiness, dullness, enervation, ennui, exhaustion, fatigue, heaviness, inertia, languor, lethargy, listlessness, sluggishness, tiredness, torpor

last[1] *adjective* 1 = **hindmost**, aftermost, at the end, rearmost 2 = **most recent**, latest 3 = **final**, closing, concluding, extreme, furthest, remotest, terminal, ultimate, utmost ♦ *adverb* 4 = **in** *or* **at the end**, after, behind, bringing up the rear, in the rear

♦ *noun* 5 = **end**, close, completion, conclusion, ending, finale, finish, termination 6 **at last** = **finally**, at length, at the end of the day, eventually, in conclusion, in the end, in the fullness of time, ultimately

➤ **Antonyms**
adjective ≠**hindmost**: first, foremost, leading ≠**final**: earliest, first, initial, introductory, opening

last[2] *verb* = **continue**, abide, carry on, endure, hold on, hold out, keep, keep on, persist, remain, stand up, survive, wear

➤ **Antonyms**
cease, depart, die, end, expire, fade, fail, stop, terminate

last-ditch *adjective* = **final**, all-out (*informal*), desperate, frantic, heroic, straining, struggling

lasting *adjective* = **continuing**, abiding, deep-rooted, durable, enduring, eternal, indelible, lifelong, long-standing, long-term, perennial, permanent, perpetual, unceasing, undying, unending

➤ **Antonyms**
ephemeral, fleeting, momentary, passing, short-lived, transient, transitory

lastly *adverb* = **finally**, after all, all in all, at last, in conclusion, in the end, to conclude, to sum up, ultimately

last-minute *adjective* = **late**, deathbed, eleventh hour, last-ditch, last-gasp

latch *noun* 1 = **fastening**, bar, bolt, catch, clamp, hasp, hook, lock, sneck (*dialect*) ♦ *verb* 2 = **fasten**, bar, bolt, lock, make fast, secure, sneck (*dialect*)

late *adjective* 1 = **overdue**, behind, behindhand, belated, delayed, last-minute, slow, tardy, unpunctual 2 = **dead**, deceased, defunct, departed, ex-, former, old, past, preceding, previous 3 = **recent**, advanced, fresh, modern, new ♦ *adverb* 4 = **belatedly**, at the last minute, behindhand, behind time, dilatorily, slowly, tardily, unpunctually

➤ **Antonyms**
adjective ≠**overdue**: beforehand, early, prompt, punctual, seasoned, timely ≠**dead**: alive, existing ≠**recent**: old ♦ *adverb* ≠**belatedly**: beforehand, early, in advance

lately *adverb* = **recently**, in recent times, just now, latterly, not long ago, of late

lateness *noun* = **delay**, advanced hour, belatedness, late date, tardiness, unpunctuality

latent *adjective* = **hidden**, concealed, dormant, inherent, invisible, lurking, potential, quiescent, secret, undeveloped, unexpressed, unrealized, unseen, veiled

➤ **Antonyms**
apparent, conspicuous, developed,
evident, expressed, manifest, obvious,
realized

later *adverb* = **afterwards**, after, by and by,
in a while, in time, later on, next,
subsequently, thereafter

lateral *adjective* = **sideways**, edgeways,
flanking, side, sideward

latest *adjective* = **up-to-date**, current,
fashionable, happening (*informal*), in,
modern, most recent, newest, now,
up-to-the-minute, with it (*informal*)

lather *noun* 1 = **froth**, bubbles, foam, soap,
soapsuds, suds 2 *Informal* = **fluster**, dither
(*chiefly Brit.*), fever, flap (*informal*), fuss,
state (*informal*), stew (*informal*), sweat,
tizzy (*informal*) ♦ *verb* 3 = **froth**, foam,
soap 4 *Informal* = **beat**, cane, drub, flog,
lambast(e), strike, thrash, whip

latitude *noun* = **scope**, a free hand,
elbowroom, freedom, indulgence, laxity,
leeway, liberty, licence, play, room, space,
unrestrictedness

latter *adjective* = **second**, closing,
concluding, last, last-mentioned, later,
latest, modern, recent
➤ **Antonyms**
antecedent, earlier, foregoing, former,
preceding, previous, prior

latterly *adverb* = **recently**, hitherto, lately,
of late

lattice *noun* = **grid**, fretwork, grating, grille,
latticework, mesh, network, openwork,
tracery, trellis, web

laud *verb Literary* = **praise**, acclaim,
approve, celebrate, crack up (*informal*),
extol, glorify, honour, sing *or* sound the
praises of

laudable *adjective* = **praiseworthy**,
admirable, commendable, creditable,
estimable, excellent, meritorious, of note,
worthy
➤ **Antonyms**
base, blameworthy, contemptible,
ignoble, lowly, unworthy

laudatory *adjective* = **eulogistic**,
acclamatory, adulatory, approbatory,
approving, commendatory,
complimentary, panegyrical

laugh *verb* 1 = **chuckle**, be convulsed
(*informal*), be in stitches, be rolling in the
aisles (*informal*), bust a gut (*informal*),
chortle, crack up (*informal*), crease up
(*informal*), giggle, guffaw, roar with
laughter, snigger, split one's sides, titter 2
laugh at = **make fun of**, belittle, deride,
jeer, lampoon, make a mock of, mock,
ridicule, scoff at, take the mickey (out of)

(*informal*), taunt ♦ *noun* 3 = **chuckle**, belly
laugh (*informal*), chortle, giggle, guffaw,
roar *or* shriek of laughter, snigger, titter 4
Informal = **clown**, card (*informal*), caution
(*informal*), comedian, comic, entertainer,
hoot (*informal*), humorist, scream
(*informal*), wag, wit 5 *Informal* = **joke**, hoot
(*informal*), lark, scream (*informal*)

laughable *adjective* = **ridiculous**, absurd,
derisive, derisory, farcical, ludicrous,
nonsensical, preposterous, risible, worthy
of scorn

laughing stock *noun* = **figure of fun**, Aunt
Sally (*Brit.*), butt, everybody's fool, fair
game, target, victim

laugh off *verb* = **disregard**, brush aside,
dismiss, ignore, minimize, pooh-pooh,
shrug off

laughter *noun* 1 = **chuckling**, cachinnation,
chortling, giggling, guffawing, laughing,
tittering 2 = **amusement**, glee, hilarity,
merriment, mirth

launch *verb* 1 = **propel**, cast, discharge,
dispatch, fire, project, send off, set afloat,
set in motion, throw 2 = **begin**,
commence, embark upon, inaugurate,
initiate, instigate, introduce, open, start

launder *verb* 1 = **wash**, clean 2 = **process**,
cook (*slang*), doctor, manipulate

laurels *plural noun* = **glory**, acclaim,
awards, Brownie points, commendation,
credit, distinction, fame, honour, kudos,
praise, prestige, recognition, renown,
reward

lavatory *noun* = **toilet**, bathroom, bog
(*slang*), can (*U.S. & Canad. slang*),
cloakroom (*Brit.*), crapper (*taboo slang*),
Gents *or* Ladies, john (*slang, chiefly U.S. &
Canad.*), khazi (*slang*), latrine, little boy's
room *or* little girl's room (*informal*), loo
(*Brit. informal*), pissoir, powder room,
privy, (public) convenience, washroom,
water closet, W.C.

lavish *adjective* 1 = **plentiful**, abundant,
copious, exuberant, lush, luxuriant,
opulent, profuse, prolific, sumptuous 2
= **generous**, bountiful, effusive, free,
liberal, munificent, open-handed,
unstinting 3 = **extravagant**, exaggerated,
excessive, immoderate, improvident,
intemperate, prodigal, thriftless,
unreasonable, unrestrained, wasteful, wild
♦ *verb* 4 = **spend**, deluge, dissipate,
expend, heap, pour, shower, squander,
waste
➤ **Antonyms**
adjective ≠**plentiful**: frugal, meagre,
miserly, scanty, stingy ≠**generous**: cheap,
miserly, parsimonious, stingy, tight-fisted
≠**extravagant**: sparing, thrifty ♦ *verb*

≠**spend**: begrudge, economize, stint, withhold

law *noun* **1** = **constitution**, charter, code, jurisprudence **2** = **rule**, act, canon, code, command, commandment, covenant, decree, demand, edict, enactment, order, ordinance, regulation, statute **3** = **principle**, axiom, canon, criterion, formula, precept, standard **4 lay down the law** = **dictate**, dogmatize, emphasize, pontificate

law-abiding *adjective* = **obedient**, compliant, dutiful, good, honest, honourable, lawful, orderly, peaceable, peaceful

law-breaker *noun* = **criminal**, convict, crook (*informal*), culprit, delinquent, felon (*formerly criminal law*), miscreant, offender, sinner, transgressor, trespasser, villain, violator, wrongdoer

lawful *adjective* = **legal**, allowable, authorized, constitutional, just, legalized, legitimate, licit, permissible, proper, rightful, valid, warranted
➤ **Antonyms**
banned, forbidden, illegal, illegitimate, illicit, prohibited, unauthorized, unlawful

lawless *adjective* = **disorderly**, anarchic, chaotic, insubordinate, insurgent, mutinous, rebellious, reckless, riotous, seditious, ungoverned, unrestrained, unruly, wild
➤ **Antonyms**
civilized, compliant, disciplined, law-abiding, obedient, orderly, restrained, well-governed

lawlessness *noun* = **anarchy**, chaos, disorder, mob rule

lawsuit *noun* = **case**, action, argument, cause, contest, dispute, industrial tribunal, litigation, proceedings, prosecution, suit, trial

lawyer *noun* = **legal adviser**, advocate, attorney, barrister, counsel, counsellor, solicitor

lax *adjective* = **slack**, careless, casual, easy-going, easy-oasy (*slang*), lenient, neglectful, negligent, overindulgent, remiss, slapdash, slipshod
➤ **Antonyms**
conscientious, disciplined, firm, heedful, rigid, scrupulous, severe, stern, strict, stringent

laxative *noun* = **purgative**, aperient, cathartic, physic (*rare*), purge, salts

lay[1] *verb* **1** = **place**, deposit, establish, leave, plant, put, set, set down, settle, spread **2** = **attribute**, allocate, allot, ascribe, assign, charge, impute **3** = **put forward**, advance,

bring forward, lodge, offer, present, submit **4** = **devise**, concoct, contrive, design, hatch, plan, plot, prepare, work out **5** = **arrange**, dispose, locate, organize, position, set out **6** = **produce**, bear, deposit **7** = **bet**, gamble, give odds, hazard, risk, stake, wager **8 lay bare** = **reveal**, disclose, divulge, explain, expose, show, unveil **9 lay hold of** = **grasp**, get, get hold of, grab, grip, seize, snatch

lay[2] *adjective* **1** = **nonclerical**, laic, laical, secular **2** = **nonspecialist**, amateur, inexpert, nonprofessional

lay[3] *noun* = **poem**, ballad, lyric, ode, song

layabout *noun* = **idler**, couch potato (*slang*), good-for-nothing, laggard, loafer, lounger, ne'er-do-well, shirker, skiver (*Brit. slang*), vagrant, wastrel

lay aside *verb* = **abandon**, cast aside, dismiss, postpone, put aside, put off, reject, shelve

lay down *verb* **1** = **sacrifice**, give up, relinquish, surrender, yield **2** = **stipulate**, affirm, assume, establish, formulate, ordain, postulate, prescribe

layer *noun* **1** = **tier**, ply, row, seam, stratum, thickness **2** = **covering**, blanket, coat, coating, cover, film, mantle, sheet

lay in *verb* = **store (up)**, accumulate, amass, build up, collect, hoard, stockpile, stock up

lay into *verb Informal* = **attack**, assail, belabour, go for the jugular, hit out at, lambast(e), let fly at, pitch into (*informal*), set about

layman *noun* = **nonprofessional**, amateur, lay person, outsider

lay-off *noun* = **unemployment**, discharge, dismissal

lay off *verb* **1** = **dismiss**, discharge, drop, give the boot to (*slang*), let go, make redundant, oust, pay off **2** *Informal* = **stop**, belay (*Nautical*), cease, desist, get off someone's back (*informal*), give it a rest (*informal*), give over (*informal*), give up, leave alone, leave off, let up, quit

lay on *verb* **1** = **provide**, cater (for), furnish, give, purvey, supply **2 lay it on thick** *Slang* = **exaggerate**, butter up, flatter, overdo it, overpraise, soft-soap (*informal*)

layout *noun* = **arrangement**, design, draft, format, formation, geography, outline, plan

lay out *verb* **1** = **arrange**, design, display, exhibit, plan, spread out **2** *Informal* = **spend**, disburse, expend, fork out (*slang*), invest, pay, shell out (*informal*) **3** *Informal* = **knock out**, kayo (*slang*), knock for six (*informal*), knock unconscious, KO or K.O. (*slang*)

lay up *verb* **1** *Informal* = **confine (to bed)**, hospitalize, incapacitate **2** = **store up**, accumulate, amass, garner, hoard, keep, preserve, put away, save, treasure

laze *verb* **1** = **idle**, hang around, loaf, loll, lounge, stand around **2** *often with* **away** = **kill time**, fool away, fritter away, pass time, veg out (*slang, chiefly U.S.*), waste time, while away the hours

laziness *noun* = **idleness**, inactivity, indolence, lackadaisicalness, slackness, sloth, slothfulness, slowness, sluggishness, tardiness

lazy *adjective* **1** = **idle**, good-for-nothing, inactive, indolent, inert, remiss, shiftless, slack, slothful, slow, workshy **2** = **lethargic**, drowsy, languid, languorous, sleepy, slow-moving, sluggish, somnolent, torpid
➤ **Antonyms**
active, assiduous, diligent, energetic, industrious, quick, stimulated

lazybones *noun Informal* = **idler**, couch potato (*slang*), loafer, lounger, shirker, skiver (*Brit. slang*), sleepyhead, slugabed, sluggard

leach *verb* = **extract**, drain, filter, filtrate, percolate, seep, strain

lead *verb* **1** = **guide**, conduct, escort, pilot, precede, show the way, steer, usher **2** = **cause**, dispose, draw, incline, induce, influence, persuade, prevail, prompt **3** = **command**, direct, govern, head, manage, preside over, supervise **4** = **be ahead (of)**, blaze a trail, come first, exceed, excel, outdo, outstrip, surpass, transcend **5** = **live**, experience, have, pass, spend, undergo **6** = **result in**, bring on, cause, conduce, contribute, produce, serve, tend ♦ *noun* **7** = **first place**, cutting edge, precedence, primacy, priority, supremacy, van, vanguard **8** = **example**, direction, guidance, leadership, model **9** = **advantage**, advance, edge, margin, start **10** = **clue**, guide, hint, indication, suggestion, tip, trace **11** = **leading role**, principal, protagonist, star part, title role ♦ *adjective* **12** = **main**, chief, first, foremost, head, leading, most important, premier, primary, prime, principal

leaden *adjective* **1** = **heavy**, cumbersome, inert, onerous **2** = **grey**, greyish, lacklustre, louring *or* lowering, lustreless, overcast, sombre **3** = **lifeless**, dismal, dreary, dull, gloomy, languid, listless, spiritless

leader *noun* = **principal**, boss (*informal*), captain, chief, chieftain, commander, conductor, director, guide, head, number one, ringleader, ruler, superior
➤ **Antonyms**
adherent, disciple, follower, hanger-on,

henchman, sidekick (*slang*), supporter

leadership *noun* **1** = **guidance**, administration, direction, directorship, domination, management, running, superintendency **2** = **authority**, command, control, influence, initiative, pre-eminence, supremacy, sway

leading *adjective* = **principal**, chief, dominant, first, foremost, governing, greatest, highest, main, number one, outstanding, pre-eminent, primary, ruling, superior
➤ **Antonyms**
following, hindmost, incidental, inferior, lesser, minor, secondary, subordinate

lead off *verb* = **begin**, commence, get going, get under way, inaugurate, initiate, kick off (*informal*), open, set out, start, start the ball rolling (*informal*)

lead on *verb* = **entice**, beguile, deceive, draw on, inveigle, lure, seduce, string along (*informal*), tempt

lead up to *verb* = **introduce**, approach, intimate, make advances, make overtures, pave the way, prepare for, prepare the way, work round to

leaf *noun* **1** = **frond**, blade, bract, flag, foliole, needle, pad **2** = **page**, folio, sheet **3** **turn over a new leaf** = **reform**, amend, begin anew, change, change one's ways, improve ♦ *verb* **4** **leaf through** = **skim**, browse, flip, glance, riffle, thumb (through) **5** = **put out leaves**, bud, green, turn green

leaflet *noun* = **booklet**, advert (*Brit. informal*), bill, brochure, circular, handbill, mailshot, pamphlet

leafy *adjective* = **green**, in foliage, leaved, shaded, shady, verdant, wooded

league *noun* **1** = **association**, alliance, band, coalition, combination, combine, compact, confederacy, confederation, consortium, federation, fellowship, fraternity, group, guild, order, partnership, union **2** *Informal* = **class**, ability group, category, level **3** **in league (with)** = **collaborating**, allied, hand in glove, in cahoots (*informal*), leagued ♦ *verb* **4** = **unite**, ally, amalgamate, associate, band, collaborate, combine, confederate, join forces

leak *noun* **1** = **hole**, aperture, chink, crack, crevice, fissure, opening, puncture **2** = **leakage**, drip, leaking, oozing, percolation, seepage **3** = **disclosure**, divulgence ♦ *verb* **4** = **escape**, discharge, drip, exude, ooze, pass, percolate, seep, spill, trickle **5** = **disclose**, blow wide open (*slang*), divulge, give away, let slip, let the cat out of the bag, make known, make public, pass on, reveal, spill the beans (*informal*), tell

leaky *adjective* = **leaking**, cracked, holey, not watertight, perforated, porous, punctured, split, waterlogged

lean[1] *verb* 1 = **rest**, be supported, prop, recline, repose 2 = **bend**, heel, incline, slant, slope, tilt, tip 3 = **tend**, be disposed to, be prone to, favour, gravitate towards, have a propensity, prefer 4 **lean on** = **depend on**, confide in, count on, have faith in, rely on, trust

lean[2] *adjective* 1 = **trim**, angular, bony, emaciated, gaunt, lank, rangy, scraggy, scrawny, skinny, slender, slim, spare, thin, unfatty, wiry 2 = **poor**, bare, barren, inadequate, infertile, meagre, pathetic, pitiful, scanty, sparse, unfruitful, unproductive
➤ **Antonyms**
≠**trim**: ample, brawny, burly, fat, full, obese, plump, portly ≠**poor**: abundant, fertile, plentiful, profuse, rich

leaning *noun* = **tendency**, aptitude, bent, bias, disposition, inclination, liking, partiality, penchant, predilection, proclivity, proneness, propensity, taste

leap *verb* 1 = **jump**, bounce, bound, caper, cavort, frisk, gambol, hop, skip, spring 2 = **jump over**, clear, vault ♦ *noun* 3 = **jump**, bound, caper, frisk, hop, skip, spring, vault 4 = **rise**, change, escalation, increase, surge, upsurge, upswing

learn *verb* 1 = **master**, acquire, attain, become able, grasp, imbibe, pick up 2 = **memorize**, commit to memory, con (*archaic*), get off pat, get (something) word-perfect, learn by heart 3 = **discover**, ascertain, detect, determine, discern, find out, gain, gather, hear, suss (out) (*slang*), understand

learned *adjective* = **scholarly**, academic, cultured, erudite, experienced, expert, highbrow, intellectual, lettered, literate, skilled, versed, well-informed, well-read
➤ **Antonyms**
ignorant, illiterate, uneducated, unlearned

learner *noun* 1 = **beginner**, apprentice, neophyte, novice, tyro 2 = **student**, disciple, pupil, scholar, trainee
➤ **Antonyms**
≠**beginner**: adept, expert, master, virtuoso, wizard ≠**student**: coach, guru, instructor, mentor, teacher, tutor

learning *noun* = **knowledge**, acquirements, attainments, culture, education, erudition, information, letters, literature, lore, research, scholarship, schooling, study, tuition, wisdom

lease *verb* = **hire**, charter, let, loan, rent

leash *noun* 1 = **lead**, rein, tether ♦ *verb* 2 = **tether**, fasten, secure, tie up

least *adjective* = **smallest**, feeblest, fewest, last, lowest, meanest, minimum, minutest, poorest, slightest, tiniest

leathery *adjective* = **tough**, durable, hard, hardened, leatherlike, rough, rugged, wrinkled

leave[1] *verb* 1 = **depart**, abandon, abscond, decamp, desert, disappear, do a bunk (*Brit. slang*), exit, flit (*informal*), forsake, go, go away, hook it (*slang*), make tracks, move, pack one's bags (*informal*), pull out, quit, relinquish, retire, set out, sling one's hook (*Brit. slang*), slope off, take off (*informal*), withdraw 2 = **forget**, lay down, leave behind, mislay 3 = **give up**, abandon, cease, desert, desist, drop, evacuate, forbear, refrain, relinquish, renounce, stop, surrender 4 = **cause**, deposit, generate, produce, result in 5 = **entrust**, allot, assign, cede, commit, consign, give over, refer 6 = **bequeath**, hand down, transmit, will
➤ **Antonyms**
≠**depart**: appear, arrive, come, emerge, stay ≠**give up**: assume, continue, hold, persist, remove, retain

leave[2] *noun* 1 = **permission**, allowance, authorization, concession, consent, dispensation, freedom, liberty, sanction 2 = **holiday**, furlough, leave of absence, sabbatical, time off, vacation 3 As in **take one's leave of** = **departure**, adieu, farewell, goodbye, leave-taking, parting, retirement, withdrawal
➤ **Antonyms**
≠**permission**: denial, prohibition, refusal, rejection ≠**holiday**: duty ≠**departure**: arrival, stay

leaven *noun* 1 = **yeast**, barm, ferment, leavening 2 = **catalyst**, influence, inspiration ♦ *verb* 3 = **ferment**, lighten, raise, work 4 = **stimulate**, elevate, imbue, inspire, permeate, pervade, quicken, suffuse

leave off *verb* = **stop**, abstain, belay (*Nautical*), break off, cease, desist, discontinue, end, give over (*informal*), give up, halt, kick (*informal*), knock off (*informal*), refrain

leave out *verb* = **omit**, bar, cast aside, count out, disregard, except, exclude, ignore, neglect, overlook, reject

leave-taking *noun* = **departure**, farewell, going, goodbye, leaving, parting, sendoff (*informal*), valediction

leavings *plural noun* = **leftovers**, bits, dregs, fragments, pieces, refuse, remains, remnants, residue, scraps, spoil, sweepings, waste

lecher noun = **womanizer**, adulterer, Casanova, debauchee, dirty old man (slang), Don Juan, fornicator, goat (informal), lech or letch (informal), libertine, profligate, rake, roué, satyr, seducer, sensualist, wanton, wolf (informal)

lecherous adjective = **lustful**, carnal, lascivious, lewd, libidinous, licentious, prurient, randy (informal, chiefly Brit.), raunchy (slang), salacious, unchaste, wanton
➤ **Antonyms**
prim, proper, prudish, puritanical, strait-laced, virginal, virtuous

lechery noun = **lustfulness**, carnality, debauchery, lasciviousness, lecherousness, leching (informal), lewdness, libertinism, libidinousness, licentiousness, lubricity, lust, profligacy, prurience, rakishness, randiness (informal, chiefly Brit.), salaciousness, sensuality, wantonness, womanizing

lecture noun 1 = **talk**, address, discourse, disquisition, harangue, instruction, lesson, speech 2 = **telling off** (informal), castigation, censure, chiding, dressing-down (informal), going-over (informal), heat (slang, chiefly U.S. & Canad.), rebuke, reprimand, reproof, scolding, talking-to (informal) ♦ verb 3 = **talk**, address, discourse, expound, give a talk, harangue, hold forth, speak, spout, teach 4 = **tell off** (informal), admonish, bawl out (informal), berate, carpet (informal), castigate, censure, chew out (U.S. & Canad. informal), chide, give a rocket (Brit. & N.Z. informal), rate, read the riot act, reprimand, reprove, scold, tear into (informal), tear (someone) off a strip (Brit. informal)

ledge noun = **shelf**, mantle, projection, ridge, sill, step

lee noun = **shelter**, cover, protection, refuge, screen, shade, shadow, shield

leech noun = **parasite**, bloodsucker (informal), freeloader (slang), hanger-on, sponger (informal), sycophant

leer noun, verb = **grin**, drool, eye, gloat, goggle, ogle, smirk, squint, stare, wink

leery adjective Slang = **wary**, careful, cautious, chary, distrustful, doubting, dubious, on one's guard, sceptical, shy, suspicious, uncertain, unsure

lees plural noun = **sediment**, deposit, dregs, grounds, precipitate, refuse, settlings

leeway noun = **room**, elbowroom, latitude, margin, play, scope, space

left adjective 1 = **left-hand**, larboard (Nautical), port, sinistral 2 Of politics = **socialist**, leftist, left-wing, liberal, progressive, radical

left-handed adjective 1 Archaic = **awkward**, cack-handed (informal), careless, clumsy, fumbling, gauche, maladroit 2 = **ambiguous**, backhanded, double-edged, enigmatic, equivocal, indirect, ironic, sardonic

leftover noun 1 = **remnant**, leaving, oddment, remains, scrap ♦ adjective 2 = **surplus**, excess, extra, remaining, uneaten, unused, unwanted

left-wing adjective = **socialist**, communist, Marxist, radical, red (informal)

leg noun 1 = **limb**, lower limb, member, pin (informal), stump (informal) 2 = **support**, brace, prop, upright 3 = **stage**, lap, part, portion, section, segment, stretch 4 **not have a leg to stand on** Informal = **have no basis**, be defenceless, be full of holes, be illogical, be invalid, be undermined, be vulnerable, lack support 5 **on one's (its) last legs** = **worn out**, about to break down, about to collapse, at death's door, dying, exhausted, failing, giving up the ghost 6 **pull someone's leg** Informal = **tease**, chaff, deceive, fool, have (someone) on, joke, kid (informal), make fun of, poke fun at, rag, rib (informal), trick, twit, wind up (Brit. slang) 7 **shake a leg** Informal = **hurry**, get a move on (informal), get cracking (informal), hasten, look lively (informal), rush, stir one's stumps 8 **stretch one's legs** = **take a walk**, exercise, go for a walk, move about, promenade, stroll, take the air ♦ verb 9 **leg it** Informal = **run**, go on foot, hotfoot, hurry, skedaddle (informal), walk

legacy noun 1 = **bequest**, devise (Law), estate, gift, heirloom, inheritance 2 = **heritage**, birthright, endowment, inheritance, patrimony, throwback, tradition

legal adjective 1 = **lawful**, allowable, allowed, authorized, constitutional, legalized, legitimate, licit, permissible, proper, rightful, sanctioned, valid 2 = **judicial**, forensic, judiciary, juridical

legality noun = **lawfulness**, accordance with the law, admissibleness, legitimacy, permissibility, rightfulness, validity

legalize verb = **permit**, allow, approve, authorize, decriminalize, legitimate, legitimize, license, sanction, validate

legal tender noun = **currency**, medium, money, payment, specie

legate noun = **messenger**, ambassador, delegate, depute (Scot.), deputy, emissary, envoy

legatee *noun* = **beneficiary**, heir, inheritor, recipient

legation *noun* = **delegation**, consulate, diplomatic mission, embassy, envoys, ministry, representation

legend *noun* **1** = **myth**, fable, fiction, folk tale, narrative, saga, story, tale, urban legend, urban myth **2** = **celebrity**, big name, celeb (*informal*), luminary, marvel, megastar (*informal*), phenomenon, prodigy, spectacle, wonder **3** = **inscription**, caption, device, motto **4** = **key**, cipher, code, table of symbols

legendary *adjective* **1** = **famous**, celebrated, famed, illustrious, immortal, renowned, well-known **2** = **mythical**, apocryphal, fabled, fabulous, fanciful, fictitious, romantic, traditional
➤ Antonyms
≠**famous**: unknown ≠**mythical**: factual, genuine, historical

legerdemain *noun* **1** = **sleight of hand**, prestidigitation **2** = **deception**, artfulness, artifice, chicanery, contrivance, craftiness, cunning, feint, hocus-pocus, manipulation, manoeuvring, subterfuge, trickery

legibility *noun* = **readability**, clarity, decipherability, ease of reading, legibleness, neatness, plainness, readableness

legible *adjective* = **readable**, bold, clear, decipherable, distinct, easily read, easy to read, neat, plain

legion *noun* **1** = **army**, brigade, company, division, force, troop **2** = **multitude**, drove, horde, host, mass, myriad, number, throng

legislate *verb* = **make laws**, codify, constitute, enact, establish, ordain, pass laws, prescribe, put in force

legislation *noun* **1** = **lawmaking**, codification, enactment, prescription, regulation **2** = **law**, act, bill, charter, measure, regulation, ruling, statute

legislative *adjective* = **law-making**, congressional, judicial, law-giving, parliamentary

legislator *noun* = **lawmaker**, lawgiver, parliamentarian

legislature *noun* = **parliament**, assembly, chamber, congress, diet, house, law-making body, senate

legitimate *adjective* **1** = **lawful**, acknowledged, authentic, authorized, genuine, kosher (*informal*), legal, legit (*slang*), licit, proper, real, rightful, sanctioned, statutory, true **2** = **reasonable**, admissible, correct, just, justifiable, logical, sensible, valid, warranted, well-founded

♦ *verb* **3** = **legitimize**, authorize, give the green light for, legalize, legitimatize, permit, pronounce lawful, sanction
➤ Antonyms
adjective ≠**lawful**: false, fraudulent, illegal, illegitimate, unlawful ≠**reasonable**: unfair, unfounded, unjustified, unreasonable, unsound

legitimize, legitimise *verb* = **legalize**, authorize, give the green light for, legitimate, permit, pronounce lawful, sanction

leisure *noun* **1** = **spare time**, breathing space, ease, freedom, free time, holiday, liberty, opportunity, pause, quiet, recreation, relaxation, respite, rest, retirement, spare moments, time off, vacation **2 at leisure: a** = **free**, available, not booked up, on holiday, unengaged, unoccupied **b at one's leisure** = **in one's own (good) time**, at an unhurried pace, at one's convenience, deliberately, unhurriedly, when it suits one, when one gets round to it (*informal*), without hurry
➤ Antonyms
≠**spare time**: business, duty, employment, labour, obligation, occupation, work

leisurely *adjective* **1** = **unhurried**, comfortable, easy, gentle, laid-back (*informal*), lazy, relaxed, restful, slow
♦ *adverb* **2** = **unhurriedly**, at one's convenience, at one's leisure, comfortably, deliberately, easily, indolently, lazily, lingeringly, slowly, without haste
➤ Antonyms
adjective ≠**unhurried**: brisk, fast, hasty, hectic, hurried, quick, rapid, rushed
♦ *adverb* ≠**unhurriedly**: briskly, hastily, hurriedly, quickly, rapidly

leitmotif *or* **leitmotiv** *noun, with recurrent or recurring* = **theme**, air, convention, device, idea, melody, motif, phrase, strain

lend *verb* **1** = **loan**, accommodate one with, advance **2** = **give**, add, afford, bestow, confer, contribute, furnish, grant, hand out, impart, present, provide, supply **3 lend an ear** = **listen**, give ear, hearken (*archaic*), heed, take notice **4 lend a hand** = **help**, aid, assist, give a (helping) hand, help out **5 lend itself to** = **be appropriate**, be adaptable, be serviceable, fit, present opportunities of, suit

length *noun* **1** *Of linear extent* = **distance**, extent, longitude, measure, reach, span **2** *Of time* = **duration**, period, space, span, stretch, term **3** = **piece**, measure, portion, section, segment **4** = **lengthiness**, elongation, extensiveness, protractedness **5 at length: a** = **at last**, at long last, eventually, finally, in the end **b = in detail**, completely, fully, in depth, thoroughly, to the full **c = for a long time**, for ages, for hours, interminably

lengthen *verb* = **extend**, continue, draw out, elongate, expand, increase, make longer, prolong, protract, spin out, stretch
➤ **Antonyms**
abbreviate, abridge, curtail, cut, cut down, diminish, shorten, trim

lengthy *adjective* = **long**, diffuse, drawn-out, extended, interminable, lengthened, long-drawn-out, long-winded, overlong, prolix, prolonged, protracted, tedious, verbose, very long
➤ **Antonyms**
brief, concise, condensed, limited, short, succinct, terse, to the point

leniency *noun* = **mercy**, clemency, compassion, forbearance, gentleness, indulgence, lenity, mildness, moderation, pity, quarter, tenderness, tolerance

lenient *adjective* = **merciful**, clement, compassionate, forbearing, forgiving, gentle, indulgent, kind, mild, sparing, tender, tolerant
➤ **Antonyms**
harsh, merciless, rigid, rigorous, severe, stern, strict, stringent

leper *noun* = **outcast**, pariah, untouchable

lesbian *noun* 1 = **dyke** (*slang*), butch (*slang*), sapphist ◆ *adjective* 2 = **homosexual**, butch (*slang*), dykey (*slang*), gay, sapphic

lesion *noun* = **injury**, abrasion, bruise, contusion, hurt, trauma (*Pathology*), wound

less *adjective* 1 = **smaller**, shorter, slighter ◆ *adverb* 2 = **to a smaller extent**, barely, little, meagrely ◆ *preposition* 3 = **minus**, excepting, lacking, subtracting, without

lessen *verb* = **reduce**, abate, abridge, contract, curtail, decrease, de-escalate, die down, diminish, downsize, dwindle, ease, grow less, impair, lighten, lower, minimize, moderate, narrow, relax, shrink, slacken, slow down, weaken, wind down
➤ **Antonyms**
add to, augment, boost, enhance, enlarge, expand, increase, magnify, multiply, raise

lessening *noun* = **reduction**, abatement, contraction, curtailment, decline, decrease, diminution, dwindling, ebbing, let-up (*informal*), minimization, moderation, petering out, shrinkage, slackening, slowing down, waning, weakening

lesser *adjective* = **lower**, inferior, less important, minor, secondary, slighter,

subordinate, under-
➤ **Antonyms**
greater, higher, major, primary, superior

lesson *noun* 1 = **class**, coaching, instruction, period, schooling, teaching, tutoring 2 = **exercise**, assignment, drill, homework, lecture, practice, reading, recitation, task 3 = **example**, deterrent, exemplar, message, model, moral, precept 4 = **punishment**, admonition, censure, chiding, rebuke, reprimand, reproof, scolding, warning

let[1] *verb* 1 = **allow**, authorize, entitle, give leave, give permission, give the go-ahead, give the green light, give the O.K. *or* okay (*informal*), grant, permit, sanction, suffer (*archaic*), tolerate, warrant 2 = **lease**, hire, rent 3 = **enable**, allow, cause, grant, make, permit

let[2] *noun* = **hindrance**, constraint, impediment, interference, obstacle, obstruction, prohibition, restriction

letdown *noun* = **disappointment**, anticlimax, bitter pill, blow, comedown (*informal*), frustration, setback, washout (*informal*), whammy (*informal, chiefly U.S.*)

let down *verb* = **disappoint**, disenchant, disillusion, dissatisfy, fail, fall short, leave in the lurch, leave stranded

lethal *adjective* = **deadly**, baneful, dangerous, deathly, destructive, devastating, fatal, mortal, murderous, noxious, pernicious, poisonous, virulent
➤ **Antonyms**
harmless, healthy, innocuous, safe, wholesome

lethargic *adjective* = **sluggish**, apathetic, comatose, debilitated, drowsy, dull, enervated, heavy, inactive, indifferent, inert, languid, lazy, listless, sleepy, slothful, slow, torpid
➤ **Antonyms**
active, alert, animated, energetic, responsive, spirited, stimulated, vigorous

lethargy *noun* = **sluggishness**, apathy, drowsiness, dullness, inaction, indifference, inertia, languor, lassitude, listlessness, sleepiness, sloth, slowness, stupor, torpidity, torpor
➤ **Antonyms**
animation, brio, energy, life, liveliness, spirit, verve, vigour, vim, vitality, vivacity, zeal, zest

let in *verb* = **admit**, allow to enter, give access to, greet, include, incorporate, receive, take in, welcome

let off *verb* 1 = **excuse**, absolve, discharge, dispense, exempt, exonerate, forgive, pardon, release, spare 2 = **fire**, detonate, discharge, explode 3 = **emit**, exude, give off, leak, release

let on *verb Informal* **1** = **reveal**, admit, disclose, divulge, give away, let the cat out of the bag (*informal*), make known, say **2** = **pretend**, act, counterfeit, dissemble, dissimulate, feign, make believe, make out, profess, simulate

let out *verb* **1** = **emit**, give vent to, produce **2** = **release**, discharge, free, let go, liberate **3** = **reveal**, betray, blow wide open (*slang*), disclose, leak, let fall, let slip, make known

letter *noun* **1** = **message**, acknowledgment, answer, billet (*archaic*), communication, dispatch, epistle, line, missive, note, reply **2** = **character**, sign, symbol **3 to the letter** = **precisely**, accurately, exactly, literally, strictly, word for word

lettered *adjective* = **educated**, accomplished, cultivated, cultured, erudite, informed, knowledgeable, learned, literate, scholarly, versed, well-educated, well-read

letters *plural noun* = **learning**, belles-lettres, culture, erudition, humanities, literature, scholarship

let-up *noun Informal* = **lessening**, abatement, break, breathing space, cessation, interval, lull, pause, recess, remission, respite, slackening

let up *verb* = **stop**, abate, decrease, diminish, ease (up), moderate, relax, slacken, subside

levee *noun* = **reception**, ceremony, entertainment, gathering, party

level *adjective* **1** = **horizontal**, as flat as a pancake, flat, plane **2** = **even**, consistent, plain, smooth, uniform **3** = **equal**, aligned, balanced, commensurate, comparable, equivalent, even, flush, in line, neck and neck, on a line, on a par, proportionate ♦ *verb* **4** = **flatten**, even off *or* out, make flat, plane, smooth **5** = **equalize**, balance, even up **6** = **direct**, aim, beam, focus, point, train **7** = **destroy**, bulldoze, demolish, devastate, flatten, knock down, lay low, pull down, raze, tear down, wreck ♦ *noun* **8** = **position**, achievement, degree, grade, rank, stage, standard, standing, status **9** = **height**, altitude, elevation, vertical position **10** = **flat surface**, horizontal, plain, plane **11 on the level** *Informal* = **honest**, above board, fair, genuine, open, sincere, square, straight, straightforward, up front (*slang*)
➤ **Antonyms**
adjective ≠**horizontal**: slanted, tilted, vertical ≠**even**: bumpy, uneven ≠**equal**: above, below ♦ *verb* ≠**destroy**: build, erect, raise, roughen

level-headed *adjective* = **calm**, balanced,

collected, composed, cool, dependable, even-tempered, reasonable, sane, self-possessed, sensible, steady, together (*slang*), unflappable (*informal*)

lever *noun* **1** = **handle**, bar, crowbar, jemmy ♦ *verb* **2** = **prise**, force, jemmy, move, pry (*U.S.*), raise

leverage *noun* = **influence**, authority, clout (*informal*), pull (*informal*), purchasing power, rank, weight

leviathan *noun* = **monster**, behemoth, colossus, hulk, mammoth, Titan, whale

levity *noun* = **light-heartedness**, buoyancy, facetiousness, flightiness, flippancy, frivolity, giddiness, light-mindedness, silliness, skittishness, triviality
➤ **Antonyms**
earnestness, gravity, seriousness, solemnity

levy *verb* **1** = **impose**, charge, collect, demand, exact, gather, tax **2** = **conscript**, call, call up, mobilize, muster, press, raise, summon ♦ *noun* **3** = **imposition**, assessment, collection, exaction, gathering **4** = **tax**, assessment, duty, excise, fee, imposition, impost, tariff, toll

lewd *adjective* = **indecent**, bawdy, blue, dirty, impure, lascivious, libidinous, licentious, loose, lustful, obscene, pornographic, salacious, smutty, unchaste, vile, vulgar, wanton, wicked, X-rated (*informal*)

lewdness *noun* = **indecency**, bawdiness, carnality, crudity, debauchery, depravity, impurity, lasciviousness, lechery, licentiousness, lubricity, obscenity, pornography, salaciousness, smut, smuttiness, unchastity, vulgarity, wantonness

lexicon *noun* = **vocabulary**, dictionary, glossary, wordbook, word list

liabilities *plural noun* = **debts**, accounts payable, expenditure, obligations

liability *noun* **1** = **disadvantage**, albatross, burden, drag, drawback, encumbrance, handicap, hindrance, impediment, inconvenience, millstone, minus (*informal*), nuisance **2** = **responsibility**, accountability, answerability, culpability, duty, obligation, onus **3** = **debt**, arrear, debit, obligation

liable *adjective* **1** = **likely**, apt, disposed, inclined, prone, tending **2** = **vulnerable**, exposed, open, subject, susceptible **3** = **responsible**, accountable, answerable, bound, chargeable, obligated

liaise *verb* = **communicate**, keep contact, link, mediate

liaison *noun* **1** = **communication**, connection, contact, go-between,

hook-up, interchange, intermediary **2**
= **affair**, amour, entanglement, fling, illicit
romance, intrigue, love affair, romance

liar *noun* = **falsifier**, fabricator, fibber,
perjurer, prevaricator, storyteller (*informal*)

libel *noun* **1** = **defamation**, aspersion,
calumny, denigration, obloquy, slander,
smear, vituperation ♦ *verb* **2** = **defame**,
blacken, calumniate, derogate, drag
(someone's) name through the mud,
malign, revile, slander, slur, smear,
traduce, vilify

libellous *adjective* = **defamatory**,
derogatory, false, injurious, malicious,
maligning, scurrilous, slanderous,
traducing, untrue, vilifying, vituperative

liberal *adjective* **1** = **progressive**, advanced,
humanistic, latitudinarian, libertarian,
politically correct or PC, radical, reformist,
right-on (*informal*) **2** = **generous**,
beneficent, bounteous, bountiful,
charitable, free-handed, kind,
open-handed, open-hearted, prodigal,
unstinting **3** = **tolerant**, advanced,
broad-minded, catholic, enlightened,
high-minded, humanitarian, indulgent,
magnanimous, permissive, politically
correct or PC, right-on (*informal*),
unbiased, unbigoted, unprejudiced **4**
= **abundant**, ample, bountiful, copious,
handsome, lavish, munificent, plentiful,
profuse, rich **5** = **flexible**, broad, free,
general, inexact, lenient, loose, not close,
not literal, not strict
➤ **Antonyms**
≠**progressive**: conservative, reactionary,
right-wing ≠**generous**: cheap, stingy
≠**tolerant**: biased, bigoted, intolerant,
prejudiced ≠**abundant**: inadequate,
limited, skimpy, small ≠**flexible**: fixed,
inflexible, literal, strict

liberalism *noun* = **progressivism**,
freethinking, humanitarianism,
latitudinarianism, libertarianism, radicalism

liberality *noun* **1** = **generosity**,
beneficence, benevolence, bounty,
charity, free-handedness, kindness,
largesse or largess, munificence,
open-handedness, philanthropy **2**
= **broad-mindedness**, breadth, candour,
catholicity, impartiality, latitude,
liberalism, libertarianism, magnanimity,
permissiveness, progressivism, toleration

liberalize *verb* = **relax**, ameliorate,
broaden, ease, expand, extend, loosen,
mitigate, moderate, modify, slacken,
soften, stretch

liberate *verb* = **free**, deliver, discharge,
emancipate, let loose, let out, redeem,
release, rescue, set free

➤ **Antonyms**
confine, detain, immure, imprison,
incarcerate, intern, jail, lock up, put away

liberation *noun* = **freeing**, deliverance,
emancipation, enfranchisement, freedom,
liberating, liberty, manumission,
redemption, release, unfettering,
unshackling

liberator *noun* = **deliverer**, emancipator,
freer, manumitter, redeemer, rescuer,
saviour

libertine *noun* **1** = **reprobate**, debauchee,
lech or letch (*informal*), lecher, loose liver,
profligate, rake, roué, seducer, sensualist,
swinger (*slang*), voluptuary, womanizer
♦ *adjective* **2** = **promiscuous**, abandoned,
corrupt, debauched, decadent,
degenerate, depraved, dissolute, immoral,
licentious, profligate, rakish, reprobate,
voluptuous, wanton

liberty *noun* **1** = **freedom**, autonomy,
emancipation, immunity, independence,
liberation, release, self-determination,
sovereignty **2** = **permission**, authorization,
blank cheque, carte blanche, dispensation,
exemption, franchise, freedom, leave,
licence, prerogative, privilege, right,
sanction **3** = **impertinence**, disrespect,
familiarity, forwardness, impropriety,
impudence, insolence, overfamiliarity,
presumption, presumptuousness **4 at**
liberty = **free**, not confined, on the loose,
unlimited, unoccupied, unrestricted
➤ **Antonyms**
≠**freedom**: captivity, constraint,
enslavement, imprisonment, restraint,
slavery, tyranny ≠**permission**:
compulsion, duress, restriction

libidinous *adjective* = **lustful**, carnal,
debauched, impure, incontinent,
lascivious, lecherous, loose, prurient, randy
(*informal, chiefly Brit.*), ruttish, salacious,
sensual, unchaste, wanton, wicked

libretto *noun* = **words**, book, lines, lyrics,
script

licence *noun* **1** = **certificate**, charter,
permit, warrant **2** = **permission**, a free
hand, authority, authorization, blank
cheque, carte blanche, dispensation,
entitlement, exemption, immunity, leave,
liberty, privilege, right **3** = **freedom**,
independence, latitude, leeway, liberty **4**
= **laxity**, abandon, anarchy, disorder,
excess, immoderation, impropriety,
indulgence, irresponsibility, lawlessness,
profligacy, unruliness
➤ **Antonyms**
≠**permission**: denial, prohibition,
restriction ≠**freedom**: constraint, restraint
≠**laxity**: moderation, strictness

license *verb* = **permit**, accredit, allow, authorize, certify, commission, empower, enable, entitle, give a blank cheque to, sanction, warrant
➤ Antonyms
ban, debar, disallow, forbid, outlaw, prohibit, proscribe, rule out, veto

licentious *adjective* = **promiscuous**, abandoned, debauched, dissolute, immoral, impure, lascivious, lewd, libertine, libidinous, lustful, profligate, sensual, uncontrollable, uncontrolled, unruly, wanton
➤ Antonyms
chaste, law-abiding, lawful, moral, principled, proper, scrupulous, virtuous

licentiousness *noun* = **promiscuity**, abandon, debauchery, dissipation, dissoluteness, lechery, lewdness, libertinism, libidinousness, lust, lustfulness, profligacy, prurience, salaciousness, salacity, wantonness

lick *verb* 1 = **taste**, brush, lap, tongue, touch, wash 2 *Of flames* = **flicker**, dart, flick, ignite, kindle, play over, ripple, touch 3 *Informal* = **beat**, best, blow out of the water (*slang*), clobber (*slang*), defeat, master, outdo, outstrip, overcome, rout, run rings around (*informal*), stuff (*slang*), surpass, tank (*slang*), top, trounce, vanquish, wipe the floor with (*informal*) 4 *Informal* = **thrash**, beat, clobber (*slang*), flog, slap, spank, strike, wallop (*informal*) ◆ *noun* 5 = **dab**, bit, brush, little, sample, speck, stroke, taste, touch 6 *Informal* = **pace**, clip (*informal*), rate, speed

lie[1] *verb* 1 = **fib**, dissimulate, equivocate, fabricate, falsify, forswear oneself, invent, misrepresent, perjure, prevaricate, tell a lie, tell untruths ◆ *noun* 2 = **falsehood**, deceit, fabrication, falsification, falsity, fib, fiction, invention, mendacity, pork pie (*Brit. slang*), porky (*Brit. slang*), prevarication, untruth, white lie

lie[2] *verb* 1 = **recline**, be prone, be prostrate, be recumbent, be supine, couch, loll, lounge, repose, rest, sprawl, stretch out 2 = **be situated**, be, be buried, be found, be interred, be located, belong, be placed, exist, extend, remain 3 *usually with* **in** = **exist**, be present, consist, dwell, inhere, pertain

liege *noun* = **feudal lord**, chieftain, master, overlord, sovereign, superior

lieu *noun* **in lieu of** = **instead of**, in place of

life *noun* 1 = **being**, animation, breath, entity, sentience, viability, vitality 2 = **existence**, being, continuance, course, duration, lifetime, span, time 3 = **person**, human, human being, individual, mortal,

soul 4 = **behaviour**, conduct, life style, way of life 5 = **biography**, autobiography, career, confessions, history, life story, memoirs, story 6 = **the human condition**, the times, the world, this mortal coil 7 = **liveliness**, activity, animation, brio, energy, get-up-and-go (*informal*), go (*informal*), high spirits, pep, sparkle, spirit, verve, vigour, vitality, vivacity, zest 8 = **spirit**, animating spirit, *élan vital*, essence, heart, lifeblood, soul, vital spark 9 = **living things**, creatures, living beings, organisms, wildlife

lifeblood *noun* = **animating force**, driving force, essence, guts (*informal*), heart, inspiration, life, stimulus, vital spark

lifeless *adjective* 1 = **dead**, cold, deceased, defunct, extinct, inanimate, inert 2 = **dull**, cold, colourless, flat, heavy, hollow, lacklustre, lethargic, listless, passive, slow, sluggish, spiritless, static, stiff, torpid, wooden 3 = **unconscious**, comatose, dead to the world (*informal*), in a faint, inert, insensate, insensible, out cold, out for the count
➤ Antonyms
≠**dead**: alive, alive and kicking, animate, live, living, vital ≠**dull**: active, animated, lively, spirited

lifelike *adjective* = **realistic**, authentic, exact, faithful, graphic, natural, photographic, real, true-to-life, undistorted, vivid

lifelong *adjective* = **long-lasting**, constant, deep-rooted, enduring, for all one's life, for life, lasting, lifetime, long-standing, perennial, permanent, persistent

lifetime *noun* = **existence**, all one's born days, career, course, day(s), life span, one's natural life, period, span, time

lift *verb* 1 = **raise**, bear aloft, buoy up, draw up, elevate, heft (*informal*), hoist, pick up, raise high, rear, upheave, uplift, upraise 2 = **exalt**, advance, ameliorate, boost, dignify, elevate, enhance, improve, promote, raise, upgrade 3 = **revoke**, annul, cancel, countermand, end, relax, remove, rescind, stop, terminate 4 = **disappear**, be dispelled, disperse, dissipate, vanish 5 *Informal* = **steal**, appropriate, blag (*slang*), copy, crib (*informal*), nick (*slang, chiefly Brit.*), pilfer, pinch (*informal*), pirate, plagiarize, purloin, take, thieve ◆ *noun* 6 = **elevator** (*chiefly U.S.*) 7 = **ride**, car ride, drive, run, transport 8 = **boost**, encouragement, fillip, gee-up, pick-me-up, reassurance, shot in the arm (*informal*), uplift
➤ Antonyms
verb ≠**raise**: dash, descend, drop, fall,

hang, lower ≠**exalt**: depress ≠**revoke**: establish, impose ♦ *noun* ≠**boost**: blow, letdown

ligature *noun* = **link**, band, bandage, binding, bond, connection, ligament, tie

light[1] *noun* 1 = **brightness**, blaze, brilliance, flash, glare, gleam, glint, glow, illumination, incandescence, luminescence, luminosity, lustre, phosphorescence, radiance, ray, scintillation, shine, sparkle 2 = **lamp**, beacon, bulb, candle, flare, lantern, lighthouse, star, taper, torch 3 = **daybreak**, broad day, cockcrow, dawn, daylight, daytime, morn (*poetic*), morning, sun, sunrise 4 = **aspect**, angle, approach, attitude, context, interpretation, point of view, slant, vantage point, viewpoint 5 = **understanding**, awareness, comprehension, elucidation, explanation, insight, knowledge 6 = **shining example**, example, exemplar, guiding light, model, paragon 7 = **match**, flame, lighter 8 **in (the) light of** = **considering**, bearing in mind, because of, in view of, taking into account, with knowledge of ♦ *adjective* 9 = **bright**, aglow, brilliant, glowing, illuminated, luminous, lustrous, shining, sunny, well-lighted, well-lit 10 = **pale**, bleached, blond, faded, fair, light-hued, light-toned, pastel ♦ *verb* 11 = **ignite**, fire, inflame, kindle, set a match to, torch 12 = **illuminate**, brighten, floodlight, flood with light, illumine, lighten, light up

➤ **Antonyms**
noun ≠**brightness**: cloud, dark, darkness, dusk, obscurity, shade, shadow ≠**understanding**: mystery ♦ *adjective* ≠**bright**: dark, dim, dusky, gloomy ≠**pale**: dark, deep ♦ *verb* ≠**ignite**: douse, extinguish, put out, quench ≠**illuminate**: cloud, darken, dull

light[2] *adjective* 1 = **insubstantial**, airy, buoyant, delicate, easy, flimsy, imponderous, lightsome, lightweight, portable, slight, underweight 2 = **weak**, faint, gentle, indistinct, mild, moderate, slight, soft 3 = **insignificant**, inconsequential, inconsiderable, minute, scanty, slight, small, thin, tiny, trifling, trivial, unsubstantial, wee 4 = **undemanding**, cushy (*informal*), easy, effortless, manageable, moderate, simple, unexacting, untaxing 5 = **light-hearted**, amusing, diverting, entertaining, frivolous, funny, gay, humorous, pleasing, superficial, trifling, trivial, witty 6 = **nimble**, agile, airy, graceful, light-footed, lithe, sprightly, sylphlike 7 = **digestible**, frugal, modest, not heavy, not rich, small 8 = **carefree**, airy, animated, blithe, cheerful,

cheery, frivolous, gay, lively, merry, sunny 9 = **dizzy**, giddy, light-headed, reeling, unsteady ♦ *verb* 10 = **settle**, alight, land, perch 11 **light on** *or* **upon** = **come across**, chance upon, discover, encounter, find, happen upon, hit upon, stumble on

➤ **Antonyms**
adjective ≠**insubstantial**: heavy ≠**weak**: forceful, strong ≠**insignificant**: deep, profound, serious, weighty ≠**undemanding**: burdensome, strenuous ≠**light-hearted**: serious, sombre ≠**nimble**: clumsy ≠**digestible**: rich, substantial

lighten[1] *verb* = **brighten**, become light, flash, gleam, illuminate, irradiate, light up, make bright, shine

lighten[2] *verb* 1 = **make lighter**, ease, reduce in weight, unload 2 = **ease**, allay, alleviate, ameliorate, assuage, facilitate, lessen, mitigate, reduce, relieve 3 = **cheer**, brighten, buoy up, encourage, gladden, hearten, inspire, lift, perk up, revive

➤ **Antonyms**
≠**make lighter**: burden, encumber, handicap ≠**ease**: aggravate, heighten, increase, intensify, make worse, worsen ≠**cheer**: depress, oppress, sadden, weigh down

light-fingered *adjective* = **thieving**, dishonest, pilfering, pinching (*informal*), stealing

light-footed *adjective* = **nimble**, agile, graceful, lithe, sprightly, spry, swift

light-headed *adjective* = **faint**, delirious, dizzy, giddy, hazy, vertiginous, woozy (*informal*)

light-hearted *adjective* = **carefree**, blithe, bright, cheerful, chirpy (*informal*), effervescent, frolicsome, gay, genial, glad, happy-go-lucky, insouciant, jocund, jolly, jovial, joyful, joyous, merry, playful, sunny, untroubled, upbeat (*informal*)
➤ **Antonyms**
cheerless, dejected, depressed, despondent, gloomy, heavy-hearted, low, melancholy, morose, sad

lightly *adverb* 1 = **moderately**, sparingly, sparsely, thinly 2 = **gently**, airily, delicately, faintly, gingerly, slightly, softly, timidly 3 = **easily**, effortlessly, readily, simply 4 = **carelessly**, breezily, flippantly, frivolously, heedlessly, indifferently, slightingly, thoughtlessly
➤ **Antonyms**
≠**moderately**: abundantly, heavily, thickly ≠**gently**: firmly, forcefully, heavily ≠**easily**: arduously, awkwardly, slowly, with difficulty ≠**carelessly**: carefully, earnestly, ponderously, seriously

lightweight *adjective* = **unimportant**,

inconsequential, insignificant, nickel-and-dime (*U.S. slang*), of no account, paltry, petty, slight, trifling, trivial, worthless
➤ **Antonyms**
important, momentous, serious, significant, substantial, weighty

likable, likeable *adjective* = **attractive**, agreeable, amiable, appealing, charming, engaging, friendly, genial, nice, pleasant, pleasing, sympathetic, winning, winsome

like [1] *adjective* **1** = **similar**, akin, alike, allied, analogous, approximating, cognate, corresponding, equivalent, identical, parallel, relating, resembling, same ♦ *noun* **2** = **equal**, counterpart, fellow, match, parallel, twin
➤ **Antonyms**
adjective ≠**similar**: contrasted, different, dissimilar, divergent, diverse, opposite, unlike ♦ *noun* ≠**equal**: opposite

like [2] *verb* **1** = **enjoy**, adore (*informal*), be fond of, be keen on, be partial to, delight in, dig (*slang*), go for, love, relish, revel in **2** = **admire**, appreciate, approve, cherish, esteem, hold dear, prize, take a shine to (*informal*), take to **3** = **wish**, care to, choose, choose to, desire, fancy, feel inclined, prefer, select, want ♦ *noun* **4** *usually plural* = **preference**, cup of tea (*informal*), favourite, liking, partiality, predilection
➤ **Antonyms**
verb ≠**enjoy**, **admire**: abominate, despise, detest, dislike, hate, loathe

likelihood *noun* = **probability**, chance, good chance, liability, likeliness, possibility, prospect, strong possibility

likely *adjective* **1** = **inclined**, apt, disposed, liable, prone, tending **2** = **probable**, anticipated, expected, odds-on, on the cards, to be expected **3** = **plausible**, believable, credible, feasible, possible, reasonable **4** = **appropriate**, acceptable, agreeable, befitting, fit, pleasing, proper, qualified, suitable **5** = **promising**, fair, favourite, hopeful, up-and-coming ♦ *adverb* **6** = **probably**, doubtlessly, in all probability, like as not (*informal*), like enough (*informal*), no doubt, presumably

like-minded *adjective* = **agreeing**, compatible, *en rapport*, harmonious, in accord, in harmony, of one mind, of the same mind, unanimous

liken *verb* = **compare**, equate, juxtapose, match, mention in the same breath, parallel, relate, set beside

likeness *noun* **1** = **resemblance**, affinity, correspondence, similarity, similitude **2** = **portrait**, copy, counterpart, depiction,

effigy, facsimile, image, model, photograph, picture, replica, representation, reproduction, study **3** = **appearance**, form, guise, semblance

likewise *adverb* **1** = **also**, besides, further, furthermore, in addition, moreover, too **2** = **similarly**, in like manner, in the same way

liking *noun* = **fondness**, affection, affinity, appreciation, attraction, bent, bias, desire, inclination, love, partiality, penchant, predilection, preference, proneness, propensity, soft spot, stomach, taste, tendency, thirst, weakness
➤ **Antonyms**
abhorrence, aversion, dislike, hatred, loathing, repugnance

Lilliputian *noun* **1** = **midget**, dwarf, homunculus, hop-o'-my-thumb, manikin, pygmy *or* pigmy ♦ *adjective* **2** = **tiny**, baby, diminutive, dwarf, little, mini, miniature, minuscule, petite, pocket-sized, pygmy *or* pigmy, small, wee

lilt *noun* = **rhythm**, beat, cadence, sway, swing

lily-livered *adjective* Old-fashioned = **cowardly**, abject, chicken (*slang*), chicken-hearted, craven, faint-hearted, fearful, gutless (*informal*), pusillanimous, scared, spineless, timid, timorous, yellow (*informal*), yellow-bellied (*slang*)

limb *noun* **1** = **part**, appendage, arm, extension, extremity, leg, member, wing **2** = **branch**, bough, offshoot, projection, spur

limber *adjective* **1** = **pliant**, elastic, flexible, plastic, pliable, supple **2** = **agile**, graceful, lissom(e), lithe, loose-jointed, loose-limbed, supple ♦ *verb* **3 limber up** = **loosen up**, exercise, get ready, prepare, warm up

limelight *noun* = **publicity**, attention, celebrity, fame, glare of publicity, prominence, public eye, public notice, recognition, stardom, the spotlight

limit *noun* **1** = **end**, bound, breaking point, cutoff point, deadline, end point, furthest bound, greatest extent, termination, the bitter end, ultimate, utmost **2** = **boundary**, border, confines, edge, end, extent, frontier, pale, perimeter, periphery, precinct **3** = **maximum**, ceiling, check, curb, limitation, obstruction, restraint, restriction **4 the limit** *Informal* = **the last straw**, enough, it (*informal*), the end ♦ *verb* **5** = **restrict**, bound, check, circumscribe, confine, curb, delimit, demarcate, fix, hem in, hinder, ration, restrain, specify, straiten

limitation *noun* = **restriction**, block, check, condition, constraint, control, curb, disadvantage, drawback, impediment, obstruction, qualification, reservation, restraint, snag

limited *adjective* **1** = **restricted**, bounded, checked, circumscribed, confined, constrained, controlled, curbed, defined, finite, fixed, hampered, hemmed in **2** = **narrow**, cramped, diminished, inadequate, insufficient, minimal, reduced, restricted, scant, short, unsatisfactory
➤ **Antonyms**
≠**restricted**: boundless, limitless, unlimited, unrestricted

limitless *adjective* = **infinite**, boundless, countless, endless, illimitable, immeasurable, immense, inexhaustible, measureless, never-ending, numberless, unbounded, uncalculable, undefined, unending, unlimited, untold, vast

limp[1] *verb* **1** = **hobble**, falter, halt (*archaic*), hirple (*Scot.*), hop, shamble, shuffle ♦ *noun* **2** = **lameness**, hirple (*Scot.*), hobble

limp[2] *adjective* **1** = **floppy**, drooping, flabby, flaccid, flexible, lax, limber, loose, pliable, relaxed, slack, soft **2** = **weak**, debilitated, enervated, exhausted, lethargic, spent, tired, worn out
➤ **Antonyms**
≠**floppy**: firm, hard, rigid, solid, stiff, taut, tense, unyielding ≠**weak**: hardy, powerful, robust, strong, sturdy, tough

limpid *adjective* **1** = **clear**, bright, crystal-clear, crystalline, pure, translucent, transparent **2** = **understandable**, clear, comprehensible, intelligible, lucid, perspicuous, unambiguous

line[1] *noun* **1** = **stroke**, band, bar, channel, dash, groove, mark, rule, score, scratch, streak, stripe, underline **2** = **wrinkle**, crease, crow's foot, furrow, mark **3** = **boundary**, border, borderline, demarcation, edge, frontier, limit, mark **4** = **outline**, configuration, contour, features, figure, profile, silhouette **5** = **string**, cable, cord, filament, rope, strand, thread, wire, wisp **6** = **trajectory**, axis, course, direction, path, route, track **7** = **approach**, avenue, belief, course, course of action, ideology, method, policy, position, practice, procedure, scheme, system **8** = **occupation**, activity, area, bag (*slang*), business, calling, department, employment, field, forte, interest, job, profession, province, pursuit, specialization, trade, vocation **9** = **row**, column, crocodile (*Brit.*), file, procession, queue, rank, sequence, series **10** *Military* = **formation**, disposition, firing line, front, front line, position, trenches **11 draw the line** = **object**, lay down the law, prohibit, put one's foot down, restrict, set a limit **12**

in line: **a** = **in alignment**, in a row, plumb, straight, true **b** = **in accord**, in agreement, in conformity, in harmony, in step **13 in line for** = **due for**, a candidate for, being considered for, in the running for, next in succession to, on the short list for ♦ *verb* **14** = **mark**, crease, cut, draw, furrow, rule, score, trace, underline **15** = **border**, bound, edge, fringe, rim, skirt, verge

line[2] *verb* = **fill**, ceil, cover, face, interline

lineage *noun* = **descent**, ancestry, birth, descendants, extraction, family, forebears, forefathers, genealogy, house, line, offspring, pedigree, progeny

lineaments *plural noun* = **features**, configuration, countenance, face, line, outline, physiognomy, visage

lined *adjective* **1** = **ruled**, feint **2** = **wrinkled**, furrowed, wizened, worn

lines *plural noun* = **words**, part, script

line-up *noun* = **arrangement**, array, row, selection, team

line up *verb* **1** = **queue up**, fall in, form ranks **2** = **produce**, assemble, come up with, lay on, obtain, organize, prepare, procure, secure

linger *verb* **1** = **stay**, hang around, hang in the air, loiter, remain, stop, tarry, wait **2** = **continue**, abide, endure, persist, remain, stay **3** = **hang on**, cling to life, die slowly, last, survive **4** = **delay**, dally, dawdle, drag one's feet *or* heels, idle, lag, procrastinate, take one's time

lingering *adjective* = **slow**, dragging, long-drawn-out, protracted, remaining

lingo *noun Informal* = **language**, argot, cant, dialect, idiom, jargon, patois, patter, speech, talk, tongue

liniment *noun* = **ointment**, balm, balsam, cream, embrocation, emollient, lotion, salve, unguent

link *noun* **1** = **component**, constituent, division, element, member, part, piece **2** = **connection**, affiliation, affinity, association, attachment, bond, joint, knot, liaison, relationship, tie, tie-up ♦ *verb* **3** = **connect**, attach, bind, couple, fasten, join, tie, unite, yoke **4** = **associate**, bracket, connect, identify, relate
➤ **Antonyms**
verb ≠**connect**: detach, disconnect, divide, separate, sever, split, sunder

lion *noun* **1** = **hero**, brave person, champion, conqueror, fighter, warrior **2** = **celebrity**, big name, celeb (*informal*), idol, luminary, megastar (*informal*), notable, prodigy, star, superstar, V.I.P., wonder

lion-hearted *adjective* = **brave**, bold,

courageous, daring, dauntless, heroic, intrepid, resolute, stalwart, valiant, valorous
➤ **Antonyms**
abject, chicken-hearted, chickenshit (*U.S. slang*), cowardly, craven, faint-hearted, gutless (*informal*), lily-livered, pusillanimous, spineless, timorous, wimpish *or* wimpy (*informal*), wussy (*slang*), yellow (*informal*)

lionize *verb* = **idolize**, acclaim, celebrate, crack up (*informal*), eulogize, exalt, fête, glorify, hero-worship, honour, make much of, sing *or* sound the praises of

lip *noun* **1** = **edge**, brim, brink, flange, margin, rim **2** *Slang* = **impudence**, backchat (*informal*), cheek (*informal*), effrontery, impertinence, insolence, rudeness, sauce (*informal*) **3 smack** *or* **lick one's lips** = **relish**, anticipate, delight in, drool over, enjoy, gloat over, savour, slaver over

liquefaction *noun* = **melting**, dissolving, thawing

liquefy *verb* = **melt**, dissolve, run, thaw

liquid *noun* **1** = **fluid**, juice, liquor, solution ◆ *adjective* **2** = **fluid**, aqueous, flowing, liquefied, melted, molten, running, runny, thawed, wet **3** = **clear**, bright, brilliant, limpid, shining, translucent, transparent **4** = **smooth**, dulcet, flowing, fluent, mellifluent, mellifluous, melting, soft, sweet **5** *Of assets* = **convertible**, negotiable

liquidate *verb* **1** = **pay**, clear, discharge, honour, pay off, settle, square **2** = **dissolve**, abolish, annul, cancel, terminate **3** = **convert to cash**, cash, realize, sell off, sell up **4** = **kill**, annihilate, blow away (*slang, chiefly U.S.*), bump off (*slang*), destroy, dispatch, do away with, do in (*slang*), eliminate, exterminate, finish off, get rid of, murder, wipe out (*informal*)

liquor *noun* **1** = **alcohol**, booze (*informal*), drink, Dutch courage (*informal*), grog, hard stuff (*informal*), hooch *or* hootch (*informal, chiefly U.S. & Canad.*), intoxicant, spirits, strong drink **2** = **juice**, broth, extract, gravy, infusion, liquid, stock

lissom(e) *adjective* = **supple**, agile, flexible, graceful, light, limber, lithe, loose-jointed, loose-limbed, nimble, pliable, pliant, willowy

list[1] *noun* **1** = **inventory**, catalogue, directory, file, index, invoice, leet (*Scot.*), listing, record, register, roll, schedule, series, syllabus, tally ◆ *verb* **2** = **itemize**, catalogue, enrol, enter, enumerate, file, index, note, record, register, schedule, set down, tabulate, write down

list[2] *verb* **1** = **lean**, cant, careen, heel, heel

over, incline, tilt, tip ◆ *noun* **2** = **tilt**, cant, leaning, slant

listen *verb* **1** = **hear**, attend, be all ears, be attentive, give ear, hang on (someone's) words, hark, hearken (*archaic*), keep one's ears open, lend an ear, prick up one's ears **2** = **pay attention**, concentrate, do as one is told, give heed to, heed, mind, obey, observe, take notice

listless *adjective* = **languid**, apathetic, enervated, impassive, inattentive, indifferent, indolent, inert, languishing, lethargic, lifeless, limp, sluggish, spiritless
➤ **Antonyms**
active, alert, alive and kicking, attentive, energetic, full of beans (*informal*), lively, sparky, spirited, wide-awake

litany *noun* **1** = **prayer**, invocation, petition, supplication **2** = **recital**, account, catalogue, enumeration, list, recitation

literacy *noun* = **education**, articulacy, articulateness, knowledge, learning, scholarship

literal *adjective* **1** = **exact**, accurate, close, faithful, strict, verbatim, word for word **2** = **unimaginative**, boring, colourless, down-to-earth, dull, factual, matter-of-fact, prosaic, prosy, uninspired **3** = **actual**, bona fide, genuine, gospel, plain, real, simple, true, unexaggerated, unvarnished

literally *adverb* = **exactly**, actually, faithfully, plainly, precisely, really, simply, strictly, to the letter, truly, verbatim, word for word

literary *adjective* = **well-read**, bookish, erudite, formal, learned, lettered, literate, scholarly

literate *adjective* = **educated**, cultivated, cultured, erudite, informed, knowledgeable, learned, lettered, scholarly, well-informed, well-read

literature *noun* **1** = **writings**, letters, lore, written works **2** = **information**, brochure, leaflet, mailshot, pamphlet

lithe *adjective* = **supple**, flexible, limber, lissom(e), loose-jointed, loose-limbed, pliable, pliant

litigant *noun* = **claimant**, contestant, disputant, litigator, party, plaintiff

litigate *verb* = **sue**, contest at law, file a suit, go to court, go to law, institute legal proceedings, press charges, prosecute

litigation *noun* = **lawsuit**, action, case, contending, disputing, process, prosecution

litigious *adjective* = **contentious**, argumentative, belligerent, disputatious, quarrelsome

litter noun **1** = **rubbish**, debris, detritus, fragments, garbage (*chiefly U.S.*), muck, refuse, shreds, trash **2** = **jumble**, clutter, confusion, disarray, disorder, mess, scatter, untidiness **3** = **brood**, family, offspring, progeny, young **4** = **bedding**, couch, floor cover, mulch, straw-bed **5** = **stretcher**, palanquin ♦ verb **6** = **clutter**, derange, disarrange, disorder, mess up **7** = **scatter**, strew

little adjective **1** = **small**, diminutive, dwarf, elfin, infinitesimal, Lilliputian, mini, miniature, minute, petite, pygmy *or* pigmy, short, slender, tiny, wee **2** = **young**, babyish, immature, infant, junior, undeveloped **3** = **mean**, base, cheap, illiberal, narrow-minded, petty, small-minded **4** = **unimportant**, inconsiderable, insignificant, minor, negligible, paltry, trifling, trivial **5** = **not much**, hardly any, insufficient, meagre, measly, scant, skimpy, small, sparse **6** = **short**, brief, fleeting, hasty, passing, short-lived ♦ adverb **7** = **hardly**, barely, not much, not quite, only just **8** = **rarely**, hardly ever, not often, scarcely, seldom **9** **little by little** = **gradually**, bit by bit, by degrees, imperceptibly, piecemeal, progressively, slowly, step by step ♦ noun **10** = **bit**, dab, dash, fragment, hint, modicum, particle, pinch, small amount, snippet, speck, spot, tad (*informal, chiefly U.S.*), taste, touch, trace, trifle
➤ **Antonyms**
adjective ≠**small**: big, colossal, considerable, enormous, giant, ginormous (*informal*), great, huge, immense, large, mega (*slang*) ≠**unimportant**: grave, important, major, momentous, serious, significant ≠**not much**: abundant, ample, much, plentiful ≠**short**: long ♦ adverb ≠**hardly**: certainly, much, surely ≠**rarely**: always, much ♦ noun ≠**bit**: lot, many, much

liturgy noun = **ceremony**, celebration, form of worship, formula, rite, ritual, sacrament, service, services, worship

livable adjective **1** = **tolerable**, acceptable, bearable, endurable, passable, sufferable **2** with **with** = **congenial**, companionable, compatible, easy, easy to live with, harmonious, sociable

live[1] verb **1** = **exist**, be, be alive, breathe, draw breath, have life **2** = **persist**, be permanent, be remembered, last, prevail, remain alive **3** = **dwell**, abide, hang out (*informal*), inhabit, lodge, occupy, reside, settle, stay (*chiefly Scot.*) **4** = **survive**, abide, continue, earn a living, endure, fare, feed, get along, lead, make ends meet, pass, remain, subsist, support oneself **5** = **thrive**,
be happy, enjoy life, flourish, luxuriate, make the most of life, prosper

live[2] adjective **1** = **living**, alive, animate, breathing, existent, quick (*archaic*), vital **2** = **topical**, active, burning, controversial, current, hot, pertinent, pressing, prevalent, vital **3** = **burning**, active, alight, blazing, connected, glowing, hot, ignited, smouldering, switched on

livelihood noun = **occupation**, bread and butter (*informal*), employment, job, living, maintenance, means, (means of) support, (source of) income, subsistence, sustenance, work

liveliness noun = **energy**, activity, animation, boisterousness, brio, briskness, dynamism, gaiety, spirit, sprightliness, vitality, vivacity

livelong adjective Chiefly poetic = **everlasting**, complete, entire, full, long-drawn-out, whole

lively adjective **1** = **vigorous**, active, agile, alert, alive and kicking, bright-eyed and bushy-tailed, brisk, chirpy (*informal*), energetic, full of beans (*informal*), full of pep (*informal*), keen, nimble, perky, quick, sprightly, spry **2** = **animated**, blithe, cheerful, chirpy (*informal*), frisky, gay, merry, sparkling, sparky, spirited, upbeat (*informal*), vivacious **3** = **busy**, astir, bustling, buzzing, crowded, eventful, moving, stirring **4** = **vivid**, bright, colourful, exciting, forceful, invigorating, racy, refreshing, stimulating
➤ **Antonyms**
≠**vigorous**: debilitated, disabled, inactive, slow, sluggish, torpid ≠**animated**: apathetic, dull, lifeless, listless ≠**busy**: dull, slow ≠**vivid**: dull

liven up verb = **stir**, animate, brighten, buck up (*informal*), enliven, pep up, perk up, put life into, rouse, vitalize

liverish adjective **1** Informal = **sick**, bilious, queasy **2** = **irritable**, crotchety (*informal*), crusty, disagreeable, grumpy, ill-humoured, irascible, like a bear with a sore head, peevish, ratty (*Brit. & N.Z. informal*), snappy, splenetic, tetchy

livery noun = **costume**, attire, clothing, dress, garb, raiment (*archaic or poetic*), regalia, suit, uniform, vestments

live wire noun Informal = **dynamo**, ball of fire (*informal*), go-getter (*informal*), hustler (*U.S. & Canad. slang*)

livid adjective **1** Informal = **angry**, beside oneself, cross, enraged, exasperated, fuming, furious, hot under the collar (*informal*), incandescent, incensed, indignant, infuriated, mad (*informal*), outraged, pissed (*taboo slang*), pissed off

(*taboo slang*) **2 = discoloured**, angry, black-and-blue, bruised, contused, purple
➤ **Antonyms**
≠**angry:** assuaged, blissful, content, delighted, enchanted, forgiving, happy, mollified, overjoyed, pleased

living *adjective* **1 = alive**, active, alive and kicking, animated, breathing, existing, lively, quick (*archaic*), strong, vigorous, vital **2 = current**, active, contemporary, continuing, developing, extant, in use, ongoing, operative, persisting ◆ *noun* **3 = existence**, animation, being, existing, life, subsistence **4 = lifestyle**, mode of living, way of life **5 = livelihood**, bread and butter (*informal*), job, maintenance, (means of) support, occupation, (source of) income, subsistence, sustenance, work **6** *Church of England* = **benefice**, incumbency, stipend
➤ **Antonyms**
adjective ≠**alive:** dead, deceased, defunct, departed, expired, late, lifeless, perished ≠**current:** obsolescent, obsolete, out-of-date, vanishing

load *noun* **1 = cargo**, bale, consignment, freight, lading, shipment **2 = burden**, affliction, albatross, encumbrance, millstone, onus, oppression, pressure, trouble, weight, worry ◆ *verb* **3 = fill**, cram, freight, heap, pack, pile, stack, stuff **4 = burden**, encumber, hamper, oppress, saddle with, trouble, weigh down, worry **5** *Of firearms* = **make ready**, charge, prepare to fire, prime

loaded *adjective* **1 = laden**, burdened, charged, freighted, full, weighted **2 = charged**, at the ready, primed, ready to shoot *or* fire **3 = tricky**, artful, insidious, manipulative, prejudicial **4 = biased**, distorted, weighted **5** *Slang* = **rich**, affluent, flush (*informal*), moneyed, rolling (*slang*), wealthy, well-heeled (*informal*), well off, well-to-do

loaf[1] *noun* **1 = lump**, block, cake, cube, slab **2** *Slang* = **head**, block (*informal*), chump (*Brit. slang*), gumption (*Brit. informal*), noddle (*informal, chiefly Brit.*), nous (*Brit. slang*), sense

loaf[2] *verb* = **idle**, laze, lie around, loiter, lounge around, take it easy

loafer *noun* = **idler**, bum (*informal*), couch potato (*slang*), drone (*Brit.*), layabout, lazybones (*informal*), lounger, ne'er-do-well, shirker, skiver (*Brit. slang*), time-waster

loan *noun* **1 = advance**, accommodation, allowance, credit, mortgage ◆ *verb* **2 = lend**, accommodate, advance, allow, credit, let out

loath, loth *adjective* = **unwilling**, against, averse, backward, disinclined, indisposed, opposed, reluctant, resisting
➤ **Antonyms**
anxious, avid, desirous, eager, enthusiastic, keen, willing

loathe *verb* = **hate**, abhor, abominate, despise, detest, dislike

loathing *noun* = **hatred**, abhorrence, abomination, antipathy, aversion, detestation, disgust, horror, odium, repugnance, repulsion, revulsion

loathsome *adjective* = **hateful**, abhorrent, abominable, detestable, disgusting, horrible, nasty, nauseating, obnoxious, odious, offensive, repugnant, repulsive, revolting, vile, yucky *or* yukky (*slang*)
➤ **Antonyms**
adorable, amiable, attractive, charming, delightful, enchanting, engaging, fetching, likable *or* likeable, lovable, lovely

lob *verb Informal* = **throw**, fling, launch, lift, loft, pitch, shy (*informal*), toss

lobby *noun* **1 = corridor**, entrance hall, foyer, hall, hallway, passage, passageway, porch, vestibule **2 = pressure group** ◆ *verb* **3 = campaign**, influence, persuade, press, pressure, promote, pull strings (*Brit. informal*), push, urge

local *adjective* **1 = regional**, community, district, neighbourhood, parish, provincial **2 = restricted**, confined, limited, narrow, parochial, provincial, small-town (*chiefly U.S.*) ◆ *noun* **3 = resident**, character (*informal*), inhabitant, local yokel (*disparaging*), native

locale *noun* = **site**, locality, location, locus, place, position, scene, setting, spot, venue

locality *noun* **1 = neighbourhood**, area, district, neck of the woods (*informal*), region, vicinity **2 = site**, locale, location, place, position, scene, setting, spot

localize *verb* = **restrict**, circumscribe, concentrate, confine, contain, delimit, delimitate, limit, restrain

locate *verb* **1 = find**, come across, detect, discover, lay one's hands on, pin down, pinpoint, track down, unearth **2 = place**, establish, fix, put, seat, set, settle, situate

location *noun* = **site**, bearings, locale, locus, place, point, position, situation, spot, venue, whereabouts

lock[1] *noun* **1 = fastening**, bolt, clasp, padlock ◆ *verb* **2 = fasten**, bolt, close, latch, seal, secure, shut **3 = unite**, clench, engage, entangle, entwine, join, link, mesh **4 = embrace**, clasp, clutch, encircle, enclose, grapple, grasp, hug, press

lock[2] *noun* = **strand**, curl, ringlet, tress, tuft

lock out *verb* = **shut out**, ban, bar, debar, exclude, keep out, refuse admittance to

lockup *noun* = **prison**, can (*slang*), cell, cooler (*slang*), jail *or* gaol, jug (*slang*), police cell

lock up *verb* = **imprison**, cage, confine, detain, incarcerate, jail, put behind bars, shut up

locomotion *noun* = **movement**, motion, moving, progress, progression, travel, travelling

locution *noun* 1 = **manner of speech**, accent, articulation, diction, inflection, intonation, phrasing, style 2 = **expression**, collocation, idiom, phrase, term, turn of speech, wording

lodestar *noun* = **guide**, beacon, model, pattern, standard

lodestone *noun* = **focus**, focal point, magnet

lodge *noun* 1 = **cabin**, chalet, cottage, gatehouse, house, hunting lodge, hut, shelter 2 = **society**, association, branch, chapter, club, group 3 = **den**, haunt, lair ♦ *verb* 4 = **stay**, board, room, sojourn, stop 5 = **accommodate**, billet, entertain, harbour, put up, quarter, shelter 6 = **stick**, become fixed, catch, come to rest, imbed, implant 7 = **register**, deposit, file, lay, place, put, put on record, set, submit

lodger *noun* = **tenant**, boarder, guest, paying guest, P.G., resident

lodging *noun, often plural* = **accommodation**, abode, apartments, boarding, digs (*Brit. informal*), dwelling, habitation, quarters, residence, rooms, shelter

lofty *adjective* 1 = **high**, elevated, raised, sky-high, soaring, tall, towering 2 = **noble**, dignified, distinguished, elevated, exalted, grand, illustrious, imposing, majestic, renowned, stately, sublime, superior 3 = **haughty**, arrogant, condescending, disdainful, high and mighty (*informal*), lordly, patronizing, proud, snooty (*informal*), supercilious, toffee-nosed (*slang, chiefly Brit.*)
➤ **Antonyms**
≠**high**: dwarfed, low, short, stunted ≠**noble**: debased, degraded, humble, low, lowly, mean ≠**haughty**: friendly, modest, unassuming, warm

log *noun* 1 = **stump**, block, bole, chunk, piece of timber, trunk 2 = **record**, account, chart, daybook, journal, logbook, tally ♦ *verb* 3 = **chop**, cut, fell, hew 4 = **record**, book, chart, make a note of, note, register, report, set down

loggerheads *plural noun* **at loggerheads**

= **quarrelling**, at daggers drawn, at each other's throats, at odds, feuding, in dispute, opposed

logic *noun* 1 = **science of reasoning**, argumentation, deduction, dialectics 2 = **reason**, good reason, good sense, sense, sound judgment 3 = **connection**, chain of thought, coherence, link, rationale, relationship

logical *adjective* 1 = **rational**, clear, cogent, coherent, consistent, deducible, reasonable, sound, valid, well-organized 2 = **reasonable**, judicious, most likely, necessary, obvious, plausible, sensible, wise
➤ **Antonyms**
≠**rational**: illogical, instinctive, irrational, unorganized, unreasonable ≠**reasonable**: illogical, implausible, unlikely, unreasonable

logistics *noun* = **organization**, coordination, engineering, management, masterminding, orchestration, plans, strategy

loiter *verb* = **linger**, dally, dawdle, delay, dilly-dally (*informal*), hang about *or* around, idle, lag, loaf, loll, skulk

loll *verb* 1 = **lounge**, flop, loaf, recline, relax, slouch, slump, sprawl 2 = **droop**, dangle, drop, flap, flop, hang, hang loosely, sag

lone *adjective* 1 = **solitary**, by oneself, one, only, separate, separated, single, sole, unaccompanied 2 = **isolated**, deserted, lonesome

loneliness *noun* = **solitude**, aloneness, desertedness, desolation, forlornness, isolation, lonesomeness, seclusion, solitariness

lonely *adjective* 1 = **abandoned**, destitute, estranged, forlorn, forsaken, friendless, lonesome, outcast 2 = **solitary**, alone, apart, by oneself, companionless, isolated, lone, single, withdrawn 3 = **desolate**, deserted, godforsaken, isolated, off the beaten track (*informal*), out-of-the-way, remote, secluded, solitary, unfrequented, uninhabited
➤ **Antonyms**
≠**abandoned**: befriended, popular ≠**solitary**: accompanied, together ≠**desolate**: bustling, crowded, frequented, populous, teeming

loner *noun Informal* = **individualist**, lone wolf, maverick, outsider, recluse

lonesome *adjective Chiefly U.S. & Canad.* = **lonely**, companionless, desolate, dreary, forlorn, friendless, gloomy

long[1] *adjective* 1 = **elongated**, expanded, extended, extensive, far-reaching, lengthy,

spread out, stretched **2 = prolonged**, dragging, interminable, late, lengthy, lingering, long-drawn-out, protracted, slow, sustained, tardy **3 by a long shot: a = by far**, easily, far and away, indubitably, undoubtedly, without doubt **b = by any means**, in any circumstances, on any account
➤ **Antonyms**
≠**elongated**: compressed, contracted, little, short, small ≠**prolonged**: abbreviated, abridged, brief, momentary, quick, short, short-lived

long² verb **= desire**, ache, covet, crave, dream of, eat one's heart out over, hanker, hunger, itch, lust, pine, set one's heart on, want, wish, yearn

longing noun **1 = desire**, ache, ambition, aspiration, coveting, craving, hankering, hope, hungering, itch, thirst, urge, wish, yearning, yen (informal) ♦ adjective **2 = yearning**, ardent, avid, craving, desirous, eager, hungry, languishing, pining, wishful, wistful
➤ **Antonyms**
noun ≠**desire**: abhorrence, antipathy, apathy, disgust, disregard, indifference, loathing, revulsion, unconcern ♦ adjective ≠**yearning**: apathetic, cold, disgusted, hateful, indifferent, loathing, unconcerned, uninterested

long-lived adjective **= long-lasting**, enduring

long shot noun **= outsider**, dark horse

long-standing adjective **= established**, abiding, enduring, fixed, long-established, long-lasting, long-lived, time-honoured

long-suffering adjective **= uncomplaining**, easy-going, forbearing, forgiving, patient, resigned, stoical, tolerant

long-winded adjective **= rambling**, garrulous, lengthy, long-drawn-out, overlong, prolix, prolonged, repetitious, tedious, tiresome, verbose, wordy
➤ **Antonyms**
brief, concise, crisp, curt, laconic, pithy, sententious, short, succinct, terse, to the point

look verb **1 = see**, behold (archaic), check, check out (informal), clock (Brit. slang), examine, eye, gaze, get a load of (informal), glance, inspect, observe, peep, regard, scan, scrutinize, study, survey, take a dekko at (Brit. slang), take a gander at (informal), view, watch **2 = stare**, gape, gawk, gawp (Brit. slang), goggle, ogle **3 = consider**, contemplate **4 = seem**, appear, display, exhibit, look like, seem to be, show, strike one as **5 = face**, front, front on, give onto, overlook **6 = search**, forage, hunt, seek **7 = hope**, anticipate, await, expect, reckon on **8 look like = resemble**, be the image of, favour, make one think of, put one in mind of, remind one of, take after ♦ noun **9 = glimpse**, examination, eyeful (informal), gander (informal), gaze, glance, inspection, observation, once-over (informal), peek, recce (slang), review, shufti (Brit. slang), sight, survey, view **10 = appearance**, air, aspect, bearing, cast, complexion, countenance, demeanour, effect, expression, face, fashion, guise, manner, mien (literary), semblance

look after verb **= take care of**, attend to, care for, guard, keep an eye on, mind, nurse, protect, sit with, supervise, take charge of, tend, watch

lookalike noun **= double**, clone, dead ringer (slang), living image, replica, spitting image (informal), twin

look down on or **upon** verb **= disdain**, contemn, despise, hold in contempt, look down one's nose at (informal), scorn, sneer, spurn, treat with contempt, turn one's nose up (at) (informal)

look forward to verb **= anticipate**, await, count on, count the days until, expect, hope for, long for, look for, set one's heart on, wait for

lookout noun **1 = watch**, guard, qui vive, readiness, vigil **2 = watchman**, guard, sentinel, sentry **3 = watchtower**, beacon, citadel, observation post, observatory, post, tower **4** Informal **= concern**, business, funeral, pigeon (Brit. informal), worry **5** Chiefly Brit. **= prospect**, chances, future, likelihood, outlook, view

look out verb **= be careful**, be alert, be on guard, be vigilant, beware, keep an eye out, keep one's eyes open, keep one's eyes peeled, keep one's eyes skinned, pay attention, watch out

look over verb **= examine**, cast an eye over, check, check out (informal), inspect, look through, peruse, scan, take a dekko at (Brit. slang), view

look up verb **1 = research**, find, hunt for, search for, seek out, track down **2 = improve**, come along, get better, perk up, pick up, progress, shape up (informal), show improvement **3 = visit**, call on, drop in on (informal), go to see, look in on, pay a visit to **4 look up to = respect**, admire, defer to, esteem, have a high opinion of, honour, regard highly, revere

loom verb **= appear**, become visible, be imminent, bulk, emerge, hover, impend, menace, take shape, threaten

loop noun **1 = curve**, bend, circle, coil, convolution, curl, eyelet, hoop, kink, loophole, noose, ring, spiral, twirl, twist, whorl ♦ *verb* 2 = **twist**, bend, circle, coil, curl, curve round, encircle, fold, join, knot, roll, spiral, turn, wind round

loophole *noun* = **let-out**, avoidance, escape, evasion, excuse, means of escape, plea, pretence, pretext, subterfuge

loose *adjective* 1 = **slack**, baggy, easy, hanging, loosened, not fitting, not tight, relaxed, slackened, sloppy 2 = **free**, floating, insecure, movable, released, unattached, unbound, unconfined, unfastened, unfettered, unrestricted, unsecured, untied, wobbly 3 = **vague**, ill-defined, imprecise, inaccurate, indefinite, indistinct, inexact, rambling, random 4 *Old-fashioned* = **promiscuous**, abandoned, debauched, disreputable, dissipated, dissolute, fast, immoral, lewd, libertine, licentious, profligate, unchaste, wanton 5 = **careless**, heedless, imprudent, lax, negligent, rash, thoughtless, unmindful ♦ *verb* 6 = **free**, detach, disconnect, disengage, ease, let go, liberate, loosen, release, set free, slacken, unbind, unbridle, undo, unfasten, unleash, unloose, untie

➤ Antonyms

adjective ≠**slack**: tight ≠**free**: bound, curbed, fastened, fettered, restrained, secured, tethered, tied ≠**vague**: accurate, clear, concise, exact, precise ≠**promiscuous**: chaste, disciplined, moral, virtuous ♦ *verb* ≠**free**: bind, cage, capture, fasten, fetter, imprison, tether

loose-jointed *adjective* = **supple**, agile, elastic, flexible, limber, lissom(e), lithe, pliable, pliant

loosen *verb* 1 = **free**, deliver, let go, liberate, release, set free 2 = **untie**, detach, let out, separate, slacken, unbind, undo, unloose, work free, work loose 3 **loosen up** = **relax**, ease up *or* off, go easy (*informal*), lessen, let up, lighten up (*slang*), mitigate, moderate, soften, weaken

loot *noun* 1 = **plunder**, booty, goods, haul, prize, spoils, swag (*slang*) ♦ *verb* 2 = **plunder**, despoil, pillage, raid, ransack, ravage, rifle, rob, sack

lop *verb* = **cut**, chop, crop, detach, dock, hack, prune, sever, shorten, trim

lope *verb* = **stride**, bound, lollop, spring

lopsided *adjective* = **crooked**, askew, asymmetrical, awry, cockeyed, disproportionate, off balance, one-sided, out of shape, out of true, skewwhiff (*Brit. informal*), squint, tilting, unbalanced, unequal, uneven, warped

loquacious *adjective* = **talkative**, babbling, blathering, chattering, chatty, gabby

(*informal*), garrulous, voluble, wordy

loquacity *noun* = **talkativeness**, babbling, chattering, chattiness, effusiveness, garrulity, volubility

lord *noun* 1 = **master**, commander, governor, king, leader, liege, monarch, overlord, potentate, prince, ruler, sovereign, superior 2 = **nobleman**, earl, noble, peer, viscount 3 **Our Lord** *or* **the Lord** = **Jesus Christ**, Christ, God, Jehovah, the Almighty, the Galilean, the Good Shepherd, the Nazarene ♦ *verb* 4 **lord it over** = **order around**, be overbearing, boss around (*informal*), domineer, pull rank, put on airs, swagger

lordly *adjective* 1 = **proud**, arrogant, condescending, dictatorial, disdainful, domineering, haughty, high and mighty (*informal*), high-handed, imperious, lofty, overbearing, patronizing, stuck-up (*informal*), supercilious, tyrannical 2 = **noble**, aristocratic, gracious, grand, imperial, lofty, majestic, princely, regal, stately

lore *noun* = **traditions**, beliefs, doctrine, experience, folk-wisdom, mythos, sayings, teaching, traditional wisdom, wisdom

lose *verb* 1 = **mislay**, be deprived of, displace, drop, fail to keep, forget, misplace, miss, suffer loss 2 = **forfeit**, fail, fall short, lose out on (*informal*), miss, pass up (*informal*), yield 3 = **be defeated**, be the loser, come a cropper (*informal*), come to grief, get the worst of, lose out, suffer defeat, take a licking (*informal*) 4 = **waste**, consume, dissipate, drain, exhaust, expend, lavish, misspend, squander, use up 5 = **stray from**, wander from 6 = **outdistance**, lap, leave behind, outrun, outstrip, overtake, pass 7 = **escape**, dodge, duck, elude, evade, give someone the slip, shake off, slip away, throw off

loser *noun* = **failure**, also-ran, dud (*informal*), flop (*informal*), no-hoper (*Austral. slang*), underdog, washout (*informal*)

loss *noun* 1 = **losing**, defeat, deprivation, disappearance, drain, failure, forfeiture, misfortune, mislaying, squandering, waste 2 = **damage**, cost, destruction, detriment, disadvantage, harm, hurt, impairment, injury, ruin 3 *sometimes plural* = **deficit**, debit, debt, deficiency, depletion, shrinkage 4 **at a loss** = **confused**, at one's wits' end, baffled, bewildered, helpless, nonplussed, perplexed, puzzled, stuck (*informal*), stumped

➤ Antonyms

≠**losing**: acquisition, finding, gain, preservation, reimbursement, saving, winning ≠**damage**: advantage, recovery, restoration ≠**deficit**: gain

lost *adjective* 1 = **missing**, disappeared, forfeited, mislaid, misplaced, missed, strayed, vanished, wayward 2 = **off-course**, adrift, astray, at sea, disoriented, off-track 3 = **bewildered**, baffled, clueless (*slang*), confused, helpless, ignorant, mystified, perplexed, puzzled 4 = **wasted**, consumed, dissipated, frittered away, misapplied, misdirected, misspent, misused, squandered 5 = **engrossed**, absent, absorbed, abstracted, distracted, dreamy, entranced, preoccupied, rapt, spellbound, taken up 6 = **fallen**, abandoned, corrupt, damned, depraved, dissolute, irreclaimable, licentious, profligate, unchaste, wanton

lot *noun* 1 = **collection**, assortment, batch, bunch (*informal*), consignment, crowd, group, quantity, set 2 = **destiny**, accident, chance, doom, fate, fortune 3 **a lot** *or* **lots** = **plenty**, abundance, a great deal, heap(s), large amount, load(s) (*informal*), masses (*informal*), numbers, ocean(s), piles (*informal*), quantities, scores, stack(s) 4 **throw in one's lot with** = **join with**, ally *or* align oneself with, join forces with, join fortunes with, support

loth *see* LOATH

lotion *noun* = **cream**, balm, embrocation, liniment, salve, solution

lottery *noun* 1 = **raffle**, draw, sweepstake 2 = **gamble**, chance, hazard, risk, toss-up (*informal*), venture

loud *adjective* 1 = **noisy**, blaring, booming, clamorous, deafening, ear-piercing, ear-splitting, forte (*Music*), piercing, resounding, rowdy, sonorous, stentorian, strident, thundering, tumultuous, vociferous 2 = **garish**, brash, flamboyant, flashy, gaudy, glaring, lurid, ostentatious, showy, tasteless, tawdry, vulgar 3 = **loud-mouthed** (*informal*), brash, brazen, coarse, crass, crude, offensive, raucous, vulgar
➤ **Antonyms**
≠**noisy**: gentle, inaudible, low, low-pitched, quiet, silent, soft, soundless, subdued ≠**garish**: conservative, dull, sober, sombre ≠**loud-mouthed**: quiet, reserved, retiring, shy, unassuming

loudly *adverb* = **noisily**, at full volume, at the top of one's voice, deafeningly, fortissimo (*Music*), lustily, shrilly, uproariously, vehemently, vigorously, vociferously

loudmouth *noun* = **bigmouth** (*slang*), blowhard (*informal*), braggart, bullshit artist (*taboo slang*), bullshitter (*taboo*

slang), windbag (*slang*)

lounge *verb* 1 = **relax**, laze, lie about, loiter, loll, make oneself at home, recline, sprawl, take it easy 2 = **pass time**, dawdle, hang out (*informal*), idle, kill time, potter, veg out (*slang, chiefly U.S.*), waste time

lour *see* LOWER[1]

louring *see* LOWERING

lousy *adjective* 1 *Slang* = **mean**, base, contemptible, despicable, dirty, hateful, low, rotten (*informal*), vicious, vile 2 *Slang* = **inferior**, awful, bad, miserable, no good, poor, poxy (*slang*), rotten (*informal*), second-rate, terrible 3 = **lice-infested**, lice-infected, lice-ridden

lout *noun* = **oaf**, bear, boor, bumpkin, churl, clod, dolt, ned (*Scot. slang*), yahoo, yob *or* yobbo (*Brit. slang*)

loutish *adjective* = **oafish**, boorish, coarse, gross, ill-bred, ill-mannered, rough, uncouth, unmannerly

lovable, loveable *adjective* = **endearing**, adorable, amiable, attractive, captivating, charming, cuddly, cute, delightful, enchanting, engaging, fetching (*informal*), likable *or* likeable, lovely, pleasing, sweet, winning, winsome
➤ **Antonyms**
abhorrent, abominable, detestable, hateful, loathsome, obnoxious, odious, offensive, revolting

love *verb* 1 = **adore**, be attached to, be in love with, cherish, dote on, have affection for, hold dear, idolize, prize, think the world of, treasure, worship 2 = **enjoy**, appreciate, delight in, desire, fancy, have a weakness for, like, relish, savour, take pleasure in ♦ *noun* 3 = **passion**, adoration, adulation, affection, ardour, attachment, devotion, fondness, friendship, infatuation, liking, rapture, regard, tenderness, warmth 4 = **liking**, delight, devotion, enjoyment, fondness, inclination, partiality, relish, soft spot, taste, weakness 5 = **beloved**, angel, darling, dear, dearest, dear one, loved one, lover, sweet, sweetheart, truelove 6 **for love or money** = **by any means**, ever, under any conditions 7 **fall in love (with)** = **lose one's heart (to)**, bestow one's affections on, be taken with, fall for, take a shine to (*informal*) 8 **in love** = **enamoured**, besotted, charmed, enraptured, infatuated, smitten
➤ **Antonyms**
verb ≠**adore**, **enjoy**: abhor, abominate, detest, dislike, hate, scorn ♦ *noun* ≠**passion**, **liking**: abhorrence, abomination, animosity, antagonism, antipathy, aversion, bad blood, bitterness, detestation, disgust, dislike, hate, hatred,

hostility, ill will, incompatibility, loathing, malice, repugnance, resentment, scorn ≠**beloved**: enemy, foe

love affair noun = **romance**, affair, affaire de coeur, amour, intrigue, liaison, relationship

loveless adjective = **unloving**, cold, cold-hearted, frigid, hard, heartless, icy, insensitive, unfeeling, unresponsive

lovelorn adjective = **lovesick**, languishing, pining, slighted, spurned, unrequited, yearning

lovely adjective 1 = **beautiful**, admirable, adorable, amiable, attractive, captivating, charming, comely, enchanting, exquisite, graceful, handsome, pretty, sweet, winning 2 = **enjoyable**, agreeable, delightful, engaging, gratifying, nice, pleasant, pleasing
  ➤ **Antonyms**
≠**beautiful**: hideous, ugly, unattractive ≠**enjoyable**: abhorrent, detestable, hateful, loathsome, odious, repellent, repugnant, revolting

lovemaking noun = **sexual intercourse**, act of love, carnal knowledge, coitus, copulation, intercourse, intimacy, sexual relations, sexual union or congress

lover noun = **sweetheart**, admirer, beau, beloved, boyfriend or girlfriend, fancy man or fancy woman (slang), fiancé or fiancée, flame (informal), mistress, paramour, suitor, swain (archaic), toy boy

lovesick adjective = **lovelorn**, desiring, languishing, longing, pining, yearning

loving adjective = **affectionate**, amorous, ardent, dear, demonstrative, devoted, doting, fond, friendly, kind, solicitous, tender, warm, warm-hearted
  ➤ **Antonyms**
aloof, cold, contemptuous, cruel, detached, distasteful, hateful, hostile, indifferent, mean, scornful, unconcerned, unloving

low[1] adjective 1 = **small**, little, short, squat, stunted 2 = **low-lying**, deep, depressed, ground-level, shallow, subsided, sunken 3 = **inexpensive**, cheap, economical, moderate, modest, reasonable 4 = **meagre**, depleted, insignificant, little, measly, paltry, reduced, scant, small, sparse, trifling 5 = **inferior**, deficient, inadequate, low-grade, mediocre, pathetic, poor, puny, second-rate, shoddy, substandard, worthless 6 = **coarse**, common, crude, disgraceful, gross, dishonourable, disreputable, gross, ill-bred, obscene, rough, rude, unbecoming, undignified, unrefined, vulgar 7 = **contemptible**, abject, base,

cowardly, dastardly, degraded, depraved, despicable, ignoble, mean, menial, nasty, scurvy, servile, sordid, unworthy, vile, vulgar 8 = **lowly**, humble, lowborn, meek, plain, plebeian, poor, simple, unpretentious 9 = **dejected**, blue, depressed, despondent, disheartened, dismal, down, downcast, down in the dumps (informal), fed up, forlorn, gloomy, glum, miserable, morose, sad, unhappy 10 = **ill**, debilitated, dying, exhausted, feeble, frail, prostrate, reduced, sinking, stricken, weak 11 = **quiet**, gentle, hushed, muffled, muted, soft, subdued, whispered ♦ adverb 12 **lie low** = **hide**, conceal oneself, go underground, hide away, hide out, hole up, keep a low profile, keep out of sight, lurk, skulk, take cover
  ➤ **Antonyms**
adjective ≠**small**: tall, towering ≠**low-lying**: elevated ≠**meagre**: important, significant ≠**contemptible**: brave, eminent, exalted, fine, grand, high-ranking, honourable, laudable, lofty, praiseworthy, superior, worthy ≠**dejected**: cheerful, elated, happy, high ≠**ill**: alert, energetic, enthusiastic, strong ≠**quiet**: loud, noisy

low[2] noun 1 = **mooing**, bellow, bellowing, lowing, moo ♦ verb 2 = **moo**, bellow

lowdown noun Informal = **information**, dope (informal), gen (Brit. informal), info (informal), inside story, intelligence

low-down adjective = **mean**, base, cheap (informal), contemptible, despicable, low, nasty, reprehensible, scurvy, ugly, underhand

lower[1] adjective 1 = **under**, inferior, junior, lesser, low-level, minor, secondary, second-class, smaller, subordinate 2 = **reduced**, curtailed, decreased, diminished, lessened, pared down ♦ verb 3 = **drop**, depress, fall, let down, make lower, sink, submerge, take down 4 = **demean**, abase, belittle, condescend, debase, degrade, deign, devalue, disgrace, downgrade, humble, humiliate, stoop 5 = **lessen**, abate, curtail, cut, decrease, diminish, minimize, moderate, prune, reduce, slash 6 = **quieten**, soften, tone down
  ➤ **Antonyms**
adjective ≠**reduced**: enlarged, higher, increased ♦ verb ≠**drop**: elevate, hoist, lift, raise ≠**lessen**: amplify, augment, boost, enlarge, extend, increase, inflate, magnify, raise

lower[2], **lour** verb = **darken**, blacken, cloud up or over, loom, menace, threaten

lowering, louring adjective = **darkening**,

black, clouded, cloudy, dark, forbidding, gloomy, grey, heavy, menacing, ominous, overcast, threatening

low-key *adjective* = **subdued**, keeping a low profile, low-pitched, muffled, muted, played down, quiet, restrained, toned down, understated

lowly *adjective* **1** = **lowborn**, ignoble, inferior, mean, plebeian, proletarian, subordinate **2** = **humble**, meek, mild, modest, unassuming **3** = **unpretentious**, average, common, homespun, modest, ordinary, plain, poor, simple

low-minded *adjective* = **vulgar**, coarse, crude, dirty, disgusting, filthy, foul, gross, indecent, obscene, rude, smutty, uncouth

low-spirited *adjective* = **depressed**, apathetic, blue, dejected, despondent, dismal, down, down-hearted, down in the dumps (*informal*), down in the mouth, fed up, gloomy, heavy-hearted, low, miserable, moody, sad, unhappy

low-tech *adjective* = **unsophisticated**, basic, simple
➤ **Antonyms**
high-tech *or* hi-tech, scientific, technical, technological

loyal *adjective* = **faithful**, constant, dependable, devoted, dutiful, immovable, patriotic, staunch, steadfast, tried and true, true, true-blue, true-hearted, trustworthy, trusty, unswerving, unwavering
➤ **Antonyms**
disloyal, false, perfidious, traitorous, treacherous, unfaithful, untrustworthy

loyalty *noun* = **faithfulness**, allegiance, constancy, dependability, devotion, fealty, fidelity, patriotism, reliability, staunchness, steadfastness, true-heartedness, trueness, trustiness, trustworthiness

lozenge *noun* = **tablet**, cough drop, jujube, pastille

lubberly *adjective* = **oafish**, awkward, clodhopping (*informal*), clownish, clumsy, loutish, lumbering, lumpen (*informal*), lumpish, uncouth, ungainly

lubricate *verb* = **oil**, grease, make slippery, make smooth, smear

lucid *adjective* **1** = **clear**, clear-cut, comprehensible, crystal clear, distinct, evident, explicit, intelligible, obvious, plain, transparent **2** = **translucent**, clear, crystalline, diaphanous, glassy, limpid, pellucid, pure, transparent **3** = **bright**, beaming, brilliant, effulgent, gleaming, luminous, radiant, resplendent, shining **4** = **clear-headed**, all there, *compos mentis,* in one's right mind, rational, reasonable, sane, sensible, sober, sound

➤ **Antonyms**
≠**clear**: ambiguous, clear as mud (*informal*), confused, equivocal, incomprehensible, indistinct, muddled, unclear, unintelligible, vague ≠**translucent**: unclear ≠**bright**: dull ≠**clear-headed**: confused, irrational, muddled, unclear, unperceptive, vague

luck *noun* **1** = **fortune**, accident, chance, destiny, fate, fortuity **2** = **good fortune**, advantage, blessing, break (*informal*), fluke, godsend, good luck, prosperity, serendipity, stroke, success, windfall

luckily *adverb* **1** = **fortunately**, favourably, happily, opportunely, propitiously, providentially **2** = **by chance**, as it chanced, as luck would have it, fortuitously

luckless *adjective* = **unlucky**, calamitous, cursed, disastrous, doomed, hapless, hopeless, ill-fated, ill-starred, jinxed, star-crossed, unfortunate, unhappy, unpropitious, unsuccessful

lucky *adjective* **1** = **fortunate**, advantageous, blessed, charmed, favoured, jammy (*Brit. slang*), on a roll (*informal*), prosperous, serendipitous, successful **2** = **fortuitous**, adventitious, auspicious, opportune, propitious, providential, timely
➤ **Antonyms**
≠**fortunate**: bad, detrimental, ominous, unfavourable, unfortunate, unhappy, unlucky, unpromising ≠**fortuitous**: unlucky, untimely

lucrative *adjective* = **profitable**, advantageous, fat, fruitful, gainful, high-income, money-making, paying, productive, remunerative, well-paid

lucre *noun Usually facetious* = **money**, gain, mammon, pelf, profit, riches, spoils, wealth

ludicrous *adjective* = **ridiculous**, absurd, comic, comical, crazy, droll, farcical, funny, incongruous, laughable, nonsensical, odd, outlandish, preposterous, silly
➤ **Antonyms**
grave, logical, sad, sensible, serious, solemn

lug *verb* = **carry**, drag, haul, heave, hump (*Brit. slang*), pull, tow, yank

luggage *noun* = **baggage**, bags, cases, gear, impedimenta, paraphernalia, suitcases, things, trunks

lugubrious *adjective* = **gloomy**, dismal, doleful, dreary, funereal, melancholy, morose, mournful, sad, serious, sombre, sorrowful, woebegone, woeful

lukewarm *adjective* **1** = **tepid**, blood-warm, warm **2** = **half-hearted**, apathetic, cold, cool, indifferent, phlegmatic, unconcerned, unenthusiastic, uninterested, unresponsive

lull *verb* 1 = **calm**, allay, compose, hush, pacify, quell, quiet, soothe, still, subdue, tranquillize ♦ *noun* 2 = **respite**, calm, calmness, hush, let-up (*informal*), pause, quiet, silence, stillness, tranquillity

lullaby *noun* = **cradlesong**, berceuse

lumber¹ *noun* 1 *Brit.* = **junk**, castoffs, clutter, jumble, refuse, rubbish, trash ♦ *verb* 2 *Brit. informal* = **burden**, encumber, impose upon, land, load, saddle

lumber² *verb* = **plod**, clump, shamble, shuffle, stump, trudge, trundle, waddle

lumbering *adjective* = **awkward**, blundering, bumbling, clumsy, elephantine, heavy, heavy-footed, hulking, lubberly, overgrown, ponderous, ungainly, unwieldy

luminary *noun* = **celebrity**, big name, celeb (*informal*), dignitary, leading light, megastar (*informal*), notable, personage, star, V.I.P., worthy

luminescent *adjective* = **glowing**, Day-Glo, fluorescent, luminous, phosphorescent, radiant, shining

luminous *adjective* = **bright**, brilliant, glowing, illuminated, lighted, lit, luminescent, lustrous, radiant, resplendent, shining, vivid

lump¹ *noun* 1 = **piece**, ball, bunch, cake, chunk, clod, cluster, dab, gob, group, hunk, mass, nugget, spot, wedge 2 = **swelling**, bulge, bump, growth, hump, protrusion, protuberance, tumescence, tumour ♦ *verb* 3 = **group**, aggregate, bunch, coalesce, collect, combine, conglomerate, consolidate, mass, pool, unite

lump² *verb* = **put up with**, bear, endure, stand, suffer, take, tolerate

lumpish *adjective* = **clumsy**, awkward, bungling, elephantine, gawky, heavy, lethargic, lumbering, oafish, ungainly

lumpy *adjective* = **bumpy**, knobbly, uneven

lunacy *noun* 1 = **foolishness**, aberration, absurdity, craziness, folly, foolhardiness, idiocy, imbecility, madness, senselessness, stupidity, tomfoolery 2 = **insanity**, dementia, derangement, idiocy, madness, mania, psychosis
➤ **Antonyms**
≠**foolishness**: prudence, reason, sense ≠**insanity**: reason, sanity

lunatic *adjective* 1 = **irrational**, barking (*slang*), barking mad (*slang*), barmy (*slang*), bonkers (*slang, chiefly Brit.*), crackbrained, crackpot (*informal*), crazy, daft, demented, deranged, insane, loopy

(*informal*), mad, maniacal, not the full shilling (*informal*), nuts (*slang*), off one's trolley (*slang*), out to lunch (*informal*), psychotic, unhinged, up the pole (*informal*), wacko *or* whacko (*informal*) ♦ *noun* 2 = **madman**, headbanger (*informal*), headcase (*informal*), loony (*slang*), maniac, nut (*slang*), nutcase (*slang*), nutter (*Brit. slang*), psychopath

lunge *noun* 1 = **thrust**, charge, cut, jab, pass, pounce, spring, stab, swing, swipe (*informal*) ♦ *verb* 2 = **pounce**, bound, charge, cut, dash, dive, fall upon, hit at, jab, leap, plunge, poke, stab, strike at, thrust

lurch *verb* 1 = **tilt**, heave, heel, lean, list, pitch, rock, roll 2 = **stagger**, reel, stumble, sway, totter, weave

lure *verb* 1 = **tempt**, allure, attract, beckon, decoy, draw, ensnare, entice, inveigle, invite, lead on, seduce ♦ *noun* 2 = **temptation**, allurement, attraction, bait, carrot (*informal*), come-on (*informal*), decoy, enticement, incentive, inducement, magnet

lurid *adjective* 1 = **sensational**, graphic, melodramatic, shock-horror (*facetious*), shocking, startling, vivid 2 = **glaring**, fiery, flaming, intense, overbright 3 = **gruesome**, disgusting, ghastly, gory, grim, grisly, macabre, revolting, savage, violent
➤ **Antonyms**
≠**sensational**: breezy, factual, jaunty, light-hearted, mild ≠**glaring**: pale, pastel, watery

lurk *verb* = **hide**, conceal oneself, crouch, lie in wait, prowl, skulk, slink, sneak

luscious *adjective* = **delicious**, appetizing, delectable, juicy, mouth-watering, palatable, rich, savoury, scrumptious (*informal*), succulent, sweet, toothsome, yummy (*slang*)

lush *adjective* 1 = **abundant**, dense, flourishing, green, lavish, overgrown, prolific, rank, teeming, verdant 2 = **luxurious**, elaborate, extravagant, grand, lavish, opulent, ornate, palatial, plush (*informal*), ritzy (*slang*), sumptuous

lust *noun* 1 = **lechery**, carnality, lasciviousness, lewdness, libido, licentiousness, randiness (*informal, chiefly Brit.*), salaciousness, sensuality, the hots (*slang*), wantonness 2 = **desire**, appetite, avidity, covetousness, craving, greed, longing, passion, thirst ♦ *verb* 3 = **desire**, be consumed with desire for, covet, crave, hunger for *or* after, need, want, yearn

lustful *adjective* = **lascivious**, carnal, horny (*slang*), hot-blooded, lecherous, lewd, libidinous, licentious, passionate, randy (*informal, chiefly Brit.*), unchaste, wanton

lustily *adverb* = **vigorously**, forcefully, hard, powerfully, strongly, with all one's might

lustre *noun* 1 = **sparkle**, burnish, gleam, glint, glitter, gloss, glow, sheen, shimmer, shine 2 = **glory**, distinction, fame, honour, illustriousness, prestige, renown

lustrous *adjective* = **shining**, bright, burnished, dazzling, gleaming, glistening, glossy, glowing, luminous, radiant, shimmering, shiny, sparkling

lusty *adjective* = **vigorous**, brawny, energetic, hale, healthy, hearty, powerful, red-blooded (*informal*), robust, rugged, stalwart, stout, strapping, strong, sturdy, virile

luxuriant *adjective* 1 = **abundant**, ample, copious, excessive, lavish, plenteous, plentiful, prodigal, profuse 2 = **lush**, dense, fecund, fertile, flourishing, fruitful, overflowing, productive, prolific, rank, rich, riotous, teeming 3 = **elaborate**, baroque, decorated, extravagant, fancy, flamboyant, ornate, rococo, sumptuous
➤ **Antonyms**
≠**abundant, lush**: meagre, scanty, sparse, thin ≠**elaborate**: plain, simple, unadorned

luxuriate *verb* 1 = **enjoy**, bask, delight, indulge, relish, revel, wallow 2 = **flourish**, grow, prosper, thrive

luxurious *adjective* 1 = **sumptuous**, comfortable, costly, de luxe, expensive, lavish, magnificent, opulent, plush (*informal*), rich, ritzy (*slang*), splendid, well-appointed 2 = **pleasure-loving**, epicurean, pampered, self-indulgent, sensual, sybaritic, voluptuous
➤ **Antonyms**
ascetic, austere, deprived, economical,

plain, poor, sparing, Spartan, thrifty

luxury *noun* 1 = **opulence**, affluence, hedonism, richness, splendour, sumptuousness, voluptuousness 2 = **pleasure**, bliss, comfort, delight, enjoyment, gratification, indulgence, satisfaction, wellbeing 3 = **extravagance**, extra, frill, indulgence, nonessential, treat
➤ **Antonyms**
≠**opulence**: austerity, deprivation, destitution, poverty, privation, want
≠**pleasure**: burden, difficulty, discomfort, hardship, infliction, misery
≠**extravagance**: necessity, need

lying *noun* 1 = **dishonesty**, deceit, dissimulation, double-dealing, duplicity, fabrication, fibbing, mendacity, perjury, prevarication, untruthfulness ◆ *adjective* 2 = **deceitful**, dishonest, dissembling, double-dealing, false, mendacious, perfidious, treacherous, two-faced, untruthful
➤ **Antonyms**
adjective ≠**deceitful**: candid, forthright, frank, honest, reliable, sincere, straight, straightforward, truthful, veracious

lynchpin, linchpin *noun* = **driving force**, chief, co-ordinator, cornerstone, director, principal

lyric *adjective* 1 *Of poetry* = **songlike**, expressive, lyrical, melodic, musical 2 *Of a voice* = **melodic**, clear, dulcet, flowing, graceful, light 3 *plural* = **words**, book, libretto, text, words of a song

lyrical *adjective* = **enthusiastic**, carried away, ecstatic, effusive, emotional, expressive, impassioned, inspired, poetic, rapturous, rhapsodic

M m

macabre *adjective* = **gruesome**, cadaverous, deathlike, deathly, dreadful, eerie, frightening, frightful, ghastly, ghostly, ghoulish, grim, grisly, hideous, horrid, morbid, unearthly, weird
➤ **Antonyms**
appealing, beautiful, charming, delightful, lovely, pleasant

machiavellian *adjective* = **scheming**, astute, crafty, cunning, cynical, double-dealing, opportunist, sly, underhand, unscrupulous

machination *noun* = **plot**, artifice, cabal, conspiracy, design, device, dodge, intrigue, manoeuvre, ploy, ruse, scheme, stratagem, trick

machine *noun* **1** = **appliance**, apparatus, contraption, contrivance, device, engine, instrument, mechanism, tool **2** = **system**, agency, machinery, organization, party, setup (*informal*), structure

machinery *noun* **1** = **equipment**, apparatus, gear, instruments, mechanism, tackle, tools, works **2** = **procedure**, agency, channels, machine, organization, structure, system

macho *adjective* = **manly**, chauvinist, masculine, virile

mad *adjective* **1** = **insane**, aberrant, as daft as a brush (*informal, chiefly Brit.*), bananas (*slang*), barking (*slang*), barking mad (*slang*), barmy (*slang*), batty (*slang*), bonkers (*slang, chiefly Brit.*), crackers (*Brit. slang*), crackpot (*informal*), crazed, crazy (*informal*), cuckoo (*informal*), delirious, demented, deranged, distracted, doolally (*slang*), flaky (*U.S. slang*), frantic, frenzied, gonzo (*slang*), loony (*slang*), loopy (*informal*), lost one's marbles (*informal*), lunatic, mental (*slang*), *non compos mentis*, not right in the head, not the full shilling (*informal*), nuts (*slang*), nutty (*slang*), off one's chump (*slang*), off one's head (*slang*), off one's nut (*slang*), off one's rocker (*slang*), off one's trolley (*slang*), of unsound mind, out of one's mind, out to lunch (*informal*), psychotic, rabid, raving, round the bend (*Brit. slang*), round the twist (*Brit. slang*), screwy (*informal*), unbalanced, unhinged, unstable, up the pole (*informal*), wacko *or* whacko (*informal*) **2** = **foolish**, absurd, as daft as a brush (*informal, chiefly Brit.*), asinine, daft (*informal*), foolhardy, imprudent, inane, irrational, ludicrous, nonsensical, preposterous, senseless, unreasonable, unsafe, unsound, wild **3** *Informal* = **angry**, ape (*slang*), apeshit (*slang*), berserk, choked, cross, enraged, exasperated, fit to be tied (*slang*), fuming, furious, in a wax (*informal, chiefly Brit.*), incandescent, incensed, infuriated, irate, irritated, livid (*informal*), pissed (*taboo slang*), pissed off (*taboo slang*), raging, resentful, seeing red (*informal*), wild, wrathful **4** = **enthusiastic**, ardent, avid, crazy (*informal*), daft (*informal*), devoted, dotty (*slang, chiefly Brit.*), enamoured, fanatical, fond, hooked, impassioned, infatuated, in love with, keen, nuts (*slang*), wild, zealous **5** = **frenzied**, abandoned, agitated, boisterous, ebullient, energetic, excited, frenetic, full-on (*informal*), gay, riotous, uncontrolled, unrestrained, wild **6 like mad** *Informal* = **energetically**, enthusiastically, excitedly, furiously, hell for leather, like greased lightning (*informal*), like lightning, like nobody's business (*informal*), like the clappers (*Brit. informal*), madly, quickly, rapidly, speedily, unrestrainedly, violently, wildly, with might and main
➤ **Antonyms**
≠**insane:** rational, sane ≠**foolish:** sensible, sound ≠**angry:** appeased, calm, composed, cool, mollified ≠**enthusiastic:** nonchalant, uncaring

madcap *adjective* = **reckless**, crazy, foolhardy, hare-brained, imprudent, impulsive, rash, thoughtless

madden *verb* = **infuriate**, aggravate (*informal*), annoy, craze, dement, derange, drive one crazy, drive one off one's head (*slang*), drive one out of one's mind, drive one round the bend (*Brit. slang*), drive one round the twist (*Brit. slang*), drive one to distraction (*informal*), enrage, exasperate, gall, get one's back up, get one's dander up (*informal*), get one's goat (*slang*), get one's hackles up, incense, inflame, irritate, make one's blood boil, make one see red (*informal*), make one's hackles rise, nark (*Brit., Austral., & N.Z. slang*), piss one off (*taboo slang*), provoke, put one's back up, raise one's hackles, unhinge, upset, vex
➤ **Antonyms**

appease, calm, mollify, pacify, soothe

made-up *adjective* = **false**, fabricated, fictional, imaginary, invented, make-believe, mythical, specious, trumped-up, unreal, untrue

madly *adverb* 1 = **insanely**, crazily, deliriously, dementedly, distractedly, frantically, frenziedly, hysterically, rabidly 2 = **foolishly**, absurdly, irrationally, ludicrously, nonsensically, senselessly, unreasonably, wildly 3 = **energetically**, excitedly, furiously, hastily, hell for leather, hotfoot, hurriedly, like greased lightning (*informal*), like lightning, like mad (*informal*), like nobody's business (*informal*), like the clappers (*Brit. informal*), quickly, rapidly, recklessly, speedily, violently, wildly 4 *Informal* = **passionately**, desperately, devotedly, exceedingly, excessively, extremely, intensely, to distraction

madman *or* **madwoman** *noun* = **lunatic**, headbanger (*informal*), headcase (*informal*), loony (*slang*), maniac, mental case (*slang*), nut (*slang*), nutcase (*slang*), nutter (*Brit. slang*), psycho (*slang*), psychopath, psychotic

madness *noun* 1 = **insanity**, aberration, craziness, delusion, dementia, derangement, distraction, lunacy, mania, mental illness, psychopathy, psychosis 2 = **foolishness**, absurdity, daftness (*informal*), folly, foolhardiness, idiocy, nonsense, preposterousness, wildness 3 *Informal* = **anger**, exasperation, frenzy, fury, ire, rage, raving, wildness, wrath 4 = **passion**, ardour, craze, enthusiasm, fanaticism, fondness, infatuation, keenness, rage, zeal 5 = **frenzy**, abandon, agitation, excitement, furore, intoxication, riot, unrestraint, uproar

maelstrom *noun* 1 = **whirlpool**, vortex 2 = **turmoil**, chaos, confusion, disorder, tumult, upheaval

maestro *noun* = **master**, expert, genius, virtuoso

magazine *noun* 1 = **journal**, pamphlet, paper, periodical 2 = **storehouse**, ammunition dump, arsenal, depot, powder room (*obsolete*), store, warehouse

magic *noun* 1 = **sorcery**, black art, enchantment, necromancy, occultism, sortilege, spell, theurgy, witchcraft, wizardry 2 = **conjuring**, hocus-pocus, illusion, jiggery-pokery (*informal, chiefly Brit.*), jugglery, legerdemain, prestidigitation, sleight of hand, trickery 3 = **charm**, allurement, enchantment, fascination, glamour, magnetism, power
♦ *adjective* 4 *Also* **magical** = **miraculous**,

bewitching, charismatic, charming, enchanting, entrancing, fascinating, magnetic, marvellous, sorcerous, spellbinding

magician *noun* 1 = **sorcerer**, archimage (*rare*), conjuror *or* conjuror, enchanter *or* enchantress, illusionist, necromancer, thaumaturge (*rare*), theurgist, warlock, witch, wizard 2 = **miracle-worker**, genius, marvel, spellbinder, virtuoso, wizard, wonder-worker

magisterial *adjective* = **authoritative**, commanding, imperious, lordly, masterful
➤ **Antonyms**
deferential, diffident, humble, servile, shy, submissive, subservient, wimpish *or* wimpy (*informal*)

magistrate *noun* = **judge**, bailie (*Scot.*), J.P., justice, justice of the peace, provost (*Scot.*)

magnanimity *noun* = **generosity**, beneficence, benevolence, big-heartedness, bountifulness, charitableness, high-mindedness, largesse *or* largess, munificence, nobility, open-handedness, selflessness, unselfishness

magnanimous *adjective* = **generous**, beneficent, big, big-hearted, bountiful, charitable, free, great-hearted, handsome, high-minded, kind, kindly, munificent, noble, open-handed, selfless, ungrudging, unselfish, unstinting
➤ **Antonyms**
miserly, petty, resentful, selfish, small, unforgiving, vindictive

magnate *noun* 1 = **tycoon**, baron, big cheese (*slang, old-fashioned*), big hitter (*informal*), big noise (*informal*), big shot (*informal*), big wheel (*slang*), bigwig (*informal*), captain of industry, chief, fat cat (*slang, chiefly U.S.*), heavy hitter (*informal*), leader, Mister Big (*slang, chiefly U.S.*), mogul, nabob (*informal*), notable, plutocrat, V.I.P. 2 = **aristocrat**, aristo (*informal*), baron, bashaw, grandee, magnifico, nob (*slang, chiefly Brit.*), noble, notable, personage, prince

magnetic *adjective* = **attractive**, alluring, captivating, charismatic, charming, enchanting, entrancing, fascinating, hypnotic, irresistible, mesmerizing, seductive
➤ **Antonyms**
disagreeable, offensive, repellent, repulsive, unappealing, unattractive, unlikable *or* unlikeable, unpleasant

magnetism *noun* = **charm**, allure, appeal, attraction, attractiveness, captivatingness, charisma, draw, drawing power, enchantment, fascination, hypnotism, magic, mesmerism, power, pull, seductiveness, spell

magnification *noun* = **increase**, aggrandizement, amplification, augmentation, blow-up (*informal*), boost, build-up, deepening, dilation, enhancement, enlargement, exaggeration, expansion, heightening, inflation, intensification

magnificence *noun* = **splendour**, brilliance, éclat, glory, gorgeousness, grandeur, luxuriousness, luxury, majesty, nobility, opulence, pomp, resplendence, stateliness, sublimity, sumptuousness

magnificent *adjective* **1** = **splendid**, august, elegant, elevated, exalted, glorious, gorgeous, grand, grandiose, imposing, impressive, lavish, luxurious, majestic, noble, opulent, princely, regal, resplendent, rich, splendiferous (*facetious*), stately, striking, sublime, sumptuous, transcendent **2** = **excellent**, brilliant, divine (*informal*), fine, outstanding, splendid, superb, superior
➤ **Antonyms**
bad, humble, ignoble, lowly, mean, modest, ordinary, petty, poor, trivial, undistinguished, unimposing

magnify *verb* **1** = **enlarge**, aggrandize, amplify, augment, blow up (*informal*), boost, build up, deepen, dilate, expand, heighten, increase, intensify **2** = **overstate**, aggravate, blow up, blow up out of all proportion, dramatize, enhance, exaggerate, inflate, make a federal case of (*U.S. informal*), make a mountain out of a molehill, make a production (out) of (*informal*), overdo, overemphasize, overestimate, overplay, overrate
➤ **Antonyms**
≠**enlarge**: decrease, diminish, lessen, lower, minimize, reduce, shrink ≠**overstate**: belittle, deflate, denigrate, deprecate, disparage, understate

magniloquent *adjective* = **pompous**, arty-farty (*informal*), bombastic, declamatory, elevated, exalted, grandiloquent, high-flown, high-sounding, lofty, orotund, overblown, pretentious, rhetorical, sonorous, stilted, turgid

magnitude *noun* **1** = **importance**, consequence, eminence, grandeur, greatness, mark, moment, note, significance, weight **2** = **size**, amount, amplitude, bigness, bulk, capacity, dimensions, enormity, expanse, extent, hugeness, immensity, intensity, largeness, mass, measure, proportions, quantity,

space, strength, vastness, volume
➤ **Antonyms**
≠**importance**: insignificance, triviality, unimportance ≠**size**: meanness, smallness

maid *noun* **1** = **servant**, abigail (*archaic*), handmaiden (*archaic*), housemaid, maidservant, serving-maid **2** *Literary* = **girl**, damsel, lass, lassie (*informal*), maiden, miss, nymph (*poetic*), wench

maiden *noun* **1** *Literary* = **girl**, damsel, lass, lassie (*informal*), maid, miss, nymph (*poetic*), virgin, wench ♦ *adjective* **2** = **unmarried**, chaste, intact, pure, undefiled, unwed, virgin, virginal **3** = **first**, inaugural, initial, initiatory, introductory

maidenly *adjective* = **modest**, chaste, decent, decorous, demure, gentle, girlish, pure, reserved, undefiled, unsullied, vestal, virginal, virtuous
➤ **Antonyms**
brazen, corrupt, defiled, depraved, dirty, immodest, immoral, impure, indecent, loose, promiscuous, shameless, sinful, unchaste, wanton, wicked

mail *noun* **1** = **letters**, correspondence, packages, parcels, post **2** = **postal service**, post, postal system ♦ *verb* **3** = **post**, dispatch, forward, send, send by mail *or* post

maim *verb* = **cripple**, disable, hamstring, hurt, impair, incapacitate, injure, lame, mangle, mar, mutilate, put out of action, wound

main *adjective* **1** = **chief**, capital, cardinal, central, critical, crucial, essential, foremost, head, leading, major, necessary, outstanding, paramount, particular, predominant, pre-eminent, premier, primary, prime, principal, special, supreme, vital ♦ *noun* **2** = **conduit**, cable, channel, duct, line, pipe **3** = **force**, effort, might, potency, power, puissance, strength **4 in the main** = **on the whole**, for the most part, generally, in general, mainly, mostly
➤ **Antonyms**
adjective ≠**chief**: auxiliary, dependent, insignificant, least, lesser, minor, secondary, subordinate, trivial, unimportant

mainly *adverb* = **chiefly**, above all, first and foremost, for the most part, generally, in general, in the main, largely, mostly, most of all, on the whole, overall, predominantly, primarily, principally, substantially, to the greatest extent, usually

mainstay *noun* = **pillar**, anchor, backbone, bulwark, buttress, chief support, lynchpin, prop

mainstream *adjective* = **conventional**,

accepted, central, current, established, general, orthodox, prevailing, received
➤ **Antonyms**
fringe, marginal, peripheral, unconventional, unorthodox

maintain verb **1** = **continue**, carry on, conserve, keep, keep up, nurture, perpetuate, preserve, prolong, retain, sustain, uphold **2** = **look after**, care for, finance, provide for, supply, support, take care of **3** = **assert**, affirm, allege, asseverate, aver, avow, claim, contend, declare, hold, insist, profess, state **4** = **support**, advocate, argue for, back, champion, defend, fight for, justify, plead for, stand by, take up the cudgels for, uphold, vindicate
➤ **Antonyms**
≠**continue**: abolish, break off, conclude, discontinue, drop, end, finish, give up, relinquish, suspend, terminate ≠**assert**: disavow ≠**support**: abandon, desert

maintenance noun **1** = **continuation**, carrying-on, continuance, perpetuation, prolongation, retainment, support, sustainment, sustention **2** = **upkeep**, care, conservation, keeping, nurture, preservation, provision, repairs, supply **3** = **allowance**, aliment, alimony, food, keep, livelihood, living, subsistence, support, sustenance, upkeep

majestic adjective = **grand**, august, awesome, dignified, elevated, exalted, grandiose, imperial, imposing, impressive, kingly, lofty, magnificent, monumental, noble, pompous, princely, regal, royal, splendid, splendiferous (facetious), stately, sublime, superb
➤ **Antonyms**
humble, ignoble, lowly, mean, modest, ordinary, unassuming, undistinguished, unimposing

majesty noun = **grandeur**, augustness, awesomeness, dignity, exaltedness, glory, imposingness, impressiveness, kingliness, loftiness, magnificence, nobility, pomp, queenliness, royalty, splendour, state, stateliness, sublimity
➤ **Antonyms**
meanness, triviality

major adjective **1** = **main**, better, bigger, chief, elder, greater, head, higher, larger, lead, leading, most, senior, superior, supreme, uppermost **2** = **important**, critical, crucial, grave, great, mega (slang), notable, outstanding, pre-eminent, radical, serious, significant, vital, weighty
➤ **Antonyms**
≠**main**: auxiliary, lesser, minor, secondary, smaller, subordinate ≠**important**:

inconsequential, insignificant, trivial, unimportant

majority noun **1** = **most**, best part, bulk, greater number, mass, more, plurality, preponderance, superiority **2** = **adulthood**, manhood or womanhood, maturity, seniority

make verb **1** = **create**, assemble, build, compose, constitute, construct, fabricate, fashion, forge, form, frame, manufacture, mould, originate, produce, put together, shape, synthesize **2** = **force**, cause, coerce, compel, constrain, dragoon, drive, impel, induce, oblige, press, pressurize, prevail upon, railroad (informal), require **3** = **produce**, accomplish, beget, bring about, cause, create, effect, engender, generate, give rise to, lead to, occasion **4** = **perform**, act, carry out, do, effect, engage in, execute, practise, prosecute **5** = **appoint**, assign, create, designate, elect, install, invest, nominate, ordain **6** = **amount to**, add up to, compose, constitute, embody, form, represent **7** = **earn**, acquire, clear, gain, get, net, obtain, realize, secure, take in, win **8** = **calculate**, estimate, gauge, judge, reckon, suppose, think **9** = **get to**, arrive at, arrive in time for, attain, catch, meet, reach **10** = **enact**, draw up, establish, fix, form, frame, pass **11 make as if** or **though** = **pretend**, act as if or though, affect, feign, feint, give the impression that, make a show of **12 make it** Informal = **succeed**, arrive (informal), be successful, come through, crack it (informal), cut it (informal), get on, get somewhere, prosper, pull through, survive ♦ noun **13** = **brand**, build, character, composition, constitution, construction, cut, designation, form, kind, make-up, mark, model, shape, sort, structure, style, type, variety **14** = **nature**, cast of mind, character, disposition, frame of mind, humour, kidney, make-up, stamp, temper, temperament

make away verb **1** = **depart**, abscond, beat a hasty retreat, clear out (informal), cut and run (informal), decamp, do a runner (slang), flee, fly, fly the coop (U.S. & Canad. informal), hook it (slang), make off, run away or off, run for it (informal), scoot, skedaddle (informal), slope off, take a powder (U.S. & Canad. slang), take it on the lam (U.S. & Canad. slang), take to one's heels **2** with **with** = **steal**, abduct, cabbage (Brit. slang), carry off, cart off (slang), filch, kidnap, knock off (slang), make off with, nab (informal), nick (slang, chiefly Brit.), pilfer, pinch (informal), purloin, swipe (slang) **3** with **with** = **kill**, blow away (*slang, chiefly U.S.*), bump off (*slang*), destroy, dispose of, do away with, do in (*slang*), eliminate, get rid of, murder, rub out (*U.S. slang*)

make-believe *noun* 1 = **fantasy**, charade, dream, imagination, play-acting, pretence, unreality ♦ *adjective* 2 = **imaginary**, dream, fantasized, fantasy, imagined, made-up, mock, pretend, pretended, sham, unreal
➤ **Antonyms**
noun ≠**fantasy**: actuality, fact, reality, truthfulness ♦ *adjective* ≠**imaginary**: authentic, genuine, real, unfeigned

make believe *verb* = **pretend**, act as if *or* though, dream, enact, fantasize, imagine, play, play-act

make do *verb* = **manage**, cope, get along *or* by, improvise, muddle through, scrape along *or* by

make for *verb* 1 = **head for**, aim for, be bound for, head towards, proceed towards, steer (a course) for 2 = **attack**, assail, assault, fall on, fly at, go for, have a go at (*informal*), lunge at, set upon 3 = **contribute to**, be conducive to, conduce to, facilitate, favour, promote

make off *verb* 1 = **flee**, abscond, beat a hasty retreat, bolt, clear out (*informal*), cut and run (*informal*), decamp, do a runner (*slang*), fly, fly the coop (*U.S. & Canad. informal*), hook it (*slang*), make away, run away *or* off, run for it (*informal*), skedaddle (*informal*), slope off, take a powder (*U.S. & Canad. slang*), take it on the lam (*U.S. & Canad. slang*), take to one's heels 2 **make off with** = **steal**, abduct, cabbage (*Brit. slang*), carry off, cart off (*slang*), filch, kidnap, knock off (*slang*), make away with, nab (*informal*), nick (*slang, chiefly Brit.*), pilfer, pinch (*informal*), purloin, run away *or* off with, swipe (*slang*)

make out *verb* 1 = **see**, descry, detect, discern, discover, distinguish, espy, perceive, recognize 2 = **understand**, comprehend, decipher, fathom, follow, grasp, perceive, realize, see, suss (out) (*slang*), work out 3 = **write out**, complete, draw up, fill in *or* out, inscribe 4 = **prove**, demonstrate, describe, represent, show 5 = **pretend**, assert, claim, let on, make as if *or* though 6 = **fare**, get on, manage, prosper, succeed, thrive

maker *noun* = **manufacturer**, author, builder, constructor, director, fabricator, framer, producer

Maker *noun* = **God**, Creator

makeshift *adjective* 1 = **temporary**, expedient, jury (*chiefly Nautical*), make-do, provisional, rough and ready, stopgap, substitute ♦ *noun* 2 = **stopgap**, expedient,

shift, substitute

make-up *noun* 1 = **cosmetics**, face (*informal*), greasepaint (*Theatre*), maquillage, paint (*informal*), powder, war paint (*informal, humorous*) 2 = **structure**, arrangement, assembly, composition, configuration, constitution, construction, form, format, formation, organization 3 = **nature**, build, cast of mind, character, constitution, disposition, figure, frame of mind, make, stamp, temper, temperament

make up *verb* 1 = **form**, compose, comprise, constitute 2 = **invent**, coin, compose, concoct, construct, cook up (*informal*), create, devise, dream up, fabricate, formulate, frame, hatch, manufacture, originate, trump up, write 3 = **complete**, fill, meet, supply 4 = **settle**, bury the hatchet, call it quits, come to terms, compose, forgive and forget, make peace, mend, reconcile, shake hands 5 **make up for** = **compensate for**, atone for, balance, make amends for, offset, recompense, redeem, redress, requite 6 **make up one's mind** = **decide**, choose, come to a decision, determine, make a decision, reach a decision, resolve, settle 7 **make up to** *Informal* = **court**, chat up (*informal*), curry favour with, flirt with, make overtures to, woo

making *noun* 1 = **creation**, assembly, building, composition, construction, fabrication, forging, manufacture, production 2 **in the making** = **budding**, coming, emergent, growing, nascent, potential

makings *plural noun* = **beginnings**, capability, capacity, ingredients, materials, potential, potentiality, qualities

maladjusted *adjective* = **disturbed**, alienated, estranged, hung-up (*slang*), neurotic, unstable

maladministration *noun* = **mismanagement**, blundering, bungling, corruption, dishonesty, incompetence, inefficiency, malfeasance (*Law*), malpractice, misgovernment, misrule

maladroit *adjective* = **clumsy**, awkward, cack-handed (*informal*), ham-fisted *or* ham-handed (*informal*), inept, inexpert, unskilful

malady *noun* = **disease**, affliction, ailment, complaint, disorder, ill, illness, indisposition, infirmity, lurgy (*informal*), sickness

malaise *noun* = **unease**, angst, anxiety, depression, discomfort, disquiet, doldrums, enervation, illness, lassitude, melancholy, sickness, weakness

malcontent *noun* 1 = **troublemaker**,

agitator, complainer, fault-finder, grouch (*informal*), grouser, grumbler, mischief-maker, rebel, stirrer (*informal*) ♦ *adjective* **2** = **discontented**, disaffected, disgruntled, disgusted, dissatisfied, dissentious, factious, ill-disposed, rebellious, resentful, restive, unhappy, unsatisfied

male *adjective* = **masculine**, manful, manlike, manly, virile
➤ Antonyms
camp (*informal*), effeminate, female, feminine, girlie, unmanly, wimpish *or* wimpy (*informal*), womanish, womanly, wussy (*slang*)

malefactor *noun* = **wrongdoer**, convict, criminal, crook (*informal*), culprit, delinquent, evildoer, felon, lawbreaker, miscreant, offender, outlaw, transgressor, villain

malevolence *noun* = **malice**, hate, hatred, ill will, maliciousness, malignity, nastiness, rancour, spite, spitefulness, vengefulness, vindictiveness

malevolent *adjective* = **spiteful**, baleful, evil-minded, hateful (*archaic*), hostile, ill-natured, maleficent, malicious, malign, malignant, pernicious, rancorous, vengeful, vicious, vindictive
➤ Antonyms
amiable, benevolent, benign, friendly, gracious, kind, warm-hearted

malformation *noun* = **deformity**, crookedness, distortion, misshape, misshapenness

malformed *adjective* = **misshapen**, abnormal, contorted, crooked, deformed, distorted, irregular, twisted

malfunction *verb* **1** = **break down**, develop a fault, fail, go wrong ♦ *noun* **2** = **fault**, breakdown, defect, failure, flaw, glitch, impairment

malice *noun* = **spite**, animosity, animus, bad blood, bitterness, enmity, evil intent, hate, hatred, ill will, malevolence, maliciousness, malignity, rancour, spitefulness, spleen, vengefulness, venom, vindictiveness

malicious *adjective* = **spiteful**, baleful, bitchy (*informal*), bitter, catty (*informal*), evil-minded, hateful, ill-disposed, ill-natured, injurious, malevolent, malignant, mischievous, pernicious, rancorous, resentful, shrewish, vengeful, vicious
➤ Antonyms
amiable, benevolent, friendly, kind, warm-hearted

malign *verb* **1** = **disparage**, abuse, asperse, bad-mouth (*slang, chiefly U.S. & Canad.*),

blacken (someone's name), calumniate, defame, denigrate, derogate, do a hatchet job on (*informal*), harm, injure, knock (*informal*), libel, revile, rubbish (*informal*), run down, slag (off) (*slang*), slander, smear, speak ill of, traduce, vilify
♦ *adjective* **2** = **evil**, bad, baleful, baneful, deleterious, destructive, harmful, hostile, hurtful, injurious, maleficent, malevolent, malignant, pernicious, vicious, wicked
➤ Antonyms
verb ≠**disparage**: commend, compliment, extol, praise ♦ *adjective* ≠**evil**: agreeable, amiable, beneficial, benevolent, benign, friendly, good, harmless, innocuous, kind, virtuous, warm-hearted, wholesome

malignant *adjective* **1** = **hostile**, baleful, bitter, destructive, harmful, hurtful, inimical, injurious, maleficent, malevolent, malicious, malign, of evil intent, pernicious, spiteful, vicious **2** *Medical* = **uncontrollable**, cancerous, dangerous, deadly, evil, fatal, irremediable, metastatic, virulent
➤ Antonyms
≠**hostile**: amicable, benevolent, benign, friendly, kind, warm-hearted

malleable *adjective* **1** = **workable**, ductile, plastic, soft, tensile **2** = **manageable**, adaptable, biddable, compliant, impressionable, pliable, tractable

malodorous *adjective* = **smelly**, fetid, mephitic, nauseating, noisome, offensive, putrid, reeking, stinking

malpractice *noun* = **misconduct**, abuse, dereliction, misbehaviour, mismanagement, negligence

maltreat *verb* = **abuse**, bully, damage, handle roughly, harm, hurt, ill-treat, injure, mistreat

mammoth *adjective* = **colossal**, Brobdingnagian, elephantine, enormous, gargantuan, giant, gigantic, ginormous (*informal*), huge, humongous *or* humungous (*U.S. slang*), immense, jumbo (*informal*), massive, mega (*slang*), mighty, monumental, mountainous, prodigious, stellar (*informal*), stupendous, titanic, vast
➤ Antonyms
diminutive, insignificant, little, miniature, minute, puny, small, tiny, trivial

man *noun* **1** = **male**, bloke (*Brit. informal*), chap (*informal*), gentleman, guy (*informal*) **2** = **human**, adult, being, body, human being, individual, one, person, personage, somebody, soul **3** = **mankind**, Homo sapiens, humanity, humankind, human race, mortals, people **4** = **manservant**, attendant, follower, retainer, servant, valet **5** = **employee**, hand, hireling, liegeman, soldier, subject, subordinate, vassal, worker, workman **6** = **boyfriend**, beau, husband, lover, partner, significant other (*U.S. informal*), spouse **7 to a man** = **without exception**, bar none, every one, one and all, unanimously ♦ *verb* **8** = **staff**, crew, fill, furnish with men, garrison, occupy, people

manacle *noun* **1** = **handcuff**, bond, chain, fetter, gyve (*archaic*), iron, shackle, tie ♦ *verb* **2** = **handcuff**, bind, chain, check, clap *or* put in irons, confine, constrain, curb, fetter, hamper, inhibit, put in chains, restrain, shackle, tie one's hands

manage *verb* **1** = **succeed**, accomplish, arrange, bring about *or* off, contrive, cope with, crack it (*informal*), cut it (*informal*), deal with, effect, engineer **2** = **administer**, be in charge (of), call the shots, call the tune, command, concert, conduct, direct, govern, handle, manipulate, oversee, preside over, rule, run, superintend, supervise **3** = **handle**, control, dominate, govern, guide, influence, manipulate, operate, pilot, ply, steer, train, use, wield **4** = **cope**, carry on, fare, get along, get by (*informal*), get on, get through, make do, make out, muddle through, shift, survive
➤ **Antonyms**
≠**succeed**: bodge (*informal*), botch, fail, make a mess of, make a nonsense of, mismanage, muff, spoil

manageable *adjective* **1** = **easy**, convenient, handy, user-friendly, wieldy **2** = **docile**, amenable, compliant, controllable, governable, submissive, tamable, tractable
➤ **Antonyms**
≠**easy**: demanding, difficult, hard ≠**docile**: disobedient, headstrong, obstinate, refractory, stubborn, ungovernable, unruly, unyielding, wild

management *noun* **1** = **directors**, administration, board, bosses (*informal*), directorate, employers, executive(s) **2** = **administration**, care, charge, command, conduct, control, direction, governance, government, guidance, handling, manipulation, operation, rule, running, superintendence, supervision

manager *noun* = **supervisor**, administrator, boss (*informal*), comptroller, conductor, controller, director, executive, gaffer (*informal, chiefly Brit.*), governor, head, organizer, overseer, proprietor, superintendent

mandate *noun* = **command**, authority, authorization, bidding, canon, charge, commission, decree, directive, edict, fiat, injunction, instruction, order, precept, sanction, warrant

mandatory *adjective* = **compulsory**, binding, obligatory, required, requisite
➤ **Antonyms**
discretionary, nonbinding, noncompulsory, nonobligatory, optional, unnecessary, voluntary

manful *adjective* = **brave**, bold, courageous, daring, determined, gallant, hardy, heroic, indomitable, intrepid, manly, noble, powerful, resolute, stalwart, stout, stout-hearted, strong, valiant, vigorous

manfully *adverb* = **bravely**, boldly, courageously, desperately, determinedly, gallantly, hard, heroically, intrepidly, like a Trojan, like one possessed, like the devil, nobly, powerfully, resolutely, stalwartly, stoutly, strongly, to the best of one's ability, valiantly, vigorously, with might and main

mangle *verb* = **crush**, butcher, cripple, cut, deform, destroy, disfigure, distort, hack, lacerate, maim, mar, maul, mutilate, rend, ruin, spoil, tear, total (*slang*), trash (*slang*), wreck

mangy *adjective* = **scruffy**, dirty, grungy (*slang, chiefly U.S.*), mean, moth-eaten, scabby (*informal*), scuzzy (*slang, chiefly U.S.*), seedy, shabby, shoddy, squalid
➤ **Antonyms**
attractive, choice, clean, de luxe, fine, splendid, spotless, superb, tidy, well-dressed, well-kept

manhandle *verb* **1** = **rough up**, handle roughly, knock about *or* around, maul, paw (*informal*), pull, push **2** = **haul**, carry, heave, hump (*Brit. slang*), lift, manoeuvre, pull, push, shove, tug

manhood *noun* = **manliness**, bravery, courage, determination, firmness, fortitude, hardihood, manfulness, masculinity, maturity, mettle, resolution, spirit, strength, valour, virility

mania *noun* **1** = **obsession**, cacoethes, craving, craze, desire, enthusiasm, fad (*informal*), fetish, fixation, partiality, passion, preoccupation, rage, thing (*informal*) **2** = **madness**, aberration, craziness, delirium, dementia, derangement, disorder, frenzy, insanity, lunacy

maniac *noun* **1** = **madman** *or* **madwoman**, headbanger (*informal*), headcase (*informal*), loony (*slang*), lunatic, nutcase (*slang*), nutter (*Brit. slang*), psycho (*slang*), psychopath **2** = **fanatic**, energumen, enthusiast, fan, fiend (*informal*), freak (*informal*)

manifest *adjective* **1** = **obvious**, apparent,

blatant, bold, clear, conspicuous, distinct, evident, glaring, noticeable, open, palpable, patent, plain, salient, unmistakable, visible ♦ *verb* **2** = **display**, declare, demonstrate, establish, evince, exhibit, expose, express, make plain, prove, reveal, set forth, show
➤ **Antonyms**
adjective ≠**obvious**: concealed, disguised, hidden, inconspicuous, indistinct, masked, suppressed, unapparent, vague, veiled ♦ *verb* ≠**display**: conceal, cover, cover up, deny, hide, mask, obscure, refute

manifestation *noun* = **display**, appearance, demonstration, disclosure, exhibition, exposure, expression, indication, instance, mark, materialization, revelation, show, sign, symptom, token

manifold *adjective Formal* = **numerous**, abundant, assorted, copious, diverse, diversified, many, multifarious, multifold, multiple, multiplied, multitudinous, varied, various

manipulate *verb* **1** = **work**, employ, handle, operate, ply, use, wield **2** = **influence**, conduct, control, direct, do a number on (*chiefly U.S.*), engineer, guide, manoeuvre, negotiate, steer, twist around one's little finger

mankind *noun* = **people**, Homo sapiens, humanity, humankind, human race, man

manliness *noun* = **virility**, boldness, bravery, courage, fearlessness, firmness, hardihood, heroism, independence, intrepidity, machismo, manfulness, manhood, masculinity, mettle, resolution, stoutheartedness, valour, vigour

manly *adjective* = **virile**, bold, brave, butch (*slang*), courageous, daring, dauntless, fearless, gallant, hardy, heroic, macho, male, manful, masculine, muscular, noble, powerful, red-blooded (*informal*), resolute, robust, stout-hearted, strapping, strong, valiant, valorous, vigorous, well-built
➤ **Antonyms**
camp (*informal*), cowardly, craven, delicate, effeminate, faint-hearted, feeble, feminine, frail, girlie, ignoble, irresolute, sickly, soft, timid, unmanly, weak, wimpish *or* wimpy (*informal*), womanish, wussy (*slang*)

man-made *adjective* = **artificial**, ersatz, manufactured, mock, plastic (*slang*), synthetic

manner *noun* **1** = **behaviour**, air, appearance, aspect, bearing, comportment, conduct, demeanour, deportment, look, mien (*literary*), presence, tone **2** = **style**, approach, custom, fashion, form, genre, habit, line,

means, method, mode, practice, procedure, process, routine, tack, tenor, usage, way, wont **3** = **type**, brand, breed, category, form, kind, nature, sort, variety

mannered *adjective* = **affected**, artificial, arty-farty (*informal*), posed, pretentious, pseudo (*informal*), put-on, stilted
➤ **Antonyms**
genuine, honest, natural, real, sincere, unaffected, unpretentious

mannerism *noun* = **habit**, characteristic, foible, idiosyncrasy, peculiarity, quirk, trait, trick

mannerly *adjective* = **polite**, civil, civilized, courteous, decorous, genteel, gentlemanly, gracious, ladylike, polished, refined, respectful, well-behaved, well-bred, well-mannered
➤ **Antonyms**
boorish, discourteous, disrespectful, ill-mannered, impertinent, impolite, impudent, insolent, rude, unmannerly

manners *plural noun* **1** = **behaviour**, bearing, breeding, carriage, comportment, conduct, demeanour, deportment **2** = **politeness**, ceremony, courtesy, decorum, etiquette, formalities, good form, polish, politesse, proprieties, protocol, p's and q's, refinement, social graces, the done thing

manoeuvre *verb* **1** = **manipulate**, contrive, devise, engineer, intrigue, machinate, manage, plan, plot, pull strings, scheme, wangle (*informal*) **2** = **move**, deploy, exercise **3** = **steer**, direct, drive, guide, handle, navigate, negotiate, pilot ♦ *noun* **4** = **movement**, deployment, evolution, exercise, operation **5** = **stratagem**, action, artifice, dodge, intrigue, machination, move, movement, plan, plot, ploy, ruse, scheme, subterfuge, tactic, trick

mansion *noun* = **residence**, abode, dwelling, habitation, hall, manor, seat, villa

mantle *noun* **1** = **cloak**, cape, hood, shawl, wrap **2** = **covering**, blanket, canopy, cloud, cover, curtain, envelope, pall, screen, shroud, veil ♦ *verb* **3** = **cover**, blanket, cloak, cloud, disguise, envelop, hide, mask, overspread, screen, shroud, veil, wrap

manual *adjective* **1** = **hand-operated**, done by hand, human, physical ♦ *noun* **2** = **handbook**, bible, guide, guidebook, instructions, workbook

manufacture *verb* **1** = **make**, assemble, build, compose, construct, create, fabricate, forge, form, mass-produce, mould, process, produce, put together, shape, turn out **2** = **concoct**, cook up (*informal*), devise, fabricate, hatch, invent, make up, think up, trump up ♦ *noun* **3** = **making**, assembly, construction, creation, fabrication, mass-production, produce, production

manufacturer *noun* = **maker**, builder, constructor, creator, fabricator, factory-owner, industrialist, producer

manure *noun* = **compost**, droppings, dung, excrement, fertilizer, muck, ordure

many *adjective* **1** = **numerous**, abundant, copious, countless, divers (*archaic*), frequent, innumerable, manifold, multifarious, multifold, multitudinous, myriad, profuse, sundry, umpteen (*informal*), varied, various ♦ *noun* **2** = **a lot**, a horde, a mass, a multitude, a thousand and one, heaps (*informal*), large numbers, lots (*informal*), piles (*informal*), plenty, scores, tons (*informal*), umpteen (*informal*) **3 the many** = **the masses**, the crowd, (the) hoi polloi, the majority, the multitude, the people, the rank and file

mar *verb* = **spoil**, blemish, blight, blot, damage, deface, detract from, disfigure, harm, hurt, impair, injure, maim, mangle, mutilate, put a damper on, ruin, scar, stain, sully, taint, tarnish, vitiate

➤ **Antonyms**

adorn, ameliorate, better, embellish, improve, ornament

maraud *verb* = **raid**, despoil, forage, foray, harry, loot, pillage, plunder, ransack, ravage, reive (*dialect*), sack

marauder *noun* = **raider**, bandit, brigand, buccaneer, cateran (*Scot.*), corsair, freebooter, mosstrooper, outlaw, pillager, pirate, plunderer, ravager, reiver (*dialect*), robber, sea wolf

march *verb* **1** = **walk**, file, footslog, pace, parade, stalk, stride, strut, tramp, tread ♦ *noun* **2** = **stride**, gait, pace, step **3** = **walk**, hike, routemarch, tramp, trek **4** = **progress**, advance, development, evolution, progression **5** = **demonstration**, demo (*informal*), parade, procession **6 on the march** = **advancing**, afoot, astir, en route, marching, on one's way, on the way, proceeding, progressing, under way

marches *plural noun* = **borders**, borderland, boundaries, confines, frontiers, limits, marchlands

margin *noun* **1** = **edge**, border, bound, boundary, brim, brink, confine, limit, perimeter, periphery, rim, side, verge **2** = **room**, allowance, compass, elbowroom, extra, latitude, leeway, play, scope, space, surplus

marginal *adjective* **1** = **borderline**, bordering, on the edge, peripheral **2** = **insignificant**, low, minimal, minor,

negligible, slight, small

marijuana *noun* = **cannabis**, bhang, blow (*slang*), charas, chronic (*U.S. slang*), dope (*slang*), gage (*U.S. old-fashioned slang*), ganja, grass (*slang*), hash (*slang*), hashish, hemp, kif, leaf (*slang*), mary jane (*U.S. slang*), pot (*slang*), sinsemilla, smoke (*informal*), stuff (*slang*), tea (*U.S. slang*), wacky baccy (*slang*), weed (*slang*)

marine *adjective* = **nautical**, maritime, naval, ocean-going, oceanic, pelagic, saltwater, sea, seafaring, seagoing, thalassic

mariner *noun* = **sailor**, bluejacket, gob (*U.S. slang*), hand, Jack Tar, matelot (*slang, chiefly Brit.*), navigator, salt, sea dog, seafarer, seafaring man, seaman, tar

marital *adjective* = **matrimonial**, conjugal, connubial, married, nuptial, spousal, wedded

maritime *adjective* **1** = **nautical**, marine, naval, oceanic, sea, seafaring **2** = **coastal**, littoral, seaside

mark *noun* **1** = **spot**, blemish, blot, blotch, bruise, dent, impression, line, nick, pock, scar, scratch, smirch, smudge, splotch, stain, streak **2** = **sign**, badge, blaze, brand, characteristic, device, earmark, emblem, evidence, feature, flag, hallmark, impression, incision, index, indication, label, note, print, proof, seal, signet, stamp, symbol, symptom, token **3** = **criterion**, level, measure, norm, par, standard, yardstick **4** = **target**, aim, end, goal, object, objective, purpose **5** = **influence**, consequence, dignity, distinction, eminence, fame, importance, notability, note, notice, prestige, quality, regard, standing **6** = **track**, footmark, footprint, sign, trace, trail, vestige **7 make one's mark** = **succeed**, achieve recognition, be a success, find a place in the sun, get on in the world, make a success of oneself, make good, make it (*informal*), make something of oneself, prosper ♦ *verb* **8** = **scar**, blemish, blot, blotch, brand, bruise, dent, impress, imprint, nick, scratch, smirch, smudge, splotch, stain, streak **9** = **characterize**, brand, flag, identify, label, stamp **10** = **distinguish**, betoken, denote, evince, exemplify, illustrate, show **11** = **observe**, attend, hearken (*archaic*), mind, note, notice, pay attention, pay heed, regard, remark, watch **12** = **grade**, appraise, assess, correct, evaluate

marked *adjective* = **noticeable**, apparent, blatant, clear, considerable, conspicuous, decided, distinct, dramatic, evident, manifest, notable, noted, obvious, outstanding, patent, prominent,

pronounced, remarkable, salient, signal, striking
➤ **Antonyms**
concealed, doubtful, dubious, hidden, imperceptible, inconspicuous, indistinct, insignificant, obscure, unclear, unnoticeable, vague

markedly *adverb* = **noticeably**, clearly, considerably, conspicuously, decidedly, distinctly, evidently, greatly, manifestly, notably, obviously, outstandingly, patently, remarkably, seriously (*informal*), signally, strikingly, to a great extent

market *noun* 1 = **fair**, bazaar, mart ♦ *verb* 2 = **sell**, offer for sale, retail, vend

marketable *adjective* = **sought after**, in demand, merchantable, saleable, vendible, wanted

marksman, markswoman *noun* = **sharpshooter**, crack shot (*informal*), deadeye (*informal, chiefly U.S.*), dead shot (*informal*), good shot

maroon *verb* = **abandon**, cast ashore, cast away, desert, leave, leave high and dry (*informal*), strand

marriage *noun* 1 = **wedding**, espousal, match, matrimony, nuptial rites, nuptials, wedding ceremony, wedlock 2 = **union**, alliance, amalgamation, association, confederation, coupling, link, merger

married *adjective* 1 = **wedded**, hitched (*slang*), joined, one, spliced (*informal*), united, wed 2 = **marital**, conjugal, connubial, husbandly, matrimonial, nuptial, spousal, wifely

marrow *noun* = **core**, cream, essence, gist, heart, kernel, pith, quick, quintessence, soul, spirit, substance

marry *verb* 1 = **wed**, become man and wife, espouse, get hitched (*slang*), get spliced (*informal*), plight one's troth (*old-fashioned*), take the plunge (*informal*), take to wife, tie the knot (*informal*), walk down the aisle (*informal*), wive (*archaic*) 2 = **unite**, ally, bond, join, knit, link, match, merge, splice, tie, unify, yoke

marsh *noun* = **swamp**, bog, fen, morass, moss (*Scot. & Northern English dialect*), quagmire, slough

marshal *verb* 1 = **arrange**, align, array, assemble, collect, deploy, dispose, draw up, gather, group, line up, muster, order, organize, rank, sequence 2 = **conduct**, escort, guide, lead, shepherd, usher

marshy *adjective* = **swampy**, boggy, fenny, miry, paludal, quaggy, spongy, waterlogged, wet

martial *adjective* = **military**, bellicose, belligerent, brave, heroic, soldierly, warlike

martinet *noun* = **disciplinarian**, drillmaster, stickler

martyrdom *noun* = **persecution**, agony, anguish, ordeal, suffering, torment, torture
➤ **Antonyms**
bliss, ecstasy, happiness, joy

marvel *verb* 1 = **wonder**, be amazed, be awed, be filled with surprise, gape, gaze, goggle ♦ *noun* 2 = **wonder**, genius, miracle, phenomenon, portent, prodigy, whizz (*informal*)

marvellous *adjective* 1 = **excellent**, awesome (*slang*), bad (*slang*), bodacious (*slang, chiefly U.S.*), boffo (*slang*), brill (*informal*), chillin' (*U.S. slang*), colossal, cracking (*Brit. informal*), crucial (*slang*), def (*slang*), divine (*informal*), fabulous (*informal*), fantastic (*informal*), glorious, great (*informal*), jim-dandy (*slang*), magnificent, mean (*slang*), mega (*slang*), sensational (*informal*), smashing (*informal*), sovereign, splendid, stupendous, super (*informal*), superb, terrific (*informal*), topping (*Brit. slang*), wicked (*informal*), wonderful 2 = **amazing**, astonishing, astounding, breathtaking, brilliant, extraordinary, jaw-dropping, miraculous, phenomenal, prodigious, remarkable, sensational (*informal*), singular, spectacular, stupendous, wondrous (*archaic or literary*)
➤ **Antonyms**
≠excellent: awful, bad, terrible
≠amazing: believable, commonplace, credible, everyday, ordinary

masculine *adjective* 1 = **male**, manful, manlike, manly, mannish, virile 2 = **strong**, bold, brave, butch (*slang*), gallant, hardy, macho, muscular, powerful, red-blooded (*informal*), resolute, robust, stout-hearted, strapping, vigorous, well-built

mask *noun* 1 = **visor**, domino, false face, vizard (*archaic*) 2 = **disguise**, blind, camouflage, cloak, concealment, cover, cover-up, façade, front, guise, screen, semblance, show, veil, veneer ♦ *verb* 3 = **disguise**, camouflage, cloak, conceal, cover, hide, obscure, screen, veil

masquerade *verb* 1 = **pose**, disguise, dissemble, dissimulate, impersonate, pass oneself off, pretend (to be) ♦ *noun* 2 = **pretence**, cloak, cover-up, deception, disguise, mask, pose, screen, subterfuge 3 = **masked ball**, fancy dress party, revel

mass *noun* 1 = **piece**, block, chunk, concretion, hunk, lump 2 = **collection**, aggregate, body, entirety, sum, sum total, totality, whole 3 = **lot**, accumulation, aggregation, assemblage, batch, bunch, collection, combination, conglomeration,

heap, load, pile, quantity, rick, stack **4
= crowd**, assemblage, band, body, bunch
(*informal*), group, horde, host, lot, mob,
number, throng, troop **5 = majority**, body,
bulk, greater part, lion's share,
preponderance **6 = size**, bulk, dimension,
greatness, magnitude **7 the masses = the
multitude**, the commonalty, the common
people, the crowd, (the) hoi polloi
♦ *adjective* **8 = large-scale**, extensive,
general, indiscriminate, pandemic,
popular, wholesale, widespread ♦ *verb* **9
= gather**, accumulate, amass, assemble,
collect, congregate, foregather, mob,
muster, rally, swarm, throng

massacre *noun* **1 = slaughter**, annihilation,
blood bath, butchery, carnage,
extermination, holocaust, killing, mass
slaughter, murder ♦ *verb* **2 = slaughter**,
annihilate, blow away (*slang, chiefly U.S.*),
butcher, cut to pieces, exterminate, kill,
mow down, murder, slay, take out (*slang*),
wipe out

massage *noun* **1 = rub-down**, acupressure,
kneading, manipulation, reflexology,
rubbing, shiatsu ♦ *verb* **2 = rub down**,
knead, manipulate, rub

massive *adjective* **= huge**, big, bulky,
colossal, elephantine, enormous,
extensive, gargantuan, gigantic,
ginormous (*informal*), great, heavy, hefty,
hulking, humongous *or* humungous (*U.S.
slang*), immense, imposing, impressive,
mammoth, mega (*slang*), monster,
monumental, ponderous, solid, stellar
(*informal*), substantial, titanic, vast,
weighty, whacking (*informal*), whopping
(*informal*)
➤ **Antonyms**
frail, light, little, minute, petty, slight,
small, thin, tiny, trivial

master *noun* **1 = head**, boss (*informal*),
captain, chief, commander, controller,
director, employer, governor, lord,
manager, overlord, overseer, owner,
principal, ruler, skipper (*informal*),
superintendent **2 = expert**, ace (*informal*),
adept, dab hand (*Brit. informal*), doyen,
genius, grandmaster, maestro, maven
(*U.S.*), past master, pro (*informal*),
virtuoso, wizard **3 = teacher**, guide, guru,
instructor, pedagogue, preceptor,
schoolmaster, spiritual leader, swami,
torchbearer, tutor ♦ *adjective* **4 = main**,
chief, controlling, foremost, grand, great,
leading, predominant, prime, principal **5
= expert**, adept, crack (*informal*), masterly,
proficient, skilful, skilled ♦ *verb* **6 = learn**,
acquire, become proficient in, get the
hang of (*informal*), grasp **7 = overcome**,
bridle, check, conquer, curb, defeat, lick

(*informal*), overpower, quash, quell,
subdue, subjugate, suppress, tame,
triumph over, vanquish **8 = control**,
command, direct, dominate, govern,
manage, regulate, rule
➤ **Antonyms**
noun ≠**head**: crew, servant, slave, subject
≠**expert**: amateur, novice ≠**teacher**:
student ♦ *adjective* ≠**main**: lesser, minor
≠**expert**: amateurish, clumsy,
incompetent, inept, novice,
unaccomplished, unskilled, untalented
♦ *verb* ≠**overcome**: cave in (*informal*), give
in, surrender, yield

masterful *adjective* **1 = skilful**, adept,
adroit, clever, consummate, crack
(*informal*), deft, dexterous, excellent,
expert, exquisite, fine, finished, first-rate,
masterly, skilled, superior, superlative,
supreme, world-class **2 = domineering**,
arrogant, authoritative, bossy (*informal*),
despotic, dictatorial, high-handed,
imperious, magisterial, overbearing,
overweening, peremptory, self-willed,
tyrannical
➤ **Antonyms**
≠**skilful**: amateurish, clumsy, incompetent,
inept, unaccomplished, unskilled,
untalented ≠**domineering**: irresolute,
meek, spineless, weak, wimpish *or* wimpy
(*informal*), wussy (*slang*)

masterly *adjective* **= skilful**, adept, adroit,
clever, consummate, crack (*informal*),
dexterous, excellent, expert, exquisite,
fine, finished, first-rate, masterful, skilled,
superior, superlative, supreme, world-class

mastermind *verb* **1 = plan**, be the brains
behind (*informal*), conceive, devise, direct,
manage, organize ♦ *noun* **2 = organizer**,
architect, authority, brain(s) (*informal*),
brainbox, director, engineer, genius,
intellect, manager, planner, virtuoso

masterpiece *noun* **= classic**, chef-d'oeuvre,
jewel, magnum opus, master work, *pièce
de résistance, tour de force*

mastery *noun* **1 = expertise**, ability,
acquirement, attainment, cleverness,
deftness, dexterity, finesse, know-how
(*informal*), proficiency, prowess, skill,
virtuosity **2 = control**, ascendancy,
authority, command, conquest,
domination, dominion, pre-eminence,
rule, superiority, supremacy, sway,
triumph, upper hand, victory, whip hand **3
= understanding**, command,
comprehension, familiarity, grasp, grip,
knowledge

match *noun* **1 = game**, bout, competition,
contest, head-to-head, test, trial **2 = equal**,
competitor, counterpart, equivalent, peer,

rival **3 = companion**, complement,
counterpart, equal, equivalent, fellow,
mate, tally **4 = replica**, copy, dead ringer
(*slang*), double, duplicate, equal, lookalike,
ringer (*slang*), spit (*informal, chiefly Brit.*),
spit and image (*informal*), spitting image
(*informal*), twin **5 = marriage**, affiliation,
alliance, combination, couple, duet, item
(*informal*), pair, pairing, partnership, union
♦ *verb* **6 = correspond**, accompany,
accord, adapt, agree, blend, coordinate,
fit, go with, harmonize, suit, tally, tone
with **7 = pair**, ally, combine, couple, join,
link, marry, mate, unite, yoke **8 = rival**,
compare, compete, contend, emulate,
equal, measure up to, oppose, pit against,
vie

matching *adjective* **= identical**, analogous,
comparable, coordinating, corresponding,
double, duplicate, equal, equivalent, like,
paired, parallel, same, toning, twin
➤ **Antonyms**
different, disparate, dissimilar, distinct,
divergent, diverse, nonparallel, other,
unequal, unlike

matchless *adjective* **= unequalled**,
consummate, exquisite, incomparable,
inimitable, peerless, perfect, superlative,
supreme, unique, unmatched,
unparalleled, unrivalled, unsurpassed
➤ **Antonyms**
average, common, commonplace,
comparable, equalled, everyday, excelled,
inferior, lesser, mediocre, no great shakes
(*informal*), ordinary, second-class,
surpassed

mate *noun* **1** *Informal* **= friend**, buddy
(*informal*), china (*Brit. slang*), chum
(*informal*), cock (*Brit. informal*), comrade,
crony, homeboy (*slang, chiefly U.S.*), pal
(*informal*) **2 = colleague**, associate,
companion, compeer, co-worker,
fellow-worker **3 = partner**, better half
(*humorous*), husband *or* wife, significant
other (*U.S. informal*), spouse **4 = assistant**,
helper, subordinate **5 = double**,
companion, fellow, match, twin ♦ *verb* **6**
= pair, breed, copulate, couple **7 = marry**,
match, wed **8 = join**, couple, match, pair,
yoke

material *noun* **1 = substance**, body,
constituents, element, matter, stuff **2**
= cloth, fabric, stuff **3 = information**, data,
evidence, facts, notes, work ♦ *adjective* **4**
= physical, bodily, concrete, corporeal,
fleshly, nonspiritual, palpable, substantial,
tangible, worldly **5 = relevant**, applicable,
apposite, apropos, germane, pertinent **6**
= important, consequential, essential,
grave, indispensable, key, meaningful,
momentous, serious, significant, vital,

weighty

materialize *verb* **= occur**, appear, come
about, come into being, come to pass,
happen, take place, take shape, turn up

materially *adverb* **= significantly**,
considerably, essentially, gravely, greatly,
much, seriously, substantially
➤ **Antonyms**
barely, hardly, insignificantly, little,
scarcely, superficially, unsubstantially

maternal *adjective* **= motherly**

maternity *noun* **= motherhood**,
motherliness

matey *adjective Brit. informal* **= friendly**,
amiable, chummy (*informal*),
companionable, comradely, free-and-easy,
hail-fellow-well-met, intimate, pally
(*informal*), palsy-walsy (*informal*), sociable,
thick (*informal*)

matrimonial *adjective* **= marital**, conjugal,
connubial, hymeneal, married, nuptial,
spousal, wedded, wedding

matrimony *noun* **= marriage**, marital rites,
nuptials, wedding ceremony, wedlock

matted *adjective* **= tangled**, knotted,
tousled, uncombed

matter *noun* **1 = substance**, body, material,
stuff **2 = situation**, affair, business,
concern, episode, event, incident, issue,
occurrence, proceeding, question, subject,
thing, topic, transaction **3 = amount**,
quantity, sum **4 = content**, argument,
purport, sense, subject, substance, text,
thesis **5** *Medical* **= pus**, discharge,
purulence, secretion **6 = importance**,
consequence, import, moment, note,
significance, weight **7** *As in* **what's the
matter? = problem**, complication,
difficulty, distress, trouble, upset, worry
♦ *verb* **8 = be important**, be of
consequence, carry weight, count, have
influence, make a difference, mean
something, signify

matter-of-fact *adjective* **= unsentimental**,
deadpan, down-to-earth, dry, dull,
emotionless, flat, lifeless, mundane, plain,
prosaic, sober, unembellished,
unimaginative, unvarnished

mature *adjective* **1 = grown-up**, adult,
complete, fit, full-blown, full-grown, fully
fledged, grown, matured, mellow, of age,
perfect, prepared, ready, ripe, ripened,
seasoned ♦ *verb* **2 = develop**, age, become
adult, bloom, blossom, come of age, grow
up, maturate, mellow, perfect, reach
adulthood, ripen, season
➤ **Antonyms**
adjective ≠**grown-up**: adolescent, childish,
green, immature, incomplete, juvenile,

puerile, undeveloped, unfinished,
unperfected, unripe, young, youthful

maturity noun = **adulthood**, completion,
experience, full bloom, full growth,
fullness, majority, manhood or
womanhood, maturation, matureness,
perfection, ripeness, wisdom
➤ **Antonyms**
childishness, immaturity, imperfection,
incompletion, juvenility, puerility,
youthfulness

maudlin adjective = **sentimental**, icky
(informal), lachrymose, mawkish, mushy
(informal), overemotional, slushy
(informal), soppy (Brit. informal), tearful,
weepy (informal)

maul verb 1 = **tear**, claw, lacerate, mangle 2
= **ill-treat**, abuse, batter, beat, beat up
(informal), handle roughly, knock about or
around, manhandle, molest, pummel,
rough up, thrash, work over (slang)

maunder verb 1 = **idle**, dawdle, dilly-dally
(informal), drift, loaf, meander, mooch
(slang), potter, ramble, straggle, stray,
traipse (informal) 2 = **chatter**, babble,
blather, blether, gabble, prattle, rabbit
(on) (Brit. informal), ramble, rattle on,
waffle (informal, chiefly Brit.), witter
(informal)

maverick noun 1 = **rebel**, dissenter,
dissentient, eccentric, heretic, iconoclast,
individualist, nonconformist, protester,
radical ◆ adjective 2 = **rebel**, dissenting,
eccentric, heretical, iconoclastic,
individualistic, nonconformist, radical
➤ **Antonyms**
noun ≠**rebel**: Babbitt (U.S.),
conventionalist, stick-in-the-mud
(informal), traditionalist, yes man

mawkish adjective = **sentimental**,
emotional, feeble, gushy (informal), icky
(informal), maudlin, mushy (informal),
schmaltzy (slang), slushy (informal), soppy
(Brit. informal), three-hankie (informal)

maxim noun = **saying**, adage, aphorism,
apophthegm, axiom, byword, dictum,
gnome, motto, proverb, rule, saw

maximum noun 1 = **top**, apogee, ceiling,
crest, extremity, height, most, peak,
pinnacle, summit, upper limit, utmost,
uttermost, zenith ◆ adjective 2 = **greatest**,
highest, maximal, most, paramount,
supreme, topmost, utmost
➤ **Antonyms**
noun ≠**top**: bottom, minimum ◆ adjective
≠**greatest**: least, lowest, minimal

maybe adverb = **perhaps**, it could be,
mayhap (archaic), peradventure (archaic),
perchance (archaic), possibly

mayhem noun = **chaos**, commotion,

confusion, destruction, disorder, fracas,
havoc, trouble, violence

maze noun 1 = **labyrinth**, convolutions,
intricacy, meander 2 = **web**,
bewilderment, confusion, imbroglio,
mesh, perplexity, puzzle, snarl, tangle,
uncertainty

meadow noun = **field**, grassland, lea
(poetic), ley, pasture

meagre adjective 1 = **insubstantial**,
deficient, exiguous, inadequate, little,
measly, paltry, pathetic, poor, puny, scant,
scanty, scrimpy, short, skimpy, slender,
slight, small, spare, sparse 2 = **thin**, bony,
emaciated, gaunt, hungry, lank, lean,
scraggy, scrawny, skinny, starved, underfed

mean[1] verb 1 = **intend**, aim, aspire,
contemplate, design, desire, have in mind,
plan, propose, purpose, set out, want,
wish 2 = **signify**, betoken, connote,
convey, denote, drive at, express, hint at,
imply, indicate, purport, represent, say,
spell, stand for, suggest, symbolize 3
= **destine**, design, fate, fit, make, match,
predestine, preordain, suit 4 = **result in**,
bring about, cause, engender, entail, give
rise to, involve, lead to, necessitate,
produce 5 = **foretell**, adumbrate, augur,
betoken, foreshadow, herald, portend,
presage, promise

mean[2] adjective 1 = **miserly**, beggarly, close
(informal), mercenary, mingy (Brit.
informal), near (informal), niggardly,
parsimonious, penny-pinching, penurious,
selfish, skimpy, snoep (S. African informal),
stingy, tight, tight-arsed (taboo slang),
tight as a duck's arse (taboo slang),
tight-assed (U.S. taboo slang), tight-fisted,
ungenerous 2 = **dishonourable**, abject,
base, callous, contemptible, degenerate,
degraded, despicable, disgraceful,
hard-hearted, ignoble, low-minded,
narrow-minded, petty, scurvy, shabby,
shameful, sordid, vile, wretched 3
= **malicious**, bad-tempered, cantankerous,
churlish, disagreeable, hostile,
ill-tempered, nasty, rude, sour, unfriendly,
unpleasant 4 = **shabby**, beggarly,
contemptible, down-at-heel, grungy
(slang, chiefly U.S.), insignificant, low-rent
(informal, chiefly U.S.), miserable, paltry,
poor, run-down, scruffy, scuzzy (slang,
chiefly U.S.), seedy, sordid, squalid,
tawdry, wretched 5 = **lowly**, base,
baseborn (archaic), common, humble,
ignoble, inferior, low, lowborn, menial,
modest, obscure, ordinary, plebeian,
proletarian, servile, undistinguished, vulgar
➤ **Antonyms**
≠**miserly**: altruistic, big, bountiful,

generous, munificent, prodigal, unselfish
≠**dishonourable**: good, honourable,
praiseworthy ≠**malicious**: compassionate,
gentle, humane, kind, sympathetic,
warm-hearted ≠**shabby**: attractive,
choice, de luxe, excellent, first-rate,
pleasing, superb, superior ≠**lowly**:
consequential, high, important, noble,
princely, significant

mean[3] *noun* **1** = **average**, balance,
compromise, happy medium, median,
middle, middle course *or* way, midpoint,
norm ♦ *adjective* **2** = **average**,
intermediate, medial, median, medium,
middle, middling, normal, standard

meander *verb* **1** = **wind**, snake, turn, zigzag
2 = **wander**, ramble, stravaig (*Scot. &
Northern English dialect*), stray, stroll
♦ *noun* **3** = **curve**, bend, coil, loop, turn,
twist, zigzag

meandering *adjective* = **winding**,
anfractuous, circuitous, convoluted,
indirect, roundabout, serpentine, snaking,
tortuous, wandering
➤ **Antonyms**
direct, straight, straightforward,
undeviating

meaning *noun* **1** = **sense**, connotation,
denotation, drift, explanation, gist,
implication, import, interpretation,
message, purport, significance,
signification, substance, upshot, value **2**
= **purpose**, aim, design, end, goal, idea,
intention, object, plan, point, trend **3**
= **force**, effect, efficacy, point, thrust, use,
usefulness, validity, value, worth
♦ *adjective* **4** = **expressive**, eloquent,
meaningful, pointed, pregnant, speaking,
suggestive

meaningful *adjective* **1** = **significant**,
important, material, purposeful, relevant,
serious, useful, valid, worthwhile **2**
= **expressive**, eloquent, meaning, pointed,
pregnant, speaking, suggestive
➤ **Antonyms**
≠**significant**: inconsequential,
insignificant, meaningless, senseless,
superficial, trivial, unimportant, useless,
worthless

meaningless *adjective* = **pointless**,
aimless, empty, futile, hollow, inane,
inconsequential, insignificant,
insubstantial, nonsensical, nugatory,
purposeless, senseless, trifling, trivial,
useless, vain, valueless, wanky (*taboo
slang*), worthless
➤ **Antonyms**
consequential, deep, evident, important,
meaningful, obvious, purposeful, sensible,
significant, useful, valuable, worthwhile

meanness *noun* **1** = **miserliness**, minginess
(*Brit. informal*), niggardliness, parsimony,
penuriousness, selfishness, stinginess,
tight-fistedness **2** = **pettiness**, abjectness,
baseness, degeneracy, degradation,
despicableness, disgracefulness,
dishonourableness, ignobility,
low-mindedness, narrow-mindedness,
scurviness, shabbiness, shamefulness,
sordidness, vileness, wretchedness **3**
= **malice**, bad temper, cantankerousness,
churlishness, disagreeableness, hostility, ill
temper, maliciousness, nastiness,
rudeness, sourness, unfriendliness,
unpleasantness **4** = **shabbiness**,
beggarliness, contemptibleness,
insignificance, paltriness, pettiness,
poorness, scruffiness, seediness,
sordidness, squalor, tawdriness,
wretchedness **5** = **lowliness**, baseness,
humbleness, obscurity, servility

means *noun* **1** = **method**, agency, avenue,
channel, course, expedient, instrument,
measure, medium, mode, process, way
♦ *plural noun* **2** = **money**, affluence,
capital, estate, fortune, funds, income,
property, resources, riches, substance,
wealth, wherewithal **3 by all means**
= **certainly**, absolutely, definitely,
doubtlessly, of course, positively, surely **4
by means of** = **by way of**, by dint of,
through, using, utilizing, via, with the aid
of **5 by no means** = **in no way**, absolutely
not, definitely not, not at all, not in the
least, not in the slightest, not the least bit,
no way, on no account

meantime, meanwhile *adverb* = **at the
same time**, concurrently, for now, for the
duration, for the moment, for then, in the
interim, in the interval, in the intervening
time, in the meantime, in the meanwhile,
simultaneously

measly *adjective* = **meagre**, miserable,
paltry, pathetic, pitiful, poor, puny, scanty,
skimpy

measurable *adjective* = **quantifiable**,
assessable, computable, determinable,
gaugeable, material, mensurable,
perceptible, quantitative, significant

measure *noun* **1** = **quantity**, allotment,
allowance, amount, amplitude, capacity,
degree, extent, magnitude, portion,
proportion, quota, range, ration, reach,
scope, share, size **2** = **gauge**, metre, rule,
scale, yardstick **3** = **standard**, criterion,
example, model, norm, par, test,
touchstone, yardstick **4** = **action**, act,
course, deed, expedient, manoeuvre,
means, procedure, proceeding, step **5**
= **law**, act, bill, enactment, resolution,

statute **6 = rhythm**, beat, cadence, foot, metre, verse **7** As in **beyond measure = limit**, bounds, control, limitation, moderation, restraint **8 for good measure = in addition**, as a bonus, besides, into the bargain, to boot ♦ verb **9 = quantify**, appraise, assess, calculate, calibrate, compute, determine, estimate, evaluate, gauge, judge, mark out, rate, size, sound, survey, value, weigh

measured adjective **1 = steady**, dignified, even, leisurely, regular, sedate, slow, solemn, stately, unhurried **2 = considered**, calculated, deliberate, reasoned, sober, studied, well-thought-out

measureless adjective **= infinite**, beyond measure, boundless, endless, immeasurable, immense, incalculable, inestimable, limitless, unbounded, vast

measurement noun **1 = calculation**, appraisal, assessment, calibration, computation, estimation, evaluation, judgment, mensuration, metage, survey, valuation **2 = size**, amount, amplitude, area, capacity, depth, dimension, extent, height, length, magnitude, volume, weight, width

measure out verb **= dispense**, allot, apportion, assign, deal out, distribute, divide, divvy up (informal), dole out, issue, mete out, parcel out, pour out, share out

measure up to verb **= fulfil the expectations**, be adequate, be capable, be equal to, be fit, be suitable, be suited, come up to scratch (informal), come up to standard, compare, cut the mustard (U.S. slang), equal, fit or fill the bill, make the grade (informal), match, meet, rival

meat noun **1 = food**, aliment, cheer, chow (informal), comestibles, eats (slang), fare, flesh, grub (slang), nosh (slang), nourishment, nutriment, provender, provisions, rations, subsistence, sustenance, viands, victuals **2 = gist**, core, essence, heart, kernel, marrow, nub, nucleus, pith, point, substance

meaty adjective **1 = brawny**, beefy (informal), burly, fleshy, heavily built, heavy, husky (informal), muscular, solid, strapping, sturdy **2 = interesting**, meaningful, pithy, profound, rich, significant, substantial **3 = substantial**, hearty, nourishing, rich

mechanical adjective **1 = automatic**, automated, machine-driven **2 = unthinking**, automatic, cold, cursory, dead, emotionless, habitual, impersonal, instinctive, involuntary, lacklustre, lifeless, machine-like, matter-of-fact, perfunctory, routine, spiritless, unconscious, unfeeling

> **Antonyms**
≠**automatic**: manual ≠**unthinking**: conscious, genuine, sincere, thinking, voluntary, warm, wholehearted

mechanism noun **1 = workings**, action, components, gears, innards (informal), machinery, motor, works **2 = machine**, apparatus, appliance, contrivance, device, instrument, structure, system, tool **3 = process**, agency, execution, functioning, means, medium, method, methodology, operation, performance, procedure, system, technique, way, workings

meddle verb **= interfere**, butt in, intermeddle, interpose, intervene, intrude, pry, put one's oar in, put one's two cents in (U.S. slang), stick one's nose in (informal), tamper

meddlesome adjective **= interfering**, intrusive, meddling, mischievous, officious, prying

mediate verb **= intervene**, act as middleman, arbitrate, bring to an agreement, bring to terms, conciliate, intercede, interpose, make peace between, moderate, reconcile, referee, resolve, restore harmony, settle, step in (informal), umpire

mediation noun **= arbitration**, conciliation, intercession, intervention, reconciliation

mediator noun **= negotiator**, advocate, arbiter, arbitrator, go-between, honest broker, interceder, intermediary, judge, middleman, moderator, peacemaker, referee, umpire

medicinal adjective **= therapeutic**, analeptic, curative, healing, medical, remedial, restorative, roborant, sanative

medicine noun **= remedy**, cure, drug, medicament, medication, nostrum, physic

medieval adjective **1 = Gothic 2** Informal **= old-fashioned**, antediluvian, antiquated, antique, archaic, primitive, unenlightened

mediocre adjective **= second-rate**, average, banal, bog-standard (Brit. & Irish slang), commonplace, fair to middling (informal), indifferent, inferior, insignificant, mean, medium, middling, no great shakes (informal), ordinary, passable, pedestrian, run-of-the-mill, so-so (informal), tolerable, undistinguished, uninspired, vanilla (slang)

> **Antonyms**
distinctive, distinguished, excellent, extraordinary, fine, incomparable, superb, superior, unexcelled, unique, unrivalled, unsurpassed

mediocrity noun **= insignificance**, commonplaceness, indifference, inferiority, meanness, ordinariness, poorness, unimportance

meditate *verb* **1** = **reflect**, be in a brown study, cogitate, consider, contemplate, deliberate, muse, ponder, ruminate, study, think **2** = **plan**, consider, contemplate, design, devise, have in mind, intend, mull over, purpose, scheme, think over

meditation *noun* = **reflection**, brown study, cerebration, cogitation, concentration, contemplation, musing, pondering, reverie, ruminating, rumination, study, thought

medium *adjective* **1** = **average**, fair, intermediate, mean, medial, median, mediocre, middle, middling, midway ♦ *noun* **2** = **middle**, average, centre, compromise, mean, middle course, middle ground, middle path, middle way, midpoint **3** = **means**, agency, avenue, channel, form, instrument, instrumentality, mode, organ, vehicle, way **4** = **spiritualist**, channeller, spiritist **5** = **environment**, atmosphere, conditions, element, habitat, influences, milieu, setting, surroundings
➤ **Antonyms**
adjective ≠**average**: curious, distinctive, extraordinary, extreme, uncommon, unique, unusual, utmost

medley *noun* = **mixture**, assortment, confusion, farrago, gallimaufry, hodgepodge, hotchpotch, jumble, *mélange*, miscellany, mishmash, mixed bag (*informal*), olio, omnium-gatherum, pastiche, patchwork, potpourri, salmagundi

meek *adjective* = **submissive**, acquiescent, compliant, deferential, docile, forbearing, gentle, humble, long-suffering, mild, modest, patient, peaceful, soft, timid, unassuming, unpretentious, yielding
➤ **Antonyms**
arrogant, bold, bossy, domineering, feisty (*informal, chiefly U.S. & Canad.*), forward, immodest, overbearing, presumptuous, pretentious, proud, self-assertive, spirited, wilful

meekness *noun* = **submissiveness**, acquiescence, compliance, deference, docility, forbearance, gentleness, humbleness, humility, long-suffering, lowliness, mildness, modesty, patience, peacefulness, resignation, softness, submission, timidity

meet *verb* **1** = **encounter**, bump into, chance on, come across, confront, contact, find, happen on, run across, run into **2** = **converge**, abut, adjoin, come together, connect, cross, intersect, join,

link up, touch, unite **3** = **gather**, assemble, collect, come together, congregate, convene, foregather, muster, rally **4** = **fulfil**, answer, carry out, come up to, comply with, cope with, discharge, equal, gratify, handle, match, measure up to, perform, satisfy **5** = **experience**, bear, encounter, endure, face, go through, suffer, undergo
➤ **Antonyms**
≠**encounter**: avoid, elude, escape, miss ≠**converge**: diverge ≠**gather**: adjourn, disperse, scatter ≠**fulfil**: fail, fall short, renege

meeting *noun* **1** = **encounter**, assignation, confrontation, engagement, introduction, rendezvous, tryst **2** = **conference**, assembly, audience, company, conclave, congregation, congress, convention, convocation, gathering, get-together (*informal*), meet, powwow, rally, reunion, session **3** = **convergence**, concourse, confluence, conjunction, crossing, intersection, junction, union

melancholy *noun* **1** = **sadness**, blues, dejection, depression, despondency, gloom, gloominess, low spirits, misery, pensiveness, sorrow, the hump (*Brit. informal*), unhappiness, woe ♦ *adjective* **2** = **sad**, blue, dejected, depressed, despondent, disconsolate, dismal, dispirited, doleful, down, downcast, downhearted, down in the dumps (*informal*), down in the mouth, gloomy, glum, heavy-hearted, joyless, low, low-spirited, lugubrious, melancholic, miserable, moody, mournful, pensive, sombre, sorrowful, unhappy, woebegone, woeful
➤ **Antonyms**
noun ≠**sadness**: delight, gladness, happiness, joy, pleasure ♦ *adjective* ≠**sad**: blithe, bright, cheerful, gay, glad, happy, jolly, joyful, joyous, light-hearted, lively, merry, sunny

melee, mêlée *noun* = **fight**, brawl, fracas, free-for-all (*informal*), rumpus, scrimmage, scuffle, set-to (*informal*), skirmish, tussle

mellifluous *adjective* = **sweet**, dulcet, euphonious, honeyed, silvery, smooth, soft, soothing, sweet-sounding

mellow *adjective* **1** = **tuneful**, dulcet, euphonic, full, mellifluous, melodious, rich, rounded, smooth, sweet, well-tuned **2** = **relaxed**, cheerful, cordial, elevated, expansive, genial, half-tipsy, happy, jolly, jovial, merry (*Brit. informal*) **3** = **ripe**, delicate, full-flavoured, juicy, mature, perfect, rich, soft, sweet, well-matured ♦ *verb* **4** = **mature**, develop, improve,

perfect, ripen, season, soften, sweeten
➤ **Antonyms**
*adjective ≠***ripe**: green, immature, raw, sour, unripe

melodious *adjective* = **musical**, concordant, dulcet, euphonic, euphonious, harmonious, melodic, silvery, sweet-sounding, sweet-toned, tuneful
➤ **Antonyms**
cacophonous, discordant, grating, harsh, unharmonious, unmelodic, unmelodious, unmusical, untuneful

melodramatic *adjective* = **theatrical**, actorly, actressy, blood-and-thunder, extravagant, hammy (*informal*), histrionic, overdramatic, overemotional, sensational, stagy

melody *noun* 1 = **tune**, air, descant, music, refrain, song, strain, theme 2 = **tunefulness**, euphony, harmony, melodiousness, music, musicality

melt *verb* 1 = **dissolve**, deliquesce, diffuse, flux, fuse, liquefy, soften, thaw 2 *often with* **away** = **disappear**, disperse, dissolve, evanesce, evaporate, fade, vanish 3 = **soften**, disarm, mollify, relax, touch

member *noun* 1 = **representative**, associate, fellow 2 = **limb**, appendage, arm, component, constituent, element, extremity, leg, organ, part, portion

membership *noun* 1 = **members**, associates, body, fellows 2 = **participation**, belonging, enrolment, fellowship

memento *noun* = **souvenir**, keepsake, memorial, relic, remembrance, reminder, token, trophy

memoir *noun* = **account**, biography, essay, journal, life, monograph, narrative, record, register

memoirs *plural noun* = **autobiography**, diary, experiences, journals, life, life story, memories, recollections, reminiscences

memorable *adjective* = **noteworthy**, catchy, celebrated, distinguished, extraordinary, famous, historic, illustrious, important, impressive, momentous, notable, remarkable, signal, significant, striking, unforgettable
➤ **Antonyms**
commonplace, forgettable, insignificant, ordinary, trivial, undistinguished, unimportant, unimpressive, unmemorable

memorandum *noun* = **note**, communication, jotting, memo, message, minute, reminder

memorial *noun* 1 = **monument**, cairn, memento, plaque, record, remembrance, souvenir ♦ *adjective* 2 = **commemorative**, monumental

memorize *verb* = **remember**, commit to memory, con (*archaic*), get by heart, learn, learn by heart, learn by rote

memory *noun* 1 = **recall**, recollection, remembrance, reminiscence, retention 2 = **commemoration**, honour, remembrance 3 = **reputation**, celebrity, fame, glory, name, renown, repute

menace *verb* 1 = **threaten**, alarm, bode ill, browbeat, bully, frighten, impend, intimidate, loom, lour *or* lower, terrorize, utter threats to ♦ *noun* 2 = **threat**, commination, intimidation, scare, warning 3 = **danger**, hazard, jeopardy, peril 4 *Informal* = **nuisance**, annoyance, pest, plague, troublemaker

menacing *adjective* = **threatening**, alarming, baleful, bodeful, dangerous, forbidding, frightening, intimidating, intimidatory, looming, louring *or* lowering, minacious, minatory, ominous
➤ **Antonyms**
auspicious, encouraging, favourable, promising

mend *verb* 1 = **repair**, cure, darn, fix, heal, patch, rectify, refit, reform, remedy, renew, renovate, restore, retouch 2 = **heal**, convalesce, get better, recover, recuperate 3 = **improve**, ameliorate, amend, better, correct, emend, rectify, reform, revise ♦ *noun* 4 = **repair**, darn, patch, stitch 5 **on the mend** = **convalescent**, convalescing, getting better, improving, recovering, recuperating

mendacious *adjective* = **lying**, deceitful, deceptive, dishonest, duplicitous, fallacious, false, fraudulent, insincere, perfidious, perjured, untrue, untruthful
➤ **Antonyms**
genuine, honest, true, truthful

menial *adjective* 1 = **unskilled**, boring, dull, humdrum, low-status, routine 2 = **humble**, abject, base, degrading, demeaning, fawning, grovelling, ignoble, ignominious, low, lowly, mean, obsequious, servile, slavish, sorry, subservient, sycophantic, vile ♦ *noun* 3 = **servant**, attendant, dogsbody (*informal*), domestic, drudge, flunky, labourer, lackey, serf, skivvy (*chiefly Brit.*), slave, underling, varlet (*archaic*), vassal
➤ **Antonyms**
*adjective ≠***humble**: aristocratic, autocratic, bossy, dignified, domineering, elevated, haughty, high, noble, overbearing, proud ♦ *noun ≠***servant**: boss, chief, commander, lord, master, superior

menstruation *noun* = **period**, catamenia (*Physiology*), courses (*Physiology*), the curse (*informal*), flow (*informal*), menses, menstrual cycle, monthly (*informal*)

mental *adjective* **1** = **intellectual**, cerebral **2** *Informal* = **insane**, as daft as a brush (*informal, chiefly Brit.*), deranged, disturbed, lunatic, mad, mentally ill, not right in the head, psychiatric, psychotic, round the bend (*Brit. slang*), unbalanced, unstable

mentality *noun* = **attitude**, cast of mind, character, disposition, frame of mind, make-up, outlook, personality, psychology, turn of mind, way of thinking

mentally *adverb* = **in the mind**, in one's head, intellectually, inwardly, psychologically, rationally, subjectively

mention *verb* **1** = **refer to**, acknowledge, adduce, allude to, bring up, broach, call attention to, cite, communicate, declare, disclose, divulge, hint at, impart, intimate, make known, name, point out, recount, report, reveal, speak about *or* of, state, tell, touch upon **2 not to mention** = **to say nothing of**, as well as, besides, not counting ♦ *noun* **3** = **reference**, allusion, announcement, indication, notification, observation, remark **4** = **acknowledgment**, citation, recognition, tribute

mentor *noun* = **guide**, adviser, coach, counsellor, guru, instructor, teacher, tutor

menu *noun* = **bill of fare**, *carte du jour*, tariff (*chiefly Brit.*)

mercantile *adjective* = **commercial**, marketable, trade, trading

mercenary *noun* **1** = **hireling**, condottiere (*History*), free companion (*History*), freelance (*History*), soldier of fortune ♦ *adjective* **2** = **greedy**, acquisitive, avaricious, bribable, covetous, grasping, money-grubbing (*informal*), sordid, venal **3** = **hired**, bought, paid, venal
➤ **Antonyms**
adjective ≠**greedy**: altruistic, benevolent, generous, idealistic, liberal, munificent, philanthropic, unselfish

merchandise *noun* **1** = **goods**, commodities, produce, products, staples, stock, stock in trade, truck, vendibles, wares ♦ *verb* **2** = **trade**, buy and sell, deal in, distribute, do business in, market, retail, sell, traffic in, vend

merchant *noun* = **tradesman**, broker, dealer, purveyor, retailer, salesman, seller, shopkeeper, supplier, trader, trafficker, vendor, wholesaler

merciful *adjective* = **compassionate**, beneficent, benignant, clement, forbearing, forgiving, generous, gracious, humane, kind, lenient, liberal, mild, pitying, soft, sparing, sympathetic, tender-hearted
➤ **Antonyms**

cruel, hard-hearted, inhumane, merciless, pitiless, uncompassionate, unfeeling

merciless *adjective* = **cruel**, barbarous, callous, fell (*archaic*), hard, hard-hearted, harsh, heartless, implacable, inexorable, inhumane, pitiless, relentless, ruthless, severe, unappeasable, unfeeling, unforgiving, unmerciful, unpitying, unsparing, unsympathetic

mercurial *adjective* = **lively**, active, capricious, changeable, erratic, fickle, flighty, gay, impulsive, inconstant, irrepressible, light-hearted, mobile, quicksilver, spirited, sprightly, temperamental, unpredictable, unstable, variable, volatile
➤ **Antonyms**
consistent, constant, dependable, predictable, reliable, stable, steady, unchanging

mercy *noun* **1** = **compassion**, benevolence, charity, clemency, favour, forbearance, forgiveness, grace, kindness, leniency, pity, quarter **2** = **blessing**, benison (*archaic*), boon, godsend, piece of luck, relief **3 at the mercy of** = **in the power of**, defenceless against, exposed to, in the clutches of, naked before, open to, prey to, subject to, threatened by, unprotected against, vulnerable to
➤ **Antonyms**
≠**compassion**: brutality, cruelty, harshness, inhumanity, pitilessness, severity

mere *adjective* = **simple**, absolute, bare, common, complete, entire, nothing more than, plain, pure, pure and simple, sheer, stark, unadulterated, unmitigated, unmixed, utter

meretricious *adjective* = **trashy**, flashy, garish, gaudy, gimcrack, showy, tawdry, tinsel

merge *verb* = **combine**, amalgamate, become lost in, be swallowed up by, blend, coalesce, consolidate, converge, fuse, incorporate, intermix, join, meet, meld, melt into, mingle, mix, tone with, unite
➤ **Antonyms**
detach, diverge, divide, part, separate, sever

merger *noun* = **union**, amalgamation, coalition, combination, consolidation, fusion, incorporation

merit *noun* **1** = **worth**, advantage, asset, excellence, good, goodness, integrity, quality, strong point, talent, value, virtue, worthiness **2** = **claim**, credit, desert, due, right ♦ *verb* **3** = **deserve**, be entitled to, be worthy of, earn, have a claim to, have a right to, have coming to one, incur, rate, warrant

meritorious *adjective* = **praiseworthy**, admirable, commendable, creditable, deserving, excellent, exemplary, good, honourable, laudable, right, righteous, virtuous, worthy

➤ Antonyms

discreditable, dishonourable, ignoble, undeserving, unexceptional, unpraiseworthy

merriment *noun* = **fun**, amusement, conviviality, festivity, frolic, gaiety, glee, hilarity, jocularity, jollity, joviality, laughter, levity, liveliness, merrymaking, mirth, revelry, sport

merry *adjective* **1** = **cheerful**, blithe, blithesome, carefree, chirpy (*informal*), convivial, festive, frolicsome, fun-loving, gay, genial, glad, gleeful, happy, jocund, jolly, joyful, joyous, light-hearted, mirthful, rollicking, sportive, upbeat (*informal*), vivacious **2** *Brit. informal* = **tipsy**, elevated (*informal*), happy, mellow, squiffy (*Brit. informal*), tiddly (*slang, chiefly Brit.*) **3** = **comical**, amusing, comic, facetious, funny, hilarious, humorous, jocular, mirthful **4 make merry** = **have fun**, carouse, celebrate, enjoy oneself, feast, frolic, have a good time, make whoopee (*informal*), revel

➤ Antonyms

≠cheerful: dejected, dismal, down in the dumps (*informal*), gloomy, miserable, sad, unhappy

mesh *noun* **1** = **net**, netting, network, plexus, reticulation, tracery, web **2** = **trap**, entanglement, snare, tangle, toils, web ◆ *verb* **3** = **entangle**, catch, enmesh, ensnare, net, snare, tangle, trap **4** = **engage**, combine, come together, connect, coordinate, dovetail, fit together, harmonize, interlock, knit

mesmerize *verb* = **entrance**, absorb, captivate, enthral, fascinate, grip, hold spellbound, hypnotize, magnetize, spellbind

mess *noun* **1** = **disorder**, balls-up (*taboo slang*), bodge (*informal*), botch, chaos, clutter, cock-up (*Brit. slang*), confusion, dirtiness, disarray, disorganization, fuck-up (*offensive taboo slang*), grot (*slang*), hash, hodgepodge (*U.S.*), hotchpotch, jumble, litter, mishmash, pig's breakfast (*informal*), shambles, state, turmoil, untidiness **2** = **difficulty**, deep water, dilemma, fine kettle of fish (*informal*), fix (*informal*), hole (*informal*), hot water (*informal*), imbroglio, jam (*informal*), mix-up, muddle, perplexity, pickle (*informal*), plight, predicament, spot (*informal*), stew

(*informal*), tight spot ◆ *verb* **3** *often with* **up** = **dirty**, befoul, besmirch, botch, bungle, clutter, cock up (*Brit. slang*), disarrange, dishevel, foul, fuck up (*offensive taboo slang*), litter, make a hash of (*informal*), make a nonsense of, make a pig's ear of (*informal*), muck up (*Brit. slang*), muddle, pollute, scramble **4** *often with* **with** = **interfere**, fiddle (*informal*), meddle, play, tamper, tinker

mess about or **around** *verb* **1** = **potter**, amuse oneself, dabble, fool (about or around), footle (*informal*), muck about (*informal*), piss about or around (*taboo slang*), play about or around, trifle **2** = **meddle**, fiddle (*informal*), fool (about or around), interfere, piss about or around (*taboo slang*), play, tamper, tinker, toy

message *noun* **1** = **communication**, bulletin, communiqué, dispatch, intimation, letter, memorandum, missive, note, notice, tidings, word **2** = **point**, idea, import, meaning, moral, purport, theme **3** *Scot.* = **errand**, commission, job, mission, task **4 get the message** = **understand**, catch on (*informal*), comprehend, get it, get the point, see, take the hint, twig (*Brit. informal*)

messenger *noun* = **courier**, agent, bearer, carrier, delivery boy, emissary, envoy, errand-boy, go-between, harbinger, herald, runner

messy *adjective* = **untidy**, chaotic, cluttered, confused, dirty, dishevelled, disordered, disorganized, grubby, littered, muddled, scuzzy (*slang, chiefly U.S.*), shambolic, sloppy (*informal*), slovenly, unkempt

➤ Antonyms

clean, meticulous, neat, ordered, orderly, shipshape, smart, squeaky-clean, tidy

metamorphosis *noun* = **transformation**, alteration, change, conversion, mutation, transmutation

metaphor *noun* = **figure of speech**, allegory, analogy, emblem, image, symbol, trope

metaphorical *adjective* = **figurative**, allegorical, emblematic, emblematical, symbolic, tropical (*rhetoric*)

metaphysical *adjective* **1** = **philosophical**, basic, esoteric, essential, eternal, fundamental, general, ideal, intellectual, profound, speculative, spiritual, subjective, universal **2** = **abstract**, abstruse, deep, high-flown, oversubtle, recondite, theoretical, transcendental **3** = **supernatural**, immaterial, impalpable, incorporeal, intangible, spiritual, unreal, unsubstantial

mete *verb* = **distribute**, administer, allot, apportion, assign, deal, dispense, divide, dole, measure, parcel, portion, ration, share

meteoric *adjective* = **spectacular**, brief, brilliant, dazzling, ephemeral, fast, flashing, fleeting, momentary, overnight, rapid, speedy, sudden, swift, transient
➤ **Antonyms**
gradual, lengthy, long, prolonged, slow, steady, unhurried

method *noun* 1 = **manner**, approach, arrangement, course, fashion, form, mode, modus operandi, plan, practice, procedure, process, programme, routine, rule, scheme, style, system, technique, way 2 = **orderliness**, design, form, order, organization, pattern, planning, purpose, regularity, structure, system

methodical *adjective* = **orderly**, businesslike, deliberate, disciplined, efficient, meticulous, neat, ordered, organized, painstaking, planned, precise, regular, structured, systematic, tidy, well-regulated
➤ **Antonyms**
casual, chaotic, confused, disordered, disorderly, haphazard, irregular, random, unmethodical

meticulous *adjective* = **thorough**, detailed, exact, fastidious, fussy, microscopic, painstaking, particular, perfectionist, precise, punctilious, scrupulous, strict
➤ **Antonyms**
careless, haphazard, imprecise, inexact, loose, negligent, slapdash, sloppy

métier *noun* 1 = **profession**, calling, craft, line, occupation, pursuit, trade, vocation 2 = **strong point**, forte, long suit (*informal*), speciality, specialty, strong suit

metropolis *noun* = **city**, capital

mettle *noun* 1 = **courage**, ardour, balls (*taboo slang*), boldness, bottle (*Brit. slang*), bravery, daring, fire, fortitude, gallantry, gameness, grit, guts (*informal*), hardihood, heart, indomitability, life, nerve, pluck, resolution, resolve, spirit, spunk (*informal*), valour, vigour 2 = **character**, calibre, disposition, kidney, make-up, nature, quality, stamp, temper, temperament

microbe *noun* = **microorganism**, bacillus, bacterium, bug (*informal*), germ, virus

microscopic *adjective* = **tiny**, imperceptible, infinitesimal, invisible, minuscule, minute, negligible, teensy-weensy, teeny-weeny
➤ **Antonyms**
enormous, gigantic, ginormous (*informal*), great, huge, immense, large, vast

midday *noun* = **noon**, noonday, noontide, noontime, twelve noon, twelve o'clock

middle *noun* 1 = **centre**, focus, halfway point, heart, inside, mean, midpoint, midsection, midst, thick 2 = **waist**, midriff, midsection ◆ *adjective* 3 = **central**, halfway, inner, inside, intermediate, intervening, mean, medial, median, medium, mid

middle-class *adjective* = **bourgeois**, conventional, petit-bourgeois, suburban, traditional

middleman *noun* = **intermediary**, broker, distributor, entrepreneur, go-between

middling *adjective* 1 = **mediocre**, indifferent, run-of-the-mill, so-so (*informal*), tolerable, unexceptional, unremarkable 2 = **moderate**, adequate, all right, average, bog-standard (*Brit. & Irish slang*), fair, medium, modest, O.K. *or* okay (*informal*), ordinary, passable, serviceable

midget *noun* 1 = **dwarf**, gnome, homuncule, homunculus, manikin, munchkin (*informal, chiefly U.S.*), pygmy *or* pigmy, shrimp (*informal*), Tom Thumb ◆ *adjective* 2 = **tiny**, baby, dwarf, Lilliputian, little, miniature, pocket, pygmy *or* pigmy, small, teensy-weensy, teeny-weeny

midnight *noun* = **twelve o'clock**, dead of night, middle of the night, the witching hour, twelve o'clock at night

midst *noun* 1 = **middle**, bosom, centre, core, depths, heart, hub, interior, thick 2 **in the midst of** = **among**, amidst, during, enveloped by, in the middle of, in the thick of, surrounded by

midway *adjective, adverb* = **halfway**, betwixt and between, in the middle

might *noun* 1 = **power**, ability, capability, capacity, clout (*informal*), efficacy, efficiency, energy, force, potency, prowess, puissance, strength, sway, valour, vigour 2 **with might and main** = **forcefully**, as hard as one can, as hard as possible, full blast, full force, lustily, manfully, mightily, vigorously, with all one's might *or* strength

mightily *adverb* 1 = **very**, decidedly, exceedingly, extremely, greatly, highly, hugely, intensely, much, seriously (*informal*), very much 2 = **powerfully**, energetically, forcefully, lustily, manfully, strongly, vigorously, with all one's might and main, with all one's strength

mighty *adjective* 1 = **powerful**, doughty, forceful, hardy, indomitable, lusty, manful, potent, puissant, robust, stalwart, stout, strapping, strong, sturdy, vigorous 2 = **great**, bulky, colossal, elephantine, enormous, gigantic, ginormous (*informal*),

grand, huge, humongous *or* humungous (*U.S. slang*), immense, large, massive, mega (*slang*), monumental, prodigious, stellar (*informal*), stupendous, titanic, towering, tremendous, vast
➤ **Antonyms**
≠**powerful**: feeble, impotent, weak, weedy (*informal*), wimpish *or* wimpy (*informal*), wussy (*slang*) ≠**great**: small, tiny, unimposing, unimpressive

migrant *noun* 1 = **wanderer**, drifter, emigrant, gypsy, immigrant, itinerant, nomad, rover, tinker, transient, traveller, vagrant ◆ *adjective* 2 = **travelling**, drifting, gypsy, immigrant, itinerant, migratory, nomadic, roving, shifting, transient, vagrant, wandering

migrate *verb* = **move**, drift, emigrate, journey, roam, rove, shift, travel, trek, voyage, wander

migration *noun* = **wandering**, emigration, journey, movement, roving, shift, travel, trek, voyage

migratory *adjective* = **nomadic**, gypsy, itinerant, migrant, peripatetic, roving, shifting, transient, travelling, unsettled, vagrant, wandering

mild *adjective* 1 = **bland**, smooth 2 = **gentle**, amiable, calm, compassionate, docile, easy, easy-going, easy-oasy (*slang*), equable, forbearing, forgiving, indulgent, kind, meek, mellow, merciful, moderate, pacific, peaceable, placid, pleasant, serene, soft, tender 3 = **temperate**, balmy, calm, clement, moderate, tranquil, warm
➤ **Antonyms**
≠**gentle**: harsh, powerful, severe, sharp, strong, unkind, unpleasant, violent ≠**temperate**: bitter, cold, fierce, harsh, rough, stormy, violent, wild

mildness *noun* = **gentleness**, blandness, calmness, clemency, docility, forbearance, indulgence, kindness, leniency, lenity, meekness, mellowness, moderation, placidity, smoothness, softness, temperateness, tenderness, tranquillity, warmth

milieu *noun* = **surroundings**, background, element, environment, locale, location, *mise en scène*, scene, setting, sphere

militant *adjective* 1 = **aggressive**, active, assertive, combative, vigorous 2 = **warring**, belligerent, combating, contending, embattled, fighting, in arms ◆ *noun* 3 = **activist**, partisan 4 = **warrior**, belligerent, combatant, fighter, gladiator
➤ **Antonyms**
adjective ≠**aggressive**, **warring**: pacific, pacifist, peaceful

military *adjective* 1 = **warlike**, armed,

martial, soldierlike, soldierly ◆ *noun* 2 = **armed forces**, army, forces, services

militate *verb* 1 **militate against** = **counteract**, be detrimental to, conflict with, contend with, count against, counter, oppose, resist, tell against, weigh against 2 **militate for** = **promote**, advance, aid, further, help

militia *noun* = **reserve(s)**, fencibles (*History*), National Guard (*U.S.*), Territorial Army (*Brit.*), trainband (*History*), yeomanry (*History*)

milk *verb* 1 = **siphon**, drain, draw off, express, extract, let out, press, tap 2 = **exploit**, bleed, drain, extract, impose on, pump, take advantage of, use, wring

milk-and-water *adjective* = **weak**, feeble, innocuous, insipid, jejune, nerdy *or* nurdy (*slang*), vapid, weedy (*informal*), wimpish *or* wimpy (*informal*), wishy-washy (*informal*), wussy (*slang*)
➤ **Antonyms**
effective, energetic, forceful, healthy, strong

milksop *noun* = **weakling**, chinless wonder (*Brit. informal*), coward, dastard (*archaic*), jessie (*Scot. slang*), namby-pamby, sissy, wimp (*informal*), wuss (*slang*)

mill *noun* 1 = **factory**, foundry, plant, shop, works 2 = **grinder**, crusher 3 **run of the mill** = **commonplace**, average, bog-standard (*Brit. & Irish slang*), everyday, fair, middling, ordinary, routine, unexceptional, unremarkable ◆ *verb* 4 = **grind**, comminute, crush, granulate, grate, pound, powder, press, pulverize 5 = **swarm**, crowd, seethe, throng

millstone *noun* 1 = **grindstone**, quernstone 2 = **burden**, affliction, albatross, dead weight, drag, encumbrance, load, weight

mime *noun* 1 = **dumb show**, gesture, mummery, pantomime ◆ *verb* 2 = **act out**, gesture, pantomime, represent, simulate

mimic *verb* 1 = **imitate**, ape, caricature, do (*informal*), impersonate, parody, take off (*informal*) 2 = **resemble**, echo, look like, mirror, simulate, take on the appearance of ◆ *noun* 3 = **imitator**, caricaturist, copycat (*informal*), impersonator, impressionist, parodist, parrot

mimicry *noun* = **imitation**, burlesque, caricature, impersonation, mimicking, mockery, parody, take-off (*informal*)

mince *verb* 1 = **cut**, chop, crumble, grind, hash 2 = **posture**, attitudinize, give oneself airs, ponce (*slang*), pose 3 *As in* **mince one's words** = **tone down**, diminish, euphemize, extenuate, hold back, moderate, palliate, soften, spare, weaken

mincing *adjective* = **affected**, arty-farty (*informal*), camp (*informal*), dainty, effeminate, foppish, lah-di-dah (*informal*), nice, niminy-piminy, poncy (*slang*), precious, pretentious, sissy

mind *noun* 1 = **brain**, head, imagination, psyche 2 = **intelligence**, brain(s) (*informal*), grey matter (*informal*), intellect, mentality, ratiocination, reason, sense, spirit, understanding, wits 3 = **memory**, recollection, remembrance 4 = **thinker**, brain (*informal*), brainbox, genius, intellect, intellectual 5 = **attitude**, belief, feeling, judgment, opinion, outlook, point of view, sentiment, thoughts, view, way of thinking 6 = **intention**, bent, desire, disposition, fancy, inclination, leaning, notion, purpose, tendency, urge, will, wish 7 = **attention**, concentration, thinking, thoughts 8 = **sanity**, judgment, marbles (*informal*), mental balance, rationality, reason, senses, wits 9 **bear** *or* **keep in mind** = **remember**, be cognizant of, be mindful of, take note of 10 **in** *or* **of two minds** = **undecided**, dithering (*chiefly Brit.*), hesitant, shillyshallying (*informal*), swithering (*Scot.*), uncertain, unsure, vacillating, wavering 11 **make up one's mind** = **decide**, choose, come to a decision, determine, reach a decision, resolve ♦ *verb* 12 = **take offence**, be affronted, be bothered, care, disapprove, dislike, look askance at, object, resent 13 = **pay attention**, adhere to, attend, comply with, follow, heed, listen to, mark, note, notice, obey, observe, pay heed to, regard, respect, take heed, watch 14 = **be sure**, ensure, make certain 15 = **guard**, attend to, have charge of, keep an eye on, look after, take care of, tend, watch 16 = **be careful**, be cautious, be on (one's) guard, be wary, take care, watch 17 **never mind** = **forget (it)**, disregard, do not concern yourself, don't bother, don't give (it) a second thought, it does not matter, it's none of your business, it's nothing to do with you, pay no attention

mindful *adjective* = **aware**, alert, alive to, attentive, careful, chary, cognizant, conscious, heedful, regardful, respectful, sensible, thoughtful, wary, watchful
➤ **Antonyms**
heedless, inattentive, incautious, mindless, oblivious, thoughtless, unaware

mindless *adjective* 1 = **unthinking**, asinine, braindead (*informal*), brutish, careless, dead from the neck up (*informal*), dumb-ass (*slang*), foolish, forgetful, gratuitous, heedless, idiotic, imbecilic, inane, inattentive, moronic, neglectful,

negligent, oblivious, obtuse, stupid, thoughtless, unintelligent, unmindful, witless 2 = **mechanical**, automatic, brainless
➤ **Antonyms**
≠**unthinking**: attentive, aware, intelligent, mindful, sane, thinking

mind out *verb* = **be careful**, be on one's guard, beware, keep one's eyes open, look out, pay attention, take care, watch

mine *noun* 1 = **pit**, coalfield, colliery, deposit, excavation, lode, shaft, vein 2 = **source**, abundance, fund, hoard, reserve, stock, store, supply, treasury, wealth ♦ *verb* 3 = **dig up**, delve, dig for, excavate, extract, hew, quarry, unearth 4 = **tunnel**, sap, subvert, undermine, weaken 5 = **lay mines in** *or* **under**, sow with mines

miner *noun* = **coalminer**, collier (*Brit.*), pitman (*Brit.*)

mingle *verb* 1 = **mix**, admix, alloy, blend, coalesce, combine, commingle, compound, intermingle, intermix, interweave, join, marry, meld, merge, unite 2 = **associate**, circulate, consort, fraternize, hang about *or* around, hang out (*informal*), hobnob, rub shoulders (*informal*), socialize
➤ **Antonyms**
≠**mix**: detach, dissolve, divide, part, separate ≠**associate**: avoid, dissociate, estrange

miniature *adjective* = **small**, baby, diminutive, dwarf, Lilliputian, little, midget, mini, minuscule, minute, pocket, pygmy *or* pigmy, reduced, scaled-down, teensy-weensy, teeny-weeny, tiny, toy, wee
➤ **Antonyms**
big, enlarged, enormous, giant, gigantic, ginormous (*informal*), great, huge, immense, large, mega (*slang*), oversize

minimal *adjective* = **minimum**, least, least possible, littlest, nominal, slightest, smallest, token

minimize *verb* 1 = **reduce**, abbreviate, attenuate, curtail, decrease, diminish, downsize, miniaturize, prune, shrink 2 = **play down**, belittle, decry, deprecate, depreciate, discount, disparage, make light *or* little of, underestimate, underrate
➤ **Antonyms**
≠**reduce**: augment, enlarge, expand, extend, heighten, increase, magnify
≠**play down**: boast about, elevate, enhance, exalt, praise, vaunt

minimum *noun* 1 = **least**, bottom, depth, lowest, nadir, slightest ♦ *adjective* 2 = **least**, least possible, littlest, lowest, minimal, slightest, smallest

> ➤ **Antonyms**

adjective ≠**least**: greatest, highest, largest, maximum, most

minion *noun* = **follower**, bootlicker (*informal*), cohort (*chiefly U.S.*), creature, darling, dependant, favourite, flatterer, flunky, hanger-on, henchman, hireling, lackey, lickspittle, parasite, pet, sycophant, toady, underling, yes man

minister *noun* 1 = **clergyman**, chaplain, churchman, cleric, divine, ecclesiastic, padre (*informal*), parson, pastor, preacher, priest, rector, vicar 2 = **official**, administrator, ambassador, cabinet member, delegate, diplomat, envoy, executive, office-holder, plenipotentiary
♦ *verb* 3 = **attend**, accommodate, administer, answer, be solicitous of, cater to, pander to, serve, take care of, tend

ministrations *plural noun* = **help**, aid, assistance, favour, patronage, relief, service, succour, support

ministry *noun* 1 = **the priesthood**, holy orders, the church, the pulpit 2 = **department**, administration, bureau, cabinet, council, government, office, quango

minor *adjective* = **small**, inconsequential, inconsiderable, inferior, insignificant, junior, lesser, light, negligible, nickel-and-dime (*U.S. slang*), paltry, petty, secondary, slight, smaller, subordinate, trifling, trivial, unimportant, younger
> ➤ **Antonyms**
appreciable, consequential, considerable, essential, grand, great, heavy, important, major, profound, serious, significant, substantial, superior, vital, weighty

minstrel *noun* = **musician**, bard, harper, jongleur, singer, songstress, troubadour

mint *noun* 1 = **fortune**, bomb (*Brit. slang*), bundle (*slang*), heap (*informal*), King's ransom, million, packet (*slang*), pile (*informal*) ♦ *adjective* 2 = **perfect**, brand-new, excellent, first-class, fresh, unblemished, undamaged, untarnished
♦ *verb* 3 = **make**, cast, coin, produce, punch, stamp, strike 4 = **invent**, coin, construct, devise, fabricate, fashion, forge, make up, produce, think up

minuscule *adjective* = **tiny**, diminutive, infinitesimal, little, microscopic, miniature, minute

minute[1] *noun* 1 = **sixty seconds**, sixtieth of an hour 2 = **moment**, flash, instant, jiffy (*informal*), second, shake (*informal*), tick (*Brit. informal*), trice 3 **any minute** = **very soon**, any moment, any second, any time, at any time, before long 4 **up to the minute** = **latest**, all the rage, in, modish,

(most) fashionable, newest, now (*informal*), smart, stylish, trendiest, trendy (*Brit. informal*), up to date, vogue, with it (*informal*)

minute[2] *adjective* 1 = **small**, diminutive, fine, infinitesimal, Lilliputian, little, microscopic, miniature, minuscule, slender, teensy-weensy, teeny-weeny, tiny 2 = **negligible**, inconsiderable, paltry, petty, picayune (*U.S.*), piddling (*informal*), puny, slight, trifling, trivial, unimportant 3 = **precise**, close, critical, detailed, exact, exhaustive, meticulous, painstaking, punctilious
> ➤ **Antonyms**
≠**small**: enormous, generous, gigantic, ginormous (*informal*), grand, great, huge, immense, mega (*slang*), monstrous ≠**negligible**: important, major, significant, vital ≠**precise**: careless, haphazard, imprecise, inexact, loose, quick, rough, superficial

minutely *adverb* = **precisely**, closely, critically, exactly, exhaustively, in detail, meticulously, painstakingly, with a fine-tooth comb

minutes *plural noun* = **record**, memorandum, notes, proceedings, transactions, transcript

minutiae *plural noun* = **details**, finer points, ins and outs, niceties, particulars, subtleties, trifles, trivia

minx *noun* = **flirt**, baggage (*informal, old-fashioned*), coquette, hoyden, hussy, jade, tomboy, wanton

miracle *noun* = **wonder**, marvel, phenomenon, prodigy, thaumaturgy

miraculous *adjective* = **wonderful**, amazing, astonishing, astounding, extraordinary, incredible, inexplicable, magical, marvellous, phenomenal, preternatural, prodigious, superhuman, supernatural, thaumaturgic, unaccountable, unbelievable, wondrous (*archaic or literary*)
> ➤ **Antonyms**
awful, bad, banal, common, commonplace, everyday, normal, ordinary, run-of-the-mill, terrible, unexceptional, unremarkable, usual

mirage *noun* = **illusion**, hallucination, optical illusion, phantasm

mire *noun* 1 = **swamp**, bog, marsh, morass, quagmire 2 = **mud**, dirt, gloop (*informal*), grot (*slang*), muck, ooze, slime, slob (*Irish*) 3 **in the mire** = **in trouble**, encumbered, entangled, in difficulties ♦ *verb* 4 = **bog down**, flounder, sink, stick in the mud 5 = **begrime**, besmirch, bespatter, cake, dirty, muddy, soil 6 = **entangle**, catch up, enmesh, involve

mirror noun 1 = **looking-glass**, glass, reflector, speculum 2 = **reflection**, copy, double, image, likeness, replica, representation, twin ◆ verb 3 = **reflect**, copy, depict, echo, emulate, follow, represent, show

mirth noun = **merriment**, amusement, cheerfulness, festivity, frolic, fun, gaiety, gladness, glee, hilarity, jocularity, jollity, joviality, joyousness, laughter, levity, merrymaking, pleasure, rejoicing, revelry, sport

mirthful adjective = **merry**, amused, amusing, blithe, cheerful, cheery, festive, frolicsome, funny, gay, glad, gladsome (archaic), happy, hilarious, jocund, jolly, jovial, laughable, light-hearted, ludic (literary), playful, sportive, uproarious, vivacious

➤ Antonyms
dejected, depressed, despondent, dismal, down in the dumps (informal), gloomy, grave, lugubrious, melancholy, miserable, morose, sad, saturnine, serious, solemn, sombre, sorrowful, unhappy

misadventure noun = **misfortune**, accident, bad break (informal), bad luck, bummer (slang), calamity, catastrophe, debacle, disaster, failure, ill fortune, ill luck, mischance, mishap, reverse, setback

misanthrope noun = **cynic**, egoist, egotist, mankind-hater, misanthropist

misanthropic adjective = **antisocial**, cynical, malevolent, unfriendly

misapprehend verb = **misunderstand**, get hold of the wrong end of the stick, get one's lines crossed, get the wrong idea or impression, misconceive, misconstrue, misinterpret, misread, mistake

misapprehension noun = **misunderstanding**, delusion, error, fallacy, false belief, false impression, misconception, misconstruction, misinterpretation, misreading, mistake, wrong idea or impression

misappropriate verb = **steal**, cabbage (Brit. slang), defalcate (Law), embezzle, misapply, misspend, misuse, peculate, pocket, swindle

misbegotten adjective 1 = **ill-conceived**, abortive, hare-brained, ill-advised, poorly thought-out 2 Literary = **illegitimate**, bastard, born out of wedlock, natural, spurious (rare)

misbehave verb = **be naughty**, act up (informal), be bad, be insubordinate, carry on (informal), get up to mischief (informal), muck about (Brit. slang)

➤ Antonyms
act correctly, be good, behave, conduct oneself properly, mind one's manners, mind one's p's and q's, toe the line

misbehaviour noun = **misconduct**, acting up (informal), bad behaviour, impropriety, incivility, indiscipline, insubordination, mischief, misdeeds, misdemeanour, monkey business (informal), naughtiness, rudeness, shenanigans (informal)

miscalculate verb = **misjudge**, blunder, calculate wrongly, err, get (it) wrong, go wrong, make a mistake, overestimate, overrate, slip up, underestimate, underrate

miscarriage noun 1 = **spontaneous abortion**, miss (informal) 2 = **failure**, botch (informal), breakdown, error, misadventure, mischance, misfire, mishap, mismanagement, nonsuccess, perversion, thwarting, undoing

miscarry verb 1 = **abort** 2 = **fail**, come to grief, come to nothing, fall through, gang agley (Scot.), go amiss, go astray, go awry, go pear-shaped (informal), go wrong, misfire

miscellaneous adjective = **mixed**, assorted, confused, diverse, diversified, farraginous, heterogeneous, indiscriminate, jumbled, manifold, many, mingled, motley, multifarious, multiform, promiscuous, sundry, varied, various

miscellany noun = **assortment**, anthology, collection, diversity, farrago, gallimaufry, hotchpotch, jumble, medley, mélange, mixed bag, mixture, omnium-gatherum, potpourri, salmagundi, variety

mischance noun = **misfortune**, accident, bad break (informal), bad luck, bummer (slang), calamity, contretemps, disaster, ill chance, ill fortune, ill luck, infelicity, misadventure, mishap

mischief noun 1 = **misbehaviour**, devilment, impishness, monkey business (informal), naughtiness, pranks, roguery, roguishness, shenanigans (informal), trouble, waywardness 2 = **harm**, damage, detriment, disadvantage, disruption, evil, hurt, injury, misfortune, trouble

mischievous adjective 1 = **naughty**, arch, bad, badly behaved, exasperating, frolicsome, impish, ludic (literary), playful, puckish, rascally, roguish, sportive, teasing, troublesome, vexatious, wayward 2 = **malicious**, bad, damaging, deleterious, destructive, detrimental, evil, harmful, hurtful, injurious, malignant, pernicious, sinful, spiteful, troublesome, vicious, wicked

misconception noun = **delusion**, error, fallacy, misapprehension, misconstruction, mistaken belief, misunderstanding, wrong end of the stick, wrong idea

misconduct *noun* = **immorality**, delinquency, dereliction, impropriety, malfeasance (*Law*), malpractice, misbehaviour, misdemeanour, mismanagement, naughtiness, rudeness, transgression, unethical behaviour, wrongdoing

misconstrue *verb* = **misinterpret**, get a false impression, get one's lines crossed, make a wrong interpretation, misapprehend, misconceive, misjudge, misread, mistake, mistranslate, misunderstand, take the wrong way (*informal*)

miscreant *noun* = **wrongdoer**, blackguard, caitiff (*archaic*), criminal, evildoer, knave (*archaic*), malefactor, rascal, reprobate, rogue, scally (*Northwest English dialect*), scoundrel, sinner, skelm (*S. African*), vagabond, villain

misdeed *noun* = **offence**, crime, fault, misconduct, misdemeanour, sin, transgression, trespass, villainy, wrong

misdemeanour *noun* = **offence**, fault, infringement, misbehaviour, misconduct, misdeed, peccadillo, transgression, trespass

miser *noun* = **hoarder**, cheapskate (*informal*), churl (*archaic*), curmudgeon, hunks (*rare*), niggard, penny-pincher (*informal*), screw (*slang*), Scrooge, skinflint, tight-arse (*taboo slang*), tight-ass (*U.S. taboo slang*), tightwad (*U.S. & Canad. slang*)

miserable *adjective* 1 = **unhappy**, afflicted, broken-hearted, crestfallen, dejected, depressed, desolate, despondent, disconsolate, dismal, distressed, doleful, down, downcast, down in the dumps (*informal*), down in the mouth (*informal*), forlorn, gloomy, heartbroken, low, melancholy, mournful, sorrowful, woebegone, wretched 2 = **despicable**, abject, bad, contemptible, deplorable, detestable, disgraceful, lamentable, low, mean, pathetic, piteous, pitiable, scurvy, shabby, shameful, sordid, sorry, squalid, vile, worthless, wretched
➤ **Antonyms**
≠**unhappy**: cheerful, happy ≠**despicable**: admirable, good, respectable

miserly *adjective* = **mean**, avaricious, beggarly, close, close-fisted, covetous, grasping, illiberal, mingy (*Brit. informal*), near, niggardly, parsimonious, penny-pinching (*informal*), penurious, snoep (*S. African informal*), sordid, stingy, tight-arsed (*taboo slang*), tight as a duck's arse (*taboo slang*), tight-assed (*U.S. taboo*

slang*), tightfisted, ungenerous
➤ **Antonyms**
charitable, extravagant, generous, prodigal, unselfish

misery *noun* 1 = **unhappiness**, agony, anguish, depression, desolation, despair, discomfort, distress, gloom, grief, hardship, melancholy, sadness, sorrow, suffering, torment, torture, woe, wretchedness 2 = **misfortune**, affliction, bitter pill (*informal*), burden, calamity, catastrophe, curse, disaster, hardship, load, ordeal, sorrow, trial, tribulation, trouble, woe 3 = **poverty**, destitution, indigence, need, penury, privation, sordidness, squalor, want, wretchedness 4 *Brit. informal* = **moaner**, grouch (*informal*), killjoy, pessimist, prophet of doom, sourpuss (*informal*), spoilsport, wet blanket (*informal*), wowser (*Austral. & N.Z. slang*)
➤ **Antonyms**
≠**unhappiness**: comfort, contentment, ease, enjoyment, happiness, joy, pleasure ≠**poverty**: luxury

misfire *verb* = **fail**, fail to go off, fall through, go pear-shaped (*informal*), go phut (*informal*), go wrong, miscarry

misfit *noun* = **nonconformist**, eccentric, fish out of water (*informal*), oddball (*informal*), square peg (in a round hole) (*informal*)

misfortune *noun* 1 = **bad luck**, adversity, evil fortune, hard luck, ill luck, infelicity 2 = **mishap**, accident, affliction, blow, bummer (*slang*), calamity, disaster, evil chance, failure, hardship, harm, loss, misadventure, mischance, misery, reverse, setback, stroke of bad luck, tragedy, trial, tribulation, trouble, whammy (*informal, chiefly U.S.*)
➤ **Antonyms**
fortune, good luck, relief

misgiving *noun* = **unease**, anxiety, apprehension, distrust, doubt, dubiety, hesitation, qualm, reservation, scruple, suspicion, trepidation, uncertainty, worry

misguided *adjective* = **unwise**, deluded, erroneous, foolish, ill-advised, imprudent, injudicious, labouring under a delusion *or* misapprehension, misled, misplaced, mistaken, uncalled-for, unreasonable, unwarranted

mishandle *verb* = **mismanage**, bodge (*informal*), botch, bungle, flub (*U.S. slang*), make a hash of (*informal*), make a mess of, make a nonsense of, mess up (*informal*), muff, screw (up) (*informal*)

mishap *noun* = **accident**, adversity, bad luck, calamity, contretemps, disaster, evil chance, evil fortune, hard luck, ill fortune, ill luck, infelicity, misadventure, mischance, misfortune

misinform verb = **mislead**, deceive, give (someone) a bum steer (informal, chiefly U.S.), give (someone) duff gen (Brit. informal), misdirect, misguide

misinterpret verb = **misunderstand**, distort, falsify, get wrong, misapprehend, misconceive, misconstrue, misjudge, misread, misrepresent, mistake, pervert

misjudge verb = **miscalculate**, be wrong about, get the wrong idea about, overestimate, overrate, underestimate, underrate

mislay verb = **lose**, be unable to find, be unable to put or lay one's hand on, forget the whereabouts of, lose track of, misplace, miss

mislead verb = **deceive**, beguile, bluff, delude, fool, give (someone) a bum steer (informal, chiefly U.S.), hoodwink, lead astray, misdirect, misguide, misinform, pull the wool over (someone's) eyes (informal), take for a ride (informal), take in (informal)

misleading adjective = **confusing**, ambiguous, casuistical, deceitful, deceptive, delusive, delusory, disingenuous, evasive, false, sophistical, specious, spurious, tricky (informal), unstraightforward
➤ **Antonyms**
candid, clear, correct, direct, explicit, frank, genuine, honest, obvious, open, plain, simple, sincere, straightforward, true, truthful

mismanage verb = **mishandle**, be incompetent, be inefficient, bodge (informal), botch, bungle, make a hash of (informal), make a mess of, make a nonsense of, maladminister, mess up, misconduct, misdirect, misgovern

misplace verb **1** = **lose**, be unable to find, be unable to put or lay one's hand on, forget the whereabouts of, lose track of, misfile, mislay, miss, put in the wrong place **2** = **place wrongly**, place unwisely

misprint noun = **mistake**, corrigendum, erratum, literal, printing error, typo (informal), typographical error

misquote verb = **misrepresent**, distort, falsify, garble, mangle, misreport, misstate, muddle, pervert, quote or take out of context, twist

misrepresent verb = **distort**, belie, disguise, falsify, garble, misinterpret, misstate, pervert, twist

misrule noun **1** = **mismanagement**, bad government, maladministration, misgovernment **2** = **disorder**, anarchy,

chaos, confusion, lawlessness, tumult, turmoil

miss[1] verb **1** = **omit**, be late for, blunder, err, fail, fail to grasp, fail to notice, forego, lack, leave out, let go, let slip, lose, miscarry, mistake, overlook, pass over, pass up, skip, slip, trip **2** = **long for**, feel the loss of, hunger for, need, pine for, want, wish, yearn for **3** = **avoid**, escape, evade
♦ noun **4** = **mistake**, blunder, error, failure, fault, loss, omission, oversight, want

miss[2] noun = **girl**, damsel, lass, lassie (informal), maid, maiden, schoolgirl, spinster, young lady

misshapen adjective = **deformed**, contorted, crippled, crooked, distorted, grotesque, ill-made, ill-proportioned, malformed, twisted, ugly, ungainly, unshapely, unsightly, warped, wry

missile noun = **rocket**, projectile, weapon

missing adjective = **absent**, astray, gone, lacking, left behind, left out, lost, mislaid, misplaced, not present, nowhere to be found, unaccounted-for, wanting
➤ **Antonyms**
accounted for, at hand, available, here, in attendance, on hand, present, there, to hand

mission noun **1** = **task**, aim, assignment, business, calling, charge, commission, duty, errand, goal, job, office, operation, purpose, pursuit, quest, trust, undertaking, vocation, work **2** = **delegation**, commission, deputation, embassy, legation, ministry, task force

missionary noun = **evangelist**, apostle, converter, preacher, propagandist, proselytizer

missive noun = **letter**, communication, dispatch, epistle, memorandum, message, note, report

misspent adjective = **wasted**, dissipated, idle, imprudent, misapplied, prodigal, profitless, squandered, thrown away
➤ **Antonyms**
active, fruitful, industrious, meaningful, profitable, unwasted, useful, worthwhile

mist noun **1** = **fog**, cloud, condensation, dew, drizzle, film, haar (Eastern Brit.), haze, smog, smur or smir (Scot.), spray, steam, vapour ♦ verb **2** = **steam (up)**, becloud, befog, blear, blur, cloud, film, fog, obscure

mistake noun **1** = **error**, bloomer (Brit. informal), blunder, boob (Brit. slang), boo-boo (informal), clanger (informal), erratum, error of judgment, false move, fault, faux pas, gaffe, goof (informal), howler (informal), inaccuracy, miscalculation, misconception, misstep, misunderstanding, oversight, slip, slip-up (*informal*), solecism ♦ *verb* **2** = **misunderstand**, get wrong, misapprehend, misconceive, misconstrue, misinterpret, misjudge, misread **3** = **confuse with**, accept as, confound, misinterpret as, mix up with, take for **4** = **miscalculate**, be wide of *or* be off the mark, be wrong, blunder, boob (*Brit. slang*), drop a clanger (*informal*), err, goof (*informal*), misjudge, put one's foot in it (*informal*), slip up (*informal*)

mistaken *adjective* = **wrong**, barking up the wrong tree (*informal*), erroneous, fallacious, false, faulty, getting the wrong end of the stick (*informal*), inaccurate, inappropriate, incorrect, in the wrong, labouring under a misapprehension, misguided, misinformed, misled, off base (*U.S. & Canad. informal*), off beam (*informal*), off target, off the mark, unfounded, unsound, way off beam (*informal*), wide of the mark
➤ **Antonyms**
accurate, correct, logical, right, sound, true

mistakenly *adverb* = **incorrectly**, by mistake, erroneously, fallaciously, falsely, inaccurately, inappropriately, in error, misguidedly, wrongly

mistimed *adjective* = **inopportune**, badly timed, ill-timed, inconvenient, unseasonable, unsynchronized, untimely

mistreat *verb* = **abuse**, brutalize, handle roughly, harm, ill-treat, ill-use, injure, knock about *or* around, maltreat, manhandle, maul, misuse, molest, rough up, wrong

mistress *noun* = **lover**, concubine, doxy (*archaic*), fancy bit (*slang*), fancy woman (*slang*), floozy (*slang*), girlfriend, inamorata, kept woman, ladylove (*rare*), paramour

mistrust *verb* **1** = **doubt**, apprehend, beware, be wary of, distrust, fear, have doubts about, suspect ♦ *noun* **2** = **suspicion**, apprehension, distrust, doubt, dubiety, fear, misgiving, scepticism, uncertainty, wariness

mistrustful *adjective* = **suspicious**, apprehensive, cautious, chary, cynical, distrustful, doubtful, dubious, fearful, hesitant, leery (*slang*), nervous, sceptical, uncertain, wary
➤ **Antonyms**
certain, definite, positive, sure, unafraid

misty *adjective* = **foggy**, bleary, blurred, cloudy, dark, dim, fuzzy, hazy, indistinct, murky, nebulous, obscure, opaque, overcast, unclear, vague
➤ **Antonyms**

bright, clear, distinct, lucid, obvious, plain, sunny, well-defined

misunderstand *verb* = **misinterpret**, be at cross-purposes, get (it) wrong, get one's lines crossed, get one's wires crossed, get the wrong end of the stick, get the wrong idea (about), misapprehend, misconceive, misconstrue, mishear, misjudge, misread, miss the point (of), mistake

misunderstanding *noun* **1** = **mistake**, error, false impression, misapprehension, misconception, misconstruction, misinterpretation, misjudgment, misreading, mix-up, wrong idea **2** = **disagreement**, argument, breach, conflict, difference, difficulty, discord, dissension, falling-out (*informal*), quarrel, rift, rupture, squabble, variance

misunderstood *adjective* = **misjudged**, misconstrued, misheard, misinterpreted, misread, unappreciated, unrecognized

misuse *noun* **1** = **waste**, abuse, barbarism, catachresis, corruption, desecration, dissipation, malapropism, misapplication, misemployment, misusage, perversion, profanation, solecism, squandering **2** = **mistreatment**, abuse, cruel treatment, exploitation, harm, ill-treatment, ill-usage, inhumane treatment, injury, maltreatment, manhandling, rough handling ♦ *verb* **3** = **waste**, abuse, corrupt, desecrate, dissipate, misapply, misemploy, pervert, profane, prostitute, squander **4** = **mistreat**, abuse, brutalize, exploit, handle roughly, harm, ill-treat, ill-use, injure, maltreat, manhandle, maul, molest, wrong
➤ **Antonyms**
verb ≠**waste**: appreciate, prize, treasure, use ≠**mistreat**: cherish, honour, respect

mitigate *verb* = **ease**, abate, allay, appease, assuage, blunt, calm, check, diminish, dull, extenuate, lessen, lighten, moderate, modify, mollify, pacify, palliate, placate, quiet, reduce the force of, remit, soften, soothe, subdue, take the edge off, temper, tone down, tranquillize, weaken
➤ **Antonyms**
aggravate, augment, enhance, heighten, increase, intensify, strengthen

mitigation *noun* = **relief**, abatement, allaying, alleviation, assuagement, diminution, easement, extenuation, moderation, mollification, palliation, remission

mix *verb* **1** = **combine**, alloy, amalgamate, associate, blend, coalesce, commingle, commix, compound, cross, fuse, incorporate, intermingle, interweave, join, jumble, meld, merge, mingle, put together, unite **2 = socialize**, associate, come together, consort, fraternize, hang out (*informal*), hobnob, join, mingle ♦ *noun* **3 = mixture**, alloy, amalgam, assortment, blend, combination, compound, fusion, medley, meld, mixed bag (*informal*)

mixed *adjective* **1 = combined**, alloyed, amalgamated, blended, composite, compound, fused, incorporated, joint, mingled, united **2 = varied**, assorted, cosmopolitan, diverse, diversified, heterogeneous, manifold, miscellaneous, motley **3 = crossbred**, hybrid, interbred, interdenominational, mongrel **4 = uncertain**, ambivalent, equivocal, indecisive
➤ Antonyms
≠**combined**: isolated, pure, straight, unmixed ≠**varied**: homogeneous, unmixed ≠**crossbred**: pure

mixed-up *adjective* **= confused**, at sea, bewildered, distraught, disturbed, maladjusted, muddled, perplexed, puzzled, upset

mixture *noun* **= blend**, admixture, alloy, amalgam, amalgamation, association, assortment, brew, combine, composite, compound, concoction, conglomeration, cross, fusion, hotchpotch, jumble, medley, *mélange*, meld, miscellany, mix, mixed bag (*informal*), potpourri, salmagundi, union, variety

mix-up *noun* **= confusion**, disorder, fankle (*Scot.*), jumble, mess, mistake, misunderstanding, muddle, snarl-up (*informal, chiefly Brit.*), tangle

mix up *verb* **1 = combine**, blend, commix, mix **2 = confuse**, confound, muddle **3 = bewilder**, confuse, disturb, fluster, muddle, perplex, puzzle, throw into confusion, unnerve, upset **4 = entangle**, embroil, implicate, involve, rope in

moan *noun* **1 = groan**, lament, lamentation, sigh, sob, sough, wail, whine **2** *Informal* **= grumble**, beef (*slang*), bitch (*slang*), complaint, gripe (*informal*), grouch (*informal*), grouse, kvetch (*U.S. slang*), protest, whine ♦ *verb* **3 = groan**, bemoan, bewail, deplore, grieve, keen, lament, mourn, sigh, sob, sough, whine **4** *Informal* **= grumble**, beef (*slang*), bitch (*slang*), bleat, carp, complain, gripe (*informal*), groan, grouch (*informal*), grouse, moan and groan, whine, whinge (*informal*)

mob *noun* **1 = crowd**, assemblage, body, collection, drove, flock, gang, gathering, herd, horde, host, mass, multitude, pack, press, swarm, throng **2 = masses**, canaille,

commonalty, great unwashed (*informal & derogatory*), hoi polloi, rabble, riffraff, scum **3** *Slang* **= gang**, class, company, crew (*informal*), group, lot, set, troop ♦ *verb* **4 = surround**, crowd around, jostle, overrun, set upon, swarm around

mobile *adjective* **1 = movable**, ambulatory, itinerant, locomotive, migrant, motile, moving, peripatetic, portable, travelling, wandering **2 = changeable**, animated, ever-changing, expressive

mobilize *verb* **= prepare**, activate, animate, call to arms, call up, get *or* make ready, marshal, muster, organize, put in motion, rally, ready

mock *verb* **1 = laugh at**, chaff, deride, flout, insult, jeer, laugh to scorn, make a monkey out of, make fun of, poke fun at, ridicule, scoff, scorn, show contempt for, sneer, take the mickey (out of) (*informal*), take the piss (out of) (*taboo slang*), taunt, tease, wind up (*Brit. slang*) **2 = mimic**, ape, burlesque, caricature, counterfeit, do (*informal*), imitate, lampoon, parody, satirize, send up (*Brit. informal*), take off (*informal*), travesty **3 = foil**, defeat, defy, disappoint, frustrate, thwart ♦ *adjective* **4 = imitation**, artificial, bogus, counterfeit, dummy, ersatz, fake, faked, false, feigned, forged, fraudulent, phoney *or* phony (*informal*), pretended, pseudo (*informal*), sham, spurious
➤ Antonyms
verb ≠**laugh at**: encourage, praise, respect, revere ♦ *adjective* ≠**imitation**: authentic, genuine, natural, real, sincere, true, unfeigned

mockery *noun* **1 = derision**, contempt, contumely, disdain, disrespect, gibes, insults, jeering, ridicule, scoffing, scorn **2 = parody**, burlesque, caricature, deception, farce, imitation, lampoon, mimicry, pretence, send-up (*Brit. informal*), sham, spoof (*informal*), take-off (*informal*), travesty **3 = farce**, apology (*informal*), disappointment, joke, laughing stock, letdown

mocking *adjective* **= scornful**, contemptuous, contumelious, derisive, derisory, disdainful, disrespectful, insulting, irreverent, sarcastic, sardonic, satiric, satirical, scoffing, taunting

mode *noun* **1 = method**, form, manner, procedure, process, style, system, technique, way **2 = fashion**, craze, look, rage, style, trend, vogue

model *noun* **1 = representation**, copy, dummy, facsimile, image, imitation, miniature, mock-up, replica **2 = pattern**, archetype, design, epitome, example,

exemplar, gauge, ideal, lodestar, mould, norm, original, par, paradigm, paragon, prototype, standard, type **3 = sitter**, poser, subject **4 = mannequin 5 = version**, configuration, design, form, kind, mark, mode, stamp, style, type, variety
♦ *adjective* **6 = ideal**, archetypal, exemplary, illustrative, paradigmatic, perfect, standard, typical **7 = imitation**, copy, dummy, facsimile, miniature ♦ *verb* **8 = shape**, carve, cast, design, fashion, form, mould, sculpt, stamp **9 = base**, pattern, plan **10 = show off**, display, sport (*informal*), wear
➤ **Antonyms**
adjective ≠**ideal**: deficient, flawed, impaired, imperfect

moderate *adjective* **1 = mild**, calm, controlled, cool, deliberate, equable, gentle, judicious, limited, middle-of-the-road, modest, peaceable, reasonable, restrained, sober, steady, temperate **2 = average**, fair, fairish, fair to middling (*informal*), indifferent, mediocre, medium, middling, ordinary, passable, so-so (*informal*), unexceptional ♦ *verb* **3 = lessen**, abate, allay, appease, assuage, calm, clear the air, control, curb, decrease, diminish, ease, mitigate, modulate, pacify, play down, quiet, regulate, relax, repress, restrain, soften, soft-pedal (*informal*), subdue, tame, temper, tone down **4 = arbitrate**, chair, judge, mediate, preside, referee, take the chair
➤ **Antonyms**
adjective ≠**mild**: extreme, intemperate, ruffled, unreasonable, wild ≠**average**: excessive, extreme, immoderate, inordinate, unusual ♦ *verb* ≠**lessen**: heighten, increase, intensify

moderately *adverb* = **reasonably**, fairly, gently, in moderation, passably, quite, rather, slightly, somewhat, to a degree, tolerably, to some extent, within limits, within reason

moderation *noun* **1 = restraint**, calmness, composure, coolness, equanimity, fairness, judiciousness, justice, justness, mildness, moderateness, reasonableness, sedateness, temperance **2 in moderation = moderately**, within limits, within reason

modern *adjective* = **current**, contemporary, fresh, late, latest, neoteric (*rare*), new, newfangled, novel, present, present-day, recent, twentieth-century, up-to-date, up-to-the-minute, with it (*informal*)
➤ **Antonyms**
ancient, antiquated, archaic, former, obsolete, old, old-fashioned, old hat, outmoded, passé, past, square (*informal*), uncool (*slang*)

modernity *noun* = **novelty**, currency, freshness, innovation, newness

modernize *verb* = **update**, bring into the twentieth century, bring up to date, face-lift, make over, rebrand, rejuvenate, remake, remodel, renew, renovate, revamp

modest *adjective* **1 = unpretentious**, bashful, blushing, coy, demure, diffident, discreet, humble, meek, quiet, reserved, reticent, retiring, self-conscious, self-effacing, shy, simple, unassuming **2 = moderate**, fair, limited, middling, ordinary, small, unexceptional

modesty *noun* = **reserve**, bashfulness, coyness, decency, demureness, diffidence, discreetness, humbleness, humility, lack of pretension, meekness, propriety, quietness, reticence, self-effacement, shyness, simplicity, timidity, unobtrusiveness, unpretentiousness
➤ **Antonyms**
arrogance, assurance, boastfulness, boldness, conceit, confidence, egotism, forwardness, haughtiness, immodesty, indecency, ostentation, presumption, pretentiousness, pride, showiness, vanity

modicum *noun* = **little**, atom, bit, crumb, dash, drop, fragment, grain, inch, iota, mite, ounce, particle, pinch, scrap, shred, small amount, speck, tad (*informal, chiefly U.S.*), tinge, touch

modification *noun* = **change**, adjustment, alteration, modulation, mutation, qualification, refinement, reformation, restriction, revision, variation

modify *verb* **1 = change**, adapt, adjust, alter, convert, recast, redo, refashion, reform, remodel, reorganize, reshape, revise, rework, transform, tweak (*informal*), vary **2 = tone down**, abate, ease, lessen, limit, lower, moderate, qualify, reduce, relax, restrain, restrict, soften, temper

modish *adjective* = **fashionable**, contemporary, current, in, smart, stylish, trendy (*Brit. informal*), up-to-the-minute, voguish

modulate *verb* = **adjust**, attune, balance, regulate, tune, vary

mogul *noun* = **tycoon**, baron, bashaw, big cheese (*slang, old-fashioned*), big gun (*informal*), big hitter (*informal*), big noise (*informal*), big shot (*informal*), big wheel (*slang*), heavy hitter (*informal*), lord, magnate, nabob (*informal*), nob (*slang, chiefly Brit.*), notable, personage, potentate, V.I.P.

moist *adjective* = **damp**, clammy, dampish, dank, dewy, dripping, drizzly, humid, not dry, rainy, soggy, wet, wettish

moisten verb = **dampen**, bedew, damp, humidify, lick, moisturize, soak, water, wet

moisture noun = **damp**, dampness, dankness, dew, humidity, liquid, perspiration, sweat, water, wateriness, wetness

molecule noun = **particle**, atom, iota, jot, mite, mote, speck

molest verb 1 = **abuse**, accost, assail, attack, harm, hurt, ill-treat, injure, interfere with, maltreat, manhandle 2 = **annoy**, abuse, afflict, badger, beset, bother, bug (informal), disturb, harass, harry, hector, irritate, persecute, pester, plague, tease, torment, upset, vex, worry

mollify verb = **pacify**, appease, calm, conciliate, placate, quiet, soothe, sweeten

mollycoddle verb = **pamper**, baby, cosset, indulge, spoil

moment noun 1 = **instant**, bat of an eye (informal), flash, jiffy (informal), minute, no time, second, shake (informal), split second, tick (Brit. informal), trice, twinkling, two shakes (informal), two shakes of a lamb's tail (informal) 2 = **time**, hour, instant, juncture, point, point in time, stage 3 = **importance**, concern, consequence, gravity, import, seriousness, significance, substance, value, weight, weightiness, worth

momentarily adverb = **briefly**, for a little while, for a minute, for a moment, for an instant, for a second, for a short time, for a short while, for the nonce, temporarily

momentary adjective = **short-lived**, brief, ephemeral, evanescent, fleeting, flying, fugitive, hasty, passing, quick, short, temporary, transitory
➤ Antonyms
lasting, lengthy, long-lived, permanent

momentous adjective = **significant**, consequential, critical, crucial, decisive, earth-shaking (informal), fateful, grave, historic, important, of moment, pivotal, serious, vital, weighty
➤ Antonyms
inconsequential, insignificant, trifling, trivial, unimportant

momentum noun = **impetus**, drive, energy, force, power, propulsion, push, strength, thrust

monarch noun = **ruler**, crowned head, emperor or empress, king, potentate, prince or princess, queen, sovereign

monarchy noun 1 = **sovereignty**, absolutism, autocracy, despotism, kingship, monocracy, royalism 2 = **kingdom**, empire, principality, realm

monastery noun = **abbey**, cloister, convent, friary, house, nunnery, priory, religious community

monastic adjective = **monkish**, ascetic, austere, celibate, cloistered, cloistral, contemplative, conventual, hermit-like, recluse, reclusive, secluded, sequestered, withdrawn

monetary adjective = **financial**, budgetary, capital, cash, fiscal, pecuniary

money noun 1 = **cash**, ackers (slang), banknotes, brass (Northern English dialect), bread (slang), capital, coin, currency, dibs (slang), dosh (Brit. & Austral. slang), dough (slang), filthy lucre (facetious), funds, gelt (slang, chiefly U.S.), green (slang), hard cash, legal tender, lolly (Brit. slang), loot (informal), mazuma (slang, chiefly U.S.), megabucks (U.S. & Canad. slang), moolah (slang), necessary (informal), needful (informal), pelf (contemptuous), readies (informal), rhino (Brit. slang), riches, shekels (informal), silver, specie, spondulicks (slang), the ready (informal), the wherewithal, tin (slang), wealth 2 **in the money** = **rich**, affluent, flush (informal), in clover (informal), loaded (slang), on Easy Street (informal), prosperous, rolling (slang), wealthy, well-heeled (informal), well-off, well-to-do

moneymaking adjective = **profitable**, gainful, going, lucrative, paying, remunerative, successful, thriving

mongrel noun 1 = **hybrid**, bigener (Biology), cross, crossbreed, half-breed, mixed breed ♦ adjective 2 = **hybrid**, bastard, crossbred, half-breed, of mixed breed

monitor noun 1 = **watchdog**, guide, invigilator, overseer, prefect (Brit.), supervisor ♦ verb 2 = **check**, follow, keep an eye on, keep tabs on, keep track of, observe, oversee, record, scan, supervise, survey, watch

monk noun = **friar** (loosely), brother, monastic, religious

monkey noun 1 = **simian**, jackanapes (archaic), primate 2 = **rascal**, devil, imp, mischief maker, pickle (Brit. informal), rogue, scamp 3 **make a monkey of** = **make a fool of**, make fun of, make (someone) a laughing stock, make (someone) look foolish, make (someone) look ridiculous, make (someone) look silly, play a trick on, ridicule ♦ verb 4 with **around** or **about with** = **fool**, fiddle (informal), interfere, meddle, mess, play, tamper, tinker, trifle

monkey business noun 1 = **mischief**, carry-on (informal, chiefly Brit.), clowning, horseplay, monkey tricks, pranks, shenanigans (informal), skylarking (*informal*), tomfoolery **2 = dishonesty**, chicanery, funny business, hanky-panky (*informal*), skulduggery (*informal*), trickery

monolithic *adjective* = **huge**, colossal, giant, gigantic, immovable, impenetrable, imposing, intractable, massive, monumental, solid, substantial, undifferentiated, undivided, unitary

monologue *noun* = **speech**, harangue, lecture, sermon, soliloquy

monopolize *verb* = **control**, corner, corner the market in, dominate, engross, exercise *or* have a monopoly of, hog (*slang*), keep to oneself, take over, take up

monotonous *adjective* = **tedious**, all the same, boring, colourless, droning, dull, flat, ho-hum (*informal*), humdrum, mind-numbing, plodding, repetitious, repetitive, samey (*informal*), soporific, tiresome, toneless, unchanging, uniform, uninflected, unvaried, wearisome
➤ **Antonyms**
animated, enjoyable, entertaining, enthralling, exciting, exhilarating, interesting, lively, sexy (*informal*), stimulating

monotony *noun* = **tedium**, boredom, colourlessness, dullness, flatness, humdrumness, monotonousness, repetitiousness, repetitiveness, routine, sameness, tediousness, tiresomeness, uniformity, wearisomeness

monster *noun* **1 = giant**, behemoth, Brobdingnagian, colossus, leviathan, mammoth, titan **2 = brute**, barbarian, beast, bogeyman, demon, devil, fiend, ghoul, ogre, savage, villain **3 = freak**, abortion, lusus naturae, miscreation, monstrosity, mutant, teratism ◆ *adjective* **4 = huge**, Brobdingnagian, colossal, elephantine, enormous, gargantuan, giant, gigantic, ginormous (*informal*), humongous *or* humungous (*U.S. slang*), immense, jumbo (*informal*), mammoth, massive, mega (*slang*), monstrous, stellar (*informal*), stupendous, titanic, tremendous

monstrosity *noun* **1 = eyesore**, abortion, freak, horror, lusus naturae, miscreation, monster, mutant, ogre, teratism **2 = hideousness**, abnormality, atrocity, dreadfulness, evil, frightfulness, heinousness, hellishness, horror, loathsomeness, obscenity

monstrous *adjective* **1 = unnatural**, abnormal, dreadful, enormous, fiendish, freakish, frightful, grotesque, gruesome, hellish, hideous, horrendous, horrible, miscreated, obscene, teratoid, terrible **2 = outrageous**, atrocious, cruel, devilish, diabolical, disgraceful, egregious, evil, fiendish, foul, heinous, horrifying, infamous, inhuman, intolerable, loathsome, odious, satanic, scandalous, shocking, vicious, villainous **3 = huge**, colossal, elephantine, enormous, gargantuan, giant, gigantic, ginormous (*informal*), great, humongous *or* humungous (*U.S. slang*), immense, mammoth, massive, mega (*slang*), prodigious, stellar (*informal*), stupendous, titanic, towering, tremendous, vast
➤ **Antonyms**
≠**unnatural**: appealing, attractive, beautiful, delightful, lovely, natural, normal, ordinary, pleasant ≠**outrageous**: admirable, decent, fine, good, honourable, humane, kind, merciful, mild ≠**huge**: diminutive, insignificant, little, meagre, miniature, minute, puny, slight, small, tiny

month *noun* = **four weeks**, moon, thirty days

monument *noun* **1 = memorial**, cairn, cenotaph, commemoration, gravestone, headstone, marker, mausoleum, obelisk, pillar, shrine, statue, tombstone **2 = testament**, memento, record, remembrance, reminder, token, witness

monumental *adjective* **1 = important**, awe-inspiring, awesome, classic, enduring, enormous, epoch-making, historic, immortal, lasting, majestic, memorable, outstanding, prodigious, significant, stupendous, unforgettable **2 = commemorative**, cyclopean, funerary, memorial, monolithic, statuary **3** *Informal* = **immense**, catastrophic, colossal, egregious, gigantic, great, horrible, indefensible, massive, staggering, terrible, tremendous, unforgivable, whopping (*informal*)
➤ **Antonyms**
≠**important**: ephemeral, inconsequential, insignificant, modest, negligible, ordinary, trivial, undistinguished, unimportant, unimpressive, unremarkable ≠**immense**: average, insignificant, mild, petty, slight, small, tiny, trivial

mood *noun* **1 = state of mind**, disposition, frame of mind, humour, spirit, temper, tenor, vein **2 = depression**, bad temper, bate (*Brit. slang*), blues, doldrums, dumps (*informal*), fit of pique, grumps (*informal*), low spirits, melancholy, sulk, the hump (*Brit. informal*), the sulks, wax (*informal, chiefly Brit.*) **3 in the mood = inclined**, disposed (towards), eager, favourable, interested, in the (right) frame of mind, keen, minded, willing

moody *adjective* **1 = sulky**, angry,

cantankerous, crabbed, crabby, cross, crotchety (*informal*), crusty, curt, huffish, huffy, ill-humoured, ill-tempered, in a huff, irascible, irritable, offended, petulant, piqued, pissed (*taboo slang*), pissed off (*taboo slang*), short-tempered, splenetic, temperamental, testy, tetchy, touchy, waspish, wounded **2 = gloomy**, broody, crestfallen, dismal, doleful, dour, downcast, down in the dumps (*informal*), down in the mouth (*informal*), frowning, glum, in the doldrums, introspective, lugubrious, melancholy, miserable, mopish, mopy, morose, out of sorts (*informal*), pensive, sad, saturnine, sullen **3 = changeable**, capricious, erratic, faddish, fickle, fitful, flighty, impulsive, inconstant, mercurial, temperamental, unpredictable, unstable, unsteady, volatile
➤ Antonyms
≠**sulky, gloomy**: amiable, cheerful, gay, happy, optimistic ≠**changeable**: constant, stable, steady

moon *noun* **1 = satellite 2 once in a blue moon = rarely**, almost never, hardly ever, very seldom ◆ *verb* **3 = idle**, daydream, languish, mooch (*slang*), mope, waste time

moor¹ *noun* **= moorland**, fell (*Brit.*), heath, muir (*Scot.*)

moor² *verb* **= tie up**, anchor, berth, dock, fasten, fix, lash, make fast, secure

moot *adjective* **1 = debatable**, arguable, at issue, contestable, controversial, disputable, doubtful, open, open to debate, undecided, unresolved, unsettled ◆ *verb* **2 = bring up**, broach, introduce, propose, put forward, suggest, ventilate

mop *noun* **1 = squeegee**, sponge, swab **2 = mane**, shock, tangle, thatch ◆ *verb* **3 = clean**, soak up, sponge, swab, wash, wipe

mope *verb* **= brood**, fret, languish, moon, pine, pout, sulk

mop up *verb* **1 = clean up**, mop, soak up, sponge, swab, wash, wipe **2** *Military* **= finish off**, account for, clean out, clear, eliminate, neutralize, pacify, round up, secure

moral *adjective* **1 = ethical 2 = good**, blameless, chaste, decent, ethical, high-minded, honest, honourable, incorruptible, innocent, just, meritorious, noble, principled, proper, pure, right, righteous, upright, upstanding, virtuous ◆ *noun* **3 = lesson**, meaning, message, point, significance
➤ Antonyms
adjective ≠**good**: amoral, dishonest, dishonourable, immoral, improper, sinful, unethical, unfair, unjust, wrong

morale *noun* **= confidence**, esprit de corps, heart, mettle, self-esteem, spirit, temper

morality *noun* **1 = integrity**, chastity, decency, ethicality, ethicalness, goodness, honesty, justice, principle, rectitude, righteousness, rightness, uprightness, virtue **2 = standards**, conduct, ethics, habits, ideals, manners, moral code, morals, mores, philosophy, principles

morals *plural noun* **= morality**, behaviour, conduct, ethics, habits, integrity, manners, mores, principles, scruples, standards

morass *noun* **1 = marsh**, bog, fen, quagmire, slough, swamp **2 = mess**, confusion, mix-up, muddle, tangle

moratorium *noun* **= postponement**, freeze, halt, respite, standstill, stay, suspension

morbid *adjective* **1 = unwholesome**, brooding, funereal, ghoulish, gloomy, grim, melancholy, pessimistic, sick, sombre, unhealthy **2 = gruesome**, dreadful, ghastly, grisly, hideous, horrid, macabre **3 = diseased**, ailing, deadly, infected, malignant, pathological, sick, sickly, unhealthy, unsound
➤ Antonyms
≠**unwholesome**: bright, cheerful, happy, healthy, wholesome ≠**diseased**: healthy, salubrious

mordant *adjective* **= sarcastic**, biting, caustic, cutting, incisive, pungent, scathing, stinging, trenchant

more *adjective* **1 = extra**, added, additional, fresh, further, new, new-found, other, spare, supplementary ◆ *adverb* **2 = to a greater extent**, better, further, longer

moreover *adverb* **= furthermore**, additionally, also, as well, besides, further, in addition, into the bargain, likewise, to boot, too, what is more, withal (*literary*)

morgue *noun* **= mortuary**

moribund *adjective* **1 = dying**, at death's door, breathing one's last, doomed, fading fast, failing, (having) one foot in the grave, *in extremis,* near death, near the end, on one's deathbed, on one's last legs **2 = declining**, at a standstill, forceless, obsolescent, on its last legs, on the way out, stagnant, stagnating, standing still, waning, weak

morning *noun* **= dawn**, a.m., break of day, daybreak, forenoon, morn (*poetic*), morrow (*archaic*), sunrise

moron *noun* **= fool**, airhead (*slang*), ass, berk (*Brit. slang*), blockhead, bonehead (*slang*), charlie (*Brit. informal*), chump, coot, cretin, dickhead (*slang*), dickwit (*slang*), dimwit (*informal*), dipstick (*Brit. slang*), divvy (*Brit. slang*), dolt, dope (*informal*), dork (*slang*), dumb-ass (*slang*), dummy (*slang*), dunce, dunderhead, dweeb (*U.S. slang*), fathead (*informal*), fuckwit (*taboo slang*), geek (*slang*), gobshite (*Irish taboo slang*), gonzo (*slang*), halfwit, idiot, imbecile, jerk (*slang, chiefly U.S. & Canad.*), lamebrain (*informal*), mental defective, muttonhead (*slang*), nerd *or* nurd (*slang*), nitwit (*informal*), numbskull *or* numskull, numpty (*Scot. informal*), oaf, pillock (*Brit. slang*), plank (*Brit. slang*), plonker (*slang*), prat (*slang*), prick (*derogatory slang*), schmuck (*U.S. slang*), simpleton, thickhead, tosser (*Brit. slang*), twit (*informal, chiefly Brit.*), wally (*slang*), weenie (*U.S. informal*)

moronic *adjective* = **idiotic**, cretinous, dumb-ass (*slang*), foolish, halfwitted, imbecilic, mindless, stupid, unintelligent

morose *adjective* = **sullen**, blue, churlish, crabbed, crabby, cross, crusty, depressed, dour, down, down in the dumps (*informal*), gloomy, glum, grouchy (*informal*), gruff, ill-humoured, ill-natured, ill-tempered, in a bad mood, low, melancholy, miserable, moody, mournful, perverse, pessimistic, saturnine, sour, sulky, surly, taciturn
➤ **Antonyms**
amiable, blithe, cheerful, chirpy (*informal*), friendly, gay, genial, good-humoured, good-natured, happy, pleasant, sweet

morsel *noun* = **piece**, bit, bite, crumb, fraction, fragment, grain, mouthful, nibble, part, scrap, segment, slice, snack, soupçon, tad (*informal, chiefly U.S.*), taste, titbit

mortal *adjective* **1** = **human**, corporeal, earthly, ephemeral, impermanent, passing, sublunary, temporal, transient, worldly **2** = **fatal**, deadly, death-dealing, destructive, killing, lethal, murderous, terminal **3** = **unrelenting**, bitter, deadly, implacable, irreconcilable, out-and-out, remorseless, sworn, to the death **4** = **great**, agonizing, awful, dire, enormous, extreme, grave, intense, serious, severe, terrible ♦ *noun* **5** = **human being**, being, body, earthling, human, individual, man, person, woman

mortality *noun* **1** = **humanity**, ephemerality, impermanence, temporality, transience **2** = **killing**, bloodshed, carnage, death, destruction, fatality, loss of life

mortification *noun* **1** = **humiliation**, abasement, annoyance, chagrin, discomfiture, dissatisfaction, embarrassment, loss of face, shame, vexation **2** = **discipline**, abasement, chastening, control, denial, subjugation **3** *Medical* = **gangrene**, corruption, festering,

necrosis, putrescence

mortified *adjective* **1** = **humiliated**, abashed, affronted, annoyed, ashamed, chagrined, chastened, confounded, crushed, deflated, discomfited, displeased, embarrassed, given a showing-up (*informal*), humbled, made to eat humble pie (*informal*), pissed (*taboo slang*), pissed off (*taboo slang*), put down, put out (*informal*), put to shame, rendered speechless, shamed, vexed **2** = **disciplined**, abased, chastened, conquered, controlled, crushed, subdued **3** *Of flesh* = **gangrenous**, decayed, necrotic, rotted

mortify *verb* **1** = **humiliate**, abase, abash, affront, annoy, chagrin, chasten, confound, crush, deflate, disappoint, discomfit, displease, embarrass, humble, make (someone) eat humble pie (*informal*), put down, put to shame, shame, take (someone) down a peg (*informal*), vex **2** = **discipline**, abase, chasten, control, deny, subdue **3** *Of flesh* = **putrefy**, become gangrenous, corrupt, deaden, die, fester, gangrene, necrose

mortuary *noun* = **morgue**, funeral home (*U.S.*), funeral parlour

mostly *adverb* = **generally**, above all, almost entirely, as a rule, chiefly, customarily, for the most part, largely, mainly, most often, on the whole, particularly, predominantly, primarily, principally, usually

moth-eaten *adjective* = **decayed**, antiquated, decrepit, dilapidated, grungy (*slang, chiefly U.S.*), obsolete, outdated, outworn, ragged, scuzzy (*slang, chiefly U.S.*), seedy, shabby, stale, tattered, threadbare, worn-out

mother *noun* **1** = **parent**, dam, ma (*informal*), mater, mom (*U.S. informal*), mum (*Brit. informal*), mummy (*Brit. informal*), old lady (*informal*), old woman (*informal*) ♦ *adjective* **2** = **native**, connate, inborn, innate, natural ♦ *verb* **3** = **give birth to**, bear, bring forth, drop, produce **4** = **nurture**, care for, cherish, nurse, protect, raise, rear, tend **5** = **pamper**, baby, fuss over, indulge, spoil

motherly *adjective* = **maternal**, affectionate, caring, comforting, fond, gentle, kind, loving, protective, sheltering, tender, warm

mother wit *noun* = **common sense**, brains, gumption (*Brit. informal*), horse sense, judgment, native intelligence, nous (*Brit. slang*), savvy (*slang*), smarts (*slang, chiefly U.S.*)

motif *noun* **1** = **theme**, concept, idea, leitmotif, subject **2** = **design**, decoration, ornament, shape

motion *noun* **1** = **movement**, action, change, flow, kinesics, locomotion, mobility, motility, move, passage, passing, progress, travel **2** = **gesture**, gesticulation, sign, signal, wave **3** = **proposal**, proposition, recommendation, submission, suggestion **4 in motion** = **moving**, afoot, functioning, going, in progress, on the go (*informal*), on the move (*informal*), operational, travelling, under way, working ♦ *verb* **5** = **gesture**, beckon, direct, gesticulate, nod, signal, wave

motionless *adjective* = **still**, at a standstill, at rest, calm, fixed, frozen, halted, immobile, inanimate, inert, lifeless, paralysed, standing, static, stationary, stock-still, transfixed, unmoved, unmoving
➤ **Antonyms**
active, agitated, animated, frantic, lively, mobile, moving, restless, travelling

motivate *verb* = **inspire**, actuate, arouse, bring, cause, draw, drive, get going, give incentive to, impel, induce, inspirit, instigate, lead, move, persuade, prod, prompt, provoke, set off, set on, stimulate, stir, trigger

motivation *noun* **1** = **inspiration**, ambition, desire, drive, hunger, interest, wish **2** = **incentive**, carrot and stick, impulse, incitement, inducement, inspiration, instigation, motive, persuasion, reason, spur, stimulus

motive *noun* **1** = **reason**, cause, design, ground(s), incentive, incitement, inducement, influence, inspiration, intention, mainspring, motivation, object, occasion, purpose, rationale, spur, stimulus, the why and wherefore, thinking ♦ *adjective* **2** = **moving**, activating, driving, impelling, motivating, operative, prompting

motley *adjective* **1** = **miscellaneous**, assorted, disparate, dissimilar, diversified, heterogeneous, mingled, mixed, unlike, varied **2** = **multicoloured**, chequered, particoloured, polychromatic, polychrome, polychromous, rainbow, variegated
➤ **Antonyms**
≠**miscellaneous**: homogeneous, similar, uniform ≠**multicoloured**: monochromatic, plain, self-coloured, solid

mottled *adjective* = **blotchy**, brindled, chequered, dappled, flecked, freckled, marbled, piebald, pied, speckled, spotted, stippled, streaked, tabby, variegated

motto *noun* = **saying**, adage, byword, cry, dictum, formula, gnome, maxim, precept, proverb, rule, saw, slogan, tag-line, watchword

mould¹ *noun* **1** = **cast**, die, form, matrix, pattern, shape, stamp **2** = **design**, brand, build, configuration, construction, cut, fashion, form, format, frame, kind, line, make, pattern, shape, stamp, structure, style **3** = **nature**, calibre, character, ilk, kidney, kind, quality, sort, stamp, type ♦ *verb* **4** = **shape**, carve, cast, construct, create, fashion, forge, form, make, model, sculpt, stamp, work **5** = **influence**, affect, control, direct, form, make, shape

mould² *noun* = **fungus**, blight, mildew, mouldiness, mustiness

mouldy *adjective* = **stale**, bad, blighted, decaying, fusty, mildewed, musty, rotten, rotting, spoiled

mound *noun* **1** = **heap**, bing (*Scot.*), drift, pile, rick, stack **2** = **hill**, bank, dune, embankment, hillock, knoll, rise **3** = **earthwork**, bulwark, motte (*History*), rampart **4** *Archaeology* = **barrow**, tumulus

mount *verb* **1** = **ascend**, clamber up, climb, escalade, go up, make one's way up, scale **2** = **get (up) on**, bestride, climb onto, climb up on, get astride, jump on **3** = **increase**, accumulate, build, escalate, grow, intensify, multiply, pile up, swell **4** = **display**, frame, set, set off **5** = **fit**, emplace, install, place, position, put in place, set up **6** = **stage**, exhibit, get up (*informal*), prepare, produce, put on **7** *Military* = **launch**, deliver, prepare, ready, set in motion, stage ♦ *noun* **8** = **backing**, base, fixture, foil, frame, mounting, setting, stand, support **9** = **horse**, steed (*literary*)
➤ **Antonyms**
verb ≠**ascend**: descend, drop, go down, make one's way down ≠**get (up) on**: climb down from, climb off, dismount, get down from, get off, jump off ≠**increase**: contract, decline, decrease, diminish, dwindle, fall, lessen, lower, reduce, shrink, wane

mountain *noun* **1** = **peak**, alp, ben (*Scot.*), berg (*S. Afr.*), elevation, eminence, fell (*Brit.*), height, mount, Munro **2** = **heap**, abundance, mass, mound, pile, stack, ton

mountainous *adjective* **1** = **high**, alpine, highland, rocky, soaring, steep, towering, upland **2** = **huge**, daunting, enormous, gigantic, great, hulking, immense, mammoth, mighty, monumental, ponderous, prodigious
➤ **Antonyms**
≠**huge**: diminutive, insignificant, little, minute, petty, puny, small, tiny, trivial, weak

mourn verb = **grieve**, bemoan, bewail, deplore, keen, lament, miss, rue, sorrow, wail, wear black, weep

mournful adjective **1** = **sad**, afflicting, calamitous, deplorable, distressing, grievous, harrowing, lamentable, melancholy, painful, piteous, plaintive, sorrowful, tragic, unhappy, woeful **2** = **dismal**, brokenhearted, cheerless, desolate, disconsolate, downcast, down in the dumps (*informal*), funereal, gloomy, grief-stricken, grieving, heartbroken, heavy, heavy-hearted, joyless, lugubrious, melancholy, miserable, rueful, sad, sombre, unhappy, woeful
➤ **Antonyms**
≠**sad**: agreeable, cheerful, fortunate, happy, lucky, pleasant, satisfying ≠**dismal**: bright, cheerful, chirpy (*informal*), genial, happy, jolly, joyful, light-hearted, sunny, upbeat (*informal*)

mourning noun **1** = **grieving**, bereavement, grief, keening, lamentation, weeping, woe **2** = **black**, sackcloth and ashes, weeds, widow's weeds

mouth noun **1** = **lips**, chops (*slang*), gob (*slang, especially Brit.*), jaws, maw, trap (*slang*), yap (*slang*) **2** *Informal* = **boasting**, braggadocio, bragging, empty talk, gas (*informal*), hot air (*slang*), idle talk **3** *Informal* = **insolence**, backchat (*informal*), cheek (*informal*), impudence, lip (*slang*), rudeness, sauce (*informal*) **4** = **opening**, aperture, cavity, crevice, door, entrance, gateway, inlet, lips, orifice, rim **5 down in** or **at the mouth** = **depressed**, blue, crestfallen, dejected, disheartened, dispirited, down, downcast, down in the dumps (*informal*), in low spirits, melancholy, miserable, sad, sick as a parrot (*informal*), unhappy

mouthful noun = **taste**, bit, bite, drop, forkful, little, morsel, sample, sip, spoonful, sup, swallow

mouthpiece noun **1** = **spokesperson**, agent, delegate, representative, spokesman or spokeswoman **2** = **publication**, journal, organ, periodical

movable adjective = **portable**, detachable, mobile, not fixed, portative, transferable, transportable

move verb **1** = **go**, advance, budge, change position, drift, march, proceed, progress, shift, stir, walk **2** = **change**, carry, shift, switch, transfer, transport, transpose **3** = **relocate**, change residence, flit (*Scot. & Northern English dialect*), go away, leave, migrate, move house, pack one's bags (*informal*), quit, remove **4** = **drive**, activate, impel, motivate, operate, prod, propel,

push, set going, shift, shove, start, turn **5** = **prompt**, actuate, cause, give rise to, impel, incite, induce, influence, inspire, instigate, lead, motivate, persuade, rouse, stimulate, urge **6** = **touch**, affect, agitate, excite, impress, make an impression on, tug at (someone's) heartstrings (*often facetious*) **7** = **propose**, advocate, put forward, recommend, suggest, urge
♦ noun **8** = **action**, act, deed, manoeuvre, measure, motion, movement, ploy, shift, step, stratagem, stroke, turn **9** = **transfer**, change of address, flit (*Scot. & Northern English dialect*), flitting (*Scot. & Northern English dialect*), migration, relocation, removal, shift **10 get a move on** = **speed up**, get cracking (*informal*), get going, hurry (up), make haste, shake a leg (*informal*), step on it (*informal*), stir oneself **11 on the move** *Informal* **a** = **in transit**, journeying, moving, on the road (*informal*), on the run, on the wing, travelling, under way, voyaging **b** = **active**, advancing, astir, going forward, moving, progressing, stirring, succeeding
➤ **Antonyms**
verb ≠**prompt**: deter, discourage, dissuade, prevent, stop

movement noun **1** = **motion**, act, action, activity, advance, agitation, change, development, displacement, exercise, flow, gesture, manoeuvre, move, moving, operation, progress, progression, shift, steps, stir, stirring, transfer **2** = **group**, camp, campaign, crusade, drive, faction, front, grouping, organization, party **3** = **trend**, current, drift, flow, swing, tendency **4** *Music* = **section**, division, part, passage **5** = **workings**, action, innards (*informal*), machinery, mechanism, works **6** = **rhythm**, beat, cadence, measure (*Prosody*), metre, pace, swing, tempo

movie noun = **film**, feature, flick (*slang*), picture

moving adjective **1** = **emotional**, affecting, arousing, emotive, exciting, impelling, impressive, inspiring, pathetic, persuasive, poignant, stirring, touching **2** = **mobile**, motile, movable, portable, running, unfixed
➤ **Antonyms**
≠**emotional**: unemotional, unexciting, unimpressive, uninspiring ≠**mobile**: fixed, immobile, immovable, stationary, still, unmoving

mow verb = **cut**, crop, scythe, shear, trim

mow down verb = **massacre**, blow away (*slang, chiefly U.S.*), butcher, cut down, cut to pieces, shoot down, slaughter

much adjective **1** = **great**, abundant, a lot

of, ample, considerable, copious, plenteous, plenty of, sizable *or* sizeable, substantial ♦ *noun* **2 = a lot**, a good deal, a great deal, an appreciable amount, heaps (*informal*), loads (*informal*), lots (*informal*), plenty ♦ *adverb* **3 = greatly**, a great deal, a lot, considerably, decidedly, exceedingly, frequently, indeed, often, regularly
➤ **Antonyms**
adjective ≠**great**: inadequate, insufficient, little, scant ♦ *noun* ≠**a lot**: hardly anything, little, next to nothing, not a lot, not much, practically nothing, very little ♦ *adverb* ≠**greatly**: barely, hardly, infrequently, irregularly, not a lot, not much, occasionally, only just, rarely, scarcely, seldom, slightly

muck *noun* **1 = dirt**, crap (*slang*), crud (*slang*), filth, grot (*slang*), gunge (*informal*), gunk (*informal*), kak (*S. African informal*), mire, mud, ooze, scum, sewage, shit (*taboo slang*), slime, slob (*Irish*), sludge **2 = manure**, crap (*taboo slang*), dung, ordure, shit (*taboo slang*) **3 make a muck of** *Slang* **= spoil**, blow (*slang*), botch, bungle, cock up (*Brit. slang*), flub (*U.S. slang*), fuck up (*offensive taboo slang*), make a mess of, make a nonsense of, make a pig's ear of (*informal*), mar, mess up, muff, ruin, screw up (*informal*)

muck up *verb* **= ruin**, blow (*slang*), bodge (*informal*), botch, bungle, cock up (*Brit. slang*), flub (*U.S. slang*), fuck up (*offensive taboo slang*), make a mess of, make a muck of (*slang*), make a nonsense of, make a pig's ear of (*informal*), mar, mess up, muff, screw up (*informal*), spoil

mucky *adjective* **= dirty**, begrimed, filthy, grimy, messy, muddy

mud *noun* **= dirt**, clay, gloop (*informal*), mire, ooze, silt, slime, slob (*Irish*), sludge

muddle *noun* **1 = confusion**, chaos, clutter, daze, disarray, disorder, disorganization, fankle (*Scot.*), hodgepodge (*U.S.*), hotchpotch, jumble, mess, mix-up, perplexity, pig's breakfast (*informal*), plight, predicament, ravel, tangle ♦ *verb* **2 = jumble**, confuse, disarrange, disorder, disorganize, make a mess of, mess, mix up, ravel, scramble, spoil, tangle **3 = confuse**, befuddle, bewilder, confound, daze, disorient, perplex, stupefy

muddled *adjective* **1 = jumbled**, chaotic, confused, disarrayed, disordered, disorganized, higgledy-piggledy (*informal*), messy, mixed-up, scrambled, tangled **2 = bewildered**, at sea, befuddled, confused, dazed, disoriented, perplexed, stupefied, vague **3 = incoherent**, confused, loose, muddleheaded, unclear, woolly

➤ **Antonyms**
≠**jumbled**: cut-and-dried (*informal*), orderly, organized ≠**incoherent**: clear, exact, precise

muddy *adjective* **1 = dirty**, bespattered, clarty (*Scot., & Northern English dialect*), grimy, mucky, mud-caked, soiled **2 = boggy**, marshy, miry, quaggy, swampy **3 = dull**, blurred, dingy, flat, lustreless, smoky, unclear, washed-out **4 = cloudy**, dirty, foul, impure, opaque, turbid **5 = confused**, fuzzy, hazy, indistinct, muddled, unclear, vague, woolly ♦ *verb* **6 = smear**, begrime, bespatter, cloud, dirty, smirch, soil

muffle *verb* **1 = deaden**, dull, gag, hush, muzzle, quieten, silence, soften, stifle, suppress **2 = wrap up**, cloak, conceal, cover, disguise, envelop, hood, mask, shroud, swaddle, swathe

muffled *adjective* **= indistinct**, dim, dull, faint, muted, stifled, strangled, subdued, suppressed

mug[1] *noun* **= cup**, beaker, flagon, jug, pot, stein, tankard, toby jug

mug[2] *noun* **1 = face**, countenance, features, visage **2 = fool**, chump (*informal*), easy *or* soft touch (*slang*), simpleton, sucker (*slang*)

mug[3] *verb* **= attack**, assault, beat up, rob, set about *or* upon

muggy *adjective* **= humid**, clammy, close, damp, moist, oppressive, sticky, stuffy, sultry

mug up *verb* **= study**, bone up on (*informal*), burn the midnight oil (*informal*), cram (*informal*), get up (*informal*), swot (*Brit. informal*)

mull *verb* **= ponder**, consider, contemplate, deliberate, examine, meditate, muse on, reflect on, review, ruminate, study, think about, think over, turn over in one's mind, weigh

multifarious *adjective* **= diverse**, different, diversified, legion, manifold, many, miscellaneous, multiform, multiple, multitudinous, numerous, sundry, varied, variegated

multiple *adjective* **= many**, collective, manifold, multitudinous, numerous, several, sundry, various

multiply *verb* **1 = increase**, accumulate, augment, build up, expand, extend, proliferate, spread **2 = reproduce**, breed, propagate
➤ **Antonyms**
≠**increase**: abate, decline, decrease, diminish, lessen, reduce

multitude *noun* **1 = mass**, army,

assemblage, assembly, collection, concourse, congregation, crowd, great number, horde, host, legion, lot, lots (*informal*), mob, myriad, sea, swarm, throng **2 = public**, commonalty, common people, herd, hoi polloi, mob, populace, proletariat, rabble

munch *verb* = **chew**, champ, chomp, crunch, masticate, scrunch

mundane *adjective* **1 = ordinary**, banal, commonplace, day-to-day, everyday, humdrum, prosaic, routine, vanilla (*slang*), workaday **2 = earthly**, fleshly, human, material, mortal, secular, sublunary, temporal, terrestrial, worldly
➤ **Antonyms**
≠**ordinary**: dramatic, exciting, extraordinary, ground-breaking, imaginative, interesting, left-field (*informal*), novel, original, special, uncommon, unusual ≠**earthly**: ethereal, heavenly, spiritual, unworldly

municipal *adjective* = **civic**, borough, city, community, public, town, urban

municipality *noun* = **town**, borough, burgh (*Scot.*), city, district, township, urban community

munificence *noun* = **generosity**, beneficence, benevolence, big-heartedness, bounteousness, bounty, generousness, largesse *or* largess, liberality, magnanimousness, open-handedness, philanthropy

munificent *adjective* = **generous**, beneficent, benevolent, big-hearted, bounteous, bountiful, free-handed, lavish, liberal, magnanimous, open-handed, philanthropic, princely, rich, unstinting
➤ **Antonyms**
cheap, mean, miserly, parsimonious, small, stingy

murder *noun* **1 = killing**, assassination, bloodshed, butchery, carnage, homicide, manslaughter, massacre, slaying **2** *Informal* = **agony**, an ordeal, a trial, danger, difficulty, hell (*informal*), misery, trouble ♦ *verb* **3 = kill**, assassinate, blow away (*slang, chiefly U.S.*), bump off (*slang*), butcher, destroy, dispatch, do in (*informal*), do to death, eliminate (*slang*), hit (*slang*), massacre, rub out (*U.S. slang*), slaughter, slay, take out (*slang*), take the life of, waste (*informal*) **4 = ruin**, abuse, butcher, destroy, mangle, mar, misuse, spoil **5** *Informal* = **beat decisively**, blow out of the water (*slang*), cream (*slang, chiefly U.S.*), defeat utterly, drub, hammer (*informal*), lick (*informal*), make mincemeat of (*informal*), slaughter, stuff (*slang*), tank (*slang*), thrash, wipe the floor with (*informal*)

murderer *noun* = **killer**, assassin, butcher, cut-throat, hit man (*slang*), homicide, slaughterer, slayer

murderous *adjective* **1 = deadly**, barbarous, bloodthirsty, bloody, brutal, cruel, cut-throat, death-dealing, destructive, devastating, fatal, fell (*archaic*), ferocious, internecine, lethal, sanguinary, savage, slaughterous, withering **2** *Informal* = **unpleasant**, arduous, dangerous, difficult, exhausting, harrowing, hellish (*informal*), killing (*informal*), sapping, strenuous

murky *adjective* = **dark**, cheerless, cloudy, dim, dismal, dreary, dull, dusky, foggy, gloomy, grey, impenetrable, misty, nebulous, obscure, overcast
➤ **Antonyms**
bright, cheerful, clear, distinct, sunny

murmur *verb* **1 = mumble**, babble, buzz, drone, hum, mutter, purr, rumble, speak in an undertone, whisper **2 = grumble**, beef (*slang*), carp, cavil, complain, gripe (*informal*), grouse, moan (*informal*) ♦ *noun* **3 = drone**, babble, buzzing, humming, mumble, muttering, purr, rumble, susurrus (*literary*), undertone, whisper, whispering **4 = complaint**, beef (*slang*), gripe (*informal*), grouse, grumble, moan (*informal*), word

muscle *noun* **1 = tendon**, muscle tissue, sinew, thew **2 = strength**, brawn, clout (*informal*), force, forcefulness, might, potency, power, stamina, sturdiness, weight ♦ *verb* **3 muscle in** *Informal* = **impose oneself**, butt in, elbow one's way in, force one's way in

muscular *adjective* = **strong**, athletic, beefy (*informal*), brawny, husky (*informal*), lusty, powerful, powerfully built, robust, sinewy, stalwart, strapping, sturdy, thickset, vigorous, well-knit

muse *verb* = **ponder**, be in a brown study, be lost in thought, brood, cogitate, consider, contemplate, deliberate, dream, meditate, mull over, reflect, ruminate, speculate, think, think over, weigh

mushroom *verb* = **expand**, boom, burgeon, flourish, grow rapidly, increase, luxuriate, proliferate, shoot up, spread, spring up, sprout

mushy *adjective* **1 = soft**, pulpy, semi-solid, slushy, squashy, squelchy, squidgy (*informal*) **2** *Informal* = **sentimental**, icky (*informal*), maudlin, mawkish, saccharine, schmaltzy (*slang*), sloppy (*informal*), slushy (*informal*)

musical *adjective* = **melodious**, dulcet, euphonic, euphonious, harmonious,

lilting, lyrical, melodic, sweet-sounding, tuneful
➤ **Antonyms**
discordant, grating, harsh, unmelodious, unmusical

musing noun = **thinking**, absent-mindedness, abstraction, brown study, cerebration, cogitation, contemplation, day-dreaming, dreaming, introspection, meditation, reflection, reverie, rumination, woolgathering

must noun = **necessity**, duty, essential, fundamental, imperative, necessary thing, obligation, prerequisite, requirement, requisite, sine qua non

muster verb 1 = **assemble**, call together, call up, collect, come together, congregate, convene, convoke, enrol, gather, group, marshal, meet, mobilize, rally, round up, summon ♦ noun 2 = **assembly**, assemblage, collection, concourse, congregation, convention, convocation, gathering, meeting, mobilization, rally, roundup 3 **pass muster** = **be acceptable**, be or come up to scratch, fill the bill (informal), make the grade, measure up, qualify

musty adjective 1 = **stale**, airless, dank, decayed, frowsty, fusty, mildewed, mildewy, mouldy, old, smelly, stuffy 2 = **old-fashioned**, ancient, antediluvian, antiquated, banal, clichéd, dull, hackneyed, hoary, moth-eaten, obsolete, stale, threadbare, trite, worn-out
➤ **Antonyms**
≠old-fashioned: current, exciting, fashionable, fresh, imaginative, interesting, lively, modern, modish, new, novel, original, unusual, up-to-date, with it (informal)

mutability noun = **change**, alteration, evolution, metamorphosis, transition, variation, vicissitude

mutable adjective = **changeable**, adaptable, alterable, changing, fickle, flexible, inconsistent, inconstant, irresolute, uncertain, undependable, unreliable, unsettled, unstable, unsteady, vacillating, variable, volatile, wavering

mutation noun 1 = **change**, alteration, deviation, evolution, metamorphosis, modification, transfiguration, transformation, variation 2 = **mutant**, anomaly, deviant

mute adjective 1 = **silent**, aphasiac, aphasic, aphonic, dumb, mum, speechless, unexpressed, unspeaking, unspoken, voiceless, wordless ♦ verb 2 = **muffle**, dampen, deaden, lower, moderate, soften, soft-pedal, subdue, tone down, turn down

mutilate verb 1 = **maim**, amputate, butcher, cripple, cut to pieces, cut up, damage, disable, disfigure, dismember, hack, injure, lacerate, lame, mangle 2 = **distort**, adulterate, bowdlerize, butcher, censor, cut, damage, expurgate, hack, mar, spoil

mutinous adjective = **rebellious**, bolshie (Brit. informal), contumacious, disobedient, insubordinate, insurgent, refractory, revolutionary, riotous, seditious, subversive, turbulent, ungovernable, unmanageable, unruly

mutiny noun 1 = **rebellion**, defiance, disobedience, insubordination, insurrection, refusal to obey orders, resistance, revolt, revolution, riot, rising, strike, uprising ♦ verb 2 = **rebel**, be insubordinate, defy authority, disobey, refuse to obey orders, resist, revolt, rise up, strike

mutter verb = **grumble**, complain, grouch (informal), grouse, mumble, murmur, rumble

mutual adjective = **shared**, common, communal, correlative, interactive, interchangeable, interchanged, joint, reciprocal, reciprocated, requited, returned

muzzle noun 1 = **jaws**, mouth, nose, snout 2 = **gag**, guard ♦ verb 3 = **suppress**, censor, choke, curb, gag, restrain, silence, stifle

myopic adjective = **short-sighted**, near-sighted

myriad adjective 1 = **innumerable**, a thousand and one, countless, immeasurable, incalculable, multitudinous, untold ♦ noun 2 = **multitude**, a million, army, a thousand, flood, horde, host, millions, mountain, scores, sea, swarm, thousands

mysterious adjective 1 = **strange**, abstruse, arcane, baffling, concealed, cryptic, curious, Delphic, enigmatic, hidden, impenetrable, incomprehensible, inexplicable, inscrutable, insoluble, mystical, mystifying, obscure, perplexing, puzzling, recondite, secret, sphinxlike, uncanny, unfathomable, unknown, veiled, weird 2 = **secretive**, cloak-and-dagger, covert, furtive
➤ **Antonyms**
apparent, clear, manifest, open, plain

mystery noun = **puzzle**, cloak and dagger, closed book, conundrum, enigma, problem, question, riddle, secrecy, secret, teaser

mystic, mystical adjective = **supernatural**, abstruse, arcane, cabalistic, cryptic, enigmatical, esoteric, hidden, inscrutable, metaphysical, mysterious, nonrational, occult, otherworldly, paranormal, preternatural, transcendental

mystify *verb* = **puzzle**, baffle, bamboozle (*informal*), be all Greek to (*informal*), beat (*slang*), befog, bewilder, confound, confuse, elude, escape, flummox, nonplus, perplex, stump

mystique *noun* = **fascination**, awe, charisma, charm, glamour, magic, spell

myth *noun* **1** = **legend**, allegory, fable, fairy story, fiction, folk tale, parable, saga, story, tradition, urban legend, urban myth **2** = **illusion**, delusion, fancy, fantasy, figment, imagination, superstition, tall story

mythical *adjective* **1** = **legendary**, allegorical, chimerical, fabled, fabulous, fairy-tale, mythological, storied **2** = **imaginary**, fabricated, fanciful, fantasy, fictitious, invented, made-up, make-believe, nonexistent, pretended, unreal, untrue

mythological *adjective* = **legendary**, fabulous, mythic, mythical, traditional

mythology *noun* = **legend**, folklore, folk tales, lore, mythos, myths, stories, tradition

N n

nab *verb* = **catch**, apprehend, arrest, capture, catch in the act, collar (*informal*), feel one's collar (*slang*), grab, lift (*slang*), nail (*informal*), nick (*slang, chiefly Brit.*), seize, snatch

nadir *noun* = **bottom**, depths, lowest point, minimum, rock bottom, zero
➤ **Antonyms**
acme, apex, climax, crest, height, high point, peak, pinnacle, summit, top, vertex, zenith

naevus *noun* = **birthmark**, mole

naff *adjective Brit. slang* = **bad**, duff (*Brit. informal*), inferior, low-grade, pants (*slang*), poor, rubbishy, second-rate, shabby, shoddy, substandard, trashy, worthless
➤ **Antonyms**
excellent, exceptional, fine, first-class, first-rate, high-quality, superior

nag[1] *verb* **1** = **scold**, annoy, badger, bend someone's ear (*informal*), be on one's back (*slang*), berate, breathe down someone's neck, chivvy, goad, harass, harry, hassle (*informal*), henpeck, irritate, nark (*Brit., Austral., & N.Z. slang*), pester, plague, provoke, torment, upbraid, vex, worry ♦ *noun* **2** = **scold**, harpy, shrew, tartar, termagant, virago

nag[2] *noun* = **horse**, hack, jade, plug (*U.S.*)

nagging *adjective* = **irritating**, continuous, critical, distressing, on someone's back (*informal*), painful, persistent, scolding, shrewish, worrying

nail *verb* = **fasten**, attach, beat, fix, hammer, join, pin, secure, tack

naive *adjective* **1** = **gullible**, as green as grass, callow, credulous, green, unsuspicious, wet behind the ears (*informal*) **2** = **innocent**, artless, candid, childlike, confiding, frank, guileless, ingenuous, jejune, natural, open, simple, trusting, unaffected, unpretentious, unsophisticated, unworldly
➤ **Antonyms**
≠**innocent**: artful, disingenuous, experienced, sly, sophisticated, urbane, worldly, worldly-wise

naivety, naïveté *noun* **1** = **gullibility**, callowness, credulity **2** = **innocence**, artlessness, candour, frankness, guilelessness, inexperience,

ingenuousness, naturalness, openness, simplicity

naked *adjective* **1** = **nude**, bare, buck naked (*slang*), denuded, disrobed, divested, exposed, in one's birthday suit (*informal*), in the altogether (*informal*), in the bare scud (*slang*), in the buff (*informal*), in the raw (*informal*), naked as the day one was born (*informal*), scuddy (*slang*), starkers (*informal*), stripped, unclothed, uncovered, undraped, undressed, without a stitch on (*informal*) **2** = **undisguised**, blatant, evident, manifest, open, overt, patent, plain, simple, stark, unadorned, unconcealed, unexaggerated, unmistakable, unqualified, unvarnished
➤ **Antonyms**
≠**nude**: clothed, concealed, covered, dressed, wrapped up ≠**undisguised**: concealed, disguised

nakedness *noun* **1** = **nudity**, baldness, bareness, undress **2** = **openness**, plainness, simplicity, starkness

namby-pamby *adjective* = **feeble**, anaemic, boneless, colourless, insipid, mawkish, niminy-piminy, prim, prissy (*informal*), sentimental, spineless, vapid, weak, weedy (*informal*), wimpish or wimpy (*informal*), wishy-washy (*informal*), wussy (*slang*)

name *noun* **1** = **title**, appellation, cognomen, denomination, designation, epithet, handle (*slang*), moniker or monicker (*slang*), nickname, sobriquet, term **2** = **fame**, distinction, eminence, esteem, honour, note, praise, renown, repute **3** = **reputation**, character, credit ♦ *verb* **4** = **call**, baptize, christen, denominate, dub, entitle, label, style, term **5** = **nominate**, appoint, choose, cite, classify, commission, designate, flag, identify, mention, select, specify

named *adjective* **1** = **called**, baptized, christened, denominated, dubbed, entitled, known as, labelled, styled, termed **2** = **nominated**, appointed, chosen, cited, classified, commissioned, designated, identified, mentioned, picked, selected, singled out, specified

nameless *adjective* **1** = **anonymous**, innominate, undesignated, unnamed, untitled **2** = **unknown**, incognito, obscure,

undistinguished, unheard-of, unsung **3**
= **horrible**, abominable, indescribable,
ineffable, inexpressible, unmentionable,
unspeakable, unutterable

namely *adverb* = **specifically**, i.e., that is to
say, to wit, viz.

nap¹ *noun* **1** = **sleep**, catnap, forty winks
(*informal*), kip (*Brit. slang*), rest, shuteye
(*slang*), siesta, zizz (*Brit. informal*) ♦ *verb* **2**
= **sleep**, catnap, doze, drop off (*informal*),
drowse, kip (*Brit. slang*), nod, nod off
(*informal*), rest, snooze (*informal*), zizz
(*Brit. informal*)

nap² *noun* = **weave**, down, fibre, grain, pile,
shag

napkin *noun* = **serviette**, cloth

narcissism *noun* = **egotism**,
self-admiration, self-love, vanity

narcotic *noun* **1** = **drug**, anaesthetic,
analgesic, anodyne, opiate, painkiller,
sedative, tranquillizer ♦ *adjective* **2**
= **sedative**, analgesic, calming, dulling,
hypnotic, Lethean, numbing, painkilling,
somnolent, soporific, stupefacient,
stupefactive, stupefying

nark *verb* = **annoy**, aggravate (*informal*),
bother, bug, exasperate, gall, get on one's
nerves (*informal*), irk, irritate, miff
(*informal*), nettle, peeve, pique, piss one
off (*taboo slang*), provoke, rile

narrate *verb* = **tell**, chronicle, describe,
detail, recite, recount, rehearse, relate,
repeat, report, set forth, unfold

narration *noun* = **telling**, description,
explanation, reading, recital, rehearsal,
relation, storytelling, voice-over (*in film*)

narrative *noun* = **story**, account, chronicle,
detail, history, report, statement, tale

narrator *noun* = **storyteller**, annalist,
author, bard, chronicler, commentator,
raconteur, reciter, relater, reporter, writer

narrow *adjective* **1** = **thin**, attenuated, fine,
slender, slim, spare, tapering **2** = **limited**,
circumscribed, close, confined,
constricted, contracted, cramped,
incapacious, meagre, near, pinched,
restricted, scanty, straitened, tight **3**
= **exclusive**, select **4** = **insular**, biased,
bigoted, dogmatic, illiberal, intolerant,
narrow-minded, partial, prejudiced,
puritan, reactionary, small-minded ♦ *verb*
5 = **tighten**, circumscribe, constrict,
diminish, limit, reduce, simplify, straiten
➤ **Antonyms**
adjective ≠**thin**: broad, wide ≠**limited**:
ample, big, broad, generous, open,
spacious, wide ≠**insular**: broad-minded,
generous, liberal, receptive, tolerant

narrowly *adverb* = **just**, barely, by a

whisker *or* hair's-breadth, by the skin of
one's teeth, only just, scarcely

narrow-minded *adjective* = **intolerant**,
biased, bigoted, conservative, hidebound,
illiberal, insular, opinionated, parochial,
petty, prejudiced, provincial, reactionary,
short-sighted, small-minded, strait-laced
➤ **Antonyms**
broad-minded, catholic, cosmopolitan,
freethinking, indulgent, open-minded,
permissive, tolerant, unprejudiced

narrows *plural noun* = **channel**, gulf,
passage, sound, straits

nastiness *noun* = **unpleasantness**,
disagreeableness, malice, meanness,
offensiveness, spitefulness

nasty *adjective* **1** = **objectionable**, dirty,
disagreeable, disgusting, filthy, foul, grotty
(*slang*), horrible, loathsome, malodorous,
mephitic, nauseating, noisome,
obnoxious, odious, offensive, polluted,
repellent, repugnant, sickening,
unappetizing, unpleasant, vile, yucky *or*
yukky (*slang*) **2** = **painful**, bad, critical,
dangerous, serious, severe **3** = **spiteful**,
abusive, annoying, bad-tempered,
despicable, disagreeable, distasteful,
malicious, mean, unpleasant, vicious, vile
➤ **Antonyms**
≠**objectionable**: admirable, agreeable,
enjoyable, nice, pleasant, sweet ≠**spiteful**:
decent, kind, nice, pleasant, sweet

nation *noun* = **country**, commonwealth,
community, people, population, race,
realm, society, state, tribe

national *adjective* **1** = **nationwide**, civil,
countrywide, governmental, public, state,
widespread **2** = **domestic**, internal, social
♦ *noun* **3** = **citizen**, inhabitant, native,
resident, subject

nationalism *noun* = **patriotism**,
allegiance, chauvinism, fealty, jingoism,
loyalty, nationality

nationality *noun* = **race**, birth, ethnic
group, nation

nationwide *adjective* = **national**,
countrywide, general, overall, widespread

native *adjective* **1** = **local**, domestic, home,
home-grown, home-made, indigenous,
mother, vernacular **2** = **original**, genuine,
real **3** = **inborn**, built-in, congenital,
endemic, hereditary, immanent, inbred,
ingrained, inherent, inherited, innate,
instinctive, intrinsic, inveterate, natal,
natural **4** = **indigenous**, aboriginal,
autochthonous ♦ *noun* **5** = **inhabitant**,
aborigine, autochthon, citizen,
countryman, dweller, national, resident

nativity *noun* **1** = **birth**, delivery,

parturition **2 = crèche**, manger scene
➤ Antonyms
≠**birth**: death, demise, dying, expiration
natter verb **1 = gossip**, blather, blether, chatter, chew the fat or rag (slang), gabble, jabber, jaw (slang), palaver, prate, prattle, rabbit (on) (Brit. informal), run off at the mouth (slang), shoot the breeze (informal), talk, talk idly, witter (informal) ♦ noun **2 = gossip**, blather, blether, chat, chinwag (Brit. informal), chitchat, confabulation, conversation, gab (informal), gabble, gabfest (informal, chiefly U.S. & Canad.), jabber, jaw (slang), palaver, prattle, talk

natty adjective **= smart**, chic, crucial (slang), dapper, elegant, fashionable, neat, snazzy (informal), spruce, stylish, trendy (Brit. informal), trim, well-dressed, well-turned-out

natural adjective **1 = normal**, common, everyday, legitimate, logical, ordinary, regular, typical, usual **2 = unaffected**, artless, candid, frank, genuine, ingenuous, open, real, simple, spontaneous, unpretentious, unsophisticated, unstudied **3 = innate**, characteristic, congenital, essential, immanent, inborn, indigenous, inherent, in one's blood, instinctive, intuitive, natal, native **4 = pure**, organic, plain, unbleached, unmixed, unpolished, unrefined, whole
➤ Antonyms
≠**normal**: abnormal, irregular, out of the ordinary, strange, untypical ≠**unaffected**: affected, artificial, assumed, counterfeit, feigned, phoney or phony (informal), unnatural ≠**pure**: manufactured, processed, synthetic, unnatural

naturalism noun **= realism**, factualism, verisimilitude

naturalist noun **1 = biologist**, botanist, ecologist, zoologist **2 = realist**, factualist

naturalistic adjective **= realistic**, lifelike, true-to-life

naturalize verb **= adopt**, acclimate, acclimatize, acculturate, accustom, adapt, domesticate, enfranchise, familiarize, grant citizenship, habituate

naturally adverb **1 = of course**, absolutely, as a matter of course, certainly **2 = genuinely**, as anticipated, customarily, informally, normally, simply, spontaneously, typically, unaffectedly, unpretentiously

nature noun **1 = creation**, cosmos, earth, environment, universe, world **2 = make-up**, attributes, character, complexion, constitution, essence, features, quality, traits **3 = kind**, category,

description, sort, species, style, type, variety **4 = temperament**, disposition, humour, mood, outlook, temper **5 = country**, countryside, landscape, natural history, scenery

naturist noun **= nudist**

naughty adjective **1 = disobedient**, annoying, bad, exasperating, fractious, impish, misbehaved, mischievous, perverse, playful, refractory, roguish, sinful, teasing, wayward, wicked, worthless **2 = obscene**, bawdy, blue, improper, lewd, off-colour, ribald, risqué, smutty, vulgar, X-rated (informal)
➤ Antonyms
≠**disobedient**: good, obedient, polite, proper, seemly, well-behaved, well-mannered ≠**obscene**: polite, proper

nausea noun **1 = sickness**, biliousness, qualm(s), queasiness, retching, squeamishness, vomiting **2 = disgust**, abhorrence, aversion, loathing, odium, repugnance, revulsion

nauseate verb **= sicken**, disgust, gross out (U.S. slang), horrify, offend, repel, repulse, revolt, turn one's stomach

nauseous adjective **= sickening**, abhorrent, disgusting, distasteful, nauseating, offensive, repugnant, repulsive, revolting

nautical adjective **= maritime**, marine, naval, oceanic, seafaring, seagoing, yachting

naval adjective **= nautical**, marine, maritime, oceanic

navel noun **= umbilicus**, bellybutton (informal), omphalos (literary)

navigable adjective **1 = passable**, clear, negotiable, traversable, unobstructed **2 = sailable**, controllable, dirigible, steerable

navigate verb **= sail**, con (Nautical), cross, cruise, direct, drive, guide, handle, journey, manoeuvre, pilot, plan, plot, skipper, steer, voyage

navigation noun **= sailing**, cruising, helmsmanship, pilotage, seamanship, steering, voyaging

navigator noun **= pilot**, mariner, seaman

navvy noun **= labourer**, ganger, worker, workman

navy noun **= fleet**, argosy (archaic), armada, flotilla, warships

near adjective **1 = close**, adjacent, adjoining, a hop, skip and a jump away (informal), alongside, at close quarters, beside, bordering, close by, contiguous, just round the corner, nearby, neighbouring, proximate, touching, within sniffing distance (informal) **2 = forthcoming**, approaching, imminent, impending, in the offing, looming, near-at-hand, next, nigh, on the cards (*informal*), upcoming **3 = intimate**, akin, allied, attached, connected, dear, familiar, related

➤ **Antonyms**

≠**close**: distant, far, faraway, far-flung, far-off, far-removed, outlying, out-of-the-way, remote, removed ≠**forthcoming**: distant, faraway, far-off, remote ≠**intimate**: distant, remote

nearby *adjective* **1 = neighbouring**, adjacent, adjoining, convenient, handy ♦ *adverb* **2 = close at hand**, at close quarters, just round the corner, not far away, proximate, within reach, within sniffing distance (*informal*)

nearly *adverb* **= almost**, about, all but, approaching, approximately, as good as, closely, just about, not quite, practically, roughly, virtually, well-nigh

nearness *noun* **1 = closeness**, accessibility, availability, contiguity, handiness, juxtaposition, propinquity, proximity, vicinity **2 = immediacy**, imminence **3 = intimacy**, dearness, familiarity

near-sighted *adjective* **= short-sighted**, myopic

near thing *noun* **= narrow escape**, close shave (*informal*), near miss

neat *adjective* **1 = tidy**, accurate, dainty, fastidious, methodical, nice, orderly, shipshape, smart, spick-and-span, spruce, straight, systematic, trim, uncluttered **2 = elegant**, adept, adroit, agile, apt, clever, deft, dexterous, efficient, effortless, expert, graceful, handy, nimble, practised, precise, skilful, stylish, well-judged **3** *Of alcoholic drinks* **= undiluted**, pure, straight, unmixed

➤ **Antonyms**

≠**tidy**: clumsy, cluttered, disarrayed, disorderly, disorganized, messy, slobby (*informal*), sloppy (*informal*), untidy ≠**elegant**: awful, bad, clumsy, incompetent, inefficient, inelegant, terrible

neatly *adverb* **1 = tidily**, accurately, daintily, fastidiously, methodically, nicely, smartly, sprucely, systematically **2 = elegantly**, adeptly, adroitly, agilely, aptly, cleverly, deftly, dexterously, efficiently, effortlessly, expertly, gracefully, handily, nimbly, precisely, skilfully, stylishly

neatness *noun* **1 = tidiness**, accuracy, daintiness, fastidiousness, methodicalness, niceness, nicety, orderliness, smartness, spruceness, straightness, trimness **2 = elegance**, adeptness, adroitness, agility, aptness, cleverness, deftness, dexterity, efficiency, effortlessness, expertness, grace, gracefulness, handiness,

nimbleness, preciseness, precision, skilfulness, skill, style, stylishness

nebulous *adjective* **= vague**, ambiguous, amorphous, cloudy, confused, dim, hazy, imprecise, indefinite, indeterminate, indistinct, misty, murky, obscure, shadowy, shapeless, uncertain, unclear, unformed

necessarily *adverb* **= certainly**, accordingly, automatically, axiomatically, by definition, compulsorily, consequently, incontrovertibly, ineluctably, inevitably, inexorably, irresistibly, naturally, *nolens volens*, of course, of necessity, perforce, undoubtedly, willy-nilly

necessary *adjective* **1 = needed**, compulsory, *de rigueur*, essential, imperative, indispensable, mandatory, needful, obligatory, required, requisite, vital **2 = certain**, fated, inescapable, inevitable, inexorable, unavoidable

➤ **Antonyms**

≠**needed**: dispensable, expendable, inessential, nonessential, superfluous, unnecessary ≠**certain**: unnecessary

necessitate *verb* **= compel**, call for, coerce, constrain, demand, entail, force, impel, make necessary, oblige, require

necessities *plural noun* **= essentials**, exigencies, fundamentals, indispensables, needs, requirements

necessity *noun* **1 = inevitability**, compulsion, destiny, fate, inexorableness, obligation **2 = essential**, desideratum, fundamental, necessary, need, prerequisite, requirement, requisite, *sine qua non*, want **3 = needfulness**, demand, exigency, indispensability, need, requirement **4 = poverty**, destitution, extremity, indigence, need, penury, privation

necromancy *noun* **= magic**, black art, black magic, demonology, divination, enchantment, sorcery, thaumaturgy (*rare*), voodoo, witchcraft, witchery, wizardry

necropolis *noun* **= cemetery**, burial ground, churchyard, God's acre, graveyard

need *verb* **1 = require**, call for, demand, entail, have occasion to *or* for, lack, miss, necessitate, want ♦ *noun* **2 = lack**, inadequacy, insufficiency, paucity, shortage **3 = requirement**, demand, desideratum, essential, necessity, requisite **4 = emergency**, exigency, necessity, obligation, urgency, want **5 = poverty**, deprivation, destitution, distress, extremity, impecuniousness, indigence, neediness, penury, privation

needed *adjective* **= necessary**, called for, desired, lacked, required, wanted

needful *adjective* = **necessary**, essential, indispensable, needed, required, requisite, stipulated, vital

needle *verb* = **irritate**, aggravate (*informal*), annoy, bait, be on one's back (*slang*), gall, get in one's hair (*informal*), get on one's nerves (*informal*), get under one's skin (*informal*), goad, harass, hassle (*informal*), irk, nag, nark (*Brit., Austral., & N.Z. slang*), nettle, pester, piss one off (*taboo slang*), prick, prod, provoke, rile, ruffle, spur, sting, taunt

needless *adjective* = **unnecessary**, causeless, dispensable, excessive, expendable, gratuitous, groundless, nonessential, pointless, redundant, superfluous, uncalled-for, undesired, unwanted, useless
➤ **Antonyms**
beneficial, essential, obligatory, required, useful

needlework *noun* = **embroidery**, fancywork, needlecraft, sewing, stitching, tailoring

needy *adjective* = **poor**, deprived, destitute, dirt-poor, disadvantaged, down at heel (*informal*), impecunious, impoverished, indigent, on the breadline (*informal*), penniless, poverty-stricken, underprivileged
➤ **Antonyms**
affluent, comfortable, moneyed, prosperous, rich, wealthy, well-off, well-to-do

ne'er-do-well *noun* = **layabout**, black sheep, good-for-nothing, idler, loafer, loser, skiver (*Brit. slang*), wastrel

nefarious *adjective* = **wicked**, abominable, atrocious, base, criminal, depraved, detestable, dreadful, evil, execrable, foul, heinous, horrible, infamous, infernal, iniquitous, monstrous, odious, opprobrious, shameful, sinful, vicious, vile, villainous
➤ **Antonyms**
admirable, good, honest, honourable, just, noble, praiseworthy, upright, virtuous

negate *verb* **1** = **invalidate**, abrogate, annul, cancel, countermand, neutralize, nullify, obviate, repeal, rescind, retract, reverse, revoke, void, wipe out **2** = **deny**, contradict, disallow, disprove, gainsay (*archaic or literary*), oppose, rebut, refute
➤ **Antonyms**
≠**deny**: affirm, assert, attest, avouch, avow, certify, confirm, declare, maintain, pronounce, ratify, state, swear, testify

negation *noun* **1** = **cancellation**, neutralization, nullification **2** = **denial**, antithesis, antonym, contradiction, contrary, converse, counterpart, disavowal, disclaimer, inverse, opposite, rejection, renunciation, reverse

negative *adjective* **1** = **contradictory**, contrary, denying, dissenting, opposing, recusant, refusing, rejecting, resisting **2** = **pessimistic**, antagonistic, colourless, contrary, cynical, gloomy, jaundiced, neutral, uncooperative, unenthusiastic, uninterested, unwilling, weak **3** = **neutralizing**, annulling, counteractive, invalidating, nullifying ♦ *noun* **4** = **contradiction**, denial, refusal
➤ **Antonyms**
adjective ≠**contradictory**: affirmative, approving, assenting, concurring, positive
≠**pessimistic**: cheerful, enthusiastic, optimistic, positive

negativeness, negativity *noun* **1** = **contradictoriness**, contradiction, contrariness, denial, dissent, opposition, recusancy, refusal, rejection, resistance **2** = **pessimism**, antagonism, colourlessness, contrariness, cynicism, gloom, neutrality, uncooperativeness, uninterestedness, unwillingness, weakness

neglect *verb* **1** = **forget**, be remiss, evade, let slide, omit, pass over, procrastinate, shirk, skimp **2** = **disregard**, contemn, discount, disdain, ignore, leave alone, overlook, pass by, rebuff, scorn, slight, spurn, turn one's back on ♦ *noun* **3** = **negligence**, carelessness, default, dereliction, failure, forgetfulness, laxity, laxness, neglectfulness, oversight, remissness, slackness, slovenliness **4** = **disregard**, disdain, disrespect, heedlessness, inattention, indifference, slight, unconcern
➤ **Antonyms**
verb ≠**disregard**: appreciate, attend to, notice, observe, regard, remember, value ♦ *noun* ≠**negligence**, **disregard**: attention, care, consideration, notice, regard, respect

neglected *adjective* **1** = **abandoned**, derelict, overgrown **2** = **disregarded**, unappreciated, underestimated, undervalued

neglectful *adjective* = **careless**, disregardful, heedless, inattentive, indifferent, lax, negligent, remiss, thoughtless, uncaring, unmindful

negligence *noun* = **carelessness**, default, dereliction, disregard, failure, forgetfulness, heedlessness, inadvertence, inattention, inattentiveness, indifference, laxity, laxness, neglect, omission, oversight, remissness, shortcoming, slackness, thoughtlessness

negligent *adjective* = **careless**, cursory,

disregardful, forgetful, heedless, inadvertent, inattentive, indifferent, neglectful, nonchalant, offhand, regardless, remiss, slack, slapdash, slipshod, thoughtless, unmindful, unthinking
➤ **Antonyms**
attentive, careful, considerate, mindful, painstaking, rigorous, thorough, thoughtful

negligible *adjective* = **insignificant**, imperceptible, inconsequential, minor, minute, nickel-and-dime (*U.S. slang*), petty, small, trifling, trivial, unimportant
➤ **Antonyms**
important, noteworthy, significant, vital

negotiable *adjective* = **debatable**, discussable *or* discussible, transactional, transferable, variable

negotiate *verb* **1** = **deal**, adjudicate, arbitrate, arrange, bargain, conciliate, confer, consult, contract, cut a deal, debate, discuss, handle, manage, mediate, parley, settle, transact, work out **2** = **get round**, clear, cross, get over, get past, pass, pass through, surmount

negotiation *noun* = **bargaining**, arbitration, debate, diplomacy, discussion, mediation, transaction, wheeling and dealing (*informal*)

negotiator *noun* = **mediator**, ambassador, delegate, diplomat, honest broker, intermediary, moderator

neighbourhood *noun* = **district**, community, confines, environs, locale, locality, precincts, proximity, purlieus, quarter, region, surroundings, vicinity

neighbouring *adjective* = **nearby**, abutting, adjacent, adjoining, bordering, connecting, contiguous, near, nearest, next, surrounding
➤ **Antonyms**
distant, far, far-off, remote

neighbourly *adjective* = **helpful**, considerate, friendly, harmonious, hospitable, kind, obliging, sociable

nemesis *noun* = **retribution**, destiny, destruction, fate, vengeance

nepotism *noun* = **favouritism**, bias, partiality, patronage, preferential treatment

nerd, nurd *noun Slang* = **bore**, anorak (*informal*), dork (*slang*), geek (*informal*), obsessive, trainspotter (*informal*), wonk (*informal*)

nerve *noun* **1** = **bravery**, balls (*taboo slang*), ballsiness (*taboo slang*), bottle (*Brit. slang*), coolness, courage, daring, determination, endurance, energy, face (*informal*), fearlessness, firmness, force, fortitude,

gameness, grit, guts (*informal*), hardihood, intrepidity, mettle, might, pluck, resolution, spirit, spunk (*informal*), steadfastness, vigour, will **2** *Informal* = **impudence**, audacity, boldness, brass (*informal*), brass neck (*Brit. informal*), brazenness, cheek (*informal*), chutzpah (*U.S. & Canad. informal*), effrontery, front, gall, impertinence, insolence, neck (*informal*), sassiness (*U.S. slang*), sauce (*informal*), temerity ♦ *verb* **3 nerve oneself** = **brace oneself**, embolden oneself, encourage oneself, fortify oneself, gee oneself up, hearten oneself, invigorate oneself, steel oneself, strengthen oneself

nerveless *adjective* **1** = **calm**, composed, controlled, cool, impassive, imperturbable, self-possessed, unemotional **2** = **fearless**, brave, courageous, daring, gutsy (*slang*), plucky, unafraid

nerve-racking *adjective* = **tense**, annoying, difficult, distressing, frightening, gut-wrenching, harassing, harrowing, maddening, stressful, trying, worrying

nerves *plural noun* = **tension**, anxiety, butterflies (in one's stomach) (*informal*), cold feet (*informal*), fretfulness, heebie-jeebies (*slang*), imbalance, nervousness, strain, stress, worry

nervous *adjective* = **apprehensive**, agitated, antsy (*informal*), anxious, edgy, excitable, fearful, fidgety, flustered, hesitant, highly strung, hyper (*informal*), hysterical, jittery (*informal*), jumpy, nervy (*Brit. informal*), neurotic, on edge, ruffled, shaky, tense, timid, timorous, twitchy (*informal*), uneasy, uptight (*informal*), weak, wired (*slang*), worried
➤ **Antonyms**
bold, calm, confident, constant, cool, equable, even, laid-back (*informal*), peaceful, relaxed, steady, together (*slang*), unfazed (*informal*)

nervous breakdown *noun* = **collapse**, breakdown, crack-up (*informal*), nervous disorder, neurasthenia (*obsolete*)

nervousness *noun* = **anxiety**, agitation, antsiness (*informal*), disquiet, excitability, fluster, perturbation, tension, timidity, touchiness, tremulousness, worry

nervy *adjective* = **anxious**, agitated, fidgety, jittery (*informal*), jumpy, nervous, on edge, tense, twitchy (*informal*)

nest *noun* = **refuge**, den, haunt, hideaway, resort, retreat, snuggery

nest egg *noun* = **reserve**, cache, deposit, fall-back, fund(s), savings, store

nestle *verb* = **snuggle**, cuddle, curl up, huddle, nuzzle

nestling *noun* = **chick**, fledgling

net[1] *noun* **1** = **mesh**, lacework, lattice, netting, network, openwork, reticulum, tracery, web ♦ *verb* **2** = **catch**, bag, capture, enmesh, ensnare, entangle, nab (*informal*), trap

net[2], **nett** *adjective* **1** = **take-home**, after taxes, clear, final **2** = **conclusive**, closing, final ♦ *verb* **3** = **earn**, accumulate, bring in, clear, gain, make, realize, reap

nether *adjective* = **lower**, basal, below, beneath, bottom, inferior, Stygian, under, underground

nether world *noun* = **hell**, Avernus, Hades, infernal regions, nether regions, underworld

nettle *verb* = **irritate**, aggravate (*informal*), annoy, chafe, exasperate, fret, gall, get on one's nerves (*informal*), goad, harass, hassle (*informal*), incense, nark (*Brit., Austral., & N.Z. slang*), pique, piss one off (*taboo slang*), provoke, ruffle, sting, tease, vex

nettled *adjective* = **irritated**, aggrieved, angry, annoyed, chafed, choked, cross, exasperated, galled, goaded, hacked (off) (*U.S. slang*), harassed, huffy, incensed, irritable, peeved, peevish, piqued, pissed (*taboo slang*), pissed off (*taboo slang*), provoked, put out, ratty (*Brit. & N.Z. informal*), riled, ruffled, stung, teased, tetchy, touchy, vexed

network *noun* = **system**, arrangement, channels, circuitry, complex, convolution, grid, grill, interconnections, labyrinth, lattice, maze, mesh, net, nexus, organization, plexus, structure, tracks, web

neurosis *noun* = **obsession**, abnormality, affliction, derangement, deviation, instability, maladjustment, mental disturbance, mental illness, phobia, psychological *or* emotional disorder

neurotic *adjective* = **unstable**, abnormal, antsy (*informal*), anxious, compulsive, deviant, disordered, distraught, disturbed, hyper (*informal*), maladjusted, manic, nervous, obsessive, overwrought, twitchy (*informal*), unhealthy
➤ **Antonyms**
calm, laid-back (*informal*), level-headed, normal, rational, sane, stable, together (*slang*), well-adjusted, well-balanced

neuter *verb* = **castrate**, doctor (*informal*), dress, emasculate, fix (*informal*), geld, spay

neutral *adjective* **1** = **unbiased**, disinterested, dispassionate, even-handed, impartial, indifferent, nonaligned, nonbelligerent, noncombatant, noncommittal, nonpartisan, sitting on the fence, unaligned, uncommitted, undecided, uninvolved, unprejudiced **2** = **indeterminate**, achromatic, colourless, dull, expressionless, indistinct, indistinguishable, intermediate, toneless, undefined
➤ **Antonyms**
≠**unbiased**: active, belligerent, biased, decided, interested, interfering, partial, participating, positive, prejudiced

neutrality *noun* = **impartiality**, detachment, disinterestedness, nonalignment, noninterference, noninterventionism, noninvolvement, nonpartisanship

neutralize *verb* = **counteract**, cancel, compensate for, counterbalance, frustrate, invalidate, negate, nullify, offset, undo

never *adverb* = **at no time**, not at all, not for love nor money (*informal*), not on your life (*informal*), not on your nelly (*Brit. slang*), no way, on no account, under no circumstances
➤ **Antonyms**
always, aye (*Scot.*), constantly, continually, every time, forever, perpetually, without exception

never-ending *adjective* = **eternal**, boundless, ceaseless, constant, continual, continuous, everlasting, incessant, interminable, nonstop, perpetual, persistent, relentless, unbroken, unceasing, unchanging, uninterrupted, unremitting

never-never *noun Informal* = **hire-purchase** (*Brit.*), H.P. (*Brit.*)

nevertheless *adverb* = **nonetheless**, but, even so, (even) though, however, notwithstanding, regardless, still, yet

new *adjective* **1** = **modern**, advanced, all-singing, all-dancing, contemporary, current, different, fresh, ground-breaking, happening (*informal*), latest, modernistic, modish, newfangled, novel, original, recent, state-of-the-art, topical, ultramodern, unfamiliar, unknown, unused, unusual, up-to-date, virgin **2** = **extra**, added, more, new-found, supplementary **3** = **changed**, altered, improved, modernized, rebranded, redesigned, renewed, restored
➤ **Antonyms**
≠**modern**: aged, ancient, antiquated, antique, hackneyed, old, old-fashioned, outmoded, passé, stale, trite

newcomer *noun* = **novice**, alien, arrival, beginner, foreigner, immigrant, incomer, Johnny-come-lately (*informal*), outsider, parvenu, settler, stranger

newfangled *adjective* = **new**, all-singing, all-dancing, contemporary, fashionable,

gimmicky, modern, new-fashioned, novel, recent, state-of-the-art
➤ **Antonyms**
antiquated, dated, obsolete, old-fashioned, outmoded, out-of-date, passé

newly *adverb* = **recently**, anew, freshly, just, lately, latterly

newness *noun* = **novelty**, freshness, innovation, oddity, originality, strangeness, unfamiliarity, uniqueness

news *noun* = **information**, account, advice, bulletin, buzz, communiqué, dirt (*U.S. slang*), disclosure, dispatch, exposé, gen (*Brit. informal*), gossip, hearsay, intelligence, latest (*informal*), leak, news flash, release, report, revelation, rumour, scandal, scuttlebutt (*U.S. slang*), statement, story, tidings, word

newsworthy *adjective* = **interesting**, arresting, important, notable, noteworthy, remarkable, significant, stimulating

next *adjective* 1 = **following**, consequent, ensuing, later, subsequent, succeeding 2 = **nearest**, adjacent, adjoining, closest, neighbouring ♦ *adverb* 3 = **afterwards**, closely, following, later, subsequently, thereafter

next world *noun* = **afterlife**, afterworld, heaven, hereafter, nirvana, paradise

nibble *verb* 1 = **bite**, eat, gnaw, munch, nip, peck, pick at ♦ *noun* 2 = **snack**, bite, crumb, morsel, peck, *soupçon*, taste, titbit

nice *adjective* 1 = **pleasant**, agreeable, attractive, charming, delightful, good, pleasurable 2 = **kind**, amiable, commendable, courteous, friendly, likable or likeable, polite, prepossessing, refined, well-mannered 3 = **neat**, dainty, fine, tidy, trim 4 = **subtle**, accurate, careful, critical, delicate, discriminating, exact, exacting, fastidious, fine, meticulous, precise, rigorous, scrupulous, strict
➤ **Antonyms**
≠**pleasant**: awful, disagreeable, dreadful, miserable, unpleasant ≠**kind**: disagreeable, mean, unfriendly, unkind, unpleasant, vulgar ≠**neat**: coarse, crude, rough, shabby, sloppy (*informal*) ≠**subtle**: careless, rough, sloppy (*informal*), vague

nicely *adverb* 1 = **pleasantly**, acceptably, agreeably, attractively, charmingly, delightfully, pleasingly, pleasurably, well 2 = **kindly**, amiably, commendably, courteously, likably, politely, prepossessingly 3 = **neatly**, daintily, finely, tidily, trimly 4 = **subtly**, accurately, carefully, critically, delicately, exactingly, exactly, fastidiously, finely, meticulously, precisely, rigorously, scrupulously, strictly

➤ **Antonyms**
≠**pleasantly**: unattractively, unpleasantly ≠**neatly**: sloppily (*informal*) ≠**subtly**: carelessly, sloppily (*informal*)

niceness *noun* 1 = **kindness**, agreeableness, amiability, attractiveness, charm, courtesy, delightfulness, friendliness, good manners, goodness, likableness or likeableness, pleasantness, pleasurableness, politeness, refinement 2 = **neatness**, daintiness, fineness, tidiness, trimness 3 = **precision**, accuracy, care, carefulness, criticalness, delicacy, discrimination, exactingness, exactitude, exactness, fastidiousness, fineness, meticulosity, meticulousness, preciseness, rigorousness, rigour, scrupulosity, scrupulousness, strictness, subtleness, subtlety

nicety *noun* 1 = **subtlety**, daintiness, delicacy, discrimination, distinction, nuance, refinement 2 = **precision**, accuracy, exactness, fastidiousness, finesse, meticulousness, minuteness

niche *noun* 1 = **alcove**, corner, hollow, nook, opening, recess 2 = **position**, calling, pigeonhole (*informal*), place, slot (*informal*), vocation

nick *verb* 1 = **cut**, chip, damage, dent, mark, notch, scar, score, scratch, snick 2 *Slang* = **steal**, finger (*slang*), knock off (*slang*), pilfer, pinch (*informal*), snitch (*slang*), swipe (*slang*) ♦ *noun* 3 = **cut**, chip, dent, mark, notch, scar, score, scratch, snick

nickname *noun* = **pet name**, diminutive, epithet, familiar name, handle (*slang*), label, moniker or monicker (*slang*), sobriquet

nifty *adjective Informal* = **neat**, agile, apt, attractive, chic, clever, deft, enjoyable, excellent, pleasing, quick, sharp, smart, spruce, stylish

niggard *noun* = **miser**, cheapskate (*informal*), cheeseparer, churl (*archaic*), meanie or meany (*informal, chiefly Brit.*), penny-pincher (*informal*), screw (*slang*), Scrooge, skinflint, tight-arse (*taboo slang*), tight-ass (*U.S. taboo slang*)

niggardliness *noun* = **miserliness**, avarice, avariciousness, closeness, covetousness, frugality, grudgingness, meanness, mercenariness, nearness (*informal*), parsimony, penuriousness, sordidness, sparingness, stinginess, thrift, tightfistedness, ungenerousness

niggardly *adjective* 1 = **stingy**, avaricious, close, covetous, frugal, grudging, mean, mercenary, miserly, near (*informal*), parsimonious, penurious, Scrooge-like,

snoep (*S. African informal*), sordid, sparing, stinging, tight-arse (*taboo slang*), tight-arsed (*taboo slang*), tight as a duck's arse (*taboo slang*), tight-ass (*U.S. taboo slang*), tight-assed (*U.S. taboo slang*), tightfisted, ungenerous **2 = paltry**, beggarly, inadequate, insufficient, meagre, mean, measly, miserable, pathetic, scant, scanty, skimpy, small, wretched
➤ **Antonyms**
≠**stingy**: bountiful, generous, lavish, liberal, munificent, prodigal ≠**paltry**: abundant, ample, bountiful, copious, generous, handsome, liberal, plentiful, profuse

niggle *verb* **1 = worry**, annoy, irritate, rankle **2 = criticize**, carp, cavil, find fault, fuss

niggling *adjective* **1 = persistent**, gnawing, irritating, troubling, worrying **2 = petty**, cavilling, finicky, fussy, insignificant, minor, nit-picking (*informal*), pettifogging, picky (*informal*), piddling (*informal*), quibbling, trifling, unimportant

night *noun* **= darkness**, dark, dead of night, hours of darkness, night-time, night watches

night and day *adverb* **= constantly**, all the time, ceaselessly, continually, continuously, day in, day out, endlessly, incessantly, interminably, unremittingly

nightfall *noun* **= evening**, crepuscule, dusk, eve (*archaic*), eventide, gloaming (*Scot. or poetic*), sundown, sunset, twilight, vespers
➤ **Antonyms**
aurora (*poetic*), cockcrow, dawn, dawning, daybreak, daylight, morning, sunrise

nightly *adjective* **1 = nocturnal**, night-time ♦ *adverb* **2 = every night**, each night, night after night, nights (*informal*)

nightmare *noun* **1 = bad dream**, hallucination, incubus, night terror, succubus **2 = ordeal**, hell on earth, horror, torment, trial, tribulation

nihilism *noun* **= nonbelief**, abnegation, agnosticism, atheism, denial, disbelief, rejection, renunciation, repudiation, scepticism

nil *noun* **= nothing**, duck, love, naught, nihil, none, zero, zilch (*slang*)

nimble *adjective* **= agile**, active, alert, bright (*informal*), brisk, deft, dexterous, lively, nippy (*Brit. informal*), pdq (*slang*), proficient, prompt, quick, quick-witted, ready, smart, sprightly, spry, swift
➤ **Antonyms**
awkward, clumsy, dull, heavy, inactive, indolent, lethargic, slow

nimbleness *noun* **= agility**, adroitness,

alacrity, alertness, dexterity, finesse, grace, lightness, nippiness (*Brit. informal*), skill, smartness, sprightliness, spryness

nimbly *adverb* **= quickly**, actively, acutely, agilely, alertly, briskly, deftly, dexterously, easily, fast, fleetly, hotfoot, pdq (*slang*), posthaste, proficiently, promptly, pronto (*informal*), quick-wittedly, readily, sharply, smartly, speedily, spryly, swiftly

nimbus *noun* **1 = cloud 2 = halo**, ambience, atmosphere, aura, aureole, corona, glow, irradiation

nincompoop *noun* **= idiot**, berk (*Brit. slang*), blockhead, charlie (*Brit. informal*), chump, coot, dickhead (*slang*), dimwit (*informal*), dipstick (*Brit. slang*), divvy (*slang*), dolt, dork (*slang*), dumb-ass (*slang*), dunce, dweeb (*U.S. slang*), fathead (*informal*), fool, fuckwit (*taboo slang*), geek (*slang*), gobshite (*Irish taboo slang*), gonzo (*slang*), jerk (*slang, chiefly U.S. & Canad.*), lamebrain (*informal*), nerd or nurd (*slang*), ninny, nitwit (*informal*), noodle, numbskull or numskull, numpty (*Scot. informal*), oaf, pillock (*Brit. slang*), plank (*Brit. slang*), plonker (*slang*), prat (*slang*), prick (*slang*), schmuck (*U.S. slang*), simpleton, twit (*informal, chiefly Brit.*), wally (*slang*)

nip[1] *verb* **1 = pinch**, bite, catch, clip, compress, grip, nibble, snag, snap, snip, squeeze, tweak, twitch **2 = thwart**, check, frustrate

nip[2] *noun* **= dram**, draught, drop, finger, mouthful, peg (*Brit.*), portion, shot (*informal*), sip, snifter (*informal*), soupçon, sup, swallow, taste

nipper *noun Informal* **= child**, ankle-biter (*Austral. slang*), baby, boy, girl, infant, kid (*informal*), little one, rug rat (*slang*), sprog (*slang*), tot

nipple *noun* **= teat**, boob (*slang*), breast, dug, mamilla, pap, papilla, tit, udder

nippy *adjective* **1 = chilly**, biting, nipping, sharp, stinging **2** *Informal* **= quick**, active, agile, fast, nimble, pdq (*slang*), spry

nirvana *noun* **= paradise**, bliss, joy, peace, serenity, tranquillity

nit-picking *adjective* **= fussy**, captious, carping, cavilling, finicky, hairsplitting, pedantic, pettifogging, quibbling

nitty-gritty *noun* **= basics**, bottom line, brass tacks (*informal*), core, crux, essence, essentials, facts, fundamentals, gist, heart of the matter, ins and outs, nuts and bolts, reality, substance

nitwit *noun Informal* **= fool**, dickhead (*slang*), dickwit (*slang*), dimwit (*informal*), dipstick (*Brit. slang*), divvy (*slang*), dork (*slang*), dummy (*slang*), fuckwit (*taboo slang*), geek (*slang*), gobshite (*Irish taboo slang*), halfwit, lamebrain (*informal*), nincompoop, ninny, numpty (*Scot. informal*), oaf, plank (*Brit. slang*), simpleton

no *interjection* **1** = **never**, nay, not at all, no way ♦ *noun* **2** = **refusal**, denial, negation, rejection, veto **3** = **objector**, dissenter, dissident, protester
➤ **Antonyms**
interjection ≠**never**: certainly, of course, yes ♦ *noun* ≠**refusal**: acceptance, assent, consent

nob *noun* *Slang* = **aristocrat**, aristo (*informal*), big hitter (*informal*), big shot (*informal*), bigwig (*informal*), celeb (*informal*), fat cat (*slang, chiefly U.S.*), heavy hitter (*informal*), nabob (*informal*), toff (*Brit. slang*), V.I.P.

nobble *verb* **1** *Brit. slang* = **bribe**, get at, influence, intimidate, outwit, win over **2** *Brit. slang* = **disable**, handicap, incapacitate, weaken **3** *Brit. slang* = **steal**, filch, knock off (*slang*), nick (*slang, chiefly Brit.*), pilfer, pinch (*informal*), purloin, snitch (*slang*), swipe (*slang*)

nobility *noun* **1** = **dignity**, eminence, excellence, grandeur, greatness, illustriousness, loftiness, magnificence, majesty, nobleness, stateliness, sublimity, superiority, worthiness **2** = **integrity**, honour, incorruptibility, uprightness, virtue **3** = **aristocracy**, elite, high society, lords, nobles, patricians, peerage, ruling class, upper class

noble *adjective* **1** = **worthy**, generous, honourable, magnanimous, upright, virtuous **2** = **aristocratic**, blue-blooded, gentle (*archaic*), highborn, lordly, patrician, titled **3** = **impressive**, august, dignified, distinguished, elevated, eminent, excellent, grand, great, imposing, lofty, splendid, stately, superb ♦ *noun* **4** = **lord**, aristo (*informal*), aristocrat, childe (*archaic*), nobleman, peer
➤ **Antonyms**
adjective ≠**worthy**: contemptible, despicable, dishonest, selfish
≠**aristocratic**: base, humble, ignoble, lowborn, lowly, peasant, plebeian, vulgar
≠**impressive**: base, humble, ignoble, insignificant, lowly, mean, modest, plain ♦ *noun* ≠**lord**: commoner, peasant, serf

nobody *pronoun* **1** = **no-one** ♦ *noun* **2** = **nonentity**, cipher, lightweight (*informal*), menial, nothing (*informal*)
➤ **Antonyms**
noun ≠**nonentity**: big name, big noise (*informal*), big shot (*slang*), celeb (*informal*), celebrity, megastar (*informal*),

personage, star, superstar, V.I.P.

nocturnal *adjective* = **nightly**, night, night-time, of the night

nod *verb* **1** = **acknowledge**, bob, bow, dip, duck, gesture, indicate, salute, signal **2** = **agree**, assent, concur, show agreement **3** = **sleep**, be sleepy, doze, droop, drowse, kip (*Brit. slang*), nap, slump, zizz (*Brit. informal*) ♦ *noun* **4** = **gesture**, acknowledgment, beck, greeting, indication, salute, sign, signal

noggin *noun* **1** *Informal* = **head**, bean (*U.S. & Canad. slang*), block (*informal*), bonce (*Brit. slang*), conk (*slang*), dome (*slang*), napper (*slang*), noddle (*informal, chiefly Brit.*), nut (*slang*) **2** = **quarter-pint**, gill **3** = **cup**, dram, mug, nip, tot

no go *adjective* = **impossible**, futile, hopeless, not on (*informal*), vain

noise *noun* **1** = **sound**, babble, blare, clamour, clatter, commotion, cry, din, fracas, hubbub, outcry, pandemonium, racket, row, rumpus, talk, tumult, uproar ♦ *verb* **2** = **report**, advertise, bruit, circulate, gossip, publicize, repeat, rumour

noiseless *adjective* = **silent**, hushed, inaudible, mute, muted, quiet, soundless, still

noisome *adjective* **1** = **offensive**, disgusting, fetid, foul, malodorous, noxious, putrid, smelly, stinking **2** = **poisonous**, bad, harmful, pernicious, pestilential, unhealthy, unwholesome

noisy *adjective* = **loud**, boisterous, cacophonous, chattering, clamorous, deafening, ear-splitting, obstreperous, piercing, riotous, strident, tumultuous, turbulent, uproarious, vociferous
➤ **Antonyms**
hushed, quiet, silent, still, subdued, tranquil, tuneful

nomad *noun* = **wanderer**, drifter, itinerant, migrant, rambler, rover, vagabond

nomadic *adjective* = **wandering**, itinerant, migrant, migratory, pastoral, peripatetic, roaming, roving, travelling, vagrant

nom de plume *noun* = **pseudonym**, alias, assumed name, nom de guerre, pen name

nomenclature *noun* = **terminology**, classification, codification, locution, phraseology, taxonomy, vocabulary

nominal *adjective* **1** = **so-called**, formal, ostensible, pretended, professed, puppet, purported, self-styled, *soi-disant*, supposed, theoretical, titular **2** = **small**, inconsiderable, insignificant, minimal, symbolic, token, trifling, trivial

nominate *verb* = **name**, appoint, assign, choose, commission, designate, elect, elevate, empower, present, propose, recommend, select, submit, suggest, term

nomination *noun* = **choice**, appointment, designation, election, proposal, recommendation, selection, suggestion

nominee *noun* = **candidate**, aspirant, contestant, entrant, favourite, protégé, runner

nonaligned *adjective* = **neutral**, impartial, uncommitted, undecided

nonchalance *noun* = **indifference**, calm, composure, cool (*slang*), equanimity, imperturbability, sang-froid, self-possession, unconcern

nonchalant *adjective* = **casual**, airy, apathetic, blasé, calm, careless, collected, cool, detached, dispassionate, indifferent, insouciant, laid-back (*informal*), offhand, unconcerned, unemotional, unfazed (*informal*), unperturbed
➤ **Antonyms**
anxious, caring, concerned, involved, worried

noncombatant *noun* = **civilian**, neutral, nonbelligerent

noncommittal *adjective* = **evasive**, ambiguous, careful, cautious, circumspect, discreet, equivocal, guarded, indefinite, neutral, politic, reserved, tactful, temporizing, tentative, unrevealing, vague, wary

non compos mentis *adjective* = **insane**, crazy, deranged, mentally ill, of unsound mind, unbalanced, unhinged
➤ **Antonyms**
all there (*informal*), compos mentis, in one's right mind, lucid, mentally sound, rational, sane

nonconformist *noun* = **maverick**, dissenter, dissentient, eccentric, heretic, iconoclast, individualist, protester, radical, rebel
➤ **Antonyms**
Babbitt (*U.S.*), conventionalist, stick-in-the-mud (*informal*), traditionalist, yes man

nonconformity *noun* = **dissent**, eccentricity, heresy, heterodoxy

nondescript *adjective* = **ordinary**, bog-standard (*Brit. & Irish slang*), characterless, common or garden (*informal*), commonplace, dull, featureless, indeterminate, mousy, nothing to write home about, run-of-the-mill, unclassifiable, unclassified, undistinguished, unexceptional, uninspiring, uninteresting, unmemorable, unremarkable, vague, vanilla (*informal*)
➤ **Antonyms**

distinctive, extraordinary, memorable, remarkable, unique, unusual

none *pronoun* = **not any**, bugger all (*slang*), diddly (*U.S. slang*), f.a. (*Brit. slang*), fuck all (*Brit. taboo slang*), nil, nobody, no-one, no part, not a bit, nothing, not one, sweet F.A. (*Brit. slang*), sweet Fanny Adams (*Brit. slang*), zero, zilch (*slang, chiefly U.S. & Canad.*)

nonentity *noun* = **nobody**, cipher, lightweight (*informal*), mediocrity, small fry, unimportant person

nonessential *adjective* = **unnecessary**, dispensable, excessive, expendable, extraneous, inessential, peripheral, superfluous, unimportant
➤ **Antonyms**
appropriate, essential, important, indispensable, significant, vital

nonetheless *adverb* = **nevertheless**, despite that, even so, however, in spite of that, yet

nonevent *noun* = **flop** (*informal*), clunker (*informal*), disappointment, dud (*informal*), failure, fiasco, washout

nonexistent *adjective* = **imaginary**, chimerical, fancied, fictional, hallucinatory, hypothetical, illusory, imagined, insubstantial, legendary, missing, mythical, unreal
➤ **Antonyms**
actual, existent, existing, genuine, real, true, veritable

nonplus *verb* = **take aback**, astonish, astound, baffle, be all Greek to (*informal*), bewilder, confound, confuse, discomfit, disconcert, discountenance, dismay, dumbfound, embarrass, faze, flummox, mystify, perplex, puzzle, stump, stun

nonsense *noun* = **rubbish**, absurdity, balderdash, balls (*taboo slang*), bilge (*informal*), blather, bollocks (*Brit. taboo slang*), bombast, bosh (*informal*), bull (*slang*), bullshit (*taboo slang*), bunk (*informal*), bunkum *or* buncombe (*chiefly U.S.*), claptrap (*informal*), cobblers (*Brit. taboo slang*), crap (*slang*), double Dutch (*Brit. informal*), drivel, eyewash (*informal*), fatuity, folly, foolishness, garbage (*informal*), gibberish, guff (*slang*), hogwash, hokum (*slang, chiefly U.S. & Canad.*), horsefeathers (*U.S. slang*), hot air (*informal*), idiocy, inanity, jest, ludicrousness, moonshine, pants (*slang*), pap, piffle (*informal*), poppycock (*informal*), rhubarb, ridiculousness, rot, senselessness, shit (*taboo slang*), silliness, stuff, stupidity, tommyrot, tosh (*slang, chiefly Brit.*), trash, tripe (*informal*), twaddle, waffle (*informal, chiefly Brit.*)

> ➤ **Antonyms**
fact, reality, reason, sense, seriousness,
truth, wisdom

nonsensical *adjective* = **senseless**, absurd,
asinine, crazy, foolish, inane,
incomprehensible, irrational, ludicrous,
meaningless, ridiculous, silly

nonstarter *noun* = **dead loss**, dud
(*informal*), lemon (*informal*), loser,
no-hoper (*informal*), turkey (*informal*),
washout (*informal*)

nonstop *adjective* 1 = **continuous**,
ceaseless, constant, direct, endless,
incessant, interminable, relentless, steady,
unbroken, unending, unfaltering,
uninterrupted, unremitting ♦ *adverb* 2
= **continuously**, ceaselessly, constantly,
directly, endlessly, incessantly,
interminably, perpetually, relentlessly,
steadily, unbrokenly, unendingly,
unfalteringly, uninterruptedly,
unremittingly, without stopping
> ➤ **Antonyms**
adjective ≠**continuous**: broken,
discontinuous, fitful, intermittent,
irregular, occasional, periodic, punctuated,
recurrent, spasmodic, sporadic, stop-go
(*informal*)

nook *noun* = **niche**, alcove, cavity, corner,
cranny, crevice, cubbyhole, hide-out,
inglenook (*Brit.*), opening, recess, retreat

noon *noun* = **midday**, high noon, noonday,
noontide, noontime, twelve noon

norm *noun* = **standard**, average,
benchmark, criterion, mean, measure,
model, par, pattern, rule, type, yardstick

normal *adjective* 1 = **usual**, accustomed,
acknowledged, average, bog-standard
(*Brit. & Irish slang*), common,
conventional, habitual, natural, ordinary,
popular, regular, routine, run-of-the-mill,
standard, typical 2 = **sane**, rational,
reasonable, well-adjusted
> ➤ **Antonyms**
≠**usual**: abnormal, exceptional, irregular,
peculiar, rare, remarkable, singular,
uncommon, unnatural, unusual

normality *noun* 1 = **regularity**,
accustomedness, averageness,
commonness, commonplaceness,
conventionality, habitualness, naturalness,
ordinariness, popularity, routineness,
typicality, usualness 2 = **sanity**,
adjustment, balance, rationality, reason

normally *adverb* = **usually**, as a rule,
commonly, generally, habitually,
ordinarily, regularly, typically

north *adjective* 1 = **northern**, Arctic, boreal,
northerly, polar ♦ *adverb* 2
= **northward(s)**, northerly

nose *noun* 1 = **snout**, beak, bill, conk
(*slang*), hooter (*slang*), neb (*archaic or
dialect*), proboscis, schnozzle (*slang, chiefly
U.S.*), snitch (*slang*) ♦ *verb* 2 = **ease
forward**, nudge, nuzzle, push, shove 3
= **pry**, meddle, snoop (*informal*)

nose-dive *verb* = **drop**, dive, plummet,
plunge

nosegay *noun* = **posy**, bouquet

nose out *verb* = **detect**, scent, search (for),
smell, sniff

nosey, nosy *adjective* = **inquisitive**,
curious, eavesdropping, interfering,
intrusive, meddlesome, prying, snooping
(*informal*)

nosh *Slang* ♦ *noun* 1 = **food**, aliment, chow
(*informal*), comestibles, eats (*slang*), fare,
feed, grub (*slang*), meal, nosebag (*slang*),
repast, scoff (*slang*), sustenance, tack
(*informal*), viands, victuals, vittles (*obsolete
or dialect*) ♦ *verb* 2 = **eat**, consume, scoff
(*slang*)

nostalgia *noun* = **reminiscence**,
homesickness, longing, pining, regret,
regretfulness, remembrance, wistfulness,
yearning

nostalgic *adjective* = **sentimental**,
emotional, homesick, longing, maudlin,
regretful, wistful

nostrum *noun* = **medicine**, cure, cure-all,
drug, elixir, panacea, patent medicine,
potion, quack medicine, remedy,
sovereign cure, specific, treatment

notability *noun* 1 = **fame**, celebrity,
distinction, eminence, esteem, renown 2
= **celebrity**, big name, celeb (*informal*),
dignitary, megastar (*informal*), notable,
personage, V.I.P., worthy

notable *adjective* 1 = **remarkable**,
celebrated, conspicuous, distinguished,
eminent, evident, extraordinary, famous,
manifest, marked, memorable,
noteworthy, noticeable, notorious,
outstanding, pre-eminent, pronounced,
rare, renowned, salient, striking,
uncommon, unusual, well-known ♦ *noun*
2 = **celebrity**, big name, celeb (*informal*),
dignitary, luminary, megastar (*informal*),
notability, personage, V.I.P., worthy
> ➤ **Antonyms**
adjective ≠**remarkable**: anonymous,
concealed, hidden, imperceptible,
obscure, unknown, vague

notably *adverb* = **particularly**,
conspicuously, distinctly, especially,
markedly, noticeably, outstandingly,
remarkably, seriously (*informal*), signally,
strikingly, uncommonly

notation *noun* = **signs**, characters, code,

script, symbols, system

notch *noun* 1 = **cut**, cleft, incision, indentation, mark, nick, score 2 *Informal* = **level**, cut (*informal*), degree, grade, step ♦ *verb* 3 = **cut**, indent, mark, nick, score, scratch

notch up *verb* = **register**, achieve, gain, make, score

note *noun* 1 = **message**, annotation, comment, communication, epistle, gloss, jotting, letter, memo, memorandum, minute, record, remark, reminder 2 = **symbol**, indication, mark, sign, token 3 *As in* **of note** = **fame**, celebrity, character, consequence, distinction, eminence, prestige, renown, reputation 4 *As in* **take note of** = **notice**, heed, observation, regard ♦ *verb* 5 = **see**, notice, observe, perceive 6 = **mark**, denote, designate, indicate, record, register 7 = **mention**, remark

notebook *noun* = **jotter**, commonplace book, diary, exercise book, Filofax (*Trademark*), journal, memorandum book, notepad, record book

noted *adjective* = **famous**, acclaimed, celebrated, conspicuous, distinguished, eminent, illustrious, notable, notorious, prominent, recognized, renowned, well-known
➤ **Antonyms**
infamous, obscure, undistinguished, unknown

notes *plural noun* = **jottings**, impressions, outline, record, report, sketch

noteworthy *adjective* = **remarkable**, exceptional, extraordinary, important, notable, outstanding, significant, unusual
➤ **Antonyms**
commonplace, insignificant, normal, ordinary, pedestrian, run-of-the-mill, unexceptional, unremarkable

nothing *noun* = **nought**, bagatelle, cipher, emptiness, naught, nil, nobody, nonentity, nonexistence, nothingness, nullity, trifle, void, zero

nothingness *noun* 1 = **oblivion**, nihility, nonbeing, nonexistence, nullity 2 = **insignificance**, unimportance, worthlessness

notice *noun* 1 = **interest**, cognizance, consideration, heed, note, observation, regard 2 = **attention**, civility, respect 3 = **announcement**, advice, communication, instruction, intelligence, intimation, news, notification, order, warning 4 = **review**, advertisement, comment, criticism, poster, sign ♦ *verb* 5 = **observe**, behold (*archaic or literary*), detect, discern, distinguish, eyeball (*slang*), heed, mark, mind, note,

perceive, remark, see, spot
➤ **Antonyms**
noun ≠**interest**: disregard, ignorance, neglect, omission, oversight ♦ *verb* ≠**observe**: disregard, ignore, neglect, overlook

noticeable *adjective* = **obvious**, appreciable, blatant, bold, clear, conspicuous, distinct, evident, manifest, observable, perceptible, plain, salient, striking, unmistakable

notification *noun* = **announcement**, advice, alert, declaration, information, intelligence, message, notice, notifying, publication, statement, telling, warning

notify *verb* = **inform**, acquaint, advise, alert, announce, apprise, declare, make known, publish, tell, warn

notion *noun* 1 = **idea**, apprehension, belief, concept, conception, impression, inkling, judgment, knowledge, opinion, sentiment, understanding, view 2 = **whim**, caprice, desire, fancy, impulse, inclination, wish

notional *adjective* = **speculative**, abstract, conceptual, fanciful, hypothetical, ideal, imaginary, theoretical, unreal, visionary
➤ **Antonyms**
actual, factual, genuine, real

notoriety *noun* = **scandal**, dishonour, disrepute, infamy, obloquy, opprobrium

notorious *adjective* = **infamous**, dishonourable, disreputable, opprobrious, scandalous

notoriously *adverb* = **infamously**, dishonourably, disreputably, opprobriously, scandalously

notwithstanding *preposition* 1 = **despite**, in spite of ♦ *adverb* 2 = **nevertheless**, although, (even) though, however, nonetheless, though, yet

nought *noun* = **zero**, naught, nil, nothing, nothingness

nourish *verb* 1 = **feed**, attend, furnish, nurse, nurture, supply, sustain, tend 2 = **encourage**, comfort, cultivate, foster, maintain, promote, support

nourishing *adjective* = **nutritious**, alimentative, beneficial, healthful, health-giving, nutritive, wholesome

nourishment *noun* = **food**, aliment, diet, nutriment, nutrition, sustenance, tack (*informal*), viands, victuals, vittles (*obsolete or dialect*)

nouveau riche *noun* = **new-rich**, arriviste, parvenu, upstart

novel[1] *noun* = **story**, fiction, narrative, romance, tale

novel[2] *adjective* = **new**, different, fresh, ground-breaking, innovative, left-field

(*informal*), original, rare, singular, strange, uncommon, unfamiliar, unusual
➤ **Antonyms**
ancient, common, customary, familiar, habitual, old-fashioned, ordinary, run-of-the-mill, traditional, usual

novelty *noun* 1 = **newness**, freshness, innovation, oddity, originality, strangeness, surprise, unfamiliarity, uniqueness 2 = **gimmick**, curiosity, gadget 3 = **knick-knack**, bagatelle, bauble, gewgaw, gimcrack, memento, souvenir, trifle, trinket

novice *noun* = **beginner**, amateur, apprentice, convert, learner, neophyte, newcomer, novitiate, probationer, proselyte, pupil, trainee, tyro
➤ **Antonyms**
ace, doyen, expert, grandmaster, guru, master, maven, old hand, professional, teacher

novitiate *noun* = **apprenticeship**, probation, training

now *adverb* 1 = **nowadays**, any more, at the moment, these days 2 = **immediately**, at once, instanter (*Law*), instantly, presently (*Scot. & U.S.*), promptly, straightaway 3 **now and again** *or* **then** = **occasionally**, at times, from time to time, infrequently, intermittently, on and off, once in a while, on occasion, sometimes, sporadically

nowadays *adverb* = **now**, any more, at the moment, in this day and age, these days, today

noxious *adjective* = **harmful**, baneful (*archaic*), corrupting, deadly, deleterious, destructive, detrimental, foul, hurtful, injurious, insalubrious, noisome, pernicious, pestilential, poisonous, unhealthy, unwholesome
➤ **Antonyms**
innocuous, innoxious, inoffensive, nontoxic, not dangerous, safe, unobjectionable

nuance *noun* = **subtlety**, degree, distinction, gradation, nicety, refinement, shade, tinge

nubile *adjective* = **marriageable**, ripe (*informal*)

nucleus *noun* = **centre**, basis, core, focus, heart, kernel, nub, pivot

nude *adjective* = **naked**, *au naturel*, bare, buck naked (*slang*), disrobed, exposed, in one's birthday suit (*informal*), in the altogether (*informal*), in the bare scud (*slang*), in the buff (*informal*), in the raw (*informal*), naked as the day one was born (*informal*), scuddy (*slang*), starkers (*informal*), stark-naked, stripped, unclad,

unclothed, uncovered, undraped, undressed, without a stitch on (*informal*)
➤ **Antonyms**
attired, clothed, covered, dressed

nudge *verb, noun* = **push**, bump, dig, elbow, jog, poke, prod, shove, touch

nudity *noun* = **nakedness**, bareness, deshabille, nudism, undress

nugget *noun* = **lump**, chunk, clump, hunk, mass, piece

nuisance *noun* = **problem**, annoyance, bore, bother, drag (*informal*), gall, hassle (*informal*), inconvenience, infliction, irritation, offence, pain in the arse (*taboo informal*), pain in the backside, pain in the butt (*informal*), pain in the neck, pest, plague, trouble, vexation
➤ **Antonyms**
benefit, blessing, delight, happiness, joy, pleasure, satisfaction

null *adjective* **null and void** = **invalid**, characterless, ineffectual, inoperative, nonexistent, powerless, useless, vain, valueless, void, worthless

nullify *verb* = **cancel**, abolish, abrogate, annul, bring to naught, counteract, countervail, invalidate, negate, neutralize, obviate, quash, rebut, render null and void, repeal, rescind, revoke, veto, void
➤ **Antonyms**
authorize, confirm, endorse, ratify, validate

nullity *noun* = **nonexistence**, characterlessness, ineffectualness, invalidity, powerlessness, uselessness, valuelessness, voidness, worthlessness

numb *adjective* 1 = **unfeeling**, benumbed, dead, deadened, frozen, immobilized, insensible, insensitive, paralysed, stupefied, torpid ♦ *verb* 2 = **deaden**, benumb, dull, freeze, immobilize, paralyse, stun, stupefy
➤ **Antonyms**
adjective ≠**unfeeling**: feeling, responsive, sensitive, sentient

number *noun* 1 = **numeral**, character, count, digit, figure, integer, sum, total, unit 2 = **quantity**, aggregate, amount, collection, company, crowd, horde, many, multitude, throng 3 = **issue**, copy, edition, imprint, printing ♦ *verb* 4 = **calculate**, account, add, compute, count, enumerate, include, reckon, tell, total
➤ **Antonyms**
noun ≠**quantity**: insufficiency, lack, scantiness, scarcity, shortage, want ♦ *verb* ≠**calculate**: conjecture, guess, theorize

numbered *adjective* 1 = **included**, categorized, contained, counted, designated, fixed, specified, totalled 2 = **limited**, limited in number

numberless *adjective* = **infinite**, countless, endless, innumerable, multitudinous, myriad, unnumbered, untold

numbness *noun* = **deadness**, dullness, insensibility, insensitivity, paralysis, stupefaction, torpor, unfeelingness

numbskull, numskull *noun* = **fool**, blockhead, clot (*Brit. informal*), dolt, dummy (*slang*), dunce, oaf, twit (*informal*)

numeral *noun* = **number**, character, cipher, digit, figure, integer, symbol

numerous *adjective* = **many**, abundant, copious, plentiful, profuse, several, thick on the ground
➤ **Antonyms**
few, not many, scarcely any

nuncio *noun* = **ambassador**, envoy, legate, messenger

nunnery *noun* = **convent**, abbey, cloister, house, monastery

nuptial *adjective* = **marital**, bridal, conjugal, connubial, hymeneal (*poetic*), matrimonial, wedded, wedding

nuptials *plural noun* = **wedding**, espousal (*archaic*), marriage, matrimony

nurse *verb* 1 = **look after**, care for, minister to, tend, treat 2 = **breast-feed**, feed, nourish, nurture, suckle, wet-nurse 3 = **foster**, cherish, cultivate, encourage, harbour, keep alive, preserve, promote, succour, support

nursery *noun* = **crèche**, kindergarten, playgroup

nurture *noun* 1 = **development**, discipline, education, instruction, rearing, training, upbringing ◆ *verb* 2 = **develop**, bring up, cultivate, discipline, educate, instruct, rear, school, train 3 = **nourish**, feed, nurse, support, sustain, tend
➤ **Antonyms**
verb ≠**develop**, **nourish**: deprive, disregard, ignore, neglect, overlook

nut *noun* 1 = **kernel**, pip, seed, stone 2 *Slang* = **madman**, crackpot (*informal*), crank (*informal*), eccentric, headbanger (*informal*), headcase (*informal*), loony (*slang*), lunatic, maniac, nutcase (*slang*), nutter (*Brit. slang*), oddball (*informal*), psycho (*slang*), wacko (*slang*) 3 *Slang* = **head**, brain, mind, reason, senses

nutrition *noun* = **food**, nourishment, nutriment, sustenance

nutritious *adjective* = **nourishing**, alimental, alimentative, beneficial, healthful, health-giving, invigorating, nutritive, strengthening, wholesome

nuts *adjective Slang* = **insane**, as daft as a brush (*informal, chiefly Brit.*), bananas (*slang*), barking (*slang*), barking mad (*slang*), batty (*slang*), crazy (*informal*), demented, deranged, doolally (*slang*), eccentric, gonzo (*slang*), irrational, loony (*slang*), loopy (*informal*), mad, not the full shilling (*informal*), nutty (*slang*), off one's trolley (*slang*), out to lunch (*informal*), psycho (*slang*), psychopathic, up the pole (*informal*), wacko *or* whacko (*informal*)

nuzzle *verb* = **snuggle**, burrow, cuddle, fondle, nestle, pet

nymph *noun* = **sylph**, damsel, dryad, girl, hamadryad, lass, maid, maiden, naiad, Oceanid (*Greek myth*), oread

O o

oaf *noun* = **dolt**, blockhead, bonehead (*slang*), brute, clod, dullard, dumb-ass (*slang*), dunce, fathead (*informal*), fool, galoot (*slang, chiefly U.S.*), gawk, geek (*slang*), gobshite (*Irish taboo slang*), goon, halfwit, idiot, jerk (*slang, chiefly U.S. & Canad.*), lout, lummox (*informal*), moron, nerd *or* nurd (*slang*), numbskull *or* numskull, numpty (*Scot. informal*), schmuck (*U.S. slang*), wally (*slang*)
➤ **Antonyms**
brain (*informal*), egghead (*informal*), genius, intellect, smart aleck (*informal*), wiseacre

oafish *adjective* = **stupid**, boneheaded (*slang*), bovine, brutish, dense, dim, dim-witted (*informal*), doltish, dozy (*Brit. informal*), dull, dumb (*informal*), dumb-ass (*slang*), loutish, lubberly, lumbering, moronic, obtuse, slow on the uptake (*informal*), thick
➤ **Antonyms**
acute, brainy (*informal*), bright, clever, intelligent, quick-witted, sharp, smart

oasis *noun* = **haven**, island, refuge, resting place, retreat, sanctuary, sanctum

oath *noun* 1 = **promise**, affirmation, avowal, bond, pledge, sworn statement, vow, word 2 = **swearword**, blasphemy, curse, cuss (*informal*), expletive, imprecation, malediction, profanity, strong language

obdurate *adjective* = **stubborn**, adamant, dogged, firm, fixed, hard, hard-hearted, immovable, implacable, inexorable, inflexible, mulish, obstinate, perverse, pig-headed, relentless, stiff-necked, unbending, unfeeling, unimpressible, unrelenting, unshakable, unyielding
➤ **Antonyms**
amenable, biddable, compliant, flexible, malleable, pliant, soft-hearted, submissive, tender, tractable, yielding

obedience *noun* = **submissiveness**, accordance, acquiescence, agreement, assent, compliance, deference, docility, dutifulness, duty, observance, respect, reverence, submission, subservience, tractability
➤ **Antonyms**
defiance, disobedience, insubordination, obstinacy, recalcitrance, stubbornness, wilfulness

obedient *adjective* = **submissive**, acquiescent, amenable, biddable, compliant, deferential, docile, duteous, dutiful, law-abiding, observant, regardful, respectful, subservient, tractable, under control, well-trained, yielding
➤ **Antonyms**
arrogant, contrary, disobedient, disrespectful, intractable, obdurate, obstinate, rebellious, stubborn, undutiful, ungovernable, unmanageable, unruly, wayward

obeisance *noun Formal* 1 = **respect**, deference, homage, reverence 2 = **bow**, bending of the knee, curtsy *or* curtsey, genuflection, salaam

obelisk *noun* = **column**, monolith, monument, needle, pillar, shaft

obese *adjective* = **fat**, corpulent, fleshy, gross, heavy, outsize, overweight, paunchy, plump, podgy, portly, roly-poly, rotund, stout, tubby, well-upholstered (*informal*)
➤ **Antonyms**
emaciated, gaunt, lean, scraggy, skeletal, skinny, slender, thin

obesity *noun* = **fatness**, beef (*informal*), bulk, corpulence, fleshiness, grossness, overweight, portliness, stoutness, tubbiness, weight problem
➤ **Antonyms**
emaciation, gauntness, leanness, skinniness, slenderness, thinness

obey *verb* 1 = **do what one is told**, bow to, cave in (*informal*), come to heel, get into line, give in, give way, knuckle under (*informal*), submit, succumb, surrender (to), take orders from, toe the line, yield 2 = **carry out**, abide by, act upon, adhere to, be ruled by, comply, conform, discharge, do what is expected, execute, follow, fulfil, heed, keep, mind, observe, perform, respond, serve
➤ **Antonyms**
≠**do what one is told:** disobey, rebel
≠**carry out:** contravene, defy, disobey, disregard, ignore, transgress, violate

obfuscate *verb Formal* = **confuse**, befog, cloud, darken, muddy the waters, obscure, perplex

object¹ *noun* 1 = **thing**, article, body, entity, fact, item, phenomenon, reality 2

= **target**, butt, focus, recipient, victim **3**
= **purpose**, aim, design, end, end purpose, goal, idea, intent, intention, motive, objective, point, reason

object² *verb* = **protest**, argue against, demur, draw the line (at something), expostulate, oppose, raise objections, take exception
➤ **Antonyms**
accept, acquiesce, agree, approve, assent, comply, concur, consent, like, take on board, welcome

objection *noun* = **protest**, cavil, censure, counter-argument, demur, doubt, exception, opposition, remonstrance, scruple
➤ **Antonyms**
acceptance, affirmation, agreement, approbation, assent, endorsement, support

objectionable *adjective* = **unpleasant**, abhorrent, deplorable, disagreeable, displeasing, distasteful, exceptionable, insufferable, intolerable, noxious, obnoxious, offensive, regrettable, repugnant, unacceptable, undesirable, unseemly, unsociable
➤ **Antonyms**
acceptable, agreeable, desirable, likable *or* likeable, pleasant, pleasing, welcome

objective *noun* **1** = **purpose**, aim, ambition, aspiration, design, end, end in view, goal, Holy Grail (*informal*), intention, mark, object, target ♦ *adjective* **2** = **unbiased**, detached, disinterested, dispassionate, equitable, even-handed, fair, impartial, impersonal, judicial, just, open-minded, unemotional, uninvolved, unprejudiced
➤ **Antonyms**
adjective ≠**unbiased**: biased, personal, prejudiced, subjective, unfair, unjust

objectively *adverb* = **impartially**, disinterestedly, dispassionately, even-handedly, with an open mind, with objectivity *or* impartiality

objectivity *noun* = **impartiality**, detachment, disinterest, disinterestedness, dispassion, equitableness, impersonality
➤ **Antonyms**
bent, bias, partiality, predisposition, prejudice, subjectivity

obligation *noun* = **duty**, accountability, accountableness, burden, charge, compulsion, culpability, liability, must, onus, pigeon (*informal*), requirement, responsibility, trust

obligatory *adjective* = **compulsory**, binding, coercive, *de rigueur*, enforced, essential, imperative, mandatory, necessary, required, requisite, unavoidable

➤ **Antonyms**
discretionary, elective, noncompulsory, optional, voluntary

oblige *verb* **1** = **compel**, bind, coerce, constrain, dragoon, force, impel, make, necessitate, obligate, railroad (*informal*), require **2** = **do (someone) a favour** *or* a **kindness**, accommodate, benefit, favour, gratify, indulge, please, put oneself out for, serve
➤ **Antonyms**
≠**do (someone) a favour** *or* a **kindness**: bother, discommode, disoblige, disrupt, inconvenience, put out, trouble

obliged *adjective* **1** = **grateful**, appreciative, beholden, gratified, indebted, in (someone's) debt, thankful **2** = **bound**, compelled, forced, required, under an obligation, under compulsion

obliging *adjective* = **cooperative**, accommodating, agreeable, amiable, civil, complaisant, considerate, courteous, eager to please, friendly, good-natured, helpful, kind, polite, willing
➤ **Antonyms**
discourteous, disobliging, inconsiderate, rude, sullen, surly, unaccommodating, uncooperative, unhelpful, unobliging

oblique *adjective* **1** = **slanting**, angled, aslant, at an angle, atilt, inclined, slanted, sloped, sloping, tilted **2** = **indirect**, backhanded, circuitous, circumlocutory, evasive, implied, roundabout, sidelong
➤ **Antonyms**
≠**indirect**: blunt, candid, direct, downright, forthright, frank, open, straightforward

obliquely *adverb* **1** = **at an angle**, aslant, aslope, diagonally, slantwise **2** = **indirectly**, circuitously, evasively, in a roundabout manner *or* way, not in so many words

obliterate *verb* = **destroy**, annihilate, blot out, cancel, delete, efface, eradicate, erase, expunge, extirpate, root out, wipe from *or* off the face of the earth, wipe out
➤ **Antonyms**
build, construct, create, establish, form, formulate, generate, make

obliteration *noun* = **annihilation**, blotting out, deletion, effacement, elimination, eradication, erasure, extirpation, rooting out, wiping out
➤ **Antonyms**
building, construction, creation, establishment, formation, generation, making

oblivion *noun* **1** = **neglect**, abeyance, disregard, forgetfulness, (waters of) Lethe **2** = **unconsciousness**, insensibility, obliviousness, unawareness

➤ **Antonyms**

≠**unconsciousness:** awareness,
consciousness, perception, realization,
recognition, sensibility

oblivious *adjective* = **unaware**, blind,
careless, deaf, disregardful, forgetful,
heedless, ignorant, inattentive, insensible,
neglectful, negligent, regardless,
unconcerned, unconscious, unmindful,
unobservant
➤ **Antonyms**
alert, attentive, aware, conscious, heedful,
mindful, observant, watchful

obloquy *noun Formal* **1** = **abuse**, aspersion,
attack, blame, censure, criticism, invective,
reproach, slander, vilification **2** = **disgrace**,
discredit, dishonour, humiliation,
ignominy, infamy, shame, stigma

obnoxious *adjective* = **offensive**,
abhorrent, abominable, detestable,
disagreeable, disgusting, foul, hateful,
horrid, insufferable, loathsome, nasty,
nauseating, objectionable, obscene,
odious, repellent, reprehensible,
repugnant, repulsive, revolting, sickening,
unpleasant
➤ **Antonyms**
agreeable, amiable, charming, congenial,
delightful, likable *or* likeable, pleasant,
pleasing

obscene *adjective* **1** = **indecent**, bawdy,
blue, coarse, dirty, filthy, foul, gross,
immodest, immoral, improper, impure,
lewd, licentious, loose, offensive,
pornographic, prurient, ribald, salacious,
shameless, smutty, suggestive, unchaste,
unwholesome, X-rated (*informal*) **2**
= **disgusting**, atrocious, evil, heinous,
loathsome, outrageous, shocking,
sickening, vile, wicked
➤ **Antonyms**
≠**indecent:** chaste, decent, decorous,
inoffensive, modest, proper, pure, refined,
respectable, seemly

obscenity *noun* **1** = **indecency**, bawdiness,
blueness, coarseness, dirtiness, filthiness,
foulness, grossness, immodesty,
impropriety, impurity, indelicacy,
lewdness, licentiousness, pornography,
prurience, salacity, smut, smuttiness,
suggestiveness, vileness **2** = **swearword**,
four-letter word, profanity, vulgarism **3**
= **atrocity**, abomination, affront, blight,
evil, offence, outrage, vileness, wrong
➤ **Antonyms**
≠**indecency:** chastity, decency, decorum,
delicacy, innocence, modesty, propriety,
purity

obscure *adjective* **1** = **little-known**,
humble, inconspicuous, lowly, minor,

nameless, out-of-the-way, remote,
undistinguished, unheard-of, unimportant,
unknown **2** = **vague**, abstruse, ambiguous,
arcane, concealed, confusing, cryptic,
deep, Delphic, doubtful, enigmatic,
esoteric, hazy, hidden, incomprehensible,
indefinite, intricate, involved, mysterious,
occult, opaque, recondite, unclear **3**
= **dark**, blurred, clouded, cloudy, dim,
faint, gloomy, indistinct, murky, shadowy,
shady, sombre ♦ *verb* **4** = **conceal**, cover,
disguise, hide, obfuscate, screen, throw a
veil over, veil **5** = **cover**, bedim, block,
block out, blur, cloak, cloud, darken, dim,
dull, eclipse, mask, overshadow, shade,
shroud
➤ **Antonyms**
adjective ≠**little-known:** celebrated,
distinguished, eminent, familiar, famous,
illustrious, important, major, prominent,
renowned, significant, well-known,
widely-known ≠**vague:** apparent, clear,
definite, distinct, evident, explicit,
intelligible, lucid, manifest, obvious, plain,
prominent, straightforward, transparent,
unmistakable ≠**dark:** bright, clear, sharp,
transparent, well-defined ♦ *verb* ≠**conceal:**
clarify, disclose, explain, explicate, expose,
interpret, reveal, show ≠**cover:** expose,
reveal, uncover, unmask, unveil

obscurity *noun* **1** = **insignificance**,
inconspicuousness, lowliness,
namelessness, nonrecognition,
unimportance **2** = **vagueness**,
abstruseness, ambiguity, complexity,
impenetrableness, incomprehensibility,
intricacy, reconditeness **3** = **darkness**,
dimness, dusk, duskiness, gloom, haze,
haziness, indistinctness, murkiness,
shadows
➤ **Antonyms**
≠**vagueness:** clarity, clearness,
comprehensibility, explicitness, lucidity,
obviousness

obsequies *plural noun Formal* = **funeral
rites**, burial, burial service, funeral, last
offices

obsequious *adjective* = **sycophantic**,
cringing, deferential, fawning, flattering,
grovelling, ingratiating, servile, submissive,
unctuous

observable *adjective* = **noticeable**,
apparent, appreciable, blatant, clear,
detectable, discernible, evident, obvious,
open, patent, perceivable, perceptible,
recognizable, visible

observance *noun* **1** = **carrying out**,
adherence to, attention, celebration,
compliance, discharge, fulfilment,
heeding, honouring, notice, observation,

performance **2 = ritual**, ceremonial, ceremony, custom, fashion, form, formality, practice, rite, service, tradition
➤ **Antonyms**
≠**carrying out:** disdain, disregard, evasion, heedlessness, inattention, neglect, nonobservance, omission, oversight

observant *adjective* = **attentive**, alert, eagle-eyed, heedful, mindful, obedient, perceptive, quick, sharp-eyed, submissive, vigilant, watchful, wide-awake
➤ **Antonyms**
distracted, dreamy, heedless, inattentive, indifferent, negligent, preoccupied, unobservant, vague

observation *noun* **1 = study**, attention, consideration, examination, experience, information, inspection, knowledge, monitoring, notice, review, scrutiny, surveillance, watching **2 = comment**, annotation, finding, note, opinion, pronouncement, reflection, remark, thought, utterance

observe *verb* **1 = see**, detect, discern, discover, espy, note, notice, perceive, spot, witness **2 = watch**, behold (*archaic or literary*), check, check out (*informal*), contemplate, eye, eyeball (*slang*), get a load of (*informal*), keep an eye on (*informal*), keep tabs on (*informal*), keep track of, keep under observation, look at, monitor, pay attention to, regard, scrutinize, study, survey, take a dekko at (*Brit. slang*), view **3 = remark**, comment, declare, mention, note, opine, say, state **4 = carry out**, abide by, adhere to, comply, conform to, follow, fulfil, heed, honour, keep, mind, obey, perform, respect **5 = celebrate**, commemorate, keep
➤ **Antonyms**
≠**carry out:** disregard, ignore, miss, neglect, omit, overlook, violate

observer *noun* = **spectator**, beholder, bystander, commentator, eyewitness, fly on the wall, looker-on, onlooker, viewer, watcher, witness

obsessed *adjective* = **preoccupied**, beset, dominated, gripped, haunted, having a one-track mind, hung up on (*slang*), infatuated, in the grip of, troubled
➤ **Antonyms**
aloof, apathetic, detached, disinterested, impassive, indifferent, uncaring, unconcerned

obsession *noun* = **preoccupation**, addiction, bee in one's bonnet (*informal*), complex, enthusiasm, fetish, fixation, hang-up (*informal*), infatuation, mania, phobia, ruling passion, thing (*informal*)

obsessive *adjective* = **compulsive**,

besetting, consuming, fixed, gripping, haunting, tormenting

obsolescent *adjective* = **becoming obsolete**, ageing, declining, dying out, not with it (*informal*), on the decline, on the wane, on the way out, past its prime, waning

obsolete *adjective* = **out of date**, anachronistic, ancient, antediluvian, antiquated, antique, archaic, bygone, dated, discarded, disused, extinct, old, old-fashioned, old hat, out, outmoded, out of fashion, out of the ark (*informal*), outworn, passé, past it
➤ **Antonyms**
à la mode, contemporary, current, fashionable, in, in vogue, modern, new, present day, trendy (*Brit. informal*), up-to-date

obstacle *noun* = **difficulty**, bar, barrier, block, check, hindrance, hitch, hurdle, impediment, interference, interruption, obstruction, snag, stumbling block
➤ **Antonyms**
advantage, aid, asset, assistance, benefit, help, support

obstinacy *noun* = **stubbornness**, doggedness, firmness, inflexibility, intransigence, mulishness, obduracy, perseverance, persistence, pertinacity, pig-headedness, resoluteness, tenacity, wilfulness
➤ **Antonyms**
compliance, cooperativeness, docility, flexibility, meekness, submissiveness, tractability

obstinate *adjective* = **stubborn**, cussed, determined, dogged, firm, headstrong, immovable, inflexible, intractable, intransigent, mulish, persistent, pertinacious, perverse, pig-headed, recalcitrant, refractory, self-willed, steadfast, stiff-necked, strong-minded, tenacious, unyielding, wilful
➤ **Antonyms**
amenable, biddable, complaisant, compliant, docile, flexible, irresolute, manageable, obedient, submissive, tractable, undecided, wavering

obstreperous *adjective* = **unruly**, boisterous, disorderly, loud, noisy, out of control, out of hand, raucous, restive, riotous, rough, rowdy, tumultuous, turbulent, uncontrolled, undisciplined, unmanageable, uproarious, vociferous, wild
➤ **Antonyms**
calm, controlled, disciplined, docile, gentle, orderly, peaceful, placid, quiet

obstruct *verb* = **block**, arrest, bar,

barricade, bring to a standstill, bung, check, choke, clog, cut off, frustrate, get in the way of, hamper, hamstring, hide, hinder, hold up, impede, inhibit, interfere with, interrupt, obscure, prevent, restrict, retard, shield, shut off, slow down, stop, thwart
➤ **Antonyms**
abet, advance, aid, assist, encourage, favour, further, gee up, help, promote, support

obstruction *noun* = **obstacle**, bar, barricade, barrier, block, blockage, check, difficulty, hazard, hindrance, impediment, occlusion, snag, stop, stoppage
➤ **Antonyms**
aid, assistance, cooperation, encouragement, favour, furtherance, geeing-up, help, support

obstructive *adjective* = **unhelpful**, awkward, blocking, delaying, difficult, hindering, inhibiting, preventative, restrictive, stalling, uncooperative
➤ **Antonyms**
cooperative, encouraging, favourable, helpful, obliging, supportive

obtain *verb* 1 = **get**, achieve, acquire, attain, come by, earn, gain, get hold of, get one's hands on, land, procure, score (*slang*), secure 2 *Formal* = **exist**, be in force, be prevalent, be the case, hold, prevail, stand
➤ **Antonyms**
≠**get**: forfeit, forgo, give up, hand over, lose, relinquish, renounce, surrender

obtainable *adjective* = **available**, achievable, at hand, attainable, on tap (*informal*), procurable, ready, to be had

obtrusive *adjective* = **noticeable**, blatant, obvious, prominent, protruding, protuberant, sticking out
➤ **Antonyms**
concealed, covert, hidden, inconspicuous, low-key, muted, unnoticeable, unobtrusive

obtuse *adjective* 1 = **stupid**, dense, dopey (*informal*), dull, dull-witted, dumb (*informal*), dumb-ass (*informal*), heavy, imperceptive, insensitive, retarded, slow, slow on the uptake (*informal*), stolid, thick, uncomprehending, unintelligent 2 = **blunt**, rounded
➤ **Antonyms**
≠**stupid**: astute, bright, clever, keen, quick, sensitive, sharp, shrewd, smart

obviate *verb Formal* = **preclude**, avert, prevent, remove

obvious *adjective* = **evident**, apparent, blatant, bold, clear, conspicuous, distinct, indisputable, manifest, much in evidence, noticeable, open, overt, palpable, patent,

perceptible, plain, plain as the nose on your face (*informal*), pronounced, recognizable, salient, self-evident, self-explanatory, staring one in the face (*informal*), sticking out a mile (*informal*), straightforward, transparent, unconcealed, undeniable, undisguised, unmistakable, visible
➤ **Antonyms**
ambiguous, clear as mud (*informal*), concealed, dark, hidden, imperceptible, inconspicuous, indistinct, invisible, obscure, unapparent, unclear, vague

obviously *adverb* = **clearly**, certainly, distinctly, manifestly, needless to say, of course, palpably, patently, plainly, undeniably, unmistakably, unquestionably, without doubt

occasion *noun* 1 = **time**, chance, convenience, incident, moment, occurrence, opening, opportunity, window 2 = **reason**, call, cause, excuse, ground(s), justification, motive, prompting, provocation 3 = **event**, affair, celebration, experience, happening, occurrence ◆ *verb* 4 *Formal* = **cause**, bring about, create, effect, elicit, engender, evoke, generate, give rise to, induce, inspire, lead to, move, produce, prompt, provoke

occasional *adjective* = **infrequent**, casual, desultory, incidental, intermittent, irregular, odd, rare, sporadic, uncommon
➤ **Antonyms**
constant, continual, customary, frequent, habitual, incessant, regular, routine, usual

occasionally *adverb* = **sometimes**, at intervals, at times, (every) now and then, every so often, from time to time, irregularly, now and again, off and on, on and off, once in a while, on occasion, periodically
➤ **Antonyms**
constantly, continually, continuously, frequently, habitually, often, regularly, routinely

occult *adjective* = **supernatural**, abstruse, arcane, cabbalistic, esoteric, magical, mysterious, mystic, mystical, preternatural, recondite, unknown

occultism *noun* = **black magic**, diabolism, magic, sorcery, supernaturalism, the black arts, witchcraft

occupancy *noun* = **tenancy**, possession, residence, tenure, use

occupant *noun* = **inhabitant**, addressee, incumbent, indweller, inmate, lessee, occupier, resident, tenant, user

occupation *noun* 1 = **profession**, activity, business, calling, craft, employment, job, line (of work), post, pursuit, trade, vocation, walk of life, work **2 = possession**, control, holding, occupancy, residence, tenancy, tenure, use **3 = invasion**, conquest, foreign rule, seizure, subjugation

occupied *adjective* **1 = busy**, employed, engaged, tied up (*informal*), working **2 = in use**, engaged, full, taken, unavailable **3 = inhabited**, full, lived-in, peopled, settled, tenanted
➤ **Antonyms**
≠**inhabited**: deserted, empty, tenantless, uninhabited, unoccupied, untenanted, vacant

occupy *verb* **1 = live in**, be established in, be in residence in, dwell in, inhabit, own, possess, reside in, stay in (*Scot.*), tenant **2** *often passive* **= take up**, absorb, amuse, busy, divert, employ, engage, engross, entertain, hold the attention of, immerse, interest, involve, keep busy *or* occupied, monopolize, preoccupy, tie up **3 = fill**, cover, hold, permeate, pervade, take up, use, utilize **4 = invade**, capture, hold, overrun, seize, take over, take possession of
➤ **Antonyms**
≠**live in**: abandon, depart, desert, evacuate, quit, vacate ≠**invade**: retreat, withdraw

occur *verb* **1 = happen**, arise, befall, betide, chance, come about, come off (*informal*), come to pass (*archaic*), crop up (*informal*), materialize, result, take place, turn up (*informal*) **2 = exist**, appear, be found, be present, develop, manifest itself, obtain, show itself **3 occur to = come to mind**, come to one, cross one's mind, dawn on, enter one's head, spring to mind, strike one, suggest itself

occurrence *noun* **1 = incident**, adventure, affair, circumstance, episode, event, happening, instance, proceeding, transaction **2 = existence**, appearance, development, manifestation, materialization

odd *adjective* **1 = unusual**, abnormal, atypical, bizarre, curious, deviant, different, eccentric, exceptional, extraordinary, fantastic, freak, freakish, funny, irregular, kinky (*informal*), left-field (*informal*), oddball (*informal*), off-the-wall (*slang*), outlandish, out of the ordinary, peculiar, quaint, queer, rare, remarkable, singular, strange, uncommon, unconventional, weird **2 = occasional**, casual, incidental, irregular, miscellaneous, periodic, random, sundry, varied, various **3 = spare**, leftover, remaining, single, solitary, surplus, unmatched, unpaired

➤ **Antonyms**
≠**unusual**: common, customary, familiar, natural, normal, ordinary, regular, typical, unexceptional, unremarkable, usual ≠**occasional**: habitual, permanent, regular, steady ≠**spare**: even, matched, paired

oddity *noun* **1 = irregularity**, abnormality, anomaly, eccentricity, freak, idiosyncrasy, kink, peculiarity, phenomenon, quirk, rarity **2 = misfit**, card (*informal*), crank (*informal*), maverick, nut (*slang*), oddball (*informal*), wacko (*slang*), weirdo *or* weirdie (*informal*) **3 = strangeness**, abnormality, bizarreness, eccentricity, extraordinariness, freakishness, incongruity, oddness, outlandishness, peculiarity, queerness, singularity, unconventionality, unnaturalness

odd man out *noun* **= misfit**, exception, freak, maverick, nonconformist, outsider, square peg in a round hole (*informal*)

oddment *noun* **= leftover**, bit, fag end, fragment, off cut, remnant, scrap, snippet

odds *plural noun* **1 = probability**, balance, chances, likelihood **2** *Brit.* **= difference**, disparity, dissimilarity **3 = advantage**, edge, lead, superiority **4 at odds = in conflict**, at daggers drawn, at loggerheads, at sixes and sevens, at variance, in disagreement, in opposition to, on bad terms, out of line

odds and ends *plural noun* **= scraps**, bits, bits and pieces, debris, leavings, litter, oddments, remnants, rubbish, sundry *or* miscellaneous items

odious *adjective* **= offensive**, abhorrent, abominable, detestable, disgusting, execrable, foul, hateful, horrible, horrid, loathsome, obnoxious, obscene, repellent, repugnant, repulsive, revolting, unpleasant, vile, yucky *or* yukky (*slang*)
➤ **Antonyms**
agreeable, charming, congenial, delightful, enchanting, enjoyable, pleasant, pleasing, winsome

odium *noun* *Formal* **= hatred**, abhorrence, antipathy, censure, condemnation, detestation, disapprobation, disapproval, disfavour, dislike, obloquy, opprobrium

odour *noun* **= smell**, aroma, bouquet, essence, fragrance, perfume, redolence, scent, stench, stink

odyssey *noun* **= journey**, crusade, peregrination, pilgrimage, quest, trek, voyage

off *adverb* **1 = away**, apart, aside, elsewhere, out ◆ *adjective* **2 = cancelled**, absent, finished, gone, inoperative, postponed, unavailable **3 = substandard**, bad, below par, disappointing, low-quality, poor, unsatisfactory **4 = bad**, decomposed, high, mouldy, rancid, rotten, sour, turned

off and on *adverb* **= occasionally**, (every) now and again, every once in a while, from time to time, intermittently, now and then, on and off, sometimes, sporadically

offbeat *adjective* **= unusual**, bizarre, eccentric, far-out (*slang*), idiosyncratic, kinky (*informal*), left-field (*informal*), novel, oddball (*informal*), off-the-wall (*slang*), outré, strange, uncommon, unconventional, unorthodox, wacko (*slang*), way-out (*informal*), weird
➤ **Antonyms**
common, conventional, normal, ordinary, orthodox, run-of-the-mill, stereotyped, traditional, unoriginal, usual

off colour *adjective* **= ill**, green about the gills, not up to par, off form, out of sorts, peaky, peely-wally (*Scot.*), poorly (*informal*), queasy, run down, sick, under par, under the weather (*informal*), unwell, washed out

offence *noun* **1 = crime**, breach of conduct, delinquency, fault, lapse, misdeed, misdemeanour, peccadillo, sin, transgression, trespass, wrong, wrongdoing **2 = annoyance**, anger, displeasure, hard feelings, huff, indignation, pique, resentment, umbrage, wounded feelings, wrath **3 = insult**, affront, displeasure, harm, hurt, indignity, injury, injustice, outrage, put-down (*slang*), slight, snub **4 take offence = be offended**, be disgruntled, go into a huff, resent, take the huff, take umbrage

offend *verb* **1 = insult**, affront, annoy, cut to the quick, disgruntle, displease, give offence, hurt (someone's) feelings, miff (*informal*), outrage, pique, piss one off (*taboo slang*), put (someone's) back up, put (someone's) nose out of joint, slight, snub, tread on (someone's) toes (*informal*), upset, wound **2 = disgust**, be disagreeable to, gross out (*U.S. slang*), make (someone) sick, nauseate, repel, repulse, sicken, turn (someone) off (*informal*)
➤ **Antonyms**
≠**insult**: appease, assuage, conciliate, delight, mollify, placate, please, soothe

offended *adjective* **= resentful**, affronted, disgruntled, displeased, huffy, in a huff, miffed (*informal*), outraged, piqued, put out (*informal*), smarting, stung, upset

offender *noun* **= criminal**, crook, culprit, delinquent, lawbreaker, miscreant, sinner, transgressor, villain, wrongdoer

offensive *adjective* **1 = disgusting**, abominable, detestable, disagreeable,

grisly, loathsome, nasty, nauseating, noisome, obnoxious, odious, repellent, revolting, sickening, unpalatable, unpleasant, unsavoury, vile, yucky *or* yukky (*slang*) **2 = insulting**, abusive, annoying, discourteous, displeasing, disrespectful, impertinent, insolent, irritating, objectionable, rude, uncivil, unmannerly **3 = attacking**, aggressive, invading ♦ *noun* **4 = attack**, campaign, drive, onslaught, push (*informal*) **5 As in** **on the offensive = aggression**, attack
➤ **Antonyms**
adjective ≠**disgusting**: agreeable, attractive, captivating, charming, delightful, pleasant ≠**insulting**: civil, conciliatory, courteous, deferential, polite, respectful ≠**attacking**: defensive ♦ *noun* ≠**aggression**: defensive

offer *verb* **1 = proffer**, bid, extend, give, hold out, put on the market, put up for sale, tender **2 = provide**, afford, furnish, make available, place at (someone's) disposal, present, purvey, show **3 = volunteer**, be at (someone's) service, come forward, offer one's services **4 = propose**, advance, extend, move, put forth, put forward, submit, suggest ♦ *noun* **5 = proposal**, attempt, bid, endeavour, essay, overture, proposition, submission, suggestion, tender
➤ **Antonyms**
verb ≠**proffer**: refuse, retract, revoke, take back, withdraw, withhold

offering *noun* **1 = contribution**, donation, gift, hand-out, present, subscription, widow's mite **2 = sacrifice**, oblation (*in religious contexts*)

offhand *adjective* **1 = casual**, abrupt, aloof, brusque, careless, cavalier, couldn't-care-less, curt, glib, informal, offhanded, perfunctory, take-it-or-leave-it (*informal*), unceremonious, unconcerned, uninterested ♦ *adverb* **2 = impromptu**, ad lib, extempore, just like that (*informal*), off the cuff (*informal*), off the top of one's head (*informal*), without preparation
➤ **Antonyms**
adjective ≠**casual**: attentive, careful, grave, intent, planned, premeditated, prepared, responsible, serious, thoughtful

office *noun* **1 = post**, business, capacity, duty, employment, function, occupation, place, responsibility, role, service, situation, station, work **2 good offices = help**, aid, backing, intercession, intervention, mediation, support

officer *noun* **= official**, agent, appointee, bureaucrat, dignitary, executive, functionary, office-holder, public servant, representative

official *adjective* 1 = **authorized**, accredited, authentic, authoritative, bona fide, certified, endorsed, formal, legitimate, licensed, proper, sanctioned, signed and sealed ♦ *noun* 2 = **officer**, agent, bureaucrat, executive, functionary, office bearer, representative
➤ **Antonyms**
adjective ≠**authorized**: casual, doubtful, dubious, informal, unauthorized, unofficial, unreliable

officiate *verb* = **preside**, chair, conduct, manage, oversee, serve, superintend

officious *adjective* = **interfering**, dictatorial, forward, impertinent, intrusive, meddlesome, meddling, obtrusive, overzealous, pushy (*informal*), self-important
➤ **Antonyms**
aloof, detached, indifferent, reserved, reticent, retiring, shy, taciturn, unforthcoming, withdrawn

offing *noun* **in the offing** = **imminent**, close at hand, coming up, hovering, in prospect, in the immediate future, in the wings, on the horizon, on the way, upcoming

off key *adjective* = **out of tune**, discordant, dissonant, inharmonious, jarring

off-load *verb* = **get rid of**, discharge, dump, jettison, shift, take off, transfer, unburden, unload

off-putting *adjective Informal* = **discouraging**, daunting, discomfiting, disconcerting, dismaying, dispiriting, disturbing, formidable, frustrating, intimidating, unnerving, unsettling, upsetting

offset *verb* = **cancel out**, balance out, compensate for, counteract, counterbalance, make up for, neutralize

offshoot *noun* 1 = **outgrowth**, branch, limb, sprout 2 = **by-product**, adjunct, appendage, development, spin-off

offspring *noun* 1 = **child**, descendant, heir, scion, successor 2 = **children**, brood, descendants, family, heirs, issue, kids (*informal*), progeny, seed (*chiefly biblical*), spawn, successors, young
➤ **Antonyms**
ancestor, begetter, forebear, forefather, forerunner, parent, predecessor, procreator, progenitor

often *adverb* = **frequently**, again and again, generally, many a time, much, oft (*archaic or poetic*), oftentimes (*archaic*), ofttimes (*archaic*), over and over again, repeatedly, time after time, time and again
➤ **Antonyms**

hardly ever, infrequently, irregularly, never, now and then, occasionally, rarely, scarcely, seldom

ogle *verb* = **leer**, eye up (*informal*), give the glad eye (*informal*), give the once-over (*informal*), make sheep's eyes at (*informal*)

ogre *noun* = **monster**, bogey, bogeyman, bugbear, demon, devil, giant, spectre

oil *verb* = **lubricate**, grease

oily *adjective* 1 = **greasy**, fatty, oleaginous 2 = **obsequious**, flattering, plausible, servile, smarmy (*Brit. informal*), smooth, unctuous

ointment *noun* = **lotion**, balm, cream, embrocation, emollient, liniment, salve, unguent

O.K., okay *Informal* ♦ *interjection* 1 = **all right**, agreed, right, roger, very good, very well, yes ♦ *adjective* 2 = **fine**, acceptable, accurate, adequate, all right, approved, convenient, correct, fair, good, in order, middling, not bad (*informal*), passable, permitted, satisfactory, so-so (*informal*), tolerable, up to scratch (*informal*) ♦ *verb* 3 = **approve**, agree to, authorize, consent to, endorse, entitle, give one's consent to, give the go-ahead, give the green light, give the thumbs up (*informal*), pass, rubber-stamp (*informal*), sanction, say yes to ♦ *noun* 4 = **approval**, agreement, approbation, assent, authorization, consent, endorsement, go-ahead (*informal*), green light, permission, sanction, say-so (*informal*), seal of approval
➤ **Antonyms**
adjective ≠**fine**: displeasing, inaccurate, inadequate, incorrect, not up to scratch (*informal*), poor, unacceptable, unsatisfactory, unsuitable

old *adjective* 1 = **aged**, advanced in years, ancient, decrepit, elderly, getting on, grey, grey-haired, hoary, mature, over the hill (*informal*), past it, past one's prime, senile, venerable 2 = **worn-out**, crumbling, done 3 = **early**, aboriginal, antique, archaic, bygone, of old, olden (*archaic*), original, primeval, primitive, primordial 4 = **out of date**, antediluvian, antiquated, antique, dated, hackneyed, obsolete, old-fashioned, outdated, outmoded, out of the ark (*informal*), passé, stale, superannuated, timeworn, unfashionable 5 = **former**, earlier, erstwhile, ex-, one-time, previous, quondam 6 = **long-established**, age-old, experienced, familiar, of long standing, practised, skilled, time-honoured, traditional, veteran, vintage
➤ **Antonyms**
≠**aged**: immature, juvenile, young, youthful ≠**out of date**: current,

fashionable, modern, modish, new, novel, recent, up-to-date

old age *noun* = **declining years**, advancing years, age, autumn *or* evening of one's life, dotage, senility, Third Age
➤ **Antonyms**
adolescence, childhood, early life, immaturity, young days, youth

old-fashioned *adjective* = **out of date**, ancient, antiquated, archaic, behind the times, dated, dead, *démodé*, not with it (*informal*), obsolescent, obsolete, old hat, old-time, outdated, outmoded, out of style, out of the ark (*informal*), passé, past, square (*informal*), unfashionable
➤ **Antonyms**
chic, contemporary, current, fashionable, happening (*informal*), modern, modish, trendy (*Brit. informal*), up-to-date, voguish, with it (*informal*)

old hand *noun* = **expert**, past master, veteran

old-time *adjective* = **old-fashioned**, ancient, antique, bygone, former, past, vintage

old-world *adjective* = **traditional**, archaic, ceremonious, chivalrous, courtly, gallant, old-fashioned, picturesque, quaint

oleaginous *adjective* = **oily**, fat, fatty, greasy, sebaceous

Olympian *adjective* = **majestic**, elevated, exalted, glorious, godlike, lofty, sublime

omen *noun* = **sign**, augury, foreboding, foretoken, indication, portent, premonition, presage, prognostication, warning

ominous *adjective* = **threatening**, baleful, dark, fateful, forbidding, foreboding, inauspicious, menacing, portentous, premonitory, sinister, unpromising, unpropitious
➤ **Antonyms**
auspicious, encouraging, favourable, promising, propitious

omission *noun* = **exclusion**, default, failure, forgetfulness, lack, leaving out, neglect, noninclusion, oversight
➤ **Antonyms**
addition, inclusion, incorporation, insertion

omit *verb* = **leave out**, disregard, drop, eliminate, exclude, fail, forget, give (something) a miss (*informal*), leave (something) undone, miss (out), neglect, overlook, pass over, skip
➤ **Antonyms**
add, enter, include, incorporate, insert, put in

omnipotence *noun* = **supremacy**, divine right, invincibility, mastery, sovereignty, supreme power
➤ **Antonyms**
frailty, impotence, inability, inferiority, powerlessness, vulnerability, weakness

omnipotent *adjective* = **almighty**, all-powerful, supreme
➤ **Antonyms**
feeble, frail, impotent, incapable, inferior, powerless, vulnerable, weak

omniscient *adjective* = **all-knowing**, all-wise

on and off *adverb* = **occasionally**, by fits and starts, discontinuously, (every) now and again, fitfully, from time to time, intermittently, now and then, off and on, sometimes, spasmodically

once *adverb* **1** = **at one time**, formerly, in the old days, in the past, in times gone by, in times past, long ago, once upon a time, previously **2 once and for all** = **for the last time**, conclusively, decisively, finally, for all time, for good, permanently, positively, with finality **3 once in a while** = **occasionally**, at intervals, at times, every now and then, from time to time, now and again, on occasion, sometimes ♦ *noun* **4 at once: a** = **immediately**, directly, forthwith, instantly, now, right away, straight away, straightway (*archaic*), this (very) minute, without delay, without hesitation **b** = **simultaneously**, at *or* in one go (*informal*), at the same time, together

oncoming *adjective* = **approaching**, advancing, forthcoming, looming, onrushing

one-horse *adjective Informal* = **small**, backwoods, inferior, minor, obscure, quiet, sleepy, slow, small-time (*informal*), tinpot (*Brit. informal*), unimportant

onerous *adjective* = **difficult**, backbreaking, burdensome, crushing, demanding, exacting, exhausting, formidable, hard, heavy, laborious, oppressive, responsible, taxing, weighty
➤ **Antonyms**
cushy (*informal*), easy, effortless, facile, light, painless, simple, trifling, undemanding, unexacting, untaxing

one-sided *adjective* = **biased**, coloured, discriminatory, inequitable, lopsided, partial, partisan, prejudiced, unequal, unfair, unjust
➤ **Antonyms**
equal, equitable, fair, impartial, just, unbiased, uncoloured, unprejudiced

one-time *adjective* = **former**, erstwhile, ex-, late, previous, quondam, sometime

one-track *adjective Informal* = **obsessed**, fanatical, fixated, single-track

ongoing *adjective* = **in progress,** continuous, developing, evolving, progressing, unfinished, unfolding

onlooker *noun* = **observer,** bystander, eyewitness, looker-on, spectator, viewer, watcher, witness

only *adjective* 1 = **sole,** exclusive, individual, lone, one and only, single, solitary, unique ♦ *adverb* 2 = **merely,** at most, barely, exclusively, just, purely, simply

onomatopoeic *adjective* = **imitative,** echoic, onomatopoetic

onrush *noun* = **surge,** charge, flood, flow, onset, onslaught, push, rush, stampede, stream

onset *noun* = **beginning,** inception, kick-off (*informal*), outbreak, start
➤ **Antonyms**
conclusion, culmination, end, ending, finish, outcome, termination, wind-up

onslaught *noun* = **attack,** assault, blitz, charge, offensive, onrush, onset
➤ **Antonyms**
defensive, escape, flight, retreat, rout, stampede, withdrawal

onus *noun* = **burden,** liability, load, obligation, responsibility, task
➤ **Antonyms**
exemption, exoneration, liberation, pardon, release, relief, remission

onward, onwards *adverb* = **ahead,** beyond, forth, forward, in front, on

ooze[1] *verb* = **seep,** bleed, discharge, drain, dribble, drip, drop, emit, escape, exude, filter, leak, sweat, weep

ooze[2] *noun* = **mud,** alluvium, mire, muck, silt, slime, sludge

opacity *noun* = **opaqueness,** cloudiness, dullness, impermeability, murkiness, obscurity

opalescent *adjective* = **iridescent,** lustrous, nacreous, opaline, pearly

opaque *adjective* 1 = **cloudy,** clouded, dim, dull, filmy, hazy, impenetrable, murky 2 = **incomprehensible,** abstruse, baffling, cryptic, difficult, enigmatic, obscure, unclear, unfathomable, unintelligible
➤ **Antonyms**
≠**cloudy:** bright, clear, crystal clear, limpid, lucid, pellucid, transparent
≠**incomprehensible:** clear, crystal clear, lucid

open *adjective* 1 = **unclosed,** agape, ajar, gaping, revealed, unbarred, uncovered, unfastened, unlocked, unobstructed, unsealed, yawning 2 = **extended,** expanded, spread out, unfolded, unfurled 3 = **unenclosed,** clear, exposed, extensive, free, rolling, spacious, sweeping,

uncrowded, wide, wide-open 4 = **accessible,** available, free, free to all, general, public, unengaged, unoccupied, unrestricted, up for grabs (*informal*), vacant 5 = **unresolved,** arguable, debatable, moot, undecided, unsettled, up in the air, yet to be decided 6 = **objective,** disinterested, free, impartial, receptive, unbiased, uncommitted, unprejudiced 7 = **frank,** above board, artless, candid, fair, guileless, honest, ingenuous, innocent, natural, sincere, transparent, unreserved 8 = **generous,** bounteous, bountiful, liberal, munificent, prodigal 9 = **obvious,** apparent, barefaced, blatant, bold, clear, conspicuous, downright, evident, flagrant, frank, manifest, noticeable, overt, plain, unconcealed, undisguised, visible 10 = **unprotected,** exposed, undefended, unfortified 11 *with* **to** = **susceptible,** an easy target for, at the mercy of, defenceless against, disposed, exposed, liable, vulnerable 12 = **gappy,** filigree, lacy, loose, porous, spongy ♦ *verb* 13 = **unfasten,** clear, throw wide, unbar, unblock, unclose, uncork, uncover, undo, unlock, unseal, untie, unwrap 14 = **unfold,** expand, spread (out), unfurl, unroll 15 = **split,** come apart, crack, rupture, separate 16 = **start,** begin, commence, get *or* start the ball rolling, inaugurate, initiate, kick off (*informal*), launch, set in motion
➤ **Antonyms**
adjective ≠**unclosed:** closed, fastened, locked, sealed, shut ≠**unenclosed:** bounded, confined, covered, crowded, enclosed, limited, obstructed, restricted ≠**accessible:** inaccessible, private, protected, restricted ≠**objective:** biased, partial, prejudiced ≠**frank:** artful, cunning, introverted, reserved, secretive, sly, withdrawn ≠**obvious:** covert, disguised, hidden, secret, veiled ≠**unprotected:** defended, protected ♦ *verb* ≠**unfasten:** block, close, fasten, lock, obstruct, seal, shut ≠**unfold:** fold ≠**start:** close, conclude, end, finish, terminate

open-air *adjective* = **outdoor,** alfresco

open-and-shut *adjective* = **straightforward,** foregone, obvious, simple

open-handed *adjective* = **generous,** bountiful, free, lavish, liberal, munificent, prodigal, unstinting
➤ **Antonyms**
avaricious, close-fisted, grasping, grudging, mean, miserly, parsimonious, penny-pinching (*informal*), penurious, stingy, tight-fisted

opening *noun* 1 = **beginning,** birth, commencement, dawn, inauguration,

inception, initiation, kickoff (*informal*), launch, launching, onset, opening move, outset, overture, start **2 = opportunity**, break (*informal*), chance, look-in (*informal*), occasion, place, vacancy, window **3 = hole**, aperture, breach, break, chink, cleft, crack, fissure, gap, orifice, perforation, rent, rupture, slot, space, split, vent ♦ *adjective* **4 = first**, beginning, commencing, early, inaugural, initial, introductory, maiden, primary
➤ **Antonyms**
noun ≠**beginning**: cessation, close, completion, conclusion, culmination, ending, finale, finish, termination, winding up (*informal*) ≠**hole**: blockage, closing, closure, obstruction, occlusion, plug, seal, stoppage

openly *adverb* **1 = candidly**, face to face, forthrightly, frankly, overtly, plainly, straight from the shoulder (*informal*), unhesitatingly, unreservedly **2 = blatantly**, brazenly, flagrantly, in full view, in public, publicly, shamelessly, unabashedly, unashamedly
➤ **Antonyms**
covertly, furtively, in camera, privately, quietly, secretly, slyly, surreptitiously

open-minded *adjective* **= unprejudiced**, broad, broad-minded, catholic, dispassionate, enlightened, free, impartial, liberal, reasonable, receptive, tolerant, unbiased, undogmatic
➤ **Antonyms**
biased, bigoted, dogmatic, intolerant, narrow-minded, opinionated, pig-headed, prejudiced, uncompromising

openness *noun* **= frankness**, candour *or* (*U.S.*) candor, honesty, sincerity *or* sincereness

operate *verb* **1 = work**, act, be in action, be in business, function, go, perform, run **2 = handle**, be in charge of, manage, manoeuvre, use, work **3 = perform surgery**
➤ **Antonyms**
≠**work**: break down, conk out (*informal*), cut out (*informal*), fail, falter, halt, seize up, stall, stop

operation *noun* **1 = procedure**, action, affair, course, exercise, motion, movement, performance, process, use, working **2 = effect**, activity, agency, force, influence **3 = undertaking**, affair, business, deal, enterprise, proceeding, transaction **4 = surgery 5 = manoeuvre**, assault, campaign, exercise **6 in operation =̇ in action**, effective, functioning, going, in business, in force, operative

operational *adjective* **= working**,

functional, going, in working order, operative, prepared, ready, up and running, usable, viable, workable
➤ **Antonyms**
broken, ineffective, inoperative, kaput (*informal*), nonfunctional, on the blink (*slang*), on the fritz (*slang*), out of order

operative *adjective* **1 = in force**, active, current, effective, efficient, functional, functioning, in business, in operation, operational, serviceable, workable **2 = relevant**, crucial, important, indicative, influential, key, significant ♦ *noun* **3 = worker**, artisan, employee, hand, labourer, machinist, mechanic
➤ **Antonyms**
adjective ≠**in force**: ineffective, inefficient, inoperative, nonfunctional, powerless, unusable, unworkable

operator *noun* **1 = worker**, conductor, driver, handler, mechanic, operative, practitioner, technician **2 = manager**, administrator, contractor, dealer, director **3** *Informal* **= manipulator**, Machiavellian, mover, shyster (*slang, chiefly U.S.*), wheeler-dealer (*informal*), worker

opiate *noun* **= narcotic**, downer (*slang*), drug, sedative, tranquillizer

opine *verb Formal* **= give as one's opinion**, believe, conjecture, declare, say, suggest, suppose, venture, volunteer

opinion *noun* **1 = belief**, assessment, conception, conjecture, estimation, feeling, idea, impression, judgment, mind, notion, persuasion, point of view, sentiment, theory, view **2 matter of opinion = debatable point**, matter of judgment, moot point, open question

opinionated *adjective* **= dogmatic**, adamant, biased, bigoted, bull-headed, cocksure, dictatorial, doctrinaire, inflexible, obdurate, obstinate, overbearing, pig-headed, prejudiced, self-assertive, single-minded, stubborn, uncompromising
➤ **Antonyms**
broad-minded, compliant, compromising, dispassionate, flexible, open-minded, receptive, tolerant, unbiased, unbigoted, unprejudiced

opponent *noun* **= adversary**, antagonist, challenger, competitor, contestant, disputant, enemy, foe, opposer, rival, the opposition
➤ **Antonyms**
accomplice, ally, associate, colleague, friend, helper, mate, supporter

opportune *adjective Formal* **= timely**, advantageous, appropriate, apt, auspicious, convenient, falling into one's

lap, favourable, felicitous, fit, fitting, fortunate, happy, lucky, proper, propitious, seasonable, suitable, well-timed
➤ **Antonyms**
inappropriate, inconvenient, inopportune, unfavourable, unfortunate, unsuitable, untimely

opportunism noun = **expediency**, exploitation, Machiavellianism, pragmatism, realism, unscrupulousness

opportunity noun = **chance**, break (informal), convenience, moment, occasion, opening, scope, time, window

oppose verb = **fight**, bar, block, check, combat, confront, contradict, counter, counterattack, defy, face, fly in the face of, hinder, obstruct, prevent, resist, set one's face against, speak against, stand up to, take a stand against, take issue with, take on, thwart, withstand
➤ **Antonyms**
advance, advocate, aid, back, defend, espouse, help, promote, support

opposed adjective = **against**, antagonistic, anti (informal), antipathetic, antithetical, at daggers drawn, averse, clashing, conflicting, contra (informal), contrary, dissentient, hostile, incompatible, inimical, in opposition, opposing, opposite

opposing adjective = **conflicting**, antagonistic, antipathetic, clashing, combatant, contrary, enemy, hostile, incompatible, irreconcilable, opposed, opposite, rival, warring

opposite adjective 1 = **facing**, corresponding, fronting 2 = **different**, adverse, antagonistic, antithetical, conflicting, contradictory, contrary, contrasted, diametrically opposed, differing, diverse, hostile, inconsistent, inimical, irreconcilable, opposed, reverse, unlike ◆ noun 3 = **reverse**, antithesis, contradiction, contrary, converse, inverse, the other extreme
➤ **Antonyms**
adjective ≠**different**: alike, consistent, corresponding, identical, like, matching, same, similar, uniform

opposition noun 1 = **hostility**, antagonism, competition, counteraction, disapproval, obstruction, obstructiveness, prevention, resistance, unfriendliness 2 = **opponent**, antagonist, competition, foe, other side, rival
➤ **Antonyms**
≠**hostility**: agreement, approval, assent, collaboration, concurrence, cooperation, friendliness, responsiveness

oppress verb 1 = **subjugate**, abuse, crush, maltreat, overpower, overwhelm, persecute, subdue, suppress, wrong 2 = **depress**, afflict, burden, dispirit, harass, lie or weigh heavy upon, sadden, take the heart out of, torment, vex
➤ **Antonyms**
≠**subjugate**: deliver, emancipate, free, liberate, loose, release, set free ≠**depress**: unburden

oppressed adjective = **downtrodden**, abused, browbeaten, burdened, disadvantaged, enslaved, harassed, maltreated, misused, slave, subject, tyrannized, underprivileged
➤ **Antonyms**
advantaged, exalted, favoured, honoured, liberated, privileged

oppression noun = **subjugation**, abuse, brutality, cruelty, hardship, harshness, injury, injustice, iron hand, maltreatment, persecution, subjection, suffering, tyranny
➤ **Antonyms**
benevolence, clemency, compassion, goodness, humaneness, justice, kindness, mercy, sympathy, tenderness

oppressive adjective 1 = **tyrannical**, brutal, cruel, despotic, harsh, heavy, inhuman, overbearing, repressive, severe, unjust 2 = **stifling**, airless, close, heavy, muggy, overpowering, stuffy, suffocating, sultry, torrid
➤ **Antonyms**
≠**tyrannical**: gentle, humane, just, lenient, merciful, soft

oppressor noun = **persecutor**, autocrat, bully, despot, scourge, slave-driver, taskmaster, tormentor, tyrant

opprobrious adjective 1 = **contemptuous**, abusive, damaging, defamatory, insulting, vitriolic 2 = **shameful**, abominable, contemptible, despicable, dishonourable, disreputable, ignominious, reprehensible

opprobrium noun Formal = **disgrace**, calumny, censure, discredit, disfavour, dishonour, disrepute, ignominy, ill repute, infamy, shame, stigma

oppugn verb Formal = **dispute**, argue, attack, call into question, cast doubt on, oppose

opt verb, often with **for** = **choose**, decide (on), elect, go for, plump for, prefer
➤ **Antonyms**
decide against, dismiss, eliminate, exclude, preclude, reject, rule out, turn down

optimistic adjective 1 = **idealistic**, Utopian 2 = **hopeful**, bright, buoyant, can-do (informal), cheerful, confident, encouraged, expectant, looking on the bright side, positive, rosy, sanguine
➤ **Antonyms**

≠**hopeful**: bleak, cynical, despairing, despondent, downhearted, fatalistic, gloomy, glum, hopeless, pessimistic, resigned

optimum *adjective* = **ideal**, best, choicest, highest, most favourable *or* advantageous, optimal, peak, perfect, superlative
➤ **Antonyms**
inferior, least, lowest, minimal, poorest, worst

option *noun* = **choice**, alternative, election, preference, selection

optional *adjective* = **voluntary**, discretionary, elective, extra, noncompulsory, open, possible, up to the individual
➤ **Antonyms**
compulsory, *de rigueur*, mandatory, obligatory, required

opulence *noun* 1 = **wealth**, affluence, big bucks (*informal, chiefly U.S.*), big money, fortune, lavishness, luxuriance, luxury, megabucks (*U.S. & Canad. slang*), plenty, prosperity, riches, richness, sumptuousness, tidy sum (*informal*) 2 = **abundance**, copiousness, cornucopia, fullness, profusion, richness, superabundance
➤ **Antonyms**
≠**wealth**: impecuniousness, indigence, lack, penury, poverty, privation, want ≠**abundance**: dearth, lack, paucity, scantiness, scarcity, want

opulent *adjective* 1 = **rich**, affluent, lavish, luxurious, moneyed, prosperous, sumptuous, wealthy, well-heeled (*informal*), well-off, well-to-do 2 = **abundant**, copious, lavish, luxuriant, plentiful, profuse, prolific
➤ **Antonyms**
≠**rich**: broke (*informal*), destitute, down and out, indigent, moneyless, needy, on the rocks, penurious, poor, poverty-stricken

opus *noun* = **work**, brainchild, composition, creation, *oeuvre*, piece, production

oracle *noun* 1 = **prophet**, seer, sibyl, soothsayer 2 = **prophecy**, answer, augury, divination, prediction, prognostication, revelation, vision 3 = **authority**, adviser, guru, high priest, horse's mouth, mastermind, mentor, pundit, source, wizard

oracular *adjective* 1 = **prophetic**, portentous, prescient, sibylline 2 = **wise**, authoritative, sage 3 = **mysterious**, ambiguous, arcane, cryptic, Delphic, equivocal, obscure, two-edged

oral *adjective* = **spoken**, verbal, viva voce, vocal

oration *noun* = **speech**, address, declamation, discourse, harangue, homily, lecture, spiel (*informal*)

orator *noun* = **public speaker**, declaimer, lecturer, rhetorician, speaker

oratorical *adjective* = **rhetorical**, bombastic, declamatory, eloquent, grandiloquent, high-flown, magniloquent, silver-tongued, sonorous

oratory *noun* = **eloquence**, declamation, elocution, grandiloquence, public speaking, rhetoric, speechifying, speech-making

orb *noun* = **sphere**, ball, circle, globe, ring, round

orbit *noun* 1 = **path**, circle, course, cycle, ellipse, revolution, rotation, track, trajectory 2 = **sphere of influence**, ambit, compass, course, domain, influence, range, reach, scope, sphere, sweep ♦ *verb* 3 = **circle**, circumnavigate, encircle, revolve around

orchestrate *verb* 1 = **score**, arrange 2 = **organize**, arrange, concert, coordinate, integrate, present, put together, set up, stage-manage

ordain *verb* 1 = **appoint**, anoint, consecrate, invest, nominate 2 *Formal* = **order**, decree, demand, dictate, establish, fix, lay down, legislate, prescribe, pronounce, rule, set, will

ordeal *noun* = **hardship**, affliction, agony, anguish, baptism of fire, nightmare, suffering, test, torture, trial, tribulation(s), trouble(s)
➤ **Antonyms**
bliss, delight, elation, enjoyment, gladness, happiness, joy, pleasure

order *noun* 1 = **instruction**, behest, command, decree, dictate, direction, directive, injunction, law, mandate, ordinance, precept, regulation, rule, say-so (*informal*), stipulation 2 = **tidiness**, arrangement, harmony, method, neatness, orderliness, organization, pattern, plan, regularity, symmetry, system 3 = **sequence**, arrangement, array, categorization, classification, codification, grouping, layout, line-up, ordering, placement, progression, series, setup (*informal*), structure, succession 4 = **peace**, calm, control, discipline, law, law and order, quiet, tranquillity 5 = **request**, application, booking, commission, requisition, reservation 6 = **class**, caste, degree, grade, hierarchy, pecking order (*informal*), position, rank, status 7 = **kind**, breed, cast, class, family, genre, genus, ilk, sort, species, subclass, taxonomic group, tribe, type 8 = **society**, association, brotherhood, community, company,

fraternity, guild, league, lodge, organization, sect, sisterhood, sodality, union **9 in order: a = tidy**, arranged, in sequence, neat, orderly, shipshape **b = appropriate**, acceptable, called for, correct, fitting, O.K. or okay (*informal*), right, suitable **10 out of order: a = not working**, broken, broken-down, bust (*informal*), gone haywire (*informal*), in disrepair, inoperative, kaput (*informal*), nonfunctional, on the blink (*slang*), on the fritz (*U.S. slang*), out of commission, U.S. (*informal*), wonky (*Brit. slang*) **b = improper**, indecorous, not cricket (*informal*), not done, not on (*informal*), out of place, out of turn, uncalled-for, wrong ♦ *verb* **11 = command**, adjure, bid, charge, decree, demand, direct, enjoin, instruct, ordain, prescribe, require **12 = request**, apply for, book, call for, contract for, demand, engage, prescribe, reserve, send away for **13 = arrange**, adjust, align, catalogue, class, classify, conduct, control, group, lay out, marshal, neaten, organize, put to rights, regulate, sequence, set in order, sort out, systematize, tabulate, tidy
➤ **Antonyms**
noun ≠**tidiness**: chaos, clutter, confusion, disarray, disorder, jumble, mess, muddle, pandemonium, shambles ♦ *verb* ≠**arrange**: clutter, confuse, disarrange, disorder, disturb, jumble up, mess up, mix up, muddle, scramble

orderly *adjective* **1 = well-organized**, businesslike, in apple-pie order (*informal*), in order, methodical, neat, regular, scientific, shipshape, systematic, systematized, tidy, trim, well-regulated **2 = well-behaved**, controlled, decorous, disciplined, law-abiding, nonviolent, peaceable, quiet, restrained
➤ **Antonyms**
≠**well-organized**: chaotic, disorderly, disorganized, higgledy-piggledy (*informal*), messy, sloppy, unsystematic ≠**well-behaved**: disorderly, riotous, uncontrolled, undisciplined

ordinance *noun* **= rule**, command, decree, dictum, edict, law, order, precept, regulation, ruling, statute

ordinarily *adverb* **= usually**, as a rule, commonly, customarily, generally, habitually, in general, in the usual way, normally
➤ **Antonyms**
hardly ever, infrequently, occasionally, rarely, scarcely, seldom, uncommonly

ordinary *adjective* **1 = usual**, accustomed, common, conventional, customary, established, everyday, familiar, habitual, normal, regular, routine, standard, stock,

typical **2 = commonplace**, banal, common or garden (*informal*), humble, humdrum, modest, mundane, pedestrian, plain, prosaic, run-of-the-mill, unremarkable, workaday **3 = average**, fair, indifferent, inferior, mean, mediocre, no great shakes (*informal*), second-rate, undistinguished, unexceptional, uninspired, unremarkable **4 out of the ordinary = unusual**, atypical, exceptional, exciting, extraordinary, noteworthy, outstanding, rare, remarkable, significant, special, striking, uncommon
➤ **Antonyms**
≠**commonplace, average**: distinguished, exceptional, extraordinary, important, impressive, inspired, notable, novel, outstanding, rare, significant, superior, uncommon, unconventional, unique, unusual

ordnance *noun* **= weapons**, arms, artillery, big guns, guns, materiel, munitions

organ *noun* **1 = part**, element, member, process, structure, unit **2 = medium**, agency, channel, forum, journal, means, mouthpiece, newspaper, paper, periodical, publication, vehicle, voice

organic *adjective* **1 = natural**, animate, biological, live, living **2 = systematic**, integrated, methodical, ordered, organized, structured

organism *noun* **= creature**, animal, being, body, entity, living thing, structure

organization *noun* **1 = group**, association, body, company, concern, confederation, consortium, corporation, federation, institution, league, outfit (*informal*), syndicate **2 = management**, construction, coordination, direction, formation, forming, formulation, methodology, organizing, planning, regulation, running, structuring **3 = structure**, arrangement, chemistry, composition, configuration, conformation, constitution, design, format, framework, grouping, make-up, pattern, plan, system, unity, whole

organize *verb* **1 = plan**, arrange, be responsible for, constitute, construct, coordinate, establish, form, frame, get going, get together, marshal, put together, run, see to (*informal*), set up, shape, take care of **2 = put in order**, arrange, catalogue, classify, codify, group, systematize
➤ **Antonyms**
≠**plan**: confuse, derange, disrupt, upset ≠**put in order**: disorganize, jumble, mix up, muddle, scramble

orgasm *noun* **= climax**, coming (*taboo slang*), pleasure

orgy *noun* **1** = **revel**, bacchanalia, carousal, debauch, revelry, Saturnalia **2** = **spree**, binge (*informal*), bout, excess, indulgence, overindulgence, splurge, surfeit

orient *verb* = **adjust**, acclimatize, adapt, align, familiarize, get one's bearings, orientate

orientation *noun* **1** = **position**, bearings, coordination, direction, location, sense of direction **2** = **adjustment**, acclimatization, adaptation, assimilation, breaking in, familiarization, introduction, settling in

orifice *noun* = **opening**, aperture, cleft, hole, mouth, perforation, pore, rent, vent

origin *noun* **1** = **root**, base, basis, cause, derivation, font (*poetic*), fount, fountain, fountainhead, provenance, roots, source, spring, wellspring **2** = **beginning**, birth, commencement, creation, dawning, early stages, emergence, foundation, genesis, inauguration, inception, launch, origination, outset, start **3** = **ancestry**, beginnings, birth, descent, extraction, family, heritage, lineage, parentage, pedigree, stirps, stock
➤ **Antonyms**
≠**beginning**: conclusion, culmination, death, end, expiry, finale, finish, outcome, termination

original *adjective* **1** = **first**, aboriginal, earliest, early, infant, initial, introductory, opening, primary, primitive, primordial, rudimentary, starting **2** = **new**, fresh, ground-breaking, innovative, innovatory, novel, seminal, unconventional, unprecedented, untried, unusual **3** = **creative**, fertile, imaginative, ingenious, inventive, resourceful **4** = **authentic**, archetypal, first, first-hand, genuine, master, primary, prototypical ♦ *noun* **5** = **prototype**, archetype, master, model, paradigm, pattern, precedent, standard, type
➤ **Antonyms**
adjective ≠**first**: final, last, latest ≠**new**: antiquated, banal, commonplace, conventional, familiar, normal, old, old-fashioned, ordinary, stale, standard, stock, traditional, typical, unimaginative, unoriginal, usual ≠**authentic**: borrowed, copied, secondary, unoriginal ♦ *noun* ≠**prototype**: copy, imitation, replica, reproduction

originality *noun* = **novelty**, creativeness, creative spirit, creativity, freshness, imagination, imaginativeness, individuality, ingenuity, innovation, innovativeness, inventiveness, new ideas, newness, unconventionality, unorthodoxy
➤ **Antonyms**

conformity, conventionality, imitativeness, normality, orthodoxy, regularity, staleness, traditionalism

originally *adverb* = **initially**, at first, at the outset, at the start, by origin, first, in the beginning, in the first place, to begin with

originate *verb* **1** = **begin**, arise, be born, come, derive, emanate, emerge, flow, issue, proceed, result, rise, spring, start, stem **2** = **introduce**, bring about, conceive, create, develop, discover, evolve, form, formulate, generate, give birth to, inaugurate, initiate, institute, invent, launch, pioneer, produce, set in motion, set up
➤ **Antonyms**
cease, conclude, end, finish, terminate, wind up

originator *noun* = **creator**, architect, author, father *or* mother, founder, generator, innovator, inventor, maker, pioneer, prime mover

ornament *noun* **1** = **decoration**, accessory, adornment, bauble, embellishment, festoon, frill, garnish, knick-knack, trimming, trinket **2** = **leading light**, flower, honour, jewel, pride, treasure ♦ *verb* **3** = **decorate**, adorn, beautify, brighten, deck, dress up, embellish, festoon, garnish, grace, prettify, trim

ornamental *adjective* = **decorative**, attractive, beautifying, embellishing, for show, showy

ornamentation *noun* = **decoration**, adornment, elaboration, embellishment, embroidery, frills, ornateness

ornate *adjective* = **elaborate**, baroque, beautiful, bedecked, busy, decorated, elegant, fancy, florid, fussy, ornamented, overelaborate, rococo
➤ **Antonyms**
austere, bare, basic, ordinary, plain, severe, simple, spartan, stark, subdued, unadorned, unfussy

orthodox *adjective* = **established**, accepted, approved, conformist, conventional, customary, kosher (*informal*), official, received, traditional, well-established
➤ **Antonyms**
eccentric, heretical, left-field (*informal*), liberal, nonconformist, novel, off-the-wall (*slang*), original, radical, unconventional, unorthodox, unusual

orthodoxy *noun* = **conformity**, authoritativeness, authority, conformism, conventionality, inflexibility, received wisdom, traditionalism
➤ **Antonyms**
flexibility, heresy, heterodoxy, impiety,

nonconformism, nonconformity, unconventionality

oscillate *verb* = **fluctuate**, seesaw, sway, swing, vacillate, vary, vibrate, waver
➤ **Antonyms**
commit oneself, decide, determine, purpose, resolve, settle

oscillation *noun* = **swing**, fluctuation, instability, seesawing, vacillation, variation, wavering

ossify *verb* = **harden**, fossilize, freeze, petrify, solidify, stiffen

ostensible *adjective* = **apparent**, alleged, avowed, exhibited, manifest, outward, pretended, professed, purported, seeming, so-called, superficial, supposed

ostensibly *adverb* = **apparently**, on the face of it, on the surface, professedly, seemingly, supposedly, to all intents and purposes

ostentation *noun* = **display**, affectation, boasting, exhibitionism, flamboyance, flashiness, flaunting, flourish, pageantry, parade, pomp, pretension, pretentiousness, show, showiness, showing off (*informal*), swank (*informal*), vaunting
➤ **Antonyms**
humility, inconspicuousness, modesty, plainness, reserve, simplicity, unpretentiousness

ostentatious *adjective* = **pretentious**, boastful, brash, conspicuous, extravagant, flamboyant, flash (*informal*), flashy, gaudy, loud, obtrusive, pompous, showy, swanky (*informal*), vain, vulgar
➤ **Antonyms**
conservative, inconspicuous, low-key, modest, plain, reserved, simple, sombre

ostracism *noun* = **exclusion**, avoidance, banishment, boycott, cold-shouldering, exile, expulsion, isolation, rejection
➤ **Antonyms**
acceptance, admission, approval, inclusion, invitation, reception, welcome

ostracize *verb* = **exclude**, avoid, banish, blackball, blacklist, boycott, cast out, cold-shoulder, excommunicate, exile, expatriate, expel, give (someone) the cold shoulder, reject, send to Coventry, shun, snub
➤ **Antonyms**
accept, admit, approve, embrace, greet, include, invite, receive, welcome

other *adjective* 1 = **additional**, added, alternative, auxiliary, extra, further, more, spare, supplementary 2 = **different**, contrasting, dissimilar, distinct, diverse, remaining, separate, unrelated, variant

otherwise *conjunction* 1 = **or else**, if not, or then ♦ *adverb* 2 = **differently**, any other way, contrarily

ounce *noun* = **shred**, atom, crumb, drop, grain, iota, particle, scrap, speck, trace, whit

oust *verb* = **expel**, depose, dislodge, displace, dispossess, eject, throw out, topple, turn out, unseat

out *adjective* 1 = **away**, abroad, absent, elsewhere, gone, not at home, outside 2 = **extinguished**, at an end, cold, dead, doused, ended, exhausted, expired, finished, used up 3 = **old-fashioned**, antiquated, behind the times, dated, dead, démodé, old hat, passé, square (*informal*), unfashionable 4 = **not allowed**, impossible, not on (*informal*), ruled out, unacceptable
➤ **Antonyms**
≠**old-fashioned**: à la mode, fashionable, in, in fashion, latest, modern, trendy (*Brit. informal*), up-to-date, with it (*informal*)

out-and-out *adjective* = **absolute**, arrant, complete, consummate, deep-dyed (*usually derogatory*), downright, outright, perfect, thorough, total, unmitigated, unqualified, utter

outbreak *noun* = **eruption**, burst, epidemic, explosion, flare-up, flash, outburst, rash, spasm, upsurge

outburst *noun* = **outpouring**, attack, discharge, eruption, explosion, fit of temper, flare-up, outbreak, paroxysm, spasm, storm, surge

outcast *noun* = **pariah**, castaway, exile, leper, *persona non grata*, refugee, untouchable, vagabond, wretch

outclass *verb* = **surpass**, be a cut above (*informal*), beat, eclipse, exceed, excel, leave *or* put in the shade, leave standing (*informal*), outdistance, outdo, outrank, outshine, outstrip, overshadow, run rings around (*informal*)

outcome *noun* = **result**, aftereffect, aftermath, conclusion, consequence, end, end result, issue, payoff (*informal*), sequel, upshot

outcry *noun* = **protest**, clamour, commotion, complaint, exclamation, hue and cry, hullaballoo, outburst, uproar

outdated *adjective* = **old-fashioned**, antiquated, antique, archaic, behind the times, démodé, obsolete, outmoded, out of date, out of style, out of the ark (*informal*), passé, unfashionable
➤ **Antonyms**
à la mode, all the rage, contemporary, current, fashionable, in vogue, modern, modish, stylish, trendy (*Brit. informal*),

up-to-date, with it (*informal*)

outdistance *verb* = **leave behind**, leave standing (*informal*), lose, outrun, outstrip, shake off

outdo *verb* = **surpass**, beat, be one up on, best, eclipse, exceed, excel, get the better of, go one better than (*informal*), outclass, outdistance, outmanoeuvre, outshine, outsmart (*informal*), overcome, run rings around (*informal*), top, transcend

outdoor *adjective* = **open-air**, alfresco, out-of-door(s), outside
➤ **Antonyms**
indoor, inside, interior, within

outer *adjective* = **external**, exposed, exterior, outlying, outside, outward, peripheral, superficial, surface
➤ **Antonyms**
central, closer, inner, inside, interior, internal, inward, nearer

outface *verb* = **outstare**, confront, defy, look straight in the eye, square up to, stare down, stare out

outfit *noun* 1 = **costume**, clothes, ensemble, garb, gear (*informal*), get-up (*informal*), kit, rigout (*informal*), suit, threads (*slang*) 2 *Informal* = **group**, company, corps, coterie, crew, organization, set, setup (*informal*), squad, team, unit

outfitter *noun* Old-fashioned = **clothier**, costumier, couturier, dressmaker, tailor

outflow *noun* = **discharge**, ebb, effluence, effusion, emanation, gush, issue, jet, outpouring, rush, spout

outgoing *adjective* 1 = **leaving**, departing, ex-, former, last, past, retiring, withdrawing 2 = **sociable**, approachable, communicative, cordial, demonstrative, easy, expansive, extrovert, friendly, genial, gregarious, informal, open, unreserved, warm
➤ **Antonyms**
≠**leaving**: arriving, entering, incoming ≠**sociable**: austere, cold, indifferent, reserved, retiring, withdrawn

outgoings *plural noun* = **expenses**, costs, expenditure, outlay, overheads

outgrowth *noun* 1 = **product**, by-product, consequence, development, result, spin-off 2 = **offshoot**, bulge, excrescence, outcrop, process, shoot, sprout

outing *noun* = **trip**, excursion, expedition, jaunt, pleasure trip, spin (*informal*)

outlandish *adjective* = **strange**, alien, bizarre, eccentric, exotic, fantastic, far-out (*slang*), foreign, freakish, grotesque, outré, preposterous, queer, unheard-of, weird
➤ **Antonyms**

banal, commonplace, everyday, familiar, humdrum, mundane, normal, ordinary, usual, well-known

outlast *verb* = **outlive**, outstay, outwear, survive

outlaw *noun* 1 *History* = **bandit**, brigand, desperado, footpad (*archaic*), fugitive, highwayman, marauder, outcast, pariah, robber ♦ *verb* 2 = **forbid**, ban, banish, bar, disallow, embargo, exclude, interdict, make illegal, prohibit, proscribe 3 = **put a price on (someone's) head**
➤ **Antonyms**
verb ≠**forbid**: allow, approve, authorize, consent, endorse, legalise, permit, sanction, support

outlay *noun* = **expenditure**, cost, disbursement, expenses, investment, outgoings, spending

outlet *noun* 1 = **release**, means of expression, safety valve, vent 2 = **shop**, market, store 3 = **opening**, avenue, channel, duct, egress, exit, orifice, release, way out

outline *noun* 1 = **summary**, bare facts, main features, recapitulation, résumé, rough idea, rundown, synopsis, thumbnail sketch 2 = **shape**, configuration, contour, delineation, figure, form, profile, silhouette ♦ *verb* 3 = **summarize**, adumbrate, delineate, draft, plan, rough out, sketch (in), trace

outlive *verb* = **survive**, outlast

outlook *noun* 1 = **attitude**, angle, frame of mind, perspective, point of view, slant, standpoint, viewpoint, views 2 = **prospect**, expectations, forecast, future 3 = **view**, aspect, panorama, prospect, scene, vista

outlying *adjective* = **remote**, backwoods, distant, far-flung, in the middle of nowhere, outer, out-of-the-way, peripheral, provincial

outmanoeuvre *verb* = **outwit**, get the better of, outdo, outflank, outsmart (*informal*), run rings round (*informal*), steal a march on (*informal*)

outmoded *adjective* = **old-fashioned**, anachronistic, antediluvian, antiquated, antique, archaic, behind the times, dated, démodé, obsolescent, obsolete, old-time, out-of-date, out of style, outworn, passé, square (*informal*), unfashionable
➤ **Antonyms**
all the rage, fashionable, fresh, in vogue, latest, modern, modish, new, recent

out-of-date *adjective* = **old-fashioned**, antiquated, archaic, dated, discarded, elapsed, expired, invalid, lapsed, obsolete, outmoded, out of the ark (*informal*),

outworn, passé, stale, unfashionable
➤ **Antonyms**
contemporary, current, fashionable, in, new, now (*informal*), trendy (*Brit. informal*), up to date, valid

out-of-the-way *adjective* = **remote**, distant, far-flung, inaccessible, isolated, lonely, obscure, off the beaten track, outlying, secluded, unfrequented
➤ **Antonyms**
accessible, close, convenient, frequented, handy, near, nearby, proximate, reachable, within sniffing distance (*informal*)

out-of-work *adjective* = **unemployed**, idle, jobless, laid off, on the dole (*Brit.*), out of a job, redundant

outpouring *noun* = **stream**, cascade, deluge, effluence, effusion, emanation, flow, flux, issue, outflow, spate, spurt, torrent

output *noun* = **production**, achievement, manufacture, product, productivity, yield

outrage *noun* **1** = **indignation**, anger, fury, hurt, resentment, shock, wrath **2** = **atrocity**, barbarism, enormity, evil, inhumanity **3** = **violation**, abuse, affront, desecration, indignity, injury, insult, offence, profanation, sacrilege, shock, violence ♦ *verb* **4** = **offend**, affront, incense, infuriate, madden, scandalize, shock

outrageous *adjective* **1** = **unreasonable**, excessive, exorbitant, extravagant, immoderate, O.T.T. (*slang*), over the top (*slang*), preposterous, scandalous, shocking, steep (*informal*) **2** = **atrocious**, abominable, barbaric, disgraceful, egregious, flagrant, heinous, horrible, infamous, inhuman, iniquitous, nefarious, offensive, scandalous, shocking, unspeakable, villainous, violent, wicked
➤ **Antonyms**
≠**unreasonable**: equitable, fair, moderate, reasonable ≠**atrocious**: just, mild, minor, tolerable, trivial

outré *adjective* = **eccentric**, bizarre, fantastic, freakish, odd, off-the-wall (*slang*), outlandish, unconventional, weird

outrider *noun* = **escort**, advance guard, attendant, bodyguard

outright *adjective* **1** = **absolute**, arrant, complete, consummate, downright, out-and-out, perfect, pure, thorough, thoroughgoing, total, unconditional, undeniable, unmitigated, unqualified, utter, wholesale **2** = **direct**, definite, flat, straightforward, unequivocal, unqualified ♦ *adverb* **3** = **absolutely**, completely, straightforwardly, thoroughly, to the full,

without hesitation, without restraint **4** = **instantly**, at once, immediately, instantaneously, on the spot, straight away, there and then, without more ado **5** = **openly**, explicitly, overtly

outrun *verb* **1** = **outdistance**, beat, escape, get away from, lose, outpace, outstrip, shake off **2** = **surpass**, exceed, leave behind, outdo

outset *noun* = **beginning**, commencement, early days, inauguration, inception, kickoff (*informal*), onset, opening, start, starting point
➤ **Antonyms**
closing, completion, conclusion, consummation, end, finale, finish, termination

outshine *verb* = **outdo**, be head and shoulders above, be superior to, eclipse, leave *or* put in the shade, outclass, outstrip, overshadow, surpass, top, transcend, upstage

outside *adjective* **1** = **external**, exterior, extraneous, extreme, out, outdoor, outer, outermost, outward, surface **2** *As in* **an outside chance** = **remote**, distant, faint, marginal, negligible, slight, slim, small, unlikely ♦ *noun* **3** = **exterior**, façade, face, front, skin, surface, topside
➤ **Antonyms**
adjective ≠**external**: in, indoor, inner, innermost, inside, interior, internal, inward

outsider *noun* = **interloper**, alien, foreigner, incomer, intruder, newcomer, nonmember, odd one out, outlander, stranger

outsize *adjective* = **extra-large**, enormous, gargantuan, giant, gigantic, huge, humongous *or* humungous (*U.S. slang*), immense, jumbo (*informal*), large, mammoth, monster, oversized
➤ **Antonyms**
baby, dwarf, micro, mini, pocket, tiny, undersized

outskirts *plural noun* = **edge**, borders, boundary, environs, periphery, purlieus, suburbia, suburbs, vicinity

outsmart *verb Informal* = **outwit**, get the better of, outfox, outmanoeuvre, pull a fast one on (*informal*), put one over on (*informal*), run rings round (*informal*), trick

outspoken *adjective* = **forthright**, abrupt, blunt, candid, direct, downright, explicit, frank, free, free-spoken, open, plain-spoken, round, unceremonious, unequivocal, unreserved
➤ **Antonyms**
diplomatic, gracious, judicious, reserved, reticent, tactful

outspread *adjective* = **outstretched**,

expanded, extended, fanlike, fanned out, flared, open, opened up, unfolded, unfurled, wide-open

outstanding *adjective* **1 = excellent**, celebrated, distinguished, eminent, exceptional, great, important, impressive, pre-eminent, special, superior, superlative, well-known **2 = unpaid**, due, owing, payable, pending, remaining, uncollected, unresolved, unsettled **3 = conspicuous**, arresting, eye-catching, marked, memorable, notable, noteworthy, prominent, salient, signal, striking
➤ **Antonyms**
≠**excellent**: dull, inferior, insignificant, mediocre, no great shakes (*informal*), ordinary, pedestrian, run-of-the-mill, unexceptional, unimpressive

outstrip *verb* **1 = surpass**, better, eclipse, exceed, excel, outdo, overtake, transcend **2 = outdistance**, outpace, outrun, shake off

outward *adjective* **= apparent**, evident, exterior, external, noticeable, observable, obvious, ostensible, outer, outside, perceptible, superficial, surface, visible
➤ **Antonyms**
inner, inside, interior, internal, invisible, inward, obscure, unnoticeable

outwardly *adverb* **= apparently**, as far as one can see, externally, officially, on the face of it, on the surface, ostensibly, professedly, seemingly, superficially, to all appearances, to all intents and purposes, to the eye

outweigh *verb* **= override**, cancel (out), compensate for, eclipse, make up for, outbalance, overcome, predominate, preponderate, prevail over, take precedence over, tip the scales

outwit *verb* **= outsmart** (*informal*), cheat, deceive, dupe, get the better of, make a fool *or* monkey of, outfox, outmanoeuvre, outthink, put one over on (*informal*), run rings round (*informal*), swindle, take in (*informal*)

outworn *adjective* **= outdated**, antiquated, behind the times, discredited, disused, hackneyed, obsolete, outmoded, out-of-date, threadbare, worn-out
➤ **Antonyms**
fresh, modish, new, recent, up to date

oval *adjective* **= elliptical**, egg-shaped, ovate, oviform, ovoid

ovation *noun* **= applause**, acclaim, acclamation, big hand, cheering, cheers, clapping, plaudits, tribute
➤ **Antonyms**
abuse, booing, catcalls, derision, heckling, jeers, jibes, mockery, ridicule

over *preposition* **1 = on top of**, above, on,

superior to, upon **2 = more than**, above, exceeding, in excess of **3 over and above = in addition to**, added to, as well as, besides, let alone, not to mention, on top of, plus ♦ *adverb* **4 = above**, aloft, on high, overhead **5 = extra**, beyond, in addition, in excess, left over **6 over and over (again) = repeatedly**, ad nauseam, again and again, frequently, often, time and again ♦ *adjective* **7 = finished**, accomplished, at an end, by, bygone, closed, completed, concluded, done (with), ended, gone, past, settled, up (*informal*) **8 = extra**, remaining, superfluous, surplus, unused

overabundance *noun* **= excess**, glut, plethora, profusion, superabundance, superfluity, surfeit, surplus

overact *verb* **= exaggerate**, ham *or* ham up (*informal*), overdo, overplay

overall *adjective* **1 = total**, all-embracing, blanket, complete, comprehensive, general, global, inclusive, long-range, long-term, overarching ♦ *adverb* **2 = in general**, generally speaking, in (the) large, in the long term, on the whole

overawe *verb* **= intimidate**, abash, alarm, browbeat, cow, daunt, frighten, scare, terrify
➤ **Antonyms**
bolster, buoy up, cheer up, comfort, console, hearten, reassure

overbalance *verb* **= topple over**, capsize, keel over, lose one's balance, lose one's footing, overturn, slip, take a tumble, tip over, tumble, turn turtle, upset

overbearing *adjective* **= dictatorial**, arrogant, autocratic, bossy (*informal*), cavalier, dogmatic, domineering, haughty, high-handed, imperious, lordly, officious, peremptory, supercilious, superior, tyrannical
➤ **Antonyms**
deferential, humble, modest, self-effacing, submissive, unassertive, unassuming

overblown *adjective* **= excessive**, disproportionate, immoderate, inflated, overdone, over the top, undue

overcast *adjective* **= cloudy**, clouded, clouded over, dismal, dreary, dull, grey, hazy, leaden, louring *or* lowering, murky, threatening
➤ **Antonyms**
bright, brilliant, clear, cloudless, fine, sunny, unclouded

overcharge *verb* **= cheat**, diddle (*informal*), do (*slang*), fleece, rip off (*slang*), rook (*slang*), short-change, skin (*slang*), sting (*informal*), surcharge

overcome *verb* **1 = conquer**, beat, crush, defeat, get the better of, lick (*informal*), master, overpower, overthrow, overwhelm, prevail, rise above, subdue, subjugate, surmount, triumph over, undo, vanquish ♦ *adjective* 2 = **affected**, at a loss for words, bowled over (*informal*), overwhelmed, speechless, swept off one's feet

overconfident *adjective* = **cocksure**, brash, foolhardy, overweening, presumptuous, riding for a fall (*informal*), uppish (*Brit. informal*)
➤ **Antonyms**
cautious, diffident, doubtful, hesitant, insecure, timid, timorous, uncertain, unsure

overcrowded *adjective* = **packed (out)**, bursting at the seams, choked, congested, crammed full, jam-packed, overloaded, overpopulated, swarming
➤ **Antonyms**
abandoned, deserted, desolate, empty, forsaken, unoccupied, vacant

overdo *verb* 1 = **exaggerate**, be intemperate, belabour, carry too far, do to death (*informal*), gild the lily, go overboard (*informal*), go to extremes, not know when to stop, overindulge, overplay, overreach, overstate, overuse 2 **overdo it** = **overwork**, bite off more than one can chew, burn the candle at both ends (*informal*), drive oneself, go too far, overload oneself, overtax one's strength, overtire oneself, strain *or* overstrain oneself, wear oneself out
➤ **Antonyms**
≠**exaggerate:** belittle, disparage, minimize, play down, underplay, underrate, understate, underuse, undervalue

overdone *adjective* 1 = **excessive**, beyond all bounds, exaggerated, fulsome, immoderate, inordinate, overelaborate, preposterous, too much, undue, unnecessary 2 = **overcooked**, burnt, burnt to a cinder, charred, dried up, spoiled
➤ **Antonyms**
≠**excessive:** belittled, minimized, moderated, played down, underdone, underplayed, understated

overdue *adjective* = **late**, behindhand, behind schedule, behind time, belated, not before time (*informal*), owing, tardy, unpunctual
➤ **Antonyms**
ahead of time, beforehand, early, in advance, in good time, punctual

overeat *verb* = **overindulge**, binge (*informal*), eat like a horse (*informal*), gorge, gormandize, guzzle, make a pig of oneself (*informal*), pig out (*slang*), stuff, stuff oneself

overemphasize *verb* = **overstress**, belabour, blow up out of all proportion, lay too much stress on, make a big thing of (*informal*), make a mountain out of a molehill (*informal*), make something out of nothing, make too much of, overdramatize
➤ **Antonyms**
belittle, downplay, make light of, minimize, play down, underplay, underrate, understate

overexert *verb* = **do too much**, burn the candle at both ends (*informal*), drive oneself, knock oneself out, overstrain oneself, overtax oneself, overtire oneself, overwork, push oneself too hard, strain oneself, wear oneself out, work oneself to death

overflow *verb* 1 = **spill**, brim over, bubble over, discharge, fall over, pour out, pour over, run over, run with, spray, surge, well over ♦ *noun* 2 = **surplus**, flood, flooding, inundation, overabundance, spill, spilling over

overhang *verb* = **project**, beetle, bulge, extend, impend, jut, loom, protrude, stick out

overhaul *verb* 1 = **check**, do up (*informal*), examine, inspect, recondition, re-examine, repair, restore, service, survey 2 = **overtake**, catch up with, draw level with, get ahead of, pass ♦ *noun* 3 = **checkup**, check, examination, going-over (*informal*), inspection, reconditioning, service

overhead *adverb* 1 = **above**, aloft, atop, in the sky, on high, skyward, up above, upward ♦ *adjective* 2 = **aerial**, overhanging, upper
➤ **Antonyms**
adverb ≠**above:** below, beneath, downward, underfoot, underneath

overheads *plural noun* = **running costs**, operating costs

overheated *adjective* = **agitated**, fiery, flaming, impassioned, inflamed, overexcited, roused
➤ **Antonyms**
calm, collected, composed, cool, dispassionate, unemotional, unexcited, unfazed (*informal*), unruffled

overindulge *verb* = **be immoderate** *or* **intemperate**, drink *or* eat too much, have a binge (*informal*), live it up (*informal*), make a pig of oneself (*informal*), overdo it, pig out (*slang*)

overindulgence *noun* = **immoderation**, excess, intemperance, overeating, surfeit

overjoyed *adjective* = **delighted**,

cock-a-hoop, deliriously happy, elated, euphoric, floating on air, happy as a lark, in raptures, joyful, jubilant, on cloud nine (*informal*), over the moon (*informal*), rapt, rapturous, thrilled, tickled pink (*informal*), transported
➤ **Antonyms**
crestfallen, dejected, disappointed, downcast, down in the dumps (*informal*), heartbroken, miserable, sad, unhappy, woebegone

overlay *verb* **1 = cover**, adorn, blanket, inlay, laminate, ornament, veneer ♦ *noun* **2 = covering**, adornment, decoration, ornamentation, veneer

overload *verb* **= overburden**, burden, encumber, oppress, overcharge, overtax, saddle (with), strain, weigh down

overlook *verb* **1 = miss**, disregard, fail to notice, forget, neglect, omit, pass, slip up on **2 = ignore**, blink at, condone, disregard, excuse, forgive, let bygones be bygones, let one off with, let pass, let ride, make allowances for, pardon, turn a blind eye to, wink at **3 = have a view of**, afford a view of, command a view of, front on to, look over *or* out on
➤ **Antonyms**
≠miss: discern, heed, mark, note, notice, observe, perceive, regard, spot

overly *adverb* **= excessively**, exceedingly, immoderately, inordinately, over, too, unduly, very much

overpower *verb* **= overwhelm**, beat, clobber (*slang*), conquer, crush, defeat, get the upper hand over, knock out, lick (*informal*), master, overcome, overthrow, quell, subdue, subjugate, vanquish

overpowering *adjective* **= overwhelming**, compelling, compulsive, extreme, forceful, invincible, irrefutable, irresistible, powerful, strong, uncontrollable

overrate *verb* **= overestimate**, assess too highly, exaggerate, make too much of, oversell, overvalue, rate too highly, think *or* expect too much of, think too highly of

overreach *verb* **overreach oneself = try to be too clever**, be hoist with one's own petard, bite off more than one can chew, defeat one's own ends, go too far, have one's schemes backfire *or* boomerang *or* rebound on one

override *verb* **= overrule**, annul, cancel, countermand, discount, disregard, ignore, nullify, outweigh, quash, reverse, set aside, supersede, take no account of

overriding *adjective* **= predominant**, cardinal, compelling, dominant, major, number one, paramount, pivotal, prevailing, primary, prime, supreme,

ultimate
➤ **Antonyms**
immaterial, inconsequential, insignificant, irrelevant, minor, negligible, paltry, petty, trifling, trivial, unimportant

overrule *verb* **= reverse**, alter, annul, cancel, countermand, disallow, invalidate, make null and void, outvote, override, overturn, recall, repeal, rescind, revoke, rule against, set aside, veto
➤ **Antonyms**
allow, approve, consent to, endorse, pass, permit, sanction

overrun *verb* **1 = overwhelm**, invade, massacre, occupy, put to flight, rout, swamp **2 = spread over**, choke, infest, inundate, overflow, overgrow, permeate, ravage, spread like wildfire, swarm over **3 = exceed**, go beyond, overshoot, run over *or* on

overseer *noun* **= supervisor**, boss (*informal*), chief, foreman, gaffer (*informal, chiefly Brit.*), manager, master, superintendent, superior

overshadow *verb* **1 = outshine**, dominate, dwarf, eclipse, excel, leave *or* put in the shade, outweigh, surpass, take precedence over, throw into the shade, tower above **2 = spoil**, blight, cast a gloom upon, mar, put a damper on, ruin, take the pleasure *or* enjoyment out of, temper

oversight *noun* **= mistake**, blunder, carelessness, delinquency, error, fault, inattention, lapse, laxity, neglect, omission, slip

overt *adjective* **= open**, apparent, blatant, bold, manifest, observable, obvious, patent, plain, public, unconcealed, undisguised, visible
➤ **Antonyms**
concealed, covert, disguised, hidden, hush-hush (*informal*), invisible, secret, surreptitious, underhand

overtake *verb* **1 = pass**, catch up with, draw level with, get past, leave behind, outdistance, outdo, outstrip, overhaul **2 = befall**, catch unprepared, come upon, engulf, happen, hit, overwhelm, strike, take by surprise

overthrow *verb* **1 = defeat**, abolish, beat, bring down, conquer, crush, depose, dethrone, do away with, master, oust, overcome, overpower, overwhelm, subdue, subjugate, topple, unseat, vanquish ♦ *noun* **2 = downfall**, defeat, deposition, destruction, dethronement, discomfiture, displacement, end, fall, ousting, rout, ruin, subversion, undoing, unseating
➤ **Antonyms**

verb ≠**defeat**: defend, guard, keep, maintain, preserve, protect, restore, support, uphold ◆ *noun* ≠**downfall**: defence, preservation, protection

overtone *noun, often plural* = **hint**, association, connotation, flavour, implication, innuendo, intimation, nuance, sense, suggestion, undercurrent

overture *noun* 1 *Music* = **introduction**, opening, prelude 2 **overtures** = **approach**, advance, invitation, offer, opening move, proposal, proposition
➤ **Antonyms**
≠**introduction**: coda, finale ≠**approach**: rejection, withdrawal

overturn *verb* 1 = **tip over**, capsize, keel over, knock over *or* down, overbalance, reverse, spill, topple, tumble, upend, upset, upturn 2 = **overthrow**, abolish, annul, bring down, countermand, depose, destroy, invalidate, obviate, repeal, rescind, reverse, set aside, unseat

overweening *adjective* = **excessive**, blown up out of all proportion, extravagant, immoderate

overweight *adjective* = **fat**, bulky, buxom, chubby, chunky, corpulent, fleshy, gross, heavy, hefty, huge, massive, obese, outsize, plump, podgy, portly, stout, tubby (*informal*)
➤ **Antonyms**
emaciated, gaunt, lean, pinched, scraggy, scrawny, skinny, thin, underweight

overwhelm *verb* 1 = **overcome**, bowl over (*informal*), devastate, knock (someone) for six (*informal*), overpower, prostrate, render speechless, stagger, sweep (someone) off his *or* her feet, take (someone's) breath away 2 = **destroy**, crush, cut to pieces, massacre, overpower, overrun, rout

overwhelming *adjective* = **overpowering**, breathtaking, crushing, devastating, invincible, irresistible, shattering, stunning, towering, uncontrollable
➤ **Antonyms**
commonplace, incidental, insignificant, negligible, paltry, resistible, trivial, unimportant

overwork *verb* 1 = **strain oneself**, burn the candle at both ends, burn the midnight oil, overstrain oneself, sweat (*informal*), work one's fingers to the bone 2 = **overuse**, drive into the ground, exhaust, exploit, fatigue, oppress, overtax, wear out, weary

overwrought *adjective* = **agitated**, beside oneself, distracted, excited, frantic, in a state, in a tizzy (*informal*), keyed up, on edge, overexcited, overworked, stirred, strung out (*informal*), tense, uptight (*informal*), wired (*slang*), worked up (*informal*), wound up (*informal*)
➤ **Antonyms**
calm, collected, controlled, cool, dispassionate, emotionless, impassive, self-contained, unfazed (*informal*), unmoved

owe *verb* = **be in debt**, be beholden to, be in arrears, be obligated *or* indebted, be under an obligation to

owing *adjective* = **unpaid**, due, outstanding, overdue, owed, payable, unsettled

owing to *preposition* = **because of**, as a result of, on account of

own *adjective* 1 = **personal**, individual, particular, private ◆ *pronoun* 2 **hold one's own** = **keep going**, compete, keep one's end up, keep one's head above water, maintain one's position 3 **on one's own** = **alone**, by oneself, independently, off one's own bat, on one's tod (*Brit. slang*), singly, unaided, unassisted, under one's own steam ◆ *verb* 4 = **possess**, be in possession of, be responsible for, enjoy, have, hold, keep, retain 5 = **acknowledge**, admit, allow, allow to be valid, avow, concede, confess, disclose, go along with, grant, recognize 6 **own up** = **confess**, admit, come clean, tell the truth

owner *noun* = **possessor**, holder, landlord *or* landlady, lord, master *or* mistress, proprietor, proprietress, proprietrix

ownership *noun* = **possession**, dominion, proprietary rights, proprietorship, right of possession, title

P p

pace *noun* 1 = **step**, gait, measure, stride, tread, walk 2 = **speed**, clip (*informal*), lick (*informal*), momentum, motion, movement, progress, rate, tempo, time, velocity ♦ *verb* 3 = **stride**, march, patrol, pound, walk back and forth, walk up and down 4 **pace out** = **measure**, count, determine, mark out, step

pacific *adjective Formal* 1 = **peacemaking**, appeasing, conciliatory, diplomatic, irenic, pacificatory, placatory, propitiatory 2 = **nonaggressive**, dovelike, dovish, friendly, gentle, mild, nonbelligerent, nonviolent, pacifist, peaceable, peace-loving 3 = **peaceful**, at peace, calm, halcyon, placid, quiet, serene, smooth, still, tranquil, unruffled
➤ **Antonyms**
≠**nonaggressive**: aggressive, antagonistic, belligerent, hostile, nonconciliatory, pugnacious, unforgiving, unfriendly, violent, warlike

pacifist *noun* = **peace lover**, conchie (*informal*), conscientious objector, dove, passive resister, peacemonger, peacenik (*informal*), satyagrahi

pacify *verb* = **calm**, allay, appease, assuage, mollify, placate, propitiate, soothe

pack *verb* 1 = **package**, batch, bundle, burden, load, store, stow 2 = **cram**, charge, compact, compress, crowd, fill, jam, mob, press, ram, stuff, tamp, throng, wedge 3 **pack off** = **send away**, bundle out, dismiss, hustle out, send packing (*informal*), send someone about his business 4 **send (someone) packing** = **send away**, discharge, dismiss, give (someone) the brushoff (*slang*), send (someone) about his *or* her business ♦ *noun* 5 = **bundle**, back pack, bale, burden, fardel (*archaic*), kit, kitbag, knapsack, load, parcel, rucksack, truss 6 = **packet**, package 7 = **group**, assemblage, band, bunch, collection, company, crew, crowd, deck, drove, flock, gang, herd, lot, mob, set, troop

package *noun* 1 = **parcel**, box, carton, container, packet 2 = **unit**, amalgamation, combination, entity, whole ♦ *verb* 3 = **pack**, batch, box, parcel (up), wrap, wrap up

packed *adjective* = **full**, brimful, bursting at the seams, chock-a-block, chock-full, congested, cram-full, crammed, crowded, filled, hoatching (*Scot.*), jammed, jam-packed, loaded *or* full to the gunwales, overflowing, overloaded, packed like sardines, seething, swarming
➤ **Antonyms**
deserted, empty, uncongested, uncrowded

packet *noun* 1 = **package**, bag, carton, container, parcel, poke (*dialect*), wrapper, wrapping 2 *Slang* = **fortune**, a bob or two (*Brit. informal*), an arm and a leg (*informal*), big bucks (*informal, chiefly U.S.*), big money, bomb (*Brit. slang*), bundle (*slang*), king's ransom (*informal*), lot(s), megabucks (*U.S. & Canad. slang*), mint, pile (*informal*), pot(s) (*informal*), pretty penny (*informal*), small fortune, tidy sum (*informal*), wad (*U.S. & Canad. slang*)

pack in *verb* 1 *Brit. informal* = **stop**, cease, chuck (*informal*), desist, give up or over, jack in, kick (*informal*), leave off 2 = **attract**, cram, draw, fill to capacity, squeeze in

pack up *verb* 1 = **put away**, store, tidy up 2 *Informal* = **stop**, call it a day (*informal*), call it a night (*informal*), finish, give up, pack in (*Brit. informal*) 3 = **break down**, conk out (*informal*), fail, give out, stall, stop

pact *noun* = **agreement**, alliance, arrangement, bargain, bond, compact, concord, concordat, contract, convention, covenant, deal, league, protocol, treaty, understanding

pad¹ *noun* 1 = **cushion**, buffer, protection, stiffening, stuffing, wad 2 = **notepad**, block, jotter, tablet, writing pad 3 = **paw**, foot, sole 4 *Slang* = **home**, apartment, flat, hang-out (*informal*), place, quarters, room ♦ *verb* 5 = **pack**, cushion, fill, line, protect, shape, stuff 6 **pad out** = **lengthen**, amplify, augment, eke, elaborate, fill out, flesh out, inflate, protract, spin out, stretch

pad² *verb* = **sneak**, creep, go barefoot, steal

padding *noun* 1 = **filling**, packing, stuffing, wadding 2 = **waffle** (*informal, chiefly Brit.*), hot air (*informal*), prolixity, verbiage, verbosity, wordiness

paddle¹ *noun* 1 = **oar**, scull, sweep ♦ *verb* 2 = **row**, oar, propel, pull, scull

paddle² *verb* 1 = **wade**, plash, slop, splash (about) 2 = **dabble**, stir

pagan *adjective* 1 = **heathen**, Gentile,

heathenish, idolatrous, infidel, irreligious, polytheistic ♦ *noun* **2 = heathen**, Gentile, idolater, infidel, polytheist, unbeliever

page[1] *noun* **1 = folio**, leaf, sheet, side **2** *Literary* **= period**, chapter, episode, epoch, era, event, incident, phase, point, stage, time ♦ *verb* **3 = paginate**, foliate, number

page[2] *noun* **1 = attendant**, bellboy (*U.S.*), footboy, pageboy, servant, squire ♦ *verb* **2 = call**, announce, call out, preconize, seek, send for, summon

pageant *noun* **= show**, display, extravaganza, parade, procession, ritual, spectacle, tableau

pageantry *noun* **= spectacle**, display, drama, extravaganza, glamour, glitter, grandeur, magnificence, parade, pomp, show, showiness, splash (*informal*), splendour, state, theatricality

pain *noun* **1 = hurt**, ache, cramp, discomfort, irritation, pang, smarting, soreness, spasm, suffering, tenderness, throb, throe (*rare*), trouble, twinge **2 = suffering**, affliction, agony, anguish, bitterness, distress, grief, hardship, heartache, misery, torment, torture, tribulation, woe, wretchedness **3** *Informal* **= nuisance**, aggravation, annoyance, bore, bother, drag (*informal*), gall, headache (*informal*), irritation, pain in the arse (*taboo informal*), pain in the neck (*informal*), pest, vexation ♦ *verb* **4 = hurt**, ail, chafe, discomfort, harm, inflame, injure, smart, sting, throb **5 = distress**, afflict, aggrieve, agonize, cut to the quick, disquiet, grieve, hurt, sadden, torment, torture, vex, worry, wound **6** *Informal* **= irritate**, annoy, exasperate, gall, harass, nark (*Brit., Austral., & N.Z. slang*), rile, vex

pained *adjective* **= distressed**, aggrieved, anguished, hurt, injured, miffed (*informal*), offended, reproachful, stung, unhappy, upset, worried, wounded

painful *adjective* **1 = distressing**, afflictive, disagreeable, distasteful, grievous, saddening, unpleasant **2 = sore**, aching, agonizing, excruciating, harrowing, hurting, inflamed, raw, smarting, tender, throbbing **3 = difficult**, arduous, hard, laborious, severe, tedious, troublesome, trying, vexatious **4** *Informal* **= terrible**, abysmal, awful, dire, dreadful, excruciating, extremely bad, godawful, gut-wrenching
➤ **Antonyms**
≠**distressing**: agreeable, enjoyable, pleasant, satisfying ≠**sore**: comforting, painless, relieving, soothing ≠**difficult**: a piece of cake (*informal*), easy, effortless, interesting, short, simple, straightforward,

undemanding

painfully *adverb* **= distressingly**, alarmingly, clearly, deplorably, dreadfully, excessively, markedly, sadly, unfortunately, woefully

painkiller *noun* **= analgesic**, anaesthetic, anodyne, drug, palliative, remedy, sedative

painless *adjective* **= simple**, easy, effortless, fast, no trouble, pain-free, quick, trouble-free

pains *plural noun* **1 = trouble**, assiduousness, bother, care, diligence, effort, industry, labour, special attention **2 = contractions**, birth-pangs, childbirth, labour

painstaking *adjective* **= thorough**, assiduous, careful, conscientious, diligent, earnest, exacting, hard-working, industrious, meticulous, persevering, punctilious, scrupulous, sedulous, strenuous, thoroughgoing
➤ **Antonyms**
careless, half-hearted, haphazard, heedless, lazy, negligent, slapdash, slipshod, thoughtless

paint *noun* **1 = colouring**, colour, dye, emulsion, pigment, stain, tint **2** *Informal* **= make-up**, cosmetics, face (*informal*), greasepaint, *maquillage*, war paint (*informal*) ♦ *verb* **3 = depict**, catch a likeness, delineate, draw, figure, picture, portray, represent, sketch **4 = coat**, apply, colour, cover, daub, decorate, slap on (*informal*) **5 = describe**, bring to life, capture, conjure up a vision, depict, evoke, make one see, portray, put graphically, recount, tell vividly **6 paint the town red** *Informal* **= celebrate**, carouse, go on a binge (*informal*), go on a spree, go on the town, live it up (*informal*), make merry, make whoopee (*informal*), revel

pair *noun* **1 = couple**, brace, combination, doublet, duo, match, matched set, span, twins, two of a kind, twosome, yoke ♦ *verb* **2 = couple**, bracket, join, marry, match (up), mate, pair off, put together, team, twin, wed, yoke

pal *noun Informal* **= friend**, buddy (*informal*), chum (*informal*), companion, comrade, crony, mate (*informal*)

palatable *adjective* **1 = delicious**, appetizing, delectable, luscious, mouthwatering, savoury, tasty, toothsome **2 = acceptable**, agreeable, attractive, enjoyable, fair, pleasant, satisfactory
➤ **Antonyms**
≠**delicious**: bland, flat, insipid, stale, tasteless, unappetizing, unpalatable

palate *noun* **1 = taste**, appetite, heart, stomach **2 = enjoyment**, appreciation, gusto, liking, relish, zest

palatial *adjective* = **magnificent**, de luxe, gorgeous, grand, grandiose, illustrious, imposing, luxurious, majestic, opulent, plush (*informal*), regal, spacious, splendid, splendiferous (*facetious*), stately, sumptuous

palaver *noun* = **fuss**, business (*informal*), carry-on (*informal, chiefly Brit.*), pantomime (*informal, chiefly Brit.*), performance (*informal*), rigmarole, song and dance (*Brit. informal*), to-do

pale *adjective* **1** = **white**, anaemic, ashen, ashy, bleached, bloodless, colourless, faded, light, like death warmed up (*informal*), pallid, pasty, sallow, wan, washed-out, whitish **2** = **poor**, feeble, inadequate, pathetic, thin, weak ◆ *verb* **3** = **become pale**, blanch, go white, lose colour, whiten **4** = **fade**, decrease, dim, diminish, dull, grow dull, lessen, lose lustre
➤ **Antonyms**
adjective ≠**white**: blooming, florid, flushed, glowing, rosy-cheeked, rubicund, ruddy, sanguine

pall¹ *noun* **1** = **cloud**, mantle, shadow, shroud, veil **2** = **gloom**, check, damp, damper

pall² *verb* = **become boring**, become dull, become tedious, cloy, glut, jade, satiate, sicken, surfeit, tire, weary

pallid *adjective* = **pale**, anaemic, ashen, colourless, pasty, wan

pallor *noun* = **paleness**, lack of colour, pallidness, wanness, whiteness

palm¹ *noun* **1** = **hand**, hook, meathook (*slang*), mitt (*slang*), paw (*informal*) **2 grease someone's palm** *Slang* = **bribe**, buy, corrupt, fix (*informal*), give a backhander (*slang*), induce, influence, pay off (*informal*), square, suborn **3 in the palm of one's hand** = **in one's power**, at one's mercy, in one's clutches, in one's control

palm² *noun* = **victory**, bays, crown, fame, glory, honour, laurels, merit, prize, success, triumph, trophy

palm off *verb* **1** = **fob off**, foist off, pass off **2 palm off on** = **foist on**, force upon, impose upon, thrust upon, unload upon

palmy *adjective* = **prosperous**, flourishing, fortunate, glorious, golden, halcyon, happy, joyous, luxurious, thriving, triumphant

palpable *adjective* **1** = **obvious**, apparent, blatant, clear, conspicuous, evident, manifest, open, patent, plain, salient, unmistakable, visible **2** = **tangible**, concrete, material, real, solid, substantial, touchable

palpitate *verb* = **beat**, flutter, pitapat, pitter-patter, pound, pulsate, pulse, quiver, shiver, throb, tremble, vibrate

palsied *adjective* = **paralysed**, arthritic, atonic (*Pathology*), crippled, debilitated, disabled, helpless, paralytic, rheumatic, sclerotic, shaking, shaky, spastic, trembling

paltry *adjective* = **insignificant**, base, beggarly, chickenshit (*U.S. slang*), contemptible, crappy (*slang*), derisory, despicable, inconsiderable, low, meagre, mean, measly, Mickey Mouse (*slang*), minor, miserable, nickel-and-dime (*U.S. slang*), petty, picayune (*U.S.*), piddling (*informal*), pitiful, poor, poxy (*slang*), puny, slight, small, sorry, toytown (*slang*), trifling, trivial, twopenny-halfpenny (*Brit. informal*), unimportant, worthless, wretched
➤ **Antonyms**
consequential, considerable, essential, grand, important, major, mega (*slang*), significant, valuable

pamper *verb* = **spoil**, baby, cater to one's every whim, coddle, cosset, fondle, gratify, humour, indulge, mollycoddle, pander to, pet, wait on (someone) hand and foot

pamphlet *noun* = **booklet**, brochure, circular, folder, leaflet, tract

pan¹ *noun* **1** = **pot**, container, saucepan, vessel ◆ *verb* **2** = **sift out**, look for, search for, separate, wash **3** *Informal* = **criticize**, blast, censure, flay, hammer (*Brit. informal*), knock (*informal*), lambast(e), put down, roast (*informal*), rubbish (*informal*), slag (off) (*slang*), slam (*slang*), slate (*informal*), tear into (*informal*), throw brickbats at (*informal*)

pan² *verb* = **move**, follow, scan, sweep, swing, track, traverse

panacea *noun* = **cure-all**, catholicon, elixir, nostrum, sovereign remedy, universal cure

panache *noun* = **style**, a flourish, brio, dash, élan, flair, flamboyance, spirit, swagger, verve

pandemonium *noun* = **uproar**, babel, bedlam, chaos, clamour, commotion, confusion, din, hubbub, hue and cry, hullabaloo, racket, ruckus (*informal*), ruction (*informal*), rumpus, tumult, turmoil
➤ **Antonyms**
calm, hush, order, peace, peacefulness, quietude, repose, stillness, tranquillity

pander *verb* **pander to** = **indulge**, cater to, gratify, play up to (*informal*), please, satisfy

pang *noun* = **twinge**, ache, agony, anguish, discomfort, distress, gripe, pain, prick, spasm, stab, sting, stitch, throe (*rare*), wrench

panic *noun* **1** = **fear**, agitation, alarm, consternation, dismay, fright, horror, hysteria, scare, terror ♦ *verb* **2** = **go to pieces**, become hysterical, be terror-stricken, have kittens (*informal*), lose one's bottle (*Brit. slang*), lose one's nerve, overreact **3** = **alarm**, put the wind up (someone) (*informal*), scare, startle, terrify, unnerve

panicky *adjective* = **frightened**, afraid, agitated, antsy (*informal*), distressed, fearful, frantic, frenzied, hysterical, in a flap (*informal*), in a tizzy (*informal*), jittery (*informal*), nervous, windy (*slang*), worked up, worried
➤ **Antonyms**
calm, collected, composed, confident, cool, imperturbable, self-controlled, together (*slang*), unexcitable, unfazed (*informal*), unflappable, unruffled

panic-stricken *adjective* = **frightened**, aghast, agitated, alarmed, appalled, fearful, frenzied, frightened out of one's wits, frightened to death, horrified, horror-stricken, hysterical, in a cold sweat (*informal*), panicky, petrified, scared, scared shitless (*taboo slang*), scared stiff, shit-scared (*taboo slang*), startled, terrified, terror-stricken, unnerved

panoply *noun* = **array**, attire, dress, garb, get-up (*informal*), insignia, raiment (*archaic or poetic*), regalia, show, trappings, turnout

panorama *noun* **1** = **view**, bird's-eye view, prospect, scenery, scenic view, vista **2** = **survey**, overall picture, overview, perspective

panoramic *adjective* = **wide**, all-embracing, bird's-eye, comprehensive, extensive, far-reaching, general, inclusive, overall, scenic, sweeping

pant *verb* **1** = **puff**, blow, breathe, gasp, heave, huff, palpitate, throb, wheeze **2** *with* **for** = **long**, ache, covet, crave, desire, eat one's heart out over, hanker after, hunger, pine, set one's heart on, sigh, suspire (*archaic or poetic*), thirst, want, yearn ♦ *noun* **3** = **puff**, gasp, huff, wheeze

panting *adjective* **1** = **out of breath**, breathless, gasping, out of puff, out of whack (*informal*), puffed, puffed out, puffing, short of breath, winded **2** = **eager**, agog, all agog, anxious, champing at the bit (*informal*), impatient, raring to go

pants *plural noun* **1** *Brit.* = **underpants**, boxer shorts, briefs, broekies (*S. African*), drawers, knickers, panties, Y-fronts (*Trademark*) **2** *U.S.* = **trousers**, slacks

pap *noun* **1** = **mush**, baby food, mash, pulp **2** = **rubbish**, drivel, trash, trivia

paper *noun* **1** = **newspaper**, blat, daily, gazette, journal, news, organ, rag (*informal*) **2** = **essay**, analysis, article, assignment, composition, critique, dissertation, examination, monograph, report, script, study, thesis, treatise **3 on paper** = **in theory**, ideally, in the abstract, theoretically **4 papers: a** = **documents**, certificates, deeds, instruments, records **b** = **letters**, archive, diaries, documents, dossier, file, records ♦ *adjective* **5** = **disposable**, cardboard, flimsy, insubstantial, paper-thin, papery, thin ♦ *verb* **6** = **wallpaper**, cover with paper, hang, line, paste up

papery *adjective* = **thin**, flimsy, fragile, frail, insubstantial, light, lightweight, paperlike, paper-thin, wafer-thin

par *noun* **1** = **average**, level, mean, median, norm, standard, usual **2** = **equivalence**, balance, equal footing, equality, equilibrium, parity **3 above par** = **excellent**, exceptional, first-rate (*informal*), outstanding, superior **4 below par: a** = **inferior**, below average, bush-league (*Austral. & N.Z. informal*), dime-a-dozen (*informal*), lacking, not up to scratch (*informal*), poor, second-rate, substandard, tinhorn (*U.S. slang*), two-bit (*U.S. & Canad. slang*), wanting **b** = **under the weather** (*informal*), not oneself, off colour (*chiefly Brit.*), off form, poorly (*informal*), sick, unfit, unhealthy **5 on a par with** = **equal to**, much the same as, the same as, well-matched with **6 par for the course** = **usual**, average, expected, ordinary, predictable, standard, typical **7 up to par** = **satisfactory**, acceptable, adequate, good enough, passable, up to scratch (*informal*), up to the mark

parable *noun* = **lesson**, allegory, exemplum, fable, moral tale, story

parade *noun* **1** = **procession**, array, cavalcade, ceremony, column, march, pageant, review, spectacle, train **2** = **show**, array, display, exhibition, flaunting, ostentation, pomp, spectacle, vaunting ♦ *verb* **3** = **flaunt**, air, brandish, display, exhibit, make a show of, show, show off (*informal*), strut, swagger, vaunt **4** = **march**, defile, process

paradigm *noun* = **model**, example, ideal, pattern

paradise *noun* **1** = **heaven**, City of God, divine abode, Elysian fields, garden of delights, Happy Valley (*Islam*), heavenly kingdom, Olympus (*poetic*), Promised Land, Zion (*Christianity*) **2** = **Garden of Eden**, Eden **3** = **bliss**, delight, felicity, heaven, seventh heaven, utopia

paradox *noun* = **contradiction**, absurdity, ambiguity, anomaly, enigma, inconsistency, mystery, oddity, puzzle

paradoxical *adjective* = **contradictory**, absurd, ambiguous, baffling, confounding, enigmatic, equivocal, illogical, impossible, improbable, inconsistent, oracular, puzzling, riddling

paragon *noun* = **model**, apotheosis, archetype, best thing since sliced bread (*informal*), criterion, cynosure, epitome, exemplar, greatest thing since sliced bread (*informal*), ideal, jewel, masterpiece, nonesuch (*archaic*), nonpareil, norm, paradigm, pattern, prototype, quintessence, standard

paragraph *noun* = **section**, clause, item, notice, part, passage, portion, subdivision

parallel *adjective* 1 = **equidistant**, aligned, alongside, coextensive, side by side 2 = **matching**, akin, analogous, complementary, correspondent, corresponding, like, resembling, similar, uniform ♦ *noun* 3 = **equivalent**, analogue, complement, corollary, counterpart, duplicate, equal, likeness, match, twin 4 = **similarity**, analogy, comparison, correlation, correspondence, likeness, parallelism, resemblance ♦ *verb* 5 = **correspond**, agree, be alike, chime with, compare, complement, conform, correlate, equal, keep pace (with), match
➤ **Antonyms**
adjective ≠**matching**: different, dissimilar, divergent, non-parallel, unlike ♦ *noun* ≠**equivalent**: opposite, reverse ≠**similarity**: difference, dissimilarity, divergence ♦ *verb* ≠**correspond**: be unlike, differ, diverge

paralyse *verb* 1 = **disable**, cripple, debilitate, incapacitate, lame 2 = **immobilize**, anaesthetize, arrest, benumb, freeze, halt, numb, petrify, stop dead, stun, stupefy, transfix

paralysis *noun* 1 = **immobility**, palsy, paresis (*Pathology*) 2 = **standstill**, arrest, breakdown, halt, inactivity, shutdown, stagnation, stoppage

paralytic *adjective* 1 = **paralysed**, crippled, disabled, immobile, immobilized, incapacitated, lame, numb, palsied 2 *Brit. informal* = **drunk**, bevvied (*dialect*), blitzed (*slang*), blotto (*slang*), bombed (*slang*), Brahms and Liszt (*slang*), canned (*slang*), flying (*slang*), inebriated, intoxicated, legless (*informal*), lit up (*slang*), out of it (*slang*), out to it (*Austral. & N.Z. slang*), pie-eyed (*slang*), pissed (*taboo slang*), plastered (*slang*), rat-arsed (*taboo slang*), sloshed (*slang*), smashed (*slang*), steamboats (*Scot. slang*), steaming (*slang*), stewed (*slang*), stoned (*slang*), tired and emotional (*euphemistic*), wasted (*slang*), wrecked (*slang*), zonked (*slang*)

parameter *noun Informal* = **limit**, constant, criterion, framework, guideline, limitation, restriction, specification

paramount *adjective* = **principal**, capital, cardinal, chief, dominant, eminent, first, foremost, main, outstanding, predominant, pre-eminent, primary, prime, superior, supreme
➤ **Antonyms**
inferior, insignificant, least, minor, negligible, secondary, slight, subordinate, trifling, unimportant

paranoid *adjective* 1 = **mentally ill**, deluded, disturbed, manic, neurotic, obsessive, paranoiac, psychotic, unstable 2 *Informal* = **suspicious**, antsy (*informal*), apprehensive, fearful, nervous, worried

paraphernalia *noun* = **equipment**, accoutrements, apparatus, appurtenances, baggage, belongings, clobber (*Brit. slang*), effects, equipage, gear, impedimenta, material, stuff, tackle, things, trappings

paraphrase *noun* 1 = **rewording**, interpretation, rehash, rendering, rendition, rephrasing, restatement, translation, version ♦ *verb* 2 = **reword**, express in other words *or* one's own words, interpret, rehash, render, rephrase, restate

parasite *noun* = **sponger** (*informal*), bloodsucker (*informal*), cadger, drone (*Brit.*), hanger-on, leech, scrounger (*informal*), sponge (*informal*)

parasitic, parasitical *adjective* = **scrounging** (*informal*), bloodsucking (*informal*), cadging, leechlike, sponging (*informal*)

parcel *noun* 1 = **package**, bundle, carton, pack, packet 2 = **group**, band, batch, bunch, collection, company, crew, crowd, gang, lot, pack 3 = **plot**, piece of land, property, tract ♦ *verb* 4 *often with* **up** = **wrap**, do up, pack, package, tie up 5 **parcel out** = **distribute**, allocate, allot, apportion, carve up, deal out, dispense, divide, dole out, mete out, portion, share out, split up

parch *verb* = **dry up**, blister, burn, dehydrate, desiccate, evaporate, make thirsty, scorch, sear, shrivel, wither

parched *adjective* = **dried out** *or* **up**, arid, dehydrated, drouthy (*Scot.*), dry, scorched, shrivelled, thirsty, torrid, waterless, withered

parching *adjective* = **drying**, baking,

blistering, burning, dry, hot, roasting (*informal*), scorching, searing, sweltering, withering

pardon *verb* 1 = **forgive**, absolve, acquit, amnesty, condone, exculpate, excuse, exonerate, free, let off (*informal*), liberate, overlook, release, remit, reprieve ♦ *noun* 2 = **forgiveness**, absolution, acquittal, allowance, amnesty, condonation, discharge, excuse, exoneration, grace, indulgence, mercy, release, remission, reprieve
➤ **Antonyms**
verb ≠**forgive**: admonish, blame, castigate, censure, chasten, chastise, condemn, discipline, fine, penalize, punish, rebuke ♦ *noun* ≠**forgiveness**: condemnation, guilt, penalty, punishment, redress, retaliation, retribution, revenge, vengeance

pardonable *adjective* = **forgivable**, allowable, condonable, excusable, minor, not serious, permissible, understandable, venial

pare *verb* 1 = **peel**, clip, cut, shave, skin, trim 2 = **cut back**, crop, cut, decrease, dock, reduce

parent *noun* 1 = **father** *or* **mother**, begetter, procreator, progenitor, sire 2 = **source**, architect, author, cause, creator, forerunner, origin, originator, prototype, root, wellspring

parentage *noun* = **family**, ancestry, birth, derivation, descent, extraction, line, lineage, origin, paternity, pedigree, race, stirps, stock

pariah *noun* = **outcast**, exile, leper, outlaw, undesirable, unperson, untouchable

parish *noun* = **community**, church, churchgoers, congregation, flock, fold, parishioners

parity *noun* 1 = **equality**, consistency, equal terms, equivalence, par, parallelism, quits (*informal*), uniformity, unity 2 = **correspondence**, affinity, agreement, analogy, conformity, congruity, likeness, resemblance, sameness, similarity, similitude

park *noun* 1 = **parkland**, estate, garden, grounds, pleasure garden, recreation ground, woodland ♦ *verb* 2 = **leave**, manoeuvre, position, station

parlance *noun* = **language**, idiom, jargon, phraseology, speech, talk, tongue

parley *Old-fashioned* ♦ *noun* 1 = **discussion**, colloquy, confab (*informal*), conference, congress, council, dialogue, meeting, palaver, powwow, seminar, talk(s) ♦ *verb* 2 = **discuss**, confabulate, confer, deliberate, negotiate, palaver, powwow, speak, talk

parliament *noun* 1 = **assembly**, congress, convention, convocation, council, diet, legislature, senate, talking shop (*informal*) 2 **Parliament** = **Houses of Parliament**, Mother of Parliaments, the House, the House of Commons and the House of Lords, Westminster

parliamentary *adjective* = **governmental**, congressional, deliberative, law-giving, law-making, legislative

parlour *noun Old-fashioned* = **sitting room**, best room, drawing room, front room, living room, lounge, reception room

parlous *adjective Archaic or humorous* = **dangerous**, chancy (*informal*), desperate, difficult, dire, hairy (*slang*), hazardous, perilous, risky

parochial *adjective* = **provincial**, insular, inward-looking, limited, narrow, narrow-minded, parish-pump, petty, restricted, small-minded
➤ **Antonyms**
all-embracing, broad, broad-minded, cosmopolitan, international, liberal, national, universal, world-wide

parodist *noun* = **mimic**, burlesquer, caricaturist, humorist, impressionist, ironist, lampooner, mocker, pasquinader, satirist

parody *noun* 1 = **takeoff** (*informal*), burlesque, caricature, imitation, lampoon, satire, send-up (*Brit. informal*), skit, spoof (*informal*) 2 = **travesty**, apology, caricature, farce, mockery ♦ *verb* 3 = **take off** (*informal*), burlesque, caricature, do a takeoff of (*informal*), lampoon, mimic, poke fun at, satirize, send up (*Brit. informal*), spoof (*informal*), take the piss out of (*taboo slang*), travesty

paroxysm *noun* = **outburst**, attack, convulsion, eruption, fit, flare-up (*informal*), seizure, spasm

parrot *noun* 1 = **mimic**, copycat (*informal*), imitator, (little) echo 2 **parrot-fashion** *Informal* = **by rote**, mechanically, mindlessly ♦ *verb* 3 = **repeat**, copy, echo, imitate, mimic, reiterate

parry *verb* 1 = **ward off**, block, deflect, fend off, hold at bay, rebuff, repel, repulse, stave off 2 = **evade**, avoid, circumvent, dodge, duck (*informal*), fence, fight shy of, shun, sidestep

parsimonious *adjective* = **mean**, cheeseparing, close, close-fisted, frugal, grasping, mingy (*Brit. informal*), miserable, miserly, near (*informal*), niggardly, penny-pinching (*informal*), penurious, saving, scrimpy, skinflinty, snoep (*S. African informal*), sparing, stingy, stinting, tight-arse (*taboo slang*), tight-arsed (*taboo*

slang), tight as a duck's arse (_taboo slang_), tight-ass (_U.S. taboo slang_), tight-assed (_U.S. taboo slang_), tightfisted
➤ **Antonyms**
extravagant, generous, lavish, munificent, open-handed, spendthrift, wasteful

parsimony _noun Formal_ = **meanness**, frugality, mininess (_Brit. informal_), miserliness, nearness (_informal_), niggardliness, penny-pinching (_informal_), stinginess, tightness

parson _noun_ = **clergyman**, churchman, cleric, divine, ecclesiastic, incumbent, man of God, man of the cloth, minister, pastor, preacher, priest, rector, reverend (_informal_), vicar

part _noun_ **1** = **piece**, bit, fraction, fragment, lot, particle, portion, scrap, section, sector, segment, share, slice **2** = **component**, branch, constituent, department, division, element, ingredient, limb, member, module, organ, piece, unit **3** _Theatre_ = **role**, character, lines **4** = **duty**, bit, business, capacity, charge, function, involvement, office, place, responsibility, role, say, share, task, work **5** = **side**, behalf, cause, concern, faction, interest, party **6** _often plural_ = **region**, airt (_Scot._), area, district, neck of the woods (_informal_), neighbourhood, quarter, territory, vicinity **7 for the most part** = **mainly**, chiefly, generally, in the main, largely, mostly, on the whole, principally **8 in good part** = **good-naturedly**, cheerfully, cordially, well, without offence **9 in part** = **partly**, a little, in some measure, partially, slightly, somewhat, to a certain extent, to some degree **10 on the part of** = **on behalf of**, for the sake of, in support of, in the name of **11 take part in** = **participate in**, associate oneself with, be instrumental in, be involved in, have a hand in, join in, partake in, play a part in, put one's twopence-worth in, take a hand in ♦ _verb_ **12** = **divide**, break, cleave, come apart, detach, disconnect, disjoin, dismantle, disunite, rend, separate, sever, split, tear **13** = **leave**, break up, depart, go, go away, go (their) separate ways, part company, quit, say goodbye, separate, split up, take one's leave, withdraw **14 part with** = **give up**, abandon, discard, forgo, let go of, relinquish, renounce, sacrifice, surrender, yield
➤ **Antonyms**
noun ≠**piece**: bulk, entirety, mass, totality, whole ♦ _verb_ ≠**divide**: adhere, close, combine, hold, join, stick, unite ≠**leave**: appear, arrive, come, gather, remain, show up (_informal_), stay, turn up

partake _verb_ **1 partake of** = **consume**, eat,

receive, share, take **2 partake in** = **participate in**, engage in, enter into, share in, take part in

partial _adjective_ **1** = **incomplete**, fragmentary, imperfect, limited, uncompleted, unfinished **2** = **biased**, discriminatory, influenced, interested, one-sided, partisan, predisposed, prejudiced, tendentious, unfair, unjust **3 be partial to** = **have a liking for**, be fond of, be keen on, be taken with, care for, have a soft spot for, have a weakness for
➤ **Antonyms**
≠**incomplete**: complete, entire, finished, full, total, whole ≠**biased**: impartial, objective, unbiased, unprejudiced

partiality _noun_ **1** = **bias**, favouritism, partisanship, predisposition, preference, prejudice **2** = **liking**, affinity, fondness, inclination, love, penchant, predilection, predisposition, preference, proclivity, taste, weakness
➤ **Antonyms**
≠**bias**: disinterest, equity, fairness, impartiality, objectivity ≠**liking**: abhorrence, antipathy, aversion, disgust, disinclination, dislike, distaste, loathing, revulsion

partially _adverb_ = **partly**, fractionally, halfway, incompletely, in part, moderately, not wholly, piecemeal, somewhat, to a certain extent _or_ degree

participant _noun_ = **participator**, associate, contributor, member, partaker, party, player, shareholder, stakeholder

participate _verb_ = **take part**, be a participant, be a party to, be involved in, engage in, enter into, get in on the act, have a hand in, join in, partake, perform, share
➤ **Antonyms**
abstain, boycott, forgo, forsake, forswear, opt out, pass up, refrain from, take no part of

participation _noun_ = **taking part**, assistance, contribution, involvement, joining in, partaking, partnership, sharing in

particle _noun_ = **bit**, atom, crumb, grain, iota, jot, mite, molecule, mote, piece, scrap, shred, speck, tittle, whit

particular _adjective_ **1** = **specific**, distinct, exact, express, peculiar, precise, special **2** = **special**, especial, exceptional, marked, notable, noteworthy, remarkable, singular, uncommon, unusual **3** = **detailed**, blow-by-blow, circumstantial, itemized, minute, painstaking, precise, selective, thorough **4** = **fussy**, choosy (_informal_), critical, dainty, demanding, discriminating, exacting, fastidious, finicky, meticulous, nice (*rare*), overnice, pernickety (*informal*), picky (*informal*) ♦ *noun* **5** *usually plural* = **detail**, circumstance, fact, feature, item, specification **6 in particular** = **especially**, distinctly, exactly, expressly, particularly, specifically

➤ **Antonyms**

adjective ≠**specific**: general, imprecise, indefinite, indistinct, inexact, unspecified, vague ≠**fussy**: casual, easy, easy to please, indiscriminate, negligent, slack, sloppy, uncritical

particularly *adverb* **1** = **especially**, decidedly, exceptionally, markedly, notably, outstandingly, peculiarly, singularly, surprisingly, uncommonly, unusually **2** = **specifically**, distinctly, especially, explicitly, expressly, in particular

parting *noun* **1** = **going**, adieu, departure, farewell, goodbye, leave-taking, valediction **2** = **division**, breaking, detachment, divergence, partition, rift, rupture, separation, split ♦ *adjective* **3** = **farewell**, departing, final, last, valedictory

partisan *noun* **1** = **supporter**, adherent, backer, champion, devotee, disciple, follower, stalwart, upholder, votary **2** = **underground fighter**, guerrilla, irregular, resistance fighter ♦ *adjective* **3** = **prejudiced**, biased, factional, interested, one-sided, partial, sectarian, tendentious **4** = **underground**, guerrilla, irregular, resistance

➤ **Antonyms**

noun ≠**supporter**: adversary, contender, critic, detractor, foe, knocker (*informal*), leader, opponent, rival ♦ *adjective* ≠**prejudiced**: bipartisan, broad-minded, disinterested, impartial, non-partisan, unbiased, unprejudiced

partition *noun* **1** = **screen**, barrier, divider, room divider, wall **2** = **division**, dividing, segregation, separation, severance, splitting **3** = **allotment**, apportionment, distribution, portion, rationing out, share ♦ *verb* **4** = **separate**, divide, fence off, screen, wall off **5** = **divide**, apportion, cut up, parcel out, portion, section, segment, separate, share, split up, subdivide

partly *adverb* = **partially**, halfway, incompletely, in part, in some measure, not fully, relatively, slightly, somewhat, to a certain degree *or* extent, up to a certain point

➤ **Antonyms**

completely, entirely, fully, in full, totally, wholly

partner *noun* **1** = **spouse**, bedfellow, better half (*Brit. informal*), consort, helpmate, her

indoors (*Brit. slang*), husband *or* wife, mate, significant other (*U.S. informal*) **2** = **companion**, accomplice, ally, associate, bedfellow, collaborator, colleague, comrade, confederate, copartner, helper, mate, participant, team-mate

partnership *noun* **1** = **company**, alliance, association, combine, conglomerate, cooperative, corporation, firm, house, society, union **2** = **cooperation**, companionship, connection, copartnership, fellowship, interest, participation, sharing

parts *plural noun* **1** *Literary* = **talents**, abilities, accomplishments, attributes, calibre, capabilities, endowments, faculties, genius, gifts, intellect, intelligence **2** = **components**, bits and pieces, spare parts, spares

party *noun* **1** = **get-together** (*informal*), at-home, bash (*informal*), beano (*Brit. slang*), celebration, do (*informal*), festivity, function, gathering, hooley *or* hoolie (*chiefly Irish & N.Z.*), knees-up (*Brit. informal*), rave (*Brit. slang*), rave-up (*Brit. slang*), reception, shindig (*informal*), social, social gathering, soirée **2** = **group**, band, body, bunch (*informal*), company, crew, detachment (*Military*), gang, gathering, squad, team, unit **3** = **faction**, alliance, association, cabal, camp, clique, coalition, combination, confederacy, coterie, grouping, league, schism, set, side **4** *Law* = **litigant**, contractor (*Law*), defendant, participant, plaintiff **5** *Informal* = **person**, individual, somebody, someone

pass *verb* **1** = **go by** *or* **past**, depart, elapse, flow, go, lapse, leave, move, move onwards, proceed, roll, run **2** = **qualify**, answer, come up to scratch (*informal*), do, get through, graduate, pass muster, succeed, suffice, suit **3** = **spend**, beguile, devote, employ, experience, fill, occupy, suffer, undergo, while away **4** = **give**, convey, deliver, exchange, hand, kick, let have, reach, send, throw, transfer, transmit **5** = **approve**, accept, adopt, authorize, decree, enact, establish, legislate, ordain, ratify, sanction, validate **6** = **pronounce**, declare, deliver, express, utter **7** = **exceed**, beat, excel, go beyond, outdistance, outdo, outstrip, overtake, surmount, surpass, transcend **8** = **ignore**, disregard, miss, neglect, not heed, omit, overlook, skip (*informal*) **9** = **excrete**, crap (*taboo slang*), defecate, discharge, eliminate, empty, evacuate, expel, shit (*taboo slang*), void **10** = **end**, blow over, cease, die, disappear, dissolve, dwindle, ebb, evaporate, expire, fade, go, melt away, terminate, vanish, wane **11** *with* **for** *or* **as**

= **be mistaken for**, be accepted as, be regarded as, be taken for, impersonate, serve as **12** *Old-fashioned* = **happen**, befall, come up, develop, fall out, occur, take place ◆ *noun* **13** = **gap**, canyon, col, defile, gorge, ravine, route **14** = **licence**, authorization, identification, identity card, passport, permission, permit, safe-conduct, ticket, warrant **15** = **thrust**, feint, jab, lunge, push, swing **16** *Informal As in* **make a pass at** = **advances**, approach, overture, play (*informal*), proposition, suggestion **17** *As in* **a pretty pass** = **predicament**, condition, juncture, pinch, plight, situation, stage, state, state of affairs, straits

➤ **Antonyms**

verb ≠**go by** *or* **past**: bring *or* come to a standstill, cease, halt, pause, stop ≠**qualify**: be inadequate, be inferior to, be unsuccessful, come a cropper (*informal*), fail, lose, suffer defeat ≠**approve**: ban, disallow, invalidate, overrule, prohibit, refuse, reject, veto ≠**ignore**: acknowledge, heed, note, notice, observe, pay attention to

passable *adjective* **1** = **adequate**, acceptable, admissible, allowable, all right, average, fair, fair enough, mediocre, middling, moderate, not too bad, ordinary, presentable, so-so (*informal*), tolerable, unexceptional **2** = **clear**, crossable, navigable, open, traversable, unobstructed

➤ **Antonyms**

≠**adequate**: A1 *or* A-one (*informal*), exceptional, extraordinary, first-class, inadequate, inadmissible, marvellous, outstanding, superb, tops (*slang*), unacceptable, unsatisfactory ≠**clear**: blocked, closed, impassable, obstructed, sealed off, unnavigable

passage *noun* **1** = **way**, alley, avenue, channel, course, lane, opening, path, road, route, thoroughfare **2** = **corridor**, aisle, doorway, entrance, entrance hall, exit, hall, hallway, lobby, passageway, vestibule **3** = **extract**, clause, excerpt, paragraph, piece, quotation, reading, section, sentence, text, verse **4** = **journey**, crossing, tour, trek, trip, voyage **5** = **movement**, advance, change, conversion, flow, motion, passing, progress, progression, transit, transition **6** = **safe-conduct**, allowance, authorization, freedom, permission, right, visa, warrant **7** = **establishment**, acceptance, enactment, legalization, legislation, passing, ratification

passageway *noun* = **corridor**, aisle, alley, hall, hallway, lane, passage

pass away *verb Euphemistic* = **die**, buy it

(*U.S. slang*), buy the farm (*U.S. slang*), check out (*U.S. slang*), croak (*slang*), decease, depart (this life), expire, go belly-up (*slang*), kick it (*slang*), kick the bucket (*slang*), pass on, pass over, peg it (*informal*), peg out (*informal*), pop one's clogs (*informal*), shuffle off this mortal coil, snuff it (*informal*)

pass by *verb* **1** = **go past**, leave, move past, pass **2** = **disregard**, miss, neglect, not choose, overlook, pass over

passé *adjective* = **out-of-date**, dated, obsolete, old-fashioned, old hat, outdated, outmoded, unfashionable

passenger *noun* = **traveller**, fare, hitchhiker, pillion rider, rider

passer-by *noun* = **bystander**, onlooker, witness

passing *adjective* **1** = **momentary**, brief, ephemeral, fleeting, short, short-lived, temporary, transient, transitory **2** = **superficial**, casual, cursory, glancing, hasty, quick, shallow, short, slight ◆ *noun* **3** = **end**, death, decease, demise, finish, loss, termination **4** *in passing* = **incidentally**, accidentally, by the bye, by the way, en passant, on the way

passion *noun* **1** = **love**, adoration, affection, ardour, attachment, concupiscence, desire, fondness, infatuation, itch, keenness, lust, the hots (*slang*) **2** = **emotion**, animation, ardour, eagerness, excitement, feeling, fervour, fire, heat, intensity, joy, rapture, spirit, transport, warmth, zeal, zest **3** = **rage**, anger, fit, flare-up (*informal*), frenzy, fury, indignation, ire, outburst, paroxysm, resentment, storm, vehemence, wrath **4** = **mania**, bug (*informal*), craving, craze, enthusiasm, fancy, fascination, idol, infatuation, obsession

➤ **Antonyms**

≠**emotion**: apathy, calmness, coldness, coolness, frigidity, hate, indifference, unconcern

passionate *adjective* **1** = **loving**, amorous, ardent, aroused, desirous, erotic, hot, lustful, sensual, sexy (*informal*), steamy (*informal*), wanton **2** = **emotional**, ablaze, animated, ardent, eager, enthusiastic, excited, fervent, fervid, fierce, flaming, frenzied, heartfelt, impassioned, impetuous, impulsive, intense, strong, vehement, warm, wild, zealous **3** = **quick-tempered**, choleric, excitable, fiery, hot-headed, hot-tempered, irascible, irritable, peppery, stormy, tempestuous, violent

➤ **Antonyms**

≠**loving**: cold, frigid, passionless, unloving,

unresponsive ≠**emotional**: apathetic, calm, cold, half-hearted, indifferent, languorous, nonchalant, unemotional, unenthusiastic ≠**quick-tempered**: agreeable, calm, easy-going, even-tempered, nonviolent, placid, unexcitable

passive *adjective* = **submissive**, acquiescent, compliant, docile, enduring, inactive, inert, lifeless, long-suffering, nonviolent, patient, quiescent, receptive, resigned, unassertive, uninvolved, unresisting
➤ Antonyms
active, alive, assertive, bossy (*informal*), defiant, domineering, energetic, feisty (*informal, chiefly U.S. & Canad.*), impatient, involved, lively, rebellious, spirited, violent, zippy (*informal*)

pass off *verb* 1 = **fake**, counterfeit, feign, make a pretence of, palm off 2 = **come to an end**, die away, disappear, fade out, vanish 3 = **take place**, be completed, go off, happen, occur, turn out

pass out *verb* 1 *Informal* = **faint**, become unconscious, black out (*informal*), drop, flake out (*informal*), keel over (*informal*), lose consciousness, swoon (*literary*) 2 = **hand out**, deal out, distribute, dole out

pass over *verb* = **disregard**, discount, forget, ignore, not dwell on, omit, overlook, pass by, take no notice of

pass up *verb Informal* = **miss**, abstain, decline, forgo, give (something) a miss (*informal*), ignore, let slip, let (something) go by, neglect, refuse, reject

password *noun* = **signal**, countersign, key word, open sesame, watchword

past *adjective* 1 = **former**, ancient, bygone, early, erstwhile, foregoing, late, long-ago, olden, preceding, previous, prior, quondam, recent 2 = **over**, accomplished, completed, done, elapsed, ended, extinct, finished, forgotten, gone, over and done with, spent ♦ *noun* 3 = **background**, experience, history, life, past life 4 **the past** = **former times**, antiquity, days gone by, days of yore, good old days, history, long ago, olden days, old times, times past, yesteryear (*literary*) ♦ *preposition* 5 = **after**, beyond, farther than, later than, outside, over, subsequent to 6 = **beyond**, across, by, on, over
➤ Antonyms
adjective ≠**former**: arrived, begun, coming, future, now, present ♦ *noun* ≠**former times**: future, now, present, time to come, today, tomorrow

paste *noun* 1 = **adhesive**, cement, glue, gum, mucilage ♦ *verb* 2 = **stick**, cement, fasten, fix, glue, gum

pastel *adjective* = **pale**, delicate, light, muted, soft, soft-hued
➤ Antonyms
bright, deep, rich, strong, vibrant, vivid

pastiche *noun* = **medley**, blend, farrago, gallimaufry, hotchpotch, *mélange*, miscellany, mixture, motley

pastille *noun* = **lozenge**, cough drop, jujube, tablet, troche (*Medical*)

pastime *noun* = **activity**, amusement, distraction, diversion, entertainment, game, hobby, leisure, play, recreation, relaxation, sport

past master *noun* = **expert**, ace (*informal*), artist, dab hand (*Brit. informal*), old hand, virtuoso, wizard

pastor *noun* = **clergyman**, churchman, divine, ecclesiastic, minister, parson, priest, rector, vicar

pastoral *adjective* 1 = **rustic**, agrestic, Arcadian, bucolic, country, georgic (*literary*), idyllic, rural, simple 2 = **ecclesiastical**, clerical, ministerial, priestly

pasture *noun* = **grassland**, grass, grazing, grazing land, lea (*poetic*), meadow, pasturage, shieling (*Scot.*)

pasty *adjective* = **pale**, anaemic, pallid, sickly, wan

pat *verb* 1 = **stroke**, caress, dab, fondle, pet, slap, tap, touch ♦ *noun* 2 = **stroke**, clap, dab, light blow, slap, tap 3 = **lump**, cake, dab, portion, small piece

patch *noun* 1 = **reinforcement**, piece of material 2 = **spot**, bit, scrap, shred, small piece, stretch 3 = **plot**, area, ground, land, tract ♦ *verb* 4 = **mend**, cover, fix, reinforce, repair, sew up 5 **patch up** = **settle**, bury the hatchet, conciliate, make friends, placate, restore, settle differences, smooth

patchwork *noun* = **mixture**, confusion, hash, hotchpotch, jumble, medley, mishmash, pastiche

patchy *adjective* = **uneven**, bitty, erratic, fitful, inconstant, irregular, random, sketchy, spotty, variable, varying
➤ Antonyms
constant, even, regular, unbroken, unvarying

patent *noun* 1 = **copyright**, invention, licence ♦ *adjective* 2 = **obvious**, apparent, blatant, clear, conspicuous, downright, evident, flagrant, glaring, indisputable, manifest, open, palpable, transparent, unconcealed, unequivocal, unmistakable

paternal *adjective* 1 = **fatherly**, benevolent, concerned, fatherlike, protective, solicitous, vigilant 2 = **patrilineal**, patrimonial

paternity *noun* **1** = **fatherhood**, fathership **2** = **parentage**, descent, extraction, family, lineage **3** = **origin**, authorship, derivation, source

path *noun* **1** = **way**, footpath, footway, pathway, road, towpath, track, trail, walkway (*chiefly U.S.*) **2** = **walk**, avenue **3** = **course**, avenue, direction, passage, procedure, road, route, track, way

pathetic *adjective* **1** = **sad**, affecting, distressing, gut-wrenching, harrowing, heartbreaking, heart-rending, melting, moving, pitiable, plaintive, poignant, tender, touching **2** = **inadequate**, deplorable, feeble, lamentable, meagre, measly, miserable, not much cop (*Brit. slang*), paltry, petty, pitiful, poor, puny, sorry, wet (*Brit. informal*), woeful **3** *Slang* = **worthless**, chickenshit (*U.S. slang*), crappy (*slang*), crummy (*slang*), pants (*informal*), poxy (*slang*), rubbishy, trashy, uninteresting, useless, wanky (*taboo slang*)
➤ **Antonyms**
≠**sad**: amusing, comical, droll, entertaining, funny, laughable, ludicrous, ridiculous

pathfinder *noun* = **pioneer**, discoverer, explorer, guide, scout, trailblazer

pathos *noun* = **sadness**, pitiableness, pitifulness, plaintiveness, poignancy

patience *noun* **1** = **forbearance**, calmness, composure, cool (*slang*), equanimity, even temper, imperturbability, restraint, serenity, sufferance, tolerance, toleration **2** = **endurance**, constancy, fortitude, long-suffering, perseverance, persistence, resignation, stoicism, submission
➤ **Antonyms**
≠**forbearance**: agitation, exasperation, excitement, impatience, irritation, nervousness, passion, restlessness

patient *adjective* **1** = **long-suffering**, calm, composed, enduring, persevering, persistent, philosophical, quiet, resigned, self-possessed, serene, stoical, submissive, uncomplaining, untiring **2** = **forbearing**, accommodating, even-tempered, forgiving, indulgent, lenient, mild, tolerant, understanding ♦ *noun* **3** = **sick person**, case, invalid, sufferer

patriot *noun* = **nationalist**, chauvinist, flag-waver (*informal*), jingo, lover of one's country, loyalist

patriotic *adjective* = **nationalistic**, chauvinistic, flag-waving (*informal*), jingoistic, loyal

patriotism *noun* = **nationalism**, flag-waving (*informal*), jingoism, love of one's country, loyalty

patrol *noun* **1** = **policing**, guarding, protecting, rounds, safeguarding, vigilance, watching **2** = **guard**, garrison, patrolman, sentinel, watch, watchman ♦ *verb* **3** = **police**, cruise, guard, inspect, keep guard, keep watch, make the rounds, pound, range, safeguard, walk the beat

patron *noun* **1** = **supporter**, advocate, angel (*informal*), backer, benefactor, champion, defender, friend, guardian, helper, philanthropist, protagonist, protector, sponsor **2** = **customer**, buyer, client, frequenter, habitué, shopper

patronage *noun* **1** = **support**, aid, assistance, backing, benefaction, championship, encouragement, espousal, help, promotion, sponsorship **2** = **custom**, business, clientele, commerce, trade, trading, traffic **3** = **condescension**, deigning, disdain, patronizing, stooping

patronize *verb* **1** = **talk down to**, be lofty with, look down on, treat as inferior, treat condescendingly, treat like a child **2** = **be a customer** *or* **client of**, buy from, deal with, do business with, frequent, shop at, trade with **3** = **support**, assist, back, befriend, foster, fund, help, maintain, promote, sponsor, subscribe to

patronizing *adjective* = **condescending**, contemptuous, disdainful, gracious, haughty, lofty, snobbish, stooping, supercilious, superior, toffee-nosed (*slang, chiefly Brit.*)
➤ **Antonyms**
deferential, humble, obsequious, respectful, servile

patter[1] *verb* **1** = **tap**, beat, pat, pelt, pitapat, pitter-patter, rat-a-tat, spatter **2** = **walk lightly**, scurry, scuttle, skip, tiptoe, trip ♦ *noun* **3** = **tapping**, pattering, pitapat, pitter-patter

patter[2] *noun* **1** = **spiel** (*informal*), line, monologue, pitch **2** = **chatter**, gabble, jabber, nattering, prattle, yak (*slang*) **3** = **jargon**, argot, cant, lingo (*informal*), patois, slang, vernacular ♦ *verb* **4** = **chatter**, babble, blab, hold forth, jabber, prate, rattle off, rattle on, spiel (*informal*), spout (*informal*), tattle

pattern *noun* **1** = **design**, arrangement, decoration, decorative design, device, figure, motif, ornament **2** = **order**, arrangement, method, orderliness, plan, sequence, system **3** = **plan**, design, diagram, guide, instructions, original, stencil, template **4** = **model**, archetype, criterion, cynosure, example, exemplar, guide, norm, original, par, paradigm, paragon, prototype, standard **5** = **sample**, example, specimen **6** = **type**, kind, shape, sort, style, variety ♦ *verb* **7** = **model**, copy, emulate, follow, form, imitate, mould, order, shape, style **8** = **decorate**, design, trim

paucity *noun Formal* = **scarcity**, dearth, deficiency, fewness, insufficiency, lack, meagreness, paltriness, poverty, rarity, scantiness, shortage, slenderness, slightness, smallness, sparseness, sparsity

paunch *noun* = **belly**, abdomen, beer-belly (*informal*), corporation (*informal*), middle-age spread (*informal*), pot, potbelly, spare tyre (*Brit. slang*), spread (*informal*)

pauper *noun* = **down-and-out**, bankrupt, beggar, have-not, indigent, insolvent, mendicant, poor person

pause *verb* **1** = **stop briefly**, break, cease, delay, deliberate, desist, discontinue, halt, have a breather (*informal*), hesitate, interrupt, rest, take a break, wait, waver ♦ *noun* **2** = **stop**, break, breather (*informal*), breathing space, caesura, cessation, delay, discontinuance, entr'acte, gap, halt, hesitation, interlude, intermission, interruption, interval, let-up (*informal*), lull, respite, rest, stay, stoppage, wait
➤ **Antonyms**
verb ≠**stop briefly**: advance, continue, proceed, progress ♦ *noun* ≠**stop**: advancement, continuance, progression

pave *verb* = **cover**, asphalt, concrete, flag, floor, macadamize, surface, tar, tile

paw *verb Informal* = **manhandle**, grab, handle roughly, maul, molest

pawn[1] *verb* **1** = **hock** (*informal, chiefly U.S.*), deposit, gage (*archaic*), hazard, mortgage, pledge, pop (*informal*), stake, wager ♦ *noun* **2** = **security**, assurance, bond, collateral, gage, guarantee, guaranty, pledge

pawn[2] *noun* = **tool**, cat's-paw, creature, dupe, instrument, plaything, puppet, stooge (*slang*), toy

pay *verb* **1** = **reimburse**, clear, compensate, cough up (*informal*), discharge, foot, give, honour, liquidate, meet, offer, recompense, remit, remunerate, render, requite, reward, settle, square up **2** *often with* **for** = **suffer**, answer for, atone, be punished, compensate, get one's deserts, make amends, suffer the consequences **3** = **give**, bestow, extend, grant, hand out, present, proffer, render **4** = **benefit**, be advantageous, be worthwhile, repay, serve **5** = **be profitable**, be remunerative, make a return, make money, provide a living **6** = **yield**, bring in, produce, profit, return **7** = **pay back**, avenge oneself for, get even with (*informal*), get revenge on, punish,

reciprocate, repay, requite, settle a score ♦ *noun* **8** = **wages**, allowance, compensation, earnings, emoluments, fee, hand-out, hire, income, meed (*archaic*), payment, recompense, reimbursement, remuneration, reward, salary, stipend, takings

payable *adjective* = **due**, mature, obligatory, outstanding, owed, owing, receivable, to be paid

pay back *verb* **1** = **repay**, refund, reimburse, return, settle up, square **2** = **get even with** (*informal*), get one's own back, hit back, reciprocate, recompense, retaliate, settle a score with

payment *noun* **1** = **paying**, defrayal, discharge, outlay, remittance, settlement **2** = **remittance**, advance, deposit, instalment, portion, premium **3** = **wage**, fee, hire, remuneration, reward

pay off *verb* **1** = **settle**, clear, discharge, liquidate, pay in full, square **2** = **succeed**, be effective, be profitable, be successful, work **3** = **dismiss**, discharge, fire, lay off, let go, sack (*informal*) **4** *Informal* = **bribe**, buy off, corrupt, get at, grease the palm of (*slang*), oil (*informal*), suborn **5** = **get even with** (*informal*), pay back, retaliate, settle a score

pay out *verb* = **spend**, cough up (*informal*), disburse, expend, fork out *or* over *or* up (*slang*), lay out (*informal*), shell out (*informal*)

peace *noun* **1** = **stillness**, calm, calmness, hush, peacefulness, quiet, quietude, repose, rest, silence, tranquillity **2** = **serenity**, calm, composure, contentment, placidity, relaxation, repose **3** = **harmony**, accord, agreement, amity, concord **4** = **truce**, armistice, cessation of hostilities, conciliation, pacification, treaty

peaceable *adjective* **1** = **peace-loving**, amiable, amicable, conciliatory, dovish, friendly, gentle, inoffensive, mild, nonbelligerent, pacific, peaceful, placid, unwarlike **2** = **calm**, balmy, peaceful, quiet, restful, serene, still, tranquil, undisturbed

peaceful *adjective* **1** = **at peace**, amicable, free from strife, friendly, harmonious, nonviolent, on friendly *or* good terms, without hostility **2** = **calm**, gentle, placid, quiet, restful, serene, still, tranquil, undisturbed, unruffled, untroubled **3** = **peace-loving**, conciliatory, irenic, pacific, peaceable, placatory, unwarlike
➤ **Antonyms**
≠**at peace**: antagonistic, bitter, hostile, unfriendly, violent, warring, wartime
≠**calm**: agitated, disquieted, disturbed, loud, nervous, noisy, raucous, restless,

upset ≠**peace-loving**: belligerent, warlike

peacemaker noun = **mediator**, appeaser, arbitrator, conciliator, pacifier, peacemonger

peak noun 1 = **point**, aiguille, apex, brow, crest, pinnacle, summit, tip, top 2 = **high point**, acme, apogee, climax, crown, culmination, maximum point, ne plus ultra, zenith ♦ verb 3 = **culminate**, be at its height, climax, come to a head, reach its highest point, reach the zenith

peal noun 1 = **ring**, blast, carillon, chime, clamour, clang, clap, crash, resounding, reverberation, ringing, roar, rumble, sound, tintinnabulation ♦ verb 2 = **ring**, chime, crack, crash, resonate, resound, reverberate, roar, roll, rumble, sound, tintinnabulate, toll

peasant noun 1 = **rustic**, churl (archaic), countryman, hind (obsolete), son of the soil, swain (archaic) 2 Informal = **boor**, churl, country bumpkin, hayseed (U.S. & Canad. informal), hick (informal, chiefly U.S. & Canad.), lout, provincial, yokel

peccadillo noun = **misdeed**, error, indiscretion, infraction, lapse, misdemeanour, petty sin, slip, trifling fault

peck verb, noun = **pick**, bite, dig, hit, jab, kiss, nibble, poke, prick, strike, tap

peculiar adjective 1 = **odd**, abnormal, bizarre, curious, eccentric, exceptional, extraordinary, far-out (slang), freakish, funny, offbeat, off-the-wall (slang), outlandish, out-of-the-way, outré, quaint, queer, singular, strange, uncommon, unconventional, unusual, wacko (slang), weird 2 = **specific**, appropriate, characteristic, distinct, distinctive, distinguishing, endemic, idiosyncratic, individual, local, particular, personal, private, restricted, special, unique
➤ Antonyms
≠**odd**: commonplace, conventional, expected, familiar, ordinary, usual
≠**specific**: common, general, indistinctive, unspecific

peculiarity noun 1 = **eccentricity**, abnormality, bizarreness, foible, freakishness, idiosyncrasy, mannerism, oddity, odd trait, queerness, quirk 2 = **characteristic**, attribute, distinctiveness, feature, mark, particularity, property, quality, singularity, speciality, trait

pedagogue noun = **teacher**, dogmatist, dominie (Scot.), educator, instructor, master or mistress, pedant, schoolmaster or schoolmistress

pedant noun = **hairsplitter**, casuist, doctrinaire, dogmatist, literalist, nit-picker (informal), pedagogue, pettifogger,

precisian, quibbler, scholastic, sophist

pedantic adjective = **hairsplitting**, abstruse, academic, bookish, didactic, donnish, erudite, formal, fussy, nit-picking (informal), overnice, particular, pedagogic, picky (informal), pompous, precise, priggish, punctilious, scholastic, schoolmasterly, sententious, stilted

pedantry noun = **hairsplitting**, bookishness, finicality, overnicety, pedagogism, pettifoggery, pomposity, punctiliousness, quibbling, sophistry, stuffiness

peddle verb = **sell**, flog (slang), hawk, huckster, market, push (informal), sell door to door, trade, vend

pedestal noun 1 = **support**, base, dado (Architecture), foot, foundation, mounting, pier, plinth, socle, stand 2 **put on a pedestal** = **worship**, apotheosize, deify, dignify, ennoble, exalt, glorify, idealize

pedestrian noun 1 = **walker**, footslogger, foot-traveller ♦ adjective 2 = **dull**, banal, boring, commonplace, flat, ho-hum (informal), humdrum, mediocre, mundane, no great shakes (informal), ordinary, plodding, prosaic, run-of-the-mill, unimaginative, uninspired, uninteresting
➤ Antonyms
noun ≠**walker**: driver, motorist ♦ adjective ≠**dull**: exciting, fascinating, imaginative, important, interesting, noteworthy, outstanding, remarkable, significant

pedigree noun 1 = **lineage**, ancestry, blood, breed, derivation, descent, extraction, family, family tree, genealogy, heritage, line, race, stemma, stirps, stock ♦ adjective 2 = **purebred**, full-blooded, thoroughbred

pedlar noun = **seller**, door-to-door salesman, hawker, huckster, vendor

peek verb 1 = **glance**, eyeball (slang), keek (Scot.), look, peep, peer, snatch a glimpse, sneak a look, spy, take a look, take or have a gander (informal) ♦ noun 2 = **glance**, blink, butcher's (Brit. slang), gander (informal), glim (Scot.), glimpse, keek (Scot.), look, look-see (slang), peep, shufti (Brit. slang)

peel verb 1 = **skin**, decorticate, desquamate, flake off, pare, scale, strip off ♦ noun 2 = **skin**, epicarp, exocarp, peeling, rind

peep[1] verb 1 = **peek**, eyeball (slang), keek (Scot.), look, look from hiding, look surreptitiously, peer, sneak a look, spy, steal a look 2 = **appear briefly**, emerge, peer out, show partially ♦ noun 3 = **look**, butcher's (Brit. slang), gander (informal), glim (Scot.), glimpse, keek (Scot.), look-see (*slang*), peek, shufti (*Brit. slang*)

peep² *verb, noun* = **tweet**, cheep, chirp, chirrup, pipe, squeak, twitter

peephole *noun* = **spyhole**, aperture, chink, crack, crevice, fissure, hole, keyhole, opening, pinhole, slit

peer¹ *noun* **1** = **noble**, aristo (*informal*), aristocrat, baron, count, duke, earl, lord, marquess, marquis, nobleman, viscount **2** = **equal**, coequal, compeer, fellow, like, match

peer² *verb* **1** = **squint**, gaze, inspect, peep, scan, scrutinize, snoop, spy, squinny **2** = **appear**, become visible, emerge, peep out

peerage *noun* = **aristocracy**, lords and ladies, nobility, peers, titled classes

peerless *adjective* = **unequalled**, beyond compare, excellent, incomparable, matchless, nonpareil, outstanding, second to none, superlative, unique, unmatched, unparalleled, unrivalled, unsurpassed
➤ **Antonyms**
commonplace, inferior, mediocre, no great shakes (*informal*), ordinary, poor, second-rate

peeved *adjective* = **irritated**, annoyed, exasperated, galled, hacked (off) (*U.S. slang*), irked, nettled, piqued, pissed (*taboo slang*), pissed off (*taboo slang*), put out, riled, sore, upset, vexed

peevish *adjective* = **irritable**, acrimonious, cantankerous, captious, childish, churlish, crabbed, cross, crotchety (*informal*), crusty, fractious, fretful, grumpy, huffy, ill-natured, ill-tempered, liverish, pettish, petulant, querulous, ratty (*Brit. & N.Z. informal*), short-tempered, shrewish, snappy, splenetic, sulky, sullen, surly, testy, tetchy, touchy, waspish, whingeing (*informal*)
➤ **Antonyms**
affable, agreeable, cheerful, cheery, easy-going, even-tempered, genial, good-natured, happy, merry, pleasant, sweet

peg *verb* **1** = **fasten**, attach, fix, join, make fast, secure **2** *with* **along** *or* **away** = **work at**, apply oneself to, beaver away (*Brit. informal*), keep at it, keep going, keep on, persist, plod along, plug away at (*informal*), stick to it, work away **3** *Of prices, etc.* = **fix**, control, freeze, limit, set

pejorative *adjective* = **derogatory**, deprecatory, depreciatory, disparaging, negative, uncomplimentary, unpleasant

pelt¹ *verb* **1** = **throw**, assail, batter, beat, belabour, bombard, cast, hurl, pepper, pummel, shower, sling, strike, thrash,

wallop (*informal*) **2** = **rush**, barrel (along) (*informal, chiefly U.S. & Canad.*), belt (*slang*), burn rubber (*informal*), career, charge, dash, hurry, run fast, shoot, speed, stampede, tear, whizz (*informal*) **3** = **pour**, bucket down (*informal*), rain cats and dogs (*informal*), rain hard, teem

pelt² *noun* = **coat**, fell, hide, skin

pen¹ *verb* = **write**, commit to paper, compose, draft, draw up, jot down

pen² *noun* **1** = **enclosure**, cage, coop, corral (*chiefly U.S. & Canad.*), fold, hutch, pound, sty ♦ *verb* **2** = **enclose**, cage, confine, coop up, fence in, hedge, hem in, hurdle, impound, mew (up), pound, shut up *or* in

penal *adjective* = **disciplinary**, corrective, penalizing, punitive, retributive

penalize *verb* = **punish**, award a penalty against (*Sport*), correct, discipline, handicap, impose a penalty on, inflict a handicap on, put at a disadvantage

penalty *noun* = **punishment**, disadvantage, fine, forfeit, forfeiture, handicap, mulct, price, retribution

penance *noun* **1** = **atonement**, mortification, penalty, punishment, reparation, sackcloth and ashes **2** *do* **penance** = **atone**, accept punishment, make amends, make reparation, mortify oneself, show contrition, suffer

penchant *noun* = **liking**, affinity, bent, bias, disposition, fondness, inclination, leaning, partiality, predilection, predisposition, proclivity, proneness, propensity, taste, tendency, turn

pending *adjective* = **undecided**, awaiting, forthcoming, hanging fire, imminent, impending, in the balance, in the offing, undetermined, unsettled, up in the air

penetrate *verb* **1** = **pierce**, bore, enter, go through, impale, perforate, prick, probe, stab **2** = **permeate**, diffuse, enter, get in, infiltrate, make inroads (into), pervade, seep, suffuse **3** = **grasp**, comprehend, decipher, discern, fathom, figure out (*informal*), get to the bottom of, suss (out) (*slang*), understand, unravel, work out **4** = **be understood**, affect, become clear, come across, get through to, impress, touch

penetrating *adjective* **1** = **sharp**, biting, carrying, harsh, intrusive, pervasive, piercing, pungent, shrill, stinging, strong **2** = **perceptive**, acute, astute, critical, discerning, discriminating, incisive, intelligent, keen, perspicacious, profound, quick, sagacious, searching, sharp, sharp-witted, shrewd
➤ **Antonyms**

≠**sharp**: blunt, dull, mild, sweet
≠**perceptive**: apathetic, dull, indifferent, obtuse, shallow, stupid, uncomprehending, unperceptive

penetration noun **1** = **piercing**, entrance, entry, incision, inroad, invasion, perforation, puncturing **2** = **perception**, acuteness, astuteness, discernment, insight, keenness, perspicacity, sharpness, shrewdness, wit

penis noun = **phallus**, chopper (Brit. slang), cock (taboo slang), dick (taboo slang), dong (slang), John Thomas (taboo slang), joystick (slang), knob (Brit. taboo slang), member, organ, pecker (U.S. & Canad. taboo slang), pizzle (archaic & dialect), plonker (slang), prick (taboo slang), schlong (U.S. slang), tadger (Brit. slang), tool (taboo slang), wang (U.S. slang), weenie (U.S. slang), whang (U.S. slang), willie or willy (Brit. informal), winkle (Brit. slang)

penitence noun = **repentance**, compunction, contrition, regret, remorse, ruefulness, self-reproach, shame, sorrow

penitent adjective = **repentant**, abject, apologetic, atoning, conscience-stricken, contrite, regretful, remorseful, rueful, sorrowful, sorry
➤ **Antonyms**
callous, impenitent, remorseless, unrepentant

penmanship noun Formal = **handwriting**, calligraphy, chirography, fist (informal), hand, longhand, script, writing

pen name noun = **pseudonym**, allonym, nom de plume

pennant noun = **flag**, banderole, banner, burgee (Nautical), ensign, jack, pennon, streamer

penniless adjective = **poor**, bankrupt, broke (informal), cleaned out (slang), destitute, dirt-poor (informal), down and out, down at heel, flat broke (informal), impecunious, impoverished, indigent, in queer street, moneyless, necessitous, needy, on one's uppers, on the breadline, penurious, poverty-stricken, ruined, short, skint (Brit. slang), stony-broke (Brit. slang), strapped (slang), without a penny to one's name, without two pennies to rub together (informal)
➤ **Antonyms**
affluent, filthy rich, loaded (slang), rich, rolling (slang), wealthy, well-heeled (informal)

penny-pinching adjective = **miserly**, cheeseparing, close, frugal, mean, mingy (Brit. informal), near (informal), niggardly, scrimping, Scrooge-like, snoep (S. African

informal), stingy, tight-arse (taboo slang), tight-arsed (taboo slang), tight as a duck's arse (taboo slang), tight-ass (U.S. taboo slang), tight-assed (U.S. taboo slang), tightfisted
➤ **Antonyms**
generous, kind, liberal, munificent, open-handed, prodigal, unstinting

pennyworth noun = **bit**, crumb, jot, little, mite, modicum, particle, scrap, small amount, tittle

pension noun = **allowance**, annuity, benefit, superannuation

pensioner noun = **senior citizen**, O.A.P., retired person

pensive adjective = **thoughtful**, blue (informal), cogitative, contemplative, dreamy, grave, in a brown study (informal), meditative, melancholy, mournful, musing, preoccupied, reflective, ruminative, sad, serious, sober, solemn, sorrowful, wistful
➤ **Antonyms**
active, carefree, cheerful, frivolous, gay, happy, joyous, light-hearted

pent-up adjective = **suppressed**, bottled up, bridled, checked, constrained, curbed, held back, inhibited, repressed, smothered, stifled

penurious adjective Formal **1** = **mean**, cheeseparing, close, close-fisted, frugal, grudging, miserly, near (informal), niggardly, parsimonious, skimping, stingy, tight-arse (taboo slang), tight-arsed (taboo slang), tight as a duck's arse (taboo slang), tight-ass (U.S. taboo slang), tight-assed (U.S. taboo slang), tightfisted, ungenerous **2** = **poor**, destitute, down and out, down at heel, impecunious, impoverished, indigent, needy, on the breadline, penniless, poverty-stricken **3** = **meagre**, beggarly, deficient, inadequate, miserable, miserly, paltry, pathetic, poor, scanty

penury noun **1** = **poverty**, beggary, destitution, indigence, need, pauperism, privation, straitened circumstances, want **2** = **scarcity**, dearth, deficiency, lack, paucity, scantiness, shortage, sparseness

people plural noun **1** = **persons**, human beings, humanity, humans, mankind, men and women, mortals **2** = **nation**, citizens, community, folk, inhabitants, population, public **3** = **family**, clan, race, tribe **4 the people** = **the public**, the commonalty, the crowd, the general public, the grass roots, the herd, (the) hoi polloi, the masses, the mob, the multitude, the plebs, the populace, the proles (derogatory slang, chiefly Brit.), the proletariat, the rabble, the rank and file ♦ verb **5** = **inhabit**, colonize, occupy, populate, settle

pepper *noun* **1** = **seasoning**, flavour, spice ♦ *verb* **2** = **sprinkle**, bespatter, dot, fleck, spatter, speck, stipple, stud **3** = **pelt**, bombard, riddle, scatter, shower

peppery *adjective* **1** = **hot**, fiery, highly seasoned, piquant, pungent, spicy **2** = **irritable**, choleric, hot-tempered, irascible, quick-tempered, snappish, testy, touchy, vitriolic, waspish **3** = **sharp**, astringent, biting, caustic, incisive, sarcastic, stinging, trenchant, vitriolic
➤ **Antonyms**
≠**hot**: bland, insipid, mild, tasteless, vapid

perceive *verb* **1** = **see**, be aware of, behold, descry, discern, discover, distinguish, espy, make out, note, notice, observe, recognize, remark, spot **2** = **understand**, appreciate, apprehend, comprehend, conclude, deduce, feel, gather, get (*informal*), get the message, get the picture, grasp, know, learn, realize, see, sense, suss (out) (*slang*)

perceptible *adjective* = **visible**, apparent, appreciable, blatant, clear, conspicuous, detectable, discernible, distinct, evident, noticeable, observable, obvious, palpable, perceivable, recognizable, tangible
➤ **Antonyms**
concealed, hidden, imperceptible, inconspicuous, indiscernible, invisible, unapparent, undetectable, unnoticeable

perception *noun* = **understanding**, apprehension, awareness, conception, consciousness, discernment, feeling, grasp, idea, impression, insight, notion, observation, recognition, sensation, sense, taste

perceptive *adjective* = **observant**, acute, alert, astute, aware, discerning, insightful, intuitive, penetrating, percipient, perspicacious, quick, responsive, sensitive, sharp
➤ **Antonyms**
dull, indifferent, insensitive, obtuse, slow-witted, stupid, thick

perch *noun* **1** = **resting place**, branch, pole, post, roost ♦ *verb* **2** = **sit**, alight, balance, land, rest, roost, settle

perchance *adverb Archaic or poetic* = **perhaps**, by chance, for all one knows, haply (*archaic*), maybe, mayhap (*archaic*), peradventure (*archaic*), possibly, probably

percipient *adjective Formal* = **perceptive**, alert, alive, astute, aware, bright (*informal*), discerning, discriminating, intelligent, observant, penetrating, perspicacious, quick-witted, sharp, wide-awake

percolate *verb* = **filter**, drain, drip, exude, filtrate, leach, ooze, penetrate, perk (*of coffee, informal*), permeate, pervade, seep, strain, transfuse

percussion *noun* = **impact**, blow, brunt, bump, clash, collision, concussion, crash, jolt, knock, shock, smash, thump

peremptory *adjective* **1** = **imperative**, absolute, binding, categorical, commanding, compelling, decisive, final, incontrovertible, irrefutable, obligatory, undeniable **2** = **imperious**, arbitrary, assertive, authoritative, autocratic, bossy (*informal*), dictatorial, dogmatic, domineering, high-handed, intolerant, overbearing

perennial *adjective* **1** = **lasting**, abiding, chronic, constant, continual, continuing, enduring, incessant, inveterate, lifelong, persistent, recurrent, unchanging **2** = **eternal**, ceaseless, deathless, everlasting, immortal, imperishable, never-ending, permanent, perpetual, unceasing, undying, unfailing, uninterrupted

perfect *adjective* **1** = **complete**, absolute, completed, consummate, entire, finished, full, out-and-out, sheer, unadulterated, unalloyed, unmitigated, utter, whole **2** = **faultless**, blameless, clean, flawless, immaculate, impeccable, pure, spotless, unblemished, unmarred, untarnished **3** = **excellent**, ideal, splendid, sublime, superb, superlative, supreme **4** = **exact**, accurate, close, correct, faithful, on the money (*U.S.*), precise, right, spot-on (*Brit. informal*), strict, true, unerring **5** = **expert**, accomplished, adept, experienced, finished, masterly, polished, practised, skilful, skilled ♦ *verb* **6** = **improve**, ameliorate, cultivate, develop, elaborate, hone, polish, refine **7** = **accomplish**, achieve, carry out, complete, consummate, effect, finish, fulfil, perform, realize
➤ **Antonyms**
adjective ≠**complete**: incomplete, partial, unfinished ≠**faultless**: damaged, defective, deficient, faulty, flawed, impaired, imperfect, impure, ruined, spoiled ≠**excellent**: bad, inferior, poor, unskilled, worthless ♦ *verb* ≠**improve**: mar

perfection *noun* **1** = **accomplishment**, achievement, achieving, completion, consummation, evolution, fulfilment, realization **2** = **completeness**, maturity **3** = **purity**, integrity, perfectness, wholeness **4** = **excellence**, exquisiteness, sublimity, superiority **5** = **exactness**, faultlessness, precision **6** = **ideal**, acme, crown, paragon

perfectionist *noun* = **stickler**, formalist, precisian, precisionist, purist

perfectly *adverb* **1** = **completely**, absolutely, altogether, consummately, entirely, every inch, fully, quite, thoroughly, totally, utterly, wholly **2** = **flawlessly**, admirably, exquisitely, faultlessly, ideally, impeccably, like a dream, superbly, superlatively, supremely, to perfection, wonderfully
➤ **Antonyms**
≠**completely**: inaccurately, incompletely, mistakenly, partially ≠**flawlessly**: badly, defectively, faultily, imperfectly, poorly

perfidious *adjective Literary* = **treacherous**, corrupt, deceitful, dishonest, disloyal, double-dealing, double-faced, faithless, false, recreant (*archaic*), traitorous, treasonous, two-faced, unfaithful, untrustworthy

perfidy *noun Literary* = **treachery**, betrayal, deceit, disloyalty, double-dealing, duplicity, faithlessness, falsity, infidelity, perfidiousness, treason

perforate *verb* = **pierce**, bore, drill, hole, honeycomb, penetrate, punch, puncture

perform *verb* **1** = **carry out**, accomplish, achieve, act, bring about, complete, comply with, discharge, do, effect, execute, fulfil, function, observe, pull off, satisfy, transact, work **2** = **present**, act, appear as, depict, enact, play, produce, put on, render, represent, stage

performance *noun* **1** = **carrying out**, accomplishment, achievement, act, completion, conduct, consummation, discharge, execution, exploit, feat, fulfilment, work **2** = **presentation**, acting, appearance, exhibition, gig (*informal*), interpretation, play, portrayal, production, representation, show **3** = **functioning**, action, conduct, efficiency, operation, practice, running, working **4** *Informal* = **carry-on** (*informal, chiefly Brit.*), act, behaviour, bother, business, fuss, pantomime (*informal, chiefly Brit.*), pother, rigmarole, to-do

performer *noun* = **artiste**, actor *or* actress, play-actor, player, Thespian, trouper

perfume *noun* = **fragrance**, aroma, attar, balminess, bouquet, cologne, essence, incense, niff (*Brit. slang*), odour, redolence, scent, smell, sweetness

perfunctory *adjective* = **offhand**, automatic, careless, cursory, heedless, inattentive, indifferent, mechanical, negligent, routine, sketchy, slipshod, slovenly, stereotyped, superficial, unconcerned, unthinking, wooden
➤ **Antonyms**
ardent, assiduous, attentive, careful, diligent, keen, spirited, thorough, thoughtful, zealous

perhaps *adverb* = **maybe**, as the case may be, conceivably, feasibly, for all one knows, it may be, perchance (*archaic*), possibly

peril *noun* = **danger**, exposure, hazard, insecurity, jeopardy, menace, pitfall, risk, uncertainty, vulnerability
➤ **Antonyms**
certainty, impregnability, invulnerability, safety, security, surety

perilous *adjective* = **dangerous**, chancy (*informal*), exposed, fraught with danger, hairy (*slang*), hazardous, parlous (*archaic*), precarious, risky, threatening, unsafe, unsure, vulnerable

perimeter *noun* = **boundary**, ambit, border, borderline, bounds, circumference, confines, edge, limit, margin, periphery
➤ **Antonyms**
central part, centre, core, heart, hub, middle, nucleus

period *noun* **1** = **time**, interval, season, space, span, spell, stretch, term, while **2** = **age**, aeon, course, cycle, date, days, epoch, era, generation, season, stage, term, time, years

periodic *adjective* = **recurrent**, at fixed intervals, cyclic, cyclical, every once in a while, every so often, infrequent, intermittent, occasional, periodical, regular, repeated, seasonal, spasmodic, sporadic

periodical *noun* = **publication**, journal, magazine, monthly, organ, paper, quarterly, review, serial, weekly, zine (*informal*)

peripheral *adjective* **1** = **incidental**, inessential, irrelevant, marginal, minor, secondary, unimportant **2** = **outermost**, exterior, external, outer, outside

perish *verb* **1** = **die**, be killed, be lost, decease, expire, lose one's life, pass away **2** = **be destroyed**, collapse, decline, disappear, fall, go under, vanish **3** = **rot**, break down, decay, decompose, disintegrate, moulder, waste, wither

perishable *adjective* = **short-lived**, decaying, decomposable, destructible, easily spoilt, liable to rot, unstable
➤ **Antonyms**
durable, lasting, long-life, long-lived, non-perishable

perjure *verb* **perjure oneself** *Criminal law* = **commit perjury**, bear false witness, forswear, give false testimony, lie under oath, swear falsely

perjured *adjective* = **lying**, deceitful, false, forsworn, mendacious, perfidious, traitorous, treacherous, untrue, untruthful

perjury *noun* = **lying under oath**, bearing false witness, false oath, false statement, false swearing, forswearing, giving false testimony, oath breaking, violation of an oath, wilful falsehood

perk *noun Brit. informal* = **bonus**, benefit, extra, fringe benefit, perquisite, plus

perk up *verb* = **cheer up**, brighten, buck up (*informal*), liven up, look up, pep up, rally, recover, recuperate, revive, take heart

permanence *noun* = **continuity**, constancy, continuance, dependability, durability, duration, endurance, finality, fixedness, fixity, immortality, indestructibility, lastingness, perdurability (*rare*), permanency, perpetuity, stability, survival

permanent *adjective* = **lasting**, abiding, constant, durable, enduring, eternal, everlasting, fixed, immovable, immutable, imperishable, indestructible, invariable, long-lasting, perennial, perpetual, persistent, stable, steadfast, unchanging, unfading
➤ **Antonyms**
brief, changing, ephemeral, finite, fleeting, impermanent, inconstant, momentary, mortal, passing, short-lived, temporary, transitory, variable

permeate *verb* = **pervade**, charge, diffuse throughout, fill, filter through, imbue, impregnate, infiltrate, pass through, penetrate, percolate, saturate, seep through, soak through, spread through

permissible *adjective* = **permitted**, acceptable, admissible, allowable, all right, authorized, kosher (*informal*), lawful, legal, legit (*slang*), legitimate, licit, O.K. *or* okay (*informal*), proper, sanctioned
➤ **Antonyms**
banned, forbidden, illegal, illicit, prohibited, unauthorized, unlawful

permission *noun* = **authorization**, allowance, approval, assent, blank cheque, carte blanche, consent, dispensation, freedom, go-ahead (*informal*), green light, leave, liberty, licence, permit, sanction, sufferance, tolerance

permissive *adjective* = **tolerant**, acquiescent, easy-going, easy-oasy (*slang*), forbearing, free, indulgent, latitudinarian, lax, lenient, liberal, open-minded
➤ **Antonyms**
authoritarian, denying, domineering, forbidding, grudging, rigid, strict

permit *verb* 1 = **allow**, admit, agree, authorize, consent, empower, enable, endorse, endure, entitle, give leave *or* permission, give the green light to, grant,

let, license, own, sanction, suffer, tolerate, warrant ♦ *noun* 2 = **licence**, authorization, liberty, pass, passport, permission, sanction, warrant

permutation *noun* = **transformation**, alteration, change, shift, transmutation, transposition

pernicious *adjective Formal* = **wicked**, bad, baleful, baneful (*archaic*), damaging, dangerous, deadly, deleterious, destructive, detrimental, evil, fatal, harmful, hurtful, injurious, maleficent, malevolent, malicious, malign, malignant, noisome, noxious, offensive, pestilent, poisonous, ruinous, venomous

pernickety *adjective Informal* 1 = **fussy**, careful, carping, difficult to please, exacting, fastidious, finicky, hairsplitting, nice, nit-picking (*informal*), overprecise, painstaking, particular, picky (*informal*), punctilious 2 = **tricky**, detailed, exacting, fiddly, fine
➤ **Antonyms**
≠**fussy**: careless, easy to please, haphazard, heedless, inattentive, lax, slack, slapdash, slipshod, sloppy, uncritical
≠**tricky**: easy, simple

peroration *noun Formal* = **summing-up**, closing remarks, conclusion, recapitulation, recapping (*informal*), reiteration

perpendicular *adjective* = **upright**, at right angles to, on end, plumb, straight, vertical

perpetrate *verb* = **commit**, be responsible for, bring about, carry out, do, effect, enact, execute, inflict, perform, wreak

perpetual *adjective* 1 = **everlasting**, abiding, endless, enduring, eternal, immortal, infinite, lasting, never-ending, perennial, permanent, sempiternal (*literary*), unchanging, undying, unending 2 = **continual**, ceaseless, constant, continuous, endless, incessant, interminable, never-ending, perennial, persistent, recurrent, repeated, unceasing, unfailing, uninterrupted, unremitting
➤ **Antonyms**
brief, ephemeral, fleeting, impermanent, momentary, passing, short-lived, temporary, transitory

perpetuate *verb* = **maintain**, continue, eternalize, immortalize, keep alive, keep going, keep up, preserve, sustain
➤ **Antonyms**
abolish, destroy, end, forget, ignore, put an end to, stamp out, suppress

perplex *verb* 1 = **puzzle**, baffle, befuddle, bemuse, beset, bewilder, confound, confuse, dumbfound, faze, flummox, mix up, muddle, mystify, nonplus, stump 2

= **complicate**, encumber, entangle, involve, jumble, mix up, snarl up, tangle, thicken

perplexing *adjective* = **puzzling**, baffling, bewildering, complex, complicated, confusing, difficult, enigmatic, hard, inexplicable, intricate, involved, knotty, labyrinthine, mysterious, mystifying, paradoxical, strange, taxing, thorny, unaccountable, weird

perplexity *noun* 1 = **puzzlement**, bafflement, bewilderment, confusion, incomprehension, mystification, stupefaction 2 = **puzzle**, can of worms (*informal*), difficulty, dilemma, enigma, fix (*informal*), how-do-you-do (*informal*), knotty problem, mystery, paradox, snarl 3 = **complexity**, difficulty, inextricability, intricacy, involvement, obscurity

perquisite *noun Formal* = **bonus**, benefit, dividend, extra, fringe benefit, icing on the cake, perk (*Brit. informal*), plus

persecute *verb* 1 = **victimize**, afflict, be on one's back (*slang*), distress, dragoon, hound, hunt, ill-treat, injure, maltreat, martyr, molest, oppress, pick on, pursue, torment, torture 2 = **harass**, annoy, badger, bait, bother, hassle (*informal*), pester, tease, vex, worry
➤ **Antonyms**
accommodate, coddle, comfort, console, cosset, humour, indulge, leave alone, let alone, mollycoddle, pamper, pet, spoil

perseverance *noun* = **persistence**, constancy, dedication, determination, diligence, doggedness, endurance, indefatigability, pertinacity, purposefulness, resolution, sedulity, stamina, steadfastness, tenacity

persevere *verb* = **keep going**, be determined *or* resolved, carry on, continue, endure, go on, hang on, hold fast, hold on (*informal*), keep on *or* at, keep one's hand in, maintain, persist, plug away (*informal*), pursue, remain, stand firm, stay the course, stick at *or* to
➤ **Antonyms**
be irresolute, dither (*chiefly Brit.*), end, falter, give in, give up, hesitate, quit, shillyshally (*informal*), swither (*Scot.*), throw in the towel, vacillate, waver

persist *verb* 1 = **continue**, abide, carry on, endure, keep up, last, linger, remain 2 = **persevere**, be resolute, continue, hold on (*informal*), insist, stand firm, stay the course

persistence *noun* = **determination**, constancy, diligence, doggedness, endurance, grit, indefatigability, perseverance, pertinacity, pluck,

resolution, stamina, steadfastness, tenacity, tirelessness

persistent *adjective* 1 = **continuous**, constant, continual, endless, incessant, interminable, lasting, never-ending, perpetual, relentless, repeated, unrelenting, unremitting 2 = **determined**, assiduous, dogged, enduring, fixed, immovable, indefatigable, obdurate, obstinate, persevering, pertinacious, resolute, steadfast, steady, stiff-necked, stubborn, tenacious, tireless, unflagging
➤ **Antonyms**
≠**continuous**: inconstant, intermittent, irregular, occasional, off-and-on, periodic ≠**determined**: changeable, flexible, irresolute, tractable, yielding

person *noun* 1 = **individual**, being, body, human, human being, living soul, soul 2 **in person** = **personally**, bodily, in the flesh, oneself

persona *noun* = **personality**, assumed role, character, façade, face, front, mask, part, public face, role

personable *adjective* = **pleasant**, affable, agreeable, amiable, attractive, charming, good-looking, handsome, likable *or* likeable, nice, pleasing, presentable, winning
➤ **Antonyms**
disagreeable, sullen, surly, ugly, unattractive, unpleasant, unsightly

personage *noun* = **personality**, big name, big noise (*informal*), big shot (*informal*), celeb (*informal*), celebrity, dignitary, luminary, megastar (*informal*), notable, public figure, somebody, V.I.P., well-known person, worthy

personal *adjective* 1 = **private**, exclusive, individual, intimate, own, particular, peculiar, privy, special 2 = **physical**, bodily, corporal, corporeal, exterior, material 3 = **offensive**, derogatory, disparaging, insulting, nasty, pejorative, slighting

personality *noun* 1 = **nature**, character, disposition, identity, individuality, make-up, psyche, temper, temperament, traits 2 = **character**, attraction, attractiveness, charisma, charm, dynamism, likableness *or* likeableness, magnetism, pleasantness 3 = **celebrity**, big name, celeb (*informal*), famous name, household name, megastar (*informal*), notable, personage, star, well-known face, well-known person

personally *adverb* 1 = **by oneself**, alone, independently, in person, in the flesh, on one's own, solely 2 = **in one's opinion**, for oneself, for one's part, from one's own viewpoint, in one's books, in one's own view **3** = **individually**, individualistically, privately, specially, subjectively

personate verb Criminal law = **impersonate**, act, depict, do (informal), enact, feign, imitate, play-act, portray, represent

personification noun = **embodiment**, epitome, image, incarnation, likeness, portrayal, recreation, representation, semblance

personify verb = **embody**, body forth, epitomize, exemplify, express, image (rare), incarnate, mirror, represent, symbolize, typify

personnel noun = **employees**, helpers, human resources, liveware, members, men and women, people, staff, workers, workforce

perspective noun **1** = **outlook**, angle, attitude, broad view, context, frame of reference, overview, way of looking **2** = **objectivity**, proportion, relation, relative importance, relativity **3** = **view**, outlook, panorama, prospect, scene, vista

perspicacious adjective Formal = **perceptive**, acute, alert, astute, aware, clear-sighted, clever, discerning, keen, observant, penetrating, percipient, sagacious, sharp, sharp-witted, shrewd

perspicacity noun Formal = **insight**, acumen, acuteness, discernment, discrimination, keenness, penetration, perceptiveness, percipience, perspicaciousness, perspicuity, sagaciousness, sagacity, sharpness, shrewdness, smarts (slang, chiefly U.S.), suss (slang), wit

perspiration noun = **sweat**, exudation, moisture, wetness

perspire verb = **sweat**, be damp, be wet, drip, exude, glow, pour with sweat, secrete, swelter

persuade verb **1** = **talk into**, actuate, advise, allure, bring round (informal), coax, counsel, entice, impel, incite, induce, influence, inveigle, prevail upon, prompt, sway, twist (someone's) arm, urge, win over **2** = **convince**, cause to believe, convert, satisfy
➤ **Antonyms**
≠**talk into**: deter, discourage, dissuade, forbid, prohibit

persuasion noun **1** = **urging**, blandishment, cajolery, conversion, enticement, exhortation, inducement, influencing, inveiglement, wheedling **2** = **persuasiveness**, cogency, force, potency, power, pull (informal) **3** = **creed**, belief, certitude, conviction, credo, faith,

firm belief, fixed opinion, opinion, tenet, views **4** = **faction**, camp, cult, denomination, party, school, school of thought, sect, side

persuasive adjective = **convincing**, cogent, compelling, credible, effective, eloquent, forceful, impelling, impressive, inducing, influential, logical, moving, plausible, sound, telling, touching, valid, weighty, winning
➤ **Antonyms**
feeble, flimsy, illogical, implausible, incredible, ineffective, invalid, unconvincing, unimpressive, weak

pert adjective = **impudent**, bold, cheeky, forward, impertinent, insolent, sassy (U.S. informal), saucy

pertain verb = **relate**, appertain, apply, be appropriate, bear on, befit, belong, be part of, be relevant, concern, refer, regard

pertinacious adjective = **determined**, bull-headed, dogged, headstrong, inflexible, intractable, mulish, obdurate, obstinate, persevering, persistent, perverse, pig-headed, relentless, resolute, self-willed, stiff-necked, strong-willed, stubborn, tenacious, unyielding, wilful

pertinent adjective = **relevant**, admissible, ad rem, applicable, apposite, appropriate, apropos, apt, fit, fitting, germane, material, pat, proper, suitable, to the point, to the purpose
➤ **Antonyms**
immaterial, inappropriate, incongruous, irrelevant, unfitting, unrelated, unsuitable

pertness noun = **impudence**, audacity, brashness, brass (informal), bumptiousness, cheek (informal), cheekiness, chutzpah (U.S. & Canad. informal), cockiness, effrontery, forwardness, front, impertinence, insolence, presumption, rudeness, sauciness

perturb verb **1** = **disturb**, agitate, alarm, bother, discompose, disconcert, discountenance, disquiet, faze, fluster, ruffle, trouble, unnerve, unsettle, upset, vex, worry **2** = **disorder**, confuse, disarrange, muddle, unsettle

perturbed adjective = **disturbed**, agitated, alarmed, antsy (informal), anxious, disconcerted, disquieted, fearful, flurried, flustered, ill at ease, nervous, restless, shaken, troubled, uncomfortable, uneasy, upset, worried
➤ **Antonyms**
assured, at ease, comfortable, composed, cool, impassive, relaxed, unperturbed, unruffled

perusal noun = **read**, browse, check,

examination, inspection, look through, scrutiny, study

peruse verb = **read**, browse, check, examine, eyeball (slang), inspect, look through, run one's eye over, scan, scrutinize, study, work over

pervade verb = **spread through**, affect, charge, diffuse, extend, fill, imbue, infuse, overspread, penetrate, percolate, permeate, suffuse

pervasive adjective = **widespread**, common, extensive, general, inescapable, omnipresent, permeating, pervading, prevalent, rife, ubiquitous, universal

perverse adjective **1** = **abnormal**, depraved, deviant, improper, incorrect, unhealthy **2** = **stubborn**, contradictory, contrary, cussed (informal), delinquent, disobedient, dogged, headstrong, intractable, intransigent, miscreant, mulish, obdurate, obstinate, pig-headed, rebellious, refractory, stiff-necked, troublesome, unmanageable, unreasonable, unyielding, wayward, wilful **3** = **ill-natured**, cantankerous, churlish, crabbed, cross, fractious, ill-tempered, peevish, petulant, shrewish, spiteful, stroppy (Brit. slang), surly
➤ Antonyms
≠**stubborn:** accommodating, agreeable, complaisant, cooperative, flexible, malleable, obedient, obliging
≠**ill-natured:** agreeable, amiable, good-natured

perversion noun **1** = **deviation**, aberration, abnormality, debauchery, depravity, immorality, kink (Brit. informal), kinkiness (slang), unnaturalness, vice, vitiation, wickedness **2** = **distortion**, corruption, falsification, misinterpretation, misrepresentation, misuse, twisting

perversity noun = **contrariness**, contradictiveness, contradictoriness, contumacy, frowardness (archaic), intransigence, obduracy, refractoriness, waywardness, wrong-headedness

pervert verb **1** = **distort**, abuse, falsify, garble, misconstrue, misinterpret, misrepresent, misuse, twist, warp **2** = **corrupt**, debase, debauch, degrade, deprave, desecrate, initiate, lead astray, subvert ♦ noun **3** = **deviant**, debauchee, degenerate, sicko (informal), sleazeball (slang), weirdo or weirdie (informal)

perverted adjective = **unnatural**, aberrant, abnormal, corrupt, debased, debauched, depraved, deviant, distorted, evil, immoral, impaired, kinky (slang), misguided, pervy (slang), sick, sicko (slang), twisted, unhealthy, vicious,

vitiated, warped, wicked

pessimism noun = **gloominess**, cynicism, dejection, depression, despair, despondency, distrust, gloom, gloomy outlook, glumness, hopelessness, melancholy, the hump (Brit. informal)

pessimist noun = **wet blanket** (informal), cynic, defeatist, doomster, gloom merchant (informal), killjoy, melancholic, misanthrope, prophet of doom, worrier

pessimistic adjective = **gloomy**, bleak, cynical, dark, dejected, depressed, despairing, despondent, distrustful, downhearted, fatalistic, foreboding, glum, hopeless, melancholy, misanthropic, morose, resigned, sad
➤ Antonyms
assured, bright, buoyant, cheerful, cheery, encouraged, exhilarated, hopeful, in good heart, optimistic, sanguine

pest noun **1** = **nuisance**, annoyance, bane, bore, bother, drag (informal), gall, irritation, pain (informal), pain in the arse (taboo informal), pain in the neck (informal), thorn in one's flesh, trial, vexation **2** = **infection**, bane, blight, bug, curse, epidemic, pestilence, plague, scourge

pester verb = **annoy**, aggravate (informal), badger, bedevil, bend someone's ear (informal), be on one's back (slang), bother, bug (informal), chivvy, disturb, drive one up the wall (slang), fret, get at, get in one's hair (informal), get on one's nerves (informal), harass, harry, hassle (informal), irk, nag, pick on, plague, ride (informal), torment, worry

pestilence noun **1** = **plague**, Black Death, epidemic, pandemic, visitation **2** = **affliction**, bane, blight, cancer, canker, curse, scourge

pestilent adjective **1** = **annoying**, bothersome, galling, irksome, irritating, plaguy (informal), tiresome, vexing **2** = **harmful**, corrupting, deleterious, destructive, detrimental, evil, injurious, pernicious, ruinous, vicious **3** = **contaminated**, catching, contagious, diseased, disease-ridden, infected, infectious, plague-ridden, tainted

pestilential adjective **1** = **deadly**, dangerous, deleterious, destructive, detrimental, evil, foul, harmful, hazardous, injurious, pernicious, ruinous **2** = **contaminated**, catching, contagious, disease-ridden, infectious, malignant, noxious, pestiferous, poisonous, venomous

pet¹ noun **1** = **favourite**, apple of one's eye, blue-eyed boy (informal), darling, fave (informal), idol, jewel, treasure ♦ adjective

2 = **tame**, domesticated, house, house-broken, house-trained (*Brit.*), trained **3** = **favourite**, cherished, dearest, dear to one's heart, fave (*informal*), favoured, particular, preferred, special ♦ *verb* **4** = **pamper**, baby, coddle, cosset, mollycoddle, spoil **5** = **fondle**, caress, pat, stroke **6** *Informal* = **cuddle**, canoodle (*slang*), kiss, neck (*informal*), smooch (*informal*), snog (*Brit. slang*)

pet² *noun* = **sulk**, bad mood, bate (*Brit. slang*), huff, ill temper, miff (*informal*), paddy (*Brit. informal*), paddywhack (*Brit. informal*), pique, pout, sulks, tantrum, temper

peter out *verb* = **die out**, come to nothing, dwindle, ebb, evaporate, fade, fail, give out, run dry, run out, stop, taper off, wane

petite *adjective* = **small**, dainty, delicate, dinky (*Brit. informal*), elfin, little, slight

petition *noun* **1** = **appeal**, address, application, entreaty, invocation, memorial, plea, prayer, request, round robin, solicitation, suit, supplication ♦ *verb* **2** = **appeal**, adjure, ask, beg, beseech, call upon, crave, entreat, plead, pray, press, solicit, sue, supplicate, urge

petrified *adjective* **1** = **terrified**, aghast, appalled, dazed, dumbfounded, frozen, horrified, numb, scared shitless (*taboo slang*), scared stiff, shit-scared (*taboo slang*), shocked, speechless, stunned, stupefied, terror-stricken **2** = **fossilized**, ossified, rocklike

petrify *verb* **1** = **terrify**, amaze, appal, astonish, astound, confound, dumbfound, horrify, immobilize, paralyse, stun, stupefy, transfix **2** = **fossilize**, calcify, harden, set, solidify, turn to stone

petty *adjective* **1** = **trivial**, contemptible, inconsiderable, inessential, inferior, insignificant, little, measly (*informal*), negligible, nickel-and-dime (*U.S. slang*), paltry, piddling (*informal*), slight, small, trifling, unimportant **2** = **small-minded**, cheap, grudging, mean, mean-minded, shabby, spiteful, stingy, ungenerous **3** = **minor**, inferior, junior, lesser, lower, secondary, subordinate
➤ **Antonyms**
≠**trivial**: consequential, considerable, essential, important, major, momentous, significant ≠**small-minded**: broad-minded, generous, liberal, magnanimous, open-minded, tolerant

petulance *noun* = **sulkiness**, bad temper, crabbiness, ill humour, irritability, peevishness, pettishness, pique, pouts, querulousness, spleen, sullenness, waspishness

petulant *adjective* = **sulky**, bad-tempered, captious, cavilling, crabbed, cross, crusty, fault-finding, fretful, huffy, ill-humoured, impatient, irritable, moody, peevish, perverse, pouting, querulous, ratty (*Brit. & N.Z. informal*), snappish, sour, sullen, ungracious, waspish
➤ **Antonyms**
affable, cheerful, congenial, easy-going, even-tempered, good-humoured, good-natured, happy, patient, smiling

phantom *noun* **1** = **spectre**, apparition, eidolon, ghost, phantasm, revenant, shade (*literary*), spirit, spook (*informal*), wraith **2** = **illusion**, chimera, figment, figment of the imagination, hallucination, vision

pharisee *noun* = **hypocrite**, canter, dissembler, dissimulator, fraud, humbug, phoney or phony (*informal*), pietist, whited sepulchre

phase *noun* = **stage**, aspect, chapter, condition, development, juncture, period, point, position, state, step, time

phase out *verb* = **wind down**, axe (*informal*), close, deactivate, dispose of gradually, ease off, eliminate, pull, pull out, remove, replace, run down, taper off, terminate, wind up, withdraw
➤ **Antonyms**
activate, begin, create, establish, form, initiate, open, set up, start

phenomenal *adjective* = **extraordinary**, exceptional, fantastic, marvellous, miraculous, notable, outstanding, prodigious, remarkable, sensational, singular, stellar (*informal*), uncommon, unique, unparalleled, unusual, wondrous (*archaic or literary*)
➤ **Antonyms**
average, common, mediocre, no great shakes (*informal*), ordinary, poor, run-of-the-mill, second-rate, unexceptional, unremarkable, usual

phenomenon *noun* **1** = **occurrence**, circumstance, episode, event, fact, happening, incident **2** = **wonder**, exception, marvel, miracle, nonpareil, prodigy, rarity, sensation, sight, spectacle

philander *verb* = **womanize** (*informal*), coquet, court, dally, flirt, fool around (*informal*), toy, trifle

philanderer *noun* = **womanizer** (*informal*), Casanova, dallier, Don Juan, flirt, gallant, gay dog, ladies' man, lady-killer (*informal*), Lothario, playboy, stud (*slang*), trifler, wolf (*informal*)

philanthropic *adjective* = **humanitarian**, almsgiving, altruistic, beneficent, benevolent, benignant, charitable, eleemosynary, generous, gracious,

humane, kind, kind-hearted, munificent, public-spirited
➤ **Antonyms**
egoistic, mean, miserly, niggardly, penurious, selfish, self-seeking, stingy

philanthropist *noun* = **humanitarian**, almsgiver, altruist, benefactor, contributor, donor, giver, patron

philanthropy *noun* = **humanitarianism**, almsgiving, altruism, beneficence, benevolence, benignity, bounty, brotherly love, charitableness, charity, generosity, generousness, kind-heartedness, largesse *or* largess, liberality, munificence, open-handedness, patronage, public-spiritedness

philistine *noun* 1 = **boor**, barbarian, bourgeois, Goth, ignoramus, lout, lowbrow, vulgarian, yahoo ♦ *adjective* 2 = **uncultured**, anti-intellectual, boorish, bourgeois, crass, ignorant, inartistic, lowbrow, tasteless, uncultivated, uneducated, unrefined

philosopher *noun* = **thinker**, dialectician, logician, mahatma, metaphysician, sage, seeker after truth, theorist, wise man

philosophical, philosophic *adjective* 1 = **rational**, abstract, erudite, learned, logical, sagacious, theoretical, thoughtful, wise 2 = **stoical**, calm, collected, composed, cool, impassive, imperturbable, patient, resigned, sedate, serene, tranquil, unruffled
➤ **Antonyms**
≠**rational**: factual, illogical, irrational, practical, pragmatic, scientific ≠**stoical**: emotional, hot-headed, impulsive, restless, upset

philosophy *noun* 1 = **thought**, aesthetics, knowledge, logic, metaphysics, rationalism, reason, reasoning, thinking, wisdom 2 = **outlook**, attitude to life, basic idea, beliefs, convictions, doctrine, ideology, principles, tenets, thinking, values, viewpoint, *Weltanschauung*, world view 3 = **stoicism**, calmness, composure, coolness, dispassion, equanimity, resignation, restraint, self-possession, serenity

phlegmatic *adjective* = **unemotional**, apathetic, bovine, cold, dull, frigid, heavy, impassive, indifferent, lethargic, listless, lymphatic, matter-of-fact, placid, sluggish, stoical, stolid, undemonstrative, unfeeling
➤ **Antonyms**
active, alert, animated, emotional, energetic, excited, hyper (*informal*), lively, passionate

phobia *noun* = **terror**, aversion, detestation, dislike, distaste, dread, fear,

hatred, horror, irrational fear, loathing, obsession, overwhelming anxiety, repulsion, revulsion, thing (*informal*)
➤ **Antonyms**
bent, fancy, fondness, inclination, liking, love, partiality, passion, penchant, soft spot

phone *noun* 1 = **telephone**, blower (*informal*) 2 = **call**, bell (*Brit. slang*), buzz (*informal*), ring (*informal, chiefly Brit.*), tinkle (*Brit. informal*) ♦ *verb* 3 = **call**, buzz (*informal*), get on the blower (*informal*), give someone a bell (*Brit. slang*), give someone a buzz (*informal*), give someone a call, give someone a ring (*informal, chiefly Brit.*), give someone a tinkle (*Brit. informal*), make a call, ring (up) (*informal, chiefly Brit.*), telephone

phoney *Informal* ♦ *adjective* 1 = **fake**, affected, assumed, bogus, counterfeit, ersatz, false, feigned, forged, imitation, pseudo (*informal*), put-on, sham, spurious, trick ♦ *noun* 2 = **fake**, counterfeit, faker, forgery, fraud, humbug, impostor, pretender, pseud (*informal*), sham
➤ **Antonyms**
adjective ≠**fake**: authentic, bona fide, genuine, original, real, sincere, unaffected, unassumed, unfeigned

photograph *noun* 1 = **picture**, image, likeness, photo (*informal*), print, shot, slide, snap (*informal*), snapshot, transparency ♦ *verb* 2 = **take a picture of**, capture on film, film, get a shot of, record, shoot, snap (*informal*), take, take (someone's) picture

photographic *adjective* 1 = **lifelike**, graphic, natural, pictorial, realistic, visual, vivid 2 *Of a person's memory* = **accurate**, detailed, exact, faithful, minute, precise, retentive

phrase *noun* 1 = **expression**, group of words, idiom, locution, motto, remark, saying, tag, utterance, way of speaking ♦ *verb* 2 = **express**, couch, formulate, frame, present, put, put into words, say, term, utter, voice, word

phraseology *noun* = **wording**, choice of words, diction, expression, idiom, language, parlance, phrase, phrasing, speech, style, syntax

physical *adjective* 1 = **bodily**, carnal, corporal, corporeal, earthly, fleshly, incarnate, mortal, somatic, unspiritual 2 = **material**, natural, palpable, real, sensible, solid, substantial, tangible, visible

physician *noun* = **doctor**, doc (*informal*), doctor of medicine, general practitioner, G.P., healer, M.D., medic (*informal*), medical practitioner, medico (*informal*), sawbones (*slang*), specialist

physique noun = **build**, body, constitution, figure, form, frame, make-up, shape, structure

pick verb **1** = **select**, cherry-pick, choose, decide upon, elect, fix upon, hand-pick, mark out, opt for, settle upon, sift out, single out, sort out **2** = **gather**, collect, cull, cut, harvest, pluck, pull **3** = **nibble**, have no appetite, peck at, play or toy with, push the food round the plate **4** = **provoke**, foment, incite, instigate, start **5** = **open**, break into, break open, crack, force, jemmy, prise open **6** **pick one's way** = **tread carefully**, be tentative, find or make one's way, move cautiously, work through ♦ noun **7** = **choice**, choosing, decision, option, preference, selection **8** = **the best**, choicest, crème de la crème, elect, elite, flower, pride, prize, the cream, the tops (slang)
➤ **Antonyms**
verb ≠**select**: cast aside, decline, discard, dismiss, reject, spurn, turn down

picket noun **1** = **protester**, demonstrator, flying picket, picketer **2** = **lookout**, guard, patrol, scout, sentinel, sentry, spotter, vedette (Military), watch **3** = **stake**, pale, paling, palisade, peg, post, stanchion, upright ♦ verb **4** = **blockade**, boycott, demonstrate **5** = **fence**, corral (U.S.), enclose, hedge in, palisade, pen in, rail in, shut in, wall in

pickle noun **1** Informal = **predicament**, bind (informal), difficulty, dilemma, fix (informal), hot water (informal), jam (informal), quandary, scrape (informal), spot (informal), tight spot ♦ verb **2** = **preserve**, cure, keep, marinade, steep

pick-me-up noun Informal = **tonic**, bracer (informal), drink, pick-up (slang), refreshment, restorative, roborant, shot in the arm (informal), stimulant

pick on verb = **torment**, badger, bait, blame, bully, goad, hector, tease

pick out verb **1** = **select**, choose, cull, hand-pick, separate the sheep from the goats, single out, sort out **2** = **identify**, discriminate, distinguish, make distinct, make out, notice, perceive, recognize, tell apart

pick up verb **1** = **lift**, gather, grasp, hoist, raise, take up, uplift **2** = **obtain**, buy, come across, find, garner, happen upon, purchase, score (slang) **3** = **recover**, be on the mend, gain, gain ground, get better, improve, make a comeback (informal), mend, perk up, rally, take a turn for the better, turn the corner **4** = **learn**, acquire, get the hang of (informal), master **5** = **collect**, call for, get, give someone a lift, go to get, uplift (Scot.) **6** Informal = **arrest**, apprehend, bust (informal), collar (informal), do (slang), feel one's collar (slang), lift (slang), nab (informal), nail (informal), nick (slang, chiefly Brit.), pinch (informal), pull in (Brit. slang), run in (slang), take into custody

pick-up noun **1** = **acceleration**, response, revving (informal), speed-up **2** = **improvement**, change for the better, gain, rally, recovery, revival, rise, strengthening, upswing, upturn

picnic noun **1** = **excursion**, fête champêtre, outdoor meal, outing **2** Informal = **walkover** (informal), breeze (U.S. & Canad. informal), cakewalk (informal), child's play (informal), cinch (slang), duck soup (U.S. slang), piece of cake (Brit. informal), pushover (slang), snap (informal)

pictorial adjective = **graphic**, expressive, illustrated, picturesque, representational, scenic, striking, vivid

picture noun **1** = **representation**, delineation, drawing, effigy, engraving, illustration, image, likeness, painting, photograph, portrait, portrayal, print, similitude, sketch **2** = **description**, account, depiction, image, impression, re-creation, report **3** = **double**, carbon copy, copy, dead ringer (slang), duplicate, image, likeness, living image, lookalike, replica, ringer (slang), spit (informal, chiefly Brit.), spit and image (informal), spitting image (informal), twin **4** = **personification**, archetype, embodiment, epitome, essence, living example, perfect example **5** = **film**, flick (slang), motion picture, movie (U.S. informal) ♦ verb **6** = **imagine**, conceive of, envision, see, see in the mind's eye, visualize **7** = **represent**, delineate, depict, describe, draw, illustrate, paint, photograph, portray, render, show, sketch

picturesque adjective **1** = **interesting**, attractive, beautiful, charming, pretty, quaint, scenic, striking **2** = **vivid**, colourful, graphic
➤ **Antonyms**
≠**interesting**: commonplace, everyday, inartistic, unattractive, uninteresting ≠**vivid**: drab, dull

piddling adjective Informal = **trivial**, chickenshit (U.S. slang), crappy (slang), derisory, fiddling, insignificant, little, measly (informal), Mickey Mouse (slang), nickel-and-dime (U.S. slang), paltry, pants (informal), petty, piffling, poxy (slang), puny, toytown (slang), trifling, unimportant, useless, wanky (taboo slang), worthless

➤ **Antonyms**
considerable, important, major,
significant, sizable or sizeable, substantial,
tidy (*informal*), useful, valuable

piebald *adjective* = **pied**, black and white,
brindled, dappled, flecked, mottled,
speckled, spotted

piece *noun* **1** = **bit**, allotment, chunk,
division, fraction, fragment, length,
morsel, mouthful, part, portion, quantity,
scrap, section, segment, share, shred, slice
2 = **instance**, case, example, occurrence,
sample, specimen, stroke **3** = **work**, article,
bit (*informal*), composition, creation, item,
production, study, work of art **4 go to
pieces** = **break down**, crack up (*informal*),
crumple, disintegrate, fall apart, lose
control, lose one's head **5 in pieces**
= **smashed**, broken, bust (*informal*),
damaged, disintegrated, in bits, in
smithereens, ruined, shattered **6 of a piece**
= **alike**, analogous, consistent, identical, of
the same kind, similar, the same, uniform
♦ *verb* **7 piece together** = **assemble**,
compose, fix, join, mend, patch, repair,
restore, unite

pièce de résistance *noun* = **masterpiece**,
chef-d'oeuvre, jewel, masterwork,
showpiece

piecemeal *adverb* **1** = **bit by bit**, at
intervals, by degrees, by fits and starts,
fitfully, gradually, intermittently, little by
little, partially, slowly ♦ *adjective* **2**
= **unsystematic**, fragmentary, intermittent,
interrupted, partial, patchy, spotty

pied *adjective* = **variegated**, dappled,
flecked, irregular, motley, mottled,
multicoloured, parti-coloured, piebald,
spotted, streaked, varicoloured

pier *noun* **1** = **jetty**, landing place,
promenade, quay, wharf **2** = **pillar**,
buttress, column, pile, piling, post,
support, upright

pierce *verb* **1** = **penetrate**, bore, drill, enter,
impale, lance, perforate, prick, probe,
puncture, run through, spike, stab, stick
into, transfix **2** = **hurt**, affect, cut, cut to
the quick, excite, move, pain, rouse, sting,
stir, strike, thrill, touch, wound

piercing *adjective* **1** *Usually of sound*
= **penetrating**, ear-splitting, high-pitched,
loud, sharp, shattering, shrill **2**
= **perceptive**, alert, aware, bright
(*informal*), keen, penetrating,
perspicacious, probing, quick-witted,
searching, sharp, shrewd **3** *Usually of
weather* = **cold**, arctic, biting, bitter,
freezing, frosty, keen, nipping, nippy,
numbing, raw, wintry **4** = **sharp**, acute,
agonizing, excruciating, exquisite, fierce,

intense, painful, powerful, racking, severe,
shooting, stabbing
➤ **Antonyms**
≠**penetrating**: inaudible, low,
low-pitched, mellifluous, quiet, soundless
≠**perceptive**: obtuse, slow, slow-witted,
thick, unperceptive

piety *noun* = **holiness**, devotion,
devoutness, dutifulness, duty, faith,
godliness, grace, piousness, religion,
reverence, sanctity, veneration

pig *noun* **1** = **hog**, boar, grunter, piggy,
piglet, porker, shoat, sow, swine **2** *Informal*
= **slob** (*slang*), animal, beast, boor, brute,
glutton, greedy guts (*slang*), guzzler, hog
(*informal*), sloven, swine

pigeon[1] *noun* **1** = **dove**, bird, culver
(*archaic*), cushat, squab **2** *Slang* = **victim**,
dupe, fall guy (*informal*), gull (*archaic*),
mug (*Brit. slang*), sitting duck, sitting
target, sucker (*slang*)

pigeon[2] *noun Brit. informal*
= **responsibility**, baby (*slang*), business,
concern, lookout (*informal*), worry

pigeonhole *noun* **1** = **compartment**,
cubbyhole, cubicle, locker, niche, place,
section **2** *Informal* = **classification**,
category, class, slot (*informal*) ♦ *verb* **3**
= **classify**, catalogue, categorize,
characterize, codify, compartmentalize,
ghettoize, label, slot (*informal*), sort **4**
= **put off**, defer, file, postpone, shelve

pig-headed *adjective* = **stubborn**,
bull-headed, contrary, cross-grained,
dense, froward (*archaic*), inflexible, mulish,
obstinate, perverse, self-willed,
stiff-necked, stupid, unyielding, wilful,
wrong-headed
➤ **Antonyms**
agreeable, amiable, complaisant,
cooperative, flexible, obliging,
open-minded, tractable

pigment *noun* = **colour**, colorant,
colouring, colouring matter, dye, dyestuff,
paint, stain, tincture, tint

pile[1] *noun* **1** = **heap**, accumulation,
assemblage, assortment, collection, hoard,
mass, mound, mountain, rick, stack,
stockpile **2** *often plural Informal* = **a lot**,
great deal, ocean, oodles (*informal*),
quantity, stacks **3** = **building**, edifice,
erection, structure **4** *Informal* = **fortune**,
big bucks (*informal, chiefly U.S.*), big
money, bomb (*Brit. slang*), megabucks
(*U.S. & Canad. slang*), mint, money,
packet (*slang*), pot, pretty penny
(*informal*), tidy sum (*informal*), wad (*U.S.
& Canad. slang*), wealth ♦ *verb* **5** = **collect**,
accumulate, amass, assemble, gather,
heap, hoard, load up, mass, stack, store **6**

= **crowd**, charge, crush, flock, flood, jam, pack, rush, stream

pile² *noun* = **foundation**, beam, column, pier, piling, pillar, post, support, upright

pile³ *noun* = **nap**, down, fibre, filament, fur, hair, plush, shag, surface

piles *plural noun* = **haemorrhoids**

pile-up *noun Informal* = **collision**, accident, crash, multiple collision, smash, smash-up (*informal*)

pilfer *verb* = **steal**, appropriate, blag (*slang*), cabbage (*Brit. slang*), embezzle, filch, knock off (*slang*), lift (*informal*), nick (*slang, chiefly Brit.*), pinch (*informal*), purloin, rifle, rob, snaffle (*Brit. informal*), snitch (*slang*), swipe (*slang*), take, thieve, walk off with

pilgrim *noun* = **traveller**, crusader, hajji, palmer, wanderer, wayfarer

pilgrimage *noun* = **journey**, crusade, excursion, expedition, hajj, mission, tour, trip

pill *noun* 1 = **tablet**, bolus, capsule, pellet, pilule 2 **the pill** = **oral contraceptive** 3 *Slang* = **trial**, bore, drag (*informal*), nuisance, pain (*informal*), pain in the neck (*informal*), pest

pillage *verb* 1 = **plunder**, depredate (*rare*), despoil, freeboot, loot, maraud, raid, ransack, ravage, reive (*dialect*), rifle, rob, sack, spoil (*archaic*), spoliate, strip ♦ *noun* 2 = **plunder**, depredation, devastation, marauding, rapine, robbery, sack, spoliation 3 = **booty**, loot, plunder, spoils

pillar *noun* 1 = **support**, column, obelisk, pier, pilaster, piling, post, prop, shaft, stanchion, upright 2 = **supporter**, leader, leading light (*informal*), mainstay, rock, torchbearer, tower of strength, upholder, worthy

pillory *verb* = **ridicule**, brand, cast a slur on, denounce, expose to ridicule, heap *or* pour scorn on, hold up to shame, lash, show up, stigmatize

pilot *noun* 1 = **airman**, aviator, captain, flyer 2 = **helmsman**, conductor, coxswain, director, guide, leader, navigator, steersman ♦ *adjective* 3 = **trial**, experimental, model, test ♦ *verb* 4 = **fly**, conduct, control, direct, drive, guide, handle, lead, manage, navigate, operate, shepherd, steer

pimple *noun* = **spot**, boil, papule (*Pathology*), plook (*Scot.*), pustule, swelling, zit (*slang*)

pin *verb* 1 = **fasten**, affix, attach, fix, join, secure 2 = **hold fast**, fix, hold down, immobilize, pinion, press, restrain

pinch *verb* 1 = **squeeze**, compress, grasp,

nip, press, tweak 2 = **hurt**, chafe, confine, cramp, crush, pain 3 *Informal* = **steal**, blag (*slang*), cabbage (*Brit. slang*), filch, knock off (*slang*), lift (*informal*), nick (*slang, chiefly Brit.*), pilfer, purloin, rob, snaffle (*Brit. informal*), snatch, snitch (*slang*), swipe (*slang*) 4 *Informal* = **arrest**, apprehend, bust (*informal*), do (*slang*), feel one's collar (*slang*), lift (*slang*), nab (*informal*), nail (*informal*), nick (*slang, chiefly Brit.*), pick up (*slang*), pull in (*Brit. slang*), run in (*slang*), take into custody 5 = **scrimp**, be stingy, distress, economize, oppress, pinch pennies, press, skimp, spare, stint, tighten one's belt ♦ *noun* 6 = **squeeze**, nip, tweak 7 = **dash**, bit, jot, mite, small quantity, soupçon, speck, taste 8 = **hardship**, crisis, difficulty, emergency, exigency, necessity, oppression, pass, plight, predicament, pressure, strait, stress
➤ **Antonyms**
verb ≠**arrest**: free, let go, let out, release, set free ≠**scrimp**: be extravagant, blow (*slang*), fritter away, spend like water, squander, waste

pinched *adjective* = **thin**, careworn, drawn, gaunt, haggard, peaky, starved, worn
➤ **Antonyms**
blooming, chubby, fat, glowing, hale and hearty, healthy, plump, radiant, ruddy, well-fed

pin down *verb* 1 = **force**, compel, constrain, make, press, pressurize 2 = **determine**, designate, home in on, identify, locate, name, pinpoint, specify 3 = **fix**, bind, confine, constrain, hold, hold down, immobilize, nail down, tie down

pine *verb* 1 *often with* **for** = **long**, ache, carry a torch for, covet, crave, desire, eat one's heart out over, hanker, hunger for, lust after, sigh, suspire (*archaic or poetic*), thirst for, wish for, yearn for 2 = **waste**, decay, decline, droop, dwindle, fade, flag, languish, peak, sicken, sink, weaken, wilt, wither

pinion *verb* = **immobilize**, bind, chain, confine, fasten, fetter, manacle, pin down, shackle, tie

pink¹ *noun* 1 = **best**, acme, height, peak, perfection, summit ♦ *adjective* 2 = **rosy**, flesh, flushed, reddish, rose, roseate, salmon

pink² *verb* = **cut**, incise, notch, perforate, prick, punch, scallop, score

pinnacle *noun* 1 = **peak**, acme, apex, apogee, crest, crown, eminence, height, meridian, summit, top, vertex, zenith 2 = **spire**, belfry, cone, needle, obelisk, pyramid, steeple

pinpoint *verb* = **identify**, define, distinguish, get a fix on, home in on, locate, spot

pint *noun Brit. informal* = **beer**, ale, jar (*Brit. informal*), jug (*Brit. informal*)

pint-size *adjective Informal* = **small**, diminutive, little, midget, miniature, pocket, pygmy *or* pigmy, teensy-weensy, teeny-weeny, tiny, wee

pioneer *noun* 1 = **settler**, colonist, colonizer, explorer, frontiersman 2 = **founder**, developer, founding father, innovator, leader, trailblazer ♦ *verb* 3 = **develop**, create, discover, establish, initiate, instigate, institute, invent, launch, lay the groundwork, map out, open up, originate, prepare, show the way, start, take the lead

pious *adjective* 1 = **religious**, dedicated, devoted, devout, God-fearing, godly, holy, reverent, righteous, saintly, spiritual 2 = **self-righteous**, goody-goody, holier-than-thou, hypocritical, pietistic, sanctimonious
➤ **Antonyms**
≠**religious:** impious, irreligious, irreverent, ungodly, unholy ≠**self-righteous:** humble, meek, sincere

pipe *noun* 1 = **tube**, conduit, conveyor, duct, hose, line, main, passage, pipeline 2 = **clay**, briar, meerschaum 3 = **whistle**, fife, horn, tooter, wind instrument ♦ *verb* 4 = **whistle**, cheep, peep, play, sing, sound, tootle, trill, tweet, twitter, warble 5 = **convey**, bring in, channel, conduct, siphon, supply, transmit

pipe down *verb Informal* = **be quiet**, belt up (*slang*), button it (*slang*), button one's lip (*slang*), hold one's tongue, hush, put a sock in it (*Brit. slang*), quieten down, shush, shut one's mouth, shut up (*informal*)

pipe dream *noun* = **daydream**, castle in the air, chimera, delusion, dream, fantasy, notion, reverie, vagary

pipeline *noun* 1 = **tube**, conduit, conveyor, duct, line, passage, pipe 2 **in the pipeline** = **on the way**, brewing, coming, getting ready, in preparation, in process, in production, under way

piquancy *noun* 1 = **spiciness**, bite (*informal*), edge, flavour, kick (*informal*), pungency, relish, sharpness, spice, tang, zest 2 = **interest**, colour, excitement, pep, pizzazz *or* pizazz (*informal*), raciness, spirit, vigour, vitality, zing (*informal*), zip (*informal*)

piquant *adjective* 1 = **spicy**, acerb, biting, highly-seasoned, peppery, pungent, savoury, sharp, stinging, tangy, tart, with a kick (*informal*), zesty 2 = **interesting**, lively, provocative, racy, salty, scintillating, sparkling, spirited, stimulating
➤ **Antonyms**
≠**spicy:** bland, insipid, mild ≠**interesting:** banal, bland, boring, dull, insipid, tame, uninteresting, vapid

pique *noun* 1 = **resentment**, annoyance, displeasure, huff, hurt feelings, irritation, miff (*informal*), offence, umbrage, vexation, wounded pride ♦ *verb* 2 = **displease**, affront, annoy, gall, get (*informal*), incense, irk, irritate, miff (*informal*), mortify, nark (*Brit., Austral., & N.Z. slang*), nettle, offend, peeve (*informal*), provoke, put out, put someone's nose out of joint (*informal*), rile, sting, vex, wound 3 = **arouse**, excite, galvanize, goad, kindle, provoke, rouse, spur, stimulate, stir, whet

piracy *noun* = **robbery**, buccaneering, freebooting, hijacking, infringement, rapine, stealing, theft

pirate *noun* 1 = **buccaneer**, corsair, filibuster, freebooter, marauder, raider, rover, sea robber, sea rover, sea wolf 2 = **plagiarist**, cribber (*informal*), infringer, plagiarizer ♦ *verb* 3 = **copy**, appropriate, borrow, crib (*informal*), lift (*informal*), plagiarize, poach, reproduce, steal

pit *noun* 1 = **hole**, abyss, cavity, chasm, coal mine, crater, dent, depression, dimple, excavation, gulf, hollow, indentation, mine, pockmark, pothole, trench ♦ *verb* 2 *often with* **against** = **set against**, match, oppose, put in opposition 3 = **scar**, dent, dint, gouge, hole, indent, mark, nick, notch, pockmark

pitch *verb* 1 = **throw**, bung (*Brit. slang*), cast, chuck (*informal*), fling, heave, hurl, launch, lob (*informal*), sling, toss 2 = **set up**, erect, fix, locate, place, plant, put up, raise, settle, station 3 = **fall**, dive, drop, stagger, topple, tumble 4 = **toss**, flounder, lurch, make heavy weather, plunge, roll, wallow, welter ♦ *noun* 5 = **sports field**, field of play, ground, park (*U.S. & Canad.*) 6 = **level**, degree, height, highest point, point, summit 7 = **slope**, angle, cant, dip, gradient, incline, steepness, tilt 8 = **tone**, harmonic, modulation, sound, timbre 9 = **sales talk**, line, patter, spiel (*informal*)

pitch-black *adjective* = **jet-black**, dark, ebony, inky, jet, pitch-dark, raven, sable, unlit

pitch in *verb* 1 = **help**, chip in (*informal*), contribute, cooperate, do one's bit, join in, lend a hand, lend a helping hand, participate 2 = **begin**, fall to, get busy, get cracking (*informal*), plunge into, set about, set to, tackle

pitch into *verb Informal* = **attack**, assail, assault, get stuck into (*informal*), tear into (*informal*)

piteous *adjective* = **pathetic**, affecting, deplorable, dismal, distressing, doleful, grievous, gut-wrenching, harrowing, heartbreaking, heart-rending, lamentable, miserable, mournful, moving, pitiable, pitiful, plaintive, poignant, sad, sorrowful, woeful, wretched

pitfall *noun* 1 = **danger**, banana skin (*informal*), catch, difficulty, drawback, hazard, peril, snag, trap 2 = **trap**, deadfall, downfall, pit, snare

pith *noun* 1 = **essence**, core, crux, gist, heart, heart of the matter, kernel, marrow, meat, nub, point, quintessence, salient point, the long and the short of it 2 = **importance**, consequence, depth, force, import, matter, moment, power, significance, strength, substance, value, weight

pithy *adjective* = **succinct**, brief, cogent, compact, concise, epigrammatic, expressive, finely honed, forceful, laconic, meaningful, pointed, short, terse, to the point, trenchant
➤ **Antonyms**
diffuse, garrulous, long, long-winded, loquacious, prolix, verbose, wordy

pitiful *adjective* 1 = **pathetic**, deplorable, distressing, grievous, gut-wrenching, harrowing, heartbreaking, heart-rending, lamentable, miserable, piteous, pitiable, sad, woeful, wretched 2 = **contemptible**, abject, base, beggarly, despicable, dismal, inadequate, insignificant, low, mean, measly, miserable, paltry, scurvy, shabby, sorry, vile, worthless
➤ **Antonyms**
≠**pathetic**: amusing, cheerful, cheering, comical, funny, happy, heartening, laughable, merry ≠**contemptible**: adequate, admirable, honourable, laudable, praiseworthy, significant, valuable

pitiless *adjective* = **merciless**, brutal, callous, cold-blooded, cold-hearted, cruel, hardhearted, harsh, heartless, implacable, inexorable, inhuman, relentless, ruthless, uncaring, unfeeling, unmerciful, unsympathetic
➤ **Antonyms**
caring, compassionate, kind, merciful, relenting, responsive, soft-hearted, sparing

pittance *noun* = **peanuts** (*slang*), allowance, chicken feed (*slang*), drop, mite, modicum, portion, ration, slave wages, trifle

pity *noun* 1 = **compassion**, charity, clemency, commiseration, condolence, fellow feeling, forbearance, kindness, mercy, quarter, sympathy, tenderness, understanding 2 = **shame**, bummer (*slang*), crime (*informal*), crying shame, misfortune, regret, sad thing, sin 3 **take pity on** = **have mercy on**, feel compassion for, forgive, melt, pardon, put out of one's misery, relent, reprieve, show mercy, spare ♦ *verb* 4 = **feel sorry for**, bleed for, commiserate with, condole with, feel for, grieve for, have compassion for, sympathize with, weep for
➤ **Antonyms**
noun ≠**compassion**: anger, apathy, brutality, cruelty, disdain, fury, hard-heartedness, indifference, inhumanity, mercilessness, pitilessness, ruthlessness, scorn, severity, unconcern, wrath

pivot *noun* 1 = **axis**, axle, fulcrum, spindle, swivel 2 = **hub**, centre, focal point, heart, hinge, kingpin ♦ *verb* 3 = **turn**, revolve, rotate, spin, swivel, twirl 4 = **rely**, be contingent, depend, hang, hinge, revolve round, turn

pivotal *adjective* = **crucial**, central, critical, decisive, vital

pixie *noun* = **elf**, brownie, fairy, peri, sprite

placard *noun* = **notice**, advertisement, *affiche*, bill, poster, public notice, sticker

placate *verb* = **calm**, appease, assuage, conciliate, humour, mollify, pacify, propitiate, satisfy, soothe, win over

place *noun* 1 = **spot**, area, location, locus, point, position, site, situation, station, venue, whereabouts 2 = **region**, city, district, hamlet, locale, locality, neighbourhood, quarter, town, vicinity, village 3 = **position**, grade, rank, station, status 4 = **space**, accommodation, room, stead 5 = **home**, abode, apartment, domicile, dwelling, flat, house, manor, mansion, pad (*slang*), property, residence, seat 6 = **duty**, affair, charge, concern, function, prerogative, responsibility, right, role 7 = **job**, appointment, berth (*informal*), billet (*informal*), employment, position, post 8 **in place of** = **instead of**, as an alternative to, as a substitute for, in exchange for, in lieu of, taking the place of 9 **put (someone) in his place** = **humble**, bring down, cut down to size, humiliate, make (someone) eat humble pie, make (someone) swallow his pride, mortify, take down a peg (*informal*) 10 **take place** = **happen**, befall, betide, come about, come to pass (*archaic*), go on, occur, transpire (*informal*) ♦ *verb* 11 = **put**, bung

(*Brit. slang*), deposit, dispose, establish, fix, install, lay, locate, plant, position, rest, set, settle, situate, stand, station, stick (*informal*) **12 = classify**, arrange, class, grade, group, order, rank, sort **13 = identify**, associate, know, put one's finger on, recognize, remember, set in context **14 = assign**, allocate, appoint, charge, commission, entrust, give

placid *adjective* = **calm**, collected, composed, cool, equable, even, even-tempered, gentle, halcyon, imperturbable, mild, peaceful, quiet, self-possessed, serene, still, tranquil, undisturbed, unexcitable, unfazed (*informal*), unmoved, unruffled, untroubled
➤ **Antonyms**
agitated, disturbed, emotional, excitable, impulsive, passionate, rough, temperamental, tempestuous

plagiarism *noun* = **copying**, borrowing, cribbing (*informal*), infringement, piracy, theft

plagiarize *verb* = **copy**, appropriate, borrow, crib (*informal*), infringe, lift (*informal*), pirate, steal, thieve

plague *noun* **1** = **disease**, contagion, epidemic, infection, lurgy (*informal*), pandemic, pestilence **2** = **affliction**, bane, blight, calamity, cancer, curse, evil, scourge, torment, trial **3** *Informal* = **nuisance**, aggravation (*informal*), annoyance, bother, hassle (*informal*), irritant, pain (*informal*), pest, problem, thorn in one's flesh, vexation ◆ *verb* **4** = **pester**, afflict, annoy, badger, bedevil, be on one's back (*slang*), bother, disturb, fret, get in one's hair (*informal*), get on one's nerves (*informal*), harass, harry, hassle (*informal*), haunt, molest, pain, persecute, tease, torment, torture, trouble, vex

plain *adjective* **1** = **clear**, apparent, bold, comprehensible, distinct, evident, legible, lucid, manifest, obvious, overt, patent, transparent, unambiguous, understandable, unmistakable, visible **2** = **straightforward**, artless, blunt, candid, direct, downright, forthright, frank, guileless, honest, ingenuous, open, outspoken, round, sincere, upfront (*informal*) **3** = **unadorned**, austere, bare, basic, discreet, modest, muted, pure, restrained, severe, simple, Spartan, stark, unembellished, unfussy, unornamented, unpatterned, unvarnished **4** = **ugly**, ill-favoured, no oil painting (*informal*), not beautiful, not striking, ordinary, unalluring, unattractive, unlovely,

unprepossessing **5** = **ordinary**, common, commonplace, everyday, frugal, homely, lowly, modest, simple, unaffected, unpretentious, workaday **6** = **flat**, even, level, plane, smooth ◆ *noun* **7** = **flatland**, grassland, llano, lowland, mesa, open country, pampas, plateau, prairie, steppe, tableland, veld
➤ **Antonyms**
adjective ≠ **clear**: ambiguous, complex, concealed, deceptive, difficult, disguised, hidden, illegible, incomprehensible, inconspicuous, indiscernible, indistinct, obscure, vague, veiled ≠ **straightforward**: circuitous, indirect, meandering, rambling, roundabout ≠ **unadorned**: adorned, decorated, fancy, ornate ≠ **ugly**: attractive, beautiful, comely, good-looking, gorgeous, handsome ≠ **ordinary**: affected, distinguished, egotistic, ostentatious, pretentious, sophisticated, worldly ≠ **flat**: bumpy, not level, uneven

plain-spoken *adjective* = **blunt**, candid, direct, downright, explicit, forthright, frank, open, outright, outspoken, straightforward, unequivocal, upfront (*informal*)
➤ **Antonyms**
diplomatic, discreet, evasive, guarded, indirect, reticent, subtle, tactful, thoughtful

plaintive *adjective* = **sorrowful**, disconsolate, doleful, grief-stricken, grievous, heart-rending, melancholy, mournful, pathetic, piteous, pitiful, rueful, sad, wistful, woebegone, woeful

plan *noun* **1** = **scheme**, contrivance, design, device, idea, method, plot, procedure, programme, project, proposal, proposition, scenario, strategy, suggestion, system **2** = **diagram**, blueprint, chart, delineation, drawing, illustration, layout, map, representation, scale drawing, sketch ◆ *verb* **3** = **devise**, arrange, concoct, contrive, design, draft, formulate, frame, invent, organize, outline, plot, prepare, represent, scheme, think out **4** = **intend**, aim, contemplate, envisage, foresee, mean, propose, purpose

plane *noun* **1** = **aeroplane**, aircraft, jet **2** = **flat surface**, level surface **3** = **level**, condition, degree, footing, position, stratum ◆ *adjective* **4** = **level**, even, flat, flush, horizontal, plain, regular, smooth, uniform ◆ *verb* **5** = **skim**, glide, sail, skate, volplane

plant *noun* **1** = **vegetable**, bush, flower, herb, shrub, weed **2** = **factory**, foundry, mill, shop, works, yard **3** = **machinery**, apparatus, equipment, gear ◆ *verb* **4** = **sow**, implant, put in the ground, scatter, seed, set out, transplant **5 = place**, establish, fix, found, imbed, insert, institute, lodge, put, root, set, settle, sow the seeds

plaque *noun* **= plate**, badge, brooch, cartouch(e), medal, medallion, panel, slab, tablet

plaster *noun* **1 = mortar**, gesso, gypsum, plaster of Paris, stucco **2 = bandage**, adhesive plaster, dressing, Elastoplast (*Trademark*), sticking plaster ♦ *verb* **3 = cover**, bedaub, besmear, coat, daub, overlay, smear, spread

plastic *adjective* **1 = manageable**, compliant, docile, easily influenced, impressionable, malleable, pliable, receptive, responsive, tractable **2 = pliant**, ductile, fictile, flexible, mouldable, pliable, soft, supple, tensile **3** *Slang* **= false**, artificial, meretricious, mock, phoney *or* phony (*informal*), pseudo (*informal*), sham, specious, spurious, superficial, synthetic
➤ **Antonyms**
≠**manageable**: intractable, rebellious, recalcitrant, refractory, unmanageable, unreceptive ≠**pliant**: brittle, hard, inflexible, rigid, stiff, unbending, unyielding ≠**false**: authentic, genuine, natural, real, sincere, true

plate *noun* **1 = platter**, dish, trencher (*archaic*) **2 = helping**, course, dish, portion, serving **3 = layer**, panel, sheet, slab **4 = illustration**, lithograph, print ♦ *verb* **5 = coat**, anodize, cover, electroplate, face, gild, laminate, nickel, overlay, platinize, silver

plateau *noun* **1 = upland**, highland, mesa, table, tableland **2 = levelling off**, level, stability, stage

platform *noun* **1 = stage**, dais, podium, rostrum, stand **2 = policy**, manifesto, objective(s), party line, principle, programme, tenet(s)

platitude *noun* **= cliché**, banality, bromide, commonplace, hackneyed saying, inanity, stereotype, trite remark, truism

platitudinous *adjective* **= clichéd**, banal, commonplace, corny (*slang*), hack, hackneyed, overworked, set, stale, stereotyped, stock, tired, trite, truistic, vapid, well-worn

platoon *noun* **= squad**, company, group, outfit (*informal*), patrol, squadron, team

platter *noun* **= plate**, charger, dish, salver, tray, trencher (*archaic*)

plaudits *plural noun* **= approval**, acclaim, acclamation, applause, approbation, clapping, commendation, congratulation, hand, kudos, ovation, praise, round of applause

plausible *adjective* **1 = believable**, colourable, conceivable, credible, likely, persuasive, possible, probable, reasonable, tenable, verisimilar **2 = glib**, fair-spoken, smooth, smooth-talking, smooth-tongued, specious
➤ **Antonyms**
≠**believable**: genuine, illogical, implausible, impossible, improbable, inconceivable, incredible, real, unbelievable, unlikely

play *verb* **1 = amuse oneself**, caper, engage in games, entertain oneself, fool, frisk, frolic, gambol, have fun, revel, romp, sport, trifle **2 = compete**, be in a team, challenge, contend against, participate, rival, take on, take part, vie with **3 = act**, act the part of, execute, impersonate, perform, personate, portray, represent, take the part of **4 = gamble**, bet, chance, hazard, punt (*chiefly Brit.*), risk, speculate, take, wager **5 play ball** *Informal* **= cooperate**, collaborate, go along, play along, reciprocate, respond, show willing **6 play by ear = improvise**, ad lib, extemporize, rise to the occasion, take it as it comes **7 play for time = stall**, delay, drag one's feet (*informal*), filibuster, hang fire, procrastinate, temporize **8 play the fool = mess about**, act the goat (*informal*), clown, clown around, horse around (*informal*), lark (about) (*informal*), monkey around, skylark (*informal*) **9 play the game** *Informal* **= play fair**, conform, follow the rules, go along with, keep in step, play by the rules, toe the line ♦ *noun* **10 = drama**, comedy, dramatic piece, entertainment, farce, masque, pantomime, performance, piece, radio play, show, soap opera, stage show, television drama, tragedy **11 = amusement**, caper, diversion, entertainment, frolic, fun, gambol, game, jest, pastime, prank, recreation, romp, sport **12 = gambling**, gaming **13 = action**, activity, employment, function, operation, transaction, working **14 = fun**, foolery, humour, jest, joking, lark (*informal*), prank, sport, teasing **15 = space**, elbowroom, give (*informal*), latitude, leeway, margin, motion, movement, range, room, scope, sweep, swing

play around *verb* **= philander**, dally, fool around, mess around, take lightly, trifle, womanize

playboy *noun* **= womanizer**, ladies' man, lady-killer (*informal*), lover boy (*slang*), man about town, philanderer, pleasure seeker, rake, roué, socialite

play down *verb* = **minimize**, gloss over, make light of, make little of, set no store by, soft-pedal (*informal*), underplay, underrate

player *noun* **1** = **sportsman** *or* **sportswoman**, competitor, contestant, participant, team member **2** = **musician**, artist, instrumentalist, music maker, performer, virtuoso **3** = **performer**, actor *or* actress, entertainer, Thespian, trouper

playful *adjective* **1** = **joking**, arch, coy, flirtatious, good-natured, humorous, jesting, jokey, roguish, teasing, tongue-in-cheek, waggish **2** = **lively**, cheerful, coltish, frisky, frolicsome, gay, impish, joyous, kittenish, larkish (*informal*), ludic (*literary*), merry, mischievous, puckish, rollicking, spirited, sportive, sprightly, vivacious
➤ **Antonyms**
despondent, gloomy, grave, morose, sedate, serious

playmate *noun* = **friend**, chum (*informal*), companion, comrade, neighbour, pal (*informal*), playfellow

play on *or* **upon** *verb* = **take advantage of**, abuse, capitalize on, exploit, impose on, milk, profit by, trade on, turn to account, utilize

plaything *noun* = **toy**, amusement, bauble, game, gewgaw, gimcrack, pastime, trifle, trinket

play up *verb* **1** = **emphasize**, accentuate, bring to the fore, call attention to, highlight, magnify, point up, stress, turn the spotlight on, underline **2** *Brit. informal* = **be awkward**, be bolshie (*Brit. informal*), be cussed (*informal*), be disobedient, be stroppy (*Brit. slang*), give trouble, misbehave **3** *Brit. informal* = **hurt**, be painful, be sore, bother, give one gyp (*Brit. & N.Z. slang*), give one trouble, pain, trouble **4** *Brit. informal* = **malfunction**, be on the blink (*slang*), be wonky (*Brit. slang*), not work properly **5 play up to** *Informal* = **butter up**, bootlick (*informal*), brown-nose (*taboo slang*), crawl to, curry favour, fawn, flatter, get in with, ingratiate oneself, keep (someone) sweet, kiss (someone's) ass (*U.S. & Canad. taboo slang*), pander to, suck up to (*informal*), toady

play with *verb* **1** = **string along**, amuse oneself with, flirt with, toy with, trifle with **2** = **fiddle with** (*informal*), fidget with, fool around, interfere with, jiggle, mess about, waggle, wiggle

playwright *noun* = **dramatist**, dramaturge, dramaturgist

plea *noun* **1** = **appeal**, begging, entreaty, intercession, overture, petition, prayer, request, suit, supplication **2** *Law* = **suit**, action, allegation, cause **3** = **excuse**, apology, claim, defence, explanation, extenuation, justification, pretext, vindication

plead *verb* **1** = **appeal**, ask, beg, beseech, crave, entreat, implore, importune, petition, request, solicit, supplicate **2** = **allege**, adduce, argue, assert, maintain, put forward, use as an excuse

pleasant *adjective* **1** = **pleasing**, acceptable, agreeable, amusing, delectable, delightful, enjoyable, fine, gratifying, lovely, nice, pleasurable, refreshing, satisfying, welcome **2** = **friendly**, affable, agreeable, amiable, charming, cheerful, cheery, congenial, engaging, genial, good-humoured, likable *or* likeable, nice
➤ **Antonyms**
≠**pleasing:** awful, disagreeable, distasteful, horrible, horrid, miserable, offensive, repulsive, unpleasant ≠**friendly:** cold, disagreeable, horrible, horrid, impolite, offensive, rude, unfriendly, unlikable *or* unlikeable

pleasantry *noun* = **joke**, badinage, banter, bon mot, good-natured remark, jest, josh (*slang, chiefly U.S. & Canad.*), quip, sally, witticism

please *verb* **1** = **delight**, amuse, charm, cheer, content, entertain, give pleasure to, gladden, gratify, humour, indulge, rejoice, satisfy, suit, tickle, tickle pink (*informal*) **2** = **want**, be inclined, choose, desire, like, opt, prefer, see fit, will, wish
➤ **Antonyms**
≠**delight:** anger, annoy, depress, disgust, displease, dissatisfy, grieve, incense, offend, provoke, sadden, vex

pleased *adjective* = **happy**, chuffed (*Brit. slang*), contented, delighted, euphoric, glad, gratified, in high spirits, over the moon (*informal*), pleased as punch (*informal*), rapt, satisfied, thrilled, tickled, tickled pink (*informal*)

pleasing *adjective* = **enjoyable**, agreeable, amiable, amusing, attractive, charming, delightful, engaging, entertaining, gratifying, likable *or* likeable, pleasurable, polite, satisfying, winning
➤ **Antonyms**
boring, disagreeable, dull, monotonous, rude, unattractive, unlikable *or* unlikeable, unpleasant

pleasurable *adjective* = **enjoyable**, agreeable, delightful, fun, good, lovely, nice, pleasant

pleasure *noun* **1** = **happiness**, amusement,

beer and skittles (*informal*), bliss, comfort, contentment, delectation, delight, diversion, ease, enjoyment, gladness, gratification, jollies (*slang*), joy, recreation, satisfaction, solace **2 = wish**, choice, command, desire, inclination, mind, option, preference, purpose, will
➤ **Antonyms**
≠**happiness**: abstinence, anger, displeasure, duty, labour, misery, necessity, obligation, pain, sadness, sorrow, suffering, unhappiness

plebeian *adjective* **1 = common**, base, coarse, ignoble, low, lowborn, lower-class, mean, non-U (*Brit. informal*), proletarian, uncultivated, unrefined, vulgar, working-class ♦ *noun* **2 = commoner**, common man, man in the street, peasant, pleb, prole (*derogatory slang, chiefly Brit.*), proletarian
➤ **Antonyms**
adjective ≠**common**: aristocratic, cultivated, highborn, high-class, patrician, polished, refined, upper-class, well-bred

pledge *noun* **1 = promise**, assurance, covenant, oath, undertaking, vow, warrant, word, word of honour **2 = guarantee**, bail, bond, collateral, deposit, earnest, gage, pawn, security, surety **3 = toast**, health ♦ *verb* **4 = promise**, contract, engage, give one's oath, give one's word, give one's word of honour, swear, undertake, vouch, vow **5 = bind**, engage, gage (*archaic*), guarantee, mortgage, plight **6 = drink to**, drink the health of, toast

plenteous *adjective* **1 = plentiful**, abundant, ample, bounteous (*literary*), bountiful, copious, generous, inexhaustible, infinite, lavish, liberal, overflowing, profuse, thick on the ground **2 = productive**, bumper, fertile, fruitful, luxuriant, plentiful, prolific

plentiful *adjective* **1 = abundant**, ample, bounteous (*literary*), bountiful, complete, copious, generous, inexhaustible, infinite, lavish, liberal, overflowing, plenteous, profuse, thick on the ground **2 = productive**, bumper, fertile, fruitful, luxuriant, plenteous, prolific
➤ **Antonyms**
≠**abundant**: deficient, inadequate, insufficient, scant, scarce, skimpy, small, sparing, sparse, thin on the ground

plenty *noun* **1 = lots** (*informal*), abundance, enough, fund, good deal, great deal, heap(s) (*informal*), mass, masses, mine, mountain(s), oodles (*informal*), pile(s) (*informal*), plethora, quantities, quantity, stack(s), store, sufficiency, volume **2**

= abundance, affluence, copiousness, fertility, fruitfulness, luxury, opulence, plenitude, plenteousness, plentifulness, profusion, prosperity, wealth

plethora *noun* **= excess**, glut, overabundance, profusion, superabundance, superfluity, surfeit, surplus
➤ **Antonyms**
dearth, deficiency, lack, scarcity, shortage, want

pliable *adjective* **1 = flexible**, bendable, bendy, ductile, limber, lithe, malleable, plastic, pliant, supple, tensile **2 = compliant**, adaptable, docile, easily led, impressionable, influenceable, like putty in one's hands, manageable, persuadable, pliant, receptive, responsive, susceptible, tractable, yielding
➤ **Antonyms**
≠**flexible**: rigid, stiff ≠**compliant**: headstrong, inflexible, intractable, obdurate, obstinate, stubborn, unadaptable, unbending, unyielding, wilful

pliant *adjective* **1 = flexible**, bendable, bendy, ductile, lithe, plastic, pliable, supple, tensile **2 = impressionable**, adaptable, biddable, compliant, easily led, influenceable, manageable, persuadable, pliable, susceptible, tractable, yielding

plight *noun* **= difficulty**, case, circumstances, condition, dilemma, extremity, hole (*slang*), hot water (*informal*), jam (*informal*), perplexity, pickle (*informal*), predicament, scrape (*informal*), situation, spot (*informal*), state, straits, tight spot, trouble

plod *verb* **1 = trudge**, clump, drag, lumber, slog, stomp (*informal*), tramp, tread **2 = slog**, drudge, grind (*informal*), grub, labour, peg away, persevere, plough through, plug away (*informal*), soldier on, toil

plot[1] *noun* **1 = plan**, cabal, conspiracy, covin (*Law*), intrigue, machination, scheme, stratagem **2 = story**, action, narrative, outline, scenario, story line, subject, theme, thread ♦ *verb* **3 = plan**, cabal, collude, conspire, contrive, hatch, intrigue, machinate, manoeuvre, scheme **4 = devise**, brew, conceive, concoct, contrive, cook up (*informal*), design, frame, hatch, imagine, lay, project **5 = chart**, calculate, compute, draft, draw, locate, map, mark, outline

plot[2] *noun* **= patch**, allotment, area, ground, lot, parcel, tract

plough *verb* **1 = turn over**, break ground, cultivate, dig, furrow, ridge, till **2** *usually with* **through = forge**, cut, drive, flounder, plod, plunge, press, push, stagger, surge, wade **3 plough into = plunge into**, bulldoze into, career into, crash into, hurtle into, shove into, smash into

ploy noun = **tactic**, device, dodge, manoeuvre, move, ruse, scheme, stratagem, trick, wile

pluck verb **1 = pull out** or **off**, collect, draw, gather, harvest, pick **2 = tug**, catch, clutch, jerk, pull at, snatch, tweak, yank **3 = strum**, finger, pick, plunk, thrum, twang ♦ noun **4 = courage**, backbone, balls (taboo slang), ballsiness (taboo slang), boldness, bottle (Brit. slang), bravery, determination, grit, guts (informal), hardihood, heart, intrepidity, mettle, nerve, resolution, spirit, spunk (informal)

plucky adjective = **courageous**, ballsy (taboo slang), bold, brave, daring, doughty, feisty (informal, chiefly U.S. & Canad.), game, gritty, gutsy (slang), hardy, have-a-go (informal), heroic, intrepid, mettlesome, spirited, spunky (informal), undaunted, unflinching, valiant
➤ **Antonyms**
afraid, chicken (slang), cowardly, dastardly, dispirited, scared, spineless, spiritless, timid, yellow (informal)

plug noun **1 = stopper**, bung, cork, spigot, stopple **2** Informal = **mention**, advert (Brit. informal), advertisement, good word, hype, publicity, puff, push **3 = wad**, cake, chew, pigtail, quid, twist ♦ verb **4 = seal**, block, bung, choke, close, cork, cover, fill, pack, stop, stopper, stopple, stop up, stuff **5** Informal = **mention**, advertise, build up, hype, promote, publicize, puff, push, write up **6** Slang = **shoot**, blow away (slang, chiefly U.S.), gun down, pick off, pop, pot, put a bullet in **7 plug away** Informal = **slog**, drudge, grind (informal), labour, peg away, plod, toil

plum noun **1 = prize**, bonus, cream, find, pick, treasure ♦ adjective **2 = choice**, best, first-class, prize

plumb verb **1 = delve**, explore, fathom, gauge, go into, measure, penetrate, probe, search, sound, unravel ♦ noun **2 = weight**, lead, plumb bob, plummet ♦ adverb **3 = vertically**, perpendicularly, up and down **4 = exactly**, bang, precisely, slap, spot-on (Brit. informal)

plume noun **1 = feather**, aigrette, crest, pinion, quill ♦ verb **2 with on** or **upon = pride oneself**, congratulate oneself, pat oneself on the back, pique oneself, preen oneself

plummet verb = **plunge**, crash, descend, dive, drop down, fall, nose-dive, stoop, swoop, tumble

plump adjective = **chubby**, beefy (informal), burly, buxom, corpulent, dumpy, fat, fleshy, full, obese, podgy, portly, roly-poly, rotund, round, stout, tubby, well-covered, well-upholstered (informal)
➤ **Antonyms**
anorexic, bony, emaciated, lanky, lean, scrawny, skinny, slender, slim, sylphlike, thin

plunder verb **1 = loot**, despoil, devastate, pillage, raid, ransack, ravage, rifle, rob, sack, spoil, steal, strip ♦ noun **2 = loot**, booty, ill-gotten gains, pillage, prey, prize, rapine, spoils, swag (slang)

plunge verb **1 = throw**, cast, pitch **2 = hurtle**, career, charge, dash, jump, lurch, rush, swoop, tear **3 = descend**, dip, dive, douse, drop, fall, go down, immerse, nose-dive, plummet, sink, submerge, tumble ♦ noun **4 = dive**, descent, drop, fall, immersion, jump, submersion, swoop

plus preposition **1 = and**, added to, coupled with, with, with the addition of ♦ adjective **2 = additional**, added, add-on, extra, positive, supplementary ♦ noun **3** Informal = **advantage**, asset, benefit, bonus, extra, gain, good point, icing on the cake, perk (Brit. informal), surplus

plush adjective = **luxurious**, costly, de luxe, lavish, luxury, opulent, palatial, rich, ritzy (slang), sumptuous
➤ **Antonyms**
cheap, cheap and nasty, inexpensive, ordinary, plain, spartan

plutocrat noun = **rich man**, capitalist, Croesus, Dives, fat cat (slang, chiefly U.S.), magnate, millionaire, moneybags (slang), tycoon

ply verb **1 = work at**, carry on, exercise, follow, practise, pursue **2 = use**, employ, handle, manipulate, swing, utilize, wield **3 = bombard**, assail, beset, besiege, harass, importune, press, urge

poach verb **1 = steal**, hunt or fish illegally, plunder, rob, steal game **2 = encroach**, appropriate, infringe, intrude, trespass

pocket noun **1 = pouch**, bag, compartment, hollow, receptacle, sack ♦ verb **2 = steal**, appropriate, cabbage (Brit. slang), filch, help oneself to, lift (informal), pilfer, purloin, snaffle (Brit. informal), take **3 = bear**, accept, brook, endure, put up with (informal), stomach, swallow, take, tolerate ♦ adjective **4 = small**, abridged, compact, concise, little, miniature, pint-size(d) (informal), portable, potted (informal)

pod noun, verb = **shell**, hull, husk, shuck

podgy adjective = **tubby**, chubby, chunky, dumpy, fat, fleshy, fubsy (archaic or *dialect*), plump, roly-poly, rotund, short and fat, squat, stout, stubby, stumpy

podium *noun* = **platform**, dais, rostrum, stage

poem *noun* = **verse**, lyric, ode, rhyme, song, sonnet

poet *noun* = **bard**, lyricist, maker (*archaic*), rhymer, versifier

poetic *adjective* = **lyrical**, elegiac, lyric, metrical, rhythmic, rhythmical, songlike

poetry *noun* = **verse**, metrical composition, poems, poesy (*archaic*), rhyme, rhyming

poignancy *noun* 1 = **sadness**, emotion, emotionalism, evocativeness, feeling, pathos, piteousness, plaintiveness, sentiment, tenderness 2 = **sharpness**, bitterness, intensity, keenness 3 = **pungency**, piquancy, sharpness

poignant *adjective* 1 = **moving**, affecting, agonizing, bitter, distressing, gut-wrenching, harrowing, heartbreaking, heart-rending, intense, painful, pathetic, sad, touching, upsetting 2 = **cutting**, acute, biting, caustic, keen, penetrating, piercing, pointed, sarcastic, severe, sharp 3 = **pungent**, acrid, piquant, sharp, stinging, tangy

point *noun* 1 = **essence**, burden, core, crux, drift, gist, heart, import, main idea, marrow, matter, meaning, nub, pith, proposition, question, subject, text, theme, thrust 2 = **aim**, design, end, goal, intent, intention, motive, object, objective, purpose, reason, use, usefulness, utility 3 = **item**, aspect, detail, facet, feature, instance, nicety, particular 4 = **characteristic**, aspect, attribute, peculiarity, property, quality, respect, side, trait 5 = **place**, location, position, site, spot, stage, station 6 = **full stop**, dot, mark, period, speck, stop 7 = **end**, apex, nib, prong, sharp end, spike, spur, summit, tine, tip, top 8 = **headland**, bill, cape, foreland, head, ness (*archaic*), promontory 9 = **stage**, circumstance, condition, degree, extent, position 10 = **moment**, instant, juncture, time, very minute 11 = **unit**, score, tally 12 **beside the point** = **irrelevant**, immaterial, incidental, inconsequential, not to the purpose, off the subject, out of the way, pointless, unimportant, without connection 13 **to the point** = **relevant**, applicable, apposite, appropriate, apropos, apt, brief, fitting, germane, pertinent, pithy, pointed, short, suitable, terse ♦ *verb* 14 = **indicate**, bespeak, call attention to, denote, designate, direct, show, signify 15 = **aim**, bring to bear, direct, level, train

point-blank *adjective* 1 = **direct**, abrupt,

blunt, categorical, downright, explicit, express, plain, straight-from-the-shoulder, unreserved ♦ *adverb* 2 = **directly**, bluntly, brusquely, candidly, explicitly, forthrightly, frankly, openly, overtly, plainly, straight, straightforwardly

pointed *adjective* 1 = **sharp**, acicular, acuminate, acute, barbed, cuspidate, edged 2 = **cutting**, accurate, acute, biting, incisive, keen, penetrating, pertinent, sharp, telling, trenchant

pointer *noun* 1 = **hint**, advice, caution, information, recommendation, suggestion, tip, warning 2 = **indicator**, guide, hand, needle

pointless *adjective* = **senseless**, absurd, aimless, dumb-ass (*slang*), fruitless, futile, inane, ineffectual, irrelevant, meaningless, nonsensical, silly, stupid, unavailing, unproductive, unprofitable, useless, vague, vain, without rhyme or reason, worthless
➤ **Antonyms**
appropriate, beneficial, desirable, fitting, fruitful, logical, meaningful, productive, profitable, proper, sensible, to the point, useful, worthwhile

point of view *noun* 1 = **perspective**, angle, orientation, outlook, position, standpoint 2 = **opinion**, approach, attitude, belief, judgment, slant, view, viewpoint, way of looking at it

point out *verb* = **mention**, allude to, bring up, call attention to, identify, indicate, remind, reveal, show, specify

poise *noun* 1 = **composure**, aplomb, assurance, calmness, cool (*slang*), coolness, dignity, elegance, equanimity, equilibrium, grace, presence, presence of mind, sang-froid, savoir-faire, self-possession, serenity ♦ *verb* 2 = **position**, balance, float, hang, hang in midair, hang suspended, hold, hover, support, suspend

poised *adjective* 1 = **ready**, all set, in the wings, on the brink, prepared, standing by, waiting 2 = **composed**, calm, collected, debonair, dignified, graceful, nonchalant, self-confident, self-possessed, serene, suave, together (*informal*), unfazed (*informal*), unruffled, urbane
➤ **Antonyms**
≠**composed**: agitated, annoyed, discomposed, disturbed, excited, irritated, ruffled, worked up

poison *noun* 1 = **toxin**, bane, venom 2 = **contamination**, bane, blight, cancer, canker, contagion, corruption, malignancy, miasma, virus ♦ *verb* 3 = **murder**, give (someone) poison, kill 4 = **contaminate**, adulterate, envenom, infect, pollute **5 = corrupt**, defile, deprave, pervert, subvert, taint, undermine, vitiate, warp ♦ *adjective* **6 = poisonous**, deadly, lethal, toxic, venomous

poisonous *adjective* **1 = toxic**, baneful (*archaic*), deadly, fatal, lethal, mephitic, mortal, noxious, venomous, virulent **2 = evil**, baleful, baneful (*archaic*), corrupting, malicious, noxious, pernicious, pestiferous, pestilential, vicious

poke *verb* **1 = jab**, butt, dig, elbow, hit, nudge, prod, punch, push, shove, stab, stick, thrust **2 = interfere**, butt in, intrude, meddle, nose, peek, poke one's nose into (*informal*), pry, put one's two cents in (*U.S. slang*), snoop (*informal*), tamper **3 poke fun at = make fun of**, chaff, jeer, make a mock of, mock, rib (*informal*), ridicule, send up (*Brit. informal*), take the mickey (*informal*), take the piss (out of) (*taboo slang*), tease ♦ *noun* **4 = jab**, butt, dig, hit, nudge, prod, punch, thrust

poky *adjective* **= small**, confined, cramped, incommodious, narrow, tiny
➤ **Antonyms**
capacious, commodious, large, open, roomy, spacious, wide

polar *adjective* **1 = freezing**, Antarctic, Arctic, cold, extreme, frozen, furthest, glacial, icy, terminal **2 = opposite**, antagonistic, antipodal, antithetical, contradictory, contrary, diametric, opposed

polarity *noun* **= opposition**, ambivalence, contradiction, contrariety, dichotomy, duality, paradox

pole[1] *noun* **= rod**, bar, mast, post, shaft, spar, staff, standard, stick

pole[2] *noun* **1 = extremity**, antipode, limit, terminus **2 poles apart = at opposite extremes**, at opposite ends of the earth, incompatible, irreconcilable, miles apart, widely separated, worlds apart

polemic *noun* **1 = argument**, controversy, debate, dispute ♦ *adjective* **2 = controversial**, argumentative, contentious, disputatious, polemical

polemics *noun* **= dispute**, argument, argumentation, contention, controversy, debate, disputation

police *noun* **1 = the law** (*informal*), boys in blue (*informal*), constabulary, fuzz (*slang*), law enforcement agency, police force, the Old Bill (*slang*) ♦ *verb* **2 = control**, guard, keep in order, keep the peace, patrol, protect, regulate, watch **3 = monitor**, check, observe, oversee, supervise

policeman *noun* **= cop** (*slang*), bizzy (*informal*), bobby (*informal*), bogey

(*slang*), constable, copper (*slang*), flatfoot (*slang*), fuzz (*slang*), gendarme (*slang*), officer, peeler (*obsolete Brit. slang*), pig (*slang*), rozzer (*slang*), woodentop (*slang*)

policy *noun* **1 = procedure**, action, approach, code, course, custom, guideline, line, plan, practice, programme, protocol, rule, scheme, stratagem, theory **2** *Archaic* **= wisdom**, discretion, good sense, prudence, sagacity, shrewdness

polish *verb* **1 = shine**, brighten, buff, burnish, clean, furbish, rub, smooth, wax **2 = perfect**, brush up, correct, cultivate, emend, enhance, finish, improve, refine, touch up ♦ *noun* **3 = varnish**, wax **4 = sheen**, brightness, brilliance, finish, glaze, gloss, lustre, smoothness, sparkle, veneer **5 = style**, breeding, class (*informal*), elegance, finesse, finish, grace, politesse, refinement, suavity, urbanity

polished *adjective* **1 = accomplished**, adept, expert, faultless, fine, flawless, impeccable, masterly, outstanding, professional, skilful, superlative **2 = shining**, bright, burnished, furbished, glassy, gleaming, glossy, slippery, smooth **3 = elegant**, civilized, courtly, cultivated, finished, genteel, polite, refined, sophisticated, urbane, well-bred
➤ **Antonyms**
≠**accomplished:** amateurish, inept, inexpert, unaccomplished, unskilled ≠**shining:** dark, dull, matt, rough ≠**elegant:** inelegant, uncivilized, uncultivated, unrefined, unsophisticated

polish off *verb Informal* **1 = finish**, consume, down, eat up, put away, shift (*informal*), swill, wolf **2 = kill**, blow away (*slang, chiefly U.S.*), bump off (*informal*), dispose of, do away with, do in (*slang*), eliminate, get rid of, liquidate, murder, take out (*slang*)

polite *adjective* **1 = mannerly**, affable, civil, complaisant, courteous, deferential, gracious, obliging, respectful, well-behaved, well-mannered **2 = refined**, civilized, courtly, cultured, elegant, genteel, polished, sophisticated, urbane, well-bred
➤ **Antonyms**
≠**mannerly:** crude, discourteous, ill-mannered, impertinent, impolite, impudent, insulting, rude ≠**refined:** uncultured, unrefined

politeness *noun* **= courtesy**, civility, courteousness, decency, etiquette, mannerliness

politic *adjective* **1 = wise**, advisable, diplomatic, discreet, expedient, in one's best interests, judicious, prudent, sagacious, sensible, tactful **2 = shrewd**, artful, astute, canny, crafty, cunning, designing, ingenious, intriguing, Machiavellian, scheming, sly, subtle, unscrupulous

political *adjective* **1 = governmental**, parliamentary, policy-making **2 = factional**, partisan, party

politician *noun* **= statesman**, legislator, Member of Parliament, M.P., office bearer, politico (*informal, chiefly U.S.*), public servant

politics *noun* **1 = statesmanship**, affairs of state, civics, government, government policy, political science, polity, statecraft **2 = power struggle**, Machiavellianism, machination, *Realpolitik*

poll *noun* **1 = canvass**, ballot, census, count, Gallup Poll, (public) opinion poll, sampling, survey **2 = vote**, figures, returns, tally, voting ♦ *verb* **3 = tally**, register **4 = question**, ballot, canvass, fly a kite, interview, sample, survey

pollute *verb* **1 = contaminate**, adulterate, befoul, dirty, foul, infect, make filthy, mar, poison, smirch, soil, spoil, stain, taint **2 = defile**, besmirch, corrupt, debase, debauch, deprave, desecrate, dishonour, profane, sully, violate
➤ **Antonyms**
≠**contaminate**: clean, cleanse, decontaminate, disinfect, purge, sanitize, sterilize ≠**defile**: esteem, honour

pollution *noun* **= contamination**, adulteration, corruption, defilement, dirtying, foulness, impurity, taint, uncleanness

poltroon *noun Obsolete* **= coward**, chicken (*slang*), craven, yellow-belly (*slang*)

polychromatic *adjective* **= multicoloured**, many-coloured, many-hued, of all the colours of the rainbow, polychrome, rainbow, varicoloured, variegated

pomp *noun* **1 = ceremony**, éclat, flourish, grandeur, magnificence, pageant, pageantry, parade, solemnity, splendour, state **2 = show**, display, grandiosity, ostentation, pomposity, vainglory

pomposity *noun* **1 = self-importance**, affectation, airs, arrogance, flaunting, grandiosity, haughtiness, pompousness, portentousness, presumption, pretension, pretentiousness, vainglory, vanity **2 = grandiloquence**, bombast, hot air (*informal*), loftiness, magniloquence, rant, turgidity

pompous *adjective* **1 = self-important**, affected, arrogant, bloated, grandiose, imperious, magisterial, ostentatious, overbearing, pontifical, portentous, pretentious, puffed up, showy, supercilious, vainglorious **2 = grandiloquent**, arty-farty (*informal*), boastful, bombastic, high-flown, inflated, magniloquent, overblown, turgid
➤ **Antonyms**
≠**self-important**: humble, modest, natural, self-effacing, simple, unaffected, unpretentious ≠**grandiloquent**: direct, plain-spoken, simple, succinct

ponce *Offensive slang, chiefly Brit. noun* **1 = fop**, beau, coxcomb (*archaic*), dandy, popinjay, swell **2 = pimp**, bawd (*archaic*), pander, procurer

pond *noun* **= pool**, dew pond, duck pond, fish pond, lochan (*Scot.*), millpond, small lake, tarn

ponder *verb* **= think**, brood, cerebrate, cogitate, consider, contemplate, deliberate, examine, excogitate, give thought to, meditate, mull over, muse, puzzle over, rack one's brains, reflect, ruminate, study, weigh

ponderous *adjective* **1 = dull**, dreary, heavy, laboured, lifeless, long-winded, pedantic, pedestrian, plodding, prolix, stilted, stodgy, tedious, tiresome, verbose **2 = unwieldy**, bulky, clunky (*informal*), cumbersome, cumbrous, heavy, hefty, huge, massive, weighty **3 = clumsy**, awkward, elephantine, graceless, heavy-footed, laborious, lumbering
➤ **Antonyms**
≠**unwieldy**: handy, light, little, small, tiny, weightless ≠**clumsy**: graceful, light, light-footed

pontifical *adjective* **1 = papal**, apostolic, ecclesiastical **2 = pompous**, dogmatic, imperious, magisterial, overbearing, portentous, pretentious, self-important

pontificate *verb* **= expound**, declaim, dogmatize, hold forth, lay down the law, pontify, preach, pronounce, sound off

pooh-pooh *verb* **= scorn**, belittle, brush aside, deride, disdain, dismiss, disregard, make little of, play down, scoff, slight, sneer, sniff at, spurn, turn up one's nose at (*informal*)
➤ **Antonyms**
exalt, extol, glorify, praise

pool¹ *noun* **1 = pond**, lake, mere, puddle, splash, tarn **2 = swimming pool**, swimming bath

pool² *noun* **1 = syndicate**, collective, combine, consortium, group, team, trust **2 = kitty**, bank, funds, jackpot, pot, stakes ♦ *verb* **3 = combine**, amalgamate, join forces, league, merge, put together, share

poor *adjective* **1 = impoverished**, badly off,

broke (*informal*), destitute, dirt-poor (*informal*), down and out, down at heel, flat broke (*informal*), hard up (*informal*), impecunious, indigent, in need, in queer street, in want, necessitous, needy, on one's beam-ends, on one's uppers, on the breadline, on the rocks, penniless, penurious, poverty-stricken, short, skint (*Brit. slang*), stony-broke (*Brit. slang*), without two pennies to rub together (*informal*) **2 = meagre**, deficient, exiguous, inadequate, incomplete, insufficient, lacking, measly, miserable, niggardly, pathetic, pitiable, reduced, scant, scanty, skimpy, slight, sparse, straitened **3 = inferior**, below par, chickenshit (*U.S. slang*), crappy (*slang*), faulty, feeble, for the birds (*informal*), low-grade, low-rent (*informal chiefly U.S.*), mediocre, no great shakes (*informal*), not much cop (*Brit. slang*), pants (*informal*), piss-poor (*taboo slang*), poxy (*slang*), rotten (*informal*), rubbishy, second-rate, shabby, shoddy, sorry, strictly for the birds (*informal*), substandard, unsatisfactory, valueless, weak, worthless **4 = unfortunate**, hapless, ill-fated, luckless, miserable, pathetic, pitiable, unhappy, unlucky, wretched
➤ **Antonyms**
≠**impoverished**: affluent, comfortable (*informal*), prosperous, rich, wealthy, well-heeled (*informal*) ≠**meagre**: abundant, adequate, ample, complete, dense, plentiful, satisfactory, sufficient, thick ≠**inferior**: excellent, exceptional, first-class, first-rate, satisfactory, superior, valuable ≠**unfortunate**: fortunate, happy, lucky, successful

poorly *adverb* **1 = badly**, crudely, inadequately, incompetently, inexpertly, inferiorly, insufficiently, meanly, shabbily, unsatisfactorily, unsuccessfully ♦ *adjective* **2** *Informal* = **ill**, ailing, below par, indisposed, off colour, out of sorts, rotten (*informal*), seedy (*informal*), sick, under the weather (*informal*), unwell
➤ **Antonyms**
adverb ≠**badly**: acceptably, adequately, competently, expertly, satisfactorily, sufficiently, well ♦ *adjective* ≠**ill**: fit, hale and hearty, healthy, in good health, in the pink, well

pop *verb* **1 = burst**, bang, crack, explode, go off, report, snap **2 = put**, insert, push, shove, slip, stick, thrust, tuck **3** *often with* **in, out,** *etc. Informal* = **call**, appear, come or go suddenly, drop in (*informal*), leave quickly, nip in or out (*Brit. informal*), visit **4** *Especially of eyes* = **protrude**, bulge, stick out ♦ *noun* **5 = bang**, burst, crack, explosion, noise, report **6** *Informal* = **soft**

drink, fizzy drink, ginger (*Scot.*), lemonade, mineral water, soda water

pope *noun* = **Holy Father**, Bishop of Rome, pontiff, Vicar of Christ

popinjay *noun* = **fop**, buck (*archaic*), coxcomb (*archaic*), dandy, peacock, swell (*informal*)

poppycock *noun* *Informal* = **nonsense**, babble, balderdash, balls (*taboo slang*), baloney (*informal*), bilge (*informal*), bollocks (*Brit. taboo slang*), bosh (*informal*), bull (*slang*), bullshit (*taboo slang*), bunk (*informal*), bunkum or buncombe (*chiefly U.S.*), cobblers (*Brit. taboo slang*), crap (*slang*), drivel, eyewash (*informal*), garbage (*informal*), hogwash, hokum (*slang, chiefly U.S. & Canad.*), hooey (*slang*), horsefeathers (*U.S. slang*), hot air (*informal*), moonshine, pants (*informal*), pap, piffle (*informal*), rot, rubbish, shit (*taboo slang*), tommyrot, tosh (*slang, chiefly Brit.*), trash, tripe (*informal*), twaddle

populace *noun* = **people**, commonalty, crowd, general public, hoi polloi, inhabitants, Joe (and Eileen) Public (*slang*), Joe Six-Pack (*U.S. slang*), masses, mob, multitude, rabble, throng

popular *adjective* **1 = well-liked**, accepted, approved, celebrated, famous, fashionable, fave (*informal*), favoured, favourite, in, in demand, in favour, liked, sought-after **2 = common**, conventional, current, general, prevailing, prevalent, public, standard, stock, ubiquitous, universal, widespread
➤ **Antonyms**
≠**well-liked**: despised, detested, disliked, hated, loathed, unaccepted, unpopular ≠**common**: infrequent, rare, uncommon, unusual

popularity *noun* = **favour**, acceptance, acclaim, adoration, approval, celebrity, currency, esteem, fame, idolization, lionization, recognition, regard, renown, reputation, repute, vogue

popularize *verb* = **make popular**, disseminate, familiarize, give currency to, give mass appeal, make available to all, simplify, spread, universalize

popularly *adverb* = **generally**, commonly, conventionally, customarily, ordinarily, regularly, traditionally, universally, usually, widely

populate *verb* = **inhabit**, colonize, live in, occupy, people, settle

population *noun* = **inhabitants**, citizenry, community, denizens, folk, natives, people, populace, residents, society

populous *adjective* = **populated**, crowded, heavily populated, overpopulated, packed, swarming, teeming, thronged

pore[1] *verb* **pore over** = **study**, brood, contemplate, dwell on, examine, go over, peruse, ponder, read, scrutinize, work over

pore[2] *noun* = **opening**, hole, orifice, outlet, stoma

pornographic *adjective* = **obscene**, blue, dirty, filthy, indecent, lewd, offensive, prurient, salacious, smutty, X-rated (*informal*)

pornography *noun* = **obscenity**, dirt, erotica, filth, indecency, porn (*informal*), porno (*informal*), smut

porous *adjective* = **permeable**, absorbent, absorptive, penetrable, pervious, spongy
➤ **Antonyms**
impenetrable, impermeable, impervious, nonporous

port *noun* = **harbour**, anchorage, haven, roads, roadstead, seaport

portable *adjective* = **light**, compact, convenient, easily carried, handy, lightweight, manageable, movable, portative

portal *noun Literary* = **doorway**, door, entrance, entrance way, entry, gateway, way in

portend *verb* = **foretell**, adumbrate, augur, bespeak, betoken, bode, foreshadow, foretoken, forewarn, harbinger, herald, indicate, omen, point to, predict, presage, prognosticate, promise, threaten, vaticinate (*rare*), warn of

portent *noun* = **omen**, augury, foreboding, foreshadowing, forewarning, harbinger, indication, premonition, presage, presentiment, prognostic, prognostication, sign, threat, warning

portentous *adjective* **1** = **significant**, alarming, bodeful, crucial, fateful, forbidding, important, menacing, minatory, momentous, ominous, sinister, threatening **2** = **pompous**, bloated, elephantine, heavy, ponderous, pontifical, self-important, solemn

porter[1] *noun* = **baggage attendant**, bearer, carrier

porter[2] *noun Chiefly Brit.* = **doorman**, caretaker, concierge, gatekeeper, janitor

portion *noun* **1** = **part**, bit, fraction, fragment, morsel, piece, scrap, section, segment **2** = **share**, allocation, allotment, allowance, division, lot, measure, parcel, quantity, quota, ration **3** = **helping**, piece, serving **4** *Literary* = **destiny**, cup, fate, fortune, lot, luck ♦ *verb* **5** = **divide**, allocate, allot, apportion, assign, deal, distribute, divvy up (*informal*), dole out, parcel out, partition, share out

portly *adjective* = **stout**, burly, corpulent, fat, fleshy, heavy, large, plump

portrait *noun* **1** = **picture**, image, likeness, painting, photograph, portraiture, representation, sketch **2** = **description**, account, characterization, depiction, portrayal, profile, thumbnail sketch, vignette

portray *verb* **1** = **represent**, delineate, depict, draw, figure, illustrate, limn, paint, picture, render, sketch **2** = **describe**, characterize, depict, paint a mental picture of, put in words **3** = **play**, act the part of, represent

portrayal *noun* = **representation**, characterization, delineation, depiction, description, impersonation, interpretation, performance, picture, rendering, take (*informal, chiefly U.S.*)

pose *verb* **1** = **position**, arrange, model, sit, sit for **2** = **put on airs**, affect, attitudinize, posture, show off (*informal*), strike an attitude **3** *often with* **as** = **impersonate**, feign, masquerade as, pass oneself off as, pretend to be, profess to be, sham **4** = **present**, advance, ask, posit, propound, put, put forward, set, state, submit ♦ *noun* **5** = **posture**, attitude, bearing, mien (*literary*), position, stance **6** = **act**, affectation, air, attitudinizing, façade, front, mannerism, masquerade, posturing, pretence, role

poser *noun* = **puzzle**, brain-teaser (*informal*), conundrum, enigma, knotty point, problem, question, riddle, teaser, tough one, vexed question

poseur *noun* = **show-off** (*informal*), exhibitionist, impostor, poser, posturer

posh *adjective Informal, chiefly Brit.* = **upper-class**, classy (*slang*), elegant, exclusive, fashionable, grand, high-class, high-toned, la-di-da (*informal*), luxurious, luxury, ritzy (*slang*), smart, stylish, swanky (*informal*), swish (*informal, chiefly Brit.*), top-drawer, up-market

posit *verb* = **put forward**, advance, assume, postulate, presume, propound, state

position *noun* **1** = **place**, area, bearings, locale, locality, location, point, post, reference, site, situation, spot, station, whereabouts **2** = **posture**, arrangement, attitude, disposition, pose, stance **3** = **attitude**, angle, belief, opinion, outlook, point of view, slant, stance, stand, standpoint, view, viewpoint **4** = **status**, caste, class, consequence, eminence, importance, place, prestige, rank, reputation, standing, station, stature **5**

= **job**, berth (*informal*), billet (*informal*), capacity, duty, employment, function, occupation, office, place, post, role, situation **6 = situation**, circumstances, condition, lie of the land, pass, plight, predicament, state, strait(s) ♦ *verb* **7** = **place**, arrange, array, dispose, fix, lay out, locate, put, sequence, set, settle, stand, stick (*informal*)

positive *adjective* **1 = certain**, assured, confident, convinced, sure **2 = definite**, absolute, actual, affirmative, categorical, certain, clear, clear-cut, conclusive, concrete, decisive, direct, explicit, express, firm, incontrovertible, indisputable, real, unequivocal, unmistakable **3 = helpful**, beneficial, constructive, effective, efficacious, forward-looking, practical, productive, progressive, useful **4** *Informal* = **absolute**, complete, consummate, downright, out-and-out, perfect, rank, thorough, thoroughgoing, unmitigated, utter
➤ **Antonyms**
≠**certain**: not confident, unassured, uncertain, unconvinced, unsure ≠**definite**: contestable, disputable, doubtful, inconclusive, indecisive, indefinite, uncertain ≠**helpful**: conservative, detrimental, harmful, impractical, reactionary, unhelpful, useless

positively *adverb* = **definitely**, absolutely, assuredly, categorically, certainly, emphatically, firmly, surely, undeniably, unequivocally, unmistakably, unquestionably, with certainty, without qualification

possess *verb* **1 = have**, be blessed with, be born with, be endowed with, enjoy, have to one's name, hold, own **2 = seize**, acquire, control, dominate, hold, occupy, take over, take possession of **3 = control**, bewitch, consume, dominate, enchant, fixate, influence, mesmerize, obsess, put under a spell

possessed *adjective* = **crazed**, bedevilled, berserk, bewitched, consumed, cursed, demented, enchanted, frenetic, frenzied, hag-ridden, haunted, maddened, obsessed, raving, under a spell

possession *noun* **1 = ownership**, control, custody, hold, occupancy, occupation, proprietorship, tenure, title **2 possessions** = **property**, assets, belongings, chattels, effects, estate, goods and chattels, things, wealth **3 = province**, colony, dominion, protectorate, territory

possessive *adjective* = **jealous**, acquisitive, controlling, covetous, dominating, domineering, grasping, overprotective, selfish

possibility *noun* **1 = feasibility**, likelihood, plausibility, potentiality, practicability, workableness **2 = likelihood**, chance, hazard, hope, liability, odds, probability, prospect, risk **3** *often plural* = **potential**, capabilities, potentiality, promise, prospects, talent

possible *adjective* **1 = conceivable**, credible, hypothetical, imaginable, likely, potential **2 = likely**, hopeful, potential, probable, promising **3 = feasible**, attainable, doable, on (*informal*), practicable, realizable, viable, within reach, workable
➤ **Antonyms**
≠**conceivable**: impossible, inconceivable, incredible, unimaginable, unlikely, unthinkable ≠**likely**: impossible, improbable ≠**feasible**: impossible, impracticable, unfeasible, unobtainable, unreasonable

possibly *adverb* **1 = perhaps**, God willing, haply (*archaic*), maybe, mayhap (*archaic*), peradventure (*archaic*), perchance (*archaic*) **2 = at all**, by any chance, by any means, in any way

post¹ *noun* **1 = mail**, collection, delivery, postal service ♦ *verb* **2 = send**, dispatch, mail, transmit **3 keep someone posted** = **notify**, advise, brief, fill in on (*informal*), inform, report to

post² *noun* **1 = support**, column, newel, pale, palisade, picket, pillar, pole, shaft, stake, standard, stock, upright ♦ *verb* **2** = **put up**, advertise, affix, announce, display, make known, pin up, proclaim, promulgate, publicize, publish, stick up

post³ *noun* **1 = job**, appointment, assignment, berth (*informal*), billet (*informal*), employment, office, place, position, situation **2 = station**, beat, place, position ♦ *verb* **3 = station**, assign, establish, locate, place, position, put, situate

poster *noun* = **notice**, advertisement, announcement, bill, placard, public notice, sticker

posterior *adjective* **1 = behind**, after, back, hind, hinder, rear **2 = later**, ensuing, following, latter, subsequent

posterity *noun* **1 = future**, future generations, succeeding generations **2** = **descendants**, children, family, heirs, issue, offspring, progeny, scions, seed (*chiefly biblical*)

posthaste *adverb* = **speedily**, at once, before one can say Jack Robinson, directly, double-quick, hastily, hotfoot, pdq (*slang*), promptly, pronto (*informal*), quickly, straightaway, swiftly

postmortem noun = **examination**, analysis, autopsy, dissection, necropsy

postpone verb = **put off**, adjourn, defer, delay, hold over, put back, put on ice (*informal*), put on the back burner (*informal*), shelve, suspend, table, take a rain check on (*U.S. & Canad. informal*)
► Antonyms
advance, bring forward, carry out, go ahead with

postponement noun = **delay**, adjournment, deferment, deferral, moratorium, respite, stay, suspension

postscript noun = **P.S.**, addition, afterthought, afterword, appendix, supplement

postulate verb Formal = **presuppose**, advance, assume, hypothesize, posit, predicate, propose, put forward, suppose, take for granted, theorize

posture noun 1 = **bearing**, attitude, carriage, disposition, mien (*literary*), pose, position, set, stance 2 = **attitude**, disposition, feeling, frame of mind, inclination, mood, outlook, point of view, stance, standpoint ♦ verb 3 = **show off** (*informal*), affect, attitudinize, do for effect, make a show, pose, put on airs, try to attract attention

posy noun = **bouquet**, boutonniere, buttonhole, corsage, nosegay, spray

pot noun 1 = **container**, bowl, pan, vessel 2 = **pool**, bank, jackpot, kitty, stakes 3 *Informal* = **trophy**, cup 4 go to pot = **decline**, deteriorate, go downhill (*informal*), go to rack and ruin, go to the dogs (*informal*), run to seed, slump, worsen ♦ verb 5 = **shoot**, hit, plug (*informal*), strike

potbelly noun = **paunch**, beer belly (*informal*), gut, middle-age spread (*informal*), pot, spare tyre (*Brit. slang*), spread (*informal*)

potency noun = **power**, authority, capacity, control, effectiveness, efficacy, energy, force, influence, might, muscle, potential, puissance, strength, sway, vigour

potent adjective 1 = **powerful**, authoritative, commanding, dominant, dynamic, influential 2 = **persuasive**, cogent, compelling, convincing, effective, forceful, impressive, telling 3 = **strong**, efficacious, forceful, mighty, powerful, puissant, vigorous
► Antonyms
≠persuasive: ineffective, unconvincing
≠strong: impotent, weak

potentate noun = **ruler**, emperor, king,

mogul, monarch, overlord, prince, sovereign

potential adjective 1 = **possible**, budding, dormant, embryonic, future, hidden, inherent, latent, likely, promising, undeveloped, unrealized ♦ noun 2 = **ability**, aptitude, capability, capacity, possibility, potentiality, power, the makings, what it takes (*informal*), wherewithal

potentiality noun = **capacity**, ability, aptitude, capability, likelihood, potential, promise, prospect, the makings

pother noun Literary = **fuss**, bother, carry-on (*informal, chiefly Brit.*), commotion, disturbance, flap (*informal*), hoo-ha, stew (*informal*), tizzy (*informal*), to-do

potion noun = **concoction**, brew, cup, dose, draught, elixir, mixture, philtre, tonic

potpourri noun = **mixture**, collection, combination, hotchpotch, medley, *mélange*, miscellany, mixed bag (*informal*), pastiche, patchwork

potter verb = **mess about**, dabble, fiddle (*informal*), footle (*informal*), fribble, fritter, poke along, tinker

pottery noun = **ceramics**, earthenware, stoneware, terracotta

potty adjective Brit. informal 1 = **crazy**, barmy (*slang*), crackers (*Brit. slang*), crackpot (*informal*), daft (*informal*), dippy (*slang*), doolally (*slang*), dotty (*slang, chiefly Brit.*), eccentric, loopy (*informal*), oddball (*informal*), off one's chump (*slang*), off one's trolley (*slang*), off the rails, off-the-wall (*slang*), touched, up the pole (*informal*), wacko or whacko (*informal*) 2 = **trivial**, footling (*informal*), insignificant, petty, piddling (*informal*), trifling

pouch noun = **bag**, container, pocket, poke (*dialect*), purse, sack

pounce verb 1 = **spring**, ambush, attack, bound onto, dash at, drop, fall upon, jump, leap at, snatch, strike, swoop, take by surprise, take unawares ♦ noun 2 = **spring**, assault, attack, bound, jump, leap, swoop

pound¹ verb 1 = **beat**, batter, beat the living daylights out of, belabour, clobber (*slang*), hammer, pelt, pummel, strike, thrash, thump 2 = **crush**, bray (*dialect*), bruise, comminute, powder, pulverize, triturate 3 with out = **thump**, bang, beat, hammer 4 = **pulsate**, beat, palpitate, pitapat, pulse, throb 5 = **stomp** (*informal*), clomp, march, thunder, tramp

pound² noun = **enclosure**, compound,

corral (*chiefly U.S. & Canad.*), pen, yard

pour *verb* 1 = **flow**, course, emit, gush, run, rush, spew, spout, stream 2 = **let flow**, decant, spill, splash 3 = **rain**, bucket down (*informal*), come down in torrents, pelt (down), rain cats and dogs (*informal*), rain hard *or* heavily, sheet, teem 4 = **stream**, crowd, swarm, teem, throng

pout *verb* 1 = **sulk**, glower, look petulant, look sullen, lour *or* lower, make a *moue*, mope, pull a long face, purse one's lips, turn down the corners of one's mouth ♦ *noun* 2 = **sullen look**, glower, long face, *moue*

poverty *noun* 1 = **pennilessness**, beggary, destitution, distress, hand-to-mouth existence, hardship, indigence, insolvency, necessitousness, necessity, need, pauperism, penury, privation, want 2 = **scarcity**, dearth, deficiency, insufficiency, lack, paucity, shortage
➤ **Antonyms**
≠**pennilessness**: affluence, comfort, luxury, opulence, richness, wealth ≠**scarcity**: abundance, plethora, sufficiency

poverty-stricken *adjective* = **penniless**, bankrupt, beggared, broke (*informal*), destitute, dirt-poor (*informal*), distressed, down and out, down at heel, flat broke (*informal*), impecunious, impoverished, indigent, in queer street, needy, on one's beam-ends, on one's uppers, on the breadline, penurious, poor, short, skint (*Brit. slang*), stony-broke (*Brit. slang*), without two pennies to rub together (*informal*)

powder *noun* 1 = **dust**, fine grains, loose particles, pounce, talc ♦ *verb* 2 = **dust**, cover, dredge, scatter, sprinkle, strew

powdery *adjective* = **fine**, chalky, crumbling, crumbly, dry, dusty, friable, grainy, granular, loose, pulverized, sandy

power *noun* 1 = **ability**, capability, capacity, competence, competency, faculty, potential 2 = **control**, ascendancy, authority, bottom, command, dominance, domination, dominion, influence, mastery, rule, sovereignty, supremacy, sway 3 = **authority**, authorization, licence, prerogative, privilege, right, warrant 4 = **strength**, brawn, energy, force, forcefulness, intensity, might, muscle, potency, vigour, weight
➤ **Antonyms**
≠**ability**: inability, incapability, incapacity, incompetence ≠**strength**: enervation, feebleness, impotence, listlessness, weakness

powerful *adjective* 1 = **controlling**, authoritative, commanding, dominant, influential, prevailing, puissant, sovereign, supreme 2 = **strong**, energetic, mighty, potent, robust, stalwart, strapping, sturdy, vigorous 3 = **persuasive**, cogent, compelling, convincing, effective, effectual, forceful, forcible, impressive, storming, striking, telling, weighty

powerfully *adverb* = **strongly**, forcefully, forcibly, hard, mightily, vigorously, with might and main

powerless *adjective* 1 = **defenceless**, dependent, disenfranchised, disfranchised, ineffective, over a barrel (*informal*), subject, tied, unarmed, vulnerable 2 = **weak**, debilitated, disabled, etiolated, feeble, frail, helpless, impotent, incapable, incapacitated, ineffectual, infirm, paralysed, prostrate
➤ **Antonyms**
≠**weak**: able-bodied, fit, healthy, lusty, powerful, robust, strong, sturdy

powwow *noun* 1 = **meeting**, confab (*informal*), confabulation, conference, congress, consultation, council, discussion, get-together (*informal*), talk ♦ *verb* 2 = **meet**, confer, discuss, get together, talk

practicability *noun* = **feasibility**, advantage, operability, possibility, practicality, use, usefulness, value, viability, workability

practicable *adjective* = **feasible**, achievable, attainable, doable, performable, possible, viable, within the realm of possibility, workable
➤ **Antonyms**
beyond the bounds of possibility, impossible, out of the question, unachievable, unattainable, unfeasible, unworkable

practical *adjective* 1 = **functional**, applied, efficient, empirical, experimental, factual, pragmatic, realistic, utilitarian 2 = **sensible**, businesslike, down-to-earth, everyday, hard-headed, matter-of-fact, mundane, ordinary, realistic, workaday 3 = **feasible**, doable, practicable, serviceable, sound, useful, workable 4 = **skilled**, accomplished, efficient, experienced, proficient, qualified, seasoned, trained, veteran, working
➤ **Antonyms**
≠**functional**: impracticable, impractical, inefficient, speculative, theoretical, unpractical, unrealistic ≠**sensible**: impractical, unrealistic ≠**feasible**: impossible, impractical, unpractical, unsound, unworkable, useless ≠**skilled**: inefficient, inexperienced, unaccomplished, unqualified, unskilled, untrained

practically *adverb* 1 = **almost**, all but,

basically, close to, essentially, fundamentally, in effect, just about, nearly, to all intents and purposes, very nearly, virtually, well-nigh **2 = sensibly**, clearly, matter-of-factly, rationally, realistically, reasonably, unsentimentally, with common sense

practice *noun* **1 = custom**, habit, method, mode, praxis, routine, rule, system, tradition, usage, use, usual procedure, way, wont **2 = rehearsal**, discipline, drill, exercise, preparation, repetition, study, training, work-out **3 = profession**, business, career, vocation, work **4 = use**, action, application, effect, exercise, experience, operation

practise *verb* **1 = rehearse**, discipline, drill, exercise, go over, go through, keep one's hand in, polish, prepare, repeat, study, train, warm up, work out **2 = do**, apply, carry out, follow, live up to, observe, perform, put into practice **3 = work at**, carry on, engage in, ply, pursue, specialize in, undertake

practised *adjective* **= skilled**, able, accomplished, experienced, expert, proficient, qualified, seasoned, trained, versed
➤ **Antonyms**
amateurish, bungling, incompetent, inexperienced, inexpert, unqualified, unskilled, untrained

pragmatic *adjective* **= practical**, businesslike, down-to-earth, efficient, hard-headed, matter-of-fact, realistic, sensible, utilitarian
➤ **Antonyms**
airy-fairy, idealistic, impractical, inefficient, starry-eyed, stupid, theoretical, unprofessional, unrealistic

praise *verb* **1 = approve**, acclaim, admire, applaud, cheer, compliment, congratulate, crack up (*informal*), cry up, eulogize, extol, honour, laud, pat on the back, pay tribute to, sing the praises of, take one's hat off to **2 = give thanks to**, adore, bless, exalt, glorify, magnify (*archaic*), pay homage to, worship ♦ *noun* **3 = approval**, acclaim, acclamation, accolade, applause, approbation, cheering, commendation, compliment, congratulation, encomium, eulogy, good word, kudos, laudation, ovation, panegyric, plaudit, tribute **4 = thanks**, adoration, devotion, glory, homage, worship

praiseworthy *adjective* **= creditable**, admirable, commendable, estimable, excellent, exemplary, fine, honourable, laudable, meritorious, worthy
➤ **Antonyms**

condemnable, deplorable, despicable, discreditable, disgraceful, dishonourable, ignoble, reprehensible

prance *verb* **1 = dance**, bound, caper, cavort, cut a rug (*informal*), frisk, gambol, jump, leap, romp, skip, spring, trip **2 = strut**, parade, show off (*informal*), stalk, swagger, swank (*informal*)

prank *noun* **= trick**, antic, caper, escapade, frolic, jape, lark (*informal*), practical joke, skylarking (*informal*)

prate *verb* **= chatter**, babble, blather, blether, go on, jaw (*slang*), rabbit (on) (*Brit. informal*), waffle (*informal, chiefly Brit.*), witter on (*informal*), yak (*slang*)

prattle *verb* **= chatter**, babble, blather, blether, drivel, gabble, jabber, rabbit (on) (*Brit. informal*), rattle on, run on, waffle (*informal, chiefly Brit.*), witter (*informal*)

pray *verb* **1 = say one's prayers**, offer a prayer, recite the rosary **2 = beg**, adjure, ask, beseech, call upon, crave, cry for, entreat, implore, importune, invoke, petition, plead, request, solicit, sue, supplicate, urge

prayer *noun* **1 = orison**, communion, devotion, invocation, litany, supplication **2 = plea**, appeal, entreaty, petition, request, suit, supplication

preach *verb* **1 = deliver a sermon**, address, evangelize, exhort, orate **2 = lecture**, admonish, advocate, exhort, harangue, moralize, sermonize, urge

preacher *noun* **= clergyman**, evangelist, minister, missionary, parson, revivalist

preamble *noun* **= introduction**, exordium, foreword, opening move, opening statement *or* remarks, overture, preface, prelude, proem, prolegomenon

precarious *adjective* **= dangerous**, built on sand, chancy (*informal*), dicey (*informal, chiefly Brit.*), dodgy (*Brit., Austral., & N.Z. informal*), doubtful, dubious, hairy (*slang*), hazardous, insecure, perilous, risky, shaky, slippery, touch and go, tricky, uncertain, unreliable, unsafe, unsettled, unstable, unsteady, unsure
➤ **Antonyms**
certain, dependable, reliable, safe, secure, stable, steady

precaution *noun* **1 = safeguard**, belt and braces (*informal*), insurance, preventative measure, protection, provision, safety measure **2 = forethought**, anticipation, care, caution, circumspection, foresight, providence, prudence, wariness

precede *verb* **= go before**, antecede, antedate, come first, forerun, go ahead of, head, herald, introduce, lead, pave the way, preface, take precedence, usher

precedence noun = **priority**, antecedence, lead, pre-eminence, preference, primacy, rank, seniority, superiority, supremacy

precedent noun = **instance**, antecedent, authority, criterion, example, exemplar, model, paradigm, pattern, previous example, prototype, standard

preceding adjective = **previous**, above, aforementioned, aforesaid, anterior, earlier, foregoing, former, past, prior

precept noun **1** = **rule**, behest, canon, command, commandment, decree, dictum, direction, instruction, law, mandate, order, ordinance, principle, regulation, statute **2** = **maxim**, axiom, byword, dictum, guideline, motto, principle, rule, saying

precinct noun **1** = **enclosure**, bound, boundary, confine, limit **2** = **area**, district, quarter, section, sector, zone

precincts plural noun = **district**, borders, bounds, confines, environs, limits, milieu, neighbourhood, purlieus, region, surrounding area

precious adjective **1** = **valuable**, choice, costly, dear, expensive, exquisite, fine, high-priced, inestimable, invaluable, priceless, prized, rare, recherché **2** = **loved**, adored, beloved, cherished, darling, dear, dearest, fave (informal), favourite, idolized, prized, treasured, valued, worth one's or its weight in gold **3** = **affected**, alembicated, artificial, chichi, fastidious, overnice, overrefined, twee (Brit. informal)

precipice noun = **cliff**, bluff, brink, cliff face, crag, height, rock face, sheer drop, steep

precipitate verb **1** = **quicken**, accelerate, advance, bring on, dispatch, expedite, further, hasten, hurry, press, push forward, speed up, trigger **2** = **throw**, cast, discharge, fling, hurl, launch, let fly, send forth ♦ adjective **3** = **hasty**, frantic, harum-scarum, heedless, hurried, ill-advised, impetuous, impulsive, indiscreet, madcap, precipitous, rash, reckless **4** = **swift**, breakneck, headlong, plunging, rapid, rushing, violent **5** = **sudden**, abrupt, brief, quick, unexpected, without warning

precipitous adjective **1** = **sheer**, abrupt, dizzy, falling sharply, high, perpendicular, steep **2** = **hasty**, abrupt, careless, harum-scarum, heedless, hurried, ill-advised, precipitate, rash, reckless, sudden

précis noun **1** = **summary**, abridgment, abstract, aperçu, compendium,

condensation, digest, outline, résumé, rundown, sketch, synopsis ♦ verb **2** = **summarize**, abridge, abstract, compress, condense, outline, shorten, sum up

precise adjective **1** = **exact**, absolute, accurate, actual, clear-cut, correct, definite, explicit, express, fixed, literal, particular, specific, strict, unequivocal **2** = **strict**, careful, ceremonious, exact, fastidious, finicky, formal, inflexible, meticulous, nice, particular, prim, punctilious, puritanical, rigid, scrupulous, stiff

➤ **Antonyms**

≠**exact**: ambiguous, equivocal, incorrect, indefinite, indistinct, inexact, loose, vague ≠**strict**: careless, flexible, haphazard, inexact, informal, relaxed, unceremonious

precisely adverb = **exactly**, absolutely, accurately, bang, correctly, just, just so, literally, neither more nor less, on the button (informal), plumb (informal), slap (informal), smack (informal), square, squarely, strictly, to the letter

precision noun = **exactness**, accuracy, care, correctness, definiteness, dotting the i's and crossing the t's, exactitude, fidelity, meticulousness, nicety, particularity, preciseness, rigour

preclude verb = **prevent**, check, debar, exclude, forestall, hinder, inhibit, make impossible, make impracticable, obviate, prohibit, put a stop to, restrain, rule out, stop

precocious adjective = **advanced**, ahead, bright, developed, forward, quick, smart ➤ **Antonyms**
backward, dense, dull, retarded, slow, underdeveloped

preconceived adjective = **presumed**, forejudged, prejudged, presupposed

preconception noun = **preconceived idea** or **notion**, bias, notion, predisposition, prejudice, prepossession, presumption, presupposition

precondition noun = **necessity**, essential, must, prerequisite, requirement, sine qua non

precursor noun **1** = **herald**, forerunner, harbinger, messenger, usher, vanguard **2** = **forerunner**, antecedent, forebear, originator, pioneer, predecessor

predatory adjective **1** = **hunting**, carnivorous, predacious, rapacious, raptorial, ravening **2** = **rapacious**, despoiling, greedy, marauding, pillaging, plundering, ravaging, thieving, voracious

predecessor noun **1** = **previous job holder**, antecedent, forerunner, former job

holder, precursor, prior job holder **2
= ancestor**, antecedent, forebear,
forefather

predestination *noun* = **fate**, destiny,
doom, election (*Theology*),
foreordainment, foreordination, lot,
necessity, predetermination

predestined *adjective* = **fated**, doomed,
foreordained, meant, predestinated,
predetermined, pre-elected, preordained

predetermined *adjective* = **prearranged**,
agreed, arranged in advance, cut and
dried (*informal*), decided beforehand,
fixed, preplanned, set, settled, set up

predicament *noun* = **fix** (*informal*), corner,
dilemma, emergency, hole (*slang*), hot
water (*informal*), how-do-you-do
(*informal*), jam (*informal*), mess, pickle
(*informal*), pinch, plight, quandary, scrape
(*informal*), situation, spot (*informal*), state,
tight spot

predicate *verb* **1** *with* **on** *or* **upon** = **base**,
build, establish, found, ground, postulate,
rest **2** = **declare**, affirm, assert, aver,
avouch, avow, contend, maintain,
proclaim, state

predict *verb* = **foretell**, augur, call, divine,
forebode, forecast, foresee, portend,
presage, prognosticate, prophesy,
soothsay, vaticinate (*rare*)

predictable *adjective* = **likely**, anticipated,
calculable, certain, expected, foreseeable,
foreseen, on the cards, reliable, sure,
sure-fire (*informal*)
➤ **Antonyms**
out of the blue, surprising, unexpected,
unforeseen, unlikely, unpredictable

prediction *noun* = **prophecy**, augury,
divination, forecast, prognosis,
prognostication, soothsaying, sortilege

predilection *noun* = **liking**, bag (*slang*),
bias, cup of tea (*informal*), fancy, fondness,
inclination, leaning, love, partiality,
penchant, predisposition, preference,
proclivity, proneness, propensity, taste,
tendency, weakness

predispose *verb* = **incline**, affect, bias,
dispose, induce, influence, lead, make
(one) of a mind to, prejudice, prepare,
prime, prompt, sway

predisposed *adjective* = **inclined**,
agreeable, amenable, given, liable,
minded, prone, ready, subject, susceptible,
willing

predisposition *noun* = **inclination**, bent,
bias, disposition, likelihood, penchant,
potentiality, predilection, proclivity,
proneness, propensity, susceptibility,
tendency, willingness

predominance *noun* = **prevalence**,
ascendancy, control, dominance,
dominion, edge, greater number, hold,
leadership, mastery, paramountcy,
preponderance, supremacy, sway, upper
hand, weight

predominant *adjective* = **main**, ascendant,
capital, chief, controlling, dominant,
important, leading, notable, paramount,
preponderant, prevailing, prevalent,
primary, prime, principal, prominent,
ruling, sovereign, superior, supreme,
top-priority
➤ **Antonyms**
inferior, minor, secondary, subordinate,
unimportant, uninfluential

predominantly *adverb* = **mainly**, chiefly,
for the most part, generally, largely,
mostly, primarily, principally

predominate *verb* = **prevail**, be most
noticeable, carry weight, get the upper
hand, hold sway, outweigh, overrule,
overshadow, preponderate, reign, rule, tell

pre-eminence *noun* = **superiority**,
distinction, excellence, paramountcy,
predominance, prestige, prominence,
renown, supremacy, transcendence

pre-eminent *adjective* = **outstanding**,
chief, consummate, distinguished,
excellent, foremost, incomparable,
matchless, paramount, peerless,
predominant, renowned, superior,
supreme, transcendent, unequalled,
unrivalled, unsurpassed

pre-empt *verb* = **anticipate**, acquire,
appropriate, arrogate, assume, seize, take
over, usurp

preen *verb* **1** *Of birds* = **clean**, plume **2**
= **smarten**, array, deck out, doll up (*slang*),
dress up, prettify, primp, prink, spruce up,
titivate, trig (*archaic or dialect*), trim **3
preen oneself (on)** = **pride oneself**,
congratulate oneself, pique oneself, plume
oneself

preface *noun* **1** = **introduction**, exordium,
foreword, preamble, preliminary, prelude,
proem, prolegomenon, prologue ◆ *verb* **2**
= **introduce**, begin, launch, lead up to,
open, precede, prefix

prefatory *adjective* = **introductory**,
antecedent, opening, precursory,
preliminary, preparatory

prefer *verb* **1** = **like better**, adopt, be partial
to, choose, desire, elect, fancy, favour, go
for, incline towards, opt for, pick, plump
for, select, single out, wish, would rather,
would sooner **2** *Law* = **put forward**, file,
lodge, place, present, press **3** = **promote**,
advance, aggrandize, elevate, move up,
raise, upgrade

preferable *adjective* = **better**, best, choice, chosen, favoured, more desirable, more eligible, superior, worthier
➤ **Antonyms**
average, fair, ineligible, inferior, mediocre, poor, second-rate, undesirable

preferably *adverb* = **rather**, as a matter of choice, by choice, first, in *or* for preference, much rather, much sooner, sooner, willingly

preference *noun* 1 = **first choice**, bag (*slang*), choice, cup of tea (*informal*), desire, election, fave (*informal*), favourite, option, partiality, pick, predilection, selection, top of the list 2 = **priority**, advantage, favoured treatment, favouritism, first place, precedence, pride of place

preferential *adjective* = **privileged**, advantageous, better, favoured, partial, partisan, special, superior

preferment *noun* = **promotion**, advancement, dignity, elevation, exaltation, rise, upgrading

prefigure *verb* 1 = **foreshadow**, foretoken, indicate, intimate, portend, presage, suggest 2 = **imagine**, consider, fancy, picture, presuppose

pregnancy *noun* = **gestation**

pregnant *adjective* 1 = **expectant**, big *or* heavy with child, enceinte, expecting (*informal*), gravid, in the club (*Brit. slang*), in the family way (*informal*), in the pudding club (*slang*), preggers (*Brit. informal*), with child 2 = **meaningful**, charged, eloquent, expressive, loaded, pointed, significant, suggestive, telling, weighty

prehistoric *adjective* = **earliest**, early, primeval, primitive, primordial

prejudge *verb* = **jump to conclusions**, anticipate, forejudge, make a hasty assessment, presume, presuppose

prejudice *noun* 1 = **bias**, jaundiced eye, partiality, preconceived notion, preconception, prejudgment, warp 2 = **discrimination**, bigotry, chauvinism, injustice, intolerance, narrow-mindedness, racism, sexism, unfairness 3 = **harm**, damage, detriment, disadvantage, hurt, impairment, loss, mischief ♦ *verb* 4 = **bias**, colour, distort, influence, jaundice, poison, predispose, prepossess, slant, sway, warp 5 = **harm**, damage, hinder, hurt, impair, injure, mar, spoil, undermine

prejudiced *adjective* = **biased**, bigoted, conditioned, discriminatory, influenced, intolerant, jaundiced, narrow-minded, one-sided, opinionated, partial, partisan,
prepossessed, unfair
➤ **Antonyms**
fair, impartial, just, neutral, not bigoted, not prejudiced, open-minded, unbiased

prejudicial *adjective* = **harmful**, counterproductive, damaging, deleterious, detrimental, disadvantageous, hurtful, inimical, injurious, undermining, unfavourable

preliminary *adjective* 1 = **first**, exploratory, initial, initiatory, introductory, opening, pilot, precursory, prefatory, preparatory, prior, qualifying, test, trial ♦ *noun* 2 = **introduction**, beginning, first round, foundation, groundwork, initiation, opening, overture, preamble, preface, prelims, prelude, preparation, start

prelude *noun* = **introduction**, beginning, commencement, curtain-raiser, exordium, foreword, intro (*informal*), overture, preamble, preface, preliminary, preparation, proem, prolegomenon, prologue, start

premature *adjective* 1 = **early**, forward, unseasonable, untimely 2 = **hasty**, ill-considered, ill-timed, impulsive, inopportune, jumping the gun, overhasty, precipitate, previous (*informal*), rash, too soon, untimely 3 = **immature**, abortive, embryonic, incomplete, predeveloped, undeveloped, unfledged

prematurely *adverb* 1 = **too early**, before one's time, too soon, untimely 2 = **overhastily**, at half-cock, half-cocked, precipitately, rashly, too hastily, too soon

premeditated *adjective* = **planned**, aforethought, calculated, conscious, considered, contrived, deliberate, intended, intentional, prepense, studied, wilful
➤ **Antonyms**
accidental, inadvertent, unintentional, unplanned, unpremeditated, unwitting

premeditation *noun* = **planning**, deliberation, design, determination, forethought, intention, malice aforethought, plotting, prearrangement, predetermination, purpose

premier *noun* 1 = **head of government**, chancellor, chief minister, P.M., prime minister ♦ *adjective* 2 = **chief**, arch, first, foremost, head, highest, leading, main, primary, prime, principal, top 3 = **first**, earliest, inaugural, initial, original

premiere *noun* = **first night**, debut, first performance, first showing, opening

premise *noun* = **assumption**, argument, assertion, ground, hypothesis, postulate, postulation, presupposition, proposition, supposition, thesis

premises *plural noun* = **building**, establishment, place, property, site

premium *noun* 1 = **bonus**, boon, bounty, fee, percentage (*informal*), perk (*Brit. informal*), perquisite, prize, recompense, remuneration, reward 2 = **regard**, appreciation, stock, store, value 3 **at a premium** = **in great demand**, beyond one's means, costly, expensive, hard to come by, in short supply, like gold dust, not to be had for love or money, rare, scarce, valuable

premonition *noun* = **feeling**, apprehension, feeling in one's bones, foreboding, forewarning, funny feeling (*informal*), hunch, idea, intuition, misgiving, omen, portent, presage, presentiment, sign, suspicion, warning

preoccupation *noun* 1 = **obsession**, bee in one's bonnet, concern, fixation, hang-up (*informal*), hobbyhorse, *idée fixe*, pet subject 2 = **absorption**, absence of mind, absent-mindedness, abstraction, brown study, daydreaming, engrossment, immersion, inattentiveness, musing, oblivion, pensiveness, prepossession, reverie, woolgathering

preoccupied *adjective* = **absorbed**, absent-minded, abstracted, caught up in, distracted, distrait, engrossed, faraway, heedless, immersed, in a brown study, intent, lost in, lost in thought, oblivious, rapt, taken up, unaware, wrapped up

preordained *adjective* = **predetermined**, destined, doomed, fated, mapped out in advance, predestined

preparation *noun* 1 = **groundwork**, development, getting ready, preparing, putting in order 2 = **readiness**, alertness, anticipation, expectation, foresight, precaution, preparedness, provision, safeguard 3 *often plural* = **arrangement**, measure, plan, provision 4 = **mixture**, composition, compound, concoction, medicine, tincture 5 *Old-fashioned* = **homework**, prep (*informal*), revision, schoolwork, study, swotting (*Brit. informal*)

preparatory *adjective* 1 = **introductory**, basic, elementary, opening, prefatory, preliminary, preparative, primary 2 **preparatory to** = **before**, in advance of, in anticipation of, in preparation for, prior to

prepare *verb* 1 = **make** *or* **get ready**, adapt, adjust, anticipate, arrange, coach, dispose, form, groom, make provision, plan, practise, prime, put in order, train, warm up 2 = **put together**, assemble, concoct, construct, contrive, draw up, fashion, fix up, get up (*informal*), make, produce, turn out 3 = **equip**, accoutre, fit, fit out, furnish,

outfit, provide, supply

prepared *adjective* 1 = **ready**, all set, all systems go (*informal*), arranged, fit, in order, in readiness, planned, primed, set 2 = **willing**, able, disposed, inclined, minded, of a mind, predisposed

preponderance *noun* = **predominance**, ascendancy, bulk, dominance, domination, dominion, extensiveness, greater numbers, greater part, lion's share, mass, power, prevalence, superiority, supremacy, sway, weight

preponderant *adjective* = **prevalent**, ascendant, dominant, extensive, foremost, greater, important, larger, paramount, predominant, prevailing, significant

preponderate *verb* = **predominate**, dominate, hold sway, outnumber, prevail, reign supreme, rule

prepossessing *adjective* = **attractive**, alluring, amiable, appealing, beautiful, bewitching, captivating, charming, engaging, fair, fascinating, fetching, glamorous, good-looking, handsome, inviting, likable *or* likeable, lovable, magnetic, pleasing, striking, taking, winning
> **Antonyms**
disagreeable, displeasing, objectionable, offensive, repulsive, ugly, unattractive, uninviting, unlikable *or* unlikeable

prepossession *noun* 1 = **partiality**, bias, inclination, liking, predilection, predisposition, prejudice 2 = **preoccupation**, absorption, engrossment

preposterous *adjective* = **ridiculous**, absurd, asinine, bizarre, crazy, excessive, exorbitant, extravagant, extreme, foolish, impossible, incredible, insane, irrational, laughable, ludicrous, monstrous, nonsensical, out of the question, outrageous, risible, senseless, shocking, unreasonable, unthinkable

prerequisite *noun* 1 = **requirement**, condition, essential, imperative, must, necessity, precondition, qualification, requisite, sine qua non ◆ *adjective* 2 = **required**, called for, essential, imperative, indispensable, mandatory, necessary, needful, obligatory, of the essence, requisite, vital

prerogative *noun* = **right**, advantage, authority, birthright, choice, claim, due, exemption, immunity, liberty, perquisite, privilege, sanction, title

presage *verb* 1 = **portend**, augur, betoken, bode, foreshadow, foretoken, signify ◆ *noun* 2 = **omen**, augury, auspice, forecast, forewarning, harbinger, intimation, portent, prediction, prognostication, prophecy, sign, warning **3 = misgiving**, apprehension, feeling, foreboding, forewarning, intuition, premonition, presentiment

prescience *noun Formal* = **foresight**, clairvoyance, foreknowledge, precognition, second sight

prescient *adjective* = **foresighted**, clairvoyant, discerning, divinatory, divining, far-sighted, perceptive, prophetic, psychic

prescribe *verb* = **order**, appoint, assign, command, decree, define, dictate, direct, enjoin, establish, fix, impose, lay down, ordain, recommend, require, rule, set, specify, stipulate

prescript *noun* = **rule**, canon, command, dictate, dictum, direction, directive, edict, instruction, law, mandate, order, ordinance, precept, regulation, requirement

prescription *noun* **1** = **instruction**, direction, formula, recipe **2** = **medicine**, drug, mixture, preparation, remedy

prescriptive *adjective* = **dictatorial**, authoritarian, didactic, dogmatic, legislating, preceptive, rigid

presence *noun* **1** = **being**, attendance, companionship, company, existence, habitation, inhabitance, occupancy, residence **2** = **personality**, air, appearance, aspect, aura, bearing, carriage, comportment, demeanour, ease, mien (*literary*), poise, self-assurance **3** = **proximity**, closeness, immediate circle, nearness, neighbourhood, propinquity, vicinity **4** = **spirit**, apparition, eidolon, ghost, manifestation, revenant, shade (*literary*), spectre, supernatural being, wraith

presence of mind *noun* = **level-headedness**, alertness, aplomb, calmness, composure, cool (*slang*), coolness, imperturbability, phlegm, quickness, sang-froid, self-assurance, self-command, self-possession, wits

present[1] *adjective* **1** = **here**, accounted for, at hand, available, in attendance, near, nearby, ready, there, to hand **2** = **current**, contemporary, existent, existing, extant, immediate, instant, present-day ♦ *noun* **3** **the present** = **now**, here and now, the present moment, the time being, this day and age, today **4 at present** = **just now**, at the moment, now, nowadays, right now **5 for the present** = **for now**, for a while, for the moment, for the nonce, for the time being, in the meantime, not for long, provisionally, temporarily

present[2] *noun* **1** = **gift**, benefaction,

bonsela (*S. African*), boon, bounty, donation, endowment, favour, grant, gratuity, hand-out, largesse *or* largess, offering, prezzie (*informal*) ♦ *verb* **2** = **introduce**, acquaint with, make known **3** = **put on**, demonstrate, display, exhibit, give, mount, put before the public, show, stage **4** = **give**, award, bestow, confer, donate, entrust, furnish, grant, hand out, hand over, offer, proffer, put at (someone's) disposal **5** = **put forward**, adduce, advance, declare, expound, extend, hold out, introduce, offer, pose, produce, proffer, raise, recount, relate, state, submit, suggest, tender

presentable *adjective* = **decent**, acceptable, becoming, fit to be seen, good enough, not bad (*informal*), O.K. *or* okay (*informal*), passable, proper, respectable, satisfactory, suitable, tolerable
➤ **Antonyms**
below par, not good enough, not up to scratch, poor, rubbishy, unacceptable, unpresentable, unsatisfactory

presentation *noun* **1** = **giving**, award, bestowal, conferral, donation, investiture, offering **2** = **performance**, demonstration, display, exhibition, production, representation, show **3** = **portrayal**, appearance, arrangement, delivery, exposition, production, rendition, staging, submission

present-day *adjective* = **current**, contemporary, latter-day, modern, newfangled, present, recent, up-to-date

presentiment *noun* = **premonition**, anticipation, apprehension, expectation, fear, feeling, foreboding, forecast, forethought, hunch, intuition, misgiving, presage

presently *adverb* = **soon**, anon (*archaic*), before long, by and by, erelong (*archaic or poetic*), in a minute, in a moment, in a short while, pretty soon (*informal*), shortly

preservation *noun* = **protection**, conservation, defence, keeping, maintenance, perpetuation, safeguarding, safekeeping, safety, salvation, security, storage, support, upholding

preserve *verb* **1** = **protect**, care for, conserve, defend, guard, keep, safeguard, save, secure, shelter, shield **2** = **maintain**, continue, keep, keep up, perpetuate, retain, sustain, uphold **3** = **keep**, conserve, put up, save, store ♦ *noun* **4** = **area**, domain, field, realm, specialism, sphere **5** *often plural* = **jam**, confection, confiture, conserve, jelly, marmalade, sweetmeat **6** = **reserve**, game reserve, reservation, sanctuary

> **Antonyms**

verb ≠**protect**: assail, assault, attack, leave unprotected ≠**maintain**: abandon, discontinue, drop, end, give up ≠**keep**: blow (*slang*), consume, fritter away, spend, squander, waste

preside *verb* = **run**, administer, be at the head of, be in authority, chair, conduct, control, direct, govern, head, lead, manage, officiate, supervise

press *verb* **1** = **compress**, bear down on, condense, crush, depress, force down, jam, mash, push, reduce, squeeze, stuff **2** = **hug**, clasp, crush, embrace, encircle, enfold, fold in one's arms, hold close, squeeze **3** = **smooth**, calender, finish, flatten, iron, mangle, put the creases in, steam **4** = **urge**, beg, entreat, exhort, implore, importune, petition, plead, pressurize, sue, supplicate **5** = **force**, compel, constrain, demand, enforce, enjoin, insist on **6** = **crowd**, cluster, flock, gather, hasten, herd, hurry, mill, push, rush, seethe, surge, swarm, throng **7 be pressed** = **be hard put**, be hurried, be pushed, be rushed (*informal*), be short of ♦ *noun* **8 the press: a** = **newspapers**, Fleet Street, fourth estate, journalism, news media, the papers **b** = **journalists**, columnists, correspondents, gentlemen of the press, journos (*slang*), newsmen, photographers, pressmen, reporters **9** = **crowd**, bunch, crush, flock, herd, horde, host, mob, multitude, pack, push (*informal*), swarm, throng

pressing *adjective* = **urgent**, burning, constraining, crucial, exigent, high-priority, imperative, important, importunate, now or never, serious, vital
> **Antonyms**
regular, routine, unimportant, unnecessary

pressure *noun* **1** = **force**, compressing, compression, crushing, heaviness, squeezing, weight **2** = **power**, coercion, compulsion, constraint, force, influence, obligation, sway **3** = **stress**, adversity, affliction, burden, demands, difficulty, distress, exigency, hassle (*informal*), heat, hurry, load, press, strain, urgency

pressurize *verb* **1** = **compress**, condense, constrict, press, squash, squeeze **2** = **force**, breathe down someone's neck, browbeat, coerce, compel, dragoon, drive, intimidate, press-gang, put the screws on (*slang*), turn on the heat (*informal*), twist one's arm (*informal*)

prestige *noun* = **status**, authority, bottom, Brownie points, cachet, celebrity, credit, distinction, eminence, esteem, fame, honour, importance, influence, kudos, regard, renown, reputation, standing, stature, weight

prestigious *adjective* = **celebrated**, eminent, esteemed, exalted, great, illustrious, important, imposing, impressive, influential, notable, prominent, renowned, reputable, respected
> **Antonyms**
humble, lowly, minor, obscure, unimportant, unimpressive, unknown

presumably *adverb* = **it would seem**, apparently, doubtless, doubtlessly, in all likelihood, in all probability, likely, most likely, on the face of it, probably, seemingly

presume *verb* **1** = **believe**, assume, conjecture, guess (*informal, chiefly U.S. & Canad.*), infer, posit, postulate, presuppose, suppose, surmise, take for granted, take it, think **2** = **dare**, go so far, have the audacity, make bold, make so bold, take the liberty, undertake, venture **3** = **depend**, bank on, count on, rely, trust

presumption *noun* **1** = **cheek** (*informal*), assurance, audacity, boldness, brass (*informal*), brass neck (*Brit. informal*), chutzpah (*U.S. & Canad. informal*), effrontery, forwardness, front, gall (*informal*), impudence, insolence, neck (*informal*), nerve (*informal*), presumptuousness, sassiness (*U.S. informal*), temerity **2** = **probability**, basis, chance, grounds, likelihood, plausibility, reason **3** = **assumption**, anticipation, belief, conjecture, guess, hypothesis, opinion, premiss, presupposition, supposition, surmise

presumptive *adjective* = **assumed**, believed, expected, hypothetical, inferred, supposed, understood

presumptuous *adjective* = **pushy** (*informal*), arrogant, audacious, bigheaded (*informal*), bold, conceited, foolhardy, forward, insolent, overconfident, overfamiliar, overweening, presuming, rash, too big for one's boots, uppish (*Brit. informal*)
> **Antonyms**
bashful, humble, modest, retiring, shy, timid, unassuming

presuppose *verb* = **presume**, accept, assume, consider, imply, posit, postulate, suppose, take as read, take for granted, take it

presupposition *noun* = **assumption**, belief, hypothesis, preconceived idea, preconception, premise, presumption, supposition, theory

pretence *noun* **1** = **deception**, acting, charade, deceit, fabrication, fakery, faking, falsehood, feigning, invention,

make-believe, sham, simulation, subterfuge, trickery 2 = **show**, affectation, appearance, artifice, display, façade, hokum (*slang, chiefly U.S. & Canad.*), posing, posturing, pretentiousness, veneer 3 = **pretext**, claim, cloak, colour, cover, excuse, façade, garb, guise, mask, masquerade, ruse, semblance, show, veil, wile
➤ **Antonyms**
≠**deception**: candour, frankness, honesty, ingenuousness, openness ≠**show**: actuality, fact, reality

pretend *verb* 1 = **feign**, affect, allege, assume, counterfeit, dissemble, dissimulate, fake, falsify, impersonate, make out, pass oneself off as, profess, put on, sham, simulate 2 = **make believe**, act, imagine, make up, play, play the part of, suppose 3 = **lay claim**, allege, aspire, claim, profess, purport

pretended *adjective* = **feigned**, alleged, avowed, bogus, counterfeit, fake, false, fictitious, imaginary, ostensible, phoney *or* phony (*informal*), pretend (*informal*), professed, pseudo (*informal*), purported, sham, so-called, spurious

pretender *noun* = **claimant**, aspirant, claimer

pretension *noun* 1 = **claim**, aspiration, assertion, assumption, demand, pretence, profession 2 = **affectation**, airs, conceit, hypocrisy, ostentation, pomposity, pretentiousness, self-importance, show, showiness, snobbery, snobbishness, vainglory, vanity

pretentious *adjective* = **affected**, arty-farty (*informal*), assuming, bombastic, conceited, exaggerated, extravagant, flaunting, grandiloquent, grandiose, highfalutin (*informal*), high-flown, high-sounding, hollow, inflated, magniloquent, mannered, ostentatious, overambitious, pompous, puffed up, showy, snobbish, specious, vainglorious
➤ **Antonyms**
modest, natural, plain, simple, unaffected, unassuming, unpretentious

pretext *noun* = **guise**, affectation, alleged reason, appearance, cloak, cover, device, excuse, mask, ploy, pretence, red herring, ruse, semblance, show, simulation, veil

prettify *verb* = **adorn**, deck out, decorate, doll up (*slang*), do up, embellish, garnish, gild, ornament, tart up (*Brit. slang*), titivate, trick out, trim

pretty *adjective* 1 = **attractive**, appealing, beautiful, bonny, charming, comely, cute, fair, good-looking, graceful, lovely, personable 2 = **pleasant**, bijou, dainty,

delicate, elegant, fine, neat, nice, pleasing, tasteful, trim ♦ *adverb* 3 *Informal* = **fairly**, kind of (*informal*), moderately, quite, rather, reasonably, somewhat
➤ **Antonyms**
adjective ≠**attractive**: plain, ugly, unattractive, unshapely, unsightly

prevail *verb* 1 = **win**, be victorious, carry the day, gain mastery, overcome, overrule, prove superior, succeed, triumph 2 = **be widespread**, abound, be current, be prevalent, exist generally, obtain, predominate, preponderate 3 **prevail on** *or* **upon** = **persuade**, bring round, convince, dispose, incline, induce, influence, prompt, sway, talk into, win over

prevailing *adjective* 1 = **widespread**, common, current, customary, established, fashionable, general, in style, in vogue, ordinary, popular, prevalent, set, usual 2 = **predominating**, dominant, influential, main, operative, preponderating, principal, ruling

prevalence *noun* = **commonness**, acceptance, common occurrence, currency, frequency, pervasiveness, popularity, profusion, regularity, ubiquity, universality

prevalent *adjective* = **common**, accepted, commonplace, current, customary, established, everyday, extensive, frequent, general, habitual, popular, rampant, rife, ubiquitous, universal, usual, widespread
➤ **Antonyms**
confined, infrequent, limited, localized, rare, restricted, uncommon, unusual

prevaricate *verb* = **evade**, beat about the bush, beg the question, cavil, deceive, dodge, equivocate, flannel (*Brit. informal*), give a false colour to, hedge, lie, palter, quibble, shift, shuffle, stretch the truth, tergiversate
➤ **Antonyms**
be blunt, be direct, be frank, be straightforward, come straight to the point, not beat about the bush

prevarication *noun* = **evasion**, cavilling, deceit, deception, equivocation, falsehood, falsification, lie, misrepresentation, pretence, quibbling, tergiversation, untruth

prevent *verb* = **stop**, anticipate, avert, avoid, balk, bar, block, check, counteract, defend against, foil, forestall, frustrate, hamper, head off, hinder, impede, inhibit, intercept, nip in the bud, obstruct, obviate, preclude, restrain, stave off, thwart, ward off
➤ **Antonyms**
allow, encourage, help, incite, permit,

support, urge

prevention noun = **elimination**, anticipation, avoidance, deterrence, forestalling, obviation, precaution, preclusion, prophylaxis, safeguard, thwarting

preventive, preventative adjective **1** = **hindering**, hampering, impeding, obstructive **2** = **protective**, counteractive, deterrent, inhibitory, precautionary, prophylactic, shielding ♦ noun **3** = **hindrance**, block, impediment, obstacle, obstruction **4** = **protection**, deterrent, neutralizer, prevention, prophylactic, protective, remedy, safeguard, shield

preview noun **1** = **sample**, advance showing, foretaste, sneak preview, taster, trailer ♦ verb **2** = **sample**, foretaste, taste

previous adjective **1** = **earlier**, antecedent, anterior, erstwhile, ex-, foregoing, former, one-time, past, preceding, prior, quondam, sometime **2** Informal = **premature**, ahead of oneself, precipitate, too early, too soon, untimely
➤ **Antonyms**
≠**earlier**: consequent, following, later, subsequent, succeeding

previously adverb = **before**, at one time, a while ago, beforehand, earlier, formerly, heretofore, hitherto, in advance, in anticipation, in days or years gone by, in the past, once, then, until now

prey noun **1** = **quarry**, game, kill **2** = **victim**, dupe, fall guy (informal), mark, mug (Brit. slang), target ♦ verb **3** = **hunt**, devour, eat, feed upon, live off, seize **4** = **worry**, burden, distress, hang over, haunt, oppress, trouble, weigh down, weigh heavily **5** = **victimize**, blackmail, bully, exploit, intimidate, take advantage of, terrorize

price noun **1** = **cost**, amount, asking price, assessment, bill, charge, damage (informal), estimate, expenditure, expense, face value, fee, figure, outlay, payment, rate, valuation, value, worth **2** = **consequences**, cost, penalty, sacrifice, toll **3 at any price** = **whatever the cost**, anyhow, cost what it may, expense no object, no matter what the cost, regardless ♦ verb **4** = **evaluate**, assess, cost, estimate, put a price on, rate, value

priceless adjective **1** = **valuable**, beyond price, cherished, costly, dear, expensive, incalculable, incomparable, inestimable, invaluable, irreplaceable, precious, prized, rare, rich, treasured, worth a king's ransom, worth one's or its weight in gold **2** Informal = **hilarious**, absurd, amusing, comic, droll, funny, killing (informal),

rib-tickling, ridiculous, riotous, side-splitting
➤ **Antonyms**
≠**valuable**: cheap, cheapo (informal), common, inexpensive, worthless

pricey, pricy adjective = **expensive**, costly, dear, high-priced, steep (informal)

prick verb **1** = **pierce**, bore, impale, jab, lance, perforate, pink, punch, puncture, stab **2** = **sting**, bite, itch, prickle, smart, tingle **3** = **distress**, cut, grieve, move, pain, stab, touch, trouble, wound **4** usually with **up** = **raise**, point, rise, stand erect ♦ noun **5** = **puncture**, cut, gash, hole, perforation, pinhole, wound **6** = **pang**, gnawing, prickle, smart, spasm, sting, twinge

prickle noun **1** = **spike**, barb, needle, point, spine, spur, thorn **2** = **tingling**, chill, goose bumps, goose flesh, pins and needles (informal), smart, tickle, tingle ♦ verb **3** = **tingle**, itch, smart, sting, twitch **4** = **prick**, jab, nick, stick

prickly adjective **1** = **spiny**, barbed, brambly, briery, bristly, thorny **2** = **itchy**, crawling, pricking, prickling, scratchy, sharp, smarting, stinging, tingling **3** = **irritable**, bad-tempered, cantankerous, edgy, fractious, grumpy, liverish, peevish, pettish, petulant, ratty (Brit. & N.Z. informal), shirty (slang, chiefly Brit.), snappish, stroppy (Brit. slang), tetchy, touchy, waspish

pride noun **1** = **satisfaction**, delight, gratification, joy, pleasure **2** = **self-respect**, amour-propre, dignity, honour, self-esteem, self-worth **3** = **conceit**, arrogance, bigheadedness (informal), egotism, haughtiness, hauteur, hubris, loftiness, morgue, presumption, pretension, pretentiousness, self-importance, self-love, smugness, snobbery, superciliousness, vainglory, vanity **4** = **gem**, boast, jewel, pride and joy, prize, treasure **5** = **elite**, best, choice, cream, flower, glory, pick ♦ verb **6 pride oneself on** = **be proud of**, boast of, brag about, congratulate oneself on, crow about, exult in, flatter oneself, glory in, revel in, take pride in
➤ **Antonyms**
noun ≠**conceit**: humility, meekness, modesty

priest noun = **clergyman**, churchman, cleric, curate, divine, ecclesiastic, father, father confessor, holy man, man of God, man of the cloth, minister, padre (informal), pastor, vicar

priestly adjective = **ecclesiastic**, canonical, clerical, pastoral, priestlike, sacerdotal

prig noun = **goody-goody** (informal), Holy

Joe (*informal*), Holy Willie (*informal*), Mrs Grundy, old maid (*informal*), pedant, prude, puritan, stuffed shirt (*informal*)

priggish *adjective* = **self-righteous**, goody-goody (*informal*), holier-than-thou, narrow-minded, pedantic, prim, prudish, puritanical, self-satisfied, smug, starchy (*informal*), stiff, stuffy

prim *adjective* = **prudish**, demure, fastidious, formal, fussy, niminy-piminy, old-maidish (*informal*), particular, precise, priggish, prissy (*informal*), proper, puritanical, schoolmarmish (*Brit. informal*), starchy (*informal*), stiff, strait-laced
➤ Antonyms
carefree, casual, easy-going, informal, laid-back, relaxed

primacy *noun* = **supremacy**, ascendancy, command, dominance, dominion, leadership, pre-eminence, superiority

prima donna *noun* = **diva**, leading lady, star

primal *adjective* 1 = **first**, earliest, initial, original, primary, prime, primitive, primordial 2 = **chief**, central, first, greatest, highest, main, major, most important, paramount, prime, principal

primarily *adverb* 1 = **chiefly**, above all, basically, especially, essentially, for the most part, fundamentally, generally, largely, mainly, mostly, on the whole, principally 2 = **at first**, at or from the start, first and foremost, initially, in the beginning, in the first place, originally

primary *adjective* 1 = **chief**, best, capital, cardinal, dominant, first, greatest, highest, leading, main, paramount, prime, principal, top 2 = **elementary**, introductory, rudimentary, simple 3 = **basic**, beginning, bog-standard (*informal*), elemental, essential, fundamental, radical, ultimate, underlying
➤ Antonyms
≠chief: inferior, lesser, lowest, subordinate, supplementary, unimportant ≠elementary: ensuing, following, later, secondary, subsequent, succeeding

prime *adjective* 1 = **main**, chief, leading, predominant, pre-eminent, primary, principal, ruling, senior 2 = **best**, capital, choice, excellent, first-class, first-rate, grade A, highest, quality, select, selected, superior, top ♦ *noun* 3 = **peak**, best days, bloom, flower, full flowering, height, heyday, maturity, perfection, zenith ♦ *verb* 4 = **inform**, brief, clue in (*informal*), fill in (*informal*), gen up (*Brit. informal*), give someone the lowdown (*informal*), notify, tell 5 = **prepare**, break in, coach, fit, get ready, groom, make

ready, train

primeval, primaeval *adjective* = **earliest**, ancient, early, first, old, original, prehistoric, primal, primitive, primordial, pristine

primitive *adjective* 1 = **early**, earliest, elementary, first, original, primary, primeval, primordial, pristine 2 = **crude**, rough, rude, rudimentary, simple, unrefined
➤ Antonyms
≠early: advanced, later, modern ≠crude: comfortable, elaborate, refined

primordial *adjective* = **primeval**, earliest, first, prehistoric, primal, primitive, pristine

primp *verb* = **preen**, deck out, doll up (*slang*), dress up

prince *noun* = **ruler**, lord, monarch, potentate, sovereign

princely *adjective* 1 = **regal**, august, dignified, grand, high-born, imperial, imposing, lofty, magnificent, majestic, noble, royal, sovereign, stately 2 = **generous**, bounteous, bountiful, gracious, lavish, liberal, magnanimous, munificent, open-handed, rich

principal *adjective* 1 = **main**, arch, capital, cardinal, chief, controlling, dominant, essential, first, foremost, highest, key, leading, most important, paramount, pre-eminent, primary, prime, strongest ♦ *noun* 2 = **headmaster** or **headmistress**, dean, director, head (*informal*), head teacher, master or mistress, rector 3 = **head**, boss (*informal*), chief, director, leader, master, ruler, superintendent 4 = **star**, first violin, lead, leader 5 = **capital**, assets, capital funds, money
➤ Antonyms
adjective ≠main: auxiliary, inferior, minor, subordinate, subsidiary, supplementary

principally *adverb* = **mainly**, above all, chiefly, especially, first and foremost, for the most part, in the main, largely, mostly, particularly, predominantly, primarily

principle *noun* 1 = **rule**, assumption, axiom, canon, criterion, dictum, doctrine, dogma, ethic, formula, fundamental, golden rule, law, maxim, moral law, precept, proposition, standard, truth, verity 2 = **morals**, conscience, integrity, probity, rectitude, scruples, sense of duty, sense of honour, uprightness 3 **in principle** = **in theory**, ideally, in essence, theoretically

principled *adjective* = **moral**, conscientious, correct, decent, ethical, high-minded, honourable, just, righteous, right-minded, scrupulous, upright, virtuous

prink *verb* **1** = **dress up**, deck, dress to kill (*informal*), dress (up) to the nines (*informal*) **2** = **preen**, adorn, doll up (*slang*), groom, primp, titivate

print *verb* **1** = **publish**, engrave, go to press, impress, imprint, issue, mark, put to bed (*informal*), run off, stamp ♦ *noun* **2** = **publication**, book, magazine, newspaper, newsprint, periodical, printed matter, typescript, zine (*informal*) **3 in print: a** = **published**, in black and white, on paper, on the streets, out, printed **b** = **available**, current, in the shops, obtainable, on the market, on the shelves **4 out of print** = **unavailable**, no longer published, o.p., unobtainable **5** = **reproduction**, copy, engraving, photo (*informal*), photograph, picture **6** = **typeface**, characters, face, font (*chiefly U.S.*), fount, lettering, letters, type

prior *adjective* **1** = **earlier**, foregoing, former, preceding, pre-existent, pre-existing, previous **2 prior to** = **before**, earlier than, preceding, previous to

priority *noun* = **precedence**, first concern, greater importance, pre-eminence, preference, prerogative, rank, right of way, seniority, superiority, supremacy, the lead

priory *noun* = **monastery**, abbey, cloister, convent, nunnery, religious house

prison *noun* = **jail**, calaboose (*U.S. informal*), can (*slang*), choky (*slang*), clink (*slang*), confinement, cooler (*slang*), dungeon, glasshouse (*Military informal*), jug (*slang*), lockup, nick (*Brit. slang*), penal institution, penitentiary (*U.S.*), poky *or* pokey (*U.S. & Canad. slang*), pound, quod (*slang*), slammer (*slang*), stir (*slang*)

prisoner *noun* **1** = **convict**, con (*slang*), jailbird, lag (*slang*) **2** = **captive**, detainee, hostage, internee

prissy *adjective* = **prim**, old-maidish (*informal*), prim and proper, prudish, strait-laced

pristine *adjective* **1** = **new**, immaculate, pure, uncorrupted, undefiled, unspoiled, unsullied, untouched, virginal **2** = **original**, earliest, first, former, initial, primal, primary, primeval, primitive, primordial

privacy *noun* **1** = **seclusion**, isolation, privateness, retirement, retreat, separateness, sequestration, solitude **2** = **secrecy**, clandestineness, concealment, confidentiality

private *adjective* **1** = **exclusive**, individual, intimate, own, particular, personal, reserved, special **2** = **secret**, clandestine, closet, confidential, covert, hush-hush (*informal*), in camera, inside, off the record, privy (*archaic*), unofficial **3**

= **nonpublic**, independent **4** = **secluded**, concealed, isolated, not overlooked, retired, secret, separate, sequestered **5** = **solitary**, withdrawn **6 in private** = **in secret**, behind closed doors, confidentially, in camera, personally, privately ♦ *noun* **7** = **enlisted man** (*U.S.*), private soldier, squaddie *or* squaddy (*Brit. slang*), tommy (*Brit. informal*), Tommy Atkins (*Brit. informal*)

➤ **Antonyms**
adjective ≠**exclusive**: common, general, open, public, unlimited, unrestricted ≠**secret**: disclosed, known, official, open, public, revealed ≠**secluded**: bustling, busy, frequented, unsecluded ≠**solitary**: outgoing, sociable

privation *noun Formal* = **want**, destitution, distress, hardship, indigence, lack, loss, misery, necessity, need, neediness, penury, poverty, suffering

privilege *noun* = **right**, advantage, benefit, birthright, claim, concession, due, entitlement, franchise, freedom, immunity, liberty, prerogative, sanction

privileged *adjective* **1** = **special**, advantaged, elite, entitled, favoured, honoured, indulged, powerful, ruling **2** = **allowed**, empowered, exempt, free, granted, licensed, sanctioned, vested

privy *adjective* **1** *Archaic* = **secret**, confidential, hidden, hush-hush (*informal*), off the record, personal, private **2 privy to** = **informed of**, apprised of, aware of, cognizant of, in on, in the know about (*informal*), in the loop, wise to (*slang*) ♦ *noun* **3** *Obsolete* = **lavatory**, latrine, outside toilet

prize[1] *noun* **1** = **reward**, accolade, award, honour, premium, trophy **2** = **winnings**, haul, jackpot, purse, stakes, windfall **3** = **goal**, aim, ambition, conquest, desire, gain, Holy Grail (*informal*), hope ♦ *adjective* **4** = **champion**, award-winning, best, first-rate, outstanding, top, top-notch (*informal*), winning

prize[2] *verb* = **value**, appreciate, cherish, esteem, hold dear, regard highly, set store by, treasure

prizefighter *noun* = **boxer**, fighter, pugilist

probability *noun* = **likelihood**, chance(s), expectation, liability, likeliness, odds, presumption, prospect

probable *adjective* = **likely**, apparent, credible, feasible, most likely, odds-on, on the cards, ostensible, plausible, possible, presumable, presumed, reasonable, seeming, verisimilar

➤ **Antonyms**
doubtful, improbable, not likely, unlikely

probably *adverb* = **likely**, as likely as not, doubtless, in all likelihood, in all probability, maybe, most likely, perchance (*archaic*), perhaps, possibly, presumably

probation *noun* = **trial period**, apprenticeship, examination, initiation, novitiate, test, trial

probe *verb* 1 = **examine**, explore, go into, investigate, look into, query, research, scrutinize, search, sift, sound, test, verify, work over 2 = **explore**, feel around, poke, prod ♦ *noun* 3 = **examination**, detection, exploration, inquest, inquiry, investigation, research, scrutiny, study

probity *noun Formal* = **integrity**, goodness, honesty, honour, morality, rectitude, righteousness, sincerity, trustworthiness, truthfulness, uprightness, virtue, worth

problem *noun* 1 = **difficulty**, can of worms (*informal*), complication, dilemma, disagreement, dispute, disputed point, doubt, Gordian knot, hard nut to crack (*informal*), how-do-you-do (*informal*), point at issue, predicament, quandary, trouble 2 = **puzzle**, brain-teaser (*informal*), conundrum, enigma, poser, question, riddle, teaser ♦ *adjective* 3 = **difficult**, delinquent, intractable, uncontrollable, unmanageable, unruly

problematic *adjective* = **tricky**, chancy (*informal*), debatable, doubtful, dubious, enigmatic, moot, open to doubt, problematical, puzzling, questionable, uncertain, unsettled
➤ **Antonyms**
beyond question, certain, clear, definite, indisputable, settled, undebatable, unquestionable

procedure *noun* = **method**, action, conduct, course, custom, form, formula, modus operandi, operation, performance, plan of action, policy, practice, process, routine, scheme, step, strategy, system, transaction

proceed *verb* 1 = **go on**, advance, carry on, continue, get going, get on with, get under way with, go ahead, make a start, move on, press on, progress, set in motion 2 = **arise**, come, derive, emanate, ensue, flow, follow, issue, originate, result, spring, stem
➤ **Antonyms**
≠go on: break off, cease, discontinue, end, get behind, halt, leave off, pack in (*Brit. informal*), retreat, stop

proceeding *noun* 1 = **action**, act, course of action, deed, measure, move, occurrence, procedure, process, step, undertaking, venture 2 **proceedings** = **business**, account, affairs, annals, archives, dealings, doings, matters, minutes, records, report, transactions

proceeds *plural noun* = **income**, earnings, gain, produce, products, profit, receipts, returns, revenue, takings, yield

process *noun* 1 = **procedure**, action, course, course of action, manner, means, measure, method, mode, operation, performance, practice, proceeding, system, transaction 2 = **development**, advance, course, evolution, formation, growth, movement, progress, progression, stage, step, unfolding ♦ *verb* 3 = **handle**, deal with, dispose of, fulfil, take care of 4 = **prepare**, alter, convert, refine, transform, treat

procession *noun* 1 = **parade**, cavalcade, column, cortege, file, march, motorcade, train 2 = **sequence**, course, cycle, run, series, string, succession, train

proclaim *verb* = **declare**, advertise, affirm, announce, blaze (abroad), blazon (abroad), circulate, enunciate, give out, herald, indicate, make known, profess, promulgate, publish, shout from the housetops (*informal*), show, trumpet
➤ **Antonyms**
conceal, hush up, keep back, keep secret, suppress, withhold

proclamation *noun* = **declaration**, announcement, decree, edict, manifesto, notice, notification, promulgation, pronouncement, pronunciamento, publication

proclivity *noun Formal* = **tendency**, bent, bias, disposition, inclination, leaning, liableness, penchant, predilection, predisposition, proneness, propensity, weakness

procrastinate *verb* = **delay**, adjourn, be dilatory, dally, defer, drag one's feet (*informal*), gain time, play a waiting game, play for time, postpone, prolong, protract, put off, retard, stall, temporize
➤ **Antonyms**
advance, expedite, get on with, hasten, hurry (up), proceed, speed up

procrastination *noun* = **delay**, dilatoriness, hesitation, slackness, slowness, temporization *or* temporisation

procreate *verb Formal* = **reproduce**, beget, breed, bring into being, engender, father, mother, produce

procure *verb* = **obtain**, acquire, appropriate, buy, come by, earn, effect, find, gain, get, get hold of, land, lay hands on, manage to get, pick up, purchase, score (*slang*), secure, win

procurer *or* **procuress** *noun* = **pimp**,

bawd (*archaic*), madam, pander, panderer, white-slaver, whoremaster (*archaic*)

prod *verb* **1** = **poke**, dig, drive, elbow, jab, nudge, prick, propel, push, shove **2** = **prompt**, egg on, goad, impel, incite, motivate, move, put a bomb under (*informal*), rouse, spur, stimulate, stir up, urge ♦ *noun* **3** = **poke**, boost, dig, elbow, jab, nudge, push, shove **4** = **prompt**, boost, cue, reminder, signal, stimulus **5** = **goad**, poker, spur, stick

prodigal *adjective* **1** = **extravagant**, excessive, immoderate, improvident, intemperate, profligate, reckless, spendthrift, squandering, wanton, wasteful **2** *often with* **of** = **lavish**, bounteous, bountiful, profuse ♦ *noun* **3** = **spendthrift**, big spender, profligate, squanderer, wastrel
➤ **Antonyms**
adjective ≠**extravagant**: economical, frugal, miserly, parsimonious, sparing, stingy, thrifty, tight ≠**lavish**: deficient, lacking, meagre, scanty, scarce, short, sparse

prodigality *noun* **1** = **wastefulness**, abandon, dissipation, excess, extravagance, immoderation, intemperance, profligacy, recklessness, squandering, wantonness, waste **2** = **lavishness**, bounteousness, profusion

prodigious *adjective* **1** = **huge**, colossal, enormous, giant, gigantic, immeasurable, immense, inordinate, mammoth, massive, monstrous, monumental, stellar (*informal*), stupendous, tremendous, vast **2** = **wonderful**, abnormal, amazing, astounding, dramatic, exceptional, extraordinary, fabulous, fantastic (*informal*), flabbergasting (*informal*), impressive, marvellous, miraculous, phenomenal, remarkable, staggering, startling, striking, stupendous, unusual
➤ **Antonyms**
≠**huge**: negligible, small, tiny ≠**wonderful**: normal, ordinary, unexceptional, unimpressive, unremarkable, usual

prodigy *noun* **1** = **genius**, brainbox, child genius, mastermind, talent, whizz (*informal*), whizz kid (*informal*), wizard, wonder child, wunderkind **2** = **wonder**, marvel, miracle, one in a million, phenomenon, rare bird (*informal*), sensation

produce *verb* **1** = **cause**, bring about, effect, generate, give rise to, make for, occasion, provoke, set off **2** = **show**, advance, bring forward, bring to light, demonstrate, exhibit, offer, present, put forward, set forth **3** = **yield**, afford, engender, furnish, give, render, supply **4** = **make**, compose, construct, create, develop, fabricate, invent, manufacture, originate, put together, turn out **5** = **bring forth**, bear, beget, breed, deliver **6** = **present**, direct, do, exhibit, mount, put before the public, put on, show, stage ♦ *noun* **7** = **fruit and vegetables**, crop, greengrocery, harvest, product, yield

producer *noun* **1** = **director**, impresario, *régisseur* **2** = **maker**, farmer, grower, manufacturer

product *noun* **1** = **goods**, artefact, commodity, concoction, creation, invention, merchandise, produce, production, work **2** = **result**, consequence, effect, end result, fruit, issue, legacy, offshoot, outcome, returns, spin-off, upshot, yield

production *noun* **1** = **producing**, assembly, construction, creation, fabrication, formation, making, manufacture, manufacturing, origination, preparation **2** = **presentation**, direction, management, staging

productive *adjective* **1** = **fertile**, creative, dynamic, energetic, fecund, fruitful, generative, inventive, plentiful, producing, prolific, rich, teeming, vigorous **2** = **useful**, advantageous, beneficial, constructive, effective, fruitful, gainful, gratifying, profitable, rewarding, valuable, worthwhile
➤ **Antonyms**
≠**fertile**: barren, poor, sterile, unfertile, unfruitful, unproductive ≠**useful**: unproductive, unprofitable, useless

productivity *noun* = **output**, abundance, mass production, production, productive capacity, productiveness, work rate, yield

profane *adjective* **1** = **sacrilegious**, disrespectful, godless, heathen, idolatrous, impious, impure, irreligious, irreverent, pagan, sinful, ungodly, wicked **2** = **secular**, lay, temporal, worldly **3** = **crude**, abusive, blasphemous, coarse, filthy, foul, obscene, vulgar ♦ *verb* **4** = **desecrate**, abuse, commit sacrilege, contaminate, debase, defile, misuse, pervert, pollute, prostitute, violate, vitiate
➤ **Antonyms**
adjective ≠**sacrilegious**: clean, holy, proper, religious, respectful, reverent, sacred, spiritual

profanity *noun* **1** = **sacrilege**, blasphemy, impiety, profaneness **2** = **swearing**, abuse, curse, cursing, execration, foul language, four-letter word, imprecation, irreverence, malediction, obscenity, swearword

profess verb 1 = **claim**, act as if, allege, call oneself, dissemble, fake, feign, let on, make out, pretend, purport, sham 2 = **state**, acknowledge, admit, affirm, announce, assert, asseverate, aver, avow, certify, confess, confirm, declare, maintain, own, proclaim, vouch

professed adjective 1 = **supposed**, alleged, apparent, ostensible, pretended, purported, self-styled, so-called, soi-disant, would-be 2 = **declared**, avowed, certified, confessed, confirmed, proclaimed, self-acknowledged, self-confessed

profession noun 1 = **occupation**, business, calling, career, employment, line, line of work, métier, office, position, sphere, vocation, walk of life 2 = **declaration**, acknowledgment, affirmation, assertion, attestation, avowal, claim, confession, statement, testimony, vow

professional adjective 1 = **expert**, ace (informal), adept, competent, crack (slang), efficient, experienced, finished, masterly, polished, practised, proficient, qualified, skilled, slick, trained ♦ noun 2 = **expert**, adept, authority, buff (informal), dab hand (Brit. informal), guru, hotshot (informal), maestro, master, maven (U.S.), past master, pro (informal), specialist, virtuoso, whizz (informal), wizard
➤ **Antonyms**
adjective ≠**expert**: amateurish, incapable, incompetent, inefficient, inept, inexperienced, unpolished, unqualified, unskilled, untrained

professor noun = **don** (Brit.), fellow (Brit.), head of faculty, prof (informal)

proffer verb Formal = **offer**, extend, hand, hold out, present, propose, propound, submit, suggest, tender, volunteer

proficiency noun = **skill**, ability, accomplishment, aptitude, competence, craft, dexterity, expertise, expertness, facility, knack, know-how (informal), mastery, skilfulness, talent

proficient adjective = **skilled**, able, accomplished, adept, apt, capable, clever, competent, conversant, efficient, experienced, expert, gifted, masterly, qualified, skilful, talented, trained, versed
➤ **Antonyms**
bad, incapable, incompetent, inept, unaccomplished, unskilled

profile noun 1 = **outline**, contour, drawing, figure, form, portrait, shape, side view, silhouette, sketch 2 = **biography**, characterization, character sketch, sketch, thumbnail sketch, vignette

profit noun 1 often plural = **earnings**, boot (dialect), bottom line, emoluments, gain, percentage (informal), proceeds, receipts, return, revenue, surplus, takings, winnings, yield 2 = **benefit**, advancement, advantage, avail, gain, good, interest, mileage (informal), use, value ♦ verb 3 = **benefit**, aid, avail, be of advantage to, better, contribute, gain, help, improve, promote, serve, stand in good stead 4 = **capitalize on**, cash in on (informal), exploit, make capital of, make good use of, make the most of, put to good use, reap the benefit of, take advantage of, turn to advantage or account, use, utilize 5 = **make money**, clean up (informal), clear, earn, gain, make a good thing of (informal), make a killing (informal), rake in (informal)

profitable adjective 1 = **money-making**, commercial, cost-effective, fruitful, gainful, lucrative, paying, remunerative, rewarding, worthwhile 2 = **beneficial**, advantageous, economic, expedient, fruitful, productive, rewarding, serviceable, useful, valuable, worthwhile
➤ **Antonyms**
disadvantageous, fruitless, unremunerative, unrewarding, useless, vain, worthless

profiteer noun 1 = **racketeer**, exploiter ♦ verb 2 = **exploit**, fleece, make a quick buck (slang), make someone pay through the nose, overcharge, racketeer, skin (slang), sting (informal)

profligacy noun 1 = **extravagance**, excess, improvidence, lavishness, prodigality, recklessness, squandering, waste, wastefulness 2 = **immorality**, abandon, corruption, debauchery, degeneracy, depravity, dissipation, dissoluteness, laxity, libertinism, licentiousness, promiscuity, wantonness

profligate adjective 1 = **extravagant**, immoderate, improvident, prodigal, reckless, spendthrift, squandering, wasteful 2 = **depraved**, abandoned, corrupt, debauched, degenerate, dissipated, dissolute, immoral, iniquitous, libertine, licentious, loose, promiscuous, shameless, sink, unprincipled, vicious, vitiated, wanton, wicked, wild ♦ noun 3 = **spendthrift**, prodigal, squanderer, waster, wastrel 4 = **degenerate**, debauchee, dissipater, libertine, rake, reprobate, roué, swinger (slang)
➤ **Antonyms**
adjective ≠**depraved**: chaste, decent, moral, principled, pure, upright, virginal, virtuous

profound adjective 1 = **wise**, abstruse,

deep, discerning, erudite, learned, penetrating, philosophical, recondite, sagacious, sage, serious, skilled, subtle, thoughtful, weighty **2** = **sincere**, abject, acute, deeply felt, extreme, great, heartfelt, heartrending, hearty, intense, keen **3** = **complete**, absolute, consummate, exhaustive, extensive, extreme, far-reaching, intense, out-and-out, pronounced, serious (*informal*), thoroughgoing, total, unqualified, utter **4** = **deep**, abysmal, bottomless, cavernous, fathomless, yawning
➤ **Antonyms**
≠**wise**: imprudent, stupid, thoughtless, uneducated, uninformed, unknowledgeable, unwise ≠**sincere**: insincere, shallow ≠**complete**: slight, superficial

profoundly *adverb* = **greatly**, abjectly, acutely, deeply, extremely, from the bottom of one's heart, heartily, intensely, keenly, seriously, sincerely, thoroughly, to the core, to the nth degree, very

profundity *noun* = **insight**, acuity, erudition, intelligence, learning, penetration, perceptiveness, perspicacity, perspicuity, sagacity, wisdom

profuse *adjective* **1** = **plentiful**, abundant, ample, bountiful, copious, luxuriant, overflowing, prolific, teeming **2** = **extravagant**, excessive, exuberant, fulsome, generous, immoderate, lavish, liberal, open-handed, prodigal, unstinting
➤ **Antonyms**
≠**plentiful**: deficient, inadequate, meagre, scanty, scarce, skimpy, sparse ≠**extravagant**: frugal, illiberal, moderate, provident, thrifty

profusion *noun* = **abundance**, bounty, copiousness, cornucopia, excess, extravagance, exuberance, glut, lavishness, luxuriance, multitude, oversupply, plenitude, plethora, prodigality, quantity, riot, superabundance, superfluity, surplus, wealth

progenitor *noun* **1** = **ancestor**, forebear, forefather, parent, primogenitor **2** = **originator**, instigator, source

progeny *noun* = **children**, breed, descendants, family, issue, lineage, offspring, posterity, race, scions, seed (*chiefly biblical*), stock, young

prognosis *noun* = **forecast**, diagnosis, prediction, prognostication, projection

prognosticate *verb* **1** = **foretell**, divine, forecast, predict, presage, prophesy **2** = **indicate**, betoken, forebode, foreshadow, point to, portend, presage

prognostication *noun* = **prediction**, forecast, prognosis, projection, prophecy, speculation

programme *noun* **1** = **schedule**, agenda, curriculum, line-up, list, listing, list of players, order of events, order of the day, plan, syllabus, timetable **2** = **show**, broadcast, performance, presentation, production ♦ *verb* **3** = **schedule**, arrange, line up, list, map out, plan, prearrange, work out

progress *noun* **1** = **development**, advance, advancement, amelioration, betterment, breakthrough, gain, gaining ground, growth, headway, improvement, increase, progression, promotion, step forward **2** = **movement**, advance, course, onward course, passage, progression, way **3** **in progress** = **going on**, being done, happening, occurring, proceeding, taking place, under way ♦ *verb* **4** = **develop**, advance, ameliorate, better, blossom, gain, grow, improve, increase, mature **5** = **move on**, advance, come on, continue, cover ground, forge ahead, gain ground, gather way, get on, go forward, make headway, make inroads (into), make one's way, make strides, proceed, travel
➤ **Antonyms**
noun ≠**development**: decline, failure, recession, regression, relapse, retrogression ≠**movement**: regression, retrogression ♦ *verb* ≠**develop**: decrease, get behind, lose, lose ground, regress, retrogress ≠**move on**: get behind, recede, regress, retrogress

progression *noun* **1** = **progress**, advance, advancement, furtherance, gain, headway, movement forward **2** = **sequence**, chain, course, cycle, order, series, string, succession

progressive *adjective* **1** = **enlightened**, advanced, avant-garde, dynamic, enterprising, forward-looking, go-ahead, liberal, modern, radical, reformist, revolutionary, up-and-coming **2** = **growing**, accelerating, advancing, continuing, continuous, developing, escalating, increasing, intensifying, ongoing

prohibit *verb* **1** = **forbid**, ban, debar, disallow, interdict, outlaw, proscribe, veto **2** = **prevent**, constrain, hamper, hinder, impede, make impossible, obstruct, preclude, restrict, rule out, stop
➤ **Antonyms**
≠**forbid**: allow, authorize, command, consent to, endure, further, give leave, let, license, order, permit, suffer, tolerate

≠**prevent:** allow, let, permit

prohibited *adjective* = **forbidden**, banned, barred, not allowed, off limits, proscribed, taboo, *verboten,* vetoed

prohibition *noun* **1** = **prevention**, constraint, disqualification, exclusion, forbiddance, interdiction, negation, obstruction, restriction **2** = **ban**, bar, boycott, disallowance, embargo, injunction, interdict, proscription, veto

prohibitive *adjective* **1** = **exorbitant**, beyond one's means, excessive, extortionate, high-priced, preposterous, sky-high, steep (*informal*) **2** = **prohibiting**, forbidding, proscriptive, repressive, restraining, restrictive, suppressive

project *noun* **1** = **scheme**, activity, assignment, design, enterprise, job, occupation, plan, programme, proposal, task, undertaking, venture, work ♦ *verb* **2** = **forecast**, calculate, call, estimate, extrapolate, gauge, predetermine, predict, reckon **3** = **stick out**, beetle, bulge, extend, jut, overhang, protrude, stand out

projectile *noun* = **missile**, bullet, rocket, shell

projection *noun* **1** = **protrusion**, bulge, eaves, jut, ledge, overhang, protuberance, ridge, shelf, sill **2** = **forecast**, calculation, computation, estimate, estimation, extrapolation, prediction, reckoning

proletarian *adjective* **1** = **working-class**, cloth-cap (*informal*), common, plebeian ♦ *noun* **2** = **worker**, commoner, Joe Bloggs (*Brit. informal*), man of the people, pleb, plebeian, prole (*derogatory slang, chiefly Brit.*)

proletariat *noun* = **working class**, commonalty, commoners, hoi polloi, labouring classes, lower classes, lower orders, plebs, proles (*derogatory slang, chiefly Brit.*), the common people, the great unwashed (*informal & derogatory*), the herd, the masses, the rabble, wage-earners
➤ **Antonyms**
aristo (*informal*), aristocracy, gentry, nobility, peerage, ruling class, upper class, upper crust (*informal*)

proliferate *verb* = **increase**, breed, burgeon, escalate, expand, grow rapidly, multiply, mushroom, run riot, snowball

proliferation *noun* = **multiplication**, build-up, concentration, escalation, expansion, extension, increase, intensification, spread, step-up (*informal*)

prolific *adjective* = **productive**, abundant, bountiful, copious, fecund, fertile, fruitful, generative, luxuriant, profuse, rank, rich, teeming
➤ **Antonyms**
barren, fruitless, infertile, sterile, unfruitful, unproductive, unprolific

prolix *adjective* = **long-winded**, boring, lengthy, long, long-drawn-out, prolonged, protracted, rambling, tedious, verbose, wordy

prologue *noun* = **introduction**, exordium, foreword, preamble, preface, preliminary, prelude, proem

prolong *verb* = **lengthen**, carry on, continue, delay, drag out, draw out, extend, make longer, perpetuate, protract, spin out, stretch
➤ **Antonyms**
abbreviate, abridge, curtail, cut, cut down, shorten

promenade *noun* **1** = **walkway**, boulevard, esplanade, parade, prom, public walk **2** = **stroll**, airing, constitutional, saunter, turn, walk ♦ *verb* **3** = **stroll**, perambulate, saunter, stretch one's legs, take a walk, walk

prominence *noun* **1** = **conspicuousness**, markedness, outstandingness, precedence, salience, specialness, top billing, weight **2** = **fame**, celebrity, distinction, eminence, greatness, importance, name, notability, pre-eminence, prestige, rank, reputation, standing **3** = **protrusion**, bulge, jutting, projection, protuberance, swelling

prominent *adjective* **1** = **noticeable**, blatant, conspicuous, easily seen, eye-catching, in the foreground, obtrusive, obvious, outstanding, pronounced, remarkable, salient, striking, to the fore, unmistakable **2** = **famous**, big-time (*informal*), celebrated, chief, distinguished, eminent, foremost, important, leading, main, major league (*informal*), notable, noted, outstanding, popular, pre-eminent, renowned, respected, top, well-known, well-thought-of **3** = **jutting**, bulging, hanging over, projecting, protruding, protrusive, protuberant, standing out
➤ **Antonyms**
≠**noticeable:** inconspicuous, indistinct, insignificant, unnoticeable ≠**famous:** insignificant, minor, secondary, undistinguished, unimportant, unknown, unnotable ≠**jutting:** concave, indented, receding

promiscuity *noun* = **licentiousness**, debauchery, immorality, looseness, permissiveness, promiscuousness, wantonness

promiscuous *adjective* **1** = **licentious**, abandoned, debauched, dissipated, dissolute, fast, immoral, lax, libertine,

loose, of easy virtue, profligate, unbridled, unchaste, wanton, wild **2** *Formal* = **mixed**, chaotic, confused, disordered, diverse, heterogeneous, ill-assorted, indiscriminate, intermingled, intermixed, jumbled, mingled, miscellaneous, motley
➤ **Antonyms**
≠**licentious:** chaste, decent, innocent, modest, moral, pure, undefiled, unsullied, vestal, virginal, virtuous ≠**mixed:** homogeneous, identical, neat, ordered, orderly, organized, shipshape, uniform, unmixed

promise *verb* **1** = **guarantee**, assure, contract, cross one's heart, engage, give an undertaking, give one's word, pledge, plight, stipulate, swear, take an oath, undertake, vouch, vow, warrant **2** = **seem likely**, augur, bespeak, betoken, bid fair, denote, give hope of, hint at, hold a probability, hold out hopes of, indicate, lead one to expect, look like, show signs of, suggest ◆ *noun* **3** = **guarantee**, assurance, bond, commitment, compact, covenant, engagement, oath, pledge, undertaking, vow, word, word of honour **4** = **potential**, ability, aptitude, capability, capacity, flair, talent

promising *adjective* **1** = **encouraging**, auspicious, bright, favourable, full of promise, hopeful, likely, propitious, reassuring, rosy **2** = **talented**, able, gifted, likely, rising, up-and-coming
➤ **Antonyms**
≠**encouraging:** discouraging, unauspicious, unfavourable, unpromising

promontory *noun* = **point**, cape, foreland, head, headland, ness (*archaic*), spur

promote *verb* **1** = **help**, advance, aid, assist, back, boost, contribute to, develop, encourage, forward, foster, further, gee up, nurture, stimulate, support **2** = **raise**, aggrandize, dignify, elevate, exalt, honour, kick upstairs (*informal*), prefer, upgrade **3** = **advertise**, beat the drum for (*informal*), hype, plug (*informal*), publicize, puff, push, sell **4** = **work for**, advocate, call attention to, champion, endorse, espouse, popularize, prescribe, push for, recommend, speak for, sponsor, support, urge
➤ **Antonyms**
≠**help:** discourage, hinder, hold back, impede, obstruct, oppose, prevent ≠**raise:** demote, downgrade, lower *or* reduce in rank

promoter *noun* **1** = **organizer**, arranger, entrepreneur, impresario **2** = **supporter**, advocate, campaigner, champion, proponent, upholder

promotion *noun* **1** = **rise**, advancement, aggrandizement, elevation, ennoblement, exaltation, honour, move up, preferment, upgrading **2** = **publicity**, advertising, advertising campaign, ballyhoo (*informal*), hard sell, hype, media hype, plugging (*informal*), propaganda, puffery (*informal*), pushing **3** = **encouragement**, advancement, advocacy, backing, boosting, cultivation, development, espousal, furtherance, progress, support

prompt *verb* **1** = **cause**, call forth, elicit, evoke, give rise to, occasion, provoke **2** = **motivate**, cause, impel, incite, induce, inspire, instigate, move, provoke, spur, stimulate, urge **3** = **remind**, assist, cue, help out, jog the memory, prod, refresh the memory ◆ *adjective* **4** = **immediate**, early, instant, instantaneous, on time, pdq (*slang*), punctual, quick, rapid, speedy, swift, timely, unhesitating **5** = **quick**, alert, brisk, eager, efficient, expeditious, ready, responsive, smart, willing ◆ *adverb* **6** *Informal* = **exactly**, on the dot, promptly, punctually, sharp ◆ *noun* **7** = **reminder**, cue, help, hint, jog, jolt, prod, spur
➤ **Antonyms**
verb ≠**motivate:** deter, discourage, prevent, restrain, talk out of ◆ *adjective* ≠**immediate:** hesitating, late, slow ≠**quick:** inefficient, remiss, slack, tardy, unresponsive

promptly *adverb* = **immediately**, at once, by return, directly, hotfoot, instantly, on the dot, on time, pdq (*slang*), posthaste, pronto (*informal*), punctually, quickly, speedily, swiftly, unhesitatingly

promptness *noun* = **swiftness**, alacrity, alertness, briskness, dispatch, eagerness, haste, promptitude, punctuality, quickness, readiness, speed, willingness

promulgate *verb* = **make known**, advertise, announce, broadcast, circulate, communicate, declare, decree, disseminate, issue, make public, notify, proclaim, promote, publish, spread

prone *adjective* **1** = **liable**, apt, bent, disposed, given, inclined, likely, predisposed, subject, susceptible, tending **2** = **face down**, flat, horizontal, lying down, procumbent, prostrate, recumbent
➤ **Antonyms**
≠**liable:** averse, disinclined, indisposed, not likely, unlikely ≠**face down:** erect, face up, perpendicular, supine, upright, vertical

prong *noun* = **point**, projection, spike, tine, tip

pronounce *verb* **1** = **say**, accent, articulate, enunciate, sound, speak, stress, utter, vocalize, voice **2** = **declare**, affirm, announce, assert, decree, deliver, judge, proclaim

pronounced *adjective* = **noticeable**, broad, clear, conspicuous, decided, definite, distinct, evident, marked, obvious, salient, striking, strong, unmistakable
➤ **Antonyms**
concealed, hidden, imperceptible, inconspicuous, unapparent, unnoticeable, vague

pronouncement *noun* = **announcement**, declaration, decree, dictum, edict, judgment, manifesto, notification, proclamation, promulgation, pronunciamento, statement

pronunciation *noun* = **intonation**, accent, accentuation, articulation, diction, elocution, enunciation, inflection, speech, stress

proof *noun* 1 = **evidence**, attestation, authentication, certification, confirmation, corroboration, demonstration, substantiation, testimony, verification 2 *As in* **put to the proof** = **test**, assay, examination, experiment, ordeal, scrutiny, trial 3 *Printing* = **trial print**, galley, galley proof, page proof, pull, slip, trial impression ♦ *adjective* 4 = **impervious**, impenetrable, repellent, resistant, strong, tight, treated 5 **be proof against** = **withstand**, hold out against, resist, stand firm against, stand up to

prop *verb* 1 = **support**, bolster, brace, buttress, hold up, maintain, shore, stay, sustain, truss, uphold 2 = **rest**, lean, set, stand ♦ *noun* 3 = **support**, brace, buttress, mainstay, stanchion, stay, truss

propaganda *noun* = **information**, advertising, agitprop, ballyhoo (*informal*), brainwashing, disinformation, hype, newspeak, promotion, publicity

propagate *verb* 1 = **spread**, broadcast, circulate, diffuse, disseminate, make known, proclaim, promote, promulgate, publicize, publish, transmit 2 = **reproduce**, beget, breed, engender, generate, increase, multiply, procreate, produce, proliferate
➤ **Antonyms**
≠**spread**: cover up, hide, hush up, keep under wraps, stifle, suppress, withhold

propagation *noun* 1 = **spreading**, circulation, communication, diffusion, dissemination, distribution, promotion, promulgation, spread, transmission 2 = **reproduction**, breeding, generation, increase, multiplication, procreation, proliferation

propel *verb* = **drive**, force, impel, launch, push, send, set in motion, shoot, shove,

start, thrust
➤ **Antonyms**
check, delay, hold back, pull, slow, stop

propensity *noun* = **tendency**, aptness, bent, bias, disposition, inclination, leaning, liability, penchant, predisposition, proclivity, proneness, susceptibility, weakness

proper *adjective* 1 = **suitable**, appropriate, apt, becoming, befitting, fit, fitting, legitimate, meet (*archaic*), right, suited 2 = **correct**, accepted, accurate, conventional, established, exact, formal, kosher (*informal*), orthodox, precise, right 3 = **polite**, *comme il faut*, decent, decorous, *de rigueur*, genteel, gentlemanly, ladylike, mannerly, punctilious, refined, respectable, seemly
➤ **Antonyms**
≠**suitable**: improper, inappropriate, unbecoming, unsuitable ≠**correct**: unconventional, unorthodox, wrong ≠**polite**: coarse, common, crude, discourteous, impolite, indecent, rude, ungentlemanly, unladylike, unrefined, unseemly

properly *adverb* 1 = **suitably**, appropriately, aptly, fittingly, rightly 2 = **correctly**, accurately 3 = **politely**, decently, decorously, respectably
➤ **Antonyms**
≠**suitably**: improperly, inappropriately, inaptly, unfittingly, unsuitably, wrongly ≠**correctly**: improperly, inaccurately, incorrectly, wrongly ≠**politely**: badly, impolitely, improperly, indecently, indecorously

property *noun* 1 = **possessions**, assets, belongings, building(s), capital, chattels, effects, estate, goods, holdings, house(s), means, resources, riches, wealth 2 = **land**, acres, estate, freehold, holding, real estate, real property, realty, title 3 = **quality**, ability, attribute, characteristic, feature, hallmark, idiosyncrasy, mark, peculiarity, trait, virtue

prophecy *noun* = **prediction**, augury, divination, forecast, foretelling, prognosis, prognostication, revelation, second sight, soothsaying, sortilege, vaticination (*rare*)

prophesy *verb* = **predict**, augur, call, divine, forecast, foresee, foretell, forewarn, presage, prognosticate, soothsay, vaticinate (*rare*)

prophet *noun* = **soothsayer**, augur, Cassandra, clairvoyant, diviner, forecaster, oracle, prognosticator, prophesier, seer, sibyl

prophetic *adjective* = **predictive**, augural, divinatory, foreshadowing, mantic, oracular, presaging, prescient, prognostic, sibylline

propinquity *noun Formal* 1 = **nearness**, adjacency, closeness, contiguity, neighbourhood, proximity, vicinity 2 = **relationship**, affiliation, affinity, blood, connection, consanguinity, kindred, kinship, relation, tie, ties of blood

propitiate *verb* = **appease**, conciliate, make peace, mollify, pacify, placate, reconcile, satisfy

propitiation *noun* = **appeasement**, conciliation, mollification, peacemaking, placation, reconciliation

propitious *adjective* 1 = **favourable**, advantageous, auspicious, bright, encouraging, fortunate, full of promise, happy, lucky, opportune, promising, prosperous, rosy, timely 2 = **well-disposed**, benevolent, benign, favourably inclined, friendly, gracious, kind

proponent *noun* = **supporter**, advocate, champion, defender, enthusiast, exponent, partisan, spokesman *or* spokeswoman, upholder

proportion *noun* 1 = **relative amount**, distribution, ratio, relationship 2 = **balance**, agreement, congruity, correspondence, harmony, symmetry 3 = **part**, amount, cut (*informal*), division, fraction, measure, percentage, quota, segment, share 4 **proportions** = **dimensions**, amplitude, breadth, bulk, capacity, expanse, extent, magnitude, measurements, range, scope, size, volume

proportional, proportionate *adjective* = **balanced**, commensurate, comparable, compatible, consistent, correspondent, corresponding, equitable, equivalent, even, in proportion, just
➤ **Antonyms**
different, discordant, disproportionate, dissimilar, incommensurable, incompatible, inconsistent, unequal

proposal *noun* = **suggestion**, bid, design, motion, offer, overture, plan, presentation, proffer, programme, project, proposition, recommendation, scheme, tender, terms

propose *verb* 1 = **put forward**, advance, come up with, present, proffer, propound, submit, suggest, tender 2 = **nominate**, introduce, invite, name, present, put up, recommend 3 = **intend**, aim, design, have every intention, have in mind, mean, plan, purpose, scheme 4 = **offer marriage**, ask for someone's hand (in marriage), pay suit, pop the question (*informal*)

proposition *noun* 1 = **proposal**, motion, plan, programme, project, recommendation, scheme, suggestion

♦ *verb* 2 = **make a pass at**, accost, make an improper suggestion, make an indecent proposal, solicit

propound *verb* = **put forward**, advance, advocate, contend, lay down, postulate, present, propose, set forth, submit, suggest

proprietor, proprietress *noun* = **owner**, deed holder, freeholder, landlord *or* landlady, landowner, possessor, titleholder

propriety *noun* 1 = **correctness**, appropriateness, aptness, becomingness, fitness, rightness, seemliness, suitableness 2 = **decorum**, breeding, courtesy, decency, delicacy, etiquette, good form, good manners, manners, modesty, politeness, protocol, punctilio, rectitude, refinement, respectability, seemliness 3 **the proprieties** = **etiquette**, accepted conduct, amenities, civilities, niceties, rules of conduct, social code, social conventions, social graces, the done thing
➤ **Antonyms**
≠**decorum**: bad form, bad manners, immodesty, impoliteness, indecency, indecorum, indelicacy, vulgarity

propulsion *noun* = **drive**, impetus, impulse, impulsion, momentum, motive power, power, pressure, propelling force, push, thrust

prosaic *adjective* = **dull**, banal, boring, commonplace, dry, everyday, flat, hackneyed, humdrum, matter-of-fact, mundane, ordinary, pedestrian, routine, stale, tame, trite, unimaginative, uninspiring, vapid, workaday
➤ **Antonyms**
entertaining, exciting, extraordinary, fascinating, imaginative, interesting, poetical, unusual

proscribe *verb* 1 = **prohibit**, ban, boycott, censure, condemn, damn, denounce, doom, embargo, forbid, interdict, reject 2 = **outlaw**, attaint (*archaic*), banish, blackball, deport, exclude, excommunicate, exile, expatriate, expel, ostracize
➤ **Antonyms**
≠**prohibit**: allow, authorize, endorse, give leave, give permission, license, permit, sanction, warrant

proscription *noun* 1 = **prohibition**, ban, boycott, censure, condemnation, damning, denunciation, dooming, embargo, interdict, rejection 2 = **banishment**, deportation, ejection, eviction, exclusion, excommunication, exile, expatriation, expulsion, ostracism

prosecute *verb* 1 *Law* = **put on trial**, arraign, bring action against, bring suit against, bring to trial, do (*slang*), indict,

litigate, prefer charges, put in the dock,
seek redress, sue, summon, take to court,
try **2 = conduct**, carry on, direct,
discharge, engage in, manage, perform,
practise, work at **3 = continue**, carry
through, follow through, persevere,
persist, pursue, see through

proselyte *noun* = **convert**, initiate,
neophyte, new believer, novice, tyro

proselytize *verb* = **convert**, bring to God,
evangelize, make converts, spread the
gospel

prospect *noun* **1 = expectation**,
anticipation, calculation, contemplation,
future, hope, odds, opening, outlook,
plan, presumption, probability, promise,
proposal, thought **2** *sometimes plural*
= **likelihood**, chance, possibility **3 = view**,
landscape, outlook, panorama,
perspective, scene, sight, spectacle, vision,
vista ♦ *verb* **4 = look for**, explore, go after,
search for, seek, survey

prospective *adjective* = **future**, about to
be, anticipated, approaching, awaited,
coming, destined, eventual, expected,
forthcoming, hoped-for, imminent,
intended, likely, looked-for, on the cards,
possible, potential, soon-to-be, -to-be, to
come, upcoming

prospectus *noun* = **catalogue**,
announcement, conspectus, list, outline,
plan, programme, scheme, syllabus,
synopsis

prosper *verb* = **succeed**, advance, be
fortunate, bloom, do well, fare well,
flourish, flower, get on, grow rich, make
good, make it (*informal*), progress, thrive

prosperity *noun* = **success**, affluence,
boom, ease, fortune, good fortune, good
times, life of luxury, life of Riley (*informal*),
luxury, plenty, prosperousness, riches, the
good life, wealth, well-being
➤ **Antonyms**
adversity, depression, destitution, failure,
indigence, misfortune, poverty, shortage,
want

prosperous *adjective* **1 = wealthy**, affluent,
in clover (*informal*), in the money
(*informal*), moneyed, opulent, rich,
well-heeled (*informal*), well-off, well-to-do
2 = successful, blooming, booming, doing
well, flourishing, fortunate, lucky, on a roll,
on the up and up (*Brit.*), palmy,
prospering, thriving
➤ **Antonyms**
≠**wealthy**: impoverished, poor
≠**successful**: defeated, failing,
inauspicious, unfavourable, unfortunate,
unlucky, unpromising, unsuccessful,
untimely

prostitute *noun* **1 = whore**, bawd
(*archaic*), brass (*slang*), call girl, camp
follower, cocotte, courtesan, fallen
woman, *fille de joie*, harlot, hooker (*U.S.
slang*), hustler (*U.S. & Canad. slang*), loose
woman, moll (*slang*), pro (*slang*), scrubber
(*Brit. & Austral. slang*), streetwalker,
strumpet, tart (*informal*), trollop, white
slave, working girl (*facetious slang*) ♦ *verb*
2 = cheapen, debase, degrade, demean,
devalue, misapply, pervert, profane

prostitution *noun* = **harlotry**, harlot's
trade, Mrs. Warren's profession,
streetwalking, the game (*slang*), the oldest
profession, vice, whoredom

prostrate *adjective* **1 = prone**, abject,
bowed low, flat, horizontal, kowtowing,
procumbent **2 = exhausted**, at a low ebb,
dejected, depressed, desolate, drained,
fagged out (*informal*), fallen, inconsolable,
overcome, spent, worn out ♦ *verb* **3**
= **exhaust**, drain, fag out (*informal*),
fatigue, sap, tire, wear out, weary **4**
prostrate oneself = **bow down to**, abase
oneself, bend the knee to, bow before,
cast oneself before, cringe, fall at
(someone's) feet, fall on one's knees
before, grovel, kneel, kowtow, submit

prosy *adjective* = **dull**, boring, flat,
humdrum, long, long-drawn-out,
long-winded, monotonous, overlong,
pedestrian, prosaic, tedious, tiresome,
unimaginative, uninteresting, wordy

protagonist *noun* **1 = supporter**,
advocate, champion, exponent, leader,
mainstay, moving spirit, prime mover,
standard-bearer, torchbearer **2 = leading
character**, central character, hero *or*
heroine, lead, principal

protean *adjective* = **changeable**,
ever-changing, many-sided, mercurial,
multiform, mutable, polymorphous,
temperamental, variable, versatile, volatile

protect *verb* = **keep safe**, care for,
chaperon, cover, cover up for, defend,
foster, give sanctuary, guard, harbour,
keep, look after, mount *or* stand guard
over, preserve, safeguard, save, screen,
secure, shelter, shield, stick up for
(*informal*), support, take under one's wing,
watch over
➤ **Antonyms**
assail, assault, attack, betray, endanger,
expose, expose to danger, threaten

protection *noun* **1 = safety**, aegis, care,
charge, custody, defence, guardianship,
guarding, preservation, protecting,
safeguard, safekeeping, security **2**
= **safeguard**, armour, barrier, buffer,
bulwark, cover, guard, refuge, screen,

shelter, shield

protective *adjective* = **protecting**, careful, covering, defensive, fatherly, insulating, jealous, maternal, motherly, paternal, possessive, safeguarding, sheltering, shielding, vigilant, warm, watchful

protector *noun* = **defender**, advocate, benefactor, bodyguard, champion, counsel, guard, guardian, guardian angel, knight in shining armour, patron, safeguard, tower of strength

protégé, protégée *noun* = **charge**, dependant, discovery, pupil, student, ward

protest *noun* **1** = **objection**, complaint, declaration, demur, demurral, disapproval, dissent, formal complaint, outcry, protestation, remonstrance ♦ *verb* **2** = **object**, complain, cry out, demonstrate, demur, disagree, disapprove, expostulate, express disapproval, kick (against) (*informal*), oppose, remonstrate, say no to, take exception, take up the cudgels **3** = **assert**, affirm, argue, asseverate, attest, avow, contend, declare, insist, maintain, profess, testify, vow

protestation *noun Formal* = **declaration**, affirmation, asseveration, avowal, oath, pledge, profession, vow

protester *noun* = **demonstrator**, agitator, dissenter, dissident, protest marcher, rebel

protocol *noun* **1** = **code of behaviour**, conventions, courtesies, customs, decorum, etiquette, formalities, good form, manners, politesse, propriety, p's and q's, rules of conduct **2** = **agreement**, compact, concordat, contract, covenant, pact, treaty

prototype *noun* = **original**, archetype, example, first, mock-up, model, norm, paradigm, pattern, precedent, standard, type

protract *verb* = **extend**, continue, drag on *or* out, draw out, keep going, lengthen, prolong, spin out, stretch out
➤ **Antonyms**
abbreviate, abridge, compress, curtail, reduce, shorten, summarize

protracted *adjective* = **extended**, dragged out, drawn-out, interminable, lengthy, long, long-drawn-out, never-ending, overlong, prolonged, spun out, time-consuming

protrude *verb* = **stick out**, bulge, come through, extend, jut, obtrude, point, pop (*of eyes*), project, shoot out, stand out, start (from), stick out like a sore thumb

protrusion *noun* = **projection**, bulge, bump, hump, jut, lump, outgrowth, protuberance, swelling

protuberance *noun* = **bulge**, bump, excrescence, hump, knob, lump, outgrowth, process, projection, prominence, protrusion, swelling, tumour

protuberant *adjective* = **bulging**, beetling, bulbous, gibbous, hanging over, jutting, popping (*of eyes*), prominent, protruding, protrusive, proud (*dialect*), swelling, swollen
➤ **Antonyms**
concave, flat, indented, receding, sunken

proud *adjective* **1** = **satisfied**, appreciative, content, contented, glad, gratified, honoured, pleased, self-respecting, well-pleased **2** = **conceited**, arrogant, boastful, disdainful, egotistical, haughty, high and mighty (*informal*), imperious, lordly, narcissistic, overbearing, presumptuous, self-important, self-satisfied, snobbish, snooty (*informal*), stuck-up (*informal*), supercilious, toffee-nosed (*slang, chiefly Brit.*), too big for one's boots *or* breeches, vain **3** = **glorious**, exalted, gratifying, illustrious, memorable, pleasing, red-letter, rewarding, satisfying **4** = **distinguished**, august, eminent, grand, great, illustrious, imposing, magnificent, majestic, noble, splendid, stately
➤ **Antonyms**
≠**satisfied**: discontented, displeased, dissatisfied ≠**conceited**: abject, ashamed, deferential, humble, meek, modest, submissive, unobtrusive ≠**distinguished**: base, humble, ignoble, ignominious, lowly, unassuming, undignified

provable *adjective* = **verifiable**, attestable, demonstrable, evincible, testable

prove *verb* **1** = **verify**, ascertain, attest, authenticate, bear out, confirm, corroborate, demonstrate, determine, establish, evidence, evince, justify, show, show clearly, substantiate **2** = **test**, analyse, assay, check, examine, experiment, put to the test, put to trial, try **3** = **turn out**, be found to be, come out, end up, result
➤ **Antonyms**
≠**verify**: discredit, disprove, give the lie to, refute, rule out

proven *adjective* = **established**, attested, confirmed, definite, proved, reliable, tested, verified

provenance *noun* = **origin**, birthplace, derivation, source

provender *noun* = **fodder**, feed, forage

proverb *noun* = **saying**, adage, aphorism, apophthegm, byword, dictum, gnome, maxim, saw

proverbial *adjective* = **conventional**, accepted, acknowledged, archetypal, axiomatic, current, customary, famed, famous, legendary, notorious, self-evident, time-honoured, traditional, typical, unquestioned, well-known

provide *verb* **1 = supply**, accommodate, cater, contribute, equip, furnish, outfit, provision, purvey, stock up **2 = give**, add, afford, bring, impart, lend, present, produce, render, serve, yield **3 provide for** *or* **against = take precautions**, anticipate, arrange for, forearm, get ready, make arrangements, make plans, plan ahead, plan for, prepare for, take measures **4 provide for = support**, care for, keep, look after, maintain, sustain, take care of
➤ **Antonyms**
≠**supply**: deprive, keep back, refuse, withhold ≠**take precautions**: disregard, fail to notice, miss, neglect, overlook ≠**support**: neglect

providence *noun* **1 = fate**, destiny, divine intervention, fortune, God's will, predestination **2 = foresight**, care, caution, discretion, far-sightedness, forethought, perspicacity, presence of mind, prudence

provident *adjective* **1 = thrifty**, economical, frugal, prudent **2 = foresighted**, canny, careful, cautious, discreet, equipped, far-seeing, far-sighted, forearmed, sagacious, shrewd, vigilant, well-prepared, wise
➤ **Antonyms**
≠**thrifty**: improvident, imprudent, prodigal, profligate, spendthrift, uneconomical, wasteful ≠**foresighted**: careless, heedless, improvident, negligent, reckless, short-sighted, thoughtless

providential *adjective* **= lucky**, fortuitous, fortunate, happy, heaven-sent, opportune, timely, welcome

provider *noun* **1 = supplier**, benefactor, donor, giver, source **2 = breadwinner**, earner, mainstay, supporter, wage earner

providing, provided *conjunction* **= on condition that**, as long as, contingent upon, given, if and only if, in case, in the event, on the assumption, subject to, upon these terms, with the proviso, with the understanding

province *noun* **1 = region**, colony, county, department, dependency, district, division, domain, patch, section, territory, tract, turf (*U.S. slang*), zone **2 = area**, business, capacity, charge, concern, duty, employment, field, function, line, orbit, part, pigeon (*Brit. informal*), post, responsibility, role, sphere, turf (*U.S. slang*)

provincial *adjective* **1 = rural**, country, hick (*informal, chiefly U.S. & Canad.*), home-grown, homespun, local, rustic **2**

= parochial, insular, inward-looking, limited, narrow, narrow-minded, parish-pump, small-minded, small-town (*chiefly U.S.*), uninformed, unsophisticated, upcountry ♦ *noun* **3 = yokel**, country cousin, hayseed (*U.S. & Canad. informal*), hick (*informal, chiefly U.S. & Canad.*), rustic
➤ **Antonyms**
adjective ≠**rural**: urban ≠**parochial**: cosmopolitan, fashionable, polished, refined, sophisticated, urbane

provision *noun* **1 = supplying**, accoutrement, catering, equipping, fitting out, furnishing, providing, victualling **2 = condition**, agreement, clause, demand, proviso, requirement, rider, specification, stipulation, term **3** *As in* **make provision for = arrangement**, plan, prearrangement, precaution, preparation

provisional *adjective* **1 = temporary**, interim, pro tem, stopgap, transitional **2 = conditional**, contingent, limited, provisory, qualified, tentative
➤ **Antonyms**
≠**temporary**: permanent ≠**conditional**: definite, fixed

provisions *plural noun* **= food**, comestibles, eatables, eats (*slang*), edibles, fare, feed, foodstuff, groceries, grub (*slang*), nosebag (*slang*), provender, rations, stores, supplies, sustenance, tack (*informal*), viands, victuals, vittles (*obsolete or dialect*)

proviso *noun* **= condition**, clause, limitation, provision, qualification, requirement, reservation, restriction, rider, stipulation, strings

provocation *noun* **1 = cause**, *casus belli*, grounds, incitement, inducement, instigation, justification, motivation, reason, stimulus **2 = offence**, affront, annoyance, challenge, dare, grievance, indignity, injury, insult, red rag, taunt, vexation

provocative *adjective* **1 = offensive**, aggravating (*informal*), annoying, challenging, disturbing, galling, goading, incensing, insulting, outrageous, provoking, stimulating **2 = suggestive**, alluring, arousing, erotic, exciting, inviting, seductive, sexy (*informal*), stimulating, tantalizing, tempting

provoke *verb* **1 = anger**, affront, aggravate (*informal*), annoy, chafe, enrage, exasperate, gall, get in one's hair (*informal*), get one's back up, get on one's nerves (*informal*), hassle (*informal*), incense, infuriate, insult, irk, irritate, madden, make one's blood boil, nark

(*Brit., Austral., & N.Z. slang*), offend, pique, piss one off (*taboo slang*), put one's back up, put out, rile, rub (someone) up the wrong way (*informal*), take a rise out of, try one's patience, vex **2 = rouse**, bring about, bring on *or* down, call forth, cause, draw forth, elicit, evoke, excite, fire, foment, generate, give rise to, incite, induce, inflame, inspire, instigate, kindle, lead to, motivate, move, occasion, precipitate, produce, promote, prompt, stimulate, stir
➤ **Antonyms**
≠**anger**: appease, calm, conciliate, mollify, pacify, placate, propitiate, quiet, soothe, sweeten ≠**rouse**: abate, allay, assuage, blunt, curb, ease, lessen, lull, mitigate, moderate, modify, relieve, temper

provoking *adjective* **= annoying**, aggravating (*informal*), exasperating, galling, irking, irksome, irritating, maddening, obstructive, offensive, tiresome, vexatious, vexing

prow *noun* **= bow(s)**, fore, forepart, front, head, nose, sharp end (*jocular*), stem

prowess *noun* **1 = skill**, ability, accomplishment, adeptness, adroitness, aptitude, attainment, command, dexterity, excellence, expertise, expertness, facility, genius, mastery, talent **2 = bravery**, boldness, courage, daring, dauntlessness, doughtiness, fearlessness, gallantry, hardihood, heroism, intrepidity, mettle, valiance, valour
➤ **Antonyms**
≠**skill**: clumsiness, inability, incapability, incompetence, ineptitude, ineptness, inexpertise ≠**bravery**: cowardice, faint-heartedness, fear, gutlessness, timidity

prowl *verb* **= move stealthily**, cruise, hunt, lurk, nose around, patrol, range, roam, rove, scavenge, skulk, slink, sneak, stalk, steal

proximity *noun* **= nearness**, adjacency, closeness, contiguity, juxtaposition, neighbourhood, propinquity, vicinity

proxy *noun* **= representative**, agent, attorney, delegate, deputy, factor, substitute, surrogate

prude *noun* **= prig**, old maid (*informal*), puritan, schoolmarm (*Brit. informal*)

prudence *noun* **1 = common sense**, canniness, care, caution, circumspection, discretion, good sense, heedfulness, judgment, judiciousness, sagacity, vigilance, wariness, wisdom **2 = thrift**, careful budgeting, economizing, economy, far-sightedness, foresight, forethought, frugality, good management, husbandry, planning, precaution,

preparedness, providence, saving

prudent *adjective* **1 = sensible**, canny, careful, cautious, circumspect, discerning, discreet, judicious, politic, sagacious, sage, shrewd, vigilant, wary, wise **2 = thrifty**, canny, careful, economical, far-sighted, frugal, provident, sparing
➤ **Antonyms**
≠**sensible**: careless, heedless, impolitic, imprudent, inconsiderate, indiscreet, injudicious, irrational, rash, thoughtless, unwise ≠**thrifty**: careless, extravagant, improvident, imprudent, wasteful

prudery *noun* **= primness**, overmodesty, priggishness, prudishness, puritanicalness, squeamishness, starchiness (*informal*), strictness, stuffiness

prudish *adjective* **= prim**, demure, formal, narrow-minded, old-maidish (*informal*), overmodest, overnice, priggish, prissy (*informal*), proper, puritanical, schoolmarmish (*Brit. informal*), squeamish, starchy (*informal*), strait-laced, stuffy, Victorian
➤ **Antonyms**
broad-minded, liberal, open-minded, permissive

prune *verb* **= cut**, clip, cut back, dock, lop, pare down, reduce, shape, shorten, snip, trim

prurient *adjective* **1 = lecherous**, lascivious, libidinous, lustful, salacious **2 = indecent**, dirty, erotic, lewd, obscene, pornographic, salacious, smutty

pry *verb* **= be inquisitive**, be a busybody, be nosy (*informal*), interfere, intrude, meddle, nose into, peep, peer, poke, poke one's nose in *or* into (*informal*), snoop (*informal*)

prying *adjective* **= inquisitive**, curious, eavesdropping, impertinent, interfering, intrusive, meddlesome, meddling, nosy (*informal*), snooping (*informal*), snoopy (*informal*), spying

psalm *noun* **= hymn**, carol, chant, paean, song of praise

pseud *noun Informal* **= poser** (*informal*), fraud, humbug, phoney *or* phony (*informal*), trendy (*Brit. informal*)

pseudo- *adjective* **= false**, artificial, bogus, counterfeit, ersatz, fake, imitation, mock, not genuine, phoney *or* phony (*informal*), pretended, quasi-, sham, spurious
➤ **Antonyms**
actual, authentic, bona fide, genuine, heartfelt, honest, real, sincere, true, unfeigned

pseudonym *noun* **= false name**, alias, assumed name, incognito, nom de guerre, nom de plume, pen name, professional name, stage name

psyche *noun* = **soul**, anima, essential nature, individuality, inner man, innermost self, mind, personality, self, spirit, subconscious, true being

psychedelic *adjective* **1** = **hallucinogenic**, consciousness-expanding, hallucinatory, mind-bending (*informal*), mind-blowing (*informal*), mind-expanding, psychoactive **2** *Informal* = **multicoloured**, crazy, freaky (*slang*), kaleidoscopic, wild

psychiatrist *noun* = **psychotherapist**, analyst, headshrinker (*slang*), psychoanalyser, psychoanalyst, psychologist, shrink (*slang*), therapist

psychic *adjective* **1** = **supernatural**, clairvoyant, extrasensory, mystic, occult, preternatural, telekinetic, telepathic **2** = **mental**, psychogenic, psychological, spiritual

psychological *adjective* **1** = **mental**, cerebral, cognitive, intellectual **2** = **imaginary**, all in the mind, emotional, irrational, psychosomatic, subconscious, subjective, unconscious, unreal

psychology *noun* **1** = **behaviourism**, science of mind, study of personality **2** *Informal* = **way of thinking**, attitude, mental make-up, mental processes, thought processes, what makes one tick

psychopath *noun* = **madman**, headbanger (*informal*), headcase (*informal*), insane person, lunatic, maniac, mental case (*slang*), nutcase (*slang*), nutter (*Brit. slang*), psychotic, sociopath

psychotic *adjective* = **mad**, certifiable, demented, deranged, insane, lunatic, mental (*slang*), *non compos mentis,* not right in the head, off one's chump, off one's head (*slang*), off one's rocker (*slang*), off one's trolley (*slang*), psychopathic, round the bend (*Brit. slang*), unbalanced

pub *or* **public house** *noun* = **tavern**, alehouse (*archaic*), bar, boozer (*Brit., Austral., & N.Z. informal*), hostelry (*archaic or facetious*), inn, local (*Brit. informal*), roadhouse, taproom, watering hole (*facetious slang*)

puberty *noun* = **adolescence**, awkward age, juvenescence, pubescence, teenage, teens, young adulthood

public *adjective* **1** = **general**, civic, civil, common, national, popular, social, state, universal, widespread **2** = **open**, accessible, communal, community, free to all, not private, open to the public, unrestricted **3** = **well-known**, important, prominent, respected **4** = **known**, acknowledged,

exposed, in circulation, notorious, obvious, open, overt, patent, plain, published, recognized ◆ *noun* **5** = **people**, citizens, commonalty, community, country, electorate, everyone, hoi polloi, Joe (and Eileen) Public (*slang*), Joe Six-Pack (*U.S. slang*), masses, multitude, nation, populace, population, society, voters **6** = **clientele**, audience, buyers, followers, following, patrons, supporters, trade
➤ **Antonyms**
adjective ≠**open**: barred, closed, exclusive, inaccessible, personal, private, restricted, unavailable ≠**known**: hidden, secluded, secret, unknown, unrevealed

publication *noun* **1** = **pamphlet**, book, booklet, brochure, handbill, hardback, issue, leaflet, magazine, newspaper, paperback, periodical, title, zine (*informal*) **2** = **announcement**, advertisement, airing, appearance, broadcasting, declaration, disclosure, dissemination, notification, proclamation, promulgation, publishing, reporting

publicity *noun* = **advertising**, attention, ballyhoo (*informal*), boost, build-up, hype, plug (*informal*), press, promotion, public notice

publicize *verb* = **advertise**, bring to public notice, broadcast, give publicity to, hype, make known, play up, plug (*informal*), promote, push, spotlight, write up
➤ **Antonyms**
conceal, contain, cover up, keep dark, keep secret, smother, stifle, suppress, withhold

public-spirited *adjective* = **altruistic**, charitable, community-minded, generous, humanitarian, philanthropic, unselfish

publish *verb* **1** = **put out**, bring out, issue, print, produce **2** = **announce**, advertise, blow wide open (*slang*), broadcast, circulate, communicate, declare, disclose, distribute, divulge, impart, leak, proclaim, promulgate, publicize, reveal, spread

pucker *verb* **1** = **wrinkle**, contract, crease, draw together, gather, knit, purse, screw up, tighten ◆ *noun* **2** = **wrinkle**, crease, fold

pudding *noun* = **dessert**, afters (*Brit. informal*), last course, pud (*informal*), second course, sweet

puerile *adjective* = **childish**, babyish, foolish, immature, inane, infantile, irresponsible, jejune, juvenile, naive, petty, ridiculous, silly, trivial, weak
➤ **Antonyms**
adult, grown-up, mature, responsible, sensible

puff *noun* **1** = **blast**, breath, draught, emanation, flurry, gust, whiff **2** = **smoke**, drag (*slang*), pull ♦ *verb* **3** = **blow**, breathe, exhale, gasp, gulp, pant, wheeze **4** = **smoke**, drag (*slang*), draw, inhale, pull at *or* on, suck **5** *usually with* **up** = **swell**, bloat, dilate, distend, expand, inflate **6** = **promote**, crack up (*informal*), hype, overpraise, plug (*informal*), praise, publicize, push

puffy *adjective* = **swollen**, bloated, distended, enlarged, inflamed, inflated, puffed up

pugilism *noun* = **boxing**, fighting, prizefighting, the noble art *or* science, the ring

pugilist *noun* = **boxer**, bruiser (*informal*), fighter, prizefighter

pugnacious *adjective* = **aggressive**, antagonistic, argumentative, bellicose, belligerent, combative, contentious, hot-tempered, irascible, irritable, quarrelsome
➤ **Antonyms**
calm, conciliatory, gentle, peaceable, peaceful, peace-loving, placatory, placid, quiet

puke *verb Slang* = **vomit**, barf (*U.S. slang*), be nauseated, be sick, chuck (up) (*slang, chiefly U.S.*), chunder (*slang, chiefly Austral.*), disgorge, heave, regurgitate, retch, spew, throw up (*informal*), upchuck (*U.S. slang*)

pukka *adjective Anglo-Indian* = **genuine**, authentic, bona fide, official, on the level (*informal*), proper, real, the real McCoy

pull *verb* **1** = **draw**, drag, haul, jerk, tow, trail, tug, yank **2** = **strain**, dislocate, rend, rip, sprain, stretch, tear, wrench **3** = **extract**, draw out, gather, pick, pluck, remove, take out, uproot, weed **4** *Informal* = **attract**, draw, entice, lure, magnetize **5 pull apart** *or* **to pieces** = **criticize**, attack, blast, find fault, lambast(e), lay into (*informal*), pan (*informal*), pick holes in, put down, run down, slam (*slang*), slate (*informal*), tear into (*informal*) **6 pull oneself together** *Informal* = **get a grip on oneself**, buck up (*informal*), get over it, regain composure, snap out of it (*informal*) ♦ *noun* **7** = **tug**, jerk, twitch, yank **8** = **puff**, drag (*slang*), inhalation **9** *Informal* = **influence**, advantage, bottom, clout (*informal*), leverage, muscle, power, weight **10** = **attraction**, drawing power, effort, exertion, force, forcefulness, influence, lure, magnetism
➤ **Antonyms**
verb ≠**draw**: drive, nudge, push, ram, shove, thrust ≠**extract**: implant, insert, plant ≠**attract**: deter, discourage, put one off, repel ♦ *noun* ≠**tug**: nudge, push, shove, thrust

pull down *verb* = **demolish**, bulldoze, destroy, raze, remove
➤ **Antonyms**
build, construct, erect, put up, raise, set up

pull in *verb* **1** = **draw in**, arrive, come in, draw up, reach, stop **2** = **attract**, bring in, draw **3** *Brit. slang* = **arrest**, bust (*informal*), collar (*informal*), feel one's collar (*slang*), lift (*slang*), nab (*informal*), nail (*informal*), pinch (*informal*), run in (*slang*), take into custody **4** = **earn**, clear, gain, gross, make, net, pocket, take home

pull off *verb Informal* = **succeed**, accomplish, bring off, carry out, crack it (*informal*), cut it (*informal*), do the trick, manage, score a success, secure one's object

pull out *verb* = **withdraw**, abandon, back off, depart, evacuate, leave, quit, rat on, retreat, stop participating

pull through *verb* = **survive**, come through, get better, get over, pull round, rally, recover, turn the corner, weather

pull up *verb* **1** = **stop**, brake, come to a halt, halt, reach a standstill **2** = **uproot**, dig out, lift, raise **3** = **reprimand**, admonish, bawl out (*informal*), carpet (*informal*), castigate, chew out (*U.S. & Canad. informal*), dress down (*informal*), rap over the knuckles, read the riot act, rebuke, reprove, slap on the wrist, take to task, tear into (*informal*), tear (someone) off a strip (*Brit. informal*), tell off (*informal*), tick off (*informal*)

pulp *noun* **1** = **paste**, mash, mush, pap, semiliquid, semisolid, triturate **2** = **flesh**, marrow, soft part ♦ *verb* **3** = **crush**, mash, pulverize, squash ♦ *adjective* **4** = **cheap**, lurid, mushy (*informal*), rubbishy, sensational, trashy

pulpy *adjective* = **soft**, fleshy, mushy, pappy, squashy, succulent

pulsate *verb* = **throb**, beat, palpitate, pound, pulse, quiver, thump

pulse *noun* **1** = **beat**, beating, oscillation, pulsation, rhythm, throb, throbbing, vibration ♦ *verb* **2** = **beat**, pulsate, throb, tick, vibrate

pulverize *verb* **1** = **crush**, granulate, grind, mill, pestle, pound **2** = **defeat**, annihilate, blow out of the water (*slang*), crush, demolish, destroy, flatten, lick (*informal*), smash, stuff (*slang*), tank (*slang*), vanquish, wipe the floor with (*informal*), wreck

pummel *verb* = **beat**, batter, hammer, pound, punch, strike, thump

pump *verb* **1** *often with* **out** = **drive out**, bail out, drain, draw off, empty, force out, siphon **2** *with* **up** = **inflate**, blow up, dilate **3** *often with* **into** = **drive**, force, inject, pour, push, send, supply **4** = **interrogate**, cross-examine, give (someone) the third degree, grill (*informal*), probe, question closely, quiz, worm out of

pun *noun* = **play on words**, double entendre, quip, witticism

punch¹ *verb* **1** = **hit**, bash (*informal*), belt (*informal*), biff (*slang*), bop (*informal*), box, clout (*informal*), pummel, slam, slug, smash, sock (*slang*), strike, swipe (*informal*), wallop (*informal*) ♦ *noun* **2** = **blow**, bash (*informal*), biff (*slang*), bop (*informal*), clout (*informal*), hit, jab, knock, sock (*slang*), swipe (*informal*), thump, wallop (*informal*) **3** *Informal* = **effectiveness**, bite, drive, force, forcefulness, impact, point, verve, vigour

punch² *verb* = **pierce**, bore, cut, drill, perforate, prick, puncture, stamp

punch-drunk *adjective* = **dazed**, confused, groggy (*informal*), in a daze, punchy (*informal*), reeling, staggering, stupefied, unsteady, woozy (*informal*)

punch-up *noun Brit. informal* = **fight**, argument, brawl, dust-up (*informal*), free-for-all (*informal*), row, scrap (*informal*), set-to (*informal*), stand-up fight (*informal*)

punchy *adjective Informal* = **effective**, dynamic, forceful, in-your-face (*slang*), storming (*informal*)

punctilious *adjective Formal* = **particular**, careful, ceremonious, conscientious, exact, finicky, formal, fussy, meticulous, nice, precise, proper, scrupulous, strict

punctual *adjective* = **on time**, early, exact, in good time, on the dot, precise, prompt, seasonable, strict, timely
➤ **Antonyms**
behind, behindhand, belated, delayed, late, overdue, tardy, unpunctual

punctuality *noun* = **promptness**, promptitude, readiness, regularity

punctuate *verb* **1** = **interrupt**, break, interject, intersperse, pepper, sprinkle **2** = **emphasize**, accentuate, lay stress on, mark, point up, stress, underline

puncture *noun* **1** = **hole**, break, cut, damage, leak, nick, opening, perforation, rupture, slit **2** = **flat tyre**, flat ♦ *verb* **3** = **pierce**, bore, cut, impale, nick, penetrate, perforate, prick, rupture

pundit *noun* = **expert**, buff (*informal*), guru, (self-appointed) expert *or* authority

pungent *adjective* **1** = **strong**, acerb, acid, acrid, aromatic, bitter, highly flavoured, hot, peppery, piquant, seasoned, sharp,

sour, spicy, stinging, tangy, tart **2** = **cutting**, acrimonious, barbed, biting, caustic, incisive, keen, pointed, sarcastic, scathing, sharp, stinging, telling, trenchant
➤ **Antonyms**
≠**strong**: bland, dull, mild, moderate, tasteless, unsavoury, unstimulating, weak ≠**cutting**: dull, inane

punish *verb* **1** = **discipline**, castigate, chasten, chastise, correct, penalize, rap someone's knuckles, sentence, slap someone's wrist, throw the book at **2** = **mistreat**, abuse, batter, give (someone) a going-over (*informal*), harm, hurt, injure, knock about, manhandle, misuse, oppress, rough up

punishable *adjective* = **culpable**, blameworthy, chargeable, convictable, criminal, indictable

punishing *adjective* = **hard**, arduous, backbreaking, burdensome, demanding, exhausting, grinding, gruelling, strenuous, taxing, tiring, uphill, wearing
➤ **Antonyms**
cushy (*informal*), easy, effortless, light, simple, undemanding, unexacting, untaxing

punishment *noun* **1** = **penalty**, chastening, chastisement, comeuppance (*slang*), correction, discipline, just deserts, penance, punitive measures, retribution, sanction, what for (*informal*) **2** *Informal* = **rough treatment**, abuse, beating, hard work, maltreatment, manhandling, pain, slave labour, torture, victimization

punitive *adjective* = **retaliatory**, in reprisal, in retaliation, retaliative, revengeful, vindictive

punt *verb* **1** = **bet**, back, gamble, lay, stake, wager ♦ *noun* **2** = **bet**, gamble, stake, wager

punter *noun* **1** = **gambler**, backer, better, punt (*chiefly Brit.*) **2** *Informal* = **person**, bloke (*Brit. informal*), fellow, guy (*informal*), man in the street **3** *Informal* = **customer**, client

puny *adjective* = **feeble**, diminutive, dwarfish, frail, little, pint-sized (*informal*), pygmy *or* pigmy, sickly, stunted, tiny, undersized, undeveloped, weak, weakly
➤ **Antonyms**
brawny, burly, healthy, hefty (*informal*), husky (*informal*), powerful, robust, strong, sturdy, well-built, well-developed

pupil *noun* = **learner**, beginner, disciple, novice, scholar, schoolboy *or* schoolgirl, student, trainee, tyro
➤ **Antonyms**
coach, guru, instructor, master *or* mistress, schoolmaster *or* schoolmistress,

schoolteacher, teacher, trainer, tutor

puppet *noun* 1 = **marionette**, doll 2 = **pawn**, cat's-paw, creature, dupe, figurehead, gull (*archaic*), instrument, mouthpiece, stooge, tool

purchase *verb* 1 = **buy**, acquire, come by, gain, get, get hold of, invest in, make a purchase, obtain, pay for, pick up, procure, score (*slang*), secure 2 = **achieve**, attain, earn, gain, realize, win ♦ *noun* 3 = **buy**, acquisition, asset, gain, investment, possession, property 4 = **grip**, advantage, edge, foothold, footing, grasp, hold, influence, lever, leverage, support, toehold
➤ **Antonyms**
verb ≠**buy**: hawk, market, merchandise, peddle, retail, sell, trade in, vend

purchaser *noun* = **buyer**, consumer, customer
➤ **Antonyms**
dealer, merchant, retailer, salesman *or* saleswoman, salesperson, seller, shopkeeper, tradesman, vendor

pure *adjective* 1 = **unmixed**, authentic, clear, flawless, genuine, natural, neat, perfect, real, simple, straight, true, unalloyed 2 = **clean**, disinfected, germ-free, immaculate, pasteurized, sanitary, spotless, squeaky-clean, sterile, sterilized, unadulterated, unblemished, uncontaminated, unpolluted, untainted, wholesome 3 = **innocent**, blameless, chaste, guileless, honest, immaculate, impeccable, maidenly, modest, squeaky-clean, true, uncorrupted, undefiled, unspotted, unstained, unsullied, upright, virgin, virginal, virtuous 4 = **complete**, absolute, mere, outright, sheer, thorough, unmitigated, unqualified, utter 5 = **theoretical**, abstract, academic, philosophical, speculative
➤ **Antonyms**
≠**unmixed**: adulterated, alloyed, flawed, imperfect, mixed ≠**clean**: contaminated, dirty, filthy, impure, infected, polluted, tainted ≠**innocent**: contaminated, corrupt, defiled, guilty, immodest, immoral, impure, indecent, obscene, sinful, unchaste, unclean, untrue ≠**complete**: qualified ≠**theoretical**: applied, practical

purebred *adjective* = **thoroughbred**, blood, full-blooded, pedigree

purely *adverb* = **absolutely**, completely, entirely, exclusively, just, merely, only, plainly, simply, solely, totally, wholly

purgative *noun* 1 = **purge**, aperient (*Medical*), cathartic, laxative ♦ *adjective* 2 = **purging**, aperient (*Medical*), cleansing, laxative

purgatory *noun* = **torment**, agony, hell (*informal*), hell on earth, misery, murder (*informal*), torture

purge *verb* 1 = **get rid of**, axe (*informal*), dismiss, do away with, eject, eradicate, expel, exterminate, kill, liquidate, remove, rid of, rout out, wipe from the face of the earth, wipe out 2 = **cleanse**, clean out, clear, expiate, purify, wash 3 = **absolve**, exonerate, forgive, pardon ♦ *noun* 4 = **removal**, cleanup, ejection, elimination, eradication, expulsion, liquidation, witch hunt 5 = **purgative** (*Medical*), aperient (*Medical*), cathartic, dose of salts, laxative

purify *verb* 1 = **clean**, clarify, cleanse, decontaminate, disinfect, filter, fumigate, refine, sanitize, wash 2 = **absolve**, cleanse, exculpate, exonerate, redeem, sanctify
➤ **Antonyms**
≠**clean**: adulterate, befoul, contaminate, corrupt, defile, foul, infect, pollute, soil, taint ≠**absolve**: stain, sully, taint, vitiate

purist *noun* = **stickler**, classicist, formalist, pedant, precisian

puritan *noun* 1 = **moralist**, fanatic, prude, rigorist, zealot ♦ *adjective* 2 = **strict**, ascetic, austere, hidebound, intolerant, moralistic, narrow, narrow-minded, prudish, puritanical, severe, strait-laced

puritanical *adjective* = **strict**, ascetic, austere, bigoted, disapproving, fanatical, forbidding, narrow, narrow-minded, prim, proper, prudish, puritan, rigid, severe, stiff, strait-laced, stuffy
➤ **Antonyms**
broad-minded, hedonistic, indulgent, latitudinarian, liberal, permissive, tolerant

purity *noun* 1 = **cleanness**, brilliance, clarity, cleanliness, clearness, faultlessness, fineness, genuineness, immaculateness, pureness, untaintedness, wholesomeness 2 = **innocence**, blamelessness, chasteness, chastity, decency, honesty, integrity, piety, rectitude, sincerity, virginity, virtue, virtuousness
➤ **Antonyms**
≠**cleanness**: cloudiness, contamination, impurity ≠**innocence**: immodesty, immorality, impurity, unchasteness, vice, wickedness

purlieu *noun Literary* 1 *usually plural* = **outskirts**, borders, confines, environs, fringes, limits, neighbourhood, periphery, precincts, suburbs, vicinity 2 *often plural* = **stamping ground**, hang-out (*informal*), haunt, patch, resort, territory

purloin *verb Formal* = **steal**, appropriate, filch, nick (*slang, chiefly Brit.*), pilfer, pinch (*informal*), swipe (*slang*), thieve

purport *verb* 1 = **claim**, allege, assert,

declare, maintain, pose as, pretend, proclaim, profess **2 = signify**, betoken, convey, denote, express, imply, import, indicate, intend, mean, point to, suggest ♦ *noun* **3 = significance**, bearing, drift, gist, idea, implication, import, meaning, sense

purpose *noun* **1 = reason**, aim, design, function, idea, intention, object, point, principle, the why and wherefore **2 = aim**, ambition, aspiration, design, desire, end, goal, Holy Grail (*informal*), hope, intention, object, objective, plan, project, scheme, target, view, wish **3 = determination**, constancy, firmness, persistence, resolution, resolve, single-mindedness, steadfastness, tenacity, will **4 = use**, advantage, avail, benefit, effect, gain, good, outcome, profit, result, return **5 on purpose = deliberately**, by design, designedly, intentionally, knowingly, purposely, wilfully, wittingly ♦ *verb* **6 = intend**, aim, aspire, contemplate, decide, design, determine, have a mind to, make up one's mind, mean, plan, propose, resolve, set one's sights on, work towards

purposeful *adjective* = **determined**, decided, deliberate, firm, fixed, immovable, resolute, resolved, settled, single-minded, steadfast, unfaltering
➤ **Antonyms**
aimless, faltering, irresolute, purposeless, undecided, undetermined, vacillating, wavering

purposeless *adjective* = **pointless**, aimless, empty, motiveless, needless, senseless, uncalled-for, unnecessary, useless, wanton

purposely *adverb* = **deliberately**, by design, calculatedly, consciously, designedly, expressly, intentionally, knowingly, on purpose, wilfully, with intent
➤ **Antonyms**
accidentally, by accident, by chance, by mistake, inadvertently, unconsciously, unintentionally, unknowingly, unwittingly

purse *noun* **1 = pouch**, money-bag, wallet **2 = money**, coffers, exchequer, funds, means, resources, treasury, wealth, wherewithal **3 = prize**, award, gift, reward ♦ *verb* **4 = pucker**, close, contract, knit, pout, press together, tighten, wrinkle

pursuance *noun Formal* = **carrying out**, bringing about, discharge, doing, effecting, execution, following, performance, pursuing

pursue *verb* **1 = follow**, accompany, attend, chase, dog, give chase to, go after, harass, harry, haunt, hound, hunt, hunt

down, plague, run after, shadow, stalk, tail (*informal*), track **2 = try for**, aim for, aspire to, desire, have as one's goal, purpose, seek, strive for, work towards **3 = engage in**, apply oneself, carry on, conduct, perform, ply, practise, wage, work at **4 = court**, chase after, pay attention to, pay court to, set one's cap at, woo **5 = continue**, adhere to, carry on, cultivate, hold to, keep on, maintain, persevere in, persist in, proceed, see through
➤ **Antonyms**
≠**follow**: avoid, flee, give (someone *or* something) a wide berth, keep away from, run away from, shun, steer clear of ≠**try for**: eschew, fight shy of

pursuit *noun* **1 = pursuing**, chase, hunt, hunting, inquiry, quest, search, seeking, tracking, trail, trailing **2 = occupation**, activity, hobby, interest, line, pastime, pleasure, vocation

purvey *verb* **1 = supply**, cater, deal in, furnish, provide, sell, trade in **2 = communicate**, make available, pass on, publish, retail, spread, transmit

purview *noun* **1 = scope**, compass, confine(s), extent, field, limit, province, range, reach, sphere **2 = understanding**, comprehension, overview, perspective, range of view

push *verb* **1 = shove**, depress, drive, poke, press, propel, ram, thrust **2 = make** *or* **force one's way**, elbow, jostle, move, shoulder, shove, squeeze, thrust **3 = promote**, advertise, boost, hype, make known, plug (*informal*), publicize **4 = urge**, egg on, encourage, expedite, gee up, hurry, impel, incite, persuade, press, prod, speed (up), spur **5 = drive**, browbeat, coerce, constrain, encourage, exert influence on, influence ♦ *noun* **6 = shove**, butt, jolt, nudge, poke, prod, thrust **7** *Informal* = **drive**, ambition, determination, dynamism, energy, enterprise, get-up-and-go (*informal*), go (*informal*), gumption (*informal*), initiative, pep, vigour, vitality **8** *Informal* = **effort**, advance, assault, attack, campaign, charge, offensive, onset, thrust **9 the push** *Informal, chiefly Brit.* = **dismissal**, discharge, marching orders (*informal*), one's books (*informal*), one's cards (*informal*), the boot (*slang*), the (old) heave-ho (*informal*), the order of the boot (*slang*), the sack (*informal*)
➤ **Antonyms**
verb ≠**shove**: drag, draw, haul, jerk, pull, tow, trail, tug, yank ≠**urge**: deter, discourage, dissuade, put off ♦ *noun* ≠**shove**: jerk, pull, tug, yank

pushed *adjective Informal, often with* **for**
= **short of**, hurried, in difficulty, pressed,
rushed, tight, under pressure, up against it
(*informal*)

pushing *adjective* = **ambitious**,
determined, driving, dynamic,
enterprising, go-ahead, on the go,
purposeful, resourceful

push off *verb Informal* = **go away**, beat it
(*slang*), depart, get lost (*informal*), hit the
road (*slang*), leave, make oneself scarce
(*informal*), make tracks, pack one's bags
(*informal*), shove off (*informal*), slope off,
take off (*informal*)

pushover *noun Informal* **1** = **piece of cake**
(*Brit. informal*), breeze (*U.S. & Canad.
informal*), cakewalk (*informal*), child's play
(*informal*), cinch (*slang*), doddle (*Brit.
slang*), picnic (*informal*), plain sailing,
walkover (*informal*) **2** = **sucker** (*slang*),
chump (*informal*), easy game (*informal*),
easy *or* soft mark (*informal*), mug (*Brit.
slang*), soft touch (*slang*), stooge (*slang*),
walkover (*informal*)
➤ **Antonyms**
≠**piece of cake**: challenge, hassle
(*informal*), ordeal, test, trial, undertaking

pushy *adjective* = **forceful**, aggressive,
ambitious, assertive, bold, brash,
bumptious, loud, obnoxious, obtrusive,
offensive, officious, presumptuous,
pushing, self-assertive
➤ **Antonyms**
diffident, inoffensive, meek, mousy, quiet,
reserved, retiring, self-effacing, shy, timid,
unassertive, unassuming, unobtrusive

pusillanimous *adjective Formal*
= **cowardly**, abject, chicken-hearted,
craven, faint-hearted, fearful, feeble,
gutless (*informal*), lily-livered, recreant
(*archaic*), spineless, timid, timorous, weak,
yellow (*informal*)
➤ **Antonyms**
bold, brave, courageous, daring,
dauntless, fearless, gallant, heroic,
intrepid, plucky, valiant, valorous

pussyfoot *verb* **1** = **creep**, prowl, slink,
steal, tiptoe, tread warily **2** = **hedge**, beat
about the bush, be noncommittal,
equivocate, flannel (*Brit. informal*), hum
and haw, prevaricate, sit on the fence

pustule *noun* = **boil**, gathering, pimple, zit
(*slang*)

put *verb* **1** = **place**, bring, deposit, establish,
fix, lay, position, rest, set, settle, situate **2**
= **impose**, commit, condemn, consign,
doom, enjoin, inflict, levy, subject **3**
= **make**, assign, constrain, employ, force,
induce, oblige, require, set, subject to **4**
= **express**, phrase, set, state, utter, word **5**

= **present**, advance, bring forward,
forward, offer, posit, propose, set before,
submit, tender **6** = **throw**, cast, fling,
heave, hurl, lob, pitch, toss

put across *or* **over** *verb* = **communicate**,
convey, explain, get across, get through,
make clear, make oneself understood, spell
out

put aside *or* **by** *verb* **1** = **save**, cache,
deposit, keep in reserve, lay by, squirrel
away, stockpile, store, stow away **2**
= **disregard**, bury, discount, forget, ignore

putative *adjective Formal* = **supposed**,
alleged, assumed, commonly believed,
imputed, presumed, presumptive,
reported, reputed

put away *verb* **1** = **save**, deposit, keep, lay
in, put by, set aside, store away **2** *Informal*
= **commit**, certify, confine, institutionalize,
lock up **3** *Informal* = **consume**, devour, eat
up, gobble, gulp down, wolf down **4** = **put
back**, replace, return to (its) place, tidy
away

put-down *noun Informal* = **humiliation**,
barb, dig, gibe, kick in the teeth (*slang*),
knock (*informal*), one in the eye (*informal*),
rebuff, slight, sneer, snub

put down *verb* **1** = **record**, enter, inscribe,
log, set down, take down, transcribe, write
down **2** = **repress**, crush, quash, quell,
silence, stamp out, suppress **3** *usually with*
to = **attribute**, ascribe, impute, set down **4**
= **put to sleep**, destroy, do away with, put
away, put out of its misery **5** *Slang*
= **humiliate**, condemn, crush, deflate,
dismiss, disparage, mortify, reject, shame,
slight, snub

put forward *verb* = **recommend**, advance,
introduce, move, nominate, prescribe,
present, press, proffer, propose, submit,
suggest, tender

put off *verb* **1** = **postpone**, defer, delay,
hold over, put back, put on ice, put on the
back burner (*informal*), reschedule, take a
rain check on (*U.S. & Canad. informal*) **2**
= **disconcert**, abash, confuse, discomfit,
dismay, distress, faze, nonplus, perturb,
rattle (*informal*), take the wind out of
someone's sails, throw (*informal*), unsettle
3 = **discourage**, dishearten, dissuade
➤ **Antonyms**
≠**discourage**: egg on, encourage, gee up,
incite, persuade, prompt, push, spur, urge

put on *verb* **1** = **don**, change into, dress,
get dressed in, slip into **2** = **fake**, affect,
assume, feign, make believe, play-act,
pretend, sham, simulate **3** = **present**, do,
mount, produce, show, stage **4** = **add**,
gain, increase by **5** = **bet**, back, lay, place,
wager

➤ **Antonyms**

≠**don**: cast off, doff, remove, shed, slip off, slip out of, take off, throw off, undress

put out *verb* **1** = **annoy**, anger, confound, disturb, exasperate, harass, irk, irritate, nettle, perturb, provoke, vex **2** = **disconcert**, discompose, discountenance, disturb, embarrass, put on the spot, take the wind out of someone's sails **3** = **extinguish**, blow out, douse, quench, smother, snuff out, stamp out **4** = **inconvenience**, bother, discomfit, discommode, disturb, impose upon, incommode, trouble, upset **5** = **issue**, bring out, broadcast, circulate, make known, make public, publish, release

putrefy *verb Formal* = **rot**, break down, corrupt, decay, decompose, deteriorate, go bad, spoil

putrescent *adjective Formal* = **rotting**, decaying, decomposing, going bad, stinking

putrid *adjective* = **rotten**, bad, contaminated, corrupt, decayed, decomposed, fetid, foul, off, putrefied, rancid, rank, reeking, rotting, spoiled, stinking, tainted

➤ **Antonyms**

clean, fresh, pure, sweet, uncontaminated, untainted, wholesome

put through *verb* = **carry out**, accomplish, achieve, bring off, conclude, do, effect, execute, manage, pull off

put up *verb* **1** = **build**, construct, erect, fabricate, raise **2** = **accommodate**, board, entertain, give one lodging, house, lodge, take in **3** = **submit**, float, nominate, offer, present, propose, put forward, recommend **4** = **provide**, advance, give, invest, pay, pledge, supply **5 put up to** = **encourage**, egg on, goad, incite, instigate, prompt, put the idea into one's head, urge **6 put up with** *Informal* = **stand**, abide, bear, brook, endure, lump (*informal*), stand for, stomach, suffer, swallow, take, tolerate

➤ **Antonyms**

≠**build**: demolish, destroy, flatten, knock down, level, pull down, raze, tear down

≠**stand**: not stand for, object to, oppose, protest against, reject, take exception to

put upon *verb* = **take advantage of**, abuse, exploit, impose upon, take for granted

puzzle *verb* **1** = **perplex**, baffle, beat (*slang*), bewilder, confound, confuse, flummox, mystify, nonplus, stump **2** *usually with* **out** = **solve**, clear up, crack, crack the code, decipher, figure out, find the key, get it, get the answer, resolve, see, sort out, suss (out) (*slang*), think through, unravel, work out **3** *usually with* **over** = **think about**, ask oneself, brood, cudgel *or* rack one's brains, mull over, muse, ponder, study, think hard, wonder ♦ *noun* **4** = **problem**, brain-teaser (*informal*), conundrum, enigma, mystery, paradox, poser, question, riddle, teaser

puzzled *adjective* = **perplexed**, at a loss, at sea, baffled, beaten, bewildered, clueless, confused, doubtful, flummoxed, in a fog, lost, mixed up, mystified, nonplussed, stuck, stumped, without a clue

puzzlement *noun* = **perplexity**, bafflement, bewilderment, confusion, disorientation, doubt, doubtfulness, mystification, questioning, surprise, uncertainty, wonder

puzzling *adjective* = **perplexing**, abstruse, ambiguous, baffling, bewildering, beyond one, enigmatic, full of surprises, hard, incomprehensible, inexplicable, involved, knotty, labyrinthine, misleading, mystifying, oracular, unaccountable, unclear, unfathomable

➤ **Antonyms**

clear, comprehensible, easy, evident, intelligible, lucid, manifest, obvious, patent, plain, simple, unambiguous, unequivocal, unmistakable

pygmy, pigmy *noun* **1** = **midget**, dwarf, Lilliputian, manikin **2** = **nonentity**, cipher, lightweight (*informal*), nobody, pipsqueak (*informal*), small fry ♦ *adjective* **3** = **small**, diminutive, dwarf, Lilliputian, midget, miniature, minuscule, tiny, undersized, wee

pyromaniac *noun* = **arsonist**, firebug (*informal*), fire raiser, incendiary

Q q

quack *noun* **1 = charlatan**, fake, fraud, humbug, impostor, mountebank, phoney *or* phony (*informal*), pretender, quacksalver (*archaic*) ♦ *adjective* **2 = fake**, counterfeit, fraudulent, phoney *or* phony (*informal*), pretended, sham

quaff *verb* **= drink**, down, gulp, imbibe, swallow, swig (*informal*)

quagmire *noun* **1 = bog**, fen, marsh, mire, morass, quicksand, slough, swamp **2 = entanglement**, difficulty, dilemma, fix (*informal*), imbroglio, impasse, jam (*informal*), muddle, pass, pickle (*informal*), pinch, plight, predicament, quandary, scrape (*informal*)

quail *verb* **= shrink**, blanch, blench, cower, cringe, droop, faint, falter, flinch, have cold feet (*informal*), quake, recoil, shake, shudder, tremble

quaint *adjective* **1 = unusual**, bizarre, curious, droll, eccentric, fanciful, fantastic, odd, old-fashioned, original, peculiar, queer, rum (*Brit. slang*), singular, strange, whimsical **2 = old-fashioned**, antiquated, antique, artful, charming, gothic, ingenious, old-world, picturesque
➤ **Antonyms**
≠**unusual**: normal, ordinary
≠**old-fashioned**: fashionable, modern, new, up-to-date

quake *verb* **= shake**, convulse, move, pulsate, quail, quiver, rock, shiver, shudder, throb, totter, tremble, vibrate, waver, wobble

qualification *noun* **1 = attribute**, ability, accomplishment, aptitude, capability, capacity, eligibility, endowment(s), fitness, quality, skill, suitability, suitableness **2 = condition**, allowance, caveat, criterion, exception, exemption, limitation, modification, objection, prerequisite, proviso, requirement, reservation, restriction, rider, stipulation

qualified *adjective* **1 = capable**, able, accomplished, adept, certificated, competent, efficient, eligible, equipped, experienced, expert, fit, knowledgeable, licensed, practised, proficient, skilful, talented, trained **2 = restricted**, bounded, circumscribed, conditional, confined, contingent, equivocal, guarded, limited, modified, provisional, reserved

➤ **Antonyms**
≠**capable**: amateur, apprentice, self-styled, self-taught, trainee, uncertificated, unqualified, untrained ≠**restricted**: categorical, outright, unconditional, unequivocal, whole-hearted

qualify *verb* **1 = certify**, capacitate, commission, condition, empower, endow, equip, fit, ground, permit, prepare, ready, sanction, train **2 = moderate**, abate, adapt, assuage, circumscribe, diminish, ease, lessen, limit, mitigate, modify, modulate, reduce, regulate, restrain, restrict, soften, temper, vary **3 = be described**, be characterized, be designated, be distinguished, be named
➤ **Antonyms**
≠**certify**: ban, debar, disqualify, forbid, preclude, prevent

quality *noun* **1 = excellence**, calibre, distinction, grade, merit, position, pre-eminence, rank, standing, status, superiority, value **2 = characteristic**, aspect, attribute, condition, feature, mark, peculiarity, property, trait **3 = nature**, character, constitution, description, essence, kind, make, sort, worth **4** *Obsolete* **= nobility**, aristocracy, gentry, ruling class, upper class

qualm *noun* **1 = misgiving**, anxiety, apprehension, compunction, disquiet, doubt, hesitation, regret, reluctance, remorse, scruple, twinge *or* pang of conscience, uncertainty, uneasiness **2 = nausea**, agony, attack, pang, queasiness, sickness, spasm, throe (*rare*), twinge

quandary *noun* **= difficulty**, bewilderment, cleft stick, delicate situation, dilemma, doubt, embarrassment, impasse, perplexity, plight, predicament, puzzle, strait, uncertainty

quantity *noun* **1 = amount**, aggregate, allotment, lot, number, part, portion, quota, sum, total **2 = size**, bulk, capacity, expanse, extent, greatness, length, magnitude, mass, measure, volume

quarrel *noun* **1 = disagreement**, affray, altercation, argument, *bagarre*, brawl, breach, broil, commotion, contention, controversy, difference (of opinion), discord, disputation, dispute, dissension, dissidence, disturbance, feud, fight, fracas,

fray, misunderstanding, row, scrap (*informal*), shindig (*informal*), shindy (*informal*), skirmish, spat, squabble, strife, tiff, tumult, vendetta, wrangle ♦ *verb* **2** = **disagree**, altercate, argue, bicker, brawl, clash, differ, dispute, fall out (*informal*), fight, fight like cat and dog, go at it hammer and tongs, row, spar, squabble, wrangle **3** = **object to**, carp, cavil, complain, decry, disapprove, find fault, take exception to
➤ **Antonyms**
noun ≠**disagreement**: accord, agreement, concord ♦ *verb* ≠**disagree**: agree, get on *or* along (with)

quarrelsome *adjective* = **argumentative**, belligerent, cantankerous, cat-and-dog (*informal*), choleric, combative, contentious, cross, disputatious, fractious, ill-tempered, irascible, irritable, litigious, peevish, petulant, pugnacious, querulous
➤ **Antonyms**
easy-going, equable, even-tempered, placid

quarry *noun* = **prey**, aim, game, goal, objective, prize, victim

quarter *noun* **1** = **district**, area, direction, locality, location, neighbourhood, part, place, point, position, province, region, side, spot, station, territory, zone **2** = **mercy**, clemency, compassion, favour, forgiveness, leniency, pity ♦ *verb* **3** = **accommodate**, billet, board, house, install, lodge, place, post, put up, station

quarters *plural noun* = **lodgings**, abode, accommodation, barracks, billet, cantonment (*Military*), chambers, digs (*Brit. informal*), domicile, dwelling, habitation, lodging, post, residence, rooms, shelter, station

quash *verb* **1** = **annul**, cancel, declare null and void, invalidate, nullify, overrule, overthrow, rescind, reverse, revoke, set aside, void **2** = **suppress**, beat, crush, destroy, extinguish, extirpate, overthrow, put down, quell, quench, repress, squash, subdue

quasi- *adverb* **1** = **almost**, apparently, partly, seemingly, supposedly ♦ *adjective* **2** = **pseudo-**, apparent, fake, mock, near, nominal, pretended, seeming, semi-, sham, so-called, synthetic, virtual, would-be

quaver *verb* **1** = **tremble**, flicker, flutter, oscillate, pulsate, quake, quiver, shake, shudder, thrill, trill, twitter, vibrate, waver ♦ *noun* **2** = **trembling**, break, quiver, shake, sob, throb, tremble, tremor, trill, vibration, warble

queasy *adjective* **1** = **sick**, bilious, green

around the gills (*informal*), ill, nauseated, off colour, squeamish, upset **2** = **uneasy**, anxious, fidgety, ill at ease, restless, troubled, uncertain, worried

queen *noun* **1** = **sovereign**, consort, monarch, ruler **2** = **ideal**, diva, doyenne, idol, mistress, model, perfection, prima donna, star

queenly *adjective* = **majestic**, grand, imperial, noble, regal, royal, stately

queer *adjective* **1** = **strange**, abnormal, anomalous, atypical, curious, disquieting, droll, eerie, erratic, extraordinary, funny, left-field (*informal*), odd, outlandish, outré, peculiar, remarkable, rum (*Brit. slang*), singular, uncanny, uncommon, unconventional, unnatural, unorthodox, unusual, weird **2** = **dubious**, doubtful, fishy (*informal*), irregular, mysterious, puzzling, questionable, shady (*informal*), suspicious **3** = **faint**, dizzy, giddy, light-headed, queasy, reeling, uneasy **4** = **eccentric**, crazy, demented, idiosyncratic, irrational, mad, odd, touched, unbalanced, unhinged ♦ *verb* **5** *As in* **queer someone's pitch** = **spoil**, bodge (*informal*), botch, endanger, harm, impair, imperil, injure, jeopardize, mar, ruin, thwart, wreck
➤ **Antonyms**
adjective ≠**strange**: believable, common, conventional, customary, natural, normal, ordinary, orthodox, rational, regular, straight, unexceptional, unoriginal ♦ *verb* ≠**spoil**: aid, boost, enhance, help

quell *verb* **1** = **suppress**, conquer, crush, defeat, extinguish, overcome, overpower, put down, quash, squelch, stamp out, stifle, subdue, vanquish **2** = **assuage**, allay, alleviate, appease, calm, compose, deaden, dull, mitigate, moderate, mollify, pacify, quiet, silence, soothe

quench *verb* **1** = **satisfy**, allay, appease, cool, sate, satiate, slake **2** = **put out**, check, crush, destroy, douse, end, extinguish, smother, snuff out, squelch, stifle, suppress

querulous *adjective* = **complaining**, cantankerous, captious, carping, censorious, critical, cross, discontented, dissatisfied, fault-finding, fretful, grouchy (*informal*), grumbling, hard to please, irascible, irritable, murmuring, peevish, petulant, plaintive, ratty (*Brit. & N.Z. informal*), sour, testy, tetchy, touchy, waspish, whining
➤ **Antonyms**
contented, easy to please, equable, placid, uncomplaining, uncritical, undemanding

query *noun* **1** = **question**, demand, doubt, hesitation, inquiry, objection, problem, reservation, scepticism, suspicion ♦ *verb* **2**

= **doubt**, challenge, disbelieve, dispute, distrust, mistrust, suspect **3 = ask**, inquire *or* enquire, question

quest *noun* = **search**, adventure, crusade, enterprise, expedition, exploration, hunt, journey, mission, pilgrimage, pursuit, voyage

question *noun* **1 = issue**, bone of contention, motion, point, point at issue, proposal, proposition, subject, theme, topic **2 = difficulty**, argument, can of worms (*informal*), confusion, contention, controversy, debate, dispute, doubt, dubiety, misgiving, problem, query, uncertainty **3 = inquiry**, examination, interrogation, investigation **4 in question** = **under discussion**, at issue, in doubt, open to debate **5 out of the question** = **impossible**, inconceivable, not to be thought of, unthinkable ♦ *verb* **6 = ask**, catechize, cross-examine, examine, grill (*informal*), inquire, interrogate, interview, investigate, probe, pump (*informal*), quiz, sound out **7 = dispute**, call into question, cast doubt upon, challenge, controvert, disbelieve, distrust, doubt, impugn, mistrust, oppose, query, suspect
➤ **Antonyms**
noun ≠**inquiry**: answer, reply ♦ *verb* ≠**ask**: answer, reply ≠**dispute**: accept, believe, buy (*slang*), swallow (*informal*), take on board, take on trust

questionable *adjective* = **dubious**, arguable, controversial, controvertible, debatable, disputable, dodgy (*Brit., Austral., & N.Z. informal*), doubtful, dubitable, equivocal, fishy (*informal*), iffy (*informal*), moot, paradoxical, problematical, shady (*informal*), suspect, suspicious, uncertain, unproven, unreliable
➤ **Antonyms**
authoritative, certain, incontrovertible, indisputable, straightforward, unequivocal

queue *noun* = **line**, chain, concatenation, file, order, progression, sequence, series, string, succession, train

quibble *verb* **1 = split hairs**, carp, cavil, equivocate, evade, pretend, prevaricate, shift ♦ *noun* **2 = objection**, artifice, cavil, complaint, criticism, duplicity, equivocation, evasion, nicety, niggle, pretence, prevarication, protest, quiddity, quirk, shift, sophism, subterfuge, subtlety

quick *adjective* **1 = fast**, active, brisk, express, fleet, hasty, headlong, pdq (*slang*), rapid, speedy, swift **2 = brief**, cursory, hasty, hurried, perfunctory **3** = **sudden**, expeditious, prompt **4** = **intelligent**, acute, alert, all there (*informal*), astute, bright (*informal*), clever,

discerning, nimble-witted, perceptive, quick on the uptake (*informal*), quick-witted, receptive, sharp, shrewd, smart **5 = deft**, able, adept, adroit, apt, dexterous, skilful **6 = excitable**, abrupt, curt, hasty, impatient, irascible, irritable, passionate, petulant, testy, touchy **7** = **nimble**, agile, alert, animated, energetic, flying, keen, lively, spirited, sprightly, spry, vivacious, winged **8** *Archaic* = **alive**, animate, existing, live, living, viable
➤ **Antonyms**
≠**fast**: slow, sluggish ≠**brief**: gradual, long ≠**intelligent**, **deft**: inexpert, maladroit, stupid, unintelligent, unskilful ≠**excitable**: calm, deliberate, patient, restrained ≠**nimble**: dull, heavy, inactive, lazy, lethargic, sluggish, unresponsive

quicken *verb* **1 = speed**, accelerate, dispatch, expedite, hasten, hurry, impel, precipitate **2 = invigorate**, activate, animate, arouse, energize, excite, galvanize, incite, inspire, kindle, refresh, reinvigorate, resuscitate, revitalize, revive, rouse, stimulate, strengthen, vitalize, vivify

quickly *adverb* = **swiftly**, abruptly, apace, at a rate of knots (*informal*), at *or* on the double, at speed, briskly, expeditiously, fast, hastily, hell for leather (*informal*), hotfoot, hurriedly, immediately, instantly, like greased lightning (*informal*), like lightning, like nobody's business (*informal*), like the clappers (*Brit. informal*), pdq (*slang*), posthaste, promptly, pronto (*informal*), quick, rapidly, soon, speedily, with all speed
➤ **Antonyms**
carefully, eventually, slowly, sluggishly, unhurriedly

quick-tempered *adjective* = **hot-tempered**, cantankerous, choleric, excitable, fiery, impatient, impulsive, irascible, irritable, petulant, quarrelsome, ratty (*Brit. & N.Z. informal*), shrewish, splenetic, testy, tetchy, waspish
➤ **Antonyms**
cool, dispassionate, phlegmatic, placid, slow to anger, tolerant

quick-witted *adjective* = **clever**, alert, astute, bright (*informal*), keen, perceptive, sharp, shrewd, smart
➤ **Antonyms**
dull, obtuse, slow, slow-witted, stupid, thick (*informal*), unperceptive

quid pro quo *noun* = **exchange**, compensation, equivalent, interchange, reprisal, retaliation, substitution, tit for tat

quiescent *adjective* = **quiet**, calm, dormant, in abeyance, inactive, latent, motionless, peaceful, placid, resting, serene, silent, smooth, still, tranquil, unagitated, undisturbed, unmoving, unruffled

quiet *adjective* **1 = silent**, dumb, hushed, inaudible, low, low-pitched, noiseless, peaceful, soft, soundless **2 = calm**, contented, gentle, mild, motionless, pacific, peaceful, placid, restful, serene, smooth, tranquil, untroubled **3 = undisturbed**, isolated, private, retired, secluded, secret, sequestered, unfrequented **4 = subdued**, conservative, modest, plain, restrained, simple, sober, unassuming, unobtrusive, unpretentious **5 = reserved**, collected, docile, even-tempered, gentle, imperturbable, meek, mild, phlegmatic, retiring, sedate, shy, unexcitable ♦ *noun* **6 = peace**, calmness, ease, quietness, repose, rest, serenity, silence, stillness, tranquillity
➤ **Antonyms**
adjective ≠**silent**: deafening, ear-splitting, high-decibel, high-volume, loud, noisy, stentorian ≠**calm**: agitated, alert, excitable, exciting, frenetic, troubled, turbulent, violent ≠**undisturbed**: bustling, busy, crowded, exciting, fashionable, lively, popular, vibrant ≠**subdued**: blatant, brash, bright, conspicuous, glaring, loud, obtrusive, ostentatious, pretentious, showy ≠**reserved**: excitable, excited, high-spirited, impatient, loquacious, passionate, restless, talkative, verbose, violent ♦ *noun* ≠**peace**: activity, bustle, commotion, din, disturbance, noise, racket

quieten *verb* **1 = silence**, compose, hush, muffle, mute, quell, quiet, shush (*informal*), stifle, still, stop, subdue **2 = soothe**, allay, alleviate, appease, assuage, blunt, calm, deaden, dull, lull, mitigate, mollify, palliate, tranquillize
➤ **Antonyms**
≠**soothe**: aggravate, exacerbate, intensify, provoke, upset, worsen

quietly *adverb* **1 = silently**, confidentially, dumbly, in a low voice *or* whisper, in an undertone, inaudibly, in hushed tones, in silence, mutely, noiselessly, privately, secretly, softly, without talking **2 = calmly**, contentedly, dispassionately, meekly, mildly, patiently, placidly, serenely, undemonstratively **3 = unobtrusively**, coyly, demurely, diffidently, humbly, modestly, unassumingly, unostentatiously, unpretentiously

quietness *noun* **= peace**, calm, calmness, hush, placidity, quiescence, quiet, quietude, repose, rest, serenity, silence, still, stillness, tranquillity

quilt *noun* **= bedspread**, comforter (*U.S.*),

continental quilt, counterpane, coverlet, doona (*Austral.*), downie (*informal*), duvet, eiderdown

quintessence *noun* **= essence**, core, distillation, extract, gist, heart, kernel, lifeblood, marrow, pith, soul, spirit

quintessential *adjective* **= ultimate**, archetypal, definitive, prototypical, typical

quip *noun* **= joke**, badinage, bon mot, counterattack, gibe, jest, pleasantry, repartee, retort, riposte, sally, wisecrack (*informal*), witticism

quirk *noun* **= peculiarity**, aberration, bee in one's bonnet, caprice, characteristic, eccentricity, fancy, fetish, foible, habit, *idée fixe*, idiosyncrasy, kink, mannerism, oddity, singularity, trait, vagary, whim

quirky *adjective* **= odd**, capricious, curious, eccentric, fanciful, idiosyncratic, offbeat, peculiar, rum (*Brit. slang*), singular, unpredictable, unusual, whimsical

quisling *noun* **= traitor**, betrayer, collaborator, fifth columnist, Judas, renegade, turncoat

quit *verb* **1 = stop**, abandon, belay (*Nautical*), cease, conclude, discontinue, drop, end, give up, halt, suspend, throw in the towel **2 = resign**, abdicate, go, leave, pull out, relinquish, renounce, retire, step down (*informal*), surrender **3 = depart**, abandon, decamp, desert, exit, forsake, go, leave, pack one's bags (*informal*), pull out, take off (*informal*), withdraw
➤ **Antonyms**
≠**stop**: complete, continue, finish, go on with, see through

quite *adverb* **1 = somewhat**, fairly, moderately, rather, reasonably, relatively, to a certain extent, to some degree **2 = absolutely**, completely, considerably, entirely, fully, in all respects, largely, perfectly, precisely, totally, wholly, without reservation **3 = truly**, in fact, in reality, in truth, really

quiver *verb* **1 = shake**, agitate, convulse, oscillate, palpitate, pulsate, quake, quaver, shiver, shudder, tremble, vibrate ♦ *noun* **2 = shake**, convulsion, oscillation, palpitation, pulsation, shiver, shudder, spasm, throb, tic, tremble, tremor, vibration

quixotic *adjective* **= unrealistic**, dreamy, fanciful, idealistic, impractical, romantic

quiz *noun* **1 = examination**, investigation, questioning, test ♦ *verb* **2 = question**, ask, catechize, examine, grill (*informal*), interrogate, investigate, pump (*informal*)

quizzical *adjective* **= mocking**, arch, questioning, sardonic, teasing

quota *noun* = **share**, allocation, allowance, assignment, cut (*informal*), part, portion, proportion, ration, slice, whack (*informal*)

quotation *noun* **1** = **passage**, citation, cutting, excerpt, extract, quote (*informal*), reference, selection **2** *Commerce*

= **estimate**, bid price, charge, cost, figure, price, quote (*informal*), rate, tender

quote *verb* = **repeat**, adduce, attest, cite, detail, extract, instance, name, paraphrase, proclaim, recall, recite, recollect, refer to, retell

R r

rabble *noun* 1 = **mob**, canaille, crowd, herd, horde, swarm, throng 2 *Derogatory* = **commoners**, canaille, common people, crowd, hoi polloi, lower classes, lumpenproletariat, masses, peasantry, populace, proletariat, riffraff, scum, the great unwashed (*informal & derogatory*), trash (*chiefly U.S. & Canad.*)
➤ **Antonyms**
≠**commoners**: aristocracy, bourgeoisie, elite, gentry, high society, nobility, upper classes

rabble-rouser *noun* = **agitator**, demagogue, firebrand, incendiary, stirrer (*informal*), troublemaker

Rabelaisian *adjective* = **bawdy**, broad, coarse, earthy, gross, lusty, raunchy (*slang*), satirical, uninhibited, unrestrained

rabid *adjective* 1 = **fanatical**, bigoted, extreme, fervent, intemperate, intolerant, irrational, narrow-minded, zealous 2 = **mad**, hydrophobic
➤ **Antonyms**
≠**fanatical**: half-hearted, moderate, wishy-washy (*informal*)

race[1] *noun* 1 = **contest**, chase, competition, contention, dash, pursuit, rivalry ◆ *verb* 2 = **compete**, contest, run 3 = **run**, career, dart, dash, fly, gallop, go like a bomb (*Brit. & N.Z. informal*), hare (*Brit. informal*), hasten, hurry, run like mad (*informal*), speed, tear, zoom

race[2] *noun* = **people**, blood, breed, clan, ethnic group, family, folk, house, issue, kin, kindred, line, lineage, nation, offspring, progeny, seed (*chiefly biblical*), stock, tribe, type

racial *adjective* = **ethnic**, ethnological, folk, genealogical, genetic, national, tribal

rack *noun* 1 = **frame**, framework, stand, structure ◆ *verb* 2 = **torture**, afflict, agonize, crucify, distress, harrow, oppress, pain, torment

racket *noun* 1 = **noise**, babel, ballyhoo (*informal*), clamour, commotion, din, disturbance, fuss, hubbub, hullabaloo, outcry, pandemonium, row, rumpus, shouting, tumult, uproar 2 = **fraud**, criminal activity, illegal enterprise, scheme 3 *Slang* = **business**, game (*informal*), line, occupation

racy *adjective* 1 = **risqué**, bawdy, blue, broad, immodest, indecent, indelicate, naughty, near the knuckle (*informal*), off colour, smutty, spicy (*informal*), suggestive 2 = **lively**, animated, dramatic, energetic, entertaining, exciting, exhilarating, heady, sparkling, spirited, stimulating, vigorous

raddled *adjective* = **run-down**, broken-down, coarsened, dilapidated, dishevelled, haggard, tattered, the worse for wear, unkempt

radiance *noun* 1 = **happiness**, delight, gaiety, joy, pleasure, rapture, warmth 2 = **brightness**, brilliance, effulgence, glare, gleam, glitter, glow, incandescence, light, luminosity, lustre, resplendence, shine

radiant *adjective* 1 = **happy**, beaming, beatific, blissful, delighted, ecstatic, gay, glowing, joyful, joyous, on cloud nine (*informal*), rapturous, sent 2 = **bright**, beaming, brilliant, effulgent, gleaming, glittering, glorious, glowing, incandescent, luminous, lustrous, resplendent, shining, sparkling, sunny
➤ **Antonyms**
≠**happy**: disconsolate, down in the dumps (*informal*), gloomy, joyless, low, miserable, sad, sombre, sorrowful ≠**bright**: black, dark, dull, gloomy, sombre

radiate *verb* 1 = **spread out**, branch out, diverge, issue 2 = **emit**, diffuse, disseminate, emanate, give off *or* out, gleam, glitter, pour, scatter, send out, shed, shine, spread

radiation *noun* = **emission**, emanation, rays

radical *adjective* 1 = **revolutionary**, extremist, fanatical 2 = **fundamental**, basic, constitutional, deep-seated, essential, innate, native, natural, organic, profound, thoroughgoing 3 = **extreme**, complete, drastic, entire, excessive, severe, sweeping, thorough, violent ◆ *noun* 4 = **extremist**, fanatic, militant, revolutionary
➤ **Antonyms**
adjective ≠**fundamental**: insignificant, minor, superficial, token, trivial ◆ *noun* ≠**extremist**: conservative, moderate, reactionary

raffish *adjective* = **dashing**, bohemian, careless, casual, devil-may-care, disreputable, jaunty, rakish, sporty, unconventional

raffle *noun* = **draw**, lottery, sweep,

sweepstake

ragamuffin *noun* = **urchin**, gamin, guttersnipe, scarecrow (*informal*), street arab (*Offensive*)

ragbag *noun* = **mixture**, confusion, hotchpotch, jumble, medley, miscellany, mixed bag (*informal*), potpourri

rage *noun* 1 = **fury**, agitation, anger, frenzy, ire, madness, mania, obsession, passion, rampage, raving, vehemence, violence, wrath 2 = **craze**, enthusiasm, fad (*informal*), fashion, latest thing, vogue
♦ *verb* 3 = **be furious**, be beside oneself, be incandescent, blow one's top, blow up (*informal*), crack up (*informal*), fly off the handle (*informal*), foam at the mouth, fret, fume, go ballistic (*slang, chiefly U.S.*), go off the deep end (*informal*), go up the wall (*slang*), lose it (*informal*), lose one's rag (*slang*), lose one's temper, lose the plot (*informal*), rant and rave, rave, see red (*informal*), seethe, storm, throw a fit (*informal*) 4 = **be at its height**, be uncontrollable, rampage, storm, surge
➤ **Antonyms**
noun ≠**fury**: acceptance, calmness, equanimity, gladness, good humour, joy, pleasure, resignation ♦ *verb* ≠**be furious**: accept, keep one's cool, remain unruffled, resign oneself to, stay calm

ragged *adjective* 1 = **shabby**, contemptible, down at heel, frayed, in holes, in rags, in tatters, mean, poor, scraggy, shaggy, tattered, tatty, threadbare, torn, unkempt, worn-out 2 = **rough**, crude, jagged, notched, rugged, serrated, uneven, unfinished
➤ **Antonyms**
≠**shabby**: fashionable, smart, well-dressed

raging *adjective* = **furious**, beside oneself, doing one's nut (*Brit. slang*), enraged, foaming at the mouth, frenzied, fuming, incandescent, incensed, infuriated, mad, raving, seething

rags *plural noun* = **old clothes**, castoffs, tattered clothing, tatters
➤ **Antonyms**
finery, gladrags, Sunday best

raid *noun* 1 = **attack**, break-in, foray, hit-and-run attack, incursion, inroad, invasion, onset, sally, sortie, surprise attack
♦ *verb* 2 = **attack**, assault, break into, foray, invade, pillage, plunder, rifle, sack, sally forth, swoop down upon

raider *noun* = **attacker**, invader, marauder, plunderer, robber, thief

rail *verb* = **complain**, attack, blast, castigate, censure, criticize, fulminate, revile, vociferate

railing *noun* = **fence**, balustrade, barrier, paling, rails

raillery *noun* = **teasing**, badinage, banter, chaff, joke, joking, kidding (*informal*), repartee, sport

rain *noun* 1 = **rainfall**, cloudburst, deluge, downpour, drizzle, fall, precipitation, raindrops, showers 2 = **shower**, deluge, flood, hail, spate, stream, torrent, volley
♦ *verb* 3 = **pour**, bucket down (*informal*), come down in buckets (*informal*), drizzle, fall, pelt (down), rain cats and dogs (*informal*), shower, teem 4 = **fall**, deposit, drop, shower, sprinkle

rainy *adjective* = **wet**, damp, drizzly, showery
➤ **Antonyms**
arid, dry, fine, sunny

raise *verb* 1 = **lift**, elevate, exalt, heave, hoist, move up, rear, set upright, uplift 2 = **increase**, advance, amplify, augment, boost, enhance, enlarge, escalate, exaggerate, heighten, hike (up) (*informal*), inflate, intensify, jack up, magnify, put up, reinforce, strengthen 3 = **collect**, assemble, form, gather, get, levy, mass, mobilize, muster, obtain, rally, recruit 4 = **cause**, bring about, create, engender, give rise to, occasion, originate, produce, provoke, start 5 = **stir up**, activate, arouse, awaken, cause, evoke, excite, foment, foster, incite, instigate, kindle, motivate, provoke, rouse, set on foot, summon up, whip up 6 = **bring up**, develop, nurture, rear 7 = **grow**, breed, cultivate, produce, propagate, rear 8 = **put forward**, advance, bring up, broach, introduce, moot, suggest 9 = **build**, construct, erect, put up 10 = **end**, abandon, give up, lift, relieve, remove, terminate 11 = **promote**, advance, aggrandize, elevate, exalt, prefer, upgrade
➤ **Antonyms**
≠**increase**: cut, decrease, diminish, drop, lessen, lower, reduce, sink ≠**stir up**: calm, depress, lessen, lower, quash, quell, reduce, sink, soothe, suppress ≠**build**: demolish, destroy, level, ruin, wreck ≠**end**: begin, establish, start ≠**promote**: demote, downgrade, reduce

rake¹ *verb* 1 = **gather**, collect, remove, scrape up 2 = **scrape**, break up, harrow, hoe, scour, scratch 3 *with* **together** *or* **up** = **collect**, assemble, dig up, dredge up, gather, scrape together 4 = **search**, comb, examine, forage, hunt, ransack, scan, scour, scrutinize 5 = **sweep**, pepper 6 = **graze**, scrape, scratch

rake² *noun* = **libertine**, debauchee, lech *or* letch (*informal*), lecher, playboy, profligate, roué, swinger (*slang*)

➤ **Antonyms**
ascetic, celibate, puritan

rakish[1] *adjective* = **dashing**, breezy, dapper, debonair, devil-may-care, flashy, jaunty, natty (*informal*), raffish, smart, snazzy (*informal*), sporty

rakish[2] *adjective* = **immoral**, abandoned, debauched, depraved, dissipated, dissolute, lecherous, licentious, loose, sinful, wanton

rally[1] *noun* 1 = **gathering**, assembly, conference, congregation, congress, convention, convocation, mass meeting, meeting, muster 2 = **recovery**, comeback (*informal*), improvement, recuperation, renewal, resurgence, revival, turn for the better ♦ *verb* 3 = **reassemble**, bring *or* come to order, re-form, regroup, reorganize, unite 4 = **gather**, assemble, bond together, bring *or* come together, collect, convene, get together, marshal, mobilize, muster, organize, round up, summon, unite 5 = **recover**, be on the mend, come round, get better, improve, perk up, pick up, pull through, recuperate, regain one's strength, revive, take a turn for the better, turn the corner

➤ **Antonyms**
noun ≠**recovery**: collapse, deterioration, relapse, turn for the worse ♦ *verb* ≠**gather**: disband, disperse, separate, split up ≠**recover**: deteriorate, fail, get worse, relapse, take a turn for the worse, worsen

rally[2] *verb* = **tease**, chaff, make fun of, mock, poke fun at, ridicule, send up (*Brit. informal*), take the mickey out of (*informal*), taunt

ram *verb* 1 = **hit**, butt, collide with, crash, dash, drive, force, impact, run into, slam, smash, strike 2 = **cram**, crowd, force, hammer, jam, pack, pound, stuff, thrust

ramble *verb* 1 = **walk**, amble, drift, perambulate, range, roam, rove, saunter, straggle, stray, stroll, traipse (*informal*), wander 2 = **babble**, chatter, digress, rabbit (on) (*Brit. informal*), rattle on, run off at the mouth (*slang*), waffle (*informal, chiefly Brit.*), wander, witter on (*informal*) 3 = **meander**, snake, twist and turn, wind, zigzag ♦ *noun* 4 = **walk**, excursion, hike, perambulation, roaming, roving, saunter, stroll, tour, traipse (*informal*), trip

rambler *noun* = **walker**, drifter, hiker, roamer, rover, stroller, wanderer, wayfarer

rambling *adjective* 1 = **sprawling**, irregular, spreading, straggling, trailing 2 = **long-winded**, circuitous, desultory, diffuse, digressive, disconnected, discursive, disjointed, incoherent, irregular, periphrastic, prolix, wordy

➤ **Antonyms**
≠**long-winded**: coherent, concise, direct, to the point

ramification *noun* **ramifications** = **consequences**, complications, developments, results, sequel, upshot

ramify *verb* 1 = **become complicated**, multiply, thicken 2 = **divide**, branch, fork, separate, split up

ramp *noun* = **slope**, grade, gradient, incline, inclined plane, rise

rampage *verb* 1 = **go berserk**, go ballistic (*slang, chiefly U.S.*), rage, run amok, run riot, run wild, storm, tear ♦ *noun* 2 **on the rampage** = **berserk**, amok, destructive, out of control, raging, rampant, riotous, violent, wild

rampant *adjective* 1 = **widespread**, epidemic, exuberant, luxuriant, prevalent, profuse, rank, rife, spreading like wildfire, unchecked, uncontrolled, unrestrained 2 *Heraldry* = **upright**, erect, rearing, standing

rampart *noun* = **defence**, barricade, bastion, bulwark, earthwork, embankment, fence, fort, fortification, guard, parapet, security, stronghold, wall

ramshackle *adjective* = **rickety**, broken-down, crumbling, decrepit, derelict, dilapidated, flimsy, jerry-built, shaky, tottering, tumbledown, unsafe, unsteady

➤ **Antonyms**
solid, stable, steady, well-built

rancid *adjective* = **rotten**, bad, fetid, foul, frowsty, fusty, musty, off, putrid, rank, sour, stale, strong-smelling, tainted

➤ **Antonyms**
fresh, pure, undecayed

rancorous *adjective* = **bitter**, acrimonious, malicious, malignant, resentful, spiteful, venomous, vindictive

rancour *noun* = **hatred**, animosity, animus, antipathy, bad blood, bitterness, chip on one's shoulder (*informal*), enmity, grudge, hate, hostility, ill feeling, ill will, malice, resentfulness, resentment, spite, spleen, venom

random *adjective* 1 = **chance**, accidental, adventitious, aimless, arbitrary, casual, desultory, fortuitous, haphazard, hit or miss, incidental, indiscriminate, purposeless, spot, stray, unplanned, unpremeditated ♦ *noun* 2 **at random** = **haphazardly**, accidentally, adventitiously, aimlessly, arbitrarily, by chance, casually, indiscriminately, irregularly, purposelessly, randomly, unsystematically, willy-nilly

➤ **Antonyms**

adjective ≠**chance**: definite, deliberate, intended, planned, premeditated, specific

randy *adjective Informal* = **lustful**, amorous, aroused, concupiscent, horny (*slang*), hot, lascivious, lecherous, raunchy (*slang*), sexually excited, sexy (*informal*), turned-on (*slang*)

range *noun* 1 = **limits**, ambit, amplitude, area, bounds, compass, confines, distance, domain, extent, field, latitude, orbit, pale, parameters (*informal*), province, purview, radius, reach, scope, span, sphere, sweep 2 = **series**, assortment, class, collection, gamut, kind, lot, order, selection, sort, variety ◆ *verb* 3 = **vary**, extend, fluctuate, go, reach, run, stretch 4 = **roam**, cruise, explore, ramble, rove, stroll, sweep, traverse, wander 5 = **arrange**, align, array, dispose, draw up, line up, order, sequence 6 = **group**, arrange, bracket, catalogue, categorize, class, classify, file, grade, pigeonhole, rank

rangy *adjective* = **long-limbed**, gangling, lanky, leggy, long-legged

rank¹ *noun* 1 = **status**, caste, class, classification, degree, division, echelon, grade, level, nobility, order, position, quality, sort, standing, station, stratum, type 2 = **row**, column, file, formation, group, line, range, series, tier ◆ *verb* 3 = **arrange**, align, array, class, classify, dispose, grade, line up, marshal, order, position, range, sequence, sort

rank² *adjective* 1 = **absolute**, arrant, blatant, complete, downright, egregious, flagrant, gross, rampant, sheer, thorough, total, undisguised, unmitigated, utter 2 = **foul**, bad, disagreeable, disgusting, fetid, fusty, musty, noisome, noxious, off, offensive, pungent, putrid, rancid, revolting, stale, stinking, strong-smelling, yucky *or* yukky (*slang*) 3 = **abundant**, dense, exuberant, flourishing, lush, luxuriant, productive, profuse, strong-growing, vigorous

rank and file *noun* = **general public**, body, Joe (and Eileen) Public (*slang*), Joe Six-Pack (*U.S. slang*), majority, mass, masses

rankle *verb* = **annoy**, anger, embitter, fester, gall, get one's goat (*slang*), get on one's nerves (*informal*), irk, irritate, rile

ransack *verb* 1 = **search**, comb, explore, forage, go through, rake, rummage, scour, turn inside out 2 = **plunder**, despoil, gut, loot, pillage, raid, ravage, rifle, sack, strip

ransom *noun* 1 = **payment**, money, payoff, price ◆ *verb* 2 = **buy the freedom of**, buy (someone) out (*informal*), deliver, liberate, obtain *or* pay for the release of, redeem, release, rescue, set free

rant *verb* 1 = **shout**, bellow, bluster, cry,

declaim, rave, roar, spout (*informal*), yell ◆ *noun* 2 = **tirade**, bluster, bombast, diatribe, harangue, rhetoric, vociferation

rap *verb* 1 = **hit**, crack, knock, strike, tap 2 = **bark**, speak abruptly, spit 3 *Slang, chiefly U.S.* = **talk**, chat, confabulate, converse, discourse 4 = **reprimand**, blast, castigate, censure, criticize, knock (*informal*), lambast(e), pan (*informal*), read the riot act, scold, tick off (*informal*) ◆ *noun* 5 = **blow**, clout (*informal*), crack, knock, tap 6 *Slang* = **rebuke**, blame, censure, chiding, punishment, responsibility, sentence

rapacious *adjective* = **greedy**, avaricious, grasping, insatiable, marauding, plundering, predatory, preying, ravenous, voracious

rapacity *noun* = **greed**, avarice, avidity, greediness, insatiableness, rapaciousness, voraciousness, voracity

rape *verb* 1 = **sexually assault**, abuse, force, outrage, ravish, violate ◆ *noun* 2 = **sexual assault**, outrage, ravishment, violation 3 = **desecration**, abuse, defilement, maltreatment, perversion, violation

rapid *adjective* = **quick**, brisk, express, fast, fleet, flying, hasty, hurried, pdq (*slang*), precipitate, prompt, quickie (*informal*), speedy, swift
➤ **Antonyms**
deliberate, gradual, leisurely, slow, tardy, unhurried

rapidity *noun* = **speed**, alacrity, briskness, celerity, fleetness, haste, hurry, precipitateness, promptitude, promptness, quickness, rush, speediness, swiftness, velocity

rapidly *adverb* = **quickly**, apace, at speed, briskly, fast, hastily, hotfoot, hurriedly, in a hurry, in a rush, in haste, like a shot, like lightning, pdq (*slang*), posthaste, precipitately, promptly, pronto (*informal*), speedily, swiftly

rapine *noun* = **pillage**, despoilment, looting, marauding, plundering, ransacking, robbery, sack

rapport *noun* = **bond**, affinity, empathy, harmony, interrelationship, link, relationship, sympathy, tie, understanding

rapprochement *noun* = **reconciliation**, detente, reconcilement, restoration of harmony, reunion
➤ **Antonyms**
antagonism, dissension, exacerbation, falling-out, quarrel, resumption of hostilities, schism

rapscallion *noun Old-fashioned* = **rogue**, blackguard, cad, disgrace, good-for-nothing, knave (*archaic*), ne'er-do-well, rascal, scallywag (*informal*), scamp, scoundrel

rapt *adjective* **1** = **spellbound**, absorbed, carried away, engrossed, enthralled, entranced, fascinated, gripped, held, intent, preoccupied **2** = **blissful**, bewitched, captivated, charmed, delighted, ecstatic, enchanted, enraptured, rapturous, transported
➤ **Antonyms**
≠**spellbound**: bored, detached, left cold, unaffected, uninterested, uninvolved, unmoved

rapture *noun* = **ecstasy**, beatitude, bliss, cloud nine (*informal*), delight, enthusiasm, euphoria, exaltation, felicity, happiness, joy, rhapsody, seventh heaven, spell, transport

rapturous *adjective* = **ecstatic**, blissful, delighted, enthusiastic, euphoric, happy, in seventh heaven, joyful, joyous, on cloud nine (*informal*), overjoyed, over the moon (*informal*), rapt, transported

rare¹ *adjective* **1** = **uncommon**, exceptional, few, infrequent, out of the ordinary, recherché, scarce, singular, sparse, sporadic, strange, unusual **2** = **superb**, admirable, choice, excellent, exquisite, extreme, fine, great, incomparable, peerless, superlative
➤ **Antonyms**
≠**uncommon**: abundant, bountiful, common, frequent, habitual, manifold, many, plentiful, profuse, regular

rare² *adjective* = **underdone**, bloody, half-cooked, half-raw, undercooked

rarefied *adjective* **1** = **exalted**, elevated, high, lofty, noble, spiritual, sublime **2** = **exclusive**, esoteric, private, select

rarely *adverb* **1** = **seldom**, almost never, hardly, hardly ever, infrequently, little, once in a blue moon, once in a while, only now and then, on rare occasions, scarcely ever **2** = **exceptionally**, extraordinarily, notably, remarkably, singularly, uncommonly, unusually
➤ **Antonyms**
≠**seldom**: commonly, frequently, often, regularly, usually

raring *adjective* As in **raring to** = **eager**, avid, champing at the bit (*informal*), desperate, enthusiastic, impatient, keen, keen as mustard, longing, ready, willing, yearning

rarity *noun* **1** = **curio**, collector's item, curiosity, find, gem, one-off, pearl, treasure **2** = **uncommonness**, infrequency, scarcity, shortage, singularity, sparseness, strangeness, unusualness **3** = **excellence**, choiceness, exquisiteness, fineness,

incomparability, peerlessness, quality, superbness

rascal *noun* = **rogue**, blackguard, devil, disgrace, good-for-nothing, imp, knave (*archaic*), miscreant, ne'er-do-well, rapscallion, reprobate, scallywag (*informal*), scamp, scoundrel, varmint (*informal*), villain

rash¹ *adjective* = **reckless**, brash, careless, foolhardy, harebrained, hasty, headlong, heedless, helter-skelter, hot-headed, ill-advised, ill-considered, impetuous, imprudent, impulsive, incautious, injudicious, precipitate, premature, thoughtless, unthinking, unwary
➤ **Antonyms**
canny, careful, cautious, considered, premeditated, prudent, well-thought-out

rash² *noun* **1** = **outbreak**, eruption **2** = **spate**, epidemic, flood, outbreak, plague, series, succession, wave

rashness *noun* = **recklessness**, carelessness, foolhardiness, hastiness, heedlessness, indiscretion, temerity, thoughtlessness

rasp *noun* **1** = **grating**, grinding, scrape, scratch ♦ *verb* **2** = **scrape**, file, grind, rub, scour **3** = **irritate**, grate (upon), irk, jar (upon), rub (someone) up the wrong way, set one's teeth on edge, wear upon

rasping or **raspy** *adjective* = **harsh**, grating, gravelly, gruff, hoarse, husky, rough

rat *Informal* ♦ *noun* **1** *Informal* = **traitor**, betrayer, double-crosser, grass (*Brit. informal*), informer, nark (*slang*), two-timer (*informal*) **2** = **rogue**, bad lot, bastard (*offensive*), bounder (*old-fashioned Brit. slang*), cad (*old-fashioned Brit. informal*), heel (*slang*), rotter (*slang, chiefly Brit.*), scoundrel ♦ *verb* **3 rat on** = **betray**, do the dirty on (*Brit. informal*), sell down the river (*informal*)

rate¹ *noun* **1** = **degree**, percentage, proportion, ratio, relation, scale, standard **2** = **speed**, gait, measure, pace, tempo, time, velocity **3** = **charge**, cost, dues, duty, fee, figure, hire, price, tariff, tax, toll **4** = **grade**, class, classification, degree, position, quality, rank, rating, status, value, worth **5 at any rate** = **in any case**, anyhow, anyway, at all events, nevertheless ♦ *verb* **6** = **evaluate**, adjudge, appraise, assess, class, classify, consider, count, esteem, estimate, grade, measure, rank, reckon, regard, value, weigh **7** = **deserve**, be entitled to, be worthy of, merit **8** *Slang* = **think highly of**, admire, esteem, respect, value

rate² *verb* = **scold**, bawl out (*informal*),

berate, castigate, censure, criticize severely, haul over the coals (*informal*), read the riot act, rebuke, reprimand, reprove, take to task, tear into (*informal*), tear (someone) off a strip (*informal*)

rather *adverb* 1 = **to some extent**, a bit, a little, fairly, kind of (*informal*), moderately, pretty (*informal*), quite, relatively, slightly, somewhat, sort of (*informal*), to some degree 2 = **preferably**, instead, more readily, more willingly, sooner

ratify *verb* = **approve**, affirm, authenticate, authorize, bear out, bind, certify, confirm, consent to, corroborate, endorse, establish, sanction, sign, uphold, validate
➤ **Antonyms**
abrogate, annul, cancel, reject, repeal, repudiate, revoke

rating *noun* = **position**, class, classification, degree, designation, estimate, evaluation, grade, order, placing, rank, rate, standing, status

ratio *noun* = **proportion**, correlation, correspondence, equation, fraction, percentage, rate, relation, relationship

ration *noun* 1 = **allowance**, allotment, dole, helping, measure, part, portion, provision, quota, share 2 **rations** = **provisions**, commons (*Brit.*), food, provender, stores, supplies ♦ *verb* 3 = **limit**, budget, conserve, control, restrict, save 4 = **distribute**, allocate, allot, apportion, deal, dole, give out, issue, measure out

rational *adjective* 1 = **sensible**, enlightened, intelligent, judicious, logical, lucid, realistic, reasonable, sagacious, sane, sound, wise 2 = **reasoning**, cerebral, cognitive, thinking 3 = **sane**, all there (*informal*), balanced, *compos mentis,* in one's right mind, lucid, normal, of sound mind
➤ **Antonyms**
insane, irrational, unreasonable, unsound

rationale *noun* = **reason**, grounds, logic, motivation, philosophy, principle, *raison d'être,* theory

rationalize *verb* 1 = **justify**, account for, excuse, explain away, extenuate, make allowance for, make excuses for, vindicate 2 = **reason out**, apply logic to, elucidate, resolve, think through 3 = **streamline**, make cuts, make more efficient, trim

rattle *verb* 1 = **clatter**, bang, jangle 2 = **shake**, bounce, jar, jiggle, jolt, jounce, vibrate 3 *Informal* = **fluster**, discomfit, discompose, disconcert, discountenance, disturb, faze, frighten, perturb, scare, shake, upset 4 *with* **off** *or* **out** = **recite**, list, reel off, run through 5 *with* **on** *or* **away** = **prattle**, blether, chatter, gabble, gibber,

jabber, rabbit (on) (*Brit. informal*), run on, witter (*informal*), yak (away) (*slang*)

ratty *adjective* = **irritable**, angry, annoyed, crabbed, cross, impatient, pissed (*taboo slang*), pissed off (*taboo slang*), short-tempered, snappy, testy, tetchy, touchy

raucous *adjective* = **harsh**, grating, hoarse, husky, loud, noisy, rasping, rough, strident
➤ **Antonyms**
dulcet, mellifluous, quiet, smooth, sweet

raunchy *adjective Slang* = **sexy**, bawdy, coarse, earthy, lecherous, lewd, lustful, lusty, ribald, salacious, sexual, smutty, steamy (*informal*), suggestive

ravage *verb* 1 = **destroy**, demolish, desolate, despoil, devastate, gut, lay waste, leave in ruins, loot, pillage, plunder, ransack, raze, ruin, sack, spoil, wreak havoc on, wreck ♦ *noun* 2 **ravages** = **damage**, demolition, depredation, desolation, destruction, devastation, havoc, pillage, plunder, rapine, ruin, ruination, spoliation, waste

rave *verb* 1 = **rant**, babble, be delirious, go mad (*informal*), rage, roar, storm, talk wildly, thunder 2 *Informal* = **enthuse**, be mad about (*informal*), be wild about (*informal*), cry up, gush, praise ♦ *noun* 3 *Informal* = **praise**, acclaim, applause, encomium

ravenous *adjective* 1 = **starving**, famished, starved, very hungry 2 = **voracious**, devouring, predatory, rapacious, ravening
➤ **Antonyms**
≠**starving**: full, glutted, sated, satiated

ravine *noun* = **canyon**, defile, gap (*U.S.*), gorge, gulch (*U.S.*), gully, pass

raving *adjective* = **mad**, berserk, crazed, crazy, delirious, frantic, frenzied, furious, hysterical, insane, irrational, out of one's mind, rabid, raging, wild

ravish *verb* 1 = **enchant**, captivate, charm, delight, enrapture, entrance, fascinate, overjoy, spellbind, transport 2 *Literary* = **rape**, abuse, force, outrage, sexually assault, violate

ravishing *adjective* = **enchanting**, beautiful, bewitching, charming, dazzling, delightful, drop-dead (*slang*), entrancing, gorgeous, lovely, radiant, stunning (*informal*)

raw *adjective* 1 = **uncooked**, bloody (*of meat*), fresh, natural, unprepared 2 = **unrefined**, basic, coarse, crude, natural, organic, rough, unfinished, unprocessed, unripe, untreated 3 = **sore**, chafed, grazed, open, scratched, sensitive, skinned, tender 4 = **inexperienced**, callow, green,

ignorant, immature, new, undisciplined, unpractised, unseasoned, unskilled, untrained, untried **5 = chilly**, biting, bitter, bleak, chill, cold, damp, freezing, harsh, parky (*Brit. informal*), piercing, unpleasant, wet **6 = frank**, bare, blunt, brutal, candid, naked, plain, realistic, unembellished, unvarnished
➤ **Antonyms**
≠**uncooked:** baked, cooked, done ≠**unrefined:** finished, prepared, refined ≠**inexperienced:** experienced, practised, professional, skilled, trained ≠**frank:** embellished, gilded

ray *noun* **1 = beam**, bar, flash, gleam, shaft **2 = trace**, flicker, glimmer, hint, indication, scintilla, spark

raze *verb* **= destroy**, bulldoze, demolish, flatten, knock down, level, pull down, remove, ruin, tear down, throw down

razzle-dazzle *or* **razzmatazz** *noun Slang* **= fuss**, carry-on (*informal, chiefly Brit.*), commotion, hullabaloo, performance (*informal*), rigmarole, song and dance (*informal*), to-do

re *preposition* **= concerning**, about, apropos, in respect of, on the subject of, regarding, respecting, with reference to, with regard to

reach *verb* **1 = arrive at**, attain, get as far as, get to, land at, make **2 = touch**, contact, extend to, get (a) hold of, go as far as, grasp, stretch to **3 = contact**, communicate with, establish contact with, find, get, get hold of, get in touch with, get through to, make contact with **4 = come to**, amount to, arrive at, attain, climb to, drop to, fall to, move to, rise to, sink to **5** *Informal* **= pass**, hand, hold out, stretch ♦ *noun* **6 = range**, ambit, capacity, command, compass, distance, extension, extent, grasp, influence, power, scope, spread, stretch, sweep

react *verb* **1 = act**, behave, conduct oneself, function, operate, proceed, work **2 = respond**, acknowledge, answer, reply, rise to the bait, take the bait

reaction *noun* **1 = response**, acknowledgment, answer, feedback, reply **2 = counteraction**, backlash, compensation, counterbalance, counterpoise, recoil **3 = conservatism**, counter-revolution, the right

reactionary *adjective* **1 = conservative**, blimpish, counter-revolutionary, right-wing ♦ *noun* **2 = conservative**, Colonel Blimp, counter-revolutionary, die-hard, rightist, right-winger
➤ **Antonyms**
adjective, noun ≠**conservative:** leftist,

progressive, radical, reformist, revolutionary, socialist

read *verb* **1 = look at**, glance at, peruse, pore over, refer to, run one's eye over, scan, study **2 = recite**, announce, declaim, deliver, speak, utter **3 = understand**, comprehend, construe, decipher, discover, interpret, perceive the meaning of, see **4 = register**, display, indicate, record, show

readable *adjective* **1 = enjoyable**, easy to read, entertaining, enthralling, gripping, interesting **2 = legible**, clear, comprehensible, decipherable, intelligible, plain, understandable
➤ **Antonyms**
≠**enjoyable:** as dry as dust, badly-written, boring, dull, heavy, heavy going, pretentious, turgid, unreadable ≠**legible:** illegible, incomprehensible, indecipherable, unintelligible, unreadable

readily *adverb* **1 = willingly**, cheerfully, eagerly, freely, gladly, quickly, voluntarily, with good grace, with pleasure **2 = promptly**, at once, easily, effortlessly, in no time, quickly, right away, smoothly, speedily, straight away, unhesitatingly, without delay, without demur, without difficulty, without hesitation
➤ **Antonyms**
≠**willingly:** reluctantly, unwillingly ≠**promptly:** hesitatingly, slowly, with difficulty

readiness *noun* **1 = preparedness**, fitness, maturity, preparation, ripeness **2 = willingness**, aptness, eagerness, inclination, keenness **3 = promptness**, adroitness, dexterity, ease, facility, quickness, rapidity, skill

reading *noun* **1 = learning**, book-learning, education, erudition, knowledge, scholarship **2 = perusal**, examination, inspection, review, scrutiny, study **3 = recital**, homily, lecture, lesson, performance, rendering, rendition, sermon **4 = interpretation**, conception, construction, grasp, impression, take (*informal, chiefly U.S.*), treatment, understanding, version

ready *adjective* **1 = prepared**, all set, arranged, completed, fit, in readiness, organized, primed, ripe, set **2 = willing**, agreeable, apt, disposed, eager, game (*informal*), glad, happy, have-a-go (*informal*), inclined, keen, minded, predisposed, prone **3 = prompt**, acute, adroit, alert, apt, astute, bright, clever, deft, dexterous, expert, handy, intelligent, keen, perceptive, quick, quick-witted, rapid, resourceful, sharp, skilful, smart **4 = available**, accessible, at *or* on hand, at

one's fingertips, at the ready, close to hand, convenient, handy, near, on call, on tap (*informal*), present **5 ready to = on the point of**, about to, close to, in danger of, liable to, likely to, on the brink of, on the verge of ♦ *noun* **6 at the ready = poised**, all systems go, in readiness, prepared, ready for action, waiting ♦ *verb* **7 = prepare**, arrange, equip, fit out, get ready, make ready, order, organize, set
➤ **Antonyms**
adjective ≠ **prepared**: immature, unequipped, unfit, unprepared ≠ **willing**: disinclined, hesitant, loath, reluctant, unprepared, unwilling ≠ **prompt**: slow ≠ **available**: distant, inaccessible, late, unavailable

real *adjective* **= genuine**, absolute, actual, authentic, bona fide, certain, essential, existent, factual, heartfelt, honest, legitimate, positive, right, rightful, sincere, true, unaffected, unfeigned, valid, veritable
➤ **Antonyms**
affected, counterfeit, fake, faked, false, feigned, imaginary, imitation, insincere

realistic *adjective* **1 = practical**, businesslike, common-sense, down-to-earth, hard-headed, level-headed, matter-of-fact, pragmatic, rational, real, sensible, sober, unromantic, unsentimental **2 = lifelike**, authentic, faithful, genuine, graphic, natural, naturalistic, representational, true, true to life, truthful, vérité
➤ **Antonyms**
≠ **practical**: fanciful, idealistic, impractical, unrealistic

reality *noun* **1 = truth**, actuality, authenticity, certainty, fact, genuineness, materiality, realism, validity, verisimilitude, verity **2 in reality = in fact**, actually, as a matter of fact, in actuality, in point of fact, in truth, really

realization *noun* **1 = awareness**, appreciation, apprehension, cognizance, comprehension, conception, consciousness, grasp, imagination, perception, recognition, understanding **2 = achievement**, accomplishment, carrying-out, completion, consummation, effectuation, fulfilment

realize *verb* **1 = become aware of**, appreciate, apprehend, be cognizant of, become conscious of, catch on (*informal*), comprehend, conceive, get the message, grasp, imagine, recognize, take in, twig (*Brit. informal*), understand **2 = achieve**, accomplish, actualize, bring about, bring off, bring to fruition, carry out or through,

complete, consummate, do, effect, effectuate, fulfil, make happen, perform **3 = sell for**, bring or take in, clear, earn, gain, get, go for, make, net, produce

really *adverb* **= truly**, absolutely, actually, assuredly, categorically, certainly, genuinely, in actuality, indeed, in fact, in reality, positively, surely, undoubtedly, verily, without a doubt

realm *noun* **1 = kingdom**, country, domain, dominion, empire, land, monarchy, principality, province, state **2 = field**, area, branch, department, orbit, patch, province, region, sphere, territory, turf (*U.S. slang*), world, zone

reap *verb* **1 = collect**, bring in, cut, garner, gather, harvest **2 = get**, acquire, derive, gain, obtain, win

rear¹ *noun* **1 = back**, back end, end, rearguard, stern, tail, tail end ♦ *adjective* **2 = back**, aft, following, hind, hindmost, last, trailing
➤ **Antonyms**
noun ≠ **back**: bow, forward end, front, nose, stem, vanguard ♦ *adjective* ≠ **back**: foremost, forward, front, leading

rear² *verb* **1 = bring up**, breed, care for, cultivate, educate, foster, grow, nurse, nurture, raise, train **2 = raise**, elevate, hoist, hold up, lift, set upright **3 = rise**, loom, soar, tower

reason *noun* **1 = cause**, aim, basis, design, end, goal, grounds, impetus, incentive, inducement, intention, motive, object, occasion, purpose **2 = sense**, apprehension, brains, comprehension, intellect, judgment, logic, mentality, mind, rationality, reasoning, sanity, sound mind, soundness, understanding **3 = justification**, argument, case, defence, excuse, explanation, ground, rationale, vindication **4 in or within reason = in moderation**, proper, reasonable, sensible, warrantable, within bounds, within limits
♦ *verb* **5 = deduce**, conclude, draw conclusions, infer, make out, resolve, solve, think, work out **6 reason with = persuade**, argue with, bring round (*informal*), debate with, dispute with, move, prevail upon, talk into or out of, urge, win over
➤ **Antonyms**
noun ≠ **sense**: emotion, feeling, instinct, sentiment

reasonable *adjective* **1 = sensible**, advisable, arguable, believable, credible, intelligent, judicious, justifiable, logical, plausible, practical, rational, reasoned, sane, sober, sound, tenable, well-advised, well-thought-out, wise **2 = fair**, acceptable, equitable, fit, just, moderate, proper, right,

within reason **3** = **average**, fair, moderate, modest, O.K. *or* okay (*informal*), tolerable
➤ **Antonyms**
≠**sensible**: impossible, irrational, unintelligent, unreasonable, unsound ≠**fair**: unfair, unreasonable

reasoned *adjective* = **sensible**, clear, judicious, logical, systematic, well-expressed, well-presented, well-thought-out

reasoning *noun* **1** = **thinking**, analysis, cogitation, deduction, logic, reason, thought **2** = **case**, argument, exposition, hypothesis, interpretation, proof, train of thought

reassure *verb* = **encourage**, bolster, buoy up, cheer up, comfort, gee up, hearten, inspirit, put *or* set one's mind at rest, relieve (someone) of anxiety, restore confidence to

rebate *noun* = **refund**, allowance, bonus, deduction, discount, reduction

rebel *verb* **1** = **revolt**, mutiny, resist, rise up, take to the streets, take up arms **2** = **defy**, come out against, dig one's heels in (*informal*), disobey, dissent, refuse to obey ♦ *noun* **3** = **revolutionary**, insurgent, insurrectionary, mutineer, resistance fighter, revolutionist, secessionist **4** = **nonconformist**, apostate, dissenter, heretic, schismatic ♦ *adjective* **5** = **rebellious**, insurgent, insurrectionary, mutinous, revolutionary

rebellion *noun* **1** = **resistance**, insurgence, insurrection, mutiny, revolt, revolution, rising, uprising **2** = **nonconformity**, apostasy, defiance, disobedience, dissent, heresy, schism

rebellious *adjective* **1** = **revolutionary**, disaffected, disloyal, disobedient, disorderly, insubordinate, insurgent, insurrectionary, mutinous, rebel, recalcitrant, seditious, turbulent, ungovernable, unruly **2** = **defiant**, difficult, incorrigible, intractable, obstinate, recalcitrant, refractory, resistant, unmanageable
➤ **Antonyms**
≠**revolutionary**: dutiful, loyal, obedient, patriotic, subordinate ≠**defiant**: dutiful, obedient, subservient

rebirth *noun* = **revival**, new beginning, regeneration, renaissance, renewal, restoration, resurgence, resurrection, revitalization

rebound *verb* **1** = **bounce**, recoil, resound, return, ricochet, spring back **2** = **misfire**, backfire, boomerang, recoil ♦ *noun* **3** = **bounce**, comeback, kickback, repercussion, return, ricochet

rebuff *verb* **1** = **reject**, brush off (*slang*), cold-shoulder, cut, decline, discourage, knock back (*slang*), put off, refuse, repulse, resist, slight, snub, spurn, turn down ♦ *noun* **2** = **rejection**, brush-off (*slang*), cold shoulder, discouragement, kick in the teeth (*slang*), knock-back (*slang*), opposition, refusal, repulse, slap in the face (*informal*), slight, snub, thumbs down
➤ **Antonyms**
verb ≠**reject**: encourage, lead on (*informal*), submit to, welcome ♦ *noun* ≠**rejection**: come-on (*informal*), encouragement, thumbs up, welcome

rebuke *verb* **1** = **scold**, admonish, bawl out (*informal*), berate, blame, castigate, censure, chide, dress down (*informal*), give a rocket (*Brit. & N.Z. informal*), haul (someone) over the coals (*informal*), lecture, read the riot act, reprehend, reprimand, reproach, reprove, take to task, tear into (*informal*), tear (someone) off a strip (*informal*), tell off (*informal*), tick off (*informal*), upbraid ♦ *noun* **2** = **scolding**, admonition, blame, castigation, censure, dressing down (*informal*), lecture, reprimand, reproach, reproof, reproval, row, telling-off (*informal*), ticking-off (*informal*)
➤ **Antonyms**
verb ≠**scold**: applaud, approve, commend, compliment, congratulate, laud, praise ♦ *noun* ≠**scolding**: commendation, compliment, laudation, praise

rebut *verb* = **disprove**, confute, defeat, invalidate, negate, overturn, prove wrong, quash, refute

rebuttal *noun* = **disproof**, confutation, defeat, invalidation, negation, refutation

recalcitrant *adjective* = **disobedient**, contrary, defiant, insubordinate, intractable, obstinate, refractory, stubborn, uncontrollable, ungovernable, unmanageable, unruly, unwilling, wayward, wilful
➤ **Antonyms**
amenable, compliant, docile, obedient, submissive

recall *verb* **1** = **recollect**, bring *or* call to mind, call *or* summon up, evoke, look *or* think back to, mind (*dialect*), remember, reminisce about **2** = **annul**, abjure, call back, call in, cancel, countermand, nullify, repeal, rescind, retract, revoke, take back, withdraw ♦ *noun* **3** = **recollection**, memory, remembrance **4** = **annulment**, cancellation, nullification, recision, repeal, rescindment, rescission, retraction, revocation, withdrawal

recant *verb* = **withdraw**, abjure, apostatize,

deny, disavow, disclaim, disown, forswear, recall, renege, renounce, repudiate, retract, revoke, take back, unsay
➤ **Antonyms**
insist, maintain, profess, reaffirm, reiterate, repeat, restate, uphold

recapitulate verb = **restate**, go over again, outline, recap (informal), recount, reiterate, repeat, review, run over, run through again, summarize, sum up

recede verb 1 = **fall back**, abate, back off, draw back, ebb, go back, regress, retire, retreat, retrogress, return, subside, withdraw 2 = **lessen**, decline, diminish, dwindle, fade, shrink, sink, wane

receipt noun 1 = **sales slip**, acknowledgment, counterfoil, proof of purchase, stub, voucher 2 = **receiving**, acceptance, delivery, reception, recipience 3 **receipts** = **takings**, gains, gate, income, proceeds, profits, return

receive verb 1 = **get**, accept, accept delivery of, acquire, be given, be in receipt of, collect, derive, obtain, pick up, take 2 = **experience**, bear, be subjected to, encounter, go through, meet with, suffer, sustain, undergo 3 = **greet**, accommodate, admit, be at home to, entertain, meet, take in, welcome 4 = **be informed of**, apprehend, be told, gather, hear, perceive

recent adjective = **new**, contemporary, current, fresh, happening (informal), late, latter, latter-day, modern, novel, present-day, up-to-date, young
➤ **Antonyms**
ancient, antique, earlier, early, former, historical, old

recently adverb = **newly**, currently, freshly, lately, latterly, not long ago, of late

receptacle noun = **container**, holder, repository

reception noun 1 = **party**, do (informal), entertainment, function, levee, soirée 2 = **response**, acknowledgment, greeting, reaction, recognition, treatment, welcome 3 = **receiving**, acceptance, admission, receipt

receptive adjective = **open**, accessible, amenable, approachable, favourable, friendly, hospitable, interested, open-minded, open to suggestions, susceptible, sympathetic, welcoming
➤ **Antonyms**
biased, narrow-minded, prejudiced, unreceptive, unresponsive

recess noun 1 = **alcove**, bay, cavity, corner, depression, hollow, indentation, niche, nook 2 = **break**, cessation of business, closure, holiday, intermission, interval, respite, rest, vacation 3 **recesses** = **depths**,

heart, innermost parts, secret places

recession noun = **depression**, decline, downturn, drop, slump
➤ **Antonyms**
boom, upturn

recherché adjective = **refined**, choice, esoteric, exotic, rare

recipe noun 1 = **directions**, ingredients, instructions 2 = **method**, formula, modus operandi, prescription, procedure, process, programme, technique

reciprocal adjective = **mutual**, alternate, complementary, correlative, corresponding, equivalent, exchanged, give-and-take, interchangeable, interdependent
➤ **Antonyms**
one-way, unilateral, unreciprocated

reciprocate verb = **return**, exchange, feel in return, interchange, reply, requite, respond, return the compliment, swap, trade

recital noun 1 = **performance**, rehearsal, rendering 2 = **recitation**, account, description, detailing, enumeration, narration, narrative, reading, relation, repetition, statement, story, tale, telling

recitation noun = **recital**, lecture, narration, passage, performance, piece, reading, rendering, telling

recite verb = **repeat**, declaim, deliver, describe, detail, enumerate, itemize, narrate, perform, recapitulate, recount, rehearse, relate, speak, tell

reckless adjective = **careless**, daredevil, devil-may-care, foolhardy, hasty, headlong, heedless, ill-advised, imprudent, inattentive, incautious, indiscreet, irresponsible, madcap, mindless, negligent, precipitate, rash, regardless, thoughtless, wild
➤ **Antonyms**
careful, cautious, heedful, mindful, observant, responsible, thoughtful, wary

reckon verb 1 Informal = **think**, assume, believe, be of the opinion, conjecture, expect, fancy, guess (informal, chiefly U.S. & Canad.), imagine, suppose, surmise 2 = **consider**, account, appraise, count, deem, esteem, estimate, evaluate, gauge, hold, judge, look upon, rate, regard, think of 3 = **count**, add up, calculate, compute, enumerate, figure, number, tally, total 4 **reckon on** or **upon** = **rely on**, bank on, calculate, count on, depend on, hope for, take for granted, trust in 5 **reckon with: a** = **deal**, cope, face, handle, settle accounts, treat **b** = **take into account**, anticipate, bargain for, bear in mind, be prepared for, expect, foresee, plan for, take cognizance of

reckoning *noun* 1 = **count**, adding, addition, calculation, computation, counting, estimate 2 = **retribution**, doom, judgment, last judgment 3 = **bill**, account, charge, due, score, settlement

reclaim *verb* = **regain**, get *or* take back, recapture, recover, redeem, reform, regenerate, reinstate, rescue, restore, retrieve, salvage

recline *verb* = **lean**, be recumbent, lay (something) down, lie (down), loll, lounge, repose, rest, sprawl, stretch out
➤ **Antonyms**
get up, rise, sit up, stand, stand up, stand upright

recluse *noun* = **hermit**, anchoress, anchorite, monk, solitary

reclusive *adjective* = **solitary**, cloistered, hermit-like, isolated, monastic, recluse, retiring, secluded, sequestered, withdrawn
➤ **Antonyms**
gregarious, sociable

recognition *noun* 1 = **identification**, detection, discovery, recall, recollection, remembrance 2 = **acceptance**, admission, allowance, avowal, awareness, concession, confession, perception, realization, understanding 3 = **approval**, acknowledgment, appreciation, gratitude, greeting, honour, salute 4 *As in* **in recognition of** = **appreciation**, cognizance, notice, respect

recognize *verb* 1 = **identify**, know, know again, make out, notice, place, put one's finger on, recall, recollect, remember, spot 2 = **acknowledge**, accept, admit, allow, avow, be aware of, concede, confess, grant, own, perceive, realize, see, take on board, understand 3 = **approve**, acknowledge, appreciate, greet, honour, salute 4 = **appreciate**, notice, respect
➤ **Antonyms**
≠**acknowledge**: be unaware of, forget, ignore, overlook

recoil *verb* 1 = **jerk back**, kick, react, rebound, spring back 2 = **draw back**, balk at, falter, flinch, quail, shrink, shy away 3 = **backfire**, boomerang, go pear-shaped (*informal*), go wrong, misfire, rebound
♦ *noun* 4 = **reaction**, backlash, kick, rebound, repercussion

recollect *verb* = **remember**, call to mind, place, recall, reminisce, summon up

recollection *noun* = **memory**, impression, mental image, recall, remembrance, reminiscence

recommend *verb* 1 = **advise**, advance, advocate, counsel, prescribe, propose, put forward, suggest, urge 2 = **commend**, approve, endorse, praise, put in a good word for, speak well of, vouch for 3 = **make attractive**, make acceptable, make appealing, make interesting
➤ **Antonyms**
≠**advise, commend**: argue against, disapprove of, reject, veto

recommendation *noun* 1 = **advice**, counsel, proposal, suggestion, urging 2 = **commendation**, advocacy, approbation, approval, endorsement, favourable mention, good word, plug (*informal*), praise, reference, sanction, testimonial

recompense *verb* 1 = **reward**, pay, remunerate 2 = **compensate**, indemnify, make amends for, make good, make restitution for, make up for, pay for, redress, reimburse, repay, requite, satisfy
♦ *noun* 3 = **compensation**, amends, damages, emolument, indemnity, pay, payment, remuneration, reparation, repayment, requital, restitution, satisfaction 4 = **reward**, meed (*archaic*), pay, payment, return, wages

reconcile *verb* 1 = **resolve**, adjust, compose, harmonize, patch up, put to rights, rectify, settle, square 2 = **make peace between**, appease, conciliate, pacify, placate, propitiate, re-establish friendly relations between, restore harmony between, reunite 3 = **accept**, get used, make the best of, put up with (*informal*), resign oneself, submit, yield

reconciliation *noun* 1 = **pacification**, appeasement, conciliation, détente, propitiation, *rapprochement*, reconcilement, reunion, understanding 2 = **accommodation**, adjustment, compromise, settlement
➤ **Antonyms**
≠**pacification**: alienation, antagonism, break-up, estrangement, falling-out, separation

recondite *adjective* = **obscure**, abstruse, arcane, cabbalistic, concealed, dark, deep, difficult, esoteric, hidden, involved, mysterious, mystical, occult, profound, secret
➤ **Antonyms**
exoteric, simple, straightforward

recondition *verb* = **restore**, do up (*informal*), fix up (*informal, chiefly U.S. & Canad.*), overhaul, remodel, renew, renovate, repair, revamp

reconnaissance *noun* = **inspection**, exploration, investigation, observation, patrol, recce (*slang*), reconnoitring, scan, scouting, scrutiny, survey

reconnoitre *verb* = **inspect**, case (*slang*),

explore, get the lie of the land, investigate, make a reconnaissance (of), observe, patrol, recce (*slang*), scan, scout, scrutinize, see how the land lies, spy out, survey

reconsider *verb* = **rethink**, change one's mind, have second thoughts, reassess, re-evaluate, re-examine, review, revise, take another look at, think again, think better of, think over, think twice

reconstruct *verb* **1** = **rebuild**, reassemble, recreate, re-establish, reform, regenerate, remake, remodel, renovate, reorganize, restore **2** = **deduce**, build up, build up a picture of, piece together

record *noun* **1** = **document**, account, annals, archives, chronicle, diary, entry, file, journal, log, memoir, memorandum, memorial, minute, register, report **2** = **evidence**, documentation, memorial, remembrance, testimony, trace, witness **3** = **disc**, album, black disc, EP, forty-five, gramophone record, LP, recording, release, seventy-eight, single, vinyl **4** = **background**, career, curriculum vitae, history, performance, track record (*informal*) **5 off the record** = **not for publication**, confidential, confidentially, in confidence, in private, private, sub rosa, under the rose, unofficial, unofficially ♦ *verb* **6** = **set down**, chalk up (*informal*), chronicle, document, enrol, enter, inscribe, log, minute, note, preserve, put down, put on file, put on record, register, report, take down, transcribe, write down **7** = **make a recording of**, tape, tape-record, video, video-tape **8** = **register**, contain, give evidence of, indicate, read, say, show

recorder *noun* = **chronicler**, annalist, archivist, clerk, diarist, historian, registrar, scorekeeper, scorer, scribe

recording *noun* = **record**, cut (*informal*), disc, gramophone record, tape, video

recount *verb* = **tell**, delineate, depict, describe, detail, enumerate, give an account of, narrate, portray, recite, rehearse, relate, repeat, report, tell the story of

recoup *verb* **1** = **regain**, make good, recover, redeem, retrieve, win back **2** = **compensate**, make redress for, make up for, refund, reimburse, remunerate, repay, requite, satisfy

recourse *noun* = **option**, alternative, appeal, choice, expedient, refuge, remedy, resort, resource, way out

recover *verb* **1** = **get better**, be on the mend, bounce back, come round, convalesce, feel oneself again, get back on

one's feet, get well, heal, improve, mend, pick up, pull through, rally, recuperate, regain one's health *or* strength, revive, take a turn for the better, turn the corner **2** = **regain**, find again, get back, make good, recapture, reclaim, recoup, redeem, repair, repossess, restore, retake, retrieve, take back, win back
➤ Antonyms
≠**get better**: deteriorate, go downhill, relapse, take a turn for the worse, weaken, worsen ≠**regain**: abandon, forfeit, lose

recovery *noun* **1** = **improvement**, convalescence, healing, mending, rally, recuperation, return to health, revival, turn for the better **2** = **revival**, amelioration, betterment, improvement, rally, rehabilitation, restoration, upturn **3** = **retrieval**, recapture, reclamation, redemption, repair, repossession, restoration

recreation *noun* = **pastime**, amusement, beer and skittles (*informal*), distraction, diversion, enjoyment, entertainment, exercise, fun, hobby, leisure activity, play, pleasure, refreshment, relaxation, relief, sport

recrimination *noun* = **bickering**, counterattack, countercharge, mutual accusation, name-calling, quarrel, retaliation, retort, squabbling

recruit *verb* **1** = **enlist**, draft, enrol, levy, mobilize, muster, raise, strengthen **2** = **win (over)**, engage, enrol, gather, obtain, procure, proselytize, round up, take on ♦ *noun* **3** = **beginner**, apprentice, convert, greenhorn (*informal*), helper, initiate, learner, neophyte, novice, proselyte, rookie (*informal*), trainee, tyro
➤ Antonyms
verb ≠**enlist**: dismiss, fire, lay off, make redundant, sack (*informal*)

rectify *verb* **1** = **correct**, adjust, amend, emend, fix, improve, make good, mend, put right, redress, reform, remedy, repair, right, set the record straight, square **2** *Chemistry* = **separate**, distil, purify, refine

rectitude *noun* = **morality**, correctness, decency, equity, goodness, honesty, honour, incorruptibility, integrity, justice, principle, probity, righteousness, scrupulousness, uprightness, virtue
➤ Antonyms
baseness, corruption, dishonesty, dishonour, immorality, scandalousness

recumbent *adjective* = **lying down**, flat, flat on one's back, horizontal, leaning, lying, prone, prostrate, reclining, resting, stretched out, supine

recuperate *verb* = **recover**, be on the

mend, convalesce, get back on one's feet, get better, improve, mend, pick up, regain one's health, turn the corner

recur *verb* 1 = **happen again**, come again, come and go, come back, persist, reappear, repeat, return, revert 2 = **return to mind**, be remembered, come back

recurrent *adjective* = **periodic**, continued, cyclical, frequent, habitual, recurring, regular, repeated, repetitive
➤ Antonyms
isolated, one-off

recycle *verb* = **reprocess**, reclaim, reuse, salvage, save

red *adjective* 1 = **crimson**, cardinal, carmine, cherry, claret, coral, maroon, pink, rose, ruby, scarlet, vermilion, wine 2 *Of hair* = **chestnut**, bay, carroty, flame-coloured, flaming, foxy, reddish, sandy, titian 3 = **flushed**, blushing, embarrassed, florid, rubicund, shamefaced, suffused 4 = **bloodshot**, inflamed, red-rimmed
♦ *noun* 5 = **redness**, colour 6 **in the red** *Informal* = **in debt**, bankrupt, in arrears, in debit, in deficit, insolvent, on the rocks, overdrawn, owing money, showing a loss 7 **see red** *Informal* = **lose one's temper**, be beside oneself with rage *(informal)*, become enraged, be *or* get pissed (off) *(taboo slang)*, be *or* get very angry, blow a fuse *(slang, chiefly U.S.)*, blow one's top, crack up *(informal)*, fly off the handle *(informal)*, go ballistic *(slang, chiefly U.S.)*, go mad *(informal)*, go off one's head *(slang)*, go off the deep end *(informal)*, go up the wall *(slang)*, lose it *(informal)*, lose one's rag *(slang)*, lose the plot *(informal)*

red-blooded *adjective Informal* = **vigorous**, hearty, lusty, manly, robust, strong, virile, vital

redden *verb* = **flush**, blush, colour (up), crimson, go red

redeem *verb* 1 = **make up for**, atone for, compensate for, defray, make amends for, make good, offset, outweigh, redress, save 2 = **reinstate**, absolve, rehabilitate, restore to favour 3 = **save**, buy the freedom of, deliver, emancipate, extricate, free, liberate, pay the ransom of, ransom, rescue, set free 4 = **buy back**, reclaim, recover, recover possession of, regain, repossess, repurchase, retrieve, win back 5 = **trade in**, cash (in), change, exchange 6 = **fulfil**, abide by, adhere to, be faithful to, carry out, discharge, hold to, keep, make good, meet, perform

redemption *noun* 1 = **compensation**, amends, atonement, expiation, reparation 2 = **salvation**, deliverance, emancipation, liberation, ransom, release, rescue 3

= **repurchase**, reclamation, recovery, repossession, retrieval 4 = **trade-in**, quid pro quo 5 = **fulfilment**, discharge, exchange, performance

red-handed *adjective* = **in the act**, bang to rights *(slang)*, (in) flagrante delicto, with one's fingers *or* hand in the till *(informal)*, with one's pants down *(U.S. slang)*

redolent *adjective* 1 = **reminiscent**, evocative, remindful, suggestive 2 = **scented**, aromatic, fragrant, odorous, perfumed, sweet-smelling

redoubtable *adjective* = **formidable**, dreadful, fearful, fearsome, mighty, powerful, strong, terrible

redound *verb* 1 **redound on** *or* **upon** = **rebound**, come back, ensue, recoil, reflect, result 2 **redound to** = **contribute to**, conduce, effect, lead to, tend towards

redress *verb* 1 = **make amends for**, compensate for, make reparation for, make restitution for, make up for, pay for, put right, recompense for 2 = **put right**, adjust, amend, balance, correct, even up, mend, rectify, regulate, relieve, remedy, repair, restore the balance, square ♦ *noun* 3 = **amends**, atonement, compensation, payment, quittance, recompense, reparation, requital, restitution 4 = **rectification**, correction, cure, ease, help, remedy

reduce *verb* 1 = **lessen**, abate, abridge, contract, curtail, cut, cut down, decrease, depress, dilute, diminish, downsize, impair, lower, moderate, shorten, slow down, tone down, truncate, turn down, weaken, wind down 2 = **degrade**, break, bring low, demote, downgrade, humble, humiliate, lower in rank, lower the status of, take down a peg *(informal)* 3 = **drive**, bring, bring to the point of, force 4 = **slim**, be *or* go on a diet, diet, lose weight, shed weight, slenderize *(chiefly U.S.)*, trim 5 = **impoverish**, bankrupt, break, pauperize, ruin
➤ Antonyms
≠**lessen**: augment, enhance, enlarge, extend, heighten, increase ≠**degrade**: elevate, enhance, exalt, promote

redundancy *noun* = **unemployment**, joblessness, layoff, the axe *(informal)*, the sack *(informal)*

redundant *adjective* = **superfluous**, de trop, excessive, extra, inessential, supernumerary, surplus, unnecessary, unwanted
➤ Antonyms
essential, necessary, needed, vital

reek *verb* 1 = **stink**, hum *(slang)*, pong *(Brit. informal)*, smell, smell to high heaven 2

reek of = be redolent of, be characterized by, be permeated by ♦ *noun* **3 = stink**, fetor, malodour, niff (*Brit. slang*), odour, pong (*Brit. informal*), smell, stench **4** *Dialect* **= smoke**, exhalation, fumes, steam, vapour

reel *verb* **1 = stagger**, falter, lurch, pitch, rock, roll, stumble, sway, totter, waver, wobble **2 = whirl**, go round and round, revolve, spin, swim, swirl, twirl

refer *verb* **1 = allude**, bring up, cite, hint, make mention of, make reference, mention, speak of, touch on **2 = relate**, apply, be directed to, belong, be relevant to, concern, pertain **3 = consult**, apply, go, have recourse to, look up, seek information from, turn to **4 = direct**, guide, point, recommend, send **5 = pass on**, commit, consign, deliver, hand over, submit, transfer, turn over

referee *noun* **1 = umpire**, adjudicator, arbiter, arbitrator, judge, ref (*informal*) ♦ *verb* **2 = umpire**, adjudicate, arbitrate, judge, mediate

reference *noun* **1 = citation**, allusion, mention, note, quotation, remark **2 = testimonial**, certification, character, credentials, endorsement, good word, recommendation **3** As in **with reference to = relevance**, applicability, bearing, concern, connection, consideration, regard, relation, respect

referendum *noun* **= public vote**, plebiscite, popular vote

refine *verb* **1 = purify**, clarify, cleanse, distil, filter, process, rarefy **2 = improve**, civilize, cultivate, hone, perfect, polish, temper

refined *adjective* **1 = cultured**, civil, civilized, courtly, cultivated, elegant, genteel, gentlemanly, gracious, ladylike, polished, polite, sophisticated, urbane, well-bred, well-mannered **2 = purified**, clarified, clean, distilled, filtered, processed, pure **3 = discerning**, delicate, discriminating, exact, fastidious, fine, nice, precise, punctilious, sensitive, sublime, subtle
➤ **Antonyms**
≠**cultured**: boorish, coarse, common, ill-bred, inelegant, uncultured, ungentlemanly, unladylike, unmannerly, unrefined ≠**purified**: coarse, impure, unrefined

refinement *noun* **1 = sophistication**, breeding, civility, civilization, courtesy, cultivation, culture, delicacy, discrimination, elegance, fastidiousness, finesse, finish, gentility, good breeding, good manners, grace, graciousness, polish, politeness, style, taste, urbanity **2**

= subtlety, fine point, fine tuning, nicety, nuance **3 = purification**, clarification, cleansing, distillation, filtering, processing

reflect *verb* **1 = throw back**, echo, give back, imitate, mirror, reproduce, return **2 = show**, bear out, bespeak, communicate, demonstrate, display, evince, exhibit, express, indicate, manifest, reveal **3 = consider**, cogitate, contemplate, deliberate, meditate, mull over, muse, ponder, ruminate, think, wonder

·**reflection** *noun* **1 = image**, counterpart, echo, mirror image **2 = consideration**, cerebration, cogitation, contemplation, deliberation, idea, meditation, musing, observation, opinion, perusal, pondering, rumination, study, thinking, thought, view **3 = criticism**, aspersion, censure, imputation, reproach, slur

reflective *adjective* **= thoughtful**, cogitating, contemplative, deliberative, meditative, pensive, pondering, ruminative

reform *noun* **1 = improvement**, amelioration, amendment, betterment, correction, rectification, rehabilitation, renovation ♦ *verb* **2 = improve**, ameliorate, amend, better, correct, emend, mend, reconstruct, rectify, rehabilitate, remodel, reorganize, repair, restore, revolutionize **3 = mend one's ways**, clean up one's act (*informal*), get back on the straight and narrow (*informal*), get it together (*informal*), get one's act together (*informal*), go straight (*informal*), pull one's socks up (*Brit. informal*), shape up (*informal*), turn over a new leaf

refractory *adjective* **= unmanageable**, difficult, disobedient, headstrong, intractable, mulish, obstinate, perverse, recalcitrant, stiff-necked, stubborn, uncontrollable, uncooperative, unruly, wilful

refrain¹ *verb* **= stop**, abstain, avoid, cease, desist, do without, eschew, forbear, give up, kick (*informal*), leave off, renounce

refrain² *noun* **= chorus**, burden, melody, song, tune

refresh *verb* **1 = revive**, brace, breathe new life into, cheer, cool, enliven, freshen, inspirit, invigorate, kick-start (*informal*), reanimate, rejuvenate, revitalize, revivify, stimulate **2 = stimulate**, brush up (*informal*), jog, prod, prompt, renew

refreshing *adjective* **1 = stimulating**, bracing, cooling, fresh, inspiriting, invigorating, revivifying, thirst-quenching **2 = new**, different, novel, original
➤ **Antonyms**
≠**stimulating**: enervating, exhausting, soporific, tiring, wearisome

refreshment noun 1 = **revival**, enlivenment, freshening, reanimation, renewal, renovation, repair, restoration, stimulation 2 **refreshments = food and drink**, drinks, snacks, titbits

refrigerate verb = **cool**, chill, freeze, keep cold

refuge noun = **shelter**, asylum, bolt hole, harbour, haven, hide-out, protection, resort, retreat, sanctuary, security

refugee noun = **exile**, displaced person, émigré, escapee, fugitive, runaway

refulgent adjective Literary = **shining**, bright, brilliant, gleaming, lustrous, radiant, resplendent

refund verb 1 = **repay**, give back, make good, pay back, reimburse, restore, return ◆ noun 2 = **repayment**, reimbursement, return

refurbish verb = **renovate**, clean up, do up (informal), fix up (informal, chiefly U.S. & Canad.), mend, overhaul, re-equip, refit, remodel, repair, restore, revamp, set to rights, spruce up

refusal noun 1 = **rejection**, defiance, denial, kick in the teeth (slang), knock-back (slang), negation, no, rebuff, repudiation, thumbs down 2 = **option**, choice, consideration, opportunity

refuse¹ verb = **reject**, abstain, decline, deny, repel, repudiate, say no, spurn, turn down, withhold
➤ Antonyms
accept, agree, allow, approve, consent, give, permit

refuse² noun = **rubbish**, dreck (slang, chiefly U.S.), dregs, dross, garbage, junk (informal), leavings, lees, litter, scum, sediment, sweepings, trash, waste

refute verb = **disprove**, blow out of the water (slang), confute, counter, discredit, give the lie to, negate, overthrow, prove false, rebut, silence
➤ Antonyms
confirm, prove, substantiate

regain verb 1 = **recover**, get back, recapture, recoup, redeem, repossess, retake, retrieve, take back, win back 2 = **get back to**, reach again, reattain, return to

regal adjective = **royal**, fit for a king or queen, kingly or queenly, magnificent, majestic, noble, princely, proud, sovereign

regale verb 1 = **entertain**, amuse, delight, divert, gratify 2 = **serve**, feast, ply, refresh

regalia plural noun = **trappings**, accoutrements, apparatus, decorations, emblems, finery, garb, gear, paraphernalia, rigout (informal)

regard verb 1 = **consider**, account, adjudge, believe, deem, esteem, estimate, hold, imagine, judge, look upon, rate, see, suppose, think, treat, value, view 2 = **look at**, behold, check, check out (informal), clock (Brit. slang), eye, eyeball (U.S. slang), gaze at, get a load of (informal), mark, notice, observe, remark, scrutinize, take a dekko at (Brit. slang), view, watch 3 = **heed**, attend, listen to, mind, note, pay attention to, respect, take into consideration, take notice of 4 **as regards** = **concerning**, pertaining to, regarding, relating to ◆ noun 5 = **respect**, affection, attachment, care, concern, consideration, deference, esteem, honour, love, store, thought 6 = **heed**, attention, interest, mind, notice 7 = **look**, gaze, glance, scrutiny, stare 8 = **relation**, bearing, concern, connection, reference, relevance

regardful adjective = **mindful**, attentive, aware, careful, considerate, dutiful, heedful, observant, respectful, thoughtful, watchful

regarding preposition = **concerning**, about, apropos, as regards, as to, in or with regard to, in re, in respect of, in the matter of, on the subject of, re, respecting, with reference to

regardless adjective 1 = **heedless**, disregarding, inattentive, inconsiderate, indifferent, neglectful, negligent, rash, reckless, remiss, unconcerned, unmindful ◆ adverb 2 = **in spite of everything**, anyway, come what may, despite everything, for all that, in any case, nevertheless, no matter what, nonetheless, rain or shine
➤ Antonyms
adjective ≠**heedless**: heedful, mindful, regardful

regards plural noun = **good wishes**, best wishes, compliments, greetings, respects, salutations

regenerate verb = **renew**, breathe new life into, change, give a shot in the arm, inspirit, invigorate, kick-start (informal), reawaken, reinvigorate, rejuvenate, renovate, restore, revive, revivify, uplift
➤ Antonyms
become moribund, decline, degenerate, stagnate, stultify

regime noun = **government**, administration, establishment, leadership, management, reign, rule, system

regimented adjective = **controlled**, disciplined, ordered, organized, regulated, systematized

region noun 1 = **area**, country, district, division, expanse, land, locality, part, patch, place, province, quarter, section, sector, territory, tract, zone **2 = sphere**, domain, field, province, realm, world **3** *As in* **in the region of = vicinity**, area, neighbourhood, range, scope, sphere

regional *adjective* **= local**, district, parochial, provincial, zonal

register *noun* **1 = list**, annals, archives, catalogue, chronicle, diary, file, ledger, log, memorandum, record, roll, roster, schedule ♦ *verb* **2 = record**, catalogue, check in, chronicle, enlist, enrol, enter, inscribe, list, note, set down, sign on *or* up, take down **3 = show**, be shown, bespeak, betray, display, exhibit, express, indicate, manifest, mark, read, reflect, reveal, say **4** *Informal* **= have an effect**, come home, dawn on, get through, impress, make an impression, sink in, tell

regress *verb* **= revert**, backslide, degenerate, deteriorate, ebb, fall away *or* off, fall back, go back, lapse, recede, relapse, retreat, retrogress, return, wane
➤ **Antonyms**
advance, improve, progress, wax

regret *verb* **1 = feel sorry about**, bemoan, be upset, bewail, cry over spilt milk, deplore, feel remorse about, grieve, lament, miss, mourn, repent, rue, weep over ♦ *noun* **2 = sorrow**, bitterness, compunction, contrition, disappointment, grief, lamentation, pang of conscience, penitence, remorse, repentance, ruefulness, self-reproach
➤ **Antonyms**
verb ≠**feel sorry about**: be happy, be satisfied, feel satisfaction, have not looked back, rejoice ♦ *noun* ≠**sorrow**: callousness, contentment, impenitence, lack of compassion, pleasure, satisfaction

regretful *adjective* **= sorry**, apologetic, ashamed, contrite, disappointed, mournful, penitent, remorseful, repentant, rueful, sad, sorrowful

regrettable *adjective* **= unfortunate**, deplorable, disappointing, distressing, ill-advised, lamentable, pitiable, sad, shameful, unhappy

regular *adjective* **1 = normal**, common, commonplace, customary, daily, everyday, habitual, ordinary, routine, typical, unvarying, usual **2 = even**, balanced, flat, level, smooth, straight, symmetrical, uniform **3 = systematic**, consistent, constant, established, even, fixed, ordered, periodic, rhythmic, set, stated, steady, uniform **4 = methodical**, dependable, efficient, formal, orderly, standardized, steady, systematic **5 = official**, approved, bona fide, correct, established, formal,

orthodox, proper, sanctioned, standard, traditional
➤ **Antonyms**
≠**normal**: abnormal, exceptional, infrequent, irregular, occasional, rare, uncommon, unconventional, unusual ≠**even**: erratic, irregular, uneven ≠**systematic**: erratic, inconsistent, inconstant, irregular, varied ≠**methodical**: disorderly, unmethodical

regulate *verb* **1 = control**, administer, arrange, conduct, direct, govern, guide, handle, manage, monitor, order, organize, oversee, rule, run, settle, superintend, supervise, systematize **2 = adjust**, balance, fit, moderate, modulate, tune

regulation *noun* **1 = rule**, canon, commandment, decree, dictate, direction, edict, law, order, ordinance, precept, procedure, requirement, standing order, statute **2 = control**, administration, arrangement, direction, governance, government, management, supervision **3 = adjustment**, modulation, tuning ♦ *adjective* **4 = conventional**, customary, mandatory, normal, official, prescribed, required, standard, usual

regurgitate *verb* **= vomit**, barf (*U.S. slang*), chuck (up) (*slang, chiefly U.S.*), chunder (*slang, chiefly Austral.*), disgorge, puke (*slang*), sick up (*informal*), spew (out *or* up), throw up (*informal*)

rehabilitate *verb* **1 = reintegrate**, adjust **2 = restore**, re-establish, reinstate **3 = redeem**, clear, reform, restore, save

rehash *verb* **1 = rework**, alter, change, make over, rearrange, refashion, rejig (*informal*), reshuffle, reuse, rewrite ♦ *noun* **2 = reworking**, new version, rearrangement, rewrite

rehearsal *noun* **1 = practice**, drill, going-over (*informal*), practice session, preparation, reading, rehearsing, run-through **2 = recital**, account, catalogue, description, enumeration, list, narration, recounting, relation, telling

rehearse *verb* **1 = practise**, act, drill, go over, prepare, ready, recite, repeat, run through, study, train, try out **2 = recite**, delineate, depict, describe, detail, enumerate, go over, list, narrate, recount, relate, review, run through, tell

reign *noun* **1 = rule**, ascendancy, command, control, dominion, empire, hegemony, influence, monarchy, power, sovereignty, supremacy, sway ♦ *verb* **2 = rule**, administer, be in power, command, govern, hold sway, influence, occupy *or* sit on the throne, wear the crown, wield the sceptre **3 = be supreme**, be rampant, be rife, hold sway, obtain, predominate, prevail

reimburse verb = **pay back**, compensate, indemnify, recompense, refund, remunerate, repay, restore, return, square up

rein noun 1 = **control**, brake, bridle, check, curb, harness, hold, restraint, restriction 2 **give (a) free rein (to)** = **give a free hand**, free, give a blank cheque (to), give carte blanche, give (someone) his or her head, give way to, indulge, let go, remove restraints ♦ verb 3 = **control**, bridle, check, curb, halt, hold, hold back, limit, restrain, restrict, slow down

reincarnation noun = **rebirth**, metempsychosis, transmigration of souls

reinforce verb = **support**, augment, bolster, buttress, emphasize, fortify, harden, increase, prop, shore up, stiffen, strengthen, stress, supplement, toughen, underline
➤ **Antonyms**
contradict, undermine, weaken

reinforcement noun 1 = **strengthening**, addition, amplification, augmentation, enlargement, fortification, increase, supplement 2 = **support**, brace, buttress, prop, shore, stay 3 **reinforcements** = **reserves**, additional or fresh troops, auxiliaries, support

reinstate verb = **restore**, bring back, recall, re-establish, rehabilitate, replace, return

reiterate verb Formal = **repeat**, do again, iterate, recapitulate, restate, retell, say again

reject verb 1 = **deny**, decline, disallow, exclude, renounce, repudiate, veto 2 = **rebuff**, jilt, refuse, repulse, say no to, spurn, turn down 3 = **discard**, bin, cast aside, eliminate, jettison, scrap, throw away or out ♦ noun 4 = **castoff**, clunker (informal), discard, failure, flotsam, second
➤ **Antonyms**
verb ≠**deny**: accept, agree, allow, approve, permit ≠**rebuff**: accept ≠**discard**: accept, receive, select ♦ noun ≠**castoff**: prize, treasure

rejection noun 1 = **denial**, dismissal, exclusion, renunciation, repudiation, thumbs down, veto 2 = **rebuff**, brushoff (slang), bum's rush (slang), kick in the teeth (slang), knock-back (slang), refusal
➤ **Antonyms**
≠**denial**: acceptance, affirmation, approval ≠**rebuff**: acceptance, selection

rejig verb Informal = **rearrange**, alter, juggle, manipulate, massage, reorganize, reshuffle, tweak

rejoice verb = **be glad**, be happy, be overjoyed, celebrate, delight, exult, glory, joy, jump for joy, make merry, revel, triumph
➤ **Antonyms**
be sad, be unhappy, be upset, grieve, lament, mourn

rejoicing noun = **happiness**, celebration, cheer, delight, elation, exultation, festivity, gaiety, gladness, joy, jubilation, merrymaking, revelry, triumph

rejoin verb = **reply**, answer, come back with, respond, retort, return, riposte

rejoinder noun = **reply**, answer, comeback (informal), counter, counterattack, response, retort, riposte

rejuvenate verb = **revitalize**, breathe new life into, give new life to, make young again, reanimate, refresh, regenerate, reinvigorate, renew, restore, restore vitality to, revivify

relapse verb 1 = **lapse**, backslide, degenerate, fail, fall back, regress, retrogress, revert, slip back, weaken 2 = **worsen**, deteriorate, fade, fail, sicken, sink, weaken ♦ noun 3 = **lapse**, backsliding, fall from grace, recidivism, regression, retrogression, reversion 4 = **worsening**, deterioration, recurrence, setback, turn for the worse, weakening
➤ **Antonyms**
verb ≠**worsen**: get better, improve, rally, recover ♦ noun ≠**worsening**: improvement, rally, recovery, turn for the better

relate verb 1 = **connect**, ally, associate, correlate, couple, join, link 2 = **concern**, appertain, apply, bear upon, be relevant to, have reference to, have to do with, pertain, refer 3 = **tell**, chronicle, describe, detail, give an account of, impart, narrate, present, recite, recount, rehearse, report, set forth
➤ **Antonyms**
≠**connect**: detach, disconnect, dissociate, divorce ≠**concern**: be irrelevant to, be unconnected, have nothing to do with

related adjective 1 = **akin**, agnate, cognate, consanguineous, kin, kindred 2 = **associated**, accompanying, affiliated, akin, allied, cognate, concomitant, connected, correlated, interconnected, joint, linked
➤ **Antonyms**
≠**akin**: unrelated ≠**associated**: separate, unconnected, unrelated

relation noun 1 = **connection**, application, bearing, bond, comparison, correlation, interdependence, link, pertinence, reference, regard, similarity, tie-in 2

= **relative**, kin, kinsman *or* kinswoman **3**
= **kinship**, affiliation, affinity,
consanguinity, kindred, propinquity,
relationship **4** = **account**, description,
narration, narrative, recital, recountal,
report, story, tale

relations *plural noun* **1** = **dealings**, affairs,
associations, connections, contact,
interaction, intercourse, rapport,
relationship, terms **2** = **family**, clan, kin,
kindred, kinsfolk, kinsmen, relatives, tribe

relationship *noun* **1** = **association**, affinity,
bond, communications, conjunction,
connection, kinship, rapport **2** = **affair**,
liaison **3** = **connection**, correlation, link,
parallel, proportion, ratio, similarity, tie-up

relative *adjective* **1** = **dependent**, allied,
associated, comparative, connected,
contingent, corresponding, proportionate,
reciprocal, related, respective **2** = **relevant**,
applicable, apposite, appropriate,
appurtenant, apropos, germane, pertinent
3 relative to = **in proportion to**,
corresponding to, proportional to ♦ *noun*
4 = **relation**, connection, kinsman *or*
kinswoman, member of one's *or* the family

relatively *adverb* = **comparatively**, in *or* by
comparison, rather, somewhat, to some
extent

relax *verb* **1** = **be** *or* **feel at ease**, calm, chill
out (*slang, chiefly U.S.*), hang loose (*slang*),
laze, let oneself go (*informal*), let one's hair
down (*informal*), lighten up (*slang*), loosen
up, make oneself at home, mellow out
(*informal*), put one's feet up, rest, take it
easy, take one's ease, unbend, unwind **2**
= **lessen**, abate, diminish, ease, ebb, let up,
loosen, lower, mitigate, moderate, reduce,
relieve, slacken, weaken
➤ **Antonyms**
≠**be** *or* **feel at ease**: be alarmed, be alert
≠**lessen**: heighten, increase, intensify,
tense, tighten, work

relaxation *noun* **1** = **leisure**, amusement,
enjoyment, entertainment, fun, pleasure,
recreation, refreshment, rest **2** = **lessening**,
abatement, diminution, easing, let-up
(*informal*), moderation, reduction,
slackening, weakening

relaxed *adjective* = **easy-going**, casual,
comfortable, downbeat (*informal*), easy,
free and easy, informal, insouciant,
laid-back (*informal*), leisurely, mellow,
mild, nonchalant, unhurried, untaxing

relay *noun* **1** = **shift**, relief, turn **2**
= **message**, communication, dispatch,
transmission ♦ *verb* **3** = **pass on**,
broadcast, carry, communicate, hand on,
send, spread, transmit

release *verb* **1** = **set free**, deliver, discharge,

disengage, drop, emancipate, extricate,
free, let go, let out, liberate, loose,
manumit, turn loose, unbridle, unchain,
undo, unfasten, unfetter, unloose,
unshackle, untie **2** = **acquit**, absolve,
dispense, excuse, exempt, exonerate, let
go, let off **3** = **issue**, break, circulate,
disseminate, distribute, launch, make
known, make public, present, publish, put
out, unveil ♦ *noun* **4** = **liberation**,
deliverance, delivery, discharge,
emancipation, freedom, liberty,
manumission, relief **5** = **acquittal**,
absolution, acquittance, dispensation,
exemption, exoneration, let-off (*informal*)
6 = **issue**, announcement, offering,
proclamation, publication
➤ **Antonyms**
verb ≠**set free**: detain, engage, fasten,
hold, imprison, incarcerate, keep ≠**issue**:
suppress, withhold ♦ *noun* ≠**liberation**:
detention, imprisonment, incarceration,
internment

relegate *verb* = **demote**, downgrade

relent *verb* **1** = **be merciful**, acquiesce,
capitulate, change one's mind, come
round, forbear, give in, give quarter, give
way, have pity, melt, show mercy, soften,
unbend, yield **2** = **ease**, die down, drop,
fall, let up, relax, slacken, slow, weaken
➤ **Antonyms**
≠**be merciful**: be unyielding, give no
quarter, remain firm, show no mercy
≠**ease**: increase, intensify, strengthen

relentless *adjective* **1** = **unremitting**,
incessant, nonstop, persistent, punishing,
sustained, unabated, unbroken,
unfaltering, unflagging, unrelenting,
unrelieved, unstoppable **2** = **merciless**,
cruel, fierce, grim, hard, harsh, implacable,
inexorable, inflexible, pitiless, remorseless,
ruthless, uncompromising, undeviating,
unforgiving, unrelenting, unstoppable,
unyielding
➤ **Antonyms**
≠**merciless**: compassionate, forgiving,
merciful, submissive, yielding

relevant *adjective* = **significant**, applicable,
apposite, appropriate, appurtenant, apt,
fitting, germane, material, pertinent,
proper, related, relative, suited, to the
point, to the purpose
➤ **Antonyms**
beside the point, extraneous, extrinsic,
immaterial, inapplicable, inappropriate,
irrelevant, unconnected, unrelated

reliable *adjective* = **dependable**, certain,
faithful, honest, predictable, regular,
reputable, responsible, safe, sound, stable,
staunch, sure, tried and true, true,

trustworthy, trusty, unfailing, upright
➤ **Antonyms**
irresponsible, undependable, unreliable, untrustworthy

reliance *noun* = **trust**, assurance, belief, confidence, credence, credit, dependence, faith

relic *noun* = **remnant**, fragment, keepsake, memento, remembrance, scrap, souvenir, survival, token, trace, vestige

relief *noun* **1** = **ease**, abatement, alleviation, assuagement, comfort, cure, deliverance, easement, mitigation, palliation, release, remedy, solace **2** = **rest**, break, breather (*informal*), diversion, let-up (*informal*), refreshment, relaxation, remission, respite **3** = **aid**, assistance, help, succour, support, sustenance

relieve *verb* **1** = **ease**, abate, allay, alleviate, assuage, calm, comfort, console, cure, diminish, dull, mitigate, mollify, palliate, relax, soften, solace, soothe **2** = **help**, aid, assist, bring aid to, succour, support, sustain **3** = **free**, deliver, discharge, disencumber, exempt, release, unburden **4** = **take over from**, give (someone) a break or rest, stand in for, substitute for, take the place of **5** = **interrupt**, break, brighten, let up on (*informal*), lighten, slacken, vary
➤ **Antonyms**
≠**ease**: aggravate, exacerbate, heighten, intensify, worsen

religious *adjective* **1** = **devout**, churchgoing, devotional, divine, doctrinal, faithful, god-fearing, godly, holy, pious, pure, reverent, righteous, sacred, scriptural, sectarian, spiritual, theological **2** = **conscientious**, exact, faithful, fastidious, meticulous, punctilious, rigid, rigorous, scrupulous, unerring, unswerving
➤ **Antonyms**
≠**devout**: godless, infidel, irreligious, rational, secular, unbelieving

relinquish *verb Formal* = **give up**, abandon, abdicate, cast off, cede, desert, drop, forgo, forsake, hand over, leave, let go, quit, release, renounce, repudiate, resign, retire from, say goodbye to, surrender, vacate, waive, withdraw from, yield

relish *verb* **1** = **enjoy**, appreciate, delight in, fancy, lick one's lips, like, look forward to, luxuriate in, prefer, revel in, savour, taste ♦ *noun* **2** = **enjoyment**, appetite, appreciation, fancy, fondness, gusto, liking, love, partiality, penchant, predilection, stomach, taste, zest, zing (*informal*) **3** = **condiment**, appetizer, sauce, seasoning **4** = **flavour**, piquancy, savour, smack, spice, tang, taste, trace
➤ **Antonyms**

verb ≠**enjoy**: be unenthusiastic about, dislike, loathe ♦ *noun* ≠**enjoyment**: dislike, distaste, loathing

reluctance *noun* = **unwillingness**, aversion, backwardness, disinclination, dislike, disrelish, distaste, hesitancy, loathing, repugnance

reluctant *adjective* = **unwilling**, averse, backward, disinclined, grudging, hesitant, loath, recalcitrant, slow, unenthusiastic
➤ **Antonyms**
eager, enthusiastic, inclined, keen, willing

rely *verb* = **depend**, bank, be confident of, be sure of, bet, count, have confidence in, lean, reckon, swear by, trust

remain *verb* **1** = **continue**, abide, bide, dwell, endure, go on, last, persist, prevail, stand, stay, survive **2** = **stay behind**, be left, delay, hang in the air, linger, stay put (*informal*), tarry, wait
➤ **Antonyms**
≠**stay behind**: depart, go, leave

remainder *noun* = **rest**, balance, butt, dregs, excess, leavings, oddment, relic, remains, remnant, residue, residuum, stub, surplus, tail end, trace, vestige(s)

remaining *adjective* = **left-over**, abiding, extant, lasting, lingering, outstanding, persisting, residual, surviving, unfinished

remains *plural noun* **1** = **remnants**, balance, crumbs, debris, detritus, dregs, fragments, leavings, leftovers, oddments, odds and ends, pieces, relics, remainder, residue, rest, scraps, traces, vestiges **2** = **corpse**, body, cadaver, carcass

remark *verb* **1** = **comment**, declare, mention, observe, pass comment, reflect, say, state **2** = **notice**, espy, make out, mark, note, observe, perceive, regard, see, take note or notice of ♦ *noun* **3** = **comment**, assertion, declaration, observation, opinion, reflection, statement, thought, utterance, word

remarkable *adjective* = **extraordinary**, conspicuous, distinguished, famous, impressive, miraculous, notable, noteworthy, odd, outstanding, phenomenal, pre-eminent, prominent, rare, signal, singular, strange, striking, surprising, uncommon, unusual, wonderful
➤ **Antonyms**
banal, common, commonplace, everyday, insignificant, mundane, ordinary, unexceptional, unimpressive, unsurprising, usual

remedy *noun* **1** = **cure**, antidote, counteractive, medicament, medicine, nostrum, panacea, relief, restorative, therapy, treatment **2** = **solution**, antidote, corrective, countermeasure, panacea, redress, relief ♦ *verb* **3** = **put right**, ameliorate, correct, fix, rectify, redress, reform, relieve, repair, set to rights, solve **4** = **cure**, alleviate, assuage, control, ease, heal, help, mitigate, palliate, relieve, restore, soothe, treat

remember *verb* **1** = **recall**, call to mind, call up, commemorate, look back (on), put one's finger on, recognize, recollect, reminisce, retain, summon up, think back **2** = **bear in mind**, keep in mind
➤ **Antonyms**
disregard, forget, ignore, neglect, overlook

remembrance *noun* **1** = **memory**, mind, recall, recognition, recollection, regard, reminiscence, retrospect, thought **2** = **souvenir**, commemoration, keepsake, memento, memorial, monument, relic, reminder, testimonial, token

remind *verb* = **call to mind**, awaken memories of, bring back to, bring to mind, call up, jog one's memory, make (someone) remember, prompt, put in mind, refresh one's memory

reminisce *verb* = **recall**, go over in the memory, hark back, live in the past, look back, recollect, remember, review, think back

reminiscence *noun* = **recollection**, anecdote, memoir, memory, recall, reflection, remembrance

reminiscent *adjective* = **suggestive**, evocative, redolent, remindful, similar

remiss *adjective Formal* = **careless**, derelict, dilatory, forgetful, heedless, inattentive, indifferent, lackadaisical, lax, neglectful, negligent, regardless, slack, slapdash, slipshod, sloppy (*informal*), slothful, slow, tardy, thoughtless, unmindful
➤ **Antonyms**
attentive, careful, diligent, painstaking, scrupulous

remission *noun* **1** = **reduction**, decrease, diminution, lessening, suspension **2** = **pardon**, absolution, acquittal, amnesty, discharge, excuse, exemption, exoneration, forgiveness, indulgence, release, reprieve **3** = **lessening**, abatement, abeyance, alleviation, amelioration, ebb, let-up (*informal*), lull, moderation, relaxation, respite

remit *verb* **1** = **send**, dispatch, forward, mail, post, transmit **2** = **cancel**, desist, halt, repeal, rescind, stop **3** = **lessen**, abate, alleviate, decrease, diminish, dwindle, ease up, fall away, mitigate, moderate, reduce, relax, sink, slacken, soften, wane, weaken **4** = **postpone**, defer, delay, put off, put on the back burner (*informal*), shelve,

suspend, take a rain check on (*U.S. & Canad. informal*) ♦ *noun* **5** = **instructions**, authorization, brief, guidelines, orders, terms of reference

remittance *noun* = **payment**, allowance, consideration, fee

remnant *noun* = **remainder**, bit, butt, end, fragment, hangover, leftovers, oddment, piece, remains, residue, residuum, rest, rump, scrap, shred, stub, tail end, trace, vestige

remonstrance *noun Formal* = **protest**, complaint, expostulation, grievance, objection, protestation, reprimand, reproof

remonstrate *verb Formal* = **protest**, argue, challenge, complain, dispute, dissent, expostulate, object, take exception, take issue

remorse *noun* = **regret**, anguish, bad *or* guilty conscience, compassion, compunction, contrition, grief, guilt, pangs of conscience, penitence, pity, repentance, ruefulness, self-reproach, shame, sorrow

remorseful *adjective* = **regretful**, apologetic, ashamed, conscience-stricken, contrite, guilt-ridden, guilty, penitent, repentant, rueful, sad, self-reproachful, sorrowful, sorry

remorseless *adjective* **1** = **pitiless**, callous, cruel, hard, hardhearted, harsh, implacable, inhumane, merciless, ruthless, savage, uncompassionate, unforgiving, unmerciful **2** = **relentless**, inexorable, unrelenting, unremitting, unstoppable

remote *adjective* **1** = **distant**, backwoods, far, faraway, far-off, godforsaken, inaccessible, in the middle of nowhere, isolated, lonely, off the beaten track, outlying, out-of-the-way, secluded **2** = **irrelevant**, extraneous, extrinsic, immaterial, outside, removed, unconnected, unrelated **3** = **aloof**, abstracted, cold, detached, distant, faraway, indifferent, removed, reserved, standoffish, unapproachable, uncommunicative, uninterested, uninvolved, withdrawn **4** = **slight**, doubtful, dubious, faint, implausible, inconsiderable, meagre, negligible, outside, poor, slender, slim, small, unlikely
➤ **Antonyms**
≠**distant**: adjacent, central, close, just round the corner, near, nearby, neighbouring ≠**irrelevant**: intrinsic, related, relevant ≠**aloof**: alert, attentive, aware, gregarious, interested, involved, outgoing, sociable ≠**slight**: considerable, good, likely, strong

removal *noun* **1** = **taking away** *or* **off** *or*

out, abstraction, dislodgment, displacement, dispossession, ejection, elimination, eradication, erasure, expunction, extraction, purging, stripping, subtraction, uprooting, withdrawal **2 = dismissal**, expulsion **3 = move**, departure, flitting (*Scot. & Northern English dialect*), relocation, transfer

remove *verb* **1 = take away** *or* **off** *or* **out**, abolish, abstract, amputate, carry off *or* away, cart off (*slang*), delete, detach, dislodge, displace, do away with, efface, eject, eliminate, erase, excise, expunge, extract, get rid of, move, pull, purge, shed, strike out, transfer, wipe from the face of the earth, wipe out, withdraw **2 = dismiss**, depose, dethrone, discharge, expel, oust, relegate, show one the door, throw out, throw out on one's ear (*informal*), unseat **3 = move**, depart, flit (*Scot. & Northern English dialect*), move away, quit, relocate, shift, transfer, transport, vacate
➤ **Antonyms**
≠**take away** *or* **off** *or* **out**: don, insert, join, link, place, put, put back, put in, put on, replace, set ≠**dismiss**: appoint, install

remunerate *verb Formal* **= pay**, compensate, indemnify, recompense, redress, reimburse, repay, requite, reward

remuneration *noun* **= payment**, compensation, earnings, fee, income, indemnity, pay, profit, recompense, reimbursement, reparation, repayment, return, reward, salary, stipend, wages

remunerative *adjective* **= profitable**, economic, gainful, lucrative, moneymaking, paying, recompensing, rewarding, rich, worthwhile

renaissance, renascence *noun* **= rebirth**, awakening, new birth, new dawn, reappearance, reawakening, re-emergence, regeneration, renewal, restoration, resurgence, resurrection, revival

renascent *adjective Literary* **= resurgent**, reanimated, reawakening, reborn, re-emerging, renewed, resurrected, reviving

rend *verb Literary* **= tear**, break, burst, cleave, crack, dissever, divide, fracture, lacerate, pierce, pull, rip, rupture, separate, sever, shatter, smash, splinter, split, sunder (*literary*), tear to pieces, wrench

render *verb* **1 = make**, cause to become, leave **2 = provide**, contribute, deliver, furnish, give, hand out, make available, pay, present, show, submit, supply, tender, turn over, yield **3 = translate**, construe, explain, interpret, put, reproduce, restate, transcribe **4**

= represent, act, depict, do, give, interpret, perform, play, portray, present **5 = give up**, cede, deliver, give, hand over, relinquish, surrender, turn over, yield

rendezvous *noun* **1 = appointment**, assignation, date, engagement, meeting, tryst (*archaic*) **2 = meeting place**, gathering point, place of assignation, trysting-place (*archaic*), venue ◆ *verb* **3 = meet**, assemble, be reunited, collect, come together, converge, gather, get together, join up, muster, rally

rendition *noun Formal* **1 = performance**, arrangement, delivery, depiction, execution, interpretation, portrayal, presentation, reading, rendering, take (*informal, chiefly U.S.*), version **2 = translation**, explanation, interpretation, reading, transcription, version

renegade *noun* **1 = deserter**, apostate, backslider, betrayer, defector, dissident, mutineer, outlaw, rebel, recreant (*archaic*), runaway, traitor, turncoat ◆ *adjective* **2 = traitorous**, apostate, backsliding, disloyal, dissident, mutinous, outlaw, rebel, rebellious, recreant (*archaic*), runaway, unfaithful

renege *verb* **= break one's word**, back out, break a promise, default, go back, repudiate, welsh (*slang*)

renew *verb* **1 = recommence**, begin again, breathe new life into, bring up to date, continue, extend, prolong, reaffirm, recreate, re-establish, regenerate, rejuvenate, reopen, repeat, restate, resume, revitalize **2 = restore**, fix up (*informal, chiefly U.S. & Canad.*), mend, modernize, overhaul, refit, refurbish, renovate, repair, transform **3 = replace**, refresh, replenish, restock

renounce *verb* **= give up**, abandon, abdicate, abjure, abnegate, abstain from, cast off, decline, deny, discard, disclaim, disown, eschew, forgo, forsake, forswear, leave off, quit, recant, reject, relinquish, renege, repudiate, resign, retract, spurn, swear off, throw off, waive, wash one's hands of
➤ **Antonyms**
assert, avow, claim, maintain, reassert

renovate *verb* **= restore**, do up (*informal*), fix up (*informal, chiefly U.S. & Canad.*), modernize, overhaul, recondition, recreate, refit, reform, refurbish, rehabilitate, remodel, renew, repair, revamp

renown *noun* **= fame**, acclaim, celebrity, distinction, eminence, glory, honour, illustriousness, mark, note, reputation, repute, stardom

renowned *adjective* = **famous**, acclaimed, celebrated, distinguished, eminent, esteemed, famed, illustrious, notable, noted, well-known
➤ **Antonyms**
forgotten, little-known, neglected, obscure, unknown

rent[1] *verb* 1 = **hire**, charter, lease, let ♦ *noun* 2 = **hire**, fee, lease, payment, rental, tariff

rent[2] *noun* = **tear**, breach, break, chink, crack, flaw, gash, hole, opening, perforation, rip, slash, slit, split

renunciation *noun* = **giving up**, abandonment, abdication, abjuration, abnegation, denial, disavowal, disclaimer, eschewal, forswearing, rejection, relinquishment, repudiation, spurning, surrender, waiver

reorganize *verb* = **rearrange**, make a clean sweep, rationalize, reshuffle, restructure, shake up, spring-clean

repair[1] *verb* 1 = **mend**, fix, heal, make good, patch, patch up, put back together, recover, renew, renovate, restore, restore to working order 2 = **put right**, compensate for, make up for, rectify, redress, retrieve, square ♦ *noun* 3 = **mend**, adjustment, darn, overhaul, patch, restoration 4 = **condition**, fettle, form, nick (*informal*), shape (*informal*), state
➤ **Antonyms**
verb ≠ **mend**: damage, destroy, harm, ruin, wreck

repair[2] *verb* = **go**, betake oneself, head for, leave for, move, remove, retire, set off for, withdraw

reparable *adjective* = **curable**, recoverable, rectifiable, remediable, restorable, retrievable, salvageable

reparation *noun* = **compensation**, amends, atonement, damages, indemnity, recompense, redress, repair, requital, restitution, satisfaction

repartee *noun* = **wit**, badinage, banter, bon mot, pleasantry, raillery, riposte, sally, witticism, wittiness, wordplay

repast *noun* = **meal**, collation, food, nourishment, spread (*informal*), victuals

repay *verb* 1 = **pay back**, compensate, make restitution, recompense, refund, reimburse, remunerate, requite, restore, return, reward, settle up with, square 2 = **reciprocate**, avenge, even *or* settle the score with, get back at, get even with (*informal*), get one's own back on (*informal*), hit back, make reprisal, pay (someone) back in his *or* her own coin, retaliate, return the compliment, revenge

repeal *verb* 1 = **abolish**, abrogate, annul, cancel, countermand, declare null and void, invalidate, nullify, obviate, recall, rescind, reverse, revoke, set aside, withdraw ♦ *noun* 2 = **abolition**, abrogation, annulment, cancellation, invalidation, nullification, rescinding, rescindment, revocation, withdrawal
➤ **Antonyms**
verb ≠ **abolish**: confirm, enact, introduce, pass, ratify, reaffirm, validate ♦ *noun* ≠ **abolition**: confirmation, enactment, introduction, passing, ratification, reaffirmation, validation

repeat *verb* 1 = **reiterate**, duplicate, echo, quote, recapitulate, recite, redo, rehearse, relate, renew, replay, reproduce, rerun, reshow, restate, retell ♦ *noun* 2 = **repetition**, duplicate, echo, recapitulation, reiteration, replay, reproduction, rerun, reshowing

repeatedly *adverb* = **over and over**, again and again, frequently, many times, often, time after time, time and (time) again

repel *verb* 1 = **disgust**, give one the creeps (*informal*), gross out (*U.S. slang*), make one shudder, make one sick, nauseate, offend, put one off, revolt, sicken, turn one off (*informal*), turn one's stomach 2 = **drive off**, beat off, check, fight, hold off, keep at arm's length, oppose, parry, put to flight, rebuff, refuse, reject, repulse, resist, ward off
➤ **Antonyms**
≠ **disgust**: attract, delight, draw, entrance, fascinate, invite, please ≠ **drive off**: submit

repellent *adjective* 1 = **disgusting**, abhorrent, abominable, discouraging, distasteful, hateful, horrid, loathsome, nauseating, noxious, obnoxious, obscene, odious, offensive, off-putting (*Brit. informal*), repugnant, repulsive, revolting, sickening, yucky *or* yukky (*slang*) 2 = **proof**, impermeable, repelling, resistant

repent *verb* = **regret**, atone, be ashamed, be contrite, be sorry, deplore, feel remorse, lament, relent, reproach oneself, rue, see the error of one's ways, show penitence, sorrow

repentance *noun* = **regret**, compunction, contrition, grief, guilt, penitence, remorse, sackcloth and ashes, self-reproach, sorriness, sorrow

repentant *adjective* = **regretful**, apologetic, ashamed, contrite, penitent, remorseful, rueful, self-reproachful, sorry

repercussion *noun* 1 **repercussions** = **consequences**, backlash, result, sequel, side effects 2 = **reverberation**, echo, rebound, recoil

repertoire *noun* = **range**, collection, list, repertory, repository, stock, store, supply

repertory *noun* = **repertoire**, collection, list, range, repository, stock, store, supply

repetition *noun* = **repeating**, duplication, echo, reappearance, recapitulation, recital, recurrence, rehearsal, reiteration, relation, renewal, replication, restatement, tautology

repetitious *adjective* = **long-winded**, pleonastic, prolix, redundant, tautological, tedious, verbose, wordy

repetitive *adjective* = **monotonous**, boring, dull, mechanical, recurrent, samey (*informal*), tedious, unchanging, unvaried

rephrase *verb* = **reword**, paraphrase, put differently, recast, say in other words

repine *verb Literary* = **complain**, brood, eat one's heart out, fret, grieve, grumble, lament, languish, moan, mope, sulk

replace *verb* 1 = **take the place of**, fill (someone's) shoes *or* boots, follow, oust, stand in lieu of, step into (someone's) shoes *or* boots, substitute, succeed, supersede, supplant, supply, take over from 2 = **put back**, re-establish, reinstate, restore

replacement *noun* = **successor**, double, fill-in, proxy, stand-in, substitute, surrogate, understudy

replenish *verb* = **refill**, fill, furnish, make up, provide, reload, renew, replace, restock, restore, stock, supply, top up
➤ **Antonyms**
consume, drain, empty, exhaust, use up

replete *adjective* 1 = **sated**, full, full up, gorged, satiated 2 = **filled**, abounding, brimful, brimming, charged, chock-full, crammed, full to bursting, glutted, jammed, jam-packed, stuffed, teeming, well-provided, well-stocked
➤ **Antonyms**
≠**sated**: empty, esurient, famished, hungry, starving ≠**filled**: bare, barren, empty, lacking, wanting

repletion *noun* 1 = **fullness**, overfullness, satiation, satiety 2 = **surfeit**, completeness, glut, plethora, superfluity

replica *noun* = **duplicate**, carbon copy (*informal*), copy, facsimile, imitation, model, reproduction
➤ **Antonyms**
master, original, prototype

replicate *verb* = **copy**, ape, duplicate, follow, mimic, recreate, reduplicate, repeat, reproduce

reply *verb* 1 = **answer**, acknowledge, come back, counter, echo, react, reciprocate, rejoin, respond, retaliate, retort, return, riposte, write back ♦ *noun* 2 = **answer**, acknowledgment, comeback (*informal*), counter, counterattack, echo, reaction, reciprocation, rejoinder, response, retaliation, retort, return, riposte

report *verb* 1 = **communicate**, air, announce, bring word, broadcast, circulate, cover, declare, describe, detail, document, give an account of, inform of, mention, narrate, note, notify, pass on, proclaim, publish, recite, record, recount, relate, relay, state, tell, write up 2 = **present oneself**, appear, arrive, be present, clock in *or* on, come, show up (*informal*), turn up ♦ *noun* 3 = **account**, announcement, communication, declaration, description, detail, information, narrative, news, note, recital, record, relation, statement, summary, tale, tidings, version, word 4 = **article**, communiqué, dispatch, message, paper, piece, story, write-up 5 = **rumour**, buzz, gossip, hearsay, talk 6 = **bang**, blast, boom, crack, crash, detonation, discharge, explosion, noise, reverberation, sound 7 = **repute**, character, eminence, esteem, fame, regard, reputation

reporter *noun* = **journalist**, announcer, correspondent, hack (*derogatory*), journo (*slang*), newscaster, newshound (*informal*), newspaperman *or* newspaperwoman, pressman, writer

repose *noun* 1 = **peace**, ease, inactivity, quiet, quietness, quietude, relaxation, respite, rest, restfulness, stillness, tranquillity 2 = **composure**, aplomb, calmness, dignity, equanimity, peace of mind, poise, self-possession, serenity, tranquillity 3 = **sleep**, slumber ♦ *verb* 4 = **rest**, drowse, lay down, lie, lie down, lie upon, recline, relax, rest upon, sleep, slumber, take it easy

repository *noun* = **store**, archive, depository, depot, magazine, receptacle, storehouse, treasury, vault, warehouse

reprehensible *adjective* = **blameworthy**, bad, censurable, condemnable, culpable, discreditable, disgraceful, ignoble, objectionable, opprobrious, remiss, shameful, unworthy
➤ **Antonyms**
acceptable, admirable, forgivable, laudable, pardonable, praiseworthy, unobjectionable

represent *verb* 1 = **stand for**, act for, be, betoken, correspond to, equal, equate with, express, mean, serve as, speak for, substitute for, symbolize 2 = **exemplify**, embody, epitomize, personify, symbolize, typify 3 = **depict**, delineate, denote, describe, designate, express, illustrate, outline, picture, portray, render, reproduce, show, sketch

representation noun 1 = **portrayal**, account, delineation, depiction, description 2 = **picture**, illustration, image, likeness, model, portrait, sketch 3 often plural = **statement**, account, argument, explanation, exposition

representative noun 1 = **delegate**, agent, commissioner, councillor, depute (Scot.), deputy, member, member of parliament, M.P., proxy, spokesman or spokeswoman 2 = **salesman**, agent, commercial traveller, rep, traveller 3 = **typical example**, archetype, embodiment, epitome, exemplar, personification, type ♦ adjective 4 = **typical**, archetypal, characteristic, emblematic, exemplary, illustrative, symbolic 5 = **chosen**, delegated, elected, elective
➤ Antonyms
adjective ≠**typical**: atypical, extraordinary, uncharacteristic

repress verb 1 = **control**, bottle up, check, curb, hold back, hold in, inhibit, keep in check, master, muffle, overcome, overpower, restrain, silence, smother, stifle, suppress, swallow 2 = **subdue**, crush, quash, quell, subjugate
➤ Antonyms
≠**control**: encourage, express, give free rein to, let out, release ≠**subdue**: free, liberate

repression noun = **subjugation**, authoritarianism, constraint, control, despotism, domination, inhibition, restraint, suppression, tyranny

repressive adjective = **oppressive**, absolute, authoritarian, despotic, dictatorial, harsh, severe, tough, tyrannical
➤ Antonyms
democratic, liberal, libertarian

reprieve verb 1 = **grant a stay of execution to**, let off the hook (slang), pardon, postpone or remit the punishment of 2 = **relieve**, abate, allay, alleviate, mitigate, palliate, respite ♦ noun 3 = **stay of execution**, abeyance, amnesty, deferment, pardon, postponement, remission, suspension 4 = **relief**, abatement, alleviation, let-up (informal), mitigation, palliation, respite

reprimand verb 1 = **blame**, admonish, bawl out (informal), carpet (informal), castigate, censure, chide, dress down (informal), give a rocket (Brit. & N.Z. informal), give (someone) a row (informal), haul over the coals (informal), lecture, rap over the knuckles, read the riot act,

rebuke, reprehend, reproach, reprove, scold, slap on the wrist (informal), take to task, tear into (informal), tear (someone) off a strip (Brit. informal), tell off (informal), tick off (informal), upbraid ♦ noun 2 = **blame**, admonition, castigation, censure, dressing-down (informal), lecture, rebuke, reprehension, reproach, reproof, row, talking-to (informal), telling-off (informal), ticking-off (informal)
➤ Antonyms
verb ≠**blame**: applaud, commend, compliment, congratulate, praise ♦ noun ≠**blame**: commendation, compliment, congratulations, praise

reprisal noun = **retaliation**, an eye for an eye, counterstroke, requital, retribution, revenge, vengeance

reproach noun 1 = **blame**, censure, condemnation, contempt, disapproval, discredit, disgrace, dishonour, disrepute, ignominy, indignity, opprobrium, rebuke, scorn, shame ♦ verb 2 = **blame**, bawl out (informal), blast, carpet (informal), censure, chide, condemn, criticize, disparage, find fault with, give a rocket (Brit. & N.Z. informal), have a go at (informal), lambast(e), read the riot act, rebuke, reprehend, reprimand, reprove, scold, take to task, tear into (informal), tear (someone) off a strip (Brit. informal), upbraid

reproachful adjective = **critical**, castigatory, censorious, condemnatory, contemptuous, disappointed, disapproving, fault-finding, reproving, scolding, upbraiding

reprobate noun 1 = **scoundrel**, asshole (U.S. & Canad. taboo slang), bad egg (old-fashioned informal), bastard (offensive), blackguard, bugger (taboo slang), degenerate, evildoer, miscreant, ne'er-do-well, profligate, rake, rascal, scumbag (slang), sinner, son-of-a-bitch (slang, chiefly U.S. & Canad.), villain, wretch, wrongdoer ♦ adjective 2 = **unprincipled**, abandoned, bad, base, corrupt, damned, degenerate, depraved, dissolute, hardened, immoral, incorrigible, profligate, shameless, sinful, vile, wicked

reproduce verb 1 = **copy**, duplicate, echo, emulate, imitate, match, mirror, parallel, print, recreate, repeat, replicate, represent, transcribe 2 Biology = **breed**, generate, multiply, procreate, produce young, proliferate, propagate, spawn

reproduction noun 1 Biology = **breeding**, generation, increase, multiplication, procreation, proliferation, propagation 2 = **copy**, duplicate, facsimile, imitation,

picture, print, replica
> **Antonyms**
≠**copy**: master, original, prototype

reproof *noun* = **rebuke**, admonition, blame, castigation, censure, chiding, condemnation, criticism, dressing-down (*informal*), reprimand, reproach, reproval, scolding, ticking-off (*informal*), tongue-lashing
> **Antonyms**
commendation, compliment, encouragement, praise

reprove *verb* = **rebuke**, admonish, bawl out (*informal*), berate, blame, carpet (*informal*), censure, chide, condemn, give a rocket (*Brit. & N.Z. informal*), read the riot act, reprehend, reprimand, scold, take to task, tear into (*informal*), tear (someone) off a strip (*Brit. informal*), tell off (*informal*), tick off (*informal*), upbraid
> **Antonyms**
applaud, commend, compliment, encourage, praise

repudiate *verb* = **reject**, abandon, abjure, cast off, cut off, deny, desert, disavow, discard, disclaim, disown, forsake, renounce, rescind, retract, reverse, revoke, turn one's back on, wash one's hands of
> **Antonyms**
accept, acknowledge, admit, assert, avow, defend, own, proclaim, ratify

repugnance *noun* = **distaste**, abhorrence, antipathy, aversion, disgust, dislike, disrelish, hatred, loathing, odium, reluctance, repulsion, revulsion

repugnant *adjective* = **distasteful**, abhorrent, abominable, disgusting, foul, hateful, horrid, loathsome, nauseating, objectionable, obnoxious, odious, offensive, repellent, revolting, sickening, vile, yucky *or* yukky (*slang*)
> **Antonyms**
agreeable, attractive, pleasant, unobjectionable

repulse *verb* 1 = **disgust**, fill with loathing, gross out (*U.S. Slang*), nauseate, offend, put off, repel, revolt, sicken, turn one's stomach 2 = **drive back**, beat off, check, defeat, fight off, rebuff, repel, throw back, ward off 3 = **reject**, disdain, disregard, give the cold shoulder to, rebuff, refuse, snub, spurn, turn down ♦ *noun* 4 = **defeat**, check, disappointment, failure, reverse 5 = **rejection**, cold shoulder, kick in the teeth (*slang*), knock-back (*slang*), rebuff, refusal, snub

repulsion *noun* = **disgust**, abhorrence, aversion, detestation, disrelish, distaste, hatred, loathing, odium, repugnance, revulsion

repulsive *adjective* = **disgusting**, abhorrent, abominable, disagreeable, distasteful, foul, hateful, hideous, horrid, loathsome, nauseating, objectionable, obnoxious, odious, offensive, repellent, revolting, sickening, ugly, unpleasant, vile
> **Antonyms**
appealing, attractive, delightful, enticing, lovely, pleasant

reputable *adjective* = **respectable**, creditable, estimable, excellent, good, honourable, honoured, legitimate, of good repute, reliable, trustworthy, upright, well-thought-of, worthy
> **Antonyms**
cowboy (*informal*), disreputable, fly-by-night, shady (*informal*), unreliable, untrustworthy

reputation *noun* 1 = **name**, character, esteem, estimation, opinion, renown, repute, standing, stature 2 = **fame**, credit, distinction, eminence, honour

repute *noun* = **reputation**, celebrity, distinction, eminence, esteem, estimation, fame, name, renown, standing, stature

reputed *adjective* = **supposed**, accounted, alleged, believed, considered, deemed, estimated, held, ostensible, putative, reckoned, regarded, rumoured, said, seeming, thought

reputedly *adverb* = **supposedly**, allegedly, apparently, ostensibly, seemingly

request *verb* 1 = **ask (for)**, appeal for, apply for, beg, beseech, call for, demand, desire, entreat, invite, petition, pray, put in for, requisition, seek, solicit ♦ *noun* 2 = **asking**, appeal, application, begging, call, demand, desire, entreaty, petition, prayer, requisition, suit
> **Antonyms**
verb ≠**ask (for)**: command, order ♦ *noun* ≠**asking**: command, order

require *verb* 1 = **need**, crave, depend upon, desire, have need of, lack, miss, stand in need of, want, wish 2 = **demand**, call for, entail, involve, necessitate, take 3 = **order**, ask, bid, call upon, command, compel, constrain, demand, direct, enjoin, exact, insist upon, instruct, oblige

required *adjective* = **needed**, called for, compulsory, demanded, *de rigueur*, essential, mandatory, necessary, obligatory, prescribed, recommended, requisite, set, unavoidable, vital
> **Antonyms**
elective, noncompulsory, not necessary, not vital, optional, unimportant, voluntary

requirement *noun* = **necessity**, demand, essential, lack, must, need, precondition, prerequisite, qualification, requisite, *sine* *qua non,* specification, stipulation, want

requisite *adjective* 1 = **necessary**, called for, essential, indispensable, mandatory, needed, needful, obligatory, prerequisite, required, vital ♦ *noun* 2 = **necessity**, condition, essential, must, need, precondition, prerequisite, requirement, *sine qua non*

requisition *verb* 1 = **demand**, apply for, call for, put in for, request 2 = **take over**, appropriate, commandeer, occupy, seize, take possession of ♦ *noun* 3 = **demand**, application, call, request, summons 4 = **takeover**, appropriation, commandeering, occupation, seizure

requital *noun* = **return**, amends, compensation, payment, recompense, redress, reimbursement, remuneration, repayment, restitution, reward

requite *verb* = **return**, compensate, get even, give in return, give tit for tat, make amends, make good, make restitution, pay, pay (someone) back in his *or* her own coin, reciprocate, recompense, redress, reimburse, remunerate, repay, respond, retaliate, return like for like, reward, satisfy

rescind *verb* = **annul**, abrogate, cancel, countermand, declare null and void, invalidate, obviate, overturn, quash, recall, repeal, retract, reverse, revoke, set aside, void
➤ **Antonyms**
confirm, enact, implement, reaffirm, support, uphold, validate

rescue *verb* 1 = **save**, deliver, extricate, free, get out, liberate, recover, redeem, release, salvage, save the life of, set free ♦ *noun* 2 = **liberation**, deliverance, extrication, recovery, redemption, release, relief, salvage, salvation, saving
➤ **Antonyms**
verb ≠ **save**: abandon, desert, leave, leave behind, lose, strand

research *noun* 1 = **investigation**, analysis, examination, experimentation, exploration, fact-finding, groundwork, inquiry, probe, scrutiny, study ♦ *verb* 2 = **investigate**, analyse, do tests, examine, experiment, explore, look into, make inquiries, probe, scrutinize, study, work over

resemblance *noun* = **similarity**, affinity, analogy, closeness, comparability, comparison, conformity, correspondence, counterpart, facsimile, image, kinship, likeness, parallel, parity, sameness, semblance, similitude
➤ **Antonyms**
difference, disparity, dissimilarity, heterogeneity, unlikeness, variation

resemble *verb* = **be like**, bear a resemblance to, be similar to, duplicate, echo, favour (*informal*), look like, mirror, parallel, put one in mind of, remind one of, take after

resent *verb* = **be bitter about**, be angry about, bear a grudge about, begrudge, be in a huff about, be offended by, be pissed (off) about (*taboo slang*), dislike, grudge, harbour a grudge against, have hard feelings about, object to, take amiss, take as an insult, take exception to, take offence at, take umbrage at
➤ **Antonyms**
accept, approve, be content with, be pleased by, feel flattered by, like, welcome

resentful *adjective* = **bitter**, aggrieved, angry, embittered, grudging, huffish, huffy, hurt, in a huff, indignant, in high dudgeon, jealous, miffed (*informal*), offended, peeved (*informal*), piqued, pissed (*taboo slang*), pissed off (*taboo slang*), put out, unforgiving, wounded
➤ **Antonyms**
content, flattered, gratified, pleased, satisfied

resentment *noun* = **bitterness**, anger, animosity, bad blood, chip on one's shoulder (*informal*), displeasure, grudge, huff, hurt, ill feeling, ill will, indignation, pique, rage, rancour, umbrage

reservation *noun* 1 = **doubt**, demur, hesitancy, scepticism, scruple 2 = **condition**, proviso, qualification, rider, stipulation 3 = **reserve**, homeland, preserve, sanctuary, territory, tract

reserve *verb* 1 = **keep**, conserve, hang on to, hoard, hold, husband, keep back, lay up, preserve, put by, retain, save, set aside, stockpile, store, withhold 2 = **book**, bespeak, engage, prearrange, pre-engage, retain, secure 3 = **delay**, defer, keep back, postpone, put off, withhold ♦ *noun* 4 = **store**, backlog, cache, capital, fall-back, fund, hoard, reservoir, savings, stock, stockpile, supply 5 = **reservation**, park, preserve, sanctuary, tract 6 = **shyness**, aloofness, constraint, coolness, formality, modesty, reluctance, reservation, restraint, reticence, secretiveness, silence, taciturnity ♦ *adjective* 7 = **substitute**, alternate, auxiliary, extra, fall-back, secondary, spare

reserved *adjective* 1 = **uncommunicative**, aloof, cautious, close-mouthed, cold, cool, demure, formal, modest, prim, restrained, reticent, retiring, secretive, shy, silent, standoffish, taciturn, unapproachable, undemonstrative, unforthcoming, unresponsive, unsociable 2 = **set aside**, booked, engaged, held, kept, restricted,

retained, spoken for, taken
➤ **Antonyms**
≠**uncommunicative**: ardent,
demonstrative, forward, open, sociable,
uninhibited, unreserved, warm

reservoir noun **1** = **lake**, basin, pond, tank
2 = **store**, accumulation, fund, pool,
reserves, source, stock, stockpile, supply

reshuffle noun **1** = **reorganization**,
change, interchange, realignment,
rearrangement, redistribution, regrouping,
restructuring, revision, shake-up (informal)
♦ verb **2** = **reorganize**, change around,
change the line-up of, interchange,
realign, rearrange, redistribute, regroup,
restructure, revise, shake up (informal)

reside verb **1** Formal = **live**, abide, dwell,
hang out (informal), have one's home,
inhabit, lodge, remain, settle, sojourn, stay
2 = **be present**, abide, be vested, consist,
dwell, exist, lie
➤ **Antonyms**
≠**live**: holiday in, visit

residence noun **1** = **home**, abode,
domicile, dwelling, flat, habitation, house,
household, lodging, pad (slang), place,
quarters **2** = **mansion**, hall, manor, palace,
seat, villa **3** = **stay**, occupancy, occupation,
sojourn, tenancy

resident noun **1** = **inhabitant**, citizen,
denizen, local, lodger, occupant, tenant
♦ adjective **2** = **inhabiting**, dwelling, living,
local, neighbourhood, settled
➤ **Antonyms**
noun ≠**inhabitant**: nonresident, visitor
♦ adjective ≠**inhabiting**: nonresident,
visiting

residual adjective = **remaining**, leftover,
net, nett, unconsumed, unused, vestigial

residue noun = **remainder**, balance, dregs,
excess, extra, leftovers, remains, remnant,
residuum, rest, surplus

resign verb **1** = **quit**, abdicate, give in one's
notice, leave, step down (informal), vacate
2 = **give up**, abandon, cede, forgo, forsake,
hand over, relinquish, renounce,
surrender, turn over, yield **3 resign oneself**
= **accept**, acquiesce, bow, give in, give up,
reconcile, submit, succumb, yield

resignation noun **1** = **leaving**,
abandonment, abdication, departure,
notice, relinquishment, renunciation,
retirement, surrender **2** = **acceptance**,
acquiescence, compliance, endurance,
forbearing, fortitude, nonresistance,
passivity, patience, submission, sufferance
➤ **Antonyms**
≠**acceptance**: defiance, dissent, kicking up
a fuss, protest, resistance

resigned adjective = **stoical**, acquiescent,

compliant, long-suffering, patient,
subdued, submissive, unprotesting,
unresisting

resilient adjective **1** = **tough**, bouncy,
buoyant, feisty (informal, chiefly U.S. &
Canad.), hardy, irrepressible, quick to
recover, strong **2** = **flexible**, bouncy,
elastic, plastic, pliable, rubbery, springy,
supple
➤ **Antonyms**
≠**tough**: delicate, effete, sensitive, sickly,
weak ≠**flexible**: flaccid, inflexible, limp,
rigid, stiff

resist verb **1** = **oppose**, battle, check,
combat, confront, contend with,
counteract, countervail, defy, dispute,
fight, hinder, hold out against, put up a
fight (against), refuse, stand up to,
struggle against, thwart, weather **2**
= **refrain from**, abstain from, avoid,
forbear, forgo, keep from, leave alone,
prevent oneself from, refuse, turn down **3**
= **withstand**, be proof against, repel
➤ **Antonyms**
≠**oppose**: accept, acquiesce, cave in
(informal), give in, submit, succumb,
surrender, welcome, yield ≠**refrain from**:
enjoy, give in to, indulge in, surrender to

resistance noun = **fighting**, battle,
combat, contention, counteraction,
defiance, fight, hindrance, impediment,
intransigence, obstruction, opposition,
refusal, struggle

Resistance noun = **freedom fighters**,
guerrillas, maquis, partisans, underground

resistant adjective **1** = **impervious**, hard,
insusceptible, proof against, strong, tough,
unaffected by, unyielding **2** = **opposed**,
antagonistic, defiant, dissident, hostile,
intractable, intransigent, recalcitrant,
unwilling

resolute adjective = **determined**, bold,
constant, dogged, firm, fixed, immovable,
inflexible, obstinate, persevering,
purposeful, relentless, set, stalwart,
staunch, steadfast, strong-willed,
stubborn, tenacious, unbending,
undaunted, unflinching, unshakable,
unshaken, unwavering
➤ **Antonyms**
doubtful, irresolute, undecided,
undetermined, unresolved, unsteady, weak

resolution noun **1** = **determination**,
boldness, constancy, courage, dedication,
doggedness, earnestness, energy,
firmness, fortitude, obstinacy,
perseverance, purpose, relentlessness,
resoluteness, resolve, sincerity,
staunchness, staying power, steadfastness,
stubbornness, tenacity, willpower **2**

= **decision**, aim, declaration, determination, intent, intention, judgment, motion, purpose, resolve, verdict **3** = **solution**, answer, outcome, settlement, solving, sorting out, upshot, working out

resolve *verb* **1** = **decide**, agree, conclude, design, determine, fix, intend, make up one's mind, purpose, settle, undertake **2** = **break down**, analyse, clear, disintegrate, dissolve, liquefy, melt, reduce, separate, solve, split up **3** = **work out**, answer, clear up, crack, elucidate, fathom, find the solution to, suss (out) (*slang*) **4** = **dispel**, banish, clear up, explain, remove ♦ *noun* **5** = **determination**, boldness, courage, earnestness, firmness, resoluteness, resolution, steadfastness, willpower **6** = **decision**, conclusion, design, intention, objective, project, purpose, resolution, undertaking

➤ **Antonyms**

noun ≠**determination**: cowardice, half-heartedness, indecision, vacillation, wavering

resonant *adjective* = **echoing**, booming, full, resounding, reverberant, reverberating, rich, ringing, sonorous, vibrant

resort *verb* **1** **resort to** = **have recourse to**, avail oneself of, bring into play, employ, exercise, fall back on, look to, make use of, turn to, use, utilize **2** = **go**, frequent, haunt, head for, visit ♦ *noun* **3** = **holiday centre**, haunt, refuge, retreat, spot, tourist centre, watering place (*Brit.*) **4** = **recourse**, reference **5** *As in* **last resort** = **course**, alternative, chance, expedient, hope, possibility

resound *verb* = **echo**, fill the air, re-echo, resonate, reverberate, ring

resounding *adjective* = **echoing**, booming, full, powerful, resonant, reverberating, rich, ringing, sonorous, sounding, vibrant

resource *noun* **1** = **supply**, hoard, reserve, source, stockpile **2** = **ingenuity**, ability, capability, cleverness, initiative, inventiveness, quick-wittedness, resourcefulness, talent **3** = **means**, course, device, expedient, resort

resourceful *adjective* = **ingenious**, able, bright, capable, clever, creative, imaginative, inventive, quick-witted, sharp, talented

➤ **Antonyms**

gormless (*Brit. informal*), unimaginative, uninventive

resources *plural noun* = **funds**, assets, capital, holdings, materials, means, money, property, reserves, riches, supplies, wealth, wherewithal

respect *noun* **1** = **regard**, admiration, appreciation, approbation, consideration, deference, esteem, estimation, honour, recognition, reverence, veneration **2** = **particular**, aspect, characteristic, detail, facet, feature, matter, point, sense, way **3** *As in* **in respect of** *or* **with respect to** = **relation**, bearing, connection, reference, regard **4** **respects** = **greetings**, compliments, good wishes, regards, salutations ♦ *verb* **5** = **think highly of**, admire, adore, esteem, defer to, esteem, have a good *or* high opinion of, honour, look up to, recognize, regard, revere, reverence, set store by, value, venerate **6** = **abide by**, adhere to, attend, comply with, follow, heed, honour, notice, obey, observe, pay attention to, regard, show consideration for

➤ **Antonyms**

noun ≠**regard**: contempt, disdain, disregard, disrespect, irreverence, scorn ♦ *verb* ≠**abide by**: abuse, disregard, disrespect, ignore, neglect, scorn

respectable *adjective* **1** = **honourable**, admirable, decent, decorous, dignified, estimable, good, honest, proper, reputable, respected, upright, venerable, worthy **2** = **reasonable**, ample, appreciable, considerable, decent, fair, fairly good, goodly, presentable, sizable *or* sizeable, substantial, tidy (*informal*), tolerable

➤ **Antonyms**

≠**honourable**: dishonourable, disreputable, ignoble, impolite, improper, indecent, unrefined, unworthy ≠**reasonable**: paltry, poor, small

respectful *adjective* = **polite**, civil, courteous, courtly, deferential, dutiful, gracious, humble, mannerly, obedient, reverent, reverential, self-effacing, well-mannered

respective *adjective* = **specific**, corresponding, individual, own, particular, personal, relevant, separate, several, various

respite *noun* **1** = **pause**, break, breather (*informal*), breathing space, cessation, halt, hiatus, intermission, interruption, interval, let-up (*informal*), lull, recess, relaxation, relief, rest **2** = **delay**, adjournment, moratorium, postponement, reprieve, stay, suspension

resplendent *adjective* = **brilliant**, beaming, bright, dazzling, effulgent, gleaming, glittering, glorious, luminous, lustrous, radiant, shining, splendid

respond *verb* = **answer**, acknowledge, act

in response, come back, counter, react, reciprocate, rejoin, reply, retort, return
➤ **Antonyms**
ignore, remain silent, turn a blind eye

response *noun* = **answer**, acknowledgment, comeback (*informal*), counterattack, counterblast, feedback, reaction, rejoinder, reply, retort, return, riposte

responsibility *noun* **1** = **authority**, importance, power **2** = **accountability**, amenability, answerability, liability **3** = **fault**, blame, burden, culpability, guilt, liability **4** = **level-headedness**, conscientiousness, dependability, maturity, rationality, reliability, sensibleness, soberness, stability, trustworthiness **5** = **duty**, care, charge, liability, obligation, onus, pigeon (*informal*), trust

responsible *adjective* **1** = **in charge**, at the helm, carrying the can (*informal*), in authority, in control **2** = **to blame**, at fault, culpable, guilty **3** = **accountable**, amenable, answerable, bound, chargeable, duty-bound, liable, subject, under obligation **4** = **sensible**, adult, conscientious, dependable, level-headed, mature, rational, reliable, sober, sound, stable, trustworthy **5** = **authoritative**, decision-making, executive, high, important
➤ **Antonyms**
≠**accountable**: unaccountable ≠**sensible**: irresponsible, unconscientious, undependable, unreliable, untrustworthy

responsive *adjective* = **sensitive**, alive, awake, aware, forthcoming, impressionable, open, perceptive, quick to react, reactive, receptive, sharp, susceptible, sympathetic
➤ **Antonyms**
apathetic, impassive, insensitive, silent, unresponsive, unsympathetic

rest[1] *noun* **1** = **relaxation**, doze, forty winks (*informal*), idleness, kip (*Brit. slang*), leisure, lie-down, nap, repose, siesta, sleep, slumber, snooze (*informal*) **2** = **inactivity**, motionlessness, standstill **3** = **refreshment**, relief **4** = **calm**, somnolence, stillness, tranquillity **5** = **pause**, break, breather (*informal*), breathing space, cessation, halt, holiday, interlude, intermission, interval, lull, respite, stop, time off, vacation **6** = **support**, base, holder, prop, shelf, stand, trestle **7 at rest: a** = **motionless**, at a standstill, still, stopped, unmoving **b** = **calm**, peaceful, tranquil **c** = **dead**, at peace **d** = **asleep**, resting, sleeping ♦ *verb* **8** = **relax**, be at ease, be

calm, doze, drowse, have a snooze (*informal*), have forty winks (*informal*), idle, kip (*Brit. slang*), laze, lie down, lie still, nap, put one's feet up, refresh oneself, sit down, sleep, slumber, snooze (*informal*), take a nap, take it easy, take one's ease **9** = **place**, be supported, lay, lean, lie, prop, recline, repose, sit, stand, stretch out **10** = **depend**, base, be based, be founded, found, hang, hinge, lie, rely, reside, turn **11** = **stop**, break off, cease, come to a standstill, desist, discontinue, halt, have a break, knock off (*informal*), stay, take a breather (*informal*)
➤ **Antonyms**
noun ≠**relaxation, pause**: activity, bustle, work ♦ *verb* ≠**relax, stop**: keep going, slog away (*informal*), work

rest[2] *noun* **1** = **remainder**, balance, excess, leftovers, others, remains, remnants, residue, residuum, rump, surplus ♦ *verb* **2** = **continue being**, be left, go on being, keep, remain, stay

restaurant *noun* = **café**, bistro, cafeteria, diner (*chiefly U.S. & Canad.*), eatery *or* eaterie, tearoom, trattoria

restful *adjective* = **relaxing**, calm, calming, comfortable, peaceful, placid, quiet, relaxed, serene, sleepy, soothing, tranquil, tranquillizing, undisturbed, unhurried
➤ **Antonyms**
agitated, busy, disturbing, restless, uncomfortable, unrelaxed

restitution *noun* **1** *Law* = **compensation**, amends, indemnification, indemnity, recompense, redress, refund, reimbursement, remuneration, reparation, repayment, requital, satisfaction **2** = **return**, restoration

restive *adjective* = **restless**, agitated, antsy (*informal*), edgy, fidgety, fractious, fretful, ill at ease, impatient, jittery (*informal*), jumpy, nervous, on edge, uneasy, unquiet, unruly
➤ **Antonyms**
at ease, calm, content, peaceful, relaxed, satisfied, serene, tranquil

restless *adjective* **1** = **moving**, active, bustling, changeable, footloose, having itchy feet, hurried, inconstant, irresolute, nomadic, roving, transient, turbulent, unsettled, unstable, unsteady, wandering **2** = **unsettled**, agitated, antsy (*informal*), anxious, disturbed, edgy, fidgeting, fidgety, fitful, fretful, ill at ease, jumpy, nervous, on edge, restive, sleepless, tossing and turning, troubled, uneasy, unquiet, unruly, worried
➤ **Antonyms**
≠**moving**: settled, stable, steady

≠**unsettled**: comfortable, composed, easy, quiet, relaxed, restful, undisturbed

restlessness noun **1** = **movement**, activity, bustle, hurry, hurry-scurry, inconstancy, instability, transience, turbulence, turmoil, unrest, unsettledness **2** = **restiveness**, agitation, ants in one's pants (slang), anxiety, disquiet, disturbance, edginess, fitfulness, fretfulness, heebie-jeebies (slang), inquietude, insomnia, jitters (informal), jumpiness, nervousness, uneasiness, worriedness

restoration noun **1** = **repair**, reconstruction, recovery, refreshment, refurbishing, rehabilitation, rejuvenation, renewal, renovation, revitalization, revival **2** = **reinstatement**, re-establishment, reinstallation, replacement, restitution, return
➤ **Antonyms**
≠**repair**: demolition, scrapping, wrecking ≠**reinstatement**: abolition, overthrow

restore verb **1** = **repair**, fix, mend, rebuild, recondition, reconstruct, recover, refurbish, rehabilitate, renew, renovate, retouch, set to rights, touch up **2** = **revive**, bring back to health, build up, reanimate, refresh, rejuvenate, revitalize, revivify, strengthen **3** = **return**, bring back, give back, hand back, recover, re-establish, reinstate, replace, send back **4** = **reinstate**, reconstitute, re-enforce, re-establish, reimpose, reintroduce
➤ **Antonyms**
≠**repair**: demolish, scrap, wreck ≠**revive**: make worse, sicken, weaken ≠**reinstate**: abolish, abrogate, repeal, rescind

restrain verb **1** = **hold back**, check, confine, constrain, contain, control, curb, curtail, hamper, have on a tight leash, hinder, hold, inhibit, keep, keep under control, limit, prevent, rein, repress, restrict, straiten, subdue, suppress **2** = **imprison**, arrest, bind, chain, confine, detain, fetter, hold, jail, lock up, manacle, pinion, tie up
➤ **Antonyms**
≠**hold back**: assist, encourage, gee up, help, incite, urge on ≠**imprison**: free, liberate, release

restrained adjective **1** = **controlled**, calm, mild, moderate, muted, reasonable, reticent, self-controlled, soft, steady, temperate, undemonstrative **2** = **unobtrusive**, discreet, quiet, subdued, tasteful
➤ **Antonyms**
≠**controlled**: fiery, hot-headed, intemperate, unrestrained, wild ≠**unobtrusive**: garish, loud, over-the-top,

self-indulgent, tasteless

restraint noun **1** = **limitation**, ban, boycott, bridle, check, curb, disqualification, embargo, interdict, limit, rein, taboo **2** = **bonds**, chains, manacles, pinions, straitjacket **3** = **self-control**, coercion, command, compulsion, constraint, control, curtailment, hindrance, hold, inhibition, limitation, moderation, prevention, pulling one's punches, restriction, self-discipline, self-possession, self-restraint, suppression **4** = **confinement**, arrest, bondage, captivity, detention, fetters, imprisonment
➤ **Antonyms**
≠**limitation**: freedom, liberty
≠**self-control**: excess, immoderation, intemperance, licence, self-indulgence

restrict verb = **limit**, bound, circumscribe, clip someone's wings, confine, contain, cramp, demarcate, hamper, handicap, hem in, impede, inhibit, keep within bounds or limits, regulate, restrain, straiten
➤ **Antonyms**
allow, broaden, encourage, foster, free, permit, promote, widen

restriction noun = **limitation**, check, condition, confinement, constraint, containment, control, curb, demarcation, handicap, inhibition, regulation, restraint, rule, stipulation

result noun **1** = **consequence**, conclusion, decision, development, effect, end, end result, event, fruit, issue, outcome, product, reaction, sequel, termination, upshot ♦ verb **2** = **arise**, appear, derive, develop, emanate, ensue, eventuate, flow, follow, happen, issue, spring, stem, turn out **3** result in = **end in**, culminate in, finish with, pan out (informal), terminate in, wind up
➤ **Antonyms**
noun ≠**consequence**: beginning, cause, germ, origin, outset, root, source

resume verb **1** = **begin again**, carry on, continue, go on, proceed, recommence, reinstitute, reopen, restart, take up or pick up where one left off **2** = **occupy again**, assume again, reoccupy, take back, take up again
➤ **Antonyms**
≠**begin again**: cease, discontinue, stop

résumé noun = **summary**, abstract, digest, epitome, précis, recapitulation, review, rundown, synopsis

resumption noun = **continuation**, carrying on, re-establishment, renewal, reopening, restart, resurgence

resurgence noun = **revival**, rebirth, re-emergence, renaissance, renascence, resumption, resurrection, return

resurrect *verb* 1 = **restore to life**, raise from the dead 2 = **revive**, breathe new life into, bring back, reintroduce, renew

resurrection *noun* 1 = **raising** *or* **rising from the dead**, return from the dead 2 = **revival**, comeback (*informal*), reappearance, rebirth, renaissance, renascence, renewal, restoration, resurgence, resuscitation, return
➤ **Antonyms**
≠**raising** *or* **rising from the dead**: burial, demise ≠**revival**: killing off

resuscitate *verb* = **revive**, bring round, bring to life, give artificial respiration to, give the kiss of life, rescue, resurrect, revitalize, revivify, save

retain *verb* 1 = **keep**, contain, detain, grasp, grip, hang *or* hold onto, hold, hold back, hold fast, keep possession of, maintain, preserve, reserve, restrain, save 2 = **hire**, commission, employ, engage, pay, reserve 3 = **remember**, memorize, recall, recollect
➤ **Antonyms**
≠**keep**: let go, lose, release, use up
≠**remember**: forget

retainer *noun* 1 = **fee**, advance, deposit 2 = **servant**, attendant, dependant, domestic, flunky, footman, henchman, lackey, supporter, valet, vassal

retaliate *verb* = **pay (someone) back**, even the score, exact retribution, get back at, get even with (*informal*), get one's own back (*informal*), give as good as one gets (*informal*), give (someone) a taste of his *or* her own medicine, give tit for tat, hit back, reciprocate, return like for like, strike back, take an eye for an eye, take revenge, wreak vengeance
➤ **Antonyms**
accept, submit, turn the other cheek

retaliation *noun* = **revenge**, an eye for an eye, a taste of one's own medicine, counterblow, counterstroke, reciprocation, repayment, reprisal, requital, retribution, tit for tat, vengeance

retard *verb* = **slow down**, arrest, brake, check, decelerate, delay, encumber, handicap, hinder, hold back *or* up, impede, obstruct, set back
➤ **Antonyms**
accelerate, advance, expedite, hasten, speed, speed up, stimulate

retch *verb* = **gag**, barf (*U.S. slang*), be sick, chuck (up) (*slang, chiefly U.S.*), chunder (*slang, chiefly Austral.*), heave, puke (*slang*), regurgitate, spew, throw up (*informal*), vomit

reticence *noun* = **silence**, quietness, reserve, restraint, secretiveness, taciturnity,

uncommunicativeness

reticent *adjective* = **uncommunicative**, close-lipped, mum, quiet, reserved, restrained, secretive, silent, taciturn, tight-lipped, unforthcoming, unspeaking
➤ **Antonyms**
candid, communicative, expansive, frank, open, talkative, voluble

retinue *noun* = **attendants**, aides, cortege, entourage, escort, followers, following, servants, suite, train

retire *verb* 1 = **stop working**, be pensioned off, (be) put out to grass (*informal*), give up work 2 = **withdraw**, absent oneself, betake oneself, depart, exit, go away, leave, remove 3 = **go to bed**, go to one's room, go to sleep, hit the hay (*slang*), hit the sack (*slang*), kip down (*Brit. slang*), turn in (*informal*) 4 = **fall back**, back off, decamp, give ground, give way, pull back, pull out, recede, retreat, withdraw

retirement *noun* = **withdrawal**, loneliness, obscurity, privacy, retreat, seclusion, solitude

retiring *adjective* = **shy**, bashful, coy, demure, diffident, humble, meek, modest, quiet, reclusive, reserved, reticent, self-effacing, shrinking, timid, timorous, unassertive, unassuming
➤ **Antonyms**
audacious, bold, brassy, forward, gregarious, outgoing, sociable

retort *verb* 1 = **reply**, answer, answer back, come back with, counter, rejoin, respond, retaliate, return, riposte ♦ *noun* 2 = **reply**, answer, comeback (*informal*), rejoinder, response, riposte

retouch *verb* = **touch up**, brush up, correct, finish, improve, recondition, renovate, restore

retract *verb* 1 = **withdraw**, abjure, cancel, deny, disavow, disclaim, disown, eat one's words, recall, recant, renege, renounce, repeal, repudiate, rescind, reverse, revoke, take back, unsay 2 = **go back on**, back out of, renege on 3 = **draw in**, pull back, pull in, reel in, sheathe

retreat *verb* 1 = **withdraw**, back away, back off, depart, draw back, fall back, give ground, go back, leave, pull back, recede, recoil, retire, shrink, turn tail ♦ *noun* 2 = **withdrawal**, departure, evacuation, flight, retirement 3 = **refuge**, asylum, den, haunt, haven, hideaway, privacy, resort, retirement, sanctuary, seclusion, shelter
➤ **Antonyms**
verb ≠**withdraw**: advance, engage, move forward ♦ *noun* ≠**withdrawal**: advance, charge, entrance

retrench *verb* = **cut back**, curtail, cut,

decrease, diminish, economize, husband, lessen, limit, make economies, reduce, save, tighten one's belt, trim

retrenchment *noun* = **cutback**, contraction, cost-cutting, curtailment, cut, economy, reduction, tightening one's belt
➤ **Antonyms**
expansion, investment

retribution *noun* = **punishment**, an eye for an eye, compensation, justice, Nemesis, reckoning, recompense, redress, repayment, reprisal, requital, retaliation, revenge, reward, satisfaction, vengeance

retrieve *verb* = **get back**, fetch back, recall, recapture, recoup, recover, redeem, regain, repair, repossess, rescue, restore, salvage, save, win back

retro *adjective* = **old-time**, antique, bygone, former, nostalgia, of yesteryear, old, old-fashioned, old-world, past, period

retrograde *adjective* 1 = **deteriorating**, backward, declining, degenerative, downward, inverse, negative, regressive, relapsing, retreating, retrogressive, reverse, waning, worsening ♦ *verb* 2 = **deteriorate**, backslide, decline, degenerate, go downhill (*informal*), regress, relapse, retreat, retrogress, revert, wane, worsen

retrogress *verb* = **deteriorate**, backslide, decline, go back, go downhill (*informal*), regress, relapse, retrocede, retrograde, return, revert, worsen

retrospect *noun* = **hindsight**, afterthought, recollection, re-examination, remembrance, reminiscence, review, survey
➤ **Antonyms**
anticipation, foresight

return *verb* 1 = **come back**, come round again, go back, reappear, rebound, recoil, recur, repair, retreat, revert, turn back 2 = **put back**, carry back, convey, give back, re-establish, reinstate, remit, render, replace, restore, send, send back, take back, transmit 3 = **give back**, pay back, reciprocate, recompense, refund, reimburse, repay, requite 4 = **earn**, bring in, make, net, repay, yield 5 = **reply**, answer, come back (with), communicate, rejoin, respond, retort 6 = **elect**, choose, pick, vote in 7 *As in* **return a verdict** = **announce**, arrive at, bring in, come to, deliver, render, report, submit ♦ *noun* 8 = **retreat**, rebound, recoil, reversion 9 = **restoration**, re-establishment, reinstatement, replacement 10 = **reappearance**, recurrence 11 = **profit**, advantage, benefit, gain, income, interest, proceeds, revenue, takings, yield 12 = **statement**, account, form, list, report,

summary 13 = **reply**, answer, comeback (*informal*), rejoinder, response, retort, riposte
➤ **Antonyms**
verb ≠**come back:** depart, disappear, go away, leave ≠**put back, give back:** hold, keep, leave, remove, retain ≠**earn:** lose ♦ *noun* ≠**restoration:** removal ≠**reappearance:** departure, leaving

revamp *verb* = **renovate**, do up (*informal*), fix up (*informal, chiefly U.S. & Canad.*), give a face-lift to, overhaul, patch up, recondition, refit, refurbish, rehabilitate, repair, restore

reveal *verb* 1 = **make known**, announce, betray, blow wide open (*slang*), broadcast, communicate, disclose, divulge, get off one's chest (*informal*), give away, give out, impart, leak, let on, let out, let slip, make public, proclaim, publish, tell 2 = **show**, bare, bring to light, display, exhibit, expose to view, lay bare, manifest, open, uncover, unearth, unmask, unveil
➤ **Antonyms**
≠**make known:** conceal, cover up, hide, keep quiet about, sweep under the carpet (*informal*) ≠**show:** conceal, cover up, hide

revel *verb* 1 **revel in** = **enjoy**, bask in, delight in, gloat about, indulge in, lap up, luxuriate in, rejoice over, relish, savour, take pleasure in, thrive on, wallow in 2 = **celebrate**, carouse, go on a spree, live it up (*informal*), make merry, paint the town red (*informal*), push the boat out (*Brit. informal*), rave (*Brit. slang*), roister, whoop it up (*informal*) ♦ *noun* 3 *often plural* = **merrymaking**, bacchanal, beano (*Brit. slang*), carousal, carouse, celebration, debauch, festivity, gala, jollification, party, rave (*Brit. slang*), rave-up (*Brit. slang*), saturnalia, spree
➤ **Antonyms**
verb ≠**enjoy:** abhor, be uninterested in, dislike, hate, have no taste for

revelation *noun* = **disclosure**, announcement, betrayal, broadcasting, communication, discovery, display, exhibition, exposé, exposition, exposure, giveaway, leak, manifestation, news, proclamation, publication, telling, uncovering, unearthing, unveiling

reveller *noun* = **merrymaker**, carouser, celebrator, partygoer, pleasure-seeker, roisterer

revelry *noun* = **merrymaking**, beano (*Brit. slang*), carousal, carouse, celebration, debauch, debauchery, festivity, fun, jollification, jollity, party, rave (*Brit. slang*), rave-up (*Brit. slang*), roistering, saturnalia, spree

revenge noun 1 = **retaliation**, an eye for an eye, reprisal, requital, retribution, satisfaction, vengeance ♦ verb 2 = **avenge**, even the score for, get even, get one's own back for (informal), hit back, pay (someone) back, repay, requite, retaliate, take an eye for an eye for, take revenge for, vindicate

revengeful adjective = **vengeful**, bitter, merciless, pitiless, resentful, unforgiving, unmerciful

revenue noun = **income**, gain, interest, proceeds, profits, receipts, returns, rewards, takings, yield
➤ **Antonyms**
expenditure, expenses, outgoings

reverberate verb = **echo**, rebound, recoil, re-echo, resound, ring, vibrate

reverberation noun = **echo**, rebound, recoil, re-echoing, reflection, resonance, resounding, ringing, vibration

revere verb = **be in awe of**, adore, defer to, exalt, have a high opinion of, honour, look up to, put on a pedestal, respect, reverence, think highly of, venerate, worship
➤ **Antonyms**
deride, despise, hold in contempt, scorn, sneer at

reverence noun = **respect**, admiration, adoration, awe, deference, devotion, high esteem, homage, honour, veneration, worship
➤ **Antonyms**
contempt, contumely, derision, disdain, scorn

reverent adjective = **respectful**, adoring, awed, deferential, devout, humble, loving, meek, pious, reverential
➤ **Antonyms**
cheeky, disrespectful, flippant, impious, irreverent, mocking, sacrilegious

reverie noun = **daydream**, absent-mindedness, abstraction, brown study, castles in the air or Spain, daydreaming, inattention, musing, preoccupation, trance, woolgathering

reverse verb 1 = **turn round**, invert, transpose, turn back, turn over, turn upside down, upend 2 = **go backwards**, back, backtrack, back up, move backwards, retreat 3 Law = **change**, annul, cancel, countermand, declare null and void, invalidate, negate, obviate, overrule, overset, overthrow, overturn, quash, repeal, rescind, retract, revoke, set aside, undo, upset ♦ noun 4 = **opposite**, antithesis, contradiction, contrary, converse, inverse 5 = **back**, flip side, other side, rear, underside, verso, wrong side 6

= **misfortune**, adversity, affliction, blow, check, defeat, disappointment, failure, hardship, misadventure, mishap, repulse, reversal, setback, trial, vicissitude
♦ adjective 7 = **opposite**, back to front, backward, contrary, converse, inverse, inverted
➤ **Antonyms**
verb ≠**go backwards**: advance, go forward, move forward ≠**change**: carry out, enforce, implement, validate ♦ noun ≠**back**: forward side, front, obverse, recto, right side

revert verb = **return**, backslide, come back, go back, hark back, lapse, recur, regress, relapse, resume, take up where one left off

review noun 1 = **critique**, commentary, critical assessment, criticism, evaluation, judgment, notice, study 2 = **magazine**, journal, periodical, zine (informal) 3 = **survey**, analysis, examination, perusal, report, scrutiny, study 4 = **inspection**, display, march past, parade, procession 5 = **re-examination**, another look, fresh look, reassessment, recapitulation, reconsideration, re-evaluation, rethink, retrospect, revision, second look ♦ verb 6 = **assess**, criticize, discuss, evaluate, give one's opinion of, judge, read through, study, weigh, write a critique of 7 = **reconsider**, go over again, look at again, reassess, recapitulate, re-evaluate, re-examine, rethink, revise, run over, take another look at, think over 8 = **look back on**, call to mind, recall, recollect, reflect on, remember, summon up 9 = **inspect**, examine, scrutinize

reviewer noun = **critic**, arbiter, commentator, connoisseur, essayist, judge

revile verb = **malign**, abuse, asperse, bad-mouth (slang, chiefly U.S. & Canad.), calumniate, defame, denigrate, knock (informal), libel, reproach, rubbish (informal), run down, scorn, slag (off) (slang), slander, smear, traduce, vilify

revise verb 1 = **change**, alter, amend, correct, edit, emend, modify, reconsider, redo, re-examine, revamp, review, rework, rewrite, update 2 = **study**, cram (informal), go over, memorize, reread, run through, swot up (Brit. informal)

revision noun 1 = **change**, alteration, amendment, correction, editing, emendation, modification, re-examination, review, rewriting, updating 2 = **studying**, cramming (informal), homework, memorizing, rereading, swotting (Brit. informal)

revitalize verb = **reanimate**, breathe new life into, bring back to life, refresh, rejuvenate, renew, restore, resurrect, revivify

revival *noun* = **renewal**, awakening, quickening, reanimation, reawakening, rebirth, refreshment, renaissance, restoration, resurgence, resurrection, resuscitation, revitalization, revivification
➤ **Antonyms**
disappearance, extinction, falling off, suppression

revive *verb* = **revitalize**, animate, awaken, breathe new life into, bring back to life, bring round, come round, comfort, invigorate, kick-start (*informal*), quicken, rally, reanimate, recover, refresh, rekindle, renew, renovate, restore, resuscitate, rouse
➤ **Antonyms**
die out, disappear, enervate, exhaust, tire out, weary

revivify *verb* = **revive**, breathe new life into, give new life to, inspirit, invigorate, kick-start (*informal*), reanimate, refresh, renew, restore, resuscitate

revoke *verb* = **cancel**, abolish, abrogate, annul, call back, countermand, declare null and void, disclaim, invalidate, negate, nullify, obviate, quash, recall, recant, renege, renounce, repeal, repudiate, rescind, retract, reverse, set aside, take back, withdraw
➤ **Antonyms**
confirm, endorse, implement, maintain, put into effect, uphold

revolt *noun* 1 = **uprising**, defection, insurgency, insurrection, mutiny, putsch, rebellion, revolution, rising, sedition ◆ *verb* 2 = **rebel**, defect, mutiny, resist, rise, take to the streets, take up arms (against) 3 = **disgust**, give one the creeps (*informal*), gross out (*U.S. slang*), make one's flesh creep, nauseate, offend, repel, repulse, shock, sicken, turn off (*informal*), turn one's stomach

revolting *adjective* = **disgusting**, abhorrent, abominable, appalling, distasteful, foul, horrible, horrid, loathsome, nasty, nauseating, nauseous, noisome, obnoxious, obscene, offensive, repellent, repugnant, repulsive, shocking, sickening, yucky *or* yukky (*slang*)
➤ **Antonyms**
agreeable, attractive, delightful, fragrant, palatable, pleasant

revolution *noun* 1 = **revolt**, coup, coup d'état, insurgency, mutiny, putsch, rebellion, rising, uprising 2 = **transformation**, drastic *or* radical change, innovation, metamorphosis, reformation, sea change, shift, upheaval 3 = **rotation**, circle, circuit, cycle, gyration,

lap, orbit, round, spin, turn, wheel, whirl

revolutionary *adjective* 1 = **rebel**, extremist, insurgent, insurrectionary, mutinous, radical, seditious, subversive 2 = **innovative**, avant-garde, different, drastic, experimental, fundamental, ground-breaking, new, novel, progressive, radical, thoroughgoing ◆ *noun* 3 = **rebel**, insurgent, insurrectionary, insurrectionist, mutineer, revolutionist
➤ **Antonyms**
adjective, noun ≠**rebel**:
counter-revolutionary, loyalist, reactionary
◆ *adjective* ≠**innovative**: conservative, conventional, mainstream, minor, traditional, trivial

revolutionize *verb* = **transform**, break with the past, metamorphose, modernize, reform, revamp

revolve *verb* 1 = **go round**, circle, gyrate, orbit, rotate, spin, turn, twist, wheel, whirl 2 = **consider**, deliberate, meditate, mull over, ponder, reflect, ruminate, study, think about, think over, turn over (in one's mind)

revulsion *noun* = **disgust**, abhorrence, abomination, aversion, detestation, distaste, loathing, odium, recoil, repugnance, repulsion
➤ **Antonyms**
attraction, desire, fascination, liking, pleasure

reward *noun* 1 = **payment**, benefit, bonus, bounty, compensation, gain, honour, merit, premium, prize, profit, recompense, remuneration, repayment, requital, return, wages 2 = **punishment**, comeuppance (*slang*), desert, just deserts, requital, retribution ◆ *verb* 3 = **compensate**, honour, make it worth one's while, pay, recompense, remunerate, repay, requite
➤ **Antonyms**
noun ≠**payment**: fine, penalty, punishment ◆ *verb* ≠**compensate**: fine, penalize, punish

rewarding *adjective* = **satisfying**, advantageous, beneficial, economic, edifying, enriching, fruitful, fulfilling, gainful, gratifying, pleasing, productive, profitable, remunerative, valuable, worthwhile
➤ **Antonyms**
barren, boring, fruitless, unproductive, unprofitable, unrewarding, vain

reword *verb* = **put in other words**, express differently, paraphrase, put another way, recast, rephrase

rewrite *verb* = **revise**, correct, edit, emend, recast, redraft, touch up

rhapsodize *verb* = **enthuse**, go into

ecstasies, gush, rave (*informal*), wax lyrical

rhetoric *noun* 1 = **oratory**, eloquence 2 = **hyperbole**, bombast, grandiloquence, hot air (*informal*), magniloquence, pomposity, rant, verbosity, wordiness

rhetorical *adjective* 1 = **oratorical**, linguistic, stylistic, verbal 2 = **high-flown**, arty-farty (*informal*), bombastic, declamatory, flamboyant, flashy, florid, flowery, grandiloquent, high-sounding, hyperbolic, magniloquent, oratorical, pompous, pretentious, showy, verbose, windy

rhyme *noun* 1 = **poetry**, ode, poem, song, verse 2 **rhyme or reason** = **sense**, logic, meaning, method, plan ♦ *verb* 3 = **sound like**, chime, harmonize

rhythm *noun* = **beat**, accent, cadence, flow, lilt, measure (*Prosody*), metre, movement, pattern, periodicity, pulse, swing, tempo, time

rhythmic, rhythmical *adjective* = **cadenced**, flowing, harmonious, lilting, melodious, metrical, musical, periodic, pulsating, throbbing

ribald *adjective* = **coarse**, bawdy, blue, broad, earthy, filthy, gross, indecent, licentious, naughty, near the knuckle (*informal*), obscene, off colour, Rabelaisian, racy, raunchy (*slang*), risqué, rude, scurrilous, smutty, vulgar, X-rated (*informal*)
➤ **Antonyms**
chaste, decent, decorous, genteel, inoffensive, polite, proper, refined, tasteful

ribaldry *noun* = **coarseness**, bawdiness, earthiness, filth, grossness, indecency, licentiousness, naughtiness, obscenity, raciness, rudeness, scurrility, smut, smuttiness, vulgarity

rich *adjective* 1 = **wealthy**, affluent, filthy rich, flush (*informal*), loaded (*slang*), made of money (*informal*), moneyed, opulent, propertied, prosperous, rolling (*slang*), stinking rich (*informal*), well-heeled (*informal*), well-off, well-to-do 2 = **well-stocked**, abounding, full, productive, well-endowed, well-provided, well-supplied 3 = **fruitful**, abounding, abundant, ample, copious, exuberant, fecund, fertile, full, lush, luxurious, plenteous, plentiful, productive, prolific 4 = **full-bodied**, creamy, delicious, fatty, flavoursome, heavy, highly-flavoured, juicy, luscious, savoury, spicy, succulent, sweet, tasty 5 = **vivid**, bright, deep, gay, intense, strong, vibrant, warm 6 = **resonant**, deep, dulcet, full, mellifluous, mellow 7 = **funny**, amusing, comical, hilarious, humorous, laughable, ludicrous,

ridiculous, risible, side-splitting
➤ **Antonyms**
≠**wealthy**: destitute, impoverished, needy, penniless, poor ≠**well-stocked**: lacking, poor, scarce, wanting ≠**fruitful**: barren, poor, unfertile, unfruitful, unproductive ≠**full-bodied**: bland, dull ≠**vivid**: dull, insipid, weak ≠**resonant**: high-pitched

riches *plural noun* = **wealth**, abundance, affluence, assets, fortune, gold, money, opulence, plenty, property, resources, richness, substance, treasure
➤ **Antonyms**
dearth, indigence, lack, need, paucity, poverty, scantiness, scarcity, want

richly *adverb* 1 = **elaborately**, elegantly, expensively, exquisitely, gorgeously, lavishly, luxuriously, opulently, palatially, splendidly, sumptuously 2 = **fully**, amply, appropriately, in full measure, properly, suitably, thoroughly, well

rickety *adjective* = **shaky**, broken, broken-down, decrepit, derelict, dilapidated, feeble, flimsy, frail, imperfect, infirm, insecure, jerry-built, precarious, ramshackle, tottering, unsound, unsteady, weak, wobbly

rid *verb* 1 = **free**, clear, deliver, disabuse, disburden, disencumber, lighten, make free, purge, relieve, unburden 2 **get rid of** = **dispose of**, dispense with, do away with, dump, eject, eliminate, expel, jettison, remove, shake off, throw away *or* out, unload, weed out, wipe from the face of the earth

riddle[1] *noun* = **puzzle**, brain-teaser (*informal*), conundrum, enigma, mystery, poser, problem, teaser

riddle[2] *verb* 1 = **pierce**, honeycomb, pepper, perforate, puncture 2 = **sieve**, filter, screen, sift, strain, winnow ♦ *noun* 3 = **sieve**, filter, screen, strainer

riddled *adjective* = **filled**, corrupted, damaged, impaired, infested, marred, permeated, pervaded, spoilt

ride *verb* 1 = **control**, handle, manage, sit on 2 = **travel**, be borne, be carried, be supported, float, go, journey, move, progress, sit 3 = **dominate**, enslave, grip, haunt, oppress, tyrannize over ♦ *noun* 4 = **journey**, drive, jaunt, lift, outing, spin (*informal*), trip, whirl (*informal*)

ridicule *noun* 1 = **mockery**, banter, chaff, derision, gibe, irony, jeer, laughter, raillery, sarcasm, satire, scorn, sneer, taunting
♦ *verb* 2 = **laugh at**, banter, caricature, chaff, deride, humiliate, jeer, lampoon, laugh to scorn, make a fool of, make a monkey out of, make fun of, make one a laughing stock, mock, parody, poke fun at,

pooh-pooh, satirize, scoff, send up (*Brit. informal*), sneer, take the mickey out of (*informal*), take the piss (out of) (*taboo slang*), taunt

ridiculous *adjective* = **laughable**, absurd, comical, contemptible, derisory, farcical, foolish, funny, hilarious, inane, incredible, ludicrous, nonsensical, outrageous, preposterous, risible, silly, stupid, unbelievable
➤ **Antonyms**
bright, clever, intelligent, logical, prudent, rational, reasonable, sagacious, sane, sensible, serious, smart, solemn, well-thought-out, wise

rife *adjective* = **widespread**, abundant, common, current, epidemic, frequent, general, plentiful, prevailing, prevalent, raging, rampant, teeming, ubiquitous, universal

riffraff *noun* = **rabble**, *canaille*, dregs of society, hoi polloi, ragtag and bobtail, scum, undesirables

rifle *verb* = **ransack**, burgle, despoil, go through, gut, loot, pillage, plunder, rob, rummage, sack, strip

rift *noun* **1** = **breach**, alienation, difference, disagreement, division, estrangement, falling out (*informal*), quarrel, schism, separation, split **2** = **split**, breach, break, chink, cleavage, cleft, crack, cranny, crevice, fault, fissure, flaw, fracture, gap, opening, space

rig *verb* **1** = **fix** (*informal*), arrange, doctor, engineer, fake, falsify, fiddle with (*informal*), gerrymander, juggle, manipulate, tamper with, trump up **2** *Nautical* = **equip**, accoutre, fit out, furnish, kit out, outfit, provision, supply, turn out ◆ *noun* **3** = **apparatus**, accoutrements, equipage, equipment, fitments, fittings, fixtures, gear, machinery, outfit, tackle

right *adjective* **1** = **just**, equitable, ethical, fair, good, honest, honourable, lawful, moral, proper, righteous, true, upright, virtuous **2** = **correct**, accurate, exact, factual, genuine, precise, satisfactory, sound, spot-on (*Brit. informal*), true, unerring, valid, veracious **3** = **proper**, appropriate, becoming, *comme il faut*, desirable, done, fit, fitting, seemly, suitable **4** = **favourable**, advantageous, convenient, deserved, due, ideal, opportune, propitious, rightful **5** = **healthy**, all there (*informal*), balanced, *compos mentis*, fine, fit, in good health, in the pink, lucid, normal, rational, reasonable, sane, sound, unimpaired, up to par, well **6** = **conservative**, reactionary, Tory ◆ *adverb* **7** = **correctly**, accurately, aright, exactly,

factually, genuinely, precisely, truly **8** = **suitably**, appropriately, aptly, befittingly, fittingly, properly, satisfactorily **9** = **straight**, directly, immediately, instantly, promptly, quickly, straightaway, without delay **10** = **exactly**, bang, precisely, slap-bang (*informal*), squarely **11** = **properly**, ethically, fairly, fittingly, honestly, honourably, justly, morally, righteously, virtuously **12** = **favourably**, advantageously, beneficially, for the better, fortunately, to advantage, well ◆ *noun* **13** = **prerogative**, authority, business, claim, due, freedom, interest, liberty, licence, permission, power, privilege, title **14** = **justice**, equity, fairness, good, goodness, honour, integrity, lawfulness, legality, morality, propriety, reason, rectitude, righteousness, truth, uprightness, virtue **15 by rights** = **in fairness**, equitably, justly, properly **16 to rights** = **in order**, arranged, straight, tidy ◆ *verb* **17** = **rectify**, compensate for, correct, fix, put right, redress, repair, settle, sort out, straighten, vindicate
➤ **Antonyms**
adjective ≠**just**: bad, dishonest, immoral, improper, indecent, unethical, unfair, unjust, wrong ≠**correct**: counterfeit, erroneous, fake, false, fraudulent, illegal, illicit, inaccurate, incorrect, inexact, invalid, mistaken, questionable, uncertain, unlawful, untruthful, wrong ≠**proper**: inappropriate, undesirable, unfitting, unseemly, unsuitable, wrong ≠**favourable**: disadvantageous, inconvenient, unfavourable ≠**healthy**: abnormal, unsound ≠**conservative**: left, leftist, left-wing, liberal, radical, socialist ◆ *adverb* ≠**correctly**: inaccurately, incorrectly ≠**suitably**: improperly, incompletely ≠**straight**: indirectly, slowly ≠**favourably**: badly, poorly, unfavourably ◆ *noun* ≠**justice**: badness, dishonour, evil, immorality, impropriety ◆ *verb* ≠**rectify**: make crooked, topple

right away *adverb* = **immediately**, at once, directly, forthwith, instantly, now, posthaste, promptly, pronto (*informal*), right off, straightaway, straight off (*informal*), this instant, without delay, without hesitation

righteous *adjective* = **virtuous**, blameless, equitable, ethical, fair, good, honest, honourable, just, law-abiding, moral, pure, squeaky-clean, upright
➤ **Antonyms**
bad, corrupt, dishonest, dishonourable, evil, false, guilty, immoral, improper, indecent, insincere, sinful, unethical, unfair, unjust, unprincipled, unrighteous,

unscrupulous, unseemly, wicked

righteousness *noun* = **virtue**,
blamelessness, equity, ethicalness,
faithfulness, goodness, honesty, honour,
integrity, justice, morality, probity, purity,
rectitude, uprightness

rightful *adjective* = **lawful**, authorized,
bona fide, due, just, legal, legitimate,
proper, real, suitable, true, valid

rigid *adjective* **1** = **strict**, adamant, exact,
fixed, harsh, inflexible, intransigent,
invariable, rigorous, set, severe, stern,
stringent, unalterable, unbending,
uncompromising, undeviating,
unrelenting, unyielding **2** = **stiff**, inelastic,
inflexible, unyielding
➤ **Antonyms**
≠**strict**: flexible, indulgent, lax, lenient,
merciful, soft, tolerant ≠**stiff**: bending,
elastic, flexible, limber, lissom(e), mobile,
pliable, pliant, soft, supple, yielding

rigmarole *noun* **1** = **procedure**, bother,
carry-on (*informal, chiefly Brit.*), fuss, hassle
(*informal*), nonsense, palaver, pantomime
(*informal*), performance (*informal*), red
tape, to-do **2** = **twaddle**, balderdash,
gibberish, jargon, trash

rigorous *adjective* **1** = **strict**, challenging,
demanding, exacting, firm, hard, harsh,
inflexible, rigid, severe, stern, stringent,
tough **2** = **thorough**, accurate,
conscientious, exact, meticulous, nice,
painstaking, precise, punctilious,
scrupulous
➤ **Antonyms**
≠**strict**: easy, flexible, friendly, genial,
gentle, humane, indulgent, kind, lax,
lenient, loose, mild, permissive, relaxed,
soft, sympathetic, tolerant, weak
≠**thorough**: careless, half-hearted,
haphazard, imperfect, inaccurate,
incorrect, inexact, loose, negligent,
slapdash, sloppy, slovenly, unscrupulous

rigour *noun* **1** = **hardship**, ordeal, privation,
suffering, trial **2** = **strictness**, asperity,
firmness, hardness, harshness, inflexibility,
rigidity, sternness, stringency **3**
= **thoroughness**, accuracy,
conscientiousness, exactitude, exactness,
meticulousness, preciseness, precision,
punctiliousness

rigout *noun Informal* = **outfit**, apparel,
clobber (*Brit. slang*), clothing, costume,
dress, garb, gear (*informal*), get-up
(*informal*), habit, togs

rig out *verb* **1** = **dress**, array, attire, clothe,
costume, kit out **2** = **equip**, accoutre, fit,
furnish, kit out, outfit, set up

rig up *verb* = **set up**, arrange, assemble,
build, cobble together, construct, erect, fix

up, improvise, put together, put up, throw
together

rile *verb* = **anger**, aggravate (*informal*),
annoy, bug (*informal*), gall, get *or* put
one's back up, get one's goat (*slang*), get
on one's nerves (*informal*), get under one's
skin (*informal*), irk, irritate, nark (*Brit.,
Austral., & N.Z. slang*), nettle, peeve
(*informal*), pique, provoke, rub one up the
wrong way, try one's patience, upset, vex

rim *noun* = **edge**, border, brim, brink,
circumference, flange, lip, margin, verge

rind *noun* = **skin**, crust, husk, integument,
outer layer, peel

ring¹ *verb* **1** = **chime**, clang, peal, resonate,
resound, reverberate, sound, toll **2**
= **phone**, buzz (*informal, chiefly Brit.*), call,
telephone ◆ *noun* **3** = **chime**, knell, peal **4**
= **call**, buzz (*informal, chiefly Brit.*), phone
call

ring² *noun* **1** = **circle**, band, circuit, halo,
hoop, loop, round **2** = **arena**, circus,
enclosure, rink **3** = **gang**, association,
band, cabal, cartel, cell, circle, clique,
combine, coterie, crew (*informal*), group,
junta, knot, mob, organization, syndicate
◆ *verb* **4** = **encircle**, circumscribe, enclose,
encompass, gird, girdle, hem in, seal off,
surround

rinse *verb* **1** = **wash**, bathe, clean, cleanse,
dip, splash, wash out, wet ◆ *noun* **2**
= **wash**, bath, dip, splash, wetting

riot *noun* **1** = **disturbance**, anarchy,
commotion, confusion, disorder, fray,
lawlessness, mob violence, quarrel, row,
street fighting, strife, tumult, turbulence,
turmoil, upheaval, uproar **2**
= **merrymaking**, blast (*U.S. slang*),
boisterousness, carousal, excess, festivity,
frolic, high jinks, jollification, revelry, romp
3 = **display**, extravaganza, flourish,
profusion, show, splash **4 run riot: a**
= **rampage**, be out of control, break *or* cut
loose, go wild, let oneself go, raise hell,
throw off all restraint **b** = **grow profusely**,
grow like weeds, luxuriate, spread like
wildfire ◆ *verb* **5** = **rampage**, fight in the
streets, go on the rampage, raise an
uproar, run riot, take to the streets

riotous *adjective* **1** = **unrestrained**,
boisterous, loud, luxurious, noisy,
orgiastic, roisterous, rollicking, saturnalian,
side-splitting, uproarious, wanton, wild **2**
= **unruly**, anarchic, disorderly, lawless,
mutinous, rampageous, rebellious,
refractory, rowdy, tumultuous,
ungovernable, uproarious, violent
➤ **Antonyms**
calm, civilized, disciplined, gentle, lawful,
mild, obedient, orderly, peaceful, quiet,

restrained, well-behaved

rip *verb* **1** = **tear**, be rent, burst, claw, cut, gash, hack, lacerate, rend, score, slash, slit, split ♦ *noun* **2** = **tear**, cleavage, cut, gash, hole, laceration, rent, slash, slit, split

ripe *adjective* **1** = **mature**, fully developed, fully grown, mellow, ready, ripened, seasoned **2** = **suitable**, auspicious, favourable, ideal, opportune, right, timely **3 ripe for** = **ready for**, eager for, in readiness for, prepared for
➤ **Antonyms**
≠**mature**: green, immature, undeveloped, unripe ≠**suitable**: disadvantageous, inappropriate, inconvenient, inopportune, unfavourable, unfitting, unseemly, unsuitable, untimely

ripen *verb* = **mature**, burgeon, come of age, come to fruition, develop, get ready, grow ripe, make ripe, prepare, season

rip-off *noun Slang* = **cheat**, con (*informal*), con trick (*informal*), daylight robbery (*informal*), exploitation, fraud, robbery, scam (*slang*), sting (*informal*), swindle, theft

rip off *verb Slang* **1** = **cheat**, con (*informal*), defraud, diddle (*informal*), dupe, fleece, rob, skin (*slang*), steal from, swindle, trick **2** = **steal**, filch, knock off (*slang*), lift (*informal*), pilfer, pinch (*informal*), swipe (*slang*), thieve

riposte *noun* **1** = **retort**, answer, comeback (*informal*), counterattack, rejoinder, repartee, reply, response, return, sally ♦ *verb* **2** = **retort**, answer, come back, rejoin, reply, respond, return

ripple *noun* **1** = **wave**, undulation **2** = **flutter**, frisson, thrill, tingle, tremor

rise *verb* **1** = **get up**, arise, get out of bed, get to one's feet, rise and shine, stand up, surface **2** = **go up**, ascend, climb, levitate, move up **3** = **advance**, be promoted, get on, get somewhere, go places (*informal*), progress, prosper, work one's way up **4** = **get steeper**, ascend, climb, go uphill, mount, slope upwards **5** = **increase**, enlarge, go up, grow, intensify, lift, mount, soar, swell, wax **6** = **rebel**, mutiny, resist, revolt, take up arms **7** = **originate**, appear, crop up, emanate, emerge, flow, happen, issue, occur, spring, turn up ♦ *noun* **8** = **upward slope**, acclivity, ascent, elevation, hillock, incline, rising ground **9** = **pay increase**, increment, raise (*U.S.*) **10** = **increase**, advance, ascent, climb, improvement, upsurge, upswing, upturn, upward turn **11** = **advancement**, aggrandizement, climb, progress, promotion **12 give rise to** = **cause**, bring about, bring on, effect, produce, provoke,

result in
➤ **Antonyms**
verb ≠**go up, get steeper**: descend, drop, fall, plunge, sink ≠**increase**: abate, abbreviate, abridge, condense, curtail, decline, decrease, descend, diminish, drop, dwindle, fall, lessen, plunge, reduce, shrink, sink, wane ♦ *noun* ≠**increase**: blip, decline, decrease, downswing, downturn, drop, fall

risible *adjective Formal* = **ridiculous**, absurd, amusing, comical, droll, farcical, funny, hilarious, humorous, laughable, ludicrous, rib-tickling (*informal*), side-splitting

risk *noun* **1** = **danger**, chance, gamble, hazard, jeopardy, peril, pitfall, possibility, speculation, uncertainty, venture ♦ *verb* **2** = **dare**, chance, endanger, expose to danger, gamble, hazard, imperil, jeopardize, put in jeopardy, take a chance on, take the plunge, venture

risky *adjective* = **dangerous**, chancy (*informal*), dicey (*informal, chiefly Brit.*), dodgy (*Brit., Austral., & N.Z. informal*), fraught with danger, hazardous, perilous, precarious, touch-and-go, tricky, uncertain, unsafe
➤ **Antonyms**
certain, reliable, safe, secure, stable, sure

risqué *adjective* = **suggestive**, bawdy, blue, daring, immodest, improper, indelicate, naughty, near the knuckle (*informal*), off colour, Rabelaisian, racy, ribald

rite *noun* = **ceremony**, act, ceremonial, custom, formality, liturgy, mystery, observance, practice, procedure, ritual, sacrament, service

ritual *noun* **1** = **ceremony**, ceremonial, liturgy, mystery, observance, rite, sacrament, service **2** = **custom**, convention, form, formality, habit, practice, procedure, protocol, red tape, routine, stereotype, tradition, usage ♦ *adjective* **3** = **ceremonial**, ceremonious, conventional, customary, formal, habitual, prescribed, routine, stereotyped

ritzy *adjective Slang* = **luxurious**, de luxe, elegant, glamorous, glittering, grand, high-class, luxury, opulent, plush (*informal*), posh (*informal, chiefly Brit.*), stylish, sumptuous, swanky (*informal*)

rival *noun* **1** = **opponent**, adversary, antagonist, challenger, competitor, contender, contestant **2** = **equal**, compeer, equivalent, fellow, match, peer ♦ *adjective* **3** = **competing**, competitive, conflicting, opposed, opposing ♦ *verb* **4** = **compete**, be a match for, bear comparison with, come up to, compare with, contend, emulate, equal, match, measure up to,

oppose, seek to displace, vie with
➤ **Antonyms**
noun ≠**opponent:** ally, friend, helper, supporter ♦ *verb* ≠**compete:** aid, back, help, support

rivalry *noun* = **competition**, competitiveness, conflict, contention, contest, duel, opposition, struggle, vying

river *noun* **1** = **stream**, beck, brook, burn (*Scot.*), creek, rivulet, tributary, waterway **2** = **flow**, flood, rush, spate, torrent

riveting *adjective* = **enthralling**, absorbing, arresting, captivating, engrossing, fascinating, gripping, hypnotic, spellbinding

road *noun* **1** = **way**, avenue, course, direction, highway, lane, motorway, path, pathway, roadway, route, street, thoroughfare, track **2** *Nautical* = **roadstead**, anchorage

roam *verb* = **wander**, drift, meander, prowl, ramble, range, rove, stray, stroll, travel, walk

roar *verb* **1** = **cry**, bawl, bay, bell, bellow, clamour, crash, howl, rumble, shout, thunder, yell **2** = **guffaw**, bust a gut (*informal*), crack up (*informal*), hoot, laugh heartily, split one's sides (*informal*) ♦ *noun* **3** = **cry**, bellow, clamour, crash, howl, outcry, rumble, shout, thunder, yell **4** = **guffaw**, belly laugh (*informal*), hoot

rob *verb* = **steal from**, burgle, cheat, con (*informal*), defraud, deprive, despoil, dispossess, do out of (*informal*), hold up, loot, mug (*informal*), pillage, plunder, raid, ransack, rifle, rip off (*slang*), sack, skin (*slang*), stiff (*slang*), swindle

robber *noun* = **thief**, bandit, brigand, burglar, cheat, con man (*informal*), fraud, fraudster, highwayman, looter, mugger (*informal*), pirate, plunderer, raider, stealer, swindler

robbery *noun* = **theft**, burglary, embezzlement, filching, hold-up, larceny, mugging (*informal*), pillage, plunder, raid, rip-off (*slang*), stealing, steaming (*informal*), stick-up (*slang, chiefly U.S.*), swindle, thievery

robe *noun* **1** = **gown**, costume, habit, vestment **2** = **dressing gown**, bathrobe, housecoat, negligee, peignoir, wrapper ♦ *verb* **3** = **clothe**, apparel (*archaic*), attire, drape, dress, garb

robot *noun* = **machine**, android, automaton, mechanical man

robust *adjective* = **strong**, able-bodied, athletic, brawny, fighting fit, fit, fit as a fiddle (*informal*), hale, hardy, healthy, husky (*informal*), in good health, lusty,

muscular, powerful, rugged, sound, staunch, stout, strapping, sturdy, tough, vigorous, well
➤ **Antonyms**
delicate, feeble, frail, hothouse (*informal, often disparaging*), infirm, sickly, slender, unfit, unhealthy, unsound, weak, weedy (*informal*), wimpish *or* wimpy (*informal*), wussy (*slang*)

rock [1] *noun* **1** = **stone**, boulder **2** = **tower of strength**, anchor, bulwark, cornerstone, foundation, mainstay, protection, support

rock [2] *verb* **1** = **sway**, lurch, pitch, reel, roll, swing, toss, wobble **2** = **shock**, astonish, astound, daze, dumbfound, shake, stagger, stun, surprise

rocky [1] *adjective* = **rough**, boulder-strewn, craggy, pebbly, rugged, stony

rocky [2] *adjective* = **unstable**, doubtful, rickety, shaky, uncertain, undependable, unreliable, unsteady, weak, wobbly

rod *noun* = **stick**, bar, baton, birch, cane, crook, mace, pole, sceptre, shaft, staff, switch, wand

rogue *noun* = **scoundrel**, blackguard, charlatan, cheat, con man (*informal*), crook (*informal*), deceiver, fraud, fraudster, knave (*archaic*), ne'er-do-well, rapscallion, rascal, scally (*Northwest English dialect*), scamp, scumbag (*slang*), skelm (*S. African*), swindler, villain

roguish *adjective* **1** = **unprincipled**, criminal, crooked, deceitful, deceiving, dishonest, fraudulent, knavish, rascally, shady (*informal*), swindling, unscrupulous, villainous **2** = **mischievous**, arch, cheeky, coquettish, frolicsome, impish, playful, waggish

roister *verb* Old-fashioned = **make merry**, carouse, celebrate, frolic, go on a spree, live it up (*informal*), paint the town red (*informal*), push the boat out (*Brit. informal*), rave (*Brit. slang*), revel, rollick, romp, whoop it up (*informal*)

role *noun* **1** = **job**, capacity, duty, function, part, position, post, task **2** = **part**, character, impersonation, portrayal, representation

roll *verb* **1** = **turn**, go round, gyrate, pivot, reel, revolve, rotate, spin, swivel, trundle, twirl, wheel, whirl **2** = **wind**, bind, coil, curl, enfold, entwine, envelop, furl, swathe, twist, wrap **3** = **flow**, run, undulate **4** = **level**, even, flatten, press, smooth, spread **5** = **toss**, billow, lurch, reel, rock, sway, swing, tumble, wallow, welter **6** = **rumble**, boom, drum, echo, grumble, resound, reverberate, roar, thunder **7** = **sway**, lumber, lurch, reel, stagger, swagger, waddle **8** = **pass**, elapse, go past

♦ *noun* **9** = **turn**, cycle, gyration, reel, revolution, rotation, run, spin, twirl, undulation, wheel, whirl **10** = **spool**, ball, bobbin, cylinder, reel, scroll **11** = **register**, annals, catalogue, census, chronicle, directory, index, inventory, list, record, roster, schedule, scroll, table **12** = **tossing**, billowing, lurching, pitching, rocking, rolling, swell, undulation, wallowing, waves **13** = **rumble**, boom, drumming, growl, grumble, resonance, reverberation, roar, thunder

rollicking *adjective* = **boisterous**, carefree, cavorting, devil-may-care, exuberant, frisky, frolicsome, full of beans (*informal*), hearty, jaunty, jovial, joyous, lively, merry, playful, rip-roaring (*informal*), romping, spirited, sprightly, swashbuckling
➤ **Antonyms**
cheerless, despondent, dull, gloomy, lifeless, melancholy, morose, sad, sedate, serious, unhappy

roly-poly *adjective* = **plump**, buxom, chubby, fat, overweight, podgy, pudgy, rotund, rounded, tubby

romance *noun* **1** = **love affair**, affair, *affaire (du coeur)*, affair of the heart, amour, attachment, intrigue, liaison, passion, relationship **2** = **excitement**, adventure, charm, colour, exoticness, fascination, glamour, mystery, nostalgia, sentiment **3** = **story**, fairy tale, fantasy, fiction, idyll, legend, love story, melodrama, novel, tale, tear-jerker (*informal*) **4** = **tall story** (*informal*), absurdity, exaggeration, fabrication, fairy tale, falsehood, fiction, flight of fancy, invention, lie, trumped-up story, urban legend, urban myth ♦ *verb* **5** = **exaggerate**, be economical with the truth, fantasize, let one's imagination run away with one, lie, make up stories, stretch the truth, tell stories

romantic *adjective* **1** = **loving**, amorous, fond, icky (*informal*), lovey-dovey, mushy (*informal*), passionate, sentimental, sloppy (*informal*), soppy (*Brit. informal*), tender **2** = **idealistic**, dreamy, high-flown, impractical, quixotic, starry-eyed, unrealistic, utopian, visionary, whimsical **3** = **exciting**, charming, colourful, exotic, fascinating, glamorous, mysterious, nostalgic, picturesque ♦ *noun* **4** = **idealist**, Don Quixote, dreamer, romancer, sentimentalist, utopian, visionary
➤ **Antonyms**
adjective ≠**loving**: cold-hearted, insensitive, unaffectionate, unimpassioned, unloving, unromantic, unsentimental ≠**idealistic**: practical, realistic ≠**exciting**: uninspiring

romp *verb* **1** = **frolic**, caper, cavort, frisk, gambol, have fun, make merry, revel, roister, skip, sport **2 romp home** *or* **in** = **win easily**, run away with it, walk it (*informal*), win by a mile (*informal*), win hands down ♦ *noun* **3** = **frolic**, caper, lark (*informal*)

rook *verb Old-fashioned slang* = **cheat**, bilk, defraud, diddle (*informal*), do (*slang*), fleece, overcharge, rip off (*slang*), skin (*slang*), sting (*informal*), swindle

room *noun* **1** = **chamber**, apartment, office **2** = **space**, allowance, area, capacity, compass, elbowroom, expanse, extent, latitude, leeway, margin, range, scope, territory, volume **3** = **opportunity**, chance, occasion, scope

roomy *adjective* = **spacious**, ample, broad, capacious, commodious, extensive, generous, large, sizable *or* sizeable, wide
➤ **Antonyms**
bounded, confined, cramped, narrow, small, tiny

root¹ *noun* **1** = **stem**, radicle, radix, rhizome, tuber **2** = **source**, base, beginnings, bottom, cause, core, crux, derivation, foundation, fountainhead, fundamental, germ, heart, mainspring, nub, nucleus, origin, seat, seed, starting point **3 roots** = **sense of belonging**, birthplace, cradle, family, heritage, home, origins **4 root and branch** = **completely**, entirely, finally, radically, thoroughly, totally, utterly, wholly, without exception ♦ *verb* **5** = **become established**, anchor, become settled, embed, entrench, establish, fasten, fix, ground, implant, moor, set, stick, take root

root² *verb* = **dig**, burrow, delve, ferret, forage, hunt, nose, poke, pry, rootle, rummage

rooted *adjective* = **deep-seated**, confirmed, deep, deeply felt, entrenched, established, firm, fixed, ingrained, radical, rigid

rootless *adjective* = **footloose**, homeless, itinerant, roving, transient, vagabond

root out *verb* = **get rid of**, abolish, cut out, destroy, dig up by the roots, do away with, efface, eliminate, eradicate, erase, exterminate, extirpate, remove, tear out by the roots, uproot, weed out, wipe from the face of the earth

rope *noun* **1** = **cord**, cable, hawser, line, strand **2 the rope** = **hanging**, capital punishment, halter, lynching, noose **3 know the ropes** = **be experienced**, be an old hand, be knowledgeable, know all the ins and outs, know one's way around, know the score (*informal*), know what's what ♦ *verb* **4** = **tie**, bind, fasten, hitch, lash, lasso, moor, tether

rope in *verb Brit.* = **persuade**, drag in, engage, enlist, inveigle, involve, talk into

ropey, ropy *adjective Informal* **1** = **inferior**, deficient, inadequate, indifferent, mediocre, no great shakes (*informal*), of poor quality, poor, sketchy, substandard **2** = **unwell**, below par, off colour, poorly (*informal*), rough (*informal*), sickish, under the weather (*informal*)

roseate *adjective* = **pink**, pinkish, red, rose-coloured, rosy

roster *noun* = **rota**, agenda, catalogue, inventory, list, listing, register, roll, schedule, scroll, table

rostrum *noun* = **stage**, dais, platform, podium, stand

rosy *adjective* **1** = **pink**, red, roseate, rose-coloured **2** = **glowing**, blooming, blushing, flushed, fresh, healthy-looking, radiant, reddish, roseate, rubicund, ruddy **3** = **promising**, auspicious, bright, cheerful, encouraging, favourable, hopeful, optimistic, reassuring, roseate, rose-coloured, sunny
➤ **Antonyms**
≠**glowing**: ashen, colourless, grey, pale, pallid, sickly, wan, white ≠**promising**: cheerless, depressing, discouraging, dismal, down in the dumps (*informal*), dull, gloomy, hopeless, miserable, pessimistic, unhappy, unpromising

rot *verb* **1** = **decay**, break down, corrode, corrupt, crumble, decompose, degenerate, deteriorate, disintegrate, fester, go bad, moulder, perish, putrefy, spoil, taint **2** = **deteriorate**, decline, degenerate, languish, waste away, wither away ♦ *noun* **3** = **decay**, blight, canker, corrosion, corruption, decomposition, deterioration, disintegration, mould, putrefaction, putrescence **4** *Informal* = **nonsense**, balderdash, balls (*taboo slang*), bilge (*informal*), bosh (*informal*), bullshit (*taboo slang*), bunk (*informal*), claptrap (*informal*), cobblers (*Brit. taboo slang*), codswallop (*Brit. slang*), crap (*slang*), drivel, garbage (*chiefly U.S.*), guff (*slang*), hogwash, hot air (*informal*), moonshine, pants (*slang*), piffle (*informal*), poppycock (*informal*), rubbish, shit (*taboo slang*), stuff and nonsense, tommyrot, tosh (*slang, chiefly Brit.*), trash, tripe (*informal*), twaddle

rotary *adjective* = **revolving**, gyratory, rotating, rotational, rotatory, spinning, turning

rotate *verb* **1** = **revolve**, go round, gyrate, pirouette, pivot, reel, spin, swivel, turn, wheel **2** = **follow in sequence**, alternate,

interchange, switch, take turns

rotation *noun* **1** = **revolution**, gyration, orbit, pirouette, reel, spin, spinning, turn, turning, wheel **2** = **sequence**, alternation, cycle, interchanging, succession, switching

rotten *adjective* **1** = **decaying**, bad, corroded, corrupt, crumbling, decayed, decomposed, decomposing, disintegrating, festering, fetid, foul, mouldering, mouldy, perished, putrescent, putrid, rank, sour, stinking, tainted, unsound **2** *Informal* = **bad**, deplorable, disappointing, regrettable, unfortunate, unlucky **3** *Informal* = **despicable**, base, contemptible, dirty, disagreeable, filthy, mean, nasty, unpleasant, vile, wicked **4** *Informal* = **inferior**, crummy (*slang*), duff (*Brit. informal*), ill-considered, ill-thought-out, inadequate, lousy (*slang*), poor, poxy (*slang*), ropey or ropy (*Brit. informal*), sorry, substandard, unacceptable, unsatisfactory **5** = **corrupt**, bent (*slang*), crooked (*informal*), deceitful, dishonest, dishonourable, disloyal, faithless, immoral, perfidious **6** *Informal* = **unwell**, bad, below par, ill, off colour, poorly (*informal*), ropey or ropy (*Brit. informal*), rough (*informal*), sick, under the weather (*informal*)
➤ **Antonyms**
≠**decaying**: fresh, good, pure, sweet, wholesome ≠**corrupt**: decent, honest, honourable, moral, scrupulous, trustworthy

rotter *noun Old-fashioned* = **scoundrel**, bad lot, blackguard, blighter (*Brit. informal*), bounder (*old-fashioned Brit. slang*), cad (*Brit. informal*), cur, louse (*slang*), rat (*informal*), scumbag (*slang*), stinker (*slang*), swine

rotund *adjective* **1** = **round**, bulbous, globular, orbicular, rounded, spherical **2** = **plump**, chubby, corpulent, fat, fleshy, heavy, obese, podgy, portly, roly-poly, rounded, stout, tubby **3** = **pompous**, full, grandiloquent, magniloquent
➤ **Antonyms**
≠**plump**: angular, gaunt, lank, lanky, lean, scrawny, skinny, slender, slight, slim, thin

roué *noun* = **libertine**, debauchee, dirty old man (*slang*), lech or letch (*informal*), lecher, profligate, rake, sensualist, swinger (*slang*), wanton

rough *adjective* **1** = **uneven**, broken, bumpy, craggy, irregular, jagged, rocky, rugged, stony **2** = **ungracious**, bluff, blunt, brusque, churlish, coarse, curt, discourteous, ill-bred, ill-mannered, impolite, inconsiderate, indelicate, loutish, rude, unceremonious, uncivil, uncouth, uncultured, unmannerly, unpolished,

unrefined **3** = **unpleasant**, arduous, difficult, hard, tough, uncomfortable **4** = **approximate**, estimated, foggy, general, hazy, imprecise, inexact, sketchy, vague **5** = **stormy**, agitated, boisterous, choppy, inclement, squally, tempestuous, turbulent, wild **6** = **basic**, crude, cursory, hasty, imperfect, incomplete, quick, raw, rough-and-ready, rough-hewn, rudimentary, shapeless, sketchy, unfinished, unpolished, unrefined **7** = **rough-hewn**, crude, raw, uncut, undressed, unhewn, unpolished, unprocessed, unwrought **8** = **grating**, cacophonous, discordant, gruff, harsh, husky, inharmonious, jarring, rasping, raucous, unmusical **9** = **harsh**, boisterous, cruel, curt, drastic, extreme, hard, nasty, rowdy, severe, sharp, tough, unfeeling, unjust, unpleasant, violent **10** *Informal* = **unwell**, below par, ill, not a hundred per cent (*informal*), off colour, poorly (*informal*), ropey *or* ropy (*Brit. informal*), rotten (*informal*), sick, under the weather (*informal*), upset **11** = **coarse**, bristly, fuzzy, hairy, shaggy ♦ *verb* **12 rough out** = **outline**, block out, delineate, draft, plan, sketch, suggest **13 rough up** *Informal* = **beat up**, bash up (*informal*), batter, do over (*Brit., Austral., & N.Z. slang*), knock about *or* around, maltreat, manhandle, mistreat, thrash, work over (*slang*) ♦ *noun* **14** = **outline**, draft, mock-up, preliminary sketch, suggestion **15** *Informal* = **thug**, bruiser, bully boy, casual, lager lout, ned (*slang*), roughneck (*slang*), rowdy, ruffian, tough
➤ **Antonyms**
adjective ≠**uneven**: even, level, regular, smooth, unbroken ≠**ungracious**: civil, considerate, courteous, courtly, delicate, elegant, graceful, gracious, pleasant, polite, refined, smooth, sophisticated, urbane, well-bred, well-mannered ≠**unpleasant**: comfortable, cushy (*informal*), easy, pleasant, soft ≠**approximate**: exact, perfected, specific ≠**stormy**: calm, gentle, quiet, smooth, tranquil ≠**basic**: complete, detailed, finished, perfected, polished, refined, specific ≠**rough-hewn**: smooth ≠**grating**: harmonious, smooth ≠**harsh**: gentle, just, kind, mild, pleasant, quiet, soft ≠**coarse**: smooth, soft

rough-and-ready *adjective* = **makeshift**, adequate, cobbled together, crude, improvised, provisional, sketchy, stopgap, thrown together, unpolished, unrefined

rough-and-tumble *noun* = **fight**, affray (*Law*), brawl, donnybrook, dust-up (*informal*), fracas, melee *or* mêlée,

punch-up (*Brit. informal*), roughhouse (*slang*), scrap (*informal*), scrimmage, scuffle, shindig (*informal*), shindy (*informal*), struggle

roughhouse *noun Slang* = **rough behaviour**, boisterousness, brawl, brawling, disorderliness, disturbance, horseplay, row, rowdiness, rowdyism

roughneck *noun Slang* = **thug**, bruiser (*informal*), bully boy, heavy (*slang*), rough (*informal*), rowdy, ruffian, tough

round *adjective* **1** = **spherical**, ball-shaped, bowed, bulbous, circular, curved, curvilinear, cylindrical, discoid, disc-shaped, globular, orbicular, ring-shaped, rotund, rounded **2** = **plump**, ample, fleshy, full, full-fleshed, roly-poly, rotund, rounded **3** = **complete**, entire, full, solid, unbroken, undivided, whole ♦ *verb* **4** = **go round**, bypass, circle, circumnavigate, encircle, flank, skirt, turn ♦ *noun* **5** = **sphere**, ball, band, circle, disc, globe, orb, ring **6** = **series**, bout, cycle, sequence, session, succession **7** = **stage**, division, lap, level, period, session, turn **8** = **course**, ambit, beat, circuit, compass, routine, schedule, series, tour, turn **9** = **bullet**, cartridge, discharge, shell, shot

roundabout *adjective* = **indirect**, circuitous, circumlocutory, devious, discursive, evasive, meandering, oblique, periphrastic, tortuous
➤ **Antonyms**
direct, straight, straightforward

round off *verb* = **complete**, bring to a close, cap, close, conclude, crown, finish off, put the finishing touch to, settle
➤ **Antonyms**
begin, commence, initiate, open, start

round on *verb* = **attack**, abuse, bite (someone's) head off (*informal*), have a go at (*Brit. slang*), lose one's temper with, retaliate, snap at, turn on, wade into

roundup *noun* **1** *Informal* = **summary**, survey **2** = **gathering**, assembly, collection, herding, marshalling, muster, rally

round up *verb* = **gather**, assemble, bring together, collect, drive, group, herd, marshal, muster, rally

rouse *verb* **1** = **wake up**, arouse, awaken, call, get up, rise, wake **2** = **excite**, agitate, anger, animate, arouse, bestir, disturb, exhilarate, galvanize, get going, incite, inflame, instigate, move, prod, provoke, startle, stimulate, stir, whip up

rousing *adjective* = **lively**, brisk, electrifying, exciting, exhilarating, inspiring, moving, spirited, stimulating, stirring, vigorous
➤ **Antonyms**

boring, dreary, dull, lifeless, sluggish,
spiritless, unenergetic, wearisome,
wishy-washy (*informal*)

rout *noun* 1 = **defeat**, beating, debacle,
disorderly retreat, drubbing, headlong
flight, hiding (*informal*), licking (*informal*),
overthrow, overwhelming defeat, pasting
(*slang*), ruin, shambles, thrashing ◆ *verb* 2
= **defeat**, beat, chase, clobber (*slang*),
conquer, crush, destroy, dispel, drive off,
drub, lick (*informal*), overpower,
overthrow, put to flight, tank (*slang*),
thrash, throw back in confusion, wipe the
floor with (*informal*), worst

route *noun* 1 = **way**, avenue, beat, circuit,
course, direction, itinerary, journey,
passage, path, road, round, run ◆ *verb* 2
= **send**, convey, direct, dispatch, forward,
steer

routine *noun* 1 = **procedure**, custom,
formula, grind (*informal*), method, order,
pattern, practice, programme, usage, way,
wont ◆ *adjective* 2 = **usual**, conventional,
customary, everyday, familiar, habitual,
normal, ordinary, standard, typical,
wonted, workaday 3 = **boring**, clichéd,
dull, hackneyed, humdrum,
mind-numbing, predictable,
run-of-the-mill, tedious, tiresome,
unimaginative, uninspired, unoriginal
➤ **Antonyms**
adjective ≠**usual**: abnormal, different,
exceptional, irregular, special, unusual

rove *verb* = **wander**, cruise, drift, meander,
ramble, range, roam, stray, stroll, traipse
(*informal*)

rover *noun* = **wanderer**, drifter, gypsy,
itinerant, nomad, rambler, ranger, rolling
stone, transient, traveller, vagrant

row[1] *noun* 1 = **line**, bank, column, file,
queue, range, rank, sequence, series,
string, tier 2 **in a row** = **consecutively**, one
after the other, successively

row[2] *noun Informal* 1 = **quarrel**, altercation,
brawl, controversy, dispute, falling-out
(*informal*), fracas, fuss, ruckus (*informal*),
ruction (*informal*), scrap (*informal*), shindig
(*informal*), shindy (*informal*), shouting
match (*informal*), slanging match (*Brit.*),
squabble, tiff, trouble 2 = **disturbance**,
commotion, noise, racket, rumpus, tumult,
uproar 3 = **telling-off** (*informal*),
castigation, dressing-down (*informal*),
lecture, reprimand, reproof, rollicking (*Brit.*
informal), talking-to (*informal*), ticking-off
(*informal*), tongue-lashing ◆ *verb* 4
= **quarrel**, argue, brawl, dispute, fight, go
at it hammer and tongs, scrap (*informal*),
spar, squabble, wrangle

rowdy *adjective* 1 = **disorderly**, boisterous,

loud, loutish, noisy, obstreperous, rough,
unruly, uproarious, wild ◆ *noun* 2
= **hooligan**, brawler, casual, lager lout,
lout, ned (*Scot. slang*), rough (*informal*),
ruffian, tearaway (*Brit.*), tough,
troublemaker, yahoo, yob *or* yobbo (*Brit.*
slang)
➤ **Antonyms**
adjective ≠**disorderly**: decorous, gentle,
law-abiding, mannerly, orderly, peaceful,
refined

royal *adjective* 1 = **regal**, imperial, kinglike,
kingly, monarchical, princely, queenly,
sovereign 2 = **splendid**, august, grand,
impressive, magnificent, majestic, stately,
superb, superior

rub *verb* 1 = **stroke**, caress, knead, massage,
smooth 2 = **polish**, clean, scour, shine,
wipe 3 = **spread**, apply, put, smear 4
= **chafe**, abrade, fray, grate, scrape 5 **rub**
up the wrong way = **annoy**, aggravate
(*informal*), anger, bug (*informal*), get one's
goat (*slang*), get on one's nerves
(*informal*), get under one's skin (*informal*),
irk, irritate, nark (*Brit., Austral., & N.Z.*
slang), peeve (*informal*), piss one off
(*taboo slang*), vex ◆ *noun* 6 = **massage**,
caress, kneading 7 = **polish**, shine, stroke,
wipe 8 *As in* **the rub** = **difficulty**, catch,
drawback, hazard, hindrance, hitch,
impediment, obstacle, problem, snag,
trouble

rubbish *noun* 1 = **waste**, crap (*slang*),
debris, dregs, dross, flotsam and jetsam,
garbage (*chiefly U.S.*), grot (*slang*), junk
(*informal*), litter, lumber, offal, refuse,
scrap, trash 2 = **nonsense**, balderdash,
balls (*taboo slang*), bollocks (*Brit. taboo*
slang), bosh (*informal*), bullshit (*taboo*
slang), bunkum *or* buncombe (*chiefly*
U.S.), claptrap (*informal*), cobblers (*Brit.*
taboo slang), codswallop (*Brit. slang*), crap
(*slang*), drivel, garbage (*chiefly U.S.*),
gibberish, guff (*slang*), hogwash, hot air
(*informal*), moonshine, pants (*slang*), piffle
(*informal*), poppycock (*informal*), rot, shit
(*taboo slang*), stuff and nonsense,
tommyrot, tosh (*slang, chiefly Brit.*), trash,
tripe (*informal*), twaddle

rubbishy *adjective* = **trashy**, cheap,
shoddy, tatty, tawdry, throwaway,
twopenny-halfpenny, valueless, worthless

rubicund *adjective Old-fashioned* = **reddish**,
blushing, florid, flushed, pink, roseate,
rosy, ruddy

rub out *verb* 1 = **erase**, cancel, delete,
efface, excise, expunge, obliterate,
remove, wipe out 2 *U.S. slang* = **murder**,
assassinate, blow away (*slang, chiefly U.S.*),
bump off (*slang*), dispatch, do in

(*informal*), eliminate (*slang*), kill, knock off (*slang*), slaughter, slay, take out (*slang*), waste (*informal*)

ructions *plural noun Informal* = **row**, altercation, brawl, commotion, dispute, disturbance, fracas, fuss, hue and cry, quarrel, racket, rumpus, scrap (*informal*), scrimmage, shindig (*informal*), shindy (*informal*), storm, to-do, trouble, uproar

ruddy *adjective* **1** = **rosy**, blooming, blushing, florid, flushed, fresh, glowing, healthy, radiant, red, reddish, rosy-cheeked, rubicund, sanguine **2** = **red**, crimson, pink, reddish, roseate, ruby, scarlet
➤ **Antonyms**
≠**rosy**: anaemic, ashen, colourless, grey, pale, pallid, sickly, wan, white

rude *adjective* **1** = **impolite**, abrupt, abusive, blunt, brusque, cheeky, churlish, curt, discourteous, disrespectful, ill-mannered, impertinent, impudent, inconsiderate, insolent, insulting, offhand, peremptory, short, uncivil, unmannerly **2** = **vulgar**, barbarous, boorish, brutish, coarse, crude, graceless, gross, ignorant, loutish, low, oafish, rough, scurrilous, uncivilized, uncouth, uncultured, uneducated, ungracious, unpolished, unrefined **3** = **unpleasant**, abrupt, harsh, sharp, startling, sudden, violent **4** = **roughly-made**, artless, crude, inartistic, inelegant, makeshift, primitive, raw, rough, rough-hewn, simple
➤ **Antonyms**
≠**impolite**: civil, considerate, cordial, courteous, courtly, decent, gentlemanly, gracious, ladylike, mannerly, polite, respectful, sociable, urbane, well-bred ≠**vulgar**: civilized, cultured, educated, elegant, learned, polished, refined, sophisticated, urbane ≠**roughly-made**: artful, even, finished, shapely, smooth, well-made

rudimentary *adjective* = **basic**, early, elementary, fundamental, immature, initial, introductory, primary, primitive, undeveloped
➤ **Antonyms**
advanced, complete, developed, higher, later, mature, refined, secondary, sophisticated, supplementary

rudiments *plural noun* = **basics**, beginnings, elements, essentials, first principles, foundation, fundamentals, nuts and bolts

rue *verb Literary* = **regret**, bemoan, be sorry for, bewail, deplore, grieve, kick oneself for, lament, mourn, repent, reproach oneself for

rueful *adjective* = **regretful**, conscience-stricken, contrite, dismal, melancholy, mournful, penitent, remorseful, repentant, sad, self-reproachful, sorrowful, sorry, woebegone, woeful
➤ **Antonyms**
cheerful, delighted, glad, happy, joyful, pleased, unrepentant

ruffian *noun* = **thug**, bruiser (*informal*), brute, bully, bully boy, casual, heavy (*slang*), hoodlum, hooligan, lager lout, ned (*Scot. slang*), rascal, rogue, rough (*informal*), roughneck (*slang*), rowdy, scoundrel, tough, tsotsi (*S. African*), villain, wretch, yardie

ruffle *verb* **1** = **disarrange**, derange, discompose, dishevel, disorder, mess up, rumple, tousle, wrinkle **2** = **annoy**, agitate, confuse, disconcert, disquiet, disturb, faze, fluster, harass, hassle (*informal*), irritate, nettle, peeve (*informal*), perturb, put out, rattle (*informal*), shake up (*informal*), stir, trouble, unnerve, unsettle, upset, vex, worry
➤ **Antonyms**
≠**annoy**: appease, calm, comfort, compose, console, ease, mollify, solace, soothe

rugged *adjective* **1** = **rocky**, broken, bumpy, craggy, difficult, irregular, jagged, ragged, rough, stark, uneven **2** = **strong-featured**, furrowed, leathery, lined, rough-hewn, weather-beaten, weathered, worn, wrinkled **3** = **stern**, austere, crabbed, dour, gruff, hard, harsh, rough, rude, severe, sour, surly **4** = **tough**, beefy (*informal*), brawny, burly, hale, hardy, husky (*informal*), muscular, robust, strong, sturdy, vigorous, well-built
➤ **Antonyms**
≠**rocky**: even, gentle, level, regular, smooth, unbroken ≠**strong-featured**: delicate, pretty, refined, smooth, unmarked, youthful ≠**tough**: delicate, feeble, fragile, frail, infirm, sickly, skinny, soft, weak

ruin *verb* **1** = **destroy**, break, bring down, bring to nothing, bring to ruin, crush, defeat, demolish, devastate, lay in ruins, lay waste, overthrow, overturn, overwhelm, raze, shatter, smash, total (*slang*), trash (*slang*), wreak havoc upon, wreck **2** = **bankrupt**, impoverish, pauperize **3** = **spoil**, blow (*slang*), botch, damage, disfigure, injure, make a mess of, mangle, mar, mess up, screw up (*informal*), undo
♦ *noun* **4** = **destruction**, breakdown, collapse, crackup (*informal*), crash, damage, defeat, devastation, downfall, failure, fall, the end, undoing, wreck **5**

= **disrepair**, decay, disintegration, ruination, wreckage **6** = **bankruptcy**, destitution, insolvency
➤ **Antonyms**
verb ≠**destroy**: build, construct, create, keep, preserve, save ≠**spoil**: enhance, enrich, improve, mend, repair, restore, strengthen, support ♦ *noun* ≠**destruction**: creation, preservation, success, triumph, victory

ruinous *adjective* **1** = **destructive**, baleful, calamitous, catastrophic, deadly, deleterious, devastating, dire, disastrous, fatal, injurious, pernicious, shattering **2** = **extravagant**, crippling, immoderate, wasteful

rule *noun* **1** = **regulation**, axiom, canon, criterion, decree, dictum, direction, guide, guideline, law, maxim, order, ordinance, precept, principle, ruling, standard, tenet **2** = **procedure**, course, formula, method, policy, way **3** = **custom**, condition, convention, form, habit, order *or* way of things, practice, procedure, routine, tradition, wont **4** = **government**, administration, ascendancy, authority, command, control, direction, domination, dominion, empire, influence, jurisdiction, leadership, mastery, power, regime, reign, supremacy, sway **5 as a rule** = **usually**, customarily, for the most part, generally, mainly, normally, on the whole, ordinarily ♦ *verb* **6** = **govern**, administer, be in authority, be in power, command, control, direct, guide, hold sway, lead, manage, preside over, regulate, reign **7** = **be pre-eminent**, be superior, dominate **8** = **be prevalent**, be customary, hold sway, obtain, predominate, preponderate, prevail **9** = **decree**, adjudge, adjudicate, decide, determine, establish, find, judge, lay down, pronounce, resolve, settle

rule out *verb* = **exclude**, ban, debar, dismiss, disqualify, eliminate, forbid, leave out, obviate, preclude, prevent, prohibit, proscribe, reject
➤ **Antonyms**
allow, approve, authorize, let, license, order, permit, sanction

ruler *noun* **1** = **governor**, commander, controller, crowned head, emperor *or* empress, head of state, king *or* queen, leader, lord, monarch, potentate, prince *or* princess, sovereign **2** = **measure**, rule, straight edge, yardstick

ruling *adjective* **1** = **governing**, commanding, controlling, dominant, leading, reigning, upper **2** = **predominant**, chief, current, dominant, main, pre-eminent, preponderant, prevailing,

prevalent, principal, supreme ♦ *noun* **3** = **decision**, adjudication, decree, finding, judgment, pronouncement, resolution, verdict
➤ **Antonyms**
adjective ≠**predominant**: auxiliary, inferior, least, minor, secondary, subordinate, subsidiary, unimportant

rum *adjective Brit, slang* = **strange**, curious, dodgy (*Brit., Austral., & N.Z. informal*), funny, odd, peculiar, queer, singular, suspect, suspicious, unusual, weird

rumbustious *adjective* = **unruly**, boisterous, disorderly, loud, noisy, obstreperous, rough, rowdy, unmanageable, uproarious, wild

ruminate *verb* = **ponder**, brood, chew over, cogitate, consider, contemplate, deliberate, meditate, mull over, muse, rack one's brains, reflect, revolve, think, turn over in one's mind, weigh

rummage *verb* = **search**, delve, examine, explore, forage, hunt, ransack, root

rumour *noun* **1** = **story**, bush telegraph, buzz, dirt (*U.S. slang*), gossip, hearsay, news, report, talk, tidings, whisper, word ♦ *verb* **2 be rumoured** = **be said**, be circulated, be passed around, be put about, be reported, be told, be whispered

rump *noun* = **buttocks**, arse (*taboo slang*), ass (*U.S. & Canad. taboo slang*), backside (*informal*), bottom, bum (*Brit. slang*), buns (*U.S. slang*), butt (*U.S. & Canad. informal*), derrière (*euphemistic*), haunch, hindquarters, posterior, rear, rear end, seat, tail (*informal*)

rumple *verb* = **ruffle**, crease, crinkle, crumple, crush, derange, dishevel, disorder, mess up, pucker, screw up, scrunch, tousle, wrinkle

rumpus *noun* = **commotion**, brouhaha, confusion, disruption, disturbance, furore, fuss, hue and cry, noise, row, shindig (*informal*), shindy (*informal*), tumult, uproar

run *verb* **1** = **race**, barrel (along) (*informal, chiefly U.S. & Canad.*), bolt, career, dart, dash, gallop, hare (*Brit. informal*), hasten, hurry, jog, leg it (*informal*), lope, rush, scamper, scramble, scurry, speed, sprint, stampede **2** = **flee**, abscond, beat a retreat, beat it (*slang*), bolt, clear out, cut and run (*informal*), decamp, depart, do a runner (*slang*), escape, fly the coop (*U.S. & Canad. informal*), leg it (*informal*), make a run for it, make off, scarper (*Brit. slang*), skedaddle (*informal*), slope off, take flight, take off (*informal*), take to one's heels **3** = **give a lift to**, bear, carry, convey, drive, manoeuvre, operate, propel, transport **4**

= **operate**, go **5** = **move**, course, glide, go, pass, roll, skim, slide **6** = **work**, function, go, operate, perform **7** = **manage**, administer, be in charge of, boss (*informal*), carry on, conduct, control, coordinate, direct, handle, head, lead, look after, mastermind, operate, oversee, own, regulate, superintend, supervise, take care of **8** = **continue**, extend, go, last, lie, proceed, range, reach, stretch **9** = **flow**, cascade, discharge, go, gush, issue, leak, move, pour, proceed, spill, spout, stream **10** = **melt**, dissolve, fuse, go soft, liquefy, turn to liquid **11** = **spread**, be diffused, bleed, lose colour, mix **12** = **unravel**, come apart, come undone, ladder, tear **13** = **circulate**, be current, climb, creep, go round, spread, trail **14** = **publish**, display, feature, print **15** *chiefly U.S. & Canad.* = **compete**, be a candidate, challenge, contend, put oneself up for, stand, take part **16** = **smuggle**, bootleg, deal in, ship, sneak, traffic in ♦ *noun* **17** = **race**, dash, gallop, jog, rush, sprint, spurt **18** = **ride**, drive, excursion, jaunt, journey, joy ride (*informal*), lift, outing, round, spin (*informal*), trip **19** = **sequence**, chain, course, cycle, passage, period, round, season, series, spell, streak, stretch, string **20** = **type**, category, class, kind, order, sort, variety **21** = **demand**, pressure, rush **22** = **tear**, ladder, rip, snag **23** = **enclosure**, coop, pen **24 in the long run** = **in the end**, at the end of the day, eventually, in the fullness of time, in time, ultimately, when all is said and done **25 on the run: a** = **escaping**, at liberty, fugitive, in flight, on the lam (*U.S. slang*), on the loose **b** = **in retreat**, defeated, falling back, fleeing, in flight, retreating, running away
➤ **Antonyms**
verb ≠**race**: crawl, creep, dawdle, walk ≠**flee**: remain, stay ≠**continue**: cease, stop

run across *verb* = **meet**, bump into, chance upon, come across, come upon, encounter, meet with, run into

runaway *noun* **1** = **fugitive**, absconder, deserter, escapee, escaper, refugee, truant ♦ *adjective* **2** = **escaped**, fleeing, fugitive, loose, out of control, uncontrolled, wild **3** = **easily won**, easy, effortless

run away *verb* **1** = **flee**, abscond, beat it (*slang*), bolt, clear out, decamp, do a bunk (*Brit. slang*), do a runner (*slang*), escape, fly the coop (*U.S. & Canad. informal*), make a run for it, run off, scarper (*Brit. slang*), scram (*informal*), skedaddle (*informal*), take flight, take it on the lam (*U.S. & Canad. slang*), take off, take to one's heels, turn tail **2 run away with: a** = **abscond**, abduct, elope **b** = **win easily**,

romp home, walk it (*informal*), win by a mile (*informal*), win hands down

rundown *noun* = **summary**, briefing, outline, précis, recap (*informal*), résumé, review, run-through, sketch, synopsis

run-down *adjective* **1** = **exhausted**, below par, debilitated, drained, enervated, fatigued, out of condition, peaky, tired, under the weather (*informal*), unhealthy, weak, weary, worn-out **2** = **dilapidated**, broken-down, decrepit, dingy, ramshackle, seedy, shabby, tumbledown, worn-out
➤ **Antonyms**
≠**exhausted**: fighting fit, fine, fit, fit as a fiddle, full of beans (*informal*), healthy, well

run down *verb* **1** = **criticize**, bad-mouth (*slang, chiefly U.S. & Canad.*), belittle, decry, defame, denigrate, disparage, knock (*informal*), put down, revile, rubbish (*informal*), slag (off) (*slang*), speak ill of, vilify **2** = **reduce**, curtail, cut, cut back, decrease, downsize, drop, pare down, trim **3** = **knock down**, hit, knock over, run into, run over, strike **4** = **weaken**, debilitate, exhaust, sap the strength of, tire, undermine the health of

run-in *noun Informal* = **fight**, altercation, argument, brush, confrontation, contretemps, dispute, face-off (*slang*), quarrel, row, set-to (*informal*), skirmish, tussle

run in *verb* **1** = **break in gently**, run gently **2** *Informal* = **arrest**, apprehend, bust (*informal*), collar (*informal*), jail, lift (*slang*), nab (*informal*), nail (*informal*), pick up, pinch (*informal*), pull in (*Brit. slang*), take into custody, take to jail, throw in jail

run into *verb* **1** = **meet**, be beset by, be confronted by, bump into, chance upon, come across or upon, encounter, meet with, run across **2** = **collide with**, bump into, crash into, dash against, hit, ram, strike

runner *noun* **1** = **athlete**, jogger, sprinter **2** = **messenger**, courier, dispatch bearer, errand boy **3** *Botany* = **stem**, offshoot, shoot, sprig, sprout, tendril

running *adjective* **1** = **continuous**, constant, incessant, in succession, on the trot (*informal*), perpetual, together, unbroken, unceasing, uninterrupted **2** = **flowing**, moving, streaming ♦ *noun* **3** = **management**, administration, charge, conduct, control, coordination, direction, leadership, organization, regulation, superintendency, supervision **4** = **working**, functioning, maintenance, operation, performance

runny *adjective* = **flowing**, diluted, fluid, liquefied, liquid, melted, streaming, watery

run off *verb* **1** = **flee**, bolt, clear out, decamp, do a runner (*slang*), escape, fly the coop (*U.S. & Canad. informal*), make off, run away, scarper (*Brit. slang*), skedaddle (*informal*), take flight, take it on the lam (*U.S. & Canad. slang*), take to one's heels, turn tail **2** = **produce**, churn out (*informal*), duplicate, print **3** = **drain**, bleed, flow away, siphon, tap **4 run off with: a** = **run away with**, abscond with, elope with **b** = **steal**, lift (*informal*), make off with, pinch (*informal*), purloin, run away with, swipe (*slang*)

run-of-the-mill *adjective* = **ordinary**, average, banal, bog-standard (*Brit. & Irish slang*), common, commonplace, dime-a-dozen (*informal*), fair, mediocre, middling, modest, no great shakes (*informal*), passable, tolerable, undistinguished, unexceptional, unexciting, unimpressive, vanilla (*informal*)
➤ **Antonyms**
excellent, exceptional, extraordinary, marvellous, out of the ordinary, splendid, unusual

run out *verb* **1** = **be used up**, be exhausted, cease, dry up, fail, finish, give out, peter out **2** = **expire**, close, come to a close, end, terminate **3 run out of** = **exhaust one's supply of**, be cleaned out, be out of, have no more of, have none left, have remaining **4 run out on** *Informal* = **desert**, abandon, forsake, leave high and dry, leave holding the baby, leave in the lurch, rat on (*informal*), run away from, strand

run over *verb* **1** = **knock down**, hit, knock over, run down, strike **2** = **overflow**, brim over, spill, spill over **3** = **review**, check, examine, go over, go through, rehearse, run through, survey

run through *verb* **1** = **rehearse**, go over, practise, read, run over **2** = **pierce**, impale, spit, stab, stick, transfix

run-up *noun* = **build-up**, approach, preliminaries

rupture *noun* **1** = **break**, breach, burst, cleavage, cleft, crack, fissure, fracture, rent, split, tear **2** = **breach**, altercation, break, bust-up (*informal*), contention, disagreement, disruption, estrangement, falling-out (*informal*), feud, hostility, quarrel, rift, schism, split **3** *Medical* = **hernia** ♦ *verb* **4** = **break**, burst, cleave, crack, fracture, puncture, rend, separate, sever, split, tear **5** = **cause a breach**, break off, come between, disrupt, divide, split

rural *adjective* = **rustic**, agrarian, agricultural, Arcadian, bucolic, countrified, country, hick (*informal, chiefly U.S. & Canad.*), pastoral, sylvan, upcountry

➤ **Antonyms**
city, cosmopolitan, town, urban

ruse *noun* = **trick**, artifice, blind, deception, device, dodge, hoax, manoeuvre, ploy, sham, stratagem, subterfuge, wile

rush *verb* **1** = **hurry**, barrel (along) (*informal, chiefly U.S. & Canad.*), bolt, burn rubber (*informal*), career, dart, dash, fly, hasten, lose no time, make haste, race, run, scramble, scurry, shoot, speed, sprint, stampede, tear **2** = **push**, accelerate, dispatch, expedite, hurry, hustle, press, quicken, speed up **3** = **attack**, capture, charge, overcome, storm, take by storm ♦ *noun* **4** = **hurry**, charge, dash, dispatch, expedition, haste, race, scramble, speed, stampede, surge, swiftness, urgency **5** = **attack**, assault, charge, onslaught, push, storm, surge ♦ *adjective* **6** = **hasty**, brisk, cursory, emergency, expeditious, fast, hurried, prompt, quick, rapid, swift, urgent
➤ **Antonyms**
verb ≠**hurry**: dally, dawdle, delay, procrastinate, slow down, tarry, wait ♦ *adjective* ≠**hasty**: careful, detailed, leisurely, not urgent, slow, thorough, unhurried

rust *noun* **1** = **corrosion**, oxidation **2** = **mildew**, blight, mould, must, rot ♦ *verb* **3** = **corrode**, oxidize **4** = **deteriorate**, atrophy, decay, decline, go stale, stagnate, tarnish

rustic *adjective* **1** = **simple**, artless, homely, homespun, plain, unaffected, unpolished, unrefined, unsophisticated **2** = **rural**, Arcadian, bucolic, countrified, country, pastoral, sylvan **3** = **uncouth**, awkward, boorish, churlish, cloddish, clodhopping (*informal*), clownish, coarse, crude, graceless, hick (*informal, chiefly U.S. & Canad.*), loutish, lumpish, rough, uncultured, unmannerly ♦ *noun* **4** = **yokel**, boor, bumpkin, clod, clodhopper (*informal*), hayseed (*U.S. & Canad. informal*), hick (*informal, chiefly U.S. & Canad.*), hillbilly, peasant, son of the soil
➤ **Antonyms**
adjective ≠**simple**: elegant, grand, polished, refined, sophisticated ≠**rural**: cosmopolitan, urban ≠**uncouth**: courtly, polished, refined, sophisticated, urbane ♦ *noun* ≠**yokel**: city slicker, cosmopolitan, courtier, sophisticate, townie, townsman

rustle *verb* **1** = **crackle**, crinkle, swish, whish, whisper, whoosh ♦ *noun* **2** = **crackle**, crinkling, rustling, whisper

rusty *adjective* **1** = **corroded**, oxidized, rust-covered, rusted **2** = **reddish-brown**, chestnut, coppery, reddish, russet, rust-coloured **3** = **out of practice**, not what it was, sluggish, stale, unpractised, weak

rut *noun* **1** = **groove**, furrow, gouge, indentation, pothole, score, track, trough, wheel mark **2** = **habit**, dead end, groove, humdrum existence, pattern, routine, system

ruthless *adjective* = **merciless**, brutal, callous, cruel, hard, hard-hearted, harsh, heartless, inexorable, inhuman, pitiless, relentless, remorseless, severe, stern, unfeeling, unmerciful, unpitying, unrelenting, without pity

➤ **Antonyms**
compassionate, forgiving, gentle, humane, kind, lenient, merciful, pitying, sparing

rutted *adjective* = **grooved**, cut, furrowed, gouged, holed, indented, marked, scored

S s

sable *adjective* = **black**, dark, dusty, ebony, jet, raven, sombre

sabotage *noun* 1 = **damage**, destruction, disruption, subversion, treachery, treason, wrecking ♦ *verb* 2 = **damage**, cripple, destroy, disable, disrupt, incapacitate, subvert, throw a spanner in the works (*Brit. informal*), undermine, vandalize, wreck

sac *noun* = **pouch**, bag, bladder, cyst, pocket, pod, vesicle

saccharine *adjective* = **oversweet**, cloying, honeyed, icky (*informal*), maudlin, mawkish, nauseating, sentimental, sickly, soppy (*Brit. informal*), sugary, syrupy (*informal*), treacly

sack¹ *noun* 1 **the sack** = **dismissal**, discharge, termination of employment, the axe (*informal*), the boot (*slang*), the chop (*Brit. slang*), the (old) heave-ho (*informal*), the order of the boot (*slang*), the push (*slang*) 2 **hit the sack** *Slang* = **go to bed**, bed down, hit the hay (*slang*), retire, turn in (*informal*) ♦ *verb* 3 *Informal* = **dismiss**, axe (*informal*), discharge, fire (*informal*), give (someone) his books (*informal*), give (someone) his cards, give (someone) the elbow, give (someone) the push (*informal*), kick out (*informal*)

sack² *noun* 1 = **plundering**, despoliation, destruction, devastation, looting, pillage, plunder, ravage, ruin, waste ♦ *verb* 2 = **plunder**, demolish, despoil, destroy, devastate, lay waste, loot, maraud, pillage, raid, ravage, rifle, rob, ruin, spoil, strip

sackcloth and ashes *noun* = **penitence**, compunction, contrition, grief, mortification, mourning, penance, remorse, repentance

sacred *adjective* 1 = **holy**, blessed, consecrated, divine, hallowed, revered, sanctified, venerable 2 = **religious**, ecclesiastical, holy, solemn 3 = **inviolable**, inviolate, invulnerable, protected, sacrosanct, secure
➤ **Antonyms**
≠**holy, religious:** lay, nonspiritual, profane, secular, temporal, unconsecrated, worldly

sacrifice *noun* 1 = **surrender**, destruction, loss, renunciation 2 = **offering**, immolation, oblation ♦ *verb* 3 = **give up**, forego, forfeit, let go, lose, say goodbye to, surrender 4 = **offer**, immolate, offer up

sacrificial *adjective* = **propitiatory**, atoning, expiatory

sacrilege *noun* = **desecration**, blasphemy, heresy, impiety, irreverence, mockery, profanation, profaneness, profanity, violation
➤ **Antonyms**
piety, respect, reverence

sacrilegious *adjective* = **profane**, blasphemous, desecrating, godless, impious, irreligious, irreverent, ungodly, unholy

sacrosanct *adjective* = **inviolable**, hallowed, inviolate, sacred, sanctified, set apart, untouchable

sad *adjective* 1 = **unhappy**, blue, cheerless, dejected, depressed, disconsolate, dismal, doleful, down, downcast, down in the dumps (*informal*), down in the mouth (*informal*), gloomy, glum, grief-stricken, grieved, heavy-hearted, low, low-spirited, lugubrious, melancholy, mournful, pensive, sick at heart, sombre, wistful, woebegone 2 = **tragic**, calamitous, dark, depressing, disastrous, dismal, grievous, harrowing, heart-rending, moving, pathetic, pitiable, pitiful, poignant, sorry, tearful, upsetting 3 = **deplorable**, bad, dismal, lamentable, miserable, shabby, sorry, to be deplored, wretched 4 = **regrettable**, distressing, unfortunate, unhappy, unsatisfactory
➤ **Antonyms**
≠**unhappy:** blithe, cheerful, cheery, chirpy (*informal*), glad, happy, in good spirits, jolly, joyful, joyous, light-hearted, merry, pleased ≠**deplorable:** good ≠**regrettable:** fortunate

sadden *verb* = **upset**, aggrieve, bring tears to one's eyes, cast a gloom upon, cast down, dash, deject, depress, desolate, dispirit, distress, grieve, make one's heart bleed, make sad

saddle *verb* = **burden**, charge, encumber, load, lumber (*Brit. informal*), task, tax

sadistic *adjective* = **cruel**, barbarous, beastly, brutal, fiendish, inhuman, perverse, perverted, ruthless, savage, vicious

sadness *noun* = **unhappiness**, bleakness, cheerlessness, dejection, depression, despondency, dolefulness, gloominess, grief, heavy heart, melancholy, misery, mournfulness, poignancy, sorrow, sorrowfulness, the blues, the dumps (*informal*), tragedy, wretchedness

safe *adjective* **1** = **secure**, free from harm, impregnable, in safe hands, in safety, out of danger, out of harm's way, out of the woods, protected, safe and sound **2** = **unharmed**, all right, intact, O.K. *or* okay (*informal*), undamaged, unhurt, unscathed **3** = **cautious**, circumspect, conservative, dependable, discreet, on the safe side, prudent, realistic, reliable, sure, tried and true, trustworthy, unadventurous **4** = **risk-free**, certain, impregnable, riskless, secure, sound **5** = **harmless**, innocuous, nonpoisonous, nontoxic, pure, tame, unpolluted, wholesome ♦ *noun* **6** = **strongbox**, coffer, deposit box, repository, safe-deposit box, vault
➤ **Antonyms**
adjective ≠**secure**: at risk, damaged, endangered, imperilled, insecure, jeopardized, put at risk, put in danger, threatened ≠**cautious**: imprudent, incautious, reckless, risky, unsafe ≠**harmless**: baneful, dangerous, harmful, hazardous, hurtful, injurious, noxious, pernicious, unsafe

safe-conduct *noun* = **permit**, authorization, licence, pass, passport, safeguard, warrant

safeguard *verb* **1** = **protect**, defend, guard, look after, preserve, screen, shield, watch over ♦ *noun* **2** = **protection**, aegis, armour, bulwark, convoy, defence, escort, guard, security, shield, surety

safekeeping *noun* = **protection**, care, charge, custody, guardianship, keeping, supervision, surveillance

safely *adverb* = **in safety**, in one piece, safe and sound, securely, with impunity, without risk, with safety

safety *noun* **1** = **security**, assurance, immunity, impregnability, protection **2** = **shelter**, cover, refuge, sanctuary

sag *verb* **1** = **sink**, bag, bulge, cave in, dip, droop, drop, fall, fall unevenly, give way, hang loosely, settle, slump, swag **2** = **tire**, decline, droop, fall, flag, slide, slip, slump, wane, weaken, wilt ♦ *noun* **3** = **drop**, decline, depression, dip, downturn, fall, lapse, slip, slump

saga *noun* = **tale**, adventure, chronicle, epic, narrative, story, yarn

sagacious *adjective Formal* = **wise**, astute, canny, clear-sighted, discerning, far-sighted, insightful, intelligent, judicious, knowing, perceptive, perspicacious, sage, sharp, sharp-witted,

shrewd, smart

sagacity *noun* = **wisdom**, acuteness, astuteness, canniness, discernment, insight, judiciousness, perspicacity, sapience, sense, sharpness, shrewdness, understanding

sage *noun* **1** = **wise man**, authority, elder, expert, guru, mahatma, man of learning, master, philosopher, pundit, savant, Solomon ♦ *adjective* **2** = **wise**, acute, canny, discerning, intelligent, judicious, learned, perspicacious, politic, prudent, sagacious, sapient, sensible

sail *verb* **1** = **go by water**, cruise, ride the waves, voyage **2** = **embark**, cast *or* weigh anchor, get under way, put to sea, set sail **3** = **pilot**, captain, navigate, skipper, steer **4** = **glide**, drift, float, fly, scud, shoot, skim, skirr, soar, sweep, wing **5 sail into** *Informal* = **attack**, assault, fall upon, get going, get to work on, lambast(e), set about, tear into (*informal*)

sailor *noun* = **mariner**, Jack Tar, lascar, marine, matelot (*slang, chiefly Brit.*), navigator, salt, sea dog, seafarer, seafaring man, seaman, tar (*informal*)

saintly *adjective* = **virtuous**, angelic, beatific, blameless, blessed, devout, god-fearing, godly, holy, pious, religious, righteous, sainted, saintlike, sinless, worthy

sake *noun* **1** *As in* **for someone's** *or* **one's own sake** = **benefit**, account, advantage, behalf, consideration, gain, good, interest, profit, regard, respect, welfare, wellbeing **2** *As in* **for the sake of** = **purpose**, aim, cause, end, motive, objective, principle, reason

salacious *adjective* = **lascivious**, bawdy, blue, carnal, erotic, indecent, lecherous, lewd, libidinous, lustful, obscene, pornographic, prurient, ribald, ruttish, smutty, steamy (*informal*), wanton, X-rated (*informal*)

salary *noun* = **pay**, earnings, emolument, income, remuneration, stipend, wage, wages

sale *noun* **1** = **selling**, auction, deal, disposal, marketing, transaction, vending **2 for sale** = **available**, in stock, obtainable, on offer, on sale, on the market

salient *adjective* = **prominent**, arresting, conspicuous, important, marked, noticeable, outstanding, projecting, pronounced, remarkable, signal, striking

sallow *adjective* = **wan**, anaemic, bilious, jaundiced-looking, pale, pallid, pasty, peely-wally (*Scot.*), sickly, unhealthy, yellowish
➤ **Antonyms**
glowing, healthy-looking, radiant, rosy,

ruddy

sally noun 1 = witticism, bon mot, crack (informal), jest, joke, quip, retort, riposte, smart remark, wisecrack (informal) 2 = attack, campaign, foray, incursion, offensive, raid, sortie, thrust 3 = excursion, frolic, jaunt, trip ♦ verb 4 = go forth, erupt, issue, rush, set out, surge

salt noun 1 = seasoning, flavour, relish, savour, taste 2 = wit, bite, dry humour, liveliness, piquancy, punch, pungency, sarcasm, sharpness 3 = sailor, mariner, sea dog, seaman, tar (informal) 4 with a grain or pinch of salt = sceptically, cynically, disbelievingly, doubtfully, suspiciously, with reservations ♦ adjective 5 = salty, brackish, briny, saline, salted

salt away verb = save, accumulate, amass, bank, cache, hide, hoard up, lay by, lay in, lay up, put by, save for a rainy day, stash away (informal), stockpile

salty adjective 1 = salt, brackish, brak (S. African), briny, over-salted, saline, salted 2 = witty, colourful, humorous, lively, piquant, pungent, racy, sharp, snappy (informal), spicy, tangy, tart, zestful

salubrious adjective = health-giving, beneficial, good for one, healthful, healthy, invigorating, salutary, wholesome

salutary adjective 1 = beneficial, advantageous, good, good for one, helpful, practical, profitable, timely, useful, valuable 2 = healthy, healthful, salubrious

salutation noun Formal = greeting, address, salute, welcome

salute verb 1 = greet, accost, acknowledge, address, doff one's cap to, hail, kiss, pay one's respects to, welcome 2 = honour, acknowledge, pay tribute or homage to, recognize ♦ noun 3 = greeting, address, recognition, salutation

salvage verb = save, glean, recover, redeem, rescue, restore, retrieve

salvation noun = saving, deliverance, escape, lifeline, preservation, redemption, rescue, restoration
> Antonyms
condemnation, damnation, doom, downfall, hell, loss, perdition, ruin

salve noun = ointment, balm, cream, dressing, emollient, liniment, lotion, lubricant, medication, unguent

same adjective 1 = aforementioned, aforesaid, selfsame, very 2 = identical, alike, corresponding, duplicate, equal, equivalent, indistinguishable, interchangeable, synonymous, twin 3 = unchanged, changeless, consistent, constant, invariable, unaltered, unfailing,

uniform, unvarying 4 all the same = nevertheless, after all, anyhow, be that as it may, in any event, just the same, nonetheless, still 5 be all the same = be unimportant, be immaterial, be of no consequence, not be worth mentioning
> Antonyms
≠identical: different, dissimilar, diverse, miscellaneous, other ≠unchanged: altered, inconsistent, variable

sameness noun 1 = similarity, identicalness, identity, indistinguishability, likeness, oneness, resemblance, standardization, uniformity 2 = lack of variety, consistency, monotony, predictability, repetition, tedium

sample noun 1 = specimen, cross section, example, exemplification, illustration, indication, instance, model, pattern, representative, sign ♦ verb 2 = test, experience, inspect, partake of, taste, try ♦ adjective 3 = test, illustrative, pilot, representative, specimen, trial

sanctify verb = consecrate, absolve, anoint, bless, cleanse, hallow, purify, set apart

sanctimonious adjective = holier-than-thou, canting, false, goody-goody (informal), hypocritical, pi (Brit. slang), pietistic, pious, priggish, self-righteous, self-satisfied, smug, too good to be true, unctuous

sanction noun 1 = permission, allowance, approbation, approval, authority, authorization, backing, confirmation, countenance, endorsement, O.K. or okay (informal), ratification, stamp or seal of approval, support 2 often plural = ban, boycott, coercive measures, embargo, penalty ♦ verb 3 = permit, allow, approve, authorize, back, countenance, endorse, entitle, lend one's name to, support, vouch for 4 = confirm, ratify, warrant
> Antonyms
noun ≠permission: ban, disapproval, embargo, prohibition, proscription, refusal, veto ≠ban: approbation, approval, authority, authorization, dispensation, licence, permission ♦ verb ≠permit: ban, boycott, disallow, forbid, refuse, reject, veto

sanctity noun 1 = sacredness, inviolability, solemnity 2 = holiness, devotion, godliness, goodness, grace, piety, purity, religiousness, righteousness, sanctitude, spirituality

sanctuary noun 1 = shrine, altar, church, Holy of Holies, sanctum, temple 2 = protection, asylum, haven, refuge, retreat, shelter 3 = reserve, conservation area, national park, nature reserve

sanctum noun 1 = **sanctuary**, Holy of Holies, shrine 2 = **refuge**, den, private room, retreat, study

sane adjective 1 = **rational**, all there (informal), compos mentis, in one's right mind, in possession of all one's faculties, lucid, mentally sound, normal, of sound mind 2 = **sensible**, balanced, judicious, level-headed, moderate, reasonable, sober, sound
➤ **Antonyms**
≠**rational**: bonkers (slang, chiefly Brit.), crackpot (informal), crazy, daft (informal), insane, loony (slang), mad, mentally ill, non compos mentis, nuts (slang), off one's head (slang), off one's trolley (slang), out to lunch (informal), round the bend or twist (slang) ≠**sensible**: dumb-ass (slang), foolish, stupid, unreasonable, unsound, up the pole (informal), wacko or whacko (informal)

sang-froid noun = **composure**, aplomb, calmness, cool (slang), cool-headedness, coolness, equanimity, imperturbability, indifference, nonchalance, phlegm, poise, self-possession

sanguinary adjective Formal 1 = **savage**, bloodthirsty, cruel, grim 2 = **bloody**, bloodied, gory

sanguine adjective 1 = **cheerful**, animated, assured, buoyant, confident, hopeful, in good heart, lively, optimistic, spirited 2 = **ruddy**, florid, red, rubicund
➤ **Antonyms**
≠**cheerful**: despondent, dispirited, down, gloomy, heavy-hearted, melancholy, pessimistic ≠**ruddy**: anaemic, ashen, pale, pallid, peely-wally (Scot.)

sanitary adjective = **hygienic**, clean, germ-free, healthy, salubrious, unpolluted, wholesome

sanity noun 1 = **mental health**, normality, rationality, reason, right mind (informal), saneness, stability 2 = **good sense**, common sense, judiciousness, level-headedness, rationality, sense, soundness of judgment
➤ **Antonyms**
≠**mental health**: craziness, dementia, insanity, lunacy, madness, mental derangement, mental illness ≠**good sense**: folly, senselessness, stupidity

sap[1] noun 1 = **vital fluid**, animating force, essence, lifeblood 2 Slang = **fool**, charlie (Brit. informal), chump (informal), dumb-ass (slang), dweeb (U.S. slang), idiot, jerk (slang, chiefly U.S. & Canad.), muggins (Brit. slang), nerd or nurd (slang), nincompoop, ninny, nitwit (informal),

numpty (Scot. informal), numskull or numbskull, oaf, plonker (slang), prat (slang), simpleton, twit (informal), wally (slang)

sap[2] verb = **weaken**, bleed, deplete, devitalize, drain, enervate, erode, exhaust, rob, undermine, wear down

sapience noun, often used ironically = **wisdom**, discernment, insight, nous (Brit. slang), perspicacity, sagacity, sense, shrewdness, understanding

sapient adjective, often used ironically = **wise**, canny, discerning, discriminating, intelligent, judicious, knowing, perspicacious, sagacious, sage, shrewd

sarcasm noun = **irony**, bitterness, contempt, cynicism, derision, mockery, mordancy, ridicule, satire, scorn, sneering, venom, vitriol

sarcastic adjective = **ironical**, acerb, acerbic, acid, acrimonious, bitchy (informal), biting, caustic, contemptuous, cutting, cynical, derisive, disparaging, mocking, mordacious, mordant, sardonic, sarky (Brit. informal), satirical, sharp, sneering, taunting, vitriolic

sardonic adjective = **mocking**, bitter, cynical, derisive, dry, ironical, jeering, malicious, mordacious, mordant, sarcastic, sneering, wry

Satan noun = **The Devil**, Beelzebub, Lord of the Flies, Lucifer, Mephistopheles, Old Nick (informal), Prince of Darkness, The Evil One

satanic adjective = **evil**, accursed, black, demoniac, demoniacal, demonic, devilish, diabolic, fiendish, hellish, infernal, inhuman, iniquitous, malevolent, malignant, wicked
➤ **Antonyms**
benevolent, benign, divine, godly, holy

sate verb = **satisfy**, indulge to the full, satiate, slake

satellite noun 1 = **sputnik**, communications satellite 2 = **moon**

satiate verb 1 = **glut**, cloy, gorge, jade, nauseate, overfill, stuff, surfeit 2 = **satisfy**, sate, slake

satiety noun Formal 1 = **surfeit**, overindulgence, saturation 2 = **fullness**, gratification, repletion, satiation, satisfaction

satire noun = **mockery**, burlesque, caricature, irony, lampoon, parody, ridicule, sarcasm, send-up (Brit. informal), skit, spoof (informal), takeoff (informal), travesty, wit

satirical, satiric adjective = **mocking**, biting, bitter, burlesque, caustic, censorious, cutting, cynical, incisive, ironical, mordacious, mordant, pungent, Rabelaisian, sarcastic, sardonic, taunting, vitriolic

satirize verb = **ridicule**, abuse, burlesque, censure, criticize, deride, hold up to ridicule, lampoon, lash, parody, pillory, send up (*Brit. informal*), take off (*informal*), travesty

satisfaction noun 1 = **contentment**, comfort, complacency, content, contentedness, ease, enjoyment, gratification, happiness, peace of mind, pleasure, pride, repletion, satiety, well-being 2 = **fulfilment**, achievement, assuaging, gratification, resolution, settlement 3 = **compensation**, amends, atonement, damages, indemnification, justice, recompense, redress, reimbursement, remuneration, reparation, requital, restitution, settlement, vindication
➤ **Antonyms**
≠**contentment**: annoyance, discontent, displeasure, dissatisfaction, frustration, grief, misgivings, pain, shame, unhappiness ≠**compensation**: injury

satisfactory adjective = **adequate**, acceptable, all right, average, competent, fair, good enough, passable, sufficient, suitable, up to scratch, up to standard, up to the mark
➤ **Antonyms**
bad, below par, inadequate, insufficient, leaving a lot to be desired, mediocre, no great shakes (*informal*), not up to scratch (*informal*), poor, sub-standard, unacceptable, unsatisfactory, unsuitable

satisfied adjective = **contented**, at ease, complacent, content, convinced, easy in one's mind, happy, like the cat that swallowed the canary (*informal*), pacified, positive, smug, sure

satisfy verb 1 = **content**, appease, assuage, feed, fill, gratify, indulge, mollify, pacify, pander to, please, quench, sate, satiate, slake, surfeit 2 = **be sufficient**, answer, be adequate, be enough, come up to expectations, do, fill the bill (*informal*), fulfil, meet, qualify, serve, serve the purpose, suffice 3 = **convince**, assure, dispel (someone's) doubts, persuade, put (someone's) mind at rest, quiet, reassure 4 = **fulfil**, answer, comply with, discharge, meet
➤ **Antonyms**
≠**content**: annoy, displease, dissatisfy, exasperate, frustrate, give cause for complaint ≠**be sufficient**: fail to meet ≠**convince**: dissuade, fail to persuade

satisfying adjective = **satisfactory**, cheering, convincing, filling, gratifying, pleasing, pleasurable

saturate verb = **soak**, douse, drench, imbue, impregnate, seep, souse, steep, suffuse, waterlog, wet through

saturated adjective = **soaked**, drenched, dripping, droukit or drookit (*Scot.*), soaked to the skin, soaking (wet), sodden, sopping (wet), waterlogged, wet through, wringing wet

saturnine adjective = **gloomy**, dour, dull, glum, grave, heavy, morose, phlegmatic, sedate, sluggish, sombre, taciturn, uncommunicative

sauce noun Informal = **impudence**, audacity, backchat (*informal*), cheek (*informal*), cheekiness, disrespectfulness, front, impertinence, insolence, lip (*slang*), nerve (*informal*), rudeness

sauciness noun = **impudence**, backchat (*informal*), brazenness, cheek (*informal*), flippancy, impertinence, insolence, lip (*slang*), pertness, rudeness, sauce (*informal*)

saucy adjective 1 = **impudent**, cheeky (*informal*), disrespectful, flip (*informal*), flippant, forward, fresh (*informal*), impertinent, insolent, lippy (*U.S. & Canad. slang*), pert, presumptuous, rude, sassy (*U.S. informal*), smart-alecky (*informal*) 2 = **jaunty**, dashing, gay, natty (*informal*), perky, rakish, sporty

saunter verb 1 = **stroll**, amble, dally, meander, mosey (*informal*), ramble, roam, rove, take a stroll, wander ♦ noun 2 = **stroll**, airing, amble, constitutional, perambulation, promenade, ramble, turn, walk

savage adjective 1 = **wild**, feral, undomesticated, untamed 2 = **cruel**, barbarous, beastly, bestial, bloodthirsty, bloody, brutal, brutish, devilish, ferocious, fierce, harsh, inhuman, merciless, murderous, pitiless, ruthless, sadistic, vicious 3 = **primitive**, in a state of nature, nonliterate, rude, unspoilt 4 = **uncultivated**, rough, rugged, uncivilized ♦ noun 5 = **primitive**, autochthon, barbarian, heathen, indigene, native 6 = **lout**, barbarian, bear, boor, roughneck (*slang*), yahoo, yob (*Brit. slang*), yobbo (*Brit. slang*) 7 = **brute**, beast, fiend, monster ♦ verb 8 = **attack**, lacerate, mangle, maul 9 = **criticise**, attack, tear into (*informal*)
➤ **Antonyms**
adjective ≠**wild**: domesticated, tame ≠**cruel**: gentle, humane, kind, merciful, mild, restrained ≠**uncultivated**: civilized,

cultivated, refined ♦ *verb* ≠**criticise**:
acclaim, celebrate, praise, rave about
(*informal*)

savagery *noun* = **cruelty**, barbarity,
bestiality, bloodthirstiness, brutality,
ferocity, fierceness, inhumanity,
ruthlessness, sadism, viciousness

savant *noun* = **sage**, authority, intellectual,
mahatma, master, mastermind,
philosopher, scholar

save *verb* **1** = **rescue**, bail (someone) out,
come to (someone's) rescue, deliver, free,
liberate, recover, redeem, salvage, save
(someone's) bacon (*British informal*), set
free **2** = **protect**, conserve, guard, keep
safe, look after, preserve, safeguard,
screen, shield, take care of **3** = **keep**, be
frugal, be thrifty, collect, economize,
gather, hide away, hoard, hold, husband,
lay by, put aside for a rainy day, put by,
reserve, retrench, salt away, set aside,
store, treasure up **4** = **prevent**, hinder,
obviate, rule out, spare
➤ Antonyms
≠**rescue**, **protect**: abandon, endanger,
expose, imperil, risk, threaten ≠**keep**: be
extravagant (with), blow (*slang*),
consume, discard, fritter away, spend,
splurge, squander, use, use up, waste

saving *noun* **1** = **economy**, bargain,
discount, reduction ♦ *adjective* **2** *As in*
saving grace = **redeeming**, compensatory,
extenuating, qualifying

savings *plural noun* = **nest egg**, fall-back,
fund, provision for a rainy day, reserves,
resources, store

saviour *noun* = **rescuer**, defender,
deliverer, friend in need, Good Samaritan,
guardian, knight in shining armour,
liberator, preserver, protector, redeemer,
salvation

Saviour *noun* = **Christ**, Jesus, Messiah,
Redeemer

savoir-faire *noun* = **social know-how**
(*informal*), accomplishment, diplomacy,
discretion, finesse, poise, social graces,
tact, urbanity

savour *verb* **1** = **enjoy**, appreciate, delight
in, drool, enjoy to the full, gloat over, like,
luxuriate in, partake, relish, revel in **2**
savour of = **suggest**, bear the hallmarks of,
be indicative of, be suggestive of, partake
of, show signs of, smack of, verge on
♦ *noun* **3** = **flavour**, piquancy, relish,
smack, smell, tang, taste, zest, zing
(*informal*) **4** = **trace**, distinctive quality

savoury *adjective* **1** = **spicy**, agreeable,
appetizing, dainty, delectable, delicious,
full-flavoured, good, luscious,
mouthwatering, palatable, piquant, rich,

scrumptious (*informal*), tangy, tasty,
toothsome **2** = **wholesome**, decent,
honest, reputable, respectable
➤ Antonyms
≠**spicy**: insipid, tasteless, unappetizing,
unpalatable, unpleasant ≠**wholesome**:
disreputable, distasteful, nasty, unpleasant,
unsavoury

savvy *Slang* ♦ *verb* **1** = **understand**,
apprehend, catch on, comprehend, get
the gist, grasp, perceive, take in ♦ *noun* **2**
= **understanding**, apprehension,
comprehension, grasp, ken, perception

saw *noun Old-fashioned* = **saying**, adage,
aphorism, apophthegm, axiom, dictum,
maxim, proverb

say *verb* **1** = **speak**, add, affirm, announce,
assert, asseverate, come out with
(*informal*), declare, express, give voice *or*
utterance to, maintain, mention,
pronounce, put into words, remark, state,
utter, voice **2** = **tell**, answer, disclose,
divulge, give as one's opinion, make
known, reply, respond, reveal **3** = **recite**,
deliver, do, orate, perform, read, rehearse,
render, repeat **4** = **report**, allege, bruit,
claim, noise abroad, put about, rumour,
suggest **5** = **suppose**, assume, conjecture,
dare say, estimate, guess, hazard a guess,
imagine, judge, presume, surmise **6**
= **express**, communicate, convey, give the
impression that, imply **7 go without
saying** = **be obvious**, be accepted, be a
matter of course, be self-evident, be taken
as read, be taken for granted, be
understood **8 to say the least** = **at the very
least**, to put it mildly, without any
exaggeration ♦ *noun* **9** = **chance to speak**,
crack (*informal*), opportunity to speak,
turn to speak, voice, vote **10** = **influence**,
authority, clout (*informal*), power, sway,
weight

saying *noun* = **proverb**, adage, aphorism,
apophthegm, axiom, byword, dictum,
maxim, saw, slogan

scale[1] *noun* = **flake**, lamina, layer, plate

scale[2] *noun* **1** = **graduation**, calibration,
degrees, gamut, gradation, graduated
system, hierarchy, ladder, progression,
ranking, register, seniority system,
sequence, series, spectrum, spread, steps **2**
= **ratio**, proportion **3** = **degree**, extent,
range, reach, scope, way ♦ *verb* **4** = **climb**,
ascend, clamber, escalade, mount,
surmount **5** = **adjust**, proportion, prorate
(*chiefly U.S.*), regulate

scam *noun Slang* = **swindle**, diddle, fiddle,
racket, stratagem

scamp *noun* = **rascal**, devil, imp,
mischief-maker, monkey, rogue, scallywag

(*informal*), scapegrace, toerag (*slang*), tyke (*informal*)

scamper *verb* = **run**, beetle, dart, dash, fly, hasten, hurry, romp, scoot, scurry, scuttle, sprint

scan *verb* 1 = **glance over**, check, check out (*informal*), clock (*Brit. slang*), examine, eye, eyeball (*slang*), get a load of (*informal*), look one up and down, look through, run one's eye over, run over, size up (*informal*), skim, take a dekko at (*Brit. slang*) 2 = **scrutinize**, con (*archaic*), investigate, recce (*slang*), scour, search, survey, sweep, take stock of

scandal *noun* 1 = **crime**, disgrace, embarrassment, offence, sin, skeleton in the cupboard, wrongdoing 2 = **shame**, calumny, defamation, detraction, discredit, disgrace, dishonour, ignominy, infamy, obloquy, offence, opprobrium, reproach, stigma 3 = **gossip**, abuse, aspersion, backbiting, dirt, dirty linen (*informal*), rumours, slander, talk, tattle

scandalize *verb* = **shock**, affront, appal, disgust, horrify, offend, outrage, raise eyebrows

scandalmonger *noun* = **gossip**, muckraker, tattler

scandalous *adjective* 1 = **shocking**, atrocious, disgraceful, disreputable, highly improper, infamous, monstrous, odious, opprobrious, outrageous, shameful, unseemly 2 = **slanderous**, defamatory, gossiping, libellous, scurrilous, untrue
➤ **Antonyms**
≠**shocking**: decent, proper, reputable, respectable, seemly, upright ≠**slanderous**: laudatory, unimpeachable

scant *adjective* = **meagre**, bare, barely sufficient, deficient, inadequate, insufficient, limited, little, minimal, sparse
➤ **Antonyms**
abundant, adequate, ample, full, generous, plentiful, satisfactory, sufficient

scanty *adjective* = **meagre**, bare, deficient, inadequate, insufficient, pathetic, poor, restricted, scant, short, skimpy, slender, sparing, sparse, thin

scapegoat *noun* = **whipping boy**, fall guy (*informal*)

scar *noun* 1 = **mark**, blemish, cicatrix, injury, trauma (*Pathology*), wound ♦ *verb* 2 = **mark**, brand, damage, disfigure, traumatize

scarce *adjective* = **rare**, at a premium, deficient, few, few and far between, infrequent, in short supply, insufficient, thin on the ground, uncommon, unusual, wanting

➤ **Antonyms**
abundant, ample, common, commonplace, frequent, numerous, plenteous, plentiful, sufficient

scarcely *adverb* 1 = **hardly**, barely, only just, scarce (*archaic*) 2 *often used ironically* = **definitely not**, by no means, hardly, not at all, on no account, under no circumstances

scarcity *noun* = **shortage**, dearth, deficiency, infrequency, insufficiency, lack, paucity, poverty, rareness, undersupply, want
➤ **Antonyms**
abundance, excess, glut, superfluity, surfeit, surplus

scare *verb* 1 = **frighten**, alarm, daunt, dismay, give (someone) a fright, give (someone) a turn (*informal*), intimidate, panic, put the wind up (someone) (*informal*), shock, startle, terrify, terrorize ♦ *noun* 2 = **fright**, alarm, alert, panic, shock, start, terror

scared *adjective* = **frightened**, fearful, panicky, panic-stricken, petrified, shaken, startled, terrified

scaremonger *noun* = **alarmist**, doom merchant (*informal*), prophet of doom

scarper *verb Brit slang* = **run away**, abscond, beat a hasty retreat, beat it (*slang*), clear off (*informal*), decamp, depart, disappear, do a bunk (*Brit. slang*), flee, go, hook it (*slang*), make off, make oneself scarce (*informal*), run for it, scram (*informal*), skedaddle (*informal*), slope off, take flight, take oneself off, take to one's heels, vamoose (*slang, chiefly U.S.*)

scary *adjective Informal* = **frightening**, alarming, bloodcurdling, chilling, creepy (*informal*), hair-raising, hairy (*slang*), horrendous, horrifying, intimidating, shocking, spine-chilling, spooky (*informal*), terrifying, unnerving

scathing *adjective* = **critical**, belittling, biting, caustic, cutting, harsh, mordacious, mordant, sarcastic, savage, scornful, searing, trenchant, vitriolic, withering

scatter *verb* 1 = **throw about**, broadcast, diffuse, disseminate, fling, litter, shower, sow, spread, sprinkle, strew 2 = **disperse**, disband, dispel, dissipate, disunite, put to flight, separate
➤ **Antonyms**
≠**throw about**: cluster, collect ≠**disperse**: assemble, congregate, converge, rally, unite

scatterbrain *noun* = **featherbrain**, bird-brain (*informal*), butterfly, flibbertigibbet, madcap

scatterbrained *adjective* = **empty-headed**, bird-brained (*informal*), careless, featherbrained, forgetful, frivolous, giddy, madcap, scatty (*Brit. informal*), silly, slaphappy (*informal*), thoughtless

scattering *noun* = **sprinkling**, few, handful, scatter, smatter, smattering

scenario *noun* = **story line**, master plan, outline, résumé, rundown, scheme, sequence of events, sketch, summary, synopsis

scene *noun* **1** = **site**, area, locality, place, position, setting, situation, spot, stage, whereabouts **2** = **setting**, backdrop, background, location, *mise en scène*, set **3** = **show**, display, drama, exhibition, pageant, picture, representation, sight, spectacle, tableau **4** = **act**, division, episode, part **5** = **view**, landscape, panorama, prospect, vista **6** = **fuss**, carry-on (*informal, chiefly Brit.*), commotion, confrontation, display of emotion, drama, exhibition, hue and cry, performance, row, tantrum, to-do, upset **7** *Informal* = **world**, arena, business, environment, field of interest, milieu

scenery *noun* **1** = **landscape**, surroundings, terrain, view, vista **2** *Theatre* = **set**, backdrop, décor, flats, setting, stage set

scenic *adjective* = **picturesque**, beautiful, breathtaking, grand, impressive, panoramic, spectacular, striking

scent *noun* **1** = **fragrance**, aroma, bouquet, niff (*Brit. slang*), odour, perfume, redolence, smell **2** = **trail**, spoor, track ♦ *verb* **3** = **detect**, be on the track *or* trail of, discern, get wind of (*informal*), nose out, recognize, sense, smell, sniff, sniff out

scented *adjective* = **fragrant**, ambrosial, aromatic, odoriferous, perfumed, redolent, sweet-smelling

sceptic *noun* = **doubter**, agnostic, cynic, disbeliever, doubting Thomas, scoffer, unbeliever

sceptical *adjective* = **doubtful**, cynical, disbelieving, doubting, dubious, hesitating, incredulous, mistrustful, questioning, quizzical, scoffing, unbelieving, unconvinced
➤ **Antonyms**
believing, certain, convinced, credulous, dogmatic, free from doubt, of fixed mind, sure, trusting, undoubting, unquestioning

scepticism *noun* = **doubt**, agnosticism, cynicism, disbelief, incredulity, suspicion, unbelief

schedule *noun* **1** = **plan**, agenda, calendar, catalogue, inventory, itinerary, list, list of appointments, programme, timetable

♦ *verb* **2** = **plan**, appoint, arrange, book, organize, programme, slot (*informal*), time

schematic *adjective* = **diagrammatic**, diagrammatical, graphic, illustrative, representational

schematize *verb* = **systematize**, arrange, catalogue, categorize, classify, file, grade, methodize, order, pigeonhole, put into order, regulate, sort, standardize, systemize, tabulate

scheme *noun* **1** = **plan**, contrivance, course of action, design, device, programme, project, proposal, strategy, system, tactics, theory **2** = **plot**, conspiracy, dodge, game (*informal*), intrigue, machinations, manoeuvre, ploy, ruse, shift, stratagem, subterfuge **3** = **diagram**, arrangement, blueprint, chart, codification, draft, layout, outline, pattern, schedule, schema, system ♦ *verb* **4** = **plan**, contrive, design, devise, frame, imagine, lay plans, project, work out **5** = **plot**, collude, conspire, intrigue, machinate, manoeuvre, wheel and deal (*informal*)

scheming *adjective* = **calculating**, artful, conniving, cunning, deceitful, designing, duplicitous, foxy, Machiavellian, slippery, sly, tricky, underhand, wily
➤ **Antonyms**
above-board, artless, guileless, honest, ingenuous, naive, straightforward, trustworthy, undesigning

schism *noun* = **division**, breach, break, discord, disunion, rift, rupture, separation, splintering, split

schmaltzy *adjective* = **sentimental**, corny (*slang*), icky (*informal*), maudlin, mawkish, mushy (*informal*), overemotional, sloppy (*informal*), slushy (*informal*), soppy (*informal*), tear-jerking

scholar *noun* **1** = **intellectual**, academic, bluestocking (*usually disparaging*), bookworm, egghead (*informal*), man of letters, savant **2** = **student**, disciple, learner, pupil, schoolboy *or* schoolgirl

scholarly *adjective* = **learned**, academic, bookish, erudite, intellectual, lettered, scholastic, studious, well-read
➤ **Antonyms**
lowbrow, middlebrow, philistine, unacademic, uneducated, unintellectual, unlettered

scholarship *noun* **1** = **learning**, accomplishments, attainments, book-learning, education, erudition, knowledge, lore **2** = **bursary**, fellowship

scholastic *adjective* = **learned**, academic, bookish, lettered, literary, scholarly

school *noun* **1** = **academy**, alma mater,

college, department, discipline, faculty, institute, institution, seminary 2 = **group**, adherents, circle, class, clique, denomination, devotees, disciples, faction, followers, following, schism, sect, set ♦ *verb* 3 = **train**, coach, discipline, drill, educate, indoctrinate, instruct, prepare, prime, tutor, verse

schooling *noun* 1 = **teaching**, book-learning, education, formal education, tuition 2 = **training**, coaching, drill, grounding, guidance, instruction, preparation

schoolteacher *noun* = **schoolmaster** *or* **schoolmistress**, instructor, pedagogue, schoolmarm (*informal*)

science *noun* 1 = **discipline**, body of knowledge, branch of knowledge 2 = **skill**, art, technique

scientific *adjective* = **systematic**, accurate, controlled, exact, mathematical, precise

scientist *noun* = **inventor**, boffin (*informal*), technophile

scintillate *verb* = **sparkle**, blaze, coruscate, flash, give off sparks, gleam, glint, glisten, glitter, twinkle

scintillating *adjective* = **brilliant**, animated, bright, dazzling, ebullient, exciting, glittering, lively, sparkling, stimulating, witty

scion *noun* 1 = **descendant**, child, heir, offspring, successor 2 = **offshoot**, branch, graft, shoot, slip, sprout, twig

scoff[1] *verb* = **scorn**, belittle, deride, despise, flout, gibe, jeer, knock (*informal*), laugh at, make light of, mock, poke fun at, pooh-pooh, revile, ridicule, slag (off) (*slang*), sneer, take the piss (out of) (*taboo slang*)

scoff[2] *verb* = **gobble (up)**, bolt, cram, devour, gollop, gorge oneself on, gulp down, guzzle, put away, stuff oneself with, wolf

scold *verb* 1 = **reprimand**, bawl out (*informal*), berate, blame, castigate, censure, chide, find fault with, give (someone) a dressing-down, give (someone) a row, give (someone) a talking-to (*informal*), go on at, haul (someone) over the coals (*informal*), lecture, nag, rebuke, reproach, reprove, slate (*informal, chiefly Brit.*), take (someone) to task, tear into (*informal*), tear (someone) off a strip (*Brit. informal*), tell off (*informal*), tick off (*informal*), upbraid ♦ *noun* 2 = **nag**, shrew, termagant (*rare*) ➤ **Antonyms** *verb* ≠ **reprimand**: acclaim, applaud, approve, commend, compliment, extol,

laud, praise

scolding *noun* = **rebuke**, dressing-down (*informal*), (good) talking-to (*informal*), lecture, piece of one's mind, row, telling-off (*informal*), ticking-off (*informal*), tongue-lashing

scoop *noun* 1 = **ladle**, dipper, spoon 2 = **exclusive**, coup, exposé, inside story, revelation, sensation ♦ *verb* 3 *often with* **up** = **lift**, clear away, gather up, pick up, remove, sweep up *or* away, take up 4 **scoop out** = **hollow**, bail, dig, dip, empty, excavate, gouge, ladle, scrape, shovel

scoot *verb* = **dash**, bolt, dart, run, scamper, scurry, scuttle, skedaddle (*informal*), skitter

scope *noun* 1 = **opportunity**, elbowroom, freedom, latitude, liberty, room, space 2 = **range**, ambit, area, capacity, orbit, outlook, purview, reach, span, sphere 3 = **extent**, compass, confines, range

scorch *verb* = **burn**, blacken, blister, char, parch, roast, sear, shrivel, singe, wither

scorching *adjective* = **burning**, baking, boiling, broiling, fiery, flaming, red-hot, roasting, searing, sizzling, sweltering, torrid, tropical, unbearably hot

score *noun* 1 = **points**, grade, mark, outcome, record, result, total 2 **the score** *Informal* = **the situation**, the equation, the facts, the lie of the land, the reality, the setup (*informal*), the truth 3 = **amount due**, account, bill, charge, debt, obligation, reckoning, tab (*U.S. informal*), tally, total 4 = **grounds**, account, basis, cause, ground, reason 5 = **grievance**, a bone to pick, grudge, injury, injustice, wrong 6 **scores** = **lots**, a flock, a great number, an army, a throng, crowds, droves, hosts, hundreds, legions, masses, millions, multitudes, myriads, swarms, very many ♦ *verb* 7 = **gain**, achieve, amass, chalk up (*informal*), make, notch up (*informal*), win 8 = **keep count**, count, keep a tally of, record, register, tally 9 = **cut**, deface, gouge, graze, indent, mar, mark, nick, notch, scrape, scratch, slash 10 *with* **out** *or* **through** = **cross out**, cancel, delete, obliterate, put a line through, strike out 11 *Music* = **arrange**, adapt, orchestrate, set 12 = **go down well with (someone)**, gain an advantage, impress, make a hit (*informal*), make an impact *or* impression, make a point, put oneself across, triumph

score off *verb* = **get the better of**, be one up on (*informal*), make a fool of

scorn *noun* 1 = **contempt**, contemptuousness, derision, despite, disdain, disparagement, mockery, sarcasm, scornfulness, slight, sneer ♦ *verb*

2 = despise, be above, consider beneath one, contemn, deride, disdain, flout, hold in contempt, look down on, make fun of, reject, scoff at, slight, sneer at, spurn, turn up one's nose at (informal)
➤ Antonyms
noun ≠**contempt**: acceptance, admiration, affection, esteem, high regard, respect, tolerance, toleration, veneration, worship ♦ verb ≠**despise**: accept, admire, esteem, look favourably on, respect, revere, tolerate, venerate, worship

scornful adjective = **contemptuous**, defiant, derisive, disdainful, haughty, insolent, insulting, jeering, mocking, sarcastic, sardonic, scathing, scoffing, slighting, sneering, supercilious, withering

scornfully adverb = **contemptuously**, disdainfully, dismissively, scathingly, slightingly, with a sneer, with contempt, with disdain, witheringly

scot-free adjective = **unharmed**, safe, undamaged, unhurt, uninjured, unpunished, unscathed, without a scratch

Scots adjective = **Scottish**, Caledonian

scoundrel noun Old-fashioned = **rogue**, bad egg (old-fashioned informal), bastard (offensive), blackguard, bugger (taboo slang), good-for-nothing, heel (slang), knave (archaic), miscreant, ne'er-do-well, rascal, reprobate, rotter (slang, chiefly Brit.), scally (Northwest English dialect), scamp, scumbag (slang), skelm (S. African), son-of-a-bitch (slang, chiefly U.S. & Canad.), swine, villain, wretch

scour[1] verb **1 = rub**, abrade, buff, burnish, clean, cleanse, polish, scrub **2 = wash**, cleanse, flush, purge

scour[2] verb = **search**, beat, comb, forage, go over with a fine-tooth comb, hunt, look high and low, rake, ransack

scourge noun **1 = affliction**, bane, curse, infliction, misfortune, pest, plague, punishment, terror, torment **2 = whip**, cat, cat-o'-nine-tails, lash, strap, switch, thong ♦ verb **3 = afflict**, curse, harass, plague, terrorize, torment **4 = whip**, beat, belt (informal), cane, castigate, chastise, discipline, flog, horsewhip, lash, leather, punish, take a strap to, tan (someone's) hide (slang), thrash, trounce, wallop (informal)
➤ Antonyms
noun ≠**affliction**: benefit, blessing, boon, favour, gift, godsend

scout noun **1 = vanguard**, advance guard, escort, lookout, outrider, precursor, reconnoitrer **2 = recruiter**, talent scout ♦ verb **3 = reconnoitre**, case (slang), check out, investigate, make a reconnaissance, observe, probe, recce (slang), see how the land lies, spy, spy out, survey, watch **4**
scout about or **around = search for**, cast around for, ferret out, hunt for, look for, rustle up, search out, seek, track down

scowl verb **1 = glower**, frown, grimace, look daggers at, lour or lower ♦ noun **2 = glower**, black look, dirty look, frown, grimace

scrabble verb = **scrape**, clamber, claw, dig, grope, paw, scramble, scratch

scraggy adjective = **scrawny**, angular, bony, emaciated, gangling, gaunt, lanky, lean, rawboned, skinny, undernourished

scram verb Informal = **go away**, abscond, beat it (slang), bugger off (taboo slang), clear off (informal), depart, disappear, get lost (informal), go to hell (informal), leave, make oneself scarce (informal), make tracks, quit, scarper (Brit. slang), scoot, skedaddle (informal), sling one's hook (Brit. slang), take oneself off, vamoose (slang, chiefly U.S.)

scramble verb **1 = struggle**, clamber, climb, crawl, move with difficulty, push, scrabble, swarm **2 = strive**, contend, hasten, jockey for position, jostle, make haste, push, run, rush, vie ♦ noun **3 = climb**, trek **4 = struggle**, commotion, competition, confusion, free-for-all (informal), hassle (informal), hustle, melee or mêlée, muddle, race, rush, tussle

scrap[1] noun **1 = piece**, atom, bit, bite, crumb, fragment, grain, iota, mite, modicum, morsel, mouthful, part, particle, portion, remnant, sliver, snatch, snippet, trace **2 = waste**, junk, off cuts **3 scraps = leftovers**, bits, leavings, remains, scrapings ♦ verb **4 = get rid of**, abandon, break up, chuck (informal), discard, dispense with, ditch (slang), drop, jettison, junk (informal), shed, throw away or out, toss out, trash (slang), write off
➤ Antonyms
verb ≠**get rid of**: bring back, recall, re-establish, reinstall, reinstate, restore, return

scrap[2] Informal ♦ noun **1 = fight**, argument, battle, brawl, disagreement, dispute, quarrel, row, scrimmage, scuffle, set-to (informal), shindig (informal), shindy (informal), squabble, tiff, wrangle ♦ verb **2 = fight**, argue, barney (informal), bicker, come to blows, fall out (informal), have a shouting match (informal), have words, row, spar, squabble, wrangle

scrape verb **1 = rub**, abrade, bark, graze, scratch, scuff, skin **2 = scour**, clean, erase, file, remove, rub **3 = grate**, grind, rasp, scratch, screech, set one's teeth on edge, squeak 4 = **scrimp**, live from hand to mouth, pinch, save, skimp, stint, tighten one's belt 5 **scrape through** = **get by** (*informal*), cut it fine (*informal*), have a close shave (*informal*), just make it, struggle ♦ *noun* 6 *Informal* = **predicament**, awkward situation, difficulty, dilemma, distress, fix (*informal*), mess, plight, spot (*informal*), tight spot, trouble

scrape together *verb* = **collect**, amass, dredge up, get hold of, glean, hoard, muster, rake up *or* together, save

scrapheap *noun* **on the scrapheap** = **discarded**, ditched (*slang*), jettisoned, put out to grass (*informal*), redundant, written off

scrappy *adjective* = **incomplete**, bitty, disjointed, fragmentary, perfunctory, piecemeal, sketchy, thrown together

scratch *verb* 1 = **mark**, claw, cut, damage, etch, grate, graze, incise, lacerate, make a mark on, rub, score, scrape 2 = **erase**, annul, cancel, cross out, delete, eliminate, strike off 3 = **withdraw**, pull out, stand down ♦ *noun* 4 = **mark**, blemish, claw mark, gash, graze, laceration, scrape 5 **up to scratch** *Informal* = **adequate**, acceptable, capable, competent, satisfactory, sufficient, up to standard ♦ *adjective* 6 = **improvised**, haphazard, hastily prepared, impromptu, rough, rough-and-ready

scrawl *verb*, *noun* = **scribble**, doodle, scratch, squiggle

scrawny *adjective* = **thin**, angular, bony, gaunt, lanky, lean, scraggy, skeletal, skin-and-bones (*informal*), skinny, undernourished

scream *verb* 1 = **cry**, bawl, holler (*informal*), screech, shriek, shrill, sing out, squeal, yell 2 = **be conspicuous**, clash, jar, shriek ♦ *noun* 3 = **cry**, howl, outcry, screech, shriek, wail, yell, yelp 4 *Informal* = **laugh**, card (*informal*), caution (*informal*), character (*informal*), comedian, comic, entertainer, hoot (*informal*), joker, riot (*slang*), sensation, wag, wit

screech *noun*, *verb* = **cry**, scream, shriek, squawk, squeal, yelp

screed *noun* = **passage**, speech

screen *noun* 1 = **cover**, awning, canopy, cloak, concealment, guard, hedge, mantle, partition, room divider, shade, shelter, shield, shroud 2 = **mesh**, net ♦ *verb* 3 = **cover**, cloak, conceal, hide, mask, shade, shroud, shut out, veil 4 = **protect**, defend, guard, safeguard, shelter, shield 5 = **vet**, cull, evaluate, examine, filter, gauge, grade, process, scan, sieve, sift, sort 6 = **broadcast**, present, put on, show

screw *verb* 1 = **turn**, tighten, twist, work in 2 *Informal* = **coerce**, bring pressure to bear on, constrain, force, hold a knife to (someone's) throat, oppress, pressurize, put the screws on (*informal*), squeeze 3 *Informal* = **contort**, contract, crumple, distort, pucker, wrinkle 4 *Informal, often with* **out of** = **extort**, extract, wrest, wring

screw up *verb* 1 *Informal* = **bungle**, bodge (*informal*), botch, make a hash of (*informal*), make a mess of (*slang*), make a nonsense of, mess up, mishandle, mismanage, spoil 2 = **contort**, contract, crumple, distort, knit, knot, pucker, wrinkle

screwy *adjective Informal* = **crazy**, batty (*slang*), cracked (*slang*), crackers (*Brit. slang*), crackpot (*informal*), dotty (*slang, chiefly Brit.*), eccentric, loopy (*informal*), nutty (*slang*), odd, oddball (*informal*), off-the-wall (*slang*), out to lunch (*informal*), queer (*informal*), round the bend (*Brit. slang*), up the pole (*informal*), wacko *or* whacko (*informal*), weird

scribble *verb* = **scrawl**, dash off, doodle, jot, pen, scratch, write

scribe *noun* = **copyist**, amanuensis, clerk, notary (*archaic*), secretary, writer

scrimmage *noun* = **fight**, brawl, disturbance, fray, free-for-all (*informal*), melee *or* mêlée, riot, row, scrap (*informal*), scuffle, set-to (*informal*), shindig (*informal*), shindy (*informal*), skirmish, struggle

scrimp *verb* = **economize**, be frugal, curtail, limit, pinch, pinch pennies, reduce, save, scrape, shorten, skimp, stint, straiten, tighten one's belt

script *noun* 1 = **text**, book, copy, dialogue, libretto, lines, manuscript, words 2 = **handwriting**, calligraphy, hand, letters, longhand, penmanship, writing

Scripture *noun* = **The Bible**, Holy Bible, Holy Scripture, Holy Writ, The Book of Books, The Good Book, The Gospels, The Scriptures, The Word, The Word of God

scroll *noun* = **roll**, parchment

Scrooge *noun* = **miser**, cheapskate (*informal*), meanie *or* meany (*informal, chiefly Brit.*), niggard, penny-pincher (*informal*), skinflint, tightwad (*U.S. & Canad. slang*)

scrounge *verb Informal* = **cadge**, beg, blag (*slang*), bum (*informal*), forage for, freeload (*slang*), hunt around (for), mooch (*slang*), sponge (*informal*), touch (someone) for (*slang*)

scrounger *adjective* = **cadger**, bum (*informal*), freeloader (*slang*), parasite, sponger (*informal*)

scrub verb 1 = **scour**, clean, cleanse, rub 2 Informal = **cancel**, abandon, abolish, call off, delete, discontinue, do away with, drop, forget about, give up

scrubby adjective = **stunted**, meagre, scrawny, spindly, underdeveloped, undersized

scruff[1] noun = **nape**, scrag (informal)

scruff[2] noun Informal = **ragamuffin**, ragbag (informal), scarecrow, sloven, tatterdemalion (rare), tramp

scruffy adjective = **tatty**, disreputable, grungy, ill-groomed, mangy, messy, ragged, run-down, scrubby (Brit. informal), seedy, shabby, sloppy (informal), slovenly, squalid, tattered, ungroomed, unkempt, untidy
➤ Antonyms
chic, dapper, natty, neat, soigné or soignée, spruce, tidy, well-dressed, well-groomed, well-turned-out

scrumptious adjective Informal = **delicious**, appetizing, delectable, exquisite, inviting, luscious, magnificent, moreish (informal), mouthwatering, succulent, yummy (slang)

scrunch verb = **crumple**, crush, ruck up, squash

scruple noun 1 = **misgiving**, caution, compunction, difficulty, doubt, hesitation, perplexity, qualm, reluctance, second thoughts, squeamishness, twinge of conscience, uneasiness ♦ verb 2 = **have misgivings about**, balk at, be loath, be reluctant, demur, doubt, falter, have qualms about, hesitate, stick at, think twice about, vacillate, waver

scrupulous adjective 1 = **moral**, conscientious, honourable, principled, upright 2 = **careful**, exact, fastidious, meticulous, minute, nice, painstaking, precise, punctilious, rigorous, strict
➤ Antonyms
≠moral: amoral, dishonest, uncaring, unconscientious, unprincipled, unscrupulous, without scruples ≠careful: careless, inexact, reckless, slapdash, superficial

scrutinize verb = **examine**, analyse, dissect, explore, go over with a fine-tooth comb, inquire into, inspect, investigate, peruse, pore over, probe, research, scan, search, sift, study, work over

scrutiny noun = **examination**, analysis, close study, exploration, inquiry, inspection, investigation, once-over (informal), perusal, search, sifting, study

scud verb = **fly**, blow, race, sail, shoot, skim, speed

scuffle verb 1 = **fight**, clash, come to blows, contend, exchange blows, grapple, jostle, struggle, tussle ♦ noun 2 = **fight**, barney (informal), brawl, commotion, disturbance, fray, ruck (slang), ruckus (informal), rumpus, scrap (informal), scrimmage, set-to (informal), shindig (informal), shindy (informal), skirmish, tussle

sculpture verb = **sculpt**, carve, chisel, cut, fashion, form, hew, model, mould, shape

scum noun 1 = **impurities**, algae, crust, dross, film, froth, offscourings 2 = **rabble**, canaille, dregs of society, dross, lowest of the low, ragtag and bobtail, riffraff, rubbish, trash (chiefly U.S. & Canad.)

scupper verb Brit. slang = **destroy**, defeat, demolish, overthrow, overwhelm, put paid to, ruin, torpedo, undo, wreck

scurrility noun = **slanderousness**, abusiveness, invective, obloquy, offensiveness, scurrilousness, vituperation

scurrilous adjective = **slanderous**, abusive, coarse, defamatory, foul, gross, indecent, infamous, insulting, low, obscene, offensive, scandalous, vituperative, vulgar
➤ Antonyms
decent, polite, proper, refined, respectful

scurry verb 1 = **hurry**, beetle, dart, dash, fly, race, scamper, scoot, scud, scuttle, sprint, whisk ♦ noun 2 = **flurry**, bustle, scampering, whirl
➤ Antonyms
verb ≠hurry: amble, mooch (slang), mosey (informal), saunter, stroll, toddle, wander

scurvy adjective Old-fashioned = **contemptible**, bad, base, despicable, dishonourable, ignoble, low, low-down (informal), mean, rotten, shabby, vile

scuttle verb = **run**, bustle, hare (Brit. informal), hasten, hurry, rush, scamper, scoot, scramble, scud, scurry

sea noun 1 = **ocean**, main, the briny (informal), the deep, the drink (informal), the waves 2 = **expanse**, abundance, mass, multitude, plethora, profusion, sheet, vast number 3 at sea = **bewildered**, adrift, astray, at a loss, baffled, confused, disoriented, lost, mystified, puzzled, upset

seafaring adjective = **nautical**, marine, maritime, naval, oceanic

seal noun 1 = **authentication**, assurance, attestation, confirmation, imprimatur, insignia, notification, ratification, stamp ♦ verb 2 = **close**, bung, cork, enclose, fasten, make airtight, plug, secure, shut, stop, stopper, stop up, waterproof 3 = **authenticate**, assure, attest, confirm, establish, ratify, stamp, validate 4 = **settle**, clinch, conclude, consummate, finalize, shake hands on (*informal*) **5 seal off** = **isolate**, board up, fence off, put out of bounds, quarantine, segregate

seam *noun* **1** = **joint**, closure, suture (*Surgery*) **2** = **layer**, lode, stratum, vein **3** = **ridge**, furrow, line, scar, wrinkle

seamy *adjective* = **sordid**, corrupt, dark, degraded, disreputable, low, nasty, squalid, unpleasant, unwholesome

sear *verb* **1** = **scorch**, brand, burn, cauterize, desiccate, dry up *or* out, sizzle **2** = **wither**, blight, shrivel, wilt

search *verb* **1** = **look**, cast around, check, comb, examine, explore, forage, hunt, inquire, inspect, investigate, look high and low, probe, ransack, scour, scrutinize, seek, sift, turn inside out, turn upside down
♦ *noun* **2** = **look**, examination, exploration, going-over (*informal*), hunt, inquiry, inspection, investigation, pursuit, quest, scrutiny

searching *adjective* = **keen**, close, intent, minute, penetrating, piercing, probing, quizzical, severe, sharp, thorough
➤ **Antonyms**
cursory, perfunctory, peripheral, sketchy, superficial

season *noun* **1** = **period**, division, interval, spell, term, time, time of year ♦ *verb* **2** = **flavour**, colour, enliven, lace, pep up, salt, salt and pepper, spice **3** = **make experienced**, acclimatize, accustom, habituate, harden, mature, prepare, toughen, train

seasonable *adjective* = **appropriate**, convenient, fit, opportune, providential, suitable, timely, welcome, well-timed

seasoned *adjective* = **experienced**, hardened, long-serving, mature, old, practised, time-served, veteran, weathered, well-versed
➤ **Antonyms**
callow, green, inexperienced, new, novice, unpractised, unseasoned, unskilled

seasoning *noun* = **flavouring**, condiment, dressing, relish, salt and pepper, sauce, spice

seat *noun* **1** = **chair**, bench, pew, settle, stall, stool, throne **2** = **base**, bed, bottom, cause, footing, foundation, ground, groundwork **3** = **centre**, axis, capital, headquarters, heart, hub, location, place, site, situation, source, station **4** = **mansion**, abode, ancestral hall, house, residence **5** = **membership**, chair, constituency, incumbency, place ♦ *verb* **6** = **sit**, deposit, fix, install, locate, place, set, settle **7** = **hold**, accommodate, cater for, contain, have room *or* capacity for, sit, take

seating *noun* = **accommodation**, chairs, places, room, seats

secede *verb* = **withdraw**, break with, leave, pull out, quit, resign, retire, separate, split from

secession *noun* = **withdrawal**, apostasy, break, defection, disaffiliation, seceding, split

secluded *adjective* = **private**, cloistered, cut off, isolated, lonely, off the beaten track, out-of-the-way, reclusive, remote, retired, sequestered, sheltered, solitary, tucked away, unfrequented
➤ **Antonyms**
accessible, busy, frequented, open, public

seclusion *noun* = **privacy**, concealment, hiding, isolation, retirement, retreat, shelter, solitude

second[1] *adjective* **1** = **next**, following, subsequent, succeeding **2** = **additional**, alternative, extra, further, other, repeated **3** = **inferior**, lesser, lower, secondary, subordinate, supporting ♦ *noun* **4** = **supporter**, assistant, backer, helper ♦ *verb* **5** = **support**, advance, aid, approve, assist, back, commend, encourage, endorse, forward, further, give moral support to, go along with, help, promote

second[2] *noun* = **moment**, bat of an eye (*informal*), flash, instant, jiffy (*informal*), minute, sec (*informal*), split second, tick (*Brit. informal*), trice

secondary *adjective* **1** = **subordinate**, inferior, lesser, lower, minor, second-rate, unimportant **2** = **resultant**, consequential, contingent, derivative, derived, indirect, resulting, second-hand **3** = **backup**, alternate, auxiliary, extra, fall-back, relief, reserve, second, subsidiary, supporting
➤ **Antonyms**
≠**subordinate:** cardinal, chief, head, larger, main, major, more important, prime, principal, superior ≠**resultant:** original, preceding ≠**backup:** only, primary

second childhood *noun* = **senility**, Alzheimer's disease, dotage

second-class *adjective* = **inferior**, déclassé, indifferent, mediocre, no great shakes (*informal*), outclassed, second-best, second-rate, undistinguished, uninspiring

second-hand *adjective* **1** = **used**, handed down, hand-me-down (*informal*), nearly new, reach-me-down (*informal*) ♦ *adverb* **2** = **indirectly**, at second-hand

second in command *noun* = **deputy**, depute (*Scot.*), number two, right-hand man, successor designate

secondly *adverb* = **next**, in the second

place, second

second-rate *adjective* = **inferior**,
bush-league (*Austral. & N.Z. informal*),
cheap, cheap and nasty (*informal*),
commonplace, dime-a-dozen (*informal*),
low-grade, low-quality, mediocre, no great
shakes (*informal*), not much cop (*Brit.
slang*), pants (*slang*), poor, rubbishy,
shoddy, substandard, tacky (*informal*),
tawdry, two-bit (*U.S. & Canad. slang*)
➤ **Antonyms**
a cut above (*informal*), choice, de luxe,
excellent, fine, first-class, first-rate, good
quality, high-class, quality, superior

secrecy *noun* **1** = **mystery**, cloak and
dagger, concealment, confidentiality,
privacy, retirement, seclusion, silence,
solitude, surreptitiousness **2**
= **secretiveness**, clandestineness,
covertness, furtiveness, stealth

secret *adjective* **1** = **concealed**, behind
someone's back, camouflaged,
cloak-and-dagger, close, closet (*informal*),
confidential, conspiratorial, covered,
covert, disguised, furtive, hidden,
hole-and-corner (*informal*), hush-hush
(*informal*), reticent, shrouded, undercover,
underground, under wraps, undisclosed,
unknown, unpublished, unrevealed,
unseen **2** = **stealthy**, close, deep, discreet,
reticent, secretive, sly, underhand **3**
= **mysterious**, abstruse, arcane, cabbalistic,
clandestine, classified, cryptic, esoteric,
occult, recondite ♦ *noun* **4** = **mystery**,
code, confidence, enigma, key, skeleton in
the cupboard **5 in secret** = **secretly**,
behind closed doors, by stealth, in camera,
incognito, slyly, surreptitiously
➤ **Antonyms**
adjective ≠**concealed, stealthy**: apparent,
candid, disclosed, frank, manifest, obvious,
open, overt, public, unconcealed, visible
≠**mysterious**: straightforward, well-known

secret agent *noun* = **spy**, nark (*Brit.,
Austral., & N.Z. slang*), undercover agent

secrete[1] *verb* = **give off**, emanate, emit,
extrude, exude

secrete[2] *verb* = **hide**, bury, cache, conceal,
cover, disguise, harbour, screen, secure,
stash (*informal*), stash away (*informal*),
stow, veil
➤ **Antonyms**
bare, display, exhibit, expose to view,
leave in the open, reveal, show, uncover,
unmask, unveil

secretion *noun* = **discharge**, emission,
excretion, exudation

secretive *adjective* = **reticent**, cagey
(*informal*), close, cryptic, deep, enigmatic,
playing one's cards close to one's chest,

reserved, tight-lipped, uncommunicative,
unforthcoming, withdrawn
➤ **Antonyms**
candid, communicative, expansive,
forthcoming, frank, open, unreserved

secretly *adverb* = **in secret**, behind closed
doors, behind (someone's) back,
clandestinely, confidentially, covertly,
furtively, in camera, in confidence, on the
fly (*slang, chiefly Brit.*), on the q.t.
(*informal*), on the sly, privately, quietly,
stealthily, surreptitiously, unobserved

sect *noun* = **group**, camp, denomination,
division, faction, party, schism, school,
school of thought, splinter group, wing

sectarian *adjective* **1** = **narrow-minded**,
bigoted, clannish, cliquish, doctrinaire,
dogmatic, exclusive, factional, fanatic,
fanatical, hidebound, insular, limited,
parochial, partisan, rigid ♦ *noun* **2** = **bigot**,
adherent, disciple, dogmatist, extremist,
fanatic, partisan, zealot
➤ **Antonyms**
adjective ≠**narrow-minded**:
broad-minded, catholic, free-thinking,
liberal, non-sectarian, open-minded,
tolerant, unbigoted, unprejudiced

section *noun* **1** = **part**, component, cross
section, division, fraction, fragment,
instalment, passage, piece, portion,
sample, segment, slice, subdivision **2**
= **district**, area, department, region,
sector, zone

sectional *adjective* = **regional**, divided,
exclusive, factional, local, localized, partial,
separate, separatist

sector *noun* = **part**, area, category, district,
division, quarter, region, stratum,
subdivision, zone

secular *adjective* = **worldly**, civil, earthly,
laic, laical, lay, nonspiritual, profane, state,
temporal
➤ **Antonyms**
divine, holy, religious, sacred, spiritual,
theological

secure *adjective* **1** = **safe**, immune,
impregnable, in safe hands, out of harm's
way, protected, sheltered, shielded,
unassailable, undamaged, unharmed **2**
= **sure**, assured, certain, confident, easy,
reassured **3** = **fixed**, dependable, fast,
fastened, firm, fortified, immovable, stable,
steady, tight **4** = **reliable**, definite, in the
bag (*informal*), solid, tried and true ♦ *verb*
5 = **obtain**, acquire, come by, gain, get,
get hold of, land (*informal*), make sure of,
pick up, procure, score (*slang*), win
possession of **6** = **fasten**, attach, batten
down, bolt, chain, fix, lash, lock, lock up,
make fast, moor, padlock, tie up **7**

= **guarantee**, assure, ensure, insure
➤ **Antonyms**
adjective ≠**safe**: endangered, unprotected, unsafe ≠**sure**: ill-at-ease, insecure, unassured, uncertain, uneasy, unsure ≠**fixed**: insecure, loose, not fastened, precarious, unfixed, unsafe, unsound ♦ *verb* ≠**obtain**: give up, let (something) slip through (one's) fingers, lose ≠**fasten**: loose, unloose, untie ≠**guarantee**: endanger, imperil, leave unguaranteed

security *noun* 1 = **precautions**, defence, guards, protection, safeguards, safety measures, surveillance 2 = **safety**, asylum, care, cover, custody, immunity, preservation, protection, refuge, retreat, safekeeping, sanctuary 3 = **assurance**, certainty, confidence, conviction, ease of mind, freedom from doubt, positiveness, reliance, sureness 4 = **pledge**, collateral, gage, guarantee, hostage, insurance, pawn, surety
➤ **Antonyms**
≠**safety**: exposure, jeopardy, vulnerability ≠**assurance**: insecurity, uncertainty

sedate *adjective* 1 = **calm**, collected, composed, cool, decorous, dignified, imperturbable, placid, proper, quiet, seemly, serene, staid, tranquil, unflappable (*informal*), unruffled 2 = **unhurried**, deliberate, slow-moving
➤ **Antonyms**
≠**calm**: agitated, antsy (*informal*), excitable, excited, flighty, impassioned, jumpy, nervous, undignified, unsteady, wild

sedative *adjective* 1 = **calming**, allaying, anodyne, calmative, lenitive, relaxing, sleep-inducing, soothing, soporific, tranquillizing ♦ *noun* 2 = **tranquillizer**, anodyne, calmative, downer or down (*slang*), narcotic, opiate, sleeping pill

sedentary *adjective* = **inactive**, desk, desk-bound, motionless, seated, sitting, torpid
➤ **Antonyms**
active, mobile, motile, moving, on the go (*informal*)

sediment *noun* = **dregs**, deposit, grounds, lees, precipitate, residue, settlings

sedition *noun* = **rabble-rousing**, agitation, disloyalty, incitement to riot, subversion, treason

seditious *adjective* = **revolutionary**, disloyal, dissident, insubordinate, mutinous, rebellious, refractory, subversive, treasonable

seduce *verb* 1 = **corrupt**, betray, debauch, deflower, deprave, dishonour, ruin (*archaic*) 2 = **tempt**, allure, attract, beguile,

deceive, decoy, ensnare, entice, inveigle, lead astray, lure, mislead

seduction *noun* 1 = **corruption**, defloration, ruin (*archaic*) 2 = **temptation**, allure, enticement, lure, snare

seductive *adjective* = **alluring**, attractive, beguiling, bewitching, captivating, come-hither (*informal*), come-to-bed (*informal*), enticing, flirtatious, inviting, irresistible, provocative, ravishing, sexy (*informal*), siren, specious, tempting

seductress *noun* = **temptress**, Circe, enchantress, *femme fatale,* Lorelei, siren, vamp (*informal*)

sedulous *adjective* = **diligent**, assiduous, conscientious, industrious, laborious, painstaking

see[1] *verb* 1 = **perceive**, behold, catch a glimpse of, catch sight of, check, check out (*informal*), clock (*Brit. slang*), descry, discern, distinguish, espy, eye, eyeball (*slang*), get a load of (*slang*), glimpse, identify, lay or clap eyes on (*informal*), look, make out, mark, note, notice, observe, recognize, regard, sight, spot, take a dekko at (*Brit. slang*), view, witness 2 = **understand**, appreciate, catch on (*informal*), comprehend, fathom, feel, follow, get, get the drift of, get the hang of (*informal*), grasp, know, make out, realize, take in 3 = **foresee**, anticipate, divine, envisage, foretell, imagine, picture, visualize 4 = **find out**, ascertain, determine, discover, investigate, learn, make inquiries, refer to 5 = **make sure**, ensure, guarantee, make certain, mind, see to it, take care 6 = **consider**, decide, deliberate, give some thought to, judge, make up one's mind, mull over, reflect, think over 7 = **visit**, confer with, consult, encounter, interview, meet, receive, run into, speak to 8 = **go out with**, consort or associate with, court, date (*informal, chiefly U.S.*), go steady with (*informal*), keep company with, walk out with (*obsolete*) 9 = **accompany**, attend, escort, lead, show, usher, walk

see[2] *noun* = **diocese**, bishopric

see about *verb* 1 = **take care of**, attend to, consider, deal with, give some thought to, look after, see to 2 = **investigate**, look into, make inquiries, research

seed *noun* 1 = **grain**, egg, egg cell, embryo, germ, kernel, ovule, ovum, pip, spore 2 = **origin**, beginning, germ, inkling, nucleus, source, start, suspicion 3 *chiefly Biblical* = **offspring**, children, descendants, heirs, issue, progeny, race, scions, spawn, successors 4 **go** or **run to seed** = **decline**, decay, degenerate, deteriorate, go downhill (*informal*), go to pieces, go to pot, go to rack and ruin, go to waste, let oneself go

seedy *adjective* **1** = **shabby**, crummy (*slang*), decaying, dilapidated, down at heel, faded, grotty (*slang*), grubby, mangy, manky (*Scot. dialect*), old, run-down, scruffy, sleazy, slovenly, squalid, tatty, unkempt, worn **2** *Informal* = **unwell**, ailing, ill, off colour, out of sorts, peely-wally (*Scot.*), poorly (*informal*), sickly, under the weather (*informal*)
➤ **Antonyms**
≠**shabby**: classy, elegant, fashionable, high-toned, posh (*informal, chiefly Brit.*), ritzy (*slang*), smart, swanky (*informal*), swish (*informal, chiefly Brit.*), top-drawer, up-market

seeing *conjunction* = **since**, as, inasmuch as, in view of the fact that

seek *verb* **1** = **look for**, be after, follow, go gunning for, go in pursuit of, go in quest of, go in search of, hunt, inquire, pursue, search for **2** = **try**, aim, aspire to, attempt, endeavour, essay, have a go (*informal*), strive

seem *verb* = **appear**, assume, give the impression, have the *or* every appearance of, look, look as if, look like, look to be, pretend, sound like, strike one as being

seeming *adjective* = **apparent**, appearing, illusory, ostensible, outward, quasi-, specious, surface

seemingly *adverb* = **apparently**, as far as anyone could tell, on the face of it, on the surface, ostensibly, outwardly, to all appearances, to all intents and purposes

seemly *adjective* = **fitting**, appropriate, becoming, befitting, *comme il faut,* decent, decorous, fit, in good taste, meet (*archaic*), nice, proper, suitable, the done thing
➤ **Antonyms**
improper, inappropriate, indecorous, in poor taste, out of keeping, out of place, unbecoming, unbefitting, unseemly, unsuitable

seep *verb* = **ooze**, bleed, exude, leach, leak, percolate, permeate, soak, trickle, well

seepage *noun* = **leakage**, exudation, leak, oozing, percolation

seer *noun* = **prophet**, augur, predictor, sibyl, soothsayer

seesaw *verb* = **alternate**, fluctuate, go from one extreme to the other, oscillate, pitch, swing, teeter

seethe *verb* **1** = **be furious**, be in a state (*informal*), be incandescent, be incensed, be livid, be pissed (off) (*taboo slang*), foam at the mouth, fume, get hot under the

collar (*informal*), go ballistic (*slang, chiefly U.S.*), rage, see red (*informal*), simmer, storm **2** = **boil**, bubble, churn, ferment, fizz, foam, froth

see-through *adjective* = **transparent**, diaphanous, filmy, fine, flimsy, gauzy, gossamer, sheer, thin, translucent

see through *verb* **1** = **be undeceived by**, be wise to (*informal*), fathom, get to the bottom of, have (someone's) number (*informal*), not fall for, penetrate, read (someone) like a book **2** **see (something) through** = **persevere (with)**, keep at, persist, see out, stay to the bitter end, stick out (*informal*) **3** **see (someone) through** = **help out**, stick by, support

see to *verb* = **take care of**, arrange, attend to, be responsible for, do, look after, manage, organize, sort out, take charge of

segment *noun* = **section**, bit, compartment, division, part, piece, portion, slice, wedge

segregate *verb* = **set apart**, discriminate against, dissociate, isolate, separate, single out
➤ **Antonyms**
amalgamate, desegregate, join together, mix, unify, unite

segregation *noun* = **separation**, apartheid, discrimination, isolation

seize *verb* **1** = **grab**, catch up, clutch, fasten, grasp, grip, lay hands on, snatch, take **2** = **confiscate**, appropriate, commandeer, impound, take possession of **3** = **take by storm**, abduct, annex, hijack **4** = **capture**, apprehend, arrest, catch, collar (*informal*), get, grasp, nab (*informal*), nail (*informal*), take captive
➤ **Antonyms**
≠**grab**: let go, loose ≠**confiscate**: hand back, relinquish ≠**capture**: free, release, set free, turn loose

seizure *noun* **1** = **attack**, convulsion, fit, paroxysm, spasm **2** = **capture**, abduction, apprehension, arrest **3** = **taking**, annexation, commandeering, confiscation, grabbing

seldom *adverb* = **rarely**, hardly ever, infrequently, not often, occasionally, once in a blue moon (*informal*), scarcely ever
➤ **Antonyms**
again and again, frequently, many a time, much, often, over and over again, time after time, time and again

select *verb* **1** = **choose**, cherry-pick, opt for, pick, prefer, single out, sort out ◆ *adjective* **2** = **choice**, excellent, first-class, first-rate, hand-picked, picked, prime, rare, selected, special, superior, top-notch (*informal*) **3** = **exclusive**, cliquish, elite, limited,

privileged
> **Antonyms**
verb ≠**choose**: eliminate, reject, turn down
♦ adjective ≠**choice**: cheap, indifferent,
inferior, ordinary, run-of-the-mill,
second-rate, shoddy, substandard,
unremarkable ≠**exclusive**: indiscriminate

selection noun **1** = **choice**, choosing,
option, pick, preference **2** = **range**,
anthology, assortment, choice, collection,
line-up, medley, miscellany, mixed bag
(informal), pick 'n' mix, potpourri, variety

selective adjective = **particular**, careful,
discerning, discriminating, discriminatory,
eclectic
> **Antonyms**
all-embracing, careless, desultory,
indiscriminate, unselective

self-assurance noun = **confidence**,
assertiveness, nerve, poise, positiveness,
self-confidence, self-possession

self-centred adjective = **selfish**, egotistic,
inward looking, narcissistic, self-absorbed,
self-seeking, wrapped up in oneself

self-confidence noun = **self-assurance**,
aplomb, confidence, high morale, nerve,
poise, self-reliance, self-respect

self-confident adjective = **self-assured**,
assured, confident, fearless, poised, secure,
self-reliant, sure of oneself

self-conscious adjective = **embarrassed**,
affected, awkward, bashful, diffident, ill at
ease, insecure, like a fish out of water,
nervous, out of countenance, shamefaced,
sheepish, uncomfortable

self-control noun = **willpower**, calmness,
cool, coolness, restraint, self-discipline,
self-mastery, self-restraint, strength of
mind or will

self-denial noun = **abstemiousness**,
asceticism, renunciation, self-abnegation,
selflessness, self-sacrifice, unselfishness

self-esteem noun = **self-respect**,
amour-propre, confidence, faith in oneself,
pride, self-assurance, self-regard, vanity

self-evident adjective = **obvious**,
axiomatic, clear, cut-and-dried (informal),
incontrovertible, inescapable, manifestly or
patently true, undeniable, written all over
(something)

self-government noun = **autonomy**,
democracy, devolution, home rule,
independence, self-determination,
self-rule, sovereignty

self-important adjective = **conceited**,
arrogant, bigheaded, bumptious, cocky,
full of oneself, overbearing, pompous,
presumptuous, pushy (informal), strutting,
swaggering, swollen-headed

self-indulgence noun = **intemperance**,
dissipation, excess, extravagance,
incontinence, self-gratification, sensualism

selfish adjective = **self-centred**, egoistic,
egoistical, egotistic, egotistical, greedy,
looking out for number one (informal),
mean, mercenary, narrow, self-interested,
self-seeking, ungenerous
> **Antonyms**
altruistic, benevolent, considerate,
generous, magnanimous, philanthropic,
self-denying, selfless, self-sacrificing,
ungrudging, unselfish

selfless adjective = **unselfish**, altruistic,
generous, magnanimous, self-denying,
self-sacrificing, ungrudging

self-possessed adjective = **self-assured**,
collected, confident, cool, cool as a
cucumber (informal), poised, sure of
oneself, together (slang), unruffled

self-possession noun = **self-assurance**,
aplomb, composure, confidence, cool
(slang), poise, sang-froid, self-command

self-reliant adjective = **independent**, able
to stand on one's own two feet (informal),
capable, self-sufficient, self-supporting
> **Antonyms**
dependent, helpless, reliant, relying on

self-respect noun = **pride**, amour-propre,
dignity, faith in oneself, morale, one's own
image, self-esteem

self-restraint noun = **self-control**,
abstemiousness, forbearance, patience,
self-command, self-discipline, willpower

self-righteous adjective = **sanctimonious**,
complacent, goody-goody (informal),
holier-than-thou, hypocritical, pharisaic, pi
(Brit. slang), pietistic, pious, priggish,
self-satisfied, smug, superior, too good to
be true

self-sacrifice noun = **selflessness**, altruism,
generosity, self-abnegation, self-denial

self-satisfaction noun = **smugness**,
complacency, contentment, ease of mind,
flush of success, glow of achievement,
pride, self-approbation, self-approval

self-satisfied adjective = **smug**,
complacent, flushed with success, like a
cat that has swallowed the canary, pleased
with oneself, proud of oneself, puffed up,
self-congratulatory, too big for one's boots
or breeches, well-pleased

self-seeking adjective = **selfish**, acquisitive,
calculating, careerist, fortune-hunting,
gold-digging, looking out for number one
(informal), mercenary, on the make
(slang), opportunistic, out for what one
can get, self-interested, self-serving

self-styled adjective = **so-called**, professed,

quasi-, self-appointed, *soi-disant,* would-be

self-willed *adjective* = **stubborn**, headstrong, intractable, obstinate, opinionated, pig-headed, refractory, stiff-necked, stubborn as a mule, ungovernable, wilful

sell *verb* 1 = **trade**, barter, dispose of, exchange, put up for sale 2 = **deal in**, be in the business of, handle, hawk, market, merchandise, peddle, retail, stock, trade in, traffic in, vend 3 = **give up**, betray, deliver up, sell down the river (*informal*), sell out (*informal*), surrender 4 = **promote**, gain acceptance for, put across
➤ **Antonyms**
≠**trade, deal in:** acquire, buy, get, invest in, obtain, pay for, procure, purchase, shop for

seller *noun* = **dealer**, agent, merchant, purveyor, rep, representative, retailer, salesman *or* saleswoman, shopkeeper, supplier, tradesman, traveller, vendor

selling *noun* 1 = **dealing**, business, commercial transactions, trading, traffic 2 = **marketing**, boosterism, merchandising, promotion, salesmanship

sell out *verb* 1 = **dispose of**, be out of stock of, get rid of, run out of, sell up 2 *Informal* = **betray**, break faith with, double-cross (*informal*), fail, give away, play false, rat on (*informal*), sell down the river (*informal*), stab in the back

semblance *noun* = **appearance**, air, aspect, bearing, façade, figure, form, front, guise, image, likeness, mask, mien, pretence, resemblance, show, similarity, veneer

semen *noun* = **sperm**, come *or* cum (*taboo*), seed (*archaic or dialect*), seminal fluid, spermatic fluid, spunk (*taboo*)

seminal *adjective* = **influential**, creative, formative, ground-breaking, imaginative, important, innovative, original, productive

seminary *noun* = **college**, academy, high school, institute, institution, school

send *verb* 1 = **dispatch**, communicate, consign, convey, direct, forward, remit, transmit 2 = **propel**, cast, deliver, fire, fling, hurl, let fly, shoot 3 *with* **off, out,** *etc.* = **emit**, broadcast, discharge, exude, give off, radiate 4 *Old-fashioned, slang* = **enrapture**, charm, delight, electrify, enthrall, excite, intoxicate, move, please, ravish, stir, thrill, titillate, turn (someone) on (*slang*)

send for *verb* = **summon**, call for, demand, order, request

sendoff *noun* = **farewell**, departure, going-away party, leave-taking, start,

valediction

send-up *noun* = **imitation**, mockery, parody, satire, skit, spoof (*informal*), take-off (*informal*)

send up *verb* = **imitate**, burlesque, lampoon, make fun of, mimic, mock, parody, satirize, spoof (*informal*), take off (*informal*), take the mickey out of (*informal*), take the piss out of (*taboo slang*)

senile *adjective* = **doddering**, decrepit, doting, failing, gaga (*informal*), imbecile, in one's dotage, in one's second childhood

senility *noun* = **dotage**, Alzheimer's disease, caducity, decrepitude, infirmity, loss of one's faculties, second childhood, senescence, senile dementia

senior *adjective* 1 = **higher ranking**, superior 2 = **older**, elder, major (*Brit.*)
➤ **Antonyms**
≠**higher ranking:** inferior, junior, lesser, lower, minor, subordinate ≠**older:** junior, younger

senior citizen *noun* = **pensioner**, elder, O.A.P., old age pensioner, old *or* elderly person, retired person

seniority *noun* = **superiority**, eldership, longer service, precedence, priority, rank

sensation *noun* 1 = **feeling**, awareness, consciousness, impression, perception, sense, tingle 2 = **excitement**, agitation, commotion, furore, scandal, stir, surprise, thrill, vibes (*slang*) 3 = **hit** (*informal*), crowd puller (*informal*), wow (*slang, chiefly U.S.*)

sensational *adjective* 1 = **exciting**, amazing, astounding, breathtaking, dramatic, electrifying, hair-raising, horrifying, lurid, melodramatic, revealing, scandalous, sensationalistic, shock-horror (*facetious*), shocking, spectacular, staggering, startling, thrilling 2 *Informal* = **excellent**, awesome (*slang*), boffo (*slang*), brill (*informal*), brilliant, chillin' (*U.S. slang*), cracking (*Brit. informal*), crucial (*slang*), def (*slang*), exceptional, fabulous (*informal*), first class, impressive, marvellous, mean (*slang*), mega (*slang*), mind-blowing (*informal*), out of this world (*informal*), smashing (*informal*), sovereign, superb
➤ **Antonyms**
≠**exciting:** boring, dull, humdrum, understated, undramatic, unexaggerated, unexciting ≠**excellent:** commonplace, mediocre, no great shakes (*informal*), ordinary, prosaic, run-of-the-mill, vanilla (*informal*)

sense *noun* 1 = **faculty**, feeling, sensation, sensibility 2 = **feeling**, appreciation, atmosphere, aura, awareness,

consciousness, impression, intuition, perception, premonition, presentiment, sentiment **3** *sometimes plural* = **intelligence**, brains (*informal*), clear-headedness, cleverness, common sense, discernment, discrimination, gumption (*Brit. informal*), judgment, mother wit, nous (*Brit. slang*), quickness, reason, sagacity, sanity, sharpness, smarts (*slang, chiefly U.S.*), tact, understanding, wisdom, wit(s) **4** = **point**, advantage, good, logic, purpose, reason, use, value, worth **5** = **meaning**, definition, denotation, drift, gist, implication, import, interpretation, message, nuance, purport, significance, signification, substance ♦ *verb* **6** = **perceive**, appreciate, apprehend, be aware of, discern, divine, feel, get the impression, grasp, have a (funny) feeling (*informal*), have a hunch, just know, notice, observe, pick up, realize, suspect, understand
➤ **Antonyms**
noun ≠**intelligence**: folly, foolishness, idiocy, nonsense, silliness, stupidity ♦ *verb* ≠**perceive**: be unaware of, fail to grasp *or* notice, miss, misunderstand, overlook

senseless *adjective* **1** = **stupid**, absurd, asinine, crazy, daft (*informal*), dumb-ass (*slang*), fatuous, foolish, halfwitted, idiotic, illogical, imbecilic, inane, incongruous, inconsistent, irrational, ludicrous, mad, meaningless, mindless, moronic, nonsensical, pointless, ridiculous, silly, simple, unintelligent, unreasonable, unwise, without rhyme or reason **2** = **unconscious**, anaesthetized, cold, deadened, insensate, insensible, numb, numbed, out, out cold, stunned, unfeeling
➤ **Antonyms**
≠**stupid**: intelligent, meaningful, rational, reasonable, sensible, useful, valid, wise, worthwhile ≠**unconscious**: conscious, feeling, sensible

sensibility *noun* **1** = **awareness**, appreciation, delicacy, discernment, insight, intuition, perceptiveness, taste **2** *often plural* = **feelings**, emotions, moral sense, sentiments, susceptibilities **3** = **sensitivity**, responsiveness, sensitiveness, susceptibility
➤ **Antonyms**
≠**awareness**: insensibility, lack of awareness, unconsciousness, unperceptiveness ≠**sensitivity**: deadness, insensibility, insensitivity, numbness, unresponsiveness

sensible *adjective* **1** = **wise**, canny, discreet, discriminating, down-to-earth, far-sighted, intelligent, judicious, matter-of-fact, practical, prudent, rational, realistic,

reasonable, sagacious, sage, sane, shrewd, sober, sound, well-reasoned, well-thought-out **2** = **perceptible**, appreciable, considerable, discernable, noticeable, palpable, significant, tangible, visible **3** *Literary, usually with* **of** = **aware**, acquainted with, alive to, conscious, convinced, mindful, observant, sensitive to, understanding
➤ **Antonyms**
≠**wise**: daft (*informal*), dumb-ass (*slang*), foolish, idiotic, ignorant, injudicious, irrational, senseless, silly, stupid, unreasonable, unwise ≠**aware**: blind, ignorant, insensible, insensitive, unaware, unmindful

sensitive *adjective* **1** = **easily hurt**, delicate, tender **2** = **susceptible**, delicate, easily affected, impressionable, reactive, responsive, sentient, touchy-feely (*informal*) **3** = **touchy**, easily offended, easily upset, irritable, temperamental, thin-skinned **4** = **precise**, acute, fine, keen, perceptive, responsive
➤ **Antonyms**
≠**easily hurt**: insensitive, tough ≠**susceptible, touchy**: callous, hard, hardened, insensitive, thick-skinned, tough, uncaring, unfeeling ≠**precise**: approximate, imprecise, inexact, unperceptive

sensitivity *noun* = **sensitiveness**, delicacy, reactiveness, reactivity, receptiveness, responsiveness, susceptibility

sensual *adjective* **1** = **physical**, animal, bodily, carnal, epicurean, fleshly, luxurious, voluptuous **2** = **erotic**, lascivious, lecherous, lewd, libidinous, licentious, lustful, randy (*informal, chiefly Brit.*), raunchy (*slang*), sexual, sexy (*informal*), steamy (*informal*), unchaste

sensuality *noun* = **eroticism**, animalism, carnality, lasciviousness, lecherousness, lewdness, libidinousness, licentiousness, prurience, salaciousness, sexiness (*informal*), voluptuousness

sensuous *adjective* = **pleasurable**, bacchanalian, epicurean, gratifying, hedonistic, lush, rich, sensory, sumptuous, sybaritic
➤ **Antonyms**
abstemious, ascetic, celibate, plain, self-denying, Spartan

sentence *noun* **1** = **punishment**, condemnation, decision, decree, judgment, order, pronouncement, ruling, verdict ♦ *verb* **2** = **condemn**, doom, mete out justice to, pass judgment on, penalize

sententious *adjective* = **pompous**, canting, judgmental, moralistic, ponderous, preachifying (*informal*), sanctimonious

sentient *adjective* = **feeling**, conscious, live, living, reactive, sensitive

sentiment *noun* **1** = **emotion**, sensibility, soft-heartedness, tender feeling, tenderness **2** *often plural* = **feeling**, attitude, belief, idea, judgment, opinion, persuasion, saying, thought, view, way of thinking **3** = **sentimentality**, emotionalism, mawkishness, overemotionalism, romanticism, slush (*informal*)

sentimental *adjective* = **romantic**, corny (*slang*), dewy-eyed, emotional, gushy (*informal*), icky (*informal*), impressionable, maudlin, mawkish, mushy (*informal*), nostalgic, overemotional, schmaltzy (*slang*), sloppy (*informal*), slushy (*informal*), soft-hearted, tearful, tear-jerking (*informal*), tender, touching, weepy (*informal*)
➤ **Antonyms**
commonsensical, dispassionate, down-to-earth, earthy, hard-headed, practical, realistic, undemonstrative, unemotional, unfeeling, unromantic, unsentimental

sentimentality *noun* = **romanticism**, bathos, corniness (*slang*), emotionalism, gush (*informal*), mawkishness, mush (*informal*), nostalgia, pathos, play on the emotions, schmaltz (*slang*), sloppiness (*informal*), slush (*informal*), sob stuff (*informal*), tenderness

sentinel *noun* = **guard**, lookout, picket, sentry, watch, watchman

separable *adjective* = **distinguishable**, detachable, divisible

separate *verb* **1** = **divide**, break off, cleave, come apart, come away, come between, detach, disconnect, disentangle, disjoin, keep apart, remove, sever, split, sunder, uncouple **2** = **part**, bifurcate, break up, disunite, diverge, divorce, estrange, go different ways, part company, set at variance *or* at odds, split up **3** = **isolate**, discriminate between, put on one side, segregate, single out, sort out ◆ *adjective* **4** = **unconnected**, detached, disconnected, discrete, disjointed, divided, divorced, isolated, unattached **5** = **individual**, alone, apart, autonomous, distinct, independent, particular, single, solitary
➤ **Antonyms**
verb ≠**divide**, **part**, **isolate**: amalgamate, combine, connect, join, link, merge, mix, unite ◆ *adjective* ≠**unconnected**, **individual**: affiliated, alike, connected, interdependent, joined, similar, unified, united

separated *adjective* = **disconnected**, apart, broken up, disassociated, disunited, divided, living apart, parted, put asunder, separate, split up, sundered

separately *adverb* = **individually**, alone, apart, independently, one at a time, one by one, personally, severally, singly
➤ **Antonyms**
as a group, as one, collectively, in a body, in concert, in unison, jointly, together

separation *noun* **1** = **division**, break, detachment, disconnection, disengagement, disjunction, dissociation, disunion, gap, segregation, severance **2** = **split-up**, break-up, divorce, estrangement, farewell, leave-taking, parting, rift, split

septic *adjective* = **infected**, festering, poisoned, pussy, putrefactive, putrefying, putrid, suppurating, toxic

sepulchral *adjective* = **gloomy**, cheerless, dismal, funereal, grave, lugubrious, melancholy, morbid, mournful, sad, sombre

sepulchre *noun* = **tomb**, burial place, grave, mausoleum, sarcophagus, vault

sequel *noun* **1** = **follow-up**, continuation, development **2** = **consequence**, conclusion, end, issue, outcome, payoff (*informal*), result, upshot

sequence *noun* = **succession**, arrangement, chain, course, cycle, order, procession, progression, series

sequestered *adjective* = **secluded**, cloistered, isolated, lonely, out-of-the-way, private, quiet, remote, retired, unfrequented

seraphic *adjective* = **angelic**, beatific, blissful, celestial, divine, heavenly, holy, pure, sublime

serene *adjective* **1** = **calm**, composed, imperturbable, peaceful, placid, sedate, tranquil, undisturbed, unruffled, untroubled **2** = **clear**, bright, cloudless, fair, halcyon, unclouded
➤ **Antonyms**
≠**calm**: agitated, anxious, disturbed, excitable, flustered, perturbed, troubled, uptight (*informal*)

serenity *noun* **1** = **calmness**, calm, composure, peace, peacefulness, peace of mind, placidity, quietness, quietude, stillness, tranquillity **2** = **clearness**, brightness, fairness

serf *noun* = **vassal**, bondsman, liegeman, servant, slave, villein

series *noun* = **sequence**, arrangement, chain, course, line, order, progression, run, set, string, succession, train

serious *adjective* **1** = **grave**, acute, alarming, critical, dangerous, severe **2** = **important**, crucial, deep, difficult, far-reaching, fateful, grim, momentous, no laughing matter, of moment *or* consequence, pressing, significant, urgent, weighty, worrying **3** = **solemn**, grave, humourless, long-faced, pensive, sedate, sober, stern, thoughtful, unsmiling **4** = **sincere**, deliberate, determined, earnest, genuine, honest, in earnest, resolute, resolved
➤ **Antonyms**
≠**important:** insignificant, minor, slight, trivial, unimportant ≠**solemn:** carefree, flippant, frivolous, jolly, joyful, light-hearted, smiling ≠**sincere:** capricious, flighty, flippant, frivolous, insincere, uncommitted, undecided

seriously *adverb* **1** = **gravely**, acutely, badly, critically, dangerously, distressingly, grievously, severely, sorely **2** = **sincerely**, all joking aside, earnestly, gravely, in all conscience, in earnest, no joking (*informal*), solemnly, thoughtfully, with a straight face

seriousness *noun* **1** = **importance**, danger, gravity, moment, significance, urgency, weight **2** = **solemnity**, earnestness, gravitas, gravity, humourlessness, sedateness, sobriety, staidness, sternness

sermon *noun* **1** = **homily**, address, exhortation **2** *Disparaging* = **lecture**, dressing-down (*informal*), harangue, talking-to (*informal*)

serpentine *adjective* = **twisting**, coiling, sinuous, snaking, snaky, tortuous, twisty, winding

serrated *adjective* = **notched**, sawlike, sawtoothed, serrate, toothed

serried *adjective Literary* = **massed**, assembled, close, compact, dense, phalanxed

servant *noun* = **attendant**, domestic, drudge, help, helper, lackey, liegeman, maid, menial, retainer, skivvy (*chiefly Brit.*), slave, varlet (*archaic*), vassal

serve *verb* **1** = **work for**, aid, assist, attend to, be in the service of, be of assistance, be of use, help, minister to, oblige, wait on **2** = **perform**, act, attend, complete, discharge, do, fulfil, go through, observe, officiate, pass **3** = **provide**, arrange, deal, deliver, dish up, distribute, handle, present, purvey, set out, supply **4** = **be adequate**, answer, answer the purpose, be acceptable, be good enough, content, do, do duty as, do the work of, fill the bill (*informal*), function as, satisfy, suffice, suit

service *noun* **1** = **help**, advantage, assistance, avail, benefit, ministrations, supply, use, usefulness, utility **2** = **work**, business, duty, employ, employment, labour, office **3** = **overhaul**, check, maintenance, servicing **4** = **ceremony**, function, observance, rite, worship ♦ *verb* **5** = **overhaul**, check, fine tune, go over, maintain, recondition, repair, tune (up)

serviceable *adjective* = **useful**, advantageous, beneficial, convenient, dependable, durable, efficient, functional, hard-wearing, helpful, operative, practical, profitable, usable, utilitarian
➤ **Antonyms**
impractical, inefficient, unserviceable, unusable, useless, worn-out

servile *adjective* = **subservient**, abject, base, bootlicking (*informal*), craven, cringing, fawning, grovelling, humble, low, mean, menial, obsequious, slavish, submissive, sycophantic, toadying, toadyish, unctuous

servility *noun* = **subservience**, abjection, baseness, bootlicking (*informal*), fawning, grovelling, meanness, obsequiousness, self-abasement, slavishness, submissiveness, sycophancy, toadyism, unctuousness

serving *noun* = **portion**, helping, plateful

servitude *noun Formal* = **slavery**, bondage, bonds, chains, enslavement, obedience, serfdom, subjugation, thraldom, thrall

session *noun* = **meeting**, assembly, conference, congress, discussion, get-together (*informal*), hearing, period, seminar, sitting, term

set[1] *verb* **1** = **put**, aim, apply, deposit, direct, embed, fasten, fix, install, lay, locate, lodge, mount, park (*informal*), place, plant, plonk, plump, position, rest, seat, situate, station, stick, turn **2** = **prepare**, arrange, lay, make ready, spread **3** = **harden**, cake, condense, congeal, crystallize, gelatinize, jell, solidify, stiffen, thicken **4** = **adjust**, coordinate, rectify, regulate, synchronize **5** = **arrange**, agree upon, allocate, appoint, conclude, decide (upon), designate, determine, establish, fix, fix up, name, ordain, regulate, resolve, schedule, settle, specify **6** = **assign**, allot, decree, impose, lay down, ordain, prescribe, specify **7** = **go down**, decline, dip, disappear, sink, subside, vanish ♦ *noun* **8** = **position**, attitude, bearing, carriage, fit, hang, posture, turn **9** = **scenery**, mise-en-scène, scene, setting, stage set, stage setting ♦ *adjective* **10** = **fixed**, agreed, appointed, arranged, customary, decided, definite, established,

firm, prearranged, predetermined, prescribed, regular, scheduled, settled, usual **11 = inflexible**, entrenched, firm, hard and fast, hardened, hidebound, immovable, rigid, strict, stubborn **12 = conventional**, artificial, formal, hackneyed, rehearsed, routine, standard, stereotyped, stock, traditional, unspontaneous **13 set on** or **upon = determined**, bent, intent, resolute
➤ **Antonyms**
adjective ≠**inflexible**: flexible, free, open, open-minded, undecided

set² noun **1 = series**, assemblage, assortment, batch, collection, compendium, coordinated group, kit, outfit **2 = group**, band, circle, class, clique, company, coterie, crew (informal), crowd, faction, gang, outfit, posse (informal)

set about verb **1 = begin**, address oneself to, attack, get cracking (informal), get down to, get to work, make a start on, put one's shoulder to the wheel (informal), roll up one's sleeves, set to, start, tackle, take the first step **2 = assault**, assail, attack, belabour

set against verb **1 = balance**, compare, contrast, juxtapose, weigh **2 = alienate**, disunite, divide, drive a wedge between, estrange, make bad blood, make mischief, oppose, set at cross purposes, set at odds

set aside verb **1 = reserve**, earmark, keep, keep back, put on one side, save, select, separate, set apart, single out **2 = reject**, abrogate, annul, cancel, discard, dismiss, nullify, overrule, overturn, quash, render null and void, repudiate, reverse

setback noun **= hold-up**, blow, bummer (slang), check, defeat, disappointment, hitch, misfortune, rebuff, reverse, upset, whammy (informal, chiefly U.S.)

set back verb **= hold up**, delay, hinder, impede, retard, slow

set off verb **1 = leave**, depart, embark, sally forth, set out, start out **2 = detonate**, explode, ignite, kick-start, light, set in motion, touch off, trigger (off) **3 = enhance**, show off, throw into relief

set on or **upon** verb **= attack**, ambush, assail, assault, beat up, fall upon, fly at, go for, lay into (informal), let fly at, mug (informal), pitch into (informal), pounce on, put the boot in (slang), set about, turn on, work over (slang)

set out verb **1 = arrange**, array, display, dispose, exhibit, expose to view, lay out, present, set forth **2 = explain**, describe, detail, elaborate, elucidate **3 = embark**, begin, get under way, hit the road (slang), sally forth, set off, start out, take to the road

setting noun **= surroundings**, backdrop, background, context, frame, locale, location, mise en scène, perspective, scene, scenery, set, site, surround

settle verb **1 = put in order**, adjust, dispose, order, regulate, set to rights, straighten out, work out **2 = make oneself comfortable**, bed down **3 = land**, alight, come to rest, descend, light **4 = move to**, dwell, inhabit, live, make one's home, put down roots, reside, set up home, take up residence **5 = colonize**, found, people, pioneer, plant, populate **6 = calm**, allay, compose, lull, pacify, quell, quiet, quieten, reassure, relax, relieve, sedate, soothe, tranquillize **7 = subside**, decline, fall, sink **8 = pay**, acquit oneself of, clear, discharge, liquidate, square (up) **9 = resolve**, clear up, complete, conclude, decide, dispose of, put an end to, reconcile **10** often with **on** or **upon = decide**, agree, appoint, arrange, choose, come to an agreement, confirm, determine, establish, fix
➤ **Antonyms**
≠**calm**: agitate, bother, discompose, disquieten, disturb, rattle, trouble, unsettle, upset

settlement noun **1 = agreement**, adjustment, arrangement, completion, conclusion, confirmation, establishment, resolution, working out **2 = payment**, clearance, clearing, defrayal, discharge, liquidation, satisfaction **3 = colony**, colonization, community, encampment, hamlet, outpost, peopling

settler noun **= colonist**, colonizer, frontiersman, immigrant, pioneer, planter

set-to noun Informal **= fight**, argument, argy-bargy (Brit. informal), barney (informal), brush, disagreement, dust-up (informal), fracas, quarrel, row, scrap (informal), slanging match (Brit.), spat, squabble, wrangle

setup noun Informal **= arrangement**, circumstances, conditions, organization, regime, structure, system

set up verb **1 = build**, assemble, construct, elevate, erect, put together, put up, raise **2 = finance**, back, build up, establish, promote, subsidize **3 = establish**, arrange, begin, compose, found, initiate, install, institute, make provision for, organize, prearrange, prepare

sever verb **1 = cut**, bisect, cleave, cut in two, detach, disconnect, disjoin, disunite, divide, part, rend, separate, split, sunder **2 = discontinue**, abandon, break off, dissociate, dissolve, put an end to, terminate

➤ **Antonyms**

≠**cut**: attach, connect, fix together, join, link, unite ≠**discontinue**: continue, maintain, uphold

several *adjective* **1** = **some**, assorted, different, disparate, diverse, manifold, many, sundry, various **2** *Formal* = **different**, distinct, individual, particular, respective, single

severe *adjective* **1** = **strict**, austere, cruel, Draconian, drastic, hard, harsh, inexorable, iron-handed, oppressive, pitiless, relentless, rigid, unbending, unrelenting **2** = **harsh**, astringent, biting, caustic, cutting, mordacious, mordant, satirical, scathing, unsparing, vitriolic **3** = **grim**, cold, disapproving, dour, forbidding, grave, serious, sober, stern, strait-laced, tight-lipped, unsmiling **4** = **plain**, ascetic, austere, chaste, classic, functional, restrained, simple, Spartan, unadorned, unembellished, unfussy **5** = **intense**, acute, bitter, critical, dangerous, distressing, extreme, fierce, violent **6** = **tough**, arduous, demanding, difficult, exacting, fierce, hard, punishing, rigorous, stringent, taxing, unrelenting

➤ **Antonyms**

≠**strict**: easy, lax, lenient, relaxed, tractable ≠**harsh**: compassionate, gentle, kind ≠**grim**: affable, genial ≠**plain**: embellished, fancy, ornamental, ornate, temperate ≠**intense**: gentle, mild, minor, moderate ≠**tough**: easy, manageable

severely *adverb* **1** = **strictly**, harshly, like a ton of bricks (*informal*), rigorously, sharply, sternly, with an iron hand, with a rod of iron **2** = **seriously**, acutely, badly, critically, dangerously, extremely, gravely, hard

severity *noun* = **strictness**, austerity, hardness, harshness, rigour, seriousness, severeness, sternness, stringency, toughness

sex *noun* **1** = **gender 2** *Informal* = **(sexual) intercourse**, coition, coitus, copulation, fornication, fucking (*taboo slang*), going to bed (with someone), intimacy, legover (*slang*), lovemaking, nookie (*slang*), rumpy-pumpy (*slang*), screwing (*taboo slang*), sexual relations, shagging (*Brit. taboo slang*), the other (*informal*) **3** = **facts of life**, desire, libido, reproduction, sexuality, the birds and the bees (*informal*)

sex appeal *noun* = **desirability**, allure, attractiveness, glamour, magnetism, seductiveness, sensuality, sexiness (*informal*), voluptuousness

sexless *adjective* = **asexual**, androgynous, epicene, hermaphrodite, neuter, nonsexual

sexual *adjective* **1** = **carnal**, coital, erotic,

intimate, of the flesh, sensual, sexy **2** = **reproductive**, genital, procreative, sex, venereal

sexual intercourse *noun* = **copulation**, bonking (*informal*), carnal knowledge, coition, coitus, congress, consummation, coupling, fucking (*taboo slang*), intimacy, legover (*slang*), mating, nookie (*slang*), penetration, rumpy-pumpy (*slang*), screwing (*taboo slang*), sex (*informal*), shagging (*Brit. taboo slang*), the other (*informal*), union

sexuality *noun* = **desire**, bodily appetites, carnality, eroticism, lust, sensuality, sexiness (*informal*), virility, voluptuousness

sexy *adjective* = **erotic**, arousing, come-hither (*informal*), flirtatious, inviting, naughty, provocative, provoking, seductive, sensual, sensuous, slinky, suggestive, titillating, voluptuous

shabby *adjective* **1** = **tatty**, dilapidated, down at heel, faded, frayed, having seen better days, mean, neglected, poor, ragged, run-down, scruffy, seedy, tattered, the worse for wear, threadbare, worn, worn-out **2** = **mean**, cheap, contemptible, despicable, dirty, dishonourable, ignoble, low, low-down (*informal*), rotten (*informal*), scurvy, shameful, shoddy, ungentlemanly, unworthy

➤ **Antonyms**

≠**tatty**: handsome, in mint condition, neat, new, smart, well-dressed, well-kept, well-to-do ≠**mean**: fair, generous, honourable, praiseworthy, worthy

shack *noun* = **hut**, cabin, dump (*informal*), hovel, lean-to, shanty

shackle *noun* **1** *often plural* = **fetter**, bond, chain, handcuff, hobble, iron, leg-iron, manacle, rope, tether ♦ *verb* **2** = **fetter**, bind, chain, handcuff, hobble, manacle, pinion, put in irons, secure, tether, tie, trammel **3** = **hamper**, constrain, embarrass, encumber, hamstring, impede, inhibit, limit, obstruct, restrain, restrict, tie (someone's) hands

shade *noun* **1** = **dimness**, coolness, dusk, gloom, gloominess, obscurity, screen, semidarkness, shadiness, shadow, shadows **2** = **screen**, blind, canopy, cover, covering, curtain, shield, veil **3** = **hue**, colour, stain, tinge, tint, tone **4** = **dash**, amount, degree, hint, nuance, suggestion, suspicion, trace **5** *Literary* = **ghost**, apparition, manes, phantom, shadow, spectre, spirit **6 put into the shade** = **outshine**, eclipse, make pale by comparison, outclass, overshadow ♦ *verb* **7** = **cover**, conceal, hide, mute, obscure, protect, screen, shield, veil **8** = **darken**, cast a shadow over, cloud, dim, shadow, shut out the light

shadow *noun* **1** = **dimness**, cover, darkness, dusk, gathering darkness, gloaming (*Scot. or poetic*), gloom, obscurity, protection, shade, shelter **2** = **trace**, hint, suggestion, suspicion **3** = **cloud**, blight, gloom, sadness ♦ *verb* **4** = **shade**, cast a shadow over, darken, overhang, screen, shield **5** = **follow**, dog, spy on, stalk, tail (*informal*), trail

shadowy *adjective* **1** = **dark**, dim, dusky, funereal, gloomy, indistinct, murky, obscure, shaded, shady, tenebrous **2** = **vague**, dim, dreamlike, faint, ghostly, illusory, imaginary, impalpable, intangible, nebulous, obscure, phantom, spectral, undefined, unreal, unsubstantial, wraithlike

shady *adjective* **1** = **shaded**, cool, dim, leafy, shadowy **2** *Informal* = **crooked**, disreputable, dodgy (*Brit., Austral., & N.Z. informal*), dubious, fishy (*informal*), questionable, shifty, slippery, suspect, suspicious, unethical, unscrupulous, untrustworthy
➤ Antonyms
≠**shaded**: bright, exposed, open, out in the open, sunlit, sunny, unshaded ≠**crooked**: above-board, ethical, honest, honourable, reputable, respectable, straight, trustworthy, upright

shaft *noun* **1** = **handle**, pole, rod, shank, stem, upright **2** *As in* **shaft of wit** *or* **humour** = **gibe**, barb, cut, dart, sting, thrust **3** = **ray**, beam, gleam, streak

shaggy *adjective* = **unkempt**, hairy, hirsute, long-haired, rough, tousled, unshorn
➤ Antonyms
close-cropped, crew-cut, cropped, neatly-trimmed, shorn, short-haired, smooth

shake *verb* **1** = **vibrate**, bump, fluctuate, jar, joggle, jolt, oscillate, quake, quiver, rock, shiver, shudder, sway, totter, tremble, waver, wobble **2** *often with* **up** = **agitate**, churn, convulse, rouse, stir **3** = **wave**, brandish, flourish **4** = **upset**, discompose, distress, disturb, frighten, intimidate, move, rattle (*informal*), shock, unnerve **5** = **undermine**, impair, weaken ♦ *noun* **6** = **vibration**, agitation, convulsion, disturbance, jar, jerk, jolt, jounce, pulsation, quaking, shiver, shock, shudder, trembling, tremor **7** *Informal* = **moment**, instant, jiffy (*informal*), second, tick (*Brit. informal*), trice

shake off *verb* = **get rid of**, dislodge, elude, get away from, get shot of (*slang*), give the slip, leave behind, lose, rid oneself of, throw off

shake up *verb* **1** = **stir (up)**, agitate, churn

(up), mix **2** = **reorganize**, overturn, turn upside down **3** *Informal* = **upset**, disturb, shock, unsettle

shaky *adjective* **1** = **unsteady**, faltering, insecure, precarious, quivery, rickety, tottering, trembling, tremulous, unstable, weak, wobbly **2** = **uncertain**, dubious, iffy (*informal*), questionable, suspect, undependable, unreliable, unsound, unsupported
➤ Antonyms
≠**unsteady**: firm, secure, stable, steady, strong ≠**uncertain**: dependable

shallow *adjective* **1** = **superficial**, empty, idle, meaningless, skin-deep, slight, surface, trivial **2** = **unintelligent**, flimsy, foolish, frivolous, ignorant, puerile, simple ♦ *noun* **3** *often plural* = **bank**, flat, sandbank, sand bar, shelf, shoal
➤ Antonyms
adjective ≠**superficial**: analytical, comprehensive, deep, in-depth, meaningful, penetrating, perceptive, profound, serious, weighty ≠**unintelligent**: serious, thoughtful

sham *noun* **1** = **phoney** *or* **phony** (*informal*), counterfeit, forgery, fraud, hoax, humbug, imitation, impostor, imposture, pretence, pretender, pseud (*informal*) ♦ *adjective* **2** = **false**, artificial, bogus, counterfeit, ersatz, feigned, imitation, mock, phoney *or* phony (*informal*), pretended, pseudo (*informal*), simulated, spurious, synthetic ♦ *verb* **3** = **fake**, affect, assume, counterfeit, feign, imitate, pretend, put on, simulate
➤ Antonyms
noun ≠**phoney** *or* **phony**: master, original, the genuine article, the real McCoy (*or* McKay), the real thing ♦ *adjective* ≠**false**: authentic, bona fide, genuine, legitimate, natural, real, sound, true, unfeigned, veritable

shambles *noun* = **chaos**, anarchy, confusion, disarray, disorder, disorganization, havoc, madhouse, mess, muddle

shambolic *adjective Informal* = **disorganized**, anarchic, at sixes and sevens, chaotic, confused, disordered, inefficient, in total disarray, muddled, topsy-turvy, unsystematic

shame *noun* **1** = **embarrassment**, abashment, chagrin, compunction, humiliation, ignominy, loss of face, mortification, shamefacedness **2** = **disgrace**, blot, contempt, degradation, derision, discredit, dishonour, disrepute, ill repute, infamy, obloquy, odium, opprobrium, reproach, scandal, skeleton in

the cupboard, smear **3 put to shame**
= **outdo**, disgrace, eclipse, outclass,
outstrip, show up, surpass ♦ *verb* **4**
= **embarrass**, abash, confound, disconcert,
disgrace, humble, humiliate, mortify,
reproach, ridicule, take (someone) down a
peg (*informal*) **5** = **dishonour**, blot,
debase, defile, degrade, discredit, smear,
stain
➤ **Antonyms**
noun ≠**embarrassment**: brass neck (*Brit.
informal*), brazenness, cheek,
shamelessness, unabashedness ≠**disgrace**:
credit, distinction, esteem, glory, honour,
pride, renown, self-respect ♦ *verb*
≠**embarrass**: do credit to, make proud
≠**dishonour**: acclaim, credit, enhance the
reputation of, honour

shamefaced *adjective* = **embarrassed**,
abashed, ashamed, chagrined,
conscience-stricken, contrite, discomfited,
humiliated, mortified, red-faced,
remorseful, sheepish

shameful *adjective* **1** = **embarrassing**,
blush-making (*informal*), cringe-making
(*Brit. informal*), degrading, humiliating,
mortifying, shaming, toe-curling (*slang*) **2**
= **disgraceful**, atrocious, base, dastardly,
degrading, dishonourable, ignominious,
indecent, infamous, low, mean,
outrageous, reprehensible, scandalous,
unbecoming, unworthy, vile, wicked
➤ **Antonyms**
≠**disgraceful**: admirable, creditable,
estimable, exemplary, honourable,
laudable, right, worthy

shameless *adjective* = **brazen**, abandoned,
audacious, barefaced, brash, corrupt,
depraved, flagrant, hardened, immodest,
improper, impudent, incorrigible,
indecent, insolent, unabashed,
unashamed, unprincipled, wanton

shanty *noun* = **shack**, bothy (*Scot.*), cabin,
hovel, hut, lean-to, shed

shape *noun* **1** = **form**, build, configuration,
contours, cut, figure, lines, make, outline,
profile, silhouette **2** = **appearance**, aspect,
form, guise, likeness, semblance **3**
= **pattern**, frame, model, mould **4**
= **condition**, fettle, health, kilter, state,
trim ♦ *verb* **5** = **form**, create, fashion,
make, model, mould, produce **6**
= **develop**, adapt, convert, define, devise,
frame, guide, modify, plan, prepare

shapeless *adjective* = **formless**,
amorphous, asymmetrical, irregular,
misshapen, unstructured
➤ **Antonyms**
well-formed, well-proportioned,
well-turned

shapely *adjective* = **well-formed**, comely,
curvaceous, elegant, graceful, neat, trim,
well-proportioned, well-turned

shape up *verb Informal* = **progress**, be
promising, come on, develop, look good,
proceed, turn out

share *noun* **1** = **part**, allotment, allowance,
contribution, cut (*informal*), division, due,
lot, portion, proportion, quota, ration,
whack (*informal*) ♦ *verb* **2** = **divide**,
apportion, assign, distribute, divvy up
(*informal*), parcel out, split **3** = **go halves**,
go Dutch (*informal*), go fifty-fifty (*informal*)
4 = **partake**, participate, receive, use in
common

sharp *adjective* **1** = **keen**, acute, cutting,
honed, jagged, knife-edged, knifelike,
pointed, razor-sharp, serrated, sharpened,
spiky **2** = **sudden**, abrupt, distinct,
extreme, marked **3** = **clear**, clear-cut, crisp,
distinct, well-defined **4** = **quick-witted**,
alert, apt, astute, bright, clever, discerning,
knowing, observant, on the ball (*informal*),
penetrating, perceptive, quick, ready,
subtle **5** = **cunning**, artful, crafty,
dishonest, fly (*slang*), shrewd, sly, smart,
unscrupulous, wily **6** = **cutting**,
acrimonious, barbed, biting, bitter,
caustic, harsh, hurtful, sarcastic, sardonic,
scathing, severe, trenchant, vitriolic **7**
= **sour**, acerbic, acetic, acid, acrid,
burning, hot, piquant, pungent, tart,
vinegary **8** = **acute**, distressing,
excruciating, fierce, gut-wrenching,
intense, painful, piercing, severe, shooting,
sore, stabbing, stinging, violent **9** *Informal*
= **stylish**, chic, classy (*slang*), dressy,
fashionable, natty (*informal*), smart,
snappy, trendy (*informal*) ♦ *adverb* **10**
= **promptly**, exactly, on the dot, on time,
precisely, punctually
➤ **Antonyms**
adjective ≠**keen**: blunt, dull, rounded,
unsharpened ≠**sudden**: even, gentle,
gradual, moderate, progressive ≠**clear**:
blurred, fuzzy, ill-defined, indistinct,
unclear ≠**quick-witted**: dim, dull-witted,
dumb (*informal*), slow, slow on the uptake,
stupid ≠**cunning**: artless, guileless,
ingenuous, innocent, naive, simple,
undesigning ≠**cutting**: amicable,
courteous, friendly, gentle, kindly, mild
≠**sour**: bland, mild, tasteless ♦ *adverb*
≠**promptly**: approximately, more or less,
roughly, round about, vaguely

sharpen *verb* = **whet**, edge, grind, hone,
put an edge on, strop

shatter *verb* **1** = **smash**, break, burst, crack,
crush, demolish, explode, implode,
pulverize, shiver, split **2** = **destroy**, blast,

blight, bring to nought, demolish, disable, exhaust, impair, overturn, ruin, torpedo, wreck **3** = **upset**, break (someone's) heart, crush, devastate

shattered *adjective Informal* **1** = **exhausted**, all in (*slang*), dead beat (*informal*), dead tired (*informal*), done in (*informal*), drained, knackered (*slang*), ready to drop, spent, tired out, weary, wiped out (*informal*), worn out, zonked (*slang*) **2** = **devastated**, crushed, gutted (*slang*)

shattering *adjective* = **devastating**, crushing, overwhelming, paralysing, severe, stunning

shave *verb* **1** = **trim**, crop, pare, plane, shear **2** = **brush**, graze, touch

shed[1] *noun* = **hut**, bothy (*chiefly Scot.*), lean-to, lockup, outhouse, shack

shed[2] *verb* **1** = **give out**, afford, cast, diffuse, drop, emit, give, pour forth, radiate, scatter, shower, spill, throw **2** = **cast off**, discard, moult, slough

sheen *noun* = **shine**, brightness, burnish, gleam, gloss, lustre, patina, polish, shininess

sheepish *adjective* = **embarrassed**, abashed, ashamed, chagrined, foolish, mortified, self-conscious, shamefaced, silly, uncomfortable
➤ **Antonyms**
assertive, audacious, bold, brash, brass-necked (*Brit. informal*), brazen, confident, unabashed, unapologetic, unembarrassed

sheer *adjective* **1** = **total**, absolute, arrant, complete, downright, out-and-out, pure, rank, thoroughgoing, unadulterated, unalloyed, unmitigated, unqualified, utter **2** = **steep**, abrupt, headlong (*archaic*), perpendicular, precipitous **3** = **fine**, diaphanous, gauzy, gossamer, see-through, thin, transparent
➤ **Antonyms**
≠**total**: moderate ≠**steep**: gentle, gradual, horizontal, slanting, sloping ≠**fine**: coarse, heavy, impenetrable, opaque, thick

sheet *noun* **1** = **coat**, film, lamina, layer, leaf, membrane, overlay, stratum, surface, veneer **2** = **piece**, folio, pane, panel, plate, slab **3** = **expanse**, area, blanket, covering, stretch, sweep

shell *noun* **1** = **case**, carapace, husk, pod **2** = **frame**, chassis, framework, hull, skeleton, structure ♦ *verb* **3** = **husk 4** = **bomb**, attack, barrage, blitz, bombard, strafe, strike

shell out *verb* = **pay out**, disburse, expend, fork out (*slang*), give, hand over, lay out (*informal*)

shelter *noun* **1** = **protection**, awning,

cover, covert, defence, guard, roof over one's head, screen, umbrella **2** = **safety**, asylum, haven, refuge, retreat, sanctuary, security ♦ *verb* **3** = **take shelter**, hide, seek refuge **4** = **protect**, cover, defend, guard, harbour, hide, safeguard, shield, take in
➤ **Antonyms**
verb ≠**protect**: expose, lay open, leave open, make vulnerable

sheltered *adjective* = **protected**, cloistered, isolated, quiet, reclusive, retired, screened, secluded, shaded, shielded, withdrawn
➤ **Antonyms**
exposed, laid bare, made public, open, public, unconcealed, unprotected, unsheltered

shelve *verb* = **postpone**, defer, dismiss, freeze, hold in abeyance, hold over, lay aside, mothball, put aside, put off, put on ice, put on the back burner (*informal*), suspend, take a rain check on (*U.S. & Canad. informal*)

shepherd *noun* **1** = **herdsman**, drover, grazier, stockman ♦ *verb* **2** = **guide**, conduct, convoy, herd, marshal, steer, usher

shield *noun* **1** = **buckler**, escutcheon (*Heraldry*) **2** = **protection**, aegis, bulwark, cover, defence, guard, rampart, safeguard, screen, shelter ♦ *verb* **3** = **protect**, cover, defend, guard, safeguard, screen, shelter, ward off

shift *verb* **1** = **move**, alter, budge, change, displace, fluctuate, move around, rearrange, relocate, remove, reposition, swerve, switch, transfer, transpose, vary, veer ♦ *noun* **2** = **move**, about-turn, alteration, change, displacement, fluctuation, modification, permutation, rearrangement, removal, shifting, switch, transfer, veering **3** = **scheme**, artifice, contrivance, craft, device, dodge, expedient, move, resource, ruse, stratagem, subterfuge, trick, wile

shiftless *adjective* = **lazy**, aimless, good-for-nothing, idle, incompetent, indolent, inefficient, inept, irresponsible, lackadaisical, slothful, unambitious, unenterprising

shifty *adjective* = **untrustworthy**, contriving, crafty, deceitful, devious, duplicitous, evasive, furtive, scheming, slippery, sly, tricky, underhand, unprincipled, wily
➤ **Antonyms**
dependable, guileless, honest, honourable, open, reliable, trustworthy, upright

shillyshally *verb Informal* = **be irresolute or indecisive**, dilly-dally (*informal*), dither (*chiefly Brit.*), falter, fluctuate, hem and haw *or* hum and haw, hesitate, seesaw, swither (*Scot.*), vacillate, waver

shimmer *verb* **1** = **gleam**, dance, glimmer, glisten, scintillate, twinkle ♦ *noun* **2** = **gleam**, diffused light, glimmer, glow, incandescence, iridescence, lustre, phosphorescence, unsteady light

shin *verb* **shin up** = **climb**, ascend, clamber, scale, scramble, swarm

shine *verb* **1** = **gleam**, beam, emit light, flash, give off light, glare, glimmer, glisten, glitter, glow, radiate, scintillate, shimmer, sparkle, twinkle **2** = **polish**, brush, buff, burnish, rub up **3** = **be outstanding**, be conspicuous, be distinguished, be pre-eminent, excel, stand out, stand out in a crowd, star, steal the show ♦ *noun* **4** = **brightness**, glare, gleam, lambency, light, luminosity, radiance, shimmer, sparkle **5** = **polish**, glaze, gloss, lustre, patina, sheen

shining *adjective* **1** = **bright**, aglow, beaming, brilliant, effulgent, gleaming, glistening, glittering, luminous, radiant, shimmering, sparkling **2** = **outstanding**, brilliant, celebrated, conspicuous, distinguished, eminent, glorious, illustrious, leading, splendid

shiny *adjective* = **bright**, agleam, burnished, gleaming, glistening, glossy, lustrous, polished, satiny, sheeny

ship *noun* = **vessel**, boat, craft

shipshape *adjective* = **tidy**, Bristol fashion, businesslike, neat, orderly, spick-and-span, trig (*archaic or dialect*), trim, uncluttered, well-ordered, well-organized, well-regulated

shirk *verb* = **dodge**, avoid, body-swerve (*Scot.*), duck (out of) (*informal*), evade, get out of, shun, sidestep, skive (*Brit. slang*), slack

shirker *noun* = **slacker**, clock-watcher, dodger, idler, malingerer, quitter, shirk, skiver (*Brit. slang*)

shiver[1] *verb* **1** = **tremble**, palpitate, quake, quiver, shake, shudder ♦ *noun* **2** = **trembling**, flutter, *frisson*, quiver, shudder, thrill, tremble, tremor **3 the shivers** = **the shakes** (*informal*), chattering teeth, chill, goose flesh, goose pimples

shiver[2] *verb* = **splinter**, break, crack, fragment, shatter, smash, smash to smithereens

shivery *adjective* = **shaking**, chilled, chilly, cold, quaking, quivery, shuddery, trembly

shoal *noun* **1** = **shallow** **2** = **sandbank**, sand bar, shelf

shock *verb* **1** = **horrify**, agitate, appal, disgust, disquiet, give (someone) a turn

(*informal*), gross out (*U.S. slang*), nauseate, offend, outrage, raise eyebrows, revolt, scandalize, sicken, traumatize, unsettle **2** = **astound**, jar, jolt, numb, paralyse, shake, shake up (*informal*), stagger, stun, stupefy ♦ *noun* **3** = **impact**, blow, clash, collision, encounter, jarring, jolt **4** = **upset**, blow, bolt from the blue, bombshell, breakdown, collapse, consternation, distress, disturbance, prostration, rude awakening, state of shock, stupefaction, stupor, trauma, turn (*informal*), whammy (*informal, chiefly U.S.*)

shocking *adjective* = **dreadful**, abominable, appalling, atrocious, detestable, disgraceful, disgusting, disquieting, distressing, foul, frightful, from hell (*informal*), ghastly, hellacious (*U.S. slang*), hideous, horrible, horrifying, loathsome, monstrous, nauseating, obscene, odious, offensive, outrageous, repulsive, revolting, scandalous, sickening, stupefying, unspeakable
➤ Antonyms
admirable, decent, delightful, excellent, fine, first-rate, gratifying, honourable, laudable, marvellous, pleasant, praiseworthy, satisfying, wonderful

shoddy *adjective* = **inferior**, cheap, cheapo (*informal*), junky (*informal*), low-rent (*informal, chiefly U.S.*), poor, rubbishy, second-rate, slipshod, tacky (*informal*), tatty, tawdry, trashy
➤ Antonyms
accurate, careful, craftsman-like, excellent, fine, first-rate, meticulous, quality, superlative, well-made

shoemaker *noun* = **cobbler**, bootmaker

shoot *verb* **1** = **hit**, bag, blast (*slang*), blow away (*slang, chiefly U.S.*), bring down, kill, open fire, pick off, plug (*slang*), pump full of lead (*slang*), zap (*slang*) **2** = **fire**, discharge, emit, fling, hurl, launch, let fly, project, propel **3** = **speed**, bolt, charge, dart, dash, flash, fly, hurtle, race, rush, scoot, spring, streak, tear, whisk, whizz (*informal*) **4** = **sprout**, bud, burgeon, germinate ♦ *noun* **5** = **sprout**, branch, bud, offshoot, slip, sprig, twig

shop *noun* = **store**, boutique, emporium, hypermarket, market, mart, supermarket

shore *noun* = **beach**, coast, lakeside, sands, seaboard (*chiefly U.S.*), seashore, strand (*poetic*), waterside

shore up *verb* = **support**, augment, brace, buttress, hold, prop, reinforce, strengthen, underpin

short *adjective* **1** = **concise**, abridged, brief, compressed, laconic, pithy, succinct, summary, terse **2** = **small**, diminutive, dumpy, knee high to a gnat, knee high to a grasshopper, little, low, petite, squat, wee **3 = brief**, fleeting, momentary, short-lived, short-term **4** *often with* **of** *or* **on = lacking**, deficient, inadequate, in need of, insufficient, limited, low (on), meagre, missing, poor, scant, scanty, scarce, sparse, strapped (for) (*slang*), tight, wanting **5 = abrupt**, blunt, brusque, curt, discourteous, gruff, impolite, offhand, sharp, terse, testy, uncivil **6** *Of pastry* **= crumbly**, brittle, crisp ♦ *adverb* **7 = abruptly**, by surprise, suddenly, unaware, without warning **8 short of = except**, apart from, other than, unless ♦ *noun* **9 in short = briefly**, in a nutshell, in a word, in essence, to come to the point, to cut a long story short, to put it briefly

➤ Antonyms

adjective ≠**concise**: diffuse, lengthy, long, long-drawn-out, long-winded, prolonged, rambling, unabridged, verbose, wordy ≠**small**: big, high, lanky, lofty, tall ≠**brief**: extended, long, long-term ≠**lacking**: abundant, adequate, ample, bountiful, copious, inexhaustible, plentiful, sufficient, well-stocked ≠**abrupt**: civil, courteous, polite ♦ *adverb* ≠**abruptly**: bit by bit, gently, gradually, little by little, slowly

shortage *noun* **= deficiency**, dearth, deficit, failure, inadequacy, insufficiency, lack, leanness, paucity, poverty, scarcity, shortfall, want

➤ Antonyms

abundance, adequate amount, excess, overabundance, plethora, profusion, sufficiency, surfeit, surplus

shortcoming *noun* **= failing**, defect, drawback, fault, flaw, foible, frailty, imperfection, weakness, weak point

shorten *verb* **= cut**, abbreviate, abridge, curtail, cut back, cut down, decrease, diminish, dock, downsize, lessen, prune, reduce, trim, truncate, turn up

➤ Antonyms

draw out, elongate, expand, extend, increase, lengthen, make longer, prolong, protract, spin out, stretch

short-lived *adjective* **= brief**, ephemeral, fleeting, impermanent, passing, short, temporary, transient, transitory

shortly *adverb* **1 = soon**, anon (*archaic*), any minute now, before long, in a little while, presently **2 = curtly**, abruptly, sharply, tartly, tersely

short-sighted *adjective* **1 = near-sighted**, blind as a bat, myopic **2 = unthinking**, careless, ill-advised, ill-considered, impolitic, impractical, improvident, imprudent, injudicious, seeing no further

than (the end of) one's nose

short-tempered *adjective* **= quick-tempered**, choleric, fiery, hot-tempered, impatient, irascible, peppery, ratty (*Brit. & N.Z. informal*), testy, touchy

shot[1] *noun* **1 = throw**, discharge, lob, pot shot **2 = pellet**, ball, bullet, lead, projectile, slug **3 = marksman**, shooter **4** *Informal* **= attempt**, chance, crack (*informal*), effort, endeavour, essay, go (*informal*), opportunity, stab (*informal*), try, turn **5** *Informal* **= guess**, conjecture, surmise **6 like a shot = at once**, eagerly, immediately, like a bat out of hell (*slang*), like a flash, quickly, unhesitatingly **7 shot in the arm** *Informal* **= boost**, encouragement, fillip, geeing-up, impetus, lift, stimulus

shot[2] *adjective* **= iridescent**, moiré, opalescent, watered

shoulder *noun* **1 put one's shoulder to the wheel** *Informal* **= work hard**, apply oneself, buckle down to (*informal*), exert oneself, get down to, make every effort, set to work, strive **2 rub shoulders with** *Informal* **= mix with**, associate with, consort with, fraternize with, hobnob with, socialize with **3 shoulder to shoulder: a = side by side b = together**, as one, in cooperation, in partnership, in unity, jointly, united ♦ *verb* **4 = bear**, accept, assume, be responsible for, carry, take on, take upon oneself **5 = push**, elbow, jostle, press, shove, thrust

shoulder blade *noun* **= scapula**

shout *noun* **1 = cry**, bellow, call, roar, scream, yell ♦ *verb* **2 = cry (out)**, bawl, bay, bellow, call (out), holler (*informal*), hollo, raise one's voice, roar, scream, yell

shout down *verb* **= silence**, drown, drown out, overwhelm

shove *verb* **= push**, crowd, drive, elbow, impel, jostle, press, propel, shoulder, thrust

shovel *verb* **= move**, convey, dredge, heap, ladle, load, scoop, shift, spoon, toss

shove off *verb* *Informal* **= go away**, bugger off (*taboo slang*), clear off (*informal*), depart, fuck off (*offensive taboo slang*), get on one's bike (*Brit. slang*), go to hell (*informal*), leave, push off (*informal*), scram (*informal*), sling one's hook (*Brit. slang*), slope off, take oneself off, vamoose (*slang, chiefly U.S.*)

show *verb* **1 = be visible**, appear **2 = present**, display, exhibit **3 = prove**, assert, clarify, demonstrate, elucidate, evince, point out **4 = instruct**, demonstrate, explain, teach **5 = indicate**, demonstrate, disclose, display, divulge,

evidence, evince, make known, manifest, register, reveal, testify to **6 = act with**, accord, bestow, confer, grant **7 = guide**, accompany, attend, conduct, escort, lead ♦ *noun* **8 = entertainment**, presentation, production **9 = exhibition**, array, demonstration, display, exposition, fair, manifestation, pageant, pageantry, parade, representation, sight, spectacle, view **10 = pretence**, affectation, air, appearance, display, illusion, likeness, ostentation, parade, pose, pretext, profession, semblance
➤ Antonyms
verb ≠**be visible**: be invisible ≠**present**, **indicate**: conceal, hide, keep secret, mask, obscure, suppress, veil, withhold ≠**prove**: deny, disprove, gainsay (*archaic or literary*), refute

showdown *noun Informal* = **confrontation**, breaking point, clash, climax, crisis, culmination, denouement, exposé, face-off (*slang*), moment of truth

shower *noun* **1 = deluge**, barrage, downpour, fusillade, rain, stream, torrent, volley **2** *Brit. slang* = **rabble**, crew ♦ *verb* **3 = inundate**, deluge, heap, lavish, load, pour, rain, spray, sprinkle

showing *noun* **1 = display**, demonstration, exhibition, presentation, staging **2 = performance**, account of oneself, appearance, demonstration, impression, show, track record

showman *noun* **1 = performer**, entertainer **2 = impresario**, publicist, stage manager

show-off *noun Informal* = **exhibitionist**, boaster, braggadocio, braggart, egotist, peacock, poseur, swaggerer

show off *verb* **1 = exhibit**, advertise, demonstrate, display, flaunt, parade **2** *Informal* = **boast**, blow one's own trumpet, brag, make a spectacle of oneself, strut one's stuff (*chiefly U.S.*), swagger

show up *verb* **1 = stand out**, appear, be conspicuous, be visible, catch the eye, leap to the eye **2 = reveal**, expose, highlight, lay bare, pinpoint, put the spotlight on, unmask **3** *Informal* = **embarrass**, let down, mortify, put to shame, shame, show in a bad light **4** *Informal* = **arrive**, appear, come, make an appearance, put in an appearance, show one's face, turn up

showy *adjective* **1 = ostentatious**, brash, flamboyant, flash (*informal*), flashy, over the top (*informal*), pompous, pretentious, splashy (*informal*) **2 = gaudy**, garish, loud, tawdry, tinselly
➤ Antonyms
discreet, low-key, muted, quiet, restrained, subdued, tasteful, unobtrusive

shred *noun* **1 = strip**, bit, fragment, piece, rag, ribbon, scrap, sliver, snippet, tatter **2 = particle**, atom, grain, iota, jot, scrap, trace, whit

shrew *noun* = **nag**, ballbreaker (*slang*), dragon (*informal*), fury, harpy, harridan, scold, spitfire, virago, vixen

shrewd *adjective* = **clever**, acute, artful, astute, calculating, canny, crafty, cunning, discerning, discriminating, far-seeing, far-sighted, fly (*slang*), intelligent, keen, knowing, perceptive, perspicacious, sagacious, sharp, sly, smart, wily
➤ Antonyms
artless, dull, gullible, imprudent, ingenuous, innocent, naive, obtuse, slow-witted, stupid, trusting, undiscerning, unsophisticated, unworldly

shrewdly *adverb* = **cleverly**, artfully, astutely, cannily, far-sightedly, knowingly, perceptively, perspicaciously, sagaciously, with all one's wits about one

shrewdness *noun* = **cleverness**, acumen, acuteness, astuteness, canniness, discernment, grasp, judgment, penetration, perspicacity, quick wits, sagacity, sharpness, smartness

shrewish *adjective* = **bad-tempered**, complaining, fault-finding, ill-humoured, ill-natured, ill-tempered, nagging, quarrelsome, scolding, sharp-tongued, vixenish

shriek *verb, noun* = **cry**, holler, howl, scream, screech, squeal, wail, whoop, yell

shrill *adjective* = **piercing**, acute, ear-piercing, ear-splitting, high, high-pitched, penetrating, piping, screeching, sharp
➤ Antonyms
deep, dulcet, mellifluous, silver-toned, soft, soothing, sweet-sounding, velvety, well-modulated

shrink *verb* **1 = decrease**, contract, deflate, diminish, downsize, drop off, dwindle, fall off, grow smaller, lessen, narrow, shorten, shrivel, wither, wrinkle **2 = recoil**, cower, cringe, draw back, flinch, hang back, quail, shy away, wince, withdraw
➤ Antonyms
≠**decrease**: balloon, dilate, distend, enlarge, expand, increase, inflate, mushroom, stretch, swell ≠**recoil**: confront, embrace, face, receive, welcome

shrivel *verb* **1 = wither**, dehydrate, desiccate, dwindle, shrink, wilt, wizen, wrinkle **2 = dry (up)**, burn, parch, scorch, sear

shrivelled *adjective* = **withered**, desiccated, dried up, dry, shrunken, wizened, wrinkled

shroud *noun* 1 = **winding sheet**, covering, grave clothes 2 = **covering**, cloud, mantle, pall, screen, veil ♦ *verb* 3 = **conceal**, blanket, cloak, cover, envelop, hide, screen, swathe, veil

shudder *verb* 1 = **shiver**, convulse, quake, quiver, shake, tremble ♦ *noun* 2 = **shiver**, convulsion, quiver, spasm, trembling, tremor

shuffle *verb* 1 = **scuffle**, drag, scrape, scuff, shamble 2 = **rearrange**, confuse, disarrange, disorder, intermix, jumble, mix, shift

shun *verb* = **avoid**, body-swerve (*Scot.*), cold-shoulder, elude, eschew, evade, fight shy of, give (someone *or* something) a wide berth, have no part in, keep away from, shy away from, steer clear of

shut *verb* 1 = **close**, bar, draw to, fasten, push to, seal, secure, slam 2 **shut in** = **confine**, cage, enclose, impound, imprison, pound, wall off *or* up 3 **shut out** = **exclude**, keep out
➤ **Antonyms**
≠**close**: open, throw wide, unbar, unclose, undo, unfasten, unlock

shut down *verb* 1 = **stop**, cease, cease operating, discontinue, halt, switch off 2 = **close**, shut up

shut out *verb* 1 = **exclude**, bar, black, blackball, debar, keep out, lock out, ostracize 2 = **conceal**, block out, cover, hide, mask, screen, veil

shuttle *verb* = **go back and forth**, alternate, commute, go to and fro, seesaw, shunt

shut up *verb* 1 *Informal* = **be quiet**, button one's lip (*slang*), fall silent, gag, hold one's tongue, hush, keep one's trap shut (*slang*), muzzle, pipe down (*slang*), put a sock in it (*Brit. slang*), silence 2 = **confine**, bottle up, box in, cage, coop up, immure, imprison, incarcerate, intern, keep in

shy [1] *adjective* 1 = **timid**, backward, bashful, coy, diffident, modest, mousy, nervous, reserved, reticent, retiring, self-conscious, self-effacing, shrinking 2 **shy of** = **cautious of**, chary of, distrustful of, hesitant about, suspicious of, wary of ♦ *verb* 3 *sometimes with* **off** *or* **away** = **recoil**, balk, buck, draw back, flinch, quail, rear, start, take fright, wince
➤ **Antonyms**
adjective ≠**timid**: assured, bold, brash, cheeky, confident, fearless, forward, pushy (*informal*), self-assured, self-confident ≠**cautious of**: rash, reckless, unsuspecting, unwary

shy [2] *verb* = **throw**, cast, chuck (*informal*), fling, hurl, lob (*informal*), pitch, propel, send, sling, toss

shyness *noun* = **timidness**, bashfulness, diffidence, lack of confidence, modesty, mousiness, nervousness, reticence, self-consciousness, timidity, timorousness

sibyl *noun* = **prophetess**, Cassandra, oracle, seer

sick *adjective* 1 = **nauseous**, green about the gills (*informal*), ill, nauseated, puking (*slang*), queasy 2 = **unwell**, ailing, diseased, feeble, indisposed, laid up (*informal*), poorly (*informal*), under par (*informal*), under the weather, weak 3 *Informal* = **morbid**, black, ghoulish, macabre, sadistic 4 **sick of** = **tired**, blasé, bored, fed up, jaded, satiated, weary
➤ **Antonyms**
≠**unwell**: able-bodied, fine, fit, fit and well, fit as a fiddle, hale and hearty, healthy, robust, up to par, well

sicken *verb* 1 = **disgust**, gross out (*U.S. slang*), make one's gorge rise, nauseate, repel, revolt, turn one's stomach 2 = **fall ill**, ail, be stricken by, contract, go down with, show symptoms of, take sick

sickening *adjective* = **disgusting**, cringe-making (*Brit. informal*), distasteful, foul, gut-wrenching, loathsome, nauseating, nauseous, noisome, offensive, putrid, repulsive, revolting, stomach-turning (*informal*), vile, yucky *or* yukky (*slang*)
➤ **Antonyms**
delightful, inviting, marvellous, mouth-watering, pleasant, tempting, wholesome, wonderful

sickly *adjective* 1 = **unhealthy**, ailing, delicate, faint, feeble, indisposed, infirm, in poor health, lacklustre, languid, pallid, peaky, wan, weak 2 = **nauseating**, cloying, icky (*informal*), mawkish, revolting (*informal*)

sickness *noun* 1 = **illness**, affliction, ailment, bug (*informal*), complaint, disease, disorder, indisposition, infirmity, lurgy (*informal*), malady 2 = **nausea**, (the) collywobbles (*slang*), puking (*slang*), queasiness, vomiting

side *noun* 1 = **border**, boundary, division, edge, limit, margin, part, perimeter, periphery, rim, sector, verge 2 = **part**, aspect, face, facet, flank, hand, surface, view 3 = **party**, camp, cause, faction, sect, team 4 = **point of view**, angle, light, opinion, position, slant, stand, standpoint, viewpoint 5 *Brit. slang* = **conceit**, airs, arrogance, insolence, pretentiousness ♦ *adjective* 6 = **lateral**, flanking 7 = **subordinate**, ancillary, incidental, indirect, lesser, marginal, minor, oblique,

roundabout, secondary, subsidiary ◆ *verb* **8** *usually with* **with = support**, ally with, associate oneself with, befriend, favour, go along with, join with, second, take the part of, team up with (*informal*)
➤ **Antonyms**
noun ≠ **border**: centre, core, heart, middle ◆ *adjective* ≠ **subordinate**: central, essential, focal, fundamental, key, main, middle, primary, principal ◆ *verb* ≠ **support**: counter, oppose, stand against, withstand

sideline *noun* = **supplement**, subsidiary

sidelong *adjective* = **sideways**, covert, indirect, oblique

side-splitting *adjective* = **hilarious**, farcical, hysterical, rollicking, uproarious

sidestep *verb* = **avoid**, body-swerve (*Scot.*), bypass, circumvent, dodge, duck (*informal*), elude, evade, find a way round, skip, skirt

sidetrack *verb* = **distract**, deflect, divert, lead off the subject

sideways *adverb* **1** = **obliquely**, crabwise, edgeways, laterally, sidelong, sidewards, to the side ◆ *adjective* **2** = **oblique**, side, sidelong, slanted

sidle *verb* = **edge**, creep, inch, slink, sneak, steal

siesta *noun* = **nap**, catnap, doze, forty winks (*informal*), kip (*Brit. slang*), rest, sleep, snooze (*informal*), zizz (*Brit. informal*)

sieve *noun* **1** = **strainer**, colander, riddle, screen, sifter ◆ *verb* **2** = **sift**, bolt, remove, riddle, separate, strain

sift *verb* **1** = **sieve**, bolt, filter, pan, part, riddle, separate **2** = **examine**, analyse, go through, investigate, pore over, probe, research, screen, scrutinize, work over

sigh *verb* **1** = **breathe**, complain, grieve, lament, moan, sorrow **2** *sigh for* = **long for**, eat one's heart out over, languish over, mourn for, pine for, yearn for

sight *noun* **1** = **vision**, eye, eyes, eyesight, seeing **2** = **view**, appearance, apprehension, eyeshot, field of vision, ken, perception, range of vision, viewing, visibility **3** = **spectacle**, display, exhibition, pageant, scene, show, vista **4** *Informal* = **eyesore**, blot on the landscape (*informal*), fright (*informal*), mess, monstrosity, spectacle **5** *catch sight of* = **spot**, descry, espy, glimpse, recognize, view ◆ *verb* **6** = **spot**, behold, discern, distinguish, make out, observe, perceive, see

sign *noun* **1** = **indication**, clue, evidence, gesture, giveaway, hint, manifestation, mark, note, proof, signal, suggestion,

symptom, token, trace, vestige **2** = **notice**, board, placard, warning **3** = **symbol**, badge, character, cipher, device, emblem, ensign, figure, logo, mark, representation **4** = **omen**, augury, auspice, foreboding, forewarning, portent, presage, warning ◆ *verb* **5** = **autograph**, endorse, initial, inscribe, set one's hand to, subscribe **6** = **gesture**, beckon, gesticulate, indicate, signal, use sign language, wave

signal *noun* **1** = **sign**, beacon, cue, gesture, go-ahead (*informal*), green light, indication, indicator, mark, token ◆ *adjective* **2** *Formal* = **significant**, conspicuous, exceptional, extraordinary, memorable, momentous, notable, noteworthy, outstanding, remarkable, serious (*informal*), striking ◆ *verb* **3** = **gesture**, beckon, communicate, gesticulate, give a sign to, indicate, motion, nod, sign, wave

sign away *verb* = **give up**, abandon, dispose of, forgo, lose, relinquish, renounce, surrender, transfer, waive

significance *noun* **1** = **importance**, consequence, consideration, impressiveness, matter, moment, relevance, weight **2** = **meaning**, force, implication(s), import, message, point, purport, sense, signification

significant *adjective* **1** = **important**, critical, material, momentous, noteworthy, serious, vital, weighty **2** = **meaningful**, denoting, eloquent, expressing, expressive, indicative, knowing, meaning, pregnant, suggestive
➤ **Antonyms**
≠ **important**: immaterial, inconsequential, insignificant, irrelevant, of no consequence, paltry, petty, trivial, unimportant, worthless ≠ **meaningful**: meaningless

signify *verb* **1** = **indicate**, announce, be a sign of, betoken, communicate, connote, convey, denote, evidence, exhibit, express, imply, intimate, matter, mean, portend, proclaim, represent, show, stand for, suggest, symbolize **2** *Informal* = **matter**, be important, carry weight, count

sign up *verb* **1** = **engage**, employ, hire, put on the payroll, recruit, take into service, take on, take on board (*informal*) **2** = **enlist**, contract with, enrol, join, join up, register, volunteer

silence *noun* **1** = **quiet**, calm, hush, lull, noiselessness, peace, quiescence, stillness **2** = **muteness**, dumbness, reticence, speechlessness, taciturnity, uncommunicativeness ◆ *verb* **3** = **quieten**, cut off, cut short, deaden, extinguish, gag,

muffle, quell, quiet, stifle, still, strike dumb, subdue, suppress
➤ **Antonyms**
noun ≠**quiet**: cacophony, din, noise, racket, sound, tumult, uproar ≠**muteness**: babble, chatter, garrulousness, hubbub, loquaciousness, prattle, speech, talk, talking, verbosity ♦ *verb* ≠**quieten**: amplify, broadcast, disseminate, encourage, foster, make louder, promote, promulgate, publicize, rouse, spread, support, ungag

silent *adjective* **1** = **quiet**, hushed, muted, noiseless, soundless, still, stilly (*poetic*) **2** = **mute**, dumb, nonvocal, not talkative, speechless, struck dumb, taciturn, tongue-tied, uncommunicative, unspeaking, voiceless, wordless **3** = **unspoken**, implicit, implied, tacit, understood, unexpressed, unpronounced

silently *adjective* = **quietly**, as quietly as a mouse (*informal*), dumbly, inaudibly, in silence, mutely, noiselessly, soundlessly, speechlessly, without a sound, wordlessly

silhouette *noun* **1** = **outline**, delineation, form, profile, shape ♦ *verb* **2** = **outline**, delineate, etch, stand out

silky *adjective* = **smooth**, silken, sleek, velvety

silly *adjective* **1** = **foolish**, absurd, asinine, brainless, childish, daft, dopy (*slang*), dozy (*Brit. informal*), dumb-ass (*slang*), fatuous, foolhardy, frivolous, giddy, idiotic, imprudent, inane, inappropriate, irresponsible, meaningless, pointless, preposterous, puerile, ridiculous, senseless, stupid, unwise, witless **2** *Old-fashioned* = **dazed**, benumbed, groggy (*informal*), in a daze, muzzy, stunned, stupefied ♦ *noun* **3** *Informal* = **fool**, clot (*Brit. informal*), ignoramus, nerd *or* nurd (*slang*), ninny, nitwit (*informal*), plonker (*slang*), prat (*slang*), simpleton, twit (*informal*), wally (*slang*)
➤ **Antonyms**
adjective ≠**foolish**: acute, aware, bright, clever, intelligent, mature, perceptive, profound, prudent, reasonable, sane, sensible, serious, smart, thoughtful, well-thought-out, wise

silt *noun* **1** = **sediment**, alluvium, deposit, ooze, residue, sludge ♦ *verb* **2 silt up** = **clog**, choke, congest, dam

silver *noun* **1** = **silverware**, silver plate ♦ *adjective* **2** = **silvery**, argent (*poetic*), pearly, silvered

similar *adjective* = **alike**, analogous, close, comparable, congruous, corresponding, homogeneous, homogenous, in agreement, like, much the same, of a piece, resembling, uniform
➤ **Antonyms**
antithetical, clashing, contradictory, contrary, different, disparate, dissimilar, diverse, heterogeneous, irreconcilable, opposite, unalike, unrelated, various, varying

similarity *noun* = **resemblance**, affinity, agreement, analogy, closeness, comparability, concordance, congruence, correspondence, likeness, point of comparison, relation, sameness, similitude
➤ **Antonyms**
antithesis, contradictoriness, difference, disagreement, discordance, discrepancy, disparity, dissimilarity, diversity, heterogeneity, incomparability, irreconcilability, unalikeness, variation, variety

similarly *adverb* = **in the same way**, by the same token, correspondingly, in like manner, likewise

simmer *verb* = **fume**, be agitated, be angry, be pissed (off) (*taboo slang*), be tense, be uptight (*informal*), boil, burn, rage, see red (*informal*), seethe, smart, smoulder

simmer down *verb Informal* = **calm down**, collect oneself, contain oneself, control oneself, cool off *or* down, grow quieter

simper *verb* = **smile coyly**, smile affectedly, smile self-consciously, smirk

simpering *adjective* = **coy**, affected, self-conscious

simple *adjective* **1** = **uncomplicated**, clear, easy, easy-peasy (*slang*), elementary, intelligible, lucid, manageable, plain, straightforward, understandable, uninvolved **2** = **plain**, classic, clean, natural, severe, Spartan, unadorned, uncluttered, unembellished, unfussy **3** = **pure**, elementary, single, unalloyed, unblended, uncombined, undivided, unmixed **4** = **artless**, childlike, frank, guileless, ingenuous, innocent, naive, natural, simplistic, sincere, unaffected, unpretentious, unsophisticated **5** = **honest**, bald, basic, direct, frank, naked, plain, sincere, stark, undeniable, unvarnished **6** = **unpretentious**, homely, humble, lowly, modest, rustic **7** *Informal* = **feeble-minded**, brainless, dense, dumb (*informal*), dumb-ass (*slang*), feeble, foolish, half-witted, moronic, obtuse, shallow, silly, slow, stupid, thick
➤ **Antonyms**
≠**uncomplicated**: advanced, complex, complicated, convoluted, difficult, elaborate, highly developed, intricate, involved, refined, sophisticated ≠**plain**:

contrived, elaborate, fussy, intricate, ornate ≠**artless**: artful, smart, sophisticated, worldly, worldly-wise ≠**unpretentious**: extravagant, fancy, flashy ≠**feeble-minded**: astute, bright, clever, intelligent, knowing, on the ball, quick, quick on the uptake, quick-witted, sharp, smart, wise

simple-minded *adjective* **1** = **unsophisticated**, artless, natural **2** = **feeble-minded**, a bit lacking (*informal*), addle-brained, backward, brainless, dim-witted, foolish, idiot, idiotic, moronic, retarded, simple, stupid

simpleton *noun* = **halfwit**, berk (*Brit. slang*), blockhead, booby, charlie (*Brit. informal*), chump, dickhead (*slang*), divvy (*Brit. slang*), dolt, dope (*informal*), dork (*slang*), dullard, dumb-ass (*slang*), dunce, fathead (*informal*), fool, geek (*slang*), gobshite (*Irish taboo slang*), gonzo (*slang*), idiot, imbecile (*informal*), jackass, jerk (*slang, chiefly U.S. & Canad.*), moron, nerd *or* nurd (*slang*), nincompoop, ninny, nitwit (*informal*), numpty (*Scot. informal*), numskull *or* numbskull, oaf, plank (*Brit. slang*), schmuck (*U.S. slang*), twerp *or* twirp (*informal*), twit (*informal, chiefly Brit.*), wally (*slang*)

simplicity *noun* **1** = **ease**, absence of complications, clarity, clearness, easiness, elementariness, obviousness, straightforwardness **2** = **plainness**, clean lines, lack of adornment, modesty, naturalness, purity, restraint **3** = **artlessness**, candour, directness, guilelessness, innocence, lack of sophistication, naivety, openness
➤ **Antonyms**
≠**ease**: complexity, complicatedness, difficulty, intricacy, lack of clarity ≠**plainness**: decoration, elaborateness, embellishment, fanciness, fussiness, ornateness, ostentation ≠**artlessness**: brains, craftiness, cunning, deviousness, guile, sharpness, slyness, smartness, sophistication, worldliness

simplify *verb* = **make simpler**, abridge, decipher, disentangle, dumb down, facilitate, make intelligible, reduce to essentials, streamline

simplistic *adjective* = **oversimplified**, naive

simply *adverb* **1** = **plainly**, clearly, directly, easily, intelligibly, modestly, naturally, straightforwardly, unaffectedly, unpretentiously, without any elaboration **2** = **just**, merely, only, purely, solely **3** = **totally**, absolutely, altogether, completely, really, unreservedly, utterly, wholly

simulate *verb* = **pretend**, act, affect, assume, counterfeit, fabricate, feign, imitate, make believe, put on, reproduce, sham

simulated *adjective* **1** = **pretended**, artificial, assumed, feigned, insincere, make-believe, phoney *or* phony (*informal*), put-on **2** = **synthetic**, artificial, fake, imitation, man-made, mock, pseudo (*informal*), sham, substitute

simultaneous *adjective* = **coinciding**, at the same time, coincident, concurrent, contemporaneous, synchronous

simultaneously *adverb* = **at the same time**, all together, concurrently, in chorus, in unison, together

sin *noun* **1** = **wrongdoing**, crime, damnation, error, evil, guilt, iniquity, misdeed, offence, sinfulness, transgression, trespass, ungodliness, unrighteousness, wickedness, wrong ♦ *verb* **2** = **transgress**, err, fall, fall from grace, go astray, lapse, offend

sincere *adjective* = **honest**, artless, bona fide, candid, earnest, frank, genuine, guileless, heartfelt, natural, no-nonsense, open, real, serious, straightforward, true, unaffected, unfeigned, upfront (*informal*), wholehearted
➤ **Antonyms**
affected, artful, artificial, deceitful, deceptive, dishonest, false, feigned, hollow, insincere, phoney *or* phony (*informal*), pretended, put on, synthetic, token, two-faced

sincerely *adverb* = **honestly**, earnestly, from the bottom of one's heart, genuinely, in all sincerity, in earnest, in good faith, really, seriously, truly, wholeheartedly

sincerity *noun* = **honesty**, artlessness, candour, frankness, genuineness, good faith, guilelessness, probity, seriousness, straightforwardness, truth, wholeheartedness

sinecure *noun* = **cushy number** (*informal*), gravy train (*slang*), money for jam *or* old rope (*informal*), soft job (*informal*), soft option

sinewy *adjective* = **muscular**, athletic, brawny, lusty, powerful, robust, strong, sturdy, vigorous, wiry

sinful *adjective* = **wicked**, bad, corrupt, criminal, depraved, erring, guilty, immoral, iniquitous, irreligious, morally wrong, ungodly, unholy, unrighteous
➤ **Antonyms**
chaste, decent, free from sin, godly, holy, honest, honourable, immaculate, moral, pure, righteous, sinless, spotless, squeaky-clean, unblemished, upright,

virtuous, without sin

sing *verb* **1** = **warble**, carol, chant, chirp, croon, make melody, pipe, trill, vocalize, yodel **2** = **hum**, buzz, purr, whine, whistle **3** *Slang, chiefly U.S.* = **inform (on)**, betray, blow the whistle (on) (*informal*), grass (*Brit. slang*), rat (on) (*informal*), shop (*slang, chiefly Brit.*), spill one's guts (*slang*), spill the beans (*informal*), squeal (*slang*), tell all

singe *verb* = **burn**, char, scorch, sear

singer *noun* = **vocalist**, balladeer, cantor, chanteuse (*fem.*), chorister, crooner, minstrel, soloist, songster *or* songstress, troubadour

single *adjective* **1** = **one**, distinct, individual, lone, only, particular, separate, singular, sole, solitary, unique **2** = **individual**, exclusive, separate, undivided, unshared **3** = **unmarried**, free, unattached, unwed **4** = **simple**, unblended, uncompounded, unmixed ♦ *verb* **5** *usually with* **out** = **pick**, choose, distinguish, fix on, pick on *or* out, put on one side, select, separate, set apart

single-handed *adverb* = **unaided**, alone, by oneself, independently, on one's own, solo, unassisted, under one's own steam, without help

single-minded *adjective* = **determined**, dedicated, dogged, fixed, hellbent (*informal*), steadfast, stubborn, tireless, undeviating, unswerving, unwavering

singly *adverb* = **one by one**, individually, one at a time, separately

sing out *verb* = **call (out)**, cooee, cry (out), halloo, holler (*informal*), make oneself heard, shout, yell

singular *adjective* **1** = **single**, individual, separate, sole **2** = **remarkable**, conspicuous, eminent, exceptional, extraordinary, notable, noteworthy, outstanding, prodigious, rare, uncommon, unique, unparalleled **3** = **unusual**, atypical, curious, eccentric, extraordinary, odd, oddball (*informal*), out-of-the-way, outré, peculiar, queer, strange, wacko (*slang*)
➤ **Antonyms**
≠**remarkable, unusual:** common, common or garden, commonplace, conventional, everyday, familiar, normal, routine, run-of-the-mill, unexceptional, unremarkable, usual

singularity *noun* **1** = **oddness**, abnormality, curiousness, extraordinariness, irregularity, peculiarity, queerness, strangeness **2** = **idiosyncrasy**, eccentricity, oddity, particularity, peculiarity, quirk, twist

singularly *adverb* = **remarkably**, conspicuously, especially, exceptionally, extraordinarily, notably, outstandingly, particularly, prodigiously, seriously (*informal*), surprisingly, uncommonly, unusually

sinister *adjective* = **threatening**, baleful, bodeful, dire, disquieting, evil, forbidding, injurious, malevolent, malign, malignant, menacing, ominous
➤ **Antonyms**
auspicious, benevolent, benign, calming, encouraging, good, heartening, heroic, honourable, just, noble, promising, propitious, reassuring, righteous, upright, worthy

sink *verb* **1** = **descend**, cave in, decline, dip, disappear, droop, drop, drown, ebb, fall, founder, go down, go under, lower, plummet, plunge, sag, slope, submerge, subside **2** = **fall**, abate, collapse, drop, lapse, relapse, retrogress, slip, slump, subside **3** = **stoop**, be reduced to, debase oneself, lower oneself, succumb **4** = **decline**, decay, decrease, degenerate, depreciate, deteriorate, die, diminish, dwindle, fade, fail, flag, go downhill (*informal*), lessen, weaken, worsen **5** = **dig**, bore, drill, drive, excavate, lay, put down
➤ **Antonyms**
≠**descend:** arise, ascend, climb, go up, move up, rise, rise up ≠**decline:** go up, grow, improve, increase, intensify, rise, rise up, swell, wax

sink in *verb* = **be understood**, get through to, make an impression, penetrate, register (*informal*), take hold of

sinner *noun* = **wrongdoer**, evildoer, malefactor, miscreant, offender, reprobate, transgressor

sinuous *adjective Literary* = **curving**, coiling, crooked, curvy, lithe, meandering, serpentine, undulating, winding

sip *verb* **1** = **drink**, sample, sup, taste ♦ *noun* **2** = **swallow**, drop, taste, thimbleful

siren *noun* = **seductress**, charmer, Circe, *femme fatale,* Lorelei, temptress, vamp (*informal*), witch

sissy *or* **cissy** *noun* **1** = **wimp** (*informal*), baby, coward, jessie (*Scot. slang*), milksop, mummy's boy, namby-pamby, pansy, softie (*informal*), weakling, wet (*Brit. informal*), wuss (*slang*) ♦ *adjective* **2** = **wimpish** *or* **wimpy** (*informal*), cowardly, effeminate, feeble, namby-pamby, soft (*informal*), unmanly, weak, wet (*Brit. informal*), wussy (*slang*)

sit *verb* **1** = **rest**, be seated, perch, settle, take a seat, take the weight off one's feet **2** = **convene**, assemble, be in session, deliberate, meet, officiate, preside

site *noun* 1 = **location**, ground, place, plot, position, setting, spot ♦ *verb* 2 = **locate**, install, place, position, set, situate

sitting *noun* = **meeting**, congress, consultation, get-together (*informal*), hearing, period, session

situation *noun* 1 = **state of affairs**, ball game (*informal*), case, circumstances, condition, equation, kettle of fish (*informal*), lie of the land, plight, scenario, state, status quo, the picture (*informal*) 2 = **location**, locale, locality, place, position, seat, setting, site, spot 3 = **status**, rank, sphere, station 4 = **job**, berth (*informal*), employment, office, place, position, post

sixth sense *noun* = **intuition**, clairvoyance, second sight

sizable, sizeable *adjective* = **large**, considerable, decent, decent-sized, goodly, largish, respectable, substantial, tidy (*informal*)

size *noun* = **dimensions**, amount, bigness, bulk, extent, greatness, hugeness, immensity, largeness, magnitude, mass, measurement(s), proportions, range, vastness, volume

size up *verb Informal* = **assess**, appraise, evaluate, eye up, get (something) taped (*Brit. informal*), get the measure of, take stock of

sizzle *verb* = **hiss**, crackle, frizzle, fry, spit, sputter

skedaddle *verb Informal* = **run away**, abscond, beat a hasty retreat, bolt, decamp, disappear, do a bunk (*Brit. slang*), flee, hop it (*Brit. slang*), scarper (*Brit. slang*), scoot, scram (*informal*)

skeletal *adjective* = **emaciated**, cadaverous, fleshless, gaunt, hollow-cheeked, lantern-jawed, skin-and-bone (*informal*), wasted

skeleton *noun* = **framework**, bare bones, bones, draft, frame, outline, sketch, structure

sketch *noun* 1 = **drawing**, delineation, design, draft, outline, plan, skeleton ♦ *verb* 2 = **draw**, block out, delineate, depict, draft, outline, paint, plot, portray, represent, rough out

sketchily *adverb* = **incompletely**, cursorily, hastily, imperfectly, patchily, perfunctorily, roughly

sketchy *adjective* = **incomplete**, cobbled together, crude, cursory, inadequate, perfunctory, rough, scrappy, skimpy, slight, superficial, unfinished, vague
➤ **Antonyms**
complete, detailed, full, thorough

skewwhiff *adjective Brit. informal*
= **crooked**, askew, aslant, cockeyed (*informal*), out of true, squint (*informal*), tilted

skilful *adjective* = **expert**, able, accomplished, adept, adroit, apt, clever, competent, dexterous, experienced, handy, masterly, practised, professional, proficient, quick, ready, skilled, trained
➤ **Antonyms**
amateurish, awkward, bungling, cack-handed, clumsy, cowboy (*informal*), ham-fisted, incompetent, inept, inexperienced, inexpert, maladroit, slapdash, unaccomplished, unqualified, unskilful, unskilled

skill *noun* = **expertise**, ability, accomplishment, adroitness, aptitude, art, cleverness, competence, craft, dexterity, experience, expertness, facility, finesse, handiness, ingenuity, intelligence, knack, proficiency, quickness, readiness, skilfulness, talent, technique
➤ **Antonyms**
awkwardness, brute force, cack-handedness, clumsiness, gaucheness, ham-fistedness, inability, incompetence, ineptitude, inexperience, lack of finesse, maladroitness, unhandiness

skilled *adjective* = **expert**, able, accomplished, a dab hand at (*Brit. informal*), experienced, masterly, practised, professional, proficient, skilful, trained
➤ **Antonyms**
amateurish, cowboy (*informal*), inexperienced, inexpert, unprofessional, unqualified, unskilled, untalented, untrained

skim *verb* 1 = **separate**, cream 2 = **glide**, brush, coast, dart, float, fly, sail, soar 3 *usually with* **through** = **scan**, glance, run one's eye over, skip (*informal*), thumb *or* leaf through

skimp *verb* = **stint**, be mean with, be niggardly, be sparing with, cut corners, pinch, scamp, scant, scrimp, tighten one's belt
➤ **Antonyms**
act as if one had money to burn, be extravagant, be generous with, be prodigal, blow (*slang*), fritter away, lavish, overspend, splurge, squander, throw money away

skimpy *adjective* = **inadequate**, exiguous, insufficient, meagre, miserly, niggardly, scant, scanty, short, sparse, thin, tight

skin *noun* 1 = **hide**, fell, integument, pelt 2 = **coating**, casing, crust, film, husk, membrane, outside, peel, rind 3 **by the skin of one's teeth** = **narrowly**, by a hair's-breadth, by a narrow margin, by a whisker (*informal*), only just **4 get under one's skin** *Informal* = **annoy**, aggravate (*informal*), get in one's hair (*informal*), get on one's nerves (*informal*), grate on, irk, irritate, needle (*informal*), nettle, piss one off (*taboo slang*), rub up the wrong way ◆ *verb* **5** = **peel**, abrade, bark, excoriate, flay, graze, scrape

skin-deep *adjective* = **superficial**, artificial, external, meaningless, on the surface, shallow, surface

skinflint *noun* = **miser**, meanie *or* meany (*informal, chiefly Brit.*), niggard, penny-pincher (*informal*), Scrooge, tightwad (*U.S. & Canad. slang*)

skinny *adjective* = **thin**, emaciated, lean, scraggy, scrawny, skeletal, skin-and-bone (*informal*), undernourished
➤ **Antonyms**
beefy (*informal*), fat, fleshy, heavy, obese, plump, podgy, portly, stout, tubby

skip *verb* **1** = **hop**, bob, bounce, caper, cavort, dance, flit, frisk, gambol, prance, trip **2** = **pass over**, eschew, give (something) a miss, leave out, miss out, omit, skim over **3** *Informal* = **miss**, bunk off (*slang*), cut (*informal*), dog it *or* dog off (*dialect*), play truant from, wag (*dialect*)

skirmish *noun* **1** = **fight**, affair, affray (*Law*), battle, brush, clash, combat, conflict, contest, dust-up (*informal*), encounter, engagement, fracas, incident, scrap (*informal*), scrimmage, set-to (*informal*), spat, tussle ◆ *verb* **2** = **fight**, clash, collide, come to blows, scrap (*informal*), tussle

skirt *verb* **1** = **border**, edge, flank, lie alongside **2** *often with* **around** *or* **round** = **avoid**, body-swerve (*Scot.*), bypass, circumvent, detour, evade, steer clear of

skit *noun* = **parody**, burlesque, sketch, spoof (*informal*), takeoff (*informal*), travesty

skittish *adjective* = **lively**, antsy (*informal*), excitable, fickle, fidgety, frivolous, highly strung, jumpy, nervous, playful, restive
➤ **Antonyms**
calm, composed, demure, laid-back, placid, relaxed, sober, staid, steady, unexcitable, unfazed (*informal*), unflappable, unruffled

skive *verb Brit. informal* = **slack**, dodge, idle, malinger, shirk, skulk, swing the lead

skiver *noun Brit. informal* = **slacker**, dodger, idler, loafer, shirker

skulduggery *noun Informal* = **trickery**, double-dealing, duplicity, machinations, shenanigan(s) (*informal*), swindling, underhandedness, unscrupulousness

skulk *verb* **1** = **sneak**, creep, pad, prowl, slink **2** = **lurk**, lie in wait, loiter

sky *noun* **1** = **heavens**, firmament, upper atmosphere, vault of heaven **2 to the skies** = **fulsomely**, excessively, extravagantly, highly, immoderately, inordinately, profusely

slab *noun* = **piece**, chunk, hunk, lump, nugget, portion, slice, wedge, wodge (*Brit. informal*)

slack *adjective* **1** = **loose**, baggy, easy, flaccid, flexible, lax, limp, not taut, relaxed **2** = **negligent**, idle, inactive, inattentive, lax, lazy, neglectful, remiss, slapdash, slipshod, tardy **3** = **slow**, dull, inactive, quiet, slow-moving, sluggish ◆ *noun* **4** = **room**, excess, give (*informal*), leeway, looseness, play ◆ *verb* **5** = **shirk**, dodge, flag, idle, neglect, relax, skive (*Brit. slang*), slacken
➤ **Antonyms**
adjective ≠**loose**: inflexible, rigid, stiff, strained, stretched, taut, tight
≠**negligent**: concerned, diligent, exacting, hard, hard-working, meticulous, stern, strict ≠**slow**: active, bustling, busy, fast-moving, hectic

slacken *verb, often with* **off** = **lessen**, abate, decrease, diminish, drop off, ease (off), let up, loosen, moderate, reduce, relax, release, slack off, slow down

slacker *noun* = **layabout**, dodger, good-for-nothing, idler, loafer, passenger, shirker, skiver (*Brit. slang*)

slag *verb Slang, often with* **off** = **criticize**, abuse, berate, deride, insult, malign, mock, slam, slander, slang, slate

slake *verb* = **satisfy**, assuage, gratify, quench, sate, satiate

slam *verb* **1** = **bang**, crash, smash, thump **2** = **throw**, dash, fling, hurl **3** *Slang* = **criticize**, attack, blast, lambast(e), pan (*informal*), pillory, shoot down (*informal*), slate (*informal*), tear into (*informal*), vilify

slander *noun* **1** = **defamation**, aspersion, backbiting, calumny, libel, misrepresentation, muckraking, obloquy, scandal, smear ◆ *verb* **2** = **defame**, backbite, blacken (someone's) name, calumniate, disparage, libel, malign, muckrake, slur, smear, traduce, vilify
➤ **Antonyms**
noun ≠**defamation**: acclaim, acclamation, approval, praise, tribute ◆ *verb* ≠**defame**: acclaim, applaud, approve, compliment, eulogize, laud, praise, sing the praises of

slanderous *adjective* = **defamatory**, abusive, calumnious, damaging, libellous, malicious

slang *verb* = **insult**, abuse, berate, call names, hurl insults at, malign, revile, vilify, vituperate

slanging match *noun* = **quarrel**, altercation, argument, argy-bargy (*Brit. informal*), barney (*informal*), battle of words, row, set-to (*informal*), spat

slant *verb* 1 = **slope**, angle off, bend, bevel, cant, heel, incline, lean, list, shelve, skew, tilt 2 = **bias**, angle, colour, distort, twist, weight ♦ *noun* 3 = **slope**, camber, declination, diagonal, gradient, incline, pitch, rake, ramp, tilt 4 = **bias**, angle, attitude, emphasis, leaning, one-sidedness, point of view, prejudice, viewpoint

slanting *adjective* = **sloping**, angled, aslant, asymmetrical, at an angle, bent, diagonal, inclined, oblique, on the bias, sideways, slanted, slantwise, tilted, tilting

slap *noun* 1 = **smack**, bang, blow, chin (*slang*), clout (*informal*), cuff, spank, swipe, wallop (*informal*), whack 2 **a slap in the face** = **insult**, affront, blow, humiliation, put-down, rebuff, rebuke, rejection, repulse, snub ♦ *verb* 3 = **smack**, bang, clap, clout (*informal*), cuff, hit, spank, strike, swipe, whack 4 *Informal, chiefly Brit.* = **plaster**, daub, plonk, spread ♦ *adverb* 5 *Informal* = **exactly**, bang, directly, plumb (*informal*), precisely, slap-bang (*informal*), smack (*informal*)

slapdash *adjective* = **careless**, clumsy, disorderly, haphazard, hasty, hurried, last-minute, messy, negligent, perfunctory, slipshod, sloppy (*informal*), slovenly, thoughtless, untidy
➤ **Antonyms**
careful, conscientious, fastidious, meticulous, ordered, orderly, painstaking, precise, punctilious, thoughtful, tidy

slaphappy *adjective* = **happy-go-lucky**, casual, haphazard, hit-or-miss (*informal*), irresponsible, nonchalant

slapstick *noun* = **knockabout comedy**, buffoonery, farce, horseplay

slap-up *adjective Brit. informal* = **luxurious**, elaborate, excellent, first-rate, lavish, magnificent, no-expense-spared, princely, splendid, sumptuous, superb

slash *verb* 1 = **cut**, gash, hack, lacerate, rend, rip, score, slit 2 = **reduce**, cut, drop, lower ♦ *noun* 3 = **cut**, gash, incision, laceration, rent, rip, slit

slate *verb Informal, chiefly Brit.* = **criticize**, berate, blame, blast, castigate, censure, haul over the coals (*informal*), lambast(e), lay into (*informal*), pan (*informal*), pitch into (*informal*), rap (someone's) knuckles, rebuke, roast (*informal*), scold, slam (*slang*), take to task, tear into (*informal*),

tear (someone) off a strip (*informal*)

slattern *noun Old-fashioned* = **sloven**, drab (*archaic*), slut, trollop

slatternly *adjective Old-fashioned* = **slovenly**, bedraggled, dirty, sluttish, unclean, unkempt, untidy

slaughter *noun* 1 = **slaying**, blood bath, bloodshed, butchery, carnage, extermination, holocaust, killing, liquidation, massacre, murder ♦ *verb* 2 = **slay**, butcher, destroy, do to death, exterminate, kill, liquidate, massacre, murder, put to the sword 3 *Informal* = **defeat**, blow out of the water (*slang*), crush, hammer (*informal*), lick (*informal*), overwhelm, rout, tank (*slang*), thrash, trounce, vanquish, wipe the floor with (*informal*)

slaughterhouse *noun* = **abattoir**, butchery, shambles

slave *noun* 1 = **servant**, bondservant, bondsman, drudge, scullion (*archaic*), serf, skivvy (*chiefly Brit.*), slavey (*Brit. informal*), varlet (*archaic*), vassal, villein ♦ *verb* 2 = **toil**, drudge, grind (*informal*), slog, sweat, work one's fingers to the bone

slaver *verb* = **drool**, dribble, salivate, slobber

slavery *noun* = **enslavement**, bondage, captivity, serfdom, servitude, subjugation, thraldom, thrall, vassalage
➤ **Antonyms**
emancipation, freedom, liberty, manumission, release

slavish *adjective* 1 = **servile**, abject, base, cringing, despicable, fawning, grovelling, low, mean, menial, obsequious, submissive, sycophantic 2 = **imitative**, conventional, second-hand, unimaginative, uninspired, unoriginal
➤ **Antonyms**
≠**servile**: assertive, domineering, masterful, rebellious, self-willed, wilful
≠**imitative**: creative, imaginative, independent, inventive, original, radical, revolutionary

slay *verb Archaic or literary* = **kill**, annihilate, assassinate, butcher, destroy, dispatch, do away with, do in (*slang*), eliminate, exterminate, massacre, mow down, murder, slaughter

sleaze *noun Informal* = **corruption**, bribery, crookedness (*informal*), dishonesty, extortion, fiddling (*informal*), fraud, shady dealings (*informal*), unscrupulousness, venality

sleazy *adjective* = **sordid**, crummy, disreputable, low, run-down, seedy, squalid, tacky (*informal*)

sleek *adjective* = **glossy**, lustrous, shiny, smooth, well-fed, well-groomed
➤ **Antonyms**
badly groomed, bedraggled, dishevelled, frowzy, ill-nourished, in poor condition, ratty (*Brit. & N.Z. informal*), rough, shaggy, sloppy, slovenly, unkempt

sleep *noun* **1** = **slumber(s)**, beauty sleep (*informal*), dormancy, doze, forty winks (*informal*), hibernation, kip (*Brit. slang*), nap, repose, rest, shuteye (*slang*), siesta, snooze (*informal*), zizz (*Brit. informal*) ♦ *verb* **2** = **slumber**, be in the land of Nod, catnap, doze, drop off (*informal*), drowse, go out like a light, hibernate, kip (*Brit. slang*), nod off (*informal*), snooze (*informal*), snore, take a nap, take forty winks (*informal*), zizz (*Brit. informal*)

sleepless *adjective* **1** = **wakeful**, disturbed, insomniac, restless, unsleeping **2** *Chiefly poetic* = **alert**, unsleeping, vigilant, watchful, wide awake

sleeplessness *noun* = **insomnia**, wakefulness

sleepwalker *noun* = **somnambulist**, noctambulist

sleepwalking *noun* = **somnambulism**, noctambulation, noctambulism, somnambulation

sleepy *adjective* **1** = **drowsy**, dull, heavy, inactive, lethargic, sluggish, somnolent, torpid **2** = **quiet**, dull, hypnotic, inactive, sleep-inducing, slow, somnolent, soporific
➤ **Antonyms**
≠**drowsy**: active, alert, animated, awake, boisterous, energetic, full of beans (*informal*), lively, wakeful, wide-awake ≠**quiet**: active, bustling, busy, lively, thriving

sleight of hand *noun* = **dexterity**, adroitness, legerdemain, manipulation, prestidigitation, skill

slender *adjective* **1** = **slim**, lean, narrow, slight, svelte, sylphlike, willowy **2** = **faint**, feeble, flimsy, fragile, poor, remote, slight, slim, tenuous, thin, weak **3** = **meagre**, inadequate, inconsiderable, insufficient, little, scant, scanty, small, spare
➤ **Antonyms**
≠**slim**: bulky, chubby, fat, heavy, large, podgy, stout, tubby, well-built ≠**faint**: good, solid, strong ≠**meagre**: ample, appreciable, considerable, generous, large, substantial

sleuth *noun Informal* = **detective**, dick (*slang, chiefly U.S.*), gumshoe (*U.S. slang*), private eye (*informal*), (private) investigator, sleuthhound (*informal*)

slice *noun* **1** = **piece**, cut, helping, portion, segment, share, sliver, wedge ♦ *verb* **2**
= **cut**, carve, divide, sever

slick *adjective* **1** = **glib**, meretricious, plausible, polished, smooth, sophistical, specious **2** = **skilful**, adroit, deft, dexterous, dextrous, polished, professional, sharp ♦ *verb* **3** = **smooth**, make glossy, plaster down, sleek, smarm down (*Brit. informal*)
➤ **Antonyms**
adjective ≠**skilful**: amateur, amateurish, clumsy, crude, inexpert, unaccomplished, unpolished, unprofessional, unskilful

slide *verb* **1** = **slip**, coast, glide, skim, slither, toboggan, veer **2 let slide** = **neglect**, forget, gloss over, ignore, let ride, pass over, push to the back of one's mind, turn a blind eye to

slight *adjective* **1** = **small**, feeble, inconsiderable, insignificant, insubstantial, meagre, measly, minor, modest, negligible, paltry, scanty, superficial, trifling, trivial, unimportant, weak **2** = **slim**, delicate, feeble, fragile, lightly-built, small, spare ♦ *verb* **3** = **snub**, affront, cold-shoulder, despise, disdain, disparage, give offence *or* umbrage to, ignore, insult, neglect, put down, scorn, show disrespect for, treat with contempt ♦ *noun* **4** = **insult**, affront, discourtesy, disdain, disregard, disrespect, inattention, indifference, neglect, rebuff, slap in the face (*informal*), snub, (the) cold shoulder
➤ **Antonyms**
adjective ≠**small**: appreciable, considerable, great, heavy, important, large, noticeable, obvious, significant, substantial ≠**slim**: muscular, solid, strong, sturdy, well-built ♦ *verb* ≠**snub**: compliment, flatter, praise, speak well of, treat considerately ♦ *noun* ≠**insult**: compliment, flattery, praise

slightly *adverb* = **a little**, marginally, on a small scale, somewhat, to some extent *or* degree

slim *adjective* **1** = **slender**, lean, narrow, slight, svelte, sylphlike, thin, trim **2** = **slight**, faint, poor, remote, slender ♦ *verb* **3** = **lose weight**, diet, reduce, slenderize (*chiefly U.S.*)
➤ **Antonyms**
adjective ≠**slender**: broad, bulky, chubby, fat, heavy, muscular, obese, overweight, sturdy, tubby, well-built, wide ≠**slight**: good, strong ♦ *verb* ≠**lose weight**: build oneself up, put on weight

slimy *adjective* **1** = **viscous**, clammy, gloopy (*informal*), glutinous, miry, mucous, muddy, oozy **2** *Chiefly Brit.* = **obsequious**, creeping, grovelling, oily, servile, smarmy (*Brit. informal*), soapy (*slang*), sycophantic, toadying, unctuous

sling verb 1 Informal = **throw**, cast, chuck (informal), fling, heave, hurl, lob (informal), shy, toss 2 = **hang**, dangle, suspend, swing

slink verb = **creep**, prowl, pussyfoot (informal), skulk, slip, sneak, steal

slinky adjective = **figure-hugging**, clinging, close-fitting, sinuous, skintight, sleek

slip¹ verb 1 = **fall**, lose one's balance, miss or lose one's footing, skid, trip (over) 2 = **slide**, glide, skate, slither 3 = **sneak**, conceal, creep, hide, steal 4 = **get away**, break away from, break free from, disappear, escape, get clear of 5 sometimes with **up** = **make a mistake**, blunder, boob (Brit. slang), drop a brick or clanger (informal), err, go wrong, miscalculate, misjudge, mistake 6 **let slip** = **give away**, blurt out, come out with (informal), disclose, divulge, leak, let out (informal), let the cat out of the bag, reveal ♦ noun 7 = **mistake**, bloomer (Brit. informal), blunder, boob (Brit. slang), error, failure, fault, faux pas, indiscretion, lapse, omission, oversight, slip of the tongue, slip-up (informal) 8 **give (someone) the slip** = **escape from**, dodge, elude, evade, get away from, lose (someone), outwit, shake (someone) off

slip² noun 1 = **strip**, piece, sliver 2 = **cutting**, offshoot, runner, scion, shoot, sprig, sprout

slippery adjective 1 = **smooth**, glassy, greasy, icy, perilous, slippy (informal or dialect), unsafe, unstable, unsteady 2 = **untrustworthy**, crafty, cunning, devious, dishonest, duplicitous, evasive, false, foxy, shifty, sneaky, treacherous, tricky, two-faced, unpredictable, unreliable

slipshod adjective = **careless**, casual, loose, slapdash, sloppy (informal), slovenly, untidy

slit noun 1 = **cut**, fissure, gash, incision, opening, rent, split, tear ♦ verb 2 = **cut (open)**, gash, impale, knife, lance, pierce, rip, slash, split open

slither verb = **slide**, glide, skitter, slink, slip, snake, undulate

sliver noun = **shred**, flake, fragment, paring, shaving, slip, splinter

slob noun Informal = **layabout**, couch potato (slang), good-for-nothing, idler, loafer, lounger

slobber verb = **drool**, dribble, drivel, salivate, slaver, water at the mouth

slobbish adjective = **messy**, slatternly, sloppy (informal), slovenly, unclean, unkempt, untidy

slog verb 1 = **work**, apply oneself to, keep one's nose to the grindstone, labour, persevere, plod, plough through, slave, toil, work one's fingers to the bone 2 = **trudge**, tramp, trek 3 = **hit**, hit for six, punch, slosh (Brit. slang), slug, sock (slang), strike, thump, wallop (informal) ♦ noun 4 = **labour**, blood, sweat, and tears (informal), effort, exertion, struggle 5 = **trudge**, hike, tramp, trek

slogan noun = **catch phrase**, catchword, jingle, motto, rallying cry, tag-line

slop verb = **spill**, overflow, slosh (informal), spatter, splash, splatter

slope noun 1 = **inclination**, brae (Scot.), declination, declivity, descent, downgrade (chiefly U.S.), gradient, incline, ramp, rise, slant, tilt ♦ verb 2 = **slant**, drop away, fall, incline, lean, pitch, rise, tilt 3 **slope off** or **away** Informal = **slink away**, creep away, make oneself scarce, skulk, slip away, steal

sloping adjective = **slanting**, atilt, bevelled, inclined, inclining, leaning, oblique

sloppy adjective 1 Informal = **careless**, amateurish, clumsy, hit-or-miss (informal), inattentive, messy, slipshod, slovenly, unkempt, untidy, weak 2 Informal = **sentimental**, gushing, icky (informal), mawkish, mushy (informal), overemotional, slushy (informal), soppy (Brit. informal) 3 = **wet**, sludgy, slushy, splashy, watery

slosh verb Informal 1 = **pour**, shower, slap, spray 2 = **splash**, flounder, slop, wade

slot noun 1 = **opening**, aperture, channel, groove, hole, slit, vent 2 Informal = **place**, niche, opening, position, space, time, vacancy ♦ verb 3 = **fit in**, adjust, assign, fit, insert, pigeonhole

sloth noun = **laziness**, idleness, inactivity, indolence, inertia, slackness, slothfulness, sluggishness, torpor

slothful adjective Formal = **lazy**, good-for-nothing, idle, inactive, indolent, inert, skiving (Brit. slang), slack, workshy

slouch verb = **slump**, droop, loll, stoop

slovenly adjective 1 = **untidy**, disorderly, slatternly, unkempt 2 = **careless**, heedless, loose, negligent, slack, slapdash, slipshod, sloppy (informal)
➤ **Antonyms**
≠**untidy**: clean, meticulous, neat, orderly, shipshape, smart, soigné or soignée, tidy, trim, well-groomed ≠**careless**: careful, conscientious, disciplined, methodical, meticulous, well-ordered

slow adjective 1 = **prolonged**, gradual, lingering, long-drawn-out, protracted, time-consuming 2 = **unhurried**, creeping, dawdling, deliberate, easy, lackadaisical, laggard, lagging, lazy, leaden, leisurely,

loitering, measured, plodding, ponderous, slow-moving, sluggardly, sluggish **3 = late**, backward, behind, behindhand, delayed, dilatory, long-delayed, tardy, unpunctual **4 = stupid**, bovine, braindead (*informal*), dense, dim, dozy (*Brit. informal*), dull, dull-witted, dumb (*informal*), obtuse, retarded, slow on the uptake (*informal*), slow-witted, thick, unresponsive **5 = dull**, boring, conservative, dead, dead-and-alive (*Brit.*), inactive, quiet, slack, sleepy, sluggish, stagnant, tame, tedious, uneventful, uninteresting, unproductive, unprogressive **6 slow to = unwilling to**, averse to, disinclined to, hesitant to, indisposed to, loath to, reluctant to ♦ *verb* **7** *often with* **up** *or* **down = reduce speed**, brake, check, curb, decelerate, delay, detain, handicap, hold up, lag, rein in, relax, restrict, retard, slacken (off)
➤ **Antonyms**
adjective ≠ **unhurried**: brisk, eager, fast, hectic, hurried, precipitate, prompt, quick, quickie (*informal*), quick-moving, sharp, speedy, swift ≠ **stupid**: bright, clever, intelligent, perceptive, quick, quick-witted, sharp, smart ≠ **dull**: action-packed, animated, exciting, interesting, lively, stimulating ♦ *verb* ≠ **reduce speed**: accelerate, advance, aid, boost, help, pick up speed, quicken, speed up

slowly *adverb* **= gradually**, at a snail's pace, at one's leisure, by degrees, in one's own (good) time, leisurely, ploddingly, steadily, taking one's time, unhurriedly

sludge *noun* **= sediment**, dregs, gloop (*informal*), mire, muck, mud, ooze, residue, silt, slime, slop, slush

sluggish *adjective* **= inactive**, dull, heavy, indolent, inert, lethargic, lifeless, listless, slothful, slow, slow-moving, torpid, unresponsive
➤ **Antonyms**
alive and kicking, animated, brisk, dynamic, energetic, enthusiastic, fast, full of beans (*informal*), full of life, industrious, lively, swift, vigorous

sluggishness *noun* **= inactivity**, apathy, drowsiness, dullness, heaviness, indolence, inertia, languor, lassitude, lethargy, listlessness, slothfulness, somnolence, stagnation, torpor

sluice *verb* **1 = drain**, flush **2 = wash out**, cleanse, drench, irrigate, wash down

slum *noun* **= hovel**, ghetto

slumber *verb* **= sleep**, be inactive, doze, drowse, kip (*Brit. slang*), lie dormant, nap, repose, snooze (*informal*), zizz (*Brit. informal*)

slump *verb* **1 = fall**, collapse, crash, decline,

deteriorate, fall off, go downhill (*informal*), plummet, plunge, sink, slip **2 = sag**, bend, droop, hunch, loll, slouch ♦ *noun* **3 = fall**, collapse, crash, decline, depreciation, downturn, drop, failure, falling-off, lapse, low, reverse, stagnation, trough **4 = recession**, depression
➤ **Antonyms**
verb ≠ **fall**: advance, boom, develop, expand, flourish, grow, increase, prosper, thrive ♦ *noun* ≠ **fall**: advance, boom, boost, development, expansion, gain, growth, improvement, increase, upsurge, upswing, upturn

slur *noun* **= insult**, affront, aspersion, calumny, discredit, disgrace, innuendo, insinuation, reproach, smear, stain, stigma

slut *noun Offensive* **= tart**, drab (*archaic*), scrubber (*Brit. & Austral. slang*), slag (*Brit. slang*), slapper (*Brit. slang*), slattern, sloven, trollop

sluttish *adjective* **= promiscuous**, coarse, dissipated, immoral, tarty (*informal*), trollopy, whorish

sly *adjective* **1 = cunning**, artful, astute, clever, conniving, covert, crafty, devious, foxy, furtive, guileful, insidious, scheming, secret, shifty, stealthy, subtle, underhand, wily **2 = roguish**, arch, impish, knowing, mischievous ♦ *noun* **3 on the sly = secretly**, behind (someone's) back, covertly, like a thief in the night, on the q.t. (*informal*), on the quiet, privately, surreptitiously, underhandedly
➤ **Antonyms**
adjective ≠ **cunning**: above-board, artless, direct, frank, guileless, honest, ingenuous, open, straightforward, trustworthy

smack *verb* **1 = slap**, box, clap, cuff, hit, pat, sock (*slang*), spank, strike, swipe, tap ♦ *noun* **2 = slap**, blow, crack, swipe **smack in the eye** *Informal, chiefly Brit.* **= snub**, rebuff, slap in the face ♦ *adverb* **4** *Informal* **= directly**, exactly, plumb, point-blank, precisely, right, slap (*informal*), squarely, straight

smack of *verb* **1 = smell of**, be redolent of, reek of **2 = be suggestive** *or* **indicative of**, bear the stamp of, betoken, have all the hallmarks of, suggest

small *adjective* **1 = little**, diminutive, immature, Lilliputian, mini, miniature, minute, petite, pint-sized (*informal*), pocket-sized, puny, pygmy *or* pigmy, slight, teeny, teeny-weeny, tiny, undersized, wee, young **2 = meagre**, inadequate, inconsiderable, insufficient, limited, measly, scant, scanty **3 = unimportant**, insignificant, lesser, minor, negligible, paltry, petty, trifling, trivial **4**

= **petty**, base, grudging, illiberal, mean, narrow **5** = **modest**, humble, small-scale, unpretentious **6 make (someone) feel small** = **humiliate**, disconcert, humble, make (someone) look foolish, mortify, put down (*slang*), show up (*informal*), take down a peg or two (*informal*)
➤ **Antonyms**
≠**little**: big, colossal, enormous, great, huge, immense, massive, mega (*slang*), sizable *or* sizeable, vast ≠**meagre**: ample, considerable, generous, substantial ≠**unimportant**: appreciable, important, major, powerful, serious, significant, urgent, vital, weighty ≠**modest**: grand, large-scale

small-minded *adjective* = **petty**, bigoted, grudging, intolerant, mean, narrow-minded, ungenerous
➤ **Antonyms**
broad-minded, far-sighted, generous, liberal, open, open-minded, tolerant, unbigoted

small-time *adjective* = **minor**, insignificant, no-account (*U.S. informal*), of no account, of no consequence, petty, piddling (*informal*), unimportant

smarmy *adjective Informal* = **obsequious**, bootlicking (*informal*), crawling, fawning, fulsome, greasy, ingratiating, oily, servile, slimy, smooth, soapy (*slang*), suave, sycophantic, toadying, unctuous

smart *adjective* **1** = **chic**, elegant, fashionable, fine, modish, natty (*informal*), neat, snappy, spruce, stylish, trendy (*Brit. informal*), trim, well turned-out **2** = **clever**, acute, adept, agile, apt, astute, bright, brisk, canny, ingenious, intelligent, keen, nimble, quick, quick-witted, ready, sharp, shrewd **3** = **impertinent**, nimble-witted, pointed, ready, saucy, smart-alecky (*informal*), witty **4** = **brisk**, cracking (*informal*), jaunty, lively, quick, spirited, vigorous **5** = **stinging**, hard, keen, painful, piercing, resounding, sharp ♦ *verb* **6** = **sting**, burn, hurt, pain, throb, tingle ♦ *noun* **7** = **sting**, burning sensation, pain, pang, smarting, soreness
➤ **Antonyms**
adjective ≠**chic**: dowdy, dull, fogeyish, naff (*Brit. slang*), old-fashioned, outmoded, out-of-date, passé, scruffy, sloppy, uncool, unfashionable, untrendy (*Brit. informal*) ≠**clever**: daft (*informal*), dense, dim-witted (*informal*), dull, dumb (*informal*), dumb-ass (*slang*), foolish, idiotic, moronic, slow, stupid, thick, unintelligent

smart aleck *noun Informal* = **know-all** (*informal*), clever-clogs (*informal*), clever Dick (*informal*), smartarse (*slang*), smarty

boots (*informal*), smarty pants (*informal*), wise guy (*informal*)

smarten *verb* = **tidy**, beautify, groom, put in order, put to rights, spruce up

smash *verb* **1** = **break**, crush, demolish, disintegrate, pulverize, shatter, shiver **2** = **collide**, crash **3** = **destroy**, defeat, lay waste, overthrow, ruin, total (*slang*), trash (*slang*), wreck ♦ *noun* **4** = **destruction**, collapse, defeat, disaster, downfall, failure, ruin, shattering **5** = **collision**, accident, crash, pile-up (*informal*), smash-up (*informal*)

smashing *adjective Informal, chiefly Brit.* = **excellent**, awesome (*slang*), boffo (*slang*), brilliant (*informal*), cracking (*Brit. informal*), crucial (*slang*), def (*slang*), exhilarating, fabulous (*informal*), fantastic (*informal*), first-class, first-rate, great (*informal*), magnificent, marvellous, mean (*slang*), mega (*slang*), out of this world (*informal*), sensational (*informal*), sovereign, stupendous, super (*informal*), superb, superlative, terrific (*informal*), wonderful, world-class
➤ **Antonyms**
abysmal, appalling, average, awful, bad, boring, crap (*slang*), disappointing, disgraceful, disgusting, dreadful, dreary, dull, hideous, horrible, mediocre, no great shakes (*informal*), ordinary, rotten, run-of-the-mill, sickening, terrible, unexciting, uninspired, vile

smattering *noun* = **modicum**, bit, dash, elements, nodding acquaintance, passing acquaintance, rudiments, smatter, sprinkling

smear *verb* **1** = **spread over**, bedaub, coat, cover, daub, plaster, rub on **2** = **dirty**, bedim, besmirch, blur, smirch, smudge, soil, stain, sully **3** = **slander**, besmirch, blacken, calumniate, drag (someone's) name through the mud, malign, vilify ♦ *noun* **4** = **smudge**, blot, blotch, daub, smirch, splotch, streak **5** = **slander**, calumny, defamation, libel, mudslinging, vilification, whispering campaign

smell *verb* **1** = **sniff**, get a whiff of, nose, scent **2** = **stink**, be malodorous, hum (*slang*), pong (*Brit. informal*), reek, stink to high heaven (*informal*) ♦ *noun* **3** = **odour**, aroma, bouquet, fragrance, niff (*Brit. slang*), perfume, scent, whiff **4** = **stink**, fetor, malodour, niff (*Brit. slang*), pong (*Brit. informal*), stench

smelly *adjective* = **stinking**, evil-smelling, fetid, foul, foul-smelling, high, malodorous, niffy (*Brit. slang*), noisome, pongy (*Brit. informal*), putrid, reeking, stinky (*informal*), strong, strong-smelling, whiffy (*Brit. slang*)

smile *noun, verb* = **grin**, beam

smirk *noun* = **smug look**, grin, simper

smitten *adjective* **1** = **afflicted**, beset, laid low, plagued, struck **2** = **infatuated**, beguiled, bewitched, bowled over (*informal*), captivated, charmed, enamoured, swept off one's feet

smoky *adjective* = **black**, begrimed, grey, grimy, hazy, murky, smoke-darkened, sooty

smooth *adjective* **1** = **even**, flat, flush, horizontal, level, plain, plane, unwrinkled **2** = **sleek**, glassy, glossy, mirror-like, polished, shiny, silky, soft, velvety **3** = **easy**, effortless, untroubled, well-ordered **4** = **flowing**, fluent, regular, rhythmic, steady, uniform **5** = **mellow**, agreeable, bland, mild, pleasant, soothing **6** = **suave**, debonair, facile, glib, ingratiating, persuasive, silky, slick, smarmy (*Brit. informal*), unctuous, urbane ◆ *verb* **7** = **flatten**, iron, level, plane, polish, press **8** = **ease**, allay, alleviate, appease, assuage, calm, extenuate, mitigate, mollify, palliate, soften, soothe **9** = **facilitate**, ease, iron out the difficulties of, pave the way
➤ **Antonyms**
adjective ≠**even**: bumpy, irregular, lumpy, rough, uneven ≠**sleek**: abrasive, coarse, jagged, rough, sharp ◆ *verb* ≠**ease**: aggravate, exacerbate, hamper, hinder, intensify, make worse, roughen

smother *verb* **1** = **extinguish**, snuff **2** = **suffocate**, choke, stifle, strangle **3** = **overwhelm**, cocoon, cover, envelop, heap, inundate, shower, surround **4** = **suppress**, conceal, hide, keep back, muffle, repress, stifle

smoulder *verb* = **seethe**, be resentful, boil, burn, fester, fume, rage, simmer

smudge *verb* **1** = **smear**, blacken, blur, daub, dirty, mark, smirch, soil ◆ *noun* **2** = **smear**, blemish, blot, blur, smut, smutch

smug *adjective* = **self-satisfied**, complacent, conceited, holier-than-thou, priggish, self-opinionated, self-righteous, superior

smuggler *noun* = **trafficker**, bootlegger, rum-runner, runner

smutty *adjective* = **obscene**, bawdy, blue, coarse, crude, dirty, filthy, improper, indecent, indelicate, lewd, off colour, pornographic, prurient, racy, raunchy (*U.S. slang*), risqué, salacious, suggestive, vulgar, X-rated (*informal*)

snack *noun* = **light meal**, bite, bite to eat, elevenses (*Brit. informal*), nibble, refreshment(s), titbit

snag *noun* **1** = **difficulty**, catch, complication, disadvantage, downside, drawback, hazard, hitch, inconvenience, obstacle, problem, stumbling block, the rub ◆ *verb* **2** = **catch**, hole, rip, tear

snaky *adjective* **1** = **twisting**, convoluted, serpentine, sinuous, tortuous, twisty **2** = **treacherous**, crafty, insidious, perfidious, sly, venomous

snap *verb* **1** = **break**, come apart, crack, give way, separate **2** = **crackle**, click, pop **3** = **bite at**, bite, catch, grip, nip, seize, snatch **4** = **speak sharply**, bark, fly off the handle at (*informal*), growl, jump down (someone's) throat (*informal*), lash out at, retort, snarl **5 snap one's fingers at** *Informal* = **defy**, cock a snook at (*Brit.*), flout, pay no attention to, scorn **6 snap out of it** *Informal* = **get over**, cheer up, get a grip on oneself, pull oneself together (*informal*), recover ◆ *noun* **7** = **crackle**, pop **8** = **bite**, grab, nip ◆ *adjective* **9** = **instant**, abrupt, immediate, spur-of-the-moment, sudden, unpremeditated

snappy *adjective* **1** = **smart**, chic, dapper, fashionable, modish, natty (*informal*), stylish, trendy (*Brit. informal*), up-to-the-minute, voguish **2** = **irritable**, apt to fly off the handle (*informal*), cross, edgy, impatient, like a bear with a sore head (*informal*), pissed (*taboo slang*), pissed off (*taboo slang*), quick-tempered, ratty (*Brit. & N.Z. informal*), snappish, testy, tetchy, touchy, waspish **3 make it snappy** = **hurry (up)**, be quick, buck up (*informal*), get a move on (*informal*), get one's skates on, look lively, make haste

snap up *verb* = **take advantage of**, avail oneself of, grab, grasp, nab (*informal*), pounce upon, seize, swoop down on

snare *noun* **1** = **trap**, catch, gin, net, noose, pitfall, wire ◆ *verb* **2** = **trap**, catch, entrap, net, seize, wire

snarl[1] *verb* = **growl**, show one's teeth (*of an animal*)

snarl[2] *verb, often with* **up** = **tangle**, complicate, confuse, embroil, enmesh, entangle, entwine, muddle, ravel

snarl-up *noun* = **tangle**, confusion, entanglement, muddle, (traffic) jam

snatch *verb* **1** = **seize**, catch up, clutch, grab, grasp, grip, pluck, pull, take, wrench, wrest ◆ *noun* **2** = **bit**, fragment, part, piece, smattering, snippet, spell

snazzy *adjective Informal* = **stylish**, attractive, dashing, flamboyant, flashy, jazzy (*informal*), showy, smart, sophisticated, swinging (*slang*), with it (*informal*)

sneak *verb* **1** = **slink**, cower, lurk, pad, sidle,

skulk, slip, steal **2** = **slip**, smuggle, spirit **3**
Informal, chiefly Brit. = **inform on**, grass on
(*Brit. slang*), shop (*slang, chiefly Brit.*), sing
(*slang, chiefly U.S.*), spill one's guts (*slang*),
tell on (*informal*), tell tales ♦ *noun* **4**
= **informer**, snake in the grass, telltale
♦ *adjective* **5** = **surprise**, clandestine,
furtive, quick, secret, stealthy

sneaking *adjective* **1** = **nagging**, intuitive,
niggling, persistent, uncomfortable,
worrying **2** = **secret**, hidden, private,
suppressed, unavowed, unconfessed,
undivulged, unexpressed, unvoiced **3**
= **underhand**, contemptible, furtive,
mean, sly, sneaky, surreptitious, two-faced

sneaky *adjective* = **sly**, base, contemptible,
cowardly, deceitful, devious, dishonest,
double-dealing, furtive, low, mean, nasty,
shifty, slippery, unreliable, unscrupulous,
untrustworthy

sneer *noun* **1** = **scorn**, derision, disdain,
gibe, jeer, mockery, ridicule ♦ *verb* **2**
= **scorn**, deride, disdain, gibe, hold in
contempt, hold up to ridicule, jeer, laugh,
look down on, mock, ridicule, scoff, sniff
at, turn up one's nose (*informal*)

snide *or* **snidey** *adjective* = **nasty**, cynical,
disparaging, hurtful, ill-natured,
insinuating, malicious, mean, sarcastic,
scornful, sneering, spiteful, unkind

sniff *verb* = **inhale**, breathe, smell, snuff,
snuffle

sniffy *adjective Informal* = **contemptuous**,
condescending, disdainful, haughty,
scornful, supercilious, superior

snigger *noun, verb* = **laugh**, giggle, smirk,
sneer, snicker, titter

snip *verb* **1** = **cut**, clip, crop, dock, nick, nip
off, shave, trim ♦ *noun* **2** *Informal, chiefly
Brit.* = **bargain**, giveaway, good buy, steal
(*informal*) **3** = **bit**, clipping, fragment,
piece, scrap, shred, snippet

snipe *verb* = **criticize**, bitch, carp,
denigrate, disparage, have a go (at)
(*informal*), jeer, knock (*informal*), put down

snippet *noun* = **piece**, fragment, part,
particle, scrap, shred, snatch

snivel *verb* = **whine**, blubber, cry, girn
(*Scot. & Northern English dialect*), gripe
(*informal*), grizzle (*informal, chiefly Brit.*),
moan, sniffle, snuffle, weep, whimper,
whinge (*informal*)

snob *noun* = **elitist**, highbrow, prig, social
climber

snobbery *noun* = **arrogance**, airs,
condescension, pretension, pride, side
(*Brit. slang*), snobbishness, snootiness
(*informal*), uppishness (*Brit. informal*)

snobbish *adjective* = **superior**, arrogant,

condescending, high and mighty
(*informal*), hoity-toity (*informal*),
patronizing, pretentious, snooty
(*informal*), stuck-up (*informal*),
toffee-nosed (*slang, chiefly Brit.*), uppish
(*Brit. informal*), uppity
➤ **Antonyms**
down to earth, humble, modest, natural,
unassuming, unostentatious,
unpretentious, without airs

snoop *verb* = **pry**, interfere, poke one's
nose in (*informal*), spy

snooper *noun* = **nosy parker** (*informal*),
busybody, meddler, pry, snoop (*informal*),
stickybeak (*Austral. informal*)

snooty *adjective Informal* = **snobbish**, aloof,
condescending, disdainful, haughty, high
and mighty (*informal*), hoity-toity
(*informal*), pretentious, proud, snotty,
stuck-up (*informal*), supercilious, superior,
toffee-nosed (*slang, chiefly Brit*), uppish
(*Brit. informal*), uppity
➤ **Antonyms**
down to earth, humble, modest, natural,
unassuming, unpretentious, without airs

snooze *Informal* ♦ *verb* **1** = **doze**, catnap,
drop off (*informal*), drowse, kip (*Brit.
slang*), nap, nod off (*informal*), take forty
winks (*informal*) ♦ *noun* **2** = **doze**, catnap,
forty winks (*informal*), kip (*Brit. slang*),
nap, siesta

snub *verb* **1** = **insult**, cold-shoulder, cut
(*informal*), cut dead (*informal*), give
(someone) the brush-off (*slang*), give
(someone) the cold shoulder, humble,
humiliate, kick in the teeth (*slang*),
mortify, put down, rebuff, shame, slight
♦ *noun* **2** = **insult**, affront, brush-off
(*slang*), humiliation, put-down, slap in the
face

snug *adjective* **1** = **cosy**, comfortable, comfy
(*informal*), homely, intimate, sheltered,
warm **2** = **close**, compact, neat, trim

snuggle *verb* = **nestle**, cuddle, nuzzle

soak *verb* **1** = **wet**, bathe, damp, drench,
immerse, infuse, marinate (*Cookery*),
moisten, saturate, steep **2** = **penetrate**,
permeate, seep **3 soak up** = **absorb**,
assimilate, drink in, take in *or* up

soaking *adjective* = **soaked**, drenched,
dripping, droukit *or* drookit (*Scot.*), like a
drowned rat, saturated, soaked to the skin,
sodden, sopping, streaming, waterlogged,
wet through, wringing wet

soar *verb* **1** = **ascend**, fly, mount, rise,
tower, wing **2** = **rise**, climb, escalate,
rocket, shoot up
➤ **Antonyms**
descend, dive, drop, fall, nose-dive,
plummet, plunge, swoop

sob verb = **cry**, bawl, blubber, greet (Scot. or archaic), howl, shed tears, snivel, weep

sober adjective 1 = **abstinent**, abstemious, moderate, on the wagon (informal), temperate 2 = **serious**, calm, clear-headed, composed, cool, dispassionate, grave, level-headed, lucid, practical, rational, realistic, reasonable, sedate, solemn, sound, staid, steady, unexcited, unruffled 3 = **plain**, dark, drab, quiet, severe, sombre, subdued ◆ verb 4 usually with **up** = **clear one's head**, come or bring to one's senses
➤ **Antonyms**
adjective ≠**abstinent**: bevvied (dialect), blitzed (slang), blotto (slang), bombed (slang), Brahms and Liszt (slang), drunk, flying (slang), fu' (Scot.), guttered (slang), having had one too many, inebriated, intoxicated, merry (Brit. informal), paralytic (informal), pie-eyed (slang), pissed (taboo slang), plastered, rat-arsed (taboo slang), sloshed (slang), smashed (slang), steamboats (Scot. slang), steaming (slang), tiddly (slang, chiefly Brit.), tight (informal), tipsy, tired and emotional (euphemistic), wasted (slang), wrecked (slang), zonked (slang) ≠**serious**: excessive, frivolous, happy, immoderate, imprudent, injudicious, irrational, lighthearted, sensational, unrealistic ≠**plain**: bright, flamboyant, flashy, garish, gaudy, light ◆ verb ≠**clear one's head**: become intoxicated, get drunk

sobriety noun 1 = **abstinence**, abstemiousness, moderation, nonindulgence, self-restraint, soberness, temperance 2 = **seriousness**, calmness, composure, coolness, gravity, level-headedness, reasonableness, sedateness, solemnity, staidness, steadiness

so-called adjective = **alleged**, ostensible, pretended, professed, self-styled, soi-disant, supposed

sociability noun = **friendliness**, affability, companionability, congeniality, conviviality, cordiality, gregariousness, neighbourliness

sociable adjective = **friendly**, accessible, affable, approachable, companionable, convivial, cordial, familiar, genial, gregarious, neighbourly, outgoing, social, warm
➤ **Antonyms**
antisocial, businesslike, cold, distant, formal, introverted, reclusive, standoffish, stiff, tense, uncommunicative, unfriendly, unsociable, uptight (informal), withdrawn

social adjective 1 = **sociable**, companionable, friendly, gregarious, neighbourly 2 = **communal**, collective, common, community, general, group, organized, public, societal ◆ noun 3 = **get-together** (informal), do (informal), gathering, party

socialize verb = **mix**, be a good mixer, entertain, fraternize, get about or around, get together, go out

society noun 1 = **civilization**, culture, humanity, mankind, people, population, social order, the community, the general public, the public, the world at large 2 = **organization**, association, brotherhood or sisterhood, circle, club, corporation, fellowship, fraternity, group, guild, institute, league, order, union 3 = **upper classes**, beau monde, elite, gentry, high society, polite society, the country set, the nobs (slang), the smart set, the top drawer, upper crust (informal) 4 Old-fashioned = **companionship**, camaraderie, company, fellowship, friendship

sodden adjective = **soaked**, drenched, droukit or drookit (Scot.), marshy, miry, saturated, soggy, sopping, waterlogged

sodomy noun = **anal intercourse**, anal sex, buggery

sofa noun = **couch**, chaise longue, chesterfield, divan, ottoman, settee

soft adjective 1 = **pliable**, bendable, ductile (of metals), elastic, flexible, impressible, malleable, mouldable, plastic, supple, tensile 2 = **yielding**, cushioned, cushiony, doughy, elastic, gelatinous, pulpy, spongy, squashy 3 = **velvety**, downy, feathery, fleecy, furry, rounded, silky, smooth 4 = **quiet**, dulcet, gentle, low, mellifluous, mellow, melodious, murmured, muted, soft-toned, soothing, subdued, sweet, understated, whispered 5 = **pale**, bland, light, mellow, pastel, subdued 6 = **dim**, diffuse, dimmed, faint, restful 7 = **mild**, balmy, delicate, temperate 8 = **lenient**, easy-going, indulgent, lax, liberal, overindulgent, permissive, spineless, weak 9 Informal = **feeble-minded**, a bit lacking (informal), daft (informal), foolish, silly, simple, soft in the head (informal) 10 = **out of condition**, effeminate, flabby, flaccid, limp, namby-pamby, out of training, overindulged, pampered, podgy, weak 11 Informal = **easy**, comfortable, cushy (informal), easy-peasy (slang), undemanding 12 = **kind**, compassionate, gentle, pitying, sensitive, sentimental, sympathetic, tender, tenderhearted, touchy-feely (informal)
➤ **Antonyms**
≠**pliable**, **yielding**: firm, hard, inflexible, rigid, solid, stiff, tough, unyielding

≠**velvety**: abrasive, coarse, grating, hard, rough ≠**quiet**: harsh, loud, noisy, strident ≠**pale**: bright, garish, gaudy, glaring, harsh ≠**dim**: bright, glaring, harsh ≠**lenient**: austere, harsh, no-nonsense, stern, strict

soften verb = **lessen**, abate, allay, alleviate, appease, assuage, calm, cushion, diminish, ease, lighten, lower, melt, mitigate, moderate, modify, mollify, muffle, palliate, quell, relax, soothe, still, subdue, temper, tone down, turn down

softhearted adjective = **kind**, charitable, compassionate, generous, indulgent, sentimental, sympathetic, tender, tenderhearted, warm-hearted
➤ **Antonyms**
callous, cold, cruel, hard, hard-hearted, heartless, insensitive, uncaring, unkind, unsympathetic

soft-pedal verb = **play down**, tone down

soggy adjective = **sodden**, dripping, heavy, moist, mushy, pulpy, saturated, soaked, sopping, spongy, waterlogged

soil[1] noun 1 = **earth**, clay, dirt, dust, ground, loam 2 = **land**, country, region

soil[2] verb = **dirty**, befoul, begrime, besmirch, defile, foul, muddy, pollute, smear, smirch, spatter, spot, stain, sully, tarnish

sojourn Literary ♦ noun 1 = **stay**, rest, stop, stopover, visit ♦ verb 2 = **stay**, abide, dwell, lodge, reside, rest, stop, tarry

solace noun 1 = **comfort**, alleviation, assuagement, consolation, relief ♦ verb 2 = **comfort**, allay, alleviate, console, mitigate, soften, soothe

soldier noun = **fighter**, enlisted man (U.S.), GI (U.S. informal), man-at-arms, military man, redcoat, serviceman, squaddie or squaddy (Brit. slang), Tommy (Brit. informal), trooper, warrior

sold on adjective Slang = **convinced of**, converted to, hooked on, persuaded of, talked into, won over to

sole adjective = **only**, alone, exclusive, individual, one, one and only, single, singular, solitary

solecism noun Formal = **blunder**, bloomer (Brit. informal), breach of etiquette, faux pas, gaffe, gaucherie, impropriety, incongruity, lapse, mistake

solely adverb = **only**, alone, completely, entirely, exclusively, merely, single-handedly, singly

solemn adjective 1 = **formal**, august, awe-inspiring, ceremonial, ceremonious, dignified, grand, grave, imposing, impressive, majestic, momentous, stately 2

= **serious**, earnest, glum, grave, portentous, sedate, sober, staid, thoughtful
➤ **Antonyms**
≠**formal**: informal, relaxed, unceremonious ≠**serious**: bright, cheerful, chirpy (informal), frivolous, genial, happy, jovial, light-hearted, merry

solemnity noun 1 = **formality**, grandeur, gravitas, impressiveness, momentousness, portentousness 2 = **seriousness**, earnestness, gravity 3 often plural = **ritual**, celebration, ceremonial, ceremony, formalities, observance, proceedings, rite

solemnize verb = **celebrate**, commemorate, honour, keep, observe, perform

solicit verb Formal = **request**, ask, beg, beseech, canvass, crave, entreat, implore, importune, petition, plead for, pray, seek, supplicate

solicitous adjective 1 = **concerned**, anxious, apprehensive, attentive, careful, caring, earnest, troubled, uneasy, worried 2 = **eager**, zealous

solicitude noun = **concern**, anxiety, attentiveness, care, considerateness, consideration, regard, worry

solid adjective 1 = **firm**, compact, concrete, dense, hard, massed 2 = **strong**, stable, sturdy, substantial, unshakable 3 = **reliable**, decent, dependable, law-abiding, level-headed, sensible, serious, sober, trusty, upright, upstanding, worthy 4 = **continuous**, complete, unalloyed, unanimous, unbroken, undivided, uninterrupted, united, unmixed 5 = **sound**, genuine, good, pure, real, reliable
➤ **Antonyms**
≠**firm**: gaseous, hollow, liquid, permeable, unsubstantial ≠**strong**: crumbling, decaying, flimsy, precarious, shaky, unstable, unsteady ≠**reliable**: flighty, irresponsible, unreliable, unsound, unstable, unsteady ≠**sound**: impure, unreliable, unsound

solidarity noun = **unity**, accord, camaraderie, cohesion, community of interest, concordance, esprit de corps, harmony, like-mindedness, singleness of purpose, soundness, stability, team spirit, unanimity, unification

solidify verb = **harden**, cake, coagulate, cohere, congeal, jell, set

solitary adjective 1 = **unsociable**, cloistered, isolated, reclusive, retired, unsocial 2 = **single**, alone, lone, sole 3 = **lonely**, companionless, friendless, lonesome 4 = **isolated**, desolate, hidden,

out-of-the-way, remote, sequestered, unfrequented, unvisited ♦ *noun* **5** = **hermit**, introvert, loner (*informal*), lone wolf, recluse
➤ **Antonyms**
adjective ≠**unsociable**: companionable, convivial, cordial, gregarious, outgoing, sociable, social ≠**isolated**: bustling, busy, frequented, public, well-frequented
♦ *noun* ≠**hermit**: extrovert, mixer, socialite

solitude *noun* = **isolation**, ivory tower, loneliness, privacy, reclusiveness, retirement, seclusion

solution *noun* **1** = **answer**, clarification, elucidation, explanation, key, resolution, result, solving, unfolding, unravelling **2** *Chemistry* = **mixture**, blend, compound, emulsion, mix, solvent, suspension **3** = **dissolving**, disconnection, dissolution, liquefaction, melting

solve *verb* = **answer**, clarify, clear up, crack, decipher, disentangle, elucidate, explain, get to the bottom of, interpret, resolve, suss (out) (*slang*), unfold, unravel, work out

solvent *adjective* = **financially sound**, in the black, solid, unindebted

sombre *adjective* **1** = **gloomy**, dismal, doleful, funereal, grave, joyless, lugubrious, melancholy, mournful, sad, sepulchral, sober **2** = **dark**, dim, drab, dull, dusky, gloomy, obscure, shadowy, shady, sober
➤ **Antonyms**
≠**gloomy**: bright, cheerful, chirpy (*informal*), effusive, full of beans, genial, happy, lively, sunny, upbeat (*informal*) ≠**dark**: bright, colourful, dazzling, garish, gaudy

somebody *noun* = **celebrity**, big hitter (*informal*), big name, big noise (*informal*), big shot (*informal*), celeb (*informal*), dignitary, heavy hitter (*informal*), heavyweight (*informal*), household name, luminary, megastar (*informal*), name, notable, personage, person of note, public figure, star, superstar, V.I.P.
➤ **Antonyms**
also-ran, cipher, lightweight (*informal*), menial, nobody, nonentity, nothing (*informal*)

someday *adverb* = **eventually**, in the fullness of time, one day, one of these (fine) days, sooner or later, ultimately

somehow *adverb* = **one way or another**, by fair means or foul, by hook or (by) crook, by some means or other, come hell or high water (*informal*), come what may

sometimes *adverb* = **occasionally**, at times, every now and then, every so often, from time to time, now and again, now

and then, off and on, once in a while, on occasion
➤ **Antonyms**
always, consistently, constantly, continually, eternally, ever, everlastingly, evermore, forever, invariably, perpetually, unceasingly, without exception

somnolent *adjective Formal* = **sleepy**, comatose, dozy, drowsy, half-awake, heavy-eyed, nodding off (*informal*), soporific, torpid

song *noun* = **ballad**, air, anthem, canticle, carol, chant, chorus, ditty, hymn, lay, melody, number, pop song, psalm, shanty, strain, tune

song and dance *noun Brit. informal* = **fuss**, ado, commotion, flap (*informal*), pantomime (*informal*), performance (*informal*), stir, to-do

sonorous *adjective* **1** = **rich**, deep, full, loud, resonant, resounding, ringing, rounded **2** = **grandiloquent**, high-flown, high-sounding

soon *adverb* = **before long**, anon (*archaic*), any minute now, in a little while, in a minute, in a short time, in the near future, shortly

soothe *verb* **1** = **calm**, allay, appease, calm down, hush, lull, mitigate, mollify, pacify, quiet, settle, smooth down, soften, still, tranquillize **2** = **relieve**, alleviate, assuage, ease
➤ **Antonyms**
≠**calm**: aggravate (*informal*), agitate, annoy, disquiet, disturb, excite, get on one's nerves (*informal*), hassle (*informal*), inflame, irritate, rouse, upset, vex, worry ≠**relieve**: exacerbate, increase, inflame, irritate, stimulate

soothing *adjective* **1** = **calming**, relaxing, restful **2** = **emollient**, easeful, lenitive, palliative

soothsayer *noun* = **prophet**, augur, diviner, fortune-teller, seer, sibyl

sophisticated *adjective* **1** = **cultured**, cosmopolitan, cultivated, jet-set, refined, urbane, worldly, worldly-wise **2** = **complex**, advanced, complicated, delicate, elaborate, highly-developed, intricate, refined, subtle
➤ **Antonyms**
≠**cultured**: naive, unrefined, unsophisticated, unworldly, wet behind the ears (*informal*) ≠**complex**: basic, old-fashioned, plain, primitive, simple, uncomplicated, unrefined, unsophisticated, unsubtle

sophistication *noun* = **savoir-faire**, finesse, poise, *savoir-vivre*, urbanity, worldliness, worldly wisdom

sophistry noun = **fallacy**, casuistry, quibble, sophism

soporific adjective 1 = **sleep-inducing**, hypnotic, sedative, sleepy, somnolent, tranquillizing ♦ noun 2 = **sedative**, anaesthetic, hypnotic, narcotic, opiate, tranquillizer

soppy adjective Brit. informal = **sentimental**, corny (slang), gushy (informal), icky (informal), lovey-dovey, mawkish, overemotional, schmaltzy (slang), silly, slushy (informal), soft (informal), weepy (informal)

sorcerer or **sorceress** noun = **magician**, enchanter, mage (archaic), magus, necromancer, warlock, witch, wizard

sorcery noun = **black magic**, black art, charm, divination, enchantment, incantation, magic, necromancy, spell, witchcraft, witchery, wizardry

sordid adjective 1 = **dirty**, filthy, foul, mean, seamy, seedy, sleazy, slovenly, slummy, squalid, unclean, wretched 2 = **base**, debauched, degenerate, degraded, despicable, disreputable, low, shabby, shameful, vicious, vile 3 = **mercenary**, avaricious, covetous, grasping, selfish, self-seeking
➤ **Antonyms**
≠**dirty**: clean, fresh, pure, spotless, squeaky-clean, unblemished, undefiled, unsullied ≠**base**: blameless, decent, honourable, noble, pure, upright

sore adjective 1 = **painful**, angry, burning, chafed, inflamed, irritated, raw, reddened, sensitive, smarting, tender 2 = **annoying**, distressing, grievous, harrowing, severe, sharp, troublesome 3 = **annoyed**, aggrieved, angry, cross, grieved, hurt, irked, irritated, pained, peeved (informal), pissed (taboo slang), pissed (off) (taboo slang), resentful, stung, upset, vexed 4 Literary = **urgent**, acute, critical, desperate, dire, extreme, pressing ♦ noun 5 = **abscess**, boil, chafe, gathering, inflammation, ulcer

sorrow noun 1 = **grief**, affliction, anguish, distress, heartache, heartbreak, misery, mourning, regret, sadness, unhappiness, woe 2 = **affliction**, blow, bummer (slang), hardship, misfortune, trial, tribulation, trouble, woe, worry ♦ verb 3 = **grieve**, agonize, bemoan, be sad, bewail, eat one's heart out, lament, moan, mourn, weep
➤ **Antonyms**
noun ≠**grief**: bliss, delight, elation, exaltation, exultation, gladness, happiness, joy, pleasure ≠**affliction**: good fortune, lucky break ♦ verb ≠**grieve**: celebrate,

delight, exult, jump for joy, rejoice, revel

sorrowful adjective = **sad**, affecting, dejected, depressed, disconsolate, dismal, distressing, doleful, down in the dumps (informal), grieving, harrowing, heartbroken, heart-rending, heavy-hearted, lugubrious, melancholy, miserable, mournful, painful, piteous, rueful, sick at heart, sorry, tearful, unhappy, woebegone, woeful, wretched

sorry adjective 1 = **regretful**, apologetic, conscience-stricken, contrite, guilt-ridden, penitent, remorseful, repentant, self-reproachful, shamefaced 2 = **sympathetic**, commiserative, compassionate, full of pity, moved, pitying 3 = **sad**, disconsolate, distressed, grieved, melancholy, mournful, sorrowful, unhappy 4 = **wretched**, abject, base, deplorable, dismal, distressing, mean, miserable, paltry, pathetic, piteous, pitiable, pitiful, poor, sad, shabby, vile
➤ **Antonyms**
≠**regretful**: impenitent, not contrite, shameless, unapologetic, unashamed, unremorseful, unrepentant ≠**sympathetic**: heartless, indifferent, uncompassionate, unconcerned, unmoved, unpitying, unsympathetic ≠**sad**: cheerful, delighted, elated, happy, joyful

sort noun 1 = **kind**, brand, breed, category, character, class, denomination, description, family, genus, group, ilk, make, nature, order, quality, race, species, stamp, style, type, variety 2 out of sorts = **in low spirits**, crotchety, down in the dumps (informal), down in the mouth (informal), grouchy (informal), not up to par, not up to snuff (informal), off colour, poorly (informal), under the weather (informal) 3 sort of = **rather**, as it were, in part, moderately, reasonably, slightly, somewhat, to some extent ♦ verb 4 = **arrange**, catalogue, categorize, choose, class, classify, distribute, divide, file, grade, group, order, put in order, rank, select, separate, systematize, tabulate

sort out verb 1 = **resolve**, clarify, clear up, put or get straight 2 = **separate**, pick out, put on one side, segregate, select, sift 3 = **organize**, tidy up

so-so adjective Informal = **average**, adequate, fair, indifferent, middling, moderate, not bad (informal), O.K. or okay (informal), ordinary, passable, run-of-the-mill, tolerable, undistinguished

soul noun 1 = **spirit**, animating principle, essence, intellect, life, mind, psyche, reason, vital force 2 = **essence**, embodiment, epitome, incarnation,

personification, quintessence, type **3**
= **feeling**, animation, ardour, courage,
energy, fervour, force, vitality, vivacity **4**
= **person**, being, body, creature,
individual, man or woman, mortal

soul-destroying adjective
= **mind-numbing**, dreary, dull, humdrum,
monotonous, tedious, tiresome, treadmill,
unvarying, wearisome

soulful adjective = **expressive**, eloquent,
heartfelt, meaningful, mournful, moving,
profound, sensitive

soulless adjective **1** = **spiritless**, dead,
lifeless, mechanical, soul-destroying,
uninteresting **2** = **unfeeling**, callous, cold,
cruel, harsh, inhuman, unkind,
unsympathetic

sound[1] noun **1** = **noise**, din, report,
resonance, reverberation, tone, voice **2**
= **impression**, drift, idea, implication(s),
look, tenor ♦ verb **3** = **resound**, echo,
resonate, reverberate **4** = **seem**, appear,
give the impression of, look, strike one as
being **5** = **pronounce**, announce,
articulate, declare, enunciate, express,
signal, utter

sound[2] adjective **1** = **perfect**, complete,
entire, firm, fit, hale, hale and hearty,
healthy, intact, robust, solid, sturdy,
substantial, undamaged, unhurt,
unimpaired, uninjured, well-constructed,
whole **2** = **safe**, established, proven,
recognized, reliable, reputable, secure,
solid, solvent, stable, tried-and-true **3**
= **sensible**, correct, fair, just, level-headed,
logical, proper, prudent, rational,
reasonable, reliable, responsible, right,
right-thinking, true, trustworthy, valid,
well-founded, well-grounded, wise **4**
= **deep**, peaceful, unbroken, undisturbed,
untroubled
➤ **Antonyms**
≠**perfect**: ailing, damaged, frail, shaky,
sketchy, superficial, unbalanced, unstable,
weak ≠**safe**: unreliable, unsound, unstable
≠**sensible**: fallacious, faulty, flawed,
irrational, irresponsible, specious ≠**deep**:
broken, fitful, shallow, troubled

sound[3] verb **1** = **fathom**, plumb, probe **2**
= **examine**, inspect, investigate, test

sound[4] noun = **channel**, passage, strait

sound out verb = **probe**, canvass,
examine, pump, put out feelers to,
question, see how the land lies, test the
water

sour adjective **1** = **sharp**, acerb, acetic, acid,
bitter, pungent, tart, unpleasant **2** = **gone
off**, curdled, fermented, gone bad, rancid,
turned, unsavoury, unwholesome **3**
= **ill-natured**, acrimonious, churlish,
cynical, disagreeable, discontented,
embittered, grouchy (informal), grudging,
ill-tempered, jaundiced, peevish, tart,
ungenerous, waspish ♦ verb **4** = **embitter**,
alienate, disenchant, exacerbate, turn off
(informal)
➤ **Antonyms**
adjective ≠**sharp**: agreeable, bland, mild,
pleasant, savoury, sugary, sweet ≠**gone
off**: fresh, unimpaired, unspoiled
≠**ill-natured**: affable, amiable, congenial,
friendly, genial, good-humoured,
good-natured, good-tempered, pleasant,
warm-hearted ♦ verb ≠**embitter**: enhance,
improve, strengthen

source noun **1** = **origin**, author, beginning,
cause, derivation, fount, fountainhead,
originator, rise, spring, wellspring **2**
= **informant**, authority

sourpuss noun Informal = **killjoy**,
crosspatch (informal), grump (informal),
misery (Brit. informal), prophet of doom

souse verb = **steep**, drench, dunk,
immerse, marinate (Cookery), pickle, soak

souvenir noun = **keepsake**, memento,
relic, reminder, token

sovereign noun **1** = **monarch**, chief,
emperor or empress, king or queen,
potentate, prince or princess, ruler, shah,
supreme ruler, tsar or tsarina ♦ adjective **2**
= **supreme**, absolute, chief, dominant,
imperial, kingly or queenly, monarchal,
paramount, predominant, principal, regal,
royal, ruling, unlimited **3** = **excellent**,
effectual, efficacious, efficient

sovereignty noun = **supreme power**,
ascendancy, domination, kingship,
primacy, supremacy, suzerainty, sway

sow verb = **scatter**, broadcast, disseminate,
implant, inseminate, lodge, plant, seed

space noun **1** = **room**, amplitude, capacity,
elbowroom, expanse, extension, extent,
leeway, margin, play, scope, spaciousness,
volume **2** = **gap**, blank, distance, interval,
lacuna, omission **3** = **time**, duration,
interval, period, span, while

spaceman or **spacewoman** noun
= **astronaut**, cosmonaut

spacious adjective = **roomy**, ample, broad,
capacious, comfortable, commodious,
expansive, extensive, huge, large, sizable
or sizeable, uncrowded, vast
➤ **Antonyms**
close, confined, cramped, crowded,
limited, narrow, poky, restricted, small

spadework noun = **preparation**,
donkey-work, groundwork, labour

span noun **1** = **extent**, amount, distance,
length, reach, spread, stretch **2** = **period**,

duration, spell, term ♦ *verb* 3 = **extend across**, arch across, bridge, cover, cross, link, range over, traverse

spank *verb* = **smack**, belt (*informal*), cuff, give (someone) a hiding (*informal*), slap, slipper (*informal*), wallop (*informal*), whack

spanking *adjective* 1 *Informal* = **smart**, brand-new, fine, gleaming 2 = **fast**, brisk, energetic, lively, quick, smart, snappy, vigorous

spar *verb* = **argue**, bicker, dispute, fall out (*informal*), have a tiff, row, scrap (*informal*), squabble, wrangle

spare *adjective* 1 = **extra**, additional, emergency, free, in excess, in reserve, leftover, odd, over, superfluous, supernumerary, surplus, unoccupied, unused, unwanted 2 = **thin**, gaunt, lank, lean, meagre, slender, slight, slim, wiry 3 **go spare** *Brit. slang* = **become enraged**, become angry, become distraught, become mad (*informal*), become upset, be or get pissed (off) (*taboo slang*), blow one's top (*informal*), do one's nut (*Brit. slang*), go mental (*slang*), go up the wall (*slang*), have or throw a fit (*informal*) ♦ *verb* 4 = **have mercy on**, be merciful to, deal leniently with, go easy on (*informal*), leave, let off (*informal*), pardon, refrain from, release, relieve from, save from 5 = **afford**, allow, dispense with, do without, give, grant, let (someone) have, manage without, part with
➤ **Antonyms**
adjective ≠**extra**: allocated, designated, earmarked, in use, necessary, needed, set aside, spoken for ≠**thin**: corpulent, fat, flabby, fleshy, generous, heavy, large, plump ♦ *verb* ≠**have mercy on**: afflict, condemn, damn, destroy, hurt, punish, show no mercy to

spare time *noun* = **leisure**, free time, odd moments, time on one's hands, time to kill

sparing *adjective* = **economical**, careful, frugal, prudent, saving, thrifty
➤ **Antonyms**
extravagant, lavish, liberal, open-handed, prodigal, spendthrift

spark *noun* 1 = **flicker**, flare, flash, gleam, glint, scintillation, spit 2 = **trace**, atom, hint, jot, scintilla, scrap, vestige ♦ *verb* 3 *often with* **off** = **start**, animate, excite, inspire, kick-start, kindle, precipitate, prod, provoke, rouse, set in motion, set off, stimulate, stir, touch off, trigger (off)

sparkle *verb* 1 = **glitter**, beam, dance, flash, gleam, glint, glisten, glow, scintillate, shimmer, shine, spark, twinkle, wink 2 = **fizz**, bubble, effervesce, fizzle ♦ *noun* 3 = **glitter**, brilliance, dazzle, flash, flicker,

gleam, glint, radiance, spark, twinkle 4 = **vivacity**, animation, brio, dash, élan, gaiety, life, liveliness, panache, spirit, vim (*slang*), vitality, zip (*informal*)

sparse *adjective* = **scattered**, few and far between, meagre, scanty, scarce, sporadic
➤ **Antonyms**
crowded, dense, lavish, lush, luxuriant, numerous, plentiful, thick

spartan *adjective* = **austere**, abstemious, ascetic, bleak, disciplined, extreme, frugal, plain, rigorous, self-denying, severe, stern, strict, stringent

spasm *noun* 1 = **convulsion**, contraction, paroxysm, twitch 2 = **burst**, access, eruption, fit, frenzy, outburst, seizure

spasmodic *adjective* = **sporadic**, convulsive, erratic, fitful, intermittent, irregular, jerky

spat *noun* = **quarrel**, altercation, bicker, contention, controversy, dispute, squabble, tiff

spate *noun* = **flood**, deluge, flow, outpouring, rush, torrent

spatter *verb* = **splash**, bespatter, daub, dirty, scatter, soil, speckle, splodge, spray, sprinkle

speak *verb* 1 = **talk**, articulate, communicate, converse, discourse, enunciate, express, make known, pronounce, say, state, tell, utter, voice 2 = **lecture**, address, argue, declaim, deliver an address, descant, discourse, harangue, hold forth, plead, spout

speaker *noun* = **orator**, lecturer, public speaker, spokesman *or* spokeswoman, spokesperson

speak for *verb* = **represent**, act for *or* on behalf of, appear for

speak up *or* **out** *verb* 1 = **speak one's mind**, have one's say, make one's position plain, sound off, stand up and be counted 2 = **speak loudly**, make oneself heard, say it loud and clear

spearhead *verb* = **lead**, blaze the trail, head, initiate, launch, lead the way, pioneer, set in motion, set off

special *adjective* 1 = **exceptional**, distinguished, especial, extraordinary, important, memorable, momentous, out of the ordinary, significant, uncommon, unique, unusual 2 = **specific**, appropriate, certain, characteristic, distinctive, especial, individual, particular, peculiar, precise, specialized 3 = **particular**, chief, main, major, primary
➤ **Antonyms**
≠**exceptional**: common, everyday, humdrum, mediocre, no great shakes

(*informal*), normal, ordinary, routine, run-of-the-mill, undistinguished, unexceptional, usual ≠**specific**: general, multi-purpose, undistinctive, unspecialized

specialist *noun* = **expert**, authority, buff (*informal*), connoisseur, consultant, guru, hotshot (*informal*), master, professional, whizz (*informal*)

speciality *noun* = **forte**, bag (*slang*), claim to fame, distinctive *or* distinguishing feature, métier, *pièce de résistance,* special, specialty

species *noun* = **kind**, breed, category, class, collection, description, genus, group, sort, type, variety

specific *adjective* **1** = **particular**, characteristic, definite, distinguishing, especial, peculiar, special **2** = **precise**, clear-cut, definite, exact, explicit, express, limited, unambiguous, unequivocal
➤ **Antonyms**
≠**particular**: common, general ≠**precise**: approximate, general, hazy, imprecise, non-specific, uncertain, unclear, vague, woolly

specification *noun* = **requirement**, condition, detail, item, particular, qualification, stipulation

specify *verb* = **state**, be specific about, cite, define, designate, detail, enumerate, indicate, mention, name, spell out, stipulate

specimen *noun* = **sample**, embodiment, example, exemplar, exemplification, exhibit, individual, instance, model, pattern, proof, representative, type

specious *adjective* = **fallacious**, casuistic, deceptive, misleading, plausible, sophistic, sophistical, unsound

speck *noun* **1** = **mark**, blemish, blot, defect, dot, fault, flaw, fleck, mote, speckle, spot, stain **2** = **particle**, atom, bit, dot, grain, iota, jot, mite, modicum, shred, tittle, whit

speckled *adjective* = **flecked**, brindled, dappled, dotted, freckled, mottled, spotted, spotty, sprinkled, stippled

spectacle *noun* **1** = **sight**, curiosity, laughing stock, marvel, phenomenon, scene, wonder **2** = **show**, display, event, exhibition, extravaganza, pageant, parade, performance, sight

spectacular *adjective* **1** = **impressive**, breathtaking, daring, dazzling, dramatic, eye-catching, fantastic (*informal*), grand, magnificent, marked, remarkable, sensational, splendid, staggering, striking, stunning (*informal*) ◆ *noun* **2** = **show**, display, extravaganza, spectacle
➤ **Antonyms**

adjective ≠**impressive**: everyday, modest, ordinary, plain, run-of-the-mill, simple, unimpressive, unostentatious, unspectacular

spectator *noun* = **onlooker**, beholder, bystander, eyewitness, looker-on, observer, viewer, watcher, witness
➤ **Antonyms**
contestant, contributor, partaker, participant, participator, party, player

spectral *adjective* = **ghostly**, insubstantial, phantom, shadowy, supernatural, wraithlike

spectre *noun* = **ghost**, apparition, phantom, presence, shade (*literary*), shadow, spirit, vision, wraith

speculate *verb* **1** = **conjecture**, cogitate, consider, contemplate, deliberate, guess, hypothesize, meditate, muse, scheme, suppose, surmise, theorize, wonder **2** = **gamble**, have a flutter (*informal*), hazard, play the market, risk, take a chance with, venture

speculation *noun* **1** = **conjecture**, consideration, contemplation, deliberation, guess, guesswork, hypothesis, opinion, supposition, surmise, theory **2** = **gamble**, gambling, hazard, risk

speculative *adjective* = **hypothetical**, abstract, academic, conjectural, notional, suppositional, tentative, theoretical

speech *noun* **1** = **communication**, conversation, dialogue, discussion, intercourse, talk **2** = **talk**, address, discourse, disquisition, harangue, homily, lecture, oration, spiel (*informal*) **3** = **language**, articulation, dialect, diction, enunciation, idiom, jargon, lingo (*informal*), parlance, tongue, utterance, voice

speechless *adjective* **1** = **mute**, dumb, inarticulate, lost for words, silent, tongue-tied, wordless **2** = **astounded**, aghast, amazed, dazed, dumbfounded, dumbstruck, shocked, thunderstruck

speed *noun* **1** = **swiftness**, acceleration, celerity, haste, hurry, momentum, pace, quickness, rapidity, rush, velocity ◆ *verb* **2** = **race**, barrel (along) (*informal, chiefly U.S. & Canad.*), belt (along) (*slang*), bomb (along), burn rubber (*informal*), career, expedite, flash, gallop, go hell for leather (*informal*), go like a bat out of hell, go like a bomb (*Brit. & N.Z. informal*), go like the wind, hasten, hurry, lose no time, make haste, press on, quicken, rush, sprint, step on it (*informal*), tear, zoom **3** = **help**, advance, aid, assist, boost, expedite, facilitate, further, impel, promote
➤ **Antonyms**

noun ≠**swiftness**: delay, slowness, sluggishness, tardiness ♦ verb ≠**race**: crawl, creep, dawdle, delay, take one's time, tarry ≠**help**: delay, hamper, hinder, hold up, retard, slow

speed up verb = **accelerate**, gather momentum, get moving, get under way, increase, increase the tempo, put on speed
➤ **Antonyms**
brake, decelerate, reduce speed, rein in, slacken (off), slow down

speedy adjective = **quick**, express, fast, hasty, headlong, hurried, immediate, pdq (slang), precipitate, prompt, quickie (informal), rapid, swift, winged
➤ **Antonyms**
dead slow and stop, delayed, dilatory, late, leisurely, lingering, long-drawn-out, plodding, slow, sluggish, tardy, unhurried, unrushed

spell[1] verb = **indicate**, amount to, augur, herald, imply, mean, point to, portend, presage, promise, signify, suggest

spell[2] noun 1 = **incantation**, abracadabra, charm, conjuration, sorcery, witchery 2 = **enchantment**, allure, bewitchment, fascination, glamour, magic, trance

spell[3] noun = **period**, bout, course, interval, patch, season, stint, stretch, term, time, turn

spellbound adjective = **entranced**, bemused, bewitched, captivated, charmed, enthralled, fascinated, gripped, hooked, mesmerized, possessed, rapt, transfixed, transported, under a spell

spelling noun = **orthography**

spell out verb 1 = **make clear** or **plain**, clarify, elucidate, explicate, make explicit, specify 2 = **puzzle out**, discern, make out

spend verb 1 = **pay out**, disburse, expend, fork out (slang), lay out, shell out (informal), splash out (Brit. informal) 2 = **pass**, fill, occupy, while away 3 = **apply**, bestow, concentrate, devote, employ, exert, invest, lavish, put in, use 4 = **use up**, consume, deplete, dissipate, drain, empty, exhaust, fritter away, run through, squander, waste
➤ **Antonyms**
≠**pay out, use up**: hoard, invest, keep, put aside, put by, save, store

spendthrift noun 1 = **squanderer**, big spender, prodigal, profligate, spender, waster, wastrel ♦ adjective 2 = **wasteful**, extravagant, improvident, prodigal, profligate
➤ **Antonyms**
noun ≠**squanderer**: meanie or meany (informal, chiefly Brit.), miser, penny-pincher (informal), Scrooge,

skinflint, tight-arse (taboo slang), tight-ass (U.S. taboo slang), tightwad (U.S. & Canad. slang) ♦ adjective ≠**wasteful**: careful, economical, frugal, parsimonious, provident, prudent, sparing, thrifty

spent adjective 1 = **used up**, consumed, expended, finished, gone 2 = **exhausted**, all in (slang), burnt out, clapped out (Austral. & N.Z. informal), dead beat (informal), debilitated, done in or up (informal), drained, knackered (slang), played out (informal), prostrate, ready to drop (informal), shattered (informal), tired out, weakened, wearied, weary, whacked (Brit. informal), wiped out (informal), worn out, zonked (informal)

sperm noun 1 = **spermatozoon**, male gamete, reproductive cell 2 = **semen**, come or cum (taboo), seed (archaic or dialect), spermatozoa

spew verb = **vomit**, barf (U.S. slang), chuck (up) (slang, chiefly U.S.), chunder (slang, chiefly Austral.), disgorge, puke (slang), regurgitate, throw up (informal), upchuck (U.S. slang)

sphere noun 1 = **ball**, circle, globe, globule, orb 2 = **field**, capacity, department, domain, function, patch, province, range, realm, scope, territory, turf (U.S. slang), walk of life 3 = **rank**, station, stratum

spherical adjective = **round**, globe-shaped, globular, orbicular, rotund

spice noun 1 = **seasoning**, relish, savour 2 = **excitement**, colour, gusto, kick (informal), pep, piquancy, tang, zap (slang), zest, zing (informal), zip (informal)

spick-and-span adjective = **neat**, clean, immaculate, impeccable, shipshape, spotless, spruce, tidy, trim

spicy adjective 1 = **hot**, aromatic, flavoursome, piquant, pungent, savoury, seasoned, tangy 2 Informal = **scandalous**, hot (informal), improper, indecorous, indelicate, racy, ribald, risqué, sensational, suggestive, titillating

spiel noun = **patter**, pitch, recital, sales patter, sales talk, speech

spike noun 1 = **point**, barb, prong, spine ♦ verb 2 = **impale**, spear, spit, stick

spill verb 1 = **pour**, discharge, disgorge, overflow, scatter, shed, slop over, spill or run over, teem, throw off, upset 2 **spill the beans** Informal = **betray a secret**, blab, give the game away, grass (Brit. slang), inform, let the cat out of the bag, shop (slang, chiefly Brit.), sing (slang, chiefly U.S.), split (slang), squeal (slang), talk out of turn, tattle, tell all ♦ noun 3 Informal = **fall**, accident, cropper (informal), tumble

spin *verb* **1** = **revolve**, birl (*Scot.*), gyrate, pirouette, reel, rotate, turn, twirl, twist, wheel, whirl **2** *As in* **spin a yarn** = **tell**, concoct, develop, invent, narrate, recount, relate, unfold **3** = **reel**, be giddy, be in a whirl, grow dizzy, swim, whirl ♦ *noun* **4** = **revolution**, gyration, roll, twist, whirl **5** *Informal* = **drive**, hurl (*Scot.*), joy ride (*informal*), ride, turn, whirl

spindly *adjective* = **lanky**, attenuated, gangling, gangly, leggy, spidery, spindle-shanked

spine *noun* **1** = **backbone**, spinal column, vertebrae, vertebral column **2** = **barb**, needle, quill, ray, spike, spur

spine-chilling *adjective* = **frightening**, bloodcurdling, eerie, hair-raising, horrifying, scary (*informal*), spooky (*informal*), terrifying

spineless *adjective* = **weak**, boneless, chickenshit (*U.S. slang*), cowardly, faint-hearted, feeble, gutless (*informal*), inadequate, ineffective, irresolute, lily-livered, pathetic, soft, submissive, vacillating, weak-kneed (*informal*), weak-willed, without a will of one's own, yellow (*informal*)
➤ **Antonyms**
ballsy (*taboo slang*), bold, brave, courageous, gritty, strong, strong-willed

spin out *verb* = **prolong**, amplify, delay, drag out, draw out, extend, lengthen, pad out, protract

spiral *noun* **1** = **coil**, corkscrew, curlicue, helix, screw, whorl ♦ *adjective* **2** = **coiled**, circular, corkscrew, helical, scrolled, whorled, winding

spirit *noun* **1** = **life force**, air, breath, life, psyche, soul, vital spark **2** = **feeling**, atmosphere, gist, humour, tenor, tone **3** = **temperament**, attitude, character, complexion, disposition, essence, humour, outlook, quality, temper **4** = **liveliness**, animation, ardour, brio, earnestness, energy, enthusiasm, fire, force, life, mettle, resolution, sparkle, vigour, warmth, zest **5** = **courage**, backbone, balls (*taboo slang*), ballsiness (*taboo slang*), dauntlessness, gameness, grit, guts (*informal*), spunk (*informal*), stoutheartedness **6** = **will**, motivation, resolution, resolve, willpower **7** = **intention**, essence, intent, meaning, purport, purpose, sense, substance **8** = **ghost**, apparition, phantom, shade (*literary*), shadow, spectre, spook (*informal*), sprite, vision **9 spirits** = **mood**, feelings, frame of mind, humour, morale ♦ *verb* **10** *with* **away** *or* **off** = **remove**, abduct, abstract, carry, convey, make away with, purloin, seize, snaffle (*Brit.*

informal), steal, whisk

spirited *adjective* = **lively**, active, animated, bold, courageous, energetic, feisty (*informal, chiefly U.S. & Canad.*), game, have-a-go (*informal*), high-spirited, mettlesome, plucky, sprightly, spunky (*informal*), vigorous, vivacious
➤ **Antonyms**
apathetic, bland, calm, dispirited, dull, feeble, half-hearted, lacklustre, lifeless, low-key, spiritless, timid, token, unenthusiastic, weary

spirits *noun* = **alcohol**, firewater, liquor, strong liquor, the hard stuff (*informal*)

spiritual *adjective* **1** = **nonmaterial**, immaterial, incorporeal **2** = **sacred**, devotional, divine, ethereal, holy, pure, religious
➤ **Antonyms**
≠**nonmaterial**: concrete, corporeal, material, nonspiritual, physical, substantial, tangible

spit *verb* **1** = **eject**, discharge, expectorate, hiss, spew, splutter, sputter, throw out ♦ *noun* **2** = **saliva**, dribble, drool, slaver, spittle

spite *noun* **1** = **malice**, animosity, bitchiness (*slang*), gall, hate, hatred, ill will, malevolence, malignity, rancour, spitefulness, spleen, venom **2 in spite of** = **despite**, (even) though, in defiance of, notwithstanding, regardless of ♦ *verb* **3** = **annoy**, gall, harm, hurt, injure, needle (*informal*), nettle, offend, pique, provoke, put out, put (someone's) nose out of joint (*informal*), vex
➤ **Antonyms**
noun ≠**malice**: benevolence, big-heartedness, charity, compassion, generosity of spirit, goodwill, kindliness, kindness, love, warm-heartedness ♦ *verb* ≠**annoy**: aid, benefit, help, please

spiteful *adjective* = **malicious**, barbed, bitchy (*informal*), catty (*informal*), cruel, ill-disposed, ill-natured, malevolent, malignant, nasty, snide, splenetic, venomous, vindictive

spitting image *noun* = **double**, clone, (dead) ringer (*slang*), likeness, living image, lookalike, picture, replica

splash *verb* **1** = **scatter**, bespatter, shower, slop, slosh (*informal*), spatter, splodge, spray, spread, sprinkle, squirt, strew, wet **2** = **dash**, batter, break, buffet, plop, smack, strike, surge, wash **3** = **publicize**, blazon, broadcast, flaunt, tout, trumpet ♦ *noun* **4** = **dash**, burst, patch, spattering, splodge, touch **5** *Informal* = **display**, effect, impact, sensation, splurge, stir **6 make a splash** *Informal* = **cause a stir**, be ostentatious, cut a dash, go overboard (*informal*), go to town, splurge

splash out *verb Informal* = **spend**, be extravagant, push the boat out (*Brit. informal*), spare no expense, splurge

spleen *noun* = **spite**, acrimony, anger, animosity, animus, bad temper, bile, bitterness, gall, hatred, hostility, ill humour, ill will, malevolence, malice, malignity, peevishness, pique, rancour, resentment, spitefulness, venom, vindictiveness, wrath

splendid *adjective* **1** = **excellent**, awesome (*slang*), boffo (*slang*), brill (*informal*), cracking (*Brit. informal*), crucial (*slang*), def (*slang*), fantastic (*informal*), fine, first-class, glorious, great (*informal*), marvellous, mean (*slang*), mega (*slang*), sovereign, wonderful **2** = **magnificent**, costly, dazzling, gorgeous, grand, imposing, impressive, lavish, luxurious, ornate, resplendent, rich, splendiferous (*facetious*), sumptuous, superb
► Antonyms
≠**excellent**: depressing, disgusting, lacklustre, mediocre, miserable, no great shakes (*informal*), ordinary, pathetic, poor, rotten, run-of-the-mill, tawdry, undistinguished, unexceptional
≠**magnificent**: beggarly, drab, dull, low, mean, plain, poor, poverty-stricken, sordid, squalid

splendour *noun* = **magnificence**, display, éclat, gorgeousness, grandeur, majesty, pomp, resplendence, richness, show, solemnity, spectacle, stateliness, sumptuousness
► Antonyms
lacklustreness, meanness, ordinariness, plainness, poverty, simplicity, squalor, tawdriness

splenetic *adjective Literary* = **irritable**, bad-tempered, choleric, crabby, cross, fretful, irascible, peevish, ratty (*Brit. & N.Z. informal*), testy, tetchy, touchy

splice *verb* = **join**, braid, entwine, graft, interlace, intertwine, intertwist, interweave, knit, marry, mesh, plait, unite, wed, yoke

splinter *noun* **1** = **sliver**, chip, flake, fragment, paring, shaving ♦ *verb* **2** = **shatter**, break into fragments, disintegrate, fracture, shiver, split

split *verb* **1** = **break**, break up, burst, come apart, come undone, crack, gape, give way, open, rend, rip, slash, slit, snap, splinter **2** = **separate**, bifurcate, branch, cleave, disband, disunite, diverge, fork, go separate ways, part, pull apart **3** = **share out**, allocate, allot, apportion, carve up,

distribute, divide, divvy up (*informal*), dole out, halve, parcel out, partition, slice up **4 split on** *Slang* = **betray**, give away, grass (*Brit. slang*), inform on, shop (*slang, chiefly Brit.*), sing (*slang, chiefly U.S.*), squeal (*slang*) ♦ *noun* **5** = **crack**, breach, damage, division, fissure, gap, rent, rip, separation, slash, slit, tear **6** = **division**, breach, break, break-up, difference, discord, disruption, dissension, disunion, divergence, estrangement, rift, rupture, schism ♦ *adjective* **7** = **divided**, ambivalent, bisected, broken, cleft, cracked, dual, fractured, ruptured

split up *verb* = **separate**, break up, disband, divorce, go separate ways, part, part company

spoil *verb* **1** = **ruin**, blemish, blow (*slang*), damage, deface, destroy, disfigure, harm, impair, injure, mar, mess up, put a damper on, scar, total (*slang*), trash (*slang*), undo, upset, wreck **2** = **overindulge**, coddle, cosset, indulge, kill with kindness, mollycoddle, pamper, spoon-feed **3** = **go bad**, addle, become tainted, curdle, decay, decompose, go off (*Brit. informal*), mildew, putrefy, rot, turn **4 spoiling for** = **eager for**, bent upon, desirous of, keen to, looking for, out to get (*informal*), raring to
► Antonyms
≠**ruin**: conserve, enhance, improve, keep, preserve, save ≠**overindulge**: be strict with, deprive, ignore, pay no attention to, treat harshly

spoils *plural noun* = **booty**, gain, loot, pickings, pillage, plunder, prey, prizes, swag (*slang*)

spoilsport *noun Informal* = **killjoy**, damper, dog in the manger, misery (*Brit. informal*), party-pooper (*U.S. slang*), wet blanket (*informal*)

spoken *adjective* = **said**, by word of mouth, expressed, oral, phonetic, put into words, told, unwritten, uttered, verbal, viva voce, voiced

spokesperson *noun* = **speaker**, mouthpiece, official, spin doctor (*informal*), spokesman or spokeswoman, voice

sponger *noun Informal* = **scrounger** (*informal*), bloodsucker (*informal*), cadge (*Brit.*), cadger, freeloader (*slang*), hanger-on, leech, parasite

spongy *adjective* = **porous**, absorbent, cushioned, cushiony, elastic, light, springy

sponsor *noun* **1** = **backer**, angel (*informal*), godparent, guarantor, patron, promoter ♦ *verb* **2** = **back**, finance, fund, guarantee, patronize, promote, put up the money for, subsidize

spontaneous *adjective* = **unplanned**, extempore, free, impromptu, impulsive, instinctive, natural, unbidden, uncompelled, unconstrained, unforced, unpremeditated, unprompted, voluntary, willing
➤ **Antonyms**
arranged, calculated, contrived, deliberate, forced, mannered, orchestrated, planned, prearranged, premeditated, preplanned, stage-managed, studied

spontaneously *adverb* = **of one's own accord**, extempore, freely, impromptu, impulsively, instinctively, in the heat of the moment, off one's own bat, off the cuff (*informal*), on impulse, quite unprompted, voluntarily

spoof *noun Informal* 1 = **parody**, burlesque, caricature, lampoon, mockery, satire, send-up (*Brit. informal*), take-off (*informal*), travesty 2 = **trick**, bluff, deception, game, hoax, joke, leg-pull (*Brit. informal*), prank

spooky *adjective* = **eerie**, chilling, creepy (*informal*), frightening, ghostly, mysterious, scary (*informal*), spine-chilling, supernatural, uncanny, unearthly, weird

spoon-feed *verb* = **mollycoddle**, cosset, overindulge, overprotect, spoil, wrap up in cotton wool (*informal*)

sporadic *adjective* = **intermittent**, infrequent, irregular, isolated, occasional, on and off, random, scattered, spasmodic
➤ **Antonyms**
consistent, frequent, recurrent, regular, set, steady, systematic

sport *noun* 1 = **game**, amusement, diversion, entertainment, exercise, pastime, physical activity, play, recreation 2 = **fun**, badinage, banter, jest, joking, kidding (*informal*), merriment, mirth, raillery, ridicule, teasing ♦ *verb* 3 *Informal* = **wear**, display, exhibit, show off

sporting *adjective* = **fair**, game (*informal*), gentlemanly, sportsmanlike
➤ **Antonyms**
unfair, unsporting, unsportsmanlike

sportive *adjective* = **playful**, frisky, frolicsome, full of beans (*informal*), full of fun, gay, joyous, lively, merry, rollicking, skittish, sprightly

sporty *adjective* 1 = **athletic**, energetic, hearty, outdoor 2 = **casual**, jazzy (*informal*), snazzy (*informal*), stylish, trendy (*Brit. informal*)

spot *noun* 1 = **mark**, blemish, blot, blotch, daub, discoloration, flaw, scar, smudge, speck, speckle, stain, taint 2 = **place**, locality, location, point, position, scene, site, situation 3 = **pimple**, plook (*Scot.*), pustule, zit (*slang*) 4 *Informal, chiefly Brit.*

= **bit**, little, morsel, splash 5 *Informal* = **predicament**, difficulty, hot water (*informal*), mess, plight, quandary, tight spot, trouble 6 **soft spot** = **fondness**, liking, partiality, weakness ♦ *verb* 7 = **see**, behold (*archaic or literary*), catch sight of, detect, discern, espy, identify, make out, observe, pick out, recognize, sight 8 = **mark**, besmirch, blot, dirty, dot, fleck, mottle, scar, smirch, soil, spatter, speckle, splodge, splotch, stain, sully, taint, tarnish

spotless *adjective* 1 = **clean**, faultless, flawless, gleaming, immaculate, impeccable, pure, shining, snowy, unblemished, unstained, unsullied, untarnished, white 2 = **blameless**, above reproach, chaste, innocent, irreproachable, squeaky-clean, unimpeachable
➤ **Antonyms**
≠**clean**: besmirched, bespattered, blemished, defiled, dirty, filthy, flawed, impure, messy, soiled, spotted, stained, sullied, tainted, tarnished ≠**blameless**: notorious, reprehensible

spotlight *noun* 1 = **attention**, fame, interest, limelight, notoriety, public attention, public eye ♦ *verb* 2 = **highlight**, accentuate, draw attention to, feature, focus attention on, give prominence to, illuminate, point up, throw into relief

spot-on *adjective Informal* = **accurate**, correct, exact, precise, right, unerring

spotted *adjective* = **speckled**, dappled, dotted, flecked, mottled, pied, polka-dot, specked

spotty *adjective* 1 = **pimply**, blotchy, pimpled, plooky-faced (*Scot.*), poor-complexioned 2 = **inconsistent**, erratic, fluctuating, irregular, patchy, sporadic, uneven

spouse *noun* = **partner**, better half (*humorous*), companion, consort, helpmate, her indoors (*Brit. slang*), husband *or* wife, mate, significant other (*U.S. informal*)

spout *verb* 1 = **stream**, discharge, emit, erupt, gush, jet, shoot, spray, spurt, squirt, surge 2 *Informal* = **hold forth**, declaim, go on (*informal*), orate, pontificate, rabbit (on) (*Brit. informal*), ramble (on), rant, speechify, talk

sprawl *verb* 1 = **loll**, flop, lounge, slouch, slump 2 = **spread**, ramble, straggle, trail

spray¹ *noun* 1 = **droplets**, drizzle, fine mist, moisture, spindrift 2 = **aerosol**, atomizer, sprinkler ♦ *verb* 3 = **scatter**, atomize, diffuse, shower, sprinkle

spray² *noun* = **sprig**, bough, branch, corsage, floral arrangement, shoot

spread verb 1 = **open (out)**, be displayed, bloat, broaden, dilate, expand, extend, fan out, sprawl, stretch, swell, unfold, unfurl, unroll, widen 2 = **proliferate**, escalate, multiply, mushroom 3 = **circulate**, advertise, broadcast, cover, diffuse, disseminate, distribute, make known, make public, proclaim, promulgate, propagate, publicize, publish, radiate, scatter, strew, transmit ♦ noun 4 = **increase**, advance, advancement, development, diffusion, dispersal, dissemination, escalation, expansion, proliferation, spreading, suffusion, transmission 5 = **extent**, compass, period, reach, span, stretch, sweep, term 6 Informal = **feast**, array, banquet, repast
➤ **Antonyms**
verb ≠**circulate**: contain, control, curb, hold back, hold in, repress, restrain, stifle

spree noun = **binge** (informal), bacchanalia, bender (informal), carousal, carouse, debauch, fling, orgy, revel, splurge

sprightly adjective = **lively**, active, agile, animated, brisk, cheerful, energetic, frolicsome, gay, jaunty, nimble, perky, playful, spirited, spry, vivacious
➤ **Antonyms**
dull, inactive, lethargic, sedentary, sluggish, torpid, unenergetic

spring verb 1 = **jump**, bounce, bound, hop, leap, rebound, recoil, vault 2 often with from = **originate**, arise, be derived, be descended, come, derive, descend, emanate, emerge, grow, issue, proceed, start, stem 3 often with up = **appear**, burgeon, come into existence or being, develop, mushroom, shoot up ♦ noun 4 = **jump**, bound, buck, hop, leap, vault 5 = **source**, beginning, cause, fount, fountainhead, origin, root, well, wellspring 6 = **elasticity**, bounce, bounciness, buoyancy, flexibility, give (informal), recoil, resilience, springiness ♦ adjective 7 Of the season = **vernal**, springlike

springy adjective = **elastic**, bouncy, buoyant, flexible, resilient, rubbery, spongy

sprinkle verb = **scatter**, dredge, dust, pepper, powder, shower, spray, strew

sprinkling noun = **scattering**, admixture, dash, dusting, few, handful, scatter, smattering, sprinkle

sprint verb = **race**, dart, dash, go at top speed, hare (Brit. informal), hotfoot, put on a burst of speed, scamper, shoot, tear, whizz (informal)

sprite noun = **spirit**, apparition, brownie, dryad, elf, fairy, goblin, imp, leprechaun, peri, pixie, sylph

sprout verb = **grow**, bud, develop, germinate, shoot, spring

spruce adjective = **smart**, dainty, dapper, elegant, natty (informal), neat, soigné or soignée, trig (archaic or dialect), trim, well-groomed, well turned out
➤ **Antonyms**
bedraggled, disarrayed, dishevelled, frowsy, messy, rumpled, uncombed, unkempt, untidy

spruce up verb = **smarten up**, groom, have a wash and brush-up (Brit.), tidy, titivate

spry adjective = **active**, agile, brisk, nimble, nippy (Brit. informal), quick, ready, sprightly, supple
➤ **Antonyms**
awkward, decrepit, doddering, inactive, lethargic, slow, sluggish, stiff

spunk noun Old-fashioned, informal = **courage**, backbone, balls (taboo slang), bottle (Brit. slang), gumption (informal), guts (informal), mettle, nerve, pluck, spirit

spur noun 1 = **stimulus**, impetus, impulse, incentive, incitement, inducement, motive 2 = **goad**, prick 3 on the spur of the moment = **on impulse**, impetuously, impromptu, impulsively, on the spot, unpremeditatedly, unthinkingly, without planning, without thinking ♦ verb 4 = **incite**, animate, drive, goad, impel, press, prick, prod, prompt, stimulate, urge

spurious adjective = **false**, artificial, bogus, contrived, counterfeit, deceitful, ersatz, fake, feigned, forged, imitation, mock, phoney or phony (informal), pretended, pseudo (informal), sham, simulated, specious, unauthentic
➤ **Antonyms**
authentic, bona fide, genuine, honest, kosher (informal), legitimate, real, sound, unfeigned, valid

spurn verb = **reject**, cold-shoulder, contemn, despise, disdain, disregard, kick in the teeth (slang), put down, rebuff, repulse, scorn, slight, snub, turn one's nose up at (informal)
➤ **Antonyms**
embrace, grasp, seize, take up, welcome

spurt verb 1 = **gush**, burst, erupt, jet, shoot, spew, squirt, surge ♦ noun 2 = **burst**, access, fit, rush, spate, surge

spy noun 1 = **undercover agent**, double agent, fifth columnist, foreign agent, mole, nark (Brit., Austral., & N.Z. slang), secret agent, secret service agent ♦ verb 2 usually with on = **watch**, follow, keep under surveillance, keep watch on, shadow, tail (informal) 3 = **catch sight of**, behold (archaic or literary), descry, espy, glimpse, notice, observe, set eyes on, spot

spying *noun* = **espionage**, secret service

squabble *verb* 1 = **quarrel**, argue, bicker, brawl, clash, dispute, fall out (*informal*), fight, have words, row, scrap (*informal*), wrangle ♦ *noun* 2 = **quarrel**, argument, barney (*informal*), difference of opinion, disagreement, dispute, fight, row, scrap (*informal*), set-to (*informal*), spat, tiff

squad *noun* = **team**, band, company, crew, force, gang, group, troop

squalid *adjective* = **dirty**, broken-down, decayed, disgusting, fetid, filthy, foul, low, nasty, poverty-stricken, repulsive, run-down, seedy, sleazy, slovenly, slummy, sordid, unclean, yucky *or* yukky (*slang*)
➤ **Antonyms**
attractive, clean, hygienic, in good condition, pleasant, salubrious, spick-and-span, spotless, tidy, well-kempt, well looked-after

squalor *noun* = **filth**, decay, foulness, meanness, sleaziness, slumminess, squalidness, wretchedness
➤ **Antonyms**
cleanliness, fine condition, luxury, neatness, order, pleasantness, splendour

squander *verb* = **waste**, be prodigal with, blow (*slang*), consume, dissipate, expend, fritter away, lavish, misspend, misuse, run through, scatter, spend, spend like water, throw away
➤ **Antonyms**
be frugal, be thrifty, economize, keep, put aside for a rainy day, save, store

square *noun* 1 *Informal* = **(old) fogey**, conservative, die-hard, dinosaur, fuddy-duddy (*informal*), traditionalist ♦ *adjective* 2 = **honest**, above board, decent, equitable, ethical, fair, fair and square, genuine, just, kosher (*informal*), on the level (*informal*), on the up and up, straight, straightforward, upfront (*informal*), upright 3 *Informal* = **old-fashioned**, behind the times, conservative, conventional, dated, out of date, out of the ark (*informal*), straight (*slang*), strait-laced, stuffy ♦ *verb* 4 = **even up**, accommodate, adapt, adjust, align, level, regulate, suit, tailor, true (up) 5 *sometimes with* **up** = **pay off**, balance, clear (up), discharge, liquidate, make even, quit, satisfy, settle 6 *often with* **with** = **agree**, accord, conform, correspond, fit, harmonize, match, reconcile, tally
➤ **Antonyms**
adjective ≠**old-fashioned**: fashionable, in vogue, modern, modish, stylish, trendy (*Brit. informal*), voguish

squash *verb* 1 = **crush**, compress, distort,
flatten, mash, pound, press, pulp, smash, stamp on, trample down 2 = **suppress**, annihilate, crush, humiliate, put down (*slang*), put (someone) in his (*or* her) place, quash, quell, silence

squashy *adjective* = **soft**, mushy, pappy, pulpy, spongy, yielding

squawk *verb* 1 = **cry**, cackle, crow, hoot, screech, yelp 2 *Informal* = **complain**, kick up a fuss (*informal*), protest, raise Cain (*slang*)

squeak *verb* = **peep**, pipe, shrill, squeal, whine, yelp

squeal *noun*, *verb* 1 = **scream**, screech, shriek, wail, yell, yelp, yowl ♦ *verb* 2 *Slang* = **inform on**, betray, blab, grass (*Brit. slang*), rat on (*informal*), sell (someone) down the river (*informal*), shop (*slang, chiefly Brit.*), sing (*slang, chiefly U.S.*), snitch (*slang*), tell all 3 *Informal, chiefly Brit.* = **complain**, kick up a fuss (*informal*), moan, protest, squawk (*informal*)

squeamish *adjective* 1 = **fastidious**, delicate, finicky, nice (*rare*), particular, prissy (*informal*), prudish, punctilious, scrupulous, strait-laced 2 = **queasy**, nauseous, qualmish, queer, sick, sickish
➤ **Antonyms**
≠**fastidious**: bold, brassy, brazen, coarse, earthy, immodest, indifferent, tough, wanton ≠**queasy**: strong-stomached

squeeze *verb* 1 = **press**, clutch, compress, crush, grip, nip, pinch, squash, wring 2 = **cram**, crowd, force, jam, jostle, pack, press, ram, stuff, thrust, wedge 3 = **hug**, clasp, cuddle, embrace, enfold, hold tight 4 = **extort**, bring pressure to bear on, lean on (*informal*), milk, oppress, pressurize, put the screws on (*informal*), put the squeeze on (*informal*), wrest ♦ *noun* 5 = **hug**, clasp, embrace, handclasp, hold 6 = **crush**, congestion, crowd, jam, press, squash

squint *adjective Informal* = **crooked**, askew, aslant, awry, cockeyed, oblique, off-centre, skew-whiff (*informal*)
➤ **Antonyms**
aligned, even, horizontal, in line, level, perpendicular, plum, square, straight, true, vertical

squire *verb Old-fashioned* = **escort**, accompany, attend, companion

squirm *verb* = **wriggle**, fidget, flounder, shift, twist, wiggle, writhe

stab *verb* 1 = **pierce**, bayonet, cut, gore, impale, injure, jab, knife, puncture, run through, spear, spill blood, stick, thrust, transfix, wound 2 **stab in the back** = **betray**, break faith with, deceive, do the dirty on (*Brit. slang*), double-cross (*informal*), let down, play false, sell, sell out (*informal*) ♦ *noun* 3 = **wound**, gash, incision, jab, puncture, rent, thrust 4 = **twinge**, ache, pang, prick 5 *Informal* = **attempt**, crack (*informal*), endeavour, essay (*informal*), go, shot (*informal*), try

stability *noun* = **firmness**, constancy, durability, permanence, solidity, soundness, steadfastness, steadiness, strength
➤ **Antonyms**
changeableness, fickleness, fragility, frailty, inconstancy, instability, unpredictability, unreliability, unsteadiness

stable *adjective* 1 = **firm**, abiding, constant, deep-rooted, durable, enduring, established, fast, fixed, immovable, immutable, invariable, lasting, permanent, secure, sound, strong, sturdy, unalterable, unchangeable, unwavering, well-founded 2 = **steady**, reliable, staunch, steadfast, sure
➤ **Antonyms**
≠**firm**: changeable, erratic, inconstant, insecure, irresolute, mercurial, mutable, shaky, shifting, temperamental, uncertain, unpredictable, unreliable, unstable, variable, volatile, wavering ≠**steady**: unsteady, unsure

stack *noun* 1 = **pile**, heap, hoard, load, mass, mound, mountain ♦ *verb* 2 = **pile**, accumulate, amass, assemble, bank up, heap up, load, stockpile

staff *noun* 1 = **workers**, employees, lecturers, officers, organization, personnel, teachers, team, workforce 2 = **stick**, cane, crook, pole, prop, rod, sceptre, stave, wand

stage *noun* 1 = **step**, division, juncture, lap, leg, length, level, period, phase, point ♦ *verb* 2 = **present**, do, give, perform, play, produce, put on 3 = **organize**, arrange, engineer, lay on, mount, orchestrate

stagger *verb* 1 = **totter**, falter, lurch, reel, sway, teeter, waver, wobble 2 = **astound**, amaze, astonish, bowl over (*informal*), confound, dumbfound, flabbergast, give (someone) a shock, nonplus, overwhelm, shake, shock, strike (someone) dumb, stun, stupefy, surprise, take (someone) aback, take (someone's) breath away, throw off balance 3 = **alternate**, overlap, step

stagnant *adjective* = **stale**, brackish, motionless, quiet, sluggish, standing, still
➤ **Antonyms**
clear, flowing, fresh, moving, pure, running, unpolluted

stagnate *verb* = **vegetate**, decay, decline, deteriorate, fester, go to seed, idle, languish, lie fallow, rot, rust, stand still

staid *adjective* = **sedate**, calm, composed, decorous, demure, grave, quiet, self-restrained, serious, set in one's ways, sober, solemn, steady
➤ **Antonyms**
adventurous, capricious, demonstrative, exuberant, flighty, giddy, indecorous, lively, rowdy, sportive, wild

stain *verb* 1 = **mark**, blemish, blot, dirty, discolour, smirch, soil, spot, tarnish, tinge 2 = **dye**, colour, tint ♦ *noun* 3 = **mark**, blemish, blot, discoloration, smirch, spot 4 = **stigma**, blemish, disgrace, dishonour, infamy, shame, slur 5 = **dye**, colour, tint

stake¹ *noun* 1 = **pole**, pale, paling, palisade, picket, post, spike, stave, stick ♦ *verb* 2 *often with* **out** = **lay claim to**, define, delimit, demarcate, mark out, outline, reserve 3 = **support**, brace, prop, secure, tie up

stake² *noun* 1 = **bet**, ante, chance, hazard, peril, pledge, risk, venture, wager 2 = **interest**, claim, concern, investment, involvement, share ♦ *verb* 3 = **bet**, chance, gamble, hazard, pledge, put on, risk, venture, wager

stale *adjective* 1 = **old**, decayed, dry, fetid, flat, fusty, hard, insipid, musty, sour, stagnant, tasteless 2 = **unoriginal**, antiquated, banal, cliché-ridden, common, commonplace, drab, flat, hackneyed, insipid, old hat, overused, repetitious, stereotyped, threadbare, trite, worn-out
➤ **Antonyms**
≠**old**: crisp, fresh ≠**unoriginal**: different, imaginative, innovative, lively, new, novel, original, refreshing

stalemate *noun* = **deadlock**, draw, impasse, standstill, tie

stalk *verb* 1 = **pursue**, creep up on, follow, haunt, hunt, shadow, tail (*informal*), track 2 = **strut**, flounce, march, pace, stride

stall *verb* = **play for time**, beat about the bush (*informal*), hedge, temporize

stalwart *adjective* 1 = **strong**, athletic, beefy (*informal*), brawny, hefty (*informal*), husky (*informal*), lusty, manly, muscular, robust, rugged, sinewy, stout, strapping, sturdy, vigorous 2 = **loyal**, dependable, reliable, staunch
➤ **Antonyms**
≠**strong**: feeble, frail, infirm, namby-pamby, puny, shilpit (*Scot.*), sickly, weak

stamina *noun* = **staying power**, endurance, energy, force, indefatigability, lustiness, power, power of endurance, resilience, resistance, strength, tenacity, vigour

stammer *verb* = **stutter**, falter, hem and haw, hesitate, pause, stumble

stamp *noun* 1 = **imprint**, brand, cast, earmark, hallmark, mark, mould, signature 2 = **type**, breed, cast, character, cut, description, fashion, form, kind, sort ♦ *verb* 3 = **trample**, beat, crush 4 = **identify**, brand, categorize, exhibit, label, mark, pronounce, reveal, show to be, typecast 5 = **imprint**, engrave, fix, impress, inscribe, mark, mould, print

stamp collecting *noun* = **philately**

stampede *noun* = **rush**, charge, flight, rout, scattering

stamp out *verb* = **eliminate**, crush, destroy, eradicate, extinguish, extirpate, put down, put out, quell, quench, scotch, suppress

stance *noun* 1 = **attitude**, position, stand, standpoint, viewpoint 2 = **posture**, bearing, carriage, deportment

stanch *see* STAUNCH[1]

stand *verb* 1 = **be upright**, be erect, be vertical, rise 2 = **put**, mount, place, position, rank, set 3 = **exist**, be in force, belong, be situated *or* located, be valid, continue, hold, obtain, prevail, remain, stay 4 = **tolerate**, abide, allow, bear, brook, cope with, countenance, endure, experience, hack (*slang*), handle, put up with (*informal*), stomach, submit to, suffer, support, sustain, take, thole (*dialect*), undergo, withstand ♦ *noun* 5 = **stall**, booth, table 6 = **grandstand** 7 = **stop**, halt, rest, standstill, stay 8 = **position**, attitude, determination, firm stand, opinion, stance, standpoint 9 = **support**, base, bracket, dais, frame, place, platform, rack, rank, stage, tripod, trivet

standard *noun* 1 = **level**, gauge, grade, measure 2 = **criterion**, average, benchmark, example, guide, guideline, model, norm, par, pattern, sample, touchstone, yardstick 3 *often plural* = **principles**, canon, code of honour, ethics, ideals, moral principles, morals, rule 4 = **flag**, banner, colours, ensign, pennant, pennon, streamer ♦ *adjective* 5 = **usual**, average, basic, customary, normal, orthodox, popular, prevailing, regular, set, staple, stock, typical 6 = **accepted**, approved, authoritative, classic, definitive, established, official, recognized

➤ **Antonyms**
adjective ≠**usual**: abnormal, atypical, exceptional, extraordinary, irregular, singular, strange, uncommon, unusual ≠**accepted**: unauthorised, unconventional, unofficial

standardize *verb* = **bring into line**, assimilate, institutionalize, mass-produce, regiment, stereotype

stand by *verb* 1 = **be prepared**, wait, wait in the wings 2 = **support**, back, befriend, be loyal to, champion, defend, stick up for (*informal*), take (someone's) part, uphold

stand for *verb* 1 = **represent**, betoken, denote, exemplify, indicate, mean, signify, symbolize 2 *Informal* = **tolerate**, bear, brook, endure, put up with, suffer

stand-in *noun* = **substitute**, deputy, locum, replacement, reserve, stopgap, surrogate, understudy

stand in for *verb* = **be a substitute for**, cover for, deputize for, do duty for, replace, represent, take the place of, understudy

standing *adjective* 1 = **permanent**, fixed, lasting, perpetual, regular, repeated 2 = **upright**, erect, perpendicular, rampant (*Heraldry*), upended, vertical ♦ *noun* 3 = **status**, eminence, estimation, footing, position, rank, reputation, repute, station 4 = **duration**, continuance, existence, experience

standoffish *adjective* = **reserved**, aloof, cold, distant, haughty, remote, unapproachable, unsociable

➤ **Antonyms**
affable, approachable, congenial, cordial, friendly, open, sociable, warm

stand out *verb* = **be conspicuous**, attract attention, be distinct, be highlighted, be obvious, be prominent, be striking, catch the eye, project, stare one in the face (*informal*), stick out a mile (*informal*), stick out like a sore thumb (*informal*)

standpoint *noun* = **point of view**, angle, position, stance, viewpoint

stand up for *verb* = **support**, champion, come to the defence of, defend, side with, stick up for (*informal*), uphold

stand up to *verb* 1 = **resist**, brave, confront, defy, oppose, tackle 2 = **withstand**, endure

staple *adjective* = **principal**, basic, chief, essential, fundamental, key, main, predominant, primary

star *noun* 1 = **heavenly body** 2 = **celebrity**, big name, celeb (*informal*), idol, lead, leading man *or* lady, luminary, main attraction, megastar (*informal*), name ♦ *adjective* 3 = **leading**, brilliant, celebrated, illustrious, major, paramount, principal, prominent, talented, well-known

starchy *adjective* = **formal**, conventional, precise, prim, punctilious, stiff, stuffy

stare *verb* = **gaze**, eyeball (*slang*), gape, gawk, gawp (*Brit. slang*), goggle, look, ogle, watch

stark *adjective* 1 = **harsh**, austere, bare, barren, bleak, cold, depressing, desolate, dreary, grim, hard, plain, severe, unadorned 2 = **absolute**, arrant, blunt, downright, entire, flagrant, out-and-out, palpable, patent, pure, sheer, simple, unalloyed, unmitigated, utter ♦ *adverb* 3 = **absolutely**, altogether, clean, completely, entirely, quite, utterly, wholly

stark-naked *adjective* = **undressed**, buck naked (*slang*), in a state of nature, in one's birthday suit (*informal*), in the altogether (*informal*), in the buff (*informal*), naked, naked as the day one was born (*informal*), nude, stark, starkers (*informal*), stripped, unclad, without a stitch on (*informal*)

start *verb* 1 = **begin**, appear, arise, come into being, come into existence, commence, get under way, go ahead, issue, originate 2 = **set about**, embark upon, make a beginning, take the first step, take the plunge (*informal*) 3 = **set in motion**, activate, engender, enter upon, get going, get (something) off the ground (*informal*), get or set the ball rolling, initiate, instigate, kick off (*informal*), kick-start, open, originate, trigger, turn on 4 = **jump**, blench, flinch, jerk, recoil, shy, twitch 5 = **establish**, begin, create, father, found, inaugurate, initiate, institute, introduce, launch, pioneer, set up ♦ *noun* 6 = **beginning**, birth, commencement, dawn, first step(s), foundation, inauguration, inception, initiation, kickoff (*informal*), onset, opening, outset 7 = **advantage**, edge, head start, lead 8 = **jump**, convulsion, jar, spasm, twitch 9 = **opportunity**, backing, break (*informal*), chance, helping hand, introduction, opening, sponsorship
➤ Antonyms
verb ≠**begin**, set about, set in motion: abandon, bring to an end, call it a day (*informal*), cease, conclude, delay, desist, end, finish, give up, put aside, put off, quit, stop, switch off, terminate, turn off, wind up ♦ *noun* ≠**beginning**: cessation, conclusion, denouement, end, finale, finish, outcome, result, stop, termination, turning off, wind-up

startle *verb* = **surprise**, agitate, alarm, amaze, astonish, astound, frighten, give (someone) a turn (*informal*), make (someone) jump, scare, shock, take (someone) aback

startling *adjective* = **surprising**, alarming, astonishing, astounding, extraordinary, jaw-dropping, shocking, staggering, sudden, unexpected, unforeseen

starving *adjective* = **hungry**, famished, ravenous, ready to eat a horse (*informal*), sharp-set, starved

stash *verb Informal* = **store**, cache, hide, hoard, lay up, secrete, stockpile, stow

state *noun* 1 = **condition**, case, category, circumstances, equation, mode, pass, plight, position, predicament, shape, situation, state of affairs 2 = **frame of mind**, attitude, humour, mood, spirits 3 = **country**, body politic, commonwealth, federation, government, kingdom, land, nation, republic, territory 4 = **ceremony**, dignity, display, glory, grandeur, majesty, pomp, splendour, style 5 **in a state** *Informal* = **distressed**, agitated, all steamed up (*slang*), anxious, disturbed, flustered, het up, panic-stricken, ruffled, upset, uptight (*informal*) ♦ *verb* 6 = **express**, affirm, articulate, assert, aver, declare, explain, expound, present, propound, put, report, say, specify, utter, voice

stately *adjective* = **grand**, august, dignified, elegant, imperial, imposing, impressive, lofty, majestic, noble, regal, royal
➤ Antonyms
common, humble, lowly, modest, simple, undignified, undistinguished, unimpressive

statement *noun* = **account**, announcement, communication, communiqué, declaration, explanation, proclamation, recital, relation, report, testimony, utterance

state-of-the-art *adjective* = **latest**, newest, up-to-date, up-to-the-minute
➤ Antonyms
obsolescent, obsolete, old-fashioned, outdated, outmoded, out of date

static *adjective* = **stationary**, changeless, constant, fixed, immobile, inert, motionless, stagnant, still, stock-still, unmoving, unvarying
➤ Antonyms
active, dynamic, kinetic, lively, mobile, moving, travelling, varied

station *noun* 1 = **headquarters**, base, depot 2 = **position**, grade, post, rank, situation, sphere, standing, status 3 = **occupation**, appointment, business, calling, employment 4 = **place**, location, position, post, seat, situation ♦ *verb* 5 = **assign**, establish, fix, garrison, install, locate, post, set

stationary *adjective* = **motionless**, at a standstill, fixed, inert, parked, standing, static, stock-still, unmoving
➤ Antonyms
changeable, changing, inconstant, mobile, moving, shifting, travelling, unstable, variable, varying, volatile

statuesque *adjective* = **well-proportioned**, dignified, imposing, Junoesque, majestic, regal, stately

stature *noun* = **importance**, consequence, eminence, high station, prestige, prominence, rank, size, standing

status *noun* = **position**, condition, consequence, degree, distinction, eminence, grade, prestige, rank, standing

statute *noun* = **law**, act, decree, edict, enactment, ordinance, regulation, rule

staunch[1], **stanch** *verb* = **stop**, arrest, check, dam, halt, plug, stay, stem

staunch[2] *adjective* = **loyal**, constant, dependable, faithful, firm, immovable, reliable, resolute, sound, stalwart, steadfast, stout, strong, sure, tried and true, true, true-blue, trustworthy, trusty

stave off *verb* = **hold off**, avert, evade, fend off, keep at arm's length, keep at bay, ward off

stay[1] *verb* **1** = **remain**, abide, bide, continue, delay, establish oneself, halt, hang around (*informal*), hover, linger, loiter, pause, reside, settle, stand, stay put, stop, tarry, wait **2** *often with* **at** = **lodge**, be accommodated at, sojourn, visit ♦ *noun* **3** = **visit**, holiday, sojourn, stop, stopover **4** = **postponement**, deferment, delay, halt, pause, remission, reprieve, stopping, suspension
➤ **Antonyms**
verb ≠**remain**: abandon, depart, exit, go, leave, move on, pack one's bags (*informal*), pass through, quit, withdraw

stay[2] *noun* = **support**, brace, buttress, prop, reinforcement, stanchion

staying power *noun* = **endurance**, stamina, strength, toughness

steadfast *adjective* = **firm**, constant, dedicated, dependable, established, faithful, fast, fixed, immovable, intent, loyal, persevering, reliable, resolute, single-minded, stable, stalwart, staunch, steady, unfaltering, unflinching, unswerving, unwavering
➤ **Antonyms**
capricious, faint-hearted, faltering, fickle, flagging, half-hearted, inconstant, irresolute, uncommitted, undependable, unreliable, unstable, vacillating, wavering

steady *adjective* **1** = **firm**, fixed, immovable, on an even keel, safe, secure, stable, substantial, unchangeable, uniform **2** = **continuous**, ceaseless, confirmed, consistent, constant, even, habitual, incessant, nonstop, persistent, regular, rhythmic, unbroken, unfaltering, unfluctuating, uninterrupted, unremitting,

unvarying, unwavering **3** = **dependable**, balanced, calm, equable, having both feet on the ground, imperturbable, level-headed, reliable, sensible, serious-minded, sober ♦ *verb* **4** = **stabilize**, balance, brace, secure, support
➤ **Antonyms**
adjective ≠**firm**: insecure, unsettled, unstable, unsteady ≠**continuous**: changeable, faltering, fluctuating, inconsistent, infrequent, intermittent, irregular, occasional, sporadic ≠**dependable**: careless, fickle, half-hearted, in two minds, uncommitted, unconscientious, undependable, unpredictable, unreliable, vacillating, wavering ♦ *verb* ≠**stabilize**: agitate, shake, tilt, upset

steal *verb* **1** = **take**, appropriate, be light-fingered, blag (*slang*), embezzle, filch, lift (*informal*), misappropriate, nick (*slang, chiefly Brit.*), pilfer, pinch (*informal*), pirate, plagiarize, poach, purloin, shoplift, swipe (*slang*), thieve, walk *or* make off with **2** = **sneak**, creep, flit, slink, slip, tiptoe

stealing *noun* = **theft**, embezzlement, larceny, misappropriation, pilfering, plagiarism, robbery, shoplifting, thieving

stealth *noun* = **secrecy**, furtiveness, slyness, sneakiness, stealthiness, surreptitiousness, unobtrusiveness

stealthy *adjective* = **secret**, clandestine, covert, furtive, secretive, skulking, sly, sneaking, sneaky, surreptitious, underhand

steamy *adjective Informal* = **erotic**, carnal, hot (*slang*), lascivious, lewd, raunchy (*slang*), sensual, sexy (*informal*), titillating

steel oneself *verb* = **brace oneself**, fortify oneself, grit one's teeth, harden oneself, make up one's mind

steep[1] *adjective* **1** = **sheer**, abrupt, headlong, precipitous **2** *Informal* = **high**, excessive, exorbitant, extortionate, extreme, overpriced, stiff, unreasonable
➤ **Antonyms**
≠**sheer**: easy, gentle, gradual, moderate, slight ≠**high**: fair, moderate, reasonable

steep[2] *verb* **1** = **soak**, damp, drench, immerse, marinate (*Cookery*), moisten, souse, submerge **2** = **saturate**, fill, imbue, infuse, permeate, pervade, suffuse

steer *verb* **1** = **drive**, control, direct, guide, handle, pilot **2** = **direct**, administer, conduct, control, govern **3 steer clear of** = **avoid**, body-swerve (*Scot.*), circumvent, eschew, evade, give a wide berth to, shun

steersman *noun* = **pilot**, cox, coxswain, helmsman

stem[1] *noun* **1** = **stalk**, axis, branch, shoot,

stock, trunk ♦ *verb* **2 stem from
= originate from**, arise from, be brought
about by, be caused by, be generated by,
derive from, develop from, emanate from,
flow from

stem² *verb* = **stop**, bring to a standstill,
check, contain, curb, dam, hold back,
oppose, resist, restrain, stanch, staunch,
withstand

stench *noun* = **stink**, foul smell, malodour,
niff (*Brit. slang*), pong (*Brit. informal*), reek,
whiff (*Brit. slang*)

stentorian *adjective* = **loud**, booming,
carrying, powerful, ringing, strident,
strong, thundering
➤ **Antonyms**
gentle, hushed, low, low-pitched, quiet,
soft, subdued

step *noun* **1** = **footstep**, footfall, footprint,
impression, pace, print, stride, trace, track
2 = **stage**, advance, advancement, move,
phase, point, process, progression **3**
= **action**, act, deed, expedient,
manoeuvre, means, measure, move,
procedure, proceeding **4** = **degree**, level,
rank **5** = **gait**, walk **6** = **stair**, doorstep,
rung, tread **7 in step** *Informal* = **in
agreement**, coinciding, conforming, in
conformity, in harmony, in line, in unison
8 out of step *Informal* = **in disagreement**,
erratic, incongruous, out of harmony, out
of line, out of phase, pulling different ways
9 take steps = **take action**, act, intervene,
move in, prepare, take measures, take the
initiative **10 watch one's step** *Informal* = **be
careful**, be canny, be cautious, be discreet,
be on one's guard, have one's wits about
one, look out, mind how one goes, mind
one's p's and q's, take care, take heed,
tread carefully ♦ *verb* **11** = **walk**, move,
pace, tread

step down *verb Informal* = **resign**,
abdicate, bow out, give up, hand over,
leave, pull out, quit, retire

step in *verb Informal* = **intervene**, become
involved, chip in (*informal*), intercede, take
action, take a hand

step up *verb Informal* = **increase**,
accelerate, augment, boost, escalate,
intensify, raise, speed up, up

stereotype *noun* **1** = **formula**, mould,
pattern, received idea ♦ *verb* **2**
= **categorize**, dub, pigeonhole,
standardize, take to be, typecast

sterile *adjective* **1** = **germ-free**, antiseptic,
aseptic, disinfected, sterilized **2** = **barren**,
abortive, bare, dry, empty, fruitless,
infecund, unfruitful, unproductive,
unprofitable, unprolific
➤ **Antonyms**

≠**germ-free**: contaminated, dirty,
germ-ridden, infected, insanitary,
unhygienic, unsterile ≠**barren**: fecund,
fertile, fruitful, productive, prolific

sterilize *verb* = **disinfect**, fumigate, purify

sterling *adjective* = **excellent**, authentic,
fine, first-class, genuine, pure, real, sound,
standard, substantial, superlative, true

stern *adjective* **1** = **strict**, austere,
authoritarian, cruel, drastic, grim, hard,
harsh, inflexible, relentless, rigid, rigorous,
unrelenting **2** = **severe**, forbidding,
frowning, serious
➤ **Antonyms**
≠**strict**: compassionate, flexible, gentle,
kind, lenient, liberal, permissive, soft,
sympathetic, tolerant ≠**severe**:
approachable, friendly, warm

stew *noun* **1** = **hash**, goulash, ragout **2 in a
stew** *Informal* = **troubled**, anxious,
concerned, fretting, in a panic, worrying

stick¹ *noun* **1** = **cane**, baton, birch, crook,
pole, rod, sceptre, staff, stake, switch,
twig, wand **2** *Slang* = **abuse**, blame,
criticism, flak (*informal*)

stick² *verb* **1** = **poke**, dig, gore, insert, jab,
penetrate, pierce, pin, prod, puncture,
spear, stab, thrust, transfix **2** = **fasten**,
adhere, affix, attach, bind, bond, cement,
cleave, cling, fix, fuse, glue, hold, hold on,
join, paste, weld **3** *with* **out, up**, *etc.*
= **protrude**, bulge, extend, jut, obtrude,
poke, project, show **4** *Informal* = **put**,
deposit, drop, fix, install, lay, place, plant,
plonk, position, set, store, stuff **5** = **catch**,
become immobilized, be embedded, clog,
come to a standstill, jam, lodge, snag, stop
6 = **stay**, linger, persist, remain **7** *Slang*
= **tolerate**, abide, endure, hack (*slang*),
stand, stomach, take

stick-in-the-mud *noun Informal* = **(old)
fogey**, conservative, die-hard, dinosaur,
fuddy-duddy (*informal*), reactionary

stickler *noun* = **fanatic**, fusspot (*Brit.
informal*), maniac (*informal*), martinet, nut
(*slang*), pedant, perfectionist, purist

stick out *verb Informal* = **endure**, bear, grin
and bear it (*informal*), put up with
(*informal*), see through, soldier on, take it
(*informal*), weather

stick to *verb* = **remain faithful**, adhere to,
cleave to, continue in, honour, keep,
persevere in, remain loyal, remain true,
stick at

stick up for *verb Informal* = **defend**,
champion, stand up for, support, take the
part *or* side of, uphold

sticky *adjective* **1** = **tacky**, adhesive,
clinging, gluey, glutinous, gooey

(*informal*), gummy, icky (*informal*), syrupy, viscid, viscous 2 *Informal* = **difficult**, awkward, delicate, discomforting, embarrassing, hairy (*slang*), nasty, painful, thorny, tricky, unpleasant 3 = **humid**, clammy, close, muggy, oppressive, sultry, sweltering

stiff *adjective* 1 = **inflexible**, brittle, firm, hard, hardened, inelastic, rigid, solid, solidified, taut, tense, tight, unbending, unyielding 2 = **unsupple**, arthritic, creaky (*informal*), rheumaticky 3 = **awkward**, clumsy, crude, graceless, inelegant, jerky (*informal*), ungainly, ungraceful 4 = **difficult**, arduous, exacting, fatiguing, formidable, hard, laborious, tough, trying, uphill 5 = **severe**, cruel, drastic, extreme, great, hard, harsh, heavy, oppressive, pitiless, rigorous, sharp, strict, stringent 6 = **unrelaxed**, artificial, chilly, cold, constrained, forced, formal, laboured, prim, standoffish, starchy (*informal*), stilted, uneasy, unnatural, wooden 7 = **powerful**, brisk, fresh, strong, vigorous
➤ **Antonyms**
≠**inflexible**: bendable, ductile, elastic, flexible, pliable, pliant, yielding ≠**unsupple**: flexible, limber, lissom(e), lithe, supple ≠**unrelaxed**: casual, easy, informal, laid-back, natural, relaxed, spontaneous

stiffen *verb* 1 = **brace**, reinforce, starch, tauten, tense 2 = **set**, coagulate, congeal, crystallize, harden, jell, solidify, thicken

stiff-necked *adjective* = **stubborn**, obstinate, opinionated, uncompromising

stifle *verb* 1 = **suppress**, check, choke back, cover up, curb, extinguish, gag, hush, muffle, prevent, repress, restrain, silence, smother, stop 2 = **suffocate**, asphyxiate, choke, smother, strangle

stigma *noun* = **disgrace**, blot, brand, dishonour, mark, reproach, shame, slur, smirch, spot, stain

stigmatize *verb* = **brand**, cast a slur upon, defame, label, mark

still *adjective* 1 = **motionless**, at rest, calm, inert, lifeless, peaceful, placid, restful, serene, smooth, stationary, tranquil, undisturbed, unruffled, unstirring 2 = **silent**, hushed, noiseless, quiet ♦ *noun* 3 *Poetic* = **stillness**, hush, peace, quiet, silence, tranquillity ♦ *verb* 4 = **quieten**, allay, alleviate, appease, calm, hush, lull, pacify, quiet, settle, silence, smooth, smooth over, soothe, subdue, tranquillize ♦ *conjunction* 5 = **however**, but, for all that, nevertheless, notwithstanding, yet
➤ **Antonyms**
adjective ≠**motionless**: active, agitated,

astir, bustling, busy, humming, lively, moving, restless, turbulent ≠**silent**: noisy ♦ *noun* ≠**stillness**: bustle, clamour, hubbub, noise, uproar ♦ *verb* ≠**quieten**: aggravate, agitate, exacerbate, increase, inflame, rouse, stir up

stilted *adjective* = **stiff**, artificial, arty-farty (*informal*), bombastic, constrained, forced, grandiloquent, high-flown, high-sounding, inflated, laboured, pedantic, pompous, pretentious, unnatural, wooden
➤ **Antonyms**
flowing, fluid, free, natural, spontaneous, unaffected, unpretentious

stimulant *noun* = **pick-me-up** (*informal*), bracer (*informal*), energizer, pep pill (*informal*), restorative, reviver, tonic, upper (*slang*)
➤ **Antonyms**
calmant, depressant, downer (*slang*), sedative, tranquilliser

stimulate *verb* = **encourage**, animate, arouse, fan, fire, foment, gee up, goad, impel, incite, inflame, inspire, instigate, prod, prompt, provoke, quicken, rouse, spur, turn on (*slang*), urge, whet

stimulating *adjective* = **exciting**, exhilarating, inspiring, intriguing, provocative, provoking, rousing, stirring, thought-provoking
➤ **Antonyms**
as dry as dust, boring, dull, mind-numbing, unexciting, unimaginative, uninspiring, uninteresting, unstimulating

stimulus *noun* = **incentive**, encouragement, fillip, geeing-up, goad, impetus, incitement, inducement, provocation, shot in the arm (*informal*), spur

sting *verb* 1 = **hurt**, burn, pain, smart, tingle, wound 2 = **anger**, gall, incense, inflame, infuriate, nettle, pique, provoke, rile 3 *Informal* = **cheat**, defraud, do (*slang*), fleece, overcharge, rip off (*slang*), skin (*slang*), swindle, take for a ride (*informal*)

stingy *adjective* = **mean**, avaricious, cheeseparing, close-fisted, illiberal, mingy (*Brit. informal*), miserly, near, niggardly, parsimonious, penny-pinching (*informal*), penurious, scrimping, snoep (*S. African informal*), tightfisted, ungenerous

stink *noun* 1 = **stench**, fetor, foulness, foul smell, malodour, pong (*Brit. informal*) 2 *Slang As in* **make, create** *or* **kick up a stink** = **fuss**, brouhaha, commotion, row, rumpus, scandal, stir, to-do, uproar ♦ *verb* 3 = **reek**, offend the nostrils, pong (*Brit. informal*), stink to high heaven (*informal*) 4

Slang = **be bad**, be abhorrent, be no good, be rotten

stinker *noun Slang* **1** = **scoundrel**, bounder (*old-fashioned Brit. slang*), cad (*Brit. informal*), cocksucker (*taboo slang*), cur, heel, nasty piece of work (*informal*), rotter (*slang, chiefly Brit.*), sod (*slang*), swine **2** = **problem**, beast, horror, poser, shocker

stinking *adjective* **1** = **foul-smelling**, fetid, ill-smelling, malodorous, noisome, pongy (*Brit. informal*), reeking, smelly, whiffy (*Brit. slang*) **2** *Informal* = **rotten**, contemptible, disgusting, low, low-down (*informal*), mean, shitty (*taboo slang*), unpleasant, vile, wretched

stint *verb* **1** = **be mean**, be frugal, begrudge, be mingy (*Brit. informal*), be parsimonious, be sparing, economize, hold back, save, scrimp, skimp on, withhold ♦ *noun* **2** = **share**, assignment, bit, period, quota, shift, spell, stretch, term, time, turn

stipulate *verb* = **specify**, agree, contract, covenant, insist upon, lay down, lay down *or* impose conditions, promise, require, settle

stipulation *noun* = **condition**, agreement, clause, contract, precondition, prerequisite, provision, proviso, qualification, requirement, restriction, rider, *sine qua non*, specification, term

stir *verb* **1** = **mix**, agitate, beat, disturb, flutter, move, quiver, rustle, shake, tremble **2** = **stimulate**, affect, animate, arouse, awaken, electrify, excite, fire, incite, inflame, inspire, instigate, kindle, move, prod, prompt, provoke, quicken, raise, rouse, spur, thrill, touch, urge **3** = **get moving**, bestir oneself, budge, exert oneself, get a move on (*informal*), hasten, look lively (*informal*), make an effort, move ♦ *noun* **4** = **commotion**, activity, ado, agitation, bustle, disorder, disturbance, excitement, ferment, flurry, fuss, movement, to-do, tumult, uproar
➤ **Antonyms**
verb ≠**stimulate**: check, curb, dampen, inhibit, restrain, stifle, suppress, throw cold water on (*informal*)

stirring *adjective* = **exciting**, dramatic, emotive, exhilarating, heady, impassioned, inspiring, intoxicating, lively, moving, rousing, spirited, stimulating, thrilling

stock *noun* **1** = **goods**, array, assortment, choice, commodities, merchandise, range, selection, variety, wares **2** = **supply**, fund, hoard, reserve, reservoir, stockpile, store **3** = **property**, assets, capital, funds, investment **4** = **livestock**, beasts, cattle, domestic animals **5** = **lineage**, ancestry,

background, breed, descent, extraction, family, forebears, house, line, line of descent, parentage, pedigree, race, strain, type, variety **6 take stock** = **review the situation**, appraise, estimate, see how the land lies, size up (*informal*), weigh up ♦ *adjective* **7** = **standard**, basic, commonplace, conventional, customary, formal, ordinary, regular, routine, run-of-the-mill, set, staple, traditional, usual **8** = **hackneyed**, banal, overused, stereotyped, trite, worn-out ♦ *verb* **9** = **sell**, deal in, handle, keep, supply, trade in **10** = **provide with**, equip, fill, fit out, furnish, kit out, provision, supply **11 stock up** = **store (up)**, accumulate, amass, buy up, gather, hoard, lay in, put away, save, supply

stocky *adjective* = **thickset**, chunky, dumpy, solid, stubby, stumpy, sturdy

stodgy *adjective* **1** = **heavy**, filling, leaden, starchy, substantial **2** = **dull**, boring, dull as ditchwater, formal, fuddy-duddy (*informal*), heavy going, ho-hum, laboured, staid, stuffy, tedious, tiresome, turgid, unexciting, unimaginative, uninspired
➤ **Antonyms**
≠**heavy**: appetizing, fluffy, insubstantial, light ≠**dull**: animated, exciting, fresh, interesting, light, lively, stimulating, up-to-date

stoical *adjective* = **resigned**, calm, cool, dispassionate, impassive, imperturbable, indifferent, long-suffering, philosophic, phlegmatic, stoic, stolid

stoicism *noun* = **resignation**, acceptance, calmness, dispassion, fatalism, forbearance, fortitude, impassivity, imperturbability, indifference, long-suffering, patience, stolidity

stolid *adjective* = **apathetic**, bovine, doltish, dozy (*Brit. informal*), dull, heavy, lumpish, obtuse, slow, stupid, unemotional, wooden
➤ **Antonyms**
acute, animated, bright, emotional, energetic, excitable, intelligent, interested, lively, passionate, sharp, smart

stomach *noun* **1** = **belly**, abdomen, gut (*informal*), inside(s) (*informal*), paunch, pot, potbelly, spare tyre (*informal*), tummy (*informal*) **2** = **inclination**, appetite, desire, mind, relish, taste ♦ *verb* **3** = **bear**, abide, endure, hack (*slang*), put up with (*informal*), suffer, swallow, take, tolerate

stony *adjective* = **cold**, adamant, blank, callous, chilly, expressionless, hard, harsh, heartless, hostile, icy, indifferent, merciless, obdurate, pitiless, unfeeling, unresponsive

stooge noun = **pawn**, butt, dupe, fall guy (informal), patsy (slang, chiefly U.S. & Canad.), puppet

stoop verb 1 = **bend**, be bowed or round-shouldered, bow, crouch, descend, duck, hunch, incline, kneel, lean, squat 2 **stoop to** = **lower oneself by**, condescend to, deign to, demean oneself by, descend to, resort to, sink to ◆ noun 3 = **slouch**, bad posture, droop, round-shoulderedness, sag, slump

stop verb 1 = **halt**, axe (informal), belay (Nautical), be over, break off, bring or come to a halt or standstill, call it a day (informal), cease, come to an end, conclude, cut out (informal), cut short, desist, discontinue, draw up, end, finish, leave off, pack in (Brit. informal), pause, peter out, pull up, put an end to, quit, refrain, run down, shut down, stall, terminate 2 = **prevent**, arrest, bar, break, check, close, forestall, frustrate, hinder, hold back, impede, intercept, interrupt, nip (something) in the bud, rein in, repress, restrain, suspend 3 = **plug**, block, bung, obstruct, seal, staunch, stem 4 = **stay**, break one's journey, lodge, rest, sojourn ◆ noun 5 = **end**, cessation, conclusion, discontinuation, finish, halt, standstill 6 = **stay**, break, rest, sojourn, stopover, visit 7 = **station**, depot, destination, halt, stage, termination, terminus 8 = **block**, bar, break, check, control, hindrance, impediment, plug, stoppage

➤ Antonyms
verb ≠**halt**: advance, begin, commence, continue, get going, get under way, give the go ahead, go, institute, keep going, keep on, kick off (informal), proceed, set in motion, set off, start ≠**prevent**: assist, boost, encourage, expedite, facilitate, further, gee up, hasten, promote, push ◆ noun ≠**end**: beginning, commencement, kick-off (informal), start ≠**block**: boost, encouragement, geeing-up, incitement

stopgap noun = **makeshift**, improvisation, resort, substitute, temporary expedient

stoppage noun 1 = **stopping**, abeyance, arrest, close, closure, cutoff, discontinuance, halt, hindrance, lay-off, shutdown, standstill 2 = **blockage**, check, curtailment, interruption, obstruction, occlusion, stopping up

store verb 1 = **put by**, accumulate, deposit, garner, hoard, husband, keep, keep in reserve, lay by or in, lock away, put aside, put aside for a rainy day, put in storage, reserve, save, stash (informal), stock,

stockpile ◆ noun 2 = **shop**, chain store, department store, emporium, hypermarket, market, mart, outlet, supermarket 3 = **supply**, accumulation, cache, fund, hoard, lot, mine, provision, quantity, reserve, reservoir, stock, stockpile 4 = **repository**, depository, depot, storehouse, storeroom, warehouse 5 set **great store by** = **value**, appreciate, esteem, hold in high regard, prize, think highly of

storm noun 1 = **tempest**, blast, blizzard, cyclone, gale, gust, hurricane, squall, tornado, whirlwind 2 = **outburst**, agitation, anger, clamour, commotion, disturbance, furore, hubbub, outbreak, outcry, passion, roar, row, rumpus, stir, strife, tumult, turmoil, violence 3 = **attack**, assault, blitz, blitzkrieg, offensive, onset, onslaught, rush ◆ verb 4 = **attack**, assail, assault, beset, charge, rush, take by storm 5 = **rage**, bluster, fly off the handle (informal), fume, go ballistic (slang, chiefly U.S.), rant, rave, thunder 6 = **rush**, flounce, fly, stalk, stamp, stomp (informal)

stormy adjective = **wild**, blustering, blustery, foul, gusty, inclement, raging, rough, squally, tempestuous, turbulent, windy

story noun 1 = **tale**, account, anecdote, chronicle, fictional account, history, legend, narration, narrative, novel, recital, record, relation, romance, urban legend, urban myth, version, yarn 2 = **report**, article, feature, news, news item, scoop 3 Informal = **lie**, falsehood, fib, fiction, pork pie (Brit. slang), porky (Brit. slang), untruth, white lie

stout adjective 1 = **fat**, big, bulky, burly, corpulent, fleshy, heavy, obese, on the large or heavy side, overweight, plump, portly, rotund, substantial, tubby 2 = **strong**, able-bodied, athletic, beefy (informal), brawny, hardy, hulking, husky (informal), lusty, muscular, robust, stalwart, strapping, sturdy, substantial, thickset, tough, vigorous 3 = **brave**, bold, courageous, dauntless, doughty, fearless, gallant, indomitable, intrepid, lion-hearted, manly, plucky, resolute, valiant, valorous

➤ Antonyms
≠**fat**: insubstantial, lanky, lean, skin-and-bones (informal), skinny, slender, slight, slim ≠**strong**: feeble, flimsy, frail, insubstantial, puny ≠**brave**: cowardly, faint-hearted, fearful, irresolute, shrinking, soft, spineless, timid, weak

stouthearted adjective Old-fashioned = **brave**, bold, courageous, dauntless, doughty, fearless, great-hearted, gutsy (*slang*), heroic, indomitable, intrepid, lion-hearted, plucky, spirited, stalwart, valiant, valorous

stow *verb* = **pack**, bundle, cram, deposit, jam, load, put away, secrete, stash (*informal*), store, stuff, tuck

straggle *verb* = **spread**, drift, ramble, range, roam, rove, stray, string out, wander

straight *adjective* 1 = **direct**, near, short, undeviating, unswerving 2 = **level**, aligned, even, horizontal, in line, right, smooth, square, true 3 = **upright**, erect, perpendicular, plumb, vertical 4 = **accurate**, authentic, fair, honest, reliable, trustworthy 5 = **frank**, blunt, bold, candid, downright, forthright, honest, outright, plain, point-blank, straightforward, unqualified, upfront (*informal*) 6 = **successive**, consecutive, continuous, nonstop, running, solid, sustained, uninterrupted, unrelieved 7 = **undiluted**, neat, pure, unadulterated, unmixed 8 = **orderly**, arranged, in order, neat, organized, put to rights, shipshape, sorted out, tidy 9 = **honest**, above board, decent, equitable, fair, fair and square, honourable, just, law-abiding, reliable, respectable, trustworthy, upright 10 *Slang* = **conventional**, bourgeois, conservative, orthodox, square (*informal*), traditional ♦ *adverb* 11 = **directly**, as the crow flies, at once, immediately, instantly 12 = **frankly**, candidly, honestly, in plain English, point-blank, pulling no punches (*informal*), with no holds barred
➤ Antonyms
adjective ≠**direct**: circuitous, indirect, roundabout, winding, zigzag ≠**level**: askew, bent, crooked, curved, skewwhiff (*Brit. informal*), twisted, uneven ≠**frank**: ambiguous, cryptic, equivocal, evasive, indirect, vague ≠**successive**: broken, discontinuous, interrupted, non-consecutive ≠**orderly**: confused, disorderly, disorganized, in disarray, messy, untidy ≠**honest**: bent (*slang*), crooked (*informal*), dishonest, dishonourable, shady (*informal*), unlawful ≠**conventional**: cool, fashionable, trendy (*Brit. informal*), voguish

straight away *adverb* = **immediately**, at once, directly, instantly, now, on the spot, right away, there and then, without any delay, without more ado

straighten *verb* = **neaten**, arrange, order, put in order, set *or* put to rights, smarten up, spruce up, tidy (up)

straighten out *verb* = **make clear**, clear up, correct, disentangle, put right, rectify, resolve, settle, sort out, work out

straightforward *adjective* 1 = **honest**, above board, candid, direct, forthright, genuine, guileless, open, sincere, truthful, upfront (*informal*) 2 *Chiefly Brit.* = **simple**, clear-cut, easy, easy-peasy (*slang*), elementary, routine, uncomplicated, undemanding
➤ Antonyms
≠**honest**: devious, disingenuous, roundabout, shady, sharp, unscrupulous
≠**simple**: complex, complicated, confused, convoluted, unclear

strain¹ *noun* 1 = **stress**, anxiety, burden, pressure, tension 2 = **exertion**, effort, force, struggle 3 = **injury**, pull, sprain, tautness, tension, wrench 4 **strains** = **tune**, air, melody, song, theme ♦ *verb* 5 = **strive**, bend over backwards (*informal*), break one's back *or* neck (*informal*), bust a gut (*informal*), do one's damnedest (*informal*), endeavour, give it one's all (*informal*), give it one's best shot (*informal*), go all out for (*informal*), go for broke (*slang*), go for it (*informal*), knock oneself out (*informal*), labour, make an all-out effort (*informal*), struggle 6 = **overexert**, drive, exert, fatigue, injure, overtax, overwork, pull, push to the limit, sprain, tax, tear, test, tire, twist, weaken, wrench 7 = **sieve**, filter, percolate, purify, screen, seep, separate, sift 8 = **stretch**, distend, draw tight, extend, tauten, tighten
➤ Antonyms
noun ≠**stress**, **exertion**: ease, effortlessness, lack of tension, relaxation ♦ *verb* ≠**strive**, **overexert**: idle, loose, pamper, relax, rest, slacken, take it easy, yield

strain² *noun* 1 = **breed**, ancestry, blood, descent, extraction, family, lineage, pedigree, race, stock 2 = **trace**, streak, suggestion, suspicion, tendency, trait

strained *adjective* 1 = **forced**, artificial, false, laboured, put on, unnatural 2 = **tense**, awkward, constrained, difficult, embarrassed, self-conscious, stiff, uncomfortable, uneasy, unrelaxed
➤ Antonyms
≠**forced**: natural ≠**tense**: comfortable, relaxed

strait *noun* 1 *often plural* = **channel**, narrows, sound 2 **straits** = **difficulty**, crisis, dilemma, distress, emergency, extremity, hardship, hole (*slang*), mess, pass, plight, predicament, pretty *or* fine kettle of fish (*informal*)

strait-laced *or* **straight-laced** *adjective* = **puritanical**, moralistic, narrow, narrow-minded, old-maidish (*informal*), prim, proper, prudish, strict, Victorian

➤ **Antonyms**
broad-minded, earthy, immoral, loose, relaxed, uninhibited, unreserved

strand *noun* = **filament**, fibre, length, lock, rope, string, thread, tress, twist, wisp

stranded *adjective* **1** = **beached**, aground, ashore, cast away, grounded, marooned, shipwrecked **2** = **helpless**, abandoned, high and dry, homeless, left in the lurch, penniless

strange *adjective* **1** = **odd**, abnormal, astonishing, bizarre, curious, eccentric, exceptional, extraordinary, fantastic, funny, irregular, left-field (*informal*), marvellous, mystifying, oddball (*informal*), off-the-wall (*slang*), out-of-the-way, outré, peculiar, perplexing, queer, rare, remarkable, rum (*Brit. slang*), singular, unaccountable, uncanny, uncommon, unheard-of, weird, wonderful **2** = **unfamiliar**, alien, exotic, foreign, new, novel, outside one's experience, unexplored, unknown, untried **3** = **out of place**, awkward, bewildered, disoriented, ill at ease, like a fish out of water, lost, uncomfortable **4 strange to** = **unaccustomed to**, a stranger to, ignorant of, inexperienced in, new to, unpractised in, unseasoned in, unused to, unversed in

➤ **Antonyms**
≠**odd**: accustomed, bog-standard (*Brit. & Irish slang*), common, commonplace, conventional, familiar, habitual, ordinary, regular, routine, run-of-the-mill, standard, typical, unexceptional, usual, well-known ≠**unfamiliar**: accustomed, familiar, habitual ≠**out of place**: at ease, at home, comfortable, relaxed

stranger *noun* = **newcomer**, alien, foreigner, guest, incomer, new arrival, outlander, unknown, visitor

strangle *verb* **1** = **throttle**, asphyxiate, choke, garrotte, smother, strangulate, suffocate **2** = **suppress**, gag, inhibit, repress, stifle

strap *noun* **1** = **belt**, leash, thong, tie ♦ *verb* **2** = **fasten**, bind, buckle, lash, secure, tie, truss

strapped *adjective* **strapped for** *Slang* = **short of**, financially embarrassed, in need of, straitened, stuck for

strapping *adjective* = **well-built**, beefy (*informal*), big, brawny, burly, hefty (*informal*), hulking, husky (*informal*), powerful, robust, stalwart, sturdy, well set-up

stratagem *noun* = **trick**, artifice, device, dodge, feint, intrigue, manoeuvre, plan, plot, ploy, ruse, scheme, subterfuge, wile

strategic *adjective* **1** = **tactical**, calculated, deliberate, diplomatic, planned, politic **2** = **crucial**, cardinal, critical, decisive, important, key, vital

strategy *noun* = **plan**, approach, grand design, planning, policy, procedure, programme, scheme

stratum *noun* **1** = **layer**, bed, level, lode, seam, stratification, tier, vein **2** = **class**, bracket, caste, category, estate, grade, group, level, rank, station

stray *verb* **1** = **wander**, be abandoned *or* lost, drift, err, go astray, lose one's way, meander, range, roam, rove, straggle **2** = **digress**, deviate, diverge, get off the point, get sidetracked, go off at a tangent, ramble ♦ *adjective* **3** = **lost**, abandoned, homeless, roaming, vagrant **4** = **random**, accidental, chance, erratic, freak, odd, scattered

streak *noun* **1** = **band**, layer, line, slash, smear, strip, stripe, stroke, vein **2** = **trace**, dash, element, strain, touch, vein ♦ *verb* **3** = **band**, daub, fleck, slash, smear, striate, stripe **4** = **speed**, barrel (along) (*informal, chiefly U.S. & Canad.*), dart, flash, fly, hurtle, sprint, sweep, tear, whizz (*informal*), zoom

stream *noun* **1** = **river**, bayou, beck, brook, burn (*Scot.*), creek (*U.S.*), freshet, rill, rivulet, tributary **2** = **flow**, course, current, drift, outpouring, run, rush, surge, tide, tideway, torrent ♦ *verb* **3** = **flow**, cascade, course, emit, flood, glide, gush, issue, pour, run, shed, spill, spout

streamer *noun* = **banner**, colours, ensign, flag, pennant, pennon, ribbon, standard

streamlined *adjective* = **efficient**, modernized, organized, rationalized, sleek, slick, smooth, smooth-running, time-saving, well-run

street *noun* **1** = **road**, avenue, boulevard, lane, roadway, row, terrace, thoroughfare **2 right up one's street** *Informal* = **to one's liking**, acceptable, compatible, congenial, familiar, one's cup of tea (*informal*), pleasing, suitable, to one's taste

strength *noun* **1** = **might**, backbone, brawn, brawniness, courage, firmness, fortitude, health, lustiness, muscle, robustness, sinew, stamina, stoutness, sturdiness, toughness, wellness **2** = **strong point**, advantage, asset, mainstay, tower of strength **3** = **power**, concentration, effectiveness, efficacy, energy, force, intensity, potency, resolution, spirit, vehemence, vigour

➤ **Antonyms**
≠**might**: debility, feebleness, frailty, infirmity, powerlessness, weakness

≠**strong point:** Achilles heel, chink in one's armour, defect, failing, flaw, shortcoming, weakness ≠**power:** feebleness, impotence, powerlessness, weakness

strengthen verb **1** = **fortify**, brace up, consolidate, encourage, gee up, give new energy to, harden, hearten, invigorate, rejuvenate, restore, stiffen, toughen **2** = **reinforce**, augment, bolster, brace, build up, buttress, confirm, corroborate, enhance, establish, give a boost to, harden, heighten, increase, intensify, justify, steel, substantiate, support
➤ **Antonyms**
crush, debilitate, destroy, dilute, enervate, render impotent, sap, subvert, undermine, weaken

strenuous adjective **1** = **demanding**, arduous, exhausting, hard, Herculean, laborious, taxing, toilsome, tough, tough going, unrelaxing, uphill **2** = **tireless**, active, bold, determined, eager, earnest, energetic, persistent, resolute, spirited, strong, vigorous, zealous
➤ **Antonyms**
≠**demanding:** easy, effortless, relaxing, undemanding, untaxing ≠**tireless:** relaxed, unenergetic

stress noun **1** = **strain**, anxiety, burden, hassle (informal), nervous tension, pressure, tension, trauma, worry **2** = **emphasis**, force, importance, significance, urgency, weight **3** = **accent**, accentuation, beat, emphasis ♦ verb **4** = **emphasize**, accentuate, belabour, dwell on, harp on, lay emphasis upon, point up, repeat, rub in, underline, underscore

stressful adjective = **worrying**, agitating, anxious, tense, traumatic

stretch verb **1** = **extend**, cover, put forth, reach, spread, unfold, unroll **2** = **pull**, distend, draw out, elongate, expand, inflate, lengthen, pull out of shape, rack, strain, swell, tighten ♦ noun **3** = **expanse**, area, distance, extent, spread, sweep, tract **4** = **period**, bit, run, space, spell, stint, term, time

strew verb = **scatter**, bestrew, disperse, litter, spread, sprinkle, toss

stricken adjective = **affected**, afflicted, hit, injured, laid low, smitten, struck, struck down

strict adjective **1** = **severe**, austere, authoritarian, firm, harsh, no-nonsense, rigid, rigorous, stern, stringent **2** = **exact**, accurate, close, faithful, meticulous, particular, precise, religious, scrupulous, true **3** = **absolute**, complete, perfect, total, utter
➤ **Antonyms**

≠**severe:** easy-going, easy-oasy (slang), flexible, laid-back (informal), lax, mild, moderate, soft, tolerant

stricture noun Formal = **criticism**, animadversion, bad press, censure, flak (informal), stick (slang)

strident adjective = **harsh**, discordant, grating, jangling, jarring, rasping, raucous, screeching, shrill, unmusical
➤ **Antonyms**
dulcet, gentle, harmonious, mellifluous, mellow, quiet, soft, soothing, sweet

strife noun = **conflict**, animosity, battle, bickering, clash, clashes, combat, contention, contest, controversy, discord, dissension, friction, quarrel, rivalry, row, squabbling, struggle, warfare, wrangling

strike verb **1** = **walk out**, down tools, mutiny, revolt **2** = **hit**, bang, beat, box, clobber (slang), clout (informal), cuff, deck (slang), hammer, knock, pound, punch, slap, smack, smite, sock (slang), swipe, thump, wallop (informal) **3** = **drive**, force, hit, impel, thrust **4** = **collide with**, be in collision with, bump into, clash, come into contact with, dash, hit, knock into, run into, smash into, touch **5** = **affect**, hit, make an impact on, reach, register (informal) **6** = **occur to**, come to, come to the mind of, dawn on or upon, hit, register (informal), seem **7** sometimes with **upon** = **discover**, come upon or across, encounter, find, happen or chance upon, hit upon, light upon, reach, stumble upon or across, turn up, uncover, unearth **8** = **reach**, achieve, arrange, arrive at, attain, effect **9 strike at** = **attack**, affect, assail, assault, deal a blow to, devastate, fall upon, hit, invade, set upon, smite

strike out verb **1** Also **strike off, strike through** = **score out**, cancel, cross out, delete, efface, erase, excise, expunge, remove **2** = **begin**, get under way, set out, start out

striking adjective = **impressive**, astonishing, conspicuous, dazzling, dramatic, drop-dead (slang), extraordinary, jaw-dropping, memorable, noticeable, out of the ordinary, outstanding, stunning (informal), wonderful
➤ **Antonyms**
average, dull, indifferent, undistinguished, unexceptional, unextraordinary, unimpressive, uninteresting, vanilla (informal)

string noun **1** = **cord**, fibre, twine **2** = **series**, chain, file, line, procession, queue, row, sequence, strand, succession ♦ verb **3** = **hang**, festoon, link, loop, sling, stretch, suspend, thread **4 = spread out**, disperse, extend, fan out, lengthen, protract, space out, straggle

string along *verb* **1** *often with* **with** = **accompany**, go along with **2 = deceive**, bluff, dupe, fool, hoax, kid (*informal*), play fast and loose with (someone) (*informal*), play (someone) false, put one over on (someone) (*informal*), take (someone) for a ride (*informal*)

stringent *adjective* = **strict**, binding, demanding, exacting, inflexible, rigid, rigorous, severe, tight, tough
➤ **Antonyms**
flexible, lax, loose, relaxed, slack, unrigorous

strings *plural noun* = **conditions**, catches (*informal*), complications, obligations, prerequisites, provisos, qualifications, requirements, riders, stipulations

stringy *adjective* = **fibrous**, gristly, sinewy, tough, wiry

strip[1] *verb* **1 = undress**, disrobe, unclothe, uncover **2 = plunder**, bare, denude, deprive, despoil, dismantle, divest, empty, lay bare, loot, peel, pillage, ransack, rob, sack, skin, spoil

strip[2] *noun* = **piece**, band, belt, bit, fillet, ribbon, shred, slip, swathe

striped *adjective* = **banded**, barred, striated, stripy

stripling *noun* = **boy**, adolescent, lad, young fellow, youngster, youth

strive *verb* = **try**, attempt, bend over backwards (*informal*), break one's neck (*informal*), compete, contend, do all one can, do one's best, do one's damnedest (*informal*), do one's utmost, endeavour, exert oneself, fight, give it one's all (*informal*), give it one's best shot (*informal*), go all out (*informal*), go for broke (*slang*), go for it (*informal*), knock oneself out (*informal*), labour, make an all-out effort (*informal*), strain, struggle, toil, try hard

stroke *verb* **1 = caress**, fondle, pat, pet, rub ♦ *noun* **2 = apoplexy**, attack, collapse, fit, seizure, shock **3 = blow**, hit, knock, pat, rap, swipe, thump **4 = feat**, accomplishment, achievement, flourish, move, movement

stroll *verb* **1 = walk**, amble, make one's way, mosey (*informal*), promenade, ramble, saunter, stretch one's legs, take a turn ♦ *noun* **2 = walk**, airing, breath of air, constitutional, excursion, promenade, ramble, turn

strong *adjective* **1 = powerful**, athletic, beefy (*informal*), brawny, burly, capable,

fighting fit, fit, fit as a fiddle, hale, hardy, healthy, Herculean, lusty, muscular, robust, sinewy, sound, stalwart, stout, strapping, sturdy, tough **2 = durable**, hard-wearing, heavy-duty, reinforced, sturdy, substantial, well-built **3 = distinct**, clear, marked, overpowering, unmistakable **4 = persuasive**, clear, clear-cut, cogent, compelling, convincing, effective, formidable, great, overpowering, potent, sound, telling, trenchant, weighty, well-established, well-founded **5 = pungent**, biting, concentrated, heady, highly-flavoured, highly-seasoned, hot, intoxicating, piquant, powerful, pure, sharp, spicy, undiluted **6 = self-confident**, aggressive, brave, courageous, determined, feisty (*informal, chiefly U.S. & Canad.*), forceful, hard as nails, hard-nosed (*informal*), plucky, resilient, resolute, resourceful, self-assertive, steadfast, stouthearted, tenacious, tough, unyielding **7 = intense**, acute, dedicated, deep, deep-rooted, eager, fervent, fervid, fierce, firm, keen, severe, staunch, vehement, violent, zealous **8 = extreme**, Draconian, drastic, forceful, severe **9 = bright**, bold, brilliant, dazzling, glaring, loud, stark
➤ **Antonyms**
≠**powerful**: delicate, feeble, frail, ineffectual, namby-pamby, puny, weak ≠**distinct**: delicate, faint, slight ≠**pungent**: bland, mild, tasteless, vapid, weak ≠**self-confident**: characterless, faint-hearted, spineless, timid, unassertive ≠**bright**: dull, insipid, pale, pastel, washed-out

strong-arm *adjective Informal* = **bullying**, aggressive, coercive, forceful, high-pressure, terror, terrorizing, threatening, thuggish, violent

stronghold *noun* = **fortress**, bastion, bulwark, castle, citadel, fastness, fort, keep, refuge

strong-minded *adjective* = **determined**, firm, independent, iron-willed, resolute, strong-willed, unbending, uncompromising

strong point *noun* = **forte**, advantage, asset, métier, speciality, strength

stroppy *adjective Brit. informal* = **awkward**, bloody-minded (*Brit. informal*), cantankerous, difficult, obstreperous, perverse, quarrelsome, uncooperative, unhelpful

structure *noun* **1 = building**, construction, edifice, erection, pile **2 = arrangement**, configuration, conformation, construction, design, form, formation, make-up, organization ♦ *verb* **3 = arrange**, assemble, build up, design, organize, put together, shape

struggle *verb* 1 = **strive**, bend over backwards (*informal*), break one's neck (*informal*), do one's damnedest (*informal*), exert oneself, give it one's all (*informal*), give it one's best shot (*informal*), go all out (*informal*), go for it (*informal*), knock oneself out (*informal*), labour, make an all-out effort (*informal*), make every effort, strain, toil, work 2 = **fight**, battle, compete, contend, grapple, scuffle, wrestle ♦ *noun* 3 = **effort**, exertion, grind (*informal*), labour, long haul, pains, scramble, toil, work 4 = **fight**, battle, brush, clash, combat, conflict, contest, encounter, hostilities, skirmish, strife, tussle

strung up *adjective Informal* = **tense**, a bundle of nerves (*informal*), antsy (*informal*), edgy, jittery (*informal*), keyed up, nervous, on edge, on tenterhooks, twitchy (*informal*), uptight (*informal*), wired (*slang*)

strut *verb* = **swagger**, parade, peacock, prance, stalk

stub *noun* 1 = **butt**, dog-end (*informal*), end, fag end (*informal*), remnant, stump, tail, tail end 2 = **counterfoil**

stubborn *adjective* = **obstinate**, bull-headed, dogged, fixed, headstrong, inflexible, intractable, mulish, obdurate, opinionated, persistent, pig-headed, recalcitrant, refractory, self-willed, stiff-necked, tenacious, unbending, unmanageable, unshakable, unyielding, wilful
► **Antonyms**
biddable, compliant, docile, flexible, half-hearted, irresolute, malleable, manageable, pliable, pliant, tractable, vacillating, wavering, yielding

stubby *adjective* = **stocky**, chunky, dumpy, short, squat, stumpy, thickset

stuck *adjective* 1 = **fastened**, cemented, fast, firm, fixed, glued, joined 2 *Informal* = **baffled**, at a loss, at a standstill, at one's wits' end, beaten, nonplussed, stumped, up against a brick wall (*informal*) 3 *Slang* **stuck on** = **infatuated with**, crazy about, for, *or* over (*informal*), enthusiastic about, hung up on (*slang*), keen on, mad about, obsessed with, wild about (*informal*) 4 **get stuck in** *Informal* = **set about**, get down to, make a start on, tackle, take the bit between one's teeth

stuck-up *adjective Informal* = **snobbish**, arrogant, bigheaded (*informal*), conceited, condescending, haughty, high and mighty (*informal*), hoity-toity (*informal*), patronizing, proud, snooty (*informal*),

swollen-headed, toffee-nosed (*slang, chiefly Brit.*), uppish (*Brit. informal*), uppity (*informal*)

stud *verb* = **ornament**, bejewel, bespangle, dot, fleck, spangle, speckle, spot, sprinkle

student *noun* = **learner**, apprentice, disciple, pupil, scholar, trainee, undergraduate

studied *adjective* = **planned**, calculated, conscious, deliberate, intentional, premeditated, purposeful, well-considered, wilful
► **Antonyms**
impulsive, natural, spontaneous, spur-of-the-moment, unplanned, unpremeditated

studio *noun* = **workshop**, atelier

studious *adjective* 1 = **scholarly**, academic, assiduous, bookish, diligent, eager, earnest, hard-working, intellectual, meditative, reflective, sedulous, serious, thoughtful 2 = **careful**, attentive, deliberate, precise
► **Antonyms**
≠**scholarly**: frivolous, idle, lazy, loafing, unacademic, unintellectual, unscholarly ≠**careful**: careless, inattentive, indifferent, negligent

study *verb* 1 = **learn**, bone up on (*informal*), burn the midnight oil, cram (*informal*), mug up (*Brit. slang*), read up, swot (up) (*Brit. informal*) 2 = **contemplate**, apply oneself (to), consider, examine, go into, meditate, ponder, pore over, read 3 = **examine**, analyse, deliberate, investigate, look into, peruse, research, scrutinize, survey, work over ♦ *noun* 4 = **learning**, academic work, application, book work, cramming (*informal*), lessons, reading, research, school work, swotting (*Brit. informal*), thought 5 = **examination**, analysis, attention, cogitation, consideration, contemplation, inquiry, inspection, investigation, perusal, review, scrutiny, survey

stuff *noun* 1 = **substance**, essence, matter, pith, quintessence 2 = **things**, belongings, bits and pieces, clobber (*Brit. slang*), effects, equipment, gear, goods and chattels, impedimenta, junk, kit, luggage, materials, objects, paraphernalia, possessions, tackle, trappings 3 = **material**, cloth, fabric, raw material, textile ♦ *verb* 4 = **cram**, compress, crowd, fill, force, jam, load, pack, pad, push, ram, shove, squeeze, stow, wedge 5 **stuff oneself** *or* **one's face** = **gorge**, gobble, gormandize, guzzle, make a pig of oneself (*informal*), overindulge, pig out (*slang*)

stuffing *noun* 1 = **forcemeat** 2 = **filling**,

kapok, packing, quilting, wadding

stuffy *adjective* **1 = airless**, close, fetid, frowsty, heavy, muggy, oppressive, stale, stifling, suffocating, sultry, unventilated **2** *Informal* **= staid**, as dry as dust, conventional, deadly, dreary, dull, fusty, old-fashioned, old-fogeyish, pompous, priggish, prim, prim and proper, stilted, stodgy, strait-laced, uninteresting
➤ **Antonyms**
≠**airless:** airy, breezy, cool, draughty, fresh, gusty, pleasant, well-ventilated

stumble *verb* **1 = trip**, blunder about, come a cropper (*informal*), fall, falter, flounder, lose one's balance, lurch, reel, slip, stagger **2 = falter**, fluff (*informal*), hesitate, stammer, stutter **3** with **across, on** or **upon = discover**, blunder upon, chance upon, come across, encounter, find, happen upon, light upon, run across, turn up

stumbling block *noun* **= obstacle**, bar, barrier, difficulty, hazard, hindrance, hurdle, impediment, obstruction, snag

stump *verb* **1 = baffle**, bewilder, bring (someone) up short, confound, confuse, dumbfound, flummox, foil, mystify, nonplus, outwit, perplex, puzzle, snooker, stop, stymie **2 = stamp**, clump, lumber, plod, stomp (*informal*), trudge

stump up *verb Brit. informal* **= pay**, chip in (*informal*), come across with (*informal*), contribute, cough up (*informal*), donate, fork out (*slang*), hand over, shell out (*informal*)

stumpy *adjective* **= stocky**, chunky, dumpy, heavy, short, squat, stubby, thick, thickset

stun *verb* **1 = overcome**, amaze, astonish, astound, bewilder, confound, confuse, dumbfound, flabbergast (*informal*), overpower, shock, stagger, strike (someone) dumb, stupefy, take (someone's) breath away **2 = knock out**, daze

stung *adjective* **= goaded**, angered, exasperated, hurt, incensed, nettled, piqued, roused, wounded

stunned *adjective* **1 = staggered**, astounded, at a loss for words, bowled over (*informal*), devastated, dumbfounded, flabbergasted (*informal*), gobsmacked (*Brit. slang*), numb, shocked, struck dumb **2 = knocked out**, dazed

stunner *noun Informal* **= beauty**, dazzler, humdinger (*slang*), knockout (*informal*), looker (*informal, chiefly U.S.*), lovely (*slang*), sensation, smasher (*informal*), wow (*slang, chiefly U.S.*)

stunning *adjective Informal* **= wonderful**, beautiful, brilliant, dazzling, devastating (*informal*), dramatic, drop-dead (*slang*), gorgeous, great (*informal*), heavenly, impressive, jaw-dropping, lovely, marvellous, out of this world (*informal*), ravishing, remarkable, sensational (*informal*), smashing (*informal*), spectacular, striking
➤ **Antonyms**
average, dreadful, horrible, mediocre, no great shakes (*informal*), ordinary, plain, poor, rotten, run-of-the-mill, ugly, unattractive, unimpressive, uninspiring, unremarkable

stunt *noun* **= feat**, act, deed, exploit, feature, trick

stunted *adjective* **= undersized**, diminutive, dwarfed, dwarfish, little, small, tiny

stupefy *verb* **= astound**, amaze, bewilder, confound, daze, dumbfound, knock senseless, numb, shock, stagger, stun

stupendous *adjective* **1 = wonderful**, amazing, astounding, breathtaking, brilliant, fabulous (*informal*), fantastic (*informal*), jaw-dropping, marvellous, mind-blowing (*informal*), mind-boggling (*informal*), out of this world (*informal*), overwhelming, phenomenal, prodigious, sensational (*informal*), staggering, stunning (*informal*), superb, tremendous (*informal*), wondrous (*archaic or literary*) **2** **= huge**, colossal, enormous, gigantic, mega (*slang*), vast
➤ **Antonyms**
≠**wonderful:** average, mediocre, modest, no great shakes (*informal*), ordinary, petty, unexciting, unimpressive, unremarkable, unsurprising ≠**huge:** diminutive, puny, tiny

stupid *adjective* **1 = unintelligent**, braindead (*informal*), brainless, crass, cretinous, dense, dim, doltish, dopey (*informal*), dozy (*Brit. informal*), dull, dumb (*informal*), dumb-ass (*slang*), gullible, half-witted, moronic, naive, obtuse, simple, simple-minded, slow, slow on the uptake (*informal*), slow-witted, sluggish, stolid, thick, thickheaded, witless, woodenheaded (*informal*) **2 = silly**, asinine, crackbrained, crackpot (*informal*), daft (*informal*), foolish, futile, half-baked (*informal*), idiotic, ill-advised, imbecilic, inane, irresponsible, laughable, ludicrous, meaningless, mindless, nonsensical, pointless, puerile, rash, senseless, short-sighted, trivial, unintelligent, unthinking **3 = dazed**, groggy, in a daze, insensate, punch-drunk, semiconscious, senseless, stunned, stupefied

> ➤ **Antonyms**

≠**unintelligent**: astute, brainy, bright, brilliant, clear-headed, clever, intelligent, lucid, on the ball (*informal*), quick, quick on the uptake, quick-witted, sensible, sharp, shrewd, smart, wise ≠**silly**: astute, prudent, realistic, reasonable, sensible, shrewd, thoughtful, well-thought-out, wise

stupidity *noun* **1** = **lack of intelligence**, asininity, brainlessness, denseness, dimness, dopiness (*slang*), doziness (*Brit. informal*), dullness, dumbness (*informal*), feeble-mindedness, imbecility, naivety, obtuseness, simplicity, slowness, thickheadedness, thickness **2** = **silliness**, absurdity, fatuousness, folly, foolhardiness, foolishness, futility, idiocy, impracticality, inanity, irresponsibility, ludicrousness, lunacy, madness, pointlessness, puerility, rashness, senselessness

stupor *noun* = **daze**, coma, inertia, insensibility, lethargy, numbness, stupefaction, torpor, trance, unconsciousness

sturdy *adjective* **1** = **robust**, athletic, brawny, firm, hardy, hearty, lusty, muscular, powerful, stalwart, staunch, thickset, vigorous **2** = **substantial**, built to last, durable, secure, solid, well-built, well-made

> ➤ **Antonyms**

≠**robust**: feeble, infirm, puny, skinny, weak ≠**substantial**: flimsy, frail, rickety, unsubstantial

stutter *verb* = **stammer**, falter, hesitate, speak haltingly, splutter, stumble

style *noun* **1** = **design**, cut, form, manner **2** = **manner**, approach, custom, method, mode, technique, way **3** = **elegance**, chic, cosmopolitanism, dash, dressiness (*informal*), élan, fashionableness, flair, grace, panache, polish, refinement, savoir-faire, smartness, sophistication, stylishness, taste, urbanity **4** = **type**, category, genre, kind, pattern, sort, spirit, strain, tenor, tone, variety **5** = **fashion**, mode, rage, trend, vogue **6** = **luxury**, affluence, comfort, ease, elegance, gracious living, grandeur **7** = **mode of expression**, expression, phraseology, phrasing, turn of phrase, vein, wording ◆ *verb* **8** = **design**, adapt, arrange, cut, dress, fashion, shape, tailor **9** = **call**, address, christen, denominate, designate, dub, entitle, label, name, term

stylish *adjective* = **smart**, à la mode, chic, classy (*slang*), dapper, dressy (*informal*), fashionable, in fashion, in vogue, modish, natty (*informal*), polished, snappy, snazzy (*informal*), trendy (*Brit. informal*), urbane,

voguish, well turned-out

> ➤ **Antonyms**

naff (*Brit. slang*), old-fashioned, outmoded, out-of-date, passé, scruffy, shabby, slovenly, tacky, tawdry, unfashionable, unstylish, untrendy (*Brit. informal*)

stymie *verb* = **frustrate**, balk, confound, defeat, flummox, foil, hinder, snooker, spike (someone's) guns, thwart

suave *adjective* = **smooth**, affable, agreeable, bland, charming, cool (*informal*), courteous, debonair, gracious, polite, smooth-tongued, sophisticated, svelte, urbane, worldly

subconscious *adjective* = **hidden**, inner, innermost, intuitive, latent, repressed, subliminal, suppressed

> ➤ **Antonyms**

aware, conscious, knowing, sensible, sentient

subdue *verb* **1** = **overcome**, break, conquer, control, crush, defeat, get the better of, get the upper hand over, get under control, master, overpower, put down, quell, tame, trample, triumph over, vanquish **2** = **moderate**, check, control, mellow, quieten down, repress, soften, suppress, tone down

> ➤ **Antonyms**

≠**moderate**: agitate, arouse, awaken, incite, provoke, stir up, waken, whip up

subdued *adjective* **1** = **quiet**, chastened, crestfallen, dejected, downcast, down in the mouth, out of spirits, sad, sadder and wiser, serious, sobered **2** = **soft**, dim, hushed, low-key, muted, quiet, shaded, sober, subtle, toned down, unobtrusive

> ➤ **Antonyms**

≠**quiet**: cheerful, enthusiastic, full of beans (*informal*), happy, lively, vivacious ≠**soft**: bright, loud, strident

subject *noun* **1** = **topic**, affair, business, issue, matter, object, point, question, subject matter, substance, theme **2** = **participant**, case, client, guinea pig (*informal*), patient, victim **3** = **citizen**, dependant, liegeman, national, subordinate, vassal ◆ *adjective* **4** = **subordinate**, captive, dependent, enslaved, inferior, obedient, satellite, subjugated, submissive, subservient **5** **subject to**: **a** = **liable to**, disposed to, prone to **b** = **vulnerable to**, at the mercy of, exposed to, in danger of, open to, susceptible to **c** = **conditional on**, contingent on, dependent on ◆ *verb* **6** = **put through**, expose, lay open, make liable, submit, treat

subjective *adjective* = **personal**, biased,

emotional, nonobjective, prejudiced
➤ **Antonyms**
detached, disinterested, dispassionate, impartial, impersonal, objective, open-minded, unbiased

subjugate verb = **conquer**, bring (someone) to his knees, crush, defeat, enslave, hold sway over, master, overcome, overpower, overthrow, put down, quell, subdue, suppress, tame, vanquish

sublimate verb = **channel**, divert, redirect, transfer, turn

sublime adjective = **noble**, elevated, eminent, exalted, glorious, grand, great, high, imposing, lofty, magnificent, majestic
➤ **Antonyms**
bad, commonplace, lowly, mundane, ordinary, poor, ridiculous

subliminal adjective = **subconscious**, unconscious

submerge verb = **immerse**, deluge, dip, drown, duck, dunk, engulf, flood, inundate, overflow, overwhelm, plunge, sink, swamp

submerged adjective = **immersed**, drowned, submarine, submersed, sunk, sunken, undersea, underwater

submission noun 1 = **surrender**, acquiescence, assent, capitulation, cave-in (informal), giving in, yielding 2 = **presentation**, entry, handing in, submitting, tendering 3 = **proposal**, argument, contention 4 = **meekness**, compliance, deference, docility, obedience, passivity, resignation, submissiveness, tractability, unassertiveness

submissive adjective = **meek**, abject, accommodating, acquiescent, amenable, biddable, compliant, deferential, docile, dutiful, humble, obedient, passive, pliant, resigned, tractable, uncomplaining, unresisting, yielding
➤ **Antonyms**
awkward, difficult, disobedient, headstrong, intractable, obstinate, stubborn, uncooperative, unyielding

submit verb 1 = **surrender**, accede, acquiesce, agree, bend, bow, capitulate, cave in (informal), comply, defer, endure, give in, knuckle under, put up with (informal), resign oneself, stoop, succumb, toe the line, tolerate, yield 2 = **present**, commit, hand in, proffer, put forward, refer, table, tender

subnormal adjective No longer in technical use = **retarded**, cretinous, feeble-minded, imbecilic, mentally defective, moronic, simple, slow

subordinate adjective 1 = **lesser**, dependent, inferior, junior, lower, minor, secondary, subject, subservient 2 = **supplementary**, ancillary, auxiliary, subsidiary ◆ noun 3 = **inferior**, aide, assistant, attendant, dependant, junior, second, subaltern, underling
➤ **Antonyms**
adjective ≠**lesser**: central, essential, greater, higher, key, main, necessary, predominant, senior, superior, vital ◆ noun ≠**inferior**: boss (informal), captain, chief, commander, head, leader, master, principal, senior, superior

subordination noun = **inferiority**, inferior or secondary status, servitude, subjection

subscribe verb 1 = **contribute**, chip in (informal), donate, give, offer, pledge, promise 2 = **support**, acquiesce, advocate, agree, consent, countenance, endorse

subscription noun 1 Chiefly Brit. = **membership fee**, annual payment, dues 2 = **contribution**, donation, gift, offering

subsequent adjective = **following**, after, consequent, ensuing, later, succeeding, successive
➤ **Antonyms**
antecedent, earlier, erstwhile, former, one-time, past, preceding, previous, prior

subsequently adverb = **later**, afterwards, at a later date, consequently, in the end

subservient adjective 1 = **servile**, abject, bootlicking (informal), deferential, inferior, obsequious, slavish, subject, submissive, sycophantic 2 = **subordinate**, ancillary, auxiliary, subsidiary
➤ **Antonyms**
≠**servile**: bolshie, bossy, disobedient, domineering, overbearing, overriding, rebellious, superior, wilful

subside verb 1 = **decrease**, abate, de-escalate, diminish, dwindle, ease, ebb, lessen, let up, level off, peter out, quieten, recede, slacken, wane 2 = **drop**, decline, descend, ebb, fall 3 = **collapse**, cave in, drop, lower, settle, sink
➤ **Antonyms**
≠**decrease, drop**: escalate, grow, heighten, increase, inflate, intensify, mount, rise, soar, swell

subsidence noun 1 = **decrease**, abatement, de-escalation, diminution, easing off, lessening, slackening 2 = **drop**, decline, descent, ebb 3 = **sinking**, collapse, settlement, settling

subsidiary adjective = **lesser**, ancillary, assistant, auxiliary, contributory, minor, secondary, subordinate, subservient, supplemental, supplementary
➤ **Antonyms**

central, chief, head, key, leading, main, major, primary, principal, vital

subsidize verb = **fund**, finance, promote, put up the money for, sponsor, support, underwrite

subsidy noun = **aid**, allowance, assistance, contribution, financial aid, grant, help, stipend, support

subsist verb = **stay alive**, continue, exist, keep going, last, live, survive, sustain oneself

subsistence noun = **living**, existence, livelihood, maintenance, survival, upkeep

substance noun 1 = **material**, body, element, fabric, stuff, texture 2 = **meaning**, essence, gist, import, main point, matter, pith, significance, subject, theme 3 = **reality**, actuality, concreteness, entity, force 4 = **wealth**, affluence, assets, estate, means, property, resources

substandard adjective = **inferior**, damaged, imperfect, inadequate, second-rate, shoddy, unacceptable

substantial adjective 1 = **big**, ample, considerable, generous, goodly, important, large, significant, sizable or sizeable, tidy (informal) 2 = **solid**, bulky, firm, hefty, massive, sound, stout, strong, sturdy 3 Formal = **real**, actual, positive, true, valid, weighty
➤ Antonyms
≠**big**: inadequate, inconsiderable, insignificant, insubstantial, meagre, niggardly, pathetic, poor, skimpy, small ≠**solid**: feeble, frail, infirm, insubstantial, light-weight, rickety, weak ≠**real**: fictitious, imaginary, imagined, insubstantial, nonexistent, unreal

substantially adverb = **essentially**, in essence, in the main, largely, materially, to a large extent

substantiate verb = **support**, affirm, attest to, authenticate, bear out, confirm, corroborate, establish, prove, validate, verify
➤ Antonyms
confute, contradict, controvert, disprove, expose, invalidate, make a nonsense of, negate, prove false, rebut, refute

substitute verb 1 = **replace**, change, commute, exchange, interchange, swap, switch 2 substitute for = **stand in for**, act for, be in place of, cover for, deputize for, fill in for, take over from ♦ noun 3 = **replacement**, agent, deputy, locum, locum tenens, makeshift, proxy, representative, reserve, stand-by, stopgap, sub, surrogate ♦ adjective 4 = **replacement**, acting, alternative, fall-back, proxy, reserve, second, surrogate

substitution noun = **replacement**, change, exchange, interchange, swap, switch

subterfuge noun = **trick**, artifice, deception, dodge, duplicity, machination, manoeuvre, ploy, pretence, pretext, ruse, stratagem

subtle adjective 1 = **faint**, delicate, implied, indirect, slight, understated 2 = **crafty**, artful, astute, cunning, devious, ingenious, Machiavellian, scheming, shrewd, sly, wily 3 = **sophisticated**, delicate, discriminating, nice, refined
➤ Antonyms
≠**faint**: overwhelming, strong ≠**crafty**: artless, blunt, direct, downright, guileless, obvious, simple, straightforward ≠**sophisticated**: crass, heavy-handed, lacking finesse, tactless, unsophisticated, unsubtle

subtlety noun 1 = **fine point**, delicacy, discernment, intricacy, nicety, refinement, sophistication 2 = **cunning**, acumen, acuteness, artfulness, astuteness, cleverness, craftiness, deviousness, guile, ingenuity, sagacity, skill, slyness, wiliness 3 = **discrimination**, discernment, finesse

subtract verb = **take away**, deduct, detract, diminish, remove, take from, take off, withdraw
➤ Antonyms
add, add to, append, increase by, supplement

suburb noun = **residential area**, environs, neighbourhood, outskirts, suburbia

subversive adjective 1 = **seditious**, destructive, insurrectionary, overthrowing, riotous, treasonous, underground, undermining ♦ noun 2 = **dissident**, fifth columnist, insurrectionary, quisling, saboteur, seditionary, seditionist, terrorist, traitor

subvert verb = **overturn**, demolish, destroy, ruin, sabotage, undermine, upset, wreck

succeed verb 1 = **make it** (informal), be successful, bring home the bacon (informal), come off (informal), crack it (informal), cut it (informal), do the trick (informal), do well, flourish, get to the top, hit the jackpot (informal), make good, make one's mark (informal), make the grade (informal), prosper, thrive, triumph, turn out well, work 2 = **follow**, be subsequent, come next, ensue, result 3 = **take over**, accede, assume the office of, come into, come into possession of, inherit, replace, step into (someone's) boots
➤ Antonyms

≠**make it**: be unsuccessful, collapse, come a cropper (*informal*), fail, fall by the wayside, fall flat, fall short, flop (*informal*), go belly up (*informal*), go by the board, not make the grade, not manage ≠**follow**: be a precursor of, come before, go ahead of, go before, pave the way, precede

succeeding *adjective* = **following**, ensuing, next, subsequent, successive
➤ **Antonyms**
antecedent, earlier, former, preceding, previous, prior

success *noun* 1 = **favourable outcome**, ascendancy, eminence, fame, fortune, happiness, luck, prosperity, triumph 2 = **hit** (*informal*), best seller, big name, celebrity, market leader, megastar (*informal*), sensation, smash (*informal*), smash hit (*informal*), somebody, star, V.I.P., winner, wow (*slang*)
➤ **Antonyms**
≠**favourable outcome**: collapse, disaster, downfall, failure, misfortune ≠**hit**: clunker (*informal*), dead duck (*slang*), fiasco, flop (*informal*), loser, nobody, no-hoper, washout

successful *adjective* 1 = **thriving**, booming, favourable, flourishing, fortunate, fruitful, lucky, lucrative, moneymaking, on a roll, paying, profitable, rewarding, top, victorious 2 = **prosperous**, wealthy
➤ **Antonyms**
≠**thriving**: defeated, failed, ineffective, losing, luckless, uneconomic, unprofitable, unsuccessful, useless

successfully *adverb* = **well**, famously (*informal*), favourably, in triumph, victoriously, with flying colours

succession *noun* 1 = **series**, chain, continuation, course, cycle, flow, order, procession, progression, run, sequence, train 2 = **taking over**, accession, assumption, elevation, entering upon, inheritance 3 **in succession** = **one after the other**, consecutively, one behind the other, on the trot (*informal*), running, successively

successive *adjective* = **consecutive**, following, in a row, in succession, succeeding

succinct *adjective* = **brief**, compact, concise, condensed, gnomic, laconic, pithy, summary, terse, to the point
➤ **Antonyms**
circuitous, circumlocutory, diffuse, discursive, long-winded, prolix, rambling, verbose, wordy

succour *noun* 1 = **help**, aid, assistance, comfort, relief, support ♦ *verb* 2 = **help**,

aid, assist, befriend, comfort, encourage, foster, minister to, nurse, relieve, render assistance to, support

succulent *adjective* = **juicy**, luscious, lush, moist, mouthwatering, rich

succumb *verb* 1 = **surrender**, capitulate, cave in (*informal*), give in, give way, go under, knuckle under, submit, yield 2 = **die**, fall, fall victim to
➤ **Antonyms**
≠**surrender**: beat, conquer, get the better of, master, overcome, rise above, surmount, triumph over

sucker *noun Slang* = **fool**, butt, cat's paw, dupe, easy game *or* mark (*informal*), mug (*Brit. slang*), nerd *or* nurd (*slang*), pushover (*slang*), sitting duck (*informal*), sitting target, victim

suck up to *verb Informal* = **ingratiate oneself with**, butter up, curry favour with, dance attendance on, fawn on, flatter, get on the right side of, keep in with (*informal*), pander to, play up to (*informal*), toady, truckle

sudden *adjective* = **quick**, abrupt, hasty, hurried, impulsive, rapid, rash, swift, unexpected, unforeseen, unusual
➤ **Antonyms**
anticipated, deliberate, expected, foreseen, gentle, gradual, slow, unhasty

suddenly *adverb* = **abruptly**, all at once, all of a sudden, on the spur of the moment, out of the blue (*informal*), unexpectedly, without warning

sue *verb Law* = **take (someone) to court**, bring an action against (someone), charge, indict, institute legal proceedings against (someone), prefer charges against (someone), prosecute, summon

suffer *verb* 1 = **undergo**, bear, endure, experience, feel, go through, sustain 2 = **be affected**, ache, agonize, be in pain, be racked, feel wretched, go through a lot (*informal*), have a bad time, hurt 3 = **deteriorate**, be impaired, fall off 4 = **tolerate**, put up with (*informal*) 5 = **be shown to disadvantage**, appear in a poor light, be handicapped

suffering *noun* = **pain**, affliction, agony, anguish, discomfort, distress, hardship, misery, ordeal, torment, torture

suffice *verb* = **be enough**, answer, be adequate, be sufficient, do, fill the bill (*informal*), meet requirements, serve

sufficient *adjective* = **adequate**, competent, enough, satisfactory
➤ **Antonyms**
deficient, inadequate, insufficient, meagre, not enough, poor, scant, short, sparse

suffocate verb = **choke**, asphyxiate, smother, stifle, strangle

suffrage noun = **right to vote**, ballot, franchise, voice, vote

suffuse verb = **spread through** or **over**, bathe, cover, flood, imbue, infuse, overspread, permeate, pervade, steep, transfuse

suggest verb 1 = **recommend**, advise, advocate, move, offer a suggestion, prescribe, propose, put forward 2 = **bring to mind**, evoke, put one in mind of 3 = **hint**, imply, indicate, insinuate, intimate, lead one to believe

suggestible adjective = **impressionable**, amenable, malleable, open, open-minded, pliant, receptive, susceptible
➤ **Antonyms**
firm, headstrong, impervious, obdurate, single-minded, unwavering

suggestion noun 1 = **recommendation**, motion, plan, proposal, proposition 2 = **hint**, breath, indication, insinuation, intimation, suspicion, trace, whisper

suggestive adjective 1 = **smutty**, bawdy, blue, immodest, improper, indecent, indelicate, off colour, provocative, prurient, racy, ribald, risqué, rude, spicy (informal), titillating, unseemly 2 **suggestive of** = **evocative of**, expressing, indicative of, redolent of, reminiscent of

suit noun 1 = **outfit**, clothing, costume, dress, ensemble, habit 2 = **lawsuit**, action, case, cause, industrial tribunal, proceeding, prosecution, trial 3 **follow suit** = **copy**, emulate ♦ verb 4 = **befit**, agree, agree with, become, be seemly, conform to, correspond, go with, harmonize, match, tally 5 = **be acceptable to**, answer, do, gratify, please, satisfy

suitability noun = **appropriateness**, aptness, fitness, opportuneness, rightness, timeliness

suitable adjective = **appropriate**, acceptable, applicable, apposite, apt, becoming, befitting, convenient, cut out for, due, fit, fitting, in character, in keeping, opportune, pertinent, proper, relevant, right, satisfactory, seemly, suited
➤ **Antonyms**
discordant, inapposite, inappropriate, incorrect, inopportune, jarring, out of character, out of keeping, unbecoming, unfitting, unseemly, unsuitable, unsuited

suite noun 1 = **rooms**, apartment 2 = **set**, collection, series 3 = **furniture**

suitor noun Old-fashioned = **admirer**, beau, follower (obsolete), swain (archaic), young man

sulk verb = **be sullen**, be in a huff, be put out, brood, have the hump (Brit. informal), pout

sulky adjective = **huffy**, cross, disgruntled, ill-humoured, in the sulks, moody, morose, petulant, put out, querulous, resentful, sullen

sullen adjective = **morose**, brooding, cross, dour, gloomy, glowering, moody, silent, sour, sulky, surly, unsociable
➤ **Antonyms**
amiable, bright, cheerful, cheery, chirpy (informal), genial, good-humoured, good-natured, pleasant, sociable, sunny, warm, warm-hearted

sullenness noun = **moroseness**, glumness, ill humour, moodiness, sourness, sulkiness, sulks

sully verb 1 = **dishonour**, besmirch, disgrace, ruin, smirch 2 = **defile**, befoul, blemish, contaminate, dirty, pollute, spoil, spot, stain, taint, tarnish

sultry adjective 1 = **humid**, close, hot, muggy, oppressive, sticky, stifling, stuffy, sweltering 2 = **seductive**, amorous, erotic, passionate, provocative, sensual, sexy (informal), voluptuous
➤ **Antonyms**
≠**humid**: cool, fresh, invigorating, refreshing

sum noun = **total**, aggregate, amount, entirety, quantity, reckoning, score, sum total, tally, totality, whole

summarily adverb = **immediately**, at short notice, forthwith, on the spot, peremptorily, promptly, speedily, swiftly, without delay

summarize verb = **sum up**, abridge, condense, encapsulate, epitomize, give a rundown of, give the main points of, outline, précis, put in a nutshell, recap, recapitulate, review

summary noun 1 = **synopsis**, abridgment, digest, outline, précis, recapitulation, résumé, review, rundown, summing-up ♦ adjective 2 = **hasty**, cursory, perfunctory

summit noun = **peak**, acme, apex, crest, crown, crowning point, culmination, head, height, pinnacle, top, zenith
➤ **Antonyms**
base, bottom, depths, foot, lowest point, nadir

summon verb 1 = **send for**, arouse, assemble, bid, call, call together, convene, convoke, invite, rally, rouse 2 often with **up** = **gather**, call into action, draw on, invoke, muster

sumptuous adjective = **luxurious**, costly, dear, de luxe, expensive, extravagant, gorgeous, grand, lavish, magnificent, opulent, plush (*informal*), posh (*informal, chiefly Brit.*), rich, ritzy (*slang*), splendid, superb

➤ **Antonyms**
austere, basic, cheap, frugal, inexpensive, meagre, mean, miserly, plain, shabby, wretched

sum up *verb* **1** = **summarize**, close, conclude, put in a nutshell, recapitulate, review **2** = **form an opinion of**, estimate, get the measure of, size up (*informal*)

sun *noun* **1** = **Sol** (*Roman myth*), Helios (*Greek myth*), Phoebus (*Greek myth*), Phoebus Apollo (*Greek myth*) ♦ *verb* **2 sun oneself** = **sunbathe**, bake, bask, tan

sunburnt *adjective* = **tanned**, bronzed, brown, brown as a berry, burnt, peeling, red, ruddy, scarlet

sundry *adjective* = **various**, assorted, different, miscellaneous, several, some, varied

sunken *adjective* **1** = **hollow**, concave, drawn, haggard, hollowed **2** = **lower**, at a lower level, below ground, buried, depressed, immersed, recessed, submerged

sunny *adjective* **1** = **bright**, brilliant, clear, fine, radiant, summery, sunlit, sunshiny, unclouded, without a cloud in the sky **2** = **cheerful**, beaming, blithe, buoyant, cheery, chirpy (*informal*), genial, happy, joyful, light-hearted, optimistic, pleasant, smiling

➤ **Antonyms**
≠**bright**: cloudy, depressing, dreary, dreich (*Scot.*), dull, gloomy, murky, overcast, rainy, shaded, shadowy, sunless, wet, wintry ≠**cheerful**: doleful, down in the dumps (*informal*), gloomy, miserable, morbid, unsmiling

sunrise *noun* = **dawn**, break of day, cockcrow, daybreak, daylight, sunup

sunset *noun* = **nightfall**, close of (the) day, dusk, eventide, gloaming (*Scot. or poetic*), sundown

super *adjective Informal* = **excellent**, awesome (*slang*), boffo (*slang*), brill (*informal*), cracking (*Brit. informal*), crucial (*slang*), def (*slang*), glorious, incomparable, magnificent, marvellous, matchless, mean (*slang*), mega (*slang*), out of this world (*informal*), outstanding, sensational (*informal*), smashing (*informal*), sovereign, superb, terrific (*informal*), top-notch (*informal*), wonderful

superannuated *adjective* **1** = **retired**, discharged, pensioned off, put out to grass (*informal*) **2** = **obsolete**, aged, antiquated, decrepit, old, past it (*informal*), senile, unfit

superb *adjective* = **splendid**, admirable, awesome (*slang*), boffo (*slang*), breathtaking, brill (*informal*), choice, divine, excellent, exquisite, fine, first-rate, gorgeous, grand, magnificent, marvellous, mega (*slang*), superior, superlative, unrivalled, world-class

➤ **Antonyms**
abysmal, awful, bad, disappointing, dreadful, inferior, mediocre, no great shakes (*informal*), pathetic, poor quality, run-of-the-mill, terrible, third-rate, uninspired, woeful

supercilious *adjective* = **scornful**, arrogant, condescending, contemptuous, disdainful, haughty, high and mighty (*informal*), hoity-toity (*informal*), lofty, lordly, overbearing, patronizing, proud, snooty (*informal*), stuck-up (*informal*), toffee-nosed (*slang, chiefly Brit.*), uppish (*Brit. informal*)

➤ **Antonyms**
deferential, humble, meek, modest, obsequious, self-effacing, submissive, unassuming, unpretentious

superficial *adjective* **1** = **hasty**, casual, cursory, desultory, hurried, passing, perfunctory, sketchy, slapdash **2** = **outward**, apparent, evident, ostensible, seeming **3** = **shallow**, empty, empty-headed, frivolous, lightweight, silly, trivial **4** = **surface**, cosmetic, exterior, external, on the surface, skin-deep, slight

➤ **Antonyms**
≠**hasty**: complete, comprehensive, detailed, exhaustive, in depth, major, penetrating, probing, thorough ≠**shallow**: earnest, serious ≠**surface**: deep, profound

superficiality *noun* = **shallowness**, emptiness, lack of depth, lack of substance, triviality

superficially *adverb* = **at first glance**, apparently, at face value, externally, on the surface, ostensibly, to the casual eye

superfluity *noun* = **excess**, glut, plethora, superabundance, surfeit, surplus

superfluous *adjective* = **excess**, excessive, extra, in excess, left over, redundant, remaining, residuary, spare, superabundant, supernumerary, surplus, surplus to requirements, uncalled-for, unnecessary, unneeded, unrequired

➤ **Antonyms**
called for, essential, imperative, indispensable, necessary, needed, requisite, vital, wanted

superhuman *adjective* **1** = **heroic**, herculean, phenomenal, prodigious, stupendous **2** = **supernatural**, divine, paranormal, preternatural

superintend *verb* = **supervise**, administer, control, direct, handle, look after, manage, overlook, oversee, run

superintendence *noun* = **supervision**, care, charge, control, direction, government, guidance, management

superintendent *noun* = **supervisor**, administrator, chief, conductor, controller, director, governor, inspector, manager, overseer

superior *adjective* 1 = **better**, grander, greater, higher, more advanced, more expert, more skilful, paramount, predominant, prevailing, surpassing, unrivalled 2 = **supercilious**, condescending, disdainful, haughty, lofty, lordly, patronizing, pretentious, snobbish, stuck-up (*informal*) 3 = **first-class**, choice, de luxe, excellent, exceptional, exclusive, fine, first-rate, good, good quality, high calibre, high-class, of the first order, world-class ♦ *noun* 4 = **boss** (*informal*), chief, director, manager, principal, senior, supervisor
➤ **Antonyms**
adjective ≠**better**: inferior, less, lesser, lower, not as good, poorer, worse ≠**first-class**: average, inferior, mediocre, no great shakes (*informal*), ordinary, second-class, second-rate, substandard, unremarkable ♦ *noun* ≠**boss**: assistant, cohort (*chiefly U.S.*), dogsbody, inferior, junior, lackey, minion, subordinate, underling

superiority *noun* = **supremacy**, advantage, ascendancy, excellence, lead, predominance, pre-eminence, prevalence

superlative *adjective* = **supreme**, consummate, excellent, greatest, highest, matchless, of the highest order, outstanding, peerless, surpassing, unparalleled, unrivalled, unsurpassed
➤ **Antonyms**
abysmal, appalling, average, dreadful, easily outclassed, inferior, ordinary, poor, rotten, run-of-the-mill, undistinguished, unexceptional, uninspired, unspectacular

supernatural *adjective* = **paranormal**, ghostly, hidden, miraculous, mysterious, mystic, occult, phantom, preternatural, psychic, spectral, uncanny, unearthly, unnatural

supernumerary *adjective* = **extra**, excess, excessive, in excess, odd, redundant, spare, superfluous, surplus, unrequired

supersede *verb* = **replace**, displace, oust, remove, supplant, take over, take the place of, usurp

supervise *verb* = **oversee**, administer, be responsible for, conduct, control, direct,

handle, have *or* be in charge of, inspect, keep an eye on, look after, manage, preside over, run, superintend

supervision *noun* = **superintendence**, administration, auspices, care, charge, control, direction, guidance, instruction, management, oversight, stewardship

supervisor *noun* = **boss** (*informal*), administrator, chief, foreman, gaffer (*informal, chiefly Brit.*), inspector, manager, overseer, steward, superintendent

supervisory *adjective* = **managerial**, administrative, executive, overseeing, superintendent

supine *adjective Formal* = **flat on one's back**, flat, horizontal, recumbent
➤ **Antonyms**
lying on one's face, prone, prostrate

supplant *verb* = **replace**, displace, oust, overthrow, remove, supersede, take over, take the place of, unseat

supple *adjective* 1 = **flexible**, limber, lissom(e), lithe, loose-limbed 2 = **pliant**, bending, elastic, plastic, pliable
➤ **Antonyms**
≠**flexible**: awkward, creaky (*informal*), graceless, inflexible, stiff, unsupple ≠**pliant**: firm, inflexible, rigid, stiff, taut, unbending, unyielding

supplement *noun* 1 = **addition**, added feature, addendum, add-on, appendix, codicil, complement, extra, insert, postscript, pull-out, sequel ♦ *verb* 2 = **add**, augment, complement, extend, fill out, reinforce, supply, top up

supplementary *adjective* = **additional**, accompanying, add-on, ancillary, auxiliary, complementary, extra, secondary, supplemental

supplicant *noun Formal* = **petitioner**, applicant, suitor

supplication *noun Formal* = **plea**, appeal, entreaty, petition, pleading, prayer, request, solicitation

supply *verb* 1 = **provide**, afford, cater to *or* for, contribute, endow, equip, furnish, give, grant, produce, purvey, stock, store, yield ♦ *noun* 2 = **store**, cache, fund, hoard, quantity, reserve, reservoir, source, stock, stockpile 3 **supplies** = **provisions**, equipment, food, foodstuff, items, materials, necessities, provender, rations, stores

support *verb* 1 = **bear**, bolster, brace, buttress, carry, hold, hold up, prop, reinforce, shore up, sustain, underpin, uphold 2 = **provide for**, finance, fund, keep, look after, maintain, subsidize, sustain, take care of 3 = **help**, aid, assist,

back, be a source of strength to, boost (someone's) morale, buoy up, champion, defend, encourage, go along with, promote, second, side with, stand up for, stick up for (*informal*), strengthen, succour, take (someone's) part, uphold **4 = bear out**, attest to, authenticate, confirm, corroborate, endorse, lend credence to, substantiate, verify ♦ *noun* **5 = help**, aid, approval, assistance, backing, blessing, encouragement, friendship, loyalty, moral support, patronage, protection, succour **6 = prop**, abutment, back, brace, foundation, pillar, post, stanchion, stiffener, underpinning **7 = supporter**, backbone, backer, mainstay, prop, second, tower of strength **8 = upkeep**, keep, livelihood, maintenance, subsistence, sustenance
➤ **Antonyms**
verb ≠**provide for**: live off, sponge off ≠**help**: go against, hinder, hold out against, oppose, reject, stab in the back, turn one's back on, undermine, walk away from ≠**bear out**: challenge, contradict, deny, refute ♦ *noun* ≠**help**: burden, encumbrance, hindrance, impediment, opposition, undermining ≠**supporter**: antagonist

supporter *noun* **= follower**, adherent, advocate, ally, champion, defender, fan, friend, helper, henchman, patron, protagonist, sponsor, well-wisher
➤ **Antonyms**
adversary, antagonist, challenger, competitor, foe, opponent, rival

supportive *adjective* **= helpful**, caring, encouraging, reassuring, sympathetic, understanding

suppose *verb* **1 = presume**, assume, calculate (*U.S. dialect*), conjecture, dare say, expect, guess (*informal, chiefly U.S. & Canad.*), imagine, infer, judge, opine, presuppose, surmise, take as read, take for granted, think **2 = imagine**, believe, conceive, conclude, conjecture, consider, fancy, hypothesize, postulate, pretend

supposed *adjective* **1 = presumed**, accepted, alleged, assumed, hypothetical, presupposed, professed, putative, reputed, rumoured **2** *usually with* **to = meant**, expected, obliged, required

supposedly *adverb* **= presumably**, allegedly, at a guess, avowedly, by all accounts, hypothetically, ostensibly, professedly, purportedly, theoretically
➤ **Antonyms**
absolutely, actually, certainly, in actuality, in fact, really, surely, truly, undoubtedly, without a doubt

supposition *noun* **= guess**, conjecture, doubt, guesswork, hypothesis, idea, notion, presumption, speculation, surmise, theory

suppress *verb* **1 = stop**, check, clamp down on, conquer, crack down on, crush, extinguish, overpower, overthrow, put an end to, quash, quell, stamp out, subdue **2 = restrain**, conceal, contain, cover up, curb, hold in *or* back, hold in check, keep secret, muffle, repress, silence, smother, stifle, withhold
➤ **Antonyms**
encourage, foster, further, gee up, incite, inflame, promote, rouse, spread, stimulate, stir up, whip up

suppression *noun* **1 = elimination**, check, clampdown, crackdown, crushing, prohibition, quashing, termination **2 = inhibition**, smothering

suppurate *verb Pathology* **= discharge**, fester, gather, ooze, weep

supremacy *noun* **= domination**, absolute rule, ascendancy, dominance, dominion, lordship, mastery, predominance, pre-eminence, primacy, sovereignty, supreme power, sway

supreme *adjective* **= highest**, cardinal, chief, crowning, culminating, extreme, final, first, foremost, greatest, head, incomparable, leading, matchless, mother of all (*informal*), paramount, peerless, predominant, pre-eminent, prevailing, prime, principal, sovereign, superlative, surpassing, top, ultimate, unsurpassed, utmost
➤ **Antonyms**
least, least successful, lowest, most inferior, most minor, most subordinate, most trivial, poorest, worst

supremo *noun Brit. informal* **= head**, boss (*informal*), commander, director, governor, leader, master, principal, ruler

sure *adjective* **1 = certain**, assured, clear, confident, convinced, decided, definite, free from doubt, persuaded, positive, satisfied **2 = reliable**, accurate, dependable, effective, foolproof, indisputable, infallible, never-failing, precise, sure-fire (*informal*), tried and true, trustworthy, trusty, undeniable, undoubted, unerring, unfailing **3 = inevitable**, assured, bound, guaranteed, inescapable **4 = secure**, fast, firm, fixed, safe, solid, stable, steady
➤ **Antonyms**
≠**certain**: distrustful, doubtful, dubious, sceptical, unassured, uncertain, unconvinced, uneasy, unsure ≠**reliable**: dodgy (*Brit., Austral., & N.Z. informal*),

dubious, fallible, iffy (*informal*), undependable, unreliable, untrustworthy, vague ≠**inevitable**: touch-and-go, unsure ≠**secure**: insecure

surely *adverb* = **undoubtedly**, assuredly, beyond the shadow of a doubt, certainly, come what may, definitely, doubtlessly, for certain, indubitably, inevitably, unquestionably, without doubt, without fail

surety *noun* 1 = **guarantor**, bondsman, sponsor 2 = **security**, bond, deposit, guarantee, indemnity, insurance, pledge, warranty

surface *noun* 1 = **outside**, covering, exterior, façade, face, facet, plane, side, skin, top, veneer 2 **on the surface** = **at first glance**, apparently, ostensibly, outwardly, seemingly, superficially, to all appearances, to the casual eye ♦ *verb* 3 = **appear**, arise, come to light, come up, crop up (*informal*), emerge, materialize, transpire

surfeit *noun* = **excess**, glut, overindulgence, plethora, superabundance, superfluity
➤ **Antonyms**
dearth, deficiency, insufficiency, lack, scarcity, shortage, shortness, want

surge *noun* 1 = **rush**, flood, flow, gush, outpouring, uprush, upsurge 2 = **wave**, billow, breaker, roller, swell ♦ *verb* 3 = **rush**, gush, rise, swell, well forth 4 = **roll**, billow, eddy, heave, swirl, undulate

surly *adjective* = **ill-tempered**, brusque, churlish, cross, grouchy (*informal*), gruff, morose, sulky, sullen, testy, uncivil, ungracious
➤ **Antonyms**
agreeable, cheerful, cheery, genial, good-natured, happy, pleasant, sunny

surmise *verb* 1 = **guess**, come to the conclusion, conclude, conjecture, consider, deduce, fancy, hazard a guess, imagine, infer, opine, presume, speculate, suppose, suspect ♦ *noun* 2 = **guess**, assumption, conclusion, conjecture, deduction, hypothesis, idea, inference, notion, possibility, presumption, speculation, supposition, suspicion, thought

surmount *verb* = **overcome**, conquer, master, overpower, prevail over, surpass, triumph over, vanquish

surpass *verb* = **outdo**, beat, best, cap (*informal*), eclipse, exceed, excel, go one better than (*informal*), outshine, outstrip, override, overshadow, put in the shade, top, transcend

surpassing *adjective* = **supreme**, exceptional, extraordinary, incomparable, matchless, outstanding, phenomenal, rare, unrivalled

surplus *noun* 1 = **excess**, balance, remainder, residue, superabundance, superfluity, surfeit ♦ *adjective* 2 = **extra**, excess, in excess, left over, odd, remaining, spare, superfluous, unused
➤ **Antonyms**
noun ≠**excess**: dearth, deficiency, deficit, insufficiency, lack, paucity, shortage, shortfall ♦ *adjective* ≠**extra**: deficient, falling short, inadequate, insufficient, lacking, limited, scant, scanty, scarce

surprise *noun* 1 = **shock**, bolt from the blue, bombshell, eye-opener (*informal*), jolt, revelation, start (*informal*), turn-up for the books (*informal*) 2 = **amazement**, astonishment, bewilderment, incredulity, stupefaction, wonder ♦ *verb* 3 = **amaze**, astonish, astound, bewilder, bowl over (*informal*), confuse, disconcert, flabbergast (*informal*), nonplus, stagger, stun, take aback, take (someone's) breath away 4 = **catch unawares** *or* **off-guard**, burst in on, catch in the act *or* red-handed, catch on the hop (*informal*), discover, spring upon, startle

surprised *adjective* 1 = **amazed**, astonished, at a loss, disconcerted, incredulous, nonplussed, speechless, startled, taken aback, thunderstruck, unable to believe one's eyes 2 = **taken by surprise**, caught on the hop (*Brit. informal*)

surprising *adjective* = **amazing**, astonishing, astounding, bewildering, extraordinary, incredible, jaw-dropping, marvellous, remarkable, staggering, startling, unexpected, unlooked-for, unusual, wonderful

surrender *verb* 1 = **give in**, capitulate, cave in (*informal*), give oneself up, give way, quit, show the white flag, submit, succumb, throw in the towel, yield 2 = **give up**, abandon, cede, concede, deliver up, forego, part with, relinquish, renounce, waive, yield ♦ *noun* 3 = **submission**, capitulation, cave-in (*informal*), relinquishment, renunciation, resignation, yielding
➤ **Antonyms**
verb ≠**give in**: defy, fight (on), make a stand against, oppose, resist, stand up to, withstand

surreptitious *adjective* = **secret**, clandestine, covert, furtive, sly, sneaking, stealthy, underhand, veiled
➤ **Antonyms**
blatant, conspicuous, frank, honest, manifest, obvious, open, overt, unconcealed, undisguised

surrogate noun = **substitute**, deputy, proxy, representative, stand-in

surround verb = **enclose**, close in on, encircle, encompass, envelop, fence in, girdle, hem in, ring

surrounding adjective = **nearby**, neighbouring

surroundings plural noun = **environment**, background, environs, location, milieu, neighbourhood, setting

surveillance noun = **observation**, inspection, scrutiny, superintendence, supervision, watch

survey verb 1 = **look over**, contemplate, examine, eyeball (slang), eye up, inspect, observe, scrutinize, view 2 = **estimate**, appraise, assess, eye up, measure, plan, plot, prospect, size up, take stock of 3 = **study**, research, review ♦ noun 4 = **examination**, inspection, once-over (informal), overview, perusal, scrutiny 5 = **study**, inquiry, review

survive verb = **remain alive**, endure, exist, hold out, last, live, live on, outlast, outlive, pull through, subsist

susceptibility noun = **vulnerability**, liability, predisposition, proneness, propensity, responsiveness, sensitivity, suggestibility, weakness

susceptible adjective 1 usually with **to** = **liable**, disposed, given, inclined, open, predisposed, prone, subject, vulnerable 2 = **impressionable**, alive to, easily moved, receptive, responsive, sensitive, suggestible, tender
➤ **Antonyms**
≠**liable**: immune, insusceptible, invulnerable, resistant, unaffected by ≠**impressionable**: insensitive, unaffected by, unmoved by, unresponsive

suspect verb 1 = **believe**, conclude, conjecture, consider, fancy, feel, guess, hazard a guess, speculate, suppose, surmise, think probable 2 = **distrust**, doubt, have one's doubts about, mistrust ♦ adjective 3 = **dubious**, dodgy (Brit., Austral., & N.Z. informal), doubtful, fishy (informal), iffy (informal), open to suspicion, questionable
➤ **Antonyms**
verb ≠**believe**: accept, be certain, be confident of, believe, buy (slang), know, swallow (informal) ≠**distrust**: have faith in, think innocent, trust ♦ adjective ≠**dubious**: above suspicion, innocent, reliable, straightforward, trustworthy, trusty

suspend verb 1 = **hang**, append, attach, dangle, swing 2 = **postpone**, adjourn, arrest, cease, cut short, debar, defer, delay, discontinue, hold off, interrupt, lay aside,

put off, shelve, stay, withhold
➤ **Antonyms**
≠**postpone**: carry on, continue, re-establish, reinstate, restore, resume, return

suspense noun = **uncertainty**, anticipation, anxiety, apprehension, doubt, expectancy, expectation, indecision, insecurity, irresolution, tension, wavering

suspension noun = **postponement**, abeyance, adjournment, break, breaking off, deferment, delay, discontinuation, interruption, remission, respite, stay

suspicion noun 1 = **distrust**, doubt, dubiety, funny feeling (informal), jealousy, misgiving, mistrust, qualm, scepticism, wariness 2 = **idea**, conjecture, guess, gut feeling (informal), hunch, impression, notion, supposition, surmise 3 = **trace**, glimmer, hint, shade, shadow, soupçon, strain, streak, suggestion, tinge, touch 4 **above suspicion** = **blameless**, above reproach, honourable, like Caesar's wife, pure, sinless, unimpeachable, virtuous

suspicious adjective 1 = **suspect**, dodgy (Brit., Austral., & N.Z. informal), doubtful, dubious, fishy (informal), funny, irregular, queer, questionable, shady (informal) 2 = **distrustful**, apprehensive, doubtful, jealous, mistrustful, sceptical, suspecting, unbelieving, wary
➤ **Antonyms**
≠**suspect**: above board, beyond suspicion, open, straight, straightforward, unquestionable ≠**distrustful**: believing, credulous, gullible, trustful, trusting, unsuspecting, unsuspicious

suss out verb Brit. & NZ slang = **work out**, figure out, find out, puzzle out, resolve, solve

sustain verb 1 = **maintain**, continue, keep alive, keep going, keep up, prolong, protract 2 = **keep alive**, aid, assist, comfort, foster, help, nourish, nurture, provide for 3 = **suffer**, bear, bear up under, endure, experience, feel, undergo, withstand 4 = **support**, bear, carry, keep from falling, keep up, uphold 5 = **uphold**, approve, confirm, endorse, ratify, validate, verify

sustained adjective = **continuous**, constant, nonstop, perpetual, prolonged, steady, unremitting
➤ **Antonyms**
broken, discontinuous, intermittent, irregular, periodic, spasmodic, sporadic

sustenance noun = **nourishment**, comestibles, daily bread, eatables, food, provender, provisions, rations, refreshments, victuals

svelte *adjective* = **slender**, graceful, lissom(e), lithe, slinky, sylphlike, willowy

swagger *verb* 1 = **show off** (*informal*), bluster, boast, brag, parade, prance, strut, swank (*informal*) ♦ *noun* 2 = **ostentation**, arrogance, bluster, braggadocio, display, pomposity, show, showing off (*informal*), swank (*informal*), swashbuckling

swallow *verb* 1 = **gulp**, absorb, consume, devour, down (*informal*), drink, eat, ingest, swig (*informal*), swill, wash down 2 *Informal* = **believe**, accept, buy (*slang*), fall for 3 = **hold in**, choke back, repress 4 **be swallowed up** = **be absorbed**, be assimilated, be consumed, be engulfed, be enveloped, be overrun, be overwhelmed

swamp *noun* 1 = **bog**, everglade(s) (*U.S.*), fen, marsh, mire, morass, quagmire, slough ♦ *verb* 2 *Naut.* = **flood**, capsize, drench, engulf, inundate, overwhelm, sink, submerge, swallow up, upset, wash over, waterlog 3 = **overwhelm**, beset, besiege, deluge, engulf, flood, inundate, overload, snow under, submerge

swampy *adjective* = **boggy**, fenny, marshy, miry, quaggy, waterlogged, wet

swank *Informal* ♦ *verb* 1 = **show off** (*informal*), give oneself airs, posture, put on side (*Brit. slang*), swagger ♦ *noun* 2 = **boastfulness**, display, ostentation, show, swagger

swanky *adjective Informal* = **ostentatious**, de luxe, exclusive, expensive, fancy, fashionable, flash, flashy, glamorous, glitzy (*slang*), gorgeous, grand, lavish, luxurious, plush (*informal*), posh (*informal, chiefly Brit.*), rich, ritzy (*slang*), showy, smart, stylish, sumptuous, swish (*informal, chiefly Brit.*)

➤ **Antonyms**

discreet, humble, inconspicuous, low-key, low-profile, modest, subdued, unassuming, unostentatious, unpretentious

swap, swop *verb* = **exchange**, bandy, barter, interchange, switch, trade, traffic

swarm *noun* 1 = **multitude**, army, bevy, crowd, drove, flock, herd, horde, host, mass, myriad, shoal, throng ♦ *verb* 2 = **crowd**, congregate, flock, mass, stream, throng 3 = **teem**, abound, be alive, be infested, be overrun, bristle, crawl

swarthy *adjective* = **dark-skinned**, black, brown, dark, dark-complexioned, dusky, tawny

swashbuckling *adjective* = **dashing**, bold, daredevil, flamboyant, gallant, spirited, swaggering

swastika *noun* = **crooked cross**, fylfot

swathe *verb* = **wrap**, bandage, bind, bundle up, cloak, drape, envelop, enwrap, fold, furl, lap, muffle up, sheathe, shroud, swaddle

sway *verb* 1 = **bend**, incline, lean, lurch, oscillate, rock, roll, swing, wave 2 = **influence**, affect, control, direct, dominate, govern, guide, induce, persuade, prevail on, win over ♦ *noun* 3 = **power**, ascendency, authority, clout (*informal*), command, control, dominion, government, influence, jurisdiction, predominance, rule, sovereignty 4 **hold sway** = **prevail**, predominate, reign, rule, run

swear *verb* 1 = **curse**, be foul-mouthed, blaspheme, cuss (*informal*), take the Lord's name in vain, utter profanities 2 = **vow**, attest, avow, give one's word, pledge oneself, promise, state under oath, take an oath, testify, warrant 3 = **declare**, affirm, assert, asseverate 4 **swear by** = **trust**, depend on, have confidence in, rely on

swearing *noun* = **bad language**, blasphemy, cursing, cussing (*informal*), foul language, imprecations, profanity

swearword *noun* = **oath**, curse, cuss (*informal*), expletive, four-letter word, obscenity, profanity

sweat *noun* 1 = **perspiration** 2 *Slang* = **labour**, backbreaking task, chore, drudgery, effort, toil 3 *Informal* = **worry**, agitation, anxiety, distress, flap (*informal*), panic, strain ♦ *verb* 4 = **perspire**, break out in a sweat, exude moisture, glow 5 *Informal* = **worry**, agonize, be on pins and needles (*informal*), be on tenterhooks, fret, lose sleep over, suffer, torture oneself 6 **sweat it out** *Informal* = **endure**, see (something) through, stay the course, stick it out (*informal*)

sweaty *adjective* = **perspiring**, bathed *or* drenched *or* soaked in perspiration, clammy, glowing, sticky, sweating

sweep *verb* 1 = **clear**, brush, clean, remove 2 = **sail**, flounce, fly, glide, hurtle, pass, scud, skim, tear, zoom ♦ *noun* 3 = **arc**, bend, curve, gesture, move, movement, stroke, swing 4 = **extent**, compass, range, scope, span, stretch, vista 5 = **lottery**, draw, raffle, sweepstake

sweeping *adjective* 1 = **wide-ranging**, all-embracing, all-inclusive, broad, comprehensive, extensive, global, overarching, radical, thoroughgoing, wide 2 = **indiscriminate**, across-the-board, blanket, exaggerated, overstated, unqualified, wholesale

➤ **Antonyms**

≠**wide-ranging**: constrained, limited, minor, narrow, restricted

sweet *adjective* **1** = **sugary**, cloying, honeyed, icky (*informal*), luscious, saccharine, sweetened, treacly **2** = **charming**, affectionate, agreeable, amiable, gentle, kind, sweet-tempered, tender, unselfish **3** = **delightful**, appealing, attractive, beautiful, cute, engaging, fair, likable *or* likeable, lovable, taking, winning, winsome **4** = **melodious**, dulcet, euphonious, harmonious, mellow, musical, silver-toned, silvery, soft, sweet-sounding, tuneful **5** = **fragrant**, aromatic, balmy, clean, fresh, new, perfumed, pure, sweet-smelling, wholesome **6 sweet on** = **in love with**, enamoured of, fond of, head over heels in love with, infatuated with, keen on, taken with, wild *or* mad about (*informal*) ♦ *noun* **7** *usually plural* = **confectionery**, bonbon, candy (*U.S.*), sweetie, sweetmeats **8** *Brit.* = **dessert**, afters (*Brit. informal*), pudding, sweet course

➤ **Antonyms**
adjective ≠**sugary**: acerbic, acetic, acid, bitter, savoury, sharp, sour, tart, vinegary ≠**charming**: bad-tempered, disagreeable, grouchy (*informal*), grumpy, ill-tempered, nasty, obnoxious ≠**delightful**: hated, loathsome, nasty, objectionable, obnoxious, unappealing, unattractive, unlovable, unpleasant ≠**melodious**: cacophonous, discordant, grating, harsh, shrill, strident, unharmonious, unmusical, unpleasant ≠**fragrant**: fetid, foul, noisome, rank, stinking

sweeten *verb* **1** = **sugar**, honey, sugar-coat **2** = **mollify**, alleviate, appease, pacify, soften up, soothe, sugar the pill

sweetheart *noun* = **love**, admirer, beau, beloved, boyfriend *or* girlfriend, darling, dear, follower (*obsolete*), inamorata *or* inamorato, lover, steady (*informal*), suitor, swain (*archaic*), sweetie (*informal*), truelove, valentine

sweet-talk *verb Informal* = **flatter**, beguile, cajole, chat up, coax, dupe, entice, inveigle, manoeuvre, persuade, seduce, soft-soap (*informal*), tempt, wheedle

swell *verb* **1** = **expand**, balloon, become bloated *or* larger, become larger, be inflated, belly, billow, bloat, bulge, dilate, distend, enlarge, extend, fatten, grow, increase, protrude, puff up, rise, round out, well up **2** = **increase**, add to, augment, enhance, heighten, intensify, mount, surge ♦ *noun* **3** = **wave**, billow, rise, surge, undulation **4** *Old-fashioned, informal* = **dandy**, beau, cockscomb (*informal*), fashion plate, fop, nob (*slang*), toff (*Brit. slang*)
➤ **Antonyms**

verb ≠**expand**: become smaller, contract, deflate, shrink ≠**increase**: decrease, diminish, ebb, fall, go down, lessen, reduce, wane

swelling *noun* = **enlargement**, blister, bulge, bump, dilation, distension, inflammation, lump, protuberance, puffiness, tumescence

sweltering *adjective* = **hot**, airless, baking, boiling, burning, humid, oppressive, roasting, scorching, steaming, stifling, sultry, torrid

swerve *verb* = **veer**, bend, deflect, depart from, deviate, diverge, incline, sheer off, shift, stray, swing, turn, turn aside, wander, wind

swift *adjective* = **quick**, abrupt, express, fast, flying, hurried, pdq (*slang*), prompt, quickie (*informal*), rapid, ready, short, short-lived, speedy, sudden, winged
➤ **Antonyms**
lingering, plodding, ponderous, slow, sluggish, tardy, unhurried

swiftly *adverb* = **quickly**, apace, (at) full tilt, double-quick, fast, hell for leather, hotfoot, hurriedly, like greased lightning (*informal*), like lightning, like the clappers (*Brit. informal*), posthaste, promptly, pronto (*informal*), rapidly, speedily, without losing time

swiftness *noun* = **speed**, celerity, fleetness, promptness, quickness, rapidity, speediness, velocity

swill *verb* **1** = **drink**, bevvy (*dialect*), consume, drain, gulp, guzzle, imbibe, quaff, swallow, swig (*informal*) **2** *Chiefly Brit., often with* **out** = **rinse**, drench, flush, sluice, wash down, wash out ♦ *noun* **3** = **waste**, mash, mush, pigswill, slops

swimmingly *adverb* = **successfully**, as planned, effortlessly, like a dream, like clockwork, smoothly, very well, with no trouble, without a hitch

swindle *verb* **1** = **cheat**, bamboozle (*informal*), bilk (of), con, deceive, defraud, diddle (*informal*), do (*slang*), dupe, fleece, hornswoggle (*slang*), rip (someone) off (*slang*), rook (*slang*), skin (*slang*), sting (*informal*), take (someone) for a ride (*informal*), take to the cleaners (*informal*), trick ♦ *noun* **2** = **fraud**, con trick (*informal*), deceit, deception, double-dealing, fiddle (*Brit. informal*), racket, rip-off (*slang*), scam (*slang*), sharp practice, sting (*informal*), swizz (*Brit. informal*), swizzle (*Brit. informal*), trickery

swindler *noun* = **cheat**, charlatan, chiseller (*informal*), confidence trickster, con man (*informal*), fraud, fraudster, grifter (*slang, chiefly U.S. & Canad.*), hustler (*U.S.*

informal), mountebank, rascal, rogue, shark, sharper, trickster

swing *verb* **1** = **sway**, fluctuate, oscillate, rock, vary, veer, vibrate, wave **2** *usually with round* = **turn**, curve, pivot, rotate, swivel, turn on one's heel, wheel **3** = **hang**, be suspended, dangle, move back and forth, suspend ♦ *noun* **4** = **swaying**, fluctuation, oscillation, stroke, sway, vibration **5 in full swing** = **at its height**, lively, on the go (*informal*), under way

swingeing *adjective Chiefly Brit.* = **severe**, Draconian, drastic, excessive, harsh, heavy, huge, oppressive, punishing, stringent

swinging *adjective* = **trendy** (*Brit. informal*), fashionable, happening (*informal*), hip (*slang*), lively, up-to-date, up to the minute, with it (*informal*)

swipe *verb* **1** *Informal* = **hit**, clip (*informal*), deck (*slang*), fetch (someone) a blow, lash out at, slap, slosh (*Brit. slang*), sock (*slang*), strike, wallop (*informal*) **2** *Slang* = **steal**, appropriate, filch, lift (*informal*), make off with, nick (*slang, chiefly Brit.*), pilfer, pinch (*informal*), purloin, snaffle (*Brit. informal*) ♦ *noun* **3** = **blow**, clip (*informal*), clout (*informal*), clump (*slang*), cuff, slap, smack, thump, wallop (*informal*)

swirl *verb* = **whirl**, agitate, boil, churn, eddy, spin, surge, twirl, twist

swish *adjective Informal, chiefly Brit.* = **smart**, de luxe, elegant, exclusive, fashionable, grand, plush *or* plushy (*informal*), posh (*informal, chiefly Brit.*), ritzy (*slang*), sumptuous

switch *noun* **1** = **change**, about-turn, alteration, change of direction, reversal, shift **2** = **exchange**, substitution, swap ♦ *verb* **3** = **change**, change course, deflect, deviate, divert, shift, turn aside **4** = **exchange**, interchange, replace by, substitute, swap, trade

swivel *verb* = **turn**, pirouette, pivot, revolve, rotate, spin, swing round

swollen *adjective* = **enlarged**, bloated, distended, inflamed, puffed up, puffy, tumescent, tumid

swoop *verb* **1** = **pounce**, descend, dive, rush, stoop, sweep ♦ *noun* **2** = **pounce**, descent, drop, lunge, plunge, rush, stoop, sweep

swop *see* SWAP

sword *noun* **1** = **blade 2 the sword: a** = **military power**, aggression, arms, war **b** = **death**, butchery, massacre, murder, slaying, violence **3 cross swords** = **fight**, argue, come to blows, dispute, spar, wrangle

swot *verb Informal* = **study**, apply oneself

to, bone up on (*informal*), cram (*informal*), mug up (*Brit. slang*), pore over, revise, toil over, work

sybarite *noun* = **hedonist**, epicure, epicurean, sensualist, voluptuary

sybaritic *adjective* = **pleasure-loving**, bacchanalian, epicurean, hedonistic, luxurious, luxury-loving, self-indulgent, sensual, voluptuous

sycophancy *noun* = **obsequiousness**, bootlicking (*informal*), fawning, flattery, grovelling, kowtowing, servility, toadyism, truckling

sycophant *noun* = **crawler**, ass-kisser (*U.S. & Canad. taboo slang*), bootlicker (*informal*), fawner, flatterer, hanger-on, parasite, toady, truckler, yes man

sycophantic *adjective* = **obsequious**, bootlicking (*informal*), crawling, fawning, flattering, grovelling, ingratiating, parasitical, servile, slimy, smarmy (*Brit. informal*), toadying, unctuous

syllabus *noun* = **course of study**, curriculum

sylphlike *adjective* = **slender**, graceful, lithe, svelte, willowy

symbol *noun* = **sign**, badge, emblem, figure, glyph, image, logo, mark, representation, token, type

symbolic *adjective* = **representative**, allegorical, emblematic, figurative, significant

symbolize *verb* = **represent**, betoken, connote, denote, exemplify, mean, personify, signify, stand for, typify

symmetrical *adjective* = **balanced**, in proportion, proportional, regular, well-proportioned

➤ **Antonyms**

asymmetrical, irregular, lopsided, unbalanced, unequal, unsymmetrical

symmetry *noun* = **balance**, agreement, correspondence, evenness, form, harmony, order, proportion, regularity

sympathetic *adjective* **1** = **caring**, affectionate, compassionate, concerned, feeling, interested, kind, kindly, pitying, responsive, supportive, tender, understanding, warm, warm-hearted **2** = **like-minded**, agreeable, companionable, compatible, congenial, friendly, responsive **3 sympathetic to** = **favourably disposed towards**, agreeable with, approving of, encouraging, friendly to, in sympathy with, pro, well-disposed towards

➤ **Antonyms**

≠**caring**: apathetic, callous, cold, cold-hearted, disinterested, indifferent, inhumane, insensitive, uncaring, uncompassionate, unfeeling, uninterested, unmoved, unsympathetic ≠**like-minded**: uncongenial, unresponsive

sympathetically *adverb* = **feelingly**, kindly, responsively, sensitively, warm-heartedly, warmly, with compassion, with feeling, with interest

sympathize *verb* **1** = **feel for**, commiserate, condole, empathize, have compassion, pity **2** = **agree**, be in accord, be in sympathy, go along with, identify with, side with, understand
➤ **Antonyms**
≠**feel for**: disdain, disregard, have no feelings for, mock, scorn ≠**agree**: disagree, fail to understand, misunderstand, oppose, reject

sympathizer *noun* = **supporter**, partisan, protagonist, well-wisher

sympathy *noun* **1** = **compassion**, commiseration, condolence(s), empathy, pity, tenderness, thoughtfulness, understanding **2** = **affinity**, agreement, congeniality, correspondence, fellow feeling, harmony, rapport, union, warmth
➤ **Antonyms**
≠**compassion**: callousness, coldness, disdain, hard-heartedness, indifference, insensitivity, lack of feeling *or* understanding *or* sympathy, pitilessness, scorn ≠**affinity**: antagonism, disapproval, hostility, opposition, resistance, unfriendliness

symptom *noun* = **sign**, expression, indication, mark, note, syndrome, token, warning

symptomatic *adjective* = **indicative**, characteristic, suggestive

synonymous *adjective* = **equivalent**, equal, identical, identified, interchangeable, one and the same, similar, tantamount, the same

synopsis *noun* = **summary**, abridgment, abstract, digest, outline, précis, résumé, review, rundown

synthesis *noun* **1** = **combining**, amalgamation, coalescence, integration, unification, welding **2** = **combination**, amalgam, blend, composite, compound, fusion, meld, union

synthetic *adjective* = **artificial**, ersatz, fake, man-made, manufactured, mock, pseudo (*informal*), sham, simulated
➤ **Antonyms**
authentic, genuine, kosher (*informal*), natural, pure, real

system *noun* **1** = **method**, fixed order, frame of reference, methodology, modus operandi, practice, procedure, routine, technique **2** = **orderliness**, definite plan, logical process, method, methodicalness, regularity, systematization **3** = **arrangement**, classification, combination, coordination, organization, scheme, setup (*informal*), structure

systematic *adjective* = **methodical**, businesslike, efficient, orderly, organized, precise, standardized, systematized, well-ordered
➤ **Antonyms**
arbitrary, disorderly, disorganized, haphazard, indiscriminate, random, slapdash, unbusinesslike, unmethodical, unsystematic

systematize *verb* = **arrange**, classify, methodize, organize, put in order, rationalize, regulate, schematize, sequence, standardize

T t

tab noun = **flap**, flag, label, marker, sticker, tag, ticket

tabby adjective = **striped**, banded, brindled, stripy

table noun 1 = **counter**, bench, board, slab, stand 2 = **list**, agenda, catalogue, chart, diagram, digest, graph, index, inventory, plan, record, register, roll, schedule, synopsis, tabulation 3 Formal = **food**, board, diet, fare, spread (informal), victuals ◆ verb 4 Brit. = **submit**, enter, move, propose, put forward, suggest

tableau noun = **picture**, representation, scene, spectacle

tableland noun = **plateau**, flat, flatland, mesa, plain, table

taboo noun 1 = **prohibition**, anathema, ban, disapproval, interdict, proscription, restriction ◆ adjective 2 = **forbidden**, anathema, banned, beyond the pale, disapproved of, frowned on, not allowed, not permitted, off limits, outlawed, prohibited, proscribed, ruled out, unacceptable, unmentionable, unthinkable
➤ Antonyms
adjective ≠**forbidden**: acceptable, allowed, permitted, sanctioned

tabulate verb = **arrange**, catalogue, categorize, chart, classify, codify, index, list, order, range, systematize

tacit adjective = **implied**, implicit, inferred, silent, taken for granted, undeclared, understood, unexpressed, unspoken, unstated, wordless
➤ Antonyms
explicit, express, spelled-out, spoken, stated

taciturn adjective = **uncommunicative**, mute, quiet, reserved, reticent, silent, tight-lipped, unforthcoming, withdrawn
➤ Antonyms
chatty, communicative, forthcoming, garrulous, loquacious, open, outgoing, sociable, talkative, verbose, voluble, wordy

tack¹ noun 1 = **nail**, drawing pin, pin, staple, thumbtack (U.S.), tintack ◆ verb 2 = **fasten**, affix, attach, fix, nail, pin, staple 3 Brit. = **stitch**, baste, sew 4 **tack on** = **append**, add, annex, attach, tag

tack² noun = **course**, approach, bearing, direction, heading, line, method, path, plan, procedure, tactic, way

tackle verb 1 = **deal with**, apply oneself to, attempt, begin, come or get to grips with, embark upon, engage in, essay, get stuck into (informal), have a go or stab at (informal), set about, take on, try, turn one's hand to, undertake 2 = **confront**, block, challenge, grab, grasp, halt, intercept, seize, stop, take hold of ◆ noun 3 = **challenge**, block, stop 4 = **equipment**, accoutrements, apparatus, gear, implements, outfit, paraphernalia, rig, rigging, tools, trappings

tacky¹ adjective = **sticky**, adhesive, gluey, gummy, icky (informal), wet

tacky² Informal adjective 1 = **vulgar**, cheap, naff (Brit. slang), sleazy, tasteless 2 = **shabby**, seedy, shoddy, tatty

tact noun = **diplomacy**, adroitness, consideration, delicacy, discretion, finesse, judgment, perception, savoir-faire, sensitivity, skill, thoughtfulness, understanding
➤ Antonyms
awkwardness, clumsiness, gaucherie, heavy-handedness, indiscretion, insensitivity, lack of consideration, lack of discretion, tactlessness

tactful adjective = **diplomatic**, careful, considerate, delicate, discreet, judicious, perceptive, polished, polite, politic, prudent, sensitive, subtle, thoughtful, understanding
➤ Antonyms
awkward, clumsy, gauche, inconsiderate, indiscreet, insensitive, tactless, tasteless, thoughtless, undiplomatic, unsubtle, untoward

tactic noun 1 = **policy**, approach, course, device, line, manoeuvre, means, method, move, ploy, scheme, stratagem, tack, trick, way 2 **tactics** = **strategy**, campaigning, generalship, manoeuvres, plans

tactical adjective = **strategic**, artful, clever, cunning, diplomatic, shrewd, skilful, smart
➤ Antonyms
blundering, clumsy, gauche, impolitic, inept

tactician noun = **strategist**, campaigner, coordinator, director, general, mastermind, planner, schemer

tactless adjective = **insensitive**, blundering,

boorish, careless, clumsy, discourteous, gauche, impolite, impolitic, inconsiderate, indelicate, indiscreet, injudicious, rude, thoughtless, undiplomatic, unfeeling, unkind, unsubtle
➤ **Antonyms**
considerate, diplomatic, discreet, polite, subtle, tactful

tag noun 1 = **label**, flap, identification, mark, marker, note, slip, tab, ticket ◆ verb 2 = **label**, earmark, flag, identify, mark, ticket 3 with **along** or **on** = **accompany**, attend, follow, shadow, tail (informal), trail 4 with **on** = **add**, adjoin, affix, annex, append, fasten, tack

tail noun 1 = **extremity**, appendage, end, rear end, tailpiece, train 2 **turn tail** = **run away**, cut and run, escape, flee, make off, retreat, run for it (informal), run off, scarper (Brit. slang), skedaddle (informal), take off (informal), take to one's heels ◆ verb 3 Informal = **follow**, dog the footsteps of, keep an eye on, shadow, stalk, track, trail

tail off or **away** verb = **decrease**, die out, drop, dwindle, fade, fall away, peter out, wane
➤ **Antonyms**
grow, increase, intensify, wax

tailor noun 1 = **outfitter**, clothier, costumier, couturier, dressmaker, garment maker, seamstress ◆ verb 2 = **adapt**, accommodate, adjust, alter, convert, customize, cut, fashion, fit, modify, mould, shape, style, suit

tailor-made adjective 1 = **made-to-measure**, cut to fit, fitted, made to order 2 = **perfect**, custom-made, ideal, just right, right, suitable

taint verb 1 = **spoil**, besmirch, blemish, blight, blot, contaminate, corrupt, damage, defile, dirty, foul, infect, poison, pollute, ruin, smear, smirch, soil, stain, sully, tarnish ◆ noun 2 = **stain**, black mark, blemish, blot, defect, demerit, fault, flaw, smear, smirch, spot 3 = **disgrace**, dishonour, shame, stigma 4 = **contamination**, contagion, infection, pollution
➤ **Antonyms**
verb ≠**spoil**: clean, cleanse, decontaminate, disinfect, purify

take verb 1 = **accompany**, bring, conduct, convoy, escort, guide, lead, usher 2 = **carry**, bear, bring, cart, convey, ferry, fetch, haul, tote (informal), transport 3 = **obtain**, acquire, carry off, catch, clutch, gain possession of, get, get hold of, grasp, grip, have, help oneself to, lay hold of, receive, secure, seize, win 4 = **steal**,

abstract, appropriate, carry off, filch, misappropriate, nick (slang, chiefly Brit.), pinch (informal), pocket, purloin, run off with, swipe (slang), walk off with 5 = **capture**, abduct, arrest, seize 6 = **choose**, book, buy, engage, hire, lease, pay for, pick, purchase, rent, reserve, select 7 = **require**, call for, demand, necessitate, need 8 = **consume**, drink, eat, imbibe, ingest, inhale, swallow 9 = **perform**, do, effect, execute, have, make 10 = **accept**, adopt, assume, enter upon, undertake 11 = **tolerate**, abide, bear, brave, brook, endure, go through, put up with (informal), stand, stomach, submit to, suffer, swallow, thole (Scot.), undergo, withstand 12 = **have room for**, accept, accommodate, contain, hold 13 = **subtract**, deduct, eliminate, remove 14 = **work**, do the trick (informal), have effect, operate, succeed 15 = **assume**, believe, consider, deem, hold, interpret as, perceive, presume, receive, regard, see as, think of as, understand
➤ **Antonyms**
≠**carry**: send ≠**steal**: give, give back, hand over, restore, return, surrender, yield ≠**capture**: free, let go, release ≠**accept**: decline, dismiss, eschew, ignore, refuse, reject, scorn, spurn ≠**tolerate**: avoid, dodge, give in, give way ≠**subtract**: add, put ≠**work**: fail, flop (informal)

take back verb 1 = **retract**, disavow, disclaim, recant, renege, renounce, unsay, withdraw 2 = **regain**, get back, recapture, reclaim, reconquer, repossess, retake 3 = **give one a refund for**, exchange

take down verb 1 = **make a note of**, minute, note, put on record, record, set down, transcribe, write down 2 = **dismantle**, demolish, disassemble, level, take apart, take to pieces, tear down 3 = **remove**, depress, drop, haul down, let down, lower, pull down, take off 4 = **humble**, deflate, humiliate, mortify, put down (slang)

take in verb 1 = **understand**, absorb, assimilate, comprehend, digest, get the hang of (informal), grasp 2 = **deceive**, bilk, cheat, con (informal), do (slang), dupe, fool, hoodwink, mislead, pull the wool over (someone's) eyes (informal), swindle, trick 3 = **include**, comprise, contain, cover, encompass 4 = **let in**, accommodate, admit, receive

takeoff noun 1 = **departure**, launch, liftoff 2 Informal = **parody**, caricature, imitation, lampoon, mocking, satire, send-up (Brit. informal), spoof (informal), travesty

take off verb 1 = **remove**, discard, divest

oneself of, doff, drop, peel off, strip off **2** = **lift off**, become airborne, leave the ground, take to the air **3** *Informal* = **depart**, abscond, beat it (*slang*), decamp, disappear, go, hit the road (*slang*), leave, set out, slope off, split (*slang*) **4** *Informal* = **parody**, caricature, imitate, lampoon, mimic, mock, satirize, send up (*Brit. informal*), spoof (*informal*), take the piss (out of) (*taboo slang*), travesty

take on *verb* **1** = **engage**, employ, enlist, enrol, hire **2** = **acquire**, assume, come to have **3** = **accept**, agree to do, have a go at (*informal*), tackle, undertake **4** = **compete against**, contend with, face, fight, oppose, pit oneself against

takeover *noun* = **merger**, change of leadership, coup, incorporation

take over *verb* = **gain control of**, assume control of, become leader of, take command of

take to *verb* **1** = **like**, become friendly with, be taken with, get on with, warm to **2** = **start**, have recourse to, make a habit of, resort to

take up *verb* **1** = **occupy**, absorb, consume, cover, extend over, fill, use up **2** = **start**, adopt, assume, become involved in, engage in

taking *adjective* = **charming**, attractive, beguiling, captivating, cute, delightful, enchanting, engaging, fascinating, fetching (*informal*), likable *or* likeable, pleasing, prepossessing, winning
➤ **Antonyms**
abhorrent, loathsome, offensive, repulsive, unattractive, unpleasant

takings *plural noun* = **revenue**, earnings, gain, gate, income, pickings, proceeds, profits, receipts, returns, take, yield

tale *noun* **1** = **story**, account, anecdote, fable, fiction, legend, narration, narrative, novel, report, romance, saga, short story, urban legend, urban myth, yarn (*informal*) **2** = **lie**, cock-and-bull story (*informal*), fabrication, falsehood, fib, gossip, rumour, tall story (*informal*), untruth

talent *noun* = **ability**, aptitude, bent, capacity, endowment, faculty, flair, forte, genius, gift, knack, power

talented *adjective* = **gifted**, able, artistic, brilliant

talisman *noun* = **charm**, amulet, fetish, lucky charm, mascot

talk *verb* **1** = **speak**, articulate, chat, chatter, communicate, converse, express oneself, gab (*informal*), give voice to, gossip, natter, prate, prattle, rap (*slang*), say, spout, utter, verbalize, witter (*informal*) **2**

= **discuss**, confabulate, confer, have a confab (*informal*), hold discussions, negotiate, parley **3** = **inform**, blab, give the game away, grass (*Brit. slang*), let the cat out of the bag, reveal information, shop (*slang, chiefly Brit.*), sing (*slang, chiefly U.S.*), spill the beans (*informal*), squeal (*slang*), tell all ♦ *noun* **4** = **speech**, address, discourse, disquisition, dissertation, lecture, oration, sermon **5** = **discussion**, confab (*informal*), confabulation, conference, consultation, dialogue **6** = **conversation**, blether, chat, chatter, chitchat, crack (*Scot. & Irish*), gab (*informal*), natter, rap (*slang*) **7** = **gossip**, hearsay, rumour, tittle-tattle **8** = **meeting**, conclave, conference, congress, negotiation, parley, seminar, symposium

talkative *adjective* = **loquacious**, big-mouthed (*slang*), chatty, effusive, gabby (*informal*), garrulous, gossipy, long-winded, mouthy, verbose, voluble, wordy
➤ **Antonyms**
quiet, reserved, reticent, silent, taciturn, tight-lipped, uncommunicative, unforthcoming

talker *noun* = **speaker**, chatterbox, conversationalist, lecturer, orator, speechmaker

talking-to *noun Informal* = **reprimand**, criticism, dressing-down (*informal*), lecture, rap on the knuckles, rebuke, reproach, reproof, row, scolding, telling-off (*informal*), ticking-off (*informal*)
➤ **Antonyms**
commendation, encouragement, praise

talk into *verb* = **persuade**, bring round (*informal*), convince, prevail on *or* upon, sway, win over

tall *adjective* **1** = **high**, big, elevated, giant, lanky, lofty, soaring, towering **2** *As in* **tall story** *Informal* = **implausible**, absurd, cock-and-bull (*informal*), exaggerated, far-fetched, incredible, preposterous, steep (*Brit. informal*), unbelievable **3** *As in* **tall order** = **difficult**, demanding, hard, unreasonable, well-nigh impossible
➤ **Antonyms**
≠**high**: short, small, squat, stumpy, tiny, wee ≠**implausible**: accurate, believable, plausible, realistic, reasonable, true, unexaggerated

tally *verb* **1** = **agree**, accord, coincide, concur, conform, correspond, fit, harmonize, match, parallel, square, suit **2** = **keep score**, compute, count up, total ♦ *noun* **3** = **record**, count, mark, reckoning, running total, score, total
➤ **Antonyms**

verb ≠**agree**: clash, conflict, contradict, differ, disagree

tame *adjective* **1** = **domesticated**, amenable, broken, cultivated, disciplined, docile, gentle, obedient, tractable **2** = **unafraid**, fearless **3** = **submissive**, compliant, docile, manageable, meek, obedient, spiritless, subdued, unresisting **4** = **unexciting**, bland, boring, dull, flat, humdrum, insipid, lifeless, prosaic, tedious, tiresome, uninspiring, uninteresting, vapid, wearisome ♦ *verb* **5** = **domesticate**, break in, house-train, make tame, pacify, train **6** = **subdue**, break the spirit of, conquer, curb, discipline, humble, master, repress, subjugate, suppress
➤ **Antonyms**
adjective ≠**domesticated**: aggressive, feral, ferocious, savage, undomesticated, untamed, wild ≠**submissive**: aggressive, argumentative, obdurate, strong-willed, stubborn, unmanageable ≠**unexciting**: exciting, frenzied, hot, interesting, lively, stimulating ♦ *verb* ≠**domesticate**: make fiercer ≠**subdue**: arouse, incite, intensify

tamper *verb* **1** = **interfere**, alter, fiddle (*informal*), fool about (*informal*), intrude, meddle, mess about, monkey around, muck about (*Brit. slang*), poke one's nose into (*informal*), tinker **2** = **influence**, bribe, corrupt, fix (*informal*), get at, manipulate, rig

tang *noun* **1** = **taste**, aroma, bite, flavour, odour, piquancy, savour, scent, smack, smell **2** = **trace**, hint, suggestion, tinge, touch, whiff

tangible *adjective* = **definite**, actual, concrete, corporeal, evident, manifest, material, objective, palpable, perceptible, physical, positive, real, solid, substantial, tactile, touchable
➤ **Antonyms**
abstract, disembodied, ethereal, immaterial, impalpable, imperceptible, indiscernible, insubstantial, intangible, theoretical, unreal

tangle *noun* **1** = **knot**, coil, entanglement, jungle, mass, mat, mesh, snarl, twist, web **2** = **confusion**, complication, entanglement, fix (*informal*), imbroglio, jam, labyrinth, maze, mess, mix-up ♦ *verb* **3** = **twist**, coil, confuse, entangle, interlace, interlock, intertwist, interweave, jam, knot, mat, mesh, ravel, snarl **4** *often with* **with** = **come into conflict**, come up against, contend, contest, cross swords, dispute, lock horns **5** = **catch**, enmesh, ensnare, entangle, entrap
➤ **Antonyms**
verb ≠**twist**: disentangle, extricate, free,

straighten out, unravel, untangle

tangled *adjective* **1** = **twisted**, entangled, jumbled, knotted, knotty, matted, messy, snarled, tousled **2** = **complicated**, complex, confused, convoluted, involved, knotty, messy, mixed-up

tangy *adjective* = **sharp**, piquant, pungent, spicy, tart

tantalize *verb* = **torment**, entice, frustrate, keep (someone) hanging on, lead on, provoke, taunt, tease, titillate, torture

tantamount *adjective* **tantamount to** = **equivalent to**, as good as, commensurate with, equal to, synonymous with, the same as

tantrum *noun* = **outburst**, fit, flare-up, hysterics, ill humour, paddy (*Brit. informal*), paroxysm, storm, temper

tap¹ *verb* **1** = **knock**, beat, drum, pat, rap, strike, touch ♦ *noun* **2** = **knock**, beat, light blow, pat, rap, touch

tap² *noun* **1** = **valve**, faucet (*U.S.*), spigot, spout, stopcock **2** = **stopper**, bung, plug **3** = **bug** (*informal*), listening device **4 on tap**: **a** *Informal* = **available**, at hand, in reserve, on hand, ready **b** = **on draught** ♦ *verb* **5** = **listen in on**, bug (*informal*), eavesdrop on **6** = **use**, draw on, exploit, make use of, milk, mine, put to use, turn to account, utilize **7** = **draw off**, bleed, broach, drain, open, siphon off

tape *noun* **1** = **strip**, band, ribbon ♦ *verb* **2** = **record**, tape-record, video **3** = **bind**, seal, secure, stick, wrap

taper *verb* **1** = **narrow**, come to a point, thin **2 taper off** = **decrease**, die away, die out, dwindle, fade, lessen, reduce, subside, thin out, wane, weaken, wind down
➤ **Antonyms**
≠**decrease**: grow, increase, intensify, step up, strengthen, swell, widen

tardiness *noun* = **lateness**, belatedness, dilatoriness, slowness, unpunctuality

tardy *adjective* **1** = **late**, behindhand, belated, dilatory, overdue, unpunctual **2** = **slow**, backward, retarded

target *noun* **1** = **goal**, aim, ambition, end, Holy Grail (*informal*), intention, mark, object, objective **2** = **victim**, butt, scapegoat

tariff *noun* **1** = **tax**, assessment, duty, excise, impost, levy, rate, toll **2** = **price list**, bill of fare, charges, menu, schedule

tarnish *verb* **1** = **stain**, blemish, blot, darken, dim, discolour, dull, lose lustre *or* shine, rust, soil, spot **2** = **damage**, blacken, smirch, sully, taint ♦ *noun* **3** = **stain**, blemish, blot, discoloration, rust, spot, taint

➤ **Antonyms**
verb ≠**stain**: brighten, enhance, polish up, shine ≠**damage**: enhance

tarry *verb Old-fashioned* **1** = **linger**, bide, dally, dawdle, delay, hang around (*informal*), loiter, pause, remain, take one's time, wait **2** = **stay**, abide, dwell, lodge, rest, sojourn
➤ **Antonyms**
≠**linger**: hasten, hurry, move on, rush, scoot, step on it (*informal*)

tart¹ *noun* = **pie**, pastry, tartlet

tart² *adjective* **1** = **sharp**, acid, acidulous, astringent, bitter, piquant, pungent, sour, tangy, vinegary **2** = **cutting**, acrimonious, barbed, biting, caustic, harsh, hurtful, nasty, scathing, sharp, short, trenchant, vitriolic, wounding
➤ **Antonyms**
≠**sharp**: honeyed, sugary, sweet, syrupy, toothsome ≠**cutting**: agreeable, delightful, gentle, kind, pleasant

tart³ *noun* = **slut**, call girl, fallen woman, floozy (*slang*), harlot, hooker (*U.S. slang*), loose woman, prostitute, scrubber (*Brit. & Austral. slang*), slag (*Brit. slang*), streetwalker, strumpet, trollop, whore, woman of easy virtue

task *noun* **1** = **job**, assignment, business, charge, chore, duty, employment, enterprise, exercise, labour, mission, occupation, toil, undertaking, work **2 take to task** = **criticize**, bawl out (*informal*), blame, blast, censure, give a rocket (*Brit. & N.Z. informal*), lambast(e), lecture, read the riot act, rebuke, reprimand, reproach, reprove, scold, tear into (*informal*), tear (someone) off a strip (*Brit. informal*), tell off (*informal*), upbraid

taste *noun* **1** = **flavour**, relish, savour, smack, tang **2** = **bit**, bite, dash, drop, morsel, mouthful, nip, sample, sip, *soupçon*, spoonful, swallow, titbit, touch **3** = **liking**, appetite, bent, desire, fancy, fondness, inclination, leaning, partiality, penchant, predilection, preference, relish **4** = **refinement**, appreciation, cultivation, culture, discernment, discrimination, elegance, grace, judgment, perception, polish, sophistication, style **5** = **propriety**, correctness, decorum, delicacy, discretion, politeness, restraint, tact, tactfulness ◆ *verb* **6** = **distinguish**, differentiate, discern, perceive **7** = **sample**, nibble, savour, sip, test, try **8** = **have a flavour of**, savour of, smack of **9** = **experience**, come up against, encounter, feel, have knowledge of, know, meet with, partake of, undergo
➤ **Antonyms**

noun ≠**flavour**: blandness, insipidity, tastelessness ≠**liking**: disinclination, dislike, distaste, hatred, loathing ≠**refinement**: lack of discernment, lack of judgment, mawkishness, tackiness, tastelessness ≠**propriety**: bawdiness, coarseness, crudeness, impropriety, indelicacy, obscenity (*informal*), tactlessness, unsubtlety ◆ *verb* ≠**distinguish**: fail to discern ≠**experience**: fail to achieve, miss, remain ignorant of

tasteful *adjective* = **refined**, aesthetically pleasing, artistic, beautiful, charming, cultivated, cultured, delicate, discriminating, elegant, exquisite, fastidious, graceful, handsome, harmonious, in good taste, polished, restrained, smart, stylish, urbane
➤ **Antonyms**
brash, flashy, garish, gaudy, inelegant, loud, objectionable, offensive, showy, sick, tacky (*informal*), tasteless, tawdry, twee, uncultured, unrefined, vulgar

tasteless *adjective* **1** = **insipid**, bland, boring, dull, flat, flavourless, mild, stale, tame, thin, watered-down, weak **2** = **vulgar**, cheap, coarse, crass, crude, flashy, garish, gaudy, graceless, gross, impolite, improper, indecorous, indelicate, indiscreet, inelegant, low, naff (*Brit. slang*), rude, tacky (*informal*), tactless, tawdry, uncouth, unseemly
➤ **Antonyms**
≠**insipid**: appetizing, delectable, delicious, flavoursome, savoury, scrumptious (*informal*), tasty ≠**vulgar**: elegant, graceful, refined, tasteful

tasty *adjective* = **delicious**, appetizing, delectable, flavourful, flavoursome, full-flavoured, luscious, palatable, savoury, scrumptious (*informal*), toothsome, yummy (*slang*)
➤ **Antonyms**
bland, flavourless, insipid, tasteless, unappetizing, unsavoury

tatters *plural noun* **1** = **rags**, bits, pieces, scraps, shreds ◆ *noun* **2 in tatters** = **ragged**, down at heel, in rags, in shreds, ripped, tattered, threadbare, torn

tattle *verb* **1** = **gossip**, babble, blab, chatter, jabber, prattle, spread rumours, tell tales, tittle-tattle ◆ *noun* **2** = **gossip**, babble, chatter, chitchat, hearsay, idle talk, jabber, prattle, small talk, tittle-tattle

tatty *adjective Chiefly Brit.* = **shabby**, bedraggled, dilapidated, down at heel, neglected, ragged, run-down, scruffy, the worse for wear, threadbare, unkempt, worn, worn out
➤ **Antonyms**

good, new, smart, well-preserved

taunt verb 1 = **jeer**, deride, insult, mock, provoke, ridicule, sneer, take the piss (out of) (taboo slang), tease, torment ♦ noun 2 = **jeer**, barb, derision, dig, gibe, insult, provocation, ridicule, sarcasm, teasing

taut adjective = **tight**, flexed, rigid, strained, stressed, stretched, tense
➤ Antonyms
loose, relaxed, slack

tautological adjective = **repetitive**, iterative, redundant, repetitious

tautology noun = **repetition**, iteration, redundancy, repetitiousness, repetitiveness

tavern noun = **inn**, alehouse (archaic), bar, boozer (Brit., Austral., & N.Z. informal), hostelry, pub (informal, chiefly Brit.), public house, taproom, watering hole (facetious slang)

tawdry adjective = **vulgar**, cheap, flashy, gaudy, gimcrack, naff (Brit. slang), plastic (slang), showy, tacky (informal), tasteless, tatty
➤ Antonyms
elegant, graceful, plain, refined, simple, stylish, tasteful, unflashy, unostentatious, well-tailored

tax noun 1 = **charge**, assessment, contribution, customs, duty, excise, imposition, impost, levy, rate, tariff, tithe, toll, tribute ♦ verb 2 = **charge**, assess, demand, exact, impose, levy a tax on, rate 3 = **strain**, burden, drain, exhaust, load, make heavy demands on, overburden, push, put pressure on, sap, stretch, test, try, weaken, wear out, weary 4 = **accuse**, arraign, blame, charge, impeach, impugn, incriminate, lay at one's door
➤ Antonyms
verb ≠accuse: acquit, clear, exculpate, exonerate, vindicate

taxing adjective = **demanding**, exacting, heavy, onerous, punishing, sapping, stressful, tiring, tough, trying, wearing, wearisome
➤ Antonyms
easy, easy-peasy (slang), effortless, light, unburdensome, undemanding

teach verb = **instruct**, advise, coach, demonstrate, direct, discipline, drill, edify, educate, enlighten, give lessons in, guide, impart, inform, instil, school, show, train, tutor

teacher noun = **instructor**, coach, don, educator, guide, guru, lecturer, master or mistress, mentor, pedagogue, professor, schoolmaster or schoolmistress, schoolteacher, trainer, tutor

team noun 1 = **group**, band, body, bunch,

company, crew, gang, line-up, posse (informal), set, side, squad, troupe 2 = **pair**, span, yoke ♦ verb 3 often with **up** = **join**, band together, cooperate, couple, get together, link, unite, work together

teamwork noun = **cooperation**, collaboration, coordination, esprit de corps, fellowship, harmony, unity

tear verb 1 = **rip**, divide, rend, run, rupture, scratch, shred, split, sunder 2 = **pull apart**, claw, lacerate, mangle, mutilate, sever 3 = **rush**, bolt, career, charge, dart, dash, fly, gallop, hurry, race, run, shoot, speed, sprint, zoom 4 = **seize**, grab, pluck, pull, rip, snatch, wrench, wrest, yank ♦ noun 5 = **hole**, laceration, rent, rip, run, rupture, scratch, split

tearaway noun Brit. = **hooligan**, delinquent, good-for-nothing, rowdy, ruffian

tearful adjective = **weeping**, blubbering, crying, in tears, lachrymose, sobbing, weepy (informal), whimpering

tears plural noun 1 = **crying**, blubbering, distress, sobbing, wailing, weeping, whimpering 2 in tears = **weeping**, blubbering, crying, distressed, sobbing, whimpering

tease verb 1 = **mock**, aggravate (informal), annoy, badger, bait, bother, chaff, goad, needle (informal), pester, plague (informal), provoke, pull someone's leg (informal), take the mickey (informal), take the piss (out of) (taboo slang), taunt, torment, vex, wind up (Brit. slang) 2 = **tantalize**, lead on

technical adjective = **scientific**, hi-tech or high-tech, skilled, specialist, specialized, technological

technique noun 1 = **method**, approach, course, fashion, manner, means, mode, modus operandi, procedure, style, system, way 2 = **skill**, adroitness, art, artistry, craft, craftsmanship, execution, facility, knack, know-how (informal), performance, proficiency, touch

tedious adjective = **boring**, banal, deadly dull, drab, dreary, dull, ho-hum (informal), humdrum, irksome, laborious, long-drawn-out, mind-numbing, monotonous, prosaic, soporific, tiresome, tiring, unexciting, uninteresting, vapid, wearisome
➤ Antonyms
enjoyable, enthralling, exciting, exhilarating, imaginative, inspiring, interesting, quickly finished, short, stimulating

tedium noun = **boredom**, banality, deadness, drabness, dreariness, dullness, ennui, monotony, routine, sameness, tediousness, the doldrums

➤ **Antonyms**

challenge, excitement, exhilaration, fascination, interest, liveliness, stimulation

teem¹ *verb* = **be full of**, abound, be abundant, bear, be crawling with, be prolific, brim, bristle, burst at the seams, overflow, produce, swarm

teem² *verb* = **pour**, bucket down (*informal*), lash, pelt (down), rain cats and dogs (*informal*), stream

teeming¹ *adjective* = **full**, abundant, alive, brimful, brimming, bristling, bursting, chock-a-block, chock-full, crawling, numerous, overflowing, packed, replete, swarming, thick

➤ **Antonyms**

deficient, lacking, short, wanting

teeming² *adjective* = **pouring**, bucketing down (*informal*), pelting, streaming

teenage *adjective* = **youthful**, adolescent, immature, juvenile

teenager *noun* = **youth**, adolescent, boy, girl, juvenile, minor

teeny *adjective Informal* = **tiny**, diminutive, microscopic, miniature, minuscule, minute, teeny-weeny, wee

teeter *verb* = **wobble**, rock, seesaw, stagger, sway, totter, waver

teetotaller *noun* = **abstainer**, nondrinker, Rechabite

telegram *noun* = **cable**, radiogram, telegraph, telex, wire (*informal*)

telegraph *noun* 1 = **cable**, telegram, telex, wire (*informal*) ◆ *verb* 2 = **cable**, send, telex, transmit, wire (*informal*)

telepathy *noun* = **mind-reading**, sixth sense, thought transference

telephone *noun* 1 = **phone**, blower (*informal*), dog and bone (*slang*), handset, line, mobile (phone) ◆ *verb* 2 = **call**, buzz (*informal*), call up, dial, give (someone) a bell (*Brit. slang*), give (someone) a buzz (*informal*), give (someone) a call, give (someone) a ring (*informal, chiefly Brit.*), give someone a tinkle (*Brit. informal*), phone, ring (*chiefly Brit.*)

telescope *noun* 1 = **glass**, spyglass ◆ *verb* 2 = **shorten**, abbreviate, abridge, capsulize, compress, condense, consolidate, contract, curtail, cut, shrink, tighten, trim, truncate

➤ **Antonyms**

verb ≠ **shorten**: amplify, draw out, elongate, extend, flesh out, lengthen, protract, spread out

television *noun* = **TV**, gogglebox (*Brit. slang*), idiot box (*slang*), receiver, small screen (*informal*), telly (*Brit. informal*), the box (*Brit. informal*), the tube (*slang*), TV set

tell *verb* 1 = **inform**, acquaint, announce, apprise, communicate, confess, disclose, divulge, express, get off one's chest (*informal*), impart, let know, make known, mention, notify, proclaim, reveal, say, speak, state, utter 2 = **instruct**, authorize, bid, call upon, command, direct, enjoin, order, require, summon 3 = **describe**, chronicle, depict, give an account of, narrate, portray, recount, relate, report 4 = **see**, comprehend, discern, discover, make out, understand 5 = **distinguish**, differentiate, discern, discriminate, identify 6 = **have** *or* **take effect**, carry weight, count, have force, make its presence felt, register, take its toll, weigh

telling *adjective* = **effective**, considerable, decisive, effectual, forceful, forcible, impressive, influential, marked, potent, powerful, significant, striking, trenchant, weighty

➤ **Antonyms**

easily ignored, inconsequential, indecisive, ineffectual, insignificant, lightweight, minor, negligible, slight, trivial, unimportant

telling-off *noun* = **reprimand**, censure, criticism, dressing-down (*informal*), lecture, rap on the knuckles, rebuke, reproach, reproof, row, scolding, slating (*informal*), talking-to, ticking-off (*informal*)

tell off *verb* = **reprimand**, bawl out (*informal*), berate, censure, chide, give (someone) a piece of one's mind, give (someone) a rocket (*Brit. & N.Z. informal*), haul over the coals (*informal*), lecture, read the riot act, rebuke, reproach, reprove, scold, take to task, tear into (*informal*), tear (someone) off a strip (*Brit. informal*), tick off (*informal*), upbraid

temerity *noun* = **audacity**, boldness, brass neck (*Brit. informal*), cheek, chutzpah (*U.S. & Canad. informal*), effrontery, front, gall (*informal*), impudence, nerve (*informal*), rashness, recklessness

temper *noun* 1 = **rage**, bad mood, fit of pique, fury, gall, paddy (*Brit. informal*), passion, tantrum 2 = **irritability**, anger, annoyance, heat, hot-headedness, ill humour, irascibility, irritation, passion, peevishness, petulance, resentment, surliness 3 = **self-control**, calm, calmness, composure, cool (*slang*), coolness, equanimity, good humour, moderation 4 = **frame of mind**, attitude, character, constitution, disposition, humour, mind, mood, nature, temperament ◆ *verb* 5 = **moderate**, allay, assuage, calm, lessen,

mitigate, mollify, palliate, restrain, soften, soft-pedal (*informal*), soothe, tone down **6 = strengthen**, anneal, harden, toughen
➤ **Antonyms**
noun ≠**irritability**: contentment, goodwill ≠**self-control**: agitation, anger, bad mood, excitability, foul humour, fury, grumpiness, indignation, irascibility, irritation, pique, vexation, wrath ♦ *verb* ≠**moderate**: aggravate, arouse, excite, heighten, intensify, provoke, stir ≠**strengthen**: soften

temperament *noun* **1 = nature**, bent, cast of mind, character, complexion, constitution, disposition, frame of mind, humour, make-up, mettle, outlook, personality, quality, soul, spirit, temper, tendencies, tendency **2 = excitability**, anger, hot-headedness, impatience, moodiness, moods, petulance, volatility

temperamental *adjective* **1 = moody**, capricious, easily upset, emotional, erratic, excitable, fiery, highly strung, hot-headed, hypersensitive, impatient, irritable, mercurial, neurotic, passionate, petulant, sensitive, touchy, volatile **2** *Informal* **= unreliable**, erratic, inconsistent, inconstant, undependable, unpredictable **3 = natural**, congenital, constitutional, inborn, ingrained, inherent, innate
➤ **Antonyms**
≠**moody**: calm, cool-headed, easy-going, even-tempered, level-headed, phlegmatic, unexcitable, unflappable, unperturbable ≠**unreliable**: constant, dependable, reliable, stable, steady

temperance *noun* **1 = moderation**, continence, discretion, forbearance, restraint, self-control, self-discipline, self-restraint **2 = teetotalism**, abstemiousness, abstinence, prohibition, sobriety
➤ **Antonyms**
≠**moderation**: excess, immoderation, intemperance, overindulgence, prodigality

temperate *adjective* **1 = mild**, agreeable, balmy, calm, clement, cool, fair, gentle, moderate, pleasant, soft **2 = moderate**, calm, composed, dispassionate, equable, even-tempered, mild, reasonable, self-controlled, self-restrained, sensible, stable
➤ **Antonyms**
≠**mild**: extreme, harsh, inclement, intemperate, severe, torrid ≠**moderate**: intemperate, uncontrolled, undisciplined, unreasonable, unrestrained, wild

tempest *noun Literary* **= storm**, cyclone, gale, hurricane, squall, tornado, typhoon

tempestuous *adjective* **1 = stormy**,

agitated, blustery, breezy, gusty, inclement, raging, squally, turbulent, windy **2 = passionate**, boisterous, emotional, excited, furious, heated, impassioned, intense, stormy, turbulent, uncontrolled, violent, wild
➤ **Antonyms**
≠**passionate**: calm, peaceful, quiet, serene, still, tranquil, undisturbed, unruffled

temple *noun* **= shrine**, church, holy place, place of worship, sanctuary

tempo *noun* **= pace**, beat, cadence, measure (*Prosody*), metre, pulse, rate, rhythm, speed, time

temporal *adjective* **1 = secular**, earthly, fleshly, lay, material, mundane, worldly **2 = temporary**, evanescent, impermanent, momentary, passing, short-lived, transient, transitory

temporarily *adverb* **= briefly**, fleetingly, for a little while, for a moment, for a short time, for a short while, for the moment, for the time being, momentarily, pro tem

temporary *adjective* **= impermanent**, brief, ephemeral, evanescent, fleeting, here today and gone tomorrow, interim, momentary, passing, pro tem, *pro tempore,* provisional, short-lived, transient, transitory
➤ **Antonyms**
durable, enduring, eternal, everlasting, long-lasting, long-term, permanent

temporize *verb* **= play for time**, beat about the bush, be evasive, delay, hum and haw, procrastinate, stall

tempt *verb* **1 = entice**, coax, decoy, inveigle, invite, lead on, lure, seduce, tantalize **2 = attract**, allure, appeal to, draw
➤ **Antonyms**
≠**entice**: deter, discourage, dissuade, hinder, inhibit, put off

temptation *noun* **1 = enticement**, allurement, bait, coaxing, come-on (*informal*), decoy, inducement, invitation, lure, pull, seduction, snare, tantalization **2 = appeal**, attraction, attractiveness, draw

tempting *adjective* **= inviting**, alluring, appetizing, attractive, enticing, mouthwatering, seductive, tantalizing
➤ **Antonyms**
off-putting (*Brit. informal*), unappetizing, unattractive, undesirable, uninviting, untempting

tenable *adjective* **= sound**, arguable, believable, defendable, defensible, justifiable, maintainable, plausible, rational, reasonable, viable
➤ **Antonyms**

indefensible, insupportable, unjustifiable, untenable

tenacious *adjective* 1 = **firm**, clinging, fast, forceful, immovable, iron, strong, tight, unshakable 2 = **stubborn**, adamant, determined, dogged, firm, immovable, inflexible, intransigent, obdurate, obstinate, persistent, resolute, staunch, steadfast, stiff-necked, strong-willed, sure, unswerving, unyielding
➤ **Antonyms**
≠**stubborn**: changeable, flexible, irresolute, vacillating, wavering, yielding

tenacity *noun* 1 = **firmness**, fastness, force, forcefulness, power, strength 2 = **perseverance**, application, determination, diligence, doggedness, firmness, inflexibility, intransigence, obduracy, obstinacy, persistence, resoluteness, resolution, resolve, staunchness, steadfastness, strength of purpose, strength of will, stubbornness
➤ **Antonyms**
≠**firmness**: looseness, powerlessness, slackness, weakness

tenancy *noun* = **lease**, holding, occupancy, occupation, possession, renting, residence

tenant *noun* = **leaseholder**, holder, inhabitant, lessee, occupant, occupier, renter, resident

tend[1] *verb* 1 = **be inclined**, be apt, be biased, be disposed, be liable, be likely, gravitate, have a leaning, have an inclination, have a tendency, incline, lean, trend 2 = **go**, aim, bear, head, lead, make for, move, point

tend[2] *verb* = **take care of**, attend, care for, cater for, control, cultivate, feed, guard, keep, keep an eye on, look after, maintain, manage, minister to, nurse, nurture, protect, see to, serve, wait on, watch, watch over
➤ **Antonyms**
disregard, ignore, neglect, overlook, shirk

tendency *noun* 1 = **inclination**, bent, disposition, leaning, liability, partiality, penchant, predilection, predisposition, proclivity, proneness, propensity, readiness, susceptibility 2 = **course**, bearing, bias, direction, drift, movement, tenor, trend

tender[1] *adjective* 1 = **gentle**, affectionate, amorous, benevolent, caring, compassionate, considerate, fond, humane, kind, loving, pitiful, sentimental, softhearted, sympathetic, tenderhearted, warm, warm-hearted 2 = **vulnerable**, immature, impressionable, inexperienced, raw, sensitive, young, youthful 3 = **sensitive**, aching, acute, bruised,

inflamed, irritated, painful, raw, smarting, sore
➤ **Antonyms**
≠**gentle**: brutal, cold-hearted, cruel, hard, hard-hearted, inhuman, insensitive, pitiless, tough, uncaring, unkind, unsympathetic ≠**vulnerable**: advanced, elderly, experienced, grown-up, mature, seasoned, sophisticated, worldly, worldly-wise

tender[2] *verb* 1 = **offer**, extend, give, hand in, present, proffer, propose, put forward, submit, suggest, volunteer ♦ *noun* 2 = **offer**, bid, estimate, proffer, proposal, submission, suggestion

tenderness *noun* 1 = **gentleness**, affection, amorousness, care, compassion, consideration, devotion, fondness, humaneness, humanity, kindness, liking, love, mercy, pity, sentimentality, softheartedness, sympathy, tenderheartedness, warm-heartedness, warmth 2 = **vulnerability**, immaturity, impressionableness, inexperience, sensitivity, youth, youthfulness 3 = **soreness**, ache, aching, bruising, inflammation, irritation, pain, painfulness, rawness, sensitiveness, sensitivity, smart
➤ **Antonyms**
≠**gentleness**: cruelty, hardness, harshness, indifference, insensitivity, unkindness

tenet *noun* = **principle**, article of faith, belief, canon, conviction, creed, doctrine, dogma, maxim, precept, rule, teaching, view

tenor *noun* = **direction**, course, drift, meaning, purport, sense, substance, tendency, theme, trend

tense *adjective* 1 = **nervous**, antsy (*informal*), anxious, apprehensive, edgy, fidgety, jittery (*informal*), jumpy, keyed up, on edge, on tenterhooks, overwrought, restless, strained, twitchy (*informal*), under pressure, uptight (*informal*), wired (*slang*), wound up (*informal*) 2 = **exciting**, moving, nerve-racking, stressful, worrying 3 = **tight**, rigid, strained, stretched, taut ♦ *verb* 4 = **tighten**, brace, flex, strain, stretch, tauten
➤ **Antonyms**
adjective ≠**nervous**: calm, collected, cool-headed, easy-going, self-possessed, serene, unconcerned, unruffled, unworried ≠**exciting**: boring, dull, uninteresting ≠**tight**: flaccid, flexible, limp, loose, pliant, relaxed ♦ *verb* ≠**tighten**: loosen, relax, slacken

tension *noun* 1 = **strain**, anxiety, apprehension, edginess, hostility, nervousness, pressure, stress, suspense, the

jitters (*informal*), unease 2 = **tightness**, pressure, rigidity, stiffness, straining, stress, stretching, tautness
> ➤ **Antonyms**
≠**strain**: calmness, peacefulness, relaxation, restfulness, serenity, tranquillity

tentative *adjective* 1 = **unconfirmed**, conjectural, experimental, indefinite, provisional, speculative, unsettled 2 = **hesitant**, cautious, diffident, doubtful, faltering, timid, uncertain, undecided, unsure
> ➤ **Antonyms**
≠**unconfirmed**: conclusive, confirmed, decisive, definite, final, fixed, resolved, settled ≠**hesitant**: assured, bold, certain, confident, unhesitating

tenuous *adjective* 1 = **slight**, doubtful, dubious, flimsy, insignificant, insubstantial, nebulous, questionable, shaky, sketchy, weak 2 = **fine**, attenuated, delicate, gossamer, slim
> ➤ **Antonyms**
≠**slight**: significant, solid, sound, strong, substantial

tenure *noun* = **holding**, occupancy, occupation, possession, residence, tenancy, term, time

tepid *adjective* 1 = **lukewarm**, slightly warm, warmish 2 = **half-hearted**, apathetic, cool, indifferent, lukewarm, unenthusiastic
> ➤ **Antonyms**
≠**half-hearted**: animated, eager, enthusiastic, excited, keen, passionate, vibrant, zealous

tergiversate *verb Formal* 1 = **prevaricate**, beat about the bush, dodge, equivocate, fence, hedge, pussyfoot (*informal*), vacillate 2 = **change sides**, defect, desert, go over to the other side, renege, turn traitor

term *noun* 1 = **word**, appellation, denomination, designation, expression, locution, name, phrase, title 2 = **period**, duration, interval, season, space, span, spell, time, while 3 = **session**, course ♦ *verb* 4 = **call**, denominate, designate, dub, entitle, label, name, style

terminal *adjective* 1 = **fatal**, deadly, incurable, killing, lethal, mortal 2 = **final**, bounding, concluding, extreme, last, limiting, ultimate, utmost ♦ *noun* 3 = **terminus**, depot, end of the line, station
> ➤ **Antonyms**
adjective ≠**final**: beginning, commencing, first, initial, introductory, opening

terminate *verb* = **end**, abort, axe (*informal*), bring *or* come to an end, cease, close, complete, conclude, cut off,

discontinue, expire, finish, issue, lapse, put an end to, stop, wind up
> ➤ **Antonyms**
begin, commence, inaugurate, initiate, instigate, introduce, open, start

termination *noun* = **ending**, abortion, cessation, close, completion, conclusion, consequence, discontinuation, effect, end, expiry, finish, wind-up
> ➤ **Antonyms**
beginning, commencement, inauguration, initiation, opening, start

terminology *noun* = **language**, argot, cant, jargon, lingo (*informal*), nomenclature, patois, phraseology, terms, vocabulary

terminus *noun* = **end of the line**, depot, garage, last stop, station

terms *plural noun* 1 = **language**, manner of speaking, phraseology, terminology 2 = **conditions**, particulars, provisions, provisos, qualifications, specifications, stipulations 3 = **price**, charges, fee, payment, rates 4 = **relationship**, footing, position, relations, standing, status 5 **come to terms with** = **learn to live with**, be reconciled to, come to accept

terrain *noun* = **ground**, country, going, land, landscape, topography

terrestrial *adjective* = **earthly**, global, worldly

terrible *adjective* 1 = **serious**, bad, dangerous, desperate, extreme, severe 2 *Informal* = **bad**, abhorrent, abysmal, awful, beastly (*informal*), dire, dreadful, duff (*Brit. informal*), foul, frightful, from hell (*informal*), godawful (*slang*), hateful, hideous, loathsome, obnoxious, obscene, odious, offensive, poor, repulsive, revolting, rotten (*informal*), unpleasant, vile 3 = **fearful**, appalling, awful, dread, dreaded, dreadful, frightful, gruesome, harrowing, hellacious (*U.S. slang*), horrendous, horrible, horrid, horrifying, monstrous, shocking, terrifying, unspeakable
> ➤ **Antonyms**
≠**serious**: harmless, insignificant, mild, moderate, paltry, small ≠**bad**: admirable, brilliant, delightful, excellent, fine, great, magic, noteworthy, pleasant, remarkable, super, superb, terrific, very good, wonderful ≠**fearful**: calming, comforting, encouraging, reassuring, settling, soothing

terribly *adverb* = **extremely**, awfully (*informal*), decidedly, desperately, exceedingly, gravely, greatly, much, seriously, thoroughly, very

terrific *adjective* 1 = **great**, awesome, awful, dreadful, enormous, excessive, extreme,

fearful, fierce, gigantic, harsh, horrific, huge, intense, monstrous, severe, terrible, tremendous **2** *Informal* = **excellent**, amazing, awesome (*slang*), boffo (*slang*), breathtaking, brilliant, cracking (*Brit. informal*), fabulous (*informal*), fantastic (*informal*), fine, great (*informal*), magnificent, marvellous, mean (*slang*), outstanding, sensational (*informal*), smashing (*informal*), stupendous, super (*informal*), superb, very good, wonderful
➤ Antonyms
≠**great**: insignificant, mild, moderate, paltry ≠**excellent**: appalling, awful, bad, dreadful, terrible

terrified *adjective* = **frightened**, alarmed, appalled, frightened out of one's wits, horrified, horror-struck, intimidated, panic-stricken, petrified, scared, scared stiff, scared to death, shocked, terror-stricken

terrify *verb* = **frighten**, alarm, appal, fill with terror, frighten out of one's wits, horrify, intimidate, make one's blood run cold, make one's flesh creep, make one's hair stand on end, petrify, scare, shock, terrorize

territory *noun* = **district**, area, country, domain, land, patch, province, region, sector, state, terrain, tract, turf (*U.S. slang*), zone

terror *noun* **1** = **fear**, alarm, anxiety, awe, consternation, dismay, dread, fright, horror, intimidation, panic, shock **2** = **scourge**, bogeyman, bugbear, devil, fiend, monster

terrorize *verb* **1** = **oppress**, browbeat, bully, coerce, intimidate, menace, threaten **2** = **terrify**, alarm, appal, fill with terror, frighten, frighten out of one's wits, horrify, intimidate, make one's blood run cold, make one's flesh creep, make one's hair stand on end, petrify, scare, shock, strike terror into

terse *adjective* **1** = **concise**, aphoristic, brief, clipped, compact, condensed, crisp, elliptical, epigrammatic, gnomic, laconic, monosyllabic, neat, pithy, short, succinct, to the point **2** = **curt**, abrupt, brusque, short, snappy
➤ Antonyms
≠**concise**: circumlocutory, confused, discursive, lengthy, long-winded, rambling, roundabout, vague, verbose, wordy ≠**curt**: chatty, polite

test *verb* **1** = **check**, analyse, assay, assess, examine, experiment, investigate, prove, put to the test, research, try, try out, verify
♦ *noun* **2** = **examination**, acid test, analysis, assessment, check, evaluation,

investigation, proof, research, trial

testament *noun* **1** = **proof**, attestation, demonstration, evidence, testimony, tribute, witness **2** = **will**, last wishes

testicles *plural noun* = **balls** (*taboo slang*), bollocks *or* ballocks (*taboo slang*), nuts (*taboo slang*)

testify *verb* = **bear witness**, affirm, assert, attest, certify, corroborate, declare, give testimony, show, state, swear, vouch, witness
➤ Antonyms
belie, contradict, controvert, disprove, dispute, gainsay (*archaic or literary*), oppose

testimonial *noun* = **tribute**, certificate, character, commendation, credential, endorsement, recommendation, reference

testimony *noun* **1** = **evidence**, affidavit, affirmation, attestation, avowal, declaration, deposition, statement, submission **2** = **proof**, corroboration, demonstration, evidence, indication, manifestation, support, verification

testing *adjective* = **difficult**, arduous, challenging, demanding, exacting, rigorous, searching, strenuous, taxing, tough
➤ Antonyms
easy, friendly, gentle, simple, straightforward, undemanding

testy *adjective* = **irritable**, bad-tempered, cantankerous, cross, fretful, grumpy, impatient, irascible, peevish, quick-tempered, ratty (*Brit. & N.Z. informal*), short-tempered, snappish, snappy, tetchy, touchy

tetchy *adjective* = **irritable**, bad-tempered, cantankerous, cross, fretful, grumpy, impatient, irascible, peevish, quick-tempered, ratty (*Brit. & N.Z. informal*), short-tempered, snappish, snappy, testy, touchy

tête-à-tête *noun* **1** = **private conversation**, chat, confab (*informal*), cosy chat, private word, talk ♦ *adverb* **2** = **in private**, intimately, privately

tether *noun* **1** = **rope**, chain, fetter, halter, lead, leash, restraint **2 at the end of one's tether** = **exasperated**, at one's wits' end, exhausted ♦ *verb* **3** = **tie**, bind, chain, fasten, fetter, secure

text *noun* **1** = **contents**, body, main body, matter **2** = **words**, wording **3** = **passage**, paragraph, sentence, verse **4** = **reference book**, source, textbook

texture *noun* = **feel**, character, composition, consistency, constitution, fabric, grain, make, quality, structure, surface, tissue, weave

thank *verb* = **say thank you**, express gratitude, show gratitude, show one's appreciation

thankful *adjective* = **grateful**, appreciative, beholden, indebted, in (someone's) debt, obliged, pleased, relieved
➤ **Antonyms**
thankless, unappreciative, ungrateful

thankless *adjective* = **unrewarding**, fruitless, unappreciated, unprofitable, unrequited, useless
➤ **Antonyms**
fruitful, productive, profitable, rewarding, useful, worthwhile

thanks *plural noun* 1 = **gratitude**, acknowledgment, appreciation, credit, gratefulness, recognition, thanksgiving 2 **thanks to** = **because of**, as a result of, by reason of, due to, owing to, through

thaw *verb* = **melt**, defrost, dissolve, liquefy, soften, unfreeze, warm
➤ **Antonyms**
chill, congeal, freeze, harden, solidify, stiffen

theatrical *adjective* 1 = **dramatic**, dramaturgic, Thespian 2 = **exaggerated**, actorly *or* actressy, affected, artificial, camp (*informal*), dramatic, histrionic, mannered, melodramatic, ostentatious, overdone, showy, stagy
➤ **Antonyms**
≠**exaggerated**: natural, plain, simple, straightforward, unaffected, unassuming, unexaggerated, unpretentious, unsophisticated

theft *noun* = **stealing**, embezzlement, fraud, larceny, pilfering, purloining, rip-off (*slang*), robbery, swindling, thievery, thieving

theme *noun* 1 = **subject**, argument, idea, keynote, matter, subject matter, text, thesis, topic 2 = **motif**, leitmotif, recurrent image, unifying idea 3 = **essay**, composition, dissertation, exercise, paper

theological *adjective* = **religious**, divine, doctrinal, ecclesiastical

theorem *noun* = **proposition**, formula, hypothesis, principle, rule, statement

theoretical *adjective* = **abstract**, academic, conjectural, hypothetical, ideal, impractical, notional, pure, speculative
➤ **Antonyms**
applied, experiential, factual, practical, realistic

theorize *verb* = **speculate**, conjecture, formulate, guess, hypothesize, project, propound, suppose

theory *noun* 1 = **hypothesis**, assumption,

conjecture, guess, presumption, speculation, supposition, surmise, thesis 2 = **system**, philosophy, plan, proposal, scheme
➤ **Antonyms**
≠**hypothesis**: certainty, experience, fact, practice, reality

therapeutic *adjective* = **beneficial**, corrective, curative, good, healing, remedial, restorative, salutary
➤ **Antonyms**
adverse, damaging, destructive, detrimental, harmful

therapist *noun* = **healer**, physician

therapy *noun* = **remedy**, cure, healing, remedial treatment, treatment

therefore *adverb* = **consequently**, accordingly, as a result, ergo, for that reason, hence, so, then, thence, thus, whence

thesaurus *noun* = **wordbook**, dictionary, encyclopedia, wordfinder

thesis *noun* 1 = **dissertation**, composition, disquisition, essay, monograph, paper, treatise 2 = **proposition**, contention, hypothesis, idea, opinion, proposal, theory, view 3 *Logic* = **premise**, assumption, postulate, proposition, statement, supposition, surmise

thick *adjective* 1 = **wide**, broad, bulky, deep, fat, solid, substantial 2 = **dense**, close, clotted, coagulated, compact, concentrated, condensed, crowded, deep, heavy, impenetrable, opaque 3 = **full**, abundant, brimming, bristling, bursting, chock-a-block, chock-full, covered, crawling, numerous, packed, replete, swarming, teeming 4 *Informal* = **stupid**, brainless, dense, dim-witted (*informal*), dopey (*informal*), dozy (*Brit. informal*), dull, dumb-ass (*informal*), insensitive, moronic, obtuse, slow, slow-witted, thickheaded 5 = **strong**, broad, decided, distinct, marked, pronounced, rich 6 *As in* **thick as thieves** *Informal* = **friendly**, chummy (*informal*), close, devoted, familiar, inseparable, intimate, matey *or* maty (*Brit. informal*), on good terms, pally (*informal*) 7 **a bit thick** *Brit. informal* = **unreasonable**, excessive, over the score (*informal*), too much, unfair, unjust ♦ *noun* 8 = **middle**, centre, heart, midst
➤ **Antonyms**
adjective ≠**wide**: narrow, slight, slim, thin ≠**dense**: clear, diluted, runny, thin, watery, weak ≠**full**: bare, clear, devoid of, empty, free from, sparse, thin ≠**stupid**: articulate, brainy, bright, clever, intellectual, intelligent, quick-witted, sharp, smart ≠**strong**: faint, slight, vague, weak

≠**friendly**: antagonistic, distant, hostile, unfriendly

thicken *verb* = **set**, cake, clot, coagulate, condense, congeal, deepen, jell
➤ **Antonyms**
dilute, thin, water down, weaken

thicket *noun* = **wood**, brake, coppice, copse, covert, grove

thickhead *noun Slang* = **idiot**, berk (*Brit. slang*), blockhead, bonehead (*slang*), chump, dimwit (*informal*), divvy (*Brit. slang*), dolt, dope (*informal*), dork (*slang*), dumb-ass (*slang*), dummy (*slang*), dunce, dunderhead, fool, imbecile, lamebrain (*informal*), moron, numbskull *or* numskull, numpty (*Scot. informal*), pillock (*Brit. slang*), plonker (*slang*), prat (*slang*), twit (*informal, chiefly Brit.*), wally (*slang*)

thickheaded *adjective* = **idiotic**, blockheaded, brainless, dense, dim-witted (*informal*), doltish, dopey (*informal*), dozy (*Brit. informal*), dumb-ass (*informal*), moronic, obtuse, slow, slow-witted, stupid, thick

thickset *adjective* 1 = **stocky**, beefy (*informal*), brawny, bulky, burly, heavy, muscular, powerfully built, strong, stubby, sturdy, well-built 2 = **dense**, closely packed, densely planted, solid, thick
➤ **Antonyms**
≠**stocky**: angular, bony, gangling, gaunt, lanky, rawboned, scraggy, scrawny, weedy (*informal*)

thick-skinned *adjective* = **insensitive**, callous, hardened, impervious, stolid, tough, unfeeling, unsusceptible
➤ **Antonyms**
concerned, feeling, sensitive, tender, thin-skinned, touchy

thief *noun* = **robber**, bandit, burglar, crook (*informal*), embezzler, housebreaker, larcenist, mugger (*informal*), pickpocket, pilferer, plunderer, shoplifter, stealer

thieve *verb* = **steal**, blag (*slang*), embezzle, filch, knock off (*slang*), lift (*informal*), misappropriate, nick (*slang, chiefly Brit.*), pilfer, pinch (*informal*), plunder, poach, purloin, rip off (*slang*), rob, run off with, swipe (*slang*)

thievish *adjective* = **thieving**, larcenous, light-fingered, rapacious

thin *adjective* 1 = **narrow**, attenuate, attenuated, fine 2 = **slim**, bony, emaciated, lank, lanky, lean, light, meagre, scraggy, scrawny, skeletal, skin and bone, skinny, slender, slight, spare, spindly, thin as a rake, undernourished, underweight 3 = **meagre**, deficient, scanty, scarce, scattered, skimpy, sparse, wispy 4 = **fine**, delicate, diaphanous, filmy, flimsy, gossamer, see-through, sheer, translucent, transparent, unsubstantial 5 = **watery**, diluted, runny, weak 6 = **unconvincing**, feeble, flimsy, inadequate, insufficient, lame, poor, scant, scanty, slight, superficial, unsubstantial, weak ♦ *verb* 7 = **reduce**, attenuate, cut back, dilute, diminish, prune, rarefy, refine, trim, water down, weaken, weed out
➤ **Antonyms**
adjective ≠**narrow**: heavy, thick ≠**slim**: bulky, corpulent, fat, heavy, obese, stout ≠**meagre**: abundant, adequate, plentiful, profuse ≠**fine**: bulky, dense, heavy, strong, substantial, thick ≠**watery**: concentrated, dense, strong, thick, viscous ≠**unconvincing**: adequate, convincing, strong, substantial

thing *noun* 1 = **object**, affair, article, being, body, circumstance, entity, fact, matter, something, substance 2 = **factor**, aspect, detail, facet, feature, item, particular, point, statement 3 = **happening**, act, deed, event, eventuality, feat, incident, occurrence, phenomenon, proceeding 4 = **device**, apparatus, contrivance, gadget, implement, instrument, machine, means, mechanism, tool 5 *Informal* = **obsession**, attitude, bee in one's bonnet, fetish, fixation, hang-up (*informal*), mania, phobia, preoccupation, quirk 6 **things** = **possessions**, baggage, belongings, bits and pieces, clobber (*Brit. slang*), clothes, effects, equipment, gear, goods, impedimenta, luggage, odds and ends, paraphernalia, stuff

think *verb* 1 = **believe**, conceive, conclude, consider, deem, determine, esteem, estimate, guess (*informal, chiefly U.S. & Canad.*), hold, imagine, judge, reckon, regard, suppose, surmise 2 = **ponder**, brood, cerebrate, cogitate, consider, contemplate, deliberate, meditate, mull over, muse, obsess, rack one's brains, reason, reflect, revolve, ruminate, turn over in one's mind, weigh up 3 **think much** *or* **a lot of** = **have a high opinion of**, admire, attach importance to, esteem, hold in high regard, rate (*slang*), respect, set store by, think highly of, value ♦ *noun* 4 *Informal* = **consideration**, assessment, contemplation, deliberation, look, reflection

thinker *noun* = **philosopher**, brain (*informal*), intellect (*informal*), mastermind, sage, theorist, wise man

thinking *noun* 1 = **reasoning**, assessment, conclusions, conjecture, idea, judgment, opinion, outlook, philosophy, position, theory, thoughts, view ♦ *adjective* 2 = **thoughtful**, contemplative, intelligent, meditative, philosophical, rational, reasoning, reflective, sophisticated

think over *verb* = **consider**, consider the pros and cons of, contemplate, give thought to, mull over, ponder, weigh up

think up *verb* = **devise**, come up with, concoct, contrive, create, dream up, imagine, improvise, invent, manufacture, trump up, visualize

thin-skinned *adjective* = **easily hurt**, hypersensitive, quick to take offence, sensitive, susceptible, touchy, vulnerable
➤ **Antonyms**
callous, hard, heartless, insensitive, obdurate, stolid, thick-skinned, tough, unfeeling

third-rate *adjective* = **mediocre**, bad, indifferent, inferior, low-grade, no great shakes (*informal*), not much cop (*informal*), poor, poor-quality, ropey *or* ropy (*Brit. informal*), shoddy

thirst *noun* 1 = **thirstiness**, craving to drink, drought, dryness 2 = **craving**, ache, appetite, desire, eagerness, hankering, hunger, keenness, longing, lust, passion, yearning, yen (*informal*)
➤ **Antonyms**
≠craving: apathy, aversion, disinclination, dislike, distaste, loathing, revulsion

thirsty *adjective* 1 = **parched**, arid, dehydrated, dry *with* **for** = **eager**, athirst, avid, burning, craving, desirous, dying, greedy, hankering, hungry, itching, longing, lusting, thirsting, yearning

thorn *noun* 1 = **prickle**, barb, spike, spine 2 **thorn in one's side** *or* **flesh** = **irritation**, affliction, annoyance, bane, bother, curse, hassle (*informal*), irritant, nuisance, pest, plague, scourge, torment, trouble

thorny *adjective* 1 = **prickly**, barbed, bristling with thorns, bristly, pointed, sharp, spiky, spiny 2 = **troublesome**, awkward, difficult, hard, irksome, problematic(al), sticky (*informal*), ticklish, tough, trying, unpleasant, worrying

thorough *adjective* 1 = **careful**, all-embracing, all-inclusive, assiduous, complete, comprehensive, conscientious, efficient, exhaustive, full, in-depth, intensive, leaving no stone unturned, meticulous, painstaking, scrupulous, sweeping 2 = **complete**, absolute, arrant, deep-dyed (*usually derogatory*), downright, entire, out-and-out, outright, perfect, pure, sheer, total, unmitigated, unqualified, utter
➤ **Antonyms**
≠careful: careless, cursory, half-hearted, haphazard, lackadaisical, sloppy
≠complete: imperfect, incomplete, partial,

superficial

thoroughbred *adjective* = **purebred**, blood, full-blooded, of unmixed stock, pedigree, pure-blooded
➤ **Antonyms**
crossbred, crossed, half-breed, hybrid, mongrel, of mixed breed

thoroughfare *noun* = **road**, access, avenue, highway, passage, passageway, roadway, street, way

thoroughly *adverb* 1 = **carefully**, assiduously, completely, comprehensively, conscientiously, efficiently, exhaustively, from top to bottom, fully, inside out, intensively, leaving no stone unturned, meticulously, painstakingly, scrupulously, sweepingly, through and through, throughout 2 = **completely**, absolutely, downright, entirely, perfectly, quite, totally, to the full, to the hilt, utterly, without reservation
➤ **Antonyms**
≠carefully: carelessly, cursorily, half-heartedly, haphazardly, lackadaisically, sloppily ≠completely: imperfectly, incompletely, in part, partly, somewhat, superficially

though *conjunction* 1 = **although**, albeit, despite the fact that, even if, even supposing, even though, granted, notwithstanding, tho' (*U.S. or poetic*), while ♦ *adverb* 2 = **nevertheless**, all the same, for all that, however, nonetheless, notwithstanding, still, yet

thought *noun* 1 = **thinking**, brainwork, cogitation, consideration, contemplation, deliberation, introspection, meditation, musing, reflection, rumination 2 = **idea**, assessment, belief, concept, conception, conclusion, conjecture, conviction, estimation, judgment, notion, opinion, thinking, view 3 = **consideration**, attention, heed, regard, scrutiny, study 4 = **intention**, aim, design, idea, notion, object, plan, purpose 5 = **expectation**, anticipation, aspiration, dream, hope, prospect

thoughtful *adjective* 1 = **considerate**, attentive, caring, helpful, kind, kindly, solicitous, unselfish 2 = **well-thought-out**, astute, canny, careful, cautious, circumspect, deliberate, discreet, heedful, mindful, prudent 3 = **reflective**, contemplative, deliberative, in a brown study, introspective, lost in thought, meditative, musing, pensive, rapt, ruminative, serious, studious, thinking, wistful
➤ **Antonyms**
≠considerate: cold-hearted, impolite,

inconsiderate, insensitive, neglectful, selfish, uncaring ≠**well-thought-out:** flippant, heedless, irresponsible, rash, thoughtless, unthinking ≠**reflective:** extrovert, shallow, superficial

thoughtless *adjective* = **inconsiderate,** impolite, indiscreet, insensitive, rude, selfish, tactless, uncaring, undiplomatic, unkind
➤ **Antonyms**
attentive, considerate, diplomatic, tactful, thoughtful, unselfish

thrall *noun* = **slavery,** bondage, enslavement, servitude, subjection, subjugation

thrash *verb* **1** = **beat,** belt (*informal*), birch, cane, flagellate, flog, give (someone) a (good) hiding (*informal*), horsewhip, leather, scourge, spank, tan (*slang*), whip **2** = **defeat,** beat, beat (someone) hollow (*Brit. informal*), blow out of the water (*slang*), clobber (*slang*), crush, drub, lick (*informal*), make mincemeat of (*informal*), overwhelm, paste (*slang*), rout, run rings around (*informal*), slaughter (*informal*), stuff (*slang*), tank (*slang*), trounce, wipe the floor with (*informal*) **3** = **thresh,** flail, heave, jerk, plunge, squirm, toss, toss and turn, writhe

thrashing *noun* **1** = **beating,** belting (*informal*), caning, drubbing, flogging, hiding (*informal*), lashing, punishment, tanning (*slang*), whipping **2** = **defeat,** beating, drubbing, hammering (*informal*), hiding (*informal*), pasting (*slang*), rout, trouncing

thrash out *verb* = **settle,** argue out, debate, discuss, have out, resolve, solve, talk over

thread *noun* **1** = **strand,** cotton, fibre, filament, line, string, yarn **2** = **theme,** course, direction, drift, plot, story line, strain, train of thought ♦ *verb* **3** = **string 4** = **pass,** ease, inch, meander, pick (one's way), squeeze through

threadbare *adjective* **1** = **shabby,** down at heel, frayed, old, ragged, scruffy, tattered, tatty, worn, worn-out **2** = **hackneyed,** clichéd, cliché-ridden, common, commonplace, conventional, corny (*slang*), familiar, overused, stale, stereotyped, stock, tired, trite, well-worn
➤ **Antonyms**
≠**shabby:** brand-new, good, new, smart, unused, well-preserved ≠**hackneyed:** different, fresh, new, novel, original, unconventional, unfamiliar, unusual

threat *noun* **1** = **menace,** intimidatory remark, threatening remark **2** = **warning,** foreboding, foreshadowing, omen,

portent, presage, writing on the wall **3** = **danger,** hazard, menace, peril, risk

threaten *verb* **1** = **intimidate,** browbeat, bully, lean on (*slang*), make threats to, menace, pressurize, terrorize, warn **2** = **endanger,** imperil, jeopardize, put at risk, put in jeopardy, put on the line **3** = **foreshadow,** be imminent, be in the air, be in the offing, forebode, impend, portend, presage, warn
➤ **Antonyms**
≠**intimidate, endanger:** defend, guard, protect, safeguard, shelter, shield

threatening *adjective* **1** = **menacing,** bullying, intimidatory, terrorizing **2** = **ominous,** baleful, bodeful, forbidding, grim, inauspicious, sinister
➤ **Antonyms**
≠**ominous:** auspicious, bright, comforting, encouraging, favourable, promising, propitious, reassuring

threesome *noun* = **trio,** triad, trilogy, trinity, triple, triplet, triptych, triumvirate

threnody *noun Formal* = **lament,** coronach (*Scot. & Irish*), dirge, elegy, funeral ode, keen, requiem

threshold *noun* **1** = **entrance,** door, doorstep, doorway **2** = **start,** beginning, brink, dawn, inception, opening, outset, starting point, verge **3** = **minimum,** lower limit
➤ **Antonyms**
≠**start:** close, decline, end, finish, twilight

thrift *noun* = **economy,** carefulness, frugality, good husbandry, parsimony, prudence, saving, thriftiness
➤ **Antonyms**
carelessness, extravagance, prodigality, profligacy, recklessness, squandering, waste

thriftless *adjective* = **spendthrift,** extravagant, improvident, imprudent, lavish, prodigal, profligate, unthrifty, wasteful
➤ **Antonyms**
careful, economical, frugal, provident, prudent, sparing, thrifty

thrifty *adjective* = **economical,** careful, frugal, parsimonious, provident, prudent, saving, sparing
➤ **Antonyms**
extravagant, free-spending, generous, improvident, prodigal, spendthrift, wasteful

thrill *noun* **1** = **pleasure,** buzz (*slang*), charge (*slang*), flush of excitement, glow, kick (*informal*), sensation, stimulation, tingle, titillation **2** = **trembling,** flutter, fluttering, quiver, shudder, throb, tremor, vibration ♦ *verb* **3** = **excite,** arouse,

electrify, flush, get a charge (*slang*), get a kick (*informal*), move, send (*slang*), stimulate, stir, tingle, titillate **4 = tremble**, flutter, quake, quiver, shake, shudder, throb, vibrate
➤ **Antonyms**
noun ≠**pleasure**: boredom, dreariness, dullness, ennui, monotony, tedium

thrilling *adjective* **1 = exciting**, electrifying, gripping, hair-raising, riveting, rousing, sensational, sexy (*informal*), stimulating, stirring **2 = trembling**, quaking, shaking, shivering, shuddering, vibrating
➤ **Antonyms**
≠**exciting**: boring, dreary, dull, monotonous, quiet, staid, tedious, tiresome, uninteresting, unmoving

thrive *verb* **= prosper**, advance, bloom, boom, burgeon, develop, do well, flourish, get on, grow, grow rich, increase, succeed
➤ **Antonyms**
decline, droop, fail, languish, perish, shrivel, stagnate, wane, wilt, wither

thriving *adjective* **= successful**, blooming, booming, burgeoning, developing, doing well, flourishing, going strong, growing, healthy, prosperous, well
➤ **Antonyms**
ailing, bankrupt, failing, impoverished, languishing, on the rocks, poverty-stricken, unsuccessful, withering

throaty *adjective* **= hoarse**, deep, gruff, guttural, husky, low, thick

throb *verb* **1 = pulsate**, beat, palpitate, pound, pulse, thump, vibrate ♦ *noun* **2 = pulse**, beat, palpitation, pounding, pulsating, thump, thumping, vibration

throes *plural noun* **1 = pains**, convulsions, fit, pangs, paroxysm, spasms, stabs **2 in the throes of = struggling with**, in the midst of, in the pangs of, suffering from

throng *noun* **1 = crowd**, assemblage, congregation, crush, horde, host, jam, mass, mob, multitude, pack, press, swarm ♦ *verb* **2 = crowd**, congregate, converge, cram, fill, flock, herd, jam, mill around, pack, swarm around
➤ **Antonyms**
verb ≠**crowd**: break up, disband, dispel, disperse, scatter, separate, spread out

throttle *verb* **1 = strangle**, choke, garrotte, strangulate **2 = suppress**, control, gag, inhibit, silence, stifle

through *preposition* **1 = from one side to the other of**, between, by, from end to end of, in and out of, past **2 = because of**, as a consequence *or* result of, by means of, by virtue of, by way of, using, via, with the help of **3 = during**, in, in the middle of, throughout ♦ *adjective* **4 with with**

= finished, done, having had enough of **5 = completed**, done, ended, finished, terminated ♦ *adverb* **6 through and through = completely**, altogether, entirely, fully, thoroughly, totally, to the core, unreservedly, utterly, wholly

throughout *preposition* **1 = through the whole of**, all over, all through, during the whole of, everywhere in, for the duration of, right through ♦ *adverb* **2 = from start to finish**, all the time, all through, from beginning to end, from the start, right through, the whole time

throw *verb* **1 = hurl**, cast, chuck (*informal*), fling, heave, launch, lob (*informal*), pitch, project, propel, put, send, shy, sling, toss **2 = bring down**, dislodge, fell, floor, hurl to the ground, overturn, unseat, upset **3** *Informal* **= confuse**, astonish, baffle, confound, disconcert, dumbfound, faze, put one off one's stroke, throw off, throw one off one's stride ♦ *noun* **4 = toss**, cast, fling, heave, lob (*informal*), pitch, put, shy, sling

throwaway *adjective Chiefly Brit.* **= casual**, careless, offhand, passing, understated

throw away *verb* **1 = discard**, bin (*informal*), cast off, chuck (*informal*), dispense with, dispose of, ditch (*slang*), dump (*informal*), get rid of, jettison, junk (*informal*), reject, scrap, throw out **2 = waste**, blow (*slang*), fail to make use of, fritter away, lose, squander
➤ **Antonyms**
≠**discard**: conserve, keep, preserve, rescue, retain, retrieve, salvage, save

throw off *verb Literary* **= free oneself of**, abandon, cast off, discard, drop, rid oneself of, shake off

throw out *verb* **1 = discard**, bin (*informal*), cast off, chuck (*informal*), dispense with, ditch (*slang*), dump (*informal*), jettison, junk (*informal*), reject, scrap, throw away **2 = expel**, dismiss, eject, evict, get rid of, kick out (*informal*), oust, show one the door, turf out (*Brit. informal*)

throw over *verb Old-fashioned* **= abandon**, break with, chuck (*informal*), desert, drop (*informal*), finish with, forsake, jilt, leave, split up with, walk out on (*informal*)

throw up *verb* **1** *Informal* **= vomit**, barf (*U.S. slang*), be sick, bring up, chuck (up) (*slang, chiefly U.S.*), chunder (*slang, chiefly Austral.*), heave, puke (*slang*), regurgitate, retch, spew **2 = give up**, abandon, chuck (*informal*), jack in, leave, quit, relinquish, renounce, resign from, step down from (*informal*) **3 = throw together**, jerry-build **4 = produce**, bring forward, bring to light, bring to the surface, reveal

thrust verb 1 = **push**, butt, drive, force, impel, jam, plunge, poke, press, prod, propel, ram, shove, urge 2 = **stab**, jab, lunge, pierce, stick 3 = **shove**, elbow or shoulder one's way, push ♦ noun 4 = **push**, drive, lunge, poke, prod, shove, stab 5 = **momentum**, impetus, motive force, motive power, propulsive force

thud noun, verb = **thump**, clunk, crash, knock, smack, wallop (informal)

thug noun = **ruffian**, bruiser (informal), bully boy, gangster, heavy (slang), hooligan, mugger (informal), tough, tsotsi (S. African)

thumb noun 1 = **pollex** 2 **all thumbs** = **clumsy**, butterfingered (informal), cack-handed (informal), ham-fisted (informal), inept, maladroit 3 **thumbs down** = **disapproval**, no, rebuff, refusal, rejection 4 **thumbs up** = **approval**, acceptance, affirmation, encouragement, go-ahead (informal), green light, O.K. or okay (informal), yes ♦ verb 5 = **handle**, dog-ear, finger, mark 6 = **hitch** (informal), hitchhike 7 **thumb one's nose at** = **show contempt for**, be contemptuous of, cock a snook at, flout, laugh in the face of, show disrespect to 8 **thumb through** = **flick through**, browse through, flip through, glance at, leaf through, riffle through, run one's eye over, scan the pages of, skim through, turn over

thumbnail adjective = **brief**, compact, concise, pithy, quick, short, succinct

thump noun 1 = **thud**, bang, clunk, crash, thwack 2 = **blow**, clout (informal), knock, punch, rap, smack, swipe, wallop (informal), whack ♦ verb 3 = **thud**, bang, crash, thwack 4 = **strike**, batter, beat, belabour, clobber (slang), clout (informal), hit, knock, pound, punch, rap, smack, swipe, thrash, wallop (informal), whack 5 = **throb**, beat

thumping adjective Slang = **huge**, colossal, enormous, excessive, gargantuan, gigantic, great, impressive, massive, monumental, terrific, titanic, tremendous, whopping (informal)
➤ Antonyms
inconsequential, insignificant, meagre, measly (informal), negligible, paltry, petty, piddling (informal), trifling, trivial

thunder noun 1 = **rumble**, boom, booming, cracking, crash, crashing, explosion, pealing, rumbling ♦ verb 2 = **rumble**, blast, boom, clap, crack, crash, explode, peal, resound, reverberate, roar 3 = **shout**, bark, bellow, roar, yell

thundering adjective Old-fashioned slang = **great**, enormous, excessive,

monumental, remarkable, unmitigated, utter

thunderous adjective = **loud**, booming, deafening, ear-splitting, noisy, resounding, roaring, tumultuous

thunderstruck adjective = **amazed**, aghast, astonished, astounded, bowled over (informal), dazed, dumbfounded, flabbergasted (informal), floored (informal), flummoxed, gobsmacked (Brit. slang), knocked for six (informal), left speechless, nonplussed, open-mouthed, shocked, staggered, struck dumb, stunned, taken aback

thus adverb 1 = **therefore**, accordingly, consequently, ergo, for this reason, hence, on that account, so, then 2 = **in this way**, as follows, in this fashion, in this manner, like so, like this, so, to such a degree

thwack verb 1 = **smack**, bash (informal), beat, clout (informal), hit, swipe, thump, wallop (informal), whack ♦ noun 2 = **smack**, bash (informal), blow, clout (informal), swipe, thump, wallop (informal), whack

thwart verb = **frustrate**, balk, check, defeat, foil, hinder, impede, obstruct, oppose, outwit, prevent, put a spoke in someone's wheel (informal), snooker, stop, stymie
➤ Antonyms
aggravate, aid, assist, encourage, exacerbate, facilitate, hasten, help, intensify, support

tic noun = **twitch**, jerk, spasm

tick¹ noun 1 = **mark**, dash, stroke 2 = **tapping**, clack, click, clicking, tap, ticktock 3 Brit. informal = **moment**, flash, instant, jiffy (informal), minute, sec (informal), second, shake (informal), split second, trice, twinkling ♦ verb 4 = **mark**, check off, choose, indicate, mark off, select 5 = **tap**, clack, click, ticktock 6 **what makes someone tick** Informal = **motivation**, drive, motive, raison d'être

tick² noun Brit. informal = **credit**, account, deferred payment, the slate (Brit. informal)

ticket noun 1 = **voucher**, card, certificate, coupon, pass, slip, token 2 = **label**, card, docket, marker, slip, sticker, tab, tag

tickle verb = **amuse**, delight, divert, entertain, excite, gratify, please
➤ Antonyms
annoy, bore, bother, irritate, pester, trouble, vex, weary

ticklish adjective = **difficult**, awkward, critical, delicate, risky, sensitive, thorny, touchy, tricky

tick off verb 1 = **mark off**, check off, put a

tick at **2** *Informal* = **scold**, bawl out
(*informal*), berate, carpet (*informal*),
censure, chide, haul over the coals
(*informal*), lecture, read the riot act,
rebuke, reprimand, reproach, reprove,
take to task, tell off (*informal*), upbraid

tide *noun* **1** = **current**, course, ebb, flow,
stream, tideway, undertow **2** = **tendency**,
course, current, direction, drift,
movement, trend

tide over *verb* = **keep one going**, aid,
assist, help, keep one's head above water,
see one through

tidings *plural noun* = **news**, bulletin,
communication, gen (*Brit. informal*),
information, intelligence, latest (*informal*),
message, report, word

tidy *adjective* **1** = **neat**, businesslike, clean,
in apple-pie order (*informal*), methodical,
ordered, orderly, shipshape,
spick-and-span, spruce, trim,
well-groomed, well-kept, well-ordered **2**
Informal = **considerable**, ample, fair,
generous, good, goodly, handsome,
healthy, large, largish, respectable, sizable
or sizeable, substantial ♦ *verb* **3** = **neaten**,
clean, groom, order, put in order, put to
rights, spruce up, straighten
➤ **Antonyms**
adjective ≠**neat**: careless, dirty, dishevelled,
disordered, disorderly, filthy, in disarray,
messy, scruffy, sloppy, slovenly,
unbusinesslike, unkempt, unmethodical,
unsystematic, untidy ≠**considerable**:
inconsiderable, insignificant, little, small,
tiny ♦ *verb* ≠**neaten**: dirty, dishevel,
disorder, mess, mess up

tie *verb* **1** = **fasten**, attach, bind, connect,
join, knot, lash, link, make fast, moor,
rope, secure, tether, truss, unite **2**
= **restrict**, bind, confine, hamper, hinder,
hold, limit, restrain **3** = **draw**, be even, be
neck and neck, equal, match ♦ *noun* **4**
= **bond**, affiliation, affinity, allegiance,
commitment, connection, duty, kinship,
liaison, obligation, relationship **5**
= **fastening**, band, bond, connection,
cord, fetter, joint, knot, ligature, link, rope,
string **6** *Brit.* = **match**, contest, fixture,
game **7** = **draw**, dead heat, deadlock,
stalemate **8** = **encumbrance**, hindrance,
limitation, restraint, restriction
➤ **Antonyms**
verb ≠**fasten**: free, loose, release, separate,
undo, unfasten, unhitch, unknot, untie
≠**restrict**: free, release

tie-in *noun* = **link**, association, connection,
relation, relationship, tie-up

tie in *verb* = **link**, be relevant, connect, fit
in, have bearing, relate

tier *noun* = **row**, bank, layer, level, line,
order, rank, series, storey, stratum

tie-up *noun* = **link**, association, connection,
linkup, relation, relationship, tie-in

tie up *verb* **1** = **bind**, attach, pinion,
restrain, tether, truss **2** = **moor**, lash, make
fast, rope, secure **3** = **occupy**, engage,
engross, keep busy

tiff *noun* = **quarrel**, difference,
disagreement, dispute, falling-out
(*informal*), row, squabble

tight *adjective* **1** = **taut**, rigid, stiff,
stretched, tense **2** = **close-fitting**, close,
compact, constricted, cramped, narrow,
snug **3** = **secure**, fast, firm, fixed **4**
= **sealed**, impervious, proof, sound,
watertight **5** = **strict**, harsh, inflexible,
rigid, rigorous, severe, stern, stringent,
tough, uncompromising, unyielding **6**
= **difficult**, dangerous, hazardous, perilous,
precarious, problematic, sticky (*informal*),
ticklish, tough, tricky **7** *Informal* = **miserly**,
close, grasping, mean, niggardly,
parsimonious, penurious, sparing, stingy,
tightfisted **8** = **close**, even,
evenly-balanced, near, well-matched **9**
Informal = **drunk**, bevvied (*dialect*),
bladdered (*slang*), blitzed (*slang*), blotto
(*slang*), half cut (*Brit. slang*), inebriated,
intoxicated, legless (*informal*), out of it
(*slang*), out to it (*Austral. & N.Z. slang*),
paralytic (*informal*), pissed (*taboo slang*),
plastered (*slang*), rat-arsed (*taboo slang*),
smashed (*slang*), sozzled (*informal*),
steamboats (*Scot. slang*), steaming (*slang*),
stoned (*slang*), tiddly (*slang, chiefly Brit.*),
tipsy, under the influence (*informal*),
wasted (*slang*), wrecked (*slang*)
➤ **Antonyms**
≠**taut**: relaxed, slack ≠**close-fitting**: loose,
spacious ≠**sealed**: loose, open, porous
≠**strict**: easy, easy-going, generous, lax,
lenient, liberal, relaxed, soft, undemanding
≠**difficult**: easy ≠**miserly**: abundant,
extravagant, generous, lavish, munificent,
open, prodigal, profuse, spendthrift
≠**close**: easy, landslide, overwhelming,
runaway, uneven ≠**drunk**: sober

tighten *verb* **1** = **stretch**, stiffen, tauten,
tense **2** = **squeeze**, close, constrict, cramp,
narrow **3** = **fasten**, fix, screw, secure
➤ **Antonyms**
≠**stretch**: loosen, relax, slacken, weaken
≠**squeeze**: ease off, let out, slacken
≠**fasten**: unbind, unfasten, unscrew

tightfisted *adjective* = **miserly**, close,
close-fisted, grasping, mean, niggardly,
parsimonious, penurious, snoep (*S. African
informal*), stingy, tight

tight-lipped *adjective* = **secretive**,

close-lipped, close-mouthed, mum, quiet, reticent, silent, taciturn, uncommunicative, unforthcoming

till¹ _verb_ = **cultivate**, dig, plough, turn over, work

till² _noun_ = **cash register**, cash box, cash drawer

tilt _verb_ 1 = **slant**, cant, heel, incline, lean, list, slope, tip 2 = **joust**, clash, contend, duel, encounter, fight ♦ _noun_ 3 = **slope**, angle, cant, inclination, incline, list, pitch, slant 4 _Medieval history_ = **joust**, clash, combat, duel, encounter, fight, lists, set-to (_informal_), tournament 5 **(at) full tilt = full speed**, for dear life, full force, headlong

timber _noun_ 1 = **wood**, beams, boards, logs, planks 2 = **trees**, forest

timbre _noun_ = **tone**, colour, resonance, ring

time _noun_ 1 = **period**, age, chronology, date, duration, epoch, era, generation, hour, interval, season, space, span, spell, stretch, term, while 2 = **occasion**, instance, juncture, point, stage 3 = **tempo**, beat, measure, metre, rhythm 4 **at one time: a = once**, for a while, formerly, hitherto, once upon a time, previously **b = simultaneously**, all at once, at the same time, together 5 **at times = sometimes**, every now and then, every so often, from time to time, now and then, occasionally, once in a while, on occasion 6 **for the time being = for now**, for the moment, for the present, in the meantime, meantime, meanwhile, pro tem, temporarily 7 **from time to time = occasionally**, at times, every now and then, every so often, now and then, once in a while, on occasion, sometimes 8 **in no time = quickly**, in a flash, in a jiffy (_informal_), in a moment, in an instant, in a trice, rapidly, speedily, swiftly 9 **in time: a = on time**, at the appointed time, early, in good time, on schedule, with time to spare **b = eventually**, by and by, in the fullness of time, one day, someday, sooner or later, ultimately 10 **on time = punctually**, in good time, on the dot 11 **time and again = frequently**, many times, often, on many occasions, over and over again, repeatedly, time after time ♦ _verb_ 12 = **measure**, clock, count, judge 13 = **schedule**, set

time-honoured _adjective_ = **long-established**, age-old, ancient, conventional, customary, established, fixed, old, traditional, usual

timeless _adjective_ = **eternal**, abiding, ageless, ceaseless, changeless, deathless, endless, enduring, everlasting, immortal, immutable, imperishable, indestructible, lasting, permanent, persistent, undying
➤ **Antonyms**
ephemeral, evanescent, momentary, mortal, passing, temporal, temporary, transitory

timely _adjective_ = **opportune**, appropriate, at the right time, convenient, judicious, prompt, propitious, punctual, seasonable, suitable, well-timed
➤ **Antonyms**
ill-timed, inconvenient, inopportune, late, tardy, unseasonable, untimely

timeserver _noun_ = **opportunist**, hypocrite, self-seeker

timetable _noun_ = **schedule**, agenda, calendar, curriculum, diary, list, order of the day, programme

timeworn _adjective_ 1 = **decrepit**, aged, ancient, broken-down, run-down, shabby, the worse for wear, weathered, worn 2 = **hackneyed**, clichéd, dated, hoary, old hat, out of date, outworn, passé, stale, stock, threadbare, tired, trite, well-worn

timid _adjective_ = **fearful**, afraid, apprehensive, bashful, cowardly, coy, diffident, faint-hearted, mousy, nervous, pusillanimous, shrinking, shy, timorous
➤ **Antonyms**
aggressive, arrogant, ballsy (_taboo slang_), bold, brave, confident, daring, fearless, fierce, forceful, forward, presumptuous, self-assured, self-confident, shameless, unabashed

timorous _adjective Literary_ = **timid**, afraid, apprehensive, bashful, cowardly, coy, diffident, faint-hearted, fearful, frightened, mousy, nervous, pusillanimous, shrinking, shy
➤ **Antonyms**
assertive, assured, audacious, bold, confident, courageous, daring, fearless

tinge _noun_ 1 = **tint**, cast, colour, dye, shade, stain, tincture, wash 2 = **bit**, dash, drop, pinch, smattering, soupçon, sprinkling, suggestion, touch, trace ♦ _verb_ 3 = **tint**, colour, dye, imbue, shade, stain, suffuse

tingle _verb_ 1 = **prickle**, have goose pimples, itch, sting, tickle ♦ _noun_ 2 = **quiver**, goose pimples, itch, itching, pins and needles (_informal_), prickling, shiver, stinging, thrill

tinker _verb_ = **meddle**, dabble, fiddle (_informal_), mess about, monkey, muck about (_Brit. slang_), play, potter, toy

tinpot _adjective Brit. informal_ = **worthless**, inferior, Mickey Mouse (_slang_), paltry, pants (_slang_), second-class, second-rate, toytown (_slang_), two-bit (_U.S. & Canad. slang_), twopenny-halfpenny, unimportant

tinsel *adjective* = **showy**, cheap, flashy, gaudy, ostentatious, plastic (*slang*), sham, specious, superficial, tawdry, trashy

tint *noun* **1** = **shade**, cast, colour, hue, tone **2** = **dye**, rinse, stain, tincture, tinge, wash ♦ *verb* **3** = **dye**, colour, rinse, stain, tincture, tinge

tiny *adjective* = **small**, diminutive, dwarfish, infinitesimal, insignificant, Lilliputian, little, microscopic, mini, miniature, minute, negligible, petite, pint-sized (*informal*), puny, pygmy *or* pigmy, slight, teeny-weeny, trifling, wee
➤ **Antonyms**
colossal, enormous, extra-large, gargantuan, giant, gigantic, great, huge, immense, mammoth, massive, monstrous, titanic, vast

tip[1] *noun* **1** = **end**, apex, cap, crown, extremity, head, peak, pinnacle, point, summit, top ♦ *verb* **2** = **cap**, crown, finish, surmount, top

tip[2] *noun* **1** = **gratuity**, gift, perquisite **2** = **hint**, gen (*Brit. informal*), information, inside information, pointer, suggestion ♦ *verb* **3** = **reward**, remunerate **4** = **advise**, give a clue, give a hint, suggest, tip (someone) the wink (*Brit. informal*)

tip[3] *verb* **1** = **tilt**, cant, capsize, incline, lean, list, overturn, slant, spill, topple over, upend, upset **2** *Brit.* = **dump**, ditch (*slang*), empty, pour out, unload ♦ *noun* **3** *Brit.* = **dump**, midden (*dialect*), refuse heap, rubbish heap

tip-off *noun* = **hint**, clue, gen (*Brit. informal*), information, inside information, pointer, suggestion, warning, word, word of advice

tip off *verb* = **advise**, caution, forewarn, give a clue, give a hint, suggest, tip (someone) the wink (*Brit. informal*), warn

tipple *verb* **1** = **drink**, bend the elbow (*informal*), bevvy (*dialect*), imbibe, indulge (*informal*), quaff, swig, take a drink, tope ♦ *noun* **2** = **alcohol**, booze (*informal*), drink, liquor, poison (*informal*)

tippler *noun* = **drinker**, boozer (*informal*), drunk, drunkard, inebriate, soak (*slang*)

tipsy *adjective* = **tiddly** (*slang, chiefly Brit.*), babalas (*S. African*), fuddled, happy (*informal*), mellow, merry (*Brit. informal*), slightly drunk, woozy (*informal*)

tirade *noun* = **outburst**, abuse, denunciation, diatribe, fulmination, harangue, invective, lecture

tire *verb* **1** = **exhaust**, drain, enervate, fatigue, knacker (*slang*), take it out of (*informal*), wear down, wear out, weary **2** = **flag**, droop, fail **3** *usually passive* = **bore**, aggravate (*informal*), annoy, exasperate, get on one's nerves (*informal*), harass, hassle (*informal*), irk, irritate, weary
➤ **Antonyms**
≠**exhaust**: energize, enliven, exhilarate, invigorate, liven up, pep up, refresh, restore, revive

tired *adjective* **1** = **exhausted**, all in (*slang*), asleep *or* dead on one's feet (*informal*), clapped out (*Austral. & N.Z. informal*), dead beat (*informal*), dog-tired (*informal*), done in (*informal*), drained, drowsy, enervated, fatigued, flagging, knackered (*slang*), ready to drop, sleepy, spent, weary, whacked (*Brit. informal*), worn out, zonked (*slang*) **2** = **bored**, annoyed, exasperated, fed up, irked, irritated, sick, weary **3** = **hackneyed**, clichéd, conventional, corny (*slang*), familiar, old, outworn, stale, stock, threadbare, trite, well-worn
➤ **Antonyms**
≠**exhausted**: alive and kicking, energetic, fresh, full of beans (*informal*), lively, refreshed, rested, wide-awake ≠**bored**: enthusiastic about, fond of, keen on ≠**hackneyed**: innovative, original

tireless *adjective* = **energetic**, determined, indefatigable, industrious, resolute, unflagging, untiring, unwearied, vigorous
➤ **Antonyms**
drained, exhausted, fatigued, flagging, tired, weak, weary, worn out

tiresome *adjective* = **boring**, annoying, dull, exasperating, flat, irksome, irritating, laborious, monotonous, tedious, trying, uninteresting, vexatious, wearing, wearisome
➤ **Antonyms**
exhilarating, inspiring, interesting, refreshing, rousing, stimulating

tiring *adjective* = **exhausting**, arduous, demanding, enervative, exacting, fatiguing, laborious, strenuous, tough, wearing, wearying

tissue *noun* **1** = **fabric**, gauze, mesh, structure, stuff, texture, web **2** = **paper**, paper handkerchief, wrapping paper **3** = **series**, accumulation, chain, collection, combination, mass, network, pack, web

titan *noun* = **giant**, colossus, leviathan

titanic *adjective* = **gigantic**, colossal, enormous, giant, herculean, huge, immense, massive, mighty, vast

titbit *noun* = **delicacy**, choice item, dainty, goody, juicy bit, morsel, scrap, snack, treat

tithe *noun* **1** = **tax**, assessment, duty, impost, levy, tariff, tenth, tribute ♦ *verb* **2** = **tax**, assess, charge, levy, rate **3** = **pay a tithe on**, give up, pay, render, surrender, turn over

titillate verb = **excite**, arouse, interest, provoke, stimulate, tantalize, tease, thrill, turn on (slang)

titillating adjective = **exciting**, arousing, interesting, lewd, lurid, provocative, sensational, stimulating, suggestive, teasing, thrilling

titivate verb = **smarten up**, doll up (slang), do up (informal), make up, preen, primp, tart up (Brit. slang), touch up

title noun 1 = **name**, appellation, denomination, designation, epithet, handle (slang), moniker or monicker (slang), nickname, nom de plume, pseudonym, sobriquet, term 2 = **heading**, caption, inscription, label, legend, name, style 3 Sport = **championship**, crown, laurels 4 Law = **ownership**, claim, entitlement, prerogative, privilege, right

titter verb = **snigger**, chortle (informal), chuckle, giggle, laugh, tee-hee

tittle noun = **bit**, atom, dash, drop, grain, iota, jot, mite, particle, scrap, shred, speck, whit

tittle-tattle noun 1 = **gossip**, blether, chatter, chitchat, dirt (U.S. slang), hearsay, idle chat, natter, rumour ♦ verb 2 = **gossip**, babble, blether, chat, chatter, chitchat, natter

titular adjective = **in name only**, honorary, nominal, putative, so-called, token
➤ Antonyms
actual, effective, functioning, real, true

toady noun 1 = **sycophant**, bootlicker (informal), crawler (slang), creep (slang), fawner, flatterer, flunkey, hanger-on, lackey, minion, parasite, yes man ♦ verb 2 = **fawn on**, be obsequious to, bow and scrape, butter up, crawl, creep, cringe, curry favour with, flatter, grovel, kowtow to, lick (someone's) boots, pander to, suck up to (informal)
➤ Antonyms
verb ≠**fawn on**: confront, defy, oppose, rebel, resist, stand against, withstand

toast[1] verb 1 = **brown**, grill, roast 2 = **warm**, heat

toast[2] noun 1 = **tribute**, compliment, drink, health, pledge, salutation, salute 2 = **favourite**, darling, hero or heroine ♦ verb 3 = **drink to**, drink (to) the health of, pledge, salute

to-do noun = **fuss**, agitation, bother, brouhaha, bustle, commotion, disturbance, excitement, furore, hue and cry, quarrel, ruction (informal), rumpus, stir, tumult, turmoil, upheaval, uproar

toe noun **tread on someone's toes**

= **offend**, affront, annoy, disgruntle, get someone's back up, hurt, hurt someone's feelings, irk, vex

together adverb 1 = **collectively**, as a group, as one, cheek by jowl, closely, hand in glove, hand in hand, in a body, in concert, in cooperation, in unison, jointly, mutually, shoulder to shoulder, side by side 2 = **at the same time**, all at once, as one, at one fell swoop, concurrently, contemporaneously, en masse, in unison, simultaneously, with one accord 3 Old-fashioned = **in succession**, consecutively, continuously, in a row, one after the other, on end, successively, without a break, without interruption ♦ adjective 4 Slang = **self-possessed**, calm, composed, cool, stable, well-adjusted, well-balanced, well-organized
➤ Antonyms
adverb ≠**collectively**: alone, apart, independently, individually, one at a time, one by one, separately, singly

toil noun 1 = **hard work**, application, blood, sweat, and tears (informal), donkey-work, drudgery, effort, elbow grease (informal), exertion, graft (informal), industry, labour, pains, slog, sweat, travail ♦ verb 2 = **labour**, bend over backwards (informal), break one's neck (informal), do one's damnedest (informal), drudge, give it one's all (informal), give it one's best shot (informal), graft (informal), grind (informal), knock oneself out (informal), make an all-out effort (informal), push oneself, slave, slog, strive, struggle, sweat (informal), work, work like a dog, work like a Trojan, work one's fingers to the bone
➤ Antonyms
noun ≠**hard work**: idleness, inactivity, indolence, inertia, laziness, sloth, torpor

toilet noun 1 = **lavatory**, bathroom, bog (slang), can (U.S. & Canad. slang), closet, convenience, gents or ladies (Brit. informal), john (slang, chiefly U.S. & Canad.), khazi (slang), ladies' room, latrine, little boy's or little girl's room (informal), loo (Brit. informal), outhouse, powder room, privy, urinal, washroom, water closet, W.C. 2 Old-fashioned = **dressing**, ablutions, bathing, grooming, toilette

toilsome adjective Literary = **laborious**, arduous, backbreaking, difficult, fatiguing, hard, herculean, strenuous, taxing, tough

token noun 1 = **symbol**, badge, clue, demonstration, earnest, evidence, expression, indication, manifestation, mark, note, proof, representation, sign ♦ adjective 2 = **nominal**, hollow, minimal, perfunctory, superficial, symbolic

tolerable *adjective* **1** = **bearable**, acceptable, allowable, endurable, sufferable, supportable **2** *Informal* = **fair**, acceptable, adequate, all right, average, fairly good, fair to middling, good enough, indifferent, mediocre, middling, not bad (*informal*), O.K. *or* okay (*informal*), ordinary, passable, run-of-the-mill, so-so (*informal*), unexceptional
➤ **Antonyms**
≠**bearable**: insufferable, intolerable, unacceptable, unbearable, unendurable ≠**fair**: awful, bad, dreadful, rotten

tolerance *noun* **1** = **broad-mindedness**, forbearance, indulgence, magnanimity, open-mindedness, patience, permissiveness, sufferance **2** = **endurance**, fortitude, hardiness, hardness, resilience, resistance, stamina, staying power, toughness **3** = **variation**, fluctuation, play, swing
➤ **Antonyms**
≠**broad-mindedness**: bigotry, discrimination, intolerance, narrow-mindedness, prejudice, sectarianism

tolerant *adjective* = **broad-minded**, catholic, fair, forbearing, latitudinarian, liberal, long-suffering, magnanimous, open-minded, patient, unbigoted, understanding, unprejudiced
➤ **Antonyms**
biased, bigoted, dogmatic, illiberal, intolerant, narrow-minded, prejudiced, sectarian

tolerate *verb* **1** = **allow**, accept, admit, brook, condone, countenance, indulge, permit, put up with (*informal*), sanction, take **2** = **endure**, abide, bear, put up with (*informal*), stand, stomach, submit to, suffer, swallow, take, thole (*Scot.*)
➤ **Antonyms**
≠**allow**: ban, disallow, disapprove, forbid, outlaw, preclude, prohibit, veto

toleration *noun* = **acceptance**, allowance, endurance, indulgence, permissiveness, sanction, sufferance

toll¹ *verb* **1** = **ring**, chime, clang, knell, peal, sound, strike **2** = **announce**, call, signal, summon, warn ♦ *noun* **3** = **ringing**, chime, clang, knell, peal, ring, tolling

toll² *noun* **1** = **charge**, assessment, customs, demand, duty, fee, impost, levy, payment, rate, tariff, tax, tribute **2** = **damage**, cost, inroad, loss, penalty

tomb *noun* = **grave**, burial chamber, catacomb, crypt, mausoleum, sarcophagus, sepulchre, vault

tombstone *noun* = **gravestone**,
headstone, marker, memorial, monument

tome *noun* = **book**, title, volume, work

tomfoolery *noun* = **foolishness**, buffoonery, childishness, clowning, fooling around (*informal*), horseplay, idiocy, messing around (*informal*), shenanigans (*informal*), silliness, skylarking (*informal*), stupidity
➤ **Antonyms**
demureness, gravity, heaviness, reserve, sedateness, seriousness, sobriety, solemnity, sternness

tone *noun* **1** = **pitch**, accent, emphasis, force, inflection, intonation, modulation, strength, stress, timbre, tonality, volume **2** = **character**, air, approach, aspect, attitude, drift, feel, manner, mood, note, quality, spirit, style, temper, vein **3** = **colour**, cast, hue, shade, tinge, tint ♦ *verb* **4** = **harmonize**, blend, go well with, match, suit

tone down *verb* = **moderate**, dampen, dim, mitigate, modulate, play down, reduce, restrain, soften, soft-pedal (*informal*), subdue, temper

tone up *verb* = **get into condition**, get in shape, shape up, trim, tune up

tongue *noun* = **language**, argot, dialect, idiom, lingo (*informal*), parlance, patois, speech, talk, vernacular

tongue-tied *adjective* = **speechless**, at a loss for words, dumb, dumbstruck, inarticulate, mute, struck dumb
➤ **Antonyms**
articulate, chatty, effusive, garrulous, loquacious, talkative, verbose, voluble, wordy

tonic *noun* = **stimulant**, boost, bracer (*informal*), fillip, livener, pick-me-up (*informal*), refresher, restorative, shot in the arm (*informal*)

too *adverb* **1** = **also**, as well, besides, further, in addition, into the bargain, likewise, moreover, to boot **2** = **excessively**, exorbitantly, extremely, immoderately, inordinately, over-, overly, unduly, unreasonably, very

tool *noun* **1** = **implement**, apparatus, appliance, contraption, contrivance, device, gadget, instrument, machine, utensil **2** = **puppet**, cat's-paw, creature, dupe, flunkey, hireling, lackey, minion, pawn, stooge (*slang*) **3** = **means**, agency, agent, intermediary, medium, vehicle, wherewithal ♦ *verb* **4** = **make**, chase, cut, decorate, ornament, shape, work

toothsome *adjective* = **appetizing**, dainty, delectable, delicious, luscious, mouthwatering, nice, palatable, savoury, scrumptious (*informal*), sweet, tasty, tempting, yummy (*slang*)

top *noun* **1** = **peak**, acme, apex, apogee, crest, crown, culmination, head, height, high point, meridian, pinnacle, summit, vertex, zenith **2** = **first place**, head, highest rank, lead **3** = **lid**, cap, cork, cover, stopper **4 over the top** = **excessive**, a bit much (*informal*), going too far, immoderate, inordinate, over the limit, too much, uncalled-for ♦ *adjective* **5** = **leading**, best, chief, crack (*informal*), crowning, culminating, dominant, elite, finest, first, foremost, greatest, head, highest, lead, pre-eminent, prime, principal, ruling, sovereign, superior, topmost, upper, uppermost ♦ *verb* **6** = **cover**, cap, crown, finish, garnish, tip **7** = **reach the top of**, ascend, climb, crest, scale, surmount **8** = **lead**, be first, be in charge of, command, head, rule **9** = **surpass**, beat, best, better, eclipse, exceed, excel, go beyond, outdo, outshine, outstrip, transcend

➤ Antonyms
noun ≠**peak**: base, bottom, foot, nadir, underneath, underside ♦ *adjective* ≠**leading**: amateurish, bottom, incompetent, inept, inferior, least, lower, lowest, second-rate, unknown, unranked, worst ♦ *verb* ≠**surpass**: fail to equal, fall short of, not be as good as

topic *noun* = **subject**, issue, matter, point, question, subject matter, text, theme, thesis

topical *adjective* = **current**, contemporary, newsworthy, popular, up-to-date, up-to-the-minute

topmost *adjective* = **highest**, dominant, foremost, leading, loftiest, paramount, principal, supreme, top, upper, uppermost
➤ Antonyms
base, basic, bottom, bottommost, last, lowest, undermost

topple *verb* **1** = **fall over**, capsize, collapse, fall, fall headlong, keel over, knock down, knock over, overbalance, overturn, tip over, totter, tumble, upset **2** = **overthrow**, bring down, bring low, oust, overturn, unseat

topsy-turvy *adjective* = **confused**, chaotic, disarranged, disorderly, disorganized, inside-out, jumbled, messy, mixed-up, untidy, upside-down
➤ Antonyms
neat, ordered, orderly, organized, shipshape, systematic, tidy

top up *verb* = **supplement**, add to, augment, boost, enhance, fill out *or* up

torment *verb* **1** = **torture**, afflict, agonize, crucify, distress, excruciate, harrow, pain,

rack **2** = **tease**, aggravate (*informal*), annoy, bedevil, bother, harass, harry, hassle (*informal*), hound, irritate, nag, persecute, pester, plague, provoke, trouble, vex, worry ♦ *noun* **3** = **suffering**, agony, anguish, distress, hell, misery, pain, torture **4** = **trouble**, affliction, annoyance, bane, bother, harassment, hassle (*informal*), irritation, nuisance, pain in the neck (*informal*), persecution, pest, plague, provocation, thorn in one's flesh *or* side, vexation, worry
➤ Antonyms
verb ≠**torture**: comfort, delight, ease, encourage, make happy, put at ease, reassure, soothe ♦ *noun* ≠**suffering**: bliss, comfort, ease, ecstasy, encouragement, happiness, joy, reassurance, rest

torn *adjective* **1** = **cut**, lacerated, ragged, rent, ripped, slit, split **2** = **undecided**, divided, in two minds (*informal*), irresolute, split, uncertain, unsure, vacillating, wavering

tornado *noun* = **whirlwind**, cyclone, gale, hurricane, squall, storm, tempest, twister (*U.S. informal*), typhoon

torpid *adjective* = **inactive**, dull, indolent, inert, lackadaisical, languid, languorous, lazy, lethargic, passive, slothful, slow, slow-moving, sluggish

torpor *noun* = **inactivity**, apathy, drowsiness, dullness, indolence, inertia, inertness, languor, laziness, lethargy, listlessness, numbness, passivity, sloth, sluggishness, stupor
➤ Antonyms
animation, energy, get-up-and-go (*informal*), go, liveliness, pep, vigour

torrent *noun* = **stream**, cascade, deluge, downpour, effusion, flood, flow, gush, outburst, rush, spate, tide

torrid *adjective* **1** = **hot**, blistering, boiling, broiling, burning, dry, flaming, parching, scorching, sizzling, stifling, sultry, sweltering, tropical **2** = **arid**, dried, parched, scorched **3** = **passionate**, ardent, fervent, intense, steamy (*informal*)

tortuous *adjective* **1** = **winding**, bent, circuitous, convoluted, crooked, curved, indirect, mazy, meandering, serpentine, sinuous, twisted, twisting, twisty, zigzag **2** = **complicated**, ambiguous, convoluted, cunning, deceptive, devious, indirect, involved, misleading, roundabout, tricky
➤ Antonyms
≠**complicated**: candid, direct, honest, ingenuous, open, reliable, straightforward, upright

torture *verb* **1** = **torment**, afflict, agonize, crucify, distress, excruciate, harrow,

martyr, pain, persecute, put on the rack, rack ♦ *noun* **2** = **agony**, affliction, anguish, distress, hell, martyrdom, misery, pain, pang(s), persecution, rack, suffering, torment
➤ **Antonyms**
verb ≠ **torment**: alleviate, comfort, console, ease, mollify, relieve, salve, solace, soothe ♦ *noun* ≠ **agony**: amusement, bliss, delight, enjoyment, happiness, joy, pleasure, well-being

toss *verb* **1** = **throw**, cast, chuck (*informal*), fling, flip, hurl, launch, lob (*informal*), pitch, project, propel, shy, sling **2** = **thrash**, agitate, disturb, jiggle, joggle, jolt, rock, roll, shake, tumble, wriggle, writhe **3** = **heave**, labour, lurch, pitch, roll, wallow ♦ *noun* **4** = **throw**, cast, fling, lob (*informal*), pitch, shy

tot *noun* **1** = **infant**, ankle-biter (*Austral. slang*), baby, child, little one, mite, rug rat (*slang*), sprog (*slang*), toddler, wean (*Scot.*) **2** = **measure**, dram, finger, nip, shot (*informal*), slug, snifter (*informal*)

total *noun* **1** = **whole**, aggregate, all, amount, entirety, full amount, mass, sum, totality ♦ *adjective* **2** = **complete**, absolute, all-out, arrant, comprehensive, consummate, deep-dyed (*usually derogatory*), downright, entire, full, gross, out-and-out, outright, overarching, sheer, sweeping, thorough, thoroughgoing, unconditional, undivided, unmitigated, unqualified, utter, whole ♦ *verb* **3** = **amount to**, come to, mount up to, reach **4** = **add up**, reckon, sum up, tot up
➤ **Antonyms**
noun ≠ **whole**: individual amount, part, subtotal ♦ *adjective* ≠ **complete**: conditional, fragmentary, incomplete, limited, mixed, part, partial, qualified, restricted, uncombined ♦ *verb* ≠ **add up**: deduct, subtract

totalitarian *adjective* = **dictatorial**, authoritarian, despotic, one-party, oppressive, tyrannous, undemocratic
➤ **Antonyms**
autonomous, democratic, egalitarian, popular, self-governing

totality *noun* **1** = **whole**, aggregate, all, entirety, everything, sum, total **2** = **completeness**, entireness, fullness, wholeness

totally *adverb* = **completely**, absolutely, comprehensively, consummately, entirely, fully, one hundred per cent, perfectly, quite, thoroughly, unconditionally, unmitigatedly, utterly, wholeheartedly, wholly
➤ **Antonyms**

incompletely, in part, partially, partly, somewhat, to a certain extent

totter *verb* = **stagger**, falter, lurch, reel, rock, shake, stumble, sway, teeter, walk unsteadily, waver, wobble

tot up *verb* = **add up**, calculate, count up, reckon, sum (up), tally, total

touch *verb* **1** = **handle**, brush, caress, contact, feel, finger, fondle, graze, lay a finger on, palpate, stroke **2** = **tap**, pat, push **3** = **come into contact**, abut, adjoin, be in contact, border, brush, come together, contact, converge, graze, impinge upon, meet **4** = **affect**, get through to, get to (*informal*), have an effect on, impress, influence, inspire, make an impression on, mark, strike **5** = **move**, disturb, stir, upset **6** = **consume**, drink, eat, partake of **7** = **match**, be a match for, be in the same league as, be on a par with, come near, come up to, compare with, equal, hold a candle to (*informal*), parallel, rival **8 touch on** = **refer to**, allude to, bring in, cover, deal with, mention, speak of ♦ *noun* **9** = **feeling**, feel, handling, palpation, physical contact **10** = **contact**, brush, caress, fondling, stroke **11** = **tap**, blow, hit, pat, push **12** = **bit**, dash, detail, drop, hint, jot, pinch, smack, small amount, smattering, soupçon, speck, spot, suggestion, suspicion, taste, tinge, trace, whiff **13** = **style**, approach, characteristic, handiwork, manner, method, technique, trademark, way

touch and go *adjective* = **risky**, close, critical, near, nerve-racking, precarious

touched *adjective* **1** = **moved**, affected, disturbed, impressed, softened, stirred, swayed, upset **2** = **mad**, barmy (*slang*), batty (*slang*), bonkers (*slang, chiefly Brit.*), crazy, daft (*informal*), loopy (*informal*), not all there, not right in the head, nuts (*slang*), nutty (*slang*), nutty as a fruitcake (*slang*), off one's rocker (*slang*), off one's trolley (*slang*), out to lunch (*informal*), soft in the head (*informal*)

touchiness *noun* = **irritability**, bad temper, fretfulness, grouchiness (*informal*), irascibility, peevishness, petulance, surliness, testiness, tetchiness

touching *adjective* = **moving**, affecting, emotive, heartbreaking, melting, pathetic, piteous, pitiable, pitiful, poignant, sad, stirring, tender

touch off *verb* = **trigger (off)**, arouse, begin, cause, foment, give rise to, initiate, provoke, set in motion, spark off

touchstone *noun* = **standard**, criterion, gauge, measure, norm, par, yardstick

touch up *verb* **1** = **enhance**, brush up, give

a face-lift to, gloss over, improve, patch up, polish up, renovate, retouch, revamp, titivate **2 = finish off**, perfect, put the finishing touches to, round off

touchy *adjective* = **oversensitive**, bad-tempered, captious, cross, easily offended, grouchy (*informal*), grumpy, irascible, irritable, peevish, petulant, querulous, quick-tempered, ratty (*Brit. & N.Z. informal*), surly, testy, tetchy, thin-skinned
➤ **Antonyms**
affable, cheerful, easy-going, genial, good-humoured, imperious, indifferent, insensitive, light-hearted, pleasant, sunny, sweet, thick-skinned, unconcerned

tough *adjective* **1 = resilient**, durable, firm, hard, inflexible, leathery, resistant, rigid, rugged, solid, stiff, strong, sturdy, tenacious **2 = strong**, brawny, fit, hard as nails, hardened, hardy, resilient, seasoned, stalwart, stout, strapping, sturdy, vigorous **3 = rough**, hard-bitten, pugnacious, ruthless, vicious, violent **4 = strict**, exacting, firm, hard, inflexible, intractable, merciless, resolute, severe, stern, unbending, unforgiving, unyielding **5 = difficult**, arduous, baffling, exacting, exhausting, hard, irksome, knotty, laborious, perplexing, puzzling, strenuous, thorny, troublesome, uphill **6** *As in* **tough luck!** *Informal* = **unlucky**, bad, lamentable, regrettable, too bad (*informal*), unfortunate ♦ *noun* **7 = ruffian**, bruiser (*informal*), brute, bully, bully boy, heavy (*slang*), hooligan, rough (*informal*), roughneck (*slang*), rowdy, thug, tsotsi (*S. African*)
➤ **Antonyms**
adjective ≠**resilient**: delicate, flexible, flimsy, fragile, soft, tender, weak ≠**strong**: delicate, soft, weak ≠**rough**: civilized, gentle, humane, soft, tender ≠**strict**: accommodating, benign, compassionate, considerate, easy, flexible, gentle, humane, indulgent, kind, lenient, merciful, mild, soft, sympathetic, tender, unexacting ≠**difficult**: easy, easy-peasy (*slang*), unexacting

tour *noun* **1 = journey**, excursion, expedition, jaunt, outing, progress, trip **2 = course**, circuit, round ♦ *verb* **3 = visit**, explore, go on the road, go round, holiday in, journey, sightsee, travel round, travel through

tourist *noun* = **traveller**, excursionist, globetrotter, holiday-maker, journeyer, sightseer, tripper, voyager

tournament *noun* **1 = competition**, contest, event, match, meeting, series **2**

Medieval = **joust**, the lists, tourney

tousle *verb* = **dishevel**, disarrange, disarray, disorder, mess up, ruffle, rumple, tangle

tout *verb* **1 = solicit**, canvass, drum up **2** *Informal* = **recommend**, approve, commend, endorse, praise, promote, speak well of

tow *verb* = **drag**, draw, hale, haul, lug, pull, trail, trawl, tug, yank

towards *preposition* **1 = in the direction of**, en route for, for, on the road to, on the way to, to **2 = regarding**, about, concerning, for, with regard to, with respect to **3 = just before**, almost, close to, coming up to, getting on for, nearing, nearly, not quite, shortly before

tower *noun* **1 = column**, belfry, obelisk, pillar, skyscraper, steeple, turret ♦ *verb* **2** *usually with* **over** = **rise**, ascend, be head and shoulders above, dominate, loom, mount, overlook, overtop, rear, soar, surpass, top, transcend

towering *adjective* **1 = tall**, colossal, elevated, high, lofty, soaring **2 = impressive**, extraordinary, imposing, magnificent, prodigious, striking, supreme, surpassing, transcendent **3 = intense**, excessive, extreme, immoderate, inordinate, intemperate, mighty, passionate, vehement, violent

toxic *adjective* = **poisonous**, deadly, harmful, lethal, noxious, pernicious, pestilential, septic
➤ **Antonyms**
harmless, invigorating, non-poisonous, nontoxic, safe, salubrious

toy *noun* **1 = plaything**, doll, game ♦ *verb* **toy with 2 = play**, amuse oneself with, dally with, flirt with, fool (about *or* around) with, sport, trifle **3 = fiddle** (*informal*), play

trace *verb* **1 = find**, ascertain, detect, determine, discover, ferret out, follow, hunt down, pursue, search for, seek, shadow, stalk, track, unearth **2 = copy 3 = outline**, chart, delineate, depict, draw, map, mark out, show, sketch ♦ *noun* **4 = track**, footmark, footprint, footstep, path, slot, spoor, trail **5 = bit**, dash, drop, hint, iota, jot, shadow, *soupçon*, suggestion, suspicion, tinge, touch, whiff **6 = remnant**, evidence, indication, mark, record, relic, remains, sign, survival, token, vestige

track *noun* **1 = path**, course, flight path, line, orbit, pathway, road, trajectory, way **2 = trail**, footmark, footprint, footstep, mark, path, scent, slipstream, spoor, trace, wake **3 = line**, permanent way, rail, rails **4 keep track of = keep up with**, follow, keep an eye on, keep in sight, keep in touch with, keep up to date with, monitor, oversee, watch **5 lose track of = lose**, lose sight of, misplace ♦ *verb* **6 = follow**, chase, dog, follow the trail of, hunt down, pursue, shadow, stalk, tail (*informal*), trace, trail

track down *verb* **= find**, apprehend, bring to light, capture, catch, dig up, discover, expose, ferret out, hunt down, run to earth *or* ground, sniff out, trace, unearth

tracks *plural noun* **1 = trail**, footprints, impressions, imprints, tyre marks, tyre prints, wheel marks **2 make tracks = leave**, beat it (*slang*), depart, get going, get moving, go, head off, hit the road (*slang*), set out, split (*slang*), take off (*informal*) **3 stop in one's tracks = bring to a standstill**, freeze, immobilize, petrify, stop dead, transfix

tract[1] *noun* **= area**, district, estate, expanse, extent, lot, plot, quarter, region, stretch, territory, zone

tract[2] *noun* **= treatise**, booklet, brochure, dissertation, essay, homily, leaflet, monograph, pamphlet

tractable *adjective Formal* **1 = manageable**, amenable, biddable, compliant, controllable, docile, governable, obedient, persuadable, submissive, tame, willing, yielding **2 = malleable**, ductile, fictile, plastic, pliable, pliant, tensile, tractile, workable
➤ **Antonyms**
≠**manageable**: defiant, headstrong, obstinate, refractory, stiff-necked, stubborn, unruly, wilful

traction *noun* **1 = pulling**, drag, draught, drawing, haulage, pull **2 = grip**, adhesion, friction, purchase, resistance

trade *noun* **1 = commerce**, barter, business, buying and selling, dealing, exchange, traffic, transactions, truck **2 = job**, avocation, business, calling, craft, employment, line, line of work, métier, occupation, profession, pursuit, skill ♦ *verb* **3 = deal**, bargain, barter, buy and sell, cut a deal, do business, exchange, have dealings, peddle, traffic, transact, truck **4 = exchange**, barter, swap, switch

trader *noun* **= dealer**, broker, buyer, marketer, merchandiser, merchant, purveyor, seller, supplier

tradesman *noun* **1 = craftsman**, artisan, journeyman, skilled worker, workman **2 = shopkeeper**, dealer, merchant, purveyor, retailer, seller, supplier, vendor

tradition *noun* **= custom**, convention, customs, established practice, folklore, habit, institution, lore, ritual, unwritten law, usage

traditional *adjective* **= customary**, accustomed, ancestral, conventional, established, fixed, historic, long-established, old, time-honoured, unwritten, usual
➤ **Antonyms**
avant-garde, contemporary, ground-breaking, innovative, modern, new, novel, off-the-wall (*slang*), original, revolutionary, unconventional, unusual

traduce *verb Formal* **= malign**, abuse, bad-mouth (*slang, chiefly U.S. & Canad.*), blacken, calumniate, decry, defame, denigrate, deprecate, depreciate, detract, disparage, knock (*informal*), revile, rubbish (*informal*), run down, slag (off) (*slang*), slander, smear, speak ill of, vilify

traffic *noun* **1 = transport**, freight, movement, passengers, transportation, vehicles **2 = trade**, barter, business, buying and selling, commerce, dealing, dealings, doings, exchange, intercourse, peddling, relations, truck ♦ *verb* **3 = trade**, bargain, barter, buy and sell, cut a deal, deal, do business, exchange, have dealings, have transactions, market, peddle, truck

tragedy *noun* **= disaster**, adversity, affliction, bummer (*slang*), calamity, catastrophe, grievous blow, misfortune
➤ **Antonyms**
fortune, happiness, joy, prosperity, success

tragic *adjective* **1 = distressing**, appalling, awful, calamitous, catastrophic, deadly, dire, disastrous, dreadful, fatal, grievous, ill-fated, ill-starred, lamentable, ruinous, sad, shocking, unfortunate, woeful, wretched **2 = sad**, anguished, dismal, doleful, heartbreaking, heart-rending, miserable, mournful, pathetic, pitiable, sorrowful
➤ **Antonyms**
≠**distressing**: beneficial, fortunate, lucky, satisfying, worthwhile ≠**sad**: cheerful, comic, happy, joyful

trail *noun* **1 = path**, beaten track, footpath, road, route, track, way **2 = tracks**, footprints, footsteps, mark, marks, path, scent, slipstream, spoor, trace, wake **3 = stream**, appendage, tail, train ♦ *verb* **4 = drag**, dangle, draw, hang down, haul, pull, stream, tow **5 = follow**, chase, hunt, pursue, shadow, stalk, tail (*informal*), trace, track **6 = lag**, bring up the rear, dawdle, fall behind, follow, hang back, linger, loiter, straggle, traipse (*informal*)

trail away *or* **off** *verb* **= fade away** *or* **out**, decrease, die away, diminish, dwindle, fall away, grow faint, grow weak, lessen, peter out, shrink, sink, subside, tail off, taper off, weaken

train *verb* **1** = **instruct**, coach, discipline, drill, educate, guide, improve, prepare, rehearse, school, teach, tutor **2** = **exercise**, prepare, work out **3** = **aim**, direct, focus, level, point ♦ *noun* **4** = **sequence**, chain, concatenation, course, order, progression, series, set, string, succession **5** = **tail**, appendage, trail

trainer *noun* = **coach**, handler

training *noun* **1** = **instruction**, coaching, discipline, education, grounding, guidance, schooling, teaching, tuition, tutelage, upbringing **2** = **exercise**, body building, practice, preparation, working out

traipse *Informal* ♦ *verb* **1** = **trudge**, drag oneself, footslog, slouch, trail, tramp ♦ *noun* **2** = **trudge**, long walk, slog, tramp, trek

trait *noun* = **characteristic**, attribute, feature, idiosyncrasy, mannerism, peculiarity, quality, quirk

traitor *noun* = **betrayer**, apostate, back-stabber, deceiver, defector, deserter, double-crosser (*informal*), fifth columnist, informer, Judas, quisling, rebel, renegade, turncoat
➤ Antonyms
defender, loyalist, patriot, supporter

traitorous *adjective* = **treacherous**, apostate, disloyal, double-crossing (*informal*), double-dealing, faithless, false, perfidious, treasonable, unfaithful, untrue
➤ Antonyms
constant, faithful, loyal, patriotic, staunch, steadfast, true, trusty

trajectory *noun* = **path**, course, flight, flight path, line, route, track

trammel *verb* **1** = **hinder**, bar, block, check, curb, fetter, hamper, handicap, impede, restrain, restrict, snag, tie ♦ *noun* **2 trammels** = **restrictions**, bars, blocks, bonds, chains, checks, curbs, fetters, handicaps, hindrances, impediments, obstacles, reins, shackles, stumbling blocks
➤ Antonyms
verb ≠**hinder**: advance, assist, expedite, facilitate, foster, further, promote, support

tramp *verb* **1** = **hike**, footslog, march, ramble, range, roam, rove, slog, trek, walk **2** = **trudge**, march, plod, stamp, stump, toil, traipse (*informal*), walk heavily ♦ *noun* **3** = **vagrant**, bag lady (*chiefly U.S.*), bum (*informal*), derelict, dosser (*Brit. slang*), down-and-out, drifter, hobo (*chiefly U.S.*), vagabond **4** = **hike**, march, ramble, slog, trek **5** = **tread**, footfall, footstep, stamp

trample *verb* **1** *often with* **on** = **crush**, flatten, run over, squash, stamp, tread, walk over **2 trample on** = **show no**
consideration for, hurt, ride roughshod over

trance *noun* = **daze**, abstraction, dream, ecstasy, hypnotic state, rapture, reverie, spell, stupor, unconsciousness

tranquil *adjective* = **calm**, at peace, composed, cool, peaceful, placid, quiet, restful, sedate, serene, still, undisturbed, unexcited, unperturbed, unruffled, untroubled
➤ Antonyms
agitated, busy, confused, disturbed, excited, hectic, restless, troubled

tranquillity *noun* = **calm**, calmness, composure, coolness, equanimity, hush, imperturbability, peace, peacefulness, placidity, quiet, quietness, quietude, repose, rest, restfulness, sedateness, serenity, stillness
➤ Antonyms
agitation, commotion, confusion, disturbance, excitement, noise, restlessness, turmoil, upset

tranquillize *verb* = **calm**, lull, pacify, quell, quiet, relax, sedate, settle one's nerves, soothe
➤ Antonyms
agitate, confuse, distress, disturb, harass, perturb, ruffle, trouble, upset

tranquillizer *noun* = **sedative**, barbiturate, bromide, downer (*slang*), opiate

transact *verb* = **carry out**, accomplish, carry on, conclude, conduct, discharge, do, enact, execute, handle, manage, negotiate, perform, see to, settle, take care of

transaction *noun* **1** = **deal**, action, affair, bargain, business, coup, deed, enterprise, event, matter, negotiation, occurrence, proceeding, undertaking **2** *plural* = **records**, affairs, doings, goings-on (*informal*), minutes, proceedings

transcend *verb* = **surpass**, eclipse, exceed, excel, go above, go beyond, leave behind, outdo, outshine, outstrip, rise above

transcendence *noun* = **greatness**, excellence, incomparability, matchlessness, pre-eminence, sublimity, superiority, supremacy

transcendent *adjective* = **unparalleled**, consummate, exceeding, extraordinary, incomparable, matchless, peerless, pre-eminent, second to none, sublime, superior, transcendental, unequalled, unique, unrivalled

transcribe *verb* **1** = **write out**, copy out, note, reproduce, rewrite, set out, take down, transfer **2** = **record**, tape, tape-record

transcript *noun* = **copy**, carbon, carbon copy, duplicate, manuscript, note, notes, record, reproduction, transcription, translation, transliteration, version

transfer *verb* **1** = **move**, carry, change, consign, convey, displace, hand over, pass on, relocate, remove, shift, translate, transmit, transplant, transport, transpose ♦ *noun* **2** = **move**, change, displacement, handover, relocation, removal, shift, transference, translation, transmission, transposition

transfigure *verb* = **change**, alter, convert, metamorphose, transform, transmute

transfix *verb* **1** = **stun**, engross, fascinate, halt *or* stop in one's tracks, hold, hypnotize, mesmerize, paralyse, petrify, rivet the attention of, root to the spot, spellbind, stop dead **2** = **pierce**, fix, impale, puncture, run through, skewer, spear, spit
➤ **Antonyms**
≠**stun**: bore, fatigue, tire, weary

transform *verb* = **change**, alter, convert, make over, metamorphose, reconstruct, remodel, renew, revolutionize, transfigure, transmogrify (*jocular*), transmute

transformation *noun* = **change**, alteration, conversion, metamorphosis, radical change, renewal, revolution, revolutionary change, sea change, transfiguration, transmogrification (*jocular*), transmutation

transfuse *verb Literary* = **permeate**, instil, pervade, spread over, suffuse

transgress *verb Formal* **1** = **break**, be out of order, break the law, contravene, defy, disobey, do *or* go wrong, err, fall from grace, go astray, infringe, lapse, misbehave, offend, sin, trespass, violate **2** = **go beyond**, encroach, exceed, overstep

transgression *noun* = **crime**, breach, contravention, encroachment, error, fault, infraction, infringement, iniquity, lapse, misbehaviour, misdeed, misdemeanour, offence, peccadillo, sin, trespass, violation, wrong, wrongdoing

transgressor *noun* = **criminal**, culprit, delinquent, evildoer, felon, lawbreaker, malefactor, miscreant, offender, sinner, trespasser, villain, wrongdoer

transience *noun* = **briefness**, brevity, ephemerality, impermanence, shortness, transitoriness

transient *adjective* = **brief**, ephemeral, evanescent, fleeting, flying, here today and gone tomorrow, impermanent, momentary, passing, short, short-lived, short-term, temporary, transitory
➤ **Antonyms**

abiding, constant, durable, enduring, eternal, imperishable, long-lasting, long-term, permanent, perpetual, persistent, undying

transit *noun* **1** = **movement**, carriage, conveyance, crossing, motion, passage, shipment, transfer, transport, transportation, travel **2 in transit** = **en route**, on the journey, on the move, on the road, on the way, while travelling

transition *noun* = **change**, alteration, changeover, conversion, development, evolution, flux, metamorphosis, passage, passing, progression, shift, transit, transmutation, upheaval

transitional *adjective* = **changing**, developmental, fluid, intermediate, passing, provisional, temporary, transitionary, unsettled

transitory *adjective* = **short-lived**, brief, ephemeral, evanescent, fleeting, here today and gone tomorrow, impermanent, momentary, passing, short, short-term, temporary, transient
➤ **Antonyms**
abiding, enduring, eternal, everlasting, lasting, long-lived, long-term, permanent, perpetual, persistent, undying

translate *verb* **1** = **interpret**, construe, convert, decipher, decode, paraphrase, render, transcribe, transliterate **2** = **convert**, alter, change, transform, transmute, turn

translation *noun* **1** = **interpretation**, decoding, gloss, paraphrase, rendering, rendition, transcription, transliteration, version **2** = **rephrasing**, elucidation, explanation, paraphrase, rewording, simplification **3** = **conversion**, alteration, change, transformation, transmutation

translator *noun* = **interpreter**, linguist

translucent *adjective* = **semitransparent**, clear, diaphanous, limpid, lucent, pellucid

transmigration *noun* = **reincarnation**, metempsychosis, migration, movement, passage, rebirth

transmission *noun* **1** = **transfer**, communication, conveyance, diffusion, dispatch, dissemination, sending, shipment, spread, transference, transport **2** = **broadcasting**, dissemination, putting out, relaying, sending, showing **3** = **programme**, broadcast, show

transmit *verb* **1** = **pass on**, bear, carry, communicate, convey, diffuse, dispatch, disseminate, forward, hand down, hand on, impart, send, spread, take, transfer, transport **2** = **broadcast**, disseminate, put on the air, radio, relay, send, send out

transmute *verb* = **transform**, alter, change, convert, metamorphose, remake, transfigure

transparency *noun* 1 = **clarity**, clearness, diaphanousness, filminess, gauziness, limpidity, limpidness, pellucidity, pellucidness, translucence, translucency, transparence 2 = **obviousness**, apparentness, distinctness, explicitness, patentness, plainness, unambiguousness 3 = **photograph**, slide
➤ Antonyms
≠**clarity**: cloudiness, murkiness, opacity, unclearness ≠**obviousness**: obscurity, unclearness, vagueness

transparent *adjective* 1 = **clear**, crystal clear, crystalline, diaphanous, filmy, gauzy, limpid, lucent, lucid, pellucid, see-through, sheer, translucent 2 = **obvious**, apparent, as plain as the nose on one's face (*informal*), bold, distinct, evident, explicit, manifest, patent, perspicuous, plain, recognizable, unambiguous, understandable, undisguised, visible
➤ Antonyms
≠**clear**: cloudy, muddy, opaque, thick, turbid, unclear ≠**obvious**: hidden, mysterious, opaque, uncertain, unclear, vague

transpire *verb* 1 = **become known**, be disclosed, be discovered, be made public, come out, come to light, emerge 2 *not universally accepted* = **happen**, arise, befall, chance, come about, come to pass (*archaic*), occur, take place

transplant *verb* = **transfer**, displace, relocate, remove, resettle, shift, uproot

transport *verb* 1 = **convey**, bear, bring, carry, fetch, haul, move, remove, run, ship, take, transfer 2 *History* = **exile**, banish, deport, sentence to transportation 3 = **enrapture**, captivate, carry away, delight, electrify, enchant, entrance, move, ravish, spellbind ♦ *noun* 4 = **vehicle**, conveyance, transportation, wheels (*informal*) 5 = **transference**, carriage, conveyance, removal, shipment, shipping, transportation 6 = **ecstasy**, bliss, cloud nine (*informal*), delight, enchantment, euphoria, happiness, heaven, rapture, ravishment, seventh heaven
➤ Antonyms
noun ≠**ecstasy**: blues (*informal*), depression, despondency, doldrums, dumps (*informal*), melancholy

transpose *verb* = **interchange**, alter, change, exchange, move, rearrange, relocate, reorder, shift, substitute, swap, switch, transfer

transverse *adjective* = **crossways**, athwart, crosswise, diagonal, oblique

trap *noun* 1 = **snare**, ambush, gin, net, noose, pitfall, springe, toils 2 = **trick**, ambush, deception, device, ruse, stratagem, subterfuge, wile ♦ *verb* 3 = **catch**, corner, enmesh, ensnare, entrap, snare, take 4 = **trick**, ambush, beguile, deceive, dupe, ensnare, inveigle

trapped *adjective* 1 = **caught**, ambushed, at bay, cornered, cut off, ensnared, in a tight corner, in a tight spot, netted, snared, stuck (*informal*), surrounded 2 = **tricked**, beguiled, deceived, duped, inveigled

trappings *plural noun* = **accessories**, accoutrements, adornments, bells and whistles, decorations, dress, equipment, finery, fittings, fixtures, fripperies, furnishings, gear, livery, ornaments, panoply, paraphernalia, things, trimmings

trash *noun* 1 = **nonsense**, balderdash, balls (*taboo slang*), bilge (*informal*), bosh (*informal*), bull (*slang*), bullshit (*taboo slang*), bunkum *or* buncombe (*chiefly U.S.*), cobblers (*Brit. taboo slang*), crap (*slang*), drivel, foolish talk, garbage (*informal*), hogwash, hot air (*informal*), kak (*S. African taboo*), moonshine, pants (*slang*), piffle (*informal*), poppycock (*informal*), rot, rubbish, shit (*taboo slang*), tommyrot, tripe (*informal*), twaddle 2 *Chiefly U.S. & Canad.* = **litter**, dreck (*slang, chiefly U.S.*), dregs, dross, garbage, junk (*informal*), offscourings, refuse, rubbish, sweepings, waste
➤ Antonyms
≠**nonsense**: logic, reason, sense, significance

trashy *adjective* = **worthless**, cheap, cheap-jack (*informal*), crappy (*slang*), inferior, poxy (*slang*), rubbishy, shabby, shoddy, tawdry, tinsel
➤ Antonyms
A1 *or* A-one (*informal*), excellent, exceptional, first-class, first-rate, outstanding, superlative

trauma *noun* 1 = **shock**, anguish, ordeal, pain, strain, suffering, torture, upheaval, upset 2 = **injury**, agony, damage, hurt, wound

traumatic *adjective* 1 = **shocking**, disturbing, painful, scarring, upsetting 2 = **wounding**, agonizing, damaging, hurtful, injurious
➤ Antonyms
≠**shocking**: calming, relaxing, therapeutic ≠**wounding**: healing, helpful, therapeutic, wholesome

travail *noun Literary* = **toil**, drudgery, effort, exertion, grind (*informal*), hardship, hard

work, labour, slog, strain, suffering, sweat
travel verb 1 = **go**, cross, journey, make a
journey, make one's way, move, proceed,
progress, ramble, roam, rove, take a trip,
tour, traverse, trek, voyage, walk, wander,
wend 2 = **be transmitted**, carry, get
through, move ♦ noun 3 usually plural
= **journey**, excursion, expedition,
globetrotting, movement, passage,
peregrination, ramble, tour, touring, trip,
voyage, walk, wandering
traveller noun 1 = **voyager**, excursionist,
explorer, globetrotter, gypsy, hiker,
holiday-maker, journeyer, migrant,
nomad, passenger, tourist, tripper,
wanderer, wayfarer 2 = **travelling
salesman**, agent, commercial traveller,
rep, representative, salesman, sales rep
travelling adjective = **itinerant**, migrant,
migratory, mobile, moving, nomadic,
peripatetic, restless, roaming, roving,
touring, unsettled, wandering, wayfaring
traverse verb = **cross**, bridge, cover, cut
across, go across, go over, make one's way
across, negotiate, pass over, range, roam,
span, travel over, wander
travesty noun 1 = **mockery**, burlesque,
caricature, distortion, lampoon, parody,
perversion, send-up (Brit. informal), sham,
spoof (informal), takeoff (informal) ♦ verb 2
= **mock**, burlesque, caricature, distort,
lampoon, make a mockery of, make fun of,
parody, pervert, ridicule, send up (Brit.
informal), sham, spoof (informal), take off
(informal)
treacherous adjective 1 = **disloyal**,
deceitful, double-crossing (informal),
double-dealing, duplicitous, faithless, false,
perfidious, traitorous, treasonable,
unfaithful, unreliable, untrue,
untrustworthy 2 = **dangerous**, deceptive,
hazardous, icy, perilous, precarious, risky,
slippery, slippy (informal or dialect), tricky,
unreliable, unsafe, unstable
➤ Antonyms
≠**disloyal**: dependable, faithful, loyal,
reliable, true, trustworthy ≠**dangerous**:
reliable, safe
treachery noun = **betrayal**, disloyalty,
double-cross (informal), double-dealing,
duplicity, faithlessness, infidelity,
perfidiousness, perfidy, stab in the back,
treason
➤ Antonyms
allegiance, dependability, faithfulness,
fidelity, loyalty, reliability
tread verb 1 = **crush underfoot**, squash,
trample 2 = **step**, hike, march, pace, plod,
stamp, stride, tramp, trudge, walk ♦ noun
3 = **step**, footfall, footstep, gait, pace,

stride, walk
treason noun = **disloyalty**, duplicity,
lese-majesty, mutiny, perfidy, sedition,
subversion, traitorousness, treachery
➤ Antonyms
allegiance, faithfulness, fidelity, loyalty,
patriotism
treasonable adjective = **disloyal**, false,
mutinous, perfidious, seditious, subversive,
traitorous, treacherous, treasonous
➤ Antonyms
dependable, faithful, loyal, patriotic,
reliable, trustworthy
treasure noun 1 = **riches**, cash, fortune,
funds, gold, jewels, money, valuables,
wealth 2 Informal = **darling**, apple of one's
eye, gem, jewel, nonpareil, paragon, pearl,
precious, pride and joy, prize ♦ verb 3
= **prize**, adore, cherish, dote upon,
esteem, hold dear, idolize, love, revere,
value, venerate, worship
treasury noun 1 = **storehouse**, bank,
cache, hoard, repository, store, vault 2
= **funds**, assets, capital, coffers, exchequer,
finances, money, resources, revenues
treat verb 1 = **behave towards**, act towards,
consider, deal with, handle, look upon,
manage, regard, use 2 = **take care of**,
apply treatment to, attend to, care for,
doctor, medicate, nurse 3 = **provide**, buy
for, entertain, foot or pay the bill, give, lay
on, pay for, regale, stand (informal) 4 **treat
of** = **deal with**, be concerned with,
contain, discuss, go into, touch upon
♦ noun 5 = **entertainment**, banquet,
celebration, feast, gift, party, refreshment
6 = **pleasure**, delight, enjoyment, fun,
gratification, joy, satisfaction, surprise, thrill
treatise noun = **paper**, disquisition,
dissertation, essay, exposition,
monograph, pamphlet, study, thesis, tract,
work, writing
treatment noun 1 = **care**, cure, healing,
medication, medicine, remedy, surgery,
therapy 2 = **handling**, action, behaviour,
conduct, dealing, management,
manipulation, reception, usage
treaty noun = **agreement**, alliance,
bargain, bond, compact, concordat,
contract, convention, covenant, entente,
pact
trek noun 1 = **journey**, expedition, footslog,
hike, long haul, march, odyssey, safari,
slog, tramp ♦ verb 2 = **journey**, footslog,
hike, march, plod, range, roam, rove, slog,
traipse (informal), tramp, trudge
tremble verb 1 = **shake**, oscillate, quake,
quiver, rock, shiver, shudder, teeter, totter,
vibrate, wobble ♦ noun 2 = **shake**,
oscillation, quake, quiver, shiver, shudder,

tremor, vibration, wobble

tremendous *adjective* **1** = **huge**, awesome, colossal, enormous, formidable, gargantuan, gigantic, great, immense, monstrous, prodigious, stupendous, terrific, titanic, towering, vast, whopping (*informal*) **2** = **excellent**, amazing, awesome (*slang*), brilliant, cracking (*Brit. informal*), exceptional, extraordinary, fabulous (*informal*), fantastic (*informal*), great, incredible, marvellous, sensational (*informal*), super (*informal*), terrific (*informal*), wonderful
➤ **Antonyms**
≠**huge:** diminutive, little, minuscule, minute, small, tiny ≠**excellent:** abysmal, appalling, average, awful, dreadful, mediocre, no great shakes (*informal*), ordinary, rotten, run-of-the-mill, so-so, terrible

tremor *noun* **1** = **shake**, agitation, quaking, quaver, quiver, quivering, shaking, shiver, tremble, trembling, vibration, wobble **2** = **earthquake**, quake (*informal*), shock

tremulous *adjective Literary* = **trembling**, aflutter, agitated, antsy (*informal*), anxious, excited, fearful, frightened, jittery (*informal*), jumpy, nervous, quavering, quivering, scared, shaking, shivering, timid

trench *noun* = **ditch**, channel, cut, drain, earthwork, entrenchment, excavation, furrow, gutter, pit, trough, waterway

trenchant *adjective* **1** = **scathing**, acerbic, acid, acute, biting, caustic, cutting, hurtful, incisive, keen, mordant, penetrating, piquant, pointed, pungent, sarcastic, severe, sharp, tart, vitriolic **2** = **effective**, driving, effectual, emphatic, energetic, forceful, potent, powerful, strong, vigorous
➤ **Antonyms**
≠**scathing:** appeasing, kind, mollifying, soothing

trend *noun* **1** = **tendency**, bias, course, current, direction, drift, flow, inclination, leaning **2** = **fashion**, craze, fad (*informal*), look, mode, rage, style, thing, vogue
♦ *verb* **3** = **tend**, bend, flow, head, incline, lean, run, stretch, swing, turn, veer

trendsetter *noun* = **leader of fashion**, arbiter of taste, pacesetter

trendy *Brit. informal* ♦ *adjective* **1** = **fashionable**, in fashion, in vogue, modish, stylish, voguish, with it (*informal*)
♦ *noun* **2** = **poser** (*informal*), pseud (*informal*)

trepidation *noun Formal* = **anxiety**, agitation, alarm, apprehension, butterflies (*informal*), cold feet (*informal*), cold sweat (*informal*), consternation, dismay, disquiet,

disturbance, dread, fear, fright, jitters (*informal*), nervousness, palpitation, perturbation, quivering, shaking, trembling, uneasiness, worry
➤ **Antonyms**
aplomb, calm, composure, confidence, coolness, equanimity, self-assurance

trespass *verb* **1** = **intrude**, encroach, infringe, invade, obtrude, poach ♦ *noun* **2** = **intrusion**, encroachment, infringement, invasion, poaching, unlawful entry, wrongful entry **3** *Old-fashioned* = **sin**, breach, crime, error, evildoing, fault, infraction, iniquity, misbehaviour, misconduct, misdeed, misdemeanour, offence, transgression, wrongdoing

trespasser *noun* **1** = **intruder**, infringer, interloper, invader, poacher, unwelcome visitor **2** *Archaic* = **sinner**, criminal, delinquent, evildoer, malefactor, offender, transgressor, wrongdoer

tresses *plural noun* = **hair**, locks

triad *noun* = **threesome**, trilogy, trinity, trio, triple, triplet, triptych, triumvirate, triune

trial *noun* **1** *Law* = **hearing**, industrial tribunal, judicial examination, litigation, tribunal **2** = **test**, audition, check, dry run (*informal*), examination, experiment, probation, proof, testing, test-run **3** = **attempt**, crack (*informal*), effort, endeavour, go (*informal*), shot (*informal*), stab (*informal*), try, venture **4** = **hardship**, adversity, affliction, burden, cross to bear, distress, grief, hard times, load, misery, ordeal, pain, suffering, tribulation, trouble, unhappiness, vexation, woe, wretchedness **5** = **nuisance**, bane, bother, drag (*informal*), hassle (*informal*), irritation, pain in the neck (*informal*), pest, plague (*informal*), thorn in one's flesh *or* side, vexation ♦ *adjective* **6** = **experimental**, exploratory, pilot, probationary, provisional, testing

tribe *noun* = **race**, blood, caste, clan, class, dynasty, ethnic group, family, house, people, seed (*chiefly biblical*), stock

tribulation *noun* = **trouble**, adversity, affliction, bummer (*slang*), burden, care, cross to bear, distress, grief, hardship, hassle (*informal*), heartache, misery, misfortune, ordeal, pain, sorrow, suffering, trial, unhappiness, woe, worry
➤ **Antonyms**
blessing, bliss, ease, good fortune, happiness, joy, pleasure, rest

tribunal *noun* = **hearing**, bar, bench, court, industrial tribunal, judgment seat, judicial examination, trial

tribute *noun* **1** = **accolade**,

acknowledgment, applause,
commendation, compliment, eulogy, gift,
gratitude, honour, panegyric, praise,
recognition, respect, testimonial **2 = tax**,
charge, contribution, customs, duty,
excise, homage, offering, payment,
ransom, subsidy, toll
➤ **Antonyms**
≠**accolade**: blame, complaint,
condemnation, criticism, disapproval,
reproach, reproof

trice *noun As in* **in a trice = moment**, flash,
instant, jiffy (*informal*), minute, second,
split second, tick (*Brit. informal*)

trick *noun* **1 = deception**, artifice, con
(*slang*), deceit, dodge, fraud, hoax,
manoeuvre, ploy, ruse, scam (*slang*), sting
(*informal*), stratagem, subterfuge, swindle,
trap, wile **2 = joke**, antic, caper, gag
(*informal*), jape, leg-pull (*Brit. informal*),
practical joke, prank, put-on (*slang*), stunt
3 = secret, art, craft, expertise, hang
(*informal*), knack, know-how (*informal*),
skill, technique **4 = sleight of hand**, device,
feat, legerdemain **5 = mannerism**,
characteristic, foible, habit, idiosyncrasy,
peculiarity, practice, quirk, trait **6 do the
trick** *Informal* **= work**, be effective *or*
effectual, have effect, produce the desired
result ♦ *verb* **7 = deceive**, cheat, con
(*informal*), defraud, delude, dupe, fool,
have (someone) on, hoax, hoodwink, kid
(*informal*), mislead, pull a fast one on
(*informal*), pull the wool over (someone's)
eyes, sting (*informal*), swindle, take in
(*informal*), trap

trickery *noun* **= deception**, cheating,
chicanery, con (*informal*), deceit,
dishonesty, double-dealing, fraud, funny
business, guile, hanky-panky (*informal*),
hoax, jiggery-pokery (*informal, chiefly
Brit.*), monkey business (*informal*),
skulduggery (*informal*), swindling
➤ **Antonyms**
artlessness, candour, directness, frankness,
honesty, openness, straightforwardness,
uprightness

trickle *verb* **1 = dribble**, crawl, creep, drip,
drop, exude, ooze, percolate, run, seep,
stream ♦ *noun* **2 = dribble**, drip, seepage

trick out *verb* **= dress up**, adorn, array,
attire, bedeck, deck out, doll up (*slang*),
do up (*informal*), get up (*informal*)

trickster *noun* **= deceiver**, cheat, chiseller
(*informal*), con man (*informal*), fraud,
fraudster, hoaxer, hustler (*U.S. informal*),
joker, practical joker, swindler

tricky *adjective* **1 = difficult**, complicated,
delicate, knotty, problematic, risky, sticky
(*informal*), thorny, ticklish, touch-and-go **2**

= crafty, artful, cunning, deceitful,
deceptive, devious, foxy, scheming,
slippery, sly, subtle, wily
➤ **Antonyms**
≠**difficult**: clear, easy, obvious, simple,
straightforward, uncomplicated ≠**crafty**:
above board, artless, direct, genuine,
honest, ingenuous, open, sincere, truthful

trifle¹ *noun* **1 = knick-knack**, bagatelle,
bauble, child's play (*informal*), gewgaw,
nothing, plaything, toy, triviality **2 = little**,
bit, dash, drop, jot, pinch, spot, touch,
trace

trifle² *verb* **= toy**, amuse oneself, dally, flirt,
mess about, play, play fast and loose
(*informal*)

trifling *adjective* **= insignificant**, empty,
footling (*informal*), frivolous,
inconsiderable, measly, minuscule,
negligible, paltry, petty, piddling
(*informal*), shallow, silly, slight, small, tiny,
trivial, unimportant, valueless, worthless
➤ **Antonyms**
considerable, crucial, important, large,
major, serious, significant, vital, weighty

trigger *verb* **= set off**, activate, bring about,
cause, elicit, generate, give rise to,
produce, prompt, provoke, set in motion,
spark off, start
➤ **Antonyms**
bar, block, hinder, impede, inhibit,
obstruct, prevent, repress, stop

trim *adjective* **1 = neat**, compact, dapper,
natty (*informal*), nice, orderly, shipshape,
smart, soigné *or* soignée, spick-and-span,
spruce, tidy, well-groomed, well
turned-out **2 = slender**, fit, shapely, sleek,
slim, streamlined, svelte, willowy ♦ *verb* **3
= cut**, barber, clip, crop, cut back, even up,
lop, pare, prune, shave, shear, tidy **4
= decorate**, adorn, array, beautify, bedeck,
deck out, dress, embellish, garnish,
ornament **5 = adjust**, arrange, balance,
distribute, order, prepare, settle ♦ *noun* **6
= decoration**, adornment, border, edging,
embellishment, frill, fringe, garnish,
ornamentation, piping, trimming **7
= condition**, fettle, fitness, form, health,
order, repair, shape (*informal*), situation,
state, wellness **8 = cut**, clipping, crop,
pruning, shave, shearing, tidying up,
trimming
➤ **Antonyms**
adjective ≠**neat**: disarrayed, disorderly,
messy, scruffy, shabby, sloppy,
ungroomed, unkempt, untidy

trimming *noun* **1 = decoration**,
adornment, border, braid, edging,
embellishment, festoon, frill, fringe,
garnish, ornamentation, piping **2**

trimmings = **extras**, accessories, accompaniments, appurtenances, frills, garnish, ornaments, paraphernalia, trappings

trinity noun = **threesome**, triad, trilogy, trio, triple, triplet, triptych, triumvirate

trinket noun = **ornament**, bagatelle, bauble, bibelot, gewgaw, gimcrack, knick-knack, toy, trifle

trio noun = **threesome**, triad, trilogy, trinity, triple, triplet, triptych, triumvirate

trip noun **1** = **journey**, errand, excursion, expedition, foray, jaunt, outing, ramble, run, tour, travel, voyage **2** = **stumble**, blunder, fall, false move, false step, misstep, slip ♦ verb **3** = **stumble**, fall, lose one's balance, lose one's footing, make a false move, misstep, slip, tumble **4** = **catch out**, confuse, disconcert, put off one's stride, throw off, trap, unsettle **5** = **skip**, caper, dance, flit, frisk, gambol, hop, spring, tread lightly **6** Informal = **take drugs**, get high (informal), get stoned (slang), turn on (slang)

tripe noun Informal = **nonsense**, balderdash, balls (taboo slang), bilge (informal), bollocks (Brit. taboo slang), bosh (informal), bull (slang), bullshit (taboo slang), claptrap (informal), cobblers (Brit. taboo slang), crap (slang), drivel, foolish talk, garbage (informal), hogwash, hot air (informal), moonshine, pants (slang), piffle (informal), poppycock (informal), rot, rubbish, shit (taboo slang), tommyrot, tosh (slang, chiefly Brit.), trash, twaddle

triple adjective **1** = **threefold**, three times as much, three-way, tripartite ♦ verb **2** = **treble**, increase threefold, triplicate ♦ noun **3** = **threesome**, triad, trilogy, trinity, trio, triplet, triumvirate

triplet noun = **threesome**, triad, trilogy, trinity, trio, triple, triumvirate

tripper noun Chiefly Brit. = **tourist**, excursionist, holiday-maker, sightseer, voyager

trite adjective = **unoriginal**, banal, clichéd, common, commonplace, corny (slang), dull, hack, hackneyed, ordinary, pedestrian, routine, run-of-the-mill, stale, stereotyped, stock, threadbare, tired, uninspired, worn
➤ **Antonyms**
exciting, fresh, interesting, new, novel, original, out-of-the-ordinary, uncommon, unexpected, unfamiliar

triumph noun **1** = **joy**, elation, exultation, happiness, jubilation, pride, rejoicing **2** = **success**, accomplishment, achievement, attainment, conquest, coup, feat, feather

in one's cap, hit (informal), mastery, sensation, smash (informal), smash hit (informal), tour de force, victory, walkover (informal) ♦ verb **3** often with **over** = **succeed**, come out on top (informal), get the better of, overcome, overwhelm, prevail, prosper, vanquish, win **4** = **rejoice**, celebrate, crow, exult, gloat, glory, jubilate, revel
➤ **Antonyms**
noun ≠**success**: catastrophe, clunker (informal), defeat, disaster, failure, fiasco, flop (informal), washout (informal) ♦ verb ≠**succeed**: come a cropper (informal), fail, fall, flop (informal), lose

triumphant adjective **1** = **victorious**, boastful, cock-a-hoop, conquering, elated, exultant, glorious, proud, successful, swaggering, undefeated, winning **2** = **celebratory**, jubilant, rejoicing, triumphal
➤ **Antonyms**
≠**victorious**: beaten, defeated, embarrassed, humbled, humiliated, shamed, unsuccessful

trivia noun = **minutiae**, details, petty details, trifles, trivialities
➤ **Antonyms**
basics, brass tacks (informal), core, essentials, fundamentals, nitty-gritty (informal), rudiments

trivial adjective = **unimportant**, commonplace, everyday, frivolous, incidental, inconsequential, inconsiderable, insignificant, little, meaningless, minor, negligible, paltry, petty, puny, slight, small, trifling, valueless, worthless
➤ **Antonyms**
considerable, crucial, essential, important, profound, serious, significant, uncommon, unusual, vital, weighty, worthwhile

triviality noun **1** = **insignificance**, frivolity, inconsequentiality, littleness, meaninglessness, negligibility, paltriness, pettiness, slightness, smallness, unimportance, valuelessness, worthlessness **2** = **trifle**, detail, no big thing, no great matter, nothing, petty detail, technicality
➤ **Antonyms**
≠**insignificance**: consequence, importance, significance, value, worth ≠**trifle**: essential, rudiment

trivialize verb = **undervalue**, belittle, laugh off, make light of, minimize, play down, scoff at, underestimate, underplay

trollop noun Derogatory = **slut**, fallen woman, floozy (slang), harlot, hussy, loose woman, prostitute, scrubber (Brit. &

Austral. slang), slag (*Brit. slang*), slattern, streetwalker, strumpet, tart (*informal*), wanton, whore

troop *noun* 1 = **group**, assemblage, band, bevy, body, bunch (*informal*), company, contingent, crew (*informal*), crowd, drove, flock, gang, gathering, herd, horde, multitude, pack, posse (*informal*), squad, swarm, team, throng, unit **2 troops = soldiers**, armed forces, army, fighting men, men, military, servicemen, soldiery ♦ *verb* 3 = **flock**, crowd, march, parade, stream, swarm, throng, traipse (*informal*)

trophy *noun* = **prize**, award, bays, booty, cup, laurels, memento, souvenir, spoils

tropical *adjective* = **hot**, humid, steamy, stifling, sultry, sweltering, torrid
➤ **Antonyms**
arctic, chilly, cold, cool, freezing, frosty, frozen, parky (*Brit. informal*)

trot *verb* 1 = **run**, canter, go briskly, jog, lope, scamper ♦ *noun* 2 = **run**, brisk pace, canter, jog, lope **3 on the trot** *Informal* = **one after the other**, consecutively, in a row, in succession, without break, without interruption

trot out *verb Informal* = **repeat**, bring forward, bring up, come out with, drag up, recite, reiterate

troubadour *noun* = **minstrel**, balladeer, poet, singer

trouble *noun* 1 = **distress**, agitation, annoyance, anxiety, bummer (*slang*), disquiet, grief, hardship, hassle (*informal*), heartache, irritation, misfortune, pain, sorrow, suffering, torment, tribulation, vexation, woe, worry **2 = ailment**, complaint, defect, disability, disease, disorder, failure, illness, malfunction, upset **3 = disorder**, agitation, bother (*informal*), commotion, discontent, discord, dissatisfaction, disturbance, hassle (*informal*), row, strife, tumult, unrest **4 = effort**, attention, bother, care, exertion, inconvenience, labour, pains, struggle, thought, work **5 = difficulty**, bother, concern, danger, deep water (*informal*), dilemma, dire straits, hassle (*informal*), hot water (*informal*), mess, nuisance, pest, pickle (*informal*), predicament, problem, scrape (*informal*), spot (*informal*), tight spot ♦ *verb* 6 = **bother**, afflict, agitate, annoy, discompose, disconcert, disquiet, distress, disturb, faze, harass, hassle (*informal*), pain, perplex, perturb, pester, plague, sadden, torment, upset, vex, worry **7 = take pains**, exert oneself, go to the effort of, make an effort, take the time **8 = inconvenience**, bother, burden, discommode, disturb, impose upon,

incommode, put out
➤ **Antonyms**
noun ≠**distress**: comfort, contentment, good fortune, happiness, pleasure, tranquillity ≠**disorder**: agreement, contentment, harmony, peace, tranquillity, unity ≠**effort**: convenience, ease, facility ♦ *verb* ≠**bother**: appease, calm, mollify, please, relieve, soothe ≠**take pains**: avoid, dodge ≠**inconvenience**: relieve

troublemaker *noun* = **mischief-maker**, *agent provocateur*, agitator, bad apple (*U.S. informal*), firebrand, incendiary, instigator, meddler, rabble-rouser, rotten apple (*Brit. informal*), stirrer (*informal*)
➤ **Antonyms**
appeaser, arbitrator, conciliator, pacifier, peace-maker

troublesome *adjective* 1 = **bothersome**, annoying, arduous, burdensome, demanding, difficult, harassing, hard, importunate, inconvenient, irksome, irritating, laborious, taxing, tiresome, tricky, trying, upsetting, vexatious, wearisome, worrisome, worrying **2 = disorderly**, insubordinate, rebellious, recalcitrant, refractory, rowdy, turbulent, uncooperative, undisciplined, unruly, violent
➤ **Antonyms**
≠**bothersome**: agreeable, calming, congenial, easy, pleasant, simple, soothing, undemanding ≠**disorderly**: disciplined, eager-to-please, obedient, well-behaved

trough *noun* 1 = **manger**, crib, water trough **2 = channel**, canal, depression, ditch, duct, flume, furrow, gully, gutter, trench, watercourse

trounce *verb* = **defeat heavily** *or* **utterly**, beat, beat (someone) hollow (*Brit. informal*), blow out of the water (*slang*), clobber (*slang*), crush, drub, give a hiding (*informal*), give a pasting (*slang*), hammer (*informal*), lick (*informal*), overwhelm, rout, run rings around (*informal*), slaughter (*informal*), tank (*slang*), thrash, wipe the floor with (*informal*)

troupe *noun* = **company**, band, cast

trouper *noun* = **performer**, actor, artiste, entertainer, player, thespian

truancy *noun* = **absence**, absence without leave, malingering, shirking, skiving (*Brit. slang*)

truant *noun* 1 = **absentee**, delinquent, deserter, dodger, malingerer, runaway, shirker, skiver (*Brit. slang*) ♦ *adjective* 2 = **absent**, absent without leave, A.W.O.L., missing, skiving (*Brit. slang*)

truce noun = **ceasefire**, armistice, break, cessation, cessation of hostilities, let-up (informal), lull, moratorium, peace, respite, stay, treaty

truckle verb = **give in**, fawn, give way, knuckle under, kowtow, lick (someone's) boots, pander to, submit, toady, yield

truculent adjective = **hostile**, aggressive, antagonistic, bad-tempered, bellicose, belligerent, combative, contentious, cross, defiant, fierce, ill-tempered, obstreperous, pugnacious, sullen
➤ **Antonyms**
agreeable, amiable, civil, co-operative, gentle, good-natured, peaceable, placid

trudge verb **1** = **plod**, clump, drag oneself, footslog, hike, lumber, march, slog, stump, traipse (informal), tramp, trek, walk heavily ♦ noun **2** = **tramp**, footslog, haul, hike, march, slog, traipse (informal), trek

true adjective **1** = **correct**, accurate, actual, authentic, bona fide, exact, factual, genuine, legitimate, natural, precise, pure, real, right, truthful, valid, veracious, veritable **2** = **faithful**, constant, dedicated, devoted, dutiful, fast, firm, loyal, reliable, sincere, staunch, steady, true-blue, trustworthy, trusty **3** = **exact**, accurate, correct, on target, perfect, precise, proper, spot-on (Brit. informal), unerring **4 come true** = **happen**, become reality, be granted, be realized, come to pass, occur ♦ adverb **5** = **truthfully**, honestly, rightly, veraciously, veritably
➤ **Antonyms**
adjective ≠correct: abnormal, artificial, atypical, bogus, counterfeit, erroneous, fake, false, fictional, fictitious, illegitimate, imaginary, inaccurate, incorrect, made-up, make-believe, phoney or phony (informal), pretended, self-styled, spurious, unofficial, untrue, untruthful ≠faithful: deceitful, disloyal, faithless, false, treacherous, unreliable, untrue, untrustworthy ≠exact: askew, awry, inaccurate, incorrect

true-blue adjective = **staunch**, confirmed, constant, dedicated, devoted, dyed-in-the-wool, faithful, loyal, trusty, uncompromising, unwavering

truism noun = **cliché**, axiom, bromide, commonplace, platitude, stock phrase, trite saying

truly adverb **1** = **correctly**, accurately, authentically, beyond doubt, beyond question, exactly, factually, genuinely, in actuality, in fact, in reality, in truth, legitimately, precisely, really, rightly, truthfully, veraciously, veritably, without a doubt **2** = **faithfully**, confirmedly, constantly, devotedly, dutifully, firmly,

loyally, sincerely, staunchly, steadily, with all one's heart, with dedication, with devotion **3** = **really**, exceptionally, extremely, greatly, indeed, of course, seriously (informal), to be sure, verily, very
➤ **Antonyms**
≠correctly: doubtfully, falsely, fraudulently, inaccurately, incorrectly, mistakenly

trump noun, verb **1** = **ruff** ♦ verb **2** = **outdo**, cap, excel, surpass, top

trumped up adjective = **invented**, concocted, contrived, cooked-up (informal), fabricated, fake, false, falsified, made-up, manufactured, phoney or phony (informal), untrue
➤ **Antonyms**
actual, authentic, bona fide, genuine, real, sound, true, veritable

trumpery noun = **trifle**, bagatelle, bauble, gewgaw, knick-knack, toy, trinket

trumpet noun **1** = **horn**, bugle, clarion **2** = **roar**, bay, bellow, call, cry **3 blow one's own trumpet** = **boast**, brag, crow, sing one's own praises ♦ verb **4** = **proclaim**, advertise, announce, broadcast, crack up (informal), extol, publish, shout from the rooftops, tout (informal)
➤ **Antonyms**
verb ≠proclaim: conceal, hide, hush up, keep secret, make light of, play down, soft pedal (informal)

trump up verb = **invent**, concoct, contrive, cook up (informal), create, fabricate, fake, make up, manufacture

truncate verb = **shorten**, abbreviate, clip, crop, curtail, cut, cut short, dock, lop, pare, prune, trim
➤ **Antonyms**
drag out, draw out, extend, lengthen, prolong, protract, spin out, stretch

truncheon noun Chiefly Brit. = **club**, baton, cudgel, staff

trunk noun **1** = **stem**, bole, stalk, stock **2** = **chest**, bin, box, case, casket, coffer, crate, portmanteau **3** = **body**, torso **4** = **snout**, proboscis

truss verb **1** = **tie**, bind, fasten, make fast, pack, secure, strap, tether ♦ noun **2** Medical = **support**, bandage **3** = **joist**, beam, brace, buttress, prop, shore, stanchion, stay, strut, support

trust verb **1** = **believe in**, bank on, count on, depend on, have faith in, lean on, pin one's faith on, place confidence in, place one's trust in, place reliance on, rely upon, swear by, take as gospel, take at face value **2** = **entrust**, assign, command, commit, confide, consign, delegate, give, put into the hands of, sign over, turn over **3**

= **expect**, assume, believe, hope, presume, suppose, surmise, think likely ♦ *noun* **4** = **confidence**, assurance, belief, certainty, certitude, conviction, credence, credit, expectation, faith, hope, reliance **5** = **responsibility**, duty, obligation **6** = **custody**, care, charge, guard, guardianship, protection, safekeeping, trusteeship
➤ **Antonyms**
verb ≠**believe in**: be sceptical of, beware, disbelieve, discredit, distrust, doubt, lack confidence in, lack faith in, mistrust, suspect ♦ *noun* ≠**confidence**: distrust, doubt, fear, incredulity, lack of faith, mistrust, scepticism, suspicion, uncertainty, wariness

trustful, trusting *adjective* = **unsuspecting**, confiding, credulous, gullible, innocent, naive, optimistic, simple, unguarded, unsuspicious, unwary
➤ **Antonyms**
cagey (*informal*), cautious, chary, distrustful, guarded, on one's guard, suspicious, wary

trustworthy *adjective* = **dependable**, ethical, honest, honourable, principled, reliable, reputable, responsible, staunch, steadfast, to be trusted, true, trusty, truthful, upright
➤ **Antonyms**
deceitful, dishonest, disloyal, irresponsible, treacherous, undependable, unethical, unprincipled, unreliable, untrustworthy

trusty *adjective* = **reliable**, dependable, faithful, solid, staunch, steady, strong, true, trustworthy
➤ **Antonyms**
dishonest, irresolute, irresponsible, undependable, unfaithful, unreliable

truth *noun* **1** = **truthfulness**, accuracy, actuality, exactness, fact, factuality, factualness, genuineness, legitimacy, precision, reality, validity, veracity, verity **2** = **fact**, axiom, certainty, law, maxim, proven principle, reality, truism, verity
➤ **Antonyms**
≠**truthfulness**: error, falsity, inaccuracy ≠**fact**: delusion, fabrication, falsehood, fiction, invention, legend, lie, make-believe, myth, old wives' tale, untruth

truthful *adjective* **1** = **honest**, candid, faithful, forthright, frank, plain-spoken, reliable, sincere, straight, straightforward, true, trustworthy, upfront (*informal*), veracious **2** = **true**, accurate, correct, exact, literal, naturalistic, precise, realistic, veritable
➤ **Antonyms**

≠**honest**: deceptive, dishonest, false, insincere, lying, untruthful ≠**true**: fabricated, false, fictional, fictitious, inaccurate, incorrect, made-up, untrue, untruthful

try *verb* **1** = **attempt**, aim, bend over backwards (*informal*), break one's neck (*informal*), do one's best, do one's damnedest (*informal*), endeavour, essay, exert oneself, give it one's all (*informal*), give it one's best shot (*informal*), go for it (*informal*), have a crack (*informal*), have a go, have a shot (*informal*), have a stab (*informal*), have a whack (*informal*), knock oneself out (*informal*), make an all-out effort (*informal*), make an attempt, make an effort, move heaven and earth, seek, strive, struggle, undertake **2** = **test**, appraise, check out, evaluate, examine, experiment, inspect, investigate, prove, put to the test, sample, taste **3** = **strain**, afflict, annoy, irk, irritate, pain, plague, stress, tax, tire, trouble, upset, vex, weary **4** = **judge**, adjudge, adjudicate, examine, hear ♦ *noun* **5** = **attempt**, crack (*informal*), effort, endeavour, essay, go (*informal*), shot (*informal*), stab (*informal*), whack (*informal*)

trying *adjective* = **annoying**, aggravating (*informal*), arduous, bothersome, difficult, exasperating, hard, irksome, irritating, stressful, taxing, tiresome, tough, troublesome, upsetting, vexing, wearisome
➤ **Antonyms**
calming, easy, no bother, no trouble, painless, simple, straightforward, undemanding

try out *verb* = **test**, appraise, check out, evaluate, experiment with, inspect, put into practice, put to the test, sample, taste

tubby *adjective* = **fat**, chubby, corpulent, obese, overweight, plump, portly, stout

tuck *verb* **1** = **push**, fold, gather, insert ♦ *noun* **2** = **fold**, gather, pinch, pleat **3** *Brit. informal* = **food**, comestibles, eats (*slang*), grub (*slang*), nosh (*slang*), scoff (*slang*), tack (*informal*), victuals, vittles (*obsolete or dialect*)

tuck in *verb* **1** = **make snug**, bed down, enfold, fold under, put to bed, swaddle, wrap up **2** *Informal* = **eat up**, chow down (*slang*), eat heartily, fall to, get stuck in (*informal*)

tuft *noun* = **clump**, bunch, cluster, collection, knot, tussock

tug *verb* **1** = **pull**, drag, draw, haul, heave, jerk, lug, tow, wrench, yank ♦ *noun* **2** = **pull**, drag, haul, heave, jerk, tow, traction, wrench, yank

tuition noun = **training**, education, instruction, lessons, schooling, teaching, tutelage, tutoring

tumble verb 1 = **fall**, drop, fall headlong, flop, pitch, plummet, roll, stumble, topple, toss, trip up ♦ noun 2 = **fall**, collapse, drop, flop, headlong fall, plunge, roll, spill, stumble, toss, trip

tumbledown adjective = **dilapidated**, crumbling, decrepit, disintegrating, falling to pieces, ramshackle, rickety, ruined, shaky, tottering
➤ Antonyms
durable, firm, solid, sound, stable, sturdy, substantial, well-kept

tumid adjective 1 = **swollen**, bloated, bulging, distended, enlarged, inflated, protuberant, puffed up, puffy, tumescent 2 = **pompous**, arty-farty (informal), bombastic, flowery, fulsome, grandiloquent, grandiose, high-flown, inflated, magniloquent, pretentious

tummy noun Informal = **stomach**, abdomen, belly, gut (informal), inside(s) (informal), paunch, pot, potbelly, spare tyre (informal), tum (informal)

tumour noun = **growth**, cancer, carcinoma (Pathology), lump, sarcoma (Medical), swelling

tumult noun = **commotion**, ado, affray (Law), agitation, altercation, bedlam, brawl, brouhaha, clamour, din, disorder, disturbance, excitement, fracas, hubbub, hullabaloo, outbreak, pandemonium, quarrel, racket, riot, row, ruction (informal), stir, stramash (Scot.), strife, turmoil, unrest, upheaval, uproar
➤ Antonyms
calm, hush, peace, quiet, repose, serenity, silence, stillness

tumultuous adjective 1 = **turbulent**, agitated, confused, disturbed, exciting, hectic, stormy 2 = **wild**, boisterous, clamorous, disorderly, excited, noisy, raging, riotous, rowdy, unrestrained, unruly, uproarious, violent
➤ Antonyms
calm, hushed, peaceful, quiet, restful, serene, still, tranquil

tune noun 1 = **melody**, air, melody line, motif, song, strain, theme 2 = **concord**, agreement, concert, consonance, euphony, harmony, pitch, unison 3 **call the tune** = **be in control**, be in charge, be in command, call the shots (slang), command, dictate, govern, lead, rule 4 **change one's tune** = **change one's attitude**, change one's mind, do an about-face, have a change of heart, reconsider, take a different tack, think

again ♦ verb 5 = **adjust**, adapt, attune, bring into harmony, harmonize, pitch, regulate
➤ Antonyms
noun ≠concord: clashing, conflict, contention, disagreement, discord, discordance, disharmony, disunity, friction

tuneful adjective = **melodious**, catchy, easy on the ear (informal), euphonic, euphonious, harmonious, mellifluous, melodic, musical, pleasant
➤ Antonyms
cacophonous, clashing, discordant, dissonant, harsh, jangly, tuneless, unmelodious

tuneless adjective = **discordant**, atonal, cacophonous, clashing, dissonant, harsh, unmelodic, unmelodious, unmusical
➤ Antonyms
harmonious, melodious, musical, pleasing, sonorous, symphonic, tuneful

tunnel noun 1 = **passage**, burrow, channel, hole, passageway, shaft, subway, underpass ♦ verb 2 = **dig**, burrow, dig one's way, excavate, mine, penetrate, scoop out

turbid adjective Literary = **murky**, clouded, cloudy, dim, muddy, opaque, unclear, unsettled

turbulence noun = **confusion**, agitation, commotion, disorder, instability, pandemonium, roughness, storm, tumult, turmoil, unrest, upheaval
➤ Antonyms
calm, peace, quiet, repose, rest, stillness

turbulent adjective 1 = **wild**, anarchic, boisterous, disorderly, lawless, mutinous, rebellious, refractory, rowdy, undisciplined, ungovernable, unruly, uproarious, violent 2 = **agitated**, blustery, choppy, confused, disordered, foaming, furious, raging, rough, tempestuous, tumultuous, unsettled, unstable
➤ Antonyms
≠agitated: calm, glassy, peaceful, quiet, smooth, still, unruffled

turf noun 1 = **grass**, clod, divot, green, sod, sward 2 **the turf** = **horse-racing**, racecourse, racetrack, racing, the flat

turf out verb Brit. informal = **throw out**, banish, cast out, chuck out (informal), discharge, dismiss, dispossess, eject, evict, expel, fire (informal), fling out, kick out (informal), show one the door

turgid adjective = **pompous**, arty-farty (informal), bombastic, flowery, fulsome, grandiloquent, grandiose, high-flown, inflated, magniloquent, overblown, pretentious, windy

turmoil noun = **confusion**, agitation,

bedlam, brouhaha, bustle, chaos, commotion, disarray, disorder, disturbance, ferment, flurry, hubbub, noise, pandemonium, row, stir, strife, trouble, tumult, turbulence, upheaval, uproar, violence
➤ **Antonyms**
calm, peace, quiet, repose, rest, serenity, stillness, tranquillity

turn verb **1 = change course**, change position, go back, move, return, reverse, shift, swerve, switch, veer, wheel **2 = rotate**, circle, go round, gyrate, move in a circle, pivot, revolve, roll, spin, swivel, twirl, twist, wheel, whirl **3 = go round**, arc, come round, corner, negotiate, pass, pass around, take a bend **4 = change**, adapt, alter, become, convert, divert, fashion, fit, form, metamorphose, mould, mutate, remodel, shape, transfigure, transform, transmute **5 = shape**, construct, execute, fashion, frame, make, mould, perform **6 = go bad**, become rancid, curdle, go off (Brit. informal), go sour, make rancid, sour, spoil, taint **7 = sicken**, nauseate, upset **8 turn to = appeal**, apply, approach, go, have recourse, look, resort ♦ noun **9 = rotation**, bend, change, circle, curve, cycle, gyration, pivot, reversal, revolution, spin, swing, turning, twist, whirl **10 = change of direction**, bend, change of course, curve, departure, deviation, shift **11 = opportunity**, chance, crack (informal), fling, go, period, round, shift, shot (informal), spell, stint, succession, time, try, whack (informal) **12 = direction**, drift, heading, tendency, trend **13 = excursion**, airing, constitutional, drive, jaunt, outing, promenade, ride, saunter, spin (informal), stroll, walk **14 = inclination**, affinity, bent, bias, leaning, propensity **15 = style**, cast, fashion, form, manner, mode, way **16** As in **good turn = act**, action, deed, favour, gesture, service **17 = twist**, bend, distortion, warp **18** Informal **= shock**, fright, scare, start, surprise **19 to a turn** Informal **= perfectly**, correctly, exactly, just right, precisely

turncoat noun **= traitor**, apostate, backslider, defector, deserter, renegade

turn down verb **1 = lower**, diminish, lessen, muffle, mute, quieten, reduce the volume of, soften **2 = refuse**, abstain from, decline, rebuff, reject, repudiate, say no to, spurn, throw out
➤ **Antonyms**
≠**lower**: amplify, augment, boost, increase, raise, strengthen, swell, turn up
≠**refuse**: accede, accept, acquiesce, agree, receive, take

turn in verb Informal **1 = go to bed**, go to

sleep, hit the hay (slang), hit the sack (slang), retire for the night **2 = hand in**, deliver, give back, give up, hand over, return, submit, surrender, tender

turning noun **= turn-off**, bend, crossroads, curve, junction, side road, turn

turning point noun **= crossroads**, change, crisis, critical moment, crux, decisive moment, moment of decision, moment of truth, point of no return

turn-off noun **= turning**, branch, exit, side road, turn

turn off verb **1 = branch off**, change direction, depart from, deviate, leave, quit, take another road, take a side road **2 = stop**, cut out, put out, shut down, switch off, turn out, unplug **3** Informal **= put off**, alienate, bore, disenchant, disgust, gross out (U.S. slang), lose one's interest, nauseate, offend, repel, sicken

turn on verb **1 = start**, activate, energize, ignite, kick-start, put on, set in motion, start up, switch on **2 = attack**, assail, assault, fall on, round on **3** Informal **= arouse**, arouse one's desire, attract, excite, please, stimulate, thrill, titillate, work up **4 = depend on**, balance on, be contingent on, be decided by, hang on, hinge on, pivot on, rest on
➤ **Antonyms**
≠**start**: cut out, put out, shut off, stop, switch off, turn off

turnout noun **1 = attendance**, assemblage, assembly, audience, congregation, crowd, gate, number, throng **2 = output**, amount produced, production, production quota, productivity, turnover, volume, yield

turn out verb **1 = turn off**, put out, switch off, unplug **2 = produce**, bring out, fabricate, finish, make, manufacture, process, put out **3 = expel**, banish, cast out, deport, discharge, dismiss, dispossess, drive out, evict, fire (informal), give one the sack (informal), kick out (informal), oust, put out, relegate, sack (informal), show one the door, throw out, turf out (Brit. informal), unseat **4 = empty**, clean out, clear, take out the contents of **5 = prove to be**, come to light, crop up (informal), develop, emerge, happen **6 = end up**, become, come about, come to be, eventuate, evolve, result, transpire (informal), work out **7 = dress**, accoutre, attire, clothe, fit, outfit, rig out **8 = come**, appear, assemble, attend, be present, gather, go, put in an appearance, show up (informal), turn up

turnover noun **1 = output**, business, flow, production, productivity, volume, yield **2 = movement**, change, coming and going, replacement

turn over *verb* **1** = **overturn**, capsize, flip over, keel over, reverse, tip over, upend, upset **2** = **consider**, contemplate, deliberate, give thought to, mull over, ponder, reflect on, revolve, ruminate about, think about, think over **3** = **hand over**, commend, commit, deliver, give over, give up, pass on, surrender, yield **4** = **start up**, activate, set going, set in motion, switch on, warm up

turn up *verb* **1** = **arrive**, appear, attend, come, put in an appearance, show (*informal*), show one's face, show up (*informal*) **2** = **find**, bring to light, come up with, dig up, disclose, discover, expose, reveal, unearth **3** = **come to light**, appear, become known, be found, come to pass, crop up (*informal*), pop up, transpire **4** = **increase**, amplify, boost, enhance, increase the volume of, intensify, make louder, raise

➤ **Antonyms**
≠**find**: hide ≠**come to light**: disappear, evaporate, fade, vanish ≠**increase**: diminish, lessen, lower, reduce, soften, turn down

turpitude *noun Formal* = **wickedness**, badness, baseness, corruption, criminality, degeneracy, depravity, evil, immorality, iniquity, sinfulness

tussle *noun* **1** = **fight**, battle, bout, brawl, competition, conflict, contention, contest, fracas, fray, punch-up (*Brit. informal*), scrap (*informal*), scrimmage, scuffle, set-to (*informal*), shindig (*informal*), shindy (*informal*), struggle ♦ *verb* **2** = **fight**, battle, brawl, contend, grapple, scrap (*informal*), scuffle, struggle, vie, wrestle

tutelage *noun Formal* = **guidance**, care, charge, custody, education, guardianship, instruction, schooling, teaching, tuition

tutor *noun* **1** = **teacher**, coach, educator, guardian, guide, guru, instructor, lecturer, master or mistress, mentor, schoolmaster or schoolmistress ♦ *verb* **2** = **teach**, coach, direct, drill, educate, guide, instruct, lecture, school, train

tutorial *noun* **1** = **seminar**, individual instruction, lesson ♦ *adjective* **2** = **teaching**, coaching, guiding, instructional

TV *noun* = **television**, gogglebox (*Brit. slang*), small screen (*informal*), television set, telly (*Brit. informal*), the box (*Brit. informal*), the tube (*slang*), TV set

twaddle *noun* **1** = **nonsense**, balderdash, balls (*taboo slang*), bilge (*informal*), bosh (*informal*), bullshit (*taboo slang*), bunkum or buncombe (*chiefly U.S.*), claptrap

(*informal*), cobblers (*Brit. taboo slang*), crap (*slang*), drivel, foolish talk, garbage (*informal*), gobbledegook (*informal*), guff (*slang*), hogwash, hot air (*informal*), moonshine, pants (*slang*), pap, piffle (*informal*), poppycock (*informal*), rot, rubbish, shit (*taboo slang*), tommyrot, tosh (*slang, chiefly Brit.*), trash, tripe (*informal*), verbiage, waffle (*informal, chiefly Brit.*)
♦ *verb* **2** = **talk nonsense**, gabble, prattle, rattle on, waffle (*informal, chiefly Brit.*)

tweak *verb, noun* = **twist**, jerk, nip, pinch, pull, squeeze, twitch

twee *adjective Informal* = **sweet**, bijou, cute, dainty, precious, pretty, quaint, sentimental

twiddle *verb* **1** = **fiddle** (*informal*), finger, jiggle, play with, twirl, wiggle **2 twiddle one's thumbs** = **be idle**, be unoccupied, do nothing, have nothing to do, mark time, sit around

twig[1] *noun* = **branch**, offshoot, shoot, spray, sprig, stick

twig[2] *verb Brit. informal* = **understand**, catch on (*informal*), comprehend, fathom, find out, get, grasp, see, tumble to (*informal*)

twilight *noun* **1** = **dusk**, dimness, evening, gloaming (*Scot. or poetic*), gloom, half-light, sundown, sunset **2** = **decline**, ebb, last phase ♦ *adjective* **3** = **evening**, crepuscular, darkening, dim **4** = **declining**, dying, ebbing, final, last

➤ **Antonyms**
noun ≠**dusk**: dawn, daybreak, morning, sunrise, sunup ≠**decline**: climax, crowning moment, height, peak

twin *noun* **1** = **double**, clone, counterpart, duplicate, fellow, likeness, lookalike, match, mate, ringer (*slang*) ♦ *verb* **2** = **pair**, couple, join, link, match, yoke

twine *noun* **1** = **string**, cord, yarn ♦ *verb* **2** = **twist together**, braid, entwine, interlace, interweave, knit, plait, splice, twist, weave **3** = **coil**, bend, curl, encircle, loop, spiral, twist, wind, wrap, wreathe

twinge *noun* = **pain**, bite, pang, pinch, prick, sharp pain, spasm, stab, stitch, throb, twist

twinkle *verb* **1** = **sparkle**, blink, coruscate, flash, flicker, gleam, glint, glisten, glitter, scintillate, shimmer, shine, wink ♦ *noun* **2** = **sparkle**, blink, coruscation, flash, flicker, gleam, glimmer, glistening, glittering, light, scintillation, shimmer, shine, spark, wink

twinkling *noun As in* **in the twinkling of an eye** = **moment**, flash, instant, jiffy (*informal*), second, shake (*informal*), split second, tick (*Brit. informal*), trice, twinkle

twirl *verb* 1 = **turn**, gyrate, pirouette, pivot, revolve, rotate, spin, turn on one's heel, twiddle, twist, wheel, whirl, wind ♦ *noun* 2 = **turn**, gyration, pirouette, revolution, rotation, spin, twist, wheel, whirl

twist *verb* 1 = **distort**, contort, screw up 2 = **wind**, coil, corkscrew, curl, encircle, entwine, intertwine, screw, spin, swivel, twine, weave, wrap, wreathe, wring 3 = **sprain**, rick, turn, wrench 4 = **misrepresent**, alter, change, distort, falsify, garble, misquote, pervert, warp 5 **twist someone's arm** = **force**, bully, coerce, persuade, pressurize, talk into ♦ *noun* 6 = **wind**, coil, curl, spin, swivel, twine 7 = **coil**, braid, curl, hank, roll 8 = **development**, change, revelation, slant, surprise, turn, variation 9 = **curve**, arc, bend, convolution, meander, turn, undulation, zigzag 10 = **distortion**, defect, deformation, flaw, imperfection, kink, warp 11 = **jerk**, pull, sprain, turn, wrench 12 **round the twist** *Brit. slang* = **mad**, barmy (*slang*), batty (*slang*), bonkers (*slang, chiefly Brit.*), crazy, cuckoo (*informal*), daft (*informal*), insane, loopy (*informal*), not all there, not right in the head, nuts (*slang*), nutty (*slang*), nutty as a fruitcake (*slang*), off one's rocker (*slang*), off one's trolley (*slang*), out to lunch (*informal*), up the pole (*informal*), wacko or whacko (*informal*)
► **Antonyms**
verb ≠**distort**: straighten, untwist ≠**wind**: straighten, uncoil, unravel, unroll, untwist, unwind

twister *noun Brit.* = **swindler**, cheat, chiseller (*informal*), con man (*informal*), crook (*informal*), deceiver, fraud, fraudster, grifter (*slang, chiefly U.S. & Canad.*), hustler (*U.S. informal*), rogue, trickster

twit[1] *verb* = **make fun of**, deride, jeer, poke fun at, scorn, taunt, tease

twit[2] *noun Informal, chiefly Brit.* = **fool**, airhead (*slang*), ass, berk (*Brit. slang*), blockhead, chump (*informal*), dickhead (*slang*), divvy (*Brit. slang*), dope (*informal*), dork (*slang*), dumb-ass (*slang*), dweeb (*U.S. slang*), geek (*slang*), gobshite (*Irish taboo slang*), halfwit, idiot, jerk (*slang, chiefly U.S. & Canad.*), nerd or nurd (*slang*), nincompoop, ninny, nitwit (*informal*), numbskull or numskull, numpty (*Scot. informal*), oaf, pillock (*Brit. slang*), plonker (*slang*), prat (*slang*), prick (*slang*), schmuck (*U.S. slang*), simpleton, twerp or twirp (*informal*), wally

twitch *verb* 1 = **jerk**, flutter, jump, squirm 2 = **pull**, pluck, snatch, tug, yank ♦ *noun* 3

= **jerk**, flutter, jump, spasm, tic, tremor, twinge

twitter *verb* 1 = **chirrup**, chatter, cheep, chirp, trill, tweet, warble, whistle 2 = **chatter**, prattle ♦ *noun* 3 = **chirrup**, call, chatter, cheep, chirp, cry, song, trill, tweet, warble, whistle 4 *As in* **in a twitter** = **nervousness**, agitation, anxiety, bustle, dither (*chiefly Brit.*), excitement, flurry, fluster, flutter, tizzy (*informal*), whirl

two-edged *adjective* = **ambiguous**, ambivalent, backhanded, double-edged, equivocal

two-faced *adjective* = **hypocritical**, deceitful, deceiving, dissembling, double-dealing, duplicitous, false, insincere, perfidious, treacherous, untrustworthy
► **Antonyms**
artless, candid, frank, genuine, honest, ingenuous, sincere, trustworthy

tycoon *noun* = **magnate**, baron, big cheese (*slang, old-fashioned*), big noise (*informal*), capitalist, captain of industry, fat cat (*slang, chiefly U.S.*), financier, industrialist, merchant prince, mogul, plutocrat, potentate, wealthy businessman

type *noun* 1 = **kind**, breed, category, class, classification, form, genre, group, ilk, order, sort, species, stamp, strain, style, subdivision, variety 2 = **print**, case, characters, face, font, fount, printing

typhoon *noun* = **storm**, cyclone, squall, tempest, tornado, tropical storm

typical *adjective* = **characteristic**, archetypal, average, bog-standard (*Brit. & Irish slang*), classic, conventional, essential, illustrative, in character, indicative, in keeping, model, normal, orthodox, representative, standard, stock, true to type, usual
► **Antonyms**
atypical, exceptional, out of keeping, out of the ordinary, singular, uncharacteristic, unconventional, unexpected, unique, unrepresentative, unusual

typify *verb* = **represent**, characterize, embody, epitomize, exemplify, illustrate, incarnate, personify, sum up, symbolize

tyrannical *adjective* = **oppressive**, absolute, arbitrary, authoritarian, autocratic, cruel, despotic, dictatorial, domineering, high-handed, imperious, overbearing, severe, tyrannous
► **Antonyms**
democratic, easy-going, lax, lenient, liberal, reasonable, tolerant, understanding

tyrannize *verb* = **oppress**, browbeat, bully, domineer, enslave, intimidate, subjugate, terrorize

tyranny *noun* = **oppression**, absolutism, authoritarianism, autocracy, cruelty, despotism, dictatorship, high-handedness, imperiousness
➤ **Antonyms**
democracy, liberality, tolerance

tyrant *noun* = **dictator**, absolutist, authoritarian, autocrat, bully, despot, Hitler, martinet, oppressor, slave-driver

tyro *noun* = **beginner**, apprentice, greenhorn (*informal*), initiate, learner, neophyte, novice, novitiate, pupil, student, trainee

U u

ubiquitous *adjective* = **everywhere**, all-over, ever-present, omnipresent, pervasive, universal

ugly *adjective* **1** = **unattractive**, homely (*chiefly U.S.*), ill-favoured, no oil painting (*informal*), not much to look at, plain, unlovely, unprepossessing, unsightly **2** = **unpleasant**, disagreeable, disgusting, distasteful, frightful, hideous, horrid, monstrous, objectionable, repugnant, repulsive, revolting, shocking, terrible, vile **3** = **ominous**, baleful, bodeful, dangerous, forbidding, menacing, sinister, threatening **4** = **bad-tempered**, angry, dark, evil, malevolent, nasty, spiteful, sullen, surly
➤ **Antonyms**
≠**unattractive**: attractive, beautiful, cute, good-looking, gorgeous, handsome, lovely, pretty ≠**unpleasant**: agreeable, pleasant ≠**ominous**: auspicious, promising ≠**bad-tempered**: good-humoured, good-natured

ulcer *noun* = **sore**, abscess, boil, fester, gathering, gumboil, peptic ulcer, pustule

ulcerous *adjective* = **festering**, cankerous, ulcerative

ulterior *adjective* = **hidden**, concealed, covert, personal, secondary, secret, selfish, undisclosed, unexpressed
➤ **Antonyms**
apparent, declared, manifest, obvious, overt, plain

ultimate *adjective* **1** = **final**, conclusive, decisive, end, eventual, extreme, furthest, last, terminal **2** = **supreme**, extreme, greatest, highest, maximum, most significant, paramount, superlative, topmost, utmost **3** = **fundamental**, basic, elemental, primary, radical ♦ *noun* **4** *As in* **the ultimate in** = **epitome**, culmination, extreme, greatest, height, mother of all (*informal*), peak, perfection, summit, the last word

ultimately *adverb* **1** = **finally**, after all, at last, at the end of the day, eventually, in due time, in the end, in the fullness of time, sooner or later **2** = **fundamentally**, basically

ultra- *prefix* = **extremely**, excessively, fanatically, immoderately, radically

ultramodern *adjective* = **advanced**, ahead of its time, avant-garde, futuristic, modernistic, progressive, way-out (*informal*)

ululate *verb* = **howl**, bawl, cry, keen, lament, wail, yowl

umbrage *noun* *As in* **take umbrage** = **offence**, anger, chagrin, displeasure, grudge, high dudgeon, huff, indignation, pique, resentment, sense of injury
➤ **Antonyms**
amity, cordiality, goodwill, harmony

umbrella *noun* **1** = **brolly** (*Brit. informal*), gamp (*Brit. informal*) **2** = **cover**, aegis, patronage, protection

umpire *noun* **1** = **referee**, adjudicator, arbiter, arbitrator, judge, ref (*informal*)
♦ *verb* **2** = **referee**, adjudicate, arbitrate, call (*Sport*), judge, mediate

umpteen *adjective* *Informal* = **very many**, a good many, considerable, countless, ever so many, millions, n, numerous

unabashed *adjective* = **unembarrassed**, blatant, bold, brazen, confident, unconcerned, undaunted, undismayed
➤ **Antonyms**
abashed, embarrassed, humbled, mortified, shamefaced, sheepish

unable *adjective* = **incapable**, impotent, inadequate, ineffectual, no good, not able, not equal to, not up to, powerless, unfit, unfitted, unqualified
➤ **Antonyms**
able, adept, adequate, capable, competent, effective, powerful

unabridged *adjective* = **uncut**, complete, full-length, uncondensed, unexpurgated, unshortened, whole

unacceptable *adjective* = **unsatisfactory**, beyond the pale, disagreeable, displeasing, distasteful, improper, inadmissible, insupportable, objectionable, offensive, unpleasant
➤ **Antonyms**
acceptable, agreeable, delightful, pleasant, pleasing

unaccompanied *adjective* **1** = **alone**, by oneself, lone, on one's own, solo, unescorted **2** *Music* = **a cappella**

unaccountable *adjective* **1** = **inexplicable**, baffling, incomprehensible, mysterious, odd, peculiar, puzzling, strange, unexplainable, unfathomable,

unintelligible 2 = **not answerable**, clear, exempt, free, not responsible, unliable
➤ **Antonyms**
≠**inexplicable**: accountable, comprehensible, explicable, intelligible, understandable

unaccounted-for *adjective* = **missing**, lost, not explained, unexplained

unaccustomed *adjective* 1 = **unfamiliar**, new, out of the ordinary, remarkable, special, strange, surprising, uncommon, unexpected, unprecedented, unusual, unwonted 2 **unaccustomed to** = **not used to**, a newcomer to, a novice at, inexperienced at, not given to, unfamiliar with, unpractised in, unused to, unversed in
➤ **Antonyms**
≠**unfamiliar**: accustomed, familiar, ordinary, regular, usual ≠**not used to**: experienced at, given to, practised in, used to, well-versed in

unadorned *adjective* = **plain**, restrained, severe, simple, stark, straightforward, unembellished, unfussy, unornamented

unadventurous *adjective* = **cautious**, cagey (*informal*), careful, chary, hesitant, prudent, safe, stay-at-home, tentative, timid, timorous, unenterprising, wary
➤ **Antonyms**
adventurous, audacious, bold, daredevil, daring, enterprising, intrepid

unaffected¹ *adjective* = **natural**, artless, genuine, honest, ingenuous, naive, plain, simple, sincere, straightforward, unassuming, unpretentious, unsophisticated, unspoilt, unstudied, without airs
➤ **Antonyms**
affected, assumed, designing, devious, insincere, mannered, pretentious, put-on, snobbish, sophisticated

unaffected² *adjective* = **impervious**, aloof, not influenced, proof, unaltered, unchanged, unimpressed, unmoved, unresponsive, untouched
➤ **Antonyms**
affected, changed, concerned, disrupted, hard-hit, influenced, interested, responsive, sympathetic, touched

unafraid *adjective* = **fearless**, confident, daring, dauntless, intrepid, unfearing, unshakable
➤ **Antonyms**
afraid, alarmed, anxious, fearful, frightened, scared

unalterable *adjective* = **unchangeable**, fixed, immovable, immutable, invariable, permanent, steadfast, unchanging
➤ **Antonyms**

alterable, changeable, changing, flexible, mutable, variable

unanimity *noun* = **agreement**, accord, assent, chorus, concert, concord, concurrence, consensus, harmony, like-mindedness, one mind, unison, unity
➤ **Antonyms**
difference, disagreement, discord, disunity, division, variance

unanimous *adjective* = **agreed**, agreeing, at one, common, concerted, concordant, harmonious, in agreement, in complete accord, like-minded, of one mind, united
➤ **Antonyms**
differing, discordant, dissident, disunited, divided, schismatic, split

unanimously *adverb* = **without exception**, by common consent, nem. con., unitedly, unopposed, with one accord, without opposition

unanswerable *adjective* 1 = **insoluble**, insolvable, unascertainable, unexplainable, unresolvable 2 = **conclusive**, absolute, incontestable, incontrovertible, indisputable, irrefutable, unarguable, undeniable

unanswered *adjective* = **unresolved**, disputed, in doubt, open, undecided, unsettled, up in the air

unappetizing *adjective* = **unpleasant**, disgusting, distasteful, insipid, off-putting (*Brit. informal*), repulsive, tasteless, unappealing, unattractive, uninteresting, uninviting, unpalatable, unsavoury
➤ **Antonyms**
agreeable, appealing, appetizing, attractive, delicious, interesting, inviting, mouthwatering, palatable, savoury, scrumptious (*informal*), succulent, tasty, tempting, toothsome

unapproachable *adjective* 1 = **unfriendly**, aloof, chilly, cool, distant, frigid, remote, reserved, standoffish, unsociable, withdrawn 2 = **inaccessible**, out of reach, out-of-the-way, remote, un-get-at-able (*informal*), unreachable
➤ **Antonyms**
≠**unfriendly**: affable, approachable, congenial, cordial, friendly, sociable

unarmed *adjective* = **defenceless**, assailable, exposed, helpless, open, open to attack, unarmoured, unprotected, weak, weaponless
➤ **Antonyms**
armed, equipped, fortified, protected, ready, strengthened

unasked *adverb* = **voluntarily**, off one's own bat, of one's own accord, without prompting

unassailable *adjective* = **impregnable**,

invincible, invulnerable, secure, well-defended

unassuming *adjective* = **modest**, diffident, humble, meek, quiet, reserved, retiring, self-effacing, simple, unassertive, unobtrusive, unostentatious, unpretentious
➤ **Antonyms**
assuming, audacious, conceited, ostentatious, overconfident, presumptuous, pretentious

unattached *adjective* **1** = **free**, autonomous, independent, nonaligned, unaffiliated, uncommitted **2** = **single**, a free agent, available, by oneself, footloose and fancy-free, left on the shelf, not spoken for, on one's own, unengaged, unmarried
➤ **Antonyms**
≠**free**: affiliated, aligned, attached, committed, dependent, implicated, involved

unattended *adjective* **1** = **abandoned**, disregarded, ignored, left alone, not cared for, unguarded, unwatched **2** = **alone**, on one's own, unaccompanied, unescorted

unauthorized *adjective* = **illegal**, off the record, unapproved, unconstitutional, under-the-table, unlawful, unofficial, unsanctioned, unwarranted
➤ **Antonyms**
authorized, constitutional, lawful, legal, official, sanctioned, warranted

unavoidable *adjective* = **inevitable**, bound to happen, certain, compulsory, fated, inescapable, inexorable, necessary, obligatory, sure

unaware *adjective* = **ignorant**, heedless, not in the loop (*informal*), oblivious, unconscious, unenlightened, uninformed, unknowing, unmindful, unsuspecting
➤ **Antonyms**
attentive, aware, conscious, informed, in the loop (*informal*), knowing, mindful

unawares *adverb* **1** = **by surprise**, aback, off guard, on the hop (*Brit. informal*), suddenly, unexpectedly, unprepared, without warning **2** = **unknowingly**, accidentally, by accident, by mistake, inadvertently, mistakenly, unconsciously, unintentionally, unwittingly
➤ **Antonyms**
≠**by surprise**: forewarned, on the lookout, prepared ≠**unknowingly**: deliberately, knowingly, on purpose, wittingly

unbalanced *adjective* **1** = **shaky**, asymmetrical, irregular, lopsided, not balanced, unequal, uneven, unstable, unsymmetrical, wobbly **2** = **biased**, inequitable, one-sided, partial, partisan, prejudiced, unfair, unjust **3** = **deranged**, barking mad (*slang*), crazy, demented, disturbed, eccentric, erratic, insane, irrational, loopy (*informal*), lunatic, mad, *non compos mentis,* not all there, not the full shilling (*informal*), off one's trolley (*slang*), out to lunch (*informal*), touched, unhinged, unsound, unstable, wacko *or* whacko (*informal*)
➤ **Antonyms**
≠**shaky**: balanced, equal, even, stable, symmetrical

unbearable *adjective* = **intolerable**, insufferable, insupportable, oppressive, too much (*informal*), unacceptable, unendurable
➤ **Antonyms**
acceptable, bearable, endurable, supportable, tolerable

unbeatable *adjective* = **invincible**, indomitable, unconquerable, unstoppable, unsurpassable

unbeaten *adjective* = **undefeated**, triumphant, unbowed, unsubdued, unsurpassed, unvanquished, victorious, winning

unbecoming *adjective* **1** = **unattractive**, ill-suited, inappropriate, unbefitting, unfit, unflattering, unsightly, unsuitable, unsuited **2** = **unseemly**, discreditable, improper, indecorous, indelicate, offensive, tasteless
➤ **Antonyms**
≠**unseemly**: becoming, decent, decorous, delicate, proper, seemly

unbelievable *adjective* **1** = **incredible**, astonishing, beyond belief, cock-and-bull (*informal*), far-fetched, implausible, impossible, improbable, inconceivable, jaw-dropping, outlandish, preposterous, staggering, unconvincing, unimaginable, unthinkable **2** = **wonderful**, awesome (*slang*), bad (*slang*), bodacious (*slang, chiefly U.S.*), boffo (*slang*), brill (*informal*), chillin' (*U.S. slang*), colossal, cracking (*Brit. informal*), crucial (*slang*), def (*slang*), divine (*informal*), excellent, fabulous (*informal*), fantastic (*informal*), glorious, great (*informal*), jim-dandy (*slang*), magnificent, mean (*slang*), mega (*slang*), sensational (*informal*), smashing (*informal*), sovereign, splendid, stupendous, super (*informal*), superb, terrific (*informal*), topping (*Brit. slang*), wicked (*informal*)
➤ **Antonyms**
≠**incredible**: authentic, believable, credible, likely, plausible, possible, probable, trustworthy ≠**wonderful**: awful, bad, terrible

unbeliever *noun* = **atheist**, agnostic, disbeliever, doubting Thomas, infidel, sceptic

unbend *verb* = **relax**, be informal, calm down, chill out (*slang, chiefly U.S.*), cool it (*slang*), ease up, let oneself go, lighten up (*slang*), loosen up, slacken, slow down, take it easy, unwind

unbending *adjective* = **inflexible**, firm, intractable, resolute, rigid, severe, strict, stubborn, tough, uncompromising, unyielding

unbiased *adjective* = **fair**, disinterested, dispassionate, equitable, even-handed, impartial, just, neutral, objective, open-minded, unprejudiced
➤ **Antonyms**
biased, bigoted, partial, prejudiced, slanted, swayed, unfair, unjust

unbidden *adjective* 1 = **uninvited**, unasked, unwanted, unwelcome 2 = **voluntary**, free, spontaneous, unforced, unprompted, willing

unbind *verb* = **free**, loosen, release, set free, unbridle, unchain, unclasp, undo, unfasten, unfetter, unloose, unshackle, unstrap, untie, unyoke
➤ **Antonyms**
bind, chain, fasten, fetter, restrain, shackle, tie, yoke

unblemished *adjective* = **spotless**, flawless, immaculate, impeccable, perfect, pure, unflawed, unspotted, unstained, unsullied, untarnished
➤ **Antonyms**
blemished, flawed, imperfect, impure, stained, sullied, tarnished

unblushing *adjective* = **shameless**, bold, brazen, forward, immodest, unabashed, unashamed, unembarrassed

unborn *adjective* = **expected**, awaited, embryonic, *in utero*

unbosom *verb* = **confide**, admit, confess, disclose, divulge, get (something) off one's chest (*informal*), get (something) out of one's system, let out, reveal, tell, unburden
➤ **Antonyms**
conceal, cover up, guard, hold back, suppress, withhold

unbounded *adjective* = **unlimited**, absolute, boundless, endless, immeasurable, infinite, limitless, unbridled, unchecked, unconstrained, uncontrolled, unrestrained, vast
➤ **Antonyms**
bounded, confined, constrained, curbed, limited, restricted

unbreakable *adjective* = **indestructible**, durable, lasting, nonbreakable, resistant, rugged, shatterproof, solid, strong, toughened
➤ **Antonyms**
breakable, brittle, delicate, flimsy, fragile

unbridled *adjective* = **unrestrained**, excessive, full-on (*informal*), intemperate, licentious, rampant, riotous, unchecked, unconstrained, uncontrolled, uncurbed, ungoverned, unruly, violent, wanton

unbroken *adjective* 1 = **intact**, complete, entire, solid, total, unimpaired, whole 2 = **continuous**, ceaseless, constant, endless, incessant, progressive, successive, uninterrupted, unremitting 3 = **undisturbed**, deep, fast, profound, sound, untroubled 4 = **untamed**, unsubdued
➤ **Antonyms**
≠**intact**: broken, cracked, damaged, fragmented, in pieces, shattered
≠**continuous**: erratic, fitful, intermittent, interrupted, irregular, occasional, off-and-on, uneven

unburden *verb* = **confess**, come clean (*informal*), confide, disclose, get (something) off one's chest (*informal*), lay bare, make a clean breast of, reveal, tell all, unbosom

uncalled-for *adjective* = **unnecessary**, gratuitous, inappropriate, needless, undeserved, unjust, unjustified, unprovoked, unwarranted, unwelcome
➤ **Antonyms**
appropriate, deserved, just, justified, necessary, needed, provoked, warranted

uncanny *adjective* 1 = **weird**, creepy (*informal*), eerie, eldritch (*poetic*), mysterious, preternatural, queer, spooky (*informal*), strange, supernatural, unearthly, unnatural 2 = **extraordinary**, astonishing, astounding, exceptional, fantastic, incredible, miraculous, prodigious, remarkable, singular, unheard-of, unusual

uncaring *adjective* = **unconcerned**, indifferent, unfeeling, uninterested, unmoved, unresponsive, unsympathetic

unceasing *adjective* = **continual**, ceaseless, constant, continuing, continuous, endless, incessant, never-ending, nonstop, perpetual, persistent, unending, unfailing, unremitting
➤ **Antonyms**
fitful, intermittent, irregular, occasional, periodic, spasmodic, sporadic

uncertain *adjective* 1 = **unpredictable**, ambiguous, chancy, conjectural, doubtful, iffy (*informal*), incalculable, indefinite, indeterminate, indistinct, questionable, risky, speculative, undetermined,

unforeseeable **2 = unsure**, doubtful, dubious, hazy, in two minds, irresolute, unclear, unconfirmed, undecided, undetermined, unfixed, unresolved, unsettled, up in the air, vacillating, vague **3 = changeable**, erratic, fitful, iffy (*informal*), inconstant, insecure, irregular, precarious, unpredictable, unreliable, variable
➤ **Antonyms**
≠**unpredictable**: certain, clear, clear-cut, decided, definite, firm, fixed, known, predictable, unambiguous ≠**unsure**: certain, positive, resolute, settled, sure, unhesitating ≠**changeable**: certain, reliable, unvarying

uncertainty *noun* **1 = unpredictability**, ambiguity, inconclusiveness, state of suspense **2 = doubt**, confusion, dilemma, dubiety, hesitancy, hesitation, indecision, irresolution, lack of confidence, misgiving, puzzlement, qualm, quandary, scepticism, vagueness
➤ **Antonyms**
≠**unpredictability**: conclusiveness, predictability ≠**doubt**: assurance, certainty, confidence, decision, resolution, sureness, trust

unchangeable *adjective* **= unalterable**, changeless, constant, fixed, immovable, immutable, inevitable, invariable, irreversible, permanent, stable, steadfast, strong
➤ **Antonyms**
changeable, inconstant, irregular, mutable, shifting, unstable, variable, wavering

unchanging *adjective* **= constant**, abiding, changeless, continuing, enduring, eternal, immutable, imperishable, lasting, permanent, perpetual, unchanged, unvarying

uncharitable *adjective* **= unkind**, cruel, hardhearted, insensitive, merciless, unchristian, unfeeling, unforgiving, unfriendly, ungenerous, unsympathetic
➤ **Antonyms**
charitable, feeling, friendly, generous, kind, merciful, sensitive, sympathetic

uncharted *adjective* **= unexplored**, not mapped, strange, undiscovered, unfamiliar, unknown, unplumbed, virgin

uncivil *adjective* **= impolite**, bad-mannered, boorish, brusque, churlish, discourteous, disrespectful, ill-bred, ill-mannered, rude, surly, uncouth, unmannerly
➤ **Antonyms**
civil, courteous, mannerly, polite, refined, respectful, well-bred, well-mannered

uncivilized *adjective* **1 = primitive**, barbarian, barbaric, barbarous, illiterate, savage, wild **2 = uncouth**, beyond the pale, boorish, brutish, churlish, coarse, gross, philistine, uncultivated, uncultured, uneducated, unmannered, unpolished, unsophisticated, vulgar

unclean *adjective* **= dirty**, contaminated, corrupt, defiled, evil, filthy, foul, impure, polluted, soiled, spotted, stained, sullied, tainted
➤ **Antonyms**
clean, faultless, flawless, pure, spotless, unblemished, unstained, unsullied

unclear *adjective* **1 = indistinct**, bleary, blurred, dim, faint, fuzzy, hazy, ill-defined, indiscernible, indistinguishable, misty, muffled, obscure, out of focus, shadowy, undefined, vague, weak **2 = doubtful**, ambiguous, confused, indefinite, indeterminate, unintelligible, vague
➤ **Antonyms**
≠**indistinct**: clear, defined, discernible, distinct, distinguishable ≠**doubtful**: determinate, evident, intelligible

uncomfortable *adjective* **1 = painful**, awkward, causing discomfort, cramped, disagreeable, hard, ill-fitting, incommodious, irritating, rough, troublesome **2 = uneasy**, awkward, confused, discomfited, disquieted, distressed, disturbed, embarrassed, ill at ease, like a fish out of water, out of place, self-conscious, troubled
➤ **Antonyms**
≠**uneasy**: at ease, at home, comfortable, easy, relaxed, serene, untroubled

uncommitted *adjective* **= uninvolved**, floating, free, free-floating, neutral, nonaligned, nonpartisan, not involved, (sitting) on the fence, unattached

uncommon *adjective* **1 = rare**, bizarre, curious, few and far between, infrequent, novel, odd, out of the ordinary, peculiar, queer, scarce, singular, strange, thin on the ground, unfamiliar, unusual **2 = extraordinary**, distinctive, exceptional, incomparable, notable, noteworthy, outstanding, rare, remarkable, singular, special, superior, unparalleled, unprecedented
➤ **Antonyms**
≠**rare**: common, familiar, frequent, regular, routine, usual ≠**extraordinary**: average, banal, commonplace, everyday, humdrum, mundane, ordinary, run-of-the-mill

uncommonly *adverb* **1 = rarely**, hardly ever, infrequently, not often, occasionally, only now and then, scarcely ever, seldom **2 = exceptionally**, extremely, particularly, peculiarly, remarkably, seriously (*informal*), strangely, unusually, very

uncommunicative *adjective* = **reticent**, close, curt, guarded, reserved, retiring, secretive, short, shy, silent, taciturn, tight-lipped, unforthcoming, unresponsive, unsociable, withdrawn
➤ **Antonyms**
chatty, communicative, forthcoming, garrulous, loquacious, responsive, talkative, voluble

uncompromising *adjective* = **inflexible**, die-hard, firm, hardline, inexorable, intransigent, obdurate, obstinate, rigid, stiff-necked, strict, stubborn, tough, unbending, unyielding

unconcern *noun* = **indifference**, aloofness, apathy, detachment, insouciance, lack of interest, nonchalance, remoteness, uninterestedness

unconcerned *adjective* **1** = **indifferent**, aloof, apathetic, cool, detached, dispassionate, distant, incurious, oblivious, uninterested, uninvolved, unmoved, unsympathetic **2** = **untroubled**, blithe, carefree, careless, easy, insouciant, nonchalant, not bothered, not giving a toss (*informal*), relaxed, serene, unperturbed, unruffled, unworried
➤ **Antonyms**
≠**indifferent**: avid, curious, eager, interested, involved ≠**untroubled**: agitated, anxious, concerned, distressed, perturbed, uneasy, worried

unconditional *adjective* = **absolute**, categorical, complete, downright, entire, full, out-and-out, outright, plenary, positive, thoroughgoing, total, unlimited, unqualified, unreserved, unrestricted, utter
➤ **Antonyms**
conditional, limited, partial, qualified, reserved, restricted

uncongenial *adjective* = **unfriendly**, antagonistic, antipathetic, disagreeable, displeasing, distasteful, incompatible, not one's cup of tea (*informal*), uninviting, unpleasant, unsuited, unsympathetic
➤ **Antonyms**
affable, agreeable, compatible, congenial, genial, pleasant, pleasing, sympathetic

unconnected *adjective* **1** = **separate**, detached, disconnected, divided, independent **2** = **incoherent**, disconnected, disjointed, illogical, irrelevant, meaningless, nonsensical, not related, unrelated
➤ **Antonyms**
≠**incoherent**: coherent, connected, intelligible, logical, meaningful, related, relevant

unconscionable *adjective* **1**

= **unscrupulous**, amoral, criminal, unethical, unfair, unjust, unprincipled **2** = **excessive**, exorbitant, extravagant, extreme, immoderate, inordinate, outrageous, preposterous, unreasonable

unconscious *adjective* **1** = **senseless**, blacked out (*informal*), comatose, dead to the world (*informal*), insensible, knocked out, numb, out, out cold, out for the count (*Boxing*), stunned **2** = **unaware**, blind to, deaf to, heedless, ignorant, in ignorance, lost to, oblivious, unknowing, unmindful, unsuspecting **3** = **unintentional**, accidental, inadvertent, unintended, unpremeditated, unwitting **4** = **subconscious**, automatic, instinctive, involuntary, latent, reflex, repressed, subliminal, suppressed, unrealized
➤ **Antonyms**
≠**senseless**: awake, conscious, sensible
≠**unaware**: alert, aware, conscious
≠**unintentional**: calculated, conscious, deliberate, intentional, planned, studied, wilful

uncontrollable *adjective* = **wild**, beside oneself, carried away, frantic, furious, irrepressible, irresistible, like one possessed, mad, strong, ungovernable, unmanageable, unruly, violent

uncontrolled *adjective* = **unrestrained**, furious, lacking self-control, out of control, out of hand, rampant, riotous, unbridled, unchecked, uncurbed, undisciplined, ungoverned, unruly, violent
➤ **Antonyms**
contained, controlled, disciplined, restrained, subdued

unconventional *adjective* = **unusual**, atypical, bizarre, bohemian, different, eccentric, far-out (*slang*), idiosyncratic, individual, individualistic, informal, irregular, left-field (*informal*), nonconformist, odd, oddball (*informal*), offbeat, off-the-wall (*slang*), original, out of the ordinary, outré, uncustomary, unorthodox, way-out (*informal*)
➤ **Antonyms**
conventional, normal, ordinary, orthodox, proper, regular, typical, usual

unconvincing *adjective* = **implausible**, cock-and-bull (*informal*), dubious, feeble, fishy (*informal*), flimsy, hard to believe, improbable, inconclusive, lame, questionable, specious, suspect, thin, unlikely, unpersuasive, weak
➤ **Antonyms**
believable, conclusive, convincing, credible, likely, persuasive, plausible, probable

uncooperative *adjective* = **unhelpful**,

awkward, bloody-minded (*Brit. informal*), cussed (*informal*), difficult, disobliging, obstructive, unaccommodating, unresponsive, unsupportive
➤ **Antonyms**
accommodating, cooperative, helpful, obliging, responsive, supportive

uncoordinated *adjective* = **clumsy**, all thumbs, awkward, bumbling, bungling, butterfingered (*informal*), graceless, lumbering, maladroit, ungainly, ungraceful

uncouth *adjective* = **coarse**, awkward, barbaric, boorish, clumsy, crude, gawky, graceless, gross, ill-mannered, loutish, oafish, rough, rude, uncivilized, uncultivated, ungainly, unrefined, unseemly, vulgar
➤ **Antonyms**
civilized, courteous, cultivated, elegant, graceful, refined, seemly, well-mannered

uncover *verb* 1 = **open**, bare, lay open, lift the lid, show, strip, unwrap 2 = **reveal**, blow wide open (*slang*), bring to light, disclose, discover, divulge, expose, lay bare, make known, unearth, unmask
➤ **Antonyms**
≠**reveal**: conceal, cover, cover up, hide, keep under wraps, suppress

uncritical *adjective* = **undiscriminating**, easily pleased, indiscriminate, undiscerning, unexacting, unfussy, unperceptive, unselective, unthinking
➤ **Antonyms**
critical, discerning, discriminating, fastidious, fussy, perceptive, selective

unctuous *adjective* = **obsequious**, glib, gushing, ingratiating, insincere, oily, plausible, slick, smarmy (*Brit. informal*), smooth, suave, sycophantic

undaunted *adjective* = **undeterred**, bold, brave, courageous, dauntless, fearless, intrepid, not discouraged, nothing daunted, not put off, resolute, steadfast, undiscouraged, undismayed

undeceive *verb* = **enlighten**, correct, disabuse, disillusion, open (someone's) eyes (to), put (someone) right, set (someone) straight, shatter (someone's) illusions

undecided *adjective* 1 = **unsure**, ambivalent, dithering (*chiefly Brit.*), doubtful, dubious, hesitant, in two minds, irresolute, swithering (*Scot.*), torn, uncertain, uncommitted, wavering 2 = **unsettled**, debatable, iffy (*informal*), indefinite, in the balance, moot, open, pending, unconcluded, undetermined, up in the air, vague
➤ **Antonyms**
≠**unsure**: certain, committed, decided,

resolute, sure ≠**unsettled**: decided, definite, determined, resolved, settled

undefined *adjective* 1 = **unspecified**, imprecise, indeterminate, inexact, unclear, unexplained 2 = **indistinct**, formless, hazy, indefinite, shadowy, tenuous, vague
➤ **Antonyms**
≠**unspecified**: clear, defined, determinate, exact, explicit, precise, specified
≠**indistinct**: clear, defined, definite

undemonstrative *adjective* = **reserved**, aloof, cold, contained, distant, formal, impassive, restrained, reticent, unaffectionate, uncommunicative, unemotional, unresponsive, withdrawn
➤ **Antonyms**
affectionate, demonstrative, emotional, expressive, friendly, outgoing, overemotional, unreserved, warm

undeniable *adjective* = **certain**, beyond (a) doubt, beyond question, clear, evident, incontestable, incontrovertible, indisputable, indubitable, irrefutable, manifest, obvious, patent, proven, sound, sure, unassailable, undoubted, unquestionable
➤ **Antonyms**
debatable, deniable, doubtful, dubious, questionable, uncertain, unproven

under *preposition* 1 = **below**, beneath, on the bottom of, underneath 2 = **subject to**, directed by, governed by, inferior to, junior to, reporting to, secondary to, subordinate to, subservient to 3 = **included in**, belonging to, comprised in ♦ *adverb* 4 = **below**, beneath, down, downward, lower, to the bottom
➤ **Antonyms**
preposition ≠**below**: above, over, up, upper, upward ♦ *adverb* ≠**below**: above, over, up, upward

underclothes *plural noun* = **underwear**, lingerie, smalls (*informal*), underclothing, undergarments, underlinen, underthings, undies (*informal*), unmentionables (*humorous*)

undercover *adjective* = **secret**, clandestine, concealed, confidential, covert, hidden, hush-hush (*informal*), intelligence, private, spy, surreptitious, underground
➤ **Antonyms**
manifest, open, overt, plain, unconcealed, visible

undercurrent *noun* 1 = **undertow**, crosscurrent, rip, rip current, riptide, tideway, underflow 2 = **undertone**, atmosphere, aura, drift, feeling, flavour, hint, murmur, overtone, sense, suggestion, tendency, tinge, trend, vibes (*slang*), vibrations

undercut verb 1 = **underprice**, sell at a loss, sell cheaply, undercharge, undersell 2 = **cut away**, cut out, excavate, gouge out, hollow out, mine, undermine

underdog noun = **weaker party**, fall guy (informal), little fellow (informal), loser, outsider, victim

underestimate verb = **underrate**, belittle, hold cheap, minimize, miscalculate, misprize, not do justice to, set no store by, think too little of, undervalue
➤ **Antonyms**
exaggerate, inflate, overdo, overestimate, overrate, overstate

undergo verb = **experience**, bear, be subjected to, endure, go through, stand, submit to, suffer, sustain, weather, withstand

underground adjective 1 = **subterranean**, below ground, below the surface, buried, covered 2 = **secret**, clandestine, concealed, covert, hidden, surreptitious, undercover 3 = **avant-garde**, alternative, experimental, radical, revolutionary, subversive ♦ noun 4 **the underground: a = the Resistance**, partisans, the Maquis **b = the tube** (Brit.), the metro, the subway

undergrowth noun = **scrub**, bracken, brambles, briars, brush, brushwood, underbrush, underwood

underhand adjective = **sly**, clandestine, crafty, crooked (informal), deceitful, deceptive, devious, dishonest, dishonourable, fraudulent, furtive, secret, secretive, sneaky, stealthy, surreptitious, treacherous, underhanded, unethical, unscrupulous
➤ **Antonyms**
above board, frank, honest, honourable, legal, open, outright, principled, scrupulous

underline verb 1 = **underscore**, italicize, mark, rule a line under 2 = **emphasize**, accentuate, bring home, call or draw attention to, give emphasis to, highlight, point up, stress
➤ **Antonyms**
≠**emphasize**: gloss over, make light of, minimize, play down, soft-pedal (informal)

underling noun Derogatory = **subordinate**, cohort (chiefly U.S.), flunky, hireling, inferior, lackey, menial, minion, servant, slave

underlying adjective 1 = **hidden**, concealed, latent, lurking, veiled 2 = **fundamental**, basic, elementary, essential, intrinsic, primary, prime, radical, root

undermine verb 1 = **weaken**, debilitate, disable, impair, sabotage, sap, subvert, threaten 2 = **wear away**, dig out, eat away at, erode, excavate, mine, tunnel, undercut
➤ **Antonyms**
≠**weaken**: fortify, promote, reinforce, strengthen, sustain ≠**wear away**: fortify, reinforce, strengthen, sustain

underpinning noun = **support**, base, footing, foundation, groundwork, substructure

underprivileged adjective = **disadvantaged**, badly off, deprived, destitute, impoverished, in need, in want, needy, on the breadline, poor

underrate verb = **underestimate**, belittle, discount, disparage, fail to appreciate, misprize, not do justice to, set (too) little store by, undervalue
➤ **Antonyms**
exaggerate, overestimate, overrate, overvalue

undersell verb = **undercut**, cut, mark down, reduce, slash, undercharge

undersized adjective = **stunted**, dwarfish, miniature, pygmy or pigmy, runtish, small, squat, teeny-weeny, tiny, underdeveloped, underweight
➤ **Antonyms**
big, colossal, giant, huge, massive, oversized, overweight

understand verb 1 = **comprehend**, appreciate, apprehend, be aware, catch on (informal), conceive, cotton on (informal), discern, fathom, follow, get, get one's head round, get the hang of (informal), get to the bottom of, grasp, know, make head or tail of (informal), make out, penetrate, perceive, realize, recognize, see, see the light, take in, tumble to (informal), twig (Brit. informal) 2 = **believe**, assume, be informed, conclude, gather, hear, learn, presume, suppose, take it, think 3 = **sympathize with**, accept, appreciate, be able to see, commiserate, empathize with, show compassion for

understandable adjective = **reasonable**, justifiable, legitimate, logical, natural, normal, to be expected

understanding noun 1 = **perception**, appreciation, awareness, comprehension, discernment, grasp, insight, intelligence, judgment, knowledge, penetration, sense 2 = **interpretation**, belief, conclusion, estimation, idea, judgment, notion, opinion, perception, view, viewpoint 3 = **agreement**, accord, common view, gentlemen's agreement, pact ♦ adjective 4 = **sympathetic**, compassionate, considerate, discerning, forbearing, forgiving, kind, kindly, patient, perceptive,

responsive, sensitive, tolerant
➤ **Antonyms**
noun ≠**perception**: ignorance, incomprehension, insensitivity, misapprehension, misunderstanding, obtuseness ≠**agreement**: disagreement, dispute ♦ *adjective* ≠**sympathetic**: inconsiderate, insensitive, intolerant, strict, unfeeling, unsympathetic

understood *adjective* **1 = implied**, implicit, inferred, tacit, unspoken, unstated **2 = assumed**, accepted, axiomatic, presumed, taken for granted

understudy *noun* **= stand-in**, double, fill-in, replacement, reserve, sub, substitute

undertake *verb* **1 = agree**, bargain, commit oneself, contract, covenant, engage, guarantee, pledge, promise, take upon oneself **2 = take on**, attempt, begin, commence, embark on, endeavour, enter upon, set about, tackle, try

undertaker *noun* **= funeral director**, mortician (*U.S.*)

undertaking *noun* **1 = task**, affair, attempt, business, effort, endeavour, enterprise, game, operation, project, venture **2 = promise**, assurance, commitment, pledge, solemn word, vow, word, word of honour

undertone *noun* **1 = murmur**, low tone, subdued voice, whisper **2 = undercurrent**, atmosphere, feeling, flavour, hint, suggestion, tinge, touch, trace, vibes (*slang*)

undervalue *verb* **= underrate**, depreciate, hold cheap, look down on, make light of, minimize, misjudge, misprize, set no store by, underestimate
➤ **Antonyms**
exaggerate, overestimate, overrate, overvalue

underwater *adjective* **= submerged**, submarine, sunken, undersea

under way *adjective* **= in progress**, afoot, begun, going on, in business, in motion, in operation, started

underwear *noun* **= underclothes**, lingerie, smalls (*informal*), underclothing, undergarments, underlinen, underthings, undies (*informal*), unmentionables (*humorous*)

underweight *adjective* **= skinny**, emaciated, half-starved, puny, skin and bone (*informal*), undernourished, undersized

underworld *noun* **1 = criminals**, criminal element, gangland (*informal*), gangsters, organized crime **2 = nether world**, abode of the dead, Hades, hell, infernal region,

nether regions, the inferno

underwrite *verb* **1 = finance**, back, fund, guarantee, insure, provide security, sponsor, subsidize **2 = sign**, countersign, endorse, initial, subscribe **3 = support**, agree to, approve, consent, O.K. *or* okay (*informal*), sanction

undesirable *adjective* **= objectionable**, disagreeable, disliked, distasteful, obnoxious, offensive, out of place, repugnant, (to be) avoided, unacceptable, unattractive, unpleasing, unpopular, unsavoury, unsuitable, unwanted, unwelcome, unwished-for
➤ **Antonyms**
acceptable, agreeable, appealing, attractive, desirable, inviting, pleasing, popular, welcome

undeveloped *adjective* **1 = immature**, embryonic, in embryo **2 = potential**, inchoate, latent

undignified *adjective* **= unseemly**, beneath one, beneath one's dignity, improper, inappropriate, indecorous, inelegant, infra dig (*informal*), lacking dignity, unbecoming, ungentlemanly, unladylike, unsuitable
➤ **Antonyms**
appropriate, becoming, decorous, dignified, elegant, proper, seemly, suitable

undisciplined *adjective* **= uncontrolled**, disobedient, obstreperous, unpredictable, unreliable, unrestrained, unruly, unschooled, untrained, wayward, wild, wilful
➤ **Antonyms**
controlled, disciplined, obedient, predictable, reliable, restrained, trained

undisguised *adjective* **= obvious**, blatant, evident, explicit, manifest, open, overt, patent, transparent, unconcealed, unfeigned, unmistakable
➤ **Antonyms**
concealed, covert, disguised, feigned, hidden, secret

undisputed *adjective* **= acknowledged**, accepted, beyond question, certain, conclusive, incontestable, incontrovertible, indisputable, irrefutable, recognized, sure, unchallenged, uncontested, undeniable, undoubted, unquestioned
➤ **Antonyms**
deniable, disputed, doubtful, dubious, inconclusive, questioned, uncertain

undistinguished *adjective* **= ordinary**, commonplace, everyday, indifferent, mediocre, no great shakes (*informal*), pedestrian, prosaic, run-of-the-mill, so-so (*informal*), unexceptional, unexciting, unimpressive, unremarkable, vanilla

(*informal*)
➤ **Antonyms**
distinguished, exceptional, exciting, extraordinary, impressive, notable, outstanding, remarkable, striking

undisturbed *adjective* 1 = **quiet**, calm, peaceful, restful, sedate, serene, still, tranquil 2 = **calm**, collected, composed, equable, placid, sedate, serene, tranquil, unagitated, unbothered, unfazed (*informal*), unperturbed, unruffled, untroubled 3 = **uninterrupted**, without interruption 4 = **untouched**, not moved
➤ **Antonyms**
≠**calm:** agitated, antsy (*informal*), bothered, disturbed, excited, flustered, nervous, perturbed, troubled, upset ≠**uninterrupted:** interrupted ≠**untouched:** interfered with, moved

undivided *adjective* 1 = **complete**, concentrated, entire, exclusive, full, thorough, total, undistracted, whole, wholehearted 2 = **united**, concerted, entire, solid, unanimous, whole

undo *verb* 1 = **open**, disengage, disentangle, loose, loosen, unbutton, unclasp, unfasten, unlock, unstrap, untie, unwrap 2 = **reverse**, annul, cancel, invalidate, neutralize, nullify, offset, wipe out 3 = **ruin**, defeat, destroy, mar, overturn, quash, shatter, subvert, undermine, upset, wreck

undoing *noun* 1 = **ruin**, collapse, defeat, destruction, disgrace, downfall, humiliation, overthrow, overturn, reversal, ruination, shame 2 = **downfall**, affliction, blight, curse, fatal flaw, misfortune, the last straw, trial, trouble, weakness

undone [1] *adjective* = **unfinished**, incomplete, left, neglected, not completed, not done, omitted, outstanding, passed over, unattended to, unfulfilled, unperformed
➤ **Antonyms**
accomplished, attended to, complete, done, finished, fulfilled, performed

undone [2] *adjective* = **ruined**, destroyed, overcome

undoubted *adjective* = **certain**, acknowledged, definite, evident, incontrovertible, indisputable, indubitable, obvious, sure, undisputed, unquestionable, unquestioned

undoubtedly *adverb* = **certainly**, assuredly, beyond a shadow of (a) doubt, beyond question, definitely, doubtless, of course, surely, undeniably, unmistakably, unquestionably, without doubt

undreamed-of *or* **undreamt-of** *adjective* = **unimagined**, astonishing, inconceivable,

incredible, miraculous, unexpected, unforeseen, unheard-of, unsuspected, unthought-of

undress *verb* 1 = **strip**, disrobe, divest oneself of, peel off (*slang*), shed, take off one's clothes ♦ *noun* 2 = **nakedness**, deshabille, disarray, nudity

undue *adjective* = **excessive**, disproportionate, extravagant, extreme, immoderate, improper, inappropriate, inordinate, intemperate, needless, overmuch, too great, too much, uncalled-for, undeserved, unjustified, unnecessary, unseemly, unsuitable, unwarranted
➤ **Antonyms**
appropriate, due, fitting, justified, necessary, proper, suitable

undulate *verb* = **wave**, billow, heave, ripple, rise and fall, roll, surge, swell

unduly *adverb* = **excessively**, disproportionately, extravagantly, immoderately, improperly, inordinately, out of all proportion, overly, overmuch, unjustifiably, unnecessarily, unreasonably
➤ **Antonyms**
duly, justifiably, moderately, ordinately, properly, proportionately, reasonably

undying *adjective* = **eternal**, constant, continuing, deathless, everlasting, infinite, perennial, permanent, perpetual, unending, unfading
➤ **Antonyms**
ephemeral, finite, fleeting, impermanent, inconstant, momentary, mortal, short-lived

unearth *verb* 1 = **discover**, bring to light, expose, ferret out, find, reveal, root up, turn up, uncover 2 = **dig up**, disinter, dredge up, excavate, exhume

unearthly *adjective* 1 = **eerie**, eldritch (*poetic*), ghostly, haunted, nightmarish, phantom, preternatural, spectral, spooky (*informal*), strange, supernatural, uncanny, weird 2 = **unreasonable**, abnormal, absurd, extraordinary, ridiculous, strange, ungodly (*informal*), unholy (*informal*)

uneasiness *noun* = **anxiety**, agitation, alarm, apprehension, apprehensiveness, disquiet, doubt, misgiving, nervousness, perturbation, qualms, suspicion, trepidation, worry
➤ **Antonyms**
calm, composure, cool, ease, peace, quiet, serenity

uneasy *adjective* 1 = **anxious**, agitated, antsy (*informal*), apprehensive, discomposed, disturbed, edgy, ill at ease, impatient, jittery (*informal*), nervous, on edge, perturbed, restive, restless, troubled, twitchy (*informal*), uncomfortable,

unsettled, upset, wired (*slang*), worried **2 = precarious**, awkward, constrained, insecure, shaky, strained, tense, uncomfortable, unstable **3 = disturbing**, bothering, dismaying, disquieting, troubling, upsetting, worrying
➤ **Antonyms**
≠**anxious**: at ease, calm, comfortable, relaxed, tranquil, unfazed (*informal*), unflustered, unperturbed, unruffled

uneconomic *adjective* = **unprofitable**, loss-making, nonpaying, non-profit-making, nonviable
➤ **Antonyms**
economic, money-making, productive, profitable, remunerative, viable

uneducated *adjective* **1 = ignorant**, illiterate, unlettered, unread, unschooled, untaught **2 = lowbrow**, benighted, uncultivated, uncultured
➤ **Antonyms**
≠**ignorant**: educated, informed, instructed, literate, schooled, taught, tutored

unemotional *adjective* = **impassive**, apathetic, cold, cool, indifferent, listless, passionless, phlegmatic, reserved, undemonstrative, unexcitable, unfeeling, unimpressionable, unresponsive
➤ **Antonyms**
demonstrative, emotional, excitable, feeling, passionate, responsive, sensitive

unemployed *adjective* = **out of work**, idle, jobless, laid off, on the dole (*Brit. informal*), out of a job, redundant, resting (*of an actor*), workless

unending *adjective* = **perpetual**, ceaseless, constant, continual, endless, eternal, everlasting, incessant, interminable, never-ending, unceasing, unremitting

unendurable *adjective* = **unbearable**, insufferable, insupportable, intolerable, more than flesh and blood can stand
➤ **Antonyms**
bearable, endurable, sufferable, tolerable

unenthusiastic *adjective* = **indifferent**, apathetic, blasé, bored, half-hearted, lukewarm, neutral, nonchalant, unimpressed, uninterested, unmoved, unresponsive
➤ **Antonyms**
ardent, eager, enthusiastic, excited, interested, keen, passionate

unenviable *adjective* = **unpleasant**, disagreeable, painful, thankless, uncomfortable, undesirable
➤ **Antonyms**
agreeable, attractive, desirable, enviable, pleasant

unequal *adjective* **1 = different**, differing,

disparate, dissimilar, not uniform, unlike, unmatched, variable, varying **2 = disproportionate**, asymmetrical, ill-matched, irregular, unbalanced, uneven **3** *with* **to = inadequate for**, found wanting, insufficient for, not up to
➤ **Antonyms**
≠**different**: equal, equivalent, identical, like, matched, similar, uniform

unequalled *adjective* = **incomparable**, beyond compare, inimitable, matchless, nonpareil, paramount, peerless, pre-eminent, second to none, supreme, unmatched, unparalleled, unrivalled, unsurpassed, without equal

unequivocal *adjective* = **clear**, absolute, black-and-white, certain, clear-cut, cut-and-dried (*informal*), decisive, definite, direct, evident, explicit, incontrovertible, indubitable, manifest, plain, positive, straight, unambiguous, uncontestable, unmistakable
➤ **Antonyms**
ambiguous, doubtful, equivocal, evasive, indecisive, noncommittal, vague

unerring *adjective* = **accurate**, certain, exact, faultless, impeccable, infallible, perfect, sure, unfailing

unethical *adjective* = **immoral**, dirty, dishonest, dishonourable, disreputable, illegal, improper, not cricket (*informal*), shady (*informal*), underhand, under-the-table, unfair, unprincipled, unprofessional, unscrupulous, wrong
➤ **Antonyms**
ethical, honest, honourable, legal, moral, proper, scrupulous, upright

uneven *adjective* **1 = rough**, bumpy, not flat, not level, not smooth **2 = variable**, broken, changeable, fitful, fluctuating, intermittent, irregular, jerky, patchy, spasmodic, unsteady **3 = unbalanced**, asymmetrical, lopsided, not parallel, odd, out of true **4 = unequal**, disparate, ill-matched, one-sided, unfair
➤ **Antonyms**
≠**rough**: even, flat, level, plane, smooth

uneventful *adjective* = **humdrum**, boring, commonplace, dull, ho-hum (*informal*), monotonous, ordinary, quiet, routine, tedious, unexceptional, unexciting, uninteresting, unmemorable, unremarkable, unvaried
➤ **Antonyms**
eventful, exceptional, exciting, interesting, memorable, momentous, remarkable

unexampled *adjective* = **unprecedented**, unequalled, unheard-of, unique, unmatched, unparalleled

unexceptional *adjective* = **ordinary**,

bog-standard (*Brit. & Irish slang*), common
or garden (*informal*), commonplace,
conventional, insignificant, mediocre, no
great shakes (*informal*), normal,
pedestrian, run-of-the-mill,
undistinguished, unimpressive,
unremarkable, usual
➤ Antonyms
distinguished, exceptional, impressive,
notable, noteworthy, outstanding,
remarkable, significant, unusual

unexpected *adjective* = **unforeseen**,
abrupt, accidental, astonishing, chance,
fortuitous, not bargained for, out of the
blue, startling, sudden, surprising,
unanticipated, unlooked-for,
unpredictable
➤ Antonyms
anticipated, awaited, expected, foreseen,
normal, planned, predictable

unfailing *adjective* 1 = **continuous**,
boundless, ceaseless, continual, endless,
inexhaustible, never-failing, persistent,
unflagging, unlimited 2 = **reliable**, certain,
constant, dependable, faithful, infallible,
loyal, staunch, steadfast, sure, tried and
true, true
➤ Antonyms
≠**reliable**: disloyal, fallible, inconstant,
uncertain, unfaithful, unreliable, unsure,
untrustworthy

unfair *adjective* 1 = **biased**, arbitrary,
bigoted, discriminatory, inequitable,
one-sided, partial, partisan, prejudiced,
unjust 2 = **unscrupulous**, crooked
(*informal*), dishonest, dishonourable,
uncalled-for, unethical, unprincipled,
unsporting, unwarranted, wrongful
➤ Antonyms
≠**unscrupulous**: ethical, fair, honest, just,
principled, scrupulous

unfaithful *adjective* 1 = **faithless**,
adulterous, fickle, inconstant, two-timing
(*informal*), unchaste, untrue 2 = **disloyal**,
deceitful, faithless, false, false-hearted,
perfidious, traitorous, treacherous,
treasonable, unreliable, untrustworthy
➤ Antonyms
≠**faithless**: constant, faithful ≠**disloyal**:
faithful, loyal, steadfast, true, trustworthy

unfamiliar *adjective* 1 = **strange**, alien,
beyond one's ken, curious, different, little
known, new, novel, out-of-the-way,
unaccustomed, uncommon, unknown,
unusual 2 **unfamiliar with** = **unacquainted
with**, a stranger to, inexperienced in,
unaccustomed to, unconversant with,
uninformed about, uninitiated in,
unpractised in, unskilled at, unversed in
➤ Antonyms

≠**strange**: accustomed, average, common,
commonplace, everyday, familiar, normal,
unexceptional, usual, well-known
≠**unacquainted with**: accustomed to,
acquainted with, conversant with,
experienced in, familiar with,
knowledgeable about, well-versed in

unfashionable *adjective* = **passé**,
antiquated, behind the times, dated,
obsolete, old-fashioned, old hat, out,
outmoded, out of date, out of fashion, out
of the ark (*informal*), square (*informal*),
unpopular
➤ Antonyms
à la mode, fashionable, modern, popular,
stylish, trendy (*Brit. informal*)

unfasten *verb* = **undo**, detach, disconnect,
let go, loosen, open, separate, unclasp,
uncouple, unlace, unlock, unstrap, untie

unfathomable *adjective* 1 = **baffling**,
abstruse, deep, esoteric, impenetrable,
incomprehensible, indecipherable,
inexplicable, profound, unknowable 2
= **immeasurable**, bottomless, unmeasured,
unplumbed, unsounded

unfavourable *adjective* 1 = **adverse**, bad,
contrary, disadvantageous, ill-suited,
inauspicious, infelicitous, inopportune,
ominous, threatening, unfortunate,
unlucky, unpromising, unpropitious,
unseasonable, unsuited, untimely,
untoward 2 = **hostile**, inimical, low,
negative, poor, unfriendly
➤ Antonyms
≠**hostile**: amicable, approving, favourable,
friendly, positive, warm, well-disposed

unfeeling *adjective* 1 = **callous**, apathetic,
cold, cruel, hardened, hardhearted,
heartless, inhuman, insensitive, pitiless,
stony, uncaring, unsympathetic 2 = **numb**,
insensate, insensible, sensationless
➤ Antonyms
≠**callous**: benevolent, caring, concerned,
feeling, gentle, humane, kind, sensitive,
sympathetic

unfettered *adjective* = **uncontrolled**, free,
unbridled, unchecked, unconfined,
unconstrained, unlimited, unrestrained,
unshackled, untrammelled

unfinished *adjective* 1 = **incomplete**,
deficient, half-done, imperfect, in the
making, lacking, unaccomplished,
uncompleted, undone, unfulfilled,
wanting 2 = **rough**, bare, crude, natural,
raw, sketchy, unpolished, unrefined
➤ Antonyms
≠**rough**: finished, flawless, perfected,
polished, refined, smooth

unfit *adjective* 1 = **incapable**, ill-equipped,
inadequate, incompetent, ineligible, no

good, not cut out for, not equal to, not up to, unprepared, unqualified, useless **2** = **unsuitable**, ill-adapted, inadequate, inappropriate, ineffective, not designed, not fit, unsuited, useless **3** = **out of shape**, debilitated, decrepit, feeble, flabby, in poor condition, out of trim, unhealthy
► **Antonyms**
≠**incapable**: able, capable, competent, equipped, qualified, ready ≠**unsuitable**: acceptable, adequate, appropriate, suitable ≠**out of shape**: fit, healthy, in good condition, strong, sturdy, well

unflappable *adjective Informal*
= **imperturbable**, calm, collected, composed, cool, impassive, level-headed, self-possessed, unfazed (*informal*), unruffled
► **Antonyms**
antsy (*informal*), excitable, flappable, hot-headed, nervous, temperamental, twitchy (*informal*), volatile

unflattering *adjective* **1** = **blunt**, candid, critical, honest, uncomplimentary **2** = **unattractive**, not shown in the best light, not shown to advantage, plain, unbecoming, unprepossessing

unfledged *adjective* = **inexperienced**, callow, green, immature, raw, undeveloped, untried, young

unflinching *adjective* = **determined**, bold, constant, firm, immovable, resolute, stalwart, staunch, steadfast, steady, unfaltering, unshaken, unshrinking, unswerving, unwavering
► **Antonyms**
cowed, faltering, scared, shaken, shrinking, wavering

unfold *verb* **1** = **open**, disentangle, expand, flatten, spread out, straighten, stretch out, undo, unfurl, unravel, unroll, unwrap **2** = **reveal**, clarify, describe, disclose, divulge, explain, illustrate, make known, present, show, uncover **3** = **develop**, bear fruit, blossom, evolve, expand, grow, mature

unforeseen *adjective* = **unexpected**, abrupt, accidental, out of the blue, startling, sudden, surprise, surprising, unanticipated, unenvisaged, unlooked-for, unpredicted
► **Antonyms**
anticipated, envisaged, expected, foreseen, predicted

unforgettable *adjective* = **memorable**, exceptional, extraordinary, fixed in the mind, impressive, never to be forgotten, notable, striking

unforgivable *adjective* = **inexcusable**, deplorable, disgraceful, indefensible, shameful, unjustifiable, unpardonable,

unwarrantable
► **Antonyms**
allowable, excusable, forgivable, justifiable, pardonable, venial

unfortunate *adjective* **1** = **disastrous**, adverse, calamitous, ill-fated, ill-starred, infelicitous, inopportune, ruinous, unfavourable, untimely, untoward **2** = **unlucky**, cursed, doomed, hapless, hopeless, luckless, out of luck, poor, star-crossed, unhappy, unprosperous, unsuccessful, wretched **3** = **regrettable**, deplorable, ill-advised, inappropriate, lamentable, unbecoming, unsuitable
► **Antonyms**
≠**disastrous**: auspicious, felicitous, fortuitous, fortunate, opportune, timely ≠**unlucky**: fortunate, happy, lucky, successful ≠**regrettable**: appropriate, becoming, unsuitable

unfounded *adjective* = **groundless**, baseless, fabricated, false, idle, spurious, trumped up, unjustified, unproven, unsubstantiated, without basis, without foundation
► **Antonyms**
attested, confirmed, factual, justified, proven, substantiated, verified

unfrequented *adjective* = **isolated**, deserted, godforsaken, lone, lonely, off the beaten track, remote, sequestered, solitary, uninhabited, unvisited

unfriendly *adjective* **1** = **hostile**, aloof, antagonistic, chilly, cold, disagreeable, distant, ill-disposed, inhospitable, not on speaking terms, uncongenial, unneighbourly, unsociable **2** = **unfavourable**, alien, hostile, inauspicious, inhospitable, inimical, unpropitious
► **Antonyms**
≠**hostile**: affable, amiable, convivial, friendly, hospitable, sociable, warm ≠**unfavourable**: auspicious, congenial, hospitable, propitious

ungainly *adjective* = **awkward**, clumsy, gangling, gawky, inelegant, loutish, lubberly, lumbering, uncoordinated, ungraceful
► **Antonyms**
attractive, comely, elegant, graceful, pleasing

ungodly *adjective* **1** = **wicked**, blasphemous, corrupt, depraved, godless, immoral, impious, irreligious, profane, sinful, vile **2** *Informal* = **unreasonable**, dreadful, horrendous, intolerable, outrageous, unearthly, unholy (*informal*), unseemly

ungovernable *adjective* **1**

= **uncontrollable**, unrestrainable, wild **2**
= **unruly**, rebellious, refractory,
unmanageable

ungracious *adjective* = **bad-mannered**,
churlish, discourteous, ill-bred, impolite,
offhand, rude, uncivil, unmannerly
➤ **Antonyms**
affable, civil, courteous, gracious,
mannerly, polite, well-mannered

ungrateful *adjective* = **unappreciative**,
selfish, thankless, unmindful, unthankful
➤ **Antonyms**
appreciative, aware, grateful, mindful,
thankful

unguarded *adjective* **1** = **unprotected**,
defenceless, open to attack, undefended,
vulnerable **2** = **frank**, artless, candid, direct,
guileless, open, straightforward **3**
= **careless**, foolhardy, heedless,
ill-considered, impolitic, imprudent,
incautious, indiscreet, rash, thoughtless,
uncircumspect, undiplomatic, unthinking,
unwary
➤ **Antonyms**
≠**careless:** cagey (*informal*), careful,
cautious, diplomatic, discreet, guarded,
prudent, wary

unhallowed *adjective* **1** = **unconsecrated**,
not sacred, unblessed, unholy,
unsanctified **2** = **wicked**, evil, godless,
irreverent, profane, sinful

unhappiness *noun* = **sadness**, blues,
dejection, depression, despondency,
discontent, dissatisfaction, gloom,
heartache, low spirits, melancholy, misery,
sorrow, wretchedness

unhappy *adjective* **1** = **sad**, blue,
crestfallen, dejected, depressed,
despondent, disconsolate, dispirited,
down, downcast, down in the dumps
(*informal*), gloomy, long-faced, low,
melancholy, miserable, mournful,
sorrowful **2** = **unlucky**, cursed, hapless,
ill-fated, ill-omened, luckless, unfortunate,
wretched
➤ **Antonyms**
≠**sad:** cheerful, chirpy (*informal*), content,
exuberant, happy, joyful, light-hearted,
overjoyed, over the moon (*informal*),
satisfied ≠**unlucky:** fortunate, lucky

unharmed *adjective* = **unhurt**, in one piece
(*informal*), intact, safe, safe and sound,
sound, undamaged, uninjured, unscarred,
unscathed, untouched, whole, without a
scratch
➤ **Antonyms**
damaged, harmed, hurt, impaired,
injured, scarred, scathed

unhealthy *adjective* **1** = **harmful**,
deleterious, detrimental, insalubrious,

insanitary, noisome, noxious,
unwholesome **2** = **sick**, ailing, delicate,
feeble, frail, infirm, in poor health, invalid,
poorly (*informal*), sickly, unsound, unwell,
weak **3** = **unwholesome**, bad, corrupt,
corrupting, degrading, demoralizing,
morbid, negative, undesirable
➤ **Antonyms**
≠**harmful:** beneficial, good, healthy,
salubrious, salutary, wholesome ≠**sick:** fit,
healthy, robust, well ≠**unwholesome:**
desirable, moral, positive

unheard-of *adjective* **1** = **unprecedented**,
ground-breaking, inconceivable, never
before encountered, new, novel, singular,
unbelievable, undreamed of, unexampled,
unique, unusual **2** = **shocking**, disgraceful,
extreme, offensive, outrageous,
preposterous, unacceptable, unthinkable **3**
= **obscure**, little known, undiscovered,
unfamiliar, unknown

unheeded *adjective* = **ignored**, disobeyed,
disregarded, forgotten, neglected,
overlooked
➤ **Antonyms**
heeded, noted, noticed, obeyed,
observed, regarded, remembered

unheralded *adjective* = **unannounced**, out
of the blue, surprise, unexpected,
unforeseen, unproclaimed, unpublicized

unhesitating *adjective* **1** = **instant**,
immediate, instantaneous, prompt, ready,
without delay **2** = **wholehearted**, implicit,
resolute, steadfast, unfaltering,
unquestioning, unreserved, unswerving,
unwavering
➤ **Antonyms**
≠**wholehearted:** diffident, hesitant,
irresolute, questioning, tentative,
uncertain, unsure, wavering

unhinge *verb* = **unbalance**, confound,
confuse, craze, dement, derange, drive out
of one's mind, madden, unsettle

unholy *adjective* **1** = **evil**, base, corrupt,
depraved, dishonest, heinous, immoral,
iniquitous, irreligious, profane, sinful,
ungodly, vile, wicked **2** *Informal*
= **outrageous**, appalling, awful, dreadful,
horrendous, shocking, unearthly, ungodly
(*informal*), unreasonable
➤ **Antonyms**
≠**evil:** devout, faithful, godly, holy, pious,
religious, saintly, virtuous

unhurried *adjective* = **leisurely**, calm,
deliberate, easy, easy-going, sedate, slow,
slow and steady, slow-paced
➤ **Antonyms**
brief, cursory, hasty, hectic, hurried, quick,
rushed, speedy, swift

unidentified *adjective* = **unnamed**,

anonymous, mysterious, nameless, unclassified, unfamiliar, unknown, unmarked, unrecognized, unrevealed
➤ **Antonyms**
classified, familiar, identified, known, marked, named, recognized

unification *noun* = **union**, alliance, amalgamation, coalescence, coalition, combination, confederation, federation, fusion, merger, uniting

uniform *noun* **1** = **outfit**, costume, dress, garb, habit, livery, regalia, regimentals, suit ♦ *adjective* **2** = **unvarying**, consistent, constant, equable, even, regular, smooth, unbroken, unchanging, undeviating **3** = **alike**, equal, identical, like, same, selfsame, similar
➤ **Antonyms**
adjective ≠ **unvarying**: changeable, changing, deviating, inconsistent, irregular, uneven, varying

uniformity *noun* **1** = **regularity**, constancy, evenness, homogeneity, invariability, sameness, similarity **2** = **monotony**, drabness, dullness, flatness, lack of diversity, sameness, tedium

unify *verb* = **unite**, amalgamate, bind, bring together, combine, confederate, consolidate, federate, fuse, join, merge
➤ **Antonyms**
alienate, disconnect, disjoin, disunite, divide, separate, sever, split

unimaginable *adjective* = **inconceivable**, beyond one's wildest dreams, fantastic, impossible, incredible, indescribable, ineffable, mind-boggling (*informal*), unbelievable, unheard-of, unthinkable

unimaginative *adjective* = **unoriginal**, banal, commonplace, derivative, dry, dull, hackneyed, lifeless, matter-of-fact, ordinary, pedestrian, predictable, prosaic, routine, tame, uncreative, uninspired, unromantic, usual, vanilla (*informal*)
➤ **Antonyms**
creative, different, exciting, fresh, ground-breaking, imaginative, innovative, inventive, original, unhackneyed, unusual

unimpeachable *adjective* = **beyond question**, above reproach, beyond criticism, blameless, faultless, impeccable, irreproachable, perfect, squeaky-clean, unassailable
➤ **Antonyms**
blameworthy, faulty, imperfect, reprehensible, reproachable, shameful

unimpeded *adjective* = **unhindered**, free, open, unblocked, unchecked, unconstrained, unhampered, unrestrained, untrammelled
➤ **Antonyms**

blocked, checked, constrained, hampered, hindered, impeded, restrained

unimportant *adjective* = **insignificant**, immaterial, inconsequential, irrelevant, low-ranking, minor, nickel-and-dime (*U.S. slang*), not worth mentioning, nugatory, of no account, of no consequence, of no moment, paltry, petty, slight, trifling, trivial, worthless
➤ **Antonyms**
essential, grave, important, major, significant, urgent, vital, weighty

uninhabited *adjective* = **deserted**, abandoned, barren, desert, desolate, empty, lonely, unoccupied, unpopulated, unsettled, untenanted, vacant, waste

uninhibited *adjective* **1** = **unselfconscious**, candid, frank, free, free and easy, informal, instinctive, liberated, natural, open, relaxed, spontaneous, unrepressed, unreserved **2** = **unrestrained**, free, unbridled, unchecked, unconstrained, uncontrolled, uncurbed, unrestricted
➤ **Antonyms**
≠ **unselfconscious**: bashful, careful, demure, inhibited, modest, self-conscious, shy, uptight (*informal*) ≠ **unrestrained**: checked, constrained, controlled, curbed, hampered, inhibited, restrained

uninspired *adjective* = **unexciting**, banal, commonplace, dull, humdrum, indifferent, ordinary, prosaic, stale, stock, unimaginative, uninspiring, uninteresting, unoriginal, vanilla (*informal*)
➤ **Antonyms**
brilliant, different, exciting, imaginative, inspired, interesting, original, outstanding

uninspiring *adjective* = **unexciting**, as dry as dust, boring, drab, dreary, dry, dull, flat, humdrum, insipid, mundane, pedestrian, plain, prosaic, spiritless, uninteresting
➤ **Antonyms**
exciting, inspiring, moving, rousing, stimulating, stirring, uplifting

unintelligent *adjective* = **stupid**, braindead (*informal*), brainless, dense, dozy (*Brit. informal*), dull, dumb-ass (*slang*), empty-headed, foolish, gormless (*Brit. informal*), obtuse, slow, thick, unreasoning, unthinking
➤ **Antonyms**
bright, clever, intelligent, sharp, smart, thinking

unintelligible *adjective* = **incomprehensible**, illegible, inarticulate, incoherent, indecipherable, indistinct, jumbled, meaningless, muddled
➤ **Antonyms**
clear, coherent, comprehensible, intelligible, legible, lucid, understandable

unintentional *adjective* = **accidental**, casual, fortuitous, inadvertent, involuntary, unconscious, undesigned, unintended, unpremeditated, unthinking, unwitting
➤ **Antonyms**
conscious, deliberate, designed, intended, intentional, premeditated, voluntary, wilful

uninterested *adjective* = **indifferent**, apathetic, blasé, bored, distant, impassive, incurious, listless, unconcerned
➤ **Antonyms**
alert, concerned, curious, enthusiastic, interested, keen

uninteresting *adjective* = **boring**, as dry as dust, commonplace, drab, dreary, dry, dull, flat, ho-hum (*informal*), humdrum, mind-numbing, monotonous, tedious, tiresome, unenjoyable, uneventful, unexciting, uninspiring, wearisome
➤ **Antonyms**
absorbing, compelling, enjoyable, exciting, gripping, inspiring, interesting, intriguing, stimulating

uninterrupted *adjective* = **continuous**, constant, continual, nonstop, steady, sustained, unbroken, undisturbed, unending

uninvited *adjective* = **unasked**, not asked, not invited, unbidden, unwanted, unwelcome

uninviting *adjective* = **unattractive**, disagreeable, offensive, off-putting (*Brit. informal*), repellent, repulsive, unappealing, unappetizing, undesirable, unpleasant, untempting, unwelcoming
➤ **Antonyms**
agreeable, appealing, appetizing, attractive, desirable, inviting, pleasant, tempting, welcoming

union *noun* 1 = **joining**, amalgam, amalgamation, blend, combination, conjunction, fusion, mixture, synthesis, uniting 2 = **alliance**, association, Bund, coalition, confederacy, confederation, federation, league 3 = **agreement**, accord, concord, concurrence, harmony, unanimity, unison, unity 4 = **intercourse**, coition, coitus, copulation, coupling, marriage, matrimony, wedlock

unique *adjective* 1 = **single**, lone, one and only, only, solitary 2 = **unparalleled**, incomparable, inimitable, matchless, nonpareil, peerless, unequalled, unexampled, unmatched, unrivalled, without equal

unison *noun* = **agreement**, accord, accordance, concert, concord, cooperation, harmony, unanimity, unity
➤ **Antonyms**
disagreement, discord, disharmony, dissension, dissidence, dissonance

unit *noun* 1 = **item**, entity, module, piece, portion, whole 2 = **part**, component, constituent, element, member, section, segment 3 = **section**, detachment, group 4 = **measure**, measurement, quantity 5 = **system**, assembly

unite *verb* 1 = **join**, amalgamate, blend, coalesce, combine, consolidate, couple, fuse, incorporate, link, marry, meld, merge, unify, wed 2 = **cooperate**, ally, associate, band, close ranks, club together, collaborate, confederate, join forces, join together, league, pool, pull together
➤ **Antonyms**
≠**join**: break, detach, disunite, divide, part, separate, sever, split ≠**cooperate**: break, divorce, part, separate, split

united *adjective* 1 = **combined**, affiliated, allied, banded together, collective, concerted, in partnership, leagued, pooled, unified 2 = **in agreement**, agreed, in accord, like-minded, of like mind, of one mind, of the same opinion, one, unanimous

unity *noun* 1 = **wholeness**, entity, integrity, oneness, singleness, undividedness, unification, union 2 = **agreement**, accord, assent, concord, concurrence, consensus, harmony, peace, solidarity, unanimity, unison
➤ **Antonyms**
≠**wholeness**: disunity, division, heterogeneity, multiplicity, separation ≠**agreement**: disagreement, discord, disunity, division, factionalism, ill will, independence, individuality, in-fighting, strife

universal *adjective* = **widespread**, all-embracing, catholic, common, ecumenical, entire, general, omnipresent, overarching, total, unlimited, whole, worldwide

universality *noun* = **comprehensiveness**, all-inclusiveness, completeness, entirety, generality, generalization, totality, ubiquity

universally *adverb* = **everywhere**, across the board, always, in all cases, in every instance, invariably, uniformly, without exception

universe *noun* = **cosmos**, creation, everything, macrocosm, nature, the natural world

unjust *adjective* = **unfair**, biased, inequitable, one-sided, partial, partisan, prejudiced, undeserved, unjustified, unmerited, wrong, wrongful
➤ **Antonyms**
equitable, fair, impartial, just, justified, right, unbiased

unjustifiable *adjective* = **inexcusable**, indefensible, outrageous, unacceptable, unforgivable, unjust, unpardonable, unwarrantable, wrong

unkempt *adjective* **1** = **uncombed**, shaggy, tousled **2** = **untidy**, bedraggled, disarranged, disarrayed, dishevelled, disordered, messy, rumpled, scruffy, shabby, slatternly, sloppy (*informal*), slovenly, sluttish, ungroomed
➤ **Antonyms**
≠**untidy**: neat, presentable, soigné *or* soignée, spruce, tidy, trim, well-groomed

unkind *adjective* = **cruel**, hardhearted, harsh, inconsiderate, inhuman, insensitive, malicious, mean, nasty, spiteful, thoughtless, uncaring, uncharitable, unchristian, unfeeling, unfriendly, unsympathetic
➤ **Antonyms**
benevolent, caring, charitable, considerate, generous, kind, soft-hearted, sympathetic, thoughtful

unkindness *noun* = **cruelty**, hardheartedness, harshness, ill will, inhumanity, insensitivity, malevolence, malice, maliciousness, meanness, spite, spitefulness, unfeeling
➤ **Antonyms**
benevolence, charity, friendliness, generosity, goodwill, kindness, sympathy, thoughtfulness

unknown *adjective* **1** = **hidden**, concealed, dark, mysterious, secret, unrecognized, unrevealed, untold **2** = **strange**, alien, new **3** = **unidentified**, anonymous, beyond one's ken, nameless, uncharted, undiscovered, unexplored, unnamed **4** = **obscure**, humble, little known, undistinguished, unfamiliar, unheard-of, unrenowned, unsung
➤ **Antonyms**
≠**obscure**: celebrated, distinguished, familiar, known, recognized, renowned, well-known

unlawful *adjective* = **illegal**, actionable, against the law, banned, criminal, forbidden, illegitimate, illicit, outlawed, prohibited, unauthorized, under-the-table, unlicensed

unleash *verb* = **release**, free, let go, let loose, unbridle, unloose, untie

unlettered *adjective* = **uneducated**, ignorant, illiterate, unlearned, unschooled, untaught, untutored
➤ **Antonyms**
educated, learned, literate, schooled, taught, tutored

unlike *adjective* = **different**, as different as chalk and cheese (*informal*), contrasted, dissimilar, distinct, divergent, diverse, ill-matched, incompatible, not alike, opposite, unequal, unrelated
➤ **Antonyms**
compatible, equal, like, matched, related, similar

unlikely *adjective* **1** = **improbable**, doubtful, faint, not likely, remote, slight, unimaginable **2** = **unbelievable**, cock-and-bull (*informal*), implausible, incredible, questionable, unconvincing

unlimited *adjective* **1** = **infinite**, boundless, countless, endless, extensive, great, illimitable, immeasurable, immense, incalculable, limitless, unbounded, vast **2** = **total**, absolute, all-encompassing, complete, full, unconditional, unconstrained, unfettered, unqualified, unrestricted
➤ **Antonyms**
≠**infinite**: bounded, confined, finite, limited ≠**total**: constrained, limited, restricted

unload *verb* = **empty**, discharge, dump, lighten, off-load, relieve, unburden, unpack

unlock *verb* = **open**, free, let loose, release, unbar, unbolt, undo, unfasten, unlatch

unlooked-for *adjective* = **unexpected**, chance, fortuitous, out of the blue, surprise, surprising, unanticipated, undreamed of, unforeseen, unhoped-for, unpredicted, unthought-of

unlovable *adjective* = **unattractive**, dislikable *or* dislikeable, obnoxious, odious, repellent, repulsive, unadorable, undesirable, unlovely, unpleasant
➤ **Antonyms**
adorable, attractive, cute, desirable, enchanting, engaging, likable *or* likeable, lovable, lovely

unloved *adjective* = **uncared-for**, disliked, forsaken, loveless, neglected, rejected, spurned, uncherished, unpopular, unwanted
➤ **Antonyms**
adored, beloved, cherished, liked, loved, popular, precious, wanted

unlucky *adjective* **1** = **unfortunate**, cursed, disastrous, hapless, luckless, miserable, unhappy, unsuccessful, wretched **2** = **ill-fated**, doomed, ill-omened, ill-starred, inauspicious, ominous, unfavourable, untimely
➤ **Antonyms**
≠**unfortunate**: blessed, favoured, fortunate, happy, lucky, prosperous

unman *verb* **1** = **unnerve**, daunt, demoralize, discourage, dispirit, intimidate, psych out (*informal*), weaken **2** = **emasculate**

unmanageable *adjective* **1 = difficult to handle**, awkward, bulky, clunky (*informal*), cumbersome, inconvenient, unhandy, unwieldy **2 = uncontrollable**, difficult, fractious, intractable, obstreperous, out of hand, refractory, stroppy (*Brit. slang*), unruly, wild
➤ **Antonyms**
≠**difficult to handle**: manageable, wieldy ≠**uncontrollable**: amenable, compliant, docile, easy, manageable, submissive, tractable

unmanly *adjective* **1 = effeminate**, camp (*informal*), feeble, sissy, soft (*informal*), weak, womanish **2 = cowardly**, abject, chicken-hearted, craven, dishonourable, ignoble, weak-kneed (*informal*), yellow (*informal*)

unmannerly *adjective* **= bad-mannered**, badly behaved, discourteous, disrespectful, ill-bred, ill-mannered, impolite, misbehaved, rude, uncivil, uncouth
➤ **Antonyms**
civil, courteous, mannerly, polite, respectful, well-behaved, well-bred, well-mannered

unmarried *adjective* **= single**, bachelor, celibate, maiden, on the shelf, unattached, unwed, unwedded, virgin

unmask *verb* **= reveal**, bare, bring to light, disclose, discover, expose, lay bare, show up, uncloak, uncover, unveil

unmatched *adjective* **= unequalled**, beyond compare, consummate, incomparable, matchless, paramount, peerless, second to none, supreme, unparalleled, unrivalled, unsurpassed

unmentionable *adjective* **= taboo**, disgraceful, disreputable, forbidden, frowned on, immodest, indecent, obscene, scandalous, shameful, shocking, unspeakable, unutterable, X-rated (*informal*)

unmerciful *adjective* **= merciless**, brutal, cruel, hard, heartless, implacable, inhumane, pitiless, relentless, remorseless, ruthless, uncaring, unfeeling, unsparing
➤ **Antonyms**
beneficent, caring, feeling, humane, merciful, pitying, sparing, tender-hearted

unmistakable *adjective* **= clear**, blatant, certain, conspicuous, decided, distinct, evident, glaring, indisputable, manifest, obvious, palpable, patent, plain, positive, pronounced, sure, unambiguous, unequivocal
➤ **Antonyms**
ambiguous, dim, doubtful, equivocal, hidden, mistakable, obscure, uncertain, unclear, unsure

unmitigated *adjective* **1 = unrelieved**, grim, harsh, intense, oppressive, persistent, relentless, unabated, unalleviated, unbroken, undiminished, unmodified, unqualified, unredeemed **2 = complete**, absolute, arrant, consummate, deep-dyed (*usually derogatory*), downright, out-and-out, outright, perfect, rank, sheer, thorough, thoroughgoing, utter

unmoved *adjective* **= unaffected**, cold, dry-eyed, impassive, indifferent, unconcerned, unfeeling, unimpressed, unresponsive, unstirred, untouched
➤ **Antonyms**
affected, concerned, impressed, moved, stirred, touched

unnatural *adjective* **1 = strange**, bizarre, extraordinary, freakish, outlandish, queer, supernatural, unaccountable, uncanny **2 = abnormal**, aberrant, anomalous, irregular, odd, perverse, perverted, unusual **3 = false**, affected, artificial, assumed, contrived, feigned, forced, insincere, laboured, mannered, phoney *or* phony (*informal*), self-conscious, stagy, stiff, stilted, strained, studied, theatrical **4 = inhuman**, brutal, callous, cold-blooded, evil, fiendish, heartless, monstrous, ruthless, savage, unfeeling, wicked
➤ **Antonyms**
≠**strange**, **abnormal**: normal, ordinary, typical ≠**false**: genuine, honest, natural, sincere, unaffected, unfeigned, unpretentious ≠**inhuman**: caring, humane, loving, warm

unnecessary *adjective* **= needless**, dispensable, expendable, inessential, nonessential, redundant, superfluous, surplus to requirements, uncalled-for, unneeded, unrequired, useless
➤ **Antonyms**
essential, indispensable, necessary, needed, required, vital

unnerve *verb* **= intimidate**, confound, daunt, demoralize, disarm, disconcert, discourage, dishearten, dismay, dispirit, faze, fluster, frighten, psych out (*informal*), rattle (*informal*), shake, throw off balance, unhinge, unman, upset
➤ **Antonyms**
arm, brace, encourage, gee up, hearten, nerve, steel, strengthen, support

unnoticed *adjective* **= unobserved**, disregarded, ignored, neglected, overlooked, undiscovered, unheeded, unperceived, unrecognized, unremarked, unseen
➤ **Antonyms**
discovered, heeded, noted, noticed,

observed, perceived, recognized, remarked

unobtrusive *adjective* = **inconspicuous**, humble, keeping a low profile, low-key, meek, modest, quiet, restrained, retiring, self-effacing, subdued, unassuming, unnoticeable, unostentatious, unpretentious
➤ **Antonyms**
blatant, bold, conspicuous, eye-catching, high-profile, noticeable, obtrusive, outgoing, prominent

unoccupied *adjective* 1 = **empty**, tenantless, uninhabited, untenanted, vacant 2 = **idle**, at a loose end, at leisure, disengaged, inactive, unemployed

unofficial *adjective* = **unauthorized**, informal, off the record, personal, private, unconfirmed, wildcat

unorthodox *adjective* = **unconventional**, abnormal, heterodox, irregular, off-the-wall (*slang*), uncustomary, unusual, unwonted
➤ **Antonyms**
conventional, customary, established, orthodox, sound, traditional, usual

unpaid *adjective* 1 = **voluntary**, honorary, unsalaried 2 = **owing**, due, not discharged, outstanding, overdue, payable, unsettled

unpalatable *adjective* = **unpleasant**, bitter, disagreeable, displeasing, distasteful, horrid, offensive, repugnant, unappetizing, unattractive, uneatable, unsavoury
➤ **Antonyms**
agreeable, appetizing, attractive, eatable, palatable, pleasant, pleasing, savoury, tasty

unparalleled *adjective* = **unequalled**, beyond compare, consummate, exceptional, incomparable, matchless, peerless, rare, singular, superlative, unique, unmatched, unprecedented, unrivalled, unsurpassed, without equal

unpardonable *adjective* = **unforgivable**, deplorable, disgraceful, indefensible, inexcusable, outrageous, scandalous, shameful, unjustifiable

unperturbed *adjective* = **calm**, as cool as a cucumber, collected, composed, cool, placid, poised, self-possessed, tranquil, undismayed, unfazed (*informal*), unflustered, unruffled, untroubled, unworried
➤ **Antonyms**
anxious, dismayed, flustered, perturbed, ruffled, troubled, worried

unpleasant *adjective* = **nasty**, abhorrent, bad, disagreeable, displeasing, distasteful, horrid, ill-natured, irksome, objectionable, obnoxious, repulsive, troublesome, unattractive, unlikable *or* unlikeable,

unlovely, unpalatable
➤ **Antonyms**
agreeable, good-natured, likable *or* likeable, lovely, nice, pleasant

unpleasantness *noun* 1 = **nastiness**, awfulness, disagreeableness, dreadfulness, grimness, horridness, ugliness 2 = **hostility**, animosity, antagonism, bad feeling, ill humour *or* will, malice, offensiveness, rudeness, unfriendliness
➤ **Antonyms**
≠**nastiness:** agreeableness, delight, enjoyment, pleasantness ≠**hostility:** friendliness, good humour *or* will, pleasantness

unpolished *adjective* 1 = **crude**, rough, rough and ready, rude, sketchy, unfinished 2 = **unrefined**, uncivilized, uncouth, uncultivated, uncultured, unsophisticated, vulgar

unpopular *adjective* = **disliked**, avoided, detested, not sought out, out in the cold, out of favour, rejected, shunned, unattractive, undesirable, unloved, unwanted, unwelcome
➤ **Antonyms**
desirable, favoured, liked, loved, popular, wanted, welcome

unprecedented *adjective* = **extraordinary**, abnormal, exceptional, freakish, ground-breaking, new, novel, original, remarkable, singular, unexampled, unheard-of, unparalleled, unrivalled, unusual

unpredictable *adjective* = **inconstant**, chance, changeable, doubtful, erratic, fickle, fluky (*informal*), hit-and-miss (*informal*), hit-or-miss (*informal*), iffy (*informal*), random, unforeseeable, unreliable, unstable, variable
➤ **Antonyms**
certain, constant, dependable, foreseeable, predictable, reliable, stable, steady, unchanging

unprejudiced *adjective* = **impartial**, balanced, even-handed, fair, fair-minded, just, nonpartisan, objective, open-minded, unbiased, uninfluenced
➤ **Antonyms**
biased, bigoted, influenced, narrow-minded, partial, prejudiced, unfair, unjust

unprepared *adjective* 1 = **taken off guard**, caught napping, caught on the hop (*Brit. informal*), surprised, taken aback, unaware, unready, unsuspecting 2 = **improvised**, ad-lib, extemporaneous, off the cuff (*informal*), spontaneous

unpretentious *adjective* = **modest**, homely, honest, humble, plain, simple,

straightforward, unaffected, unassuming, unimposing, unobtrusive, unostentatious, unspoiled
➤ **Antonyms**
affected, arty-farty (*informal*), conceited, obtrusive, ostentatious, pretentious, showy

unprincipled *adjective* = **dishonest**, amoral, corrupt, crooked, deceitful, devious, dishonourable, immoral, tricky, unconscionable, underhand, unethical, unprofessional, unscrupulous
➤ **Antonyms**
decent, ethical, honest, honourable, moral, righteous, scrupulous, upright, virtuous

unproductive *adjective* 1 = **useless**, fruitless, futile, idle, ineffective, inefficacious, unavailing, unprofitable, unremunerative, unrewarding, vain, valueless, worthless 2 = **barren**, dry, fruitless, sterile, unprolific
➤ **Antonyms**
≠**useless:** effective, fruitful, profitable, remunerative, rewarding, useful, worthwhile ≠**barren:** abundant, fertile, fruitful, productive, prolific

unprofessional *adjective* 1 = **unethical**, improper, lax, negligent, unfitting, unprincipled, unseemly, unworthy 2 = **amateurish**, amateur, cowboy (*informal*), incompetent, inefficient, inexperienced, inexpert, slapdash, slipshod, untrained
➤ **Antonyms**
≠**amateurish:** adept, competent, efficient, experienced, expert, professional, skilful

unpromising *adjective* = **inauspicious**, adverse, discouraging, doubtful, gloomy, infelicitous, ominous, unfavourable, unpropitious

unprotected *adjective* = **vulnerable**, defenceless, exposed, helpless, naked, open, open to attack, unarmed, undefended, unguarded, unsheltered, unshielded
➤ **Antonyms**
defended, guarded, immune, protected, safe, secure, shielded

unqualified *adjective* 1 = **unfit**, ill-equipped, incapable, incompetent, ineligible, not equal to, not up to, unprepared 2 = **unconditional**, categorical, downright, outright, unmitigated, unreserved, unrestricted, without reservation 3 = **total**, absolute, complete, consummate, deep-dyed (*usually derogatory*), downright, out-and-out, outright, thorough, thoroughgoing, utter

unquestionable *adjective* = **certain**,

absolute, beyond a shadow of doubt, clear, conclusive, definite, incontestable, incontrovertible, indisputable, indubitable, irrefutable, manifest, patent, self-evident, sure, undeniable, unequivocal, unmistakable
➤ **Antonyms**
ambiguous, doubtful, dubious, inconclusive, questionable, uncertain, unclear

unravel *verb* 1 = **undo**, disentangle, extricate, free, separate, straighten out, unknot, untangle, unwind 2 = **solve**, clear up, explain, figure out (*informal*), get straight, get to the bottom of, interpret, make out, puzzle out, resolve, suss (out) (*slang*), work out

unreadable *adjective* 1 = **illegible**, crabbed, undecipherable 2 = **turgid**, badly written, dry as dust, heavy going

unreal *adjective* 1 = **imaginary**, chimerical, dreamlike, fabulous, fanciful, fictitious, hypothetical, illusory, make-believe, mythical, phantasmagoric, storybook, visionary 2 = **insubstantial**, immaterial, impalpable, intangible, nebulous 3 = **fake**, artificial, false, insincere, mock, ostensible, pretended, seeming, sham
➤ **Antonyms**
≠**fake:** authentic, bona fide, genuine, real, realistic, sincere, true, veritable

unrealistic *adjective* 1 = **impractical**, half-baked (*informal*), impracticable, improbable, quixotic, romantic, starry-eyed, theoretical, unworkable 2 = **unauthentic**, non-naturalistic, unlifelike, unreal
➤ **Antonyms**
≠**impractical:** practical, pragmatic, probable, realistic, sensible, unromantic, workable

unreasonable *adjective* 1 = **excessive**, absurd, exorbitant, extortionate, extravagant, far-fetched, immoderate, irrational, preposterous, steep (*informal*), too great, uncalled-for, undue, unfair, unjust, unwarranted 2 = **biased**, arbitrary, blinkered, headstrong, illogical, opinionated
➤ **Antonyms**
≠**excessive:** fair, just, justified, moderate, reasonable, warranted ≠**biased:** fair-minded, flexible, open-minded

unregenerate *adjective* = **unrepentant**, hardened, intractable, obdurate, obstinate, recalcitrant, refractory, self-willed, stubborn, unconverted, unreformed
➤ **Antonyms**
converted, reformed, regenerate,

repentant

unrelated *adjective* **1** = **unconnected**, different, dissimilar, not kin, not kindred, not related, unlike **2** = **irrelevant**, beside the point, extraneous, inapplicable, inappropriate, not germane, unassociated, unconnected

unrelenting *adjective* **1** = **merciless**, cruel, implacable, intransigent, pitiless, relentless, remorseless, ruthless, stern, tough, unsparing **2** = **steady**, ceaseless, constant, continual, continuous, endless, incessant, perpetual, unabated, unbroken, unremitting, unwavering

unreliable *adjective* **1** = **undependable**, irresponsible, not conscientious, treacherous, unstable, untrustworthy **2** = **uncertain**, deceptive, erroneous, fake, fallible, false, implausible, inaccurate, mistaken, specious, unconvincing, unsound
➤ **Antonyms**
≠**undependable**: conscientious, dependable, reliable, responsible, stable, trustworthy ≠**uncertain**: accurate, infallible

unremitting *adjective* = **constant**, continual, continuous, incessant, indefatigable, perpetual, relentless, remorseless, unabated, unbroken, unceasing, unwavering

unrepentant *adjective* = **impenitent**, abandoned, callous, hardened, incorrigible, not contrite, shameless, unregenerate, unremorseful, unrepenting
➤ **Antonyms**
ashamed, contrite, penitent, remorseful, repentant, rueful, sorry

unreserved *adjective* **1** = **total**, absolute, complete, entire, full, unconditional, unlimited, unqualified, wholehearted, without reservation **2** = **uninhibited**, demonstrative, extrovert, forthright, frank, free, open, open-hearted, outgoing, outspoken, unrestrained, unreticent
➤ **Antonyms**
≠**uninhibited**: demure, inhibited, reserved, restrained, reticent, shy, undemonstrative

unresolved *adjective* = **undecided**, doubtful, moot, open to question, pending, problematical, unanswered, undetermined, unsettled, unsolved, up in the air, vague, yet to be decided

unrest *noun* **1** = **discontent**, agitation, disaffection, discord, dissatisfaction, dissension, protest, rebellion, sedition, strife, tumult, turmoil, upheaval **2** = **uneasiness**, agitation, anxiety, disquiet, distress, perturbation, restlessness, trepidation, worry

➤ **Antonyms**
calm, contentment, peace, relaxation, rest, stillness, tranquillity

unrestrained *adjective* = **uncontrolled**, abandoned, free, immoderate, inordinate, intemperate, natural, unbounded, unbridled, unchecked, unconstrained, unhindered, uninhibited, unlimited, unrepressed
➤ **Antonyms**
checked, constrained, frustrated, hindered, inhibited, repressed, restrained

unrestricted *adjective* **1** = **unlimited**, absolute, free, free-for-all (*informal*), open, unbounded, uncircumscribed, unhindered, unregulated **2** = **open**, clear, public, unobstructed, unopposed

unrivalled *adjective* = **unparalleled**, beyond compare, incomparable, matchless, nonpareil, peerless, supreme, unequalled, unexcelled, unmatched, unsurpassed, without equal

unruffled *adjective* **1** = **calm**, collected, composed, cool, peaceful, placid, sedate, serene, tranquil, undisturbed, unfazed (*informal*), unflustered, unmoved, unperturbed **2** = **smooth**, even, flat, level, unbroken

unruly *adjective* = **uncontrollable**, disobedient, disorderly, fractious, headstrong, insubordinate, intractable, lawless, mutinous, obstreperous, rebellious, refractory, riotous, rowdy, turbulent, ungovernable, unmanageable, wayward, wild, wilful
➤ **Antonyms**
amenable, biddable, docile, governable, manageable, obedient, orderly, tractable

unsafe *adjective* = **dangerous**, hazardous, insecure, perilous, precarious, risky, threatening, treacherous, uncertain, unreliable, unsound, unstable
➤ **Antonyms**
harmless, reliable, safe, secure, sound

unsaid *adjective* = **unspoken**, left to the imagination, tacit, undeclared, unexpressed, unstated, unuttered, unvoiced

unsatisfactory *adjective* = **not good enough**, deficient, disappointing, displeasing, inadequate, insufficient, mediocre, no great shakes (*informal*), not much cop (*Brit. slang*), not up to par, not up to scratch (*informal*), pathetic, poor, unacceptable, unsuitable, unworthy
➤ **Antonyms**
acceptable, adequate, passable, pleasing, satisfactory, sufficient, suitable

unsavoury *adjective* **1** = **unpleasant**, distasteful, nasty, objectionable,

obnoxious, offensive, repellent,
repugnant, repulsive, revolting 2
= **unappetizing**, disagreeable, distasteful,
nauseating, sickening, unpalatable
➤ **Antonyms**
≠**unappetizing**: agreeable, appetizing,
palatable, pleasant, savoury, tasteful, tasty,
toothsome

unscathed *adjective* = **unharmed**, in one
piece, safe, sound, unhurt, uninjured,
unmarked, unscarred, unscratched,
untouched, whole

unscrupulous *adjective* = **unprincipled**,
corrupt, crooked (*informal*), dishonest,
dishonourable, immoral, improper,
ruthless, unethical
➤ **Antonyms**
ethical, honest, honourable, moral,
principled, proper, scrupulous, upright

unseasonable *adjective* = **untimely**,
ill-timed, inappropriate, inopportune,
mistimed, out of keeping, unsuitable

unseat *verb* 1 = **throw**, unhorse, unsaddle 2
= **depose**, dethrone, discharge, dismiss,
displace, oust, overthrow, remove

unseemly *adjective* = **improper**,
discreditable, inappropriate, indecorous,
indelicate, in poor taste, out of keeping,
out of place, unbecoming, unbefitting,
undignified, unsuitable
➤ **Antonyms**
acceptable, appropriate, becoming,
decorous, fitting, proper, seemly, suitable

unseen *adjective* 1 = **hidden**, concealed,
invisible, obscure, veiled 2 = **unobserved**,
undetected, unnoticed, unobtrusive,
unperceived

unselfish *adjective* = **generous**, altruistic,
charitable, devoted, disinterested,
humanitarian, kind, liberal, magnanimous,
noble, self-denying, selfless, self-sacrificing

unsettle *verb* = **disturb**, agitate, bother,
confuse, discompose, disconcert, disorder,
faze, fluster, perturb, rattle (*informal*),
ruffle, throw (*informal*), throw into
confusion, throw off balance, trouble,
unbalance, unnerve, upset

unsettled *adjective* 1 = **unstable**,
disorderly, insecure, shaky, unsteady 2
= **restless**, agitated, anxious, confused,
disturbed, flustered, on edge, perturbed,
restive, shaken, tense, troubled, uneasy,
unnerved, wired (*slang*) 3 = **inconstant**,
changeable, changing, uncertain,
unpredictable, variable 4 = **unresolved**,
debatable, doubtful, moot, open,
undecided, undetermined, up in the air 5
= **owing**, due, in arrears, outstanding,
payable, pending

unshakable *adjective* = **firm**, absolute,

certain, constant, fixed, immovable,
resolute, secure, staunch, steadfast, sure,
unassailable, unswerving, unwavering,
well-founded
➤ **Antonyms**
insecure, shaky, uncertain, unsure,
wavering, wobbly

unshaken *adjective* = **unmoved**, calm,
collected, composed, impassive,
unaffected, unalarmed, undaunted,
undismayed, undisturbed, unfazed
(*informal*), unperturbed, unruffled

unsightly *adjective* = **ugly**, disagreeable,
hideous, horrid, repulsive, revolting
(*informal*), unattractive, unpleasant,
unprepossessing
➤ **Antonyms**
agreeable, attractive, beautiful, comely,
cute, handsome, pleasing, prepossessing,
pretty

unskilled *adjective* = **unprofessional**,
amateurish, cowboy (*informal*),
inexperienced, uneducated, unqualified,
untalented, untrained
➤ **Antonyms**
adept, expert, masterly, professional,
qualified, skilled, talented

unsociable *adjective* = **unfriendly**, chilly,
cold, convivial, distant, hostile,
introverted, reclusive, retiring, standoffish,
uncongenial, unforthcoming,
unneighbourly, unsocial, withdrawn
➤ **Antonyms**
congenial, convivial, friendly, gregarious,
neighbourly, outgoing, sociable

unsolicited *adjective* = **unasked for**,
free-will, gratuitous, spontaneous,
uncalled-for, unforced, uninvited,
unrequested, unsought, unwelcome,
voluntary, volunteered

unsophisticated *adjective* 1 = **natural**,
artless, childlike, guileless, inexperienced,
ingenuous, innocent, naive, unaffected,
unworldly 2 = **simple**, plain,
straightforward, uncomplex,
uncomplicated, uninvolved, unrefined,
unspecialized
➤ **Antonyms**
≠**simple**: advanced, complex,
complicated, intricate, sophisticated

unsound *adjective* 1 = **unhealthy**, ailing,
defective, delicate, deranged, diseased,
frail, ill, in poor health, unbalanced,
unhinged, unstable, unwell, weak 2
= **invalid**, defective, erroneous, fallacious,
false, faulty, flawed, ill-founded, illogical,
shaky, specious, unreliable, weak 3
= **unstable**, flimsy, insecure, not solid,
rickety, shaky, tottering, unreliable, unsafe,
unsteady, wobbly

➤ **Antonyms**
≠**unstable:** reliable, safe, solid, sound, stable, steady, strong, sturdy

unsparing *adjective* **1** = **lavish**, abundant, bountiful, generous, liberal, munificent, open-handed, plenteous, prodigal, profuse, ungrudging, unstinting **2** = **severe**, cold-blooded, hard, harsh, implacable, relentless, ruthless, stern, stringent, uncompromising, unforgiving, unmerciful

unspeakable *adjective* **1** = **indescribable**, beyond description, beyond words, inconceivable, ineffable, inexpressible, overwhelming, unbelievable, unimaginable, unutterable, wonderful **2** = **dreadful**, abominable, abysmal, appalling, awful, bad, evil, execrable, frightful, from hell (*informal*), heinous, hellacious (*U.S. slang*), horrible, loathsome, monstrous, odious, repellent, shocking, too horrible for words

unspoiled, unspoilt *adjective* **1** = **undamaged**, intact, perfect, preserved, unaffected, unblemished, unchanged, unharmed, unimpaired, untouched **2** = **natural**, artless, innocent, unaffected, unassuming, unstudied, wholesome
➤ **Antonyms**
≠**undamaged:** affected, blemished, changed, damaged, harmed, impaired, imperfect, spoilt, touched

unspoken *adjective* **1** = **tacit**, assumed, implicit, implied, inferred, left to the imagination, not put into words, not spelt out, taken for granted, undeclared, understood, unexpressed, unstated **2** = **unsaid**, mute, silent, unuttered, voiceless, wordless
➤ **Antonyms**
≠**tacit:** clear, declared, explicit, expressed, spoken, stated

unstable *adjective* **1** = **insecure**, not fixed, precarious, rickety, risky, shaky, tottering, unsettled, unsteady, wobbly **2** = **changeable**, fitful, fluctuating, inconstant, unpredictable, unsteady, variable, volatile **3** = **unpredictable**, capricious, changeable, erratic, inconsistent, irrational, temperamental, unreliable
➤ **Antonyms**
≠**changeable:** constant, predictable, stable, steady ≠**unpredictable:** consistent, level-headed, rational, reliable, stable

unsteady *adjective* **1** = **unstable**, infirm, insecure, precarious, reeling, rickety, shaky, tottering, treacherous, unsafe, wobbly **2** = **erratic**, changeable, flickering, fluctuating, inconstant, irregular, temperamental, unreliable, unsettled, variable, volatile, wavering

unsubstantial *adjective* **1** = **flimsy**, airy, fragile, frail, inadequate, light, slight, thin **2** = **immaterial**, dreamlike, fanciful, illusory, imaginary, impalpable, visionary

unsubstantiated *adjective* = **unconfirmed**, open to question, unattested, uncorroborated, unestablished, unproven, unsupported
➤ **Antonyms**
attested, confirmed, corroborated, established, proven, substantiated, supported

unsuccessful *adjective* **1** = **useless**, abortive, failed, fruitless, futile, ineffective, unavailing, unproductive, vain **2** = **unlucky**, balked, defeated, foiled, frustrated, hapless, ill-starred, losing, luckless, unfortunate
➤ **Antonyms**
≠**useless:** flourishing, fruitful, productive, prosperous, remunerative, successful, thriving, useful, worthwhile ≠**unlucky:** fortunate, lucky, triumphant, victorious, winning

unsuitable *adjective* = **inappropriate**, improper, inapposite, inapt, incompatible, incongruous, ineligible, infelicitous, out of character, out of keeping, out of place, unacceptable, unbecoming, unbefitting, unfit, unfitting, unseasonable, unseemly, unsuited
➤ **Antonyms**
acceptable, apposite, appropriate, apt, compatible, eligible, fitting, proper, suitable

unsung *adjective* = **unacknowledged**, anonymous, disregarded, neglected, unacclaimed, unappreciated, uncelebrated, unhailed, unhonoured, unknown, unnamed, unrecognized

unsure *adjective* **1** = **lacking in confidence**, insecure, unassured, unconfident **2** = **doubtful**, distrustful, dubious, hesitant, in a quandary, irresolute, mistrustful, sceptical, suspicious, unconvinced, undecided
➤ **Antonyms**
assured, certain, confident, convinced, decided, persuaded, resolute, sure

unsurpassed *adjective* = **supreme**, consummate, exceptional, incomparable, matchless, nonpareil, paramount, peerless, second to none, superlative, transcendent, unequalled, unexcelled, unparalleled, unrivalled, without an equal

unsuspecting *adjective* = **unconscious**, credulous, gullible, inexperienced, ingenuous, innocent, naive, off guard, trustful, trusting, unsuspicious, unwarned, unwary

unswerving *adjective* = **constant**, dedicated, devoted, direct, firm, resolute, single-minded, staunch, steadfast, steady, true, undeviating, unfaltering, unflagging, untiring, unwavering

unsympathetic *adjective* = **hard**, apathetic, callous, cold, cruel, harsh, heartless, indifferent, insensitive, soulless, stony-hearted, uncompassionate, unconcerned, unfeeling, unkind, unmoved, unpitying
➤ Antonyms
caring, compassionate, concerned, kind, pitying, sensitive, supportive, sympathetic, understanding

untamed *adjective* = **wild**, barbarous, feral, fierce, not broken in, savage, unbroken, uncontrollable, undomesticated, untameable

untangle *verb* 1 = **disentangle**, extricate, unravel, unsnarl 2 = **solve**, clear up, explain, straighten out
➤ Antonyms
≠disentangle: enmesh, entangle, jumble, muddle, snarl, tangle ≠solve: complicate, confuse, muddle, puzzle

untenable *adjective* = **unsustainable**, fallacious, flawed, groundless, illogical, indefensible, insupportable, shaky, unreasonable, unsound, weak
➤ Antonyms
defensible, justified, logical, rational, reasonable, sensible, sound, supportable, unarguable, uncontestable, valid, verifiable, well-grounded

unthinkable *adjective* 1 = **impossible**, absurd, illogical, improbable, not on (*informal*), out of the question, preposterous, unlikely, unreasonable 2 = **inconceivable**, beyond belief, beyond the bounds of possibility, implausible, incredible, insupportable, unbelievable, unimaginable

unthinking *adjective* 1 = **thoughtless**, blundering, inconsiderate, insensitive, rude, selfish, tactless, undiplomatic 2 = **unconscious**, careless, heedless, impulsive, inadvertent, instinctive, mechanical, negligent, oblivious, unmindful
➤ Antonyms
≠unconscious: careful, conscious, deliberate, heedful, mindful

untidy *adjective* = **messy**, bedraggled, chaotic, cluttered, disarrayed, disordered, higgledy-piggledy (*informal*), jumbled, littered, muddled, muddly, rumpled, shambolic, slatternly, slipshod, sloppy (*informal*), slovenly, topsy-turvy, unkempt
➤ Antonyms
methodical, neat, orderly, presentable, ship-shape, spruce, systematic, tidy, well-kept

untie *verb* = **undo**, free, loosen, release, unbind, unbridle, unclasp, unfasten, unknot, unlace, unstrap

untimely *adjective* 1 = **early**, premature, unseasonable 2 = **ill-timed**, awkward, badly timed, inappropriate, inconvenient, inopportune, mistimed, unfortunate, unsuitable
➤ Antonyms
≠early: seasonable, timely ≠ill-timed: appropriate, convenient, opportune, suitable, well-timed

untiring *adjective* = **tireless**, constant, determined, dogged, incessant, indefatigable, persevering, persistent, steady, unfaltering, unflagging, unremitting, unwearied

untold *adjective* 1 = **indescribable**, inexpressible, undreamed of, unimaginable, unspeakable, unthinkable, unutterable 2 = **countless**, incalculable, innumerable, measureless, myriad, numberless, uncountable, uncounted, unnumbered 3 = **undisclosed**, hidden, private, secret, unknown, unpublished, unrecounted, unrelated, unrevealed

untouched *adjective* 1 = **unharmed**, intact, safe and sound, undamaged, unhurt, uninjured, unscathed, without a scratch 2 = **unmoved**, indifferent, unaffected, unconcerned, unimpressed, unstirred
➤ Antonyms
≠unmoved: affected, concerned, impressed, moved, softened, stirred, touched

untoward *adjective* 1 = **troublesome**, annoying, awkward, disastrous, ill-timed, inconvenient, irritating, unfortunate, vexatious 2 = **unfavourable**, adverse, contrary, inauspicious, inopportune, unlucky, untimely

untrained *adjective* = **amateur**, green, inexperienced, raw, uneducated, unpractised, unqualified, unschooled, unskilled, untaught, untutored
➤ Antonyms
educated, experienced, expert, qualified, schooled, skilled, taught, trained

untried *adjective* = **untested**, in the experimental stage, new, novel, unattempted, unessayed, unproved

untroubled *adjective* = **undisturbed**, calm, composed, cool, peaceful, placid, sedate, serene, steady, tranquil, unagitated, unconcerned, unfazed (*informal*),

unflappable (*informal*), unflustered, unperturbed, unruffled, unstirred, unworried
➤ **Antonyms**
agitated, anxious, concerned, disturbed, flustered, perturbed, ruffled, troubled, worried

untrue *adjective* 1 = **false**, deceptive, dishonest, erroneous, fallacious, inaccurate, incorrect, lying, misleading, mistaken, sham, spurious, untruthful, wrong 2 = **unfaithful**, deceitful, disloyal, faithless, false, forsworn, inconstant, perfidious, traitorous, treacherous, two-faced, untrustworthy
➤ **Antonyms**
≠**false**: accurate, correct, factual, right, true ≠**unfaithful**: constant, dependable, faithful, loyal

untrustworthy *adjective* = **unreliable**, deceitful, devious, dishonest, disloyal, fair-weather, faithless, false, fly-by-night (*informal*), not to be depended on, slippery, treacherous, tricky, two-faced, undependable, unfaithful, untrue, untrusty
➤ **Antonyms**
dependable, faithful, honest, loyal, reliable, steadfast, true, trustworthy, trusty

untruth *noun* = **lie**, deceit, fabrication, falsehood, falsification, fib, fiction, pork pie (*Brit. slang*), porky (*Brit. slang*), prevarication, story, tale, whopper (*informal*)

untruthful *adjective* = **dishonest**, crooked (*informal*), deceitful, deceptive, dissembling, false, fibbing, hypocritical, lying, mendacious
➤ **Antonyms**
candid, honest, sincere, true, truthful, veracious

untutored *adjective* 1 = **uneducated**, ignorant, illiterate, unlearned, unschooled, untrained, unversed 2 = **unsophisticated**, artless, inexperienced, simple, unpractised, unrefined

unused *adjective* 1 = **unutilized**, available, extra, left, leftover, remaining, unconsumed, unexhausted 2 = **new**, fresh, intact, pristine, untouched 3 *with* **to** = **unaccustomed to**, a stranger to, inexperienced in, new to, unfamiliar with

unusual *adjective* = **extraordinary**, abnormal, atypical, bizarre, curious, different, exceptional, left-field (*informal*), notable, odd, out of the ordinary, phenomenal, queer, rare, remarkable, singular, strange, surprising, uncommon, unconventional, unexpected, unfamiliar, unwonted
➤ **Antonyms**

average, banal, commonplace, conventional, everyday, familiar, normal, routine, traditional, typical, unremarkable, usual

unutterable *adjective* = **indescribable**, beyond words, extreme, ineffable, overwhelming, unimaginable, unspeakable

unvarnished *adjective* = **plain**, bare, candid, frank, honest, naked, pure, pure and simple, simple, sincere, stark, straightforward, unadorned, unembellished

unveil *verb* = **reveal**, bare, bring to light, disclose, divulge, expose, lay bare, lay open, make known, make public, uncover
➤ **Antonyms**
cloak, conceal, cover, disguise, hide, mask, obscure, veil

unwanted *adjective* = **undesired**, *de trop*, going begging, outcast, rejected, superfluous, surplus to requirements, unasked, uninvited, unneeded, unsolicited, unwelcome, useless
➤ **Antonyms**
desired, necessary, needed, useful, wanted, welcome

unwarranted *adjective* = **unnecessary**, gratuitous, groundless, indefensible, inexcusable, uncalled-for, unjust, unjustified, unprovoked, unreasonable, wrong

unwary *adjective* = **careless**, heedless, imprudent, incautious, indiscreet, rash, reckless, thoughtless, uncircumspect, unguarded, unwatchful
➤ **Antonyms**
cautious, chary, circumspect, discreet, guarded, prudent, wary, watchful

unwavering *adjective* = **steady**, consistent, dedicated, determined, immovable, resolute, single-minded, staunch, steadfast, undeviating, unfaltering, unflagging, unshakable, unshaken, unswerving, untiring

unwelcome *adjective* 1 = **unwanted**, excluded, rejected, unacceptable, undesirable, uninvited, unpopular, unwished for 2 = **disagreeable**, displeasing, distasteful, thankless, undesirable, unpleasant
➤ **Antonyms**
acceptable, agreeable, desirable, pleasant, pleasing, popular, wanted, welcome

unwell *adjective* = **ill**, ailing, at death's door, indisposed, in poor health, off colour, out of sorts, poorly (*informal*), sick, sickly, under the weather (*informal*), unhealthy
➤ **Antonyms**
fine, healthy, robust, sound, well

unwholesome *adjective* **1** = **harmful**, deleterious, insalubrious, insanitary, noxious, poisonous, tainted, unhealthy, unnourishing **2** = **wicked**, bad, corrupting, degrading, demoralizing, depraving, evil, immoral **3** = **sickly**, anaemic, pale, pallid, pasty, wan
➤ **Antonyms**
≠**harmful**: beneficial, germ-free, healthy, hygienic, salubrious, sanitary, wholesome ≠**wicked**: moral

unwieldy *adjective* **1** = **awkward**, burdensome, cumbersome, inconvenient, unhandy, unmanageable **2** = **bulky**, clumsy, clunky (*informal*), hefty, massive, ponderous, ungainly, weighty

unwilling *adjective* = **reluctant**, averse, disinclined, grudging, indisposed, loath, not in the mood, opposed, resistant, unenthusiastic
➤ **Antonyms**
amenable, compliant, disposed, eager, enthusiastic, inclined, voluntary, willing

unwind *verb* **1** = **unravel**, disentangle, slacken, uncoil, undo, unreel, unroll, untwine, untwist **2** = **relax**, calm down, let oneself go, loosen up, mellow out (*informal*), sit back, slow down, take a break, take it easy, wind down

unwise *adjective* = **foolish**, asinine, foolhardy, ill-advised, ill-considered, ill-judged, impolitic, improvident, imprudent, inadvisable, inane, indiscreet, injudicious, irresponsible, rash, reckless, senseless, short-sighted, silly, stupid
➤ **Antonyms**
discreet, judicious, politic, prudent, responsible, sensible, shrewd, wise

unwitting *adjective* **1** = **unintentional**, accidental, chance, inadvertent, involuntary, undesigned, unintended, unmeant, unplanned **2** = **unknowing**, ignorant, innocent, unaware, unconscious, unsuspecting
➤ **Antonyms**
≠**unintentional**: deliberate, designed, intended, intentional, meant, planned ≠**unknowing**: conscious, deliberate, knowing, witting

unwonted *adjective* = **unusual**, atypical, extraordinary, infrequent, out of the ordinary, peculiar, rare, singular, unaccustomed, uncommon, uncustomary, unexpected, unfamiliar

unworldly *adjective* **1** = **spiritual**, abstract, celestial, metaphysical, nonmaterialistic, religious, transcendental **2** = **naive**, as green as grass, green, idealistic, inexperienced, innocent, raw, trusting, unsophisticated, wet behind the ears

(*informal*) **3** = **otherworldly**, ethereal, extraterrestrial, unearthly

unworthy *adjective* **1** = **undeserving**, ineligible, not deserving of, not fit for, not good enough, not worth **2** = **dishonourable**, base, contemptible, degrading, discreditable, disgraceful, disreputable, ignoble, shameful **3** **unworthy of** = **unbefitting**, beneath, improper, inappropriate, out of character, out of place, unbecoming, unfitting, unseemly, unsuitable
➤ **Antonyms**
≠**undeserving**: deserving, eligible, fit, meritorious, worthy ≠**dishonourable**: commendable, creditable, honourable

unwritten *adjective* **1** = **oral**, unrecorded, vocal, word-of-mouth **2** = **customary**, accepted, conventional, tacit, traditional, understood

unyielding *adjective* = **firm**, adamant, determined, hardline, immovable, inflexible, intractable, obdurate, obstinate, relentless, resolute, rigid, staunch, steadfast, stiff-necked, stubborn, tough, unbending, uncompromising, unwavering
➤ **Antonyms**
adaptable, compliant, compromising, cooperative, flexible, movable, tractable, yielding

up-and-coming *adjective* = **promising**, ambitious, eager, go-getting (*informal*)

upbeat *adjective Informal* = **cheerful**, buoyant, cheery, encouraging, favourable, forward-looking, heartening, hopeful, looking up, optimistic, positive

upbraid *verb* = **scold**, admonish, bawl out (*informal*), berate, blame, castigate, censure, chew out (*U.S. & Canad. informal*), chide, condemn, dress down (*informal*), give (someone) a rocket (*Brit. & N.Z. informal*), lecture, rap (someone) over the knuckles, read the riot act, rebuke, reprimand, reproach, reprove, slap on the wrist, take to task, tear into (*informal*), tear (someone) off a strip (*Brit. informal*), tell off (*informal*), tick off (*informal*)

upbringing *noun* = **education**, breeding, bringing-up, care, cultivation, nurture, raising, rearing, tending, training

update *verb* = **bring up to date**, amend, modernize, rebrand, renew, revise

upgrade *verb* = **promote**, advance, ameliorate, better, elevate, enhance, improve, raise
➤ **Antonyms**
degrade, demote, downgrade, lower

upheaval *noun* = **disturbance**, cataclysm, disorder, disruption, eruption, overthrow, revolution, turmoil, violent change

uphill *adjective* **1** = **ascending**, climbing, mounting, rising **2** = **arduous**, difficult, exhausting, gruelling, hard, laborious, punishing, strenuous, taxing, tough, wearisome
➤ **Antonyms**
≠**ascending**: descending, downhill, lowering

uphold *verb* = **support**, advocate, aid, back, champion, defend, encourage, endorse, hold to, justify, maintain, promote, stand by, stick up for (*informal*), sustain, vindicate

upkeep *noun* **1** = **maintenance**, conservation, keep, preservation, repair, running, subsistence, support, sustenance **2** = **running costs**, expenditure, expenses, operating costs, outlay, overheads

uplift *verb* **1** = **raise**, elevate, heave, hoist, lift up **2** = **improve**, advance, ameliorate, better, civilize, cultivate, edify, inspire, raise, refine, upgrade ◆ *noun* **3** = **improvement**, advancement, betterment, cultivation, edification, enhancement, enlightenment, enrichment, refinement

upper *adjective* **1** = **higher**, high, loftier, superior, top, topmost **2** = **superior**, elevated, eminent, greater, important
➤ **Antonyms**
≠**higher**: bottom, inferior, low, lower
≠**superior**: inferior, junior, low, lower

upper-class *adjective* = **aristocratic**, blue-blooded, highborn, high-class, noble, patrician, top-drawer, well-bred

upper hand *noun* = **control**, advantage, ascendancy, dominion, edge, mastery, superiority, supremacy, sway, whip hand

uppermost *adjective* **1** = **top**, highest, loftiest, most elevated, topmost, upmost **2** = **supreme**, chief, dominant, foremost, greatest, leading, main, paramount, predominant, pre-eminent, primary, principal
➤ **Antonyms**
≠**top**: bottom, bottommost, lowermost, lowest ≠**supreme**: humblest, least, lowliest, slightest

uppish *adjective Brit. informal* = **conceited**, affected, arrogant, cocky, high and mighty (*informal*), hoity-toity (*informal*), overweening, presumptuous, putting on airs, self-important, snobbish, stuck-up (*informal*), supercilious, toffee-nosed (*slang, chiefly Brit.*), uppity (*informal*)
➤ **Antonyms**
diffident, humble, lowly, meek, obsequious, servile, unaffected, unassertive

uppity *adjective Informal* = **conceited**, bigheaded (*informal*), bumptious, cocky,

full of oneself, impertinent, on one's high horse (*informal*), overweening, self-important, too big for one's boots *or* breeches (*informal*), uppish (*Brit. informal*)

upright *adjective* **1** = **vertical**, erect, on end, perpendicular, straight **2** = **honest**, above board, conscientious, ethical, faithful, good, high-minded, honourable, incorruptible, just, principled, righteous, straightforward, true, trustworthy, unimpeachable, virtuous
➤ **Antonyms**
≠**vertical**: flat, horizontal, lying, prone, prostrate, supine ≠**honest**: corrupt, devious, dishonest, dishonourable, unethical, unjust, untrustworthy, wicked

uprightness *noun* = **honesty**, fairness, goodness, high-mindedness, incorruptibility, integrity, justice, probity, rectitude, righteousness, trustworthiness, virtue

uprising *noun* = **rebellion**, disturbance, insurgence, insurrection, mutiny, outbreak, putsch, revolt, revolution, rising, upheaval

uproar *noun* = **commotion**, bagarre, brawl, brouhaha, clamour, confusion, din, furore, hubbub, hullabaloo, hurly-burly, mayhem, noise, outcry, pandemonium, racket, riot, ruckus (*informal*), ruction (*informal*), rumpus, turbulence, turmoil

uproarious *adjective* **1** = **hilarious**, hysterical, killing (*informal*), rib-tickling, rip-roaring (*informal*), screamingly funny, side-splitting, very funny **2** = **boisterous**, loud, rollicking, unrestrained
➤ **Antonyms**
≠**hilarious**: mournful, sad, serious, tragic
≠**boisterous**: peaceful, quiet

uproot *verb* **1** = **pull up**, dig up, pull out by the roots, rip up, root out, weed out **2** = **displace**, disorient, exile **3** = **destroy**, do away with, eliminate, eradicate, extirpate, remove, wipe out

ups and downs *plural noun* = **fluctuations**, changes, ebb and flow, moods, vicissitudes

upset *adjective* **1** = **distressed**, agitated, bothered, confused, disconcerted, dismayed, disquieted, disturbed, frantic, grieved, hassled (*informal*), hurt, overwrought, put out, ruffled, troubled, worried **2** = **sick**, disordered, disturbed, ill, poorly (*informal*), queasy **3** = **disordered**, at sixes and sevens, chaotic, confused, disarrayed, in disarray, in disorder, messed up, muddled, topsy-turvy **4** = **overturned**, capsized, spilled, tipped over, toppled, tumbled, upside down ◆ *verb* **5** = **tip over**, capsize, knock over, overturn, spill, topple over **6** = **mess up**, change, disorder, disorganize, disturb, mix up, put out of order, spoil, turn topsy-turvy **7** = **distress**, agitate, bother, discompose, disconcert, dismay, disquiet, disturb, faze, fluster, grieve, hassle (*informal*), perturb, ruffle, throw (someone) off balance, trouble, unnerve ♦ *noun* **8** = **reversal**, defeat, shake-up (*informal*), sudden change **9** = **distress**, agitation, bother, discomposure, disquiet, disturbance, hassle (*informal*), shock, trouble, worry **10** = **illness**, bug (*informal*), complaint, disorder, disturbance, indisposition, malady, queasiness, sickness

upshot *noun* = **result**, conclusion, consequence, culmination, end, end result, event, finale, issue, outcome, payoff (*informal*), sequel

upside down *adjective* **1** = **inverted**, bottom up, on its head, overturned, upturned, wrong side up **2** *Informal* = **confused**, chaotic, disordered, higgledy-piggledy (*informal*), in chaos, in confusion, in disarray, in disorder, jumbled, muddled, topsy-turvy

upstanding *adjective* **1** = **honest**, ethical, good, honourable, incorruptible, moral, principled, true, trustworthy, upright **2** = **sturdy**, firm, hale and hearty, hardy, healthy, robust, stalwart, strong, upright, vigorous
➤ Antonyms
≠**honest**: bad, corrupt, dishonest, false, immoral, unethical, unprincipled, untrustworthy ≠**sturdy**: delicate, feeble, frail, infirm, puny, unhealthy, weak

upstart *noun* = **social climber**, arriviste, nobody, *nouveau riche*, parvenu, status seeker

uptight *adjective Informal* = **tense**, anxious, edgy, nervy (*Brit. informal*), neurotic, on edge, uneasy, wired (*slang*)

up-to-date *adjective* = **modern**, all the rage, current, fashionable, happening (*informal*), in, in vogue, newest, now (*informal*), stylish, trendy (*Brit. informal*), up-to-the-minute, with it (*informal*)
➤ Antonyms
antiquated, dated, *démodé*, obsolete, old fashioned, outmoded, out of date, out of the ark (*informal*), passé

upturn *noun* = **rise**, advancement, boost, improvement, increase, recovery, revival, upsurge, upswing

urban *adjective* = **civic**, city, inner-city, metropolitan, municipal, town

urbane *adjective* = **sophisticated**, civil, civilized, cosmopolitan, courteous, cultivated, cultured, debonair, elegant, mannerly, polished, refined, smooth, suave, well-bred, well-mannered
➤ Antonyms
boorish, clownish, discourteous, gauche, impolite, rude, uncivilized, uncouth, uncultured

urbanity *noun* = **sophistication**, charm, civility, courtesy, culture, elegance, grace, mannerliness, polish, refinement, suavity, worldliness

urchin *noun* = **ragamuffin**, brat, gamin, guttersnipe, street Arab (*offensive*), waif

urge *noun* **1** = **impulse**, compulsion, desire, drive, fancy, itch, longing, thirst, wish, yearning, yen (*informal*) ♦ *verb* **2** = **beg**, appeal to, beseech, entreat, exhort, implore, plead, press, solicit **3** = **advocate**, advise, counsel, insist on, push for, recommend, support **4** = **drive**, compel, constrain, egg on, encourage, force, gee up, goad, hasten, impel, incite, induce, instigate, press, prompt, propel, push, spur, stimulate
➤ Antonyms
noun ≠**impulse**: aversion, disinclination, distaste, indisposition, reluctance, repugnance ♦ *verb* ≠**advocate**, **drive**: caution, deter, discourage, dissuade, warn

urgency *noun* = **importance**, extremity, gravity, hurry, imperativeness, necessity, need, pressure, seriousness, stress

urgent *adjective* **1** = **crucial**, compelling, critical, immediate, imperative, important, instant, not to be delayed, now or never, pressing, top-priority **2** = **insistent**, clamorous, earnest, importunate, intense, persistent, persuasive
➤ Antonyms
≠**crucial**: low-priority, minor, trivial, unimportant ≠**insistent**: apathetic, casual, feeble, half-hearted, lackadaisical, perfunctory, weak

urinate *verb* = **pee** (*slang*), make water, pass water, piddle (*informal*), piss (*taboo slang*), spend a penny (*Brit. informal*), tinkle (*Brit. informal*), wee (*informal*), wee-wee (*informal*)

usable *adjective* = **serviceable**, at one's disposal, available, current, fit for use, functional, in running order, practical, ready for use, utilizable, valid, working

usage *noun* **1** = **use**, control, employment, handling, management, operation, regulation, running, treatment **2** = **practice**, convention, custom, form, habit, matter of course, method, mode, procedure, regime, routine, rule, tradition, wont

use *verb* **1** = **employ**, apply, avail oneself of, bring into play, exercise, exert, find a use for, make use of, operate, ply, practise, put to use, turn to account, utilize, wield, work **2 = take advantage of**, exploit, manipulate, misuse **3 = consume**, exhaust, expend, run through, spend, waste ♦ *noun* **4 = usage**, application, employment, exercise, handling, operation, practice, service, treatment **5 = good**, advantage, application, avail, benefit, help, mileage (*informal*), point, profit, service, usefulness, utility, value, worth **6 = purpose**, call, cause, end, necessity, need, object, occasion, point, reason

used *adjective* **= second-hand**, cast-off, hand-me-down (*informal*), nearly new, not new, reach-me-down (*informal*), shopsoiled, worn
➤ **Antonyms**
brand-new, fresh, new, pristine, unused

used to *adjective* **= accustomed to**, at home in, attuned to, familiar with, given to, habituated to, hardened to, in the habit of, inured to, wont to

useful *adjective* **= helpful**, advantageous, beneficial, effective, fruitful, of help, of service, of use, practical, profitable, serviceable, valuable, worthwhile
➤ **Antonyms**
inadequate, ineffective, pants (*slang*), unbeneficial, unhelpful, unproductive, useless, vain, worthless

usefulness *noun* **= helpfulness**, benefit, convenience, effectiveness, efficacy, help, practicality, profit, service, use, utility, value, worth

useless *adjective* **1 = worthless**, disadvantageous, fruitless, futile, hopeless, idle, impractical, ineffective, ineffectual, of no use, pants (*slang*), pointless, profitless, unavailing, unproductive, unworkable, vain, valueless **2** *Informal* **= inept**, hopeless, incompetent, ineffectual, no good, pants (*slang*), stupid, weak
➤ **Antonyms**
≠**worthless**: advantageous, effective, fruitful, practical, productive, profitable, useful, valuable, workable, worthwhile

use up *verb* **= consume**, absorb, burn up, deplete, devour, drain, exhaust, finish, fritter away, run through, squander, waste

usher *noun* **1 = attendant**, doorkeeper, doorman, escort, guide, usherette ♦ *verb* **2 = escort**, conduct, direct, guide, lead, show in *or* out, steer **3** *usually with* **in = introduce**, bring in, herald, inaugurate, initiate, launch, open the door to, pave the way for, precede

usual *adjective* **= normal**, accustomed, bog-standard (*Brit. & Irish slang*), common, customary, everyday, expected, familiar, general, habitual, ordinary, regular, routine, standard, stock, typical, wonted
➤ **Antonyms**
exceptional, extraordinary, new, novel, off-beat, out of the ordinary, peculiar, rare, singular, strange, uncommon, unexpected, unique, unorthodox, unusual

usually *adverb* **= normally**, as a rule, as is the custom, as is usual, by and large, commonly, for the most part, generally, habitually, in the main, mainly, mostly, most often, on the whole, ordinarily, regularly, routinely

usurp *verb* **= seize**, appropriate, assume, commandeer, take, take over, wrest

utility *noun* **= usefulness**, advantageousness, avail, benefit, convenience, efficacy, mileage (*informal*), point, practicality, profit, service, serviceableness, use

utilize *verb* **= use**, avail oneself of, employ, have recourse to, make the most of, make use of, profit by, put to use, resort to, take advantage of, turn to account

utmost *adjective* **1 = greatest**, chief, extreme, highest, maximum, paramount, pre-eminent, supreme **2 = farthest**, extreme, final, last, most distant, outermost, remotest, uttermost ♦ *noun* **3 = greatest**, best, hardest, highest, most

Utopia *noun* **= paradise**, bliss, Eden, Garden of Eden, heaven, ideal life, perfect place, seventh heaven, Shangri-la

Utopian *adjective* **1 = perfect**, dream, fanciful, fantasy, ideal, idealistic, illusory, imaginary, impractical, romantic, visionary ♦ *noun* **2 = dreamer**, Don Quixote, idealist, romanticist, visionary

utter[1] *verb* **= express**, articulate, enunciate, pronounce, put into words, say, speak, verbalize, vocalize, voice

utter[2] *adjective* **= absolute**, arrant, complete, consummate, deep-dyed (*usually derogatory*), downright, entire, out-and-out, outright, perfect, sheer, stark, thorough, thoroughgoing, total, unmitigated, unqualified

utterance *noun* **1 = speech**, announcement, declaration, expression, opinion, remark, statement, words **2 = expression**, articulation, verbalization, vocalization, vociferation

utterly *adverb* **= totally**, absolutely, completely, entirely, extremely, fully, one hundred per cent, perfectly, thoroughly, to the core, to the nth degree, wholly

uttermost *adjective* **= farthest**, extreme, final, last, outermost, remotest, utmost

V v

vacancy *noun* **1** = **job**, opening, opportunity, position, post, room, situation **2** = **emptiness**, gap, space, vacuum, void

vacant *adjective* **1** = **unoccupied**, available, disengaged, empty, free, idle, not in use, to let, unemployed, unengaged, unfilled, untenanted, void **2** = **blank**, absent-minded, abstracted, ditzy *or* ditsy (*slang*), dreaming, dreamy, expressionless, idle, inane, thoughtless, unthinking, vacuous, vague
➤ **Antonyms**
≠**unoccupied**: busy, engaged, full, inhabited, in use, occupied, taken ≠**blank**: animated, engrossed, expressive, lively, reflective, thoughtful

vacate *verb* = **leave**, evacuate, quit

vacillate *verb* = **keep changing one's mind**, be irresolute *or* indecisive, blow hot and cold (*informal*), chop and change, dither (*chiefly Brit.*), shillyshally (*informal*), swither (*Scot.*), waver

vacillating *adjective* = **irresolute**, in two minds (*informal*), shillyshallying (*informal*), uncertain, unresolved, wavering

vacillation *noun* = **indecisiveness**, dithering (*chiefly Brit.*), fluctuation, irresoluteness, irresolution, shillyshallying (*informal*), wavering

vacuity *noun* = **unintelligence**, blankness, emptiness, inanity, incognizance, incomprehension, vacuousness

vacuous *adjective* = **unintelligent**, blank, inane, stupid, uncomprehending, vacant

vacuum *noun* = **emptiness**, free space, gap, nothingness, space, vacuity, void

vagabond *noun* = **vagrant**, bag lady (*chiefly U.S.*), beggar, bum (*informal*), down-and-out, hobo (*U.S.*), itinerant, migrant, nomad, rover, tramp, wanderer, wayfarer

vagary *noun* = **whim**, caprice, crotchet, fancy, humour, notion, whimsy

vagina *noun* = **vulva**, beaver (*taboo slang*), cunt (*taboo*), fanny (*Brit. taboo slang*), muff (*taboo slang*), pussy (*taboo slang*), snatch (*taboo slang*)

vagrant *noun* **1** = **tramp**, bag lady (*chiefly U.S.*), beggar, bum (*informal*), drifter, hobo (*U.S.*), itinerant, person of no fixed address, rolling stone, wanderer
♦ *adjective* **2** = **itinerant**, nomadic, roaming, rootless, roving, unsettled, vagabond
➤ **Antonyms**
adjective ≠**itinerant**: established, fixed, purposeful, rooted, settled

vague *adjective* **1** = **unclear**, doubtful, generalized, hazy, imprecise, indefinite, loose, uncertain, unspecified, woolly **2** = **indistinct**, amorphous, blurred, dim, fuzzy, hazy, ill-defined, indeterminate, nebulous, obscure, shadowy, unclear, unknown
➤ **Antonyms**
≠**unclear**: clear, clear-cut, definite, distinct, exact, explicit, precise, specific ≠**indistinct**: clear, distinct, lucid, well-defined

vaguely *adverb* **1** = **imprecisely**, dimly, evasively, in a general way, obscurely, slightly **2** = **absent-mindedly**, vacantly

vagueness *noun* = **impreciseness**, ambiguity, inexactitude, lack of preciseness, looseness, obscurity, undecidedness, woolliness
➤ **Antonyms**
clarity, clearness, definition, exactness, obviousness, preciseness, precision

vain *adjective* **1** = **proud**, arrogant, bigheaded (*informal*), cocky, conceited, egotistical, inflated, narcissistic, ostentatious, overweening, pleased with oneself, self-important, stuck-up (*informal*), swaggering, swollen-headed (*informal*) **2** = **futile**, abortive, empty, fruitless, hollow, idle, pointless, senseless, time-wasting, trifling, trivial, unavailing, unimportant, unproductive, unprofitable, useless, worthless **3 be vain** = **have a high opinion of oneself**, have a swelled head (*informal*), think a lot of oneself, think oneself the cat's whiskers *or* pyjamas (*slang*) ♦ *noun* **4 in vain** = **to no avail**, fruitless(ly), ineffectual(ly), to no purpose, unsuccessful(ly), useless(ly), vain(ly), wasted, without success
➤ **Antonyms**
adjective ≠**proud**: bashful, humble, meek, modest, self-deprecating ≠**futile**: fruitful, profitable, serious, successful, useful, valid, worthwhile, worthy

valediction *noun* = **farewell**, adieu, goodbye, leave-taking, sendoff (*informal*)

valedictory *adjective* = **farewell**, final, parting

valiant *adjective* = **brave**, bold, courageous, dauntless, doughty, fearless, gallant, heroic, indomitable, intrepid, lion-hearted, plucky, redoubtable, stouthearted, valorous
➤ **Antonyms**
cowardly, craven, fearful, shrinking, spineless, timid, weak

valid *adjective* 1 = **sound**, acceptable, cogent, conclusive, convincing, good, just, logical, powerful, sensible, substantial, telling, weighty, well-founded, well-grounded 2 = **legal**, authentic, bona fide, genuine, lawful, legally binding, legitimate, official, signed and sealed
➤ **Antonyms**
≠**sound**: baseless, bogus, fallacious, false, illogical, sham, spurious, unacceptable, unfounded, unrealistic, unrecognized, untrue, weak ≠**legal**: illegal, inoperative, invalid, unlawful, unofficial

validate *verb* 1 = **confirm**, certify, corroborate, prove, substantiate 2 = **authorize**, authenticate, endorse, ratify

validity *noun* 1 = **soundness**, cogency, force, foundation, grounds, point, power, strength, substance, weight 2 = **legality**, authority, lawfulness, legitimacy, right

valley *noun* = **hollow**, coomb, cwm (*Welsh*), dale, dell, depression, dingle, glen, strath (*Scot.*), vale

valorous *adjective* = **brave**, bold, courageous, dauntless, doughty, fearless, gallant, heroic, intrepid, lion-hearted, plucky, valiant

valour *noun* = **bravery**, boldness, courage, doughtiness, fearlessness, gallantry, heroism, intrepidity, lion-heartedness, spirit
➤ **Antonyms**
cowardice, dread, fear, timidity, trepidation, weakness

valuable *adjective* 1 = **precious**, costly, dear, expensive, high-priced 2 = **useful**, beneficial, cherished, esteemed, estimable, held dear, helpful, important, prized, profitable, serviceable, treasured, valued, worth one's *or* its weight in gold, worthwhile, worthy ♦ *noun* 3 **valuables** = **treasures**, heirlooms
➤ **Antonyms**
adjective ≠**precious**: cheap, cheapo (*informal*), chickenshit (*U.S. slang*), crappy (*slang*), inexpensive, worthless ≠**useful**: insignificant, pointless, silly, trifling, trivial, unimportant, useless, worthless

value *noun* 1 = **importance**, advantage, benefit, desirability, help, merit, mileage (*informal*), profit, serviceableness, significance, use, usefulness, utility, worth 2 = **cost**, equivalent, market price, monetary worth, rate 3 **values** = **principles**, code of behaviour, ethics, (moral) standards ♦ *verb* 4 = **evaluate**, account, appraise, assess, compute, estimate, price, put a price on, rate, set at, survey 5 = **regard highly**, appreciate, cherish, esteem, hold dear, hold in high regard *or* esteem, prize, respect, set store by, treasure
➤ **Antonyms**
noun ≠**importance**: insignificance, unimportance, uselessness, worthlessness ♦ *verb* ≠**regard highly**: disregard, have no time for, hold a low opinion of, underestimate, undervalue

valued *adjective* = **highly regarded**, cherished, dear, esteemed, loved, prized, treasured

valueless *adjective* = **worthless**, no good, of no value, useless

vamoose *Slang, chiefly U.S. verb* = **go away**, bugger off (*taboo slang*), clear off (*informal*), fuck off (*offensive taboo slang*), make off, make oneself scarce (*informal*), run away, scarper (*Brit. slang*), scram (*informal*)

vandal *noun* = **hooligan**, delinquent, rowdy, yob *or* yobbo (*Brit. slang*)

vanguard *noun* = **forefront**, advance guard, cutting edge, forerunners, front, front line, front rank, leaders, spearhead, trailblazers, trendsetters, van
➤ **Antonyms**
back, rear, rearguard, stern, tail, tail end

vanish *verb* = **disappear**, become invisible, be lost to sight, die out, disappear from sight *or* from the face of the earth, dissolve, evanesce, evaporate, fade (away), melt (away), vanish off the face of the earth
➤ **Antonyms**
appear, arrive, become visible, come into view, materialize, pop up

vanity *noun* = **pride**, affected ways, airs, arrogance, bigheadedness (*informal*), conceit, conceitedness, egotism, narcissism, ostentation, pretension, self-admiration, self-love, showing off (*informal*), swollen-headedness (*informal*)
➤ **Antonyms**
humility, meekness, modesty, self-abasement, self-deprecation

vanquish *verb Literary* = **defeat**, beat, blow out of the water (*slang*), clobber (*slang*), conquer, crush, lick (*informal*), master, overcome, overpower, overwhelm, put down, quell, rout, run rings around (*informal*), triumph over, wipe the floor with (*informal*)

vapid *adjective* = **dull**, bland, boring, flat, insipid, tame, uninspiring, uninteresting, weak, wishy-washy (*informal*)

vapour *noun* = **mist**, breath, dampness, exhalation, fog, fumes, haze, miasma, smoke, steam

variable *adjective* = **changeable**, capricious, fitful, flexible, fluctuating, inconstant, mercurial, mutable, shifting, temperamental, uneven, unstable, unsteady, vacillating, wavering
➤ **Antonyms**
constant, firm, fixed, settled, stable, steady, unalterable, unchanging

variance *noun* **at variance** = **in disagreement**, at loggerheads, at odds, at sixes and sevens (*informal*), conflicting, in opposition, out of harmony, out of line

variant *adjective* **1** = **different**, alternative, derived, divergent, exceptional, modified ♦ *noun* **2** = **variation**, alternative, derived form, development, modification, sport (*Biology*)

variation *noun* = **difference**, alteration, break in routine, change, departure, departure from the norm, deviation, discrepancy, diversification, diversity, innovation, modification, novelty, variety
➤ **Antonyms**
dullness, monotony, sameness, tedium, uniformity

varied *adjective* = **different**, assorted, diverse, heterogeneous, manifold, miscellaneous, mixed, motley, sundry, various
➤ **Antonyms**
homogeneous, repetitive, similar, standardized, uniform, unvarying

variegated *adjective* = **mottled**, diversified, many-coloured, motley, parti-coloured, pied, streaked, varicoloured

variety *noun* **1** = **diversity**, change, difference, discrepancy, diversification, many-sidedness, multifariousness, variation **2** = **range**, array, assortment, collection, cross section, intermixture, medley, miscellany, mixed bag (*informal*), mixture, multiplicity **3** = **type**, brand, breed, category, class, kind, make, order, sort, species, strain
➤ **Antonyms**
≠**diversity**: homogeneity, invariability, monotony, similarity, similitude, uniformity

various *adjective* = **different**, assorted, differing, disparate, distinct, diverse, diversified, heterogeneous, manifold,

many, miscellaneous, several, sundry, varied
➤ **Antonyms**
alike, equivalent, matching, same, similar, uniform

varnish *noun, verb* **1** = **lacquer**, glaze, gloss, japan, polish, shellac ♦ *verb* **2** = **adorn**, decorate, embellish, gild

vary *verb* **1** = **change**, alter, fluctuate, transform **2** = **differ**, be unlike, depart, disagree, diverge **3** = **alternate**, diversify, permutate, reorder **4** = **modify**

varying *adjective* **1** = **changing**, fluctuating, inconsistent **2** = **different**, distinct, distinguishable, diverse
➤ **Antonyms**
≠**changing**: consistent, fixed, monotonous, regular, settled, unchanging, unvarying

vassal *noun* = **serf**, bondservant, bondsman, liegeman, retainer, slave, subject

vassalage *noun* = **serfdom**, bondage, dependence, servitude, slavery, subjection

vast *adjective* = **huge**, astronomical, boundless, colossal, elephantine, enormous, extensive, gigantic, great, illimitable, immeasurable, immense, limitless, mammoth, massive, measureless, mega (*slang*), monstrous, monumental, never-ending, prodigious, sweeping, tremendous, unbounded, unlimited, voluminous, wide
➤ **Antonyms**
bounded, limited, microscopic, narrow, negligible, paltry, puny, small, tiny, trifling

vault[1] *noun* **1** = **strongroom**, depository, repository **2** = **crypt**, catacomb, cellar, charnel house, mausoleum, tomb, undercroft **3** = **arch**, ceiling, roof, span

vault[2] *verb* = **jump**, bound, clear, hurdle, leap, spring

vaulted *adjective* = **arched**, cavernous, domed

vaunt *verb* = **boast about**, brag about, exult in, flaunt, give oneself airs about, make a display of, make much of, parade, show off

veer *verb* = **change direction**, be deflected, change, change course, sheer, shift, swerve, tack, turn

vegetate *verb* = **stagnate**, be inert, deteriorate, go to seed, idle, languish, loaf, moulder, veg out (*slang, chiefly U.S.*)
➤ **Antonyms**
accomplish, develop, grow, participate, perform, react, respond

vehemence *noun* = **forcefulness**, ardour, eagerness, earnestness, emphasis, energy,

enthusiasm, fervency, fervour, fire, force, heat, intensity, keenness, passion, verve, vigour, violence, warmth, zeal
➤ **Antonyms**
apathy, coolness, indifference, inertia, lethargy, listlessness, passivity, stoicism, torpor

vehement *adjective* = **strong**, ablaze, ardent, eager, earnest, emphatic, enthusiastic, fervent, fervid, fierce, flaming, forceful, forcible, impassioned, intense, passionate, powerful, violent, zealous
➤ **Antonyms**
apathetic, calm, cool, dispassionate, half-hearted, impassive, lukewarm, moderate

vehicle *noun* 1 = **transport**, conveyance, means of transport, transportation 2 = **medium**, apparatus, channel, means, means of expression, mechanism, organ

veil *noun* 1 = **cover**, blind, cloak, curtain, disguise, film, mask, screen, shade, shroud ◆ *verb* 2 = **cover**, cloak, conceal, dim, disguise, hide, mantle, mask, obscure, screen, shield
➤ **Antonyms**
verb ≠**cover**: disclose, display, divulge, expose, lay bare, reveal, uncover, unveil

veiled *adjective* = **disguised**, concealed, covert, hinted at, implied, masked, suppressed

vein *noun* 1 = **blood vessel** 2 = **seam**, course, current, lode, stratum, streak, stripe 3 = **trait**, dash, hint, strain, streak, thread 4 = **mood**, attitude, bent, character, faculty, humour, mode, note, style, temper, tenor, tone, turn

velocity *noun* = **speed**, pace, quickness, rapidity, swiftness

velvety *adjective* = **soft**, delicate, downy, smooth

venal *adjective* = **corrupt**, bent (*slang*), corruptible, crooked (*informal*), dishonourable, mercenary, unprincipled
➤ **Antonyms**
honest, honourable, incorruptible, law-abiding, principled, upright

vendetta *noun* = **feud**, bad blood, blood feud, quarrel

veneer *noun* 1 = **layer**, finish, gloss 2 = **mask**, appearance, façade, false front, front, guise, pretence, semblance, show

venerable *adjective* = **respected**, august, esteemed, honoured, revered, reverenced, sage, wise, worshipped
➤ **Antonyms**
discredited, disdained, disgraced, dishonourable, disreputable, ignominious,

inglorious, scorned

venerate *verb* = **respect**, adore, esteem, hold in awe, honour, look up to, revere, reverence, worship
➤ **Antonyms**
deride, dishonour, disregard, execrate, mock, scorn, spurn

veneration *noun* = **respect**, adoration, awe, deference, esteem, reverence, worship

vengeance *noun* 1 = **revenge**, an eye for an eye, avenging, reprisal, requital, retaliation, retribution, settling of scores 2 **with a vengeance** = **to the utmost**, and no mistake, extremely, greatly, to the full, to the nth degree, with no holds barred
➤ **Antonyms**
≠**revenge**: absolution, acquittal, exoneration, forbearance, forgiveness, mercy, pardon, remission

vengeful *adjective* = **unforgiving**, avenging, retaliatory, revengeful, thirsting for revenge

venial *adjective* = **forgivable**, allowable, excusable, insignificant, minor, pardonable, slight, trivial

venom *noun* 1 = **malice**, acidity, acrimony, bitterness, gall, grudge, hate, ill will, malevolence, maliciousness, rancour, spite, spitefulness, spleen, virulence 2 = **poison**, bane, toxin
➤ **Antonyms**
≠**malice**: benevolence, charity, compassion, favour, goodwill, kindness, love, mercy

venomous *adjective* 1 = **malicious**, baleful, hostile, malignant, rancorous, savage, spiteful, vicious, vindictive 2 = **poisonous**, baneful (*archaic*), mephitic, noxious, poison, toxic, virulent
➤ **Antonyms**
≠**malicious**: affectionate, benevolent, compassionate, forgiving, harmless, loving, magnanimous ≠**poisonous**: harmless, nonpoisonous, nontoxic, nonvenomous

vent *noun* 1 = **outlet**, aperture, duct, hole, opening, orifice, split ◆ *verb* 2 = **express**, air, come out with, discharge, emit, empty, give expression to, give vent to, pour out, release, utter, voice
➤ **Antonyms**
verb ≠**express**: bottle up, curb, hold back, inhibit, quash, quell, repress, stifle, subdue

ventilate *verb* = **discuss**, air, bring out into the open, broadcast, debate, make known, talk about

venture *noun* 1 = **undertaking**, adventure, chance, endeavour, enterprise, fling, gamble, hazard, jeopardy, project, risk, speculation ♦ *verb* 2 = **risk**, chance, endanger, hazard, imperil, jeopardize, put in jeopardy, speculate, stake, wager 3 = **go**, embark on, plunge into, set out 4 = **dare**, advance, dare say, hazard, make bold, presume, take the liberty, volunteer

venturesome *adjective* = **daring**, adventurous, bold, courageous, enterprising, fearless, intrepid, plucky, spirited

veracious *adjective* = **truthful**, ethical, frank, high-principled, honest, trustworthy

veracity *noun* 1 = **truthfulness**, candour, frankness, honesty, integrity, probity, rectitude, trustworthiness, uprightness 2 = **accuracy**, credibility, exactitude, precision, truth

verbal *adjective* = **spoken**, literal, oral, unwritten, verbatim, word-of-mouth

verbally *adverb* = **orally**, by word of mouth

verbatim *adverb* = **word for word**, exactly, precisely, to the letter

verbiage *noun* = **verbosity**, circumlocution, periphrasis, pleonasm, redundancy, repetition, tautology

verbose *adjective* = **long-winded**, circumlocutory, diffuse, garrulous, periphrastic, pleonastic, prolix, tautological, windy, wordy
➤ **Antonyms**
brief, brusque, concise, curt, quiet, reticent, short, succinct, terse, untalkative

verbosity *noun* = **long-windedness**, garrulity, loquaciousness, prolixity, rambling, verbiage, verboseness, windiness, wordiness

verdant *adjective Literary* = **green**, flourishing, fresh, grassy, leafy, lush

verdict *noun* = **decision**, adjudication, conclusion, finding, judgment, opinion, sentence

verge *noun* 1 = **border**, boundary, brim, brink, edge, extreme, limit, lip, margin, roadside, threshold ♦ *verb* 2 **verge on** = **come near to**, approach, border

verification *noun* = **proof**, authentication, confirmation, corroboration, substantiation, validation

verify *verb* 1 = **check** 2 = **prove**, attest, attest to, authenticate, bear out, confirm, corroborate, substantiate, support, validate
➤ **Antonyms**
≠**prove**: deny, discount, discredit, dispute, invalidate, nullify, undermine, weaken

verisimilitude *noun* = **realism**, credibility, plausibility, resemblance, semblance, show of

vernacular *noun* 1 = **dialect**, argot, cant,

idiom, jargon, native language, parlance, patois, speech, vulgar tongue ♦ *adjective* 2 = **colloquial**, common, indigenous, informal, local, mother, native, popular, vulgar

versatile *adjective* = **adaptable**, adjustable, all-purpose, all-round, all-singing, all-dancing, flexible, functional, handy, many-sided, multifaceted, resourceful, variable
➤ **Antonyms**
fixed, inflexible, invariable, limited, one-sided, unadaptable

versed *adjective* = **knowledgeable**, accomplished, acquainted, competent, conversant, experienced, familiar, practised, proficient, qualified, seasoned, skilled, well informed, well up in (*informal*)
➤ **Antonyms**
callow, green, ignorant, inexperienced, new, raw, unacquainted, unfledged, unpractised, unschooled, unskilled, unversed

version *noun* 1 = **form**, design, kind, model, style, type, variant 2 = **account**, interpretation, side, take (*informal, chiefly U.S.*) 3 = **adaptation**, portrayal, reading, rendering, translation

vertex *noun* = **top**, acme, apex, apogee, crest, crown, culmination, extremity, height, pinnacle, summit, zenith

vertical *adjective* = **upright**, erect, on end, perpendicular
➤ **Antonyms**
flat, horizontal, level, plane, prone

vertigo *noun* = **dizziness**, giddiness, light-headedness, loss of equilibrium

verve *noun* = **enthusiasm**, animation, brio, dash, élan, energy, force, get-up-and-go (*informal*), gusto, life, liveliness, pep, punch (*informal*), sparkle, spirit, vigour, vim (*slang*), vitality, vivacity, zeal, zip (*informal*)
➤ **Antonyms**
apathy, disdain, half-heartedness, indifference, inertia, lack of enthusiasm, languor, lethargy, lifelessness, reluctance, torpor

very *adverb* 1 = **extremely**, absolutely, acutely, awfully (*informal*), decidedly, deeply, eminently, exceedingly, excessively, greatly, highly, jolly (*Brit.*), noticeably, particularly, profoundly, really, remarkably, seriously (*informal*), superlatively, surpassingly, terribly, truly, uncommonly, unusually, wonderfully ♦ *adjective* 2 = **exact**, actual, appropriate, express, identical, perfect, precise, real, same, selfsame, unqualified

vessel *noun* 1 = **ship**, barque (*poetic*), boat,

craft **2** = **container**, pot, receptacle, utensil

vest *verb, with* **in** *or* **with** = **place**, authorize, be devolved upon, bestow, confer, consign, empower, endow, entrust, furnish, invest, lodge, put in the hands of, settle

vestibule *noun* = **hall**, anteroom, entrance hall, foyer, lobby, porch, portico

vestige *noun* = **trace**, evidence, glimmer, hint, indication, relic, remainder, remains, remnant, residue, scrap, sign, suspicion, token

vet *verb* = **check**, appraise, check out, examine, give (someone *or* something) the once-over (*informal*), investigate, look over, pass under review, review, scan, scrutinize, size up (*informal*)

veteran *noun* **1** = **old hand**, master, old stager, old-timer, past master, pro (*informal*), trouper, warhorse (*informal*) ♦ *adjective* **2** = **long-serving**, adept, battle-scarred, expert, old, proficient, seasoned
➤ **Antonyms**
noun ≠**old hand**: apprentice, beginner, freshman, initiate, neophyte, novice, recruit, tyro

veto *noun* **1** = **ban**, boycott, embargo, interdict, nonconsent, prohibition ♦ *verb* **2** = **ban**, boycott, disallow, forbid, give the thumbs down to, interdict, prohibit, put the kibosh on (*slang*), refuse permission, reject, rule out, turn down
➤ **Antonyms**
noun ≠**ban**: approval, endorsement, go-ahead (*informal*), ratification ♦ *verb* ≠**ban**: approve, endorse, O.K. *or* okay (*informal*), pass, ratify

vex *verb* = **annoy**, aggravate (*informal*), agitate, bother, bug (*informal*), displease, distress, disturb, exasperate, gall, get one's back up, get on one's nerves (*informal*), grate on, harass, hassle (*informal*), irritate, nark (*Brit., Austral., & N.Z. slang*), needle (*informal*), nettle, offend, peeve (*informal*), pester, pique, plague, provoke, put one's back up, put out, rile, torment, trouble, upset, worry
➤ **Antonyms**
allay, appease, comfort, console, gratify, hush, mollify, please, quiet, soothe

vexation *noun* **1** = **annoyance**, aggravation (*informal*), chagrin, displeasure, dissatisfaction, exasperation, frustration, irritation, pique **2** = **problem**, bother, difficulty, hassle (*informal*), headache (*informal*), irritant, nuisance, thorn in one's flesh, trouble, upset, worry

vexatious *adjective* = **annoying**, aggravating (*informal*), bothersome,

burdensome, disagreeable, distressing, exasperating, harassing, irksome, irritating, nagging, provoking, tormenting, troublesome, trying, unpleasant, upsetting, worrisome, worrying
➤ **Antonyms**
agreeable, balmy, calming, comforting, pleasant, reassuring, relaxing, soothing

vexed *adjective* **1** = **annoyed**, aggravated (*informal*), agitated, bothered, confused, displeased, distressed, disturbed, exasperated, fed up, hacked (off) (*U.S. slang*), harassed, irritated, miffed (*informal*), nettled, peeved (*informal*), pissed (*taboo slang*), pissed off (*taboo slang*), provoked, put out, riled, ruffled, tormented, troubled, upset, worried **2** = **controversial**, contested, disputed, moot, much debated

viable *adjective* = **workable**, applicable, feasible, operable, practicable, usable, within the bounds of possibility
➤ **Antonyms**
hopeless, impossible, impracticable, inconceivable, out of the question, unthinkable, unworkable

vibes *plural noun Informal* **1** = **feelings**, emotions, reaction, response **2** = **atmosphere**, aura, emanation, vibrations

vibrant *adjective* = **energetic**, alive, animated, colourful, dynamic, electrifying, full of pep (*informal*), sparkling, spirited, storming, vigorous, vivacious, vivid

vibrate *verb* = **shake**, fluctuate, judder (*informal*), oscillate, pulsate, pulse, quiver, resonate, reverberate, shiver, sway, swing, throb, tremble, undulate

vibration *noun* = **shake**, judder (*informal*), oscillation, pulsation, pulse, quiver, resonance, reverberation, throb, throbbing, trembling, tremor

vicarious *adjective* **1** = **indirect**, at one remove **2** = **substituted**, surrogate **3** = **delegated**, deputed

vice *noun* **1** = **wickedness**, corruption, degeneracy, depravity, evil, evildoing, immorality, iniquity, profligacy, sin, turpitude, venality **2** = **fault**, blemish, defect, failing, imperfection, shortcoming, weakness
➤ **Antonyms**
≠**wickedness**: honour, morality, virtue ≠**fault**: gift, good point, strong point, talent

vice versa *adverb* = **conversely**, contrariwise, in reverse, the other way round

vicinity *noun* = **neighbourhood**, area, district, environs, locality, neck of the woods (*informal*), precincts, proximity, purlieus

vicious *adjective* 1 = **savage**, abhorrent, atrocious, bad, barbarous, cruel, diabolical, ferocious, fiendish, foul, heinous, monstrous, vile, violent 2 = **malicious**, backbiting, bitchy (*informal*), cruel, defamatory, mean, rancorous, slanderous, spiteful, venomous, vindictive
➤ **Antonyms**
≠**savage**: docile, friendly, gentle, good, honourable, kind, playful, tame, upright, virtuous ≠**malicious**: appreciative, complimentary, congratulatory

viciousness *noun* 1 = **savagery**, cruelty, ferocity 2 = **malice**, bitchiness (*slang*), rancour, spite, spitefulness, venom
➤ **Antonyms**
≠**malice**: gentleness, goodness, goodwill, graciousness, kindness, mercy, virtue

vicissitudes *plural noun* = **changes of fortune**, alterations, life's ups and downs (*informal*), shifts

victim *noun* 1 = **casualty**, fatality, injured party, martyr, sacrifice, scapegoat, sufferer 2 = **prey**, dupe, fall guy (*informal*), innocent, patsy (*slang, chiefly U.S. & Canad.*), sitting duck (*informal*), sitting target, sucker (*slang*)
➤ **Antonyms**
≠**casualty**: survivor ≠**prey**: assailant, attacker, culprit, guilty party, offender

victimize *verb* = **persecute**, discriminate against, have a down on (someone) (*informal*), have it in for (someone) (*informal*), pick on

victor *noun* = **winner**, champ (*informal*), champion, conquering hero, conqueror, first, prizewinner, top dog (*informal*), vanquisher
➤ **Antonyms**
also-ran, dud (*informal*), failure, flop (*informal*), loser, vanquished

victorious *adjective* = **winning**, champion, conquering, first, prizewinning, successful, triumphant, vanquishing
➤ **Antonyms**
beaten, conquered, defeated, failed, losing, overcome, unsuccessful, vanquished

victory *noun* = **win**, conquest, laurels, mastery, success, superiority, the prize, triumph
➤ **Antonyms**
defeat, failure, loss

victuals *plural noun Old-fashioned* = **food**, comestibles, eatables, eats (*slang*), grub (*slang*), meat, nosh (*slang*), provisions, rations, stores, supplies, tack (*informal*), viands, vittles (*obsolete*)

vie *verb* = **compete**, contend, strive, struggle

view *noun* 1 *sometimes plural* = **opinion**, attitude, belief, conviction, feeling, impression, judgment, notion, point of view, sentiment, thought, way of thinking 2 = **scene**, aspect, landscape, outlook, panorama, perspective, picture, prospect, spectacle, vista 3 = **vision**, range or field of vision, sight 4 = **look**, contemplation, . display, examination, inspection, recce (*slang*), scan, scrutiny, sight, survey, viewing 5 **with a view to** = **with the aim or intention of**, in order to, in the hope of, so as to ♦ *verb* 6 = **regard**, consider, deem, judge, look on, think about 7 = **look at**, behold, check, check out (*informal*), clock (*Brit. slang*), contemplate, examine, explore, eye, eyeball (*slang*), gaze at, get a load of (*informal*), inspect, observe, recce (*slang*), regard, scan, spectate, stare at, survey, take a dekko at (*Brit. slang*), watch, witness

viewer *noun* = **watcher**, observer, onlooker, spectator, TV watcher

viewpoint *noun* = **attitude**, angle, frame of reference, perspective, point of view, position, slant, stance, standpoint, vantage point, way of thinking

vigilance *noun* = **watchfulness**, alertness, attentiveness, carefulness, caution, circumspection, observance

vigilant *adjective* = **watchful**, alert, Argus-eyed, attentive, careful, cautious, circumspect, on one's guard, on one's toes, on the alert, on the lookout, on the qui vive, on the watch, unsleeping, wakeful, wide awake
➤ **Antonyms**
careless, inattentive, lax, neglectful, negligent, remiss, slack

vigorous *adjective* = **energetic**, active, alive and kicking, brisk, dynamic, effective, fighting fit, fit as a fiddle (*informal*), forceful, forcible, full of beans (*informal*), full of energy, hale, hale and hearty, hardy, healthy, intense, lively, lusty, powerful, red-blooded, robust, sound, spirited, strenuous, strong, vital
➤ **Antonyms**
apathetic, effete, enervated, feeble, frail, inactive, indolent, lethargic, lifeless, spiritless, torpid, weak, weedy (*informal*), wimpish or wimpy (*informal*), wishy-washy, wussy (*slang*)

vigorously *adverb* = **energetically**, eagerly, forcefully, hammer and tongs, hard, like mad (*slang*), lustily, strenuously, strongly, with a vengeance, with might and main

vigour *noun* = **energy**, activity, animation, brio, dash, dynamism, force, forcefulness,

gusto, liveliness, might, oomph (*informal*), pep, power, punch (*informal*), robustness, spirit, strength, verve, vim (*slang*), vitality
➤ **Antonyms**
apathy, feebleness, fragility, frailty, impotence, inactivity, inertia, infirmity, lethargy, sluggishness, weakness

vile *adjective* 1 = **wicked**, abandoned, appalling, bad, base, contemptible, corrupt, debased, degenerate, depraved, despicable, disgraceful, evil, impure, loathsome, low, mean, nefarious, perverted, shocking, sinful, ugly, vicious, vulgar 2 = **disgusting**, foul, horrid, loathsome, nasty, nauseating, noxious, obscene, offensive, repellent, repugnant, repulsive, revolting, sickening, yucky *or* yukky (*slang*)
➤ **Antonyms**
≠**wicked**: chaste, cultured, genteel, honourable, noble, polite, pure, refined, righteous, upright, worthy ≠**disgusting**: agreeable, delicate, lovely, marvellous, pleasant, splendid, sublime

vileness *noun* 1 = **wickedness**, corruption, degeneracy, depravity, dreadfulness, enormity, evil, heinousness, turpitude, ugliness 2 = **foulness**, noxiousness, offensiveness

vilification *noun* = **denigration**, abuse, aspersion, calumniation, calumny, defamation, disparagement, invective, mudslinging, scurrility, vituperation

vilify *verb* = **malign**, abuse, asperse, bad-mouth (*slang, chiefly U.S. & Canad.*), berate, calumniate, decry, defame, denigrate, disparage, knock (*informal*), pull to pieces (*informal*), revile, rubbish (*informal*), run down, slag (off) (*slang*), slander, smear, speak ill of
➤ **Antonyms**
adore, commend, esteem, exalt, glorify, honour, praise, revere, venerate

villain *noun* 1 = **evildoer**, blackguard, criminal, knave (*archaic*), malefactor, miscreant, rapscallion, reprobate, rogue, scoundrel, wretch 2 = **antihero**, baddy (*informal*)
➤ **Antonyms**
≠**antihero**: goody, hero, heroine

villainous *adjective* = **wicked**, bad, base, criminal, cruel, degenerate, depraved, detestable, diabolical, evil, fiendish, hateful, heinous, infamous, inhuman, nefarious, sinful, terrible, vicious, vile
➤ **Antonyms**
angelic, good, heroic, humane, moral, noble, righteous, saintly, virtuous

villainy *noun* = **wickedness**, baseness, crime, criminality, delinquency, depravity,

devilry, iniquity, sin, turpitude, vice

vindicate *verb* 1 = **clear**, absolve, acquit, exculpate, exonerate, free from blame, rehabilitate 2 = **justify**, defend, excuse
➤ **Antonyms**
≠**clear**: accuse, blame, condemn, convict, incriminate, punish, reproach

vindication *noun* 1 = **exoneration**, exculpating, exculpation 2 = **justification**, defence, excuse

vindictive *adjective* = **vengeful**, implacable, malicious, malignant, rancorous, relentless, resentful, revengeful, spiteful, unforgiving, unrelenting, venomous
➤ **Antonyms**
forgiving, generous, magnanimous, merciful, relenting, unvindictive

vintage *noun* 1 = **harvest**, crop 2 = **era**, epoch, generation, time of origin, year ♦ *adjective* 3 = **best**, choice, classic, mature, prime, rare, ripe, select, superior

violate *verb* 1 = **break**, contravene, disobey, disregard, encroach upon, infract, infringe, transgress 2 = **desecrate**, abuse, befoul, defile, dishonour, invade, outrage, pollute, profane 3 = **rape**, abuse, assault, debauch, ravish
➤ **Antonyms**
≠**break**: honour, obey, respect, uphold ≠**desecrate**: defend, honour, protect, respect, revere, set on a pedestal

violation *noun* 1 = **infringement**, abuse, breach, contravention, encroachment, infraction, transgression, trespass 2 = **desecration**, defilement, profanation, sacrilege, spoliation

violence *noun* 1 = **force**, bloodshed, bloodthirstiness, brutality, brute force, cruelty, destructiveness, ferocity, fierceness, fighting, frenzy, fury, passion, savagery, strong-arm tactics (*informal*), terrorism, thuggery, vehemence, wildness 2 = **intensity**, abandon, acuteness, fervour, force, harshness, severity, sharpness, vehemence 3 = **power**, boisterousness, raging, roughness, storminess, tumult, turbulence, wildness

violent *adjective* 1 = **destructive**, bloodthirsty, brutal, cruel, fiery, flaming, forcible, furious, hot-headed, intemperate, murderous, passionate, powerful, raging, riotous, rough, savage, strong, tempestuous, uncontrollable, ungovernable, unrestrained, vehement, vicious, wild 2 = **intense**, acute, agonizing, biting, excruciating, extreme, inordinate, painful, severe, sharp 3 = **powerful**, boisterous, devastating, gale force, raging, storming, strong, tempestuous,

tumultuous, turbulent, wild
➤ **Antonyms**
≠**destructive**: calm, composed, gentle, mild, peaceful, placid, quiet, rational, sane, serene, unruffled, well-behaved
≠**powerful**: calm, gentle, mild, placid, serene

V.I.P. *noun* = **celebrity**, big hitter (*informal*), big name, heavy hitter (*informal*), luminary, somebody, star

virago *noun* = **harridan**, ballbreaker (*slang*), battle-axe (*informal*), fury, scold, shrew

virgin *noun* **1** = **maiden** (*archaic*), damsel (*archaic*), girl, maid (*archaic*), vestal, virgo intacta ♦ *adjective* **2** = **pure**, chaste, immaculate, maidenly, modest, uncorrupted, undefiled, unsullied, vestal, virginal **3** = **fresh**, new, pristine, unsullied, untouched, unused
➤ **Antonyms**
adjective ≠**pure**: corrupted, defiled, impure
≠**fresh**: contaminated, dirty, impure, polluted, spoiled, used

virginal *adjective* **1** = **pure**, celibate, chaste, immaculate, maidenly, uncorrupted, undefiled, virgin **2** = **fresh**, immaculate, pristine, pure, snowy, spotless, undisturbed, untouched, white

virginity *noun* = **chastity**, maidenhood

virile *adjective* = **manly**, forceful, lusty, macho, male, manlike, masculine, potent, red-blooded, robust, strong, vigorous
➤ **Antonyms**
camp (*informal*), effeminate, emasculate, feminine, girlie, impotent, unmanly, weak, weedy (*informal*), wimpish *or* wimpy (*informal*), wussy (*slang*)

virility *noun* = **masculinity**, machismo, manhood, potency, vigour
➤ **Antonyms**
effeminacy, femininity, impotence, softness, unmanliness, weakness

virtual *adjective* = **practical**, essential, implicit, implied, in all but name, indirect, tacit, unacknowledged

virtually *adverb* = **practically**, almost, as good as, effectually, for all practical purposes, in all but name, in effect, in essence, nearly, to all intents and purposes

virtue *noun* **1** = **goodness**, high-mindedness, incorruptibility, integrity, justice, morality, probity, quality, rectitude, righteousness, uprightness, worth, worthiness **2** = **merit**, advantage, asset, attribute, credit, good point, good quality, plus (*informal*), strength **3** = **chastity**, honour, innocence, purity, virginity **4 by virtue of** = **because of**, as a result of, by dint of, by reason of, in view

of, on account of, owing to, thanks to
➤ **Antonyms**
≠**goodness**: corruption, debauchery, depravity, dishonesty, dishonour, evil, immorality, sin, sinfulness, turpitude, vice
≠**merit**: drawback, failing, frailty, shortcoming, weak point ≠**chastity**: promiscuity, unchastity

virtuosity *noun* = **mastery**, brilliance, craft, éclat, expertise, finish, flair, panache, polish, skill

virtuoso *noun* **1** = **master**, artist, genius, grandmaster, maestro, magician, master hand ♦ *adjective* **2** = **masterly**, bravura (*Music*), brilliant, dazzling

virtuous *adjective* **1** = **good**, blameless, ethical, excellent, exemplary, high-principled, honest, honourable, incorruptible, just, moral, praiseworthy, pure, righteous, squeaky-clean, upright, worthy **2** = **chaste**, celibate, clean-living, innocent, pure, spotless, virginal
➤ **Antonyms**
≠**good**: corrupt, debauched, depraved, dishonest, evil, immoral, sinful, unrighteous, vicious, wicked ≠**chaste**: impure, loose, promiscuous, unchaste

virulence *noun* **1** = **bitterness**, acrimony, antagonism, hatred, hostility, ill will, malevolence, malice, rancour, resentment, spite, spleen, venom, viciousness, vindictiveness **2** = **deadliness**, harmfulness, hurtfulness, infectiousness, injuriousness, malignancy, noxiousness, poisonousness, toxicity, virulency

virulent *adjective* **1** = **bitter**, acrimonious, envenomed, hostile, malevolent, malicious, rancorous, resentful, spiteful, splenetic, venomous, vicious, vindictive **2** = **deadly**, baneful (*archaic*), infective, injurious, lethal, malignant, pernicious, poisonous, septic, toxic, venomous
➤ **Antonyms**
≠**bitter**: amiable, benign, compassionate, kind, magnanimous, sympathetic, warm
≠**deadly**: harmless, innocuous, nonpoisonous, nontoxic

viscous *adjective* = **thick**, gelatinous, gluey, glutinous, gooey (*informal*), icky (*informal*), sticky, syrupy, viscid

visible *adjective* = **apparent**, bold, clear, conspicuous, detectable, discernible, discoverable, distinguishable, evident, in sight, in view, manifest, not hidden, noticeable, observable, obvious, palpable, patent, perceivable, perceptible, plain, to be seen, unconcealed, unmistakable
➤ **Antonyms**
concealed, hidden, imperceptible, invisible, obscured, unnoticeable, unseen

vision *noun* 1 = **sight**, eyes, eyesight, perception, seeing, view 2 = **image**, castle in the air, concept, conception, daydream, dream, fantasy, idea, ideal, mental picture, pipe dream 3 = **hallucination**, apparition, chimera, delusion, ghost, illusion, mirage, phantasm, phantom, revelation, spectre, wraith 4 = **foresight**, breadth of view, discernment, farsightedness, imagination, insight, intuition, penetration, prescience 5 = **picture**, dream, sight, sight for sore eyes, spectacle

visionary *adjective* 1 = **idealistic**, dreaming, dreamy, impractical, quixotic, romantic, speculative, starry-eyed, unrealistic, unworkable, utopian, with one's head in the clouds 2 = **prophetic**, mystical 3 = **imaginary**, chimerical, delusory, fanciful, fantastic, ideal, idealized, illusory, unreal ♦ *noun* 4 = **idealist**, daydreamer, Don Quixote, dreamer, romantic, theorist, utopian, zealot 5 = **prophet**, mystic, seer
➤ **Antonyms**
adjective ≠**idealistic**: pragmatic, realistic ≠**imaginary**: actual, mundane, real, unimaginary ♦ *noun* ≠**idealist**: cynic, pessimist, pragmatist, realist

visit *verb* 1 = **call on**, be the guest of, call in, drop in on (*informal*), go to see, inspect, look (someone) up, pay a call on, pop in (*informal*), stay at, stay with, stop by, take in (*informal*) 2 *Old-fashioned* = **afflict**, assail, attack, befall, descend upon, smite, trouble 3 *with* **on** *or* **upon** = **inflict**, bring down upon, execute, impose, wreak ♦ *noun* 4 = **call**, sojourn, stay, stop

visitation *noun* 1 = **inspection**, examination, visit 2 = **catastrophe**, bane, blight, calamity, cataclysm, disaster, infliction, ordeal, punishment, scourge, trial

visitor *noun* = **guest**, caller, company, visitant

vista *noun* = **view**, panorama, perspective, prospect

visual *adjective* 1 = **optical**, ocular, optic 2 = **observable**, discernible, perceptible, visible
➤ **Antonyms**
≠**observable**: imperceptible, indiscernible, invisible, out of sight, unnoticeable, unperceivable

visualize *verb* = **picture**, conceive of, conjure up a mental picture of, envisage, imagine, see in the mind's eye

vital *adjective* 1 = **essential**, basic, cardinal, fundamental, imperative, indispensable, necessary, radical, requisite 2 = **important**, critical, crucial, decisive, key, life-or-death,

significant, urgent 3 = **lively**, animated, dynamic, energetic, forceful, full of beans (*informal*), full of the joy of living, sparky, spirited, vibrant, vigorous, vivacious, zestful
➤ **Antonyms**
≠**essential**: dispensable, inessential, nonessential, unnecessary ≠**important**: minor, trivial, unimportant ≠**lively**: apathetic, lethargic, listless, uninvolved

vitality *noun* = **energy**, animation, brio, exuberance, go (*informal*), life, liveliness, lustiness, pep, robustness, sparkle, stamina, strength, vigour, vim (*slang*), vivaciousness, vivacity
➤ **Antonyms**
apathy, inertia, lethargy, listlessness, sluggishness, weakness

vitiate *verb* = **spoil**, harm, impair, injure, invalidate, mar, undermine, water down

vitiation *noun* = **spoiling**, deterioration, devaluation, dilution, impairment, marring, reduction, undermining

vitriolic *adjective* = **bitter**, acerbic, acid, bitchy (*informal*), caustic, envenomed, sardonic, scathing, venomous, virulent, withering

vituperation *noun* = **abuse**, blame, castigation, censure, fault-finding, flak (*informal*), invective, rebuke, reprimand, reproach, tongue-lashing, vilification
➤ **Antonyms**
acclaim, approval, commendation, eulogy, flattery, praise, tribute

vituperative *adjective* = **abusive**, belittling, calumniatory, censorious, defamatory, denunciatory, derogatory, harsh, insulting, opprobrious, scurrilous, withering

vivacious *adjective* = **lively**, animated, bubbling, cheerful, chirpy (*informal*), ebullient, effervescent, full of beans (*informal*), full of life, gay, high-spirited, jolly, light-hearted, merry, scintillating, sparkling, sparky, spirited, sprightly, upbeat (*informal*), vital
➤ **Antonyms**
boring, dull, languid, lifeless, listless, melancholy, spiritless, unenthusiastic

vivacity *noun* = **liveliness**, animation, brio, ebullience, effervescence, energy, gaiety, high spirits, life, pep, quickness, sparkle, spirit, sprightliness
➤ **Antonyms**
apathy, ennui, fatigue, heaviness, inertia, languor, lethargy, listlessness, weariness

vivid *adjective* 1 = **bright**, brilliant, clear, colourful, glowing, highly-coloured, intense, rich 2 = **clear**, distinct, dramatic, graphic, lifelike, memorable, powerful, realistic, sharp, sharply-etched, stirring,

strong, telling, true to life
➤ **Antonyms**
≠**bright:** colourless, cool, drab, dull, pale, pastel, sombre ≠**clear:** unclear, unmemorable, vague

vividness noun 1 = **brightness**, brilliancy, glow, radiance, resplendence 2 = **clarity**, distinctness, intensity, realism, sharpness, strength 3 = **liveliness**

vixen noun = **shrew**, ballbreaker (slang), fury, harpy, harridan, hellcat, scold, spitfire, termagant (rare), virago

viz. adverb = **namely**, that is to say, to wit, videlicet

vocabulary noun = **words**, dictionary, glossary, language, lexicon, wordbook, word stock

vocal adjective 1 = **spoken**, articulate, articulated, oral, put into words, said, uttered, voiced 2 = **outspoken**, articulate, blunt, eloquent, expressive, forthright, frank, free-spoken, noisy, plain-spoken, strident, vociferous
➤ **Antonyms**
≠**outspoken:** inarticulate, quiet, reserved, reticent, retiring, shy, silent, uncommunicative

vocation noun = **profession**, business, calling, career, employment, job, life's work, life work, métier, mission, office, post, pursuit, role, trade

vociferous adjective = **noisy**, clamorous, loud, loudmouthed (informal), obstreperous, outspoken, ranting, shouting, strident, uproarious, vehement, vocal
➤ **Antonyms**
hushed, muted, noiseless, quiet, silent, still

vogue noun 1 = **fashion**, craze, custom, dernier cri, last word, mode, style, the latest, the rage, the thing (informal), trend, way 2 As in **in vogue** = **popularity**, acceptance, currency, fashionableness, favour, prevalence, usage, use ♦ adjective 3 = **fashionable**, in, modish, now (informal), popular, prevalent, trendy (Brit. informal), up-to-the-minute, voguish, with it (informal)

voice noun 1 = **sound**, articulation, language, power of speech, tone, utterance, words 2 = **say**, decision, expression, part, view, vote, will, wish 3 = **instrument**, agency, medium, mouthpiece, organ, spokesman, spokesperson, spokeswoman, vehicle ♦ verb 4 = **express**, air, articulate, assert, come out with (informal), declare, divulge, enunciate, give expression or utterance to, put into words, say, utter

void noun 1 = **emptiness**, blank, blankness,

gap, lack, opening, space, vacuity, vacuum, want ♦ adjective 2 = **invalid**, dead, ineffective, ineffectual, inoperative, nonviable, null and void, useless, vain, worthless 3 Old-fashioned = **empty**, bare, clear, drained, emptied, free, tenantless, unfilled, unoccupied, vacant 4 with **of** = **devoid**, destitute, lacking, without ♦ verb 5 = **invalidate**, abnegate, cancel, nullify, rescind 6 = **empty**, discharge, drain, eject, eliminate (Physiology), emit, evacuate
➤ **Antonyms**
adjective ≠**empty:** abounding, complete, filled, full, occupied, replete, tenanted

volatile adjective 1 = **changeable**, explosive, inconstant, unsettled, unstable, unsteady, variable 2 = **temperamental**, airy, erratic, fickle, flighty, inconstant, lively, mercurial, up and down (informal), whimsical
➤ **Antonyms**
≠**changeable:** constant, inert, settled, stable, steady ≠**temperamental:** calm, consistent, cool-headed, dependable, reliable, self-controlled, sober

volition noun = **free will**, choice, choosing, determination, discretion, option, preference, purpose, resolution, will

volley noun = **barrage**, blast, bombardment, burst, cannonade, discharge, explosion, fusillade, hail, salvo, shower

volubility noun = **talkativeness**, fluency, garrulity, gift of the gab, glibness, loquaciousness, loquacity

voluble adjective = **talkative**, articulate, blessed with the gift of the gab, fluent, forthcoming, glib, loquacious
➤ **Antonyms**
hesitant, inarticulate, reticent, succinct, taciturn, terse, tongue-tied, unforthcoming

volume noun 1 = **capacity**, compass, cubic content, dimensions 2 = **amount**, aggregate, body, bulk, mass, quantity, total 3 = **book**, publication, title, tome, treatise

voluminous adjective 1 = **large**, ample, big, billowing, bulky, capacious, cavernous, full, massive, roomy, vast 2 = **copious**, prolific
➤ **Antonyms**
≠**large:** skimpy, slight, small, tiny ≠**copious:** inadequate, insufficient, scanty

voluntarily adverb = **willingly**, by choice, freely, off one's own bat, of one's own accord, of one's own free will, without being asked, without prompting

voluntary adjective = **unforced**, discretional, discretionary, free, gratuitous,

honorary, intended, intentional, optional, spontaneous, uncompelled, unconstrained, unpaid, volunteer, willing
➤ **Antonyms**
automatic, conscripted, forced, instinctive, involuntary, obligatory, unintentional

volunteer *verb* **1** = **offer**, offer one's services, present, proffer, propose, put oneself at (someone's) disposal, step forward **2** = **suggest**, advance, put forward, tender
➤ **Antonyms**
≠**offer:** begrudge, deny, keep, refuse, retain, withdraw, withhold

voluptuary *noun* = **sensualist**, *bon vivant*, epicurean, hedonist, luxury-lover, pleasure seeker, sybarite

voluptuous *adjective* **1** = **buxom**, ample, curvaceous (*informal*), enticing, erotic, full-bosomed, provocative, seductive, shapely **2** = **sensual**, epicurean, hedonistic, licentious, luxurious, pleasure-loving, self-indulgent, sybaritic
➤ **Antonyms**
≠**sensual:** abstemious, ascetic, celibate, rigorous, self-denying, Spartan

voluptuousness *noun* **1**
= **curvaceousness** (*informal*), seductiveness, shapeliness **2** = **sensuality**, carnality, licentiousness, opulence

vomit *verb* = **be sick**, barf (*U.S. slang*), bring up, chuck (up) (*slang, chiefly U.S.*), chunder (*slang, chiefly Austral.*), disgorge, eject, emit, heave, puke (*slang*), regurgitate, retch, sick up (*informal*), spew out *or* up, throw up (*informal*)

voracious *adjective* **1** = **gluttonous**, devouring, greedy, hungry, insatiable, omnivorous, ravening, ravenous **2** = **avid**, hungry, insatiable, prodigious, rapacious, uncontrolled, unquenchable
➤ **Antonyms**
≠**avid:** moderate, sated, satisfied, self-controlled, temperate

voracity *noun* **1** = **greed**, hunger, ravenousness **2** = **avidity**, eagerness, hunger, rapacity

vortex *noun* = **whirlpool**, eddy, maelstrom

votary *noun* = **devotee**, adherent, aficionado, believer, disciple, follower

vote *noun* **1** = **poll**, ballot, franchise, plebiscite, referendum, show of hands **2**

= **right to vote**, suffrage ♦ *verb* **3** = **cast one's vote**, ballot, elect, go to the polls, opt, return **4** *Informal* = **declare**, judge, pronounce, propose, recommend, suggest

voucher *noun* = **ticket**, coupon, token

vouch for *verb* **1** = **guarantee**, answer for, back, certify, give assurance of, go bail for, stand witness, swear to **2** = **confirm**, affirm, assert, attest to, support, uphold

vouchsafe *verb Old-fashioned* = **grant**, accord, condescend to give, confer, deign, favour (someone) with, yield

vow *noun* **1** = **promise**, oath, pledge, troth (*archaic*) ♦ *verb* **2** = **promise**, affirm, pledge, swear, undertake solemnly

voyage *noun* = **journey**, crossing, cruise, passage, travels, trip

vulgar *adjective* **1** = **crude**, blue, boorish, cheap and nasty, coarse, common, common as muck, dirty, flashy, gaudy, gross, ill-bred, impolite, improper, indecent, indecorous, indelicate, low, nasty, off colour, ribald, risqué, rude, suggestive, tasteless, tawdry, uncouth, unmannerly, unrefined **2** = **vernacular**, general, native, ordinary, unrefined
➤ **Antonyms**
≠**crude:** aristocratic, classical, decorous, elegant, genteel, high-brow, polite, refined, sophisticated, tasteful, upper-class, urbane, well-mannered

vulgarian *noun* = **upstart**, arriviste, boor, churl, *nouveau riche*, parvenu, philistine

vulgarity *noun* = **crudeness**, bad taste, coarseness, crudity, gaudiness, grossness, indecorum, indelicacy, lack of refinement, ribaldry, rudeness, suggestiveness, tastelessness, tawdriness
➤ **Antonyms**
decorum, gentility, good breeding, good manners, good taste, refinement, sensitivity, sophistication, tastefulness

vulnerable *adjective* **1** = **susceptible**, sensitive, tender, thin-skinned, weak **2** = **exposed**, accessible, assailable, defenceless, open to attack, unprotected, wide open
➤ **Antonyms**
≠**susceptible:** immune, impervious, insensitive, thick-skinned ≠**exposed:** guarded, invulnerable, unassailable, well-protected

W w

wad *noun* = **mass**, ball, block, bundle, chunk, hunk, lump, plug, roll

wadding *noun* = **padding**, filler, lining, packing, stuffing

waddle *verb* = **shuffle**, rock, sway, toddle, totter, wobble

wade *verb* **1** = **walk through**, ford, paddle, splash **2 wade in** *or* **into** = **launch oneself at**, assail, attack, get stuck in (*informal*), go for, light into (*informal*), set about, tackle, tear into (*informal*) **3 wade through** = **plough through**, drudge at, labour at, peg away at, toil at, work one's way through

waffle *verb* **1** = **prattle**, blather, jabber, prate, rabbit (on) (*Brit. informal*), verbalize, witter on (*informal*) ♦ *noun* **2** = **verbosity**, blather, jabber, padding, prating, prattle, prolixity, verbiage, wordiness

waft *verb* **1** = **carry**, bear, be carried, convey, drift, float, ride, transmit, transport ♦ *noun* **2** = **current**, breath, breeze, draught, puff, whiff

wag *verb* **1** = **wave**, bob, flutter, nod, oscillate, quiver, rock, shake, stir, vibrate, waggle, wiggle ♦ *noun* **2** = **wave**, bob, flutter, nod, oscillation, quiver, shake, toss, vibration, waggle, wiggle

wage *noun* **1** *Also* **wages** = **payment**, allowance, compensation, earnings, emolument, fee, hire, pay, recompense, remuneration, reward, stipend ♦ *verb* **2** = **engage in**, carry on, conduct, practise, proceed with, prosecute, pursue, undertake

wager *noun* **1** = **bet**, flutter (*Brit. informal*), gamble, pledge, punt (*chiefly Brit.*), stake, venture ♦ *verb* **2** = **bet**, chance, gamble, hazard, lay, pledge, punt (*chiefly Brit.*), put on, risk, speculate, stake, venture

waggle *verb* = **wag**, flutter, oscillate, shake, wave, wiggle, wobble

waif *noun* = **stray**, foundling, orphan

wail *verb* **1** = **cry**, bawl, bemoan, bewail, deplore, grieve, howl, keen, lament, ululate, weep, yowl ♦ *noun* **2** = **cry**, complaint, grief, howl, keen, lament, lamentation, moan, ululation, weeping, yowl

wait *verb* **1** = **remain**, abide, bide one's time, cool one's heels, dally, delay, hang fire, hold back, hold on (*informal*), kick one's heels, linger, mark time, pause, rest, stand by, stay, tarry ♦ *noun* **2** = **delay**, entr'acte, halt, hold-up, interval, pause, rest, stay
➤ **Antonyms**
verb ≠**remain**: depart, go, go away, leave, move off, quit, set off, take off (*informal*)

waiter, waitress *noun* = **attendant**, server, steward *or* stewardess

wait on *or* **upon** *verb* = **serve**, attend, minister to, tend

waive *verb* = **set aside**, abandon, defer, dispense with, forgo, give up, postpone, put off, refrain from, relinquish, remit, renounce, resign, surrender
➤ **Antonyms**
claim, demand, insist, maintain, press, profess, pursue, uphold

waiver *noun* = **renunciation**, abandonment, abdication, disclaimer, giving up, relinquishment, remission, resignation, setting aside, surrender

wake¹ *verb* **1** = **awaken**, arise, awake, bestir, come to, get up, rouse, rouse from sleep, stir **2** = **activate**, animate, arouse, awaken, enliven, excite, fire, galvanize, kindle, provoke, quicken, rouse, stimulate, stir up ♦ *noun* **3** = **vigil**, deathwatch, funeral, watch
➤ **Antonyms**
verb ≠**awaken**: catnap, doze, drop off (*informal*), hibernate, nod off (*informal*), sleep, snooze (*informal*), take a nap

wake² *noun* = **slipstream**, aftermath, backwash, path, track, trail, train, wash, waves

wakeful *adjective* **1** = **sleepless**, insomniac, restless, unsleeping **2** = **watchful**, alert, alive, attentive, heedful, observant, on guard, on the alert, on the lookout, on the qui vive, unsleeping, vigilant, wary
➤ **Antonyms**
≠**sleepless**: asleep, dormant, dozing ≠**watchful**: dreamy, drowsy, heedless, inattentive, off guard, sleepy

waken *verb* = **awaken**, activate, animate, arouse, awake, be roused, come awake, come to, enliven, fire, galvanize, get up, kindle, quicken, rouse, stimulate, stir
➤ **Antonyms**
be inactive, doze, lie dormant, nap,

repose, sleep, slumber, snooze (*informal*)

walk *verb* **1** = **go**, advance, amble, foot it, go by shanks's pony (*informal*), go on foot, hike, hoof it (*slang*), march, move, pace, perambulate, promenade, saunter, step, stride, stroll, traipse (*informal*), tramp, travel on foot, tread, trek, trudge **2** = **escort**, accompany, convoy, take ♦ *noun* **3** = **stroll**, constitutional, hike, march, perambulation, promenade, ramble, saunter, traipse (*informal*), tramp, trek, trudge, turn **4** = **gait**, carriage, manner of walking, pace, step, stride **5** = **path**, aisle, alley, avenue, esplanade, footpath, lane, pathway, pavement, promenade, sidewalk, trail **6 walk of life** = **profession**, area, arena, calling, career, course, field, line, métier, sphere, trade, vocation

walker *noun* = **pedestrian**, footslogger, hiker, rambler, wayfarer

walkout *noun* = **strike**, industrial action, protest, stoppage

walk out *verb* **1** = **leave suddenly**, flounce out, get up and go, storm out, take off (*informal*), vote with one's feet **2** = **go on strike**, down tools, stop work, strike, take industrial action, withdraw one's labour **3 walk out on** = **abandon**, chuck (*informal*), desert, forsake, jilt, leave, leave in the lurch, pack in (*informal*), run away from, strand, throw over
➤ **Antonyms**
≠**abandon**: be loyal to, defend, remain, stand by, stay, stick with, support, uphold

walkover *noun* = **pushover** (*slang*), breeze (*U.S. & Canad. informal*), cakewalk (*informal*), child's play (*informal*), cinch (*slang*), doddle (*Brit. slang*), duck soup (*U.S. slang*), easy victory, picnic (*informal*), piece of cake (*informal*), snap (*informal*)
➤ **Antonyms**
effort, grind (*informal*), labour, ordeal, strain, struggle, trial

wall *noun* **1** = **partition**, divider, enclosure, panel, screen **2** = **barricade**, breastwork, bulwark, embankment, fortification, palisade, parapet, rampart, stockade **3** = **barrier**, block, fence, hedge, impediment, obstacle, obstruction **4 go to the wall** *Informal* = **fail**, be ruined, collapse, fall, go bust (*informal*), go under **5 drive up the wall** *Slang* = **infuriate**, aggravate (*informal*), annoy, dement, derange, drive crazy (*informal*), drive insane, exasperate, get on one's nerves (*informal*), irritate, madden, piss one off (*taboo slang*), send off one's head (*slang*), try

wallet *noun* = **holder**, case, notecase, pocketbook, pouch, purse

wallop *verb* **1** = **hit**, batter, beat, clobber (*slang*), pound, pummel, strike, swipe, thrash, thump, whack ♦ *noun* **2** = **blow**, bash, punch, slug, smack, swipe, thump, thwack, whack

wallow *verb* **1** = **revel**, bask, delight, glory, indulge oneself, luxuriate, relish, take pleasure **2** = **roll about**, lie, splash around, tumble, welter
➤ **Antonyms**
≠**revel**: abstain, avoid, do without, eschew, forgo, give up, refrain

wan *adjective* **1** = **pale**, anaemic, ashen, bloodless, cadaverous, colourless, discoloured, ghastly, like death warmed up (*informal*), livid, pallid, pasty, sickly, washed out, waxen, wheyfaced, white **2** = **dim**, faint, feeble, pale, weak
➤ **Antonyms**
≠**pale**: blooming, bright, flourishing, glowing, healthy, roseate, rosy, rubicund, ruddy, vibrant

wand *noun* = **stick**, baton, rod, sprig, twig, withe, withy

wander *verb* **1** = **roam**, cruise, drift, knock about or around, meander, mooch around (*slang*), peregrinate, ramble, range, rove, straggle, stravaig (*Scot. & Northern English dialect*), stray, stroll, traipse (*informal*) **2** = **deviate**, depart, digress, divagate (*rare*), diverge, err, get lost, go astray, go off at a tangent, go off course, lapse, lose concentration, lose one's train of thought, lose one's way, swerve, veer **3** = **rave**, babble, be delirious, be incoherent, ramble, speak incoherently, talk nonsense ♦ *noun* **4** = **excursion**, cruise, meander, peregrination, ramble, traipse (*informal*)
➤ **Antonyms**
verb ≠**deviate**: comply, conform, fall in with, follow, run with the pack, toe the line

wanderer *noun* = **traveller**, bird of passage, drifter, gypsy, itinerant, nomad, rambler, ranger, rolling stone, rover, stroller, vagabond, vagrant, voyager

wandering *adjective* = **nomadic**, drifting, homeless, itinerant, migratory, peripatetic, rambling, rootless, roving, strolling, travelling, vagabond, vagrant, voyaging, wayfaring

wane *verb* **1** = **decline**, abate, atrophy, decrease, die out, dim, diminish, draw to a close, drop, dwindle, ebb, fade, fade away, fail, lessen, sink, subside, taper off, weaken, wind down, wither ♦ *noun* **2 on the wane** = **declining**, at its lowest ebb, dropping, dwindling, dying out, ebbing, fading, lessening, obsolescent, on its last legs, on the decline, on the way out, subsiding, tapering off, weakening,

withering
> **Antonyms**
verb ≠**decline**: blossom, brighten, develop,
expand, grow, improve, increase, rise,
strengthen, wax

wangle *verb* = **contrive**, arrange, engineer,
fiddle (*informal*), fix (*informal*),
manipulate, manoeuvre, pull off

want *verb* 1 = **desire**, covet, crave, eat
one's heart out over, feel a need for,
hanker after, have a fancy for, have a yen
for (*informal*), hope for, hunger for, long
for, pine for, set one's heart on, thirst for,
wish, would give one's eyeteeth for, yearn
for 2 = **need**, be able to do with, be
deficient in, be short of, be without, call
for, demand, fall short in, have need of,
lack, miss, require, stand in need of ◆ *noun*
3 = **wish**, appetite, craving, demand,
desire, fancy, hankering, hunger, longing,
necessity, need, requirement, thirst,
yearning, yen (*informal*) 4 = **lack**, absence,
dearth, default, deficiency, famine,
insufficiency, paucity, scantiness, scarcity,
shortage 5 = **poverty**, destitution,
indigence, need, neediness, pauperism,
penury, privation
> **Antonyms**
verb ≠**desire**: detest, dislike, hate, loathe,
reject, spurn ≠**need**: be sated, have, own,
possess ◆ *noun* ≠**lack**: abundance,
adequacy, excess, plenty, sufficiency,
surfeit, surplus ≠**poverty**: comfort, ease,
luxury, wealth

wanting *adjective* 1 = **lacking**, absent,
incomplete, less, missing, short, shy 2
= **inadequate**, defective, deficient,
disappointing, faulty, imperfect, inferior,
leaving much to be desired, not good
enough, not much cop (*Brit. slang*), not up
to expectations, not up to par, patchy,
pathetic, poor, sketchy, substandard,
unsound
> **Antonyms**
≠**lacking**: complete, full, replete, saturated
≠**inadequate**: adequate, enough,
satisfactory, sufficient

wanton *adjective* 1 = **unprovoked**,
arbitrary, cruel, evil, gratuitous,
groundless, malevolent, malicious,
motiveless, needless, senseless, spiteful,
uncalled-for, unjustifiable, unjustified,
vicious, wicked, wilful 2 = **promiscuous**,
abandoned, dissipated, dissolute, fast,
immoral, lecherous, lewd, libertine,
libidinous, licentious, loose, lustful, of easy
virtue, rakish, shameless, unchaste 3
= **reckless**, careless, devil-may-care,
extravagant, heedless, immoderate,
intemperate, lavish, outrageous, rash,
unrestrained, wild ◆ *noun* 4 = **slut**, harlot,

loose woman, prostitute, scrubber (*Brit. &
Austral. slang*), slag (*Brit. slang*), strumpet,
swinger (*informal*), tart, trollop, whore,
woman of easy virtue
> **Antonyms**
adjective ≠**unprovoked**: called-for,
excusable, justified, legitimate, motivated,
provoked, warranted ≠**promiscuous**:
overmodest, priggish, prim, prudish,
puritanical, rigid, strait-laced, stuffy,
Victorian ≠**reckless**: cautious,
circumspect, guarded, inhibited,
moderate, prudent, reserved, restrained,
temperate

war *noun* 1 = **fighting**, armed conflict,
battle, bloodshed, combat, conflict,
contention, contest, enmity, hostilities,
hostility, strife, struggle, warfare ◆ *verb* 2
= **fight**, battle, campaign against, carry on
hostilities, clash, combat, conduct a war,
contend, contest, make war, strive,
struggle, take up arms, wage war
> **Antonyms**
noun ≠**fighting**: accord, armistice,
ceasefire, co-existence, compliance,
co-operation, harmony, peace,
peace-time, treaty, truce ◆ *verb* ≠**fight**:
call a ceasefire, co-exist, co-operate, make
peace

warble *verb* = **sing**, chirp, trill, twitter

war cry *noun* = **battle cry**, rallying cry,
slogan, war whoop

ward *noun* 1 = **room**, apartment, cubicle 2
= **district**, area, division, precinct, quarter,
zone 3 = **dependant**, charge, minor,
protégé, pupil

warden *noun* = **keeper**, administrator,
caretaker, curator, custodian, guardian,
janitor, ranger, steward, superintendent,
warder, watchman

warder, wardress *noun* = **jailer**,
custodian, guard, keeper, prison officer,
screw (*slang*), turnkey (*archaic*)

ward off *verb* = **repel**, avert, avoid, beat
off, block, deflect, fend off, forestall, keep
at arm's length, keep at bay, parry, stave
off, thwart, turn aside, turn away
> **Antonyms**
accept, admit, allow, embrace, permit,
receive, take in, welcome

wardrobe *noun* 1 = **clothes cupboard**,
closet, clothes-press 2 = **clothes**, apparel,
attire, collection of clothes, outfit

warehouse *noun* = **store**, depository,
depot, stockroom, storehouse

wares *plural noun* = **goods**, commodities,
lines, manufactures, merchandise,
produce, products, stock, stuff

warfare *noun* = **war**, armed conflict, armed

struggle, arms, battle, blows, campaigning, clash of arms, combat, conflict, contest, discord, fighting, hostilities, passage of arms, strategy, strife, struggle
➤ **Antonyms**
accord, amity, armistice, ceasefire, cessation of hostilities, conciliation, harmony, peace, treaty, truce

warily *adverb* = **cautiously**, cagily (*informal*), carefully, charily, circumspectly, distrustfully, gingerly, guardedly, suspiciously, vigilantly, watchfully, with care
➤ **Antonyms**
carelessly, hastily, heedlessly, irresponsibly, rashly, recklessly, thoughtlessly, unwarily

wariness *noun* = **caution**, alertness, attention, caginess (*informal*), care, carefulness, circumspection, discretion, distrust, foresight, heedfulness, mindfulness, prudence, suspicion, vigilance, watchfulness
➤ **Antonyms**
carelessness, heedlessness, inattention, mindlessness, negligence, oblivion, recklessness, thoughtlessness

warlike *adjective* = **belligerent**, aggressive, bellicose, bloodthirsty, combative, hawkish, hostile, inimical, jingoistic, martial, militaristic, military, pugnacious, sabre-rattling, unfriendly, warmongering
➤ **Antonyms**
amicable, conciliatory, friendly, nonbelligerent, pacific, peaceable, peaceful, placid, unwarlike

warlock *noun* = **magician**, conjuror, enchanter, sorcerer, wizard

warm *adjective* 1 = **heated**, balmy, lukewarm, moderately hot, pleasant, sunny, tepid, thermal 2 = **affectionate**, affable, amiable, amorous, cheerful, congenial, cordial, friendly, genial, happy, hearty, hospitable, kindly, likable *or* likeable, loving, pleasant, tender ◆ *verb* 3 = **heat**, heat up, melt, thaw, warm up 4 = **rouse**, animate, awaken, excite, get going, interest, make enthusiastic, put some life into, stimulate, stir, turn on (*slang*)
➤ **Antonyms**
adjective ≠**heated**: chilly, cold, cool, freezing, icy ≠**affectionate**: aloof, apathetic, cold, cool, distant, half-hearted, hostile, phlegmatic, remote, stand-offish, uncaring, unenthusiastic, unfriendly, unwelcoming ◆ *verb* ≠**heat**: chill, cool, cool down, freeze ≠**rouse**: alienate, depress, sadden

warm-blooded *adjective* = **passionate**,

ardent, earnest, emotional, enthusiastic, excitable, fervent, impetuous, lively, rash, spirited, vivacious

warm-hearted *adjective* = **kindly**, affectionate, compassionate, cordial, generous, kind-hearted, loving, sympathetic, tender, tender-hearted
➤ **Antonyms**
callous, cold, cold-hearted, hard, hard-hearted, harsh, heartless, insensitive, mean, merciless, unfeeling, unsympathetic

warmonger *noun* = **hawk**, belligerent, jingo, militarist, sabre-rattler

warmth *noun* 1 = **heat**, hotness, warmness 2 = **affection**, affability, amorousness, cheerfulness, cordiality, happiness, heartiness, hospitableness, kindliness, love, tenderness
➤ **Antonyms**
≠**heat**: chill, chilliness, cold, coldness, coolness, iciness ≠**affection**: aloofness, apathy, austerity, cold-heartedness, hard-heartedness, hostility, indifference, insincerity, lack of enthusiasm, remoteness, sternness

warn *verb* = **notify**, admonish, advise, alert, apprise, caution, forewarn, give fair warning, give notice, inform, make (someone) aware, put one on one's guard, summon, tip off

warning *noun* 1 = **caution**, admonition, advice, alarm, alert, augury, caveat, foretoken, hint, notice, notification, omen, premonition, presage, sign, signal, threat, tip, tip-off, token, word, word to the wise ◆ *adjective* 2 = **cautionary**, admonitory, bodeful, monitory, ominous, premonitory, threatening

warp *verb* 1 = **twist**, bend, contort, deform, distort ◆ *noun* 2 = **twist**, bend, contortion, distortion, kink

warrant *noun* 1 = **authorization**, assurance, authority, carte blanche, commission, guarantee, licence, permission, permit, pledge, sanction, security, warranty ◆ *verb* 2 = **call for**, approve, authorize, commission, demand, deserve, empower, entail, entitle, excuse, give ground for, justify, license, necessitate, permit, require, sanction 3 = **guarantee**, affirm, answer for, assure, attest, avouch, certify, declare, pledge, secure, stand behind, underwrite, uphold, vouch for

warrantable *adjective* = **justifiable**, accountable, allowable, defensible, lawful, necessary, permissible, proper, reasonable, right
➤ **Antonyms**
indefensible, uncalled-for, undue,

unjustifiable, unnecessary, unreasonable, unwarrantable, wrong

warranty noun = **guarantee**, assurance, bond, certificate, contract, covenant, pledge

warrior noun = **soldier**, champion, combatant, fighter, fighting man, gladiator, man-at-arms

wary adjective = **cautious**, alert, attentive, cagey (informal), careful, chary, circumspect, distrustful, guarded, heedful, leery (slang), on one's guard, on the lookout, on the qui vive, prudent, suspicious, vigilant, watchful, wide-awake
➤ Antonyms
careless, foolhardy, imprudent, negligent, rash, reckless, remiss, unguarded, unsuspecting, unwary

wash verb 1 = **clean**, bath, bathe, cleanse, launder, moisten, rinse, scrub, shampoo, shower, wet 2 = **sweep away**, bear away, carry off, erode, move, wash off 3 Informal = **be plausible**, bear scrutiny, be convincing, carry weight, hold up, hold water, stand up, stick 4 **wash one's hands of** = **have nothing to do with**, abandon, accept no responsibility for, give up on, leave to one's own devices ♦ noun 5 = **cleaning**, ablution, bath, bathe, cleansing, laundering, rinse, scrub, shampoo, shower, washing 6 = **coat**, coating, film, layer, overlay, screen, stain, suffusion 7 = **swell**, ebb and flow, flow, roll, surge, sweep, wave

washed-out adjective 1 = **exhausted**, all in (slang), clapped out (Austral. & N.Z. informal), dead on one's feet (informal), dog-tired (informal), done in (informal), drained, drawn, fatigued, haggard, knackered (slang), pale, spent, tired-out, wan, weary, wiped out (informal), worn-out, zonked (slang) 2 = **faded**, blanched, bleached, colourless, etiolated, flat, lacklustre, mat, pale
➤ Antonyms
≠exhausted: alert, chirpy, energetic, full of beans (informal), full of pep (informal), lively, perky, refreshed, sprightly, zippy (informal)

washout noun 1 = **failure**, clunker (informal), disappointment, disaster, dud (informal), fiasco, flop (informal), mess 2 = **loser**, failure, incompetent
➤ Antonyms
≠failure: conquest, feat, success, triumph, victory, winner

waspish adjective = **bad-tempered**, cantankerous, captious, crabbed, crabby, cross, crotchety (informal), fretful, grumpy, ill-tempered, irascible, irritable, liverish,

peevish, peppery, pettish, petulant, ratty (Brit. & N.Z. informal), snappish, splenetic, testy, tetchy, touchy, waxy (informal, chiefly Brit.)
➤ Antonyms
affable, agreeable, cheerful, easy-going, genial, good-humoured, good-natured, jovial, pleasant

waste verb 1 = **squander**, blow (slang), dissipate, fritter away, frivol away (informal), lavish, misuse, run through, throw away 2 **waste away** = **decline**, atrophy, consume, corrode, crumble, debilitate, decay, deplete, disable, drain, dwindle, eat away, ebb, emaciate, enfeeble, exhaust, fade, gnaw, perish, sap the strength of, sink, undermine, wane, wear out, wither ♦ noun 3 = **squandering**, dissipation, expenditure, extravagance, frittering away, loss, lost opportunity, misapplication, misuse, prodigality, unthriftiness, wastefulness 4 = **rubbish**, debris, dregs, dross, garbage, leavings, leftovers, litter, offal, offscourings, refuse, scrap, sweepings, trash 5 **wastes** = **desert**, solitude, void, wasteland, wild, wilderness ♦ adjective 6 = **unwanted**, leftover, superfluous, supernumerary, unused, useless, worthless 7 = **uncultivated**, bare, barren, desolate, devastated, dismal, dreary, empty, uninhabited, unproductive, wild 8 **lay waste** = **devastate**, depredate (rare), despoil, destroy, pillage, rape, ravage, raze, ruin, sack, spoil, total (slang), trash (slang), undo, wreak havoc upon
➤ Antonyms
verb ≠**squander**: conserve, economize, husband, preserve, protect, save ≠**decline**: build, develop, increase, rally, strengthen ♦ noun ≠**squandering**: economy, frugality, good housekeeping, saving, thrift ♦ adjective ≠**unwanted**: necessary, needed, utilized ≠**uncultivated**: arable, developed, fruitful, habitable, in use, productive, verdant

wasteful adjective = **extravagant**, improvident, lavish, prodigal, profligate, ruinous, spendthrift, thriftless, uneconomical, unthrifty
➤ Antonyms
economical, frugal, money-saving, parsimonious, penny-wise, provident, sparing, thrifty

waster noun = **layabout**, good-for-nothing, idler, loafer, ne'er-do-well, shirker, skiver (Brit. slang), wastrel

wastrel noun 1 = **layabout**, drone, good-for-nothing, idler, loafer, loser, malingerer, ne'er-do-well, shirker, skiver (Brit. slang), waster 2 = **spendthrift**, prodigal, profligate, squanderer

watch *verb* **1** = **look at**, check, check out (*informal*), clock (*Brit. slang*), contemplate, eye, eyeball (*slang*), feast one's eyes on, gaze at, get a load of (*informal*), look, look on, mark, note, observe, pay attention, peer at, regard, see, stare at, take a dekko at (*Brit. slang*), view **2** = **guard**, keep, look after, mind, protect, superintend, take care of, tend **3** = **be vigilant**, attend, be on the alert, be on the lookout, be wary, be watchful, keep an eye open (*informal*), look out, take heed, wait ♦ *noun* **4** = **wristwatch**, chronometer, clock, pocket watch, timepiece **5** = **lookout**, alertness, attention, eye, heed, inspection, notice, observation, supervision, surveillance, vigil, vigilance, watchfulness

watchdog *noun* **1** = **guard dog 2** = **guardian**, custodian, inspector, monitor, protector, scrutineer

watcher *noun* = **viewer**, fly on the wall, looker-on, lookout, observer, onlooker, spectator, spy, witness

watchful *adjective* = **alert**, attentive, circumspect, guarded, heedful, observant, on one's guard, on one's toes, on the lookout, on the qui vive, on the watch, suspicious, vigilant, wary, wide awake
➤ **Antonyms**
careless, inattentive, reckless, thoughtless, unaware, unguarded, unmindful, unobservant, unwary

watchfulness *noun* = **vigilance**, alertness, attention, attentiveness, caution, cautiousness, circumspection, heedfulness, wariness
➤ **Antonyms**
carelessness, heedlessness, inattention, indiscretion, irresponsibility, neglect, recklessness, thoughtlessness

watchman *noun* = **guard**, caretaker, custodian, security guard, security man

watch out *verb* = **be careful**, be alert, be on one's guard, be on the alert, be on (the) watch, be vigilant, be watchful, have a care, keep a sharp lookout, keep a weather eye open, keep one's eyes open, keep one's eyes peeled *or* skinned (*informal*), look out, mind out, watch oneself

watch over *verb* **1** = **look after**, defend, guard, keep safe, preserve, protect, shelter, shield, stand guard over **2** = **superintend**, direct, keep an eye on, oversee, preside over

watchword *noun* **1** = **motto**, battle cry, byword, catch phrase, catchword, maxim, rallying cry, slogan, tag-line **2** = **password**, countersign, magic word, shibboleth

water *noun* **1** = **liquid**, Adam's ale *or* wine, aqua, H_2O **2 hold water** = **be sound**, bear examination *or* scrutiny, be credible, be logical, make sense, pass the test, ring true, work **3 of the first water** = **excellent**, of the best, of the best quality, of the finest quality, of the highest degree, of the highest grade ♦ *verb* **4** = **moisten**, damp, dampen, douse, drench, flood, hose, irrigate, soak, souse, spray, sprinkle **5** = **dilute**, add water to, adulterate, put water in, thin, water down, weaken

water down *verb* **1** = **dilute**, add water to, adulterate, put water in, thin, water, weaken **2** = **weaken**, adulterate, mitigate, qualify, soften, tone down
➤ **Antonyms**
≠**dilute**: fortify, purify, strengthen, thicken

waterfall *noun* = **cascade**, cataract, chute, fall, force (*Northern English dialect*), linn (*Scot.*)

waterlogged *adjective* = **soaked**, drenched, dripping, droukit *or* drookit (*Scot.*), saturated, sodden, sopping, streaming, wet through, wringing wet

watertight *adjective* **1** = **waterproof**, sound **2** = **foolproof**, airtight, firm, flawless, impregnable, incontrovertible, sound, unassailable
➤ **Antonyms**
≠**waterproof**: leaky ≠**foolproof**: defective, flawed, questionable, shaky, tenuous, uncertain, unsound, weak

watery *adjective* **1** = **wet**, aqueous, damp, fluid, humid, liquid, marshy, moist, soggy, squelchy **2** = **tearful**, rheumy, tear-filled, weepy **3** = **diluted**, adulterated, dilute, flavourless, insipid, runny, tasteless, thin, washy, watered-down, waterish, weak, wishy-washy (*informal*)
➤ **Antonyms**
≠**diluted**: concentrated, condensed, dense, fortified, solid, strong, thick

wave *verb* **1** = **signal**, beckon, direct, gesticulate, gesture, indicate, sign **2** = **brandish**, flap, flourish, flutter, move to and fro, oscillate, quiver, ripple, shake, stir, sway, swing, undulate, wag, waver, wield ♦ *noun* **3** = **ripple**, billow, breaker, comber, ridge, roller, sea surf, swell, undulation, unevenness **4** = **outbreak**, current, drift, flood, ground swell, movement, rash, rush, stream, surge, sweep, tendency, trend, upsurge

waver *verb* **1** = **hesitate**, be indecisive, be irresolute, be unable to decide, be unable to make up one's mind, blow hot and cold (*informal*), dither (*chiefly Brit.*), falter, fluctuate, hum and haw, seesaw, shillyshally (*informal*), swither (*Scot.*),

vacillate **2 = tremble**, flicker, fluctuate, quiver, reel, shake, sway, totter, undulate, vary, wave, weave, wobble
➤ **Antonyms**
≠**hesitate**: be decisive, be determined, be of fixed opinion, be resolute, determine, resolve, stand firm

wax *verb* = **increase**, become fuller, become larger, develop, dilate, enlarge, expand, fill out, get bigger, grow, magnify, mount, rise, swell
➤ **Antonyms**
contract, decline, decrease, diminish, dwindle, fade, lessen, narrow, shrink, wane

way *noun* **1 = method**, approach, course of action, fashion, manner, means, mode, plan, practice, procedure, process, scheme, system, technique **2 = style**, characteristic, conduct, custom, habit, idiosyncrasy, manner, nature, personality, practice, trait, usage, wont **3 = aspect**, detail, feature, particular, point, respect, sense **4 = route**, access, avenue, channel, course, direction, highway, lane, path, pathway, road, street, thoroughfare, track, trail **5 = journey**, advance, approach, march, passage, progress **6 = distance**, journey, length, stretch, trail **7 = room**, elbowroom, opening, space **8** *As in* **get one's own way = will**, aim, ambition, choice, demand, desire, goal, pleasure, wish **9** *As in* **in a bad way = condition**, circumstance, fettle, shape (*informal*), situation, state, status **10 by the way = incidentally**, by the bye, en passant, in parenthesis, in passing **11 give way: a = collapse**, break down, cave in, crack, crumple, fall, fall to pieces, give, go to pieces, subside **b = concede**, accede, acknowledge defeat, acquiesce, back down, make concessions, withdraw, yield **12 under way = in progress**, afoot, begun, going, in motion, moving, on the go (*informal*), on the move, started

wayfarer *noun* = **traveller**, bird of passage, globetrotter, gypsy, itinerant, journeyer, nomad, rover, trekker, voyager, walker, wanderer

wayfaring *adjective* = **roving**, drifting, itinerant, journeying, nomadic, peripatetic, rambling, travelling, voyaging, walking, wandering

waylay *verb* = **attack**, accost, ambush, catch, hold up, intercept, lie in wait for, pounce on, set upon, surprise, swoop down on

wayward *adjective* = **erratic**, capricious, changeable, contrary, contumacious, cross-grained, disobedient, fickle, flighty, froward (*archaic*), headstrong, inconstant,

incorrigible, insubordinate, intractable, mulish, obdurate, obstinate, perverse, rebellious, refractory, self-willed, stubborn, undependable, ungovernable, unmanageable, unpredictable, unruly, wilful
➤ **Antonyms**
complaisant, compliant, dependable, good-natured, malleable, manageable, obedient, obliging, predictable, reliable, submissive, tractable

weak *adjective* **1 = feeble**, anaemic, debilitated, decrepit, delicate, effete, enervated, exhausted, faint, fragile, frail, infirm, languid, puny, shaky, sickly, spent, tender, unsound, unsteady, wasted, weakly **2 = deficient**, faulty, inadequate, lacking, pathetic, poor, substandard, under-strength, wanting **3 = unsafe**, defenceless, exposed, helpless, unguarded, unprotected, untenable, vulnerable, wide open **4 = irresolute**, boneless, cowardly, impotent, indecisive, ineffectual, infirm, namby-pamby, pathetic, powerless, soft, spineless, timorous, weak-kneed (*informal*) **5 = unconvincing**, feeble, flimsy, hollow, inconclusive, invalid, lame, pathetic, shallow, slight, unsatisfactory **6 = faint**, distant, dull, imperceptible, low, muffled, poor, quiet, slight, small, soft **7 = tasteless**, diluted, insipid, milk-and-water, runny, thin, under-strength, waterish, watery, wishy-washy (*informal*)
➤ **Antonyms**
≠**feeble**: energetic, hardy, healthy, hefty, mighty, strong, tough ≠**deficient**: able, capable, effective ≠**unsafe**: invulnerable, safe, secure, well-defended ≠**irresolute**: firm, resolute ≠**unconvincing**: conclusive, convincing, forceful, incontrovertible, obvious, powerful, solid, trustworthy, valid ≠**tasteless**: flavoursome, intoxicating, potent, tasty

weaken *verb* **1 = lessen**, abate, debilitate, depress, diminish, droop, dwindle, ease up, enervate, fade, fail, flag, give way, impair, invalidate, lower, mitigate, moderate, reduce, sap, sap the strength of, soften up, take the edge off, temper, tire, undermine, wane **2 = dilute**, adulterate, cut, debase, thin, thin out, water down
➤ **Antonyms**
≠**lessen**: boost, enhance, grow, improve, increase, invigorate, revitalize, strengthen

weakling *noun* = **sissy**, coward, doormat (*slang*), drip (*informal*), jellyfish (*informal*), jessie (*Scot. slang*), milksop, mouse, wet (*Brit. informal*), wimp (*informal*), wuss (*slang*)

weakness *noun* **1** = **frailty**, debility, decrepitude, enervation, faintness, feebleness, fragility, impotence, infirmity, irresolution, powerlessness, vulnerability **2** = **failing**, Achilles heel, blemish, chink in one's armour, defect, deficiency, fault, flaw, imperfection, lack, shortcoming **3** = **liking**, fondness, inclination, partiality, passion, penchant, predilection, proclivity, proneness, soft spot
➤ **Antonyms**
≠**frailty**: hardiness, health, impregnability, potency, power, stamina, sturdiness, validity, vigour, virtue, vitality ≠**failing**: advantage, forte, strength, strong point ≠**liking**: aversion, dislike, hatred, loathing

wealth *noun* **1** = **riches**, affluence, assets, big bucks (*informal, chiefly U.S.*), big money, capital, cash, estate, fortune, funds, goods, lucre, means, megabucks (*U.S. & Canad. slang*), money, opulence, pelf, possessions, pretty penny (*informal*), property, prosperity, resources, substance, tidy sum (*informal*), wad (*U.S. & Canad. slang*) **2** = **plenty**, abundance, bounty, copiousness, cornucopia, fullness, plenitude, profusion, richness, store
➤ **Antonyms**
≠**riches**: deprivation, destitution, indigence, penury, poverty ≠**plenty**: dearth, lack, need, paucity, poverty, scarcity, shortage, want

wealthy *adjective* = **rich**, affluent, comfortable, filthy rich, flush (*informal*), in the money (*informal*), loaded (*slang*), made of money (*informal*), moneyed, on Easy Street (*informal*), opulent, prosperous, quids in (*informal*), rolling in it (*slang*), stinking rich (*slang*), well-heeled (*informal*), well-off, well-to-do
➤ **Antonyms**
broke (*informal*), deprived, destitute, dirt-poor (*informal*), down and out, down at heel, flat broke (*informal*), impoverished, indigent, needy, on the breadline, penniless, poor, poverty-stricken, short, skint (*Brit. slang*), without two pennies to rub together (*informal*)

wear *verb* **1** = **be dressed in**, bear, be clothed in, carry, clothe oneself, don, dress in, have on, put on, sport (*informal*) **2** = **show**, display, exhibit, fly **3** = **deteriorate**, abrade, consume, corrode, erode, fray, grind, impair, rub, use, wash away, waste **4** *Brit. informal* = **accept**, allow, brook, countenance, fall for, permit, put up with (*informal*), stand for, stomach, swallow (*informal*), take **5 wear well** = **last**, bear up, be durable, endure, hold up, stand up ♦ *noun* **6** = **clothes**, apparel, attire, costume, dress, garb, garments, gear (*informal*), habit, outfit, things, threads (*slang*) **7** = **damage**, abrasion, attrition, corrosion, depreciation, deterioration, erosion, friction, use, wear and tear **8** = **usefulness**, employment, mileage (*informal*), service, use, utility
➤ **Antonyms**
noun ≠**damage**: conservation, maintenance, preservation, repair, upkeep

wear down *verb* **1** = **erode**, abrade, be consumed, consume, corrode, grind down, rub away **2** = **undermine**, chip away at (*informal*), fight a war of attrition against, overcome gradually, reduce

weariness *noun* = **tiredness**, drowsiness, enervation, exhaustion, fatigue, languor, lassitude, lethargy, listlessness, prostration
➤ **Antonyms**
drive, energy, freshness, get-up-and-go (*informal*), liveliness, stamina, vigour, vitality, zeal, zest

wearing *adjective* = **tiresome**, exasperating, exhausting, fatiguing, irksome, oppressive, taxing, tiring, trying, wearisome
➤ **Antonyms**
easy, effortless, light, no bother, painless, refreshing, stimulating, undemanding

wearisome *adjective* = **tedious**, annoying, boring, bothersome, burdensome, dull, exasperating, exhausting, fatiguing, humdrum, irksome, mind-numbing, monotonous, oppressive, pestilential, prosaic, tiresome, troublesome, trying, uninteresting, vexatious, wearing
➤ **Antonyms**
agreeable, delightful, enjoyable, exhilarating, interesting, invigorating, pleasurable, refreshing, stimulating

wear off *verb* **1** = **subside**, abate, decrease, diminish, disappear, dwindle, ebb, fade, lose effect, lose strength, peter out, wane, weaken **2** = **rub away**, abrade, disappear, efface, fade
➤ **Antonyms**
≠**subside**: grow, increase, intensify, magnify, persist, step up, strengthen, wax

wear out *verb* **1** = **deteriorate**, become useless, become worn, consume, erode, fray, impair, use up, wear through **2** *Informal* = **exhaust**, enervate, fag out (*informal*), fatigue, frazzle (*informal*), knacker (*slang*), prostrate, sap, tire, weary
➤ **Antonyms**
≠**exhaust**: buck up (*informal*), energize, invigorate, pep up, perk up, refresh, revitalize, stimulate, strengthen

weary *adjective* **1** = **tired**, all in (*slang*), asleep *or* dead on one's feet (*informal*),

clapped out (*Austral. & N.Z. informal*),
dead beat (*informal*), dog-tired (*informal*),
done in (*informal*), drained, drooping,
drowsy, enervated, exhausted, fagged
(*informal*), fatigued, flagging, jaded,
knackered (*slang*), ready to drop, sleepy,
spent, wearied, whacked (*Brit. informal*),
worn out, zonked (*slang*) **2 = fed up**,
bored, browned-off (*informal*),
discontented, impatient, indifferent, jaded,
sick (*informal*), sick and tired (*informal*) **3
= tiring**, arduous, enervative, irksome,
laborious, taxing, tiresome, wearing,
wearisome ♦ *verb* **4 = tire**, burden,
debilitate, drain, droop, enervate, fade, fag
(*informal*), fail, fatigue, grow tired, sap,
take it out of (*informal*), tax, tire out, wear
out **5 = bore**, annoy, become bored,
exasperate, have had enough, irk, jade,
make discontented, plague, sicken, try the
patience of, vex
➤ **Antonyms**
adjective ≠**tired**: energetic, fresh, full of
beans (*informal*), full of get-up-and-go
(*informal*), invigorated, lively, refreshed,
stimulated ≠**fed up**: amused, excited,
forebearing, patient ≠**tiring**: exciting,
invigorating, original, refreshing ♦ *verb*
≠**tire**: enliven, invigorate, refresh, revive,
stimulate ≠**bore**: amuse, excite, interest

weather *noun* **1 = climate**, conditions **2
under the weather: a = ill**, ailing, below
par, indisposed, nauseous, not well,
off-colour, out of sorts, poorly (*informal*),
seedy (*informal*), sick **b = hung over**
(*informal*), crapulent, crapulous, drunk,
groggy (*informal*), inebriated, intoxicated,
one over the eight (*slang*), rat-arsed (*taboo
slang*), the worse for drink, three sheets in
the wind (*informal*), under the influence
(*informal*) ♦ *verb* **3 = toughen**, expose,
harden, season **4 = withstand**, bear up
against, brave, come through, endure, get
through, live through, make it (*informal*),
overcome, pull through, resist, ride out,
rise above, stand, stick it out (*informal*),
suffer, surmount, survive
➤ **Antonyms**
verb ≠**withstand**: cave in, collapse, fail,
fall, give in, go under, succumb, surrender,
yield

weave *verb* **1 = knit**, blend, braid, entwine,
fuse, incorporate, interlace, intermingle,
intertwine, introduce, mat, merge, plait,
twist, unite **2 = create**, build, construct,
contrive, fabricate, make, make up, put
together, spin **3 = zigzag**, crisscross, move
in and out, weave one's way, wind **4 get
weaving** *Informal* **= start**, get a move on,
get going, get one's finger out (*Brit.
informal*), get under way, hurry, make a

start, shake a leg (*slang*)

web *noun* **1 = spider's web**, cobweb **2
= network**, interlacing, lattice, mesh, net,
netting, screen, tangle, toils, weave,
webbing

wed *verb* **1 = marry**, become man and wife,
be married to, espouse, get hitched
(*slang*), get married, join, make one, plight
one's troth (*old-fashioned*), splice
(*informal*), take as one's husband, take as
one's wife, take the plunge (*informal*), take
to wife, tie the knot (*informal*), unite **2
= unite**, ally, blend, coalesce, combine,
commingle, dedicate, fuse, interweave,
join, link, marry, merge, unify, yoke
➤ **Antonyms**
≠**unite**: break up, disunite, divide, divorce,
part, separate, sever, split

wedding *noun* **= marriage**, espousals,
marriage ceremony, nuptial rite, nuptials,
wedlock

wedge *noun* **1 = block**, chock, chunk,
lump, wodge (*Brit. informal*) ♦ *verb* **2
= squeeze**, block, cram, crowd, force, jam,
lodge, pack, ram, split, stuff, thrust

wedlock *noun* **= marriage**, matrimony

weed out *verb* **= eliminate**, dispense with,
eradicate, extirpate, get rid of, remove,
root out, separate out, shed, uproot

weedy *adjective* **= weak**, feeble, frail,
ineffectual, namby-pamby, puny, skinny,
thin

weekly *adjective* **1 = once a week**,
hebdomadal, hebdomadary ♦ *adverb* **2
= every week**, by the week, hebdomadally,
once a week

weep *verb* **= cry**, bemoan, bewail, blub
(*slang*), blubber, boohoo, complain, greet
(*Scot. or archaic*), keen, lament, moan,
mourn, shed tears, snivel, sob, ululate,
whimper, whinge (*informal*)
➤ **Antonyms**
be glad, celebrate, delight, exult, make
merry, rejoice, revel, triumph

weigh *verb* **1 = have a weight of**, measure
the weight of, put on the scales, tip the
scales at (*informal*) **2 = measure**,
apportion, deal out, dole out **3 = consider**,
contemplate, deliberate upon, evaluate,
examine, eye up, give thought to,
meditate upon, mull over, ponder, reflect
upon, study, think over **4 = matter**, be
influential, carry weight, count, cut any ice
(*informal*), have influence, impress, tell

weigh down *verb* **= burden**, bear down,
depress, get down, oppress, overburden,
overload, press down, trouble, weigh
upon, worry
➤ **Antonyms**

alleviate, ease, hearten, help, lift, lighten, refresh, relieve, unburden

weigh on *verb* = **oppress**, bear down, burden, prey

weight *noun* **1** = **heaviness**, avoirdupois, burden, gravity, heft (*informal*), load, mass, poundage, pressure, tonnage **2** = **load**, ballast, heavy object, mass **3** = **preponderance**, greatest force, main force, onus **4** = **importance**, authority, bottom, clout (*informal*), consequence, consideration, efficacy, emphasis, impact, import, influence, moment, persuasiveness, power, significance, substance, value **5** = **burden**, albatross, load, millstone, oppression, pressure, strain ♦ *verb* **6** = **load**, add weight to, ballast, charge, freight, increase the load on, increase the weight of, make heavier **7** = **bias**, load, slant, unbalance **8** = **burden**, encumber, handicap, impede, oppress, overburden, weigh down

weighty *adjective* **1** = **important**, consequential, considerable, critical, crucial, forcible, grave, momentous, portentous, serious, significant, solemn, substantial **2** = **heavy**, burdensome, cumbersome, dense, hefty (*informal*), massive, ponderous **3** = **onerous**, backbreaking, burdensome, crushing, demanding, difficult, exacting, oppressive, taxing, worrisome, worrying
➤ **Antonyms**
≠**important**: frivolous, immaterial, incidental, inconsequential, insignificant, minor, petty, trivial, unimportant

weird *adjective* = **strange**, bizarre, creepy (*informal*), eerie, eldritch (*poetic*), far-out (*slang*), freakish, ghostly, grotesque, mysterious, odd, outlandish, queer, spooky (*informal*), supernatural, uncanny, unearthly, unnatural
➤ **Antonyms**
common, mundane, natural, normal, ordinary, regular, typical, usual

welcome *verb* **1** = **greet**, accept gladly, bid welcome, embrace, hail, meet, offer hospitality to, receive, receive with open arms, roll out the red carpet for, usher in ♦ *noun* **2** = **greeting**, acceptance, entertainment, hospitality, reception, salutation ♦ *adjective* **3** = **acceptable**, accepted, agreeable, appreciated, delightful, desirable, gladly received, gratifying, pleasant, pleasing, pleasurable, refreshing, wanted **4** = **free**, at home, invited, under no obligation
➤ **Antonyms**
verb ≠**greet**: exclude, rebuff, refuse, reject, slight, snub, spurn, turn away ♦ *noun*

≠**greeting**: cold shoulder, exclusion, ostracism, rebuff, rejection, slight, snub ♦ *adjective* ≠**acceptable**: disagreeable, excluded, rebuffed, rejected, unacceptable, undesirable, unpleasant, unwanted, unwelcome

weld *verb* = **join**, bind, bond, connect, fuse, link, solder, unite

welfare *noun* = **wellbeing**, advantage, benefit, good, happiness, health, interest, profit, prosperity, success

well[1] *adverb* **1** = **satisfactorily**, agreeably, capitally, famously (*informal*), happily, in a satisfactory manner, like nobody's business (*informal*), nicely, pleasantly, smoothly, splendidly, successfully **2** = **skilfully**, ably, adeptly, adequately, admirably, conscientiously, correctly, effectively, efficiently, expertly, proficiently, properly, with skill **3** = **carefully**, accurately, attentively, closely **4** = **prosperously**, comfortably, flourishingly **5** = **suitably**, correctly, easily, fairly, fittingly, in all fairness, justly, properly, readily, rightly **6** = **intimately**, closely, completely, deeply, fully, personally, profoundly, thoroughly **7** = **favourably**, approvingly, glowingly, graciously, highly, kindly, warmly **8** = **considerably**, abundantly, amply, completely, fully, greatly, heartily, highly, substantially, sufficiently, thoroughly, very much **9 as well** = **also**, besides, in addition, into the bargain, to boot, too **10 as well as** = **including**, along with, at the same time as, in addition to, over and above ♦ *adjective* **11** = **healthy**, able-bodied, alive and kicking, fighting fit (*informal*), fit, fit as a fiddle, hale, hearty, in fine fettle, in good health, robust, sound, strong, up to par **12** = **satisfactory**, advisable, agreeable, bright, fine, fitting, flourishing, fortunate, good, happy, lucky, pleasing, profitable, proper, prudent, right, thriving, useful
➤ **Antonyms**
adverb ≠**satisfactorily**: badly, inadequately, poorly, wrongly ≠**skilfully**: badly, ham-fistedly, incompetently, incorrectly, ineptly, inexpertly, sloppily, unskilfully ≠**suitably**: unfairly, unjustly, unsuitably ≠**intimately**: slightly, somewhat, vaguely ≠**favourably**: coldly, disapprovingly, gracelessly, unkindly, unsympathetically ♦ *adjective* ≠**healthy**: ailing, at death's door, below par, feeble, frail, green about the gills, ill, infirm, poorly, run-down, sick, sickly, under-the-weather, unwell, weak ≠**satisfactory**: going badly, improper, unfitting, unsatisfactory, unsuccessful, wrong

well[2] *noun* **1** = **hole**, bore, pit, shaft **2**

= **waterhole**, fount, fountain, pool, source, spring **3** = **source**, fount, mine, repository, wellspring ♦ *verb* **4** = **flow**, exude, gush, jet, ooze, pour, rise, run, seep, spout, spring, spurt, stream, surge, trickle

well-balanced *adjective* **1** = **sensible**, judicious, level-headed, rational, reasonable, sane, sober, sound, together (*slang*), well-adjusted **2** = **well-proportioned**, graceful, harmonious, proportional, symmetrical
➤ **Antonyms**
≠**sensible**: erratic, insane, irrational, neurotic, unbalanced, unreasonable, unsound, unstable, volatile

well-bred *adjective* **1** = **polite**, civil, courteous, courtly, cultivated, cultured, gallant, genteel, gentlemanly, ladylike, mannerly, polished, refined, sophisticated, urbane, well-brought-up, well-mannered **2** = **aristocratic**, blue-blooded, gentle, highborn, noble, patrician, well-born
➤ **Antonyms**
≠**polite**: bad-mannered, base, coarse, discourteous, ill-bred, rude, uncivilized, uncouth, uncultured, vulgar

well-fed *adjective* **1** = **well-nourished**, healthy, in good condition **2** = **plump**, chubby, fat, fleshy, podgy, portly, rotund, rounded, stout

well-groomed *adjective* = **smart**, dapper, neat, soigné *or* soignée, spruce, tidy, trim, well-dressed, well turned out

well-known *adjective* = **famous**, celebrated, familiar, illustrious, notable, noted, on the map, popular, renowned, widely known

well-nigh *adverb* = **almost**, all but, just about, more or less, nearly, next to, practically, virtually

well-off *adjective* **1** = **rich**, affluent, comfortable, flush (*informal*), loaded (*slang*), moneyed, prosperous, wealthy, well-heeled (*informal*), well-to-do **2** = **fortunate**, comfortable, flourishing, lucky, successful, thriving
➤ **Antonyms**
≠**rich**: badly off, broke (*informal*), destitute, dirt-poor (*informal*), down and out, down at heel, flat broke (*informal*), hard up (*informal*), impoverished, indigent, needy, on the breadline, on the rocks (*informal*), penniless, poor, poverty-stricken, short, without two pennies to rub together (*informal*)

well-thought-of *adjective* = **respected**, admired, esteemed, highly regarded, of good repute, reputable, revered, venerated
➤ **Antonyms**

abhorred, derided, despised, disdained, reviled, scorned, spurned

well-to-do *adjective* = **rich**, affluent, comfortable, flush (*informal*), loaded (*slang*), moneyed, prosperous, wealthy, well-heeled (*informal*), well-off
➤ **Antonyms**
bankrupt, broke (*informal*), destitute, down at heel, hard up (*informal*), indigent, insolvent, needy, on the breadline, poor, ruined

well-worn *adjective* = **stale**, banal, commonplace, hackneyed, overused, stereotyped, trite

welt *noun* = **mark**, contusion, streak, stripe, wale, weal

welter *noun* = **jumble**, confusion, hotchpotch, mess, muddle, tangle, web

wet *adjective* **1** = **damp**, aqueous, dank, drenched, dripping, humid, moist, moistened, saturated, soaked, soaking, sodden, soggy, sopping, waterlogged, watery, wringing wet **2** = **rainy**, clammy, dank, drizzling, humid, misty, pouring, raining, showery, teeming **3** *Informal* = **feeble**, boneless, effete, foolish, ineffectual, irresolute, namby-pamby, nerdy *or* nurdy (*slang*), silly, soft, spineless, timorous, weak, weedy (*informal*), wussy (*slang*) **4 wet behind the ears** *Informal* = **naïve**, as green as grass, born yesterday, callow, green, immature, inexperienced, innocent, new, raw ♦ *noun* **5** = **rain**, damp weather, drizzle, rains, rainy season, rainy weather **6** *Informal* = **weakling**, drip (*informal*), milksop, weed (*informal*), wimp (*informal*), wuss (*slang*) **7** = **moisture**, clamminess, condensation, damp, dampness, humidity, liquid, water, wetness ♦ *verb* **8** = **moisten**, damp, dampen, dip, douse, drench, humidify, irrigate, saturate, soak, splash, spray, sprinkle, steep, water
➤ **Antonyms**
adjective ≠**damp**: bone-dry, dried, dry, hardened, parched, set ≠**rainy**: arid, dry, fine, sunny ♦ *noun* ≠**rain**: dry weather, fine weather ≠**moisture**: dryness ♦ *verb* ≠**moisten**: dehydrate, desiccate, dry, parch

whack *verb* **1** = **strike**, bang, belt (*informal*), clobber (*slang*), hit, smack, swipe, thrash, thump, thwack, wallop (*informal*) ♦ *noun* **2** = **blow**, bang, belt (*informal*), hit, smack, stroke, swipe, thump, thwack, wallop (*informal*) **3** *Informal* = **share**, bit, cut (*informal*), part, portion, quota **4** *As in* **have a whack** = **attempt**, bash (*informal*), crack (*informal*), go (*informal*), shot (*informal*), stab (*informal*), try, turn

wharf noun = **dock**, jetty, landing stage, pier, quay

wheedle verb = **coax**, butter up, cajole, charm, court, draw, entice, flatter, inveigle, persuade, talk into, worm

wheel noun 1 = **circle**, gyration, pivot, revolution, roll, rotation, spin, turn, twirl, whirl 2 **at the wheel** = **in control**, at the helm, driving, in charge, in command, in the driving seat, steering ♦ verb 3 = **turn**, circle, gyrate, orbit, pirouette, revolve, roll, rotate, spin, swing, swivel, twirl, whirl

wheeze verb 1 = **gasp**, breathe roughly, catch one's breath, cough, hiss, rasp, whistle ♦ noun 2 = **gasp**, cough, hiss, rasp, whistle 3 *Brit. slang* = **trick**, expedient, idea, plan, ploy, ruse, scheme, stunt, wrinkle (*informal*) 4 *Informal* = **joke**, anecdote, chestnut (*informal*), crack (*slang*), gag (*informal*), old joke, one-liner (*slang*), story

whereabouts noun = **position**, location, site, situation

wherewithal noun = **resources**, capital, equipment, essentials, funds, means, money, ready (*informal*), ready money, supplies

whet verb 1 *As in* **whet someone's appetite** = **stimulate**, animate, arouse, awaken, enhance, excite, incite, increase, kindle, pique, provoke, quicken, rouse, stir 2 = **sharpen**, edge, file, grind, hone, strop ► **Antonyms** ≠**stimulate**: blunt, dampen, deaden, depress, dull, numb, smother, stifle, subdue, suppress ≠**sharpen**: blunt, dull

whiff noun 1 = **smell**, aroma, blast, breath, draught, gust, hint, niff (*Brit. slang*), odour, puff, scent, sniff ♦ verb 2 *Brit. slang* = **stink**, hum (*slang*), malodour, niff (*Brit. slang*), pong (*Brit. informal*), reek

whim noun = **impulse**, caprice, conceit, craze, crotchet, fad (*informal*), fancy, freak, humour, notion, passing thought, quirk, sport, sudden notion, urge, vagary, whimsy

whimper verb 1 = **cry**, blub (*slang*), blubber, grizzle (*informal, chiefly Brit.*), mewl, moan, pule, snivel, sob, weep, whine, whinge (*informal*) ♦ noun 2 = **sob**, moan, snivel, whine

whimsical adjective = **fanciful**, capricious, chimerical, crotchety, curious, droll, eccentric, fantastic, fantastical, freakish, funny, mischievous, odd, peculiar, playful, quaint, queer, singular, unusual, waggish, weird

whine noun 1 = **cry**, moan, plaintive cry, sob, wail, whimper 2 = **complaint**, beef (*slang*), gripe (*informal*), grouch

(*informal*), grouse, grumble, moan, whinge (*informal*) ♦ verb 3 = **cry**, moan, sniffle, snivel, sob, wail, whimper 4 = **complain**, beef (*slang*), bellyache (*slang*), bleat, carp, cry, gripe (*informal*), grizzle (*informal, chiefly Brit.*), grouch (*informal*), grouse, grumble, kvetch (*U.S. slang*), moan, sob, wail, whimper, whinge (*informal*)

whinge *Informal* ♦ verb 1 = **complain**, bleat, carp, gripe (*informal*), grouse, grumble, moan ♦ noun 2 = **complaint**, gripe (*informal*), grouch, grouse, grumble, moan, whine

whip noun 1 = **lash**, birch, bullwhip, cane, cat-o'-nine-tails, crop, horsewhip, knout, rawhide, riding crop, scourge, switch, thong ♦ verb 2 = **lash**, beat, birch, cane, castigate, flagellate, flog, give a hiding (*informal*), lambast(e), leather, lick (*informal*), punish, scourge, spank, strap, switch, tan (*slang*), thrash 3 *Informal* = **dash**, dart, dive, flit, flounce, fly, rush, shoot, tear, whisk 4 = **whisk**, beat 5 = **incite**, agitate, compel, drive, foment, goad, hound, instigate, prick, prod, provoke, push, spur, stir, urge, work up 6 *Informal* = **beat**, best, blow out of the water (*slang*), clobber (*slang*), conquer, defeat, drub, hammer (*informal*), lick (*informal*), make mincemeat out of (*informal*), outdo, overcome, overpower, overwhelm, rout, run rings around (*informal*), stuff (*slang*), take apart (*slang*), thrash, trounce, wipe the floor with (*informal*), worst

whip out verb = **pull out**, exhibit, flash, jerk, produce, remove, seize, show, snatch, whisk

whipping noun = **beating**, birching, caning, castigation, flagellation, flogging, hiding (*informal*), lashing, leathering, punishment, spanking, tanning (*slang*), the strap, thrashing

whirl verb 1 = **spin**, circle, gyrate, pirouette, pivot, reel, revolve, roll, rotate, swirl, turn, twirl, twist, wheel 2 = **feel dizzy**, reel, spin ♦ noun 3 = **revolution**, birl (*Scot.*), circle, gyration, pirouette, reel, roll, rotation, spin, swirl, turn, twirl, twist, wheel 4 = **bustle**, flurry, merry-go-round, round, series, succession 5 = **confusion**, agitation, commotion, daze, dither (*chiefly Brit.*), giddiness, hurly-burly, spin, stir, tumult 6 **give (something) a whirl** *Informal* = **attempt**, have a bash, have a crack (*informal*), have a go (*informal*), have a shot (*informal*), have a stab (*informal*), have a whack (*informal*), try

whirlwind noun 1 = **tornado**, dust devil,

waterspout ♦ *adjective* 2 = **rapid**, hasty, headlong, impetuous, impulsive, lightning, quick, quickie (*informal*), rash, short, speedy, swift
➤ **Antonyms**
adjective ≠**rapid**: calculated, cautious, considered, deliberate, measured, prudent, slow, unhurried

whisk *verb* 1 = **speed**, barrel (along) (*informal, chiefly U.S. & Canad.*), burn rubber (*informal*), dart, dash, fly, hasten, hurry, race, rush, shoot, sweep, tear 2 = **flick**, brush, sweep, whip, wipe 3 = **beat**, fluff up, whip ♦ *noun* 4 = **flick**, brush, sweep, whip, wipe 5 = **beater**

whisky *noun* = **Scotch**, barley-bree (*Scot.*), bourbon, firewater, John Barleycorn, malt, rye, usquebaugh (*Gaelic*)

whisper *verb* 1 = **murmur**, breathe, say softly, speak in hushed tones, utter under the breath 2 = **rustle**, hiss, murmur, sigh, sough, susurrate (*literary*), swish 3 = **gossip**, hint, insinuate, intimate, murmur, spread rumours ♦ *noun* 4 = **murmur**, hushed tone, low voice, soft voice, undertone 5 *Informal* = **rumour**, buzz, dirt (*U.S. slang*), gossip, innuendo, insinuation, report, scuttlebutt (*U.S. slang*), word 6 = **rustle**, hiss, murmur, sigh, sighing, soughing, susurration *or* susurrus (*literary*), swish 7 = **hint**, breath, fraction, shadow, suggestion, suspicion, tinge, trace, whiff
➤ **Antonyms**
verb ≠**murmur**: bawl, bellow, clamour, roar, shout, thunder, yell

white *adjective* 1 = **pale**, ashen, bloodless, ghastly, grey, like death warmed up (*informal*), pallid, pasty, wan, waxen, wheyfaced 2 *Of hair* = **silver**, grey, grizzled, hoary, snowy 3 **whiter than white** = **immaculate**, clean, impeccable, innocent, pure, spotless, squeaky-clean, stainless, unblemished, unsullied
➤ **Antonyms**
≠**pale**: black, dark

white-collar *adjective* = **clerical**, executive, nonmanual, office, professional, salaried

whiten *verb* = **pale**, blanch, bleach, blench, etiolate, fade, go white, turn pale
➤ **Antonyms**
blacken, colour, darken

whitewash *noun* 1 = **cover-up**, camouflage, concealment, deception, extenuation ♦ *verb* 2 = **cover up**, camouflage, conceal, extenuate, gloss over, make light of, suppress
➤ **Antonyms**
verb ≠**cover up**: disclose, expose, lay bare, reveal, uncover, unmask, unveil

whittle *verb* 1 = **carve**, cut, hew, pare, shape, shave, trim 2 **whittle down** *or* **away** = **reduce**, consume, destroy, eat away, erode, undermine, wear away

whole *adjective* 1 = **complete**, entire, full, in one piece, integral, total, unabridged, uncut, undivided 2 = **undamaged**, faultless, flawless, good, in one piece, intact, inviolate, mint, perfect, sound, unbroken, unharmed, unhurt, unimpaired, uninjured, unmutilated, unscathed, untouched 3 *Archaic* = **healthy**, able-bodied, better, cured, fit, hale, healed, in fine fettle, in good health, recovered, robust, sound, strong, well ♦ *adverb* 4 = **in one piece**, in one ♦ *noun* 5 = **total**, aggregate, all, everything, lot, sum total, the entire amount 6 = **totality**, ensemble, entirety, entity, fullness, piece, unit, unity 7 **on the whole**: **a** = **all in all**, all things considered, by and large, taking everything into consideration **b** = **generally**, as a rule, for the most part, in general, in the main, mostly, predominantly
➤ **Antonyms**
adjective ≠**complete**: cut, divided, fragmented, incomplete, in pieces, partial ≠**undamaged**: broken, damaged ≠**healthy**: ailing, diseased, ill, sick, sickly, under-the-weather, unwell ♦ *noun* ≠**totality**: bit, component, constituent, division, element, fragment, part, piece, portion

wholehearted *adjective* = **sincere**, committed, complete, dedicated, determined, devoted, earnest, emphatic, enthusiastic, genuine, heartfelt, hearty, real, true, unfeigned, unqualified, unreserved, unstinting, warm, zealous
➤ **Antonyms**
cool, grudging, half-hearted, insincere, qualified, reserved, unreal

wholesale *adjective* 1 = **extensive**, all-inclusive, broad, comprehensive, far-reaching, indiscriminate, mass, sweeping, wide-ranging ♦ *adverb* 2 = **extensively**, all at once, comprehensively, indiscriminately, on a large scale, without exception
➤ **Antonyms**
adjective ≠**extensive**: confined, discriminate, limited, partial, restricted, selective

wholesome *adjective* 1 = **healthy**, beneficial, good, healthful, health-giving, helpful, hygienic, invigorating, nourishing, nutritious, salubrious, salutary, sanitary, strengthening 2 = **moral**, apple-pie (*informal*), clean, decent, edifying, ethical, exemplary, honourable, improving,

innocent, nice, pure, respectable,
righteous, squeaky-clean, uplifting,
virtuous, worthy
➤ **Antonyms**
≠**healthy:** putrid, rotten, unhealthy,
unhygienic, unwholesome ≠**moral:** blue,
corrupt, degrading, dirty, dishonest, evil,
filthy, immoral, lewd, obscene, pernicious,
pornographic, tasteless, trashy,
unprincipled, unwholesome, X-rated
(*informal*)

wholly *adverb* **1 = completely,** all,
altogether, comprehensively, entirely,
fully, heart and soul, in every respect, one
hundred per cent (*informal*), perfectly,
thoroughly, totally, utterly **2 = solely,**
exclusively, only, without exception
➤ **Antonyms**
≠**completely:** incompletely, in part,
moderately, partially, partly, relatively,
slightly, somewhat

whoop *noun* **= cry,** cheer, halloo, holler
(*informal*), hoot, hurrah, scream, shout,
shriek, yell

whopper *noun* **1 = giant,** colossus,
crackerjack (*informal*), jumbo (*informal*),
leviathan, mammoth, monster **2 = big lie,**
fabrication, falsehood, tall story (*informal*),
untruth

whopping *adjective* **= gigantic,** big,
enormous, giant, great, huge, mammoth,
massive

whore *noun* **1 = prostitute,** brass (*slang*),
call girl, cocotte, courtesan,
demimondaine, demirep (*rare*), fallen
woman, *fille de joie*, harlot, hooker (*U.S.
slang*), hustler (*U.S. & Canad. slang*), lady
of the night, loose woman, scrubber (*Brit.
& Austral. slang*), slag (*Brit. slang*),
streetwalker, strumpet, tart (*informal*),
trollop, woman of easy virtue, woman of ill
repute, working girl (*facetious slang*)
♦ *verb* **2 = prostitute oneself,** be on the
game (*slang*), hustle (*U.S. & Canad. slang*),
sell one's body, sell oneself, solicit, walk
the streets **3 = sleep around** (*informal*),
fornicate, lech *or* letch (*informal*), wanton,
wench (*archaic*), womanize

wicked *adjective* **1 = bad,** abandoned,
abominable, amoral, atrocious,
black-hearted, corrupt, debased,
depraved, devilish, dissolute, egregious,
evil, fiendish, foul, guilty, heinous,
immoral, impious, iniquitous, irreligious,
maleficent, nefarious, scandalous,
shameful, sinful, sink, unprincipled,
unrighteous, vicious, vile, villainous,
worthless **2 = mischievous,** arch, impish,
incorrigible, naughty, rascally, roguish **3
= harmful,** acute, agonizing, awful,

crashing, destructive, dreadful, fearful,
fierce, gut-wrenching, injurious, intense,
mighty, painful, severe, terrible **4
= troublesome,** bothersome, difficult,
distressing, galling, offensive, trying,
unpleasant **5** *Slang* **= expert,** adept, adroit,
deft, masterly, mighty, outstanding,
powerful, skilful, strong
➤ **Antonyms**
≠**bad:** benevolent, ethical, good,
honourable, moral, noble, principled,
virtuous ≠**mischievous:** good, mannerly,
obedient, well-behaved ≠**harmful:**
harmless, innocuous, mild, pleasant,
wholesome

wide *adjective* **1 = broad,** ample, catholic,
comprehensive, distended, encyclopedic,
expanded, expansive, extensive,
far-reaching, general, immense, inclusive,
large, overarching, sweeping, vast **2
= spacious,** ample, baggy, capacious,
commodious, full, loose, roomy **3
= expanded,** dilated, distended, fully
open, outspread, outstretched **4 = distant,**
away, off, off course, off target, remote
♦ *adverb* **5 = fully,** as far as possible,
completely, right out, to the furthest
extent **6 = off target,** astray, nowhere
near, off course, off the mark, out
➤ **Antonyms**
adjective ≠**broad:** narrow, strict, tight
≠**spacious:** confined, constricted,
cramped, tight ≠**expanded:** closed,
limited, restricted, shut ♦ *adverb* ≠**fully:**
narrowly, partially, partly

wide-awake *adjective* **1 = conscious,** fully
awake, roused, wakened **2 = alert,** aware,
heedful, keen, observant, on one's toes, on
the alert, on the ball (*informal*), on the qui
vive, vigilant, wary, watchful
➤ **Antonyms**
≠**alert:** distracted, dreamy, heedless,
inattentive, negligent, oblivious,
preoccupied, unaware, unobservant

wide-eyed *adjective* **= naive,** as green as
grass, credulous, green, impressionable,
ingenuous, innocent, simple, trusting,
unsophisticated, unsuspicious, wet behind
the ears (*informal*)

widen *verb* **= broaden,** dilate, enlarge,
expand, extend, open out *or* up, open
wide, spread, stretch
➤ **Antonyms**
compress, constrict, contract, cramp,
diminish, narrow, reduce, shrink, tighten

wide-open *adjective* **1 = outspread,** fully
extended, fully open, gaping,
outstretched, splayed, spread **2
= unprotected,** at risk, defenceless,
exposed, in danger, in peril, open,

susceptible, vulnerable **3 = uncertain**, anybody's guess (*informal*), indeterminate, unpredictable, unsettled, up for grabs (*informal*)

widespread *adjective* = **common**, broad, epidemic, extensive, far-flung, far-reaching, general, pervasive, popular, prevalent, rife, sweeping, universal, wholesale
➤ Antonyms
confined, exclusive, limited, local, narrow, rare, sporadic, uncommon

width *noun* = **breadth**, compass, diameter, extent, girth, measure, range, reach, scope, span, thickness, wideness

wield *verb* **1 = brandish**, employ, flourish, handle, manage, manipulate, ply, swing, use **2** *As in* **wield power = exert**, apply, be possessed of, command, control, exercise, have, have at one's disposal, hold, maintain, make use of, manage, possess, put to use, utilize

wife *noun* = **spouse**, better half (*humorous*), bride, helpmate, helpmeet, her indoors (*Brit. slang*), little woman (*informal*), mate, old lady (*informal*), old woman (*informal*), partner, significant other (*U.S. informal*), (the) missis *or* missus (*informal*), vrou (*S. African*), woman (*informal*)

wiggle *verb, noun* = **jerk**, jiggle, shake, shimmy, squirm, twitch, wag, waggle, writhe

wild *adjective* **1 = untamed**, feral, ferocious, fierce, savage, unbroken, undomesticated **2 = uncultivated**, free, indigenous, native, natural **3 = desolate**, desert, deserted, empty, godforsaken, lonely, trackless, uncivilized, uncultivated, uninhabited, unpopulated, virgin **4 = uncivilized**, barbaric, barbarous, brutish, ferocious, fierce, primitive, rude, savage **5 = uncontrolled**, boisterous, chaotic, disorderly, impetuous, lawless, noisy, riotous, rough, rowdy, self-willed, turbulent, unbridled, undisciplined, unfettered, ungovernable, unmanageable, unrestrained, unruly, uproarious, violent, wayward **6 = stormy**, blustery, choppy, furious, howling, intense, raging, rough, tempestuous, violent **7 = excited**, agog, avid, crazy (*informal*), daft (*informal*), delirious, eager, enthusiastic, frantic, frenzied, hysterical, mad (*informal*), nuts (*slang*), potty (*Brit. informal*), raving **8 = outrageous**, extravagant, fantastic, flighty, foolhardy, foolish, giddy, ill-considered, impracticable, imprudent, madcap, preposterous, rash, reckless **9 = dishevelled**, disordered, straggly, tousled, unkempt, untidy, windblown

♦ *adverb* **10 run wild: a = grow unchecked**, ramble, spread, straggle **b = go on the rampage**, abandon all restraint, cut loose, kick over the traces, rampage, run free, run riot, stray ♦ *noun* **11 wilds = wilderness**, back of beyond (*informal*), desert, middle of nowhere (*informal*), uninhabited area, wasteland
➤ Antonyms
adjective ≠**untamed**: broken, domesticated, tame ≠**uncultivated**: cultivated, farmed, planted ≠**desolate**: civilized, inhabited, populated, urban ≠**uncivilized**: advanced, civilized ≠**uncontrolled**: calm, careful, controlled, disciplined, domesticated, friendly, genteel, gentle, lawful, mild, ordered, orderly, peaceful, polite, quiet, restrained, self-controlled, thoughtful, well-behaved ≠**excited**: unenthusiastic, uninterested ≠**outrageous**: logical, practical, realistic, well-thought-out

wilderness *noun* **1 = desert**, jungle, waste, wasteland, wilds **2 = tangle**, clutter, confused mass, confusion, congeries, jumble, maze, muddle, welter

wildlife *noun* = **flora and fauna**

wiles *plural noun* **1 = trickery**, artfulness, artifice, cheating, chicanery, craft, craftiness, cunning, fraud, guile, slyness **2 = ploys**, artifices, contrivances, devices, dodges, impositions, lures, manoeuvres, ruses, stratagems, subterfuges, tricks

wilful *adjective* **1 = obstinate**, adamant, bull-headed, determined, dogged, froward (*archaic*), headstrong, inflexible, intractable, intransigent, mulish, obdurate, persistent, perverse, pig-headed, refractory, self-willed, stiff-necked, stubborn, uncompromising, unyielding **2 = intentional**, conscious, deliberate, intended, purposeful, volitional, voluntary, willed
➤ Antonyms
≠**obstinate**: biddable, complaisant, compromising, docile, flexible, good-natured, obedient, pliant, tractable, yielding ≠**intentional**: accidental, involuntary, uncalculated, unconscious, unintentional, unplanned, unwitting

will *noun* **1 = determination**, aim, intention, purpose, resolution, resolve, willpower **2 = wish**, choice, decision, decree, desire, fancy, inclination, mind, option, pleasure, preference, volition **3 = testament**, declaration, last wishes **4 at will = as one pleases**, as one thinks fit, as one wishes, at one's desire, at one's discretion, at one's inclination, at one's pleasure, at one's whim, at one's wish

♦ *verb* **5** = **decree**, bid, bring about, cause, command, determine, direct, effect, ordain, order, resolve **6** = **wish**, choose, desire, elect, opt, prefer, see fit, want **7** = **bequeath**, confer, give, leave, pass on, transfer

willing *adjective* = **ready**, agreeable, amenable, compliant, consenting, content, desirous, disposed, eager, enthusiastic, favourable, game (*informal*), happy, inclined, in favour, in the mood, nothing loath, pleased, prepared, so-minded
➤ **Antonyms**
averse, disinclined, grudging, indisposed, loath, not keen, reluctant, unenthusiastic, unwilling

willingly *adverb* = **readily**, by choice, cheerfully, eagerly, freely, gladly, happily, lief (*rare*), of one's own accord, of one's own free will, voluntarily, with all one's heart, without hesitation, with pleasure
➤ **Antonyms**
grudgingly, hesitantly, involuntarily, reluctantly, unwillingly

willingness *noun* = **inclination**, agreeableness, agreement, consent, desire, disposition, enthusiasm, favour, goodwill, volition, will, wish
➤ **Antonyms**
aversion, disagreement, disinclination, hesitation, loathing, reluctance, unwillingness

willowy *adjective* = **slender**, graceful, lithe, slim, supple, svelte, sylphlike

willpower *noun* = **self-control**, determination, drive, firmness of purpose *or* will, fixity of purpose, force *or* strength of will, grit, resolution, resolve, self-discipline, single-mindedness
➤ **Antonyms**
apathy, hesitancy, indecision, irresolution, languor, lethargy, shilly-shallying (*informal*), torpor, uncertainty, weakness

wilt *verb* **1** = **droop**, become limp *or* flaccid, sag, shrivel, wither **2** = **weaken**, diminish, dwindle, ebb, fade, fail, flag, languish, lose courage, melt away, sag, sink, wane, wither

wily *adjective* = **cunning**, arch, artful, astute, cagey (*informal*), crafty, crooked, deceitful, deceptive, designing, fly (*slang*), foxy, guileful, intriguing, scheming, sharp, shifty, shrewd, sly, tricky, underhand
➤ **Antonyms**
artless, candid, dull, guileless, honest, ingenuous, naive, simple, straightforward

wimp *noun Informal* = **weakling**, coward, drip (*informal*), mouse, sissy, softy *or* softie, wuss (*slang*)

win *verb* **1** = **triumph**, achieve first place,

achieve mastery, be victorious, carry all before one, carry the day, come first, conquer, finish first, gain victory, overcome, prevail, succeed, sweep the board, take the prize **2** = **gain**, accomplish, achieve, acquire, attain, bag (*informal*), catch, collect, come away with, earn, get, land, net, obtain, pick up, procure, receive, secure ♦ *noun* **3** = **victory**, conquest, success, triumph
➤ **Antonyms**
verb ≠**triumph**: fail, fall, suffer defeat, suffer loss ≠**gain**: forfeit, lose, miss ♦ *noun* ≠**victory**: beating, defeat, downfall, failure, loss, washout (*informal*)

wince *verb* **1** = **flinch**, blench, cower, cringe, draw back, quail, recoil, shrink, start ♦ *noun* **2** = **flinch**, cringe, start

wind[1] *noun* **1** = **air**, air-current, blast, breath, breeze, current of air, draught, gust, zephyr **2** = **breath**, puff, respiration **3** = **flatulence**, flatus, gas **4** = **talk**, babble, blather, bluster, boasting, empty talk, gab (*informal*), hot air, humbug, idle talk, verbalizing **5** *As in* **get wind of** = **hint**, clue, inkling, intimation, notice, report, rumour, suggestion, tidings, warning, whisper **6** **get** *or* **have the wind up** *Informal* = **be afraid**, be alarmed, be frightened, be scared, fear, take fright **7** **in the wind** = **imminent**, about to happen, approaching, close at hand, coming, impending, in the offing, near, on the cards (*informal*), on the way **8** **put the wind up** *Informal* = **scare**, alarm, discourage, frighten, frighten off, scare off

wind[2] *verb* **1** = **coil**, curl, encircle, furl, loop, reel, roll, spiral, turn around, twine, twist, wreathe **2** = **meander**, bend, curve, deviate, ramble, snake, turn, twist, zigzag ♦ *noun* **3** = **twist**, bend, curve, meander, turn, zigzag

wind down *verb* = **subside**, cool off, decline, diminish, dwindle, lessen, reduce, relax, slacken, taper off, unwind
➤ **Antonyms**
accelerate, amplify, escalate, expand, heat up, increase, intensify, magnify, step up

winded *adjective* = **out of breath**, breathless, gasping for breath, out of puff, out of whack (*informal*), panting, puffed, puffed out

windfall *noun* = **godsend**, bonanza, find, jackpot, manna from heaven, pot of gold at the end of the rainbow, stroke of luck
➤ **Antonyms**
bad luck, disaster, infelicity, misadventure, mischance, misfortune, mishap

winding *noun* **1** = **twist**, bend, convolution, curve, meander, turn,

undulation ♦ *adjective* **2 = twisting**, anfractuous, bending, circuitous, convoluted, crooked, curving, flexuous, indirect, meandering, roundabout, serpentine, sinuous, spiral, tortuous, turning, twisty
➤ **Antonyms**
adjective ≠**twisting**: direct, even, level, plumb, smooth, straight, undeviating, unswerving

wind up *verb* **1 = end**, bring to a close, close, close down, conclude, finalize, finish, liquidate, settle, terminate, tie up the loose ends (*informal*), wrap up **2 = end up**, be left, end one's days, find oneself, finish up **3** *Informal* **= excite**, make nervous, make tense, put on edge, work up
➤ **Antonyms**
≠**end**: begin, commence, embark on, initiate, instigate, institute, open, start

windy *adjective* **1 = breezy**, blowy, blustering, blustery, boisterous, gusty, inclement, squally, stormy, tempestuous, wild, windswept **2 = pompous**, boastful, bombastic, diffuse, empty, garrulous, long-winded, loquacious, meandering, prolix, rambling, turgid, verbose, wordy **3** *Old-fashioned slang* **= frightened**, afraid, antsy (*informal*), chicken (*slang*), chickenshit (*U.S. slang*), cowardly, fearful, nervous, nervy (*informal*), scared, timid
➤ **Antonyms**
≠**breezy**: becalmed, calm, motionless, smooth, still, windless ≠**pompous**: modest, quiet, reserved, restrained, reticent, shy, taciturn, unforthcoming ≠**frightened**: bold, brave, courageous, daring, fearless, gallant, unafraid, undaunted

wing *noun* **1 = organ of flight**, pennon (*poetic*), pinion (*poetic*) **2 = annexe**, adjunct, ell, extension **3 = faction**, arm, branch, cabal, circle, clique, coterie, group, grouping, schism, section, segment, set, side ♦ *verb* **4 = fly**, glide, soar **5 = fly**, fleet, hasten, hurry, race, speed, zoom **6 = wound**, clip, hit, nick

wink *verb* **1 = blink**, bat, flutter, nictate, nictitate **2 = twinkle**, flash, gleam, glimmer, sparkle ♦ *noun* **3 = blink**, flutter, nictation, nictitation **4 = twinkle**, flash, gleam, glimmering, sparkle **5 = moment**, instant, jiffy (*informal*), second, split second, twinkling

wink at *verb* **= condone**, allow, blink at, connive at, disregard, ignore, overlook, pretend not to notice, put up with (*informal*), shut one's eyes to, tolerate, turn a blind eye to

winkle out *verb* **= extract**, dig out, dislodge, draw out, extricate, force out, prise out, smoke out, worm out

winner *noun* **= victor**, champ (*informal*), champion, conquering hero, conqueror, first, master, vanquisher

winning *adjective* **1 = victorious**, conquering, successful, triumphant **2 = charming**, alluring, amiable, attractive, bewitching, captivating, cute, delectable, delightful, disarming, enchanting, endearing, engaging, fascinating, fetching, likable *or* likeable, lovely, pleasing, prepossessing, sweet, taking, winsome
➤ **Antonyms**
≠**charming**: disagreeable, irksome, offensive, repellent, tiresome, unappealing, unattractive, unpleasant

winnings *plural noun* **= spoils**, booty, gains, prize, proceeds, profits, takings

winnow *verb* **= separate**, comb, cull, divide, fan, part, screen, select, separate the wheat from the chaff, sift, sort out

win over *verb* **= convince**, allure, attract, bring *or* talk round, charm, convert, disarm, influence, persuade, prevail upon, sway

wintry *adjective* **1 = cold**, brumal, chilly, freezing, frosty, frozen, harsh, hibernal, hiemal, icy, snowy **2 = bleak**, cheerless, cold, desolate, dismal
➤ **Antonyms**
balmy, bright, mild, pleasant, summery, sunny, warm

wipe *verb* **1 = clean**, brush, dry, dust, mop, rub, sponge, swab **2 = erase**, clean off, get rid of, remove, rub off, take away, take off ♦ *noun* **3 = rub**, brush, lick, swab

wipe out *verb* **= destroy**, annihilate, blot out, blow away (*slang, chiefly U.S.*), efface, eradicate, erase, expunge, exterminate, extirpate, kill to the last man, massacre, obliterate, take out (*slang*), wipe from the face of the earth

wiry *adjective* **1 = lean**, sinewy, strong, tough **2 = stiff**, bristly, kinky
➤ **Antonyms**
≠**lean**: fat, feeble, flabby, fleshy, frail, podgy, puny, spineless, weak

wisdom *noun* **= understanding**, astuteness, circumspection, comprehension, discernment, enlightenment, erudition, foresight, insight, intelligence, judgment, judiciousness, knowledge, learning, penetration, prudence, reason, sagacity, sapience, sense, smarts (*slang, chiefly U.S.*), sound judgment
➤ **Antonyms**

absurdity, daftness (*informal*), folly,
foolishness, idiocy, injudiciousness,
nonsense, senselessness, silliness, stupidity

wise *adjective* **1** = **sensible**, aware, clever,
clued-up (*informal*), discerning,
enlightened, erudite, informed, intelligent,
in the loop (*informal*), judicious, knowing,
perceptive, politic, prudent, rational,
reasonable, sagacious, sage, sapient,
shrewd, sound, understanding,
well-advised, well-informed **2** put wise
Slang = **inform**, alert, apprise, clue in *or* up
(*informal*), let (someone) into the secret,
notify, tell, tip off, warn
➤ **Antonyms**
≠**sensible**: daft (*informal*), foolish,
injudicious, rash, silly, stupid, unintelligent,
unwise

wisecrack *noun* **1** = **joke**, barb, funny
(*informal*), gag (*informal*), jest, jibe, pithy
remark, quip, sally, sardonic remark, smart
remark, witticism ♦ *verb* **2** = **joke**, be
facetious, jest, jibe, quip, tell jokes

wish *verb* **1** = **want**, aspire, covet, crave,
desiderate, desire, hanker, hope, hunger,
long, need, set one's heart on, sigh for,
thirst, yearn **2** = **require**, ask, bid,
command, desire, direct, instruct, order **3**
= **bid**, greet with ♦ *noun* **4** = **desire**,
aspiration, hankering, hope, hunger,
inclination, intention, liking, longing,
thirst, urge, want, whim, will, yearning **5**
= **request**, bidding, command, desire,
order, will
➤ **Antonyms**
noun ≠**desire**: aversion, disinclination,
dislike, distaste, loathing, reluctance,
repulsion, revulsion

wispy *adjective* = **thin**, attenuated, delicate,
fine, flimsy, fragile, frail

wistful *adjective* = **melancholy**,
contemplative, disconsolate, dreaming,
dreamy, forlorn, longing, meditative,
mournful, musing, pensive, reflective, sad,
thoughtful, yearning

wit *noun* **1** = **humour**, badinage, banter,
drollery, facetiousness, fun, jocularity,
levity, pleasantry, raillery, repartee,
wordplay **2** = **humorist**, card (*informal*),
comedian, epigrammatist, *farceur*, joker,
punster, wag **3** = **cleverness**, acumen,
brains, common sense, comprehension,
discernment, ingenuity, insight, intellect,
judgment, mind, nous (*Brit. slang*),
perception, practical intelligence, reason,
sense, smarts (*slang, chiefly U.S.*),
understanding, wisdom
➤ **Antonyms**
≠**humour**: dullness, gravity,
humourlessness, seriousness, sobriety,

solemnity ≠**cleverness**: folly, foolishness,
ignorance, lack of perception, obtuseness,
silliness, stupidity

witch *noun* = **enchantress**, crone, hag,
magician, necromancer, occultist, sorceress

witchcraft *noun* = **magic**, black magic,
enchantment, incantation, necromancy,
occultism, sorcery, sortilege, spell, the
black art, the occult, voodoo, witchery,
witching, wizardry

withdraw *verb* **1** = **remove**, draw back,
draw out, extract, pull, pull out, take away,
take off **2** = **retreat**, absent oneself, back
off, back out, cop out (*slang*), depart,
detach oneself, disengage, drop out, fall
back, go, leave, make oneself scarce
(*informal*), pull back, pull out, retire,
secede **3** = **retract**, abjure, disavow,
disclaim, recall, recant, rescind, revoke,
take back, unsay
➤ **Antonyms**
≠**retreat**: advance, forge ahead, go on,
move forward, persist, press on, proceed,
progress

withdrawal *noun* **1** = **removal**, extraction
2 = **retreat**, departure, disengagement,
exit, exodus, retirement, secession **3**
= **retraction**, abjuration, disavowal,
disclaimer, recall, recantation, repudiation,
rescission, revocation

withdrawn *adjective* **1**
= **uncommunicative**, aloof, detached,
distant, introverted, quiet, reserved,
retiring, shrinking, shy, silent, taciturn,
timorous, unforthcoming **2** = **secluded**,
hidden, isolated, out-of-the-way, private,
remote, solitary
➤ **Antonyms**
≠**uncommunicative**: extrovert, forward,
friendly, gregarious, open, outgoing,
sociable ≠**secluded**: easily accessible

wither *verb* **1** = **wilt**, atrophy, blast, blight,
decay, decline, desiccate, disintegrate,
droop, dry, fade, languish, perish, shrink,
shrivel, wane, waste **2** = **humiliate**, abash,
blast, mortify, put down, shame, snub
➤ **Antonyms**
≠**wilt**: bloom, blossom, develop, flourish,
increase, prosper, succeed, thrive, wax

withering *adjective* **1** = **scornful**, blasting,
blighting, devastating, humiliating,
hurtful, mortifying, snubbing **2**
= **destructive**, deadly, death-dealing,
devastating, killing, murderous,
slaughterous

withhold *verb* **1** = **keep back**, check,
conceal, deduct, hide, hold back, keep,
keep secret, refuse, repress, reserve, resist,
restrain, retain, sit on (*informal*), suppress **2**
with **from** = **refrain**, forbear, keep oneself,

stop oneself
➤ Antonyms
≠**keep back:** accord, expose, get off one's
chest (*informal*), give, grant, hand over, let
go, release, relinquish, reveal

withstand *verb* = **resist**, bear, brave,
combat, confront, cope with, defy,
endure, face, grapple with, hold off, hold
out against, oppose, put up with
(*informal*), stand firm against, stand up to,
suffer, take, take on, thwart, tolerate,
weather
➤ Antonyms
capitulate, falter, give in, give way, relent,
succumb, surrender, weaken, yield

witless *adjective* = **foolish**, dumb-ass
(*slang*), halfwitted, idiotic, inane, moronic,
senseless, silly, stupid

witness *noun* 1 = **observer**, beholder,
bystander, eyewitness, looker-on,
onlooker, spectator, viewer, watcher 2
= **testifier**, attestant, corroborator,
deponent 3 **bear witness: a = give
evidence**, depone, depose, give
testimony, testify **b = confirm**, attest to,
bear out, be evidence of, be proof of,
betoken, constitute proof of, corroborate,
demonstrate, evince, prove, show, testify
to, vouch for ♦ *verb* 4 = **see**, attend,
behold (*archaic or literary*), be present at,
look on, mark, note, notice, observe,
perceive, view, watch 5 = **sign**,
countersign, endorse 6 **witness to**
= **testify**, attest, authenticate, bear out,
bear witness, confirm, corroborate,
depone, depose, give evidence, give
testimony

wits *plural noun* 1 = **intelligence**, acumen,
astuteness, brains (*informal*), cleverness,
comprehension, faculties, ingenuity,
judgment, nous (*Brit. slang*), reason, sense,
smarts (*slang, chiefly U.S.*), understanding
2 **at one's wits' end = in despair**, at a loss,
at the end of one's tether, baffled,
bewildered, lost, stuck (*informal*), stumped

witter *verb* = **chatter**, babble, blather, chat,
gabble, jabber, prate, prattle, waffle
(*informal, chiefly Brit.*)

witticism *noun* = **quip**, bon mot, clever
remark, epigram, one-liner (*slang*), play on
words, pleasantry, pun, repartee, riposte,
sally, witty remark

witty *adjective* = **humorous**, amusing,
brilliant, clever, droll, epigrammatic,
facetious, fanciful, funny, gay, ingenious,
jocular, lively, original, piquant, sparkling,
waggish, whimsical
➤ Antonyms
boring, dull, humourless, stupid, tedious,
tiresome, unamusing, uninteresting, witless

wizard *noun* 1 = **magician**, conjuror,
enchanter, mage (*archaic*), magus,
necromancer, occultist, shaman, sorcerer,
thaumaturge (*rare*), warlock, witch 2
= **virtuoso**, ace (*informal*), adept, buff
(*informal*), expert, genius, guru, hotshot
(*informal*), maestro, master, maven (*U.S.*),
prodigy, star, whizz (*informal*), whizz kid
(*informal*), wiz (*informal*)

wizardry *noun* = **magic**, sorcery, voodoo,
witchcraft

wizened *adjective* = **wrinkled**, dried up,
gnarled, lined, sere (*archaic*), shrivelled,
shrunken, withered, worn
➤ Antonyms
bloated, plump, rounded, smooth,
swollen, turgid

wobble *verb* 1 = **shake**, quake, rock,
seesaw, sway, teeter, totter, tremble,
vibrate, waver 2 = **hesitate**, be unable to
make up one's mind, be undecided, dither
(*chiefly Brit.*), fluctuate, shillyshally
(*informal*), swither (*Scot.*), vacillate, waver
♦ *noun* 3 = **unsteadiness**, quaking, shake,
tremble, tremor, vibration

wobbly *adjective* = **unsteady**, rickety,
shaky, teetering, tottering, uneven

woe *noun* = **grief**, adversity, affliction,
agony, anguish, burden, curse, dejection,
depression, disaster, distress, gloom,
hardship, heartache, heartbreak,
melancholy, misery, misfortune, pain,
sadness, sorrow, suffering, trial, tribulation,
trouble, unhappiness, wretchedness
➤ Antonyms
bliss, elation, felicity, fortune, happiness,
joy, jubilation, pleasure, prosperity, rapture

woeful *adjective* 1 = **sad**, afflicted,
agonized, anguished, calamitous,
catastrophic, cruel, deplorable, disastrous,
disconsolate, dismal, distressing, doleful,
dreadful, gloomy, grieving, grievous,
harrowing, heartbreaking, heart-rending,
lamentable, miserable, mournful, pathetic,
piteous, pitiable, pitiful, plaintive,
sorrowful, tragic, unhappy, wretched 2
= **pitiful**, abysmal, appalling, awful, bad,
deplorable, disappointing, disgraceful,
dreadful, duff (*Brit. informal*), feeble,
godawful (*slang*), hopeless, inadequate,
lousy (*slang*), mean, miserable, not much
cop (*Brit. slang*), paltry, pathetic, pitiable,
poor, rotten (*informal*), shitty (*taboo
slang*), shocking, sorry, terrible, wretched
➤ Antonyms
≠**sad:** carefree, cheerful, chirpy (*informal*),
contented, delighted, glad, happy, jolly,
joyful, jubilant, light-hearted ≠**pitiful:**
abundant, ample, bountiful, enviable,
extensive, generous, lavish, luxurious,

profuse, prosperous

wolf *verb with* **down** = **devour**, bolt, cram, eat like a horse, gobble, gollop, gorge, gulp, pack away (*informal*), pig out (*slang*), scoff (*slang*), stuff
> **Antonyms**
bite, nibble, nip, peck, pick at

woman *noun* 1 = **lady**, bird (*slang*), chick (*slang*), dame (*slang*), female, gal (*slang*), girl, ho (*U.S. derogatory slang*), lass, lassie (*informal*), maid (*archaic*), maiden (*archaic*), miss, she, wench (*facetious*) 2 = **maid**, chambermaid, char (*informal*), charwoman, domestic, female servant, handmaiden, housekeeper, lady-in-waiting, maidservant 3 *Informal* = **girlfriend**, bride, girl, ladylove, mate, mistress, old lady (*informal*), partner, significant other (*U.S. informal*), spouse, sweetheart, wife
> **Antonyms**
≠**lady**: bloke (*Brit. informal*), boy, chap (*informal*), gentleman, guy (*informal*), lad, laddie, male, man

womanizer *noun* = **philanderer**, Casanova, Don Juan, lady-killer, lech *or* letch (*informal*), lecher, Lothario, seducer, wolf (*informal*)

womanly *adjective* = **feminine**, female, ladylike, matronly, motherly, tender, warm

wonder *verb* 1 = **think**, ask oneself, be curious, be inquisitive, conjecture, cudgel one's brains (*informal*), doubt, inquire, meditate, ponder, puzzle, query, question, speculate 2 = **be amazed**, be astonished, be awed, be dumbstruck, be flabbergasted (*informal*), boggle, gape, gawk, marvel, stand amazed, stare ♦ *noun* 3 = **phenomenon**, curiosity, marvel, miracle, nonpareil, portent, prodigy, rarity, sight, spectacle, wonderment 4 = **amazement**, admiration, astonishment, awe, bewilderment, curiosity, fascination, stupefaction, surprise, wonderment

wonderful *adjective* 1 = **excellent**, ace (*informal*), admirable, awesome (*slang*), bodacious (*slang, chiefly U.S.*), boffo (*slang*), brill (*informal*), brilliant, chillin' (*U.S. slang*), cracking (*Brit. informal*), fabulous (*informal*), fantastic (*informal*), great (*informal*), jim-dandy (*slang*), like a dream come true, magnificent, marvellous, mean (*slang*), out of this world (*informal*), outstanding, sensational (*informal*), smashing (*informal*), sovereign, stupendous, super (*informal*), superb, terrific, tiptop, topping (*Brit. slang*), tremendous 2 = **remarkable**, amazing, astonishing, astounding, awe-inspiring, awesome, extraordinary, fantastic,

incredible, jaw-dropping, marvellous, miraculous, odd, peculiar, phenomenal, staggering, startling, strange, surprising, unheard-of, wondrous (*archaic or literary*)
> **Antonyms**
≠**excellent**: abominable, abysmal, appalling, average, awful, bad, depressing, dire, dreadful, frightful, grim, hellacious (*U.S. slang*), indifferent, lousy (*slang*), mediocre, miserable, modest, no great shakes (*informal*), rotten, terrible, unpleasant, vile ≠**remarkable**: common, commonplace, ordinary, run-of-the-mill, uninteresting, unremarkable, usual

wonky *adjective* = **shaky**, unsteady, wobbly

wont *adjective* 1 = **accustomed**, given, in the habit of, used ♦ *noun* 2 = **habit**, custom, practice, rule, use, way

wonted *adjective* 1 = **in the habit of**, accustomed, given, habituated, used 2 = **customary**, accustomed, common, conventional, familiar, frequent, habitual, normal, regular, usual

woo *verb* = **court**, chase, cultivate, importune, pay court to, pay one's addresses to, pay suit to, press one's suit with, pursue, seek after, seek the hand of, seek to win, solicit the goodwill of, spark (*rare*)

wood *noun* 1 = **timber**, planks 2 *Also* **woods** = **woodland**, coppice, copse, forest, grove, hurst (*archaic*), thicket, trees 3 **out of the wood(s)** = **safe**, clear, home and dry (*Brit. slang*), in the clear, out of danger, safe and sound, secure

wooded *adjective* = **tree-covered**, forested, sylvan (*poetic*), timbered, tree-clad, woody

wooden *adjective* 1 = **woody**, ligneous, made of wood, of wood, timber 2 = **expressionless**, blank, colourless, deadpan, dull, emotionless, empty, glassy, lifeless, spiritless, unemotional, unresponsive, vacant 3 = **awkward**, clumsy, gauche, gawky, graceless, inelegant, maladroit, rigid, stiff, ungainly
> **Antonyms**
≠**awkward**: agile, comely, elegant, flexible, flowing, graceful, lissom(e), nimble, supple

wooden-headed *adjective* = **stupid**, dense, dim, dim-witted (*informal*), dozy (*Brit. informal*), dull, dull-witted, obtuse, slow, thick, witless

wool *noun* 1 = **fleece**, hair, yarn 2 **dyed in the wool** = **hardened**, confirmed, diehard, fixed, inflexible, inveterate, settled, unchangeable, uncompromising, unshakable 3 **pull the wool over someone's eyes** = **deceive**, bamboozle (*informal*), con (*slang*), delude, dupe, fool, hoodwink, kid (*informal*), lead (someone) up the garden path (*informal*), pull a fast one (on someone) (*informal*), put one over on (*slang*), take in (*informal*), trick

woolgathering *noun* = **daydreaming**, absent-mindedness, abstraction, building castles in the air, dreaming, inattention, musing, preoccupation, reverie
➤ **Antonyms**
alertness, attention, awareness, concentration, heed, observation, thoughtfulness, vigilance, watchfulness

woolly *adjective* **1** = **fleecy**, flocculent, hairy, made of wool, shaggy, woollen **2** = **vague**, blurred, clouded, confused, foggy, fuzzy, hazy, ill-defined, indefinite, indistinct, muddled, nebulous, unclear
➤ **Antonyms**
≠**vague**: clear, clear-cut, definite, distinct, exact, obvious, precise, sharp, well-defined

word *noun* **1** = **term**, expression, locution, name, vocable **2** = **chat**, brief conversation, chitchat, colloquy, confab (*informal*), confabulation, consultation, discussion, talk, tête-à-tête **3** = **remark**, brief statement, comment, declaration, expression, utterance **4** = **message**, account, advice, bulletin, communication, communiqué, dispatch, gen (*Brit. informal*), information, intelligence, intimation, latest (*informal*), news, notice, report, tidings **5** = **promise**, affirmation, assertion, assurance, guarantee, oath, parole, pledge, solemn oath, solemn word, undertaking, vow, word of honour **6** = **command**, bidding, commandment, decree, edict, go-ahead (*informal*), mandate, order, ukase (*rare*), will **7 in a word** = **briefly**, concisely, in a nutshell, in short, succinctly, to put it briefly, to sum up **8 last word: a** = **final say**, finis, summation, ultimatum **b** = **epitome**, best, cream, crème de la crème, crown, mother of all (*informal*), ne plus ultra, perfection, quintessence, ultimate **c** = **vogue**, dernier cri, fashion, latest, newest, rage ♦ *verb* **9** = **express**, couch, phrase, put, say, state, utter

wording *noun* = **phraseology**, language, phrasing, terminology, words

wordplay *noun* = **puns**, punning, repartee, wit, witticisms

words *plural noun* **1** = **text**, lyrics **2** As in **have words** ♦ *noun* = **argument**, altercation, angry exchange, angry speech, barney (*informal*), bickering, disagreement, dispute, falling-out (*informal*), quarrel, row, run-in (*informal*), set-to (*informal*), squabble

wordy *adjective* = **long-winded**, diffuse, discursive, garrulous, loquacious, pleonastic, prolix, rambling, verbose, windy
➤ **Antonyms**
brief, concise, laconic, pithy, short, succinct, terse, to the point

work *noun* **1** = **effort**, drudgery, elbow grease (*facetious*), exertion, grind (*informal*), industry, labour, slog, sweat, toil, travail (*literary*) **2** = **employment**, bread and butter (*informal*), business, calling, craft, duty, job, line, livelihood, métier, occupation, office, profession, pursuit, trade **3** = **task**, assignment, chore, commission, duty, job, stint, undertaking **4** = **creation**, achievement, composition, handiwork, oeuvre, opus, performance, piece, production **5 out of work** = **unemployed**, idle, jobless, on the dole (*Brit. informal*), on the street, out of a job ♦ *verb* **6** = **labour**, break one's back, drudge, exert oneself, peg away, slave, slog (away), sweat, toil **7** = **be employed**, be in work, do business, earn a living, have a job **8** = **operate**, act, control, direct, drive, handle, manage, manipulate, move, ply, use, wield **9** = **function**, go, operate, perform, run **10** = **cultivate**, dig, farm, till **11** = **manipulate**, fashion, form, handle, knead, make, mould, process, shape **12** = **progress**, force, make one's way, manoeuvre, move **13** *Informal* = **manipulate**, arrange, bring off, contrive, exploit, fiddle (*informal*), fix (*informal*), handle, pull off, swing (*informal*) **14** = **accomplish**, achieve, bring about, carry out, cause, contrive, create, effect, encompass, execute, implement **15** = **move**, be agitated, convulse, twitch, writhe
➤ **Antonyms**
noun ≠**effort**: ease, leisure, relaxation, rest ≠**employment**: entertainment, hobby, holiday, play, recreation, retirement, spare time, unemployment ♦ *verb* ≠**labour**: have fun, mark time, play, relax, skive (*Brit. slang*), take it easy ≠**function**: be broken, be out of order

workable *adjective* = **viable**, doable, feasible, possible, practicable, practical
➤ **Antonyms**
hopeless, impossible, impractical, inconceivable, unattainable, unthinkable, unworkable, useless

workaday *adjective* = **ordinary**, bog-standard (*Brit. & Irish slang*), common, commonplace, everyday, familiar, humdrum, mundane, practical, prosaic, routine, run-of-the-mill
➤ **Antonyms**
atypical, different, exciting, extraordinary,

rare, special, uncommon, unfamiliar, unusual

worker *noun* = **employee**, artisan, craftsman, hand, labourer, proletarian, tradesman, wage earner, working man *or* working woman, workman

working *adjective* **1** = **employed**, active, in a job, in work, labouring **2** = **functioning**, going, operative, running **3** = **effective**, practical, useful, viable ♦ *noun* **4** = **mine**, digging, excavation, pit, quarry, shaft **5** **workings** = **operation**, action, functioning, manner, method, mode of operation, running

workman *noun* = **labourer**, artificer, artisan, craftsman, employee, hand, journeyman, mechanic, operative, tradesman, worker

workmanlike, workmanly *adjective* = **efficient**, adept, careful, expert, masterly, painstaking, professional, proficient, satisfactory, skilful, skilled, thorough
➤ **Antonyms**
amateurish, botchy, careless, clumsy, cowboy (*informal*), incompetent, slap-dash, slipshod, unprofessional, unskilful

workmanship *noun* = **skill**, art, artistry, craft, craftsmanship, execution, expertise, handicraft, handiwork, manufacture, technique, work

work out *verb* **1** = **solve**, calculate, clear up, figure out, find out, puzzle out, resolve, suss (out) (*slang*) **2** = **plan**, arrange, construct, contrive, develop, devise, elaborate, evolve, form, formulate, put together **3** = **happen**, come out, develop, evolve, go, pan out (*informal*), result, turn out **4** = **succeed**, be effective, flourish, go as planned, go well, prosper, prove satisfactory **5** = **exercise**, do exercises, drill, practise, train, warm up **6** **work out at** = **amount to**, add up to, come to, reach, reach a total of

works *plural noun* **1** = **factory**, mill, plant, shop, workshop **2** = **writings**, canon, *oeuvre*, output, productions **3** = **deeds**, actions, acts, doings **4** = **mechanism**, action, guts (*informal*), innards (*informal*), insides (*informal*), machinery, movement, moving parts, parts, workings

workshop *noun* **1** = **studio**, atelier, factory, mill, plant, shop, workroom, works **2** = **seminar**, class, discussion group, masterclass, study group

work up *verb* = **excite**, agitate, animate, arouse, enkindle, foment, generate, get (someone) all steamed up (*slang*), incite, inflame, instigate, move, rouse, spur, stir

up, wind up (*informal*)

world *noun* **1** = **earth**, earthly sphere, globe **2** = **mankind**, everybody, everyone, humanity, humankind, human race, man, men, the public, the race of man **3** = **universe**, cosmos, creation, existence, life, nature **4** = **planet**, heavenly body, star **5** = **sphere**, area, domain, environment, field, kingdom, province, realm, system **6** = **period**, age, days, epoch, era, times **7** **for all the world** = **exactly**, in every respect, in every way, just as if, just like, precisely, to all intents and purposes **8** **on top of the world** *Informal* = **overjoyed**, beside oneself with joy, cock-a-hoop, ecstatic, elated, exultant, happy, in raptures, on cloud nine (*informal*), over the moon (*informal*) **9** **out of this world** *Informal* = **wonderful**, awesome (*slang*), bodacious (*slang, chiefly U.S.*), excellent, fabulous (*informal*), fantastic (*informal*), great (*informal*), incredible, indescribable, marvellous, superb, unbelievable

worldly *adjective* **1** = **earthly**, carnal, fleshly, lay, mundane, physical, profane, secular, sublunary, temporal, terrestrial **2** = **materialistic**, avaricious, covetous, grasping, greedy, selfish, worldly-minded **3** = **worldly-wise**, blasé, cosmopolitan, experienced, knowing, politic, sophisticated, urbane, well versed in the ways of the world
➤ **Antonyms**
≠**earthly**: divine, ethereal, heavenly, immaterial, noncorporeal, spiritual, transcendental, unworldly ≠**materialistic**: moral, nonmaterialistic, unworldly ≠**worldly-wise**: ingenuous, innocent, naive, unsophisticated, unworldly

worldwide *adjective* = **global**, general, international, omnipresent, pandemic, ubiquitous, universal
➤ **Antonyms**
confined, insular, limited, local, narrow, national, parochial, provincial, restricted

worn *adjective* **1** = **ragged**, frayed, shabby, shiny, tattered, tatty, the worse for wear, threadbare **2** = **haggard**, careworn, drawn, lined, pinched, wizened **3** = **exhausted**, fatigued, jaded, played-out (*informal*), spent, tired, tired out, wearied, weary, worn-out

worn-out *adjective* **1** = **run-down**, broken-down, clapped out (*Brit., Austral., & N.Z. informal*), decrepit, done, frayed, moth-eaten, on its last legs, ragged, shabby, tattered, tatty, threadbare, used, used-up, useless, worn **2** = **exhausted**, all in (*slang*), clapped out (*Austral. & N.Z. informal*), dead *or* out on one's feet

(*informal*), dog-tired (*informal*), done in (*informal*), fatigued, fit to drop, jiggered (*dialect*), knackered (*slang*), played-out, prostrate, shagged out (*Brit. slang*), spent, tired, tired out, weary, wiped out (*informal*), zonked (*slang*)
➤ **Antonyms**
≠**exhausted**: fresh, refreshed, relaxed, renewed, rested, restored, revived, strengthened

worried *adjective* = **anxious**, afraid, antsy (*informal*), apprehensive, bothered, concerned, distracted, distraught, distressed, disturbed, fearful, fretful, frightened, hot and bothered, ill at ease, nervous, on edge, overwrought, perturbed, tense, tormented, troubled, uneasy, unquiet, upset, wired (*slang*)
➤ **Antonyms**
calm, fearless, peaceful, quiet, tranquil, unafraid, unconcerned, unfazed (*informal*), unworried

worry *verb* **1** = **be anxious**, agonize, brood, feel uneasy, fret, obsess **2** = **trouble**, annoy, badger, bother, disquiet, distress, disturb, harass, harry, hassle (*informal*), hector, importune, irritate, make anxious, perturb, pester, plague, tantalize, tease, torment, unsettle, upset, vex **3** = **attack**, bite, gnaw at, go for, harass, harry, kill, lacerate, savage, tear ♦ *noun* **4** = **anxiety**, annoyance, apprehension, care, concern, disturbance, fear, irritation, misery, misgiving, perplexity, torment, trepidation, trouble, unease, vexation, woe **5** = **problem**, annoyance, bother, care, hassle (*informal*), irritation, pest, plague, torment, trial, trouble, vexation
➤ **Antonyms**
verb ≠**be anxious**: be apathetic, be unconcerned, be unperturbed ≠**trouble**: calm, comfort, console, solace, soothe ♦ *noun* ≠**anxiety**: calm, comfort, consolation, peace of mind, reassurance, serenity, solace, tranquillity

worsen *verb* **1** = **aggravate**, damage, exacerbate **2** = **deteriorate**, decay, decline, degenerate, get worse, go downhill (*informal*), go from bad to worse, retrogress, sink, take a turn for the worse
➤ **Antonyms**
≠**aggravate**: ameliorate, enhance, improve, mend, rectify, upgrade ≠**deteriorate**: be on the mend, improve, mend, recover

worship *verb* **1** = **praise**, adore, adulate, deify, exalt, glorify, honour, laud, pray to, respect, revere, reverence, venerate **2** = **love**, adore, idolize, put on a pedestal ♦ *noun* **3** = **praise**, adoration, adulation, deification, devotion, exaltation,

glorification, glory, homage, honour, laudation, love, prayer(s), regard, respect, reverence
➤ **Antonyms**
verb ≠**praise**: blaspheme, deride, dishonour, flout, mock, revile, ridicule, scoff at ≠**love**: despise, disdain, spurn

worst *verb* = **beat**, best, blow out of the water (*slang*), clobber (*slang*), conquer, crush, defeat, gain the advantage over, get the better of, lick (*informal*), master, overcome, overpower, overthrow, run rings around (*informal*), subdue, subjugate, undo, vanquish, wipe the floor with (*informal*)

worth *noun* **1** = **value**, cost, price, rate, valuation **2** = **importance**, aid, assistance, avail, benefit, credit, desert(s), estimation, excellence, goodness, help, merit, quality, usefulness, utility, value, virtue, worthiness
➤ **Antonyms**
≠**importance**: futility, insignificance, paltriness, triviality, unworthiness, uselessness, worthlessness, wretchedness

worthless *adjective* **1** = **useless**, a dime a dozen, chickenshit (*U.S. slang*), futile, ineffectual, insignificant, inutile, meaningless, measly, miserable, nickel-and-dime (*U.S. slang*), not much cop (*Brit.slang*), not worth a hill of beans (*chiefly U.S.*), no use, nugatory, paltry, pants (*slang*), pointless, poor, poxy (*slang*), rubbishy, trashy, trifling, trivial, two a penny (*informal*), unavailing, unimportant, unusable, valueless, wanky (*taboo slang*), wretched **2** = **good-for-nothing**, abandoned, abject, base, contemptible, depraved, despicable, ignoble, useless, vile
➤ **Antonyms**
≠**useless**: consequential, effective, fruitful, important, precious, productive, profitable, significant, useful, valuable, worthwhile ≠**good-for-nothing**: decent, honourable, noble, upright, worthy

worthwhile *adjective* = **useful**, beneficial, constructive, expedient, gainful, good, helpful, justifiable, productive, profitable, valuable, worthy
➤ **Antonyms**
inconsequential, pointless, trivial, unimportant, unworthy, useless, vain, valueless, wasteful, worthless

worthy *adjective* **1** = **praiseworthy**, admirable, commendable, creditable, decent, dependable, deserving, estimable, excellent, good, honest, honourable, laudable, meritorious, reliable, reputable, respectable, righteous, upright, valuable, virtuous, worthwhile ♦ *noun* **2** = **dignitary**,

big hitter (*informal*), big shot (*informal*), bigwig (*informal*), heavy hitter (*informal*), luminary, notable, personage
➤ **Antonyms**
adjective ≠**praiseworthy**: demeaning, disreputable, dubious, ignoble, undeserving, unproductive, untrustworthy, unworthy, useless ♦ *noun* ≠**dignitary**: member of the rank and file, nobody, pleb, punter (*informal*)

would-be *adjective* = **budding**, self-appointed, self-styled, unfulfilled, wannabe (*informal*)

wound *noun* 1 = **injury**, cut, damage, gash, harm, hurt, laceration, lesion, slash, trauma (*Pathology*) 2 = **insult**, anguish, distress, grief, heartbreak, injury, offence, pain, pang, sense of loss, shock, slight, torment, torture, trauma ♦ *verb* 3 = **injure**, cut, damage, gash, harm, hit, hurt, irritate, lacerate, pierce, slash, wing 4 = **offend**, annoy, cut (someone) to the quick, distress, grieve, hurt, hurt the feelings of, mortify, pain, shock, sting, traumatize

wrangle *verb* 1 = **argue**, altercate, bicker, brawl, contend, disagree, dispute, fall out (*informal*), fight, have words, quarrel, row, scrap, spar, squabble ♦ *noun* 2 = **argument**, altercation, angry exchange, argy-bargy (*Brit. informal*), bagarre, barney (*informal*), bickering, brawl, clash, contest, controversy, dispute, falling-out (*informal*), quarrel, row, set-to (*informal*), slanging match (*Brit.*), squabble, tiff

wrap *verb* 1 = **cover**, absorb, bind, bundle up, cloak, encase, enclose, enfold, envelop, fold, immerse, muffle, pack, package, roll up, sheathe, shroud, surround, swathe, wind ♦ *noun* 2 = **cloak**, cape, mantle, shawl, stole
➤ **Antonyms**
verb ≠**cover**: disclose, open, strip, uncover, unfold, unpack, unwind, unwrap

wrapper *noun* = **cover**, case, envelope, jacket, packaging, paper, sheath, sleeve, wrapping

wrap up *verb* 1 = **giftwrap**, bundle up, enclose, enwrap, pack, package 2 = **dress warmly**, muffle up, put warm clothes on, wear something warm 3 *Informal* = **end**, bring to a close, conclude, finish off, polish off, round off, terminate, tidy up, wind up 4 *Slang* = **be quiet**, be silent, button it (*slang*), button one's lip (*slang*), hold one's tongue, put a sock in it (*Brit. slang*), shut one's face (*Brit. slang*), shut one's mouth (*slang*), shut one's trap (*slang*), shut up

wrath *noun* = **anger**, choler, displeasure, exasperation, fury, indignation, ire,

irritation, passion, rage, resentment, temper
➤ **Antonyms**
amusement, contentment, delight, enjoyment, gladness, gratification, happiness, joy, pleasure, satisfaction

wrathful *adjective* = **angry**, beside oneself with rage, choked, displeased, enraged, furious, incandescent, incensed, indignant, infuriated, irate, on the warpath (*informal*), pissed (*taboo slang*), pissed off (*taboo slang*), raging, wroth (*archaic*)
➤ **Antonyms**
amused, calm, contented, delighted, glad, gratified, happy, joyful, pleased, satisfied

wreath *noun* = **garland**, band, chaplet, coronet, crown, festoon, loop, ring

wreathe *verb* = **surround**, adorn, coil, crown, encircle, enfold, engarland, entwine, envelop, enwrap, festoon, intertwine, interweave, twine, twist, wind, wrap, writhe

wreck *verb* 1 = **destroy**, blow (*slang*), break, cock up (*Brit. slang*), dash to pieces, demolish, devastate, fuck up (*offensive taboo slang*), mar, play havoc with, ravage, ruin, screw up (*informal*), shatter, smash, spoil, total (*slang*), trash (*slang*), undo 2 = **go** or **run aground**, founder, run onto the rocks, shipwreck, strand ♦ *noun* 3 = **shipwreck**, derelict, hulk, sunken vessel 4 = **ruin**, desolation, destruction, devastation, disruption, mess, overthrow, undoing
➤ **Antonyms**
verb ≠**destroy**: build, conserve, create, fulfil, make possible, preserve, reconstruct, salvage, save ♦ *noun* ≠**ruin**: conservation, creation, formation, fulfilment, preservation, restoration, salvage, saving

wreckage *noun* = **remains**, debris, fragments, hulk, pieces, rubble, ruin, wrack

wrench *verb* 1 = **twist**, force, jerk, pull, rip, tear, tug, wrest, wring, yank 2 = **sprain**, distort, rick, strain ♦ *noun* 3 = **twist**, jerk, pull, rip, tug, yank 4 = **sprain**, strain, twist 5 = **blow**, ache, pain, pang, shock, upheaval, uprooting 6 = **spanner**, adjustable spanner, shifting spanner

wrest *verb* = **seize**, extract, force, take, win, wrench

wrestle *verb* = **fight**, battle, combat, contend, grapple, scuffle, strive, struggle, tussle

wretch *noun* 1 = **scoundrel**, asshole (*U.S. & Canad. taboo slang*), asswipe (*U.S. & Canad. taboo slang*), bad egg (*old-fashioned informal*), bastard (*offensive*), blackguard, bugger (*taboo slang*), cocksucker (*taboo slang*), cur, good-for-nothing, miscreant, mother (*taboo slang, chiefly U.S.*), motherfucker (*taboo slang, chiefly U.S.*), outcast, profligate, rascal, rat (*informal*), rogue, rotter (*slang, chiefly Brit.*), ruffian, scumbag (*slang*), shit (*taboo slang*), son-of-a-bitch (*slang, chiefly U.S. & Canad.*), swine, turd (*taboo slang*), vagabond, villain, worm **2** = **poor thing**, poor soul, unfortunate

wretched *adjective* **1** = **unhappy**, abject, brokenhearted, cheerless, comfortless, crestfallen, dejected, deplorable, depressed, disconsolate, dismal, distressed, doleful, downcast, down in the dumps (*informal*), forlorn, funereal, gloomy, hapless, hopeless, melancholy, miserable, pathetic, pitiable, pitiful, poor, sorry, unfortunate, woebegone, woeful, worthless **2** = **worthless**, calamitous, deplorable, inferior, miserable, paltry, pathetic, poor, sorry **3** = **shameful**, base, contemptible, crappy (*slang*), despicable, low, low-down (*informal*), mean, paltry, poxy (*slang*), scurvy, shabby, vile
➤ **Antonyms**
≠**unhappy**: carefree, cheerful, contented, happy, jovial, light-hearted, untroubled ≠**worthless**: excellent, flourishing, great, splendid, successful, thriving ≠**shameful**: admirable, decent, noble, worthy

wriggle *verb* **1** = **twist**, jerk, jiggle, squirm, turn, wag, waggle, wiggle, writhe **2** = **crawl**, slink, snake, twist and turn, worm, zigzag **3** *As in* **wriggle out of** = **manoeuvre**, crawl, dodge, extricate oneself, sneak, talk one's way out, worm ♦ *noun* **4** = **twist**, jerk, jiggle, squirm, turn, wag, waggle, wiggle

wring *verb* = **twist**, coerce, extort, extract, force, screw, squeeze, wrench, wrest

wrinkle[1] *noun* **1** = **crease**, corrugation, crinkle, crow's-foot, crumple, fold, furrow, gather, line, pucker, rumple ♦ *verb* **2** = **crease**, corrugate, crinkle, crumple, fold, furrow, gather, line, pucker, ruck, rumple
➤ **Antonyms**
verb ≠**crease**: even out, flatten, iron, level, press, smooth, straighten, unfold

wrinkle[2] *noun* = **trick**, device, dodge, gimmick, idea, plan, ploy, ruse, scheme, stunt, tip, wheeze (*Brit. slang*)

writ *noun* = **summons**, court order, decree, document

write *verb* = **record**, author (*nonstandard*), commit to paper, compose, copy, correspond, create, draft, draw up, indite, inscribe, jot down, pen, put down in black and white, put in writing, scribble, set down, take down, tell, transcribe

write off *verb* **1** = **cancel**, cross out, disregard, forget about, give up for lost, score out, shelve **2** *Informal* = **wreck**, crash, damage beyond repair, destroy, smash up, total (*slang*), trash (*slang*)

writer *noun* = **author**, columnist, essayist, hack, littérateur, man of letters, novelist, penman, penny-a-liner (*rare*), penpusher, scribbler, scribe, wordsmith

writhe *verb* = **squirm**, contort, convulse, distort, jerk, struggle, thrash, thresh, toss, twist, wiggle, wriggle

writing *noun* **1** = **script**, calligraphy, chirography, hand, handwriting, penmanship, print, scrawl, scribble **2** = **document**, book, composition, letter, opus, publication, title, work **3** = **literature**, belles-lettres, letters

wrong *adjective* **1** = **incorrect**, erroneous, fallacious, false, faulty, inaccurate, in error, mistaken, off base (*U.S. & Canad. informal*), off beam (*informal*), off target, out, unsound, untrue, way off beam (*informal*), wide of the mark **2** = **bad**, blameworthy, criminal, crooked, dishonest, dishonourable, evil, felonious, illegal, illicit, immoral, iniquitous, not cricket (*informal*), reprehensible, sinful, under-the-table, unethical, unfair, unjust, unlawful, wicked, wrongful **3** = **inappropriate**, funny, improper, inapt, incongruous, incorrect, indecorous, infelicitous, malapropos, not done, unacceptable, unbecoming, unconventional, undesirable, unfitting, unhappy, unseemly, unsuitable **4** = **defective**, amiss, askew, awry, faulty, not working, out of commission, out of order **5** = **opposite**, inside, inverse, reverse ♦ *adverb* **6** = **incorrectly**, badly, erroneously, inaccurately, mistakenly, wrongly **7** = **amiss**, askew, astray, awry **8** **go wrong: a** = **fail**, come to grief (*informal*), come to nothing, fall through, flop (*informal*), go pear-shaped (*informal*), miscarry, misfire **b** = **make a mistake**, boob (*Brit. slang*), err, go astray, slip up (*informal*) **c** = **break down**, cease to function, conk out (*informal*), fail, go kaput (*informal*), go on the blink (*slang*), go phut (*informal*), malfunction, misfire **d** = **lapse**, err, fall from grace, go astray, go off the straight and narrow (*informal*), go to the bad, sin ♦ *noun* **9** = **offence**, abuse, bad *or* evil deed, crime, error, grievance, infraction, infringement, injury, injustice, misdeed, sin, transgression, trespass **10** = **wickedness**, immorality, inequity, iniquity, injustice, sinfulness, unfairness **11** **in the wrong** = **guilty**, at fault, blameworthy, in error, mistaken, off beam (*informal*), off course, off target, to be

blamed ♦ *verb* **12** = **mistreat**, abuse, cheat, discredit, dishonour, dump on (*slang, chiefly U.S.*), harm, hurt, ill-treat, ill-use, impose upon, injure, malign, maltreat, misrepresent, oppress, shit on (*taboo slang*), take advantage of
➤ **Antonyms**
adjective ≠**incorrect**: accurate, correct, precise, right, true ≠**bad**: ethical, fair, fitting, godly, honest, honourable, just, lawful, legal, moral, righteous, rightful, square, upright, virtuous ≠**inappropriate**: appropriate, apt, becoming, commendable, correct, fitting, laudable, praiseworthy, proper, seemly, sensible, suitable ♦ *adverb* ≠**incorrectly**: accurately, correctly, exactly, precisely, properly, squarely, truly ♦ *noun* ≠**offence**: favour, good deed, good turn ≠**wickedness**: decency, fairness, good, goodness, high-mindedness, honesty, lawfulness, legality, morality, propriety, virtue ♦ *verb* ≠**mistreat**: aid, do a favour, help, support, treat well

wrongdoer *noun* = **offender**, criminal, culprit, delinquent, evildoer, lawbreaker, malefactor, miscreant, sinner, transgressor, trespasser (*archaic*), villain

wrongful *adjective* = **improper**, blameworthy, criminal, dishonest, dishonourable, evil, felonious, illegal, illegitimate, illicit, immoral, reprehensible, under-the-table, unethical, unfair, unjust, unlawful, wicked
➤ **Antonyms**
ethical, fair, honest, honourable, just, lawful, legal, legitimate, moral, proper, rightful

wry *adjective* **1** = **ironic**, droll, dry, mocking, mordacious, pawky (*Scot.*), sarcastic, sardonic **2** = **contorted**, askew, aslant, awry, crooked, deformed, distorted, off the level, skewwhiff (*Brit. informal*), twisted, uneven, warped
➤ **Antonyms**
≠**contorted**: aligned, even, level, smooth, straight, unbent

Xx, Yy, Zz

Xmas *noun* = **Christmas**, Christmastide, festive season, Noel, Yule (*archaic*), Yuletide (*archaic*)

X-rays *plural noun* = **Röntgen rays** (*old name*)

yank *verb, noun* = **pull**, hitch, jerk, snatch, tug, wrench

yardstick *noun* = **standard**, benchmark, criterion, gauge, measure, par, touchstone

yarn *noun* **1** = **thread**, fibre **2** *Informal* = **story**, anecdote, cock-and-bull story (*informal*), fable, tale, tall story, urban legend, urban myth

yawning *adjective* = **gaping**, cavernous, chasmal, vast, wide, wide-open

yearly *adjective* **1** = **annual** ♦ *adverb* **2** = **annually**, every year, once a year, per annum

yearn *verb* = **long**, ache, covet, crave, desire, eat one's heart out over, hanker, have a yen for (*informal*), hunger, itch, languish, lust, pant, pine, set one's heart upon, suspire (*archaic or poetic*), would give one's eyeteeth for

yell *verb* **1** = **scream**, bawl, holler (*informal*), howl, screech, shout, shriek, squeal ♦ *noun* **2** = **scream**, cry, howl, screech, shriek, whoop
➤ **Antonyms**
verb, noun ≠**scream**: mumble, murmur, mutter, whisper

yelp *verb* = **cry**, yammer (*informal*), yap, yip (*chiefly U.S.*), yowl

yen *noun* = **longing**, ache, craving, desire, hankering, hunger, itch, passion, thirst, yearning

yes man *noun* = **sycophant**, ass-kisser (*U.S. & Canad. taboo slang*), bootlicker (*informal*), bosses' lackey, company man, crawler (*slang*), creature, minion, timeserver, toady

yet *conjunction* **1** = **nevertheless**, however, notwithstanding, still ♦ *adverb* **2** = **so far**, as yet, thus far, until now, up to now **3** = **still**, additionally, as well, besides, further, in addition, into the bargain, moreover, over and above, to boot **4** = **now**, already, just now, right now, so soon

yield *verb* **1** = **produce**, afford, bear, bring forth, bring in, earn, furnish, generate, give, net, pay, provide, return, supply **2** = **surrender**, abandon, abdicate, admit defeat, bow, capitulate, cave in (*informal*), cede, cry quits, give in, give up the struggle, give way, knuckle under, lay down one's arms, lose, part with, raise the white flag, relinquish, resign, resign oneself, submit, succumb, throw in the towel **3** = **comply**, accede, agree, allow, bow, concede, consent, go along with, grant, permit ♦ *noun* **4** = **profit**, crop, earnings, harvest, income, output, produce, return, revenue, takings
➤ **Antonyms**
verb ≠**produce**: consume, use, use up ≠**surrender**: appropriate, commandeer, grab, hold on to, hold out, keep, maintain, reserve, retain, seize, struggle ≠**comply**: combat, counterattack, defy, oppose, resist ♦ *noun* ≠**profit**: consumption, input, loss

yielding *adjective* **1** = **submissive**, accommodating, acquiescent, biddable, compliant, docile, easy, flexible, obedient, pliant, tractable **2** = **soft**, elastic, pliable, quaggy, resilient, spongy, springy, supple, unresisting
➤ **Antonyms**
≠**submissive**: dogged, headstrong, mulish, obstinate, opinionated, perverse, stiff-necked, stubborn, tenacious, wilful

yob, yobbo *noun* = **thug**, hooligan, lout, roughneck (*slang*), ruffian

yoke *noun* **1** = **bond**, chain, coupling, ligament, link, tie **2** = **oppression**, bondage, burden, enslavement, helotry, serfdom, service, servility, servitude, slavery, thraldom, vassalage ♦ *verb* **3** = **link**, bracket, connect, couple, harness, hitch, join, tie, unite

yokel *noun* = **peasant**, boor, bucolic, clodhopper (*informal*), (country) bumpkin, country cousin, countryman, hayseed (*U.S. & Canad. informal*), hick (*informal, chiefly U.S. & Canad.*), hillbilly, hind (*obsolete*), rustic

young *adjective* **1** = **immature**, adolescent, callow, green, growing, infant, in the springtime of life, junior, juvenile, little, unfledged, youthful **2** = **new**, at an early stage, early, fledgling, newish, not far advanced, recent, undeveloped ♦ *plural*

noun **3** = **offspring**, babies, brood, family, issue, litter, little ones, progeny
➤ **Antonyms**
adjective ≠**immature**: adult, aged, elderly, full-grown, grown-up, mature, old, senior ≠**new**: advanced, developed, old ♦ *plural noun* ≠**offspring**: adults, grown-ups, parents

youngster *noun* = **youth**, boy, cub, girl, juvenile, kid (*informal*), lad, lass, pup (*informal, chiefly Brit.*), teenager, teenybopper (*slang*), urchin, young adult, young hopeful, young person, young shaver (*informal*), young 'un (*informal*)

youth *noun* **1** = **immaturity**, adolescence, boyhood *or* girlhood, early life, girlhood, juvenescence, salad days, young days **2** = **boy**, adolescent, kid (*informal*), lad, shaveling (*archaic*), stripling, teenager, young man, young shaver (*informal*), youngster **3** = **young people**, teenagers, the rising generation, the young, the younger generation
➤ **Antonyms**
≠**immaturity**: adulthood, age, later life, manhood *or* womanhood, maturity, old age ≠**boy**: adult, grown-up, OAP, pensioner, senior citizen ≠**young people**: the aged, the elderly, the old

youthful *adjective* **1** = **fresh**, active, spry, vigorous, young at heart, young looking **2** = **young**, boyish, childish, girlish, immature, inexperienced, juvenile, pubescent, puerile
➤ **Antonyms**
≠**fresh**: aged, ancient, decaying, decrepit, hoary, over the hill, tired, waning, weary ≠**young**: adult, aged, ageing, elderly, grown-up, mature, old, senile

zany *adjective* = **comical**, clownish, crazy, eccentric, goofy (*informal*), madcap, wacky (*slang*)

zeal *noun* = **enthusiasm**, ardour, devotion, eagerness, earnestness, fanaticism, fervency, fervour, fire, gusto, keenness, militancy, passion, spirit, verve, warmth, zest
➤ **Antonyms**
apathy, coolness, indifference, passivity, stoicism, torpor, unresponsiveness

zealot *noun* = **fanatic**, bigot, energumen, enthusiast, extremist, fiend (*informal*), maniac, militant

zealous *adjective* = **enthusiastic**, ablaze, afire, ardent, burning, devoted, eager, earnest, fanatical, fervent, fervid, impassioned, keen, militant, passionate, rabid, spirited

➤ **Antonyms**
apathetic, cold, cool, half-hearted, indifferent, lackadaisical, lacklustre, languorous, listless, low-key, torpid, unenthusiastic, unimpassioned

zenith *noun* = **height**, acme, apex, apogee, climax, crest, high noon, high point, meridian, peak, pinnacle, summit, top, vertex
➤ **Antonyms**
base, bottom, depths, lowest point, nadir, rock bottom

zero *noun* **1** = **nothing**, cipher, naught, nil, nought **2** = **bottom**, lowest point *or* ebb, nadir, nothing, rock bottom

zero hour *noun* = **moment of truth**, appointed hour, crisis, moment of decision, turning point, vital moment

zest *noun* **1** = **enjoyment**, appetite, delectation, gusto, keenness, relish, zeal, zing (*informal*) **2** = **flavour**, charm, interest, kick (*informal*), piquancy, pungency, relish, savour, smack, spice, tang, taste
➤ **Antonyms**
≠**enjoyment**: abhorrence, apathy, aversion, disinclination, distaste, indifference, lack of enthusiasm, loathing, repugnance, weariness

zing *noun Informal* = **vitality**, animation, brio, dash, energy, go (*informal*), life, liveliness, oomph (*informal*), pep, pizzazz *or* pizazz (*informal*), spirit, vigour, zest, zip (*informal*)

zip *noun* **1** *Informal* = **energy**, brio, drive, get-up-and-go (*informal*), go (*informal*), gusto, life, liveliness, oomph (*informal*), pep, pizzazz *or* pizazz (*informal*), punch (*informal*), sparkle, spirit, verve, vigour, vim (*slang*), vitality, zest, zing (*informal*)
♦ *verb* **2** = **speed**, barrel (along) (*informal, chiefly U.S. & Canad.*), burn rubber (*informal*), dash, flash, fly, hurry, rush, shoot, tear, whizz (*informal*), zoom
➤ **Antonyms**
noun ≠**energy**: apathy, indifference, inertia, laziness, lethargy, listlessness, sloth, sluggishness

zone *noun* = **area**, belt, district, region, section, sector, sphere

zoom *verb* = **speed**, barrel (along) (*informal, chiefly U.S. & Canad.*), burn rubber (*informal*), buzz, dash, dive, flash, fly, hare (*Brit. informal*), hum (*slang*), hurtle, pelt, rip (*informal*), rush, shoot, streak, tear, whirl, whizz (*informal*), zip (*informal*)

WORD POWER

POWER

Supplement

CONTENTS

WORD POWER

CONTENTS

WORD POWER

Male

Woody Allen (*U.S.*)
Fred Astaire (*U.S.*)
Richard Attenborough
  (*English*)
Jean-Louis Barrault (*French*)
John Barrymore (*U.S.*)
Alan Bates (*English*)
Warren Beatty (*U.S.*)
Jean-Paul Belmondo
  (*French*)
Alan Bennett (*English*)
Dirk Bogarde (*English*)
Humphrey Bogart (*U.S.*)
Charles Boyer (*French*)
Kenneth Branagh (*English*)
Marlon Brando (*U.S.*)
Mel Brooks (*U.S.*)
Richard Burbage (*English*)
Richard Burton (*Welsh*)
Glen Byam Shaw (*English*)
James Cagney (*U.S.*)
Michael Caine (*English*)
Simon Callow (*English*)
Robert Carlyle (*Scottish*)
Jim Carrey (*U.S.*)
Charlie Chaplin (*English*)
Maurice Chevalier (*French*)
Colley Cibber (*English*)
John Cleese (*English*)
George Clooney (*U.S.*)
Sean Connery (*Scottish*)
Peter Cook (*English*)
Gary Cooper (*U.S.*)
Kevin Costner (*U.S.*)
Noel Coward (*English*)
Michael Crawford (*English*)
Tom Cruise (*U.S.*)
James Dean (*U.S.*)
Robert De Niro (*U.S.*)
Gerard Depardieu (*French*)
Vittorio de Sica (*Italian*)
John Dexter (*English*)
Leonardo DiCaprio (*U.S.*)
Kirk Douglas (*U.S.*)
Michael Douglas (*U.S.*)
Clint Eastwood (*U.S.*)
Douglas Fairbanks Jr. (*U.S.*)
Douglas Fairbanks Snr.
  (*U.S.*)
Fernandel (*French*)
WC Fields (*U.S.*)

Albert Finney (*English*)
Errol Flynn (*Australian*)
Henry Fonda (*U.S.*)
Harrison Ford (*U.S.*)
Jean Gabin (*France*)
Clark Gable (*U.S.*)
David Garrick (*English*)
Mel Gibson (*Australian*)
John Gielgud (*English*)
Cary Grant (*English-U.S.*)
Alec Guinness (*English*)
Gene Hackman (*U.S.*)
Tom Hanks (*U.S.*)
Oliver Hardy (*U.S.*)
Rex Harrison (*English*)
Dustin Hoffman (*U.S.*)
Bob Hope (*U.S.*)
Anthony Hopkins (*Welsh*)
Michael Hordern (*English*)
Leslie Howard (*English*)
Trevor Howard (*English*)
Rock Hudson (*U.S.*)
Barry Humphries
  (*Australian*)
John Hurt (*English*)
Jeremy Irons (*English*)
Henry Irving (*English*)
Derek Jacobi (*English*)
Al Jolson (*U.S.*)
Boris Karloff (*English*)
Edmund Kean (*English*)
Buster Keaton (*U.S.*)
Harvey Keitel (*U.S.*)
Gene Kelly (*U.S.*)
John Kemble (*English*)
Ben Kingsley (*English*)
Burt Lancaster (*U.S.*)
Charles Laughton (*English-
  U.S.*)
Stan Laurel (*English-U.S.*)
Bruce Lee (*U.S.*)
Christopher Lee (*English*)
Harold Lloyd (*U.S.*)
Bela Lugosi (*Hungarian*)
Ewan McGregor (*Scottish*)
Ian McKellen (*English*)
Steve McQueen (*U.S.*)
William Macready (*English*)
James Mason (*English*)
Raymond Massey
  (*Canadian*)

Marcello Mastroianni
  (*Italian*)
Bernard Miles (*English*)
John Mills (*English*)
Robert Mitchum (*U.S.*)
Dudley Moore (*English*)
Robert Morley (*English*)
Sam Neill (*N.Z.*)
Paul Newman (*U.S.*)
Jack Nicholson (*U.S.*)
Liam Neeson (*Irish*)
David Niven (*English*)
Gary Oldman (*English*)
Laurence Olivier (*English*)
Peter O'Toole (*Irish-British*)
Al Pacino (*U.S.*)
Gregory Peck (*U.S.*)
Donald Pleasence (*English*)
Anthony Quayle (*English*)
Anthony Quinn (*U.S.*)
Ronald Reagan (*U.S.*)
Robert Redford (*U.S.*)
Michael Redgrave (*English*)
Fernando Rey (*Spanish*)
Ralph Richardson (*English*)
Paul Robeson (*U.S.*)
Edward G Robinson (*U.S.*)
Tim Roth (*English*)
Arnold Schwarzenegger
  (*Austrian-U.S.*)
Paul Scofield (*English*)
Peter Sellers (*English*)
Sam Shepard (*U.S.*)
Sylvester Stallone (*U.S.*)
Konstantin Stanislavsky
  (*Russian*)
James Stewart (*U.S.*)
Donald Sutherland
  (*Canadian*)
Jacques Tati (*French*)
Spencer Tracy (*U.S.*)
John Travolta (*U.S.*)
Peter Ustinov (*English*)
Rudolph Valentino (*Italian-
  U.S.*)
Max Von Sydow (*Swedish*)
John Wayne (*U.S.*)
Johnny Weissmuller (*U.S.*)
Orson Welles (*U.S.*)

WORD POWER

4

Female

Yvonne Arnaud (*French*)
Peggy Ashcroft (*English*)
Tallulah Bankhead (*U.S.*)
Brigitte Bardot (*French*)
Ingrid Bergman (*Swedish-U.S.*)
Sarah Bernhardt (*French*)
Clara Bow (*U.S.*)
Fanny Brice (*U.S.*)
Glenn Close (*U.S.*)
Claudette Colbert (*French-U.S.*)
Joan Crawford (*U.S.*)
Bette Davis (*U.S.*)
Geena Davis (*U.S.*)
Judy Davis (*Australian*)
Judi Dench (*English*)
Catherine Deneuve (*French*)
Marlene Dietrich (*German*)
Faye Dunaway (*U.S.*)
Edith Evans (*English*)
Jane Fonda (*U.S.*)
Jodie Foster (*U.S.*)
Greta Garbo (*Swedish*)
Ava Gardner (*U.S.*)
Judy Garland (*U.S.*)
Lillian Gish (*U.S.*)
Joyce Grenfell (*English*)
Jean Harlow (*U.S.*)

Audrey Hepburn (*Belgian-U.S.*)
Katharine Hepburn (*U.S.*)
Wendy Hiller (*English*)
Holly Hunter (*U.S.*)
Isabelle Huppert (*French*)
Glenda Jackson (*English*)
Jian Qing (*Chinese*)
Diane Keaton (*U.S.*)
Grace Kelly (*U.S.*)
Fanny Kemble (*English-U.S.*)
Nicole Kidman (*Australian*)
Jessica Lange (*U.S.*)
Gertrude Lawrence (*English*)
Vivien Leigh (*English*)
Lotte Lenya (*Austrian*)
Margaret Lockwood (*English*)
Jennifer Lopez (*Puerto Rican*)
Sophia Loren (*Italian*)
Siobhan McKenna (*Irish*)
Shirley MacLaine (*U.S.*)
Melina Mercouri (*Greek*)
Liza Minnelli (*U.S.*)
Helen Mirren (*English*)
Marilyn Monroe (*U.S.*)
Jeanne Moreau (*French*)
Michelle Pfeiffer (*U.S.*)

Mary Pickford (*U.S.*)
Joan Plowright (*English*)
Vanessa Redgrave (*English*)
Julia Roberts (*U.S.*)
Flora Robson (*English*)
Ginger Rogers (*U.S.*)
Margaret Rutherford (*English*)
Susan Sarandon (*U.S.*)
Delphine Seyrig (*French*)
Sarah Siddons (*English*)
Simone Signoret (*French*)
Maggie Smith (*English*)
Meryl Streep (*U.S.*)
Barbra Streisand (*U.S.*)
Janet Suzman (*South African*)
Elizabeth Taylor (*English-U.S.*)
Shirley Temple (*U.S.*)
Ellen Terry (*English*)
Emma Thompson (*English*)
Sybil Thorndike (*English*)
Sigourney Weaver (*U.S.*)
Raquel Welch (*U.S.*)
Mae West (*U.S.*)
Billie Whitelaw (*English*)
Kate Winslet (*English*)
Peg Woffington (*Irish*)

WORD POWER

French regions

Alsace	Corsica	Nord-Pas-de-Calais
Aquitaine	Franche-Comté	Pays de Loire
Auvergne	Haute-Normandie	Picardie
Basse-Normandie	Île-de-France	Poitou-Charentes
Brittany	Languedoc-Roussillon	Provence-Alpes-Côte
Burgundy	Limousin	d'Azur
Centre	Lorraine	Rhône-Alpes
Champagne-Ardenne	Midi-Pyrénées	

French départements

Ain	Gers	Morbihan
Aisne	Gironde	Moselle
Allier	Guadeloupe	Niveres
Alpes de Haute Provence	Haut Rhin	Nord
Alpes Maritimes	Haute Garonne	Oise
Ardèche	Haute Loire	Orne
Ardennes	Haute Marne	Paris
Ariège	Haute Savoie	Pas de Calais
Aube	Haute Vienne	Puy de Dôme
Aude	Hautes Alpes	Pyrénées Atlantiques
Aveyron	Hautes Pyrénées	Pyrénées Orientales
Bas Rhin	Hauts de Seine	Réunion
Bouches du Rhône	Hérault	Rhône
Calvados	Ille et Vilaine	Saône
Cantal	Indre	Saône et Loire
Charente	Indre et Loire	Sarthe
Charente Maritime	Isère	Savoie
Cher	Jura	Seine et Marne
Corrèze	Landes	Seine Maritime
Corse	Loir et Cher	Seine Saint Denis
Cote d'Or	Loire	Somme
Côtes du Nord	Loire Atlantique	Tarn
Creuse	Loiret	Tarn et Garonne
Deux Sèvres	Lot	Territoire de Belfort
Dordogne	Lot et Garonne	Val d'Oise
Doubs	Lozère	Val de Marne
Drôme	Maine et Loire	Var
Essone	Manche	Vaucluse
Eure	Marne	Vendée
Eure et Loir	Martinique	Vienne
Finistère	Mayenne	Vosges
Gard	Meurthe et Moselle	Yonne
Gayane	Meuse	Yvelines

German states

Baden-Württemberg	Hessen	Saarland
Bavaria	Lower Saxony	Saxony
Berlin	Mecklenburg-West	Saxony-Anhalt
Brandenburg	Pomerania	Schleswig-Holstein
Bremen	North Rhine-Westphalia	Thuringia
Hamburg	Rhineland-Palatinate	

WORD POWER

ADMINISTRATIVE REGIONS

Italian regions

Abruzzo	Friuli-Venezia Giulia	Molise	Trentino-Alto Adige
Basilicata	Lazio	Piedmont	Tuscany
Calabria	Liguria	Puglia	Umbria
Campania	Lombardy	Sardinia	Valle d'Aosta
Emilia-Romagna	Marche	Sicily	Veneto

Italian provinces

Agrigento	Catanzaro	Lecce	Pesaro	Siracusa
Alessandria	Chieti	Lecco	Pescara	Sondrio
Ancona	Como	Livorno	Piacenza	Taranto
Aosta	Cosenza	Lodi	Pisa	Teramo
Arezzo	Cremona	Lucca	Pistoia	Terni
Ascoli Piceno	Crotone	Macerata	Pordenone	Torino
Asti	Cuneo	Mantova	Potenza	Trapani
Avellino	Enna	Massa Carrara	Prato	Trento
Bari	Ferrara	Matera	Ragusa	Treviso
Belluno	Firenze	Messina	Ravenna	Trieste
Benevento	Foggia	Milano	Reggio di	Udine
Bergamo	Forlì	Modena	Calabria	Varese
Bologna	Frosinone	Napoli	Reggio Emilia	Venezia
Bolzano	Genova	Novara	Rieti	Verbania
Brescia	Gorizia	Nuoro	Rimini	Vercelli
Brindisi	Grosseto	Oristano	Roma	Verona
Cagliari	Imperia	Padova	Rovigo	Vibo Valentia
Caltanissetta	Isernia	Palermo	Salerno	Vicenza
Campobasso	L'Aquila	Parma	Sassari	Viterbo
Caserta	La Spezia	Pavia	Savona	Repubblica di
Catania	Latina	Perugia	Siena	San Marino

Spanish regions

Andalucía	Castilla-La Mancha	Murcia
Aragón	Castilla-León	Navarra
Asturias	Catalonia	Valencian Community
Balearic Islands	Extremadura	Ceuta
Basque Country	Galicia	Melilla
Canary Islands	La Rioja	
Cantabria	Madrid	

Spanish provinces

Álava	Cádiz	Huelva	Murcia	Teruel
Albacete	Cantabria	Huesca	Navarra	Toledo
Alhucemas	Castellón	Jaén	Orense	Valencia
Alicante	Chafarinas	La Coruna	Palencia	Valladolid
Almeria	Cordoba	La Rioja	Pontevedra	Vélez de la
Asturias	Cuenca	Las Palmas	Salamanca	Gomera
Ávila	Ceuta	León	Santa Cruz de	Vizcaya
Badajoz	Ciudad Real	Lleida	Tenerife	Zamora
Balearics	Girona	Lugo	Segovia	Zaragoza
Barcelona	Granada	Madrid	Sevilla	
Burgos	Gualalajara	Málaga	Soria	
Cácares	Guipúzcoa	Melilla	Tarragona	

WORD POWER

Agostino di Duccio (*Italian*)
Josef Albers (*German-U.S.*)
Leon Battista Alberti
 (*Italian*)
Washington Allston (*U.S.*)
Lawrence Alma-Tadema
 (*Dutch-English*)
Albrecht Altdorfer (*German*)
Fra Angelico (*Italian*)
Pietro Annigoni (*Italian*)
Antonello da Messina
 (*Italian*)
Apelles (*Greek*)
Karel Appel (*Dutch*)
Aleksandr Porfiryevich
 Archipenko (*Russian*)
Giuseppe Arcimboldo
 (*Italian*)
Jean *or* Hans Arp (*French*)
John James Audubon (*U.S.*)
Frank Auerbach (*English-
 German*)
Francis Bacon (*Irish*)
Leon Nikolayevich Bakst
 (*Russian*)
Balthus (*Polish-French*)
Frédéric August Bartholdi
 (*French*)
Fra Bartolommeo (*Italian*)
Max Beckmann (*German*)
Vanessa Bell (*English*)
Giovanni Bellini (*Italian*)
Thomas Hart Benton
 (*U.S.*)
Gian Lorenzo Bernini
 (*Italian*)
Joseph Beuys (*German*)
Peter Blake (*English*)
William Blake (*English*)
Umberto Boccioni (*Italian*)
David Bomberg (*English*)
Rosa Bonheur (*French*)
Pierre Bonnard (*French*)
Richard Parkes Bonnington
 (*English*)
Gutzon Borglum (*U.S.*)
Hieronymus Bosch (*Dutch*)
Sandro Botticelli (*Italian*)
Francois Boucher (*French*)
Eugène Boudin (*French*)
Arthur Boyd (*Australian*)
Donato Bramante (*Italian*)
Constantin Brancusi
 (*Romanian*)
Georges Braque (*French*)
Brassaï (*French*)
Agnolo Bronzino (*Italian*)

Ford Madox Brown
 (*English*)
Jan Brueghel (*Flemish*)
Pieter Brueghel the Elder
 (*Flemish*)
Pieter Brueghel the Younger
 (*Flemish*)
Bernard Buffet (*French*)
Edward Burne-Jones
 (*English*)
Edward Burra (*English*)
Reg Butler (*English*)
Alexander Calder (*U.S.*)
Callimachus (*Greek*)
Robert Campin (*Flemish*)
Antonio Canova (*Italian*)
Michelangelo Merisi da
 Caravaggio (*Italian*)
Anthony Caro (*English*)
Vittore Carpaccio (*Italian*)
Agostino Carracci (*Italian*)
Annibale Carracci (*Italian*)
Ludovico Carracci (*Italian*)
Mary Cassatt (*U.S.*)
Pietro Cavallini (*Italian*)
Benvenuto Cellini (*Italian*)
Lynn Chadwick (*English*)
Marc Chagall (*Russian-
 French*)
Philippe de Champaigne
 (*French*)
Jean-Baptiste Siméon
 Chardin (*French*)
Giorgio de Chirico (*Italian*)
Giovanni Cimabue (*Italian*)
Claude Lorrain (*French*)
François Clouet (*French*)
Jean Clouet (*French*)
John Constable (*English*)
John Copley (*U.S.*)
Jean Baptiste Camille Corot
 (*French*)
Antonio Allegri da
 Corregio (*Italian*)
Gustave Courbet (*French*)
David Cox (*English*)
Antoine Coypel (*French*)
Lucas Cranach (*German*)
Walter Crane (*English*)
John Crome (*English*)
Aelbert Cuyp *or* Kuyp (*Dutch*)
Paul Cézanne (*French*)
Richard Dadd (*English*)
Salvador Dalí (*Spanish*)
Francis Danby (*Irish*)
Charles François Daubigny
 (*French*)

Honoré Daumier (*French*)
Jacques Louis David
 (*French*)
Peter de Wint (*English*)
Hilaire Germain Edgar
 Degas (*French*)
Eugène Delacroix (*French*)
Paul Delaroche (*French*)
Robert Delaunay (*French*)
Paul Delvaux (*Belgian*)
Maurice Denis (*French*)
André Derain (*French*)
William Dobell (*Australian*)
Domenichino (*Italian*)
Domenico del Barbiere
 (*Italian*)
Donatello (*Italian*)
Gerrit Dou (*Dutch*)
George Russell Drysdale
 (*Australian*)
Jean Dubuffet (*French*)
Duccio di Buoninsegna
 (*Italian*)
Marcel Duchamp (*French-
 U.S.*)
Raoul Dufy (*French*)
Albrecht Dürer (*German*)
Thomas Eakins (*U.S.*)
El Greco (*Greek-Spanish*)
James Ensor (*Belgian*)
Jacob Epstein (*British*)
Max Ernst (*German*)
Henri Fantin-Latour (*French*)
Lyonel Feininger (*U.S.*)
John Flaxman (*English*)
Jean Fouquet (*French*)
Jean Honoré Fragonard
 (*French*)
Lucian Freud (*English*)
Caspar David Friedrich
 (*German*)
Roger Fry (*English*)
Henry Fuseli (*Swiss*)
Naum Gabo (*Russian-U.S.*)
Thomas Gainsborough
 (*English*)
Henri Gaudier-Brzeska
 (*French*)
Paul Gauguin (*French*)
Gentile da Fabriano (*Italian*)
Lorenzo Ghiberti (*Italian*)
Domenico Ghirlandaio
 (*Italian*)
Alberto Giacometti (*Swiss*)
Giambologna (*Italian*)
Grinling Gibbons (*Dutch*)
Gilbert (Proesch) and

ARTISTS

George (Passmore) (*English*)
Eric Gill (*English*)
Giorgione da Castelfranco (*Italian*)
Giotto di Bondone (*Italian*)
Giulio Romano (*Italian*)
Hugo van der Goes (*Flemish*)
Julio González (*Spanish*)
Arshile Gorky (*U.S.*)
Francisco de Goya (*Spanish*)
Jan van Goyen (*Dutch*)
Duncan Grant (*Scottish*)
Jean Baptiste Greuze (*French*)
Juan Gris (*Spanish*)
Antoine Jean Gros (*French*)
George Grosz (*German-U.S.*)
Grünewald (*German*)
Francesco Guardi (*Italian*)
François Gérard (*French*)
Théodore Géricault (*French*)
Frans Hals (*Dutch*)
Richard Hamilton (*English*)
Ando Hiroshige (*Japanese*)
Damien Hirst (*English*)
Meindert Hobbema (*Dutch*)
David Hockney (*English*)
Hans Hofmann (*German-U.S.*)
William Hogarth (*English*)
Katsushika Hokusai (*Japanese*)
Hans Holbein (*German*)
Winslow Homer (*U.S.*)
Pieter de Hooch *or* Hoogh (*Dutch*)
Edward Hopper (*U.S.*)
Jean Antoine Houdon (*French*)
William Holman Hunt (*English*)
Jean Auguste Dominique Ingres (*French*)
Augustus John (*Welsh*)
Gwen John (*Welsh*)
Jasper Johns (*U.S.*)
Johan Barthold Jongkind (*Dutch*)
Jacob Jordaens (*Flemish*)
Wassily Kandinsky (*Russian*)
Angelica Kauffmann (*Swiss*)
Ernst Ludwig Kirchner (*German*)
Ron B. Kitaj (*U.S.*)

Paul Klee (*Swiss*)
Gustav Klimt (*Austrian*)
Franz Kline (*U.S.*)
Godfrey Kneller (*German-English*)
Laura Knight (*English*)
Oscar Kokoschka (*Austrian*)
Willem de Kooning (*Dutch-U.S.*)
Leon Kossoff (*English*)
Georges de La Tour (*French*)
Edwin Landseer (*English*)
Thomas Lawrence (*English*)
Charles Lebrun (*French*)
Fernand Léger (*French*)
Wilhelm Lehmbruck (*German*)
Frederic Leighton (*English*)
Peter Lely (*Dutch-English*)
Leonardo da Vinci (*Italian*)
Wyndham Lewis (*British*)
Roy Lichtenstein (*U.S.*)
Norman Alfred William Lindsay (*Australian*)
Jacques Lipchitz (*Lithuanian-U.S.*)
Filippino Lippi (*Italian*)
L(awrence) S(tephen) Lowry (*English*)
Lysippus (*Greek*)
Jan Mabuse (*Flemish*)
Charles Rennie Mackintosh (*Scottish*)
René Magritte (*Belgian*)
Aristide Maillol (*French*)
Kasimir Severinovich Malevich (*Russian*)
Edouard Manet (*French*)
Andrea Mantegna (*Italian*)
Franz Marc (*German*)
John Martin (*English*)
Simone Martini (*Italian*)
Masaccio (*Italian*)
Quentin Massys (*Flemish*)
Henri Matisse (*French*)
Hans Memling *or* Memlinc (*Flemish*)
Franz Xavier Messerschmidt (*Austrian*)
Ivan Mestrovic (*Yugoslav-U.S.*)
Michelangelo Buonarroti (*Italian*)
Michelozzi Michelozzo (*Italian*)
John Everett Millais (*English*)

Jean François Millet (*French*)
Joan Miró (*Spanish*)
Amedeo Modigliani (*Italian*)
László Moholy-Nagy (*Hungarian*)
Piet Mondrian (*Dutch*)
Claude Oscar Monet (*French*)
Henry Moore (*British*)
Gustave Moreau (*French*)
Berthe Morisot (*French*)
William Morris (*English*)
Samuel Finley Breese Morse (*U.S.*)
Grandma Moses (*U.S.*)
Edvard Munch (*Norwegian*)
Alfred Munnings (*English*)
Bartolomé Esteban Murillo (*Spanish*)
Myron (*Greek*)
Paul Nash (*English*)
Ernst Wilhelm Nay (*German*)
Barnett Newman (*U.S.*)
Ben Nicholson (*English*)
Sidney Nolan (*Australian*)
Emil Nolde (*German*)
Joseph Nollekens (*Dutch-English*)
Georgia O'Keefe (*U.S.*)
Claes Oldenburg (*Swedish-U.S.*)
Orcagna (*Italian*)
José Clemente Orozco (*Mexican*)
Jean Baptiste Oudry (*French*)
Palma Vecchio (*Italian*)
Samuel Palmer (*English*)
Eduardo Paolozzi (*Scottish*)
Parmigianino (*Italian*)
Victor Pasmore (*English*)
Joachim Patinir *or* Patenier (*Flemish*)
Perugino (*Italian*)
Baldassare Peruzzi (*Italian*)
Antoine Pevsner (*Russian-French*)
Phidias (*Greek*)
Francis Picabia (*French*)
Pablo Picasso (*Spanish*)
Piero della Francesca (*Italian*)
Piero di Cosimo (*Italian*)
Pietro da Cortona (*Italian*)
Jean Baptiste Pigalle (*French*)
Germain Pilon (*French*)
Pinturicchio (*Italian*)

John Piper (*English*)
Pisanello (*Italian*)
Andrea Pisano (*Italian*)
Giovanni Pisano (*Italian*)
Nicola Pisano (*Italian*)
Camille Pissarro (*French*)
Antonio del Pollaiuolo
 (*Italian*)
Piero del Pollaiuolo (*Italian*)
Jackson Pollock (*U.S.*)
Polyclitus (*Greek*)
Polygnotus (*Greek*)
Pontormo (*Italian*)
Paulus Potter (*Dutch*)
Nicolas Poussin (*French*)
Praxiteles (*Greek*)
Pierre Paul Prud'hon
 (*French*)
Pierre Puget (*French*)
Pierre Puvis de Chavannes
 (*French*)
Jacopa della Quercia
 (*Italian*)
Arthur Rackham (*English*)
Henry Raeburn (*Scottish*)
Allan Ramsay (*Scottish*)
Raphael (*Italian*)
Robert Rauschenberg (*U.S.*)
Man Ray (*U.S.*)
Odilon Redon (*French*)
Rembrandt Harmensz van
 Rijn (*Dutch*)
Guido Reni (*Italian*)
Pierre Auguste Renoir
 (*French*)
Joshua Reynolds (*English*)
José de Ribera (*Spanish*)
Bridget Riley (*English*)
Diego Rivera (*Mexican*)
Andrea della Robbia
 (*Italian*)
Luca della Robbia (*Italian*)
Alexander Mikhailovich
 Rodchenko (*Russian*)
Auguste Rodin (*French*)
George Romney (*English*)
Salvator Rosa (*Italian*)
Dante Gabriel Rossetti
 (*English*)
Mark Rothko (*U.S.*)
Geroges Rouault (*French*)
Louis-François Roubiliac *or*
 Roubillac (*French*)
Henri Julien Rousseau
 (*French*)

Théodore Rousseau (*French*)
Peter Paul Rubens (*Flemish*)
Rublyov *or* Rublev Andrei
 (*Russian*)
Jacob van Ruisdael (*Dutch*)
Philipp Otto Runge
 (*German*)
Salomen van Ruysdael
 (*Dutch*)
John Singer Sargent (*U.S.*)
Egon Schiele (*Austrian*)
Martin Schongauer
 (*German*)
Kurt Schwitters (*German*)
Scopas (*Greek*)
Maurice Sendak (*U.S.*)
Sesshu (*Japanese*)
Georges Seurat (*French*)
Ben Shahn (*U.S.*)
Walter Richard Sickert
 (*British*)
Paul Signac (*French*)
Luca Signorelli (*Italian*)
David Alfaro Siqueiros
 (*Mexican*)
Alfred Sisley (*French*)
John Sloan (*U.S.*)
Claus Sluter (*Dutch*)
David Smith (*U.S.*)
Chaim Soutine (*Lithuanian-
 French*)
Stanley Spencer (*English*)
Jan Steen (*Dutch*)
Veit Stoss (*German*)
George Stubbs (*English*)
Graham Sutherland
 (*English*)
Yves Tanguy (*French*)
Vladimir Tatlin (*Russian*)
David Teniers the Elder
 (*Flemish*)
David Teniers the Younger
 (*Flemish*)
Gerard Ter Borch *or*
 Terborch (*Dutch*)
Hendrik Terbrugghen
 (*Dutch*)
James Thornhill (*English*)
Bertel Thorvaldsen (*Danish*)
Giambattista Tiepolo
 (*Italian*)
Jacopo Tintoretto (*Italian*)
James Jacques Joseph Tissot
 (*French*)
Titian (*Italian*)

Henri Marie Raymond de
 Toulouse-Lautrec (*French*)
J(oseph) M(allord) W(illiam)
 Turner (*English*)
Paolo Uccello (*Italian*)
Utagawa Kuniyoshi
 (*Japanese*)
Maurice Utrillo (*French*)
Adriaen van de Velde
 (*Dutch*)
Willem van de Velde the
 Elder (*Dutch*)
Willem van de Velde the
 Younger (*Dutch*)
Rogier van der Weyden
 (*Flemish*)
Anthony Van Dyck
 (*Flemish*)
Jan van Eyck (*Flemish*)
Vincent van Gogh (*Dutch*)
Victor Vasarely (*Hungarian-
 French*)
Giorgio Vasari (*Italian*)
Diego Rodríguez de Silva y
 Velázquez (*Spanish*)
Jan Vermeer (*Dutch*)
Paolo Veronese (*Italian*)
Andrea del Verrocchio
 (*Italian*)
Élisabeth Vigée-Lebrun
 (*French*)
Jacques Villon (*French*)
Maurice de Vlaminck
 (*French*)
Andy Warhol (*U.S.*)
Jean Antoine Watteau
 (*French*)
George Frederick Watts
 (*English*)
Benjamin West (*U.S.*)
James Abbott McNeill
 Whistler (*U.S.*)
Richard Wilson (*Welsh*)
Joseph Wright (*English*)
Xia Gui *or* Hsia Kuei
 (*Chinese*)
Zeuxis (*Greek*)
Johann Zoffany (*German*)
Anders Zorn (*Swedish*)
Gaetano Giulio Zumbo
 (*Italian*)
Francisco Zurbarán
 (*Spanish*)

─AUSTRALIAN STATES AND TERRITORIES─

Australian Capital Territory
New South Wales
Northern Territory

Queensland
South Australia
Tasmania

Victoria
Western Australia

─── BAYS ───

Aboukir *or* Abukir Bay
Bay of Acre
Algoa Bay
Ariake Bay
Baffin Bay
Bay of Bengal
Bay of Biscay
Biscayne Bay
Bombetoka Bay
Botany Bay
Buzzards Bay
Bay of Cádiz
Caernarvon Bay
Callao Bay
Bay of Campeche
Cape Cod Bay
Cardigan Bay
Carmarthen Bay
Casco Bay
Chesapeake Bay
Cienfuegos Bay
Colwyn Bay
Corpus Christi Bay
Delagoa Bay
Delaware Bay
Discovery Bay
Dublin Bay
Dundalk Bay
Dvina Bay
Encounter Bay
Bay of Espírito Santo
False Bay
Famagusta Bay

Florida Bay
Bay of Fundy
Galway Bay
Bay of Gdansk
Georgian Bay
Bay of Gibraltar
Guanabara Bay
Guantánamo Bay
Hangzhou Bay
Hawke Bay
Hudson Bay
Inhambane Bay
Ise Bay
James Bay
Jervis Bay
Jiazhou Bay
Bay of Kaválla
Korea Bay
Kuskokwim Bay
Lobito Bay
Lützow-Holm Bay
Magdalena Bay
Manila Bay
Massachusetts Bay
Milne Bay
Mobile Bay
Montego Bay
Morecambe Bay
Moreton Bay
Narragansett Bay
Newark Bay
Bay of Naples
New York Bay

Omura Bay
Osaka Bay
Passamaquoddy Bay
Bay of Pigs
Bay of Plenty
Port Phillip Bay
Poverty Bay
Quiberon Bay
San Francisco Bay
San Pedro Bay
Santiago Bay
Setúbal Bay
Sligo Bay
St Austell Bay
Bay of St Michel
Swansea Bay
Table Bay
Tampa Bay
Tasman Bay
Thunder Bay
Tokyo Bay
Toyama Bay
Tralee Bay
Bay of Trincomalee
Ungava Bay
Urado Bay
Vigo Bay
Bay of Vlorë
Vyborg Bay
Walvis *or* Walfish Bay
Whitley Bay
Wick Bay

WORD POWER

CANADIAN PROVINCES

Province	Abbreviation	Province	Abbreviation
Alberta	AB	Nunavut	NU
British Columbia	BC	Ontario	ON
Manitoba	MB	Prince Edward Island	PE
New Brunswick	NB	Quebec	PQ
Newfoundland	NF	Saskatchewan	SK
Northwest Territories	NWT	Yukon Territory	YT
Nova Scotia	NS		

CANALS

Berezina Canal
Bridgewater Canal
Caledonian Canal
Champlain Canal
Corinth Canal
Dortmund-Ems Canal
Erie Canal
Göta Canal
Grand Canal

Grand Union Canal
Houston Ship Canal
Kiel Canal
Manchester Ship Canal
Canal du Midi
Mittelland Canal
Moscow Canal
New York State Barge
  Canal

Canal do Norte
Panama Canal
Rhine-Herne Canal
Canal de São Gonçalo
Suez Canal
Twente Canal
Welland Canal

WORD POWER

─── CAPITAL CITIES ───

City	Country	City	Country
Abu Dhabi	United Arab	Caracas	Venezuela
Emirates		Cardiff	Wales
Abuja	Nigeria	Castries	St. Lucia
Accra	Ghana	Cayenne	French Guiana
Addis Ababa	Ethiopia	Colombo	Sri Lanka
Astana	Kazakhstan	Conakry *or* Konakry	Guinea
Algiers	Algeria	Copenhagen	Denmark
Amman	Jordan	Dakar	Senegal
Amsterdam	Netherlands	Damascus	Syria
Andorra la Vella	Andorra	Delhi	India
Ankara	Turkey	Dhaka *or* Dacca	Bangladesh
Antananarivo	Madagascar	Dili	East Timor
Apia	Samoa	Djibouti *or* Jibouti	Djibouti *or* Jibouti
Ashkhabad	Turkmenistan	Dodoma	Tanzania
Asmara	Eritrea	Doha	Qatar
Asunción	Paraguay	Douglas	Isle of Man
Athens	Greece	Dublin	Republic of Ireland
Baghdad	Iraq	Dushanbe	Tajikistan
Baku	Azerbaijan	Edinburgh	Scotland
Bamako	Mali	Fort-de-France	Martinique
Bandar Seri Begawan	Brunei	Freetown	Sierra Leone
Bangkok	Thailand	Funafuti	Tuvalu
Bangui	Central African	Gaborone	Botswana
	Republic	Georgetown	Guyana
Banjul	Gambia	Guatemala City	Guatemala
Basseterre	St. Kitts and Nevis	Hanoi	Vietnam
Beijing	People's Republic	Harare	Zimbabwe
	of China	Havana	Cuba
Beirut *or* Beyrouth	Lebanon	Helsinki	Finland
Belfast	Northern Ireland	Honiara	Solomon Islands
Belgrade	Yugoslavia (Serbia	Islamabad	Pakistan
	and Montenegro)	Jakarta *or* Djakarta	Indonesia
Belmopan	Belize	Jerusalem	Israel
Berlin	Germany	Kabul	Afghanistan
Berne	Switzerland	Kampala	Uganda
Bishkek	Kyrgyzstan	Katmandu *or*	Nepal
Bissau	Guinea-Bissau	Kathmandu	
Bloemfontein	judicial capital of	Khartoum *or* Khartum	Sudan
	South Africa	Kiev	Ukraine
Bogotá	Colombia	Kigali	Rwanda
Brasília	Brazil	Kingston	Jamaica
Bratislava	Slovakia	Kingstown	St. Vincent and the
Brazzaville	Congo (Republic of)		Grenadines
Bridgetown	Barbados	Kinshasa	Congo
Brussels	Belgium		(Democratic
Bucharest	Romania		Republic of)
Budapest	Hungary	Kishinev	Moldova
Buenos Aires	Argentina	Palikir	Micronesia
Bujumbura	Burundi	Koror	Palau
Cairo	Egypt	Kuala Lumpur	Malaysia
Canberra	Australia	Kuwait	Kuwait
Cape Town	legislative capital	La Paz	administrative
	of South Africa		capital of Bolivia

City	Country	City	Country
Libreville	Gabon	Prague	Czech Republic
Lilongwe	Malawi	Praia	Cape Verde
Lima	Peru	Pretoria	administrative
Lisbon	Portugal		capital of South
Ljubljana	Slovenia		Africa
Lomé	Togo	Pristina	Kosovo (Federal
London	United Kingdom		Republic of
Luanda	Angola		Yugoslavia)
Lusaka	Zambia	Pyongyang	North Korea
Luxembourg	Luxembourg	Quito	Ecuador
Madrid	Spain	Rabat	Morocco
Majuro	Marshall Islands	Reykjavik	Iceland
Malabo	Equatorial Guinea	Riga	Latvia
Malé	Maldives	Riyadh	Saudi Arabia
Managua	Nicaragua	Rome	Italy
Manama	Bahrain	Roseau	Dominica
Manila	Philippines	San`a	Yemen
Maputo	Mozambique	San José	Costa Rica
Maseru	Lesotho	San Juan	Puerto Rico
Mbabane	Swaziland	San Marino	San Marino
Mexico City	Mexico	San Salvador	El Slavador
Minsk	Belarus	Santiago	Chile
Mogadishu	Somalia	Santo Domingo	Dominican
Monaco-Ville	Monaco	Republic	
Monrovia	Liberia	São Tomé	São Tomé and
Montevideo	Uruguay		Principe
Moroni	Comoros	Sarajevo	Bosnia and
Moscow	Russia		Herzegovina
Muscat	Oman	Seoul	South Korea
Nairobi	Kenya	Singapore	Singapore
Nassau	Bahamas	Skopje	Macedonia
Ndjamena	Chad	Sofia	Bulgaria
Niamey	Niger	St. George's	Grenada
Nicosia	Cyprus	St. John's	Antigua and
Nouakchott	Mauritania		Barbuda
Nuku'alofa	Tonga	Stockholm	Sweden
Nuuk	Greenland	Sucre	legislative and
Oslo	Norway		judicial capital
Ottawa	Canada		of Bolivia
Ouagadougou	Burkina-Faso	Suva	Fiji
Panama City	Panama	Taipei	Taiwan
Paramaribo	Suriname	Tallinn	Estonia
Paris	France	Tarawa	Kiribati
Phnom Penh	Cambodia	Tashkent	Uzbekistan
Pishpek	Kirghizia	Tbilisi	Georgia
Port-au-Prince	Haiti	Tegucigalpa	Honduras
Port Louis	Mauritius	Tehran	Iran
Port Moresby	Papua New	Tel Aviv	Israel
Guinea		Thimphu	Bhutan
Port of Spain	Trinidad and	Tirana	Albania
	Tobago	Tokyo	Japan
Porto Novo	Benin	Tripoli	Libya

CAPITAL CITIES

City	Country	City	Country
Tunis	Tunisia	Washington DC	United States of
Ulan Bator	Mongolia		America
Vaduz	Liechtenstein	Wellington	New Zealand
Valletta	Malta	Windhoek	Namibia
Vatican City	Vatican City	Yamoussoukro	Côte d'Ivoire
Victoria	Seychelles	Yangon (Rangoon)	Myanmar (Burma)
Vienna	Austria	Yaoundé *or* Yaunde	Cameroon
Vientiane	Laos	Yaren	Nauru
Port Vila	Vanuatu	Yerevan	Armenia
Vilnius	Lithuania	Zagreb	Croatia
Warsaw	Poland		

CASTLES

Aberystwyth	Chillon	Leeds
Amboise	Colditz	Leicester
Arundel	Conwy	Lincoln
Ashby de la Zouch	Crathes	Ludlow
Ashford	Culzean	Malahide
Aydon	Darnaway	Monmouth
Ballindalloch	Dinan	Otranto
Balmoral	Drum	Pembroke
Balvenie	Dublin	Pendennis
Barnard	Dunnottar	Pontefract
Beaumaris	Dunsinane	Portlick
Beeston	Dunstaffnage	Rait
Belvoir	Durham	Restormel
Berkeley	Edinburgh	Richmond
Berkhamstead	Eilean Donan	Rock of Cashel
Berwick-upon-Tweed	Esterháza	Rithes
Blarney	Farney	St Mawes
Blois	Forfar	Sherborne
Braemar	Fotheringhay	Scarborough
Brodie	Glamis	Skipton
Bunraity	Harlech	Stirling
Cabra	Heidelberg	Stuart
Caerlaverock	Herstmonceux	Taymouth
Caernarfon	Inverness	Tintagel
Caerphilly	Kenilworth	Torún
Cahir	Kilkea	Trausnitz
Canossa	Kilkenny	Trim
Carisbrooke	Killaghy	Urquhart
Carmarthen	Kilravock	Vaduz
Carrickfergus	Lancaster	Vincennes
Château-Raoul	Leamaneh	Wartburg
Cheb	Launceston	Warwick

WORD POWER

Classical composers

Adolphe Adam (*French*)
John Adams (*U.S.*)
Isaac Albéniz (*Spanish*)
Tomaso Albinoni (*Italian*)
Gregorio Allegri (*Italian*)
William Alwyn (*British*)
George Antheil (*U.S.*)
Thomas Arne (*English*)
Malcolm Arnold (*British*)
Daniel François Espirit Auber (*French*)
Georges Auric (*French*)
Carl Philipp Emanuel Bach (*German*)
Johann Christian Bach (*German*)
Johann Christoph Friedrich Bach (*German*)
Johann Sebastian Bach (*German*)
Wilhelm Friedemann Bach (*German*)
Mily Alexeyevich Balakirev (*Russian*)
Granville Bantock (*British*)
Samuel Barber (*U.S.*)
Béla Bartók (*Hungarian*)
Arnold Bax (*British*)
Ludwig van Beethoven (*German*)
Vincenzo Bellini (*Italian*)
Arthur Benjamin (*Australian*)
Richard Rodney Bennett (*British*)
Alban Berg (*Austrian*)
Luciano Berio (*Italian*)
Lennox Berkeley (*British*)
Hector Berlioz (*French*)
Leonard Bernstein (*U.S.*)
Heinrich Biber (*German*)
Harrison Birtwhistle (*British*)
Georges Bizet (*French*)
Arthur Bliss (*British*)
Ernest Bloch (*U.S.*)
Luigi Boccherini (*Italian*)
Arrigo Boito (*Italian*)
Francesco Antonio Bonporti (*Italian*)
Aleksandr Porfirevich Borodin (*Russian*)
Pierre Boulez (*French*)
William Boyce (*English*)
Johannes Brahms (*German*)
Havergal Brian (*British*)
Frank Bridge (*British*)
Benjamin Britten (*British*)
Max Bruch (*German*)
Anton Bruckner (*Austrian*)
John Bull (*English*)
George Butterworth (*British*)
Dietrich Buxtehude (*Danish*)
William Byrd (*English*)
John Cage (*U.S.*)

Joseph Canteloube (*French*)
John Alden Carpenter (*U.S.*)
Eliot Carter (*U.S.*)
Robert Carver (*Scottish*)
Pablo Casals (*Spanish*)
Emmanuel Chabrier (*French*)
Gustave Charpentier (*French*)
Marc-Antoine Charpentier (*French*)
Ernest Chausson (*French*)
Luigi Cherubini (*Italian*)
Frédéric Chopin (*Polish-French*)
Domenico Cimarosa (*Italian*)
Jeremiah Clarke (*English*)
Samuel Coleridge-Taylor (*British*)
Aaron Copland (*U.S.*)
Arcangelo Corelli (*Italian*)
François Couperin (*French*)
Karl Czerny (*Austrian*)
Luigi Dallapiccola (*Italian*)
Peter Maxwell Davies (*British*)
Claude Debussy (*French*)
Léo Delibes (*French*)
Frederick Delius (*British*)
Josquin des Prés (*Flemish*)
Vincent d'Indy (*French*)
Ernst von Dohnányi (*Hungarian*)
Gaetano Donizetti (*Italian*)
Antal Doráti (*U.S.*)
John Dowland (*English*)
Paul Dukas (*French*)
John Dunstable (*English*)
Henri Duparc (*French*)
Marcel Dupré (*French*)
Maurice Duruflé (*French*)
Henri Dutilleux (*French*)
Antonín Dvořák (*Czech*)
Edward Elgar (*British*)
Georges Enesco (*Romanian*)
Manuel de Falla (*Spanish*)
John Farmer (*English*)
Gabriel Fauré (*French*)
John Field (*Irish*)
Gerald Finzi (*British*)
Friedrich von Flotow (*German*)
César Franck (*Belgian-French*)
Girolamo Frescobaldi (*Italian*)
Wilhelm Fürtwangler (*German*)
Andrea Gabrieli (*Italian*)
Giovanni Gabrieli (*Italian*)
George Gershwin (*U.S.*)
Carlo Gesualdo (*Italian*)
Orlando Gibbons (*English*)

Classical composers (continued)

Alberto Ginastera (*Argentinian*)
Philip Glass (*U.S.*)
Aleksandr Konstantinovich Glazunov (*Russian*)
Mikhail Ivanovich Glinka (*Russian*)
Christoph Willibald Gluck (*German*)
Eugene Goossens (*Belgian-British*)
Henryk Górecki (*Polish*)
Charles François Gounod (*French*)
Percy Grainger (*Australian*)
Enrique Granados (*Spanish*)
Edvard Grieg (*Norwegian*)
Ivor Gurney (*British*)
Fromental Halévy (*French*)
George Frederick Handel (*German*)
Roy Harris (*U.S.*)
Franz Joseph Haydn (*Austrian*)
Michael Haydn (*Austrian*)
Hans Werner Henze (*German*)
Hildegard of Bingen (*German*)
Paul Hindemith (*German*)
Heinz Holliger (*Swiss*)
Gustav Holst (*British*)
Arthur Honegger (*French*)
Johann Nepomuk Hummel (*German*)
Englebert Humperdinck (*German*)
Jacques Ibert (*French*)
John Ireland (*British*)
Charles Ives (*U.S.*)
Leoš Janáček (*Czech*)
Émile Jaques-Dalcroze (*Swiss*)
Joseph Joachim (*Hungarian*)
Daniel Jones (*British*)
Aram Ilich Khachaturian (*Armenian*)
Otto Klemperer (*German*)
Oliver Knussen (*British*)
Zoltán Kodály (*Hungarian*)
Erich Korngold (*Austrian*)
Franz Krommer (*Moravian*)
Raphael Kubelik (*Czech*)
Édouard Lalo (*French*)
Constant Lambert (*British*)
Roland de Lassus (*Flemish*)
Henry Lawes (*English*)
William Lawes (*English*)
Franz Lehár (*Hungarian*)
Ruggiero Leoncavallo (*Italian*)
György Ligeti (*Hungarian*)
Franz Liszt (*Hungarian*)
George Lloyd (*British*)
Matthew Locke (*English*)
Karl Loewe (*German*)

Jean Baptiste Lully (*Italian-French*)
Witold Lutosławski (*Polish*)
Elisabeth Lutyens (*British*)
Guillaume de Machaut (*French*)
James MacMillan (*British*)
Elizabeth Maconchy (*British*)
Gustav Mahler (*Austrian*)
Luca Marenzio (*Italian*)
Frank Martin (*Swiss*)
Bohuslav Martinů (*Czech*)
Steve Martland (*British*)
Pietro Mascagni (*Italian*)
Jules Émile Frédéric Massenet (*French*)
Fanny Mendelssohn (*German*)
Felix Mendelssohn (*German*)
Gian Carlo Menotti (*Italian*)
André Messager (*French*)
Olivier Messiaen (*French*)
Giacomo Meyerbeer (*German*)
Darius Milhaud (*French*)
Claudio Monteverdi (*Italian*)
Thomas Morley (*English*)
Leopold Mozart (*Austrian*)
Wolfgang Amadeus Mozart (*Austrian*)
Thea Musgrave (*British*)
Modest Petrovich Mussorgsky (*Russian*)
Carl Otto Ehrenfried Nicolai (*German*)
Carl Nielsen (*Danish*)
Luigi Nono (*Italian*)
Michael Nyman (*British*)
Johannes Ockeghem (*Flemish*)
Jacques Offenbach (*German-French*)
John Ogdon (*British*)
Carl Orff (*German*)
Johann Pachelbel (*German*)
Ignace Jan Paderewski (*Polish*)
Niccolò Paganini (*Italian*)
Giovanni Pierluigi da Palestrina (*Italian*)
Andrzej Panufnik (*Polish-British*)
Hubert Parry (*British*)
Arvo Pärt (*Estonian*)
Krzystof Penderecki (*Polish*)
Giovanni Battista Pergolesi (*Italian*)
Francis Poulenc (*French*)
Michael Praetorius (*German*)
Sergei Sergeyevich Prokofiev (*Russian*)
Giacomo Puccini (*Italian*)
Henry Purcell (*English*)
Sergei Vassilievich Rachmaninov (*Russian*)
Jean Philippe Rameau (*French*)
Maurice Ravel (*French*)
Alan Rawsthorne (*British*)

WORD POWER

Classical composers (continued)

Max Reger (*German*)
Steve Reich (*U.S.*)
Ottorino Respighi (*Italian*)
Vittorio Rieti (*Italian*)
Nikolai Andreyevich Rimsky-Korsakov
  (*Russian*)
Joaquín Rodrigo (*Spanish*)
Sigmund Romberg (*U.S.*)
Gioacchino Antonio Rossini (*Italian*)
Mstislav Leopoldovich Rostropovich
  (*Russian*)
Claude Joseph Rouget de Lisle (*French*)
Albert Roussel (*French*)
Edmund Rubbra (*British*)
Anton Grigorevich Rubinstein (*Russian*)
Camille Saint-Saëns (*French*)
Antonio Salieri (*Italian*)
Erik Satie (*French*)
Alessandro Scarlatti (*Italian*)
Domenico Scarlatti (*Italian*)
Artur Schnabel (*Austrian-U.S.*)
Alfred Schnittke (*Russian*)
Arnold Schoenberg (*Austrian*)
Franz Schubert (*Austrian*)
William Schuman (*U.S.*)
Clara Schumann (*German*)
Robert Schumann (*German*)
Heinrich Schütz (*German*)
Aleksandr Nikolayvich Scriabin (*Russian*)
Peter Sculthorpe (*Australian*)
Roger Sessions (*U.S.*)
Dmitri Dmitriyevich Shostakovich (*Russian*)
Jean Sibelius (*Finnish*)
Robert Simpson (*English*)
Bedřich Smetana (*Czech*)
Ethel Smyth (*British*)
John Philip Sousa (*U.S.*)
John Stainer (*British*)
Charles Stanford (*Irish*)
Karlheinz Stockhausen (*German*)

Oscar Straus (*French*)
Johann Strauss, the elder (*Austrian*)
Johann Strauss, the younger (*Austrian*)
Richard Strauss (*German*)
Igor Fyodorovich Stravinsky (*Russian-U.S.*)
Jan Pieterszoon Sweelinck (*Dutch*)
Karol Szymanowski (*Polish*)
Toru Takemitsu (*Japanese*)
Thomas Tallis (*English*)
John Tavener (*British*)
John Taverner (*English*)
Pyotr Ilyich Tchaikovsky (*Russian*)
Georg Philipp Telemann (*German*)
Mikis Theodorakis (*Greek*)
Ambroise Thomas (*French*)
Virgil Thomson (*U.S.*)
Michael Tippett (*British*)
Paul Tortelier (*French*)
Edgar Varèse (*French-U.S.*)
Ralph Vaughan Williams (*British*)
Giuseppi Verdi (*Italian*)
Tomás Luis de Victoria (*Spanish*)
Heitor Villa-Lobos (*Brazilian*)
Antonio Vivaldi (*Italian*)
Richard Wagner (*German*)
William Walton (*British*)
David Ward (*British*)
Peter Warlock (*British*)
Carl Maria von Weber (*German*)
Anton Webern (*Austrian*)
Thomas Weelkes (*English*)
Judith Weir (*British*)
Egon Wellesz (*Austrian-British*)
Gillian Whitehead (*New Zealand*)
Malcolm Williamson (*Australian*)
Hugo Wolf (*Austrian*)
Ermanno Wolf-Ferrari (*Italian*)
Yannis Xenakis (*Romanian-Greek*)
Alexander Zemlinsky (*Austrian*)

Popular composers, songwriters and lyricists

Harold Arlen (*U.S.*)
Burt Bacharach (*U.S.*)
Joan Baez (*U.S.*)
John Barry (*British*)
Lionel Bart (*British*)
Irving Berlin (*Russian-U.S.*)
Leonard Bernstein (*U.S.*)
David Bowie (*English*)
Jacques Brel (*Belgian*)
Nacio Herb Brown (*U.S.*)
Sammy Cahn (*U.S.*)
Hoagy Carmichael (*U.S.*)
George Cohan (*U.S.*)
Leonard Cohen (*Canadian*)
Noel Coward (*English*)
Willie Dixon (*U.S.*)
Lamont Dozier (*U.S.*)
Vernon Duke (*Russian-U.S.*)
Bob Dylan (*U.S.*)
Duke Ellington (*U.S.*)
Stephen Foster (*U.S.*)
George Gershwin (*U.S.*)
W(illiam) S(chwenck) Gilbert (*British*)
Gerry Goffin (*U.S.*)
Jerry Goldsmith (*U.S.*)
Woody Guthrie (*U.S.*)
W(illiam) C(hristopher) Handy (*U.S.*)
Marvin Hamlisch (*U.S.*)
Oscar Hammerstein (*U.S.*)
Lorenz Hart (*U.S.*)
Jerry Herman (*U.S.*)
Brian Holland (*U.S.*)
Eddie Holland (*U.S.*)
Mick Jagger (*British*)
Maurice Jarre (*French*)
Antonio Carlos Jobim (*Brazilian*)
Elton John (*British*)
Robert Johnson (*U.S.*)
Jerome (David) Kern (*U.S.*)
Carole King (*U.S.*)
Kris Kristofferson (*U.S.*)
Huddie 'Leadbelly' Ledbetter (*U.S.*)
Tom Lehrer (*U.S.*)
John Lennon (*British*)
Alan Jay Lerner (*U.S.*)

Jerry Lieber (*U.S.*)
Jay Livingston (*U.S.*)
Andrew Lloyd-Webber (*British*)
Frank Loesser (*U.S.*)
Frederick Loewe (*Austrian-U.S.*)
Paul McCartney (*British*)
Ewan McColl (*British*)
Kirsty McColl (*British*)
Jimmy McHugh (*U.S.*)
Henry Mancini (*U.S.*)
Barry Manilow (*U.S.*)
Barry Mann (*U.S.*)
Joni Mitchell (*Canadian*)
Thelonious (Sphere) Monk (*U.S.*)
Van Morrison (*Irish*)
Willie Nelson (*U.S.*)
Ivor Novello (*British*)
Doc Pomus (*U.S.*)
Cole Porter (*U.S.*)
Keith Richards (*British*)
William 'Smokey' Robinson (*U.S.*)
Tim Rice (*British*)
Richard Rodgers (*U.S.*)
Sigmund Romberg (*Hungarian-U.S.*)
Howard Shore (*Canadian*)
Paul Simon (*U.S.*)
Stephen Sondheim (*U.S.*)
Mike Stoller (*U.S.*)
Billy Strayhorn (*U.S.*)
Barrett Strong (*U.S.*)
Jule Styne (*U.S.*)
Arthur Sullivan (*British*)
Allen Toussaint (*U.S.*)
Johnny Van Heusen (*U.S.*)
Tom Waites (*U.S.*)
Harry Warren (*U.S.*)
Jimmy Webb (*U.S.*)
Cynthia Weil (*U.S.*)
Kurt Weill (*German-U.S.*)
Norman Whitfield (*U.S.*)
Hank Williams (*U.S.*)
John Williams (*U.S.*)
Brian Wilson (*U.S.*)
Vincent Youmans (*U.S.*)

WORD POWER

CONTINENTS

Africa	Australia	South America
Antarctica	Europe	
Asia	North America	

COUNTIES

English counties

Bedfordshire
Berkshire
Bristol
Buckinghamshire
Cambridgeshire
Cheshire
Cornwall
Cumbria
Derbyshire
Devon
Dorset
Durham
East Riding of Yorkshire
East Sussex
Essex
Gloucestershire

Greater London
Greater Manchester
Hampshire
Herefordshire
Hertfordshire
Isle of Wight
Kent
Lancashire
Leicestershire
Lincolnshire
Merseyside
Norfolk
Northamptonshire
Northumberland
North Yorkshire
Nottinghamshire

Oxfordshire
Rutland
Shropshire
Somerset
South Yorkshire
Staffordshire
Suffolk
Surrey
Tyne and Wear
Warwickshire
West Midlands
West Sussex
West Yorkshire
Wiltshire
Worcestershire

Scottish counties

Aberdeen City
Aberdeenshire
Angus
Argyll and Bute
City of Edinburgh
Clackmannanshire
Dumfries and Galloway
Dundee City
East Ayrshire
East Dunbartonshire
East Lothian

East Renfrewshire
Falkirk
Fife
Glasgow City
Highland
Inverclyde
Midlothian
Moray
North Ayrshire
North Lanarkshire
Orkney

Perth and Kinross
Renfrewshire
Scottish Borders
Shetland
South Ayrshire
South Lanarkshire
Stirling
West Dunbartonshire
Western Isles (Eilean Siar)
West Lothian

Welsh counties

Clwyd
Dyfed
Gwent

Gwynedd
Mid Glamorgan
Powys

South Glamorgan
West Glamorgan

Northern Irish counties

Antrim
Armagh
Belfast City

Down
Fermanagh
Londonderry

Londonderry City
Tyrone

Republic of Ireland counties

Carlow
Cavan
Clare
Cork
Donegal
Dublin
Galway
Kerry
Kildare

Kilkenny
Laois
Leitrim
Limerick
Longford
Louth
Mayo
Meath
Monaghan

Offaly
Roscommon
Sligo
Tipperary
Waterford
Westmeath
Wexford
Wicklow

COUNTRIES

Afghanistan
Albania
Algeria
American Samoa
Andorra
Angola
Antigua and Barbuda
Argentina
Armenia
Australia
Austria
Azerbaijan
Bahamas
Bahrain
Bangladesh
Barbados
Belarus
Belau
Belgium
Belize
Benin
Bhutan
Bolivia
Bosnia and Herzegovina
Botswana
Brazil
Brunei
Bulgaria
Burkina-Faso
Burundi
Cambodia
Cameroon
Canada
Cape Verde
Central African Republic
Chad
Chile
Colombia
Comoros
Congo (Republic of)
Congo (Democratic
  Republic of)
Costa Rica
Côte d'Ivoire
Croatia
Cuba
Cyprus
Czech Republic
Denmark
Djibouti
Dominica
Dominican Republic
East Timor
Ecuador

Egypt
El Salvador
England
Equatorial Guinea
Eritrea
Estonia
Ethiopia
Fiji
Finland
France
Gabon
Gambia
Georgia
Germany
Ghana
Greece
Greenland
Grenada
Guatemala
Guinea
Guinea-Bissau
Guyana
Haiti
Honduras
Hungary
Iceland
India
Indonesia
Iran
Iraq
Israel
Italy
Jamaica
Japan
Jordan
Kazakhstan
Kenya
Kirghizia
Kiribati
Kuwait
Laos
Latvia
Lebanon
Lesotho
Liberia
Libya
Liechtenstein
Lithuania
Luxembourg
Macedonia
Madagascar
Malawi
Malaysia
Mali

Malta
Marshall Islands
Mauritania
Mauritius
Mexico
Micronesia
Moldova
Monaco
Mongolia
Morocco
Mozambique
Myanmar
Namibia
Nauru
Nepal
Netherlands
New Zealand
Nicaragua
Niger
Nigeria
Northern Ireland
North Korea
Norway
Oman
Pakistan
Panama
Papua New Guinea
Paraguay
People's Republic of China
Peru
Philippines
Poland
Portugal
Puerto Rico
Qatar
Republic of Ireland
Republic of Maldives
Romania
Russia
Rwanda
St Kitts and Nevis
St Lucia
St Vincent and the
  Grenadines
Samoa
San Marino
São Tomé and Principe
Saudi Arabia
Scotland
Senegal
Seychelles
Sierra Leone
Singapore
Slovakia

COUNTRIES

Slovenia
Solomon Islands
Somalia
South Africa
South Korea
Spain
Sri Lanka
Sudan
Surinam
Swaziland
Sweden
Switzerland
Syria
Taiwan

Tajikistan
Tanzania
Thailand
Togo
Tonga
Trinidad and Tobago
Tunisia
Turkey
Turkmenistan
Tuvalu
Uganda
Ukraine
United Arab Emirates
United Kingdom

United States of America
Uruguay
Uzbekistan
Vanuatu
Vatican City
Venezuela
Vietnam
Wales
Yemen
Yugoslavia (Serbia and
  Montenegro)
Zambia
Zimbabwe

CURRENCIES

Country	Currency	Country	Currency
Afghanistan	afghani	Dominican Republic	peso
Albania	lek	East Timor	US dollar
Algeria	Algerian dinar	Ecuador	US dollar
Andorra	euro	Egypt	pound
Angola	kwanza	El Salvador	cólon
Antigua and Barbuda	East Caribbean dollar	Equatorial Guinea	CFA franc
		Eritrea	nakfa
Argentina	peso	Estonia	kroon
Armenia	dram	Ethiopia	birr
Australia	Australian dollar	Fiji	Fiji dollar
Austria	euro	Finland	euro
Azerbaijan	manat	France	euro
Bahamas	Bahamian dollar	French Guiana	French franc
Bahrain	dinar	Gabon	CFA franc
Bangladesh	taka	Gambia	dalasi
Barbados	Barbados dollar	Germany	euro
Belarus	rouble	Ghana	cedi
Belgium	euro	Greece	euro
Belize	Belize dollar	Greenland	Danish krone
Benin	CFA franc	Grenada	East Caribbean dollar
Bhutan	ngultrum		
Bolivia	boliviano	Guatemala	quetzal
Bosnia-Herzegovina	convertible marka	Guinea	Guinea franc
Botswana	pula	Guinea-Bissau	CFA franc
Brazil	real	Guyana	Guyana dollar
Brunei	Brunei dollar	Haiti	gourde
Bulgaria	lev	Honduras	lempira
Burkina-Faso	CFA franc	Hungary	forint
Burundi	Burundi franc	Iceland	krona
Cambodia	riel	India	rupee
Cameroon	CFA franc	Indonesia	rupiah
Canada	Canadian dollar	Iran	rial
Cape Verde	escudo	Iraq	dinar
Central African Republic	CFA franc	Ireland (Republic of)	euro
		Israel	shekel
Chad	CFA franc	Italy	euro
Chile	peso	Jamaica	Jamaican dollar
China	yuan	Japan	yen
Colombia	peso	Jordan	dinar
Comoros	Comorian franc	Kazakhstan	tenge
Congo (Republic of)	CFA franc	Kenya	shilling
Congo (Democratic Republic of)	Congolese franc	Kirghizia	som
		Kiribati	Australian dollar
Costa Rica	cólon	Kosovo	dinar; euro
Côte d'Ivoire	CFA franc	Kuwait	dinar
Croatia	kuna	Kyrgyzstan	som
Cuba	peso	Laos	kip
Cyprus	pound	Latvia	lat
Czech Republic	koruna	Lebanon	pound
Denmark	krone	Lesotho	loti
Djibouti	Djibouti franc	Liberia	Liberian dollar
Dominica	East Caribbean dollar	Libya	dinar
		Liechtenstein	Swiss franc

23

CURRENCIES

Country	Currency	Country	Currency
Lithuania	litas	Samoa	tala
Luxembourg	euro	San Marino	euro
Macedonia	denar	São Tomé and Principe	dobra
Madagascar	Malagasy franc	Saudi Arabia	riyal
Malawi	kwacha	Senegal	CFA franc
Malaysia	ringgit	Seychelles	rupee
Maldives (Republic of)	rufiyaa	Sierra Leone	leone
Mali	CFA franc	Singapore	Singapore dollar
Malta	lira	Slovakia	koruna
Marshall Islands	U.S. dollar	Slovenia	tolar
Mauritania	ouguiya	Solomon Islands	Solomon Islands dollar
Mauritius	rupee		
Mexico	peso	Somalia	shilling
Micronesia	U.S. dollar	South Africa	rand
Moldova	leu	South Korea	won
Monaco	French franc	Spain	euro
Mongolia	tugrik	Sri Lanka	rupee
Montenegro	euro	Sudan	dinar
Montserrat	East Caribbean dollar	Surinam	guilder
		Swaziland	lilangeni
Morocco	dirham	Sweden	krona
Mozambique	metical	Switzerland	Swiss franc
Myanmar	kyat	Syria	pound
Namibia	Namibian dollar	Taiwan	Taiwan dollar
Nauru	Australian dollar	Tajikistan	somoni
Nepal	rupee	Tanzania	shilling
Netherlands	euro	Thailand	baht
New Zealand	New Zealand dollar	Togo	CFA franc
Nicaragua	córdoba	Tonga	pa'anga
Niger	CFA franc	Trinidad and Tobago	Trinidad and Tobago dollar
Nigeria	naira		
North Korea	won	Tunisia	dinar
Norway	krone	Turkey	Turkish lira
Oman	rial	Turkmenistan	manat
Pakistan	rupee	Tuvalu	Australian dollar
Palau	U.S. dollar	Uganda	shilling
Panama	balboa	Ukraine	hryvna
Papua New Guinea	kina	United Arab Emirates	dirham
Paraguay	guarani	United Kingdom	pound sterling
Peru	new sol	United States of America	U.S. dollar
Philippines	Philippine peso		
Poland	zloty	Uruguay	peso
Portugal	euro	Uzbekistan	sum
Qatar	riyal	Vanuatu	vatu
Romania	leu	Vatican City	euro
Russia	rouble	Venezuela	bolívar
Rwanda	Rwanda franc	Vietnam	dong
St. Kitts and Nevis	East Caribbean dollar	Yemen	riyal
		Yugoslavia (Serbia)	dinar
St. Lucia	East Caribbean dollar	Zambia	kwacha
		Zimbabwe	Zimbabwe dollar
St. Vincent and the Grenadines	East Caribbean dollar		

WORD POWER

DESERTS

Arabian
Atacama
Dasht-i-Lut *or* Dasht-e-Lut
Death Valley
Gibson
Gobi

Great Sandy
Great Victoria
Kalahari
Kara Kum
Kyzyl Kum
Libyan

Mohave *or* Mojave
Nubian
Rub'al Khali
Sahara
Taklimakan Shama
Thar

DRAMA

Types of Drama

comedy
comedy of manners
commedia dell'arte
costume piece *or* costume
 drama
farce
Grand Guignol
Jacobean
kabuki

Kathakali
kitchen sink
melodrama
morality play
mystery play
No *or* Noh
passion play
Restoration Comedy
revenge tragedy

shadow play
situation comedy *or* sitcom
sketch
soap opera
street theatre
theatre of cruelty
theatre of the absurd
tragedy
tragicomedy

Dramatists

Aeschylus (*Greek*)
Edward Albee (*U.S.*)
Robert Amos (*Australian*)
Jean Anouilh (*French*)
Aristophanes (*Greek*)
Alan Ayckbourn (*English*)
Pierre Augustin Caron de Beaumarchais
 (*French*)
Francis Beaumont (*English*)
Samuel Beckett (*Irish*)
Brendan Behan (*Irish*)
Richard Beynon (*Australian*)
Alan Bleasdale (*English*)
Edward Bond (*English*)
Bertolt Brecht (*German*)
Eugene Brieux (*French*)
Pedro Calderón de la Barca (*Spanish*)
George Chapman (*English*)
Anton Pavlovich Chekhov (*Russian*)
William Congreve (*English*)
Pierre Corneille (*French*)
Noël (Pierce) Coward (*English*)
Thomas Dekker (*English*)
John Dryden (*English*)
T(homas) S(tearns) Eliot (*U.S.-British*)
Louis Esson (*Australian*)
Euripides (*Greek*)
John Fletcher (*English*)
Dario Fo (*Italian*)
John Ford (*English*)
Brian Friel (*Irish*)
John Galsworthy (*English*)
Jean Genet (*French*)
W(illiam) S(chwenk) Gilbert (*English*)
(Hippolyte) Jean Giraudoux (*French*)
Johann Wolfgang von Goethe (*German*)
Nikolai Gogol (*Russian*)
Oliver Goldsmith (*Irish*)
Oriel Gray (*Australian*)
Robert Greene (*English*)

David Hare (*English*)
Gerhart Johann Robert Hauptmann
 (*German*)
Václav Havel (*Czech*)
Alfred Hayes (*U.S.*)
(Christian) Friedrich Hebbel (*German*)
Dorthy Hewett (*Australian*)
Thomas Heywood (*English*)
Jack Hibberd (*Australian*)
Sidney Howard (*U.S.*)
Henrik Ibsen (*Norwegian*)
William Motter Inge (*U.S.*)
Eugène Ionesco (*Romanian-French*)
Ben Jonson (*English*)
George Kaiser (*German*)
Tony Kushner (*U.S.*)
Thomas Kyd (*English*)
Ray Lawler (*Australian*)
Liz Lochhead (*Scottish*)
Lope de Vega (*Spanish*)
Federico Garcia Lorca (*Spanish*)
Maurice Maeterlinck (*Belgian*)
David Mamet (*U.S.*)
Christopher Marlowe (*English*)
John Marston (*English*)
Menander (*Greek*)
Arthur Miller (*U.S.*)
Molière (*French*)
Barry Oakley (*Australian*)
Sean O'Casey (*Irish*)
Eugene (Gladstone) O'Neill (*U.S.*)
Joe Orton (*English*)
John Osborne (*English*)
Thomas Otway (*English*)
John Patrick (*U.S.*)
Arthur Wing Pinero (*English*)
Harold Pinter (*English*)
Luigi Pirandello (*Italian*)
Titus Maccius Plautus (*Roman*)
Hal Porter (*Australian*)

WORD POWER

Dramatists (continued)

Aleksander Sergeyevich Pushkin (*Russian*)
Jean Baptiste Racine (*French*)
Terence Mervyn Rattigan (*English*)
John Romeril (*Australian*)
Willy Russell (*English*)
Thomas Sackville (*English*)
Jean-Paul Sartre (*French*)
Johann Christoph Friedrich von Schiller
  (*German*)
Lucius Annaeus Seneca (*Roman*)
Alan Seymour (*Australian*)
Peter Shaffer (*English*)
William Shakespeare (*English*)
George Bernard Shaw (*Irish*)

Sam Shepard (*U.S.*)
Richard Brinsley Sheridan (*Irish*)
Robert Sherwood (*U.S.*)
Sophocles (*Greek*)
Wole Soyinka (*Nigerian*)
Tom Stoppard (*Czech-English*)
August Strindberg (*Swedish*)
John Millington Synge (*Irish*)
John Webster (*English*)
Oscar Wilde (*Irish*)
Thornton Wilder (*U.S.*)
Tennessee Williams (*U.S.*)
David Keith Williamson (*Australian*)
William Wycherly (*English*)

MEMBER STATES OF THE EU

1958 Belgium	1958 The Netherlands	1986 Portugal
1958 France	1973 Denmark	1986 Spain
1958 Germany	1973 Republic of Ireland	1995 Finland
1958 Italy	1973 United Kingdom	1995 Sweden
1958 Luxembourg	1981 Greece	1995 Austria

EU applications under consideration

Cyprus	Hungary	Switzerland
Estonia	Poland	Czech Republic

WORD POWER

Place	Inhabitant	Place	Inhabitant
Aberdeen	Aberdonian	Bolivia	Bolivian
Afghanistan	Afghan	Bordeaux	Bordelais
Alabama	Alabaman or Alabamian	the Borders	Borderer
		Bosnia	Bosnian
Alaska	Alaskan	Boston	Bostonian or (U.S. slang) Bean-eater
Albania	Albanian		
Alberta	Albertan	Botswana	Botswanan
Algeria	Algerian	Brazil	Brazilian
Alsace	Alsatian	Bristol	Bristolian
American continent	American	Brittany	Breton
American Samoa	American Samoan	British Columbia	British Columbian
Amsterdam	Amsterdammer	Bulgaria	Bulgarian
Anatolia	Anatolian	Burgundy	Burgundian
Andorra	Andorran	Burkina-Faso	Burkinabe
Angola	Angolan	Burma	Burmese
Anjou	Angevin	Burundi	Burundian
Antigua	Antiguan	Byzantium	Byzantine
Argentina	Argentine or Argentinian	California	Californian
		Cambridge	Cantabrigian
Arizona	Arizonan	Cambodia	Cambodian
Arkansas	Arkansan or (informal) Arkie	Cameroon	Cameroonian
		Canada	Canadian or (informal) Canuck
Armenia	Armenian		
Asia	Asian	Canada, Maritime Provinces	Downeaster
Assam	Assamese		
Assyria	Assyrian	Cape Verde	Cape Verdean
Australia	Australian or (informal) Aussie	Castile	Castilian
		Catalonia	Catalan
Austria	Austrian	the Caucasus	Caucasian
Azerbaijan	Azerbaijani or Azeri	Cayman Islands	Cayman Islander
		Chad	Chadian or Chadean
Babylon	Babylonian		
Bahamas	Bahamian	Chicago	Chicagoan
Bahrain	Bahraini	Chile	Chilean
Bangladesh	Bangladeshi	China	Chinese
Bali	Balinese	Circassia	Circassian
Barbados	Barbadian, Bajan (informal), or Bim (informal)	Colombia	Colombian
		Colorado	Coloradan
		Connecticut	Nutmegger
Barbuda	Barbudan or Barbudian	Cork	Corkonian
		Comoros Islands	Comorian
		Congo Republic	Congolese
Bavaria	Bavarian	Cornwall	Cornishman, Cornishwoman
Belarus or Byelorussia	Belarussian or Byelorussian		
		Corsica	Corsican
Belau	Belauan	Costa Rica	Costa Rican
Belgium	Belgian	Côte d'Ivoire	Ivorian or Ivorean
Benin	Beninese or Beninois	Croatia	Croat or Croatian
		Cuba	Cuban
Berlin	Berliner	Cumbria	Cumbrian
Bhutan	Bhutanese	Cyprus	Cypriot
Birmingham	Brummie	Czech Republic	Czech
Bohemia	Bohemian		

INHABITANTS

WORD POWER

Place	Inhabitant	Place	Inhabitant
Czechoslovakia	Czechoslovak *or* Czechoslovakian	Gascony	Gascon
		Genoa	Genoese
Delaware	Delawarean	Georgia (country)	Georgian
Denmark	Dane	Georgia (U.S. state)	Georgian
Delphi	Pythian	Germany	German
Devon	Devonian	Ghana	Ghanaian *or* Ghanian
Djibouti	Djiboutian *or* Djiboutien		
		Glasgow	Glaswegian
Dominica	Dominican	Greece	Greek
Dominican Republic	Dominican	Greenland	Greenlander
Dublin	Dubliner	Grenada	Grenadian
Dundee	Dundonian	Guam	Guamanian
East Timor	East Timorese	Guatemala	Guatemalan
Ecuador	Ecuadorean *or* Ecuadoran	Guinea	Guinean
		Guyana	Guyanese *or* Guyanan
Edinburgh	Edinburgher		
Egypt	Egyptian	Haiti	Haitian
El Salvador	Salvadoran, Salvadorean, *or* Salvadorian	Hawaii	Hawaiian
		Havana	Habanero
		Hesse	Hessian
England	Englishman, Englishwoman	Hungary	Hungarian *or* Magyar
Ephesus	Ephesian	Honduras	Honduran
Estonia	Estonian	Hyderabad state	Mulki
Eritrea	Eritrean	Ibiza	Ibizan
Ethiopia	Ethiopian	Iceland	Icelander
Equatorial Guinea	Equatorian	Idaho	Idahoan
Eritrea	Eritrean	Illinois	Illinoian *or* Illinoisian
Estonia	Estonian		
Ethiopia	Ethiopian	India	Indian
Europe	European	Indiana	Indianan, Indianian, *or* (*informal*) Hoosier
Euzkadi	Basque		
Faeroe Islands	Faeroese		
Falkland Islands	Falkland Islanders *or* Falklander	Indonesia	Indonesian
		Iowa	Iowan
Fife	Fifer	Iran	Iranian
Fiji	Fijian	Iraq	Iraqi
Finland	Finn	Ireland	Irishman, Irishwoman
Flanders	Fleming		
Florence	Florentine	Israel	Israeli
Florida	Floridian	Italy	Italian
France	Frenchman, Frenchwoman	Jamaica	Jamaican
		Japan	Japanese
French Guiana	Guianese	Java	Javanese
Friesland	Frisian	Jordan	Jordanian
Friuili	Friulian	Kansas	Kansan
Gabon	Gabonese	Karelia	Karelian
Galicia	Galician	Kazakhstan	Kazakh
Galilee	Galilean	Kent (East)	Man, Woman of Kent
Galloway	Gallovidian		
Galway	Galwegian	Kent (West)	Kentish Man, Woman
Gambia	Gambian		

30

Place	Inhabitant	Place	Inhabitant
Kentucky	Kentuckian	Mauritania	Mauritanian
Kenya	Kenyan	Mauritius	Mauritian
Kirghizia	Kirghiz	Melanesia	Melanesian
Korea	Korean	Melbourne	Melburnian
Kuwait	Kuwaiti	Mexico	Mexican
Lancashire	Lancastrian	Michigan	Michigander,
Lancaster	Lancastrian		Michiganite, or
Laos	Laotian		Michiganian
Latvia	Latvian or Lett	Micronesia	Micronesian
Lebanon	Lebanese	Milan	Milanese
Liberia	Liberian	Minnesota	Minnesotan
Libya	Libyan	Mississippi	Mississippian
Liechtenstein	Liechtensteiner	Missouri	Missourian
Lincolnshire	yellow belly	Moldavia	Moldavian
	(dialect)	Monaco	Monegasque
Lithuania	Lithuanian	Mongolia	Mongolian
Liverpool	Liverpudlian or	Montana	Montanan
	(informal) Scouse	Montenegro	Montenegrin
	or Scouser	Montserrat	Montserratian
Lombardy	Lombard	Moravia	Moravian
London	Londoner or	Morocco	Moroccan
	Cockney	Moscow	Muscovite
Los Angeles	Angeleno	Mozambique	Mozambican
Louisiana	Louisianan or	Namibia	Namibian
	Louisianian	Nauru	Nauruan
Luxembourg	Luxembourger	Naples	Neapolitan
Lyon	Lyonnais	Nebraska	Nebraskan
Macao	Macaonese	the Netherlands	Dutchman,
Macedonia	Macedonian		Dutchwoman
Madagascar	Madagascan or	New Brunswick	New Brunswicker
	Malagasy	Newcastle upon Tyne	Geordie
Madrid	Madrileño,	New England	New Englander or
	Madrileña		(informal) Yankee
Maine	Mainer or		or Downeaster
	Downeaster	Newfoundland	Newfoundlander
Majorca	Majorcan		or (informal)
Malawi	Malawian		Newfie
Malaya	Malayan	Newfoundland fishing	Outporter
Malaysia	Malaysian	village	
Maldive Islands	Maldivian	New Hampshire	New Hampshirite
Malta	Maltese	New Jersey	New Jerseyan or
Man, Isle of	Manxman,		New Jerseyite
	Manxwoman	New Mexico	New Mexican
Manchester	Mancunian	New South Wales	New South
Manitoba	Manitoban		Welshman, New
Marquesas Islands	Marquesan		South
Mars	Martian		Welshwoman
Marseilles	Marsellais	New York	New Yorker or
Marshall Islands	Marshall Islander		Knickerbocker
Martinique	Martiniquean	New Zealand	New Zealander or
Maryland	Marylander		(informal) Kiwi or
Massachusetts	Bay Stater		Enzedder

WORD POWER

WORD POWER

Place	Inhabitant	Place	Inhabitant
Nicaragua	Nicaraguan	Queensland	Queenslander
Niger	Nigerien	Rhode Island	Rhode Islander
Nigeria	Nigerian	Rhodes	Rhodian
Normandy	Norman	Rhodesia	Rhodesian
North Carolina	North Carolinian or Tarheel	Rio de Janeiro	Cariocan
		Romania	Romanian
North Dakota	North Dakotan	Rome	Roman
Northern Ireland	Northern Irishman, Northern Irishwoman	Russian Federation	Russian
		Ruthenia	Ruthenian
		Rwanda	Rwandan
		Samaria	Samaritan
Northern Territory	Territorian	San Marino	San Marinese or Sammarinese
Northern Territory, northern part of	Top Ender		
		Sardinia	Sardinian
North Korea	North Korean	Saskatchewan	Saskatchewanian
Northumbria	Northumbrian	Saxony	Saxon
Norway	Norwegian	Saudi Arabia	Saudi or Saudi Arabian
Nova Scotia	Nova Scotian or (informal) Bluenose	Savoy	Savoyard
		Scandinavia	Scandinavian
Ohio	Ohioan	Scotland	Scot, Scotsman, Scotswoman, or Caledonian
Okinawa	Okinawan		
Oklahoma	Oklahoman or (slang) Okie		
Oman	Omani	Scottish Highlands	Highlander or (old-fashioned) Hielanman
Ontario	Ontarian or Ontarioan		
Oregon	Oregonian	Senegal	Senegalese
Orkney	Orcadian	Serbia	Serb or Serbian
Oxford	Oxonian	Seychelles	Seychellois
Pakistan	Pakistani	Shetland	Shetlander
Palestine	Palestinian	Sierra Leone	Sierra Leonean
Panama	Panamanian	Sind	Sindhi
Papua New Guinea	Papua	Singapore	Singaporean
Paraguay	Paraguayan	Slovakia	Slovak
Paris	Parisian or Parisienne	Slovenia	Slovene or Slovenian
		Solomon Islands	Solomon Islander
Pennsylvania	Pennsylvanian	South Africa	South African
Persia	Persian	South Australia	South Australian or (informal) Croweater
Perth	Perthite		
Peru	Peruvian		
the Philippines	Filipino	South Carolina	South Carolinian
Poland	Pole	South Dakota	South Dakota
Pomerania	Pomeranian	South Korea	South Korean
Portugal	Portuguese	Spain	Spaniard
Prince Edward Island	Prince Edward Islander	Sri Lanka	Sri Lankan
		Sudan	Sudanese
Provence	Provençal	Suriname	Surinamese
Prussia	Prussian	Swaziland	Swazi
Puerto Rico	Puerto Rican	Switzerland	Swiss
Qatar	Qatari	Sweden	Swede
Quebec	Quebecer, Quebecker, or Quebecois	Sydney	Sydneysider
		Sydney, Western suburbs of	Westie (informal)

Place	Inhabitant	Place	Inhabitant
Syria	Syrian	Uruguay	Uruguayan
Taiwan	Taiwanese	Utah	Utahan *or* Utahn
Tajikistan	Tajik	Uzbekistan	Uzbek
Tanzania	Tanzanian	Venezuela	Venezuelan
Tasmania	Tasmanian *or* (*informal*) Tassie *or* Apple Islander	Venice	Venetian
		Vermont	Vermonter
		Victoria	Victorian
Tennessee	Tennessean	Vienna	Viennese
Texas	Texan	Vietnam	Vietnamese
Thailand	Thai	Virginia	Virginian
Thessalonika	Thessalonian	Wales	Welshman, Welshwoman
Tibet	Tibetan		
Togo	Togolese	Washington	Washingtonian
Tonga	Tongan	Wearside	Mackem
Trinidad	Trinidadian	Wessex	West Saxon
Tobago	Tobagan *or* Tobagonian	Western Australia	Western Australian, Westralian, *or* (*informal*) Sandgroper
Troy	Trojan		
Tuscany	Tuscan		
Tunisia	Tunisian		
Turkey	Turk	Western Sahara	Sahwari
Turkmenistan	Turkmen	West Virginia	West Virginian
Tuvalu	Tuvaluan	Winnipeg	Winnipegger
Tyneside	Geordie	Wisconsin	Wisconsinite
Tyre	Tyrian	Wyoming	Wyomingite
Uganda	Ugandan	Yemen	Yemeni
Ukraine	Ukrainian	Yorkshire	Yorkshireman, Yorkshirewoman
Ulster	Ulsterman, Ulsterwoman		
		the Yukon	Yukoner
Umbria	Umbrian	Zaire	Zairean
United Kingdom	Briton, Brit (*informal*), *or* Britisher	Zambia	Zambian
		Zanzibar	Zanzibari
		Zimbabwe	Zimbabwean
United States of America	American *or* (*informal*) Yank *or* Yankee		

WORD POWER

ISLANDS AND ISLAND GROUPS

Achill
Admiralty
Aegean
Aegina
Alcatraz
Aldabra
Alderney
Aleutian
Alexander
Amboina
Andaman
Andaman and Nicobar
Andreanof
Andros
Anglesey
Anguilla
Anticosti
Antigua
Antilles
Antipodes
Aran
Arran
Aru or Arru
Aruba
Ascension
Auckland
Azores
Baffin
Bahamas
Balearic
Bali
Banaba
Bangka
Banks
Baranof
Barbados
Barbuda
Bardsey
Barra
Basilan
Basse-Terre
Batan
Belau
Belle
Benbecula
Bermuda
Biak
Billiton
Bioko
Bohol
Bonaire
Bonin
Bora Bora
Borneo

Bornholm
Bougainville
British
Bute
Butung
Caicos
Caldy
Calf of Man
Campobello
Canary
Canna
Canvey
Cape Breton
Capri
Caroline
Cayman
Cebú
Ceylon
Channel
Chatham
Cheju
Chichagof
Chiloé
Chios
Choiseul
Christmas
Cocos
Coll
Colonsay
Coney
Cook
Corfu
Corregidor
Corsica
Crete
Cuba
Curaçao
Cyclades
Cyprus
Cythera
Delos
D'Entrecasteaux
Diomede
Disko
Diu
Djerba or Jerba
Dodecanese
Dominica
Dry Tortugas
Easter
Eigg
Elba
Ellesmere
Espíritu Santo

Euboea
Faeroes
Faial or Fayal
Fair
Falkland
Falster
Farquhar
Fernando de Noronha
Fiji
Flannan
Flinders
Flores
Florida Keys
Foula
Foulness
Franz Josef Land
French West Indies
Frisian
Fyn
Galápagos
Gambier
Gigha
Gilbert
Gotland, Gothland, or
  Gottland
Grand Bahama
Grand Canary
Grande-Terre
Grand Manan
Greater Antilles
Greater Sunda
Greenland
Grenada
Grenadines
Guadalcanal
Guam
Guernsey
Hainan or Hainan Tao
Handa
Hawaii
Hayling
Heard and McDonald
Hebrides
Heimaey
Heligoland
Herm
Hispaniola
Hokkaido
Holy
Hong Kong
Honshu
Hormuz or Ormuz
Howland
Ibiza

Icaria
Iceland
Imbros
Iona
Ionian
Ireland
Ischia
Islay
Isle Royale
Ithaca
Iwo Jima
Jamaica
Jan Mayen
Java
Jersey
Jolo
Juan Fernández
Jura
Kangaroo
Kauai
Keos
Kerrera
Kiritimati
Kodiak
Kos or Cos
Kosrae
Krakatoa or Krakatau
Kuril or Kurile
Kyushu or Kiushu
La Palma
Labuan
Lakshadweep
Lampedusa
Lanai
Lavongai
Leeward
Lemnos
Lesbos
Lesser Antilles
Levkás, Leukas, or Leucas
Lewis with Harris or Lewis
  and Harris
Leyte
Liberty
Lindisfarne
Line
Lipari
Lismore
Lolland or Laaland
Lombok
Long
Longa
Lord Howe
Luing

Lundy
Luzon
Mackinac
Macquarie
Madagascar
Madeira
Madura
Maewo
Mahé
Mainland
Majorca
Maldives
Malé
Malta
Man
Manhattan
Manitoulin
Marajó
Margarita
Marie Galante
Marinduque
Marquesas
Marshall
Martinique
Masbate
Mascarene
Matsu or Mazu
Maui
Mauritius
May
Mayotte
Melanesia
Melos
Melville
Mersea
Micronesia
Mindanao
Mindoro
Minorca
Miquelon
Molokai
Moluccas
Montserrat
Mount Desert
Muck
Mull
Mykonos
Nantucket
Nauru
Naxos
Negros
Netherlands Antilles
Nevis
New Britain

New Caledonia
Newfoundland
New Georgia
New Guinea
New Ireland
New Providence
New Siberian
Nicobar
Niue
Norfolk
North
North Uist
Nusa Tenggara
Oahu
Oceania
Okinawa
Orkneys or Orkney
Palawan
Palmyra
Panay
Pantelleria
Páros
Patmos
Pelagian
Pemba
Penang
Pescadores
Philae
Philippines
Phoenix
Pitcairn
Polynesia
Ponape
Pribilof
Prince Edward
Prince of Wales
Principe
Qeshm or Qishm
Queen Charlotte
Queen Elizabeth
Quemoy
Raasay
Ramsey
Rarotonga
Rathlin
Réunion
Rhodes
Rhum
Rialto
Roanoke
Robben
Rockall
Rona
Ross

WORD POWER

Ryukyu
Saba
Safety
Saipan
Sakhalin
Salamis
Saltee
Samar
Samoa
Samos
Samothrace
San Cristóbal
San Juan
San Salvador
Santa Catalina
Sao Miguel
Sao Tomé
Sardinia
Sark
Savaii
Scalpay
Schouten
Scilly
Sea
Seil
Seram *or* Ceram
Seychelles
Sheppey
Shetland
Sicily
Singapore
Sjælland
Skikoku
Skokholm
Skomer
Skye
Skyros *or* Scyros
Society
Socotra
South
Southampton

South Georgia
South Orkney
South Shetland
South Uist
Spitsbergen
Sporades
Sri Lanka
St. Croix
St. Helena
St. John
St. Kilda
St. Kitts *or* St. Christopher
St. Lucia
St. Martin
St. Tudwal's
St. Vincent
Staffa
Staten
Stewart
Stroma
Stromboli
Sulawesi
Sumatra
Sumba *or* Soemba
Sumbawa *or* Soembawa
Summer
Sunda *or* Soenda
Tahiti
Taiwan
Tasmania
Tenedos
Tenerife
Terceira
Thanet
Thásos
Thera
Thousand
Thursday
Timor
Tiree
Tobago

Tokelau
Tombo
Tonga
Tortola
Tortuga
Trinidad
Tristan da Cunha
Trobriand
Truk
Tsushima
Tuamotu
Tubuai
Turks
Tutuila
Tuvalu
Ulva
Unimak
Upolu
Ushant
Vancouver
Vanua Levu
Vanuatu
Vestmannaeyjar
Victoria
Virgin
Visayan
Viti Levu
Volcano
Walcheren
Walney
West Indies
Western
Wight
Windward
Wrangel
Yap
Youth
Zante
Zanzibar

Allen
Annecy
Aral Sea or Lake Aral
Ard
Athabaska
Averno
Awe
Baikal
Bala
Balaton
Balkhash
Bangweulu
Bassenthwaite
Belfast
Biel
Bodensee
Buttermere
Caspian Sea
Chad
Champlain
Como
Coniston Water
Constance
Crummock Water
Dead Sea
Derwentwater
Dongting
Earn
Edward
Ennerdale Water
Erie
Erne
Eyre
Frome
Fyne
Garda
Gatún
Geneva
Grasmere
Great Bear
Great Bitter
Great Lakes
Great Salt
Great Slave
Hawes Water
Huron
Ijsselmeer or Ysselmeer
Iliamna

Ilmen
Issyk-Kul
Kariba
Katrine
Kivu
Koko Nor or Kuku Nor
Kootenay
Ladoga
Laggan
Lake of the Woods
Leven
Linnhe
Little Bitter
Lochy
Lomond
Lucerne
Lugano
Léman
Maggiore
Malawi
Managua
Manitoba
Maracaibo
Mead
Meech
Memphremagog
Menteith
Michigan
Miraflores
Mistassini
Mobutu
Morar
Mweru
Nam Co or Nam Tso
Nasser
Neagh
Ness
Neuchâtel
Nicaragua
Nipigon
Nipissing
No
Nyasa
Okanagan
Okeechobee
Onega
Oneida
Onondaga

Ontario
Patos
Peipus
Pontchartrain
Poopó
Poyang or P'o-yang
Pskov
Rannoch
Reindeer
Rudolf
Saint Clair
Saint John
Sea of Galilee
Sevan
Stanley Pool
Superior
Sween
Taal
Tahoe
Tana
Tanganyika
Taupo
Tay
Thirlmere
Thun
Tien
Titicaca
Tonle Sap
Torrens
Torridon
Trasimene
Tummel
Turkana
Ullswater
Urmia
Van
Victoria
Volta
Waikaremoana
Washington
Wast Water
Windermere
Winnebago
Winnipeg
Zug
Zürich

WORD POWER

Aconcagua
Adams
Albert Edward
Anai Mudi
Aneto
Annapurna
Apo
Aragats
Aran Fawddwy
Ararat
Arber
Argentera
Belukha
Ben Lomond
Ben Macdhui
Ben Nevis
Blackburn
Blanca Peak
Blue Mountain Peak
Bona
Brocken
Carmarthen Van
Carmel
Cerro de Mulhacén
Citlaltépetl
Clingman's Dome
Cook
Corcovado
Corno
Croagh Patrick
Demavend
Dhaulagiri
Eiger
Elbert
Elbrus
El Capitan
Emi Koussi
Estrella
Everest
Finsteraarhorn
Fuji
Gannet Peak
Gerlachovka
Grand Teton
Gran Paradiso
Harney Peak
Helicon
Helvellyn
Hermon

Humphreys Peak
Hymettus
Ida
Illimani
Isto
Jebel Musa
Jungfrau
K2 or Godwin Austen
Kamet
Kangchenjunga
Kenya
Kilimanjaro
Kinabalu
Kings Peak
Klínovec
Kommunizma Peak
Kongur Shan
Kosciusko
Lenin Peak
Leone
Logan
Longs Peak
Mansfield
Marcy
Markham
Marmolada
Masharbrum
Matterhorn
McKinley
Mitchell
Mont Blanc
Mount of Olives
Mulhacén
Munku-Sardyk
Musala
Nanda Devi
Nanga Parbat
Narodnaya
Nebo
Negoiu
Olympus
Ossa
Palomar
Parnassus
Pelion
Pentelikon
Perdido
Petermann Peak
Pikes Peak

Pilatus
Piz Bernina
Pobeda Peak
Puy de Dôme
Rainier
Rigi
Robson
Rock Creek
Rosa
Rushmore
Scafell Pike
Schneekoppe
Scopus
Sinai
Siple
Sir Sandford
Sir Wilfrid Laurier
Skalitsy
Slide Mountain
Smólikas
Snowdon
Sorata
Stanley
Sugar Loaf Mountain
Table Mountain
Tabor
Teide
Tengri Khan
Thabana Ntlenyana
Timpanogos
Tirich Mir
Toubkal
Troglav
Ulugh Muztagh
Uncompahgre Peak
Venusberg
Victoria
Viso
Waddington
Washington
Waun Fach
Weisshorn
White Mountain
Whitney
Wrangell
Zard Kuh
Zugspitze

NEW ZEALAND TERRITORIES

Cook Islands
Niue

the Ross Dependency
Tokelau *or* Union Islands

WORD POWER

Peter Abrahams (*South African*)
Chinua Achebe (*Nigerian*)
Peter Ackroyd (*English*)
Douglas Adams (*English*)
Richard Adams (*English*)
Alain-Fournier (*French*)
Brian Aldiss (*English*)
James Aldridge (*Australian*)
Al Alvarez (*English*)
Eric Ambler (*English*)
Kingsley Amis (*English*)
Martin Amis (*English*)
Mulk Raj Anand (*Indian*)
Maya Angelou (*U.S.*)
Lucius Apuleius (*Roman*)
Jeffrey Archer (*English*)
Isaac Asimov (*U.S.*)
Margaret Atwood (*Canadian*)
Louis Auchincloss (*U.S.*)
Jane Austen (*English*)
Beryl Bainbridge (*English*)
R M Ballantyne (*Scottish*)
J G Ballard (*English*)
Honoré de Balzac (*French*)
Iain Banks (*Scottish*)
Lynne Reid Banks (*English*)
Elspeth Barker (*Scottish*)
Pat Barker (*English*)
Julian Barnes (*English*)
Stanley Barstow (*English*)
John Barth (*U.S.*)
H E Bates (*English*)
Nina Bawden (*English*)
Simone de Beauvoir (*French*)
Sybille Bedford (*British*)
Max Beerbohm (*English*)
Aphra Behn (*English*)
Saul Bellow (*Canadian*)
Andrei Bely (*Russian*)
David Benedictus (*English*)
(Enoch) Arnold Bennett (*English*)
John Berger (*English*)
Thomas Berger (*U.S.*)
Maeve Binchy (*Irish*)
R(ichard) D(oddridge) Blackmore (*English*)
Alan Bleasdale (*English*)
Heinrich Böll (*German*)
Elizabeth Bowen (*Irish*)
Paul Bowles (*U.S.*)

William Boyd (*Scottish*)
Malcolm Bradbury (*English*)
Barbara Taylor Bradford (*English*)
Melvin Bragg (*English*)
John Braine (*English*)
André Brink (*South African*)
Vera Brittain (*English*)
Louis Bromfield (*U.S.*)
Anne Brontë (*English*)
Charlotte Brontë (*English*)
Emily (Jane) Brontë (*English*)
Christina Brooke-Rose (*English*)
Anita Brookner (*English*)
Brigid Brophy (*English*)
George Douglas Brown (*Scottish*)
George Mackay Brown (*Scottish*)
John Buchan (*Scottish*)
Pearl Buck (*U.S.*)
Mikhail Afanaseyev Bulgakov (*Russian*)
John Bunyan (*English*)
Anthony Burgess (*British*)
Fanny Burney (*English*)
Edgar Rice Burrows (*U.S.*)
William Burroughs (*U.S.*)
Samuel Butler (*English*)
A S Byatt (*English*)
Italo Calvino (*Italian*)
Albert Camus (*French*)
Elias Canetti (*Bulgarian*)
Truman Capote (*U.S.*)
Peter Carey (*Australian*)
Angela Carter (*English*)
Barbara Cartland (*English*)
Willa Cather (*U.S.*)
Camilo José Cela (*Spanish*)
Miguel de Cervantes (*Spanish*)
Raymond Chandler (*U.S.*)
G K Chesterton (*English*)
Agatha (Mary Clarissa) Christie (*English*)
Arthur C Clarke (*English*)
James Clavell (*U.S.*)
Jon Cleary (*Australian*)
J M Coatzee (*South African*)
Colette (*French*)
(William) Wilkie Collins (*English*)

Ivy Compton-Burnett (*English*)
Richard Condon (*U.S.*)
Evan Connell (*U.S.*)
Joseph Conrad (*Polish-British*)
Catherine Cookson (*English*)
James Fenimore Cooper (*U.S.*)
Jilly Cooper (*English*)
William Cooper (*English*)
Maria Correlli (*English*)
Stephen Crane (*U.S.*)
Lionel Davidson (*English*)
(William) Robertson Davies (*Canadian*)
Daniel Defoe (*English*)
Len Deighton (*English*)
E M Delafield (*English*)
Don DeLillo (*U.S.*)
Thomas de Quincy (*English*)
Anita Desai (*Indian*)
Peter De Vries (*U.S.*)
Charles (John Huffam) Dickens (*English*)
Monica Dickens (*English*)
Joan Didion (*U.S.*)
Isak Dinesen (*Danish*)
Benjamin Disraeli (*English*)
J P Donleavy (*Irish*)
John Roderigo Dos Passos (*U.S.*)
Fyodor Mikhailovich Dostoevsky (*Russian*)
Arthur Conan Doyle (*Scottish*)
Roddy Doyle (*Irish*)
Margaret Drabble (*English*)
Maureen Duffy (*English*)
Alexandre Dumas (*French*)
Daphne Du Maurier (*English*)
Nell Dunn (*English*)
Gerald Durrell (*English*)
Laurence Durrell (*English*)
Umberto Eco (*Italian*)
Maria Edgeworth (*English*)
George Eliot (*English*)
Stanley Elkin (*U.S.*)
Alice Thomas Ellis (*English*)
Ben Elton (*English*)
Zöe Fairbairns (*English*)

NOVELISTS

Philip José Farmer (*U.S.*)
Howard Fast (*U.S.*)
William Faulkner (*U.S.*)
Elaine Feinstein (*English*)
Helen Fielding (*English*)
Henry Fielding (*English*)
Eva Figes (*British*)
F(rancis) Scott (Key) Fitzgerald (*U.S.*)
Penelope Fitzgerald (*English*)
Gustave Flaubert (*French*)
Ian Fleming (*English*)
Ford Madox Ford (*English*)
Richard Ford (*U.S.*)
C S Forester (*English*)
E M Forster (*English*)
Frederick Forsyth (*English*)
John Fowles (*English*)
Janet Paterson Frame (*New Zealand*)
Dick Francis (*English*)
Antonia Fraser (*English*)
Michael Frayn (*English*)
Nicholas Freeling (*English*)
Marilyn French (*U.S.*)
Roy Fuller (*English*)
William Gaddis (*U.S.*)
Janice Galloway (*Scottish*)
John Galsworthy (*English*)
Gabriel García Márquez (*Colombian*)
Helen Garner (*Australian*)
Elizabeth Gaskell (*English*)
William Alexander Gerhardie (*English*)
Lewis Grassic Gibbon (*Scottish*)
Stella Gibbons (*English*)
André Gide (*French*)
Penelope Gilliat (*English*)
George Gissing (*English*)
Ellen Glasgow (*U.S.*)
(Margaret) Rumer Godden (*English*)
William Godwin (*English*)
Johann Wolfgang von Goethe (*German*)
Nikolai Vasilievich Gogol (*Russian*)
Herbert Gold (*U.S.*)
William (Gerald) Golding (*English*)
William Goldman (*U.S.*)

Oliver Goldsmith (*Anglo-Irish*)
Ivan Aleksandrovich Goncharov (*Russian*)
Nadine Gordimer (*South African*)
Maxim Gorky (*Russian*)
Edmund Gosse (*English*)
Winston Graham (*English*)
Günter (Wilhelm) Grass (*German*)
Robert Graves (*English*)
Alasdair Gray (*Scottish*)
Graham Greene (*English*)
John Grisham (*U.S.*)
George Grossmith (*English*)
Weedon Grossmith (*English*)
David Guterson (*U.S.*)
Rider Haggard (*English*)
Arthur Hailey (*Anglo-Canadian*)
Thomas Hardy (*English*)
L(eslie) P(oles) Hartley (*English*)
Nathaniel Hawthorne (*U.S.*)
Shirley Hazzard (*U.S.*)
Robert A Heinlein (*U.S.*)
Joseph Heller (*U.S.*)
Ernest Hemingway (*U.S.*)
Hermann Hesse (*German*)
Georgette Heyer (*English*)
Patricia Highsmith (*U.S.*)
Susan Hill (*English*)
James Hilton (*English*)
Barry Hines (*English*)
Russell Hoban (*U.S.*)
James Hogg (*Scottish*)
Winifred Holtby (*English*)
Anthony Hope (*English*)
Paul Horgan (*U.S.*)
Elizabeth Jane Howard (*English*)
Thomas Hughes (*English*)
Victor (Marie) Hugo (*French*)
Keri Hulme (*New Zealand*)
Evan Hunter (*U.S.*)
Zora Neale Hurston (*U.S.*)
Aldous Huxley (*English*)
Hammond Innes (*English*)
John Irving (*U.S.*)
Christopher Isherwood (*English-U.S.*)

Kazuo Ishiguro (*British*)
Henry James (*U.S.-British*)
P D James (*English*)
Ruth Prawer Jhabvala (*Anglo-Polish*)
Erica Jong (*U.S.*)
James Joyce (*Irish*)
Franz Kafka (*Czech*)
Johanna Kaplan (*U.S.*)
Nikos Kazantzakis (*Greek*)
Molly Keane (*Anglo-Irish*)
James Kelman (*Scottish*)
Thomas Keneally (*Australian*)
Margaret Kennedy (*English*)
Jack Kerouac (*U.S.*)
Ken Kesey (*U.S.*)
Francis King (*English*)
Stephen King (*U.S.*)
Charles Kingsley (*English*)
Rudyard Kipling (*English*)
Milan Kundera (*French-Czech*)
Pierre Choderlos de Laclos (*French*)
George Lamming (*Barbadian*)
Guiseppe Tomasi di Lampedusa (*Italian*)
D H Lawrence (*English*)
John Le Carré (*English*)
Harper Lee (*U.S.*)
Laurie Lee (*English*)
Sheridan Le Fanu (*Irish*)
Ursula Le Guin (*U.S.*)
Rosamond Lehmann (*English*)
Mikhail Yurievich Lermontov (*Russian*)
Doris Lessing (*Rhodesian*)
Primo Levi (*Italian*)
(Harry) Sinclair Lewis (*U.S.*)
Penelope Lively (*English*)
David Lodge (*English*)
Jack London (*U.S.*)
(Clarence) Malcolm Lowry (*English*)
Alison Lurie (*U.S.*)
Rose Macauley (*English*)
Carson McCullers (*U.S.*)
George MacDonald (*Scottish*)
Ian McEwan (*English*)

WORD POWER

NOVELISTS

WORD POWER

William McIlvanney
(*Scottish*)
Colin MacInnes (*English*)
Compton MacKenzie
(*English*)
Henry MacKenzie (*Scottish*)
Bernard McLaverty (*Irish*)
Alistair MacLean (*Scottish*)
Naguib Mahfouz (*Egyptian*)
Norman Mailer (*U.S.*)
Bernard Malamud (*U.S.*)
David Malouf (*Australian*)
(Cyril) Wolf Mankowitz
(*English*)
Thomas Mann (*German*)
Olivia Manning (*English*)
Kamala Markandaya
(*Indian*)
Frederick Marryat (*English*)
Ngaio Marsh (*New
Zealand*)
Allan Massie (*Scottish*)
Somerset Maugham
(*English*)
Guy de Maupassant
(*French*)
Francois Mauriac (*French*)
Herman Melville (*U.S.*)
George Meredith (*English*)
James A Michener (*U.S.*)
Henry Miller (*U.S.*)
Yukio Mishima (*Japanese*)
Julian Mitchell (*English*)
Margaret Mitchell (*U.S.*)
Naomi Mitchison (*Scottish*)
Nancy Mitford (*English*)
Timothy Mo (*British*)
Nicholas Monsarrat
(*English*)
Michael Moorcock (*English*)
Brian Moore (*Irish-
Canadian*)
Toni Morrison (*U.S.*)
John Mortimer (*English*)
Penelope Mortimer (*Welsh*)
Nicholas Mosley (*English*)
Iris Murdoch (*Irish*)
Vladimir Vladimirovich
Nabokov (*Russian-U.S.*)
V S Naipaul (*Trinidadian*)
P H Newby (*English*)
Ngugi wa Thiong'o
(*Kenyan*)
Robert Nye (*English*)

Joyce Carol Oates (*U.S.*)
Edna O'Brien (*Irish*)
Kenzaburo Oë (*Japanese*)
Liam O'Flaherty (*Irish*)
John O'Hara (*U.S.*)
Ben Okri (*Nigerian*)
Margaret Oliphant (*Scottish*)
Michael Ondaatje
(*Canadian*)
Baroness Emmuska Orczy
(*Hungarian-British*)
George Orwell (*English*)
Ouida (*English*)
Cynthia Ozick (*U.S.*)
Boris Leonidovich
Pasternak (*Russian*)
Allan Paton (*South African*)
Thomas Love Peacock
(*English*)
Mervyn Peake (*English*)
Harold Porter (*Australian*)
Katherine Anne Porter
(*U.S.*)
Anthony Powell (*English*)
John Cowper Powys
(*English*)
Terry Pratchett (*English*)
J B Priestley (*English*)
V S Pritchett (*English*)
E Annie Proulx (*U.S.*)
Marcel Proust (*French*)
Mario Puzo (*U.S.*)
Thomas Pynchon (*U.S.*)
Ellery Queen (*U.S.*)
Ann Radcliffe (*English*)
Raja Rao (*Indian*)
Frederic Raphael (*U.S.*)
Piers Paul Read (*English*)
Erich Maria Remarque
(*German*)
Mary Renault (*English*)
Ruth Rendell (*English*)
Jean Rhys (*British*)
Dorothy Richardson
(*English*)
Samuel Richardson (*English*)
Mordecai Richler
(*Canadian*)
Harold Robbins (*U.S.*)
Frederick William Rolfe
(*English*)
Henry Roth (*U.S.*)
(Ahmed) Salman Rushdie
(*Indian-British*)

Vita Sackville-West (*English*)
Marquis de Sade (*French*)
Antoine de Saint-Exupéry
(*French*)
Saki (*British*)
J D Salinger (*U.S.*)
George Sand (*French*)
William Saroyan (*U.S.*)
Jean-Paul Sartre (*French*)
Dorothy L Sayers (*English*)
Olive Schreiner (*South
African*)
Walter Scott (*Scottish*)
Hubert Selby Jr (*U.S.*)
Tom Sharpe (*English*)
Mary Shelley (*English*)
Carol Shields (*Canadian-
American*)
Mikhail Alexandrovich
Sholokhov (*Russian*)
Nevil Shute (*Anglo-Austrian*)
Alan Sillitoe (*English*)
Georges Simenon (*Belgian*)
Claude Simon (*French*)
Isaac Bashevis Singer (*U.S.*)
Iain Crichton Smith
(*Scottish*)
Zadie Smith (*British*)
Tobias George Smollett
(*Scottish*)
C P Snow (*English*)
Alexander Isayevich
Solzhenitsyn (*Russian*)
Muriel Spark (*Scottish*)
Howard Spring (*Welsh*)
C K Stead (*New Zealand*)
Gertrude Stein (*U.S.*)
John Steinbeck (*U.S.*)
Stendhal (*French*)
Laurence Sterne (*Irish-
British*)
Robert Louis Stevenson
(*Scottish*)
J I M Stewart (*Scottish*)
Mary Stewart (*English*)
Bram Stoker (*Irish*)
Robert Stone (*U.S.*)
David Storey (*English*)
Harriet Elizabeth Beecher
Stowe (*U.S.*)
William Styron (*U.S.*)
Patrick Süskind (*German*)
Graham Swift (*English*)
Jonathan Swift (*Irish*)

Julian Symons (*English*)
Emma Tennant (*English*)
William Makepeace
  Thackeray (*English*)
Paul Theroux (*U.S.*)
J(ohn) R(onald) R(euel)
  Tolkien (*English*)
Leo Tolstoy (*Russian*)
John Kennedy Toole (*U.S.*)
Nigel Tranter (*Scottish*)
Rose Tremain (*English*)
William Trevor (*Irish*)
Anthony Trollope (*English*)
Joanna Trollope (*English*)
Frank Tuohy (*English*)
Ivan Sergeyevich Turgenev
  (*Russian*)
Amos Tutuola (*Nigerian*)
Mark Twain (*U.S.*)
Anne Tyler (*U.S.*)
John Updike (*U.S.*)
Edward (Falaise) Upward
  (*English*)
Leon Uris (*U.S.*)
Laurens Van der Post (*South
  African*)

Peter Vansittart (*English*)
Mario Vargos Llosa
  (*Peruvian*)
Jules Verne (*French*)
Gore Vidal (*U.S.*)
Voltaire (*French*)
Kurt Vonnegut (*U.S.*)
John Wain (*English*)
Alice Walker (*U.S.*)
Horace Walpole (*English*)
Marina Warner (*English*)
Robert Penn Warren (*U.S.*)
Keith Waterhouse
  (*English*)
Evelyn Waugh (*English*)
Fay Weldon (*English*)
H G Wells (*English*)
Irvine Welsh (*Scottish*)
Eudora Welty (*U.S.*)
Mary Wesley (*English*)
Morris West (*Australian*)
Rebecca West (*Irish*)
Edith Wharton (*U.S.*)
Antonia White (*English*)
Patrick White
  (*Australian*)

T H White (*English*)
Oscar Wilde (*Irish*)
Thornton Wilder (*U.S.*)
Michael Wilding
  (*Australian*)
A(ndrew) N(orman) Wilson
  (*English*)
Jeanette Winterson (*English*)
P(elham) G(renville)
  Wodehouse (*English-U.S.*)
Thomas Clayton Wolfe
  (*U.S.*)
Tom Wolfe (*U.S.*)
Tobias Wolff (*U.S.*)
Virginia Woolf (*English*)
Herman Wouk (*U.S.*)
Richard Nathaniel Wright
  (*U.S.*)
Frank Yerby (*U.S.*)
Marguerite Yourcenar
  (*French*)
Evgeny Ivanovich
  Zamyatin (*Russian*)
Emile Zola (*French*)

PLACES AND THEIR NICKNAMES

Place	Nickname	Place	Nickname
Aberdeen	the Granite City	London	the Big Smoke or the Great Wen
Adelaide	the City of Churches		
Amsterdam	the Venice of the North	Los Angeles	L.A.
		New Jersey	the Garden State
Birmingham	Brum or the Venice of the North	New Orleans	the Crescent City or the Big Easy
Boston	Bean Town	New South Wales	Ma State
Bruges	the Venice of the North	New York (City)	the Big Apple
		New York (State)	the Empire State
California	the Golden State	New Zealand	Pig Island
Chicago	the Windy City	North Carolina	the Tarheel State
Dallas	the Big D	Nottingham	Queen of the Midlands
Detroit	the Motor City		
Dresden	Florence on the Elbe	Oklahoma	the Sooner State
Dublin	the Fair City	Pennsylvania	the Keystone State
Dumfries	Queen of the South	Philadelphia	Philly
Edinburgh	Auld Reekie or the Athens of the North	Portsmouth	Pompey
		Prince Edward Island	Spud Island
Florida	the Sunshine State		
Fraserburgh	the Broch	Queensland	Bananaland or the Deep North (both derogatory)
Fremantle	Freo		
Glasgow	the Dear Green Place		
Hamburg	the Venice of the North	Rome	the Eternal City
		San Francisco	Frisco
Indiana	the Hoosier State	Southeastern U.S.A.	Dixie, Dixieland, or the Deep South
Iowa	the Hawkeye State		
Ireland	the Emerald Isle	Tasmania	Tassie or the Apple Isle
Jamaica	J.A. or the Yard		
Jerusalem	the Holy City	Texas	the Lone Star State
Kentucky	the Bluegrass State	Utah	the Beehive State
Kuala Lumpur	K.L.	Venice	La Serenissima

Poetry and prosody terms

accentual metre
accentual-syllabic metre *or* stress-syllabic metre
Adonic
Alcaic
Alexandrine
alliteration
amoebaean *or* amoebean
amphibrach
amphimacer
anacrusis
arsis
anapaest *or* anapest
anapaestic *or* anapestic
antistrophe
assonance
bacchius
ballad stanza
blank verse
bob
cadence *or* cadency
caesura *or* cesura
canto
catalectic
choriamb *or* choriambus
closed couplet
common measure
common metre
consonance *or* consonancy
couplet
cretic *or* amphimacer
dactyl
dactylic
diaeresis *or* dieresis
dipody
distich
elision
end-stopped

enjambement
envoy *or* envoi
epode
eye rhyme
feminine ending
feminine rhyme
foot
free verse *or* vers libre
half-rhyme
hemistich
heptameter
heptastich
heroic couplet
hexameter
hypermeter
iamb *or* iambus
iambic
ictus
internal rhyme
ionic
jabberwocky
leonine rhyme
long metre
macaronic
masculine ending
masculine rhyme
metre
octameter
octave *or* octet
onomatopoeia
ottava rima
paeon
paeonic
pararhyme
pentameter
pentastich
perfect rhyme *or* full rhyme
Pindaric

pyhrric
quantitative metre
quatrain
quintain *or* quintet
refrain
rhyme
rhyme royal
rhyme scheme
rhythm
rime riche
Sapphic
scansion
septet
sestet
sestina *or* sextain
short metre
Spenserian stanza
spondee
spondaic
sprung rhythm
stanza
stichic
strophe
syllabic metre
tercet
terza rima
tetrabrach
tetrameter
tetrapody
tetrastich
triplet
trochaic
trochee
unstopped
verse paragraph
wheel

Poetry movements and groupings

Alexandrians
Decadents
Georgian Poets
imagists

Lake Poets
Liverpool Poets
Metaphysical Poets
the Movement

Petrarchans
Romantics
Scottish Chaucerians
symbolists

Dannie Abse (*Welsh*)
(Karen) Fleur Adcock (*New Zealander*)
Conrad (Potter) Aiken (*U.S.*)
Anna Akhamatova (*Russian*)
Maya Angelou (*U.S.*)
Guillaume Apollinaire (*French*)
Ludovico Ariosto (*Italian*)
Matthew Arnold (*English*)
W(ystan) H(ugh) Auden (*English-U.S.*)
Charles Pierre Baudelaire (*French*)
Patricia Beer (*English*)
Hilaire Belloc (*British*)
John Berryman (*U.S.*)
John Betjeman (*English*)
Elizabeth Bishop (*U.S.*)
William Blake (*English*)
Edmund Blunden (*English*)
Joseph Brodsky (*Russian-American*)
Rupert (Chawner) Brooke (*English*)
Gwendolyn Brooks (*U.S.*)
Elizabeth Barrett Browning (*English*)
Robert Browning (*English*)
Robert Burns (*Scottish*)
(George Gordon) Byron (*British*)
Callimachus (*Greek*)
Luis Vaz de Camoëns (*Portuguese*)
Thomas Campion (*English*)
Raymond Carver (*U.S.*)
Gaius Valerius Catullus (*Roman*)
Charles Causley (*English*)
Geoffrey Chaucer (*English*)
Amy Clampitt (*U.S.*)
John Clare (*English*)
Samuel Taylor Coleridge (*English*)
William Cowper (*English*)
George Crabbe (*English*)
e(dward) e(stlin) cummings (*U.S.*)
Dante (Alighieri) (*Italian*)
Cecil Day Lewis (*Irish*)
Walter de la Mare (*English*)
Emily Dickinson (*U.S.*)
John Donne (*English*)
H D (Hilda Doolittle) (*U.S.*)
John Dryden (*English*)
Carol Ann Duffy (*Scottish*)
William Dunbar (*Scottish*)
Douglas Dunn (*Scottish*)
Geoffrey Dutton (*Australian*)
T(homas) S(tearns) Eliot (*U.S.-British*)
Ebenezer Elliot (the Corn Law Rhymer)
  (*English*)
Paul Éluard (*French*)
Ralph Waldo Emerson (*U.S.*)
William Empson (*English*)

Edward Fitzgerald (*English*)
Robert Fitzgerald (*Australian*)
Robert (Lee) Frost (*U.S.*)
Allen Ginsberg (*U.S.*)
Johann Wolfgang von Goethe (*German*)
Robert Graves (*English*)
Thomas Gray (*English*)
Thom Gunn (*English*)
Seamus Heaney (*Irish*)
Adrian Henri (*English*)
Robert Henryson (*Scottish*)
George Herbert (*English*)
Robert Herrick (*English*)
Hesiod (*Greek*)
Geoffrey Hill (*English*)
Ralph Hodgson (*English*)
Homer (*Greek*)
Thomas Hood (*English*)
Gerard Manley Hopkins (*English*)
Horace (*Roman*)
A(lfred) E(dward) Housman (*English*)
Ted Hughes (*English*)
Elizabeth Jennings (*English*)
Samuel Johnson (*English*)
Ben Jonson (*English*)
Juvenal (*Roman*)
Patrick Kavanagh (*Irish*)
John Keats (*English*)
Sidney Keyes (*English*)
(Joseph) Rudyard Kipling (*English*)
Jean de La Fontaine (*French*)
Alphonse Marie Louis de Prat de Lamartine
  (*French*)
Walter Savage Landor (*English*)
William Langland (*English*)
Philip Larkin (*English*)
Tom Leonard (*Scottish*)
Henry Wadsworth Longfellow (*U.S.*)
Amy Lowell (*U.S.*)
Robert Lowell (*U.S.*)
Richard Lovelace (*English*)
Lucretius (*Roman*)
Thomas Macauley (*English*)
Norman MacCaig (*Scottish*)
Hugh MacDiarmid (*Scottish*)
Roger McGough (*English*)
Sorley MacLean (*Scottish*)
Louis MacNeice (*Irish*)
Stéphane Mallarmé (*French*)
Martial (*Roman*)
Andrew Marvell (*English*)
John Masefield (*English*)
Edna St Vincent Millay (*U.S.*)
John Milton (*English*)

WORD POWER

Marianne Moore (*U.S.*)
Edwin Morgan (*Scottish*)
Andrew Motion (*English*)
Edwin Muir (*Scottish*)
Ogden Nash (*U.S.*)
Pablo Neruda (*Chilean*)
Frank O'Hara (*U.S.*)
Omar Khayyam (*Persian*)
Ovid (*Roman*)
Wilfred Owen (*British*)
Brian Patten (*English*)
Octavio Paz (*Mexican*)
Petrarch (*Italian*)
Pindar (*Greek*)
Sylvia Plath (*U.S.*)
Alexander Pope (*English*)
Peter Porter (*Australian*)
Ezra (Loomis) Pound (*U.S.*)
Sextus Propertius (*Roman*)
Aleksander Sergeyevich Pushkin (*Russian*)
Kathleen Raine (*English*)
Adrienne Rich (*U.S.*)
Laura Riding (*U.S.*)
Rainer Maria Rilke (*Austro-German*)
Arthur Rimbaud (*French*)
(John Wilmot) Rochester (*English*)
Theodore Huebner Roethke (*U.S.*)
Isaac Rosenberg (*English*)
Christina Georgina Rossetti (*English*)
Dante Gabriel Rossetti (*English*)
Saint-John Perse (*French*)
Sappho (*Greek*)
Siegfried Sassoon (*English*)
Johann Christoph Friedrich von Schiller (*German*)

Delmore Schwarz (*U.S.*)
Sir Walter Scott (*Scottish*)
Jaroslav Seifert (*Czech*)
William Shakespeare (*English*)
Percy Bysshe Shelley (*English*)
Sir Philip Sidney (*English*)
Edith Sitwell (*English*)
John Skelton (*English*)
Christopher Smart (*English*)
Stevie Smith (*English*)
Robert Southey (*English*)
Stephen Spender (*English*)
Edmund Spenser (*English*)
Wallace Stevens (*U.S.*)
Algernon Charles Swinburne (*English*)
Wislawa Szymborska (*Polish*)
Torquato Tasso (*Italian*)
Alfred, Lord Tennyson (*English*)
Dylan (Marlais) Thomas (*Welsh*)
Edward Thomas (*English*)
R(onald) S(tuart) Thomas (*Welsh*)
James Thomson (*Scottish*)
Paul Verlaine (*French*)
Alfred Victor de Vigny (*French*)
François Villon (*French*)
Virgil (*Roman*)
Derek Walcott (*West Indian*)
Francis Charles Webb (*Australian*)
Walt Whitman (*U.S.*)
William Wordsworth (*English*)
Judith Wright (*Australian*)
Thomas Wyatt (*English*)
W(illiam) B(utler) Yeats (*Irish*)

WORD POWER

POLITICAL PARTIES

Australia
Australian Labor Party
Liberal Party of Australia
National Party of Australia

Austria
Freedom Party (FPÖ)
People's Party (ÖVP)
Socialist Party (SPÖ)

Belgium
Flemish Bloc (VB)
Flemish Green Party (Agalev)
French Green Party (Ecolo)
Flemish Liberal Party (PVV)
French Liberal Reform Party (PRL)
Flemish Social Christian Party (CVP)
French Social Christian Party (PSC)
Flemish Socialist Party (SP)
French Socialist Party (PS)

Canada
Bloc Quebecois
Liberal Party
New Democratic Party
Progressive Conservative
Reform Party
Social Credit Party

Denmark
Centre Democrats (CD)
Christian People's Party (KrF)
Conservative People's Party (KF)
Left Socialists
Liberals (V)
Progress Party (FP)
Radical Liberals (RV)
Social Democrats (SD)
Socialist People's Party (SF)

Finland
Centre Party (KP)
Democratic Alternative
Finnish People's Democratic League (SKDL)
Finnish Rural Party (SMP)
Green Party
National Coalition Party (KOK)
Social Democratic Party (SD)
Swedish People's Party (SFP)

France
Communist Party (PC)
National Front
Rally for the Republic (RDR)
Republican Party (PR)
Socialist Party (PS)
Union for French Democracy (UDF)

Germany
Christian-Democratic Union (CDU)
Christian-Social Union (CSU)
Free Democratic Party (FDP)
Green Party
Party of Democratic Socialism (PDS)
Social Democratic Party (SPD)

Greece
Greek Communist Party
New Democracy (ND)
Pan-Hellenic Socialist Movement (PASOK)
Political Spring (Politiki Aniksi)

India
Congress (I)
Janata Dal
Bharitiya Janata Party (BJP)

Irish Republic
Democratic Left
Fianna Fáil
Fine Gael
Labour Party
Progressive Democrats

Israel
Labour Party
Likud

Italy
Centre Union
Christian Democrat Party
Democratic Party of the Left (PDS)
Forza Italia
National Alliance
Northern League

Japan
Democratic Socialist Party
Liberal Democratic Party
Komeito
Social Democratic Party

POLITICAL PARTIES

Luxembourg
Communist Party
Democratic Party (PD)
Luxembourg Socialist Workers' Party
  (POSL)
Christian Social Party (PCS)

Malta
Malta Labour Party
Nationalist Party

Mexico
Institutional Revolutionary Party (PRI)
National Action Party (PAN)
Party of the Democratic Revolution (PRD)
Revolutionary Workers' Party

the Netherlands
Christian Democratic Appeal (CDA)
Labour Party (PvdA)
People's Party for Freedom and Democracy
  (VVD)

New Zealand
Labour Party
National Party

Northern Ireland
Democratic Unionist Party
Official Ulster Unionist Party
Sinn Féin
Social Democratic and Labour Party (SDLP)

Portugal
Democratic Renewal Party (PRD)
Democratic Social Centre Party (CDS)
Social Democratic Party (PSD)
Socialist Party (PS)

South Africa
African National Congress (ANC)
Inkatha Freedom Party
National Party
Pan-Africanist Congress (PAC)

Spain
Basque Nationalist Party (PNV)
Convergencia i Uni (CiU)
Herri Batasuna (HB)
People's Party (PP)
Socialist Workers' Party (PSOE)
United Left (IU)

Sweden
Centre Party
Christian Democratic Party
Green Party
Left Party
Liberal Party
Moderate Party
Social Democratic Labour Party (SAP)

Turkey
Motherland Party (ANAP)
Kurdish Workers' Party (PKK)
Social Democratic Populist Party
True Path Party

United Kingdom (mainland)
Conservative and Unionist Party
Labour Party
Liberal Democrats
Plaid Cymru
Scottish National Party

United States of America
Democratic Party
Republican Party

WORD POWER

49

Major World Ports

Abidjan	Chicago	Kingston
Accra	Chittagong	Kobe
Aden	Colombo	Kowloon
Alexandria	Colón	Kuwait
Algiers	Conakry	La Coruña
Alicante	Copenhagen	Lagos
Amsterdam	Corinth	La Guaira
Anchorage	Dakar	Las Palmas
Antwerp	Dar es Salaam	Launceston
Apia	Darwin	Le Havre
Aqaba	Dieppe	Limassol
Archangel	Djibouti	Lisbon
Ashdod	Dubrovnik	Liverpool
Auckland	Duluth	Livorno
Baku	Dunedin	Lomé
Baltimore	Dunkerque	London
Bangkok	Durban	Los Angeles
Barcelona	East London	Luanda
Basra	Eilat *or* Elat	Lübeck
Bathurst	Esbjerg	Macao
Batum	Europoort	Madras
Beira	Fray Bentos	Malmo
Beirut	Freetown	Manama
Belize	Fremantle	Manaus
Benghazi	Gdańsk	Manila
Bergen	Genoa	Maputo
Bilbao	Georgetown	Mar del Plata
Bissau	Gijón	Marseille
Bombay	Göteborg *or* Gothenburg	Melbourne
Bordeaux	Guayaquil	Mobile
Boston	Haifa	Mogadiscio *or* Mogadishu
Boulogne	Halifax	Mombasa
Bridgetown	Hamburg	Monrovia
Brindisi	Hamilton	Montego Bay
Brisbane	Havana	Montevideo
Bristol	Helsinki	Montreal
Buenaventura	Hobart	Murmansk
Buenos Aires	Ho Chi Minh City	Muscat
Cádiz	Honolulu	Nagasaki
Cagliari	Hook of Holland	Naples
Calais	Inchon	Nassau
Calcutta	Istanbul	New Orleans
Callao	Izmir	New York
Cannes	Jacksonville	Oakland
Canton	Jaffa	Odense
Cape Town	Jidda *or* Jedda	Odessa
Cap-Haitien	Juneau	Oporto
Casablanca	Kaohsiung *or* Kao-hsiung	Osaka
Catania	Karachi	Oslo
Cebu	Kawasaki	Ostend
Charleston	Keflavik	Phnom Penh
Cherbourg	Kiel	Piraeus

Major world ports (continued)

Port Adelaide
Port au Prince
Port Elizabeth
Portland
Port Louis
Port Moresby
Port Said
Portsmouth
Port Sudan
Punta Arenas
Pusan
Recife
Reykjavik
Riga
Rimini
Rio de Janeiro
Rostock
Rotterdam
Saint Petersburg
Salvador
San Diego
San Francisco
San Juan

San Sebastian
Santander
Santo Domingo
Santos
Savannah
Seattle
Sevastopol
Seville
Shanghai
Singapore
Southampton
Split
Stavanger
Stockholm
Suez
Suva
Sydney
Szczecin
Takoradi
Tallinn *or* Tallin
Tampa
Tandjungpriok
Tangier

Tokyo
Townsville
Trieste
Tripoli
Trondheim
Tunis
Turku
Tyre
Valencia
Valparaíso
Vancouver
Venice
Veracruz
Vigo
Vishakhapatnam
Vladivostok
Volgograd
Walvis Bay
Wellington
Yangon
Yokohama
Zeebrugge

Main British and Irish ports

Aberdeen
Arbroath
Ayr
Barry
Belfast
Birkenhead
Bristol
Caernarfon
Cardiff
Cóbh
Cork
Dover
Dundee
Dún Laoghaire
Ellesmere Port
Fishguard
Fleetwood
Folkestone
Galway
Glasgow
Grangemouth
Gravesend
Great Yarmouth

Greenock
Grimsby
Harwich
Holyhead
Hull
Immingham
Kirkcaldy
Larne
Leith
Lerwick
Limerick
Liverpool
London
Londonderry *or* Derry
Lowestoft
Milford Haven
Morecambe
Newcastle upon Tyne
Newhaven
Newport
Newry
Oban
Penzance

Plymouth
Poole
Portsmouth
Port Talbot
Ramsgate
Rosslare
Scarborough
Sheerness
Sligo
Southampton
South Shields
Stornoway
Stranraer
Sunderland
Swansea
Tynemouth
Waterford
Wexford
Weymouth
Whitby
Wicklow

WORD POWER

PRIME MINISTERS

British Prime Ministers

Prime Minister	Party	Term of office
Robert Walpole	Whig	1721–42
Earl of Wilmington	Whig	1742–43
Henry Pelham	Whig	1743–54
Duke of Newcastle	Whig	1754–56
Duke of Devonshire	Whig	1756–57
Duke of Newcastle	Whig	1757–62
Earl of Bute	Tory	1762–63
George Grenville	Whig	1763–65
Marquess of Rockingham	Whig	1765–66
Duke of Grafton	Whig	1766–70
Lord North	Tory	1770–82
Marquess of Rockingham	Whig	1782
Earl of Sherbourne	Whig	1782–83
Duke of Portland	Coalition	1783
William Pitt	Tory	1783–1801
Henry Addington	Tory	1801–04
William Pitt	Tory	1804–06
Lord Grenville	Whig	1806–1807
Duke of Portland	Tory	1807–09
Spencer Perceval	Tory	1809–12
Earl of Liverpool	Tory	1812–27
George Canning	Tory	1827
Viscount Goderich	Tory	1827–28
Duke of Wellington	Tory	1828–30
Earl Grey	Whig	1830–34
Viscount Melbourne	Whig	1834
Robert Peel	Conservative	1834–35
Viscount Melbourne	Whig	1835–41
Robert Peel	Conservative	1841–46
Lord John Russell	Liberal	1846–52
Earl of Derby	Conservative	1852
Lord Aberdeen	Peelite	1852–55
Viscount Palmerston	Liberal	1855–58
Earl of Derby	Conservative	1858–59
Viscount Palmerston	Liberal	1859–65
Lord John Russell	Liberal	1865–66
Earl of Derby	Conservative	1866–68
Benjamin Disraeli	Conservative	1868
William Gladstone	Liberal	1868–74
Benjamin Disraeli	Conservative	1874–80
William Gladstone	Liberal	1880–85
Marquess of Salisbury	Conservative	1885–86
William Gladstone	Liberal	1886
Marquess of Salisbury	Conservative	1886–92
William Gladstone	Liberal	1892–94
Earl of Roseberry	Liberal	1894–95
Marquess of Salisbury	Conservative	1895–1902
Arthur James Balfour	Conservative	1902–05
Henry Campbell-Bannerman	Liberal	1905–08
Herbert Henry Asquith	Liberal	1908–15

WORD POWER

British Prime Ministers (continued)

Prime Minister	Party	Term of office
Herbert Henry Asquith	Coalition	1915–16
David Lloyd George	Coalition	1916–22
Andrew Bonar Law	Conservative	1922–23
Stanley Baldwin	Conservative	1923–24
James Ramsay McDonald	Labour	1924
Stanley Baldwin	Conservative	1924–29
James Ramsay McDonald	Labour	1929–31
James Ramsay McDonald	Nationalist	1931–35
Stanley Baldwin	Nationalist	1935–37
Arthur Neville Chamberlain	Nationalist	1937–40
Winston Churchill	Coalition	1940–45
Clement Atlee	Labour	1945–51
Winston Churchill	Conservative	1951–55
Anthony Eden	Conservative	1955–57
Harold Macmillan	Conservative	1957–63
Alec Douglas-Home	Conservative	1963–64
Harold Wilson	Labour	1964–70
Edward Heath	Conservative	1970–74
Harold Wilson	Labour	1974–76
James Callaghan	Labour	1976–79
Margaret Thatcher	Conservative	1979–90
John Major	Conservative	1990–97
Tony Blair	Labour	1997–

Australian Prime Ministers

Prime Minister	Party	Term of office
Edmund Barton	Protectionist	1901–03
Alfred Deakin	Protectionist	1903–04
John Christian Watson	Labor	1904
George Houston Reid	Free Trade	1904–05
Alfred Deakin	Protectionist	1905–08
Andrew Fisher	Labor	1908–09
Alfred Deakin	Fusion	1909–10
Andrew Fisher	Labor	1910–13
Joseph Cook	Liberal	1913–14
Andrew Fisher	Labor	1914–15
William Morris Hughes	National Labor	1915–17
William Morris Hughes	Nationalist	1917–23
Stanley Melbourne Bruce	Nationalist	1923–29
James Henry Scullin	Labor	1929–32
Joseph Aloysius Lyons	United	1932–39
Earle Christmas Page	Country	1939
Robert Gordon Menzies	United	1939–41
Arthur William Fadden	Country	1941
John Joseph Curtin	Labor	1941–45
Joseph Benedict Chiffley	Labor	1945–49
Robert Gordon Menzies	Liberal	1949–66
Harold Edward Holt	Liberal	1966–67
John McEwen	Country	1967–68

Australian Prime Ministers (continued)

Prime Minister	Party	Term of office
John Grey Gorton	Liberal	1968–71
William McMahon	Liberal	1972–72
Edward Gough Whitlam	Labor	1972–75
John Malcolm Fraser	Liberal	1975–83
Robert James Lee Hawke	Labor	1983–91
Paul Keating	Labor	1991–96
John Howard	Liberal	1996–

Canadian Prime Ministers

Prime Minister	Party	Term of office
John A. MacDonald	Conservative	1867–73
Alexander Mackenzie	Liberal	1873–78
John A. MacDonald	Conservative	1878–91
John J.C. Abbot	Conservative	1891–92
John S.D. Thompson	Conservative	1892–94
Mackenzie Bowell	Conservative	1894–96
Charles Tupper	Conservative	1896
Wilfred Laurier	Liberal	1896–1911
Robert Borden	Conservative	1911–20
Arthur Meighen	Conservative	1920–21
William Lyon McKenzie King	Liberal	1921–1926
Arthur Meighen	Conservative	1926
William Lyon McKenzie King	Liberal	1926–30
Richard Bedford Bennet	Conservative	1930–35
William Lyon McKenzie King	Liberal	1935–48
Louis St. Laurent	Liberal	1948–57
John George Diefenbaker	Conservative	1957–63
Lester Bowles Pearson	Liberal	1963–68
Pierre Elliott Trudeau	Liberal	1968–79
Joseph Clark	Conservative	1979–80
Pierre Elliott Trudeau	Liberal	1968–79
Joseph Clark	Conservative	1979–80
Pierre Elliott Trudeau	Liberal	1980–84
John Turner	Liberal	1984
Brian Mulroney	Conservative	1984–93
Kim Campbell	Conservative	1993
Joseph Jacques Jean Chrétien	Liberal	1993–

New Zealand Prime Ministers

Prime Minister	Party	Term of office
Henry Sewell	–	1856
Henry Fox	–	1856
Edward William Stafford	–	1856–61
William Fox	–	1861–62
Alfred Domett	–	1862–63
Frederick Whitaker	–	1863–64
Frederick Aloysius Weld	–	1864–65

New Zealand Prime Ministers (continued)

Prime Minister	Party	Term of office
Edward William Stafford	–	1865–69
William Fox	–	1869–72
Edward William Stafford	–	1872
William Fox	–	1873
Julius Vogel	–	1873–75
Daniel Pollen	–	1875–76
Julius Vogel	–	1876
Harry Albert Atkinson	–	1876–77
George Grey	–	1877–79
John Hall	–	1879–82
Frederic Whitaker	–	1882–83
Harry Albert Atkinson	–	1883–84
Robert Stout	–	1884
Harry Albert Atkinson	–	1884
Robert Stout	–	1884–87
Harry Albert Atkinson	–	1887–91
John Ballance	–	1891–93
Richard John Sneddon	Liberal	1893–1906
William Hall-Jones	Liberal	1906
Joseph George Ward	Liberal/National	1906–12
Thomas Mackenzie	National	1912
William Ferguson Massey	Reform	1912–25
Francis Henry Dillon Bell	Reform	1925
Joseph Gordon Coates	Reform	1925–28
Joseph George Ward	Liberal/National	1928–30
George William Forbes	United	1930–35
Michael Joseph Savage	Labour	1935–40
Peter Fraser	Labour	1940–49
Sidney George Holland	National	1949–47
Keith Jacka Holyoake	National	1957
Walter Nash	Labour	1957–60
Keith Jacka Holyoake	National	1960–72
John Ross Marshall	National	1972
Norman Eric Kirk	Labour	1972–74
Wallace Edward Rowling	Labour	1974–75
Robert David Muldoon	National	1975–84
David Russell Lange	Labour	1984–89
Geoffrey Palmer	Labour	1989–90
Mike Moore	Labour	1990
Jim Bolger	National	1990–97
Jenny Shipley	National	1997–99
Helen Clark	Labour	1999–

WORD POWER

RIVERS

Adige
Ain
Aire
Aisne
Alabama
Albany
Aldan
Allier
Amazon
Amu Darya
Amur
Anadyr
Anderson
Angara
Apure
Apurimac
Araguaia
Aras
Arkansas
Arno
Aruwimi
Assiniboine
Atbara
Athabaska
Aube
Avon
Back
Barrow
Beni
Benue
Berezina
Bermejo
Bío-Bío
Black Volta
Blue Nile
Bomu
Boyne
Brahmaputra
Bug
Cam
Canadian
Caquetá
Cauca
Cauvery *or* Kaveri
Chagres
Chao Phraya
Charente
Chari *or* Shari
Chenab
Cher
Chindwin
Churchill
Clutha
Clyde

Colorado
Columbia
Congo
Connecticut
Cooper's Creek
Courantyne
Cuiaba
Damodar
Danube
Darling
Dee
Delaware
Demerara
Derwent
Des Moines
Detroit
Dnieper
Dniester
Don
Donets
Dordogne
Doubs
Douro
Drava *or* Drave
Drin
Durance
Dvina
Ebro
Elbe
Ems
Erne
Essequibo
Euphrates
Fly
Forth
Fraser
Ganges
Garonne
Glomma
Godavari
Gogra
Göta
Granta
Green
Guadalquivir
Guadiana
Guaporé
Han
Havel
Helmand
Hooghly
Hudson
Iguaçú *or* Iguassú
IJssel *or* Yssel

Illinois
Indus
Inn
Irrawaddy
Irtysh *or* Irtish
Isar
Isère
Isis
Japurá
Javari
Jhelum
Jordan
Juba
Jumna
Juruá
Kabul
Kagera
Kama
Kasai
Kentucky
Kizil Irmak
Klondike
Kolyma
Komati
Kootenay *or*
   Kootenai
Krishna
Kuban
Kura
Kuskokwim
Lachlan
Lech
Lee
Lena
Liao
Liard
Liffey
Limpopo
Lippe
Little Bighorn
Loire
Lot
Lualaba
Mackenzie
Macquarie
Madeira
Madre de Dios
Magdalena
Mahanadi
Main
Mamoré
Marañón
Maritsa
Marne

Medway
Mekong
Menderes
Mersey
Meta
Meuse
Minnesota
Miño
Mississippi
Missouri
Mohawk
Molopo
Monongahela
Morava
Moselle
Moskva
Murray
Murrumbidgee
Narmada
Neckar
Negro
Neisse
Nelson
Neman *or* Nyeman
Neva
Niagara
Niger
Nile
Ob
Oder
Ogooué *or* Ogowe
Ohio
Oise
Okanagan
Okavango
Orange
Ord
Orinoco
Orontes
Ottawa
Ouachita *or*
   Washita
Ouse
Paraguay
Paraíba
Paraná
Parnaíba *or*
   Parnahiba
Peace
Pearl
Pechora
Pecos
Piave
Pilcomayo

RIVERS

Plate
Po
Potomac
Pripet
Prut
Purús
Putamayo
Red
Rhine *or* Rhein
Rhône
Ribble
Richelieu
Rio Branco
Rio Grande
Rubicon
Saar
Sacramento
Safid Rud
Saguenay
Saint Croix
Saint John
Saint Lawrence
Salado
Salambria
Salween
Sambre
San
Santee
Saône
Saskatchewan

Sava *or* Save
Savannah
Scheldt
Seine
Severn
Shannon
Shatt-al-Arab
Shiré
Siret
Skien
Slave
Snake
Snowy
Somme
Songhua
Spey
Struma
Susquehanna
Sutlej
Suwannee *or*
  Swanee
Swan
Swat
Syr Darya
Tagus
Tana
Tanana
Tapajós
Tarim
Tarn

Tarsus
Tay
Tees
Tennessee
Thames
Tiber
Ticino
Tigris
Tisza
Tobol
Tocantins
Trent
Tugela
Tunguska
Tweed
Tyne
Ubangi
Ucayali
Uele
Ural
Usk
Ussuri
Vaal
Var
Vardar
Vienne
Vistula
Vltava
Volga
Volta

Volturno
Waal
Wabash
Waikato
Warta
Wear
Weser
White Volta
Wisconsin
Xi, Hsi, *or* Si
Xiang, Hsiang, *or*
  Siang
Xingú
Wye
Yalu
Yangtze
Yaqui
Yarra
Yellow
Yellowstone
Yenisei
Yonne
Yser
Yüan *or* Yüen
Yukon
Zambezi *or*
  Zambese
Zhu Jiang

SEAS AND OCEANS

Seas

Adriatic
Aegean
Amundsen
Andaman
Arabian
Arafura
Aral
Azov
Baltic
Banda
Barents
Beaufort
Bellingshausen
Bering
Bismarck
Black *or* Euxine
Caribbean
Caspian
Celebes

Ceram
China
Chukchi
Coral
East China
East Siberian
Flores
Icarian
Inland
Ionian
Irish
Japan
Java
Kara
Laptev
Ligurian
Lincoln
Marmara *or* Marmora
Mediterranean

Nordenskjöld
North
Norwegian
Okhotsk
Philippine
Red
Ross
Sargasso
Scotia
Solomon
South China
Sulu
Tasman
Timor
Tyrrhenian
Weddell
White
Yellow *or* Hwang Hai

Oceans

Antarctic *or* Southern
Arctic

Atlantic
Indian

Pacific

SOUTH AFRICAN PROVINCES

Province	Capital	Province	Capital
Eastern Cape	Bisho	Mpumalanga	Nelspruit
Free State	Bloemfontein	North-West	Mafikeng
Gauteng	Johannesburg	Northern Cape	Kimberley
KwaZulu-Natal	Pietermaritzburg	Western Cape	Cape Town
Limpopo	Pietersburg		

U.S. PRESIDENTS

President	Party	Term of office
1. George Washington	Federalist	1789–97
2. John Adams	Federalist	1797–1801
3. Thomas Jefferson	Democratic Republican	1801–1809
4. James Madison	Democratic Republican	1809–1817
5. James Monroe	Democratic Republican	1817–25
6. John Quincy Adams	Democratic Republican	1825–29
7. Andrew Jackson	Democrat	1829–37
8. Martin Van Buren	Democrat	1837–41
9. William Henry Harrison	Whig	1841
10. John Tyler	Whig	1841–45
11. James K. Polk	Democrat	1845–49
12. Zachary Taylor	Whig	1849–50
13. Millard Fillmore	Whig	1850–53
14. Franklin Pierce	Democrat	1853–57
15. James Buchanan	Democrat	1857–61
16. Abraham Lincoln	Republican	1861–65
17. Andrew Johnson	Republican	1865–69
18. Ulysses S. Grant	Republican	1869–77
19. Rutherford B. Hayes	Republican	1877–81
20. James A. Garfield	Republican	1881
21. Chester A. Arthur	Republican	1881–85
22. Grover Cleveland	Democrat	1885–89
23. Benjamin Harrison	Republican	1889–93
24. Grover Cleveland	Democrat	1893–97
25. William McKinley	Republican	1897–1901
26. Theodore Roosevelt	Republican	1901–1909
27. William Howard Taft	Republican	1909–13
28. Woodrow Wilson	Democrat	1913–21
29. Warren G. Harding	Republican	1921–23
30. Calvin Coolidge	Republican	1923–29
31. Herbert C. Hoover	Republican	1929–33
32. Franklin D. Roosevelt	Democrat	1933–45
33. Harry S. Truman	Democrat	1945–53
34. Dwight D. Eisenhower	Republican	1953–61
35. John F. Kennedy	Democrat	1961–63
36. Lyndon B. Johnson	Democrat	1963–69
37. Richard M. Nixon	Republican	1969–74
38. Gerald R. Ford	Republican	1974–77
39. James E. Carter, Jr	Democrat	1977–81
40. Ronald W. Reagan	Republican	1981–89
41. George H. W. Bush	Republican	1989–93
42. William J. Clinton	Democrat	1993–2001
43. George W. Bush	Republican	2001–

U.S. STATES

State	Abbreviation	Zip code
Alabama	Ala.	AL
Alaska	Alas.	AK
Arizona	Ariz.	AZ
Arkansas	Ark.	AR
California	Cal.	CA
Colorado	Colo.	CO
Connecticut	Conn.	CT
Delaware	Del.	DE
District of Columbia	D.C.	DC
Florida	Fla.	FL
Georgia	Ga.	GA
Hawaii	Haw.	HI
Idaho	Id. *or* Ida.	ID
Illinois	Ill.	IL
Indiana	Ind.	IN
Iowa	Ia. *or* Io.	IA
Kansas	Kan. *or* Kans.	KS
Kentucky	Ken.	KY
Louisiana	La.	LA
Maine	Me.	ME
Maryland	Md.	MD
Massachusetts	Mass.	MA
Michigan	Mich.	MI
Minnesota	Minn.	MN
Mississippi	Miss.	MS
Missouri	Mo.	MO
Montana	Mont.	MT
Nebraska	Neb.	NE
Nevada	Nev.	NV
New Hampshire	N.H.	NH
New Jersey	N.J.	NJ
New Mexico	N.M. *or* N.Mex.	NM
New York	N.Y.	NY
North Carolina	N.C.	NC
North Dakota	N.D. *or* N.Dak.	ND
Ohio	O.	OH
Oklahoma	Okla.	OK
Oregon	Oreg.	OR
Pennsylvania	Pa., Penn., *or* Penna.	PA
Rhode Island	R.I.	RI
South Carolina	S.C.	SC
South Dakota	S.Dak.	SD
Tennessee	Tenn.	TN
Texas	Tex.	TX
Utah	Ut.	UT
Vermont	Vt.	VT
Virginia	Va.	VA
Washington	Wash.	WA
West Virginia	W.Va.	WV
Wisconsin	Wis.	WI
Wyoming	Wyo.	WY

WORD POWER

VOLCANOES

Antisana
Apo
Askja
Cameroon
Chimborazo
Citlaltépetl
Corcovado
Cotopaxi
Egmont
Elgon
El Misti
Erciyas Dagi
Erebus
Etna
Fuji
Haleakala

Hekla
Helgafell
Huascarán *or* Huascán
Iliamna
Ixtaccihuatl *or* Iztaccihuatl
Katmai
Kazbek
Kenya
Krakatoa *or* Krakatau
Lassen Peak
Mauna Kea
Mauna Loa
Mayon
Mount St. Helens
Nevado de Colima
Nevado de Toluca

Paricutín
Pelée
Popocatépetl
Santa Maria
Semeru *or* Semeroe
Soufrière
Stromboli
Suribachi
Taal
Tambora
Teide *or* Teyde
Tolima
Tristan da Cunha
Vesuvius

WATERFALLS

Angel Falls
Churchill Falls
Cleve-Garth
Cuquenan
Iguaçú Falls
Itatinga

Kaieteur Falls
Niagara Falls
Ormeli
Pilao
Ribbon
Roraima

Sutherland Falls
Tysse
Vestre Mardola
Victoria Falls
Yellowstone Falls
Yosemite Falls

WRITERS

Children's writers

Louisa May Alcott (*U.S.*)
Hans Christian Andersen (*Danish*)
Lynn Reid Banks (*English*)
J(ames) M(atthew) Barrie (*Scottish*)
Judy Blume (*U.S.*)
Enid (Mary) Blyton (*English*)
Elinor M(ary) Brent-Dyer (*English*)
Lewis Carroll (*English*)
Babette Cole (*British*)
Eoin Colfer (*Irish*)
Susan Coolidge (*U.S.*)
Karen Cushman (*U.S.*)
Roald Dahl (*British*)
Anne Digby (*English*)
Dr Seuss (*U.S.*)
Ann Fine (*English*)
Kenneth Grahame (*Scottish*)
Laura Ingalls Wilder (*U.S.*)

Mike Inkpen (*English*)
Robin Jarvis (*English*)
Diana Wynne Jones (*Welsh*)
C(live) S(taples) Lewis (*English*)
A(lan) A(lexander) Milne (*English*)
Michael Morpurgo (*English*)
Jill Murphy (*English*)
E(dith) Nesbit (*English*)
Terry Pratchett (*English*)
Philip Pullman (*English*)
Chris Riddell (*English*)
J K Rowling (*British*)
Louis Sachar (*U.S.*)
Dick King Smith (*English*)
Paul Stewart (*English*)
Noel Streatfield (*English*)
Jacqueline Wilson (*English*)

Short story writers

Giovanni Boccaccio (*Italian*)
Jorge Luis Borges (*Argentinian*)
Stephen Crane (*U.S.*)
Arthur Conan Doyle (*British*)
Joel Chandler Harris (*U.S.*)
Nathaniel Hawthorne (*U.S.*)
Washington Irving (*U.S.*)
Carson McCullers (*U.S.*)
Katherine Mansfield (*N.Z.-British*)

Herman Melville (*U.S.*)
W(illiam) Somerset Maugham (*English*)
(Henri René Albert) Guy de Maupassant (*French*)
H(ector) H(ugh) Munro (*Scottish*)
O. Henry (*U.S.*)
Dorothy Parker (*U.S.*)
Edgar Allan Poe (*U.S.*)

Non-fiction writers

Joseph Addison (*English*)
Aesop (*Greek*)
Roger Ascham (*English*)
James Boswell (*Scottish*)
John Bunyan (*English*)
Edmund Burke (*British*)
Jane Welsh Carlyle (*Scottish*)
Thomas Carlyle (*Scottish*)
William Godwin (*English*)
Marcus Tullius Cicero (*Roman*)
William Cobbett (*English*)
Desiderius Erasmus (*Dutch*)
Edward Gibbon (*English*)
William Hazlitt (*English*)
R.H. Hutton (*English*)
Thomas Jefferson (*U.S.*)

Jerome K(lapka) Jerome (*English*)
Samuel Johnson (*English*)
Margery Kempe (*English*)
Lord Chesterfield (*English*)
John Lyly (*English*)
Thomas Malory (*English*)
Michel Eyquem de Montaigne (*French*)
Tom Paine (*English-U.S.*)
Samuel Pepys (*English*)
François Rabelais (*French*)
John Ruskin (*English*)
Richard Steele (*English*)
Leslie Stephen (*English*)
Thomas Traherne (*English*)
Izaac Walton (*English*)
Mary Wollstonecraft (*English*)

WORD POWER